5th Edition
GUITAR AMPLIFIERS

Edited by Ryan Triggs

$39.95
Publisher's Softcover
Suggested List Price

5th Edition Blue Book of
GUITAR AMPLIFIERS

Publisher's Note: This book is the result of nonstop and continual guitar amplifier research obtained by attending guitar shows, communicating with dealers and collectors throughout the country each year, following the marketplace through want ads and web sites, and staying on top of trends as they occur. This book represents an analysis of prices for which both recently manufactured and collectible amplifiers have actually been selling for during that period at an average retail level.

Although every reasonable effort has been made to compile an accurate and reliable guide, guitar amplifier prices may vary significantly depending on such factors as the locality of the sale, the number of sales we were able to consider, famous musician endorsement of certain makes/models, regional economic conditions, and other critical factors.

Accordingly, no representation can be made that the guitar amplifiers listed may be bought or sold at prices indicated, nor shall the editor or publisher be responsible for any error made in compiling and recording such values.

Blue Book Publications, Inc.
8009 34th Avenue South, Suite 250
Minneapolis, MN 55425 U.S.A.

Orders only: 800-877-4867 (U.S.A. and Canada only)
Phone: 952-854-5229
Fax: 952-853-1486
www.bluebookofguitarvalues.com
support@bluebookinc.com

ISBN-10 1-936120-88-7, ISBN-13 978-1-936120-88-8
Library of Congress ISSN Number - 1542-0655
Published and printed in the United States of America

Cover Design and Layout – Clint H. Schmidt
Cover images courtesy – Supro and Savage Audio
Art Director and Production Manager – Clint H. Schmidt
Editor and Manuscript Supervisor – Ryan Triggs
Manuscript Contributing Editor and Previous Author – Zachary R. Fjestad
Proofing – Sarah Peterson, Lisa Beuning, Ryan Triggs
Publisher – S.P. Fjestad
Printer – Bang Printing, Brainerd, MN

ABOUT THE COVER

Adorning the cover of this newest 5th Edition *Blue Book of Guitar Amplifiers* are both the front and back sides of a currently manufactured Supro Titan and an older, vintage Mesa Boogie MK-IIB amplifier. The publisher would like to thank David Koltai from Supro Amps (www.suprousa.com) and Savage Audio (www.savageamps.com) for providing Blue Book Publications with these great cover images.

TABLE OF CONTENTS

GENERAL INFORMATION

While many of you have probably dealt with our company for years, it may be helpful for you to know a little bit more about our operation, including information on how to contact us regarding our various titles and other informational services.

Blue Book Publications, Inc.
8009 34th Avenue South, Suite 250
Minneapolis, MN 55425 USA
GPS Coordinates: N44° 51 28.44, W93° 13.1709

Phone No.: 952-854-5229 • Customer Service: 800-877-4867, ext. 3 (domestic only)
Fax No.: 952-853-1486 (available 24 hours a day)
Website: www.bluebookofguitarvalues.com

General Email: support@bluebookinc.com - we check our email at 9am, 12pm, and 4pm M - F (excluding major U.S. holidays). Please refer to individual email addresses listed below with phone extension numbers.

To find out the latest information on our products, including availability and pricing, consumer related services, and up-to-date industry information (blogs, trade show recaps with photos/captions, upcoming events, feature articles, etc.), please check our website, as it is updated on a regular basis. Surf us - you'll have fun!

Images of BBP's staff with contact information is provided below:

Ryan Triggs – Editor
(ryant@bluebookinc.com)

Beth Schreiber – Ext. 1000
(beths@bluebookinc.com)

Karl Stoffels – Ext. 1200
(karls@bluebookinc.com)

S.P. Fjestad – Ext. 1300
(stevef@bluebookinc.com)

Kayla McCarthy – Ext. 1400
(kaylaM@bluebookinc.com)

Clint H. Schmidt – Ext. 1500
(clints@bluebookinc.com)

John B. Allen – Ext. 1600
(johna@bluebookinc.com)

Tom Stock – Ext. 1800
(toms@bluebookinc.com)

Sarah Peterson – Ext. 1900
(sarahp@bluebookinc.com)

Adam Burt – Ext. 2000
(adamb@bluebookinc.com)

Shauna Ritter – Ext. 2200
(shaunar@bluebookinc.com)

Lisa Beuning
(lisab@bluebookinc.com)

Office hours are: 8:30am - 5:00pm CST, Monday - Friday.

Additionally, an after-hours message service is available for ordering. All orders are processed within 24 hours of receiving them, assuming payment and order information is correct. Depending on the product, we typically ship UPS, Media Mail, or Priority Mail. Expedited shipping services are also available domestically for an additional charge. Please contact us directly for an expedited shipping quotation.

ACKNOWLEDGEMENTS

CONTRIBUTING EDITORS

Contributing Editors are the people who take certain sections of the book and physically revise it. Aside from the author and editors, the contributing editors are the next in line for providing critical information and pricing updates. Without these contributors, many sections of this book would be a lot skinnier and we appreciate the time they take to help us out.

Zachary R. Fjestad (previous author)
John Beeson, The Music Shoppe
Dave Boze
Steve Brown, www.vintaxe.com
Walter Carter
Steve Cherne
Barry Clark
Chris Emery
Tim Fletcher

Dave Hinson, Killer Vintage
Gregg Hopkins - Vintage Amp Restoration
The late Stan Jay, Mandolin Brothers
Michael Jones, Michael Jones Vintage Guitars
Jeff Krumm - Savage Audio
Wallace Marx Jr.

Larry Meiners, Flying Vintage
Nick Meuwese
Willie G. Moseley
Walter Murray, Frankenstein Fretworks
David Nordschow
Dave Rogers, Dave's Guitar Shop
Steve Russell
Mark Sampson

Chris Trider, Blue Chip Guitars
Jay Wolfe, Wolfe Guitars
The late Jack Wadsworth
John R. Wiley
David Wilson - The Tonequest Report
Rick Wilkiewicz

FRIENDS OF BLUE BOOK

The following people don't necessarily have an active role in the actual content of the book, but they are important friends of ours in the industry. Whether seeing these people at shows, talking on the phone, or emailing, they are helpful in their own way and it's a privilege to have such nice friends!

Jeff Bober - Budda Amps
Reinhold Bogner - Bogner Amps
Larry Briggs
Gurney Brown
John Brown - Brown's Guitar Factory
Dean Campbell - Campbell American Guitars
The late Zebuelon Cash-Lane
Bill Compeau - Ark Amplifiers/Armstrong Amps
Dave Crocker
Eric Dahl
Seymour Duncan

Dale Evans - Tech 21
S.J. "Frog" Forgey - Elderly Instruments
Andy Fuchs - Fuchs Audio Technology
Richard Goodsell - Goodsell Amps
George Gruhn
Norm Harris
James Heidrich - Bad Cat Amplification
Paul Jernigan - Gibson
Dave King - Naylor Engineering
John Kinnemeyer - JK Lutherie
Don & Jeff Lace - Lace Music Products

Joe Lamond, NAMM
Henry Lowenstein
Adam Moore - Premier Guitar
Willie Moseley
Joe Naylor, Reverend
Mike van Stipnout
Hartley Peavey, Peavey
Andreas Pichler
The late Mark Pollock
Eugene Robertson
Matt Schellenberg - Ark Amplifiers/Armstrong Amps
Jason Scheuner
Michael Soldano - Soldano Custom Amplification

Paul Reed Smith - PRS Guitars
Chad Speck - Encore Guitars
Jimmy "Wilbur" Triggs - Triggs Guitars
Larry Urie - PRS Guitars
Pete Wagener
Jimmy Wallace - Jimmy Wallace Guitars/Dallas Guitar Show
Gerald Weber - Kendrick Amplifiers
Nate Westgor - Willie's American Guitars

PHOTO ACKNOWLEDGEMENTS

All of the images in this book and on our website would not be possible without the following people's contributions. Many photos are taken at shows, and these dealers are nice enough and allow us to photograph them during the often hectic shows. Other people below have welcomed us to their stores/homes, allowed us to set up shop, and photograph their entire inventory/collection. Also, many thanks to the manufacturers who allow us to use the images they have spent much time and money on in our products.

Bruce Barnes - solidbody-guitar.com, Inc.
David J. Brass - Fretted Americana, Inc
John Beeson - The Music Shoppe
Steve Berge
Big Jim's Guitars
Christian Brooks
Steve Brown
Harry Browning
David Chandler, R & R Guitars

Barry Clark
Competition Music
Don's Music
Murray Dychtwald
Chris Emery
Ferris Wheel Music
S.P. Fjestad
Zachary R. Fjestad
Jimmy Gravity
Dale Hanson
Harry Harris – GuitarTracker
Kaler Hendricks

Kelly Jones Violin Shop
Wallace Marx Jr.
Steve Matacia
George McGuire
Nick Meuwese
Dave Rogers - Dave's Guitar Shop
Shake Rag
Jason Scheuner
Allen Swan
Austin Thomelson
Tommy Thorson
TLC Guitars

Jack Wadsworth
Jimmy Wallace - Jimmy Wallace Guitars
Nate Westgor - Willie's American Guitars
Glenn Wetterland
Rick Wilkiewicz

FOREWORD

Welcome to the 5th Edition *Blue Book of Guitar Amplifiers*, now with 840 pages. You can be assured that no guitar amplifier book/database on this planet has more information and up-to-date values!

Since it's been six years since the 4th Edition was published, a lot of things have changed. The biggest change is that my nephew, Zachary, has opted out of further amplifier research and providing content. He developed this database from scratch starting in 2003, and the 1st Edition of the *Blue Book of Guitar Amplifiers* was published in October of 2004. While in Kansas City for a gun show in late July of last year, noted luthier, Jimmy Triggs came to the show to discuss the design and manufacture of a "guntar", an instrument that when completed will look and play like a guitar, but shoot like a gun (more news about this in the future). I mentioned to him that Zach was no longer involved with the database, and he looked at me and said, "How about Ryan?" his son, who was working full time at Triggs Guitars making both electric/acoustic guitars and mandolins. "Do you think he would be interested?" was my caught off guard response. So the three of us put our heads together and made a deal where Ryan would work on amplifier research and data entry approximately 25 hours a week, and spend the rest hand building fretted instruments.

Looking back, all of us were fortunate to take advantage of this unique situation, and this is a bigger, better book because of Ryan's involvement. Being a musician/guitarist, song writer, and luthier with an unusual set of credentials made him the perfect job candidate because he was already familiar with the technical aspects and technology unique to guitar amplifiers. While no doubt it was a daunting task to reel in six years worth of information/updates, this is proof that he did an amazing job!

So What's Changed During the Last Six Years?

- Many companies/manufacturers who were concentrating their focus on modeling amplifiers at the beginning of this decade have now moved on to making reissues of their most popular (and now spendy) amps from the 1950s and '60s. One of the biggest reasons for bringing back reissues is that the originals have gotten so expensive that offering these reissues makes them more affordable to the consumer. The jury is still out on how long this portion of the marketplace might last, however.

- Most of the guitar-playing baby boomers are now senior citizens who due to back problems, knee/hip replacements, and other medical issues are no longer strong enough to man handle the 40+ lb. Super Reverb and Marshall Twin Stacks of yesteryear. Accordingly, values on these older larger vintage amplifiers are down considerably, and this book addresses this trend. Also, today's newer crop of guitar players also prefers smaller amplifiers that are a lot more affordable, portable, and still strong on tone.

- Chinese/Pacific Rim manufactured amps from major companies are now the norm, and are in their third generation of manufacturing development. Twenty years from now, it will be interesting if any collectors and/or musicians will pay a premium for U.S. manufactured major trademark makes/models. In the guitar marketplace, this separation has already occurred.

The legendary Jim Marshall during a past Nashville NAMM show signing a 1st Edition *Blue Book of Guitar Amplifiers* for the publisher. Jim will long be remembered for his "iron-man" performances on signing and personalizing Marshall t-shirts during NAMM shows. He once told me that he autographed 1,000 t-shirts in two days!

Now I Have to Thank Some Folks Besides the Editor!

This title certainly would've never had the popularity and success without the dedication and non-stop research by my nephew Zachary. Also, I didn't find out until this edition how much work and effort Kelsey (niece) put in to making it the best publication possible. Once again, Clint Schmidt has done a fantastic job in the design and layout – no easy job when there are over 3,650 images that have to be manually placed within the manuscript. Lisa Beuning, long-term BBP data entry and proofing specialist, once again got involved in both the final editing and proofing guaranteeing this newest edition is as error-free as possible. Another well-deserved gracci goes to Sarah Peterson for her proofing contributions. A huge thanks to all the contributing editors and people/companies who have provided us with either information or images and have helped immensely with this project over the years (see Acknowledgements section).

In closing, don't forget that this entire database is available as an online subscription, now updated monthly - please visit www.bluebookofguitarvalues.com for more information and sample pages. Finally, thanks to you, the consumer for all your help and support in this project. We will continue to provide you with the most up-to-date information and accurate pricing for both new and vintage guitar amplifiers.

Sincerely,

S.P. Fjestad
Publisher
Blue Book of Guitar Amplifiers

INTRODUCTION

Welcome to the 5th Edition *Blue Book of Guitar Amplifiers*! Since this is the first title I've worked on for Blue Book Publications, Inc. I figured I should give you a little background about myself. I've been surrounded by musical instruments and gear my whole life. I grew up sweeping sawdust in my father Jim's workshop. You may be familiar with Jim from his tenure at the Gibson Guitar Corporation or seen one of the 700 guitars or mandolins he's handmade over the past 25 years. I've been helping him create custom stringed instruments for the last 15 years and I also spend a lot of time writing songs and playing live gigs in the Kansas City area. In 2015, the opportunity to take over as the Editor for the Guitar and Amps Division at Blue Book Publications, Inc. presented itself and I jumped at the chance. There will always be room for more music related work in my life.

While the scope of this publication is still the same as previous editions in offering you the most information and up-to-date values on new and used guitar and bass amplifiers, over time, we've made some changes to the book; I think you'll agree for the better. We now have over 3,500 amplifier images within our database, and it is just not possible to include every picture within the pages of the book. We've included several black and white images – mostly of "popular" or brand new models – but you can find all of our images in full color on our website for free. Within the text, you'll notice a ↓ that indicates one or more images of that model are available for viewing on our website. This can all be viewed in our Online Subscriptions on our website. If we don't embrace technology, we'll be left behind, besides, don't many of you look for guitars and guitar amplifiers online anyway? We have also included the Trademark Index contact information directly in the listing for most current manufacturers, eliminating cumbersome page flipping. This is the most complete and easiest-to-use *Blue Book of Guitar Amplifiers* yet!

It has been six years since the last printed version of the *Blue Book of Guitar Amplifiers* was published, but that doesn't mean it hasn't been worked on since then. Since this entire book is available for sale on our website as an Online Subscription that is updated quarterly, I'm constantly updating, editing, and adding to the database. This includes adding new models released each year, updating vintage guitar amp values, and fixing sections that may be wrong or need clarification. Some readers may be surprised that our sales are split nearly 50/50 today between selling books and online subscriptions. What this tells me is that our readers want their information and values the most-up-to-date as possible and wherever they go. We've offered Online Subscriptions for many years now, but we also have a website designed specifically for mobile devices. Using your web browser on your mobile device, you can view your Online Subscriptions anywhere you go. Also, don't forget that you can inventory your entire guitar and amp collection using Gear Tracker, a free service with the purchase of our Online Subscription that you use through our website that includes automatic value and information updates. Check our website at www.BlueBookofGuitarValues.com for more information.

One of the biggest changes in the amp industry since the 4th Edition was published is the growing popularity of smaller amplifiers. Gone are the days of needing a full stack to be considered a serious guitar player. The majority of today's musicians are looking for portability, functionality, and versatility in a lightweight amp at a reasonable price point. In addition, many current live music venues have invested in high quality PA systems that don't require guitarists to load in 100-watt tube heads with accompanying speaker cabinets. If you play in smaller clubs or listening rooms, it's likely that you can mic your amp or run direct to a stage console. With all those things considered, even a micro or "lunchbox" size amplifier would be adequate for most situations these days.

Since I began working on the 5th Edition I've focused on entering new models for the larger manufacturers, expanding the image database, and updating the values of many popular vintage models. My next goal as editor is to spend more time updating the entries for our boutique manufacturers. It can be a little more difficult to track down a list of their current models with pricing information or determine their used values, but boutique builders are a growing segment in the amplifier industry and I believe it's important to have their listings as up-to-date

as possible. As previously mentioned, this book is also available on our website, so you'll be able to see these updates as they take place if you take advantage of our Online Subscriptions.

As always, we want to hear from you! Whether it is positive or negative feedback, we want to know how we're doing (please be constructive in your criticism). Remember, if something is wrong or missing within these pages, we won't know about it if you don't tell us! A simple email can not only answer your question, but it also allows me to add it to the database so others will benefit as well.

I'd like to thank the following people for their assistance with this book: Zachary R. Fjestad, the previous author, for creating and maintaining such an incredible resource for the amplifier community over the last 14 years, trusting me enough to take the reins of the guitar and amplifier books, giving me an immeasurable amount of advice on how to do my job, and providing a substantial amount of the information in this Introduction; Jim Triggs, my father, for being so flexible with my schedule and allowing me the countless hours every week to work on the 5th Edition even though it slowed down our production at Triggs Guitars; Jessica Triggs, my wife, for being Supermom to our two beautiful daughters while I've been updating the amplifier database nearly every night and weekend for the last year; Rick Wilkiewicz for his guidance on updating vintage amp pricing; Clint H. Schmidt, our production manager and art director, for taking an incredible amount of data and thousands of images and turning it into something so beautiful; Sarah Peterson and Lisa Beuning for proofing this book from cover to cover and reminding me why I never excelled in literature class; Tom, Adam, Karl, Beth, Shauna and the rest of the Blue Book team that has helped me out along the way; and S.P. Fjestad for the opportunity to work for Blue Book Publications, Inc. and believing that I could handle this project and the tremendous amount of responsibility that comes along with it. There are also many contributing editors and other people who make this book what it is and I couldn't do it without you!

Sincerely,

Ryan Triggs
Editor
Blue Book of Guitar Amplifiers

HOW TO USE THIS BOOK

When used properly, the 5th Edition *Blue Book of Guitar Amplifiers* will provide you with more up-to-date guitar amplifier information and pricing than any other single source. With over 840 pages of specific amp models and pricing, this publication continues to be more of a complete informational source than strictly a "hold-your-hand" pricing guide. In theory, you should be able to identify the trademark/name off of the amp (where applicable), and find out the country of origin, date(s) produced, and other company/model-related facts for that amp. Many smaller, out-of-production trademarks and/or companies that are only infrequently encountered in the secondary marketplace are intentionally not priced in this text, as it is pretty hard to pin the tail on a donkey that is nowhere in sight. Unfortunately, this lack of information can be a disadvantage to sellers, who may find buyers saying, "Would you take any less? After all, nobody seems to know anything about it." In other words, don't confuse rarity with desirability when it comes to these informational voids. As in the past, if you own this current 5th Edition of the *Blue Book of Guitar Amplifiers* and still have questions, we will try to assist you in identifying/evaluating your amplifier(s). Please refer to page 30 for this service.

The values listed in the 5th Edition *Blue Book of Guitar Amplifiers* are based on average national selling prices for both currently manufactured and vintage amplifiers. This is **NOT** a wholesale pricing guide – prices reflect what you should expect to pay for a amplifier. More importantly, do not expect to walk into a music store, guitar shop, or pawn shop, and think that the proprietor should pay you the retail price listed in this text. Dealer offers on most models could be 20%-50% less than the values listed, depending upon desirability, locality, and profitability.

In other words, if you want to receive 100% of the value listed in the book, then you have to do 100% of the work (become the retailer, which also includes assuming 100% of the risk). Business is business, and making regular bank deposits usually means turning a profit every once in a while.

Currently manufactured amplifiers are typically listed with the manufacturer's suggested retail (MSR), a 100% value (reflecting standard market place discounting if applicable), and in most cases, values for both Excellent and Average condition factors are included. Please consult the revised digital color Photo Grading System (pages 33-48) to learn more about the condition of your amplifier(s). The *Blue Book of Guitar Amplifiers* will continue using selected photos to illustrate real world condition factors and/or problems. Since condition is the overriding factor in price evaluation, study these photos carefully. As the saying goes, one picture can be worth a thousand words.

For your convenience, an explanation of factors that can affect condition and pricing, amplifier grading systems, how to convert them, and descriptions of individual condition factors appear on page 32 to assist you in learning more about guitar grading systems and individual condition factors. Please read these pages carefully, as the values in this publication are based on the grading/condition factors listed. This will be especially helpful when evaluating older vintage amplifiers. Remember, the price is wrong if the condition factor isn't right.

All values within this text assume original condition. The grading lines within the *Blue Book of Guitar Amplifiers* reflect the 100%, Excellent, and Average condition factors only. From the vintage marketplace or (especially) a collector's point of view, any repairs, alterations, modifications, "enhancements," "improvements," "professionally modified to a more desirable configuration," or any other non-factory changes usually detract from an amplifier's value. Please refer to page 31 regarding an explanation to coverings, repairs, alterations/modifications, and other elements which have to be factored in before determining the correct condition. Depending on the seriousness of the modification/alteration, you may have to lower the condition factor when re-computing prices for these alterations. Determining values for damaged and/or previously repaired amplifiers will usually depend on the parts and labor costs necessary to return them to playable and/or original specifications.

A new feature for the 5th Edition is that all 3,250+ color amplifier images are available for viewing on our website. Within the text, a small guitar icon ♩ appears whenever a corresponding image(s) is available and you can refer to our Online Subscription on our website to see a full color image(s).

The 5th Edition *Blue Book of Guitar Amplifiers* provides many company histories, notes on influential luthiers and designers, and other bits of knowledge as a supplement to the make/model format. Hopefully, this information will alleviate those "gray areas" of the unknown, and shed light on many new luthiers who have emerged within the past several decades, and produce excellent quality amplifiers.

We reformatted and redesigned the *Blue Book of Guitar Amplifiers* to maximize the value of the book. We utilize as much white space as possible (paper isn't cheap) and instead of including all images, we have included select black and white images, but every image in our database is available on our website. We hope that this is still an easy-to-use (and consistent) text format that will assist you in quickly finding specific information. The following pages detail every component that you will encounter in the 5th Edition *Blue Book of Guitar Amplifiers*.

- Add $45 for a Celestion G12M-70 speaker.
- Add $45 for a Celestion Classic Lead speaker.
- Add $55 for tweed covering.

- Add $100 for a Celestion Century 80W speaker.
- Add $200 for a Celestion Blue 15W speaker (disc.).
- Add $275 for a hard shell case (disc.).

EGNATER

Amplifiers and speaker cabinets currently produced in Berkley, MI. Previously produced in Pontiac, MI from 1980 to 2003. Distributed by Boutique Amps Distribution in Huntington Park, CA.

CONTACT INFORMATION
EGNATER
3383 Gage Ave.
Huntington Park, CA 90255
Phone No.: 323-277-4119
Phone No.: 877-346-2837
Fax No.: 323-277-4110
www.egnateramps.com
info@egnateramps.com

Bruce Egnater founded Egnater Custom Amplification in 1980. Egnater started out like many amp builders: he was looking for a certain tone out of a guitar amp and no product existed in the market, so he set out to create his own. In the 1970s, true tube saturation was only achieved by running a Marshall amp wide open. Egnater took a small Gibson amp book and replaced the speaker with a resistor and inserted the output from the Gibson amp into the input of a Marshall 200 Watt head that allowed the guitarist to add distortion without turning up volume. Egnater later came up with a channel switching amp that could produce both clean and overdrive tones from the same unit. Egnater received a patent for his modular musical amplification system where the pre-amp sections of an amp are modular and can be changed out of an amp. In the late 2000s, Egnater introduced a full line of standard tube amplifiers. They currently produce custom modular amplifier combos, heads, pre-amps and speaker cabinets. For more information, visit Egnater's website or contact the company directly.

ELECTRIC TUBE AMPS: MOD SERIES

Egnater offers modular tube amplifiers in head or combo versions. Both of these models have the same specifications, which include: High power 50W and Low power 10W, two channels, a power tube section that is able to be self biased with any tube, (but is sold only with 5881) with serial and parallel effects loops. Reverb is optional and a footswitch is included. The **Mod 50** has 50W/10W power and is available as a head-unit (MSR $2,250), 1-12 in. combo (MSR $2,995). The **Mod 100** has 100W power with six channel modules and is now discontinued

The **M4 Preamp** (MSR $2,100) follows the technology that has taken amplifier companies into the 21st Century. This certain model is different than most amps that are out there because you can actually plug in four different all tube module units. This system works as a rack-mounted pre amp and the four module units can be taken out by two simple screws and switched with another for a different sound. Additional modules are available for $400 a piece (see website for full listing of modules).

1. Manufacturer/Trademark Name - The manufacturer, trademark, brand name, builder, company, importer, or distributor is listed in uppercase and bold type. These are centered on each page and listed alphabetically throughout the book.

2. Manufacturer/Trademark Status - Any information regarding the production status of the manufacturer is listed directly below the manufacturer name. This includes whether amplifiers are currently or were previously produced, when they were produced, where they were produced, and any distributor and/or importer information.

3. Manufacturer/Trademark Description - This area typically describes the history of the manufacturer and/or trademark/brand. If the section is small enough, all following information may be included in this area including model descriptions and pricing.

4. Category Name - When a manufacturer/trademark is long enough, the section may be split up into categories. Category names appear in bold uppercase and are centered on each page. Categories are typically broken up into the amplifiers' primary configuration (Electric Tube Amps, Electric Solid-State Amps, Acoustic Amplifiers, etc.). Categories may also include general information, identification, options, etc.

5. Category Description - Some categories may have a description (some categories may only have a description with no models). This description contains information specific to the category.

6. Contact Information – On most current manufacturers and a select few previous manufacturers who still are accessible, their contact information will appear in a gray box below the manufacturer name and justified to the right. This used to appear in the Trademark Index at the back of the book, but it is included directly in the text now.

7. Model Name and Description - Categories are typically comprised of individual model listings and descriptions. A model name is listed in bold uppercase text, flush left, and they are typically listed alpha-numerically. Manufacturer model designations/codes may appear in parentheses after the model name (i.e. Fender has a number code for every model). A model name is followed by the description, and contains important information specific to the model name. Typically, this includes wattage, configuration, speakers, tube complement, chassis type, controls, effects, features, covering and grille cloth options, dimensions, specifications, year of mfg., finishes, etc. The following list explains in detail what appears in the model description:

Wattage - Indicates the RMS wattage of an amp (or peak when noted) or the handling power of a speaker cabinet. Whenever possible all wattages are listed at different impedances. For example, 35W, 70W, 50W (2 X 25W Stereo), 150W peak power, 350W @ 2 ohms (200W @ 4 ohms, 75W @ 8 ohms).

Speakers - If the amp is a combo unit or sold as a piggyback unit, the speakers will be listed here. If the amp is only a head unit, this section will not be included. For example, 1-12 in. speaker, 2-15 in. speakers, 2-12 in. speakers in a separate cabinet.

Configuration - Amps come as head units, combos, piggyback units, and speaker cabinets. Amps are also typically designated for guitar (lead), bass, acoustic, or other applications. If the amp is in head-unit configuration, the information and price will reflect only the head. If the amp is a piggyback, the information assumes that both the head and the speaker cabinet are combined, but the *Blue Book of Guitar Amplifiers* often lists separate prices for head units, cabinets, and both. For example, head-unit lead configuration, combo bass configuration, piggyback guitar configuration, combo acoustic configuration.

Chassis Design - Amps typically come as one of three chassis: tube, solid-state, or hybrid. If it is a tube chassis, the number of tubes will be listed (dual purpose tubes are only counted as one) followed by a tube layout when possible. Most of the time, solid-state chassis will only read "solid-state chassis" unless the number of diodes and/or transistors is known. For hybrid chassis, the different components will be labeled depending on what is tube and what is solid-state. For example, nine tube chassis, preamp: 4 X 12AX7, power: 4 X 6L6, rectifier: 5AR4, solid-state chassis (9 diodes, 15 transistors), hybrid chassis, preamp: 2 X 12AX7, power: solid-state, rectifier: solid-state.

Channels - All amps have at least one channel, but many have more than one. The number of channels on a guitar amp will be listed here. Refer to Appendix B: Glossary for what defines a separate channel. If an amp has channels plus different modes, this will be listed here as well. For example, single channel, two channels, three channels, two channels with four modes.

Built-In Effects - Since many guitar amps are different based on their effects, they will be listed next. These will only include factory installed effects. For example: reverb, tremolo, vibrato, echo, chorus, distortion, delay, flange, etc.

Location and color of the control panel - Control panels are found in many different areas of an amp, and it is helpful to identify when these are known. Control panels can be mounted in the front, back, top, or bottom of an amp, and they come in a variety of colors. For example: front black control panel, top chrome control panel, rear black control panel, front silver and red control panel.

Number of Inputs - Guitar amplifier inputs range from one and up. The number all depends upon the complexity, purpose, and number of channels the amp has. For example: single input, two inputs, four inputs (two normal, two vibrato), six inputs (two per channel).

Knobs - Whenever possible, the *Blue Book of Guitar Amplifiers* will list all the knobs on the control panel (and other knobs if applicable). Almost all knobs are abbreviated to save space and redundancy in listings (refer to the abbreviations section for more information).

Switches, buttons, displays, and other items on the control panel - Any other miscellaneous amp controls that are not knobs will be listed after the knobs. Since there are so many other controls this section can contain just about anything. For example, bright switch, deep switch, channel switch, polarity switch, programmable buttons, digital display, impedance selectors, etc.

Misc. jacks - Most guitar amplifiers have jacks besides the guitar input jacks. Any of these jacks will be included after all other controls. For example, effects loop, tuner out, preamp out, power amp in, headphone jack, external speaker jacks, etc.

Footswitch - If the amp has a footswitch, it will be listed here and display the number of buttons it has. If available, the *Blue Book of Guitar Amplifiers* will indicate what functions the footswitch serves. For example: two button footswitch, two one button footswitches (one for reverb, one for tremolo), four-button footswitch, six-button footswitch with MIDI, etc.

Any other features - Anything else that does not fall into the previous categories as far as amp features may be included. For example, tilt-back legs, angled cabinet design, construction styles, handles, wheels/casters, trim features, etc.

Covering - The color and type of covering will be indicated next. If the amp's cabinet is a hardwood without covering, this will be noted here as well. If more than one covering is available, more than one covering style was available for the same model during different years, or not all coverings are known, the *Blue Book of Guitar Amplifiers* will make note of this whenever possible. For example, black Tolex covering, two-tone brown and gray covering, tweed covering (1958-1961) or brown leatherette covering (1962-1964), various color coverings, etc.

Grille Cloth - After the covering is listed, the grille cloth should come next if applicable (some head units may not have a grille so nothing will be listed). If more than one grille is available, more than one grille style was available for the same model during different years, or not all grilles are known, the Blue *Book of Guitar Amplifiers* will make note of this whenever possible. For example, brown grille cloth, silver grille cloth with blue accents, gray grille cloth (1957-1960) or black grille cloth (1961-1967), various grille cloths, etc.

Dimensions/weight - Whenever possible/applicable the *Blue Book of Guitar Amplifiers* will list the dimensions and weight of the amp. Width is the measurement from one side to the other when looking at the amp from the front. Height (tall) is the measurement from the bottom to the top. Depth is the measurement from the front to the back. It will be noted when the amp does not have square dimensions. All measurements are listed in inches and decimals (no fractions) unless otherwise noted, and they usually come from the manufacturer's catalogs or specs (the *Blue Book of Guitar Amplifiers* does not take a tape measure to every amp we encounter). Weight is measured in pounds (lbs.) and is also taken from the manufacturer's catalogs of specs. For example, 24 in. wide, 20 in. tall, 10.5 in. deep, 35.5 lbs, 22.375 in. wide, 28.125 in. tall, 9.875 in. deep, 45.6 lbs.

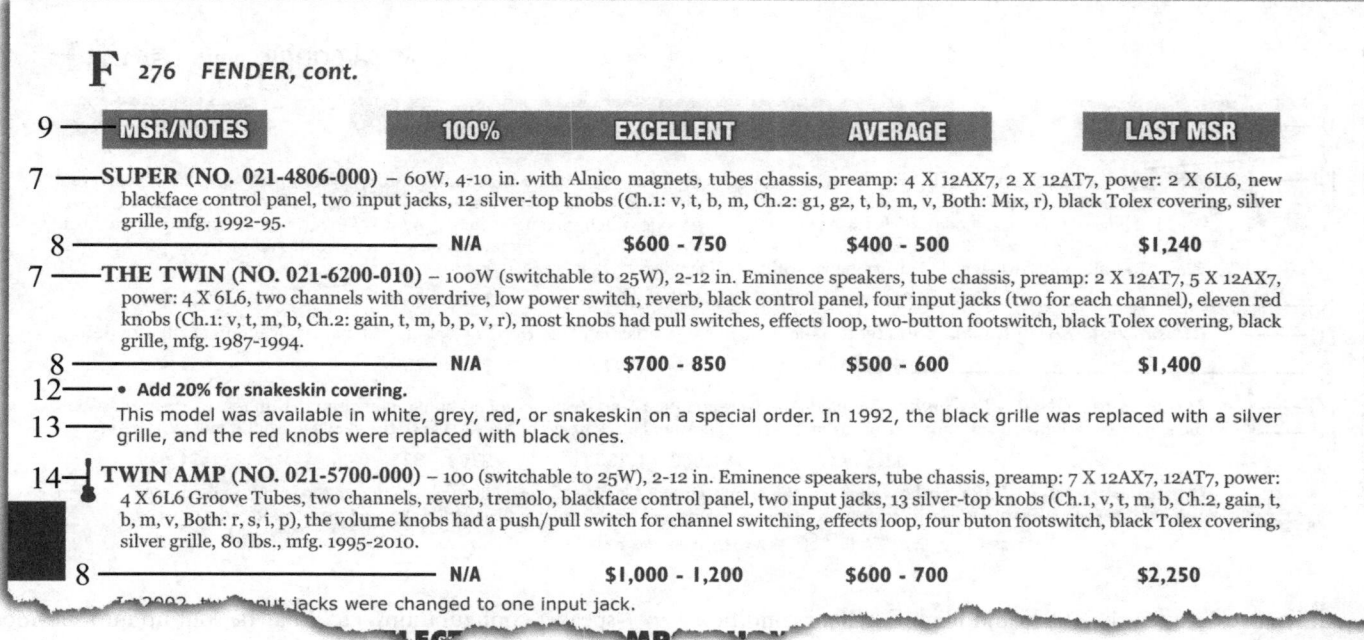

F 276 FENDER, cont.

9 MSR/NOTES	100%	EXCELLENT	AVERAGE	LAST MSR

7 **SUPER (NO. 021-4806-000)** – 60W, 4-10 in. with Alnico magnets, tubes chassis, preamp: 4 X 12AX7, 2 X 12AT7, power: 2 X 6L6, new blackface control panel, two input jacks, 12 silver-top knobs (Ch.1: v, t, b, m, Ch.2: g1, g2, t, b, m, v, Both: Mix, r), black Tolex covering, silver grille, mfg. 1992-95.

8 ——— N/A $600 - 750 $400 - 500 $1,240

7 **THE TWIN (NO. 021-6200-010)** – 100W (switchable to 25W), 2-12 in. Eminence speakers, tube chassis, preamp: 2 X 12AT7, 5 X 12AX7, power: 4 X 6L6, two channels with overdrive, low power switch, reverb, black control panel, four input jacks (two for each channel), eleven red knobs (Ch.1: v, t, m, b, Ch.2: gain, t, m, b, p, v, r), most knobs had pull switches, effects loop, two-button footswitch, black Tolex covering, black grille, mfg. 1987-1994.

8 ——— N/A $700 - 850 $500 - 600 $1,400

12 • **Add 20% for snakeskin covering.**

13 This model was available in white, grey, red, or snakeskin on a special order. In 1992, the black grille was replaced with a silver grille, and the red knobs were replaced with black ones.

14 **TWIN AMP (NO. 021-5700-000)** – 100 (switchable to 25W), 2-12 in. Eminence speakers, tube chassis, preamp: 7 X 12AX7, 12AT7, power: 4 X 6L6 Groove Tubes, two channels, reverb, tremolo, blackface control panel, two input jacks, 13 silver-top knobs (Ch.1, v, t, m, b, Ch.2, gain, t, b, m, v, Both: r, s, i, p), the volume knobs had a push/pull switch for channel switching, effects loop, four buton footswitch, black Tolex covering, silver grille, 80 lbs., mfg. 1995-2010.

8 ——— N/A $1,000 - 1,200 $600 - 700 $2,250

In 2002, the input jacks were changed to one input jack.

Fraction-to-decimal equivalent - 1/8: 0.125, 1/4: 0.25, 3/8: 0.375, 1/2: 0.5, 5/8: 0.625, 3/4: 0.75, 7/8: 0.875

Year of Manufacture - The year of manufacture is very important in identifying the amplifier. Since the actual years of manufacture, the selling dates, and advertised dates may all vary quite a bit, the *Blue Book of Guitar Amplifiers* needs to clarify this issue. With the exception of Gibson, actual shipping/selling dates are not known or considered in the year of manufacture. The advertised dates (by catalog and price list whenever possible) are used most often. For instance, if an amplifier was actually produced between 1957 and 1961, it could have shipped through 1962, and advertised until 1963 depending upon how often they updated their catalog. Which one is correct then? That is up to you to decide! The *Blue Book of Guitar Amplifiers* strives for consistency and the best way to do that is use the most available information, which is usually from catalogs and price lists. If the start or end of production dates is unknown, they will be listed differently. For example, mfg. 1956-1962, mfg. 1964-67, mfg. 1985-disc. (used when the production end date is unknown), disc. 1996 (used when the start production date is unknown, and it means 1996 was the last year of production/availability), mfg. late 1980s-early 1990s (used when an approximate range of years is known), mfg. 1990s (used when a wide range of years is known), etc.

8. Price Lines - Price lines are typically located directly under a model description. These are used to evaluate the individual model, and price ranges appear in Excellent and Average condition factors. A grading bar appears on the top of all pages that contain at least one price line. Many price lines in the *Blue Book of Guitar Amplifiers* include either an amp's MSR or Notes line (see Grading Line, #9), 100% price, Excellent price range, Average price range, and last MSR (if known). These five areas make up all pricing for the book:

MSR/Notes: If the model is currently manufactured, and has a factory retail price, the MSR price will appear flush left. If a model justifies more than one price line, the Notes will indicate what features or years of manufacture are represented by the additional price lines.

100%: The 100% condition factor (new), when encountered in a currently manufactured amp, assumes the amp has not been previously sold at retail and includes a factory warranty. A currently manufactured new amplifier must include EVERYTHING the factory originally provided with the amp – including the cover (if originally included), warranty card, instruction manual (if any), hanging tags (if any), footswitch, etc. If the model is currently or recently manufactured (2012 or later), the value will appear in this column. This is the price a consumer should expect to pay on an amplifier, which includes all standard discounting, and usually takes into consideration factory MAP (Minimum Advertised Pricing). Nearly all manufacturers establish retail pricing, but instruments rarely sell for the MSR, and sell closer to the MAP. If the instrument is 2011 or older, or is currently not available for sale, an N/A (Not Applicable) will appear in this field.

Excellent: If the model is in excellent condition, the value range will be displayed in this column. The lowest value in this range represents Low Excellent condition while the higher one represents High Excellent condition. The High Excellent condition factor represents a slightly used instrument that appears new but no longer qualifies for 100% since it has already sold at retail, and may be worth only 50%-90% of its current MSR, depending on the overall desirability factor. On currently/recently manufactured amplifiers, there usually is a fairly large price

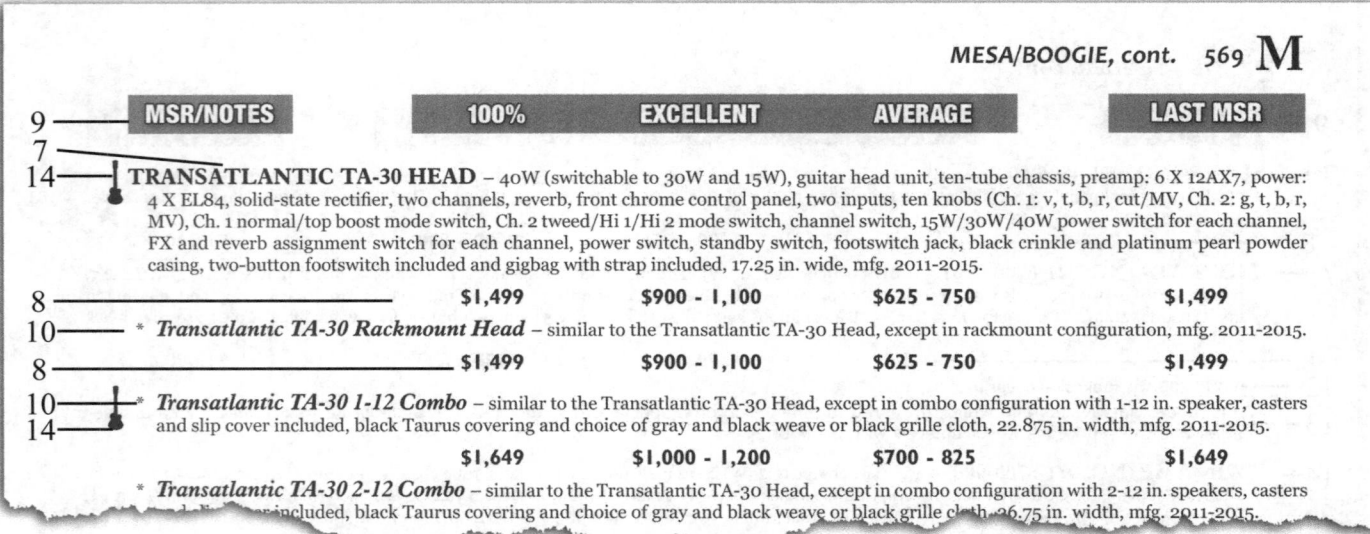

MSR/NOTES	100%	EXCELLENT	AVERAGE	LAST MSR
TRANSATLANTIC TA-30 HEAD – 40W (switchable to 30W and 15W), guitar head unit, ten-tube chassis, preamp: 6 X 12AX7, power: 4 X EL84, solid-state rectifier, two channels, reverb, front chrome control panel, two inputs, ten knobs (Ch. 1: v, t, b, r, cut/MV, Ch. 2: g, t, b, r, MV), Ch. 1 normal/top boost mode switch, Ch. 2 tweed/Hi 1/Hi 2 mode switch, channel switch, 15W/30W/40W power switch for each channel, FX and reverb assignment switch for each channel, power switch, standby switch, footswitch jack, black crinkle and platinum pearl powder casing, two-button footswitch included and gigbag with strap included, 17.25 in. wide, mfg. 2011-2015.				
	$1,499	$900 - 1,100	$625 - 750	$1,499
* Transatlantic TA-30 Rackmount Head – similar to the Transatlantic TA-30 Head, except in rackmount configuration, mfg. 2011-2015.				
	$1,499	$900 - 1,100	$625 - 750	$1,499
* Transatlantic TA-30 1-12 Combo – similar to the Transatlantic TA-30 Head, except in combo configuration with 1-12 in. speaker, casters and slip cover included, black Taurus covering and choice of gray and black weave or black grille cloth, 22.875 in. width, mfg. 2011-2015.				
	$1,649	$1,000 - 1,200	$700 - 825	$1,649
* Transatlantic TA-30 2-12 Combo – similar to the Transatlantic TA-30 Head, except in combo configuration with 2-12 in. speakers, casters and slip cover included, black Taurus covering and choice of gray and black weave or black grille cloth, 26.75 in. width, mfg. 2011-2015.				

difference between the 100% and High Excellent condition factors due to used instrument pricing, which typically is affected by dealer replacement costs. Refer to the Photo Grading System on pages 33-48 to determine the condition of your amplifier. An N/A may also appear in this condition factor indicating the amp's rarity precludes accurate pricing.

Average: If the model is in average condition, the value range will be displayed in this column. The lowest value in this range represents Low Average condition while the higher one represents High Average condition. Refer to the Photo Grading System on pages 33-48 to determine the condition of your amplifier.

Last MSR: Once a model is discontinued, the MSR will be moved to this column. While the last MSR of a model is generally used for historical purposes, it is also useful for determining used values, especially on run-of-the-mill amplifiers. Many guitar amp dealers look at the last MSR and base the used value off of that.

9. Grading Line - This grading line is the typical page header, and provides three distinct column locations (left to right) including the manufacturer's suggested retail (MSR) on currently manufactured amplifiers (if published). Important notes may also be part of this column, which include year/period of manufacture, identifying features, options, etc. that may result in multiple price lines per model. The wide middle column includes all pertinent new/used evaluating including the 100%/New value, the Excellent value range, and the Average value range. The last column indicates the Last MSR whenever applicable. Once a model is discontinued, the MSR will be moved to this column, which is helpful in determining used values.

10. Sub-model Name and Description - Models that have several variations (i.e. combo, head-unit, piggyback, multiple speaker configurations, etc.) may be split up into sub-models. In this case, any sub-models would be listed directly below the model. These are displayed in lowercase and italics, are indented more than the model name, and a have an asterisk before the model name. All other listings are the same as the model name.

11. Sub-Sub-model Name and Description (not picutred) - Sub-models that have several variations (i.e. combos, head-units, limited editions, multiple speaker configurations, etc.) may be split up into sub-sub-models. In this case, any sub-sub-models would be listed directly below the submodel. These are displayed in lowercase, and are slightly more indented than the sub-model. All other listings are the same as the model name.

12. Model Price Adjustment - Options, special orders, and other value add/subtract items apply to many models. This may include optional reverb, tremolo, coverings, unique features, etc. These price adjustments will be displayed as an add or subtract value to and an amount or a percentage. Actual dollar amounts are typically added on currently or recently manufactured instruments (mostly referring to the current or last MSR of that option) and percentages are used on many vintage instruments. Percentages may also be used on currently or recently manufactured amplifiers in certain situations (i.e. A custom color covering option of $250 on a $1,000 amplifier only applies the amount to the MSR price because the amp in 60-70% condition is only worth $500 and you can only apply 50% of the covering option to the current value. In other words you can't apply a 100% price to a covering, when the finish devalues along with the entire amp. There may be several model price adjustments after each model, sub-model, or sub-sub-model.

13. Model Notes - Any additional information pertaining to the model, sub-model, or sub-sub-model description will

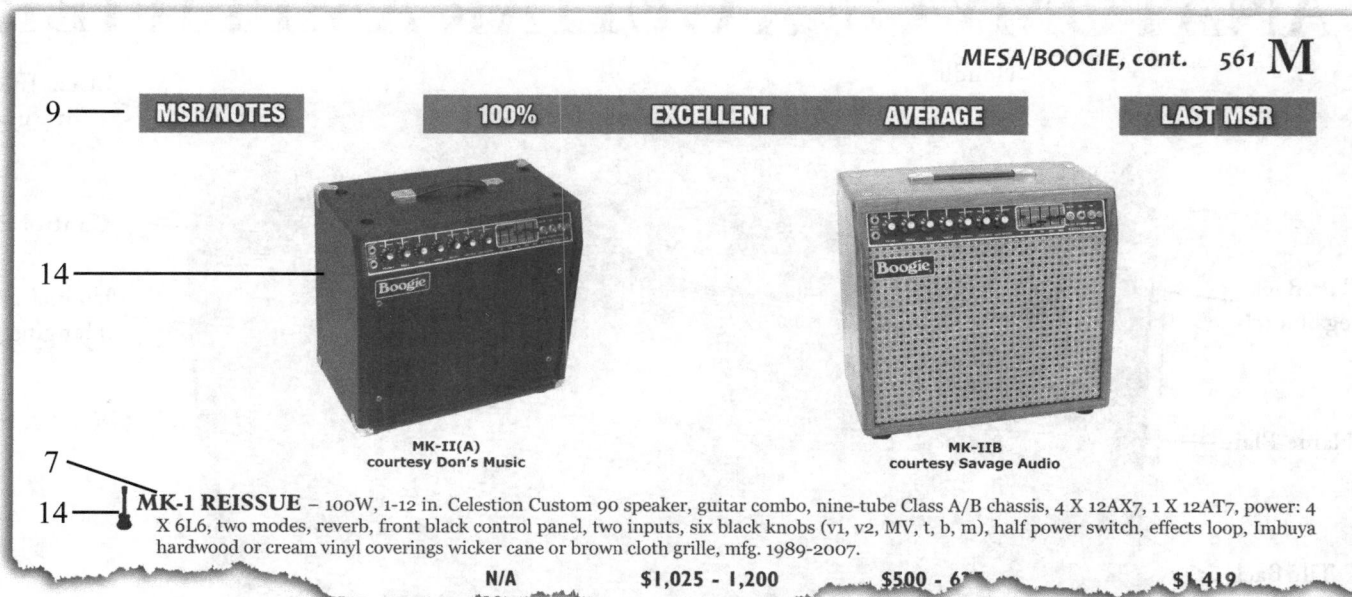

MESA/BOOGIE, cont.   561 M

9 —— | MSR/NOTES | 100% | EXCELLENT | AVERAGE | LAST MSR |

14 ——

MK-II(A)
courtesy Don's Music

Boogie

MK-IIB
courtesy Savage Audio

7 ——
14 —— **MK-1 REISSUE** – 100W, 1-12 in. Celestion Custom 90 speaker, guitar combo, nine-tube Class A/B chassis, 4 X 12AX7, 1 X 12AT7, power: 4 X 6L6, two modes, reverb, front black control panel, two inputs, six black knobs (v1, v2, MV, t, b, m), half power switch, effects loop, Imbuya hardwood or cream vinyl coverings wicker cane or brown cloth grille, mfg. 1989-2007.

| N/A | $1,025 - 1,200 | $500 - 6?? | $1,419 |

be displayed last including changes to the model during its production, finish changes, and other information pertinent to the model.

14. Images – Images of amplifiers are shown whenever possible and whenever sensible. Since images of guitar amplifiers come in several different sizes, it is difficult to stay consistent with one format. In order to save space and make the most of our book, we may have to place the images at a distance from the actual model. Normally, we try to group images at the top of the page or at the beginning of a category. For most vintage amplifiers, a front and back image (when available) will appear between the model description and the price line. For many new amplifiers, only the front image

will be displayed at the top of the respective page or section (along with up to two others per line). Whenever the image does not fall directly between the model description and the price line, a caption with courtesy will appear directly below each image. If the image falls between the model description and the price line only a courtesy caption will not appear.

The guitar icon ⌁ indicates that there is an amplifier image or images available for that manufacturer or model on our website through our Online Subscription. Our Online Subscription is formatted exactly like the book where you select the letter of manufacturer, the manufacturer, category, and model. Visit our website at guitars.bluebookinc.com for more information.

ABBREVIATIONS

Due to space constraints, the *Blue Book of Guitar Amplifiers* utilizes an abbreviation system to shorten lengthy and redundant listings. Abbreviations are most often used in the model description (see How To Use section) when describing the amp's features including the control panel. For instance, a control panel with 9 knobs may be listed like this: (Ch. 1: v, b, t, Ch. 2: v, b, t, r, s, i). The control panel has nine knobs with a volume, bass, and treble control for channel 1, and a volume, bass, treble, reverb, speed, and intensity for channel 2. If an amp has more than three channels and knobs for each one, the abbreviations may get more compact. For instance a control with 21 knobs with six knobs the same for each channel may be listed like this: (v, b, m, t, p, g for each channel, All: r, MV, FX level). For this amp, each of the three channels has a volume, bass, mid, treble, presence, and gain, along with three master channels. If the amp has separate channels but they share common controls, they may be listed like this: (v1, v2, tone) or (Ch. 1: v, tone, Ch. 2: v, tone, All: r, s, i).

b..............Bass	**h** ....High	**MSR** ....Manufacturer's	**Ser. No.** ..Serial number
bs ....Bright Switch	**i** ....Intensity (tremolo	Suggested Retail	**t** ....Treble
c..............Contour	or vibrato)	**MV** ....Master Volume	**trem** ....Tremolo
Ch...........Channel	**in.** ....Inch	**N/A**.........Not Applicable	**v**..............Volume
d..............Depth (tremolo	**inst.**..........instrument	**OD** ....Overdrive	**vib**...........vibrato
or vibrato)	**l**...............Low	**p**..............Presence	**W**...........Watt or wattage
ds ....Deep Switch	**l/m**...........Low/Mid	**PGS** ....Photo Grading	**w/** ....with
e..............Edge	**m** ....Middle	System	**w/o**.........without
EQ ....Equalizer	**m/h** ....Mid/High	**r** ....Reverb	**w/in** ....within
freq. ....Frequency	**mic**..........Microphone	**s** ....Speed (tremolo	
FS ....Footswitch	**mfg** ....Manufactured	or vibrato)	
g..............Gain	(typically dates)	**ss**..............Solid-state	

ANATOMY OF A GUITAR AMPLIFIER

Handle

Black Tolex Covering

Control Panel

Tilt Back Legs Notch

Original Factory Hanging Tag

Name Plate

Grille Cloth

Tilt Back Legs

Owner's Manual

Metal Corners

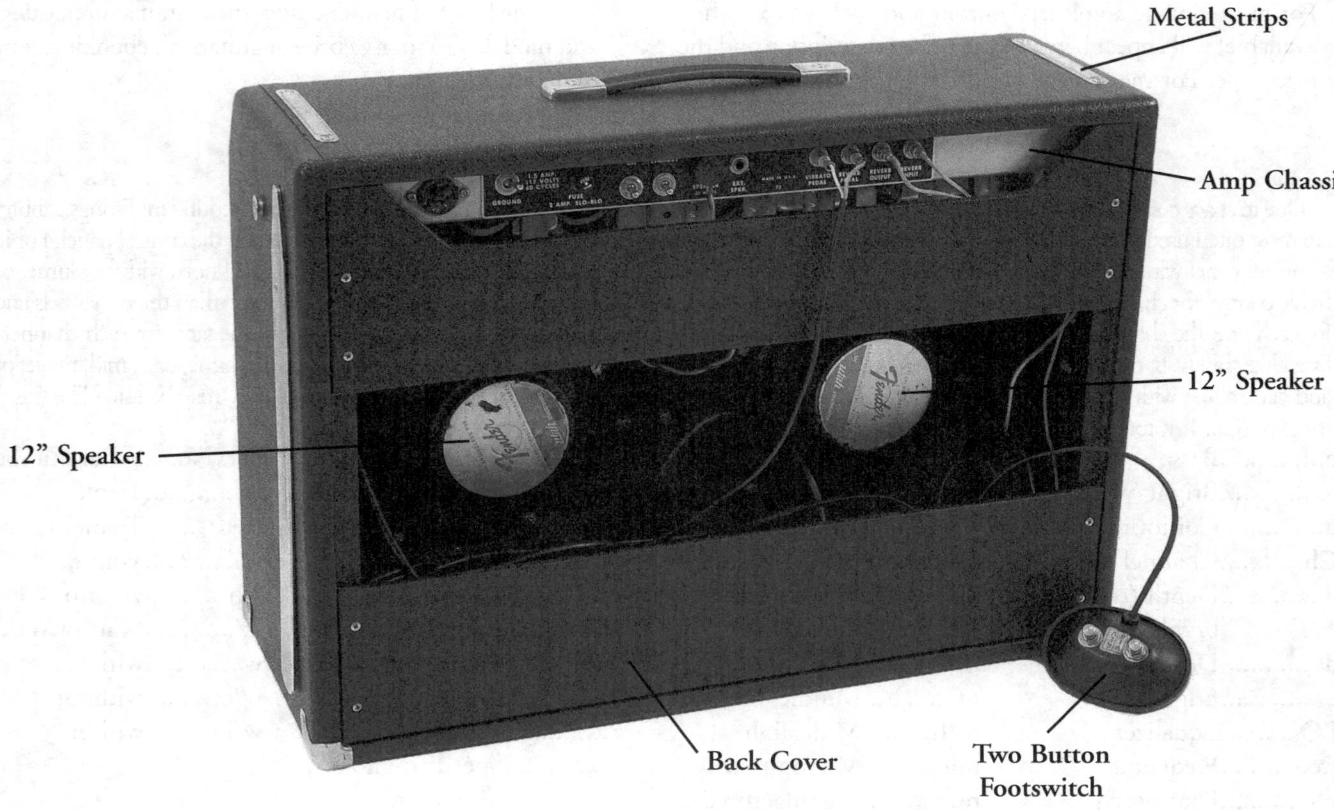

Metal Strips

Amp Chassis

12" Speaker

12" Speaker

Back Cover

Two Button Footswitch

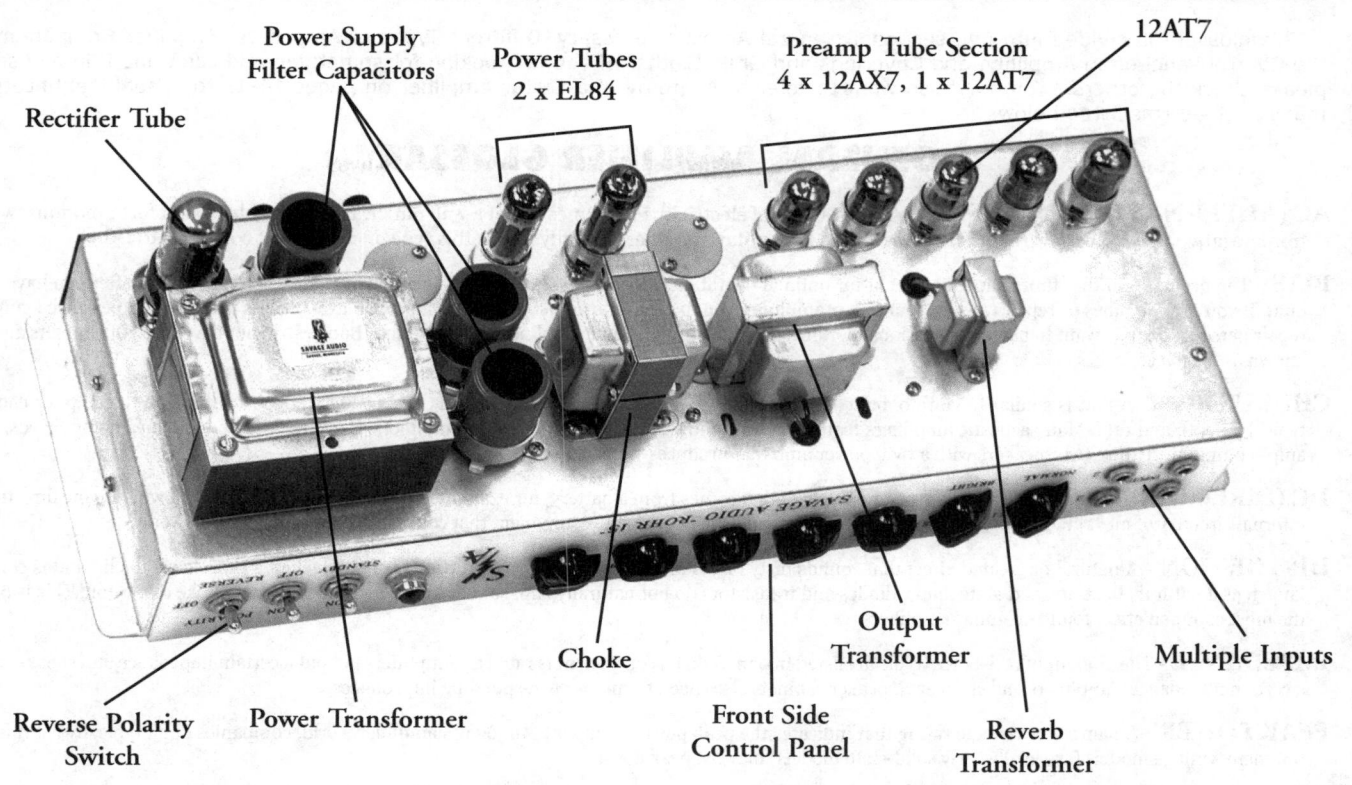

Power Supply Filter Capacitors

Rectifier Tube

Power Tubes 2 x EL84

Preamp Tube Section 4 x 12AX7, 1 x 12AT7

12AT7

Output Transformer

Multiple Inputs

Choke

Reverse Polarity Switch

Power Transformer

Front Side Control Panel

Reverb Transformer

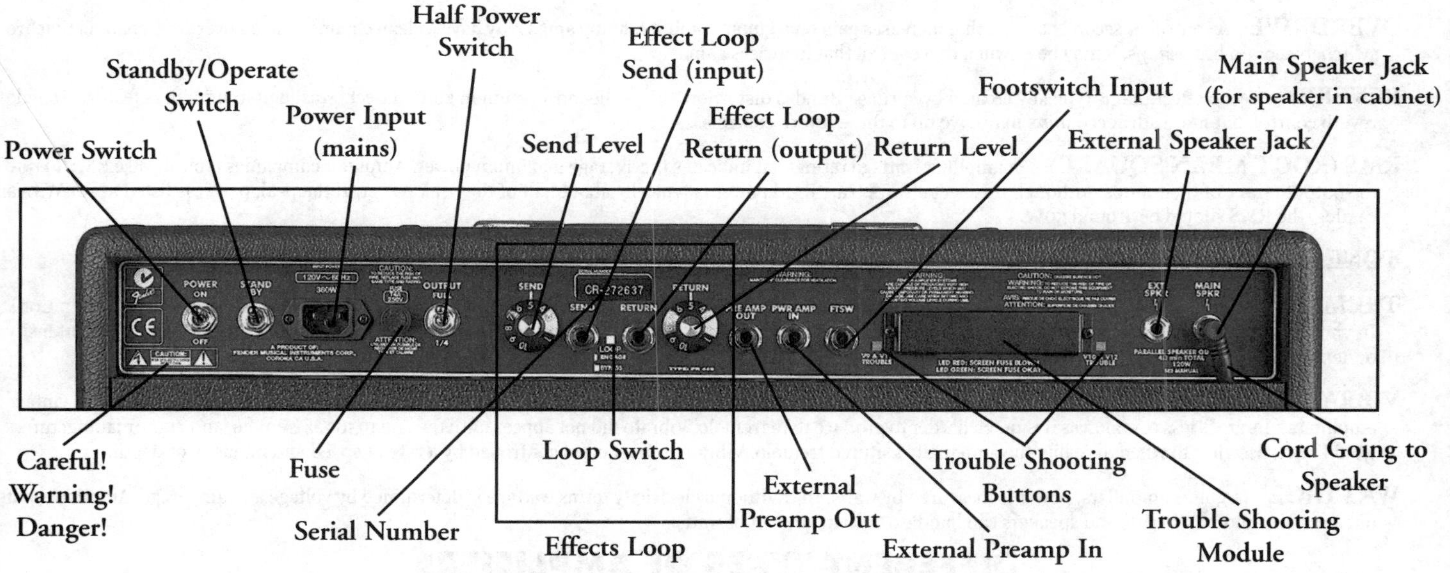

Half Power Switch

Standby/Operate Switch

Effect Loop Send (input)

Footswitch Input

Main Speaker Jack (for speaker in cabinet)

Power Switch

Power Input (mains)

Send Level

Effect Loop Return (output)

Return Level

External Speaker Jack

Careful! Warning! Danger!

Fuse

Loop Switch

Cord Going to Speaker

Serial Number

External Preamp Out

Trouble Shooting Buttons

Trouble Shooting Module

Effects Loop

External Preamp In

Bright Boost Switch

Bass (Low Range)

Gain (Pre-amp Distortion)

Tremolo Intensity

Treble (High Range)

Middle Range

Tremolo Speed

Presence Control

Volume

Reverb Knob

Channel 2

Pro Reverb Amp

FENDER MUSICAL INSTRUMENTS

INPUT

VOLUME TREBLE BASS MIDDLE   GAIN TREBLE BASS MIDDLE VOLUME CH SELECT   REVERB SPEED INTENSITY PRESENCE

Single Input

Channel 1

Treble (High Range)

Bass (Low Range)

Middle Range

Volume

Channel Selecter Switch

Controls for both Channels

Pilot Light

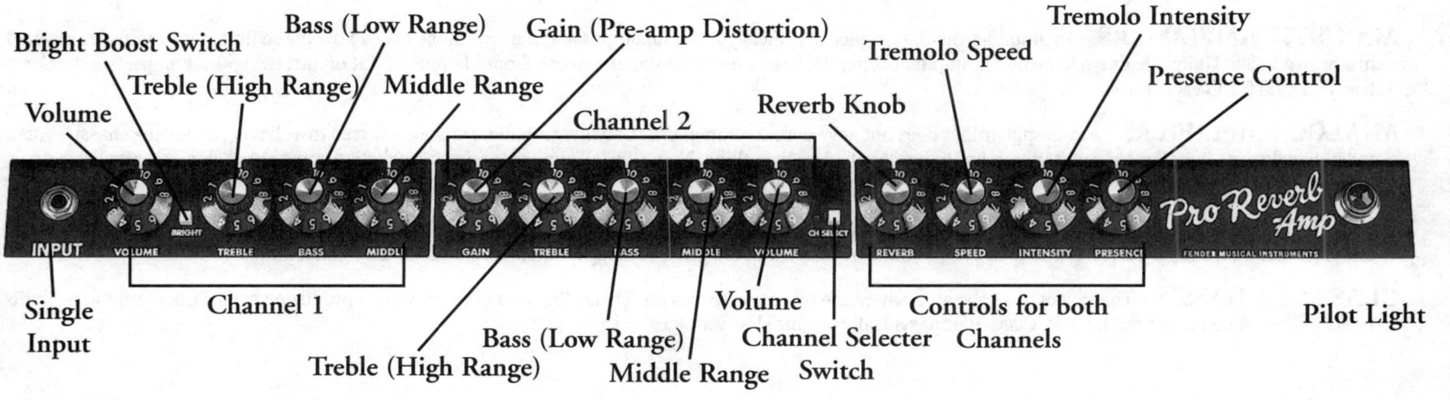

AMP GLOSSARY

This glossary is divided into five sections: General Amplifier Glossary, Different Types of Amplifiers, Amplifier Components, On the Control Panel of an Amplifier, and Coverings and Grille Cloths. If you are looking for something and can't find it in one section, please check the others. You may also want to refer to Anatomy of a Guitar Amplifier on pages 14-15 for visual identification on many of the terms listed below.

GENERAL AMPLIFIER GLOSSARY

AC (ALTERNATING CURRENT) - This is a type of electricity that comes out of a wall outlet. It flows in a back and forth motion, switching from negative to positive several times in a second. Most guitar amplifiers initially utilize this type of current but convert it to DC.

BIAS - The proper level that tubes should be set at for optimal operation. Setting the bias is much like adjusting a carburetor in a car after you have worked on it. If you replace tubes or repair work in your guitar amplifier, you may have to adjust the bias to a proper level. Unless you are an experienced guitar amp repair person, you may want to have a professional perform this adjustment. Some amplifiers, such as Mesa Boogies, do not have bias adjustments and this is known as fixed bias.

CHORUS - An effect that is similar to vibrato, but combined with reverb. When engaged it sounds like a watery effect. Controls on the amp for chorus are typically depth and rate. Many acoustic amplifiers feature chorus, and when included on guitar amplifiers, they are designed specifically for chorus. Chorus amps commonly feature two speakers with a twin power amp that produces stereo sound.

DC (DIRECT CURRENT) - This is a type of electricity that comes from a battery, for example. The current is consistently flowing in one direction. The internal circuitry of most guitar amplifiers utilize DC current, and a rectifier is the component that converts AC power into DC power.

DISTORTION - A natural or created effect that sounds dirty or distorted. In tube amps, distortion is created when a tube starts to clip and is commonly known as a natural effect. In solid-state amps, diodes and transistors do not naturally clip, so they are programmed to sound like distortion. This is probably the most common effect found on guitar amplifiers.

IMPEDANCE - The amount of resistance (typically listed in ohms) that a component is rated at. Amplifiers put out a certain impedance and speakers receive a certain impedance. Amplifiers and speakers (speaker cabinets also) need to run on corresponding impedances.

PEAK POWER - An amplifier wattage rating that indicates the peak power of an amp. In today's amplifier world, companies don't typically list this rating, but many vintage models (especially early solid-state models) may list peak power.

OHMS - A measure of electrical resistance. Impedance is listed in ohms, and this symbol is represented by the Greek letter Omega.

OVERDRIVE - A control or second channel that increases gain on a guitar amplifier. Many amps may have a clean channel and an overdrive channel that are switchable, or on basic amps, it may be a switch or a control that increases gain.

REVERB - An echo effect that is typically created by springs. Besides distortion, this is the most common guitar effect. Most guitar amplifiers feature a single reverb control, but more advanced units may have up to three reverb controls.

RMS (ROOT MEAN SQUARE) - An amplifier wattage rating that indicates the average maximum power. Amplifier companies typically use RMS to rate the output power of their amps. Although this isn't always true, RMS power is typically about half of the peak power. If the peak power is listed at 100W in a catalog, the RMS should be around 50W.

TONE - The different pitch of a sound that an amplifier produces.

TREMOLO - A pulsating effect created by altering the volume from loud to soft. Tremolo is very similar and is often confused with vibrato (see definition). In vintage amplifiers, tremolo is more common as it is much easier to produce than vibrato. Tremolo is most often controlled by a rate or speed and intensity or depth.

VIBRATO - A pulsating effect created by altering the pitch of the tone. Vibrato is very similar and is often confused with tremolo (see definition). In vintage amplifiers, vibrato is less common as it is much harder to produce than tremolo. Vibrato did not appear until the late 1950s as tremolo, and many manufacturers would advertise vibrato when in reality the amp really featured tremolo. Vibrato is most often controlled by a rate or speed and intensity or depth.

WATTAGE - In guitar amplifiers, power is measured by watts. In traditional electricity terms wattage is determined by voltage and amperage. Amplifiers put out a certain amount of watts and speakers can handle a certain amount of watts.

DIFFERENT TYPES OF AMPLIFIERS

ACOUSTIC AMPLIFIERS - An amplifier that is designed specifically for acoustic guitar and microphone use. 99.9% of the time, these amps are covered in a brown finish. Unique features for acoustic amplifiers often include separate guitar and microphone channels, XLR inputs, twin power amps, two speakers, tweeters, and feedback controls.

ANALOG AMPLIFIERS - Any amplifier that does not have digital components. Usually, amplifiers are not referred to as having an analog chassis, but in today's analog vs. digital world a guitar amp has to be classified as something. Naturally, all vintage tube and solid-state amps are analog as digital processing did not come around until the 1980s.

BASS AMPS - An amplifier that is designed specifically for bass guitars. There are certain controls on a bass amp such as limiter and compression that are unique to the instrument. Can be either tube or solid-state in design and are generally bigger and more powerful than guitar amps.

CLASS "A" CHASSIS - This refers to a tube amp where the tubes are always on. This is the least efficient way of producing sound from amplifiers, but is typically considered to sound the best. Class A amps typically produce low wattages.

CLASS "B" CHASSIS - This refers to an amp where the tubes switch on and off. This chassis usually uses a push/pull design, which means the tubes turn on and off. When one tube is working the other is off. Tubes are usually placed in pairs. These amps put out much more wattage than Class A. This is a more efficient way to operate a guitar amplifier because it creates less heat.

CLASS "A/B" CHASSIS - A combination of both Class A and Class B amps. When the volume is low the tubes will remain on in Class A. When the volume is higher it switches to Class B to create more power. Most guitar amplifiers are like this today.

CLASS "C" - This refers to an amp where the tubes are off most of the time. This creates a lot of power and is used for radio and other amplification where the sound isn't as important. Class C amps are not very common in guitar amplifiers.

DIGITAL AMPS - Any amplifier that has digital components that typically appear in the effects section, modeling section, or any programmable applications the amp may have. A digital amp will have at least some kind of computer chip to function.

GUITAR AMPS - Amplifiers that are designed specifically for electric guitars. Most amplifiers produced on the market today are usually aimed solely for guitars. Early amplifiers were often designed for multiple applications such as guitars, microphones, and accordions.

HYBRID AMPS - An amplifier that employs both tube and solid-state circuitry. Typically in a hybrid amp, the preamp stage is run by tubes and the power section is solid-state. The advantage of a hybrid chassis is sound is created with tubes, but money is saved by amplifying it with solid-state. Most companies advertise tube sound at a solid-state price.

KEYBOARD AMPLIFIERS - An amplifier that is designed specifically for keyboards. Unique features for keyboard amplifiers often include separate multiple channels and limited distortion, tremolo, and other effects.

MODELING AMPS - A design where several different amp sounds are programmed into one amplifier to produce literally hundreds of sounds available at your fingertips. This design is extremely popular as many popular amp sounds can be included in just one amp. Most of these amps use digital technology, but the first modeling amps were analog. Amps, speaker cabinets, and even effects are all modeled today. Some modeling amps even have digital read outs and motorized knobs to be set to a pre-programmed desired sound.

PUBLIC ADDRESS AMPLIFIERS (PA) - An amplifier that is designed specifically for multiple applications. Typically, they feature at least four channels and eight channels are common. They usually have high wattages and several speaker outputs. Many early European tube manufacturers such as Marshall, HiWatt, and Sound City featured a PA model. PA systems are typically a separate division of amplifier companies today as they serve a different purpose than they did in the 1960s and 1970s.

SOLID-STATE (ALSO KNOWN AS TRANSISTOR) - An amplifier that uses diodes and semiconductors instead of vacuum tubes to create and produce sound. These amps feature several more components than a tube amp. Traditionally, solid-state amps are viewed as budget models that aren't as sonically pleasing, or have the response of a tube.

TUBE AMPLIFIERS (ALSO KNOWN AS VALVE AMPLIFIERS IN EUROPE) - A glass "tube" that is sealed containing electrodes and cathodes (among other components) that generates sound by passing electrons back and forth. Tubes were used in all amps until solid-state came around in the '60s. Today, tubes are considered superior and are used in higher priced amps as they generally produce a warmer sound.

AMPLIFIER COMPONENTS

CABINET - A box (or other enclosure) that houses the amplifier, speakers, or both, and it is usually constructed out of wood. Cheap, but stable, woods are often used for construction such as plywood, particleboard, or birch since most cabinets are covered in a fabric. Some boutique amplifier companies offer cabinets built out of fancier-grade woods.

CHANNEL - A circuit in an amplifier that is in some way separate from one set of controls to another. A channel is used for creating different sounds from one amp without having to change the settings on the dials. The *Blue Book of Guitar Amplifiers* only considers an individual channel for each volume or gain knob. If an amplifier only has one volume knob, but separate inputs, it is not a multi-channel amp. If an amplifier has two volume knobs but a boost switch, it has two channels - not three.

CHASSIS - The chassis is where all the electronic components, tubes, and controls for the amp is housed. Typically, the chassis consists of one piece of metal folded into a box. Some amps have split designs where the reverb unit is separate or the preamp and power amp sections are separate. Refer to Anatomy of an Amp for pictures of a chassis.

COMBO - An amplifier that houses both the chassis and the speaker in one enclosure.

COVERING - The material that wraps the cabinet on an amplifier.

FOOTSWITCH - A remote box or control connected by a cord that has buttons to turn certain effects on or change channels on the amp. Footswitches can range from a single button to a digital processing board that can select channels, effects, and amp models.

GRILLE - The covering on the front of the amp that is usually made of cloth or metal. This covers the speaker and protects it from damage and dust.

HEAD UNIT - An amplifier where the chassis is housed in its own enclosure. There are no speakers within the cabinet. Head units were originally designed to keep the heat and frequencies of the tube chassis from interfering with the speakers, but they caught on for several reasons. As guitar amplifiers became more powerful and larger, combo units with 4-12 in. speakers were not very practical. Head units are also easier to service on their own. Separate head units and speaker cabinets also allow the player to use different combinations. This is especially evident with Marshall.

MODE - A specific sound that can be switched within a single channel. Many amplifiers are advertised with four unique channels, when in reality, there are only two channels with a mode switch on each one. For example a two channel amp will have a clean channel and an overdrive channel; the clean channel has two modes: clean and crunch, and the overdrive channel has two modes: overdrive and hi-gain.

NEODYMIUM - A specific type of magnet used in speakers designed to make them more lightweight. Many bass speaker cabinets now have speakers with Neodymium magnets to reduce weight.

POWER-AMP TUBE - A specific type of vacuum tube that turns the audio wave into physical sound. In this stage of the amplifier, the low power audio signal is amplified many times to produce several watts. These tubes actually produce the amplified sound in the guitar amplifier. In small Class A guitar amplifiers, a single tube may be used, but most often they are mounted in pairs. Examples: 6L6, EL34, KT88, 6550, EL84, 6V6, etc.

PRE-AMP TUBE - A specific type of vacuum tube that shapes and tones the audio wave. In this stage of the amplifier the signal from the guitar is shaped into the amplifier's unique style depending upon how many pre-amp tubes it has. All of a guitar amplifier's natural effects are shaped by preamp tubes: tremolo, vibrato, reverb, etc. A tube guitar amplifier has at least one pre-amp tube, but they typically have many more. Many pre-amp tubes can be split in half to serve as dual purpose. Examples: 12AX7, 12AT7, ECC81, 7025, 12AY7, etc.

RECTIFIER - A solid-state or tube unit that converts AC power into DC power, which an amplifier can use. On old and small-wattage amps the rectifier is usually a tube. On newer designs and high-watt amps the rectifier is usually solid-state. The rectifier has no direct contact with the sound, therefore a reliable solid-state rectifier can be used and no sound difference is noticed, although tubes produce an effect referred to as sag when the signal is attacked hard. In tube applications, a single tube is typically used (with the exception of Mesa/Boogie's double and triple rectifier amps). Examples (tubes): 5AR4, GZ34, 5U4.

SPEAKER - The component that the sound is projected from. Most of the time it is a round unit with an 8-,10-,12- or 15-inch speaker (excluding models such as the Fender Bantam Bass, the Ampeg Echo unit, and various early Harmony, Kay, and Supro models).

SPEAKER ENCLOSURE - A cabinet that consists of speakers only or speakers and a power amp. Although Marshall is mainly credited with inventing the 4-12 in. speaker cabinet, Fender was experimenting with piggyback units consisting of 1-12, 1-15, and 2-15 in. speaker cabinets. Some companies in the 1970s installed power amps in the speaker cabinets, and in these types of designs, only the preamp is separate. Several speaker cabinet configurations exist and some of the most popular include, 1-10 in., 1-12 in., 1-15 in., 1-18 in., 2-10 in., 2-12 in., 2-15 in., 4-10 in., 4-12 in., 6-10 in., and 8-10 in.

TILT-BACK DESIGN - An amplifier design that features tilt-back legs or a cabinet designed to sit at an angle facing upward. Many guitar players desire their sound to be projected upward as well as outward and this beats finding blocks to position your amp the way you want it. This design is usually found on smaller combo amps and acoustic amps.

ON THE CONTROL PANEL OF AN AMPLIFIER

BASS - Part of the equalization stage of the amp that represents the low end of the frequency spectrum. The frequency level varies depending upon the model. Traditionally, the bass control is one of two, three, or more sections of equalization in the guitar amp.

BOOST SWITCH - A switch that typically boosts the middle part of the tonal equalization range on the amp. Boost is a generic term and may be applied to other parts of the amp such as boost in the distortion circuit or boost for an entire channel.

BRIGHT SWITCH - A switch that boosts the high end of the tonal range on an amp. Early models sometimes had a push-pull feature on the volume or treble knob.

COMPRESSION - A control that compresses the range of sound to make the loud and soft sounds not so far apart. This control is almost always found on bass amplifiers.

CONTROL KNOBS - Knobs that control many of the features on a guitar amp. These are usually mounted on the control panel, but may also appear on the back of the amp or on footswitches and other satellite components. Common control knobs may include volume, gain, bass, mid, treble, reverb, rate, speed, intensity, and master volume.

CONTROL PANEL - The panel where the inputs, control knobs, switches and other buttons are located. On many amps there is a front and back control panel. The back control panel is for less used equipment such as the effects loop, footswitch jack, and fuses. The front control panel usually has volume and tone knobs along with input jacks. Control panels may be located in the front, back, top, or bottom of the amp depending on the location of the chassis. Most of the time that control panel is part of the chassis.

DEEP SWITCH - A switch that typically boosts the low or bass part of the tonal equalization range on the amp. Deep switches are most often found on bass amplifiers.

EFFECTS LOOP - A circuit that can be used for effects. Many effects feature in and out jacks that run directly between the guitar and the amp. The effects loop isolates the effect for use in different stages of the amp. This loop may have a level control to limit the amount of gain/volume.

FEEDBACK/NOTCH - A control that is typically used on acoustic amplifiers to limit the amount of unwanted feedback that can easily be generated by acoustic instruments. This control has been called several things by several manufacturers, but Feedback and Notch seem to be the most common.

GAIN - The technical definition of gain is the amount of distortion that goes into the preamp stage. Gain may either complement or replace the volume control depending on the complexity of the amp. Although gain appears to control the volume of the amp, it really only controls the amount of distortion or overdrive. If the gain is turned to "0" no sound will come from the amp, regardless of volume level, because nothing is being allowed into the pre-amp stage.

GRAPHIC EQUALIZER - A combination of slider switches, usually grouped in 5, 7, or 9 controls that provides ultimate tonal adjustment in the amplifier. A graphic equalizer (EQ) allows the user to precisely dial in their desired tone when simple bass, mid, and treble controls aren't enough. This is a common feature of bass amplifiers, and it is often accompanied by an on/off switch.

HALF POWER SWITCH - A switch that can take the power of an amplifier and reduce it to half or less power. This is usually accomplished by only utilizing two of four power tubes, or the amp may have a "Power Break" component built in to reduce power. Many guitar players run their amps wide open to maximize the sound, but sometimes full volume level is not required. A half-power switch lets the amp be run wide open but at a lower volume.

INPUT/INSTRUMENT JACKS - The place where the instrument or other object is plugged into the amplifier. Most input jacks are ¼ in. in diameter, but XLR jacks may be used in acoustic amplifiers for microphones. Every guitar amplifier has to have at least one input jack, but can have several depending on the number of channels and the function of the amp.

INTENSITY - A knob that controls the amount a certain effect is used. This is most often used on tremolo, vibrato, or any other pulsating effect. Speed may also be referred to as depth. This knob is optional for most pulsating effects while speed is standard.

JACKS - Besides input/instrument jacks, guitar amplifiers may have other jacks for separate purposes. Some examples of jacks include a pre-amp out, power amp in, footswitch, effects loop, external speaker(s), headphones, RCA inputs (for CD players, etc.), auxiliary input, XLR out, and MIDI connections.

LIMITER - A control that limits the sound of an amp from going too high. The limiter may have a level control or it may be a button with a built-in preset level. This feature saves the amp from getting too loud. Limiters are usually only found on bass amplifiers.

MAINS - A voltage selector/power input on a guitar amplifier that is mainly used in Europe. Different countries use different voltages and many manufacturers provided a Mains selector to allow different voltages to be utilized. Many amps today are built for specific markets, and mains controls are not used as often anymore.

MASTER VOLUME - A volume knob that controls the overall volume of the amplifier. Master volume controls were added around the 1970s on most guitar amps as many people requested the ability to lessen the volume of an amp without losing any tonal characteristics gained by running the amp wide open. While there is some argument over how this control works, this is what it was designed for. The master volume control can also govern the volume over more than one channel.

MIDDLE - Part of the equalization stage that usually cuts or boosts the mid-range of the equalization. The middle control may not be present on basic amps or may appear on one channel but not another. The middle control may also be controlled by a switch. Traditionally, the middle control is one of two, three, or more sections of equalization in the guitar amp.

PILOT LIGHT (ALSO JEWEL LIGHT) - Indicates that the amplifier is turned "on." If the amp features a standby switch, the pilot light will light when the standby switch is in the operate or idle positions. Some amps may feature separate lights for the power and standby switches. The pilot light is typically found on the front control panel.

POWER SWITCH - Turns the amp on and off.

PRESENCE - A control that typically adjusts the upper frequencies on an amp equalization circuit. The Presence control may replace the bright switch.

SPEAKON/NEUTRIK - A specific type of speaker connector often used to connect amplifiers to speaker cabinets. Unlike standard 1/4 inch and XLR jacks, Speakon/Neutrik connectors can only be connected one way and users are completely shielded from human touch.

SPEED - A knob that controls the speed a certain effect is used. This is most often used on tremolo, vibrato, or any other pulsating effect. Speed may also be referred to as rate. This knob is standard for most pulsating effects while intensity is optional.

STANDBY SWITCH - A switch that enables a tube amp to be shut off from emitting sound, but the tubes are still on. A tube takes a long time to heat up and this switch allows the amp to be shut off from operation but is still running (like a car in neutral).

TONE - If the amplifier has simple features or is an early vintage model, it may only have a tone knob instead of separate bass and treble knobs. Typically, the tone knob will have a "0" at the 12 o'clock position with more bass sound to the left and more treble sound to the right. Tone knobs were phased out in the 1960s when more tonal varieties became desirable.

TREBLE - Part of the equalization stage that controls the high end of the equalization. The frequency level varies depending upon the model. Traditionally, the middle control is one of two, three, or more sections of equalization in the guitar amp.

VOLUME - The technical term is the amount of sound allowed into the preamp or power amp stage depending on the location of the control. When it gets down to it, all guitar amps have some kind of volume control. Many advanced amps will have several volume knobs for preamp volume, power amp volume, and master volume. All these volume knobs control the amount of volume.

COVERINGS AND GRILLE CLOTHS

REFER TO INDIVIDUAL MANUFACTURERS SECTION'S FOR MAKER - specific coverings and grille cloths.

CARPET - Many bass amplifiers, keyboard amplifiers, and speaker cabinets may have carpet coverings. A carpet covering has a fuzzy feel to it and wears well when used in large applications.

LEATHERETTE - A fake leather covering used by many manufacturers in the 1950s and 1960s. Gibson used a lot of leatherettes during the 1950s.

LEVANT - Marshall's first covering that has a unique pattern and texture to it. Many companies have used variations of this covering, but it is not usually referred to as Levant.

TOLEX - A covering used by Fender starting in the late 1950s that was developed by a rubber company. Many other companies have used a covering like Tolex or call their covering Tolex, but true Tolex is the rubber covering used by Fender.

TWEED - A brown/yellow diagonal woven fabric covering used on amps in the 1950s and 1960s. Fender is probably the first and most famous user of tweed, but many other companies have used variations of this covering. Tweed is not very durable and is subject to a lot of wear.

VINYL - Probably the most common and generic covering used on guitar amplifiers. Vinyl is a cheap covering that wears well and looks good. Since it is so economical, many manufacturers opt for vinyl.

AMP DATING TOOLS

Guitar amplifiers can be dated by several different components including the speakers, potentiometers, transformers, tube charts, and serial numbers. With the exception of Marshall and a period of Ampeg production during the late 1960s, most large companies do not have a record of serialization. In fact, Fender's first kept serial number records start in 1994! More information and charts are appearing on the Internet and in magazines that are mostly compiled by collectors and enthusiasts, but much of it is not from the factory so question credibility on your own. Dating your amp by the major components (if they are original) is the best and/or most reliable way to do so.

One of the first steps to correctly date your amplifier is to figure out the manufacturer and model name or number. The manufacturer name should be present, but the model name/number may not be listed anywhere on the amplifier so you may have to do some research (this happens a lot with House Brand amplifiers such as Supro, Kay, Airline, etc.). There are many vintage catalog websites available (www.vintaxe.com), which is a great way to compare your model to others. All listings in the *Blue Book of Guitar Amplifiers* include the approximate year of production, so once you've identified the make and model name/number, you should be able to narrow it down to a few years.

Most guitar amplifier companies produced amplifiers in series (a group of models with different wattages, speakers, and features that share common cosmetics/coverings). Usually with the large companies, series were introduced and discontinued at the same time. For instance, Fender brown Tolex-covered amplifiers were produced between late 1959 through 1963. Guitar amplifiers are usually valued between the series and not individual years, but this may vary if features were only available for certain years. For instance, Fender silverface amplifiers were produced between 1968 and 1980, but a master volume knob was introduced circa 1976 meaning silverface amps produced between 1968 and 1976 will be valued different than amps produced between 1976 and 1980. In the *Blue Book of Guitar Amplifiers*, features added during production are typically noted and valued accordingly.

SPEAKER DATE CODES

If you would like to try and pinpoint exactly when your amplifier was produced, there are other ways to narrow it down. Refer to individual manufacturer sections within the *Blue Book of Guitar Amplifiers* to see if there is individual serialization or other dating methods (i.e. Fender, Marshall, Ampeg). If major components are original in your amplifier, you can also use those to help date. Speakers are probably the easiest component to locate and find a date code. Remember - if the speaker has been replaced, the date represented on the speaker will not coincide with the date of your amp! Also keep in mind that although the speaker dates 1961 it does not necessarily mean your amp is from 1961. Many large manufacturers purchased components in large quantities and used them as they needed. Speakers could sit on the shelf for months if not years before they were installed. Every American-made speaker should have a date code stamped on it, which is usually located on the edge of the frame. This date code consists of six, seven, or eight digits and will tell you the manufacturer and week and year of production. The first two, three, or occasionally four digits indicate the manufacturer (see chart for information). The next one or two digits indicate the last one or two digits of the year (most speakers built in the 1950s and 1960s have a one-digit year and after 1970 they are usually two digits, but there are variations and exceptions). The last two digits indicate the week of the year. The date code may be split with a hyphen between the manufacturer code and the year/week numbers. Many manufacturers also added other numbers or letters on the speaker to help identify it. The date code was a mandatory number the Electronics Industries Alliance (EIA) made speaker manufacturers apply, but any other date coding was done strictly by the manufacturer.

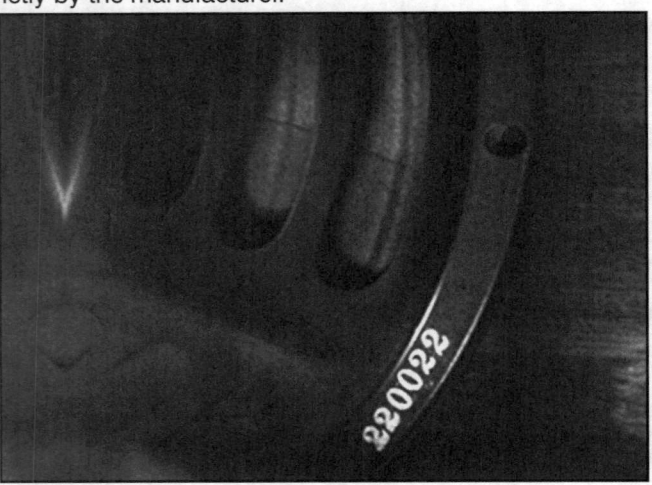

Examples:

220022: Jensen Speaker built in the 22nd week of 1950 or 1960.

465-831: Oxford Speaker built in the 31st week of 1958 or 1968.

677145: Eminence Speaker built in the 45th week of 1971.

24: Becker
34: Cornell-Dubilier
67: Eminence
101: Admiral
106: Allen-Bradley
117: Credence Speakers
119: Automatic Manufacturing
124: Alpha Wire
125: Bendix
130: Matsushita/Panasonic
132: Talk-A-Phone
134: Mepco/CentraLab/NA Philips
137: CTS
140: Clarostat
145: Cinaudagraph/Consolidated/Illinois Capacitor
150: Crescent
169: Hitachi
185: Motorola
188: General Electric (GE)
213: Dearborn Wire
220: Jensen/Viking
230: Littlefuse
232: Magnavox
235: Mallory/North American Capacitor
240: JW Davis
244: Muter
245: National
251: Ohmite
252: Dukane/Operadio
258: Perm-O-Flex
260: Philco
270: Quam-Nichols
274: RCA
277: Emerson/Radio Speaker
280: Raytheon
285: Rola
286: Ross
296: Solar
300: Speer
304: Stackpole
308: Stromberg-Carlson
312: Sylvania
328: Utah/Oxford
336: Western Electric
343: Zenith

371: Best
374: Cletron
381: Bourns
391: Altec-Lansing
394: Foster Transformer
416: Heath
423: North American Philips/Norelco
433: Cleveland
449: Wilder
465: Oxford/McGregor
466: Delco
532: Ward Leonard
549: Midwest
550: Valco/National/Supro/Airline/Oahu
555: Waldom Electronics
575: Heppner
579: Beldon/Cooper
589: Bogen
649: Electro-Voice
706: Pioneer
719: Carbonneau
722: Milwaukee Resistor
736: Sprague/Allegro MicroSystem
742: Esquire
748: Russell
756: Universal
767: Quincy
787: Sonatone
789: McGregor
794: Harman Kardon
795: Atlas
816: Dale
828: Midland
840: Ampex
847: University
918: Oaktron
932: Atlas
1056: Fisher
1059: Channel
1098: Pyle
1113: Acoustic Fiber Sounde
1149: Curtis Mathes
1191: Micro Magnet
1279: WeberVST

SPECIAL SPEAKER DATE CODES:

JENSEN

Along with the typical date code found on American-made speakers, Jensen used another proprietary code strictly for their speakers. Since Jensen was one of the most popular supplier of speakers in the 1950s and 1960s and they built several different models, this code was useful to identify what kind of speaker it was. Jensen used a letter number combination along with their own numbering system. The first letter indicates the magnet type. The next one or two numbers indicate the speaker size (typically from 6 in. to 18 in.). The last letter indicates the quality of the speaker ranging from J through X. The closer the letter is to J the better quality it is; the closer the letter is to X the lesser quality it is. The remaining letter and numbers are more than likely a Jensen production number, and no information on these numbers is available. Note: Jensen stopped using AlNiCo magnets in the 1960s, but continued use of the P prefix.

Magnet Code Letters

C: Ceramic
EM: Electronic musical
F: Field Coil magnet
P: AlNiCo V

Speaker Quality Letters:

J, K, L: Part of the Professional Series
N, P, Q, R: Part of the Concert Series
S, T, U, V, W, X: Part of the Standard Series, letters V, W, and X are all 8 in. and smaller.

Examples:

C12R: A 12 in. Jensen speaker with a ceramic magnet and is part of the Concert Series.
P10R: A 10 in. Jensen speaker with an AlNiCo magnet and is part of the Concert Series.

CELESTION

Since Celestion is a European company, many European guitar amplifier manufacturers have used their speakers. However, Celestion does not follow the American dating system. Early date codes were stamped on the gasket of the speaker, and on later models the number was stamped onto the frame itself. There are four types of date codes that have been stamped onto the speakers dating back to the 50s. Type 1 ran from 1956-1967, type 2 ran from 1968-1991, type 3 from 1992-2014, and type 4 from 2015-present. For type 1 there are two numbers first followed by two letters. The first two numbers indicate the day of the month the speaker was made (i.e. 1-31 are the numbers). Then the first letter is month and the second letter is the year, which can be found by the corresponding chart. Type 2 date codes are reversed. The letters come first followed by the numbers which are the day of the month again. Type 3 date codes follow the same system as Type 1; they just had to start over with letters as they ran out. The letters are also the same. Type 4 date codes follow the same system as Type 2. In 1962, they discontinued using the letter I because of confusion with the number 1. Examples of this system are 20 CG would be a speaker made March 20, 1962. A date code of FQ 26 would be a speaker made on June 26, 1982.

MONTH 1956-1962

A - January	D - April	G - July	J - October
B - February	E - May	H - August	K - November
C - March	F - June	I - September	L - December

MONTH 1963-CURRENT

A - January	D - April	G - July	K - October
B - February	E - May	H - August	L - November
C - March	F - June	J - September	M - December

YEAR TYPE 1956-1967

A - 1956	D - 1959	G - 1962	K - 1965
B - 1957	E - 1960	H - 1963	L - 1966
C - 1958	F - 1961	J - 1964	M - 1967

YEAR TYPE *2 1968-1991*

A - 1968/1991	G - 1974	N - 1980	U - 1986
B - 1969	H - 1975	P - 1981	V - 1987
C - 1970	J - 1976	Q - 1982	W - 1988
D - 1971	K - 1977	R - 1983	X - 1989
E - 1972	L - 1978	S - 1984	Y - 1990
F - 1973	M - 1979	T - 1985	Z - 1991

YEAR TYPE *3 1992-2014*

B - 1992	H - 1998	P - 2004	V - 2010
C - 1993	J - 1999	Q - 2005	W - 2011
D - 1994	K - 2000	R - 2006	X - 2012
E - 1995	L - 2001	S - 2007	Y - 2013
F - 1996	M - 2002	T - 2008	Z - 2014
G - 1997	N - 2003	U - 2009	

YEAR TYPE *4 2015-PRESENT*

A - 2015	B - 2016	C - 2017

The date codes after 2005 have not been verified by Celestion and may not be accurate. However, based on their dating code system, the chart provided is based on the continuation of existing numbers.

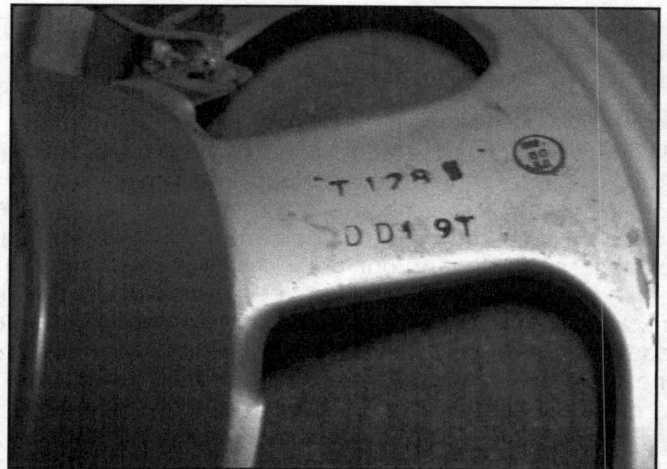 

Examples:

DD19T: A Celestion T1281 Greenback speaker manufactured on April 19, 1971. Image courtesy Douglas Phillips.

HP12: A Celestion T3054 speaker manufactured on August 12, 1981. Image courtesy Gary Borowitz.

OXFORD

Oxford used a date code similar to Jensen, but the letter indicated the power handling of the speaker. The higher the number, the higher peak power the speaker was rated at. Letters range from K to T.

POTENTIOMETER DATE CODES

On every American made potentiometer (pot), there should be a date and manufacturer code similar to speaker codes. This code consists of six or seven digits. The first three indicate the company or manufacturer who made the pot and the last three or four indicate the date it was made. If there are six digits, the fourth digit indicates the last number of the year, and the fifth and sixth digit indicate the week of that year. If there are seven digits, the fourth and fifth indicate the last two digits of the year it was made and the sixth and seventh indicate the week of that year. Usually the numbers were separated by a hyphen after the third digit. When there are possibilities of two different years, refer to the actual amplifier and see what years it was manufactured to narrow it down.

There are several instances to make sure that this system is accurate. The pots must be original. If they have been replaced, they are not going to be an accurate way to determine the date of the amplifier. The pots show that the amp was not made before the date on the pot, but could be made much later than that date. Many large manufacturers purchased components in large quantities and used them as they needed. Pots could sit on the shelf for months if not years before they were installed. If your amp has mainly 1961 pots, it only means it was produced in or after 1961.

Examples:

140-6421: Calrostat pot made in the 21st week of 1964,

137-711= a CTS pot made in the 11th week of 1947 or 1957.

106: Allen-Bradley
134: CentraLab
137: CTS
140: Clarostat

304: Stackpole
381: Bourns Networks
615: IRC

Examples:

1377918: A CTS potentiometer pot built in the 18th week of 1979.

TRANSFORMER/COIL DATE CODES

Many power transformers and coils on amps are still original and can also be used to help date amplifiers because they should also have a date code. The transformer code should be stamped into the actual metal, and will follow the system that potentiometers and speakers use. Remember - if the transformer has been replaced, the date represented on the frame will not coincide with the date of your amp! Also keep in mind that although the transformer dates to 1961 it does not necessarily mean your amp is from 1961. Many large manufacturers purchased components in large quantities and used them as they needed. Transformers could sit on the shelf for months if not years before they were installed. Every American-made transformer should have a date code stamped into the metal casing. This date code consists of six, seven, or eight digits and will tell you the manufacturer and week and year of production. The first three (and occasionally four) digits indicate the manufacturer (see chart for information). The next one or two digits indicate the last one or two digits of the year (most speakers built in the 1950s and 1960s have a one-digit year and after 1970 they are usually two digits, but there are variations and exceptions). The last two digits indicate the week of the year. The date code may be split with a hyphen between the manufacturer code and the year/week numbers. Many manufacturers also added other numbers or letters on the speaker to help identify it. The date code was a mandatory number the Electronics Industries Alliance (EIA) made speaker manufacturers apply, but any other date coding was done strictly by the manufacturer.

Examples:

549-6221: A Midwest Coil & Transformer unit built in the 21st week of 1962.

138: Stancor
141: Coil Engineering

172: Ensign Coil
183: Freed

194: General Radio

218: Jefferson Electric

238: Thordarsen-Meissner

239: Merit Coil & Transformer

305: Standard Coil

352: Essex

366: New York Transformer

391: Altec-Lansing/Peerless

394: Foster Transformer

412: General Transformer

418: United Transformer Corporation

452: Empire Coil

489: Radio-Television Products Corporation

503: Caledonia

524: Triwec Transformer

549: Midwest Coil & Transformer

550: Standard Winding Company

572: F&V Coil Winding

606: Woodward-Schumacher

637: Central Coil

682: Electrical Windings

757: Grand Transformers

773: Forest Electric

776: Ogden Coil & Transformers

830: Triad

831: Better Coil & Transformers

843: Klipsch

878: Acro Products

883: Mohawk

892: American Transformer

897: Tresco

906: Coilcraft

908: Aerocoil

928: Acme Coil & Transformer

933: Magnetic Coil Manufacturing

934: Oaktron

1005: Northlake

1052: Pacific

Several other components such as tubes, transistors, capacitors, and filter caps also utilize date codes similar to speakers, pots, and transformers. However, most of these are replaced over the years due to routine maintenance. If you are positive that these parts are original, you can try dating them. There are separate manufacturer codes for these, but they generally follow the same pattern.

Please remember that all the information included above is intended as a guide only. THERE ARE ALWAYS EXCEPTIONS TO THE RULES!!! These charts were put together from a number of sources, including Dave Funk's *Tube Amp Workbook*, and several online websites.

AMPLIFIER TUBES EXPLANATION

VACUUM TUBES - possibly the single most important component in a guitar amplifier as far as determining tone. Tone junkies love tube talk simply because there are so many options in choosing tubes. Although the *Blue Book of Guitar Amplifiers* is not dedicated solely to tube guitar amplifiers, a large part of this book contains information on this subject. We are not experts by any means in this field, but we thought a brief explanation about tubes would be helpful. NOTE: If you are seriously interested in tubes, modifications, and any other tube-related project you should refer to some other books. Several authors have written thorough books entirely on tubes and guitar tube amplifiers. Many magazines also run monthly columns and have featured articles on tubes. That said, the *Blue Book of Guitar Amplifiers* Tube Theory/Explanation section should not be taken any further than a novice view on guitar tubes. Also note that guitar amplifiers contain lethal amounts of voltage and if you don't know what you are doing, do not start poking around as you could get a nasty and even lethal shock.

Vacuum tubes were first used in electronic applications during the 1920s and 1930s simply because they were the only way engineers knew how to produce sound. All early radios, amplifiers, and related products use vacuum tubes to amplify sound. The same can be said about guitar amplifiers - vacuum tubes were the only means of shaping and amplifying sound. Little did these inventors know that over fifty years down the road vacuum tubes would be the preferred choice among tone junkies. Along with many years of improvements and adjustments, hundreds of different tubes are now available, and all of them have a unique sound. It is useful to know how a vacuum tube works first though.

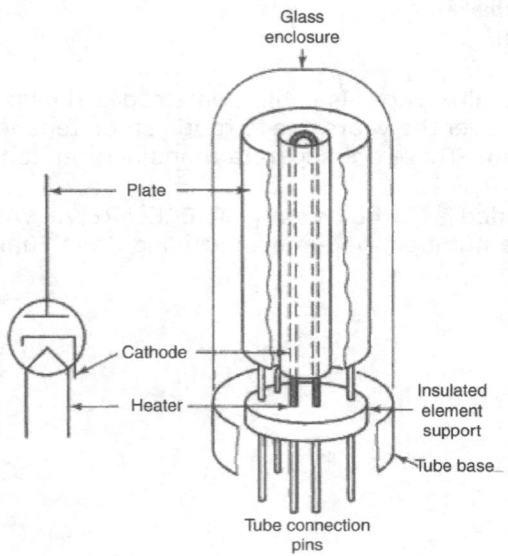

Components of a Vacuum Tube
courtesy Justin Holdon

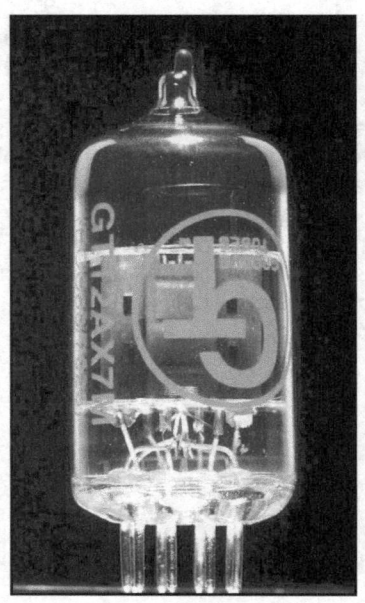

Groove Tube GT12AX7M Preamp Tube
courtesy Groove Tubes

Groove Tube GT6V6C Power Tube
courtesy Groove Tubes

A vacuum tube is constructed of a sealed glass tube with four active elements inside. The four main elements include the plate, grid, cathode, and heater (filament). Each of these components is connected to a series of pins that are all numbered. The tube works in this order: First the heater (filament) is warmed which in turn heats the cathode. When the cathode is warm, it begins emitting electrons that flow to the plate. The cathode has a negative charge and the plate has a positive charge. The grid controls the flow of this so electrons do not move too fast. All of these components are in a sealed vacuum tube with no air so none of them burn up. Needless to say, there is a lot of electricity that flows through these tiny tubes.

How does this translate into guitar sound? Well, when a small signal, such as the magnetic waves from a guitar pickup, is applied to the grid, it causes the electrons between the cathode and plate to flow at different rates. The plate end of the tube is connected to an output transformer that puts sound out to one or more speakers. There is a lot more that happens between all of this and a lot more technical information, but we'll let the more advanced authors handle that.

There are three main types of guitar amplifier vacuum tubes: preamp, power, and rectification. Each serves a unique purpose in a guitar amplifier, and even the most basically designed guitar amplifier must have at least one of each. A guitar signal passes through the preamp tube(s) first, followed by the power tube(s) and AC current is converted to DC current with a rectifier tube. Early on, the U.S. and Europe used different named/numbered tubes, but they are very similar and identical in some cases. However, most tubes have unique sounds that players prefer.

PREAMP TUBES:

Once a guitar signal enters the amplifier, it must be amplified to a level the guitar amp can work with, which is what a preamp tube(s) do(es). This is sometimes referred to as line-level strength. Even though this stage of the amp only produces a very small volume, it is still louder than when it entered the guitar amplifier. If the guitar amplifier has tone controls, effects, and other features, more preamp tubes will shape the sound. This stage of the amplifier is commonly referred to as the signal processing stage. The amount of features the amplifier employs will determine the number of preamp tubes. The most basic amp with no tone control will probably only have one preamp tube (i.e. Fender Champ, Harmony 303, etc.). Amps with two channels (separate bass, treble, and mid controls), tremolo, and reverb may have six or more preamp tubes.

Examples and conversions:

American	European	Industrial
12AT7	ECC81	6201/6679
12AU7	ECC82	6189/6680/7730
12AX7	ECC83	6681/7025/7729
12AY7	N/A	6072
12DW7	N/A	7247

POWER TUBES:

Once the sound of the guitar (or other instrument) has been shaped by the preamp tubes, it needs to be amplified to a level that is audible. Power tubes take the relatively weak signal from the preamp/signal processing stage and amplify it into several watts. This signal is then transmitted to a power transformer to match impedance with a speaker, and finally connected to a speaker(s). Power amp tubes are generally much larger than preamp tubes and they run a lot hotter because of the energy that passes through them. Small Class A amps may only utilize one power tube that is always on, but the majority of tube guitar amplifiers have power tubes mounted in pairs that work in a push/pull format. When one tube is on, the other one is off. Most tube configurations consist of either two (25W-50W output power) or four (50W-100W output power) tubes, but some larger amps may have six or even eight power tubes.

Examples and conversions:

American	European	Industrial
6AU6	N/A	6136/7543
6BQ5	EL84	N/A
6CA4	EZ81	N/A
6CA7	EL34/KT77	N/A
6L6	KT66	5881
6V6	N/A	5871/7184/7408
N/A	KT88	6550

RECTIFIER TUBES:

In order to convert standard house power (120V AC in the US) to power a guitar amplifier can utilize (DC), a tube or solid-state rectifier needs to be used. The rectifier provides power to the other tubes when they are being used. Almost all early and small tube amps will have a tube rectifier, while newer and larger amps have solid-state transistors. Since the rectifier has no direct contact with the sound, there really is no advantage for tubes in this section. However, a tube rectifier can sag when a large amount of power is needed at the other tubes resulting in a lack of power/sound that is actually desirable to some guitarists. A few amplifier companies, including Mesa/Boogie, use multiple tube rectifiers in their design to provide power to the tubes.

Examples and conversions:

American	European	Industrial
5AR4	GZ34/GZ37/U54/U77	N/A
5U4	GZ31/GZ32/U51/U52	N/A
5Y3	GZ30/U50	6087/6853

As the above charts indicate, many tubes have European and Industrial counterparts. Most of the time, tubes can be switched if desired with matching counterparts as long as they have the same pin layout. Experimenting with different tubes can provide many different sounds. For example, a schematic may call for 2 X 12AX7 and 2 X 7025 preamp tubes. By looking at the above charts, we can see that they are indeed the same tubes. Back in the 1950s and 1960s, industrial tubes were built sturdier and are regarded as more durable. Certain stages of the guitar amplifier may call for more durable tubes in a demanding position. There are many tricks to learning about tubes.

Replacing tubes often is recommended and sometimes necessary if they are too old. Tubes wear out after use, and after many years (like light bulbs) they can burn out. Tubes that are old or burnt out will make the amplifier sound really bad with a hiss, low output, or other unwanted sound. Replacing tubes and a correct bias job can make your amp sound like new again, but there are other places to look when it comes to trouble in the amplifier. Look for more information on tubes and tube maintenance in further editions of the *Blue Book of Guitar Amplifiers*.

HOUSE BRANDS/BUDGET BRANDS

In the *Blue Book of Guitar Amplifiers*, the terms House Brand and Budget Brand are referred to quite often. A House Brand is defined as a trademark used by distributors, wholesalers, and retailers to represent their respective company instead of the manufacturer. These brands are found (for the most part) on budget amplifiers, although some models are currently sought after by players and collectors on the basis of features, tone, or relative degree of "coolness" they project.

A budget brand is defined as a trademark used by a large manufacturer to produce a line of guitar amplifiers similar to the large manufacturer, but sold at a lesser price. These budget brands may be produced by the manufacturer or they can be outsourced in order to bring costs down. Many vintage guitar amplifiers that are budget brands may have only slight differences from the large manufacturer.

In the 1800s, many guitar manufacturers were located in New York and Philadelphia; by the early 1900s large guitar factories were centered in Chicago. The "Big Three" that evolved out of the early 1930s were Harmony, Kay, and Valco. As electric instruments became popular in the late 1930s and 1940s, many of these companies introduced guitar amplifiers. Like their guitar counterpart, these new guitar amplifiers were labeled House Brands.

One of the best examples to explain House Brands and Budget Brands is Valco, who produced National, Supro, Airline, and Oahu guitar amplifiers. Valco only produced a handful of amplifiers branded by their own name; almost all Valco-made amplifiers brandish the National, Supro, Airline, or Oahu name. Many models between the four brands feature identical chassis and features but different cosmetics and logos. This was very economical for Valco as they could produce a thousand identical chassis and install them into different branded cosmetics as they needed to. Airline guitars and guitar amplifiers were produced and advertised exclusively for the Montgomery Wards catalogs, which makes them a house brand. National guitar amplifiers represent Valco's big instrument line. They introduced Supro as a budget brand to National amplifiers. This can all be summed up as this:

Valco: Manufacturer

National: Large/main brand

Supro: Budget Brand to National.

Airline: House Brand for Montgomery Wards.

Many other House Brands exist, but there are only a few big ones that many people are familiar with. Danelectro was a large builder/supplier to Sears & Roebuck under the brand Silvertone. Many Danelectros and Silvertones are identical beyond cosmetics, and at one point up to 85% of Danelectro's production was reserved for Silvertone. Harmony and Kay are two other large builders/suppliers, but they don't have a large name they used exclusively.

Prior to World War II, Harmony and Kay sold straight to wholesalers like catalog houses and large distributors. In turn, these wholesalers would send their salesmen and "reps" out on the road to generate sales - no territories, no music store chains - just straight sales. Business was fierce, and companies used their own private labels to denote "their" product. House Brands were typically used as a marketing tool for distributors, wholesalers, and/or retailers to try to eliminate consumer shopping for the best price on popular makes and models of the time. How could you shop a trademark that didn't exist anywhere else? Tom Wheeler, in his book, *American Guitars*, quoted former Harmony president Charles A. Rubovits' recollection that the company built 57 private brands for the wholesalers - and sold over five million guitars.

An informative essay about House Brands and their place in the vintage guitar spectrum can be found in *Stellas & Stratocasters* (Vintage Guitar Books) by Willie G. Moseley, feature writer/columnist for *Vintage Guitar* Magazine. Moseley's commentary includes a listing of thirty-eight brands and their retailers/distributors, brief anecdotes about the major American manufacturers of budget instruments (Harmony, Kay, etc.) and photos of twenty-five American-made House Brand instruments. As Moseley states, "It's my opinion, and I dare say the opinion of most vintage guitar enthusiasts, that a good rule of thumb concerning the collectibility of House Brands would be something along the lines of 'If it was a budget instrument then, it's proportionally a budget instrument now.' Regrettably, as the interest in vintage guitars and guitar amplifiers continues to grow, some individuals and/or businesses tend to assume that simply because an instrument is 'old' and/or 'discontinued' and/or 'American-made,' that automatically makes it a 'collector's item' and/or 'valuable.' That's certainly not the case, especially with House Brands.

It's disheartening to walk into a pawn shop and see a Kay-made Silvertone archtop electric from the Sixties labeled as an 'antique' and priced at $799, when the instrument is worth no more than $250 in the vintage guitar market, and such incidents are apparently on the increase. And that's unfortunate for everybody."

In the 1990s, many House Brand guitar amplifiers could be grouped into one category as there was not much difference in pricing. However, in the 2000s, this is becoming less evident as House Brands are becoming more popular. Despite what we just stated in the previous paragraph about House Brand guitars being worth budget brand prices, they are becoming more popular among collectors and players. With the spike in prices of high-end vintage guitar amplifiers, House Brands are becoming more available to the collector or player. A Fender blackface Deluxe that could be purchased under $500 in the 1990s is around the $1,500 mark now; a Fender blackface Champ that could be purchased for around $250 is now $600. During this period of increase, many House Brand guitar amplifiers have moved very little in the vintage market, which collectors have taken notice of. Keep an eye on popular House Brand guitar amplifiers as they may creep up in value.

Almost any large company has a budget brand to complement their more expensive line. Fender has Squier, Gibson has Epiphone, Eden Electronics has Nemesis, and so on. Early on in guitar amplifier history, many of the large companies realized they had to produce a lower priced version of their amplifier to remain competitive. Usually this was done one of two ways. The first was to introduce a new series of budget amplifiers under the main trademark (i.e. Marshall's MG Series). The second way manufacturers could expand their market share was to introduce an entirely new brand that was distributed by the large company (i.e. Fender/Squier, National/Supro). A debate will always exist to what is more valuable: an independent trademark that does not connect with the large manufacturer versus a series within a trademark that may bring the credibility down with the large manufacturer. Most budget brands are heavily discounted and dealer cost can be quite a bit under the standard 50% benchmark for most other brands. Keep this in mind when determining value.

APPRAISALS/INTERESTED IN CONTRIBUTING?

The *Blue Book of Guitar Amplifiers* is the result of non-stop, and continual amp research carried out by obtaining relevant information from both manufacturers and boutique builders. Also of major importance is speaking directly with experts (both published and unpublished), reading books, catalogs, and company promo materials, gathering critical and up-to-date manufacturer/builder information obtained from the semi-annual NAMM trade shows and the makers themselves, and observing and analyzing market trends by following major vintage dealer and collector pricing and trends.

We also have a great batch of contributing editors and advisory board members that pump out a lot of good information annually - including vintage pricing updates. Going to a lot of guitar and trade shows, in addition to visiting a variety of music stores, guitar shops, pawn shops, and second-hand stores, also hones our chops.

If you feel that you can contribute in any way to the materials published herein, you are encouraged to submit hard copy regarding your potential additions, revisions, corrections, or any other pertinent information that you feel would enhance the benefits this book provides to its readers. Unfortunately, we are unable to take your information over the phone (this protects both of us)! Earn your way into the ranks of the truly twisted, join the motley crew of contributing editors, and see that your information can make a difference! We thank you in advance for taking the time to make this a better publication.

All materials sent in for possible inclusion into upcoming editions of the *Blue Book of Guitar Amplifiers* should be emailed to the editor at: Ryant@bluebookinc.com. We also have a new Interested in Contributing link on our website with directions on how to submit information. Each new edition should be an improvement on the last. Even though you can't do it all in one, ten, or even twenty editions.

ADDITIONAL SERVICES
(CORRESPONDENCE INQUIRIES, APPRAISALS, AND BUYING/SELLING)

Aside from publishing the *Blue Book of Guitar Amplifiers*, Blue Book Publications offers additional services that are helpful in identifying and evaluating amplifiers. It is literally impossible to list every amplifier that has ever been produced in one book – if we continued doing this for 100 years, there would still be information missing. Because of this, and our continued commitment to help the customer, we offer a full guitar amplifier correspondence policy. If you own the current *Blue Book of Guitar Amplifiers* and either have a question about an amp in our book or can't find something that you are looking for, contact the editor at: Ryant@bluebookinc.com and we'll do our best to answer your questions. Whenever possible, please include pictures of the amplifier(s) in question – the results will be a lot more accurate. Please allow 5 – 7 business days for a response.

For those who don't own an edition of the *Blue Book of Guitar Amplifiers*, we can help you out with a value and some quick information either over the phone or through email for only $10 per amplifier. This service is also available on our website through a secure online submittal form.

We also offer full written amplifier appraisals that are extremely useful for insurance purposes and other situations where written documentation is necessary. Appraisals are $25 per amplifier or 2% of the appraised value, whichever is higher. These can be submitted via email, and images of the amplifier must be included to determine condition and configuration. You will receive an email response within two business days. Appraisals will be completed as soon as possible in the order they are received. Please email guitars@bluebookinc.com if you'd like to receive an estimated completion date prior to submitting your appraisal request. This service is also available on our website through an online submittal form.

Another service that comes with the purchase of the *Blue Book of Guitar Amplifiers* is buying and selling assistance. If you are looking for a specific amplifier to buy, or have an amp you want to sell, we can provide you with trusted guitar and guitar amp dealers in your area. We have a wide network of dealers that we can recommend virtually anywhere in the U.S.A. This is strictly a confidential referral service and no commission is involved, nor is Blue Book Publications involved in any part of the transaction, other than the initial referral. To take advantage of this service, please contact the editor at: RyanT@bluebookinc.com.

When submitting images, please send images in .jpg format that are no larger than 1 mb per image in size. Images should include a complete frontal and back shot of the amplifier, a picture of the serial number/label, and any other important features of the amplifier. Also, please submit clear high res images of your amps – if you can't see the amplifier clearly in the picture, then we're not going to be either.

Vintage Guitar Amplifiers -
What to Look For by Dave Boze

Originally published in *The ToneQuest Report*.

An increasing number of amplifiers are being purchased today over the Internet without the new owners seeing or hearing them. Most of these transactions involve older amps (Fenders, Ampegs, Marshalls, Voxs, etc.) and aside from the varying descriptions offered by the sellers, who really knows what may be going on inside these purported cream puffs? What potential surprises should a prospective buyer look for? What are the questions you need to ask before you buy?

As many of the most desirable vintage guitars have become increasingly rare and expensive, it was inevitable that amplifiers would attract the attention of collectors. However, during the last ten years, the collecting frenzy has truly caught up with vintage guitar amps. People are finally starting to realize that in many cases, these older amplifiers are much rarer than the vintage guitars that they're spending $2,000 - $300,000 for!

Now that the word is out, the potential for some unpleasant problems exists. You'll notice that most vintage instrument dealers won't sell an amp with a warranty, for example. Why? Well, aside from the fact that amplifiers can be unexpectedly temperamental even after having been serviced, shipping can wreak havoc on an amp, even in the absence of any visible signs of damage. And unfortunately, a lot of people don't pack amplifiers properly. So the mint, just serviced, killer amp that you bought on eBay could arrive looking mint and sounding like a cat on fire!

LOOKING UNDER THE HOOD

If you want to a buy one of the more valuable and collectible models, it is crucial to know what you're getting "under the hood." For example, Blackface control panels can be bought today for around $150, along with some new grille cloth and poof - someone's Silverface amp worth $1,650 is now cosmetically transformed to a Blackface model worth $2,500. Does this go on? It must. Transformers can be changed (and they often are), speakers reconed, cabinets recovered and even new cabinets aged and recovered to look 30 years old. Would someone really do that? Think of the money involved when you're dealing with an $8,500 Vibroverb or a $10,000 '59 Bassman. Now, I'm not crying wolf and telling you that everyone who has an amp for sale is out to screw you, but sometimes I wonder if many of the sellers of all of these suddenly hot amps know if the amp they are selling is "original."

The point is I'd want to know before I spent $1,000 or more on an amplifier, or anything else. So know what you're buying, or pass!

When it comes to evaluating an amp before you buy, there are several critical things you want to verify to the best of your ability. Amps are different from guitars in that changed parts in guitars will usually reduce the selling price, but changed, missing, or altered parts in amps can be hard to detect and they can dramatically alter the tone of the amp (as well as the selling price, if you know). Some things are more important than others and in some cases an altered amp may even be more desirable than an original! More on that in a moment…

THE CABINET

Does it have the original covering? Is the Tolex or tweed in good condition? Tweed is tough to recondition, but black Tolex can usually be brought back to life with a little know-how. Even if the covering is shot and unsalvageable, you may wish to consider buying the amp at a bargain price and having it professionally restored. I run across a lot of amps with missing back panels. Not to worry, you can get some made if needed, and they will look perfect.

TRANSFORMERS

One of the key components in the classic sound of old tube amps is the way that the original transformers were made. Most were manufactured using paper bobbins and the coils were carefully interleaved together to allow the maximum transfer of sound. You'll find that in almost all new boutique amps, transformer construction is quite similar to those found in vintage amplifiers

of yesteryear. To me, original transformers have been a very important consideration, especially in 1950s amps, since exact repro copies were more difficult to find. Having said that, a much better selection of new reproduction transformers is now available and they are very close to OEM transformers. In regard to power transformers, it is critical that the voltages match the specs of the original, and in output transformers, you certainly want to have the correct impedance to match your speakers and similar construction to the original to produce authentic vintage sound. Virtually all transformers are dated, so you can verify their originality.

SPEAKERS

Original speakers can be a significant benefit to tone, or not, and almost always a determining factor in price. Most people who really know amps will tell you that the sound of an original Celestion in a Marshall, a Bulldog in a Vox, or a Jensen in a Fender is the sound that defines those amps.

Reconed speakers are highly variable. Be cautious in this area, because I have heard some reconed speakers that sound fantastic, and others that sound horrible, depending on the type of voice coil and paper that were used. There are also instances when original speakers may not be desirable. A new speaker can dramatically enhance the sound of many amps, sometimes even those with their original speakers.

INTERNAL CIRCUITRY

This is an area rife with controversy, but here's my two cents' worth:

Electronic parts wear out, primarily as a result of age, use, and heat. Also remember that in the 1950s, electronic parts were not manufactured to nearly the same tolerances that they are today; plus or minus 20% was the norm for some parts. Electrolytic capacitors definitely have a shelf life, and when they leak, they can wreak havoc in an amp in terms of tone and noise, and they can even cause transformers to fail. With time, coupling caps can leak DC into tone circuits - not good. Power resistors can drift, especially those that are near a heat source, and when they do, they can disrupt voltages throughout the amp, negatively affecting tone. Some manufacturers used cheap parts to cut costs (the brown chocolate drop coupling and tone capacitors are an example). So, if some parts are changed, that can be a good thing.

TUBES

Original tubes are in almost all cases absolutely worthless unless the amp was hardly ever played. Occasionally, I'll see lots of life left in original tubes, but for the most part, an amp that has been played will need new tubes. Tubes are mechanical components that wear out.

GRILLE CLOTH

The new repro cloth is very good and you can even acquire aged cloth now. Contrary to what anybody tells you, Fender never used black grille cloth on any Tweed, Brown, White, or Black Tolex amp (from the 1950s through 1970s).

Don't get too hung up on "changed" amps that you intend to play - especially if you have access to a good amp tech. Just be aware that originality should normally affect the final purchase price. Most players have Silverface Fender amps converted to Blackface circuits because many people believe that doing so tremendously improves the tone. So here's a case where an altered amp may have more value than an amp in original condition.

Above all, keep in mind that amps are for TONE! I've heard many absolute beaters produce the most fabulous tone that you could imagine. As a player rather than a collector, I get much less hung up on cosmetic condition and internal changes as long as the amp is running great and produces killer tone.

But it is important to know what you're buying, particularly when you're dealing with an amp you haven't seen or heard, and won't, until it's yours.

EXPLANATION AND CONVERTING GUITAR AMPLIFIER GRADING SYSTEMS

Rating the condition factors of guitar amplifiers can be very subjective if done properly while using the grading perimeters listed in this section. When grading vintage amplifiers, many things must be taken into consideration to get the correct grade, and the following descriptions will help you out when sorting through these grading criteria. Remember, the price will be wrong if the grade isn't right!

This 5th Edition *Blue Book of Guitar Amplifiers* lists 100%, Excellent, and Average condition factors, followed by the equivalent numerical grades/percentages, and ending with the corresponding page number(s) where that grade can be seen. While not listed in this text, Mint, Below Average, and Poor condition are also defined below.

Included in this section are examples of things that can affect the pricing and desirability of vintage guitar amplifiers, but it's almost impossible to accurately ascertain the correct condition factor (especially true on older models) without knowing what to look for - that means having the amplifier available for a physical inspection. Even then, three experienced amp dealers/collectors may come up with slightly different grades, not to mention different values, based on different reasons. Described below are the major condition factors to consider when accurately grading an amplifier. Also, please study the Photo Grading System digital color photos carefully on pages 33-48 to learn more about the factors described below.

GUITAR AMPLIFIER CONDITION FACTORS WITH EXPLANATIONS

100%/New - New with all factory materials, including warranty card, owner's manual, cover (if included), and other items that were originally included by the manufacturer. On currently manufactured amplifiers, the 100% value refers to an amp not previously sold at retail. Even if a new amp has been used only once and traded in a week later, it no longer qualifies at 100% - no dealer is going to buy the same amp at the 100%/New price since they can buy it from the dealer at wholesale price. Likewise, no independent buyer would buy a used amp when they could buy one brand new from the same dealer. The 100%/New condition factor only applies to amps that are currently manufactured or that have been discontinued no sooner/earlier than 2012 since it may take a while for inventory to sell out. It is instinctive to consider the 100%/New condition factor a "mint" category, but the reality on vintage amps is that if it is truly mint, it needs to be evaluated and appraised individually.

Excellent - the Excellent condition range is represented by both High Excellent and Low Excellent condition. High Excellent refers to an amplifier that is very clean, looks almost new (perhaps a few light nicks/scuffs only), and has hardly been used. Low Excellent refers to an amp that has been played/used, and has accumulated some minor wear in the form of light scratches, scuffs, tears, etc. The older an amplifier, the less likely it will be in High Excellent condition. Even Low Excellent is seldom encountered on amps over 50 years old, since most amps were originally purchased to be used. High Excellent condition also includes currently manufactured amps that have been previously sold at retail, even though they may have only played a few times. On recently manufactured amps, there usually is a fairly large price difference between the 100% and High Excellent condition factors due to used amplifier pricing which typically is affected by dealer replacements costs. Amps in this condition may not have the original manufacturer's warranty card, depending on the age of the amp, but should include the original cover if it was included when new.

Average - The Average amp condition factor indicates an amplifier that has been used extensively and has wear due to player use (hopefully, no abuse). High Average condition amps have normal scuffs, rips, and tears on the cabinet, and oxidation on metal parts. However, there should be no problems unless indicated separately. Low Average condition amps may reflect major covering problems, replacement parts, previous repairs (especially on older amps), alterations, and wear is typically visible. No excuses as a player, however. May or may not have a cover.

Below Average (this condition factor not covered in this book) - Covering and or grille cloth are still discernible, some parts possibly missing/replaced/repaired, could be either refinished or repaired, structurally sound, though frequently encountered with non-factory alterations and other problems. Must be playable.

Poor (this condition factor not covered in this book) - Ending a life sentence of hard labor, must still be playable, most of the wattage has left, family members should be notified immediately, normally not worthy unless the ad also mentions a Narrow Panel Tweed Bassman. May have to double as kindling if in a tight spot on a cold night.

100% NEW CONDITION

CIRCA 2016 SUPRO TITAN
Courtesy: Supro

Original Supro amplifiers were built in the 1950s and 1960s by Valco in Chicago, IL. Although they were popular with legendary guitar players like Jimi Hendrix and Jimmy Page, Supro amplifiers went out of production for nearly 40 years. Fortunately, with the help of former Fender amplifier designer Bruce Zinky, Absara Audio LLC of Fort Jefferson Station, NY brought Supro Brand Amplifiers back to life in 2014. This brand new 1642RT Titan Combo made its debut in 2016. The Titan is a vintage inspired, USA made combo amp featuring 50W of power, a ten-inch speaker, reverb, tremolo, and Supro's distinctive Blue Rhino Hide Tolex covering with a silver mesh grille. This 100% New Condition amplifier is fresh out of assembly and in perfect condition. Any rip, tear, scuff, or blemish in the covering or grille cloth would move this model out of the 100% New Condition category.

CIRCA 2007 SAVAGE THE ROHR 15
Courtesy: Savage Audio

Savage amplifiers are built in Savage, MN, by Jeff Krumm and his crew at Savage Audio. This particular model is called the Rohr 15 and is based on Marshall's famous 18 watt models produced in the mid-1960s. This amp was brand new and at the time it was photographed, and hadn't left their shop yet. A 100% New Condition amplifier assumes the model has never been sold at retail, and should include all accessories that were included originally including footswitches and covers. Once a currently manufactured amp has been sold to a consumer and used (regardless of how little), it is no longer considered 100% New Condition – and the value is at the upper end of the Excellent Condition value range.

EXCELLENT HIGH CONDITION

1967 FENDER PRO REVERB
Courtesy: solidbodyguitars.com, Inc.

This may be the cleanest Blackface Fender on this planet. The dealer actually found this amplifier in a church where it had spent most of its life. Since this was property of the church, it rarely found its way outside of the building. As we all know, transporting an amplifier damages and wears it more than anything else. This amplifier has no visual blemishes to speak of. The original hanging tags, owners manual, and footswitch are not only present, they are in cherry condition as well! This Pro Reverb is graded as Excellent High, but since it is so clean, it will bring a lot more money than what is listed. Extremely clean examples are the holy grail of amplifiers, and they command a premium!

EXCELLENT HIGH CONDITION

LATE 1990s MATCHLESS SC-30 and LATE 1990s MATCHLESS DC-30
Courtesy: Dave Rogers/Dave's Guitar Shop

Matchless is one of the earliest and best-known boutique amplifier companies on the market. Mark Sampson and Rick Perotta started the company in 1989, and anybody who knows Sampson knows that he is the master at Class A tube amplifier design. These two amplifiers share the same chassis, but they feature different speaker configurations. An amplifier in excellent condition will have no major rips, tears, scuffs, or any other blemishes in the covering or speaker grille. The chassis should be clean and everything in proper working order. What makes these examples different from 100% New Condition is the fact that they have been sold at retail and used for a number of years.

EXCELLENT CONDITION

1990 MARSHALL SILVER JUBILEE MODEL 2555
Courtesy: Savage Audio

The Marshall Silver Jubilee Series was introduced to commemorate twenty-five years of amplifier business and fifty years of music for Jim Marshall. For 1987, these models were covered in silver, but they were black for the remainder of the production run. This amplifier is very clean for being over twenty-five years old. Only minor covering scuffs that take close inspection to find are apparent. An Excellent Condition amplifier should be extremely clean, but is allowed minor imperfections.

1991/1992 MARSHALL JCM-900 MODEL 4500
Courtesy: Savage Audio

Marshall started to experiment with more gain, distortion, and effects loops with the JCM-900 Series. These amplifiers would prove to be very popular for Marshall, especially during the guitar boom of the 1990s. This model is another clean example of a Marshall head with minor finish blemishes. The discoloration on the back grille is due to heat from the tubes, indicating this amplifier has utilized its maximum wattage!

EXCELLENT LOW CONDITION

1960 FENDER SUPER BROWNFACE
Courtesy: Savage Audio

The older amplifiers get, the harder they are to find in Excellent Condition. This Fender Super has survived many years without too much damage. It is also one of the first Tolex Supers that Fender built after switching from tweed covering. The metal knobs may look non-original, but Fender used them very early on and they can be seen in Fender catalogs. It also features the desirable early control panel layout with the volume knob between the tone and tremolo controls. Later models featured the volume knob to the left next to the input jacks. This amplifier has a few blemishes as can be seen on the front and back edges and corners. Overall, everything else is intact and original, placing it in the Excellent Low Condition category.

AVERAGE HIGH CONDITION

MID-1960s AIRLINE MODEL 62-9026A
Courtesy: Savage Audio

Airline amplifiers were built by many big-name manufacturers including Harmony, Kay, and Valco, and sold exclusively out of Montgomery Wards catalogs and stores. Believe it or not, department stores actually sold quality guitars and amplifiers at one point! This Airline features an all-tube chassis, reverb, and tremolo – everything the Fenders and Ampegs had, but at a lesser price. The problem with budget brand amplifiers is they built thousands of them, supply far outweighs demand, and they are still considered a budget brand today. This amplifier is built like a tank with a split chassis (preamp on the top and the power section on the bottom), but has seen its share of use over the years. The covering has several noticeable scuffs and nicks throughout the amplifier, but the grille is clean and the chassis looks respectable. This amplifier falls in the Average High Condition category because it is too beat up to be considered excellent, yet still cleaner than most straight Average amplifiers.

AVERAGE CONDITION

VOX PATHFINDER TUBE MODEL V-101
Courtesy: Savage Audio

Unlike most companies at the time, Vox used the same model name on both tube and solid-state chassis amplifiers. This Pathfinder is a tube model, and it will bring about three times as much as its solid-state counterpart. This example has a fair amount of covering wear, the speaker grille is ripped in places, and part of the grille trim is missing (bottom). The amplifier is also dirty on the backside, indicating it hasn't had a good cleaning in some time.

CIRCA 1952-54 GIBSON GA-40 (FIRST VERSION)
Courtesy: John Beeson/The Music Shoppe

The Gibson GA-40 Les Paul is one of Gibson's most popular amplifiers due to its association with Les Paul and his solidbody guitar. The "LP" wooden logo on the grille cloth is a unique touch that no other model featured. The ends of the amplifier where the coverings splice show heavy wear and splitting. Part of the Gibson logo is missing, and overall the covering indicates normal use over the years.

AVERAGE CONDITION

1962/1963 SUPRO DUAL TONE MODEL 1624A
Courtesy: Savage Audio

Supro was the budget brand of National Amplifiers during the 1960s, and surprisingly, people seem to be more interested in Supro than National. Supro amplifiers were just cooler than their National counterpart and other major brands. In 1964, they released many of their amplifiers in blue, red, and white vinyl coverings – very untraditional in a traditional amplifier world. This model shows heavy wear all over the covering to the point where the cabinet is showing, the grille is worn and dirty, and the "Supro" logo from the grille is missing altogether. With this much wear and use, this Supro falls right in the middle of the Average Condition category.

AVERAGE CONDITION

EARLY 1960s AMPEG M-15 BIG M
Courtesy: Savage Audio

Everett Hull designed all his amplifiers for accordions – guitars and rock n' roll music were not acceptable to him and he didn't want his products used for that. By the 1960s, that idea was thrown out the window as guitars were the craze and marketing accordion amplifiers just didn't make sense anymore. This amplifier features two channels with individual controls and a monster fifteen-inch speaker. Heavy wear on the corners and bottom front indicates this amplifier has seen its share of use on the road. The stained grille also shows the numerous drinks spilled over the front. Many amplifiers in average condition like this Ampeg haven't survived. This model is lucky, and as long as it still works, it falls in the Average Condition category.

AVERAGE LOW CONDITION

LATE 1950s OR EARLY 1960s RICKENBACKER M-8
Courtesy: John Beeson/The Music Shoppe

Although the true guitar amplifier "pioneer" remains in question, many people credit Rickenbacker with having built one of the first amplifiers in the late 1920s. When F.C. Hall bought Rickenbacker in 1953, major changes happened in the company including the introduction of a full line of amplifiers. The M Series was very popular and it merged into the B Series a decade later. This M-8 was the entry-level amplifier of the series that probably puts out 5W in an 8-inch speaker. Whoever used this as a practice amplifier did not take very good care of it. The covering is heavily worn and dirty and the bottom of the amplifier looks as though it sat in water for some period of time. You could get away with the bottom as no one really sees it, but the tears extend to the sides indicating there are problems.

POOR CONDITION/RE-COVERING

1959 FENDER VIBROLUX
Courtesy: Willie's American Guitars

This Vibrolux would be a very expensive amplifier had it not spent most of its life with an abusive guitar player. As you can see from the picture, the tweed frays much like denim jeans do. This amplifier is also quite a bit lighter in color than it was originally and there is way too much covering missing for it to even bring average prices. Although this amplifier is in rough shape, it still is a narrow panel tweed by Fender, which is from a very desirable era of amplifiers. We do not list these amplifiers in this condition because much negotiation goes on between the buyer and seller and a solid value is difficult to determine.

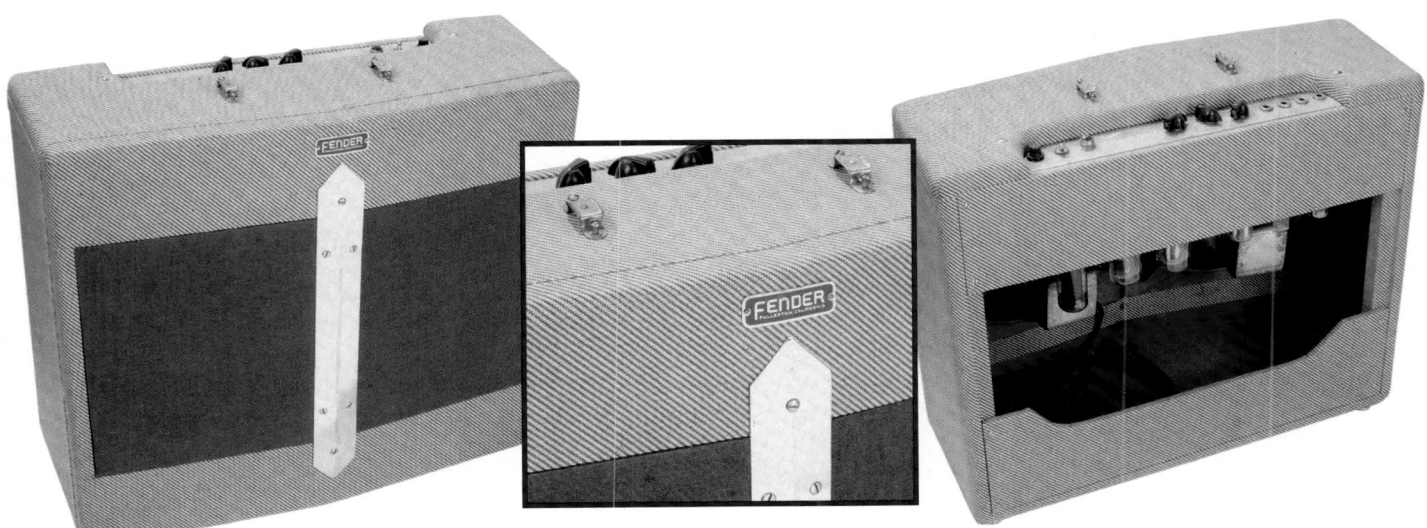

LATE 1940s/EARLY 1950s FENDER DUAL PROFESSIONAL (SUPER)
Courtesy: Savage Audio

At first glance, this amplifier looks to be a very clean example of a Fender narrow panel tweed. Actually, it is too clean – something is not right here. This amplifier has been re-covered in original tweed to make it look new, but there are other signs that show this amplifier's age. The logo, front metal strip, and chrome control panel are heavily oxidized and worn. The handle is also missing. This amplifier reeks of a restoration project that was never finished. All values in this book assume original condition, and a re-covered amplifier generally reduces the price by 50%.

FENDER COVERINGS/GRILLE CLOTHS

Fender Light Tweed

Fender Dark Tweed

Fender White Tolex

Fender Brown Tolex

Fender Black Tolex

Fender Wide Panel Tweed Grille

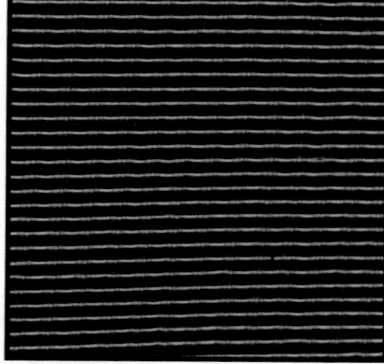

Fender Narrow Panel Tweed Grille

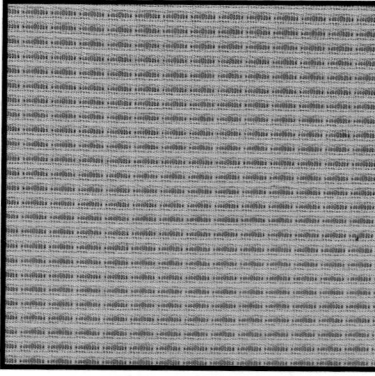

Fender Brownface Wheat Grille

Fender Brownface Brown Grille

Fender Brownface Oxblood Grille

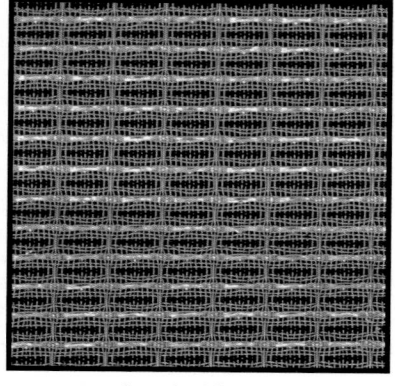

Fender Blackface Grille

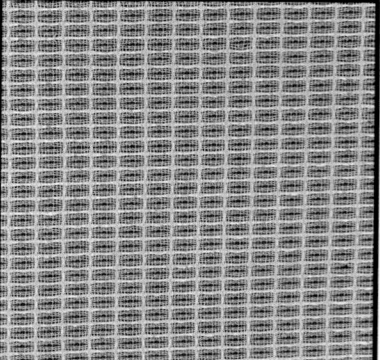

Fender Silverface Grille

MARSHALL COVERINGS/GRILLE CLOTHS

Marshall Black Levant

Marshall Red Levant

Marshall White Levant

Marshall Blue Levant

Marshall Purple Levant

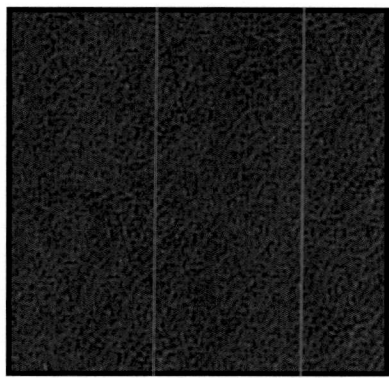

Marshall Black Elephant

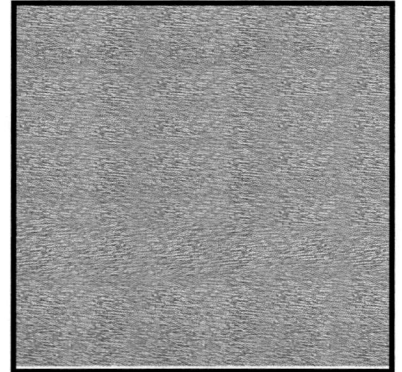

Marshall Early White Grille

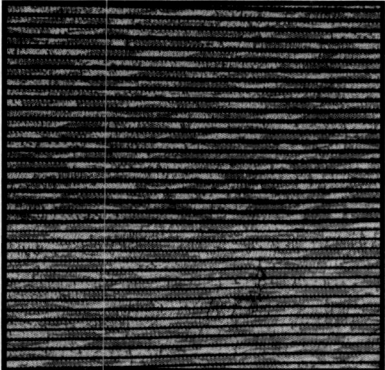

Brown Bluesbreaker Grille

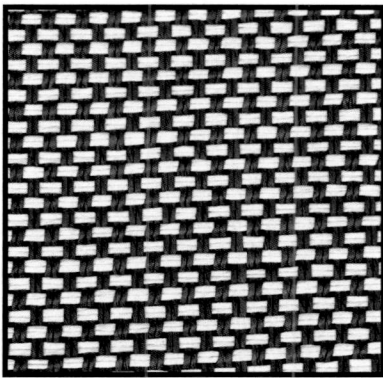

Marshall Basketweave Grille

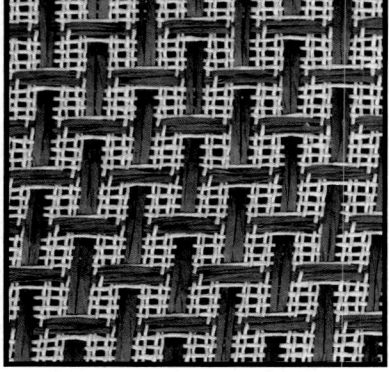

Marshall Chequerboard Grille

Marshall Black Grille

MISC. AMPLIFIER COVERINGS/GRILLE CLOTHS

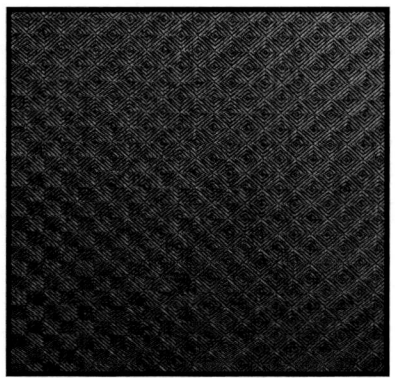

Ampeg Blue Check Covering

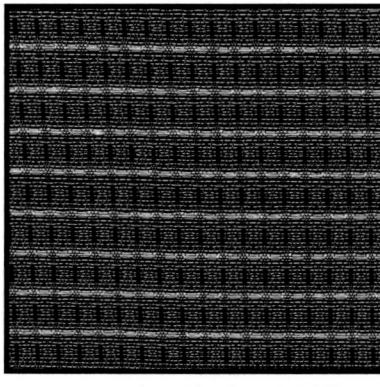

Ampeg Blue Check Era Grille

Ampeg 1970s Era Grille

Gibson Mid-1960s Brown Covering

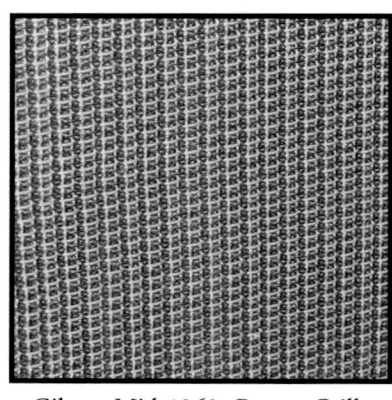

Gibson Mid-1960s Brown Grille

Gibson Late 1960s Grille

Vox Black Covering

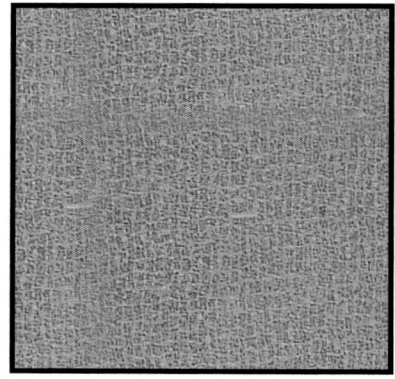

Vox Brown Covering

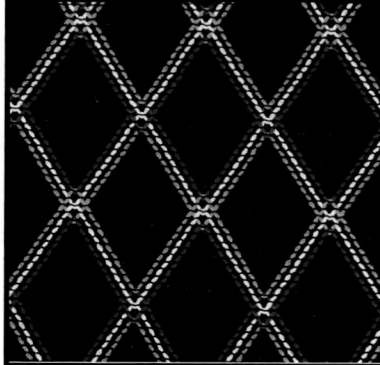

Vox Grille

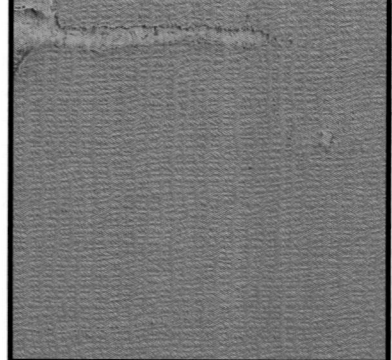

Orange Covering

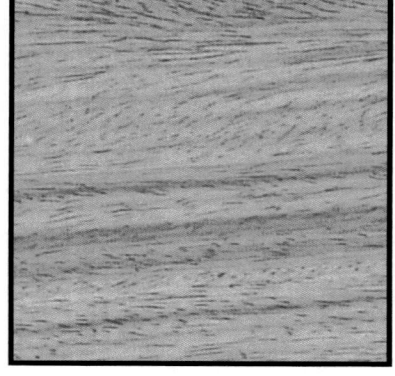

Mesa Boogie Wood Cabinet Covering

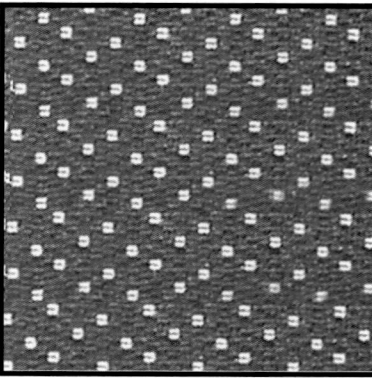

Gretsch Late 1950s Covering

AMPLIFIER CHASSIS

MID-1960s FENDER TWIN REVERB CHASSIS (ORIGINAL)

An amplifier that has been properly maintained can still use all of its original components and still function properly. This is the case with this chassis as the major components are original. The only parts that are non-original are the tubes, and tubes need to be changed over time. Notice that four of the six preamp tubes are missing – this amplifier would not work if you plugged it in right now. All original amplifiers (including chassis) typically command a premium in value.

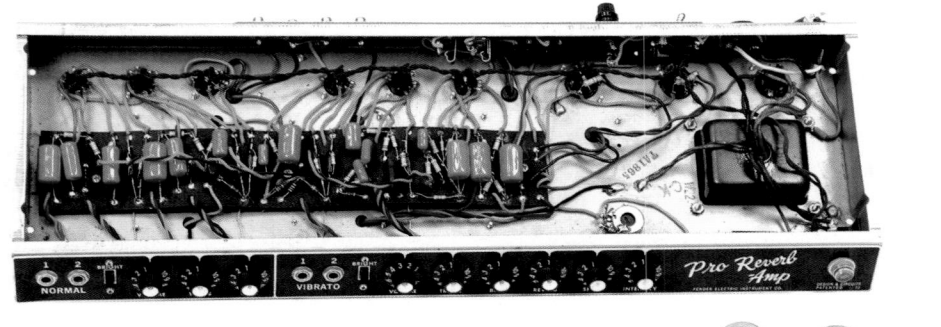

MID-1960s FENDER PRO REVERB (OVERHAULED)

Amplifiers utilize several electronic components, and after time, certain parts are going to wear out. When electric signal paths start leaking, voltage levels are off, and the amplifier just doesn't sound as good, an amplifier may require an "overhaul." Like this example, an overhaul includes replacing faulty and old wiring, filter capacitors, resistors, and any other permanent pieces. This chassis also received new tubes and a thorough cleaning. As far as value, originality is the most important factor, but an amplifier that sounds bad or doesn't work is worth far less than an overhauled model.

AMPLIFIER CHASSIS

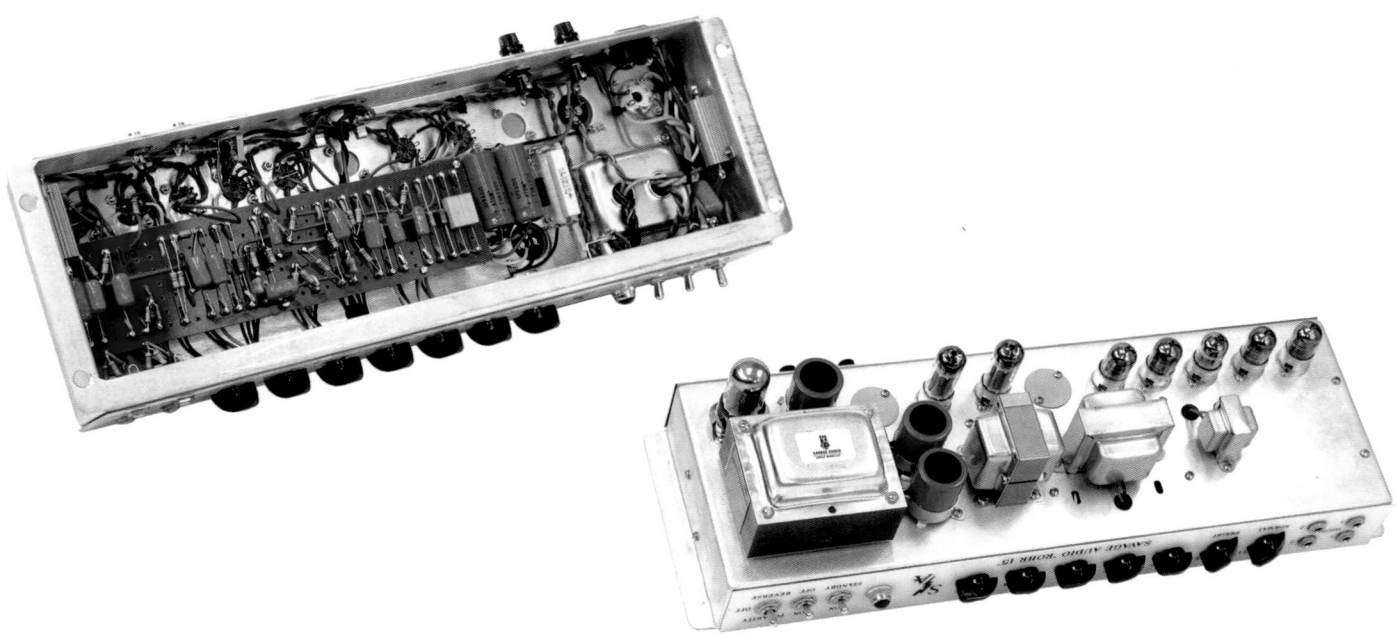

CIRCA 2002 SAVAGE ROHR 15 CHASSIS

Technology has come a long way since the 1960s, and this Savage Rohr 15 Chassis shows it. Note how organized this chassis looks compared to the Fender models on the previous page. Savage builds all their amplifiers by hand with point-to-point connections and wiring. The more organized a chassis is and the less waste it has (excess wiring, unnecessary components, etc.), the better it is going to sound. Amplifiers today are often built with more durable and lightweight parts such as the aluminum casing this chassis uses. This amplifier, at the time it was photographed, was brand new and was awaiting installation into a cabinet.

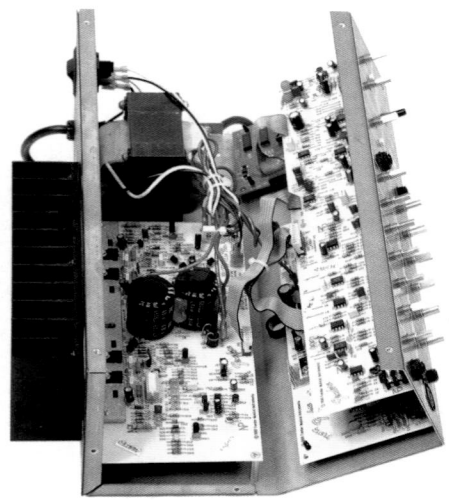

LATE 1990s FENDER ACOUSTASONIC CHASSIS

Which one of these amplifiers is not like the other? Which one of these amplifiers just isn't the same? Sure, this chassis looks more like the inside of a PC, but it really amplifies guitars – honest! Solid-state amplifiers first appeared in the 1960s and were advertised as a more durable option versus tube amplifiers. Instead of using tubes to amplify and shape the tone of the guitar, a series of diodes and transistors does the work. We all know how unpopular these amplifiers were in the 1960s and 1970s, and they really never became a reliable alternative to tube amplifiers until the 1980s. This Fender Acoustasonic has many of the bells and whistles that solid-state amplifiers can provide with digital effects (DFX), instrument and microphone channels, and reverb. A solid-state chassis is often very difficult to repair as the problem often lies in the middle of that circuit board jungle.

A SECTION
3 MONKEYS AMPS

Amplifiers currently built in Raleigh, NC since 2007.

3 Monkeys was founded by guitar tech Greg Howard, former Blockhead amp builder Ossie Ahsen, and Aermosmith guitarist Brad Whitford. Howard began working as Whitford's touring guitar tech in 2002 and as Howard was searching for gear per Whitford's request in 2003, he came in contact with Ahsen who was still building Blockhead amps. Whitford began using Blockhead amps and in 2005 they began discussing building a custom amp and Howard starting his own amp company. Toward the end of 2006, the three of them decided to start building amplifiers, and Ahsen builds an amp specifically for Whitford that becomes the first 3 Monkeys prototype. Howard stopped touring in 2007 and Ahsen moved to North Carolina to focus solely on building guitar amplifiers. Prototypes and revisions were produced through 2007 and by the summer of 2008, 3 Monkeys Amps was taking orders for production models. For more information visit 3 Monkeys' website or contact them directly.

ELECTRIC TUBE AMPLIFIERS

3 Monkeys first amp offering was **The Orangutan** (Street Price $2,499) that has 30-35W output from 4 X 6V6 power tubes and a unique six-position rotary voice switch. The Orangutan is also available as a **The Orangutan 1-12 Combo** (Street Price $2,699) and as the **Super Orangutan** (Street Price $2,999). **Zé Prototype** (Street Price $3,000) is 3 Monkeys' version of the 100W José-modded Marshall that was popular in the 1980s. The **Grease Monkey** (Street Price $2,749) is a British-voiced 30W amp powered by 4 X EL84 power tubes. The **Virgil** (Street Price $2,699) is a 30W master volume model based on Brad Whitford's BW119 model.

3RD POWER AMPLIFICATION

Amplifiers currently produced in Nashville, TN. Previously produced in Franklin, TN beginning in 2009.

3rd Power Amplification founder and designer Jamie Scott builds handmade tube amps in his Franklin, TN shop. His amplifiers include the Dream Series, the Dream Solo Series, and the HLH Series that feature triangle-shaped speaker cabinets. For more information, visit 3rd Power's website or contact Scott directly.

65 AMPS

Amplifiers and speaker cabinets currently produced in North Hollywood, CA since 2010. Previously produced in Valley Village, CA between 2004 and 2010.

65 Amps was founded by Dan Boul and Peter Stroud in 2004. They build tube amps that are designed to blend vintage and new tones in one modern reliable and road-worthy amp. The name 65 Amps comes from the era of amps that many people consider to be the epitome of amp production in 1965. Their amps are all point-to-point hand-wired and built in the U.S. Their amps and cabinets feature a unique style covering as well. For more information, visit 65 Amps' website or contact them directly.

ELECTRIC TUBE AMPLIFIERS

65 Amps produces a variety of models. The **London** features an 18W chassis, two channels, and is available as a head-unit (MSR $2,495), 1-12 in. speaker combo (MSR $3,195), 2-10 in. speaker combo (disc., last MSR was $2,895), or a 2-12 in. speaker combo (MSR $3,295). The **Marquee Club** features a 35W chassis, two channels, and is available as a head-unit (disc., last MSR was $2,895), 1-12 in. speaker combo (disc., last MSR was $3,395), 2-10 in. speaker combo (disc., last MSR was $3,395), or a 2-12 in. speaker combo (disc., last MSR was $3,495). The **Lil' Elvis** is a 12W amp powered by 2 X EL84 power tubes with tremolo and is available as a head-unit (MSR $2,495) or 1-12 in. combo (MSR $2,395). The **Tupleo** is a super versatile cousin to the Lil' Elvis with 20W output from 2 X 6V6 power tubes, and is available as a head-unit (MSR $2,195) or 1-12 in. combo (MSR $2,495). The **Stone Pony** is powered by EF86 and 12AX7 preamp tubes and 7591 power tubes. It is available as a low 25W power version in a head-unit (MSR $2,595) or 1-12 in. combo (MSR $3,195), or a high 50W power version in a head-unit (MSR $2,995) or 2-12 in. combo (MSR $3,295). The **SoHo** is an amp for players who desire a variety of tones and is powered by EL84 tubes. It is available as a low 20W power version in a head-unit (MSR $1,895) or 1-12 in. combo (MSR $3,195), or a high 35W power version in a head-unit (MSR $2,995) or 2-12 in. combo (MSR $3,295). The **Monterey** (formerly called the Memphis) is designed to maximize the potential of American 6V6 tubes. It is available as a low 22W power version in a head-unit (MSR $2,595) or 2-12 in. combo (MSR $3,295), or a high 38W power version in a head-unit (MSR $3,195) or 2-12 in. combo (MSR $3,650). The **Royal Albert** is a British-sounding amp that is powered by KT77 tubes with a choice of tube or solid-state rectification. It is only available as a head-unit (MSR $3,295). The **Apollo Bass** Head (MSR $2,595) is a 50W head unit designed for use with basses and driven by 6L6 power tubes.

Speaker cabinets are available in 1-12 in. (MSR $649), 2-12 in. (MSR $979), and 4-12 in. (MSR $1,950) speaker configurations. A 1-15 in. bass speaker cabinet is also available for the Apollo Bass (MSR $649).

MSR/NOTES		100%	EXCELLENT	AVERAGE		LAST MSR

ACCUGROOVE

Amplifiers and speaker cabinets currently produced in Redding, CA. Previously produced in Cupertino, CA. Distributed by Accugroove.

AccuGroove manufactures extremely high-end lightweight amps and speaker cabinets for guitar, bass, keyboards, and PA systems. Whatever you hear in the studio you can now hear live. There are several cabinets available from a three-way 1-10 in. to a 21 in. subwoofer. Retail prices start at $961. In 2010, Accugroove introduced their Synergy line of amplifiers. For more information visit AccuGroove's website or contact them directly.

CONTACT INFORMATION
ACCUGROOVE
PO Box 990697
Redding, CA 96099
Phone No.: 530-710-8403
Fax No.: 970-680-7130
www.accugroovellc.com
accugroovellc@gmail.com

ACE TONE

Amplifiers and other effects previously produced by Sakata Shokai, Limited in Osaka, Japan between circa 1963 and the 1970s.

Ikutaro Kakehashi founded Ace Electronic Industries, Inc. (better known as Ace Tone) in 1960 as a joint venture with Sakata Shokai in Osaka Japan. Ace Tone produced a variety of musical instruments including organs, drum machines, effects, and amplifiers, but the brand is better known as being the front runner to the Roland corporation. While many of the details are still uncovered and unknown, there are too many similarities between Ace Tone products and what became Roland in the 1970s. Ace Tone offered a guitar amplifiers in both solid-state and tube variations, bass guitar amplifiers, and vocal/channel mixer amplifiers. Most used Ace Tone amplifiers range in value between $50 and $200 depending on the amount of features and condition.

ACOUSTIC

Amplifiers currently produced in China since 2007. Amplifiers previously produced by the Acoustic Control Company in the late 1960s through the mid-1980s, and between 2001 and circa 2005 by Samick in the City of Industry, CA. Currently distributed by Guitar Center Inc.

CONTACT INFORMATION
ACOUSTIC
13659 Victory Blvd. #1-360
Van Nuys, CA 91401
acousticamplification.com
info@acousticamplification.com

Acoustic tube and solid-state amplifiers were introduced in the late 1960s. Their claim to fame was the 360 bass amp, which could efficiently relocate a small house, if needed. The 360 could power up to four speaker cabinets (the 360 is strictly a preamp, and each speaker cabinet had a 200W power amp), thus producing up to 800W of bass.

Acoustic, at its time, was a very futuristic amplifier company. They found themselves in the middle of the transistor versus tube war that was going on in the 1970s. Essentially, they were the only company that had solid-state products that could compete with the big companies (Marshall, Fender, Sunn) of the day. Acoustic established themselves as a bass amp company (even though they made several guitar amps). The bass amps were extremely clean sounding and Acoustic had several innovations including the "Variamp" control and the "Electronic Tuning Fork." There were distortion effects, which were supposed to be fuzz sounds, but became more annoying than anything.

The company folded in the mid-1980s as not many guitar players were drawn in by their products and other companies such as SWR and Hartke were coming around. Acoustic was more "old school" and offered the deep bass sound when bass players were starting to look for the more mid-range sound. With the movie *Josie and the Pussycats*, the Acoustic trademark was revived in 2001 by Samick with the re-introduction of the 360. The Acoustic trademark was reintroduced a third time in 2007. The Author would like to thank Mark Dupree for his contributions to this section.

ELECTRIC TUBE AMPLIFIERS: 1960S & 1970S MODELS

160 – wattage unknown, tubes chassis preamp: 3 X 7025, 12AT7, power: 4 X 6L6, mfg. late 1970s-mid-1980s.

	N/A	$250 - 300	$150 - 200

For a while the tubes used were 2 X 7025 and 2 X 12AT7.

164/165 – 100W (switchable to 60W), 1-12 in. combo, all tube chassis, preamp: 12AX7s, power: 6L6s, dual channels, reverb, front control panel, various contols and switches, wood cabinet, mfg. late 1970s-mid-1980s.

	N/A	$300 - 350	$175 - 225

The 164 and 165 are the same amp with minor differences.

G-60T – 60W, 1-12 in. speaker, all-tube chassis, preamp: 1 X 12AT7, 2 X 12AX7, power: 2 X 6L6, two switchable channels, reverb, front brown control panel, two inputs (low and high), seven brown knobs (v1, v2, t, m, b, r, MV), effects loop, footswitch, external speaker jacks, brown tolex covering, brown grille, mfg. late 1970s.

	N/A	$300 - 375	$200 - 250

G-100T – 100W (switchable to 50W), head-unit only, tube chassis, preamp: 3 X 7025, 12AT7, power: 4 X 6L6, dual channels, reverb, copper control panel, two inputs (high and low), eight black and silver knobs (v1, v2, t, m, b, presence, reverb, master), five-band equalizer, parallel effects loop, black covering, brown grille, mfg. late 1970s-mid-1980s.

	N/A	$350 - 425	$250 - 300

MSR/NOTES	100%	EXCELLENT	AVERAGE	LAST MSR

ELECTRIC SS AMPLIFIERS: 1960S & 1970S MODELS

Although very little information exists about Acoustic amplifiers, it appears that models built in the 1970s typically featured black covering, and models in the 1980s have brown covering. There may also be some variance in specs from different years of the same model.

114 – 50W, 2-10 in. speakers, solid-state combo, reverb, bright, master volume, black Tolex covering, black grille, mfg. late 1970s-mid-1980s.

N/A $200 - 250 $120 - 150

115 – similar to the 114 except has 1-12 in. speaker, mfg. late 1970s.

N/A $250 - 300 $135 - 175

116 – 75W, 1-15 in. speaker, solid-state combo, bright, boost, black Tolex covering, black grille, mfg. late 1970s-mid-1980s.

N/A $250 - 300 $135 - 175

120 – 125W, head-unit only, solid-state, black control panel with blue stripe, four knobs (v, t, m, b), five-band equalizer, mfg. late 1970s-early 1980s.

N/A $175 - 225 $100 - 135

123 – 100W, 1-12 in. speaker, solid-state combo, reverb, master volume, five-band equalizer, bright switch, black Tolex covering, black grille, mfg. late 1970s-mid-1980s

N/A $250 - 300 $135 - 175

124 – 100W, 4-10 in. speaker, solid-state combo, reverb, master volume, five-band equalizer, bright switch, black Tolex covering, black grille, mfg. late 1970s-mid-1980s.

N/A $250 - 300 $135 - 175

125 – similar to the 124 except has 2-12 in. speakers, mfg. late 1970s-mid-1980s.

N/A $250 - 300 $135 - 175

126 – similar to the 124 except is a bass amp with 1-15 in. speaker, mfg. late 1970s-mid-1980s.

N/A $250 - 300 $135 - 175

127 – approx. 100W, combo unit, 2-12 in. speakers, solid-state chassis, two channels, reverb, front brown control panel, single input, 11 brown and gold knobs (Ch. 1: v, t, m, b, Ch.2 v/drive, t, m, b, Both: p, r, MV), preamp in, power out, ext. speaker out, optional footswitch, brown covering, brown grille, mfg. late 1970s-mid 1980s.

courtesy Tommy Thorson   courtesy Tommy Thorson

N/A $300 - 350 $175 - 225

134 – 100W, 4-10 in. speakers, solid-state combo, dual channels, reverb, vibrato, front black control panel with blue stripe, four inputs (two per channel), nine black knobs (Ch. 1: v, b, t, Ch. 2: v, b, t, r, s, i), bright switches, black covering, mfg. 1972-76.

N/A $300 - 350 $175 - 225

135 – 100W, 2-12 in. speakers, solid-state combo, dual channels, reverb, vibrato, front black control panel with blue stripe, four inputs (two per channel), nine black knobs (Ch. 1: v, b, t, Ch. 2: v, b, t, r, s, i), bright switches, black covering, mfg. 1972-76.

N/A $300 - 350 $175 - 225

136 – 110W, 1-15 in. Eminence speaker with folded horn-cabinet, solid-state combo, dual channels, front black control panel with blue stripe, four inputs (two per channel), six black knobs (v, b, t, for each channel), black covering, mfg. 1972-76.

N/A $350 - 425 $200 - 250

140 BASS AMP – 125W, head unit and one speaker cabinet with 2-15 in. speakers, solid-state chassis, mfg. 1972-76.

| Head & Cabinet | N/A | $300 - 350 | $175 - 225 | |
| Head Only | N/A | $175 - 225 | $100 - 135 | |

MSR/NOTES	100%	EXCELLENT	AVERAGE	LAST MSR

150 – 110W, head-unit only, solid-state chassis, two channels, vibrato, reverb, front black control panel with blue stripe, two inputs, nine knobs (Ch. 1: v, t, b, Ch. 2: v, t, b, r, s, i), black covering, mfg. 1960s-late 1970s.

	N/A	$175 - 225	$100 - 135	

Later models had black knobs and these models had 125W output. The 150 was one of Acoustic's most popular models and show up quite often in the used marketplace.

* ***150B Bass*** – similar to the 150, except designed for bass use, mfg. 1960s-late 1970s.

	N/A	$175 - 225	$100 - 135	

220 BASS – 160W/170W, head-unit only, solid-state, high and low gain, bright, boost, 5-band equalizer, black control panel, black covering, black grille, mfg. mid 1970s-early 1980s.

160/170W	N/A	$200 - 250	$120 - 150	
200W	N/A	$200 - 250	$120 - 150	

In 1981, the amp was increased to 200W.

230 – similar to the 220 Bass except is a guitar amp without boost or high/low inputs, but has reverb and master volume, mfg. mid 1970s.

	N/A	$200 - 250	$120 - 150	

260 – 275W, head-unit only, solid-state chassis, two channels, tremolo, front black and blue control panel, four inputs, seventeen silver knobs, various buttons and switches, black covering, mfg. 1960s-mid 1970s.

	N/A	$275 - 325	$150 - 200	

270 – 275W with one cabinet (375W with two cabinets), guitar head-unit only, solid-state chassis, two channels, fuzz, reverb, tremolo, front black control panel, two inputs, seven knobs (v, t, m, b, s, i, reverb/fuzz), five-band graphic EQ, channel switch, fuzz/reverb switch, ground switch, power switch, rear panel: two speaker jacks, two monitor out jacks, black covering, mfg. 1970s.

	N/A	$300 - 350	$175 - 225	

320 BASS – 300W, head-unit only, solid-state, 5-band equalizer, preamp in/out, dual channels, black covering, mfg. 1970s.

	N/A	$300 - 375	$175 - 225	

330 – similar to the 320 Bass except is a guitar amp with reverb, mfg. 1970s.

	N/A	$300 - 375	$175 - 225	

360 – Preamp head-unit only (power amp is in the speaker cabinet), solid-state chassis, single channel, fuzz, front black control panel with blue stripe, two inputs (high and low), nine knobs (v, t, b, variamp balance, effect, fuzz attack, fuzz gain, electronic tuning fork course, and fine), bright/normal switch, switch for tuning fork and ground rocker, black covering, mfg. 1960s-early 1970s.

courtesy Savage Audio

courtesy Savage Audio

	N/A	$425 - 500	$250 - 300	

The 360 was the flagship model for Acoustic. This amp is known for pumping out large amounts of bass that could be heard clearly at great distances. This amplifier (and cabinet) utilized the folded-horn cabinet design and the power-amp was built in the bottom of the cabinet with the speakers. This meant that the head only housed the preamp. With the speaker(s) mounted backwards inside of a chamber the sound directed into a giant bin creating a lot of bass in a little space. This amp was so loud that there was a warning label on the back that stated "prolonged use could lead to hearing loss." Although the 360 head is valued by itself, the head is virtually only a preamp without a companion speaker cabinet. Since Acoustic offered several speaker cabinets, please refer to the Speaker cabinet section for more information.

370 – 375W (275W on later models), bass head unit, solid-state chassis, single channel, front black control panel, two inputs, four knobs (v, t, m, b), five-band graphic equalizer, ground switch, power switch, black covering, mfg. early 1970s-late 1970s.

	N/A	$500 - 600	$300 - 350	

MSR/NOTES	100%	EXCELLENT	AVERAGE	LAST MSR

400 – 375W, stereo power amp only, solid-state, dual power supplies, high speed fan cooling, rack mount, black control panel, mfg. 1970s.

| | N/A | $250 - 300 | $135 - 175 | |

450 LEAD/BASS – 175W, head-unit only, solid-state chassis, dual channels, front black control panel, two inputs, six black knobs (v, t, m, b, distortion control, aux. v), lead/bass switch, normal/bright switch, five-band equalizer, black covering, mfg. mid-1970s.

| | N/A | $275 - 325 | $150 - 200 | |

470 BASS – 170W, head-unit only, solid-state, dual channels, reverb, tremolo, built in distortion, black control panel, 12 black or white knobs including bass, treble, and mid controls, 5-band equalizer, line in & out, black covering, no grille, mfg. mid-1970s.

| | N/A | $300 - 375 | $175 - 225 | |

833 – 200W, power amp only, solid-state, rack mount, mfg. late 1970s.

| | N/A | $135 - 175 | $80 - 100 | |

ELECTRIC SS AMPS: MISC MODELS (CURRENT/RECENT MFG.)

260 MINI-STACK (CURRENT MFG.) – 100W, 1-10 in. speaker in a separate custom-designed cabinet, mini-stack piggyback bass configuration, solid-state chassis, front black control panel with blue accents, two inputs (passive, active), four knobs (v, l, m, h), aux. in jack, headphone jack, power switch, black covering, black grille with a large blue stripe in the middle and white trim (cabinet only), towel bar handle with built-in casters on the cabinet, head dimensions: 12 in. wide, 5 in. tall, 8 in. deep, 8 lbs., cabinet dimensions: 13 in. wide, 24.5 in. tall, 11.75 in. deep, 36.2 lbs., mfg. 2007-disc.

| | $300 | $175 - 225 | $100 - 135 | $600 |

360 BASS AMPLIFIER (EARLY 2000S MFG.) – 950W (2 475W power amps), head-unit only, dual channels, black and blue control panel, high and low inputs, 16 silver knobs (Ch A: level, low, mid, contour, high, fuzz level and attack, tuning fork level and pitch, Ch B: level, low, mid, high, direct out level, low and high crossovers), harmonically time aligned, convection cooled, effects loop, foot pedal, mfg. 2001-02.

| | N/A | $475 - 600 | $300 - 350 | |

Four speaker cabinets were produced to match up with the series 360 bass head. The numbers correspond to the number and how big the speakers are in the cabinet. The **FH-118** has 1-18 in. speaker and a flat front, the **FL-410T** has 4-10 in. speakers with a tweeter and a flat front, the **VL-215** has 2-15 in. speakers and an angled front, and the **VL-810T** has 8-10 in. speakers with a tweeter and an angled front. The FH-118 is recommended to match up with the VL-810T and the VL-215 with the FL-410T.

ACOUSTIC/ACOUSTIC BASS SS AMPS: AG/AB SERIES (CURRENT MFG.)

AB50
courtesy Acoustic

AG30
courtesy Acoustic

AG120S
courtesy Acoustic

AB50 – 50W, 1-10 in. speaker and a 2 in. tweeter, acoustic bass combo, solid-state chassis, two channels, front black control panel with blue accents, two combination XLR/standard 1/4 in. inputs (one per channel), five knobs (Ch. 1 v, Ch. 2 v, l, m, h), line out jack, aux. in jack, headphone jack, rear panel: power switch, angled cabinet design, black covering, black grille with white trim, 15.5 in. wide, 16 in. tall, 15.5 in. deep, 33 lbs., mfg. 2007-disc.

| | $200 | $120 - 150 | $75 - 95 | $400 |

AG15 – 15W, 1-8 in. speaker and a coaxial tweeter, acoustic guitar combo, solid-state chassis, single channel, chorus, front black control panel with blue accents, single input, five knobs (v, l, m, h, chorus depth), chorus on/off switch, aux. in jack, headphone jack, line out jack, power switch, angled cabinet design, black covering, black grille with white trim, 16 in. wide, 16.75 in. tall, 15 in. deep, 32 lbs., mfg. 2007-disc.

| | $100 | $60 - 80 | $35 - 50 | $200 |

AG30 – 30W, 1-8 in. speaker and a coaxial tweeter, acoustic guitar combo, solid-state chassis, two channels, 16 digital effects, front black control panel with blue accents, two combination Speakon/standard 1/4 in. inputs (one per channel), eight knobs (Ch. 1 v, Ch. 2 v, l, m, mid-freq., h, effects level, effects select), aux. in jack, headphone jack, line out jack, angled cabinet design, black covering, black grille with white trim, 18 in. wide, 18.75 in. tall, 17 in. deep, 44 lbs., mfg. 2007-disc.

| | $200 | $120 - 150 | $75 - 95 | $400 |

MSR/NOTES	100%	EXCELLENT	AVERAGE	LAST MSR

AG60 – 60W, 2-8 in. speakers and a coaxial tweeter, acoustic guitar combo, solid-state chassis, two channels, 16 digital effects, front black control panel with blue accents, four combination XLR/standard 1/4 in. inputs (two per channel, each with their own level control), 18 knobs (Ch. 1: v1, v2, l, m, mid-freq., h, DSP level, DSP select, Ch. 2: v1, v2, l, m, mid-freq., h, DSP level, DSP select, All: aux. in level, MV), aux. in jack, headphone jack, rear panel: power switch, effects loop, XLR balanced line out, 1/4 in. unbalanced line out, line out level control, ground lift switch, tilt-back cabinet design, black covering, black grille with white trim, 21.25 in. wide, 20.75 in. tall, 15 in. deep, 58 lbs., mfg. 2007-disc.

	$350	$225 - 275	$120 - 150	$700

AG120S – 120W (60W for each power amp), 2-8 in. speakers and a coaxial tweeter, acoustic guitar combo, solid-state chassis, two channels, 16 digital effects, front black control panel with blue accents, four combination XLR/standard 1/4 in. inputs (two per channel, each with their own level control), 18 knobs (Ch. 1: v1, v2, l, m, mid-freq., h, DSP level, DSP select, Ch. 2: v1, v2, l, m, mid-freq., h, DSP level, DSP select, All: aux. in level, MV), aux. in jack, headphone jack, rear panel: power switch, effects loop, stereo line outs, tilt-back cabinet design, black covering, black grille with white trim, mfg. 2007-disc.

	$500	$300 - 375	$175 - 225	$1,000

BASS SS AMPS: B SERIES (CURRENT MFG.)

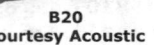

B20
courtesy Acoustic

B200
courtesy Acoustic

B600H
courtesy Acoustic

B10 – 10W, 1-10 in. speaker, bass combo, solid-state chassis, single channel, front black control panel with blue accents, single input, four knobs (v, l, m, h), aux. in jack, headphone jack, power switch, black covering, black grille with white piping, 16.75 in. wide, 20 in. tall, 13 in. deep, 23 lbs., mfg. 2007-disc.

	$100	$60 - 80	$35 - 50	$200

B20 – 20W, 1-12 in. speaker, bass combo, solid-state chassis, single channel, front black control panel with blue accents, two inputs, five knobs (v, l, l/m, m/h, h), aux. in jack, headphone jack, power switch, black covering, black grille with white piping, 13 in. wide, 15.75 in. tall, 10 in. deep, 31.5 lbs., mfg. 2007-disc.

	$150	$95 - 120	$50 - 75	$300

B100 – 100W, 1-15 in. speaker, bass combo, solid-state chassis, single channel, front black control panel with blue accents, two inputs (passive, active), seven knobs (g, v, freq. notch, l, l/m, m/h, h), power switch, rear panel: effects loop, external speaker jack, black covering, black grille with white piping, mfg. 2007-present.

MSR $500	$250	$160 - 200	$100 - 130	

B200 – 200W, 1-15 in. speaker with a built-in horn, bass combo, solid-state chassis, single channel, front black control panel with blue accents, two inputs (passive, active), nine knobs (g, v, freq. notch, 63, 150, 350, 800, 2k, 5k), power switch, rear panel: effects loop, external speaker jack, XLR balanced line out with level control and ground/lift switch, tweeter on/off switch, recessed side handles, black covering, black grille with white piping, mfg. 2007-present.

MSR $700	$350	$225 - 275	$120 - 150	

* *B200H* – similar to the B200, except in head-unit configuration with one side handle, mfg. 2007-present.

MSR $500	$250	$160 - 200	$100 - 130	

B450 – 450W (600W with an external speaker cabinet), 2-10 in. speakers with a built-in horn, bass combo, solid-state chassis, single channel, front black control panel with blue accents, two inputs (passive, active), nine knobs (g, v, freq. notch, 63, 150, 350, 800, 2k, 5k), mute switch, freq. notch on/off switch, power switch, rear panel: effects loop with mix control, external speaker jack, XLR balanced line out with level control and ground/lift and pre/post EQ switches, recessed side handles, black covering, black grille with white piping, mfg. 2007-present.

MSR $1,200	$600	$400 - 475	$250 - 300	

B600H – 600W, bass head-unit, solid-state chassis, single channel, front black control panel with blue accents, two inputs (passive, active), nine knobs (g, v, freq. notch, 63, 150, 350, 800, 2k, 5k), mute switch, freq. notch on/off switch, power switch, rear panel: effects loop with mix control, external speaker jack, XLR balanced line out with level control and ground/lift and pre/post EQ switches, single side handle, black covering, mfg. 2007-present.

MSR $1,000	$500	$300 - 375	$175 - 225	

MSR/NOTES	100%	EXCELLENT	AVERAGE	LAST MSR

B115 SPEAKER CABINET – 250W, 1-15 in. speaker with a high-freq. horn, 8 ohm impedance, two 1/4 in. parallel inputs, horn on/off switch, recessed spring-loaded side-mounted handles, caster sockets, black covering, black grille with blue accents and white trim, mfg. 2007-present.

MSR $400	$200	$120 - 150	$75 - 95	

B410 SPEAKER CABINET – 400W, 4-10 in. speakers with a high-freq. horn, 8 ohm impedance, two 1/4 in. parallel inputs, horn on/off switch, recessed spring-loaded side-mounted handles, caster sockets, black covering, black grille with blue accents and white trim, mfg. 2007-present.

MSR $600	$300	$175 - 225	$100 - 135	

B810 SPEAKER CABINET – 800W, 8-10 in. speakers with a high-freq. horn, 4 ohm impedance, 1/4 in. and Speakon inputs, horn on/off switch, recessed spring-loaded side-mounted handles, built-in rear casters with a steel kick plate and skid rails, black covering, black grille with a large blue stripe, blue accents, and white trim, mfg. 2007-present.

MSR $1,200	$600	$400 - 475	$250 - 300	

SPEAKER AND P.A. CABINETS: 1960S & 1970S MODELS

The 800 series are all PA cabinets with these following models and corresponding speakers: The 804 has 2-12 in. and 3-8 in. speakers with two piezo horns and a sealed column. The 806 has 1-15 in., a midrange horn, a piezo horn, and a front loaded tuned reflex. The 807 has 2-12 in., a midrange horn, two piezo horns, and a front loaded tuned reflex cabinet. The 808 has 2-15 in. speakers with three midrange horns, two piezo horns, and a front loaded tuned reflex. The 811 has one sectional horn with six piezo horns. The 812 has 4-15 in. speakers and front loaded tuned reflex. The 813 has 2-15 in. speakers with one midrange horn and two piezo horns. All of the models are PA cabinets and have black Tolex covering and a black grille.

301 POWERED CAB – 200W powered cab, speaker cabinet that matches the 360 head-unit, 1-18 in. speaker in a baffle unit, large blue panel front, black covering, mfg. 1960s-early 1970s.

	N/A	$425 - 500	$250 - 300	

301 SPEAKER CAB – 300W, passive cab speaker cabinet that matches the 370 head-unit, 1-18" speaker in a baffle unit, small blue panel front, black covering, mfg. early 1970s-late 1970s.

	N/A	$325 - 400	$200 - 250	

401 – 2-12 in. speaker cabinet, front loaded sealed horn, black Tolex covering, black grille, mfg. 1970s.

	N/A	$200 - 250	$120 - 150	

402 – 2-15 in. speaker cabinet, front loaded vented baffle, tuned reflex, black Tolex covering, black grille, mfg. 1970s.

	N/A	$250 - 300	$135 - 175	

403 – 4-12 in. speaker cabinet, sealed system, black Tolex covering, black grille, mfg. 1970s.

	N/A	$225 - 275	$135 - 175	

404 – 6-12 in. speaker cabinet, sealed system, black Tolex covering, black grille, mfg. 1970s.

	N/A	$325 - 400	$175 - 225	

407 – 2-15 in. speaker cabinet with midrange horns, front loaded sealed horn, black Tolex covering, black grille, mfg. 1970s.

	N/A	$250 - 300	$150 - 200	

408 – 4-15 in. speaker cabinet, tuned combination reflex, black Tolex covering, black grille, mfg. 1970s.

	N/A	$275 - 325	$175 - 225	

ACOUSTIC IMAGE

Amplifiers currently produced in Raleigh, NC. Distributed by Acoustic Image.

Acoustic Image produces amplifiers for acoustic and electric guitars and basses. Dr. Rick Jones is the founder and president of the company, and he felt that the amplifiers available for acoustic instruments were not good enough and that the public demand was great enough to develop a product that was of the finest quality. Acoustic Image uses this philosophy: "Acoustic Image products are designed and built to meet the specific needs of professionals for natural, powerful and practical sound reinforcement." Although their name suggests only acoustic amplifiers, their products are designed for all types of instruments including electric guitars and basses. For more information, visit Acoustic Image's website or contact them directly.

GUITAR AND BASS SS AMPLIFIERS AND CABINETS

The **Clarus 1** (MSR $839) features 400W output power in a simple, single-channel, small, lightweight (5 lbs.) amp. The **Clarus 1R** has added reverb (disc.). The **Clarus 2R** (disc. 2009, last MSR was $1,099) features two channels and reverb. The **Clarus SL** (disc. 2007, last MSR was $949) and **Clarus SL-R** (disc. 2007, last MSR was $1,099) have 350W output power and weigh less than the other Clarus models (40 oz). The **Clarus+** (MSR $1,149) has 800W output with two channels and effects. The **Coda R**

MSR/NOTES	100%	EXCELLENT	AVERAGE	LAST MSR

Ten 2
courtesy Acoustic Image

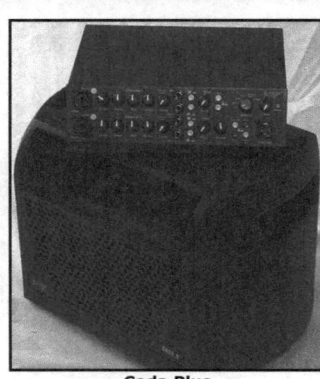

Coda Plus
courtesy Acoustic Image

Focus 2R
courtesy Acoustic Image

(disc. 2009, last MSR was $1,439) has the Clarus 2R chassis built in combo form with 1-10 in. downfiring woofer, 5 in. mid-range speaker, and a 1 in. tweeter all in a 20 lbs. lightweight package. The **Coda+** (MSR $1,549) has 800W output, two channels, effects, and a removable head. The **Contra** (MSR $1,169) has the Clarus 1 chassis built in combo form with 1-10 in. downfiring woofer, 5 in. mid-range speaker, and a 1 in. tweeter all in a 20 lbs. lightweight package. The **Contra EX** (MSR $519) is an extension speaker cabinet meant to match up with the Contra. It features all of the same speakers as the Contra without any amplifier. The Focus line of amplifiers are based on the Clarus, but with 800W of power. The **Corus** (disc. 2009, last MSR was $1,439) is similar to the Coda R, except it has slightly less bass response. The **Chorus+** (MSR $1,589) is similar to the Coda+, except has a more forward sound and a slightly reduced bass response. The **Focus 1** (disc. 2009, last MSR was $1,299) has a single channel, and the **Focus 2** (disc. 2009, last MSR was $1,549) has two channels and reverb. The **Focus SA** (disc. 2007, last MSR was $999) is strictly a power amp version of the Focus (800W). The **Ten2** (MSR $1,769) has 800W output in a 2-10 in. speaker combo that is advertised as the world's smallest and lightest 2-10 in. combo. The **Ten2 EX** (MSR $749) is an extension speaker cabinet for the Ten2 with 2-10 in. speakers.

ADA

Analog/Digital Associates. Amplifiers and speaker cabinets previously produced in Berkeley and Oakland, CA, from 1977 to 2002.

ADA started by building effects pedals, including Flanger and Final Phase. Later on, they became well-known for their preamps and power amps. ADA also produced various speaker cabinets, combo units, and signal processors.

PREAMPS

- Add $30 for MIDI program changer (Model MPC).
- Add $50 for MIDI foot controller (Model MC-1).
- Add $75 for MIDI expandable controller (Model MXC).

MP-1 – preamp only, rack-mount unit, tube chassis with 12AX7s, 128 MIDI-programmable channels, front control panel, various functions including tone controls, noise gate, chorus, tube voices, effects loop, and stereo outputs, black casing, mfg. late 1980s-mid-1990s.

	N/A	$200 - 250	$120 - 150

MP-2 – preamp only, rack-mount unit, tube chassis with 12AX7s, 128 MIDI-programmable channels, front control panel, various functions including tone controls, nine-band graphic EQ, chorus, ten tube voices, effects loop, and stereo outputs, black casing, mfg. late 1980s-mid-1990s.

	N/A	$250 - 300	$135 - 175

MB-1 BASS – bass preamp only, rack-mount unit, tube and solid-state parallel circuits chassis, MIDI-programmable, front control panel, various functions including 256 user programs, 79 factory presets, five-band programmable semi-parametric EQ, programmable compressor, effects loop, and limiting circuit for speaker protection, black casing, mfg. late 1980s-mid-1990s.

	N/A	$200 - 250	$120 - 150

AER

Audio Electric Research. Amplifiers currently produced in Germany. AER has been producing amplifiers since 1992. Currently distributed in the U.S. by SFM in Montreal, Quebec, Canada. Previously distributed in the U.S. by Musiquip, Inc. in Dorval, Quebec, Canada.

AER has been producing acoustic amplifiers and other acoustic products since the mid-1990s. AER's goal is to provide acoustic players with the best possible amplified sound. Their biggest feats to date are the Acousticube and Compact 60 models. For more information, contact the U.S. distributor directly.

CONTACT INFORMATION
AER
U.S. Distributor: Musicquip Inc.
325 Bouchard Blvd.
Dorval, Quebec H9S 1A9 Canada
Phone No.: 866-832-8679
Fax No.: 800-563-2948
www.aer-amps.de
info@musiquip.com

ACOUSTIC AMPLIFIERS

AER features amplifiers, subwoofers, speaker enclosures, and other accessories. The **Acousticube III** (MSR $3,499) is the third version of the Acousticube Series the company originally launched for acoustic guitars in 1992. It features 120W power, 1-8 in. speaker with a tweeter, two channels, programmable digital effects, and other options. The Acousticube III is also available with

MSR/NOTES	100%	EXCELLENT	AVERAGE	LAST MSR

a Natural or Mahogany oak-stained cabinet (MSR $4,399). AER also produces the **Compact 60/2** (MSR $1,299, 100% price new $1,099, also available with Red or Gray covering and Natural or Mahogany oak-stained cabinet MSR $1,599), **Compact Mobile** (MSR $1,999, 100% new price $1,699), **Compact Classic Pro** (MSR $2,099, 100% price new $1,799), the **Compact-XL** (MSR $2,199), **Domino-2** (MSR $2,099, 100% new price $1,799), **Domino-3** (MSR $2,799), and the small-sized **Alpha** (MSR $1,029, 100% new price $899) for acoustic instruments that is also available with Red or Gray covering, and the **Alpha Plus** (MSR $1,129) that has 50W output and a different look than the Alpha. For bass guitars, AER offers the **Basscube** (disc. 2006) and the **Basic Performer** (disc. 2006, last MSR was $2,399), and in 2007, AER introduced the **Bottomline Bass System** that was first offered as a head (MSR $2,999), but has expanded to the combo **Amp One** (MSR $1,999), combo **Amp Two** (MSR $2,599) and three cabinets (**Cab One**: MSR $1,499, **Cab Two**: $1,299, and **Cab Three**: $1,099). The **Basic Performer** (MSR $2,499) is designed for acoustic basses and has two channels. The **BassCube2** (MSR $4,499) is another amp designed for acoustic basses and has 550W output. AER also offers an amp for electric guitars called the **Cheeky D.** (MSR $2,299) that has 200/240W output, 1-10 in. speaker, and two channels.

AGUILAR

Amplifers currently produced in New York City, NY, since 1995.

Aguilar makes a wide variety of bass power amps, preamps, and speaker cabinets. They also have some effects such as the Direct Box. The head amplifiers are tube along with one hybrid. These are high quality amplifiers but they also cost a premium. All of the amps are rack mount, but can be used otherwise such as with the Aguilar cabinets. For more information, visit Aguilar's website or contact them directly.

CONTACT INFORMATION
AGUILAR
599 Broadway, 7th Floor
New York, NY 10012
Phone No.: 212-431-9109
Fax No.: 212-431-8201
www.aguilaramp.com
info@aguilaramp.com

ELECTRIC BASS AMPLIFIERS: AG SERIES

AG 500 Head
courtesy Aguilar

AG 500SC Head
courtesy Aguilar

AG 500 HEAD – 500W @ 4 ohms (250W @ 8 ohms), two-space rack-mount or regular head-unit, solid-state chassis, two channels, front black or brown control panel, single input, 15 black knobs (Ch. 1: g, t, h/m, l/m, b, MV, Ch. 2: saturation, contour, t, m, b, p, MV, FX: effects send level with push/pull -20dB, effects return level with push/pull series), -10dB switch, bright switch, two deep switches (one per channel), channel switch, effects loop, XLR direct line out with pre/post EQ and ground/lift switches, footswitch jack, mute switch, power switch, rear panel: two Speakon and two 1/4 in. standard speaker jacks, tuner out jack, available in black or Boss Brown casing, 17 in. wide, 3.5 in. tall, 10 in. deep, 18 lbs., mfg. 2005-present.

MSR $1,749	$1,300	$750 - 900	$475 - 550	

• **Add $115 (MSR $149) for head case.**

* *AG 500-112C Combo* – similar to the AC 500 Head, except in combo form with 1-12 in. speaker and a tweeter, black covering, black grille, 60 lbs., mfg. 2005-07.

	$1,650	$1,050 - 1,200	$600 - 700	$2,195

* *AG 500-212C Combo* – similar to the AC 500 Head, except in combo form with 2-12 in. speakers and a tweeter, black covering, black grille, 95 lbs., mfg. 2005-07.

	$1,950	$1,200 - 1,400	$700 - 800	$2,595

AG 500SC HEAD – 500W @ 4 ohms (250W @ 8 ohms), two-space rack-mount or regular head-unit, solid-state chassis, single channel, front black or brown control panel, single input, eight black knobs (g, t, h/m, l/m, b, MV, FX: effects send level with push/pull -20dB, effects return level with push/pull series), -10dB switch, bright switch, deep switch, effects loop, XLR direct line out with pre/post EQ and ground/lift switches, footswitch jack, mute switch, power switch, rear panel: two Speakon and two 1/4 in. standard speaker jacks, tuner out jack, available in black or Boss Brown casing, 17 in. wide, 3.5 in. tall, 10 in. deep, 18 lbs., mfg. 2005-present.

MSR $1,449	$1,100	$625 - 775	$400 - 475	

• **Add $115 (MSR $149) for head case.**

* *AG 500SC-112C Combo* – similar to the AC 500SC Head, except in combo form with 1-12 in. speaker and a tweeter, black covering, black grille, 60 lbs., mfg. 2005-07.

	$1,450	$900 - 1,050	$550 - 650	$1,895

* *AG 500SC-212C Combo* – similar to the AC 500 Head, except in combo form with 2-12 in. speakers and a tweeter, black covering, black grille, 95 lbs., mfg. 2005-07.

	$1,650	$1,050 - 1,200	$600 - 700	$2,195

ELECTRIC BASS AMPLIFIERS: DB SERIES

MSR/NOTES	100%	EXCELLENT	AVERAGE	LAST MSR

The **DB900** (disc. 2007, last MSR was $629) is a tube direct box with 1 X 12AX7 tube. The **DB924** (disc. 2007, last MSR was $229) is an unattached preamp with volume, treble, and bass controls. The **OBP1** (MSR $155, 100% new price is $120) is an onboard preamp that mounts right onto a bass guitar and has two bands of boost for the guitar. The **OPB2** (MSR $169, 100% new price is $130) was introduced in 2007 and has two bands of boost and cut. The **OBP3** (MSR $189-$199, 100% new price is $145-$150) was introduced in 2004 and has three bands of boost and cut.

DB 359 – 200W, rack-mount head-unit only, tube chassis, preamp: 2 X 12AX7, 1 X 12AU7, power: 4 X 6550, single channel, front silver control panel, two inputs, seven black knobs (v, t, m, b, MV, two FX knobs), bs, ds, direct line out, effects loop, black casing, 50 lbs., mfg. 1998-2004.

	N/A	$1,650 - 2,000	$1,100 - 1,350	$3,795

DB 659 PRE-AMP – preamp only, one-space rack-mount head-unit only, tube chassis, preamp: 2 X 12AX7, 1 single channel, front silver control panel, single input, seven black knobs (v, t, m, b, MV, two FX knobs), bs, ds, direct line out, effects loop, black casing, 6 lbs., disc. 2006.

	$950	$600 - 700	$375 - 450	$1,250

DB 680 PRE-AMP – preamp only, two-space rack-mount head-unit only, tube chassis, preamp: 3 X 12AX7, 2X 12AU7, two channels, front silver control panel, single input, 16 black knobs, bs, ds, direct line out, effects loop, black casing, 17 lbs., mfg. 1996-2006.

	$1,500	$950 - 1,100	$500 - 600	$1,995

DB 728 POWER AMP – 400W, four-space rack-mount bass power amp only, ten tube chassis, preamp: 1 X 12AX7, 1 X 12AU7, power: 8 X 6550, front silver control panel, single volume knob, power switch, standby switch, rear panel: two inputs (one regular, one thru), two Speakon and two 1/4 in. standard speaker jacks, 57 lbs., disc. 2004.

	N/A	$1,300 - 1,650	$950 - 1,100	

DB 750 – 975W @ 2 ohms (750W @ 4 ohms), three-space rack-mount head-unit only, hybrid chassis, preamp: 3 X 12AX7, 1 X 12AU7, power: 12 MOSFETs, single channel, front silver control panel, single input, seven black knobs (v, t, m, b, MV, two FX knobs), bs, ds, direct line out, effects loop, black casing, 46 lbs., disc. 2008.

	$2,400	$1,400 - 1,700	$950 - 1,100	$2,995

DB 751 – 975W @ 2 ohms (750W @ 4 ohms), three-space rack-mount bass head-unit, hybrid chassis, preamp: 3 X 12AX7, power: 12 MOSFETs, single channel, front silver control panel, single input, seven black knobs (g, t, m, b, MV, effects send level with push/pull -20dB, effects return level with push/pull series), -6dB switch, bright switch, deep switch, effects loop, XLR balanced line out with pre/post EQ and lift/ground switches, footswitch jack, mute switch, power switch, rear panel: two Speakon jacks, tuner out jack, black casing, 19 in. wide, 5.25 in. tall, 14 in. deep, 42 lbs., mfg. 2009-present.

courtesy Aguilar   *courtesy Aguilar*

MSR $2,795	$2,250	$1,300 - 1,600	$900 - 1,050	

  • **Add $135 (MSR $175) for head case.**

BASS SPEAKER CABINETS

The GS Series speaker cabinets represent the standard companions to other Aguilar amps. The GS Series feature cast-frame drivers, phenolic tweeters with an integral phase plug and variable tweeter level control, seven-ply void-free Philippine mahogany construction, and interlocking corners. The S Series are an outstanding value for working bassists, and they are smaller and have different construction materials. The DB Series feature more traditional looking cabinets that are available in three covering/grille schemes.

  • **Add $99-$139 for speaker cabinet covers depending on size.**

DB112 SPEAKER CABINET – 300W, 1-12 in. speaker with a tweeter, custom crossover with variable tweeter control, 8 ohm impedance, 13-ply void-free baltic birch construction, rubber feet, available in Boss Tweed (Tweed covering with a brown grille), Classic Black (black covering with a silver grille), Chocolate Thunder (brown covering with a black/brown grille), or Monster Green (dark green covering with a black grille), 45 lbs., mfg. 2007-present.

MSR $799	$600	$350 - 425	$200 - 250	

  * *DB112NT Speaker Cabinet* – similar to the DB112 Speaker Cabinet, except has no tweeter, 45 lbs., mfg. 2007-present.

MSR $739	$560	$300 - 375	$175 - 225	

DB115 SPEAKER CABINET – 400W, 1-15 in. speaker with a tweeter, 8 ohm impedance, 13-ply void-free baltic birch construction, rubber feet, available in Classic Black (black covering with a silver grille), Chocolate Thunder (brown covering with a black/brown grille), or Monster Green (dark green covering with a black grille), 71 lbs., mfg. 2008-present.

MSR $1,099	$830	$500 - 575	$300 - 350	

MSR/NOTES	100%	EXCELLENT	AVERAGE	LAST MSR

DB210 SPEAKER CABINET – 350W, 2-10 in. speakers with a tweeter, custom crossover with variable tweeter control, 8 ohm impedance, 13-ply void-free baltic birch construction, rubber feet, available in Classic Black (black covering with a silver grille), Chocolate Thunder (brown covering with a black/brown grille), or Monster Green (dark green covering with a black grille), 59 lbs., mfg. 2007-present.

MSR $979	$740	$425 - 500	$250 - 300	

DB212 SPEAKER CABINET – 600W, 2-12 in. speakers with a tweeter, custom crossover with variable tweeter control, 4 or 8 ohm impedance, 13-ply void-free baltic birch construction, rubber feet, available in Boss Tweed (Tweed covering with a brown grille), Classic Black (black covering with a silver grille), Chocolate Thunder (brown covering with a black/brown grille), or Monster Green (dark green covering with a black grille), 70 lbs., mfg. 2008-present.

MSR $1,299	$980	$600 - 700	$350 - 425	

DB285JC JACK CASADY SPEAKER CABINET – 300W, 2-8 in. speakers and 1-5 in. midrange driver, 4 ohm impedance, 13-ply void-free baltic birch construction, rubber feet, available in Classic Black (black covering with a silver grille), Chocolate Thunder (brown covering with a black/brown grille), or Monster Green (dark green covering with a black grille), 50 lbs., mfg. 2008-present.

MSR $949	$700	$425 - 500	$250 - 300	

DB410 SPEAKER CABINET – 700W, 4-10 in. speakers with a tweeter, custom crossover with variable tweeter control, 4 or 8 ohm impedance, 13-ply void-free baltic birch construction, rubber feet, available in Classic Black (black covering with a silver grille), Chocolate Thunder (brown covering with a black/brown grille), or Monster Green (dark green covering with a black grille), casters included, 98 lbs., mfg. 2007-present.

MSR $1,459	$1,100	$625 - 750	$375 - 450	

DB412 SPEAKER CABINET – 1200W, 4-12 in. speakers with a tweeter, custom crossover with variable tweeter control, 4 ohm impedance, 13-ply void-free baltic birch construction, rubber feet, available in Boss Tweed (Tweed covering with a brown grille), Classic Black (black covering with a silver grille), Chocolate Thunder (brown covering with a black/brown grille), or Monster Green (dark green covering with a black grille), 149 lbs., mfg. 2008-present.

MSR $1,999	$1,500	$900 - 1,050	$550 - 650	

DB810 SPEAKER CABINET – 1400W, 8-10 in. speakers with a tweeter, custom crossover with variable tweeter control, 4 or 8 ohm impedance, 13-ply void-free baltic birch construction, rubber feet, available in Classic Black (black covering with a silver grille), Chocolate Thunder (brown covering with a black/brown grille), or Monster Green (dark green covering with a black grille), rear wheels and a tiltback handle, 184 lbs., mfg. 2007-present.

MSR $2,149	$1,600	$950 - 1,100	$600 - 700	

GS112 SPEAKER CABINET – 300W, 1-12 in. speaker with a tweeter, 8 ohm impedance, two inputs, black covering, black metal grille, 42 lbs., current mfg.

MSR $699	$540	$300 - 375	$175 - 225	

* ***GS112 NT Speaker Cabinet*** – similar to the GS112, except has no tweeter, current mfg.

MSR $639	$480	$275 - 325	$150 - 200	

GS115 SPEAKER CABINET – 400W, 1-15 in. speaker with a tweeter, 8 ohm impedance, two inputs, casters, black covering, black metal grille, 80 lbs., disc. 2007.

	$600	$350 - 425	$225 - 275	$799

GS210 SPEAKER CABINET – 350W, 2-10 in. speaker with a tweeter, 4 or 8 ohm impedance, two inputs, black covering, black metal grille, 62 lbs., disc. 2007.

	$600	$350 - 425	$225 - 275	$799

GS212 SPEAKER CABINET – 600W, 2-12 in. speaker with a tweeter, 4 or 8 ohm impedance, two inputs, casters, black covering, black metal grille, 70 lbs., current mfg.

MSR $1,079	$800	$475 - 550	$300 - 350	

GS410 SPEAKER CABINET – 700W, 4-10 in. speaker with a tweeter, 4 or 8 ohm impedance, two inputs, casters, black covering, black metal grille, 98 lbs., current mfg.

MSR $1,349	$1,000	$600 - 700	$325 - 400	

GS412 SPEAKER CABINET – 1,200W, 4-12 in. speaker with a tweeter, 4 ohm impedance, two inputs, casters, black covering, black metal grille, 116 lbs., mfg. 2004-present.

MSR $1,749	$1,300	$750 - 900	$450 - 525	

S210 SPEAKER CABINET – 250W, 2-10 in. speaker with a tweeter, 4 or 8 ohm impedance, two inputs, black covering, black metal grille, 52 lbs., mfg. 2004-06.

	$420	$250 - 300	$150 - 190	$549

S410 SPEAKER CABINET – 500W, 4-10 in. speaker with a tweeter, 4 or 8 ohm impedance, two inputs, casters, black covering, black metal grille, 83 lbs., mfg. 2004-06.

	$650	$375 - 450	$225 - 275	$849

MSR/NOTES	100%	EXCELLENT	AVERAGE	LAST MSR

S810 SPEAKER CABINET – 1000W, 8-10 in. speaker with a tweeter, 4 ohm impedance, two inputs, casters, black covering, black metal grille,131 lbs., mfg. 2005-06.

	100%	EXCELLENT	AVERAGE	LAST MSR
	$1,025	$625 - 725	$325 - 400	$1,349

AIKEN AMPLIFICATION

Amplifiers currently produced in Greenwood, SC, since 2006. Previously produced in Buford, GA, from 2000 to 2005, and Pensacola, FL, from 2005 to early 2006.

CONTACT INFORMATION
AIKEN AMPLIFICATION
Greenwood, SC
Phone No.: 864-993-8383
Fax No.: 864-223-7136
www.aikenamps.com
contact@aikenamps.com

Randall Aiken has been involved in electronics since he was young. In high school and college he made money by repairing guitar amplifiers. He has two engineering degrees from Clemson University. Randall feels that vacuum tube amplification has become a lost art and many companies are just taking old designs and changing minute things to make their own product. Because of this, Aiken amplification was created. They produce Head units, combo units, and speaker cabinets to satisfy everyone's needs. For more information, refer to Aiken's website or contact them directly.

ELECTRIC TUBE AMPLIFIERS

The **Invader** (disc. 2005) was available in 18W and 30W versions. The Invader series featured 2 X EL34 or 2 X EL84 power tubes, reverb, and an attenuator. Last MSR prices for the Invader series were $1,995 for the 18W head, $2,195 for the 18W 1-12 in. combo, $2,395 for the 18W 2-12 in. combo, $2,195 for the 30W head, $2,395 for the 30W 1-12 in. combo, and $2,595 for the 30W 2-12 in. combo. The **Intruder** series was introduced in 2004 and discontinued in 2008 with 18W (Last MSR was$1,695) and 30W variations that were available in head and 1-12 in. combo versions. The 30W was replaced by a 50W head-unit only (Last MSR was $1,895). The Intruder series features 2 X EL34 power tubes, an effects loop, and master volume. The **Corsair** (MSR TBA) was introduced in 2005 and features a small-box design, high-gain, 2 X EL34 power tubes, gain/volume boost, and an effects loop. The **Europa** (disc. 2004) was a Class A tube amp with 10/20 W output, EL84/KT88 power tube, reverb, and an attenuator. Last MSR on the Europa head unit was $1,795 and for the 1-12 in. combo was $1,995. The **Sabre** (MSR TBA) is a 50W head unit only with 2 X EL34 power tubes, switchable channels, seperate equalizers, and two effects loops. The **Tomcat** (disc. 2007, last MSR was $1,595 for the head unit, last MSR was $1,795 for the 1-12 in. combo) features Class A power with 2 X EL84 power tubes and standard features.

Speaker cabinets are available in 1-12, 2-12, and 4-12 in. configurations. All amps and speaker cabinets are available in Aiken's custom colors at no additional charge. Gold piping and bluesbreaker grille cloth are standard.

AIMS

Amplifiers previously produced in the 1970s. Distributed by Randall Instruments.

Randall Instruments distributed a line of guitars, basses, and amplifiers in the mid-1970s (between approximately 1972 and 1976). Guitar and bass amplifiers were modeled on popular American designs. One known example is the Aims Producer, which is a dual channel solid-state head unit guitar amp with standard features (no reverb, tremolo, vibrato, etc.). Any information on the AIMS brand can be submitted directly to Blue Book Publications.

AIRLINE

Amplifiers previously produced by various manufacturers including Harmony, Kay, and Valco. Distributed by Montgomery Wards througout their retail stores and catalogs. See chapter on House Brands.

Airline was a house brand name used for Montgomery Wards during the late 1950s and most of the 1960s. Most of these amps were built by Harmony, Kay, and Valco. These amps were simply styled a little different than their Harmony, Kay, or Valco counterparts and an Airline logo was affixed to the outside. In some instances the same amp may appear with three or four different brand names! Individual models are not listed because of the inconsistancy in Airline history - the only account of these models appear in Montgomery Wards catalogs! As far as values, these

Model 62-9012A
courtesy Competition Music

Model 62-9022A
courtesy Randy Rodden/R&R Guitars

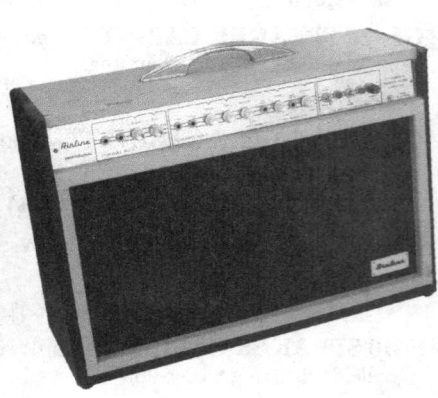

Model 62-9026A
courtesy Savage Audio

amplifiers were typically budget models, although many are of very high quality. Nonetheless, they do not command a premium in today's used marketplace. Most models are valued between $150 and $400 depending on features and condition.

AIRTIGHT GARAGE, THE

Amplifiers currently produced in New Iberia, LA.

The Airtight Garage builds custom guitar amplifiers and speaker cabinets in Acadiana, South Louisiana. Their amps are built around Airtight's own sound as opposed to cloning other amps that many other builders are doing today. All Airtight amps feature tube chassis' and are available in various configurations. Amps start at $1,500 and their higher end models are priced over $3,500, and speaker cabinets start at $500. For more information, visit Airtight's website or contact them directly.

CONTACT INFORMATION
AIRTIGHT GARAGE, THE
200 Ann St.
New Iberia, LA 70560
Phone No.: 337-257-2586
www.theairtightgarage.com

ALAMO

Amplifiers previously produced in San Antonio, Texas. The Alamo trademark was established circa 1947 and lasted to circa 1982.

Alamo was founded around 1947 by Charles Eilenberg. He started the company Southern Music in San Antonio, Texas, and began making guitars and amplifiers. By 1950, the company was producing instrument cases, tube amplifiers, and lap steel guitars. Alamo continued to produce tube amplifiers throughout the fifties and sixties. In 1970, they stopped producing tube amps and jumped on the solid-state bandwagon. The company produced amps and guitars through the 1970s when the company folded in 1982. There are numerous guitar amplifier models under the Alamo name. Look for more information on Alamo amplifiers in upcoming editions of the *Blue Book of Guitar Amplifiers*. Source: Michael Wright, *Vintage Guitar Magazine* and *Guitar Stories:* Volume Two.

Electra 25-70
courtesy Savage Audio

Electra 25-70
courtesy David Chandler/R&R Guitars

Electra 2570
courtesy Christian Brooks

ALDEN

Amplifiers previously produced in China, but other instruments are currently produced in China with their headquarters based in Korea. Distributed in the U.S. by Alden Guitar, USA in Plympton, MA.

Alden guitars is a collaboration between British luthier Alan Entwhistle and the Korean-based guitar company Muse R&D, Inc. Alden currently offers a variety of solidbody and semi-hollowbody electric guitars. They have also produced electric basses, acoustic guitars, mandolins, guitar amplifiers, and other guitar-related accessories. For more information, visit Alden's website or contact the distributor directly.

CONTACT INFORMATION
ALDEN
U.S. Distributor: Alden Guitar, USA
221 Main St.
Plympton, MA 02367
Phone No.: 781-588-9282
www.aldenguitarsales.com
info@aldenguitarsales.com

ALEMBIC

Amplifiers, guitars, basses, and other products currently produced in Santa Rosa, CA. The Alembic trademark was established in 1969. Distributed by Alembic.

The Alembic company was founded in San Francisco in 1969, primarily to incorporate new ways to clarify and amplify the sound of the rock group Grateful Dead. The Alembic workshop covered three main areas: a recording studio, PA/sound reinforcement, and guitar electronics. Wickersham was developing a low impedance pickup coupled with active electronics. Up until this point all electronics in production guitars and basses were passive systems. Artists using these "Alembicized" instruments early on include David Crosby (a Guild 12-string), Jack Casady (Guild bass), and Phil Lesh (SG and Guild basses). Both Bob Weir's and Jerry Garcia's guitars were converted as well. Wickersham found that mounting the active circuitry in the instrument itself gave the player a greater degree of control over his tone than ever before. The first F-2B preamp unit shipped out of the factory in 1969. For a complete history, refer to the *Blue Book of Electric Guitars*. For further information and complete specs, visit Alembic's website or contact them directly.

CONTACT INFORMATION
ALEMBIC
3005 Wiljan Court
Santa Rose, CA 95407 USA
Phone No.: 707-523-2611
Fax No.: 707-523-2935
www.alembic.com
alembic@alembic.com

MSR/NOTES	100%	EXCELLENT	AVERAGE	LAST MSR

PRE-AMPLIFIERS

The **F-1X** (MSR $1,375) is a tube driven preamp with a 12AX7 tube. It features bright and boost switches along with tone controls and gain effect. The F-1X along with all of the Alembic amps are rack-mount units and take up one space. The **F-2B** (MSR $1,475) was introduced in the late 1960s. This amp is generally used as a stereo amp and has a complete tube preamp section. Originally this amp was inspired by the Fender Dual Showman. The F-2B has some more controls and features than its younger brother the F-1X. There are two channels to get the stereo effect. The other Alembic preamp is the **SF-2** (MSR $1,375), which stands for the Superfilter. There are two tunable active filters in the amp which gives a large range. There are a possible three channels, and the stereo mode can mix two of them together. It is a switchable mono/stereo amplifier that can also be used as a stand-alone unit.

ALESIS

Amplifiers, effects, and other digital products currently produced overseas since 1992. Distributed by Alesis in Cumberland RI, and Culver City, CA.

Alesis is most famous for pioneering recording products. They started building recording products in 1992 and have expanded since to produce synths, monitors, mixers, sound reinforcement, signal processors, and a few guitar products. The Wildfild guitar amplifier series features Alesis GuitarFX technology. They also produce guitar sound effect pedals. For more information, contact Alesis directly.

CONTACT INFORMATION
ALESIS
200 Scenic View Drive
Cumberland, RI 02864
Phone No.: 401-658-5760
Fax No.: 401-658-3640
www.alesis.com
info@alesis.com

ACOUSTIC, BASS, AND ELECTRIC AMPLIFIERS

Bassfire 60
courtesy Alesis

Roadfire 15
courtesy Alesis

Wildfire 30
courtesy Alesis

BASSFIRE 60 – 60W, 1-12 in. speaker basscombo, solid-state chassis, designed for basses, several effect types, over 80 presets, single channel, front silver and black control panel, single input, six knobs (effect select, effect value, drive, t, b, v), digital display with up/down selector buttons, headphone jack, True-Stereo processing, RCA inputs, black covering, silver grille, disc. 2006.

$200	$125 - 150	$70 - 90	$300

COOLFIRE 15 – 15W, 1-8 in. speaker combo with a 1 in. tweeter, solid-state chassis, designed for acoustic guitar use, over 20 effect types, over 80 presets, single channel, front silver and brown control panel, single input, three knobs (effect select, effect value, v), digital display with up/down selector buttons, headphone jack, True-Stereo processing, RCA inputs, brown Tolex-style covering, brown grille, disc. 2006.

$130	$80 - 100	$40 - 55	$200

ROADFIRE 15 – 15W, 1-8 in. speaker combo, solid-state chassis, rechargeable battery for AC/DC portable operation, several effect types, over 80 presets, single channel, front silver control panel, single input, three knobs (effect select, effect value, v), digital display with up/down selector buttons, headphone jack, True-Stereo processing, RCA inputs, optional footswitch, expression pedal input, stereo link output, speaker out, heavy duty silver covering with aluminum corners and edges, silver grille, mfg. 2006-07.

$200	$125 - 150	$70 - 90	$300

WILDFIRE 15 – 15W, 1-8 in. speaker combo, solid-state chassis, Alesis GuitarFX technology with 40 effects, 80 editable presets, 9 effects modules, single channel, front silver control panel, single input, three knobs (effects, drive, v), digital display, headphone jack, built-in chromatic tuner, black covering, black grille, disc. 2006.

$130	$80 - 100	$40 - 55	$200

WILDFIRE 30 – 30W, 1-10 in. speaker combo, solid-state chassis, Alesis GuitarFX technology with 40 effects, 80 editable presets, 9 effects modules, single channel, front silver control panel, single input, four knobs (effects, value, drive, v), digital display, headphone jack, built-in chromatic tuner, black covering, black grille, disc. 2006.

$165	$100 - 125	$60 - 80	$249

MSR/NOTES	100%	EXCELLENT	AVERAGE	LAST MSR

WILDFIRE 60 – 60W, 1-12 in. speaker combo, solid-state chassis, Alesis GuitarFX technology with 40 effects, 80 editable presets, 9 effects modules, single channel, front silver control panel, single input, six knobs (effects, value, drive, b, t, v), digital display, headphone jack, built-in chromatic tuner, black covering, black grille, disc. 2006.

	$200	$125 - 150	$70 - 90	$299

ALESSANDRO

Amplifiers, speaker cabinets, and other accesories currently produced in Huntington Valley, PA since 1998. Distributed by Alessandro.

CONTACT INFORMATION
ALESSANDRO
PO Box 253
Huntington Valley, PA 19006
Phone No.: 215-355-6424
www.alessandro-products.com
hounddogcorp@msn.com

George Alessandro founded Hound Dog amps in 1994 (see Hound Dog), and changed the company name to Alessandro in 1998. Once the company switched to Alessandro, George started using high-end products such as high-purity grain oriented copper and silver conductors, and improved circuit boards in his amplifiers. All amps feature a tube chassis with circuits developed by George himself, and they come in head only or combo units (speaker cabinets are also available). All of the cabinets for the amps and speakers are made of high-grade woods that can be upgraded and changed on request. In 2001, the Working Dog brand was introduced (see Working Dog). Alessandro also offers speaker cables, instrument cables, parts, components, and vacuum tubes. For more information, visit Alessandro's website or contact them directly.

ELECTRIC TUBE AMPLIFIERS

The Redbone and Bloodhound series were first introduced under the Hound Dog trademark and are the only two models that carried over to Alessandro. The **Redbone** (MSR $2,600) has 55W output with 2 X 6550 power tubes. The **Redbone Special** (MSR $3,200) is similar to the Redbone, except has a different preamp, which gives it more options for more range between clean and distortion. The **Bloodhound** (MSR $2,400) has 55W output with 12AX7 preamp and 2 X 6550 power tubes. The **Beagle** (MSR $2,400) is a 10W amp with 2 classic EL84 output tubes. The **Basset Hound** (MSR $2,600) is a bass amp with 60W output coming from 2 X 6550 power tubes. This model helps electric basses sound more like an upright. The **English Coonhound** (MSR $2,800) is a Class-A, English sounding amp with 20W output coming from 4 X EL84 output tubes. The **Plott Hound** (MSR $2,400) has 10W output coming from 2 X 6V6 tubes and is one of the most advanced amplifiers in the Alessandro range with a cross between English and American sounds. Recent additions to the Alessandro line include the Black 'n Tan, Blue, Trick, and the Italian. The **Black 'n Tan** (MSR $2,600) is a Class A amp with 15W of power and 2 X EL34, 6L6, or KT66 power tubes can be used for a variety of sounds. The **Blue Trick** (MSR $2,800) is a Class A amp with 20W of power and 4 X 6V6 power tubes. The **Italian** (MSR $2,600) is a high-powered jazz-style amp with 60W output power from 2 X 6550 power tubes. The **American Coonhound** (2008-present, MSR $5,000) puts out 15W, features the highly regarded Western Electric 300B power triode, and is housed in a solid hand-rubbed oak cabinet. The **Rhodesian** (MSR $2,800) has a sound that is a cross between mid-60s British tones and late 50s American tones and it features 30W output from 2 X KT66 tubes.

Custom woods are available on all amps and speaker cabinets: curly maple, flame maple, quilted maple, mahogany, quilted mahogany, walnut, cherry, and rosewood are all options.

- **Custom wood cabinets start at $300 (contact Alessandro for exact price).**
- **Add $300 for Audioquest functionally-perfect silver wire.**
- **Add $500 for Black Gate Filter capacitors.**
- **Add $800 for 24kt. gold-plated solid copper chassis.**
- **Add $1,000 for preamp and power tube upgrade.**
- **Add $1,200 for combo-unit upgrade with 1-12 in. Celestion Bulldog speaker.**
- **Add $4,000 for a solid pure silver chassis.**
- **Add $50,000 for a solid gold chassis.**

SPEAKER CABINETS

Like the amp heads, Alessandro produces matching speaker cabinets of the same caliber wood. There are four models available including configurations of 1-12, 2-12, 4-10, and 4-12. All of these cabinets come unloaded without any speakers at a base price of $800 for an oak cabinet or $1,200 for curly or flame maple. The speakers used in the cabinets are either Celestion G12H or Celestion "Bulldog" Alnico speakers. Contact Alessandro for exact specifications and prices.

ALLEN AMPLIFICATION

Amplifiers and speaker cabinets currently produced in Walton, KY since 1998. Distributed by Allen Amplification.

CONTACT INFORMATION
ALLEN AMPLIFICATION
1325 Richwood Road
Walton, KY 41094 USA
Phone No.: 859-485-6423
Fax No.: 859-485-6424
www.allenamps.com
david@allenamps.com

The Allen Amplification company makes tube amplifiers similar to the blackface Fender amps of the mid-1960s. They are known for making quality amplifiers with the vintage edge to them. Allen amplifiers are available to buy completely assembled or as a kit where the customer can assemble them at a discounted price. This is because all Allen amps assembled at the factory are wired point-to-point by hand and is quite time consuming. If the customer provides his/her own tubes, speakers, etc. there is also a discount in price. For more information, visit Allens' website or contact them directly.

ELECTRIC TUBE AMPLIFIERS

The **Accomplice** features 22W (35W or 40W with different tubes/transformers) and has a striking resemblance to a Blues Jr. The Accomplice is available as a head unit (MSR $1,499), 1-12 in. combo (MSR $1,699), 1-15 in. combo (MSR $1,749), 2-10 in. combo (MSR $1,749), and a 2-12 in. combo (MSR $1,899). The **Accomplice Jr.** has the same power output as the Accomplice but does not have reverb or the impedance switch. The Accomplice Jr. is available as a head unit (MSR $1,349), 1-10 in. combo (MSR $1,499), 1-12 in. combo (MSR $1,549), or 2-12 in. combo (MSR $1,749). The **Old Flame** was updated in 2007 with a new angled front stainless steel chassis and new knobs. It features 25W or 40W depending on tubes/transformers and is available as a head unit (MSR $1,499), 1-12 in. combo (MSR $1,699), 1-15 in. combo (MSR $1,749), 2-10 in. combo (MSR $1,699), 2-12 in. combo (MSR $1,899), or 4-10 in. combo (MSR $1,899). The **Tone Savor** (disc.) is an 80W amp that is similar to the mid 1960s blackface Fender models. It was available as a head (last MSR $1,349) or a 2-12 in. combo (last MSR $1,649). The **Sweet Spot** was introduced in 2003, and features 18W with 6V6 tubes or 25W with 6L6 tubes. The Sweet Spot is available as a head unit (MSR $1,399), a 1-10 in. combo (MSR $1,549), 1-12 in. combo (MSR $1,599), 1-15 in. combo (MSR $1,649), or 2-12 in. combo (MSR $1,799). The **Class Act** (disc.) is the smallest amp with 10W ouptut max. The Class Act was available as a head (last MSR $899) or a 1-12 in. combo with a bottom-mounted chassis, (last MSR $999). The **Encore** has 35W power with tremolo and is available in a head unit (MSR $1,599), 1-12 in. combo (MSR $1,799), 1-15 in. combo (MSR $1,849), 2-10 in. combo (MSR $1,799), 2-12 in. combo (MSR $1,999), and a 4-10 in. combo (MSR $1,999). Blonde and brown covering are optional on the Encore. The **Brown Sugar** features brown tolex covering with 15W or 30W output and is available as a head unit (MSR $1,499), 1-12 in. combo (MSR $1,699), 1-15 in. combo (MSR $1,799), 2-10 in. combo (MSR $1,799), and 2-12 in. combo (MSR $1,899). The **Hot Fudge** (also Hot Fudge w/nuts) is based on a brownface Princeton, has 15W (20W, 30W Hot Fudge w/nuts), vibrato, and is available as a head unit (MSR $1,199 regular, $1,299 w/nuts), 1-10 in. combo (MSR $1,299 regular only), 1-12 in. combo (MSR $1,349 regular, $1,449 w/ nuts), 1-15 in. combo (MSR $1,449, w/nuts only), and 2-12 in. combo (MSR $1,599 w/nuts only). The **Classic 10** (MSR $799) is a 10W single-ended Class A amp with 1-10 in. speaker, a single channel with a volume and tone control, and has standard blackface appointments. The **Chihuahua** is a 10W single-ended Class A amp with 1-10 in. speaker, a single channel with volume, treble, mid/ raw, and bass controls and reverb. The Chihuahua is available as a head-unit (MSR $849), 1-10 in. combo (MSR $949), or 2-6 in. combo (MSR $999).

ALOHA

Amplifiers previously built in San Antonio, TX, and Chicago, IL. Distributed by the Aloha Publishing and Musical Instrument Company of Chicago, IL.

The Aloha company was founded in 1935 by J.M. Raleigh. True to the nature of a House Brand distributor, Raleigh's company distributed both Aloha instruments and amplifiers and Raleigh brand instruments through his Chicago office. Acoustic guitars were supplied by Harmony, and initial amplifiers and guitars were supplied by the Alamo company of San Antonio. By the mid-1950s, Aloha was producing its own amps, but continued using Alamo products (source: Michael Wright, *Vintage Guitar Magazine*). Aloha amplifiers typically sell for $50-$150 in the used marketplace.

AMERICAN ACOUSTIC DEVELOPMENT (AAD)

Amplifiers currently produced in China. Distributed by AAD in St. Louis, MO. Showroom in Clifton, NJ.

Phil Jones fell in love with the bass guitar at the early age of 13, and ever since then, he has been involved in playing bass guitar and building his own equipment. In 1990, he moved from England to the U.S. and worked for Boston Acoustics for a short while. In 1994, he developed Platinum Audio, which specialized in building hi-fi home speakers and studio monitors. In 1998, he founded American Acoustic Development, which also specializes in hi-fi speakers and other products. Circa 2003, Phil took what had worked so well for professional audio and presented it to the bass guitar player. Recently, AAD introduced a small, portable acoustic guitar amplifier. For more information visit AAD's website or contact them directly.

ACOUSTIC/ELECTRIC AMPLIFIERS

The **Cub AG-100** (MSR $608) is a portable acoustic amplifier with 100W output power and 2-5 in. speakers. The **Super Cub AG-300** (MSR $1,450) is a portable acoustic/electric guitar amplifier with 250W output power and 6-5 in. speakers.

AMP (AMPLIFIED MUSIC PRODUCTS)

Amplifiers and speaker cabinets previously produced in Chatsworth, CA between circa 1981 and 1988.

AMP (Amplified Music Products) was founded in Chatsworth, California in 1981 by Russ Allee and Roger Smith. This is verified, according to California records, that AMP was registered as a corporation in 1981 in California listing Russell V Allee as president. Before AMP, Allee earned his reputation when he worked for the Acoustic amplifier company and designed the 360 and 370 Series of bass amplifiers. After forming AMP, he had another former Acoustic employee named Steve Rabe design the preamp for the new AMP Model 420 bass heads.

Rabe left AMP to found his own company called SWR, which stood for Steve W. Rabe, where he developed his own preamp. Allee continued on with AMP until the company folded in 1988. Gibson reportedly bought AMP after they closed and began offering their "new" GB 440 bass amp that was nearly identical to the AMP Model 420. While unverified, Allee either designed Gibson's GB 440 Bass or Gibson simply used Allee's Model 420 and called it the GB

MSR/NOTES	100%	EXCELLENT	AVERAGE	LAST MSR

440. Allee also worked with David Nordschow of Eden Electronics to develop Eden's World Tour Series of bass amps. Regardless, AMP's Model 420, SWR's SM-400, Eden's WT-800, and Gibson's GB 440 are all very similar in design and appearance, but users all agree that each amp sounds different and has varying amounts of pros and cons.

The author would like to thank Neil Springer for his AMP contributions.

BASS AMPLIFIERS

AMP offered four main bass amp heads including three single-channel amps, the **BH-220**, the **BH-260**, and the **BH-420**, and one two-channel amp, the **BH-250**. AMP also offered the **Model 8000** power amp that last retailed for $825.

BH-220 HEAD – 240W output @ 4 ohms (150W output @ 8 ohms), solid-state chassis, bass head-unit, single channel, front black and gray control panel, two inputs, seven knobs (v, b, l/m, midrang, h/m, t, tonal balance), enhance switch, power switch, rear panel: two speaker outputs, headphone jack, power amp input jack, effects loop, balanced direct pre-EQ XLR jack, post EQ line out, black casing, 17 in. wide, 4 in. tall, 9.5 in. deep, 16 lbs., mfg. circa 1981-88.

	N/A	$250 - 300	$150 - 200	$599

* *CX-220 Combo* – similar to the BH-220 Head, except in combo configuration with 1-15 in. speaker in a telescoping cabinet, black covering, black grille, mfg. circa 1981-88.

	N/A	$325 - 400	$200 - 250	$849

BH-250 HEAD – 250W output @ 4 ohms (180W output @ 8 ohms), solid-state chassis, bass head-unit, two channels, limiter, front black and gray control panel, two inputs, 10 knobs (g, Ch. A: b, m, t, v, Ch. B: edge, b, m, t, v), Ch. A/Ch. B effects loop switch, channel selector switch, footswitch for channel selection, power switch, rear panel: two speaker outputs, headphone jack, power amp input jack, effects loop, balanced direct pre-EQ XLR jack, post EQ line out, black casing, mfg. circa 1981-84.

	N/A	$275 - 325	$175 - 225	

BH-260 HEAD – 260W output @ 4 ohms (150W output @ 8 ohms), solid-state chassis, bass head-unit, single channel, front black and gray control panel, two inputs, 10 knobs (v, b, six-band semi-parametric bass EQ, t, tonal balance), enhance switch, power switch, footswitch jack, rear panel: two speaker outputs, headphone jack, power amp input jack, lo freq. and high freq. bi-amp outputs, effects loop, balanced direct pre-EQ XLR jack, post EQ line out, black casing, 17 in. wide, 4 in. tall, 9.5 in. deep, mfg. circa 1981-84.

	N/A	$275 - 325	$175 - 225	

BH-420 HEAD – 400W output @ 4 ohms (200W output @ 8 ohms), solid-state chassis, bass head-unit, single channel, limited, compressor, front black and gray control panel, two inputs, 15 knobs (g, limiter, b, eight semi-parametric EQ knobs, t, tonal balance, v, crossover), enhance switch, power switch, rear panel: two speaker outputs, headphone jack, power amp input jack, low freq. and high freq. bi-amp output jacks, effects loop, balanced direct pre-EQ XLR jack, post EQ line out, black casing, 17 in. wide, 4 in. tall, 9.5 in. deep, mfg. circa 1981-88.

	N/A	$300 - 350	$200 - 250	$799

SL-1 PREAMP – preamp only, solid-state chassis, bass head-unit, single channel, limited, compressor, front black and gray control panel, two inputs, 15 knobs (g, limiter, b, eight semi-parametric EQ knobs, t, tonal balance, v, crossover), enhance switch, power switch, rear panel: low freq. and high freq. bi-amp output jacks, effects loop, balanced direct pre-EQ XLR jack, post EQ line out, black casing, 17 in. wide, 2 in. tall, 9.5 in. deep, mfg. circa 1981-88.

	N/A	$175 - 225	$95 - 125	$425

SPEAKER CABINETS

AMP also offered a Model B-12 speaker enclosure with a 12 inch speaker (last retail was $295) and a Model B-15 speaker enclosure with a 15 inch speaker (last retail was $449).

XB-15 – 250W, 1-15 in. speaker, 8 ohm impedance, combination speaker cabinet and traveling case: speaker cabinet is stored inside case during travel and sits atop the case during performance making the case part of the cabinet, black covering with a black grille on the cabinet, black case covering with anodized aluminum edges, 22.5 in. wide, 26.875 in. tall, 17.125 in. deep, 81 lbs., mfg. circa 1981-88.

MSR $699	N/A	$250 - 300	$150 - 200	

AMPEG

Amplifiers currently produced in China, South Korea, and Woodinville, WA (Heritage Series). Previously produced in a variety of locations in the U.S. including New York, NY and St. Louis, MO. Distributed by LOUD Technologies in Woodinville, WA since 2005. Previously distributed by St. Louis Music of St. Louis, MO from 1985 to 2005. The Ampeg trademark was established circa 1945 in Chicago, IL.

See categories in history for company biography.

CONTACT INFORMATION
AMPEG
Distributed by LOUD Technologies, Inc.
16220 Wood-Red Road NE
Woodinville, WA 98072
Phone No.: 425-892-6500
Phone No.: 866-858-5832
Fax No.: 425-487-4337
www.ampeg.com

HISTORY: 1904-1979

Charles Everett Hull was born on January 17, 1904 in Wisconsin. A constructive and energetic young man, Everett developed an interest in playing bass guitar when he could find no one else to do the job in his band. He had played around in the 20s and 30s with numerous bands and his own orchestra. After playing an upright bass for some time, he noticed that during bass solos the sound was remarkably quiet. He knew that a microphone would work on the outside of the instrument, but would pick up unwanted sounds such as hitting it with his bow. A light went on in Hull's head and one late night he took out the peg that holds up the bass guitar on the bottom, fixed up a microphone inside of the bass with coat hangers, ran it through a radio, and the Amplifier-Peg was born. Everett's wife, Gertrude, named the new invention "ampeg," which was short for Amplifier Peg. Popularity picked up on the invention and in 1946 Everett applied for a patent, which was granted a year and a half later.

In 1946, Everett moved to Newark, New Jeresy to pursue his amplifier invention. Everett had been selling a Dynaco hi-fi amp, but wanted to design his own amp specifically for bass instruments. Everett met Stanley Michael in New York and the two of them opened The Michael-Hull Electronics Labs in 1946. Here they offered the "ampeg" for the bass and the Michael-Hull Bassamp. This partnership that seemed to be a good matchup dissolved in 1948 as they were both unhappy. Everett ended up with the company and moved it to New York where the company was renamed The Ampeg Bassamp Co.

After a few years of rough times and small business, the Ampeg company started to expand and grow. This involved a move to a new factory in New York in 1954, and another move in 1957. In 1956, the name was shortened to simply the Ampeg Company. That year Everett's right hand man to work for Ampeg, Jess Oliver, came into Ampeg when they were still a cramped little shop to buy an Ampeg. Everett offered him a job, and he accepted in 1956, as they became friends. With Oliver, Ampeg amps began to sell regularly and business appeared to be booming. Money had always been a problem at Ampeg and continued up into the 60s. Ampeg had grown so much that they had to move to Linden, New Jersey. Models were rolling off of the shelf at this point, and in the early '60s Ampeg released their first guitar, a stand-up bass.

Times began to get rough as Oliver and Hull's partnership went sour over a compensation deal. Oliver was then fired or quit, and still we don't really know what happened. Avnet was in the process of buying, but they pulled out in fall of 1966. The company, Unimusic, then bought out more than 50 percent of Ampeg's stock in the fall of 1967. The company was under new ownership, but Everett was still president. As many top-officials left Ampeg, Hull began to get upset with the way things were going and still didn't like Rock & Roll music. He ended up resigning in the fall of 1968. This was the start of the downward spiral for Unimusic. Things going askew, Unimusic sold to Magnavox in 1971 as part of the Selmer division.

In the '70s, Ampeg was still of good quality, but they didn't keep up with the times. Their tube amps were hardly updated over the time when Magnavox was in charge. A few solid-state amps were introduced, but not enough. The Linden factory was closed in 1974 and manufacturing was moved to Jefferson City, Tennessee. Magnavox just wasn't a good "marriage" with Ampeg and they never made any money on them. Lots of things changed at this point. Ampeg did have a lot of endorsers, including The Rolling Stones and Fleetwood Mac, but without new product, Ampeg made no large impact in the 1970s. The only breakthrough Ampeg had in this decade was what Dan Armstrong created.

HISTORY: 1980-PRESENT

Ernie Breifel started Music Technology Inc. (MTI) in 1977 as a wholesaler that imported instruments. MTI was looking to expand the corporation and in 1980 Ernie and MTI bought Ampeg from Selmer-Magnavox. This finished a deal that Ernie had tried to do back in the late '50s, but he didn't like how Hull worked and refused to deal with Ampeg. At this point, the Japanese market was in high swing for instrument makers. Ampeg followed suit and started to make amps overseas. These new amps that they were making just didn't have the same sound that the old Ampeg amps had, and they weren't well received by the public. MTI ended up filing for bankruptcy and the name was up for sale again. Gene Kornblum of St. Louis Music (SLM) was there to purchase the company in the bankruptcy court. When SLM went to move all of the stock out of Long Island, all Ampeg had was two truckloads of odds and ends, and very little inventory. In short, SLM had very little to go on. SLM had started to distribute Crate amps in the '70s and Ampeg was brought in for the higher end of amplifiers. It only took one model, the SVT-100 made of old MTI heads, but it brought Ampeg back into the market. In 1987, Ampeg introduced 14 new bass and guitar amps at the NAMM show. The sign that Ampeg was back into the majors was their new "Monster" bass amp. This amp stood nine feet tall, weighed in at 718 lbs, and had 600W running into 32 10 in. speakers! It is now a world record.

As the 1990s rolled around SLM, and Ampeg were both going strong with new products and endorsers joining consistently. Ampeg was keeping up with technology and what other companies were doing. That is something that they really failed to do in the '70s and early '80s. Now Ampeg amps are distributed throughout 40 countries, they have made reissue amps from the glory days and continue to take the Ampeg pride into the new century. Ampeg also reissued the Dan Armstrong Ampeg lucite guitar. In 2005, LOUD Technologies, Inc. purchased St. Louis Music, Inc. and all of their trademarks. With this acquisition, the headquarters of St. Louis Music was moved to Woodinville, WA and production of all amplifiers moved overseas shortly thereafter. In 2010, Ampeg introduced a new American-made line of amplifiers called the Heritage Series. Jess Oliver passed away on June 30, 2011.

Source for Ampeg History: *Ampeg The Story Behind the Sound* by Gregg Hopkins & Bill Moore.

DATING AMPEG AMPLIFIERS

In dating Ampeg Amplifiers, there are several different schemes to be used. The good thing about Ampeg is that when they changed their models, they all changed at the same time. This means that it is fairly easy to determine the range of year by just looking at the outside of the amp. Like all U.S.A. made amps, the speakers, transformers, and potentiometers have date codes on them. This along with the serial number on the amp can help narrow down the year of manufacture.

There are six distinctive periods in the Ampeg line. Each period has a different way of identifying the year made. Note that each different period is approximately during each different ownership. The chart here should be of some help.

Pre 1953 - These amps can only be dated by the EIA (Electronics Industries Association) codes on the speakers and other parts. No serial numbers were used during this time. Michael-Hull amplifiers were made between 1946-48. When Hull started on his own, the name was switched to Ampeg and were mostly wooden amps with Ampeg written across the grille.

1953-Mid 1965 - In 1953, the first Serialization system was introduced. This was a six-digit number like this: YMMNNN, which was the last digit of the year, month, and number of production. Since there is a possibility of overlap here, cosmetics are a huge factor in determining the year. The year 1953 could be 1963 since only the last digit was used. Ampeg changed their cosmetics several times in the late '50s and by determining whether the amp is black, blue, grey, or tan will identify the year.

MSR/NOTES	100%	EXCELLENT	AVERAGE	LAST MSR

1965-1969 - In early 1965 a new serialization system went into effect. The old one lasted on certain models for about six months. This system was also six digits. This system here was strictly numerical and started at 000001. It ran for about five years and ended with 092000. This chart is fairly accurate:

000001-020000 - 1965	075000-080000 - 1968
020000-049000 - 1966	080000-090000 - 1969
049000-075000 - 1967	

1970-1979 - By 1970, Ampeg was in turmoil and in the process of selling to Magnavox. It was only fitting to introduce a third serialization system. At this point in time there isn't enough information about the serial numbers to accurately date with them. The best way to do that is by the cosmetics and when they were used over the decade. There is a small list of what Selmer and Ampeg changed during this time. The first feature is the control panel. From 1968-1972, a blue control panel was used. In 1972 until 1975, the control panel was changed to black with square corners.

In 1976, the panel was horizontally split with rounded corners (This was started in 1973 on solid-state models). The second feature is the addition of a distortion knob which occured in 1976. The third are the "white rocker switches," which replaced the "black rocker switches." These were changed on solid-state amps in 1973 and on tube amps in 1976. The final feature was the "a" logo. It was metal from 1968-1972, and plastic from 1973 on.

1985-2005 - These are the amps during the St. Louis Music period. A new serialization system was developed and it became a code used for many years. This is the best way to identify the date of manufacture during this period. A 10 digit number is used as a serial number, which contains lots of information. The number is set up like this: LLLCYMNNNN. LLL stands for the model, C stands for the country. (U is U.K., Y is Europe, W is Worldwide, and D stands for domestic or U.S.). The Y is a year code that is a letter. (A is 1988, B is 1989, C is 1990, and so on. What happened before 1987 for the year is unclear as very few amps were made because of bankruptcy for MTI). The M is a number code for January-October. (Jan is 1, Feb is 2, Oct is 10, fill in the blanks.) For November and December the letters A and B were used respectively. The last 4 numbers (N) are the actual serial number for the instrument. Example? Certainly. Serial number on a B-15R is AJYDB60626. This is a U.S. amp made in June of 1989 and its serial number 626.

ELECTRIC TUBE AMPS: OVERVIEW

Our greatest attempt has been made to try to break up the Tube amps into sensible categories. Ampeg really didn't have model series until the early '60s when the Universal series was released. We have broken up the early models into time periods, as are miscellaneous amps in the sixties and amps throughtout the seventies and eighties. There are series of amplifiers that begin to show up in the 1960s, and most of these are pretty self-explanatory. If a certain amp isn't listed under a series, check the misc. models for that time period. Every attempt has been made to include every Ampeg amp in an easy format.

ELECTRIC TUBE AMPS: EARLY MODELS, MICHAEL-HULL SERIES

The Michael-Hull Series refers to the amps that Stanley Michael and Everett Hull built when they opened their shop. There were two models, the **Michael-Hull Bassamp** and the **Model 770 Bassamp** and these were designed to be used with Hull's "Ampeg" pickup inside of a stand up bass. Only two amps from the Michael-Hull Series are known to have survived. The early model Bassman had a plywood cabinet with mahogany veneer making it very classy in appearance, and the chassis was mounted on one side of the cabinet with the controls mounted to a slanted control panel on the back of the amp. It featured 1-12 in. GE Alnico V speaker that was covered by a bass clef sign, two channels, 18W output, and tubes consisting of 2 X 6SC7 preamps, 2 X 6L6 outputs, and a 5U4 rectifier.

The Model 770 Bassman was very similar to the Michael-Hull Bassamp, except for the the covering many Ampeg enthusiasts refer to as "mother-of-toilet-seat" that was much shinier than mahogany. The preamp tubes were also changed from 2 X 6SC7s to 3 X 6SN7s. This version had an even more elaborate control panel and a new vent to let heat escape out the back.

ELECTRIC TUBE AMPS: EARLY MODELS BASSAMP/GUITARAMP MODELS

The **Model 500/700** Guitar amps were introduced in 1950 as the first guitar amps for Ampeg. These amps were very similar to the Super 800 Bassman and Model 815 Bassman, but there is only one known survivor of these models. The **Model 600 Guitaramp** was offered between 1955 and 1957 and featured 10W with 1-12 in. Jensen Concert Alnico V speaker but no examples are known to exist today.

There are other models of Bassamps such as the **Model 824**, **Model 825**, and **Model 825D** that have been discovered, but they were never in an Ampeg catalog. Keep in mind this may happen to other models as well.

MODEL 800 SUPER BASSAMP – 18W, 1-12 in. GE Alnico V speaker, five-tube chassis, preamp: 2 X 6BG6 power: 2 X 6SN7, rectifier: 5U4, top control panel, three "chicken head" knobs (v, b, t), all controls on the panel, a sensitivity control, brown cocoa vinyl covering, brown grille with Ampeg logo silk-screened onto it, mfg. 1949-1951.

	N/A	$800 - 1,000	$425 - 525	

The chassis on the Model 800 Super Bassman was mounted on the bottom and speedometer cables ran between the chassis and control panel instead of wires to change the volume, bass, and treble settings.

MODEL 815 BASSAMP – similar to the Super 800 Bassman except has 1-15 in. Alnico V Jensen speaker, new engraved polished aluminum control panel, mfg. 1951-55.

	N/A	$725 - 900	$375 - 475	

There are three different versions of the Model 815 Bassamp. The first one was produced between 1951 and 1952. The second one was produced between 1952 and 1954 and featured a change to 3 X 6SJ7 preamp tubes and 4 X 6V6 power tubes, and the vinyl covering was changed to a dot tweed. The third version was produced from 1954 until 1955, went back to the 6BG6 tubes, and a voltage regulator was added. The speedometer cables for controls were finally discontinued and replaced with wires.

MSR/NOTES	100%	EXCELLENT	AVERAGE	LAST MSR

MODEL 820 BASSAMP – 20W, 1-15 in. speaker, five-tube chassis, preamp: 3 X 6SN7, power: 2 X 6L6/5881, Stancor transformers, top control panel with knobs for one channel, sensitivity control, black vinyl covering, square plastic grille with horizontal bar, mfg. 1956-58.

| | N/A | $725 - 900 | $375 - 475 | |

MODEL 822 BASSAMP – similar to the Model 820 Bassamp, except has two channels, mfg. 1957-58.

| | N/A | $775 - 900 | $375 - 475 | |

MODEL 830 BASSAMP – similar to the Model 820 Bassamp, except has 30W output, mfg. 1956-58.

| | N/A | $750 - 950 | $500 - 600 | |

MODEL 833 SUPER COMBOAMP/COMBOAMP/MODEL 950-C SUPERCOMBO – 30W (early models) 40W (later models), 2-15 in. Jensen Alnico speakers, guitar/bass combo, 10 tube chassis, power: 4 X 6L6GC power tubes, three channels, rear control panel, four inputs (one for each channel 1 and 2 and two for Channel 3), nine knobs (Ch. 1: v, t, b, Ch. 2: v, t, b, Ch. 3: v, t, b), mfg. 1956-1960.

| | N/A | $1,050 - 1,250 | $525 - 650 | |

The Model 833 Super Comboamp was changed to the Model 833 Comboamp in 1958 and to the 950-C Supercombo amp in 1959. Approximately six of these amps were ever made. This amp appears to be two Model 835 Bassamps welded together.

MODEL 835 BASSAMP – similar to the Super Comboamp except it is only about half of that since the Super Comboamp appears to be two Model 835 amps welded together, mfg. 1959-1961.

courtesy Shaped Music

courtesy Shaped Music

| | N/A | $800 - 1,000 | $425 - 525 | |

TONY MOTTOLA "DANGER" GUITARAMP – 20W, 1-12 in. Jensen Concert Speaker, different from the Super 800 and Model 500 Guitaramps as it was shallower and the speaker sat higher, each amp was made differently, used by jazz guitarist Tony Mottola, mfg. 1953-55.

| | N/A | $875 - 1,025 | $425 - 550 | |

ELECTRIC TUBE AMPS: EARLY MODELS, JS/FOUNTAIN OF SOUND MODELS

JS-20 FOUNTAIN OF SOUND – similar to the JS-35, except the preamp tubes were changed to 6SJ7s and an OC3 voltage regulator was added, mfg. 1957-58.

| | N/A | $1,000 - 1,400 | $650 - 800 | |

JS-30 FOUNTAIN OF SOUND – similar to the JS-20 Fountain of Sound, except has 30W output, mfg. 1957-58.

| | N/A | $1,000 - 1,400 | $650 - 800 | |

JS-35 FOUNTAIN OF SOUND – 20W or 30W, 15 in. JBL speaker, tube chassis, preamp: 3 X 6SJ7, power: 2 X 6L6/5881, silver control panel, five black knobs, three inputs, navy blue covering, gray grille, sat on four legs, upward pointing speaker, mfg. 1955-1960.

| | N/A | $1,000 - 1,400 | $650 - 800 | |

The JS-35 stood for Johnny Smith as this amp replaced the old one in his name. This amp looks like a pool table.

ELECTRIC TUBE AMPS: EARLY MODELS, GUITARAMP/ACCORDIAMP MODELS

In 1956, Ampeg introduced their Guitaramp/Accordiamp Series, but many of these amps were still built one at a time as opposed to on a production line. The problem with amps produced in the late 1950s is that around this time Ampeg was using the same chassis for many different amps, and it was difficult to decipher model numbers as they weren't often listed on the amp. Model numbers were listed by the type of amp. If it was a Bassamp, the series were numbered 800 or 8000, Accordiamps used 400 or 7000 numbers, and Guitaramps used 6000. In 1958, the model numbers were converted to all three-digits (the 6000 changed to 600 and the 7000 changed to 700). Tremolo was only available in the guitar and accordion amps and Bassamps had deeper cabinets with a slanted control panel. In 1956, the logo changed and the "p" in Ampeg now went through the line underneath the logo. The Dolphin, Zephyr, and Continental amps were all voiced for guitars and the Jupiter, Rhapsody, and New Yorker are all identical respectively, except they are voiced for accordions.

MSR/NOTES	100%	EXCELLENT	AVERAGE	LAST MSR

Ampeg produced other models without much information on them including the **518 Dolphin Special**, the **Model 435 SN**, the **Model 635-S Zephyr**, the **Model 720-SN Jupiter II**, and the **625-SN Constellation**. Most of these amps were submodels of more popular models and often only have minor differences or were made at a different time period.

DOLPHIN I (S-6015/615)/JUPITER (S-7015/715) – 15W, 1-12 in. Jensen Alnico speaker, guitar (Dolphin I) or accordion (Jupiter) combo, five tube chassis, preamp: 2 X 6SN7, power: 2 X 6V6 outputs, rectifier: 5Y3, single channel, tremolo, top control panel, chrome control panel, six control knobs (pickup matching, tremolo intensity, tremolo speed, v, t, b,) footswitch jack, black vinyl covering, square plastic grille cloth with a horizontal bar in the middle, mfg. 1956-1960.

N/A $475 - 550 $235 - 290

In 1957, the covering changed to gray bookbinding-type and a dark grey swirl grille. In 1958, the covering was changed to the Navy Random Flair. This amp along with the Zephyr and the Continental were all in a "series" together.

* ***Dophin II (D-6015/615)*** – similar to the Dolphin, except only available in a guitar combo, has two channels, four inputs (two per channel), and nine knobs (Ch. 1: ultra high, s, i, v, t, b, Ch. 2: v, t, b), mfg. 1956-1960.

courtesy Willie's American Guitars

courtesy Willie's American Guitars

N/A $600 - 700 $300 - 375

ZEPHYR I (S-6020/620)/RHAPSODY (S-7020/435-S) – 20W, 1-15 in. Jensen speaker, guitar (Zephyr I) or accordion (Rhapsody) combo, six-tube chassis, preamp: 3 X 6SN7, power: 2 X 6L6/5881, rectifier: 5U4 rectifier, single channel, top chrome control panel, controls for one channel, black vinyl covering, square plastic grille cloth with horizontal bar in the middle, mfg. 1956-59.

N/A $625 - 750 $325 - 400

In 1957, the ouptut was raised to 25W, the covering changed to grey bookbinding-type, and a dark grey swirl grille. In 1958, the covering was changed to the Navy Random Flair.

* ***Zephyr Duette (D-6020/620)*** – similar to the Zephyr I, except has two channels, mfg. 1956-58.

N/A $625 - 750 $325 - 400

CONTINENTAL I (S-6030/630)/NEW YORKER (S-7030/440-S) – 30W, 1-15 in. Jensen coaxial speaker, guitar (Continental I) or accordion (New Yorker) combo, six-tube chassis, preamp: 3 X 6SN7, power: 2 X 6L6/5881, rectifier: 5U4, single channel, top chrome control panel, controls for one channel, black vinyl covering, square plastic grille cloth with horizontal bar in the middle, mfg. 1956-59.

N/A $625 - 750 $325 - 400

In 1957, the output was raised to 35W, the covering changed to grey bookbinding-type, and a dark grey swirl grille. In 1958, the covering was changed to the Navy Random Flair.

* ***Continental Duette (D-6030/630)*** – similar to the Continental I, except has two channels, mfg. 1956-58.

N/A $725 - 850 $350 - 450

ELECTRIC TUBE AMPS: UNIVERSAL SERIES (JET, MERCURY, & ROCKET MODELS)

The Universal Series was the first official organized series of amplifiers released by Ampeg, and they referred to them as Universal because they could be used for guitar, accordion, and microphones. The first two amps from the Universal Series appeared in 1957: the R-12 Rocket and M-12 Mercury. The Universal Series expanded slowly throughout the late 1950s and early 1960s with the introduction of the J-12 Jet in 1958, the M-15 "Big M" in 1959, the R-12R Reverberocket in 1961, and the R-15R Superbreverb in 1963. In 1964, Ampeg began updating and improving the electronics of various Universal Series amps and these new variations often had a suffix letter of "A" or "B" attached to the model number to denote these changes. In 1965, the Universal Series was discontinued, but the J-12 Jet was offered intermittently through 1970.

J-12 JET (FIRST VERSION) – 12W, 1-12 in. speaker, five tube chassis, preamp: 2 X 6SN7, power: 2 X 6V6GT, rectifier: 5Y3, one channel, tremolo top black control panel, two inputs, three black knobs (v, tone, tremolo), power switch, available in cream or yellow bookbinding covering with red or watermelon colored grilles (1957-mid-1958), Navy Random Flair with a gray grille with white swirls (mid-1958-1962), or Blue Check with a gray grille (1962-63, 1967-1970) mfg. 1958-1963, 1967-1970.

	100%	EXCELLENT	AVERAGE
1958 Cream/Yellow Covering	N/A	$675 - 800	$475 - 550
1958-1963 Blue Covering	N/A	$500 - 600	$300 - 350
1967-1970	N/A	$375 - 450	$225 - 275

MSR/NOTES	100%	EXCELLENT	AVERAGE	LAST MSR

Jet J-12
courtesy Savage Audio

Jet J-12
courtesy Savage Audio

Jet J-12A
courtesy Willie's American Guitars

In 1958, the Jet changed to the Navy Random Flair covering like all Ampeg amps at that time. In 1962, the Blue Check covering was introduced. There were a few models made in 1959 and 1960 with the Tin logos.

* **J-12A Jet** – similar to the J-12 Jet, except has 7591A power tubes, mfg. 1964 only.

| | N/A | $425 - 500 | $275 - 325 | |

* **J-12T Jet** – similar to the J-12A, except has 2 X 6BK11 preamp tubes, mfg. 1965 only.

| | N/A | $425 - 500 | $275 - 325 | |

* **J-12D Jet** – similar to the J-12T Jet, except has a solid-state rectifier instead of a 5Y3GT, mfg. 1965-66.

| | N/A | $400 - 500 | $225 - 275 | |

This model was changed back to the J-12 Jet in 1966 until it was discontinued in 1967. Some J-12D's had 7868 preamp tubes. For the J-12R Reverbojet see the Golden Glo series in the Ampeg tube section along with the Jet II.

J-12 JET (SECOND VERSION) – 18W, 1-12 in. speaker, four-tube chassis, preamp: 2 X 12AX7, power: 2 X 7591, solid-state rectifier, single channel, tremolo, top chrome control panel, two inputs (bright, normal), three black knobs (v, tone, tremolo), power switch, single button footswitch, available in black vinyl covering with a silver grille and large "a" ampeg logo badge, mfg. 1967-1970.

| | N/A | $375 - 450 | $225 - 275 | |

* **J-12R Jet** – similar to the J-12 Jet (Second Version) except has reverb with an additional 6U10 preamp tube and a reverb control, mfg. 1968-1970.

| | N/A | $425 - 500 | $250 - 300 | |

M-12 MERCURY – 15W, 1-12 in. speaker, six tube chassis, preamp: 3 X 6SL7, power: 2 X 6V6GT, rectifier: 5Y3, two channels, tremolo, top black control panel, four inputs (two instruments, two accordions), six black knobs (Ch. 1: v, tone, Ch. 2: v, tone, Both: s, i), power switch, available in cream or yellow bookbinding covering with red or watermelon colored grilles (1957-mid-1958), Navy Random Flair with a gray grille with a white swirl (mid-1958-1962), or Blue Check covering with a gray grille (1962-63), mfg. 1957-1963.

| | N/A | $550 - 650 | $375 - 450 | |

* **M-12A Mercury** – similar to the M-12 Mercury except has an updated chassis, mfg. 1964-65.

| | N/A | $550 - 650 | $375 - 450 | |

M-15 BIG M – 20W (early models) or 25W (later models), 1-15 in. Jensen speaker, guitar combo, six tube chassis, preamp: 3 X 6SL7, power: 2 X 6L6 outputs, rectifier: 5U4, two channels, top control channel, six inputs (three for instruments, three for accordions), six black knobs (Ch. 1: v, tone, Ch. 2: v, tone, s, i), power switch, available in Navy Random Flair covering with a gray grille cloth with white swirls (1959-1962) or Blue Check covering with a gray grille (1962-65), mfg. 1959-1965.

courtesy Savage Audio

courtesy Savage Audio

| | N/A | $625 - 750 | $450 - 525 | |

MSR/NOTES	100%	EXCELLENT	AVERAGE	LAST MSR

R-12 ROCKET – 12W, 1-12 in. speaker combo, guitar or accordion application, five tube chassis, preamp 2 X 6SL7, power: 2 X 6V6GT, rectifier: 5Y3, single channel, tremolo, top black control panel, three inputs (guitar, accordion, mic), four black knobs (v, tone, s, i), power switch, available in cream or yellow bookbinding covering with red or watermelon colored grilles (1957-mid-1958), Navy Random Flair covering with a gray grille with white swirls (mid-1958-1962), or Blue Check covering with a gray grille (1962-63), mfg. 1957-1963.

| | N/A | $600 - 700 | $425 - 500 | |

* ***R-12A Rocket*** – similar to the R-12 Rocket, except has an updated chassis, mfg. 1964-65.

| | N/A | $600 - 700 | $425 - 500 | |

R-12R REVERBEROCKET – 15W, 1-12 in. speaker, guitar or accordion combo, seven tube chassis, preamp 2 X 6SL7, 2 X 6SN7, power: 2 X 6V6GT, rectifier: 5Y3, single channel, tremolo, echo dimension (reverb), top black control panel, three inputs (guitar, accordion, mic), five black knobs (v, tone, echo dimension, s, i), power switch, two-button footswitch, available in Navy Random Flair covering with a gray grille with white swirls (1961-62), or Blue Check covering with a gray grille (1962-63), mfg. 1961-63.

| | N/A | $675 - 800 | $475 - 550 | |

* ***R-12R-B Reverberocket*** – similar to the R-12R Reverberocket, except has 7591A power tubes, mfg. 1964 only.

| | N/A | $675 - 800 | $475 - 550 | |

* ***R-12R-T Reverberocket*** – similar to the R-12R Reverberocket, except has a revised chassis with either 7591A or 7868 power tubes, mfg. 1965 only.

| | N/A | $675 - 800 | $475 - 550 | |

R-15R SUPEREVERB/SUPERBREVERB – 25W, 1-15 in. speaker, guitar or accordion combo, six tube chassis, preamp 2 X 6SL7, 1 X 6SN7, 1 X 7025, power: 2 X 6V6GT (1963 only) or 2 X 7591A (late 1963-64), solid-state rectifier, single channel, tremolo, echo dimension (reverb) top black control panel, three inputs (guitar, accordion, mic), five black knobs (v, tone, echo dimension, s, i), power switch, two-button footswitch, available in Blue Check covering with a gray grille, mfg. 1963-64.

| | N/A | $850 - 1,000 | $650 - 750 | |

The R-15R was initially called the Supereverb, but due to the similarity in the name to Fender's Super Reverb, Ampeg changed the name to Superbreverb shortly after production started.

GS-12 ROCKET 2 – 12W, 1-12 in. speaker, guitar combo, four-tube chassis: preamp: 2 X 12AX7, power: 2 X 7591A, solid-state rectifier, single channel, tremolo, front control panel, two inputs, five black knobs (v, t, b, s, i), available in Blue Check covering with a gray grille, mfg. 1965-67.

| | N/A | $625 - 750 | $325 - 400 | |

This amp replaced the R-12 Rocket and it featured Ampeg's new Repeat Percussion effect. Ampeg also offered a model identical to this one with four inputs instead of two called the Gemini IV.

GS-12R REVERBEROCKET 2 – 18W, 1-12 in. speaker, guitar combo, five-tube chassis: preamp: 1 X 12AX7, 1 X 6U10, 1 X 7199, power: 2 X 7591A, solid-state rectifier, single channel, reverb, tremolo, front chrome control panel, two inputs, six black knobs (v, t, b, r, s, i), two-button footswitch, available in Blue Check covering with a gray grille (1965-67) or black vinyl covering with a gray grille (1967-1970), mfg. 1965-1970.

| | N/A | $725 - 850 | $350 - 450 | |

ELECTRIC TUBE AMPS: B-25, B-25B, B-22X JUPITER 22, & B-42X JUPITER 42 MODELS

B-25 – 55W, 2-15 in. speakers in a separate cabinet, piggyback guitar configuration, six-tube chassis: preamp: 2 X 12AX7, 1 X 7199, power: 2 X 7027A, rectifirer: 5AR4, two channels, front silver control panel, four inputs (two per channel with one each for bright and normal), six black knobs (Ch 1: v, t, b, Ch 2: v, t, b), ultra high and ultra low switches for each channel, power switch, black covering, blue/gray grille, mfg. 1969 only.

| courtesy The Music Shoppe | | courtesy The Music Shoppe | |

| **Head Only** | N/A | $475 - 550 | $300 - 350 |
| **Head & Cabinet** | N/A | $850 - 1,100 | $550 - 700 |

* ***B-25B*** – similar to the B-25, except designed for bass guitars with heavier duty speakers, mfg. 1969-1980.

| **Head Only** | N/A | $475 - 550 | $300 - 350 |
| **Head & Cabinet** | N/A | $850 - 1,100 | $550 - 700 |

MSR/NOTES	100%	EXCELLENT	AVERAGE	LAST MSR

B-22X JUPITER 22 – 55W, 2-12 in. speakers, guitar combo, nine tube chassis, preamp: 4 X 12AX7, 1 X 6CG7, 1 X 7199, power: 2 X 7027A, rectifier: 5AR4, single channel, reverb, vibrato, front control panel, four inputs (two per channel, and one each for bright and normal), nine knobs (v, t, b, Ultra high, Ultra Lo, tremolo, vibrato, reverb, afterbeat) black covering, blue/gray grille, mfg. 1969-1971.

	N/A	$700 - 900	$500 - 600	

Altec 417B speakers were optional.

B-42X JUPITER 42 – similar to the B-22X Jupiter 22, except in piggyback configuration with a 4-12 in. speaker cabinet, mfg. 1969-1970.

Head Only	N/A	$500 - 600	$325 - 400	
Head & Cabinet	N/A	$850 - 1,100	$550 - 700	

Altec 417B speakers were optional.

ELECTRIC TUBE AMPS: ECHO SERIES

In 1961, Ampeg began offering reverb on their amplifiers and the first was the R-12R Reverberocket followed by the ET-1 Echo Twin. Ampeg also developed a unit that would allow users to add reverb to their existing amp. The ES-1 Echo Satellite attached to the speaker lugs of another separate amp with alligator clips and used the signal from the other amplifier to produce a reverb effect. In 1962, Ampeg introduced their extremely popular ET-2 Super Echo Twin that featured two amplifiers housed in the same unit that produced stereo sound with reverb.

EJ-12 ECHO JET – 12W, 1-12 in. speaker, add-on reverb unit that can also be used as a stand alone guitar amplifier, four tube chassis, preamp: 1 X 6D10, power: 2 X 7591, rectifier: 5Y3GT, single channel, top control panel, two inputs, two knobs (v, tone), power switch, one-button footswitch, available in Blue Check covering with a gray grille, mfg. 1963-64.

	N/A	$500 - 600	$325 - 400	

The EJ-12 Echo Jet was designed to be used as reverb unit that could be added to any amplifier that did not have reverb. However, it could also be used as a stand alone guitar amplifier similar in performance to the J-12 Jet, but when used as just a guitar amplifier reverb could not be utilized.

* *EJ-12A/EJ-12D Echo Jet* – similar to the EJ-12 Echo Jet, except has revised electronics/preamp sections, EJ-12A replaced the EJ-12 in early 1965 and the EJ-12D followed, mfg. 1965 only.

	N/A	$500 - 600	$325 - 400	

ES-1 ECHO SATELLITE – 6W, 1-8 in. oval speaker (early models), 2-4 in. speakers (later models), add-on reverb unit that attaches to a separate amplifier with alligator clips, three tube chassis: preamp: 1 X 6SL7, power: 1 X 6V6GT, rectifier: 5Y3, single channel, top control panel, single reverb knob, available in Navy Random Flair covering with a gray grille (1961-62) or Blue Check covering with a gray grille (1962-63), mfg. 1961-63.

Oval Speaker	N/A	$500 - 600	$325 - 400	
Round Speakers	N/A	$375 - 450	$225 - 275	

ET-1 ECHO TWIN – 30W (2 x 15W stereo with two separate power amps), 2-12 in. Jensen speakers, guitar/accordion combo, 10 tube chassis (two power tubes and one rectifier for each power amp), preamp: 4 X 6SL7, power: 4 X 6V6, rectifier: 2 X 5Y3, two channels, tremolo, stereo echo (reverb), top chrome control panel, three inputs, eight knobs (Ch. 1: v, tone, s, i, Ch. 2: v, tone, s, i), echo switch, power switch, two-button footswitch, available in Navy Random Flair covering with a gray grille cloth (1961-62) or Blue Check covering with a gray grille (1962-63), mfg. 1961-63.

	N/A	$850 - 1,050	$600 - 700	

* *ET-1-B Echo Twin* – similar to the ET-1 Echo Twin, except has an eight-tube chassis with 4 X 6SL7 preamp tubes, 4 X 7591A power tubes and solid-state rectifiers, available in Blue Check covering with a gray grille, mfg. 1963-64.

	N/A	$850 - 1,050	$600 - 700	

ET-2 SUPER ECHO TWIN – 30W (2 x 15W stereo with two separate power amps), 2-12 in. Jensen speakers, guitar/accordion combo, 10 tube chassis (two power tubes and one rectifier for each power amp), preamp: 4 X 6SL7, power: 4 X 6V6, rectifier: 2 X 5Y3, two channels, vibrato, stereo echo (reverb), top chrome control panel, five inputs (two inputs per channel and one stereo input), seven knobs (Ch. 1: v, tone, s, i, Ch. 2: v, tone, echo dimension), channel selector switch (Channel 1 only or Channel 1 and 2), power switch, two-button footswitch, available in Navy Random Flair covering with a gray grille cloth (1962 only) or Blue Check covering with a gray grille (1962-63), mfg. 1961-63.

courtesy Rick Wilkiewicz

courtesy Rick Wilkiewicz

courtesy Rick Wilkiewicz

	N/A	$1,100 - 1,400	$750 - 900	

MSR/NOTES	100%	EXCELLENT	AVERAGE	LAST MSR

* *ET-2-B Super Echo Twin* – similar to the ET-2 Super Echo Twin, except has an eight-tube chassis with 4 X 6SL7 preamp tubes, 4 X 7591A power tubes and solid-state rectifiers, available in Blue Check covering with a gray grille, mfg. 1964 only.

	N/A	$1,100 - 1,400	$750 - 900	

ELECTRIC TUBE AMPS: DIAMOND BLUE SERIES

In 1995, Ampeg began reissuing amps with the vintage "Blue Check" covering that was extremely popular during the 1960s. Models retained their vintage names such as Jet and Reverberocket and general features generally remained the same, although some minor modifications were performed to make the circuits more modern.

J20 Jet
courtesy Ampeg

SJ-12R "Super Jet"
courtesy Ampeg

Sr-212RT Superrocket
courtesy Ampeg

J-12R "JET II" – 15W, 1-12 in. Ampeg vintage speaker, guitar/accordion combo, four-tube chassis, preamp: 2 X 12AX7, power: 2 X EL84, solid-state rectifier, single channel, reverb, top chrome control panel, two inputs (guitar, accordion), four black knobs (v, t, b, r), power switch, vintage diamond blue vinyl covering, sparkle-weave grille cloth, 18.75 in. wide, 16 in. tall, 10 in. deep, 30 lbs., mfg. 1995-98.

	N/A	$225 - 275	$135 - 175	$499

J-12T "JET II" – 15W, 1-12 in. Ampeg vintage speaker, guitar/accordion combo, four-tube chassis, preamp: 2 X 12AX7, power: 2 X EL84, single channel, reverb, tremolo, top chrome control panel, two inputs (guitar, accordion), five black knobs (v, tone, s, i, r), power switch, vintage diamond blue vinyl covering, sparkle-weave grille cloth, 18.75 in. wide, 16 in. tall, 10 in. deep, 30 lbs., mfg. 1995-2006.

	$475	$325 - 375	$200 - 250	$649

J20 JET – 20W, 1-12 in. Alnico speaker, guitar combo, six-tube chassis, preamp: 3 X 12AX7, power: 2 X 6V6, rectifier: 1 X 5AR4, single channel, tremolo, front chrome control panel, two inputs, four black knobs (v, tone, s, i), footswitch for tremolo on/off, vintage diamond blue vinyl covering, sparkle-weave grille cloth, 25 lbs., 20 in. wide, 17.5 in. tall, 9.75 in. deep, mfg. 2007-09.

	N/A	$500 - 600	$300 - 350	$1,190

SJ-12R "SUPER JET" – 50W, 1-12 in. speaker, guitar combo, four-tube chassis, preamp: 2 X 12AX7, power: 2 X 6L6, single channel, reverb, top chrome control panel, two inputs, five black knobs (v, t, m, b, r), power switch, footswitch included, vintage diamond blue vinyl covering, sparkle-weave grille cloth, 21 in. wide, 17 in. tall, 10 in. deep, 35 lbs., mfg. 1996-2003.

	N/A	$325 - 400	$200 - 250	$829

SJ-12T "SUPER JET" – 50W, 1-12 in. speaker, guitar combo, four-tube chassis, preamp: 2 X 12AX7, power: 2 X 6L6, single channel, reverb, tremolo, top chrome control panel, two inputs, five black knobs (v, tone, s, i, r), power switch, footswitch included, vintage diamond blue vinyl covering, sparkle-weave grille cloth, 21 in. wide, 17 in. tall, 10 in. deep, 35 lbs., mfg. 1996-2006.

	$650	$375 - 450	$225 - 275	$879

R-12R REVERBEROCKET – 50W, 1-12 in. speaker, guitar/accordion combo, five-tube chassis, preamp: 3 X 12AX7, power: 2 X 6L6, solid-state rectifier, two channels, reverb, top chrome control panel, two inputs (guitar and accordion), seven black knobs (g, v, t, m, b, MV, r), line out, line in, footswitch jack, channel select switch, standby switch, power switch, vintage diamond blue vinyl covering, sparkle-weave grille cloth, 24 in. wide, 19 in. tall, 11 in. deep, 45 lbs., mfg. 1996-2006.

	$700	$450 - 525	$275 - 325	$999

* *R-212R Reverberocket* – similar to the R-12R Reverberocket, except has 2-12 in. speakers, 25 in. wide, 19 in. tall, 11 in. deep, 55 lbs., mfg. 1996-2006.

	$775	$500 - 575	$300 - 350	$1,099

* *R-50H Reverberocket* – similar to the R-12R Reverberocket, except in head-unit configuration, front mounted control panel, 29.5 in. wide, 10.5 in. tall, 9 in. deep, 36 lbs., mfg. 1997-2003.

	N/A	$425 - 500	$275 - 325	$949

R-412TA/BA SPEAKER CABINET – 120W, 4-12 in. Ampeg Vintage speakers, 16 ohm impedance, straight (R-412BA) or angled (R-412TA) front, designed for use with the R-50H Reverberocket, recessed side handles, removable casters, vintage diamond blue vinyl covering, sparkle-weave grille cloth, 30 in. wide, 32 in. tall, 14 in. deep, 102 lbs., mfg. 1997-2003.

	N/A	$300 - 350	$175 - 225	$749

MSR/NOTES	100%	EXCELLENT	AVERAGE	LAST MSR

SR-212RT SUPERROCKET – 100W, 2-12 in. Celestion Vintage 30 speakers, guitar/accordion combo, seven-tube chassis, preamp: 3 X 12AX7, power: 4 X 6L6, solid-state rectifier, two channels, reverb, tremolo, top chrome control panel, two inputs (guitar and accordion), nine black knobs (g, v, t, m, b, MV, s, i, r), line out jack, line in jack, two footswitch jacks, channel switch, standby switch, power switch, rear panel: two speaker jacks with impedance selector, vintage diamond blue vinyl covering, sparkle-weave grille cloth, 28 in. wide, 21 in. tall, 10.5 in. deep, 77 lbs., mfg. 2002-06.

	$1,050	$700 - 800	$425 - 500	$1,499

ELECTRIC TUBE AMPS: GEMINI SERIES

The Gemini Series was introduced in 1964 after a year in development and was named after the space program. It was Ampeg's first series of amps to have a front-mounted control panel and a horizontally-mounted chassis besides the Portaflex Series. Parts of the back panel on the Gemini amps could be removed to alter the sound and tone. The Gemini name was used on a variety of different amplifiers through the early 1970s.

G-12 GEMINI I – 22W, 1-12 in. speaker, guitar/accordion combo, seven-tube chassis, preamp: 3 X 6SL7/12AX7, 1 X 6SN7, 1 X 7199, power: 2 X 7591A, solid-state rectifier, two channels, reverb, tremolo, front chrome control panel, four inputs (two per channel with one each for accordion and one for guitar), nine black knobs (Ch. 1: s, i, v, t, b, echo, Ch. 2: v, t, b), two-button footswitch, available in Blue Check covering with a gray grille, mfg. 1964-68.

	N/A	$625 - 750	$325 - 400	

The treble control had a click stop feature that acted as a bright switch when clicked past. Reverb was only available on the first channel, but models have been observed between 1966-67 with another reverb control for the second channel on the back of the amp - it is likely that this was a non-cataloged factory option. This model was also available with a Lansing speaker and called the G-12L.

G-15 GEMINI II – 30W, 1-15 in. speaker, guitar/accordion combo, seven-tube chassis, preamp: 3 X 6SL7/12AX7, 1 X 6SN7, 1 X 7868, power: 2 X 7591A, solid-state rectifier, two channels, reverb, tremolo, front chrome control panel, four inputs (two per channel with one each for accordion and one for guitar), nine black knobs (Ch. 1: s, i, v, t, b, echo, Ch. 2: v, t, b), two-button footswitch, available in Blue Check covering with a gray grille, mfg. 1965-68.

	N/A	$625 - 750	$325 - 400	

G-20 GEMINI 20 – 35W, 2-10 in. speakers, guitar combo, eight-tube chassis: preamp: 4 X 12AX7, 1 X 6CG7, 1 X 7199, power: 2 X 6L6GC, solid-state rectifier, two channels, reverb, tremolo, silver front control panel, four inputs (two per channel, one each for normal and bright), nine black knobs (Ch. 1: v, t, b, r, tremolo speed, afterbeat, Ch. 2: v, t, b), ultra high and ultra low switches for each channel, black covering, blue/gray grille, mfg. 1969-1972.

	N/A	$700 - 825	$350 - 425	

GS-15R GEMINI VI – 22W, 1-12 in. speaker, accordion combo, six-tube chassis, preamp: 2 X 12AX7, 1 X 6CG7, 1 X 7199, power: 2 X 7591A, solid-state rectifier, single channel, reverb, tremolo, front chrome control panel, four inputs (guitar, accordion, aux., mic.), six black knobs (v, t, b, r, s, i), two-button footswitch, available in Blue Check covering with a gray grille, mfg. 1966-67.

courtesy Shaped Music   courtesy Shaped Music

	N/A	$600 - 700	$425 - 500	

GV-15 GEMINI V (FIRST VERSION) – 30W, 1-15 in. speaker, guitar/accordion combo, seven-tube chassis, preamp: 3 X 6SL7/12AX7, 1 X 6SN7, 1 X 7868, power: 2 X 7591A, solid-state rectifier, two channels, reverb, tremolo, vibrato, front chrome control panel, four inputs (two per channel), nine black knobs (Ch. 1: tremolo, vibrato, v, t, b, echo, Ch. 2: v, t, b), two-button footswitch, available in Blue Check covering with a gray grille, mfg. 1967 only.

	N/A	$625 - 750	$325 - 400	

Later in 1968, the Gemini V changed to a printed circuit board, ultra high and lo controls, output was raised to 35W, and an Altec 418B speaker available as an option.

GV-15 GEMINI V (SECOND VERSION) – 35W, 1-15 in. speaker, guitar/accordion combo, seven-tube chassis, preamp: 3 X 6SL7/12AX7, 1 X 6SN7, 1 X 7868, power: 2 X 7591A, solid-state rectifier, printed circuit board, two channels, reverb, tremolo, vibrato, front chrome control panel, four inputs (two per channel), nine black knobs (Ch. 1: tremolo, vibrato, v, t, b, echo, Ch. 2: v, t, b), ultra high and ultra low switches for

MSR/NOTES	100%	EXCELLENT	AVERAGE	LAST MSR

each channel, two-button footswitch, available in black vinyl covering with a gray grille, mfg. 1968-1972.

| | N/A | $625 - 750 | $325 - 400 | |

This model had an optional Altec 418B speaker.

GV-22 GEMINI 22 – 35W, 2-12 in. speakers, guitar combo, eight-tube chassis: preamp: 4 X 12AX7, 1 X 6CG7, 1 X 7199, power: 2 X 6L6GC, solid-state rectifier, two channels, reverb, tremolo, vibrato, silver front control panel, four inputs (two per channel, one each for normal and bright), nine black knobs (Ch. 1: v, t, b, Ch. 2: v, t, b, r, s, i), ultra high and ultra low switches for each channel, black covering, blue/gray grille, mfg. 1969-1972.

| | N/A | $700 - 825 | $350 - 425 | |

The GV-22 Gemini 22 utilized the chassis from the GV-15 Gemini 15. Altec speakers were optional.

GEMINI 12 – 22W, 1-12 in. speaker, guitar/accordion combo, seven-tube chassis, preamp: 3 X 6SL7/12AX7, 1 X 6SN7, 1 X 7199, power: 2 X 7591A, solid-state rectifier, two channels, reverb, tremolo, front chrome control panel, four inputs (two per channel), nine black knobs (Ch. 1: s, i, v, t, b, echo, Ch. 2: v, t, b), ultra hi switch, ultra low switch, two-button footswitch, available in black vinyl covering with a gray grille, mfg. 1968-1971.

| | N/A | $625 - 750 | $325 - 400 | |

ELECTRIC TUBE AMPS: GOLDEN-GLO SERIES

Ampeg introduced the Golden-Glo Series in 1967 and featured revamped designs of some of their most popular amps with brand new cosmetics. These amps were covered in black covering with a brown/copper straw-like grille stuck out about three inches from the rest of the amp. On top of this protusion was the copper-plated control panel with controls pointing toward the sky. The top of the amp rises another six inches from the control panel, and is finished in wood-grain with the Ampeg logo.

JET II – 15W, 1-12 in. speaker, guitar combo, tube chassis, preamp: 12AX7s, power: 2 X 6V6GT, solid-state rectifier, single channel, tremolo, top gold control panel, two inputs, three black knobs (v, tone, s), black covering, brown straw grille, mfg. 1967-68.

| | N/A | $475 - 550 | $235 - 290 | |

J-12R REVERBOJET – 18W, 1-12 in. speaker, guitar combo, five-tube chassis: preamp: 2 X 12AX7, 1 X 6U10, power: 2 X 7591A, solid-state rectifier, single channel, tremolo, reverb, top gold control panel, two inputs, four black knobs (v, t, b, r), VU meter on control panel, black covering, brown straw grille, mfg. 1967-68.

courtesy John Beeson/The Music Shoppe

courtesy John Beeson/The Music Shoppe

| | N/A | $500 - 600 | $255 - 325 | |

GSC-12R REVERBEROCKET III – 18W, 1-12 in. speaker, guitar combo, six-tube chassis: preamp: 3 X 12AX7, 1 X 6SL7, power: 2 X 7591, solid-state rectifier, single channel, reverb, tremolo, repeat percussion, top gold control panel, two inputs, eight black knobs (v, t, b, r, s, i, repeat percussion, rate echo control), black covering, brown straw grille, light-up lucite logo (red) mfg. 1967-68.

| | N/A | $675 - 800 | $350 - 425 | |

The Reverberocket III was the only Golden Glo model to have a light-up lucite logo similar to the Portaflex amps. There have also been examples found of this model spelled "Reverborocket".

ELECTRIC TUBE AMPS: GVT SERIES

GVT5H HEAD – 5W (switchable to 2.5W), guitar head-unit, two-tube chassis, preamp: 1 X 12AX7, power: 1 X 6V6, solid-state rectifier, single channel, Baxandall tone controls, front brushed aluminum control panel, single input, three knobs (v, t, b), half-power switch, power switch, rear panel: five speaker jacks (two 4 ohm, two 8 ohm, one 16 ohm), black covering, black with silver accents grille cloth, 15.5 in. wide, 9.1 in. tall, 9.1 in. deep, 20 lbs., mfg. summer 2011-2014.

| $350 | $200 - 250 | $120 - 150 | | $490 |

* *GVT5-110 Combo* – similar to the GVT5H Head, except in combo configuration with 1-10 in. Celestion speaker, black covering, black with silver accents grille cloth, 15.5 in. wide, 16 in. tall, 9.1 in. deep, 28.5 lbs., mfg. summer 2011-2014.

| $400 | $250 - 300 | $150 - 190 | | $560 |

MSR/NOTES	100%	EXCELLENT	AVERAGE	LAST MSR

GVT15H HEAD – 15W (switchable to 7.5W), guitar head-unit, four-tube chassis, preamp: 2 X 12AX7, power: 2 X 6V6, solid-state rectifier, single channel, reverb, Baxandall tone controls, front brushed aluminum control panel, single input, six knobs (g, t, m, b, v, r), half-power switch, power switch, rear panel: effects loop, footswitch jack, five speaker jacks (two 4 ohm, two 8 ohm, one 16 ohm), black covering, black with silver accents grille cloth, 18 in. wide, 9.8 in. tall, 10 in. deep, 27.5 lbs., optional two-button footswitch (Model GTV-FS2), mfg. summer 2011-2014.

	$500	$300 - 375	$175 - 225	$700

* **GVT15-112 Combo** – similar to the GVT15H Head, except in combo configuration with 1-12 in. Celestion speaker, black covering, black with silver accents grille cloth, 18 in. wide, 19.1 in. tall, 10 in. deep, 42 lbs., mfg. summer 2011-2014.

	$600	$350 - 425	$200 - 250	$840

GVT52-112 COMBO – 50W (switchable to 25W), guitar combo, 1-12 in. Celestion speaker, five-tube chassis, preamp: 3 X 12AX7, power: 2 X 6V6, solid-state rectifier, two channels, reverb, Baxandall tone controls, front brushed aluminum control panel, single input, 12 knobs (Ch. 1: g, t, m, b, v, Ch. 2: g, t, m, b, v, All: r, MV), channel switch, standby switch, power switch, rear panel: channel switch footswitch jack, reverb/effects loop footswitch jack, effects loop, five speaker jacks (two 4 ohm, two 8 ohm, one 16 ohm), black covering, black with silver accents grille cloth, 24 in. wide, 19.5 in. tall, 11 in. deep, 52 lbs., single button footswitch included (Model GVT-FS1) or optional two-button footswitch (Model GTV-FS2), mfg. summer 2011-2014.

	$750	$475 - 550	$275 - 325	$1,050

* **GVT52-212 Combo** – similar to the GVT52-112 Combo, except has 2-12 in. Celestion speakers, 26.5 in. wide, 21 in. tall, 11 in. deep, 63 lbs., mfg. summer 2011-2014.

	$900	$550 - 650	$325 - 400	$1,260

GVT112E SPEAKER CABINET – 60W, 1-12 in. Celestion Vintage 30 speaker, sealed cabinet, two inputs, designed for use with the GVT5H and GVT15H heads, black covering, black with silver accents grille cloth, 18 in. wide, 16.5 in. tall, 11 in. deep, 31 lbs., mfg. summer 2011-2014.

	$250	$150 - 190	$95 - 120	$350

* **GVT112EW Speaker Cabinet** – similar to the GVT112E, except has a wide double baffle design, black covering, black with silver accents grille cloth, 24 in. wide, 16.5 in. tall, 11 in. deep, 38 lbs., mfg. summer 2011-2014.

	$300	$175 - 225	$105 - 130	$420

ELECTRIC TUBE AMPS: HERITAGE SERIES

The Heritage Series was introduced in 2010 and at the time was the only American-built Ampeg amplifiers offered.

Heritage B-15N
courtesy Ampeg

Heritage R-12R Combo Amp
courtesy Ampeg

HERITAGE B-15 – 25W (1964 bias) or 30W (1966 bias), 1-15 in. custom designed Eminence speaker, Portaflex design flip-top combo, six-tube chassis, preamp: 3 X SL7, power: 2 X 6L6GC, rectifier: 1 X 5AR4 or 5U4G, two channels (1964 and 1966), front chrome control panel, four inputs (two per channel), six knobs (v, t, b for each channel), standby switch, 1964/1966 channel switch, power switch, rear panel: external amp out, four speaker jacks, baltic birch and poplar construction with double baffle cabinet design, black diamond Tolex covering, black/silver vintage-style grille cloth, removable dolly with casters, 96 lbs., limited edition run of 50 individually numbered/matched amp/cabinet units in 2011 and 100 units in 2012, mfg. 2011-2012.

	$4,000	N/A	N/A	$5,600

The Heritage B-15 Portaflex contains two distinct channels based on two of the most desirable configurations of the original B-15. One channel is based on the 1964 cathode bias B-15NC and the other is based on the 1966 fixed bias B-15NF.

* **Heritage B-15N** – 25W (1964 bias) or 30W (1966 bias), 1-15 in. custom designed Eminence speaker, Portaflex flip-top combo, six-tube chassis, preamp: 3 X 12AX7, power: 2 X 6L6GC, rectifier: 1 X 5AR4, two channels (1964 and 1966), front black control panel, four inputs (two per channel), six knobs (v, t, b for each channel), 1964/1966 channel/standby switch, power switch, rear panel: external amp out, three speaker jacks, baltic birch and poplar construction with double baffle cabinet design, vinyl covering, black/silver vintage-style grille cloth, removable casters, 82.5 lbs., limited edition run of 250 individually numbered/matched amp/cabinet units, mfg. 2013-present.

MSR $4,200	$3,000	$1,950 - 2,250	$975 - 1,200	

MSR/NOTES	100%	EXCELLENT	AVERAGE	LAST MSR

**Heritage SVT-CL
courtesy Ampeg**

**Heritage SVT-410LF Speaker Cabinet
courtesy Ampeg**

**Heritage SVT-810E Speaker Cabinet
courtesy Ampeg**

HERITAGE R-12R COMBO AMP – 15W Vintage or 30W Full, 1-12 in. Celestion Alnico Gold speaker, guitar combo, seven tube chassis, preamp 2 X 6SL7, 2 X 6SN7, power: 2 X 6L6GC, rectifier: 1 X 5AR4, single channel, tremolo, echo dimension (reverb), top white control panel, two inputs (bright, normal), five black knobs (v, tone, echo dimension, s, i), power switch, full/standby/vintage switch, two-button footswitch, external speaker jack, available in black diamond Tolex covering with vintage gray grille, baltic birch and poplar construction, limited run of 100 units, 55 lbs., mfg. 2012 only.

	$4,500	$2,950 - 3,400	$1,475 - 1,800	$6,300

HERITAGE SVT-CL – 300W @ 2 or 4 ohms, bass head unit, 11 tube chassis, preamp: 3 X 12AX7, 2 X 12AU7, power: "Winged C" 6 X 6550, single channel, front brushed aluminum control panel, two inputs (0dB and -15dB), six black knobs (g, b, m, five-position mid-range freq., t, MV), ultra hi switch, ultra lo switch, power switch standby switch, rear panel: transformer balanced line out, Neutrik Speakon and 1/4 in. speaker jacks, recessed side handles, black Tolex covering, Heritage black sparkle grille cloth with "Ampeg" logo in upper left corner and "Heritage" logo in lower right corner, 80 lbs., mfg. 2010-present.

MSR $3,360	$2,400	$1,450 - 1,750	$850 - 1,050	

HERITAGE SVT-410HLF SPEAKER CABINET – 500W @ 4 ohms, 4-10 in. U.S.-built Eminence LF drivers and a 1 in. Eminence APT:50 HF driver with L-Pad level control, 15mm birch construction, recessed side handles, black Tolex covering, Heritage black sparkle grille cloth with "Ampeg" badge in upper left corner and "Heritage" logo in lower right corner, 76 lbs., mfg. 2010-present.

MSR $1,260	$900	$575 - 650	$325 - 400	

HERITAGE SVT-810E SPEAKER CABINET – 800W @ 4 ohms mono (400W @ 8 ohms stereo), 8-10 in. U.S.-built Eminence LF drivers, 15mm birch construction, recessed side handles, black Tolex covering, Heritage black sparkle grille cloth with "Ampeg" badge in upper left corner and "Heritage" logo in lower right corner, 137 lbs., mfg. 2010-present.

MSR $1,820	$1,300	$800 - 950	$475 - 550	

ELECTRIC TUBE AMPS: PORTAFLEX SERIES

Ampeg's Portaflex or "flip top" series of amplifiers debuted in 1960. Combo amplifiers were convenient because of their portability, but the space was limited inside the cabinet and the tubes often overheated due to the lack of cooling. Piggyback amplifiers (separate amplifier heads and speaker cabinets) solved this problem, but the portability was gone. The new Portaflex design combined elements from both of these designs to solve these problems. In the Portaflex, the amplifier chassis was mounted on a removable panel that acted as the top of the cabinet. When the player was using the amplifier, the chassis locked onto the cabinet like a Piggback unit and allowed the tubes and transformers to properly cool. For storage or transport, the chassis was unlocked and flipped over to sit inside the cabinet. When the chassis was stored, it looked like a regular combo amp or speaker cabinet. The chassis connected to the cabinet through a single cable, and nearly all Portaflex amplifiers were sold with the optional four-wheel dolly. Part of the chassis included a light up lucite Ampeg name plate that would illuminate when the amplifier was in use. Ampeg also allowed owners to personalize the name plate with their name to let others now whose amp it was!

The Portaflex design was a constant model in the Ampeg line between 1960 and 1980, but each model underwent several revisions that were often noted by a letter suffix such as "B", "C", or "Y". Please note that the amplifiers themselves often did not include the suffix letter. For instance, the B-15N with a solid-state rectifier is still called a B-15N although according to Ampeg's service records, it is referred to as the B-15NB.

B-12N PORTAFLEX – 25W, 1-12 in. speaker, guitar or accordion combo/piggyback Portaflex design, six-tube chassis, preamp: 2 X 6SL7, 1 X 6SL7, power: 2 X 6L6GC, rectifier: 5U4G, two channels, front silver control panel, three input jacks (two for Ch. 1, one for Ch. 2), six black knobs (Ch. 1: v, t, b, Ch. 2: v, t, b), standby switch, ground switch, power switch, rear panel: two inputs for 8 ohm extension speaker and extension amplifier, illuminated lucite panel with Ampeg logo and optional owner's monogram, detachable leg support for tilt cabinet, available in Navy Random Flair covering with a gray grille (1961-62) or Blue Check covering with a gray grille (1962-65), mfg. 1961-65.

	N/A	$1,100 - 1,400	$750 - 900	

Later models were available with a Lansing speaker and called the B-12NL.

B-12X PORTAFLEX – 30W, 1-12 in. speaker and either an oval 4 X 8 in. speaker or 2-4 in. speakers enclosed in a separate cabinet for echo, multi-purpose piggyback/combo Portaflex design, 10-tube chassis: preamp: 5 X 6SL7, 1 X 6SN7, power: 2 X 6L6GC, 1 X 6V6, rectifier: 5U4, two

MSR/NOTES	100%	EXCELLENT	AVERAGE	LAST MSR

channels, vibrato, reverb, front chrome control panel, five inputs (two per channel and one for stereo), nine knobs (Ch. 1: v, t, b, echo dimension [reverb], s, i, Ch. 2: v, t, b), footswitch jack, rear panel: power switch, ground switch, standby switch, extension speaker jack, echo speaker jack, extension amplifier jack, illuminated lucite panel with Ampeg logo and optional owner's monogram, two-button footswitch, available in Navy Random Flair covering with a gray grille (1961-62) or Blue Check covering with a gray grille (1962-65), mfg. 1961-65.

| | N/A | $1,000 - 1,300 | $650 - 800 | |

This was the first Portaflex amplifier specifically designed for guitars, and it had a separate speaker cabinet for echo dimension (reverb) that had an oval speaker (early models) or 2-4 in. speakers (later models) that would fit inside the Portaflex cabinet. The reverb circuit was driven by one 6SN7 preamp tube and one 6V6 power tube. Later models were available with a Lansing speaker and called the B-12XL.

* **B-12XY Portaflex** – similar to the B-12X Portaflex, except had a revised circuit with a 6D10 preamp tube replacing the 6SL7, a 7591A power tube replacing the 6V6 for the reverb unit, and 2 X 7027A power tubes for the main unit, and output raised from 30W to 50W, mfg. late 1964-65.

| | N/A | $1,000 - 1,300 | $650 - 800 | |

B-12XT PORTAFLEX – 50W, 2-12 in. Jensen speakers, guitar/accordion combo/piggyback Portaflex design, nine-tube chassis, preamp: 4 X 12AX7, 1 X 6CG7, 1 X 7199, power: 2 X 7027A, rectifier: 5AR4, two channels, vibrato, reverb, front chrome control panel, four input jacks (two per channel), 10 black knobs (Ch. 1: v, t, b, Ch. 2: v, t, b, i, s, r, reverb channel selector), footswitch jack, rear panel: standby switch, ground switch, power switch, input for 8 ohm extension speaker, output jack for external amplifier, hum balance control, illuminated lucite panel with Ampeg logo and optional owner's monogram, available in Blue Check covering with a gray grille (1965-67) or black covering with a blue/gray grille with chrome trim (1965-68), mfg. 1965-68.

| 1965-1967 Blue Check | N/A | $1,000 - 1,300 | $650 - 800 | |
| 1967-1968 Black | N/A | $800 - 1,000 | $550 - 650 | |

* **B-12XTC Portaflex** – similar to the B-12XT, except has a 4-12 in. speaker cabinet, available in black covering with a blue/gray grille and chrome trim, mfg. 1967 only.

| | N/A | $800 - 1,000 | $550 - 650 | |

A-15/B-15 PORTAFLEX – 25W, 1-15 in. speaker, accordion (A-15) or guitar (B-15) combo/piggyback configuration Portaflex design, six-tube chassis, preamp: 3 X 6SL7, power: 2 X 6L6GC, rectifier: 5U4G, two channels, chrome control panel, three input jacks (one for stereo), four black knobs (Ch. 1 v, Ch. 2 v, t, b), available in Navy Random Flair covering with a gray grille, mfg. 1960-61 (B-15 was produced in 1961 only).

| | N/A | $1,200 - 1,500 | $800 - 1,000 | |

B-15N PORTAFLEX (FIRST VERSION) – 25W, 1-15 in. speaker, guitar or accordion combo/piggyback Portaflex design, six-tube chassis, preamp: 2 X 6SL7, 1 X 6SL7, power: 2 X 6L6GC, rectifier: 5U4G, two channels, front silver control panel, three input jacks (two for Ch. 1, one for Ch. 2), six black knobs (Ch. 1: v, t, b, Ch. 2: v, t, b), standby switch, ground switch, power switch, rear panel: two inputs for 8 ohm extension speaker and extension amplifier, illuminated lucite panel with Ampeg logo and optional owner's monogram, detachable leg support for tilt cabinet, available in Navy Random Flair covering with a gray grille, mfg. 1961-62.

| | N/A | $1,200 - 1,500 | $800 - 1,000 | |

* **B-15NB Portaflex** – similar to the B-15N Portaflex, except had a slightly revised preamp/power amp circuit and a solid-state rectifier, available in Blue Check covering with a gray grille cloth, mfg. 1962-64.

courtesy Savage Audio

courtesy Savage Audio

courtesy Savage Audio

| | N/A | $1,200 - 1,500 | $800 - 1,000 | |

* **B-15NC Portaflex (First Version)** – similar to the B-15NB Portaflex, except utilized a printer circuit board and the solid-state rectifier was replaced by a 5AR4 rectifier tube, available in Blue Check covering with a gray grille cloth, mfg. late 1964-mid-1965.

| | N/A | $1,200 - 1,500 | $800 - 1,000 | |

* **B-15NF Portaflex** – similar to the B-15NC Portaflex except output power was raised to 30W, power tubes were changed to fixed-bias 2 X 6L6GC, a new printed circuit board was introduced and the inside of the cabinet was changed to a single baffle, available in Blue Check with a gray grille (mid-1965-1967) or black vinyl covering with chrome trim and a gray grille (1967 only), mfg. mid-1965-67.

| | N/A | $1,200 - 1,500 | $800 - 1,000 | |

B-15X PORTAFLEX – 50W, 1-15 in. speaker with a horn tweeter and 2-4 in. "echo" speakers, multi-purpose piggyback/combo Portaflex design, 10-tube chassis: preamp: 1 X 6SL7, 1 X 6SN7, 1 X 7199, 2 X 6D10, 1 X 7591, power: 2 X 7027A, 1 X 6V6, rectifier: 5AR4, two channels, vibrato, reverb, front chrome control panel, five inputs (two per channel and one for stereo), nine knobs (Ch. 1: v, t, b, echo dimension [reverb], s, i, Ch. 2: v, t, b), footswitch jack, rear panel: power switch, ground switch, standby switch, extension speaker jack, echo speaker jack, extension amplifier jack, illuminated lucite panel with Ampeg logo and optional owner's monogram, two-button footswitch, available in Blue Check covering with a gray grille, mfg. 1964-67.

| | N/A | $1,200 - 1,500 | $800 - 1,000 | |

This model was also available with a Lansing speaker and called the B-15XL.

B-15NC PORTAFLEX (SECOND VERSION) – 50W, 2-15 in. CTS speakers mounted in a tall vertical cabinet, Portaflex design, five tube chassis, preamp: 2 X 6SL7, 1 X 7199, power: 2 X 7027A, rectifier: 5AR4, two channels, front chrome control panel, six black knobs (Ch. 1: v, b, t, Ch. 2: v, b, t), illuminated lucite panel with Ampeg logo and optional owner's monogram, available in black vinyl covering with a blue and silver grille, mfg. 1967-68.

| | N/A | $950 - 1,200 | $650 - 800 | |

B-15ND PORTAFLEX – 50W, 1-15 in. speaker mounted in a regular cabinet and 1-15 in. speaker mounted in an extension cabinet, Portaflex design, five tube chassis, preamp: 2 X 6SL7, 1 X 7199, power: 2 X 7027A, rectifier: 5AR4, two channels, front chrome control panel, six black knobs (Ch. 1: v, b, t, Ch. 2: v, b, t), illuminated lucite panel with Ampeg logo and optional owner's monogram, available in black vinyl covering with a blue and silver grille, mfg. 1967 only.

| | N/A | $1,000 - 1,300 | $650 - 800 | |

B-15N PORTAFLEX (SECOND VERSION) – 50W, 1-15 in. speaker, Portaflex design, six-tube chassis, preamp: 3 X 6SL7, power: 2 X 6L6GC, rectifier: 5AR4, front silver control panel, four input jacks (two per channel), six knobs (Ch. 1: v, b, t, Ch. 2: v, b, t), ultra high boost and ultra low boost switches for each channel, power switch, standby switch, black vinyl covering, blue/silver grille, mfg. 1968-1980.

courtesy John Beeson/The Music Shoppe   courtesy John Beeson/The Music Shoppe

| | N/A | $950 - 1,200 | $650 - 800 | |

B-15S PORTAFLEX – 60W, 1-15 in. speaker, Portaflex design, six-tube chassis, preamp: 2 X 12AX7, 1 X 12DW7, 1 X 12AU7, power: 2 X 7027A, solid-state rectifier, front silver control panel, four input jacks (two per channel), seven knobs (three-position response knob, Ch. 1: v, b, t, Ch. 2: v, b, t), ultra high boost and ultra low boost switches for each channel, power switch, standby switch, extension speaker jack, output jack for external amplifier, black vinyl covering, blue/silver grille, mfg. 1971-77.

| | N/A | $850 - 1,000 | $425 - 525 | |

B-18N PORTAFLEX – 50W, 1-18 in. speaker, bass combo/piggyback, six-tube chassis, preamp: 2 X 6SL7, 1 X 7199, power: 2 X 7027A, rectifier: 5AR4, two channels, front chrome control panel, three input jacks (two for Ch. 1, one for Ch. 2), six black knobs (Ch. 1: v, t, b, Ch. 2: v, t, b), standby switch, ground switch, power switch, rear panel: input for 8 ohm extension speaker, output jack for external amplifier, hum balance control, illuminated lucite panel with Ampeg logo and optional owner's monogram, available in Blue Check covering with a gray grille, mfg. 1963-67.

courtesy John Beeson/The Music Shoppe   courtesy John Beeson/The Music Shoppe

courtesy John Beeson/The Music Shoppe

| 1963-1965 | N/A | $1,700 - 2,000 | $850 - 1,050 | |
| 1966-1967 | N/A | $1,525 - 1,800 | $775 - 950 | |

MSR/NOTES	100%	EXCELLENT	AVERAGE	LAST MSR

B-18X PORTAFLEX – 50W, 1-18 in. Fane speaker with a Jensen mid-range horn, keyboard/guitar/bass combo/piggyback Portaflex design, nine-tube chassis, preamp: 4 X 12AX7, 1 X 6CG7, 1 X 7199, power: 2 X 7027A, rectifier: 5AR4, two channels, vibrato, reverb, front chrome control panel, four input jacks (two per channel), 10 black knobs (Ch. 1: v, t, b, Ch. 2: v, t, b, i, s, r, reverb channel selector), footswitch jack, rear panel: standby switch, ground switch, power switch, input for 8 ohm extension speaker, output jack for external amplifier, hum balance control, illuminated lucite panel with Ampeg logo and optional owner's monogram, available in Blue Check covering with a gray grille (1966-67) or black covering with a blue/gray grille with chrome trim (1967-68), mfg. 1966-68.

1966-1967 Blue Check	N/A	$1,000 - 1,300	$650 - 800	
1967-1968 Black	N/A	$800 - 1,000	$550 - 650	

SB-12 PORTAFLEX – 25W, 1-12 in. Jensen C12N speaker, mulit-purpose combo/piggyback Portaflex design, five-tube chassis: preamp: 2 X 12AX7, power: 2 X 7868/7591A (early models)or 2 X 6L6GC (later models), single channel, front silver control panel, two inputs, three knobs (v, b, t), power switch, standby switch, available in Blue Check covering with a gray grille (1965-67) or black vinyl covering with a blue/silver grille (1967-1971), mfg. 1965-1971.

	N/A	$700 - 850	$500 - 600	

This was a close but not an exact replacement for the B-12N. This amp was specifically designed for the Ampeg Baby Bass.

ELECTRIC TUBE AMPS: SVT SERIES

Ampeg's flagship model, the SVT (Super Vacuum Tube), was introduced in 1969 and has been produced in one form or another by Ampeg ever since. At 300 watts powered by a 14-tube chassis, it was easily the most powerful production amplifier at the time when the "power race" was in full force. At first, the SVT was described as an all-purpose amp like most Ampegs, but by the mid-1970s it was clear that it was best suited for bass guitars and Ampeg began considering it a bass amp. When St. Louis Music pruchased Ampeg, they began developing several other amplifiers called the SVT including tube amps, solid-state amps, hybrid amps, preamps, and power amps. Please refer to other SVT categories for non-tube SVT amps.

SVT (1969-1985 MFG.) – 300W, 16-10 in. speakers (two 8-10 in. speaker cabinets with four seperate compartments for each pair of speakers), bass piggyback configuration, 14 tube chassis: preamp: 4 X 12DW7, 1 X 12AX7, 2 X 12BH7, 1 X 6C4, power: 6 X 6550 (early models featured 6146), solid-state rectifier, two channels, front silver (1969-1980) or black (1981-85) control panel, four inputs (two per channel with one each for normal and bright), seven knobs (Ch.1: v, t, m, b, Ch. 2: v, t, b), ultra-high and ultra low switches for each channel, three-way mid-range selector switch on Channel 1, black covering, blue/gray grille (1969-1980) or black grille (1981-85), mfg. 1969-1985.

courtesy Savage Audio

courtesy Savage Audio

1969-1972 Head Only	N/A	$2,000 - 2,500	$1,200 - 1,500	
1969-1972 Head & Two Cabinets	N/A	$3,250 - 4,250	$2,000 - 2,500	
1973-1980 Head Only	N/A	$1,650 - 2,000	$1,050 - 1,300	
1973-1980 Head & Two Cabinets	N/A	$2,750 - 3,500	$1,750 - 2,250	
1981-1985 Head Only	N/A	$1,500 - 1,850	$950 - 1,200	
1981-1985 Head & Two Cabinets	N/A	$2,500 - 3,000	$1,500 - 1,850	

Early models were equipped with 6 X 6146 power tubes, but were discontinued shortly after the SVT was introduced because they ran too hot. There was a recall issued in 1972 to update all of the amps with the more reliable 6550 tubes and other modifications. It should be noted that any model still equipped with 6146 tubes are worth significantly less because the amp does not run properly. When MTI took over in the early 1980s they produced the SVTs in Japan with Japanese parts and the 12DW7 preamp tubes were replaced with 12AX7s.

SVT-HD (1986-89 MFG.) – 300W, bass head unit, 14 tube chassis: preamp: 5 X 12AX7, 2 X 12BH7, 1 X 6C4WA, power: 6 X 6550, solid-state rectifier, two channels, front black control panel, four inputs (two per channel with one each for normal and bright), seven knobs (Ch.1: v, t, m, b, Ch. 2: v, t, b), ultra-high and ultra low switches for each channel, three-way mid-range selector switch on Channel 1, black covering, black grille, limited edition run of 500 instruments, mfg. 1986-89.

	N/A	$1,500 - 1,850	$950 - 1,200	

When St. Louis Music took over in 1986, the production of the SVT moved back to the U.S and only 500 were made over a five year period in the "Skunkworks" department. The amp became known as the SVT-HD, although only SVT appeared on the control panel. The SVT-HD was sold separately from any speaker cabinets.

MSR/NOTES	100%	EXCELLENT	AVERAGE	LAST MSR

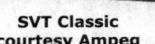

SVT Classic
courtesy Ampeg

SVT-AV
courtesy Ampeg

SVT-VR
courtesy Ampeg

SVT CLASSIC (1994-PRESENT) – 300W, bass head-unit, 11-tube chassis: preamp: 3 X 12AX7, 2 X AU7, power: 6 X 6550, solid-state rectifier, two channels, two inputs, six black knobs (g, b, m, five-position mid-range freq, t, MV), standby switch, power switch, transformer balanced line out, recessed side handles, black covering, black grille, 80 lbs., mfg. 1994-present.

MSR $2,520	$1,800	$1,175 - 1,350	$575 - 725	

   • Add 10% for Limited Edition models with Blue, Red, or White coverings (offered late 1990s only).

SVT-AV (1999-2005 MFG.) – 300W, bass head unit, 11 tube chassis: preamp: 3 X 12AX7, 2 X 12AU7, power: 6 X 6550, solid-state rectifier, single channel, front silver control panel, two inputs, six knobs (g, b, m, five-position mid-range freq., t, MV), ultra-high and ultra low switches, power switch, standby switch, recessed side handles, black covering, blue/gray grille, mfg. 1999-2005.

	N/A	$1,000 - 1,200	$600 - 700	$2,299

SVT-VR (VINTAGE REISSUE, 2006-PRESENT MFG.) – 300W, bass head-unit only, 12-tube chassis, preamp: 3 X 12AX7, 3 X 12AU7, power: 6 X 6550, two channels, front silver control panel with blue lines, four inputs (two per channel with one each for normal and bright), seven knobs (Ch. 1: v, t, m, b, Ch. 2: v, t, b), ultra hi and ultra lo switches for each channel, three-way mid-range selector switch, polarity switch, power switch, rear panel: preamp out, power amp in, recessed side handles, black covering, silver grille, 85 lbs., mfg. 2006-present.

MSR $3,080	$2,200	$1,425 - 1,650	$725 - 875	

This is a reissue of the original SVT head from the 1970s.

SVT-II – 300W, bass three-space rack-mount head, 12-tube chassis: preamp: 4 X 12AX7, 2 X 12AU7, power: 6 X 6550, solid-state rectifier, single channel, front black control panel, two inputs (normal, bright), five knobs (v, t, m, five-position mid-range freq. selector, b), six-band graphic EQ with level adjustment and footswitch jack, balanced out pre/post switch, ultra hi switch, graphic EQ switch, ultra lo switch, standby switch, power switch, rear panel: convenience outlet, polarity switch, line out, line in, XLR balanced line out, two speaker jacks, hum balance control, impedance switch, 80 lbs., mfg. 1989-1994.

	N/A	$1,050 - 1,250	$525 - 650	

The SVT-II is similar to the SVT, except it has only a single channel and a six-band graphic EQ.

SVT-100 – 100W, bass head unit, seven-tube chassis: preamp: 3 X 12AX7, power: 4 X 6550, solid-state rectifier, single channel, front black control panel, two inputs, six black knobs (pre v, MV, b, m, t, p), ultra hi switch, ultra lo switch, power switch, standby switch, black covering, black grille, mfg. 1986-1992.

	N/A	$650 - 750	$475 - 550	

The SVT-100 was a modified V5 amp that St. Louis Music received through the MTI purchase and made into a new bass amp.

ELECTRIC TUBE AMPS: V/VT SERIES

V-2 – 60W, 4-12 in. speakers, guitar piggyback unit with a ported cabinet containing Eminence or CTS speakers, nine-tube chassis: preamp: 3 X 12AX7, 1 X 6K11, 1 X 12DW7, 1 X 6CG7, 1 X 12AU7, power: 2 X 7027A, solid-state rectifier, two channels, reverb, front silver control panel, two inputs, six silver knobs (v1, v2, t, m, b, r), black covering, blue/gray grille, mfg. 1971-1980.

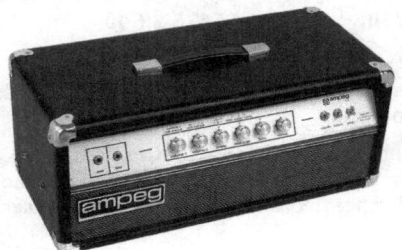

V-2
courtesy Savage Audio

V-2
courtesy Savage Audio

Head Only	N/A	$475 - 550	$300 - 350	
Head & Cabinet	N/A	$900 - 1,100	$625 - 750	

This model was derived from the VT-22 to put out smaller wattages but to retain the piggyback design and Altec 417-8C speakers were optional.

V-3 – 55W, 4-12 in. speakers, guitar piggyback configuration, six-tube chassis: preamp: 2 X 12AX7, 1 X 7199, power: 2 X 7027A, rectifier: 5AR4, two channels, front control panel, six silver knobs (Ch 1: v, b, t, Ch 2: v, b, t), ultra high and lo switches, black covering, blue/gray grille, mfg. 1970-71.

Head Only	N/A	$475 - 550	$300 - 350	
Head & Cabinet	N/A	$950 - 1,200	$650 - 800	

This amp was derived from the circuit of the B-25 made a year earlier. The only two changes were the cabinet was changed to 4-12 in. and the negative feedback loop was removed.

MSR/NOTES	100%	EXCELLENT	AVERAGE	LAST MSR

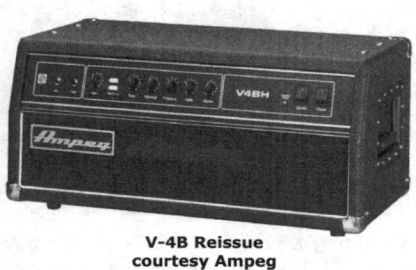

V-4B Reissue
courtesy Ampeg

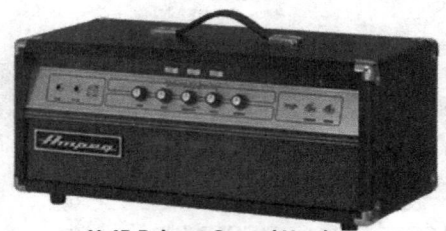

V-4B Reissue Second Version
courtesy Ampeg

V-4 – 100W, 4-12 in. CTS or Eminence speakers, guitar piggyback unit with a sealed cabinet, 11-tube chassis: preamp: 2 X 12AX7, 1 X 6K11, 1 X 12DW7, 1 X 6AN8, 1 X 6CG7, power: 4 X 7027A, solid-state rectifier, two channels, front silver control panel, two inputs, six silver knobs (Ch. 1 v, Ch. 2 v, t, m, b, r), sensitivity switches for each channel, ultra hi switch, three-position mid-range freq. switch, standby switch, polarity switch, power switch, black covering, blue/gray grille, mfg. 1970-1980.

Head Only	N/A	$625 - 750	$425 - 500	
Head & Cabinet	N/A	$1,000 - 1,300	$650 - 800	

This model is similar to the VT-22 except in piggyback configuration with 4-12 in. CTS or Eminece ceramic magnet speakers in a cabinet that is totally sealed, and Altec 417-8C speakers were optional.

* V-4B – similar to the V-4, except is designed for bass use and has 2-15 in. speakers in a separate cabinet, mfg. 1971-1980.

Head Only	N/A	$725 - 850	$425 - 500	
Head & Cabinet	N/A	$1,050 - 1,200	$650 - 800	

The V-4B had Altec 421A speakers initially and later were switched to Electo-Voice 200W speakers.

V-4B REISSUE FIRST VERSION – 100W, bass head-unit, seven-tube chassis, preamp: 3 X 12AX7, power: 4 X 6L6GC/5881, solid-state rectifier, single channel, front black control panel, two inputs, six black knobs (g, b, m, five-position mid-range freq. selector, t, MV), ultra hi switch, ultra lo switch, standby switch, power switch, rear panel: preamp out jack, power amp in jack, slave output jack, XLR balanced line out, power amp presence boost switch, two 1/4 in. speaker jacks with impedance selector, recessed side handles, black Tolex covering, black grille with white trim, 23.75 in. wide, 11 in. tall, 12.75 in. deep, 40 lbs., mfg. 1995-2006.

	N/A	$550 - 675	$350 - 425	$1,299

The V-4B Reissue utilizes the same circuitry as the original V-4B produced in the 1970s.

V-4B REISSUE SECOND VERSION – 100W, bass head-unit, eight-tube chassis, preamp: 2 X 12AX7, driver: 1 X 12AX7, 1 X 12AU7, power: 4 X 6L6GC, single channel, front black control panel, two inputs, five black/silver knobs (g, b, m, t, MV), ultra low switch, 1/2/3 mid tone switch, ultra hi switch, standby switch, power switch, rear panel: AC line in, fuse, preamp out jack, power amp in jack, slave output jack, XLR balanced line out, lift/ground switch, five 1/4 in. speaker jacks, top handle, black covering, blue/gray grille, 24 in. wide, 11 in. tall, 11 in. deep, 41 lbs., mfg. 2014-present.

MSR $1,820	$1,300	$850 - 975	$425 - 525	

V-9 – 300W, 9-10 in. speakers, guitar/keyboard piggyback configuration, 14-tube chassis: preamp: 2 X 12BH7, 4 X 12DW7, 1 X 12AX7, 1 X 6CG7, power: 6 X 6550, solid-state rectifier, two channels, reverb, distortion, front silver control panel, two inputs, seven knobs (v1, distortion, v, b, m, t, r), three-position mid-range freq. switch, ultra hi switch, footswitch jack, power switch, black covering, blue/gray grille, mfg. 1975-1980.

Head Only	N/A	$600 - 750	$425 - 500	
Head & Cabinet	N/A	$1,200 - 1,500	$800 - 950	

This amp was very similar to the SVT, but designed for guitars and keyboards instead of bass. The speaker cabinet was divided up into three compartments and each one was sealed from the others.

VT-22 – 100W, 2-12 in. CTS or Eminence speakers, guitar combo, 11-tube chassis: preamp: 2 X 12AX7, 1 X 6K11, 1 X 12DW7, 1 X 6AN8, 1 X 6CG7, power: 4 X 7027A, solid-state rectifier, two channels, front silver control panel, two inputs, six silver knobs (Ch. 1 v, Ch. 2 v, t, m, b, r), sensitivity switches for each channel, ultra hi switch, three-position mid-range freq. switch, standby switch, polarity switch, power switch, black covering, blue/gray grille, mfg. 1970-1980.

	N/A	$675 - 800	$350 - 425	

Altec 417-8C speakers were optional. Later models may have a 10-tube chassis, preamp: 1 X 12AX7, 3 X 12DW7, 1 X 6CG7, 1 X 6AN8, power: 4 X 7027 and seven knobs.

VT-40 – 50W, 4-10 in. CTS speakers, guitar combo, nine-tube chassis: preamp: 3 X 12AX7, 1 X 6K11, 1 X 12AU7, 1 X 12DW7, 1 X 6CG7, power: 2 X 7027A, solid-state rectifier, two channels, front silver control panel, two inputs, seven silver knobs (Ch. 1 v, Ch. 2 v, t, m, b, r), sensitivity switches for each channel, ultra hi switch, three-position mid-range freq. switch, standby switch, polarity switch, power switch, black covering, blue/gray grille, mfg. 1971-1980.

	N/A	$675 - 800	$350 - 425	

This model was derived from the V-4 to put out smaller wattages but to retain the piggyback design, and the VT-40 had optional Altec 425-8A speakers. The early VT-40 had a top mounted control panel and a vertical chassis.

ELECTRIC TUBE AMPS: V SERIES (V3, V5, & V7)

When MTI bought Magnavox/Ampeg in 1980, they completely overhauled the entire Ampeg line. They introduced new lines including the V Series and all the amps had a cosmetic makeover to black covering with a black grille. MTI released six new tube amps at this time the V3SC, V3HD, V5SC, V5HD, V7SC, and the V7HD. The model description here stood for what each one had in terms of speakers. the SCs were combos and the HDs were head units. The combos had 1-12 in. speaker for the V3SC and 2-12 in. for the V5SC and V7SC. The heads were designed to be used with 4-12 in. V series speaker cabinets.

V3SC – 50W, 1-12 in. speaker, guitar combo, seven-tube chassis, preamp: 4 X 12AX7, 1 X 12AT7, power: 2 X 6550, two channels, reverb, front black control panel, two inputs, nine black and silver knobs (Ch. 1: pre v, post v, Ch.2: v, Both: b, m, t, p, r, MV), mid-shift switch, EQ shift switch, power switch, standby switch, black covering, black grille, mfg. 1981-85.

| | N/A | $475 - 550 | $275 - 325 | |

* **V3HD** – similar to the V3SC except in head-unit configuration, mfg. 1981-85.

| | N/A | $325 - 400 | $200 - 250 | |

V5SC – 100W, 2-12 in. speakers, guitar combo, seven-tube chassis: preamp: 3 X 12AX7, power: 4 X 6550, single channel, front black control panel, two inputs, six black and silver knobs (pre v, MV, b, m, t, p), bright switch, gain switch, black covering, black grille, mfg. 1981-85.

| | N/A | $500 - 600 | $300 - 350 | |

* **V5HD** – similar to the V5SC, except in head unit configuration, mfg. 1981-85.

| | N/A | $375 - 450 | $225 - 275 | |

V7SC – 100W, 2-12 in. speakers, guitar combo, nine-tube chassis, preamp: 4 X 12AX7, 1 X 12AT7, power: 4 X 6550, two channels, reverb, front black control panel, two inputs, nine black and silver knobs (Ch. 1: pre v, post v, Ch.2: v, Both: b, m, t, p, r, MV), mid-shift switch, EQ shift switch, power switch standby switch, black covering, black grille, mfg. 1981-85.

| | N/A | $600 - 700 | $375 - 450 | |

* **V7HD** – similar to the V7SC except in head unit configuration, mfg. 1981-85.

| | N/A | $425 - 500 | $275 - 325 | |

ELECTRIC TUBE AMPS: VT "TRI-AX" SERIES

Ampeg's Tri-Ax Series featured a "Multi-stage Musical Instrument Amplifier Having Distortion Modes" that meant the user could change between distortion and normal modes while using the gain stage in both modes. St. Louis Music/Ampeg received a patent for this design.

VT-60 – 60W, 1-12 in. speaker, guitar combo, seven-tube chassis, preamp: 4 X 12AX7, 1 X 12AU7, power: 2 X 6L6GC, solid-state rectifier, three channels, reverb, front black control panel, two inputs, 11 black knobs (Ch. A: g, h with push/pull low boost, ultra mid, level with push/pull channel select, Ch. B: g, level with push/pull channel select, Ch. C: g, l, m, h with push/pull bright switch, All: r with push/pull bright switch), standby switch, power switch, rear panel: convenience outlet, polarity switch, line out, line in, presence control with low/high damping switch, triode/pentode switch, reverb and channel select footswitch jacks, five speaker jacks, black covering, black grille, mfg. 1989-1992.

| | N/A | $475 - 550 | $235 - 290 | |

* **VT-60H** – similar to the VT-60, except in head-unit configuration, mfg. 1989-1992.

| | N/A | $400 - 475 | $275 - 325 | |

VT-120 – 120W, 1-12 in. speaker, guitar combo, nine-tube chassis, preamp: 4 X 12AX7, 1 X 12AU7, power: 4 X 6L6GC, solid-state rectifier, three channels, reverb, front black control panel, two inputs, 11 black knobs (Ch. A: g, h with push/pull low boost, ultra mid, level with push/pull channel select, Ch. B: g, level with push/pull channel select, Ch. C: g, l, m, h with push/pull bright switch, All: r with push/pull bright switch), standby switch, power switch, rear panel: presence control with low/high damping switch, triode/pentode switch, 60W/120W power switch, reverb and channel select footswitch jacks, five speaker jacks, black covering, black grille, mfg. 1989-1992.

| | N/A | $475 - 550 | $235 - 290 | |

* **VT-120H** – similar to the VT-120, except in head-unit configuration, mfg. 1989-1992.

| | N/A | $375 - 450 | $190 - 235 | |

ELECTRIC TUBE AMPS: VL SERIES

Ampeg brought in electrical and amplifier engineer Lee Jackson to design the VL Series of guitar amplifiers. These amplifiers featured channel switching (except the VL-501/VL-1001), switchable 6550/EL34 power tubes, and a lock and key system to prevent unauthorized use. Ampeg also offered four speaker cabinets for use with the VL amplifiers including the **V412TV** with 4-12 in. Celestion Vintage 30s, **V412TC** with 4-12 in. Celestion G12T-75s, the **SS412A** with 4-12 in. Ampeg Custom speakers, and the **SS212** with Celestion G12K-85 speakers.

VL-501 – 50W, guitar head-unit, six-tube chassis, preamp: 4 X 12AX7, power: 2 X EL34/6550, single channel, front black control, single input, eight black knobs (preamp, g, MV, l, m, h, level, p), power switch, standby switch, effects loop, black covering, black grille, mfg. 1991-92.

| | N/A | $375 - 450 | $225 - 275 | |

MSR/NOTES	100%	EXCELLENT	AVERAGE	LAST MSR

VL-502 – 50W, guitar head-unit, eight-tube chassis, preamp: 6 X 12AX7, power: 2 X EL34/6550, two channels, front black control, single input, 16 black knobs (Ch. 1: preamp, l, m, h, Ch. 2: preamp, g, l, m, five-position mid-range freq. selector, h, All: r1, r2, MV1, MV2, power attenuator level, p), channel select switch, power attenuator switch, lock, power switch, standby switch, rear panel: speaker output impedance selector, two speaker jacks, effects loop with on/off switch and pad switch, footswitch jack, black covering, black grille, mfg. 1991-95.

| | N/A | $425 - 500 | $250 - 300 | |

VL-503 – 75W (6550 power tubes) or 50W (EL34 power tubes), 1-12 in. speaker, guitar combo, tube chassis, power: 2 X 6550 or EL34, three channels, reverb, front black control panel, 23 knobs (Ch. 1: v, l, m, h, Ch. 2: preamp, g, l, m, h, MV, Ch. 3: preamp, g, l, m, five-position mid-range selector, All: r1, r2, r3, attenuator level, power amp slope, power amp presence, three channel switches, Ch. 2 mid-boost switch, reverb on/off switch, attenuator on/off switch, effects loop on/off switch, standby switch, power switch, rear panel: bias select switch (6550/EL34), hum balance, two bias adj. knobs with LED indicators, impedance switch, two speaker jacks, line out switch, 1/4 in. unbalanced line out jack, recording output switch, effects loop pad switch, effects loop, footswitch jack, five-button footswitch, black covering, black grille, 21.75 in. wide, 19.75 in. tall, 11.5 in. deep, 85 lbs., mfg. 1993-95.

| | N/A | $600 - 700 | $350 - 425 | |

VL-1001 – 100W, guitar head-unit, eight-tube chassis, preamp: 4 X 12AX7, power: 4 X EL34/6550, single channel, front black control, single input, eight black knobs (preamp, g, MV, l, m, h, level, p), power switch, standby switch, effects loop, black covering, black grille, mfg. 1991-93.

| | N/A | $400 - 500 | $250 - 300 | |

VL-1002 – 100W, guitar head-unit, ten-tube chassis, preamp: 6 X 12AX7, power: 4 X EL34/6550, two channels, front black control, single input, 16 black knobs (Ch. 1: preamp, l, m, h, Ch. 2: preamp, g, l, m, five-position mid-range freq. selector, h, All: r1, r2, MV1, MV2, power attenuator level, p), channel select switch, power attenuator switch, lock, power switch, standby switch, rear panel: speaker output impedance selector, two speaker jacks, effects loop with on/off switch and pad switch, footswitch jack, black covering, black grille, mfg. 1991-95.

| | N/A | $425 - 500 | $215 - 265 | |

ELECTRIC TUBE AMPS: MISC. MODELS

625-D MANHATTEN – 25W, 2-12 in. Jensen speakers, six-tube chassis: preamp: 2 X 6CG7, 1 X 12AU7, 1 X 6SL7, power: EL37, rectifier: 5U4, two channels, top chrome control panel, six black knobs (v, b, t, for each channel), Navy Random Flair covering, gray grille, mfg. 1959-1961.

| | N/A | $950 - 1,200 | $650 - 800 | |

AC-12 – 20W, 1-12 in. speaker, accordion combo, five-tube chassis, preamp: 1 X 12AX7, 1 X 6U10, 1 X 12DW7, power: 2 X 7591A, solid-state rectifier, single channel, reverb, tremolo, silver front control panel, two inputs, six black knobs (v, b, t, reverb, s, i), black covering, blue/gray grille, mfg. 1970 only.

| | N/A | $325 - 375 | $160 - 195 | |

The AC-12 was a new Ampeg specifically designed for Accoridans that did not sell well. After one year, Ampeg took the circuit from this and developed it into a new guitar amplifier that replaced the Rocket II. This was the last amp that Ampeg made especially for accordians.

GU-12 – 20W, 1-12 in. speaker, guitar combo, five-tube chassis, preamp: 1 X 12AX7, 1 X 6U10, 1 X 12DW7, power: 2 X 7591A, solid-state rectifier, single channel, reverb, tremolo, silver front control panel, two inputs, six black knobs (v, t, b, i, s, echo dimension [reverb]), standby switch, power switch, black covering, blue/gray grille, mfg. 1971-73.

| | N/A | $325 - 375 | $160 - 195 | |

The GU-12 is similar to the AC-12, except it doesn't have a negative-feedback loop and was specifically designed for guitar use.

ELECTRIC SS AMPS: FIRST SERIES PORTAFLEX MODELS (1966-1968)

Ampeg introduced its first line of solid-state amplifiers at the 1966 Summer NAMM show and they were officially launched in 1967, which was right around the time that Fender and other amplifier builders were also beginning to experiment with solid-state designs. Ampeg's first series of solid-state amps featured their patented combo/piggyback Portaflex design available in several different wattage and speaker configurations. These amps had traditional blue Ampeg covering with a silver/blue grille cloth, but the control panels on the head units were much different and solid-state badging was very prominent. According to Jess Oliver, the very first solid-state Ampegs were prone to overheating that often caused components to fail, however, Ampeg quickly fixed this problem and by mid-1967, their solid-state amps were more reliable. Ampeg's first solid-state amps also utilized an electroluminescent control panel that glowed blue when the amp was on. The first series of solid-state amps was produced through 1968. Some of the earliest solid-state models may have black covering.

BT-15 FIRST VERSION – 50W, 1-15 in. speaker, multi-purpose piggyback Portaflex design, solid-state chassis, two channels, front chrome control panel, four inputs (two per channel), six knobs (Ch. 1: v, t, b, Ch. 2: v, t, b), ultra hi switches for each channel, polarity switch, power switch, external speaker jack, external amp/line out jack, dark blue covering, blue/gray grille cloth, 20.125 in. wide, 22.75 in. tall, 14 in. deep, 65 lbs., four-wheel dolly included, mfg. 1966-68.

| | N/A | $350 - 425 | $225 - 275 | |

* **BT-15C** – similar to the BT-15, except has 100W output, and a column-style speaker cabinet with 2-15 in. speakers, 21 in. wide, 39 in. tall, 14 in. deep, 108 lbs., mfg. 1967-68.

| | N/A | $500 - 600 | $325 - 400 | |

MSR/NOTES	100%	EXCELLENT	AVERAGE	LAST MSR

* ***BT-15D*** – similar to the BT-15, except has 85W output, and a matching extension speaker cabinet with another 15 in. speaker, 20.125 in. wide, 45.5 in. tall, 14 in. deep, 112 lbs., mfg. 1966-68.

| | N/A | $475 - 550 | $300 - 375 | |

BT-18 – 50W, 1-18 in. speaker, multi-purpose piggyback Portaflex design, solid-state chassis, two channels, front chrome control panel, four inputs (two per channel), six knobs (Ch. 1: v, t, b, Ch. 2: v, t, b), ultra hi switches for each channel, polarity switch, power switch, external speaker jack, external amp/line out jack, dark blue covering, blue/gray grille cloth, mfg. 1966-68.

| | N/A | $350 - 425 | $225 - 275 | |

* ***BT-18C*** – similar to the BT-18, except has 100W output, and a column-style speaker cabinet with 2-18 in. speakers, 24 in. wide, 42 in. tall, 14 in. deep, 132 lbs., mfg. 1967-68.

| | N/A | $500 - 600 | $325 - 400 | |

T-12T – 100W, 2-12 in. speaker, multi-purpose piggyback Portaflex design, solid-state chassis, two channels, reverb, vibrato, front chrome control panel, four inputs (two per channel), nine knobs (Ch. 1: v, t, b, Ch. 2: v, t, b, s, i, dimension), ultra hi switches for each channel, polarity switch, power switch, external speaker jack, external amp/line out jack, dark blue covering, blue/gray grille cloth, 26.75 in. wide, 21 in. tall, 12 in. deep, four-wheel dolly included, mfg. 1967-68.

| | N/A | $475 - 550 | $300 - 375 | |

* ***T-12D*** – similar to the T-12T, except has a matching extension speaker cabinet with another 2-12 in. speakers, 26.75 in. wide, 42 in. tall, 12 in. deep, 101 lbs., mfg. 1967-68.

| | N/A | $500 - 600 | $325 - 400 | |

T-15 – 50W, 1-15 in. speaker, multi-purpose piggyback Portaflex design, solid-state chassis, two channels, reverb, vibrato, front chrome control panel, four inputs (two per channel), nine knobs (Ch. 1: v, t, b, Ch. 2: v, t, b, s, i, dimension), ultra hi switches for each channel, polarity switch, power switch, external speaker jack, external amp/line out jack, dark blue covering, blue/gray grille cloth, 20.125 in. wide, 22.75 in. tall, 14 in. deep, four-wheel dolly included, mfg. 1966-67.

| | N/A | $425 - 500 | $275 - 325 | |

* ***T-15D*** – similar to the T-15, except has 85W output, and a matching extension speaker cabinet with another 15 in. speaker, 20.125 in. wide, 45.5 in. tall, 14 in. deep, 99 lbs., mfg. 1966-68.

| | N/A | $550 - 650 | $375 - 450 | |

ELECTRIC SS AMPS: SECOND SERIES PORTAFLEX MODELS (1968-1969)

In 1968, Ampeg introduced their second series of solid-state amps and like the first series, all of these used Portaflex cabinet designs. The second series featured amplifiers that were much larger, especially the three ST models. All models in this series were very short lived and few of them exist today. However, the BT-140, ST-22L Gladiator, ST-25L Olympian, and ST-42L Colossus all moved on to Ampeg's unofficial third series in 1969. Since the Portaflex cabinet design was primarily used to allow the tubes to dissipate heat, it was not needed in solid-state design and Ampeg pretty much abandoned use of the Portaflex cabinet with solid-state amplifiers after 1968.

BT-140 FIRST VERSION – 100W, 2-15 in. JBL D-140F speakers in a column style cabinet, piggyback-style bass amp with separate head and cabinet, solid-state chassis, two channels, front silver electroluminescent control panel, four inputs (two per channel), six knobs (Ch. 1: v, t, b, Ch. 2: v, t, b), hi and lo switches for each channel, black covering, blue/gray grille, mfg. 1968-69.

| **Head Only** | N/A | $250 - 300 | $150 - 200 | |
| **Head & Cabinet** | N/A | $425 - 500 | $275 - 325 | |

The BT-140 was essentially a GT-15C but made for bassists.

GT-15C – 100W, 2-15 in. Altec speakers in a column style cabinet, combo/piggyback Portaflex guitar amp, solid-state chassis, two channels, front silver electroluminescent control panel, four inputs (two per channel), six knobs (Ch. 1: v, t, b, Ch. 2: v, t, b), hi and lo switches for each channel, black covering, blue/gray grille, mfg. 1967-68.

| | N/A | $425 - 500 | $275 - 325 | |

ST-22L GLADIATOR – 120W, 2-12 in. Altec 417A speakers in a column-style cabinet, combo/piggyback Portaflex design, solid-state chassis, two channels, tremolo, vibrato, reverb, front bottom silver electroluminescent control panel, four inputs (two per channel), nine black and silver knobs (Ch. 1: v, t, b, s, i, r, Ch. 2: v, t, b), polarity switch, power switch, dark blue covering, blue/gray grille, mfg. 1967-68.

| | N/A | $500 - 600 | $325 - 400 | |

ST-25L OLYMPIAN – 120W, 2-12 in. Altec 418A speakers in a column-style cabinet, combo/piggyback Portaflex design, solid-state chassis, two channels, tremolo, vibrato, reverb, front bottom silver electroluminescent control panel, four inputs (two per channel), nine black and silver knobs (Ch. 1: v, t, b, s, i, r, Ch. 2: v, t, b), polarity switch, power switch, dark blue covering, blue/gray grille, mfg. 1967-68.

| | N/A | $525 - 625 | $350 - 425 | |

ST-42L COLOSSUS – 120W, 4-12 in. Altec 417A speakers, combo/piggyback Portaflex design, solid-state chassis, two channels, tremolo, vibrato, reverb, front bottom silver electroluminescent control panel, four inputs (two per channel), nine black and silver knobs (Ch. 1: v, t, b, s, i, r, Ch. 2: v, t, b), polarity switch, power switch, dark blue covering, blue/gray grille, mfg. 1967-68.

| | N/A | $550 - 650 | $375 - 450 | |

MSR/NOTES	100%	EXCELLENT	AVERAGE	LAST MSR

ELECTRIC SS AMPS: THIRD SERIES PIGGYBACK MODELS (1969-1971)

In 1969, Ampeg introduced their third series of solid-state amps, and they also went away from the Portaflex design to a more traditional piggyback design with separate heads and cabinets (because of this, amps in this section are evaluated with separate head and cabinet prices because they are often sold in the vintage market without one another). The third series featured a mixture of carryover models from 1968 (BT-15, BT-140, ST-22, ST-25, and ST-42) as well as new models (BT-25, BT-25L, SBT, and SST). Ampeg also introduced their "70s" cosmetics with black covering, a blue/silver grille, and large Ampeg logo with shield. Most amps in this series weren't produced very long and only lasted through the late 1960s or early 1970s.

BT-15 SECOND VERSION – 85W, 1-15 in. speaker, multi-purpose combo/piggyback Portaflex design, solid-state chassis, two channels, front chrome control panel, four inputs (two per channel), six knobs (Ch. 1: v, t, b, Ch. 2: v, t, b), ultra hi switches for each channel, polarity switch, power switch, external speaker jack, external amp/line out jack, black covering, blue/gray grille cloth, 21 in. wide, 24 in. tall (closed), 14 in. deep, 70 lbs., four-wheel dolly included, mfg. 1968-69.

	N/A	$350 - 425	$225 - 275	

BT-25 – 120W, 2-15 in. CTS speakers in a column style cabinet, piggyback-style bass amp with separate head and cabinet, solid-state chassis, two channels, front silver control panel, four inputs (two per channel), six knobs (Ch. 1: v, t, b, Ch. 2: v, t, b), hi and lo switches for each channel, polarity switch, power switch, black covering, blue/gray grille, mfg. 1969-1971.

Head Only	N/A	$250 - 300	$150 - 200	
Head & Cabinet	N/A	$425 - 500	$250 - 300	

* **BT-25L** – similar to the BT-25, except has 2-15 in. Altec Lansing speakers, mfg. 1969-1970.

Head Only	N/A	$250 - 300	$150 - 200	
Head & Cabinet	N/A	$425 - 500	$250 - 300	

BT-140 SECOND VERSION – 100W, 2-15 in. JBL D-140F speakers in a column style cabinet, piggyback-style bass amp with separate head and cabinet, solid-state chassis, two channels, front top silver control panel, four inputs (two per channel), six knobs (Ch. 1: v, t, b, Ch. 2: v, t, b), hi and lo switches for each channel, black covering, blue/gray grille, mfg. 1969-1971.

Head Only	N/A	$250 - 300	$150 - 200	
Head & Cabinet	N/A	$425 - 500	$275 - 325	

SBT – 120W, 4-15 in. 421A Altec speakers (2-15 in. speakers in each cabinet), bass piggyback with two speaker cabinets, solid-state chassis, two channels, silver front control panel, four inputs (two for each channel), seven knobs (Ch 1: v, t, b, mid-range, Ch. 2: v, t, b), ultra hi and ultra lo switches for each channel, Ch. 1 mid-range freq. select, black covering, blue/gray grille, mfg. 1969-1971.

Head Only	N/A	$120 - 150	$75 - 95	
Head & Cabinet	N/A	$650 - 800	$450 - 550	

Ampeg borrowed a design from the Acoustic 360 in the SBT by including only the preamp in the head unit and adding a separate power amp to drive each speaker cabinet. The speaker cabinets featured input jacks, a level control, and an on/off switch as well as a four-wheel dolly. Because the head alone is unable to drive a normal speaker cabinet, it is virtually worthless without the cabinets it was sold with originally.

SST – 120W, 4-12 in. 417B Altec speakers (2-12 in. speakers in each cabinet), guitar piggyback with two speaker cabinets, solid-state chassis, two channels, reverb, tremolo, vibrato, silver front control panel, four inputs (two for each channel), 10 knobs (Ch 1: v, t, m, b, vibrato s/vibrato i, tremolo s/tremolo i, Ch. 2: v, t, b, All: echo dimension), switches for Ch. 1: midrange cut, midrange boost, ultra hi switch, midrange freq. selector, three-way ultra lo switch, reverb on/off switches for Ch. 2: reverb on/off control, ultra hi, ultra lo, black covering, blue/gray grille, mfg. 1969-1970.

Head Only	N/A	$150 - 200	$95 - 120	
Head & Cabinet	N/A	$700 - 900	$500 - 600	

Ampeg borrowed a design from the Acoustic 360 in the SST by including only the preamp in the head unit and adding a separate power amp to drive each speaker cabinet. The speaker cabinets featured input jacks, a level control, and an on/off switch as well as a four-wheel dolly. Because the head alone is unable to drive a normal speaker cabinet, it is virtually worthless without the cabinets it was sold with originally.

ST-22 GLADIATOR – 120W, 2-12 in. Altec Lansing speakers in a column-style cabinet, piggyback configuration, solid-state chassis, two channels, tremolo, vibrato, reverb, front top silver control panel, four inputs (two per channel), nine black and silver knobs (Ch. 1: v, t, b, s, i, r, Ch. 2: v, t, b), polarity switch, power switch, black covering, blue/gray grille, mfg. 1969 only.

	N/A	$500 - 600	$325 - 400	

ST-25 OLYMPIAN – 120W, 2-15 in. Altec Lansing speakers in a column-style cabinet, piggyback configuration, solid-state chassis, two channels, tremolo, vibrato, reverb, front top silver control panel, four inputs (two per channel), nine black and silver knobs (Ch. 1: v, t, b, s, i, r, Ch. 2: v, t, b), polarity switch, power switch, black covering, blue/gray grille, mfg. 1969-1970.

	N/A	$525 - 625	$350 - 425	

ST-42 COLOSSUS – 120W, 4-12 in. Altec Lansing speakers, piggyback configuration, solid-state chassis, two channels, tremolo, vibrato, reverb, front top silver control panel, four inputs (two per channel), nine black and silver knobs (Ch. 1: v, t, b, s, i, r, Ch. 2: v, t, b), polarity switch, power switch, black covering, blue/gray grille, mfg. 1969-1970.

	N/A	$550 - 650	$375 - 450	

MSR/NOTES	100%	EXCELLENT	AVERAGE	LAST MSR

ELECTRIC SS AMPS: COMBO MODELS (1971-1980)

In 1971, Ampeg released their first solid-state combo amp with the GT-10. They followed in 1973 with five more new solid-state amps that shared similar chassis. Models with "B" prefixes were designed for bass use and models with "G" prefixes were designed for guitar use. Ampeg also used the model number to indicate the speaker configuration. For example, the G-412 was a guitar amp with 4-12 in. speakers. Many amps in this series were prouduced throughout the 1970s and discontinued in 1980.

B-100 – 20W, 1-10 in. speaker, bass combo, solid-state channel, single channel, front silver control panel, two input jacks, three black and silver knobs (v, b, t), power switch, black covering, blue/gray grille, mfg. 1976-1980.

	N/A	$120 - 150	$75 - 95	

The B-100 and G-100 shared the same chassis, except the B-100 had a heavier magnet in the speaker for bass applications.

B-115 – 120W, 1-15 in. speaker, bass combo, solid-state chassis, two channels, front silver control panel, four inputs (two per channel), eight black and silver knobs (Ch. 1: v, b, m, t, Ch 2: v, b, m, t), selective midrange switch and ultra-hi switch for each channel, polarity switch, power switch, tuned reflex speaker design, black covering, black grille, mfg. 1973-1980.

	N/A	$325 - 400	$175 - 225	

The B-115 and the B-410 shared the same chassis.

B-410 – 120W, 4-10 in. speakers, bass combo, solid-state chassis, two channels, front silver control panel, four inputs (two per channel), eight black and silver knobs (Ch. 1: v, b, m, t, Ch 2: v, b, m, t), selective midrange switch and ultra-hi switch for each channel, polarity switch, power switch, sealed cabinet, black covering, black grille, mfg. 1973-1980.

	N/A	$350 - 475	$200 - 250	

The B-115 and the B-410 shared the same chassis.

G-18 – 10W, 1-8 in. speaker, guitar combo, solid-state chassis, single channel, front silver control panel, two input jacks, three black and silver knobs (v, t, b), power switch, black covering, blue/gray grille, mfg. 1977-1980.

	N/A	$80 - 100	$40 - 60	

G-100 – 20W, 1-10 in. speaker, guitar combo, solid-state channel, single channel, front silver control panel, two input jacks, three black and silver knobs (v, b, t), power switch, black covering, blue/gray grille, mfg. 1976-1980.

	N/A	$120 - 150	$75 - 95	

The B-100 and G-100 shared the same chassis, except the B-100 had a heavier magnet in the speaker for bass applications.

G-110 – 20W, 1-10 in. speaker, guitar combo, solid-state channel, single channel, reverb, tremolo, front silver control panel, two input jacks, three black and silver knobs (v, t, b, s, i, r), footswitch jack, power switch, black covering, blue/gray grille, mfg. 1978-1980.

	N/A	$150 - 200	$95 - 120	

The G-110 was very similar to the G-100 with the addition of reverb and tremolo.

G-115 – 175W, 1-15 in. JBL speaker, guitar combo, solid-state chassis, single channel, front silver control panel, two input jacks, ten black and silver knobs (v, t, m, b, mid-freq., p, sensitivity, r, s, i), black covering, blue/gray grille, mfg. 1979-1980.

	N/A	$150 - 200	$100 - 120	

G-212 – 120W, 2-12 in. speakers, guitar combo, solid-state chassis, two channels, reverb, tremolo, front silver control panel, four inputs, two per channel, eleven black and silver knobs (Ch 1: v, t, m, b, Ch 2: v, t, m, b, Both: r, s, i), midrange and ultra hi switch for each channel, polarity switch, power switch, open back, black covering, black grille with white piping, mfg. 1973-1980.

	N/A	$250 - 300	$150 - 200	

Altec speakers were optional. The G-212, G-410, and G-412 all shared the same chassis.

G-410 – 120W, 4-10 in. speakers, guitar combo, solid-state chassis, two channels, reverb, tremolo, front silver control panel, four inputs, two per channel, eleven black and silver knobs (Ch 1: v, t, m, b, Ch 2: v, t, m, b, Both: r, s, i), midrange and ultra hi switch for each channel, polarity switch, power switch, sealed cabinet, casters included, black covering, black grille with white piping, mfg. 1973-1980.

	N/A	$300 - 350	$175 - 225	

Altec speakers were optional. The G-212, G-410, and G-412 all shared the same chassis.

G-412 – 120W, 4-12 in. speakers, guitar combo, solid-state chassis, two channels, reverb, tremolo, front silver control panel, four inputs, two per channel, eleven black and silver knobs (Ch 1: v, t, m, b, Ch 2: v, t, m, b, Both: r, s, i), midrange and ultra hi switch for each channel, polarity switch, power switch, sealed cabinet, casters included, black covering, black grille with white piping, mfg. 1973-1980.

	N/A	$300 - 350	$175 - 225	

Altec speakers were optional. The G-212, G-410, and G-412 all shared the same chassis.

GT-10 – 15W, 1-10 in. speaker, guitar combo, solid-state chassis, single channel, reverb, silver top control panel, two inputs, four black knobs (v, t, b, r), power switch, black covering, blue/gray grille, mfg. 1971-1980.

	N/A	$135 - 175	$75 - 100	

MSR/NOTES	100%	EXCELLENT	AVERAGE	LAST MSR

ELECTRIC SS AMPS: G/B SERIES (MTI MFG., 1981-1985)

When MTI purchased Ampeg from Magnavox, they discontinued all production of current models in 1980 and introduced a new line of amps in 1981. The solid-state models included two guitar combos (G-30 and G-50) and three bass combos (B-30, B-50, and B-80N). These amps were produced in Japan by Benidai.

G-30 – 30W, 1-12 in. speaker, guitar combo, solid-state chassis, two channels, distortion, reverb, front black control panel, two inputs, six black knobs (v, b, m, t, MV, reverb), distortion switch, black covering, black grille, mfg. 1981-1985.

| | N/A | $175 - 225 | $110 - 140 | |

G-50 – 50W, 1-12 in. speaker, guitar combo, solid-state chassis, two channels, distortion, reverb, front black control panel, two inputs, six black knobs (v, b, m, t, MV, reverb), distortion switch, black covering, black grille, mfg. 1981-1985.

| | N/A | $200 - 250 | $120 - 150 | |

B-30 – 30W, 1-15 in. speaker, bass combo, solid-state chassis, single channel, front black control panel, two inputs, four black knobs (v, b, m, t), black covering, black grille, mfg. 1981-1985.

| | N/A | $175 - 225 | $110 - 140 | |

B-50 – 50W, 1-15 in. speaker, bass combo, solid-state chassis, single channel, front black control panel, two inputs, four black knobs (v, b, m, t), black covering, black grille, mfg. 1981-1985.

| | N/A | $200 - 250 | $120 - 150 | |

B-80N – 80W, 1-12 in. or 1-15 in. speaker, bass combo, solid-state chassis, single channel, top/rear black control panel, two inputs, four knobs (v, t, m, b), EQ shift switch, power switch, rear panel: external speaker jack, line out jack, pre/post EQ line out switch, headphone jack, black covering, black grille, 17 in. wide, 20 in. tall, 12 in. deep, 39.5 lbs. (12 in. speaker) or 42.5 lbs. (15 in. sepaker), mfg. 1981-85.

| | N/A | $225 - 275 | $135 - 175 | |

ELECTRIC SS AMPS: SS SERIES

SS-35 – 35W @ 8 omhs, 1-12 in. Ampeg Custom (SS-35A) speaker, solid-state chassis, two channels, reverb, front black control panel, two inputs, nine knobs (Ch. A: g, level with push/pull channel select, p, Ch. B: l, m, h, level with push/pull bright switch, r), footswitch jack, headphone jack, line out, power switch, external speaker jack on rear panel, black covering, black and blue speaker grille (early models) or black grille (later models), 19.25 in. wide, 17.5 in. tall, 9.75 in. deep, mfg. 1987-1992.

| | N/A | $170 - 200 | $85 - 105 | |

SS-70 – 70W @ 8 omhs (90W @ 4 ohms), 1-12 in. Celestion G12K-85 (SS-70) or 1-12 in. Ampeg Custom (SS-70A) speaker, solid-state chassis, two channels, reverb, front black control panel, two inputs, 12 knobs (Ch. A: g, l, ultra mid, h, level with push/pull channel switch, Ch. B: g, l, m, h, level with push/pull bright switch, All: reverb A, reverb B), power switch, rear panel: 1/4 in. preamp out, 1/4 in. power amp in, footswitch jack, two speaker jacks, AC convenience outlet, polarity switch, headphone jack, speaker mute switch, black covering, black and blue speaker grille (early models) or black grille (later models), 20.75 in. wide, 20.5 in. tall, 11.75 in. deep, mfg. 1987-1990.

| | N/A | $215 - 250 | $105 - 130 | |

• **Add 10% for Celestion G12K-85 speaker.**

* ***SS-70 Head*** – similar to the SS-70, except in head-unit configuration, 20.5 in. wide, 10.75 in. tall, 9.125 in. deep, mfg. 1987-88.

| | N/A | $150 - 175 | $75 - 90 | |

SS-70C – 70W @ 8 omhs (2 X 35W stereo), 2-10 in. Celestion (SS-70C) or 2-10 in. Ampeg Custom (SS-70C) speakers, solid-state chassis, two channels, chorus, reverb, front black control panel, two inputs, 11 knobs (Ch. A: g, level with push/pull channel switch, p, All: l, m, h, level with push/pull bright switch, r, chorus depth, chorus rate), effects loop, headphone jack, power switch, rear panel: two footswitch jacks, left and right 1/4 in. and balanced XLR line outs, two speaker jacks, black covering, black and blue speaker grille (early models) or black grille (later models), 23.75 in. wide, 17.5 in. tall, 9.75 in. deep, mfg. 1987-1992.

| | N/A | $235 - 275 | $115 - 145 | |

• **Add 10% for Celestion speaker.**

SS-140C – 140W @ 8 omhs (2 X 70W stereo, or 180W @ 4 ohms 2 X 90W stereo), 2-12 in. Ampeg Custom speakers, solid-state chassis, two channels (overdrive and clean), chorus, reverb, front black control panel, two inputs, 15 knobs (Ch. A: g, l, ultra mid, h, level with push/pull channel switch, Ch. B: g, l, m, h, level with push/pull bright switch, All: reverb A, reverb B, chorus depth A, chorus depth B, chorus rate), effects loop, power switch, rear panel: two footswitch jacks, left and right power amp line out/line in jacks, left and right balanced XLR line outs, four speaker jacks, 1/4 in. mono mix jack, AC convenience outlet, polarity switch, black covering, black and blue speaker grille (early models) or black grille (later models), 27.75 in. wide, 19.75 in. tall, 11.75 in. deep, mfg. 1987-1990.

| | N/A | $275 - 325 | $140 - 170 | |

* ***SS-140C Head*** – similar to the SS-140C, except in head-unit configuration, 27.75 in. wide, 10.75 in. tall, 9.125 in. deep, mfg. 1987-89.

| | N/A | $225 - 275 | $135 - 175 | |

SS-150 – 150W @ 8 omhs (200W @ 4 ohms), 1-12 in. Celestion Sidewinder (SS-150) or 1-12 in. Ampeg Custom (SS-150A) speaker, solid-state chassis, two channels, reverb, front black control panel, two inputs, 12 knobs (Ch. A: g, l, ultra mid, h, level with push/pull channel switch, Ch. B: g, l, m, h, level with push/pull bright switch, All: reverb A, reverb B), power switch, rear panel: 1/4 in. preamp out, 1/4 in. power amp in,

MSR/NOTES	100%	EXCELLENT	AVERAGE	LAST MSR

footswitch jack, two speaker jacks, AC convenience outlet, polarity switch, black covering, black and blue speaker grille (early models) or black grille (later models), 20.75 in. wide, 20.5 in. tall, 11.75 in. deep, mfg. 1987-1991.

| | N/A | $375 - 450 | $190 - 235 | |

- **Add 10% for Celestion Sidewinder speaker.**

* *SS-150 Head* – similar to the SS-150, except in head-unit configuration, 20.5 in. wide, 10.75 in. tall, 9.875 in. deep, mfg. 1987-1990.

| | N/A | $300 - 350 | $150 - 185 | |

SS-212EC SPEAKER CABINET – 140W mono/70W per side stereo, 2-12 in. Ampeg Custom speakers in separate infinite baffle housings, 4 ohm impedance mono/8 ohm impedance stereo, straight front, black covering, black and blue grille cloth, 27.75 in. wide, 17.5 in. tall, 11.75 in. deep, mfg. 1987-88.

| | N/A | $200 - 250 | $120 - 150 | |

SS-412ER/ES SPEAKER CABINET – 280W mono, 4-12 in. Celestion G12M-70 speakers, 4 ohm or 16 ohm switchable impedance mono, angled front (SS-412ES) or straight front (SS-412ER), recessed side handles, casters, black covering, black and blue speaker grille (early models) or black grille (later models), 30.25 in. wide, 30.25 in. tall, 14.25 in. deep, mfg. 1987-1990.

| | N/A | $300 - 350 | $175 - 225 | |

ELECTRIC SS AMPS: SVT SERIES

When St. Louis Music purchased Ampeg, they began expanding the line and introduced a variety of SVT amps including utilizing solid-state technology.

MICRO-CL STACK – Head: 100W @ 8 ohms, bass head-unit, solid-state chassis, single channel, front black control panel, two inputs, five black knobs (mv, t, m, bass, aux), aux input jack, headphone jack, power switch, rear panel: AC power input, unbalanced line out, two effects loop jacks, speaker jack, black covering with white piping, black grille cloth, 12.2 in. wide, 7 in. tall, 10 in. deep, 13.8 lbs., Cabinet: 100W @ 8 ohms, 2-10 in. speakers LF drivers, black vinyl covering, black grille with Ampeg badge in upper left hand corner, 13 in. wide, 24 in. tall, 11 in. deep, 33.2 lbs., mfg. 2012-present.

Micro-CL Stack
courtesy Ampeg

| MSR $490 | $350 | $230 - 265 | $115 - 140 | |

SVT-15T – similar to the SVT-70T, except has a 1-15 in. tuned-port cabinet, mfg. 1989-1992.

| | N/A | $300 - 350 | $175 - 225 | |

SVT-70T – 70W, 1-15 in. speaker, bass combo, solid-state chassis, single channel, front black control panel, two inputs (low and high), seven knobs (gain, low with push/pull ultra low, low mid with push/pull shift, high mid with push/pull shift, high with push/pull ultra high, master level, line out level), boost, line out/line in jacks, power switch, rear panel: XLR line out, line out/line in level, headphone jack, two speaker jacks, speaker mute switch, polarity switch, AC convenience outlet, black covering, black grille, 21 in. wide, 24.75 in. tall, 12 in. deep, mfg. 1987-89.

| | N/A | $300 - 350 | $175 - 225 | |

SVT-100T – 100W, 2-8 in. speakers, bass combo, solid-state chassis, single channel, front black control panel, two inputs (low and high), seven knobs (gain, low with push/pull ultra low, low mid with push/pull shift, high mid with push/pull shift, high with push/pull ultra high, master level, line out level), boost, line out/line in jacks, power switch, rear panel: XLR line out, line out/line in level, headphone jack, two speaker jacks, speaker mute switch, polarity switch, AC convenience outlet, black covering, black grille, mfg. 1990-92.

| | N/A | $400 - 475 | $275 - 325 | |

SVT-140TC – 140W (2 X 70W stereo), 4-10 in. speakers (2 pairs of 2-10 in. speakers), bass combo, solid-state chassis, single channel, chorus, front black control panel, two inputs (low and high), nine knobs (gain, low with push/pull ultra low, low mid with push/pull shift, high mid with push/pull shift, high with push/pull ultra high, stage volume with push/pull limiter, line out level, chorus rate, chorus depth with push/pull chorus on/off), line out/line in jacks, power switch, rear panel: chrorus footswitch jack, stereo left and right XLR line out, left and right line out/line in level, mono output jack, four speaker jacks, polarity switch, AC convenience outlet, black covering, black grille, 23.25 in. wide, 33 in. tall, 16 in. deep, optional dolly, mfg. 1987 only.

| | N/A | $350 - 425 | $200 - 250 | |

* *SVT-140TC Head* – similar to the SVT-140TC, except in head-unit configuration, 24 in. wide, 10.75 in. tall, 12.75 in. deep, mfg. 1987 only.

| | N/A | $200 - 250 | $120 - 150 | |

SVT-150H – 150W, bass head-unit, solid-state chassis, single channel, front black control panel, single input, six black knobs (g, drive, b, ultra mid, t, MV), nine-band graphic EQ, input pad switch, power switch, rear panel: effects loop, XLR balanced line out with pre/post EQ switch, black covering, black grille with white piping, 19 in. wide, 9.5 in. tall, 12.5 in. deep, 30 lbs., mfg. 1997-98.

| | N/A | $300 - 350 | $175 - 225 | $599 |

MSR/NOTES	100%	EXCELLENT	AVERAGE	LAST MSR

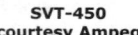

SVT-450
courtesy Ampeg

SVT-1000
courtesy Ampeg

SVT Micro-VR Head
courtesy Ampeg

SVT-200T – 200W @ 8 ohms (300W @ 4 ohms), 4-10 in. speakers, bass combo, solid-state chassis, single channel, front black control panel, two inputs (low and high), 11 knobs (gain, 62 Hz with push/pull ultra low, 125 Hz, 300 Hz push/pull 400 Hz, 600 Hz push/pull 850Hz, 1.3k Hz, 3k Hz with push/pull ultra high, stage volume with push/pull limiter, bi-amp freq., bi-amp balance, line out level), effects loop, power switch, rear panel: bi-amp high jack, bi-amp low jack, XLR balanced send, 1/4 in. unbalanced line out jack, two speaker jacks, polarity switch, AC convenience outlet, black covering, black grille, 23.25 in. wide, 33 in. tall, 16 in. deep, optional dolly, mfg. 1987 only.

	N/A	$500 - 600	$255 - 325	

* ***SVT-200T Head*** – similar to the SVT-200T, except in head-unit configuration, 24 in. wide, 10.75 in. tall, 12.75 in. deep, mfg. 1987-1994.

	N/A	$350 - 450	$150 - 200	

SVT-350T – 200W @ 8 ohms (350W @ 4 ohms), 2-10 in. speakers with a horn in an infinite baffle enclosure, bass combo, solid-state chassis, single channel, front black control panel, two inputs (low and high), 11 knobs (gain, 62 Hz with push/pull ultra low, 125 Hz, 300 Hz push/pull 400 Hz, 600 Hz push/pull 850Hz, 1.3k Hz, 3k Hz with push/pull ultra high, stage volume with push/pull limiter, bi-amp freq., bi-amp balance, line out level), effects loop, power switch, rear panel: bi-amp high jack, bi-amp low jack, XLR balanced send, 1/4 in. unbalanced line out jack, two speaker jacks, polarity switch, AC convenience outlet, black covering, black grille, 24 in. wide, 24 in. tall, 15.75 in. deep, removable casters, mfg. 1989-1991.

	N/A	$450 - 525	$300 - 350	

SVT-350H – 350W, bass head-unit, solid-state chassis, single channel, front black control panel, single input, five knobs (g, b, ultra mid, t, MV), nine-band graphic equalizer, input pad switch, limiter switch, graphic EQ on/off switch, power switch, rear panel: one Speakon jack, two 1/4 in. speaker jacks, power amp in jack, preamp out jack, effects loop, XLR balanced line out with -20dB and pre/post EQ switches, recessed side handles, black Tolex covering, black grille with white trim, mfg. 1995-2005.

	N/A	$425 - 500	$275 - 325	$949

SVT-400T HEAD – 250W @ 8 ohms (400W @ 4 ohms or 600W @ 2 ohms), two-space rack-mount bass head with removable ears, solid-state chassis, single channel, front black control panel, two inputs (low and high), 10 knobs (gain, sustain, low with push/pull ultra low, mid with push/pull graphic EQ on/off, mid sweep, high with push/pull ultra high, line out send level, stage volume with push/pull limiter on/off, bi-amp freq., bi-amp balance), six-band graphic EQ with EQ level, graphic EQ footswitch jack, power switch, rear panel: effects loop, send/return level balance, bi-amp high jack, bi-amp low jack, XLR balanced send, 1/4 in. preamp out and power amp in jacks, two speaker jacks, polarity switch, black casing, 19 in. wide, 5.25 in. tall, 15 in. deep, mfg. 1987-1997.

	N/A	$425 - 500	$300 - 350	

SVT-450 – 450W @ 4 ohms (275W @ 8 ohms), bass head-unit, solid-state chassis, MOSFET power section, single channel, front black control panel, single input, five black knobs (g, b, ultra mid, t, MV), nine-band graphic equalizer, input pad switch, limit switch, EQ on/off switch, power switch, rear panel: one Speakon and two 1/4 in. speaker jacks, power amp in, preamp out, effects loop, XLR balanced line out with -20dB/0dB and pre/post EQ switches, variable speed fan, black Tolex covering, black grille, 24 in. wide, 11.5 in. tall, 13 in. deep, 44 lbs., mfg. 2006-2012.

$750	$475 - 550	$300 - 350	$1,050	

SVT-1000 – 1000W @ 4 ohms (750W @ 8 ohms), bass head-unit, solid-state chassis, MOSFET power amp, single channel, front black control panel, two inputs, seven knobs (g, five-position style selector, b, ultra mid, t, effects mix, MV), nine-band graphic EQ with level slider control, mute switch, texture switch, graphic EQ on/off switch, limit defeat switch, power switch, rear panel: footswitch jack, preamp out, power amp in, two Speakon and two 1/4 in. speaker jacks, tuner out, effects loop, 1/4 in. unbalanced line out, XLR balanced line out with level control and ground/lift and pre/post EQ switches, black covering, black grille, 24 in. wide, 11.5 in. tall, 13 in. deep, 48 lbs., mfg. 2005-06.

	N/A	$725 - 850	$450 - 525	$1,599

SVT-GS GENE SIMMONS PUNISHER SIGNATURE – limited edition head and cabinet unit, 350W @ 4 ohms, bass head unit, solid-state chassis, Mosfet power section, single channel, front brushed stainless steel panel with "Ampeg Punisher" logo and Gene Simmons signature, single input, five black knobs (g, b, ultra mid, t, MV), nine-band graphic EQ with on/off switch, pad switch, limiter switch, rear panel: two speaker jacks, power amp in, preamp out, effects loop, XLR balanced line out with pre/post EQ switch and -20dB switch, black covering, 24 in. wide, 13 in. tall, 13 in. deep, 44 lbs., speaker cabinet: 400W, 2-15 in. cast frame JBL drivers that are housed in two seperate chambers, 4 ohm impedance, 3 in. dolly-style casters, tilt-back bar handle, black covering, steel grille, 48 in. tall, 26 in. wide, 16 in. deep, 148 lbs., mfg. late 1990s.

	N/A	$1,500 - 1,800	$1,000 - 1,200	

This was a limited edition and it is rumored that only 100 head and cabinet sets were produced.

SVT MICRO-VR HEAD – 150W @ 8 ohms, 200W @ 4 ohms, bass head-unit, solid-state chassis, MOSFET power section, single channel, front brushed aluminum control panel, single input, five black and silver knobs (g, b, ultramid, t, v), -15 dB pad switch, limiter switch, audio in jack, headphone jack, power switch, rear panel: balanced XLR line out, effects loop, two speaker jacks, black covering, blue/gray grille cloth, 12 in. wide, 5.5 in. tall, 10 in. deep, 9 lbs., mfg. 2008-present.

MSR $420	$300	$175 - 225	$110 - 140	

MSR/NOTES	100%	EXCELLENT	AVERAGE	LAST MSR

ELECTRIC SS AMPS: VARYING HARMONIC (VH) SERIES

Ampeg's patented Varying Harmonic Series was designed to make solid-state amps sound like tube amps by utilizing many harmonic textures.

VH-70 – 70W @ 8 ohms (90W @ 4 ohms), 1-12 in. Celestion G12K-85 (VH-70) or 1-12 in. Ampeg Custom (VH-70A) speaker, guitar combo, solid-state chassis with Varying Harmonic circuitry, two channels, reverb, front black control panel, two inputs (low and high), 12 knobs (Ch. A: g, l, ultra mid, h, level with push/pull channel switch, Ch. B: g, l, m, h, level with push/pull bright switch, All: reverb A, reverb B, power switch, rear panel: preamp out jack, power amp in jack, two footswitch jacks, convenience outlet, polarity switch, black covering, black grille, 20.5 in. wide, 20.75 in. tall, 11.75 in. deep, mfg. 1991-92.

| | N/A | $325 - 400 | $200 - 250 | |

VH-140C – 140W (2 X 70W per side stereo @ 8 ohms), 2-12 in. Celestion G12K-85 (VH-140C) or 2-12 in. Ampeg (VH-140CA) speakers, guitar combo, solid-state chassis utilizing Varying Harmonic circuitry, two channels, stereo chorus, reverb, front black control panel, two inputs, 15 black knobs (Chorus: Rate, Depth Ch. A, Depth Ch. B, Reverb: Ch. A, Ch. B, Ch. B: lead, h, m, l, g, Ch. A: lead, h, m, l, g), effects loop, speaker compensated XLR line out, black covering, black grille with white piping and scripted Ampeg logo, 27 in. wide, 21 in. tall, 12 in. deep, mfg. 1992-98.

| | N/A | $375 - 450 | $225 - 275 | $1,099 |

* **VH-140C Head** – similar to the VH-140C, except in head-unit configuration, 27 in. wide, 10 in. tall, 11 in. deep, 48 lbs., mfg. 1992-98.

| | N/A | $275 - 325 | $150 - 200 | $949 |

VH-150 – 150W, guitar head-unit, solid-state chassis with Varying Harmonic circuitry, two channels, reverb, front black control panel, two inputs (low and high), 12 knobs (Ch. A: g, l, ultra mid, h, level with push/pull channel switch, Ch. B: g, l, m, h, level with push/pull bright switch, All: reverb A, reverb B, power switch), rear panel: preamp out jack, power amp in jack, two footswitch jacks, convenience outlet, polarity switch, black covering, black grille, mfg. 1991-92.

| | N/A | $300 - 375 | $175 - 225 | |

VH-412TA/VH-412TB SPEAKER CABINET – 120W (240W mono), 4-12 in. speakers, Infinite Baffle design, tuned sound post, angled (VH-412TA) or straight (VH-412TB) front, side-mounted handles, black covering, black grille with white piping and scripted Ampeg logo, 2 in. removable casters, 30 in. wide, 32 in. tall, 14 in. deep, 102 lbs., disc. 1998.

| | N/A | $250 - 300 | $150 - 200 | $699 |

ELECTRIC SS AMPS: MISC. MODELS

B-15T PORTAFLEX – 100W, 1-15 in. EVM (B-15TEV) or 1-15 in. Ampeg Custom (B-15T) speaker mounted in a ported bass reflex cabinet, bass combo/piggyback Portaflex design, solid-state chassis, single channel, front black control panel, two inputs, seven knobs (g, low with push/pull ultra low, low mid with push/pull shift, high mid with push/pull shift, high with push/pull ultra high, stage volume with push/pull limiter, line out level), effects loop, power switch, rear panel: XLR balanced sends, 1/4 in. unbalanced, line out/line in jacks, speaker jack, headphone jack, speaker mute switch, polarity switch, removable casters, tilt-back leg, black covering, black grille, 21 in. wide, 24.75 in. tall, 15.75 in. deep, mfg. 1988-1992.

| | N/A | $325 - 400 | $175 - 225 | |

The B-15T utilized the same chassis as the SVT-70T in a Portaflex cabinet.

B-40 – 120W, 4-10 in. speakers in a sealed cabinet, bass piggyback configuration, solid-state chassis, two channels, front silver control panel, four inputs (two per channel), eight black and silver knobs (Ch. 1: v, b, m, t, Ch 2: v, b, m, t), three-way mid-range and ultra-hi switches for each channel, tuned reflex speaker design, black covering, black grille, mfg. 1975-1980.

| Head Only | N/A | $300 - 350 | $175 - 225 | |
| Head & Cabinet | N/A | $600 - 700 | $425 - 500 | |

The B-40 utilizes the chassis of the B115 and B410.

G-60 – 120W, 6-10 in. speakers in a ported speaker cabinet, guitar piggyback configuration, solid-state chassis, two channels, reverb, tremolo, front control panel, four inputs (two per channel), 11 knobs (Ch.1: v, b, m, t, Ch 2: v, b, m, t, r, s, i), mid-range freq. switches and ultra hi switches for each channel, power switch, black covering, black grille, mfg. 1975-1980.

| Head Only | N/A | $300 - 350 | $175 - 225 | |
| Head & Cabinet | N/A | $700 - 850 | $500 - 600 | |

V-6B – 240W, 2-15 in. speakers, bass piggyback configuration with a separate head and cabinet, solid-state chassis, single channel, front white control panel, two inputs, four knobs (v, b, m, t), mid-range freq. switch, Ultra-hi switch, modular components, black covering, blue/gray grille (cabinet only, cabinet also has a "towel bar" handle on top), mfg. 1974-1980.

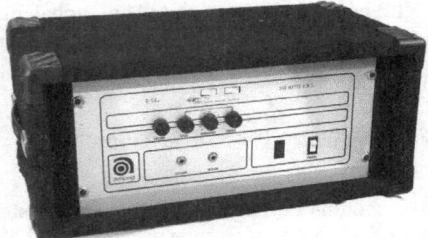

courtesy John Beeson/The Music Shoppe

| Head Only | N/A | $300 - 350 | $175 - 225 | |
| Head & Cabinet | N/A | $600 - 750 | $425 - 500 | |

MSR/NOTES	100%	EXCELLENT	AVERAGE	LAST MSR

SOUNDCUBE (MODEL 8850) & BUSTER (MODEL 8851) – these are two amps that were listed as mini amps. Each of these amps operated on AC or DC power. The soundcube was in the shape of a cube with the "a" logo on the side and the Buster is taller and looks a lot like a Pignose. Each amp has one knob and one input. Both of these amps were introduced in 1975. The Buster was discontinued by the end of the year, while the Soundcube lasted until 1977.

N/A   N/A   N/A

ELECTRIC HYBRID AMPS: AX SERIES

Ampeg introduced their first hybrid amplifiers with the AX Series in 1990. Hybrid technology utilizes a mixture of tube and solid-state technology - most often with one or two preamp tubes to shape the sound and a solid-state power section. Both the AX-44C and AX-70 featured a 12AX7 preamp tube. These amps did not last in Ampeg's line very long, but they did go on to use hybrid technology in many of their bass amps later on.

AX-44C – 44W (2 X 22W stereo), 2-8 in. speakers, guitar combo, hybrid chassis, 12AX7 preamp tube, solid-state power amp, two channels, chorus, reverb, front black control panel, two inputs (low and high), 11 knobs (Ch. A: g, ultra mid with push/pull shift, level with push/pull channel switch, Ch. B: g, l, m, h, level with push/pull bright switch, All: r, chorus depth with push/pull chorus on/off, chorus rate), effects loop insert jack, power switch, rear panel: right and left line outs, two footswitch jacks, black covering, black grille, mfg. 1990-92.

N/A $200 - 250 $120 - 150

Celestion G8L-35 speakers were optional.

AX-70 – 70W, 1-12 in. speaker, guitar combo, hybrid chassis, 12AX7 preamp tube, solid-state power amp, two channels, reverb, front black control panel, two inputs (low and high), 10 knobs (Ch. A: g, p with push/pull low, ultra mid, level with push/pull channel switch, Ch. B: g, l, m, h, level with push/pull bright switch, All: r), footswitch jack, line out, line in, power switch, black covering, black grille, mfg. 1990-91.

N/A $250 - 300 $135 - 175

ELECTRIC HYBRID AMPS: SVT SERIES

SVT-III – 350W, two-space rack-mount head-unit, hybrid chassis with a tube preamp and MOSFET power amp, single channel, front black control panel, two inputs (normal and bright), five knobs (v, b, m, five-position mid-range freq. selector, t), six-band graphic EQ with level slider control, ultra low switch, balance line out switch, ultra high switch, graphic EQ switch, footswitch jack, power switch, black casing, mfg. 1991-94.

N/A $425 - 500 $250 - 300

ELECTRIC HYBRID AMPS: SVT PRO SERIES

Rack space kits are also available for SVT Pro head units. The **PR-RC4** is a four space and retails for $349. The **PR-RC3** is a three space, which retails for $249.

SVT-II Pro/SVT-2Pro
courtesy Ampeg

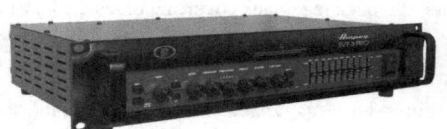
SVT-III Pro/SVT-3Pro
courtesy Ampeg

SVT-IV Pro/SVT-4Pro
courtesy Ampeg

SVT-II PRO/SVT-2PRO – 300W, three-space rack-mount bass head unit, 14-tube chassis, preamp: 6 X 12AX7, 2 X 12AU7; power: 6 X 6550, single channel, front black control panel with white lines and blue accents (1992-99) or black with gray insert (2000-present), single input, seven black knobs (g, drive, b, m, five-position mid-range selector, t, MV), nine-band graphic equalizer with level slider control, input pad switch, mute switch, ultra lo switch, bright switch, ultra hi switch, graphic EQ on/off switch, standby switch, power switch, rear panel: polarity switch, two tube bias adjustment screws, slave out jack, power amp in, preamp out, XLR balanced line out and 1/4 in. unbalanced line out with level control and pre/post EQ switch, effects loop, tuner out, footswitch jack, two 1/4 in. speaker jacks with two red/black speaker connectors, black casing, 19.5 in. wide, 15.75 in. deep, 7.375 in. tall, 70 lbs., mfg. 1992-2012.

$2,000 $1,100 - 1,350 $675 - 825 $2,600

SVT-III PRO/SVT-3PRO – 450W @ 4 ohms (275W @ 9 ohms), two-space rack-mount bass head unit, hybrid chassis, preamp: 3 X 12AX7, power: tube driven MOSFET, single channel, front black control panel with white lines and blue accents (1994-99) or black with gray insert (2000-present), single input, seven black knobs (g, b, m, five-position mid-range selector, t, MV, tube gain), nine-band graphic equalizer with level slider control, input pad switch, bright switch, ultra hi switch, ultra lo switch, mute switch, graphic EQ on/off switch, power switch, rear panel: convenience outlet, two 1/4 in. speaker jacks with two red/black speaker connectors, XLR balanced line out and 1/4 in. unbalanced line out with level control and pre/post EQ switch, power amp in, preamp out, effects loop, tuner out, footswitch jack, black casing, 19.5 in. wide, 16.5 in. deep, 5.25 in. tall, mfg. 1994-present.

MSR $1,540 $1,100 $725 - 825 $350 - 450

While this has essentially been the same model since it was introduced in 1994, the badging on the front changed from SVT-III Pro to SVT-3 Pro in 1999.

SVT-IV PRO/SVT-4PRO – 1600W @ 4 ohms mono (1200W @ 8 ohms mono, 2 X 900W @ 2 ohms stereo, 2 X 625W @ 4 ohms stereo, or 2 X 350W @ 9 ohms stereo), two-space rack-mount bass head-unit, hybrid chassis, preamp: 3 X 12AX7, power: tube driven MOSFET, single channel, front black control panel (1997-99) or black and gray control panel (1999-present), ten black knobs (g, compression, b, m, five-position mid-range freq. selector, t, line out level, MV, crossover freq., crossover balance), nine-band graphic EQ with level slider control, mute switch,

MSR/NOTES	100%	EXCELLENT	AVERAGE	LAST MSR

SVT-6Pro
courtesy Ampeg

SVT-7Pro
courtesy Ampeg

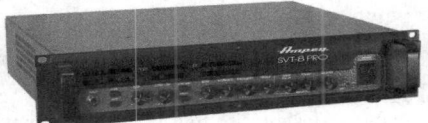

SVT-8Pro
courtesy Ampeg

input pad switch, ultra high switch, ultra low switch, bright switch, graphic EQ on/off switch, effects bypass switch, limit defeat switch, power switch, rear panel: convenience outlet, bi-amp high and low outputs, two XLR balanced line outs and two unbalanced 1/4 in. line outs (one per channel each) with stereo/mono and pre/post EQ switches, effects loop with two returns (one per channel), tuner out, four 1/4 in. speaker jacks, and two sets of red/black speaker connectors, stereo/mono power amp switch, two power amp inputs and two preamp outputs (one per channel each), two footswitch jacks, black casing, 19 in. wide, 3.5 in. tall, 15.5 in. deep, 42 lbs., mfg. 1997-present.

MSR $2,170	**$1,550**	**$1,000 - 1,150**	**$500 - 625**	

While this has essentially been the same model since it was introduced in 1997, the badging on the front changed from SVT-IV Pro to SVT-4 Pro in circa 1999.

SVT-5PRO – 1000W @ 4 ohms mono (680W @ 8 ohms mono, 2 X 500W @ 2 ohms stereo, 2 X 340W @ 4 ohms stereo, or 2 X 255W @ 8 ohms stereo), three-space bass rack-mount head-unit, hybrid chassis with 1 X 12AX7 preamp tube, MOSFET power amp, two channels, front black and gray control panel, single input, 15 black knobs (Clean Ch.: g, b, m, t, v, octave, OD Ch.: g, b, m, mid-range freq., t, v, All: MV, crossover freq., crossover balance), mute switch, input pad switch, ultra high switch, ultra low switch, bright switch, compression switch, combine switch, channel switch, limit defeat switch, OD Ch. boost switch, OD Ch. gate switch, power switch, rear panel: convenience outlet, bi-amp high and low outputs, two XLR balanced line outs with clean pre/post switch and OD/mix switches, two effects loops (one per channel), tuner out, three Speakon jacks, four 1/4 in. speaker jacks, full range/biamp switch, stereo/mono power amp switch, two power amp inputs (one per channel) and three preamp outputs (OD, Clean/Mix, Octave), clean/mix separate switch, two footswitch jacks, black casing, 19 in. wide, 5.75 in. tall, 15.5 in. deep, mfg. 2002-05.

	N/A	**$750 - 900**	**$500 - 600**	**$1,799**

SVT-6PRO – 1100W @ 4 ohms (750W @ 8 ohms), two-space bass rack-mount head unit, hybrid chassis, preamp: 4 X 12AX7, 2 X 12AU7, power: MOSFET, single channel, front black and gray control panel, single input, 14 black knobs (compression, g, b, four semi-parametric mid tone controls each with a freq. selector, t, tube volume, MV), input pad switch, mute switch, ultra lo switch, ultra hi switch, bright switch, power switch, rear panel: convenience outlet, one Speakon and two 1/4 in. speaker jacks, XLR balanced line out with level control and pre/post switch, unbalanced 1/4 in. line out, tuner out, power amp in, preamp out, effects loop, footswitch jack, black casing, 19 in. wide, 3.5 in. tall, 15 in. deep, 41 lbs., mfg. 2005-09.

	N/A	**$675 - 800**	**$350 - 425**	**$1,820**

SVT-7PRO – 600W @ 8 ohms (1000W @ 4 omhs), bass head, one-space rack mount, hybrid chassis, preamp: 1 X JJ 12AX7, power: solid-state Class D, single channel, dark gray front control panel, single input, eight black knobs (compression, g, b, m, five-position mid-freq., t, FX mix, MV), mute switch, -15dB switch, ultra hi switch, ultra lo switch, power switch, headphone jack, rear panel: footswitch jack, power amp in, preamp out, effects loop, tuner out, two Speakon speaker jacks, tube direct XLR output, post/pre EQ switch, 0dB/-40dB switch, ground/lift switch, RCA aux. inputs, black casing, removable rack ears, 15.5 lbs., mfg. 2010-present.

MSR $1,000	**$800**	**$450 - 550**	**$275 - 325**	

SVT-8PRO – 800W @ 8 ohms (1300W @ 4 omhs, 2500W @ 2 ohms), bass head, one-space rack mount, hybrid chassis, preamp: 2 X 12AX7, 1 X 12AU7 (2010-present) or 2 X 12AU7 (2006-08), power: solid-state Class D, single channel, dark gray front control panel, single input, 10 black knobs (g, five-position ultra low, b, m, five-position mid-freq, t, drive with pull on switch, power, MV), mute switch, -12dB switch, ultra hi switch, bright switch, power switch, rear panel: balanced XLR line out, pre/post EQ switch, ground/lift switch, tuner out, power amp in, preamp out, effects loop, footswitch jack, two Speakon speaker jacks, black casing, 23 lbs., mfg. 2006-08, 2010-2012.

	$2,400	**$1,400 - 1,750**	**$850 - 1,050**	**$3,360**

PR-15H SPEAKER CABINET – 400W, 1-15 in. speaker, 1 in. horn with variable level attenuator, 8 ohm impedance, Bass reflex cabinet design, baltic birch plywood construction, multi-coat urethane polymer finish/sealant, black metal grille, side handles, 99 lbs., disc. 2001.

	N/A	**$500 - 575**	**$300 - 375**	**$1,149**

PR-210H SPEAKER CABINET – 300W, 2-10 in. speakers, 1 in. horn with variable level attenuator, 8 ohm impedance, Bass reflex cabinet design, baltic birch plywood construction, multi-coat urethane polymer finish/sealant, black metal grille, side handles, 84 lbs., disc. 2000.

	N/A	**$500 - 575**	**$300 - 375**	**$1,149**

PR-212H SPEAKER CABINET – 400W, 2-12 in. speakers, 1 in. horn with variable level attenuator, 8 ohm impedance, Bass reflex cabinet design, baltic birch plywood construction, multi-coat urethane polymer finish/sealant, black metal grille, side handles, 110 lbs., disc. 2000.

	N/A	**$500 - 575**	**$300 - 375**	**$1,149**

PR-410H SPEAKER CABINET – 600W, 4-10 in. speakers, 1 in. horn with variable level attenuator, 8 ohm impedance, Bass reflex cabinet design, baltic birch plywood construction, multi-coat urethane polymer finish/sealant, black metal grille, side handles, 118 lbs., disc. 2001.

	N/A	**$575 - 675**	**$350 - 425**	**$1,299**

MSR/NOTES	100%	EXCELLENT	AVERAGE	LAST MSR

* PR-410HLF Speaker Cabinet – similar to the PR-410H Speaker Cabinet, except has a extended low end design and 4 ohm impedance, 128 lbs., disc. 2006.

	N/A	$625 - 725	$375 - 450	$1,399

PR-810H SPEAKER CABINET – 1200W, 8-10 in. speakers, 2-1 in. horns with variable level attenuator, 8 ohm impedance, Bass reflex cabinet design with four separate cabinet compartments, baltic birch plywood construction, multi-coat urethane polymer finish/sealant, black metal grille, side handles, 212 lbs., disc. 2003.

	N/A	$1,100 - 1,300	$725 - 875	$2,499

ELECTRIC BASS AMPS: DIAMOND BLUE SERIES

B-15R Portaflex
courtesy Ampeg

B-50R Rocket Bass
courtesy Ampeg

B-200R Rocket Bass
courtesy Ampeg

B-15R PORTAFLEX – 100W (switchable to 60W), 1-15 in. speaker with a tweeter, guitar/bass combo/piggyback Portaflex combo, seven-tube chassis, preamp: 1 X 12AU7, 2 X 12AX7, power: 4 X 6L6/EL34, solid-state rectifier, front chrome control panel, two inputs (guitar and bass), six black knobs (g, b, m, mid-range freq., t, MV), ultra hi switch, ultra lo switch, 100W/60W half power switch, standby switch, power switch, rear panel: tube bias switch, one Speakon and one 1/4 in. speaker jack, impedance selector, line out with level control, line in, balanced XLR line out with post/pre EQ and ground/lift switches, removable dolly board with casters included, vintage diamond blue vinyl covering, sparkle-weave grille cloth, 21 in. wide, 21 in. tall, 14 in. deep, 87 lbs., mfg. 1997-2006.

	N/A	$1,050 - 1,250	$525 - 650	$2,899

B-50R ROCKET BASS – 50W, 1-12 in. speaker, bass combo, solid-state chassis, single channel, top chrome control panel, single input, five black knobs (v, b, low mid, high mid, t), headphone jack, power switch, vintage diamond blue vinyl covering, sparkle-weave grille cloth, 18.5 in. wide, 21.25 in. tall, 14.25 in. deep, 48 lbs., mfg. 1996-2003.

	N/A	$325 - 375	$175 - 210	$549

B-100R ROCKET BASS – 100W, 1-15 in. speaker, bass combo, solid-state chassis, single channel, top chrome control panel, two inputs, six black knobs (g, b, low mid, high mid, t, MV), ultra low switch, ultra mid switch, ultra high switch, line out jack, headphone jack, power switch, vintage diamond blue vinyl covering, sparkle-weave grille cloth, 19 in. wide, 21.25 in. tall, 14.25 in. deep, 65 lbs., mfg. 1996-2009.

	N/A	$325 - 375	$160 - 195	$812

B-200R ROCKET BASS – 220W, 1-15 in. speaker, bass combo, hybrid chassis with a single 12AU7 preamp tube, single channel, top rear chrome control panel, two inputs, six black knobs (g, b, low mid, high mid, t, MV, line out/headphones level), ultra low switch, ultra mid switch, ultra high switch, XLR line out jack, headphone jack, power switch, vintage diamond blue vinyl covering, sparkle-weave grille cloth, 22.25 in. wide, 22.25 in. tall, 14.25 in. deep, 69 lbs., mfg. 2006-09.

	N/A	$350 - 425	$180 - 225	$910

B-15E SPEAKER CABINET – 200W, 1-15 in. speaker, 8 ohm impedance, three-way horn level switch, removable dolly board with casters, side-mounted handles, diamond blue covering, gray striped grille, designed for use with the B-15R Portaflex (Diamond Blue), 21 in. wide, 21 in. tall, 14 in. deep, 72 lbs., disc. 2000.

	N/A	$250 - 300	$150 - 200	$699

ELECTRIC BASS AMPS: PORTAFLEX SERIES

Ampeg's Portaflex Series combines the vintage styling and flip-top design of the 1960s Portaflex design with modern circuitry and features.

PF20T ALL TUBE HEAD – 20W @ 4 or 8 ohms, all tube head-unit, four-tube chassis, preamp: 2 X 12AX7, power: 2 X 6V6, single channel, front brushed aluminum control panel, single input, five knobs (g, b, m, t, v), rear panel: power switch, standby switch, fuse, impedance selector switch, bias section, post-eq/pre-eq, preamp out, lift/ground switch, speaker jack, transformer balanced line out, black covering, no speaker load required, 13 in. wide, 7.3 in. tall, 10.4 in. deep, 16 lbs., new 2016.

MSR $840	$600	$400 - 450	$195 - 240	

MSR/NOTES	100%	EXCELLENT	AVERAGE		LAST MSR

PF20T All Tube Head
courtesy Ampeg

PF50T All Tube Head
courtesy Ampeg

PF112HLF Portaflexx Speaker Cabinet
courtesy Ampeg

PF50T ALL TUBE HEAD – 50W @ 4 or 8 ohms, all tube head-unit, five-tube chassis, preamp: 2 X 12AX7, power: 1 X 12AU7, 2 X 6V6, single channel, front brushed aluminum control panel, two inputs, six knobs (g, b, m, five-way frequency selector, t, v), ultra hi switch, ultra low switch, rear panel: power switch, standby switch, fuse, impedance selector switch, bias section, post-eq/pre-eq, preamp out, lift/ground switch, speaker jack, transformer balanced line out, black covering, no speaker load required, 13.9 in. wide, 7.3 in. tall, 10.4 in. deep, 19.4 lbs., new 2016.

MSR $1,260	$900	$575 - 675	$295 - 350

PF350 PORTAFLEX HEAD – 350W @ 4 ohms (250W @ 8 ohms), bass head-unit, solid-state chassis with a Class D power amp, single channel, front brushed aluminum control panel, single input, input pad switch, 5 knobs (g, b, m, t, v), limiter switch, audio in jack, headphone jack, rear panel: power switch, two speaker jacks, XLR line out, effects loop, black casing, 8 lbs, 2011-present.

MSR $560	$300	$175 - 225	$100 - 135

PF500 PORTAFLEX HEAD – 500W @ 4 ohms (300W @ 8 ohms), bass head-unit, solid-state chassis with a MOSFET preamp and Class D power amp, single channel, front brushed aluminum control panel, single input, mute switch, input pad switch, eight knobs (comp., g, b, m, five-position mid control, t, FX blend, v), ultra hi switch, ultra lo switch, rear panel: power switch, two speaker jacks (single 1/4 in. and single Speakon), footswitch jack, power amp in, pre amp out, XLR line out with pre/post EQ, -40dB pad, and ground/lift switches, tuner out, effects loop, black casing, 11 lbs, mfg. 2011-present.

MSR $700	$400	$250 - 300	$150 - 190

PF800 PORTAFLEX HEAD – 800W @ 4 ohms, bass head-unit, solid-state chassis with a MOSFET preamp and Class D power amp, single channel, front brushed aluminum control panel, single input, mute switch, input pad switch, eight knobs (comp., g, b, m, five-position mid control, t, FX blend, v), ultra hi switch, ultra lo switch, audio in, headphone in, rear panel: power switch, two speaker jacks (single 1/4 in. and single Speakon), footswitch jack, power amp in, pre amp out, XLR line out with pre/post EQ, -40dB pad, and ground/lift switches, tuner out, effects loop, black casing, 11.8 lbs, mfg. 2013-present.

MSR $840	$600	$400 - 450	$195 - 240

PF112HLF PORTAFLEX SPEAKER CABINET – 200W, 1-12 in. ceramic Eminence LF driver, 1-1 in. HF compression driver with L-pad level control, 8 ohm impedance, two inputs, tweeter switch, ported Portaflex design, 15 mm poplar ply construction, integrated side handles, black diamond Tolex covering, vintage B-15-style black and silver grille cloth, 30.8 lbs., new 2016.

MSR $560	$400	$260 - 300	$130 - 160

PF115HE PORTAFLEX SPEAKER CABINET – 450W, 1-15 in. ceramic Eminence LF driver, 1-1 in. compression driver, 8 ohm impedance, three-position high-freq. attenuator, two inputs, vintage Portaflex flip-top design, 15 mm poplar ply construction, inegrated skid rails, removable casters, designed for use with the PF350 and PF500 Portaflex heads, black diamond Tolex covering, vintage B-15-style black and silver grille cloth, 45 lbs., mfg. 2011-present.

MSR $520	$400	$250 - 300	$150 - 190

PF115LF PORTAFLEX SPEAKER CABINET – 400W, 1-15 in. ceramic Eminence LF driver, 8 ohm impedance, two inputs, low-frequency shelf ports, 15 mm poplar ply construction, integrated side handles, removable casters, black diamond Tolex covering, vintage B-15-style black and silver grille cloth, 55.8 lbs., mfg. 2012-present.

MSR $490	$350	$230 - 265	$115 - 140

PF210HE PORTAFLEX SPEAKER CABINET – 450W, 2-10 in. ceramic Eminence LF drivers, 1-1 in. compression driver, 8 ohm impedance, three-position high-freq. attenuator, two inputs, vintage Portaflex flip-top design, 15 mm poplar ply construction, inegrated skid rails, removable casters, designed for use with the PF350 and PF500 Portaflex heads, black diamond Tolex covering, vintage B-15-style black and silver grille cloth, 48 lbs., mfg. 2011-present.

MSR $520	$400	$250 - 300	$150 - 190

PF410HLF PORTAFLEX SPEAKER CABINET – 800W, 4-10 in. ceramic Eminence LF driver, 1-1 in. HF compression driver with L-pad level control, 8 ohm impedance, two inputs, high-frequency three-position attenuator switch, low-frequency shelf ports, 15 mm poplar ply construction, integrated side handles, removable casters, black diamond Tolex covering, vintage B-15-style black and silver grille cloth, 73.4 lbs., mfg. 2012-present.

MSR $770	$550	$350 - 400	$180 - 220

MSR/NOTES	100%	EXCELLENT	AVERAGE	LAST MSR

ELECTRIC BASS SS AMPS: B SERIES

Ampeg changed the cosmetics of their amplifiers in the late 1990s, but it doesn't appear that there was a clear cut date when the change was made. Their B Bass combos and heads appear to change throughout 1999, so models produced in 1999 and before will have black control panels with blue accents and a black cloth grille with white piping and a large square Ampeg logo in the upper left corner. Models produced in 1999 and later will have black and gray control panels with white accents and a black metal grille with a small oval Ampeg logo at the bottom. In 1998, Ampeg advertised a B-1000R amp in their catalog and price list, but the price was listed as TBA (to be announced) and it appears that this amp never went into production as it did not appear in the 1999 catalog.

B-2
courtesy Ampeg

B-3
courtesy Ampeg

B-4R
courtesy Ampeg

B-1 – 150W, 1-12 in. Ampeg Custom speaker with a 4 in. high freq. horn, bass combo, hybrid chassis, preamp: 3 X 12AX7, power: solid-state, two channels, front black and gray control panel, single input, seven knobs (g, bass with push/pull shift, mid-range, treble with push/pull shift, solo voice, solo boost, MV), input pad switch, ultra low switch, ultra high switch, balance out switch, solo channel switch, limit switch, power switch, rear panel: two 1/4 in. speaker jacks, power amp in jack, preamp out jack, effects loop, XLR balanced line out, footswitch jack, cabinet controls: high-freq. attenuator, normal input, contour input, black covering, black grille, 21 in. wide, 18.5 in. tall, 13 in. deep, 63 lbs., mfg. 1992-95.

| N/A | $275 - 325 | $140 - 170 | |

* **B-1R Head** – similar to the B-1, except in a one-space rack-mount head-unit configuration, 19 in. wide, 1.75 in. tall, 12.75 in. deep, 15 lbs., mfg. 1992-95.

| N/A | $190 - 225 | $95 - 120 | |

B-1RE – 300W @ 4 ohms (175W @ 8 ohms), two-space bass rack-mount head-unit, solid-state chassis, MOSFET power amp, single channel, front black and gray control panel, single input, five black knobs (g, b, ultra mid , t, MV), input pad switch, limit switch, power switch, rear panel: two speaker jacks, power amp in, preamp out, effects loop, XLR balanced line out with -20dB/0dB and pre/post EQ switches, black casing, 19 in. wide, 3.5 in. tall, 15 in. deep, 22 lbs., mfg. 2005-09.

| N/A | $255 - 300 | $130 - 160 | $700 |

B-2 – 200W @ 8 ohms (350W @ 4 ohms), 1-15 in. speaker, bass combo, solid-state chassis, single channel, front black control panel (1994-99) or gray control panel (1999-2001), single input, five black knobs (g, b, ultra mid, t, MV), nine-band graphic EQ, input pad switch, limiter on/off switch, graphic EQ on/off switch, power switch, rear panel: two speaker jacks, power amp in jack, preamp out jack, effects loop, XLR balanced line out with pad switch and pre/post EQ switch, recessed side handles, black Tolex covering, black grille, 24 in. wide, 24.5 in. tall, 16 in. deep, 87 lbs., mfg. 1994-2001.

| N/A | $475 - 550 | $235 - 290 | $1,099 |

* **B-248** – similar to the B-2, except has 4-8 in. speakers, 94 lbs., mfg. 1997-2000.

| N/A | $425 - 500 | $215 - 265 | $949 |

* **B-2R Head** – similar to the B-2, except in a two-space rack-mount head-unit configuration, black casing, 19 in. wide, 3.5 in. tall, 15 in. deep, 15 lbs., mfg. 1994-2004.

| N/A | $350 - 400 | $170 - 210 | $769 |

»**B-2RE Head** – similar to the B-2R, except has 450W @ 4 ohms (250W @ 8 ohms), 26 lbs., mfg. 2005-2010.

| N/A | $300 - 350 | $150 - 185 | $840 |

B-3 – 150W, 1-15 in. speaker, bass combo, solid-state chassis, single channel, front black control panel (1995-99) or gray control panel (1999-2001), single input, six black knobs (g, drive, b, ultra-mid, t, MV), nine-band graphic equalizer, XLR balanced line out, effects loop, preamp out/power amp in, optocoupler limiter, black Tolex covering, black metal grille, 68 lbs., mfg. 1995-2001.

| N/A | $400 - 475 | $200 - 250 | $879 |

* **B-3158** – similar to the B-3, except has 1-8 in. and 1-15 in. speakers that are bi-amped (100W to the 15 in. and 50W to the 8 in.) and an additional biamp level balance knob, 84 lbs., mfg. 1995-2001.

| N/A | $475 - 550 | $235 - 290 | $1,099 |

MSR/NOTES	100%	EXCELLENT	AVERAGE		LAST MSR

B-500DR
courtesy Ampeg

B-410HE Speaker Cabinet
courtesy Ampeg

BSE-410H Speaker Cabinet
courtesy Ampeg

* B-328 – similar to the B-3 except has 2-8 in. speakers with a tweeter, 57 lbs., mfg. 2000-01.

N/A	$400 - 475	$200 - 250	$879

* B-3 Head – similar to the B-3, except in head-unit configuration, mfg. 1998 only.

N/A	$170 - 200	$85 - 105	$499

B-4R – 1000W @ 4 ohms (700W @ 8 ohms mono or 2 X 500W @ 2 ohms, 2 X 350W @ 4 ohms, or 2 X 200W @ 8 ohms stereo), three-space rack-mount bass head-unit, solid-state chassis with two power amps, single channel, front all black control panel (1998-99) or black and gray control panel (1999-2008), two inputs, nine black knobs (g, five-position style selector, b, ultra mid, t, effects mix, master, crossover freq. crossover balance), nine band graphic equalizer with slider level control, power switch, XLR balanced line out, effects loop, preamp out/power amp in, rear panel: bi-amp high output and low output jacks, balanced XLR and unbalanced 1/4 in. line outs with level control, pre/post switch, and ground/lift switch, effects loop, tuner out jack, four 1/4 in. speaker jacks and three Speakon jacks (Ch. A, Ch. B, or bridged), power amp in and preamp out jacks for each power amp channel, full range and stereo/mono switches, footswitch jack, black metal covering, 19 in. wide, 5.25 in. tall, 19 in. deep, 39 lbs., mfg. 1998-2008.

N/A	$600 - 700	$300 - 375	$1,540

B-5R – 500W @ 2 ohms (340W @ 4 ohms or 205W @ 8 ohms), two-space bass rack-mount head-unit, two channels, black and gray control panel, two inputs, 11 knobs (Clean Ch.: v, five-position style selector, b, ultra mid, t, OD Ch.: g, five-position style selector, v, All: octave volume, FX blend, MV), mute switch, combine switch, channel select switch, OD boost switch, power switch, rear panel: one Speakon and two 1/4 in. speaker jacks, 1/4 in. unbalanced line out, XLR balanced line out, effects loop, tuner out, power amp in, preamp out, two footswitch jacks, black metal casing, 19 in. wide, 3.75 in. tall, 15 in. deep, 32 lbs., mfg. 2000-05.

N/A	$500 - 600	$255 - 325	$1,299

B-500DR – 500W @ 2 ohms (350W @ 4 ohms and 200W @ 8 ohms), two-space bass rack-mount head-unit, solid-state chassis, single channel, front gray control panel, two inputs, six knobs (g, b, ultra mid, t, FX blend, MV), four programmable presets, input switch, input pad switch, limit defeat switch, power switch, rear panel: one Speakon and two 1/4 in. speaker jacks, multi-pin footswitch jack, XLR balanced line out with level control and pre/post EQ switch, effects loop, power amp in, preamp out, black metal casing, four-button footswitch included, 19 in. wide, 3.5 in. tall, 15 in. deep, 32 lbs., mfg. 2005-06.

N/A	$500 - 600	$255 - 325	$1,299

The B500DR has four presets that can be programmed and saved by the user.

B-115E SPEAKER CABINET – 200W, 1-15 in. speaker, 8 ohm impedance, baltic birch plywood construction, black covering, black metal grille, handles on the side, 2 in. swivel casters, 72 lbs., mfg. 2006-2012.

$300	$175 - 225	$100 - 135	$390

B-410HE SPEAKER CABINET – 200W, 4-10 in. speakers with a 1 in. horn, 8 ohm impedance, three-way horn switch, baltic birch plywood construction, black covering, black metal grille, handles on the side, 2 in. swivel casters, 72 lbs., mfg. 2006-2012.

$400	$225 - 275	$140 - 175	$520

* B-410HLF Speaker Cabinet – similar to the B-410HE Speaker Cabinet, except has a low-end design, 400W handling, and 4 ohm impedance, 88 lbs., mfg. 2006-2012.

$500	$300 - 375	$175 - 225	$650

BSE-115 SPEAKER CABINET – 200W, 1-15 in. speaker, 8 ohm impedance, black covering, black metal grille, handles on the side, 2 in. swivel casters, 75 lbs., mfg. 2000-05.

N/A	$225 - 275	$140 - 175	$499

BSE-410H SPEAKER CABINET – 200W, 4-10 in. speakers with a horn, 8 ohm impedance, three-way horn switch, black covering, black metal grille, handles on the side, 2 in. swivel casters, 75 lbs., mfg. 2000-05.

N/A	$300 - 375	$175 - 225	$699

MSR/NOTES	100%	EXCELLENT	AVERAGE	LAST MSR

* ***BSE-410HS Speaker Cabinet*** – similar to the BSE-410H Speaker Cabinet, except has a slanted top and 400W handling, 91 lbs., mfg. 2003-05.

	N/A	$350 - 425	$200 - 250	$799

* ***BSE-410HLF Speaker Cabinet*** – similar to the BSE-410H Speaker Cabinet, except has an extended low-end design with 400W handling and 4 ohm impedance, 91 lbs., mfg. 2000-05.

	N/A	$375 - 450	$225 - 275	$879

BXT-115HL4/8 SPEAKER CABINET – 300W, 1-15 in. speaker with a horn, 4 or 8 ohm impedance, extended low-end design, variable "L" pad, 2 in. swivel casters, black covering, black metal grille, handles on the side, stackable corners, 105 lbs., mfg. 2000-06.

	N/A	$450 - 525	$275 - 325	$999

BXT-210M SPEAKER CABINET – 400W, 2-10 in. speakers with a Tractrix wave-guide coaxial horn, 4 ohm impedance, extended low-end design, variable "L" pad, tilt-back cabinet design, black covering, black metal grille, handles on the side, stackable corners, 61 lbs., mfg. 2002-06.

	N/A	$350 - 425	$200 - 250	$799

BXT-410HL4/8 SPEAKER CABINET – 600W, 4-10 in. speakers with a horn, 4 or 8 ohm impedance, extended low-end design, variable "L" pad, 2 in. swivel casters, black covering, black metal grille, handles on the side, stackable corners, 122 lbs., mfg. 2000-06.

	N/A	$525 - 625	$300 - 350	$1,199

ELECTRIC BASS SS AMPS: BASSAMP SERIES

The Bassamp Series was introduced in the late 1990s, and they pay tribute to Ampeg's original Bassamp line of amplifiers from the 1950s. The Bassamp Series was completely redesigned in 2015 and now features front-facing controls, 60-degree monitoring angle, and a Bass Scrambler Overdrive Circuit (except the BA-108).

BA-108 First Version
courtesy Ampeg

BA-108 Second Version
courtesy Ampeg

BA-110 Third Version
courtesy Ampeg

BA-108 FIRST VERSION – 25W, 1-8 in. speaker, bass combo, solid-state chassis, single channel, top/rear black control panel, two inputs, five knobs (v, b, m, t, CD in level), power switch, RCA cd input, headphone jack, line out, effects loop, tilt back cabinet design, black Tolex covering, black cloth grille with white trim, 27 lbs., mfg. 2011-2014.

	$100	$60 - 75	$35 - 45	$140

BA-108 SECOND VERSION – 20W, 1-8 in. custom Ampeg speaker, bass combo, solid-state chassis, single channel, front black control panel, two inputs (1/4 in., 1/8 in. auxillary), five black knobs (v, b, m, t, aux level), power switch, -15db switch, headphone jack, metal corners, black Tolex covering, black grille, 15mm poplar ply construction, 28 lbs., mfg. 2015-present.

MSR $140	$100	$65 - 75	$35 - 40	

BA-110 FIRST VERSION – 30W, 1-10 in. speaker, bass combo, solid-state chassis, single channel, top/rear black control panel, two inputs, four knobs (v, b, m, t), contour switch, power switch, RCA CD input, line out, headphone jack, tilt back cabinet design, black Tolex covering, black cloth grille with white trim, 15 in., 16 in. tall, 12 in. deep, 32 lbs., mfg. 2001-03.

	N/A	$150 - 200	$95 - 120	$379

BA-110 SECOND VERSION – 35W, 1-10 in. speaker, bass combo, solid-state chassis, single channel, top/rear black control panel, two inputs, five knobs (v, b, m, t, CD in level), power switch, RCA cd input, headphone jack, line out, effects loop, tilt back cabinet design, black Tolex covering, black cloth grille with white trim, 32 lbs., mfg. 2011-2014.

	$180	$100 - 135	$60 - 75	$252

BA-110 THIRD VERSION – 40W, 1-10 in. custom Ampeg speaker, bass combo, solid-state chassis, two channels, front black control panel, two inputs (1/4 in., 1/8 in. auxillary), seven black knobs (drive, blend, v, b, m, t, aux level), power switch, -15db switch, headphone jack, metal corners, black Tolex covering, black grille, 15mm poplar ply construction, 34 lbs., mfg. 2015-present.

MSR $252	$180	$115 - 135	$60 - 70	

| MSR/NOTES | 100% | EXCELLENT | AVERAGE | LAST MSR |

BA-112 First Version
courtesy Ampeg

BA-112 Second Version
courtesy Ampeg

BA-115 Second Version
courtesy Ampeg

BA-112 FIRST VERSION – 50W, 1-12 in. speaker, bass combo, solid-state chassis, single channel, top/rear black control panel, two inputs, five knobs (v, five-position style selector, b, ultra mid, t), power switch, RCA cd input, headphone jack, line out, tilt back cabinet design, black Tolex covering, black cloth grille with white trim, 17.25 in., 18 in. tall, 13 in. deep, 39 lbs., mfg. 1999-2014.

| | $280 | $175 - 225 | $110 - 140 | $392 |

- **Add 10% for Anniversary Model Limited Edition appointments (offered in 2001 only).**

BA-112 SECOND VERSION – 75W, 1-12 in. custom Ampeg speaker, bass combo, solid-state chassis, two channels, front black control panel, two inputs (1/4 in., 1/8 in. auxillary), seven black knobs (drive, blend, v, b, m, t, aux level), power switch, -15db switch, ultra hi switch, ultra lo switch, headphone jack, footswitch jack, external speaker out, metal corners, black Tolex covering, black grille, 15mm poplar ply construction, 42 lbs., mfg. 2015-present.

| MSR $420 | $300 | $195 - 225 | $100 - 120 | |

BA-115 FIRST VERSION – 100W, 1-15 in. speaker with a high-freq. tweeter, bass combo, solid-state chassis, single channel, top/rear black control panel, two inputs, six knobs (g, MV, five-position style selector, b, ultra mid, t), power switch, RCA cd input, headphone jack, XLR line out, tilt back cabinet design, black Tolex covering, black cloth grille with white trim, 21 in., 21 in. tall, 16 in. deep, 62 lbs., mfg. 1999-2014.

| | $380 | $225 - 275 | $140 - 175 | $532 |

* *BA-115T* – similar to the BA-115, except has a single 12AU7 preamp tube, mfg. 2006-08.

| | N/A | $300 - 350 | $175 - 225 | $700 |

BA-115 SECOND VERSION – 150W, 1-15 in. custom Ampeg speaker and a 1 in. HF tweeter, bass combo, solid-state chassis, two channels, front black control panel, two inputs (1/4 in., 1/8 in. auxillary), seven black knobs (drive, blend, v, b, m, t, aux level), mute switch, power switch, -15db switch, ultra hi switch, ultra lo switch, headphone jack, XLR line out, footswitch jack, effects return jack, effects send jack, metal corners, black Tolex covering, black grille, 15mm poplar ply construction, 45 lbs., mfg. 2015-present.

| MSR $560 | $400 | $260 - 300 | $130 - 160 | |

BA-115HP – 220W, 1-15 in. custom Eminence LF driver and a 1 in. compression driver, bass combo, solid-state chassis, single channel, top/rear black control panel, two inputs, six black knobs (g, five-position style selector, l, m, h, MV), mute switch, power switch, RCA CD input, digital tuner, headphone jack, XLR line out, HF level control (back panel), removable casters, black Tolex covering, black cloth grille with white trim, 21 in. wide, 21 in. tall, 15.5 in. deep, 80 lbs., mfg. 2004-2014.

| | $500 | $300 - 350 | $175 - 225 | $650 |

* *BA-115HPT* – similar to the BA-115HP, except has a single 12AU7 preamp tube, mfg. 2006-08.

| | N/A | $400 - 475 | $250 - 300 | $952 |

BA-115SP – 100W, 1-15 in. speaker with a high freq. tweeter, bass combo, solid-state chassis, 16 digital effects, single channel, top/rear black control panel, two inputs, nine black knobs (v, five-position style selector, l, m, h, level, Effects: select, adjust, level), power switch, RCA CD input, headphone jack, footswitch jack, XLR line out, tilt back cabinet design, black Tolex covering, black cloth grille with white trim, 21 in. wide, 21 in. tall, 15.5 in. deep, 62 lbs., mfg. 2001-03.

| | N/A | $325 - 400 | $200 - 250 | $789 |

BA-210 FIRST VERSION – 220W, 2-10 in. custom Ampeg speakers and a 1 in. compression driver, bass combo, solid-state chassis, single channel, top/rear black control panel, two inputs, six black knobs (g, five-position style selector, l, m, h, MV), mute switch, power switch, RCA CD input, digital tuner, headphone jack, XLR line out, HF level control (back panel), removable casters, black Tolex covering, black cloth grille with white trim, 21 in. wide, 21 in. tall, 15.5 in. deep, 86 lbs., mfg. 2004-06.

| | N/A | $450 - 525 | $275 - 325 | $999 |

MSR/NOTES	100%	EXCELLENT	AVERAGE	LAST MSR

BA-210 Second Version
courtesy Ampeg

BA300-115
courtesy Ampeg

BA600-115
courtesy Ampeg

BA-210 SECOND VERSION – 450W, 2-10 in. custom Ampeg speakers and a 1 in. HF tweeter, bass combo, solid-state chassis, two channels, front black control panel, two inputs (1/4 in., 1/8 in. auxillary), seven black knobs (drive, blend, v, b, m, t, aux level), mute switch, power switch, -15db switch, ultra hi switch, ultra lo switch, headphone jack, XLR line out, footswitch jack, effects return jack, effects send jack, external speaker out (back panel), metal corners, black Tolex covering, black grille, 15mm poplar ply construction, 48 lbs., mfg. 2015-present.

MSR $700	$500	$325 - 375	$165 - 200	

BA-210SP – 200W (2001-03) or 220W (2004-08), 2-10 in. speakers with a high freq. tweeter, bass combo, solid-state chassis, 16 digital effects, single channel, top/rear black control panel, two inputs, nine black knobs (v, five-position style selector, l, m, h, level, Effects: select, adjust, level), power switch, RCA CD input, headphone jack, footswitch jack, XLR line out, tilt back cabinet design, black Tolex covering, black cloth grille with white trim, 21 in. wide, 21 in. tall, 15.5 in. deep, 76 lbs., mfg. 2001-2008.

	N/A	$425 - 500	$275 - 325	$980

BA300-115 – 300W, 1-15 in. speaker and a 1 in. horn, bass combo, hybrid chassis with a single 12AU7 preamp tube, single channel, top/rear black control panel, two inputs, seven knobs (compression threshold, v, five-position style selector, b, m, t, MV), mute switch, compression on/off switch, ultra hi switch, ultra lo switch, power switch, rear panel: effects loop, 1/4 in. unbalanced line out, XLR balanced line out, line out level control and pre/post EQ and ground/lift switches, tuner out jack, horn level control, removable casters, black covering, dark gray grille with white trim, 21.25 in. wide, 21.5 in. tall, 16 in. deep, 60 lbs., mfg. 2007-2010.

	N/A	$400 - 475	$250 - 300	$910

* **BA300-210** – similar to the BA-300 115, except has 2-10 in. speakers, 65 lbs., mfg. 2007-2010.

	N/A	$475 - 550	$300 - 350	$1,050

BA500 – 500W @ 2 ohms (350W @ 4 ohms), 2-10 in. speakers with a 1 in. compression driver horn, bass combo, solid-state chassis, single channel, front black control panel, single input, five black knobs (g, b, ultra mid, t, MV), nine-band graphic EQ, mute switch, input pad switch, limit switch, graphic EQ on/off switch, power switch, single Speakon and two 1/4 in. speaker jacks, footswitch jack, tuner out, power amp in, preamp in out, effects loop, XLR balanced line out with -20dB/0dB and pre/post EG switches, ported cabinet with tilt-back design, recessed side handles, black covering, black grille with white piping, 24 in. wide, 23.5 in. tall, 17.25 in. deep, 95 lbs., mfg. 2004-2007.

	N/A	$575 - 675	$325 - 400	$1,300

BA600-115 – 600W, 1-15 in. speaker and a 1 in. horn, bass combo, hybrid chassis with 1 X 12AU7 and 1 X 12AX7 preamp tubes, two channels (Vintage and Modern), top/rear black control panel, two inputs, nine knobs (compression threshold, Vintage Ch.: v, t, b, Modern Ch.:, g, b, m, t, MV), channel select switch, mute switch, compression on/off switch, ultra hi switch, ultra lo switch, power switch, rear panel: effects loop, 1/4 in. unbalanced line out, XLR balanced line out, line out level control and pre/post EQ and ground/lift switches, tuner out jack, footswitch jack, horn level control, removable casters, black covering, dark gray grille with white trim, 23 in. wide, 21 in. tall, 15.25 in. deep, 50 lbs., mfg. 2007-2010.

	N/A	$525 - 600	$300 - 375	$1,190

* **BA600-210** – similar to the BA600-115, except has 2-10 in. speakers, 55 lbs., mfg. 2007-2010.

	N/A	$600 - 700	$375 - 450	$1,330

ELECTRIC BASS SS AMPS: PORTABASS SERIES

Ampeg's Portbass Series were designed as a lightweight, portable option for bass guitarists who dislike the task of moving heavy equipment wherever they play. The Portabass Series also featured an MDT power amp that stands for Micro Dynamic Technology.

PORTABASS 228 COMBO (PBC-228) – 200W @ 4 ohms, 2-8 in. Eminence speakers, bass combo, solid-state chassis with MDT power amp, two channels, top/rear gray control panel, four inputs (two normal and two padded), 12 black knobs (Ch. 1: g, l, l/m, h/m, h, Ch. 2: g, l, l/m, h/m, h, All: effects blend, MV), two ultra low switches and two ultra high switches (one each per channel), power switch, rear panel: line out jack, effects loop, transformer XLR balanced line out with level control and pre/post EQ and ground/lift switches, black covering, dark gray metal grille, 16 in. wide, 16 in. tall, 10 in. deep, 35 lbs., mfg. 2004-2006.

	N/A	$325 - 375	$160 - 195	$849

MSR/NOTES	100%	EXCELLENT	AVERAGE	LAST MSR

Portabass 228 Combo (PBC-228)
courtesy Ampeg

Portabass 800 Head (PB-800)
courtesy Ampeg

Portabass 212H Speaker Cabinet (PB-212H)
courtesy Ampeg

PORTABASS 250 HEAD (PB-250) – 250W @ 4 ohms (150W @ 8 ohms), bass head-unit, solid-state chassis with MDT power amp, single channel, front gray control panel, two inputs (normal and padded), seven black knobs (gain, l, l/m, h/m, h, effects blend, MV), ultra low switch, low/mid shift switch, high/mid shift switch, ultra high switch, rear panel: one Speakon and one 1/4 in. speaker jacks, line out jack, effects loop, transformer XLR balanced line out with level control and pre/post EQ and ground/lift switches, silver casing, 12.5 in. wide, 3.75 in. tall, 10.5 in. deep, 14 lbs., mfg. 2002-05.

	N/A	$350 - 400	$170 - 210	$899

* Add $40 for padded gig bag.

PORTABASS 800 HEAD (PB-800) – 800W @ 2 ohms (550W @ 4 ohms, 300W @ 2 ohms), bass head-unit, solid-state chassis with MDT power amp, two channels, front gray control panel, four inputs (two normal and two padded), 12 black knobs (Ch. 1: g, l, l/m, h/m, h, Ch. 2: g, l, l/m, h/m, h, All: effects blend, MV), two ultra low switches and two ultra high switches (one each per channel), power switch, rear panel: two Speakon and two 1/4 in. speaker jacks, line out jack, effects loop, transformer XLR balanced line out with level control and pre/post EQ and ground/lift switches, silver casing, 15 in. wide, 3.75 in. tall, 12 in. deep, 20 lbs., mfg. 2003-06.

	N/A	$600 - 700	$300 - 375	$1,599

* Add $50 for padded gigbag.

PORTABASS 2210 COMBO (PBC-2210) – 250W @ 4 ohms, 2-10 in. speakers and a 1 in. compression driver horn, bass combo, solid-state chassis with MDT power amp, single channel, front gray control panel, two inputs (normal and padded), seven black knobs (gain, l, l/m, h/m, h, effects blend, MV), ultra low switch, low/mid shift switch, high/mid shift switch, ultra high switch, rear panel: line out jack, effects loop, transformer XLR balanced line out with level control and pre/post EQ and ground/lift switches, high freq. volume level control, removable telescoping handle, black covering, dark gray metal grille, 17 in. wide, 26 in. tall, 13.75 in. deep, 53 lbs., mfg. 2002-05.

	N/A	$550 - 650	$275 - 350	$1,499

* Add $70 for padded slip cover.

PORTABASS 110H SPEAKER CABINET (PB-110H) – 300W, 1-10 in. Neo driver, 1 horn, 4 ohm impedance, variable L-Pad control, black covering, gray metal grille, 20 lbs., mfg. 2002-04.

	N/A	$215 - 250	$105 - 130	$569

* Add $40 for padded slip cover.

PORTABASS 112H SPEAKER CABINET (PB-112H) – 300W, 1-12 in. Neo driver, 1 horn, 4 ohm impedance, variable L-Pad control, removable Dolly-style handle with wheels, black covering, gray metal grille, 24 lbs., mfg. 2002-04.

	N/A	$235 - 275	$115 - 145	$649

* Add $50 for padded slip cover.

PORTABASS 210H SPEAKER CABINET (PB-210H) – 600W, 2-10 in. Neo drivers, 1 horn, 4 ohm impedance, variable L-Pad control, removable telescoping Dolly-style handle with wheels, black carpet covering, gray metal grille, 32 lbs., mfg. 2002-06.

	N/A	$500 - 575	$245 - 300	$799

* Add $60 for padded slip cover.

PORTABASS 212H SPEAKER CABINET (PB-212H) – 600W, 2-12 in. Neo drivers, 1 horn, 4 ohm impedance, variable L-Pad control, removable telescoping Dolly-style handle with wheels, black carpet covering, gray metal grille, 38 lbs., mfg. 2003-06.

	N/A	$325 - 375	$160 - 195	$899

* Add $70 for padded slip cover.

PREAMPS/POWER AMPS

As rack systems became more popular in the 1980s, Ampeg began offering components for their amplifiers. Most of their preamps and power amps are simply one component of a regular model, but they also offered original models such as the AP3550 and AP6500. Although some of these preamps and power amps were part of other series, they are listed in their own section to eliminate confusion. Ampeg also produced a preamp called the **SVT-4** that put out 1600W and featured tubes.

| MSR/NOTES | 100% | EXCELLENT | AVERAGE | LAST MSR |

SVP-CL Preamp
courtesy Ampeg

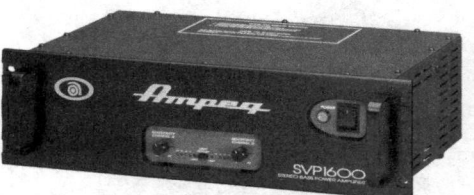

SVP-1600 Power Amp
courtesy Ampeg

AP3550 POWER AMP – 350W, power amp only, two-space rack-mount head-unit, solid-state chassis, front black control panel, two knobs (v, p), power switch, rear panel: polarity switch, convenience outlet, two 1/4 in. speaker jacks and a pair of red/black speaker wire connections, two inputs, black casing, mfg. 1992-93.

N/A $275 - 325 $150 - 200

AP6500 POWER AMP – 1300W mono (650W per side stereo), stereo power amp only, two-space rack-mount head-unit, solid-state chassis, front black control panel, four knobs (Ch. 1: v, p, Ch. 2: v, p), power switch, rear panel: polarity switch, convenience outlet, two 1/4 in. speaker jacks and a pair of red/black speaker wire connections, two inputs, black casing, mfg. 1992-95.

N/A $425 - 500 $300 - 350

SVP-BSP PREAMP – preamp only, single-space bass rack-mount head-unit, single 12AX7 preamp tube, two channels, front black and gray control panel, single input, 12 knobs (Clean: g, bass with push/pull low boost, mid, treble with push/pull high boost, volume push/pull compression, OD: gain with push/pull boost, b, m, mid-range freq., t, v with push/pull gate, MV), input pad switch, mute switch, channel select switch, combine switch, power switch, rear panel: footswitch jack, two preamp out jacks (OD, Clean/Mix), two effects loop (one per channel), two XLR balanced line outs with level controls (one per channel), tuner out jack, black casing, 19 in. wide, 1.75 in. tall, 10 in. deep, 10 lbs., mfg. 1999-2005.

N/A $300 - 375 $200 - 250 $699

SVP-CL PREAMP – preamp only, single-space bass rack-mount head-unit, four-tube chassis: 2 X 12AX7, 2 X 12AU7, single channel, front black and gray control panel, single input, seven black knobs (g, five-position ultra low, b, m, five-position mid-range freq. selector, t, MV), input pad switch, mute switch, ultra high switch, bright switch, power switch, rear panel: footswitch jack, two preamp out jacks, XLR transformer balanced line out with pre/post and ground/lift switches, tuner out, black casing, 19 in. wide, 1.75 in. tall, 10 in. deep, 7 lbs., mfg. 2004-06.

N/A $325 - 375 $200 - 250 $699

SVP-PRO PREAMP – preamp only, single-space rack-mount head-unit, five-tube chassis, preamp: 5 X 12AX7, single channel, front black control panel (1994-99) or black and gray control panel (1999-2006), single input, seven knobs (g, drive, b, m, five-position mid-range freq. selector, t, MV), nine-band graphic equalizer with level slider control, input pad switch, mute switch, ultra lo switch, bright switch, ultra hi switch, graphic EQ on/off switch, power switch, rear panel: footswitch jack, two preamp out jacks, effects loop, tuner out jack, XLR balanced line out with pre/post EQ switch, black casing, 19 in. wide, 1.75 in. tall, 10 in. deep, 9 lbs., mfg. 1994-2006.

N/A $325 - 375 $200 - 250 $699

SVP-1500 POWER AMP – 560W @ 16 ohms mono (960W @ 8 ohms mono, 1560W @ 4 ohms mono, 2 X 780 @ 2 ohms stereo, 2 X 480W @ 4 ohms stereo, or 2 X 280W @ 8 ohms stereo), three-space rackmount head, bass power amp, MOSFET chassis, two channels (A & B), front black control panel, power switch, reset button, 1/4 in. balanced inputs and blind post outputs, black casing, 19 in. wide, 5.25 in. tall, 12.5 in. deep, 33 lbs., mfg. 1996-98.

N/A $425 - 500 $250 - 300 $949

SVP-1600 POWER AMP – 900W @ 8 ohms (1200W @ 4 ohms mono, 2 X 600 @ 2 ohms), three-space rack-mount head-unit, bass power amp, MOSFET chassis, two channels, front black control panel, two black knobs (Ch. A v, Ch. B v), limiter button, power switch, rear panel: convenience outlet, three Speakon jacks (Ch. A, Ch. B, mono/bridged), four 1/4 in. speaker jacks, stereo/mono switch, power amp A and B inputs and outputs, black casing, 19 in. wide, 5.75 in. tall, 10 in. deep, 39 lbs., mfg. 2004-06.

N/A $625 - 725 $375 - 450 $1,399

The SVP-1600 utilizes the power section out of the SVT-4Pro.

SVT-IIP PREAMP – preamp only, one-space rack-mount head-unit, hybrid chassis with a tube preamp, single channel, front black control panel, two inputs (normal and bright), five knobs (v, b, m, five-position mid-range freq. selector, t), six-band graphic EQ with level slider control, ultra low switch, balance line out switch, ultra high switch, graphic EQ switch, footswitch jack, power switch, black casing, mfg. 1991-95.

N/A $250 - 300 $135 - 175

SVT-300 POWER AMP – 300W, power amp only, similar to the SVT original with 6 X 6550 power tubes, mfg. 1991-95.

N/A $750 - 900 $600 - 675

This amp was designed to be mated with the SVT-IIP preamp to create a complete rack system.

MSR/NOTES	100%	EXCELLENT	AVERAGE	LAST MSR

SPEAKER CABINETS: PRO NEO SERIES

Pro Neo PN-115HLF Speaker Cabinet
courtesy Ampeg

Pro Neo PN-210HLF Speaker Cabinet
courtesy Ampeg

Pro Neo PN-410HLF Speaker Cabinet
courtesy Ampeg

PRO NEO PN-115HLF SPEAKER CABINET – 575W @ 8 ohms, 1-15 in. U.S.-built Eminence LF driver and a 1 in. Eminence APT:50 HF driver with L-Pad level control, 15mm birch construction, bottom ported, side-mounted recessed handles, black paint and splatter covering, black metal grille with white trim, Ampeg badge logo in upper left-hand corner, and Pro Neo logo in lower right-hand corner, 59 lbs., mfg. 2010-present.

| MSR $1,232 | $875 | $575 - 650 | $285 - 350 | |

PRO NEO PN-210HLF SPEAKER CABINET – 550W @ 8 ohms, 2-10 in. U.S.-built Eminence LF drivers and a 1 in. Eminence APT:50 HF driver with L-Pad level control, 15mm birch construction, bottom ported, top handle, black paint and splatter covering, black metal grille with white trim, Ampeg badge logo in upper left-hand corner, and Pro Neo logo in lower right-handcorner, 44 lbs., mfg. 2010-present.

| MSR $1,232 | $875 | $575 - 650 | $285 - 350 | |

PRO NEO PN-410HLF SPEAKER CABINET – 850W @ 8 ohms, 2-10 in. U.S.-built Eminence LF drivers and a 1 in. Eminence APT:50 HF driver with L-Pad level control, 15mm birch construction, bottom ported, side-mounted recessed handles, black paint and splatter covering, black metal grille with white trim, Ampeg badge logo in upper left-hand corner, and Pro Neo logo in lower right-hand corner, 64 lbs., mfg. 2010-present.

| MSR $1,750 | $1,250 | $800 - 925 | $400 - 500 | |

SPEAKER CABINETS: SVT SERIES

SVT-12HE Speaker Cabinet
courtesy Ampeg

SVT-15E Speaker Cabinet
courtesy Ampeg

SVT-18 Speaker Cabinet
courtesy Ampeg

SVT-12HE SPEAKER CABINET – 300W, 1-12 in. speaker with a 1 in. horn/driver, 8 ohm impedance, variable "L" pad, baltic birch plywood construction, black vinyl covering, black grille with Classic logo in lower right corner, side handles, 46 lbs., mfg. 2006 only.

| | N/A | $275 - 325 | $150 - 200 | $599 |

SVT-15E SPEAKER CABINET – 200W, 1-15 in. speaker, 8 ohm impedance, baltic birch plywood construction, 2 in. swivel casters, black vinyl covering, black grille with Classic logo in lower right corner, side handles, 72 lbs., current mfg.

| MSR $742 | $525 | $350 - 400 | $170 - 210 | |

SVT-18 SPEAKER CABINET – 500W, 1-18 in. speaker, 4 ohm impedance, baltic birch plywood construction, 2 in. swivel casters, black vinyl covering, black grille with Classic logo in lower right corner, side handles, 86 lbs., mfg. 2003-06.

| | N/A | $400 - 475 | $250 - 300 | $899 |

SVT-18E SPEAKER CABINET – 200W, 1-18 in. speaker, 8 ohm impedance, baltic birch plywood construction, 2 in. removable swivel casters, bottom ported, black vinyl covering, black grille with Classic logo in lower right corner, side handles, 85 lbs., mfg. 1986-1998.

| | N/A | $250 - 300 | $150 - 200 | $599 |

MSR/NOTES	100%	EXCELLENT	AVERAGE	LAST MSR

SVT-112AV Speaker Cabinet
courtesy Ampeg

SVT-212AV Speaker Cabinet
courtesy Ampeg

SVT-410HE Speaker Cabinet
courtesy Ampeg

SVT-48HE SPEAKER CABINET – 200W @ 8 ohms stereo or 400W @ 4 ohms mono, 4-8 in. speakers, 8 ohm impedance, switchable high-freq. level, baltic birch plywood construction, 2 in. removable swivel casters, black vinyl covering, black grille with Classic logo in lower right corner, 70 lbs., disc. 1998.

	N/A	$250 - 300	$150 - 200	$499

SVT-112AV SPEAKER CABINET – 300W @ 8 ohms, 1-12 in. speaker custom Eminence LF driver, black vinyl covering, blue/gray grille with Ampeg badge in upper left hand corner, recessed side handles, 24 in. wide, 17 in. tall, 16 in. deep, 45 lbs., mfg. 2013-present.

MSR $700	$500	$325 - 375	$165 - 200	

SVT-210AV SPEAKER CABINET – 200W @ 8 ohms, 2-10 in. speakers custom Eminence LF drivers, black vinyl covering, black and silver vintage-style grille with Ampeg badge in upper right hand corner, designed for use with Micro-VR Head, 13 in. wide, 24 in. tall, 11 in. deep, 26 lbs., mfg. 2008-present.

MSR $420	$300	$175 - 225	$110 - 140	

SVT-210HE SPEAKER CABINET – 200W, 2-10 in. speakers with a 1 in. horn/driver, 8 ohm impedance, variable "L" pad, baltic birch plywood construction, black vinyl covering, black grille with Classic logo in lower right corner, side handles, 60 lbs., disc. 2006.

	N/A	$275 - 325	$150 - 200	$599

SVT-212AV SPEAKER CABINET – 600W @ 4 ohms, 2-12 in. speakers custom Eminence LF drivers, black vinyl covering, blue/gray grille with Ampeg badge in upper left hand corner, recessed side handles, 24 in. wide, 25 in. tall, 16 in. deep, 66 lbs., mfg. 2013-present.

MSR $979	$700	$450 - 525	$230 - 280	

SVT-215E SPEAKER CABINET – 400W, 2-15 in. speakers, 4 ohm impedance, 3 in. swivel casters, baltic birch plywood construction, tilt-back handle bar, black vinyl covering, black grille with Classic logo in lower right corner, 148 lbs., disc. 2006.

	N/A	$575 - 675	$350 - 425	$1,299

SVT-410AV SPEAKER CABINET – 500W, 4-10 in. speakers with a 1 in. horn/driver, 8 ohm impedance, variable "L" pad, baltic birch plywood construction, 2 in. swivel casters, black vinyl covering, black and silver vintage-style grille, side handles, 91 lbs., mfg. 1999-2000.

	N/A	$375 - 450	$225 - 275	

SVT-410E SPEAKER CABINET – 175W, 4-10 in. speakers, 8 ohm impedance, cabinet is split into two separate compartments with two speakers in each compartment, two inputs, baltic birch plywood construction, 2 in. swivel casters, black vinyl covering, black grille, recessed side handles, 69 lbs., mfg. 1986-disc.

	N/A	$250 - 300	$135 - 175	

SVT-410HE SPEAKER CABINET – 500W, 4-10 in. speakers with a 1 in. horn/driver, 8 ohm impedance, variable "L" pad, baltic birch plywood construction, 2 in. swivel casters, black vinyl covering, black grille with Classic logo in lower right corner, side handles, 91 lbs., current mfg.

MSR $952	$675	$450 - 500	$220 - 270	

* *SVT-410HLF Speaker Cabinet* – similar to the SVT-410HE Speaker Cabinet, except is front ported, has 4 ohm impedance, and has 3 in. dolly-style casters, 110 lbs., current mfg.

MSR $1,120	$800	$525 - 600	$260 - 325	

SVT-412HE SPEAKER CABINET – 400W, 4-12 in. speakers with a 1 in. compression driver, 4 ohm impedance, variable "L" pad, baltic birch plywood construction, 2 in. swivel casters, black vinyl covering, black grille with Classic logo in lower right corner, side handles, 91 lbs., mfg. 2003-05.

	N/A	$450 - 525	$275 - 325	$999

MSR/NOTES	100%	EXCELLENT	AVERAGE		LAST MSR

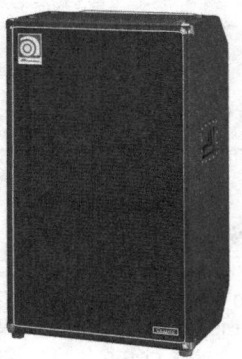
SVT-610HLF Speaker Cabinet
courtesy Ampeg

SVT-810E Speaker Cabinet
courtesy Ampeg

SVT-810AV Speaker Cabinet
courtesy Ampeg

SVT-610HLF SPEAKER CABINET – 600W, 6-10 in. speakers with a 1 in. horn/driver, 4 ohm impedance, variable "L" pad, front ported designed for low-end, baltic birch plywood construction, 3 in. dolly-style casters, black vinyl covering, black grille with Classic logo in lower right corner, side handles, 115 lbs., mfg. 2000-present.

MSR $1,400	$1,000	$625 - 725	$375 - 450		

SVT-806HE SPEAKER CABINET – 400W @ 8 ohms stereo or 800W @ 4 ohms mono, 8-6.5 in. speakers, 4 ohm impedance, infinite baffle design, baltic birch plywood construction, 2.5 in. dolly-style casters, tilt-back handle, protective skid rails, black vinyl covering, black grille with Classic logo in lower right corner, 85 lbs., disc. 1998.

	N/A	$325 - 400	$200 - 250		$649

SVT-808HE SPEAKER CABINET – 600W @ 8 ohms stereo or 1200W @ 4 ohms mono, 8-8 in. speakers, 4 ohm impedance, baltic birch plywood construction, 3 in. dolly-style casters, tilt-back handle, protective skid rails, black vinyl covering, black grille with Classic logo in lower right corner, 130 lbs., disc. 1998.

	N/A	$500 - 600	$300 - 375		$999

SVT-810E SPEAKER CABINET – 400W @ 8 ohms stereo or 800W @ 4 ohms mono, 8-10 in. speakers, 4 or 8 ohm impedance, baltic birch plywood construction, 3 in. dolly-style casters, tilt-back handle, protective skid rails, black vinyl covering, black grille with Classic logo in lower right corner, 165 lbs., mfg. 1986-present.

MSR $1,400	$1,000	$625 - 725	$375 - 450		

* **Add 10% for Limited Edition models with Blue, Red, or White coverings (offered late 1990s only).**

SVT-810AV SPEAKER CABINET – 400W @ 8 ohms stereo or 800W @ 4 ohms mono, 8-10 in. speakers, 4 or 8 ohm impedance, baltic birch plywood construction, 3 in. dolly-style casters, tilt-back handle, protective skid rails, black vinyl covering, black and silver vintage-style grille, 165 lbs., mfg. 1999-present.

MSR $1,750	$1,250	$800 - 925	$400 - 500		

SVT-810HPC SPEAKER CABINET – 1500W, 8-10 in. speakers (6-10 in. regular speakers, 2-10 in. Tractrix wave-guide coaxial speakers), 1 in. horn, 4 or 8 ohm impedance, variable "L" pad, baltic birch plywood construction, black vinyl covering, black grille with a horizontal bar across the middle and "Ultra" logo in lower right corner, 205 lbs., mfg. 2002-05.

	N/A	$900 - 1,050	$600 - 700		$2,000

SVT-1510E SPEAKER CABINET – 175W, 1-15 in. and 1-10 in. speakers, 8 ohm impedance, cabinet is split into two separate compartments with one speaker in each compartment, two inputs, baltic birch plywood construction, 2 in. swivel casters, black vinyl covering, black grille, recessed side handles, 67 lbs., mfg. 1986-disc.

	N/A	$250 - 300	$135 - 175		

SVT-1540HE SPEAKER CABINET – 550W, 1-15 in. (lower) and 4-10 in. (upper) speakers, 1 in. horn/driver, 2 X 4 or 8 ohm impedance, variable high-freq. level, 3 in. swivel casters, baltic birch plywood construction, tilt-back handle bar, black vinyl covering, black grille with Classic logo in lower right corner, 153 lbs., disc. 2000.

	N/A	$650 - 750	$425 - 500		

AMP-U-PLUG-N-PLAY

Amplifiers currently produced overseas. Distributed by Amp-U-Plug-N-Play in Kissimmee, FL.

The Amp-U-Plug-N-Play is a mini-amp that plugs directly into the guitar jack (the 1/4 in. jack is part of the amp - there is no cord). Essentially, the amp becomes part of the guitar. It is small enough to fit in guitar cases, and runs on regular batteries. In 2010, they introduced an upgraded model with an MP3 input, headphone jack, and clean/overdrive switch, MSR is $29.95. For more information, visit their website or contact them directly.

ANDERSON AMPLIFIERS

Amplifiers and speaker cabinets currently built in Gig Harbor, WA since 1993. Distributed by Anderson Amplifiers.

CONTACT INFORMATION
ANDERSON AMPLIFIERS
13518 94th St. KPN
Gig Harbor, WA 98329
Phone No.: 253-857-5154
www.andersonamps.com
andersonamps@harbornet.com

Jack Anderson founded Anderson Amplifiers in 1993, and he builds custom tube amplifiers as head units and combos and also offers speaker cabinets. Anderson's amps are based on Marshall's classic designs of the 1960s and 1970s. All work is done in house, with the exception of bending the aluminum chassis. For more information, individual specs, or pricing information, visit Anderson Amplifiers' website or contact them directly.

ELECTRIC TUBE AMPS/SPEAKER CABINETS

Anderson offers several models that each come in several configurations. The **18 Watt Model** (head starts at $775) has EL84 power tubes and a rectifier tube. The **20 Watt Model** (head starts at $775) has 6V6 power tubes and a rectifier tube. The **45/50 Watt Model** (head starts at $875) has a choice of 6L6 or EL34 power tubes and a tube rectifier on the 45 Watt model. All four of the 18, 20, 45, and 50 Watt models have a choice of a single tone control or individual bass, mid, and treble controls. The **20/45 Watt Model** (head starts at $1,000) has a custom Pacific output transformer that can handle a variety of tubes and speaker impedance loads. The **100 Watt Model** (head starts at $1,025) has a choice of either 6L6 or EL34 power tubes and also has a choice of a single tone control or individual bass, mid, and treble controls. All amps are available in combo configurations as well with a variety of speaker options. Speaker cabinets start at $250 and are also available in a variety of speaker options. Anderson also offers a tremolo/reverb unit ($800).

ANIMAL, THE

Amplifiers previously produced in Korea during the mid-1990s. Distributed by Vega Music International (VMI).

Vega Music International (VMI) offered The Animal line of amplifiers for a short while during the 1990s. These small guitar amplifiers were available in guitar and bass configurations and are of all solid-state design. Models included **The Original** (AG 5), the **Dual Power** (AG-6), the **Dual Gain** (AG-20), and the **Bass Model** (AB-20). Used prices on these amps are typically between $25 and $50.

ARACOM AMPLIFIERS

Amplifiers currently produced in Morgan Hill, CA since 1996.

CONTACT INFORMATION
ARACOM AMPLIFIERS
Morgan Hill, CA
Phone No.: 408-778-9597
www.aracom-amps.com
info@aracom-amps.com

ARACOM Amplifiers was founded in 1996 by Jeff Aragaki in Northern California's Silicon Valley. Aragaki has a degree in electrical engineering, and prior to forming ARACOM, he held a number of key positions within high-tech companies, where he learned many aspects of the business including manufacturing techniques, customer service, management, sales, and marketing.

ARACOM Amplifiers is a small "boutique" amplifier company that specializes in "old school" handwired all-tube guitar amplifiers and high end power attenuators. Their amplifiers feature premium components that are hand soldered onto their custom designed turret boards, and are handwired into a special designed chassis using transformers custom wound to vintage specifications. All of this adds up to sonically rich and versatile amps.

ARACOM offers their Custom Series amplifiers that utilize both ARACOM and Marshall inspired designs that incorporate modern design features. They also offer their Tribute Series amplifiers that are essentially reproductions of Marshall's classics from the 1960s and early 1970s. Additionally, ARACOM offers their Power Rox PRX150 line of power attenuators that provide up to 40dB of attenuation, while maintaining a high level of transparency. All of ARACOM's guitar amplifier products are hand-built and hand soldered with components designed to their specifications and are offered in head or combo configuration. Extension speaker cabinets are also available. For more information, visit ARACOM's website or contact them directly.

ELECTRIC TUBE AMPS

Custom 45R
courtesy Aracom Amplifiers

Evolver 45 Head
courtesy Aracom Amplifiers

Vintage Rox VRX 22 Combo
courtesy Aracom Amplifiers

ARACOM offers two distinct series: the Custom Series that feature the Vintage Rox, Evolver, and Custom 45R amps, and the Tribute Series that include PLX BB 18 (Bluesbreaker), PLX 45, PLX 50, and MPL 50. The **Vintage Rox** is available in either 18W

(EL84 power tubes) or 22W (6V6 power tubes) variations and prices start at $895. The **Evolver** features Plexi/JTM tone with channel switching, a MV control bypass, built-in tube overdrive feature and is available in 45W or 50W variations with prices starting at $1,895. The **Custom 45R** has Marshall JTM45 tone with reverb, 45/22 watt switch, MV control, a bright switch, a bite switch, and prices start at $1,725.

The **PLX BB 18** is based on Marshall's 18W amp from 1967 called the Mini Bluesbreaker and is available in reverb and non-reverb versions with pricing starting at $1,345. The **PLX 45** is based on Marshall's JTM45 from the 1960s and prices start at $1,525. The **PLX 50** is based on Marshall's JTM50 from the late 1960s and prices start at $1,525. The **MPL 50** is based on Marshall's JMP amps from the late 1960s and early 1970s with prices starting at $1,525.

Additionally, ARACOM offers their **Power Rox, PRX150** line of power attenuators. The PRX150 is a power attenuator designed to be used with tube amplifiers and it allows guitarist to achieve the much desired "fully cranked up" tone from their tube amp, but at more practical volume levels. Utilizing its unique and innovative "Speaker Reactance Thru" (SRT) technology, the PRX150-Pro allows the speaker to fully maintain its natural reactance. As a result, the PRX150-Pro allows the amplifier's original, "cranked up" tone to be maintained at reduced volume levels, with prices starting at $660.

ARIA/ARIA PRO II

Amplifiers currently produced in Japan beginning in the late 1970s. Current instruments currently produced in the U.S., Japan, Korea, China, Indonesia, and Spain. Distributed in the U.S. by Dana B. Goods in Ventura, CA. Previously distributed by Hanser Music Group (previously HHI) in Hebron, KY and by Aria USA/NHF in Pennsauken, NJ.

CONTACT INFORMATION
ARIA/ARIA PRO II
U.S. Distributor: Dana B. Goods
4054 Transport St., Unit A
Ventura, CA 93003
Phone No.: 800-741-0109
www.danabgoods.com

Factory/Headquarters
www.ariaguitars.com

Aria is the trademark of the Arai Company of Japan, which began producing guitars in 1956. Prior to 1975, the trademark was either Aria, or Aria Diamond. Original designs in the 1960s gave way to a greater emphasis on replicas of American designs in the late 1970s. Ironically, the recognition of these well-produced replicas led to success in later years as the company returned to producing original designs. The Aria trademark has always reflected high production quality, and currently there has been more emphasis on stylish designs (such as the Fullerton guitar series, or in bass designs such as the AVB-SB).

The Aria company has produced instruments under their Aria/Aria Diamond/Aria Pro II trademark for a number of years. The first guitar amplifiers appeared on the market around 1979. Most amplifiers only had a run of a year or two and was replaced by a new series.

Note: Aria usually releases catalogs and price lists, but the two often don't coincide with one another, since distributors only offer certain items. Currently Aria's U.S. distributor does not offer any guitar amplifiers although they may be offered in other countries. The dates of production listed on the amplifiers in this section are based on their availability through distributors in the U.S.

ELECTRIC: AG SERIES

AG-20REC
courtesy Aria/Aria Pro II

AG-25RX
courtesy Aria/Aria Pro II

AG-30REC
courtesy Aria/Aria Pro II

AG-10X – 3W, 1-4 in. speaker, distortion, single input, four knobs, black covering, silver slat grille, disc. 2006.

$50	$25 - 35	$10 - 20	$70

AG-20REC – 10W, 1-8 in. speaker, two channels, red control panel, six knobs, EZ recording controls, two button footswitch, black covering, silver slat grille, disc. 2006.

$160	$100 - 125	$60 - 80	$220

AG-20X – 10W, 1-6 in. speaker, distortion, single input, five knobs, black covering, silver slat grille, mfg. 1989-2006.

$65	$40 - 50	$20 - 30	$90

This model was originally known as the AG-20.

MSR/NOTES	100%	EXCELLENT	AVERAGE	LAST MSR

AG-25X – 13W, 1-8 in. speaker, distortion, single input, five knobs, black covering, silver slat grille, disc. 2006.

	$95	$60 - 75	$35 - 45	$130

* AG-25RX – similar to the AG-25X, except has reverb (six overall knobs), disc. 2006.

	$120	$75 - 90	$40 - 55	$170

AG-30AT – 15W, 1-8 in. speaker, two channels, single input, seven knobs, digital tuner, black covering, silver slat grille, disc. 2006.

	$120	$75 - 90	$40 - 55	$170

AG-30REC – 15W, 1-8 in. speaker, two channels, red control panel, seven knobs, EZ recording controls, two button footswitch, black covering, silver slat grille, disc. 2006.

	$210	$130 - 160	$75 - 100	$296

AG-35RX – 17W, 1-10 in. speaker, two channels, reverb, single input, eight knobs, black covering, silver slat grille, mfg. 1989-2006.

	$170	$100 - 130	$60 - 80	$240

This model was originally known as the AG-35R.

ELECTRIC: AX SERIES

The AX Series looks to be the revamped and more expanded line after the MX series. These amps were introduced in 1983 and only lasted until 1984. Guitar amps included the AX-5, AX-15, AX-40, AX-60, and the AX-100. Bass amps included the AX-15B, AX-40B, AX-60B, and the AX-100B. Specs and pricing are still under research.

ELECTRIC: MX SERIES

The MX series is apparently the first series of amplifiers to come from Aria. The models that were available are the MX-60, the MX-100, the MX-100R, and the MXB-120 Bass Amp. These models debuted circa 1979 and were discontinued shortly thereafter in the early 1980s. Specs and pricing are still under research.

ELECTRIC BASS: AB SERIES

AB-25
courtesy Aria/Aria Pro II

AB-30
courtesy Aria/Aria Pro II

AB-50
courtesy Aria/Aria Pro II

AB-20 – 10W, 1-6 in. speaker, silver control panel, single input, four knobs, black covering, brown grille, disc. 2006.

	$79	$45 - 60	$25 - 40	$110

AB-25 – 13W, 1-8 in. speaker, silver control panel, single input, five knobs, black covering, brown grille, disc. 2006.

	$85	$50 - 65	$30 - 45	$120

AB-30 – 20W, 1-10 in. speaker, silver control panel, single input, seven knobs, black covering, brown grille, mfg. 1989-2006.

	$129	$80 - 100	$50 - 65	$180

AB-50 – 30W, 1-12 in. speaker, silver control panel, single input, seven knobs, black covering, brown grille, mfg. 1989-2006.

	$165	$95 - 125	$60 - 80	$230

ARK AMPS

Amplifiers currently produced in Farmington Hills, MI and Windsor, Ontario, Canada since 2005.

Ark Amps was started by Bill Compeau and Matt Schellenberg in 2005. Compeau is the co-artist designer and also co-designs the circuits (with amp wiz Randy Fay of Windsor) and Schellenberg is the main artist designer/CEO. All of Ark's amplifiers are housed in uniquely-styled high-grade wood cabinets that make them different

CONTACT INFORMATION
ARK AMPS
Farmington Hills, MI
Phone No.: 519-979-0951
kinaxis@hotmail.com

than any other amp builder out there. The cabinets are constructed in Michigan and the chassis/electronics are assembled in Canada. For more information, visit Ark's website or contact them directly.

ELECTRIC TUBE AMPLIFIERS

Ark offers a variety of amps and configurations but just about everything starts with a base model. All models are in piggyback configuration with a head and separate speaker cabinet and the base price listed is just for the head. The **Aviator** (base price $4,000) is Ark's most traditional amplifier with a mainly rectangular head shape, it is a 50 watt master volume into 2 EL34's design. The **Model A** (base price is $4,750) is the first of Ark's organic looking amplifiers and it features the same circuitry as the Aviator. The **Model A-28** (base price is $3,250) is the baby brother of the Model A with a smaller power section driven by a pair of 6V6 tubes. The Model **B-20** (base price is $2,950) is Ark's first non-master volume amp and has a simple three knob control panel. The Model **C-15** (base price is $2,950) has 15W output (max) that uses 6L6, 6V6 or EL34 power tubes. The Model **D-24** (base price is $3,250) is a 6V6 powered fixed bias model that produces a variety of tones. The **Rhino** is a 70W all-tube bass amp, and it has a matching and unique "resonant" 300 watt 1x12 ported cab. Speaker cabinets price around $1,750 each.

Aviator Head
courtesy Ark Amps

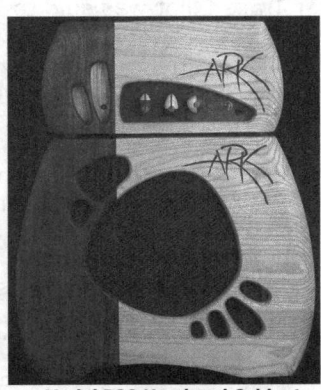

Model B20 Head and Cabinet
courtesy Ark Amps

Rhino Head and Cabinet
courtesy Ark Amps

ARMSTRONG AMPLIFICATION

Amplifiers currently produced in Windsor, Ontario, Canada since 2010.

CONTACT INFORMATION
ARMSTRONG AMPLIFICATION
Phone No.: 519-979-0951
kinaxis@hotmail.com

Bill Compeau, who is also the co-founder of Ark Amplifiers, started Armstrong Amplification in 2010 that builds guitar amplifiers geared toward the working man's budget. Using the same ultra high quality components and true "hi-fi" level point to point construction that Compeau uses with Ark, Armstrong Amps satisfies the desire for ultra high quality guitar tone in a more traditional rectangle box head shell. Compeau's own distinctive visual style and love for famous war planes helps to set these amps apart in this now very crowded boutique market. Two-channel foot-switchable models (hardware based switching-without relay switches) and transparent tube effects loops are offered as well to satisfy the gigging guitarists need for more versatility in a live situation. According to Compeau, it is only because they now have their new ultra transparent tube effects loop and hardware based (non-relay switch) channel switching system, that they have decided to start offering these very popular features themselves since there is now no compromise to the high sound quality that their reputation is built on. Armstrong's first model is the **P-51** and is a 50W amp with KT77 power tubes and no master volume. The amp retails for $1,299 and a $500 down payment is required to start a new build. For more information, contact Compeau directly.

ART

Applied Research and Technology. Amplifiers and professional audio signal processing equipment currently produced in China and in Rochester, NY. Distributed by The Yorkville Group in Rochester, NY. The A.R.T. trademark was established in 1984.

CONTACT INFORMATION
ART
Yorkville Sound USA
Distributed by The Yorkville Group
4625 Witmer Industrial Estate
Niagra Falls, NY 14305 USA
Phone No.: 716-297-2920
Fax No.: 716-297-3689
www.artproaudio.com
support@artproaudio.com

ART was created in 1984 by former employees of the original MXR innovations, and they started with pro audio processing poducts. In 1996, ART released the Tube MP Microphone Preamp, which set a new standard in this field. During the mid-1990s, ART produced the Attack and DST series. The Attack Series were basic guitar amps with "Quad-S" special effects. The DST Series were some of the first modeling amplifiers to appear on the market. Currently, ART produces a full line of audio equipment including rack-mounted equalizers, reverb units, tube processors, microphone preamps, and other audio products. Artists such as Robben Ford and Eric Johnson have used these effects and processors over the years. For more information, visit ART's website or contact them directly.

MSR/NOTES	100%	EXCELLENT	AVERAGE	LAST MSR

ASHDOWN ENGINEERING

Amplifiers currently produced in Essex, England and China (All Access Series) since 1997. Distributed in the U.S. by Korg USA in Melville, NY since mid-2013. Previously distributed in the U.S. by Musiquip, Inc. in Dorval, Quebec, Canada between mid-2011 and mid-2013, Power Group Ltd. in Mississauga, Ontario, Canada, the Musical Distributors Group of Boonton, NJ, EMD Music in Lavergne, TN, and in North and South America by HHB Communications in Los Angeles, CA and Toronto, Ontario Canada.

CONTACT INFORMATION
ASHDOWN ENGINEERING
Ashdown Design & Marketing Ltd
The Old Maltings, Hall Road, Heybridge,
Maldon
Essex, CM9 4NJ United Kingdom
Phone No.: 01621 858800
Fax No.: 01621 857200
www.ashdownmusic.co.uk
sales@hhbusa.com

U.S. Distributor: Korg USA
316 S. Service Road
Melville, NY 11747
Phone No.: 631-390-6800
www.korg.com

Ashdown Engineering is a relatively young company with an array of models ranging from acoustic amps to bass amps. Mark Gooday was the managing director of Trace Elliot back in the mid-1980s. After Trace Elliot was sold to Kaman Music in 1992, he worked for Kaman for the next five years on a contract. After his tenure at Kaman and Trace Elliot, Mark left the company in 1997. He took the skills and knowledge he had, and decided to develop a bass amp that brought back real tone and style. Mark worked with old friends and started up his new company, which he called Ashdown after his wife's family name. The first amps made were named as Klystron Bass Magnifier from a movie. The Klystron name had to be dropped as another company of years ago had used it. Only 200 units were shipped with the Klystron name. After this, the Acoustic Radiator amps made their debut. Now Ashdown Engineering is a world-known amplifier maker and their company grows daily. Ashdown Amplifiers have a VU meter on almost every one of their models, which is almost unique to the company. In September, 2013, Korg USA became the U.S. distributor of Ashdown. For more information, visit Ashdown's website or contact them directly.

ACOUSTIC AMPLIFIERS: ACOUSTIC RADIATOR SERIES

Acoustic Radiator
courtesy Ashdown Engineering

Acoustic Radiator 2
courtesy Ashdown Engineering

Acoustic Reso 2
courtesy Ashdown Engineering

ACOUSTIC RADIATOR 1 (AAR-1V-R) – 60W, 1-8" driver speaker with dual tweeter array, solid-state combo, single channel, vertical control panel on right side of amp, one input, six cream knobs (output, reverb, notch frequency, t, b, input level), numerous buttons for acoustic effects, wood cabinet, black vinyl covering, basket weave grille, 13 lbs., mfg. 1999-disc.

$525	$325 - 400	$175 - 225	$750

- **Add 25% (MSR $980) for cherry wood covering.**
- **Add 10% for burgundy bookbound covering.**
- **Add 20% for cherry and walnut wood covering.**

This model is available in walnut, cherry, and burgundy bookbound wood coverings. A black vinyl and polished "Bakelite" finish is also available. The burgundy bookbound covering has a hinged mesh grille. Walnut and burgundy bookbound covering were both discontinued in 2002. Cherry Model is known as the AAR-1C-R.

* *Reso 1 (AAR-1RESO)* – similar to the Acoustic Radiator 1 except is finished in a classic, polished metal "Resonator" style cabinet, 14 lbs., mfg. 1999-2006.

$1,800	$1,250 - 1,450	$700 - 800	$2,699

ACOUSTIC RADIATOR 2 FIRST VERSION (AAR-2V) – 120W, 1-8 in.driver speaker with dual tweeter array and 1-8 in.bass radiator, solid-state combo, dual channels, reverb, top cream control panel, four inputs (Ch.1: active, piezo, Ch. 2: Low 1/4", XLR), 17 cream knobs (Ch. 1: input level, b, m, t, Ch. 2: input level, tube selector, b, m, t, Both: Mid Feedback Notch (F & Q), Low Feedback Notch (F & Q), reverb level for each channel, reverb type, output level), equlizer, VU meter, phase shifter, various other buttons, wood cabinet finish, basket weave grille, 34 lbs., mfg. 1999-2006.

$700	$425 - 500	$300 - 350	$980

- **Add 10% for burgundy bookbound covering.**
- **Add 20% for cherry or walnut wood covering.**

This model is available in walnut, cherry, burgundy bookbound, carbon fibre, polished "bakelite", and black vinyl. Walnut and burgundy bookbound covering were both discontinued in 2002. The Cherry Model is known as the AAR-2C.

MSR/NOTES	100%	EXCELLENT	AVERAGE	LAST MSR

* **Acoustic Radiator 2-12H** – similar to the Acoustic Radiator 2 except has 1-12" speaker with a high-frequency horn, mfg. 1999-2001.

	N/A	$500 - 600	$325 - 400	

* **Reso 2 (AAR-2RESO)** – similar to the Acoustic Radiator 2 except is finished in a classic, polished metal "Resonator" style cabinet, 35 lbs., mfg. 1999-2004.

	N/A	$850 - 1,000	$600 - 700	$1,999

ACOUSTIC RADIATOR 3 (AAR3-10) – 350W (bi-amped), 1-10 in. dual concentric speaker, acoustic combo, solid-state chassis, two channels, 16 digital reverb settings, front/side cream control panel, three inputs (Ch. 1 XLR and 1/4 in., Ch. 2 1/4 in.), 10 knobs (Ch. 1: level, b, t, Ch. 2: level, b, t, All: notch freq., reverb selector, reverb level, output level), phantom power in/out switch, clip switch, channel switch, notch freq. switch, rear panel: XLR balanced direct line out, line out & link jack, effects loop, reverb mute footswitch jack, wedge cabinet design that can be mounted on a stand, black covering, black metal grille, mfg. 2009-disc.

	$650	$425 - 500	$235 - 280	$930

* **Acoustic Radiator 3 (AAR3-12)** – similar to the Acoustic Radiator 3 (AAR3-10), except has 1-12 in. speaker, mfg. 2009-disc.

	$700	$450 - 550	$250 - 300	$1,000

ACOUSTIC AMPLIFIERS: WOODSMAN SERIES

Woodsman Classic Combo
courtesy Ashdown Engineering

Woodman Jumbo Combo
courtesy Ashdown Engineering

Woodman Perlour Combo
courtesy Ashdown Engineering

WOODSMAN CLASSIC COMBO – 40W, 1-8 in. speaker with tweeter, acoustic guitar combo, solid-state chassis, dual channels (mic, guitar), front cream control panel, four inputs, nine knobs (Mic.: v, tone, Instr.: v, b, t, All: freq., depth, reverb, MV), aux. input, XLR DI out, power switch, top handle, brown covering, brown grille, 16.10 lbs., mfg. 2015-present.

MSR $580	$400	$260 - 300	$130 - 160	

WOODSMAN JUMBO COMBO – 65W, 2-8 in. speakers with tweeter, acoustic guitar combo, solid-state chassis, dual channels (mic, guitar), front cream control panel, three inputs, ten knobs (Mic.: v, b, t, Aux.: level, Instr.: v, b, t, All: freq., reverb, MV), aux. input, XLR DI out, effect loop, power switch, top handle, brown covering, brown grille, 26.46 lbs., mfg. 2015-present.

MSR $740	$525	$350 - 400	$170 - 210	

WOODSMAN PARLOUR COMBO – 25W, 1-8 in. speaker, acoustic guitar combo, solid-state chassis, single channel, top cream control panel, two input, seven knobs (Mic.: v, Instr.: v, b, m, t, All: reverb, MV), aux. input, power switch, top handle, brown covering, brown grille, 9.37 lbs., mfg. 2015-present.

MSR $340	$250	$165 - 190	$80 - 100	

BASS AMPLIFIERS: AAA EVO SERIES

AAA-30-8 Combo
courtesy Ashdown Engineering

AAA-60-10T Combo
courtesy Ashdown Engineering

AAA-120-15T Combo
courtesy Ashdown Engineering

MSR/NOTES	100%	EXCELLENT	AVERAGE	LAST MSR

AAA-300-210T Combo
courtesy Ashdown Engineering

AAA-115T Speaker Cabinet
courtesy Ashdown Engineering

AAA-Tour Bus 10 Combo
courtesy Ashdown Engineering

AAA-30-8 COMBO – 30W, 1-8 in. speaker, bass combo, solid-state chassis, single channel, top black control panel, single input, five white knobs (v, b, m, t, aux. mix), AppTek jack, line in jack, headphone jack, power switch, speaker mute switch, AppTek cable and socket included, top handle, black covering, vintage red grille, 19.84 lbs., new 2016.

| MSR $204 | $150 | $100 - 115 | $50 - 60 | |

AAA-60-10T COMBO – 60W, 1-10 in. speaker, bass combo, solid-state chassis, single channel, top black control panel, two input (high, low), seven white knobs (input, drive, b, m, t, aux. mix, v), aux. input, AppTek jack, line in jack, headphone jack, DI XLR jack, power switch, speaker mute switch, external speaker jack, AppTek cable and socket included, top handle, black covering, vintage red grille, 18.11 in. tall, 17.52 in. wide, 15.16 in. deep, 26.46 lbs., new 2016.

| MSR $340 | $250 | $165 - 190 | $80 - 100 | |

AAA-120-15T COMBO – 120W, 1-15 in. speaker with tweeter, bass combo, solid-state chassis, 4 ohm impedance, single channel, top black control panel, two inputs (high, low), nine white knobs (input, app/fx mix, drive, b, low m, mid sweep, hi mid, t, v), aux. input, AppTek jack, line in jack, headphone jack, DI XLR jack, footswitch jack, effects loop, power switch, speaker mute switch, tweeter mute switch, external speaker jack, AppTek cable and socket included, top handle, black covering, vintage red grille, 25 in. tall, 21.26 in. wide, 16.14 in. deep, 37.47 lbs., new 2016.

| MSR $480 | $350 | $230 - 265 | $115 - 140 | |

AAA-300-210T COMBO – 300W, 2-10 in. speakers with tweeter, bass combo, solid-state chassis, 8 ohm impedance, single channel, top black control panel, two inputs (high, low), nine white knobs (input, app/fx mix, drive, b, low m, mid sweep, hi mid, t, v), aux. input, AppTek jack, line in jack, headphone jack, DI XLR jack, footswitch jack, effects loop, power switch, speaker mute switch, tweeter mute switch, external speaker jack, AppTek cable and socket included, top handle, black covering, vintage red grille, 25 in. tall, 21.26 in. wide, 16.14 in. deep, 37.47 lbs., new 2016.

| MSR $680 | $500 | $325 - 375 | $165 - 200 | |

AAA-115T SPEAKER CABINET – 300W, 1-15 in. Ashdown speaker, horn tweeter with control switch, 8 ohm impedance, lightweight ply cabinet, recessed handles, black covering, vintage red grille, 25 in. tall, 21.26 in. wide, 16.14 in. deep, 32.62 lbs., new 2016.

| MSR $316 | $230 | $150 - 175 | $75 - 90 | |

AAA-TOUR BUS 10 COMBO – 10W, 1-6.5 in. speaker, bass combo, solid-state chassis, single channel, top black control panel, single input, three black knobs (v, b, t), line in jack, headphone jack, power switch, top handle, black covering, black grille, 6.61 lbs., mfg. 2012-present.

| MSR $112 | $80 | $50 - 60 | $25 - 30 | |

BASS AMPLIFIERS: ALL ACCESS SERIES

After Eight
courtesy Ashdown Engineering

Five Fifteen
courtesy Ashdown Engineering

Perfect Ten
courtesy Ashdown Engineering

AFTER EIGHT – 15W, 1-8 in. speaker bass combo, solid-state chassis, single channel, top silver control panel, single input, five black knobs (input g, b, m, t, output level), deep switch, headphone jack, external speaker jack, black covering, silver grille, 32.25 lbs., mfg. 2004-disc.

| | $175 | $95 - 125 | $50 - 70 | $250 |

MSR/NOTES	100%	EXCELLENT	AVERAGE	LAST MSR

FIVE FIFTEEN – 100W, 1-15 in. speaker bass combo, solid-state chassis, single channel, top silver control panel, single input, five black knobs (input g, b, m, t, output level), deep switch, headphone jack, external speaker jack, black covering, silver grille, 59 lbs., mfg. 2004-disc.

	$300	$175 - 225	$110 - 140	$430

PERFECT TEN – 30W, 1-10 in. speaker bass combo, solid-state chassis, single channel, top silver control panel, single input, five black knobs (input g, b, m, t, output level), deep switch, headphone jack, external speaker jack, black covering, silver grille, 47.25 lbs., mfg. 2004-disc.

	$245	$150 - 190	$95 - 120	$350

BASS AMPLIFIERS: ABM (ASHDOWN BASS MAGNIFICATION) SERIES

The first ABM models produced in 1998 featured "Klystron Bass Magnifier" across the front control panel, and the original output was at 200W. After a few hundered were produced, they removed the Kylstron trademark at the request of another manufacturer who had already registered it and began producing amps with "Ashdown Bass Magnifier" across the front. The output power was also increased to 300W around this time.

Originally, these models all had pale blue control panels along with black speakers. In 2002, the speakers were changed to the Ashdown Blueline speakers that appear blue through the grille, and the whole series was designated with an EVO behind the model number (i.e. ABM-C110-300 EVO). In 2005, the third series of the EVO models was issued called the EVO II Series. Noticeable changes include combining the inputs into one with an active/passive input switch. The power sections were also upgraded. In 2008, the fourth version of the ABM was introduced as the EVO III that features a new built-in compressor with compression level knob and switch.

• **Add $90 for the grille cloth option on all of the following models.**

ABM-C110-300 (EVO)
courtesy Ashdown Engineering

ABM-C115-300 (EVO)
courtesy Ashdown Engineering

ABM-C210-300 (EVO)
courtesy Ashdown Engineering

ABM-C110-300 (EVO) – 300W, 1-10 in., solid-state combo, one channel, blue control panel, two inputs (high and low), seven black knobs (input, input mix, b, m, t, sub-harmonic level, output level), 4-band equalizer, various push buttons, two outputs, black vinyl covering, black grille, 55 lbs., mfg. 2000-04.

	N/A	$600 - 700	$375 - 450	$1,449

In 2002, the output was raised to 320W.

ABM-C115-300 (EVO) – 300W, 1-15 in., solid-state combo, one channel, blue control panel, two inputs (high and low), seven black knobs (input, input mix, b, m, t, sub-harmonic level, output level), 4-band equalizer, various push buttons, two outputs, black vinyl covering, black grille, 57.2 lbs., mfg. 2000-04.

	N/A	$625 - 750	$400 - 475	$1,579

In 2002, the output was raised to 320W.

* *ABM-C115-500 (EVO, EVO II, EVO III)* – similar to the ABM-C115-300 except has 500W output, 61.6 lbs., mfg. 1999-disc.

	$1,050	$675 - 800	$400 - 475	$1,500

In 2002, the output was raised to 575W.

ABM-C210-300 (EVO) – 300W, 2-10 in. speakers, solid-state combo, one channel, blue control panel, two inputs (high and low), seven black knobs (input, input mix, b, m, t, sub-harmonic level, output level), 4-band equalizer, various push buttons, two outputs, black vinyl covering, black grille, 77 lbs., mfg. 2000-04.

	N/A	$625 - 750	$400 - 475	$1,599

In 2002, the output was raised to 320W.

* *AMB-C210T-500 (EVO, EVO II, EVO III)* – similar to the ABM-C210-500 except has 500W output and a horn along with the speaker, 83.6 lbs., mfg. 2000-disc.

	$1,100	$700 - 825	$425 - 500	$1,550

In 2002, the output was raised to 575W.

MSR/NOTES	100%	EXCELLENT	AVERAGE	LAST MSR

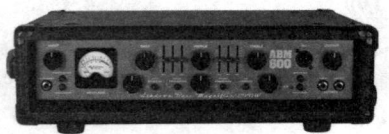

ABM-600-EVO IV
courtesy Ashdown Engineering

ABM-1200-EVO IV
courtesy Ashdown Engineering

ABM 115-EVO IV Speaker Cabinet
courtesy Ashdown Engineering

ABM-C410H-500 (EVO, EVO II) – 500W, 4-10 in. speakers & high-fidelity horn, solid-state combo, one channel, blue control panel, two inputs (high and low), seven black knobs (input, input mix, b, m, t, sub-harmonic level, output level), 4-band equalizer, various push buttons, two outputs, black vinyl covering, black grille, mfg. 2000-06.

	$1,250	$800 - 950	$500 - 600	$1,799

In 2002, the output was raised to 575W.

ABM-300 (EVO, EVO II) – 300W, head-unit only, solid-state combo, one channel, blue control panel, two inputs (high and low), seven black knobs (input, input mix, b, m, t, sub-harmonic level, output level), 4-band equalizer, various push buttons, two outputs, black vinyl covering, black grille, mfg. 2000-06.

	$700	$450 - 525	$275 - 325	$999

Output was increased to 320W in 2002.

* ABM-500 (EVO, EVO II, EVO III) – similar to the ABM-300 except has 500W output, mfg. 2000-disc.

	$810	$500 - 575	$300 - 375	$1,150

Output was increased to 575W in 2002. This model is also available in a rack-mount configuration (ABM-500-RC EVO).

* ABM-900 (EVO, EVO II, EVO III) – similar to the ABM-300 except has 900W output and cooling slits on the front control panel, mfg. 2000-disc.

	$1,025	$650 - 750	$400 - 475	$1,450

Output was increased to 575W + 575W in 2002.

ABM-600-EVO IV – 600W, head-unit only, hybrid chassis, Preamp: 1 X 12AX7 tube, one channel, blue control panel, one 1/4 in. input, eight black knobs (input, b, m, t, drive plus, compression, harmonics, output level), 9-band equalizer, VU meter, shape switch, active/passive switch, pre/post switch, mute switch, DI XLR jack, two outputs (tuner/line out), power switch, footswitch jack, line in jack, effects loop, two speaker output jacks, two cooling fans, side handle, black covering, 5.27 in. tall, 18.66 in. wide, 12.4 in. deep, 33.07 lbs., mfg. 2015-present.

MSR $1,250	$900	$575 - 675	$295 - 350	

Also available in rackmount configuration (Model ABM-600-RC-EVO IV).

ABM-1200-EVO IV – 1200W, head-unit only, hybrid chassis, Preamp: 1 X 12AX7 tube, one channel, blue control panel, one 1/4 in. input, eight black knobs (input, b, m, t, drive plus, compression, harmonics, output level), 9-band equalizer, VU meter, shape switch, active/passive switch, pre/post switch, mute switch, DI XLR jack, two outputs (tuner/line out), power switch, footswitch jack, line in jack, effects loop, four speaker out jacks, four cooling fans, side handle, black covering, 6.22 in. tall, 24 in. wide, 13.98 in. deep, 61.73 lbs., mfg. 2015-present.

MSR $2,650	$1,800	$1,175 - 1,350	$575 - 725	

ABM 115 SPEAKER CABINET – 300W, 1-15 in. speaker, 8 ohm impedance, high-grade birch plywood construction, black covering, black grille, disc.

	$435	$275 - 325	$150 - 200	$620

* ABM 115 Compact Speaker Cabinet – similar to the ABM 115 Speaker Cabinet, except has a compact cabinet design, disc.

	$410	$250 - 300	$140 - 180	$580

ABM-115H-EVO IV SPEAKER CABINET – 300W, 1-15 in. Ashdown Blueline speaker with a horn tweeter, 8 ohm impedance, high-grade birch plywood construction, recessed handles, black buffalo leather cloth covering, black steel grille, 19.69 in. tall, 24 in. wide, 16.53 in. deep, 55.12 lbs., mfg. 2015-present.

MSR $600	$450	$295 - 325	$145 - 180	

• Add $800 (MSR $1,400) for Model AMB-115H-UK which is handmade in England.

MSR/NOTES	100%	EXCELLENT	AVERAGE	LAST MSR

ABM-210-EVO IV Speaker Cabinet
courtesy Ashdown Engineering

ABM 210T Speaker Cabinet
courtesy Ashdown Engineering

ABM 410H-EVO IV Speaker Cabinet
courtesy Ashdown Engineering

ABM-210H-EVO IV SPEAKER CABINET – 300W, 2-10 in. Ashdown Blueline speakers with a horn tweeter, 8 ohm impedance, high-grade birch plywood construction, recessed handles, black buffalo leather cloth covering, black steel grille, 18.66 in. tall, 24 in. wide, 16.73 in. deep, 61.73 lbs., mfg. 2015-present.

MSR $600	$450	$295 - 325	$145 - 180	

ABM 210T SPEAKER CABINET – 400W, 2-10 in. speaker with a tweeter, 8 ohm impedance, high-grade birch plywood construction, black covering, black grille, disc.

	$485	$300 - 350	$175 - 225	$690

ABM 212T SPEAKER CABINET – 400W, 2-12 in. speaker with a tweeter, 8 ohm impedance, high-grade birch plywood construction, black covering, black grille, mfg. 2005-06.

	$700	$450 - 525	$275 - 325	$1,029

ABM 215 SPEAKER CABINET – 800W, 2-15 in. speakers, 4 ohm impedance, high-grade birch plywood construction, black covering, black grille, mfg. 2005-06.

	$1,300	$800 - 950	$550 - 650	$1,799

ABM 410H-EVO IV SPEAKER CABINET – 650W, 4-10 in. Ashdown Blueline speakers with a horn tweeter, 8 ohm impedance, high-grade birch plywood construction, recessed handles, black buffalo leather cloth covering, black steel grille, 26 in. tall, 24 in. wide, 16.5 in. deep, 79.4 lbs., mfg. 2015-present.

MSR $700	$500	$325 - 375	$165 - 200	

* Add $1,150 (MSR $1,850) for Model AMB-410H-UK which is **handmade in England.**

ABM 410T/414T SPEAKER CABINET – 650W, 4-10 in. speaker with a tweeter, 4 ohm (414T) or 8 ohm (410T) impedance, high-grade birch plywood construction, black covering, black grille, disc.

	$630	$400 - 475	$250 - 300	$900

ABM 810 SPEAKER CABINET – 1200W, 8-10 in. speakers, 4 ohm impedance, high-grade birch plywood construction, black covering, black grille, current mfg.

MSR $1,400	$1,000	$600 - 700	$375 - 450	

* Add $1,500 (MSR $2,900) for Model AMB-810H-UK which is handmade in England.

BASS AMPLIFIERS: CLASSIC (KLYSTRON/NEO) SERIES

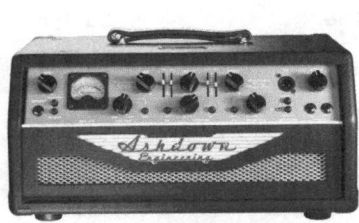

Klystron 500 Head
courtesy Ashdown Engineering

Klystron C210T-500 Combo
courtesy Ashdown Engineering

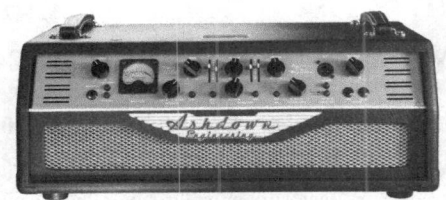

Klystron 1000 Head
courtesy Ashdown Engineering

KLYSTRON 500 HEAD – 575W, bass head unit, solid-state chassis, single channel, EVO III preamp, front light blue control panel, single input, eight black knobs (input, b, m, t, output level, wave drive, compression, sub-harmonics), four slider switches (two in between the b and m knobs and two in between the m and t knobs for more tonal options), various buttons, two outputs, XLR direct line out, four-button footswitch, black covering, silver grille, 35.25 lbs., mfg. 2006-disc.

	$1,260	$800 - 950	$550 - 650	$1,800

MSR/NOTES	100%	EXCELLENT	AVERAGE	LAST MSR

Neo 115T Speaker Cabinet
courtesy Ashdown Engineering

Neo 410T/414T Speaker Cabinet
courtesy Ashdown Engineering

Neo Mini 48 Speaker Cabinet
courtesy Ashdown Engineering

* ***Klystron C115-500 Combo*** – similar to the Klystron 500 Head, except in combo configuration with 1-15 in. Neo Superdrive Lite speaker, top control panel, black covering, black lower grille and silver upper grille, two top handles and built-in side handles, 79.4 lbs., mfg. 2006-disc.

	$1,960	$1,200 - 1,500	$850 - 1,000	$2,800

* ***Klystron C210T-500 Combo*** – similar to the Klystron 500 Head, except in combo configuration with 2-10 in. Neo Superdrive Lite speakers and a horn, top control panel, black covering, black lower grille and silver upper grille, two top handles and built-in side handles, 81.6 lbs., mfg. 2006-disc.

	$2,100	$1,300 - 1,650	$900 - 1,100	$3,000

* ***Klystron C410T-500 Combo*** – similar to the Klystron 500 Head, except in combo configuration with 4-10 in. Neo Superdrive Lite speakers and a horn, top control panel, black covering, black lower grille and silver upper grille, two top handles and built-in side handles, 103.6 lbs., mfg. 2006-disc.

	$3,250	$1,400 - 1,750	$950 - 1,150	$3,200

KLYSTRON 1000 HEAD – 575W + 575W, bass head unit, solid-state chassis, single channel, EVO III preamp, front light blue control panel, single input, eight black knobs (input, b, m, t, output level, wave drive, compression, sub-harmonics), four slider switches (two in between the b and m knobs and two in between the m and t knobs for more tonal options), various buttons, two outputs, XLR direct line out, four-button footswitch, black covering, silver grille, 52.9 lbs., mfg. 2006-disc.

	$1,590	$1,000 - 1,200	$675 - 800	$2,260

NEO 115T SPEAKER CABINET – 500W, 1-15 in. Neo Superdrive Lite speaker with a horn, 8 ohm impedance, black covering, black upper grille, silver lower grille, built-in side handles, mfg. 2006-disc.

	$1,085	$675 - 800	$425 - 500	$1,550

NEO 210T SPEAKER CABINET – 500W, 2-10 in. Neo Superdrive Lite speakers with a horn, 8 ohm impedance, black covering, black upper grille, silver lower grille, built-in side handles, mfg. 2006-disc.

	$1,085	$675 - 800	$425 - 500	$1,550

NEO 410T/414T SPEAKER CABINET – 800W, 4-10 in. Neo Superdrive Lite speakers with a horn, 8 ohm (410T) or 4 ohm (414T) impedance, black covering, black upper grille, silver lower grille, built-in side handles, 81.6 lbs., mfg. 2006-disc.

	$1,475	$900 - 1,100	$600 - 700	$2,100

NEO 810 SPEAKER CABINET – 1050W, 8-10 in. Neo Superdrive Lite speakers with a horn, 4 ohm impedance, black covering, black upper grille, silver lower grille, built-in side handles, 132.3 lbs., mfg. 2006-disc.

	$2,425	$1,450 - 1,800	$950 - 1,100	$3,450

NEO MINI 15 SPEAKER CABINET – 500W, 1-15 in. Neo Superdrive Lite speaker, 8 ohm impedance, super compact cabinet, black covering, black upper grille, silver lower grille, built-in side handles, 46.3 lbs., mfg. 2006-08.

	$1,200	$675 - 800	$425 - 500	$1,500

NEO MINI 48 SPEAKER CABINET – 600W, 4-8 in. Neo Superdrive Lite speakers, 8 ohm impedance, super compact cabinet, black covering, black upper grille, silver lower grille, built-in side handles, 55.1 lbs., mfg. 2006-08.

	$1,400	$750 - 900	$500 - 600	$1,770

BASS AMPLIFIERS: ELECTRIC BLUE SERIES

These amplifiers are what you could call the entry level for Ashdown. These are basic combo amplifiers that are solid-state and have the basic features. There is rumor that these amplifiers exist in 130W form but aren't found in the catalogs.

EB12-150 – 150W, 1-12 in. speaker, solid-state combo, single channel, front blue control panel, two inputs, eight black knobs (input, b, m, t, two other equalizers, output, level), various buttons and switches, black carpet covering, black metal grille, 36.3 lbs., mfg. 2001-03.

	N/A	$300 - 350	$175 - 225	$699

MSR/NOTES	100%	EXCELLENT	AVERAGE	LAST MSR

* **EB-15-150** – similar to the EB12-150 except has a 15 in. speaker, 41.8 lbs., mfg. 2001-03.

	N/A	$325 - 400	$200 - 250	$749

* **EB-210T-150** – similar to the EB12-150 except has 2-10 in. speakers and a tweeter, 58.3 lbs., mfg. 2001-03.

	N/A	$375 - 450	$225 - 275	$899

EB-180 HEAD – similar to the EB 12-150, except has 180W output and in head-unit only configuration,16.5 lbs., mfg. 2004-06.

	$220	$140 - 170	$70 - 90	$319

* **EB12-180** – similar to the EB 180 Head, except in combo form with 1-12 in. speaker, black covering, black metal grille, 36.4 lbs., mfg. 2004-disc.

	$415	$250 - 300	$135 - 175	$590

* **EB15-180** – similar to the EB 180 Head, except in combo form with 1-15 in. speaker, black covering, black metal grille, 42 lbs., mfg. 2004-disc.

	$455	$275 - 325	$150 - 200	$650

BASS AMPLIFIERS: MAG SERIES

This series is designed for the player who doesn't need all the bells and whistles of the ABM series. For a reasonable price, bass players get a classic sound. Like the ABM series, there is a wide variety of combos, heads, and speaker cabinets. All combo models have black metal grilles. The older models only had 200W output and in 2002 they switched them over to 265W.

MAG-300
courtesy Ashdown Engineering

MAG C210T 300 Combo
courtesy Ashdown Engineering

MAG 210T Deep Speaker Cabinet
courtesy Ashdown Engineering

MAG-200 – 200W, head-unit only, solid-state chassis, one channel, black control panel, two inputs (high and low), eight black knobs (input, b, 220Hz, m, 1.6KHz, t, Sub-harmonics level, output), effects loop, deep, bright, and EQ switches, output D.I post EQ XLR input, gray carpet covering, mfg. 2000-01.

	N/A	$300 - 375	$175 - 225	

* **MAG-250** – similar to the Mag-200 except has 265W output, white control panel, 18.7 lbs., mfg. 2002-04.

	N/A	$325 - 400	$200 - 250	$699

»**MAG-C115-250 Combo** – similar to the MAG-250 head, except is in combo configuration with 1-15 in. speaker, mfg. 2000-01.

	N/A	$425 - 500	$250 - 300	$999

»**MAG-C210T-250 Combo** – similar to the MAG-250 head, except is in combo configuration with 2-10 in. speakers and a tweeter, mfg. 2000-01.

	N/A	$475 - 550	$275 - 325	$1,099

»**MAG-C410T-250 Combo** – similar to the MAG-250 head, except is in combo configuration with 4-10 in. speakers and a tweeter, mfg. 2000-01.

	N/A	$500 - 600	$300 - 350	$1,299

MAG-300 – 307W, head-unit only, solid-state chassis, single input, front chrome control panel, two inputs, eight black knobs (pre g, five-band EQ, sub-hamonics level, MV), effects loop, black covering, mfg. 2004-disc.

	$400	$250 - 300	$135 - 175	$570

This unit is available in either a rack-mount or standard head-unit configuration. In 2008, the MAG-300 was upgraded to the EVO II with a compression circuit with compression control level and switch.

* **Mag C115 300 Combo** – similar to the Mag 300, except in combo form with 1-15 in. speaker, black covering, gray metal grille, mfg. 2004-disc.

	$500	$300 - 375	$175 - 225	$720

MSR/NOTES	100%	EXCELLENT	AVERAGE	LAST MSR

* *Mag C210T 300 Combo* – similar to the Mag 300, except in combo form with 2-10 in. speakers and a tweeter, black covering, gray metal grille, mfg. 2004-disc.

	$595	$375 - 450	$200 - 250	$850

* *Mag C410T 300 Combo* – similar to the Mag 300, except in combo form with 2-10 in. speakers and a tweeter, black covering, gray metal grille, mfg. 2004-disc.

	$665	$425 - 500	$250 - 300	$950

MAG-400 – 500W, head-unit only, solid-state chassis, single channel, black control panel, two inputs (high and low), eight black knobs (input, b, 220Hz, m, 1.6KHz, t, Sub-harmonics level, output), effects loop, deep, bright, and EQ switches, output D.I post EQ XLR input, gray carpet covering, mfg. 2000-04.

	N/A	$375 - 450	$225 - 275	$899

MAG 600R – 575W/600W, rack-mount head-unit only, solid-state chassis, single input, front chrome control panel, two inputs, eight black knobs (pre g, five-band EQ, sub-hamonics level, MV), effects loop, black casing, mfg. 2005-disc.

	$490	$300 - 350	$175 - 225	$700

This unit is available in either a rack-mount or standard head-unit configuration.

MAG-MON-10-200 – 200W, 1-10 in. speaker, wedge monitor combo, solid-state combo, one channel, black control panel, two inputs (high and low), eight black knobs (input, b, 220Hz, m, 1.6KHz, t, Sub-harmonics level, output), effects loop, deep, bright, and EQ switches, output D.I post EQ XLR input, gray carpet covering, black metal grille, mfg. 2000-01.

	N/A	$325 - 400	$200 - 250	

* *MAG-MON-12-200* – similar to the MAG-MON-10-200 except has 1-12 in. speaker, mfg. 2000-01.

	N/A	$350 - 425	$225 - 275	$1,169

* *MAG-MON-15-200* – similar to the MAG-MON-10-200 except has 1-15 in. speaker, mfg. 2000-01.

	N/A	$375 - 450	$225 - 275	

MAG 115 DEEP SPEAKER CABINET – 150W, 1-15 in. speaker, 8 ohm impedance, black carpet covering, metal grille, disc.

	$260	$150 - 190	$95 - 120	$370

MAG 210T DEEP SPEAKER CABINET – 200W, 2-10 in. speakers and a tweeter, 8 ohm impedance, black carpet covering, metal grille, 42 lbs., disc.

	$260	$150 - 190	$95 - 120	$370

MAG 410T/414T DEEP SPEAKER CABINET – 350W, 4-10 in. speakers and a tweeter, 4 ohm (414T) or 8 ohm (410T) impedance, black carpet covering, metal grille, 61 lbs., disc.

	$300	$175 - 225	$110 - 140	$430

MAG 810 DEEP SPEAKER CABINET – 640W, 8-10 in. speakers, 8 ohm impedance, black carpet covering, metal grille, disc.

	$590	$375 - 450	$225 - 275	$840

BASS AMPLIFIERS: ROOTMASTER SERIES

RM-500-EVO Head
courtesy Ashdown Engineering

RM-800-EVO Head
courtesy Ashdown Engineering

RM-500-EVO HEAD – 500W, head-unit only, solid-state chassis, one channel, front silver control panel, two inputs (passive, active), eleven black knobs (input, b, m, t, drive, compression, sub, line mix, 240Hz, 1K5Hz, output level), 5-band equalizer, VU meter, shape switch, mute switch, EQ switch, comp. switch, drive switch, rear panel: DI XLR out jack, two speaker out jacks, power switch, footswitch jack, line in jack, effects loop, cooling fan, black covering, 3.07 in. tall, 12.32 in. wide, 8.86 in. deep, 9.92 lbs., new 2016.

MSR $700	$500	$325 - 375	$165 - 200	

RM-800-EVO HEAD – 800W, head-unit only, solid-state chassis, one channel, front silver control panel, two inputs (passive, active), eleven black knobs (input, b, m, t, drive, compression, sub, line mix, 240Hz, 1K5Hz, output level), 5-band equalizer, VU meter, shape switch, mute switch, EQ switch, comp. switch, drive switch, rear panel: DI XLR out jack, two speaker out jacks, power switch, footswitch jack, line in jack, effects loop, cooling fan, black covering, 3.07 in. tall, 12.32 in. wide, 8.86 in. deep, 9.92 lbs., mfg. 2015-present.

MSR $950	$700	$450 - 525	$230 - 280	

RM-C112T-500-EVO COMBO – 500W, 1-12 in. White Line speaker, solid-state combo, one channel, front silver control panel, two inputs (passive, active), eleven black knobs (input, b, m, t, drive, compression, sub, line mix, 240Hz, 1K5Hz, output level), 5-band equalizer, VU meter, shape switch, mute switch, EQ switch, comp. switch, drive switch, rear panel: DI XLR out jack, two speaker out jacks, power switch, footswitch jack, line in jack, effects loop, cooling fan, black covering, black grille, 20.79 in. tall, 21.26 in. wide, 15.75 in. deep, 36.38 lbs., new 2016.

MSR $890	$650	$425 - 475	$210 - 260	

MSR/NOTES	100%	EXCELLENT	AVERAGE	LAST MSR

RM-C115T-500-EVO Combo
courtesy Ashdown Engineering

RM-C210T-500-EVO Combo
courtesy Ashdown Engineering

RM-115T-EVO Speaker Cabinet
courtesy Ashdown Engineering

RM-C115T-500-EVO COMBO – 500W, 1-15 in. White Line speaker, solid-state combo, one channel, front silver control panel, two inputs (passive, active), eleven black knobs (input, b, m, t, drive, compression, sub, line mix, 240Hz, 1K5Hz, output level), 5-band equalizer, VU meter, shape switch, mute switch, EQ switch, comp. switch, drive switch, rear panel: DI XLR out jack, two speaker out jacks, power switch, footswitch jack, line in jack, effects loop, cooling fan, black covering, black grille, 25.79 in. tall, 20.79 in. wide, 15.75 in. deep, 38.58 lbs., new 2016.

| MSR $990 | $725 | $475 - 550 | $235 - 290 | |

RM-C210T-500-EVO COMBO – 500W, 2-10 in. White Line speakers, solid-state combo, one channel, front silver control panel, two inputs (passive, active), eleven black knobs (input, b, m, t, drive, compression, sub, line mix, 240Hz, 1K5Hz, output level), 5-band equalizer, VU meter, shape switch, mute switch, EQ switch, comp. switch, drive switch, rear panel: DI XLR out jack, two speaker out jacks, power switch, footswitch jack, line in jack, effects loop, cooling fan, black covering, black grille, 25.79 in. tall, 20.79 in. wide, 15.75 in. deep, 37.48 lbs., new 2016.

| MSR $990 | $725 | $475 - 550 | $235 - 290 | |

RM-112T-EVO SPEAKER CABINET – 300W, 1-12 in. Ashdown speaker, horn tweeter with control switch, 8 ohm impedance, compact ply cabinet, recessed handles, black covering, black grille, 22.13 in. tall, 18.90 in. wide, 17.13 in. deep, 22.04 lbs., new 2016.

| MSR $400 | $300 | $195 - 225 | $100 - 120 | |

RM-115T-EVO SPEAKER CABINET – 300W, 1-15 in. Ashdown speaker, horn tweeter with control switch, 8 ohm impedance, compact ply cabinet, recessed handles, black covering, black grille, 23.15 in. tall, 22.13 in. wide, 17.13 in. deep, 32.62 lbs., new 2016.

| MSR $400 | $300 | $195 - 225 | $100 - 120 | |

RM-210T-EVO SPEAKER CABINET – 300W, 2-10 in. Ashdown speakers, horn tweeter with control switch, 8 ohm impedance, compact ply cabinet, recessed handles, black covering, black grille, 18.43 in. tall, 23.74 in. wide, 13.19 in. deep, 34.17 lbs., new 2016.

| MSR $400 | $300 | $195 - 225 | $100 - 120 | |

RM-610T-EVO SPEAKER CABINET – 900W, 6-10 in. Ashdown speakers, horn tweeter with control switch, 4 ohm impedance, compact ply cabinet, recessed handles, black covering, black grille, 35.55 in. tall, 23.74 in. wide, 13.19 in. deep, 81.57 lbs., new 2016.

| MSR $890 | $650 | $425 - 475 | $210 - 260 | |

BASS AMPLIFIERS: VALVE SERIES

427 Small Block
courtesy Ashdown Engineering

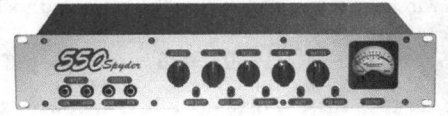

550 Spyder
courtesy Ashdown Engineering

BTA 400
courtesy Ashdown Engineering

427 SMALL BLOCK – 427W, bass head-unit, tube chassis, preamp: ECC83s, power: 8 X KT88, single channel, front chrome control panel, two inputs (high and low), five knobs (m, b, t, g, MV), effects loop, mid shift button, bass shift button, bright switch, mute switch, pre/post switch, output level gauge, rear panel: footswitch jack, line in jack, effects loop, 4/8 ohm impedance selector, two Speakon speaker jacks, power switch standby switch, black covering, black grille, 24 in. wide, 14.25 in. tall, 11.75 in. deep, 77 lbs., mfg. 2010-disc.

| | $3,500 | $2,250 - 2,750 | $1,250 - 1,500 | N/A |

550 SPYDER – 500W, bass head-unit, hybrid chassis, preamp: ECC83s, power: AMB solid-state section, single channel, front chrome control panel, two inputs (high and low), five knobs (m, b, t, g, MV), effects loop, mid shift button, bass shift button, bright switch, mute switch, pre/post switch, output level gauge, rear panel: power switch, effects loop, two Speakon speaker jacks, red casing, 20.625 in. wide, 7.625 in. tall, 12.75 in. deep, 30.8 lbs., mfg. 2010-disc.

| | $1,000 | $650 - 775 | $350 - 425 | N/A |

MSR/NOTES	100%	EXCELLENT	AVERAGE	LAST MSR

* **550 Touring** – similar to the 550 Spyder, except in combo configuration with 2-10 in. speakers, recessed side handles, black covering, black grille, 30.125 in. wide, 28.75 in. tall, 18.125 in. deep, 81.4 lbs., mfg. 2010-disc.

	100%	EXCELLENT	AVERAGE	LAST MSR
$1,200	$775 - 950	$425 - 525	N/A	

BTA 200 – 200W, bass head-unit, hybrid chassis with Ashdown's ABM solid-state preamp section and 6 X 6550 power tubes, single channel, front black control panel, single input, eight knobs (input level, b, m, t, valve drive, compression level, sub-harmonics level, output level), four-band graphic EQ, flat/sharp switch, passive/active input switch, valve drive switch, EQ in/out switch, compression in/out switch, sub-harmonics in/out switch, XLR direct line out with pre/post EQ switch, mute switch, tuner out, line out, input level gauge, rear panel: power switch, effects loop, one Speakon and one standard 1/4 in. speaker jacks, black covering, black grille, 24 in. wide, 14.25 in. tall, 11.75 in. deep, 72.5 lbs., mfg. 2010-disc.

	100%	EXCELLENT	AVERAGE	LAST MSR
$2,700	$1,750 - 2,150	$950 - 1,150	N/A	

BTA 300 – 300W, bass head-unit, hybrid chassis with Ashdown's ABM solid-state preamp section and 6 X KT88 power tubes, single channel, front black control panel, single input, eight knobs (input level, b, m, t, valve drive, compression level, sub-harmonics level, output level), four-band graphic EQ, flat/sharp switch, passive/active input switch, valve drive switch, EQ in/out switch, compression in/out switch, sub-harmonics in/out switch, XLR direct line out with pre/post EQ switch, mute switch, tuner out, line out, input level gauge, rear panel: power switch, effects loop, one Speakon and one standard 1/4 in. speaker jacks, black covering, black grille, 24 in. wide, 14.25 in. tall, 11.75 in. deep, 73.7 lbs., mfg. 2010-disc.

	100%	EXCELLENT	AVERAGE	LAST MSR
$2,800	$1,800 - 2,200	$975 - 1,175	N/A	

BTA 400 – 400W, bass head-unit, hybrid chassis with Ashdown's ABM solid-state preamp section and 8 X KT88 power tubes, single channel, front black control panel, single input, eight knobs (input level, b, m, t, valve drive, compression level, sub-harmonics level, output level), four-band graphic EQ, flat/sharp switch, passive/active input switch, valve drive switch, EQ in/out switch, compression in/out switch, sub-harmonics in/out switch, XLR direct line out with pre/post EQ switch, mute switch, tuner out, line out, input level gauge, rear panel: power switch, effects loop, one Speakon and one standard 1/4 in. speaker jacks, black covering, black grille, 24 in. wide, 14.25 in. tall, 11.75 in. deep, 77 lbs., mfg. 2010-present.

MSR/NOTES	100%	EXCELLENT	AVERAGE	LAST MSR
MSR $5,600	$4,000	$2,600 - 3,000	$1,300 - 1,600	

LITTLE BASTARD 30 (LB30WB) – 30W, bass head-unit, tube chassis, preamp: ECC82/ECC83s, single channel, front chrome control panel, two inputs (high and low), four knobs (m, b, t, v), effects loop, mid shift button, bass shift button, bright switch, mute switch, output level gauge, rear panel: power switch, one Speakon and two standard 1/4 in. speaker jacks, black covering, chrome grille, 15.75 in. wide, 8.625 in. tall, 8.875 in. deep, 30.8 lbs., mfg. 2010-disc.

	100%	EXCELLENT	AVERAGE	LAST MSR
$630	$400 - 475	$225 - 275	$850	

BASS AMPLIFIERS: MISC. MODELS

B-Social Wireless Combo
courtesy Ashdown Engineering

CTM-100 Head
courtesy Ashdown Engineering

CTM-300 Head
courtesy Ashdown Engineering

B-SOCIAL WIRELESS COMBO – 75W, 2-5 in. speakers, bass combo, solid-state chassis, two channels, top black control panel, two inputs (high, low), ten black knobs (input 1 level, input 2 level, Instrument: b, m, t, v, Audio: b, m, t, v), AppTek jack, line in jack, line out jack, headphone jack, USB connection, Bluetooth wireless, power switch, AppTek cable and socket included, top handles, available in black, natural wood, or white covering, 16.7 lbs., mfg. 2015-present.

MSR/NOTES	100%	EXCELLENT	AVERAGE	
MSR $900	$625	$400 - 475	$205 - 250	

CTM-100 HEAD – 100W, bass head-unit, all-tube chassis, preamp: 2 X 12AX7, 2 X 12AU7, Power: 2 X KT88, single channel, front black control panel, two inputs (high, low), five cream knobs (g, b, m, t, MV), 3-band EQ, mellow switch, deep switch, shift switch, bright switch, mute switch, audio/bias switch, tube selector switch, XLR direct line out with pre/post EQ switch, VU meter, effects loop, rear panel: preheat switch, power switch, three external speaker jacks, black covering, top handles, 42 lbs., mfg. 2012-present.

MSR/NOTES	100%	EXCELLENT	AVERAGE	
MSR $1,820	$1,300	$850 - 975	$425 - 525	

CTM-300 HEAD – 300W, bass head-unit, all-tube chassis, preamp: 2 X ECC832, 2 X ECC82, 1 X ECC99, Power: 6 X KT88, single channel, front black control panel, two inputs (high, low), five cream knobs (g, b, m, t, MV), 3-band EQ, mellow switch, deep switch, shift switch, bright switch, mute switch, audio/bias switch, tube selector switch, XLR direct line out with pre/post EQ switch, VU meter, effects loop, rear panel: preheat switch, power switch, three external speaker jacks, black covering, top handles, 72.75 lbs., mfg. 2012-present.

MSR/NOTES	100%	EXCELLENT	AVERAGE	
MSR $3,780	$2,700	$1,750 - 2,025	$875 - 1,075	

DH-15-C110 COMBO – 15W, vintage style bass combo, all-tube chassis head, boutique style 1-10 in. cabinet, preamp: 2 X 12AX7, Power: 2 X EL84, single channel, front black control panel, one input, five white knobs (g, b, m, t, MV), 3-band EQ, VU meter, black grille, black covering, mfg. 2014-present.

MSR/NOTES	100%	EXCELLENT	AVERAGE	
MSR $1,400	$1,000	$650 - 750	$325 - 400	

MSR/NOTES	100%	EXCELLENT	AVERAGE	LAST MSR

Little Giant 350
courtesy Ashdown Engineering

Little Giant 1000
courtesy Ashdown Engineering

Mark King Signature Head
courtesy Ashdown Engineering

LB-30 DROPHEAD 15H COMBO – 30W, vintage style bass combo, all-tube chassis head, boutique style 1-15 in. cabinet with tweeter, preamp: 1 X ECC83, 1 X ECC82, Power: 4 X EL84, single channel, front silver control panel, two inputs (high, low), four black knobs (b, m, t, MV), 3-band EQ, mid-shift switch, bass-shift switch, bright switch, mute switch, VU meter, effects loop, black covering, mfg. 2011-present.

| MSR $2,500 | $1,800 | $1,175 - 1,350 | $575 - 725 | |

LITTLE GIANT 350 – 350W, bass compact head-unit, solid-state chassis, single channel, front green control panel, single input, five knobs (input v, three freq. knobs, output v), four-band graphic EQ (b, l/m, h/m, t), active/passive input switch, deep switch, shape switch, EQ in/out switch, power switch, rear panel: XLR balanced line out with pre/post EQ switch, effects loop, line input and output, two combination Speakon/standard speaker jacks, dark gray casing, 8.25 in. wide, 2.625 in. tall, 12.25 in. deep, 6.6 lbs., mfg. 2009-disc.

| | $475 | $300 - 375 | $175 - 225 | $680 |

LITTLE GIANT 1000 – 1000W, bass compact head-unit, solid-state chassis, single channel, front orange control panel, single input, five knobs (input v, three freq. knobs, output v), four-band graphic EQ (b, l/m, h/m, t), active/passive input switch, deep switch, shape switch, EQ in/out switch, power switch, rear panel: XLR balanced line out with pre/post EQ switch, effects loop, line input and output, two combination Speakon/standard speaker jacks, dark gray casing, 8.25 in. wide, 2.625 in. tall, 12.25 in. deep, 7.7 lbs., mfg. 2009-disc.

| | $650 | $425 - 500 | $235 - 280 | $930 |

MARK KING SIGNATURE HEAD (AL-MK500) – 575W, rack-mount bass head unit, solid-state chassis, single channel, front red control panel, two inputs (one 1/4 in. one XLR), three black knobs (input level, harmonic emphasis, output level), 12-band graphic EQ, XLR line out, red casing/covering, 30.9 lbs., mfg. 2004-disc.

| | $1,050 | $650 - 775 | $400 - 475 | $1,500 |

* *Mark King Signature Combo (MK500 Combo)* – similar to the Mark King Signature Head, except in combo configuration with 2-10 in. speakers with a horn, recessed side handles, black covering, black grille, disc.

| | $1,610 | $1,000 - 1,200 | $675 - 800 | $2,300 |

RETROGLIDE-800 HEAD – 800W, head-unit only, solid-state chassis, one channel, front silver control panel, two inputs (passive, active), two black knobs (input, output), 12-band equalizer, mute switch, EQ switch, rear panel: DI XLR out jack, one speaker out jack, power switch, line in jack, effects loop, cooling fan, black covering, 2.56 in. tall, 10.63 in. wide, 8.46 in. deep, 6.61 lbs., mfg. 2015-present.

| MSR $1,220 | $850 | $550 - 625 | $275 - 350 | |

ELECTRIC GUITAR AMPLIFIERS: PEACEMAKER SERIES

Peacemaker 40
courtesy Ashdown Engineering

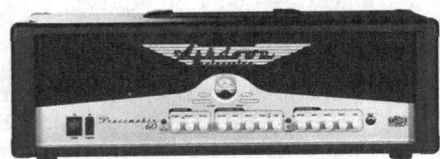

Peacemaker 60R Head
courtesy Ashdown Engineering

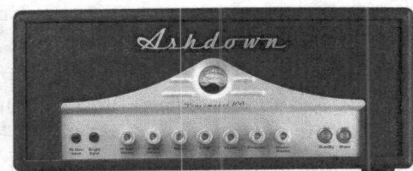

Peacemaker 100
courtesy Ashdown Engineering

PEACEMAKER 20 – 20W, 1-10 in. Celestion V10 speaker, all tube Class A chassis, three channels (gain boost on channel 2), front silver control panel, single input, 12 silver knobs (Ch.1: gain, t, m, b, v, Ch. 2: gain, t, m, b, v, Master: r, v), black Tolex covering, silver grille, 28.6 lbs., mfg. 2001-04.

| | N/A | $400 - 475 | $250 - 300 | $899 |

PEACEMAKER 40 – 40W, 1-12 in. Celestion Vintage 30 speaker, all tube Class A chassis, three channels (gain boost on channel 2), front silver control panel, single input, 13 silver knobs (Ch.1: gain, t, m, b, v, Ch. 2: gain, t, m, b, v, Master: r, v1, v2), black Tolex covering, silver grille, 37.4 lbs., mfg. 2001-04.

| | N/A | $450 - 525 | $300 - 350 | $999 |

PEACEMAKER 50 – 70W, head-unit only, all-tube chassis, hand-wired, preamp: 5 X 12AX7, power: 2 X 6550, front silver control panel, two inputs, seven silver knobs (g1, g2, b, m, t, p, MV), standby and mains switches, black Tolex covering, 68.2 lbs., mfg. 2001-02.

| | N/A | $1,300 - 1,600 | $900 - 1,050 | |

MSR/NOTES	100%	EXCELLENT	AVERAGE	LAST MSR

PEACEMAKER 60R HEAD – 60W, guitar head unit, all tube Class A chassis, three channels (gain boost on channel 2), front silver control panel, single input, 13 silver knobs (Ch.1: gain, t, m, b, v, Ch. 2: gain, t, m, b, v, Master: r, v1, v2), black Tolex covering, 30.8 lbs., mfg. 2001-04.

	N/A	$450 - 525	$300 - 350	$999

* *Peacemaker 60 Combo* – similar to the Peacemaker 60R Head, except in combo configuration with 2-12 in. Celestion Vintage 30 speakers and a silver grille, 46.2 lbs., mfg. 2001-04.

	N/A	$650 - 750	$425 - 500	$1,399

PEACEMAKER 100 – 130W, head-unit only, all-tube chassis, hand-wired, preamp: 5 X 12AX7, power: 4 X EL34, front silver control panel, two inputs, seven silver knobs (g1, g2, b, m, t, p, MV), standby and mains switches, black Tolex covering, 70.4 lbs., mfg. 2001-06.

$2,500	$1,600 - 1,900	$1,100 - 1,300	$3,599

SPEAKER CABINETS: USA SERIES

Ashdown's USA Series amps are built at Ashdown's factory in Kentucky.

USA 115 SPEAKER CABINET (US-115) – 500W, 1-15 in. Eminence speaker, 8 ohm impedance, 3/4 in. birch construction, recessed side handles, black Tolex covering, black grille, 24 in. wide, 29 in. tall, 16.5 in. deep, mfg. 2009-disc.

$910	$575 - 675	$325 - 400	$1,300

USA 410 SPEAKER CABINET (US-410H/414H) – 1050W, 4-10 in. Eminence speakers with a horn, 4 ohm (US-414H) or 8 ohm (US-410H) impedance, 3/4 in. birch construction, recessed side handles, black Tolex covering, black grille, 24 in. wide, 29 in. tall, 16.5 in. deep, mfg. 2009-disc.

$1,110	$700 - 850	$400 - 475	$1,580

USA 610 SPEAKER CABINET (US-610) – 1200W, 6-10 in. Eminence speakers, 4 ohm impedance, 3/4 in. birch construction, recessed side handles, black Tolex covering, black grille, 24 in. wide, 29 in. tall, 36.625 in. deep, mfg. 2009-disc.

$1,575	$1,000 - 1,200	$550 - 675	$2,250

USA 810 SPEAKER CABINET (US-810) – 1600W, 8-10 in. Eminence speakers, 4 ohm impedance, 3/4 in. birch construction, recessed side handles, black Tolex covering, black grille, 24 in. wide, 45.25 in. tall, 36.625 in. deep, mfg. 2009-disc.

$1,825	$1,150 - 1,400	$650 - 775	$2,600

ASHTON

Amplifiers currently produced overseas. Currently, there is no U.S. Distributor.

Ashton amplifiers are designed in Australia and produced overseas. These amps are priced and built for the beginner guitar player and the amp line includes a wide range of guitar, bass, acoustic, and keyboard amps. They also produce a wide variety of other musical products including acoustic guitars, electric guitars, bass guitars, sound reinforcement, keyboards, and accessories. Guitar packs (guitar, amplifier, accessories, etc.) are also available. For more information, visit Ashton's website.

CONTACT INFORMATION
ASHTON
www.ashtonmusic.com

ASLIN DANE

Amplifiers currently produced overseas. Currently distributed by Codel Enterprises, LLC in Bethel, CT. Previously distributed by David Burns Musical Instruments Inc.

Aslin Dane produces amplifiers that have the looks of classic boutique designs with great sound as well as high performance. They produce electric, acoustic, and bass amplifiers. The electric models are covered in rain forest tolex green. MSR prices range between $99 and $249. In 2005, Codel Enterprises (formerly Burns USA) started distributing Aslin Dane products. For more information visit Aslin Dane's website or contact them directly.

CONTACT INFORMATION
ASLIN DANE
Distributed by Codel Enterprises, LLC
PO Box 269
Bethel, CT 06801
Phone No.: 203-205-0056
Fax No.: 203-205-9062
www.aslindane.com
iamjoncoates@gmail.com

ATOMIC AMPLIFIERS

Powered speaker cabinets and template kits currently produced in Orange, CT. Distributed by Atomic Amplifiers.

Tom King, president of Atomic Amplifiers, liked using his Line 6 POD modular so much that he set out to design a powered speaker cabinet that could act as a docking station for a POD (or other modeling device). Before, there was no way to utilize a POD on-stage or in other live settings (PODs are really designed for headphone use). If you plug a POD directly into another guitar amplifier, the tone and signal path is changed from the natural effects an amp has. You also can't plug it directly into a speaker cabinet, since the POD strictly acts as a preamp. King went to the best designer he knew, Harry Kolbe, presented the idea, and after a product was developed, he started Atomic. The Atomic Reactor houses the modeling unit and drives the sound through a tube-chassis power section

CONTACT INFORMATION
ATOMIC AMPLIFIERS
476 Grace Trail
Orange, CT 06477
Phone No.: 212-426-1090
www.atomicamps.com
info@atomicamps.com

out to either 1-12 in. or 2-12 in. speakers. Currently several modeling devices can be used including: the Line 6 POD Classic, XT, and Pro, the Behringer V-Amp, the Vox ToneLab, and others. In 2010, Atomic introduced their new Reactor Series that replaced all previous models. For more information, visit Atomic's website or contact them directly.

POWERED SPEAKER CABINETS: REACTOR SERIES

The **Reactor 112** (disc. 2009, last MSR was $699) features 18W, 1-12 in. Atomic G12 Mega-Ton speaker, tube chassis, preamp: 1 X 12AX7, power: 2 X EL84, and weighs 54 lbs. The **Reactor 212** (disc. 2009, last MSR was $1,299) features 55W, 2-12 in. Atomic G12 Mega-Ton speaker, tube chassis, preamp: 1 X 12AX7, power: 2 X 6L6, and weighs 74 lbs. Both models come standard with the DS-1 docking unit. Extra docking units retailed for $69, and all template kits retailed for $40. Covers are also available for the amps.

In 2010, Atomic introduced their new Reactor Series with a cabinet, wedge, and power amp. The **Reactor FR Cabinet** is available in active (50W power amp, MSR $799) or passive (no amp, MSR $349) configurations. The **Reactor FR Wedge** is available in active (50W power amp, MSR $849) or passive (no amp, MSR $399) configurations. The **Reactor FR Mono Block Power Amp** (MSR $499) features the same power amp as the active Reactor FR Cabinet and Wedge with 50W ouput, a single 12AX7 preamp tube, and 2 X 6L6GC power tubes.

AURALUX

Amplifiers and effects currently built in Highland Park (Chicago), IL since 2000. Distributed by Auralux.

Auralux was founded in 2000 by Mitchell Omori and David Salzmann. They produce custom-made tube amps and effects. They currently offer the StageKing amp available as a head-unit or combo, the Cleargain effect, and the KingTrem effect. For more information, visit Auralux's website or contact them directly.

AUSTIN

Amplifiers and other instruments currently built in Korea and China since 1999. Distributed by U.S. Band & Orchestra in St. Louis, MO since late 2008. Previously distributed by LOUD Technologies, Inc. in Woodinville, WA between 2005 and 2008 and by St. Louis Music Inc., in St. Louis, MO between 1999 and 2005.

St. Louis Music introduced the Austin line of guitars as budget models to complement their other lines. Instead of adding a budget line to Alvarez and Alvarez Yairi, they did like many other brands have done and added an entirely new trademark. Austin has a wide variety of products including acoustic, acoustic electric, banjos, electric guitars, electric basses, mandolins, and amplifiers. In 2005, LOUD Technologies, Inc. purchased St. Louis Music, Inc. and all of their trademarks. With this acquisition, the headquarters of St. Louis Music was moved to Woodinville, WA. However, the guitar repair and set-up shop were still located in St. Louis. In late 2008, Mark Ragin and U.S. Band & Orchestra bought the Austin brand from LOUD Technologies, and in 2010, U.S. Band & Orchestra purchased the St. Louis Music brand from LOUD Technologies, which Austin has once again become part of. For more information, visit Austin's website or contact them directly.

AMPLIFIERS

Austin offers amplifiers for acoustic guitars, bass guitars, and electric guitars. The **AU15GS2** (disc. last MSR was $99) has 15W output, 1-8 in. speaker, and two channels. The **AU35GS2** (disc. last MSR was $219) has 35W output, 1-10 in. speaker, two channels, reverb, and an effects loop. The **AU35AS2** (disc. last MSR was $199) is an acoustic amplifier with 35W output, 1-8 in. speaker with a tweeter, and seperate guitar/mic inputs. The **AU20BS2** (disc. last MSR was $119) is a bass amplifier with 20W output, 1-8 in. speaker, and one channel. The **AU40BS2** (disc. last MSR was $239) is a larger bass amplifier with 40W output, 1-10 in. speaker, and a compression level control.

In 2010, Austin introduced a new line of guitar amplifiers that includes three guitar amps and one bass amp. The **Super 10** (MSR $79) is a 10W guitar amp with 1-6.5 in. speaker, a single channel, and overdrive control. The **Super 15** (MSR $99) is a 15W guitar amp with 1-8 in. speaker, a single channel, and overdrive control. The **Super 25** (MSR $129) is a 25W guitar amp with 1-8 in. speaker, a single channel, and overdrive control. The **Boomer 25** (MSR $129) is a 25W bass amp with 1-10 in. speaker, a single channel, and three-band passive EQ section.

AXL

Amplifiers previously built and other instruments currently built in China since 2001. Distributed by the Music Link in Brisbane, CA.

The Axl trademark was introduced in 2001 as a line of electric and acoustic guitars as well as a line of guitar amplifiers. The first line of instruments were based on popular American designs (Stratocaster, Telecaster, etc.). In 2005, Axl discontinued their copy-brand and acoustic instruments and introduced the Mayhem series. These guitars have radical designs that are mainly original and are finished in black including hardware. In 2006, the Bloodshed series was introduced. These guitars are similar to the Mayhem models, but they feature two tone red and black finish. In 2007, the Marquee Series was introduced. Axl no longer manufactures amplifiers. For more information contact Axl directly or visit their website.

ELECTRIC TUBE AMPS: AKITA SERIES

AKITA AT20 – 20W, 1-10 in. speaker guitar combo, three-tube chassis, preamp: 1 X 12AX7, power: 2 X EL84, two switchable channels, reverb, top brushed aluminum copper control panel, single input, seven copper knobs (clean v, OD g, OD level, b, m, t, r), effects loop, speaker out,

MSR/NOTES	100%	EXCELLENT	AVERAGE	LAST MSR

Akita AT20
courtesy Axl

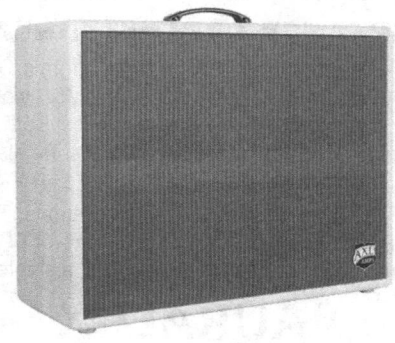

Akita AT40
courtesy Axl

Akita AT50 & 412C Speaker Cabinet
courtesy Axl

optional footswitch, available in Blonde Tolex or Birch plywood veneer covering, brown vintage-style grille, 18 in. wide, 16 in. tall, 10 in. deep, 32 lbs., mfg. fall 2007-disc.

$325	$175 - 225	$110 - 140		$430

• Add 15% (MSR $500) for Birch veneer covering.

AKITA AT30 – 30W, 1-12 in. speaker guitar combo, four-tube chassis, preamp: 2 X 12AX7, power: 2 X 6L6GC, two switchable channels, reverb, top brushed aluminum copper control panel, single input, seven copper knobs (clean v, OD g, OD level, b, m, t, r), effects loop, speaker out, optional footswitch, available in Blonde Tolex or Birch plywood veneer covering, brown vintage-style grille, 19.5 in. wide, 18 in. tall, 11 in. deep, 40 lbs., mfg. fall 2007-disc.

$420	$250 - 300	$150 - 190		$560

• Add 7.5% (MSR $600) for Birch veneer covering.

AKITA AT40 – 40W, 2-12 in. speaker guitar combo, eight-tube chassis, preamp: 4 X 12AX7, power: 4 X EL84, two switchable channels, reverb, top brushed aluminum copper control panel, single input, eight copper knobs (clean v, OD g, OD level, b, m, t, r, MV), effects loop, speaker out, optional footswitch, available in Blonde Tolex or Birch plywood veneer covering, brown vintage-style grille, 26.25 in. wide, 22 in. tall, 13.5 in. deep, 62 lbs., mfg. fall 2007-disc.

$600	$325 - 400	$175 - 225		$800

• Add 7.5% (MSR $800) for Birch veneer covering.

AKITA AT50 – 50W, guitar head unit, six-tube chassis, preamp: 4 X 12AX7, power: 2 X 6L6GC, two switchable channels, reverb, top brushed aluminum copper control panel, single input, eight copper knobs (clean v, OD g, OD level, b, m, t, r, MV), effects loop, speaker out, optional footswitch, available in Blonde Tolex or Birch plywood veneer covering, brown vintage-style grille, 26 in. wide, 8.5 in. tall, 10.75 in. deep, 38 lbs., mfg. fall 2007-disc.

$490	$275 - 325	$160 - 200		$650

• Add 7.5% (MSR $700) for Birch veneer covering.

AKITA 412C SPEAKER CABINET – 200W, 4-12 in. speakers, closed back design, available in Blonde Tolex or Birch plywood veneer covering, brown vintage-style grille, built-in side handles, 29 in. wide, 29 in. tall, 13.75 in. deep, 70 lbs., mfg. fall 2007-disc.

$375	$200 - 250	$120 - 150		$500

• Add 10% (MSR $550) for Birch veneer covering.

ELECTRIC TUBE AMPS: MEDWAY SERIES

MEDWAY SPECIAL 1GN – 18W, 1-12 in. G12M Celestion speaker guitar combo, four-tube chassis, preamp: 2 X 12AX7, power: 2 X EL84, single channel, reverb, top black control panel, two inputs (hi/lo), six white chickenhead knobs (g, b, m, t, r, MV), effects loop, speaker out, footswitch jack, finger-jointed cabinet, green tolex covering, basket weave-style brown grille cloth, 43 lbs., mfg. 2008-disc.

$600	$350 - 425	$200 - 250		$800

ELECTRIC SS AMPS: RAPTURE SERIES

RAPTURE 20T – 15W, 1-8 in. speaker guitar combo, solid-state chassis, two channels, top brushed aluminum control panel, single input, six black knobs (MV, drive v, g, t, m, b), drive select switch, chromatic tuner, RCA inputs, headphone jack, black covering, black grille, disc.

$105	$50 - 75	$30 - 40		$140

* *Rapture 20TR* – similar to the Rapture 20T, except has reverb with an additional reverb knob, disc.

$120	$60 - 85	$35 - 50		$160

RAPTURE 25TR – 25W, 1-10 in. speaker guitar combo, solid-state chassis, two channels, top brushed aluminum control panel, single input, seven black knobs (MV, drive v, g, t, m, b, r), drive select switch, chromatic tuner, RCA inputs, footswitch, headphone jack, black covering, black grille, disc.

$175	$95 - 120	$50 - 70		$230

MSR/NOTES	100%	EXCELLENT	AVERAGE	LAST MSR

RAPTURE 70R – 70W, 1-12 in. speaker guitar combo, solid-state chassis, two channels, front brushed aluminum control panel, two inputs, nine black knobs (Clean Ch.: v, t, b, OD Ch.: v, g, t, m, b, Both: r), channel select switch, mid-gain switch, footswitch, black covering, black grille, disc.

$275	$150 - 190	$95 - 120		$360

RAPTURE 100R – 70W, 2-10 in. speaker guitar combo, solid-state chassis, two channels, front brushed aluminum control panel, two inputs, nine black knobs (Clean Ch.: v, t, b, OD Ch.: v, g, t, m, b, Both: r), channel select switch, mid-gain switch, footswitch, black covering, black grille, disc.

$295	$160 - 200	$100 - 125		$391

RAPTURE 150HR HEAD – 100W, guitar head unit, solid-state chassis, two channels, front brushed aluminum control panel, two inputs, ten black knobs (Clean Ch.: v, t, m, b, OD Ch.: v, g, t, m, b, Both: r), channel select switch, gain boost switch, mid-cut switch, footswitch, black covering, black grille, disc.

$225	$120 - 150	$75 - 95		$299

Rapture150R Combo – similar to the Rapture 150HR Head, except in combo configuration with 2-12 in. speakers, disc.

$325	$175 - 225	$110 - 140		$433

RAPTURE 412C SPEAKER CABINET – 200W, 4-12 in. speakers, angled cabinet design, black covering, black grille, built-in side handles, disc.

$290	$160 - 200	$100 - 125		$381

ELECTRIC SS AMPS: MISC. MODELS

Rapture 20T
courtesy Axl

Rapture 25TR
courtesy Axl

Rapture 150HR Head
courtesy Axl

REPTONE DSP – 10W, 1-6.5 in. speaker guitar combo, solid-state chassis, single channel, 16 digital effects, front black control panel, single input, eight black knobs (g, v, t, m, b, effects select, FX, FX level), headphone jack, black Tolex covering, black metal grille, 12.5 lbs., mfg. 2008-disc.

$130	$70 - 95	$35 - 50		$170

THINAMP – 10W, 2-4 in. high output speakers, solid-state chassis, front brushed aluminum control panel, various knobs and buttons, rechargable battery pack, purple covering, silver grille, tilt-back legs, 2 in. deep, 5.3 lbs., disc. 2007.

N/A	$85 - 110	$50 - 65		$196

BASS SS AMPS: TYRANT SERIES

TYRANT 100B – 100W, 1-15 in. speaker bass combo, solid-state combo, single channel, front brushed aluminum control panel, two inputs (passive, active), five silver knobs (v, b, l/m, h/m, b), tone cut switch, RCA aux. inputs, effects loop, XLR line-out with control, tilt-back cabinet design, black covering, black grille, built-in side handles, disc.

$325	$175 - 225	$110 - 140		$430

TYRANT 200B – 200W, 2-10 in. speakers bass combo, solid-state combo, single channel, front brushed aluminum control panel, two inputs (passive, active), five silver knobs (v, b, l/m, h/m, b), tone cut switch, RCA aux. inputs, effects loop, XLR line-out with control, tilt-back cabinet design, black covering, black grille, built-in side handles, mfg. 2008-disc.

$495	$275 - 325	$150 - 200		$660

NOTES

B SECTION
BACINO AMPLIFIER COMPANY

Amplifiers currently produced in Arlington Heights, IL since 2002. Distributed by Bacino Amplifier Company.

CONTACT INFORMATION
BACINO AMPLIFIER COMPANY
Arlington Heights, IL 60005
Phone No.: 847-736-4987
www.bacinoamp.com
mike@bacinoamp.com

Mike Bacino founded the Bacino Amplifier Company in 2002, and he builds tube head-unit and combo amplifiers and speaker cabinets. The Bacino design is based on the Marshall 18 Watt combo models from the mid-1960s and Bacino advertises them as "the most faithful recreation of the legendary Marshall 18 watt combos." All components are built from original specifications of the original Marshall amplifiers, and no so-called improvements are used to alter these replicas. For more information including detailed specifications, visit Bacino's website, or contact them directly.

ELECTRIC TUBE AMPLIFIERS

The Bacino replica of the Marshall 18W Model 1958 is available as a head-unit or combo. The head-unit (MSR $2,395) has a front-mounted control panel. The combo units have top-mounted control panels and are available as a 1-12 in. combo (MSR $2,595), 2-10 in. combo (MSR $2,695), or 2-12 in. combo (MSR $2,695). A 2-12 in. extension speaker cabinet (MSR $749) is also available.

BACKLINE ENGINEERING

Amplifiers currently produced in Camarillo, CA since 2004.

CONTACT INFORMATION
BACKLINE ENGINEERING
www.backline-eng.com
support@backline-eng.com

Gary Lee founded BackLine Engineering in 2004 and they offer tube guitar amp heads, guitar effects, and a guitar amp app for the iPhone. BackLine's **Zentone 7** (MSR $995) is a programmable 7 watt guitar amp head that can utilize a variety of pre-amp and power tubes and it can be used with a regular speaker cab via standard 1/4 inch speaker jacks, in the studio with the balanced XLR direct out, and as a pre-amp for use with an external power amp. For more information, visit BackLine's website or contact them directly.

Zen Tone 7
courtesy Backline Engineering

Zen Tone 7
courtesy Backline Engineering

BAD CAT

Amplifiers currently produced in Anaheim, CA since 2009. Previously produced in Corona, CA between 2000 and 2009. Distributed by Bad Cat.

CONTACT INFORMATION
BAD CAT
1092 N. Armando St.
Anaheim, CA 92806
Phone No.: 714-630-0101
Fax No.: 714-630-0106
www.badcatamps.com
james@badcatamps.com

Bad Cat amplifiers was founded in 2000 by James and Debbie Heidrich. Bad Cat produces Class A and Class A/B all-tube amplifiers that are hand-built and hand wired to ensure perfection. They also offer speaker cabinets and effects pedals. In 2009, production moved from Corona, CA to Anaheim, CA. For more information, visit Bad Cat's website or contact them directly.

COLOR OPTIONS

Bad Cat offers a wide variety of colors for cabinet and grille coverings. Models come standard with a Black grille with silver thread and piping, and light gold grille with gold piping is available on request. Additional cabinet coverings include leather embossed vinyl: Black, Turquoise, Burgundy, Gray, Flame, Green, Cream, Red, and White. Sparkle vinyl coverings are also available: Cascade, Blue, Gold, Green, Red, Silver, Charcoal, Hot Pink, and Fuschia. Tolex coverings have also been introduced in Black, Red, and Tan finishes.

- **Add $49 for a reverb footswitch.**
- **Add $109 for an A/B mix footswitch.**
- **Add $79 for 2-10 in. speakers.**
- **Add $100 for custom coverings including Sparkle, Flame, Hammered, Black Snake, and Everglade (Mini II and Alley Cat models only).**
- **Add $200 for custom coverings including Sparkle, Flame, Hammered, Black Snake, and Everglade (all other models).**
- **Add $75 for custom front coverings including Sparkle, Flame, Hammered, Black Snake, and Everglade (all other models).**

MSR/NOTES	100%	EXCELLENT	AVERAGE	LAST MSR

ELECTRIC TUBE AMPLIFIERS: BLACK CAT & WILD CAT SERIES

In 2003, a separate bass and treble control was added to each model in addition to the five-way rotary tone switch.

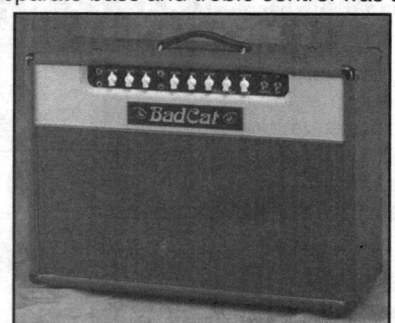

**Black Cat Reverb 212 Combo
courtesy Bad Cat**

**Wild Cat Reverb Head
courtesy Bad Cat**

BLACK CAT 15 HEAD – 15W, head-unit only, Class A all tube chassis, preamp: 1 X 12AX7, 1 X EF86, power: 2 X EL84, GZ34 rectifier, dual channels, front control panel, ten chicken knobs (Ch 1: v, b, t, MV, Ch. 2: v, tone, b, t, MV, presence), choice of color covering, corresponding grille, 32 lbs., current mfg.

MSR $2,034	$1,850	$1,200 - 1,375	$600 - 750	

• Add $274 (MSR $2,308) for reverb.

* *Black Cat 15 112 Combo* – 15W, 1-12 in. custom Celestion speaker, Class A all tube chassis, preamp: 1 X 12AX7, 1 X EF86, power: 2 X EL84, GZ34 rectifier, dual channels, front control panel, ten chicken knobs (Ch 1: v, b, t, MV, Ch. 2: v, tone, b, t, MV, presence), choice of color covering, corresponding grille, 54 lbs., current mfg.

MSR $2,419	$2,200	$1,425 - 1,650	$725 - 875	

• Add $279 (MSR $2,698) for reverb.

BLACK CAT 30 HEAD – 30W, head-unit only, Class A all tube chassis, preamp: 3 X 12AX7, EF86, power: 4 X EL84, 5AR4 rectifier, dual channels, front control panel, four inputs (two per channel), nine chicken knobs (Ch 1: v, b, t, Ch. 2: v, 5-position tone, b, t, cut, master volume), choice of color covering, corresponding grille, 58 lbs., mfg. 2000-present.

MSR $2,419	$2,200	$1,425 - 1,650	$725 - 875	

* *Black Cat 30 112 Combo* – similar to the Black Cat Head, except in combo configuration with 1-12 in. speaker, mfg. 2000-present.

MSR $2,808	$2,550	$1,650 - 1,900	$825 - 1,025	

* *Black Cat 30 212 Combo* – similar to the Black Cat Head, except in combo configuration with 2-12 in. speakers that are dissimilar, 85 lbs., mfg. 2000-disc.

	$2,659	$1,650 - 1,900	$1,000 - 1,200	$2,659

* *Black Cat 30 Reverb Head* – similar to the Black Cat Head except has reverb, two additional 12AX7 tubes, and ten control knobs (Ch. 1: v, b, t, Ch. 2: v, tone, b, t, r, cut MV), 58 lbs., mfg. 2000-present.

MSR $2,698	$2,450	$1,600 - 1,825	$800 - 975	

» *Black Cat 30 Reverb 112 Combo* – similar to the Black Cat Reverb Head, except in combo configuration with 1-12 in. Celestion speaker, mfg. 2000-present.

MSR $3,079	$2,700	$1,750 - 2,025	$875 - 1,075	

» *Black Cat 30 Reverb 212 Combo* – similar to the Black Cat Reverb Head, except in combo configuration with 2-12 in. Celestion speakers that are dissimilar, 85 lbs., mfg. 2000-disc.

	$2,999	$1,850 - 2,100	$1,200 - 1,400	$2,999

BLACK CAT 40 HEAD – 40W, head-unit only, Class A all tube chassis, preamp: 1 X 12AX7, 1 X EF86, power: 2 X EL34, solid state rectifier, dual channels, front control panel, ten chicken head knobs (Ch 1: v, b, t, K-Master, Ch. 2: v, 5-position tone, b, t, K-master, presence), choice of color covering, corresponding grille, 39 lbs., mfg. 2014-present.

MSR $2,969	$2,450	$1,600 - 1,825	$800 - 975	

• Add $110 (MSR $3,079) for reverb.

* *Black Cat X Head* – similar to the Black Cat Head except has two switchable channels, dual reverb, dual MV, and effects loop, mfg. 2008-09.

	$3,679	$2,400 - 2,750	$1,475 - 1,750	$3,679

» *Black Cat X 212 Combo* – similar to the Black Cat X Head, except in combo configuration with 2-12 in. Celestion speakers that are dissimilar, mfg. 2008-09.

	$3,989	$2,600 - 3,000	$1,600 - 1,900	$3,989

WILD CAT REVERB HEAD – similar to the Black Cat Reverb except has 40W Class A output and 2 X EL34 tubes instead of EL84, 58 lbs., mfg. 2000-disc.

	$2,639	$1,700 - 1,950	$1,050 - 1,250	$2,639

MSR/NOTES	100%	EXCELLENT	AVERAGE	LAST MSR

Wild Cat Reverb 212 Combo
courtesy Bad Cat

Cub (II) Reverb 112/210 Combo
courtesy Bad Cat

* *Wild Cat Reverb 112 Combo* – similar to the Wild Cat, except in combo configuration with 1-12 in. Celestion speaker, mfg. 2000-disc.

	$2,839	$1,775 - 2,075	$1,125 - 1,325	$2,839

* *Wild Cat Reverb 212 Combo* – similar to the Wild Cat, except in combo configuration with 2-12 in. Celestion speakers, mfg. 2000-disc.

	$2,999	$1,900 - 2,200	$1,200 - 1,400	$2,999

ELECTRIC TUBE AMPLIFIERS: BOBCAT SERIES

BOBCAT 5 COMBO – 5W, 1-12 in. custom Celestion speaker, all tube chassis, preamp: 1 X 6SL7, power: 1 X 6V6, front control panel, four chicken head knobs (g, tone, reverb, MV), rip switch, effects loop, black covering, light brown grille, 40 lbs., current mfg.

MSR N/A	$1,000	$650 - 750	$325 - 400	

BOBCAT 20 COMBO – 20W, 1-12 in. custom Celestion speaker, all tube chassis, preamp: 1 X 6SL7, power: 2 X 6V6, front control panel, four chicken head knobs (g, tone, reverb, MV), rip switch, boost switch, effects loop, black covering, light brown grille, 40 lbs., current mfg.

MSR N/A	$1,500	$975 - 1,125	$475 - 600	

BOBCAT 5/100 COMBO – 100W (switchable to 5W), 1-12 in. custom Celestion speaker, all tube chassis, preamp: 1 X 6SL7, power: 1 X 6V6, front control panel, four chicken head knobs (g, tone, reverb, MV), rip switch, effects loop, black covering, light brown grille, 40 lbs., current mfg.

MSR N/A	$1,500	$975 - 1,125	$500 - 600	

ELECTRIC TUBE AMPLIFIERS: CLASSIC SERIES

CLASSIC CAT – 20W, 1-12 in. Bad Cat proprietary Celestion speaker combo, Class A all-tube chassis, preamp: 2 X 12AY7, power: 2 X 6V6, single channel, front control panel, two inputs, two knobs (v, tone), line out, available in various finishes, mfg. 2006-disc.

	$1,449	$850 - 1,000	$550 - 625	$1,449

* *Classic Cat Reverb* – similar to the Classic Cat, except has a reverb circuit, mfg. 2006-disc.

	$1,789	$1,100 - 1,300	$675 - 800	$1,789

CLASSIC DELUXE – 20W, 1-12 in. speaker, guitar combo, seven-tube chassis, preamp: 1 X 12AT7, 2 X 12AX7, power: 2 X 6V6, GZ34 rectifier, front black control panel, single input, four knobs (v, t, b, r), standby switch, power switch, available in various coverings and grille cloths, 20 in. wide, 18.5 in. tall, 10.5 in. deep, 48 lbs., mfg. 2009-disc.

	$1,999	$1,300 - 1,500	$800 - 950	$1,999

ELECTRIC TUBE AMPLIFIERS: CUB SERIES

In 2002, the original Cub model added a switch for tone defeat and was renamed the Cub II. In 2014, Bad Cat released the Cub III models that feature a switchable A/B valve, gain select, and K Master volume control.

CUB (II) HEAD – 15W, head-unit only, Class A six tube chassis, preamp: 3 X 12AX7, power: 2 X EL84, 5AR4 rectifier, single channel, front control panel, two inputs, five chicken head knobs (v, b, t, cut, master), choice of color covering, corresponding grille, mfg. 2002-present.

MSR $1,549	$1,549	$1,000 - 1,150	$650 - 750	

* *Cub (II) 112/210 Combo* – similar to the Cub (II) Head, except in combo form with 1-12 in. or 2-10 in. (disc. 2005) speakers, mfg. 2002-present.

MSR $1,699	$1,699	$1,050 - 1,250	$700 - 800	

* *Cub (II) Reverb Head* – similar to the Cub (II) Head, except has a reverb circuit with two more 12AX7 preamp tubes, and an additional knob for reverb, mfg. 2002-present.

MSR $1,889	$1,889	$1,200 - 1,400	$750 - 900	

» *Cub (II) Reverb 112/210 Combo* – similar to the Cub (II) Reverb Head, except has 1-12 in. or 2-10 in. (disc. 2005) speakers, current mfg.

MSR $2,039	$2,039	$1,250 - 1,500	$800 - 950	

MSR/NOTES	100%	EXCELLENT	AVERAGE	LAST MSR

CUB III 15 HEAD – 15W, head-unit only, four tube chassis, preamp: 1 X 12AX7, 1 X EF86, power: 2 X EL84, GZ34 rectifier, single channel, front control panel, six chicken head knobs (v, b, t, tone, presence, K-master), effects loop, choice of color covering, corresponding grille, 32 lbs., mfg. 2014-present.

MSR $1,759	$1,600	$1,050 - 1,200	$525 - 650	

• Add $275 (MSR $2,034) for reverb.

* *Cub III 15 112 Combo* – 15W, 1-12 in. Celestion speaker, four tube chassis, preamp: 1 X 12AX7, 1 X EF86, power: 2 X EL84, GZ34 rectifier, single channel, front control panel, six chicken head knobs (v, b, t, tone, presence, K-master), effects loop, choice of color covering, corresponding grille, 54 lbs., mfg. 2014-present.

MSR $2,199	$1,950	$1,275 - 1,450	$625 - 775	

• Add $100 (MSR $2,299) for reverb.

CUB III 30 HEAD – 30W, head-unit only, six tube chassis, preamp: 1 X 12AX7, 1 X EF86, power: 4 X EL84, 5AR4 rectifier, single channel, front control panel, six chicken head knobs (v, b, t, tone, presence, K-master), effects loop, footswitch included, choice of color covering, corresponding grille, 41 lbs., mfg. 2014-present.

MSR $2,034	$1,850	$1,200 - 1,375	$600 - 750	

• Add $265 (MSR $2,299) for reverb.

* *Cub III 30 112 Combo* – 30W, 1-12 in. Celestion speaker, six tube chassis, preamp: 1 X 12AX7, 1 X EF86, power: 4 X EL84, 5AR4 rectifier, single channel, front control panel, six chicken head knobs (v, b, t, tone, presence, K-master), effects loop, footswitch included, choice of color covering, corresponding grille, 65 lbs., mfg. 2014-present.

MSR $2,419	$2,200	$1,425 - 1,650	$725 - 875	

• Add $550 (MSR $2,969) for reverb.

CUB III 40 HEAD – 40W, head-unit only, four tube chassis, preamp: 1 X 12AX7, 1 X EF86, power: 2 X EL34, solid state rectifier, single channel, front control panel, six chicken head knobs (v, b, t, tone, presence, K-master), effects loop, footswitch included, choice of color covering, corresponding grille, 41 lbs., mfg. 2014-present.

MSR $2,299	$2,100	$1,375 - 1,575	$675 - 850	

• Add $285 (MSR $2,584) for reverb.

ELECTRIC TUBE AMPLIFIERS: HOT CAT SERIES

Hot Cat 30W Head
courtesy Bad Cat

Hot Cat 30W 112/210 Combo
courtesy Bad Cat

HOT CAT 15W HEAD – 15W, head-unit only, Class A power, seven tube chassis, preamp: 4 X 12AX7, power: 2 X EL84, 5AR4/solid-state rectifier, dual channels, front control panel, two inputs, eight chicken head knobs (v, g, e, level, b, t, brilliance, MV), choice of color covering, corresponding grille, 44 lbs., mfg. 2003-present.

MSR $2,034	$1,850	$1,200 - 1,375	$600 - 750	

• Add $165 (MSR $2,199) for reverb.

* *Hot Cat 15W 112/210 Combo* – similar to the Hot Cat 15W, except in combo configuration with 1-12 in. or 2-10 in. (disc.) speakers, 61 lbs., mfg. 2003-present.

MSR $2,419	$2,200	$1,425 - 1,650	$725 - 875	

• Add $215 (MSR $2,634) for reverb.

HOT CAT 30W HEAD – 30W, head-unit only, Class A power, seven tube chassis, preamp: 4 X 12AX7, power: 2 X EL34, 5AR4/solid-state rectifier, dual channels, front control panel, two inputs, eight chicken head knobs (v, g, e, level, b, t, brilliance, MV), choice of color covering, corresponding grille, 44 lbs., mfg. 2002-present.

MSR $2,419	$2,200	$1,425 - 1,650	$725 - 875	

* *Hot Cat 30W 112/210 Combo* – similar to the Hot Cat 30W, except in combo configuration with 1-12 in. or 2-10 in.(disc.) speakers, 61 lbs., mfg. 2002-present.

MSR $2,808	$2,550	$1,650 - 1,900	$825 - 1,025	

* *Hot Cat 30W 212 Combo* – similar to the Hot Cat 30W, except in combo configuration with 2-12 in. speakers, mfg. 2002-disc.

	$2,659	$1,650 - 1,900	$1,000 - 1,200	$2,659

MSR/NOTES	100%	EXCELLENT	AVERAGE	LAST MSR

* *Hot Cat 30W Reverb Head* – similar to the Hot Cat 30W Head, except has a tube buffered reverb circuit, two switchable channels, 10 control knobs (Ch. 1: v, five-way tone selector, r, Ch. 2: g, edge, level, b, t, brilliance, MV), a mid-cut boost switch, and a tube buffered effects loop, mfg. 2004-present.

MSR $2,634	$2,400	$1,550 - 1,800	$775 - 950	

»*Hot Cat 30W Reverb 112 Combo* – similar to the Hot Cat 30W Reverb Head, except in combo configuration with 1-12 in. speaker, mfg. 2004-present.

MSR $3,079	$2,800	$1,825 - 2,100	$900 - 1,125	

HOT CAT 50W HEAD – 50W, Class A/B head-unit only, four tube chassis, preamp: 2 X 12AX7, power: 2 X EL34, solid-state rectifier, dual channels, front control panel, ten chicken head knobs (Ch. 1: v, b, t, K-Master, Ch. 2: g, b, m, t, MV, presence), choice of color covering, corresponding grille, 52 lbs., mfg. 2014-present.

MSR $2,699	$2,500	$1,625 - 1,875	$800 - 1,000	

- Add $270 (MSR $2,969) for reverb.

HOT CAT 100W HEAD – 100W, head unit only, Class A power, nine tube chassis, preamp: 4 X 12AX7, power: 4 X EL34, 5AR4/solid-state rectifier, dual channels, front control panel, two inputs, eight chicken head knobs (v, g, e, level, b, t, brilliance, MV), choice of color covering, corresponding grille, mfg. 2003-05.

	N/A	$1,800 - 2,150	$1,150 - 1,350	$3,199

* *Hot Cat 100W Reverb Head* – similar to the Hot Cat 100W Head, except has a tube buffered reverb circuit, two switchable channels, 10 control knobs (Ch. 1: v, five-way tone selector, r, Ch. 2: g, edge, level, b, t, brilliance, MV), a mid-cut boost switch, and a tube buffered effects loop, mfg. 2005-disc.

	$3,229	$2,000 - 2,350	$1,250 - 1,450	$3,229

ELECTRIC TUBE AMPLIFIERS: MINI CAT SERIES

MINI CAT HEAD – 5W, head-unit only, Class A, single channel, all-tube chassis, preamp: 12AX7, power: EL84, front black control panel, single input, four black chickenhead knobs (v, b, t, MV), speaker outputs, line outputs, available in various color coverings, 10 lbs., mfg. 2003-05.

	N/A	$425 - 500	$275 - 325	$799

* *Mini Cat Combo* – similar to the Mini Cat Head, except has 1-10 in. Jensen speaker, 18 lbs., mfg. 2003-05.

	N/A	$500 - 600	$300 - 350	$869

MINI CAT II 112 COMBO – 5W, 1-12 in. speaker combo, Class A, single channel, all-tube chassis, preamp: 2 X 12AX7, power: EL84, front black control panel, single input, four black chickenhead knobs (v, b, t, MV), speaker outputs, line outputs, available in various color coverings, 25 lbs., mfg. 2004-disc.

	$869	$550 - 650	$325 - 375	$869

ELECTRIC TUBE AMPLIFIERS: PANTHER SERIES

PANTHER HEAD – 35W, guitar head unit, 10 tube chassis, preamp: 4 X 12AX7, 1 X EF86, power: 4 X 6V6, rectifier: 5AR4, two channels, front black control panel, two inputs (one per channel), 12 black knobs (Ch. 1: v, b, m, five-way mid sweep, t, Ch. 2: v, tone, b, t, All: cut, Ch. 1 MV, Ch. 2 MV), half-power switch, multiple taps, two-way voicing switch, line out, speaker outputs, available in various coverings and grille cloths, mfg. 2007-disc.

	$2,869	$1,800 - 2,100	$1,050 - 1,250	$2,869

* *Panther 112 Combo* – similar to the Panther Head, except in combo configuration with 1-12 in. speaker, mfg. 2007-disc.

	$3,069	$1,900 - 2,200	$1,100 - 1,300	$3,069

* *Panther 212 Combo* – similar to the Panther Head, except in combo configuration with 2-12 in. speakers, mfg. 2007-disc.

	$3,229	$2,000 - 2,300	$1,200 - 1,400	$3,229

* *Panther Reverb Head* – similar to the Panther Head, except has reverb, mfg. 2007-disc.

	$3,209	$2,000 - 2,300	$1,200 - 1,400	$3,209

»*Panther Reverb 112 Combo* – similar to the Panther Reverb Head, except in combo configuration with 1-12 in. speaker, mfg. 2007-disc.

	$3,409	$2,100 - 2,450	$1,250 - 1,500	$3,409

»*Panther Reverb 212 Combo* – similar to the Panther Reverb Head, except in combo configuration with 2-12 in. speakers, mfg. 2007-disc.

	$3,569	$2,150 - 2,550	$1,300 - 1,550	$3,569

ELECTRIC TUBE AMPLIFIERS: TONE CAT & TREM CAT SERIES

TONE CAT HEAD – 30W, head-unit only, Class A, two channels, all-tube chassis, preamp: 9 X 12AX7 (4 preamp, 2 reverb, 1 phase inverter, 2 effects loop), power: 4 X EL84 (Ch. 1) and 2 X EL34 (Ch. 2), rectifier: 5AR4, front black control panel, two inputs, 11 black chickenhead knobs (Ch. 1: v, b, t, Ch. 2: g, e, level, b, t, r, brilliance MV), effects loop, various color coverings, 58 lbs., mfg. 2005-disc.

	$3,299	$2,050 - 2,400	$1,250 - 1,500	$3,299

MSR/NOTES	100%	EXCELLENT	AVERAGE	LAST MSR

Tone Cat 112 Combo – similar to the Tone Cat Head, except in combo form with 1-12 in. speaker, 70 lbs., mfg. 2005-disc.

| | $3,459 | $2,150 - 2,550 | $1,300 - 1,600 | $3,459 |

TREM CAT HEAD – 30W, head-unit only, Class A, single channel, tremolo, reverb, all-tube chassis, preamp: 5 X 12AX7 and EF86, power: 4 X EL84, rectifier: GZ34, front black control panel, two inputs, 10 black chickenhead knobs (v, tone, select, b, t, s, d, r, cut, MV), impedance switch, speaker phase switch, Hi/Lo power switch, available in various color coverings, 58 lbs., mfg. 2004-disc.

| | $2,869 | $1,800 - 2,100 | $1,050 - 1,250 | $2,869 |

Trem Cat 112 Combo – similar to the Trem Cat, except in combo form with 1-12 in. speaker, available in various color coverings, 70 lbs., mfg. 2004-disc.

| | $3,029 | $1,900 - 2,200 | $1,100 - 1,300 | $3,029 |

ELECTRIC TUBE AMPLIFIERS: MISC. MODELS

ALLEY CAT – 7.5W, 1-12 in. Bad Cat proprietary Celestion speaker combo, Class A all-tube chassis, preamp: 2 X 12AX7, power: 2 X EL84, two switchable channels, front control panel, single input, five knobs (Ch. 1: v, Ch. 2: g, b, t, MV), line out, multi-ohm tap switch, available in various finishes, mfg. 2006-09.

| | $1,199 | $725 - 850 | $475 - 550 | $1,199 |

BC-50 – 50W, guitar head-unit, five-tube chassis, preamp: 3 X 12AX7, power: 2 X EL34, solid-state rectifier, two channels, front black control panel, single input, seven black knobs (off/standby/on power, p, b, m, t, v1, v2), rear panel: two speaker jacks with impedance selector, standard black covering with black corners and Bad Cat logo, mfg. 2008-disc.

| MSR $1,599 | $1,599 | $1,050 - 1,200 | $650 - 750 | |

LIL' 15 – 15W, guitar head-unit, Class A/B five-tube chassis, preamp: 2 X 12AX7, 1 X EF86, power: 2 X EL84, two channels, front black control panel, single input, five black knobs (v, g, tone, cut, MV), channel switch, rear panel: off/standby/on power knob, footswitch jack, line out jack, speaker jack with impedance selector, standard black covering with black corners and a black handle, 14 in. wide, 7 in. tall, 7 in. deep, 21 lbs., mfg. 2009-disc.

| | $1,449 | $950 - 1,100 | $575 - 675 | $1,449 |

Lil' 15 1-12 Combo – similar to the Lil' 15 Head, except in combo configuration with 1-12 in. speaker and an expanded control panel that has individual power and standby switches on the front, standard black covering with black corners and a black handle, 14 in. wide, 18.5 in. tall, 10.5 in. deep, 46 lbs., mfg. 2009 only.

| | $1,699 | $1,100 - 1,275 | $675 - 800 | $1,699 |

LYNX – 50W, guitar head unit, seven tube chassis, preamp: 4 X 12AX7, power: 2 X EL34, rectifier: 1 X 5AR4, two channels, front black control panel, two inputs (one per channel), 10 black knobs (v, five-way tone, g, edge, b, m, five-way mid boost, t, p, MV), half power switch, two-way voicing switch, tube/solid-state rectifier switch, multiple taps, line out, available in various coverings and grille cloths, mfg. 2007-disc.

| | $2,869 | $1,800 - 2,100 | $1,050 - 1,250 | $2,869 |

SPEAKER CABINETS

S112 – 30W, 1-12 in. Bad Cat proprietary Celestion speaker, various color coverings, large or small size, 40 lbs., mfg. 2000-present.

| MSR $599 | $599 | $375 - 450 | $225 - 275 | |

S212 – 60W, 2-12 in. Celestion dissimilar speakers, various color coverings, mfg. 2000-present.

| MSR $799 | $799 | $475 - 550 | $275 - 325 | |

* Add 15% for the vertical cabinet (disc. 2007, last MSR was $849).

S410 – 140W, 4-10 in. Celestion speakers, various color coverings, mfg. 2000-09.

| | $839 | $500 - 600 | $325 - 375 | $839 |

* Add 15% for Jensen speakers (last MSR was $969).

S412 – 120W, 4-12 in. Celestion speakers, various color coverings, mfg. 2000-present.

| MSR $1,149 | $1,149 | $675 - 800 | $450 - 525 | |

MINI CAT CABINET 110 – 5W, 1-10 in. speaker, various color coverings, designed for use with the Mini Cat, 12 lbs., mfg. 2004-06.

| | $299 | $150 - 200 | $95 - 125 | $299 |

BAG END

Speaker cabinets currently produced in Algonquin, IL. Previously produced in Barrington, IL. Distributed by Bag End.

Bag End produces a variety of loudspeakers and speaker cabinets for guitars, basses, acoustics, and keyboards. They also produce several loudspeakers for other industries such as the studio and cinema. Their musical cabinets come in the traditional 10, 12, 15, and 18 in. speaker configurations and handle a variety of wattages. For more information, visit Bag End's website, or contact them directly.

CONTACT INFORMATION
BAG END
1201 Armstrong St.
Algonquin, IL 60102
Phone No.: 847-658-8888
Fax No.: 847-658-5008
www.bagend.com
lit@bagend.com

BAKOS AMP WORKS

Amplifiers were previously produced in Atlanta, GA from the mid-2000s to the early-2010s.

Jeff Bakos founded Bakos Amp Works several years ago, and for many years he repaired and restored amps before he began building his own designs. Bakos' first design was based on a tube-rectified Marshall JTM-45 called the **Plus 45**. All of Bakos amps are built on request and can usually be voiced specifically for the user's requests.

BALDWIN

Amplifiers previously produced between 1965 and 1970. Baldwin amplifiers were initially built in England by Burns; later models were assembled in Booneville, AR. Distributed by the Baldwin Piano Company of Cincinnati, OH.

Baldwin has been a big name in pianos dating back to 1862 when Dwight Hamilton Baldwin opened a music store in Cincinnati. In 1866, Lucien Wulsin came to work for Baldwin as a bookkeeper. The store became so successful, he started manufacturing pianos in 1890. In 1899, Baldwin died, and left the company to Wulsin. The Baldwin company stayed in Wulsin's name for several generations, and by the early 1960s, Baldwin was ready to get into guitars and amplifiers. Their first attempt was to buy Fender Electric Instruments. Negotiations began with Fender in April of 1964, who offered $5 million (minus Fender's liabilities). When talks bogged down over acoustic guitar and electric piano operations, Randall met with representatives of the Columbia Broadcasting System (CBS). An agreement with CBS was signed in October, 1964, for $13 million that took effect in January of 1965.

Baldwin, outbid by CBS but still looking to diversify its product lines, then bought the Burns manufacturing facilities from Jim Burns (regarded as "the British Leo Fender") in September, 1965. U.S. distributed models bore the Baldwin trademark. During Baldwin's first year of ownership, only the logos were changed on the amplifiers. Many amplifiers were only changed cosmetically (the names Baldwin and Burns appear separately on the exact same amp several times), whereas some series were completely redesigned. The Baldwin company then began assembling the imported Burns parts in Booneville, Arkansas. By the late 1960s, all Baldwin amps were different than what Burns models were produced before Burns was sold. Amplifier (and guitar) production ceased in 1970.

Baldwin acquired the Gretsch trademark when Fred Gretsch, Jr. sold the company in 1967. As part of a business consolidation, the New York Gretsch operation was moved to the Arkansas facility in 1970. Baldwin then concentrated its corporate interests in the Gretsch product line, discontinuing further Baldwin/Burns models. For further Baldwin/Gretsch history, see Gretsch (source: Paul Day, *The Burns Book*, Per Gjorde, *Pearls and Crazy Diamonds: Fifty Years of Burns Guitars 1952-2002*, and Michael Wright, *Vintage Guitar Magazine*).

ELECTRIC SS AMPLIFIERS

The Orbit and Sonic series of guitar amplifiers carried over from Burns to the new Baldwin trademark. They also underwent an overhaul with their new name. Models after the Baldwin buyout include the **Orbit 75**, **Sonic 25**, **Sonic 35**, and **Sonic 55**. Look for more information on these models in further editions of the *Blue Book of Guitar Amplifiers*.

MODEL B1 BASS – 45W, bass combo unit, 1-15 in. and 1-12 in. speakers, solid-state chassis, two channels, top brushed aluminum control panel, four inputs (two per channel), six knobs (v, b, t, per each channel), timbre switch, line out, blue sides, black grille, mfg. circa mid-1960s-1970.

	N/A	$250 - 300	$135 - 175	

MODEL B2 BASS – 35W, bass combo unit, 1-15 in. speaker, solid-state chassis, two channels, top brushed aluminum control panel, four inputs (two per channel), six knobs (v, b, t, per each channel), timbre switch, line out, different cosmetics than the B1 that were to make the B2 look more professional, mfg. circa mid-1960s-1970.

	N/A	$225 - 275	$120 - 150	

MODEL C1 CUSTOM – 45W, guitar combo unit, 2-12 in. speakers, solid-state chassis, two channels, reverb, tremolo, top brushed aluminum control panel, four inputs (two per channel), nine knobs (Ch. 1: v, b, t, Ch. 2: v, b, t, s, i, r), five multi-color pre-set "Supersound" push button switches, line out, optional footswitch, blue sides, black grille, mfg. circa mid-1960s-1970.

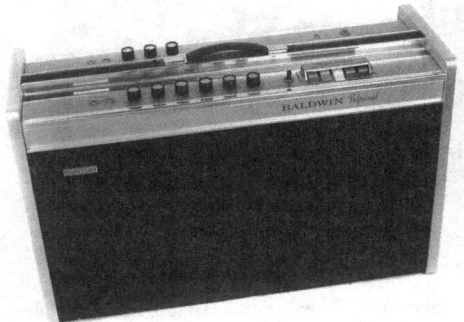

courtesy John Beeson/The Music Shoppe

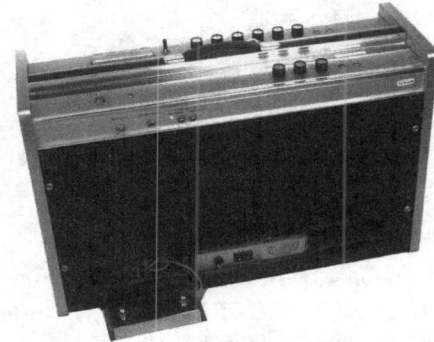

courtesy John Beeson/The Music Shoppe

	N/A	$300 - 375	$175 - 225	

MSR/NOTES	100%	EXCELLENT	AVERAGE	LAST MSR

MODEL C2 – 40W, guitar combo unit, 2-12 in. speakers, solid-state chassis, two channels, reverb, tremolo, top brushed aluminum control panel, four inputs (two per channel), nine knobs (Ch. 1: v, b, t, Ch. 2: v, b, t, s, i, r), five multi-color pre-set "Supersound" push button switches, line out, optional footswitch, different cosmetics than the C1 that were to make the C2 look more professional, mfg. circa mid-1960s-1970.

	N/A	$300 - 350	$175 - 225	

MODEL D1 DELUXE – 30W, guitar combo unit, 1-12 in. speaker, solid-state chassis, two channels, reverb, tremolo, top brushed aluminum control panel, four inputs (two per channel), nine knobs (Ch. 1: v, b, t, Ch. 2: v, b, t, s, i, r), five multi-color pre-set "Supersound" push button switches, line out, optional footswitch, blue sides, black grille, mfg. circa mid-1960s-1970.

	N/A	$275 - 325	$150 - 200	

MODEL E1 "THE EXTERMINATOR" – 100W, large guitar combo unit, six speakers (2-15 in., 2-12 in., and 2-7 in.), solid-state chassis, two channels, reverb, tremolo, top brushed aluminum control panel, four inputs (two per channel), nine knobs (Ch. 1: v, b, t, Ch. 2: v, b, t, s, i, r), five multi-color pre-set "Supersound" push button switches, line out, optional footswitch, blue sides, black grille, mfg. circa mid-1960s-1970.

	N/A	$500 - 600	$300 - 350	

MODEL S1 THE SLAVE – 40W, power amplifier and speaker cabinet only, two speakers (1-15 in. and 1-12 in.), top control panel, two inputs, single volume knob, mfg. circa mid-1960s-1970.

	N/A	$200 - 250	$120 - 150	

This model was meant to be a powered extension speaker cabinet of any other Baldwin model from this era.

BARCUS-BERRY

Amplifiers previously produced in the late 1970s. Pickups and other electronics currently produced since 1963. Distributed by Musicorp, Inc. in Louisville, KY.

Violinist John Berry and electronics guru Les Barcus founded Barcus Berry in 1963 with the first piezo-crystal transducer for musical instruments. This revolutionary design led to many other feats and firsts by the company such as the electric violin, piezo transducers for guitars, pianos, and harps, and the first under-saddle piezo pickup. In the late 1970s, Barcus-Berry introduced a line of guitar amplifiers. They currently produce a line of pickups, electronics, and accessories.

BASSON SOUND EQUIPMENT

Amplifiers and speaker cabinets previously produced in Carlsbad, CA from 2001-2010. Distributed by Basson Sound Equipment.

Basson Sound Equipment was founded by Victor Basson in 2001. They specialized in guitar, bass, and PA speaker cabinets. In 2006, they introduced a line of guitar amplifiers. For more information, visit Basson's website or contact them directly.

ELECTRIC TUBE AMPLIFIERS

BGA1 HEAD – 120W, guitar head unit, eight tube chassis, preamp: 4 X 12AX7A, power: 4 X 6CA7, solid-state rectifier, two channels, front white control panel, single input, 11 black or silver knobs, effects loop, footswitch, available in black covering with a silver grille (BGA1GR) or black covering with a black grille and white piping (BGA1BK), mfg. 2006-present.

MSR $1,395	$850	$600 - 700	$375 - 450	

GUITAR SPEAKER CABINETS

B112 Speaker Cabinet
courtesy Basson Sound Equipment

B212 Speaker Cabinet
courtesy Basson Sound Equipment

B412 Speaker Cabinet
courtesy Basson Sound Equipment

B112 SPEAKER CABINET – 75W, 1-12 in. Eminence Legend speaker, 8 ohm impedance, air-tight cabinet, available in black Tolex covering, black or silver grille, 27 lbs., current mfg.

MSR $259	$200	$120 - 150	$70 - 95	

MSR/NOTES	100%	EXCELLENT	AVERAGE	LAST MSR

B212 SPEAKER CABINET – 150W, 2-12 in. Eminence Legend speakers, 8 ohm impedance, air-tight straight cabinet, available in black Tolex covering, black or silver grille, built-in side handles, 68 lbs., current mfg.

| MSR $465 | $350 | $225 - 275 | $120 - 150 | |

B212SL Speaker Cabinet – similar to the B212 Speaker Cabinet, except has a slanted tall cabinet design, 74 lbs., current mfg.

| MSR $489 | $380 | $250 - 300 | $135 - 175 | |

B410 SPEAKER CABINET – 300W, 4-10 in. Eminence Legend speakers, 8 ohm impedance, air-tight straight cabinet, available in black Tolex covering, black or silver grille, built-in side handles, removable casters, 72 lbs., disc. 2008.

| | $525 | $300 - 375 | $200 - 250 | $705 |

B412 SPEAKER CABINET – 300W, 4-12 in. Eminence Legend speakers, 8 ohm impedance, air-tight slanted or straight cabinet, available in black Tolex covering, black or silver grille, built-in side handles, removable casters, 106 lbs., current mfg.

| MSR $640 | $500 | $300 - 375 | $175 - 225 | |

• Add 10% (MSR $950) for 480W handling power.

BASS SPEAKER CABINETS

B15B – 300W, 1-15 in. Eminence Delta speaker with a piezo horn, 8 ohm impedance, recessed side handles, black carpet covering, black grille with white trim or gray grille, 24.25 in. wide, 30.25 in. tall, 18.25 in. deep, 84 lbs., current mfg.

| MSR $395 | $340 | $200 - 250 | $125 - 150 | |

B210B – 500W, 2-10 in. BS1075 speakers with a horn, 4 ohm impedance, horn on/off switch, recessed side handles, removable casters, black carpet covering, black grille with white trim or gray grille, 24.25 in. wide, 33.25 in. tall, 18.25 in. deep, 110 lbs., current mfg.

| MSR $550 | $450 | $250 - 300 | $135 - 175 | |

B410B – 1000W, 4-10 in. BS1075 speakers with a horn, 8 ohm impedance, horn on/off switch, recessed side handles, removable casters, black carpet covering, black grille with white trim or gray grille, 28.625 in. wide, 35.25 in. tall, 17.25 in. deep, 148 lbs., current mfg.

| MSR $740 | $600 | $325 - 400 | $200 - 250 | |

B810B – 2000W, 8-10 in. BS1075 speakers, 4 ohm impedance, recessed side handles, 1.5 in. wide grab bar and fixed casters, black carpet covering, black grille with white trim or gray grille, 26.25 in. wide, 55 in. tall, 18 in. deep, 228 lbs., current mfg.

| MSR $1,100 | $900 | $500 - 600 | $300 - 375 | |

BC AUDIO

Amplifiers currently produced in San Francisco, CA since 2009.

Bruce Clement builds his unique Amplifier No. 7 amp in a military .50 caliber ammo canister. Clement built a few prototype tube preamps in the ammo cans during the 1990s, but he began building a full guitar amplifier in the canister in 2004. After gigging with the prototype for five years, he introduced the Amplifier No. 7 in 2009. The **Amplifier No. 7** (MSR $1,795) and **Amplifier No. 8** (MSR $1,895) has a 100% all-tube signal path with true point-to-point wiring, a tube rectifier, and puts out either 15W or 25W depending on the selected power tubes. For more information, visit BC Audio's website or contact them directly.

CONTACT INFORMATION
BC AUDIO
San Francisco, CA
Phone No.: 415-310-3087
www.bcaudio.com

B.C. RICH

Amplifiers produced overseas. Distributed by Hanser Music Group in Hebron, KY. Previously distributed by B.C. Rich, HHI, and Davitt & Hanser Music in Cincinnati, OH.

B.C. Rich does not have a dedicated line of amplifiers - they only offer an amp as part of their guitar and amp packages including the Metal Master Warlock, Son of Beast, and Red Bevel Warlock pack with red Insinerator amp. The B.C. Rich **BCL-10** (12W, 1-6.5 in. speaker, solid-state chassis, headphone jack, and Warlock headstock design in sides) amplifier comes with said guitar, strap, gigbag, pickups, and cord. For a full history on B.C. Rich guitars, refer to the *Blue Book of Electric Guitars*. For more information visit B.C. Rich's website or contact them directly.

CONTACT INFORMATION
B.C. RICH
Distributed by Hanser Music Group
3015 Kustom Drive
Hebron, KY 41048
Phone No.: 859-817-7100
Fax No.: 859-817-7199
www.bcrich.com

BEDROCK AMPLIFICATION, INC.

Amplifiers previously produced in Nashua, NH between 1984 and 1991 and in Farmington, MA between 1991 and 1997. Distributed by Bedrock Amplification, Inc.

Brad Jeter and Ron Pinto founded Bedrock Amplification in 1984, and they first produced amplifiers under the brand name Fred, but changed the name to Bedrock after about fifty amplifiers were built by circa 1986. In 1988, Jay Abend joined Bedrock and eventually became president, and Evan Cantor was hired as a designer. In the early 1990s, the two founding members, Jeter and Pinto, left the company leaving Abend and Cantor to run it until they went out of business in 1997. They also moved to Farmington, MA in the early 1990s.

MSR/NOTES	100%	EXCELLENT	AVERAGE	LAST MSR

Bedrock produced amplifiers that were based on designs of the Vox AC-30 and other English type amplifiers. They produced several guitar combo amps, heads, and speaker cabinets. After they went out of business, a few other boutique builders obtained the equipment. Information courtesy of Steve Cherne.

BEHRINGER

Amplifiers, speaker cabinets, and other audio electronics currently produced in Germany and in Asia, since 1989. Distributed by Behringer USA, Inc. in Bothell, WA.

CONTACT INFORMATION
BEHRINGER
18912 North Creek Parkway, Suite 200
Bothell, WA 98011
Phone No.: 425-672-0816
Fax No.: 425-673-7647
www.behringer.com
support@behringer.com

Behringer was founded by Uli Behringer in 1989, but Uli actually built his first synthesizer in 1978. The Germany-based company's first product was the Studio Exciter D. Throughout the early and mid-1990s, Behringer continued to introduce new audio products from synthesizers to mixers. In 1998, Behringer introduced guitar and bass amplifiers. In 2001, they introduced the V-AMP guitar digital modeler (similar to the Line-6 POD). In 2003, they introduced guitars and guitar/amp combo packs.

Behringer currently produces a wide range of analog and digital guitar modeling amplifiers, as well as solid-state amps, tube amps, acoustic amps, and bass amps. They also offer speaker cabinets, microphones, stomp boxes (effects), and a variety of audio accessories and electronics. For more information, visit Behringer's website or contact them directly.

ACOUSTIC AMPLIFIERS: ULTRACOUSTIC SERIES

Ultracoustic ACX900
courtesy Behringer

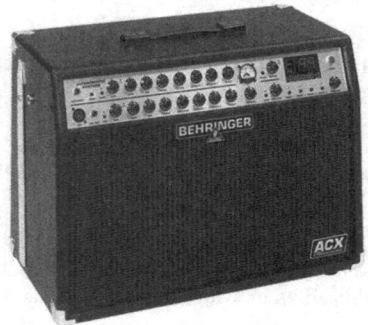

Ultracoustic ACX1000
courtesy Behringer

Ultracoustic AT108
courtesy Behringer

ULTRACOUSTIC ACX450 – 45W, 1-8 in. Bugera dual-cone speaker, acoustic combo, solid-state chassis, two channels, two integrated 24-bit digital FX processesors (one per channel), 16 digital effects, front gold control panel, three inputs (1/4 in. standard on Ch. 1, 1/4 in. line and XLR mic. on Ch. 2), six knobs (Ch. 1: g, FX select, FX level, Ch. 2: g, FX select, FX level), two five-band graphic EQs (one per channel), FBQ Feedback detection system on each channel, power switch, rear pane: RCA inputs with level control, footswitch jack, brown leatherette covering, dark brown covering, mfg. 2007-present.

MSR $270	$180	$120 - 150	$70 - 95

ULTRACOUSTIC ACX900 – 90W (2 X 45W stereo), 2-8 in. Bugera dual-cone speakers, acoustic combo, solid-state chassis, two channels, two integrated 24-bit digital FX processesors (one per channel), 16 digital effects, front gold control panel, three inputs (1/4 in. standard on Ch. 1, 1/4 in. line and XLR mic. on Ch. 2), six knobs (Ch. 1: g, FX select, FX level, Ch. 2: g, FX select, FX level), two seven-band graphic EQs (one per channel), FBQ Feedback detection system on each channel, tuner switch on each channel, power switch, rear panel: RCA inputs with level control, tuner out jack, footswitch jack, two balanced XLR line outs (stereo) with ground/lift switch, two effects loop (one per channel), brown leatherette covering, dark brown covering, mfg. 2007-present.

MSR $440	$300	$175 - 225	$110 - 140

ULTRACOUSTIC ACX1000 – 120W (2 X 60W stereo), 2-8 in. high-resolution speakers with a HF driver, acoustic combo, solid-state chassis with tube emulator, two channels, stereo 24-bit muliti FX processesor, 16 digital effects, 99 programmable presets, front gold control panel, three inputs (1/4 in. standard on Ch. 1, 1/4 in. line and XLR mic. on Ch. 2), 19 knobs (Ch. 1: g, b, m, t, attack, feedback 1, feedback 2, effect, Ch. 2: g, b, m, t, enahancer, feedback 1, feedback 2, effect, All: warmth, aux. level, MV), two phase switches, tuner switch, +48V switch, mute switch, four preset buttons, program button, LED digital display, meter, rear panel: mutable stereo aux. input, tuner out jacks, channel and master inserts, stereo tap in/out, black leatherette covering, dark brown grille, four-button FS114 footswitch included, mfg. 2003-07.

	$300	$175 - 225	$110 - 140	$440

ULTRACOUSTIC ACX1800 – 180W (2 X 90W stereo), 2-8 in. Bugera dual-cone speakers, acoustic combo, solid-state chassis, two channels, two integrated 24-bit digital FX processesors (one per channel), 16 digital effects, front gold control panel, three inputs (1/4 in. standard on Ch. 1, 1/4 in. line and XLR mic. on Ch. 2), 12 knobs (Ch. 1: g, compression in/out, FX select, paramter, FX level, Ch. 2: g, compression, FX select, parameter, FX level, All: MV, CD input level), two nine-band graphic EQs (one per channel), FBQ Feedback detection system on each channel, phase switch, compression limit switch on each channel, parameter in/out switch on each channel, tuner switch on each channel, mute switch, power switch, rear panel: RCA CD inputs, tuner out jack, footswitch jack, two balanced XLR line outs (stereo) with ground/lift switch, two effects loop (one per channel), brown leatherette covering, dark brown covering, mfg. 2007-present.

MSR $590	$400	$250 - 300	$135 - 175

ULTRACOUSTIC AT108 – 15W, 1-8 in. dual-cone speaker, acoustic combo, solid-state chassis with Virtual Tube Circuitry (VTC), two channels, front black control panel, two inputs (XLR mic on Ch. 1, standard 1/4 in. on Ch. 2), five knobs (mic. v, inst. v, l, m, h), CD input, headphone jack, power switch, brown leatherette covering, brown grille, mfg. 2006-present.

MSR $100 $70 $45 - 55 $25 - 35

ELECTRIC GUITAR AMPLIFIERS: V-TONE SERIES

V-Tone GM108
courtesy Behringer

V-Tone GMX112
courtesy Behringer

V-Tone GMX212
courtesy Behringer

V-TONE GM108 – 15W, 1-8 in. speaker, electric guitar combo, solid-state chassis, authentic V-Tone analog modeling, single channel, front black control panel, single input, five knobs (drive, l, m, h, MV), three classic guitar amp selector switch, three gain mode selector switch, three speaker simulation model selector switch, CD input, headphone jack, black covering, dark gray grille, mfg. 2004-present.

MSR $80 $60 $35 - 45 $20 - 25

V-TONE GMX110 – 30W, 1-10 in. Bugera speaker, electric guitar combo, solid-state chassis, authentic V-Tone analog modeling, 24-bit FX processor, 99 programmable presets, two channels, front dark gray control panel, single input, eight knobs (clean level, drive level, l, m, h, MV, preset selector, FX selector), channel selector, three classic guitar amp selector switch, three gain mode selector switch, three speaker simulation model selector switch, LED digital display, tuner and MIDI control, black covering, black grille, mfg. 2004-present.

MSR $220 $150 $95 - 120 $50 - 70

V-TONE GMX112 – 60W, 1-12 in. Bugera speaker, electric guitar combo, solid-state chassis, authentic V-Tone analog modeling, 24-bit FX processor, 99 programmable presets, two channels, front dark gray control panel, single input, 12 knobs (Ch. 1: drive, l, m, h, level, Ch. 2: drive, l, m, h, All: MV, preset selector, FX selector), three classic guitar amp selector switch, three gain mode selector switch, and three speaker simulation model selector switch (one for each channel), channel switch, in/out FX switch, power switch, LED digital display, rear panel: headphone jack, CD input, stereo line outputs, effects loop, footswitch jack, two-button FS112 footswitch included, black covering, black grille, mfg. 2005-08.

                            $200 $120 - 150 $70 - 95 $300

V-TONE GMX210 – 60W (2 X 30W stereo), 2-10 in. Bugera speakers, electric guitar combo, solid-state chassis, authentic V-Tone analog modeling, 24-bit FX processor, 99 programmable presets, two channels, front dark gray control panel, single input, 12 knobs (Ch. 1: drive, l, m, h, level, Ch. 2: drive, l, m, h, All: MV, preset selector, FX selector), three classic guitar amp selector switch, three gain mode selector switch, and three speaker simulation model selector switch (one for each channel), channel switch, in/out FX switch, power switch, LED digital display, rear panel: footswitch jack, MIDI input, two speaker jacks (stereo), headphone jack, stereo slave in, RCA tape in/out, stereo line outputs, CD input, effects loop, two-button FS112 footswitch included, black covering, black grille, mfg. 2005-2010.

                            $200 $120 - 150 $70 - 95 $300

V-TONE GMX212 – 120W (2 X 60W stereo), 2-12 in. Bugera speakers, electric guitar combo, solid-state chassis, authentic V-Tone analog modeling, 24-bit FX processor, 99 programmable presets, two channels, front dark gray control panel, single input, 14 knobs (Ch. 1: drive, l, m, h, MV, level, Ch. 2: drive, l, m, h, level, All: preset selector, FX selector, p, MV), three classic guitar amp selector switch, three gain mode selector switch, and three speaker simulation model selector switch (one for each channel), channel switch, in/out FX switch, power switch, LED digital display, rear panel: footswitch jack, MIDI input, two speaker jacks (stereo), headphone jack, stereo slave in, RCA tape in/out, stereo line outputs, CD input, effects loop, two-button FS112 footswitch included, black covering, black grille, mfg. 2004-present.

MSR $380 $260 $150 - 200 $95 - 120

V-TONE GMX1200H – 120W (2 X 60W stereo), electric guitar head unit, solid-state chassis, authentic V-Tone analog modeling, 24-bit FX processor, 99 programmable presets, two channels, front dark gray control panel, single input, 14 knobs (Ch. 1: drive, l, m, h, MV, level, Ch. 2: drive, l, m, h, level, All: preset selector, FX selector, p, MV), three classic guitar amp selector switch, three gain mode selector switch, and three speaker simulation model selector switch (one for each channel), channel switch, in/out FX switch, power switch, LED digital display, rear panel: footswitch jack, MIDI input, two speaker jacks (stereo), headphone jack, stereo slave in, RCA tape in/out, stereo line outputs, CD input, effects loop, two-button FS112 footswitch included, black covering, black grille, mfg. 2005-2010.

                            $200 $120 - 150 $70 - 95 $300

MSR/NOTES	100%	EXCELLENT	AVERAGE	LAST MSR

BELCAT

Amplifiers, preamps, effects, and other electronic products produced in China and Indonesia since 1988. Distributed by Belcat, Co. LTD. in Korea.

CONTACT INFORMATION
BELCAT
www.belcat.com
belcat@belcat.com

Belcat has been producing preamps, amplifiers, pickups, and other accessories since 1988. They offer a wide variety of guitar, acoustic, and bass amplifiers. For more information, visit Belcat's website.

BELTONE

Amplifiers previously produced in Japan by TEISCO during the 1960s and/or 1970s. Distributed in Canada by various companies.

While there is no documentation of where these amps were actually built, many people believe (and have researched) that Beltone amplifiers were manufactured in Japan and imported for sale in Canada. They were probably built by Teisco in Japan because the Beltone chassis' are very similar to the Teiscos. Any further information can be submitted directly to Blue Book Publications. Initial information courtesy: Tales From The Tone Lounge (www.tone-lizard.com).

ELECTRIC TUBE AMPLIFIERS

Early Beltone models feature a purple covering with a gold-style grille. One early example, which appears to be an extremely popular model by Beltone, features 2-8 in. speakers, 6AV6 preamp tubes and 6AR5 power tubes, tremolo, and four inputs. This model was also available as a piggy-back unit with separate head-units and speaker cabinets. Although these amps appear to be low-end beginner models, they are valued today between $250 and $350 depending upon condition.

BENNETT MUSIC LABS

Amplifiers and effects pedals currently produced in Chattanooga, TN.

CONTACT INFORMATION
BENNETT MUSIC LABS
6921 Middle Valley Rd.
Ste 107
Hixson, TN 37343
Phone No.: 423-760-0618
www.bennettmusiclabs.com
bmlinc@epbfi.com

Luthier Bruce Bennett started building custom guitars in 1979 in Chattanooga, TN. After having apprenticed for shops like Griffin Guitars, Steinburger/Tobias Guitars, and Gibson Guitars, Bennett designed and helped create the Warrior Instrument line in 1995 in Rossville, GA along with Micheal Shawn, William Fix, and J.D. Lewis. In 2001, a new Prototyping style shop was opened inside called The Pickers Exchange (a local Chattanooga music store) and continues to this day where one-of-a-kind creations are built to exact specifications. Bennett Music Labs builds guitars, tube amps, and effect pedals. For more information on Bennett electric guitars, please refer to the *Blue Book of Electric Guitars*. For more information in general, visit Bennett's website or contact him directly.

ELECTRIC TUBE AMPLIFIERS

The **AD-7** (MSR $999) is a small 7W amp with 6V6 power tubes, 1-10 in. speaker, and single volume knob. Each model is numbered and hand-signed as each color series is run in a limited number of 25. The **AD-30** (MSR $3,299) is a 30W Class A/B amp with unique styling and tremolo and reverb. The **AD-412** speaker cabinet (MSR $1,799) features 4-12 in. speakers in a uniquely-shaped cabinet.

B-52

Amplifiers and other pro audio equipment currently produced in Huntington Park, CA since 2000.

CONTACT INFORMATION
B-52
3383 Gage Ave.
Huntington Park, CA 90255
Phone No.: 323-277-4100
Phone No.: 800-344-4384
Fax No.: 323-277-4108
www.b-52stealthseries.com
information@b-52pro.com

B-52 produces both guitar amplifiers and pro audio equipment. All of their products are manufactured in the U.S. Guitar amps are called the Stealth Series and feature tube and solid-state designs. They also keep their prices low, so many people can afford their products. For more information, refer to their website or contact them directly.

ELECTRIC TUBE AMPLIFIERS: AT SERIES

AT-100 HEAD – 100W, head-unit only, all-tube chassis, preamp:7 X 12AX7, power: 4 X 6L6/5881, rectifier: 5AR4, three channels, reverb, front silver control panel, two inputs, 15 knobs (OD: g1, g2, b, m, t, c, v1, v2, Clean: b, m, t, v, All: MV, resonance, r), effects loop with level controls, footswitch, black covering, black grille with silver outline, 53 lbs., mfg. 2005-08.

$600	$425 - 500	$275 - 325	$1,400

* **AT-112 Combo** – similar to the AT-100 head-unit, except in combo configuration with 1-12 in. speakers and 60W output, seven-tube chassis, preamp: 5 X 12AX7, 2 X 6L6/5881, 40 lbs., mfg. 2005-08.

$550	$325 - 400	$200 - 250	$1,099

* **AT-212 Combo** – similar to the AT-100 head-unit, except in combo configuration with 2-12 in. speakers, 78 lbs., mfg. 2005-08.

$700	$475 - 550	$300 - 350	$1,700

MSR/NOTES	100%	EXCELLENT	AVERAGE	LAST MSR

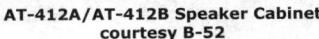

AT-412A/AT-412B Speaker Cabinet
courtesy B-52

ST-60A Head
courtesy B-52

LG-200A Head
courtesy B-52

ATX-100 HEAD – 100W, guitar head-unit, 10-tube chassis, preamp: 6 X 12AX7, power: 4 X 6L6/5881, solid-state rectifier, three channels (Clean, Overdrive 1, Overdrive 2), reverb, front chrome control panel, two inputs (high and low), 15 knobs (Master: r, low res, MV, Clean Ch.: v, t, m, b, OD1/OD2 Ch.: v2, v1, mid-cut, t, m, b, g2, g1), clean channel bright switch, channel select switch, two mid-cut switches (Ch. 1, Ch.2), gain select switch, power switch, standby switch, rear panel: effects loop, two footswitch jacks, two speaker jacks with impedance selector, black covering, black grille with silver piping, four-button footswitch included, mfg. 2009-present.

| MSR $1,200 | $600 | $425 - 500 | $275 - 325 | |

AT-412A/AT-412B SPEAKER CABINET – 480W, 4-12 in. Custom B-52 speakers, mono/stereo switchable, straight or angled cabinet, removable casters, black covering, black grille, 93 lbs., mfg. 2005-present.

| MSR $800 | $400 | $275 - 325 | $150 - 200 | |

ELECTRIC TUBE AMPLIFIERS: ST SERIES

ST-60A HEAD – 60W, head-unit only, all-tube chassis, preamp: 6 X 12AX7, power: 2 X 6L6/5881, rectifier: 5AR4, two channels, reverb, front silver control panel, two inputs, 13 knobs (OD: g1, g2, c, b, m, t, v, Clean: v, b, m, t, All: MV, r), effects loop, line out with level control, headphone jack, footswitch, black covering, black metal grille with silver flame accents, 51 lbs., disc. 2008.

| | $550 | $325 - 400 | $200 - 250 | $1,000 |

* ST-6012 Combo – similar to the ST-60A Head, except in combo form with 2-12 in. Celestion Vintage 30 speakers, black covering, black grille, 84 lbs., disc. 2008.

| | $750 | $500 - 575 | $325 - 375 | $1,600 |

ST-100A HEAD – 100W, head-unit only, all-tube chassis, preamp: 6 X 12AX7, power: 4 X 6L6/5881, rectifier: 5AR4, two channels, reverb, front silver control panel, two inputs, 13 knobs (OD: g1, g2, c, b, m, t, v, Clean: v, b, m, t, All: MV, r), effects loop, line out with level control, headphone jack, footswitch, black covering, black metal grille with silver flame accents, 56 lbs., disc. 2008.

| | $600 | $425 - 500 | $275 - 325 | $1,600 |

ST-212S SPEAKER CABINET – 140W, 2-12 in. Celestion Vintage 30 speakers, 16 or 8 ohm impedance, black covering, black grille, 63 lbs., disc. 2008.

| | $400 | $275 - 325 | $150 - 200 | $800 |

ST-412V/ST-412S SPEAKER CABINET – 280W, 4-12 in. Celestion Vintage 30 speakers, 16 or 8 ohm impedance, straight or angled front, black covering, black grille, 98/100 lbs., disc. 2008.

| | $600 | $425 - 500 | $275 - 325 | $1,100 |

ELECTRIC SS AMPLIFIERS: LG SERIES

LG-100A HEAD – 100W, head-unit only, solid-state chassis, two channels, reverb, front gold control panel, single input, 13 black knobs (OD: g1, g2, c, b, m, t, level, Clean: level, b, m, t, All: r, MV), effects loop, headphone jack, line out with level control, footswitch, black covering, black grille, 33 lbs., disc. 2008.

| | $350 | $200 - 250 | $120 - 150 | $600 |

LG-200A HEAD – 200W, head-unit only, solid-state chassis, two channels, reverb, chorus, front gold control panel, single input, 15 black knobs (OD: g1, g2, c, b, m, t, level, Clean: level, b, m, t, All: r, MV, rate, depth), effects loop, headphone jack, line out with level control, footswitch, black covering, black grille, 41 lbs., disc. 2006.

| | $400 | $275 - 325 | $150 - 200 | $800 |

LG-7512 COMBO – 75W, 1-12 in. speaker combo, solid-state chassis, two channels, reverb, front gold control panel, single input, 13 black knobs (OD: g1, g2, c, b, m, t, level, Clean: level, b, m, t, All: r, MV), effects loop, headphone jack, line out with level control, footswitch, black covering, black grille, 51 lbs., disc. 2008.

| | $300 | $175 - 225 | $95 - 125 | $600 |

LG-10012S Combo
courtesy B-52

LS-100 Head
courtesy B-52

LS-412A/LS-412B Speaker Cabinet
courtesy B-52

LG-10012S COMBO – 200W, 2-12 in. speaker combo, solid-state chassis, two channels, reverb, chorus, front gold control panel, single input, 15 black knobs (OD: g1, g2, c, b, m, t, level, Clean: level, b, m, t, All: r, MV, rate, depth), effects loop, headphone jack, line out with level control, footswitch, black covering, black grille, 63 lbs., disc. 2008.

	$400	$275 - 325	$150 - 200	$800

LG-412V/LG-412S SPEAKER CABINET – 400W, 4-12 in. B-52 speakers, rear-ported, straight or angled front, black covering, black metal grille, 94 lbs., disc. 2008.

	$350	$200 - 250	$120 - 150	$600

ELECTRIC SS AMPLIFIERS: LS SERIES

LS-100 HEAD – 100W, guitar head unit, solid-state chassis, three channels, reverb, front silver control panel, single input, 14 black knobs (Clean Ch.: v, t, m, b, OD Ch.: v2, v1, c, t, m, b, g2, g1, All: MV, r), mid-cut switch (Clean Ch.), channel select switch, two contour switches, gain switch, effects loop with level controls, line out with level control, two speaker outs, voltage switch, black Tolex covering, black metal grille, 34 lbs., mfg. 2007-present.

MSR $600	$300	$175 - 225	$95 - 125	

LS-412A/LS-412B SPEAKER CABINET – 400W, 4-12 in. speakers, mono/stereo switchable, rear-ported, straight (LS-412B) or angled (LS-412A) cabinet, black vinyl covering, black metal grille, built-in side handles, removable casters, mfg. 2007-present.

MSR $600	$300	$175 - 225	$95 - 125	

BGW

Amplifiers and other audio equipment currently produced in Montebello, CA by Amplifier Technologies, Inc. since 2003. Previously produced in Hawthorne, CA. The BGW trademark was established in 1971.

BGW makes a full line of rack-mount amplifiers along with other audio equipment including computers, subwoofers, and other rack-mount accessories. In 2003, Amplifier Technologies, Inc. aquired BGW. For the full product line, options, and prices visit BGW's website or contact them directly.

CONTACT INFORMATION
BGW
1749 Chapin Road
Montebello, CA 90640
Phone No.: 323-278-0001
Phone No.: 800-468-2677
Fax No.: 323-278-0083
www.bgw.com
info@bgw.com

BIG M

Amplifiers previously produced in England by Marshall between 1966 and 1968, and in Long Island, NY in 1975.

Big M is one of five other brands Marshall produced in the 1960s (CMI, Park, Kitchen Marshall, and Narb were the other four). As Marshall grew as a company, they began selling amplifiers in different countries, including Germany. However, a German company was already using the name Marshall on a line of trumpets, and Jim Marshall wasn't able to use the brand on his amplifiers. In 1966, he started building amps for Germany under the name "Big M" that were simply Marshall amplifiers with a different name on the front. The Big M trademark was relatively short-lived since by 1968, Jim bought the rights to Marshall trumpets in Germany and stopped producing Big M amplifiers since he could now sell Marshall amplifiers there.

Big M reappeared in 1975, in the American market. Marshall/Rose-Morris marketing executives decided that building amps in America would be cheaper, and thus boost sales so the second run of Big M amplifiers were manufactured in Long Island, NY. The new Big M built both solid-state and tube heads, for lead and bass applications. They also made some speaker cabinets with some new features, such as the extended frequency enclosure. These units were cheaper and used Eminence speakers, instead of Celestions. The second run of Big M lasted less than a year and they were discontinued. Big M never made a third comeback. Source: Michael Doyle, *The History of Marshall.*

| MSR/NOTES | 100% | EXCELLENT | AVERAGE | LAST MSR |

BLACKHEART

Amplifiers previously produced in China from 2008-2013. Distributed by LOUD Technologies in Woodinville, WA and a division of Crate Amps.

Amp designer and builder Pyotr Belov and LOUD Technologies (Crate, Ampeg, Alvarez, etc.) introduced the Blackheart line of amplifiers in late 2007. Belov has built custom order amplifiers and has also designed amps for Gibson and Epiphone. Blackheart amps are all-tube boutique amps that were built in China and offered at a reasonable price. Belov traveled to China and personally selected and inspected the factory that built these amps. LOUD Technologies distributed the Blackheart trademark through their Crate brand.

ELECTRIC TUBE AMPLIFIERS

BH1H "KILLER ANT" HEAD – 1W, guitar head-unit, tube chassis, solid-state rectifier, single channel, front silver control panel, single

BH5H "Little Giant" Head
courtesy Blackheart

BH15-112 "Handsome Devil" Combo
courtesy Blackheart

BH100H "Hot Head" Head
courtesy Blackheart

input, single black volume knob, three speaker out jacks, black covering, gray grille with white piping, mfg. 2008-disc.

$180	$100 - 130	$60 - 80	$273

BH5H "LITTLE GIANT" HEAD – 5W, guitar head-unit, two-tube chassis, preamp: 1 X 12AX7, power: 1 X EL34, solid-state rectifier, single channel, front silver control panel, single input, four black knobs (v, t, m, b), pentode (5W)/triode (3W) switch, multiple speaker out jacks, black covering, gray grille with white piping, mfg. 2008-disc.

$200	$120 - 150	$70 - 95	$303

* BH5-112 "Little Giant" Combo – similar to the BH5H Head, except in combo configuration with 1-12 in. Eminence speaker, a top-mounted control panel, and no speaker out jacks, mfg. 2008-disc.

$350	$200 - 250	$120 - 150	$531

BH15H "HANDSOME DEVIL" HEAD – 15W, guitar head-unit, tube chassis, solid-state rectifier, single channel, front silver control panel, single input, six black knobs (drive, level, t, m, b, p), pentode (15W)/triode (7W) switch, multiple speaker out jacks, black covering, gray grille with white piping, mfg. 2008-disc.

$350	$200 - 250	$120 - 150	$531

* BH15-112 "Handsome Devil" Combo – similar to the BH15H Little Giant Head, except in combo configuration with 1-12 in. Eminence speaker, a top-mounted control panel, and no speaker out jacks, mfg. 2008-disc.

$450	$275 - 325	$150 - 200	$683

BH100H "HOT HEAD" HEAD – 100W, guitar head-unit, tube chassis, solid-state rectifier, two channels (Loud, F'N Loud), front silver control panel, single input, 12 black knobs (Ch. 1: d, level, t, m, b, Ch. 2: g, level, t, m, b, All: p, MV), channel select switch, Class A/Class AB switch, full power/half power switch, line out jack, five speaker out jacks, footswitch, effects loop with send and return levels and series/parallel switch, black covering, gray grille with white piping, mfg. 2008-disc.

$900	$500 - 600	$300 - 350	$1,365

SPEAKER CABINETS

BH110 SPEAKER CABINET – 30W, 1-10 in. Eminence British-voiced speaker, 16 ohm impedance, closed back design, two speaker jacks, 18mm thick plywood construction, black covering, black and silver grille cloth with white piping, mfg. 2008-present.

MSR $228	$150	$95 - 120	$50 - 70

BH112 SPEAKER CABINET – 75W, 1-12 in. Eminence British-voiced speaker, 16 ohm impedance, closed back design, two speaker jacks, 18mm thick plywood construction, black covering, black and silver grille cloth with white piping, mfg. 2008-present.

MSR $243	$160	$100 - 130	$60 - 80

MSR/NOTES	100%	EXCELLENT	AVERAGE	LAST MSR

BH412SL/BH412ST SPEAKER CABINET – 300W, 4-12 in. Eminence British-voiced speakers, 16 ohm impedance, closed back design, angled (BH412SL) or straight (BH412ST) front, two speaker jacks, 18mm thick plywood construction, metal side-mounted handles, black covering, black and silver grille cloth with white piping, mfg. 2008-present.

MSR $834	$550	$325 - 400	$175 - 225

BLACKSTAR AMPLIFICATION

Amplifiers currently produced in Korea and headquartered and designed in Northampton, England since 2007. Distributed in the U.S. by Korg USA in Melville, NY.

Ian Robinson and Bruce Keir founded Blackstar Amplification in 2007. Robinson and Keir are both former employees in Marshall's research and development department, who wanted to create amplifiers and effects pedals that didn't quite fit the Marshall brand. Blackstar started out with a line of valve-powered effects pedals and they have expanded to a full series of tube amplifiers and hand-wired amps. All of Blackstar's design and engineering happens in England, but the production actually happens in Korea. For more information, visit Blackstar's website or contact them directly.

CONTACT INFORMATION
BLACKSTAR AMPLIFICATION
Headquarters
Beckett House, 14 Billing Road
Northampton, NN1 5AW United
Kingdom
Phone No.: +44 (0) 1604 652844
www.blackstaramps.com
enquiries@blackstaramps.com

U.S. Distribution: Korg USA
316 S. Service Road
Melville, NY 11747
Phone No.: 631-390-6800
www.korg.com

ELECTRIC TUBE AMPS: ARTISAN SERIES

Blackstar's Artisan Series are all hand-wired and they represent the top-of-the-line amplifiers for Blackstar.

Artisan 15H Head
courtesy Blackstar Amplification

Artisan 30 Combo
courtesy Blackstar Amplification

Artisan 100 Head
courtesy Blackstar Amplification

ARTISAN 15 COMBO – 15W, 1-12 in. Vintage G12M Celestion speaker, guitar combo, six-tube chassis, preamp: 2 X ECC83, 1 X EF86, power: 2 X EL84, rectifier: 1 X EZ81, two channels (one based on an ECC83 and one based on an EF86), top/rear black control panel, four inputs (two per channel, one high, one low), four knobs (Ch. 1: v, tone, Ch. 2: v, tone), 5W/15W switch, standby switch, power switch, rear panel: impedance selector, two speaker jacks, dark brown covering, black grille, mfg. 2008-present.

MSR $2,380	$2,000	$1,200 - 1,450	$800 - 950

* ***Artisan 15H Head*** – similar to the Artisan 15 Combo, except in head-unit configuration, front control panel, and all dark brown covering, mfg. 2008-present.

MSR $1,800	$1,200	$775 - 900	$400 - 475

ARTISAN 30 COMBO – 30W, 2-12 in. Celestion Vintage 30 speakers, guitar combo, nine-tube chassis, preamp: 3 X ECC83, 1 X EF86, power: 4 X EL84, rectifier: 1 X GZ34, two channels (one based on an ECC83 and one based on an EF86), top/rear black control panel, four inputs (two per channel, one high, one low), nine knobs (Ch. 1: v, tone, five-position bass shape, Ch. 2: g, two-position warm/bright voice, b, m, t, v), 10W/30W switch, standby switch, power switch, rear panel: impedance selector, two speaker jacks, dark brown covering, black grille, mfg. 2008-present.

MSR $2,800	$1,900	$1,225 - 1,425	$625 - 750

* ***Artisan 30H Head*** – similar to the Artisan 30 Combo, except in head-unit configuration, front control panel, and all dark brown covering, mfg. 2008-present.

MSR $2,500	$1,700	$1,100 - 1,275	$550 - 675

ARTISAN 100 HEAD – 100W, guitar head-unit, seven-tube chassis, preamp: 3 X ECC83, power: 4 X EL34, solid-state rectifier, two channels, front black control panel, four inputs (two per channel, one high, one low), seven knobs (v1, v2, b, m, t, four-position voice, p), standby switch, power switch, rear panel: impedance selector, two speaker jacks, dark brown covering, mfg. 2008-present.

MSR $3,000	$1,900	$1,225 - 1,425	$625 - 750

ARTISAN 212 SPEAKER CABINET – 120W, 2-12 in. Celestion Vintage 30 speakers mounted vertically, 16 ohm impedance, designed for use with the Artisan 15H and Artisan 30H heads, finger-jointed birch plywood construction, recessed side handles, brown covering, black grille, mfg. 2008-present.

MSR $812	$600	$375 - 450	$250 - 300

MSR/NOTES	100%	EXCELLENT	AVERAGE	LAST MSR

Artisan 412A/412B Speaker Cabinet
courtesy Blackstar Amplification

Artist 15 Combo
courtesy Blackstar Amplification

Artist 30 Combo
courtesy Blackstar Amplification

ARTISAN 412A/412B SPEAKER CABINET – 240W, 4-12 in. Celestion Vintage 30 speakers, 16 ohm impedance, angled (412A) or straight (412B) front, designed for use with the Artisan 100H head, finger-jointed birch plywood construction, recessed side handles, brown covering, black grille, mfg. 2008-present.

MSR $1,540 $900 $575 - 675 $295 - 350

ELECTRIC TUBE AMPS: ARTIST SERIES

ARTIST 15 COMBO – 15W, 1-12 in. Celestion V speaker, guitar combo, four-tube chassis, preamp: 2 X ECC83, power: 2 X 6L6, two channels, top/rear black control panel, single input, ten knobs (Ch.1: v, tone, Ch. 2: g, v, All: b, m, t , ISF, MV, reverb), channel switch, power switch, rear panel: three speaker jacks, emulated speaker jack, effect loop with level, footswitch jack, footswitch included, black covering, black grille, 39.7 lbs., new 2016.

MSR $1,080 $800 $525 - 600 $260 - 325

ARTIST 30 COMBO – 30W, 2-12 in. Celestion V speakers, guitar combo, four-tube chassis, preamp: 2 X ECC83, power: 2 X 6L6, two channels, digital reverb, top black control panel, single input, ten knobs (Ch.1: v, tone, Ch. 2: g, v, All: b, m, t , ISF, MV, reverb), channel switch, standby switch, power switch, rear panel: three speaker jacks, emulated speaker jack, effect loop with level, footswitch jack, footswitch included, black covering, black grille, 49.6 lbs., new 2016.

MSR $1,540 $1,100 $725 - 825 $350 - 450

ELECTRIC TUBE AMPS: HT-1 SERIES

HT-1 Combo
courtesy Blackstar Amplification

HT-1RH Head
courtesy Blackstar Amplification

HT-408 Speaker Cabinet
courtesy Blackstar Amplification

HT-1 COMBO – 1W, guitar combo amp, 1-8 in. Blackbird 15 speaker, two-tube chassis, preamp: 1 X ECC83. 1 X ECC82, two channels, Infinite Shape Feature, top black control panel, single input, three knobs (g, v, EQ), OD switch, power switch, emulated output/headphone jack, MP3/line input jack, speaker output jack, top handle, black covering, black grille, 13.23 lbs., mfg. 2011-present

MSR $337 $250 $165 - 190 $80 - 100

HT-1R COMBO – 1W, guitar combo amp, 1-8 in. Blackbird 15 speaker, two-tube chassis, preamp: 1 X ECC83. 1 X ECC82, two channels, Infinite Shape Feature, stereo reverb, top black control panel, single input, four knobs (g, v, EQ, reverb), OD switch, power switch, emulated output/headphone jack, MP3/line input jack, speaker output jack, top handle, black covering, black grille, 13.23 lbs., mfg. 2011-present

MSR $400 $325 $215 - 250 $105 - 130

Also available in Limited Edition White covering (model HT-1RW).

HT-1RH HEAD – 1W, guitar head unit, two-tube chassis, preamp: 1 X ECC83. 1 X ECC82, two channels, Infinite Shape Feature, stereo reverb, front black control panel, single input, four knobs (g, v, EQ, reverb), OD switch, power switch, emulated output/headphone jack, MP3/line input jack, speaker output jack, top handle, black covering, black grille, 8.82 lbs., mfg. 2011-present

MSR $320 $250 $165 - 190 $80 - 100

Also available in Limited Edition White covering (model HT-1RHW).

HT-408 SPEAKER CABINET – 60W, 4-8 in. Blackbird 15 speakers, 8 ohm impedance, designed for use with the HT-1RH head unit, top handle, black covering, black grille, 28.66 lbs., mfg. 2011-present.

MSR $337 $270 $175 - 205 $90 - 110

Also available in Limited Edition with White covering (model HT-408W).

MSR/NOTES	100%	EXCELLENT	AVERAGE	LAST MSR

ELECTRIC TUBE AMPS: HT-5 SERIES

HT-5 Head
courtesy Blackstar Amplification

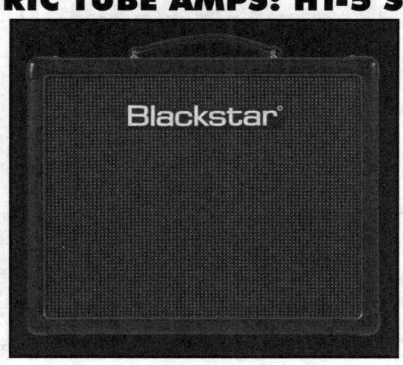

HT-5 Combo
courtesy Blackstar Amplification

HT-5S Mini-Stack
courtesy Blackstar Amplification

HT-5 HEAD – 5W, guitar head-unit, two-tube chassis, preamp: 1 X ECC83, power: 1 X 12BH7, solid-state rectifier, two channels, Infinite Shape Feature, front black control panel, single input, seven knobs (clean Ch. v, OD Ch. g, OD Ch. v, b, m, t, ISF), OD switch, emulated speaker/headphone jack with 1x12 or 4x12 voicing switch, standby switch, power switch, rear panel: two speaker jacks, footswitch jack, effects loop with level control, single-button footswitch included, black covering, mfg. 2008-2010.

	$350	$225 - 275	$135 - 175	$500

* **HT-5 Combo** – similar to the HT-5 Head, except in combo configuration with 1-10 in. Celestion speaker, top control panel, and a dark gray grille with white trim, mfg. 2008-2010.

	$400	$275 - 325	$150 - 200	$630

* **HT-5S Mini-Stack** – similar to the HT-5 Head, except in mini-stack configuration with the HT-5 Head unit and two cabinets equipped with 1-10 in. Celestion speaker each, and a dark gray grille with white trim on the cabinets, mfg. 2008-2010.

	$600	$375 - 450	$225 - 275	$880

HT-5C COMBO – 5W, guitar combo amp, 1-12 in. Blackbird 50 speaker, two-tube chassis, preamp: 1 X ECC83, power: 1 X 12BH7, two channels, Infinite Shape Feature, top black control panel, single input, eight knobs (clean Ch. v, clean Ch, tone, OD Ch. g, OD Ch. v, b, m, t, ISF), OD switch, emulated speaker with 1x12 or 4x12 voicing switch, standby switch, power switch, footswitch jack, effects loop with level control, footswitch included, top handle, black covering, black grille, 27.1 lbs., mfg. 2011-2015.

	$350	$225 - 260	$115 - 140	$450

HT-5R COMBO – 5W, guitar combo amp, 1-12 in. Blackbird 50 speaker, two-tube chassis, preamp: 1 X ECC83, power: 1 X 12BH7, two channels, Infinite Shape Feature, stereo reverb, top black control panel, single input, nine knobs (clean Ch. v, clean Ch. tone, OD Ch. g, OD Ch. v, b, m, t, ISF, reverb), OD switch, emulated speaker with 1x12 or 4x12 voicing switch, standby switch, power switch, footswitch jack, effects loop with level control, MP3 input jack, footswitch included, top handle, black covering, black grille, 27.1 lbs., mfg. 2011-present.

MSR $625	$500	$325 - 375	$165 - 200	

In 2012, Blackstar issued a Limited Edition (2500 units) 5th Anniversary version (model HT-5TH) with cream covering.

Also available in Limited Edition with White (model HT-5RW) or Red (model HT-5R RED) covering.

* **HT-5RH Head** – 5W, guitar head unit, two-tube chassis, preamp: 1 X ECC83, power: 1 X 12BH7, two channels, Infinite Shape Feature, stereo reverb, front black control panel, single input, nine knobs (clean Ch. v, clean Ch, tone, OD Ch. g, OD Ch. v, b, m, t, ISF, reverb), OD switch, emulated speaker with 1x12 or 4x12 voicing switch, standby switch, power switch, footswitch jack, effects loop with level control, MP3 input jack, footswitch included, top handle, black covering, 16.5 lbs., mfg. 2011-present.

MSR $500	$400	$260 - 300	$130 - 160	

Also available in Limited Edition with White covering (model HT-5RHW).

* **HT-5RS Mini-Stack** – mini-stack configuration, 5W guitar head unit, 2 X 1-12 in. 50W cabinets with Blackbird 50 speakers, two-tube chassis, preamp: 1 X ECC83, power: 1 X 12BH7, two channels, Infinite Shape Feature, stereo reverb, front black control panel, single input, nine knobs (clean Ch. v, clean Ch, tone, OD Ch. g, OD Ch. v, b, m, t, ISF, reverb), OD switch, emulated speaker with 1x12 or 4x12 voicing switch, standby switch, power switch, footswitch jack, effects loop with level control, MP3 input jack, footswitch included, top handle, black covering, black grille, mfg. 2011-present.

MSR $937	$750	$475 - 550	$245 - 300	

Also available in Limited Edition with White covering (model HT-5RSW).

HT-5210 COMBO – 5W, guitar combo amp, 2-10 in. Celestion speakers, two-tube chassis, preamp: 1 X ECC83, power: 1 X 12BH7, two channels, Infinite Shape Feature, stereo reverb, top black control panel, single input, nine knobs (clean Ch. v, clean Ch. tone, OD Ch. g, OD Ch. v, b, m, t, ISF, reverb), OD switch, emulated speaker with 1x12 or 4x12 voicing switch, standby switch, power switch, footswitch jack, effects loop with level control, MP3 input jack, footswitch included, top handle, black covering, black grille, 37.48 lbs., mfg. 2013-present.

MSR $700	$550	$350 - 400	$180 - 220	

MSR/NOTES	100%	EXCELLENT	AVERAGE	LAST MSR

HT-5R Combo
courtesy Blackstar Amplification

HT-5210 Combo
courtesy Blackstar Amplification

HT-112 Speaker Cabinet
courtesy Blackstar Amplification

HT-110 SPEAKER CABINET – 40W, 1-10 in. Celestion speaker, 16 ohm impedance, designed for use with the HT-5 Head, black covering, dark gray grille with white trim, mfg. 2008-2010.

	$180	$110 - 140	$65 - 85	$250

HT-112 SPEAKER CABINET – 50W, 1-12 in. Blackbird 50 speaker, 16 ohm impedance, designed for use with the HT-5 series head units, top handle, black covering, dark gray grille with white trim, 23.63 lbs., mfg. 2011-present.

MSR $300	$190	$125 - 145	$60 - 75	

Also available in Limited Edition with White covering (model HT-112W).

ELECTRIC TUBE AMPS: HT METAL SERIES

HT Metal 1 Combo
courtesy Blackstar Amplification

HT Metal 5 Head
courtesy Blackstar Amplification

HT Metal 60 Combo
courtesy Blackstar Amplification

HT METAL 1 COMBO – 1W, guitar combo amp, 1-8 in. speaker, two-tube chassis, preamp: 1 X ECC83, 1 X ECC82, two channels, Infinite Shape Feature, stereo reverb, top control panel, single input, four knobs (g, v, EQ, reverb), OD switch, emulated speaker/headphone jack, MP3/line input jack, power switch, speaker output jack, top handle, black covering, black grille, 13 lbs., mfg. 2013-present.

MSR $489	$375	$245 - 280	$120 - 150	

HT METAL 1 HEAD – 1W, guitar head-unit, two-tube chassis, preamp: 1 X ECC83, 1 X ECC82, two channels, Infinite Shape Feature, stereo reverb, front gray control panel, single input, four knobs (g, v, EQ, reverb), OD switch, emulated speaker/headphone jack, MP3/line input jack, power switch, speaker output jack, top handle, black covering, black grille, 8.38 lbs., mfg. 2013-present.

MSR $392	$300	$195 - 225	$100 - 120	

HT METAL 5 COMBO – 5W, guitar combo amp, 1-12 in. Blackbird 50 speaker, two-tube chassis, preamp: 1 X ECC83, power: 1 X 12BH7, two channels, Infinite Shape Feature, stereo reverb, top gray control panel, single input, nine knobs (clean Ch. v, clean Ch. tone, OD Ch. g, OD Ch. v, b, m, t, ISF, reverb), OD switch, emulated speaker with 1x12 or 4x12 voicing switch, standby switch, power switch, footswitch jack, effects loop with level control, MP3 input jack, footswitch included, top handle, black covering, black grille, 31 lbs., mfg. 2013-present.

MSR $742	$500	$325 - 375	$165 - 200	

HT METAL 5 HEAD – 5W, guitar head-unit, two-tube chassis, preamp: 1 X ECC83, power: 1 X 12BH7, two channels, Infinite Shape Feature, stereo reverb, front gray control panel, single input, nine knobs (clean Ch. v, clean Ch. tone, OD Ch. g, OD Ch. v, b, m, t, ISF, reverb), OD switch, emulated speaker with 1x12 or 4x12 voicing switch, standby switch, power switch, footswitch jack, effects loop with level control, MP3 input jack, footswitch included, top handle, black covering, black grille, 16.75 lbs., mfg. 2013-present.

MSR $600	$425	$280 - 325	$140 - 170	

HT METAL 60 COMBO – 60W, closed-back guitar combo amp, 2-12 in. Celestion speakers, four-tube chassis, preamp: 2 X ECC83, power: 2 X 6L6, three channels, Infinite Shape Feature, digital reverb, top gray control panel, single input, fifteen knobs (clean Ch.: v, b, t, OD Ch. 1: g, v, OD Ch. 2: g, v, OD: b, m, t, ISF, All: reverb, resonance, presence, MV), voice switch, OD 1 switch, OD 2 switch, emulated speaker with 1x12 or 4x12 voicing switch, standby switch, power switch, footswitch jack, effects loop with level control, five speaker output jacks, footswitch included, top handle, black covering, black grille, 64.8 lbs., mfg. 2014-present.

MSR $1,610	$1,150	$750 - 850	$375 - 450	

MSR/NOTES	100%	EXCELLENT	AVERAGE	LAST MSR

HT Metal 100 Head
courtesy Blackstar Amplification

HT Metal 112 Speaker Cabinet
courtesy Blackstar Amplification

HT Metal 412 Speaker Cabinet
courtesy Blackstar Amplification

HT METAL 100 HEAD – 100W, head-unit, seven-tube chassis, preamp: 2 X ECC83, 1 X ECC82 power: 4 X 6L6, three channels, Infinite Shape Feature, digital reverb, front gray control panel, single input, fifteen knobs (clean Ch.: v, b, t, OD Ch. 1: g, v, OD Ch. 2: g, v, OD: b, m, t, ISF, All: reverb, resonance, presence, MV), voice switch, OD 1 switch, OD 2 switch, emulated speaker with 1x12 or 4x12 voicing switch, standby switch, power switch, footswitch jack, effects loop with level control, five speaker output jacks, footswitch included, top handle, black covering, black grille, 43.2 lbs., mfg. 2014-present.

| MSR $1,540 | $1,100 | $725 - 825 | $350 - 450 | |

HT METAL 112 SPEAKER CABINET – 50W, 1-12 in. Blackbird 50 speaker, 16 ohm impedance, top handle, black covering, black grille, 28.66 lbs., mfg. 2013-present.

| MSR $292 | $220 | $145 - 165 | $70 - 90 | |

HT METAL 408 SPEAKER CABINET – 60W, 4-8 in. Blackbird 15 speakers, 8 ohm impedance, top handle, black covering, black grille, 33.95 lbs., mfg. 2013-present.

| MSR $337 | $270 | $175 - 205 | $90 - 110 | |

HT METAL 412 SPEAKER CABINET – 320W, 4-12 in. Celestion speakers, 4/16 ohm mono/8 ohm stereo impedance, angled front (412A) or straight front (412B), designed for use with the HT Metal Series amps, black covering, black grille, mfg. 2013-present.

| MSR $910 | $650 | $425 - 475 | $210 - 260 | |

ELECTRIC TUBE AMPS: HT VENUE SERIES

HT Club 40
courtesy Blackstar Amplification

HT Studio 20 Head
courtesy Blackstar Amplification

HT Club 40
courtesy Blackstar Amplification

HT STUDIO 20 – 20W, 1-12 in. Celestion speaker, guitar combo, four-tube chassis, preamp: 2 X ECC83, power: 2 X EL34, solid-state rectifier, two channels, reverb, Infinite Shape Feature (ISF), front black control panel, single input, 10 knobs (Clean Ch.: g, v, OD Ch.: g, v, All: b, m, t, ISF, MV, r), channel switch, power switch, rear panel: speaker emulated output, effects loop, footswitch jack, one-button footswitch included, black covering, black grille with silver specks, mfg. 2010-present.

| MSR $840 | $550 | $350 - 400 | $180 - 220 | |

* *HT Studio 20 Head* – similar to the HT Studio 20 Combo, except in head-unit configuration and all black covering, mfg. 2010-present.

| MSR $630 | $500 | $325 - 400 | $200 - 250 | |

HT CLUB 40 – 40W, 1-12 in. Celestion speaker, guitar combo, four-tube chassis, preamp: 2 X ECC83, power: 2 X EL34, solid-state rectifier, two channels, reverb, Infinite Shape Feature (ISF), front black control panel, single input, 10 knobs (Clean Ch.: g, v, OD Ch.: g, v, All: b, m, t, ISF, MV, r), channel switch, clean channel voice switch, overdrive channel voice switch, standby switch, power switch, rear panel: speaker emulated output, reverb dark/bright switch, effects loop, footswitch jack, two-button footswitch included, black covering, black grille with silver specks, mfg. 2010-present.

| MSR $980 | $600 | $375 - 450 | $225 - 275 | |

Also available in Limited Edition models HT Club 40 RED, HT Club 40 VP and HT Club 40 SE.

MSR/NOTES	100%	EXCELLENT	AVERAGE	LAST MSR

HT Club 50 Head
courtesy Blackstar Amplification

HT Stage 60
courtesy Blackstar Amplification

HTV-112 Speaker Cabinet
courtesy Blackstar Amplification

HT CLUB 50 HEAD – 50W, guitar head unit, four-tube chassis, preamp: 2 X ECC83, power: 2 X EL34, two channels, reverb, Infinite Shape Feature (ISF), front black control panel, single input, 10 knobs (Clean Ch.: g, v, OD Ch.: g, v, All: b, m, t, ISF, MV, r), channel switch, standby switch, power switch, rear panel: speaker emulated output, reverb dark/bright switch, effects loop, footswitch jack, two-button footswitch included, black covering, black grille with silver specks, 30 lbs., mfg. 2012-present.

MSR $1,120 $800 $525 - 600 $260 - 325

HT SOLOIST 60 – 60W, 1-12 in. Celestion speaker, guitar combo, four-tube chassis, preamp: 2 X ECC83, power: 2 X EL34, solid-state rectifier, two channels, reverb, Infinite Shape Feature (ISF), front black control panel, single input, 12 knobs (Clean Ch.: g, v, OD Ch.: g, v, All: b, m, t, ISF, r, p, MV, solo boost), channel switch, clean channel voice switch, overdrive channel voice switch, body switch, standby switch, power switch, rear panel: speaker emulated output, 1x12/4x12 speaker cabinet switch, two speaker jacks, reverb dark/light switch, effects loop, footswitch jack, footswitch mode switch, four-button footswitch included, black covering, black grille with silver specks, mfg. 2010-present.

MSR $1,260 $900 $575 - 675 $295 - 350

HT STAGE 60 – 60W, 2-12 in. Celestion speakers, guitar combo, five-tube chassis, preamp: 2 X ECC83, 1 X ECC82, power: 2 X EL34, solid-state rectifier, three channels (clean, OD1, OD2), reverb, Infinite Shape Feature (ISF), front black control panel, single input, 15 knobs (Clean Ch.: v, b, t, OD1/OD2 Ch.: OD1 g, OD1 v, OD2 g, OD2 v, b, m, t, ISF, r, resonance, p, MV, solo boost), three channel switches, three channel voice switches, standby switch, power switch, rear panel: speaker emulated output, 1x12/4x12 speaker cabinet switch, two speaker jacks, reverb dark/light switch, effects loop, footswitch jack, footswitch mode switch, four-button footswitch included, black covering, black grille with silver specks, mfg. 2010-present.

MSR $1,400 $1,000 $650 - 750 $325 - 400

HT STAGE 100 HEAD – 100W, guitar head-unit, seven-tube chassis, preamp: 2 X ECC83, 1 X ECC82, power: 4 X EL34, solid-state rectifier, three channels (clean, OD1, OD2), reverb, Infinite Shape Feature (ISF), front black control panel, single input, 15 knobs (Clean Ch.: v, b, t, OD1/OD2 Ch.: OD1 g, OD1 v, OD2 g, OD2 v, b, m, t, ISF, r, resonance, p, MV, solo boost), three channel switches, three channel voice switches, standby switch, power switch, rear panel: speaker emulated output, 1x12/4x12 speaker cabinet switch, two speaker jacks, reverb dark/light switch, effects loop, footswitch jack, footswitch mode switch, four-button footswitch included, black covering, black grille with silver specks, mfg. 2010-present.

MSR $1,260 $900 $575 - 675 $295 - 350

HTV-112 SPEAKER CABINET – 80W, 1-12 in. Celestion speaker, 16 ohm mono impedance, designed for use with the HT Venue Series amps, black covering, black grille with silver specks, mfg. 2010-present.

MSR $290 $230 $150 - 175 $75 - 90

HTV-212 SPEAKER CABINET – 160W, 2-12 in. Celestion speakers, 8 ohm mono/16 ohm stereo impedance, designed for use with the HT Venue Series amps, black covering, black grille with silver specks, mfg. 2010-present.

MSR $412 $325 $215 - 250 $105 - 130

HTV-412A/412B SPEAKER CABINET – 320W, 4-12 in. Celestion speakers, 16 ohm mono/8 ohm stereo impedance, angled front (412A) or straight front (412B), designed for use with the HT Venue Series amps, black covering, black grille with silver specks, mfg. 2010-present.

MSR $840 $600 $375 - 450 $250 - 300

ELECTRIC TUBE AMPS: SERIES ONE SERIES

SERIES ONE 45 COMBO – 45W, 2-12 in. Celestion custom designed Neo speakers, guitar combo, six-tube chassis, preamp: 3 X ECC83, 1 X ECC82, power: 2 X EL34, solid-state rectifier, two channels (clean, overdrive), four modes (warm, bright, crunch, super crunch), Infinite Shape Feature (ISF), dynamic power reduction (DPR), front black control panel, single input, 12 knobs (Clean Ch.: g, v, OD Ch.: g, v, All: b, m, t, ISF, r, p, MV, DPR), warm clean mode switch, bright clean mode switch, crunch mode switch, super crunch mode switch, standby switch, power switch, rear panel: effects loop with level control, XLR and 1/4 in. emulated speaker output, two speaker jacks with impedance selector, MIDI in, MIDI thru, footswitch jack, black covering, black grille, mfg. 2008-present.

MSR $2,375 $1,600 $1,050 - 1,200 $525 - 650

MSR/NOTES	100%	EXCELLENT	AVERAGE	LAST MSR

Series One 50 Head
courtesy Blackstar Amplification

Series One 1046L6 Head
courtesy Blackstar Amplification

Series One 104EL34 Head
courtesy Blackstar Amplification

SERIES ONE 50 HEAD – 50W, guitar head-unit, six-tube chassis, preamp: 3 X ECC83, 1 X ECC82, power: 2 X EL34, solid-state rectifier, two channels (clean, overdrive), four modes (warm, bright, crunch, super crunch), Infinite Shape Feature (ISF), dynamic power reduction (DPR), front black control panel, single input, 12 knobs (Clean Ch.: g, v, OD Ch.: g, v, All: b, m, t, ISF, r, p, MV, DPR), warm clean mode switch, bright clean mode switch, crunch mode switch, super crunch mode switch, standby switch, power switch, rear panel: effects loop with level control, XLR and 1/4 in. emulated speaker output, two speaker jacks with impedance selector, MIDI in, MIDI thru, footswitch jack, black covering, black metal grille, mfg. 2011-present.

| MSR $2,000 | $1,300 | $850 - 975 | $425 - 525 | |

SERIES ONE 100 HEAD – 100W, guitar head-unit, eight-tube chassis, preamp: 3 X ECC83, 1 X ECC82, power: 4 X EL34, solid-state rectifier, two channels (clean, overdrive), four modes (warm, bright, crunch, super crunch), Infinite Shape Feature (ISF), dynamic power reduction (DPR), front black control panel, single input, 12 knobs (Clean Ch.: g, v, OD Ch.: g, v, All: b, m, t, ISF, r, p, MV, DPR), warm clean mode switch, bright clean mode switch, crunch mode switch, super crunch mode switch, standby switch, power switch, rear panel: effects loop with level control, XLR and 1/4 in. emulated speaker output, two speaker jacks with impedance selector, MIDI in, MIDI thru, footswitch jack, black covering, black metal grille, mfg. 2008-present.

| MSR $2,250 | $1,500 | $975 - 1,125 | $500 - 600 | |

SERIES ONE 1046L6 HEAD – 100W, guitar head-unit, nine-tube chassis, preamp: 4 X ECC83, 1 X ECC82, power: 4 X 6L6, solid-state rectifier, four channels (clean, crunch, OD1, OD2), six modes, Infinite Shape Feature (ISF), dynamic power reduction (DPR), front black control panel, single input, 20 knobs (Clean Ch.: g, v, Crunch Ch.: g, v, OD 1 Ch.: g, v, OD 2 Ch.: g, v, All: b1, b2, m1, m2, t1, t2, ISF1, ISF2, r, p, MV, DPR), warm bright mode switch, clean mode switch, crunch mode switch, super crunch mode switch, OD1 switch, OD2 switch, standby switch, power switch, rear panel: effects loop with level control, XLR and 1/4 in. emulated speaker output, two speaker jacks with impedance selector, MIDI in, MIDI thru, footswitch jack, black covering, black metal grille, 60 lbs., mfg. 2011-present.

| MSR $2,200 | $1,600 | $1,050 - 1,200 | $525 - 650 | |

SERIES ONE 104EL34 HEAD – 100W, guitar head-unit, nine-tube chassis, preamp: 4 X ECC83, 1 X ECC82, power: 4 X EL34, solid-state rectifier, four channels (clean, crunch, OD1, OD2), six modes, Infinite Shape Feature (ISF), dynamic power reduction (DPR), front black control panel, single input, 20 knobs (Clean Ch.: g, v, Crunch Ch.: g, v, OD 1 Ch.: g, v, OD 2 Ch.: g, v, All: b1, b2, m1, m2, t1, t2, ISF1, ISF2, r, p, MV, DPR), warm bright mode switch, clean mode switch, crunch mode switch, super crunch mode switch, OD1 switch, OD2 switch, standby switch, power switch, rear panel: effects loop with level control, XLR and 1/4 in. emulated speaker output, two speaker jacks with impedance selector, MIDI in, MIDI thru, footswitch jack, black covering, black metal grille, 60 lbs., mfg. 2011-present.

| MSR $2,200 | $1,600 | $1,050 - 1,200 | $525 - 650 | |

SERIES ONE 200 HEAD – 200W, guitar head-unit, nine-tube chassis, preamp: 4 X ECC83, 1 X ECC82, power: 4 X KT88, solid-state rectifier, four channels (clean, crunch, overdrive 1, overdrive 2), four modes (Clean Ch.: warm, and bright, Crunch Ch.: crunch, super crunch), Infinite Shape Feature (ISF), dynamic power reduction (DPR), front black control panel, single input, 20 knobs (Clean Ch.: g, v, Crunch Ch.: g, v, OD1 Ch.: g, v, OD2 Ch.: g, v, Clean/Crunch Ch.: b, m, t, ISF, OD1/OD2 Ch.: b, m, t, ISF, All: r, p, MV, DPR), four channel switches, bright/warm clean mode switch, crunch/super crunch mode switch, standby switch, power switch, rear panel: effects loop with level control, XLR and 1/4 in. emulated speaker output, two speaker jacks with impedance selector, MIDI in, MIDI thru, footswitch jack, black covering, black metal grille, mfg. 2008-present.

| MSR $2,600 | $1,900 | $1,225 - 1,425 | $625 - 750 | |

SERIES ONE 212 SPEAKER CABINET – 120W, 2-12 in. Celestion Vintage 30 speakers, 8/16 ohm impedance, switchable mono/stereo operation, straight front, designed for use with the Series One heads, finger-jointed birch plywood construction, top handle, black covering, black grille, 46.3 lbs., mfg. 2011-present.

| MSR $900 | $600 | $400 - 450 | $195 - 240 | |

SERIES ONE 412A/412B SPEAKER CABINET – 240W, 4-12 in. Celestion Vintage 30 speakers, 16 ohm impedance, switchable mono/stereo operation, angled (412A) or straight (412B) front, designed for use with the Series One 100 and 200 heads, finger-jointed birch plywood construction, recessed side handles, black covering, black grille, mfg. 2008-present.

| MSR $1,375 | $900 | $575 - 675 | $295 - 350 | |

SERIES ONE 412A/412B PRO SPEAKER CABINET – 240W, 4-12 in. Celestion Vintage 30 speakers, 8/16 ohm impedance, switchable mono/stereo operation, 1960's standard size cabinet, angled (412A) or straight (412B) front, designed for use with the Series One heads, finger-jointed birch plywood construction, recessed side handles, black covering, black grille, mfg. 2011-2015.

| | $900 | $575 - 675 | $295 - 350 | $1,375 |

MSR/NOTES	100%	EXCELLENT	AVERAGE	LAST MSR

Gus G. Signature Blackfire 200 Head
courtesy Blackstar Amplification

Fly 3 Mini Combo
courtesy Blackstar Amplification

Fly 3 Stereo Pack
courtesy Blackstar Amplification

ELECTRIC TUBE AMPS: SIGNATURE SERIES

GUS G. SIGNATURE BLACKFIRE 200 HEAD – 200W, guitar head-unit, nine-tube chassis, preamp: 4 X ECC83, 1 X ECC82, power: 4 X KT88, solid-state rectifier, four channels (clean, crunch, overdrive 1, overdrive 2), six modes, Infinite Shape Feature (ISF), dynamic power reduction (DPR), front black control panel, single input, 20 knobs (Clean Ch.: g, v, Crunch Ch.: g, v, OD1 Ch.: g, v, OD2 Ch.: g, v, Clean/Crunch Ch.: b, m, t, ISF, OD1/OD2 Ch.: b, m, t, ISF, All: r, p, MV, DPR), six channel switches, standby switch, power switch, rear panel: effects loop with level control, XLR and 1/4 in. emulated speaker output, two speaker jacks with impedance selector, MIDI in, MIDI thru, footswitch jack, limited run of 225 units, black covering, black metal grille, 60 lbs., mfg. 2013-present.

MSR $3,300 $2,500 $1,625 - 1,875 $825 - 1,000

GUS G. SIGNATURE BLACKFIRE 412 SPEAKER CABINET – 240W, 4-12 in. Celestion Vintage 30 speakers, 4/16 ohm impedance, switchable mono/stereo operation, angled (412A) or straight (412B) front, designed for use with the Blackfire 200 head unit, finger-jointed birch plywood construction, recessed side handles, black covering, black grille, 108 lbs., mfg. 2013-2015.

$1,150 $750 - 850 $375 - 450 $1,610

ELECTRIC SS AMPS: FLY SERIES

FLY 3 MINI COMBO – 3W, guitar mini combo amp, 1-3 in. speaker, solid-state chassis, two channels, Infinite Shape Feature, tape delay effect, single input, top black control panel, four black knobs (g, v, EQ, delay), power switch, emulated speaker/headphone out, MP3/line in jack, battery or DC powered, top handle, black covering, black grille, 2 lbs., mfg. 2015-present.

MSR $70 $60 $40 - 45 $20 - 25

Also available in Limited Edition Cream, Union Flag, or Green covering.

FLY 103 MINI SPEAKER CABINET – 3W, 1-3 in. speaker, designed to pair with the Fly 3 mini combo amp to create a 6W stereo speaker system, black covering, black grille, 2 lbs., mfg. 2015-present.

MSR $40 $30 $20 - 25   N/A - 10

FLY 3 STEREO PACK – 6W total (2 X 3W) stereo amp, 3W Fly combo amp, 3W Fly extension cabinet, power supply included, top black control panel, black covering, black grille, 4 lbs., mfg 2015-present.

MSR $140 $100 $65 - 75 $35 - 40

ELECTRIC SS AMPS: ID SERIES

ID:15 TVP COMBO – 15W, 1-10 in. speaker, digital guitar combo amp, solid-state chassis, True Valve Power, six amp models, six channels, 12 effects, ISF, front black control panel, ten black knobs (voice selector, g, v, b, t, ISF, TVP selector, effect type, effect level, MV), power switch, emulated speaker/headphone out, MP3/line in jack, footswitch jack, various switches, USB connector, top handle, black covering, black grille, 24.25 lbs., mfg. 2013-present.

MSR $340 $230 $150 - 175 $75 - 90

ID:30 TVP COMBO – 30W, 1-12 in. speaker, digital guitar combo amp, solid-state chassis, True Valve Power, six amp models, six channels, 12 effects, ISF, front black control panel, ten black knobs (voice selector, g, v, b, t, ISF, TVP selector, effect type, effect level, MV), power switch, emulated speaker/headphone out, MP3/line in jack, footswitch jack, various switches, USB connector, top handle, black covering, black mesh grille, 28.66 lbs., mfg. 2013-present.

MSR $510 $350 $230 - 265 $115 - 140

ID:60 TVP COMBO – 60W, 1-12 in. speaker, digital guitar combo amp, solid-state chassis, True Valve Power, six amp models, six channels, 12 effects, ISF, front black control panel, single input, 13 black knobs (voice selector, g, v, b, m, t, ISF, TVP selector, effect type, effect level, resonance, presence, MV), power switch, emulated speaker out, MP3/line in jack, footswitch jack, MIDI in, speaker output jack, various switches, USB connector, top handle, black covering, black mesh grille, 39.68 lbs., mfg. 2013-present.

MSR $740 $500 $325 - 375 $165 - 200

MSR/NOTES	100%	EXCELLENT	AVERAGE	LAST MSR

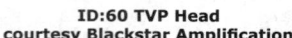

ID:60 TVP Head
courtesy Blackstar Amplification

ID:260 TVP Combo
courtesy Blackstar Amplification

ID:Core Beam Combo
courtesy Blackstar Amplification

ID:60 TVP HEAD – 60W, digital guitar head unit, solid-state chassis, True Valve Power, six amp models, six channels, 12 effects, ISF, front black control panel, single input, 13 black knobs (voice selector, g, v, b, m, t, ISF, TVP selector, effect type, effect level, resonance, presence, MV), power switch, emulated speaker out, MP3/line in jack, footswitch jack, MIDI in, speaker output jacks, various switches, USB connector, top handle, black covering, black mesh grille, 23.8 lbs., mfg. 2013-present.

MSR $600	$400	$260 - 300	$130 - 160

ID:100 TVP HEAD – 100W, digital guitar head unit, solid-state chassis, True Valve Power, six amp models, six channels, 12 effects, ISF, front black control panel, single input, 13 black knobs (voice selector, g, v, b, m, t, ISF, TVP selector, effect type, effect level, resonance, presence, MV), power switch, emulated speaker out, MP3/line in jack, footswitch jack, MIDI in, speaker output jacks, various switches, USB connector, top handle, black covering, black mesh grille, 28.22 lbs., mfg. 2013-present.

MSR $610	$450	$295 - 325	$145 - 180

ID:260 TVP COMBO – 2 X 60W, 2-12 in. speaker, digital guitar combo amp, solid-state chassis, True Valve Power, six amp models, six channels, 12 effects, ISF, front black control panel, single input, 13 black knobs (voice selector, g, v, b, m, t, ISF, TVP selector, effect type, effect level, resonance, presence, MV), power switch, emulated speaker out, MP3/line in jack, footswitch jack, MIDI in, speaker output jacks, various switches, USB connector, top handle, black covering, black mesh grille, 53.35 lbs., mfg. 2013-present.

MSR $879	$600	$400 - 450	$195 - 240

ID:412 SPEAKER CABINET – 320W, 4-12 in. Celestion speakers, angled front (412A) or straight front (412B), designed for use with the ID Series amps, black covering, black grille, 108 lbs., mfg. 2013-present.

MSR $700	$500	$325 - 375	$165 - 200

ID:CORE STEREO 10 COMBO – 2 X 5W stereo digital guitar combo amp, solid-state chassis, six channels, 12 effects, ISF, top black control panel, single input, six black knobs (voice selector, g, v, EQ, effect type, effect level), power switch, emulated speaker/headphone out, MP3/line in jack, various switches, USB connector, top handle, black covering, black grille, 8.16 lbs., mfg. 2014-present.

MSR $143	$100	$65 - 75	$30 - 40

ID:CORE STEREO 20 COMBO – 2 X 10W stereo digital guitar combo amp, solid-state chassis, six channels, 12 effects, ISF, top black control panel, single input, six black knobs (voice selector, g, v, EQ, effect type, effect level), power switch, emulated speaker/headphone out, MP3/line in jack, footswitch jack, various switches, USB connector, top handle, black covering, black grille, 11.46 lbs., mfg. 2014-present.

MSR $210	$150	$100 - 115	$50 - 60

ID:CORE STEREO 40 COMBO – 2 X 20W stereo digital guitar combo amp, solid-state chassis, six channels, 12 effects, ISF, top black control panel, single input, six black knobs (voice selector, g, v, EQ, effect type, effect level), power switch, emulated speaker/headphone out, MP3/line in jack, footswitch jack, various switches, USB connector, top handle, black covering, black grille, 13.67 lbs., mfg. 2014-present.

MSR $240	$200	$130 - 150	$65 - 80

ID:CORE STEREO 40 HEAD – 2 X 20W stereo digital guitar head unit, solid-state chassis, six channels, 12 effects, ISF, top black control panel, single input, six black knobs (voice selector, g, v, EQ, effect type, effect level), power switch, emulated speaker/headphone out, MP3/line in jack, footswitch jack, various switches, USB connector, top handle, black covering, black grille, 5.5 lbs., new 2016.

MSR $250	$180	$115 - 135	$60 - 70

ID:CORE BEAM COMBO – 20W, digital guitar/bass combo amp, 2-3 in. speakers, solid-state chassis, ISF, top black control panel, single input, six black knobs (voice selector, g, v, EQ, effect type, effect level), emulated speaker/headphone out, MP3/line in jack, various switches, USB connector, Bluetooth, black covering, black grille, 8.6 lbs., mfg. 2015-present.

MSR $390	$280	$180 - 210	$90 - 110

BLANKENSHIP AMPLIFICATION

Amplifiers currently produced in Van Nuys, CA since 2011. Previously produced in Houston, TX between 2009 and 2011 and in North Hollywood, CA between 2005 and 2009.

Roy Blankenship built one-off guitar amplifiers for many years before he founded Blankenship Amplification in 2005. According to Blankenship, he felt that there were so many boutique amplifiers around to justify building his own line. However, several of his clients who owned one of his one-off amplifiers, continued to request that Blankenship start his own line, and in 2005, Blankenship Amplification was founded in Houston, TX. Blankenship's amplifiers are custom, hand-built units that deliver the pre-1964 tonal architecture that many players cherish, and he focuses more on playability than bells and whistles. In 2009, Blankenship moved from North Hollywood, CA to Houston, TX and in 2011 returned to the Los Angeles area (Van Nuys) where he continues to build amplifiers. For more information, visit Blankenship's website or contact him directly.

ELECTRIC TUBE AMPLIFIERS

Blankenship currently offers the FATBoy Series, LEEDS21 Series, and the VariPlex Series. The **FATBoy** (MSR $1,495) is based on a late 1950s Fender Deluxe Narrow Panel Tweed with 25W (switchable to 18, 15, or 10W), 1-12 in. speaker, and can use either 6L6 or 6V6 power tubes and 5AR4 or 5Y3 rectifier. The **FATBoy Supreme With Sour Cream** (MSR $2,295) is similar to the FATBoy, except it has reverb and a six-way bright switch and it features 36W or 25W and 1-15 in. or 3-10 in. speakers.

The **LEEDS21 Head** (MSR $1,695) is based on the early 1960s British model with 21W, 2 X EL84 power tubes, two channels, and tremolo. The LEEDS21 is also available in a 2-10 in. combo (MSR $1,795) or 1-12 in. Celestion Blue speaker combo (MSR $1,995). The **Mini-LEEDS21 Carry On** (MSR $1,495) is a miniature version of the LEEDS21 Head that only has one channel and no tremolo. The **Mini-LEEDS21 System** features the LEEDS21 Head with only one channel and tremolo that is available in a piggyback head and 2-10 in. speaker cabinet (MSR $1,995) or 1-12 in. Celestion Blue speaker cabinet (MSR $2,195). Extension speaker cabinets are also available in 1-12 in. (MSR $595) or 2-12 in. (MSR $895) configurations.

The **VariPlex** Head is based on Blankenship's friends 1968 Marshall Plexi head and is available in 50W (MSR $2,500) or 100W (MSR $2,800) variations. It features two channels with one designed for single coil use and the other for humbucker use, and Variac that modulates the power output.

BLOCKHEAD AMPLIFICATION

Amplifiers previously produced in Putnam Valley, NY during the 2000s.

Blockhead Amplification built replica Marshall amps, specializing on the Plexi-JTM-45 amps of the early 1960s that have a very unique tone and are some of the most sought after amps. Blockhead took the original Marshall designs, blueprints, and parts and recreated them to exact replicas. If replica parts aren't available as standard production, Blockhead had them custom built. Prices started around $2,200 for most head units and $2,350 for combo units, and they also offered speaker cabinets. Designer and builder Ossie Ahsen is now buiding amps with Aerosmith guitarist Brad Whitford and his guitar tech Greg Howard under the trademark 3 Monkeys Amps.

BLUDOTONE AMP WORKS

Amplifiers currently produced in Littleton, CO.

Brandon Montgomery builds his Bludotone amplifiers in Littleton, Colorado. Bludotone mainly builds the **Bludo-Drive** guitar amp head (prices start at $4,150) that has standard output of 100W, but several customizable features are available. Bludotone also builds one-offs and encourages players to contact them for quotes on amplifiers. For more information, visit Bludotone's website or contact them directly.

BLUESLAND AMPLIFIERS

Amplifiers previously produced between circa 1994 and the early 2000s.

Bluesland Amplifiers were built by Woody Wolfe between circa 1994 and the early 2000s. Most of Bluesland's amplifiers were of early Fender vintage (late 1940s/ 1950s) with mainly tweed coverings. Some models include the **B-30**, **B-40**, **Baby Blues**, **BluesMaster**, and **KR100**. Bluesland amplifiers are usually reported to be of high-quality, however, there have been several complaints about their customer service and business practices. It is unknown when Bluesland ceased production of amplifiers, but it is estimated to be around the early 2000s. Any further information can be submitted directly to Blue Book Publications.

BLUES PEARL

Amplifiers previously produced in Kodak, TN from 2009 to early-2010s and in Soddy Daisy, TN between the late 1980s and early 2000s.

Robert Hudson opened a music shop in the 1980s and guitarists would come into his shop requesting him to turn their amplifier into something that it could never be stock from the factory. Therefore, he began building his own amplifiers under the name of Blues Pearl that began in the late 1980s. Most of his designs are based on vintage Fender amps from the 1950s and 1960s. Unfortunately, a serious illness forced Hudson to retire from Blues Pearl in the early 2000s and they halted production of amplifiers for much of the 2000s decade. In the late 2000s, Hudson was approached by another company who was interested in producing Blues Pearl amplifiers again. Working with Hudson, they developed a new line of Blues Pearl amplifiers and effects pedals.

ELECTRIC TUBE AMPLIFIERS

The **Texas Tornado** (last MSR was $1,295) is a 20W model with either 2-10 in. or 1-12 in. speakers. The **Verbrasonic** (last MSR was $1,395) has 40W, 2-10 in. Jensen speakers, 6L6 power tubes, and is a bigger brother to the Texas Tornado. The **Blues Master** (last MSR was $1,495) is a dual channel amp that is driven by 6L6GC power tubes to deliver 40W of power with 3-10 in. Jensen speakers. The **Diablo** (last MSR was $1,595), which appears to be like the Blues Master has 40W of power, but has 4-10 in. Jensen speakers. The **Hombre** (last MSR was $1,495) is an amp that has 1-15 in. speaker, dual channels, and 40W from 6L6GC tubes. Other models previously available include the **Brittone**, **Classic Glass**, **Copperhead**, and **Shred Head** models. Blues Pearl's new amplifiers introduced in 2009 include the Texas Tornado, Vebrasonic, and new **Diamond Back**.

BLUE TONE

Amplifiers previously produced in the United Kingdom, between 2002 and the late 2000s.

Blue Tone Amplifiers LTD., was founded by Alex Cooper in the United Kingdom. Blue Tone offered the **Pro 30M** amplifiers that utilized Virtual Valve Technology, and it simulated the complex interactions that happend between the guitar and the amplifier with a solid-state chassis. The Pro 30M combo amp featured 30W output power, one channel, and basic controls, and it last retailed for $910 plus delivery. Blue Tone stopped producing amplifiers in the late 2000s.

Pro 30M
courtesy Blue Tone

Pro 30M
courtesy Blue Tone

BLUETRON

Amplifiers and speaker cabinets previously produced in Boston, MA in the early-2010s and in Brentwood, TN from 2004 to 2009. Distributed by Bluetron.

DM "Smitty" Smith founded Bluetron in 2004 to improve on Fender's vintage amps from the 1960s. Smith knows that the Blackface Fender amps from the '60s are great amps, but when pushed hard, they left something to desire. After extensive research and experimentation, Smith found that great distortion is created when the gain is controlled at each stage. The Blueverb is Bluetron's only amp as well as the world's first amp to control the drive at every gain stage. Smith also builds his amps to the same specifications that Leo Fender was so well-known for, with a few minor improvements.

ELECTRIC TUBE AMPLIFIERS/SPEAKER CABINETS

Bluetron produced the **Blueverb** model, and it was available as a raw chassis ($2,000) with several power transformers including the Bandmaster, Super Reverb, Bassman, Twin Reverb, and Bukoverb. Smitty offers five amp voices including Super Clean, Clean, Standard, Overdrive, and Super Overdrive. All head-units previously listed can be fitted with a speaker as a 1-12 in., 1-15 in., 2-10 in., 2-12 in., or a 4-10 in. combo. Extension speaker cabinets were also available starting at $65 with a wide range of speakers available for each amp.

BOGNER

Amplifiers currently produced in North Hollywood, CA since 1989. Distributed by Bogner.

Reinhold Bogner moved from Germany to Los Angeles in 1989 and started Bogner Amplification. He had been building amplifiers in Germany for some time before he came to the US. After earning the trust of many famed musicians, including overhauling Eddie Van Halen's #1 Plexi Marshall, he started Bogner Amplification. They build top-end tube amplifiers and speaker cabinets. For more information, visit Bogner's website or contact them directly.

ELECTRIC TUBE AMPLIFIERS

Bogner produces amplification in combo, head, and speaker cabinet forms. The **Metropolis** was introduced in 1999 and features a 15 or 30W chassis, has a single channel, and is available as a head, 1-12 in., or 2-12 in. combo. The **Shiva** is a 65W unit available in a head, has two channels, and is available as a 1-12 in. or 2-12 in. combo. The **Ecstasy** has 100W (switchable to 50W), three channels, and is available as a head unit or 2-12 in. speaker combo. The **Ubershcall** has 120W power from 4 X EL34 tubes, two channels, a fiber-optic backlight, and is available only as a head. The **Duende** has 18W power from 2 X 6V6 tubes, two channels that can be combined or separated individually, and is available as a head or a 1-12 in. speaker combo.

MSR/NOTES	100%	EXCELLENT	AVERAGE	LAST MSR

ELECTRIC TUBE AMPS: ALCHEMIST SERIES

Alchemist Head
courtesy Bogner

Alchemist 2-12 Combo
courtesy Bogner

Alchemist 2-12 Speaker Cabinet
courtesy Bogner

ALCHEMIST HEAD – 40W, guitar head-unit, seven-tube chassis, preamp: 5 X 12AX7, power: 2 X 6L6, solid-state rectifier, two channels (gold/mercury), reverb, delay, front black control panel, single input, 13 black knobs (Ch. 1: g, t, m, b, v, Ch. 2: g, t, m, b, v, All: delay, repeats, reverb), Ch. 1 bright switch, Ch. 1 deep switch, Ch. 1 clean/crunch switch, Ch. 2 punch switch, Ch. 2 bright switch, Ch. 2 mid shift switch, boost switch, channel select switch, ducking/analong/tape switch, tap tempo button, plate/spring/hall reverb selector switch, 40W/standby/20W switch, power switch, rear panel: effect level control, effects loop, footswitch jack, three speaker jacks (one eight ohm, two four ohm), four-button footswitch included, black covering, black grille, 25.75 in. wide, 12.25 in. tall, 10.25 in. deep, 41 lbs., mfg. 2009-present.

| MSR $1,750 | $900 | $600 - 700 | $375 - 450 | |

* *Alchemist 1-12 Combo* – similar to the Alchemist Head, except in combo configuration with 1-12 in. Celestion Vintage 30 speaker, 25.75 in. wide, 21.75 in. tall, 10.25 in. deep, 65 lbs., mfg. 2009-present.

| MSR $1,960 | $1,000 | $625 - 750 | $400 - 475 | |

* *Alchemist 2-12 Combo* – similar to the Alchemist Head, except in combo configuration with 1-12 in. Celestion G12M Greenback and 1-12 in. Celestion G12H Anniversary speakers, 25.75 in. wide, 26 in. tall, 10.25 in. deep, 80 lbs., mfg. 2009-present.

| MSR $2,240 | $1,100 | $650 - 800 | $425 - 500 | |

ALCHEMIST 2-12 SPEAKER CABINET – 55W, 1-12 in. Celestion G12M Greenback and 1-12 in. Celestion G12H Anniversary speakers, 8 ohm impedance, open-back cabinet, designed for use with the Alchemist Head, black covering, black grille, 25.75 in. wide, 26 in. tall, 10.25 in. deep, 58 lbs., mfg. 2009-present.

| MSR $980 | $500 | $350 - 425 | $225 - 275 | |

BOLT

Amplifiers previously produced in Salt Lake City, UT between 2009 and 2012. Distributed by XP Audio, Inc. in Salt Lake City, UT.

John Fisher, Rick Bos, and John Johnson formed Bolt Guitar Amplification Systems in 2009. Bos and Johnson founded XP Audio in 2007 to develop top-line highly innovative audio products that now include the trademarks Motion Sound, Forge, and Morpheus. Bolt guitar amplifiers utilize tube electronics but they employ a computer chip, similar to the chip found in modern automobiles, that controls the preamp and power amp tubes to maximize their tone. Bolt offers a variety of head and combo units as well as speaker cabinets, and all products are designed and produced in the U.S.

BRAND X

Amplifiers previously produced between 2004 and 2008. Distributed by FMIC (Fender Musical Instrument Corporation) in Scottsdale, AZ.

Fender introduced the trademark Brand X on a line of budget, entry-level solid-state amps in 2004. They featured a unique look with black covering, black metal grilles, brushed aluminum control panels, metal knobs, a headphone output, and a bright red pilot light. Fender also offered a limited warranty on these amps. Fender produced Brand X amplifiers through the mid- to late 2000s.

ELECTRIC SOLID-STATE AMPLIFIERS

Brand X offered four models: the **X-10** (last MSR was $100), the **X-15R** with reverb (last MSR was $150), the **X-25R** with reverb (last MSR was $220), and the **X-15 B** bass amp (last MSR was $200). All amps feature a variety of controls and options.

BRONX

Amplifiers and speaker cabinets previously produced in Korea between 2004 and the late 2000s. Distributed in the U.S. by Pro-Link Sales in Fullerton, CA.

Bronx produced a line of tube and solid-state guitar amps and speaker cabinets in Korea. Tube amplifiers were built with either Electro-Harmonix or Sovtek tubes, and speakers used were either Celestion or Eminence. Tube amps feature traditional two-channel function controls and have black covering with a brown grille cloth. Solid-state amplifiers feature DSP technologies and have traditional black covering with silver grilles.

BROOKLYN GEAR

Speaker cabinets and other accessories previously produced in Brooklyn, NY. Distributed by Brooklyn Gear in Brooklyn, NY.

Brooklyn Gear distributes a wide range of products including speaker cabinets, strings, capos, and guitar straps. The Perfect Series speaker cabinets are designed and built by Doyle Audio. All cabinets are hand-built to exact specifications. Their cabinets are designed for guitar and bass use. A monitor is also available. Prices start at $1,095 and $995 for the monitor.

BROWN NOTE AMPS

Amplifiers previously produced in Fair Oaks, CA.

Brown Note Amps produces guitar amplifiers focusing on bringing legendary tone to guitarists, both professional and aspiring. Brown Note utilizes hand-wired craftsmanship on their amplifiers as well as premium components including custom U.S.-built transformers. Their models include the D'Lite, Brown Fox, and the Lite 18, which is based on Marshall's 18-Watt amps of the mid-1960s.

BRUNETTI

Amplifiers currently produced in Modena, Italy. Distributed in the U.S. by GuitarX in Denver, CO. Previously distributed in the U.S. by Salwender International of Orange, CA until 2004.

Brunetti Amplifiers are hand-made in Italy by Marco Brunetti. Each amplifier is hand crafted from start to finish and tested at the factory. Marco has designed each model according to the market needs and the best design out there. Brunetti makes a full variety of tube amplifiers, rack-mount amplifiers, rack-mounted effects, preamps, and speaker cabinets. Brunetti amplifiers are distributed in many countries in Europe and were distributed by Salwender until circa 2004. For more information, visit their website or contact them directly.

CONTACT INFORMATION

BRUNETTI
Headquarters
Via De' Bonomini 25/31
Modena, 41100 Italy
Phone No.: +39059243404
Fax No.: +39059216464
www.brunetti.it
info@brunetti.it

U.S. Distributor: GuitarX
Denver, CO
Phone No.: 303-282-9800
www.guitarx.com
sales@guitarx.com

ELECTRIC TUBE AMPLIFIERS

The first version of the **059** (last U.S. MSR $3,250) is a 120W head-unit amp that has a 10-tube chassis with 6 X 12AX7A preamp tubes and 4 X EL34 power tubes, three channels (clean, crunch, and solo) and a number of features and effects on its red control panel (18 black knobs in all!). The second version of the **059** (MSR $3,240) features 100W output in Class AB operation that is switchable to 20W output in Class A operation, a 10-tube chassis with 6 X 12AX7 preamp tubes and 4 X EL34 power tubes, three independent channels and a number of features and effects on a black control panel with 18 black knobs in all. The **XL R-evo** (MSR $2,881) is an improved version of the **XL** Series amp (now discontinued), with 120W output (switchable to 60W) a nine-tube chassis with 5 X 12AX7A preamp tubes and 2 X EL34 power tubes, three switchable channels (clean, boost, X-lead) and a number of effects and features. The **Pirata 141** (MSR $2,141) is a two-channel hi gain head available in two variations: the Valvemix (50-75W with 2 X EL34, 2 X 6L6, or all four tubes combined with the Valvemix knob) and the Impact (130W with 4 X 6L6 tubes), and five 12AX7 preamp tubes. The **Mark 6L6** (MSR $4,185) is a two-channel handwired head with 50W output, a nine-tube chassis with 5 X 12AX7 and 1 X 12AT7 preamp tubes, 2 X 6L6GC power tubes, and 1 X 5U4 rectifier that is switchable to solid-state, and a series/parallel effects loop. The **Mercury EL34** is a two-channel handwired head with either 50W output (MSR $4,185) or 100W output (MSR $4,520), an eight or ten-tube chassis with 5 X 12AX7 preamp tubes, 2 X EL34/4 X EL34 power tubes, and a 5U4GB rectifier, which is also switchable to solid-state, two indepednent channels, and a series/parallel effects loop. The **Wizard 6V6 Reverb** Head (MSR $4,185) has 35W output, a 10-tube chassis with 4 X 12AX7A and 1 X 12AT7 preamp tubes, 4 X 6V6GTB power tubes, and 1 X 5AR4/GZ34 rectifier tube, two independent channels, and reverb.

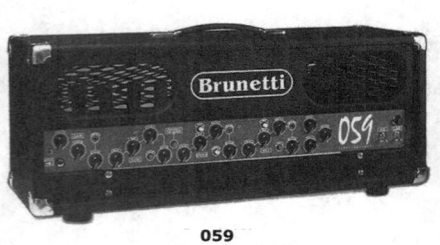

059
courtesy Brunetti

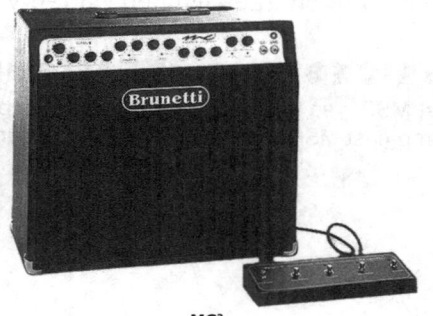

MC²
courtesy Brunetti

Silver Bullet
courtesy Brunetti

The **Maranello** (MSR $1,442) is a combo amp with 20W output, 1-12 in. Jensen speaker, a five-tube chassis with 3 X 12AX7 preamp tubes and 2 X EL84 power tubes, two channels, and an array of features and effects. The **MC2** (MSR $2,349) has 60W output, 1-12 in. Celestion speaker, a six-tube chassis with 4 X 12AX7 preamp tubes and 2 X EL34 power tubes, three channels, reverb, a Harmonic Shape Mirror, and a foot pedal microprocessor. The **Mercury EL34** (MSR $5,017) is based on the Mercury EL34 head and has 50W output, 1-12 in. Celestion Vintage 30 speaker, a eight-tube chassis with 5 X 12AX7 preamp tubes, 2 X EL34 power tubes, and a 5U4GB rectifier, which is also switchable to solid-state, two indepdendent channels, and a series/parallel effects loop. The **Wizard 6V6 Reverb** Combo (MSR $5,336) has 35W output, 1-12 in Celestion Vintage 30 speaker, a 10-tube chassis with 4 X 12AX7A and 1 X 12AT7 preamp tubes, 4 X 6V6GTB power tubes, and 1 X 5AR4/GZ34 rectifier tube, two independent channels, and reverb. The **Singleman** is new from Brunetti and features 35W output in Class AB operation (MSR $2,006) or 16W in Class A operation (MSR $1,847), 1-12 in. Celestion Vintage 30 speaker, four-tube chassis with 2 X 12AX7 preamp tubes and 2 X 6V6GT or 2 X 6L6WGC power tubes, and a single channel.

The **Silver Bullet** (last U.S. MSR $1,850) is a 120W (60W per side), two channel power amp, that has 2 X 12AX7 and 1 X 5814A preamp tubes and 4 X EL34 power tubes with volume and presence controls for each channel. The **Rockit** (last U.S. MSR $1,250) is a 120W output power amp (switchable to 60W and 40W). The tubes are 2 X 5814As and this has power level and spectral response controls. Both the Silver Bullet and the Rockit are rack units.

There are a wide variety of preamps also available. The **Mille** (last U.S. MSR $1,999), has three channels (clean, crunch, and lead shine) with a fourth branching out (lead fat). The tubes for this are 6 X 12AX7s. The control panel is blue with several silver knobs, and the unit takes up two rack spaces. The **Centouno** (last U.S. MSR $1,150) is a three channel preamp driven by 3 X 12AX7 and 1 X PCF82 tubes. The control panel on this is silver with blue knobs and it takes up one rack space. Other units include the **Matrix** (last U.S. MSR $1,599), the **RPS 300** (last U.S. MSR $850), the **Mister B** (last U.S. MSR $1,999), and the **Van der Graal** (last U.S. MSR $2,850).

SPEAKER CABINETS

Brunetti offers three different speaker cabinets that can be matched up with any one of their heads. The **XL-Cab** (last U.S. MSR $1,390) is a 4-12 in. speaker cabinet that can handle 400W and has 12 in. Jensen Custom speakers. The XL-Cab can be run at 400W in mono or 200W in stereo. The **Dual-Cab** has either 2-12 in. Jensen Custom speakers (MSR $829) or 2-12 in. Celestion speakers (MSR $986) and can handle 200W in mono and 100W in stereo. The **XL-Mini Cab** (MSR $645) has 1-12 in. Jensen Custom or 1-12 in. Celestion speaker and can handle 100W. The **Neo 1512 Cab** (MSR $1,478) has one 12 in. Celestion Vintage 30 speaker and one 15 in. Jensen Neodymium speaker that can handle 250W. The **Custom Work 412 Cabinet** (MSR $1,890) has 4-12 in. Celestion Vintage 30 speakers. All cabinets are designed with a "Half Back Open" system and are constructed of hard-plywood that is hand assembled. Most cabinets are covered with black Tolex covering and have black grilles with the Brunetti Logo in white letters on the middle with the exception of the Custom Work 412 Cabinet that has a gray grille.

BUDDA

Amplifiers currently produced in San Francisco, CA. Previously produced in San Rafael, CA. Budda was introduced in 1995. Distributed by Peavey.

Budda amplifiers was founded in the hills of northern California by Scot Sier, Paul Lamb, and amp designer Jeff Bober. Scot was inspired by Jeff's amp design, and Paul's cabinet design brought the company together in 1995. Budda currently offers tube amps, speaker cabinets, effects, and various accessories. They are best known for their Superdrive series. For more information visit Budda's website or contact them directly.

CONTACT INFORMATION
BUDDA
5022 Hwy 493 N
Meridian, MS 39305
Phone No.: 877-612-8332
Phone No.: 877-866-3439
Fax No.: 601-486-1254
www.budda.com
support@budda.com

Superdrive Combo
courtesy Budda

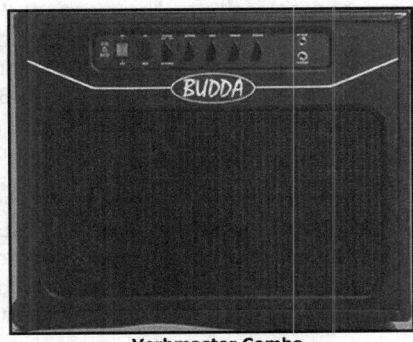

Verbmaster Combo
courtesy Budda

ELECTRIC TUBE AMPLIFIERS

The Verbmaster series (disc.) has six different models in the line. The Verbmaster 18 came as a head unit (last MSR $1,450), 1-12 in. combo (last MSR $1,650), or a 2-12 in. combo (last MSR $1,800). The **Verbmaster 18** sports 18W of power, has a tube section of: 3 X 12AX7 & 1 X 12AU7 for the preamp, 2 X EL84 power tubes, and a 5U4 rectifier tube. Features include dual reverb settings, normal and high gain inputs, treble, bass, and volume controls and an effects loop with Slave out. The **Verbmaster 30** has 30W output coming from 2 X 6L6 high grade tubes. The preamps are the same as the Verbmaster 18 as are the controls. The 30 is also available as a head-unit (last MSR $1,700), a 1-12 in. combo (last MSR $1,900) and a 2-12 in. combo (last MSR $2,050).

The **Twinmaster** (disc.) is the smaller brother to the Verbmaster. This model has 18W and came in three versions: a head-unit (last MSR $1,200), 1-12 in. combo (last MSR $1,400), and a 2-12 in. combo (last MSR $1,500). The tube section in this series consists of: 2 X 12AX7 preamps, 2 X EL84 power tubes, and a 5U4 rectifier. The features on these amps include: normal & high inputs, treble, bass, volume controls, and effects loop with slave out, and a custom purple anodized chassis. Budda is offering a **10th Anniversary Twinmaster** model in a 1-12 in. combo (MSR $4,995), and only 100 of these limited editions will be produced.

MSR/NOTES	100%	EXCELLENT	AVERAGE	LAST MSR

The Superdrive series features the current line of amplifiers from Budda, and there are four different wattage models including 18, 30, 45 and the massive 80. In 2002, they updated everything to be the series 2. The **Superdrive 18** has 18W output power, 2 X EL84, a 5U4 rectifier, and is available as a head unit (MSR $1,595), 1-12 in. combo (MSR $1,795), and 2-12 in. combo (disc., last MSR $1,700). The **Superdrive 30** has 30W output power, 4 X EL84 power tubes, a 5U4 rectifier, and is available as a head unit (MSR $1,995), 1-12 in. combo (MSR $2,195), and 2-12 in. combo (MSR $2,395). The **Superdrive 45** has 45W output power, 2 X KT66 power tubes, a tube rectifier, and is available as a head unit (MSR $2,495), 1-12 in. combo (MSR $2,695), and 2-12 in. combo (MSR $2,895). The **Superdrive 80** has 80W output power, 4 X 6L6GC power tubes a solid-state rectifier, and is available as a head unit (MSR $2,995), 1-12 in. combo (disc., last MSR $2,300), and 2-12 in. combo (MSR $3,395). All superdrive models feature 3 X 12AX7 preamp tubes, two channels (rhythm and drive), six knobs (MV, t, m, b, drive, rhythm volume), and effects loop.

SPEAKER CABINETS

Budda makes their own speaker cabinets to match the amplifier heads. All the cabinets are made of pine with great durability. The following cabinets are available, 1-12 in. speaker cabinet with an open or closed back (MSR $425), a 2-12 in. speaker cabinet with an open or closed back (MSR $750), or a 4-12 in. speaker cabinet (MSR $1,100).

BUGERA

Amplifiers currently produced since 2006. Distributed by Behringer in Bothell, WA.

The Bugera trademark was developed by the Red Chip Company LTD., in the British Virgin Islands. Behringer, who produces a variety of amplifiers and other guitar related accessories, is the exclusive distributor for Bugera amplifiers. Bugera amps feature tube chassis, high-quality cabinets, and are available in head/speaker cabinet or combo configurations. For more information, visit Bugera's website or contact them directly.

CONTACT INFORMATION
BUGERA
U.S. Distributor: Behringer USA
18912 North Creek Parkway, Suite 200
Bothell, WA 98011
Phone No.: 425-672-0816
Fax No.: 425-673-7647
www.bugera-amps.com
info@bugera-amps.com

BURNS

Amplifiers previously produced in England from circa 1961-1970. Baldwin-built Burns were produced from 1965-1970 in Booneville, AR. Amplifiers were produced again in England circa 1979-1983.

James O. Burns has produced many guitars and amplifiers in Britain from the 1940s-1980s. More known for his guitars, Burns has many original ideas such as the 24-fret fingerboard and other features on the guitar. For a full history on Burns Guitars, refer to the *Blue Book of Electric Guitars*.

After making guitars for many years, Burns released his first line of amplifiers in 1961. The idea for an amplifier came from the first Hawaiian guitar that Burns made. An amplifier would be needed to amplify the sound of the guitar. In the 1950s, Burns made a number of one-time amplifiers, but nothing that went into production as a model line. In the early 1960s, Burns had become a very big name in guitars in Britain so they tried their luck with a line of guitar amplifiers. Jim Burns bought a slug of empty TV cabinets to encase his new amplifiers, which became the Tele-Amp models. The Orbit and Sonic series were released in the early to mid-1960s. In September, 1965, Baldwin, bought the Burns manufacturing facilities from Jim Burns (regarded as "the British Leo Fender"). Many amplifiers were only changed cosmetically to the name Baldwin-Burns, and later to strictly Baldwin, whereas completely new and redesigned series were introduced. The Baldwin company then began assembling the imported Burns parts in Booneville, Arkansas. Amplifier (and guitar) production ceased in 1970. When Burns revived the company as Jim Burns Actualizers LTD in the late 1970s/early 1980s four models debuted: The Steer 50 (a combo amp made for the Steer guitar), the mini Snake, the Bullfrog Bass, and the practice Bee. (Courtesy: Paul Day, *The Burns Book* and Per Gjorde, *Pearls and Crazy Diamonds: Fifty Years of Burns Guitars*, 1952-2002).

ELECTRIC SOLID-STATE AMPLIFIERS: EARLY MODELS

Information on a lot of these models are scarce. The *Blue Book of Guitar Amplifiers* strongly suggests getting a second opinion when buying or selling any Burns amplifiers as the market pricing on these amps has not been established. Along with the models listed here there have been some models that were prototypes that never went into production. The "Bassmaster" Bass amp was a piggyback amp designed by Gordon Chandler. Because of a lot of problems in the prototype stage, the amp never went into production.

TELE-AMP – 15W, 1-12 in. speaker with a treble and mid-range units, dual channels, tremolo, top control panel, four inputs (two per channel), five controls (v1, v2, tone, tremolo depth, tremolo speed), cabinet that was designed for televisions, grille that resembles the front of a T.V., mfg. 1961-63.

	N/A	$425 - 500	$425 - 500	

This was the first production model Burns. The name comes partly from the fact that the housing for the amplifier was an empty television cabinet. There were some modifications done to the amp as production went on, including the addition of the treble and mid-range speaker units (early models didn't have them).

BISON – 24W, 1-15 in. Jensen speaker, solid-state, dual channels, top control panel, four inputs (two per channel), six controls (Ch. 1: v, tone, tremolo depth, tremolo speed, Ch. 2: v, tone), tone switches, grayish covering, light cloth grille, mfg. 1962-63.

	N/A	$425 - 500	$425 - 500	

MSR/NOTES	100%	EXCELLENT	AVERAGE	LAST MSR

BISON BASS COMBO – 35W, 2-12 in. Jensen Bass speakers, solid-state, tremolo, dual channels, top control panel, four inputs (two per channel), six controls (Ch. 1: v, tone, tremolo depth, tremolo speed, Ch. 2: volume, tone), grayish covering, light grille cloth, mfg. 1962-63.

	N/A	$500 - 600	$325 - 400	

The Bison and Bison Bass models were both manufactured by the Supro company in U.S.A. and imported by the Barnes & Mullins company. The only thing separating the Supro from the Burns models was the name of "Burns Bison" on the amp.

ELECTRIC SOLID-STATE AMPLIFIERS: ORBIT & DOUBLE 12 SERIES

Even though these two series have separate names, they share many of the same features. Their cabinets are very similar, they both have the leather handles, and the Orbital and Super Orbital speakers were made by the Fane company. Essentially these amps are all in the same series with the differences mainly coming from wattages, and speaker configurations. When the Orbit 75 was released by Baldwin-Burns in 1966, the amp was available with 10 different cabinet color options. A new Automatic Power Control was featured.

ORBIT 2 COMBO – 40W, 1-12 in. "Orbital" speaker, solid-state, dual channels, vibrato, rear-top control panel, four inputs (two per channel), seven silver knobs (Ch 1: v, b, t, s, i, Ch 2: v, t), black covering, aluminum metal grille, mfg. 1963-65.

	N/A	$600 - 750	$425 - 500	

ORBIT 3 COMBO – 60W, 3-10 in. speakers, solid-state, dual channels, vibrato, rear-top silver control panel, four inputs (two per channel), seven silver knobs (Ch. 1: v, 6-way tone select, t, s, i, Ch. 2: v, t), black covering, aluminum metal grille, mfg. 1963-65.

	N/A	$700 - 850	$450 - 550	

* *Orbit 3 Reverb Combo* – similar to the Orbit 3 Combo except has reverb and reverb dimension control on channel 1, mfg. 1963-65.

	N/A	$800 - 950	$550 - 650	

DOUBLE 12 COMBO – 60W, 2-12 in. speakers, solid-state, dual channels, vibrato, rear-top silver control panel, four inputs (two per channel), eight silver knobs (Ch.1: v, 6-way tone select, t, s, i, Ch. 2: v, b, t), black covering, aluminum metal grille, mfg. 1963-65.

	N/A	$700 - 850	$450 - 550	

* *Double 12 Reverb Combo* – similar to the Double 12 Combo except has reverb with a reverb dimension control, mfg. 1963-65.

	N/A	$800 - 950	$550 - 650	

ORBIT 75 COMBO – 75W, 2-12 in. heavy-duty speakers, solid-state, dual channels, top front control panel, four inputs (two per channel), nine black and silver knobs (Ch. 1: v, b, t, i, s, reverb dimension, Ch. 2: t, b, v), light covering, black cloth grille, mfg. 1966-late 1960s.

	N/A	$800 - 950	$550 - 650	

The Orbit 75 was the first model released under the Baldwin-Burns name after the buyout in 1965. The Orbit Series and the Double 12 Series were condensed to become the Orbit 75. This new model was quite different then the earlier Burns models including the changes of: a front control panel, back-mounted speakers, and a new cloth grille. The cost of this model in 1966 was 156 pounds (in England).

ELECTRIC SOLID-STATE AMPLIFIERS: SONIC SERIES

The Sonic series was a line of amplifiers that were marketed as more of a budget model. These models were targeted to be used with the budget guitars of the same caliber. Most of these amps have only a few controls and features.

SONIC 20 COMBO – 20W, 2-10 in. Orbital speakers, solid-state, dual channels, top black control panel, two inputs (one per channel), six silver knobs (Ch. 1: v, t, i, s, Ch. 2: t, v), dark covering, light cloth grille, mfg. 1964-65.

	N/A	$300 - 375	$175 - 225	

SONIC 25 COMBO – 25W, 2-10 in. speakers, solid-state, dual channels, front black control panel, two inputs (one per channel), six black and silver knobs (Ch. 1: v, t, i, s, Ch. 2: v, t), dark covering, black cloth grille, mfg. 1966.

	N/A	$300 - 375	$175 - 225	

SONIC 30 COMBO – 30W, 1-12 in. Orbital speaker, solid-state, top black control panel, two inputs (one per channel), six silver knobs (Ch. 1: v, t, i, s, Ch. 2: t, v), dark or light covering, light cloth grille, mfg. 1963-65.

	N/A	$350 - 425	$200 - 250	

SONIC 35 COMBO – 35W, 1-12 in. heavy-duty speaker, solid-state, dual channels, vibrato, front control panel, three inputs (two for channel one, one for channel two), eight black and silver knobs (Ch. 1: v, b, m, t, i, s, Ch. 2: v, t), dark covering, dark grille cloth, mfg. 1966.

	N/A	$350 - 425	$200 - 250	

SONIC 50 COMBO – 50W, 2-12 in. Orbital speakers, solid-state, dual channels, vibrato, top black control panel, four inputs (two per channel), eight black and silver knobs (Ch. 1: v, b, t, i, s, Ch. 2: v, b, t), dark covering, light grille cloth, mfg. 1963-65.

	N/A	$425 - 500	$250 - 300	

SONIC 55 COMBO – 55W, 2-12 in. heavy-duty speakers, solid-state, dual channels, vibrato, top front control panel, four inputs (two per channel), nine black and silver knobs (Ch. 1: v, b, t, i, s, 3-way tone select, Ch. 2: v, b, t), various coverings with various cloth grilles, mfg. 1966.

	N/A	$425 - 500	$250 - 300	

MSR/NOTES	100%	EXCELLENT	AVERAGE	LAST MSR

ELECTRIC SOLID-STATE AMPLIFIERS: MISC. MODELS

Burns has also made several P.A. amplifiers and speaker cabinets to go along with their amplifier line. There is also a wide assortment of vibrato units, cases, strings, machine heads, and pickups that they made.

DOUBLE B BASS AMPLIFIER – 75W, piggyback and cabinet with 2-18 in. speakers, solid-state, single channel, front black and silver control panel, two inputs, three black and silver knobs (v, b, t), black covering, dark grille cloth for cabinet, mfg. 1965-66.

N/A	$650 - 800	$450 - 550

INTERNATIONAL COMBO – 80W, 3-12 in. speakers, solid-state, dual channels, vibrato, front control panel, four inputs (two per channel), various knobs, mfg. 1965-66.

N/A	$650 - 800	$450 - 550

* *International Reverb Combo* – similar to the International except has reverb and a reverb dimension control, mfg. 1965-66.

N/A	$700 - 900	$500 - 600

SNAKE – 0.6W, 1-5 in. speaker mini-combo, solid-state chassis, single channel, front control panel, single input, three knobs (v, b, t), DC powered, optional rechargable unit, suede leather/paint covering, carrying-type handle, mfg. circa 1979-1983.

N/A	$120 - 150	$70 - 90

STEER 50 – 50W, 1-12 in. speaker combo, solid-state chassis, single channel, reverb, front silver control panel, two inputs, eight knobs (v, b, m, t, p, r, MV, power), preamp out, power in, black covering, silver or metal grille, mfg. circa 1979-1983.

N/A	$200 - 250	$120 - 150

BURRISS

Amplifiers and speaker cabinets currently produced in Lexington, KY since 2001. Distributed by Burriss/QED, Inc.

Bob Burriss founded Burriss in 2001 in Lexington, KY. They produce tube amplifiers, speaker cabinets and effects pedals. Circa 2005, Burriss merged with QED, Inc. For more information visit Burriss' website or contact them directly.

CONTACT INFORMATION
BURRISS
750 Enterprise Dr.
Lexington, KY 40510
Phone No.: 859-381-0152
Phone No.: 866-997-4546
Fax No.: 859-231-0376
www.burrissamps.com
bob@burrissamps.com

ELECTRIC TUBE AMPLIFIERS

The **Shadow** features 28W power, a tube rectifier, single channel, on-board reverb, optional vibrato, and comes with 1-12 in. speaker (MSR $2,610), 2-10 in. speakers (MSR $2,665), or 2-12 in. speakers (MSR $2,685). The **dB Special** features 38W power, a solid-state rectifier, a single channel, and comes with 1-12 in. speaker (MSR $2,340), 2-10 in. speakers (MSR $2,395), or 2-12 in. speakers (MSR $2,415). The **Switch Master** features 30W power, a solid-state rectifier, two channels, optional vibrato and reverb, and comes with 1-12 in. speaker (MSR $2,880), 2-10 in. speakers (MSR $2,935), or 2-12 in. speakers (MSR $2,955). The **Royal Bluesman** is a small compact full-featured hand-wired amp that features a class A chassis with 18W power, 2 X EL84 power tubes, and is available only as a head unit (MSR $1,195, the VIB+ pedal is included, and the OPI switch for operation through headphones or low power speakers retails for $65). The **Dirty Red** is another small compact full-featured amp that is designed for the rock and roller that features 18W power, 2 X EL84 power tubes, footswitchable effects loop, and only weighs 12.7 lbs. The Dirty Red is available only as a head unit and it retails for $1,195 including the Power Loop pedal. Burriss has also introduced a new speaker cabinet design that allows the user to swap out the speaker in a few seconds. The **DC Cab** is available with no speaker (MSR $445) or loaded with 1-12 in. speaker (MSR $495).

* **Add $125 for Vibrato (Shadow and SwitchMaster only).**
* **Add $225 for Reverb (Switchmaster only).**

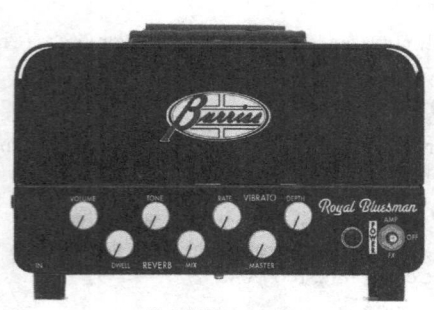
Royal Bluesman
courtesy Burriss

DC Cabinet
courtesy Burriss

Dirty Red
courtesy Burriss

BYERS AMPLIFIERS

Amplifiers previously produced in Corona, CA during the mid- to late 2000s.

Trevor Byers worked at the Fender Custom Shop in Corona, CA for many years before he began building his own amplifiers in the 2000s. Byers' first amp was his original creation called the Model 10 and he followed that up with a recreation of one of Leo Fender's earliest K&F amps. Byers specialized in K&F amps and early Fender amps from the late 1940s. The price for a reproduction K&F Byers amp was around $1,000.

C SECTION
CALIFORNIA AMPLIFIERS

Amplifiers and other accessories currently produced in China since 2004. Distributed by Eleca International Inc. in Chino, CA.

Eleca International Inc. offers the California trademark of amplifiers that are produced in China and distributed throughout the United States. California produces a variety of combo guitar and bass amplifiers. California also offers a line of Strat-style electric solidbody guitars. For more information please refer to Eleca's website or contact them directly.

CONTACT INFORMATION
CALIFORNIA AMPLIFIERS
Distributed by Eleca International, Inc.
21088 Commerce Pointe Drive
Walnut, CA 91789
Phone No.: 909-468-1382
Phone No.: 888-463-5322
Fax No.: 909-468-1652
www.calamplifiers.com
info@elecaamps.com

CALLAHAM VINTAGE AMPLIFIERS

Amplifiers previously produced in Winchester, VA between 1989 and 2008.

Callaham Vintage Guitars builds solidbody electric guitars and offers a variety of replacement parts. Callaham produced tube amplifiers until 2008, and they felt that these amps were not copies of existing designs, but original models that were some of the best sounding amplifiers on the market. Rather than pay extreme prices on the vintage market, Callaham figures to offer reproduction amplifiers that people want at a more reasonable price. These amps feature hand point-to-point wiring, all-tube chassis, wooden cabinets, and components that are of the finest quality. Callaham is currently focusing on solidbody electric guitars and replacement parts.

CONTACT INFORMATION
CALLAHAM VINTAGE AMPLIFIERS
217 Park Center Drive
Winchester, VA 22603
Phone No.: 540-955-0294
Fax No.: 540-678-8779
www.callahamguitars.com
callaham@callahamguitars.com

ELECTRIC TUBE AMPLIFIERS

Callaham amplifiers are named after the power tubes used in the design. All cabinets are built of .75 in. Honduran mahogany or cherry with flamed birch or maple trim. The **EL34** (last base MSR was $1,750) model has 28W Class AB power, 3 X 12AX7 preamp tubes, 2 X EL34 power tubes, optional GZ34 rectifier tube (Add $60), and five knobs. The **EL84R** (last base MSR was $1,800) model has 25W Class A power, 3 X 12AX7 preamp tubes, 4 X EL84 power tubes, optional GZ34 rectifier tube (Add $60), and five knobs. The **EL84V** (last base MSR was $1,850) model has 20W Class A power, 3 X 12AX7 preamp tubes, 4 X EL84 power tubes, a standard GZ34 rectifier tube, and four knobs.

CARL MARTIN

Amplifiers and effects pedals currently produced in Denmark since 1990. Distributed in the U.S. by Gary Castelluccio & Associates in Clifton, NJ.

Carl Martin amplifiers and effects are produced by East Sound Research in Denmark. East Sound was founded as a professional PA rental company in 1990. Shortly thereafter, they began building their own custom made audio equipment. In 1993, they introduced their first guitar pedal called the Hot Drive'n Boost. In 2005, they introduced the Custom Shop 50 tube combo amp. This amp was designed to compete with any other combo tube amp on the market, and it can also handle high-gain overdrive pedals without breaking out. Carl Martin also offers a Custom Shop 30 combo and a Custom Shop 200 Bass amp. For more information, visit Carl Martin's website or contact them directly.

CONTACT INFORMATION
CARL MARTIN
Factory/Headquarters
Raadmandsvej 24
Grenaa, DK 8500 Denmark
Phone No.: +45 86 32 51 00
Fax No.: +45 86 32 51 99
www.carlmartin.com
info@carlmartin.com

Distributed by Gary Castelluccio & Associates
57 Crooks Ave.
Clifton, NJ 07011
Phone No.: 973-772-3333
Phone No.: 800-888-1899
Fax No.: 973-772-5410
info@castelluccio.com

CARLSBRO

Amplifiers, speaker cabinets, and other accessories currently produced in Derbyshire, United Kingdom. The Carlsbro trademark was founded in 1959.

Carlsbro was founded in 1959 in the United Kingdom. They have produced several products over the years including tube and solid-state guitar amplifiers, PA systems, speaker cabinets, microphones, and a variety of other accessories. For more information visit Carlsbro's website or contact them directly.

CONTACT INFORMATION
CARLSBRO
Evolution House Unit 6, The Village, Maisies Way
South Normanton, Derbyshire DE55 2DS United Kingdom
Phone No.: 0845 258 2910
www.carlsbro.com
info@carlsbro.com

CAROL-ANN AMPLIFIERS

Amplifiers currently produced in Pelham, NH. Previously produced in North Andover, MA beginning in 2003.

Alan Phillips founded Carol-Ann Custom Amplifiers as a full service custom boutique tube amp builder in 2003. All of their amplifiers are hand-built point-to-point using high quality materials and components. Carol-Ann's flagship model is the **OD2** Series of amplifiers that have two footswitchable channels and are available in regular head and recording head models. Carol-Ann also offers the 75W 6550 tube driven **Tucana** and the 50/100W EL34 tube driven single channel **Revo 1**, as well as the **JB-100** Joe Bonamassa signature model. For more information, visit Carol-Ann's website or contact them directly.

CONTACT INFORMATION
CAROL-ANN AMPLIFIERS
302 Old Gage Hill Road
Pelham, NH 03076
Phone No.: 978-222-3120
Phone No.: 888-930-2226
www.carolannamps.com
info@carolannamps.com

MSR/NOTES	100%	EXCELLENT	AVERAGE	LAST MSR

CARR AMPLIFIERS, INC.

Amplifiers currently produced in Pittsboro, NC since 1998.

Carr Amplifiers began when Steve Carr started producing amps out of his repair shop in 1998. Steve Carr is a guitarist and engineer, and he repaired amps in Chapel Hill before producing his own. Carr Amplifiers is now located in a converted 1950s chicken hatchery located 15 miles south of Chapel Hill. The company employs twelve craftsmen builders, including a dedicated cabinet shop. Carr's philosophy is to combine the best vintage sound with the modern technology and products. They spend hours selecting components and testing amplifiers to get the best sound possible out of an amplifier. For more information, visit Carr's website or contact them directly.

CONTACT INFORMATION
CARR AMPLIFIERS, INC.
433 W. Salisbury St.
Pittsboro, NC 27312
Phone No.: 919-545-0747
Fax No.: 919-545-0739
www.carramps.com
info@carramps.com

ELECTRIC TUBE AMPLIFIERS

The standard covering on Carr amps is black Tolex.

- Add $100 for Custom Colors including Blue, Coco, Cowboy (black with swirled accents), Cream, Green, Orange (disc.), Purple, Red, and Wine.

ARTEMUS HEAD – 30W (switchable to 15W), guitar head unit, seven-tube chassis, preamp: 2 X 12AX7, power: 4 X EL84, rectifier: 1 X 5AR4/GZ34, single channel, top control panel, single input, three knobs (v, t, b), edge (bright and upper mid-boost) switch, mid (flat or scooped) switch, 15/30W switch, available in standard Black covering or a variety of covering and grille cloths, 31 lbs., new 2010.

MSR $1,890	$1,875	$1,200 - 1,450	$850 - 1,000

* *Artemus 1-12 Combo* – similar to the Artemus Head, except in combo configuration with 1-12 in. Eminence Red, White, & Blues speaker, 40 lbs., new 2010.

MSR $1,990	$1,975	$1,250 - 1,550	$900 - 1,050

* *Artemus 1-15 Combo* – similar to the Artemus Head, except in combo configuration with 1-15 in. Eminence Legend 151 speaker, new 2010.

MSR $2,130	$2,100	$1,350 - 1,650	$950 - 1,100

* *Artemus 2-12 Combo* – similar to the Artemus Head, except in combo configuration with 2-12 in. Eminence Red, White, & Blues speakers, 52 lbs., new 2010.

MSR $2,130	$2,100	$1,350 - 1,650	$950 - 1,100

EL MOTO – 88W, head-unit only, all-tube chassis, preamp: 4 X 12AX7, power: 4 X EL34, two channels, front black control panel, single input, nine black knobs (Ch. 1: v, MV, t, m, b, Ch. 2: v, t, b, overall MV), reverse trapezoid head shape, various color covering, brown grille, mfg. 2000-02.

	N/A	$1,400 - 1,750	$1,000 - 1,150	$2,295

- Add $200 for FX loop.

HAMMERHEAD 1-12 COMBO – 25W, 1-12 in. speaker combo, all-tube chassis, preamp: 2 X 12AX7EH, power: 2 X EL-34, single channel, top control panel, single input, four black knobs (v, MV, impact, grip), various color covering, diamond shaped grille cloth, mfg. 2000-04.

	N/A	$900 - 1,050	$650 - 750	$1,595

* *Hammerhead 2-10 Combo* – similar to the Hamerhead 1-12 Combo except has 2-10 in. speakers, mfg. 2000-04.

	N/A	$1,000 - 1,200	$725 - 850	$1,795

* *Hammerhead 2-12 Combo* – similar to the Hammerhead 1-12 Combo except has 2-12 in. speakers, mfg. 2000-04.

	N/A	$1,100 - 1,300	$750 - 900	$1,795

HAMMERHEAD MKII HEAD – 28W, head-unit only, tube chassis, preamp: 2 X 12AX7, power: 2 X EL34, single channel, front black control panel, single input, five black knobs (v, impact, MV, grip, tone), black covering, 24 lbs., mfg. 2004-09.

$1,750	$1,100 - 1,350	$750 - 900	$1,750

* *Hammerhead MKII 1-12 Combo* – similar to the Hammerhead MKII, except in combo form with 1-12 in. speaker, brown grille, 38 lbs., mfg. 2004-09.

$1,850	$1,150 - 1,400	$800 - 950	$1,850

* *Hammerhead MKII 2-10/2-12 Combo* – similar to the Hammerhead MKII, except in combo form with 2-10 in. or 2-12 in. speakers, two circle brown grille, 49 lbs., mfg. 2004-09.

$1,950	$1,200 - 1,500	$850 - 1,000	$1,950

IMPERIAL HEAD – 60W, head-unit only, all-tube chassis, preamp: 3 X 12AX7, 1 X 12AT7, power: 4 X 6L6GC, single channel, reverb, tremolo, top control panel, single input, seven black knobs (v, b, t, m, r, depth, s), pentode/triode switch, footswitch, various color covering, pointed shaped grille cloth, mfg. 2000-02.

	N/A	$1,400 - 1,750	$1,000 - 1,150	$2,395

* *Imperial 2-12 & 1-15 Combo* – similar to the Imperial head except in combo form with 2-12 in. or 1-15 in. speakers respectively, mfg. 2000-03.

	N/A	$1,650 - 2,000	$1,150 - 1,350	$2,795

MSR/NOTES	100%	EXCELLENT	AVERAGE	LAST MSR

Hammerhead MKII 1-12 Combo
courtesy Carr Amplifiers, Inc.

Mercury
courtesy Carr Amplifiers, Inc.

Raleigh 1-10 Combo
courtesy Carr Amplifiers, Inc.

* *Imperial 4-10 Combo* – similar to the Imperial head except in combo form with 4-10 in. speakers, mfg. 2000-03.

| | N/A | $1,700 - 2,100 | $1,150 - 1,400 | $2,995 |

MERCURY – 8W (switchable to 2, .5, & .1W), 1-12 in. combo, all tube Class A chassis: preamp: 1 X 12AX7EH, 1 X 12AX7C, 1 X 12AT7, power: 1 X EL34, single channel, reverb, top control panel, six knobs (v, 3-position boost, t, b, r, power selection), treble cut switch, dark blue covering, brown circle grille, 35 lbs., mfg. 2003-present.

| MSR $2,290 | $2,250 | $1,450 - 1,750 | $1,000 - 1,200 | |

• Add 15% for a Two-Tone color cabinet available in Coco/Cream/Coco, Black/Cream/Black, Green/Cream/Green, or Wine/Cream/Wine (MSR $150).

* *Mini-Merc* – similar to the Mercury, except has 1-10 in. Eminence Lil Buddy speaker and a smaller cabinet, 35 lbs., mfg. 2007-present.

| MSR $2,390 | $2,350 | $1,500 - 1,800 | $1,050 - 1,250 | |

RALEIGH 1-10 COMBO – 3W, 1-10 in. Eminence Lil' buddy hemp cone speaker, guitar combo, three-tube chassis, preamp: 2 X 12AX7, power: 1 X EL84, single channel with overdrive circuit, top control panel, single input, three knobs (v, tone, MV), clean/overdrive switch, available in a variety of covering and grille cloths, 21 lbs., new 2010.

| MSR $1,250 | $1,250 | $800 - 950 | $550 - 650 | |

• Add $100 for custom color covering/panels.
• Add $250 for hardwood maple or cherry cabinet.

RAMBLER HEAD – 28W, guitar head-unit, all-tube chassis, preamp: 3 X 12AX7, 1 X 12AT7, power: 2 X 6L6GC, single channel, reverb, tremolo, top control panel, single input, seven black knobs (v, b, t, m, r, tremolo depth, tremolo speed), pentode/triode switch, footswitch, various color covering, parallelogram shaped grille cloth, 34 lbs., mfg. 2009-present.

| MSR $2,330 | $2,300 | $1,475 - 1,775 | $1,025 - 1,225 | |

* *Rambler 1-12 Combo* – similar to the Rambler Head, except in combo configuration with 1-12 in. speaker, 40 lbs., mfg. 1999-present.

| MSR $2,430 | $2,400 | $1,500 - 1,850 | $1,050 - 1,250 | |

* *Rambler 2-12, 2-10, or 1-15 Combo* – similar to the Rambler 1-12 Combo except have 2-12 in., 2-10 in., or 1-15 in. speakers, 52 lbs., 49 lbs., and 48 lbs., respectively, mfg. 1999-present.

| MSR $2,530 | $2,500 | $1,550 - 1,900 | $1,100 - 1,300 | |

SLANT 6V HEAD – 40W, head-unit only, all-tube chassis, preamp: 4 X 12AX7, 2 X 12AT7, power: 4 X 6V6, dual channels, reverb, front control panel, single input, ten black knobs (Ch.1: v, t, m, b, r, Ch. 2: v, MV, t, m, b), pentode/triode switch, gain-mode switch, footswitch, various color covering, brown grille cloth, 38 lbs., mfg. 1998-present.

| MSR $3,150 | $3,100 | $2,000 - 2,400 | $1,300 - 1,600 | |

• Add $100 for 1.5X power (55W, fixed bias, and solid-state rectifier).
• Add $140 for reverb on both channels.
• Add $230 for boost control on footswitch.

Carr Amplifiers have expanded the Slant 6V line to include the Slant 6VLt that only has the first channel, the Slant 6VHP that is a 100W version of the Slant 6V, and the Slant 6VLtHP that is a 100W version of the Slant 6V with only the first channel.

* *Slant 6V 1-12 Combo* – similar to the Slant 6V head except in combo form with 1-12 in. speaker, 55 lbs., mfg. 1998-present.

| MSR $3,250 | $3,200 | $2,050 - 2,450 | $1,325 - 1,625 | |

• Add $100 for 1.5X power (55W, fixed bias, and solid-state rectifier).
• Add $140 for reverb on both channels.
• Add $230 for boost control on footswitch.

* *Slant 6V 2-12, 2-10, or 1-15 Combo* – similar to the Slant 6V 1-12 Combo except have 2-12 in., 2-10 in., or 1-15 in. speakers, 65 lbs., 61 lbs., and 59 lbs. respectively, mfg. 1998-present.

| MSR $3,350 | $3,300 | $2,100 - 2,500 | $1,350 - 1,650 | |

MSR/NOTES	100%	EXCELLENT	AVERAGE	LAST MSR

Slant 6V Head
courtesy Carr Amplifiers, Inc.

Slant 6V 2-12
courtesy Carr Amplifiers, Inc.

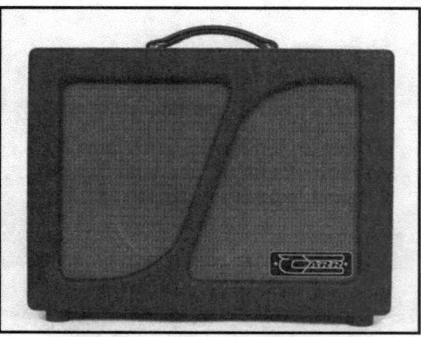
The Vincent/Viceroy Head
courtesy Carr Amplifiers, Inc.

- Add $100 for 1.5X power (55W, fixed bias, and solid-state rectifier).
- Add $140 for reverb on both channels.
- Add $230 for boost control on footswitch.

DOUBLE POWER 6V HEAD – 80W, head-unit only, all-tube chassis, preamp: 4 X 12AX7, 2 X 12AT7, power: 4 X 6L6, dual channels, reverb, front control panel, single input, ten black knobs (Ch.1: v, t, m, b, r, Ch. 2: v, MV, t, m, b), pentode/triode switch, gain-mode switch, footswitch, various color covering, brown grille cloth, mfg. 1998-2005.

	N/A	$2,100 - 2,500	$1,500 - 1,750	$2,690

* *Double Power 6V 2-12 Combo* – similar to the Double Power 6V head except in combo form with 2-12 in.speakers, mfg. 1998-2005.

	N/A	$2,250 - 2,750	$1,600 - 1,950	$3,090

THE VINCENT/VICEROY HEAD – 33W (switchable to 7W), guitar head unit, Class A six-tube chassis, preamp:3 X 12AX7, 1 X 12AT7, power: 2 X 6L6GC, single channel, reverb, top white control panel, single input, seven black knobs (v, t, m, b, r, drive, 7W/33W power level), mid-boost switch, power output switch, footswitch for boost on/off included, solid pine dovetailed cabinet, available in Black or other custom color coverings, 21 in. wide, 10.5 in. tall, 11 in. deep, 34 lbs., mfg. 2007-present.

MSR $2,530	$2,500	$1,550 - 1,900	$1,100 - 1,300	

The Vincent was renamed the Viceroy shortly after it was introduced.

* *The Vincent/Viceroy 1-12 Combo* – similar to The Vincent Head, except in combo configuration with 1-12 in. Eminence Wizard speaker, 21 in. wide, 16.25 in. tall, 10 in. deep at base, 45 lbs., mfg. 2007-present.

MSR $2,630	$2,600	$1,650 - 2,000	$1,150 - 1,350	

* *The Vincent/Viceroy 2-12 Combo* – similar to The Vincent Head, except in combo configuration with 2-12 in. Eminence Wizard speakers, 27.5 in. wide, 17.5 in. tall, 10 in. deep at base, 62 lbs., mfg. 2007-present.

MSR $2,830	$2,800	$1,800 - 2,200	$1,200 - 1,450	

SPEAKER CABINETS

HAMMERHEAD 1-12 SPEAKER CABINET – 1-12 in. Eminence Cannabis Rex speaker, closed back with asymmetrical curved backs, pine construction with dovetail corners, 30 lbs., disc. 2009.

	$650	$400 - 475	$250 - 300	$650

HAMMERHEAD 2-12 SPEAKER CABINET – 2-12 in. Eminence Cannabis Rex speaker, closed back with asymmetrical curved backs, pine construction with dovetail corners, 48 lbs., disc. 2009.

	$750	$475 - 550	$300 - 350	$750

SLANT 6V 1-12 SPEAKER CABINET – 1-12 in. Eminence Cannabis Rex speaker, closed or open back, current mfg.

MSR $715	$700	$475 - 550	$300 - 350	

- Add 25% for a closed back cabinet (MSR $900).

SLANT 6V 2-12 SPEAKER CABINET – 2-12 in. Eminence Cannabis Rex speaker, closed or open back, current mfg.

MSR $850	$825	$550 - 650	$350 - 425	

- Add 22.5% for closed back cabinet (MSR $1,050).

SLANT 6V 1-15/2-10 SPEAKER CABINET – 1-15 in. or 2-10 in. (disc.) Eminence Cannabis Rex speaker, open back, current mfg.

MSR $850	$825	$550 - 650	$350 - 425	

- Add 22.5% for closed back cabinet (MSR $1,050).

CARVIN

Amplifiers, speaker cabinets, and various other accessories currently produced in San Diego, CA since 1946. Carvin instruments are sold through direct catalog sales, as well as through five factory stores in CA: Covina, Hollywood, Sacramento, San Diego, and Santa Ana.

CONTACT INFORMATION
CARVIN
12340 World Trade Drive
San Diego, CA 92128 USA
Phone No.: 858-487-1600
Phone No.: 800-854-2235
www.carvin.com

In 1946, Lowell Kiesel founded Kiesel Electronics in Los Angeles, CA. In 1947, they had produced their first guitar amplifiers. Two years later, the Kiesel family settled in Covina, CA, and began the original catalog business of manufacturing and distributing lap steel guitars, small tube amps, and pickups. The Carvin trademark was derived from Kiesel's two oldest sons, Carson and Gavin. Guitars were originally offered in kit form, or by parts since 1949, and Carvin began building complete guitars in 1956. By 1978, the glued set-neck design replaced the bolt-on necks. The majority of the current guitar and bass models currently feature a neck-through design.

Carvin started out as a mail-order-only company, and they continue to offer players a wide range of options on their individual models through their catalog and website. However, Carvin now has five retail stores in California where products can be tested before purchase, but they do not sell to independent dealers.

The Carvin company also offers mixing boards, power amplifiers, power mixers, P.A. speakers, monitor speakers, guitar combo amps/heads/cabinets, and bass amps/cabinets. Lowell Kiesel passed away on December 28, 2009. For more information, visit Carvin's website or contact them directly.

ELECTRIC TUBE AMPLIFIERS: MTS (MASTER TUBE) SERIES

The MTS (Master Tube Series) featured two fully independent channels (clean, lead), a 100/50W half output power switch, and reverb. Carvin offered half-stack and full-stack packages for a special price. The **MTS412** half-stack last sold new for $850, and the **MTS812** full-stack last sold new for $1,150.

MTS 3200 Head
courtesy Carvin

G412T MTS Speaker Cabinet
courtesy Carvin

MTS 3200 HEAD – 100W (switchable to 50W), guitar head-unit, nine-tube chassis, preamp: 5 X 12AX7A power: 4 X 5881, 6L6, or EL34, solid-state rectifier, two channels (clean, crunch), reverb, silver control panel, single input, 11 silver knobs (All: r, p, Ch. 2: t, m, b, v, Ch. 1: t, m, b, drive, v), channel switch, power switch, standby switch, rear panel: two speaker jacks with 4/8/16 ohm impedance selector, 100/50W half output power switch, 5881/6L6/EL34 tube bias switch, cabinet voiced line out, footswitch jack, effects loop, optional two-button footswitch, seven-ply poplar cabinet, black vinyl covering and black vinyl front with white piping and Carvin logo, 24.25 in. wide, 10.5 in. tall, 9.5 in. deep, 40 lbs, mfg. 1997-2008.

$675	$425 - 500	$275 - 325	$1,195

* Add $15 for cover (CV3200).
* Add $20 for two-button footswitch (FS22).

* *MTS 3200 Combo (MTS 3212)* – similar to the MTS 3200 Head, except in combo configuration with 2-12 in. British BR12 (1997-2001, 2007-08), GT12 (2002-04), or GS12 (2005-06) speakers, 26 in. wide, 17.5 in. tall, 10.25 in. deep, 62 lbs., mfg. 1997-2008.

$750	$475 - 550	$300 - 350	$1,395

* Add $20 for cover (CV3212).
* Add $20 for two-button footswitch (FS22).

VE212 MTS SPEAKER CABINET – 150W, 2-12 in. British BR12 (1997-2001), GT12 (2002-04), or GS12 (2005 only) speakers, 8 ohm impedance, designed for use with the MTS 3200 Combo (MTS3212), black covering, black grille, 26 in. wide, 17.5 in. tall, 10.25 in. deep, 40 lbs., mfg. 1997-2005.

N/A	$150 - 200	$95 - 120	

G412B/G412T MTS SPEAKER CABINET – 300W, 4-12 in. 2-12 in. British BR12 (1997-2001, 2007-08), GT12 (2002-04), or GS12 (2005-06) speakers, 8 ohm stereo or 16 ohm mono impedance, straight (G412B) or angled (G412T) front, cabinet, black covering, black grille with white piping and Carvin block logo, 30 in. wide, 30 in. tall, 14.5 in. deep, 90 lbs., mfg. 1997-2008.

$400	$250 - 300	$150 - 200	$895

MSR/NOTES	100%	EXCELLENT	AVERAGE	LAST MSR

ELECTRIC TUBE AMPLIFIERS: VALVE MASTER (VM) SERIES

The Valve Master Series was offered in special half-stack and full-stack packages. The **VM212** Single Tube Stack featured the VM100 head and one V212 Cabinet (Last MSR was $1,495, sold new for $725), the **VM212-2** Dual Tube Stack featured the VM100 head and two V212 Cabinets (Last MSR was $1,995, sold new for $925), the **VM412** Single Tube Stack featured the VM100 head and one V412 Cabinet (Last MSR was $1,695, sold new for $825), and the **VM812** Double Tube Stack featured the VM100 head and two V412 Cabinets (Last MSR was $2,395, sold new for $1,150).

VALVE MASTER HEAD (VM100) – 100W (switchable to 50W), guitar head unit, nine-tube chassis, preamp: 5 X 12Ax7, power: 4 X 5881, EL84, or 6L6, solid-state rectifier, two channels (rhythm, lead), reverb, front black control panel, single input, 10 black chickenhead knobs (Rhythm Ch.: v, m, b, t, Lead Ch.: drive, v, b, m, t, All: r), channel switch, rear panel: two speaker out jacks with 4/8/16 ohm impedance selector, 100/50W half-power output switch, cabinet voiced line out jack, footswitch jack, effects loop, rhythm channel acoustic presence knob, lead channel presence knob, power tube bias switch, power switch standby switch, optional two-button footswitch, black DuraTuff II covering with white piping and a small black metal grille with Carvin block logo, mfg. 1995-97.

	N/A	$300 - 375	$175 - 225	$1,195

* Add $20 for two-button footswitch (FS22).

* *Valve Master 1-12 Combo (CM112 Club Master)* – similar to the Valve Master Head (VM100), except in combo configuration with 1-12 in. BR12 speaker, black DuraTuff II covering with Carvin block logo, black metal grille, 19.5 in. wide, 17.75 in. tall, 10.25 in. deep, mfg. 1995-97.

	N/A	$350 - 450	$200 - 250	$1,195

* Add $20 for two-button footswitch (FS22).
* Add $20 for cover (CV211BLK).

* *Valve Master 2-12 Combo (SM212 Stage Master)* – similar to the Valve Master Head (VM100), except in combo configuration with 2-12 in. BR12 speakers, black DuraTuff II covering with Carvin block logo, black metal grille, 26 in. wide, 17.75 in. tall, 10.25 in. deep, mfg. 1995-97.

	N/A	$375 - 450	$225 - 275	$1,295

* Add $20 for two-button footswitch (FS22).
* Add $20 for cover (CV221BLK).

VALVE MASTER 2-12 SPEAKER CABINET (V212) – 200W, 2-12 in. BR12 speakers mounted vertically, 4 or 16 ohm impedance, recessed side handles, black DuraTuff II covering, black metal grille with Carvin block logo, 16 in. wide, 30 in. tall, 14 in. deep, 54 lbs., mfg. 1995-97.

	N/A	$150 - 200	$95 - 120	$495

VALVE MASTER 4-12 SPEAKER CABINET (V412B/V412T) – 400W, 4-12 in. BR12 speakers, 4 or 8 ohm impedance, angled front (V412T) or straight front (V412B), recessed side handles, black DuraTuff II covering with white piping, black metal grille with Carvin block logo, 30 in. wide, 30 in. tall, 14.5 in. deep, 54 lbs., mfg. 1995-97.

	N/A	$225 - 275	$120 - 150	$695

ELECTRIC TUBE AMPLIFIERS: VINTAGE TUBE SERIES

BEL AIR 212 – 50W, 2-12 in. VL12 (1995-2001, 2008-09), GT12 (2002-04, 2010-present), or Celestion Vintage 30 (2005-07, optional 2010-present) speakers, guitar combo, nine-tube chassis, preamp: 5 X 12AX7, power: 4 X EL84, solid-state rectifier, two channels, reverb, front brown control panel, single input, 10 cream chickenhead knobs (Ch. 1: v1, b, m, t, Ch. 2: soak, v2, b, m, t, All: MV), channel switch, rear panel: power switch, standby switch, Channel 1 acoustic presence knob, effects loop, footswitch jack, cabinet voiced line out, two speaker jacks with 4/8/16 ohm impedance selector, available in standard vintage tweed diagonal covering with a brown cloth grille (several other color options available), optional two-button footswitch, 26 in. wide, 17.75 in. tall, 10.25 in. deep, 50 lbs., mfg. 1995-present.

MSR N/A	$700	$450 - 525	$230 - 280	

* Add $20 for cover.
* Add $30 for two-button footswitch (FS22).
* Add $100 for Celestion Vintage 30 speakers.

NOMAD 112 – 50W, 1-12 in. VL12 (1995-2001, 2008-09), GT12 (2002-04, 2010-present), or Celestion Vintage 30 (2005-07, optional 2010-present) speaker, guitar combo, nine-tube chassis, preamp: 5 X 12AX7, power: 4 X EL84, solid-state rectifier, two channels, reverb, front brown control panel, single input, 10 cream chickenhead knobs (Ch. 1: v1, b, m, t, Ch. 2: soak, v2, b, m, t, All: MV), channel switch, rear panel: power switch, standby switch, Channel 1 acoustic presence knob, effects loop, footswitch jack, cabinet voiced line out, two speaker jacks with 4/8/16 ohm impedance selector, available in standard vintage tweed diagonal covering with a brown cloth grille (several other color options available), optional two-button footswitch, 19.5 in. wide, 17.75 in. tall, 10.25 in. deep, 40 lbs., mfg. 1995-present.

MSR N/A	$650	$325 - 400	$175 - 225	

* Add $35 for cover.
* Add $30 for two-button footswitch (FS22).
* Add $50 for a Celestion Vintage 30 speaker.

MSR/NOTES	100%	EXCELLENT	AVERAGE	LAST MSR

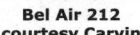
Bel Air 212
courtesy Carvin

Vintage 16
courtesy Carvin

Vintage 50 Head
courtesy Carvin

VINTAGE 16 – 16W (switchable to 5W), 1-12 in. GT12 (2002-04, 2010-present), Celestion Vintage 30 (2005-07, optional 2010-present), or VL12 (2008-09) speaker, guitar combo, five-tube chassis, preamp: 3 X 12AX7, power: 2 X EL84, single channel, reverb, front brown control panel, single input, six creme chickenhead knobs (soak, v, b, m, t, reverb), power switch, rear panel: triode (5W)/normal (16W) output power switch, 8 ohm speaker output (for internal use), available in standard vintage tweed diagonal covering with a brown cloth grille (other color coverings also available), 16 in. wide, 17.75 in. tall, 8.5 in. deep, 31 lbs., mfg. 2002-present.

MSR N/A	$450	$250 - 300	$150 - 200	

* Add $20 for cover.
* Add $50 for a Celestion Vintage 30 speaker.

VINTAGE 16 MICRO HEAD – 16W (switchable to 5W), guitar head-unit, four-tube chassis, preamp: 2 X 12AX7, power: 2 X EL84, single channel, reverb, front brown control panel, single input, six creme chickenhead knobs (soak, v, b, m, t, reverb), power switch, rear panel: triode (5W)/normal (16W) output power switch, 8 ohm speaker output (for internal use), available in standard vintage tweed diagonal covering with a brown cloth grille (other color coverings also available), 16 in. wide, 8.25 in. tall, 8.5 in. deep, 18 lbs., mfg. 2012-present.

MSR N/A	$400	$260 - 300	$130 - 160	

VINTAGE 33 – 33W, 1-12 in. VL speaker, guitar combo, nine-tube chassis, preamp: 5 X 12AX7, power: 4 X EL84, solid-state rectifier, two channels, reverb, front brown control panel, single input, 10 cream chickenhead knobs (Ch. 1: v1, b, m, t, Ch. 2: soak, v2, b, m, t, All: MV), channel switch, rear panel: power switch, standby switch, footswitch jack, cabinet voiced line out, two speaker jacks with 4/8/16 ohm impedance selector, available in standard vintage tweed diagonal covering with a brown cloth grille, optional two-button footswitch, 19.5 in. wide, 17.75 in. tall, 10.25 in. deep, 42 lbs., mfg. 1995-99.

	N/A	$300 - 350	$175 - 225	$695

* Add $20 for cover (CV211).
* Add $30 for two-button footswitch (FS22).

VINTAGE 50 HEAD (VT50) – 50W, guitar head unit, nine-tube chassis, preamp: 5 X 12AX7, power: 4 X EL84, solid-state rectifier, two channels, reverb, front brown control panel, single input, 10 cream chickenhead knobs (Ch. 1: v1, b, m, t, Ch. 2: soak, v2, b, m, t, All: MV), channel switch, rear panel: power switch, standby switch, Channel 1 acoustic presence knob, effects loop, footswitch jack, cabinet voiced line out, two speaker jacks with 4/8/16 ohm impedance selector, available in standard vintage tweed diagonal covering, optional two-button footswitch, 22.5 in. wide, 9 in. tall, 10.5 in. deep, 28 lbs., mfg. 1995-99, reintroduced 2009-present.

1995-1999	N/A	$325 - 400	$200 - 250	
2009-Present MSR N/A	$550	$325 - 400	$200 - 250	

* Add $20 for cover.
* Add $30 for two-button footswitch (FS22).

112E VINTAGE EXTENSION CABINET – 60W, 1-12 in. VL12 (1997-2001, 2008-09), GT12 (2002-04, 2010-present), or Celestion Vintage 30 (2005-07, optional 2010-present) speaker, 8 ohm impedance, designed for use as an extension cabinet with the Nomad 112, vintage tweed diagonal covering, brown cloth grille, 19.5 in. wide, 17.5 in. tall, 10.25 in. deep, 24 lbs., mfg. 1997-present.

MSR N/A	$220	$135 - 175	$80 - 105	

* Add $50 for a Celestion Vintage 30 speaker.

212E VINTAGE EXTENSION CABINET – 120W, 2-12 in. VL12 (1997-2001, 2008-09), GT12 (2002-04, 2010-present), or Celestion Vintage 30 (2005-07, optional 2010-present) speakers, 8 ohm impedance, designed for use as an extension cabinet with the Bel Air 212, vintage tweed diagonal covering, brown cloth grille, 26 in. wide, 17.5 in. tall, 10.25 in. deep, 33 lbs., mfg. 1997-present.

MSR N/A	$300	$150 - 200	$95 - 120	

* Add $100 for Celestion Vintage 30 speakers.

410 VINTAGE SPEAKER CABINET – 260W, 4-10 in. VL10 speakers, designed for use as an extension cabinet with the Vintage 50 Head (VT50), vintage tweed diagonal covering, brown cloth grille, 22.5 in. wide, 22.5 in. tall, 10.5 in. deep, 41 lbs., mfg. 1995-99.

	N/A	$150 - 200	$95 - 120	$395

MSR/NOTES	100%	EXCELLENT	AVERAGE	LAST MSR

VL300 Vai Legacy III Head
courtesy Carvin

VL2100 Vai Legacy II Head
courtesy Carvin

C212E VAI Legacy Speaker Cabinet
courtesy Carvin

ELECTRIC TUBE AMPLIFIERS: VL (VAI LEGACY) SERIES

The Steve Vai Legacy Series was introduced in 1999, and was developed with virtuoso guitarist Steve Vai. These amps are built by Carvin along with Steve's specifications and ideas. Unique features include a rear panel half power switch and bias switch that allow the use of three different power tubes (6L6, EL34, 5881) In 2009, Carvin introduced the Legacy II Series that features three individual channels and a half/quarter power switch.

Carvin offers a special price for both the Legacy and Legacy II Series in a half or full stack package. These packages come with the head, one or two speaker cabinets, and cables to connect them. For the Legacy Series, the half stack **VL412** last retailed for $3,000 and sold for $1,400, and the full stack **VL812** retailed for $4,200 and sold for $2,050. For the Legacy II Series, the half stack **VL2412** retails for $3,700 and sells for $1,800, and the full stack **VL2812** retails for $4,900 and sells for $2,450.

VL100 VAI LEGACY HEAD – 100W (switchable to 50W), guitar head-unit, nine-tube chassis, preamp: 5 X 12AX7, power: 4 X EL84, solid-state chassis, two channels (clean, overdrive/sustain), reverb, black control panel, single input, 11 white chickenhead knobs (All: r, Clean Ch.: t, m, b, v2, Overdrive Ch.: p, t, m, b, drive1, v1), clean channel presence switch, channel switch, power switch, standby switch, rear panel: two speaker jacks with a 4/8/16 ohm impedance selector, 50/100W output power switch, bias switch, line out jack, footswitch jack, effects loop, optional two-button footswitch (FS22), available in standard black covering (white, blue, gray, red, and other optional color coverings also available), black metal grille with a red background and Steve Vai Legacy logo, 24.5 in. wide, 9.5 in. tall, 10.5 in. deep, 37 lbs., mfg. 1999-2009.

	$800	$525 - 625	$325 - 375	$1,800

* Add $20 for cover (CV2300).
* Add $30 for two-button footswitch (FS22).

* VL212 Vai Legacy Combo – similar to the VL100 Vai Legacy Head, except in combo configuration with 2-12 in. Celestion G12 Vintage 30 speakers, closed or open back cabinet, 26 in. wide, 21 in. tall, 10.25 in. deep, 74 lbs., mfg. 1999-2009.

	$1,100	$675 - 800	$400 - 475	$2,195

* Add $30 for two-button footswitch (FS22).

VL300 VAI LEGACY III HEAD – 100W (switchable to 50W and 15W), guitar head unit, eight-tube chassis, preamp: 4 X 12AX7, power: 4 X EL34, solid-state rectifier, three channels (clean, drive, drive with high-gain), front brown control panel, single input, 16 cream chickenhead knobs (Ch. 1: t, m, b, v, Ch. 2: presence, drive, v, Ch. 3: p, drive, v, Ch. 2/3: t, b, m, All: MV, boost, reverb), presence switch for Ch. 1, gain switch for Ch. 3, three channel switches, power switch standby switch, rear panel: two speaker jacks with 4/8/16 ohm impedance switch, 15/50/100W power switch, bias switch, line out jack, two footswitch jacks, MIDI in, MIDI through, effects loop, master out jack, power amp in jack, optional four-button FS44M footswitch, available in brown or green covering/grille, Steve Vai Legacy logo, 17 in. wide, 8.5 in. tall, 9 in. deep, 29 lbs., mfg. 2012-present.

MSR N/A	$1,000	$650 - 750	$325 - 400	

VL2100 VAI LEGACY II HEAD – 100W (switchable to 50W and 25W), guitar head unit, nine-tube chassis, preamp: 5 X 12AX7, power: 4 X EL34, solid-state rectifier, three channels (clean, clean boost, lead), front black control panel, single input, 14 white chickenhead knobs (Ch. 1: t, m, b, v, Ch. 2: tone, drive, v, Ch. 3: p, t, m, b, drive, v, All: MV), presence switches for Channel 1 and Channel 2, three channel switches, power switch standby switch, rear panel: two speaker jacks with 4/8/16 ohm impedance switch, 25/50/100W power switch, bias switch, line out jack, footswitch jack, MIDI in, MIDI through, effects loop, seven-ply poplar cabinet, optional three-button FS33 footswitch, available in standard black covering (white, blue, gray, red, and other optional color coverings also available), black metal grille with a green background and Steve Vai Legacy logo, 24.5 in. wide, 9.5 in. tall, 10.5 in. deep, 39 lbs., mfg. 2009-2012.

	$1,500	$1,000 - 1,200	$650 - 800	$2,995

* Add $40 for three-button footswitch (Model FS33).

* VL2122 Vai Legacy II Combo – similar to the VL2100 Vai Legacy II Head, except in combo configuration with 2-12 in. Celestion G12 Vintage 30 speakers, closed or open back cabinet, 30 in. wide, 28 in. tall, 14 in. deep, 79 lbs., mfg. 2009-2012.

	$1,800	$1,200 - 1,450	$850 - 1,000	$2,900

* Add $40 for three-button footswitch (Model FS33).

C212E VAI LEGACY SPEAKER CABINET – 60W, 2-12 in. Celestion G12 Vintage 30 speakers, 8 ohm impedance, designed for use with the VL212 combo, black metal grille with a red baffle/background and Steve Vai Legacy logo, 26 in. wide, 17.5 in. tall, 10.25 in. deep, 40 lbs., mfg. 1999-2009.

	$450	$275 - 325	$150 - 200	$650

MSR/NOTES	100%	EXCELLENT	AVERAGE	LAST MSR

C212GE/C212BE Legacy III Speaker Cabinet courtesy Carvin

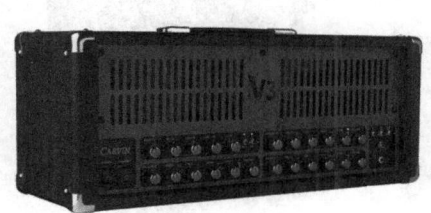

V3 Head courtesy Carvin

V3MC Micro Combo courtesy Carvin

C212GE/C212BE LEGACY III SPEAKER CABINET – 120W, 2-12 in. Celestion G12 Vintage 30 speakers, 16 ohm mono impedance, closed back, straight front, recessed side-mounted handles, tilt back stand, standard brown country western vinyl covering with chrome metal corners, other custom coverings available, green (C212GE) or tan (C212BE) metal grille with Steve Vai Legacy logo, 26 in. wide, 17.5 in. tall, 10.25 in. deep, 40 lbs., mfg. 2012-present.

MSR N/A	$475	$300 - 350	$155 - 190	

C412B/C412T VAI LEGACY SPEAKER CABINET – 240W, 4-12 in. Celestion G12 Vintage 30 speakers, 16 ohm impedance, closed back, angled front (C412T) or straight front (C412B), recessed side-mounted handles, black covering with chrome metal corners, black metal grille with a red baffle/background and Steve Vai Legacy logo, 30 in. wide, 30 in. tall, 14.5 in. deep, 92 lbs., mfg. 1999-2009, 2012-present.

MSR N/A	$675	$425 - 500	$220 - 270	

* Add $20 for removable casters (CTS4).
* Add $25 for cover (CVS412B/CVS412T).

C412B2/C412T2 VAI LEGACY II SPEAKER CABINET – 240W, 4-12 in. Celestion G12 Vintage 30 speakers, 16 ohm impedance, closed back, angled front (C412T2) or straight front (C412B2), recessed side-mounted handles, black covering with chrome metal corners, black metal grille with a green baffle/background and Steve Vai Legacy logo, 30 in. wide, 30 in. tall, 14.5 in. deep, 92 lbs., mfg. 2009-2012.

	$800	$425 - 500	$250 - 300	$1,200

* Add $20 for removable casters (CTS4).
* Add $25 for cover (CVS412B/CVS412T).

ELECTRIC TUBE AMPLIFIERS: V3 SERIES

The V3 is a rugged amp with 100% tube signal path that was built to withstand a lot of wear and tear. Carvin offers the V3 at a special price in half-stack and full-stack variations. The **V3412** half-stack with G12T-75 speakers retails for $2,995 and sells for $1,250, and the **V3412-30** with Vintage 30 speakers retails for $2,995 and sells for $1,400. The **V3812** full-stack with G12T-75 speakers retails for $3,995 and sells for $1,650, and the **V3812-30** with Vintage 30 speakers retails for $3,995 and sells for $1,950.

V3 HEAD – 100W, guitar head-unit, nine-tube chassis, preamp: 5 X 12AX7, power: 4 X EL34 (or 5881/6L6GC), solid-state rectifier, three channels, front black control panel, single input, 23 knobs (Ch. 1, Ch.2, and Ch.3: p, t, m, b, drive, v, All: MV, boost, bright, mid cut, deep), three momentary channel switches, EQ switch for each channel, Channel 1 and 2 three-way Thick/Center/Intense switch, Channel 3 three-way Soak/Center/Bright switch, two smart loop switches, power switch, standby switch, rear panel: two speaker jacks with 4/8/16 ohm impedance selector, 50/100W output power switch, bias switch, line out with level control and cabinet voicing switch, two effects loops (series and parallel with level control), MIDI in, MIDI through, two footswitch jacks, standard black covering (blue, Country Western vinyl, red, white, and other colors available), gray metal or optional diamond plate front panel, 24.25 in. wide, 10.5 in. tall, 9.5 in. deep, 35 lbs., mfg. 2006-present.

MSR N/A	$900	$575 - 675	$290 - 350	

* Add $40 for four-button footswitch (FS44).

This model is also available with an LED backlit front panel.

V3MC MICRO COMBO – 50W, 1-12 in. GT12 speaker, guitar combo amp, eight-tube chassis, preamp: 4 X 12AX7, power: 4 X EL84, three channels, front silver control panel, single input, 20 knobs (Ch. 1, Ch.2, and Ch.3: p, t, m, b, drive, v, All: MV, reverb), two momentary channel switches, EQ switch for each channel, Channel 1 and 2 three-way Thick/Center/Intense switch, Channel 3 three-way Soak/Center/Bright switch, power switch, standby switch, rear panel: two speaker jacks with 4/8/16 ohm impedance selector, 50/22/7W output power switch, line out jack, effects loop, two footswitch jacks, standard black covering, black grille, top handle, 16 in. wide, 17.75 in. tall, 9.3 in. deep, 36 lbs., mfg. 2011-present.

MSR N/A	$800	$525 - 600	$260 - 325	

V3M MICRO HEAD – 50W, guitar micro head-unit, eight-tube chassis, preamp: 4 X 12AX7, power: 4 X EL84, three channels, front black control panel, single input, 20 knobs (Ch. 1, Ch.2, and Ch.3: p, t, m, b, drive, v, All: MV, reverb), two momentary channel switches, EQ switch for each channel, Channel 1 and 2 three-way Thick/Center/Intense switch, Channel 3 three-way Soak/Center/Bright switch, power switch, standby switch, rear panel: two speaker jacks with 4/8/16 ohm impedance selector, 50/22/7W output power switch, line out jack, effects loop, two footswitch jacks, standard silver covering (gold covering also available), 15 in. wide, 7 in. tall, 8.5 in. deep, 19 lbs., mfg. 2011-present.

MSR N/A	$700	$450 - 525	$230 - 280	

MSR/NOTES	100%	EXCELLENT	AVERAGE	LAST MSR

V3212 Combo
courtesy Carvin

VX112 Speaker Cabinet
courtesy Carvin

412VB Speaker Cabinet
courtesy Carvin

V3212 COMBO – similar to the V3 Head, except in combo configuration with 2-12 in. Celestion GT12 or Celestion Vintage 30 speakers, black covering, black metal grille, 30 in. wide, 28 in .tall, 14 in. deep, 82 lbs., mfg. 2006-disc.

	$1,200	$800 - 950	$500 - 575	$2,495

* Add $40 for four-button footswitch (FS44).
* Add $80 for Celestion Vintage 30 speakers.

VX112 SPEAKER CABINET – 100W, 1-12 in. Celestion GT12 speaker, 16 ohm impedance, straight front, tilt back option, recessed handles, metal corners, black covering, black metal grille, 17 in. wide, 17 in. tall, 12.5 in. deep, 34 lbs., current mfg.

MSR N/A	$350	$235 - 270	$115 - 145	

VX212 SPEAKER CABINET – 200W, 2-12 in. Celestion GT12 speakers, 8 ohm stereo or 16 ohm mono impedance, straight front, recessed handles, metal corners, black covering, black metal grille, 17 in. wide, 30 in. tall, 13 in. deep, 60 lbs., current mfg.

MSR N/A	$450	$295 - 325	$145 - 180	

VX212S SPEAKER CABINET – 200W, 2-12 in. Celestion GT12 speakers, 8 ohm stereo or 16 ohm mono impedance, angled stacked front, recessed handles, metal corners, black covering, black metal grille, 17 in. wide, 30 in. tall, 13 in. deep, 60 lbs., current mfg.

MSR N/A	$450	$295 - 325	$145 - 180	

VX412T/VX412B SPEAKER CABINET – 400W, 4-12 in. Celestion GT12 speakers, 8 ohm stereo or 16 ohm mono impedance, straight (VX412B) or angled (VX412T) front, recessed handles, metal corners, black covering, black metal grille, 30 in. wide, 30 in. tall, 14.5 in. deep, 90 lbs., current mfg.

MSR N/A	$600	$400 - 450	$195 - 240	

412VB/412VT SPEAKER CABINET – 300W, 4-12 in. Celestion G12T-75 speakers, 8 ohm stereo or 16 ohm mono impedance, straight (412VB) or angled (412VT) front, recessed handles, metal corners, black covering, black metal grille, 30 in. wide, 30 in. tall, 14.5 in. deep, 90 lbs., mfg. 2006-disc.

	$600	$375 - 450	$225 - 275	$1,099

412VB-30/412VT-30 SPEAKER CABINET – 300W, 4-12 in. Celestion Vintage 30 speakers, 8 ohm stereo or 16 ohm mono impedance, straight (412VB-30) or angled (412VT-30) front, recessed handles, metal corners, black covering, black metal grille, 30 in. wide, 30 in. tall, 14.5 in. deep, 90 lbs., mfg. 2006-disc.

	$750	$425 - 500	$250 - 300	$1,099

ELECTRIC TUBE AMPLIFIERS: X100B SERIES IV

This Series IV is a reissue of the original X100B amps from the 1980s. Carvin offers the X100B Series IV in half-stack and full-stack configurations for a special price. The **XB412** half-stack retails for $1,899 and sells new for $1,150, and the **XB812** full-stack retails for $2,695 and sells new for $1,600.

X-50B HEAD – 50W, guitar head unit, five-tube chassis, preamp: 3 X 12AX7, power: 2 X EL34, solid-state rectifier, two channels, reverb, front black control panel, single input (1981-82) or two inputs (1983-1994), eight knobs (r, p, t, m, b, MV, lead drive, rhyhtm), five-band graphic EQ, push/pull hot rod switch on Master knob, push/pull drive switch on lead drive knob, power switch, standby switch, channel switch, rear panel: two speaker out jacks with 4/8/16 ohm impedance selector, 25/50/100% output power switch, effects loop, XLR preamp out, 120/240V switch, gray DuraTuff covering with white piping and block logo, mfg. 1991 only.

	N/A	$325 - 400	$200 - 250	$995

X-60B HEAD – 60W, guitar head unit, five-tube chassis, preamp: 3 X 12AX7, power: 2 X EL34, solid-state rectifier, two channels, reverb, front black control panel, single input (1981-82) or two inputs (1983-88), eight knobs (r, p, t, m, b, MV, lead drive, rhyhtm), five-band graphic EQ, push/pull hot rod switch on Master knob, push/pull drive switch on lead drive knob, power switch, standby switch, channel switch, rear panel: two speaker out jacks with 4/8/16 ohm impedance selector, 25/50/100% output power switch, effects loop, XLR preamp out, 120/240V switch, black Tolex covering with white piping and cursive logo (1981-87) or block logo (1988 only), mfg. 1981-88.

	N/A	$325 - 400	$200 - 250	

MSR/NOTES	100%	EXCELLENT	AVERAGE	LAST MSR

X100-B Series IV Head
courtesy Carvin

X100-B Series IV 2-12 Combo
courtesy Carvin

GX412B Speaker Cabinet
courtesy Carvin

X-100A HEAD – 100W, guitar head unit, seven-tube chassis, preamp: 3 X 12AX7, power: 4 X EL34, solid-state rectifier, two channels, reverb, front black control panel, single input (1981-82) or two inputs (1983-1994), eight knobs (r, p, t, m, b, MV, lead drive, rhyhtm), push/pull hot rod switch on Master knob, push/pull drive switch on lead drive knob, power switch, standby switch, rear panel: two speaker out jacks with 4/8/16 ohm impedance selector, 25/50/100% output power switch, effects loop, XLR preamp out, 120/240V switch, black Tolex covering with white piping and block logo, mfg. 1988 only.

	N/A	$325 - 400	$200 - 250	

X-100B HEAD – 100W, guitar head unit, seven-tube chassis, preamp: 3 X 12AX7, power: 4 X EL34, solid-state rectifier, two channels, reverb, front black control panel, single input (1981-82) or two inputs (1983-1994), eight knobs (r, p, t, m, b, MV, lead drive, rhyhtm), five-band graphic EQ, push/pull hot rod switch on Master knob, push/pull drive switch on lead drive knob, power switch, standby switch, channel switch, rear panel: two speaker out jacks with 4/8/16 ohm impedance selector, 25/50/100 output power switch, effects loop, XLR preamp out, 120/240V switch, available in black Tolex covering with white piping (1981-88) or gray DuraTuff covering with white piping (1989-1994) and cursive logo (1981-87) or block logo (1988-1994), mfg. 1981-1994.

	N/A	$375 - 450	$225 - 275	$1,195

X100-B SERIES IV HEAD – 100W (switchable to 50W or 25W), guitar head-unit configuration, seven tube chassis, preamp: 3 X 12AX7, power: 4 X EL34 (5881s or 6L6GCs can also be used), solid-state rectifier, two channels, reverb, front black control panel, single input, nine black and silver skirted knobs (r, p, t, m, b, MV, lead, drive, rhythm), five-band graphic EQ, power switch, standby switch, graphic EQ channel assignment switch, MV/boost switch, lead/gain switch, channel/drive switch, bright switch, rear panel: two speaker jacks with 4/8/16 ohm impedance selector, 25/50/100W output power switch, tube bias switch, cabinet voiced XLR balanced output, effects loop with +4/0/-10 loop level selector, two footswitch jacks, available in standard black covering with white piping (other color coverings are also available), optional two-button or four-button footswitch, 24.25 in. wide, 10.5 in. tall, 9.5 in. deep, 35 lbs., mfg. 2008-present.

MSR N/A	$800	$475 - 550	$300 - 375	

- Add $10 (MSR $20) for cover.
- Add $25 (MSR $40) for four-button footswitch (FS44).

X100-B SERIES IV 2-12 COMBO (X212B) – similar to the X100B Series IV Head, except in combo configuration with 2-12 in. Rocket 50 (2008-09), GT12 (2010-disc.), or Celestion Vintage 30 speakers (optional, 2010-disc.) and a black grille cloth, 26 in. wide, 17.5 in. tall, 10.25 in. deep, 58 lbs., mfg. 2008-disc.

	$900	$525 - 600	$325 - 400	$1,395

- Add $10 (MSR $20) for cover.
- Add $25 (MSR $40) for four-button footswitch (FS44).
- Add $100 for Celestion Vintage 30 speakers.

GX412T/GX412B SPEAKER CABINET – 200W, 4-12 in. Rocket 50 (2008-09), GT12 (2010-disc.), or Celestion Vintage 30 (optional 2010-disc.) speakers, 4 ohm impedance stereo/8 ohm impedance mono, multi-laminated plywood closed back constructed straight (GX412B) or angled (GX412T) front, black covering, black metal grille with white piping, 30 in. wide, 30 in. tall, 14.5 in. deep, 90 lbs., mfg. 2008-disc.

	$600	$300 - 350	$175 - 225	$799

- Add $150 for Celestion Vintage 30 speakers.

ELECTRIC SS AMPLIFIERS: SX SERIES

The SX Series was introduced in 1987 and were noted for being compact studio amplifiers driven by a MOSFET solid-state power section. The first three models were the SX60, SX100, and SX200 and they featured two channels with independent EQ sections. The old wavy Carvin logo was used on these amplifiers for 1987 only, and the new block-style Carvin logo was introduced in 1988. In 1989, the black vinyl covering was changed to a dark gray carpet covering, and BR "British" speakers were introduced. In 1992, a black metal grille replaced the black cloth grille and the logo moved to the center bottom of the amp. In mid-1997, the second series of the SX Series was introduced that featured four digital effects and Carvin's Tube Technology. The second series is also distinguishable by their brown Lavant vinyl covering and black metal grille. In 2002, the third and current series of the SX Series was introduced that featured digital effects and tube emulation. Carvin offers the SX Series as a half-stack and a full-stack. The **SX3412** half-stack retails for $1,390 and sells new for $600, and the **SX3812** full-stack retails for $1,995 and sells new for $900.

SX100 Third Version
courtesy Carvin

SX200 2-12 Combo Third Version
courtesy Carvin

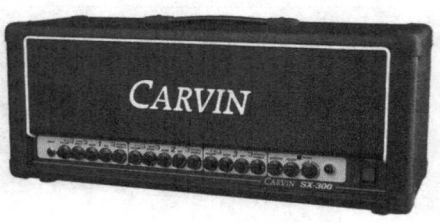

SX300H
courtesy Carvin

SX50 – 50W, 1-12 in. speaker, guitar combo, solid-state chassis, four digital effects (echo, reverb, chorus, flanger) with SmartEffects, 256 programmable variations, two channels, front silver and black control panel, single input, 12 black knobs (Ch. 1: v, drive, b, m, t, Ch. 2: v, b, m, t, All: effects selector, effects level, adjust level), Ch. 1 blues switch, channel switch, rear panel: footswitch jack, line out jack, headphone jack, external speaker jack, available in standard black covering with a black grille (other custom colors also available), 28 lbs., mfg. 2002-06.

* Add $20 for cover.

| | $275 | $175 - 225 | $95 - 125 | $495 |

SX60 – 60W, 1-12 in. BR-12 speaker, guitar combo, solid-state chassis with Tube Simulator, two channels, front black control panel, two inputs (A/B, B), 12 black knobs with silver tips (Ch. A: v, OD, b, m, t, p, Ch. B: v, b, m, t, p, All: r), channel switch, headphone jack, power switch, rear panel: pre-amp out, effects loop, footswitch jack, two speaker jacks, optional two-button footswitch, black vinyl covering (1987-88) or black Duratuff II covering (1989-1992), black cloth grille with white piping and a Carvin logo in lower right hand corner (1987-1991) or black metal grille with a Carvin logo centered at the bottom (1992 only), 46 lbs., mfg. 1987-1992.

* Add $20 for cover (CV100).

| | N/A | $175 - 225 | $110 - 140 | $595 |

SX100 FIRST VERSION – 100W, 1-12 in. BR-12 speaker, guitar combo, solid-state chassis with Tube Simulator, two channels, front black control panel, two inputs (A/B, B), 12 black knobs with silver tips (Ch. A: v, OD, b, m, t, p, Ch. B: v, b, m, t, p, All: r), channel switch, headphone jack, power switch, rear panel: pre-amp out, effects loop, footswitch jack, two speaker jacks, optional two-button footswitch, black vinyl covering (1987-88) or black Duratuff II covering (1989-1997, black cloth grille with white piping and a Carvin logo in lower right hand corner (1987-1991) or black metal grille with a Carvin logo centered at the bottom (1992-97), 46 lbs., mfg. 1987-mid-1997.

* Add $20 for cover (CV100).

| | N/A | $200 - 250 | $120 - 150 | $695 |

SX100 SECOND VERSION – 100W, 1-12 in. BR-12 speaker, guitar combo, solid-state chassis with Tube Technology, four digital effects (flanger, reverb, chorus, echo), two channels, front black control panel, two inputs (A/B, B), 13 black knobs with silver tips (Ch. A: v, OD, b, m, t, p, Ch. B: v, b, m, t, p, All: effects level, effects selector), channel switch, power switch, rear panel: effects loop, line out, footswitch jack, headphone jack, external speaker jack, optional two-button footswitch, available tan Lavant covering, black metal grille, 36 lbs., mfg. mid-1997-2001.

* Add $20 for cover (CV211).
* Add $30 for two-button footswitch (FS22).

| | N/A | $200 - 250 | $120 - 150 | $695 |

SX100 THIRD VERSION – 100W, 1-12 in. speaker, guitar combo, solid-state chassis, four digital effects (echo, reverb, chorus, flanger) with SmartEffects, 256 programmable variations, two channels, front silver and black control panel, single input, 12 black knobs (Ch. 1: v, drive, b, m, t, Ch. 2: v, b, m, t, All: effects selector, effects level, adjust level), Ch. 1 blues switch, channel switch, rear panel: footswitch jack, line out jack, headphone jack, external speaker jack, available in standard black covering with a black grille (other custom colors also available), 19.5 in. wide, 17.75 in. tall, 10.25 in. deep, 37 lbs., mfg. 2002-09.

* Add $20 for cover (CV211).
* Add $30 for two-button footswitch (FS22).

| | $300 | $175 - 225 | $110 - 140 | $595 |

SX200 FIRST VERSION – 100W, 2-12 in. BR-12 speakers, guitar combo, solid-state chassis with Tube Simulator, two channels, front black control panel, two inputs (A/B, B), 12 black knobs with silver tips (Ch. A: v, OD, b, m, t, p, Ch. B: v, b, m, t, p, All: r), channel switch, headphone jack, power switch, rear panel: pre-amp out, effects loop, footswitch jack, two speaker jacks, optional two-button footswitch, black vinyl covering (1987-88) or black Duratuff II covering (1989-1997, black cloth grille with white piping and a Carvin logo in lower right hand corner (1987-1991) or black metal grille with a Carvin logo centered at the bottom (1992-97), 58 lbs., mfg. 1987-mid-1997.

* Add $20 for cover (CV200).

| | N/A | $225 - 275 | $135 - 175 | $795 |

SX200 SECOND VERSION – 100W, 2-12 in. BR-12 speakers, guitar combo, solid-state chassis with Tube Technology, four digital effects (flanger, reverb, chorus, echo), two channels, front black control panel, two inputs (A/B, B), 13 black knobs with silver tips (Ch. A: v, OD, b, m, t, p, Ch. B: v, b, m, t, p, All: effects level, effects selector), channel switch, power switch, rear panel: effects loop, footswitch jack, preamp jack, headphone jack, optional two-button footswitch, available in tan Lavant covering, black metal grille, 49 lbs., mfg. mid-1997-2001.

| | N/A | $225 - 275 | $135 - 175 | $795 |

* Add $20 for cover (CV3212).
* Add $30 for two-button footswitch (FS22).

MSR/NOTES	100%	EXCELLENT	AVERAGE	LAST MSR

SX200 2-12 Combo Third Version
courtesy Carvin

G212 Speaker Cabinet
courtesy Carvin

G412B Speaker Cabinet
courtesy Carvin

SX200H – 200W, guitar head unit, solid-state chassis, four digital effects (echo, reverb, chorus, flanger) with SmartEffects, 256 programmable variations, two channels, front silver and black control panel, single input, 14 black knobs (Ch. 1: v, drive, b, m, t, p, Ch. 2: v, b, m, t, p, All: effects selector, effects level, adjust level), Ch. 1 blues switch, channel switch, effects switch, rear panel: effects loop, voiced line out jack, footswitch jack, headphone jack, two speaker jacks with 4/8/16 ohm impedance selector, optinal two-button footswitch, available in standard black covering with a black grille (other custom colors also available), mfg. summer 2002-03.

	N/A	$175 - 225	$110 - 140	$599

- Add $20 for cover.

*** SX200 2-12 Combo Third Version** – similar to the SX200H, except in combo configuration with 2-12 in. speakers, available in standard black covering with a black grille (other custom colors also available), 26 in. wide, 17.75 in. tall, 10.25 in. deep, 39 lbs., mfg. 2002-disc.

	$350	$200 - 250	$120 - 150	$795

- Add $20 for cover (CV3212).
- Add $30 for two-button footswitch (FS22).

SX300H – 300W, guitar head unit, solid-state chassis, four digital effects (echo, reverb, chorus, flanger) with SmartEffects, 256 programmable variations, three channels, front silver and black control panel, single input, 17 black knobs (Ch. 1: v, drive, b, m, t, Ch. 2: v, drive, b, m, t, Ch. 3: v, b, m, t, All: effects selector, effects level, adjust level), Ch. 1 channel switch, high gain switch, and presence switch, Ch. 2 channel switch, blues switch, and presence switch, Ch. 3 channel switch and presence switch, All: reverb switch, rear panel: effects loop, voiced line out jack, footswitch jack, headphone jack, two speaker jacks with 4/8/16 ohm impedance selector, optinal four-button footswitch, available in standard black covering with a black grille (other custom colors also available), 24.5 in. wide, 10.5 in. tall, 9.5 in. deep, mfg. 2003-disc.

	$350	$200 - 250	$120 - 150	$695

- Add $20 for cover (CV3200)
- Add $40 for four-button footswitch (FS44).

*** SX300 2-12 Combo** – similar to the SX300H, except in combo configuration with 2-12 in. speakers, available in standard black covering with a black grille (other custom colors also available), 26 in. wide, 17.75 in. tall, 10.25 in. deep, 50 lbs., mfg. 2003-present.

MSR N/A	$400	$225 - 275	$135 - 175	

- Add $20 for cover (CV3212).
- Add $40 for four-button footswitch (FS44).

SC212E SPEAKER CABINET – 160W, 2-12 in. Celestion Seventy 80 speakers, 8 ohm impedance, closed back, black covering, black metal grille, top handle, 33 lbs., disc. 2006.

	$250	$150 - 200	$90 - 120	$560

SC412B/SC412T SPEAKER CABINET – 320W, 4-12 in. Celestion Seventy 80 speakers, 4 or 8 ohm impedance, closed back, straight (B) or angled (T) front, black covering, black metal grille, recessed handles, 90 lbs., disc.

	$400	$250 - 300	$150 - 190	$695

G212 SPEAKER CABINET – 140W, 2-12 in. Carvin British BR12 speakers, 8 ohm impedance, closed back, top handle, available in standard black covering with a black metal grille (other custom color coverings also available), 26 in. wide, 17.5 in. tall, 10.25 in. deep, 33 lbs., mfg. 2007-09.

	$225	$120 - 150	$75 - 95	$595

G412B/G412T SPEAKER CABINET – 280W, 4-12 in. Carvin British BR12 speakers, 4 ohm stereo or 8 ohm mono impedance, straight (G412B) or angled (G412T) front, closed back, recessed side handles, available in standard black covering with a black metal grille (other custom color coverings also available), top handle, 30 in. wide, 30 in. tall, 14.5 in. deep, 90 lbs., mfg. 2007-disc.

	$400	$250 - 300	$150 - 200	$695

ELECTRIC BASS SS AMPLIFIERS: B SERIES

Carvin offers a special price for both the B and BX Series in a variety of head and speaker cabinet packages. These packages come with the head, one or two speaker cabinets, and cables to connect them. The **SBR810** (retail price $2,695, new price is $1,050) includes the BX1500 head, BR810 speaker cabinet, and a C5S cable. The **SBR1018** (retail price $2,795, new price is $1,200) includes the BX1500 head, a BR410 speaker cabinet, a BR118N speaker cabinet, and a C5S cable. The **BX500-10.2N** (retail price $2,490, new price is $900) includes the BX500 head, a BRX10.2NEO speaker cabinet, and a C5S cable. The **BX1500-**

MSR/NOTES	100%	EXCELLENT	AVERAGE	LAST MSR

**B1000 Head
courtesy Carvin**

**BX250 Micro Head
courtesy Carvin**

**BX500 Head
courtesy Carvin**

10.4N (retail price $2,890, new price is $1,000) includes the BX1500 head, a BRX10.4NEO speaker cabinet, and a C5S cable. The **B2000-10.4N** (retail price $3,190, new price is $1,130) includes the B2000 head, a BRX10.4NEO speaker cabinet, and a C5S cable. In 2006, Carvin redesigned the B/BRX series with built in casters and combo units.

B500 HEAD – 500W at 2 ohms (350W at 4 ohms, 225W at 8 ohms), rack-mount head-unit only, solid-state chassis, single channel, front black control panel, single input, eight chrome knobs (sub b, b, l/m, m, h/m, t, drive, v), effects loop, line out with level control, black casing, 25 lbs., mfg. 2003-05.

	N/A	$325 - 375	$200 - 250	$995

B800 HEAD – 800W at 2 ohms (500W at 4 ohms, 300W at 8 ohms), head-unit only, solid-state chassis, single channel, front black control panel, single input, eight chrome knobs (sub b, b, l/m, m, h/m, t, drive, MV), effects loop, line out with level control, black covering, 22 lbs., mfg. 2006 only.

	$450	$325 - 375	$200 - 250	$995

B1000 HEAD – 900W at 2 ohms (600W at 4 ohms, 325W at 8 ohms), head-unit only, hybrid chassis with 1 X 12AX7 preamp tube, single channel, front black control panel, single input, nine chrome knobs (drive, sub b, b, l/m, m, h/m, t, DI out level, v), mute switch, active switch, fx loop switch, pre/post switch, power switch, effects loop, tuner jack, line out with level control, footswitch jack, two speaker jacks, black casing, 14 in. wide, 9 in. deep, 3.15 in. tall, 6.4 lbs., mfg. 2014-present.

MSR N/A	$500	$325 - 375	$165 - 200	

B1500 HEAD – 1900W at 2 ohms (1250W at 4 ohms, 700W at 8 ohms), rack-mount head-unit only, solid-state chassis, single channel, front black control panel, single input, eight chrome knobs (sub b, b, l/m, m, h/m, t, drive, v), effects loop, line out with level control, black casing, 33 lbs., mfg. 2003-09.

	$800	$450 - 525	$275 - 325	$1,595

B2000 HEAD – 2050W @ 2 ohms (1300W @ 4 ohms, 700W @ 8 ohms), two-space rack-mount bass head-unit, hybrid chassis with 1 X 12AX7 preamp tube, single channel, black front control panel, single input, eight chrome knobs (drive, sub b, b, l/m, m, h/m, t, drive, v), mute switch, active/passive input switch, effects loop on/off switch, power switch, rear panel: footswitch jack, tuner out, tube bypass switch, effects loop, XLR balanced direct line out with level control, pre/post EQ switch, and ground/lift switch, two Speakon jacks, black casing, 19 in. wide, 3.5 in. tall, 10.5 in. deep, 13 lbs., mfg. 2010-present.

MSR N/A	$750	$450 - 525	$275 - 325	

* Add $30 for two-button footswitch (FS22).
* Add $40 for two-space rack-mount case (SV2).

BX120 HEAD – 120W, non-rackmount head-unit, solid-state chassis, single channel, front gray control panel, single input, nine knobs, five-band graphic EQ, XLR direct out, effects loop, black covering, 9 lbs., mfg. 2007-08.

	$250	$150 - 200	$95 - 120	$595

BX250 MICRO HEAD – 250W @ 4 ohms (200W @ 8 ohm), bass head unit, solid-state chassis, single channel, front gray control panel, single input, 11 black knobs (drive, contour, b, lo/mid, hi/mid, t, DI level, compressor, lo freq., hi freq., MV), ground/lift switch, pre/post switch, mute switch, active/passive input switch, rear panel: power switch, two speaker jacks, XLR direct out, tuner out, black casing, 10 in. wide, 3.7 in. tall, 7.15 in. deep, 3.2 lbs., mfg. 2011-present.

MSR N/A	$300	$195 - 225	$100 - 120	

BX500 HEAD – 500W @ 4 or 2 ohms (300W @ 8 ohms), bass head unit, hybrid chassis with a 12AX7 preamp tube and solid-state power section, single channel, front gray control panel, single input, 11 black knobs (drive, contour, b, lo/mid, hi/mid, t, DI level, compressor, lo freq., hi freq., MV), nine-band graphic EQ, mute switch, active/passive input switch, graphic EQ in switch, power switch, rear panel: effects loop, footswitch jack, speaker jacks, optional two-button footswitch jack, black casing, 14 in. wide, 2.8 in. tall, 9 in. deep, 5.8 lbs., mfg. 2009-present.

MSR N/A	$400	$260 - 300	$130 - 160	

* Add $30 for two-button footswitch (FS22).
* Add $35 for rackmount faceplate.

* BR510N Combo – similar to the BX500 Bass Head, except in combo configuration with 2-10 in. Neodymium speakers and a titanium tweeter, available in standard black covering with a black metal grille (other optional colors also available), 20.75 in. wide, 23.75 in. tall, 18.5 in. deep, 48 lbs., mfg. 2009-disc.

	$725	$400 - 475	$225 - 275	$1,095

* Add $30 for two-button footswitch (FS22).

| MSR/NOTES | 100% | EXCELLENT | AVERAGE | LAST MSR |

BX700 Head
courtesy Carvin

BX1600 Head
courtesy Carvin

BR15 Combo
courtesy Carvin

* *BR515N Combo* – similar to the BX500 Bass Head, except in combo configuration with 1-15 in. Neodymium speaker and a titanium tweeter, available in standard black covering with a black metal grille (other optional colors also available), 20.75 in. wide, 23.75 in. tall, 18.5 in. deep, 40 lbs., mfg. 2009-disc.

| | $725 | $400 - 475 | $225 - 275 | $1,095 |

- Add $30 for two-button footswitch (FS22).

BX600 HEAD – 600W @ 2 ohm (400W @ 4 ohm, 225W @ 8 ohm), non-rackmount head-unit, solid-state chassis, single channel, front gray control panel, single input, 13 knobs (d, c, b, l/m, m, h/m, t, compression, three freq. knobs, direct level, MV), nine-band graphic EQ, active/passive switch, XLR direct out, effects loop, black covering, 20 lbs., mfg. summer 2006-08.

| | $400 | $300 - 350 | $175 - 225 | $995 |

BX700 HEAD – 700W @ 2 ohm (550W @ 4 ohm, 300W @ 8 ohm), head-unit, hybrid chassis with 1 X 12AX7 preamp tube, single channel, front red control panel, single input, 11 knobs (d, c, b, l/m, h/m, t, direct level, compression, freq. 1, freq. 2, MV), nine-band graphic EQ, mute switch, active/passive switch, pre/post switch, graphic EQ switch, two speaker output jacks, footswitch jack, XLR direct out, tuner jack, effects loop, black covering, 14 in. wide, 3.25 in. tall, 9 in. deep, 5.9 lbs., mfg. 2014-present.

| MSR N/A | $450 | $295 - 325 | $145 - 180 | |

BX1200 HEAD – 600W per channel @ 2 ohm (400W per channel @ 4 ohm, 275W per channel @ 8 ohm), rackmount or regular head-unit, solid-state chassis, single channel, front gray control panel, single input, 15 knobs (d, c, b, l/m, m, h/m, t, compression, three freq. knobs, crossover freq., power lo, power high, MV), nine-band graphic EQ, active/passive switch, XLR direct out with level control, effects loop, black covering, 23 lbs., mfg. summer 2006-09.

| | $700 | $375 - 450 | $225 - 275 | $1,395 |

BX1500 HEAD – 750W per channel @ 2 ohm (450W per channel @ 4 ohm, 300W per channel @ 8 ohm), two-space rack-mount bass head-unit, hybrid chassis with 1 X 12AX7 preamp tube, single channel, front gray and black control panel, single input, 15 knobs (drive, contour, b, l/m, m, h/m, t, compression, l/m freq., m freq., h/m freq., crossover freq., power amp lo level, power amp high level, MV), nine-band graphic EQ, mute switch, active/passive input switch, graphic EQ in/out switch, effects on/off switch, crossover on/off switch, power switch, rear panel: footswitch jack with two switches to select footswitch functions, power amp bridge switch, tuner out jack, effects loop, two stereo amp patch inserts, XLR balanced direct line out with level control, pre/post EQ switch, and ground/lift switch, three Speakon jacks (two regulard, one bridged), black casing, 19 in. wide, 3.5 in. tall, 10.5 in. deep, 10 lbs., mfg. 2010-present.

| MSR N/A | $550 | $350 - 400 | $180 - 220 | |

- Add $30 for two-button footswitch (FS22).
- Add $40 for two-space rack-mount case (SV2).

BX1600 HEAD – 800W per channel @ 2 ohm (500W per channel @ 4 ohm, 325W per channel @ 8 ohm), two-space rack-mount bass head-unit, hybrid chassis with 1 X 12AX7 preamp tube, single channel, front red and black control panel, single input, 15 knobs (drive, contour, b, l/m, m, h/m, t, compression, l/m freq., m freq., h/m freq., crossover freq., power amp lo level, power amp high level, MV), nine-band graphic EQ, mute switch, active/passive input switch, graphic EQ in/out switch, effects on/off switch, crossover on/off switch, power switch, rear panel: footswitch jack with two switches to select footswitch functions, power amp bridge switch, tuner out jack, effects loop, two stereo amp patch inserts, XLR balanced direct line out with level control, pre/post EQ switch, and ground/lift switch, three Speakon jacks (two regular, one bridged), black casing, 19 in. wide, 3.5 in. tall, 10.5 in. deep, 8.5 lbs., mfg. 2014-present.

| MSR N/A | $650 | $425 - 475 | $210 - 260 | |

BR12 COMBO – 120W, 1-12 in. speaker, solid-state chassis, single channel, front gray control panel, single input, nine knobs (d, c, b, m, t, compression, freq., direct level, MV), five-band graphic EQ, active/passive switch, XLR direct out, HF control, black covering, black metal grille, retractable handles, 36 lbs., mfg. summer 2006 only.

| | $375 | $225 - 275 | $120 - 150 | $595 |

BR15 COMBO – 120W, 1-15 in. speaker, solid-state chassis, single channel, front gray control panel, single input, nine knobs (d, c, b, m, t, compression, freq., direct level, MV), five-band graphic EQ, active/passive switch, XLR direct out, HF control, black covering, black metal grille, retractable handles, 46 lbs., mfg. summer 2006-09.

| | $400 | $250 - 300 | $135 - 175 | $795 |

MSR/NOTES	100%	EXCELLENT	AVERAGE	LAST MSR

BR615 Combo
courtesy Carvin

BRX212 Combo
courtesy Carvin

BR118N-4 Speaker Cabinet
courtesy Carvin

BR610 COMBO – 600W @ 2 ohm (400W @ 4 ohm, 225W @ 8 ohm), 2-10 in. speakers, solid-state chassis, single channel, front gray control panel, single input, 13 knobs (d, c, b, l/m, m, h/m, t, compression, three freq. knobs, direct level, MV), nine-band graphic EQ, active/passive switch, XLR direct out, effects loop, black covering, 61 lbs., mfg. summer 2006-08.

	$575	$375 - 450	$225 - 275	$1,095

BR615 COMBO – 600W @ 2 ohm (400W @ 4 ohm, 225W @ 8 ohm), 1-15 in. speaker, solid-state chassis, single channel, front gray control panel, single input, 13 knobs (d, c, b, l/m, m, h/m, t, compression, three freq. knobs, direct level, MV), nine-band graphic EQ, active/passive switch, XLR direct out, effects loop, black covering, 64 lbs., mfg. summer 2006-08.

	$575	$350 - 425	$200 - 250	$1,095

BRX112 COMBO – 800W at 2 ohms (500W at 4 ohms, 300W at 8 ohms), 1-12 in. Neo speaker combo, solid-state chassis, single channel, front black control panel, single input, eight chrome knobs (sub b, b, l/m, m, h/m, t, drive, MV), effects loop, line out with level control, tilt-back cabinet design, black covering, black metal grille, 47 lbs., mfg. 2006 only.

	$700	$525 - 600	$325 - 375	$1,195

BRX212 COMBO – 800W at 2 ohms (500W at 4 ohms, 300W at 8 ohms), 2-12 in. Neo speaker combo, 1 in. Titanium horn, solid-state chassis, single channel, front black control panel, single input, eight chrome knobs (sub b, b, l/m, m, h/m, t, drive, MV), effects loop, line out with level control, built-in casters, tilt-back pull-behind handle, recessed handles, black covering, black metal grille, 69 lbs., mfg. 2005-06.

	$850	$550 - 650	$375 - 450	$1,695

BR115 SPEAKER CABINET – 600W, 1-15 in. heavy duty woofer, 1-1 in. driver, 4 ohm impedance, black covering, black metal grille, retractable handles, 56 lbs., mfg. summer 2006-08, reintroduced-present.

MSR N/A	$300	$175 - 225	$110 - 140	

BR115N-4/BR115N-8 SPEAKER CABINET – 600W, 1-15 in. Neodymium driver, 1-1 in. titanium HF horn, 4 ohm (BR115N-4) or 8 ohm (BR115N-8) impedance, Speakon and 1/4 in. inputs, black covering, black metal grille, recessed handles, 23.5 in. wide, 25.5 in. tall, 18.25 in. deep, 52 lbs., mfg. 2009-disc.

	$400	$200 - 250	$120 - 150	$595

BR118 SPEAKER CABINET – 800W, 1-18 in. heavy duty woofer, 1-1 in. driver, 4 ohm impedance, black covering, black metal grille, retractable handles, 62 lbs., mfg. summer 2006-08.

	$350	$200 - 250	$120 - 150	$695

BR118N-4/BR118N-8 SPEAKER CABINET – 800W, 1-18 in. Neodymium driver, 4 ohm (BR118N-4) or 8 ohm (BR118N-8) impedance, Speakon and 1/4 in. inputs, black covering, black metal grille, recessed handles, 23.5 in. wide, 25.5 in. tall, 18.25 in. deep, 59 lbs., mfg. 2009-disc.

	$420	$225 - 275	$135 - 175	$695

BR210 SPEAKER CABINET – 400W, 2-10 in. heavy duty woofers, 1-1 in. driver, 4 ohm impedance, precision crossover with five-position HF knob, black covering, black metal grille, retractable handles, 43 lbs., mfg. summer 2006-present.

MSR N/A	$270	$150 - 200	$95 - 120	

BR210N-4/BR210N-8 SPEAKER CABINET – 600W, 2-10 in. Neodymium drivers, 1-1 in. titanium HF horn, 4 ohm (BR210N-4) or 8 ohm (BR210N-8) impedance, Speakon and 1/4 in. inputs, black covering, black metal grille, recessed handles, 23.5 in. wide, 17.5 in. tall, 18.25 in. deep, 43 lbs., mfg. 2009-disc.

	$380	$225 - 275	$135 - 175	$795

BR410 SPEAKER CABINET – 800W, 4-10 in. heavy duty woofers, 1-1 in. driver, 8 ohm impedance, precision crossover with five-position HF knob, black covering, black metal grille, retractable handles, 68 lbs., mfg. summer 2006-present.

MSR N/A	$370	$225 - 275	$135 - 175	

MSR/NOTES	100%	EXCELLENT	AVERAGE	LAST MSR

BR410N-4 Speaker Cabinet
courtesy Carvin

BRX10 Speaker Cabinet
courtesy Carvin

BRX10.4Neo Speaker Cabinet
courtesy Carvin

BR410N-4/BR410N-8 SPEAKER CABINET – 1200W, 4-10 in. Neodymium drivers, 1-1 in. titanium HF horn, 4 ohm (BR410N-4) or 8 ohm (BR410N-8) impedance, Speakon and 1/4 in. inputs, black covering, black metal grille, recessed handles, 23.5 in. wide, 25.5 in. tall, 18.25 in. deep, 65 lbs., mfg. 2009-disc.

	$600	$325 - 400	$175 - 225	$995

BR810 SPEAKER CABINET – 1200W, 8-10 in. heavy duty woofers, 1-1 in. driver, 4 ohm impedance, precision crossover with five-position HF knob, black covering, black metal grille, retractable handles, 118 lbs., mfg. summer 2006-disc.

	$700	$375 - 450	$225 - 275	$1,295

BRX10 SPEAKER CABINET – 1200W, 4-10 in. woofers with a tweeter, 8 ohm impedance, bottom ported, recessed handles, black covering, black metal grille, 99 lbs., mfg. 2003-06.

	$725	$550 - 650	$350 - 425	$1,495

BRX12 SPEAKER CABINET – 600W, 2-12 in. woofers with a tweeter, 8 ohm impedance, bottom ported, recessed handles, black covering, black metal grille, 83 lbs., mfg. 2003-06.

	$500	$350 - 425	$200 - 250	$995

BRX18 SPEAKER CABINET – 800W, 1-18 in. woofer with a tweeter, 8 ohm impedance, bottom ported, recessed handles, black covering, black metal grille, 95 lbs., mfg. 2003-05.

	N/A	$425 - 500	$300 - 350	$1,195

BRX10.2NEO SPEAKER CABINET – 600W, 2-10 in. 300W Neodymium woofers, 1-1 in. horn, 4 ohm impedance, six-position horn knob, DuraTex scratch resistant finish, black metal grille, built-in handles, 46 lbs., mfg. summer 2006-present.

MSR $370	$375	$240 - 280	$120 - 150	

BRX10.4NEO SPEAKER CABINET – 1200W, 4-10 in. 300W Neodymium woofers, 1-1 in. horn, 4 ohm impedance, six-position horn knob, DuraTex scratch resistant finish, black metal grille, built-in handles, 76 lbs., mfg. summer 2006-present.

MSR N/A	$575	$375 - 425	$185 - 230	

ELECTRIC BASS SS AMPLIFIERS: MB MICRO BASS SERIES

BX MICRO BASS MB10 – 200W @ 8 ohms (250W @ 4 ohms with extension speaker), 1-10 in. driver with a NEO titanium tweeter, bass combo, solid-state chassis, single channel, top black control panel, single input, 11 black knobs (drive, contour, b, lo/mid, hi/mid, t, DI level, compressor, lo/mid freq., hi/mid freq., MV), mute switch, active/passive input switch, XLR balanced direct line out with lift/ground switch and pre/post switch, headphone/tuner jack, external speaker jack, tweeter full/DIM switch, power switch, standard black covering, black grille, 12.75 in. wide, 18.5 in. tall, 11.5 in. deep, 23 lbs., mfg. 2010-present.

MSR N/A	$350	$230 - 265	$115 - 140	

BX MICRO BASS MB12 – 200W @ 8 ohms (250W @ 4 ohms with extension speaker), 1-12 in. woofer with 1-6 in. mid-range driver, and a NEO titanium tweeter, bass combo, solid-state chassis, single channel, top black control panel, single input, 11 black knobs (drive, contour, b, lo/mid, hi/mid, t, DI level, compressor, lo/mid freq., hi/mid freq., MV), mute switch, active/passive input switch, XLR balanced direct line out with lift/ground switch and pre/post switch, headphone/tuner jack, external speaker jack, tweeter full/DIM switch, power switch, standard black covering, black grille, 17 in. wide, 19 in. tall, 12 in. deep, 30 lbs., mfg. 2010-present.

MSR N/A	$475	$300 - 350	$155 - 190	

BX MICRO BASS MB15 – 200W @ 8 ohms (250W @ 4 ohms with extension speaker), 1-15 in. woofer with a NEO titanium tweeter, bass combo, solid-state chassis, single channel, top black control panel, single input, 11 black knobs (drive, contour, b, lo/mid, hi/mid, t, DI level, compressor, lo/mid freq., hi/mid freq., MV), mute switch, active/passive input switch, XLR balanced direct line out with lift/ground switch and pre/post switch, headphone/tuner jack, external speaker jack, tweeter full/DIM switch, power switch, standard black covering, black grille, 17 in. wide, 19 in. tall, 12 in. deep, 30 lbs., mfg. 2010-present.

MSR N/A	$400	$260 - 300	$130 - 160	

MSR/NOTES	100%	EXCELLENT	AVERAGE	LAST MSR

BX Micro Bass MB210
courtesy Carvin

115MBE Micro Bass Speaker Cabinet
courtesy Carvin

115MBE Micro Bass Speaker Cabinet
courtesy Carvin

BX MICRO BASS MB210 – 250W @ 8 ohms, 2-10 in. drivers with a NEO titanium tweeter, bass combo, solid-state chassis, single channel, top black control panel, single input, 11 black knobs (drive, contour, b, lo/mid, hi/mid, t, DI level, compressor, lo/mid freq., hi/mid freq., MV), mute switch, active/passive input switch, XLR balanced direct line out with lift/ground switch and pre/post switch, headphone/tuner jack, external speaker jack, tweeter full/DIM switch, power switch, standard black covering, black grille, 12.75 in. wide, 24.5 in. tall, 11.5 in. deep, 36.4 lbs., mfg. 2011-present.

| MSR N/A | $400 | $260 - 300 | $130 - 160 | |

115MBE MICRO BASS SPEAKER CABINET – 400W, 1-15 in. bass speaker cabinet, 8 ohm impedance, black covering, black grille, top handle, 17 in. wide, 12 in. deep, 19 in. tall, 30 lbs., mfg. 2015-present.

| MSR N/A | $230 | $150 - 175 | $75 - 90 | |

210MBE MICRO BASS SPEAKER CABINET – 400W, 2-10 in. speaker, bass extension cabinet, 8 ohm impedance, black covering, black grille, top handle, 12.75 in. wide, 11.5 in. deep, 24.5 in. tall, 33.6 lbs., mfg. 2010-present.

| MSR N/A | $230 | $150 - 175 | $75 - 90 | |

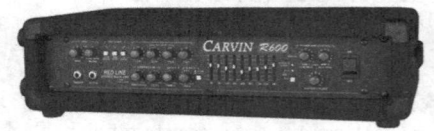

Pro Bass 100-10
courtesy Carvin

RC210 Red Eye Combo
courtesy Carvin

R600 Head
courtesy Carvin

ELECTRIC BASS SS AMPLIFIERS: PRO SERIES

PRO BASS 100-10 – 100W, 1-10 in.speaker, solid-state bass combo, black control panel, one input, seven black and red knobs (v, b, g, freq, t, comp, gate), three white push buttons, black Dura Tuff II covering, black metal grille, 30 lbs., disc. 2005.

| | N/A | $150 - 200 | $90 - 120 | $395 |

* Pro Bass 100-15 – similar to the Pro Bass 100-10, except has 1-15 in. speaker, 48 lbs., disc. 2008.

| | $275 | $150 - 200 | $90 - 120 | $395 |

PRO BASS 200 – 160W, 1-15 in., solid-state bass combo, black control panel, one input, seven black and red knobs (v, b, g, freq, t, comp, gate) 5-band equalizer, three white push buttons, tweeter pad control on back, black Dura Tuff II covering, black metal grille, 46 lbs., disc. 2006.

| | $350 | $275 - 325 | $175 - 225 | $695 |

ELECTRIC BASS SS AMPLIFIERS: RED EYE SERIES

RC210 RED EYE COMBO – 600W, 2-10 in. heavy-duty drivers plus red eye horn, solid-state bass combo, tilt-back cabinet, black front control panel, two inputs, 13 red knobs, 9-band equalizer, various white buttons, black Dura Tuff II covering, black metal grille, disc. 2004.

| | N/A | $600 - 700 | $325 - 400 | $1,395 |

RC210-18 – similar to the RC210 except has an 18 in. extension cabinet, disc. 2004.

| | N/A | $750 - 900 | $425 - 500 | $2,090 |

• **Add $20 for cover.**

The RC210 features the series III R600 bass amp head.

MSR/NOTES	100%	EXCELLENT	AVERAGE	LAST MSR

R1010 Combo
courtesy Carvin

RL115T Speaker Cabinet
courtesy Carvin

RL410T Speaker Cabinet
courtesy Carvin

RL6815 CYCLOPS – similar to the RC210 Red Eye except has different speaker configuration of 1-15 in. woofer, 2-8 in. mid-range drivers, and the red-eye horn driver, disc.

	N/A	$675 - 800	$375 - 450	$1,495

• Add $25 for cover.

ELECTRIC BASS SS AMPLIFIERS: RED LINE SERIES

R600 HEAD – 600W bridged, head-unit only, solid-state bass amp, black front control panel, two inputs, 13 red knobs, 9-band equalizer, various white buttons, black Dura Tuff II covering, disc. 2006.

$525	$400 - 475	$275 - 325	$1,195

R1000 HEAD – similar to the R600 except has 1000W output bridged, 31 lbs., disc. 2006.

$600	$450 - 525	$325 - 400	$1,295

R1010 COMBO – 1000W (R1000 head), 2-10 in. drivers, 1 in. horn, recessed handles, tilt-back cabinet, black carpet covering, black metal grille, 68 lbs., mfg. 2005-06.

$700	$525 - 625	$325 - 400	$1,395

R1015 COMBO – 1000W (R1000 head), 1-15 in. driver and 2-8 in. mid-range speakers, 1 in. horn, recessed handles, black carpet covering, black metal grille, 93 lbs., mfg. 2005-06.

$800	$600 - 700	$375 - 450	$1,495

RL115 SPEAKER CABINET – 600W, 1-15 in. speaker, 4 ohm impedance, bottom port, recessed handles, casters, black carpet covering, black metal grille, 70 lbs., disc. 2005.

	N/A	$175 - 225	$95 - 125	$595

RL115T SPEAKER CABINET – 600W, 1-15 in. speaker with a 1 in. horn, 4 ohm impedance, bottom port, recessed handles, black carpet covering, black metal grille, 63 lbs., mfg. 2005-06.

$325	$200 - 250	$120 - 150	$695

RL118 SPEAKER CABINET – 800W, 1-18 in. speaker, 4 ohm impedance, bottom port, recessed handles, black carpet covering, black metal grille, 74 lbs., disc. 2006.

$350	$225 - 275	$150 - 180	$695

RL210T SPEAKER CABINET – 400W, 2-10 in. speaker with a 1 in. horn, 4 ohm impedance, bottom port, recessed handles, black carpet covering, black metal grille, 40 lbs., disc. 2006.

$225	$150 - 200	$70 - 95	$495

RL410T SPEAKER CABINET – 800W, 4-10 in. speakers with a 1 in. horn, 8 ohm impedance, bottom port, recessed handles, black carpet covering, black metal grille, 69 lbs., disc. 2006.

$325	$225 - 275	$150 - 180	$695

RL810T SPEAKER CABINET – 1200W, 8-10 in. speakers with a 1 in. horn, 4 ohm impedance, bottom port, recessed handles, casters, black carpet covering, black metal grille, 118 lbs., disc. 2006.

$500	$400 - 475	$275 - 325	$1,295

ACOUSTIC SS AMPLIFIERS

AG100 – 100W, 1-12 in. PS12 200W driver with a switchable horn tweeter, acoustic guitar combo, solid-state chassis, three channels, reverb, black front control panel, three inputs (Ch. 1 and Ch. 2 1/4 in. and Ch. 3 XLR mic input), 14 gray knobs (Ch. 1: lo, g, freq., high, v, reverb/effect level, Ch. 2: lo, high, v, Ch. 3: lo, high, v, reverb/effect level, All: master reverb/effects level), five-band graphic equalizer, Ch. 1 mid switch, Ch. 1 acoustic/electric switch, power switch, effects loop, Duratuff II dark gray carpet covering, black metal grille, 17.5 in. wide, 22 in. tall, 12 in. deep, 40 lbs., mfg. 1996-98.

	N/A	$250 - 300	$135 - 175	$795

• Add $20 for cover (CV155).
• Add $90 for speaker stand (TS30BN).

MSR/NOTES	100%	EXCELLENT	AVERAGE	LAST MSR

AG200 Combo
courtesy Carvin

AG300 Combo
courtesy Carvin

300AGE Speaker Cabinet
courtesy Carvin

AG100D SERIES I – 100W, 1-12 in. PS12 200W driver with a horn tweeter, acoustic guitar combo, solid-state chassis, three channels, four digital effects (echo, reverb, chorus, flange) with two assignable channels, black front control panel, four inputs (one 1/4 in. per channel and Ch. 3 XLR mic input), 16 gray knobs (Ch. 1: lo, freq., g, high, effect level, v, Ch. 2: lo, high, effect level, v, Ch. 3: lo, high, effect level, v, All: effects select, effects level), five-band graphic equalizer, Ch. 1 mid switch, Ch. 1 high switch, Ch. 2 bass switch, Ch. 2 mid switch, power switch, rear panel: stereo line out, headphone jack, effects loop, two speaker jacks, footswitch jack, optional two-button footswitch, available in standard hunter green vinyl covering with a black metal grille (other custom color coverings also available), 17 in. wide, 22 in. tall, 12 in. deep, 43 lbs., mfg. mid-1997-2001.

	N/A	$275 - 325	$150 - 200	$895

- Add $20 for cover (CV155).
- Add $30 for two-button footswitch (FS22).
- Add $40 for folding amp stand (MA12).
- Add $60 for speaker stand (SS20).

AG100D SERIES II – 100W, 1-12 in. AG12 200W driver with a horn tweeter, acoustic guitar combo, solid-state chassis, three channels, four digital effects (echo, reverb, chorus, flange) with two assignable channels, black front control panel, four inputs (one 1/4 in. per channel and Ch. 3 XLR mic input), 21 gray knobs (Ch. 1: lo, freq., g, high, v, effect level, Ch. 2: lo, high, effect level, v, Ch. 3: lo, high, effect level, v, All: effect 1 select, effect 2 select, parameter 1, parameter 2, level 1, level 2, MV), five-band graphic equalizer, Ch. 1 mid switch, Ch. 1 high switch, Ch. 2 mid switch, Ch. 2 high switch, power switch, rear panel: stereo line out, headphone jack, effects loop, two speaker jacks, footswitch jack, optional two-button footswitch, available in standard hunter green vinyl covering with a black metal grille (other custom color coverings also available), 17 in. wide, 22 in. tall, 12 in. deep, 35 lbs., mfg. 2002-present.

MSR N/A	$440	$300 - 350	$175 - 225	

- Add $20 for cover (CV155).
- Add $30 for two-button footswitch (FS22).
- Add $60 for speaker stand (SS20).

AG112 EXTENSION SPEAKER CABINET – 300W, 1-12 in. speaker, 8 ohm impedance, available in standard hunter green vinyl covering with a black metal grille (other custom color coverings are also available), 17 in. wide, 19 in. tall, 12 in. deep, 26 lbs., disc.

	$250	$160 - 210	$105 - 130	$399

- Add $20 for cover (CVS112).

AG200 COMBO – 200W, 2-6.5 in. drivers with a titanium tweeter, acoustic guitar combo, solid-state chassis, three channels, digital effects with two assignable channels, black top control panel, six inputs (one 1/4 in. and one XLR per channel), 22 gray knobs (DI out level, Ch. 1: lo, freq., mid, high, v, effect level, Ch. 2: lo, freq, mid, high, effect level, v, Ch. 3: lo, high, effect level, v, All: effect 1 select, effect 2 select, level 1, level 2, MV), Ch. 1 phantom switch, Ch. 1 gain switch, Ch. 2 gain switch, Ch. 2 phantom switch, Ch. 2 high switch, power switch, XLR DI out jack, headphone jack, effects loop, two speaker jacks, footswitch jack, external speaker jack, USB charge port, available in standard Brown Marvelon vinyl covering with a black metal grille (other custom color coverings also available), 12.75 in. wide, 18.5 in. tall, 11.5 in. deep, 29 lbs., mfg. 2014-present.

MSR N/A	$500	$325 - 375	$165 - 200	

AG300 COMBO – 200W, 1-12 in. driver and 1-6.5 in. driver with a titanium tweeter, acoustic guitar combo, solid-state chassis, three channels, digital effects with two assignable channels, black top control panel, six inputs (one 1/4 in. and one XLR per channel), 22 gray knobs (DI out level, Ch. 1: lo, freq., mid, high, v, effect level, Ch. 2: lo, freq, mid, high, effect level, v, Ch. 3: lo, high, effect level, v, All: effect 1 select, effect 2 select, level 1, level 2, MV), Ch. 1 phantom switch, Ch. 1 gain switch, Ch. 2 gain switch, Ch. 2 phantom switch, Ch. 2 high switch, power switch, XLR DI out jack, headphone jack, effects loop, two speaker jacks, footswitch jack, external speaker jack, USB charge port, available in standard Brown Marvelon vinyl covering with a black metal grille (other custom color coverings also available), 17 in. wide, 18.5 in. tall, 12 in. deep, 30.5 lbs., mfg. 2014-present.

MSR N/A	$600	$400 - 450	$195 - 240	

300AGE SPEAKER CABINET – 300W, 1-12 in. driver, 1-6.5 in. driver, Titanium 1 in. tweeter, 8 ohm impedance, available in standard brown vinyl covering with a black metal grille (other custom color coverings are also available), 17 in. wide, 18.5 in. tall, 12 in. deep, 30.5 lbs., mfg. 2014-present.

MSR N/A	$350	$230 - 265	$115 - 140	

CATEGORY 5 AMPLIFICATION

Amplifiers currently produced in Farmers Branch, TX since 2005.

CONTACT INFORMATION
CATEGORY 5 AMPLIFICATION
3517 Pinehurst Circle
Farmers Branch, TX 75234
Phone No.: 469-556-3757, 214-244-1900
Fax No.: 972-406-0939
www.category5amps.com
don@category5amps.com, stvnscott@category5amps.com

Steven Scott began building amps as a hobby in 2001 although he had built a few amps before when his kept breaking down. As word of mouth spread, Scott was building a few amps a month and in 2004 he met Don Ritter after he built an amp for him. When the tsunami happened in Asia, Scott built an amp to benefit a few charities helping with the tsunami recovery, and they began throwing around the idea of actually starting an amp company. Hurricanes Rita and Katrina struck around the same time they began building amps, so they decided to name their company and their amps after natural disasters. Category 5 is still actively involved in charities and they donate 10% of all their sales to charities - customers can also specify what charity they would like to donate to. Ritter is currently the Director of Artist Relations while Scott is the Director of Product Development. For more information, visit Category 5's website or contact them directly.

ELECTRIC TUBE AMPLIFIERS

The **Tsunami** is an 18 watt amp with 2 X EL84 power tubes, two independent channels, a tube rectifier, and reverb and it is available as a head unit (MSR $2,399), 1-12 in. combo (MSR $2,579), and a 2-10 in. combo (MSR $2,679). The **Ivan** is a 20 watt amp with two separate preamps (one voiced like Jimi Hendrix, one voiced for Stevie Ray Vaughun), 2 X 6V6 power tubes, and reverb and it is available as a head unit (MSR $2,450), 1-12 in. combo (MSR $2,699), and a 2-10 in. combo (MSR $2,799). Category 5 describes the **1900** as the loudest amp they make with three gain stages, a single channel, various wattage outputs depending on the power tubes (6V6, EL34, or KT77), and reverb, and is available only as a head unit (MSR $2,850). The **Andrew** is Ivan's bigger brother with more power from either 2 X 5881 or 2 X 6L6 power tubes and it is available as a head unit (MSR $2,795), 2-10 in. combo (MSR $2,995), 2-12 in. combo (MSR $3,195), and a 4-10 in. combo (MSR $3,350). Category 5 also offers the **Katrina** (pricing starting at $2,995), the **Allen** (pricing starting at $3,250), the **Tempest** (pricing starting at $3,250), the **Camille** (pricing starting at $3,250), the **Isabelle** (pricing starting at $3,495), the **Joe Bonamassa JB-50** (pricing starting at $3,250) and **JB-100** (pricing starting at $3,750), the **Tad Benoit VOW-45** (pricing starting at $3,350) and **VOW-90** (pricing starting at $3,495). Category 5 also offers a variety of speaker cabinets.

CAUBLE AMPLIFICATION

Amplifiers and speaker cabinets currently produced in Arlington, TX.

CONTACT INFORMATION
CAUBLE AMPLIFICATION
3007-B Pleasant Valley Lane, Suite B
Arlington, TX 76015-2929
Phone No.: 817-472-0279
www.caubleamps.com
caubleamps@caubleamps.com

Cauble Custom Amplifiers produces point-to-point hand-wired guitar amplifiers using premium components. They use Groove Tubes, but others can be specified. Models are available as a head-unit or combo and speaker cabinets are also available. For more information, visit Cauble's website or contact them directly.

ELECTRIC TUBE AMPLIFIERS

The **Omni-Tone 25** is available as a head-unit or combo with 1-12 in. Celestion speaker, selectable 2 X 6V6 or 2 X EL84 power tubes, two independent channels, and an all-tube effects loop. The Omni-Tone 25 head lists for $2,950 ($3,100 for the two-channel option). The Omni-Tone 25 1-12 Combo lists for $3,100 for a non-removable back and $3,250 for a removable back. The **Omni-Tone 60** Head (list $3,595) is the bigger brother of the 25 with selectable 2 X 6L6 or 2 X EL34 power tubes. The **Super 50** and **Super 100** heads are 50W and 100W output power respectively. The 50 has 2 X EL34 power tubes and lists for $1,995 for shared EQ, or $2,595 for independent channel EQ. The 100 has 2 X EL34 and 2 X 6L6 power tubes and lists for $2,195 for shared EQ, or $2,795 for independent channel EQ. The **Blue Ghost** (disc.) is a Class A 40W combo. The **Little Blue Ghost** (disc.) is a smaller version of the Blue Ghost and is a Class A 15W combo. The Blue Ghost amps were replaced by the GigaTone models. The **Gigatone 15** (list $1,400) is a Class A 15W 1-12 in. combo amp with a 12 in. Celestion Vintage 30 speaker, 2 X EL84 power tubes, and a 5U4 tube rectifier. The **Gigatone 30** (list $1,600 is also available.

Cauble also produces a 2-12 in. and a 4-12 in. speaker cabinet. Cabinets are built of baltic birch and Celestion Vintage 30 speakers are used.

C.B. EVANS AMPLIFICATION

Amplifiers previously produced in Oklahoma City, OK.

Berry Evans is the founder of C.B. Evans Amplification and he built hand made boutique tube amplifiers in his Oklahoma City shop. Evans named the company after his grandfather, Charles Berry Evans, because of his theory that "actions speak louder than words" and he applied that to the amplifiers he built. Evans offered the **Corsair**, **Mustang**, and **Spitfire** and prices started at $1,799.

CENTAUR

Amplifiers currently produced in San Bernandino County, CA since 1977.

CONTACT INFORMATION
CENTAUR
Phone No.: 760 964-2670
Fax No.: 760 949-0127
www.centauramp.com
centauramp@aol.com

Centaur produces a variety of acoustic, bass, and keyboard amps. Centaur began producing powered mixers in the late 1970s and early 1980s, and they introduced acoustic amplifiers shortly thereafter. For more information, visit Centaur's website or contact them directly.

CHARVEL

Amplifiers previously produced in South Korea during the early to mid-1990s. Distributed by Charvel.

For a complete history of Charvel and its guitar operations, please refer to the *Blue Book of Electric Guitars*. In the early 1990s, Charvel introduced a line of student amplifiers known as the CH series. These amplifiers lasted through the mid-1990s, but it appears they were discontinued before all guitar production stopped in 1999.

Jackson purchased the rights to Charvel and by 2002 were producing guitars once again, but no amplifiers. In the fall of 2002, Fender (FMIC) purchased the Jackson/Charvel corporation. Currently Jackson/Charvel still produces guitars in their manufacturing facilities and these are distributed by FMIC.

ELECTRIC SS AMPLIFIERS

CH200 – 20W, 1-8 in. speaker combo, solid-state chassis, two channels, front black control panel, single input, seven black knobs (Ch. 1: g, v, Ch. 2: v, Both: t, m, b, p), headphone jack, effects loop, black covering, black grille, mfg. early 1990s-mid-1990s.

| | N/A | $50 - 75 | $25 - 40 | $135 |

* *CH200R* – similar to the CH200, except has a reverb circuit with control knob, mfg. early 1990s-mid-1990s.

| | N/A | $70 - 95 | $35 - 50 | $165 |

CH200B BASS – 20W, 1-10 in. speaker bass combo, solid-state chassis, one channel, front black control panel, single input, five black knobs (v, t, h/m, l/m, b), headphone jack, effects loop, ported cabinet, black covering, black grille, mfg. early 1990s-mid-1990s.

| | N/A | $60 - 85 | $30 - 45 | $150 |

CH400(RC) STEREO CHORUS – 40W (20W per channel), 2-10 in. speaker combo, solid-state chassis, two channels, reverb, chorus, front black control panel, two inputs, 10 black knobs (Ch. 1: g, v, Ch. 2: g, v, Both: t, m, b, r, chorus depth, chorus rate), headphone jack, effects loop, black covering, black grille, mfg. early 1990s-mid-1990s.

| | N/A | $150 - 200 | $95 - 120 | $375 |

CH600(RC) STEREO CHORUS – 60W (30W per channel), 2-12 in. speaker combo, solid-state chassis, two channels, reverb, chorus, front black control panel, two inputs, 10 black knobs (Ch. 1: g, v, Ch. 2: g, v, Both: t, m, b, r, chorus depth, chorus rate), headphone jack, effects loop, black covering, black grille, mfg. early 1990s-mid-1990s.

| | N/A | $200 - 250 | $120 - 150 | $475 |

CHICAGO BLUES BOX

Amplifiers currently produced in Lombard (Chicago), IL since 2001. Distributed by Chicago Blues Box/Butler Custom Sound.

Chicago Blues Box amplifiers are produced by Butler Custom Sound. President Dan Butler builds these amplifiers in a suburb of Chicago, IL. Butler was inspired by the circuitry of vintage amplifiers and merging it with the technologies of today. After extensive testing and tweaking, Butler came up with a new breed of blues amplification that is known as the Chicago Blues Box. Since starting the company in 2001, Buddy Guy asked Butler to design him an amp. Chicago Blues Box now produces the Buddy Guy Signature Amp. Every amplifier requires over 60 hours of hand-built construction, along with another 60 hours of testing time. For more information, visit Chicago Blues Box's website, or contact them directly.

CICOGNANI

Amplifiers previously produced in Italy until 2012. Distributed by FBT USA, Inc. in Palm Coast, FL.

Cicognani amplifiers were built in Italy by pro audio manufacturer FBT. They produced a variety of guitar and bass amplifiers that are powered and toned by tubes giving their amplifiers their own identity. For guitar amplifiers they produced the Imperium, Dragon, and Brutus, and for bass amplifiers they offered the Indy Series.

CLARK AMPLIFICATION

Amplifiers, effects, and other amplifier accessories currently produced in Mauldin, SC since 2010 and in Cayce, SC between 1995 and 2010. Distributed in the U.S. by The Perfect Note, Guitar Adoptions, and J. Hale Music.

Michael Clark builds vintage replica tube amplifiers based on Fender tweed-era models from the 1950s and blackface-era models from the 1960s. Each amp is built per order, and Clark doesn't build models in advance. Clark also offers various vintage parts for amplifiers. For a complete list and for more information, visit Clark's website, or contact him directly.

ELECTRIC TUBE AMPLIFIERS

Clark produces a variety of Fender narrow panel tweed-era amps and the following all from this era. The **Tyger** (MSR $2,925) is based on the Fender 5E7 Bandmaster with 30W power, and 3-10 in. speakers. The **Low Country** (Low Power MSR $3,395, High Power MSR $3,675) is based on the Fender Twin with a 45W 5E8-A low power circuit or 80W 5F8-A high power circuit through 2-12 in. speakers. The **Piedmont** (MSR $3,195) is based on the late 1950s Bassman Model 5F6-A circuit with 4-10 in. speakers. The **Penrose** (MSR $2,795) is based on the Super Model 5F4 circuit with 2-10 in. speakers. The **Beaufort** (MSR $2,250) is based on the Fender 5E3 Deluxe Narrow Panel model with 15W power, 1-12 in. speaker, and two channels. The **Clark Special** (disc., last MSR was $1,395) is a modified modern Deluxe Model 5E3. The **Lil' Bit** (MSR $1,275/$1,375) is based on the narrow panel Champ Model 5F1 with 5W and 1-12 in. speaker. The **Webster** (MSR $1,700 with a 10 in. speaker, $1,800 with a 12 in. speaker) is based on the narrow panel Harvard Model 5F10 10W amp with either 1-10 in. or 1-12 in. speaker.

Clark also produces a series of blackface era amps from the 1960s. The **Belmont Reverb** (MSR $2,100) is based on a blackface Vibrolux Reverb with 35W output, 2-10 in. speakers, reverb, and tremolo. The **Beaufort Reverb** (MSR $1,850) is based on a blackface Deluxe Reverb with 22W output and 1-12 in. speaker. The **Kanee Reverb** (MSR $1,700) features 20W output, 1-10 in. speaker, reverb, and tremolo.

Clark also builds a Marshall JTM-45 replica called the **MTC-45** (MSR $2,200) that features 45W and comes as a head unit only.

CLUB AMPLIFIERS

Amplifiers currently produced in Scotts Valley, CA since 2005.

CONTACT INFORMATION
CLUB AMPLIFIERS
PO Box 67357
Scotts Valley, CA 95067
www.clubamps.com
info@clubamps.com

While Club Amplifiers were founded by Don Anderson in 2005, he has been building amplifiers since the mid-1960s. Anderson graduated from Oregon State University with a degree in engineering. Throughout the years he has built several amplifiers for himself and local musicians, and in 2005 he started Club Amplifiers with the intention of offering club-sized amplifiers to gigging musicians. All Club Amplifiers are built custom to order with a base price depending on the power output (20W is $1,350, 30W is $1,475, and 50W is $1,600) and the customer can specify a head or combo. For more information or a specific quote on an amplifier, visit Club's website or contact Don Anderson directly.

CMI (GIBSON)

Chicago Musical Instruments. Amplifiers produced in Chicago, IL between the late 1960s and early 1970s.

Chicago Musical Instruments (CMI) purchased Gibson in 1944 and owned the company until 1969. In 1967, Gibson stopped producing amplifiers in Kalamazoo and production of all amps was moved to Chicago. CMI, Norlin, and Gibson all marketed amplifiers after 1967, but they were never produced by Gibson in Kalamazoo. Not much is known about individual CMI models, but they are generally budget model solid-state amps. Any information can be submitted directly to Blue Book Publications. Source: Walter Carter, *Gibson Guitars, 100 Years of an American Icon*, and George Gruhn and Walter Carter, *Gruhn's Guide to Vintage Guitars*.

CMI (MARSHALL)

Cleartone Musical Instruments, Ltd. Amplifiers previously made in Birmingham, England from 1976 to 1977. The CMI label was a part of Marshall.

The Cleartone Musical Instrument Ltd. Company (CMI) was a distribution company established in 1965. Jim Marshall bought into the company in 1967, and took over the company in 1969 when it was financially indebted to him. Later in the 1970s, Marshall decided to introduce a new line of amps to run alongside its other sibling called Park. Park amplifiers had been made for Johnny Jones since 1965, but were essentially Marshall amps with a different name on them. CMI amplifiers were introduced around 1976 and also followed Marshall's design very closely. To this day, there is speculation as to why Marshall would introduce a new line of amplifiers that were almost identical to Park. Most of CMI amplifiers were designed for PA use, but they also made a few guitar amps. CMI proved to be unsuccessful as another Marshall line and was discontinued around 1977. Source for CMI history: Michael Doyle, *The History of Marshall: The Illustrated Story of "The Sound of Rock"*.

ELECTRIC TUBE AMPLIFIERS

The CMI line did not last very long and only a few models were made. CMI models were designed to be a budget model of Marshall, but because they are so rare and associated with Marshall, they are fairly collectible. However, very few CMI amps appear on the used market making it difficult to attach a value to them.

MODEL 1037 – 50W, head-unit only, lead & bass application, tubes: preamp: 3 X ECC83, power: 2 X EL34, dual channels, two inputs per channel for a total of four, silver control panel, six black and silver knobs (presence, b, m, t, v1, v2), black covering, mfg. 1976-77.

| | N/A | N/A | N/A | |

Some of these models were available with 12AX7 preamp tubes. Blue vinyl covering was also available.

MODEL 1038 – 100W, head-unit only, lead & bass application, tubes: preamp: 3 X ECC83, power: 4 X EL34, dual channels, two inputs per channel for a total of four, silver control panel, six black and silver knobs (presence, b, m, t, v1, v2), black covering, mfg. 1976-77.

| | N/A | N/A | N/A | |

Some of these models were available with 12AX7 preamp tubes. Blue vinyl covering was also available.

MSR/NOTES	100%	EXCELLENT	AVERAGE	LAST MSR

MODEL 1070 – 50W, combo, tubes: 3 X ECC83, power: 2 X EL34, tremolo, dual channels, two inputs per channel, black covering, mfg. 1976-77.

courtesy Solidbodyguitar.com, Inc.

courtesy Solidbodyguitar.com, Inc.

N/A   N/A   N/A

COMINS GUITARS

Amplifiers currently produced in Willow Grove, PA since 2003.

Bill Comins began playing guitar at an early age, and later went on to major in Jazz Guitar at Temple University. During this time, along with performing and teaching privately, Comins cultivated an interest in Luthery. Eventually he took a job in a violin shop where he worked for four years while building his own repair/custom shop business. In 1991, Comins met Master Luthier Bob Benedetto whose shared knowledge inspired Comins to develop his own line of archtop guitars. In the time since Comins has carved out a reputation as one of the more highly regarded contemporary archtop guitar builders, he has built over 200 instruments for international clientele consisting of players, educators, and collectors. His work has appeared in numerous books and collections, including the Chinery "Blue Guitar" project. Well versed in both traditional and contemporary approaches, Comins offers personalized collaborations with dedicated attention to design and detail.

In 2003, Bill collaborated with George Allesandro from Allesandro to develop a Comins amplifier. Bill feels that an amplifier should be an extension of the guitar, and there was not a good tube jazz amplifier on the market. After extensive trial and error Allesandro and Comins produced a line of Comins amplifiers for the Jazz guitarist. For acoustic models, refer to the *Blue Book of Acoustic Guitars*, and for electric models, refer to the *Blue Book of Electric Guitars*. For more information, contact Comins directly or visit his website.

CONTACT INFORMATION
COMINS GUITARS
PO Box 611
Willow Grove, PA 19090
Phone No.: 215-376-0595
www.cominsguitars.com
bill@cominsguitars.com

ELECTRIC TUBE AMPLIFIERS

The **Comins Jazz Guitar Amplifier** is available as a head-unit (MSR $1,250), 1-12 in. combo (MSR $1,600), and 2-12 in. combo (MSR $1,600), and features 60W output power, 3 X 12AX7 preamp tubes, 2 X 6550 power tubes, a single channel, top control panel, single input, six knobs (v, r, t, m, b, MV), and a Jangly/Creamy switch. All amps are hand-wired and hand-assembled and are lightweight in construction.

CORAL

Amplifiers previously produced in Neptune City, NJ between 1967 and 1969 by the Danelectro Corporation. Distributed by MCA, after buying the Danelectro company and trademark.

In 1967, after MCA purchased the Danelectro Corporation, the Coral trademark was introduced. The Coral line was MCA's marketing strategy for direct wholesale selling to individual dealers, instead of selling to Sears & Roebuck. Once the company went that route, however, they came up against competition from the larger guitar manufacturers at the dealer level. The Coral line of guitars and amplifiers was only produced for about three years. The Coral amplifier line included a variety of tube and solid-state models as well as PA units. Coral's Kilowatt amp was advertised at putting out 1000 watts of peak power (300 RMS) and included a head with two speaker cabinets each containing 8-12 in. speakers.

CORNELL

Amplifiers currently produced in Essex, United Kingdom. Cornell is part of DC Developments.

Denis Cornell builds Cornell amplifiers (many that have the brand Plexi on the front) in Essex, United Kingdom. Cornell has always been interested in guitars and amplifiers, and he has worked for many amplifier builders including Sound City, Vox, and Fender. All models are hand-built with high-quality parts. Although Cornell offers several different models, his flagship model is the 30W Journeyman. He also custom built an amp for Eric Clapton that has turned into a regular production model. Cornell's amplifiers are all listed in English pounds, but he does sell to the U.S. and has a few dealers in the U.S. For more information, visit Cornell's website, or contact him directly.

CONTACT INFORMATION
CORNELL
60 Eastcote Grove
Southend on Sea, Essex SS2 4QB
United Kingdom
Phone No.: +44 (0)1702 610964
Fax No.: +44 (0)1702 610964
www.dcdevelopments.com
den_cornell@dc-developments.com

| MSR/NOTES | 100% | EXCELLENT | AVERAGE | LAST MSR |

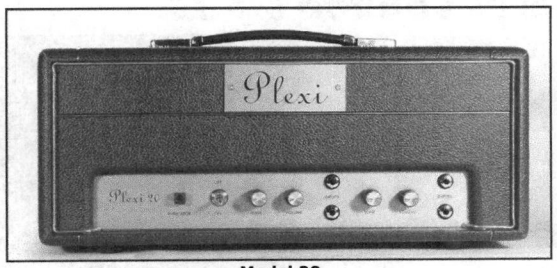

Model 20
courtesy Musician's Friend

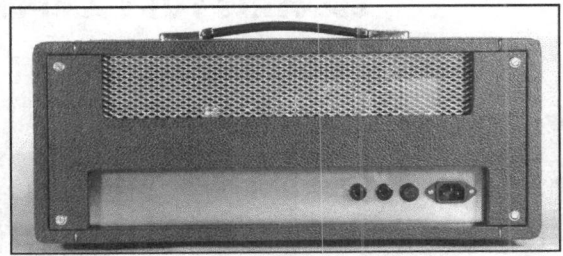

Model 20
courtesy Musician's Friend

CORNFORD AMPLIFICATION

Amplifiers and speaker cabinets previously produced in Kent, England until 2013. Distributed in the U.S. by Cornford USA, Inc. in Minneapolis, MN.

Paul Cornford produced Cornford amplifiers in England. They had been available for many years in England, but only in the U.S. as regular distribution since the early 2000s. Cornford amplifiers are all hand-built one at a time, with absolutely no machines putting components together. A variety of amplifiers and speaker cabinets were available.

ELECTRIC TUBE AMPLIFIERS/SPEAKER CABINETS

The **Harlequin** (street price $1,499) is a 6W 1-12 in. combo. The **Carrera** (street price $1,999) is a 1-12 in. combo. The **Hurricane** (street price $2,499) is a 20W 1-12 in. combo. The **Hellcat** is a 35W amp available as a head (street price $3,499) or a 1-12 in. combo (disc., last MSR was $3,999). The **MK50H** (street price $3,299) is a single channel 50W head, and the **MK50H MKII** (street price $3,999) is a two channel 50W head. The **RK100** (street price $3,699) is a 100W head. The Roadhouse Series of guitars amps are designed to be a more affordable version by stripping them down and keeping them simple. The **Roadhouse 30** is a 30W cathode-based amp and is available as a head (street price $1,399) or a 1-12 in. combo (street price $1,499), and the **Roadhouse 50** is a 50W fixed biased amp and is available as a head (street price $1,899) or a 1-12 in. combo (street price $2,199).

Cornford also offers a variety of speaker cabinets including their regular cabs in 2-12 in. (street price $1,199), 4-12 in. (street price $1,499), or an angled 4-12 in. (street price $1,699) configurations, the RK Series of cabs in 2-12 in. (street price $1,349) or 4-12 in. (street price $1,699) configurations, and the Roadhouse Series designed for use with the Roadhouse heads in 1-12 in. (street price $749), 2-12 in. (street price $1,199), and 4-12 in. (street price $1,499) configurations.

Model 20
courtesy Cornford Amplifiers

CRATE

Amplifiers most recently produced in China. Previously produced in St. Louis, MO. Most recently distributed by LOUD Technologies, Inc. in Woodinville, WA since 2005. Previously distributed by St. Louis Music in St. Louis, MO from 1979 to 2004. The Crate Trademark was established in 1979. LOUD Technologies has discontinued production of Crate Amplifiers.

The Crate trademark was founded in 1979 by St. Louis Music (SLM) during a time when the entire guitar industry was at a time of rebuilding. SLM had distributed amplifiers in the past (Magnatone and EMC), but they have never built them before. The first Crate amps were actually built into a wood cabinet that resembled a wooden crate - hence the name. The amplifiers were also affordable and very successful at a young age. However, the public always considered Crate to be a budget line of inexpensive models since that is how they were introduced. In 1986, (SLM) bought Ampeg from MTI. SLM decided to keep Crate as more of an entry-level line of amps and make Ampeg their top-end models. By 1989, Crate had received its first award as an amplifier maker. Since the mid-1980s, Crate has continued to produce student amps, but they have also built several tube models, as well as a full line of PA products. In 2005, LOUD Technologies, Inc. purchased St. Louis Music, Inc. and all of their trademarks. With this acquisition, the headquarters of St. Louis Music was moved to Woodinville, WA. However, the guitar repair and set-up shop is still located in St. Louis. For more information, visit Crate's website or contact them directly. Source: Gregg Hopkins and Bill Moore, *Ampeg: The Story Behind the Sound*.

| MSR/NOTES | 100% | EXCELLENT | AVERAGE | LAST MSR |

ELECTRIC TUBE AMPLIFIERS: BLUE VOODOO SERIES

BV120H Head
courtesy Crate

BV150HB Head
courtesy Crate

BV412 SVB Speaker Cabinet
courtesy Crate

BV120H/HB/HR HEAD – 120W, full-size head unit only, all tube chassis, preamp: 4 X 12AX7, power: 4 X 6L6, dual selectable channels, dual reverb, black front control panel, one input, 12 black and silver knobs (Ch. 1: v, h, m, l, Ch. 2: g, h, m, l, v, Both: r1, r2, p), effects loop, line out, footswitch, available in blue covering with gold cosmetics (H, disc.), black covering with silver cosmetics (HB), or "Red Rocker" covering with silver cosmetics (HR, disc.), 52 lbs., mfg. 1996-2009.

| | **$750** | **$500 - 575** | **$300 - 350** | **$1,083** |

- Add $50 for the Sammy Hagar "Red Rocker" covering.

BV150HB HEAD – 150W, full-size head unit only, all tube chassis, preamp: 8 X 12AX7, power: 6 X 6L6, three channels, dual reverb, black front control panel, one input, 12 black and silver knobs (Ch. 1: v, h, m, l, Ch. 2: g, h, m, l, v, Both: r1, r2, p), effects loop, line out, footswitch, (HB), black covering with silver cosmetics, mfg. 2003-06.

| | **$1,350** | **$850 - 950** | **$600 - 675** | **$1,800** |

BV300HB HEAD – 300W, full-size head unit only, all tube chassis, preamp: 8 X 12AX7, 2 X 12AU7, power: 6 X 6550, three channels, black front control panel, one input, 20 black and silver knobs (Eek, Ugh, Each channel has these six knobs: level, mid-freq, mid-boost, or high freq. select, b, m, t), effects loop, line out, footswitch, (HB), black covering with silver cosmetics, 90 lbs., mfg. 2003-06.

| | **$1,900** | **$1,150 - 1,350** | **$800 - 950** | **$2,500** |

BV412 RVB/SVB SPEAKER CABINET – 280W, 4-12 in. Celestion Vintage 30 speaker, mono/stereo capability, impedance selector switch, .75 in. void free birch construction, fixed casters, angled or straight front, black, blue (disc.), or red (disc.) covering, black metal grille, 85 lbs. (slant) or 87 lbs. (straight), disc. 2006.

| | **$750** | **$425 - 500** | **$275 - 325** | **$980** |

ELECTRIC TUBE AMPLIFIERS: VINTAGE CLUB SERIES

This series of amps was introduced in 1994. These are combo amps that are all Class A or Class AB chassis and come in up to 50W output. Some of these amplifier models were available in blonde covering instead of black and had a brown grille.

VC508 Combo
courtesy Crate

VC3112B Combo
courtesy Crate

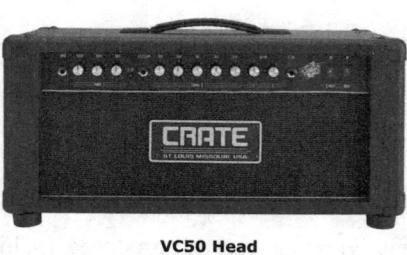

VC50 Head
courtesy Crate

VC508 COMBO – 5W, 1-8 in. Celestion speaker, all tube Class A chassis, preamp: 12AX7, power: EL84, single channel, top silver control panel, one input, three silver knobs (g, tone, v), line out, painted black cabinet, black metal grille, 18 lbs., mfg. 1994-2002.

| | **N/A** | **$150 - 180** | **$95 - 120** | **$280** |

VC3112B COMBO – 30W, 1-12 in. Crate Vintage speaker, all tube Class A chassis, preamp: 4 X 12AX7, power: 4 X EL84, dual selectable channels, dual reverb, top silver control panel, one input, 10 silver knobs (Ch. A: v, t, b, Ch. B: g, t, m, b, level, rA, rB), effects loop, footswitch, black Tolex covering, black cloth grille, 48 lbs., mfg. 1994-2001.

| | **N/A** | **$325 - 400** | **$175 - 225** | **$800** |

VC50 HEAD – 50W, head-unit only, all tube Class AB chassis, preamp: 4 X 12AX7, power: 4 X EL84, dual selectable channels, dual reverb, top silver control panel, one input, 10 silver knobs (Ch. A: v, t, b, Ch. B: g, t, m, b, level, rA, rB), effects loop, footswitch, black or white (early models) Tolex covering, mfg. 1994-99.

| | **N/A** | **$300 - 350** | **$150 - 200** | |

MSR/NOTES	100%	EXCELLENT	AVERAGE	LAST MSR

* **VC5212B Combo** – similar to the VC50 Head, except in combo configuration with 2-12 in. speakers, 63 lbs., mfg. 1994-99.

N/A	$375 - 450	$225 - 275	$900

VC6112 COMBO – 60W, 1-12 in. Crate Vintage Speaker, all tube chassis, preamp: 5 X 12AX7, power: 2 X EL34, dual selectable channels, dual reverb, silver front control panel, two inputs, 14 silver knobs (g, b, m, t, MV, r, p all for each channel), mid, bass, and boost switches, parallel effects loop, footswitch, black or white (early models) Tolex covering, black grille, mfg. 1994-2000.

N/A	$425 - 500	$275 - 325

* **VC6212 Combo** – similar to the VC6112 except has 2-12 in. speakers, mfg. 1994-2000.

N/A	$475 - 550	$300 - 350

ELECTRIC TUBE AMPLIFIERS: V SERIES

In 2003, the V series replaced the Vintage Club amps. These amps featured the DSP digital modeling effects along with new cosmetics. All of these amps have tube circuits equipped with Groove Tubes. In 2007, all production of the V Series was moved overseas to China and along with this, Crate discontinued most of the older V Series amps and introduced an entirely new line.

V5 Combo
courtesy Crate

V18-112 Combo
courtesy Crate

V33H Head
courtesy Crate

V5 COMBO – 5W, 1-8 in. speaker, single tube chassis, power: 1 X EL84, single channel, top gray control panel, single input, two knobs (v, tone), speaker out, black covering, black grille with a "5" on the upper part, made in China, mfg. 2007-08.

$200	$120 - 150	$75 - 95	$289

V58 COMBO – 5W, 1-8 in. Celestion speaker, all tube Class A chassis, preamp: 12AX7, power: EL84, single channel, top silver control panel, one input, three silver knobs (g, tone, v), line out, painted black cabinet, black cloth grille with "5" logo, 18 lbs., mfg. 2003-06.

$275	$150 - 180	$115 - 135	$380

V1512 COMBO – 15W, 1-12 in. V-series speaker, all tube Class A chassis, preamp: 3 X 12AX7A, power: 2 X EL84, single channel, reverb, top black control panel, single input, six silver knobs (g, t, m, b, level, r), black covering, black grille, "15" logo on front, 38 lbs., mfg. 2002-06.

$420	$275 - 325	$215 - 240	$600

* Add 15% for Tone Tubby speaker (Last MSR was $700).

V18-112 COMBO – 18W, 1-12 in. speaker, hybrid chassis, power: 2 X EL84, single channel, reverb, top gray control panel, single input, six knobs (g, level, t, m, b, r), line out, speaker out, black covering, black grille with an "18" on the upper part, made in China, mfg. 2007-08.

$330	$200 - 250	$120 - 150	$477

* Add $15 (Last MSR was $22) for Burgundy, Cream, or Turquoise skin.

* **V18-212 Combo** – similar to the V18-112 Combo, except has 2-12 in. speakers, made in China, mfg. 2007-08.

$380	$225 - 275	$135 - 175	$549

* Add $20 (Last MSR was $29) for Burgundy, Cream, or Turquoise skin.

V30H HEAD – 30W, head-unit only, all tube Class A chassis, preamp: 3 X 12AX7A, power: 4 X EL84, dual channels, top black control panel, single input, seven knobs (clean v, OD g, t, m, b, OD level, r), black covering, black grille "30" logo on front, 25 lbs., mfg. 2005-06.

$575	$350 - 425	$200 - 250	$800

* **V3112 Combo** – similar to the V30H Head, except in combo configuration with 1-12 in. V-Series speaker, mfg. 2003-06.

$575	$400 - 450	$250 - 300	$800

* Add 10% for a Tone Tubby speaker (Last MSR was $900).

V33H HEAD – 33W, guitar head unit, tube chassis, power: 4 X EL84, single channel, reverb, front gray control panel, single input, seven knobs (v, g, level, t, m, b, r), channel select switch, boost switch, presence switch, footswitch, effects loop, extension speaker jack, speaker out jack, black covering, black grille with a "33" on the lower part, made in China, mfg. 2007-08.

$330	$200 - 250	$120 - 150	$477

MSR/NOTES	100%	EXCELLENT	AVERAGE	LAST MSR

V33-212 Combo – similar to the V33H Head, except in combo configuration with 2-12 in. speakers and a black grille with a "33" on the upper part, made in China, mfg. 2007-08.

| | $450 | $300 - 350 | $175 - 225 | $650 |

V50-112 COMBO – 50W, 1-12 in. speaker guitar combo, tube chassis, power: 2 X 6L6, single channel, reverb, top gray control panel, single input, seven knobs (v, g, level, t, m, b, r), channel select switch, boost switch, presence switch, footswitch, effects loop, extension speaker jack, speaker out jack, black covering, black grille with a "50" on the upper part, made in China, mfg. 2007-08.

| | $380 | $225 - 275 | $135 - 175 | $549 |

* Add $15 (Last MSR was $22) for Burgundy, Cream, or Turquoise skin.

VFX5112 COMBO – 50W, 1-12 in. V-Series speaker, all tube Class AB chassis, preamp: 4 X 12AX7A, power: 2 X EL34, dual channels, DSP effects, top black control panel, single input, 12 silver knobs (Ch A: v, t, m, b, Ch. B: g, t, m, b, level, Master: DSP mode, DSP level, p), 16 digital effects, footswitch, line in/out, 16 or 8 Ohm, extension speaker jack, black covering, black grille "50" logo on front, 48 lbs., mfg. 2002-06.

| | $700 | $500 - 600 | $400 - 450 | $1,000 |

* Add 10% for a Tone Tubby speaker (Last MSR was $1,100).

VFX5212 Combo – similar to the VFX5112 except has 2-12 in. speakers, 58 lbs., mfg. 2002-06.

| | $775 | $525 - 625 | $425 - 475 | $1,100 |

* Add 20% for Tone Tubby speakers (Last MSR was $1,300).

V100H HEAD – 100W, guitar configuration head-unit, eight tube chassis, preamp: 4 X 12AX7, power: 4 X EL34, two channels (clean, overdrive), reverb, front black control panel, two inputs (bright/normal), 12 knobs (Clean Ch.: level, t, m, b, OD Ch.: g, level, t, m, b, All: boost, p, r), channel select switch, flat/vintage voice switch, presence switch, half-power switch, effects loop, extension speaker jack, two speaker out jacks with selectable impedance, optional two button footswitch, black covering, black grille with a "100" on the upper part, made in China, mfg. 2008 only.

| | $500 | $300 - 375 | $175 - 225 | $722 |

V212B SPEAKER CABINET – 100W, 2-12 in. speakers, 8 ohm impedance, meant for use with the V33H Head, removable casters, black covering, black grille, 47 lbs., mfg. 2007-08.

| | $300 | $175 - 225 | $110 - 140 | $433 |

V212T SPEAKER CABINET – 160W, 2-12 in. Tone Tubby speakers, 8 ohm impedance, tilt legs, meant for use with the V30H Head, removable casters, black covering, black grille, 67 lbs., mfg. 2005-06.

| | $575 | $350 - 425 | $200 - 250 | $800 |

V412A/V412B SPEAKER CABINET – 240W, 4-12 in. speakers, angled (V412A) or straight (V412B) front, designed for use with the V100H Head, black covering, black grille, mfg. 2008 only.

| | $400 | $250 - 300 | $135 - 175 | $578 |

ELECTRIC SS AMPLIFIERS: CR SERIES (WOOD CABINETS)

These amps were named crates because they look like wooden crates. All early Crate amplifiers were built in either a Ponderosa pine or oak wood cabinet, which gives these models a unique look. There are other CR models that are missing here, but we do not have any information on them. It is a safe assumption that these amplifiers are generally priced between $50 and $150 depending upon the size and condition. Any further information on CR model amplifiers can be submitted directly to Blue Book Publications.

CR-1 – 20W, 1-12 in. speaker, solid-state combo, single channel, front green control panel, two inputs, four black knobs (g, b, t, MV), line out, Ponderosa pine wood cabinet, black metal grille, mfg. late 1970s-early 1980s.

courtesy John Beeson/The Music Shoppe

courtesy John Beeson/The Music Shoppe

| | N/A | $75 - 100 | $35 - 50 | |

CR-1D Deluxe – similar to the CR-1 except has a distortion control with a footswitch option and a bright switch, mfg. late 1970s-early 1980s.

| | N/A | $85 - 110 | $45 - 60 | |

MSR/NOTES	100%	EXCELLENT	AVERAGE	LAST MSR

* **CR-1R Reverb** – similar to the CR-1 except has reverb circuit with a reverb control (five total knobs), mfg. late 1970s-early 1980s.

| | N/A | $95 - 120 | $50 - 70 | |

»**CR-1RD Deluxe Reverb** – similar to the CR-1R except has a distortion control with with a footswitch option and a bright switch, mfg. late 1970s-early 1980s.

| | N/A | $105 - 135 | $60 - 80 | |

CR-II – 60W, 1-12 in. Crate or optional Celestion speaker, solid-state combo, single channel, front control panel, two inputs, six black knobs (g, t, mid-freq, m, b, MV), bright switch, line in, line out, ext. speaker jack, Ponderosa pine cabinet, black metal grille, mfg. late 1970s-early 1980s.

| | N/A | $120 - 150 | $70 - 90 | |

• **Add 10% for a Celestion speaker.**

* **CR-IIR Reverb** – similar to the CR-II, except has a reverb circuit with control (seven knobs), and is available in a Ponderosa pine, solid oak (Scandanavian style), or Rich Oriental Teak stained solid oak cabinet, black metal grille, mfg. late 1970s-early 1980s.

| | N/A | $130 - 175 | $80 - 100 | |

• **Add 10% for a Celestion speaker.**
• **Add 20% for a solid oak or stained oak cabinet.**

»**CR-IIRH Reverb Head** – similar to the CR-IIR Reverb, except in head-unit configuration, mfg. late 1970s-early 1980s.

| | N/A | $95 - 120 | $50 - 70 | |

• **Add 10% for a Celestion speaker.**
• **Add 20% for a solid oak or stained oak cabinet.**

CR-65 – 60W, 1-12 in. Crate Magnum projection or optional Celestion speaker, solid-state combo, two switchable or combineable channels, reverb, front black and silver control panel, two inputs, seven knobs on front (g, b, mid-freq, m, t, r, MV), bright switch, and contour switch, Channel Two's controls mounted on back with five knobs (g, t, b, MV, combine volume), footswitch included, solid oak stained wood cabinet, black grille, mfg. late 1970s-early 1980s.

| | N/A | $175 - 225 | $110 - 140 | |

• **Add 10% for a Celestion speaker.**

* **CR-65DL Deluxe** – similar to the CR-65, except is housed in a solid elmwood, dovetailed corner cabinet that has smooth sides, mfg. late 1970s-early 1980s.

| | N/A | $200 - 250 | $120 - 150 | |

• **Add 10% for a Celestion speaker.**

CR-110 – wattage unknown, 1-10 in. speaker, solid-state combo, dual channels (normal and overdrive), black and white front control panel, two inputs (high and low), six black and silver knobs (OD: level, g, Clean: level, b, m, t), footswitch, black covering, black grille with wood bar, mfg. early 1980s.

| | N/A | $100 - 135 | $75 - 90 | |

CR-112 – similar to the CR-110 except has 1-12 in. speaker and reverb, circuit with control, mfg. early 1980s.

| | N/A | $125 - 150 | $85 - 105 | |

CRI-B BASS – 20W, 1-12 in. speaker, solid-state bass chassis, front-mounted control panel, two inputs, four knobs (g, t, b, MV), line out, Ponderosa pine cabinet, black covering, mfg. early 1980s.

| | N/A | $75 - 100 | $35 - 50 | |

CR-M "MINI CRATE" – 20W, 1-10 in. speaker, solid-state chassis, top-mounted control panel, single input, four knobs (g, t, b, MV), line out, Ponderosa pine cabinet, black covering, mfg. late 1970s-early 1980s.

| | N/A | $75 - 100 | $35 - 50 | |

ELECTRIC SS AMPLIFIERS: DX DIGITAL MODELING SERIES

The DX series was introduced in 1999 and won the Amplifier of the Year in 2000. These amps have on board digital modeling technology that provides 16 different amp voices and 16 effects. You can then program 10 channels with these different effects. Crate also sells the DXJFC footpedal (last MSR $150) to control the channels. The DXFC MIDI Footpedal (last MSR $280) can store up to 128 channels.

• **Add $100 for the DXJFC footpedal.**
• **Add $200 for the DXFC MIDI footpedal.**

DXB112 – 30W, 1-12 in. Crate Guitar Driver speaker, solid-state combo, 10 user-programmable channels, 16 digital effects, 16 amp voices, top brushed copper control panel, single input, ten black knobs (MV, Amp voice selection, g, b, m, t, channel level, effects selection, effect adjust, r), footswitch, MIDI in, external speaker, headphone jack, CD input, black covering, black with copper grille, mfg. 2001-02.

| | N/A | $225 - 275 | $120 - 150 | $550 |

DXJ112 – 60W, 1-12 in. Crate Vintage Driver speaker, solid-state combo, 10 user-programmable channels, 16 digital effects, 16 amp voices, front brushed copper control panel, single input, eleven black knobs (MV, Amp voice selection, g, b, m, t, channel level, effects selection, effect adjust, r level, r depth), footswitch, MIDI in/out, stereo line in, line out, stereo headphone jack, black covering, black with copper grille, mfg. 1999-2002.

| | N/A | $300 - 350 | $175 - 225 | $700 |

MSR/NOTES	100%	EXCELLENT	AVERAGE	LAST MSR

DXB112
courtesy John Beeson/The Music Shoppe

DXJ112
courtesy Crate

DX212
courtesy Crate

* **DX212** – similar to the DXJ112, except has 100W output and 2-12 in. speakers, mfg. 2000-02.

N/A	$375 - 450	$225 - 275	$900

ELECTRIC SS AMPLIFIERS: FLEXWAVE (FW) SERIES

Crate offers a FlexWave Half Stack option with the FW120H Head and the FW412A Speaker Cabinet that retails for $867 (same price as the components priced separately) but sells new for $500 ($100 less than the 100%/New value priced separately).

FW120/212
courtesy Crate

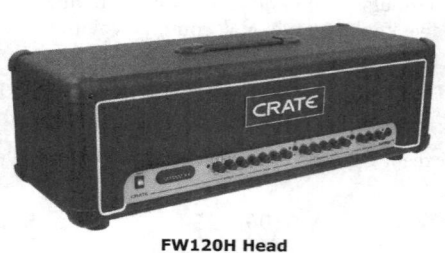

FW120H Head
courtesy Crate

FW412A Speaker Cabinet
courtesy Crate

FW15 – 15W, 1-8 in. speaker guitar combo, solid-state chassis, two channels, front gray control panel, single input, six knobs (OD: g, level, Clean: v, l, m, h), OD switch, CD input, headphone jack, speaker out, black covering, dark gray grille, mfg. 2007-disc.

$80	$45 - 60	$25 - 35	$110

* **FW15R** – similar to the FW15, except has a reverb circuit, mfg. 2007-disc.

$100	$65 - 80	$40 - 50	$160

FW65/112 – 65W, 1-12 in. speaker guitar combo, solid-state chassis, DSP, three channels, front gray control panel, single input, 15 knobs (High Gain: g, shape, level, OD: g, l, m, h, level, Clean: v, l, m, h, All: r, mod, delay), High Gain switch, OD switch, CD input, speaker out, two footswitch jacks, insert jack, black covering, dark gray grille, mfg. 2007-disc.

$300	$175 - 225	$100 - 135	$450

FW120/212 – similar to the FW65, except has 2-12 in. speakers, mfg. 2007-disc.

$400	$250 - 300	$150 - 200	$600

FW120H HEAD – 120W, guitar head unit, solid-state chassis, DSP, three channels, front gray control panel, single input, 15 knobs (High Gain: g, shape, level, OD: g, l, m, h, level, Clean: v, l, m, h, All: r, mod, delay), High Gain switch, OD switch, CD input, chromatic tuner, speaker out, two footswitch jacks, insert jack, black covering, dark gray grille, mfg. 2007-disc.

$300	$175 - 225	$100 - 135	$500

FW412A/FW412B SPEAKER CABINET – 120W, 4-12 in. speakers, mono/stereo operation, designed for use with the FW120H Head, angled (FW412A) or straight (FW412B) cabinet design, black covering, dark gray grille, removable casters, built-in side handles, mfg. 2007-disc.

$300	$175 - 225	$100 - 135	$500

ELECTRIC SS AMPLIFIERS: GFX SERIES

This series of amps include the "Flexwave Evolution 5" preamp in each model. Introduced in 2002, the upper three models now have a built in chromatic tuner and the model names have a T at the end of them now. The 2200HT head unit can be matched up with cabinets from the GX series (see GX series).

MSR/NOTES	100%	EXCELLENT	AVERAGE	LAST MSR

GFX20
courtesy Crate

GF50TT (Two Tone)
courtesy Crate

GFX120
courtesy Crate

GFX15 – 12+W, 1-8 in. Crate speaker, solid-state combo, two selectable channels, DSP, front black control panel, single input, seven gray knobs (OD: g, level, Clean: level, l, m, h, DSP mode), headphone jack, external speaker jack, black covering, gray grille, 15 lbs., mfg. 1990s-2002.

| | N/A | $75 - 100 | $45 - 60 | $200 |

GFX20 – 20W, 1-10 in. Crate speaker, solid-state combo, two selectable channels, DSP, front black control panel, single input, seven gray knobs (OD: g, level, Clean: level, l, m, h, DSP mode), headphone jack, external speaker jack, black covering, gray grille, 21 lbs., mfg. 1990s-2002.

| | N/A | $150 - 150 | $75 - 95 | $330 |

GFX30 – 30W, 1-12 in. Crate speaker, solid-state combo, two selectable channels, DSP, front black control panel, single input, seven gray knobs, two blue knobs, (OD: g, shape, level, Clean: level, l, m, h, DSP mode, level), headphone jack, external speaker jack, footswitch, black covering, gray grille, 24 lbs., mfg. 1990s-2002.

| | N/A | $135 - 175 | $95 - 115 | $380 |

GFX50TT (TWO TONE) – 50W, 1-12 in. Crate speaker, solid-state combo, independent two player operation (two channels), DSP, front black control panel, two inputs, 15 gray knobs, 2 blue knobs (Ch. A & Ch. B each have v, g, t, m, b, level, effects, DSP mode, DSP level, CD input level), headphone jacks, black covering, gray grille, 34 lbs., mfg. 1997-2002.

| | N/A | $200 - 250 | $120 - 150 | $530 |

GFX65/GFX65T – 65W, 1-12 in. Crate Custom speaker, solid-state combo, three selectable channels, DSP, front black control panel, single input, 10 gray knobs, 2 blue knobs (OD: g1, g2, shape, l, h, level, Clean: level, l, m, h, DSP: level, mode), 16 digital effects, footswitch, external speaker jack, chromatic tuner, black covering, gray grille, 44 lbs., mfg. 1997-2002.

| | N/A | $225 - 275 | $135 - 175 | $540 |

This model used to be strictly the GFX65 without the Chromatic tuner. The GFX65T was introduced in 2002.

GFX120/GFX120T – 120W, 1-12 in. Crate Custom speaker, solid-state combo, three selectable channels, DSP, front black control panel, single input, 10 gray knobs, 2 blue knobs (OD: g1, g2, shape, l, h, level, Clean: level, l, m, h, DSP: level, mode), 16 digital effects, footswitch, external speaker jack, chromatic tuner, black covering, gray grille, 34 lbs., mfg. 1997-2002.

| | N/A | $225 - 275 | $135 - 175 | $580 |

In 2002, a chromatic tuner was introduced and the model name was changed to the GFX120T.

* GFX212/GFX212T – similar to the GFX120T except has 2-12 in. speakers, 50 lbs., mfg. 1997-2002.

| | N/A | $250 - 300 | $150 - 200 | $660 |

In 2001, a chromatic tuner was introduced and the model name was changed to the GFX212T.

GFX2200H HEAD – 220W, solid-state full size head, three switchable channels, DSP, front black control panel, single input, 13 black and silver knobs (Ch A: g1, g2, l, m, h, level, Ch. B: l, m, h, level, DSP: mode, level A, level B), footswitch, bright switch, chromatic tuner, black covering, black grille, 41 lbs., mfg. 2002-03.

| | N/A | $300 - 375 | $175 - 225 | $780 |

ELECTRIC SS AMPLIFIERS: GLX SERIES

The Crate GLX Series features "live effects" that are designed for live performances. Crate also offers half- and full-stack units with their GLX1200H head and 4-12 in. G speaker cabinets.

GLX15 – 15W, 1-8 in. Crate speaker, solid-state combo, two selectable channels, DSP, front black control panel, single input, seven black knobs (OD: g, level, Clean: level, l, m, h, DSP mode), headphone jack, external speaker jack, black, camo, or python redcovering, black grille, 15 lbs., mfg. 2003-06.

| $175 | $100 - 125 | $60 - 80 | | $250 |

In 2005, a backlit control panel was introduced.

MSR/NOTES	100%	EXCELLENT	AVERAGE	LAST MSR

GLX15
courtesy Crate

GLX50TT (Two Tone)
courtesy Crate

GLX120
courtesy Crate

GLX30 – 30W, 1-12 in. Crate speaker, solid-state combo, two selectable channels, DSP, front black control panel, single input, nine black knobs, (OD: g, shape, level, Clean: level, l, m, h, DSP mode, level), headphone jack, external speaker jack, footswitch, black covering, black grille, 21 lbs., mfg. 2003-06.

$260	$150 - 200	$95 - 120		$370

In 2005, a backlit control panel was introduced.

GLX50TT (TWO TONE) – 50W, 1-12 in. Crate speaker, solid-state combo, independent two player operation (two channels), DSP, front black control panel, two inputs, 17 black knobs (Ch. A & Ch. B each have v, g, t, m, b, level, effects, DSP mode, DSP level, CD input level), headphone jacks, black covering, black grille, 34 lbs., mfg. 2003-05.

N/A	$200 - 250	$120 - 150		$570

GLX65 – 65W, 1-12 in. Crate Custom speaker, solid-state combo, three selectable channels, DSP, front black backlit control panel, single input, 12 black knobs (OD: g1, g2, shape, l, h, level, Clean: level, l, m, h, DSP: level, mode), 16 digital effects, footswitch, external speaker jack, chromatic tuner, black covering, black grille, 32 lbs., mfg. 2003-06.

$400	$275 - 325	$150 - 200		$560

GLX120 – 120W, 1-12 in. Crate Custom speaker, solid-state combo, three selectable channels, DSP, front black backlit control panel, single input, 12 black knobs (OD: g1, g2, shape, l, h, level, Clean: level, l, m, h, DSP: level, mode), 16 digital effects, footswitch, external speaker jack, chromatic tuner, black covering, black grille, 42 lbs., mfg. 2003-05.

N/A	$275 - 325	$150 - 200		$650

* **GLX212** – similar to the GLX120 except has 2-12 in. speakers, 48 lbs., mfg. 2003-06.

$490	$325 - 375	$225 - 275		$700

GLX1200H HEAD – 120W, solid-state full size head, three switchable channels, DSP, front black control panel, single input, 14 black knobs (Ch A: g1, g2, l, m, h, level, Ch. B: l, m, h, level, DSP: mode, level A, level B), footswitch, bright switch, chromatic tuner, black covering, black grille, 30 lbs., mfg. 2003-06.

$420	$275 - 325	$150 - 200		$600

ELECTRIC SS AMPLIFIERS: GT SERIES

Crate also offers half- and full-stack units with their GT1200H and GT3500H Shockwave heads with 4-12 in. GT speaker cabinets.

GT15
courtesy Crate

GT65
courtesy Crate

GT350H Head Shockwave
courtesy Crate

GT15 – 15W, 1-8 in. speaker combo, solid-state chassis, two channels, front black control panel, single input, six black knobs (solo: g, level, clean: v, l, m, h), RCA inputs, headphone jack, external speaker jack, black covering, black grille, 15 lbs., mfg. 2003-06.

$85	$45 - 60	$25 - 35		$120

MSR/NOTES	100%	EXCELLENT	AVERAGE	LAST MSR

* **GT15R** – similar to the GT15, except has reverb, mfg. 2003-06.

| | $115 | $65 - 85 | $35 - 45 | $160 |

GT30 – 30W, 1-12 in. speaker combo, solid-state chassis, two channels, reverb, front black control panel, single input, 10 black knobs (solo: g, shape, level, clean: level, l, m, h, All: r, depth, rate), RCA inputs, headphone jack, external speaker jack, black covering, black grille, 24 lbs., mfg. 2003-06.

| | $210 | $120 - 150 | $70 - 90 | $300 |

GT65 – 65W, 1-12 in. speaker combo, solid-state chassis, three channels, reverb, front black control panel, single input, 13 black knobs (solo: g, shape, level, OD: g, l, m, h, level, Clean: v, l, m, h, r), RCA inputs, external speaker jack, black covering, black grille, 34 lbs., mfg. 2003-06.

| | $280 | $150 - 200 | $95 - 120 | $400 |

GT212 – 120W, 2-12 in. speaker combo, solid-state chassis, three channels, reverb, front black control panel, single input, 13 black knobs (solo: g, shape, level, OD: g, l, m, h, level, Clean: v, l, m, h, r), RCA inputs, external speaker jack, footswitch, black covering, black grille, 50 lbs., mfg. 2003-06.

| | $350 | $200 - 250 | $120 - 150 | $500 |

GT1200H HEAD – 120W, head-unit only, solid-state chassis, three channels, reverb, front black control panel, single input, 13 black knobs (solo: g, shape, level, OD: g, l, m, h, level, Clean: v, l, m, h, r), RCA inputs, external speaker jack, footswitch, black covering, black grille, 29 lbs., mfg. 2003-06.

| | $350 | $200 - 250 | $120 - 150 | $500 |

GT3500H HEAD SHOCKWAVE – 350W, head-unit only, solid-state chassis, three channels, reverb, front black control panel, single input, 13 black knobs (solo: g, shape, level, OD: g, l, m, h, level, Clean: v, l, m, h, r), effects loop, external speaker jack, footswitch, black covering, black metal grille, 41 lbs., mfg. 2004-06.

| | $575 | $350 - 425 | $200 - 250 | $800 |

ELECTRIC SS AMPLIFIERS: GTX SERIES

The Crate GTX is a "tech effects" amplifier. These amplifiers are designed mainly for practice, rehearsal, and other places where the effects need to be fine-tuned. This series is very similar to the GFX series.

GTX15
courtesy Crate

GTX30
courtesy Crate

GTX65
courtesy Crate

GTX15 – 15W, 1-8 in. Crate speaker, solid-state combo, two selectable channels, DSP, front silver control panel, single input, seven black knobs (OD: g, level, Clean: level, l, m, h, DSP mode), headphone jack, external speaker jack, black covering, black grille, 15 lbs., mfg. 2003-06.

| | $150 | $95 - 120 | $55 - 75 | $200 |

GTX30 – 30W, 1-12 in. Crate speaker, solid-state combo, two selectable channels, DSP, front silver control panel, single input, nine black knobs, (OD: g, shape, level, Clean: level, l, m, h, DSP mode, level), headphone jack, external speaker jack, footswitch, black covering, black grille, 22 lbs., mfg. 2003-06.

| | $230 | $140 - 170 | $80 - 100 | $330 |

GTX65 – 65W, 1-12 in. Crate Custom speaker, solid-state combo, three selectable channels, DSP, front silver control panel, single input, 15 black knobs, 16 digital effects, footswitch, external speaker jack, chromatic tuner, black covering, black grille, 34 lbs., mfg. 2003-06.

| | $330 | $200 - 250 | $120 - 160 | $470 |

GTX212 – 120W, 2-12 in. Crate Custom speakers, solid-state combo, three selectable channels, DSP, front black backlit control panel, single input, 15 black knobs, 16 digital effects, footswitch, external speaker jack, chromatic tuner, black covering, black grille, 50 lbs., mfg. 2003-06.

| | $450 | $275 - 325 | $125 - 175 | $600 |

MSR/NOTES	100%	EXCELLENT	AVERAGE	LAST MSR

ELECTRIC SS AMPLIFIERS: GX SERIES

This series of amps have been very popular for Crate as far as solid-state goes. Along with the combos there are a couple of head-units that they make. There are also speaker cabinets to match up with these. There are two full size cabs the **GX412S** and the **GX412R**, which each include 4-12 in. Crate speakers and weigh 74 lbs. These each retail for $659.99. There are two compact sized cabs (to match the compact 1200H head) which are the **GX412XS** and the **GX 412XR**, which have 4-12 in. speakers, and weigh 54 lbs. These retail for $469.99. The only difference between the two in each set is one is slanted (S) and the other is straight (R). Note that this series has changed cosmetically from year to year but the electronics are generally the same.

GX15
courtesy John Beeson/The Music Shoppe

GX30M
courtesy Crate

GX900H Head
courtesy Crate

GX10 – 10W, 1-6.5 in. Crate speaker, solid-state combo, dual selectable channels, front black control panel, six gray knobs (OD: g, level, Clean: level, l, m, h), headphone jack, ext. speaker jack, black covering, black grille, mfg. 2002 only.

	N/A	$30 - 40	$15 - 25	$100

GX15 – 12+W, 1-8 in. Crate speaker, solid-state combo, dual selectable channels, front black control panel, six gray knobs (OD: g, level, Clean: level, l, m, h), headphone jack, ext. speaker jack, black covering, black grille, 15 lbs., mfg. 1990s-2003.

	N/A	$35 - 50	$20 - 30	$110

* **GX15R** – similar to the GX15 except has reverb effect and control for reverb, 16 lbs., mfg. 1990s-2003.

	N/A	$40 - 60	$25 - 35	$150

GX20M – 20W, 1-10 in. Crate speaker, solid-state combo, dual selectable channels, reverb, mono chorus, front black control panel, seven gray knobs (OD: g, level, Clean: level, l, m, h, r), headphone jack, ext. speaker jack, black covering, 21 lbs., black grille, disc. 2003.

	N/A	$75 - 100	$45 - 60	$250

* **GX20C** – similar to the GX20M except has 2-6 in. speakers for stereo chorus, mfg. late 1980s-early 1990s.

	N/A	$95 - 120	$60 - 75	

GX30M – 30W, 1-12 in. Crate speaker, solid-state combo, dual selectable channels, reverb, mono chorus, front gray control panel, single input, ten gray knobs (OD: g, shape, level, Clean: level, l, m. h, Both: r, d, rate), footswitch, headphone jack, external speaker jack, black covering, black grille, 24 lbs., mfg. 1990s-2003.

	N/A	$95 - 120	$60 - 75	$300

GX65 – 65W, 1-12 in. Crate speaker, solid-state combo, three selectable channels, reverb, front gray control panel, single input, eleven gray knobs (OD: g1, g2, shape, l, h, level, Clean: level, l, m, h, level), footswitch, headphone jack, external speaker jack, black covering, black grille, 34 lbs., mfg. 1990s-2003.

	N/A	$120 - 150	$75 - 95	$400

* **GX212** – similar to the GX65 except has 120W output and 2-12 in. Crate speakers, 50 lbs., mfg. 1990s-2003.

	N/A	$150 - 200	$95 - 120	$500

GX900H HEAD – 90W, head-unit only, solid-state, three selectable channels, reverb, front black control panel, single input, 12 black and silver knobs (rA, rB, Ch B: level, h, m, l, Ch A: l, h, m, l, g2, g1), effects loop, footswitch, bright switch, black covering, black grille, 33 lbs., mfg. 1990s-2003.

	N/A	$200 - 250	$120 - 150	$590

GX1200H HEAD – 120W, compact head-unit, solid-state, three selectable channels, reverb, front black control panel, single input, eleven gray knobs (OD: g, shape, l, h, level, Clean: level, l, m, h, r1, r2), effects loop, footswitch, black covering, black grille, 25 lbs., mfg. 1990s-2003.

	N/A	$135 - 175	$80 - 100	$460

GX2200H HEAD – similar to the 900H except has 220W output, 41 lbs., mfg. 1990s-2003.

	N/A	$225 - 275	$135 - 175	$660

MSR/NOTES	100%	EXCELLENT	AVERAGE	LAST MSR

ELECTRIC SS AMPLIFIERS: TAXI & LIMO SERIES

The Taxi & Limo amps are battery operated for use on the go. The first amps were introduced in 1998 and more have been added along the way. These amps have a 120V AC wall charger and some have a 12V DC car charger. The TX50DBE even has Crate's DSP effect.

TX15
courtesy Crate

TX30BE
courtesy Crate

TX50DBE
courtesy Crate

TX15 – 15W, 1-8 in. Crate woofer with Crate piezo tweeter, solid-state combo, angled cabinet (3 positions), dual channels, top black control panel, two inputs (one per channel, one normal, one 1/4 in./XLR combo), six black and yellow knobs (v1, v2, l, l/m, h/m, h), CD input, headphone jack, 120V Wall charger/adapter, black covering, black steel grille, 20 lbs., mfg. 2002-disc.

	$170	$100 - 130	$65 - 85	$238

TX30BE/TX30E – 30W, 1-8 in. Crate woofer with Crate piezo tweeter, solid-state combo, angled cabinet (3 positions), dual channels, top black control panel, two inputs, seven black and yellow knobs (Ch 1: level, tone, Ch 2: g, l, m, h, level), insert/effects loop, headphone jack, black or yellow covering, black steel grille, 17 lbs., mfg. 1998-2006.

	$230	$155 - 175	$110 - 125	$330

TX50DBE – 50W, 1-10 in. Crate woofer with Crate piezo tweeter, solid-state combo, angled cabinet (3 positions), three channels (two instrument, one mic), top silver control panel, three inputs (one XLR, two normal), ten gray and three blue knobs (Ch 1: g, level, shape, Ch 2: l, m, h, level, Mic: level, l, m, h, three blue DSP knobs), insert/effects loop, headphone jack, footswitch, CD inputs, black covering, black steel grille, 17 lbs., mfg. 1998-disc.

	$400	$250 - 300	$150 - 200	$578

* **TXB50E** – similar to the TX50DBE, except is specified for bass instruments, has no piezo tweeters, smaller control panel, 22 lbs., mfg. 2002-05.

	N/A	$250 - 300	$150 - 200	$530

ELECTRIC SS AMPLIFIERS: VTX SERIES

The VTX Series stands for Vintage Tech Effects.

VTX15B
courtesy Crate

VTX65B
courtesy Crate

VTX212B
courtesy Crate

VTX15B – 15W, 1-8 in. speaker combo, solid-state chassis, two channels, top black control panel, single input, seven knobs (g, level, v, l, m, h, DSP) RCA inputs, headphone jack, external speaker jack, black covering, black grille, 19 lbs., mfg. 2005-07.

	$140	$95 - 120	$50 - 70	$230

VTX30B – 30W, 1-10 in. speaker combo, solid-state chassis, two channels, top black control panel, single input, nine knobs (g, shape, level 1, level 2, l, m, h, DSP level, DSP select) RCA inputs, headphone jack, external speaker jack, black covering, black grille, 20 lbs., mfg. 2005-07.

	$200	$150 - 180	$95 - 120	$360

VTX65B – 65W, 1-12 in. speaker combo, solid-state chassis, three channels, top black control panel, single input, 15 knobs (Solo: g, shape, level, Rhythm: g, l, m, h, level, Clean: v, l, m, h, All: DSP multi, DSP delay, r) RCA inputs, external speaker jack, footswitch, black covering, black grille, 34 lbs., mfg. 2005-07.

	$300	$225 - 275	$120 - 150	$540

MSR/NOTES	100%	EXCELLENT	AVERAGE	LAST MSR

VTX200SH HEAD – 200W stereo, guitar head unit, solid-state chassis, three channels, front black control panel, single input, 18 knobs (l, m, h, g, level per channel, DSP effects, DSP delay, r) effects loop, external speaker jack, footswitch, black leather covering, top-mounted leather handles, mfg. 2007 only.

	$500	$300 - 375	$150 - 200	$700

* *VTX200S Combo* – similar to the VTX200SH Head, except in combo configuration with 2-12 in. speakers, top black control panel, a brown grille, and removable casters, mfg. 2005-07.

	$500	$400 - 475	$250 - 300	$900

VTX212B – 120W, 2-12 in. speaker combo, solid-state chassis, three channels, top black control panel, single input, 15 knobs (Solo: g, shape, level, Rhythm: g, l, m, h, level, Clean: v, l, m, h, All: DSP multi, DSP delay, r) RCA inputs, effects loop, external speaker jack, footswitch, removable casters, black covering, black grille, 46 lbs., mfg. 2005-07.

	$440	$300 - 375	$175 - 225	$680

VTX350H HEAD – 350W, head-unit configuration, solid-state chassis, FlexWave Evolution 5 Preamp, three channels, Vintage Tech Effects, front black control panel, single input, 15 knobs (r, delay, effects, Each Ch. has: level, g, h, m, l), effects loop, external speaker jack, three-button footswitch, black covering, 46 lbs., mfg. 2005-06.

	$700	$450 - 525	$275 - 325	$1,000

ELECTRIC SS AMPLIFIERS: MISC. SERIES

Powerblock CPB150
courtesy Crate

Profiler Model 5
courtesy Crate

G-600
courtesy Dave's Guitar Shop

POWERBLOCK CPB150 – 150W, small head-unit only, single channel, front control panel, single input, five knobs (g, l, m, h, level), line out, headphone jack, external speaker jacks, RCA inputs, effects loop, black casing, 4.6 lbs., mfg. 2005-06.

	$200	$120 - 150	$70 - 90	$300

PROFILER MODEL 5 – 5W (2.5W per channel stereo), 2-3 in. speakers, guitar combo, single channel, top black control panel, single input, seven black knobs (g, tone, master, profiles, delay, effects, r), headphone jack, audio input, USB connection, battery or AC operation, black covering, black grille, made in China, mfg. 2007-09.

	$150	$90 - 110	$55 - 70	$216

G-60 – 60W, 1-12 in. Crate speaker or optional Celestion G12M-70 speaker (G-60/GT), guitar combo, solid-state chassis, two channels, reverb, front black control panel, two inputs, eight knobs (Ch. A: g, shape, level, Ch. B: v, l, m, h, All: r), channel switch, bright switch, power switch, rear panel: two external speaker jacks, line in jack, line out jack, footswitch jack, black covering, black grille, mfg. 1986-89.

	N/A	$120 - 150	$75 - 95	

G-600 – wattage unknown, head-unit only, front black control panel, eleven knobs, black covering, mfg. 1980s-1990s.

	N/A	$100 - 150	$50 - 75	

ELECTRIC BASS AMPLIFIERS: BT SERIES

BT10 – 10W, 1-8 in. speaker combo, solid-state chassis, single channel, front black control panel, single input, four knobs (g, l, m, h), external speaker jack, headphone jack, black covering, black metal grille, mfg. 2007 only.

	$55	$35 - 45	$20 - 30	$80

BT15 – 12W, 1-8 in. speaker combo, solid-state chassis, single channel, front black control panel, single input, five knobs (g, l, l/m, h/m, h), RCA inputs, external speaker jack, headphone jack, black covering, black metal grille, 21 lbs., mfg. 2004-07.

	$70	$45 - 60	$25 - 35	$110

BT25 – 25W, 1-10 in. speaker combo, solid-state chassis, two channels, front black control panel, single input, 10 knobs (Distortion: g, shape, level, Clean: level, l, l/m, h/m, h, All: octave, MV), chromatic tuner, RCA inputs, headphone jack, black covering, black metal grille, 30 lbs., mfg. 2004-07.

	$130	$90 - 110	$55 - 70	$200

MSR/NOTES	100%	EXCELLENT	AVERAGE	LAST MSR

BT25
courtesy Crate

BT100
courtesy Crate

BT220H Head
courtesy Crate

BT50 – 50W, 1-12 in. speaker combo, solid-state chassis, two channels, front black control panel, single input, 10 knobs (Distortion: g, shape, level, Clean: level, l, l/m, h/m, h, All: octave, MV), chromatic tuner, RCA inputs, headphone jack, footswitch, black covering, black metal grille, 46 lbs., mfg. 2004-07.

| | $180 | $120 - 150 | $80 - 100 | $280 |

BT100 – 100W, 1-15 in. speaker combo, solid-state chassis, two channels, front black control panel, single input, 10 knobs (Distortion: g, shape, level, Clean: level, l, l/m, h/m, h, All: octave, MV), chromatic tuner, RCA inputs, headphone jack, footswitch, black covering, black metal grille, 69 lbs., mfg. 2004-07.

| | $250 | $150 - 200 | $95 - 120 | $380 |

BT220 – 220W, 1-15 in. speaker combo, solid-state chassis, two channels, front black control panel, single input, 10 knobs (Distortion: g, shape, level, Clean: level, l, l/m, h/m, h, All: octave, MV), chromatic tuner, RCA inputs, headphone jack, footswitch, casters, side handles, black covering, black metal grille, 87 lbs., mfg. 2004-07.

| | $500 | $275 - 325 | $150 - 200 | $600 |

BT220H HEAD – 220W, head-unit only, solid-state chassis, two channels, front black control panel, single input, 10 knobs (Distortion: g, shape, level, Clean: level, l, l/m, h/m, h, All: octave, MV), chromatic tuner, RCA inputs, headphone jack, footswitch, black covering, black metal grille, 30 lbs., mfg. 2004-05.

| | N/A | $200 - 250 | $120 - 150 | $500 |

BT1000 – 100W, 1-12 in. speaker combo, solid-state chassis, single channel, front black control panel, single input, eight knobs (level, l, l/m, m/h, h, Expander: slope, level, MV), pad switch, mute, expander switch, headphone jack, tilt-back cabinet design, black covering, black metal grille, 53 lbs., mfg. 2005-07.

| | $275 | $160 - 210 | $100 - 125 | $400 |

BT115E SPEAKER CABINET – 1-15 in. ProBass American driver, 8 ohm impedance, removable casters, black covering, black metal grille, 44 lbs., mfg. 2004-05.

| | N/A | $150 - 200 | $95 - 120 | $400 |

BT215E SPEAKER CABINET – 2-15 in. ProBass American drivers, 4 ohm impedance, removable casters, black covering, black metal grille, 82 lbs., mfg. 2004-05.

| | N/A | $250 - 300 | $150 - 200 | $600 |

BT410E SPEAKER CABINET – 4-10 in. ProBass American drivers, 4 ohm impedance, removable casters, black covering, black metal grille, 76 lbs., mfg. 2004-05.

| | N/A | $225 - 275 | $135 - 175 | $550 |

ELECTRIC BASS AMPLIFIERS: BX/BFX SERIES

BX15 – 12W, 1-8 in. speaker, solid-state combo, front black control panel, five gray knobs (v, l, l/m, l/h, h), black Tolex covering, black grille, 19 lbs., disc. 2004.

| | N/A | $60 - 80 | $35 - 50 | $160 |

* BFX15 – similar to the BX15, except has digital effects with an additional blue DSP knob, gray grille, 19 lbs., disc. 2004.

| | N/A | $75 - 100 | $45 - 60 | $260 |

BX25DLX – 25W, 1-10 in. speaker, solid-state combo, front black control panel, ten gray knobs, built in tuner, black Tolex covering, black grille, 30 lbs., disc. 2004.

| | N/A | $120 - 150 | $75 - 95 | $320 |

MSR/NOTES	100%	EXCELLENT	AVERAGE	LAST MSR

BFX25
courtesy Crate

BX50DLX
courtesy Crate

BX200H Head
courtesy John Beeson/The Music Shoppe

* *BFX25* – similar to the BX25DLX, except has digital effects with seven gray knobs and two blue knobs, gray grille, 30 lbs., disc. 2004.

	N/A	$135 - 175	$80 - 100	$400

BX50DLX – 50W, 1-12 in. speaker, solid-state combo, front black control panel, ten gray knobs, built in tuner, black Tolex covering, black grille, 43 lbs., disc. 2004.

	N/A	$135 - 175	$80 - 100	$390

* *BFX50* – similar to the BFX50DLX, except has digital effects with seven gray knobs, and two blue knobs, gray grille, 43 lbs., disc. 2004.

	N/A	$150 - 200	$95 - 120	$460

BX100 – 100W, 1-15 in. speaker, solid-state combo, front black control panel, four gray knobs, 8 band EQ, black Tolex covering, black grille, 60 lbs., disc. 2004.

	N/A	$175 - 225	$110 - 140	$530

* *BFX100* – similar to the BX100, except has digital effects with three gray knobs and two blue knobs, gray grille, 60 lbs., disc. 2004.

	N/A	$200 - 250	$120 - 150	$650

• **Add $75 for Tiltback compact portable cabinet.**

BX200H HEAD – 200W, head-unit only, solid-state chassis, black covering, mfg. 1990s.

	N/A	$175 - 225	$110 - 140	

BXH220 HEAD – 220W, head-unit only, solid-state chassis, front black control panel, single input, six silver knobs, 8 band EQ, black covering, 30 lbs., disc. 2004.

	N/A	$200 - 250	$120 - 150	$580

BFX220H HEAD – 220W, head-unit only, solid-state chassis, DSP with 9 digital effects, front black control panel, single input, eight silver knobs, 8 band EQ, black covering, 30 lbs., disc. 2004.

	N/A	$250 - 300	$135 - 175	$730

ACOUSTIC SS AMPLIFIERS

The Acoustic Series have a lot of the features that the electric counterparts have, including the DSP effect. The models that don't have DSP have a darker covering. All the models from the CA60 up have the ability to have an instrument as well as a microphone to be in use at the same time.

CA-10 – 10W, 1-8 in. speaker combo with tweeter, solid-state chassis, single channel, chorus, top brown control panel, single input, five knobs (level, l, m, h, chorus rate), chorus switch, headphone jack, green covering, brown wicker grille, mfg. 2007-disc.

	$100	$60 - 75	$40 - 50	$144

CA-15 CIMARRON – 15W, 1-8 in. speaker combo with tweeter, solid-state chassis, two channels, reverb, top brown control panel, two inputs, six knobs (g1, g2, l, m, h, r), RCA inputs, headphone jack, external speaker jack, green covering, brown wicker grille, 21 lbs., mfg. 2005-disc.

	$150	$90 - 110	$50 - 70	$217

CA30 – 30W, 1-8 in. High Fidelity speaker with a Crate special design tweeter, solid-state slanted front combo, dual channels, spring reverb, brown control panel, two inputs, seven black knobs (g1, g2, l, m, c, h, r), line out, effects loop, mahogany Tolex covering, brown grille, 28 lbs., mfg. 1995-2003.

	N/A	$135 - 175	$80 - 100	$360

* *CA30D* – similar to the CA30 except has the DSP digital effect (more knobs), spruce Tolex covering, mfg. 1997-2003.

	N/A	$150 - 200	$95 - 120	$400

MSR/NOTES	100%	EXCELLENT	AVERAGE	LAST MSR

CA-30DG TAOS
courtesy Crate

CA60
courtesy Crate

CA-6110DG Gunnison
courtesy Crate

CA-30DG TAOS – 30W, 1-8 in. speaker combo with tweeter, solid-state chassis, DSP effects, two channels, reverb, top brown control panel, two inputs, eight knobs (g1, g2, l, m, c, h, mode, level), line out, insert, effects loop, green covering, brown wicker grille, 26 lbs., mfg. 2004-disc.

	$250	$150 - 190	$95 - 120	$361

CA60 – 60W, 2-6.5 in. Crate High Fidelity speakers, Crate tweeter, solid-state slanted front combo, dual channels, stereo chorus, reverb, feedback elimination circuit, front brown control panel, three inputs, 15 brown knobs (Inst: g, l, m, h, f, cut, rev/eff send, d, rate, Vocal: g, l, h, rev/eff send, Master: rev return, level), line out, footswitch, mahogany Tolex, brown grille, 38 lbs., mfg. 1995-2003.

	N/A	$225 - 275	$135 - 175	$650

* CA60D – similar to the CA60 except has the DSP digital effect (more knobs), spruce Tolex covering, mfg. 1997-2003.

	N/A	$250 - 300	$150 - 200	$730

CA112D – 125W, 1-12 in. Dual Voice Coil sub with tweeter, solid-state tilt back cabinet combo, three channels, feedback elimination circuit, stereo chorus, DSP effects, front brown control panel, four inputs, 18 brown knobs (Inst: g, l, m, c, h, f, cut, rev/eff send, Mic: g, rev/eff send, Aux: g, rev/eff send, Chorus: d, rate, Effects mode, rev/ret, eff/ret, level out) 5-band equalizer, effects loop. Line out with knobs, footswitch, spruce Tolex covering, brown grille, 42 lbs., mfg. 1997-2003.

	N/A	$350 - 425	$200 - 250	$970

* CA125D – smilar to the CA112D except has 2-8 in. high-fi speakers with tweeters, mfg. 1997-2003.

	N/A	$350 - 425	$200 - 250	$970

CA-6110DG GUNNISON – 60W, 1-10 in. speaker combo with tweeter, solid-state chassis, DSP effects, two channels, reverb, top brown control panel, two inputs, 17 knobs (Ch. 1: g, l, m, c, h, effects, Ch. 2: g, l, m, c, h, effects, All: CD level, tweeter level, effects mode, r, level), feedback filters, RCA inputs, line out, effects loop, footswitch, green covering, brown wicker grille, 37 lbs., mfg. 2004-disc.

	$380	$225 - 275	$135 - 175	$549

CA-120DG DURANGO – 120W, 1-12 in. speaker combo with tweeter, solid-state chassis, DSP effects, two channels, reverb, top brown control panel, two inputs, 20 knobs (Ch. 1: g1, g2, l, m, c, h, effects, Ch. 2: g1, g2, l, m, c, h, effects, All: CD level, tweeter level, effects mode, r, effects return, level), feedback filters, RCA inputs, line out, effects loop, footswitch, green covering, brown wicker grille, 45 lbs., mfg. 2004-disc.

	$500	$300 - 375	$175 - 225	$722

CA-125DG TELLURIDE – 125W (2 x 50 + 25W tweeter), 2-8 in. speaker combo with tweeter, solid-state chassis, chorus, DSP effects, three channels, reverb, front brown control panel, two inputs, 18 knobs (Instrument: g, l, m, c, h, freq, cut, Vocal: g, effects send, Aux: g, effects send, effects mode, effects level, effects return, level, chorus depth, chorus rate), five-band EQ, line out, effects loop, footswitch, green covering, brown wicker grille, 44 lbs., mfg. 2004-disc.

	$600	$350 - 425	$225 - 275	$867

SPEAKER CABINETS

Crate produces several different speaker cabinets to match up with their heads. Oftentimes they are sold in sets (head and speaker cabinet). The Blue Voodoo, GLX, GX, and BX Bass series all have their own speaker cabinets in various sizes and configurations. Look for more information in future editions of the *Blue Book of Guitar Amplifiers*.

G412 SPEAKER CABINET – 100W, 4-12 in. speakers, straight or angled cabinet, black covering, black metal grille, 54 lbs., mfg. 2003-06.

	$350	$200 - 250	$120 - 150	$500

GT112SL SPEAKER CABINET – 100W, 1-12 in. Celestion speakers, 8 ohm impedance, open back, fixed covering, black covering, black grille, 36 lbs., mfg. 2005-06.

	$175	$100 - 130	$50 - 70	$250

MSR/NOTES	100%	EXCELLENT	AVERAGE	LAST MSR

G412 Speaker Cabinet
courtesy Crate

GT112SL Speaker Cabinet
courtesy Crate

GT412 Speaker Cabinet
courtesy Crate

GT212S SPEAKER CABINET – 160W, 2-12 in. Celestion speakers, impedance selector switch, .75 in. plywood construction, angled front, black covering, black grille, 47 lbs., mfg. 2006 only.

	$225	$130 - 170	$75 - 100	$320

GT412 SPEAKER CABINET – 300W, 4-12 in. Celestion speakers, straight or angled cabinet, fixed covering, black covering, black metal grille, 75 lbs. (77 straight front), mfg. 2004-06.

	$420	$250 - 300	$125 - 175	$600

CRUISE AUDIO SYSTEMS

Amplifiers and speaker cabinets previously produced in Cuyahoga Falls, OH between 1999 and circa 2003.

Mark Altekruse founded Cruise Audio Systems in 1999, and he built traditional vacuum tube amps with high engineering and ultra-modern manufacturing practices. The first amp produced was the **MQ4**, which had four independent channels, and it was available as a combo or a head with speaker cabinet.

CUSTOM KRAFT

Amplifiers previously produced in Chicago, IL by Valco during the early 1960s and possibly Japan in the late 1960s. See chapter on House Brands.

The Custom Kraft trademark was a House Brand of St. Louis Music. The St. Louis Music Supply Company was founded in 1922 by Bernard Kornblum, originally as an importer of German violins. The St. Louis, MO-based company has been a distributor, importer, and manufacturer of musical instruments since the 1920s.

In the mid-1950s, St. Louis Music distributed amplifiers and guitars from other producers such as Alamo, Harmony, Kay, Magnatone, Rickenbacker, and Supro. By 1960, the focus was on Harmony, Kay, and Supro: all built "upstream" in Chicago, IL. 1960 was also the year that St. Louis Music began carrying Kay's Thinline single cutaway electric guitar.

Custom Kraft was launched in 1961 as St. Louis Music's own House Brand. The first series of semi-hollowbody Custom Kraft Color Dynamic Electric guitars were built by Kay, and appear to be Thinline models in Black, Red, and White. In 1963, a line of solid body double cutaway electrics built by Valco were added to the catalog under the Custom Kraft moniker, as well as Kay-built archtop and flattop acoustic. By 1966, a line of guitar amplifiers had appeared in their catalogs as well.

In 1967, Valco purchased Kay, a deal that managed to sink both companies by 1968. St. Louis Music continued advertising both companies models through 1970, perhaps with NOS supplies from their warehouse. St. Louis Music continued to offer Custom Kraft guitars into the early 1970s, but as their sources had dried up so did the trademark name. St. Louis Music's next trademark guitar line was Electra, followed by Westone, and Alvarez. Source: Michael Wright, *Vintage Guitar Magazine*.

ELECTRIC TUBE AMPS

Custom Kraft's 1966 catalog advertises five models and interestingly enough, the higher the model number doesn't neccessarily mean a better model. The **No. 600C "Fire Ball Special"** is the chepest model and has 1-8 in. speaker with three inputs and a single volume knob. The **No. 500C "Tremolo Deluxe"** also has 1-8 in. speaker but is equipped with tremolo. The **No. 900C "Power-Sonic"** has 30W output, 1-12 in. speaker, and individual tremolo rate and depth controls. The **No. 800C Bass Amp** is designed for bass use with 40W output, 1-15 in. speaker, and individual bass and treble controls. The **No. 875 Custom Kraft Amp** has 1-12 in. speaker, reverb, tremolo, a six-tube chassis, all with individual controls. Values on used Custom Kraft amplifiers is still relatively unknown.

D SECTION
DAAB AMPS

Amplifiers previously produced in Spartanburg, SC.

Fred Daab built guitar amplifiers in his Spartanburg, SC shop. Daab's philosophy was that it was the player's unique perspective and character that creates tone. His goal as an amp builder/designer is to produce the most responsive guitar amplifier possible. From his point of view, an amplifier should be an extension of how one plays the guitar and not just a louder, tacked-on sound that the speakers emit. Everything, from the angle of your pick/fingernail to the dynamics you feel, should be coming out of the speaker and reaching your audience. Daab offered the Tupelo Honey, which was a 30W amp available in a head or combo configuration and powered by EL84 power tubes. Pricing started at $1,650 for head and $2,050 for a combo.

DANELECTRO

Amplifiers previously produced in Red Bank, NJ from 1953 to 1958, Neptune, NJ from 1958 to 1969, and in Asia from the mid-1990s to the present. Currently distributed by the Evets Corporation in San Clemente, CA.

CONTACT INFORMATION
DANELECTRO
PO Box 5030
San Clemente, CA 92674 USA
www.danelectro.com

The Danelectro company was started by Nathan I. Daniels in 1948. Danelectro only produced amplifiers for the first five years that the company was in business. The first guitar was released in 1953. Daniels also built amps for Sears that were branded Silvertone. Danelectro thrived during the guitar boom of the 1950s and 1960s, but they could not keep up with all the competition in the guitar industry in the late 1960s. Danelectro closed its doors by 1969, and no guitars or amps were produced for another 25 years. The Evets Corporation bought Danelectro in the mid-1990s, and released new budget-line guitar amplifiers in 1996, along with guitars and effects. In 2003, Danelectro discontinued all guitar and amplifiers (besides the Honeytone Mini-Amp), and focused strictly on effects. In 2005, Danelectro started offering guitars again, as part of a limited edition. A certain number of one model is produced, and when they are gone, a new model is introduced. Source for Danelectro history: Paul Bechtoldt and Doug Tulloch, *GuitarsFromNeptune*; and Mark Wollerman, Wollerman Guitars.

ELECTRIC TUBE AMPLIFIERS: EARLY MODELS

MSR/NOTES	100%	EXCELLENT	AVERAGE	LAST MSR

CHALLENGER – 30W, 1-15 in. Alnico speaker, seven tube chassis, dual channels, eight control knobs, light brown simulated leather covering, dark grille cloth, mfg. 1950s.

	N/A	$375 - 450	$250 - 300	

COMMANDO – 30W, 8-8 in. speakers, nine tube chassis, dual channels, control panel on inside of amp, six total inputs (three per channel), six knobs (v, b, t for each channel), electronic vibrato with two controls, dual cabinets that swing apart, brown simulated leather covering, brown cloth grille, mfg. 1956-1960.

	N/A	$1,100 - 1,400	$700 - 900	

In later 1956, the covering was changed to gray, but there are a few white ones out there as well.

This model had a massive number of speakers at eight. To get this all into a combo amp, they placed two cabinets (each cabinet with four speakers enclosed), that were placed back to back. In another words, it was a double faced amp with sound projecting from the front and the back. The amp would separate in the middle for access to the controls and the guts of the amp.

ENVOY – 10W, 1-12 in. speaker, six tube chassis, AC/DC power supply, top control panel, three inputs, two knobs (v, tone), brown simulated leather covering, light brown four-leaf clover grille cloth design, mfg. 1948-1952.

	N/A	$425 - 500	$250 - 300	

LEADER – 10W, 1-12 in. Alnico V speaker, five tube chassis, single channel, top control panel, three inputs, two knobs (v, tone), brown simulated leather covering, light brown four-leaf clover grille cloth design, mfg. 1948-1958

	N/A	$600 - 750	$375 - 450	

In 1956, a model number (#48) was assigned to the amp.

MAESTRO (SUPER VIBRAVOX) – 20W, 1-12 in. speaker, seven tube chassis, dual channels, top mounted control panel, three inputs, brown simulated leather covering, light brown four-leaf clover grill design, leather handle, Danelectro emblem on bottom of amp, mfg. 1948-1958.

	N/A	$550 - 650	$325 - 400	

In 1952, the Maestro output was increased to 25W. In 1956, a model number (#78) was assigned to the amp.

MASTER/SLAVE SYSTEM – 30W, 1-15 in. Alnico V speaker, seven-tube chassis (four preamp, three power), dual channels, vibrato, six total inputs (three per channel), eight knobs (two vibrato controls, v, t, b for each channel), light covering, dark grille, mfg. 1956-late 50s.

	100%	EXCELLENT	AVERAGE	
Master	N/A	$500 - 600	$300 - 375	
Slave	N/A	$250 - 300	$150 - 200	

This model was a cousin of the stack system. The Master amp came with the amp and a speaker. The Master could be used by

MSR/NOTES	100%	EXCELLENT	AVERAGE	LAST MSR

itself for a total output of 30W. A slave, as the name states, operates from the Master. The master had a power amp in it and hooks up to the master amp as an extension cabinet except the power was then increased to another 30W. More and more slave cabinets could be added for an unlimited number of watts or cabinets. Not exactly a Marshall stack, but it was a start.

SPECIAL (VIBRAVOX) – 15W, 1-12 in. Alnico V speaker, six tube chassis, 3 X 6SJ7, 2 X 6V6GT, 6X5GT single channel, top mounted control panel, three inputs, four knobs (v, tone, s, vibrato strength), brown simulated leather covering, four-leaf clover design light brown speaker grille, mfg. 1948-1958.

	N/A	$500 - 600	$300 - 375	

SUPER CONSOLE – 50W, 3-12 in. auditorium type loudspeakers, dual channels, rear control panel, six inputs (three per channel), six knobs (v, b, t for each channel), brown simulated leather covering, diagonal woven light brown grille, four leaf clover speaker opening, mfg. 1951-55.

	N/A	$800 - 1,000	$550 - 650	

The Super Console had three removable speaker cabinets that could be placed as extension cabinets. This is truly a unique design as the amp was supplied with 100 feet of cable to move the speakers or keep them in the cabinet.

TWIN TWELVE (SUPER VIBRAVOX) – 30W, 2-12 in. diagonally-mounted heavy-duty speakers, guitar combo, eight tube diagonally-mounted chassis, preamp: 1 X 12AX7, 1 X 6AU6, 1 X 6FQ7, power: 4 X 6L6GC, rectifier: 5U4GB, two channels, vibrato, rear control panel, six inputs (three per channel), seven control knobs (Ch. A v, Ch. B v, amplification, b, t, s, i), brown simulated leather covering, two light brown four-leaf clover grille cloth designs, mfg. 1949-1969.

	N/A	$800 - 1,000	$500 - 600	

In 1952, output was increased to 50W.

ELECTRIC TUBE AMPLIFIERS: MODELS INTRODUCED IN 1962

All models were changed at this point in time to reflect the familiar Danelectro look. The upper line models, such as the Twins, the Centurion, and the Explorer all had a piggyback design without the seperate units. Inside the combo unit, the tube chassis was separated on the top from the speaker cabinet, which was on the bottom. This way the entire chassis was shielded from any foreign hum or noise.

CADET (MODEL 123) – 5W, 1-6 in. speaker, three tube chassis combo, single channel, rear control panel, two inputs, two knobs (v, and tone), white covering, dark grille cloth, mfg. 1962-69.

1962-1964	N/A	$200 - 250	$120 - 150	
1965-1969	N/A	$175 - 225	$110 - 140	

CENTURION (MODEL 275) – 15W, 1-12 in. speaker, seven tube chassis combo, dual channels, vibrato, reverb, top control panel, four inputs (two per channel), eight black knobs (v, b, t for each channel, vibrato, reverb), black covering, light diagonal grille cloth, mfg. 1962-64.

courtesy Willie's American Guitars

courtesy Willie's American Guitars

	N/A	$450 - 550	$300 - 375	

CORPORAL (MODEL 132) – 10W, 2-8 in. speakers, four tube chassis combo, single channel, back control panel, three inputs, two knobs (v, and tone), white covering, dark grille cloth, mfg. 1962-64.

	N/A	$450 - 550	$250 - 300	

EXPLORER (MODEL 291) – 30W, 1-15 in. speaker, seven tube chassis combo, dual channels, vibrato, top control channel, four inputs (two per channel), eight black knobs (v, b, t for each channel, vibrato controls), black covering, light diagonal grille cloth, mfg. 1962-64.

	N/A	$550 - 700	$350 - 425	

TWIN FIFTEEN (MODEL 217) – 60W, 2-15 in. speakers, nine tube chassis combo, 5 preamp tubes, 4 X 6L6 output tubes, dual channels, vibrato, top control panel, various control knobs, black covering, light diagonal grille cloth, mfg. 1962-64.

	N/A	$750 - 900	$475 - 600	

TWIN TWELVE (MODEL 300) – 30W, 2-12 in. speakers, eight tube chassis combo, dual channels, vibrato, reverb, top control panel, nine black knobs, black covering, light diagonal grille cloth, mfg. 1962-64.

	N/A	$750 - 900	$500 - 575	

In 1964, output was raised to 40W.

MSR/NOTES	100%	EXCELLENT	AVERAGE	LAST MSR

VISCOUNT (MODEL 143) – 12W, 1-12" speaker, six tube chassis combo, single channel, vibrato, back mounted control panel, three input jacks, various control knobs, white covering, dark grille cloth, mfg. 1962-64.

courtesy Harry Browning

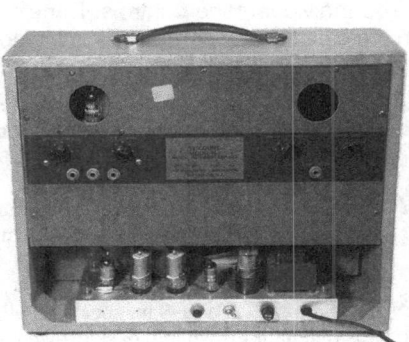
courtesy Harry Browning

| | N/A | $450 - 550 | $250 - 300 | |

ELECTRIC TUBE AMPLIFIERS: D SERIES

In 1965, Danelectro introduced a whole new line of amplifiers. All old amplifiers were discontinued except for the small Cadet model. These new models had new true Piggyback designs with an amp head sitting on top of the speaker cabinet. This differs from the earlier "piggyback" design as there are two separate cabinets instead of a separation in one cabinet. The D series are the most desirable and collectible Danelectro amplifiers on the market.

DM-10 – 10W, 1-8 in. Jensen speaker, tube combo, single channel, vibrato, top silver control panel, two inputs, four knobs (v, tone, vibrato speed, vibrato strength), black covering, brown cloth grille, mfg. 1965-69.

| | N/A | $275 - 350 | $150 - 200 | |

DM-25 – 25W, 1-12 in. Jensen speaker, piggyback design, tubes: 6X4, 3 X 12AX7, 2 X 7189, 6FQ7 or 6C67, dual channels, reverb, vibrato, top silver control panel, four inputs (two per channel), nine knobs (Ch. 1: v, b, t, Ch. 2: v, b, t, r, vibrato speed, vibrato strenth), two button footswitch, black covering, brown cloth grille, mfg. 1965-69.

courtesy Harry Browning

courtesy Harry Browning

| | N/A | $600 - 750 | $400 - 450 | |

DS-50 – 50W, 3-10 in. Jensen speakers, piggyback design, tubes, dual channels, reverb, vibrato, top silver control panel, four inputs (two per channel), nine knobs (Ch. 1: v, b, t, Ch. 2: v, b, t, r, vibrato speed, vibrato strength), black covering, brown cloth grille, mfg. 1965-69.

| | N/A | $1,000-1,250 | $600 - 800 | |

DS-100 – 100W, 6-10 in. Jensen speakers, piggyback design, tubes, dual channels, reverb, vibrato, top silver control panel, four inputs (two per channel), nine knobs (Ch. 1: v, b, t, Ch. 2: v, b, t, r, vibrato speed, vibrato strength), black covering, brown cloth grille, mfg. 1965-69.

| | N/A | $1,100 - 1,400 | $700 - 900 | |

ELECTRIC SS AMPLIFIERS

Danelectro put out only one model (that we know about) that was solid-state in the 1960s. They did come roaring back in the 1990s with their new transistor models (see corresponding sections below).

DTR-40 – 40W, 2-10 in. speakers, solid-state combo, dual channels, vibrato, top silver control panel, four inputs (two per channel), eight knobs (Ch. 1: v, b, t, Ch. 2: v, b, t, vibrato speed, vibrato strength), black covering, brown grille, mfg. 1965-69.

| | N/A | $350 - 450 | $175 - 225 | |

MSR/NOTES	100%	EXCELLENT	AVERAGE	LAST MSR

ELECTRIC SS AMPLIFIERS: 1996-2003 MFG.

The **Honeytone** (last MSR was $39), is a small portable amp powered by a 9-volt battery (optional AC/DC adapter) that features a small speaker and individual tone controls. Danelectro also offered the **Amp in a Bag** (last MSR $39), is a throw back to the Silvertone amp in the case (however no guitar is included in this version). The entire package comes with a white with brown swirl gig-bag that has a small, removable amp attached to the case.

DIRTY THIRTY – approx. 10W, 1-8 in. speaker, solid-state chassis, top brown control panel, single input, three knobs (distortion, level, tone), two-tone light brown and dark brown covering, round plaid speaker grille, mfg. late 1990s-2003.

	N/A	$35 - 50	$15 - 25	$99

NIFTY FIFTY – approx. 15W, 1-8 in. speaker, solid-state chassis, top brown control panel, single input, five knobs (dirty-sweet, level, b, m, t), headphone jack, two-tone light brown and dark brown covering, round plaid speaker grille, mfg. mid-1990s-2003.

	N/A	$40 - 60	$20 - 30	$129

NIFTY SEVENTY – approx. 15W, 1-8 in. speaker, solid-state bass chassis, top brown control panel, single input, four knobs (level, b, m, t), headphone jack, two-tone light brown and dark brown covering, round plaid speaker grille, mfg. mid-1990s-2003.

	N/A	$45 - 65	$25 - 35	$149

DEAN

Amplifiers previously produced in Japan, Korea, or China since 1998 (earliest models produced in the early 1990s). Distributed by Armadillo Enterprises in Tampa, FL, previously located in Clearwater, FL.

Like many guitar/amp manufacturers, Dean started out building guitars in 1977. By the late 1980s, a majority of their guitar production was located in Japan and they began catering more to student/entry-level guitar players. As their instruments became more popular in the early 1990s, they decided to introduce a line of amplifiers. The first amplifiers appeared in the early 1990s, but they did not become a steady fixture in the Dean line until circa 1998. They currently offer electric, bass, and acoustic amplifiers in a variety of configurations that are targeted to the student or entry-level guitar player. For a complete history on Dean, refer to the *Blue Book of Electric Guitars*. For more information on Dean products, visit their website or contact them directly.

GUITAR AMPLIFIERS

In the early 1990s, Dean produced at least one model named the D-1025 that featured 25W, 1-10 in. speaker, distortion and reverb was optional. The last MSR on this amp was $180 ($250 with reverb).

GA 40 – 40W, 1-12 in. speaker, solid-state guitar combo, two channels, reverb front silver control panel, two inputs, nine black knobs (Ch. 1: g, shape, p, level, Ch. 2: level, t, m, b, r), channel select switch, headphone jack, external speaker jack, black covering, black grille, mfg. 2000-06.

	$195	$120 - 150	$70 - 90	$300

MEAN 10 – 10W, 1-6.5 in. speaker, solid-state guitar combo, front silver control panel, single input, five black knobs (g, v, t, m, b), boost switch, headphone jack, black covering, black grille, mfg. 2002-disc.

	$50	$30 - 40	$15 - 25	$83

MEAN 16 – 16W, 1-8 in. speaker, solid-state guitar combo, two channels, front silver control panel, two inputs, seven black knobs (Ch. 1: v, Ch. 2: drive, shift, v, All: b, m, t), channel select switch, headphone jack, external speaker jack, black covering, black grille, mfg. 1998-disc.

	$75	$50 - 60	$30 - 40	$123

The Mean 16 was the first amp to be introduced as part of Dean guitar/amp packages.

* *Mean 16-R Reverb* – similar to the Mean 16, except has a reverb circuit with reverb control, mfg. 2002-08.

	$90	$60 - 70	$35 - 50	$140

MICHAEL SCHENKER ALL ACCESS AMP – 15W, 1-8 in. speaker, solid-state guitar combo, single channel, front illuminated control panel, two inputs, six black knobs (g, t, m, b, p, MV), headphone jack, white Tolex covering with black accents, black metal grille, mfg. 2005-06.

	$110	$60 - 85	$35 - 50	$173

BASS AMPLIFIERS

BASSOLA 10 – 10W, 1-8 in. speaker, solid-state bass combo, single channel, front silver control panel, single input, five black knobs (v, t, m, b, p), headphone jack, black covering, black grille, mfg. 2002-disc.

	$50	$30 - 40	$15 - 25	$81

BASSOLA 15 – 15W, 1-10 in. speaker, solid-state bass combo, single channel, front silver control panel, single input, five black knobs (v, t, low m, high m, b), headphone jack, black covering, black grille, current mfg.

MSR $99	$80	$50 - 60	$25 - 30	

MSR/NOTES	100%	EXCELLENT	AVERAGE	LAST MSR

Bassola 15
courtesy Dean

DA15C
courtesy Dean

DA25C
courtesy Dean

BASSOLA 25 – 25W, 1-10 in. speaker, solid-state bass combo, single channel, front silver control panel, two inputs, six black knobs (g, v, t, m, b, p), headphone jack, effects loop, black covering, black grille, mfg. 2002-06.

	$90	$60 - 70	$35 - 50	$140

BASSOLA 40 – 40W, 1-12 in. speaker, solid-state bass combo, single channel, front silver control panel, two inputs, seven black knobs (g, shape, t, m, b, p, level), headphone jack, oversized enclosure, black covering, black grille, mfg. 2000-06.

	$190	$120 - 150	$70 - 90	$290

ACOUSTIC AMPLIFIERS

DA15C – 15W, solid-state acoustic guitar chassis, single channel, chorus, top brown control panel, one input, five black knobs, headphone jack, simulated brown leather covering with gold accents, brown speaker grille, current mfg.

MSR $139	$100	$65 - 75	$35 - 40	

DA15-2 – 15W, 2-5 in. speakers, solid-state acoustic guitar chassis, two channels (guitar, mic), reverb, front gold control panel, three inputs (two guitar, one XLR mic), six black knobs (guitar level, mic level, t, m, b, r), headphone jack, simulated brown leather covering with gold accents, brown speaker grille split into two sections, mfg. 2000-06.

	$160	$100 - 125	$60 - 80	$250

DA20 – 20W, 2-5 in. speakers, solid-state acoustic guitar chassis, single channel, top brown control panel, one input, five black knobs (v, t, m, b, p), headphone jack, simulated brown leather covering with gold accents, brown speaker grille, mfg. 2004-present.

MSR $100	$80	$50 - 60	$25 - 30	

DA30-4 – 30W, 4-5 in. speakers, solid-state acoustic guitar chassis, two channels (guitar, mic), reverb, front gold control panel, three inputs (two guitar, one XLR mic), six black knobs (guitar level, mic level, t, m, b, r), headphone jack, simulated brown leather covering with gold accents, brown speaker grille split into four sections, mfg. 2000-08.

	$200	$130 - 160	$80 - 100	$320

DA25C – 25W, solid-state acoustic guitar chassis, dual channel, chorus, top brown control panel, one input, seven black knobs, headphone jack, simulated brown leather covering with gold accents, brown speaker grille, top handle, current mfg.

MSR $211	$150	$100 - 115	$50 - 60	

DEAN MARKLEY

Amplifiers currently produced in Asia. Previously produced in the U.S. during the 1980s. Distributed by Dean Markley Strings, Inc. in Santa Clara, CA.

Dean Markley is most known for their strings, pickups, and various other accessories. In 1983, they introduced their first amplifiers with several more lines coming out in the mid-1980s. The K-Series became very popular among student guitarists, however they did produce a line of all-tube amplifiers. They discontinued their entire line of amplifiers in the 1990s, but they currently offer mini-practice amps that run on 12-volt batteries. Many schematics and user manuals are posted on their website. For more information, visit Dean's website or contact them directly.

CONTACT INFORMATION
DEAN MARKLEY
3350 Scott Blvd. Ste #45
Santa Clara, CA 95054 USA
Phone No.: 408-988-2456
Phone No.: 800-800-1008
Fax No.: 408-988-0441
www.deanmarkley.com
info@deanmarkley.com

ELECTRIC SS AMPLIFIERS: K SERIES

DMC-40 – 50W (2 X 25W stereo), 2-8 in. speakers, solid-state chassis, two channels, chorus, front black control panel, two inputs, nine knobs (OD: g, level, Clean: v, t, m, b, r, Chorus: speed, depth), line in/out, footswitch jack, headphone jack, effects loop, Drive Voicing Module, black covering, black grille, 37 lbs., mfg. 1990s.

	N/A	$120 - 150	$80 - 100	

MSR/NOTES	100%	EXCELLENT	AVERAGE	LAST MSR

DMC-80 – 100W (2 X 50W stereo), 2-10 in. speakers, solid-state chassis, two channels, chorus, front black control panel, two inputs, nine knobs (OD: g, level, Clean: v, t, m, b, r, Chorus: speed, depth), line in/out, footswitch jack, headphone jack, effects loop, Drive Voicing Module, black covering, black grille, 52 lbs., mfg. 1990s.

| | N/A | $150 - 200 | $100 - 120 | |

K15 – 10W, 1-6.5 in. speaker, solid-state chassis, front black control panel, single input, three black knobs (v, t, b), headphone jack, yellow or black covering, black grille, mfg. 1980s-1990s.

| | N/A | $40 - 60 | $20 - 30 | |

K15-X – 9W, 1-6 in. speaker, solid-state chassis, front black control panel, single input, four black knobs (g, level, t, b), headphone jack, black covering, black grille, mfg. 1990s.

| | N/A | $45 - 65 | $25 - 35 | |

K20 – 15W, 1-8 in. speaker, solid-state chassis, front black control panel, five black knobs (v, MV, t, m, b), single input, yellow or black covering, black grille, mfg. 1980s-1990s.

courtesy Kaler Hendricks   courtesy Kaler Hendricks

| | N/A | $50 - 75 | $30 - 40 | |

K20-X – 10W, 1-8 in. speaker, solid-state chassis, two channels, front black control panel, six black knobs (OD: g, level, Clean: v, t, m, b), single input, black covering, black grille, 13 lbs., mfg. 1990s.

| | N/A | $60 - 85 | $35 - 50 | |

K20-B – 25W, 1-8 in. speaker, bass application, solid-state chassis, front black control panel, single input, four black knobs (v, t, m, b), line out, headphone jack, yellow or black covering, black grille, mfg. 1980s-1990s.

| | N/A | $70 - 90 | $40 - 60 | |

K20-BX – 27W, 1-8 in. speaker, solid-state chassis, single channel, front black control panel, single input, five black knobs (g, b, m/h, m/l, t), black covering, black grille, 13 lbs., mfg. 1990s.

| | N/A | $75 - 100 | $50 - 65 | |

K30-RX – 17W, 1-10 in. speaker, solid-state chassis, two channels, front black control panel, single input, seven black knobs (OD: g, level, Clean: v, t, m, b, r), black covering, black grille, 15 lbs., mfg. 1990s.

| | N/A | $80 - 100 | $40 - 60 | |

K50 – 35W, 1-10 in. speaker, solid-state chassis, front black control panel, two channels, reverb, single input, seven black knobs (drive, v2, v1, t, m, b, r), line out/in, headphone jack, footswitch jack, yellow or black covering, black grille, mfg. 1980s-1990s.

 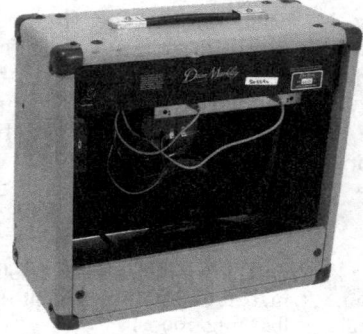

courtesy John Beeson/The Music Shoppe   courtesy John Beeson/The Music Shoppe

| | N/A | $100 - 120 | $60 - 80 | |

MSR/NOTES	100%	EXCELLENT	AVERAGE	LAST MSR

K65 – 50W, 1-10 in. speaker, solid-state chassis, front black control panel, two channels, reverb, single input, seven black knobs (drive, v2, v1, t, m, b, r), line out/in, headphone jack, footswitch jack, yellow or black covering, black grille, mfg. 1980s-1990s.

	N/A	$110 - 130	$70 - 85	

K75 – 50W, 1-12 in. speaker, solid-state chassis, front black control panel, two channels, reverb, single input, seven black knobs (drive, v2, v1, t, m, b, r), line out/in, headphone jack, footswitch jack, yellow or black covering, black grille, mfg. 1980s-1990s.

	N/A	$125 - 150	$80 - 100	

K100-B – 50W, 1-10 in. speaker, bass application, solid-state chassis, front black control panel, two channels, reverb, single input, five black knobs (v, t, m, mid shift, b), line out/in, headphone jack, footswitch jack, yellow or black covering, black grille, 36 lbs., mfg. 1980s-1990s.

	N/A	$100 - 125	$60 - 80	

K150 – 100W, 1-12 in. speaker, solid-state chassis, front black control panel, two channels, reverb, single input, seven black knobs (drive, v2, v1, t, m, b, r), line out/in, headphone jack, footswitch jack, yellow or black covering, black grille, mfg. 1980s-1990s.

	N/A	$125 - 150	$80 - 100	

K200-B – 100W, 1-12 in. speaker, bass application, solid-state chassis, front black control panel, one channel, compressor, single input, five black knobs (v, t, m, mid shift, b), line out/in, headphone jack, footswitch jack, yellow or black covering, black grille, 44 lbs., mfg. 1980s-1990s.

	N/A	$120 - 150	$80 - 100	

K300-B – 150W, 1-15 in. speaker, bass application, solid-state chassis, front black control panel, one channel, compressor, single input, five black knobs (v, t, m, mid shift, b), nine-band EQ, line out/in, headphone jack, footswitch jack, yellow or black covering, black grille, 60 lbs., mfg. 1980s-1990s.

	N/A	$120 - 150	$80 - 100	

ELECTRIC SS AMPLIFIERS: SIGNATURE SERIES

All of these amplifiers are available in rack-mount configuration.

SR30/40 SR – 30W (early models, SR30) or 40W, 1-12 in. speaker combo, hybrid chassis (tube preamp, solid-state power section), single channel, front black control panel, single input, eight black knobs (v, MV, drive, b, m, t, p, r), effects loop, preamp out, power amp in, yellow or cream color covering, black grille, mfg. 1983-mid-1980s.

	N/A	$120 - 150	$80 - 100	

80 SR – 80W, 1-12 in. speaker combo, hybrid chassis (tube preamp, solid-state power section), single channel, front black control panel, single input, eight black knobs (v, MV, drive, b, m, t, p, r), effects loop, preamp out, power amp in, yellow or cream color covering, black grille, mfg. 1983-mid-1980s.

	N/A	$150 - 180	$100 - 125	

40 DR – 40W, 1-12 in. speaker combo, hybrid chassis (tube preamp, solid-state power section), two channels, reverb, front black control panel, single input, 14 black knobs (v, MV, b, m, t, p, r for each channel), effects loop, preamp out, power amp in, yellow or cream color covering, black grille, 46 lbs., mfg. 1983-mid-1980s.

	N/A	$150 - 200	$100 - 125	

80 DR – 80W, 1-12 in. speaker combo, hybrid chassis (tube preamp, solid-state power section), two channels, reverb, front black control panel, single input, 14 black knobs (v, MV, b, m, t, p, r for each channel), effects loop, preamp out, power amp in, yellow or cream color covering, black grille, 50 lbs., mfg. 1983-mid-1980s.

	N/A	$175 - 225	$120 - 150	

150 DR – 150W, 1-12 in. speaker combo, hybrid chassis (tube preamp, solid-state power section), two channels, reverb, front black control panel, single input, 14 black knobs (v, MV, b, m, t, p, r for each channel), effects loop, preamp out, power amp in, yellow or cream color covering, black grille, 54 lbs., mfg. 1983-mid-1980s.

	N/A	$200 - 250	$140 - 170	

ELECTRIC SS AMPLIFIERS: SPECTRA SERIES

SPECTRA 80A – 15W, 1-8 in. speaker, solid-state combo, single channel, front black control panel, two inputs, five black knobs (v, t, m, b, MV), overdrive switch, effects loop, line in/line out, headphone jack, black covering, black grille, 17 lbs., mfg. 1983-mid-1980s.

	N/A	$40 - 60	$25 - 35	

SPECTRA 110A – 20W, 1-10 in. speaker, solid-state combo, single channel, front black control panel, two inputs, five black knobs (v, t, m, b, MV), overdrive switch, effects loop, line in/line out, headphone jack, black covering, black grille, 24 lbs., mfg. 1983-mid-1980s.

	N/A	$60 - 80	$40 - 50	

SPECTRA 112A – 20W, 1-12 in. speaker, solid-state combo, single channel, reverb, front black control panel, two inputs, six black knobs (v, t, m, b, MV, r), overdrive switch, effects loop, line in/line out, headphone jack, black covering, black grille, 26 lbs., mfg. 1983-mid-1980s.

	N/A	$80 - 100	$50 - 70	

MSR/NOTES	100%	EXCELLENT	AVERAGE	LAST MSR

SPECTRA 122A – 30W, 1-12 in. speaker, solid-state combo, single channel, reverb, front black control panel, two inputs, six black knobs (v, t, m, b, MV, r), overdrive switch, effects loop, line in/line out, headphone jack, black covering, black grille, 28 lbs., mfg. 1983-mid-1980s.

	N/A	$80 - 100	$40 - 60	

SPECTRA 125A – 75W, 1-12 in. speaker, solid-state combo, single channel, reverb, front black control panel, two inputs, nine black knobs (drive level, v, t, m, b, p, r, MV), overdrive switch, effects loop, line in/line out, headphone jack, footswitch included, black covering, black grille, 47 lbs., mfg. 1983-mid-1980s.

	N/A	$100 - 120	$60 - 80	

SPECTRA 180A – 130W, 1-12 in. speaker, solid-state combo, single channel, reverb, chorus, front black control panel, two inputs, 11 black knobs (drive, level, v, t, m, b, p, MV, chorus rate, chorus intensity, r), overdrive switch, effects loop, line in/line out, headphone jack, footswitch included, black covering, black grille, 54 lbs., mfg. 1983-mid-1980s.

	N/A	$120 - 150	$80 - 100	

SPECTRA 210A – 85W, 2-10 in. speakers, solid-state combo, two channels, reverb, chorus, front black control panel, two inputs, 16 black knobs (Ch. 1: v, t, m, b, MV, Ch. 2: drive, level, v, t, m, b, p, MV, chorus rate, chorus intensity, r), overdrive switch, effects loop, line in/line out, headphone jack, footswitch included, black covering, black grille, 48 lbs., mfg. 1983-mid-1980s.

	N/A	$125 - 150	$80 - 100	

SPECTRA 225A – 160W, 2-12 in. speakers, solid-state combo, two channels, reverb, chorus, front black control panel, two inputs, 16 black knobs (Ch. 1: v, t, m, b, MV, Ch. 2: drive, level, v, t, m, b, p, MV, chorus rate, chorus intensity, r), overdrive switch, effects loop, line in/line out, headphone jack, footswitch included, black covering, black grille, 77 lbs., mfg. 1983-mid-1980s.

	N/A	$125 - 150	$80 - 100	

SPECTRA 515S – 150W, 1-15 in. speaker, solid-state combo, single channel, reverb, front black control panel, two inputs, nine black knobs (v, p, t, m, midshift, b, r, MV, crossover), black covering, black grille, special order only, mfg. 1983-mid-1980s.

	N/A	$100 - 125	$60 - 80	

This model was designed for use with keyboards, steel guitars, drum machines, or any other kind of instrument that requires high clarity.

ELECTRIC TUBE AMPLIFIERS: SIGNATURE SERIES

CD30 – 40W, 1-12 in. speaker combo, tube chassis, two channels, reverb, front black control panel, various knobs and controls, yellow (early) or black (later) covering, black grille, 52 lbs., mfg. 1984-mid-1980s.

	N/A	$125 - 150	$80 - 100	

CD60 – 60W, 1-12 in. speaker combo, tube chassis, two channels, reverb, front black control panel, various knobs and controls, yellow (early) or black (later) covering, black grille, 57 lbs., mfg. 1984-mid-1980s.

	N/A	$150 - 200	$100 - 125	

CD120 – 120W, 1-12 in. speaker combo, tube chassis, two channels, reverb, front black control panel, various knobs and controls, yellow (early) or black (later) covering, black grille, 60 lbs., mfg. 1984-mid-1980s.

	N/A	$175 - 225	$120 - 150	

CD212 – 120W, 2-12 in. speakers, tube chassis, front black control panel, two inputs, various knobs and controls, wheel casters, yellow or black covering, black grille, mfg. 1984-mid-1980s.

courtesy Dave Rogers/Dave's Guitar Shop

courtesy Dave Rogers/Dave's Guitar Shop

	N/A	$200 - 250	$100 - 150	

T-60 HEAD – 50W, cabinet or rack-mounted configuration, tube chassis, single channel, front black control panel, single input, six black knobs (pre g, MV, b, m, t, p), effects loop, preamp out, power amp in, multiple speaker outputs, yellow cabinet or black casing (rack-mount), 32 lbs., mfg. 1983-mid-1980s.

	N/A	$100 - 125	$60 - 80	

MSR/NOTES	100%	EXCELLENT	AVERAGE	LAST MSR

* **T-60R Head Reverb** – similar to the T-60 Head, except has a reverb circuit with reverb control (seven knobs) 33 lbs., mfg. 1983-mid-1980s.

| | N/A | $150 - 180 | $100 - 125 | |

T-120 HEAD – 100W, cabinet or rack-mounted configuration, tube chassis, single channel, front black control panel, single input, six black knobs (pre g, MV, b, m, t, p), effects loop, preamp out, power amp in, multiple speaker outputs, yellow cabinet or black casing (rack-mount), 36 lbs., mfg. 1983-mid-1980s.

| | N/A | $150 - 200 | $100 - 125 | |

* **T-120R Head Reverb** – similar to the T-120 Head, except has a reverb circuit with reverb control (seven knobs) 37 lbs., mfg. 1983-mid-1980s.

| | N/A | $175 - 225 | $125 - 150 | |

ELECTRIC TUBE AMPLIFIERS: SPECTRA SERIES

SPECTRA 30-T – 30W, 1-12 in. speaker combo, tube chassis, single channel, reverb, front black control panel, two inputs, nine knobs (v, t, m, b, MV, lead g, lead master, r, p), effects loop, extension speaker jack, cream vinyl, black grille, 33 lbs., mfg. 1984-mid-1980s.

| | N/A | $120 - 150 | $80 - 100 | |

SPECTRA H60-T HEAD – 60W, head-unit configuration, tube chassis, single channel, reverb, front black control panel, two inputs, nine knobs (v, t, m, b, MV, lead g, lead master, r, p), effects loop, extension speaker jack, cream vinyl, black grille, mfg. 1984-mid-1980s.

| | N/A | $125 - 175 | $80 - 100 | |

* **Spectra 60-T Combo** – similar to the Spectra H60-T Head, except in combo configuration with 1-12 in. speaker, mfg. 1984-mid-1980s.

| | N/A | $150 - 180 | $100 - 120 | |

SPECTRA H120-T HEAD – 60W, head-unit configuration, tube chassis, single channel, reverb, front black control panel, two inputs, nine knobs (v, t, m, b, MV, lead g, lead master, r, p), effects loop, extension speaker jack, cream vinyl, black grille, mfg. 1984-mid-1980s.

| | N/A | $175 - 225 | $120 - 150 | |

* **Spectra 120-T Combo** – similar to the Spectra H120-T Head, except in combo configuration with 1-12 in. speaker, mfg. 1984-mid-1980s.

| | N/A | $200 - 250 | $125 - 150 | |

SPECTRA 212-T COMBO – similar to the Spectra H120-T Head, except in combo configuration with 2-12 in. speakers and two independent channels, mfg. 1984-mid-1980s.

| | N/A | $200 - 250 | $125 - 150 | |

DEARMOND

Amplifiers previously produced in Toledo, OH during the late 1950s and early 1960s. Previously distributed by Rowe Industries.

DeArmond was well-known by their stringed instrument pickups by the 1950s, and they decided to expand their line with a series or amplifiers that were built by Rowe Instruries, in Toledo, OH. DeArmond amps were not highly powerful (typically less than 10W), but they were built with quality components, have Jensen speakers, and are highly regarded as an early high-end boutique amp to many collectors/players. Configurations exist in a 1-10 in. combo (R5, R5T), a 1-12 in. combo (R15, R15T), a 1-15 in. combo, and a 2-10 in. combo (R25T). The R5 1-10 in. combo appears to be the most popular. Unlike many other cheaper amps at the time (Supro, Kay, Harmony, etc.), DeArmond's were not cheap. An advertisement from circa 1961 lists prices at $100 for the R5 to $275 for the R25T! It is unknown when they stopped producing amps during the heyday of the guitar boom, but a majority of examples found were produced in either 1959 or 1960. Rowe also built amplifiers for Martin with a C.F. Martin & Co. logo on the front, that were identical in design to the DeArmonds. Jeff Krumm and Savage Audio designed their Macht 6 and Macht 12 amplifiers on the original DeArmond chassis. Any additional information can be submitted directly to Blue Book Publications. Initial information courtesy: *The Tonequest Report*, July 2004.

ELECTRIC TUBE AMPLIFIERS

MODEL R5 – ~5W, 1-10 in. speaker combo, tube chassis, preamp: 12AX7, power: 6V6, rectifier: 6X4, single channel, top control panel, two inputs, two knobs (v, tone), copper covering, brown slanted grille, mfg. circa 1959-1962.

| | N/A | $600 - 700 | $375 - 450 | |

* **Model R5T** – similar to the Model R5, except has a tremolo circuit with an additional 12AX7 preamp tube, four knobs (v, tone, tremolo depth, tremolo rate), and a footswitch, mfg. circa 1959-1962.

| | N/A | $725 - 850 | $475 - 550 | |

MODEL R15 – ~15W, 1-12 in. speaker combo, tube chassis, preamp: 2 X 12AX7, power: 2 X 6V6, rectifier: 5Y3, two channels, top control panel, four inputs, three knobs (tone, Ch. 1 v, Ch. 2 v), external speaker jack, copper covering, brown slanted grille, mfg. circa 1959-1962.

| | N/A | $625 - 750 | $400 - 475 | |

* **Model R15T** – similar to the Model R15, except has a tremolo circuit with an additional 12AX7 preamp tube, five knobs (tremolo depth, tremolo rate, tone, Ch. 1 v, Ch. 2 v), and a footswitch, mfg. circa 1959-1962.

| | N/A | $750 - 900 | $500 - 600 | |

MSR/NOTES	100%	EXCELLENT	AVERAGE	LAST MSR

MODEL R25T – ~25W, 2-12 in. Jensen speaker combo, tube chassis, preamp: 3 X 12AX7, power: 2 X 6L6GC, rectifier: 5AR4/GZ34, two channels, tremolo, top control panel, four inputs, six knobs (tremolo rate, tremolo depth, b, t, Ch. 1 v, Ch. 2 v), external speaker jack, copper covering, brown slanted grille, footswitch, mfg. circa 1959-1962.

	N/A	$800 - 1,000	$550 - 650	

DECCA

Amplifiers previously produced in Japan during the 1960s. Distributed by Decca Records.

Decca imported a line of amplifiers from Japan that were built by Teisco in the 1960s. Most models were small and designed for the student/entry-level player, but they produced at least one tube amplifier. Any further information can be submitted directly to Blue Book Publications. Initial information courtesy: Michael Wright, *Guitar Stories*, Volume One.

DEMETER

A.KA. Innovative Audio Systems from 1980 to 1989. Amplifiers currently produced in Templeton, CA, since 2006. Previously produced in Van Nuys, CA from 1980 to 2005. Distributed by Demeter.

CONTACT INFORMATION
DEMETER
6990 Kingsbury Road
Templeton, CA 93465 USA
Phone No.: 805-461-4100
Fax No.: 805-267-4079
www.demeteramps.com
sales@demeteramps.com

The roots of Demeter date back to 1980 when John Demeter, Rob Robinetter, and Phil Van Allen designed their first FET direct box. They started the company called Innovative Audio Systems and continued to produce different audio products. In 1990, the company was renamed Demeter Amplification, and more guitar related amplifiers started to surface in the early 1990s. Now in the 21st century, Demeter has a full range of products which include guitar combo amps, power amps, preamps, and other audio effects. For more information, visit Demeter's website or contact them directly.

ELECTRIC TUBE AMPLIFIERS

The **TGA-3** was Demeter's first amplifier that was introduced around 1985 and included features such as three channels and a stereo effects loop. This amp lasted into the 1990s.

Demeter replaced the TGA-3 amplifier with the TGA-2 series of amplifiers in the 1990s. The TGA-2 had many features of the TGA-3, except only two discreet channels are available. These amps were available in six different combinations including the choice between 50 and 100 Watt power outage and as a head unit, or a 1-12 inch or 2-12 inch combo. The TGA-2 Series of amplifiers were discontinued in 2004 and last retail prices for these amps are as follows: **TGA2-T50** - $1,799, the **TGA2-T100** - $1,999, the **TGA2-C50-112** $1,999, the **TGA2-C50-212** - unknown, the **TGA2-100-112** - $2,299, the **TGA2-100-212** - $2,499. In 2005, the TGA-2 series was replaced with the TGA-2.1 Series. Demeter's speaker cabinets include the **GSC-212** (MSR $949/selling price of $800) with 2-12 in. Eminence speakers, and the **GSC-412** (last MSR was $999) with 4-12 in. Eminence speakers.

TGA2.1-T50 HEAD – 50W, guitar head-unit, six-tube chassis, preamp: 4 X 12AX7A, power: 2 X 5881, solid-state rectifier, two channels, front black control panel, single input, 11 knobs (Ch. 1: clean gain with push/pull bright switch, MV, Ch. 2: edge gain with push/pull boost switch, solo gain, MV, All: t, m, b, p, effects send, effects return), channel switch, power switch, standby switch, rear panel: footswitch jack, effects loop, pentode/triode switch, three speaker jacks, black covering with white piping, mfg. 2005-present.

courtesy Demeter

MSR $2,399	$2,050	$1,450 - 1,675	$1,025 - 1,200

* **TGA2.1-T50C-112 Combo** – similar to the TGA2.1-T50 Head, except in combo configuration with 1-12 in. Eminence speaker, black covering, gray grille with white piping, mfg. 2005-present.

MSR $2,549	$2,150	$1,525 - 1,775	$1,075 - 1,275

* **TGA2.1-T50C-210 Combo** – similar to the TGA2.1-T50 Head, except in combo configuration with 2-10 in. Eminence speakers, black covering, gray grille with white piping, mfg. 2005-present.

MSR $2,599	$2,200	$1,550 - 1,850	$1,100 - 1,300

MSR/NOTES	100%	EXCELLENT	AVERAGE	LAST MSR

TGA2.1-T100 HEAD – 100W, guitar head-unit, eight-tube chassis, preamp: 4 X 12AX7A, power: 4 X 5881, solid-state rectifier, two channels, front black control panel, single input, 11 knobs (Ch. 1: clean gain with push/pull bright switch, MV, Ch. 2: edge gain with push/pull boost switch, solo gain, MV, All: t, m, b, p, effects send, effects return), channel switch, power switch, standby switch, rear panel: footswitch jack, effects loop, pentode/triode switch, three speaker jacks, black covering with white piping, mfg. 2005-present.

| MSR $2,599 | $2,200 | $1,550 - 1,850 | $1,100 - 1,300 | |

* ***TGA2.1-T100C-112 Combo*** – similar to the TGA2.1-T100 Head, except in combo configuration with 1-12 in. Eminence speaker, black covering, gray grille with white piping, mfg. 2005-present.

| MSR $2,749 | $2,350 | $1,650 - 1,925 | $1,175 - 1,375 | |

* ***TGA2.1-T100C-210 Combo*** – similar to the TGA2.1-T100 Head, except in combo configuration with 2-10 in. Eminence speakers, black covering, gray grille with white piping, mfg. 2005-present.

| MSR $2,799 | $2,400 | $1,675 - 1,975 | $1,200 - 1,400 | |

DIAMOND AMPLIFICATION

Amplifiers and speaker cabinets currently produced in Houston, TX. Distributed by Diamond Amplification.

CONTACT INFORMATION
DIAMOND AMPLIFICATION
8637 Windfern Rd.
Houston, TX 77064
Phone No.: 713-934-0100
Fax No.: 713-934-0155
www.diamondamplification.com
sales@diamondamplification.com

Jeff Diamant started Diamond Amplification, based in Houston, TX. The first Diamond amps were designed by Diamant and Martin Golub at Custom Audio Electronics. Diamond is a boutique builder that produces tube amp heads and speaker cabinets. They focus on a small number of products so they can concentrate on testing each model thoroughly. Diamond offers a variety of guitar amp head-units and speaker cabinets. Recently, Diamant has collaborated with Roy Blankenship of Blankenship Amplifiers to produce a few lower wattage models. For more information, visit Diamond Amplification's website or contact them directly.

ELECTRIC TUBE AMPS/SPEAKER CABINETS

The **Spec Op** (MSR $3,999) is Diamond's flagship amplifier with 100W power, 2.5 channels, and EL34 power tubes. Matching Spec Op speaker cabinets include the **Spec Op 2 x 12 Cab** (MSR $999) has 2-12 in. Celestion Vintage 30 speakers and the **Spec Op 4 x 12 Cab** (MSR $1,499) has 4-12 in. Celestion Vintage 30 speakers. The **Decada** (MSR $4,199) was introduced in 2009 and is an updated and refined version of the Spec Op. Matching Decada speaker cabinets include the **Decada 2 x 12 Cab** (MSR $999) with 2-12 in. Celestion Vintage 30 speakers and the **Decada 4 x 12 Cab** (MSR $1,399) with 4-12 in. Celestion Vintage 30 speakers. The **Spitfire** (MSR $2,449) has 100W, 1.5 channels with a clean channel and dual volume/gain controls, and is powered by EL34 tubes. The **Spitfire II** (MSR $3,599) is similar to the Spitfire, except has two independent channels. Matching Spitfire speaker cabinets include the **Spitfire 2 x 12 Cab** (MSR $999) with 2-12 in. Celestion Vintage 30 speakers and the **Spitfire 4 x 12 Cab** (MSR $1,399) with 4-12 in. Celestion Vintage 30 speakers. The Spitfire was also available as a combo unit (disc. 2008, last MSR was $2,499) with 2-12 in. Celestion Vintage 30 speakers. The **Phantom** (MSR $3,499) is a 100W head voiced to a more traditional high gain sound with more saturation and driven by EL34 power tubes. The matching Phantom speaker cabinet includes the **Phantom 4 x 12 Cab** (MSR $1,399) with 4-12 in. Celestion Vintage 30 speakers. The **Nitrox** (MSR $2,799) is Diamond's most high-gain head with 100W output, two channels, and powered by EL34 tubes. The matching Nitrox speaker cabinet includes the **Nitrox 4 x 12 Cab** (MSR $1,349) with 4-12 in. Celestion Vintage 30 speakers. The **Immortal** (MSR $1,999) is a 50W head that was developed with Roy Blankenship and driven by EL34 power tubes. The **Del Fuego** (MSR $1,699) is a 22W class A amp that was also developed with Blankenship and is available in black or snakeskin Tolex covering. The Del Fuego is also offered as a 1-12 in. combo (MSR $1,949) and a 2-12 in. combo (MSR $2,149). The **Balinese** (MSR $1,599) is a small combo amp that has various power settings depending on the use of 6L6 or 6V6 tubes. The Balinese R15 (MSR $2,299) is similar to the Balinese, but has the addition of reverb. Diamond also offers a 1-12 in. speaker cabinet (MSR $699) or a 2-12 in. speaker cabinet (MSR $999).

DIAZ

Amplifiers previously produced in California between the early 1980s and 2002.

Cesar Diaz was a native of Puerto Rico, and he was involved in the music business since he was six years old. He came to the United States with Johnny Nash in 1969 where he became one of the best "amp doctors" for many musicians including Stevie Ray Vaughan, Eric Clapton, and Keith Richards. He was also the amp technician for Bob Dylan (Dylan's guitarist G.E. Smith, who was Diaz's long-time friend), and later the guitar player in Dylan's band. Cesar left Dylan in 1993 to concentrate on making Diaz amps. Diaz amplifiers were hand-built tube amplifiers previously made by Cesar Diaz himself. Several musicians who own and use Diaz amps include Billy Gibbons, Jimmy Vivino, R.E.M., Collective Soul, and Joan Osborne. Diaz also produced effects pedals including a tremolo device called the Tremodillo. Cesar Diaz passed away on April 26, 2002. In late 2002, Diaz Musical Products began producing amplifiers and pedals again and they are currently offering a full line of gear.

ELECTRIC TUBE AMPLIFIERS

Diaz built a number of different tube amplifiers over the years, some which may not be listed here. The **Vibramaster** (last MSR $1,500) is a tremolo and reverb unit only, which means it doesn't have an internal power amplifier. The **P-XX** (last MSR $2,500) is a 20W amp that can serve as a practice amp as well as a performer. The **CD-30** (last MSR $3,500) is an amp that has 35W of output. The **Classic Twin** (last MSR $4,500) is a 100W performer amp. The top of the line model was the **CD-100** (last MSR $5,000). Most of Diaz's amplifiers were available as combos or head-units and extension speaker cabinets were also available.

DICKERSON

Amplifiers previously produced in the U.S. during the late 1930s and early 1940s.

The Dickerson brand was developed by the Dickerson brothers in 1937 and they originally produced electric lap steels with matching amplifiers. These amps were very similar to Oahu models of the same era, and there is speculation as to whether they were built by the same company. In 1947, Dickerson was sold to what would become Magnatone. Dickerson amps are typically low-wattage all-tube amps with small speakers, and limited controls. Any further information can be submitted directly to Blue Book Publications.

DIEZEL

CONTACT INFORMATION
DIEZEL
Donaustrasse 5 1/2
Dillingen, 89407 Germany
Phone No.: +49 (0) 9071 718 80
Fax No.: +49 (0) 9071 728 656
www.diezelamplification.com
usa@diezelamplification.com

Amplifiers currently produced in Munich, Germany since 1993.

In the 1980s, Peter Diezel began modifying Marshall amps and he met Peter Stapfer, who was a pro-musician. They came together to form Diezel Amplification in 1993. In 1994, the first VH4 was introduced. In 2002, the Herbert was introduced. In 2003, Diezel moved from Munich to Bad Steban (Bavaria). In 2005, the Einstein model (named after Diezel's dog) was introduced, and they started production on a bassamp model called Lucy. In 2006, they started work on a Class A model called the Schmidt. They offer all-tube amplifier heads and combos, as well as speaker cabinets. Diezel amplifiers were distributed in the U.S. by Salwender and later by Diezel USA, LLC in Dawsonville, GA. In 2009, Diezel started their own distribution in the U.S. under Diezel USA, LLC, but they are setting up a network of dealers in the U.S. to ship amplifiers directly to them. For more information, visit Diezel's website or contact them directly.

ELECTRIC TUBE AMPLIFIERS

The **VH4** (MSR $4,399) is a mono amplifier with 90 or 160W output. There are four channels with bass, mid, treble, and volume in each. The Chassis consists of an all-tube circuit, and in the 4-tube power section, there are several different tubes that can be used including EL34s, 6L6s, and 5881s among others. The **VH4S** (MSR $4,699) is the same in set-up as the VH4 except in a stereo version. This amp puts out 45W per side and a total combination of 80W. The **Herbert** (MSR $4,299) was introduced in 2002, and is a 180W head with three distinctive channels. The **Einstein** was introduced in 2005 and is available as a 50W head (MSR $2,999), 100W head (MSR $3,199), or a 1-12 in. combo (MSR $3,299). The Einstein features two channels.

The **V112** speaker cabinet (MSR $550) has 1-12 in. speaker and is available with an open back or closed back version. The **V212** speaker cabinet (MSR $995) has 2-12 in. speakers and is available in front- or rear-loaded versions. The **V412** speaker cabinet (MSR $1,299) has 4-12 in. speakers and is available in front-, rear-, or NYC rear-loaded versions.

DINOSAUR

Amplifiers and other products previously produced in China. Distributed by Eleca International Inc. in Walnut, CA.

Dinosaur amplifiers are built overseas in China and sold throughout the United States and many other countries. Dinosaur builds tube and solid-state amplifiers at a competitive price. They also offer guitars, pedals, effects, and a number of accessories.

ELECTRIC TUBE AMPLIFIERS

Dinosaur offered two tube amplifiers. The **DG-30VR** (disc.) is a 30W amp with an 8 in. speaker and a tube chassis that consists of 1 X 12AX7 & 1 X 6F2 for preamp and 2 X 6V6GT for power. There is a simple three band equalizer. The **DG-60VR** (disc.) is a 60W unit with a 10 in. speaker, and a tube chassis of: 3 X 12AX7 preamp, 2 X 6L6GC power. This amp has more features such as gain, reverb, and presence added to the three band EQ. These amps are covered in an attractive wood covering, with a gold control panel, and a black grille.

ELECTRIC SOLID-STATE AMPLIFIERS

Dinosaur had several models in the solid-state genre. The **DG-Series** are guitar amps that come in all varieties of sizes and wattages. Models range from the DG-10 (10W, 1-6 in. speaker, Last MSR $60) to the DG-200R (200W, 1-12 in. speaker, two channels, Last MSR $600). The **DB-Series** features several models as well. Models range from the DB-15 (20W, 1-5 in. speaker, Last MSR $114) to the DB-100 (100W, 1-15 in. speaker, Last MSR $342). There are also Stereo Chorus Amps, Guitar Effect Amps, and Lead Amplifiers.

DIVIDED BY THIRTEEN

Amplifiers currently produced in Southern California. Distributed by Divided by Thirteen.

CONTACT INFORMATION
DIVIDED BY THIRTEEN
437 W. 6th Street
San Pedro, CA 90731
Phone No.: 949-631-1330
Fax No.: 310-519-1300
www.dividedby13.com
info@dividedby13.com

Fredric Taccone describes himself as being a gearhead all his life. He has been playing guitar since he was 12, and during school, he worked for Risson Amplifiers building power amps. Taccone toured the Los Angeles area for many years repairing many amplifiers. After talking to a few people who requested their amplifier perform a certain way, Taccone decided to start building his own models that could fulfill the void many other amps left. All of his amps are of tube design and are hand-built one at a time. He has built amps for many people, including Billy Gibbons of ZZ Top. For more information, visit Divided By Thirteen's website or contact them directly.

MSR/NOTES	100%	EXCELLENT	AVERAGE	LAST MSR

DR. BASS

Amplifiers and speaker cabinets currently produced in Myrtle Beach, SC.

Marc and Tony Serio build high-quality durable bass speaker cabinets in Myrtle Beach, SC. All cabinets are sprayed with a Pure Polyurea coating that is also used on the decks of submarines making it a very durable substance, and grilles are constructed from 18 gauge steel. Dr. Bass offers a variety of cabinets with different speakers and configurations. For more information, visit Dr. Bass's website or contact them directly.

CONTACT INFORMATION
DR. BASS
4517 Thomas St. #145
Myrtle Beach, SC 29588
Phone No.: 843-467-6896
Fax No.: 843-580-9257
www.drbasscabs.com
drbass@drbasscabs.com

DRIVE

Amplifiers previously produced in Asia during the 2000s. Distributed by Switchmusic.com, Inc. in Ontario, CA.

Drive amplifiers were produced overseas and distributed in the U.S. by Switchmusic.com, Inc. They produced a wide range of guitar, bass, and keyboard amplifiers in a variety of configurations. Most Drive amps are designed for the student/entry-level guitar player with many MSRs starting below $100.

AMPLIFIERS

The Drive **DSP Series** features an on-board DSP processor that delivers a possible 250 combinations of effects and blends, and prices started at $279. The **CD Series** are mainly practice amps with basic controls and prices started at $59. The **B Series** are bass amplifiers that started at $399. The **Vintage Series** feature designs meant to sound like amps of yesterday and the cosmetics feature round speaker openings. Prices started at $69. The **EA Electric Acoustic Series** are designed for acoustic guitars and models started at $159. A Keyboard series and an Elite Guitar series were also available.

DR. Z

Amplifiers currently produced in Maple Heights, OH, since 1991. Distributed by Dr. Z.

Mike Zaite founded Dr. Z amplifiers out of his basement in 1991. All amplifiers use tube chassis and are wired point-to-point. Dr. Z has produced several different models over the years. Brad Paisley became an endorser in 2001, and Zaite has established a great relationship with him collaborating on several amplifiers including the Stang Ray and Prescription Extra Strength. Head-units, combos, and speaker cabinets are all available, and they come in Black, Blonde, or Red cabinets. For more information, visit Dr. Z's website or contact them directly.

CONTACT INFORMATION
DR. Z
17011 Broadway Ave.
Maple Heights, OH 44137
Phone No.: 216-475-1444
Fax No.: 216-475-4333
www.drzamps.com
sales@drzamps.com

ELECTRIC TUBE AMPLIFIERS: OVERVIEW

Starting December 1, 2001, all amplifiers and cabinets were available in either Black, Blonde, or Red covering.

- **Add $50 for a Celestion Heritage 65 speaker.**
- **Add $90 for an adjustable direct out.**
- **Add $90 for an effects loop (where an effects loop is a non-standard option).**
- **Add $139 for an Eminence Red Fang Alnico speaker.**
- **Add $189 for a Celestion Alnico "Blue Bell" speaker.**
- **Add $229 for a Celestion Alnico "Gold" speaker.**
- **Add $249 and up for hardwood fronts.**

ELECTRIC TUBE AMPLIFIERS: MAZ SERIES

- **Subtract 10-15% for models without reverb (all models without reverb retail for $200 less than the models listed below).**

MAZ 8 HEAD – 8W, head-unit only, all tube chassis, preamp: 4 X 12AX7, 1 X 12AT7, power: 1 X EL84, 5AR4 rectifier, single channel, reverb, front black control panel, two inputs, seven cream knobs (v, t, m, b, cut, MV, r), choice of color covering, 32 lbs., current mfg.

MSR $1,675	$1,675	$1,100 - 1,250	$550 - 675

* *MAZ 8 1-12 Combo* – 8W, 1-12 in. speaker, guitar combo, all tube chassis, preamp: 4 X 12AX7, 1 X 12AT7, power: 1 X EL84, 5AR4 rectifier, single channel, reverb, front black control panel, two inputs, seven cream knobs (v, t, m, b, cut, MV, r), choice of color covering, 60 lbs., current mfg.

MSR $1,825	$1,825	$1,175 - 1,375	$600 - 725

* *MAZ 8 2-10 Combo* – 8W, 2-10 in. speakers, guitar combo, all tube chassis, preamp: 4 X 12AX7, 1 X 12AT7, power: 1 X EL84, 5AR4 rectifier, single channel, reverb, front black control panel, two inputs, seven cream knobs (v, t, m, b, cut, MV, r), choice of color covering, 60 lbs., current mfg.

MSR $1,825	$1,825	$1,175 - 1,375	$600 - 725

MAZ-18 JUNIOR HEAD – 18W, head-unit only, all tube chassis, preamp: 4 X 12AX7, 1 X 12AT7, power: 2 X EL84, GZ34 rectifier, single channel, reverb, front black control panel, single input, seven black knobs (v, t, m, b, cut, MV, r), choice of color covering, current mfg.

MSR $1,825	$1,825	$1,175 - 1,375	$600 - 725

* *MAZ-18 Junior 1-12* – similar to the head-unit except in combo form with 1-12 in. speaker, current mfg.

MSR $2,050	$2,050	$1,325 - 1,525	$675 - 825

MSR/NOTES	100%	EXCELLENT	AVERAGE	LAST MSR

* **MAZ-18 Junior 2-10** – similar to the head-unit except in combo form with 2-10 in. speakers, current mfg.

| MSR $2,050 | $2,050 | $1,325 - 1,525 | $675 - 825 | |

* **MAZ-18 Junior 2-12** – similar to the head-unit except in combo form with 2-12 in. speakers, mfg. 2003-present.

| MSR $2,275 | $2,275 | $1,475 - 1,700 | $750 - 900 | |

MAZ-38 SENIOR – 38W, head-unit only, all tube chassis, preamp: 4 X 12AX7, 1 X 12AT7, power: 4 X EL84, GZ34 rectifier, single channel, reverb, front black control panel, single input, seven black knobs (v, t, m, b, MV, cut, r), choice of color covering, gray grille, current mfg.

| MSR $2,000 | $2,000 | $1,300 - 1,500 | $650 - 800 | |

* **MAZ-38 Senior 1-12 (Studio Deluxe)** – similar to the MAZ-38 head-unit except in combo form with 1-12 in. speaker, current mfg.

| MSR $2,250 | $2,250 | $1,450 - 1,675 | $725 - 900 | |

* **MAZ-38 Senior 2-10** – similar to the MAZ-38 head-unit except in combo form with 2-10 in. speakers, mfg. 2001-present.

| MSR $2,250 | $2,250 | $1,450 - 1,675 | $725 - 900 | |

* **MAZ-38 Senior 2-12 (Invasion)** – similar to the MAZ-38 head-unit except in combo form with 2-12 in. speakers, current mfg.

| MSR $2,450 | $2,450 | $1,600 - 1,825 | $800 - 975 | |

* **MAZ-38 Senior 3-10 (Non-Reverb, Super Z)** – similar to the MAZ-38 head-unit except in combo form with 3-10 in. speakers and no reverb, disc. 2006.

| | $1,749 | $1,175 - 1,375 | $825 - 925 | $1,749 |

ELECTRIC TUBE AMPLIFIERS: PRESCRIPTION SERIES

Prescription Head
courtesy Dave Rogers/Dave's Guitar Shop

Prescription Extra Strength Head
courtesy Dr. Z

Prescription Jr. Head
courtesy Dr. Z

PRESCRIPTION HEAD – 45W, head-unit only, all tube chassis, preamp: 3 X 12AX7, power: 4 X EL84, GZ34 rectifier, dual channels, front black control panel, four black knobs (v, t, m, b), 3-way bright switch, expand switch, footswitch boost, choice of color covering, gray grille, disc. 2004.

| | N/A | $1,000 - 1,200 | $725 - 850 | $1,499 |

* **Prescription 2-12 Combo** – similar to the Prescription head except in combo form with 2-12 in.speakers, disc. 2004.

| | N/A | $1,200 - 1,400 | $800 - 950 | $1,899 |

There is also a 1-12 combo advertised but no price was listed.

PRESCRIPTION EXTRA STRENGTH HEAD – 45W, head-unit only, all tube chassis, preamp: 2 X 12AX7, EF86, power: 4 X EL84, rectifier: 5AR4, dual channels, front black control panel, four black knobs (v, t, m, b), overdose switch, footswitch, choice of color covering, gray grille, 22 lbs., mfg. 2004-disc.

| | $1,649 | $1,075 - 1,250 | $750 - 875 | $1,649 |

This amp was designed by Mike Zaite with input from Brad Paisley. Even though this amp is named like a souped-up version of the Prescription, it contains an entirely new chassis than the old model.

* **Prescription Extra Strength 1-12 Combo** – similar to the Prescription Extra Strength Head except in combo form with 1-12 in. Celestion Alnico Gold speaker, mfg. 2007-disc.

| | $1,949 | $1,225 - 1,475 | $875 - 1,025 | $1,949 |

* **Prescription Extra Strength 2-12 Combo** – similar to the Prescription Extra Strength head except in combo form with 2-12 in. speakers, 65 lbs., mfg. 2004-disc.

| | $1,949 | $1,225 - 1,475 | $875 - 1,025 | $1,949 |

PRESCRIPTION JR. HEAD – 18W, guitar head unit, six-tube chassis, preamp: 2 X 12AX7, 1 X EF86, power: 2 X EL84, rectifier: 1 X 5Y3, single channel, front black control panel, two inputs, four knobs (v, t, m, b), power switch, standby switch, available in Black, Blonde, or Red covering, 19 in. wide, 9.75 in. tall, 9.5 in. deep, mfg. 2007-disc.

| | $1,499 | $975 - 1,125 | $675 - 800 | $1,499 |

MSR/NOTES	100%	EXCELLENT	AVERAGE	LAST MSR

* Prescription Jr. 1-12 Combo – similar to the Prescription Jr. head-unit except in combo configuration with 1-12 in. speaker, 23 in. wide, 20.125 in. tall, 10 in. deep, mfg. 2007-disc.

	$1,699	$1,100 - 1,275	$775 - 900	$1,699

ELECTRIC TUBE AMPLIFIERS: MISC. MODELS

6545 – wattage unknown, head-unit only, tube chassis, preamp: EF86, 12AX7, power: 2 X EL34, two switchable channels, front silver control panel, single input, eight black knobs (Ch. 1: t, b, v, Ch. 2: b, m, t, MV, g), black covering, 22 lbs., disc. 2006.

	$1,799	$1,150 - 1,350	$700 - 800	$1,799

This amp has two switchable channels, and the preamps for each of these channels come from other amp designs: the KT45 and the SRZ-65.

ANTIDOTE HEAD – 45W, guitar head unit, five-tube chassis, preamp: 3 X 12AX7, power: 2 X KT66, 5AR4 rectifier, two channels, front black control panel, single input, six knobs (presence, b, m, t, high v, low v), power switch, standby switch, available in Black, Blonde, or Red covering, 19 in. wide, 9.75 in. tall, 9.5 in. deep, 27 lbs., current mfg.

MSR $1,950	$1,950	$1,275 - 1,450	$625 - 775	

CARMEN GHIA HEAD – 18W, head-unit only, all-tube chassis, preamp: 5751, 12AX7, power: 2 X EL84, 5Y3 rectifier, single channel, front black control panel, single input, two white chicken head knobs (v, tone), choice of color covering, gray grille, current mfg.

MSR $1,275	$1,275	$825 - 950	$425 - 500	

* Carmen Ghia 1-10 Combo – similar to the Carmen Ghia head-unit except in combo configuration with 1-10 in. speaker, mfg. 2008-present.

MSR $1,400	$1,400	$900 - 1,050	$450 - 550	

* Carmen Ghia 1-12 Combo – similar to the Carmen Ghia head-unit except in combo configuration with 1-12 in. speaker, mfg. 2001-present.

MSR $1,500	$1,500	$975 - 1,125	$475 - 600	

* Carmen Ghia 2-10 Combo – similar to the Carmen Ghia head-unit except in combo configuration with 2-10 in. speakers, mfg. 2001-present.

MSR $1,500	$1,500	$975 - 1,125	$475 - 600	

DB4 HEAD – 38W (switchable to 18W), head-unit configuration, all-tube chassis, preamp: 1 X 12AX7, 1 X 5879, power: 4 X EL84, rectifier: 5AR4, single channel, front control panel, two inputs, three knobs (v, tone, cut), power switch, standby switch, available in Black, Blonde, or Red finish, 26 lbs., current mfg.

MSR $1,800	$1,800	$1,175 - 1,350	$575 - 725	

* DB4 1-12 Combo – 38W (switchable to 18W), 1-12 in. Celestion Alnico Gold speaker, guitar combo, all-tube chassis, preamp: 1 X 12AX7, 1 X 5879, power: 4 X EL84, rectifier: 5AR4, single channel, front control panel, two inputs, three knobs (v, tone, cut), power switch, standby switch, available in Black, Blonde, or Red finish, 42 lbs., current mfg.

MSR $2,200	$2,200	$1,425 - 1,650	$725 - 875	

* DB4 2-12 Combo – 38W (switchable to 18W), 2-12 in. Celestion Alnico Blue speakers, guitar combo, all-tube chassis, preamp: 1 X 12AX7, 1 X 5879, power: 4 X EL84, rectifier: 5AR4, single channel, front control panel, two inputs, three knobs (v, tone, cut), power switch, standby switch, available in Black, Blonde, or Red finish, 68 lbs., current mfg.

MSR $2,900	$2,900	$1,875 - 2,175	$950 - 1,150	

DELTA 88 – 88W (32W clean), head-unit only, tube chassis, preamp: 1 X EF86, power: 2 X KT66, solid-state rectifier, single channel, front control panel, single input, three knobs (v, b, t), Black, Blonde, Red, or other wood finishes, diagonal grille, 22 lbs., mfg. 2005-06.

	$1,599	$1,050 - 1,200	$750 - 850	$1,599

GALAXIE HEAD – 40W (switchable to 30W), six-tube chassis, preamp: 3 X 12AX7, power: 2 X 6L6, rectifier: 1 X 5U4, two channels, front black control panel, single input, five white knobs (v1, v2, t, b, p), back panel: accessory outlet, pentode/triode switch, line out, footswitch jack, channel select footswitch, available in Black, Blonde, or Red covering, mfg. 2007-disc.

	$1,599	$1,025 - 1,200	$725 - 850	$1,599

* Galaxie 1-12 Combo – similar to the Galaxie Head, except in combo configuration with 1-12 in. speaker and a brown grille, mfg. 2007-disc.

	$1,849	$1,200 - 1,400	$825 - 975	$1,849

* Galaxie 2-10 Combo – similar to the Galaxie Head, except in combo configuration with 2-10 in. speakers and a brown grille, mfg. 2007-disc.

	$1,849	$1,200 - 1,400	$825 - 975	$1,849

EZG-50 HEAD – 50W, guitar head unit, seven-tube chassis, preamp: 2 X 12AX7, 2 X 12AT7, power: 2 X 6L6, rectifier: 1 X GZ34, single channel, front black control panel, two inputs, seven knobs (pre v, post v, t, m, b, reverb dwell, reverb mix), power switch, standby switch, rear panel: three speaker jacks, available in Black, Blonde, or Red covering, 22.75 in. wide, 10.125 in. tall, 10 in. deep, 40 lbs., mfg. 2009-present.

MSR $2,100	$2,100	$1,375 - 1,575	$675 - 850	

MSR/NOTES	100%	EXCELLENT	AVERAGE	LAST MSR

Galaxie 2-10 Combo
courtesy Dr. Z

EZG-50 1-12 Combo
courtesy Dr. Z

JAZ 20/40 2-10
courtesy Dr. Z

* ***EZG-50 1-12 Combo*** – similar to the EZG-50 head-unit except in combo configuration with 1-12 in. speaker, mfg. 2009-present.

| MSR $2,350 | $2,350 | $1,525 - 1,750 | $775 - 950 | |

* ***EZG-50 2-10 Combo*** – similar to the EZG-50 head-unit except in combo configuration with 2-10 in. speakers, mfg. 2009-present.

| MSR $2,350 | $2,350 | $1,525 - 1,750 | $775 - 950 | |

JAZ 20/40 HEAD – 20/40W, guitar head unit, ten-tube chassis, preamp: 5 X 12AX7, 1 X 12AT7, power: 4 X 6V6, solid-state rectifier, single channel, reverb, tremolo, front black control panel, single input, eight knobs (v, t, m, b, MV, r, s, d), power switch, standby switch, rear panel: 20/40W half-power switch, three speaker jacks, footswitch jack, two-button footswitch included, available in Black, Blonde, or Red covering, mfg. 2009-disc.

| | $1,949 | $1,225 - 1,475 | $875 - 1,025 | $1,949 |

* ***JAZ 20/40 1-12 Combo*** – similar to the JAZ 20/40 head-unit except in combo configuration with 1-12 in. speaker, mfg. 2009-disc.

| | $2,199 | $1,425 - 1,650 | $975 - 1,150 | $2,199 |

* ***JAZ 20/40 2-10 Combo*** – similar to the JAZ 20/40 head-unit except in combo configuration with 2-10 in. speakers, mfg. 2009-disc.

| | $2,199 | $1,425 - 1,650 | $975 - 1,150 | $2,199 |

KT-45 – 45W, head-unit only, all-tube chassis and solid state rectifier, preamp: EF86, 12AX7, power: 2 X EL34, single channel, front black control panel, single input, three white knobs (v, b, t), choice of color covering, gray grille, disc.

| | $1,649 | $1,075 - 1,250 | $750 - 875 | $1,649 |

M12 HEAD – 12W, head-unit only, all tube chassis, preamp: 1 X EF86, 1 X 12AX7, power: 2 X EL84, 5Y3 rectifier, two channels, front black control panel, single input, three black knobs (v, t, b), channel switch, standby switch, power switch, choice of color covering, gray grille, 29 lbs., current mfg.

| MSR $1,350 | $1,350 | $875 - 1,000 | $450 - 550 | |

* ***M12 1-10 Combo*** – 12W, 1-10 in. Z10 speaker, guitar combo, all tube chassis, preamp: 1 X EF86, 1 X 12AX7, power: 2 X EL84, 5Y3 rectifier, two channels, front black control panel, single input, three black knobs (v, t, b), channel switch, standby switch, power switch, choice of color covering, gray grille, 45 lbs., current mfg.

| MSR $1,500 | $1,500 | $975 - 1,125 | $500 - 600 | |

* ***M12 1-12 Combo*** – 12W, 1-12 in. Celestion Greenback speaker, guitar combo, all tube chassis, preamp: 1 X EF86, 1 X 12AX7, power: 2 X EL84, 5Y3 rectifier, two channels, front black control panel, single input, three black knobs (v, t, b), channel switch, standby switch, power switch, choice of color covering, gray grille, 60 lbs., current mfg.

| MSR $1,600 | $1,600 | $1,050 - 1,200 | $525 - 650 | |

* ***M12 2-10 Combo*** – 12W, 2-10 in. Z10 speakers, guitar combo, all tube chassis, preamp: 1 X EF86, 1 X 12AX7, power: 2 X EL84, 5Y3 rectifier, two channels, front black control panel, single input, three black knobs (v, t, b), channel switch, standby switch, power switch, choice of color covering, gray grille, 66 lbs., current mfg.

| MSR $1,600 | $1,600 | $1,050 - 1,200 | $525 - 650 | |

MAZERATI HEAD – 30W, head-unit only, all tube chassis, preamp: 1 X 5751, 1 X 12AX7, power: 4 X EL84, 5Y3 rectifier, single channel, front black control panel, single input, two knobs (v, tone), choice of color covering, disc. 2006.

| | $1,249 | $750 - 850 | $500 - 575 | $1,249 |

* ***Mazerati 1-12 Combo*** – similar to the Mazerati Head, except in combo form with 1-12 in. speaker, mfg. 2003-06.

| | $1,499 | $950 - 1,100 | $650 - 750 | $1,499 |

* ***Mazerati 2-10 Combo*** – similar to the Mazerati Head, except in combo form with 2-10 in. speakers, mfg. 2003-06.

| | $1,499 | $950 - 1,100 | $650 - 750 | $1,499 |

* ***Mazerati 2-12 Combo*** – similar to the Mazerati Head, except in combo form with 2-12 in. speakers, mfg. 2003-06.

| | $1,699 | $1,150 - 1,350 | $800 - 900 | $1,699 |

Mini-Z Head
courtesy Dr. Z

Mona 1-10 Combo
courtesy Dr. Z

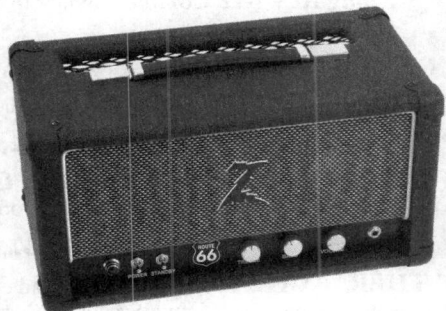

Route 66
courtesy Dave Rogers/Dave's Guitar Shop

MAZERATI GT HEAD – 38W, guitar head unit, seven-tube chassis, preamp: 2 X 12AX7, power: 4 X EL84, rectifier: 1 X 5AR4, single channel, front black control panel, single input, two knobs (v, tone), power switch, standby switch, available in Black, Blonde, or Red covering, 19 in. wide, 9.75 in. tall, 9.5 in. deep, 25 lbs., mfg. 2007-disc.

| | $1,699 | $1,100 - 1,275 | $775 - 900 | $1,699 |

MINI-Z 1-8 COMBO – 5W, 1-8 in. speaker combo, tube chassis, preamp: 1 X 12AX7M, power: 1 X EL84, single channel, front control panel, single input, volume control, black covering, brown grille, 22 lbs., mfg. 2005-06.

| | $699 | $475 - 550 | $325 - 375 | $699 |

MINI-Z HEAD – 5W, guitar head-uni, two-tube chassis, preamp: 1 X 12AX7M, power: 1 X EL84, single channel, front black control panel, single input, two knobs (v, five-position attenuator), power switch, rear panel: 8/4 ohm impedance switch, single speaker jack, available in Black, Blonde, or Red covering, 17.5 in. wide, 9 in. tall, 9.5 in. deep, mfg. 2010-present.

| MSR $850 | $850 | $550 - 625 | $275 - 350 | |

* Mini Z 1-10 Combo – similar to the Mini Z head-unit except in combo configuration with 1-10 in. speaker, 17.5 in. wide, 17 in. tall, 10 in. deep, 30 lbs., mfg. 2010-present.

| MSR $1,000 | $1,000 | $650 - 750 | $325 - 400 | |

MONZA HEAD – 20W, guitar head unit, five-tube chassis, preamp: 2 X 12AX7, power: 2 X EL84, rectifier: 1 X 5AR4, single channel, front black control panel, single input, three knobs (v, drive, tone), power switch, standby switch, rear panel: two speaker jacks, available in Black, Blonde, or Red covering, 17.5 in. wide, 9 in. tall, 9.5 in. deep, 23 lbs., mfg. 2010-present.

| MSR $1,500 | $1,500 | $975 - 1,125 | $475 - 600 | |

* Monza 1-10 Combo – similar to the Monza head-unit except in combo configuration with 1-10 in. Eminence Red Fang speaker, 17.5 in. wide, 17 in. tall, 10 in. deep, 37 lbs., mfg. 2010-present.

| MSR $1,650 | $1,650 | $1,075 - 1,225 | $525 - 650 | |

* Monza 1-12 Combo – similar to the Monza head-unit except in combo configuration with 1-12 in. speaker, 23 in. wide, 20.125 in. tall, 10 in. deep, 50 lbs., mfg. 2010-present.

| MSR $1,750 | $1,750 | $1,125 - 1,300 | $575 - 700 | |

* Monza 2-10 Combo – similar to the Monza head-unit except in combo configuration with 2-10 in. speakers, 23 in. wide, 20.125 in. tall, 10 in. deep, 54 lbs., mfg. 2010-present.

| MSR $1,750 | $1,750 | $1,125 - 1,300 | $575 - 700 | |

REMEDY HEAD – 40W, guitar head unit, seven-tube chassis, preamp: 3 X 12AX7, power: 4 X 6V6, solid-state rectifier, single channel, front black control panel, single input, five knobs (b, m, t, high v, low v), power switch, standby switch, rear panel: three speaker jacks, half-power switch, available in Black, Blonde, or Red covering, 19 in. wide, 9.75 in. tall, 9.5 in. deep, 33 lbs., mfg. 2010-present.

| MSR $1,875 | $1,875 | $1,225 - 1,400 | $600 - 750 | |

ROUTE 66 – 32W, head-unit only, all tube chassis, preamp: 1 X EF86, 1 X 12AX7, power: 2 X KT66, GZ34 rectifier, single channel, front black control panel, single input, three black knobs (v, t, b), choice of color covering, gray grille, current mfg.

| MSR $1,850 | $1,850 | $1,200 - 1,375 | $600 - 750 | |

SRZ-65 HEAD – this amp is still available, only in a limited production.

STANG RAY HEAD – 30W, head-unit configuration, all-tube chassis, preamp: 1 X 12AX7, 1 X EF86, power: 4 X EL84, rectifier: GZ34, single channel, front control panel, two inputs, three knobs (v, tone, cut), available in Black, Blonde, or Red finish, black grille, mfg. 2006-disc.

| | $1,799 | $1,175 - 1,350 | $800 - 950 | $1,799 |

This model is the second collaboration between Dr. Z and Brad Paisley. This amp was meant to have the top-boost sound from the early Vox AC-30s.

MSR/NOTES	100%	EXCELLENT	AVERAGE	LAST MSR

* ***Stang Ray 1-12 Combo*** – similar to the Stang Ray Head, except in combo configuration with 1-12 in. Celestion Alnico Gold speaker, mfg. 2007-disc.

| | $2,049 | $1,325 - 1,550 | $925 - 1,075 | $2,049 |

* ***Stang Ray 2-12 Combo*** – similar to the Stang Ray Head, except in combo configuration with 2-12 in. Celestion Blues speakers, mfg. 2006-disc.

| | $2,399 | $1,550 - 1,800 | $1,075 - 1,250 | $2,399 |

* ***Stang Ray 2-12 Piggyback Head & Cabinet*** – similar to the Stang Ray Head, except comes with a matching 2-12 in. speaker cabinet with Celestion Blues speakers, mfg. 2006-disc.

| | $2,599 | $1,675 - 1,950 | $1,175 - 1,350 | $2,599 |

THERAPY HEAD – 35W, guitar head unit, four-tube chassis, preamp: 2 X 12AX7, power: 2 X 6L6, 5AR4 rectifier, single channel, front black control panel, single input, five knobs (b, m, t, v, Master), power switch, standby switch, available in Black, Blonde, or Red covering, 19 in. wide, 9.75 in. tall, 9.5 in. deep, 30 lbs., current mfg.

| MSR $1,750 | $1,750 | $1,125 - 1,300 | $575 - 700 | |

Z-28 HEAD – 22W, head-unit only, all tube chassis, preamp: 1 X EF86, 1 X 12AX7, power: 2 X 6V6, tube rectifier, single channel, front black control panel, one input, three knobs (v, b, t), choice of color covering, mfg. 2000-present.

| MSR $1,600 | $1,600 | $1,050 - 1,200 | $525 - 650 | |

* ***Z-28 1-10 Combo*** – similar to the Z-28 head-unit except in combo configuration with 1-10 in. speaker, mfg. 2008-present.

| MSR $1,750 | $1,750 | $1,125 - 1,300 | $575 - 700 | |

* ***Z-28 1-12 Combo*** – similar to the Z-28 head-unit except in combo form with 1-12 in. speaker, mfg. 2003-present.

| MSR $1,850 | $1,850 | $1,200 - 1,375 | $600 - 750 | |

* ***Z-28 2-10 Combo*** – similar to the Z-28 head-unit except in combo form with 2-10 in. speakers, mfg. 2003-present.

| MSR $1,850 | $1,850 | $1,200 - 1,375 | $600 - 750 | |

* ***Z-28 4-10 Combo*** – similar to the Z-28 head-unit except in combo form with 4-10 in. speakers, mfg. 2000-06.

| | $1,679 | $1,100 - 1,300 | $750 - 850 | $1,679 |

Z-LUX HEAD – 40W (switchable to 20W), guitar head unit, nine-tube chassis, preamp: 4 X 12AX7, 1 X 12AT7, power: 4 X 6V6, solid-state rectifier, single channel, front black control panel, single input, eight knobs, power switch, standby switch, half-power switch, available in Black, Blonde, or Red covering, 35 lbs., current mfg.

| MSR $2,050 | $2,050 | $1,325 - 1,525 | $675 - 825 | |

* ***Z-LUX 1-12 Combo*** – 40W (switchable to 20W), 1-12 in. speaker, guitar combo, nine-tube chassis, preamp: 4 X 12AX7, 1 X 12AT7, power: 4 X 6V6, solid-state rectifier, single channel, front black control panel, single input, eight knobs, power switch, standby switch, half-power switch, available in Black, Blonde, or Red covering, 42 lbs., current mfg.

| MSR $2,400 | $2,400 | $1,550 - 1,800 | $775 - 950 | |

SPEAKER CABINETS

1-10 SPEAKER CABINET – 1-10 in. speaker, open cabinet in the back, available in Black, Blonde, or Red covering, brown grille, 17.5 in. wide, 17 in. tall, 10 in. deep, mfg. 2010-present.

| MSR $475 | $475 | $300 - 350 | $155 - 190 | |

1-12 SPEAKER CABINET – 1-12 in. Celestion Vintage 30 speaker standard (other speakers available), convertible design that allows for a closed or open cabinet in the back, available in Black, Blonde, or Red covering, brown grille, 22.75 in. wide, 19.5 in. tall, 10.25 in. deep, 38 lbs., current mfg.

| MSR $575 | $575 | $375 - 425 | $190 - 230 | |

In 2007, the new convertible closed/open back cabinet design replaced the previous open back only design.

2-10 SPEAKER CABINET – 2-10 in. Z speakers standard (other speakers available), convertible design that allows for a closed or open cabinet in the back, available in Black, Blonde, or Red covering, brown grille, 22.75 in. wide, 19.5 in. tall, 10.25 in. deep, 41 lbs., current mfg.

| MSR $575 | $575 | $375 - 425 | $190 - 230 | |

In 2007, the new convertible closed/open back cabinet design replaced the previous open back only design.

2-12 SPEAKER CABINET – 2-12 in. Celestion speakers standard (other speakers available), open back cabinet design, available in Black, Blonde, or Red covering, brown grille, 27.5 in. wide, 22.25 in. tall, 10.25 in. deep, 54 lbs., current mfg.

| MSR $800 | $800 | $525 - 600 | $260 - 325 | |

2-12 "Z-BEST" THIELE PORTED SPEAKER CABINET – 1-12 in. Celestion Vintage 30 and 1-12 in. Celestion G12H30 speakers standard (other speakers available), closed back cabinet design with a Thield Ported system, can be used horizontally or vertically for different sound frequencies, available in Black, Blonde, or Red covering, brown grille, 19.25 in. wide, 28.25 in. tall, 13.75 in. deep, 60 lbs., current mfg.

| MSR $799 | $799 | $500 - 575 | $325 - 375 | |

MSR/NOTES	100%	EXCELLENT	AVERAGE	LAST MSR

2-12 BACKLINE SPEAKER CABINET – 2-12 in. Z speakers standard (other speakers available), available in Black, Blonde, or Red covering, brown grille, 24 in. wide, 24 in. tall, 10 in. deep, 53 lbs., current mfg.

MSR $779	$779	$425 - 500	$250 - 300	

4-10 BACKLINE SPEAKER CABINET – 4-10 in. Z speakers standard (other speakers available), available in Black, Blonde, or Red covering, brown grille, 24 in. wide, 24 in. tall, 10 in. deep, 53 lbs., current mfg.

MSR $779	$779	$425 - 500	$250 - 300	

DST ENGINEERING

Amplifiers and speaker cabinets currently produced in Beverly, MA since 2003. Distributed by DST Engineering.

CONTACT INFORMATION
DST ENGINEERING
4 Clipper Way
Beverly, MA 01915
Phone No.: 978-578-0532
www.dst-engineering.com, www.swansoncabinets.com
jeff@dst-engineering.com, jeff@swansoncabinets.com

Jeff Swanson and Bob Dettorre started DST Engineering in 2003 just north of Boston. They produce guitar tube amplifiers and speaker cabinets. Bob is mainly in charge of amplifier design, while Jeff concentrates on building the speaker cabinets. Prices on their head units range from $999 to $2,699. There are many heads, combos, and speaker cabinet combinations available. Currently building under the name Swanson Custom Sound. For more information, visit DST's website or contact them directly. Source: *The Tonequest Report*, October, 2005.

DUMBLE

Amplifiers currently produced in California since circa 1963.

Alexander "Howard" Dumble began producing amplifiers circa 1963 and he has become one of the best boutique amplifier manufacturers in the industry. The durability and tone of Dumble's amp is what makes them famous - many players consider it to be the best tone that they have ever heard. Many people (and companies) have copied Dumble's schematic piece by piece. In the 1980s, Dumble started covering his circuitry with a layer of epoxy to keep people from copying the exact design. Dumble also builds most amps to a player's own specs, and he has built models for many famous players including Carlos Santana, Robben Ford, and Eric Johnson to name a few. While exact numbers are unknown, it is speculated that less than 300 Dumble amplifiers have been produced. For more information, search the Internet - Dumble does not have his own website, but there is a lot of information out there on the subject.

ELECTRIC TUBE AMPLIFIERS

Dumble has produced a variety of models over the years, but the **Overdrive Special** is the best known and probably most produced Dumble amp. Other Dumble amps include the **Dumbleland**, **Mega PLX**, **Odyssey**, **Overdrive Reverb**, **Sidewinder**, **Small Special**, **Steel String Singer** (SSS), and the **Winterland**.

Due to Dumble's popularity as a builder, the rarity of the amps, and the overall quality, these amps command a huge premium in the used market. Most models in excellent condition are valued around $30,000 and several examples have sold for $40,000 or more. We suggest getting a second opinion on a Dumble amp if you encounter one. When a specific model becomes this valuable, the threat of fakes showing up is always possible.

NOTES

E SECTION
EARTH SOUND RESEARCH

Amplifiers and speaker cabinets previously produced in the 1970s.

The history of Earth Sound Research (ESR) is not definitive by any means, but several people have weighed in with their information and experience. ESR was started as an amplifier brand by ISC Audio in Huntington, NY, and the two owners were Marc Neumann and Dave Garrett. ESR amps were all copies of popular brands especially Fender tube amps and Peavey solid-state models. ESR never had their own factory or engineering department and all amps were built by subcontractors at various locations. However, ESR amps were built much cheaper than their Fender and Peavey copies, and they had a lot of problems with amps not working. The output transistors in particular were built cheaply and they failed often. At one time, Peavey was going to sue ESR because of their design infringement, but they told ESR to change their design as it was cheaper than taking the small company to court. Andy Fuchs of Fuchs Amplifiers actually worked at ESR for a year in the early 1970s.

There is also a lot of speculation that ESR and Plush Amplifiers are one in the same company. The theory is Plush started out building amplifiers in New York, they built a second factory on the West Coast in Los Angeles, and throughout the East Coast company going under the amps in the West Coast were renamed Earth Sound Research. Currently there is no proof that ESR and Plush were the same company, built the same amps, or operated in the same building. There seems to be a lot of crossover between these two names, and any additional information about Earth Sound Research can be submitted directly to Blue Book Publications.

AMPLIFIERS

Even though ESR's amps were mainly copies of popular American designs, they did build some interesting amplifiers. The most collectible is the **G-2000** half-stack with a head-unit and speaker cabinet with values ranging between $550 and $700 in excellent condition. These amps resemble the Kustom Tuck-N-Roll covering models. Later models are very similar in appearance to early Peavey models and a few Fender tweed narrow-panel amps exist as well.

EBS

Amplifiers currently produced in Solna, Sweden, since 1988. Distributed in the U.S. by Musical Distributors Group, LLC in Boonton, NJ.

EBS was founded in 1988 by Bo Engberg and Mats Kristoffersson to build high-end products for bass guitars/players. Based in Sweden, the staff consists mostly of bass players. This way they are able to work with the product and perfect the sound. EBS makes combo amplifiers, head units, speaker cabinets, pedal effects, and preamps. For more information, visit EBS's website or contact their U.S. Distributor.

ELECTRIC BASS AMPLIFIERS & SPEAKER CABINETS

EBS offers rack-mounted preamps and heads, combos, and speaker cabinets. **Fafner the Dragon** (street price $1,749) is a tube loaded amp head. This model was previously named the **TD600** and has a continuous output of 500W (600W at a 2 Ohm load). The **HD350** (street price $1,299) is a high-definition bass head that puts out 350W of MOSFET power in a compact design. The **TD650** (MSR $1,839) is a professional tube-definition bass head that uses hybrid technology and puts out 650W of MOSFET power. The **EBS Classic T90** (disc., last street price $1,299) is an all-tube bass amp that puts out 90W with 6550 tubes. The **EBS Classic 450** (street price $999) is a solid-state bass amp head that puts out 450W. The **EBS-1** series are preamps for rack units. The EBS combo units are split into two series, the **Drome** and the **Gorm**. The Drome series are 150W amplifiers with either 1-12 in. (disc. last MSR was $1,969) or 1-15 in. (disc. last MSR was $2,499) speaker, and a variety of controls. The Gorm amps have 350W power and a few more options. The Gorm were available in three different configurations, with 1-15 in. speaker (disc. last MSR was $2,295), 2-10 in. speakers (disc. last MSR was $1,199), or 4-10 in. speakers (disc. last MSR was $3,399). There are several different speaker cabinets currently available. They start out with a cabinet of 1-15 in. and go along the line with 2-10 in., 4-10 in. and at the "super size" an 8-10 in. or 4-12 in. giant cabinet are available.

CONTACT INFORMATION
EBS
Factory/Headquarters
Grindstuvägen 44-46,
Bromma, SE-167 33 Sweden
Phone No.: +46-8-735 00 10
Fax No.: +46-8-735 00 15
www.ebssweden.com
info@ebssweden.com

U.S. Distributor: Musical Distributors Group
9 Mars Court, Suite C-3
Boonton, NJ 07005
Phone No.: 973-335-7888
Phone No.: 866-632-8346
Fax No.: 973-335-7779
www.musicaldistributors.com
sales@musicaldistributors.com

EDEN ELECTRONICS

Amplifiers and speaker cabinets currently produced in Mundelein, IL since 2003 and China since the mid-2000s. Previously produced in Montrose, MN between 1976 and the mid-2000s. Eden amplifiers are distributed by Marshall Amplification USA. Distributed in the U.S. by U.S. Music Corporation in Mundelein, IL since 2003.

David Nordschow founded Eden Electronics in 1976 to build high-quality bass amplifiers and speaker cabinets in Montrose, MN. Eden's World Tour Series is very popular among bass players as well as the many combos and speaker cabinets. In 2003, U.S. Music Corporation acquired Eden Electronics and moved the location to suburban Chicago, IL and they have moved some of their production overseas. Nordschow is no longer with the company. In late 2011, Marshall Amplification purchased Eden Electronics from U.S. Music Corp; however, U.S. Music Corp continues to be the U.S. distributor. For more information visit the Eden Electronics website or contact U.S. Music Corp. directly.

CONTACT INFORMATION
EDEN ELECTRONICS
444 E. Courtland St.
Mundelein, IL 60060
Phone No.: 847-949-0444
Phone No.: 800-877-6863
Fax No.: 847-949-8444
www.eden-electronics.com
info@eden-electronics.com

MSR/NOTES	100%	EXCELLENT	AVERAGE	LAST MSR

E300T Head
courtesy Eden Electronics

EC8 Combo Amp
courtesy Eden Electronics

EC8 Combo Amp
courtesy Eden Electronics

E300T Head
courtesy Eden Electronics

ELECTRIC BASS AMPLIFIERS: E SERIES

Eden Electronics' E Series are manufactured in the U.S. and the speaker enclosures are tuned a little higher than Eden's D Series speaker cabinets.

E300 HEAD – 300W at 4 ohms, head-unit only, solid-state chassis, single channel, front black control panel, single input, six black knobs (gain, enhance, b, m, t, v), auxillary input, line out, headphone jack, MP3 in, power switch, speaker out, black casing, 16.5 lbs., mfg. 2010-present.

| MSR $480 | $350 | $230 - 265 | $115 - 140 | |

E300T HEAD – 300W @ 4 ohms, bass application, four-space self-enclosed head configuration, tube chassis, power: 6 X KT88, single channel, front black control panel, single input, five chrome knobs (g, b, m, t, MV), low shift switch, overdrive switch, mid-shift switch, mute switch, tuner out jack, balanced XLR direct out, speaker outputs with 4/8 ohm selector switch, footswitch included, black covering, black grille with brown accents, 40 lbs., mfg. 2008 only.

| | $1,360 | $750 - 900 | $500 - 600 | $1,700 |

E115 SPEAKER CABINET – 300W, 1-15 in. EC1503E8 Eden speaker, E 2700 tweeter with a level control, 8 ohm impedance, front ported cabinet, black covering, black grille with brown accents, 23 in. wide, 25.5 in. tall, 18.5 in. deep, 56 lbs., mfg. 2008 only.

| | $480 | $275 - 325 | $150 - 200 | $600 |

E210 SPEAKER CABINET – 300W, 2-10 in. ES1040E16 Eden speakers, E 2700 tweeter with a level control, 8 ohm impedance, front ported cabinet, black covering, black grille with brown accents, 23 in. wide, 17.5 in. tall, 18.5 in. deep, 60 lbs., mfg. 2008 only.

| | $480 | $275 - 325 | $150 - 200 | $600 |

E410 SPEAKER CABINET – 650W, 4-10 in. ES1040E16 Eden speakers, E 2700 tweeter with level control, 4 ohm impedance, front ported cabinet, black covering, black grille with brown accents, 23 in. wide, 27.5 in. tall, 18.5 in. deep, 98 lbs., mfg. 2008 only.

| | $840 | $500 - 575 | $300 - 375 | $1,050 |

E810 SPEAKER CABINET – 1000W, 8-10 in. ES1040XSV8 Eden speakers, E 2700 tweeter with level control, 4 ohm impedance, rear ported cabinet, black covering, two black grilles with brown accents, 23 in. wide, 52.5 in. tall, 18.25 in. deep, 140 lbs., mfg. 2008 only.

| | $1,040 | $600 - 700 | $350 - 425 | $1,300 |

EC8 COMBO AMP – 20W, 1-8 in. Eden designed speaker, bass combo, solid-state chassis, single channel, top rear black control panel, single input, three black knobs (g, enhance, t), power switch, headphone jack, MP3 jack, black covering, black metal grille, 8.5 in. wide, 12.6 in. tall, 10.5 in. deep, 11 lbs., mfg. 2014-present.

| MSR $140 | $100 | $65 - 75 | $35 - 40 | |

EC10 COMBO AMP – 50W, 1-10 in. Eden designed speaker, bass combo, solid-state chassis, single channel, top rear black control panel, single input, six black knobs (g, enhance, b, m, t, MV), rear panel: power switch, headphone jack, MP3 jack, tuner, send jack, return jack, black covering, black metal grille, 12.5 in. wide, 15.6 in. tall, 13 in. deep, 24.2 lbs., mfg. 2014-present.

| MSR $270 | $200 | $130 - 150 | $65 - 80 | |

EC15 COMBO AMP – 180W, 1-15 in. Eden designed speaker, bass combo, solid-state chassis, single channel, top rear black control panel, single input, eight black knobs (g, compressor, enhance, b, m, mid sweep, t, MV), rear panel: power switch, headphone jack, MP3 jack, tuner jack, send jack, return jack, XLR out, external speaker out jack, black covering, black metal grille, 14.5 in. wide, 20.6 in. tall, 20 in. deep, 42.9 lbs., mfg. 2014-present.

| MSR $590 | $400 | $260 - 300 | $130 - 160 | |

EC28 COMBO AMP – 180W, 2-8 in. Eden designed speakers, bass combo, solid-state chassis, single channel, top rear black control panel, single input, eight black knobs (g, compressor, enhance, b, m, mid sweep, t, MV), rear panel: power switch, headphone jack, MP3 jack, tuner jack, XLR out, effects loop, external speaker out, black covering, black metal grille, 14.5 in. wide, 14.6 in. tall, 18.5 in. deep, 37.4 lbs., mfg. 2014-present.

| MSR $680 | $500 | $325 - 375 | $165 - 200 | |

MSR/NOTES	100%	EXCELLENT	AVERAGE	LAST MSR

EC210 Combo Amp
courtesy Eden Electronics

EX112 Speaker Cabinet
courtesy Eden Electronics

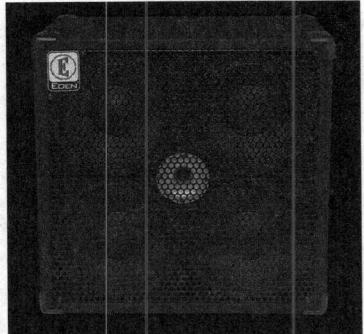
EX410 Speaker Cabinet
courtesy Eden Electronics

EC210 COMBO AMP – 180W, 2-10 in. Eden designed speakers, bass combo, solid-state chassis, single channel, top rear black control panel, single input, eight black knobs (g, compressor, enhance, b, m, mid sweep, t, MV), rear panel: power switch, headphone jack, MP3 jack, tuner jack, XLR out, effects loop, external speaker out, black covering, black metal grille, 14.5 in. wide, 20.6 in. tall, 20 in. deep, 46.3 lbs., mfg. 2014-present.

MSR $590	$400	$260 - 300	$130 - 160

EX110 SPEAKER CABINET – 300W, 1-10 in. Eden designed speaker, 4 or 8 ohm impedance, one 1/4 in. speaker jack, black covering, black metal grille, 25 lbs., mfg. 2010-present.

MSR $300	$200	$130 - 150	$65 - 80

EX112 SPEAKER CABINET – 300W, 1-12 in. Eden designed speaker, 4 or 8 ohm impedance, one 1/4 in. speaker jack, black covering, black metal grille, 30.3 lbs., mfg. 2010-present.

MSR $375	$250	$165 - 190	$80 - 100

EX115 SPEAKER CABINET – 300W, 1-15 in. Eden designed speaker, 4 or 8 ohm impedance, one 1/4 in. speaker jack, black covering, black metal grille, 41.1 lbs., mfg. 2013-present.

MSR $550	$400	$260 - 300	$130 - 160

EX210 SPEAKER CABINET – 300W, 2-10 in. Eden designed speakers with a tweeter, 4 or 8 ohm impedance, one 1/4 in. speaker jack, two Speakon speaker jacks, tweeter level control, black covering, black metal grille, 44.9 lbs., mfg. 2013-present.

MSR $675	$450	$295 - 325	$145 - 180

EX410 SPEAKER CABINET – 600W, 4-10 in. Eden designed speakers with a tweeter, 4 ohm impedance, one 1/4 in. speaker jack, two Speakon speaker jacks, tweeter level control, black covering, black metal grille, 65 lbs., mfg. 2011-present.

MSR $750	$550	$350 - 400	$180 - 220

EX410SC4 SPEAKER CABINET – 400W, 4-10 in. Eden designed speakers, 4 ohm impedance, 1/4 in. speaker jack, black covering, black metal grille, 62 lbs., mfg. 2011-present.

MSR $410	$300	$195 - 225	$100 - 120

ELECTRIC BASS AMPLIFIERS: METROMIX SERIES

EM15 Combo
courtesy Eden Electronics

EM25 Combo
courtesy Eden Electronics

EM275 Combo
courtesy Eden Electronics

EM15 COMBO – 15W at 4 ohms, 1-8 in. Eden designed extended range speaker, bass combo, solid-state chassis, single channel, front black control panel, dual inputs with individual volume/tone controls, speaker mute, two headphone jacks, MP3 jack, black covering, black metal grille, 11 lbs., mfg. 2011-present.

MSR $200	$150	$100 - 115	$50 - 60

MSR/NOTES	100%	EXCELLENT	AVERAGE	LAST MSR

EM25 COMBO – 25W , 1-8 in. Eden designed extended range speaker, bass combo, solid-state chassis, single channel, front black control panel, dual inputs, eight knobs (gain 1, gain 2, b, m, t, MV, headphone 1, headphone 2), dual headphone jacks, MP3 jack, power switch, rear panel: line out, two RCA inputs, black covering, black metal grille, 17 lbs., mfg. 2011-present.

MSR $270	$200	$130 - 150	$65 - 80	

EM275 COMBO – 150W, 2-10 in. Eden designed extended range speaker, bass combo, solid-state chassis, two channels, front black control panel, dual inputs, 1/4 in. stereo input, 3.5mm stereo input, three headphone jacks, eighteen knobs (gain 1, gain 2, distortion, b1, b2, m1, m2, t1, t2, pan 1, pan 2, volume 1, volume 2, stereo volume, MV, headphone 1, headphone 2, headphone 3), power switch, black covering, black metal grille, 68.3 lbs., mfg. 2011-present.

MSR $680	$500	$325 - 375	$165 - 200	

ELECTRIC BASS AMPLIFIERS: TERRA NOVA SERIES

In January of 2016, Eden introduced the Terra Nova Series at the Winter NAMM show in Anaheim, CA. This line features head units (TN501, TN226), speaker cabinets (TN410, TN210, TN110), and combo amps (TN2252, TN2251). All head units and combo amps in this series feature active and passive instrument inputs, 4-band EQ, compressor, DI output, effects loop, mute switch, and tuner output.

ELECTRIC BASS AMPLIFIERS: WORLD TOUR SERIES

Eden offers a full-upgrade service on many of their head-units, meaning you can upgrade your old model to current specs.

WT-405 Time Traveler
courtesy Eden Electronics

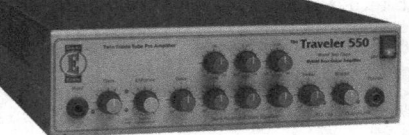

WT-550 Traveler
courtesy Eden Electronics

WT-800 World Tour
courtesy Eden Electronics

WT-330 TIME TRAVELER – 330W, head-unit only, solid-state chassis, single channel, front gold control panel, two inputs, two blue knobs, two gray knobs, three red knobs, various buttons, various outputs, headphone jack, black casing, 15 lbs., mfg. 2002-04.

	N/A	$475 - 550	$300 - 350	$1,000

Eden offered an upgrade of this model to WT405 specs (Last MSR was $199).

WT-400 TRAVELER PLUS – 400W, head-unit only, solid-state chassis, single channel, compressor, front gold control panel, single input, two blue knobs, one gray knob, eight red knobs, headphone jack, black casing, 13 lbs., disc. 2004.

	N/A	$550 - 650	$350 - 425	$1,250

Eden can upgrade this model to 2004 low noise specs ($199), add pre/post-EQ selector to Direct Input circuit ($85), and add a B version high-flow cover ($59).

WT-405 TIME TRAVELER – 405W at 4 ohms (650W at 2 ohms, 250W at 8 ohms), head-unit only, solid-state chassis, single channel, front gold control panel, two inputs, two blue knobs, two gray knobs, four red knobs, various buttons, various outputs, headphone jack, black casing, 15 lbs., mfg. 2005-2012.

$1,100	$625 - 750	$400 - 475	$1,400

WT-500 HIGHWAYMAN – 500W (2 X 250W), head-unit only, solid-state chassis, single channel, compressor, front gold control panel, single input, two blue knobs, two gray knobs, eight red knobs, various buttons, headphone jack, various outputs, effects loop, black casing, 20 lbs., disc. 2002.

	N/A	$650 - 800	$425 - 500	$1,440

Eden can upgrade this model to the WT600 specs ($125), or to the WT800 specs ($295).

WT-550 TRAVELER – 500W (2 X 250W), head-unit only, solid-state chassis, single channel, compressor, front gold control panel, single input, two blue knobs, one gray knobs, eight red knobs, various buttons, headphone jack, various outputs, effects loop, black casing, 18 lbs., mfg. 2003-present.

MSR $1,350	$900	$575 - 675	$295 - 350	

Eden can upgrade this model with the B version high-flow cover ($59).

WT-600 ROADRUNNER – 600W (2 X 300W), head-unit only, solid-state chassis, single channel, crossover, compressor, front gold control panel, single input, two blue knobs, two gray knobs, nine red knobs, various buttons, headphone jack, various outputs, effects loop, black casing, 22 lbs., disc. 2004.

	N/A	$850 - 1,000	$600 - 700	$1,750

Eden can upgrade this model to the WT800A power specs ($195), upgrade to the 2004 noise reduction specs ($295), or both for $445.

MSR/NOTES	100%	EXCELLENT	AVERAGE	LAST MSR

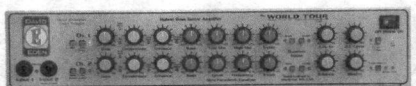

WT-1205 World Tour
courtesy Eden Electronics

WT-1250 Bass Power Amp
courtesy Eden Electronics

WTX-260
courtesy Eden Electronics

WT-800 WORLD TOUR – 800W (2 X 400W), head-unit only, solid-state chassis, single channel, crossover, compressor, front gold control panel, single input, two blue knobs, two gray knobs, nine red knobs, various buttons, headphone jack, various outputs, effects loop, black casing, 26 lbs., current mfg.

| MSR $2,250 | $1,500 | $975 - 1,125 | $500 - 600 | |

Eden can upgrade this model to the 2004 low noise specs ($295), uprade to early 2005 model with full B version specs ($150), upgrade to pre-2005 models with B version specs ($495), or add a pre/post-EQ selector on the direct input circuit ($85).

WT-1205 WORLD TOUR – 1200W bridged at 4 ohms (1000W bridged at 8 ohms), head-unit only, hybrid chassis, preamp: 2 X 7025, two channels, crossover, compressor, front gold control panel, two inputs, four blue knobs, four gray knobs, ten red knobs, various buttons, headphone jack, various outputs, effects loop, black casing, 28 lbs., mfg. 2005-2012.

| | $2,000 | $1,150 - 1,350 | $700 - 850 | $2,500 |

WT-1000 BASS POWER AMP – 1000W (2 X 450W), head-unit only, solid-state chassis, single channel, front gold control panel, single input, two blue knobs, two red knobs, various buttons, various outputs, black casing, 28 lbs., disc. 2004.

| | N/A | $550 - 650 | $350 - 425 | $1,200 |

WT-1250 BASS POWER AMP – 1250W at 4 ohms bridged (2 X 625 at 2 ohms, 2 X 430W at 4 ohms), head-unit only, solid-state chassis, single channel, front gold control panel, single input, two blue knobs, two red knobs, various buttons, various outputs, black casing, 28 lbs., mfg. 2004-08.

| | $1,200 | $750 - 900 | $525 - 625 | $1,500 |

WT-1400 BASS POWER AMP – 1400W (2 X 700W), head-unit only, hybrid chassis (2 X 7025), single channel, front gold control panel, single input, two blue knobs, two red knobs, various buttons, various outputs, black casing, 32 lbs., mfg. 2003 only.

| | N/A | $550 - 650 | $350 - 425 | $1,200 |

WT-1550 BASS POWER AMP – 1550W bridged (2 X 750W at 2 ohms, 2 X 430W at 4 ohms), head-unit only, hybrid chassis (2 X 7025), single channel, front gold control panel, single input, two blue knobs, two red knobs, various buttons, various outputs, black casing, 32 lbs., mfg. 2004-06.

| | $1,200 | $800 - 900 | $525 - 625 | $1,500 |

WTX-260 – 260/300W @ 4 ohms, compact head-unit bass configuration, solid-state chassis, single channel, front gold control panel, single input, six knobs (g, enhance, b, m, h, MV), effects loop, stereo aux. inputs, tuner out, mute switch, XLR direct in with level control, headphone jack, optional footswitch, black casing, 8 in. wide, 2.5 in. tall, 9 in. deep, 3.8 lbs., mfg. 2006-08.

| | $700 | $425 - 500 | $250 - 300 | $900 |

WTX-264 – 260 @ 4 ohms, compact bass head-unit, solid-state chassis, single channel, front gold control panel, single input, six knobs (g, enhance, b, m, h, MV), effects loop, stereo aux. inputs, tuner out, mute switch, rear panel: footswitch jack, XLR direct out with level control and ground/lift switch, headphone jack, one Speakon and two 1/4 in. standard speaker jacks, black casing, 8 in. wide, 2.5 in. tall, 9 in. deep, 3.8 lbs., mfg. 2010-present.

| MSR $731 | $500 | $300 - 400 | $175 - 225 | |

WTX-500 – 500W @ 4 ohms, bass head unit, solid-state chassis, single channel, front brushed aluminum gold control panel, single input, six black chrome knobs (g, enhance, b, m, h, MV), mute switch, effects loop, two aux. inputs (left and right), tuner out jack, black casing, rear panel: headphone jack, two 1/4 in. speaker jacks and one Speakon jack, optional footswitch, 8 in. wide, 2.5 in. tall, 9 in. deep, 4.8 lbs., mfg. 2009-present.

| MSR $890 | $650 | $350 - 425 | $200 - 250 | |

WTX-1000 "THE NAVIGATOR 1000" – 1000W @ 4 ohms (2 X 500W stereo), bass head unit, solid-state chassis with a stereo power amp, single channel, front brushed gold aluminum control panel, single input, three blue knobs, eight gray knobs, and ten red knobs (g, compressor: threshold, ratio, tube, enhance, b, l, m, h, t, three semi-parametric EQ knobs, DI level, crossover, balance, MV), mute switch, compressor bypass switch, enhance bypass switch, normal gain/turbo boost switch, DI select comp switch and EQ switch, power switch, stereo headphone jack, black casing, 17 in. wide, 3.5 in. tall, 12 in. deep, 11.2 lbs., mfg. 2009-2012.

| | $1,100 | $625 - 750 | $400 - 475 | $1,450 |

MSR/NOTES	100%	EXCELLENT	AVERAGE	LAST MSR

VT-300A All Tube Bass Amp
courtesy Eden Electronics

WP-100 Navigator
courtesy Eden Electronics

World Tour Black WTB-700
courtesy Eden Electronics

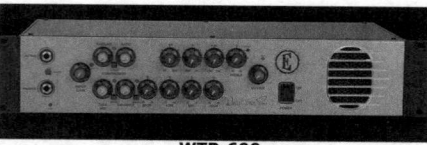

WTP-600
courtesy Eden Electronics

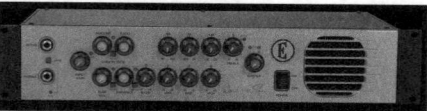

WTP-900
courtesy Eden Electronics

WP-100 NAVIGATOR – preamp only, head-unit, solid-state chassis, single channel, compression, front gold control panel, two blue knobs, eight gray knobs, eight red knobs, various buttons, headphone jack, various outputs, effects loop, black casing, 12 lbs., current mfg.

| MSR $1,100 | $880 | $550 - 650 | $450 - 500 | |

VT-300A ALL TUBE BASS AMP – 300W, head-unit only, all tube chassis, 4 X EL34 or 4 X 6550 power tubes, single channel, front gold control panel, two inputs, two blue knobs, six red knobs, black casing, 40 lbs., disc. 2008.

| | $2,500 | $1,400 - 1,750 | $1,000 - 1,150 | $3,090 |

Eden can upgrade this model 2006 low-noise specs ($50), or a re-tube, bias, and cleaning ($335).

ELECTRIC BASS AMPLIFIERS: WORLD TOUR BLACK SERIES

World Tour Black amplifiers are produced in China.

WORLD TOUR BLACK WT-300V (WTB300V) – 300W @ 4 ohms, bass head unit, tube chassis, power: 6 X KT88, single channel, front black control panel, single input, five chrome knobs (g, b, m, t, MV), -10dB input switch, overdrive switch, mid-shift switch, standby switch, power switch, rear panel: two speaker jacks with a 4/8 ohm impedance selector, power tube bias adjustments, effects loop, footswitch jack, XLR balanced line out, footswitch included, black covering, black grille, 42 lbs., mfg. 2009-2011.

| | $1,400 | $800 - 950 | $500 - 600 | $1,800 |

WORLD TOUR BLACK WTB-400 – 400W @ 4 ohms, bass head unit, solid-state chassis, single channel, front black control panel, single input, nine knobs (gain with push/pull -12dB input pad, distortion, enhance with push/pull compressor bypass, semi-parametric EQ level, semi-parametric EQ freq., b, m, t, MV), semi-parametric on/off switch, D.I. level pre/post EQ switch, power switch, headphone jack, rear panel: footswitch jack, one Speakon jacks and one standard 1/4 in. jack, XLR direct line out with level control and ground/lift switch, tuner out jack, pre EQ effects loop, black casing, 26 lbs., mfg. 2010-2011.

| | $500 | $300 - 350 | $175 - 225 | $750 |

WORLD TOUR BLACK WTB-700 – 700W @ 2 ohms, bass head unit, solid-state chassis, single channel, front black control panel, single input, nine knobs (g, distortion, enhance, semi-parametric EQ level, semi-parametric EQ freq., b, m, t, D.I. level, MV), gain boost switch, compression bypass switch, mute switch, semi-parametric on/off switch, D.I. level pre/post EQ switch, power switch, headphone jack, rear panel: two Speakon jacks and two standard 1/4 in. jacks, XLR direct line out with lift/ground switch, pre EQ effects loop, stereo EQ post effects loop, tuner out jack, footswitch jack, black casing, 33 lbs., mfg. 2010-2011.

| | $750 | $500 - 575 | $300 - 350 | $1,125 |

WORLD TOUR BLACK WTB-1000 – 1100W bridged @ 4 ohms (880W @ 8 ohms), bass head unit, solid-state chassis with a dual power amp, single channel, front black control panel, single input, nine knobs (gain with push/pull -12dB input pad, tube, compressor, enhance, b, graphic EQ level, graphic freq., t, MV) nine-band graphic EQ with graphic on/off switch, mute switch, dynamic boost bass switch, dynamic boost treble switch, bridged mono on/off switch, stereo headphone jack, power switch, rear panel: two Speakon jacks and two standard 1/4 in. jacks, XLR direct line out with level control and lift/ground switch, stereo recording output, pre effects loop, stereo post effects loop, tuner out jack, one Speakon and two standard 1/4 in. stereo amp out lines, black casing, 26 lbs., mfg. 2009-2011.

| | $1,500 | $950 - 1,100 | $625 - 750 | $2,100 |

ELECTRIC BASS AMPLIFIERS: WORLD TOUR PRO SERIES

WTP-600 – 600W, head-unit only, solid-state chassis, single channel, compressor, front gold control panel, two inputs (active, passive), two blue knobs, four gray knobs, eight red knobs, mute switch, auxillary input, DI out, crossover control, tuner out, headphone jack, various outputs, effects loop, black casing, 29 lbs., mfg. 2015-present.

| MSR $1,790 | $1,175 | $750 - 875 | $375 - 475 | |

WTP-900 – 900W (2 X 450W), head-unit only, solid-state chassis, single channel, compressor, front gold control panel, two inputs (active, passive), two blue knobs, four gray knobs, eight red knobs, mute switch, auxillary input, DI out, crossover control, tuner out, headphone jack, various outputs, effects loop, black casing, 33 lbs., mfg. 2015-present.

| MSR $2,450 | $1,800 | $1,175 - 1,350 | $575 - 725 | |

MSR/NOTES	100%	EXCELLENT	AVERAGE	LAST MSR

DC112XLT Metro Combo
courtesy Eden Electronics

CXC1015
courtesy Eden Electronics

ECX112N
courtesy Eden Electronics

WTP-PRE PREAMP – preamp only, single channel, compressor, front gold control panel, two inputs (active, passive), two blue knobs, four gray knobs, eight red knobs, mute switch, auxillary input, DI out, crossover control, tuner out, headphone jack, various outputs, effects loop, black casing, mfg. 2015-present.

MSR $1,360 $1,000 $650 - 750 $325 - 400

ELECTRIC BASS AMPLIFIERS: COMBO UNITS

- Add $80 (MSR $100) for the 390W RMS amp option (600W at 2 ohms, 390W at 4 ohms, and 200W at 8 ohms). This option is typically used on the Signature products and is indicated by an S after the model name.

DC112XLT METRO COMBO – 330W at 4 ohms (420W at 2 ohms, 200W at 8 ohms), 1-12 in. speaker combo, solid-state chassis, two channels, front gold control panel, single input, two blue knobs, one gray knob, four red knobs, black carpet covering, black metal grille, 49 lbs., mfg. 2005-09.

          $1,200 $700 - 800 $425 - 500 $1,550

DC210XLT METRO COMBO – 400W at 4 ohms, 2-10 in. speaker combo, solid-state chassis, two channels, front gold control panel, single input, three blue knobs, two gray knobs, eleven red knobs, black carpet covering, black metal grille, 78 lbs., disc. 2009.

          $1,600 $950 - 1,150 $650 - 750 $2,100

CXC110 – features WT-330 head unit in a 1-10 in.speaker combo, black carpet covering, black metal grille, 39 lbs., disc. 2007.

          $925 $550 - 650 $375 - 450 $1,190

CXC112 – features WT-330 head unit in a 1-12 in. speaker combo, black carpet covering, black metal grille, 49 lbs., disc. 2004.

          N/A $625 - 725 $425 - 500 $1,300

CXC210 – features WT-330 head unit in a 2-10 in. speaker combo, black carpet covering, black metal grille, 68 lbs., disc. 2006.

          $1,125 $675 - 775 $475 - 550 $1,400

CXC212 – features WT-330 head unit in a 2-12 in. speaker combo, black carpet covering, black metal grille, 78 lbs., disc. 2004.

          N/A $725 - 825 $525 - 600 $1,500

CXC1015 – features WT-330 head unit in a 1-12 in. and 1-15 in. speaker combo, black carpet covering, black metal grille, 80 lbs., disc. 2006.

          $1,295 $750 - 850 $550 - 625 $1,600

CXC410 – features WT-330 head unit in a 4-10 in. speaker combo, black carpet covering, black metal grille, 100 lbs., disc. 2005.

          N/A $800 - 900 $600 - 675 $1,650

ECX110N – 250W, 1-10 in. XST Neodynium speaker with a E-2700 Cast Bell tweeter, bass combo, solid-state chassis, single channel, front brushed aluminum gold control panel, single input, six black chrome knobs (g, enhance, b, m, h, MV), mute switch, power switch, rear panel: effects loop, two aux. inputs (left and right), tuner out jack, black casing, rear panel: headphone jack, two 1/4 in. speaker jacks and one Speakon jack, optional footswitch, black covering, black metal grille, removable handle/caster set, 15 in. wide, 22.5 in. tall, 14.5 in. deep, 42.75 lbs., mfg. 2009 only.

          $1,230 $700 - 825 $450 - 525 $1,600

This model features the WTX260 head.

ECX112N – 250W, 1-12 in. XST Neodynium speaker with a E-2700 Cast Bell tweeter, bass combo, solid-state chassis, single channel, front brushed aluminum gold control panel, single input, six black chrome knobs (g, enhance, b, m, h, MV), mute switch, power switch, rear panel: effects loop, two aux. inputs (left and right), tuner out jack, black casing, rear panel: headphone jack, two 1/4 in. speaker jacks and one Speakon jack, optional footswitch, black covering, black metal grille, removable handle/caster set, 15 in. wide, 24.5 in. tall, 14.5 in. deep, 45 lbs., mfg. 2009 only.

          $1,280 $725 - 875 $475 - 550 $1,700

This model features the WTX260 head.

MSR/NOTES	100%	EXCELLENT	AVERAGE	LAST MSR

Microtour Miniamp
courtesy Eden Electronics

CX110
courtesy Eden Electronics

D118XL
courtesy Eden Electronics

MICROTOUR MINIAMP – 2W, bass amp, solid state chassis, gold front control plate, single input, blue volume knob, red tone knob, power switch, headphone jack, black cover, black metal grille, 2.5 lbs., mfg. 2015-present.

MSR $82	$60	$40 - 45	$20 - 25	

SPEAKER CABINETS

Eden is probably equally as famous for their speaker cabinets in comparison to the amplifiers.

CX110 – 200W, 1-10 in. speaker with tweeter, 8 ohm impedance, black covering, black grille, 26 lbs., mfg. 2003-06.

	$340	$175 - 225	$95 - 125	$420

CX112 – 200W, 1-12 in. speaker with tweeter, 8 ohm impedance, black covering, black grille, 35 lbs., mfg. 2003-04.

	N/A	$225 - 275	$125 - 175	$500

CX210 – 250W, 2-10 in. speaker with tweeter, 8 ohm impedance, black covering, black grille, 48 lbs., mfg. 2003-06.

	$440	$250 - 300	$140 - 180	$550

CX212 – 250W, 2-12 in. speaker with tweeter, 8 ohm impedance, black covering, black grille, 52 lbs., mfg. 2003-04.

	N/A	$300 - 350	$150 - 200	$650

CX410 – 500W, 4-10 in. speaker with tweeter, 4 ohm impedance, black covering, black grille, 80 lbs., mfg. 2003-04.

	N/A	$350 - 425	$200 - 250	$800

CX1015 – 250W, 1-15 in. and 1-10 in. speaker with tweeter, 8 ohm impedance, black covering, black grille, 55 lbs., mfg. 2003-06.

	$560	$325 - 375	$175 - 225	$700

D210MBX – 350W, 2-10 in. speaker with a tweeter, 4 or 8 ohm impedance, black covering, black metal grille, mounted in a tilt-back montitor-style cabinet, 50 lbs., mfg. 2005-09, 2015-present.

MSR $1,250	$850	$550 - 625	$275 - 350	

D115XL – 400W, 1-15 in. speaker, 8 ohm impedance, black covering, black metal grille, 58 lbs., disc 2010.

	$500	$275 - 325	$150 - 200	$620

D118XL – 500W, 1-18 in. speaker, 8 ohm impedance, black covering, black metal grille, 75 lbs., disc. 2009.

	$675	$350 - 425	$200 - 250	$830

D215XL – 400W, 2-15 in. speaker, 4 or 8 ohm impedance, rear casters and handle, dual ported, black covering, black metal grille, 100 lbs., disc. 2006.

	$680	$375 - 450	$225 - 275	$850

D112XLT – 250W, 1-12 in. speaker with a tweeter, 8 ohm impedance, black covering, black metal grille, 38 lbs., mfg. 2003-2011.

	$500	$275 - 325	$150 - 200	$620

* ***D112XLTN*** – similar to the D112XLT, except has a Neodynium speaker with a tweeter, 32 lbs., mfg. 2009-2011.

	$530	$300 - 350	$175 - 225	$700

D115XLT – 400W, 1-15 in. speaker with a tweeter, 8 ohm impedance, black covering, black metal grille, 59 lbs., current mfg.

MSR $1,250	$850	$550 - 625	$275 - 350	

D210XLT – 350W, 2-10 in. speakers with a tweeter, 4 or 8 ohm impedance, casters, black covering, black metal grille, 68 lbs., current mfg.

MSR $1,250	$850	$550 - 625	$275 - 350	

MSR/NOTES	100%	EXCELLENT	AVERAGE	LAST MSR

D210XLT
courtesy Eden Electronics

D112XST
courtesy Eden Electronics

D212XST
courtesy Eden Electronics

D212XLT – 400W, 2-12 in. speakers with a tweeter, 4 or 8 ohm impedance, casters, black covering, black metal grille, 74 lbs., disc. 2011.

| MSR $930 | $750 | $400 - 475 | $250 - 300 | |

D215XLT – 800W, 2-15 in. speakers with a tweeter, 4 or 8 ohm impedance, casters, black covering, black metal grille, 100 lbs., disc. 2009.

| | $780 | $425 - 500 | $275 - 325 | $980 |

D410XLT – 700W, 4-10 in. speakers with a tweeter, 4 or 8 ohm impedance, casters, black covering, black metal grille, 98 lbs., current mfg.

| MSR $1,700 | $1,200 | $775 - 900 | $400 - 475 | |

D610XLT – 1050W, 6-10 in. speakers with a tweeter, 6 ohm impedance, casters, black covering, black metal grille, 130 lbs., mfg. 2005-09.

| | $1,325 | $750 - 900 | $450 - 525 | $1,700 |

D810XLT (D810XT) – 1400W, 8-10 in. speakers with a tweeter, 4 or 8 ohm impedance, casters, black covering, black metal grille, 250 lbs., disc. 2005, reintroduced 2009-present.

| MSR $2,600 | $1,800 | $1,175 - 1,350 | $575 - 725 | |

D810RP – 1200W, 8-10 in. hand-built XSV speakers, E-2700 horn, 4 ohm impedance, AA void-free plywood construction with massive internal bracing, rear-ported, back wheels and corner mount handles, locking corners, black carpet covering, black metal grille, 125 lbs., mfg. 2006-08.

| | $1,490 | $775 - 925 | $525 - 600 | $1,860 |

D112XST – 300W, 1-12 in. speaker with a tweeter, studio quality, 8 ohm impedance, black covering, black metal grille, 38 lbs., mfg. 2013-present.

| MSR $820 | $525 | $350 - 400 | $170 - 210 | |

D210XST – 500W, 2-10 in. speakers with a tweeter, studio quality, 4 or 8 ohm impedance, casters, black covering, black metal grille, 65 lbs., mfg. 2003-present.

| MSR $1,220 | $850 | $550 - 625 | $275 - 350 | |

* **D210XSTN** – similar to the D210XST, except has Neodynium speakers with a tweeter, 4 ohm impedance only, 49 lbs., mfg. 2009 only.

| | $700 | $475 - 550 | $300 - 350 | $1,080 |

D212XST – 600W, 2-12 in. speakers with a tweeter, studio quality, 4 or 8 ohm impedance, casters, black covering, black metal grille, 74 lbs., mfg. 2013-present.

| MSR $1,230 | $900 | $575 - 675 | $295 - 350 | |

D410XST – 1000W, 4-10 in. speakers with a tweeter, studio quality, 8 ohm impedance, casters, black covering, black metal grille, 95 lbs., mfg. 2002-present.

| MSR $1,620 | $1,200 | $775 - 900 | $400 - 475 | |

* **D410XSTN** – similar to the D210XST, except has Neodynium speakers with a tweeter, 8 ohm impedance only, 75 lbs., mfg. 2009 only.

| | $1,150 | $650 - 750 | $400 - 475 | $1,600 |

D610XST – 1500W, 6-10 in. speakers with a tweeter, studio quality, 6 ohm impedance, casters, black covering, black metal grille, 130 lbs., mfg. 2010-present.

| MSR $2,450 | $1,600 | $1,050 - 1,200 | $525 - 650 | |

EDGERTON

Amplifiers previously produced in Kansas during the mid-1990s.

Bud Ross, who founded Kustom Electronics in 1965, started another amplifier company called Edgerton in the 1990s. Egderton designed and produced guitar and P.A. amplifiers, and one of their most popular models were octagon shaped amps that sounded a lot like Kustoms of the 1960s and 1970s. The son of the owner went on to form KrossRoads, which were good tuck and roll versions of Kustom amps for the 1990s. It is unknown what happened to the Edgerton brand, but by the late 1990s and early 2000s, they were no longer being produced. Any further information on Edgerton amplifiers can be submitted directly to Blue Book Publications.

EDWARD AMPLIFICATION

Amplifiers currently produced in Burlington, Ontario, Canada. Distributed by Edward Amplification.

Edward Amplifiers builds low-wattage tube amplifiers with high quality components available with many options. They produce head-units, combos, and speaker cabinets. The Edward Amplification company describes their amplifiers as "products for those who want low power amplification for harmonically rich distortion created by driving the output tubes to the edge." Edward amplifiers are all available with a variety of color and grille options along with electronic options. For more information visit Edward Amplification's website or contact them directly.

CONTACT INFORMATION
EDWARD AMPLIFICATION
3100 Driftwood Dr.
Burlington, Ontario L7M 1X6 Canada
Phone No.: 289-237-5691
www.edwardamp.com
eds@edwardamp.com

ELECTRIC AMPLIFIERS & SPEAKER CABINETS

Edward Amplification produces one amplifier chassis available as a head unit or a combo. The **HED** (MSR $1,200) is a 14W amp in head-unit configuration, with a single channel, six knobs (v, b, t, r, tremolo speed, tremolo depth), a low and high gain stage to get that distortion factor, line in and out, external speaker jacks, footswitch with assignable options, and a wide array of colors for the covering. The **ED** is the same as the HED except in combo configuration with with a single Celestion 25W Greenback speaker and is available designed for guitars (MSR $1,400) or harmonicas (MSR $1,450). The **Shoulder** (MSR $450) is a separate 1-12 in. speaker cabinet.

Edward also offers several options, including two or three spring reverb, numerous speaker choices (Celestion Greenback, Celestion Blue, etc.), handle and grille color, cabinet color, and optional footswitch configurations (12 different combinations that control the gain, boost, reverb, and tremolo). There are also hard and soft covers available for Edward amps.

* Add $40 for a Celestion G12H 30W speaker.
* Add $40 for a Celestion Vintage 30 60W speaker.
* Add $45 for a Celestion G12M-70 speaker.
* Add $45 for a Celestion Classic Lead speaker.
* Add $55 for tweed covering.
* Add $65 for a soft vinyl cover.
* Add $100 for a Celetion Century 80W speaker (disc.).
* Add $200 for a Celestion Blue 15W speaker (disc.).
* Add $275 for a hard shell case (disc.).

EGNATER

Amplifiers and speaker cabinets currently produced in Berkley, MI. Previously produced in Pontiac, MI from 1980 to 2003. Distributed by Boutique Amps Distribution in Huntington Park, CA.

Bruce Egnater founded Egnater Custom Amplification in 1980. Egnater started out like many amp builders: he was looking for a certain tone out of a guitar amp and no product existed in the market, so he set out to create his own. In the 1970s, true tube saturation was only achieved by running a Marshall amp wide open. Egnater took a small Gibson amp book and replaced the speaker with a resistor and inserted the output from the Gibson amp into the input of a Marshall 200 Watt head that allowed the guitarist to add distortion without turning up volume. Egnater later came up with a channel switching amp that could produce both clean and overdrive tones from the same unit. Egnater received a patent for his modular musical amplification system where the pre-amp sections of an amp are modular and can be changed out of an amp. In the late 2000s, Egnater introduced a full line of standard tube amplifiers. They currently produce custom modular amplifier combos, heads, pre-amps and speaker cabinets. For more information, visit Egnater's website or contact the company directly.

CONTACT INFORMATION
EGNATER
3383 Gage Ave.
Huntington Park, CA 90255
Phone No.: 323-277-4119
Phone No.: 877-346-2837
Fax No.: 323-277-4110
www.egnateramps.com
info@egnateramps.com

ELECTRIC TUBE AMPS: MOD SERIES

Egnater offers modular tube amplifiers in head or combo versions. Both of these models have the same specifications, which include: High power 50W and Low power 10W, two channels, a power tube section that is able to be self biased with any tube, (but is sold only with 5881) with serial and parallel effects loops. Reverb is optional and a footswitch is included. The **Mod 50** has 50W/10W power and is available as a head-unit (MSR $2,250), 1-12 in. combo (MSR $2,995). The **Mod 100** has 100W power with six channel modules and is now discontinued.

The **M4 Preamp** (MSR $2,100) follows the technology that has taken amplifier companies into the 21st Century. This certain model is different than most amps that are out there because you can actually plug in four different all tube module units. This system works as a rack-mounted pre amp and the four module units can be taken out by two simple screws and switched with another for a different sound. Additional modules are available for $400 a piece (see website for full listing of modules).

MSR/NOTES	100%	EXCELLENT	AVERAGE	LAST MSR

Egnater also offers speaker cabinets available in the form of an oversized ported 1-12 in. (MSR $660). Other cabinets are special order only.

- Add $10 for a blank module cover.
- Add $30 for a cover.
- Add $50 for cabinet wheels.
- Add $125 for a four-button footswitch.
- Add $250 for spring reverb.

ELECTRIC TUBE AMPS

REBEL-20 – 20W, guitar head unit, seven-tube chassis, preamp: 3 X 12AX7, power: 2 X EL84/2 X 6V6, solid-state rectifier, single channel, front black control panel, single input, seven knobs (tube mix, variable wattage, MV, t, m, b, g), bright switch, tight switch, power switch, standby switch, rear panel: effects loop, three speaker jacks, two-tone Black and Blonde Tolex covering, salt and pepper grille, padded cover included, 14 in. wide, 7.5 in. tall, 8 in. deep, mfg. 2009-present.

| MSR N/A | $550 | $350 - 425 | $200 - 250 | |

REBEL-30 – 30W, guitar head unit, nine-tube chassis, preamp: 5 X 12AX7, power: 2 X EL84/2 X 6V6, solid-state rectifier, two channels, reverb, front black control panel, single input, 11 knobs (Ch. 1: v, b, t, Ch. 2: g, b, m, t, v, Ch. 1 variable wattage, Ch. 2 variable wattage, tube mix), channel switch, two bright switches (one per channel), two tight switches (one per channel), standby switch, rear panel: power switch, two speaker jacks with impedance selector, XLR balanced line out, Ch. 1 reverb level, Ch. 2 reverb level, effects loop, two-tone Black and Blonde Tolex covering, salt and pepper grille, padded cover included, 17 in. wide, 8.5 in. tall, 10.75 in. deep, 23 lbs., mfg. 2009-present.

| MSR N/A | $750 | $500 - 575 | $300 - 375 | |

* **Rebel-30 1-12 Combo** – similar to the Rebel-30 Head, except in combo configuration with 1-12 in. Celestion Elite-80 speaker, 18.5 in. wide, 15.5 in. tall, 12.75 in. deep, 43 lbs., mfg. 2009-present.

| MSR N/A | $900 | $600 - 700 | $375 - 450 | |

* **Rebel-30 2-12 Combo** – similar to the Rebel-30 Head, except in combo configuration with 1-12 in. Celestion Elite-80 speaker and 1-12 in. Celestion Vintage 30 speaker, 26 in. wide, 21 in. tall, 12.75 in. deep, 73 lbs., mfg. 2009-present.

| MSR N/A | $1,100 | $700 - 850 | $425 - 500 | |

REBEL 112X SPEAKER CABINET – 1-12 in. Celestion Elite-80 speaker, 16 ohm impedance, birch construction, two-tone Black and Blonde Tolex covering, 18.75 in. wide, 15.5 in. tall, 12.75 in. deep, 31 lbs., mfg. 2009-present.

| MSR N/A | $280 | $175 - 225 | $110 - 140 | |

RENEGADE – 65W, guitar head unit, ten-tube chassis, preamp: 6 X 12AX7, power: 2 X EL34/2 X 6L6, solid-state rectifier, two channels, reverb, front black control panel, single input, 18 knobs (Ch. 1: g, b, m, t, tube mix, v, Ch. 2: g, b, m, t, tube mix, v, All: Ch. 1 r, Ch. 2 r, density, presence, main 1, main 2), channel switch, two 65W/18W power switches (one per channel), two tight/deep switches (one per channel), two bright/normal switches (one per channel), power switch, standby switch, rear panel: two footswitch jacks, tube bias controls, two speaker jacks with impedance selector switch, XLR direct line out, effects loop, two-tone Black and Blonde Tolex covering, salt and pepper grille, four-button footswitch and padded cover included, 25 in. wide, 9.5 in. tall, 10.5 in. deep, mfg. 2009-present.

| MSR N/A | $1,000 | $650 - 750 | $400 - 475 | |

* **Renegade 1-12 Combo** – similar to the Renegade Head, except in combo configuration with 1-12 in. Celestion Elite-100 speaker, 25 in. wide, 19.5 in. tall, 10.5 in. deep, mfg. 2009-present.

| MSR N/A | $1,100 | $700 - 850 | $425 - 500 | |

* **Renegade 2-12 Combo** – similar to the Renegade Head, except in combo configuration with 1-12 in. Celestion Elite-80 speaker and 1-12 in. Celestion Vintage 30 speaker, recessed side handles, casters, 26.5 in. wide, 21.5 in. tall, 10.5 in. deep, mfg. 2009-present.

| MSR N/A | $1,200 | $750 - 900 | $450 - 525 | |

* **Renegade 4-10 Combo** – similar to the Renegade Head, except in combo configuration with 4-10 in. Celestion Elite-1065 speakers, recessed side handles, casters, 25 in. wide, 27.5 in. tall, 10.5 in. deep, mfg. 2009-present.

| MSR N/A | $1,500 | $950 - 1,150 | $600 - 700 | |

TOURMASTER 4100 – 100W, guitar head unit, 12-tube chassis, preamp: 8 X 12AX7, power: 4 X 6L6, solid-state rectifier, four channels (Clean/Vintage 1, Clean/Vintage 2, OD1, OD2), reverb, front black control panel, single input, 28 knobs (Clean/Vintage 1 Ch.: v, contour, t, m, b, g, Clean/Vintage 2 Ch.: v, contour, t, m, b, g, OD 1 Ch.: v, contour, t, m, b, g, OD 2 Ch.: v, contour, t, m, b, g, All: MV, r, density, p), four channel switches, four classic/modern voicing switches (one per channel), power switch, standby switch, rear panel: effects loop assignable to various channels and send and return levels, footswitch jack, power grid with various power settings for each channel, record out with level control, tube bias controls, two speaker jacks with impedance selector switch, two-tone Black and Blonde Tolex covering, salt and pepper grille, six-button footswitch and padded cover included, 27 in. wide, 10.5 in. tall, 11 in. deep, 60 lbs., mfg. 2009-present.

| MSR N/A | $1,400 | $875 - 1,075 | $550 - 650 | |

* **Tourmaster 4212 Combo** – similar to the Renegade Head, except in combo configuration with 1-12 in. Celestion Elite-80 speaker and 1-12 in. Celestion Vintage 30 speaker, recessed side handles, casters, 26.5 in. wide, 21.5 in. tall, 10.5 in. deep, mfg. 2009-present.

| MSR N/A | $1,600 | $1,025 - 1,225 | $625 - 750 | |

TOURMASTER 212X SPEAKER CABINET – 2-12 in. Celestion Elite-80 speakers, 8 ohm impedance mono, 16 ohm impedance stereo, birch construction, removable back panel, two-tone Black and Blonde Tolex covering, mfg. 2009-present.

| MSR N/A | $450 | $300 - 350 | $175 - 225 | |

MSR/NOTES	100%	EXCELLENT	AVERAGE	LAST MSR

TOURMASTER 412A/412B SPEAKER CABINET – 4-12 in. Celestion Vintage 30 speakers, 8 ohm impedance mono, 16 ohm impedance stereo, birch construction, angled (412A) or straight (412B) front, recessed side handles, detachable casters, two-tone Black and Blonde Tolex covering, mfg. 2009-present.

| MSR N/A | $600 | $375 - 450 | $225 - 275 | |

TWEAKER – 15W, guitar head unit, five-tube chassis, preamp: 3 X 12AX7, power: 2 X 6V6, solid-state rectifier, single channel, front black control panel, single input, five knobs (MV, t, m, b, g), vintage/modern switch, USA/AC/Brit switch, hot/clean switch, bright/normal switch, tight/deep switch, power switch, standby switch, rear panel: effects loop, two speaker jacks with impedance selector, Black Tolex covering, brown cloth grille, 14 in. wide, 7.5 in. tall, 8 in. deep, new 2010.

| MSR N/A | $400 | $275 - 325 | $150 - 200 | |

* *Tweaker 1-12 Combo* – similar to the Tweaker Head, except in combo configuration with 1-12 in. Celestion G12H-30 speaker, new 2010.

| MSR N/A | $580 | $375 - 450 | $225 - 275 | |

TWEAKER 112X SPEAKER CABINET – 30W, 1-12 in. Celestion Vintage 30 speaker, birch construction, partial open back cabinet, Black Tolex covering, brown cloth grille, new 2010.

| MSR N/A | $250 | $150 - 200 | $95 - 120 | |

EKO

Amplifiers currently produced since circa 2000 in Asia. Distributed by the EKO Music Group in Italy and in the U.S. by IBC Trading USA LLC in New Jersey. Amplifiers and speaker cabinets previously produced in Recanati, Italy from circa 1967 through the 1970s. Previously distributed by LoDuca Brothers in Milwaukee, WI.

CONTACT INFORMATION
EKO
EKO Music Group S.p.A.
Via Falleroni, 92 , PO Box 58
Recanati, MC 62019 Italy
Phone No.: +39 0733 227 1
Fax No.: +39 0733 227 250
www.ekomusicgroup.com
info@ekomusicgroup.com

U.S. Distributor: IBC Trading USA LLC
NJ
Phone No.: 978 255-2334
Fax No.: 978 255-2334
www.ekoguitarsusa.com
sales@ekoguitarsusa.com

The LoDuca Bros. musical distribution company was formed in 1941 by brothers Tom and Guy LoDuca. Capitalizing on money made through their accordion-based vaudeville act, lessons, and accordion repair, the LoDucas began importing and selling Italian accordions. Throughout the 1940s and 1950s, the LoDucas built up a musical distributorship with accordions and sheet music. By the late 1950s, they were handling Magnatone amplifiers and guitars.

In 1961, the LoDucas teamed up with Italy-based Oliviero Pigini & Company to import guitars. Pigini, one of the LoDuca's accordion manufacturers, had formed the EKO company in anticipation of the boom in the guitar market.

By 1967, EKO had established dealers in 57 countries around the world. In the later 1960s, Eko started to produce their own amplifiers (at least with their name on them). Amplifiers only lasted a short time compared to how long their guitars were on the market (it is unsure if LoDuca ever offered them). During the late 1960s and early 1970s the guitar market began to get soft, and many guitar builders began to go out of business. EKO continued on, but cut back the number of models offered.

The EKO company kept producing models until 1985. By the mid-1980s, the LoDuca Bros. company had begun concentrating on guitar case production, and stopped importing the final Alembic-styled set-neck guitars that were being produced. The original EKO company's holdings were liquidated in 1987.

Currently, the EKO trademark has again been revived in Italy, and appears on entry level solid body guitars and now amplifiers built in various countries. The revived company is offering a wide range of acoustic, classical, and solid body electric guitars and amplifiers - all with contemporary market designs. In the late 2000s, EKO introduced their higher-end Lorenz line of tube amplifiers. EKO history source: Michael Wright, *Guitar Stories*, Volume One.

ELECTRIC TUBE AMPLIFIERS

A line of amps were produced with EKO on the front in the early 1960s, but it is unknown if any of them were ever distributed in the U.S.

DUKE – 50W, 1-12 in. speaker combo designed for bass or electronic organ, tube chassis, single channel, front black control panel, two inputs, three knobs (v, b, t), black covering, black and white checkered grille, mfg. late 1960s.

| | N/A | N/A | N/A | |

PRINCE – 50W, 1-12 in. speaker combo guitar amp, tube chassis, two channels, vibrato, front black control panel, four inputs, eight knobs (Ch. 1: vibrato speed, vibrato intensity, v, t, m/l, Ch. 2: v, t, m/l), black covering, black and white checkered grille, mfg. late 1960s.

| | N/A | N/A | N/A | |

* *Prince Reverb* – similar to the Prince, except has a reverb circuit, reverb controls, and ten knobs (Ch. 1: vibrato speed, vibrato intensity, v, t, m/l, r intensity, r brilliance, Ch. 2: v, t, m/l), mfg. late 1960s.

| | N/A | N/A | N/A | |

SUPER DUKE – 100W, 2-12 in. speaker piggyback configuration designed for bass or electronic organ, tube chassis, single channel, front black control panel, two inputs, three knobs (v, b, t), black covering, black and white checkered grille, mfg. late 1960s.

| | N/A | N/A | N/A | |

MSR/NOTES	100%	EXCELLENT	AVERAGE	LAST MSR

VALET – 30W, 1-10 in. speaker combo guitar amp, tube chassis, single channel, vibrato, front black control panel, two inputs, four knobs (v, tone, s, i), black covering, black and white checkered grille, mfg. late 1960s.

N/A   N/A   N/A

VISCOUNT – 100W, 2-12 in. speaker piggyback configuration guitar amp, tube chassis, two channels, front black control panel, four inputs, eight knobs (Ch. 1: vibrato speed, vibrato intensity, v, t, m/l, Ch. 2: v, t, m/l), black covering, black and white checkered grille, mfg. late 1960s.

N/A   N/A   N/A

* ***Viscount Reverb*** – similar to the Viscount, except has a reverb circuit, reverb controls, and ten knobs (Ch. 1: vibrato speed, vibrato intensity, v, t, m/l, r intensity, r brilliance, Ch. 2: v, t, m/l), mfg. late 1960s.

N/A   N/A   N/A

ELECTRIC SS AMPLIFIERS

HERALD I – 10W, 1-10 in. speaker guitar combo, solid-state chassis, single channel, vibrato, front silver control panel, two inputs, four knobs (v, tone, i, s), footswitch jack, green/brown covering, brown grille, mfg. early 1970s.

N/A   N/A   N/A

HEARLD JUNIOR – 10W, 1-10 in. speaker guitar combo, solid-state chassis, single channel, vibrato, front silver control panel, two inputs, four knobs (v, tone, i, s), footswitch jack, brown covering, brown grille, mfg. early 1970s.

N/A   N/A   N/A

HEARLD III BASS – 30W, 1-12 in. speaker bass combo, solid-state chassis, single channel, front silver control panel, two inputs, three knobs (v, t, b), black covering, brown grille, mfg. early 1970s.

N/A   N/A   N/A

ELECA

Amplifiers and other accessories currently produced in China since 2004. Distributed by Eleca International Inc. in Walnut, CA.

Eleca instruments are produced in China and distributed throughout the United States. They produce a variety of guitar amplifiers including head units, combo units, and speaker cabinets. Eleca also produces a line of effects pedals. Most of their products are offered at a competitive price. For more information please refer to Eleca's website or contact them directly.

CONTACT INFORMATION
ELECA
Distributed by Eleca International, Inc.
21088 Commerce Pointe Drive
Walnut, CA 91789
Phone No.: 909-468-1382
Phone No.: 888-463-5322
Fax No.: 909-468-1652
www.elecaamps.com
info@elecaamps.com

ELECTAR

Amplifiers and PA equipment currently produced in Korea since circa 1996. Distributed by Gibson in Nashville, TN.

Electar is a trademark used on various amplifiers by Gibson Guitar Corp. In the mid-1990s, Gibson released a series of PA amps, solid-state and tube guitar amps, and wireless microphone systems branded Electar. Electar was also used on a line of Epiphone amplifiers during the 1930s, and when Gibson purchased Epiphone, the rights to this name came with.

ELECTRO-HARMONIX

Amplifiers and other products currently produced in New York City, NY. The Electro-Harmonix trademark was first established in 1968 and existed to circa 1984, and was revived in 1991.

Mike Matthews founded Electro-Harmonix in 1968, and they first produced the LPB-1 (Linear Power Boost). Jimi Hendrix was one of the first big-name guitar players to use an Electro-Harmonix product in the late 1960s. Hartley Peavey also received his inspiration after attending a NAMM show where Matthews was demonstrating his LPB-1. Peavey started building channel-switching amplifiers after this design. In 1970, they introduced the Big Muff Pi fuzz effect pedal. In 1971, EH introduced their first guitar amplifier - the AC/DC Freedom Amp. In the late-1970s, EH released an amp named after the president - The Mike Matthews Dirt Road Special. Electro-Harmonix thrived throughout the 1970s and early 1980s reporting at least one year of five million dollars in sales. However, in 1979, a union group attempted to get Matthews to make the company unionized. Matthews declined the move, but in 1981, the union came back and offered money to employees to join the union. Things did not go well, and six employees attacked Matthews in 1981. Matthews exposed the union group behind the entire situation on a local television station. The union went away, but the damage had been done. EH could not return to their previous production capacity and Matthews filed for bankruptcy in 1982. He bought the company back shortly thereafter, but ran into more trouble with the increasing Japanese market. EH filed for bankruptcy again in 1984. In 1988, he decided to start producing vacuum tubes in a Russian factory. He was able to utilize all the Russian military factories that were not producing anymore to build tubes for him. The first tube company he made was New Sensor Corporation and in 1989, he introduced Sovtek. After a few years of trying other ventures, Matthews bought the company one more time in 1991, however, the first

CONTACT INFORMATION
ELECTRO-HARMONIX
32-33 47th Ave.
Long Island City, NY 11101
Phone No.: 718-937-8300
Phone No.: 800-633-5477
Fax No.: 718-937-9222
www.ehx.com
info@ehx.com

MSR/NOTES	100%	EXCELLENT	AVERAGE	LAST MSR

new product released wasn't until 2001. They reintroduced a Freedom amp in the 2000s, but they currently focus on effects pedals and other accessories. For more information, visit Electro-Harmonix's website or contact the company directly.

ELECTRIC SOLID-STATE AMPLIFIERS

Electro-Harmonix recently offered the **Freedom** Amplifier. The Freedom amp is based off of the original Freedom amp back in the 1970s that was one of the first guitar amplifiers to be battery-operated. This is a reissue of the original Freedom amp with an 8 in. speaker that is battery operated and can be recharged. The controls on the amp are volume, tone, and bite to get a lot of sound out of a little amp. The amplifier also features a preamp output and comes in a hand crafted pine cabinet with a brown grille. Electro-Harmonix also offered a speaker cabinet with 4-10 in. speakers. This enclosure features a hand-crafted pine box, four Electro-Harmonix 10CS speakers and a removable brown grille.

FREEDOM AMP – low wattage, 2-5.5 in. speakers, solid-state chassis, AC/DC operation, wood cabinet, mfg. 1971-late 1970s.

N/A	$150 - 200	$95 - 120

MIKE MATTHEWS DIRT ROAD SPECIAL – 25W, 1-12 in. Celestion speaker, solid-state chassis, phase shifter, single channel, top black control panel, single input, four black knobs, black covering, black grille, mfg. mid- to late 1970s.

courtesy S.P. Fjestad

courtesy S.P. Fjestad

courtesy S.P. Fjestad

N/A	$250 - 300	$150 - 200

ELK

Amplifiers previously produced in Japan during the 1960s.

Elk amplifiers were built by Elk Gakki in Japan during the 1960s. Not much history is known about Elk, but their designs are based very closely on Fender Bassman and early Marshall models of the 1960s. Like many copied amplifiers produced in the 1960s, these models seem to have a weak spot in the output transformer. Any additional information can be submitted directly to Blue Book Publications. Source: Rittor Books, *60s Bizzare Guitars*.

ELECTRIC TUBE AMPLIFIERS

Elk produced two distinctive series. The Custom Series, which included the **EL-30** (Custom 30), the **EL-50** (Custom 50), the **EL-150L** (Custom 150-L), and the **EL-150S** (Custom 150-S). The EL-30 and EL-50 are very similar to blackface Fender Bassmans. The EL-150s have early Marshall style heads with large vertical speaker cabinets. The Viking Series consists of the **Viking-100** and the **Viking-50**. These models are also similar to early Marshall models with tall speaker cabinets. They also produced a Twin-Amp that came in 50W and 60W variations. These amps tend to sell between $300 and $400 in excellent condition.

ELMWOOD AMPS

Amplifiers previously produced in Sweden between 1998 and 2014.

Jan Alm founded Elmwood Amps in 1998 to build tube guitar amplifiers with the most outstanding sound and functionality available. Elmwood produced a variety of tube guitar amps including head units, combos, and accompanying speaker cabinets.

ELPICO

Amplifiers previously produced in London, England between the early 1950s and the late 1960s.

Elpico amplifiers were originally produced by the Lee Products Company. In the late 1960s, Lee became Elizabethan Electronics, and by 1970 they had stopped producing amplifiers. Elpico built radios, record players, and small amplifiers that were meant to amplify tape decks, etc. However, many Elpico models were used by guitar players (as there is not that much difference in early guitar amps). They also gained a bit of popularity due to Paul McCartney and Dave Davis of the Kinks using them occasionally. Information courtesy: Tim Fletcher and Steve Russell.

ELECTRIC TUBE AMPLIFIERS

The most popular Elpico models are the **AC-52** and **AC-55**, which can be easily identified by their blue/green covering, trapezoid-shaped grille, and round holes in the back cabinet. The AC-52 has a rear and side-mounted control panel with three knobs. The AC-55 has a top-mounted control panel with five knobs. Elpico also offered the **AC-85** and **AC-88** PA systems. Very few of these amplifiers show up in the used marketplace, especially since many of them never left England. However they appear to be valued between $200 and $400 depending upon features and condition.

EMC

Electronics Music Corporation. Amplifiers and speaker cabinets previously produced in Cleveland, OH during the early 1970s.

The Electronics Music Corporation (EMC) produced solid-state amplifiers in Cleveland, OH during the early 1970s (catalogs exist from 1971 to 1973). They produced a wide range of guitar, bass, organ, and PA amplifiers. The configurations EMC used are very similar to Kustom of the same era (minus the cool Tuck 'N Roll covering). Most amps are piggybacks with separate heads and cabinets, but they did produce combo units as well.

ELECTRIC SS AMPLIFIERS

EMC borrowed an idea from Fender and produced the Zodiac series of amps. The Virgo series was designed for bass guitars, the Leo series for organs, the Aries series for combo guitars, the Sagittarius series for piggyback guitars, and the Gemini series for PA systems. Just about every imagineable configuration was available in this line, but it was discontinued shortly after inception (did Fender have something to do with that?!). In 1972, a new series of bass and guitar amplifiers was released. Although there were not specific amps designed for PA or organ use, it is safe to say the bass models could be used for more than one application. The B series featured four models the **B-150** combo, **B-250** combo, **B-350** piggyback, and **B-450** piggyback. The G series featured four models the **G-150** combo, **G-250** combo, **G-350** piggyback, and **G-450** piggyback.

B-150 – 65W, 1-15 in. speaker, bass combo, solid-state chassis, two channels, front black and blue control panel, four inputs (two per channel), six black and silver knobs (v, b, t, for each channel), black covering, blue/gray grille cloth, 70 lbs., mfg. early 1970s.

courtesy S.P. Fjestad

	N/A	$100 - 150	$50 - 75	

B-250 – 110W, 1-15 in. speaker, bass combo, solid-state chassis, two channels, front black and blue control panel, four inputs (two per channel), eight black and silver knobs (v, b, m, t for each channel), brite switches, black covering, blue/gray grille cloth, 100 lbs., mfg. early 1970s.

	N/A	$150 - 200	$90 - 120	

G-150 – 65W, 2-12 in. speakesr, guitar combo, solid-state chassis, two channels, reverb, vibrato, front black and blue control panel, four inputs (two per channel), 10 black and silver knobs (Ch. 1: v, t, b, Ch. 2: v, t, m, b, r, s, i), brite switches, black covering, blue/gray grille cloth, footswitch, 75 lbs., mfg. early 1970s.

	N/A	$140 - 175	$90 - 115	

G-250 – 110W, 2-12 in. speakesr, guitar combo, solid-state chassis, two channels, reverb, vibrato, front black and blue control panel, four inputs (two per channel), 11 black and silver knobs (Ch. 1: v, t, m, b, Ch. 2: v, t, m, b, r, s, i), brite switches, black covering, blue/gray grille cloth, footswitch, 90 lbs., mfg. early 1970s.

	N/A	$150 - 200	$90 - 120	

EMERY SOUND

Amplifiers currently produced in El Cerrito, CA, since 1997. Direct Sales by Emery Sound.

Curt Emery started Emery Sound Amplifiers in 1997. Emery produces hand-built, low-wattage, tube-chassis models that are sold direct (no dealers). Low-wattage is a lot lower than most amps with a 6G6 power tube running wide open, the output is about 2W. Emery offers his amplifiers as chassis only, head-units, or combos, and speaker cabinets are also available. His heads and cabinets are finished in solid mahogany. For more information or how to order, visit Emery Sound's website or contact them directly.

CONTACT INFORMATION
EMERY SOUND
2651 Tamalpais Ave
El Cerrito, CA 94530
Phone No.: 510-236-1176
Fax No.: 510-236-1176
www.emerysound.com
amps@emerysound.com

ELECTRIC TUBE AMPLIFIERS

The **Microbaby** is a class A amp with 2W of power (and a half power switch), 6G6 tubes (optional 6K6 or 6V6 tubes), two knobs (v, tone), and the normal jacks for a head-unit. The Microbaby is available as a chassis (MSR $1,200, 100% $700), enclosed head-unit (MSR $1,580, 100% $950), a 1-10 in. speaker combo (MSR $2,000, 100% $1,200), or a 1-12 in. speaker combo (MSR $2,250, 100% $1,350). The **Superbaby** is a 6-12W amp depending upon the tube setup (several combinations are available). The Superbaby is available as a chassis (MSR $1,200, 100% $700), enclosed head-unit (MSR $1,580, 100% $950), a 1-10 in. speaker combo (MSR $2,000, 100% $1,200), or a 1-12 in. speaker combo (MSR $2,250, 100% $1,350), The **Spotlight** (disc., last 100% $1,350) featured the same chassis as the Superbaby, but was in combo configuration with 1-10 in. Jensen speaker and a unique-shaped cabinet. The **Stagebaby** (MSR $2,670, 100% $1,700) is similar to the Superbaby in that you can use a variety of tube configurations to put out 12W-35W and the amp will bias itself. The **Bassbaby** (MSR $2,670, 100% $1,700) is designed for bass guitars and puts out 20W-40W of power. Emery offers a **Mad Scientist** kit that includes 12 different tubes to experiment with different sounds. Emery also offers speaker cabinets available in 1-10 in. speaker (MSR $830, 100% $500) or 1-12 in. speaker (MSR $1,080, 100% $650) configurations.

courtesy Emery Sound

EMPERADOR

Amplifiers and other instruments previously built in Japan by the Kasuga company between circa 1966 and 1992. Distributed by Westheimer Musical Instruments in Chicago, IL.

The Emperador trademark was a brand name used in the U.S. market by the Westheimer Musical Instruments of Chicago, IL. The Emperador trademark was the Westheimer company's entry level line to their Cort products line through the years. Emperador models are usually shorter-scaled entry level instruments, and the trademark can be found on both jazz-style thinline acoustic/electric archtops, solid body electric guitars and basses, and a line of solid-state amplifiers.

ELECTRIC SS AMPS

Emperador's 1969 catalog displays four solid-state amplifiers available. The **P-10R** is a piggyback amp with 10W output and 2-10 in. speakers. The **P-30R** is a piggyback amp with 30W output, 1-8 in. and 1-12 in. speaker, and two independent channels. The **P-100ST** is a piggyback amp with 100W output and has two speaker cabinets each containing 2-12 in. speakers. The **B-2015** is a piggyback bass amp with 20W output, 1-15 in. speaker, and volume, bass, and treble controls. Used values on these amps are generally between $100 and $200.

ENGL

Amplifiers, speaker cabinets, and accessories currently produced in Germany, since 1984. Distributed in the U.S. by Velvet Distribution in Naples, FL. Previously distributed in the U.S. by JI Concept.

Edmund Engl to this day still believes in building the most innovative, cutting edge amplifiers. Engl debuted their first amplifier, The Straight, at the Frankfurt Music Fair in 1984. Engl has been producing fine tube amplification for over two decades now, and have added to their arsenal immensely. Engl produces amplifiers, speaker cabinets, and accessories. For more information, visit Engl's website or contact them directly.

CONTACT INFORMATION

ENGL
Germany
www.engl-amps.com
info@engldistribution.com

U.S. Distributor: Velvet Distribution
1079 Jardin Drive
Naples, FL 34104
Phone No.: 239-877-7757
Fax No.: 239-262-5499
velvetdistribution@comcast.net

ELECTRIC TUBE AMPLIFIERS: CLASSIC SERIES

CLASSIC SERIES HEAD (E 355C) – 50W, guitar head-unit, six-tube chassis, preamp: 3 X ECC83, power: 1 X ECC83, 2 X 5881, two channels (lo gain/hi gain), reverb, front black control panel, single input, nine cream chicken head knobs (lo gain 1, hi gain 2, b, m, t, r1, r2, MV1, MV2), bright and depth switches, lo/hi switch, line out, effects loop with level control, balanced line out with level control, various speaker outputs, dual footswitch jacks, cream covering, brown grille, disc.

100%	EXCELLENT	AVERAGE	LAST MSR
$1,500	$900 - 1,050	$600 - 700	$1,875

* *Classic Series 210 Combo (E 350C)* – similar to the Classic Series Head except in combo form with 2-10 in. Celestion Vintage speakers, disc.

100%	EXCELLENT	AVERAGE	LAST MSR
$1,800	$1,050 - 1,250	$725 - 850	$2,250

* *Classic Series 212 Combo (E 358)* – similar to the Classic Series Head except in combo form with 2-12 in. Celestion Greenback 25 speakers, disc.

100%	EXCELLENT	AVERAGE	LAST MSR
$2,000	$1,100 - 1,350	$775 - 925	$2,500

CLASSIC 210 SPEAKER CABINET (E 210C) – 100W, 2-10 in. Celestion Vintage 10 speakers, 16 ohm impedance, cream covering, brown grille, top handle, disc.

100%	EXCELLENT	AVERAGE	LAST MSR
$590	$350 - 425	$225 - 275	$737

MSR/NOTES	100%	EXCELLENT	AVERAGE	LAST MSR

CLASSIC 410 SPEAKER CABINET (E 410C) – 100W, 4-10 in. Celestion Vintage 10 or Jensen Alnico speakers, 16 ohm impedance, cream covering, brown grille, recessed side handles, disc.

	$800	$475 - 550	$275 - 325	$1,000

ELECTRIC TUBE AMPLIFIERS: MISC. MODELS

The original Engl amp was the **Straight 50**, which was introduced in the '80s, but is no longer in production.

ARTIST EDITION HEAD (E 651) – 100W, guitar head-unit, eight-tube chassis, preamp: 4 X ECC83, power: 4 X EL34, two channels (clean/lead) with gain control for each, front silver control panel, single input, nine black chicken head knobs (clean gain, lead gain, b, m, t, presence, volume, MV A, MV B), bright switch, shape switch, gain switch, channel switch, standby switch, power switch, rear panel: three footswitch jacks, noise gate threshold, effects loop with balance control, five poweramp jacks, black covering with a silver grille, current mfg.

MSR $2,500	$2,000	$1,300 - 1,500	$650 - 800	

FIREBALL (E 625) – 60W, head-unit only, six-tube chassis, preamp: 3 X ECC83, power: 1 X ECC83, 2 X 6L6GC, two channels (crunch/ultra lead), front silver control panel, single input, seven black chicken head knobs (g, b, m, t, p, MVA, MVB), bright switch, depth switch, ultra gain switch, effects loop with balance control, various speaker outputs, footswitch jacks, black covering with a criss-cross black grille, current mfg.

MSR $1,845	$1,475	$950 - 1,100	$475 - 600	

FIREBALL 100 (E 635) – 100W, guitar head-unit, eight-tube chassis, preamp: 4 X ECC83, power: 4 X 6L6GC, two channels (clean/lead), front black control panel, single input, nine black chicken head knobs (Clean Ch. g, Lead Ch. g, b, m, t, Lead v, MV A, MV B, p), Clean Ch. bright switch, bottom switch, mid boost switch, channel switch, standby switch, power switch, rear panel: two footswitch jacks, noise gate threshold, effects loop with balance control, five poweramp jacks, black covering with a criss-cross black grille, mfg. 2010-present.

MSR $2,313	$1,850	$1,200 - 1,375	$600 - 750	

GIG MASTER 15 HEAD (E 315) – 15W, guitar head-unit, three-tube chassis, preamp: 1 X ECC83, power: 2 X EL84, two channels, front gray control panel, single input, seven knobs (input g, lead drive, b, m, t, lead v, MV), mid-boost switch, channel switch, standby switch, power switch, rear panel: four-way power soak selector, footswitch jack, effects loop, balanced line out, three poweramp (speaker) jacks, black covering, black crisscross grille, mfg. summer 2010-present.

MSR $937	$750	$425 - 500	$250 - 300	

* *Gig Master 15 Combo (E 310)* – similar to the Gig Master 15 Head, except in combo configuration with 1-10 in. Celestion G10N-40 speaker, black covering, black crisscross grille, mfg. summer 2010-present.

MSR $1,062	$850	$500 - 600	$300 - 350	

GIG MASTER 30 HEAD (E 305) – 30W, guitar head-unit, five-tube chassis, preamp: 1 X ECC83, power: 4 X EL84, two channels, front gray control panel, single input, seven knobs (input g, lead drive, b, m, t, lead v, MV), mid-boost switch, gain-boost switch, channel switch, standby switch, power switch, rear panel: four-way power soak selector, footswitch jack, effects loop, balanced line out, three poweramp (speaker) jacks, black covering, black crisscross grille, current mfg.

MSR $1,186	$950	$625 - 700	$300 - 375	

* *Gig Master 30 Combo (E 300)* – 30W, 1-12 in. Celestion speaker, guitar combo amp, five-tube chassis, preamp: 1 X ECC83, power: 4 X EL84, two channels, front gray control panel, single input, seven knobs (input g, lead drive, b, m, t, lead v, MV), mid-boost switch, gain-boost switch, channel switch, standby switch, power switch, rear panel: four-way power soak selector, footswitch jack, effects loop, balanced line out, three poweramp (speaker) jacks, black covering, black crisscross grille, current mfg.

MSR $1,250	$1,000	$650 - 750	$325 - 400	

INVADER 100 HEAD (E 642) – 100W, guitar head-unit, ten-tube chassis, preamp: 4 X ECC83, power: 4 X EL34, four channels, front brushed aluminum control panel, single input, 24 black chickenhead knobs (one of each of the following for each channel: g, b, m, t, v, All: p, depth punch, MV A, MV B), channel switches, effects loop switch, noise gate switch, Master A/B switch, write/copy switch, various jacks and outputs on back, black covering with five dark gray bars running horizontal across the front, current mfg.

MSR $4,000	$3,200	$2,075 - 2,400	$1,050 - 1,275	

INVADER 150 HEAD (E 640) – 150W, guitar head-unit, ten-tube chassis, preamp: 4 X ECC83, power: 6 X EL34, four channels, front brushed aluminum control panel, single input, 24 black chickenhead knobs (one of each of the following for each channel: g, b, m, t, v, All: p, depth punch, MV A, MV B), channel switches, effects loop switch, noise gate switch, Master A/B switch, write/copy switch, various switches on front, various jacks and outputs on back, black covering with five dark gray bars running horizontal across the front, current mfg.

MSR $3,937	$3,150	$2,050 - 2,350	$1,025 - 1,250	

IRONBALL (E 606) – 20W, guitar head-unit, six-tube chassis, preamp: 4 X ECC83, power: 2 X EL84, two channels, reverb, front gray control panel, single input, eight knobs (clean g, lead g, b, m, t, presence, lead v, MV), gain boost switch, channel switch, standby switch, power switch, rear panel: four-way power soak selector, two footswitch jacks, reverb level control, effects loop, balanced line out, headphone jack, three external speaker jacks, black covering, black grille, current mfg.

MSR $1,500	$1,200	$775 - 900	$400 - 475	

METALMASTER 20 HEAD (E 309) – 20W, guitar head-unit, four-tube chassis, preamp: 2 X ECC83, power: 2 X EL84, two channels, reverb, front black control panel, single input, eight knobs (clean g, lead g, b, m, t, reverb, lead v, MV), mid-scoop switch, channel switch, standby switch, power switch, rear panel: four-way power soak selector, footswitch jack, effects loop, balanced line out, black covering, black grille, current mfg.

MSR $1,250	$1,000	$650 - 750	$325 - 400	

MSR/NOTES	100%	EXCELLENT	AVERAGE	LAST MSR

**Invader 150 Head
courtesy Engl**

**Raider 100 Combo
courtesy Engl**

**Steve Morse Signature 100 Head
courtesy Engl**

* ***Metalmaster 20 Combo (E 304)*** – 20W, 1-10 in. G10N-40 Celestion speaker, guitar combo, four-tube chassis, preamp: 2 X ECC83, power: 2 X EL84, two channels, reverb, front black control panel, single input, eight knobs (clean g, lead g, b, m, t, reverb, lead v, MV), mid-scoop switch, channel switch, standby switch, power switch, rear panel: four-way power soak selector, footswitch jack, effects loop, balanced line out, black covering, black grille, current mfg.

MSR $1,375	$1,100	$725 - 825	$350 - 450	

POWERBALL HEAD (E 645) – 100W, guitar head-unit, nine-tube chassis, preamp: 4 X ECC83, power: 1 X ECC83, 4 X 6L6GC, four channels (clean, crunch, low gain lead, high gain lead), front chrome control panel, single input, 18 black chickenhead knobs, various switches on front, various jacks and outputs on back, black covering with black criss-cross grille, disc. 2009.

	$2,000	$1,175 - 1,400	$800 - 950	$2,500

POWERBALL II HEAD (E 645/2) – 100W, guitar head-unit, eight-tube chassis, preamp: 4 X ECC83, power: 4 X 6L6GC, four channels (clean Ch. 1, crunch Ch. 2, lead Ch. 3, lead Ch. 4), front black control panel, single input, 20 black chickenhead knobs (Ch. 1/Ch. 2: clean Ch. 1 g, clean Ch. 2 g, b, m, clean Ch. 1 t, crunch Ch. 2 t, clean Ch. 1 v, crunch Ch. 2 v, Ch. 3/Ch. 4: lead Ch. 3 g, lead Ch. 4 g, b, m, mid-boost, t, lead Ch. 3 v, lead Ch. 4, All: p, depth punch, MV A, MV B), Ch. 1/2 bright switch, Ch. 1/2 bottom switch, Ch. 3 bottom switch, Ch. 4 bottom switch, mid boost switch, two channel switches, standby switch, power switch, rear panel: S.A.C. footswitch jack, three standard footswitch jacks, noise gate threshold level, effects loop with balance control, five poweramp (speaker) jacks, black covering with black criss-cross grille, mfg. 2010-present.

MSR $3,000	$2,400	$1,550 - 1,800	$775 - 950	

RAIDER 100 COMBO (E 344) – 100W, 1-12 in. Celestion Vintage 30 speaker, guitar combo, eight-tube chassis, preamp: 4 X ECC83, power: 4 X 5881, two channels, front black control panel, single input, 16 black chickenhead knobs (Ch. 1: g, b, m, t, r, v, Ch. 2: g, b, m, t, r, v, All: p, depth punch, MV A, MV B), bright switch, clean/bright switch, presence/depth punch on/off switch, mid boost switch, Master A/B switch, channel switch, hi gain switch, FX loop switch, LED power tube monitor, effects loop with balance control, footswitch jacks, speaker jacks, black covering, dark chrome criss-cross grille, mfg. 2008-present.

MSR $2,500	$2,000	$1,100 - 1,350	$775 - 925	

RETRO 50 HEAD (E 762) – 50W, guitar head-unit, six-tube chassis, preamp: 2 X ECC83, power: 2 X EL34, two channels (clean, lead) with gain control for each, front black control panel, single input, eleven black knobs (Ch. 1: g, b, m, t, v, Ch. 2: g, b, m, t, v, All: MV), standby switch, power switch, black covering, black grille, available with black, red, or gold faceplate, current mfg.

MSR $2,440	$1,950	$1,275 - 1,450	$625 - 775	

RITCHIE BLACKMORE SIGNATURE 100 (E 650) – 100W, guitar head-unit, eight-tube chassis, preamp: 3 X ECC83, power: 1 X ECC83, 4 X 5881, four channels (clean, crunch, lead, heavey lead), front silver control panel, single input, nine black chicken head knobs (clean, lead, b, m, t, p, MV, Master A Lo Gain, Master B Hi Gain), bright switch, contour switch, two channel switches, effects loop with balance control, line out, multiple speaker jacks, footswitch jack, black covering with four silver bars running horizontal across the front, current mfg.

MSR $2,250	$1,800	$1,175 - 1,350	$575 - 725	

ROCKMASTER 20 HEAD (E 307) – 20W, guitar head-unit, four-tube chassis, preamp: 2 X ECC83, power: 2 X EL84, two channels, reverb, front gray control panel, single input, eight knobs (clean g, lead g, b, m, t, reverb, lead v, MV), mid-scoop switch, channel switch, standby switch, power switch, rear panel: four-way power soak selector, footswitch jack, effects loop, balanced line out, black covering, silver grille, current mfg.

MSR $1,250	$1,000	$650 - 750	$325 - 400	

* ***Rockmaster 20 Combo (E 302)*** – 20W, 1-10 in. Celestion G10N-40 speaker, guitar combo, four-tube chassis, preamp: 2 X ECC83, power: 2 X EL84, two channels, reverb, front gray control panel, single input, eight knobs (clean g, lead g, b, m, t, reverb, lead v, MV), mid-scoop switch, channel switch, standby switch, power switch, rear panel: four-way power soak selector, footswitch jack, effects loop, balanced line out, black covering, silver grille, current mfg.

MSR $1,375	$1,100	$725 - 825	$350 - 450	

SAVAGE 120 (E 610) – 120W, head-unit only, eight-tube chassis, preamp: 5 X ECC83, power: 1 X ECC83, 2 X 6550, four channels, six basic sounds, 19 black and gray knobs, various switches and jacks, line out, black Tolex covering, current mfg.

MSR $3,250	$2,600	$1,700 - 1,950	$850 - 1,050	

MSR/NOTES	100%	EXCELLENT	AVERAGE	LAST MSR

SAVAGE SPECIAL EDITION (E 660) – 100W, head-unit only, ten-tube chassis, preamp: 5 X ECC83, power: 1 X ECC83, 4 X 6L6GC, four channels (clean, crunch, crunch 2, lead), reverb, front control panel, single input, 22 black and gray knobs, line out, several jacks, black Tolex covering, disc.

	$2,350	$1,800 - 2,050	$1,400 - 1,550	$2,899

SOVEREIGN 100 VINTAGE 112 COMBO (E 365) – 100W, 1-12 in. Celestion Vintage 30 speaker combo, 10-tube chassis, preamp: 5 X ECC83, power: 1 X ECC83, 4 X 5881, four channels (clean, crunch, soft lead, heavy lead), reverb, front silver control panel, single input, 18 black and silver knobs (Ch. 1/Ch. 2: clean g, crunch g, b, m, t clean, t crunch, clean v, crunch v, Ch. 3/Ch. 4: lead g, heavy lead g, b, m, t, p, lead v, heavy lead v, MV A, MV B), bright switch, soft/heavy switch, six additional channel switches, effects loop with balance control, balanced line out with level control, various speaker output jacks, dual footswitch jacks, MIDI port, black covering, black metal criss-cross grille, current mfg.

MSR $3,250	$2,600	$1,500 - 1,800	$1,050 - 1,200	

* *Sovereign 100 Vintage 212 Combo (E 368)* – similar to the Sovereign 100 Vintage 112 Combo, except has 2-12 in. Celestion Vintage 30 speakers, current mfg.

MSR $3,625	$2,900	$1,700 - 2,000	$1,150 - 1,350	

SCREAMER 50 HEAD (E 335) – 50W, guitar head-unit, six-tube chassis, preamp: 3 X ECC83, power: 1 X ECC83, 2 X 5881, four channels (clean, crunch, lead, heavy lead), reverb, front silver control panel, single input, nine black knobs (clean, lead, b, m, t, p, r, MV1, MV2), bright switch, two channel switches, effects loop with balance control, balanced line out with freq. control, various speaker outputs, dual footswitch jacks, black covering, black metal criss-cross grille, current mfg.

MSR $1,625	$1,300	$775 - 900	$500 - 575	

* *Screamer 50 Combo (E 330)* – similar to the Screamer 50 Head unit except in combo configuration with 1-12 in. Celstion Vintage 30 speaker (early models may have V80 speaker), current mfg.

MSR $1,845	$1,475	$950 - 1,100	$475 - 600	

SPECIAL EDITION HEAD (E 670/E 670EL34) – 100W, guitar head-unit, nine-tube chassis, preamp: 5 X ECC83, power: 4 X 6L6GC (or 4 X EL34), four channels (clean, crunch, lead 1, lead 2), front black control panel, single input, 22 chrome knobs, various switches on front, various jacks and outputs on back, black covering with five silver bars running horizontal across the front, current mfg.

MSR $5,250	$4,200	$2,750 - 3,150	$1,375 - 1,675	

STEVE MORSE SIGNATURE 100 HEAD (E 656) – 100W, guitar configuration head-unit, eight-tube chassis, preamp: 4 X ECC83/12AX7, power: 4 X EL34, three channels, front blue control panel, single input, 23 black knobs (Ch. 1: g, b, m, t, v, Ch. 2: g, b, m, t, v, Ch. 3: g, b, lo m 1, lo mid 2, hi mid 1, hi mid 2, t, v, All: p, depth punch, MV A, MV B), three channel switches, tone switch, hi gain switch, lo mid switch, hi mid switch, effects loop switch, noise gate switch, Master A/B switch, write/copy switch, MIDI control, two effects loops, footswitch jacks, speaker jacks, black covering, dark chrome bars running across front, mfg. 2008-present.

MSR $3,250	$2,600	$1,500 - 1,800	$1,050 - 1,200	

THUNDER HEAD (E 325) – 50W, guitar head-unit, six-tube chassis, preamp: 3 X ECC83, power: 1 X ECC83, 2 X 5881, three channels (clean, crunch, lead), front silver control panel, single input, seven black knobs (g, b, m, t, crunch v, lead v, MV), crunch/lead switch, clean/lead switch, various output jacks, black covering, criss-cross metal grille, current mfg.

MSR $1,250	$1,000	$575 - 675	$375 - 450	

* *Thunder 50 Combo (E 322)* – similar to the Thunder 50 Head, except in combo form with 1-12 in. Celestion Vintage V30 speaker (older models may have a V80 speaker), current mfg.

MSR $1,437	$1,150	$750 - 850	$375 - 450	

* *Thunder 50 Combo Reverb (E 320)* – similar to the Thunder 50 Head, except in combo form with 1-12 in. Celestion Vintage V30 speaker (older models may have a V80 speaker), and has a reverb circuit where the crunch volume knob is replaced with a reverb knob, current mfg.

MSR $1,625	$1,300	$775 - 900	$500 - 575	

VICTOR SMOLSKI LTD (E 646) – 100W, guitar head-unit, eight-tube chassis, preamp: 4 X ECC83, power: 4 X 6L6GC, four channels (clean, crunch, lead, heavey lead), front black control panel, single input, twenty black chicken head knobs, standby switch, power switch, effects loop with balance control, multiple speaker jacks, footswitch jack, black covering with black grille, current mfg.

MSR $3,125	$2,500	$1,625 - 1,875	$825 - 1,000	

ELECTRIC TUBE AMPLIFIERS: PREAMPS/POWER AMPS

MIDI TUBE PREAMP (E 580) – preamp only, two-space rack-mount guitar head-unit, four-tube chassis: 4 X ECC83, MIDI capabilities with 256 MIDI presets (40 factory presets), front chrome control panel, single input, eight chrome knobs (g, b, l/m, h/m, t, effect, v, MV), preamp defeat switch, clean/lead switch, gain lo/hi switch, bottom switch, contour switch, bright switch, ultra bright switch, modern/classic switch, rec. out bass switch, rec. out treble switch, three number digital display with four MIDI buttons, back panel: ground lift switch, stereo line out, line out level, two XLR line outs (left and right), stereo out (left/right) with level control, effects loop, aux. input, four MIDI inputs, black casing, current mfg.

MSR $3,937	$3,150	$1,850 - 2,300	$1,250 - 1,500	

PREAMP (E 530) – preamp only, one-space rack-mount guitar head-unit, two-tube chassis: 2 X ECC83, four channels (clean, crunch, soft lead, heavy lead), front black control panel, single input, eleven black knobs (Ch. 1/Ch. 2: clean g, b, m, t, clean v, Ch. 3/Ch. 4: lead g, b, l/m, h/m, t, lead v), bright switch, contour switch, gain lo/hi switch, clean/lead switch, preamp defeat switch, instrument output, effects loop (mono send, stereo return), stereo line out with level control, stereo line out, dual footswitch jacks, black casing, current mfg.

MSR $750	$600	$350 - 425	$200 - 250	

MSR/NOTES	100%	EXCELLENT	AVERAGE	LAST MSR

SPECIAL EDITION PREAMP (E 570) – preamp only, two-space rack-mount guitar head-unit, four-tube chassis: 4 X ECC83, four channels (clean, crunch, lead 1, lead 2), front black control panel, single input, 17 chrome knobs (Ch. 1/Ch. 2: clean g, crunch g, b, m, clean t, crunch t, clean v, crunch v, Ch. 3/Ch. 4: lead 1 g, lead 2 g, b, m, lead 1 t, lead 2 t, lead 1 v, lead 2 v, MV), various switches, MIDI in/thru, stereo out, balanced line outs, footswitch jacks, black casing, current mfg.

MSR $2,375	$1,900	$1,100 - 1,300	$750 - 900	

POWERAMP (E 840/50) – 100W (50W per side), two-space rack-mount guitar poweramp only, six-tube chassis: 2 X ECC83, 4 X 5881 (1 X ECC83 and 2 X 5881 per each side), two channels, front black control panel, eight black knobs (left v A, left v B, right v A, right v B, left p A, left p B, right p A, right p B), various speaker outputs, dual footswitch jacks, black casing, current mfg.

MSR $1,812	$1,450	$850 - 1,000	$600 - 700	

POWERAMP (E 850/100) – 200W (100W per side), two-space rack-mount guitar poweramp only, 11-tube chassis: 3 X ECC83, 8 X 6L6GC, two channels, front black control panel, eight black knobs (left v A, left v B, right v A, right v B, left p A, left p B, right p A, right p B), various speaker outputs, dual footswitch jacks, black casing, current mfg.

MSR $2,937	$2,350	$1,400 - 1,700	$950 - 1,100	

POWERAMP (E 930/60) – 120W (60W per side), three-space rack-mount guitar poweramp only, seven-tube chassis: 3 X ECC83, 4 X 6L6GC (1 X ECC83 and 2 X 6L6GC per each side), two channels, front black control panel, eight black knobs (left v A, left v B, right v A, right v B, left p A, left p B, right p A, right p B), input A/B switch, depth boost switch, MIDI port, various speaker outputs, dual footswitch jacks, black casing, disc.

N/A	$900 - 1,100	$600 - 725	$1,699	

SPEAKER CABINETS

110 GIGBOX SPEAKER CABINET (E 110) – 40W, 1-10 in. Celestion G10N-40 speaker, black covering, black metal criss-cross grille, mfg. summer 2010-present.

MSR $375	$300	$175 - 225	$110 - 140	

112 PRO SPEAKER CABINET (E 112V) – 60W, 1-12 in. Celestion Vintage 30 speaker, 8 ohm impedance, Siberian birch construction, black covering, black metal criss-cross grille, current mfg.

MSR $712	$575	$375 - 425	$185 - 230	

112 STANDARD SPEAKER CABINET (E 112S) – 60W, 1-12 in. Celestion V80 speaker, 8 ohm impedance, Siberian birch construction, black covering, black metal criss-cross grille, current mfg.

MSR $625	$500	$300 - 350	$175 - 225	

212 PRO SPEAKER CABINET (E 212V) – 120W, 2-12 in. Celestion Vintage 30 speakers, 16 ohm impedance, Siberian birch construction, black covering, black metal criss-cross grille, current mfg.

MSR $1,000	$800	$450 - 525	$275 - 325	

* *212 Pro Speaker Cabinet Horizontal (E 212VH(B))* – similar to the 212 Pro Speaker Cabinet, except has a horizontal speaker configuration, current mfg.

MSR $1,125	$900	$575 - 675	$295 - 350	

212 STANDARD SPEAKER CABINET (E 212S) – 120W, 2-12 in. Celestion V60 speakers, 16 ohm impedance, Siberian birch construction, black covering, black metal criss-cross grille, current mfg.

MSR $1,000	$800	$450 - 525	$275 - 325	

412 PRO SPEAKER CABINET (E 412GG/E 412GS) – 100W mono (50W per side stereo), 4-12 in. Celestion Greenback 25 speakers, 8 ohm impedance mono (16 ohm impedance stereo), straight (SG) or angled (SS) front, Siberian birch construction, black covering, black metal criss-cross grille, current mfg.

MSR $1,562	$1,250	$725 - 875	$500 - 575	

412 PRO SPEAKER CABINET (E 412VG/E 412VS) – 240W mono (120W per side stereo), 4-12 in. Celestion Vintage 30 speakers, 8 ohm impedance mono (16 ohm impedance stereo), straight (SG) or angled (SS) front, Siberian birch construction, black covering, black metal criss-cross grille, current mfg.

MSR $1,686	$1,350	$875 - 1,000	$450 - 550	

* *412 Pro XXL Speaker Cabinet (E 412 XXL)* – similar to the 412 Pro Speaker Cabinet, except has a larger cabinet, current mfg.

MSR $1,687	$1,350	$800 - 950	$525 - 625	

412 STANDARD SPEAKER CABINET (E 412SG/E 412SS) – 240W mono (120W per side stereo), 4-12 in. Celestion V60 speakers, 8 ohm impedance mono (16 ohm impedance stereo), straight (SG) or angled (SS) front, black covering, black metal criss-cross grille, current mfg.

MSR $1,250	$1,000	$650 - 750	$325 - 400	

MSR/NOTES	100%	EXCELLENT	AVERAGE	LAST MSR

EPIFANI CUSTOM SOUND

Amplifiers and speaker cabinets currently produced in Staten Island, NY. Previously produced in Brooklyn, NY beginning in 1992.

Epifani started producing bass amplifiers and speaker cabinets in 1992. They have worked closely with bassists to create some of the finest bass products out there. In 2004, they introduced their first bass combos. For more information, please contact Epifani directly.

CONTACT INFORMATION
EPIFANI CUSTOM SOUND
4442 Arthur Kill Rd.
Staten Island, NY 10309
Phone No.: 718-569-5588
www.epifani.com
info@epifani.com

ELECTRIC BASS AMPLIFIERS

UL 502 HEAD – 600W, head-unit only, solid-state chassis, two channels, front control panel, two inputs, eleven black knobs, black casing, 16 lbs., mfg. 2004-09.

$1,600	$1,000 - 1,200	$650 - 750	$1,999

UL 902 HEAD – 900W, head-unit only, solid-state chassis, two channels, front control panel, two inputs, eleven black knobs, black casing, 18 lbs., mfg. 2004-09.

$2,400	$1,400 - 1,700	$850 - 1,000	$2,899

UL 112C COMBO – 600W, 1-12 in. speaker combo, solid-state chassis, two channels, front control panel, two inputs, eleven black knobs, black casing, 48 lbs., mfg. 2004-07.

$1,900	$1,200 - 1,400	$700 - 800	$2,499

UL 115C COMBO – 600W, 1-15 in. speaker combo, solid-state chassis, two channels, front control panel, two inputs, eleven black knobs, black casing, 58 lbs., mfg. 2004-07.

$2,000	$1,300 - 1,500	$700 - 850	$2,599

UL 210C COMBO – 600W, 2-10 in. speaker combo, solid-state chassis, two channels, front control panel, two inputs, eleven black knobs, black covering, black grille, 58 lbs., mfg. 2004-07.

$2,200	$1,400 - 1,600	$800 - 950	$2,849

SPEAKER CABINETS

PS-112 SPEAKER CABINET – 300W, 1-12 in. speaker with a 1 in. tweeter, 17-ply baltic birch construction, black covering, black metal grille, top handle, 19.5 in. wide, 16.5 in. tall, 16.5 in. deep, 36 lbs., mfg. 2006-present.

MSR $550	$400	$250 - 300	$150 - 200

PS-115 SPEAKER CABINET – 400W, 1-15 in. speaker with a 1 in. tweeter, 17-ply baltic birch construction, black covering, black metal grille, recessed side handles, 23 in. wide, 21.5 in. tall, 18 in. deep, 52 lbs., mfg. 2006-present.

MSR $649	$500	$300 - 350	$175 - 225

PS-210 SPEAKER CABINET – 400W, 2-10 in. speakers with a 1 in. tweeter, 17-ply baltic birch construction, black covering, black metal grille, recessed side handles, 23 in. wide, 18.5 in. tall, 18 in. deep, 49 lbs., mfg. 2006-present.

MSR $699	$500	$300 - 375	$200 - 250

PS-410 SPEAKER CABINET – 800W, 4-10 in. speakers with a 1 in. tweeter, 17-ply baltic birch construction, black covering, black metal grille, recessed side handles, 23 in. wide, 28.5 in. tall, 18.5 in. deep, 79 lbs., mfg. 2006-present.

MSR $999	$700	$475 - 550	$300 - 375

UL2-110 SPEAKER CABINET – 300W, 1-10 in. 250W cast aluminum frame speaker with a 100W tweeter, 8 ohm impedance, top handle, black covering, black metal grille, 17 in. wide, 13.75 in. tall, 12.5 in. deep, 22 lbs., mfg. 2006-present.

MSR $599	$450	$275 - 325	$150 - 200

UL2-112 SPEAKER CABINET – 300W, 1-12 in. 300W cast aluminum frame speaker with a 100W tweeter, 8 ohm impedance, recessed side handles, black covering, black metal grille, 19.5 in. wide, 16.5 in. tall, 16.25 in. deep, 30 lbs., mfg. 2006-present.

MSR $799	$600	$350 - 425	$200 - 250

UL2-115 SPEAKER CABINET – 400W, 1-15 in. 400W cast aluminum frame speaker with a 100W tweeter, 8 ohm impedance, recessed side handles, black covering, black metal grille, 23 in. wide, 21.5 in. tall, 17.75 in. deep, 43 lbs., mfg. 2006-present.

MSR $1,149	$900	$550 - 625	$350 - 425

UL2-210 SPEAKER CABINET – 500W, 2-10 in. 250W cast aluminum frame speakers with a 100W tweeter, 8 or 4 ohm impedance, recessed side handles, black covering, black metal grille, 23 in. wide, 18.5 in. tall, 17.75 in. deep, 38 lbs., mfg. 2006-present.

MSR $1,149	$900	$550 - 625	$350 - 425

UL2-212 SPEAKER CABINET – 700W, 2-12 in. 300W cast aluminum frame speakers with a 100W tweeter, 4 or 8 ohm impedance, recessed side handles, black covering, black metal grille, 23 in. wide, 26.25 in. tall, 17.75 in. deep, 53 lbs., mfg. 2006-present.

MSR $1,299	$1,000	$600 - 700	$375 - 450

MSR/NOTES	100%	EXCELLENT	AVERAGE	LAST MSR

UL2-310 SPEAKER CABINET – 750W, 3-10 in. 250W cast aluminum frame speakers with a 100W tweeter, 4 ohm impedance, recessed side handles, black covering, black metal grille, 21.5 in. wide, 23 in. tall, 16.5 in. deep, 47 lbs., mfg. 2006-present.

| MSR $1,299 | $1,000 | $600 - 700 | $375 - 450 | |

UL2-410 SPEAKER CABINET – 1000W, 4-10 in. 250W cast aluminum frame speakers with a 100W tweeter, 8 or 4 ohm impedance, recessed side handles, black covering, black metal grille, 23 in. wide, 26.25 in. tall, 17.75 in. deep, 57 lbs., mfg. 2006-present.

| MSR $1,499 | $1,150 | $675 - 800 | $425 - 500 | |

UL2-610 SPEAKER CABINET – 1500W, 6-10 in. 250W cast aluminum frame speakers with a 100W tweeter, 4 ohm impedance, recessed side handles, black covering, black metal grille, 23 in. wide, 42 in. tall, 18.25 in. deep, 76 lbs., mfg. 2006-present.

| MSR $1,999 | $1,500 | $950 - 1,100 | $600 - 700 | |

EPIPHONE

Amplifiers and speaker cabinets currently produced in China, Japan, or Korea since the late 1980s. Previously produced in Kalamazoo, MI by Gibson between 1959 and 1967. Epiphone is a division of Gibson Musical Instruments in Nashville, TN. The Epiphone trademark was established in 1930 and was purchased in 1958 by Gibson.

CONTACT INFORMATION
EPIPHONE
645 Massman Drive
Nashville, TN 37210
Phone No.: 800-444-2766
www.epiphone.com

The Epiphone company was founded in the late 1920s as the The Epiphone Banjo Co. Anastasios Stathopoulo, his wife Marianthe, and son Epaminondas (Epi) were the three that started making instruments when they moved to the U.S. from Greece in 1903. Their first products were banjos, ukuleles and other instruments of the like. In 1931, the Masterbuilt series of guitars released and this was the first line of guitars for Epiphone. When the first band of electric guitars came out in the mid-1930s, there was a need to amplify the sound. In 1941, the first line of Epiphone amplifiers made their debut. These first three models were the Dreadnaught, Zephyr, and Century.

Shortly after the release of the amplifiers, Epi Strathopoulo, the founder of Epiphone, died of Leukemia in 1943. In a sense this was the beginning of the end for Epiphone. Orthie Stathopoulo took over as president, but couldn't get things going as well again. Frixo Stathopoulo, his brother, and Ortho were in constant friction and it took its toll on the company. In 1951, there was a labor strike at the plant that stopped production for several months. After this Ortho sold part of his share and the production moved to Philadelphia. The 1950s were especially rough for Epiphone. Frixo died leaving the rest of the company already in turmoil to Orphie. New guitar manufacturers and the lack of Epiphone to keep up with that led Orphie going to Ted McCarty, Gibson's president, to talk about selling the company. Gibson and Epiphone signed a deal and Gibson got a lot more than what they bargained for! Instead of going to New York and Philadelphia to get just the bass violin production, the trucks returned with the bass violin material, and all the jigs and what not for making guitars and some works in progress. For less than the cost of a mid-sized car today, Gibson bought its rival for $20,000. This would turn out to be the most profitable assest of Gibson.

After Gibson bought Epiphone in 1957/1958 the entire line went under renovation. The old amps were all discontinued and a new line was introduced in 1959. Some of these models carried the old names with a new twist (i.e. EA-5 Emperor, EA-25 Triumph, etc.), while some new ones were introduced (i.e. EA-30 Triumph). By 1961, all old model names were dropped in favor of Gibson's letter and number system (i.e. EA-10RV, EA-32RVT, etc.). Gibson produced Epiphone amplifiers through 1967 when all models were discontinued (a few amps still appeared on the price list through 1968 though). By 1970, Epiphone production had moved to Japan and an entire new line of guitars were introduced, but no amps. In the late 1980s, as Epiphone once again became Gibson's budget line, they introduced a new line of solid-state amplifiers. Currently they produce tube and solid-state guitar and bass amplifiers. For more information, visit Epiphone's website, or contact them directly. Information courtesy Walter Carter, *Epiphone: The Complete History*, shipping total information courtesy: *Gibson Shipment Totals 1948-1979*.

LTD. ED. 75th Anniversary Inspired By "1939" Electar Century Amplifier Special-II courtesy Epiphone

ELECTRIC TUBE AMPLIFIERS: CURRENT MODELS

LTD. ED. 75TH ANNIVERSARY INSPIRED BY "1939" ELECTAR CENTURY AMPLIFIER SPECIAL-II – 18 Watt, 1-12 in. speaker, four tube chassis, 2 X 6V6, 2 X 12AX7, three inputs, master volume control with push/pull boost, master tone control, vintage grille, internal bias adjustment, mfg. 2014-2015.

| | $400 | $260 - 300 | $130 - 160 | $665 |

ELECTRIC TUBE AMPLIFIERS: EARLY MODELS

Epiphone jumped into the electric guitar market under the Electar name in 1935. Shortly thereafter, Electar amplifiers emerged for Epiphone. Nat Daniels was responsible for making the first Epiphones. These first Electar models were made by Daniels and a suitcase company. The suitcase company supplied the cabinets and Daniels made the chassis to go inside of them.

MSR/NOTES	100%	EXCELLENT	AVERAGE	LAST MSR

ELECTAR MODEL – unspecified wattage, 1-8 in. speaker, tube chassis, single channel, rear control panel, three inputs (two for instruments, one for microphone), on/off switch, later models have volume and tone controls, black leatherette covering, black grille, mfg. 1936-37.

| | N/A | $425 - 500 | $250 - 300 | |

This model was available as an AC model or as an AC/DC power supply. The front and rear panels were detachable.

ELECTAR MODEL C – unspecified wattage, 1-10 in. speaker, tube chassis, single channel, rear control panel, on/off switch, volume control, grey linen covering, airplane cloth grille, "E" logo on the grille, mfg. 1936-39.

| | N/A | $550 - 700 | $350 - 425 | |

This model was available as an AC/DC power input. In 1937, a tone control was added and an AC only model was made available.

ELECTAR MODEL M – 15W (AC), 10W (AC/DC), 1-12 in. speaker, tube chassis, rear control panel, two input jacks, on/off switch, grey linen airplane cloth, brown grille with metal "E" logo, mfg. 1936-39.

| | N/A | $550 - 700 | $300 - 375 | |

In 1937, the output of the DC version was raised to 15W and a special AC/DC model was available, which had a high fidelity speaker and an additional filter. In 1938, a volume control was added.

ELECTAR SUPER AC/DC – 30W (AC/DC power), 1-12 in. speaker, tube chassis, rear control panel, three inputs (two for instruments, one for microphone), on/off switch, tone control, black Keratol covering, brown speaker covering with metal "E" logo, mfg. 1936-39.

| | N/A | $700 - 850 | $375 - 450 | |

In 1937, an AC only model was available. In 1938, a volume control was added.

CORONET – unspecified wattage, unspecified speaker, unspecified tubes, single channel, two input jacks, on/off switch, volume control, gray linen covering, "E" logo on the grille, mfg. 1939-1949.

| | N/A | $325 - 400 | $200 - 250 | |

In 1941, the cabinet was changed to a wood with walnut finish. We promise that this amp was "specified."

CENTURY – unspecified wattage (until 1949), 1-12 in. speaker, tube chassis, single channel, three inputs, on/off switch, volume control, wood maple covering with "E" logo on grille, mfg. 1939-1957.

1939-1948	N/A	$475 - 550	$275 - 325	
1949-1954	N/A	$500 - 600	$300 - 350	
1955-1957	N/A	$550 - 650	$300 - 375	

In 1949, wattage was found at 14W, vibrato was added to some models, covering was changed to a tweed plastic fabric with the "E" logo, tone control was added, cabinet size was increased, and it was only available as an AC model. In 1954, vertical slots were added to the grille. In 1955, output was increased to 15W, a channel was added, another input jack was added (two per channel), covering was changed to a yellow plastic linen, and a footswitch for the vibrato was available.

DREADNAUGHT (ZEPHYR DREADNAUGHT) – unspecified wattage (until 1949), 1-12 in. speaker, tube chassis, single channel, three input jacks (two for instrument, one for microphone), on/off switch, volume and tone controls, wood cabinet, "E" logo on grille, mfg. 1939-1957.

1939-1949	N/A	$625 - 750	$350 - 425	
1950-1954	N/A	$650 - 800	$375 - 450	
1955-1957	N/A	$500 - 600	$300 - 350	

When the Dreadnaught was released in 1939, it was a Zephyr that had more power. In 1949, it became its own name, the Dreadnaught, vibrato was an option, AC/DC was discontinued, covering was changed to a walnut veneer and output was stated to be 30W. In 1950, Vibrato was standard. In 1954, the speaker was upgraded to 1-15", the covering was changed to a tweed plastic linen, and a footswitch was available. In 1955, output was increased to 50W, the speaker configuration was change to 2-12", and the covering was changed to a yellow plastic linen.

KENT – 6.5W, 1-10 in. speaker, tubes, single channel, two input jacks, on/off switch, volume control, tweed plastic covering, "E" logo on the grille, mfg. 1949-1950.

| | N/A | $325 - 400 | $175 - 225 | |

ZEPHYR – unspecified wattage (until 1949), 1-12 in. speaker, AC/DC power, tube chassis, single channel, on/off switch, three input jacks, volume and tone controls, wood cabinet, "E" logo on grille, mfg. 1939-1957.

1939-1949	N/A	$600 - 700	$325 - 400	
1950-1954	N/A	$650 - 800	$350 - 425	
1955-1957	N/A	$500 - 600	$300 - 350	

In 1949, wattage set at 20W, vibrato available as an option with controls for speed and intensity, and the AC/DC option was discontinued. In 1950, vibrato was standard, and wood cabinet was made of walnut veneer. In 1954, a footswitch for vibrato was an option. In 1955, output was increased to 30W, the speaker was upped to 1-15", a second channel was added with another input jack, volume and tone controls for each channel, and covering was changed to a yellow plastic linen with a brown grille.

ELECTRIC TUBE AMPLIFIERS: EA SERIES

Many (if not all) Epiphone EA-Series amps are Gibson models with an Epiphone logo and cosmetics. When available, the corresponding Gibson model is listed. An interesting note: Gibson amplifiers are numbered as their entry level model starting with a low number (GA1) and climbing to high numbers (GA-100) while Epiphones are exactly the opposite (with the exception of amps over EA-70). Their low model started with a high number (EA-50) and the high end model is a low number (EA-4T). Since exact Epiphone specs are hard to come by, any additional information would be appreciated and can be submitted directly to Blue Book Publications.

EA-2T – specifications unknown, 48 shipped, mfg. 1964-65.

	N/A	N/A	N/A

EA-4T EMPEROR – 35W, 1-15 in. and 1-10 in. speaker with crossover, eight tube chassis, preamp: 3 X 6EU7, 1 X 6C4, 1 X 6FQ7, power: 2 X 6L6, 0A2 rectifier, dual channels, tremolo, ten control knobs (Ch. 1: v, b, m, t, depth, freq, Ch. 2: v, b, m, t), gray covering, light grille, 139 shipped, mfg. 1963-65.

	N/A	$500 - 600	$300 - 375

This model is the same as the Gibson Mercury II.

*   ***EA-4TL Emperor*** – similar to the EA-4T, except has Lansing speakers, 54 shipped, mfg. 1963-65.

	N/A	$550 - 650	$325 - 400

EA-5 EMPEROR – unknown wattage, 1-12 in. speaker, six tube chassis, 55 shipped, mfg. 1959-1961.

	N/A	$500 - 600	$300 - 375

EA-5RVT EMPEROR – 25W, 1-15 in. speaker, nine tube chassis, preamp: 4 X 6EU7, 1 X 7199, 1 X 12AU7, power: 2 X 7591, 5AR4 rectifier, two channels, tremolo, reverb, front mounted control panel, four inputs, nine control knobs (Ch. 1: v, b, t, r, depth, freq, Ch. 2: v, b, t), gray covering, brown grille, 97 shipped, mfg. 1962-63.

	N/A	$600 - 700	$375 - 450

*   ***EA-5RVTL Emperor*** – similar to the EA-5, except has Lansing speakers, 12 shipped, mfg. 1963 only.

	N/A	$650 - 800	$400 - 475

EA-6T EMPEROR – 35W, 2-12 in. speakers with crossover, eight tube chassis, preamp: 3 X 6EU7, 1 X 6C4, 1 X 6FQ7, power: 2 X 6L6, 0A2 rectifier, dual channels, tremolo, ten control knobs (Ch. 1: v, b, m, t, depth, freq, Ch. 2: v, b, m, t), gray covering, light grille, 70 shipped, mfg. 1964-65.

	N/A	$550 - 650	$325 - 400

This model is the same as the Gibson Mercury I, and similar to the EA-4T Emperor with 2-12 in. speakers.

EA-7P PROFESSIONAL – 15W, 1-12 in. speaker, six tube chassis: 2 X 6EU7, 1 X 6C4, 2 X 6BQ5, 1 X 6CA4 rectifier, single channel, top control panel, no controls on the amp, 287 shipped, mfg. 1962-66.

EA-5RVT Emperor
courtesy S.P. Fjestad

courtesy S.P. Fjestad

Amp Only	N/A	$375 - 450	$225 - 275
Amp & Guitar	N/A	$2,000 - 2,500	$1,200 - 1,500

This amp came paired with the Professional guitar, which had all the controls mounted on the pickguard of the guitar, and controlled the amp through the cable attached to the multiprong jack. The amp will not work without the Professional guitar.

EA-8P PROFESSIONAL – 35W, 1-12 in. speaker, seven tube chassis: 3 X 6EU7, 1 X 12AU7, 2 X 7591, 1 X 5AR4 rectifier, single channel, reverb, tremolo, top control panel, no controls on the amp, 139 shipped, mfg. 1963-65.

Amp Only	N/A	$425 - 500	$250 - 300
Amp & Guitar	N/A	$2,100 - 2,600	$1,250 - 1,550

This amp came paired with the Professional guitar, which had all the controls mounted on the pickguard of the guitar, and controlled the amp through the cable attached to the multiprong jack. The amp will not work without the Professional guitar.

MSR/NOTES	100%	EXCELLENT	AVERAGE	LAST MSR

EA-10 DELUXE – ~25W, 1-15 in. speaker, six tube chassis, preamp: 2 X 12AX7, 1 X 12AU7, power: 2 X 6L6GB, 5AR4 rectifier, two channels, four inputs, five control knobs (v1, v2, t, m, b), gray covering, light grille, 24 shipped, mfg. 1959-1961.

courtesy George McGuire

courtesy George McGuire

| | N/A | $500 - 600 | $300 - 375 | |

* **EA-10RV** – similar to the EA-10 Deluxe, except has a reverb circuit with control, 76 shipped, mfg. 1961-63.

| | N/A | $550 - 650 | $325 - 400 | |

EA-12RVT FUTURA – 50W, 4-10 in. speakers, eight tube chassis, preamp: 4 X 6EU7, 1 X 12AU7, power: 2 X 7591, 5AR4 rectifier, two channels, reverb, tremolo, front control panel, four inputs, two volume controls, two tone controls, reverb on one channel, tremolo on both channels, gray covering, light grille, 1,951 shipped, mfg. 1962-67.

| | N/A | $600 - 700 | $375 - 450 | |

This model is the same as the Gibson GA-30RVT Invader.

EA-14RVT FUTURA – similar to the EA-12RVT Futura, except has 2-10 in. speakers, 642 shipped, mfg. 1965-67.

| | N/A | $500 - 600 | $300 - 375 | |

This model is the same as the Gibson GA-45RVT Saturn.

EA-15 ZEPHYR – 14W or 20W, 1-12 in. speaker, two channels, tremolo, 58 shipped, mfg. 1959-1961.

| | N/A | $475 - 550 | $300 - 350 | |

This model is the same as the Gibson GA-40.

* **EA-15RV** – similar to the the EA-15 Zephyr, except has reverb and no tremolo circuit, 384 shipped, mfg. 1961-63.

| | N/A | $500 - 600 | $300 - 375 | |

* **EA-15RVT** – similar to the the EA-15 Zephyr, except has an eight tube chassis, preamp: 4 X 6EU7, 1 X 12AU7, power: 2 X 6V6, 5Y3 rectifier, dual channels, reverb, tremolo, four inputs, two volume controls, two tone controls, reverb on one channel, tremolo on both channels, gray covering, light grille, 890 shipped, mfg. 1962-65.

| | N/A | $500 - 600 | $300 - 400 | |

EA-16RVT REGENT – 35W, 1-12 in. speaker, eight tube chassis, 2 X 6EU7, 12AX7, 2 X 12AU7, 2 X 7591, 0A2 rectifier, dual channels, tremolo, reverb, front control panel, four inputs (two per channel), eight knobs (Ch.1: v, b, t, Ch. 2: v, b, t, depth, freq, reverb), gray Tolex covering, light grille, 756 shipped, mfg. 1965-67.

| | N/A | $350 - 450 | $250 - 300 | |

This model is the same as the Gibson GA-35RVT Lancer.

EA-22RVT – wattage unknown, 1-12 in. speaker, six tubes chassis: 2 X 12AU7, 2 X EU7, 2 X EL34, single channel, tremolo, reverb, front control panel, three inputs, six knobs (v, b, t, depth, speed, r), gray Tolex covering, light grille, 211 shipped, mfg. mid 1964-67.

| | N/A | $800 - 1,000 | $550 - 700 | |

EA-25 CENTURY – 14W or 20W, 1-12 in. speaker, seven tube chassis, preamp: 1 X 5879, 1 X 12AY7, 1 X 12AX7, 1 X 6SQ7, power: 2 X 6V6, 5Y3 rectifier, dual channels, four inputs, two volume controls, one tone control, gray covering, light grille, 127 shipped, mfg. mid 1959-1960.

| | N/A | $375 - 450 | $225 - 275 | |

This model is the same as the Gibson GA-20 Crest.

* **EA-25T** – similar to the EA-25 Century, except has a tremolo circuit, 157 shipped, mfg. mid 1961-63.

| | N/A | $425 - 500 | $250 - 300 | |

This model is the same as the Gibson GA-20T.

MSR/NOTES	100%	EXCELLENT	AVERAGE	LAST MSR

EA-28RVT Pathfinder
courtesy John Beeson/The Music Shoppe

EA-50 Pacemaker
courtesy George McGuire

EA-26RVT ELECTRA – 12.5W, 1-12 in. speaker, eight tubes, 3 X 6EU7, 2 X 12AU7, 2 X EL84, 5Y3 rectifier, dual channels, reverb, tremolo, white front control panel, four inputs (two per channel), eight knobs (Ch. 1: v, b, t, Ch. 2: v, b, t, s, i, r), footswitch, gray Tolex covering, gray light grille, 1,275 shipped, mfg. 1965-67.

N/A	$400 - 450	$250 - 300

This model is the same as the Gibson GA-20RVT Minuteman.

EA-28RVT PATHFINDER – wattage unknown, 1-12 in. speaker, seven tube chassis: 3 X 6EU7, 1 X 6C4, 2 X 6V6, 5Y3 rectifier, reverb, tremolo, single channel, front control panel, two inputs, six knobs (v, b, t, r, s, i), gray Tolex covering, light grille, 3,026 shipped, mfg. 1961-65.

N/A	$475 - 550	$300 - 350

This model is the same as the Gibson GA-19RVT Falcon.

EA-30 TRIUMPH – 1-12 in. speaker, five tube chassis, preamp: 2 X 12AX7, power: 2 X 6V6, 5Y3 rectifier, dual channels, four inputs, two volume controls, one tone control, gray covering, light grille, 78 shipped, mfg. 1959-1961.

N/A	$600 - 750	$350 - 450

This model is the same as the Gibson GA-14 Titan.

EA-32RVT COMET – 12.5W, 1-10 in. speaker, five tube chassis, preamp: 2 X 6EU7, 12AU7, power: 2 X 6BQ5, single channel, tremolo, reverb, front white control panel, three inputs, six control knobs (v, b, t, r, depth, freq.), coarse gray Tolex covering, gray grille cloth, 1,883 shipped, mfg. 1961, 1965-67.

N/A	$375 - 450	$225 - 275

This model is the same as the Gibson GA-15RVT Explorer.

EA-33RVT GALAXIE – output unkown, 1-10 in. speaker, six tube chassis, preamp: 2 X 6EU7, 12AX7, power: 2 X 6AQ5, 6CA4 rectifier, single channel, tremolo, reverb, top silver control panel, two inputs, four black and silver knobs (v, r, tremolo freq., power switch), gray covering, gray cloth grille, 1,810 shipped, mfg. 1963-65.

N/A	$375 - 450	$225 - 275

This model is the same as the Gibson GA-17RVT Scout.

EA-35 DEVON – 10W, 1-12 in. speaker, four tube chassis: 6EU7, 6C4, 2 X 6BQ5 power, 6CA4, single channel, top nickel plated control panel, two instrument inputs, one volume and one tone control, gray vinyl covering, light cloth grille, 680 shipped, mfg. 1959-1963.

N/A	$425 - 500	$250 - 300

This model is the same as the Gibson GA-8 Discoverer.

* *EA-35T Devon Tremolo* – similar to the EA-35 except has tremolo circuit, tube complement: 2 X 6EU7, 1 X 6CA4, 2 X 6BQ5, and the addition of tremolo controls, 1,736 shipped, mfg. 1960-65.

N/A	$450 - 525	$275 - 325

This model is the same as the Gibson GA-8T Discoverer.

EA-50 PACEMAKER – 12.5W, 1-10 in. speaker, five tube chassis, preamp: 1 X 6EU7, 6C4, power: 2 X 6BQ5, 6X4 rectifier, single channel, front control panel, two inputs, single volume knob, coarse gray Tolex covering, gray grille cloth, 4,350 shipped, mfg. 1959-1967.

N/A	$250 - 300	$135 - 175

Early models only had one volume knob while later models had v, b, and t. Later tube complements have 2 X 6EU7 and 2 X 6AQ5. This model is the same as the Gibson GA-5 Skylark.

* *EA-50T Pacemaker Tremolo* – similar to the EA-50 Pacemaker, except has tremolo, tube complement of 2 X 6EU7, 2 X 6AQ5, and 1 X 6X4, 4,997 shipped, mfg. 1961-67.

N/A	$275 - 325	$150 - 200

This model is the same as the Gibson GA-5T Skylark. The Pacemaker Tremolo had volume, bass, treble, and depth controls on later models.

MSR/NOTES	100%	EXCELLENT	AVERAGE	LAST MSR

EA-65 RIVOLI – 20W, single speaker combo, five tube chassis, preamp: 2 X 6EU7, power: 2 X 7591, 5AR4 rectifier, single channel, two inputs, unusual high frequency feedback loop, gray covering, light grille, 99 shipped, mfg. 1962-63.

	N/A	$300 - 350	$175 - 225	

This model is the same as the Gibson GA-60 Hercules.

EA-70 BASS AMPLIFIER – 35W, 1-12 in. speaker, piggy-back design, nine tube chassis, 6EU7, 2 X 6BD6, 2 X 6FM8, 2 X 6L6, GZ34, 0A2, single channel, front silver control panel, two inputs, three black chicken head knobs (v, t, b), head-unit is mounted in gray covering, cabinet is gray covering with light cloth grille, logo, 160 shipped, mfg. 1960-63.

	N/A	$600 - 700	$375 - 450	

This model is the same as the Gibson GA-100 Bass Amplifier.

EA-71 CONSTELLATION V – 50W, 1-15 in. speaker combo, five tube chassis, preamp: 2 X 6EU7, 6C4, power: 2 X 6L6, single channel, two inputs, three controls, (v, b, t), covering unknown, 473 shipped, mfg. 1964-67.

	N/A	$475 - 550	$300 - 350	

This model is the same as the Gibson Atlas Medalist.

EA-72 CONSTELLATION BASS AMP – similar to the EA-71 Constellation V, except in piggyback configuration, 574 shipped, mfg. 1964-67.

	N/A	$475 - 550	$300 - 350	

This model is the same as the Gibson Atlas IV. Five models were produced with Lansing speakers.

EA-300RVT EMBASSY – 90W, 2-12 in. speaker combo, ten tube chassis: 2 X 6EU7, 3 X 12AU7, 4 X 6L6, 0A2 rectifier, two channels, reverb, tremolo, four inputs, eleven knobs (Ch. 1: v, b, m, t, Ch. 2: v, b, m, t, r, s, depth), 233 shipped, mfg. 1965-67.

	N/A	$500 - 600	$300 - 400	

This amp was Epiphone's answer to Fender's Twin Reverb. Five models were produced with Lansing speakers. This model is the same as the Gibson GA-95RVT Apollo.

EA-400T PANORAMA V – 65W, 1-10 in. and 1-15 in. speaker combo, eleven tube chassis: 3 X 6EU7, 2 X 12AU7, 1 X 6FG7, 4 X 6L6, 0A2 rectifier, two channels, tremolo, four inputs, eight knobs (Ch. 1: v, b, t, Ch. 2: v, b, m, t, s, depth), 37 shipped, mfg. mid 1964-67.

	N/A	$500 - 600	$300 - 375	

EA-500T PANORAMA – similar to the EA-400T, except in piggyback configuration with a speaker cabinet configuration of 1-15 in. and 2-10 in. speakers, 106 shipped, mfg. mid 1963-66.

	N/A	$450 - 550	$300 - 375	

This model is the same as the Gibson Titan III.

ELECTRIC TUBE AMPLIFIERS: GALAXIE SERIES

Galaxie 10
courtesy Epiphone

Galaxie 25
courtesy Epiphone

GALAXIE 10 – 10W, 1-10 in. Celestion speaker, guitar combo, Class A two-tube chassis, preamp: 1 X 12AX7, power: 1 X 6L6, single channel, top control panel, single input, five black knobs (v, t, m, b, g), black or blue Tolex covering, gray grille, mfg. 2001-04.

	N/A	$135 - 175	$80 - 100	$332

GALAXIE 25 – 25W, 1-12 in. Celestion speaker, guitar combo, six-tube chassis, preamp: 3 X 12AX7, 1 X 12AT7, power: 2 X EL34, solid-state rectifier, single channel, reverb, top control panel, single input, five black knobs (v, t, m, b, r), black or blue Tolex covering, gray grille, mfg. 2003-04.

	N/A	$225 - 275	$120 - 150	$582

MSR/NOTES	100%	EXCELLENT	AVERAGE	LAST MSR

ELECTRIC TUBE AMPLIFIERS: VALVE SERIES

- Add $25 (MSR $40) for two-button (channel select, reverb) footswitch (Blues Custom 30 and So-Cal models only).

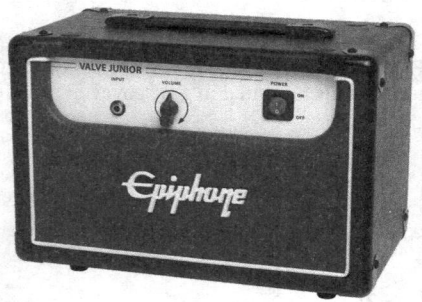

Valve Junior Head
courtesy Epiphone

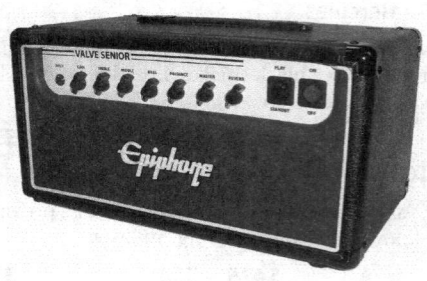

Valve Senior Head
courtesy Epiphone

Valve Standard
courtesy Epiphone

BLUES CUSTOM 30 (EPA-BKBC30) – 30W (Class AB) or 15W (Class A), 2-12 in. Lady Luck by Eminence speakers, guitar combo, all tube chassis, preamp: 5 X 12AX7, power: 2 X 5881, rectifier: 5AR4, two channels, reverb, front control panel, single input, eight black knobs (Ch. 1: v, Ch. 2: drive, mid, level, all: t, m, b, r), EQ switch, external speaker jacks, half power switch, optional footswitch, black covering, brown grille split diagonally, mfg. 2006-disc.

| | $580 | $350 - 425 | $200 - 250 | $1,100 |

SO-CAL 50H HEAD (EPA-BKSC50H) – 50W (switchable to 25W), Class AB, head-unit configuration, tube chassis, preamp: 5 X 12AX7, power: 2 X EL34, rectifier: solid-state, two channels, reverb, front white control panel, single input, nine black knobs (Ch. 1: v, Ch. 2: g, c, level, All: t, m, b, r, p), EQ switch, mulitple speaker outs, half-power switch, optional footswitch, black covering, black metal grille, mfg. 2006-disc.

| | $500 | $300 - 375 | $175 - 225 | $800 |

SO-CAL 412S SPEAKER CABINET (EPA-BKVS412SL) – 280W, 4-12 in. Lady Luck by Eminence speakers, stereo/mono operation, slanted front, black covering, black metal grille, mfg. 2006-disc.

| | $350 | $175 - 225 | $110 - 140 | $550 |

VALVE JUNIOR HEAD (EPA-EMJRMH) – 5W, head-unit configuration, Class A tube chassis, preamp: 1 X 12AX7, power: 1 X EL84, single channel, front control panel, single input, single volume control, 4, 8, or 16 ohm speaker out, black covering, brown front, mfg. 2006-disc.

| | $150 | $80 - 100 | $50 - 65 | $280 |

* Valve Junior Combo (EPA-BKJR) – similar to the Valve Junior Head except in combo configuration with 1-8 in. speaker, black covering, brown grille, mfg. 2004-disc.

| | $200 | $100 - 130 | $55 - 75 | $350 |

VALVE JUNIOR HOT-ROD HEAD (EPA-VJHR) – 5W, guitar head-unit, Class A three-tube chassis, preamp: 2 X 12AX7, power: 1 X EL84, solid-state rectifier, single channel, reverb, front control panel, single input, three knobs (g, v, r), standby switch, power switch, 4, 8, or 16 ohm speaker out, dummy load out for reverb use only, black leather covering, red leather front with Epiphone logo, mfg. 2008-disc.

| | $220 | $110 - 140 | $70 - 90 | $370 |

VALVE JUNIOR 112 SPEAKER CABINET (EPA-EMJREC) – 70W, 1-12 in. Eminence Lady Luck speaker, birch plywood construction, black covering, brown grille with red leather bar on top with "Epiphone" logo, designed for use with the Valve Junior Head or Valve Junior Combo, 18.25 in. wide, 18.75 in. tall, 10.75 in. deep, 26 lbs., mfg. 2007-disc.

| | $160 | $85 - 110 | $50 - 65 | $300 |

VALVE SENIOR HEAD (EPA-VSH) – 18W, guitar head-unit, Class AB six-tube chassis, preamp: 4 X 12AX7, power: 2 X 6V6GT, solid-state rectifier, single channel, reverb, front control panel, single input, seven black chickenhead knobs (g, t, m, b, p, MV, r), standby switch, power switch, 4, 8, and 16 ohm speaker outs, black leather covering, red leather front with Epiphone logo, mfg. 2008-disc.

| | $300 | $150 - 200 | $95 - 120 | $500 |

* Valve Senior Combo (EPA-VSC) – similar to the Valve Senior Head, except in combo configuration with 1-12 in. Eminence Lady Luck speaker, black leather covering, split red leather/brown cloth grille with Epiphone logo, mfg. 2008-disc.

| | $360 | $200 - 250 | $120 - 150 | $600 |

VALVE SPECIAL (EPA-BKSPDSP) – 5W, 1-10 in. speaker, Class A tube chassis, preamp: 2 X 12AX7, power: 1 X EL84, single channel, DSP, front control panel, single input, seven black knobs (g, t, m, b, DSP, r, MV), black covering, brown grille, mfg. 2004-08.

| | $240 | $150 - 180 | $95 - 120 | $400 |

VALVE STANDARD (EPA-BKSTDSP) – 15W, 1-12 in. speaker, Class A tube chassis, preamp: 2 X 12AX7, power: 2 X EL84, single channel, DSP, front control panel, single input, seven black knobs (g, t, m, b, DSP, r, MV), black covering, brown grille, mfg. 2004-08.

| | $300 | $175 - 225 | $110 - 140 | $500 |

MSR/NOTES	100%	EXCELLENT	AVERAGE	LAST MSR

ELECTRIC SS AMPLIFIERS: EARLY MODELS

Although there is not much information on the EA-100 and EA-101, they are probably solid-state models as no schematics exist on the design and most models produced in 1967 were solid-state.

EA-100 – unknown wattage, 1-10 in. speaker, solid-state chassis, 208 shipped, mfg. 1967 only.

	N/A	$75 - 100	$50 - 65	

EA-101 – unknown wattage, 1-10 in. speaker, solid-state chassis, tremolo, 630 shipped, mfg. 1967 only.

	N/A	$95 - 120	$60 - 75	

EA-550RVT SUPERBA – 50W, 2-10 in. speakers, guitar combo, solid-state chassis, 15 transistors, nine diodes, two channels, reverb, tremolo, front control panel, four inputs, 11 knobs (Ch. 1: v, b, m, t, r, s, i, Ch. 2: v, b, m, t), two-button footswitch, black covering, light grille, 127 shipped, mfg. 1966-67.

	N/A	$325 - 400	$200 - 250	

ES-600RVT MAXIMA – 100W, 4-10 in. speakers, guitar piggyback configuration with two horizontal 2-10 in. speaker cabinets, solid-state chassis, 26 transistors, nine diodes, two channels, reverb, tremolo, vibrato, front control panel, four inputs, 11 knobs two-button footswitch, black covering, light grille, 272 shipped, mfg. 1965-67.

	N/A	$275 - 350	$150 - 200	

E-20B – 20W, 1-15 in. speaker, bass combo, solid-state chassis, single channel, front black and silver control panel, two inputs, three knobs (v, t, b), three-way on/off/polarity power switch, black covering, black grille, 19 in. wide, 29 in. tall, 10 in. deep, 41 lbs., mfg. mid-1970s.

	N/A	$120 - 150	$75 - 95	

E-65 – 5W, 1-10 in. speaker, guitar combo, solid-state chassis, single channel, front black and silver control panel, two inputs, two knobs (v, tone), black covering, black grille, 16.5 in. wide, 19 in. tall, 8.5 in. deep, 16 lbs., mfg. mid-1970s.

	N/A	$95 - 120	$55 - 75	

E-75 – 5W, 1-10 in. speaker, guitar combo, solid-state chassis, single channel, tremolo, front black and silver control panel, two inputs, three knobs (v, tremolo, tone), black covering, black grille, 16.5 in. wide, 19 in. tall, 8.5 in. deep, 16 lbs., mfg. mid-1970s.

	N/A	$105 - 135	$65 - 85	

E-85 – 8W, 1-12 in. speaker, guitar combo, solid-state chassis, single channel, reverb, tremolo, front black and silver control panel, two inputs, four knobs (v, r, tremolo, tone), black covering, black grille, 18 in. wide, 23 in. tall, 8 in. deep, 23 lbs., mfg. mid-1970s.

	N/A	$120 - 150	$75 - 95	

ELECTRIC SS AMPLIFIERS: FIREFLY & TRIGGERMAN SERIES

* Add $25 (MSR $37) for two-button (channel select, DSP) footswitch.

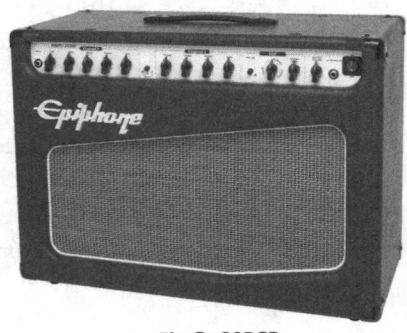

Firefly 30DSP
courtesy Epiphone

Triggerman 60DSP
courtesy Epiphone

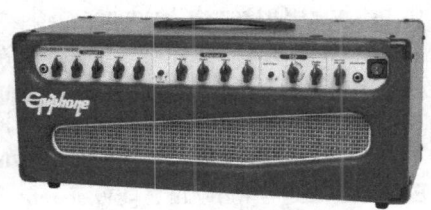

Triggerman 100DSP
courtesy Epiphone

FIREFLY 30DSP (EPA-DRF30DSP) – 30W, 1-10 in. speaker, guitar combo, solid-state chassis, two channels, DSP effects, front control panel, single input, 12 black knobs (Ch. 1: g, level, t, m, b, Ch. 2: v, t, m, b, All: DSP, r, MV), channel select switch, DSP on/off switch, power switch, headphone jack, rear panel: two speaker jacks, aux. in with level control, footswitch jack, red covering, brown grille with white piping, mfg. 2004-07.

	N/A	$110 - 140	$70 - 90	$320

TRIGGERMAN 60DSP (EPA-DRT60DSP) – 60W, 1-12 in. speaker, solid-state chassis, two channels, DSP effects (delay, flanger, chorus), front control panel, single input, 12 black knobs (Ch. 1: g, level, t, m, b, Ch. 2: v, t, m, b, All: DSP, r, MV), channel select switch, DSP on/off switch, power switch, headphone jack, rear panel: two speaker jacks, XLR DI out with level control, aux. in with level control, aux. out, footswitch jack, effects loop, red leather covering, brown cloth grille, mfg. 2004-06.

	N/A	$150 - 200	$90 - 120	$390

MSR/NOTES	100%	EXCELLENT	AVERAGE	LAST MSR

TRIGGERMAN 100DSP (EPA-DR100HDSP) – 100W, guitar head unit, solid-state chassis, two channels, DSP effects (delay, flanger, chorus), front control panel, single input, 12 black knobs (Ch. 1: g, level, t, m, b, Ch. 2: v, t, m, b, All: DSP, r, MV), channel select switch, DSP on/off switch, power switch, headphone jack, rear panel: two speaker jacks, XLR DI out with level control, aux. in with level control, aux. out, footswitch jack, effects loop with return level, red leather covering, brown cloth grille with white piping, mfg. 2004-disc.

	N/A	$140 - 180	$80 - 100	$400

TRIGGER 412 SPEAKER CABINET (EPA-DRT412S) – 280W, 4-12 in. special design speakers, mono/stereo operation, red covering, brown grille, mfg. 2005-08.

	N/A	$130 - 160	$80 - 100	$390

ELECTRIC SS AMPLIFIERS: REGENT SERIES

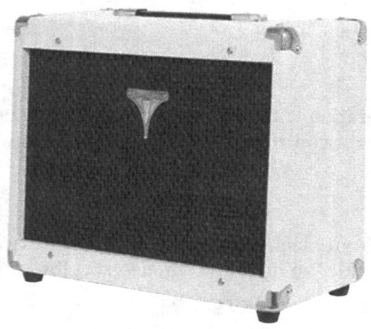

Acoustic Regent 30
courtesy Epiphone

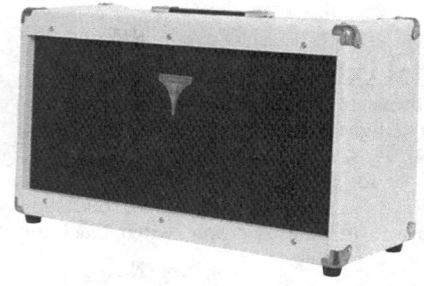

Acoustic Regent 220
courtesy Epiphone

ACOUSTIC REGENT 30 – 30W, 4-5 in. Electar speakers, solid-state chassis, two channels, reverb, top gold control panel, three inputs, six black knobs (guitar level, mic level, t, m, b, r), cream Tolex covering, brown grille, mfg. 1997-2004.

	N/A	$95 - 120	$60 - 75	$298

ACOUSTIC REGENT 220 – 40W (2 X 20W stereo), 1-8 and 2-5 in. Electar speakers, solid-state chassis, two channels, reverb, chorus, top gold control panel, three inputs, 10 black knobs (guitar level, mic level, t, m, b, anti-feedback freq, level, r, d, rate), cream Tolex covering, brown grille, mfg. 1995-2004.

	N/A	$175 - 225	$95 - 125	$499

ACOUSTIC REGENT 230 – 60W (2 X 30W stereo), 1-10 and 4-5 in. Electar speakers, solid-state chassis, two channels, reverb, chorus, top gold control panel, three inputs, 10 black knobs (guitar level, mic level, t, m, b, anti-feedback freq, level, r, d, rate), cream Tolex covering, brown grille, mfg. 1995-2004.

	N/A	$225 - 275	$120 - 150	$615

REGENT 20 – 50W, 1-12 in. Electar speaker combo, solid-state chassis, single channel, top gold control panel, single input, five black knobs (b, m, t, v, g), OD switch, headphone jack, cream Tolex covering, brown grille, mfg. 1995-2000.

	N/A	$75 - 100	$40 - 55	$189

REGENT 50R – 50W, 1-12 in. Electar speaker combo, solid-state chassis, single channel, reverb, top gold control panel, single input, five black knobs (r, b, t, v, g), OD switch, headphone jack, cream Tolex covering, brown grille, mfg. 1995-2000.

	N/A	$125 - 175	$70 - 90	$399

REGENT 250 – 100W (2 X 50W stereo), 2-12 in. Electar speaker combo, solid-state chassis, two channels, reverb, chorus, top gold control panel, two inputs, 10 black knobs (Ch. 1: g, v, Ch. 2: g, v, t, m, b, r, Chorus: d, rate), OD switch, Chorus switch, headphone jack, cream Tolex covering, brown grille, mfg. 1995-2000.

	N/A	$350 - 425	$175 - 225	$949

REGENT BASS 50 – 50W, 1-15 in. Electar speaker combo, solid-state chassis, single channel, top gold control panel, two inputs, six black knobs (g, v, t, m, b, p), headphone jack, cream Tolex covering, brown grille, mfg. 1995-2000.

	N/A	$175 - 225	$95 - 125	$475

ELECTRIC SS AMPLIFIERS: STANDARD (EP) SERIES

The Standard Series were the first amplifiers built under the new Epiphone ownership. The Standard Series were introduced in the late 1980s with the models EP-10, EP-25R, EP-60R, and EP-25 Bass. In 1993, the modern Standard Series were introduced. These amps were produced for more then a decade and the electronics did not change during this period. However, the cosmetics were changed a few times. The Standard Series were first built with a black Tolex and a black grille. In 1994, they began offering a Tweed covering with a black grille, but the black version was still available. By 1999, all of the Tweed models were discontinued. Circa 2001, they changed the control panel to a gold, altered the grille to look a bit more brown, and used a new "Flying E" logo.

MSR/NOTES	100%	EXCELLENT	AVERAGE	LAST MSR

EP-800R
courtesy Epiphone

EP-1000R
courtesy Epiphone

EP-SC210
courtesy Epiphone

EP-800 – 15W, 1-8 in. speaker combo, solid-state chassis, front control panel, single input, five knobs (g, v, b, m, t), headphone jack, black Tolex or Tweed covering, black or brown grille, mfg. 1993-2000.

| | N/A | $50 - 70 | $30 - 40 | $139 |

* **EP-800R** – similar to the EP-800, except has a reverb circuit with a reverb level, mfg. 1993-2004.

| | N/A | $60 - 80 | $35 - 45 | $165 |

* **EP-800B** – similar to the EP-800, except designed for bass application, five black knobs (v, b, m1, m2, t), mfg. 1993-2000.

| | N/A | $65 - 85 | $40 - 50 | $180 |

EP-1000 – 25W, 1-10 in. speaker combo, solid-state chassis, two channels, front control panel, single input, six knobs (g, v, b, m, t), headphone jack, black Tolex or Tweed covering, black or brown grille, mfg. 1993-2000.

| | N/A | $70 - 90 | $40 - 50 | $199 |

* **EP-1000R** – similar to the EP-1000, except has reverb circuit and reverb level, mfg. 1993-2004.

| | N/A | $95 - 120 | $50 - 70 | $245 |

* **EP-1000B** – similar to the EP-1000, except designed for bass application, six black knobs (g, v, b, m1, m2, t), mfg. 1993-2004.

| | N/A | $95 - 120 | $50 - 70 | $239 |

EP-SC28 – 40W (2 X 20W stereo), 2-8 in. speaker combo, solid-state chassis, two channels, reverb, chorus, front control panel, two inputs, 10 knobs (Ch. 1: g, v, Ch. 2: v, b, m, t, p, r, Chorus: d, rate), headphone jack, black Tolex or Tweed covering, black or brown grille, mfg. 1993-2000.

| | N/A | $150 - 200 | $95 - 120 | $399 |

EP-SC210 – 60W (2 X 30W stereo), 2-10 in. speaker combo, solid-state chassis, two channels, reverb, chorus, front control panel, two inputs, 10 knobs (Ch. 1: g, v, Ch. 2: v, b, m, t, p, r, Chorus: d, rate), headphone jack, effects loop, black Tolex or Tweed covering, black or brown grille, mfg. 1993-2004.

| | N/A | $175 - 225 | $120 - 150 | $499 |

EUPHONIC AUDIO

Amplifiers and speaker cabinets currently produced in Robbinsville, NJ. Previously produced in Princeton Junction, NJ beginning in 1995. Distributed by Euphonic Audio in Jackson, NJ.

Euphonic Audio (EA) began designing musical equipment in 1995. Larry Ullman, Gary Gibilisco, and John Dong are at the helm of the company, and they believe to get the best possible sound out of their products, they're going to need feedback from players. Real life situations are what make these products unique. EA offers an odd yet captivating philosophy with "at EA, we believe that neither amps nor speakers should have their tone." EA offers power amps, preamps, combos, and speaker cabinets. For more information, visit Euphonic Audio's website or contact them directly.

ELECTRIC BASS SS AMPLIFIERS

iAMP 200 HEAD – 200W @ 4 ohms, head-unit configuration, solid-state chassis, single channel, front black control panel, two inputs, mini-stereo input, nine black knobs (level, mini stereo levell, l/m, m/h, h, MV, effects loop level, direct out level), four EQ presets, effects loop, link in/link out, selectable voltage, black casing, 8.5 lbs., disc. 2006.

| $750 | $475 - 550 | $300 - 350 | $995 |

* **iAMP 200 Wizzy Combo** – similar to the iAMP 200 Head, except in combo configuration with 1-12 in. speaker, black covering, black grille, 44 lbs., disc. 2006.

| $1,225 | $775 - 900 | $500 - 575 | $1,645 |

MSR/NOTES	100%	EXCELLENT	AVERAGE	LAST MSR

iAMP MICRO 300 HEAD – 300W @ 4 ohms, bass head-unit configuration, solid-state chassis, two channels, front black control panel, two inputs, 10 black knobs (Ch. 1: g, l, m, h, Ch. 2: g, l, m, h, All: MV, effects loop blend), channel switch (intelligent Input Switching), mute switch, effects loop, direct line out jack, footswitch jack, black casing, 2.5 lbs., mfg. 2006-present.

MSR $795	$600	$375 - 450	$225 - 275	

iAMP 500 HEAD – 500W @ 4 ohms (350W @ 8 ohms, 800W @ 2 ohms), head-unit configuration, solid-state chassis, single channel, front black control panel, two inputs, nine black knobs (level, mini stereo levell, l/m, m/h, h, MV, effects loop level, direct out level), four EQ presets, effects loop, limiter, selectable voltage, black casing, 13 lbs., current mfg.

MSR $1,195	$900	$575 - 675	$350 - 425	

* ***iAMP 500 Wizzy Combo*** – similar to the iAMP 500 Head, except in combo configuration with 1-12 in. speaker, black covering, black grille, 44 lbs., current mfg.

MSR $1,845	$1,390	$875 - 1,025	$550 - 650	

iAMP 800 HEAD – 800W @ 4 ohms (1000W @ 2 ohms), head-unit configuration, solid-state chassis, single channel, front black control panel, gold plated input and output jacks, two inputs, ten black knobs (level, mini stereo levell, l/m, m/h, h, MV, 2 effects loop level, direct out level), four EQ presets, two effects loop, limiter, selectable voltage, black casing, 19 lbs., current mfg.

MSR $1,495	$1,125	$725 - 850	$475 - 550	

* ***iAMP 800 Combo*** – similar to the iAMP 800 Head, except in combo configuration with 1-12 in. Custom Kevlar speaker, black covering, black grille, 58 lbs., current mfg.

MSR $2,445	$1,840	$1,175 - 1,375	$750 - 850	

SPEAKER CABINETS

CM-208 – 400W, 2-8 in. proprietary speakers with a 1 in. phenolic compression driver, 8 ohm impedance, two Speakon combo connectors, black covering, black metal grille, side handles, 16 in. wide, 19.5 in. tall, 12.75 in. deep, 41 lbs., mfg. 2007-present.

MSR $1,195	$900	$550 - 650	$325 - 400	

CXL-110 – 350W, 1-10 in. speaker with a 1 in. titanium compression driver tweeter, 8 ohm impedance, one Speakon combo and one 1/4 in. jack connectors, black covering, black metal grille, top handle, 14.75 in. wide, 13.5 in. tall, 12.5 in. deep, 29 lbs., disc. 2005.

	N/A	$275 - 325	$150 - 200	$600

CXL-112 – 350W, 1-12 in. Custom Kevlar speaker with a 1 in. high efficiency phenolic compression driver, 8 ohm impedance, two Speakon combo connectors, black covering, black metal grille, side handles, 17 in. wide, 19 in. tall, 15 in. deep, 37 lbs., current mfg.

MSR $895	$675	$425 - 500	$250 - 300	

M-LINE WIZZY 112 – 200W, 1-12 in. EA Neodymium driver with Whizzer cone, 4 or 8 ohm (special order) impedance, two Speakon combo connectors, black covering, black metal grille, side handles, 16 in. wide, 19.5 in. tall, 12.75 in. deep, 34 lbs., current mfg.

MSR $745	$575	$325 - 400	$200 - 250	

NL-210 – 500W, 2-10 in. custom Neodymium Kevlar speakers with a 1 in. phenolic compression driver, 4 (special order) or 8 ohm impedance, two Speakon combo connectors, black covering, black metal grille, side handles, tilt-back cabinet, 17 in. wide, 22.5 in. tall, 15 in. deep, 37 lbs., mfg. 2006-present.

MSR $1,195	$900	$550 - 650	$325 - 400	

NM-410 – 1000W, 4-10 in. custom Neodymium Kevlar speakers with a 1 in. titanium compression driver, 8 ohm impedance, two Speakon combo connectors, black covering, black metal grille, side handles, 25 in. wide, 22 in. tall, 18 in. deep, 69 lbs., current mfg.

MSR $1,795	$1,350	$850 - 1,000	$500 - 600	

WIZZY 110 – 250W, 1-10 in. EA Neodymium driver with Whizzer cone, 4 ohm impedance, two Speakon combo connectors, black covering, black metal grille, side handle, tilt-up cabinet design, 12.5 in. wide, 15 in. tall, 11 in. deep, 18 lbs., mfg. 2007-present.

MSR $595	$450	$275 - 325	$150 - 200	

WIZZY 112 – 200W, 1-12 in. EA Neodymium driver with Whizzer cone, 4 or 8 ohm (special order) impedance, two Speakon combo connectors, black covering, black metal grille, side handles, 17 in. wide, 17 in. tall, 12.5 in. deep, 29 lbs., current mfg.

MSR $645	$490	$300 - 350	$175 - 225	

WIZZY 112 POWERED CABINET – 200W powered extension cabinet designed for use with the iAMP 200, 1-12 in. EA Neodymium driver with Whizzer cone, two XLR connectors, black covering, black metal grille, side handles, tilt-back cabinet, 17 in. wide, 19.25 in. tall, 12.5 in. deep, 43 lbs., disc. 2006.

	$1,095	$675 - 800	$425 - 500	$1,445

MSR/NOTES	100%	EXCELLENT	AVERAGE	LAST MSR

EVANS CUSTOM AMPLIFIERS

Amplifiers currently produced in Burlington, NC. Direct sales by Evans. The Evans trademark was established in 1962.

The Evans Custom Amplifier has been producing amplifiers for nearly fifty years. They produce solid-state amps and hybrid amps with all-tube preamps. Evans specializes in amplifiers for archtops, jazz, and steel guitars. They also have a full line of speaker cabinets. Head units start at $1,274 and combo units start at $1,548. For more information, visit Evans' website or contact them directly.

EVH

Amplifiers currently produced in Corona, CA since 2009. Distributed by FMIC in Scottsdale, AZ.

The EVH (Eddie Van Halen) brand was launched in 2007 as a joint-venture between Van Halen and Fender. The first project released under the EVH brand was a replica of his original Frankenstein guitar built by the Fender Custom Shop. The EVH Frankenstein (Last MSR was $25,000) has all the oddball features Eddie's guitar had including the cutout pickup cavity with humbucker, masking tape pick holder, truck reflectors on the back, and handcrafted black pickguard. Every scratch, ding, stripe, and cigarette burn are accounted for as well. This Frankenstein was a limited edition with 300 guitars scheduled for production. In 2009, EVH introduced the new Wolfgang model, which was completely developed with Eddie Van Halen around his famous Wolfgang design body. EVH also produces the third installment of the EVH 5150 guitar amplifier. For more information visit EVH's website or contact them directly.

ELECTRIC TUBE AMPS: 5150 III SERIES

5150 III 50W HEAD – 50W, guitar head-unit, eight-tube chassis, preamp: 6 X 12AX7, power: 2 X 6L6, solid-state rectifier, three channels, front white control panel, single input, 11 white knobs (Ch. 1/2: g, l, m, h, v, Ch. 3: g, l, m, h, v, All: p), channel switches, rear panel: power switch, standby switch, headphone jack, MIDI footswitch jack, 1/4 in. footswitch jack, effects loop, preamp out jack, resonance control, two speaker jacks with 4/8/16 ohm impedance selector switch, available in Black or Ivory covering and a black metal grille with "EVH" and "5150 III" logos, 25 lbs., mfg. 2011-present.

MSR $1,333 $1,000 $650 - 800 $400 - 475

5150 III 100W HEAD – 100W, guitar head-unit, 12-tube chassis, preamp: 8 X 12AX7, power: 4 X 6L6, solid-state rectifier, three channels, front white control panel, single input, 18 white knobs (g, l, m, h, v, p for each channel), channel switches, rear panel: power switch, standby switch, effects loop, preamp out jack, MIDI footswitch jack, two speaker jacks with 4/8/16 ohm impedance selector switch, available in Black or Ivory covering and a black metal grille with "EVH" and "5150 III" logos, 29.75 in. wide, 10.25 in. tall, 11.5 in. deep, 55 lbs., four-button footswitch included, mfg. 2007-present.

MSR $2,400 $1,800 $1,100 - 1,350 $675 - 825

5150 III 1-12 SPEAKER CABINET – 25W, 1-12 in. Celestion EVH speaker, 16 ohm impedance, birch construction, single 1/4 in. input, top handle, available in Black or Ivory textured vinyl covering, black cloth grille with "EVH" and "5150 III" logos, mfg. 2010-present.

MSR $493 $370 $200 - 250 $120 - 150

5150 III 2-12 SPEAKER CABINET – 50W, 2-12 in. Celestion EVH speakers, 16 ohm impedance, birch construction, single 1/4 in. input, recessed side handles, tilt-back legs, removable casters, available in Black or Ivory textured vinyl covering, black cloth grille with "EVH" and "5150 III" logos, 60 lbs., mfg. 2010-present.

MSR $666 $500 $300 - 350 $175 - 225

5150 III 4-12 SPEAKER CABINET – 100W, 4-12 in. Celestion EVH speakers, 16 ohm impedance, birch construction, single 1/4 in. input, recessed side handles, removable casters, available in Black or Ivory textured vinyl covering, black cloth grille with "EVH" and "5150 III" logos, 29.25 in. wide, 30 in. tall, 14 in. deep, 88 lbs., mfg. 2007-present.

MSR $1,333 $1,000 $650 - 800 $400 - 475

NOTES

F SECTION
FARGEN AMPLIFICATION

Amplifiers currently produced in Sacramento, CA since 1997. Re-branded as Exclusive Amps by Fargen.

Ben Fargen founded Fargen Amplification in 1997, and they produce all-tube hand-wired guitar amplifiers and speaker cabinets. Along with his standard models, Fargen also has a custom shop where each amp is personally built by Ben Fargen. In 2005, Fargen teamed up with Soloway guitars to produce the Fargen Soloway Classic, which is designed to be a match with the Soloway Swan long-neck guitars. For more information, visit Fargen's website or contact him directly.

CONTACT INFORMATION
FARGEN AMPLIFICATION
PO Box 601042
Sacramento, CA 95860
Phone No.: 916-971-4992
Fax No.: 916-338-4992
www.fargenamps.com, www.
exclusiveamps.com
bf-amps@sbcglobal.net

ELECTRIC TUBE AMPLIFIERS

The **'49 X '54** (disc., last price was $1,899) is a dual channel combo amp with one channel voiced for a 1940s-era Fender Deluxe TV Front amp, and one voiced for a 1950s-era Fender Deluxe Narrow Panel amp. Features include 15W, 1-12 in. Celestion Greenback speaker, a six tube chassis (preamp: 1 X 6SL7, 1 X 12AY7, 1 X 12AX7, power: 2 X 6V6, rectifier: 5AR4/GZ34, and independent inputs and controls for each channel. The **Blackbird** is based on an early 1960s Fender Deluxe Reverb Blackface. The Blackbird is available as a 20W 1-12 in. speaker combo with 2 X 6V6 tubes, a 30W 1-12 in. speaker combo with 4 X 6V6 tubes, and a 40W 1-12 in. speaker combo with 2 X 6L6 tubes. In 2007, to celebrate Fargen's 10th Anniversary, they began offering the Blackbird with a new cabinet style/cosmetics. The **Blackbird VS2** (Head $1,895) is Fargen's most current Blackbird that puts out 40W. The **Olde 800** (Head $1,699) is voiced for the high-gain British sound. Features include 50W, a head or combo configuration, and a five tube chassis (preamp: 3 X 12AX7, power: 2 X EL34). Other models include the **JW40** Jim Weider Signature (disc.), the **El Bastage** (disc.), the **Mini Plex MK II**, and the **AC Duo-Tone**.

**JW40 Jim Weider Signature
courtesy Fargen Amplification**

FATBOY AMPLIFIERS

Amplifiers previously produced in Deerfield, IL during the 1990s.

Fatboy produced a line of amplifiers in the 1990s. The personnel of the company in 1995 consisted of Norb Funk, Howard Kaufman, Jeff Thirey, Jeff Demuth, and Dan Saviano. They produced at least two different models in different configurations. The **Chubby C-2** featured 80W from an all-tube chassis and was available in a head-unit or combo. The **F-3** was also 80W and available in a head-unit or combo. They also produced a 4-10 in. and a 4-12 in. speaker cabinets. Any further information would be appreciated, and can be submitted directly to Blue Book Publications.

FENDER

Amplifiers currently produced in Scottsdale, AZ (Amplifier Custom Shop), Corona, CA (U.S.), Indonesia, Mexico, Japan, Tianjin (China), and Korea. Distributed by the Fender Musical Instruments Corporation in Scottsdale, AZ. The Fender trademark was established circa 1946 in Fullerton, CA.

CONTACT INFORMATION
FENDER
17600 North Perimeter Drive
Scottsdale, AZ 85255
Phone No.: 480-596-9690
Fax No.: 480-367-5262
www.fender.com
custserv@fenderusa.com

Clarence Leonidas Fender was born in 1909, and raised in Fullerton, California. As a teenager he developed an interest in electronics, and soon was building and repairing radios for fellow classmates. After high school, Leo Fender became a bookkeeper for employment while he still did radio repair at home. After holding a series of jobs, Fender opened up a full scale radio repair shop in 1939. In addition to service work, Leo's Fender Radio Service store soon became a general electronics retail outlet. However, the forerunner to the Fender Electric Instruments company was a smaller two-man operation that was originally started as the K&F company in 1945. Leo Fender began building small amplifiers and electric lap steels with his partner, Clayton Orr "Doc" Kaufman. Leo and Doc produced their first amplifier and steel guitar in 1945. Kauffman left K&F in early 1946 and Leo Fender took over. Leo then formed the Fender Electric Instrument Company in 1946, located on South Pomona Avenue in Fullerton, California. By 1947, Fender introduced the Model 26 guitar amp and shortly thereafter came the Super. In 1948, the new Fender amps featured a new cabinet construction. The Champion student amplifier was also introduced at this time. With all the increased demand, Fender had no choice but to move to a new building.

Soon Fender's inventive genius began designing new models through the early 1950s and early 1960s. The Fender Bassman Amp was unveiled in 1951, which paved the way to an entire line of tweed amplifiers. In 1952, the Twin Amplifier was introduced that consisted of two 12 in. speakers and became the top model of the line. With the success of this line, Fender was forced to move again in 1953. In 1955, Fender developed an amp using the new effect of tremolo that they named the Tremolux. Fender also had a tendency to introduce guitars with corresponding amplifiers. One example was in 1958, the Jazzmaster was released along with the Vibrasonic amp, which was truly an entirely new design. It featured a front facing control panel and its covering was made by the General Tire & Rubber Company. This allowed for these amps to take a lot of abuse and not a lot of wear. The Reverb Unit, Twin Reverb, and the Showman debuted in the early '60s.

By 1964, Fender's line of products included electric guitars, basses, steel guitars, effects units, acoustic guitars, electric pianos, and a variety of accessories. However, Leo's faltering health in the mid-1960s prompted him to put the company up for sale. It was first offerd to Don Randall, the head of Fender Sales, for a million and a half dollars. Randall opened negotiations with the Baldwin Piano & Organ company, but when those negotiations fell through, Fender offered it to the conglomerate CBS (who was looking to diversify the company holdings). Fender (FEIC) was purchased by CBS in December of 1964 for thirteen million dollars. Leo Fender was kept on as a special consultant for five years, and then left when the contract was up in 1970. Due to a ten year no compete clause, the next Leo Fender designed guitars or amplifiers did not show up in the music industry until 1976 (Music Man).

While Fender was just another division of CBS, a number of key figures left the company. Forrest White, the production manager, left in 1967 after a dispute in producing solid-state amplifiers. Don Randall left in 1969, because he was not impressed with corporate life. George Fullerton, one of the people involved with the Stratocaster design, left in 1970. Many people seem to think that quality dropped drastically the day CBS took over. Dale Hyatt, another veteran of the early Fender days, figured that the quality on the products stayed relatively stable until around 1968 (Hyatt left in 1972). But a number of cost-cutting strategies, and attempts to produce more products had a deteriorating effect. This reputation leads right to the classic phrase heard at vintage guitar shows, "Is the amp pre-CBS?"

In the early 1980s, the Fender guitar empire began to crumble. Many cost-cutting factors and management problems forced CBS to try various last ditch efforts to salvage the instrument line. In March of 1982, Fender (with CBS' blessing) negotiated with Kanda Shokai and Yamano Music to establish Fender Japan. After discussions with Tokai (who built a great Fender Strat replica, among other nice guitars), Kawai, and others, Fender finally chose Fuji Gen Gakki (based in Matsumoto, about 130 miles northwest of Tokyo) to build guitars for them. In 1983, the Squier Series was built in Japan, earmarked for European distribution. The Squier trademark came from a string-making company in Michigan (V.C. Squier) that CBS had acquired in 1965.

HISTORY: 1984-PRESENT

In 1984, CBS decided to sell Fender. Offers came in from IMC (Hondo, Charvel/Jackson) and the Kaman Music Corporation (Ovation). Finally, CBS sold Fender to an investment group led by William "Bill" Schultz in March for twelve and a half million dollars. This investment group formally became the Fender Musical Instruments Corporation (FMIC). As the sale did not include production facilities, USA guitar and amplifier production ceased for most of 1985. It has been estimated that 80% of the amplifiers sold between late 1984 and mid 1986 were made in Japan. Many other amplifiers were from leftover stock. Soon after, a new factory was built in Corona, California, and USA production was restored in 1986.

In 1990, the Fender (FMIC) company built an assembly facility in Mexico to offset rising costs of Asian production due to the weakening of the American dollar in the international market. Fender also experimented with production based in India from 1989 to 1990. The Fender (FMIC) company currently manufactures instruments in China, Japan, Korea, Mexico, and the U.S.

By the early 1990s, Fender had regained their status as one of the top guitar and amplifier manufacturers in the country. Much of this can be attributed to Bill Schultz's aggressive and effective business and production decisions. Fender was one of the first companies to introduce minimum advertised pricing (MAP), which is the lowest price that any dealer advertising Fender products can advertise at. Fender also started expanding their line by buying Sunn Amplifiers in the late 1980s. Many Fender bass amplifiers currently produced today still utilize the Sunn circuitry.

In August of 2002, Fender expanded its power once again by buying the Gretsch company. This buy-out went into effect January 1, 2003. In 2003, Fender aquired the rights to SWR Amplifiers. In 2005, Fender expanded their vast line once again by aquiring Tacoma/Olympia/Orpheum. Fender's line now includes Fender, Squier, Gretsch, Guild, Benedetto, Jackson, Charvel, Tacoma, Olympia, Orpheum, Sunn, and SWR. Bill Schultz also stepped down as CEO of FMIC and Bill Mendello stepped into the position. Schultz remained the Chairman of the Board. On September 21, 2006, Bill Schultz passed away in his Arizona home.

In 2007, FMIC purchased Kaman Music, which includes the brands Ovation, Takamine, Hamer, Applause, and Genz Benz amplifiers.

In 2008, FMIC purchased Groove Tubes and introduced an entirely new line of American Standard guitars that included the Stratocaster, Telecaster, Jazz Bass, and Precision Bass.

In 2009, Fender introduced their new Road Worn Series that features more affordable versions of their popular Custom Shop Relic instruments. The Stratocaster, Telecaster, Jazz Bass, and Precision Bass are all available as a Road Worn instrument. Fender also revamped their Standard line of instruments that are made in Mexico and targeted as Fender's entry-level model.

In 2010, Larry Thomas was appointed CEO at FMIC.

In 2011, Fender celebrated their 60th Anniversary of the Telecaster and Precision Bass models.

In mid-2014, Fender discontinued use of the MSRP pricing and simply went to using only MAP (Minimum Advertised Pricing) or the "Street" price on their amplifiers.

(Source for earlier Fender history: Richard R. Smith, *Fender: The Sound Heard 'Round the World*.)

DATING FENDER AMPLIFIERS

When trying to determine the date of an Fender amplifier, it is useful to know a few things about feature changes that have occurred over the years. Serialization on Fender amps is not a reliable way to date them as records of these were not kept until 1994; however, Greg Gagliano has compiled several hundred serial numbers on Fender amplifiers and has put together an extensive list. Currently, Gagliano's serialization is a six-piece article that was first published in *20th Century Guitar* magazine in 1997 with the most recent addition appearing in *Vintage Guitar* magazine.

The following information may help you to determine the approximate date of manufacture of a Fender amplifier by visual observation, without having to handle (or disassemble) the instrument for serial number verification. Check a number of these procedures together to try to get the right year. Sometimes parts weren't used for a time and the amps are actually newer than the dates on certain procedures may indicate.

1946-1948: Several variations including uncovered wood cabinets, early tweed variants, and gray.

1948-1953 TV Front: Vertical or diagonal tweed (some two-tone brown) covering with a brown speaker grille that looks like the front of the TV.

1953-1954/1955 Wide Panel: Diagonal Tweed covering with a brown grille (no stripes) and wide panels above and below the speaker grille.

1954/1955-1959/1960 Narrow Panel: Tweed covering with a brown striped grille and a narrow panel front where the grille is larger than earlier models.

1957: Fender introduced the use of treble, bass, middle, and presence controls.

1959/1960-1963/1964 Brownface: Brown or white Tolex covering with white, brown, or Oxblood red grilles and a front facing brown control panel.

1963/1964-1967 Blackface: Black Tolex covering with a brown/silver grille and a front facing black control panel.

1967/1968-1980 Silverface: Black Tolex covering with a silver/blue grille and a front facing silver control panel.

1976: Introduction of the Master Volume control/feature.

1980/1981-1982 New Blackface: A black control panel was re-introduced again with slight changes from the 1960s Blackface models.

DATE CODES ON TRANSFORMERS

The power transformer inside Fender amps can also be used to date the model. NOTE: If the transformer has been replaced it will not represent the actual year the amp was built (the transformer needs to be original to use this system). Also keep in mind that transformers were often bought in large quantities, and they often sat on the shelf for a period of six months to one year (or longer). This means a transformer dated 1964 might really be used in an amp that is a 1965 or 1966 model.

On transformers there is an EIA number that always starts with 606 and is followed by three or four additional digits. Similar to speaker and pot date codes, the first digit (for three additional numbers) or first two digits (for four additional numbers) indicates the year of production. The last two digits indicate the week of the year of production. Examples: 606-4-21 is a transformer produced in the 21st week of 1964. 606-66-36 is a tranformer produced in the 36th week of 1966.

DATE CODES ON TUBE CHARTS

On Fender Amplifiers made after 1953, there is a date code stamped onto their tube charts. These charts are found on the inside cabinet of combo models, and on the amp head of piggy-back models. This date code is rubber stamped in ink, and consists of two, small letters. The first letter stands for the year, and the second letter indicates the month of manufacture. The procedure can be found by this chart:

A - 1951/January	F - 1956/June	K - 1961/November	P - 1966
B - 1952/February	G - 1957/July	L - 1962/December	Q - 1967
C - 1953/March	H - 1958/August	M - 1963	R - 1968
D - 1954/April	I - 1959/September	N - 1964	S - 1969
E - 1955/May	J - 1960/October	O - 1965	

This code starts on January 1951, even though it was not introduced/used until 1953.

 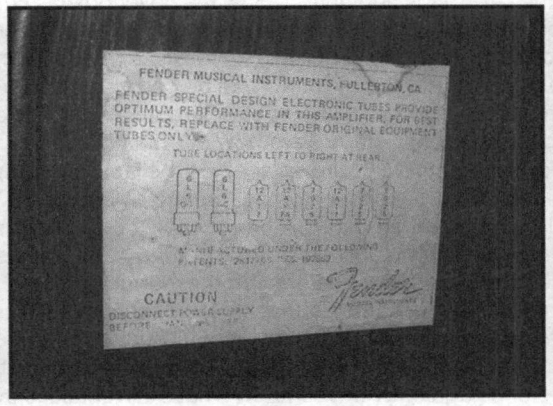 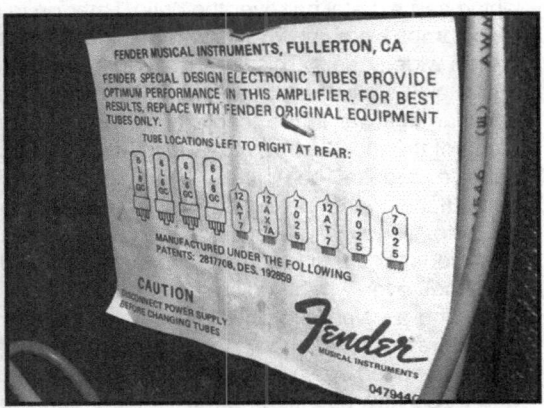

Here are some examples of what Fender tube charts look like. The Super Reverb has a date code of QH, which means it was produced August of 1967. The other two tube charts are from later models (Silverface's). Production dates on tube charts was discontinued around 1969 or 1970.

Fender started using a date code again in 1990 that was very similar to the one used in the 1960s and 70s. The code is located on the black and silver QA (Quality Assurance) sticker on the back of the amp. Among all the lines/numbers on this sticker, the last two letters indicate the date - the first letter indicating the year and the second letter indicating the month. Here is a chart for these amplifiers:

A - 1990/January	F - 1995/June	L - 2001/December	R - 2007
B - 1991/February	G - 1996/July	M - 2002	S - 2008
C - 1992/March	H - 1997/August	N - 2003	T - 2009
D - 1993/April	I - 1998/September	O - 2004	U - 2010
E - 1994/May	J - 1999/October	P - 2005	V - 2011
	K - 2000/November	Q - 2006	

MSR/NOTES	100%	EXCELLENT	AVERAGE	LAST MSR

MODEL NUMBERS & TUBE SCHEMATICS

Along with the tube chart that is supposed to be on the inside of every Fender tube amp, there is a model number that tells a lot about what the amp is. Fender started using this model number as the tube schematic and circuit date of the amp. Fender would change the chassis of their amplifier from time to time but the average person could not tell the difference. This can also work as a dating tool as well as figuring out what specific chassis your amp may be. Fender used two different variations of this system. The first that was introduced in 1951 consisted of the number 5 or 6, a letter, and another digit or two (i.e. 5G13). The first number indicates the decade that the specific chassis was used (5 for 1950s and 6 for 1960s). The letter indicates the variation of the chassis (this started with A and went up alphabetically, however if an amp was introduced in the late 1950s, the letter would be the specific letter being used at that time). The final number indicated the model name. Each model that Fender introduced in the 1950s had a specific number and here is a table to code:

1 - Champ	5 - Pro	9 - Tremolux	13 - Vibrasonic
2 - Princeton	6 - Bassman	10 - Harvard	14 - Showman
3 - Deluxe	7 - Bandmaster	11 - Vibrolux	
4 - Super	8 - Twin	12 - Concert	

The way this numbering system worked is Fender made chassis' numerically and each chassis they made was the next number in the series. This means the Champ was their first amp when they went to this system. An example is: (5E6 would be a 1950s variation E Bassman, 6G11 would be a 1960s variation G Vibrolux).

When Blackface was introduced (circa mid 1963), they went to a new system. This system had two letters (typically AA, AB, or AC, followed by three or four digits). The AA refered to the variation of the chassis. AA was the original and when they were changed or altered it would be AB followed by AC, etc. The next number or two was strictly the number for the amp (several numbers were the same on different amps). The last two numbers were the last two numbers of the year. For instance AA763 was the first variation of (what amp?!) the Pro, Super Reverb, Concert, Deluxe, or Deluxe Reverb, that was introduced in 1963. The only problem with this system is you don't know what model it is by looking at it. This system lasted until the early 1970s when model numbers were discontinued.

The model numbering is used mainly for schematics and matching. Since the tube date chart is easier to use and gives you a more specific date it makes more sense to use that. This is why it is so important to have that tube chart still on the inside of your prized blackface!

ELECTRIC TUBE AMPS: OVERVIEW

Fender amplifiers are what started Leo's business. The first amplifier was a simple tube amp with a small speaker. To this date, there are literally hundreds of different amplifiers, including many tube amps. Throughout the years there have been many variations in the different series of Fender amps. Most amp gurus know what a Blackface is from a Silverface and so on. For eveyone else, here's a brief overview. The first Fender amps (excluding oddballs) were the wood cabinets, dubbed "woodies," which had a metal bar over the grille. Later on in the late 1940s and early 1950s, the covering was changed to a vinyl and the look of the amps were known as TV front, since they looked like a TV set of that era. Around 1952-53 Tweed amplifiers were introduced, first as wide panels. This meant the top and bottom panels on the amplifiers were wider (than a narrow model in the late 1950s). The late '50s had the look of the narrow panel. Wide panel and narrow panel can be compared and a difference noticed. Tolex is a covering that was introduced around 1959 on some amps and by 1961 was standard on almost all Fenders. A Tolex amp featured some of the most extreme changes that Fender has ever done. Amps were now in a Tolex covering, had a front mounted control panel, and looked completely different than any Fender amp before. Brownface was the first Tolex amp. This meant that the control panel (face) was a brown in color and the actual covering was either a white, cream, or brown. 1964 brought the most popular amps for Fender, the Blackface look. The control panel was then black with black Tolex covering, and a silver grille. These were only made for about five years and are the most desirable among collectors. In or around 1968 Silverface was phased in (right after CBS took over, what a coincidence), and this lasted up until 1980. Features on these models had a silver control panel on black Tolex and a silver/blue grille. These amps were practically the same as Blackface in schematics, but not nearly as desireable to collectors (In fact we had a tough time finding someone with a Silverface collection!). During the limbo years of the '80s, Blackface was introduced again to try and revive Fender, but to little or no avail. After many other experiments, the '90s brought Blackface in with vigor. Now all Fender amplifiers are Blackface once again. Even you know what a Silverface is from a Blackface now!

ELECTRIC TUBE AMPS: BANDMASTER SERIES

BANDMASTER (TV FRONT) – 15W, 1-15 in. Jensen, tube chassis: 2 X 6SJ7,6SN7 or 6SL7, 2 X 6L6, top control panel, two pointer knobs (v, tone), early tweed covering, cloth grille, mfg. 1952 only.

	N/A	N/A	N/A	

This model would be almost identical to the Bassman of the same time. It is extremely rare, and there are doubts that it actually exists.

BANDMASTER (WIDE PANEL, 1-15 IN. SPEAKER) – 15W, 1-15 in. Jensen speakers, tube chassis: 2 X 6SJ7, 6SN7, or 6SL7, 2 X 6L6, top chrome control panel, two black pointer knobs, (v, tone), diagonal tweed covering, brown cloth grille, mfg. 1952-54.

	N/A	$3,600 - 4,500	$2,150 - 2,700	

In 1954, model 5D7 replaced the model 5C7 with 12AY7 and 12AX7 tubes.

BANDMASTER (NARROW PANEL, 3-10 IN. SPEAKERS) – 15W, 3-10 in. Jensen speakers, tube chassis: preamp: 12AY7, 12AX7, power: 2 X 6L6G, 5U4G rectifier, top control panel, five pointer knobs, (Mic v, Inst v, t, b, p), diagonal tweed covering, brown tweed-era grille, mfg. 1954-1960.

courtesy Dave Rogers/Dave's Guitar Shop   *courtesy Dave Rogers/Dave's Guitar Shop*

	100%	EXCELLENT	AVERAGE
1954-1956	N/A	$7,500 - 10,000	$4,750 - 6,000
1957-1960	N/A	$8,000 - 10,500	$5,750 - 7,250

This model is known as the 5E7.

BANDMASTER (BROWNFACE) – 30W, 3-10 in. Jensen speakers, vibrato, tube chassis, preamp: 5 X 7025, power: 2 X 6L6GC, silicon rectifier, two channels, vibrato, front brownface control panel, nine brown knobs (Norm: b, t, v, Vibr: b, t, v, s, i, Both, p), brown Tolex covering, brown tweed-era grille, mfg. 1960-61.

	100%	EXCELLENT	AVERAGE
	N/A	$4,800 - 6,000	$2,875 - 3,600

This model is known as the 6G7. The 1960 version has controls in reverse order. This model has virtually the identical chassis to the Concert, Pro, and Vibrasonic.

BANDMASTER (PIGGYBACK BROWNFACE) – 40W, 1-12 or 2-12 in. speakers in a seperate cabinet, tubes: 4 X 7025, 2 X 12AX7, 2 X 5881, silicon rectifiers, two channels, vibrato, brownface control panel, nine brown or cream knobs, (Norm: v, b, t, Vibrato: v, b, t, s, i, Both: p), cream Tolex covering, maroon grille, mfg. 1961-64.

courtesy Dave Rogers/Dave's Guitar Shop   *courtesy Dave Rogers/Dave's Guitar Shop*

	100%	EXCELLENT	AVERAGE
1961 Head & 1-12 in. Cab	N/A	$2,400 - 3,000	$1,450 - 1,800
1962-1964 Head & 2-12 in. Cab	N/A	$2,000 - 2,500	$1,200 - 1,500
1961-1964 Head Only	N/A	$950 - 1,200	$575 - 725
1961-1964 Cab Only	N/A	$850 - 1,050	$500 - 625

Known as models 6G7-A and AA763. In late 1962, the 2-12 in. cabinet was introduced.

BANDMASTER (PIGGYBACK BLACKFACE) – 40W, 1-12 or 2-12 in. speakers in a separate cabinet, tubes: 4 X 7025, 2 X 12AX7, 2 X 5881, silicon rectifiers, two channels, vibrato, blackface control panel, nine black knobs, (Norm: v, b, t, Vibrato: v, b, t, s, i, Both: p), black Tolex covering, silver grille, mfg. 1964-67.

	100%	EXCELLENT	AVERAGE
1964-1965 Head & Cab	N/A	$1,175 - 1,450	$650 - 800
1964-1965 Head Only	N/A	$525 - 650	$325 - 400
1966-1967 Head & Cab	N/A	$1050 - 1,300	$575 - 725
1966-1967 Head Only	N/A	$475 - 600	$275 - 350
Cab Only	N/A	$400 - 500	$250 - 300

This model is known as the AA763.

MSR/NOTES	100%	EXCELLENT	AVERAGE	LAST MSR

BANDMASTER (PIGGYBACK SILVERFACE) – 40W, 2-12 in. speakers in a separate cab, tube chassis preamp: 2 X 7025, 12AX7, 12AT7, power: 2 X 6L6GC, silicon rectifiers, two channels, vibrato, silverface control panel, eight silver top knobs, (Norm: v, b, t, Vibrato: v, b, t, s, i), black Tolex covering, silver grille, mfg. 1968-1974.

courtesy Savage Audio   *courtesy Savage Audio*

	100%	EXCELLENT	AVERAGE
1968-1970 Head & Cab	N/A	$725 - 900	$425 - 550
1971-1974 Head & Cab	N/A	$600 - 750	$350 - 475
1968-1970 Head Only	N/A	$350 - 450	$225 - 275
1971-1974 Head Only	N/A	$325 - 400	$190 - 240
Cab Only	N/A	$275 - 350	$170 - 210

Models include AA 568 and AA 1069. In 1970, output was increased to 45W.

* ***Bandmaster Reverb (Piggback Silverface)*** – similar to Silverface Bandmaster, except has 45W output, tubes: 3 X 7025, 2 X 12AT7, 12AX7, 2 X 6L6GC, rectifier 5U4GB, ten silver knobs, and an added bright switch, mfg. 1968-1981.

courtesy George McGuire

	100%	EXCELLENT	AVERAGE
1968-1975 Head & Cab	N/A	$1000 - 1,250	$575 - 725
1976-1981 Head & Cab	N/A	$975 - 1,200	$525 - 650
1970-1975 Head Only	N/A	$450 - 550	$275 - 325
1976-1981 Head Only	N/A	$375 - 450	$225 - 275
Cab Only	N/A	$300 - 350	$175 - 225

In 1976, underlining in name plate is removed, and a master volume switch with distortion switch is added. Speakers are mounted diagonally as well. In 1981, output is raised to 70W.

ELECTRIC TUBE AMPS: BASSBREAKER SERIES

BASSBREAKER 007 HEAD – 7W, guitar head-unit, three-tube chassis, preamp: 2 X 12AX7, power: 1 X EL34, single channel, top black control panel, single input, 5 black knobs (g, b, m, t, MV), treble boost switch, power switch, rear panel: speaker output jack, line output jack, footswitch jack, Dark Gray Lacquered tweed covering, black grille cloth, block Fender logo, top handle, 8.94 in. tall, 15.81 in. wide, 8 in. deep, 16.6 lbs., new 2016.

MSR N/A	$400	$260 - 300	$130 - 160

* ***Bassbreaker 007 Combo*** – 7W, guitar combo amp, 1-10 in. Celestion Ten Thirty speaker, three-tube chassis, preamp: 2 X 12AX7, power: 1 X EL34, single channel, top black control panel, single input, 5 black knobs (g, b, m, t, MV), treble boost switch, power switch, rear panel: speaker output jack, line output jack, footswitch jack, Dark Gray Lacquered tweed covering, black grille cloth, block Fender logo, top handle, 14.75 in. tall, 15.81 in. wide, 8.5 in. deep, 25.5 lbs., new 2016.

MSR N/A	$450	$295 - 325	$145 - 180

BASSBREAKER 15 HEAD – 15W, guitar head-unit, five-tube chassis, preamp: 3 X 12AX7, power: 2 X EL34, single channel with selectable amp voice, top black control panel, single input, seven black knobs (g level, g structure selector, b, m, t, MV, reverb), bright switch, power switch, rear panel: ohm impedance selector switch (4/8/16), main speaker output jack, extension speaker jack, effect loop jacks, XLR line out jack, Dark Gray Lacquered tweed covering, black grille cloth, block Fender logo, top handle, 9.75 in. tall, 19.58 in. wide, 8.81 in. deep, 25.5 lbs., new 2016.

MSR N/A	$600	$400 - 450	$195 - 240

MSR/NOTES	100%	EXCELLENT	AVERAGE	LAST MSR

Bassbreaker 007 Head
courtesyFender

Bassbreaker 18/30Combo
courtesy Fender

Bassbreaker 1x12 Speaker Cabinet
courtesy Fender

* *Bassbreaker 15 Combo* – 15W, guitar combo amp, 1-12 in. Celestion G12V-70 speaker, five-tube chassis, preamp: 3 X 12AX7, power: 2 X EL34, single channel with selectable amp voice, top black control panel, single input, seven black knobs (g level, g structure selector, b, m, t, MV, reverb), bright switch, power switch, mute switch, rear panel: ohm impedance selector switch (4/8/16), main speaker output jack, extension speaker jack, effect loop jacks, XLR line out jack, Dark Gray Lacquered tweed covering, black grille cloth, block Fender logo, top handle, 17.5 in. tall, 19.56 in. wide, 10.5 in. deep, 40 lbs., new 2016.

| MSR N/A | $650 | $425 - 475 | $210 - 260 | |

BASSBREAKER 18/30 COMBO – 18/30W, guitar combo amp, 2-12 in. Celestion G12V-70 speakers, five-tube chassis, preamp: 3 X 12AX7, power: 2 X EL84, dual channels, top black control panel, single input, six black knobs (Ch. 1: v, b, m, t, Ch. 2: v, tone), power switch, standby switch, rear panel: power amp line out, ohm impedance selector switch (4/8/16), main speaker output jack, extension speaker jack, footswitch jack, channel-switching footswitch included, Dark Gray Lacquered tweed covering, black grille cloth, block Fender logo, top handle, 21.875 in. tall, 26.25 in. wide, 10 in. deep, 50 lbs., new 2016.

| MSR N/A | $850 | $550 - 625 | $275 - 350 | |

BASSBREAKER 45 HEAD – 45W, guitar head unit, five-tube chassis, preamp: 3 X 12AX7, power: 2 X EL34, dual channels, top black control panel, three inputs (normal, bright, both), seven black knobs (normal v, bright v, output selector, t, b, m, presence), power switch, standby switch, rear panel: ohm impedance selector switch (4/8/16), main speaker output jack, extension speaker jack, Dark Gray Lacquered tweed covering, black grille cloth, block Fender logo, top handle, 10.75 in. tall, 26.22 in. wide, 10.5 in. deep, 32 lbs., new 2016.

| MSR N/A | $900 | $575 - 675 | $295 - 350 | |

* *Bassbreaker 45 Combo* – 45W, guitar combo amp, 2-12 in. Celestion G12V-70 speakers, five-tube chassis, preamp: 3 X 12AX7, power: 2 X EL34, dual channels, top black control panel, three inputs (normal, bright, both), seven black knobs (normal v, bright v, output selector, t, b, m, presence), power switch, standby switch, rear panel: ohm impedance selector switch (4/8/16), main speaker output jack, extension speaker jack, Dark Gray Lacquered tweed covering, black grille cloth, block Fender logo, top handle, 22 in. tall, 26.22 in. wide, 8.5 in. deep, 55 lbs., new 2016.

| MSR N/A | $1,000 | $650 - 750 | $325 - 400 | |

BASSBREAKER 1-12 SPEAKER CABINET – 70W, 1-12 in. Celestion G12V-70 speaker, speaker cabinet designed for use with the Bassbreaker 007 head, 15 head, or 15 combo, semi-closed back, 8 ohms, 1/4 in. speaker jack, 19.5 in. wide, 16.88 in. tall, 9 in. deep, 21 lbs., top handle, available in dark gray lacquered tweed covering, black grille cloth, new 2016.

| MSR N/A | $250 | $165 - 190 | $80 - 100 | |

BASSBREAKER 2-12 SPEAKER CABINET – 140W, 2-12 in. Celestion G12V-70 speakers, speaker cabinet designed for use with the Bassbreaker 18/30 combo, 45 head, or 45 combo, semi-closed back, 16 ohms total, 1/4 in. speaker jack, 26.25 in. wide, 22.13 in. tall, 10.63 in. deep, 36 lbs., top handle, available in dark gray lacquered tweed covering, black grille cloth, new 2016.

| MSR N/A | $350 | $230 - 265 | $115 - 140 | |

ELECTRIC TUBE AMPS: BASSMAN SERIES

For the Bassman 300 PRO (Current Mfg.) refer to the Bass Tube Amps category.

BASSMAN (T.V. FRONT) – 26W, 1-15 in. Jensen speaker, tube chassis, preamp: 2 X 6SJ7, 6SL7, power: 2 X 6L6, top chrome control panel, two pointer knobs (v, tone), closed back with circle ports, chassis is on the bottom of the cabinet, early tweed covering, cloth grille, mfg. 1951-52.

| | N/A | $2,500 - 3,000 | $1,500 - 2,000 | |

BASSMAN (WIDE PANEL) – 26W, 1-15 in. Jensen speaker, tube chassis, preamp: 2 X 6SJ7, 6SL7, power: 2 X 6L6, top chrome control panel, two pointer knobs (v, tone), closed back with circle ports, chassis is on the bottom of the cabinet, wide panel tweed covering, brown grille, mfg. 1952-54.

| | N/A | $2,600 - 3,200 | $1,800 - 2,200 | |

MSR/NOTES	100%	EXCELLENT	AVERAGE	LAST MSR

BASSMAN (NARROW PANEL) – 50W, 4-10 in. Jensen P-10R speakers, tube chassis, preamp: 12AY7, 2 X 12AX7, power: 2 X 6L6G, rectifiers: 2 X 5U4G, top chrome control panel, four pointer knobs (v, b, t, p), diagonal tweed covering, brown tweed-era grille, mfg. 1954-1961.

courtesy solidbodyguitar.com, Inc.

courtesy solidbodyguitar.com, Inc.

1954-1956	N/A	$8,000 - 10,000	$4,800 - 6,000
1957-1961	N/A	$9,000 - 11,000	$5,750 - 7,250

Especially clean models may command a premium. Model 5E6 was used until 1955 when the 5F6 was introduced, which had four inputs, a middle control knob, and a single rectifier. In 1958 the 5F6-A was introduced and the GZ34 rectifier was replaced and an added "swamper resistor" was added.

BASSMAN (BROWNFACE) – 50W, 1-12 in. Jensen speaker in a seperate cabinet, tube chassis: preamp: 4 X 7025, power: 2 X 5881, GZ34 rectifier, two channels, brownface control panel, seven brown knobs (Ch. 1: v, t, b; Ch 2: v, t, b, Both: p), cream Tolex covering, maroon grille, mfg. 1961-64.

1961 Head & 1-12 in. Cab	N/A	$2,300 - 2,850	$1,800 - 2,100
1962-1964 Head & 2-12 in. Cab	N/A	$2,250 - 2,750	$1,650 - 1,950
1961 Head Only	N/A	$1,400 - 1,750	$850 - 1,050
1962-1964 Head Only	N/A	$800 - 1,000	$475 - 600
Cab Only	N/A	$675 - 850	$400 - 500

• **Add $150-200 for GZ34 rectifier model.**

The 1-12 in. cabinet was model 6G6. In 1962, the 2-12 in. cabinet is introduced (Model 6G6-A). Around 1962, a solid-state rectifier was introduced. Tubes in later models may be different, and include preamp: 3 X 7025, 12AT7, and power: 2 X 6L6GC. Silicon rectifiers were also used. In 1964, the presence switchwas repalced by abright switch (Model AA864).

BASSMAN (BLACKFACE) – 50W, 2-12 in. Jensen speakers, tube chassis, preamp: 3 X 7025, 12AT7, power: 6L6GC, GZ34 rectifier, two channels, blackface control panel, dual inputs, six silver knobs (Ch. 1: v, t, b; Ch. 2: v, t, b), black Tolex covering, silver grille, mfg. 1964-68.

courtesy John Beeson/The Music Shoppe

courtesy Dave Rogers/Dave's Guitar Shop

courtesy John Beeson/The Music Shoppe

1964-65 Head & Cab	N/A	$1,400 - 1,750	$850 - 1,050
1964-65 Head Only	N/A	$550 - 700	$350 - 425
1966-67 Head & Cab	N/A	$1,275 - 1,600	$750 - 950
1966-67 Head Only	N/A	$525 - 650	$325 - 400
Cab Only	N/A	$400 - 500	$250 - 300

In 1967, the speaker cabinet was replaced by a larger, vertical design. Some early models may still have the presence control instead of the bright switch.

MSR/NOTES	100%	EXCELLENT	AVERAGE	LAST MSR

BASSMAN (SILVERFACE) – 50W, 2-12 in. Jensen speakers in a separate enclosure, tube chassis, preamp: 3 X 7025, 12AT7, power: 6L6GC, GZ34 rectifier, two channels, silverface control panel, dual inputs, six silver knobs (Ch. 1: v, t, b; Ch. 2: v, t, b), black Tolex covering, silver grille, mfg. 1968-1972.

1968-1969 Head & Cab	N/A	$725 - 900	$425 - 550
1968-1969 Head Only	N/A	$475 - 600	$275 - 350
1970-1972 Head & Cab	N/A	$600 - 750	$350 - 450
1970-1972 Head Only	N/A	$400 - 500	$250 - 300
Cab Only	N/A	$325 - 400	$225 - 275

In 1968, the entire design was changed to the model AA568 (this was probably introduced when models switched to Silverface control panels). In 1970, a 2-15 speaker cab was introduced. The Silverface was renamed the Bassman 50 in 1972.

SUPER BASSMAN/SUPER BASSMAN II – 100W, 2-15 in. speakers in a separate cabinet (Super Bassman II has two cabinets, 4-15 in. speakers), tube chassis: 2 X 7025, 12AT7, power: 4 X 6LGC, silicon rectifiers, two channels, silverface control panel, four inputs (two bass and two normal), seven silver-top knobs (Bass: v, t, b, Norm: v, t, m, b) deep and bright switches for both channels, black Tolex covering, silver grille, mfg. 1969-1971.

Super Bassman	N/A	$500 - 650	$375 - 450
Super Bassman II	N/A	$650 - 850	$450 - 600

This model was renamed the Bassman 100 in 1972.

BASSMAN 10 – 50W, 4-10 in. Jensen speakers, tube chassis, preamp: 2 X 7025, 12AT7, power: 2 X 6L6GC, solid-state rectifiers, two channels, silver control panel, four inputs, eight silver-top numbered knobs (Ch. 1: v, t, b; Ch. 2: v, t, b, m, MV), bs, ds, black Tolex covering, silver grille, mfg. 1972-1982.

	N/A	$600 - 750	$350 - 425

In 1981, the blackface control panel became standard, and the output was increased to 70W.

BASSMAN 20 – 20W, 1-15 in. Jensen speaker, tube chassis, preamp: 2 X 7025, power: 2 X 6V6GTA, blackface control panel, single input, one channel, four silver-top numbered knobs (v, t, b, m), black Tolex covering, silver grille, mfg. 1982-85.

	N/A	$450 - 550	$250 - 300

BASSMAN 50 – 50W, 2-15 in. speakers in a separate cabinet, tube chassis, preamp: 2 X 7025, 12AT7, power: 2 X 6L6GC, solid-state rectifier, silverface control panel, four inputs, six silver-top numbered knobs (Bass, v, t, b, Norm, v, t, b), bright switch, deep switch, black Tolex covering, silver grille, mfg. 1972-76.

courtesy Savage Audio

courtesy Savage Audio

Head & Cab	N/A	$500 - 600	$275 - 325
Head Only	N/A	$300 - 375	$180 - 225

In 1974, a Master Volume control was added.

BASSMAN 70 – 70W, 4-10 in. speakers in a separate cabinet, tube chassis, preamp: 3 X 7025, 12AT7, power: 2 X 6L6GC, silicon rectifier, two channels, silverface control panel, seven silver-top knobs (Bass: v, t, b, Norm: v, t, b MV), bright switch, deep switch, black Tolex covering, silver grille, mfg. 1977-79.

Head & Cab	N/A	$700 - 850	$350 - 450
Head Only	N/A	$450 - 550	$250 - 300

BASSMAN 100 – 100W, 4-12 in. speakers in a separate cabinet, tube chassis, preamp: 2 X 7025, 12AT7, power: 2 X 6L6, solid-state rectifier, silverface control panel, four inputs, eight silver-top numbered knobs (Bass: v, t, b, Norm: v, t, b, m, MV), black Tolex covering, silver grille, mfg. 1972-79.

Head & Cab	N/A	$700 - 850	$375 - 475
Head Only	N/A	$400 - 500	$250 - 300

MSR/NOTES	100%	EXCELLENT	AVERAGE	LAST MSR

BASSMAN 135 – 135W, 4-10 in. speakers in a cabinet, tube chassis, preamp: 2 X 7025, 12AT7, power: 4 X 6L6, solid-state rectifier, two channels, silverface control panel, four inputs, nine silver-top numbered knobs (Bass: v, t, m, b, Norm: v, b, m, t, MV), bright switch, black Tolex covering, silver grille, mfg. 1979-1983.

Head & Cab	N/A	$650 - 800	$350 - 450	
Head Only	N/A	$400 - 500	$250 - 300	

ELECTRIC TUBE AMPS: BLUES/HOT ROD SERIES

In 2011, Fender introduced the "III" Series of Blues/Hot Rod amps. Upgrades to these amps include easier to read black control panels with forward-facing text, a new Fender badge, vintage Fender "dog bone" handle, and a vintage-size jewel light.

**Blues Deluxe Reissue
courtesy Fender**

**Blues Deville Reissue
courtesy Fender**

**Blues Junior
courtesy Rick Wilkiewicz**

BLUES DELUXE (NO. 021-3102-000) – 40W, 1-12 in. Eminence speaker, tube chassis, preamp: 3 X 12AX7, power: 2 X GT 6L6, two channels, reverb, top chrome control panel, two inputs, eight black chickenhead knobs (v, drive, t, b, m, MV, r, p), channel select switches, effects loop, one-button footswitch, tweed covering, brown/gold grille, 45 lbs., mfg. 1994-96.

	N/A	$425 - 500	$250 - 300	$610

BLUES DELUXE REISSUE (NO. 223-2200-000) – 40W, 1-12 in. Eminence speaker, tube chassis, preamp: 3 X 12AX7, power: 2 X 6L6, two channels, reverb, top chrome control panel, two inputs, eight black chickenhead knobs (v, drive, t, b, m, MV, r, p), channel select switches, effects loop, one-button footswitch, tweed covering, brown/gold grille, 45 lbs., mfg. summer 2005-present.

MSR N/A	$770	$450 - 550	$275 - 325	

BLUES DEVILLE (NO. 021-3101-000) – 60W, 4-10 in. speakers, tube chassis: preamp: 3 X 12AX7, power: 2 X 6L6, top chrome control panel, eight black chickenhead knobs (p, r, MV, m, b, t, drive), effects loop, diagonal tweed covering, brown tweed-era grille, 58 lbs., mfg. 1994-96.

	N/A	$550 - 700	$350 - 425	$900

* *Blues DeVille 2-12 (No. 021-3100-000)* – similar to the Blues Deville, except has 2-12 in. Eminence speakers, mfg. 1994-96.

	N/A	$525 - 650	$325 - 400	$840

BLUES DEVILLE REISSUE (NO. 223-2100-000) – 60W, 4-10 in. Blue Alnico Eminence speakers, tube chassis: preamp: 3 X 12AX7, power: 2 X 6L6, top chrome control panel, eight black chickenhead knobs (p, r, MV, m, b, t, drive), effects loop, diagonal tweed covering, brown tweed-era grille, 50 lbs., mfg. summer 2005-2013.

	$1,050	$600 - 750	$375 - 450	$1,470

BLUES JUNIOR (NO. 021-3205-000/223-0500-000) – 15W, 1-12 in. Eminence speaker (1997-2010) or 1-12 in. Fender Special Design "Lightning Bolt" speaker by Eminence (2011-present), tube chassis, preamp: 3 X 12AX7, power: 2 X EL-84 Groove Tubes, reverb, top silver control panel, one input, FAT switch, six black pointer knobs (r, MV, m, b, t, v,), one button footswitch, narrow panel vintage cabinet, available in Black Tolex covering with a silver grille, Blonde Tolex covering with an oxblood grille, Brown Tolex covering with an oxblood grille, Surf Green with a silver grille, Texas Red with a silver grille, Tweed with a brown grille, Two-Tone Blonde/Brown Tolex covering with a wheat grille, or White Blonde Tolex covering with an oxblood grille, 31 lbs., mfg. 1997-present.

MSR N/A	$530	$300 - 375	$175 - 225	

The Blues Junior lists black Tolex covering with a silver grille as standard equipment, but this amp has been produced in various other coverings including Blonde, Brown, Surf Green, and Texas Red. In 2011, the Blues Junior III was introduced and replaced the previous Blues Junior with minor differences.

* *Blues Junior Lacquered Tweed LTD C12N (No. 021-320-5700)* – similar to the Blues Junior, except has a Jensen 12-in. speaker and available in lacquered tweed covering with a vintage-style brown and gold grille cloth, mfg. 2015-present.

MSR N/A	$600	$325 - 425	$200 - 250	

* *Blues Junior NOS* – similar to the Blues Junior, except has a vintage 1-12 in. Jensen C12-N speaker and lacquered tweed covering with a pinstripe grille cloth, disc..

	$580	$350 - 425	$200 - 250	$790

This model is produced for and sold exclusively through various music retailers including Guitar Center and Musician's Friend.

MSR/NOTES	100%	EXCELLENT	AVERAGE	LAST MSR

Hot Rod Deville 410
courtesy Fender

Pro Junior
courtesy Fender

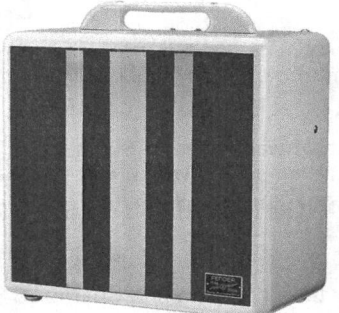

Pro Junior 60th Anniversary Woody
courtesy Fender

* ***Blues Junior ProGuitarShop Limited Edition*** – similar to the Blues Junior, except has a Celestion Vintage 30 speaker and red Tolex covering with a wheat grille cloth, limited edition run of 150 amps, mfg. late 2010.

	$530	$350 - 425	$200 - 250	

This model is produced for and sold exclusively through ProGuitarShop.com.

HOT ROD DELUXE (NO. 021-3202-000/223-0200-000) – 40W, 1-12 in. Eminence speaker (1997-2010) or 1-12 in. Celestion G12P-80 speaker, tube chassis, preamp: 3 X 12AX7, power: 2 X GT 6L6, three channels, reverb, top chrome control panel, two inputs, eight black chickenhead knobs (v, drive, t, b, m, MV, r, p), channel select switches, effects loop, two button footswitch, black vinyl covering, silver grille, cover included, 45 lbs., mfg. 1997-present.

MSR N/A	$730	$425 - 525	$275 - 325	

• Add 10-20% for limited editions of this model.

In 2011, the Hot Rod Deluxe III was introduced and replaced the previous Hot Rod Deluxe with minor differences. Fender has produced several limited editions of the Hot Rod Deluxe including one in a 3-Color Sunburst cabinet (2003/04), a natural maple cabinet (2003/04), the White Lightning with white Tolex (2006/07), the Texas Red with red Tolex covering (2008), the Emerald Green version, The Giddy Up with Brown faux tooled-leather vinyl covering and Wheat grille cloth (2014-present), and a Blonde Tolex version.

HOT ROD DELUXE 112 SPEAKER CABINET (NO. 223-1000-XXX/223-1010-XXX) – 80W, 1-12 in. Celestion G12T-100-8 speaker (2008-2010) or 1-12 in. Celestion G12P-80 speaker (2011-present), extension speaker cabinet designed for use with the Hot Rod Deluxe, closed back, removable glide cups for stacking, 22.5 in. wide, 18 in. tall, 11 in. deep, 41 lbs., includes black nylon cover and speaker cable, available in Black textured vinyl with a silver grille cloth, Blonde textured vinyl with an Oxblood grille cloth (2008-09), Blonde textured vinyl with a Wheat grille cloth (2008-09), Emerald textured vinyl with a dark black/silver grille cloth (2008-09), Lacquered Tweed with an Oxblood grille cloth, Texas Red textured vinyl with a Wheat grille cloth (2008-09), Tweed with an Oxblood grille cloth, or White Lightning textured vinyl with a dark black/silver grille cloth (2008-09), mfg. 2008-present.

MSR N/A	$300	$175 - 225	$110 - 135	

• Add 20% (MAP: $350) for Lacquered Tweed covering with an Oxblood grille cloth.

HOT ROD DEVILLE 212 (NO. 021-3200-000/223-0000-000) – 60W, 2-12 in. Eminence speakers (1997-2010) or 2-12 in. Celestion G12P-80 speakers (2011-present), tube chassis, preamp: 3 X 12AX7, power: 2 X GT 6L6, three channels, reverb, top chrome control panel, two inputs, eight black chickenhead knobs (v, drive, t, b, m, MV, r, p), channel select switches, effects loop, two button footswitch, black vinyl covering, silver grille, cover included, 53.5 lbs., mfg. 1997-present.

MSR N/A	$930	$500 - 625	$300 - 375	

In 2011, the Hot Rod Deville 212 III was introduced and replaced the previous Hot Rod Deville 212 with minor differences.

HOT ROD DEVILLE 410 (NO. 021-3201-000/223-0100-000) – 60W, 4-10 in. Eminence speaker, tube chassis, preamp: 3 X 12AX7, power: 2 X GT 6L6, three channels, reverb, top chrome control panel, two inputs, eight black chickenhead knobs (v, drive, t, b, m, MV, r, p), channel select switches, effects loop, two button footswitch, black vinyl covering, silver grille, cover included, 50 lbs., mfg. 1997-present.

MSR N/A	$950	$525 - 650	$325 - 400	

In 2011, the Hot Rod Deville 410 was introduced and replaced the previous Hot Rod Deville 410 with minor differences.

PRO JUNIOR (NO. 021-3203-000/223-0300-000) – 15W, 1-10 in. Eminence speaker, tube chassis, preamp: 2 X 12AX7, power: 2 X EL84 Groove Tubes, single channel, top chrome control panel, one input, two pointer knobs (volume, tone), narrow panel vintage cabinet, black textured vinyl or tweed with silver or brown/gold grille cloth, 20 lbs., mfg. 1994-present.

MSR N/A	$420	$250 - 315	$145 - 175	

In 1997, the covering was changed to black textured vinyl with a silver grille. It was part of the change from the Blues series to the Hot Rod series. However, the Pro Junior retained the same name. In 2011, the Pro Junior III was introduced and replaced the previous Pro Junior with minor differences.

PRO JUNIOR 60TH ANNIVERSARY WOODY (NO. 223-2300) – 15W, 1-10 in. Jensen speaker, tube chassis, preamp: 2 X 12AX7, power: 2 X EL84, single channel, top chrome control panel, one input, two pointer knobs (volume, tone), solid ash construction (semi-opaque wood finish) with wood handle, red grille covering with three vertical chrome strips, 22 lbs., cover included, limited mfg. from July-November 2006.

	N/A	$625 - 750	$375 - 475	$1,200

ELECTRIC TUBE AMPS: BRONCO SERIES

BRONCO – 5W, 1-8 in. speaker, tube chassis, preamp: 2 X 12AX7A, power: 6V6GTA, solid-state rectifier, single channel, vibrato, silverface control panel, two inputs, five pointer knobs (v, b, t, s, i), black Tolex covering, silver grille, mfg. 1968-1974.

| | N/A | $350 - 450 | $225 - 275 | $94.50 |

Output was raised to 6W in 1972. The Bronco matches the schematics and manuals of the Vibro-Champ. These are basically the same amplifiers with a different name on them. The Bronco has red lettering while the Vibro-Champ has blue lettering.

BRONCO (SOLID STATE) – refer to the Solid-State listing in the Fender section.

ELECTRIC TUBE AMPS: CHAMP/CHAMPION SERIES

For the Champ 25 and Champ 25 S/E models see the Hybrid section. For the Champion 110, see the Solid State Standard/Third Series section.

CHAMPION 600 (TV FRONT) – 4W, 1-6 in. Jensen, tube chassis, preamp: 6SJ7, power: 6V6, 5Y3 rectifier, two inputs one volume pointer knob, two-tone brown and white textured vinyl covering, brown clothe grille, mfg. 1949-1953.

courtesy Dave Rogers/Dave's Guitar Shop   courtesy Dave Rogers/Dave's Guitar Shop

| | N/A | $1,000 - 1,250 | $600 - 750 |

This model was also known as the Student or the Student 600.

CHAMPION 800 (TV FRONT) – 4W, 1-8 in. Jensen, tube chassis, preamp: 6SJ7, power: 6V6, 5Y3 rectifier, two inputs one volume pointer knob, gray-green Hammerloid finish with white marking, gray-green linen, gray grille, mfg. 1948-49.

| | N/A | $1,125 - 1,400 | $675 - 850 |

This is the rare version that came before the Champion 600. It is estimated that only 100 of these amps were produced.

CHAMP (STUDENT, WIDE PANEL) – 4W, 1-6 in. Jensen, tube chassis, preamp: 6SJ7, power: 6V6, 5Y3 rectifier, two inputs one volume pointer knob, diagonal tweed covering, brown cloth grille, mfg. 1953-54.

courtesy Dave Rogers/Dave's Guitar Shop   courtesy Dave Rogers/Dave's Guitar Shop

| | N/A | $1,200 - 1,500 | $725 - 900 |

This model was called the student in the catalog, and was renamed due to other claimants to that name. Earlier versions of this model had the "600" logo on the control plate, later ones had "Champ Amp" on the plate.

MSR/NOTES	100%	EXCELLENT	AVERAGE	LAST MSR

CHAMP (NARROW PANEL) – 4W, 1-6 in Jensen speaker, tube chassis, preamp: 12AX7, power: 6V6GT, 5Y3GT rectifier, top control panel, two inputs, one volume pointer knob, tweed covering, brown tweed-era grille, mfg. 1954-1964.

courtesy Dave Rogers/Dave's Guitar Shop   courtesy Dave Rogers/Dave's Guitar Shop   courtesy Dave Rogers/Dave's Guitar Shop

Tweed (1954-1964)	N/A	$1,325 - 1,650	$800 - 1,000
Black (1964)	N/A	$1,000 - 1,250	$600 - 750

Some later models came with black Tolex covering, and a silver sparkle grille (circa 1963/64).In 1951, a choke was added to the high-voltage filter section and the use of negative feedback was used (Model 5E1). In 1956, the choke was removed (Model 5F1, and the chassis remained unchanged until 1964.

CHAMP (BLACKFACE/SILVERFACE) – 4W, 1-8 in. speaker, tube chassis, preamp: 12AX7, power: 6V6GT, 5YTGT rectifier, single channel, blackface/silverface control panel, two input jacks, three silver-top knobs (v, t, b), black Tolex covering, silver grille, mfg. 1964-1980.

Champ Blackface   **Champ Blackface**   **Champ Silverface**
courtesy solidbodyguitar.com, Inc.   courtesy solidbodyguitar.com, Inc.   courtesy Savage Audio

1964-1967 Blackface	N/A	$550 - 700	$350 - 425
1968-1971 Silverface	N/A	$400 - 500	$250 - 300
1972-1980 Silverface	N/A	$325 - 400	$190 - 240

In 1964, separate bass and treble controls were introduced (Model AA764). In 1965, output increased to 5W. In 1968, Silverface was introduced. In 1972, output increased to 6W . Chassis remained unchanged until 1982

VIBRO CHAMP – 4W, 1-8 in. speaker, tube chassis, preamp: 2 X 12AX7, power: 6V6GT, 5Y3GT rectifier, single channel, vibrato, blackface/silverface control panel, two input jacks, five silver-top knobs (v, t, b, s, i), black Tolex covering, silver grille, mfg. 1964-1980.

courtesy solidbodyguitar.com, Inc.   courtesy solidbodyguitar.com, Inc.

1964-1967 Blackface	N/A	$600 - 750	$350 - 450
1968-1971 Silverface	N/A	$450 - 550	$275 - 325
1972-1980 Silverface	N/A	$400 - 500	$250 - 300

Model number is AA764, the same as the Champ. In 1965, output increased to 5W. In 1969, silverface was introduced. In 1972, output increased to 6W.

MSR/NOTES	100%	EXCELLENT	AVERAGE	LAST MSR

CHAMP II – 18W, 1-10 in. speaker, tube chassis, preamp: 2 X 7025, power: 2 X 6V6GTA, solid-state rectifiers, bs, new blackface control panel, four silver-top knobs (v, t, b, mv), black Tolex covering, silver grille, mfg. 1982-85.

	N/A	$400 - 500	$250 - 300	

This model was a cheaper version of the Super Champ and featured completely new circuitry.

CHAMP 12 – 12W, 1-12 in. Eminence speaker, tube chassis, preamp: 2 X 12AX7, power: 6L6, solid-state rectifier, blackface control panel, two inputs, six red knobs (t, b, v, overdrive gain, v, r), tape inputs, line output, headphone jack, black Tolex covering, black grille, mfg. 1986-1992.

courtesy Savage Audio   courtesy Savage Audio

	N/A	$275 - 350	$170 - 210	

• **Add 15% for custom coverings including red, white, gray, or snakeskin.**

This model came with five custom coverings, including red, white, gray, and snakeskin besides the standard black.

SUPER CHAMP – 18W, 1-10 in. speaker, tube chassis, preamp: 2 X 7025, power: 2 X 6V6GTA, solid-state rectifiers, reverb, hot rod lead channel, new blackface control panel, one input jack, six silver-top knobs (v, t, b, r, lead level, MV), black Tolex covering, silver grille, mfg. 1982-85.

	N/A	$800 - 1,000	$475 - 600	

This amp uses reverb and switching lead sound using the reverb drive as an extra pre-amp.

* *Super Champ Deluxe* – similar to the Super Champ except, has an Electro-voice speaker, solid oak cabinet, brown cloth grille, brown knobs, brown control panel, padded cover included, mfg. 1982-85.

	N/A	$1,200 - 1,500	$725 - 900	

ELECTRIC TUBE AMPS: CONCERT SERIES

For the Concert made between 1992 and 1995, and 2002-present, refer to the Pro-Tube series.

CONCERT (BROWNFACE) – 40W, 4-10 in. Jensen speakers, seven-tube chassis, preamp: 5 X 7025, power: 2 X 6L6GC, two channels, vibrato, brownface control panel, four inputs, (two normal, two vibrato), nine brown knobs (Norm: v, t, b, Vibrato: v, t, b, s, i, Both: p), brown Tolex covering, light brown grille, mfg. 1959-1963.

courtesy Dave Rogers/Dave's Guitar Shop   courtesy Dave Rogers/Dave's Guitar Shop

1959-1960	N/A	$2,200 - 2,750	$1,325 - 1,650	
1961-1963	N/A	$2,000 - 2,500	$1,200 - 1,500	

• **Add 25% for 1960 Tweed grille.**

The earliest Concerts had a center volume control, which was a transition period. First model number was 6G12 and in late 1960, a tremolo circuit was added (Model 6G12-A). In 1961, the light brown grille was changed to maroon, which was then changed to a richer shade of brown. In 1962, one 7025 tube was replaced with two 12AX7's, and the 6L6GC tube was replaced by a 5881. The grille also changed to a wheat-colored cloth. In 1963, the Model AA763 was introduced.

MSR/NOTES	100%	EXCELLENT	AVERAGE	LAST MSR

CONCERT (BLACKFACE) – 40W, 4-10 in. Jensen speakers, tube chassis, preamp: 1 X 12AX7, 2 X 7025, 1 X 12AT7, power: 2 X 6L6GC, two channels, vibrato, blackface control panel, four inputs, (two normal, two vibrato), eight brown knobs (Norm: v, t, b, Vibrato: v, t, b, s, i), bright switch, black Tolex covering, silver grille, mfg. 1963-65.

courtesy Dave Rogers/Dave's Guitar Shop   courtesy Dave Rogers/Dave's Guitar Shop

| | N/A | $2,000 - 2,600 | $1,175 - 1,450 | |

CONCERT II (112) – 60W, 1-12 in. speaker, tube chassis, preamp: 5 X 7025, 2 X 12AT7, power: 2 X 6L6GC, two switchable channels, new blackface control panel, two inputs, eleven silver-top knobs (Ch.1, v, t, m, b, Ch.2, v, g, MV, t, m, b, r, p), effects loop, black Tolex covering, silver grille, mfg. 1982-85.

| | N/A | $800 - 1,000 | $400 - 500 | |

This model was available as a combo or with a separate head.

* *Concert II (210)* – similar to the Concert II 112, except has 2-10 in. speakers, mfg. 1982-85.

| | N/A | $800 - 1,000 | $400 - 500 | |

* *Concert II (410)* – similar to Concert II 112, except has 4-10 in. speakers, mfg. 1982-85.

| | N/A | $850 - 1,050 | $425 - 550 | |

ELECTRIC TUBE AMPS: DELUXE SERIES

Deluxe (Model 26)
courtesy solidbodyguitar.com, Inc.

Deluxe (TV Front)
courtesy Dave Rogers/Dave's Guitar Shop

DELUXE (MODEL 26) – 10W, 1-10 in. Jensen speaker, tube chassis, preamp: 6SC7, 6N7, power: 2 X 6F6, 5Y3 rectifier, top black control panel with white lettering, three pointer knobs (inst. v, mic. v, tone), polished wood cabinet, colored felt with vertical chrome strips, mfg. 1946-48.

| | N/A | $1,800 - 2,250 | $1,075 - 1,350 | |

Also known as the "Woodie." Some of these models had two strips instead of the more common three on the front. This model was sometimes called the Model 26. This name appears on the control panel of the Deluxe and Professional amps. Later models have a 6V6 power tube instead of the 6F6.

DELUXE (TV FRONT) – 10W, 1-12 in. Jensen speaker, tube chassis, preamp: 6SC7/6N7, power: 2 X 6V6, 5Y3 rectifier, top control panel, three pointer knobs (inst. v, mic. v, tone), early tweed covering, dark brown cloth grille, mfg. 1948-1953.

| | N/A | $2,800 - 3,600 | $1,450 - 1,800 | |

Some of these models have a deep back panel. In 1949, the vertical tweed and dark brown grille was replaced with diagonal tweed and brown linen cloth. This model was 5A3.

DELUXE (WIDE FRONT) – 10W, 1-12 in. Jensen speaker, tube chassis, preamp: 2 X 6SC7, power: 2 X 6V6, 5Y3 rectifier, top control panel, three pointer knobs (inst. v, mic. v, tone), a separate on/off switch, extra speaker jack, negative feedback loop, diagonal tweed covering, dark brown grille cloth, mfg. 1953-55.

courtesy Dave Rogers/Dave's Guitar Shop

courtesy Dave Rogers/Dave's Guitar Shop

| N/A | $2,800 - 3,500 | $1,675 - 2,100 |

Model numbers 5B3 and 5C3 are virtually identical, which were introduced with the wide panel tweed. The 5C3 featured a separate on/off switch, spare speaker jack, and a negative feedback loop. In 1954 the 5D3 Models was intrdouced and used minature 12AX7 and 12AY7 preamp tubes, and the negative feedback loop was removed. This was the end of metal tubes that were replaced by glass tubes.

DELUXE (NARROW PANEL) – 15W, 1-12 in. Jensen speaker, tube chassis, preamp: 12AX7, 12AY7, power: 2 X 6V6, 5Y3 rectifier, top control panel, four inputs, three pointer knobs (inst. v, mic. v, tone), ground switch, diagonal tweed covering, brown tweed-era grille, mfg. 1955-1960.

courtesy Dave Rogers/Dave's Guitar Shop

courtesy Dave Rogers/Dave's Guitar Shop

| N/A | $4,500 - 5,500 | $2,400 - 3,000 |

The 5E3 Model was introduced when it switched to Narrow Panel. This model had a new ground switch and four inputs. When the model was changed to 5F3 from 5E3 the half of the 12AX7 tube was being used, leaving the other half as another preamp stage. This means the other half could be used to create higher gain. Musicians know the Deluxe as a model to distort at low volumes.

DELUXE (BROWNFACE) – 15W, 1-12 in. Jensen speaker, tube chassis, preamp: 7025, 2 X 12AX7, power: 2 X 6V6, GZ34 rectifier, two channels, front brown control panel, four inputs (two normal, two bright), six brown knobs (Norm: v, t, Bright: v, t, Both: s, i), external speaker jack, brown Tolex covering, light brown grille, mfg. 1961-63.

courtesy Dave Rogers/Dave's Guitar Shop

courtesy Dave Rogers/Dave's Guitar Shop

| N/A | $2,500 - 3,000 | $1,325 - 1,650 |

Tremolo operates on both channels. In 1961, Model 6G3 was introduced and had the channels reversed.

MSR/NOTES	100%	EXCELLENT	AVERAGE	LAST MSR

DELUXE (BLACKFACE) – 20W, 1-12 in. Jensen speaker, tube chassis, preamp: 2 X 7025, 12AX7, 12AY7, power: 2 X 6V6, GZ34 rectifier, two channels, blackface control panel, four inputs, (two normal, two vibrato), eight silver-top knobs (Norm: v, b, t, Vib: v, b, t, s, i), black Tolex covering, silver grille, mfg. 1963-66.

courtesy Savage Audio courtesy Savage Audio

| | N/A | $2,400 - 3,000 | $1,075 - 1,350 | |

When the Blackface was introduced (Model AA763), it had separate bass and treble controls. Models AA763 and AB763 are almost identical. In 1966, some amps get the underlined Fender nameplates on the grilles.

Tremolo operates on bright channel only.

DELUXE REVERB (BLACKFACE) – 20W, 1-12 in. speaker, tube chassis, preamp: 3 X 7025, 2 X 12AT7, 12AX7, power: 2 X 6V6, GZ34 rectifier, two channels, tremelo, reverb, front blackface control panel, four inputs, (two normal, two vibrato), nine silver-top knobs (Norm: v, b, t, Vibrato: v, b, t, r, s, i), black Tolex covering, silver grille, mfg. 1963-68.

courtesy Dave Rogers/Dave's Guitar Shop courtesy Dave Rogers/Dave's Guitar Shop

| | N/A | $2,500 - 3,000 | $1,325 - 1,650 | |

This amp was introduced at the same time as the Blackface Deluxe but lasted longer. The model name was the same as the Deluxe (AA763). In 1966, the Fender nameplate was put on the front.

DELUXE REVERB (SILVERFACE) – 20W, 1-12 in. speaker, tube chassis, preamp: 3 X 7025, 2 X 12AT7, 12AX7, power: 2 X 6V6, solid-state rectifier, two channels, tremelo, reverb, front silverface control panel, four inputs, (two normal, two vibrato), nine silver-top knobs (Norm: v, b, t, Vibrato: v, b, t, r, s, i), black Tolex covering, silver grille, mfg. 1968-1979.

 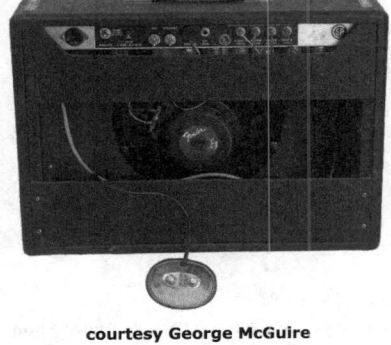

courtesy George McGuire courtesy George McGuire

1968-1969	N/A	$1,800 - 2,250	$850 - 1,050	
1970-1972	N/A	$1,200 - 1,500	$675 - 850	
1973-1979	N/A	$1,000 - 1,250	$600 - 750	

A 1200 pF capacitor was placed on the grids of each of the power tubes, which cures instability that was on earlier blackface models.

MSR/NOTES	100%	EXCELLENT	AVERAGE	LAST MSR

DELUXE REVERB II – 20W, 1-12 in. speaker, tube chassis, preamp: 5 X 7025, 12AT7, power: 2 X 6V6GTA, tremolo, two switchable channels, distortion, front blackface control panel, two inputs, 11 silver-top control knobs (Ch.1: v, t, b, Ch.2: v, g, MV, t, m, b, r, p), preamp output and power amp input jacks, hum balance control, black Tolex covering, silver grille, mfg. 1982-85.

N/A $800 - 1,000 $475 - 600

ELECTRIC TUBE AMPS: HARVARD SERIES

For the Harvard model produced between 1982 and 1985, see the Solid State Second Series section.

HARVARD – 10W, 1-8 or 1-10 in. speaker, tube chassis, preamp: 6AT6, 12AX7, power: 2 X 6V6, 5Y3 rectifier, top numbered chrome control panel, three inputs, two pointer knobs (v, tone), diagonal tweed covering, brown tweed-era grille, mfg. 1955-1961.

courtesy Dave Rogers/Dave's Guitar Shop   courtesy Dave Rogers/Dave's Guitar Shop   courtesy Dave Rogers/Dave's Guitar Shop

N/A $2,300 - 2,800 $1,325 - 1,600

The model number was 5F10. The Harvard is shown in some catalogs with 8 in. speakers and some with 10 in. speakers. Both were used at different times during the production of the amp. The Harvard was discontinued in 1961 when the Princeton and the Champ were too close in price to justify another amp in between. A 6G10 was shown in schematics, but never made it into production. Late models only have one 6V6 power tube.

ELECTRIC TUBE AMPS: PRINCETON SERIES

It is known that 200 Princetons were taken apart and used for the first Mesa Boogie amps.

PRINCETON (MODEL 26) – 4.5W, 1-8 in. Jensen or Utah speaker, tube chassis, preamp: 6SL7, power: 6V6, 5Y3 rectifier, no control panel, only two jacks in the back, no on/off switch, polished wood cabinet, colored cloth grille with vertical chrome strips, mfg. 1946-48.

N/A $1,050 - 1,300 $625 - 775

This model never had the name "Princeton" on the amp, this model was named this because it is very close to the Princeton amps to follow. The chassis was quite similar to that of the earlier K&F model.

PRINCETON (TV FRONT) – 4.5W, 1-8 in. Jensen speaker, tube chassis, preamp: 6SL7, power: 6V6, 5Y3 rectifier, top control panel, two input jacks, two pointer knobs (volume and tone, on/off switch was part of the tone control), fuse holder, new jeweled control pilot light, early tweed covering, brown cloth grille, mfg. 1948-1952.

N/A $1,125 - 1,400 $675 - 850

This model's circuitry is virtually identical to that of the Model 26 Princeton.

PRINCETON (WIDE PANEL) – 4.5W, 1-8 in. Jensen spealer, tube chassis, preamp: 6SL7, power: 6V6, 5Y3 rectifier, top control panel, two input jacks, two pointer knobs (v, tone), diagonal tweed covering, brown cloth grille, mfg. 1952-54.

courtesy Dave Rogers/Dave's Guitar Shop   courtesy Dave Rogers/Dave's Guitar Shop

N/A $1,125 - 1,400 $675 - 850

This model also had the same circuitry of earlier Princetons with the exception of the preamp tubes becoming 6SC7 in 1953 and 12AX7 (Model 5D2) in 1954.

MSR/NOTES	100%	EXCELLENT	AVERAGE	LAST MSR

PRINCETON (NARROW PANEL) – 4.5W, 1-8 in. Jensen spealer, tube chassis, preamp: 6SL7, power: 6V6, 5Y3 rectifier, top control panel, two input jacks, two pointer knobs (v, tone), narrow panel diagonal tweed covering, brown tweed-era grille, mfg. 1954-1961.

courtesy solidbodyguitar.com, Inc.

courtesy solidbodyguitar.com, Inc.

| N/A | $1,600 - 1,950 | $850 - 1,050 |

Model 5E2 had a choke and negative loop (circa 1954/55). The choke was removed in 1956 and named the Model 5F2. This model's cabinet was enlarged in 1956, which was also used for the Harvard. The Champ then used the old Princeton box.

PRINCETON (BROWNFACE) – 12W, 1-10 in. Jensen speaker, tube chassis, preamp: 7025, 12AX7, power: 2 X 6V6, 5Y3 rectifier, tremolo, front brownface control panel, two input jacks, four brown knobs (v, t, s, i), ground switch on back, completely new design from earlier Princeton, brown Tolex covering, light brown grille, mfg. 1961-63.

courtesy Dave Rogers/Dave's Guitar Shop

courtesy Dave Rogers/Dave's Guitar Shop

| N/A | $1,600 - 2,050 | $850 - 1,050 |

With the introduction of the Brownface, the model was changed to 6G2. There were about 100 Model 5E2 Princetons made, which are the rarest.

PRINCETON (BLACKFACE) – 12W, 1-10 in. Jensen speaker, tube chassis, preamp: 7025, 12AX7, power: 2 X 6V6, 5Y3 rectifier, tremolo, front brownface control panel, two input jacks, five black knobs (v, t, b, s, i), ground switch on back, black Tolex covering, silver grille, mfg. 1963-67.

courtesy Dave Rogers/Dave's Guitar Shop

courtesy Dave Rogers/Dave's Guitar Shop

courtesy Dave Rogers/Dave's Guitar Shop

| 1963-1965 | N/A | $1,600 - 2,050 | $850 - 1,050 |
| 1965-1967 | N/A | $1,275 - 1,600 | $750 - 950 |

Models produced in 1963 still have only four knobs (single tone knob), and some of these amps may still have the white knobs. In 1964 model AA964 was introduced with separate bass and treble controls. Around 1966, the Fender nameplate was put on the grille.

MSR/NOTES	100%	EXCELLENT	AVERAGE	LAST MSR

PRINCETON (SILVERFACE) – similar to the blackface Princeton except has a silverface control panel, five silver-top knobs (bass and treble were now separate knobs), mfg. 1968-1979.

1968-1969	N/A	$800 - 1,000	$475 - 600
1970-1979	N/A	$650 - 800	$375 - 475

In 1970, Model AA1270 was introduced that featured a 3-way ground switch.

PRINCETON REVERB – 12W, 1-10 in. speaker, tube chassis, preamp: 7025, 2 X 12AX7, 12AT7, power: 2 X 6V6, 5U4 rectifier, single channel, reverb, tremolo, blackface control panel, two inputs, six silver-top knobs (v, t, b, r, s, i), black Tolex covering, silver grille, mfg. 1964-1981.

  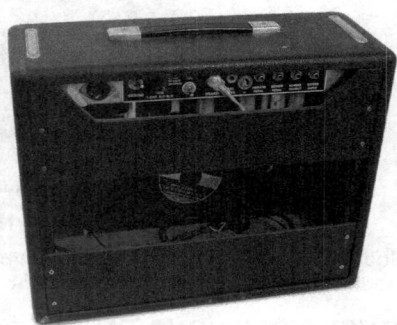

courtesy Dave Rogers/Dave's Guitar Shop	courtesy Dave Rogers/Dave's Guitar Shop	courtesy Dave Rogers/Dave's Guitar Shop

1964-1967 Blackface	N/A	$1,800 - 2,250	$1,075 - 1,350
1968-1973 Silverface	N/A	$1,075 - 1,350	$650 - 800
1974-1981 Silverface	N/A	$950 - 1,200	$575 - 725

The Model number was AA764. In 1966, the Fender underlined nameplate is added on the grille, In 1968, the control panel was changed to silver, blue cloth, and aluminum trim was added. In 1970, a three position ground switch was added. The underline on the namplate was dropped in the mid-seventies. Around 1978, a boost-pull knob pot was added. In 1980, blackface with silver grille was re-introduced and became an option.

ELECTRIC TUBE AMPS: PRO SERIES

For the current mfg. Pro Reverb, refer to the Pro-Tube series.

PROFESSIONAL (MODEL 26) – 15W, 1-15 in. Jensen speaker, tube chassis, preamp: 6SC7/6N7, power: 2 X 6L6, 5Y3 rectifier, two channels, back control panel, three inputs, (one mic, two inst.), three pointer knobs (mic. v, inst. v, tone), polished wood cabinet, red, blue, or gold grilles, with vertical chrome strips, mfg. 1946-47.

	N/A	$2,800 - 3,500	$1,675 - 2,100

This model was also known as the Model 26 which was the same as the Princeton and Deluxe. Some of these models use a field-coil speaker, which has no permanent magnet. There were approx. 30 of these amps produced.

PRO AMP (TV FRONT) – 15W, 1-15 in. Jensen speaker, tube chassis, preamp: 3 X 6SC7, power: 2 X 6L6G, 5U4G rectifier, two channels, top black control panel, four inputs, (two inst., two mic), three pointer knobs (mic. v, inst. v, tone), early tweed covering, brown cloth grille, formerly known as the Professional, mfg. 1948-1952.

courtesy David Chandler/R&R Guitars	courtesy David Chandler/R&R Guitars

	N/A	$3,000 - 3,600	$1,925 - 2,400

In 1950, the removable back paneling, which was originally a solid rectangle, had two holes cut in it, to let heat escape from the tubes.

PRO AMP (WIDE PANEL) – 15W, 1-15 in. Jensen, tube chassis, preamp: 12AY7, 12AX7, power: 2 X 6L6G, 5U5G rectifier, top control panel, four inputs, (two inst., two mic), three pointer knobs (mic. v, inst. v, tone), spare speaker jack in back, standby switch, diagonal tweed covering, brown cloth grille, mfg. 1952-1954.

	N/A	$3,200 - 4,050	$2,050 - 2,550

PRO AMP (NARROW PANEL) – 26W, 1-15 in. Jensen, tube chassis, preamp: 2 X 12AY7, 12AX7, power: 2 X 6L6, 5U4G rectifier, top control panel, four inputs, (two inst., two mic), three pointer knobs (mic. v, inst. v, tone), ground switch added to panel, negative feedback removed, diagonal tweed covering, brown tweed-era grille, mfg. 1954-1960.

courtesy Savage Audio		courtesy Savage Audio
N/A	$3,900 - 4,900	$2,150 - 2,700

Circa 1955/56, the choke was removed (Model 5C5). A standby switch was added for Model 5D5. Model 5E5 had the negative feedback loop removed, and 5E5-A had a fixed bias supply. The circuitry in this model was still linked with earlier models. In 1956, bass, treble, and presence controls were added. In 1957, a new nameplate was introduced.

PRO AMP (BROWNFACE) – 25W, 1-15 in. Jensen speaker, tube chassis, preamp: 5 X 7025, power: 2 X 6L6GC, tremolo, brownface control panel, four inputs, (two normal, two vibrato), nine brown knobs (Norm: v, t, b, s, i, Vibrato: v, t, b, Both: p), brown Tolex covering, light brown grille, mfg. 1960-63.

 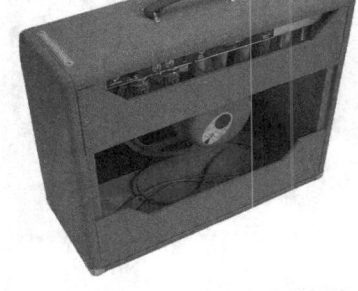

courtesy Dave Rogers/Dave's Guitar Shop		courtesy Dave Rogers/Dave's Guitar Shop
N/A	$2,200 - 2,750	$1,325 - 1,650

The Brownface was Model 6G5. In late 1960, the tubes were changed and included preamp: 4 X 7025, 2 X 12AX7, power: 2 X 5881 (Model 6G5-A). This amp is almost identical to the Vibrasonic, except for the speaker, which was about $200 cheaper than the Vibrasonic.

PRO AMP (BLACKFACE) – 25W, 1-15 in. speaker, tube chassis, preamp: 2 X 7025, 12AX7, 12AT7, power: 2 X 6L6GC, 5U4GB rectifier, tremolo, front black control panel, four inputs, (two normal, two vibrato), bright switches, eight silver-top knobs (Norm: bs, v, t, b, Vibrato: bs, v, t, b, s, i), AC outlet on back panel, black Tolex covering, silver grille, mfg. 1963-65.

courtesy Savage Audio		courtesy Savage Audio
N/A	$2,000 - 2,650	$1,075 - 1,350

The blackface Pro was the Model AA763 and featured a revised tremolo unit. This model faded out after the Pro Reverb amp was introduced. The Pro-Amp was on the cover of any Fender owner's manual for amps.

MSR/NOTES	100%	EXCELLENT	AVERAGE	LAST MSR

PRO REVERB (BLACKFACE) – 40W, 2-12 in. speakers, tube chassis, preamp: 3 X 7025, 12AX7, 2 X 12AT7, power: 2 X 6L6GC, 5U4GB rectifier, tremolo, reverb, black control panel, four inputs, (two normal, two vibrato), nine silver-top knobs (Norm: bs, v, t, b, Vibrato: bs, v, t, b, r, s, i), tilt back legs, black Tolex covering, silver grille, mfg. 1965-67.

courtesy solidbodyguitar.com, Inc. courtesy solidbodyguitar.com, Inc.

| | N/A | $2,200 - 2,600 | $1,150 - 1,450 | |

This was the Model AA165.

PRO REVERB (SILVERFACE) – 40W, 2-12 in. speakers, tube chassis, preamp: 3 X 7025, 12AX7, 2 X 12AT7, power: 2 X 6L6GC, GZ34 rectifier, tremolo, reverb, silverface control panel, four inputs, (two normal, two vibrato), nine silver-top knobs (Norm: bs, v, t, b, Vibrato: bs, v, t, b, r, s, i), tilt back legs, black Tolex covering, silver grille, mfg. 1967-1981.

courtesy David Chandler/R&R Guitars courtesy David Chandler/R&R Guitars

1967-1969	N/A	$1,525 - 1,850	$800 - 1,000	
1970-1973	N/A	$1,050 - 1,300	$625 - 775	
1974-1981	N/A	$800 - 1,000	$475 - 600	

In 1968, a change in the bias section occured (Model AB6686). In 1969, the cathode was brought back to ground (Model AA1069). In 1972, the output is increased to 45W by using a different rectifier, and increased voltage in the output stage. In 1976, a master volume knob is added and a pull distortion switch. In 1981, the Pro Reverb went back to the blackface. At this time the output was raised to 70W, the tubes were changed to: preamp: 4 X 7025, 2 X 12AT7, power: 2 X 6L6, and had twelve black knobs with a middle added to each channel.

ELECTRIC TUBE AMPS: PRO-TUBE SERIES

Concert
courtesy David Chandler/R&R Guitars

Concert Reverb
courtesy Fender

"Custom" Vibolux Reverb
courtesy Fender

CONCERT (NO. 021-4802-000) – 60W, 1-12 in. speaker, tube chassis, preamp: 2 X 12AT7, 4 X 12AX7, power: 2 X 6L6, two-selectable channels, new blackface control panel, two inputs, 12 silver-top knobs (Ch.1: v, t, m, b, Ch. 2: g1, g2, v, t, b, m, Both: mix, r), effects loop, line out jack, footswitch, black Tolex covering, silver grille, mfg. 1992-95.

| | N/A | $600 - 750 | $350 - 450 | $1,030 |

This model was also available with a Celestion G1280 speaker.

| MSR/NOTES | 100% | EXCELLENT | AVERAGE | LAST MSR |

Machete
courtesy Fender

Princeton Recording
courtesy Fender

Prosonic
courtesy Dave Rogers/Dave's Guitar Shop

CONCERT REVERB (NO. 021-5900-000) – 50W (switchable to 12W), 4-10 in. Special design Fender Eminence speakers, tubes: preamp: 7 X 12AX7, 12AT7, power: 2 X 6L6 Groove Tubes, dual selectable channels (normal and drive), tremolo, reverb, blackface control panel, 13 silver-top knobs, (Ch. 1, v, t, m, b, Ch. 2, gain, t, b, m, v, Both: r, s, i, p), footswitchable FX loop with send and return level controls, external speaker jack, tilt-back legs, four-button footswitch, black Tolex covering, silver grille, cover included, 85 lbs., mfg. 2002-05.

| | N/A | $675 - 850 | $400 - 500 | $1,800 |

"CUSTOM" VIBRASONIC (NO. 021-5200-000) – 100W, 1-15 in. speaker, guitar/steel combo, tube chassis, preamp: 12AX7s, power: 4 X 6L6GC, solid-state rectifier, two independent channels (steel/guitar), reverb, vibrato, front blackface control panel, four inputs (two per channel), 11 black skirted knobs (Steel Ch.: v, t, m, b, Guitar Ch.: v, t, m, b, r, s, i), Steel Ch. sweet switch, Guitar Ch. fat switch, rear panel: power switch, standby switch, two speaker jacks, footswitch jack, tilt-back legs, two-button footswitch included, black Tolex covering, silver grille, 71 lbs., mfg. 1995-96.

| | N/A | $650 - 800 | $400 - 500 | $1,500 |

"CUSTOM" VIBROLUX REVERB (NO. 021-5100-000) – 40W, 2-10 in. Jensen P-10R speakers, tubes chassis, preamp: 5 X 12AX7, 12AT7, power: 2 X 6L6 Groove Tubes, two independent channels (normal and bright), reverb, vibrato, front black control panel, four inputs, nine white knobs (Norm: v, t, b, Bright: v, t, b, r, Both: s, i), tilt-back legs, two-button footswitch, black Tolex covering, silver grille, 46 lbs., mfg. 1995-2013.

| | $1,200 | $675 - 800 | $450 - 525 | $1,600 |

DUAL SHOWMAN (SR) (NO. 021-6108-010) – 100W (switchable to 25W), 4-12 in. speakers in a separate cabinet, tube chassis, preamp: 4 X 12AX7, 1 X 12AT7, power: 4 X 6L6GC, two switchable channel, black control panel, four inputs, ten red knobs (Ch.1: v, t, m, b, Ch. 2: gain, t, m, b, p, v), effects loop, high gain preamp, three-position damping control, black Tolex covering, black grille, mfg. 1987-1994.

| | N/A | $625 - 750 | $450 - 525 | $1,100 |

In 1990, the Dual Showman was changed to the Dual Showman SR, which had reverb. In 1992, a 25 watt switch and parallel channel mode was installed. This made it possible for all the controls to be working at once.

MACHETE (NO. 216-3000-000) – 50W, 1-12 in. Celestion Vintage 30 speaker, guitar combo, seven-tube chassis, preamp: 5 X 7025/12AX7A, power: 2 X 6L6GC, solid-state rectifier, two channels, reverb, front black control panel, single input, 14 chrome knobs (Ch. 1: g, v, l, m, h, tune, Ch. 2: g, v, l, m, h, notch, all: r, damping), 6dB pad switch, rear panel: power switch, standby switch, effects loop with send and return level controls, power amp mute switch, XLR line out with cabinet emulation switch, MIDI in, footswitch jack, two speaker jacks with impedance selector, black covering with a gray middle stripe, black and white pepper grille with white piping, 24.5 in. wide, 22 in. tall, 11.5 in. deep, 71 lbs., four-button footswitch and cover included, mfg. 2012-disc.

| | $1,900 | $1,075 - 1,350 | $650 - 800 | $2,600 |

PRINCETON RECORDING (NO. 215-2000) – 20W, 1-10 in. Jensen C-10R speaker combo, tube chassis, preamp: 3 X 12AX7, 12AT7, power: 2 X 6V6, one channel, reverb, front split control panel (black on top/silver below it), two inputs, six knobs (v, t, b, r, compressor: sensitivity, level, overdrive: OD, tone, level, Trans-Impedance Power Attenuator), headphone jack, XLR line out with level and ground control, speaker output, effects loop, four-button footswitch, black textured vinyl covering, silver grille, 45 lbs., mfg. summer 2006-09.

| | $1,400 | $575 - 725 | $350 - 475 | $1,750 |

PRO REVERB (NO. 021-5500-000) – 50W (switchable to 12), 1-12 in. Jensen C12N speaker, tube chassis, preamp: 7 X 12AX7, 12AT7, power: 2 X 6L6 Groove Tubes, two channels, tremolo, reverb, front black control panel, one input, 13 silver-top knobs (Ch. 1, v, t, m, b, Ch. 2, gain, t, b, m, v, Both: r, s, i, p), switchable channels, external speaker jack, effects, loop preamp jacks, tilt-back legs, black Tolex covering, silver grille, cover included, 75 lbs., mfg. 2002-05.

| | N/A | $650 - 775 | $400 - 500 | $1,500 |

PROSONIC (NO. 021-1007-000) – 60W, 2-10 in. Celestion speakers, all-tube circuitry, three-way rectifier switch, dual selectable channels (normal and drive), all-tube reverb, blackface control panel, two inputs, channel switch, eight black knobs (v, gain 1, gain 2, t, b, m, master, r), effects loop, two button footswitch, black Tolex, red lizard, or green lizard covering, silver or black grille, 54 lbs., mfg. 1996-2001.

| | N/A | $700 - 850 | $500 - 600 | $1,600 |

* *Prosonic Head (No. 021-2007-000)* – similar to Pronsonic except head unit only, 35 lbs., mfg. 1996-2001.

| | N/A | $550 - 700 | $325 - 400 | $1,300 |

Refer to the Custom Shop Series section for the Prosonic/Tone-Master enclosure.

MSR/NOTES	100%	EXCELLENT	AVERAGE	LAST MSR

SUPER (NO. 021-4806-000) – 60W, 4-10 in. with Alnico magnets, tubes chassis, preamp: 4 X 12AX7, 2 X 12AT7, power: 2 X 6L6, new blackface control panel, two input jacks, 12 silver-top knobs (Ch.1: v, t, b, m, Ch.2: g1, g2, t, b, m, v, Both: Mix, r), black Tolex covering, silver grille, mfg. 1992-95.

	N/A	$600 - 750	$400 - 500	$1,240

THE TWIN (NO. 021-6200-010) – 100W (switchable to 25W), 2-12 in. Eminence speakers, tube chassis, preamp: 2 X 12AT7, 5 X 12AX7, power: 4 X 6L6, two channels with overdrive, low power switch, reverb, black control panel, four input jacks (two for each channel), eleven red knobs (Ch.1: v, t, m, b, Ch.2: gain, t, m, b, p, v, r), most knobs had pull switches, effects loop, two-button footswitch, black Tolex covering, black grille, mfg. 1987-1994.

	N/A	$700 - 850	$500 - 600	$1,400

- **Add 20% for snakeskin covering.**

This model was available in white, grey, red, or snakeskin on a special order. In 1992, the black grille was replaced with a silver grille, and the red knobs were replaced with black ones.

TWIN AMP (NO. 021-5700-000) – 100 (switchable to 25W), 2-12 in. Eminence speakers, tube chassis, preamp: 7 X 12AX7, 12AT7, power: 4 X 6L6 Groove Tubes, two channels, reverb, tremolo, blackface control panel, two input jacks, 13 silver-top knobs (Ch.1, v, t, m, b, Ch.2, gain, t, b, m, v, Both: r, s, i, p), the volume knobs had a push/pull switch for channel switching, effects loop, four buton footswitch, black Tolex covering, silver grille, 80 lbs., mfg. 1995-2010.

	N/A	$1,000 - 1,200	$600 - 700	$2,250

In 2002, two input jacks were changed to one input jack.

ELECTRIC TUBE AMPS: SHOWMAN SERIES

The Showman is virtually the Twin amplifer in Piggyback version. For the Showman 112/212/115/210 and refer to the Solid State Second series. For the Dual Showman SR that was produced in the late 1980s and early 1990s, refer to the Pro-Tube series.

Showman (Brownface)
courtesy Dave Rogers/Dave's Guitar Shop

Showman (Blackface)
courtesy Dave Rogers/Dave's Guitar Shop

Dual Shownman (Blackface) w/ JBL Speaker
courtesy Dave Rogers/Dave's Guitar Shop

SHOWMAN (BROWNFACE) – 85W, 1-12 in. or 1-15 in. JBL speaker in separate cabinet, tube chassis, preamp: 4 X 7025, 2 X 12AX7, power: 4 X 5881, two channels, tremolo, brownface control panel, four inputs, (two normal, two vibrato), nine white or brown knobs (Norm: v, t, b, Vibrato: v, t, b, s, i, Both: p), elaborate porting system, tilt-back legs, cream Tolex covering, maroon grille, mfg. 1961-63.

1961 Head & Cab Oxblood	N/A	$3,450 - 4,250	$2,500 - 3,000
1962-1963 Head & Cab Wheat	N/A	$3,000 - 3,750	$2,000 - 2,500
1961 Head Only Oxblood	N/A	$1,650 - 2,000	$1,100 - 1,300
1962-1963 Head Only Wheat	N/A	$1,300 - 1,750	$1,000 - 1,200
Cab Only	N/A	$750 - 1,000	$500 - 650

This model was available with a 12 in. or 15 in. speaker. Some early models (6G14) have a 6 X 7025 and 4 X 6L6GC tube configuration. In 1962, the grille was changed to a wheat color. Later models were labeled Model 6G14-A.

Double/Dual Showman (Brownface) – similar to the Showman, except has 2-15 in. JBL speakers, mfg. 1961-63.

1961 Oxblood	N/A	$4,000 - 5,000	$2,750 - 3,500
1962-1963 Wheat	N/A	$2,750 - 3,500	$2,000 - 2,500
Cab Only	N/A	$1,200 - 1,500	$700 - 850

This model was originally called the Double Showman, and in 1963, it was renamed the Dual Showman. However, it is unknown if any brownface amps were called Dual Showmans. Brownface Dual Showmans are extremely rare with approx. 25 total production between 1961 and 1963. This amp is very popular with surf music.

SHOWMAN (BLACKFACE) – 85W, 1-12 in. or 1-15 in. JBL speaker in separate cabinet, tube chassis, preamp:2 X 7025, 12AT7, 12AX7, power: 4 X 6L6GC, two channels, tremolo, blackface control panel, four inputs, (two normal, two vibrato), nine silver-top knobs (Norm: v, t, b, Vibrato: v, t, b, s, i, Both: p), elaborate porting system, tilt-back legs, black Tolex covering, silver grille, mfg. 1963-67.

Head & Cab	N/A	$1,750 - 2,250	$1,100 - 1,400
Head Only	N/A	$750 - 1,000	$500 - 650
Cab Only	N/A	$425 - 500	$275 - 325

This is the model AA763. In 1963, the bright switch replaced the presence control.

MSR/NOTES	100%	EXCELLENT	AVERAGE	LAST MSR

* *Dual Showman (Blackface)* – similar to the Showman, except has 2-15 in. JBL speakers, mfg. 1963-67.

Head & Horizontal Cab	N/A	$2,250 - 2,750	$1,400 - 1,750
Head & Vertical Cab	N/A	$1,200 - 1,500	$950 - 1,050
Horizontal Cab Only	N/A	$850 - 1,000	$600 - 700
Vertical Cab Only	N/A	$375 - 450	$225 - 275

SHOWMAN (SILVERFACE)

SHOWMAN (SILVERFACE) – 85W, 1-15 in. JBL speaker in separate cabinet, tube chassis, preamp: 2 X 7025, 12AT7, 12AX7, power: 4 X 6L6GC, two channels, tremolo, silverface control panel, four inputs, (two normal, two vibrato), nine black knobs (Norm: v, t, b, Vibrato: v, t, b, s, i, Both: p), elaborate porting system, tilt-back legs, black Tolex covering, silver grille, mfg. 1968-69.

Head & Cab	N/A	$800 - 1,000	$550 - 700
Head Only	N/A	$550 - 650	$350 - 425
Cab Only	N/A	$325 - 400	$200 - 250

* *Dual Showman (Silverface)* – similar to the Showman, except has 2-15 in. JBL speakers, mfg. 1968-69.

Head & Cab	N/A	$900 - 1,100	$700 - 800
Cab Only	N/A	$375 - 450	$225 - 275

DUAL SHOWMAN REVERB (SILVERFACE)

DUAL SHOWMAN REVERB (SILVERFACE) – 100W, 2-15 in. JBL speakers in a separate cabinet, tube chassis, preamp: 3 X 7025, 2 X 12AT7, 12AX7, power: 4 X 6L6GC, two channels, reverb, vibrato, silverface control panel, four inputs, (two normal and two vibrato), 11 silver-top knobs (Norm: bs, v, b, m, t, Vibrato: bs, v, b, m, t, s, i, r), bright switches on each channel, remote footswitches for vibrato and reverb, black Tolex covering, silver grille, mfg. 1969-1980.

1969-1972	N/A	$1,000 - 1,300	$550 - 700
1973-1980	N/A	$1,000 - 1,200	$500 - 625
Head Only	N/A	$650 - 800	$450 - 525
Cab Only	N/A	$375 - 450	$225 - 275

Model AA768. This model was also sold as the Dual Showman Reverb Bass. In 1972, master volume was added. In 1976, a distortion switch was added. This amp is virtually the Twin in piggy-back form. There has also been a model AC568.

ELECTRIC TUBE AMPS: SUPER (DUAL PROFESSIONAL) SERIES

This series started out with the Dual Professional. In 1947, after only one year of production, the name was changed to the Super. Wide panel was introduced in 1952. Narrow panel was introduced in 1954. Brownface and brown Tolex was introduced in 1960. This model was disc. in 1964 and replaced by the Super Reverb. The original Super never received the blackface change. For the Super Six Reverb, see the Twin series, since the Super Six is really a Twin chassis. For the Super produced in the 1990s, refer to the Pro-Tube series.

DUAL PROFESSIONAL (SUPER) – 16W, 2-10 in. Jensen speakers, tube chassis, preamp: 3 X 6SJ7, power: 2 X 6L6, 5U4 rectifier, top numbered control panel, four inputs (two instruments, one mic, one lo-gain), three pointer knobs (mic v, inst. v, tone), fuse holder, and red pilot light, V-front cabinet, early tweed covering, dark brown grille with vertical chrome strip in middle, mfg. 1946-1952.

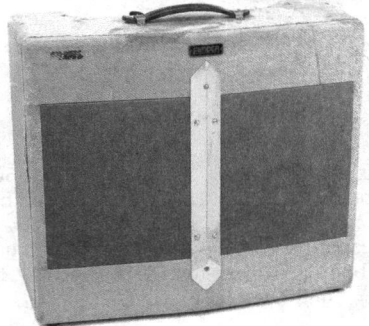

courtesy solidbodyguitar.com, Inc.   courtesy solidbodyguitar.com, Inc.

1946	N/A	$4,700 - 5,700	$2,900 - 3,500
1947-1949	N/A	$3,500 - 4,000	$2,250 - 2,750
1950-1952	N/A	$3,950 - 4,800	$2,700 - 3,250

This amp was renamed the Super in 1947, and the 3 X 6SJ7 preamp tubes were changed to 3 X 6SC7. The tubes are converted over to 12AX7 and 12AY7 as soon as they were available (Model 5C4). A TV front Super was never made. In 1952, the V front is taken away, There are some Super amplifiers of this time with 6V6 tubes. The Dual Professional was the first two-speaker amp for Fender.

SUPER (WIDE PANEL) – 20W, 2-10 in. Jensen speakers, tube chassis: 2 X 12AY7, 12AX7, power: 2 X 6L6G, 5U4G rectifier, top numbered control panel, four inputs, three pointer knobs (mic v, inst. v, tone), diagonal tweed covering, brown tweed-era grille, mfg. 1952-54.

	N/A	$3,750 - 4,750	$2,500 - 3,000

MSR/NOTES	100%	EXCELLENT	AVERAGE	LAST MSR

SUPER (NARROW PANEL) – 20W, 2-10 in. Jensen speakers, tube chassis, preamp: 2 X 12AY7, 12AX7, power: 2 X 6L6G, 5U4G rectifier, top numbered control panel, four input jacks, four pointer knobs (mic v, inst. v, t, b), ground switch, diagonal tweed covering, brown tweed-era grille, mfg. 1954-1960.

courtesy Dave Rogers/Dave's Guitar Shop   courtesy Dave Rogers/Dave's Guitar Shop

1954-1956	N/A	$4,500 - 5,500	$3,000 - 3,500	
1957-1960	N/A	$6,000 - 7,500	$3,500 - 4,000	

This model has a self-balancing paraphrase inverter circuit (Model 5D4). In 1955, 6V6 tubes were introduced (Model 5E4), and the nameplate changed to script type. In 1956, the tubes were changed back to 6L6 (Model 5F4), and the namplate is changed to Super Amp script. In 1958, a presence control was added.

SUPER (BROWNFACE) – 30W, 2-10 in. Jensen speakers, tube chassis, preamp: 5 X 7025, power: 2 X 6L6GC, 5U4G rectifier, two channels, tremolo, brownface control panel, four inputs, (two normal two vibrato), nine brown knobs (Norm: v, b, t, Vibrato: v, b, t, s, i, Both: p), brown Tolex covering, brown grille, mfg. 1960-64.

courtesy Dave Rogers/Dave's Guitar Shop   courtesy Dave Rogers/Dave's Guitar Shop

1960-1962 Oxblood	N/A	$2,250 - 2,800	$1,500 - 1,850	
1962-1964 Wheat	N/A	$2,250 - 2,800	$1,200 - 1,800	

* **Add 50% for reverse knobs on the control panel.**

Circa 1961-62, a GZ34 rectifier was intrdouced (6G4). In 1961, a 7025 was replaced by 2 X 12AX7 (Model 6G14-A). From 1962, some amps were made with 5881 output tubes and could produce 45W output. The Super amp was replaced by the Super Reverb.

SUPER REVERB (BLACKFACE) – 40W, 4-10 in.speakers, tube chassis, preamp: 3 X 7025, 12AX7, 2 X 12AT7, power: 2 X 6L6GC, two channels, tremolo, reverb, blackface control panel, four inputs (two normal, two vibrato), 10 silver-top knobs (Norm: v, t, b, Vibrato: v, t, m, b, r, s, i), two bright switches (one per channel), black Tolex covering, silver grille, mfg. 1964-67.

courtesy Dave Rogers/Dave's Guitar Shop   courtesy Dave Rogers/Dave's Guitar Shop

	N/A	$2,200 - 2,700	$1,200 - 1,500	

Introduced as Model AA763.

MSR/NOTES	100%	EXCELLENT	AVERAGE	LAST MSR

SUPER REVERB (SILVERFACE) – 40W, 4-10 in. speakers, tube chassis, preamp:4 X 7025, 2 X 12AT7, power: 2 X 6L6GC, two channels, tremolo, reverb, silverface control panel, four inputs (two normal, two vibrato), 10 silver-top knobs (Norm: v, t, b, Vibrato: v, t, m, b, r, s, i), two bright switches (one per channel), black Tolex covering, silver grille, mfg. 1968-1980.

courtesy S.P. Fjestad   courtesy S.P. Fjestad

1968	N/A	$1,500 - 1,750	$900 - 1,050	
1969	N/A	$1,300 - 1,600	$800 - 950	
1970-1975	N/A	$1,200 - 1,500	$700 - 850	
1976-1980	N/A	$900 - 1,200	$600 - 700	

The Silverface was introduced as the Model AB568. In 1969, Model AA1069 was introduced. In 1970, the output was raised to 45W. In 1976, a master volume knob and distortion switch was added. In the late 1970s, some models may appear with a mid control in the normal channel. Silver Reverbs come in three different control layouts. The first has 10 knobs, which is listed in the above description. The second features an added Master Volume knob for a total of 11 knobs. The third version has both a Master Volume and a mid control in the Normal channel for a total of 12 knobs.

SUPER REVERB (NEW BLACKFACE) – 70W, 4-10 in. speakers, tube chassis, preamp: 4 X 7025, 2 X 12AT7, power: 2 X 6L6GC, two channels, tremolo, reverb, blackface control panel, four inputs (two normal, two vibrato), bright switch, 11 silver-top knobs (Norm: v, t, b, Vibrato: v, t, m, b, r, s, i, MV), black Tolex covering, silver grille, mfg. 1981-82.

	N/A	$950 - 1,200	$500 - 600

SUPER SIX REVERB – see the Twin Series listing in the Fender section.

SUPER 60 COMBO – 60W, 1-12 in. Eminence speaker, tubes chassis, preamp: 2 X 12AX7, 12AT7, power: 2 X 6L6, black control panel, two input jacks, eight red knobs (Ch. 1: v, t, m, b, Ch. 2: v, g, Both: p, r), black Tolex covering, black grille, mfg. 1988-1992.

	N/A	$350 - 450	$250 - 300

The red knobs on this amp were replaced by black ones shortly after the amp was introduced. This unit was available as a head-unit only or as a combo.

* *Super 60 Head (No. 021-6408)* – similar to the Super 60, except in a head-unit four-space rack mount enclosure or regular head, mfg. 1988-1992.

	N/A	$225 - 300	$135 - 175

* *Super 112 Combo* – similar to the Super 60, except has overdrive channel, and a notch filter, Celestian speakers an option, mfg. 1990-93.

	N/A	$300 - 375	$175 - 225

* *Super 210 Combo* – similar to Super 210, except has 2-10 in. speakers, mfg. 1990-93.

	N/A	$350 - 425	$250 - 300

ELECTRIC TUBE AMPS: SUPER-SONIC SERIES

SUPER-SONIC HEAD (NO. 216-0100) – 60W, head-unit only, tube chassis, preamp: 5 X 12AX7, 2 X 12AT7, power: 2 X 6L6GC, two channels (Vintage/Burn), reverb, blackface or brownface control panel, one input jack, nine black or cream knobs (Ch.1 [Vintage]: v, t, b, Ch.2 [Burn] g1, g2, t, m, b, r), effects loop, pre-amp out, power-amp in, two speaker jacks, standby switch, three-buton footswitch, black textured vinyl covering with a peppered silver grille or Blonde textured vinyl covering with a brown Oxblood grille, 32 lbs., cover included, mfg. 2006-2010.

	N/A	$800 - 950	$475 - 550	$1,700

* *Super-Sonic 112 Combo (No. 216-0100)* – similar to the Super-Sonic Head, except is in combo form with 1-12 in. Celestion V30 speaker, 54 lbs., cover included, mfg. 2006-2010.

	N/A	$850 - 1,000	$500 - 600	$1,780

* *Super-Sonic 212 Speaker Cabinet (No. 216-1200)* – speaker cabinet companion to the Super-Sonic series, 120W, 2-12 in. Celestion V30 speakers, 8 ohm impedance, closed back, 74 lbs., mfg. 2006-2010.

	N/A	$400 - 475	$250 - 300	$900

MSR/NOTES	100%	EXCELLENT	AVERAGE	LAST MSR

Super-Sonic Head
courtesy Fender

Super-Sonic 60 Combo
courtesy Fender

Super-Sonic 100 Head
courtesy Fender

Super-Sonic 60 Head
courtesy Fender

Super-Sonic 100 Head
courtesy Fender

* **Super-Sonic 412 Speaker Cabinet (No. 216-1400)** – speaker cabinet companion to the Super-Sonic series, 240W, 4-12 in. Celestion V30 speakers, 16 ohm impedance, closed back, side handles, 88 lbs., mfg. 2006-2010.

N/A	$475 - 550	$300 - 350	$1,100

SUPER-SONIC 22 COMBO (NO. 216-0000) – 22W, 1-12 in. Fender Lightning Bolt speaker by Eminence, seven-tube chassis, preamp: 3 X 12AX7, 2 X 12AT7, power: 2 X 6V6, two channels (Vintage/Burn), reverb, blackface or brownface control panel, single input, 10 cream knobs (Ch.1 [Vintage]: v, t, b, Ch.2 [Burn] g1, g2, t, b, m, v, All: r), Vintage Ch. voicing switch, channel switch, rear panel: effects loop, extension speaker jack, standby switch, power switch, footswitch jack, available in black textured vinyl covering with a peppered silver grille or blonde textured vinyl covering with a brown Oxblood grille, cover and four-buton footswitch included, 24 in. wide, 17.25 in. tall, 8.5 in. deep, 40 lbs., mfg. summer 2010-present.

MSR N/A	$1,050	$625 - 775	$350 - 425

SUPER-SONIC 22 HEAD (NO. 216-1000) – 22W, guitar head-unit, seven-tube chassis, preamp: 3 X 12AX7, 2 X 12AT7, power: 2 X 6V6, two channels (Vintage/Burn), reverb, blackface or brownface control panel, single input, 10 cream knobs (Ch.1 [Vintage]: v, t, b, Ch.2 [Burn] g1, g2, t, b, m, v, All: r), Vintage Ch. voicing switch, channel switch, rear panel: effects loop, extension speaker jack, standby switch, power switch, footswitch jack, available in black textured vinyl covering with a peppered silver grille or blonde textured vinyl covering with a brown Oxblood grille, cover and four-buton footswitch included, 24 in. wide, 9.4 in. tall, 8.7 in. deep, 27 lbs., mfg. 2013-present.

MSR N/A	$1,000	$600 - 750	$350 - 450

SUPER-SONIC 60 HEAD (NO. 216-0100) – 60W, guitar head-unit, eight-tube chassis, preamp: 5 X 12AX7, 1 X 12AT7, power: 2 X 6L6, two channels (Vintage/Burn), blackface or brownface control panel, single input, nine cream knobs (Ch.1 [Vintage]: v, t, b, Ch.2 [Burn] g1, g2, t, b, m, v), Vintage Ch. voicing switch, channel switch, rear panel: effects loop with send and return level controls, extension speaker jack, pre-amp out jack, power amp in jack, standby switch, power switch, footswitch jack, available in black textured vinyl covering with a peppered silver grille or blonde textured vinyl covering with a brown Oxblood grille, cover and three-buton footswitch included, 25.25 in. wide, 8.625 in. tall, 9.625 in. deep, 32 lbs., mfg. summer 2010-2014.

	$1,200	$725 - 900	$475 - 550	$1,700

SUPER-SONIC 60 COMBO (NO. 216-0500) – 60W, 1-12 in. Celestion Vintage 30 speaker, guitar combo, 10-tube chassis, preamp: 6 X 12AX7, 2 X 12AT7, power: 2 X 6L6, two channels (Vintage/Burn), reverb, blackface or brownface control panel, single input, 10 cream knobs (Ch.1 [Vintage]: v, t, b, Ch.2 [Burn] g1, g2, t, b, m, v, All: r), Vintage Ch. voicing switch, channel switch, rear panel: effects loop with send and return level controls, extension speaker jack, pre-amp out jack, power amp in jack, standby switch, power switch, footswitch jack, available in black textured vinyl covering with a peppered silver grille or blonde textured vinyl covering with a brown Oxblood grille, cover and four-button footswitch included, 25.25 in. wide, 17.75 in. tall, 10.25 in. deep, 54 lbs., mfg. summer 2010-2014.

	$1,400	$800 - 1,000	$525 - 625	$1,900

SUPER-SONIC 60 212 SPEAKER CABINET (NO. 216-1200-010/410) – 2-12 in. speakers, single input, closed back, designed for use with the Super-Sonic 60 Head, available in black textured vinyl covering with a silver grille or blonde textured vinyl covering with a brown grille, mfg. summer 2010-present.

MSR N/A	$700	$375 - 475	$250 - 300

SUPER-SONIC 100 HEAD (NO. 216-0100) – 100W, guitar head-unit, 13-tube chassis, preamp: 7 X 12AX7, 2 X 12AT7, power: 4 X 6L6, two channels (Vintage/Burn), blackface or brownface control panel, single input, 13 cream knobs (Ch.1 [Vintage]: g, t, b, m, v, Ch.2 [Burn] g1, g2, t, b, m, notch tune, v, All: r), Vintage Ch. Showman/Bassman voicing switch, channel switch, rear panel: areana/club 100W/25W power switch, effects loop with send and return level controls, pre-amp out jack, power amp in jack, three-way loose/normal/tight damping control, two speaker jacks, standby switch, power switch, footswitch jack, available in black textured vinyl covering with a peppered silver grille or blonde textured vinyl covering with a brown Oxblood grille, cover and four-buton footswitch and cover included, 26.25 in. wide, 10.5 in. tall, 10.5 in. deep, 53 lbs., mfg. summer 2011-13.

	$1,800	$1,075 - 1,350	$650 - 800	$2,500

MSR/NOTES	100%	EXCELLENT	AVERAGE	LAST MSR

SUPER-SONIC 100 412 SPEAKER CABINET (NO. 216-2400/2450) – 100W, 4-12 in. Celestion Vintage 30 speakers, single input, closed back, straight (No. 216-2400) or slanted (No. 216-2450) front, designed for use with the Super-Sonic 100 Head, available in black textured vinyl covering with a silver grille or blonde textured vinyl covering with a brown grille, 30 in. wide, 29.25 in. tall, 14 in. deep, casters included, mfg. summer 2011-13.

	$700	$375 - 475	$250 - 300	$900

SUPER-SONIC TWIN COMBO (NO. 216-2000) – 100W, 2-12 in. Celestion Vintage 30 speakers, guitar combo, 13-tube chassis, preamp: 7 X 12AX7, 2 X 12AT7, power: 4 X 6L6, solid-state rectifier, two channels (Vintage/Burn), blackface or brownface control panel, single input, 13 cream knobs (Ch.1 [Vintage]: g, t, b, m, v, Ch.2 [Burn] g1, g2, t, b, m, notch tune, v, All: r), Vintage Ch. Showman/Bassman voicing switch, channel switch, rear panel: areana/club 100W/25W power switch, effects loop with send and return level controls, pre-amp out jack, power amp in jack, three-way loose/normal/tight damping control, two speaker jacks, standby switch, power switch, footswitch jack, available in black textured vinyl covering with a peppered silver grille or blonde textured vinyl covering with a brown Oxblood grille, casters, cover, and four-buton footswitch included, 26.25 in. wide, 20.25 in. tall, 11.3 in. deep, 83 lbs., mfg. summer 2011-13.

	$2,000	$1,200 - 1,500	$725 - 900	$2,800

ELECTRIC TUBE AMPS: TREMOLUX SERIES

TREMOLUX (NARROW PANEL) – 15W, 1-12 in. Jensen speaker, tube chassis, preamp: 12AY7, 2 X 7025, power: 2 X 6L6, 5AR4 rectifier, tremolo, top numbered control panel, four input jacks, five pointer knobs (mic v, inst. v, tone, s, d), tremolo foot control switch, diagonal tweed covering, brown tweed-era grille, mfg. 1955-1960.

courtesy solidbodyguitar.com, Inc.　　courtesy solidbodyguitar.com, Inc.　　courtesy solidbodyguitar.com, Inc.

	N/A	$3,500 - 4,250	$2,500 - 3,000	

First model was the 5E9. In 1957, output was changed to 18W (Model 5G9). In the later models, they may have different phase inverter and tremolo circuits. The nameplate changed in 1957. This was the first Fender amp with an electric tremolo unit.

TREMOLUX (BROWNFACE) – 30W, 1-10 in. speaker, tube chassis, preamp: 4 X 7025, power: 2 X 6L6GC, 5AR4 rectifier, tremolo, front brownface control panel, four input jacks (two bright, two normal), tremolo works on both channels, eight cream knobs (Bright: v, t, b, Norm: v, t, b, Both: s, i), cream Tolex covering, maroon or wheat grille, mfg. 1961-63.

Tremolux (Brownface)　　Tremolux (Brownface)　　Tremolux (Blackface)
courtesy Dave Rogers/Dave's Guitar Shop　　courtesy Dave Rogers/Dave's Guitar Shop　　courtesy Dave Rogers/Dave's Guitar Shop

1961-1962 1-10 in. Cab	N/A	$2,250 - 2,750	$1,450 - 1,800
1962-1963 2-10 in. Cab Maroon	N/A	$2,250 - 2,750	$1,300 - 1,650
1963-1964 2-10 in. Cab Wheat/Gold	N/A	$2,250 - 2,750	$1,300 - 1,800

Model 6G9-A was first to have 6L6 tubes. In 1962, the 1-10 in. speaker was changed to 2-10 in. (Model 6G9-B). In 1963, the maroon grille was changed to a wheat grille and later that year the handle was changed to black.

TREMOLUX (BLACKFACE) – 30W, 2-10 in. speaker, tube chassis, preamp: 3 X 7025, 12AT7, power: 2 X 6L6GC, 5AR4 rectifier, tremolo, front blackface control panel, four input jacks (two bright, two normal), tremolo works on both channels, eight cream knobs (Bright: v, t, b, Norm: v, t, b, Both: s, i), black Tolex covering, silver grille, mfg. 1964-66.

	N/A	$1,600 - 2,000	$950 - 1,100	

The Blackface was introduced as the Model AA763. In 1964, a bright switch was added. This amp used the same chassis as the Bandmaster, Concert, Pro, and Vibrolux of the same era.

MSR/NOTES	100%	EXCELLENT	AVERAGE	LAST MSR

ELECTRIC TUBE AMPS: TWIN SERIES

For "The Twin" model made in the late 1980s and early 1990s, see the Pro-Tube series.

TWIN (WIDE PANEL) – 15W, 2-12 in. Jensen Concert Series speakers, tube chassis, preamp: 3 X 6SC7, 6J5, power: 2 X 6L6, 5U4 rectifier, top numbered control panel, four input jacks, four pointer knobs (mic v, inst. v, b, t), diagonal tweed covering, brown cloth grille, mfg. 1952-54.

	N/A	$6,500 - 8,000	$4,000 - 5,250	

This was the first wide panel amp for Fender and the first to offer dual tone controls. Model 5D8 featured a 12AY7 tube.

TWIN (NARROW PANEL) – 50W, 2-12 in. Jensen speakers, tube chassis, preamp: 3 X 12AY7, 12AX7, power: 2 X 6L6, rectifer: 2 X 5Y3GY, top numbered control panel, four input jacks, five pointer knobs (mic v, inst. v, b, t, p), diagonal tweed covering, brown tweed-era grille, mfg. 1954-1960.

courtesy Dave Rogers/Dave's Guitar Shop

courtesy Dave Rogers/Dave's Guitar Shop

1954-1955 5 Knobs	N/A	$10,000 - 12,000	$7,000 - 8,500
1956-1957 6 Knobs	N/A	$12,000 - 14,000	$8,500 - 10,000
1958-1960 6 Knobs	N/A	$14,000 - 17,000	$9,000 - 12,000

Model 5E8 was the first to have 50W. In 1955, the rectifers were changed to 2 X 5U4G (Model 5F8) and later on to a5AR4 (Model 5F8-A). In 1956, a mid-range control is added along with bright and normal inputs. In 1958, the pre-amp and driver tubes were changed to a 12AY7 and 2 X 12AX7, and the output tubes are changed to 4 X 5881. This is model 5F8-A, and power output was reported at 85W. The control panel now had six knobs. A few of the very late (1960) models were covered in brown Tolex with the top control panel. Some collectors say early Twin's had 2-10 in. speakers.

TWIN (BROWNFACE) – 90W, 2-12 in. Jensen speakers, tube chassis, preamp: 6 X 7025, power: 4 X 6L6GC, solid state rectifier, two channels, tremolo, front brownface control panel, four input jacks (two normal, two vibrato), nine cream knobs (Norm: v, t, b, Vibrato: v, t, b, s, i, Both: p), available in brown (1960 only) or cream Tolex covering, maroon or wheat colored grille, mfg. 1960-63.

courtesy Willie's American Guitars

courtesy Willie's American Guitars

1960 Brown Tolex	N/A	$10,000 - 12,000	$7,500 - 9,000
1960-1961 Cream Tolex, Maroon Grille	N/A	$6,500 - 8,000	$5,000 - 6,000
1961-1963 Cream Tolex, Wheat Grille	N/A	$6,000 - 7,500	$4,500 - 5,500

Model number 6G8A changed the tube schematics to 6 X 7025 and 4 X 6L6. There are many different variants of this model over its 11 year existence. There are a few amps made with brown Tolex covering and a smaller box. The Twin was phased out when the Twin Reverb was introduced.

TWIN REVERB (BLACKFACE) – 85W, 2-12 in. Jensen speakers, tube chassis, preamp: 3 X 7025, 2 X 12AT7, 12AX7, power: 4 X 6L6GC, solid-state rectifier, two channels, reverb, vibrato, front blackface control panel, four input jacks (two normal, two vibrato), bright and middle switches, 11 silver-top knobs (Norm: v, t, m, b, Vibrato: v, t, m, b, r, s, i), black Tolex covering, silver grille, mfg. 1963-67.

	N/A	$2,000 - 2,500	$1,100 - 1,400	

MSR/NOTES	100%	EXCELLENT	AVERAGE	LAST MSR

Twin Reverb (Blackface)
courtesy Dave Rogers/Dave's Guitar Shop

Twin Reverb (Blackface)
courtesy Dave Rogers/Dave's Guitar Shop

Twin Reverb (Silverface)
courtesy S.P. Fjestad

TWIN REVERB (SILVERFACE) – 85W, 2-12 in. Jensen speakers, tube chassis, preamp: 3 X 7025, 2 X 12AT7, 12AX7, power: 4 X 6L6GC, solid-state rectifier, two channels, reverb, vibrato, front silverface control panel, four input jacks (two normal, two vibrato), bright and middle switches, 11 silver-top knobs (Norm: v, t, m, b, Vibrato: v, t, m, b, r, s, i), black Tolex covering, silver grille, mfg. 1968-1980.

1968-1972	N/A	$1,525 - 1,800	$775 - 950	
1973-1976	N/A	$1,050 - 1,250	$525 - 650	
1976-1980	N/A	$1,000 - 1,250	$500 - 625	

In 1968, the Silverface is introduced with silver control panel, blue cloth grille, and aluminum trim. The Silverface is the same as the Blackface in the schematics. In 1973, the output was raised to 100W and a master volume control was added. In 1976, a push/pull distortion switch was added to the master volume control and JBL speakers became an option.

TWIN REVERB (NEW BLACKFACE) – 135W, 2-12 in. Jensen speakers, tube chassis, preamp: 4 X 7025, 2 X 12AX7, power: 4 X 6L6GC, solid-state rectifier, two channels, reverb, vibrato, front blackface control panel, four input jacks (two normal, two vibrato), bright and middle switches, 12 silver-top knobs (Norm: v, t, m, b, Vibrato: v, t, m, b, r, s, i, MV), black Tolex covering, silver grille, mfg. 1981-83.

	N/A	$1,000-1,250	$500 - 700

QUAD REVERB – 100W, 4-12 in. Jensen speakers, tube chassis, preamp: 4 X 7025, 2 X 12AT7, power: 4 X 6L6, solid-state rectifier, two channels, reverb, vibrato, front silverface control panel, four input jacks (two normal, two vibrato), bright and middle switches, 12 silver-top knobs (Norm: v, t, m, b, Vibrato: v, t, m, b, r, s, i, MV), black Tolex covering, silver grille, mfg. 1970-79.

	N/A	$750 - 900	$500 - 600

The Quad Reverb has the same chassis as the Twin Reverb.

SUPER SIX REVERB – 100W, 6-10 in. Jensen speakers, tube chassis, preamp: 4 X 7025, 2 X 12AT7, power: 4 X 6L6, solid-state rectifier, two channels, reverb, vibrato, front silverface control panel, four input jacks (two normal, two vibrato), bright and middle switches, 12 silver-top knobs (Norm: v, t, m, b, Vibrato: v, t, m, b, r, s, i, MV), black Tolex covering, silver grille, mfg. 1970-79.

	N/A	$900 - 1,100	$600 - 700

The Super Six Reverb has the same chassis as the Twin Reverb. It features removable casters on the side and uses a series-parallel connection.

SUPER TWIN – 180W, 2-12 in. speakers, tube chassis, preamp: 2 X 7025, 12AT7, 6CX8, 6C10, power: 6 X 6L6, solid-state rectifier, front black control panel, two inputs, elaborate equilization system, new active electronics, 12 silver-top knobs, (v, t, m, b, p, distortion, output level, and five-way equilization), black Tolex covering, black grille with white trim, casters, mfg. 1975-76.

	N/A	$800 - 950	$475 - 625

* *Super Twin Reverb* – similar to Super Twin except has reverb unit, tube schematics were changed to: one 7025 was replaced with two sections of a 6C10 triple triode, the reverb driver was a 6CX8 pentode, mfg. 1977-1980

	N/A	$850 - 1,000	$475- 650

This model replaced the Super Twin in 1977.

TWIN REVERB II COMBO – 105W, 2-12 in. speakers, tube chassis, preamp: 5 X 7025, 2 X 12AT7, power: 4 X 6L6GC, new blackface control panel, two inputs, 12 silver-top knobs (Ch.1: v, t, m, b, Ch.2: v, g, MV, t, m, b, r, p), three-stage distortion, channel switching, rear mounted effects loop, black Tolex covering, silver grille, mfg. 1982-85.

	N/A	$675 - 800	$450 - 525

Note: production of this amp stopped in 1985 at the end of CBS ownership, but was still sold through 1986.

* *Twin Reverb II Piggyback* – similar to the Twin Reverb II Combo, except in piggyback configuration with a separate head and speaker cabinet, black Tolex covering, silver grille, mfg. 1982-85.

Head & Cabinet	N/A	$850 - 1,000	$600 - 700	
Head Only	N/A	$550 - 650	$375 - 400	
Cab Only	N/A	$250 - 300	$140 - 175	

Note: production of this amp stopped in 1985 at the end of CBS ownership, but was still sold through 1986.

ELECTRIC TUBE AMPS: VIBRASONIC/VIBROSONIC SERIES

VIBRASONIC (BROWNFACE) – 25W, 1-15 in. JBL speaker, tube chassis, preamp: 5 X 7025, power: 2 X 6L6GC, two channels, tremolo, brownface control panel, four inputs (two normal, two vibrato), nine brown knobs (Norm: v, t, b, Vibrato: v, t, b, s, i, Both: p), brown Tolex covering, brown tweed-era grille, mfg. 1959-1963.

courtesy Dave Rogers/Dave's Guitar Shop

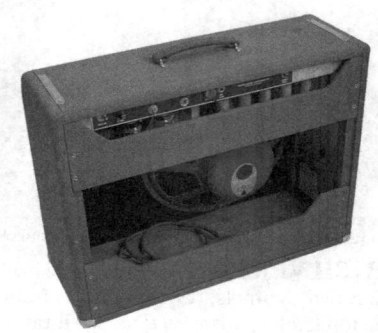

courtesy Dave Rogers/Dave's Guitar Shop

1959-1960 Brown	N/A	$2,500 - 3,000	$1,650 - 2,000
1961 Maroon	N/A	$2,000 - 2,500	$1,300 - 1,650
1962-1963 Wheat	N/A	$1,800 - 2,250	$1,100 - 1,400

Introduced as the Model 5G13. This amp had a reversed control layout at first but went back to the original design shortly thereafter. In 1961, the grille turned to maroon, and in 1962, it turned to wheat. Later models used 2 X 12AX7 tubes in the tremolo circuit rather than the 7025 and 5881 tubes (Model 6G13-A). This amp was a very close relative to the Pro amp with vibrato and a 15 in. JBL speaker.

VIBROSONIC (SILVERFACE) – 100W, 1-15 in. speaker, tube chassis, preamp: 3 X 7025, 2 X 12AT7, 12AX7, power: 4 X 6L6GC, two channels, reverb, vibrato, silverface control panel, four inputs (two normal, two vibrato), bright switches, 12 silver-top knobs (Norm: v, t, m, b, Vibrato: v, t, m ,b, r, s, i, Both: MV), black Tolex covering, silver grille, mfg. 1972-1981.

	N/A	$750 - 900	$500 - 600

No, that is not an error in spelling, it is the Vibr-O-sonic. This amp was released nine years after the original Vibrasonic was released, but it is more similar to the Twin, Quad, and Super-Six Reverb amps. It doesn't have a lot to do with the original Vibrasonic. In 1974, a less expensive JBL D-130F was offered for a speaker. In 1976, a distortion switch was added to the master volume knob. In 1979, the JBL speaker was replaced with a 15 in. Electro-voice.

ELECTRIC TUBE AMPS: VIBROLUX SERIES

VIBROLUX (NARROW PANEL) – 10W, 1-10 in. Jensen, tube chassis, preamp: 2 X 12AX7, power: 2 X 6V6, 5Y3 rectifier, tremolo, top black control panel, three inputs, four pointer knobs (v, tone, s, d), diagonal tweed covering, brown tweed-era grille, mfg. 1954-1961.

courtesy Dave Rogers/Dave's Guitar Shop

courtesy Dave Rogers/Dave's Guitar Shop

courtesy Willie's American Guitars

	N/A	$2,600 - 3,250	$1,550 - 1,950

The early variations were Model 5E11. Model 5F11 featured three inputs, and the four controls.

VIBROLUX (BROWNFACE) – 30W, 1-12 in. Jensen speakers, tube chassis, preamp: 2 X 7025, 2 X 12AX7, power: 2 X 6L6GC, two channels, vibrato, front blackface control panel, four inputs, two normal, two bright, eight brown knobs (Norm: v, t, b, Vibrato: v, t, b, Both: s, i), tremolo works on both channels, brown Tolex covering, light brown grille, mfg. 1961-63.

	N/A	$2,600 - 3,200	$1,650 - 1,900

This model was introduced as the 6G11.

MSR/NOTES	100%	EXCELLENT	AVERAGE	LAST MSR

Vibrolux (Brownface)
courtesy Dave Rogers/Dave's Guitar Shop

Vibrolux (Brownface)
courtesy Dave Rogers/Dave's Guitar Shop

Vibrolux (Blackface)
courtesy Dave Rogers/Dave's Guitar Shop

VIBROLUX (BLACKFACE) – 30W, 1-12 in. Jensen speakers, tube chassis, preamp: 4 X 7025, power: 2 X 6L6GC, two channels, vibrato, front blackface control panel, four inputs (two normal, two bright), eight black knobs (Norm: v, t, b, Vibrato: v, t, b, s, i), tremolo works only on Vibrato channel, black Tolex covering, silver grille, mfg. 1964-65.

| | N/A | $2,200 - 2,750 | $1,325 - 1,650 | |

VIBROLUX REVERB (BLACKFACE) – 35W, 2-10 in. Jensen speakers, tube chassis, preamp: 3 X 7025, 2 X 12AT7, 12AX7, power: 2 X 6L6GC, two channels, vibrato, reverb, blackface control panel, four inputs (two normal, two vibrato), bright switches, nine silver-top knobs (Norm: v, t, b, Vibrato: v, t, b, r, s, i), black Tolex covering, silver grille, mfg. 1964-67.

courtesy solidbodyguitar.com, Inc.

courtesy solidbodyguitar.com, Inc.

| 1964-1965 | N/A | $2,500 - 3,200 | $1,600 - 1,950 | |
| 1966-1967 | N/A | $2,200 - 2,750 | $1,325 - 1,650 | |

This model was introduced as the AA964.

VIBROLUX REVERB (SILVERFACE) – 40W, 2-10 in. Jensen speakers, tube chassis, preamp: 3 X 7025, 2 X 12AT7, 12AX7, power: 2 X 6L6GC, two channels, vibrato, reverb, silverface control panel, four inputs (two normal, two vibrato), bright switches, nine silver-top knobs (Norm: v, t, b, Vibrato: v, t, b, r, s, i), black Tolex covering, silver grille, mfg. 1967-1979.

courtesy David Chandler/R&R Guitars

courtesy David Chandler/R&R Guitars

| 1967-1974 | N/A | $1,325 - 1,650 | $800 - 1,000 | |
| 1975-1979 | N/A | $1,075 - 1,350 | $650 - 800 | |

ELECTRIC TUBE AMPS: VIBROVERB SERIES

VIBROVERB (BROWNFACE) – 35W, 2-10 in. Oxford speakers, tube chassis, preamp: 4 X 7025, 2 X 12AX7, power: 2 X 6L6GC, 5U4 rectifier, two channels, reverb, vibrato, brownface control panel, four input jacks (two normal, two bright), nine brown knobs (Norm: v, t, b, Bright: v, t, b, r, Both: s, i), tilt-back legs, brown Tolex covering, light brown grille, mfg. 1963 only.

| | N/A | $7,000 - 8,500 | $4,750 - 6,000 | |

MSR/NOTES	100%	EXCELLENT	AVERAGE	LAST MSR

Vibroverb (Brownface)
courtesy Dave Rogers/Dave's Guitar Shop

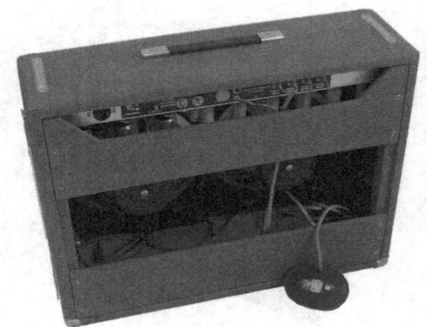

Vibroverb (Brownface)
courtesy Dave Rogers/Dave's Guitar Shop

Vibroverb (Blackface)
courtesy Dave Rogers/Dave's Guitar Shop

VIBROVERB (BLACKFACE) – 40W, 1-15 in. speaker, tube chassis, preamp: 3 X 7025, 12AX7, 2 X 12AT7, power: 2 X 6L6GC, 5U4 rectifier, two channels (normal and vibrato), four input jacks (two for each channel), blackface control panel, nine silver-top knobs (Norm: v, t, b, Vibrato: v, t, b, r, s, i), bright switches, black Tolex covering, silver grille, mfg. 1963-64.

| | N/A | $3,800 - 4,800 | $2,500 - 3,000 | |

Blackface introduced as Model AA763. This version of the Vibroverb was completely different from the first version with different circuitry in the phase inverter and tremolo. Fender stopped making this amp in fall of 1964, however models were still sold through early 1965. This model was replaced by the Vibrolux Reverb.

ELECTRIC TUBE AMPS: VINTAGE MODIFIED SERIES

Band-Master VM Head
courtesy Fender

Champion 600
courtesy Fender

Deluxe VM
courtesy Fender

'68 CUSTOM DELUXE REVERB (NO. 227-4000) – 22W, guitar combo, 1-12 in. Celestion G12V-70 speaker, eight-tube chassis, preamp: 4 X 12AX7, 2 X 12AT7, power: 2 X 6V6, two channels (Vintage for traditional Silverface tonality and Custom for tweed-era Bassman), reverb, tremolo, front silver control panel, four inputs (two per channel), nine black skirted knobs (Custom: v, t, b, Custom: v, t, b, All: r, s, i), black Tolex covering, silver with turquoise accents grille cloth, two-button footswitch and cover included, mfg. 2014-present.

| MSR N/A | $1,050 | $675 - 775 | $350 - 425 | |

'68 CUSTOM PRINCETON REVERB (NO. 227-2000) – 12W, guitar combo, 1-10 in. Celestion Ten 30 speaker, six-tube chassis, preamp: 3 X 12AX7, 1 X 12AT7, power: 2 X 6V6, single channel voiced for a tweed-era Bassman, reverb, tremolo, front silver control panel, two inputs, six black skirted knobs (v, t, b, r, s, i), black Tolex covering, silver with turquoise accents grille cloth, two-button footswitch and cover included, mfg. 2014-present.

| MSR $1,200 | $900 | $500 - 625 | $300 - 375 | |

'68 CUSTOM TWIN REVERB (NO. 227-3000) – 85W, guitar combo, 2-12 in. Celestion G12V-70 speakers, 10-tube chassis, preamp: 4 X 12AX7, 2 X 12AT7, power: 4 X 6L6, two channels (Vintage for traditional Silverface tonality and Custom for tweed-era Bassman), reverb, tremolo, front silver control panel, four inputs (two per channel), 11 black skirted knobs (Custom: v, t, m, b, Custom: v, t, m, b, All: r, s, i), bright switches for each channel, black Tolex covering, silver with turquoise accents grille cloth, two-button footswitch and cover included, mfg. 2014-present.

| MSR $1,800 | $1,300 | $775 - 925 | $450 - 575 | |

'68 CUSTOM VIBROLUX REVERB (NO. 227-5000) – 35W, guitar combo, 2-10 in. Celestion Ten 30 speakers, eight-tube chassis, preamp: 4 X 12AX7, 2 X 12AT7, power: 2 X 6L6, two channels (Vintage for traditional Silverface tonality and Custom for tweed-era Bassman), reverb, tremolo, front silver control panel, four inputs (two per channel), nine black skirted knobs (Custom: v, t, b, Custom: v, t, b, All: r, s, i), two bright switches, black Tolex covering, silver with turquoise accents grille cloth, two-button footswitch and cover included, mfg. 2015-present.

| MSR N/A | $1,200 | $650 - 800 | $375 - 475 | |

Super Champ XD
courtesy Fender

'Super Champ X2 Combo
courtesy Fender

Super Champ SC112 Speaker Cabinet
courtesy Fender

BAND-MASTER VM HEAD (NO. 222-0200) – 40W, guitar head-unit, four-tube chassis, preamp: 2 X 12AX7, power: 2 X 6L6GC, solid-state rectifier, two channels (clean/drive), new DSP platform with chorus and delay, front black control panel, single input, 12 black knobs with silver tops (Ch. 1: v, t, b, Ch. 2: g, v, t, m, b, r, chorus/delay time/rate, delay mix, chorus depth), drive switch, effects adjust switch (chorus/delay), chorus switch, effects loop, two speaker out jacks, standby switch, four-button footswitch included (drive, reverb, delay, chorus), black textured vinyl covering, silver grille cloth with Vintage Modified logo on lower right-hand corner, 24 in. wide, 10 in. tall, 10 in. deep, 26 lbs., black cover included, mfg. 2009-2012.

	$700	$400 - 500	$250 - 300	$960

BAND-MASTER VM 212 SPEAKER CABINET (NO. 222-1200) – 160W, 2-12 in. Celestion G12P-80 16 ohm speakers, 8 ohm impedance, 13-ply baltic birch/maple plywood cabinet, closed back, black textured vinyl covering, silver grille cloth with Vintage Modified logo in lower right-hand corner, designed for use with the Band-Master VM Head, 32 in. wide, 21.5 in. tall, 12 in. deep, 48.5 lbs., black cover included, mfg. 2009-2012.

	$375	$225 - 275	$135 - 170	$500

CHAMPION 600 (NO. 233-0100) – 5W, 1-6 in. speaker, two tube chassis, preamp: 1 X 12AX7A, power: 1 X 6V6, solid-state rectifier, single channel, rear brown control panel, two inputs (high and low), single volume knob, two-tone brown/blonde vinyl covering, TV-style brown grille, 12 in. wide, 11 in. tall, 7.5 in. deep, 15 lbs., mfg. 2007-2012.

	$150	$95 - 120	$50 - 75	$240

DELUXE VM (NO. 222-0000) – 40W, 1-12 in. Celestion G12P-80 speaker, guitar combo, four-tube chassis, preamp: 2 X 12AX7, power: 2 X 6L6, solid-state rectifier, two channels (clean/drive), new DSP platform with chorus and delay, front black control panel, single input, 12 black knobs with silver tops (Ch. 1: v, t, b, Ch. 2: g, v, t, m, b, r, chorus/delay time/rate, delay mix, chorus depth), drive switch, effects adjust switch (chorus/delay), chorus switch, effects loop, two speaker out jacks, standby switch, four-button footswitch included (drive, reverb, delay, chorus), black textured vinyl covering, silver grille cloth with Vintage Modified logo on lower right-hand corner, 24 in. wide, 17.5 in. tall, 10 in. deep, 40 lbs., black cover included, mfg. 2009-2012.

	$800	$450 - 550	$275 - 325	$1,080

SUPER CHAMP XD (NO. 233-1100) – 15W, 1-10 in. special design speaker, guitar combo, three-tube chassis, preamp: 1 X 12AX7A, power: 2 X 6V6, solid-state rectifier, two channels (normal/amp voice), 16 amp voicings, 16 DSP effects, front black control panel, single input, eight black knobs with silver tops (Ch. 1: v, Ch. 2: g, v, voice, t, b, FX level, FX select), line out jack, optional footswitch, black textured vinyl covering, silver grille cloth, 17.5 in. wide, 15 in. tall, 9 in. deep, 24 lbs., mfg. late 2007-mid-2011.

	$300	$175 - 225	$110 - 140	$420

* Add $25 for two-button footswitch.

SUPER CHAMP X2 HD (NO. 222-3100) – 15W, guitar head unit, three-tube chassis, preamp: 1 X 12AX7, power: 2 X 6V6, solid-state rectifier, two channels (normal/amp voice), 16 amp voicings, 15 DSP effects, front black control panel, single input, eight black knobs with silver tops (Ch. 1: v, Ch. 2: g, v, voice, t, b, FX adj., FX select), tap button, line out jack, USB out, optional footswitch, black textured vinyl covering, silver grille cloth, 17.5 in. wide, 8 in. tall, 8.5 in. deep, 18.5 lbs., mfg. 2012-present.

MSR N/A	$300	$175 - 225	$105 - 130	

* Add $25 for two-button footswitch.

* ***Super Champ X2 Combo (No. 222-3000)*** – similar to the Super Champ X2 HD, except in combo configuration with 1-10 in. speaker, 17.5 in. wide, 15 in. tall, 9.25 in. deep, 24 lbs., mfg. 2012-present.

MSR N/A	$380	$225 - 275	$135 - 170	

* Add $25 for two-button footswitch.

SUPER CHAMP SC112 SPEAKER CABINET (NO. 222-3200) – 80W, 1-10 in. Celestion G12P-80 speaker, 8 ohm impedance, closed back, designed for use with the Super Champ X2 HD, black covering, silver grille cloth, 17.5 in. wide, 17 in. tall, 9.15 in. deep, 28 lbs., mfg. 2012-present.

MSR N/A	$200	$120 - 150	$75 - 95	

MSR/NOTES	100%	EXCELLENT	AVERAGE	LAST MSR

VIBRO CHAMP XD (NO. 233-1000) – 5W, 1-8 in. special design speaker, guitar combo, two-tube chassis, preamp: 1 X 12AX7A, power: 1 X 6V6, solid-state rectifier, single channel, 16 amp voicings, 16 DSP effects, front black control panel, single input, seven black knobs with silver tops (g, v, voice, t, b, FX level, FX select), line out jack, black textured vinyl covering, silver grille cloth, 17 in. wide, 14 in. tall, 8.7 in. deep, 23 lbs., mfg. late 2007-2011.

| | $240 | $140 - 175 | $85 - 105 | $340 |

ELECTRIC TUBE AMPS: VINTAGE REISSUE SERIES

'59 Bassman LTD Vintage Reissue courtesy Fender

'65 Deluxe Reverb Vintage Reissue courtesy Fender

'65 Super Reverb Vintage Reissue courtesy Fender

'59 BASSMAN VINTAGE REISSUE (NO. 021-7100-000) – 45W, 4-10 in. 8 Ohm Jensen P10R speakers, tubes chassis: preamp: 2 12AX7, power: 2 X 6L6 Groove Tube, plug in 8 pin tube rectifier (can plug in a 5AR4 or 5U4), dual channels (normal and bright), top chrome control panel with numbers to 12, 4 inputs, two per channel, six chickenhead knobs (p, m, b, t, v bright, v norm), diagonal tweed covering, Oxblood grille cloth, 53 lbs., mfg. 1990-2003.

| | N/A | $800 - 1,000 | $475 - 600 | $1,420 |

'59 BASSMAN LTD VINTAGE REISSUE (NO. 217-1000-010) – 50W, 4-10 in. 8 Ohm Jensen P10R speakers, tube chassis: preamp: 2 12AX7, power: 2 X GT6L6-GE , 5AR4 rectifier, dual channels (normal and bright), top chrome control panel with numbers to 12, 4 inputs, two per channel, six chickenhead knobs (p, m, b, t, v bright, v norm), diagonal tweed covering, Oxblood grille cloth, 53 lbs., mfg. 2004-present.

| MSR $1,950 | $1,450 | $800 - 1,000 | $475 - 600 | |

* Add $25 for Limited Edition Blonde textured vinyl covering

'63 FENDER REVERB VINTAGE REISSUE (NO. 021-7500-000) – reverb unit that can be added to any other amp, tube chassis, preamp: 12AX7, 12AT7, power: 6V6, top black control panel, single input and output, three black knobs (dwell, mixer, tone), available in Black Tolex covering with a silver grille (1995-late 1990s), Blonde Tolex covering with an oxblood grille (1995-late 1990s), Brown Tolex covering with a wheat grille, Lacquered Tweed covering with a brown pinstripe grille (2009-present), or Tweed covering with an oxblood grille and chickenhead knobs (1995-late 1990s), 13 lbs., mfg. 1995-present.

| MSR $950 | $700 | $400 - 500 | $250 - 300 | |

* Add 15% (MSR $1,070) for lacquered tweed covering with a brown pinstripe grille.

'63 VIBROVERB VINTAGE REISSUE (NO. 021-7200-000) – 40W, 2-10 in. speakers, tube chassis, preamp: 4 X 12AX7, 2 X 12AT7, power: 2 X 6L6GC, solid-state rectifier, vibrato, reverb, two channels (normal and bright), brownface control panel, four input jacks, two for each channel, nine brown knobs (Norm: v, t, b, Bright: v, t, b, r, Both: s, i), brown Tolex covering, light brown grille, mfg. 1990-95.

| | N/A | $725 - 900 | $425 - 550 | $1,080 |

'65 DELUXE REVERB VINTAGE REISSUE (NO. 021-7400-000) – 22W, 1-12 in. speaker, all-tube chassis: preamp: 4 X 12AX7, 2 X 12AT7, power: 2 X 6V6, 5AR4 rectifier, two channels, reverb, vibrato, front blackface control panel, four inputs, two normal, two vibrato, nine silver-top knobs (Norm, v, b, t, Vibrato, v, b, t, r, s, i), two-button footswitch, black Tolex covering, silver grille, 42 lbs., mfg. 1993-present.

| MSR $1,500 | $1,100 | $650 - 800 | $375 - 475 | |

This amp was available in other coverings other than black Tolex in the 1990s.

* **'65 Deluxe Reverb Head Vintage Reissue (No. 021-7400-010)** – similar to the '65 Deluxe Reverb Vintage Reissue, except in head configuration with no speakers, mfg. 2014-present.

| MSR $1,400 | $1,000 | $550 - 700 | $350 - 425 | |

This amp was available in other coverings other than black Tolex in the 1990s.

'65 PRINCETON REVERB VINTAGE REISSUE (NO. 217-2000) – 15W, 1-10 in. Jensen C-10R 40W speaker with a ceramic magnet, seven-tube chassis: preamp:3 X 12AX7, 1 X 12AT7, power: 2 X 6V6, rectifier: 5AR4, single channel, reverb, vibrato, front blackface control panel, two inputs, two normal, two vibrato, six black knobs with silver tops (v, t, b r, s, i), footswitch jack, power switch on back panel, external speaker jack, two-button footswitch included (reverb, vibrato), black Tolex covering, silver grille, 19.875 in. wide, 16 in. tall, 9.5 in. deep, 34 lbs., cover included, mfg. summer 2008-present.

| MSR N/A | $1,000 | $550 - 700 | $350 - 425 | |

* Subtract 10-15% for models built in Mexico.

MSR/NOTES	100%	EXCELLENT	AVERAGE	LAST MSR

'65 SUPER REVERB VINTAGE REISSUE (NO. 021-7600-000) – 40W, 4-10 in. Jensen P-10R Alnico speakers, tubes chassis: preamp: 4 X 12AX7, 2 X 12AT7, power: 2 X 6L6 Groove Tube, 5AR4 rectifier, dual channels, vibrato, reverb, black control panel, four inputs, two normal, two vibrato, 10 silver-top knobs (Norm: v, t, b, Vibrato: v, t, m, b, r, s, i), two-button footswitch (reverb and vibrato), tilt back legs, black textured vinyl, silver grille, 65 lbs., mfg. 2001-present.

MSR $2,050	$1,550	$850 - 1,050	$500 - 625	

In 2002, the output was increased to 45W.

'65 TWIN REVERB VINTAGE REISSUE (NO. 021-7300-000) – 85W, 2-12 in. Jensen speakers, tubes chassis: preamp: 4 X 12AX7, 2 X 12AT7, power: 4 X 6L6GC, two channels, reverb, vibrato, blackface control panel, four inputs, two normal, two vibrato, bright switches, 11 silver-top knobs (Norm: v, t, m, b, Vibrato: v, t, m, b, r, s, i), two button footswitch for reverb and vibrato, tilt-back legs, black Tolex covering, silver grille, 64 lbs., mfg. 1992-present.

MSR $2,000	$1,450	$800 - 1,000	$475 - 600	

'65 TWIN CUSTOM 15 VINTAGE REISSUE (NO. 217-3000-010) – 85W, 1-15 in. Eminence speaker, tubes chassis: preamp: 4 X 12AX7, 2 X 12AT7, power: 4 X 6L6GC, two channels, reverb, vibrato, blackface control panel, four inputs, two normal, two vibrato, bright switches, 11 silver-top knobs (Norm: v, t, m, b, Vibrato: v, t, m, b, r, s, i), two button footswitch for reverb and vibrato, tilt-back legs, black Tolex covering, silver grille, casters, 64 lbs., mfg. 2004-present.

MSR $2,050	$1,550	$850 - 1,050	$500 - 625	

ELECTRIC TUBE AMPS: CUSTOM SHOP SERIES

The Fender Custom shop was introduced in 1993, and was formed to reissue vintage models and to create some new and unique designs. In 2000, Fender introduced their Custom shop Master Built Guitar Amplifiers. These amps are all-tube amps, hand crafted, and are true custom shop creations usually built in limited quantities. The **Woody Junior Exotic** and **Woody Pro Exotic** are both built out of wood cabinets with the metal strips on the panel. The **Woody Junior Ash** and **Woody Pro Ash** are 50s-style models covered in ash and white gloss paint, with a narrow panel front and a brown grille. The **Bass Breaker** is similar to the mid-50s Bassman with narrow panel tweed cosmetics, but with Celestian speakers. The **Two Tone** is a completely different amp than what Fender has ever done before. It has top control panel, but the controls are in the front, the grille is slanted at the top and the covering is black on the sides, and white on the top and bottom.

**'57 Bandmaster
courtesy Fender**

**'57 Champ
courtesy Fender**

**'57 Deluxe Amp
courtesy Fender**

'57 BANDMASTER (NO. 817-0500) – 26W, 3-10 in. Special-Design Jensen P10R-F speakers, five tube chassis, preamp: 3 X 12AX7, power: 2 X 6L6, rectifier: 5AR4, two channels, top chrome control panel, four inputs (two inst., two mic.), five black chickenhead knobs (presence, bass, treble, inst. v, mic. v), standby switch, tweed covering, brown/gold grille cloth, 20.37 in. wide, 20.87 in. tall, 10.87 in. deep, 45 lbs., mfg. 2013-present.

MSR N/A	$2,500	$1,625 - 1,875	$825 - 1,000	

'57 CHAMP (NO. 816-0500) – 5W, 1-8 in. Weber Special Design 10W speaker, guitar combo, hand-wired 5F1 three tube chassis, preamp: 1 X 12AX7, power: 1 X 6V6GT, rectifier: 5Y3GT, single channel, top chrome control panel, two inputs (input 1: full sensitivity, input 2: lower sensitivity), single black chickenhead volume knob, power switch, finger-jointed solid pine cabinet, lacquered tweed covering, oxblood grille cloth, brown cover included, 12.5 in. wide, 13.5 in. tall, 7.8 in. deep, 16.5 lbs., mfg. summer 2009-mid-2011.

	$1,000	$600 - 700	$325 - 400	$1,300

This model is based on the 1957 Fender Champ with Model 5F1 circuitry.

'57 DELUXE AMP (NO. 815-0500) – 12W, 1-12 in. Alnico Jensen P-12Q speaker, five tube chassis, preamp: 2 X 12AX7 (or 12AY7), power: 2 X GT6V6, rectifier: 5Y3GT, two channels, top chrome control panel, four inputs (two inst., two mic.), three black chickenhead knobs (tone, inst. v, mic. v), standby switch, tweed covering, brown/gold grille cloth, cover included, 20 in. wide, 16.75 in. tall, 9.5 in. deep, 30 lbs., mfg. 2007-mid-2011.

	$2,000	$1,050 - 1,300	$800 - 950	$2,700

This model is based on the 1957 Fender Deluxe with Model 5E3 circuitry. Original models featured a polarity switch and in place of that, this new model has a standby switch.

MSR/NOTES	100%	EXCELLENT	AVERAGE	LAST MSR

'57 Deluxe Head
courtesy Fender

'57 Twin Amp
courtesy Fender

'64 Vibroverb Custom
courtesy Fender

'57 DELUXE HEAD (NO. 815-050-0010) – 12W, guitar head unit, five tube chassis, 8 ohms, preamp: 2 X 12AX7, power: 2 X 6V6, rectifier: 5Y3GT, two channels, top chrome control panel, four inputs (two inst., two mic.), three black chickenhead knobs (tone, inst. v, mic. v), standby switch, leather top handle, tweed covering, brown/gold grille cloth, cover included, 20 in. wide, 10 in. tall, 8.25 in. deep, 17.5 lbs., mfg. 2014-present.

| MSR N/A | $1,900 | $1,225 - 1,425 | $625 - 750 | |

This model is based on the 1957 Fender Deluxe with Model 5E3 circuitry. Original models featured a polarity switch and in place of that, this new model has a standby switch.

'57 TWIN AMP (NO. 814-0500-000) – 40W, 2-12 in. Alnico speakers, all-tube chassis, preamp: 4 X 12AX7, power:2 X GT6L6-GE, 2 X 5U4 rectifiers, two channels, top chrome control panel, four inputs, five black chickenhead knobs (p, b, t, v bright, v norm), tweed covering, brown/gold grille cloth, cover included, 44 lbs., mfg. 2004-mid-2011.

| | $3,000 | $1,500 - 1,800 | $1,000 - 1,200 | $4,000 |

'64 VIBROVERB CUSTOM (NO. 814-0000-000) – 50W, 1-15 in. Eminence speaker, tube chassis, preamp: 4 X 12AX7, 2 X 12AT7, power: 2 X GT 6L6-GE, 5AR4 rectifier (switchable to a diode), two channels, vibrato, reverb, front blackface control panel, four inputs, nine silver top knobs (Ch. 1: v, t, b, Ch. 2: v, t, b, r, s, i), tilt-back legs, two-button footswitch, black Tolex covering, silver grille, cover included, 52 lbs., mfg. 2003-08.

| | $2,500 | $1,300 - 1,700 | $900 - 1,100 | $3,500 |

The late Cesar Diaz, the amp doctor, provided insight in the development of this amp.

DUAL PROFESSIONAL (NO. 081-1005-000) – 100W, into 4 or 2 Ohms, 2-12 in. Celestion Vintage 30 speakers, tubes chassis: preamp: 4 X 12AX7, 6V6 reverb, dual channels, reverb, vibrato, brownface control panel, two inputs, ten cream knobs (dwell, mix, tone, volume A, volume B, t, m, b, s, i) three switches for FAT and channel switching, two button footswitch, effects loop, cream Tolex covering, oxblood grille, 76 lbs., mfg. 1995-2002.

| | N/A | $1,300 - 1,500 | $900 - 1,100 | $3,000 |

EC TREMOLUX (NO. 815-1500-000) – 12W, 1-12 in. Celestion Heritage G12-65 speaker, guitar combo, six-tube chassis, preamp: 3 X 12AX7, power: 2 X 6V6, rectifier: 5Y3GT, single channel, tremolo, top chrome control panel, two inputs, three black chickenhead knobs (v, tone, speed), high/low output switch, standby switch, power switch, Narrow Panel-style tweed covering, vintage-style brown/gold grille cloth, 20 in. wide, 16.75 in. tall, 9.5 in. deep, 25 lbs., deluxe cover included, mfg. late 2011-disc.

| | $2,000 | $1,200 - 1,500 | $725 - 900 | $2,800 |

The EC Tremolux features a circuit based on a late 1950s Fender Deluxe Model 5E3.

EC TWINOLUX (NO. 814-1500-000) – 40W, 2-12 in. Weber-designed Eminence speakers, guitar combo, eight-tube chassis, preamp: 4 X 12AX7, power: 2 X 6L6, rectifier: 2 X 5U4, single channel, tremolo, top chrome control panel, two inputs, seven black chickenhead knobs (v, t, b, s, i, p, three-way 1 Sp Lo/2 Sp Lo/Full output power selector), standby switch, power switch, Narrow Panel-style tweed covering, vintage-style brown/gold grille cloth, 24.5 in. wide, 20.5 in. tall, 9 in. deep, 53 lbs., deluxe cover included, mfg. late 2011-present.

| MSR $4,200 | $3,000 | $1,800 - 2,250 | $1,075 - 1,350 | |

The EC Twinolux features a circuit based on a late 1950s Fender Twin Model 5E8-A.

EC VIBRO-CHAMP (NO. 816-1500-000) – 5W, 1-8 in. Weber speaker, guitar combo, four-tube chassis, preamp: 2 X 12AX7, power: 1 X 6V6, rectifier: 5Y3GT, single channel, tremolo, top chrome control panel, two inputs, two black chickenhead knobs (v, speed), high/low output switch, power switch, Narrow Panel-style tweed covering, vintage-style brown/gold grille cloth, 12.5 in. wide, 13.5 in. tall, 7.8 in. deep, 16.5 lbs., deluxe cover included, mfg. late 2011-disc.

| | $1,000 | $600 - 750 | $350 - 450 | $1,400 |

The EC Vibro-Champ features a circuit based on a late 1950s Fender Champ Model 5F1.

MSR/NOTES	100%	EXCELLENT	AVERAGE	LAST MSR

GB Hot Rod Deluxe Combo
courtesy Fender

Hot Rod Deville ML 212
courtesy Fender

The Edge Deluxe
courtesy Fender

GB HOT ROD DELUXE COMBO (NO. 223-0400) – 40W, 1-12 in. Jensen C12K speaker, tube chassis, preamp: 2 X 12AX7, 1 X 12AT7, power: 2 X 6L6, solid-state rectifier, three channels, reverb, top black control panel, two inputs, eight black chickenhead knobs (v, drive, t, b, m, MV, r, p), channel select switches, effects loop, two button footswitch, gray/black vinyl covering, silver strand grille with George Benson "GB" logo badge on lower right corner, 18.75 in. tall, 23.5 in. wide, 10.5 in. deep, cover included, 43 lbs., mfg. 2012-present.

| MSR N/A | $900 | $575 - 675 | $295 - 350 | |

GB HOT ROD DELUXE 112 ENCLOSURE (NO. 223-1400) – 100W, 1-12 in. Jensen C12K speaker, extension speaker cabinet designed for use with the GB Hot Rod Deluxe, closed back, 23.5 in. wide, 18.75 in. tall, 10.5 in. deep, 30.5 lbs., includes cover and speaker cable, available in gray/black textured vinyl with a silver strand grille cloth, George Benson "GB" logo badge on lower right corner of grille, mfg. 2012-present.

| MSR N/A | $400 | $260 - 300 | $130 - 160 | |

GB TWIN REVERB (NO. 217-3400) – 85W, 2-12 in. Jensen Tornado speakers, 8 ohms, tube chassis, preamp: 3 X 12AX7, 2 X 12AT7, 1 X 12AY7, power: 4 X 6L6, solid-state rectifier, two channels, reverb, vibrato, front black control panel, four input jacks (two normal, two vibrato), bright and middle switches, 11 silver-top knobs (Norm: v, t, m, b, Vibrato: v, t, m, b, r, s, i), gray vinyl covering, silver sparkle grille, George Benson "GB" badge on lower right corner of front panel, cover included, 19.875 in. tall, 10.25 in. wide, 20.5 in. deep, 50 lbs., new 2016.

| MSR N/A | $1,700 | $1,100 - 1,275 | $550 - 675 | |

HOT ROD DEVILLE ML 212 (NO. 223-2400) – 60W, 2-12 in. Celestion V-Type speakers, tube chassis, preamp: 3 X 12AX7, power: 2 X 6L6, solid-state rectifier, two channels, reverb, top black control panel, two inputs, seven black chickenhead knobs (v1,v2, t, b, m, r, p), channel select switches, preamp out, power amp in, footswitch jack, standby switch, power switch, two button footswitch included, black vinyl covering, black/silver grille, cover included, 21 in. tall, 24.25 in. wide, 10.75 in.deep, 54 lbs., mfg. 2015-present.

| MSR N/A | $1,100 | $725 - 825 | $350 - 450 | |

RUMBLE BASS (NO. 081-2100-000) – 300W at 2 or 4 Ohms, head unit only, tubes, dual channels, brownface control panel, nine cream knobs, three inputs, cream Tolex covering, brown grille, mfg. 1994-98.

| | N/A | $1,100 - 1,400 | $1,100 - 1,350 | $2,400 |

Designed to run with a Rumble-Bass 410 Full-Range Speaker Enclosure (No. 081-3100-000), which has 4-10 in. special design cast-frame speakers, and can handle 600W. It was also designed for the Rumble-Bass 410 SUB Speaker enclosure (No. 081-3101-000) which has 4-10 in. special Fender design steel frame speakers, and can also handle 600W. They both last retailed for $800.

THE EDGE DELUXE (NO. 815-1700) – 12W, 1-12 in. Celestion Alnico Blue speaker, five tube chassis, preamp: 2 X 12AX7, power: 2 X 6V6, rectifier: 5Y3, two channels, top chrome control panel, four inputs (two inst., two mic.), three black chickenhead knobs (tone, inst. v, mic. v), standby switch, tweed covering, brown/gold grille cloth, The Edge badge on lower right corner of grille, 20.5 in. wide, 17 in. tall, 9.5 in. deep, 30.5 lbs., new 2016.

| MSR N/A | $2,400 | $1,550 - 1,800 | $775 - 950 | |

THE FENDER '57 AMP (NO. 815-0600) – 12W, 1-12 in. Celestion Alnico Blue speaker, five tube chassis, preamp: 2 X 12AX7 (or 12AY7), power: 2 X GT6V6, rectifier: 5Y3GT, two channels, top chrome control panel, four inputs (two inst., two mic.), three chrome Tele-style knobs with "57" engraved logo (tone, inst. v, mic. v), standby switch, solid maple cabinet with Black piano laquer finish, horizontally-split unique-shaped black/silver grille, cover included, 20 in. wide, 18.75 in. tall, 9.5 in. deep, 36 lbs., limited edition of 300, mfg. 2007 only.

| | N/A | $1,200 - 1,400 | $750 - 1,000 | $4,000 |

This model is based on the 1957 Fender Deluxe with Model 5E3 circuitry. Only 300 of these amps were produced and each one has a "One of only 300" badge on the rear panel. This amp is shipped with a Meguiar's Mist & Wipe Kit, leather collectors' portfolio with certificate of authenticity, designer's notes, factory photos, and other accessories.

TONE-MASTER (NO. 081-2000-000) – 100W into 4, 8, or 16 Ohms, head-unit only, tube chassis, preamp: 3 X 12AX7, dual channels, brownface control panel, one input, nine cream knobs (Ch. 1 v, t, b, m, Ch. 2 gain, t, b, m, v), FAT switches, effects loops, footswitch, one-button footswitch, cream Tolex covering, brown grille, 45 lbs., mfg. 1994-2002.

| | N/A | $1,000 - 1,200 | $650 - 800 | $2,300 |

MSR/NOTES	100%	EXCELLENT	AVERAGE	LAST MSR

The Fender '57 Amp
courtesy Fender

Two-Tone Amp
courtesy Dave Rogers/Dave's Guitar Shop

Vibro-King
courtesy Fender

* *Tone Master 212 Enclosure (No. 081-3000-000)* – 2-12 in. Celestion G1280 speakers, speaker cabinet for Tone Master heads, 13-ply birch cabinet, blonde Tolex covering, oxblood grille, 74 lbs., mfg. 1994-2002.

N/A	$350 - 425	$225 - 275	$700

Also available as the Tone Master 212 V30 (No. 081-3003-000) enclosure, which has 2-12 in. Celestion Vintage 30 speakers.

* *Tone Master 412 Enclosure (No. 081-3001-000)* – 4-12 in. Celestion Vintage 30 speakers, speaker cabinet for Tone Master heads, 13-ply birch cabinet, blonde Tolex covering, oxblood grille, 88 lbs., mfg. 1994-2002.

N/A	$425 - 500	$250 - 300	$900

Earlier models may have Greenback speakers.

TWO-TONE AMP (NO. 082-2000) – 15W, 1-10 in. and 1-12 in. Eminence speakers, preamp: 3 X 12AX7, power: 2 X EL-84, solid-state rectifier, single channel, reverb, top chrome control panel, single input, six black pointer knobs (r, MV, m, b, t, v,), FAT switch, single-button footswitch, solid pine cabinet, two-tone blonde and black Tolex covering, trapezoid-shaped speaker opening with wheat grille cloth, 23.5 in. wide, 20 in. tall, 10.5 in. deep, 51 lbs., limited production, each amp signed and dated by the Custom Shop Master Builder, mfg. 2001 only.

N/A	$850 - 1,000	$600 - 700	$1,650

VIBRO-KING (NO. 081-1000-000) – 60W into 2 Ohms, 3-10 in. Celestion speakers, tube chassis, preamp: 5 X 12AX7, reverb: 6V6, power: 2 X 6V6-GE Groove Tubes, reverb, vibrato, brownface control panel, two inputs, nine cream knobs (dwell, mix, tone, v, t, b, m, s, i), FAT switch, footswitch, cream Tolex covering, brown grille, 72 lbs., mfg. 1993-present.

MSR $5,000	$3,600	$2,100 - 2,500	$1,175 - 1,400

In 2003, they changed the covering to a black Tolex with silver grille and the model was changed to the Vibro King Custom. The Vibro King has been offered as a limited edition with various cabinet/covering choices such as 3-Tone Sunburst, Dark Stained Maple, or Alligator leather.

* *Vibro King 212 Enclosure (No. 081-3004-000/811-0000-010)* – speaker enclosure for the Vibro-King amp, handles 140W, 2-12 Celestion Vintage 30 speakers, 55 lbs., available in Black Tolex covering with a silver grille or Blonde Tolex covering with a brown grille (2010-2012), mfg. 1993-2012.

$500	$300 - 375	$175 - 225	$700

• Add $20 for cover.

ELECTRIC TUBE AMPS: MISC. MODELS

30 – 30W, 2-10 in. or 1-12 in. speakers, tube chassis, preamp: 4 X 7025, 2 X 12AT7, power: 2 X 6L6, 5U4 rectifier, two channels, reverb, front black control panel, two inputs, nine silver-top knobs (Ch. 1: v, t, b, Ch. 2: g, t, m, b, r, v), some knobs have push/pull switches, bright switches, two-button footswitch, black Tolex covering, silver or black grille, mfg. 1979-1982.

N/A	$450 - 550	$300 - 350	

In 1981, the grille cloth was changed to silver.

75 – 75W, 1-15 in. speaker, tube chassis, preamp: 4 X 7025, 2 X 12AT7, power: 2 X 6L6, solid-state rectifiers, two channels, reverb, front black control panel, two inputs, eight silver-top knobs (Ch. 1: g, t, m, b, Ch. 2: lead drive, r, lead level, MV), some knobs have push/pull switches, bright switches, black Tolex covering, silver grille, mfg. 1979-1982.

N/A	$500 - 650	$325 - 400	

In 1981, the grille cloth was changed to silver.

* *75 Piggy-Back* – similar to the 75 Combo, except in a separate head and cabinet unit that had either 1-15 in. or 4-10 in. speakers, mfg. 1979-1982.

Head & Cabinet	N/A	$600 - 700	$375 - 450	
Head Only	N/A	$300 - 375	$200 - 250	

140 – 135W, 4-12 in. speakers in a separate cab, tube chassis, preamp: 4 X 7025, 2 X 12AT7, power: 4 X 6L6, solid-state rectifier, two channels, reverb, front black control panel, two inputs, eight silver-top knobs (Ch. 1: g, t, m, b, Ch. 2: lead drive, r, lead level, MV), some knobs have push/pull switches, bright switches, black Tolex covering, silver grille, mfg. 1979-1982.

Head & Cabinet	N/A	$500 - 600	$300 - 350	
Head Only	N/A	$350 - 425	$200 - 250	

In 1981, the grille cloth was changed to silver.

MSR/NOTES	100%	EXCELLENT	AVERAGE	LAST MSR

75
courtesy Ferris Wheel Music

Bantam Bass
courtesy George Wells

Musicmaster Bass
courtesy Savage Audio

300PS – 300W, head-unit with a metal stand, 4-12 in. cabinet that is separate, tube chassis, preamp: 2 X 7025, 12AT7, 6V6, power: 4 X 6550, black control panel, two input jacks, 12 silver-top numbered knobs (v, t, m, b, p, 5-way equalizer, distortion, output), black Tolex covering, black foam grille, mfg. 1975-79.

N/A	$625 - 750	$450 - 525

This amp was also available as the 300PS Bass with a larger cabinet. This amp was offered through the release of the B-300, which is a solid state amp.

400 PS BASS – 435W, head-unit that has a metal stand, 18 in. horn cabinet separate from the head, tube chassis, preamp: 6 X 7025, 12AT7, power: 6 X 6550, black control panel, four input jacks (two bass, two normal), bass and bright switches, 11 numbered knobs (Bass: v, t, b, Norm: v, t, m, b, r, s, i, MV), three power output jacks, black Tolex covering, black foam grille, mfg. 1970-75.

N/A	$600 - 750	$425 - 500

The three output jacks boasted to have each 145W output, when you could get all the power out of one. There were three amplifers within the model and they all came together to drive the massive cabinet. This was Fender's response to the power race in bass amplifiers in the 1970s.

BANTAM BASS – 50W, Yamaha plastic cone non-circular speaker, tube chassis, preamp: 2 X 7025, 12AT7, power: 2 X 6L6, 5U4 rectifier, two channels (bass and normal), silverface control panel, four input jacks (two per channel), seven silver-top knobs (Norm: v, b, t, Vibrato: v, b, t, s, i, r), bright switches, black Tolex covering, silver grille, mfg. 1969-1971.

N/A	$500 - 600	$300 - 350

- **Subtract 50% for non-original speaker.**

The Bantam Bass was replaced by the Bassman Ten in 1972. This amp featured a very oddly-shaped speaker made by Yamaha (see picture). It is very rare to find a replacement speaker and working Bantam amps with original speakers are very rare in today's market.

K&F – 3W, 1-8 in. or 1-10 in. speaker, tube chassis, preamp: 6N7, power: 6V6, 5Y3 rectifier, no controls, gray crackle paint, corse mesh or cloth, mfg. 1945-46.

N/A	$850 - 1,000	$600 - 700

This amp was the first produced by Leo Fender. The K&F was meant for steel type guitars. Some models would have one volume knob. This model was found with two different sized speakers. This is an extremely rare amplifier.

MUSICMASTER BASS – 12W, 1-12 in. speaker, tube chassis preamp: 12AX7, power: 2 X 6V6GTA, silverface control panel, two black plastic knobs with silver skirts, (v, tone), black Tolex covering, silver grille, mfg. 1970-1982.

N/A	$400 - 500	$250 - 300

The Musicmaster is one of the earliest versions using a phase inverter. Around 1976, the nameplate lost the tail. In 1982, blackface was reintroduced for its final year of existence. This model was replaced by the Bassman 20. Later models may utilize 6AQ5A power tubes.

STUDIO BASS – 200W, 1-15 in. Electrovoice, tube chassis, preamp: 2 X 7025, 12AT7, 12AU7A, 12AX7A, power: 6 X 6L6, new blackface control panel, two inputs, 12 silver-top knobs (v, t, m, b, p, distortion, output level, five-way equalization), black Tolex covering, black grille, mfg. 1977-1980.

N/A	$375 - 450	$250 - 300

This amp combined the equalization system of the 300 PS with the Super Twin chassis.

WHITE – 3W, 1-8 in. speaker, tube chassis, preamp: 12AX7, power: 6V6, 5Y3 rectifier, top numbered control panel, two pointer knobs (v, tone), grey fabric covering, blue-black grille, mfg. 1955 only.

N/A	$850 - 1,000	$600 - 700

This was an amp produced by Leo Fender, but didn't bear the Fender name. The White was a student amp that came with a matching steel guitar, and was a tribute to Forest White.

MSR/NOTES	100%	EXCELLENT	AVERAGE	LAST MSR

ELECTRIC SS AMPS: FIRST SERIES (1966-1971)

Fender released its first solid-state series under CBS management in the summer of 1966. This series of amplifiers featured some of Fender's most popular tube amps and transformed them into solid-state versions. The first three models were the Dual Showman, Twin Reverb, and Bassman. A solid-state reverb unit and PA system were also introduced in this series. These amps were completely different than anything Fender had tried before and sported a silver control panel at a 45 degree angle, cylindrical flat-topped knobs, and aluminum trim around the speaker cabinets that would become standard for all Fender amps later on. These models had "Fender" spelled in black letters along the top of the grille and the words SOLID STATE printed in bold red letters. In 1967, Fender announced four new solid-state combos. These amps did not last long, and the entire line was discontinued in 1971.

Fender then began to start to experimenting with other solid-state ideas after the first series was discontinued. The Super Showman replaced the Dual Showman in 1969. This amp had many features including new technology with powered speakers. This was an amp that was designed for everyone in the band to use that same amp. The head had a built in E tuner, and a master volume the could control the combine the output of the three individual preamps. Fender used the idea of channel patching as well with the Super Showman. If only one person was using the amp, they could patch the channels together with short cords and use all the effects at the same time. Each speaker cabinet had a volume control on it. This amp had a lot of power, however, it was very expensive and very large. It only lasted for two years and was discontinued with the rest of the first series of solid-state amplifiers.

BASSMAN (SOLID-STATE) – 100W, 3-12 in. JBL speakers, piggy-back style, solid-state chassis, silver control panel, two inputs, four silver-top knobs (style, v, t, b), the style controlled the tone for four positions: Bass Boost 1, Bass Boost 2, Guitar Normal, and Guitar Bright, black Tolex covering, silver grille with aluminum trim, mfg. 1966-1971.

Bassman
courtesy Allen Swan/Steve Berge

Bassman
courtesy Allen Swan/Steve Berge

Bassman
courtesy Allen Swan/Steve Berge

	N/A	$375 - 475	$225 - 275	

DELUXE REVERB (SOLID-STATE) – 25W, 1-12 in. speaker, solid-state chassis, vibrato, reverb, dual channels, silver control panel, four inputs, two per channel, bright switches, nine silver-top knobs (Norm: v, t, b, Vibrato: v, t, b, s, i, r), black Tolex covering, silver grille with aluminum trim, mfg. 1967-69.

	N/A	$425 - 500	$275 - 325	

DUAL SHOWMAN (SOLID-STATE) – 100W, 2-15 in. JBL speakers, solid-state chassis, piggy-back style, two channels, normal and vibrato, silverface control panel, two inputs for each channel, bright switches, 11 silver-top knobs (Norm: style, v, t, b, Vibrato: style, v, t, b, s, i, r), the style control gives tone settings of pop/normal/CW-RR, black Tolex covering, silver grille with aluminum trim, mfg. 1966-68.

	N/A	$425 - 500	$250 - 300	

PRO REVERB (SOLID-STATE) – 50W, 2-12 in. speakers, solid-state chassis, two channels, vibrato and normal, four inputs, two per channel, ten silver-top control knobs (Norm: v, t, b, Vibrato: style, v, t, b, reverb, s, i), the style control switches to three tone settings: pop, normal, CW/RR, bright switches, black Tolex covering, silver grille, aluminum trim, mfg. 1967-69.

	N/A	$450 - 525	$300 - 350	

SUPER REVERB (SOLID-STATE) – 50W, 4-10 in. speakers, solid-state chassis, two channels, vibrato and normal, four inputs, two per channel, ten silver-top control knobs (Norm: v, t, b, Vibrato: style, v, t, b, reverb, s, i), the style control switches to three tone settings: pop, normal, CW/RR, bright switches, black Tolex covering, silver grille, aluminum trim, mfg. 1967-69.

	N/A	$425 - 500	$250 - 300	

SUPER SHOWMAN XFL-1000 – 140W, 4-12 in. speakers, solid state chassis (49 transistors and 19 diodes), reverb, vibrato, new dimension IV effect, black/aluminum control panel, three channels, six inputs, two per channel, 18 silver numbered knobs (Ch 1.: v, b, m, t, fuzz, Ch. 2.: v, b, m, t, dimension IV, Ch. 3: s, i, r, t, m, b, v, MV), black Tolex covering, silver grille, mfg. 1969-1971.

	N/A	$400 - 475	$250 - 300	

SUPER SHOWMAN XFL-2000 – similar to the Super Showman XFL-1000, except has 8-10 in. speakers, mfg. 1969-1971.

	N/A	$425 - 500	$250 - 325	

TWIN REVERB (SOLID-STATE) – 100W, 2-12 in. speakers mounted on top of each other, solid-state chassis, piggy-back style, two channels, normal and vibrato, silverface control panel, two inputs for each channel, bright switches, 11 silver-top knobs (Norm: style, v, t, b, Vibrato: style, v, t, b, s, i, r), the style control gives tone settings of pop/normal/CW-RR, black Tolex covering, silver grille with aluminum trim, mfg. 1966-68.

	N/A	$400 - 525	$275 - 325	

MSR/NOTES	100%	EXCELLENT	AVERAGE	LAST MSR

VIBROLUX REVERB (SOLID-STATE) – 35W, 2-10 in. speakers, solid-state chassis, reverb, vibrato, silver control panel, dual channels, four inputs, two per channel, bright switches, nine silver-top knobs (Norm: v, t, b, Vibrato: v, t, b, s, i, reverb), black Tolex covering, silver grille with aluminum trim, mfg. 1967-69.

N/A $375 - 475 $225 - 275

ELECTRIC SS AMPS: ZODIAC SERIES

The Zodiac series was designed after the first series of solid-state amps and were supposedly designed better and more reliable than the first models. There were four models in the series all named after Zodiac signs including the Libra, Capricorn, Scorpio, and the Taurus. These amps featured JBL speakers, alligator skin covering, and a new control panel. Other than that there were few changes beside cosmetics from the old amps. These amps were offered just under two years and very few of them were actually manufactured. They are very rare today, but hardly collectible. All models came with a remote footswitch for vibrato and reverb.

CAPRICORN – 105W, 3-12 in. JBL speakers, solid-state chassis (28 transistors, 13 diodes), two channels, reverb, vibrato, black/aluminum control panel, four inputs, two for each channel, bright switches, ten numbered black knobs with silver skirts (Norm: v, t, b, Vibrato: v, t, m, b, reverb, s, i), ground and power switch on front, optional casters, black alligator covering, silver grille, mfg. 1969-1971.

N/A $475 - 575 $300 - 350

LIBRA – 105W, 4-12 in. JBL speakers, solid-state chassis (28 transistors, 13 diodes), two channels, reverb, vibrato, black/aluminum control panel, four inputs, two for each channel, bright switches, ten numbered black knobs with silver skirts (Norm: v, t, b, Vibrato: v, t, m, b, reverb, s, i), ground and power switch on front, optional casters, black alligator covering, silver grille, mfg. 1969-1971.

N/A $475 - 575 $300 - 350

SCORPIO – 56W, 2-12 in. JBL speakers, solid-state chassis (26 transistors, 10 diodes), two channels, reverb, vibrato, black/aluminum control panel, four inputs, two for each channel, bright switches, ten numbered black knobs with silver skirts (Norm: v, t, b, Vibrato: v, t, m, b, reverb, s, i), ground and power switch on front, optional casters, black alligator covering, silver grille, mfg. 1969-1971.

Scorpio
courtesy John Beeson/The Music Shoppe   **Scorpio**
courtesy John Beeson/The Music Shoppe

N/A $475 - 575 $300 - 350

TAURUS – 42W, 2-10 in. JBL speakers, solid-state chassis (26 transistors, 10 diodes), two channels, reverb, vibrato, black/aluminum control panel, four inputs, two for each channel, bright switches, nine numbered black knobs with silver skirts (Norm: v, t, b, Vibrato: v, t, b, reverb, s, i), ground and power switch on front, optional casters, black alligator covering, silver grille, mfg. 1969-1971.

N/A $375 - 475 $250 - 300

ELECTRIC SS AMPS: SECOND SERIES (1981-1987)

Fender went ten years without a solid-state amp, after they discontinued the First-Series and Zodiac lines in 1971. In 1981, Fender started building small solid-state amps and snuck them in with the tube amps with little fanfare. The first two amps were the Harvard (MSR $189) and the Harvard Reverb (MSR $239), which were marketed for the student player and offered the amp with the new Fender Bullet guitar. When the Harvard solid-state amp was introduced, the tube Champ was available for the same price. In the early 1980s, you could get a fully-loaded solid-state Harvard for the same price of a basic Champ. The Harvard sold very well, and shortly after the Champ was switched to the Super Champ, and the entry line of Fender amplifiers have been solid-state ever since. At the same time a Bassman Compact amp was released and lasted until 1983. In 1982, Fender released a whole new line of solid-state amplifiers. These amplifiers were mixed right in with the tube amps for the 1983 catalog. These models included the Harvard Reverb II, Yale Reverb, Studio Lead, Stage Lead, the Montreux, London Reverb, and the Showman 112/212/115/210. Fender stopped producing these amps in 1985, but they were sold through 1987.

B-300 – 300W, head only, solid-state chassis, black control panel, 10 black knobs (v, b, low mid, mid, effects, 3-way equalizer, compressor), rack-mountable, built-in compressor, variable crossover, blanaced line out, no covering just a metal case, mfg. 1979-82.

N/A   N/A   N/A

This was actually Fender's first solid-state amp in almost 10 years. Even though it didn't mark the start of the second line, it was released before the Second Series, and it replaced the 300PS Bass. It was a good effort and sounded decent, but it was very expensive. With the deluxe bass enclosure along with 2-15 in. speakers it cost over $1,600! It was simply too much for the public at that time.

MSR/NOTES	100%	EXCELLENT	AVERAGE	LAST MSR

BASSMAN COMPACT – 50W, 1-15 in. speaker, solid state, chassis new blackface control panel, six silver-top knobs (v, t, m, b, compressor, MV), black Tolex covering, silver grille, mfg. 1981-84.

	N/A	$150 - 200	$95 - 120	

HARVARD (SOLID-STATE) – 20W, 1-10 in. speaker, solid-state chassis, new blackface control panel, two inputs, four black knobs (v, b, t, MV with distortion), black Tolex covering, silver grille, mfg. 1981-82.

	N/A	$120 - 150	$70 - 95	

* *Harvard Reverb (Solid-State)* – similar to the Harvard, except has reverb and reverb control, mfg. 1979-1982.

	N/A	$135 - 175	$85 - 110	

HARVARD REVERB II – 20W, 1-10 in. speaker, solid-state chassis, new blackface control panel, seven silver-top knobs (v, g, MV, t, m, b, r), black Tolex covering, silver grille, mfg. 1983-85.

	N/A	$125 - 175	$75 - 100	

LONDON REVERB HEAD – 100W, head-unit only, solid-state chassis, reverb, two channels, front new black control panel, single input, 12 silver-top knobs (Ch. 1: v, t, b, Ch. 2: v, g, MV, t, mid1, mid2, b, r1, r2), 5-band EQ, black Tolex covering, silver grille, mfg. 1983-85.

	N/A	$250 - 300	$135 - 175	

* *London Reverb 112 Combo* – similar to the London Reverb, except has 1-12 in. speaker, mfg. 1983-85.

	N/A	$300 - 375	$175 - 225	

* *London Reverb 210 Combo* – similar to the London Reverb, except has 2-10 in. speakers, mfg. 1983-85.

	N/A	$325 - 400	$200 - 250	

MONTREUX – 100W, 1-12 in. speaker, solid-state chassis, new black control panel, 12 silver-top knobs (Ch. 1: v, t, b, Ch. 2: v, g, MV, t, mid 1, mid 2, b, r1, r2), black Tolex covering, silver grille, mfg. 1983-85.

	N/A	$300 - 375	$175 - 225	

SHOWMAN 112/212/115/210 – 200W, 1-12 in., 2-12 in., 1-15 in. or 2-10 in. speakers, the model number (112) refers to 1-12 in. speaker, etc., solid-state chassis, new blackface control panel, 12 silver-top knobs (Ch. 1: v, t, b, Ch. 2: v, g, MV, t, mid1, mid2, b, r1, r2), 5-way equlizer, black Tolex covering, silver grille, mfg. 1983-85.

112	N/A	$375 - 450	$225 - 275	
210	N/A	$400 - 475	$250 - 300	
115	N/A	$400 - 475	$250 - 300	
212	N/A	$425 - 525	$275 - 325	

STAGE LEAD – 100W, 1-12 in. speaker, solid-state chassis, reverb, new black control panel, two inputs, 11 silver-top knobs (Ch. 1: v, t, m, b, Ch. 2: v, g, MV, t, m, b, r), black Tolex covering, silver grille, mfg. 1983-85.

	N/A	$225 - 275	$135 - 175	

* *Stage Lead II* – similar to the Stage Lead, except has 2-12 in. speakers, mfg. 1983-85.

	N/A	$250 - 300	$150 - 200	

STUDIO LEAD – 50W, 1-12 in. speaker, solid-state chassis, new blackface control panel, dual channels, 11 silver-top knobs, (Ch. 1: v, t, m, b, Ch. 2: v, g, MV, t, m, b, r), black Tolex covering, silver grille, mfg. 1983-85.

	N/A	$225 - 275	$135 - 175	

YALE REVERB – 50W, 1-12 in. speaker, solid-state chassis, new blackface control panel, seven silver-top knobs (v, g, MV, t, m, b, r), black Tolex covering, silver grille, mfg. 1982-85.

	N/A	$275 - 325	$140 - 175	

ELECTRIC SS AMPS: SIDEKICK SERIES (1983-1992)

The Sidekick series are entry-level instruments and their prices reflect that. Most of these amps were produced in Japan at Fender Japan. Squier amps were also produced in Japan. This is why these amps could have either Fender or Squier on the grille. A few of these amps may have been built in Taiwan. For Squier amps see the Squier section of the *Blue Book of Guitar Amplifiers*.

SIDEKICK 10 – 10W, 1-8 in. speaker, solid-state chassis, front black control panel, single input, five black knobs (v, MV, t, m, b), black Tolex covering, silver grille, mfg. 1983-85.

	N/A	$40 - 60	$25 - 35	

SIDEKICK 15R (NO. 023-4100) – 15W, 1-8 in. speaker, solid-state chassis, reverb, front black control panel, seven black knobs (v, g, MV, t, m, b, r), power shift switch, black Tolex covering, silver grille, mfg. 1986-1992.

	N/A	$60 - 80	$30 - 40	

SIDEKICK 20 CHORUS (NO. 023-2600) – 20W (2 X 10W Stereo), 2-8 in. speakers, solid-state chassis, reverb, front black control panel, ten red knobs (OD, g, v, t, m, b, p, chorus rate, chorus depth), overdrive switch, effects loop, black Tolex covering, silver grille, mfg. 1991-92.

	N/A	$95 - 120	$50 - 75	

MSR/NOTES	100%	EXCELLENT	AVERAGE	LAST MSR

SIDEKICK 20 REVERB – 20W, 1-10 in. speaker, solid-state chassis, reverb, front black control panel, single input, six black knobs (v, MV, t, m, b, r), black Tolex covering, silver grille, mfg. 1983-85.

	N/A	$70 - 90	$45 - 55	

SIDEKICK 25R (NO. 023-4200) – 25W, 1-10 in. speaker, solid-state chassis, reverb, front black control panel, eight black knobs (v, g, MV, t, m, b, p, r), power shift switch, effects loop, black Tolex covering, silver grille, mfg. 1986-1992.

	N/A	$75 - 100	$50 - 65	

This model may also be listed as the Squier Sidekick 25R instead of Fender.

SIDEKICK 30 REVERB – 30W, 1-12 in. speaker, solid-state chassis, reverb, front black control panel, single input, seven black knobs (v, MV, t, m, b, p, r), black Tolex covering, silver grille, mfg. 1983-85.

	N/A	$80 - 100	$45 - 60	

SIDEKICK 35R (NO. 023-4300) – 35W, 1-12 in. speaker, solid-state chassis, reverb, front black control panel, eight black knobs (v, g, MV, t, m, b, p, r), power shift switch, effects loop, black Tolex covering, silver grille, mfg. 1986-1992.

	N/A	$95 - 120	$50 - 75	

This model may also be listed as the Squier Sidekick 35R instead of Fender.

SIDEKICK 65 REVERB – 65W, 1-12 in. speaker, solid-state chassis, reverb, two channels, front black control panel, single input, 11 black knobs (Ch. 1: v, t, b, Ch. 2: v, g, MV, t, m, b, p, r), black Tolex covering, silver grille, mfg. 1986-88.

	N/A	$100 - 135	$60 - 80	

SIDEKICK BASS (NO. 023-2000) – 30W, 1-10 in. speaker, solid-state, front black control panel, five black knobs (v, MV, t, m, b), black Tolex covering, silver grille, mfg. 1988-1992.

	N/A	$60 - 80	$40 - 50	

SIDEKICK BASS 30 – 30W, 1-12 in. speaker, solid-state, front black control panel, six black-top knobs (v, MV, t, m, b, p), black Tolex covering, silver grille, mfg. 1983-85.

	N/A	$75 - 95	$50 - 60	

SIDEKICK BASS 35 – 35W, 1-12 in. speaker, solid-state, front black control panel, six black-top knobs (g, t, m, freq, b, MV), black Tolex covering, silver grille, mfg. 1986-89.

	N/A	$75 - 95	$50 - 60	

SIDEKICK BASS 50 – 50W, 1-15 in. speaker, solid-state, front black control panel, six black-top knobs (v, MV, t, m, b, p), black Tolex covering, silver grille, mfg. 1983-85.

	N/A	$95 - 120	$50 - 75	

SIDEKICK BASS 65 – 65W, 1-15 in. speaker, solid-state, front black control panel, six black-top knobs (g, t, m, freq, b, MV), black Tolex covering, silver grille, mfg. 1986-89.

	N/A	$95 - 120	$50 - 75	

SIDEKICK BASS 100/100 BASS HEAD (NO. 023-1800) – 100W, piggy-back unit, 1-15 in. Eminence speaker, solid-state, front black control panel, six black-top knobs (g, v, m, t, m, b), limiter, effects loop, black Tolex covering, silver grille, mfg. 1986-1993.

Head & Cab	N/A	$120 - 150	$75 - 95	
Head Only	N/A	$70 - 90	$40 - 50	

SIDEKICK BASSMAN/BASSMAN 60 (NO. 023-2400) – 60W, 1-15 in. speaker, solid-state chassis, front black control panel, six black knobs (v, MV, t, m, b, limiter), effects loop, black Tolex covering, silver grille, mfg. 1989-1992.

	N/A	$95 - 120	$50 - 75	

SIDEKICK SWITCHER – 35W, 1-12 in. speaker, solid-state chassis, reverb, two switchable channels, front black control panel, 11 black knobs (Ch. 1: v, t, b, Ch. 2: v, g, MV, t, b, m, p, r), black Tolex covering, silver grille, mfg. 1988-89.

	N/A	$95 - 120	$50 - 75	

This model may have Squier for nameplate instead of Fender.

ELECTRIC SS AMPS: THIRD/STANDARD SERIES (1988-2001)

After CBS sold to Schultz and crew in 1985, Fender Musical Instrument Corporation (FMIC), took over without an amp manufacturing facility. Fender then used up their old-stock and started to import some solid-state amps including the Squier 15 and Sidekicks. By 1987, FMIC started to release a few new models, which were American bass BXR amps. In 1988 FMIC released an entire new line of American solid-state amps, which unofficially became Fender's third line of solid-state products. This new line of amps used names from vintage tube models, like the Deluxe-85, Princeton Chorus, and Pro-185, but were nothing like the amps of the same name. In 1989, gray covered amps were introduced with names like the M-80, and Power Chorus. Other amps made their debut in 1990 in gray with the H.O.T., J.A.M.,and the R.A.D.,which were geared toward younger students. By 1992, there were over 25 models in the solid-state line. By this time certain models were phased out, but the whole line was going strong. There are now all kinds of models and variations in this line. Finally after over 20 years of trial and error, Fender has stabilized the solid-state market.

FENDER, cont.

F 298

MSR/NOTES	100%	EXCELLENT	AVERAGE	LAST MSR

BRONCO (NO. 022-3104-000) – 15W, 1-8 in. speaker, top chrome control panel, single input, six black chickenhead knobs (v1, g, v2, t, m, b), overdrive switch, headphone jack, tweed covering, brown grille, 14 lbs., mfg. 1994-2001.

| | N/A | $100 - 125 | $65 - 85 | $230 |

BULLET (NO. 022-6705-000) – 15W, 1-8 in. speaker, solid-state chassis, front black control panel, single input, six black knobs (v1, g, v2, t, m, b), overdrive switch, headphone jack, black Tolex covering, silver grille, 15 lbs., mfg. 1994-99.

| | N/A | $40 - 60 | $20 - 30 | $170 |

* *Bullet Reverb (No. 022-6706-000)* – similar to the Bullet, except has reverb and reverb knob, mfg. 1994-2001.

| | N/A | $40 - 60 | $20 - 30 | |

CHAMPION 110 (NO. 022-6703-000) – 25W, 1-10 in. speaker, solid-state chassis, two selectable channels, reverb, black control panel, single input, seven black knobs (v, g, v, t, m, b, r), black Tolex covering. silver grille, 25 lbs., mfg. 1993-97.

| | N/A | $100 - 120 | $70 - 85 | |

DELUXE 85 (NO. 022-5100) – 85W, 1-12 in. speaker, solid-state, dual channels, 11 red knobs (Ch 1: v, t, b, Ch. 2: g, b, m, t, limiter, p, r, v), black Tolex covering, black grille, mfg. 1988-1993.

| | N/A | $250 - 300 | $140 - 175 | |

* *85 (No. 022-5000)* – similar to the Deluxe 85, except only has nine red knobs and only one channel, knobs include (v, t, m, b, r, gain, limiter, p, v), mfg. 1988-1992.

| | N/A | $200 - 250 | $120 - 150 | |

DELUXE 112 (NO. 022-6702-000) – 65W, 1-12 in. speaker, solid-state chassis, two selectable channels, reverb, front black control panel, two inputs, ten knobs (Ch. 1: v, t, m, b, g, contour, Ch. 2: v, t, b, r), effects loop, headphone jack, 2-button footswitch, black Tolex covering, silver grille, mfg. 1992-94.

| | N/A | $175 - 225 | $120 - 150 | $430 |

* *Deluxe 112 Plus (No. 022-6702-010)* – similar to the Deluxe 112, except has 90W output, 33 lbs., mfg. 1995-99.

| | N/A | $200 - 250 | $140 - 175 | $490 |

POWER CHORUS (U.S. NO. 022-5800) – 130W (2 X 65W Stereo), 2-12 in. speakers, two channels, reverb, chorus, front black control panel, two inputs, 15 red knobs (Ch. 1: v, t, m, b, Ch. 2: g, boost, t, m, b, contour, p, v, r, chorus rate, chorus depth), effects loop, four-button footswitch, black Tolex covering, black grille, mfg. 1991-92.

| | N/A | $200 - 250 | $140 - 175 | |

This model evolved into the Ulitmate Chorus in 1993.

PRINCETON 112 (NO. 022-6704-000) – 35W, 1-12 in. speaker, solid-state chassis, two selectable channels, reverb, front black control panel, two inputs, ten knobs (Ch. 1: v, t, m, b, g, contour, Ch. 2: v, t, b, r), effects loop, headphone jack, footswitch jack, black Tolex covering, silver grille, mfg. 1993-94.

| | N/A | $150 - 200 | $75 - 100 | $340 |

* *Princeton 112 Plus (No. 022-6704-010)* – similar to the Princeton 112, except has 65W output, 28 lbs., mfg. 1995-99.

| | N/A | $150 - 200 | $95 - 120 | $370 |

PRINCETON STEREO CHORUS (NO. 022-5700-010) – 50W, (2 X 25W Stereo), 2-10 in. speakers, solid-state chassis, reverb, chorus, front black control panel, two inputs, 11 black knobs (v, t, m, b, r, g, limiter, presence, v, chorus rate, chorus depth), stereo and mono effects loop, two-button footswitch, black Tolex covering, silver grille, 39 lbs., mfg. 1988-2001.

courtesy Zachary R. Fjestad

courtesy Zachary R. Fjestad

| 1988-1992 | N/A | $200 - 250 | $120 - 150 | |
| 1993-2001 | N/A | $200 - 250 | $120 - 150 | $600 |

MSR/NOTES	100%	EXCELLENT	AVERAGE	LAST MSR

PRO 185 (NO. 022-5600-010) – 160W, 2-12 in. speakers, solid-state chassis, reverb, front black control panel, two inputs, 14 red knobs (Ch. 1: v, t, m, b, Ch. 2: g, boost, t, m, b, contour, p, v, r), mid boost, tilt button, adjustable effects loop, 3-button footswitch, black Tolex covering, black grille, mfg. 1989-1994.

	N/A	$275 - 325	$150 - 200	$690

In 1993, a silver grille replaced the black one and black knobs replaced the red ones.

STAGE 112 SE (NO. 022-6700-000) – 160W, 1-12 in. speaker, solid-state chassis, two selectable channels, reverb, front black control panel, two inputs, ten knobs (Ch. 1: v, t, m, b, g, contour, Ch. 2: v, t, b, r), effects loop, headphone jack, 2-button footswitch, black Tolex covering, silver grille, 45 lbs., mfg. 1993-99.

	N/A	$225 - 275	$140 - 175	

STAGE 185 (NO. 022-5200-000) – 160W, 1-12 in. speaker, solid-state chassis, reverb, front black control panel, two inputs, 12 red knobs (Ch. 1: v, t, b, Ch. 2: g, boost, t, m, b, contour, p, v, r), mid boost, tilt button, adjustable effects loop, 3-button footswitch, black Tolex covering, black grille, mfg. 1989-1992.

	N/A	$250 - 300	$140 - 175	

This model was replaced by the Stage 112 SE.

ULTRA CHORUS/ULTIMATE CHORUS (NO. 022-6701-000/010) – 130W (2 X 65W Stereo), 2-12 in. speakers, two channels, reverb, chorus, front black control panel, two inputs, 14 black knobs (Ch. 1: v, t, m, b, r Ch. 2: g, contour, v, t, m, b, r, chorus rate, chorus depth, mono and stereo effects loop, two-button footswitch, black Tolex covering, black grille, 48 lbs., mfg. 1993-2001.

	N/A	$200 - 250	$140 - 175	$730

This model started out as the Ultra Chorus but was changed to the Ultimate Chorus in 1995.

X-15 (NO. 022-1100-000) – 15W, 1-8 in. speaker, solid-state chassis, front black control panel, five red knobs (g, v, t, b, contour), headphone jack, black Tolex covering, black grille, mfg. 1991-93.

	N/A	$50 - 70	$30 - 40	$140

ELECTRIC SS AMPS: M-80, RAD, HOT, & JAM SERIES

This series was introduced in 1989 and was first produced in early 1990. The most identifying feature about this series was the gray carpet covering on them. Fender hadn't had any covering other than Tolex in over 20 years. The M-80 amps were discontinued by 1995. The RAD/JAM/HOT models were phased out in 1997 and replaced by the Frontman Series.

H.O.T. (NO. 022-6100-010) – 25W, 1-10 in. speaker, solid-state chassis, reverb, front black control panel, two inputs, four preprogrammed sounds, three black knobs (contour, v, r), tape/CD input, effects loop, headphone jack, gray carpet covering, black grille, 23 lbs., mfg. 1990-96.

	N/A	$75 - 100	$45 - 60	$280

In 1992, the gray carpet was changed to black and other minor cosmetic changes appeared. In 1996, the covering was changed to black Tolex.

J.A.M. (NO. 022-6200-010) – 25W, 1-12 in. speaker, solid-state chassis, reverb, chorus, front black control panel, two inputs, four preprogrammed sounds, three black knobs (contour, v, r, chorus rate, chorus depth), tape/CD input, effects loop, headphone jack, gray carpet covering, black grille, 27 lbs., mfg. 1990-96.

	N/A	$65 - 85	$40 - 55	$330

In 1992, the gray carpet was changed to black and other minor cosmetic changes appeared. In 1996, the covering was changed to black Tolex.

M-80 (NO. 022-5900-010) – 90W, 1-12 in. speaker combo, solid-state chassis, two switchable channels, front black control panel, two inputs, nine red knobs (Ch. 1: v, t, m, b, Ch. 2: v, g, c, p, r), effects loop, headphone jack, one-button footswitch, gray carpet or black Tolex covering, black grille, mfg. 1990-94.

	N/A	$175 - 225	$110 - 140	$470

This model was available with either the carpet or Tolex before 1992. In 1992, black covering or Tolex replaced the gray carpet and black knobs replaced the red ones.

* **M-80 Head (No. 022-5907-010)** – similar to the M-80, except is in head-unit only, mfg. 1990-94.

	N/A	$150 - 200	$95 - 120	$470

* **M-80 Pro (No. 022-5909-010)** – similar to the M-80, except is in a rack-mount unit, the unit is mounted in a four-space rack mount cabinet, with three spaces left for other units, mfg. 1990-93.

	N/A	$150 - 200	$95 - 120	$460

* **M-80 Pre Amp (No. 022-5901-000)** – similar to the M-80, except is the pre-amp version only, mfg. 1992-93.

	N/A	$120 - 150	$70 - 95	$300

M-80 BASS (NO. 022-4200-010) – 160W, 1-15 in. speaker, solid-state chassis, front black control panel, two inputs, six red knobs (v, t, m, b, chorus rate, chorus depth), effects loop, gray carpet covering, black grille, mfg. 1991-94.

	N/A	$175 - 225	$120 - 150	$620

MSR/NOTES	100%	EXCELLENT	AVERAGE	LAST MSR

* M-80 Bass Head (No. 022-4207-010) – similar to the M-80 Bass, except in head-unit only, mfg. 1991-94.

| | N/A | $150 - 200 | $95 - 120 | $500 |

M-80 CHORUS (NO. 022-5905-010) – 130W (2 X 65W Stereo), 2-12 in. speakers, solid-state chassis, reverb, chorus, two selectable channels, front black control panel, two inputs, 11 red knobs (Ch. 1: v, b, t, m, Ch. 2: v, g, c, p, r, chorus rate, chorus depth), effects loop, headphone jack, two-button footswitch, gray carpet or Tolex covering, black grille, mfg. 1990-94.

| | N/A | $225 - 275 | $140 - 175 | $720 |

This model was available with either the carpet or Tolex before 1992. In 1992, black covering or Tolex replaced the gray carpet and black knobs replaced the red ones.

* M-80 Chorus Head (No. 022-5908-010) – similar to the M-80 Chorus, except in head-unit only, mfg. 1990-94.

| | N/A | $175 - 225 | $110 - 140 | $620 |

R.A.D. (NO. 022-6000-010) – 20W, 1-8 in. speaker, solid-state chassis, front black control panel, two inputs, four preprogrammed sounds, two black knobs (contour, v), tape/CD input, effects loop, headphone jack, gray carpet covering, black grille, 20 lbs., mfg. 1990-96.

| | N/A | $60 - 80 | $35 - 50 | $200 |

In 1992, the gray carpet was changed to black and other minor cosmetic changes appeared. In 1996, the covering was changed to black Tolex.

R.A.D. BASS (NO. 022-4300-010) – 25W, 1-10 in. speaker, solid-state chassis, front black control panel, two inputs, four red knobs (v, l, m, h), tape/CD input, effects loop, headphone jack, gray carpet covering, black grille, mfg. 1992-94.

| | N/A | $60 - 80 | $40 - 50 | $280 |

In 1992, the gray carpet was changed to black and black knobs were introduced. This model was changed to the BXR25 in 1995.

ELECTRIC SS AMPS: AUTOMATIC SERIES

These amps can be classified as modeling amps in the most basic way. They each have five programmed sounds that are of Fender vintage. However, instead of listing specific amp models such as a Deluxe Reverb '65, they just have pictures of what different sounds would sound like.

AUTOMATIC SE (NO. 022-6400-000) – 25W, 1-12 in. speaker, solid-state chassis, five programmed sounds classic Fender sound, front black control panel, single input, seven white pushbuttons, five black knobs (v, t, b, r, chorus), tape/CD inputs, footswitch, black Tolex covering, silver grille, 28 lbs., mfg. 1998-99.

| | N/A | $100 - 125 | $65 - 85 | $300 |

• Add $25 for footswitch.

AUTOMATIC GT (NO. 022-6300-000) – 25W, 1-12 in. speaker, solid-state chassis, five programmed sounds Born To Rock Hard, front silver control panel, single input, seven white pushbuttons, five black knobs (v, t, b, r, chorus), tape/CD inputs, footswitch, black Tolex covering, black grille, 28 lbs., mfg. 1998-99.

| | N/A | $125 - 175 | $75 - 100 | $340 |

• Add $25 for footswitch.

ELECTRIC SS AMPS: CHAMPION SERIES

Champion 20 Combo
courtesy Fender

Champion 40 Combo
courtesy Fender

Champion 100 Combo
courtesy Fender

CHAMPION 20 COMBO – 20W, 1-8 in. speaker, guitar combo, solid-state chassis, single channel, front black control panel, single input, seven black knobs (g, v, voice, t, b, effect level, effect selector) tap tempo button, 1/8 in. stereo aux. input, 1/8 in. headphone jack, power switch, black textured vinyl covering, silver grille cloth, 13.75 in. wide, 12.75 in. tall, 7.5 in. deep, 12 lbs., mfg. 2013-present.

| MSR N/A | $100 | $65 - 75 | $35 - 40 | |

CHAMPION 40 COMBO – 40W, 1-12 in. speaker, guitar combo, solid-state chassis, dual channel, front black control panel, single input, eight black knobs (V1, g, V2, voice, t, b, effect level, effect selector), footswitch jack, tap tempo button, 1/8 in. stereo aux. input, 1/8 in. headphone jack, power switch, black textured vinyl covering, silver grille cloth, 17.25 in. wide, 17.25 in. tall, 9 in. deep, 19 lbs., mfg. 2013-present.

| MSR N/A | $180 | $115 - 135 | $60 - 70 | |

MSR/NOTES	100%	EXCELLENT	AVERAGE	LAST MSR

CHAMPION 100 COMBO – 100W, 2-12 in. speakers, guitar combo, solid-state chassis, dual channel, front black control panel, single input, 13 black knobs (Ch. 1: v, t, b, effect level, effect selector, Ch. 2: g, v, voice, t, m, b, effect level, effect selector), footswitch jack, tap tempo button for each channel, channel select button, effects loop, 1/8 in. stereo aux. input, 1/8 in. headphone jack, power switch, black textured vinyl covering, silver grille cloth, 26 in. wide, 19 in. tall, 10.25 in. deep, 40 lbs., mfg. 2013-present.

| MSR N/A | $350 | $230 - 265 | $115 - 140 | |

ELECTRIC SS AMPS: CYBER-TWIN SERIES

Cyber-Champ
courtesy Fender

Cyber-Deluxe
courtesy Fender

CYBER-CHAMP (NO. 229-0300-000) – 65W, 1-12 in. Celestion G12T-100 speaker, 21 presets, digital tuner, programmable noise gate and compressor, new blackface control panel, one input, nine silver-top knobs (g, v, t, m, b, MV, r, mod f/x), black Tolex covering, silver grille, mfg. 2003-05.

| | N/A | $200 - 250 | $135 - 165 | $640 |

- **Add $150 for the Cyber Foot Controller.**

CYBER-DELUXE (NO. 022-9001-000) – 65W, 1-12 in.Celestion G12T-100 speaker, 64 presets, 16 reverbs, 16 modulation effects, 16 delay types, digital tuner, programmable noise gate and compressor, new blackface control panel, one input, fourteen silver-top knobs (trim, g, v, t, m, b, MV, r, mod f/x, delay, amp type, and three others for digital processing), four-button footswitch, black Tolex covering, silver grille, mfg. 2002-05.

| | N/A | $350 - 425 | $200 - 250 | $1,000 |

ELECTRIC SS AMPS: DYNA-TOUCH SERIES (1999-2006)

The Dyna-Touch series were introduced in summer, 1999. These amps replaced the Standard Series of solid-state amplifiers. In 2002, Fender introduced the Dyna-Touch Plus series with Digital Signal Processing (DSP). DSP are hand-crafted Fender sounds that are digitally produced in the amplifier. Effects may include reverb, delay, chorus, flange, tremolo, etc. In 2004, they revamped the Dyna-Touch series again to produce the Dyna-Touch III Series. These amps are based off the models before but have different electronics and digital tuners on the higher models. The grille was also changed to a darker gray. The Dyna-Touch series has used the same model names through the changes, but have made minor refinements to each one.

- **Add $20 for cover on any amp for Dyna-Touch series.**

BULLET REVERB (NO. 022-6706-049) – 15W, 1-8" speaker, solid-state chassis, two selectable channels, reverb, front black control panel, single input, seven silver-top knobs (v, g, v, t, m, b, r), headphone jack, external speaker jack, black vinyl covering, silver grille, 15 lbs., mfg. 1999-2002.

| | N/A | $50 - 70 | $30 - 40 | $200 |

BULLET 15 DSP (NO. 22-67700-23) – 15W, 1-8 in.speaker, solid-state chassis, DSP effects, blackface control panel, seven black knobs (v, g, v, t, m, b, effects), tape/CD inputs, headphone jack, black vinyl covering, silver grille, 15 lbs., mfg. summer 2002-2004.

| | N/A | $75 - 100 | $40 - 60 | $229 |

BULLET 150 (NO. 236-7700-033) – 15W, 1-8 in. speaker, solid-state chassis, DSP effects, blackface control panel, seven black knobs (v, g, v, t, m, b, effects), tape/CD inputs, headphone jack, black vinyl covering, dark gray grille, mfg. summer 2004-05.

| | N/A | $75 - 100 | $40 - 60 | $229 |

CHAMPION 30 (NO. 022-6703-010) – 30W, 1-10 in. speaker, solid-state chassis, two switchable channels, reverb, front black control panel, two inputs, seven silver-top knobs (v, g, v, t, m, b, r), external speaker jack, black vinyl covering, silver grille, 25 lbs., mfg. 1999-2002.

| | N/A | $75 - 100 | $40 - 60 | $310 |

CHAMPION 30 DSP (NO. 22-67300-020) – 30W, 1-10 in. speaker, solid-state chassis, two switchable channels, DSP effects, front black control panel, eight black knobs (v, g, v, t, m, b, FX level, FX select), black vinyl covering, silver grille, 25 lbs., mfg. summer 2002-04.

| | N/A | $75 - 100 | $40 - 60 | $329 |

- **Add $30 for footswitch.**

CHAMPION 300 (NO. 236-7300-030) – 30W, 1-10 in. speaker, solid-state chassis, two switchable channels, DSP effects, front black control panel, eight silver top knobs (v, g, v, t, m, b, FX level, FX select), black vinyl covering, dark gray grille, 25 lbs., mfg. summer 2004-06.

| | N/A | $120 - 150 | $70 - 95 | $329 |

- **Add $30 for footswitch.**

MSR/NOTES	100%	EXCELLENT	AVERAGE	LAST MSR

Champion 30
courtesy Fender

Deluxe 900
courtesy Fender

Princeton 650
courtesy Fender

DELUXE 90 (NO. 022-6702-020) – 90W, 1-12 in. Celestion speaker, solid-state chassis, three selectable channels, reverb, front black control panel, two inputs, 10 silver-top knobs (Ch. 1: v, t, m, b, Ch. 2 & 3: drive, v, t, m, b, r), effects loop, two-button footswitch, black vinyl covering, silver grille, 33 lbs., mfg. 1999-2002.

	N/A	$175 - 225	$100 - 125	$570

DELUXE 90 DSP (NO. 22-67200-030) – 90W, 1-12 in. Celestion speaker, solid-state chassis, three switchable channels, DSP effects, front blackcontrol panel, two inputs, 12 black knobs (Ch. 1: v, t, m, b, Ch. 2 & 3: drive, v, t, m, b, FX level, FX select, FX time/rate), three-button footswitch, black vinyl covering, silver grille, 33 lbs., mfg. summer 2002-04.

	N/A	$200 - 250	$125 - 150	$571

DELUXE 900 (NO. 236-7200-040) – 90W, 1-12 in. Celestion speaker, solid-state chassis, three switchable channels, DSP effects, front black control panel, single input, nine silver-top and three black knobs (Ch. 1: v, t, m, b, Ch. 2: drive, v, Ch. 3: drive, v, t, m, b, FX level, FX select, FX time/rate), digital tuner, three-button footswitch, black vinyl covering, dark gray grille, 37 lbs., mfg. summer 2004-06.

	N/A	$250 - 300	$150 - 200	$670

PRINCETON 65 (NO. 022-6704-020) – 65W, 1-12 in. speaker, solid-state chassis, reverb, two switchable channels, front black control panel, two inputs, nine silver-top knobs (Ch.1: v, t, b, Ch. 2: level, v, t, m, b, r), effects loop, black vinyl covering, silver grille, 28 lbs., mfg. 1999-2002.

	N/A	$150 - 200	$95 - 120	$420

PRINCETON 65 DSP (NO. 22-67400-030) – 65W, 1-12 in. speaker, solid-state chassis, two switchable channels, DSP effects, front black control panel, two inputs, 10 silver-top knobs (Ch.1: v, t, b, Ch. 2: level, v, t, m, b, FX level, FX select), effects loop, black vinyl covering, silver grille, 28 lbs., mfg. summer 2002-04.

	N/A	$175 - 225	$120 - 150	$480

- Add $40 for footswitch.

PRINCETON 650 (NO. 236-7400-040) – 65W, 1-12 in. Celestion speaker, solid-state chassis, two switchable channels, DSP effects, front black control panel, two inputs, eight silver-top and three black knobs (Ch.1: v, t, b, Ch. 2: d, v, t, m, b, FX level, FX select, FX time/rate), digital tuner, effects loop, black vinyl covering, silver grille, 28 lbs., mfg. summer 2004-06.

	N/A	$150 - 200	$100 - 125	$570

- Add $40 for footswitch.

PRINCETON CHORUS DSP (NO. 022-5700-020) – 50W (2 X 25W stereo), 2-10 in. speakers, solid-state chassis, two channels, DSP effects, front black control panel, two inputs, 13 black knobs (v, g, limiter, p, v, t, m, b, r level, r type, chorus level, chorus type, chorus rate), three-button footswitch, black vinyl covering, silver grille, 48 lbs., mfg. 1999-2002.

	N/A	$200 - 250	$120 - 150	$720

STAGE 100 (NO. 022-6700-010) – 100W, 1-12 in. Celestion G12T-100 speaker, solid-state chassis, three channels, reverb, front black control panel, two inputs, 11 silver-top knobs (Ch. 1: v, t, m, b, r, Ch. 2: drive, v, t, m, b, r), effects loop, two-button footswitch, black vinyl covering, silver grille, 42 lbs., mfg. 1999-2002.

	N/A	$275 - 325	$150 - 200	$650

Stage 100 Head (No. 022-6900-000) – similar to the Stage 100 except is the head unit only, 24 lbs., mfg. 2000-02.

	N/A	$200 - 250	$110 - 140	$580

STAGE 100 DSP (NO. 22-67000-020) – 100W, 1-12 in. Celestion G12T-100 speaker, solid-state chassis, DSP effects, three channels, reverb, front black control panel, single input, 14 black knobs (Ch. 1: v, t, m, b, Ch. 2 & 3: drive, v, t, m, b, r, r, FX level), mid/contour button, effects loop, black vinyl covering, silver grille, 42 lbs., mfg. summer 2002-04.

	N/A	$275 - 325	$150 - 200	$700

Stage 100 Head DSP (No. 22-69000-010) – similar to the Stage 100 except is the head unit only, 24 lbs., mfg. summer 2002-04.

	N/A	$175 - 225	$110 - 140	$650

MSR/NOTES	100%	EXCELLENT	AVERAGE	LAST MSR

Stage 1000
courtesy Fender

Stage 1600
courtesy Fender

STAGE 1000 (NO. 236-7000-030) – 100W, 1-12 in. Celestion G12T-100 speaker, solid-state chassis, DSP effects, three channels, reverb, front black control panel, single input, 11 silver-top and 5 black knobs (Ch. 1: v, t, m, b, Ch. 2: drive, v, Ch. 3: drive, v, t, m, b, r level, r, FX level, FX select, FX time/rate), effects loop, four-button footswitch, black vinyl covering, dark gray grille, 47 lbs., mfg. summer 2004-06.

	N/A	$300 - 375	$175 - 225	$714

STAGE 160 (NO. 022-6800-010) – 160W, 2-12 in. Celestion G12T-100 speakers, solid-state chassis, three channels, reverb, front black control panel, two inputs, 11 silver-top knobs (Ch. 1: v, t, m, b, r, Ch. 2: drive, v, t, m, b, r), effects loop, two-button footswitch, black vinyl covering, silver grille, 53 lbs., mfg. 1999-2002.

	N/A	$250 - 300	$150 - 200	$760

STAGE 160 DSP (NO. 22-68000-020) – 160W, 2-12 in. Celestion G12T-100 speakers, solid-state chassis, three channels, DSP effects, reverb, front black control panel, single input, 14 black knobs (Ch. 1: v, t, m, b, Ch. 2 & 3: drive, v, t, m, b, r, r, FX level), mid/contour button, effects loop, black vinyl covering, silver grille, 53 lbs., mfg. summer 2002-04.

	N/A	$250 - 300	$150 - 200	$786

STAGE 1600 (NO. 236-8000-030) – 160W, 2-12 in. Celestion G12T-100 speakers, solid-state chassis, three channels, DSP effects, reverb, front black control panel, single input, 11 silver-top and five black knobs (Ch. 1: v, t, m, b, Ch. 2: drive, v, Ch. 3: drive, v, t, m, b, r level, r, FX level, FX select, FX time/rate), digital tuner, effects loop, four-button footswitch, black vinyl covering, dark gray grille, 58 lbs., mfg. summer 2004-06.

	N/A	$275 - 325	$175 - 225	$810

ULTIMATE CHORUS DSP (NO. 022-6701-020) – 130W (2 X 65W stereo), 2-12 in. Eminence speakers, solid-state chassis, two channels, DSP effects, front black control panel, two inputs, 16 black knobs (Ch. 1: v, t, m, b, r/d, Ch. 2: g, p, v, t, m, b, r/d, r type, chorus level, chorus type, chorus rate), effects loop, three-button footswitch, black vinyl covering, silver grille, casters included, 47 lbs., mfg. 2000-05.

	N/A	$200 - 250	$125 - 150	$850

DT 112 SPEAKER CABINET (NO. 021-1664-000) – 1-12 in. Celestion G12T-100 speaker, black vinyl covering, silver grille, 38 lbs., mfg. 2000-04.

	N/A	$120 - 150	$70 - 95	$300

This model is designed to team up with the Stage 100 Head or Stage 100 Combo.

DT 412 SPEAKER CABINET (NO. 021-1665-000) – 4-12 in. Celestion G12T-100 speakers, black vinyl covering, silver grille, casters, 67 lbs., mfg. 2000-04.

	N/A	$120 - 150	$70 - 95	$300

This model is designed to team up with the Stage 100 Head.

ELECTRIC SS AMPS: FM SERIES

* **Add $15 for cover.**

FM 15DSP (NO. 231-8000-003) – 15W, 1-8 in. Special Design speaker, solid-state chassis, DSP effects, two channels, front black control panel, single input, eight black knobs (Ch. 1 v, g, Ch. 2 v, amp type, t, m, b, FX), headphone jack, RCA inputs, black covering, black grille, 14 lbs., mfg. summer 2005-07.

	N/A	$75 - 100	$40 - 60	$250

FM 25DSP (NO. 231-8500-000) – 25W, 1-10 in. Special Design speaker, solid-state chassis, DSP effects, two channels, front black control panel, single input, eight black knobs (Ch. 1 v, g, Ch. 2 v, amp type, t, m, b, FX), headphone jack, RCA inputs, black covering, black grille, 23 lbs., mfg. summer 2005-2010.

	N/A	$75 - 100	$40 - 60	$170

* **Add $25 for one-button footswitch.**

MSR/NOTES	100%	EXCELLENT	AVERAGE	LAST MSR

FM 15DSP
courtesy Fender

FM 65R
courtesy Fender

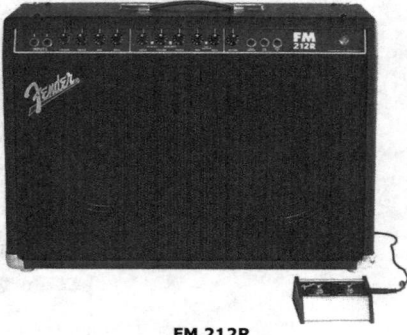
FM 212R
courtesy Fender

FM 65R (NO. 231-6000-000) – 65W, 1-12 in. Special Design speaker, two channels, reverb, solid-state chassis, front black control panel, two inputs, nine black knobs (Ch. 1: v, t, b, Ch. 2: drive, v, t, m, b, r), footswitch jack, pre-amp in/out, black covering, black grille, 32 lbs., mfg. 2003-07.

| | N/A | $160 - 210 | $105 - 130 | $450 |

* **Add $25 for one-button footswitch.**

In 2008, the cosmetics of this amp were changed and it was moved to the Frontman Series.

* *FM 65DSP (No. 231-6100)* – similar to the FM 65R, except has DSP effects with two additional knobs (FX select, FX level) and an amp type knob instead of reverb for a total of 11 knobs, RCA input and headphone jack on the front, and only one input, two-button footswitch included, 32 lbs., mfg. summer 2006-2010.

| | N/A | $130 - 160 | $75 - 100 | $300 |

FM 100H (NO. 231-7000-000) – 100W, head-unit only, two channels, reverb, solid-state chassis, front black control panel, two inputs, ten black knobs (Ch. 1: v, t, m, b, Ch. 2: drive, v, t, m, b, r), footswitch jack, pre-amp in/out, black covering, black grille, 27 lbs., mfg. summer 2005-2010.

| | N/A | $120 - 150 | $75 - 95 | $280 |

FM 210R (NO. 231-6300-000) – 65W, 2-10 in. Special Design speakers, two channels, reverb, solid-state chassis, front black control panel, two inputs, nine black knobs (Ch. 1: v, t, b, Ch. 2: drive, v, t, m, b, r), footswitch jack, pre-amp in/out, black covering, black grille, 36 lbs., mfg. summer 2005-07.

| | N/A | $175 - 225 | $110 - 140 | $483 |

* **Add $25 for one-button footswitch.**

FM 212R (NO. 231-6500-000) – 100W, 2-12 in. Special Design speakers, two channels, reverb, solid-state chassis, front black control panel, two inputs, ten black knobs (Ch. 1: v, t, m, b, Ch. 2: drive, v, t, m, b, r), footswitch jack, pre-amp in/out, black covering, black grille, 48 lbs., mfg. 2003-07.

| | N/A | $200 - 250 | $120 - 150 | $550 |

In 2008, the cosmetics of this amp were changed and it was moved to the Frontman Series.

* *FM 212DSP (No. 231-6600)* – similar to the FM 212R, except has DSP effects with 16 knobs (g, v, amp type, t, m, b, FX type, FX level for each channel) headphone jack, and only one input, two-button footswitch included, 43 lbs., mfg. summer 2006-2010.

| | N/A | $200 - 250 | $110 - 140 | $480 |

FM 412SL SPEAKER CABINET (NO. 231-7800-000) – 100W, 4-12 in. Special Design speakers, 4 ohm impedance, side handles, casters, black covering, black grille, meant for use with the FM 100H, 82 lbs., mfg. summer 2005-2010.

| | N/A | $175 - 225 | $100 - 125 | $400 |

ELECTRIC SS AMPS: FRONTMAN SERIES

The Frontman Series was introduced in 1997. These amps replaced the H.O.T., J.A.M., and R.A.D. models. In 2003, the Frontman Series was renamed the Frontman II Series. With the change of series the amps received a facelift with a silver grille and silver-top knobs to look like the blackface amps of vintage. The external speaker jack was also replaced with an auxillary RCA input.

FRONTMAN 10G (NO. 231-1000-000) – 10W, 1-6 in. speaker, guitar combo, solid-state chassis, single channel with overdrive effect, front black control panel, single input, four black knobs (g, v, t, b), overdrive/gain switch, 1/8 in. aux. in jack, 1/8 in. headphone jack, black textured vinyl covering, silver grille, 10.25 in. wide, 11 in. tall, 5.75 in. deep, 8.5 lbs., mfg. late 2007-present.

| MSR $80 | $60 | $35 - 50 | $20 - 30 | |

FRONTMAN 15(G) (NO. 022/023-1500-049) – 15W, 1-8 in. speaker, solid-state chassis, two selectable channels, front black control panel, single input, six black knobs (t, m, b, v, g, drive), headphone jack, black vinyl covering, black metal or silver grille, 15 lbs., mfg. 1997-2010.

| | N/A | $40 - 55 | $25 - 35 | $90 |

* *Frontman 15R (No. 022/023-1501-049)* – similar to the Frontman 15(G), except has reverb and reverb knob, mfg. 1997-2010.

| | N/A | $45 - 60 | $30 - 40 | $110 |

MSR/NOTES	100%	EXCELLENT	AVERAGE	LAST MSR

Frontman 15(G)
courtesy Fender

Frontman 25R
courtesy Fender

Frontman 65R
courtesy Fender

FRONTMAN 25R (NO. 022/023-1502-049) – 25W, 1-10 in. speaker, solid-state chassis, two selectable channels, front black control panel, single input, seven black knobs (v, g, drive, t, m, b, r), headphone jack, available in black or red vinyl covering with a black metal or silver grille, 25 lbs., mfg. 1997-2013.

	$100	$50 - 70	$35 - 45	$130

- Add $25 for footswitch.

Red vinyl covering is available on this amp and is sold only through select retailers including Musician's Friend and Guitar Center.

FRONTMAN 65R (NO. 231-6000-000) – 65W, 1-12 in.Special Design speaker, solid-state chassis, two channels, reverb, front black control panel, two inputs, nine black knobs (Ch. 1: v, t, b, Ch. 2: drive, v, t, m, b, r), footswitch jack (one-button channel switch footswitch included), pre-amp out, power amp in, black textured vinyl covering, silver grille, 18.75 in. wide, 16.8 in. tall, 9 in. deep, 32 lbs., made in China, mfg. late 2007-09.

	N/A	$120 - 150	$75 - 95	$260

FRONTMAN 212R (NO. 231-6500-000) – 100W, 2-12 in.Special Design speakers, guitar combo, solid-state chassis, two channels, reverb, front black control panel, two inputs, ten black knobs (Ch. 1: v, t, m, b, Ch. 2: drive, v, t, m, b, r), channel select switch, more drive switch, mid contour switch, footswitch jack (two-button three function footswitch included), pre-amp out, power amp in, black textured vinyl covering, silver grille, 26 in. wide, 19.5 in. tall, 9.5 in. deep, 48 lbs., made in China, mfg. late 2007-2013.

	$330	$185 - 235	$115 - 140	$460

ELECTRIC SS AMPS: G-DEC SERIES

G-DEC
courtesy Fender

G-DEC 30
courtesy Fender

G-DEC 3 Fifteen
courtesy Fender

G-DEC (NO. 235-000-000) – 15W, 1-8 in. speaker combo, solid-state chassis, MIDI synthesizer, front black control panel, single input, two knobs (v, tone), digital processor with various buttons and display, headphone jack, MIDI in and out, aux in and out, black Tolex covering, silver grille, 16 lbs., mfg. 2005-09.

	N/A	$135 - 175	$80 - 110	$350

G-DEC stands for Guitar Digital Entertainment Center. This amp is a practice amp with the effects of a modeling amp and the drum beats of a MIDI processor. This amp can provide a drum and bass background that the guitar can play over.

* G-DEC EXEC (No. 235-0000-005) – similar to the G-DEC, except has a maple cabinet with a sunburst finish, oxblood grille cloth, shoulder strap, and deluxe padded cover, 16 lbs., mfg. summer 2006-08.

	N/A	$225 - 275	$130 - 170	$533

G-DEC 30 (NO. 235-0500) – 30W, 1-10 in. speaker combo, solid-state chassis, MIDI synthesizer, front black control panel, single input, three knobs (v, guitar tone, backing level), digital processor with various buttons, data wheel, and display, headphone jack, MIDI in and out, aux in and out, black Tolex covering, silver grille, 19.5 lbs., mfg. summer 2006-09.

	N/A	$200 - 240	$110 - 135	$450

- Add $60 (Last MSR was $75) for ULT 4 four-button footswitch.

MSR/NOTES	100%	EXCELLENT	AVERAGE	LAST MSR

G-DEC JUNIOR (NO. 235-1000-000/010) – 15W, 1-8 in. speaker, guitar combo configuration, solid-state chassis, single channel, 16 amp types, 15 special effects presets, 15 loops, 14 keys, top black control panel, single input, nine knobs (g, v, tone, amp select, FX select, loop v, tempo, key select, loop select), start/stop button, metronome, tuner, headphone jack/line out, MIDI connector, aux in, narrow panel black textured vinyl covering (2007-2010, 000) or Carbon Tweed covering (2011 only, 010), silver grille, 13.25 in. wide, 12.5 in. tall, 7.25 in. deep, 15 lbs., mfg. 2007-2011.

| | N/A | $75 - 95 | $45 - 55 | $200 |

G-DEC 3 FIFTEEN (NO. 235-4000) – 15W, 1-8 in. Fender speaker, digital modeling guitar combo, solid-state chassis, single channel, 100 factory and user presets with digital amp modeling and DSP effects, MP3 and Wav file storage and playback, front black control panel, single input, three black knobs with silver insets (guitar tone, band level, v), digital display with various buttons including start/stop, quick access, tap/tuner, phrase sampler, four soft keys, save key, and exit/utility mode key, chromatic tuner, SD card slot, headphone jack, USB port, black textured vinyl covering with black metal corners, silver grille cloth, USB cable included, optional four-button footswitch and cover, 15.25 in. wide, 13.75 in. tall, 7.25 in. deep, 21.5 lbs., mfg. spring 2010-disc.

| | $200 | $120 - 150 | $75 - 95 | $400 |

- Add $75 for ULT-4 four-button footswitch.

G-DEC 3 THIRTY (NO. 235-4500) – 30W, 1-10 in. Fender speaker with high-frequency tweeter, digital modeling guitar combo, solid-state chassis, single channel, 100 factory and user presets with digital amp modeling and DSP effects, MP3 and Wav file storage and playback, front black control panel, single input, three black knobs with silver insets (guitar tone, band level, v), digital display with various buttons including start/stop, quick access, tap/tuner, phrase sampler, four soft keys, save key, and exit/utility mode key, chromatic tuner, SD card slot, headphone jack, USB port, stereo line out jacks, black textured vinyl covering with black metal corners, silver grille cloth, USB cable included, optional four-button footswitch and cover, 16.75 in. wide, 16.25 in. tall, 8.25 in. deep, 27.3 lbs., mfg. spring 2010-disc.

| | $300 | $175 - 225 | $105 - 130 | $550 |

- Add $75 for ULT-4 four-button footswitch.

*** G-DEC 3 Thirty Country (No. 235-4500-800)** – similar to the G-DEC 3 Thirty, except has onboard backing tracks recorded by several country artists and has a brown Western "cowboy tooled" vinyl covering with a wheat grille, mfg. mid-2011-disc.

| | $300 | $175 - 225 | $105 - 130 | $550 |

- Add $75 for ULT-4 four-button footswitch.

*** G-DEC 3 Thirty Metal (No. 235-4500-666)** – similar to the G-DEC 3 Thirty, except has onboard backing tracks recorded by several metal artists and has a black/white/gray camo covering, mfg. mid-2011-disc.

| | $300 | $175 - 225 | $105 - 130 | $550 |

- Add $75 for ULT-4 four-button footswitch.

ELECTRIC SS AMPS: MH (METALHEAD) SERIES

MH-500 Metalhead
courtesy Fender

MH-412SL Speaker Cabinet
courtesy Fender

MH-412ST Speaker Cabinet
courtesy Fender

MH-500 METALHEAD (NO. 228-2000-000) – 550W into 2 ohms (400W into 4 ohms), head-unit only, solid-state chassis, three channels, front black control panel, single input, 19 chrome knobs (Clean: v, t, m, b, Tight Drive: drive, v, p, t, m, b, Loose Drive: drive, v, p, t, m, b, boost, All: FX level, FX select), effects loop, cooling fan, four-button footswitch, black Tolex covering, large "MH" logo on front, 50 lbs., mfg. 2005-08.

| | N/A | $425 - 500 | $325 - 375 | $1,400 |

MH-412SL/MH-412ST SPEAKER CABINET (NO. 228-2800/2900-000) – 400W, 4-12 in. 100W Celestion speakers, 4 ohm impedance, slant or straight design, black Tolex covering, black perforated metal grille, angled nickel-plated steel edge reinforcement, 106 lbs., mfg. 2005-08.

| | N/A | $300 - 350 | $200 - 250 | $1,100 |

ELECTRIC SS AMPS: MUSTANG SERIES

Fender's Mustang Series of amplifiers feature built-in amp models and effects as well as USB connectivity with Fender's Fuse software.

In 2013, the Mustang Series was revamped. The new models (V.2) feature Tolex covering, a modern control panel, pitch shifting, five new amp models (Studio Preamp, '57 Twin, '60s Thrift, British Watts, British Colour) and five new stomp box effects (Ranger Boost, Green Box, Orange Box, Black Box, Big Fuzz).

MSR/NOTES	100%	EXCELLENT	AVERAGE	LAST MSR

Mustang I
courtesy Fender

Mustang II
courtesy Fender

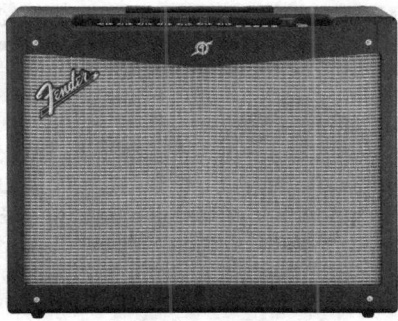

Mustang IV
courtesy Fender

- Add $90 (MSR $120) for the Fender Mustang EXP-1 Expression pedal.
- Add $300 (MSR $400) for the Fender Mustang Floor controller.

MUSTANG I (NO. 230-0010) – 20W, 1-8 in. speaker, guitar combo, solid-state chassis, single channel, 24 presets, top black control panel, single input, five black skirted knobs (g, v, t, b, MV), three black dome knobs (preset select, modulation select, delay/reverb select), save button, exit button, tap tempo button, power switch, footswitch jack, 1/8 in. stereo aux. input, 1/8 in. headphone/speaker emulated line out, speaker emulated USB, carbon tweed textured vinyl covering, silver grille cloth, 15.5 in. wide, 14.5 in. tall, 7.6 in. deep, 17 lbs., optional one-button footswitch, mfg. 2011-present.

MSR N/A	$120	$80 - 90	$40 - 50	

- **Add $20 for one-button footswitch.**

In 2013, the V.2 model was introduced and features a Tolex covering, a modern control panel, pitch shifting, five new amp models (Studio Preamp, '57 Twin, '60s Thrift, British Watts, British Colour) and five new stomp box effects (Ranger Boost, Green Box, Orange Box, Black Box, Big Fuzz).

MUSTANG II (NO. 230-0020) – 40W, 1-12 in. speaker, guitar combo, solid-state chassis, single channel, 24 presets, top black control panel, single input, five black skirted knobs (g, v, t, b, MV), three black dome knobs (preset select, modulation select, delay/reverb select), save button, exit button, tap tempo button, power switch, footswitch jack, 1/8 in. stereo aux. input, 1/8 in. headphone/speaker emulated line out, speaker emulated USB, carbon tweed textured vinyl covering, silver grille cloth, 17.25 in. wide, 18.25 in. tall, 8.75 in. deep, 24 lbs., optional one-button footswitch, mfg. 2011-present.

MSR N/A	$200	$120 - 160	$70 - 95	

- **Add $20 for one-button footswitch.**

In 2013, the V.2 model was introduced and features a Tolex covering, a modern control panel, pitch shifting, five new amp models (Studio Preamp, '57 Twin, '60s Thrift, British Watts, British Colour) and five new stomp box effects (Ranger Boost, Green Box, Orange Box, Black Box, Big Fuzz).

MUSTANG III (NO. 230-0030) – 100W, 1-12 in. Celestion G12T-100 speaker, guitar combo, solid-state chassis, single channel, 100 presets, 12 amp models, seven stomp effects, 11 modulation effects, nine delay effects, ten reverb effects, top black control panel, single input, seven black skirted knobs (g, v, t, m, b, r, MV), large data wheel knob, digital display, amp select button, stomp edit button, modulation edit button, delay edit button, reverb edit button, utility button, save button, exit button, tap tuner button, power switch, 1/8 in. stereo aux. input, 1/8 in. headphone/speaker emulated line out, speaker emulated USB, footswitch jack, mono effects loop, carbon tweed textured vinyl covering, silver grille cloth, 20.5 in. wide, 17.75 in. tall, 10.75 in. deep, 36 lbs., two-button footswitch included, optional four-button footswitch, mfg. 2011-present.

MSR N/A	$330	$180 - 240	$105 - 140	

- **Add $60 (MSR $63) for four-button footswitch.**

In 2013, the V.2 model was introduced and features a Tolex covering, a modern control panel, pitch shifting, five new amp models (Studio Preamp, '57 Twin, '60s Thrift, British Watts, British Colour) and five new stomp box effects (Ranger Boost, Green Box, Orange Box, Black Box, Big Fuzz).

MUSTANG IV (NO. 230-0040) – 150W (2 X 75W stereo), 2-12 in. Celestion G12P-80 speakers, guitar combo, solid-state chassis, single channel, 100 presets, 12 amp models, seven stomp effects, 11 modulation effects, nine delay effects, ten reverb effects, top black control panel, single input, seven black skirted knobs (g, v, t, m, b, r, MV), large data wheel knob, digital display, amp select button, stomp edit button, modulation edit button, delay edit button, reverb edit button, utility button, save button, exit button, tap tuner button, power switch, 1/8 in. stereo aux. input, 1/8 in. headphone/speaker emulated line out, speaker emulated USB, footswitch jack, stereo effects loop, carbon tweed textured vinyl covering, silver grille cloth, 26.5 in. wide, 21.5 in. tall, 10.75 in. deep, 47 lbs., four-button footswitch included, optional two-button footswitch, mfg. 2011-present.

MSR $700	$500	$300 - 375	$175 - 225	

- **Add $30 for two-button programmable footswitch.**

In 2013, the V.2 model was introduced and features a Tolex covering, a modern control panel, pitch shifting, five new amp models (Studio Preamp, '57 Twin, '60s Thrift, British Watts, British Colour) and five new stomp box effects (Ranger Boost, Green Box, Orange Box, Black Box, Big Fuzz).

MSR/NOTES	100%	EXCELLENT	AVERAGE	LAST MSR

MUSTANG V HEAD (NO. 230-0050) – 150W (2 X 75W stereo), guitar head-unit, solid-state chassis, single channel, 100 presets, 12 amp models, seven stomp effects, 11 modulation effects, nine delay effects, ten reverb effects, top black control panel, single input, seven black skirted knobs (g, v, t, m, b, r, MV), large data wheel knob, digital display, amp select button, stomp edit button, modulation edit button, delay edit button, reverb edit button, utility button, save button, exit button, tap tuner button, power switch, 1/8 in. stereo aux. input, 1/8 in. headphone/speaker emulated line out, speaker emulated USB, footswitch jack, stereo effects loop, carbon tweed textured vinyl covering, silver grille cloth, 26.5 in. wide, 21.5 in. tall, 10.75 in. deep, 47 lbs., four-button footswitch included, optional two-button footswitch, mfg. 2011-present.

| MSR $420 | $300 | $180 - 240 | $105 - 140 | |

• **Add $30 for two-button programmable footswitch.**

In 2013, the V.2 model was introduced and features a Tolex covering, a modern control panel, pitch shifting, five new amp models (Studio Preamp, '57 Twin, '60s Thrift, British Watts, British Colour) and five new stomp box effects (Ranger Boost, Green Box, Orange Box, Black Box, Big Fuzz).

MUSTANG V 412 SPEAKER CABINET (NO. 230-1400) – 200W (2 X 100W stereo), 4-12 in. Celestion Rocket 50 speakers, 8 ohm impedance stereo, 4 ohm impedance mono, center baffle bracing post, casters included, designed for use with the Mustang V Head, 30 in. wide, 30.5 in. tall, 12.5 in. deep, 78 lbs., mfg. 2011-present.

| MSR $400 | $300 | $180 - 240 | $105 - 140 | |

MUSTANG MINI (NO. 230-0060) – 7W, 1-6.5 in. speaker, guitar combo, solid-state chassis, single channel, 24 presets, top black control panel, single input, four black skirted knobs (g, v, t, MV), two black dome knobs (preset select, effects select), save button, exit button, tap tempo button, power switch, footswitch jack, 1/8 in. stereo aux. input, 1/8 in. headphone/speaker emulated line out, speaker emulated USB, carbon tweed textured vinyl covering, silver grille cloth, 9.5 in. wide, 9.5 in. tall, 6.7 in. deep, 7.25 lbs., optional one-button footswitch, mfg. mid-2011-disc.

| | $130 | $75 - 95 | $45 - 60 | $175 |

• **Add $20 for one-button footswitch.**

ELECTRIC SS AMPS: MISC. MODELS

Amp Can
courtesy Fender

Jazzmaster Ultralight 112 Speaker Cabinet
courtesy Fender

Steel King
courtesy Fender

AMP CAN (NO. 022/023-1200-000) – 15W, 1-4 in. speaker, solid-state chassis, two channels (guitar and mic), two inputs, four knobs (v1, tone1, v2, tone2), gain switch, rechargable battery, power pack (120V) supply, round black canister cabinet with handle, black metal grille, 13 lbs., mfg. 1998-2008.

| | N/A | $150 - 200 | $75 - 100 | $250 |

Replacement batteries can be purchased new for $40 (Last MSR was $55).

JAZZ KING (NO. 228-9700-000) – 140W, jazz guitar amp, 1-15 in. Eminence Legend speaker, solid-state chassis, reverb, front black control panel, single input, eight black knobs (g, EQ tilt, t, mid level, mid freq, b, r, MV), effects loop, three-button footswitch, black vinyl covering, silver grille, casters, 66 lbs., mfg. summer 2005-08.

| | N/A | $500 - 575 | $300 - 375 | $1,100 |

JAZZMASTER ULTRALIGHT HEAD (NO. 227-7000) – 250W (125 X 2), head-unit only, solid-state chassis, two channels (Normal and Drive), DSP effects, black control panel that looks like a rack-mount, two inputs (one Mic, one Inst.), 13 knobs (Norm Ch.: v, t, m, b, FX level, FX select, Drive Ch.: g, v, t, m, b, FX level, FX select), XLR line out with level control, headphone jack, tuner out, black anodized aluminum casing with maple side panels and top trim pieces finished in Sunburst, gig-bag included, optional footswitch, 7.5 lbs., mfg. 2006-09.

| | N/A | $500 - 575 | $300 - 350 | $1,100 |

* *Jazzmaster Ultralight 112 Speaker Cabinet (No. 227-7700)* – speaker cabinet companion to the Jazzmaster Ultralight Head, 250W, 1-12 in. Eminence speaker, 2 ohm impedance, Black textured vinyl covering with a black grille, 17 lbs., mfg. 2006-09.

| | N/A | $200 - 250 | $110 - 140 | $450 |

MSR/NOTES	100%	EXCELLENT	AVERAGE	LAST MSR

PAWN SHOP SPECIAL EXCELSIOR (NO. 301-3000) – 13W, 1-15 in. speaker, guitar combo, four-tube chassis, preamp: 2 X 12AX7, power: 2 X 6V6, solid-state rectifier, single channel, tremolo, top silver control panel, three inputs (guitar, mic, accordion), two brown knobs (v, tremolo), bright/dark switch, rear panel: single speaker jack, brown textured vinyl covering, "E-shaped" light brown grille, 19.5 in. wide, 21 in. tall, 9 in. deep, 33 lbs., mfg. 2012-2013.

	$300	$175 - 225	$105 - 130	$400

PAWN SHOP SPECIAL GRETA (NO. 230-3000) – 2W, 1-4 in. speaker, small guitar combo, two-tube chassis, preamp: 1 X 12AX7, power: 1 X 12AT7, solid-state rectifier, single channel, front panel: two gold knobs (v, tone) and a VU meter with clean to overload indicator, rear panel: single input, aux. in jack, line out, speaker jack, power switch, bright red painted front with round speaker opening and "Greta" logo, bright red painted back, gold-finished metal top, 10 in. wide, 6.75 in. tall, 7.25 in. deep, 8.7 lbs., mfg. 2012-2013.

	$200	$110 - 140	$65 - 85	$260

STEEL KING (NO. 228-9500-000) – 200W, pedal steel amp, 1-15 in. Eminence speaker, solid-state chassis, reverb, front black control panel, single input, eight black knobs (g, EQ tilt, t, mid level, mid freq, b, MV, r), effects loop, three-button footswitch, black vinyl covering, silver grille, casters, 70 lbs., mfg. 2004-09.

	N/A	$500 - 650	$275 - 350	$1,349

ELECTRIC HYBRID AMPS: CHAMP & PERFORMER SERIES

CHAMP 25 S/E (NO. 021-6600-000) – 25W, 1-10 in. speaker, used new "hybrid" circuitry, which combines tubes with transistors, solid-state preamp, 2 X 5881 / 6L6 power output tubes, black control panel, 11 black knobs (norm, v, t, b, m, drive, gain, overdrive, v, t, b, r), black or custom Tolex covering, mfg. 1992-94.

	N/A	$200 - 250	$120 - 150	$510

* **Add $15 for footswitch.**

This model came with five custom coverings, including red, white, gray, and snakeskin.

* *Champ 25 (No. 021-6601-000)* – similar to the Champ 25 S/E, except doesn't have tape inputs, line out, master volume, and standby switch, mfg. 1992-94.

	N/A	$175 - 225	$110 - 140	$410

PERFORMER 1000 (NO. 022-6800-000) – 100W, 1-12" speaker, 12AX7 preamp tube, otherwise solid-state, reverb, new blackface control panel, 11 black knobs (Ch. 1: v, t, m, b, Ch. 2: gain, t, m, b, v, Both: reverb and effects mix), black Tolex covering, silver grille, three button footswitch, mfg. 1993-95.

	N/A	$200 - 250	$100 - 150	$590

Was also available in head only version (No. 022-6801-000) for $510

* *Performer 650 (No. 022-6805-000)* – similar to Performer 1000 except output is 70W and two button footswitch, mfg. 1993-95.

	N/A	$175 - 225	$120 - 150	$460

ELECTRIC HYBRID AMPS: CYBER TWIN SERIES

The Cyber Twin Series represents Fender's latest step into hybrid technology. Fender took a wide selection of their vintage amplifiers and by using modern technology were able to put them all into one monster amp. The new technology is called Cybernetic Amp Design. There is a mixture of tubes, capacitors, and resistors, along with analog drive circuits, and the DSP circuits in the stereo amps. There are three preset sections including: your amp collection, Fender Custom Shop, and Player's Lounge. There is a total of 205 different preset possibilites. This amp also makes it possible to create your own amp by mixing the possibilities. There is a Cyber foot controller (No. 022-9100-000) for the amp that retails for $349.00. For the Cyber Deluxe (no tubes) see solid-state section.

Cyber-Twin
courtesy Fender

Cyber-Twin SE
courtesy Fender

Cyber-Twin SE Foot Controller
courtesy Fender

CYBER-TWIN (NO. 022-9000-000) – 130W, 2-12 in. Celestian G12 T-100 speakers, 2 X 12AX7 preamp tubes, solid-state power amp, new blackface control panel with digital display, one input, nine black knobs (trim, gain, v, t, m, b, presence, reverb, master), various buttons and knobs for the digital processor, black Tolex covering, silver grille, 55 lbs., mfg. 2001-04.

	N/A	$450 - 550	$325 - 400	$1,750

* *Cyber-Twin SE (No. 229-0000-010)* – similar to the Cyber-Twin, except is upgraded from the first version with new cosmetics including a black control panel with blue jewel, white LEDs, and silver buttons, new effects, more presets, and other accessories, 55 lbs., mfg. 2005-09.

	N/A	$450 - 550	$300 - 350	$1,698

* **Add $250 (Last MSR was $350) for foot controller.**

MSR/NOTES	100%	EXCELLENT	AVERAGE	LAST MSR

CYBER-TWIN HEAD UNIT ONLY (NO. 022-9002-000) – similar to the Cyber-Twin Combo but in the head unit configuration, 30 lbs., mfg. 2001-04.

	N/A	$375 - 450	$250 - 300	$1,500

SHOWMAN 412S ENCLOSURE (NO. 021-1675-010) – 4-12 in. Celestion G12T-75 speakers in a black Tolex covering silver grille cabinet, matches the Cyber Twin Head to create a piggy-back unit, 97 lbs., mfg. 2001-04.

	N/A	$275 - 325	$150 - 200	$750

ELECTRIC HYBRID AMPS: ROC-PRO SERIES

- Add $15 for cover.

ROC PRO 700 (NO. 022-6806-000) – 70W, 1-12 in. speaker, hybrid design, 12AX7 preamp, solid-state power, two switchable channels, front chrome control panel, single input, 10 black knobs (Ch. 1: v, t, m, b, Ch. 2: g, t, m, b, v, master r), effects loop, two-button footswitch, black Tolex covering, black steel grille, 33 lbs., mfg. 1996-2000.

	N/A	$150 - 200	$100 - 125	$550

ROC PRO 1000 HEAD (NO. 022-6807-000) – 100W, head-unit only, hybrid design, 12AX7 preamp, solid-state power, two switchable channels, front silver control panel, single input, 12 black knobs (Ch. 1: v, t, m, b, Ch. 2: g1, g2, t, m, b, v, master r, effects mix), effects loop, three-button footswitch, black Tolex covering, black steel grille, 24 lbs., mfg. 1996-2000.

	N/A	$150 - 200	$100 - 125	$570

* *Roc Pro 1000 Combo (No. 022-6808-000)* – similar to the Roc Pro 1000 Head, except in combo form with 1-12 in. speaker, 41 lbs., mfg. 1996-2000.

	N/A	$175 - 225	$100 - 125	$650

ROC PRO GE-112 SPEAKER CABINET (NO. 021-1660-000) – 80W, 1-12 in. speaker, 8 Ohm impedance, closed back, stacking cups, black Tolex covering, black steel grille, 41 lbs., mfg. 1996-2000.

	N/A	$120 - 150	$70 - 95	$230

ROC PRO GE-412 SPEAKER CABINET (NO. 021-1662-000) – 300W, 4-12 in. speaker, 8 Ohm impedance, closed back, inset slant baffle, stacking cups, black Tolex covering, black steel grille, casters, 60 lbs., mfg. 1996-2000.

	N/A	$225 - 275	$135 - 175	$500

ACOUSTIC AMPLIFIERS: ACOUSTASONIC SERIES

- Add $15 for cover.

**Acoustasonic SFX II
courtesy Fender**

**Acoustasonic Jr. DSP
courtesy Fender**

**Acoustasonic 15
courtesy Fender**

ACOUSTASONIC SFX (NO. 022-1301-000) – 2 X 80W into 8 ohms, 1-8 in. 8 ohm Fender Special Design Foster Culver speaker, 1-10 in. Fender Special Design speaker, solid state combo, two independent channels (instrument and microphone), XLR input for mic, onbard digital signal processor with 32 stereo digital presets, insert patch points for external signal processors, one input for instrument channel, two for mic, seventeen black-top knobs (Instrument: gain, t, m, b, string dynamics, feedback notch, DSP send, SFX, DSP return, MV, Mic: gain, t, m, b, feedback notch, DSP send, DSP effects), bypass switches, brown textured vinyl, wheat grille cloth, mfg. 1998-2002.

	N/A	$375 - 450	$250 - 300	$930

* *Acoustasonic SFX II (No. 221-3100-010)* – similar to the Acoustasonic SFX, except has a redesigned cabinet and updated DSP, mfg. 2003-mid-2011.

	N/A	$400 - 500	$300 - 350	$1,200

ACOUSTASONIC PRO (NO. 022-1300-000) – 160W (2 X 80), 2-8 in. special design & high frequency horn, dual notch filters, 1 special piezo horn, solid-state combo, dual processing, 99 digital multi-effect presets two independent channels (instrument and microphone), XLR input for mic, 18 black-top knobs (Inst: gain, t, m, b, channel send, return, attack, string dynamics, feedback notch 1 & 2, Mic: gain, t, m, b, channel send, return, both: Master and auxillary level), auxillary inputs, presets, four button footswitch, brown Tolex covering, wheat grille, 45 lbs., mfg. 1998-2001.

	N/A	$400 - 450	$275 - 325	$1,400

MSR/NOTES	100%	EXCELLENT	AVERAGE	LAST MSR

**Acoustasonic 90
courtesy Fender**

**Acoustasonic 150
courtesy Fender**

**Acoustasonic Ultralight Head and Stereo
Speaker Cabinet courtesy Fender**

ACOUSTASONIC JR. (NO. 022-1302-000) – 2 X 40W, 2-8 in. Fender special design Foster Culver speakers, 1 piezo horn, solid state combo, two independent channels (Inst. and Mic/Inst), reverb, stereo chorus, stereo FX loop, brownface control panel, three inputs, one 1/4 in. for each channel and a XRL on the mic, 13 black knobs (Inst: v, t, m, b, feedback notch, string dynamics, Mic: v, t, b, reverb send, both: r, depth, master volume) three switches, brown Tolex covering, wheat grille, 43 lbs., mfg 1998-2003.

	N/A	$250 - 300	$135 - 175	$620

* Acoustasonic Jr. DSP (No. 221-3200-010) – similar to the Acoustasonic Jr., except has DSP effects, 43 lbs., mfg. 2004-mid-2011.

	N/A	$250 - 300	$150 - 200	$700

• Add $50 (Last MSR was $66) for two-button footswitch.

ACOUSTASONIC 15 (NO. 231-3700) – 15W, 1-6 in. speaker, acoustic combo, solid-state chassis, two channels, chorus, front brown control panel, two inputs, six black knobs (Inst Ch.: v, t, m, b, chorus, Mic Ch.: v), power switch, headphone jack, brown textured vinyl covering, black grille cloth, 11.19 in. wide, 11.5 in. tall, 7.13 in. deep, 10.5 lbs., mfg. 2013-present.

MSR N/A	$100	$65 - 75	$35 - 40	

ACOUSTASONIC 30 (NO. 022-1303-000) – 30W, 1-8" Fender special design Foster Culver speaker & 1 piezo horn, solid state combo, two independent channels (Inst. and Mic),chorus, reverb, two inputs, XRL for mic, brownface control panel, ten black knobs (v, t, m, b, string dynamics, chorus, Mic: v, t, b, Both: reverb) optional footswitch, line out, portable floor wedge design (sits at an angle), brown Tolex covering, wheat grille, 34 lbs., mfg. 2000-03.

	N/A	$150 - 200	$95 - 120	$450

* Acoustasonic 30 DSP (No. 221-3300-010) – similar to the Acoustasonic 30, except has DSP effects, 34 lbs., mfg. 2004-mid-2011.

	N/A	$225 - 275	$120 - 150	$490

• Add $50 (Last MSR was $66) for two-button footswitch.

ACOUSTASONIC 90 (NO. 231-3800) – 90W, 1-8 in. speaker with a high-freq. tweeter, acoustic combo, solid-state chassis, two channels, vibratone, chorus, reverb, delay, front brown control panel, two inputs, 13 brown knobs (Inst Ch.: v, t, m, b, FX select, FX level, Mic/Inst. Ch.: v, t, b, FX select, FX level), feedback elimination switches on each channel, mute switch, rear panel: balanced line out with ground lift, aux in jack, power switch, footswitch jack, brown textured vinyl covering, black grille cloth, 19.375 in. wide, 15.375 in. tall, 9.8125 in. deep, 18 lbs., optional two-button footswitch, mfg. 2014-present.

MSR N/A	$325	$215 - 250	$105 - 130	

ACOUSTASONIC 100 (NO. 231-3500) – 100W, 1-8 in. speaker with a high-freq. tweeter, acoustic combo, solid-state chassis, two channels, vibratone, chorus, reverb, delay, voicing control with dreadnought, parlor, and jumbo acoustic tones and tweed, Blackface, and British electric tones, front brown control panel, two inputs, 13 brown knobs (Inst Ch.: v, t, m, b, voicing select, string dynamics, FX select, FX level, Mic/Inst. Ch.: v, t, b, FX select, FX level), feedback elimination switches on each channel, mute switch, rear panel: balanced line out with ground lift and level control, power switch, built-in kickstand, brown textured vinyl covering, black grille cloth, 19.375 in. wide, 15.375 in. tall, 9.8125 in. deep, 18 lbs., optional two-button footswitch, mfg. late 2011-disc.

	$400	$250 - 300	$150 - 190	$560

ACOUSTASONIC 150 (NO. 231-3600) – 150W (75W per side), 2-8 in. speakers with a piezo horn, acoustic combo, solid-state chassis, two channels, vibratone, chorus, reverb, delay, voicing control with dreadnought, parlor, and jumbo acoustic tones and tweed, Blackface, and British electric tones, front brown control panel, two inputs, 13 brown knobs (Inst Ch.: v, t, m, b, voicing select, string dynamics, FX select, FX level, Mic/Inst. Ch.: v, t, b, FX select, FX level), feedback elimination switches on each channel, mute switch, rear panel: balanced line out with ground lift and level control, power switch, built-in kickstand, brown textured vinyl covering, black grille cloth, 22.375 in. wide, 16 in. tall, 10.125 in. deep, 22.5 lbs., optional two-button footswitch, mfg. late 2011-present.

MSR N/A	$500	$300 - 375	$175 - 225	

ACOUSTASONIC ULTRALIGHT HEAD (NO. 227-1000) – acoustic configuration, 250W (125 X 2), head-unit only, solid-state chassis, two channels, DSP effects, black control panel that looks like a rack-mount, two inputs (one Mic, one Inst.), 14 knobs (Inst. Ch.: v, t, m, b, notch, string dynamics, FX level, FX select, Mic. Ch.: v, t, m, b, FX level, FX select), XLR line out with level control, headphone jack, tuner out, black anodized aluminum casing with maple side panels and top trim pieces finished in Honey Blonde, 7.5 lbs., mfg. 2006-09.

	N/A	$500 - 575	$300 - 375	$1,100

| MSR/NOTES | 100% | EXCELLENT | AVERAGE | LAST MSR |

Acoustic Pro
courtesy Fender

Acoustic SFX
courtesy Fender

Bassman 300 Pro
courtesy Fender

* *Acoustasonic Ultralight Stereo Speaker Cabinet (No. 227-1700)* – speaker cabinet companion to the Acoustasonic Ultralight Head, 250W, 2-8 in. Eminence drivers and 1-1 in. dome tweeter, Blonde textured vinyl covering with a black grille, 17 lbs., mfg. 2006-09.

N/A $250 - 300 $135 - 175 $700

ACOUSTIC AMPLIFIERS: ACOUSTIC PRO SERIES

ACOUSTIC PRO – 200W, 1-12 in. speaker with high-frequency horn, acoustic combo, solid-state chassis, two channels, reverb, top black control panel, two inputs, 12 black knobs (Each Ch.: v, reverb, l, mid level, mid freq., high), phase switch on each channel, aux. in, phone jack, rear panel: balanced line out with ground lift, mic/line switch, power switch, effects loop, footswitch jack, built-in kickstand, cover included, optional footswitch, stained amber wood covering, brown grille cloth, 21 in. wide, 17.5 in. tall, 10.5 in. deep, 27 lbs., new 2016.

MSR N/A $1,000 $650 - 750 $325 - 400

ACOUSTIC SFX – 160W (2x80W), 1-8 in. low-frequency driver and 1-6.5 in side-radiating speaker with high-frequency horn, acoustic combo, solid-state chassis, two channels, reverb, echo, delay, chorus, vibratone, top black control panel, two inputs, 13 black knobs (Each Ch.: v, reverb, effects level, low, mid, high, All: SFX level), phase switch on each channel, aux. in, phone jack, rear panel: balanced line out with ground lift, mic/line switch, power switch, footswitch jack, cover included, optional footswitch, stained amber wood covering, brown grille cloth, 17.5 in. wide, 19.5 in. tall, 10.5 in. deep, 25 lbs., new 2016.

MSR N/A $900 $575 - 675 $295 - 350

BASS TUBE AMPS

BASSMAN 300 PRO (NO. 021-3302-010) – 300W, bass head-unit, tube chassis, preamp: 2 X 12AX7, power: 6 X 6550, two channels, compression, front black control panel, single input, eleven black knobs, 10-band graphic equalizer, black covering, black metal grille, 75 lbs., mfg. 2002-2012.

$1,700 $975 - 1,200 $575 - 725 $2,350

TBP-1 TUBE BASS PRE-AMP (NO. 21-4700-000/010) – preamp only, tube chassis, preamp: 2 X 12AX7, two channels, front silver control panel, single input, 11 black knobs (Ch. 1: v, b, m, t, Ch. 2: g, v, blend, Vari Q: freq, level, room balance, MV), rear panel: footswitch jack, active crossover with balance and freq controls, main output, line out with level control, effects loop with trim level, tuner out, optional input jack, black casing, 13 lbs., mfg. 2005-disc.

$800 $450 - 575 $275 - 325 $1,100

BASS SS AMPS: BASSMAN SERIES (2000-09 MFG.)

The Bassman Series have always been popular for Fender. They started to make solid-state models many years after the original tube Bassmans were phased out. At the 2002 Summer NAMM show, Fender started to get back into the tube Bassmans. Fender purchased Sunn sometime in the late 1980s and had been producing SUNN amps for a while. Now they are putting Fender's name on SUNN amps. What used to be the SUNN 1200s and 300T are now the Fender Bassman 1200 and 300, respectively. For the Bassman 300, see the Electric Tube Amplifiers: Bassman Series section. For the Bassman 1200 see the Hybrid Amplifiers: Bassman Series section. The Bassman 400 Series was replaced with the Pro series.

BASSMAN 25 (NO. 022-4501-000) – 25W, 1-10 in. Eminence speaker, solid-state combo, active and passive inputs, FX loop, headphone jack, aux. input, black control panel, five silver-top knobs (v, t, m, b, aux level), tuner out jack, tuner mute switch with indicator, enhance switch, wedge cabinet design, black Tolex covering, black metal grille, 33 lbs., mfg. 2000-04.

N/A $75 - 100 $40 - 60 $386

BASSMAN 60 (NO. 022-4502-000) – 60W, 1-12 in. Eminence speaker, piezo horn, solid-state combo, active/passive input pad selector, gain, black control panel, one input, five silver-top knobs (gain, bass, mid level, mid frequency, treble), tuner out jack, indicators for tuner mute, power amp, and preamp clip, XLR line-out, FX loop, wedge cabinet design, black Tolex covering, black metal grille, 50 lbs., mfg. 2000-04.

N/A $125 - 175 $75 - 100 $557

MSR/NOTES	100%	EXCELLENT	AVERAGE	LAST MSR

Bassman 100 Combo Second Version
courtesy Fender

Bassman 150 Combo
courtesy Fender

Bassman 250HD
courtesy Fender

BASSMAN 100 COMBO FIRST VERSION (NO. 022-4503-000) – 100W, 1-15 in. Eminence speaker, Piezo horn, solid-state combo, active/passive input pad selector, gain, black control panel, one input, seven silver-top knobs (gain, bass, mid level, mid frequency, treble, compressor, mv), tuner out jack, indicators for tuner mute, power amp, compressor level, and preamp clip, XLR line-out, FX loop, black Tolex covering, black metal grille, 65 lbs., mfg. 2000-04.

	N/A	$225 - 275	$120 - 150	$714

• Add $15 for cover.

BASSMAN 100 COMBO SECOND VERSION (NO. 23-45700-010) – 100W, 1-10 in. speaker combo with piezo horn, solid-state chassis, single channel, front silver control panel, single input, seven black knobs (v, c, b, m/h, m/l, t, line level), effects loop, RCA inputs, headphone jack, tuner out, XLR out, tilt-back cabinet, black covering, black metal grille, 25 lbs., mfg. 2005-09.

	N/A	$225 - 275	$120 - 150	$550

BASSMAN 150 COMBO (NO. 23-45500-010) – 150W, 1-12 in. speaker combo with piezo horn, solid-state chassis, single channel, compressor, front silver control panel, single input, 11 black knobs (v, compressor, c, b, m/h, m/l, 2 levels, t, line level, MV), effects loop, RCA inputs, headphone jack, tuner out, XLR out, tilt-back cabinet, black covering, black metal grille, 39 lbs., mfg. 2005-09.

	N/A	$200 - 275	$100 - 150	$750

BASSMAN 200 (NO. 022-4504-000) – 200W, 1-15 in. Eminence speaker, 1 8 Ohm compression driver horn, solid-state combo, black control panel, one input, eight silver-top knobs (gain, room balance, b, m, mid frequency, t, compressor, master volume), tuner out jack, FX loop, black Tolex covering, black metal grille, 68 lbs., mfg. 2000-04.

	N/A	$225 - 275	$125 - 175	$929

BASSMAN 250HD (NO. 23-45900 -010) – 250W, head-unit only, solid-state chassis, single channel, compressor, front silver control panel, single input, 13 black knobs (v, compressor, balanc, c, b, m/h, m/l, 2 levels, t, line level, effects loop, MV), effects loop, RCA inputs, headphone jack, tuner out, XLR out, black carpet covering, mfg. 2005-09.

	N/A	$250 - 300	$125 - 175	$700

Bassman 250/115 Combo (No. 23-45300-010) – similar to the Bassman 250HD, except in combo form with 1-15 in. speaker with a compression driver horn, casters, black metal grille, 63 lbs., mfg. 2005-09.

	N/A	$325 - 400	$200 - 250	$1,000

Bassman 250/210 Combo (No. 23-45100-010) – similar to the Bassman 250HD, except in combo form with 2-10 in. speakers with a compression driver horn, casters, black metal grille, 63 lbs., mfg. 2005-09.

	N/A	$375 - 450	$275 - 325	$1,100

BASSMAN 400 (NO. 022-4505-000) – 350W, 2-10 in. Eminence speakers, 1 8 Ohm compression driver horn, solid-state combo, black control panel, one input, 13 silver-top knobs (gain, room balance, b, t, 6 knob equalizer, compressor, MV), FX loop, mute switch, casters, one-button footswitch, black Tolex covering, black metal grille, mfg. 2000-03.

	N/A	$325 - 400	$200 - 250	$1,429

Bassman 400 Head Only (No. 022-4506-000) – similar to the Bassman 400, except it is the head unit only, and has two speaker out jacks, mfg 2000-03.

	N/A	$250 - 300	$150 - 200	$800

Bassman 410H Enclosure (No. 021-1671-010) – this enclosure matches up exactly to the Bassman 400 Head, as is designed for that application. There are 4-10 in. Eminence speakers with one compression driver horn with level control, mfg. 2000-03.

	N/A	$250 - 300	$150 - 200	$643

Bassman 115 Enclosure (No. 021-1670-010) – this enclosure sits perfectly underneath the Bassman 410, but it can be used for other applications as well. There is 1-15 in. Eminence speaker with a ported enclosure, mfg. 2000-03.

	N/A	$150 - 200	$95 - 120	$471

MSR/NOTES	100%	EXCELLENT	AVERAGE	LAST MSR

Bassman 115 Speaker Cabinet
courtesy Fender

Bassman 410 Speaker Cabinet
courtesy Fender

BASSMAN 115 SPEAKER CABINET (NO. 43-47200-000) – 250W, 1-15 in. speaker with compression driver horn, 8 ohm impedance, casters, black carpet covering, black metal grille, 66 lbs., mfg. 2005-09.

	N/A	$225 - 275	$125 - 150	$500

BASSMAN 410 SPEAKER CABINET (NO. 43-47000-000) – 250W, 1-15 in. speaker with compression driver horn, 8 ohm impedance, casters, black carpet covering, black metal grille, 71 lbs., mfg. 2005-09.

	N/A	$325 - 375	$175 - 210	$700

BASS SS AMPS: BXR SERIES

The BXR series was introduced in 1987 as part of Fender's first attempt into amplifiers after the CBS sale. BXR stands for Bass Extended Range.

- **Add $15 for original cover.**

BXR 15 (NO. 022-4402-000) – 15W, 1-8 in. speaker, solid-state combo, black control panel, one input, four black knobs (v, l, m, h), headphone jack, external speaker jack, black Tolex covering, black grille, 21 lbs., mfg. 1995-96.

	N/A	$70 - 95	$50 - 60	$200

BXR 25 (NO. 022-4403-000) – 25W, 1-10 in. speaker, solid-state combo, blackface control panel, two inputs hi/lo, four black-top knobs (v, l, m, h), tape inputs, effects loop, headphone jack, black Tolex covering, black grille, 32 lbs., mfg. 1995-99.

	N/A	$120 - 150	$70 - 95	$300

BXR 60 (NO. 022-4404-000) – 60W, 1-10 in. speaker, solid-state combo, blackface control panel, two inputs, five black knobs (v, l, low mid, high mid, high), tape inputs, effects loop, headphone jack, line out, black Tolex covering, black grille, 45 lbs., mfg. 1994-99.

	N/A	$150 - 200	$95 - 120	$430

BXR 100 (NO. 022-4401-000) – 100W, 1-15 in. speaker, solid-state combo, blackface control panel, two inputs, enhancement buttons, four black knobs (g, low and high shelving, v), 7-band equalizer, effects loop, headphone jack, line out, black Tolex covering, black grille, mfg. 1993-99.

	N/A	$225 - 275	$150 - 200	$530

BXR 200 (NO. 022-4405-000) – 200W, 1-15 in. speaker, solid-state combo, chorus, blackface control panel, enhancement buttons, five black knobs (gain, low and high shelving, rate, depth), 9-band equalizer, delta comp switch, footswitch, effects loop, black Tolex covering, black grille, 72 lbs., mfg. 1995-99.

	N/A	$300 - 350	$175 - 225	$730

* ***BXR 200 HD (No. 022-4406-000)*** – similar to the BXR 200 except is the head unit only, 27 lbs., mfg. 1995-99.

	N/A	$200 - 250	$135 - 175	$530

BXR 300C (NO. 022-4100-010) – 300W, 1-15 in. speaker, solid-state combo, blackface control panel, two inputs, five red knobs (v, t, m, mid-frequency, b), effects loop, Delta-Comp Limiter, fan cooling, black Tolex covering, black grille, 107 lbs., mfg. 1987-1999.

	N/A	$300 - 375	$175 - 225	$800

In 1993, this amp was remodeled with different cosmetics including a new control panel and black knobs.

* ***BXR 300R Head (No. 022-4107-010)*** – similar to the BXR 300C except is the head unit two-space rack mount, mfg. 1987-1994.

	N/A	$225 - 275	$135 - 175	$640

BXR 400 DUAL BASS HEAD (NO. 022-4000-000) – 400W (Twin 200W amps), head three-space rack mount, solid-state chassis, 11 bands of equalization, compressor, only a couple of knobs, black metal casing, mfg. 1987-1993.

	N/A	$375 - 450	$250 - 300	$900

BXR 115B SPEAKER CABINET (NO. 021-1670-000) – 300W, 1-15 in. speaker, 8 Ohm impedance, black carpet covering, black metal grille, 62 lbs., mfg. 1995-99.

	N/A	$135 - 175	$85 - 110	$320

MSR/NOTES	100%	EXCELLENT	AVERAGE	LAST MSR

BXR 210H SPEAKER CABINET (NO. 021-1671-000) – 300W, 2-10 in. speaker, horn tweeter, 8 Ohm impedance, black carpet covering, black metal grille, 58 lbs., mfg. 1995-99.

	N/A	$150 - 200	$95 - 120	$400

BXR 410H SPEAKER CABINET (NO. 021-1672-000) – 600W, 4-10 in. speaker, horn tweeter, 8 Ohm impedance, black carpet covering, black metal grille, 75 lbs., mfg. 1995-99.

	N/A	$225 - 275	$125 - 175	$550

BASS SS AMPS: FRONTMAN SERIES

The Frontman series was introduced in 1997. These amps replaced the H.O.T., J.A.M., and R.A.D. models.

FRONTMAN 15B (NO. 022-1503-049) – 15W, bass amp, 1-8 in. speaker, solid-state chassis, front black control panel, single input, four black knobs (v, l, m, h), headphone jack, black vinyl covering, black metal grille, 21 lbs., mfg. 1997-2003.

	N/A	$50 - 70	$30 - 40	$200

FRONTMAN 25B (NO. 022-1504-049) – 25W, bass amp, 1-10 in. speaker, solid-state chassis, front black control panel, two inputs, four black knobs (v, l, m, h), headphone jack, aux. RCA inputs, effects loop, black vinyl covering, black metal grille, 32 lbs., mfg. 2000-03.

	N/A	$75 - 100	$40 - 60	$300

FRONTMAN 60B (NO. 023-1505-049) – 60W, bass amp, 1-12 in. speaker, solid-state chassis, front control panel, two inputs, five black knobs (v, l, lm, hm, h), headphone jack, aux. RCA inputs, effects loop, black vinyl covering, silver grille, 45 lbs., mfg. 2003 only.

	N/A	$125 - 175	$75 - 100	$383

BASS SS AMPS: PRO SERIES

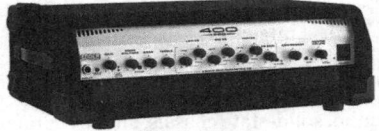

400 Pro Head
courtesy Fender

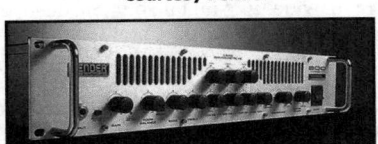

800 Pro Head
courtesy Fender

400 Pro Combo
courtesy Fender

410 Pro Cabinet SL
courtesy Fender

400 PRO HEAD (NO. 224-5600-010) – 500W @ 2 Ohms, 350W @ 4 Ohms, head-unit only, solid-state chassis, single channel, front silver control panel, single input, 12 black knobs (room balance, b, t, 2 lows, 2 mids, 2 highs, g, compressor, MV), black carpet covering, space for an available tuner, 42 lbs., mfg. 2004-08.

	N/A	$250 - 300	$150 - 200	$900

* 400 Pro Combo (No. 224-5500-010) – similar to the 400 Pro Head, except in combo form with 2-10 in. Eminence speakers and a compression driver HF horn, mfg. 2004-08.

	N/A	$450 - 550	$300 - 350	$1,500

800 PRO HEAD (NO. 214-6800-000) – 1200W @ 2 Ohms, 800W @ 4 Ohms, two-space rack-mount head-unit only, solid-state chassis, single channel, front silver control panel, single input, 12 black knobs (room balance, b, t, 2 lows, 2 mids, 2 highs, g, compressor, MV), black casing, 36 lbs., mfg. 2004-08.

	N/A	$375 - 475	$250 - 300	$1,500

115 PRO CABINET (NO. 221-7700-000) – 700W program, 350W RMS, 1-15 in. speaker, 8 Ohm impedance, black covering, black grille, removable casters, 64 lbs., mfg. 2004-08.

	N/A	$300 - 350	$175 - 225	$700

* 115 Pro EXT Cabinet (No. 221-7800-000) – similar to the 115 Pro, except has a smaller cabinet to match up with the 400 Pro Combo, 500W program, 250W RMS, 4 Ohm impedance, 60 lbs., mfg. 2004-08.

	N/A	$275 - 325	$150 - 200	$650

210 PRO CABINET (NO. 221-7500-000) – 700W program, 350W RMS, 2-10 in. speakers, 8 Ohm impedance, black covering, black grille, removable casters, 61 lbs., mfg. 2004-08.

	N/A	$300 - 350	$175 - 225	$700

410 PRO CABINET SL/ST (NO. 221-7000/7100-000) – 600W program, 300W RMS, 4-10 in. speakers, 8 ohm impedance, black covering, black grille, removable casters, straight or slanted cab, 78 lbs., mfg. 2004-08.

	N/A	$375 - 450	$200 - 250	$900

MSR/NOTES	100%	EXCELLENT	AVERAGE	LAST MSR

810 PRO CABINET (NO. 221-7200-000) – 1200W program, 600W RMS, 8-10 in. speakers, 4 ohm impedance, black covering, black grille, removable casters, 160 lbs., mfg. 2004-07.

	N/A	$650 - 800	$400 - 500	$1,600

BASS SS AMPS: RUMBLE BASS SERIES

In 2014, Fender completely revamped the Rumble Series. The new models are lighter, louder, and feature a new footswitchable overdrive circuit, three-button voicing palette, Eminence drivers, premium HF compression tweeters, soft-touch radio knobs, and classic Fender styling.

Rumble 15 First Version courtesy Fender

Rumble 15 Second Version courtesy Fender

Rumble 25 courtesy Fender

RUMBLE 15 FIRST VERSION (NO. 023-15300-010) – 15W, 1-8 in. speaker combo, solid-state combo, front black control panel, single input, four knobs (v, b, m, t), CD inputs, headphone jack, black fuzzy covering, black metal grille, 19 lbs., mfg. 2003-09.

	N/A	$75 - 100	$40 - 60	$230

RUMBLE 15 SECOND VERSION (NO. 231-5300) – 15W, 1-8 in. Fender speaker, bass combo, solid-state chassis, single channel, Delta Comp Adaptive Compression Circuitry, front black control panel, single input, four black knobs (v, b, m, t), RCA aux. input, headphone jack, power switch, sealed cabinet, black textured vinyl covering with nickel corners, black metal grille, 14 in. wide, 16.5 in. tall, 9.25 in. deep, 22 lbs., mfg. 2010-present.

MSR N/A	$80	$50 - 60	$25 - 30	

In 2014, this model was upgraded to be lighter, louder, and feature a new footswitchable overdrive circuit, three-button voicing palette, Eminence drivers, premium HF compression tweeters, soft-touch radio knobs, and classic Fender styling.

RUMBLE 25 (NO. 023-15400-010) – 25W, 1-10 in. speaker combo, solid-state combo, front black control panel, two inputs, four knobs (v, b, m, t), CD inputs, speaker loop, headphone jack, black fuzzy covering, black metal grille, 32 lbs., mfg. 2003-09, 2014-present.

MSR N/A	$100	$65 - 75	$35 - 40	

In 2014, this model was upgraded to be lighter, louder, and feature a new footswitchable overdrive circuit, three-button voicing palette, Eminence drivers, premium HF compression tweeters, soft-touch radio knobs, and classic Fender styling.

RUMBLE 30 (NO. 231-5400) – 30W, 1-10 in. Fender speaker, bass combo, solid-state chassis, single channel, Delta Comp Adaptive Compression Circuitry, front black control panel, two inputs, six black knobs (v, OD g, OD blend, b, m, t), OD switch, RCA aux. input, headphone jack, power switch, vented tilt-back cabinet design, black textured vinyl covering with nickel corners, black metal grille, 15.25 in. wide, 17.5 in. tall, 14.25 in. deep, 30 lbs., mfg. 2010-disc.

	$180	$100 - 125	$60 - 75	$250

RUMBLE 40 COMBO (NO. 237-0300) – 40W, 1-10 in. speaker, bass combo, solid-state chassis, single channel, top black control panel, single input, eight knobs (g, drive, level, b, low mid, high mid, t, MV), OD switch, bright/contour/vintage buttons, aux. input, headphone jack, footswitch jack, XLR line out jack with ground lift switch, power switch, black textured vinyl covering, silver grille, optional one-button footswitch, 16.5 in. wide, 16.5 in. tall, 12. in. deep, 18 lbs., mfg. 2014-present.

MSR N/A	$200	$130 - 150	$65 - 80	

RUMBLE 60 (NO. 023-15500-010) – 60W, 1-12 in. speaker combo, solid-state combo, front black control panel, two inputs, five knobs (v, b, h/m, l/m, t), CD inputs, speaker loop, headphone jack, line out, black fuzzy covering, black metal grille, 46 lbs., mfg. 2003-09.

	N/A	$150 - 200	$95 - 120	$500

RUMBLE 75 (NO. 231-5500) – 75W, 1-12 in. Fender speaker, bass combo, solid-state chassis, single channel, Delta Comp Adaptive Compression Circuitry, front black control panel, two inputs, seven black knobs (v, OD g, OD blend, b, l/m, h/m, t), OD switch, punch shape filter switch, scoop shape filter switch, RCA aux. input, headphone jack, line out jack, footswitch jack, power switch, bottom vented tilt-back cabinet design, black textured vinyl covering with nickel corners, black metal grille, optional one-button footswitch, 22.875 in. wide, 25.5 in. tall, 16.75 in. deep, 47 lbs., mfg. 2010-disc.

	$250	$140 - 175	$85 - 105	$330

• Add $40 (MSR $55) for one-button footswitch.

MSR/NOTES	100%	EXCELLENT	AVERAGE	LAST MSR

Rumble 100 Combo
courtesy Fender

Rumble 150 Combo
courtesy Fender

Rumble 200 Combo
courtesy Fender

RUMBLE 100 115 (NO. 023-15600-010) – 100W, 1-15 in. speaker combo, solid-state combo, front black control panel, single input, six knobs (v, b, h/m, l/m, t, line level), CD inputs, speaker loop, headphone jack, line out, black fuzzy covering, black metal grille, 60 lbs., mfg. 2003-09.

N/A	$210 - 260	$120 - 150	$600

RUMBLE 100 210 (NO. 023-15700-010) – 100W, 2-10 in. speaker combo, solid-state combo, front black control panel, single input, six knobs (v, b, h/m, l/m, t, line level), CD inputs, speaker loop, headphone jack, line out, black fuzzy covering, black metal grille, casters, 62 lbs., mfg. 2006-09.

N/A	$225 - 275	$130 - 160	$650

RUMBLE 100 COMBO (NO. 237-0400) – 100W, 1-12 in. Eminence speaker, bass combo, solid-state chassis, single channel, top black control panel, single input, eight knobs (g, drive, level, b, low mid, high mid, t, MV), OD switch, bright/contour/vintage buttons, effects loop, aux. input, headphone jack, footswitch jack, XLR line out jack with ground lift switch, power switch, black textured vinyl covering, silver grille, optional one-button footswitch, 16.5 in. wide, 18.5 in. tall, 14. in. deep, 22 lbs., mfg. 2014-present.

MSR N/A	$300	$195 - 225	$100 - 120

RUMBLE 150 COMBO (NO. 231-5600) – 150W, 1-15 in. Fender speaker with a piezo horn, bass combo, solid-state chassis, single channel, Delta Comp Adaptive Compression Circuitry, front black control panel, single input with passive/active switch, seven black knobs (v, OD g, OD blend, b, l/m, h/m, t), OD switch, punch shape filter switch, scoop shape filter switch, effects loop, RCA aux. input, headphone jack, footswitch jack, XLR line out jack with ground lift switch, horn on/off switch, power switch, bottom vented cabinet design, black textured vinyl covering with nickel corners, black metal grille, spring-loaded rubber handles, removable casters, optional one-button footswitch, 23 in. wide, 23.5 in. tall, 14.25 in. deep, 65 lbs., mfg. 2010-disc.

$350	$200 - 250	$120 - 150	$450

- Add $40 (MSR $55) for one-button footswitch.

RUMBLE 150 HEAD (NO. 231-5800) – 150W, bass head-unit, solid-state chassis, single channel, Delta Comp Adaptive Compression Circuitry, front black control panel, single input with -6dB switch, seven black knobs (v, OD g, OD blend, b, l/m, h/m, t), OD switch, punch shape filter switch, scoop shape filter switch, power switch, rear panel: two speaker jacks, effects loop, RCA aux. input, headphone jack, footswitch jack, XLR line out jack with ground lift switch, black casing, optional one-button footswitch, 12.75 in. wide, 3 in. tall, 7 in. deep, 5.5 lbs., mfg. 2011-disc.

$250	$140 - 175	$85 - 105	$400

- Add $40 (MSR $55) for one-button footswitch.

RUMBLE 200 COMBO (NO. 237-0500) – 200W, 1-15 in. Eminence speaker with compression horn, bass combo, solid-state chassis, single channel, top black control panel, single input, eight knobs (g, drive, level, b, low mid, high mid, t, MV), OD switch, bright/contour/vintage buttons, effects loop, aux. input, headphone jack, footswitch jack, XLR line out jack with ground lift switch, horn on/off switch, power switch, black textured vinyl covering, silver grille, optional one-button footswitch, 19 in. wide, 23 in. tall, 14. in. deep, 34.5 lbs., mfg. 2014-present.

MSR N/A	$450	$295 - 325	$145 - 180

RUMBLE 200 HEAD (NO. 237-0700) – 200W, bass head-unit, solid state chassis, single channel, front black control panel, single input, eight knobs (g, drive, level, b, low mid, high mid, t, MV), OD switch, bright/contour/vintage buttons, effects loop, aux. input, headphone jack, footswitch jack, XLR line out jack with ground lift switch, power switch, external speaker jacks, black covering, optional one-button footswitch, 13.8 in. wide, 2.68 in. tall, 7.2 in. deep, 4.5 lbs., mfg. 2014-present.

MSR N/A	$300	$195 - 225	$100 - 120

RUMBLE 350 (NO. 231-5700) – 350W, 2-10 in. Fender speakers with a piezo horn, bass combo, solid-state chassis, single channel, Delta Comp Adaptive Compression Circuitry, front black control panel, single input with passive/active switch, seven black knobs (v, OD g, OD blend, b, l/m, h/m, t), OD switch, punch shape filter switch, scoop shape filter switch, effects loop, RCA aux. input, headphone jack, footswitch jack, XLR line out jack with ground lift switch, horn on/off switch, power switch, bottom vented cabinet design, black textured vinyl covering with nickel corners, black metal grille, spring-loaded rubber handles, removable casters, optional one-button footswitch, 23 in. wide, 21.5 in. tall, 14.25 in. deep, 67 lbs., mfg. 2010-disc.

$500	$300 - 350	$175 - 225	$650

- Add $40 (MSR $55) for one-button footswitch.

MSR/NOTES	100%	EXCELLENT	AVERAGE	LAST MSR

Rumble 500 Head
courtesy Fender

Rumble 115 Speaker Cabinet
courtesy Fender

Rumble 410 Speaker Cabinet
courtesy Fender

RUMBLE 350 HEAD (NO. 231-5900) – 350W, bass head-unit, solid-state chassis, single channel, Delta Comp Adaptive Compression Circuitry, front black control panel, single input with -6dB switch, seven black knobs (v, OD g, OD blend, b, l/m, h/m, t), OD switch, punch shape filter switch, scoop shape filter switch, power switch, rear panel: two speaker jacks, effects loop, RCA aux. input, headphone jack, footswitch jack, XLR line out jack with ground lift switch, black casing, optional one-button footswitch, 12.75 in. wide, 3 in. tall, 7 in. deep, 5.6 lbs., mfg. 2011-disc.

	$400	$225 - 275	$135 - 170	$550

• Add $40 (MSR $55) for one-button footswitch.

RUMBLE 500 COMBO (NO. 237-0600) – 500W, 2-10 in. Eminence speakers with a compression horn, bass combo, solid-state chassis, single channel, front black control panel, single input, eight knobs (g, drive, level, b, low mid, high mid, t, MV), OD switch, bright/contour/vintage buttons, effects loop, aux. input, headphone jack, footswitch jack, XLR line out jack with ground lift switch, horn on/off switch, power switch, external speaker jack, black textured vinyl covering, silver grille, optional one-button footswitch, 19 in. wide, 23 in. tall, 14. in. deep, 36.5 lbs., mfg. 2014-present.

MSR N/A	$600	$400 - 450	$195 - 240	

RUMBLE 500 HEAD (NO. 237-0800) – 500W, bass head-unit, solid state chassis, single channel, front black control panel, single input, eight knobs (g, drive, level, b, low mid, high mid, t, MV), OD switch, bright/contour/vintage buttons, effects loop, aux. input, headphone jack, footswitch jack, XLR line out jack with ground lift switch, power switch, external speaker jacks, black covering, optional one-button footswitch, 13.75 in. wide, 2.68 in. tall, 7.2. in. deep, 5 lbs., mfg. 2014-present.

MSR N/A	$400	$260 - 300	$130 - 160	

RUMBLE 112 SPEAKER CABINET (NO. 224-7012) – 250W, 1-12 in. Eminence speaker with a Neodymium magnet, 8 ohm impedance, piezoelectric tweeter, three-position high-freq. level control switch, two 1/4 in. jacks, ported enclosure, Okume cabinet material, black covering, black metal grille, 19.75 in. wide, 15 in. tall, 12 in. deep, 24 lbs., mfg. 2011-present.

MSR N/A	$300	$195 - 225	$100 - 120	

In 2014, this model was upgraded to be lighter, louder, and feature a new footswitchable overdrive circuit, three-button voicing palette, Eminence drivers, premium HF compression tweeters, soft-touch radio knobs, and classic Fender styling.

RUMBLE 115 SPEAKER CABINET (NO. 237-0900) – 600W, 1-15 in. Eminence speaker, 8 ohm impedance, compression tweeter, one 1/4 in. jack, one Speakon jack, lightweight plywood cabinet material, black vinyl covering, silver grille, recessed handles, magnetic locking system to hold Rumble Head in place, 23 in. wide, 20.75 in. tall, 14 in. deep, 39 lbs., mfg. 2014-present.

MSR N/A	$300	$195 - 225	$100 - 120	

RUMBLE 2X8 SPEAKER CABINET (NO. 224-7008) – 250W, 2-8 in. Eminence speakers with Neodymium magnets, 8 ohm impedance, piezoelectric tweeter, three-position high-freq. level control switch, two 1/4 in. jacks, ported enclosure, Okume cabinet material, black covering, black metal grille, 19.75 in. wide, 15 in. tall, 12 in. deep, 28 lbs., mfg. 2011-disc.

	$400	$250 - 300	$150 - 190	$560

RUMBLE 210 SPEAKER CABINET (NO. 238-0100) – 700W, 2-10 in. Eminence speakers, 8 ohm impedance, compression tweeter, one 1/4 in. jack, one Speakon jack, lightweight plywood cabinet material, black vinyl covering, silver grille, recessed handles, magnetic locking system to hold Rumble Head in place, 19 in. wide, 23 in. tall, 14 in. deep, 39 lbs., mfg. 2014-present.

MSR N/A	$350	$230 - 265	$115 - 140	

RUMBLE 410 SPEAKER CABINET (NO. 224-7000) – 500W, 4-10 in. Fender Special Design speakers, 4 ohm impedance, piezoelectric tweeter, three-position high-freq. level control switch, two 1/4 in. jacks, Okume cabinet material, black covering, black metal grille, recessed spring-loaded handles, removable casters, magnetic locking system to hold Rumble Head in place, 23 in. wide, 25 in. tall, 14.375 in. deep, 76 lbs., mfg. 2011-present.

MSR N/A	$400	$260 - 300	$130 - 160	

In 2014, this model was upgraded to be lighter, louder, and feature a new footswitchable overdrive circuit, three-button voicing palette, Eminence drivers, premium HF compression tweeters, soft-touch radio knobs, and classic Fender styling.

MSR/NOTES	100%	EXCELLENT	AVERAGE	LAST MSR

BASS SS AMPS: MISC. MODELS

B-DEC 30
courtesy Fender

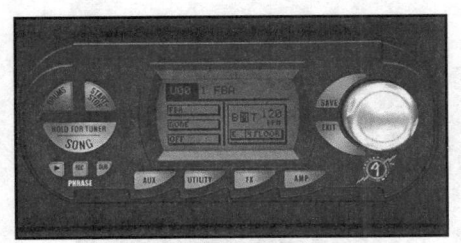

B-DEC 30 Digital Display
courtesy Fender

MB-1200 Power Amp
courtesy Fender

B-DEC 30 (NO. 235-4200) – 30W, bass combo, 1-10 in. speaker, 1 high frequency piezo horn, solid-state chassis, single channel, MIDI synthesizer, front black control panel, single input, four knobs (v, b, m, t), digital processor with various buttons, data wheel, and display, headphone jack, MIDI in and out, aux in and out, optional footswitch, tilt-back cabinet design, black carpet covering, black grille, 33 lbs., mfg. summer 2006-09.

	N/A	$200 - 250	$120 - 150	$550

• **Add $70 (Last MSR was $82) for the ULT-4 Footswitch.**

BRONCO 40 (NO. 230-2000) – 40W, 1-10 in. speaker, bass combo, solid-state chassis, single channel, eight amp models (Rumble, '59 Bassman, Bassman TV, Bassman 300, Redhead, Rockin' Peg, KGB800, Monster), multiple effects (Modern Bass Overdrive, Overdrive, Fuzz, Greenbox, chrorus, flanger, phaser, Vibratone, Envelope Control filter, octave, step filter, delay, reverb), 24 presets, top black control panel, single input, eight black knobs (g, b, m, t, MV, preset select, Compression select, FX select), save button, exit button, tap button, USB jack, aux. in jack, headphone jack, rear panel: XLR direct out, footswitch jack, black powder coated covering, black metal grille, 18 in. wide, 15.25 in. tall, 11.25 in. deep, 30 lbs., mfg. mid-2011-present.

MSR $350	$250	$150 - 190	$95 - 115	

MB-1200 POWER AMP (NO. 214-7500-000/224-7500-000) – 1200W at 2 ohms, two-space rack-mount head only, mono-power block solid-state chassis, front brushed chrome control panel, single volume knob, six speaker outputs, black casing, 35 lbs., mfg. summer 2005-disc.

	$1,000	$600 - 750	$375 - 450	$1,400

BASS HYBRID AMPS: BASSMAN/BASSMAN PRO SERIES

Bassman 1200
courtesy Fender

Bassman 500 Head
courtesy Fender

Super Bassman Head
courtesy Fender

BASSMAN 1200 (NO. 022-4505-000/021-3300-010) – 1200W, two-space rack mount head-unit only, hybrid design, preamp: 2 X 12AX7, solid-state power amp, dual channels, compression, front black control panel, single input, eleven black knobs, 10-band graphic equalizer, various buttons black covering, black grille, 35 lbs., mfg. 2002-07.

	N/A	$650 - 800	$400 - 500	$1,643

BASSMAN 100T HEAD (NO. 224-9100) – 100W (switchable to 25W), bass head-unit, seven-tube chassis, preamp: 2 X 12AX7, power: 1 X 12AT7, 4 X 6L6, solid-state rectifier, two channels (vintage, overdrive), front black control panel, two inputs, 12 black skirted knobs (Ch. 1: v, b with push/pull deep switch, m, t with push/pull bright switch, Ch. 2: g, blend, v, b with push/pull deep switch, mid-freq., mid level, t with push/pull bright switch, All: MV with push/pull mute switch), channel switch, rear panel: pre-amp out, power amp in, XLR line out with level and ground lift, speaker jack with impedance switch, footswitch jack, 100W/25W power switch, black Tolex covering, silver grille cloth, side spring-loaded handles and top handle, 24.5 in. wide, 10 in. tall, 10.625 in. deep, 48.5 lbs., single-button footswitch included, mfg. 2012-present.

MSR $2,000	$1,450	$850 - 1,050	$500 - 625	

BASSMAN 500 HEAD (NO. 224-9600) – 500W, bass head-unit, hybrid chassis, preamp: 2 X 12AX7, power: Class D power amp, solid-state rectifier, two channels (vintage, overdrive), front black control panel, two inputs, 12 black skirted knobs (Ch. 1: v, b with push/pull deep switch, m, t with push/pull bright switch, Ch. 2: g, blend, v, b with push/pull deep switch, mid-freq., mid level, t with push/pull bright switch, All: MV with push/pull mute switch), channel switch, rear panel: pre-amp out, power amp in, XLR line out with level and ground lift, parallel speaker jacks, footswitch jack, tuner output jack, black Tolex covering, silver grille cloth, top handle, 22.7 in. wide, 8.94 in. tall, 10.5 in. deep, 16 lbs., single-button footswitch included, mfg. 2015-present.

MSR N/A	$800	$525 - 600	$260 - 325	

MSR/NOTES	100%	EXCELLENT	AVERAGE	LAST MSR

Bassman 115 Neo Speaker Cabinet
courtesy Fender

Bassman 410 Neo Speaker Cabinet
courtesy Fender

Bassman 810 Speaker Cabinet
courtesy Fender

SUPER BASSMAN HEAD (NO. 224-9000) – 300W, bass head-unit, 10-tube chassis, preamp: 2 X 12AX7, 1 X 12AT7, power: 1 X 12AT7, 6 X 6550, solid-state rectifier, two channels (vintage, overdrive), front black control panel, two inputs, 12 black skirted knobs (Ch. 1: v, b with push/pull deep switch, m, t with push/pull bright switch, Ch. 2: g, blend, v, b with push/pull deep switch, mid-freq., mid level, t with push/pull bright switch, All: MV with push/pull mute switch), channel switch, rear panel: pre-amp out, power amp in, XLR line out with level and ground lift, speaker jack with impedance switch, footswitch jack, black Tolex covering, silver grille cloth, side spring-loaded handles and top handle, 24.5 in. wide, 10 in. tall, 13.5 in. deep, 65 lbs., single-button footswitch included, mfg. 2012-present.

| MSR $2,400 | $1,800 | $1,000 - 1,250 | $600 - 750 | |

BASSMAN 115 NEO SPEAKER CABINET (NO. 224-9500) – 350W, 1-15 in. Eminence Neodymium speaker and compression driver tweeter, 8 ohm impedance, high-freq. horn attenuator, lightweight plywood construction, black Tolex covering, silver grille cloth, side-mounted steel flip handles, removable casters, 26 in. wide, 20.75 in. tall, 16.25 in. deep, 45 lbs., mfg. 2012-present.

| MSR N/A | $650 | $425 - 475 | $210 - 260 | |

BASSMAN 410 NEO SPEAKER CABINET (NO. 224-9400) – 500W, 4-10 in. Eminence Neodymium speakers and compression driver tweeter, 8 ohm impedance, high-freq. horn attenuator, lightweight plywood construction, black Tolex covering, silver grille cloth, side-mounted steel flip handles, removable casters, 26 in. wide, 24.5 in. tall, 16.25 in. deep, 55 lbs., mfg. 2012-present.

| MSR N/A | $800 | $525 - 600 | $260 - 325 | |

BASSMAN 610 NEO SPEAKER CABINET (NO. 224-9300) – 800W, 6-10 in. Eminence Neodymium speakers and compression driver tweeter, 4 ohm impedance, high-freq. horn attenuator, lightweight plywood construction, black Tolex covering, silver grille cloth, top, rear-mounted steel bar handles and bottom-mounted steel-flip handles, bottom rear-mounted wheels, 26 in. wide, 36.625 in. tall, 16.25 in. deep, 90 lbs., mfg. 2012-present.

| MSR N/A | $1,400 | $900 - 1,050 | $450 - 550 | |

BASSMAN 810 NEO SPEAKER CABINET (NO. 224-9200) – 1000W, 8-10 in. Eminence Neodymium speakers and compression driver tweeter, 4 ohm impedance, high-freq. horn attenuator, lightweight plywood construction, black Tolex covering, silver grille cloth, top, rear-mounted steel bar handles and bottom-mounted steel-flip handles, bottom rear-mounted wheels, 26 in. wide, 48 in. tall, 16.25 in. deep, 115 lbs., mfg. 2012-present.

| MSR N/A | $1,500 | $975 - 1,125 | $500 - 600 | |

BASS HYBRID AMPS: BASSMAN TV SERIES

Bassman TV Ten
courtesy Fender

Bassman TV Twelve
courtesy Fender

Bassman TV Fifteen
Cabinet courtesy Fender

BASSMAN TV TEN (NO. 224-8100) – 150W, 1-10 in. Celestion Green Label Ferrite 200W bass speaker, bass combo, hybrid chassis with 1 X 12AX7 preamp tube and Class D solid-state power amp, single channel, top chrome control panel, two inputs, four chickenhead knobs (v, b, m, t), XLR output jack with ground lift, rear ported reinforced vintage-style TV cabinet, dog bone handle, lacquered tweed covering, brown pinstripe grille, 20 in. wide, 18 in. height, 11.75 in. deep, 38 lbs., mfg. summer 2009-2011.

| | N/A | $550 - 625 | $300 - 350 | $1,190 |

MSR/NOTES	100%	EXCELLENT	AVERAGE	LAST MSR

BASSMAN TV TWELVE (NO. 224-8200) – 150W, 1-12 in. Celestion Green Label Ferrite 200W bass speaker, bass combo, hybrid chassis with 1 X 12AX7 preamp tube and Class D solid-state power amp, single channel, top chrome control panel, two inputs, five chickenhead knobs (g, b, m, t, v), deep and bright switches, XLR output jack with ground lift, rear ported reinforced vintage-style TV cabinet, dog bone handle, lacquered tweed covering, brown pinstripe grille, 22 in. wide, 20 in. tall, 12.75 in. deep, 44.6 lbs., mfg. summer 2009-2011.

N/A	$575 - 675	$325 - 400		$1,190

BASSMAN TV FIFTEEN (NO. 224-8300) – 350W, 1-15 in. Celestion Green Label Ferrite 400W bass speaker, bass combo, hybrid chassis with 1 X 12AX7 preamp tube and Class D solid-state power amp, single channel, top chrome control panel, two inputs, five chickenhead knobs (g, b, m, t, v), deep and bright switches, XLR output jack with ground lift, rear ported reinforced vintage-style TV cabinet, dog bone handle, removable casters, lacquered tweed covering, brown pinstripe grille, 25 in. wide, 23 in. tall, 14 in. deep, 59.5 lbs., mfg. summer 2009-2011.

N/A	$675 - 800	$375 - 450		$1,400

BASSMAN TV DUO TEN (NO. 224-8400) – 350W, 2-10 in. Celestion Green Label Ferrite 200W bass speakers, bass combo, hybrid chassis with 1 X 12AX7 preamp tube and Class D solid-state power amp, single channel, top chrome control panel, two inputs, five chickenhead knobs (g, b, m, t, v), deep and bright switches, XLR output jack with ground lift, rear ported reinforced vintage-style TV cabinet, dog bone handle, removable casters, lacquered tweed covering, brown pinstripe grille, 25 in. wide, 23 in. tall, 14 in. deep, 61.5 lbs., mfg. summer 2009-2011.

N/A	$675 - 800	$375 - 450		$1,400

BASS HYBRID AMPS: PRO SERIES

In 2008, the solid-state line of Pro Series bass amps was discontinued and replaced by the hybrid Pro Bass Series (tube preamp/solid-state power amp).

* Add $30 (MSR $35) for speaker cabinet cover.

TB-600 Head
courtesy Fender

TB-1200 Head
courtesy Fender

TB-600 Combo
courtesy Fender

215 Pro Speaker Cabinet
courtesy Fender

TB-600 HEAD (NO. 224-5800) – 600W @ 4ohms (400W @ 8 ohms), two-space rack-mount head-unit bass amplifier, hybrid chassis with 2 X 12AX7 preamp tubes and a solid state power amp, single channel, front brushed aluminum panel, two inputs (one in front, one in back), 11 black knobs (Vintage Tube Tone: v, b, m, t, Tube Overdrive: g, v, blend, Vari Q: freq., level, room balance, MV), balanced line out with ground lift, pre/post switches, and level control, tuner out, effects loop, full range 1/4 in. and Speakon speaker jacks, footswitch jack, black casing, 19 in. wide, 3.5 in. tall, 15 in. deep, 32 lbs., optional four-button footswitch, mfg. summer 2008-disc.

$1,100	$650 - 800	$400 - 500		$1,500

* Add $60 (MSR $80) for the TBFS-4 four-button footswitch with built-in tuner.

* TB-600 Combo (No. 224-6000) – similar to the TB-600 Head, except in combo configuration with 2-10 in. Fender Special Design Eminence cast frame speakers and a Foster high-frequency compression driver horn with rear attenuator, black textured vinyl covering, black metal grille with large Fender logo, casters, 23.5 in. wide, 25.5 in. tall, 16.5 in. deep, 102 lbs., optional four-button footswitch with built-in tuner (Model TBFS-4) and cover, mfg. summer 2008-disc.

$1,500	$850 - 1,050	$500 - 625		$2,050

* Add $30 (MSR $35) for matching cover.
* Add $60 (MSR $80) for the TBFS-4 four-button footswitch with built-in tuner.

TB-1200 HEAD (NO. 224-5700) – 1200W @ 2ohms (800W @ 4 ohms or 550W @ 8 ohms), two-space rack-mount head-unit bass amplifier, hybrid chassis with 2 X 12AX7 preamp tubes and a solid state power amp, single channel, front brushed aluminum panel, two inputs (one in front, one in back), 11 black knobs (Vintage Tube Tone: v, b, m, t, Tube Overdrive: g, v, blend, Vari Q: freq., level, room balance, MV), balanced line out with ground lift, pre/post switches, and level control, tuner out, effects loop, full range 1/4 in. and Speakon spaker jacks, footswitch jack, black casing, 19 in. wide, 3.5 in. tall, 15 in. deep, 34 lbs., four-button footswitch with built in tuner included (Model TBFS-4), mfg. summer 2008-disc.

$1,300	$750 - 925	$450 - 575		$1,800

* Add $60 (MSR $80) for the TBFS-4 four-button footswitch with built-in tuner.

115 PRO SPEAKER CABINET (NO. 221-7800) – 400W continuous (800W max), 1-15 in. Fender Special Design cast frame Eminence speaker, Foster horn, horn attenuator, Speakon connector, and parallel wired 1/4 in. speaker jacks on back panel, 3/4 in. 13-ply Baltic Birch plywood construction, heavy duty recessed spring-loaded handles, black textured vinyl covering, black metal grille with large Fender logo, 23.5 in. wide, 21.5 in. tall, 16.5 in. deep, 71 lbs., optional cover, mfg. summer 2009-disc.

$700	$400 - 500	$250 - 300		$950

MSR/NOTES	100%	EXCELLENT	AVERAGE	LAST MSR

215 PRO SPEAKER CABINET (NO. 221-5200) – 800W continuous (1600W max), 2-15 in. Fender Special Design cast frame Eminence speakers, Foster horn, horn attenuator, Speakon connector, and parallel wired 1/4 in. speaker jacks on back panel, 3/4 in. seven-ply Baltic Birch plywood construction, corner-mounted recessed handles, heavy duty skid rails, diamond plated rear kick plate, recessed casters, black textured vinyl covering, black metal grille with large Fender logo, 26 in. wide, 36.625 in. tall, 16.25 in. deep, 108 lbs., optional cover, mfg. summer 2008-disc.

	$1,100	$625 - 775	$375 - 475	$1,500

610 PRO SPEAKER CABINET (NO. 221-6200) – 800W continuous (1600W max), 6-10 in. Fender Special Design cast frame Eminence speakers, Foster horn, horn attenuator, Speakon connector, and parallel wired 1/4 in. speaker jacks on back panel, 3/4 in. seven-ply Baltic Birch plywood construction, corner-mounted recessed handles, heavy duty skid rails, diamond plated rear kick plate, recessed casters, black textured vinyl covering, black metal grille with large Fender logo, 26 in. wide, 36.625 in. tall, 16.25 in. deep, 117 lbs., optional cover, mfg. summer 2008-disc.

	$1,100	$625 - 775	$375 - 475	$1,500

810 PRO SPEAKER CABINET (NO. 221-7200) – 1000W continuous (2000W max), 8-10 in. Fender Special Design cast frame Eminence speakers, Foster horn, horn attenuator, Speakon connector, and parallel wired 1/4 in. speaker jacks on back panel, 3/4 in. seven-ply Baltic Birch plywood construction, corner-mounted recessed handles, heavy duty skid rails, diamond plated rear kick plate, recessed casters, black textured vinyl covering, black metal grille with large Fender logo, 26 in. wide, 48 in. tall, 16 in. deep, 160 lbs., optional cover, mfg. summer 2008-disc.

	$1,300	$750 - 925	$450 - 575	$1,800

KEYBOARD SS AMPLIFIERS: KXR SERIES

The KXR series was designed by Fender for keyboards or self contained P.A. systems. The KXR series was introduced circa 1995 but they offered keyboard amplifiers before that. The Sidekick Keyboard and Keyboard 60 were available in the early 1990s. There was also an SFX Keyboard amp produced in 1999.

KXR 60 (NO. 022-8500-000) – 50W, keyboard amp, 1-12 in. Eminence speaker, piezo electric HF horn, solid-state chassis, two channels, front black control panel, two inputs, eight black knobs with white tops (v1, v2, l, lm, hm, h, r, MV), effects loop, aux. RCA inputs, headphone jack, Delta Comp limiter, black Tolex covering, black grille, 51 lbs., mfg. 1996-2002.

	N/A	$175 - 225	$100 - 140	$470

KXR 100 (NO. 022-8501-000) – 90W, keyboard amp, 1-15 in. speaker, piezo dual electric HF horn, solid-state chassis, three channels, front black control panel, four inputs, nine black knobs with white tops (v1, v2, v3, l, lm, hm, h, r, MV), effects loop, aux. RCA inputs, headphone jack, Delta Comp limiter, black Tolex covering, black grille, 55 lbs., mfg. 1995-2002.

	N/A	$225 - 275	$125 - 175	$570

KXR 200 (NO. 022-8502-000) – 200W, keyboard amp, 1-15 in. speaker, piezo dual electric HF horn, solid-state chassis, four channels, front black control panel, five inputs, 28 black knobs with white tops, effects loop, Delta Comp limiter, black Tolex covering, black grille, pop-in casters, 88 lbs., mfg. 1995-2000.

	N/A	$325 - 400	$200 - 250	$850

SPEAKER CABINETS

2-12(S) SLANT (NO. 021-1616-010) – 2-12 in. Eminence speakers, 8 Ohm mono/16 Ohm stereo impedance, black Tolex covering, mfg. late 1980s-1993.

	N/A	$150 - 200	$95 - 125	$390

4-12(S) SLANT/STRAIGHT (NO. 021-1620/1621-010) – 4-12 in. Eminence speakers, 8 Ohm mono/16 Ohm stereo impedance, straight or slanted cab, black Tolex covering, mfg. late 1980s-1993.

	N/A	$175 - 225	$110 - 140	$560

CB-112 STD (NO. 021-1608-010) – 1-12 in. Eminence speaker, 8 Ohm impedance, black Tolex covering, mfg. late 1980s-1993.

	N/A	$95 - 125	$50 - 70	$260

HM 1-12 (NO. 021-1609-010) – 1-12 in. Eminence speaker, 8 Ohm impedance, gray carpet covering, mfg. late 1980s-1993.

	N/A	$95 - 125	$50 - 70	$260

HM 2-12 S SLANT (NO. 021-1613-010) – 2-12 in. Eminence speakers, 8 Ohm mono/16 Ohm stereo impedance, gray carpet covering, mfg. late 1980s-1993.

	N/A	$140 - 175	$85 - 110	$390

HM 4-12A/B SLANT/STRAIGHT (NO. 021-1618/1619-010) – 4-12 in. Eminence speakers, 8 Ohm mono/16 Ohm stereo impedance, straight or slanted cab, gray carpet covering, mfg. late 1980s-1993.

	N/A	$175 - 225	$110 - 140	$560

FENTON WEILL

Amplifiers previously produced in London, England between circa 1960 and 1965.

Henry Weill built Fenton-Weill amplifiers in the early 1960s. In 1959, Weill and Jim Burns (see Burns) produced a few guitars under the name Burns-Weill. This partnership didn't last long and by the end of 1959, the two had each

MSR/NOTES	100%	EXCELLENT	AVERAGE	LAST MSR

gone their own way. Weill continued to build guitars under the name Weill-London, but soon changed it to Fenton-Weill (Fenton comes from a name of a Burns-Weill guitar model). Weill started building guitar amplifiers around this time as well. By 1963, Weill operated out of his own factory in London and employed up to fifteen people. He also built guitars and amplifiers for other companies such as Hohner and Selmer. However, Weill couldn't manage the financial aspect of his company and filed bankruptcy in 1965. After Fenton-Weill went under, he continued to produce PA units and other miscellaneous amplifiers in his basement. Information courtesy: Tim Fletcher and Steve Russell.

ELECTRIC TUBE AMPLIFIERS

Fenton-Weill produced several models in the early 1960s, however very few seem to appear in the used marketplace. Models include the **Auditorium**, **Black Star**, **Cadet**, **Dualmaster Compact**, **Dualmaster Packaway**, **Golden Arrow**, **Hornet**, **Porta-Bass 15**, and the **Stereo Amplifier** head. Prices seem to fall between $200 and $400; however, most models reside in England.

FERNANDES

Amplifiers previously produced in Japan, China, Korea, and Taiwan during the late 1980s and 1990s. Distributed by Fernandes Guitars International Inc., in Chatsworth, CA. The Fernandes trademark was established in 1969, and they currently produce a variety of electric guitars and basses.

Fernandes has been building guitars overseas since 1969. For a full history on Fernandes, refer to the *Blue Book of Electric Guitars*. In the late 1980s, Fernandes introduced three entry level amplifiers. They continued to produce amplifiers throughout the 1990s further expanding their line. In the mid-1990s, Fernandes purchased HIWATT and in 1999, they discontinued production of all Fernandes amplifiers and concentrated on developing/producing HIWATT products. By 2000, HIWATT amplifiers were featured on Fernandes guitar price lists. Many catalogs in the late 1990s and early 2000s feature a double listing of Fernandes guitars and HIWATT amplifiers. In the 2000s, Fernandes offered the Skel-Zo, which is shaped like the popular Nomad guitar. Currently Fernandes only offers a small 10W practice amp as part of their guitar packages, and their built-in amp Nomad models. For more information, visit Fernandes or HIWATT's website or contact the company directly.

CONTACT INFORMATION
FERNANDES
11044 Weddington St., Suite 13
North Hollywood, CA 91601
www.fernandesguitars.com

U.S. Distributor: Musical Distributors Group
9 Mars Court, Suite C-3
Boonton, NJ 07005
Phone No.: 973-335-7888
Phone No.: 866-632-8346
Fax No.: 973-335-7779
www.musicaldistributors.com
sales@musicaldistributors.com

ELECTRIC SS AMPLIFIERS

FA-15 – 15W, 1-8 in. speaker, guitar combo, solid-state chassis, single channel, front black control panel, single input, seven black knobs (g1, g2, MV, t, m, b, p), effects loop, headphone jack, black covering, black grille, mfg. late 1980s-1998.

	N/A	$50 - 70	$30 - 40	$129

FA-15B BASS AMP – 15W, 1-8 in. speaker, guitar combo, solid-state chassis, single channel, front black control panel, single input, five black knobs (v, t, m, b, p), effects loop, headphone jack, black covering, black grille, mfg. late 1980s-1998.

	N/A	$55 - 75	$30 - 40	$149

FA-20D – 20W, 1-8 in. speaker and 2-2 in. tweeters, guitar combo, solid-state chassis, two channels, front black control panel, single input, eight black knobs (Ch. 1: g, level, Ch. 2: g, level, All: t, m, b, p), effects loop, headphone jack, aux. input, black covering, black grille, mfg. late 1980s-1994.

	N/A	$60 - 80	$40 - 50	$149

FA-50DSR – 50W (25W per channel), 2-6 in. speakers and 2-2 in. tweeters, guitar combo, solid-state chassis, two channels, reverb, front black control panel, single input, eight black knobs (Ch. 1: level, Ch. 2: g, level, All: t, m, b, p, r), effects loop, headphone jack, aux. input, black covering, black grille, mfg. 1994-95.

	N/A	$70 - 95	$45 - 60	$199

GC-20 – 20W, 1-6 in. (16 cm) speaker, guitar combo, solid-state chassis, single channel, front gold control panel, single input, six black knobs (g, fine, t, m, b, MV), effects return only, headphone jack, footswitch, black covering, black grille, mfg. 1995-98.

	N/A	$60 - 80	$40 - 50	$179

* **GC-20R** – similar to the GC-20, except has reverb with control (seven total knobs), mfg. 1995-98.

	N/A	$70 - 95	$45 - 60	$199

TX-10 – 10W, 1-6 in. (16 cm) speaker, guitar combo, solid-state chassis, single channel, front black control panel, single input, five black knobs (g, MV, t, m, b), headphone jack, black covering, black grille, mfg. 1995-98.

	N/A	$40 - 50	$20 - 30	$99

MSR/NOTES	100%	EXCELLENT	AVERAGE	LAST MSR

FIREBELLY AMPS

Amplifiers currently produced in Santa Monica, CA since 2008.

Father Steven Cohen and his son Scott Cohen build vintage-style tube guitar amplifiers in their Santa Monica shop. The Cohens set out to recreate the tone of Fender amps from the 1950s and 1960s while upgrading them and enhancing them wherever possible. Their line includes three vintage hand-wired Blackface combo amps based on the Fender Princeton Reverb, Deluxe Reverb, and Vibrolux Reverb. They also offer a Standard line of amplifiers that are similar to their vintage recreations but have printed circuit boards instead and prices start at $995. For more information, visit Firebelly Amps' website or contact them directly.

CONTACT INFORMATION
FIREBELLY AMPS
2530 Wilshire Blvd., 3rd Floor
Santa Monica, CA 90403
Phone No.: 310-701-1950
www.firebellyamps.com
info@firebellyamps.com

FIRST ACT

Amplifiers currently produced in China since 1995. Distributed by First Act of Boston, MA.

First Act Inc. produces a full line of musical instruments ranging from guitars to amplifiers. They produce a line of guitars built in the U.S., a custom shop in the U.S., and a line of guitars and amplifiers built in China. The company's custom products are matched by a commitment to make music more accessible for everyone - challenging the idea that quality instruments have to be expensive and sold in a handful of places. First Act makes it possible for people from all backgrounds to play music. Amplifiers utilize V-Stack technology. You may also recognize many First Act guitars in 2006-07 model Volkswagons, as they teamed together to sell cars and guitars packaged together. Anybody who bought a Volkswagon model in the last quarter of 2006, got a First Act guitar (matching color) that could be plugged into the VW's aux. input on the radio. For more information visit First Act's website or contact the company directly.

CONTACT INFORMATION
FIRST ACT
745 Boylston Street
Boston, MA 02116
Phone No.: 617-226-7888
Phone No.: 888-551-1115
Fax No.: 617-226-7890
www.firstact.com
support@firstact.com

ELECTRIC SS AMPLIFIERS

All First Act amplifiers utilize V-Stack Technology that emulates tube sound in an analog solid-state design.
- **Add $50 for VFC001 Footswitch.**
- **Add $100 for VFC002 Footswitch.**

VA850
courtesy First Act

VA851
courtesy First Act

VA881
courtesy First Act

VA850 – 30W, 1-10 in. speaker, guitar combo, solid-state chassis, V-Stack technology, four directly selectable channels, reverb, echo, tremolo, front black control panel, single input, 12 black knobs, Black vinyl covering with a cream stripe running on the left/center side, brown grille cloth, 20.5 in. wide, 19.75 in. tall, 11 in. deep, 39.5 lbs., disc. 2009.

	100%	EXCELLENT	AVERAGE	LAST MSR
	$300	$175 - 225	$110 - 140	$435

VA851 – 50W, 1-12 in. speaker, guitar combo, solid-state chassis, V-Stack technology, four directly selectable channels, reverb, echo, tremolo, front black control panel, single input, 12 black knobs, Black vinyl covering with a cream stripe running on the left/center side, brown grille cloth, 20.5 in. wide, 20.5 in. tall, 17.9 in. deep, 44 lbs., current mfg.

MSR $500	$350	$200 - 250	$120 - 150	

VA852 – 75W, 1-12 in. speaker, guitar combo, solid-state chassis, V-Stack technology, four directly selectable channels, reverb, echo, tremolo, front black control panel, single input, 12 black knobs, Black vinyl covering with a cream stripe running on the left/center side, brown grille cloth, 24.8 in. wide, 22.5 in. tall, 13.75 in. deep, 57.5 lbs., disc. 2006.

	$400	$240 - 290	$140 - 180	$579

VA881 – 75W, 1-12 in. speaker, guitar combo, solid-state chassis, V-Stack technology, four directly selectable channels, reverb, echo, tremolo, front black control panel, single input, 15 black knobs, Black vinyl covering with a cream stripe running on the left/center side, tan grille cloth, 30.75 in. wide, 23.5 in. tall, 13 in. deep, 72.75 lbs., disc. 2009.

	$600	$375 - 450	$225 - 275	$865

MSR/NOTES	100%	EXCELLENT	AVERAGE	LAST MSR

VA882 – 100W, 2-12 in. speaker, guitar combo, solid-state chassis, V-Stack technology, four directly selectable channels, reverb, echo, tremolo, front black control panel, single input, 15 black knobs, Black vinyl covering with a cream stripe running on the left/center side, tan grille cloth, 31.5 in. wide, 24.5 in. tall, 13 in. deep, 86 lbs., disc. 2006.

	N/A	$375 - 450	$225 - 275	$1,080

FIRST MAN

Amplifiers and other instruments previously manufactured in Japan during the late 1960s and early 1970s.

First Man amplifiers were produced in Japan during the late 1960s and possibly into the 1970s. The "F" in the First Man logo is very similar to the reverse "F" in Fender's logo and First Man's line of amplifiers are very similar to Fender's first solid-state line of amplifiers in the late 1960s. First Man also offered a variety of semi-hollowbody electrics and violin basses as well as a line of electric organs. First Man also had an unknown relationship with Mosrite and was possibly Mosrite's distributor in Japan as they appear in Japanese catalogs together.

FISHMAN

Amplifiers currently produced in China since 2003. Distributed by Fishman Transducers, Inc. in Wilmington, MA. The Fishman trademark was established in 1981.

CONTACT INFORMATION
FISHMAN
6 Riverside Drive
Andover, MA 01810
Phone No.: 978-988-9199
Fax No.: 978-988-0770
www.fishman.com

Larry Fishman founded Fishman Transducers, Inc. in 1981 as an acoustic pickup manufacturer. Fishman played acoustic bass in jazz venues throughout the 1970s and early 1980s, and he found it was increasingly difficult to amplify the sound from the guitar. He then started to develop pickups for acoustic guitars. This experimentation led to a full-time job and in the early 1980s he was supplying OEM pickups for Guild and built the Thin Line pickup for Martin. At the summer 2003 NAMM show, Fishman introduced the Loudbox series of acoustic amplifiers. These amplifiers are designed for the particular acoustic player with high-quality features. In 2010, Fishman introduced the **SA220** (MSR $1,540) Solo Performance System and Acoustic Guitar Combo. For more information, visit Fishman's website or contact them directly.

ACOUSTIC SS AMPLIFIERS

LOUDBOX – 250W (tri-amped), 1-8 in woofer (160W), 1-4 in. midrange cone (60W), and 2-1 in. neodymium soft dome tweeters (30W), solid-state chassis, reverb, single channel, front dark gray control panel, one input, 16 black knobs (v, l, m, h, brilliance, anti-feedback, r), mute switch, notch filter, effects loop, XLR D.I. output, adj. kickstand, black covering, dark gray grille, 15.5 in. wide, 19.25 in. tall, 13.75 in. deep, 55.5 lbs., mfg. 2004-05.

	N/A	$300 - 350	$175 - 225	$700

LOUDBOX 100 – 100W (bi-amped), 1-8 in woofer and a 1 in. neodymium soft dome tweeter, solid-state chassis, digital effects including chorus, front dark gray control panel, three inputs (two 1/4 in. and one XLR), 16 black knobs (Ch. 1: g, l m, h, anti-feedback, FX level, Ch. 2: g, l m, h, anti-feedback, FX level, All: digital FX select, digital FX level, aux. level, MV), two notch filters (one per channel), two phase switches (one per channel), dedicated effects loop, mute switch, tuner out, headphone jack, black covering, dark gray grille, 15.5 in. wide, 16 in. tall, 11.2 in. deep, 23 lbs., mfg. 2006-present.

MSR $930	$600	$375 - 450	$225 - 275	

LOUDBOX PERFORMER – 130W (tri-amped), 2-6.5 in woofers and a 1 in. neodymium soft dome tweeter, solid-state chassis, digital effects including chorus, front dark gray control panel, three inputs (two 1/4 in. and one XLR), 16 black knobs (Ch. 1: g, l m, h, anti-feedback, FX level, Ch. 2: g, l m, h, anti-feedback, FX level, All: digital FX select, digital FX level, aux. level, MV), two notch filters (one per channel), two phase switches (one per channel), dedicated effects loop, mute switch, tuner out, headphone jack, single-position kickstand, black covering, dark gray grille, 15.5 in. wide, 19.2 in. tall, 11.2 in. deep, 35 lbs., mfg. 2005-present.

MSR $1,050	$700	$475 - 550	$300 - 350	

LOUDBOX PRO – 600W (tri-amped), 1-12 in woofer (380W), 1-4 in. midrange cone (160W), and 3-1 in. neodymium soft dome tweeters (60W), solid-state chassis, digital effects including chorus, front dark gray control panel, three inputs (two 1/4 in. and one XLR), 16 black knobs (Ch. 1: g, l m, h, anti-feedback, FX level, Ch. 2: g, l m, h, anti-feedback, FX level, All: digital FX select, digital FX level, aux. level, MV), two notch filters (one per channel), two phase switches (one per channel), dedicated effects loop, mute switch, tuner out, headphone jack, adj. kickstand, black covering, dark gray grille, 25 in. wide, 19.25 in. tall, 11.75 in. deep, 77 lbs., mfg. 2005-09.

	$1,800	$1,100 - 1,300	$675 - 800	$2,580

FLITE SOUND INNOVATIONS, INC.

Speaker cabinets previously produced in Plainfield, CT and Danielson, CT. The Flite Sound trademark was established in 1987.

Flite Sound had been building professional, lightweight speaker enclosures since 1987. They make a wide variety of bass, guitar, P.A., monitors, and keyboard speakers. All cabinets were hand-built one at a time.

FLOT-A-TONE

Amplifiers previously produced in Milwaukee, WI between the late 1940s and the early 1960s.

Flot-A-Tone produced a wide variety of tube amplifiers between the late 1940s and the early 1960s. They were based in Milwaukee, WI, and possibly distributed by the LoDuca brothers (also of EKO fame). There are a few variations in story about what happened to the company, but the general opinion seems to be that the Koss Corporation bought the company or Flot-A-Tone turned into Koss in the mid-1960s. When the company changed hands, Flot-A-Tone amps were discontinued.

There are several Flot-A-Tone different models out there, and most often, no two are alike as rumor has it that they built these amps as they were ordered. They are known for having a great tremolo system and being built well. Most models feature a red and white covering with a refridgerator-style handle on top. Noted artists G.E. Smith of the Saturday Night Live band and Ry Cooder are known for playing Flot-A-Tones. Any information on Flot-A-Tone can be submitted directly to Blue Book Publications.

Model 500-600
courtesy George McGuire

Model 500-600
courtesy George McGuire

FLUXTONE SPEAKERS

Speakers and speaker cabinets currently produced in Lafayette, CO.

Steve Carey invented the variable efficiency speaker that makes it behave the way a master volume control should. With a Fluxtone speaker, the player can reduce the volume at the speaker level without losing any tone. Fluxtone offers their speakers as stand-alone units, in Fluxtone speaker cabinets, and as retrofits in existing amplifiers. Fluxtone's speaker cabinets are built by MojoTone and come in a variety of configurations. For more information, visit Fluxtone's website or contact them directly.

CONTACT INFORMATION
FLUXTONE SPEAKERS
301 East Cannon St.
Lafayette, CO 80026
Phone No.: 303-907-9078
www.fluxtonespeakers.com
fluxtone@gmail.com

FORGE

Amplifiers previously produced in Salt Lake City, UT. Distributed by XP Audio, Inc. in Salt Lake City, UT.

Forge Active Bass Amplification builds bass amplifiers and speaker cabinets. Rick Bos and John Johnson founded XP Audio in 2007 to develop top-line highly innovative audio products that include Forge as well as the trademarks Motion Sound, Bolt, and Morpheus. Forge's systems include the AXB Bass tube preamp head and a variety of powered speaker cabinets.

FRAMUS

Amplifiers currently produced in Markneukirchen, Germany since 1996. Distributed by Warwick GmbH & Co. Music Equipment Kg of Markneukirchen, Germany, and in the U.S. by Dana B. Goods in Ventura, CA. The Framus trademark was produced from the late 1940s to the late 1970s and reintroduced in 1996.

When Frederick Wilfer returned to his home town of Walthersgrun at the end of World War II, he realized that the American-controlled Sudetenland area was soon to fall under control of the Russian forces. With the help of the Americans, Wilfer succeeded in resettling a number of violin makers from Schonbach to Franconia (later in the district of Erlangen). Between 1945 to 1947, Wilfer continued to find homes and employment for the Schonbach violin makers.

CONTACT INFORMATION
FRAMUS
Factory
PO Box 10100 Gewerbegebiet
Wohlhausen
Markneukirchen, D-08258 Germany
Phone No.: 49-37422-555-0
Fax No.: 49-37422-55599
www.framus.de

In 1946, Wilfer founded the Framus production company, the company name an acronym for Franconian Musical instruments. As the company established itself in 1946, Wilfer drew on the knowledge of his violin builder from Schonbach to produce a range of musical instruments including violins and cellos. The new Framus company expanded out of its first couple of production buildings, eventually building a new factory in Bubenreuth in 1955.

The first Framus electric guitars appeared in the 1950s. Due to the presence of American servicemen stationed there, the influence of rock 'n' roll surfaced earlier in Germany than other European countries. As a result, German guitar builders had a headstart on answering the demand caused by the proliferation of pop groups during the 1960s. Furthermore, as the German production increased, they began exporting their guitars to other countries

MSR/NOTES	100%	EXCELLENT	AVERAGE	LAST MSR

(including the U.S.) The Framus company stayed active in producing acoustic and electric guitars, and electric basses until the mid-1970s.

In the 1970s, increased competition and serious price undercutting from firms in the Asian market had a serious effect on established companies. Unfortunately, one aspect was to force a number of firms into bankruptcy - and Framus was one of those companies in 1975. However, Wilfer did have the opportunity to watch his son, Hans-Peter Wilfer, establish his own company in 1982 (see Warwick). Warwick's success allowed Hans-Peter to re-introduce the Framus trademark to the European musical market in 1996. In honor of his father Frederick, Hans-Peter chose to use the world famous Framus trademark when he began offering guitar models in 1996 Source: Hans Peter Wilfer, Warwick GmbH & Co. Music Equipment Kg; and Tony Bacon and Paul Day, *The Guru's Guitar Guide*.

Current Framus instruments (including electric guitars, acoustics, and hand wired tube guitar amps) are produced at the Warwick facility. Currently, Framus instruments are available in England, Germany, Sweden, Switzerland, and the United States. For more information, visit Framus' website.

AMPLIFIERS & SPEAKER CABINETS

A Classic Stack is available with a 30W class A head and cabinet set that is set in black Tolex covering (MSR $2,799) or dovetail-jointed bubinga cabinet (MSR $5,999).

COBRA HEAD – 100W, head-unit only, all-tube chassis, three channels, front silver control panel, single input, 22 knobs, effects loop, integrated MIDI interface, impedance selector, black or blue covering, gray metal grille, current mfg.

| MSR $4,966 | N/A | $1,500 - 1,750 | $950 - 1,100 | |

COBRA CABINET – 100W, 4-12 in. Celestion Vintage 25 Greenback speakers, 8 or 16 ohm impedance, straight or angled cabinet, black or blue covering, gray metal grille, current mfg.

| MSR $1,562 | N/A | $550 - 650 | $325 - 400 | |

DRAGON HEAD – 100W, head-unit only, all-tube chassis, three channels, front black control panel, single input, 22 knobs, effects loop, integrated MIDI interface, impedance selector, black covering, brown grille, current mfg.

| MSR $4,530 | N/A | $1,450 - 1,700 | $950 - 1,100 | |

DRAGON CABINET – 200W, 4-12 in. Celestion Vintage 30 speakers, 8 or 16 ohm impedance, straight or angled cabinet, black covering, brown grille, current mfg.

| MSR $1,228 | N/A | $450 - 525 | $275 - 325 | |

RUBY RIOT I/II COMBO – 30W, 2-12 in. mismatched Celestion speakers, tube chassis, two channels, reverb, top black control panel, single input, eleven knobs, effects loop, top handles, black or red covering, brown grille, current mfg.

| MSR $4,836 | N/A | $1,550 - 1,800 | $1,000 - 1,150 | |

The Ruby Riot II is voiced for British Class A sounds.

FRED

See Bedrock Amplification, Inc.

FRYETTE AMPLIFICATION

Amplifiers currently produced in Burbank, CA since 2009.

Steven Fryette, who founded VHT Amplification in 1989, sold the trademark to The Music Link in 2009, but continues to build his amplifiers under the Fryette brand. The Music Link is now building their own models under the VHT brand while Fryette kept all of the model designs and moved them to the Fryette line. For more information, visit their website or contact them directly.

FUCHS AUDIO TECHNOLOGY

Amplifiers currently produced in Clifton NJ; company founded in Bloomfield, NJ in 1999.

Fuchs Audio Technology was founded in 1999 by Andy Fuchs. Fuchs started repairing and modifying amplifiers in the NYC area in the late 1970s. He worked for a number of amp manufacturers including Plush, Earth Sound Research, and New York Audio Labs, and he began building amps under the Fuchs brand in 1999. The original Overdrive Supreme influenced by the legendary Overdrive Special by Dumble has been in continuous production since 1999. Fuchs Audio Technology now produces a full line of amplifiers from 7 to 150 watts and from one to three channels. All models are now CE certified and RoHs for export. Fuchs also owns and manufactures effects pedals under the PLUSH brand name. A partial list of Fuchs endorsers includes Kenny Wayne Shepherd, Al Di Meola, Paul Jackson Jr., Jeff Golub, Dweezil Zappa, Joe Bonamassa, Jake Cinninger, Shane Gibson (Korn), Vic Juris, and Matt O'Ree. For more information visit Fuch's website or contact them directly.

ELECTRIC TUBE AMPLIFIERS

The **Lucky 7** features 7W output, 2 X 12AX7 preamp tubes, 1 X EL34 power tube, and is available in a head-unit (MSR $989), 1-8 in. speaker combo (MSR $1,098), a 2-8 in. speaker combo (MSR $1,195), and a 1-12 in. speaker combo (MSR $1,550). The **Blackjack 21** features 21W output, 2 X 12AX7 preamp tubes, 2 X 6V6 power tubes, and is available as a head-unit (MSR $1,320), 1-8 in. speaker combo (MSR $1,430), 2-8 in. speaker combo (MSR $1,525), and 1-12 in. speaker combo (MSR $1,750). The **Train 45** is a single channel amp inspired by legendary Trainwreck amps. This amp has 35W output and is available as a head-unit (MSR $2,199), hardwood head (disc., last MSR was $2,495) or 1-12 in. speaker combo (MSR $2,475). The **Overdrive Supreme** features several configurations with output power ranges from 30W to 150W. The Overdrive 30 head unit starts at $2,855. The **Triple Drive Supreme** features distinct three channels. It comes in 50W, 100W, and 150W configurations and head-unit, 1-12 in. combo, and 2-12 in. combo versions. Prices start at $3,955. The **Frost 100** was produced during 2006 and 2007 and featured 100W output power and is available in one or two channel configurations. The **Viper** Series was produced in 2008 and 2009, features 120W output power and two distinct channel voices as well as a "thrust" control for low frequency extension and presence for increased high end clarity. The **Clean Machine** was introduced in 2009 and features the "A" channel from the Tripledrive that sounds very much like a blackface Fender. It is available in three power levels (75, 100, and 150) and is available as a head-unit (75W MSR $3,000, 100W MSR $3,200, 150W MSR $3,300) and a 1-12 in. combo (75W MSR $3,500, 100W MSR $3,700, 150W MSR $3,900). The **Mantis** was introduced in 2010, is designed for use with the rock and metal genre, and is available as a 50W head (MSR $3,185) or a 100W head (MSR $3,000). Fuchs also manufactures a series of 112, 212 and 412 speaker cabinets featuring Birch plywood construction and internal acoustic treatment for improved performance. Eminence speakers are standard and Celestion and EV speakers are optional.

FULTON-WEBB

Amplifiers previously produced in Austin, TX beginning in 1998.

Fulton-Webb was founded by Steve Fulton and Bill Webb in 1998. Their amplifiers are completely hand-built and are usually delivered eight to ten weeks from the time when ordered. Fulton-Webb offers a variety of models including the 17 Watt, 31 Watt, 50 Watt, 100 Watt, D'Luxe 18, D'Luxe 36, DR45, Imperial Reverb, and Viola models. These amps are all tube, point-to-point wired, and have either a tube or solid-state rectifier switch.

G SECTION
GABRIEL SOUND GARAGE

Amplifiers and speaker cabinets currently produced in Arlington Heights (Chicago), IL since 2001.

CONTACT INFORMATION
GABRIEL SOUND GARAGE
Arlington Heights, IL 60005
Phone No.: 847-394-5091
www.gabtone.com

Gabriel Bucataru started building Gabriel amps around 2000, but he has been involved in guitar amplifiers and electronics ever since he was a young boy. Bucataru grew up in communist Romania where western products (mainly amplifiers) were forbidden, and the only amps he had to use were from Romania and Russia. In 2000, Gabriel moved to the U.S. where he became very interested in the low-wattage Marshall amps of the 1960s and 1970s. Along with Graydon Stuckey of GDS Amplification, Mark Durham, and Jeff Swanson, Bucataru started www.18watt.com. This site is entirely dedicated to the 18W Marshall amps. In 2001, he built his first prototype 18W guitar amp with a Gabriel Logo. Since then he has introduced the Grand and Voxer (later renamed the V-18) 18 Watt models, as well as a new 33W model based on the V-18. For more information, visit Gabriel's website or contact the company directly. Information courtesy *The Tonequest Report*, October 2005.

ELECTRIC TUBE AMPLIFIERS

The **V-18** (previously called the Voxer) is an 18W tube amp with two channels. It is available as a head-unit (MSR $1,990), 1-12 in. speaker combo (MSR $2,590), or 2-12 in. speaker combo (MSR $2,680). The **V-18 LowCarb** version (MSR $1,870) with only one channel and less controls is also available. The **V-33** is a higher-power version of the V-18 with a cathode biased 33W output from 4 X EL84 power tubes and is available as a head unit (MSR $2,350), 1-12 in. combo (MSR $2,820), or 2-12 in. combo (MSR $2,980). The **Grand** model also has 18W power, but features a tremolo circuit. This model is available as a head-unit (disc., last MSR was $2,090), 1-12 in. speaker combo (disc. last MSR was $2,715), or 2-12 in. speaker combo (disc. last MSR was $2,890). A LowCarb version with only one channel and less controls is also available as a head-unit (disc., last MSR was $2,000) or 1-12 in. speaker combo (disc. last MSR was $2,110). They also offer speakers cabinets in 1-12 in. (MSR $550), a regular 2-12 in. (MSR $860), and a slanted 2-12 in. (MSR $910) configuration.

GALLIEN-KRUEGER

Amplifiers and speaker cabinets currently produced in Stockton, CA. Distributed by Gallien-Krueger. The Gallien-Krueger trademark was established in 1968.

CONTACT INFORMATION
GALLIEN-KRUEGER
2234 Industrial Drive
Stockton, CA 95206 USA
Phone No.: 209-234-7300
Fax No.: 209-234-8420
www.gallien-krueger.com
support@gallien.com

Robert Gallien is a graduate of Stanford University circa the late 1960s, and he took his first hand-built amplifier to a local music store in 1968. Carlos Santana happened to be around when Gallien introduced this amplifier, and he bought it the following day. The rest, as we say, is history. Gallien-Krueger has successfully been building quality bass amplifiers and speaker cabinets for almost 40 years now. Some of the artists that play their products include Tom Hamilton of Aerosmith, Tony Kanal of No Doubt, and Flea of the Red Hot Chili Peppers. In 2003, the company moved from San Jose to Stockton, California. For more information visit Gallien-Krueger's website or contact them directly.

MSR/NOTES	100%	EXCELLENT	AVERAGE	LAST MSR

ELECTRIC BASS AMPLIFIERS: ARTIST, FUSION, & RB SERIES

All head units except for the 400RB-III have dual amplifiers, one to run the woofer, and one to run the horn unit. The 800RB has been in the family for over two decades. This amp differs from the others in the line as it has a gray control panel instead of silver. There are cooling fans in the larger amplifiers. The combo units have a tilt-back cabinet design as well as a regular design.

400RB-III (302-0051-A) – 240W (150W), head-unit only, solid-state chassis, single channel, front silver control panel, single input, nine black knobs (v, c, p, t, h/m, l/m, b, boost, master), direct out line effects loop, voicing filters, black metal covering, 15 lbs., disc. 2002.

	N/A	$300 - 350	$175 - 225	$649

* **400RB/210 (303-0150-A)** – similar to the 400RB-III except in combo form with 2-10 in. speakers, black covering, black metal grille, 65 lbs., disc. 2003.

	N/A	$425 - 500	$275 - 325	$999

* **400RB/115 (303-0140-A)** – similar to the 400RB-III except in combo form with 1-15 in. speaker, black covering, black metal grille, 65 lbs., disc. 2003.

	N/A	$425 - 500	$275 - 325	$999

* **400RB/112 (303-0130-A)** – similar to the 400RB-III except in combo configuration with 1-12 in. speaker, black covering, black metal grille, 65 lbs., disc. 2002.

	N/A	$425 - 500	$275 - 325	$999

400RB-IV – 280W at 4 ohm (180W at 8 ohm), rack-mount head-unit only, solid-state chassis, single channel, front silver control panel, single input, nine black knobs (v, c, p, t, h/m, l/m, b, boost, master), direct out line, effects loop, voicing filters, black metal casing, 16.5 lbs., mfg. 2003-09, 2011-present.

MSR $714	$500	$300 - 375	$175 - 225	

MSR/NOTES	100%	EXCELLENT	AVERAGE	LAST MSR

700RB II
courtesy Gallien-Krueger

400RB-IV/115 Combo
courtesy Gallien-Krueger

800RB
courtesy Gallien-Krueger

700RB II/210 Combo
courtesy Gallien-Krueger

* **400RB-IV/115 Combo** – similar to the 400RB IV, except in combo form with 1-15 in. speaker, 65 lbs., mfg. 2003-06.

	N/A	$425 - 525	$250 - 325	$999

* **400RB-IV/210 Combo** – similar to the 400RB IV, except in combo form with 1-15 in. speaker, 65 lbs., mfg. 2003-06.

	N/A	$425 - 525	$250 - 325	$999

700RB (302-0020-A) – 380W + 50W, head-unit only, solid-state chassis, single channel, front silver control panel, single input, eleven black knobs (direct out level, v, c, p, t, h/m, l/m, b, boost, tweeter, woofer), effects loop, voicing filters, black metal covering, 16.5 lbs., disc. 2002.

	N/A	$350 - 425	$200 - 250	$799

* **700RB/112 (303-0100-A)** – similar to the 700RB except in combo form with 1-12 in. speaker, black covering, black metal grille, 77 lbs., disc. 2002.

	N/A	$625 - 750	$375 - 450	$1,499

* **700RB/115 (303-0110-A)** – similar to the 700RB except in combo form with 1-15 in. speaker, black covering, black metal grille, 77 lbs., disc. 2003.

	N/A	$625 - 750	$375 - 450	$1,499

* **700RB/210 (303-0120-A)** – similar to the 700RB except in combo form with 2-10 in. speakers, black covering, black metal grille, 82 lbs., disc. 2003.

	N/A	$625 - 750	$375 - 450	$1,499

700RB II – 480W + 50W at 4 ohms (320W at 8 ohms), head-unit only, solid-state chassis, single channel, front silver control panel, single input, eleven black knobs (direct out level, v, c, p, t, h/m, l/m, b, boost, tweeter, woofer), effects loop, voicing filters, black metal covering, 25 lbs., mfg. 2003-present.

MSR $928	$650	$425 - 475	$210 - 260	

* **700RB II/115 Combo** – similar to the 700RB II, except in combo form with 1-15 in. speaker, tilt-back cabinet design, black covering, black metal grille, 75 lbs., mfg. 2003-08.

	$900	$550 - 650	$325 - 400	$1,279

* **700RB II/210 Combo** – similar to the 700RB II, except in combo form with 2-10 in. speaker, tilt-back cabinet design, black covering, black metal grille, 78 lbs., mfg. 2003-09.

	$900	$550 - 650	$325 - 400	$1,279

800RB (302-0060-0) – 300W +100W, head-unit only, solid-state chassis, single channel, front silver and black control panel, single input, nine black and gray knobs (v, t, h/m, l/m, b, boost, f, MV 300, MV100), effects loop, voicing filters, black metal covering, 25 lbs., disc.

	$800	$500 - 600	$425 - 475	$1,142

1001RB (302-0030-A) – 540W + 50W, head-unit only, solid-state chassis, single channel, front silver control panel, single input, eleven black knobs (direct out level, v, c, p, t, h/m, l/m, b, boost, tweeter, woofer), effects loop, voicing filters, black metal covering, 18 lbs., disc. 2002.

	N/A	$450 - 525	$275 - 325	$999

* **1001RB/115 (303-0160-A)** – similar to the 1001RB except in combo form with 1-15 in. speaker, black covering, black metal grille, 77 lbs., disc. 2003.

	N/A	$750 - 900	$475 - 550	$1,699

* **1001RB/210 (303-0170-A)** – similar to the 1001RB except in combo form with 2-10 in. speakers, black covering, black metal grille, 83 lbs., disc. 2003.

	N/A	$750 - 900	$475 - 550	$1,699

MSR/NOTES	100%	EXCELLENT	AVERAGE		LAST MSR

1001RB II
courtesy Gallien-Krueger

1001RB II/115 Combo
courtesy Gallien-Krueger

2001RB
courtesy Gallien-Krueger

1001RB II/210 Combo
courtesy Gallien-Krueger

1001RB II – 700W + 50W, head-unit only, solid-state chassis, single channel, front silver control panel, single input, eleven black knobs (direct out level, v, c, p, t, h/m, l/m, b, boost, tweeter, woofer), effects loop, voicing filters, black metal covering, 22 lbs., mfg. 2003-present.

MSR $1,069	$750	$475 - 550	$300 - 350		

* **1001RB II/115 Combo** – similar to the 1001RB II, except in combo form with 1-15 in. speaker, tilt-back cabinet design, black covering, black metal grille, 77 lbs., mfg. 2003-06.

	N/A	$650 - 800	$375 - 425		$1,499

* **1001RB II/210 Combo** – similar to the 1001RB II, except in combo form with 2-10 in. speakers, tilt-back cabinet design, black covering, black metal grille, 80 lbs., mfg. 2003-06.

	N/A	$650 - 800	$375 - 425		$1,499

2001RB (302-0090-A) – 2 X 500W, 2 X 50W, head-unit only, solid-state chassis, dual channels, front silver control panel, single input, 14 black knobs (Ch. B: g, e, bottom, level B, Ch. A: level A, c, p, t, h/m, l/m, b), boost, tweeter, woofer, effects loop, distortion circuits, voicing filters, 42.5 lbs., current mfg.

MSR $1,926	$1,350	$850 - 1,000	$550 - 650		

2001RBP PREAMP – preamp section from the 2001RB, single space rack-mount unit, two channels, front silver control panel, single input, 14 black knobs (Ch. B: g, e, bottom, level B, Ch. A: level A, c, p, t, h/m, l/m, b), boost, tweeter, woofer, effects loop, distortion circuits, voicing filters, black casing, 19 in. wide, 1.65 in. tall, 6 in. deep, 5 lbs., disc. 2009.

	$599	$350 - 425	$200 - 250		$599

FUSION 550 – 500W @ 4 ohms (350W @ 8 ohms), 50W horn bi-amp system, three-space rack-mount bass head-unit, hybrid chassis, preamp: 3 X 12AX7, power: solid-state, two channels, front black control panel, single input, eight black knobs (g, c, t, h/m, l/m, b, horn bi-amp level, MV), active/passive switch, channel switch, freq. switch, bright switch, deep switch, mute switch, rear panel: effects loop, tuner out, transformer isolated active DI with level control, pre/post/ground switch, two speakon outputs and two 1/4 in. outputs, 19 in. wide, 5.25 in. tall, 9.75 in. deep, 25 lbs., mfg. 2007-present.

MSR $1,498	$1,050	$600 - 750	$350 - 450		

ELECTRIC BASS AMPLIFIERS: BACKLINE SERIES

The Backline Series was introduced at the NAMM show in 2002. The Backline 115 was introduced in 2001, but the rest of the models were introduced in 2002. Originally, these models featured a gray front with red lettering, but in 2005, GK changed it to a black front with white lettering.

BACKLINE 110 – 70W, 1-10 in. speaker, solid-state combo, dual channels, front silver control panel, single input, ten black knobs (g, level B, level A, c, t, h/m, l/m, b), boost, master, effects loop, footswitch, direct out line, black covering, black metal grille, 30 lbs., mfg. 2002-09.

	$200	$120 - 150	$75 - 95		$285

BACKLINE 112 – 70W, 1-12 in. speaker, solid-state combo, dual channels, front silver control panel, single input, ten black knobs (g, level B, level A, c, t, h/m, l/m, b), boost, master, effects loop, footswitch, direct out line, black covering, black metal grille, 40 lbs., mfg. 2002-09.

	$250	$150 - 200	$95 - 120		$356

BACKLINE 115 – 125W, 1-15 in. speaker, solid-state combo, dual channels, front silver control panel, single input, ten black knobs (g, level B, level A, c, t, h/m, l/m, b), boost, master, effects loop, footswitch, direct out line, black covering, black metal grille, 55 lbs., mfg. 2001-08.

	$300	$175 - 225	$110 - 140		$426

BACKLINE 210 – 175W, 2-10 in speakers, solid-state combo, dual channels, front silver control panel, single input, ten black knobs (g, level B, level A, c, t, h/m, l/m, b), boost, master, effects loop, footswitch, direct out line, black covering, black metal grille, 65 lbs., mfg. 2003-09.

	$500	$300 - 375	$175 - 225		$714

MSR/NOTES	100%	EXCELLENT	AVERAGE	LAST MSR

Backline 112
courtesy Gallien-Krueger

Backline 115
courtesy Gallien-Krueger

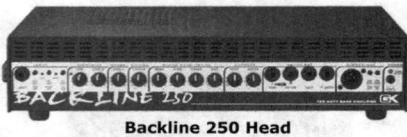

Backline 250 Head
courtesy Gallien-Krueger

Backline 600 Head
courtesy Gallien-Krueger

BACKLINE 250 HEAD – 125W, head-unit only, solid-state chassis, two channels, front silver control panel, single input, 10 black knobs (g, level B, level A, c, t, h/m, l/m, b), boost, master, effects loop, footswitch, direct out line, tuner out, black covering, black metal grille, 12 lbs., mfg. 2002-05.

	N/A	$135 - 175	$85 - 110	$299

BACKLINE 350 HEAD – 175W, head-unit/rack-mount configuration, solid-state chassis, two channels, front silver control panel, single input, 10 black knobs (g, level B, level A, c, t, h/m, l/m, b), boost, master, effects loop, footswitch, tuner out, direct out line, tuner out, black covering, 13 lbs., mfg. 2003-04.

	N/A	$150 - 200	$95 - 120	

BACKLINE 600 HEAD – 300W, head-unit/rack-mount configuration, solid-state chassis, two channels, front black and silver control panel, single input, 10 black knobs (g, level B, level A, c, t, h/m, l/m, b), boost, master, effects loop, footswitch, direct out line, tuner out, black covering, 16.5 lbs., mfg. 2005-2010.

	$300	$175 - 225	$110 - 140	$426

115 BLX SPEAKER CABINET – 200W, 1-15 in. speaker, 8 ohm impedance, MDF construction, black carpet covering, gray grille with red lettering, or black grille with white lettering, 69 lbs., mfg. 2002-09.

	$200	$120 - 150	$75 - 95	$285

210 BLX SPEAKER CABINET – 200W, 2-10 in. speaker, 8 ohm impedance, MDF construction, black carpet covering, gray grille with red lettering or black grille with white lettering, 58 lbs., mfg. 2002-09.

	$200	$120 - 150	$75 - 95	$285

410 BLX SPEAKER CABINET – 400W, 4-10 in. speaker, 8 ohm impedance, MDF construction, black carpet covering, gray grille with red lettering or black grille with white lettering, 93 lbs., mfg. 2002-09.

	$300	$175 - 225	$110 - 140	$426

810 BLX SPEAKER CABINET – 600W, 8-10 in. speakers, 4 ohm impedance, MDF construction, black carpet covering, gray grille with red lettering or black grille with white lettering, 158 lbs., mfg. 2005-08.

	N/A	$400 - 500	$250 - 300	$899

ELECTRIC BASS AMPLIFIERS: MICROBASS SERIES

MB 108 COMBO – 25W, 1-8 in. speaker, bass combo, solid-state chassis with a digital power amp, single channel, top black control panel, one input, four black knobs (g, t, mid, b), aux. in jack, headphones jack, power switch, black covering, black grille, mfg. 2014-present.

MSR $213	$150	$100 - 115	$50 - 60	

MB 110 COMBO – 100W, 1-10 in. speaker, bass combo, solid-state chassis with a digital power amp, single channel, top black control panel, one input, five black knobs (g, t, hi-mid, low-mid, b), contour on/off switch, -10dB on/off switch, aux. in jack, headphones jack, power switch, XLR direct line out, XLR chain out, black covering, black grille, 12.5 in. wide, 14.5 in. tall, 12.5 in. deep, 21 lbs., mfg. 2012-present.

MSR $500	$350	$230 - 265	$115 - 140	

MB 112 COMBO – 200W, 1-12 in. speaker, bass combo, solid-state chassis with a digital power amp, single channel, top silver control panel, two inputs (passive, active), five black knobs (g, t, hi-mid, low-mid, b), contour on/off switch, aux. in jack, headphones jack, XLR direct line out power switch, black covering, silver metal grille, 15.5 in. wide, 17.5 in. tall, 14.75 in. deep, 28 lbs., mfg. 2010-present.

MSR $570	$400	$260 - 300	$130 - 160	

MSR/NOTES	100%	EXCELLENT	AVERAGE	LAST MSR

MB 108 Combo
courtesy Gallien-Krueger

MB 110 Combo
courtesy Gallien-Krueger

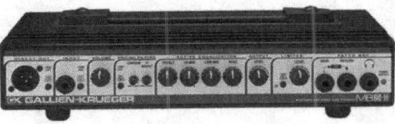
MB150S III Head
courtesy Gallien-Krueger

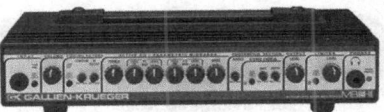
MB150E III Head
courtesy Gallien-Krueger

MB 115 COMBO – 200W, 1-15 in. speaker with a horn, bass combo, solid-state chassis with a digital power amp, two channels (normal, boost), top silver control panel, two inputs (passive, active), seven black knobs (g, t, hi-mid, low-mid, b, boost Ch. MV, normal Ch. MV), contour on/off switch, limiter on/off switch, horn on/off switch, aux. in jack, headphones jack, XLR direct line out, power switch, black covering, silver metal grille, 19.5 in. wide, 23.5 in. tall, 14.75 in. deep, 35 lbs., new 2010.

| MSR $714 | $450 | $295 - 325 | $145 - 180 | |

MB150S III HEAD – 150W, head-unit configuration, solid-state chassis, single channel, front gray control panel, single input, seven black knobs (v, t, h/m, h/l, b, output level, limiter level), effects loop, black covering, 10 lbs., disc. 2008.

| | $450 | $250 - 300 | $125 - 175 | $589 |

* *MB150S112 Combo (303-0006-0)* – similar to the MB150S-III Head, except in combo configuration with 1-12 in. speaker, black covering, black metal grille, 26 lbs., current mfg.

| MSR $1,018 | $700 | $475 - 550 | $300 - 350 | |

MB150E III HEAD – 150W, head-unit configuration, solid-state chassis, single channel, stereo chorus (with knobs), front gray control panel, single input, nine black knobs (v, t, h/m (freq & level), h/l (freq & level), b, output level, limiter level), effects loop, black covering, 10 lbs., disc. 2008.

| | $550 | $325 - 375 | $175 - 225 | $749 |

* *MB150E112 Combo (303-0011-0)* – similar to the MB150E-III Head, except in combo configuration with 1-12 in. speaker, black metal grille, 26 lbs., disc.

| | $800 | $525 - 600 | $325 - 400 | $1,176 |

MB 200 HEAD – 200W @ 4 ohms (140W @ 8 ohms), light-weight bass head unit, solid-state chassis, single channel, front silver control panel with two chrome handles, single input, five black knobs (g, t, hi-mid, low-mid, b), -10dB input pad switch, contour on/off switch, power switch, rear panel: headphone/line out jack with usage switch, XLR balanced line out with pre/post EQ switch, aux. in jack, Speakon speaker jack, silver casing with black feet, 7.75 in. wide, 1.75 in. tall, 8 in. deep, 2 lbs., mfg. 2010-present.

| MSR $356 | $250 | $150 - 200 | $95 - 120 | |

MB 210 COMBO – 350W @ 8 ohms (500W with an extension speaker cabinet), 2-10 in. Neodymium speakers with a horn, bass combo, solid-state chassis with a digital power amp, two channels (normal, boost), top silver control panel, two inputs (passive, active), seven black knobs (g, t, hi-mid, low-mid, b, boost Ch. MV, normal Ch. MV), contour on/off switch, limiter on/off switch, horn on/off switch, aux. in jack, headphones jack, XLR direct line out, power switch, black covering, silver metal grille, 19.5 in. wide, 23.5 in. tall, 14.75 in. deep, 33 lbs., mfg. 2010-present.

| MSR $855 | $600 | $375 - 450 | $225 - 275 | |

MB 212 COMBO – 350W @ 8 ohms (500W with an extension speaker cabinet), 2-12 in. Neodymium speakers with a horn, bass combo, solid-state chassis with a digital power amp, two channels (normal, boost), top silver control panel, two inputs (passive, active), seven black knobs (g, t, hi-mid, low-mid, b, boost Ch. MV, normal Ch. MV), contour on/off switch, limiter on/off switch, horn on/off switch, aux. in jack, headphones jack, XLR direct line out, power switch, black covering, silver metal grille, 19.5 in. wide, 26.75 in. tall, 14.75 in. deep, 37 lbs., mfg. 2010-present.

| MSR $1,142 | $800 | $525 - 600 | $260 - 325 | |

MB 410 COMBO – 500W, 4-10 in. Neodymium speakers, bass combo, solid-state chassis with a digital power amp, one channel, top black control panel, one input, seven black knobs (g, t, hi-mid, low-mid, b, boost Ch. MV, normal Ch. MV), contour on/off switch, limiter on/off switch, horn on/off switch, aux. in jack, headphones jack, XLR direct line out, power switch, black covering, black grille, 23 in. wide, 26.5 in. tall, 14.5 in. deep, 64 lbs., mfg. 2011-present.

| MSR $1,284 | $900 | $575 - 675 | $295 - 350 | |

MB 500 HEAD – 500W @ 4 ohms (350W @ 8 ohms), light-weight bass head unit, solid-state chassis, two channels (normal, boost), front silver control panel with two chrome handles, single input, nine black knobs (g, c, t, hi-mid, low-mid, b, boost, boost Ch. MV, normal Ch. MV), -10dB pad switch, mute switch, boost (channel switch), power switch, rear panel: XLR out with pre/post EQ and ground/lift switches, boost footswitch jack, tuner out, effects loop, switchable line out/headphone jack with usage switch, two Speakon jacks, silver casing with black feet, 10.75 in. wide, 1.75 in. tall, 8.5 in. deep, 3.75 lbs., mfg. 2010-present.

| MSR $714 | $500 | $300 - 375 | $175 - 225 | |

MSR/NOTES	100%	EXCELLENT	AVERAGE	LAST MSR

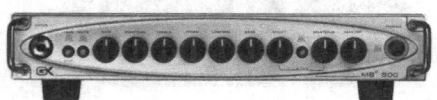

MB² 500 Head
courtesy Gallien-Krueger

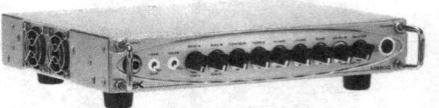

MB 800 Head
courtesy Gallien-Krueger

MB Fusion 500 Head
courtesy Gallien-Krueger

MB Fusion 800 Head
courtesy Gallien-Krueger

CX 210 Speaker Cabinet
courtesy Gallien-Krueger

MB² 500 HEAD – 500W @ 4 ohms (350W @ 8 ohms), light-weight bass head unit, solid-state chassis with a digital power amp, two channels (normal, boost), front silver control panel with two chrome handles, single input, nine black knobs (g, c, t, hi-mid, low-mid, b, boost, boost v, MV), 10dB pad switch, mute switch, boost (channel switch), power switch, rear panel: effects loop, switchable line out/headphone jack, XLR out with pre/post EQ and ground lift switch, boost footswitch jack, tuner out, two Speakon jacks, silver casing with black feet, 10.75 in. wide, 1.75 in. tall, 8.5 in. deep, 3.75 lbs., mfg. 2008-09.

	$500	$300 - 375	$175 - 225	$714

* **MB² 500 210 Combo** – similar to the MB² 500 Head, except in combo configuration with 2-10 in. neodymium speakers, black covering, silver metal grille with GK logo, 33 lbs., mfg. 2008-09.

	$600	$375 - 450	$225 - 275	$855

* **MB² 500 212 Combo** – similar to the MB² 500 Head, except in combo configuration with 2-12 in. neodymium speakers, black covering, silver metal grille with GK logo, 39 lbs., mfg. 2008-09.

	$700	$450 - 525	$275 - 325	$999

MB 800 HEAD – 800W @ 4 ohms (500W @ 8 ohms), light-weight bass head unit, solid-state chassis, single channel, front silver control panel with two chrome handles, single input, nine black knobs (g 1, g 2, c, t, hi-mid, low-mid, b, level, MV), -10dB pad switch, mute switch, power switch, rear panel: XLR out with pre/post EQ switch, footswitch jack, tuner out, effects loop, switchable line out/headphone jack with usage switch, two Speakon jacks, silver casing with black feet, 10.75 in. wide, 1.75 in. tall, 8.5 in. deep, 4.9 lbs., mfg. 2011-present.

MSR $1,000	$700	$450 - 525	$230 - 280	

MB FUSION 500 HEAD – 500W @ 4 ohms (350W @ 8 ohms), lightweight bass head unit, hybrid chassis, preamp: 3 X 12AX7, power: solid-state, two channels, front black control panel, single input, nine black knobs (g1, g2, c, t, h/m, l/m, b, MV A, MV B), 14 dB pad switch, mute switch, channel switch, bright switch, deep switch, mute switch, rear panel: effects loop, tuner out, XLR out with pre/post EQ and ground lift, two speakon outputs, 4.5 lbs., mfg. 2009-present.

MSR $999	$700	$450 - 525	$275 - 325	

MB FUSION 800 HEAD – 800W, lightweight bass head unit, hybrid chassis, preamp: 3 X 12AX7, power: solid-state, two channels, front black control panel, single input, nine black knobs (g1, g2, c, t, h/m, l/m, b, level B, MV), 10 dB pad switch, mute switch, power switch, rear panel: effects loop, tuner out, XLR out with pre/post EQ and ground lift, two Speakon outputs, 5.5 lbs., mfg. 2012-present.

MSR $1,284	$900	$575 - 675	$295 - 350	

CX 115 SPEAKER CABINET – 300W, 1-15 in. speaker with a high frequency transducer, 8 ohm impedance, Speakon speaker jack, horn on/off switch, black covering, black grille, 23 in. wide, 19 in. tall, 14.5 in. deep, 35 lbs., mfg. 2014-present.

MSR $500	$350	$230 - 265	$115 - 140	

CX 210 SPEAKER CABINET – 400W, 2-10 in. speakers with a high frequency transducer, 8 ohm impedance, Speakon speaker jack, horn on/off switch, black covering, black grille, 23 in. wide, 19 in. tall, 14.5 in. deep, 35 lbs., mfg. 2014-present.

MSR $500	$350	$230 - 265	$115 - 140	

CX 410 SPEAKER CABINET – 800W, 4-10 in. speakers with a high frequency transducer, 8 ohm impedance, Speakon speaker jack, horn on/off switch, black covering, black grille, 23 in. wide, 26.5 in. tall, 14.5 in. deep, 67 lbs., mfg. 2014-present.

MSR $714	$500	$325 - 375	$165 - 200	

MBE 115 SPEAKER CABINET – 400W, 1-15 in. Neodymium speaker, 8 ohm impedance, one Speakon and one regular 1/4 in. jack, black covering, silver metal grille, 19.5 in. wide, 23.5 in. tall, 14.75 in. deep, 35 lbs., mfg. 2010-disc.

	$300	$175 - 225	$110 - 140	$426

MBE 210 SPEAKER CABINET – 400W, 2-10 in. Neodymium speakers, 8 ohm impedance, one Speakon and one regular 1/4 in. jack, black covering, silver metal grille, 19.5 in. wide, 23.5 in. tall, 14.75 in. deep, 30 lbs., mfg. 2010-disc.

	$300	$175 - 225	$110 - 140	$426

MSR/NOTES	100%	EXCELLENT	AVERAGE	LAST MSR

MBP 112 Speaker Cabinet
courtesy Gallien-Krueger

MBP 212 Speaker Cabinet
courtesy Gallien-Krueger

MBP 410 Speaker Cabinet
courtesy Gallien-Krueger

MBE 212 SPEAKER CABINET – 600W, 2-12 in. Neodymium speakers, available in 4 or 8 ohm impedance, one Speakon and one regular 1/4 in. jack, black covering, silver metal grille, 19.5 in. wide, 26.75 in. tall, 14.75 in. deep, 34 lbs., mfg. 2010-disc.

	$400	$250 - 300	$150 - 200	$570

MBE 410 SPEAKER CABINET – 800W, 4-10 in. Neodymium speakers, available in 4 or 8 ohm impedance, one Speakon and one regular 1/4 in. jack, black covering, silver metal grille, 23.5 in. wide, 24.5 in. tall, 14.75 in. deep, 41 lbs., mfg. 2010-disc.

	$450	$300 - 350	$175 - 225	$641

MBP 112 SPEAKER CABINET – 200W, 1-12 in. speaker, straight front, one XLR input, poplar construction , black covering, black grille, 17 in. tall, 15 in. wide, 14.5 in. deep, 30 lbs., mfg. 2012-present.

MSR $500	$350	$230 - 265	$115 - 140	

MBP 115 SPEAKER CABINET – 200W, 1-15 in. speaker, horn tweeter, straight front, one XLR input, poplar construction , black covering, black grille, 23.5 in. tall, 19.5 in. wide, 14.75 in. deep, 37 lbs., mfg. 2012-present.

MSR $641	$450	$295 - 325	$145 - 180	

MBP 212 SPEAKER CABINET – 500W, 2-12 in. speakers, horn tweeter, straight front, one XLR input, poplar construction, black covering, black grille, 26.75 in. tall, 14.75 in. wide, 19.5 in. deep, 39 lbs., mfg. 2012-present

MSR $1,069	$750	$475 - 550	$245 - 300	

MBP 410 SPEAKER CABINET – 500W, 4-10 in. speakers, horn tweeter, straight front, one XLR input, poplar construction, black covering, black grille, 24.5 in. tall, 23.5 in. wide, 14.75 in. deep, 48 lbs., mfg. 2012-present

MSR $1,213	$850	$550 - 625	$275 - 350	

MBX 112 SPEAKER CABINET – 100W, 1-12 in. speaker, 8 ohm impedance, black covering, black grille, 16 lbs., current mfg.

MSR $426	$300	$175 - 225	$110 - 140	

MBX 115 SPEAKER CABINET – 200W, 1-15 in. speaker with a piezo tweeter, 8 ohm impedance, Speakon and 1/4 in. standard speaker jacks, tweeter defeat button, plywood construction, black Tolex covering, gray metal grille, 23.5 in. wide, 19.5 in. tall, 18.5 in. deep, 41 lbs., mfg. 2010-disc.

	$250	$150 - 200	$95 - 120	$356

MBX 210 SPEAKER CABINET – 200W, 2-10 in. speakers with a piezo tweeter, 8 ohm impedance, Speakon and 1/4 in. standard speaker jacks, tweeter defeat button, plywood construction, black Tolex covering, gray metal grille, 23.5 in. wide, 16.5 in. tall, 18.5 in. deep, 40 lbs., mfg. 2010-disc.

	$250	$150 - 200	$95 - 120	$356

MBX 410 SPEAKER CABINET – 400W, 4-10 in. speakers with a piezo tweeter, 8 ohm impedance, Speakon and 1/4 in. standard speaker jacks, tweeter defeat button, plywood construction, black Tolex covering, gray metal grille, 23.5 in. wide, 26.5 in. tall, 18.5 in. deep, 74 lbs., mfg. 2010-disc.

	$350	$225 - 275	$135 - 175	$499

ELECTRIC BASS AMPLIFIERS: NEO SERIES

NEO 700/112 COMBO – 320W + 50W horn amp, 1-12 in. speaker combo, solid-state chassis, single channel, front silver control panel, single input, eleven black knobs (direct out level, v, c, p, t, h/m, l/m, b, boost, tweeter, woofer), effects loop, voicing filters, black casing, black covering, gray metal grille, 55 lbs., mfg. 2005-08.

	$900	$550 - 650	$325 - 400	$1,199

NEO 1001/212 COMBO – 700W + 50W horn amp, 2-12 in. speaker combo, solid-state chassis, single channel, front silver control panel, single input, eleven black knobs (direct out level, v, c, p, t, h/m, l/m, b, boost, tweeter, woofer), effects loop, voicing filters, extendable handle and wheels, black covering, gray metal grille, 81 lbs., mfg. 2005-08.

	$1,200	$700 - 850	$475 - 550	$1,599

MSR/NOTES	100%	EXCELLENT	AVERAGE	LAST MSR

Neo 700/112 Combo
courtesy Gallien-Krueger

Neo 1001/212 Combo
courtesy Gallien-Krueger

Neo 115 Speaker Cabinet
courtesy Gallien-Krueger

NEO 112 SPEAKER CABINET – 300W, 1-12 in. speaker and horn, 8 ohm impedance, 11-ply poplar cabinet, black covering, gray metal grille, mfg. 2004-present.

MSR $641	$450	$295 - 325	$145 - 180	

NEO 115 SPEAKER CABINET – 400W, 1-15 in. speaker and horn, 8 ohm impedance, 11-ply poplar cabinet, casters, black covering, gray metal grille, mfg. 2004-present.

MSR $714	$500	$325 - 375	$165 - 200	

NEO 210 SPEAKER CABINET – 400W, 2-10 in. speakers and a horn, 8 ohm impedance, 11-ply poplar cabinet, casters, black covering, gray metal grille, mfg. 2007-disc.

	$450	$300 - 350	$175 - 225	$641

NEO 212 SPEAKER CABINET – 600W, 2-12 in. speaker and horn, 8 ohm impedance, 11-ply poplar cabinet, casters, black covering, gray metal grille, mfg. 2004-present.

MSR $855	$600	$400 - 450	$195 - 240	

NEO 410 SPEAKER CABINET – 800W, 4-10 in. speakers and a horn, 8 ohm impedance, 11-ply poplar cabinet, casters, black covering, gray metal grille, mfg. 2007-present.

MSR $1,069	$750	$475 - 550	$245 - 300	

NEO 412 SPEAKER CABINET – 1200W, 4-12 in. speaker and horn, 4 ohm impedance, 11-ply poplar cabinet, casters, black covering, gray metal grille, mfg. 2004-present.

MSR $1,498	$1,050	$675 - 775	$350 - 425	

NEO 810 SPEAKER CABINET – 1600W, 8-10 in. speakers and a horn, 4 ohm impedance, 11-ply poplar cabinet, casters, black covering, gray metal grille, mfg. 2010-disc.

	$1,000	$600 - 725	$350 - 425	$1,427

SPEAKER CABINETS: RBH, RBX, & SBX SERIES

115 RBH Speaker Cabinet
courtesy Gallien-Krueger

115 SBX II Speaker Cabinet
courtesy Gallien-Krueger

810 SBX Speaker Cabinet
courtesy Gallien-Krueger

115 RBH SPEAKER CABINET – 400W, 1-15 in. speaker and horn, 8 ohm impedance, front-slot ported on the sides, casters, black covering, gray metal grille, 66 lbs., current mfg.

MSR $913	$640	$375 - 450	$225 - 275	

210 RBH SPEAKER CABINET – 400W, 2-10 in. speaker and horn, 8 ohm impedance, tilt-back cabinet, front-slot ported on the bottom, black covering, gray metal grille, 60.5 lbs., disc.

	$600	$350 - 425	$200 - 250	$855

MSR/NOTES	100%	EXCELLENT	AVERAGE	LAST MSR

410 RBH SPEAKER CABINET – 800W, 4-10 in. speaker and horn, available in either 4 or 8 ohm impedance, front-slot ported on the sides, casters, black covering, gray metal grille, 96 lbs., current mfg.

| MSR $1,356 | $950 | $625 - 700 | $300 - 375 | |

115 RBX SPEAKER CABINET – 400W, 1-15 in. speaker plus a horn, 8 ohm impedance, 11-ply poplar construction, front ported, one speakon and one 1/4 in. connector, black carpet covering, dark gray steel grille, spring-loaded side handles, interlocking corners, removable casters, 23.5 in. wide, 26.5 in. tall, 18.5 in. deep, 77.5 lbs., mfg. 2007-09.

| | $450 | $275 - 325 | $150 - 200 | $599 |

210 RBX SPEAKER CABINET – 400W, 2-10 in. speakers plus a horn, 8 ohm impedance, 11-ply poplar construction, front ported, one speakon and one 1/4 in. connector, black carpet covering, dark gray steel grille, spring-loaded side handles, interlocking corners, tilt-back cabinet design, 23.5 in. wide, 19.5 in. tall, 16.5 in. deep, 54.5 lbs., mfg. 2007-09.

| | $400 | $225 - 275 | $130 - 175 | $529 |

410 RBX SPEAKER CABINET – 800W, 4-10 in. speakers plus a horn, 8 ohm impedance, 11-ply poplar construction, front ported, one speakon and one 1/4 in. connector, black carpet covering, dark gray steel grille, spring-loaded side handles, interlocking corners, removable casters, 23.5 in. wide, 26.5 in. tall, 18.5 in. deep, 92.5 lbs., mfg. 2007-09.

| | $525 | $300 - 375 | $175 - 225 | $699 |

810 RBX SPEAKER CABINET – 1600W, 8-10 in. speakers plus a horn, 4 ohm impedance, 11-ply poplar construction, sealed cabinet, one speakon and one 1/4 in. connector, black carpet covering, dark gray steel grille, spring-loaded side handles, interlocking corners, tilt-back handle with wheels, rear-mounted slide rails, 26.5 in. wide, 49 in. tall, 18.5 in. deep, 149 lbs., mfg. 2007-09.

| | $900 | $550 - 625 | $350 - 425 | $1,199 |

115 SBX II SPEAKER CABINET – 400W, 1-15 in. speaker and horn, 8 ohm impedance, casters, black covering, gray metal grille, 64 lbs., disc. 2006.

| | $450 | $275 - 325 | $150 - 200 | $599 |

210 SBX II SPEAKER CABINET – 400W, 2-10 in. speaker and horn, 8 ohm impedance, casters, black covering, gray metal grille, 49 lbs., disc. 2006.

| | $420 | $250 - 300 | $125 - 175 | $549 |

410 SBX SPEAKER CABINET – 400W, 4-10 in. speaker and horn, 8 ohm impedance, casters, black covering, gray metal grille, 84 lbs., disc. 2006.

| | $490 | $300 - 350 | $150 - 200 | $649 |

* **410 SBX+ Speaker Cabinet** – similar to the 410 SBX, except has 800W handling capabilities, disc. 2006.

| | $600 | $350 - 425 | $200 - 250 | $799 |

810 SBX SPEAKER CABINET – 600W, 8-10 in. speaker and horn, 4 ohm impedance, skid rails and kick plate, handlebar with wheels, black covering, gray metal grille, 149 lbs., disc. 2006.

| | $900 | $550 - 650 | $325 - 400 | $1,199 |

GARNET

Amplifiers previously produced in Canada between the mid-1960s and 1989.

Gar Gillies was involved in electronics all his life. During the mid-1960s, the radio and T.V. repair business Gillies had been running evolved into the Garnet Amplifier Company. With the help of Gillies' two sons, Russell and Garnet, they formed a partnership and began producing their first amplifiers in the late 1960s. Garnet produced quality tube amplifiers, while Gar was the roadie for the Guess Who in the 1970s. P.A. equipment was also a product offered by Garnet. The late 1970s and 1980s were the heyday for Garnet until 1989. Because of financial hardship after an expansion project, Garnet stopped producing amps. However, Gar continued to work on amplifiers, fixing, upgrading, and designing some amplifiers in Winnipeg, Canada until he passed away in 2007. For a complete history, specs, and more information on Garnet amplifiers, visit Garnet's website. Information for Garnet history from Russell Gillies and www.gartnetamps.com.

CONTACT INFORMATION
GARNET
Currently Not Produced
Winnipeg, Manitoba Canada
www.garnetamps.com
info@garnetamps.com

ELECTRIC TUBE AMPLIFIERS

Garnet produced some interesting amplifiers over the years. The first models to be released were the **Pro**, **Rebel**, and **BTO** (stood for Big Time Operator) series. These models had two guitar heads and a P.A. system. The Pro series evolved into the **Pro 200**, **400**, and **600** models. After this, three Deputy models were released. They also had combo amps such as the **Banshee**, **Gnome**, **L'il Rock**, **Mach 5**, **Enforcer**, **Sessionman**, and three **Revolution** models. Gar also produced reverb units.

MSR/NOTES	100%	EXCELLENT	AVERAGE	LAST MSR

GDS AMPLIFICATION

Amplifiers, speaker cabinets, parts, and amp kits currently produced in Fenton, MI since 1998.

CONTACT INFORMATION
GDS AMPLIFICATION
7518 Driftwood Drive
Fenton, MI 48430
Phone No.: 810-750-3477
www.gdsamps.com
graydon@gdsamps.com

Graydon Stuckey founded GDS Amplification in 1998 focusing on recreating the tone of the Marshall 18W "Mini Bluesbreaker" from the mid-1960s. Interest is high regarding Marshall's 18W models, and several craftsmen are offering variations of them, including Stuckey. GDS amps are available as head-units, combos, speaker cabinets, and build-it-yourself amp kits are also available. Graydon is also the one who started the 18W enthusiast web community at www.18watt.com. For more information, visit GDS Amplification's website or contact the company directly.

ELECTRIC TUBE AMPLIFIERS

The GDS 18W models are available in traditional Marshall configurations including the Model 1974-style 1-12 in. combo (MSR $2,400, street price $2,000), Model 1958-style 2-10 in. combo (MSR $2,400, street price $2,000), and Model 1973 2-12 in. combo (MSR $2,600, street price $2,200). They also offer the 18W model as a head-unit (MSR $2,100, street price $1,700), offset chassis head unit similar to early Marshall JTM-45 heads (MSR $2,400, street price $2,000), a S/C single channel head (MSR $1,500, street price $1,200), and a new Mini 18W combo with 1-12 in. speaker and a single channel (MSR $1,200, street price $1,100). The GDS 18 Watt kits are available as a head unit (MSR $770), combo unit (MSR $820), and the S/C kit that can be used in a head or combo (MSR $620). These kits do not include the cabinet or speakers.

GENESIS

Amplifiers and other electric products previously produced in Sydney, Australia.

Robert Ang started Genesis Amplifiers. With a degree from the UWA (University of Western Australia), he started work in medicine, and then moved into another field after moving to Sydney. There, he built some tube amplifiers and preamps. Not much is known about Genesis, and any further information can be submitted directly to Blue Book Publications.

GENESIS (GIBSON)

Amplifiers previously produced during the mid- to late 1980s. Distributed by Gibson in Nashville, TN.

In 1984, Norlin (Gibson) introduced a budget-line of guitar and bass amplifiers branded Genesis. These amps did not last very long as Gibson was sold by 1985 and the new owners did not continue to produce these models. Little else is known about the Genesis brand, and any further information on Genesis amps can be submitted directly to Blue Book Publications.

ELECTRIC SS AMPLIFIERS

B40 – 40W, 1-12 in. speaker, bass combo, solid-state chassis, single channel, front black control panel, two inputs, four black knobs (g, t, m, b), black covering, black grille, 29 lbs., mfg. mid-1980s.

	N/A	$95 - 120	$60 - 80	

B70 – 70W, 1-15 in. speaker, bass combo, solid-state chassis, single channel, front black control panel, two inputs, four black knobs (g, t, m, b), black covering, black grille, mfg. mid-1980s.

	N/A	$120 - 150	$75 - 95	

G10 – 10W, 1-8 in. speaker, guitar combo, solid-state chassis, single channel, front black control panel, two inputs, three black knobs (g, tone, overdrive), optional footswitch, black covering, black grille, 17 lbs., mfg. mid-1980s.

	N/A	$60 - 80	$35 - 50	

G25 – 25W, 1-10 in. speaker, guitar combo, solid-state chassis, single channel, front black control panel, two inputs, five black knobs (g, t, m, b, overdrive), optional footswitch, black covering, black grille, 25 lbs., mfg. mid-1980s.

	N/A	$85 - 110	$55 - 70	

* **G25R** – similar to the G25, except has reverb with reverb control (six total knobs), 25 lbs., mfg. mid-1980s.

	N/A	$95 - 120	$60 - 80	

G40R – 40W, 2-10 in. speakers, guitar combo, solid-state chassis, single channel, reverb, front black control panel, two inputs, six black knobs (g, t, m, b, overdrive, r), optional footswitch, black covering, black grille, 30 lbs., mfg. mid-1980s.

	N/A	$120 - 150	$75 - 95	

MSR/NOTES	100%	EXCELLENT	AVERAGE	LAST MSR

GENZ BENZ

Amplifiers previously produced in Scottsdale, AZ since 1984 and Taiwan since the mid-2000s. Previously distributed by Kaman Music Corporation in Bloomfield, CT.

Genz Benz was founded by Jeff and Cathy Genzler in 1984. Benz built acoustic guitar, electric guitar, and bass amplifiers and speaker cabinets, as well as many accessories. In 2003, Kaman Music purchased Genz Benz and became the exclusive distributor. In late 2007, the Fender Musical Instrument Corporation (FMIC) purchased the Kaman Music Corporation, which included Genz Benz. Amplifiers were built in Arizona as well as other foreign countries. In 2013, it was announced that Genz Benz would discontinue operations.

ACOUSTIC AMPLIFIERS: SHENANDOAH SERIES

Shenandoah 60
courtesy Genz Benz

Shenandoah 60 LT
courtesy Genz Benz

Shenandoah 100
courtesy Genz Benz

SHENANDOAH 60 – 60W Stereo (30W per side), 2-6.5 in. speakers and tweeters, solid-state chassis, Alesis digital processor, two channels, front control panel, three inputs (one XLR, two 1/4 in.), 15 knobs, tilt-back cabinet, brown covering, metal grille, 38 lbs., mfg. 2005-07.

$550	$300 - 350	$150 - 200	$679

SHENANDOAH 60 LT – 60W (30W per side stereo), 2-6.5 in. woofers with built in tweeters, acoustic guitar combo, solid-state chassis, two channels, 16 preset digital effects, front brown control panel, three inputs (Ch. 1: XLR and 1/4 in. instrument, Ch. 2: 1/4 in.), 15 knobs (Ch. 1: v, effects level, l, l/m, m/h, h, Ch. 2: v, effects level, l, l/m, m/h, h, All: digital effects select, effects level, MV), power switch, rear panel: two speaker jacks (internal use), headphone jack with on/off switch, effects cancel jack, left and right direct outs with XLR and 1/4 in. jacks for each side, ground/lift switch, plywood monitor-shaped cabinet, brown covering, silver metal grille, 19 in. wide, 17.5 in. tall, 12 in. deep, 29 lbs., mfg. 2008-disc.

$580	$325 - 400	$180 - 220	$729

SHENANDOAH 100 – 100W,1-12 in. speaker and tweeter with level control, solid-state chassis, Alesis digital processor, two channels, front control panel, four inputs (two XLR, two 1/4 in.), 15 knobs, 15 digital effects, effects loop, tilt-back cabinet, brown covering, metal grille, 47 lbs., mfg. 2002-06.

$690	$400 - 475	$225 - 275	$859

* Shenandoah 100 Ext 12 Speaker Cabinet – 100W, 1-12 in. speaker and a tweeter, 8 ohm impedance, extension cabinet for the Shenandoah 100, brown covering, metal grille, 30 lbs., disc. 2006.

$320	$175 - 225	$95 - 125	$389

SHENANDOAH 150LT – 150W, 1-12 in. speaker and tweeter with level control, solid-state chassis, two channels, built-in digital effects, front brown control panel, four inputs (two XLR, two 1/4 in., one of each per channel), 15 knobs (Ch. 1: v, effects, l, l/m, m/h, h, Ch. 2: v, effects, l, l/m, m/h, h, All: digital effects select, digital effects level, MV), 15 digital effects, effects loop, three direct outputs, extension speaker jack, tilt-back cabinet design, brown covering, brown metal grille, 19 in. wide, 18.25 in. tall, 13 in. deep, 26.5 lbs., mfg. 2007-disc.

$750	$425 - 500	$250 - 300	$939

* Shenandoah 150LT Ext 12 Speaker Cabinet – 150W, 1-12 in. speaker and tweeter, 8 ohm impedance, extension speaker cabinet for the Shenandoah 150LT, bottom-mounted stand adapter, brown covering, brown metal grille, 18.25 in. wide, 15.75 in. tall, 13 in. deep, 21 lbs., mfg. 2007-disc.

$330	$175 - 225	$110 - 140	$419

SHENANDOAH 200 – 200W stereo (100W per side), 2-10 in. speakers and tweeters with level controls, solid-state chassis, Alesis digital processor, two channels, front control panel, four inputs (two XLR, two 1/4 in.), 26 knobs, effects loop, four direct out XLR jacks, tilt-back cabinet, removable casters, brown covering, metal grille, 70 lbs., mfg. 2002-07.

$1,230	$700 - 825	$425 - 500	$1,539

* Shenandoah 200 Ext L/R Speaker Cabinets – 100W, pair of 1-10 in. speakers and tweeters in separate cabinets, 8 ohm impedance, extension cabinet for the Shenandoah 200, brown covering, metal grille, 23 lbs. each, mfg. 2002-07.

$630	$350 - 425	$200 - 250	$789

MSR/NOTES	100%	EXCELLENT	AVERAGE	LAST MSR

**Shenandoah 200
courtesy Genz Benz**

**Shenandoah 300 LT
courtesy Genz Benz**

**Shenandoah Junior
courtesy Genz Benz**

SHENANDOAH 300 LT – 300W (150W per side @ 8 ohms and 100W per side @ 4 ohms stereo), 2-10 in. woofers with built in tweeters, acoustic guitar combo, solid-state chassis, two channels, 16 preset digital effects, front brown control panel, four inputs (XLR and 1/4 in. per channel), 26 knobs, input phase switch for each channel, power switch, rear panel: four speaker jacks, effects cancel jack, tuner out, four effects loops, four XLR and four 1/4 in. direct out jacks, ground/lift switch, aux. input jacks, two three-way tweeter level controls, plywood monitor-shaped cabinet, brown covering, silver metal grille, 26 in. wide, 21 in. tall, 13 in. deep, 51 lbs., mfg. 2008-disc.

	$1,600	$900 - 1,050	$600 - 700	$1,999

* **Shenandoah 300 Ext L/R Speaker Cabinets** – 200W, pair of 1-10 in. speakers and tweeters in separate cabinets, 8 ohm impedance, extension cabinets designed for use with the Shenandoah 300 LT, brown covering, metal grille, 13 in. wide, 17 in. tall, 13 in. deep, 22 lbs. each, mfg. 2008-disc.

	$800	$450 - 525	$250 - 300	$999

SHENANDOAH JUNIOR – 35W, 1-10 in. speaker and a tweeter, solid-state chassis, Alesis digital processor, two channels, front control panel, three inputs (one XLR, two 1/4 in.), 11 knobs, tilt-back cabinet, brown covering, metal grille, 35 lbs., mfg. 2002-09.

	$450	$250 - 300	$125 - 175	$559

SHENANDOAH JUNIOR LT – 45W, 1-10 in. woofer with built in tweeter, acoustic guitar combo, solid-state chassis, two channels, 15 preset digital effects, front brown control panel, three inputs (Ch. 1: XLR and 1/4 in. instrument, Ch. 2: 1/4 in.), 11 knobs (Ch. 1: v, effects level, Ch. 2: v, effects level, All: l, l/m, m/h, h, digital effects select, effects level, MV), power switch, rear panel: speaker jack (internal use), headphone jack, direct out with XLR and 1/4 in. jacks, ground/lift switch, plywood monitor-shaped cabinet, brown covering, silver metal grille, 16 in. wide, 18 in. tall, 11.5 in. deep, 25 lbs., mfg. 2010-disc.

	$480	$250 - 300	$135 - 175	$579

SHENANDOAH PRO – 200W, 1-12 in. speaker and tweeter with level control, hybrid chassis, 12AX7 tube/FET preamp, Alesis digital processor, two channels, front control panel, four inputs (two XLR, two 1/4 in.), 20 knobs, 15 digital effects, effects loop, direct out XLR jacks, tilt-back cabinet, removable casters, brown covering, metal grille, 50 lbs., mfg. 2005-07.

	$1,030	$600 - 700	$350 - 425	$1,289

SHENANDOAH PRO LT – 300W @ 4 ohms (175W @ 8 ohms), 1-12 in. woofers with built-in tweeter, acoustic guitar combo, hybrid chassis with a 12AX7 preamp tube/FET preamp and Class D solid-state power amp, two channels, 15 preset digital effects, front brown control panel, four inputs (XLR and 1/4 in. per channel), 20 knobs (Ch. 1: v, preamp blend, effects level, l, l/m, m/h, h, digital effects program, digital effects level, Ch. 2: v, preamp blend, effects level, l, l/m, m/h, h, digital effects program, digital effects level, All: aux. level, MV), input phase switch for each channel, power switch, rear panel: two speaker jacks, headphone jack with on/off switch, three effects jacks, three XLR and 1/4 in. direct out jacks, ground/lift switch, RCA and 1/4 in. aux. inputs, three-way tweeter level switch, plywood monitor-shaped cabinet, brown covering, silver metal grille, 21.5 in. wide, 20 in. tall, 12 in. deep, 37 lbs., mfg. 2008-disc.

	$1,250	$675 - 800	$425 - 500	$1,549

SHENANDOAH COMPAK 300 HEAD (SHEN-CPK-H) – 175W @ 8 ohms (300W @ 4 ohms with an extension cabinet), acoustic guitar head, solid-state chassis with Class D power amp, two channels, digital effects with 15 preset programs, front brown control panel, three inputs (Ch. 1: 1/4 in., Ch. 2: XLR and 1/4 in.), 15 chrome knobs (Ch. 1: v, effects, l, mid-gain, mid-freq., h, Ch. 2: v, effects, l, mid-gain, mid-freq., h, All: program selector, effects v, MV), phase switch for each channel, rear panel: power switch, two speaker jacks, aux. input, headphone jack, effects loop with cancel jack, three XLR and two 1/4 in. direct out jacks with ground/lift switch, black casing, 10 in. wide, 3.5 in. tall, 10.25 in. deep, 3.5 lbs., mfg. 2009-disc.

	$680	$375 - 475	$200 - 250	$849

* **Shenandoah Compak 300 1-8 Combo (SHEN-CPK-8T)** – similar to the Shenandoah Compak 300 Head, except in combo configuration with 1-8 in. Neodymium speaker and a soft dome tweeter with a level control, removable chassis, brown vinyl covering, black metal grille, leather handle, bottom-mounted tilt foot, 11.25 in. wide, 13.25 in. tall, 11.375 in. deep, 16.5 lbs., mfg. 2009-disc.

	$900	$500 - 600	$300 - 350	$1,149

MSR/NOTES	100%	EXCELLENT	AVERAGE	LAST MSR

Shenandoah Junior LT
courtesy Genz Benz

Shenandoah Pro
courtesy Genz Benz

Shenandoah Compak 300 1-10 Combo
courtesy Genz Benz

* *Shenandoah Compak 300 1-10 Combo (SHEN-CPK-10T)* – similar to the Shenandoah Compak 300 Head, except in combo configuration with 1-10 in. Neodymium speaker and a soft dome tweeter with a level control, removable chassis, brown vinyl covering, black metal grille, leather handle, bottom-mounted tilt foot, 12 in. wide, 16.375 in. tall, 11.375 in. deep, 19 lbs., mfg. 2009-disc.

	$1,000	**$550 - 650**	**$325 - 400**	**$1,249**

SHENANDOAH COMPAK 300 1-8 SPEAKER CABINET (SHEN-CPK-EXT8) – 175W, 1-8 in. Neodymium speaker and soft dome tweeter with level control, 8 ohm impedance, brown vinyl covering, black metal grille, leather handle, 11.25 in. wide, 13.5 in. tall, 11.375 in. deep, 12 lbs., mfg. 2009-disc.

	$400	**$225 - 275**	**$125 - 150**	**$499**

SHENANDOAH COMPAK 300 1-10 SPEAKER CABINET (SHEN-CPK-EXT10) – 200W, 1-10 in. Neodymium speaker and soft dome tweeter with level control, 8 ohm impedance, brown vinyl covering, black metal grille, leather handle, 12 in. wide, 13.5 in. tall, 11.375 in. deep, 12 lbs., mfg. 2009-disc.

	$480	**$275 - 325**	**$150 - 200**	**$599**

ELECTRIC GUITAR AMPLIFIERS: BLACK PEARL SERIES

Black Pearl 30 Head
courtesy Genz Benz

Black Pearl 30 112 Combo
courtesy Genz Benz

Black Pearl 30 310 Combo
courtesy Genz Benz

BLACK PEARL 30 HEAD (BP30) – 30W (switchable to 15W and 8W), guitar head-unit, Class A 10 tube chassis, preamp: 4 X 12AX7, 1 X 12AU7, power: 4 X EL84, rectifier: 5AUR4, single channel, reverb, front gray control panel, single input, 10 black knobs (v, three-way mode selector, b. level, five-way voicing selector, b, m, t, tap, r, MV), half-power switch, footswitch jack, effects loop, line out, selectable speaker jack outputs, black leatherette covering, gray grille, 22 in. wide, 11 in. tall, 12 in. deep, 38 lbs., mfg. 2007-disc.

	$1,200	**$650 - 775**	**$400 - 475**	**$1,499**

* *Black Pearl 30 112 Combo (BP30-112)* – similar to the Black Pearl 30 Head, except in combo configuration with 1-12 in. Eminence Red Fang Alnico speaker, 22 in. wide, 20.5 in. tall, 12 in. deep, 53 lbs., mfg. 2007-disc.

	$1,480	**$800 - 950**	**$500 - 600**	**$1,849**

* *Black Pearl 30 212 Combo (BP30-212)* – similar to the Black Pearl 30 Head, except in combo configuration with 2-12 in. Eminence Red Fang Alnico speakers, 27 in. wide, 20.5 in. tall, 12 in. deep, 68 lbs., mfg. 2007-disc.

	$1,700	**$950 - 1,100**	**$600 - 700**	**$2,129**

* *Black Pearl 30 310 Combo (BP30-310)* – similar to the Black Pearl 30 Head, except in combo configuration with 3-10 in. Eminence Red Fang Alnico speakers, 27 in. wide, 25.5 in. tall, 12 in. deep, 80 lbs., mfg. 2007-disc.

	$2,020	**$1,050 - 1,300**	**$700 - 825**	**$2,529**

BLACK PEARL 212 SPEAKER CABINET (BP30-212CAB) – 100W, 2-12 in. Eminence Red Fang Alnico speakers, 4 or 16 ohm impedance, black covering with white piping, gray grille, 27 in. wide, 18 in. tall, 12 in. deep, 43 lbs., mfg. summer 2006-disc.

	$950	**$525 - 600**	**$325 - 400**	**$1,189**

MSR/NOTES	100%	EXCELLENT	AVERAGE	LAST MSR

BLACK PEARL 410 SPEAKER CABINET (BP30-410CAB) – 120W, 4-10 in. Eminence Red Fang Alnico speakers, 16 ohm impedance, top handles, black covering with white piping, gray grille, 27 in. wide, 26 in. tall, 12 in. deep, 65 lbs., mfg. summer 2007-disc.

$1,380 $750 - 900 $475 - 550 $1,729

ELECTRIC GUITAR AMPLIFIERS: EL DIABLO SERIES

El Diablo 60C 112 Combo
courtesy Genz Benz

El Diablo 60
courtesy Genz Benz

El Diablo 100
courtesy Genz Benz

El Diablo 100C 212 Combo
courtesy Genz Benz

EL DIABLO 60 – 60W (switchable to 30W), head-unit only, tube chassis, preamp: 3 X 12AX7, power: 2 X EL34 or 2 X 6L6, two channels, reverb, front black control panel, single input, 16 knobs, black covering, gray metal grille, mfg. summer 2004-disc.

$1,100 $600 - 700 $350 - 425 $1,379

• Add 5% (MSR $1,429) for grille cloth that matches the Tribal Series.

* *El Diablo 60C 112 Combo* – similar to the El Diablo 60, except has 1-12 in. GBE 1240-V75 speaker, 62 lbs., mfg. summer 2004-disc.

$1,250 $650 - 800 $400 - 475 $1,549

EL DIABLO 100 – 100W (switchable to 50W), head-unit only, tube chassis, preamp: 3 X 12AX7, power: 4 X EL34, 4 X 6L6, or 4 X 5881, two channels, reverb, front black control panel, single input, 16 knobs, footswitch included, black covering, gray metal grille and chrome front cover, mfg. 2004-disc.

$1,420 $800 - 950 $525 - 600 $1,779

* *El Diablo 100C 212 Combo* – similar to the El Diablo 100, except in combo form with 2-12 in. GBE 1240-V75 speakers, black covering, metal speaker grille, removable casters, 95 lbs., mfg. 2004-disc.

$1,780 $1,000 - 1,200 $600 - 700 $2,229

ELECTRIC GUITAR AMPLIFIERS: SPEAKER CABINETS

GB 212 G-FLEX SPEAKER CABINET – 150W mono, (75W stereo), 2-12 in. GBE 1240-V75 speakers, 4 or 16 ohm impedance (mono) or 8 ohm impedance (stereo), front ported, black covering, black metal grille, top corner handles, 30 in. wide, 21 in. tall, 14 in. deep, 62 lbs., disc.

$700 $375 - 450 $225 - 275 $869

GB 412 G-FLEX SPEAKER CABINET – 300W mono, (150W stereo), 4-12 in. GBE 1240-V75 speakers, 8 ohm impedance (mono) or 4 ohm impedance (stereo), front ported, black covering, black metal grille, side handles, removable casters, 30 in. wide, 34.25 in. tall, 14 in. deep, 93 lbs., disc.

$1,200 $650 - 775 $400 - 475 $1,499

TS 112 SPEAKER CABINET – 50W, 1-12 in. Eminence Private Jack speaker, 8 ohm impedance, birch plywood construction, black vinyl covering with white piping, black or wheat grille, 24 in. wide, 18 in. tall, 12 in. deep, 34 lbs., mfg. summer 2004-08.

$480 $275 - 325 $150 - 200 $599

TS 212 SPEAKER CABINET – 100W, 2-12 in. Eminence Private Jack speakers, 4 or 16 ohm impedance, birch plywood construction, black vinyl covering with white piping, black or wheat grille, 30 in. wide, 19 in. tall, 12 in. deep, 45 lbs., mfg. summer 2004-disc.

$680 $375 - 450 $225 - 275 $849

TS 412 SL/ST SPEAKER CABINET – 200W, 4-12 in. Eminence Private Jack speakers, 8 ohm impedance, slanted (SL) or straight (ST) front, birch plywood construction, black vinyl covering with white piping, black or wheat grille, 30 in. wide, 29.5 in. tall, 14 in. deep, 78 lbs., mfg. summer 2004-disc.

$980 $525 - 625 $325 - 375 $1,229

BASS AMPLIFIERS: GBE SERIES

GBE 100 115T COMBO – 100W, 1-15 in. speaker with tweeter combo, solid-state chassis, front silver control panel, seven knobs, RCA CD in, headphone jack, tuner out, black vinyl covering, black metal grille, 55 lbs., mfg. 2002-07.

$499 $300 - 350 $175 - 225 $629

MSR/NOTES	100%	EXCELLENT	AVERAGE	LAST MSR

GBE 400 Head
courtesy Genz Benz

GBE 600 Head
courtesy Genz Benz

GBE 1200 Head
courtesy Genz Benz

GBE 100 210T COMBO – 100W, 2-10 in. speaker with tweeter combo, solid-state chassis, front silver control panel, seven knobs, RCA CD in, headphone jack, tuner out, black vinyl covering, black metal grille, 62 lbs., mfg. 2002-07.

$560	$325 - 375	$200 - 250		$699

GBE 400 HEAD – 450W at 2 ohms, 330W at 4 ohms, and 200W at 2 ohms, two-space rack-mount head-unit only, solid-state chassis, front silver control panel, single input, seven knobs (g, five-band EQ, MV), tuner out, XLR direct out, effects loop, black casing, 23 lbs., mfg. 2002-05.

N/A	$325 - 400	$200 - 250		$789

GBE 600 HEAD – 625W at 2 ohms, 425W at 4 ohms, and 275W at 2 ohms, two-space rack-mount head-unit only, hybrid chassis, 12AX7 tube/FET preamp, two channels, front silver control panel, single input, 12 knobs, tuner out, XLR direct out, effects loop, two-button footswitch (four-button optional) black casing, 25 lbs., mfg. 2002-05.

N/A	$500 - 600	$300 - 350		$1,199

GBE 750 HEAD – 750W @ 2 ohms, (675W @ 4 ohms, and 400W @ 2 ohms), two-space rack-mount head-unit only, hybrid chassis, 12AX7 tube/FET preamp, two channels, front silver control panel, single input, 18 knobs, tuner out, XLR direct out, effects loop, two-button footswitch (four-button optional) black casing, 33 lbs., mfg. 2006-disc.

$1,150	$625 - 750	$375 - 450		$1,439

- **Add $80 (MSR $99) for two-space carpeted carrying case (ES-SLV).**

GBE 1200 HEAD – 1200W at 2 ohms, 1000W at 4 ohms, and 550W at 2 ohms, three-space rack-mount head-unit only, hybrid chassis, 12AX7 tube/FET preamp, Powerflex circuitry, two channels, front silver control panel, single input, 18 knobs, tuner out, XLR direct out, effects loop, five-button footswitch, black casing, 42 lbs., mfg. 2005-disc.

$1,450	$800 - 950	$525 - 600		$1,829

- **Add $100 (MSR $129) for three-space carpeted carrying case (ES-SLV3).**

BASS AMPLIFIERS: ML SERIES

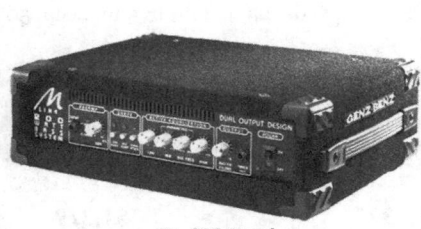

ML 200 Head
courtesy Genz Benz

ML 200 112T Combo
courtesy Genz Benz

ML 200 210T Combo
courtesy Genz Benz

ML 200 HEAD – 200W, head-unit only, solid-state chassis, single channel, front black control panel, single input, six chrome knobs (g, l, m, m freq., h, MV), tuner out, effects loop, black covering, side handles, 20 lbs., mfg. 2002-07.

$400	$225 - 275	$125 - 175		$499

* ***ML 200 112T Combo*** – similar to the ML 200 Head, except in combo form with 1-12 in. speaker and a tweeter, tilt-up cabinet, black metal grille, 48 lbs., mfg. 2002-07.

$630	$350 - 425	$200 - 250		$789

* ***ML 200 115T Combo*** – similar to the ML 200 Head, except in combo form with 1-15 in. speaker and a tweeter, tilt-up cabinet, black metal grille, 57 lbs., mfg. 2002-07.

$680	$375 - 450	$225 - 275		$849

* ***ML 200 210T Combo*** – similar to the ML 200 Head, except in combo form with 2-10 in. speakers and a tweeter, tilt-up cabinet, black metal grille, 60 lbs., mfg. 2002-07.

$750	$425 - 500	$250 - 300		$939

MSR/NOTES	100%	EXCELLENT	AVERAGE	LAST MSR

Neo-Pak 3.5 Head
courtesy Genz Benz

NeoX 112T Speaker Cabinet
courtesy Genz Benz

NeoX 210T Speaker Cabinet
courtesy Genz Benz

BASS AMPLIFIERS: NEOX SERIES

NEO-PAK 3.5 HEAD – 350W (switchable to 225W), head-unit/rack-mount configuration, hybrid chassis, preamp: 12AX7, power: digital SMPS, single channel, front silver control panel, single input, seven silver knobs (g, v, l, m, mid-freq., h, MV), signal shape buttons, tuner out, XLR direct out, gray casing, optional shoulder bag, 8.5 lbs., mfg. 2006-07.

	$740	$400 - 475	$250 - 300	$919

* Add $25 (MSR $29) for rack-mount hardware.
* Add $40 (MSR $49) for padded shoulder bag.

NEOX400-112T COMBO – 425W @ 4 ohms (300W @ 8 ohms), 1-12 in. speaker and a tweeter combo, hybrid chassis, preamp: FET & 12AX7, power: solid-state, single channel, front silver control panel, single input, 12 silver knobs (FET g, Tube g, Tube v, three signal shape knobs, five EQ knobs, MV), signal shape buttons, tuner out, XLR direct out, black covering, black metal grille, 57 lbs., mfg. 2006-07.

	$1,250	$700 - 850	$425 - 500	$1,539

* *NeoX400-210T Combo* – similar to the NeoX400-112T Combo, except has 2-10 in. speakers with a tweeter, 66 lbs., mfg. 2006-07.

	$1,400	$800 - 950	$525 - 600	$1,749

NEOX 112T SPEAKER CABINET – 300W, 1-12 in. GNX 12300 Neodymium speaker and a compact compression tweeter, 8 ohm impedance, dual edge porting, top handle, black covering, black metal grille, 21.25 in. wide, 18 in. tall, 16.5 in. deep, 37 lbs., mfg. summer 2003-disc.

	$640	$350 - 425	$200 - 250	$799

NEOX 210T SPEAKER CABINET – 450W, 2-10 in. GNX 10250 Neodymium speakers and a compact compression tweeter, 4 ohm impedance, dual edge porting, top corner edge lift handles, black covering, black metal grille, 21.25 in. wide, 25 in. tall, 16.5 in. deep, 50 lbs., mfg. summer 2005-disc.

	$900	$500 - 575	$300 - 350	$1,099

NEOX 212T SPEAKER CABINET – 600W, 2-12 in. GNX 12300 Neodymium speakers and a compact compression tweeter, 4 ohm impedance, dual edge porting, top corner edge lift handles, kick back casters, black covering, black metal grille, 21.25 in. wide, 31 in. tall, 16.5 in. deep, 62 lbs., mfg. summer 2003-disc.

	$880	$475 - 550	$275 - 325	$1,029

BASS AMPLIFIERS: SHUTTLE SERIES

SHUTTLE 3.0 HEAD (STL3-0) – 175W @ 4 ohms (300W @ 8 ohms), bass guitar head unit, solid-state chassis with FET preamp and Class D power amp, single channel, front silver control panel, single input, six silver knobs (v, l, m, mid freq., h, MV), mute switch, three-band push button signal shape circuit (low freq. boost, mid scoop, high freq. attack), LED status indicators, rear panel: power switch, 1/4 in. and Speakon speaker out jacks, aux in. jack, headphone jack, effects loop, tuner out jack, XLR balanced direct out jack with level, EQ, and ground/lift switches, black casing, 8.5 in. wide, 2.375 in. tall, 9.25 in. deep, 2.75 lbs., mfg. 2008-disc.

	$550	$300 - 375	$175 - 225	$689

* Add $40 (MSR $49) for padded carrying bag (STL-BAG).

* *Shuttle 3.0 1-8 Combo (STL3.0-8T)* – similar to the Shuttle 3.0 Head, except in combo configuration with 1-8 in. Neodymium speaker and a soft dome Neodymium tweeter, removable chassis, rear-ported cabinet, black covering, black metal grille, 11.875 in. wide, 13.5 in. tall, 10.75 in. deep, 13.5 lbs., mfg. 2008-disc.

	$700	$375 - 450	$225 - 275	$879

* *Shuttle 3.0 1-10 Combo (STL3.0-10T)* – similar to the Shuttle 3.0 Head, except in combo configuration with 1-10 in. Neodymium speaker and a soft dome Neodymium tweeter, removable chassis, rear-ported cabinet, black covering, black metal grille, 14 in. wide, 15.5 in. tall, 11.75 in. deep, 18 lbs., mfg. 2008-disc.

	$800	$450 - 525	$275 - 325	$999

MSR/NOTES	100%	EXCELLENT	AVERAGE	LAST MSR

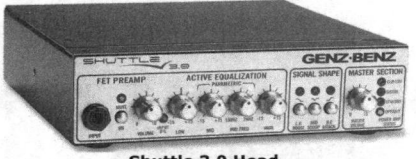

**Shuttle 3.0 Head
courtesy Genz Benz**

**Shuttle 6.0 Head
courtesy Genz Benz**

**Shuttle 3.0 1-10 Combo
courtesy Genz Benz**

**Shuttle 6.0 2-10 Combo
courtesy Genz Benz**

SHUTTLE 6.0 HEAD (STL6-0) – 375W @ 4 ohms (600W @ 8 ohms), bass guitar head unit, hybrid chassis with 1 X 12AX7 preamp tube and Class D power amp, digital SMPS (Switch Mode Power Supply), single channel, front silver control panel, single input, seven silver knobs (g, v, l, m, mid freq., h, MV), mute switch, input switch, three-band push button signal shape circuit (low freq. boost, mid scoop, high freq. attack), LED status indicators, rear panel: power switch, two Speakon jacks, headphone jack, footswitch jack, effects loop, aux in. jack, tuner out jack, XLR balanced direct out jack with level, EQ, and ground/lift switches, optional four-button footswitch (mute, three signal shape buttons), black casing, 10 in. wide, 2.5 in. tall, 10.5 in. deep, 3.75 lbs., mfg. 2008-disc.

	$700	$375 - 450	$225 - 275	$879

* Add $40 (MSR $49) for padded carrying bag (STL-BAG).
* Add $40 (MSR $49) for rack mount kit (STL6-0RK).
* Add $80 (MSR $99) for four-button footswitch (F/S-SLT6-0)

Shuttle 6.0 1-12 Combo (STL6.0-12T) – similar to the Shuttle 6.0 Head, except in combo configuration with 1-12 in. Neodymium GNX12300 speaker and a soft dome Neodymium tweeter, removable chassis, rear-ported cabinet, tilt-back kickstand, black covering, black metal grille, 18.375 in. wide, 21.75 in. tall, 14.25 in. deep, 32 lbs., mfg. 2008-disc.

	$1,200	$650 - 775	$375 - 400	$1,499

Shuttle 6.0 2-10 Combo (STL6.0-210T) – similar to the Shuttle 6.0 Head, except in combo configuration with 2-10 in. Neodymium GNX10250 speakers and a compression tweeter, removable chassis, rear-ported cabinet, tilt-back kickstand, black covering, black metal grille, 18.375 in. wide, 27.75 in. tall, 14.25 in. deep, 41 lbs., mfg. 2008-disc.

	$1,300	$675 - 825	$375 - 450	$1,629

SHUTTLE 9.0 HEAD (STL9-0) – 500W @ 4 ohms (900W @ 8 ohms), bass guitar head unit, hybrid chassis with 1 X 12AX7 preamp tube and Class D power amp, digital SMPS (Switch Mode Power Supply), PHAT (Proprietary Heat Abatement Technology), single channel, front black control panel, single input, seven silver knobs (g, v, l, m, mid freq., h, MV), mute switch, input switch, three-band push button signal shape circuit (low freq. boost, mid scoop, high freq. attack), LED status indicators, rear panel: power switch, two Speakon jacks, headphone jack, footswitch jack, effects loop, aux in. jack, tuner out jack, XLR balanced direct out jack with level, EQ, and ground/lift switches, optional four-button footswitch (mute, three signal shape buttons), black casing, 10 in. wide, 2.5 in. tall, 10.5 in. deep, 4 lbs., mfg. late 2009-disc.

	$830	$500 - 575	$300 - 350	$1,099

* Add $40 (MSR $49) for padded carrying bag (STL-BAG).
* Add $40 (MSR $49) for rack mount kit (STL6-0RK).
* Add $80 (MSR $99) for four-button footswitch (F/S-SLT6-0)

SHUTTLE MAX 6.0 HEAD (STL-MAX-6-0) – 375W @ 4 ohms (600W @ 8 ohms), bass guitar head unit, hybrid chassis with a blendable 1 X 12AX7 tube/FET preamp and Class D power amp, two channels, front silver control panel, single input, 20 silver knobs (FET Ch.: g, v, l, l/m gain, l/m freq., h/m, gain h/m freq., h, Tube Ch.: g, v, l, l/m gain, l/m freq., h/m, gain h/m freq., h, All: low freq. boost, mid scoop, high freq. attack, MV), mute switch, FET/Tube channel switch, mix channel switch, high gain/low gain switch per channel, three-band push button signal shape circuit (low freq. boost, mid scoop, high freq. attack), LED status indicators, rear panel: power switch, voltage selector switch, two parallel Speakon jacks, footswitch jack, mute switch jack, headphone jack, three effects loop (Master, Tube Ch., FET Ch.), aux in. jack, tuner out jack, XLR balanced direct out jack with level, EQ, and ground/lift switches, five-button footswitch (tube, mix, three signal shape buttons), black casing, 13.5 in. wide, 3.5 in. tall, 13 in. deep, 5.75 lbs., mfg. 2009-disc.

	$900	$500 - 600	$300 - 350	$1,149

* Add $45 (MSR $59) for padded carrying bag (STL-MAX-BAG).
* Add $40 (MSR $49) for rack mount kit (STL-MAX-RK).
* Add $100 (MSR $139) for cabinet mounting saddle (SLT-MAX-SDL).

SHUTTLE MAX 12.0 HEAD (STL-MAX-12-0) – 375W-1200W depending on power amp and cabinet load usage, bass guitar head unit, hybrid chassis with a blendable 1 X 12AX7 tube/FET preamp and two Class D power amps, two channels, front silver control panel, single input, 20 silver knobs (FET Ch.: g, v, l, l/m gain, l/m freq., h/m, gain h/m freq., h, Tube Ch.: g, v, l, l/m gain, l/m freq., h/m, gain h/m freq., h, All: low freq. boost, mid scoop, high freq. attack, MV), mute switch, FET/Tube channel switch, mix channel switch, high gain/low gain switch per channel, three-band push button signal shape circuit (low freq. boost, mid scoop, high freq. attack), LED status indicators, rear panel: power switch, voltage selector switch, two Speakon jacks (one for each power amp), footswitch jack, mute switch jack, headphone jack, three

MSR/NOTES	100%	EXCELLENT	AVERAGE	LAST MSR

**Shuttle 9.0 Head
courtesy Genz Benz**

**Shuttle 12.0 Max Head
courtesy Genz Benz**

**Shuttle 1-12 Speaker Cabinet
courtesy Genz Benz**

**Shuttle 6.0 2-10 Combo
courtesy Genz Benz**

effects loop (Master, Tube Ch., FET Ch.), aux in. jack, tuner out jack, XLR balanced direct out jack with level, EQ, and ground/lift switches, five-button footswitch (tube, mix, three signal shape buttons), black casing, 13.5 in. wide, 3.5 in. tall, 13 in. deep, 6.75 lbs., mfg. 2009-disc.

$1,100	$600 - 700	$350 - 425		$1,379

* Add $45 (MSR $59) for padded carrying bag (STL-MAX-BAG).
* Add $40 (MSR $49) for rack mount kit (STL-MAX-RK).
* Add $100 (MSR $139) for cabinet mounting saddle (SLT-MAX-SDL).

SHUTTLE 1-8 SPEAKER CABINET (STL-8T) – 175W, 1-8 in. Neodymium speaker and a soft dome tweeter, 8 ohm impedance, Speakon and 1/4 in. inputs, black covering with black metal corners, black metal grille, 11.75 in. wide, 10.5 in. tall, 11.25 in. deep, 11 lbs., mfg. summer 2008-disc.

$380	$225 - 275	$120 - 150		$479

SHUTTLE 1-10 SPEAKER CABINET (STL-10T) – 200W, 1-10 in. Neodymium speaker and a soft dome tweeter, 8 ohm impedance, Speakon and 1/4 in. inputs, black covering with black metal corners, black metal grille, 14 in. wide, 12.5 in. tall, 11.75 in. deep, 16 lbs., mfg. summer 2008-disc.

$480	$275 - 325	$150 - 200		$599

SHUTTLE 1-12 SPEAKER CABINET (STL-12T) – 300W, 1-12 in. Neodymium speaker and a soft dome tweeter with level control, 8 ohm impedance, Speakon and 1/4 in. inputs, black covering with black metal corners, black metal grille, 18.5 in. wide, 18 in. tall, 14.25 in. deep, 27 lbs., mfg. summer 2008-disc.

$580	$300 - 375	$175 - 225		$729

SHUTTLE 2-10 SPEAKER CABINET (STL-210T) – 400W, 2-10 in. Neodymium speakers and a soft dome tweeter with level control, 8 ohm impedance, Speakon and 1/4 in. inputs, black covering with black metal corners, black metal grille, 18.5 in. wide, 24 in. tall, 14.25 in. deep, 37 lbs., mfg. summer 2008-disc.

$680	$350 - 425	$200 - 250		$859

BASS SPEAKER CABINETS: LS SERIES

LS 112T SPEAKER CABINET – 200W, 1-12 in. GBE 1241C woofer, a GBE 4941 tweeter, and a GBE 2937 crossover with tweeter level control, 8 ohm impedance, top handle, black covering, black metal grille, 22 in. wide, 18 in. tall, 16 in. deep, 36 lbs., mfg. 2002-07.

$380	$200 - 250	$120 - 150		$479

LS 115B SPEAKER CABINET – 150W, 1-15 in. GBE 1540 woofer, designed for low-end use - typically used under the LS 210T or LS410T cabinet, 8 ohm impedance, top corner edge lift handles, black covering, black metal grille, 25 in. wide, 24.5 in. tall, 18 in. deep, 61 lbs., mfg. 2002-07.

$400	$225 - 275	$135 - 175		$499

LS 210T SPEAKER CABINET – 200W, 2-10 in. GBE 1030 woofer, a GBE 4941 tweeter, and a GBE 2937 crossover with tweeter level control, 8 ohm impedance, top corner edge lift handles, black covering, black metal grille, 25 in. wide, 15.5 in. tall, 18 in. deep, 49 lbs., mfg. 2002-07.

$400	$225 - 275	$135 - 175		$499

LS 410T SPEAKER CABINET – 400W, 4-10 in. GBE 1030 woofers, a GBE 4941 tweeter, and a GBE 2937 crossover with tweeter level control, 8 ohm impedance, top corner edge lift handles, black covering, black metal grille, 25 in. wide, 24 in. tall, 18 in. deep, 72 lbs., mfg. 2002-07.

$600	$325 - 400	$175 - 225		$749

MSR/NOTES	100%	EXCELLENT	AVERAGE	LAST MSR

**LS 115B Speaker Cabinet
courtesy Genz Benz**

**Über 2-10 Speaker Cabinet
courtesy Genz Benz**

**Über 8-10 Speaker Cabinet
courtesy Genz Benz**

BASS SPEAKER CABINETS: ÜBER SERIES

ÜBER 2-10 SPEAKER CABINET (GB210T-UB) – 450W, 2-10 in. GNX-10250 Neodymium speakers and a compression bullet tweeter, 8 ohm impedance, Speakon and 1/4 in. input jacks, tweeter level control, bottom ported cabinet, black "nubby-textured" vinyl covering with black metal corners, silver/black wire mesh grille cloth, top side-mounted recessed handles, 24.5 in. wide, 20 in. tall, 18 in. deep, 50 lbs., mfg. summer 2008-disc.

$930	$525 - 625	$300 - 350		$1,159

ÜBER 2-12 SPEAKER CABINET (GB212T-UB) – 600W, 2-12 in. GNX-12300 Neodymium speakers and a compression bullet tweeter, 4 ohm impedance, Speakon and 1/4 in. input jacks, tweeter level control, bottom ported cabinet, black "nubby-textured" vinyl covering with black metal corners, silver/black wire mesh grille cloth, top side-mounted recessed handles, 24.5 in. wide, 28 in. tall, 18.25 in. deep, 63 lbs., mfg. 2009-disc.

$1,040	$575 - 675	$325 - 400		$1,299

ÜBER 4-10 SPEAKER CABINET (GB410T-UB) – 1000W, 4-10 in. GNX-10250 Neodymium speakers and a compression bullet tweeter, 4 (GB410T-UB-4) or 8 (GB410T-UB-8) ohm impedance, Speakon and 1/4 in. input jacks, tweeter level control, bottom ported cabinet, black "nubby-textured" vinyl covering with black metal corners, silver/black wire mesh grille cloth, top side-mounted recessed handles, rear-mounted casters, skid rails, 24.5 in. wide, 28 in. tall, 18.25 in. deep, 72 lbs., mfg. 2008-disc.

$1,160	$625 - 750	$350 - 425		$1,449

ÜBER 8-10 SPEAKER CABINET (GB810T-UB) – 1600W, 8-10 in. GNX-10250 Neodymium speakers and a compression bullet tweeter, 4 ohm impedance, Speakon and 1/4 in. input jacks, tweeter level control, bottom ported cabinet, black "nubby-textured" vinyl covering with black metal corners, silver/black wire mesh grille cloth, top side-mounted recessed handles, rear-mounted casters, skid rails, 24 in. wide, 49.75 in. tall, 18.25 in. deep, 120 lbs., mfg. 2008-disc.

$1,600	$900 - 1,050	$500 - 600		$1,999

BASS SPEAKER CABINETS: XB SERIES

GB 115T-XB2 SPEAKER CABINET – 400W, 1-15 in. GBE 1580 woofer, 1-4 in. GBE 4410 tweeter, and a 3560 crossover, 8 ohm impedance, front ported, side handles, black covering, black metal grille, 25 in. wide, 30 in. tall, 16 in. deep, 75 lbs., disc. 2008.

$750	$425 - 500	$250 - 300		$949

* *GB 115B-XB2 Speaker Cabinet* – similar to the GB 115T-XB2, except has no tweeter, disc. 2008.

$650	$350 - 425	$200 - 250		$829

GB 210T-XB2 4/8 SPEAKER CABINET – 350W, 2-10 in. GXB 1040 woofers, 1-4 in. GBE 4410 tweeter, and a 3560 crossover, available in 4 or 8 ohm impedance, front ported, top corner handles, black covering, black metal grille, 25 in. wide, 21 in. tall, 16 in. deep, 69 lbs., disc. 2008.

$650	$350 - 425	$200 - 250		$829

GB 410T-XB2 4/8 SPEAKER CABINET – 700W, 4-10 in. GXB 1040 woofers, 1-4 in. GBE 4410 tweeter, and a 3560 crossover, available in 4 or 8 ohm impedance, front ported, rear-mounted edge lift handle, kick back casters, black covering, black metal grille, 25 in. wide, 31 in. tall, 16 in. deep, 90 lbs., disc. 2008.

$900	$500 - 600	$300 - 350		$1,129

GB 610T-XB2 SPEAKER CABINET – 900W, 6-10 in. GXB 1040 woofers, 1-4 in. GBE 4410 tweeter, and a 3560 crossover, 4 ohm impedance, front ported, rear-mounted edge lift handle, kick back casters, black covering, black metal grille, 25 in. wide, 44 in. tall, 18 in. deep, 130 lbs., disc. 2008.

$1,160	$625 - 750	$375 - 450		$1,449

MSR/NOTES	100%	EXCELLENT	AVERAGE	LAST MSR

GB 210T-XB2 4/8 Speaker Cabinet
courtesy Genz Benz

GB 610T-XB2 Speaker Cabinet
courtesy Genz Benz

GB 210T-XB3 Speaker Cabinet
courtesy Genz Benz

GB 115T-XB3 SPEAKER CABINET – 400W, 1-15 in. speaker and a compression bullet tweeter, 8 ohm impedance, Speakon and 1/4 in. inputs, bottom "shelf" ported cabinet, black covering with black metal corners, black grille with "XB3" logo, top mounted recessed handles, casters included, 24 in. wide, 28 in. tall, 18.25 in. deep, 70 lbs., mfg. 2009-disc.

$720	$400 - 475	$225 - 275		$899

GB 210T-XB3 SPEAKER CABINET – 350W, 2-10 in. speakers and a compression bullet tweeter, 8 ohm impedance, Speakon and 1/4 in. inputs, bottom "shelf" ported cabinet, black covering with black metal corners, black grille with "XB3" logo, top mounted recessed handles, 24 in. wide, 19.75 in. tall, 18.25 in. deep, 53 lbs., mfg. 2009-disc.

$750	$425 - 200	$250 - 300		$929

GB 410T-XB3 SPEAKER CABINET – 700W, 4-10 in. speakers and a compression bullet tweeter, 4 ohm impedance, Speakon and 1/4 in. inputs, bottom "shelf" ported cabinet, black covering with black metal corners, black grille with "XB3" logo, top mounted recessed handles, casters included, 24 in. wide, 28 in. tall, 18.25 in. deep, 79 lbs., mfg. 2009-disc.

$900	$500 - 575	$300 - 350		$1,129

GB 810T-XB3 SPEAKER CABINET – 1200W, 8-10 in. speakers and a compression bullet tweeter, 4 ohm impedance, Speakon and 1/4 in. inputs, bottom "shelf" ported cabinet, black covering with black metal corners, black grille with "XB3" logo, top mounted recessed handles, tilt-back casters and skid rails included, 24 in. wide, 50.5 in. tall, 18.25 in. deep, 130 lbs., mfg. 2009-disc.

$1,360	$725 - 875	$425 - 500		$1,699

GEORGE DENNIS LTD.

Amplifiers, speaker cabinets, and effects currently produced in the Czech Republic since 1991. Previously distributed in the U.S. by European Musical Imports, Inc. in Hillsdale, NJ.

George Dennis amplifiers have been produced since 1996, but the story of the company goes back to 1973. The president of the company today, George Burgerstein, was playing in a band with Alex Bajger, who is the designer and developer of the company. Alex showed George an amp he had designed, and George liked it so much he sold his Vox AC-30 and used Alex's exclusively. In 1983, after the band had broken up, George and another friend, Martin, worked to create "The Blue Amplifier," until Martin was killed in a car accident. The amplifier project was put on hold, but in 1991, George started producing effects pedals under the George Dennis trademark. In 1996, George met up with Alex again and the two became partners to create the Blue Amplifier once again. Since these two men have so much experience in the music industry, their prototype amplifier, "The Blue," is a "truly terrific guitar amplifier." Currently, George Dennis Ltd. produces a full line of amplifiers, speaker cabinets, and effect pedals. For more information, visit George Dennis' website or contact them directly.

CONTACT INFORMATION
GEORGE DENNIS LTD.
Factory
Nostrasnicka 39
Prague 10, CZ-100 00 Czech Republic
Phone No.: 420-2-7822758/9
Fax No.: 420-2-7822584
www.georgedennis.eu
georgede@volny.cz

ELECTRIC TUBE AMPLIFIERS

The Blue Series is the flagship of George Dennis and there are several variations of this model. The **Blue 60** and **Blue 100** both feature four channels, reverb, 5-button footswitch, 12AX7 preamp tubes, EL34 power tubes, and Celestion speakers for all the combos. They are available as a the 60W Head, 60W 1-12 in. speaker combo, 60W 2-12 in. speaker combo, 100W Head, and 100W 2-12 in. speaker combo.

The **Blue Beetle** is a 15W tube amp powered by 2 X EL84 tubes, and is available as a head-unit or as a combo with 1-10 in. Celestion speaker. The **Mighty Mouse** has 30W output from 4 X EL84 tubes, and is available as a head-unit or as a combo with 1-12 in. Celestion speaker. Controls are identical on the Blue Beetle and Mighty Mouse with dual channels, and reverb.

The **Vintage Blue** model features 80W power, 4 X 12AX7 preamp tubes, 2 X EL34 power tubes, two channels, and a front panel built of Canadian cherry. This model is available as a head-unit or a 2-12 in. speaker combo.

The **Bluesman 40** model features 40W power, 3 X 12AX7 preamp tubes, 4 X EL84 power tubes, a tube rectifier, and a single channel. This model is available as a 1-12 in. speaker combo or a 2-12 in. speaker combo. The **Bluesman 60** model features 60W power, 4 X 12AX7 preamp tubes, 2 X EL34 power tubes, two channels, and an effects loop. This model is available as a head-unit or a 2-12 in. speaker combo.

The **Spit-Fire** model features 50W power, 3 X 12AX7 preamp tubes, 4 X EL84 power tubes, a dual rectifier, two channels, and an effects loop. This model is available as a 1-12 in. or 2-10 in. speaker combo.

George Dennis also produces a line of bass amplifiers. The Bassic Tube is offered in two versions, the only difference being wattage and tubes. The **Bassic Tube 120** has 120W output from 4 X EL34 tubes. The **Bassic Tube 200** has 200W from 4 X KT88 tubes.

All amplifiers are covered in a blue vinyl covering. In 2002, to mark their 10 year anniversary, they offered all of their tube amps with denim covering and a polished stainless steel control panel. They also have a silver plate on the lower right corner stating the 10 year anniversary.

SPEAKER CABINETS

George Dennis offers speaker cabinets in 1-12 in., 2-10 in., 2-12 in., 4-10 in., and 4-12 in. speaker configurations. Several speaker types are available as well including Celestion G12s, Celestion Vintage 30s, Celestion Greenbacks, and Jensen Alnicos. The 4-12 in. speaker cabinet comes in a straight or slanted version. Many speaker types are available on combos as well.

GERHART AMPLIFICATION

Amplifiers currently produced in Tulsa, OK. Previously produced in West Hills, CA. The Gerhart trademark was established in 2000.

Gary Gerhart founded Gerhart Amplification in 2000. They specialize in guitar and bass tube amplifiers and speaker cabinets. Models range in a variety of sizes from 1/2W up to 100W. Gerhart also offers a tube amp kit of his popular Gilmore model. For more information, visit Gerhart's website or contact the company directly.

GERLITZ

Amplifiers and speaker cabinets previously produced in Salem, OR.

Harvey Gerlitz started building custom cabinets for other manufacturers including Matchless for their Exotic cabinets. The Gerlitz amplifier company was founded to create one specific design by combining two other products into one. The G1 "Revelator" Dual Amp has the sounds of a Marshall Plexi unit and a Fender Blackface all in one amp. The Blackface is based around a Deluxe Super Reverb (mid-1960s) and the Marshall Plexi around a 50 Watt Lead (late 1960s). The Revelator is available as a head-unit or combo and speaker cabinets are also available. Gerlitz is no longer building amplifiers as of circa 2007.

GERMINO AMPLIFICATION

Amplifiers currently produced in North Carolina since 2002.

Greg Germino founded Germino Amplification in 2002, but he has been working with tube amplifiers since the 1970s. While playing in several bands over the years, Greg also worked for The Tube Farm, Fat Sound Guitars, Bull City Sound, Shomaker Guitars, and Mojo Musical Supply. By the late 1990s and early 2000s, Greg really had a handle on how tube amps worked, especially Marshalls. In 2002, he started building Germino amps, and they are all inspired by Marshall plexi models from the late 1960s and early 1970s. Each model is hand-built by Greg with the finest components, and he offers a transferable limited lifetime warranty on most parts and labor. Head-units, combos, and speaker cabinets are all available. For more information, visit Germino Amplification's website or contact them directly.

ELECTRIC TUBE AMPLIFIERS

The Germino **Classic 45** is based on the Marshall JTM-45 of the mid 1960s. This amp is available as a head-unit (MSR $2,200), 1-12 in. speaker combo (MSR $2,350), or a 2-12 in. speaker combo (MSR $2,650). The **Club 40** is based on Marshall's JTM-50 and JMP-50 bass 50W heads and are available as a head-unit (MSR $2,200), 1-12 in. speaker combo (MSR $2,350), or a 2-12 in. speaker combo (MSR $2,650). The **Lead 55** was discontinued in 2009 and was a JMP-50 design with 2 X EL34 power tubes, a solid-state rectifier, and lead circuit values. This model is available as a head-unit (disc. 2009, last MSR was $2,100), 1-12 in. speaker combo (disc. 2009, last MSR was $2,300), or a 2-12 in. speaker combo (disc. 2009, last MSR was $2,500). This model is

Classic 45 Orange Head
courtesy Germino Amplification

Club 40 Purple Head
courtesy Germino Amplification

Lead 55 Black
courtesy Germino Amplification

also available as the **Lead 55 LV** with a different power transformer and is available as a head-unit (MSR $2,200), 1-12 in. speaker combo (MSR $2,350), or a 2-12 in. speaker combo (MSR $2,500). The **Monterey 100** (previously called the Monterey Classic, MSR $2,650) is built on a full-size aluminum chassis as the original "Super Amp" from circa 1966. The **Fillmore 100** (previously called the Fillmore Classic, MSR $2,650) is a 100W amp based on the early 1967 JTM-100 Marshall. The **Headroom 100** (MSR $2,650) is based on the late 1967/early 1968 100W Marshall and is available in Super Lead or Super Bass versions. 2-12 in. and 4-12 in. speaker cabinets are also available. All amps and cabinets are available in late 1960s/early 1970s Marshall-style colored coverings in Black, Orange, Purple, Red, and White.

GIANNINI

Amplifiers previously produced in Brazil between circa 1960s and the 1980s.

In 1890, Tranquillo Giannini left Italy and migrated to San Paulo, Brazil where he began manufacturing guitars. The company eventually became one of the largest manufacturers of guitars in Brazil. In the 1960s, Giannini released a line of tube amplifiers that were basically copies of many Fender designs including models Tremendao (copy of Twin Reverb), Thunder Sound Bass (copy of Bassman), and the Jet Sound (copy of Tremolux). In the early 1970s, Giannini was distributed in the U.S. by Giannini Guitars at 75 Frost Street, Westbury (New York 11590). If that address seems somewhat familiar, that may be because it was shared by Westbury Guitars, the Merson company, and currently Korg USA (Marshall, Parker, Korg, and Vox). Giannini also produced a line of solid-state amps in the 1970s and/or 1980s but very little information is known about them.

GIBSON

Amplifiers currently produced since the early 1990s. Gibson previously produced amplifiers in Kalamazoo, MI from the mid-1930s-1967, and various other locations including Chicago, IL from 1968 through the mid-1970s. Distributed by the Gibson Guitar Corporation in Nashville, TN.

CONTACT INFORMATION
GIBSON
309 Plus Park Blvd.
Nashville, TN 37217
Phone No.: 615-871-4500
Fax No.: 615-884-9411
www.gibson.com

The roots of Gibson go way back to Orville Gibson when he and other men founded the company in 1902. Gibson guitars were made with the Gibson logo starting in 1896 (for more information on Gibson electric guitars, refer to the *Blue Book of Electric Guitars*). Gibson amplifiers didn't come into the picture until the late 1930s, however. With the release of the first Gibson electric guitar, the ES-150, a guitar amplifier would be needed to make the new electric pickup useful. The first Gibson amplifiers were the EH series, which debuted in the late 1930s. With World War II going on in the early 1940s, Gibson amplifiers didn't really become a steady production item until circa 1948. Shipment totals from Gibson were first tracked on amplifiers starting in 1948. In 1948, all amplifier production was moved into the Kalamazoo factory and the first GA Series models were released. These popular models were produced in all shapes and sizes through 1967, when all production of amplifiers at the Kalamazoo plant halted. When Gibson bought Epiphone in 1957, they started to produce Epiphone amplifiers. Almost all Epiphone amps between 1957 and 1970 are copies of Gibson models (see Epiphone for more information and corresponding models). Gibson also introduced the Maestro brand on amps specifically designed for accordions (see Maestro).

Other companies started building amps for Gibson, and by 1968 a new line of tube amplifiers with some familiar old names were released. These lasted only a short time through 1969, when only various solid-state models were available. In the early 1970s, a new series was introduced called the G Series with some models featuring a phase shift. In 1977, the Lab Series was introduced (see Lab Series). These amps were designed by Moog, which was a division of Gibson's parent company, Norlin. These amps all have an L prefix and come in a variety of power and speaker configurations. The first Lab series was produced through the late 1970s, but was replaced by the Lab Series 2 in 1980 (also see Lab Series). These amps have a GA prefix for guitars and a B prefix for bass amps. In 1980, the Genesis series was released as well, which are amps that are targeted for practice and entry level models. These amps also have G and B prefixes for their guitar and bass models (see Genesis).

Another series of Gibson amplifiers appeared in the early 1990s, with the revival of the Lab series again. These amps featured a gold and orange cover and came in the Classic Gold, Gold Chorus, and GB 440 bass amp models. Currently Gibson produces a line of tube amps called the Goldtone Series.

Information courtesy Wallace Marx Jr., *Gibson Amplifiers 1933-2008 - 75 Years of the Gold Tone*, George Gruhn/Walter Carter, *Gruhn's Guide to Vintage Guitars*, Walter Carter, *Gibson Guitars: 100 Years of an American Icon*; Aspen Pittman, *The Tube Amp Book "Deluxe Revised Edition,"* and Larry Meiners: *Gibson Shipment Totals*), and various Gibson catalogs.

AMPLIFIER ABBREVIATIONS

Gibson used many abbreviations to organize their models.

BR: Barnes & Reinecke
E: Echo
EH: Electric Hawaiian
GA: Gibson Tube Amplifier
GSS: Gibson Solid-State Amplifier

L: Lansing speaker(s)
R or RV: Reverb
T: tremolo

For Example a GA-77RETL is a Gibson Tube Amplifier Model 77 with reverb, echo, tremolo, and has Lansing speakers. This works for almost all Gibson amplifiers. This system essentially started around 1948 when the GA amplifiers were introduced.

• **Add 10% for original cover on amplifier.**

MSR/NOTES	100%	EXCELLENT	AVERAGE	LAST MSR

COVERING AND STYLING OVERVIEW

Gibson generally changed styles across their lines when they introduced new styling. However, this usually only applies to most larger models. The GA-5, GA-6, GA-9 and similar models generally had their own styling and it is noted in the model descriptions. For most other models, this general year range can be used to date amplifiers. This is only a guide.

1935-1942: Various tweeds and aeroplane coverings, mostly specific to each model.

1947-1954: Medium brown bookbinding covering (occasionally tan or cream color was used instead of the brown). Light brown grille cloth and many often had the speaker opening split by one or more slats (see early GA-20, GA-50, and GA-75).

1955-1957: Two tone covering with lower half a mottled gray/brown and the top half with a brown leatherette. Logos placed above the grille with "Gibson" and respective GA model number (i.e. 20, 30, 40, etc.). The speaker grille is entirely under the top brown leatherette. Leather handles are used.

1958-1959: Two-tone covering with lower half a light tweed-style covering and the top half a brown leatherette. Logo above the grille is only "Gibson." The speaker grille extends into the top brown leatherette. Metal handles with plastic inserts are used.

1960-1962: Tweed-style covering with the speaker grille covering all of the front except for the edge that the tweed creates. Brown grille with "Gibson" logo in upper right grille, metal handle with Gibson plastic insert.

1963-1965: Advertised as "Indian Brown" coarse vinyl covering, "Spanish Crush" brown grille with "Gibson" in upper right corner, control panel moved to the front and angles towards the top. Some models may have a gray vinyl covering during this time.

1965-1967: Black coarse alligator style vinyl covering, silver grille with "Gibson" mainly in upper left corner but does appear other places, white control panel that faces front, mostly rubber handles. Very similar to Fender Silverfaces of the time.

1968-1969: Black vinyl, black grille cloth, cabinets are all taller than they are wider and have extended sides into the top. Most control panels face up (some forward).

1970-1975: Black vinyl, black grille cloth. These models are again similar to Fender's blackface models with the control panel facing front.

ELECTRIC TUBE AMPLIFIERS: ELECTRIC HAWAIIAN (EH) SERIES

The Electric Hawaiian (EH) series of guitars and amps were produced between 1935 and 1942. The first Gibson Electric Steel Guitar was produced in 1935 that came with a matching amplifier, the **EH-150** (the **EH-100** followed a year later). These first EH-Series amplifiers were built by Lyon and Healy. Oftentimes, the guitar was sold with the matching amplifier. The EH-Series were produced up until the start of World War II when all amplifier production halted (along with most guitar production). After the war, an entirely new line of amps was released (the BR Series).

EH-100 – 8W, 1-8 in. (1936-37) or 1-10 in. (1937-1941) speaker, guitar combo, varying tube chassis, 6N7, 6C8, 6C5, & others for preamp, mainly 6V6 power, single channel, two inputs, no controls, black aeroplane cloth (1936-37), tan aeroplane cloth (1937-38), dark brown aeroplance with yellow horizontal stripes (1938-1940), or natural wood finish (1940-41) covering, mfg. 1936-1941.

	N/A	$600 - 700	$375 - 450	

The EH-100 changed almost every year that it was in production and there are at least five distinct versions of it. In mid-1937, the chassis was increased to five tubes, a microphone input replaced one instrument input, a volume control was added, and the covering was changed to a tan aeroplane cloth with vertical, dark stripes. In mid-1938, the chassis was increased to six tubes, and the covering was changed to a brown aeroplane cloth with horizontal, yellow stripes. In mid-1939, the covering was changed to a green/gray cloth with horizontal white stripes. In mid-1940, the cabinet was changed to be narrower (12 in.) but taller (14.75 in.) with an open back and the top part of the amp seperated from the chassis, the covering was changed to a wood natural mahogany finish (most were covered in the gray/green cloth).

EH-110 – similar to the EH-100, except designed to operate on AC/DC power, mfg. 1937-1942.

	N/A	$625 - 725	$400 - 475	

EH-125 – wattage unknown, 1-12 in. speaker, six tube chassis, preamp: 2 X 6SQ7, 1 X 6J5, power: 2 X 6V6, rectifier: 5Y3, three inputs (two instruments, one microphone), microphone volume control, round shouldered cabinet, brown aeroplane (1941-early 1942) or dark green aeroplane (early 1942-late 1942) cloth covering, 10.625 in. round speaker opening, black metal grille, 16.5 in. wide, 15.375 in. tall, 8.625 in. deep, mfg. 1941-42.

	N/A	$675 - 800	$425 - 500	

EH-126 – similar to the EH-125, except designed to operate on 6 volt DC power, five produced, mfg. 1941 only.

	N/A	$1,050 - 1,250	$525 - 650	

EH-135 – similar to the EH-125, except designed to run on AC/DC power, seven produced, mfg. 1941 only.

	N/A	$1,100 - 1,300	$550 - 675	

EH-150 – 15W, 1-10 in. speaker, guitar combo, various tube chassis, 1st version (1935-36): four tubes (1 X 6A6, power: 2 X 6F6, rectifier: 1 X 5Z4), 2nd version (1936-37): six tubes (1 X 6F5, 1 X 6N7, 1 X 6C5, power: 2 X 6N6, rectifier: 5Z3), 3rd version (1937-1941): seven tubes (3 X 6SQ7, 1 X 6N7, power: 2 X 6L6, rectifier: 5U4), 4th version (1941-42): seven tubes (3 X 6C5, 1 X 6F5, power: 2 X 6L6, rectifier: 5U4), rear control panel, three inputs (two instruments, one microphone), two volume controls, tone switch, echo speaker jack, square cabinet, aeroplane cloth covering, dark grille, mfg. 1935-1942.

	N/A	$1,200 - 1,500	$725 - 900	

The original model produced between late 1935 and early 1936 featured a cabinet with a gold/brown tweed covering with vertical

MSR/NOTES	100%	EXCELLENT	AVERAGE	LAST MSR

courtesy solidbodyguitar.com, Inc.

courtesy solidbodyguitar.com, Inc.

courtesy solidbodyguitar.com, Inc.

orange and black stripes in the center, a leather suitcase-style handle, a removable back, alligator grained material on the inside, four rubber feet, and is 13.75 in. wide, 13.75 in. tall, and 7.25 in. deep.

In late 1936, the control panel consisted of this from left to right (power, echo input, mic v, pilot light, inst. v, three inputs (one mic, two inst.) and normal/bass tone toggle switch below the inputs), the chassis was changed to six tubes, and the cabinet sized changed to 15.25 in. wide, 14.75 in. tall, and 8 in. deep.

In early 1937, the chassis was increased to seven tubes and the cabinet was changed to 8.5 in. deep and a .75 in. thick front.

In mid-1937, the cabinet was changed where the sides rounded at the top, the speaker hole was changed to 10.625 in. round with a metal grille, the inside was covered with a black grained material, and the dimensions changed to 16.5 in. wide, 15.375 in. tall, 8.625 in. deep.

In mid-1941, the amp was changed one last time with a new control panel consisting of from left to right (power cord, power switch, tone control, mic v, inst. v, three inputs (one mic, two inst.), pilot light, model, and serial number), a speaker hole with a rounded front edge, inside covering of cream colored paper, and dimensions of 17.25 in. wide, 15.625 in. tall, and 9 in. deep. Two models in 1937 were finished in White and labeled Smeck in the lower right corner.

EH-160 – similar to the EH-150, except designed to operate on AC/DC power, mfg. 1936-1942.

	N/A	$1,200 - 1,500	$725 - 900	

EH-185 – 15W, 1-12 in. speaker, six-tube chassis, preamp: 1 X 6SN7, 1 X 6SC7, 1 X 6SJ7, power: 2 X 6L6, rectifier: 5U4, two channels, front black control panel, three inputs (mic, two inst.), four knobs (t, b, mic v, inst. v), echo speaker jack, gold tweed covering with vertical black and orange stripes in the center, round speaker hole and oblong opening to cool chassis above speaker hole, black metal grilles, top of amp flips up to access controls and the chassis lifts out of cabinet to become seperated by a 13 ft. cord, mfg. mid-1939-1942.

	N/A	$1,050 - 1,250	$725 - 850	

This model was introduced as the new Model EH-150. Approx. the first 60 units built have EH-150 in the model name or scratched in over another name. The first control panel consisted of from left to right (power cord, power switch, echo speaker jack, t, b, pilot light, mic v, inst. v, three inputs). In late 1941, the control panel changed to the EH-150's of the same era with controls left to right (power cord, power switch, tone, mic v, inst. v, three inputs (mic, two inst.), pilot light, model and serial number.

* EH-185C – similar to the EH-185, except designed to operate on 6 volt DC power, mfg. mid-1939-1942.

	N/A	$1,200 - 1,400	$600 - 725	

EH-195 – similar to the EH-185, except has a tremolo circuit with controls and designed to operate on AC/DC power, mfg. mid-1939-1942.

	N/A	$1,525 - 1,800	$775 - 950	

EH-250 – similar to the EH-185, except has a natural maple cabinet, two produced, mfg. 1940 only.

	N/A	$1,875 - 2,200	$925 - 1,150	

EH-275 – similar to the EH-185, except has a natural maple cabinet with tortoiseshell celluloid binding, approx. 30 produced, mfg. 1940-42.

	N/A	$1,875 - 2,200	$925 - 1,150	

ELECTRIC TUBE AMPLIFIERS: BARNES & REINECKE (BR) SERIES

After World War II, Gibson went back to work producing amplifiers again. Barnes Reinecke designed these new amps, and they were produced in Kalamazoo. All of these amps were designed to be used with the Electric Hawaiian guitars. These models lasted only a few years as the GA series was released in 1948. The BR-6 and BR-9 both lasted until the mid-1950s when they both evolved into the GA-6 and GA-9 respectively. The BR named was used because the electric Hawaiian models were still produced. It is unknown if the BR-6 and BR-9 were produced at the same time as the GA-6 and GA-9 .

BR-1 – 15-18W, 1-12 in. speaker, guitar combo, six tube chassis, preamp: 1 X 6SJ7, 1 X 6SC7, 1 X 6SN7, power: 2 X 6L6, rectifier: 5U4, two channels, top-mounted chassis, rear cream control panel, three inputs (two instrument, one microphone), three control knobs (mic v, inst. v, tone), pilot light, fuse cap, power switch, rectangular grille made of perforated aluminum with a large sytilzied G, brown leatherette covering, mfg. late 1945-48.

	N/A	$675 - 800	$350 - 425	

MSR/NOTES	100%	EXCELLENT	AVERAGE	LAST MSR

BR-3 – 12-15W, 1-12 in. speaker, guitar combo, six tube chassis, preamp: 2 X 7B4, 1 X 6J5, power: 2 X 6V6, rectifier: 5Z4, two channels, rear control panel, three inputs (two inst., one mic), three control knobs (inst. v, mic v, tone), round speaker hole, modern "G" stenciled on grille, hinged cabinet, early models have a darker aeroplane cloth with stripes, a dark grille cloth and stenciled gold capital G, later models have a light tweed covering with no stripes and a green stenciled capital G, 79 shipped, mfg. 1946 only.

	N/A	$675 - 800	$350 - 425	

BR-4 – 14W, 1-12 in. speaker, guitar combo, six tube chassis, preamp: 1 X 6SJ7, 1 X 6SL7, 1 X 6SN7, power: 2 X 6V6, rectifier: 5Y3, two channels, bottom-mounted chassis, rear control panel, three inputs (two inst., one mic), three black control knobs (inst. v, mic v, tone), pilot light, fuse cap, power switch, two-tone brown leatherette covering with a wide cream strip in the center, square grille with swirl grille cloth and two vertical wooden strips, mfg. 1946-47.

	N/A	$600 - 700	$300 - 375	

BR-6 – 8-10W (1946-47) or 12W (1948-1956), 1-10 in. speaker, five tube chassis, preamp: 1 X 6SL7 (1946-47) or 1 X 6SJ7 (1948-1956), 1 X 6SN7, power: 2 X 6V6, rectifier: 5Y3, single channel, bottom-mounted chassis, rear control panel, two (1946-47) or three (1948-1952) inputs, one volume knob, two or three horizontal grille openings, brown leatherette covering, approx. 8,443 shipped, mfg. 1946-1954.

courtesy solidbodyguitar.com, Inc. *courtesy solidbodyguitar.com, Inc.*

1946-1947 BR-6	N/A	$600 - 700	$300 - 375	
1948-1954 BR-6F	N/A	$500 - 600	$255 - 325	

In 1948, the model was changed to the BR-6F, the wattage increased to 12W, a 10 in. dynamic speaker replaced the field coil, a 6SJ7 preamp tube replaced the 6SL7, an input was added, and the cabinet changed to a horizontal design with a lighter brown covering, tan grille cloth, and a two hole rectangle speaker hole with a stylized "G." This model was renamed the GA-6 in 1956. Shipping totals reflect the total number shipped through the end of 1955 (regardless if models were still shipped into 1956).

BR-9 – 10W, 1-8 in. speaker, four-tube chassis, preamp: 1 X 6SN7, power: 2 X 6V6, rectifier: 5Y3, single channel, rear control panel, two inputs, one volume control, power switch, fuse cap, cabinet narrows at top, round speaker hole with multi-piece brown trim over the speaker hole, logo under speaker inside of trim, cream leatherette covering, approx. 11,798 shipped, mfg. 1948-1954.

courtesy Harry Browning

	N/A	$425 - 500	$215 - 265	

This model was renamed the GA-9 in 1954. Shipping totals reflect the total number shipped through the end of 1954 (regardless if the amp was called the GA-9 by then).

ELECTRIC TUBE AMPLIFIERS: GA (GA-5 - GA-20) SERIES

GA-5 LES PAUL JUNIOR – 4W, 5 X 7 in. special oval type speaker (1954-56) or 1-8 in. round speaker (1957), three-tube chassis: preamp: 1 X 6SJ7, power: 1 X 6V6, rectifier: 5Y3, single channel, rear control panel, two inputs, single volume knob, earlier models have a light gray covering with a tan grille cloth, later models have tan covering with a brown grille cloth, 13.5 in. wide, 11.5 in. tall, 10,420 shipped, mfg. 1954-57.

1954-1956 Oval Speaker	N/A	$550 - 650	$325 - 400	
1957 Round Speaker	N/A	$500 - 600	$300 - 375	

In 1957, the "Les Paul" and "TV model" logos began appearing on this amp.

MSR/NOTES	100%	EXCELLENT	AVERAGE	LAST MSR

GA-Les Paul Junior
courtesy solidbodyguitar.com, Inc.

GA-Les Paul Junior
courtesy solidbodyguitar.com, Inc.

GA-Les Paul Junior
courtesy Savage Audio

GA-5 SKYLARK (FIRST VERSION) – 4.5W, 1-8 in. Jensen speaker, three tube chassis: preamp: 1 X 7025, power: 1 X 6V6, rectifier: 5Y3, single channel, rear control panel, two instrument inputs, one volume control, light brown grained covering, gold grille fabric, 13.5 in. wide, 13.5 in. tall, 16,618 shipped, mfg. 1958-1962.

courtesy Atomic Guitars

courtesy Atomic Guitars

N/A	$425 - 500	$215 - 265	

The GA-5 Skylark essentially replaced the Les Paul Junior amplifier with a wider cabinet.

* **GA-5T Skylark (First Version)** – similar to the GA-5 Skylark except has built-in tremolo, five tube chassis, preamp: 2 X 6EU7, power: 6AQ7, rectifier: 6X4, and controls for tremolo speed and intensity, 4,464 shipped, mfg. 1960-62.

N/A	$375 - 450	$225 - 275	

GA-5 SKYLARK (SECOND VERSION) – 10W, 1-10 in. speaker, five tube chassis, preamp: 1 X 6EU7, 1 X 6C4, power: 2 X 6AQ5, rectifier: 6X4, single channel, front silver control panel, two inputs, two knobs (v, power switch), brown covering, brown grille, 19.5 in. wide, 15 in. tall, 7 in. deep, 9,515 shipped, mfg. 1963-65.

courtesy Dave Rogers/Dave's Guitar Shop

courtesy Dave Rogers/Dave's Guitar Shop

N/A	$350 - 400	$170 - 210	

The second version of the GA-5 Skylark featured a higher and wider cabinet than the first version and power was increased to 10W.

* **GA-5T Skylark (Second Version)** – similar to the GA-5 Skylark (Second Version) except has built in tremolo, five-tube chassis, preamp: 2 X 6EU7, power: 6AQ7, rectifier: 6X4, and controls for tremolo speed and intensity, 10,315 shipped, mfg. 1963-65.

N/A	$300 - 375	$175 - 225	

MSR/NOTES	100%	EXCELLENT	AVERAGE	LAST MSR

GA-5T Skylark (Second Version)
courtesy TLC Guitars

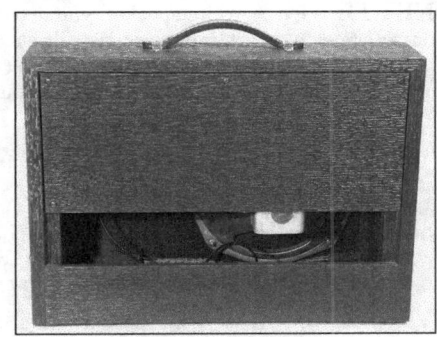

GA-5T Skylark (Second Version)
courtesy TLC Guitars

GA-5 SKYLARK (THIRD VERSION) – 10W, 1-10 in. speaker, three tube chassis, preamp: 6EU7, power: 6BQ5, rectifier: 6X4, two diodes, single channel, front silver control panel, two inputs, four knobs (v, t, b, power), black alligator covering, gray grille, 17 in. wide, 14.75 in. tall, 8.5 in. deep, 2,624 shipped, mfg. 1966-67.

	N/A	$250 - 300	$140 - 175	

The third version of the GA-5 Skylark featured an even larger cabinet than the first two versions.

* *GA-5T Skylark (Third Version)* – similar to the GA-5 Skylark (Third Version) except has built in-tremolo, a four-tube chassis, preamp: 2 X 6EU7, power: 6AQ7, rectifier: 6X4, and six knobs (v, t, b, depth, freq., power), 4,993 shipped, mfg. 1966-67.

	N/A	$300 - 350	$175 - 225	

GA-6 – 12W, 1-12 in. Jensen speaker, guitar/microphone combo, five-tube chassis: preamp: 1 X 12AX7, 1 X 6SL7, power: 2 X 6V6, rectifier: 5Y3, two channels, top control panel, four inputs (three instrument, one mic), three black chicken head knobs (tone, inst v, mic v), available in two-tone "oatmeal" buffalo grain fabric covering with a woven Saran grille (1956-57) or dark brown buffalo covering with a light brown woven Saran grille (1958-59), 5,845 shipped, mfg. 1956-59.

courtesy Willie's American Guitars

	N/A	$550 - 650	$275 - 350	

This amp was originally the BR-6 and in 1956 was renamed the GA-6. The original cabinet featured a mottled gray/brown covering and dimensions were 20 in. wide, and 11.25 in. tall. In 1958, the covering was changed to a dark brown, and the dimensions changed to 20 in. wide, 16 in. tall, 9 in. deep, and 24 lbs. In 1960, this model was renamed the GA-6 Lancer, the covering changed to a tweed with a Gibson logo in the upper right corner of the grille, and the power increased to 14W.

GA-6 LANCER – 14W, 1-12 in. Jensen speaker, five-tube chassis: preamp: 2 X 12AX7, power: 2 X 6V6, rectifier: 5Y3, two channels, top control panel, four inputs (two per channel), three black chicken head knobs (tone, inst v, mic v), tweed covering, full face dark brown grille cloth, 821 shipped, mfg. 1960-61.

	N/A	$700 - 850	$425 - 500	

This amp was originally the BR-6 and in 1956 was renamed the GA-6. The original cabinet featured a mottled gray/brown covering and dimensions were 20 in. wide, and 11.25 in. tall. In 1958, the covering was changed to a dark brown, and the dimensions changed to 20 in. wide, 16 in. tall, 9 in. deep, and 24 lbs. In 1960, this model was renamed the GA-6 Lancer, the covering changed to a tweed with a Gibson logo in the upper right corner of the grille, and the power increased to 14W.

GA-7 LES PAUL TV MODEL – 4W, 1-10 in. speaker, guitar combo, three-tube chassis, preamp: 1 X 6SJ7, power: 1 X 6V6, rectifier: 5Y3, single channel, rear control panel, two inst. inputs, single volume knob, two-tone "oatmeal" buffalo grain covering, gold grille fabric, 469 shipped, mfg. 1954-56.

	N/A	$525 - 625	$325 - 400	

This model is identical to the GA-5 Les Paul Junior in construction and the only difference is "Les Paul TV Model" logo included in the graphics.

MSR/NOTES	100%	EXCELLENT	AVERAGE	LAST MSR

GA-8 GIBSONETTE – 8W, 1-10 in. speaker, guitar combo, four-tube chassis, preamp: 1 X 12AX7, power: 2 X 6V6, rectifier: 5Y3, single channel, top control panel, two inst. inputs, single volume knob, available in brown covering with a round metal speaker grille (1952-53), light brown grained fabric with a square dark brown grille cloth (1954-57), or light tan covering with narrow sides, large speaker opening, and a metal handle, Gibsonette logo above grille, 17.5 in. wide, 13 in. tall, 7,365 shipped, mfg. 1952-59.

1952-1953	N/A	$475 - 550	$300 - 350	
1954-1957	N/A	$500 - 575	$325 - 375	
1958-1959	N/A	$525 - 600	$325 - 400	

In 1958, the output was raised to 9W, the Gibson logo was moved above the grille, the handle was metal with a plastic middle, the covering was changed to a gold fabric, the grille was a dark brown, and the cabinet size was increased to 20 in. wide, 16 in. tall, 9 in. deep, and 20 lbs. Most of these amps don't actually have GA-8 stamped on them.

GA-8 DISCOVERER – 9-10W, 1-12 in. speaker, guitar combo, five-tube chassis, preamp: 1 X 6EU7, 1 X 6C4, power: 2 X 6BQ5, rectifier: 6CA4, single channel, top nickel-plated control panel (1960-62) or front control panel (1963), two inst. inputs, two knobs (v, tone), available in tweed covering with a full face slanted dark brown grille (1960-62) or Indian brown Tolex covering with a Spanish Crush brown grille (1963), 3,294 shipped, mfg. 1960-63.

	N/A	$475 - 550	$300 - 375	

In 1962, the output was increased to 10W.

* GA-8T Discoverer – similar to the GA-8 Discoverer, except has built-in tremolo, five-tube chassis, preamp: 2 X 6EU7, power: 2 X 6BQ5, rectifier: 6CA4, four knobs (v, tone, s, i, 1960-62) or five knobs (v, t, b, s, i), available in tweed covering with a full face slanted dark brown grille (1960-62) or Indian brown Tolex covering with a Spanish Crush brown grille (1963-66) in 8,532 shipped, mfg. 1960-66.

courtesy solidbodyguitar.com, Inc.

courtesy solidbodyguitar.com, Inc.

1960-1962 Tweed	N/A	$500 - 575	$325 - 400	
1963-1966 Brown	N/A	$375 - 450	$225 - 275	

In 1963, the output was increased to 15W.

GA-9 – 10W, 1-8 in. (1954-56) or 1-10 in. Jensen (1956-59) speaker, four-tube chassis: preamp: 6SJ7, power: 2 X 6V6, rectifier: 5Y3, single channel, top-mounted chrome control panel, two inst. inputs, two knobs (v, tone), available in light brown covering with a square brown cloth grille and "Gibson 9" logo centered above the grille (1954-56) or tweed covering with a large dark brown grille and "Gibson" centered above the grille (1956-59), 4,319 shipped, mfg. 1954-59.

1954-1956 8 in. Speaker	N/A	$475 - 550	$300 - 375	
1958-1959 10 in. Speaker	N/A	$425 - 500	$275 - 325	

This model was sold with the BR-9 Steel Guitar also. This model was originally named the BR-9 and was changed to the GA-9 in 1954. In 1956, the cabinet size was increased to 17.5 in. wide and 13 in. tall, the speaker was changed to 1-10 in. Jensen from an 8 in., and the Gibson 9 logo was mounted above the grille. In 1958, a Gibson logo was placed above the grille, the handle became metal with a plastic middle, and the cabinet dimensions changed to 20 in. wide, 16 in. tall, 9 in. deep, and 20 lbs.

GA-14 TITAN – 14W, 1-10 in. Jensen speaker, guitar/microphone combo, five-tube chassis, preamp: 2 X 12AX7, power: 2 X 6V6, rectifier: 5Y3, two channels, top control panel, four inputs (two per channel), three control knobs (v1, v2, tone), tweed covering, full-faced brown grille with Gibson logo in upper right hand corner, 20 in. wide, 16 in. high, 493 shipped, mfg. 1959-1961.

	N/A	$550 - 650	$350 - 425	

This model is identical to the GA-6 except has a 10 in. speaker.

GA-15 EXPLORER – 14W, 1-10 in. speaker, guitar combo, five-tube chassis, preamp: 1 X 12AX7, 1 X 6SL7, power: 2 X 6V6, rectifier: 5Y3, two channels, three inputs (Ch. 1: two inst., Ch. 2: one inst./mic), three knobs (two v, tone), light tweed covering, dark cloth grille, 175 shipped, mfg. 1955-58.

	N/A	$600 - 700	$375 - 450	

GA-15RVT EXPLORER – 18W, 1-10 in. speaker, guitar combo, five-tube chassis, preamp: 2 X 6EU7, 1 X 12AU7, power: 2 X 6BQ5, solid-state rectifier, single channel, tremolo, reverb, front white control panel, three inputs, seven knobs (v, t, b, r, depth, freq., power), black alligator covering, gray grille cloth, 20.5 in. wide, 16.75 in. tall, 9.625 in. deep, 6,003 shipped, mfg. 1965-67.

courtesy John Beeson/The Music Shoppe   *courtesy John Beeson/The Music Shoppe*

N/A	$400 - 475	$250 - 300	

GA-17RVT SCOUT – wattage unknown, 1-10 in. speaker, six-tube chassis, preamp: 2 X 6EU7, 1 X 12AX7, power: 2 X 6AQ5, rectifier: 6CA4, single channel, tremolo, reverb, top silver control panel, two inputs, four black and silver knobs (v, r, tremolo freq., power switch), Indian Brown covering, Spanish Crush brown cloth grille, 5,197 shipped, mfg. 1963-67.

N/A	$475 - 550	$300 - 375	

Only two GA-17RVT Scouts were produced after 1965, but it is possible this amp was covered with black alligator covering and a silver grille. However, we have never encountered a black GA-17RVT.

GA-18 EXPLORER – 14W, 1-10 in. speaker, guitar/microphone combo, five-tube chassis, preamp: 1 X 12AX7, 1 X 6SL7, power: 2 X 6V6, rectifier: 1 X 5Y3, single channel, top silver control panel, three inputs, two black chicken head knobs (v, tone), tweed covering, brown cloth grille, 1,421 shipped, mfg. 1959 only.

N/A	$725 - 850	$450 - 525	

GA-18T EXPLORER – 14W, 1-10 in. speaker, guitar combo, six-tube chassis, preamp: 2 X 6EU7, 1 X 12AX7, power: 2 X 6AQ5, rectifier: 1 X 6CA4, single channel, tremolo, top rear-mounted control panel, three inputs, four black chickenhead knobs (v, tone, tremolo depth, tremolo freq.), tweed covering, full front slanted dark brown grille cloth with Gibson logo in upper right-hand corner, metal handle with plastic middle, 20 in. wide, 16.5 in. tall, 3,092 shipped, mfg. 1960-63.

N/A	$750 - 900	$475 - 550	

GA-19RVT FALCON – 15W, 1-12 in. speaker, guitar combo, seven-tube chassis, preamp: 3 X 6EU7, 1 X 7199, power: 2 X 6V6, rectifier: 5Y3, two channels, tremolo, reverb, top silver control panel, two inputs, five black knobs (v, tone, depth, freq, r), footswitch, available in tweed covering with a full-front dark brown grille cloth (1961-62) or Indian Brown covering with a Spanish Crush brown grille cloth, 13,914 shipped, mfg. 1961-67.

courtesy John Beeson/The Music Shoppe   *courtesy John Beeson/The Music Shoppe*

1961-1962 Tweed	N/A	$1,000 - 1,200	$675 - 800
1963-1967 Brown	N/A	$500 - 600	$300 - 375

From 1961 to 1962, this model featured a tweed covering with brown grille. In 1963, a cabinet with brown covering and a light brown grille was introduced, and the dimensions changed to 22 in. wide, 18 in. tall, and 10.5 in. deep. It is possible that models produced after 1965 featured black alligator covering and a silver grille cloth, although all examples we have encountered do not have this. Only 12 GA-19RVT Falcons were shipped after 1965.

MSR/NOTES	100%	EXCELLENT	AVERAGE	LAST MSR

GA-20 FIRST VERSION – 12-14W, 1-12 in. Jensen speaker, six-tube chassis, preamp: 2 X 6SC7, 1 X 6SL7, output: 2 X 6V6, rectifier: 5Y3, two channels, top rear-mounted control panel, four inputs (three inst., one mic), three controls (inst. v, mic v, tone), brown leatherette covering with a light brown grille cloth split horizontally with a thin bar containing a "G" logo in the middle, 20 in. wide, 17 in. tall, 5,117 shipped, mfg. 1950-53.

courtesy solidbodyguitar.com, Inc.   courtesy solidbodyguitar.com, Inc.

| | N/A | $650 - 800 | $450 - 525 | |

GA-20/GA-20 CREST SECOND VERSION – 16W, 1-12 in. Jensen Concert Series speaker, guitar combo, five-tube chassis, preamp: 2 X 12AX7, output: 2 X 6V6, rectifier: 5Y3, two channels, top rear control panel, four inputs (three inst., one mic 1954-56, two per channel 1957-1961), three controls (inst. v, mic v, tone), available in two-tone Buffalo grain covering with a woven Saran grille and "Gibson 20" logo centered above the grille (1954-56), two-tone Buffalo grain covering with a woven Saran grille and "Gibson" logo centered above the grille (1957-59), or tweed covering with a dark brown grille cloth, 4,271 shipped, mfg. 1954-1961.

1954-1956	N/A	$850 - 1,000	$600 - 700	
1957-1959 Brown	N/A	$925 - 1,100	$650 - 775	
1960-1961 Tweed	N/A	$1,000 - 1,200	$725 - 850	

In 1954, Gibson introduced the second version of the GA-20 and changed to a two-tone brown covering with a rectangle brown speaker grille, the logo "Gibson 20" moved above the grille, and dimensions of 20 in. wide, 16 in. tall, 8.625 in. deep, and 24 lbs. In 1958, the cabinet was changed slightly to a different two-tone brown covering, only the "Gibson" logo appeared on the front, and the dimensions changed to 20 in. wide, 16 in. tall, 9 in. deep, and 24 lbs. In 1960, the name Crest was added to GA-20 and the cabinet changed again to a tweed covering with a brown grille and the "Gibson" logo in the upper right corner.

GA-20T/GA-20T Ranger – similar to the GA-20/GA-20 Crest Second Version, except has a tremolo circuit with a seven-tube chassis, preamp: 1 X 12AY7, 1 X 7025, 1 X 5879, 1 X 6SQ7, power: 2 X 6V6, rectifier: 5Y3, five knobs (tone, s, v1, i, v2), available in two-tone Buffalo grain covering with a woven Saran grille and "Gibson 20T" logo centered above the grille (1956 only), two-tone Buffalo grain covering with a woven Saran grille and "Gibson" logo centered above the grille (1957-59), or tweed covering with a dark brown grille cloth (1960-61), 4,224 shipped, mfg. 1956-61.

courtesy Blue Book Archive   courtesy Blue Book Archive

1956	N/A	$675 - 800	$475 - 550	
1957-1959 Brown	N/A	$850 - 1,000	$600 - 700	
1960-1961 Tweed	N/A	$1,050 - 1,300	$750 - 900	

Originally, this amp cabinet featured a two-tone brown covering with a rectangle brown speaker grille, the logo "Gibson 20T" above the grille, and dimensions of 20 in. wide, 16 in. tall, 8.625 in. deep, and 24 lbs. In 1958, the cabinet was changed slightly to a different two-tone brown covering, only the "Gibson" logo appeared on the front, and the dimensions changed to 20 in. wide, 16 in. tall, 9 in. deep, and 24 lbs. In 1960, the name Ranger was added to GA-20T and the cabinet changed again to a tweed covering with a brown grille and the "Gibson" logo in the upper right corner.

MSR/NOTES	100%	EXCELLENT	AVERAGE	LAST MSR

GA-20RVT MINUTEMAN – 12.5W, 1-12 in. speaker, guitar combo, eight-tube chassis, preamp: 3 X 6EU7, 2 X 12AU7, power: 2 X EL84, rectifier: 5Y3, two channels, reverb, tremolo, white front control panel, four inputs (two per channel), 10 knobs (Ch. 1: v, t, b, Ch. 2: v, t, b, r, depth, freq., power switch), footswitch, black alligator covering, silver grille, two-button footswitch included, 5,457 shipped, mfg. 1965-67.

courtesy John Beeson/The Music Shoppe

courtesy John Beeson/The Music Shoppe

| N/A | $425 - 500 | $215 - 265 | |

ELECTRIC TUBE AMPLIFIERS: GA (GA-25 - GA-50) SERIES

GA-25 – 15W, 1-12 in. Jensen P12R and 1-8 in. speakers, guitar combo, six-tube chassis, preamp: 1 X 6SJ7, 2 X 6J5, power: 2 X 6V6GT, rectifier: 5Y3, single channel, bottom rear-mounted control panel, four inputs (three inst., one mic), two knobs (v, tone), brown mottled leather covering with two different sized circular brown speaker grilles and a gold "Gibson" logo in the lower right-hand corner, mfg. 1947-48.

*courtesy Wallace Marx Jr.
and Steve Matacia*

*courtesy Wallace Marx Jr.
and Steve Matacia*

| N/A | $675 - 800 | $450 - 525 | |

GA-25RVT HAWK – approx. 15W, 1-15 in. speaker (early models) or 2-10 in. speakers (later models), guitar combo, eight-tube chassis, preamp: 4 X 6EU7, 1 X 12AU7, power: 2 X 6V6, rectifier: 5Y3, two channels, tremolo, reverb, top front control panel, four inputs (two per channel), seven control knobs (early models: v1, v2, tone, depth, freq., r, power), or nine control knobs (later models: Ch. 1: v, b, t, Ch. 2: v, b, t, s, i, r), footswitch, Indian Brown covering with a Spanish Crush brown grille (early models) or black covering with a light tan grille (later models), 26 in. wide, 20 in. tall, 10.5 in. deep, 3,783 shipped, mfg. 1963-67.

courtesy Steve Brown

courtesy Steve Brown

| N/A | $500 - 600 | $300 - 375 | |

Late in production, the Hawk had independent tone controls for each channel and the tubes were changed to 2 X 6EU7, 3 X 12AU7, 2 X 7591. Although this amp was shipped through 1967, it doesn't appear that it adopted the style between 1965 and 1967 that featured black covering, a silver grille, and front white control panel.

GA-30 – 14W, 1-12 in. Jensen P12R and 1-8 in. Jensen speakers, guitar combo, six-tube chassis, preamp: 1 X 6SC7, 2 X 6SJ7, power: 2 X 6V6, rectifier: 5Y3, two channels, rear bottom control panel (1949-1954) or rear top control panel (1954-1961), four inputs (three inst., one mic), three knobs (tone, inst. v, mic v), tone expander switch, available in brown leatherette covering with a wide rectangular light brown grille cloth and centered "Gibson" logo (1949-1954), two-tone Buffalo grain covering with a woven Saran grille and "Gibson 30" logo centered above the grille (1954-56), two-tone Buffalo grain covering with a woven Saran grille and "Gibson" logo centered above the grille (1957-59), or tweed covering with a dark brown grille cloth (1960-61), 5,996 shipped, mfg. 1948-1961.

courtesy solidbodyguitar.com, Inc.   courtesy solidbodyguitar.com, Inc.

1948-1954 Brown	N/A	$775 - 900	$475 - 550
1955-1959 Two-Tone Brown	N/A	$850 - 1,000	$600 - 700
1960-1961 Tweed	N/A	$1,000 - 1,200	$725 - 850

Originally, the covering on this amp was a medium brown with a light brown rectangle grille cloth and a "Gibson" logo in the center. In 1956, the chassis was moved to to the top, the cabinet changed to a two-tone brown covering with a rectangle brown speaker grille, the logo "Gibson 30" was placed above the grille, and dimensions were 22 in. wide, 20 in. tall, 10.175 in. deep, and 32 lbs. In 1958, the cabinet was changed slightly to a different two-tone brown covering, only the "Gibson" logo appeared on the front, and a metal handle with plastic middle replaced the leather one. In 1960, the name Invader was added to GA-30, a standby pointer knob was added, and the cabinet changed again to a tweed covering with a brown grille and the "Gibson" logo in the upper right corner.

* ***GA-30RV Invader*** – similar to the GA-30 Invader, except has a reverb circuit with a seven-tube chassis, preamp: 3 X 6EU7, 1 X 12AU7, power: 2 X 6V6 power, rectifier: 5Y3, top mounted silver control panel, four inputs (two per channel), four black and silver knobs (v1, v2, tone, r), tweed covering with a full front slanted brown cloth grille, 715 shipped, mfg. 1961 only.

N/A	$1,025 - 1,200	$500 - 625

GA-30RVT INVADER – 25W, 1-12 in. and 1-10 in. speakers, guitar combo, nine-tube chassis, preamp: 4 X 6EU7, 2 X 12AU7, power: 2 X 7591, rectifier: 0A2/5AR4, two channels, top silver control panel, four inputs (two per channel), eight black and silver knobs (1962-late 1963: Ch. 1: v, tone, Ch. 2: v, tone, r, depth, freq., power), or 10 knobs (late 1963-67: Ch. 1: v, t, b, Ch. 2: v, t, b, r, depth, freq., power), available in Indian Brown covering with a Spanish Crush brown grille, 2,601 shipped, mfg. 1962-67.

courtesy S.P. Fjestad   courtesy S.P. Fjestad

N/A	$625 - 750	$425 - 500

In late 1963, independent volume and bass tone controls were introduced for each channel. Although this amp was introduced in 1962 and shipped through 1967, it doesn't appear that it was produced in tweed covering nor did it adopt the style between 1965 and 1967 that featured black alligator covering, a silver grille, and front white control panel.

GA-35RVT LANCER – 35W, 1-12 in. speaker, guitar combo, eight-tube chassis, preamp: 2 X 6EU7, 12AX7, 2 X 12AU7, power: 2 X 7591, rectifer: 0A2, two channels, tremolo, reverb, front white control panel, four inputs (two per channel), 10 knobs (Ch.1: v, t, b, Ch. 2: v, t, b, r, depth, freq, power), black alligator covering, silver sparkle grille, 25.5 in. wide, 17.5 in. tall, 9.625 in. deep, 2,322 shipped, mfg. 1966-67.

N/A	$425 - 500	$215 - 265

GA-40 LES PAUL FIRST VERSION – 14W, 1-12 in. Jensen speaker, guitar combo, eight-tube chassis, preamp: 3 X 6SJ7, 1 X 6SN7, 1 X 6V6, power: 2 X 6V6, rectifier: 5V4, two channels, tremolo, top rear-mounted black control panel, four inputs (three inst., one mic), four black chicken head knobs (Ch. 1 v, Ch. 2 v, tone, tremolo), two tone brown covering, rectangular basket weave grille cloth with large "LP" letters across the front, footswitch, 22 in. wide, 15.5 in. tall, 3,261 shipped, mfg. 1952-54.

courtesy John Beeson/The Music Shoppe   courtesy John Beeson/The Music Shoppe

| | N/A | $1,275 - 1,500 | $650 - 800 | |

Shipping totals reflect the total number shipped through the end of 1954 (regardless if first version models were still shipped into 1955).

GA-40 LES PAUL SECOND VERSION – 14W (1955-57) or 16W (1958-1960), 1-12 in. Jensen speaker, guitar/microphone combo, seven-tube chassis, preamp: 2 X 5879, 1 X 7025, 1 X 6SQ7, power: 2 X 6V6, rectifier: 5Y3, two channels, tremolo, top rear-mounted control panel, four inputs (two per channel), five black chicken head knobs (Ch. 1 v, Ch. 2 v, tone tremolo depth, tremolo freq.), available in two-tone Buffalo grain covering with a woven Saran grille and "Gibson 40" logo centered above the grille (1955-56), two-tone Buffalo grain covering with a woven Saran grille and "Gibson" logo centered above the grille (1957-59), or tweed covering with a dark brown grille cloth (1960), 22 in. wide, 20 in. tall, 10.125 in. deep, 4,275 shipped, mfg. 1955-1960.

courtesy Savage Audio   courtesy Savage Audio

| 1955-1959 Two-Tone Brown | N/A | $1,200 - 1,500 | $800 - 1,000 |
| 1960 Tweed | N/A | $1,200 - 1,500 | $800 - 1,000 |

In 1956, the chassis was upgraded to eight tubes (tubes unknown). In 1958, the design changed to a two-tone brown, only a "Gibson" logo above the grille, and a metal handle with a plastic middle replaced the leather one. Shipping totals reflect the total number shipped from the start of 1955 (regardless if first version models were still shipped into 1955).

GA-40T LES PAUL – 25W, 1-12 in. Jensen speaker, guitar combo, seven-tube chassis, preamp: 3 X 6EU7, 1 X 12AU7, power: 2 X 7591, rectifier: 5AR4, two channels, tremolo, top silver control panel, four inputs (two per channel), five black and silver knobs (Ch. 1 v, C. 2 v, tone, tremolo depth, tremolo freq.), tweed covering, brown grille with Gibson logo in upper right corner, 22 in. wide, 20 in. tall, 10.5 in. deep, 928 shipped, mfg. 1961-62.

| | N/A | $1,650 - 2,000 | $1,050 - 1,300 | |

Shipping totals reflect the total number shipped through the end of 1962 (regardless if GA-40T Les Paul models were still shipped into 1963).

GA-40T MARINER – 25W, 1-12 in. speaker, guitar combo, six-tube chassis, 1962-63 preamp: 3 X 6EU7, 1 X 12AU7, power: 2 X 7591, rectifier: GZ34, 1964-67 preamp: 3 X 6EU7, 1 X 6C4, power: 2 X 7591, rectifier: GZ34, two channels, tremolo, top/front silver control panel, four inputs (two per channel), six knobs (Ch. 1 v, Ch. 2 v, tone, tremolo depth, tremolo freq., power), Indian Brown covering, Spanish Crush brown grille with Gibson logo in upper right-hand corner, leather handle, 26 in. wide, 20 in. tall, 10.5 in. deep, 987 shipped, mfg. 1962-67.

| | N/A | $500 - 600 | $255 - 325 | |

This is the same model as the GA-40T Les Paul, but Gibson changed the name of it when they stopped using the Les Paul brand on their products (see the Gibson Les Paul Guitar). Shipping totals reflect the total number shipped from the start of 1962 (regardless if GA-40T Les Paul models were still shipped into 1962). Although this amp was shipped through 1967, it doesn't appear that it adopted the style between 1965 and 1967 that featured black covering, a silver grille, and front white control panel.

MSR/NOTES	100%	EXCELLENT	AVERAGE	LAST MSR

GA-45RVT SATURN – Wattage unknown, 2-10 in. speakers, guitar combo, nine-tube chassis, preamp: 4 X 6EU7, 1 X 12AU7, 1 X 6CG7, power: 2 X 6L6, rectifier: 0A2, three diodes, two channels, reverb, tremolo, front white control panel, four inputs (two per channel), 10 black knobs (Ch. 1: v, t, b, Ch. 2: v, t, b, r, depth, freq., power), two bright switches, external speaker jack, black alligator covering, silver sparkle grille, 25.5 in. wide, 17.5 in. tall, 9.625 in. deep, 2,524 shipped, mfg. 1965-67.

| | N/A | $475 - 550 | $235 - 290 | |

14 models were shipped with Lansing speakers.

GA-50 – 18W, 1-12 in and 1-8 in. Jensen speakers, seven-tube chassis, preamp: 2 X 6SJ7, 2 X 6J5, power: 2 X 6550, rectifier: 5AR4, two channels, bottom rear control panel, four inputs (three inst., one mic), four knobs (Ch. 1 v, Ch. 2 v, b, t), brown mottled leather covering, two different-sized speaker holes with vertical slats , removable back to access chassis and controls, 26 in. wide, 20.5 in. tall, 1,033 shipped, mfg. 1948-1955.

courtesy Harry Browning   courtesy Harry Browning   courtesy Harry Browning

| | N/A | $1,550 - 1,900 | $1,000 - 1,200 | |

* **GA-50T** – similar to the GA-50, except has a tremolo circuit with an eight-tube chassis, preamp: 3 X 6SJ7, 1 X 6SN7, 1 X 6SL7, power: 2 X 6L6, rectifier: 5V4, and six knobs (Ch. 1 v, Ch. 2 v, b, t, s, i), 1,717 shipped, mfg. 1948-1955.

| | N/A | $1,650 - 2,000 | $1,050 - 1,300 | |

ELECTRIC TUBE AMPLIFIERS: GA (GA-55 - GA-79) SERIES

GA-55 RANGER – 18W, 2-12 in. speakers, guitar combo, six-tube chassis, preamp: 2 X 12AY7, 1 X 6SC7, power: 2 X 6L6, rectifier: 5V4, two channels, top rear-mounted control panel, four inputs (two per channel), five knobs (Ch. 1 v, Ch. 2 v, b, t, power), two-tone buffalo-grained covering with a woven Saran grille and "Gibson 55" logo centered above the grille, 26.5 in. wide, 20 in. tall, 10.125 in. deep, 203 shipped, mfg. 1954-58.

courtesy C.W. Green   courtesy C.W. Green

| | N/A | $2,125 - 2,500 | $1,075 - 1,325 | |

* **GA-55V Ranger** – similar to the GA-55, except has vibrato circuit with a remote vibrato switch and control that plugged into the player's guitar, 473 shipped, mfg. 1954-58.

| | N/A | $2,000 - 2,400 | $1,300 - 1,600 | |

The vibrato controls were mounted on a small plastic box that had a guitar plug fastened to it so the vibrato controls could be adjusted on the guitar while a person was playing without having to go back to the amp.

GA-55RVT RANGER – approx. 35-40W, 4-10 in. speakers, guitar combo, nine-tube chassis, preamp: 4 X 6EU7, 1 X 12AU7, 1 X 6CG7, power: 2 X 6L6, rectifier: 0A2, two channels, reverb, tremolo, front white control panel, four inputs (two per channel), 12 black knobs (Ch. 1: v, t, m, b, Ch. 2: v, t, m, b, r, depth, freq., power), two presence swithces, external speaker jack, black alligator covering, silver/gray sparkle grille, 28 in. wide, 25.25 in. tall, 10.75 in. deep, 2,087 shipped, mfg. 1965-67.

| | N/A | $500 - 600 | $255 - 325 | |

101 models were shipped as the GA-55RVTL with Lansing speakers (1967 only).

GA-60 HERCULES – 25W, 1-15 in. speaker, bass combo, five-tube chassis, preamp: 2 X 6EU7, power: 2 X 7591, rectifier: 5AR4, single channel, top silver control panel, two inputs, three knobs (v, b, t), brown covering, light brown grille, 493 shipped, mfg. 1962-63.

| | N/A | $550 - 650 | $375 - 450 | |

GA-70 COUNTRY WESTERN FIRST VERSION – 25W, 1-15 in. Jensen speaker, guitar combo, six tube chassis, preamp: 1 X 7025, 1 X 12AY7, 1 X 12AU7, power: 2 X 6L6, rectifier: 5V4, two channels, top control panel, four inputs (two per channel), four black chicken head knobs (Ch. 1 v, Ch. 2 v, tone, power), two-tone brown buffalo-grain covering, narrow rectangular woven Saran brown grille with "Gibson" logo and Texas longhorn logo on front, 20 in. wide, 22 in. tall, 10.125 in. deep, 40 lbs, 160 shipped, mfg. 1955-56.

	N/A	$1,650 - 2,000	$1,050 - 1,300	

A fidelity knob and "bell-like" treble are what set this country western amp aside from standard models. Unlike most Gibson models from this era, this model had a rectangle speaker opening that ran vertical leaving large strips of covering on either sides of the speaker.

GA-70 COUNTRY WESTERN SECOND VERSION – 25W, 1-15 in. Jensen speaker, guitar combo, six-tube chassis, preamp: 1 X 12AX7, 1 X 12AY7, 1 X 12AU7, power: 2 X 5881, rectifier: 5V4G, two channels, top control panel, four inputs (two per channel), six black chicken head knobs (Ch. 1 v, Ch. 2 v, b, t, fidelity, power), two-tone brown buffalo-grain covering, narrow rectangular woven Saran brown grille with "Gibson" logo and Texas longhorn logo on front, 20 in. wide, 22 in. tall, 10.125 in. deep, 40 lbs, 172 shipped, mfg. 1957-58.

	N/A	$1,800 - 2,200	$1,150 - 1,400	

GA-75 – 25W, 1-15 in. Jensen speaker, guitar/bass combo, seven-tube chassis, preamp: 1 X 6SJ7, 2 X 6SC7, 1 X 7025, power: 2 X 6L6, rectifier: 5V4, two channels, rear top-mounted control panel, five inputs (four inst., one mic), four knobs (Ch. 1 v, Ch. 2 v, b, t), brown mottled leather covering, brown speaker grille made up of six vertical slats in a circle pattern, "Gibson" logo on upper right corner, 1,247 shipped, mfg. 1950-55.

courtesy Jimmy Gravity   courtesy Jimmy Gravity

	N/A	$1,350 - 1,600	$675 - 850	

Later models used a 12AX7 in place of the 7025 in the pre-amp section.

GA-75/GA-75L RECORDING – approx. 25W, 2-10 in. speakers standard (GA-75) or 1-15 in. Lansing (Model GA-75L) speaker optional, guitar/bass combo, six-tube chassis, preamp: 2 X 6EU7, 1 X 6CG7 (6FQ7), power: 2 X 6L6, rectifier: 6C4, three diodes, two channels, top/rear control panel, four inputs (two per channel), seven knobs (Ch. 1: v, t, b, Ch. 2: v, t, b, power), available in brown covering with a brown grille (1964) or black alligator covering with a silver/gray sparkle grille (1965-67), 20 in. wide, 21.875 in. tall, 9.75 in. deep, 255 shipped (74 shipped with Lansing speakers), mfg. 1964-67.

	N/A	$475 - 550	$235 - 290	

GA-77/GA-77 VANGUARD – 25W, 1-15 in. Jensen speaker, six-tube chassis, preamp: 1 X 12AX7, 1 X 12AY7, 1 X 12AU7, power: 2 X 6L6, rectifier: 5V4, two channels, top control panel, four inputs (two per channel), six black chicken head knobs (1954-57: v1, v2, b, t, tone, power), or six black chickenhead knobs (1958-1961: v1, v2, b, t, tone, fidelity, power), available in two-tone Buffalo grain covering with a woven Saran grille and "Gibson 77" logo centered above the grille (1954-56), two-tone Buffalo grain covering with a woven Saran grille and "Gibson" logo centered above the grille (1957-59), or tweed covering with a dark brown grille cloth (1960-61), 1,220 shipped, mfg. 1954-1961.

1954-1959 Two-Tone Brown	N/A	$1,100 - 1,300	$550 - 675	
1960-1961 Tweed	N/A	$1,275 - 1,500	$650 - 850	

Originally, the covering on this amp was a two-tone mottled gray/brown leatherette covering with a rectangle brown speaker grille, the logo "Gibson 77" was above the grille, and dimensions were 24 in. wide, 20 in. tall, 10.175 in. deep, and 40 lbs. In 1958, the cabinet was changed slightly to a different two-tone brown covering, only the "Gibson" logo appeared on the front, and a metal handle with plastic middle replaced the leather one. In 1960, the name Vanguard was added to GA-77, the cabinet changed again to a tweed covering with a brown grille and the "Gibson" logo was moved in the upper right corner.

* **GA-77RV Vanguard Reverb** – similar to the GA-77 Vanguard, except has a reverb circuit with six knobs (Ch. 1: v, b, t, Ch. 2: v, tone, r), tweed covering, full front slanted dark brown grille, 337 shipped, mfg. 1961 only.

	N/A	$1,700 - 2,000	$850 - 1,050	

GA-77RET/GA-77RETL VANGUARD – 50W, 2-10 in. standard speakers (GA-77RET) or 1-15 in. JBL optional speaker (GA-77RETL), guitar combo, nine-tube chassis, preamp: 3 X 6EU7, 2 X 12AU7, 1 X 6CG7, power: 2 X 6L6, rectifier: 0A2, two channels, tremolo, echo, front white control panel, four inputs (two per channel), 13 black and silver knobs (Ch. 1: v, t, m, b, Ch. 2: v, t, m, b, echo switch, echo level, depth, freq, power switch), black alligator covering, silver/gray sparkle grille cloth, 28 in. wide, 20.5 in. tall, 10.75 in. deep, 640 shipped (180 shipped with JBL speakers), mfg. 1964-67.

	N/A	$600 - 700	$300 - 375	

The GA-77RET differed from the GA-77RVT in that it did not have reverb, but an oil can type echo that was manufactured by Tel-Ray. There was no reverb control but it had a three-position echo switch used in conjunction with a level knob instead.

MSR/NOTES	100%	EXCELLENT	AVERAGE	LAST MSR

GA-77RVT/GA-77RVTL VANGUARD – 50W, 1-15 in. regular speaker (GA-77RVT) or optional 1-15 in. Lansing speaker (GA-77RVTL), guitar combo, eight-tube chassis, preamp: 4 X 6EU7, 1 X 12AU7, 1 X 7199, power: 2 X 6L6, rectifier: 5V4, two channels, tremolo, reverb, top/front silver control panel, four inputs (two per channel), 10 black and silver knobs (first version: Ch. 1: v, b, t, Ch. 2: v, b, t, r, depth, freq., power switch) or 12 black and silver knobs (second version: Ch. 1: v, t, m, b, Ch. 2: v, t, m, b, r, depth, freq., power switch), Indian Brown covering, Spanish Crush brown grille, 26 in. wide, 20 in. tall, 10.5 in. deep, 1,229 shipped (310 shipped with JBL speakers), mfg. 1962-67.

	N/A	$600 - 700	$300 - 375	

The earliest models built in 1962 may have featured an old-style cabinet covered in tweed. In 1963/64 a middle tone control was introduced to each channel. Although this amp was shipped through 1967, it doesn't appear that it adopted the style between 1965 and 1967 that featured black covering, a silver grille, and front white control panel.

GA-79(T) – 30W mono (2 X 15 Stereo), 2-10 in. Jensen speakers, stereo guitar combo, eight-tube chassis, preamp: 4 X 6EU7 power: 4 X 6BQ5, solid-state rectifier, two channels, tremolo, top silver control panel, five inputs (four mono, one stereo), six knobs (Ch. 1: v, tone, depth, freq., Ch. 2: v, tone), mono-stereo switch, footswitch for tremolo, six sided trapezoid-shaped cabinet with tweed covering, woven brown Saran grille cloth, two oblong holes in the front, 25.75 in. wide in back, 11 in. wide in front, 18.75 in. tall, 10.5 in. deep, 210 shipped, mfg. 1960-61.

	N/A	$1,875 - 2,200	$925 - 1,150	

The original GA-79 model was advertised as having reverb, but the control panel in the catalog clearly shows knobs for tremolo (depth, freq.), and none for reverb. All Gibson amps during this era only used one knob for reverb. The GA-79 was replaced by the GA-79RV with reverb in 1961.

* GA-79RV – similar to the GA-79(T) except has a reverb circuit with a reverb knob, 409 shipped (1 shipped in 1967), mfg. 1961 only.

	N/A	$2,050 - 2,400	$1,025 - 1,250	

GA-79RVT – 30W mono (2 X 15 Stereo), 2-10 in. Jensen speakers, stereo guitar combo, nine-tube chassis, preamp: 3 X 6EU7, 1 X 7199, 1 X 12AU7, power: 4 X 6BQ5, solid-state rectifier, two channels, tremolo, top silver control panel, five inputs (four mono, one stereo), six knobs (Ch. 1: v, Ch. 2 v, r, three stacked knobs: Ch. 1 t/b, Ch. 2 t/b, tremolo depth/freq.), mono-stereo switch, footswitch for tremolo, six sided trapezoid-shaped cabinet with two oblong holes in the front, available in tweed covering with woven brown Saran grille cloth (1961-62), Indian Brown covering with a Spanish Crush brown grille cloth (1963-65), or black alligator covering with a silver/gray grille cloth (1965-67), 25.75 in. wide in back, 11 in. wide in front, 18.75 in. tall, 10.5 in. deep, 1,134 shipped, mfg. 1960-67.

courtesy solidbodyguitar.com, Inc.   courtesy solidbodyguitar.com, Inc.   courtesy John Beeson/The Music Shoppe

1961-1962 Tweed	N/A	$2,050 - 2,400	$1,025 - 1,250	
1963-1965 Brown	N/A	$1,700 - 2,000	$850 - 1,050	
1965-1967 Black	N/A	$1,650 - 1,950	$825 - 1,025	

ELECTRIC TUBE AMPLIFIERS: GA (GA-80 - GA-400) SERIES

GA-80(T) VARI-TONE – 25W, 1-15 in. Jensen speaker, guitar combo, seven-tube chassis, preamp: 2 X 12AX7, 2 X 5879, power: 2 X 6L6, rectifier: GZ34, two channels, top rear-mounted silver control panel, four inputs (two per channel), four black chicken head knobs (Ch.1: v, tone, Ch. 2: v, tone), six button Vari-tone selector switch, tweed covering, brown cloth grille with Gibson logo in upper right corner, 22 in. wide, 20 in. tall, 10.125 in. deep, 594 shipped, mfg. 1959-1961.

	N/A	$1,450 - 1,700	$725 - 900	

A revised model GA-80T with tremolo was advertised in 1962, but none were ever shipped. A plain GA-80 without Vari-Tone may exist as well.

GA-83 STEREO VIBRATO – 36W (2 X 18W stereo), 4-8 in. and 1-12 in. Jensen speakers, 13-tube chassis, preamp: 4 X 12AX7, 1 X 12AU7, 3 X 6CG7, power: 4 X 6BQ5, rectifer: GZ34, two channels, stereo pitch shifting vibrato, top rear-mounted silver control panel, four inputs (two stereo, two mono), six black knobs (three stacked knobs: Ch. 1 v/Ch. 2 v, Ch. 1 b/Ch. 2 b, Ch. 1 t/Ch. 2 t, trem depth, tremolo freq, stereo/mono switch), cabinet has 2-8 in. speakers on each side and the 12 in. speaker facing front, tweed covering, dark brown grille cloth, 26.25 in. wide, 21.5 in. tall, 279 shipped, mfg. 1959-1961.

	N/A	$2,200 - 2,600	$1,100 - 1,375	

MSR/NOTES	100%	EXCELLENT	AVERAGE	LAST MSR

GA-85 – 25W, 1-12 in. Jensen speaker, guitar combo with a removable chassis, six-tube chassis, preamp: 2 X 12AX7, 1 X 5V6, power: 2 X 5881, rectifier: 5V4, two channels, front silver control panel, four inputs (two per channel), six black chicken head knobs (Ch. 1 v, Ch. 2 v, b, t, voicing, power switch), two-tone buffalo-grain covering, Spanish gold grille cloth with Gibson logo, 17.25 in. wide, 26 in. tall, 10 in. deep, 39 lbs, 60 shipped, mfg. 1957-58.

| | N/A | $1,000 - 1,200 | $675 - 800 | |

This model was essentially Gibson's first piggyback unit where the tube chassis/control panel detached and could be placed away from the amp with a supplied 15 foot extension cord.

GA-86 ENSEMBLE – 25W, 1-12 in. Jensen speaker, guitar combo with a removable chassis/control panel, six-tube chassis, preamp: 2 X 12AX7, 1 X 6V6, power: 2 X 5881, rectifier: 5AR4, two channels, front control panel, four inputs (two per channel), seven knobs (Ch. 1: v, b, t, Ch. 2: v, b, t, power switch), tweed covering, dark brown grille with Gibson logo, 17.25 in. wide, 26 in. tall, 52 shipped, mfg. 1959-1961.

| | N/A | $1,275 - 1,500 | $650 - 800 | |

GA-88S STEREO TWIN – 35W, 2-12 in. Jensen speakers, piggyback unit with a separate chassis and two speaker cabinets, eight-tube chassis, preamp: 3 X 12AX7, power: 4 X 6BQ5, rectifier: 5AR4, two channels, top control panel, four inputs (two per channel), seven knobs (Ch.1: v, b, t, Ch. 2: v, b, t, stereo/mono switch), chassis is enclosed in black casing, cabinets have tweed covering with a brown grille with "Gibson" logo in upper right-hand corner, 22.75 in. wide, 22 in. tall, 236 shipped, mfg. 1959-1961.

| | N/A | $3,000 - 3,500 | $1,500 - 1,850 | |

GA-90 HIGH FIDELITY – 25W, 6-8 in. speakers, guitar combo, eight-tube chassis, preamp: 2 X 5879, 1 X 12AU7, 2 X 6SN7, power: 2 X 6L6, rectifier: 5V4, two channels, top silver control panel, four inputs (two per channel), five black knobs (first version: Ch. 1: v, tone, Ch. 2: v, tone, power switch) or seven black knobs (second version: Ch. 1: v, t, b, Ch. 2: v, t, b, power switch), gain switch, available in dark brown buffalo-grained fabric covering with either a large rectangular see-through grille with a small "G" logo on the right-hand side (1953-54), large rectangular grille with a centered "Gibson" logo (1955-56), or a large rectangular woven Saran grille with a "Gibson 90" logo (1957-1960), 24.5 in. wide, 20 in. tall, 9.5 in. deep, 38 lbs., 947 shipped, mfg. 1953-1960.

| | N/A | $1,200 - 1,425 | $600 - 750 | |

GA-95RVT APOLLO – 90W, 2-12 in. regular speakers (GA-95RVT) or Lansing speakers (GA-95RVTL), guitar combo, ten-tube chassis, preamp: 2 X 6EU7, 2 X 12AU7, 1 X 12AX7, power: 4 X 6L6, rectifier: OA2, three diodes, two channels, reverb, tremolo, four input jacks, 12 knobs (Ch. 1: v, t, m, b, Ch. 2: v, t, m, b, r, freq, depth, power switch), external speaker jack, two-button footswitch, black alligator covering with two air vents on top, silver/gray sparkle grille, 28 in. wide, 20.5 in. tall, 10.75 in. tall, 772 shipped (24 shipped with Lansing speakers), mfg. 1965-67.

| | N/A | $600 - 700 | $425 - 500 | |

GA-100 BASS AMPLIFIER – 35W, 1-12 in. Jensen speaker, guitar/bass combo/piggyback design with a removable chassis that could be mounted on a tripod stand, nine-tube chassis, preamp: 1 X 6EU7, 2 X 6BD6, 2 X 6FM8, power: 2 X 6L6, rectifier: GZ34, 0C2 AS voltage regulator, single channel, front silver control panel, two inputs, three black chicken head knobs (v, t, b), head-unit is enclosed in dark covering, cabinet is covered in tweed with a brown cloth grille and "Gibson" logo in upper right corner, 22 in. wide, 20 in. tall, 10 in. deep, 409 shipped, mfg. 1960-61.

  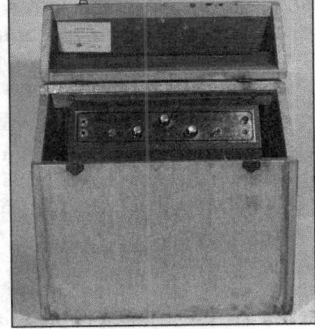

courtesy Steve Brown   courtesy Steve Brown   courtesy Steve Brown

| | N/A | $1,000 - 1,200 | $675 - 800 | |

• Add 10% for tripod stand for the tube chassis and control panel (head-unit).

GA-100 BASS AMPLIFIER CRESTLINE TUCK-A-WAY – 35W, 1-12 in. Jensen speaker, guitar/bass piggyback design with a removable head that was stored in the back of the cabinet, eight-tube chassis, preamp: 1 X 6EU7, 2 X 6BD6, 2 X 6FM8, power: 2 X 6L6, rectifier: GZ34, 0C2 AS voltage regulator, single channel, front silver control panel, two inputs, four knobs (v, t, b, power switch), head-unit is enclosed in metal casing, cabinet is covered in Indian Brown with a Spanish Crush brown cloth grille and "Gibson" logo in upper right corner, 478 shipped, mfg. 1962-63.

| | N/A | $500 - 600 | $255 - 325 | |

GA-200 RHYTHM KING – 60W, 2-12 in. Norelco/Phillips dual voice cone speakers, guitar combo, 11-tube chassis, preamp: 2 X 12AX7, 1 X 12AY7, 2 X 6BJ8, 2 X 6SK7, 6V6, power: 2 X 6550, rectifer: GZ34, two channels, top control panel, four inputs (two per channel), seven black knobs (Ch. 1: v, b, t, Ch. 2: v, b, t, power switch), available in two-tone brown buffalo grained covering (1956-59) or tweed covering (1960-61), brown cloth grille with "Gibson 200" logo centered at top of grille, top and side handles, Gada-Kart wheel standard between 1956-59, 28 in. wide, 20 in. tall, 10.5 in. deep, 62 lbs., 799 shipped, mfg. 1956-1961.

1956-1959 Two-Tone Brown	N/A	$1,800 - 2,250	$1,250 - 1,500	
1960-1961 Tweed	N/A	$2,000 - 2,500	$1,350 - 1,650	

• Add 15% for the Gada-Kart.

MSR/NOTES	100%	EXCELLENT	AVERAGE	LAST MSR

GA-200 RHYTHM KING CRESTLINE TUCK-A-WAY – 60W, 2-12 in. Norelco/Phillips dual voice cone speakers, guitar/bass piggyback design with a removable head that was stored in the back of the cabinet, 11-tube chassis, preamp: 2 X 12AX7, 1 X 12AY7, 2 X 6BJ8, 2 X 6SK7, 6V6, power: 2 X 6550, rectifer: GZ34, two channels, front control panel, four inputs (two per channel), seven black knobs (Ch. 1: v, b, t, Ch. 2: v, b, t, power switch), head-unit is enclosed in metal casing, cabinet is covered in Indian Brown with a Spanish Crush brown cloth grille and "Gibson" logo in upper right corner, 569 shipped, mfg. 1962-63.

| | N/A | $1,650 - 2,000 | $1,050 - 1,300 | |

GA-300RVT SUPER 300 – 60W, 2-12 in. Norelco/Phillips dual voice cone speakers, guitar piggyback unti with "tuck-a-way" design, nine tube chassis, preamp: 2 X 6EU7, 3 X 12AU7, 1 X 7199, power: 2 X 6L6, rectifer: 0A2, six diodes, two channels, reverb, tremolo, top control panel, four inputs (two per channel), 11 black and silver knobs (Ch. 1: v, t, m, b, tremolo depth, tremolo freq., r, Ch. 2: v, t, m, b), Indian Brown covering, Spanish Crush brown grille with "Gibson" logo in upper right-hand corner, 541 shipped, mfg. 1962-63.

| | N/A | $1,525 - 1,800 | $775 - 950 | |

GA-400 SUPER 400 – 60W, 2-12 in. Norelco/Phillips dual voice cone speakers, guitar combo, 12-tube chassis, preamp: 3 X 12AX7, 1 X 12AY7, 2 X 6BJ8, 2 X 6SK7, 6V6, power: 2 X 6550, rectifer: GZ34, three channels, top control panel, six inputs (two per channel), nine black and silver knobs (v, b, t, for each channel), available in two-tone brown buffalo grained covering (1956-59) or tweed covering (1960-61), brown cloth grille with "Gibson 400" logo centered at the top of the grille, top and side handles, Gada-Kart wheel standard 1956-59, 28 in. wide, 20 in. tall, 10.5 in. deep, 62 lbs., 660 shipped, mfg. 1956-1963.

| 1956-1959 Two-Tone Brown | N/A | $2,000 - 2,500 | $1,350 - 1,650 | |
| 1960-1963 Tweed | N/A | $2,250 - 2,750 | $1,450 - 1,800 | |

• **Add 15% for the Gada-Kart.**

GA-CB – 25-30W, 1-15 in. Jensen speaker with a built-in tweeter, ten-tube chassis, preamp: 3 X 6SJ7, 2 X SQ7, 2 X 6J5, power: 2 X 6L6, rectifer: 5T4, two channels, tremolo, bottom mounted chassis/control panel, four inputs (three inst., one mic), six black control knobs (b, t, tremolo freq., tremolo i, inst. v, mic v), four-way freq. selector, footswitch, six-sloted metal tan grille, leather or plastic handle, brown leatherette or brown aeroplane covering with green piping, 108 shipped, mfg. 1949-1953.

| | N/A | $1,700 - 2,000 | $850 - 1,050 | |

The CB stands for Custom-Built.

ELECTRIC TUBE AMPLIFIERS: POWER PLUS SERIES

The Power-Plus Series offered the guitar/bass player flexibility with a separate chassis that could be placed away from the cabinet for ease of use and maneuverability with snap on wheels. They are also all-tube amps with fairly new designs and some cabinets feature tilt-back legs. These amps were named after rockets that NASA had used. The piggyback models were released in 1963, and combo Medalist models were introduced in 1964. There are also two different styles of these models with the first version running from approx. 1963 to 1965 and the second version from late 1965 to 1967. The first version featured Indian brown covering, a Spanish crush brown grille cloth with gold thread, no logo on the grille, a trapezoid-shaped cabinet (wider at the bottom), and dimensions of 38 in. wide at the bottom, 24.75 in. tall, and 12.25 in. deep. The second version featured coarse black covering, a silver grille cloth, "Gibson" logo on the upper right corner of the grille (except for the Medalist), a standard rectangle-shaped cabinet, handles on the cabinet, and dimensions of 31.5 in. wide, 33.5 in. tall (including head and cabinet), and 11.75 in. deep.

ATLAS IV – 50W, 1-15 in. speaker (Atlas IV) or optional Lansing speaker (Atlas IV-L), guitar/bass piggyback with separate head and cabinet, five-tube chassis, preamp: 2 X 6EU7, 1 X 6C4, power: 2 X 6L6, solid-state rectifer, single channel, two inputs, four knobs, (v, b, t, power switch), available in Indian Brown covering with a Spanish Crush grille cloth (1963-65) or black alligator covering with a silver/gray sparkle grille cloth (1965-67), 1,949 shipped, mfg. 1963-67.

| | N/A | $525 - 600 | $350 - 425 | |

37 Atlas IVs were shipped in 1967 with Lansing speakers (model Atlas IVL).

* *Atlas Medalist* – similar to the Atlas IV, except in combo combo configuration, 26.5 in. wide, 28.5 in. tall, 11.5 in. deep, 1,328 shipped, mfg. 1964-67.

| | N/A | $525 - 600 | $350 - 425 | |

MERCURY I – 35W, 2-12 in. speakers, guitar piggyback unit with separate head and speaker cabinet, eight-tube chassis, preamp: 3 X 6EU7, 1 X 6C4, 1 X 6FQ7, power: 2 X 6L6, rectifer: 0A2, two channels, tremolo, 11 knobs (Ch. 1: v, b, m, t, tremolo depth, tremolo freq., Ch. 2: v, b, m, t, power switch), footswitch, available in Indian Brown covering with a Spanish Crush grille cloth (1963-65) or black alligator covering with a silver/gray sparkle grille cloth (1965-67), 643 shipped, mfg. 1963-67.

| Head & Cab | N/A | $450 - 525 | $300 - 350 | |
| Head Only | N/A | $250 - 300 | $135 - 175 | |

* *Mercury II* – similar to the Mercury I, except in piggyback configuration with 1-15 in. and 1-10 in. speakers (optional Lansing speakers), 709 shipped, mfg. 1963-67.

| | N/A | $525 - 600 | $350 - 425 | |

6 Mercury IIs were shipped with Lansing speakers (model Mercury II-L).

* *Mercury Medalist* – similar to the Mercury I, except in combo configuration with 2-12 in. speakers, 327 shipped, mfg. 1964-67.

| | N/A | $550 - 650 | $350 - 425 | |

MSR/NOTES	100%	EXCELLENT	AVERAGE	LAST MSR

TITAN I – approx. 90W, 2-12 in. speakers, guitar piggyback unit with a separate head and speaker cabinet, eleven-tube chassis, preamp: 3 X 6EU7, 2 X 12AU7, 6FQ7, power: 4 X 6L6, rectifier: 0A2, three diodes, two channels, tremolo, four inputs (two per channel), 11 knobs (Ch. 1: v, b, m, t, depth, freq, Ch. 2: v, b, m, t, power switch), footswitch, available in Indian Brown covering with a Spanish Crush grille cloth (1963-65) or black alligator covering with a silver/gray sparkle grille cloth (1965-67), 255 shipped, mfg. 1963-67.

| | N/A | $475 - 550 | $300 - 375 | |

* **Titan III** – similar to the Titan I, except in piggyback configuration with 1-15 in. and 2-10 in. speakers, 399 shipped, mfg. 1963-67.

| | N/A | $525 - 625 | $350 - 425 | |

* **Titan V** – similar to the Titan I, except in piggyback configuration with 2-15 in. JBL speakers, 191 shipped, mfg. 1963-67.

| | N/A | $575 - 675 | $375 - 450 | |

* **Titan Medalist** – similar to the Titan I, except in combo configuration with 1-10 in. and 1-15 in. speakers, 26.5 in. wide, 28.5 in. tall, 11.5 in. deep, 148 shipped, mfg. 1964-67.

| | N/A | $525 - 625 | $350 - 425 | |

ELECTRIC TUBE AMPLIFIERS: LATE 1960S MODELS

DUO MEDALIST – 30W, 1-12 in. Jensen speaker, guitar combo, eight-tube chassis, preamp: 3 X 6EU7, 1 X 7025, 2 X 12AU7, power: 2 X 7591, solid-state rectifier, two channels (Normal and Reverb), reverb, tremolo, top silver/woodgrain control panel, four inputs (two per channel), 10 knobs (Normal Ch.: v, t, b, Reverb Ch.: v, t, b, r, tremolo s, tremolo depth, power switch), external speaker jack, cabinet with extended sides and a handle, black vinyl covering, black grille, 19.5 in. wide, 37.5 in. tall, 9.5 in. deep, 69 lbs., mfg. 1968-early 1970s.

| | N/A | $450 - 525 | $225 - 275 | |

FALCON – wattage unknown, 1-12 in. speaker, guitar combo, eight-tube chassis, preamp: 3 X 6EU7, 1 X 7025, 2 X 12AU7, power: 2 X 7591, solid-state rectifier, two channels, reverb, tremolo, front silver/woodgrain control panel, four inputs, nine knobs, pilot light, cabinet has raised sides, black vinyl covering, black grille, mfg. 1968-69.

| | N/A | $255 - 300 | $130 - 160 | |

Later models may have a six tube chassis with preamp: 4 X 7025 and power: 2 X EL84 (6BQ5).

❚ **HAWK** – 12W, 1-10 in. speaker, guitar combo, five-tube chassis, preamp: 3 X 7025, power: 2 X EL84 (6BQ5), solid-state rectifier, single channel, reverb, tremolo, front silver/woodgrain control panel, two inputs, four knobs (v, tone, tremolo, reverb), fuse cap, pilot light, cabinet has raised sides, black vinyl covering, black grille, 14.75 in. wide, 24.5 in. tall, 8 in. deep, 24 lbs., mfg. 1968-69.

courtesy Murray Dychtwald

courtesy Jimmy Gravity

| | N/A | $225 - 275 | $135 - 175 | |

MEDALIST 2/12 – 60W, 2-12 in. speakers in a vertical cabinet, guitar combo, nine-tube chassis, two channels (Normal and Reverb), reverb, tremolo, top silver/woodgrain control panel, four inputs (two per channel), 12 knobs (Normal Ch.: v, t, m, b, Reverb Ch.: v, t, m, b, r, tremolo speed, tremolo depth), two presence switches, external speaker jack, monitor jack, cabinet with extended sides and handles, black vinyl covering, black grille, 21.5 in. wide, 43.5 in. tall, 9.5 in. deep, 93 lbs., 9 shipped 1967 (shipping totals after 1968 unknown), mfg. 1968-early 1970s.

| | N/A | $425 - 500 | $275 - 325 | |

MEDALIST 4/10 – 60W, 4-10 in. speakers in a vertical cabinet, guitar combo, nine-tube chassis, two channels (Normal and Reverb), reverb, tremolo, top silver/woodgrain control panel, four inputs (two per channel), 12 knobs (Normal Ch.: v, t, m, b, Reverb Ch.: v, t, m, b, r, tremolo speed, tremolo depth), two presence switches, external speaker jack, monitor jack, cabinet with extended sides and handles, black vinyl covering, black grille, 21.5 in. wide, 43.5 in. tall, 9.5 in. deep, 93 lbs., 9 shipped 1967 (shipping totals after 1968 unknown), mfg. 1968-early 1970s.

| | N/A | $475 - 550 | $300 - 350 | |

SKYLARK – 5W, 1-10 in. speaker, guitar combo, four-tube chassis, preamp: 1 X 7025, 1 X 6X4, power: 1 X EL84 (6BQ5), rectifier: 5V4, single channel, front silver/woodgrain control panel, two inputs, three knobs (v, tone, power switch), pilot light, cabinet has raised sides, black vinyl covering, black grille, 13.25 in. wide, 18.75 in. tall, 7 in. deep, 16 lbs., mfg. 1968-69.

| | N/A | $200 - 250 | $120 - 150 | |

* **Skylark T Tremolo** – similar to the Skylark, except has a tremolo circuit with a five-tube chassis, preamp: 2 X 7025, 1 X 6X4, power: 1 X EL84 (6BQ5), rectifier: 5V4, and an additional tremolo control for a total of four knobs, mfg. 1968-69.

| | N/A | $225 - 275 | $140 - 175 | |

G 368 GIBSON, cont.

MSR/NOTES	100%	EXCELLENT	AVERAGE	LAST MSR

SUPER MEDALIST – 30W, 2-12 in. Jensen speakers in a vertical cabinet, guitar combo, eight-tube chassis, preamp: 2 X 6EU7, 1 X 6AU7, 1 X 7025, 2 X 12AU7, power: 2 X 7591, solid-state rectifier, two channels, reverb, tremolo, top silver/woodgrain control panel, four inputs (two per channel), 10 knobs (Normal Ch.: v, t, b, Reverb Ch.: v, t, b, r, tremolo speed, tremolo depth, power switch), external speaker jack, cabinet with extended sides and a handle, black vinyl covering, black grille, 19.5 in. wide, 37.5 in. tall, 9.5 in. deep, 69 lbs., mfg. 1968-early 1970s.

	N/A	$375 - 450	$225 - 275	

THOR – 50W, 2-10 in. speakers in a vertical cabinet, bass amp combo, four-tube chassis, preamp: 2 X 6EU7, power: 2 X 6CA7, solid-state rectifier, single channel, front silver/woodgrain control panel, two inputs, four knobs (v, t, b, power switch), cabinet has raised sides, black vinyl covering, black grille, 16 in. wide, 33.75 in. tall, 10 in. deep, 55.5 lbs., 493 shipped in 1967 (shipping totals unknown for 1968-69), mfg. 1967-69.

	N/A	$350 - 400	$170 - 210	

ELECTRIC TUBE AMPLIFIERS: GOLDTONE SERIES

- Add $30 for 2-button footswitch.
- Add $125 for Super Goldtone 5-button footswitch.

GA-5 Les Paul Junior
courtesy Gibson

GA-15RV
courtesy Gibson

GA-20RVT
courtesy Gibson

GA-5 LES PAUL JUNIOR (TGA-GA5) – 5W, 1-8 in. speaker, guitar combo, three-tube chassis, preamp: 1 X 12AX7, 1 X ECC83, power: 1 X EL84 or 1 X 6BQ5, solid-state rectifier, single channel, rear control panel, two inputs, single volume knob, light brown covering, brown grille, mfg. 2004-08.

	N/A	$300 - 350	$150 - 185	$1,000

GA-15 (TGA-BK15) – 15W, 1-10 in. speaker combo, four-tube chassis, preamp: 2 X 12AX7, power: 2 X EL84, solid-state rectifier, single channel, rear-mounted control panel, single input, two gold knobs (v, tone), bright switch, external speaker jack, available in black or brown leatherette covering, round gold metal grille, mfg. 1999-2003.

	N/A	$375 - 450	$225 - 275	$859

* GA-15RV (TGA-BK15RV) – similar to the GA-15, except has 1-12 in. Celestion Vintage speaker, a reverb circuit with reverb control knob, and a triode/pentode switch, mfg. 1999-2004.

	N/A	$500 - 600	$300 - 350	$1,149

GA-20RVT (TGA-GA20RVT) – 15W, 1-12 in. Eminence Legend speaker, guitar combo, seven-tube chassis, preamp: 5 X 12AX7, power: 2 X 6V6, solid-state rectifier, two channels, reverb, tremolo, front control panel, three inputs (two instrument with one per channel, one aux.), 10 knobs (Ch. 1: v, t, b, Ch. 2: v, t, m, b, r, tremolo s, tremolo d), two-tone light brown/dark brown covering, dark brown grille, two leather handles, mfg. 2004-07.

	N/A	$600 - 700	$375 - 450	$1,200

GA-30RVH (TGA-BK30RVH) – 30W, guitar head-unit, eight-tube chassis, preamp: 4 X 12AX7, power: 4 X EL84, solid-state rectifier, two channels, reverb, front brown control panel, single input, 12 gold knobs (Ch. 1: v, t, m, b, Ch. 2: g, level, t, m, b, r1, r2, MV), preamp switch, boost switch, rear panel: effects loop with controls, speaker out jack, available in brown or black leatherette covering, mfg. 2000-04.

	N/A	$750 - 900	$500 - 575	$1,995

* GA-30RV (TGA-BK30RV) – similar to the GA-30RVH head, except in combo configuration with 1-10 in. and 1-12 in. Celestion speakers, available in black or brown leatherette covering with two different-sized gold round speaker grilles, mfg. 2000-04.

	N/A	$1,000 - 1,200	$675 - 800	$2,395

GA-30RVS (TGA-BK30RVS) – 30W (15W per side stereo), 2-12 in. speakers, stereo guitar combo, eight-tube chassis, preamp: 4 X 12AX7, power: 4 X EL84, two channels, reverb, rear-mounted brown control panel, two inputs, three gold knobs (v with push/pull gain boost, tone, r), bright switch, effects loop, footswitch, external speaker jack, available in black or brown leatherette covering, two-round gold metal grilles, mfg. 1999-2004.

	N/A	$850 - 1,000	$425 - 525	$1,826

MSR/NOTES	100%	EXCELLENT	AVERAGE	LAST MSR

GA-40RVT
courtesy Gibson

GA-42RVT
courtesy Gibson

GA-50H
courtesy Gibson

GA-40RVT (TGA-40RVT) – 30W (switchable to 15W), 1-12 in. Eminence Legend speaker, guitar combo, seven-tube chassis, preamp: 5 X 12AX7, power: 2 X 6L6, solid-state rectifier, two channels, reverb, tremolo, front control panel, three inputs (two instrument with one per channel, one aux.), 10 knobs (Ch. 1: v, t, b, Ch. 2: v, t, m, b, r, tremolo s, tremolo d), standby switch, power switch, rear panel: pentode/triode switch, speaker jacks, two-tone light brown/dark brown covering, brown grille, two leather handles, mfg. 2004-2011.

2004-2006	N/A	$700 - 850	$425 - 500	
2007-2011	N/A	$425 - 500	$275 - 325	$1,500

GA-42RVT (TGA-42RVT) – 30W (switchable to 15W), 2-12 in. Eminence Legend speakers, guitar combo, seven-tube chassis, preamp: 5 X 12AX7, power: 2 X 6L6, solid-state rectifier, two channels, reverb, tremolo, front control panel, three inputs (two instrument with one per channel, one aux.), 10 knobs (Ch. 1: v, t, b, Ch. 2: v, t, m, b, r, tremolo s, tremolo d), standby switch, power switch, rear panel: pentode/triode switch, speaker jacks, two-tone light brown/dark brown covering, brown grille, two leather handles, mfg. 2008-2011.

	N/A	$450 - 525	$300 - 350	$1,600

GA-50H – 50W, guitar head-unit, eight-tube chassis, preamp: 5 X 12AX7, power: 2 X EL34, rectifier: 5V4, two channels, reverb, tremolo, front control panel, three inputs, 10 knobs (Ch. 1: v, t, b, Ch. 2: v, t, m, b, r, tremolo s, tremolo d), standby switch, power switch, rear panel: effects loop, two-tone light brown/dark brown covering, mfg. 2004-05.

	N/A	$625 - 750	$425 - 500	$1,560

GA-60RV (TGA-BK60RV) – 60W, 2-12 in. Celestion speakers, seven-tube chassis, preamp: 5 X 12AX7, power: 2 X EL34, two channels, reverb, front brown control panel, single input, 12 gold knobs (Ch. 1: v, t, m, b, Ch. 2: g, level, t, m, b, r1, r2, MV), preamp switch, boost switch, rear panel: effects loop with controls, speaker out jack, available in black or brown leatherette covering, two same-sized round gold metal speaker grilles, mfg. 2000-04.

	N/A	$925 - 1,075	$450 - 575	$2,495

SGT/CAB SPEAKER CABINET – 240W mono (120W per side stereo), cabinet is split into two cabinets with 2-10 in. Vintage Celestion speakers the top half with an open back design, and 2-12 in. Vintage Celestion speakers in the bottom half with a closed back design, designed for use with the GA-30RVH and GA-60RV heads, available in black or brown leatherette covering with four round gold metal grilles, mfg. 2000-04.

	N/A	$525 - 600	$350 - 425	$1,295

ELECTRIC SS AMPLIFIERS: EARLY MODELS

GSS-50 – 50W, 2-10 in. speakers, guitar combo, solid state chassis (15 transistors, 10 diodes), two channels, reverb, tremolo, front silver control panel, four inputs (two per channel), 11 knobs (three red, eight black, Ch. 1: v, b, t, mid/presence, r, depth, freq., Ch. 2: v, b, t, mid/presence), two-button footswitch, black vinyl covering, silver grille, 23.75 in. wide, 20 in. tall, 9.5 in. deep, 836 shipped, mfg. 1966-67.

	N/A	$325 - 375	$160 - 195

GSS-100 FIRST VERSION – 100W, 4-10 in. speakers, guitar piggyback unit with a head and two separate horizontal speaker cabinets with 2-10 in. speakers in each one, solid state chassis (26 transistors, 9 diodes), two channels, reverb, tremolo, vibrato, front silver control panel, four inputs, 11 knobs (three red, eight black, Ch. 1: v, b, t, Ch. 2: v, b, t, m, three unknown red, MV), two-button footswitch, black vinyl covering, silver grille, head dimensions: 24.5 in. wide, 6.5 in. tall, 11.5 in. deep, speaker cabinet dimensions: 24 in. wide, 12 in. tall, 12 in. deep, 2,921 shipped, mfg. 1966-67.

Head & Two Cabinets	N/A	$425 - 500	$275 - 325
Head Only	N/A	$200 - 250	$120 - 150
Cab Only	N/A	$150 - 200	$95 - 120

GSS-100 SECOND VERSION – similar to the GSS-100 First Version, except has a total of 8-10 in. speakers in two 4-10 in. speaker column cabinets, mfg. 1970 only.

	N/A	$475 - 550	$300 - 350

* **GSS-100HC** – similar to the GSS-100 Second Version, except has two speaker cabinets with 2-12 in. speakers and 1-14 in. horn in each one, mfg. 1970 only.

	N/A	$425 - 500	$275 - 325

» **GSS-100HCL** – similar to the GSS-100HC, except has Lansing speakers, mfg. 1970 only.

	N/A	$450 - 525	$275 - 325

MSR/NOTES	100%	EXCELLENT	AVERAGE	LAST MSR

LP-12 – amp system composed of an LP-1 head and an LP-2 cabinet, the head features a 35W preamp, dual channels, tremolo, reverb, vibrato, vibrola, five inputs, front control panel, 12 knobs (Normal: v, p, b, t, Effects: v, p, b, t, All: tremolo depth, vibrato depth, rate, r), the cabinet features 4-12 in. speakers with 2 horns and a 190W power amp, black covering, black grille, mfg. early 1970s.

LP-1 Head & LP-2 Cabinet	N/A	$375 - 450	$250 - 300	

More cabinets could be hooked up to the head, since each cabinet had its own power amp. This concept is similar to Acoustic's 360 and 370 bass heads and cabinets.

PLUS-50 – 50W, 2-10 in. speakers, extension/add-on amp, solid state chassis (6 transistors, 8 diodes), single channel, rear control panel, single input, one volume knob, black vinyl covering, silver grille, 24 in. wide, 12 in. tall, 12 in. deep, 835 shipped, mfg. 1966-67.

	N/A	$450 - 525	$275 - 325	

This unit could be used for either an add-on or extension to another amplifier.

SUPER THOR – 65W, 2-15 in. speakers in a vertical cabinet, bass combo, solid-state chassis, two channels, front black control panel, four inputs, six knobs (v, t, b per channel), black vinyl covering, black grille, casters, 24.75 in. wide, 44.5 in. tall, 12 in. deep, 80 lbs., mfg. 1970-74.

	N/A	$350 - 425	$200 - 250	

TR-1000T STARFIRE – 40W, 1-12 in. speaker, guitar combo, solid-state chassis (12 transistors, 2 diodes), single channel, top/front silver control panel, two inputs, seven knobs (v, t, m, b, depth, freq., power switch), charcoal gray covering, light gray grille cloth with silver thread, 22 in. wide, 18 in. tall, 10.5 in. deep, 330 shipped, mfg. 1962-67.

	N/A	$300 - 350	$200 - 250	

* **TR-1000RVT Starfire Reverb** – similar to the TR-1000T Starfire, except has a reverb circuit with 15 transistors, and eight knobs (v, t, m, b, depth, freq., r, power switch), 550 shipped, mfg. 1963-66.

	N/A	$325 - 400	$225 - 275	

THOR – 50W, 2-10 in. speakers in a vertical cabinet, bass amp combo, solid-state chassis, single channel, front black control panel, two inputs, three knobs (v, t, b), black vinyl covering, black grille, 18.75 in. wide, 31.25 in. tall, 11.25 in. deep, 51 lbs., mfg. 1970-74.

	N/A	$350 - 400	$170 - 210	

ELECTRIC SS AMPLIFIERS: G SERIES

G-10 – 10W, 1-10 in. speaker, solid-state chassis, single channel, tremolo, front black control panel, two inputs, five knobs (v, t, b, s, i), black vinyl covering, black grille, 20 in. wide, 15 in. tall, 8 in. deep, 16 lbs., mfg. 1972-75.

	N/A	$85 - 100	$45 - 55	

G-20 – 10W, 1-10 in. speaker, solid-state chassis, single channel, reverb, tremolo, front black control panel, two inputs, six knobs (v, t, b, r, s, i), black vinyl covering, black grille, 21 in. wide, 17 in. tall, 8 in. deep, 20 lbs., mfg. 1972-75.

	N/A	$105 - 125	$55 - 65	

G-30 – 15W, 1-12 in. speaker, guitar combo, solid-state chassis, single channel, reverb, tremolo, front black control panel, two inputs, six knobs (v, t, b, r, s, i), black vinyl covering, black grille, mfg. 1972-73.

	N/A	$175 - 225	$110 - 140	

G-35 – 15W, 1-12 in. speaker, guitar combo, solid-state chassis, single channel, reverb, tremolo, front black control panel, two inputs, six knobs (v, t, b, r, s, i), black vinyl covering, black grille, optional footswitch, 22 in. wide, 19 in. tall, 8 in. deep, 22 lbs., mfg. 1974-75.

	N/A	$175 - 225	$110 - 140	

G-40 – 20W, 1-12 in. speaker, guitar combo, solid-state chassis, single channel, tremolo, reverb, front black control panel, two inputs, six knobs (v, t, b, r, s, i), black vinyl covering, black grille, mfg. 1972-73.

	N/A	$225 - 275	$140 - 175	

G-50 – 40W, 1-12 in. speaker, guitar combo, solid-state chassis, two channels, tremolo, reverb, front control panel, four inputs, nine knobs (Ch. 1: v, t, b, Ch. 2: v, t, b, r, s, i), black vinyl covering, black grille, mfg. 1972-73.

	N/A	$250 - 300	$150 - 200	

G-55 – 50W, 1-12 in. speaker, guitar combo, solid-state chassis, single channel, reverb, front silver control panel, two inputs, seven knobs (harmonic distortion, v, r, t, m, b, phase), phase switch, black vinyl covering, black grille, two-button footswitch, 24.5 in. wide, 20 in. tall, 9.5 in. deep, 30 lbs., mfg. 1974-75.

	N/A	$275 - 325	$150 - 200	

G-60 – 60W, 1-15 in. speaker, guitar combo, solid-state chassis, two channels, tremolo, reverb, front black control panel, four inputs (two per channel), nine knobs (Ch. 1: v, t, b, Ch. 2: v, t, b, r, s, i), black vinyl covering, black grille, mfg. 1972-73.

	N/A	$300 - 350	$175 - 225	

G-70 – 60W, 2-12 in. speakers, guitar combo, solid-state chassis, two channels, tremolo, reverb, front black control panel, four inputs (two per channel), nine knobs (Ch. 1: v, t, b, Ch. 2: v, t, b, r, s, i), black vinyl covering, black grille, mfg. 1972-73.

	N/A	$300 - 375	$175 - 225	

G-80 – 60W, 4-10 in. speakers, guitar combo, solid-state chassis, two channels, tremolo, reverb, front black control panel, four inputs (two per channel), nine knobs (Ch. 1: v, t, b, Ch. 2: v, t, b, r, s, i), black vinyl covering, black grille, mfg. 1972-73.

	N/A	$325 - 400	$200 - 250	

MSR/NOTES	100%	EXCELLENT	AVERAGE	LAST MSR

G-105 – 100W, 2-12 in. speakers, guitar combo, solid-state chassis, single channel, phase shift, reverb, front silver control panel, two inputs, eight knobs (harmonic distortion, v, r, t, m, b, MV, phase), phase switch, black vinyl covering, black grille, two-button footswitch, 27.5 in. wide, 22.5 in. tall, 10 in. deep, 50 lbs., mfg. 1974-75.

N/A $350 - 425 $225 - 275

G-115 – 100W, 4-10 in. speakers, guitar combo, solid-state chassis, single channel, phase shift, reverb, front silver control panel, two inputs, eight knobs (harmonic distortion, v, r, t, m, b, MV, phase), phase switch, black vinyl covering, black grille, two-button footswitch, wheels, 27.375 in. wide, 29.5 in. tall, 10 in. deep, 60 lbs., mfg. 1974-75.

N/A $375 - 450 $250 - 300

GINELLE AMPLIFICATION

Amplifiers previously produced in West Berlin, NJ beginning in 1996. Distributed by Ginelle Amplification.

Ginelle Amplification was founded by Rick Emery in 1996. Ginelle's amplifiers are all-tube combo units that are hand-wired, and hand-built one at a time. They only have one current production model called the **El Toro Pequena**, which is a 20W combo amp with 1-12 in. speaker and powered by EL84 power tubes. Cabinets are available in a black or purple Tolex, and an effects loop is optional. Each amp is custom-built as it is ordered and takes approximately four to five weeks for delivery.

GLOCKENKLANG

Amplifiers and speaker cabinets currently produced in Germany. Distributed in the U.S. through various dealers.

Glockenklang amplifiers are designed and manufactured by Udo Klempt-Giessing in Germany, and distributed through a network of select dealers in the United States. Udo developed a reference bass amplifier at someone's request, and the rest, as they say, is history. The Bugatti system is the preamp system that was used in the first Glockenklang Bass System. Today Glockenklang offers the Bassware line and the Soul amplifier. For more information, visit Glockenlang's website.

CONTACT INFORMATION
GLOCKENKLANG
Eimterstrasse 147
Herford, D-32049 Germany
Phone No.: 49-5221-51506
Fax No.: 49-5221-108755
www.glockenklang.com
info@glockenklang.de

BASS AMPLIFIERS

The **Soul** is a 440W head unit with a single channel, and various controls. The **Heart Rock** is a 750W head unit with a MOSFET power section, and the same features/controls as the Soul. The **Bass Art Classic** Head has 400W, and various other features based on Class A technology. The Bass Art Classic Preamp is the preamp section from the full head unit. The **Bugatti 400** Stereo Power amp is strictly the power section from the Bass Art Classic Head. The Soul chassis is available in combo units as well. The **Soul Combo** features 2-10 in. speakers. There are several speaker cabinets available as well.

GOMEZ AMPLIFICATION

Amplifiers previously produced in Rancho Santa Margarita, CA from 2005-2016.

Dario G. Gomez founded Gomez Amplification in 2005 and he built Fender brownface-style guitar tube amps. Gomez started building amps to provide an affordable alternative to the costly vintage guitar amps on the market. All amps are hand-wired and are designed to sound like a vintage amp. Gomez offered the Bassman-inspired **El Sonido**, the Princeton Reverb-inspired **"G" Reverb-Amp**, the Showman-inspired **Surfer Amp**, and the **"G-Spring"** reverb unit based on Fender's reverb unit. All amps have brownface features and appointments.

GOODSELL

Amplifiers currently produced in Atlanta, GA since the early 2000s. Distributed by Goodsell.

When it comes to repairing Hammond organs, Richard Goodsell is one of the best. He has always been interested in Hammond and Leslie organ amplifiers, even though he didn't know how to play organ very well. During the 1990s, he became known as one of the best repairers with Hammonds and Leslie. In the early 2000s, Goodsell decided to do something with all the leftover parts he had from many B3 Hammond models over the years, and he started work on the Super 17 amplifier. There was a lot of trial and error to make a bunch of parts from an organ amplifier into a guitar amplifier, and the original model with serial #0001 featured all organ parts (an idea he dropped shortly thereafter). Goodsell appreciates the quality of parts and craftsmanship used on amps over 50 years old and applies this to all the amps he builds. He also believes in simplicity - his amps have as few controls as possible. For more information, visit Goodsell's website or contact them directly. Initial information courtesy *The Tonequest Report*, Nov. 2005.

CONTACT INFORMATION
GOODSELL
1841-M Marietta Blvd.
Atlanta, GA 30318
Phone No.: 678-488-8176
www.superseventeen.com
richard@goodsellamps.com

ELECTRIC TUBE AMPLIFIERS

The **Super 17** (MSR $1,299) was Goodsell's first amplifier. It features 17W power from 2 X EL84 tubes, with three control knobs (v, gain, tone), and is available as a head-unit only. The **Super 17 MK II** (MSR $1,999) was introduced in 2006, and is an an evolution of the Super 17W with reverb and tremolo and is available as a 1-12 in. combo with a Goodsell RGH speaker. The **33 Custom** is also based on the Super 17, but it has 4 X EL34 power tubes to double the power. The 33 Custom is available as a head-unit (MSR

| MSR/NOTES | 100% | EXCELLENT | AVERAGE | LAST MSR |

$1,599), a head-unit with reverb and tremolo (MSR $1,899), or three combo units that all have reverb and tremolo: 1-12 in. combo (MSR $2,299), 2-10 in. combo (MSR $2,399), or 2-12 in. combo (MSR $2,499). The **Black Dog 20** and **Black Dog 50** have a more complex two-stage gain structure and are voiced on early 1970s medium to high-gain amps. Introduced in 2009, they are available as the Black Dog 20 head (MSR $1,399) and Black Dog 20 1-12 in. combo (MSR $1,999) as well as the Black Dog 50 head (MSR $1,799). The **Unibox 10** (MSR $999, MSR $1,399 with reverb) is a 10-watt 1-12 in. combo based on the Unibox U-45B and has an unsual tube layout of 1 X 12AX7 preamp tube, 2 X 6BM8/ECL82 power tubes, and a 6X5GT rectifier. The **Dominatrix 18** (MSR $1,899) is based on the Watkins Dominator with 18W power and 1-12 in. speaker. The **Valpreaux** (MSR $1,999) is a 1-12 in. combo based on a popular Valco/Supro design with a 6973 power tube. Goodsell also offers speaker cabinets as well.

GOODTONE

Amplifiers currently produced in Pasadena, MD since 2004.

Goodtone was started in 2004 in Pasadena, Maryland. After several all tube protoyptes, the first custom amp was built for Danny Morris of the Danny Morris Band. In 2006, two standard models were offered, the **Elmira** (single channel reverb) and the **Tandem** (dual channel high gain) combos. In 2007, a head version of the Tandem model was offered, and in 2008, a custom designed model available as a head or combo was offered through Jim's Guitar's of Baltimore under their "Screaming Man" label. In 2010, a custom model "Twang-o-Verb" was built for Andy Rutherford of Ruthie and The Wranglers. A new model "Toneslinger" with a clean channel and high gain channel with variable tube/solid state drive will be available in 2011. For more information, visit Goodtone's website or contact them directly.

CONTACT INFORMATION
GOODTONE
www.goodtone.com
goodtone@verizon.net

GORILLA

Amplifiers currently produced in Asia. Distributed by Pignose in Las Vegas, NV.

Gorilla is a brand used on a line of amps distributed by Pignose. An early Gorilla model was dubbed as one of the first modeling amps. In the owner's manual it showed how to set the tone controls and such to get it to sound like other amplifiers. These amps were produced in the 1980s when supposedly Peavey sued them for patented circuitry. They changed their designs and continue to produce amplifiers today. All models are practice or entry-level amplifiers and retail prices fall between $75 and $200. For more information, visit Gorilla's website or contact them directly.

CONTACT INFORMATION
GORILLA
570 W. Cheyenne Ave
Suite 80
North Las Vegas, NV 89030
Phone No.: 702-648-2444
Fax No.: 702-648-2440
www.pignoseamps.com
hchatt@aol.com

GOYA

Amplifiers previously produced in the U.S. during the late 1960s. Distributed by Goya in New York, NY.

The Goya trademark was originally used by the Hershman Musical Instrument Company of New York City, New York in the 1950s on models built by Sweden's Levin company (similar models were sold in Europe under the company's Levin trademark). Levin built high quality acoustic flattop, classical, and archtop guitars as well as mandolins. A large number of rebranded Goya instruments were imported to the U.S. market.

In the late 1950s, solid body electric guitars and basses built by Hagstrom (also a Swedish company) were rebranded Goya and distributed in the U.S. as well. In 1963 the company changed its name to the Goya Musical Instrument Corporation. It was around this same time that Goya started offering guitar amplifiers. Not much is known about Goya amps, but they only appear to have been offered during the 1960s.

Goya was purchased by Avnet (see Guild) in 1966, and continued to import instruments such as the Rangemaster in 1967. By the late 1960s, electric solid body guitars and basses were then being built in Italy by the EKO company. Avnet then sold the Goya trademark to Kustom Electronics. It has been estimated that the later Goya instruments of the 1970s were built in Japan.

The C.F. Martin company later acquired the Levin company, and bought the rights to the Goya trademark from a company named Dude, Inc. in 1976. Martin imported a number of guitar, mandolin, and banjo string instruments from the 1970s through to 1996. While this trademark is currently discontinued, the rights to the name are still held by the Martin Guitar company.

ELECTRIC/BASS AMPLIFIERS

BARRACUDA – 75W, 2-12 in. speakers, guitar piggyback unit, solid-state chassis, two channels, reverb, tremolo, fuzz tone, front brushed aluminum control panel, four inputs, 12 multi-colored knobs (Ch. 1: v, b, t, Ch. 2: v, b, t, s, i, r, anti-hum, power, one unknown), various switches and lights, monitor jacks, remote control jacks, black covering, gray grille, mfg. mid-1960s.

| N/A | $425 - 500 | $300 - 350 |

BOMBARDIER – 75W, 1-18 in. speaker, bass piggyback unit, solid-state chassis, two channels, front brushed aluminum control panel, four inputs, seven multi-colored knobs (Ch. 1: v, b, t, Ch. 2: v, b, t, power), various switches and lights, black covering, gray grille, mfg. mid-1960s.

| N/A | $325 - 400 | $200 - 250 |

GREEN

See MatAmp.

GRETSCH

Amplifiers currently produced in Naperville, IL since 2005. Distributed by Fender Musical Instruments Corporation in Scottsdale, AZ. Amplifiers previously produced by Valco in New York City, NY until 1970, and later produced in Booneville, AR until the late 1970s.

Gretsch dates way back to 1883 when Friedrich Gretsch began manufacturing instruments as the Fred Gretsch Company. Friedrich died on a trip overseas, and his son Fred took over the company in 1895 at the age of 15. Business boomed and the company had expanded to percussion, ukuleles, and banjos. In the early 1930s Gretsch introduced their archtop guitars. Fred Gretsch Sr. retired in 1942, and William Walter Gretsch took over until 1948 when Fred Gretsch Jr. became president. The 1950-60s became the heyday for Gretsch as their instruments became endorsed by Chet Atkins and George Harrison. Gretsch Jr., Jimmy Webster, and Charles "Duke" Kramer were all responsible for the success. Kramer was involved with the company until he retired in 1980. In the early 1950s, Gretsch decided to bring in an amplifier line to go with their guitars. Valco, a company that made amplifiers for many companies (Supro, National, Airline, & Oahu), also started to make amplifiers for Gretsch. Naturally, these amps were quite similar to other Valco made amplifiers.

Gretsch went through five distinct changes over the years to the amplifier line. In 1967, Gretsch was bought out by Baldwin, where Gretsch Jr. was made a director. Rumor has it that Baldwin slowed amplifier production after the buyout. Valco continued to make amplifiers for Gretsch until Valco went out of business in 1968-69. Amplifiers were then probably manufactured by Multivox/Premier and the Reverb units were made by OC Electronics. In 1972, Gretsch released the solid-state Sonax series that was relatively short lived. There was a big fire that pretty much wiped out everything in January 1973 (Booneville). This halted guitar production for three months when Bill Hagner of Hagner Musical Instruments formed an agreement with Baldwin to build and sell Gretsch guitars. Baldwin kept the trademark rights, and everything was good until another fire in December of 1973. However, they recovered and squeeked through the 1970s, when Baldwin came in 1978 and took over again. Baldwin bought the Kustom amplifier company in 1978, and it is rumored that some Gretsch amps were actually Kustoms in disguise!

The 1970s took their toll on Gretsch for a number of reasons. Quality control went downhill in a hurry, and it is rumored that disgruntled employees were sabatoging product. Sales were way down and Chet Atkins withdrew his endorsement in 1979. Gretsch stopped producing everything except for drums (produced in Tennessee) in 1981. There were some attempts to get Gretsch going again in the early 1980s, but to no avail. Amplifier production had been long gone by this time. Kramer got Baldwin to sell the rights back to the family and Gretsch III was in charge again. He started producing guitars from Japan that were mainly offered in the U.S. In 1995, Gretsch introduced three reissue models built in the U.S. In 2005, Gretsch contracted Mark Baier from Victoria Amplifiers to build a new line of U.S.-built Gretsch-branded tube amplifiers. In 2008, Gretsch introduced a small tube amp called the Electromatic that is produced overseas, and they also produced a limited edition Variety amp for Gretsch's 125th Anniversary. Source for Gretsch History: Michael Wright, *Guitar Stories:*Volume 1; *The Gretsch Pages.*

DATE CODES ON GRETSCH AMPLIFIERS

Since Gretsch Amplifiers were produced by Valco, the numbers reflect Valco's date codes. Below is a chart of date codes from 1940-1964 for Valco made amplifiers (This works for all amplifiers produced by Valco).

G Suffix - 1940-42	X17000-X30000 - 1953	T25000-T50000 - 1960
V100-V7500 - 1947	X30000-X43000 - 1954	T50000-T75000 - 1961
V7500-V15000 - 1948	X43000-X57000 - 1955	T75000-T90000 - 1962
V15000-V25000 - 1949	X57000-X71000 - 1956	T90000-T99000 - 1963
V25000-V35000 - 1950	X71000-X85000 - 1957	G5000-G15000 - 1963
V35000-V38000 - 1951	X85000-X99000 - 1958	G15000-G40000 - 1964
X100-X7000 - 1951	T100-T5000 - 1958	
X7000-X17000 - 1952	T5000-T25000 - 1959	

STYLES AND COVERINGS ON GRESTCH AMPLIFIERS

Just like many other big amp manufacturers, Gretsch went through style changes every so often. Between the early 1950s and 1968 there were about six significant style/covering changes. This is helpful for a dating tool, but there is still some overlap between years - This is only a rough guide!

Early 1950s-1955 Tweed: Most amps are covered in tweed and feature various speaker openings. Most control panels are located on the back or top of the amp. The logo features the long T but no tail below the word Gretsch on the G letter. Models produced towards the end of this style were actually labeled Electromatic.

Circa 1955-1958 First style Electromatic: The first "official" Electromatic Series. Models were covered in a black/gray covering with silver accents and the grille cloth was typically a rectangle opening that wrapped around the left side of the amp. Some models feature small openings for tweeters, etc.

Circa 1958-1962 Second style Electromatic: The second Electromatic Series: Models still had a black/gray covering but it was slightly different than the mid-1950s models. The grille cloth is angled instead of straight and it still wraps around the left side of the amp. The logo now has a tail on the G in Gretsch.

MSR/NOTES	100%	EXCELLENT	AVERAGE	LAST MSR

Circa 1962-1966 Standard Box: A entirely new cabinet was introduced that was much less elaborate than previous models. Many models feature updated chassis and speaker configurations. Cabinets are covered in a black coarse vinyl with silver accents. There are actually two variations within this general range. The first version generally have slightly taller cabinets and the logo appears in the lower right corner. This version lasted from approx. 1962 to 1964. The second version have cabinets that are slightly shorter (they look wider, even though most of the widths change less than an inch), and the Gretsch logo moved to the upper left on smaller models. This version lasted from approx. 1964 to 1966.

Circa 1966-1968 Piggyback/Combo style: On tube amplifiers, large models are all converted to piggyback style. All models feature a new control panel that faces front, and the smaller models are taller than they are wide. Compact and reverb models do not change at all. Solid-state amplifiers are introduced around this time and feature very tall, large cabinets. Solid-state models all have model numbers starting with 7, and the logo does not have the tail on the G of Gretsch.

1972: The Sonax Series is introduced briefly. These amps are covered in a black vinyl.

2005-present: The new Gretsch tube amps are covered in a two-tone black/burgundy vinyl with a wheat brown grille.

ELECTRIC TUBE AMPLIFIERS: EARLY MODELS

Although there isn't a definitive date to when Gretsch amps first appeared, it seems the early 1950s is a close approximation. Refer to "Styles and Coverings on Gretsch Amplifiers" for specific information on coverings available for certain years.

6144 PRE-AMP REVERB – pre-amp only, no speaker, top control panel, three-way tone switch, reverb intensity knob, footswitch, available in one variation (black covering, brown grille), 15.625 in. wide, 8.75 in. tall, 7.375 in. deep, 8 lbs., mfg. circa 1967-68.

	N/A	$200 - 250	$120 - 150	

This amp has no speaker or power section. It is designed to add reverb to any standard amplifier. Essentially, this is a very large, tube-driven, effect pedal.

6149 DELUXE REVERB – 17W, 1-10 in. Jensen speaker, reverb or guitar amp combo, five tube chassis, top control panel, volume knob/reverb intensity, reverb contrast tone switch, remote footswitch, available in one variation (black covering, brown grille), 19.25 in. wide, 8.75 in. tall, 7.5 in. deep, 19.5 lbs., mfg. circa 1965-68.

	N/A	$325 - 400	$200 - 250	

This amp is designed to add reverb to any standard amplifier or be used as a stand alone amplifier. When used as a regular amp the knob controls the volume. When used as a reverb unit, the knob controls the reverb intensity.

6150 COMPACT – 5W, 1-8 in. speaker, all tube chassis, preamp: 12AX7, power: 6V6, rectifier: 5V3, single channel, back brown control panel, two or three inputs, one volume knob, available in at least three variations (1st Electromatic style, 2nd Electromatic style, Standard Box style), mfg. mid 1950s-1968.

courtesy Blue Book Archive

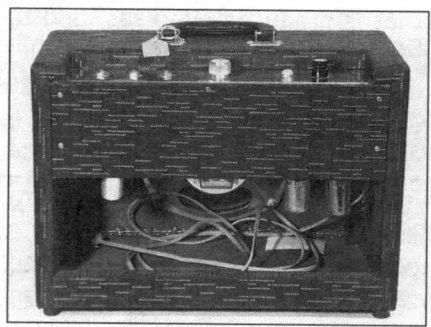

courtesy Blue Book Archive

	N/A	$425 - 500	$200 - 250	

It is possible that the 6150 Compact and the 6151 Electromatic Standard are the same models with different numbers. In the *Blue Book of Guitar Amplfiers*, we assume that the Compact did not appear until after 1955 therefore the first covering would be the 1st Electromatic style.

* 6150T Compact Tremolo – similar to the 6150 except has tremolo circuit, four tubes, tremolo control, tone control, line reversing switch, and footswitch, mfg. mid 1950s-1964.

	N/A	$350 - 425	$225 - 275	

6151 COMPACT TREMOLO – similar to the 6150T except model number changed to 6151 by 1965, mfg. 1965-68.

	N/A	$500 - 600	$225 - 275	

This model replaced the 6150. The 8 in. speaker was replaced by a 10 in. in 1967.

6151 ELECTROMATIC STANDARD – 5-6W, 1-8 in. speaker, guitar combo, three tube chassis, single channel, rear control panel, three inputs, two white plastic pointer knobs (v, tone), available in two variations (tweed and first style Electromatic gray/black), mfg. mid 1950s.

	N/A	$500 - 650	$250 - 325	

This model is probably the same as the 6150 Compact, or at least the model that preceded the Compact.

MSR/NOTES	100%	EXCELLENT	AVERAGE	LAST MSR

6152 COMPACT TREMOLO REVERB – 5W, 11 X 6 in. Jensen elliptical or 1-12 in. speaker, six tube chassis, preamp: 3 X 12AX7, power: 2 X 6V6, rectifier: 5Y3, single channel, top control panel, reverb, tremolo, three inputs, four control knobs (v, tone, r, s), three-way power switch, two footswitch inputs, available in one variation (standard box style), mfg. 1964-68.

| | N/A | $550 - 650 | $300 - 350 | |

In 1967, a 12 in. Maximum performance speaker replaced the Elliptical Jensen. The cabinet size and weight also changed slightly. Earlier models have dimensions of 19.25 in. wide, 14 in. tall, 7.5 in. deep, and 19.5 lbs. Later models are more square in shape with dimensions of 19.875 in. wide, 17.25 in. tall, 7.5 in. deep, and 25 lbs. This model was also sold as the Supro S6422TR/S6522TR, National N6422TR, and the Airline 62-9025A.

6154 SUPER BASS – 70W, 2-12 in. Jensen speakers, bass combo, eight tube chassis, top control panel, two inputs, three knobs (v, tone, three-way tone switch), available in one variation (standard box style), 27.5 in. wide, 18.75 in. tall, 9 in. deep, 53 lbs., mfg. circa 1964-67.

| | N/A | $650 - 800 | $400 - 500 | |

6155 ELECTROMATIC ARTIST – 10-12W, 1-10 in. speaker, guitar combo, five tube chassis, single channel, rear control panel, three inputs, two white plastic pointer knobs (v, tone), available in two variations (tweed and first style Electromatic gray/black), mfg. mid-1950s.

courtesy Blue Book Archive

courtesy Blue Book Archive

| | N/A | $550 - 700 | $300 - 400 | |

This model is probably the same as the 6150 Compact, or at least the model that preceded the Compact.

6156 PLAYBOY – 17W, 1-10 in. or 1-12 in. speaker, six tube chassis, preamp: 3 X 12AX7, power: 2 X 6973, rectifier: 5Y3GT, single channel, tremolo (later models), back control panel, three inputs, three knobs (tone, v, i for later models), available in at least three variations (first style Electromatic, second style Electromatic, and standard box style), mfg. mid-1950s-1966.

courtesy John Beeson/The Music Shoppe

courtesy John Beeson/The Music Shoppe

| 10 in. Speaker | N/A | $500 - 600 | $300 - 375 | |
| 12 in. Speaker | N/A | $600 - 700 | $375 - 450 | |

Circa 1961, the speaker was changed from a 1-10 in. to 1-12 in. Jensen. Early 1960s dimensions are 18 in. wide, 16 in. tall, and 8.5 in. deep. Circa 1964/65, the dimensions changed to 19.25 in. wide, 14 in. tall, 7.5 in. deep, and 19.5 lbs.

6157 SUPER BASS – 35W, 2-15 in. Maximum performance speakers, bass piggyback design, five tube chassis, single channel, front control panel, three inputs, three knobs (v, tone, tone range selector), high/low bass switch, power switch with polarity reversal, available in one variation (piggyback style), circa 1967-68.

| | N/A | $500 - 600 | $275 - 325 | |

This model replaced the 6154 Super Bass.

6159 DUAL BASS – 35/37W, 2-12 in. Jensen speakers, bass combo, seven tube chassis, two channels, tremolo, top control panel, four inputs, six knobs (Ch. 1: v, tone, s, i, Ch. 2: v, tone), power/standby switch, available in one variation (standard box style), mfg. early 1960s-1966.

| | N/A | $650 - 800 | $375 - 450 | |

MSR/NOTES	100%	EXCELLENT	AVERAGE	LAST MSR

6159 DUAL PLAYBOY TREMOLO – 35W, 2-12 in Jensen speakers, tall combo unit, six tube chassis, four diodes, two channels, tremolo, front control panel, four inputs, six knobs (Ch. 1: v, tone, s, i, Ch. 2: v, tone), available in one variation (tall combo style), mfg. circa 1967-68.

N/A — $550 - 650 — $350 - 425

6160 CHET ATKINS COUNTRY GENTLEMAN – 35/37W, 2-12 in. Jensen speakers, nine tube chassis, preamp: 6 X 12AX7, power: 2 X 7027, rectifier: 5U4G, two channels, two control panels, top panel has six knobs (Ch. 1: v, b, t, Ch. 2: v, b, t), rear panel has five inputs plus one for phonograph, two knobs (s, i), treble brilliance switch, standby switch, polarity switch, footswitch, available in one variation (standard box style), 26 in. wide, 18 in. tall, 10.5 in. deep, 44.5 lbs., mfg. early 1960s-1966.

N/A — $700 - 850 — $375 - 450

6161 ELECTROMATIC TWIN – 14W, 2 11 X 6 in. Elliptical speakers plus a 3 in. tweeter, six tube chassis preamp: 3 X 12AX7, power: 2 X 6973 (or 6L6), rectifier: 5U4, two channels, tremolo, rear or top control panel, three knobs, three knobs (v, tone, s), footswitch, available in three variations (tweed, first style Electromatic, and second style Electromatic), mfg. early 1950s-early 1960s.

 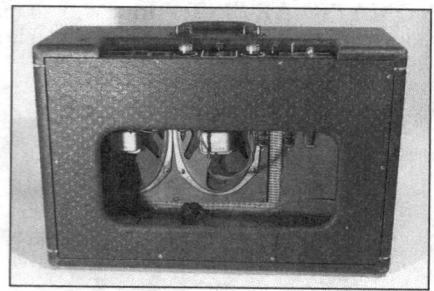

courtesy Blue Book Archive — courtesy Blue Book Archive

N/A — $625 - 775 — $400 - 475

6161 DUAL TWIN (FIRST VERSION) – 17W, 2-10 in. Jensen speakers plus a 5 in. tweeter, six tube chassis preamp: 3 X 12AX7, power: 2 X 6973 (or 6L6), rectifier: 5U4, two channels, tremolo, top control panel, four inputs, four knobs, (v1, v2, tone, s), footswitch, available in one variation (standard box style), 23.5 in. wide, 16 in. tall, 8 in. deep, 26.5 lbs., mfg. circa 1962-66.

courtesy Willie's American Guitars — courtesy Willie's American Guitars

N/A — $700 - 900 — $375 - 450

6161 DUAL TWIN (SECOND VERSION) – 17W, 2-10 in. speakers, six tube chassis preamp: 3 X 12AX7, power: 2 X 6973 (or 6L6), rectifier: 5U4, four diodes, two channels, tremolo, reverb, front control panel, four inputs, five knobs, (Ch. 1: v, tone, Ch. 2: v, tone, s), footswitch, available in one variation (tall combo style), 19 in. wide, 26.5 in. tall, 9.25 in. deep, 34 lbs., mfg. circa 1966-68.

N/A — $700 - 900 — $400 - 500

6162 DUAL TWIN REVERB (FIRST VERSION) – 19/17W, 2-10 in. Jensen speakers, eight tube chassis preamp: 5 X 12AX7, power: 2 X 6973 (or 6L6), rectifier: 5U4, one channel, tremolo, reverb, top control panel, three inputs, five knobs, (v, tone, s, i), footswitch, available in one variations (standard box style), 23.625 in. wide, 16 in. tall, 8.5 in. deep, 35.5 lbs., mfg. circa 1964-66.

N/A — $700 - 900 — $400 - 475

6162 DUAL TWIN REVERB (SECOND VERSION) – 17W, 2-10 in. speakers, eight tube chassis preamp: 5 X 12AX7, power: 2 X 6973 (or 6L6), rectifier: 5U4, four diodes, two channels, tremolo, reverb, front control panel, four inputs, seven knobs, (Ch. 1: v, tone, Ch. 2: v, tone, s, i, r), footswitch, external speaker jack, available in one variation (tall combo style), 19 in. wide, 26.5 in. tall, 9.25 in. deep, 40 lbs., mfg. circa 1966-68.

N/A — $500 - 600 — $300 - 375

6162 Dual Twin Reverb
(Second Version)
courtesy John Beeson/The Music Shoppe

MSR/NOTES	100%	EXCELLENT	AVERAGE	LAST MSR

6163 ELECTROMATIC DELUXE – 20-25W, 1-15 in. Jensen speaker, six tube chassis, power: 2 X 6L6, two channels, tremolo, rear or top control panel, four inputs (three of Ch. 1, one for Ch. 2), three knobs (v, tone, s), footswitch, available in at least two variations (tweed and first style Electromatic), mfg. early 1950s-late 1950s.

N/A $1,200 - 1,500 $800 - 950

* **6163W Electromatic Deluxe Western** – similar to the 6163 Electromatic Deluxe, except has a Western Motif design with a white covering, brown leather trim, and longhorn bull graphic on grille, mfg. mid-1950s-late 1950s.

N/A $1,800 - 2,250 $1,100 - 1,400

6163 CHET ATKINS PIGGYBACK – 70W, 1-15 in. and 1-12 in. Maximum performance speakers, guitar piggyback unit, tube chassis, four diodes, two channels, reverb, tremolo, front control panel, five inputs, ten knobs, (Ch. 1: v, t, b, Ch. 2: v, t, b, Both: brilliance switch, s, i, r), built in tuner, line reversing switch, available in one version (piggyback style), head dimensions: 26.5 in. wide, 9.5 in. tall, 9.5 in. deep, 30 lbs., cabinet dimensions: 32.175 in. wide, 20 in. tall, 11.25 in. deep, 45 lbs, mfg. circa 1966-68.

N/A $600 - 750 $350 - 450

This amp replaced the 6160 Chet Atkins. Supposedly, the 12 in. speaker is driven by the reverb/tremolo channel, and the 15 in. speaker is driven by the second channel. There was an input to combine the two channels as well.

6164 VARIETY – 35W, 2-12 in. Jensen speakers, nine tube chassis, power: 2 X 6L6, two channels, tremolo, top control panel, four inputs, eight knobs (Ch. 1: v, b, t, Ch. 2: v, b, t, s, i) hi/lo gain switch, available in one variation (standard box style), 26 in. wide, 18.5 in. tall, 9 in. deep, 45.5 lbs., mfg. circa 1964-66.

N/A $700 - 900 $300 - 375

6165 VARIETY PLUS – 35W, 2-12 in. Jensen speakers, 11 tube chassis, power: 2 X 6L6, two channels, reverb, tremolo, top control panel, four inputs, nine knobs (Ch. 1: v, b, t, Ch. 2: v, b, t, s, i, r) hi/lo gain switch, available in one variation (standard box style), 27.625 in. wide, 18.75 in. tall, 9.5 in. deep, 47.5 lbs., mfg. circa 1964-66.

N/A $750 - 950 $500 - 600

6166 ELECTROMATIC HI-FI – 30W, 2-12 in. Jensen speakers and two tweeters, 10 tube chassis, two channels, top control panel, five inputs (two in Ch. 1, three in Ch. 2), five knobs (v1, v2, t, b, tone-range selector), available in at least two variations (tweed and first style Electromatic), mfg. early 1950s-mid-1950s.

N/A $675 - 800 $450 - 525

6166 FURY – 70W, 2-12 in. Jensen speakers, guitar combo, 12 tube chassis, power: 4 X 6V6, two channels, tremolo, reverb, top control panel, four inputs, 10 knobs (Ch. 1: v, b, t, Ch. 2: v, b, t, tone range selector, s, i, r), footswitch, availble in one variation (standard box style), 27.375 in. wide, 18.75 in. tall, 9.5 in. deep, 57 lbs., mfg. circa 1964-66.

N/A $750 - 950 $450 - 550

This amplifier was a unique amp in that it was essentially two amps in one. Each channel was controlled individually into its own preamp and driven to its own speaker. It was also all Class A and it featured a split-chassis.

6169 ELECTROMATIC TWIN WESTERN – similar to the 6161, except has a Western Motif design with a white covering, brown leather trim, and longhorn bull graphic on grille, mfg. mid-1950s-early 1960s.

N/A $4,500 - 5,500 $2,000 - 3,000

6169 FURY PIGGYBACK – 70W, 2-12 in. speakers, guitar piggyback unit, 11 tube chassis, four diodes, two channels, reverb, tremolo, front black and silver control panel, five inputs (two per each channel, one dual purpose), 10 knobs (Ch. 1: v, b, t, Ch. 2: v, b, t, tone selector, s, i, r), external speaker jack, available in one variation (piggyback style), head dimensions: 26.5 in. wide, 9.5 in. tall, 9.5 in. deep, 30 lbs., cabinet dimensions: 32.175 in. wide, 20 in. tall, 11.25 in. deep, 45 lbs., mfg. circa 1966-68.

N/A $700 - 900 $450 - 550

This model replaced the 6166 Fury.

6170 PRO BASS – 25W (Later models 35W), 1-15 in. Maximum Performance speaker, five tube chassis, four diodes, single channel, front control panel, three inputs, three knobs (v, b, t), line reverse switch, available in one variation (tall combo style), 19 in. wide, 27.5 in. tall, 9.5 in. deep, 39 lbs., mfg. circa 1966-68.

N/A $500 - 600 $250 - 300

ELECTRIC TUBE AMPLIFIERS: CURRENT MODELS

In 2005, Gretsch introduced a new line of amplifiers that feature all-tube, point-to-point wired chassis with single channels, and basic features. All cabinets are made of finger-jointed pine and covered in a two-tone vinyl covering with the back, sides, top, and bottom finished in black and the front in burgundy. The grille cloth is a wheat brown. In 2008, Gretsch expanded their amp line with an entry-level Electromatic model that is built overseas but has a tube chassis.

G5222 ELECTROMATIC COMPACT AMP (NO. 230-1030) – 5W, 1-6 in. Special Design speaker, guitar combo, two-tube chassis, preamp: 1 X 12AX7, power: 1 X 6V6, two channels (high and low sensitivity), rear brown control panel, two inputs, single volume knob, pilot light, on/off switch, external speaker jack, Vintage Tweed covering with a TV-style speaker opening, dark brown grille with narrow light brown horizontal stripes and "Gretsch" and "Electromatic" logos, leather strap handle, 12 in. wide, 11 in. tall, 7.5 in. deep, 15 lbs., mfg. 2008-disc.

N/A $90 - 110 $55 - 70 $195

• **Add $20 (MSR $25) for cover.**

MSR/NOTES	100%	EXCELLENT	AVERAGE	LAST MSR

G6156 Playboy
courtesy Gretsch

G6163 Executive
courtesy Gretsch

G6164 Variety
courtesy Gretsch

G6156 PLAYBOY (NO. 230-1000-100) – 15W, 1-12 in. Eminence Legend speaker, guitar combo, tube chassis, preamp: 3 X 12AX7, power: 2 X EL34, single channel, tremolo, top chrome control panel, single input, six knobs (i, s, m, b, t, v), power switch, pilot light, two-tone black and burgundy vinyl covering, triangle-shaped brown grille, 23 in. wide, 21 in. tall, 10 in. deep, 35 lbs., mfg. 2005-2008.

N/A	$1,100 - 1,400	$700 - 900	$2,950

G6163 EXECUTIVE (NO. 230-1010-100) – 20W, 1-15 in. Eminence Legend speaker, guitar combo, tube chassis, preamp: 3 X 12AX7, 2 X 12AT7, power: 2 X 6V6, rectifier: 5AR4, single channel, reverb, tremolo, top chrome control panel, two inputs, seven knobs (i, s, r, m, b, t, v), power switch, standby switch, pilot light, two-tone black and burgundy vinyl covering, triangle-shaped brown grille, two-button footswitch included, 26 in. wide, 24 in. tall, 11 in. deep, 50 lbs., mfg. 2005-2008.

N/A	$1,400 - 1,700	$900 - 1,100	$3,650

G6164 VARIETY (NO. 230-1020-100) – 40W, 3-10 in. Jensen speakers, guitar combo, tube chassis, preamp: 3 X 12AX7, 3 X 12AT7, power: 2 X 6L6, rectifier: 5AR4, single channel, reverb, tremolo, top chrome control panel, two inputs, seven knobs (i, s, r, m, b, t, v), power switch, standby switch, pilot light, two-tone black and burgundy vinyl covering, parallelogram-shaped brown grille, two-button footswitch included, mfg. 2005-09.

N/A	$1,600 - 1,900	$1,200 - 1,400	$3,950

G6164 VARIETY 125TH ANNIVERSARY (NO. 230-1250-100) – 40W, 3-10 in. Jensen speakers, guitar combo, tube chassis, preamp: 3 X 12AX7, 3 X 12AT7, power: 2 X 6L6, rectifier: 5AR4, single channel, reverb, tremolo, top chrome control panel, two inputs, seven knobs (i, s, r, m, b, t, v), power switch, standby switch, pilot light, silver sparkle on white vinyl covering with gold piping, parallelogram-shaped white grille with gold "g" logo, two-button footswitch included, limited production of 25 amplifiers, mfg. late 2008 only.

N/A	$2,350 - 2,850	N/A	$4,700

ELECTRIC SS AMPLIFIERS

It is estimated that all the solid-state amplifiers produced by Gretsch were manufactured by Multivox/Premier or GSM. In 1972, Gretsch debuted the Sonax series that were built in Canada. Models include the **775G**, **750G**, **730G**, **720G**, **550B**, and **530B**. There is also a 330P/480C head unit, which can be used as a guitar or PA system. See Sonax for individual model listings.

7154 NASHVILLE – 75W, 2-15 in. Maximum Performance or optional Lansing speakers, guitar/bass combo unit, solid-state chassis, reverb, tremolo, magic echo, front silver control panel, five inputs (Ch. 1: two, Ch. 2: three), eight knobs (Ch. 1: v, b, t, Ch. 2: v, b, t, r, s), magic echo speed control, three-button footswitch, 24 in. wide, 50 in. tall, 11 in. deep, 70 lbs., mfg. circa 1968-1970.

N/A	$475 - 550	$300 - 350	

7155 TORNADO – 150W, 4-15 in. Lansing speakers, guitar/bass head and two speaker cabinets with 2-15 in. speakers in each one, solid-state chassis, reverb, tremolo, magic echo, front silver control panel, five inputs (Ch. 1: two, Ch. 2: three), eight knobs (Ch. 1: v, b, t, Ch. 2: v, b, t, r, s), magic echo speed control, three-button footswitch, head dimensions: 22 in. wide, 9 in. tall, 10 in. deep, 20 lbs., speaker cabinet dimensions: 15 in. wide, 60 in. tall, 12 in. deep, 60 lbs., mfg. circa 1968-1970.

Head & Cabinets	N/A	$600 - 700	$375 - 450	
Head Only	N/A	$250 - 300	$150 - 200	
Speaker Cabinet	N/A	$200 - 250	$120 - 150	

7157 ROGUE – 35W, 2-12 in. Maximum Performance speakers, guitar/bass combo unit, solid-state chassis, reverb, tremolo, magic echo, front silver control panel, five inputs (Ch. 1: two, Ch. 2: three), eight knobs (Ch. 1: v, b, t, Ch. 2: v, b, t, r, s), magic echo speed control, three-button footswitch, 19 in. wide, 42 in. tall, 11 in. deep, 40 lbs., mfg. circa 1968-1970.

N/A	$250 - 300	$150 - 200	

7763 EXPANDER-G – 300W, head-unit plus two cabinets "single-but-split" either 2-12 in. or 1-15 in. speakers, solid-state chassis, two or three channels, tremolo, fuzz control, reverb, front silver control panel, various controls and knobs, black covering, black grille, mfg. 1970s.

N/A	$500 - 600	$325 - 400	

This was a huge unit with two speaker cabinets, which may also have tweeters. On the reverb tank on this model it reads "O.C. Electronics, Folded Line reverb unit. Manufactured by beautiful girls in Milton, Wisconsin under controlled atmospheric conditions."

MSR/NOTES	100%	EXCELLENT	AVERAGE	LAST MSR

BROADKASTER MINI LEAD 50 – 50W, 1-12 in. speaker, guitar combo, solid-state chassis, single channel, reverb, front silver control panel, two inputs, four knobs (v, b, t, r), black covering, black grille, mfg. early 1970s.

	N/A	$250 - 300	$135 - 175	

GROOVE TUBES

Amplifiers previously produced in San Fernando, CA between 1989 and 2008. The Groove Tubes trademark was established in 1979.

In the late 1970s, Aspen Pittman hired a few technicians to figure out why tubes acted and performed the way they did. What these people found were new ways to test and perfect tubes. From this research and new information, Pittman started Groove Tubes (GT) as a tube manufacturing company. GT is probably best known for their excellent guitar amp tubes, but they have also ventured in other areas as well. In 1985, GT patented the Fathead, which was a weight that clamped onto the headstock to add weight and sustain. In fall of 1985, The Speaker Emulator was born along with Pittman's new company called GT Electronics that was formed to develop guitar pre-amps, tube guitar amps, and guitar speaker systems. The first Groove Tubes amps were introduced in 1989. In 1997, the SFX design was debuted, which stands for Stereo Field Expansion and is used in the Fender Acoustisonic series. Possibly the best achievement for Aspen and GT is the *Tube Amp Book*. It is currently in its fifth edition, and there are over 110,000 copies in print. GT sells all kinds of replacement tubes and tube related products for American and British amplifiers. In summer 2008, the Fender Musical Instrument Corporation (FMIC) purchased Groove Tubes; however, Pittman remains part of GT as a consultant. Fender has reorganized Groove Tubes to focus on tube production and they no longer produce amplifiers. For more information, visit GT's website or contact them company directly.

ELECTRIC TUBE AMPLIFIERS

The first Groove Tube amplifier (not including the Speaker Emulator) was the **D-75 Dual** amp and **Trio Preamp**. The idea behind the Dual 75 was for an amp that could use Fender tubes (6L6) and Marshall tubes (EL34). This amp was designed by Red Rhodes, and it was designed so that flipping between the two channels was in fact switching tubes. The Trio preamp was designed to work in conjunction with the Dual 75. The Trio had three channels (clean, mean, and scream), and when used with the Dual 75, nine possible sounds were available. These amps are still available through the GT custom shop. Also offered are the **D-120 Dual** amp, which has more power.

In 1992, Red Rhodes designed the Soul-o amps. These amps could switch between Class A and Class A/B. The **Solo 75** featured 4 preamp tubes, and a duet of power tubes. The **Solo 150** was essentially the same except with twice the power output. These amps are also available through the custom shop. There are some other amplifiers, including the **STP-B**, and the **STP-G**. Besides these two models, the rest are available to accept many different tube types. The preamp, phase inverter, and power stage are all subject for a number of different tubes.

In 2002, the **SINGLE** was designed. This is a guitar amp with a 10 in. combo, or head unit. Different tubes are acceptable for this amp as well, and it is Class A. There are also speaker cabinets available for these products.

* **Add $79 for one-button footswitch (boost only, Single amps only).**
* **Add $99 for two-button footswitch (boost and reverb, S30 and S50 amps only).**

SOUL-O SINGLE HEAD – various wattages, head-unit only, tube chassis, preamp: 2 X 12AX7, 5751, or 12AT7, power: 1 X KT66, 6L6, EL34, KT88, or 6550, single channel, front chrome control panel, single input, six black knobs (g, t, m, b, p, MV), effects loop, impedance selector, black covering, brown grille, mfg. 2002-08.

	$1,299	$800 - 950	$550 - 650	$1,299

* *Soul-O Single Laptop* – similar to the Soul-O Head, except has 2-4 in. speakers in the head cabinet, mfg. 2004-08.

	$1,399	$850 - 1,000	$575 - 675	$1,399

* *Soul-O Single 10 in. Combo* – similar to the Soul-O Head, except has 1-10 in. speaker, mfg. 2002-08.

	$1,399	$850 - 1,000	$575 - 675	$1,399

* *Soul-O Single 12 in. Combo* – similar to the Soul-O Head, except has 1-12 in. speaker, mfg. 2002-08.

	$1,399	$850 - 1,000	$575 - 675	$1,399

SOUL-O 30 HEAD – 30W, head-unit only, tube chassis, power: 2 X 6L6, single channel, reverb, front chrome control panel, single input, eight black knobs (bias, g, t, m, b, p, r, MV), effects loop, impedance selector, black covering, brown grille, mfg. 2003-08.

	$1,649	$1,050 - 1,250	$700 - 850	$1,649

* *Soul-O 30 12 in. Combo* – similar to the Soul-O 30, except in combo form with 1-12 in. speaker, mfg. 2003-08.

	$1,749	$1,100 - 1,300	$725 - 875	$1,749

* *Soul-O 30 15 in. Combo* – similar to the Soul-O 30, except in combo form with 1-15 in. speaker, mfg. 2003-08.

	$1,799	$1,150 - 1,350	$750 - 900	$1,799

MSR/NOTES	100%	EXCELLENT	AVERAGE	LAST MSR

SOUL-O 50 HEAD – 50W, head-unit only, tube chassis, power: 2 X EL34/6CA7, single channel, reverb, front chrome control panel, single input, eight black knobs (bias, g, t, m, b, p, r, MV), effects loop, impedance selector, black covering, brown grille, mfg. 2004-08.

	100%	EXCELLENT	AVERAGE	LAST MSR
	$1,649	$1,050 - 1,250	$700 - 850	$1,649

* *Soul-O 50 12 in. Combo* – similar to the Soul-O 50, except in combo form with 1-12 in. speaker, mfg. 2004-08.

	$1,749	$1,100 - 1,300	$725 - 875	$1,749

* *Soul-O 50 15 in. Combo* – similar to the Soul-O 50, except in combo form with 1-15 in. speaker, mfg. 2004-08.

	$1,799	$1,150 - 1,350	$750 - 900	$1,799

SPEAKER CABINETS

EX112 SPEAKER CABINET – unknown wattage, 1-12 in. Celestion speaker, removable rear panel, black covering, brown grille, disc. 2008.

	$599	$375 - 450	$225 - 275	$599

EX115 SPEAKER CABINET – unknown wattage, 1-15 in. Celestion speaker, removable rear panel, black covering, brown grille, disc. 2008.

	$699	$450 - 525	$275 - 325	$699

EX212 SPEAKER CABINET – unknown wattage, 2-12 in. Celestion speakers, removable rear panel, black covering, brown grille, disc. 2008.

	$599	$500 - 575	$300 - 350	$749

EX410 SPEAKER CABINET – unknown wattage, 4-10 in. Celestion speakers, removable rear panel, black covering, brown grille, disc. 2006.

	$599	$550 - 650	$325 - 400	$849

GT ELECTRONICS

See Groove Tubes.

GUILD

Amplifiers previously produced in New York City from 1952 to 56; production moved to Hoboken, New Jersey from late 1956-1968, and from Westerly, Rhode Island in 1969-current.

The Guild Guitar company was started in 1952 by Alfred Dronge. They are most known for building fine acoustic and electric guitars. For a full history on acoustic guitars, refer to the *Blue Book of Acoustic Guitars* and for a full history on electric guitars, refer to the *Blue Book of Electric Guitars*. As electric guitars became popular in the early to mid-1950s, Guild started to build guitar amplifiers with the Masteramp Series. The company moved to Hoboken, New Jersey in late 1956 to expand the rapidly growing company. Guild enjoyed their best amplifier production between the late 1950s and mid-1960s when they built several tube amplifiers and other electronic accessories. In 1966, Avnet bought the Guild company, and around this time they introduced the "Thunder" line of guitar amplifiers. In 1969, Avnet moved the entire Guild corporation to Westerly, RI. By the end of the 1960s, most standard amplifier production had stopped, with the exception of a few new models trickling into the 1970s. Alfred Dronge, president of the company since the 1960s, was killed in a plane crash in 1973. The vice president, Leon Tell, took over the company until 1983. During the 1970s and early 1980s, Guild produced mainly solid-state amplifiers in limited runs. In 1986, Avnet sold Guild to a management/investment group. This ownership lasted until 1988 when the Faas company of New Berlin, WI bought them out. This ownership eventually evolved into U.S. Music Corporation during the early 1990s. At one point, Guild was distributed along with Randall and Matchless amplifiers!

During the early 1990s, Guild gave one more run at amplifiers and this time they focused on acoustic models only. These amps were built by Randall amps located in Anaheim, CA because Guild was a partner of U.S. Music Corporation that also owned Randall. These amps lasted just before the company was sold again, and Guild has not produced another guitar amplifier since. In 1995, Guild finally found a real home with the Fender Musical Instrument Corporation (FMIC). Fender continued to produce instruments in the Westerly, RI factory until the late 1990s and early 2000s, when all production was moved to other Fender locations. Eventually, acoustic guitars moved to the Tacoma plant that Fender also bought in 2005, and electric guitar production was discontinued altogether. Information courtesy Hans Moust, *The Guild Guitar Book*, and early factory catalogs.

STYLING AND COVERING ON GUILD AMPLIFIERS

Over the years, Guild went through several style and covering changes on their amps, and they often did not change the chassis or specs of the amp at all. Therefore the same model may appear in three or more covering styles. This is generally a helpful dating tool when it comes to identifying Guild amplifiers. This is only a rough guide!

Early 1950s-mid-1950s: Early models are generally covered in a two-tone brown with a light brown top half and dark brown lower half. The grille cloth is square with rounded corners and sits center in the front of the amp. Control panels are on top and a leather handle is used. Little information is known on specific models, but this style was used on the Masteramp Models 60 and 110.

Late 1950s-1959: New two-tone brown covering. Approx. the top 1/4 is covered in a light brown and the lower 3/4 is covered in a dark brown. The speaker grille is trapezoid-shaped with it being wider at the bottom, and is brown in color with white swirls. The

MSR/NOTES	100%	EXCELLENT	AVERAGE	LAST MSR

top of the speaker grille is the line where the covering changes color. A "GUILD" logo is placed center above the speaker grille. Control panels are still on top and leather handles are used.

Circa 1960-62: New two-tone blue/gray covering. Approx. the top 1/4 is covered in a blue vinyl and the lower 3/4 is covered in a gray. The speaker grille is a light brown, trapezoid-shaped, and extends into the top blue vinyl covering making the forehead of the amp not so large. The "GUILD" logo is still center above the speaker, but the letters are more blocked-shaped. Control panels still on top and leather handles still used.

Circa 1963-65: Revision of the two-tone blue/gray covering. Guild still uses the two-tone from the early 1960s, but the speaker grille is changed to a square and the edge of the front is very narrow (similar to many standard box style amps from this era).

Circa 1965-68: Brown coverings and brown grilles. There are two variations of this type of styling and it is unknown when either or were used. The 1966 catalog indicates a dark brown covering with a light brown grille. The other variation is a light brown covering with a two-tone light brown/dark brown grille cloth that is split approx. 75/25. This entire series featres entirely new models, new chassis, control panels are in the front, and logos are on the grille.

ELECTRIC TUBE AMPLIFIERS

MASTERAMP 60 – 14W, 1-12 in. RCA speaker, guitar combo, six-tube chassis, preamp: 1 X 6SN7GT, 2 X 12AX7, power: 2 X 50L6GT, rectifier: 35Z5GT, two channels, tremolo, top chrome control panel, four inputs (one for Ch. 1, three for Ch. 2), six knobs (Ch. 1 v, Ch. 2 v, b, t, s, i), tremolo selector switch, two-tone brown vinyl/simulated woodgrain covering, brown grille cloth, mfg. mid-1950s.

	N/A	$450 - $575	$275 - 325	

MASTERAMP 110 – 14W, 1-15 in. speaker, guitar combo, six-tube chassis, preamp: 1 X 6SN7GT, 2 X 12AX7, power: 2 X 50L6GT, rectifier: 35Z5GT, two channels, tremolo, top chrome control panel, four inputs (one for Ch. 1, three for Ch. 2), six knobs (Ch. 1 v, Ch. 2 v, b, t, s, i), tremolo selector switch, two-tone brown vinyl/simulated woodgrain covering, brown grille cloth, mfg. mid-1950s.

	N/A	$500 - 650	$275 - 325	

MAVERICK – 25W, 2-10 in. CTS speakers, guitar combo, six-tube chassis, preamp: 1 X 12DW7, 1 X 6GW8, 2 X 12AX7, power: 2 X 7591A, solid-state rectifier, single channel, reverb, tremolo, front red control panel, two inputs, six knobs (b, t, v, s, i, r), bass/bright switch, standby switch, power switch, black covering, two-tone gray/black sparkle grille cloth, mfg. late 1960s-early 1970s.

	N/A	$400 - 500	$275 - 325	

MAVERICK BASS – 25W, 1-15 in. CTS speaker, bass combo, four-tube chassis, preamp: 1 X 12DW7, 1 X 12AX7, power: 2 X 7591A, solid-state rectifier, single channel, front blue control panel, two inputs, three knobs (b, t, v), bass/bright switch, standby switch, power switch, black covering, two-tone gray/black sparkle grille cloth, mfg. late 1960s-early 1970s.

	N/A	$225 - 275	$135 - 175	

MODEL 50-J – 14W, 1-12 In. Jensen speaker, guitar combo, six tube chassis, single channel, tremolo, top control panel, three inputs, four knobs (v, tone, s, i), available in second version blue/gray two-tone covering, 19 in. wide, 18 in. tall, 8.75 in. deep, 23.5 lbs., mfg. circa 1962-65

	N/A	$400 - 500	$235 - 275	

MODEL 66-J – 20W, 1-12 in. Jensen speaker, guitar combo, six tube chassis, preamp: 3 X 12AX7, power: 2 X 6V6GT, rectifier: 1 X 5Y3GT, two channels, tremolo, top control panel, four inputs, six knobs (v1, v2, b, t, s, i), available in at least four covering variations/styles (TV style two-tone brown, trapezoid two-tone brown, first version two-tone blue/gray and second version two-tone blue/gray), mfg. mid-1950s-1965

	N/A	$450 - 575	$325 - 375	

The earliest models had 15W output and an RCA speaker.

MODEL 98-RT – 30W, 1-12 in. speaker, guitar combo, seven tube chassis, preamp: 3 X 6SN7, 1 X 6SL7, power: 2 X 6V6GT, rectifier: 5Y3GT, single channel, reverb, tremolo, top chrome control panel, three inputs, five knobs (v, tone, r, s, i), two-button footswitch, available in one variation (two-tone blue/gray covering), 22 in. wide, 20 in. tall, 9.5 in. deep, 56 lbs., mfg. circa 1962-65.

	N/A	$600 - 700	$425 - 500	

MODEL 99-J – 30W, 1-12 in. Jensen speaker, guitar combo, seven tube chassis, two channels, tremolo, top control panel, four inputs, six knobs (v1, v2, b, t, s, i), available in at least four variations of coverings/styles (TV style two-tone brown, trapezoid two-tone brown, first version two-tone blue/gray and second version two-tone blue/gray), mfg. mid-1950s-1965.

	N/A	$450 - 600	$300 - 350	

The earliest models had 25W output and three speakers with 1-12 in. Jensen driver and two Jensen tweeters.

* *Model 99-U Ultra Piggyback* – similar to the Model 99-J, except is in piggyback configuration with either 1-12 in. speaker or 1-15 in. speaker, head locks onto cabinet, mfg. circa 1962-65.

1-12 in. Cab	N/A	$500 - 600	$375 - 450	
1-15 in. Cab	N/A	$550 - 650	$400 - 450	

MODEL 100-J – 35W, 1-15 in. Jensen speaker, guitar combo, seven tube chassis, two channels, tremolo, top control panel, four inputs, six knobs (v1, v2, b, t, s, i), available in three variations of coverings, mfg. late 1950s-1965.

	N/A	$500 - 650	$350 - 425	

MSR/NOTES	100%	EXCELLENT	AVERAGE	LAST MSR

MODEL 200S/DOUBLE TWIN – 50W (25W per amplifier/side), 2-12 in. Jensen speakers, guitar combo, nine tube chassis, two channels, tremolo, top control panel, four inputs, eight knobs (Ch. 1: v, b, t, Ch. 2: v, b, t, s, i), available in at least three variations of coverings/styles (TV style two-tone brown, trapezoid two-tone brown, and second version two-tone blue/gray with a middle slat), mfg. mid-1950s-1965.

| | N/A | $750 - 950 | $500 - 600 | |

MODEL RC-20 REVERB CONVERTER – 8W, 1-10 in. speaker, reverb converter unit, two tube chassis, two silicon rectifiers, single channel, reverb, tremolo, top chrome control panel, two inputs, two knobs (v, s), one-button footswitch, available in one variation (two-tone blue/gray covering), 18 in. wide, 15.5 in. tall, 8 in. deep, 19.5 lbs., mfg. circa 1962-65.

| | N/A | $475 - 550 | $325 - 375 | |

This reverb unit connects to the main amp with two wires hooked directly up to the speaker.

THUNDER 1 – ~14W, 1-12 in. speaker, seven tube chassis, guitar combo, single channel, tremolo, front control panel, two inputs, four knobs (tremolo, v, t, b), available in two variations of coverings (dark brown with brown grille or light brown with two-tone brown grille), mfg. circa 1965-68.

courtesy John Beeson/The Music Shoppe

courtesy John Beeson/The Music Shoppe

| | N/A | $300 - 350 | $175 - 225 | |

THUNDER 1 RVT – ~18W, 1-12 in. speaker and one smaller speaker for reverb, seven tube chassis, preamp: 3 X 12AX7, 1 X 6BM8, power: 2 X GW8, rectifier: 6CA4, guitar combo, single channel, reverb, tremolo, front control panel, three inputs, six knobs (r, s, i, b, t, v), available in two variations of coverings (dark brown with brown grille or light brown with two-tone brown grille), mfg. circa 1965-68.

| | N/A | $475 - 600 | $275 - 325 | |

THUNDERBASS – ~45W (23W per channel), 2-12 in. or 2-15 in. speakers, bass piggyback unit, two channels, front control panel, four inputs, seven knobs (Ch. 1: v, b, t, Ch. 2: v, b, t, MV), crossover, available in two variations of coverings (dark brown with brown grille or light brown with two-tone brown grille), mfg. circa 1965-68.

| **Head & Cab** | N/A | $500 - 700 | $400 - 450 | |
| **Head Only** | N/A | $275 - 325 | $210 - 240 | |

THUNDERBIRD – ~25W, 1-12 in. and 1-8 in. speakers, guitar/bass combo, two channels, front control panel, four inputs, 10 knobs, available in two variations of coverings (dark brown with brown grille or light brown with two-tone brown grille), mfg. circa 1965-68.

| | N/A | $450 - 550 | $275 - 325 | |

THUNDERSTAR BASS – ~45W (23W per channel), 2-12 in. or 2-15 in. speakers, bass piggyback unit, four-tube chassis, preamp: 1 X 12AX7, 1 X 12DW7, power: 2 X 6L6GC, solid-state rectifier, single channel, front control panel, two inputs, three knobs (v, b, t), bass/bright switch, crossover, black covering, mfg. late 1970s.

| **Head & Cab** | N/A | $525 - 600 | $375 - 425 | |
| **Head Only** | N/A | $250 - 300 | $150 - 200 | |

MODEL U-101 – 10W, 1-12 in. Jensen P12S speaker, guitar combo, six-tube chassis, preamp: 1 X 6AU6, 2 X 12AX7, power: 2 X 6AQ5A, rectifier: 1 X 6CA4, single channel, tremolo, top chrome control panel, three inputs (accordion, guitar, auxillary), four knobs (v, tone, tremolo strength, tremolo speed), dark gray covering, light gray grille cloth, mfg. early 1960s.

| | N/A | $200 - 250 | $120 - 150 | |

ELECTRIC SS AMPLIFIERS

In the mid-1970s and early 1980s, Guild released various solid-state amps. They followed similar suit in model designation with their early 1960s counterparts and were named Model One, Model Two, etc. The first series was released in the mid-1970s and they featured tall vertical cabinets. The **Model One** features 30W power and 1-12 in. speaker. The **Model Two** features 50W power and 2-10 in. speakers. The **Model Three** features 60W power and 1-15 in. speaker. In the early 1980s, they continued on with this series with a line of practice/beginner solid-state models. Models include the **Model Four**, **Model Five**, **Model Six**, and **Model Seven**.

MSR/NOTES	100%	EXCELLENT	AVERAGE	LAST MSR

ACOUSTIC SS AMPLIFIERS

In the early 1990s, Guild released a line of acoustic amplifiers called the Timberline Series. A G-500 bi-powered amp was also produced with the G-1000, but it probably evolved into the G600 Aspen.

G300 TAMARACK – 40W (20W per side), 2-8 in. speakers plus a tweeter, acoustic guitar combo, solid-state chassis, single channel, reverb, chorus, front gold control panel, single input, 11 knobs (sensitivity, level, t, m, b, plectron, notch, r, MV, chorus level, chorus speed), headphone jack, solid oak cabinet, gold/brown grille cloth with Guild Acoustic logo in lower right corner, mfg. circa 1992-94.

	N/A	$250 - 300	$150 - 200	$749

G600 ASPEN – 60W (30W per side), 2-10 in. speakers plus a tweeter, acoustic guitar combo, solid-state chassis, single channel, reverb, chorus, Rototron, front gold control panel, single input, 12 knobs (sensitivity, level, t, m, b, plectron, notch, r, MV, chorus level, chorus speed, Rototron), isolated effects loop, two-button footswitch, solid oak cabinet, gold/brown grille cloth with Guild Acoustic logo in lower right corner, mfg. circa 1992-94.

	N/A	$300 - 375	$200 - 250	$879

Add 20% for digital reverb with delay.

G700 SEQUOIA – 160W (80W per side), 4-8 in. speakers plus a tweeter, acoustic guitar combo, solid-state chassis, two channels, reverb, chorus, Rototron, front gold control panel, regular and XLR inputs, 16 knobs, five-band graphic EQ, isolated effects loop, two-button footswitch, solid oak cabinet, gold/brown grille cloth with Guild Acoustic logo in lower right corner, mfg. circa 1992-94.

	N/A	$400 - 500	$275 - 325	$1,199

Add 25% for digital reverb with delay.

G1000 – 90W (30W per side), 4-6 in. speakers plus 1-10 in. subwoofer, acoustic guitar combo, solid-state chassis, two channels, reverb, chorus, rear black control panel, regular and XLR inputs, 11 knobs (mic level, MV, sensitivity, line out level, level, h, m, l, r, chorus speed, chorus depth), five-band graphic EQ, isolated effects loop, direct outs, two-button footswitch, hexagon-shaped cabinet with three sides of speaker grille, and three sides of solid material, six removable casters, cushioned seat, available in black ebony with black grille or mahogany with brown grille, MOP Guild inlaid logo, mfg. circa 1992-94.

courtesy S.P. Fjestad

courtesy S.P. Fjestad

	N/A	$600 - 750	$400 - 500	$1,499

This amp is designed for the guitar player to sit on it and play. There are three separate 30W amplifiers with two of them driving 2-6 in. speakers each and the third driving the 10 in. subwoofer.

GUYATONE

Amplifiers previously produced in Japan from the late 1940s through the early 1970s. The Guyatone trademark was established circa 1933, and they currently produce a full line of effects pedals.

The original company was founded by Mitsou Matsuki, an apprentice cabinet maker in the early 1930s. Matsuki, who studied electronics in night classes, was influenced by listening to Hawaiian music. A friend and renowned guitar player, Atsuo Kaneko, requested that Matsuki build a Hawaiian electric guitar. The two entered into business as a company called Matsuki Seisakujo, and produced guitars under the Guya trademark.

In 1948, a little after World War II, Matsuki founded his new company, Matsuki Denki Onkyo Kenkyujo. This company produced electric Hawaiian guitars, amplifiers, and record player cartridges. In 1951, this company began using the Guyatone trademark for its guitars. By the next year the corporate name evolved into Tokyo Sound Company. They produced their first solid body electric in the late 1950s. Original designs dominated the early production, albeit entry level quality. Later quality improved, but at the sacrifice of originality as Guyatone began building medium quality designs based on Fender influences. Some Guyatone guitars also were imported under such brandnames as Star or Antoria. Many amplifiers produced in the 1960s resemble Fender Blackface or Silverface designs. The Guyatone trademark is currently used on a line of effects pedals. Source: Michael Wright, *Guitar Stories, Volume One*.

ELECTRIC AMPLIFIERS

Early amplifiers typically have original designs, but once they moved into the 1960s, they began copying popular designs. Models made in the 1960s are numbered like this; they have a GA prefix followed by a three or four-digit number. It is not known what each model features or the specifications. Later models (1970s and possibly early 1980s) are known as the Flip models. Most Guyatone amplifiers are solid-state but the Flips are also of hybrid design. Any further information on Guyatone can be submitted directly to Blue Book Publications.

GUYTRON

Amplifiers and speaker cabinets currently built in Fenton, MI. Distributed by Guytron. Previously produced in Troy, MI. The Guytron trademark was established in 1995.

CONTACT INFORMATION
GUYTRON
7518 Driftwood Drive
Fenton, MI 48430
Phone No.: 810-955-1151
Fax No.: 810-750-3477
www.guytron.com
graydon@guytron.com

Guytron was founded by Guy Hendrick in 1995, with the introduction of the GT100 amplifier. Guytron's amplifiers are designed to give the player total tone control without having thirty different amps and the simplicity of switching between sounds with little modifications of the control knobs. Essentially this amp has everything a player needs and nothing he or she doesn't need. The result is an amp that sounds fully cranked at any volume and the right features and controls to make it sound good. Guytron produces heads, speaker cabinets, and combos, which they released in 2006. In 2008, GDS Amplification LLC purchased Guytron and is now operated by Graydon Stuckey. For more information, visit Guytron's website or contact them directly.

ELECTRIC TUBE AMPLIFIERS

The original **GT100** was produced between 1995 and 2003. In 2003, the **GT100-FV** (MSR $3,295) was introduced, which is a multi-voiced version of the GT-100. Upgraded features include a stainless steel chassis, switchable effects loop level, focus and voicing controls, and the ability to mod the amplifier on the go. The **GT-20** (MSR was $2,395) was introduced in 2006 and is a 1-12 in. speaker combo based on the GT-100FV. The **GT212** speaker cabinet is also available with a closed (MSR $895) or open back (MSR $845). All Guytron combos and cabinets are loaded with Guytron's proprietary Bigtone speakers. New models including the GT20 Head and the GT40 in both head and combo configurations.

H SECTION
HAGSTROM

Amplifiers previously produced in Sweden. Early distributors included the Hershman Musical Instrument Company of New York (under Goya logo) and Selmer, U.K. (under Futurama logo). In the mid-1970s, Ampeg became the U.S. distributor. Hagstrom was produced in Sweden 1957-1983, and reintroduced in 2004 as an overseas product.

Hagstrom first began building guitars and basses in 1957 and continued through 1983. The brand was reintroduced as an overseas product in 2004. For a complete history on Electric Guitars, refer to the *Blue Book of Electric Guitars*.

In the late 1950s or early 1960s, Hagstrom started to produce tube guitar amplifiers, and it is also rumored that Hagstrom built amps for Guild. Hagstrom continued to produce tube and solid-state amplifiers throughout the 1960s and into the 1970s. Even though Hagstrom produced a number of amplifiers, many of them never made it to the U.S. and very few are found in the used marketplace. This makes used evaluating very difficult, and at this point we do not have a solid pricing scheme. Some popular models seem to be the **GA-225** and the briefcase amp, which are both pictured. Any further information on Hagstrom amplifiers can be submitted directly to Blue Book Publications. Information courtesy Kwinn Kastrosky, Yesterday's Guitars.

GA-220
courtesy Yesterday's Guitars

Model 26 (Suitcase Amp)
courtesy Yesterday's Guitars

Model 310
courtesy Yesterday's Guitars

HARMONY

Amplifiers currently produced in China since 2007. Previously produced in Chicago, IL between the late 1940s and the mid-1970s and in various Asian locations during the 1980s and early 2000s. Currently distributed by The Original Harmony Guitar Company, Inc. in Palatine, IL. Previously distributed by Sears & Roebuck between the late 1940s and the mid-1970s, JC Penney and possibly other distributors in the 1980s, and by MBT International during the early 2000s.

CONTACT INFORMATION
HARMONY
532 South Hicks Road
Palatine, IL 60067
Phone No.: 847-221-5086
Fax No.: 847-221-5091
www.harmonyguitars.com
info@harmonyguitars.com

The Harmony Company of Chicago, IL was one of the largest American musical instrument manufacturers. Harmony has the historical distinction of being the largest "jobber" house in the nation, producing stringed instruments for a number of different wholesalers. Individual dealers or distributors could get stringed instruments with their own brand name on them if they ordered more than 100 pieces. At one time, Harmony was producing the largest percentage of stringed instruments in the U.S. market.

The company was founded by Wilhelm J.F. Shultz in 1892. Business expanded exponentially and by 1915 the company already had a 125 person workforce and $250,000 in annual sales. In 1916, Sears, Roebuck & Company purchased Harmony and in 1925 they produced 250,000 units. Most of these guitars were sold through Sears in their catalog (about 35%-40% in 1930). In 1930, they sold 500,000 units, and only sold to wholesalers. Harmony became sort of a steamroller, bought trademarks and kept selling guitars and other equipment faster than they could make them.

In the 1940s, Harmony introduced guitar amplifiers to complement the increasingly popular electric guitar. Through the 1950s and 1960s Harmony continued to sell guitars, amplifiers, and other instruments at a rapid pace. Unlike many companies that went bankrupt by the end of the 1960s, Harmony managed to survive and thrive in the guitar industry. However, the 1970s finally took its toll on the large company and they closed in 1976.

In the late 1970s, the Harmony trademark was sold and licensed for use on a line of Asian-built guitars. From the late 1970s through the 1990s, Harmony was mainly used on cheap entry-level guitars that were often sold through mass merchandisers. The trademark and licensing agreements were also bought and sold several times throughout this period. In 2000, MBT International began to distribute Harmony guitars with a line of acoustic and electric instruments, as well as unbranded amplifiers, mainly based on popular American designs; however, by 2001, this licensing agreement was dissolved.

Current Harmony president Charlie Subecz bought the Harmony trademark in the mid-1990s, and by the mid-2000s, he decided to reintroduce the Harmony guitar line. Instead of using Harmony as simply a budget brand of copied models, Subecz went to work on offering vintage Harmony guitars that were reminiscent of the 1950s and 1960s. Unfortunately, no blueprints or records existed on Harmony's vintage guitars, so Subecz and his crew had to obtain physical examples of these guitars. Examples were then sent to Korea where they were precisely duplicated and readied for production. Harmony is currently offering a line of small guitar and bass amps with tweed coverings. For more information, visit Harmony's website or contact them directly.

MSR/NOTES	100%	EXCELLENT	AVERAGE	LAST MSR

ELECTRIC TUBE AMPLIFIERS: H100 & H200 SERIES

Throughout the late 1940s and 1950s, Harmony produced several different models of amplifiers. It seems when they changed the covering style of their amp, they called it a different number even though the chassis probably stayed the same. Therefore, the same chassis (or at least mild variations) were used in several different style cabinets. If your model is not listed, you can probably compare specs to one that is listed (or in the H300 Series) to get an estimate of value. Any further information can be submitted directly to Blue Book Publications.

MODEL 195 – wattage unknown, speaker size unknown, four tube chassis, single channel, rear control panel, two inputs, two-tone brown imitation leather covering, metal decorative grille, mfg. late 1940s.

	N/A	$250 - 300	$150 - 200	

H189 STUDENT – wattage unknown, 1-6 in. or 1-8 in. speaker, guitar combo, three tube chassis, single channel, rear control panel, two inputs, single volume knob, black covering, octagon brown grille, mfg. mid-1950s.

	N/A	$200 - 250	$100 - 150	

H191 – wattage unknown, 1-6 in. or 1-8 in. speaker, guitar combo, three tube chassis, single channel, rear control panel, two inputs, single volume knob, red ribbed covering on front and top, ivory covering on sides, square brown grille with rounded corners, mfg. mid-1950s.

	N/A	$400 - 500	$200 - 275	

H193 – wattage unknown, 1-6 in. speaker, guitar combo, three tube chassis, single channel, rear control panel, two inputs, one volume control, brown simulated leather covering with Harmony logo in upper right corner above grille, large rectangle brown gille that wraps around both sides, mfg. mid-1950s-late 1950s.

	N/A	$300 - 375	$150 - 200	

H194 – wattage unknown, 1-8 in. speaker, guitar combo, four tube chassis, single channel, rear control panel, two inputs, two knobs (v, tone), brown pig grain covering with Harmony logo in upper right corner above grille, large rectangle brown gille that wraps around both sides, mfg. mid-1950s-late 1950s.

	N/A	$275 - 350	$150 - 200	

H200 – wattage unknown, 1-12 in. speaker, guitar combo, six-tube chassis, two channels, rear control panel, three inputs, three knobs (v1, v2, tone), two-tone light brown/dark brown covering, square two-tone red/light tan grille cloth with Harmony logo and notes, mfg. mid-1940s-1950.

	N/A	$400 - 500	$200 - 275	

H204 – wattage unknown, 1-12 in. speaker, guitar combo, five tube chassis, two channels, rear control panel, three inputs, three knobs (v1, v2, tone), brown pig grain covering with Harmony logo in upper right corner above grille, large rectangle brown gille that wraps around both sides, mfg. mid-1950s-late 1950s.

	N/A	$400 - 500	$250 - 300	

H205 – wattage unknown, 1-12 in. speaker, guitar combo, five tube chassis, two channels, rear control panel, three inputs, three knobs (v1, v2, tone), tweed covering with blue saddlehide ends, rectangle brown grille with Harmony logo and notes in lower right corner, mfg. mid-1950s.

	N/A	$350 - 450	$200 - 250	

H210 – wattage unknown, 1-12 in. speaker, guitar combo, six tube chassis, two channels, tremolo, rear control panel, four inputs, six knobs (v1, tone 1, v2, tone 2, s, i), footswitch, brown pig grain covering with Harmony logo in upper right corner above grille, large rectangle brown gille that wraps around both sides, mfg. mid-1950s-late 1950s.

	N/A	$375 - 450	$200 - 275	

ELECTRIC TUBE AMPLIFIERS: H300 SERIES

All models in this series feature a blue/gray simulated covering with a gray grille, rear-mounted chassis/control panels, and a block Harmony logo in the upper left corner.

H303(A) – wattage unknown, 1-6 in. speaker, guitar combo, three tube chassis, single channel, rear control panel, two or three inputs, single volume knob, blue/gray simulated leather, gray grille, mfg. late 1950s-mid-1960s.

H303
courtesy S.P. Fjestad

H303
courtesy S.P. Fjestad

	N/A	$200 - 250	$100 - 150	

In 1960, the model H303A was introduced with three inputs.

MSR/NOTES	100%	EXCELLENT	AVERAGE	LAST MSR

H304(A) – wattage unknown, 1-10 in. Jensen speaker, guitar combo, four tube chassis, single channel, rear/top control panel, two inputs, two knobs (v, tone), blue/gray simulated leather, gray grille, 18 in. wide, 15 in. tall, 9.5 in. deep, mfg. late 1950s-1965.

	N/A	$200 - 250	$100 - 150	

Early models may have an 8 in. speaker.

H305(A) – wattage unknown, 1-12 in. Jensen speaker, guitar combo, five tube chassis, two channels, rear/top control panel, three inputs (two regular, one high gain), three knobs (v1, v2, tone), blue/gray simulated leather, gray grille, mfg. late 1950s-1965.

	N/A	$200 - 250	$100 - 150	

H306(A) – wattage unknown, 1-12 in. Jensen speaker, guitar combo, six tube chassis, two channels, vibrato (later models refer to it as tremolo), rear/top control panel, four inputs (three regular, one mic), six knobs (v1, v2, tone 1, tone 2, s, i), one-button footswitch, blue/gray simulated leather, gray grille, mfg. late 1950s-1965.

	N/A	$300 - 375	$200 - 250	

ELECTRIC TUBE AMPLIFIERS: H400 SERIES

All models in this series feature a black ostrich grained leather covering, a brown wheat grille, top mounted control panels, and on the larger models, the Harmony logo and model number appear on a metal strip that runs along the top.

H400(A) – wattage unknown, 1-8 in. Jensen speaker, guitar combo, three tube chassis, single channel, top mounted control panel, three inputs, one volume control or one volume and one tone knob, black ostrich grained leather covering, brown grille, 15.75 in. wide, 16 in. tall, 7.75 in. deep, mfg. 1965-67.

	N/A	$200 - 250	$125 - 150	

• **Add 10% for a tone knob.**

In 1966, the model H400A was introduced with two knobs (v, tone).

H410(A) – ~8W, 1-8 in. Jensen speaker, guitar combo, four tube chassis, single channel, tremolo, top mounted control panel, three inputs, four knobs (v, tone, s, i), black ostrich grained leather covering, brown grille, 18.75 in. wide, 16 in. tall, 7.75 in. deep, mfg. 1965-67.

	N/A	$375 - 475	$250 - 300	

H415 – wattage unknown, 2-12 in. Jensen special design speakers, guitar combo, six tube chassis, two channels, tremolo, top mounted control panel, four inputs, six knobs (v1, v2, tone 1, tone 2, s, i), one button footswitch, black ostrich grained leather covering, brown grille, 26.5 in. wide, 18.5 in. tall, 9.5 in. deep, mfg. 1966-67.

	N/A	$600 - 750	$400 - 500	

H420 – 35W, 1-15 in. Jensen Special Design speaker, guitar, accordion or voice combo, four tube chassis with four diode rectifiers, two channels, tremolo, top mounted control panel, three inputs, three knobs (v, t, b), black ostrich grained leather covering, brown grille, 19.25 in. wide, 23.75 in. tall, 11.5 in. deep, mfg. 1965-66.

	N/A	$400 - 500	$200 - 275	

H430 – wattage unknown, 2-10 in. Jensen special design speakers, guitar combo, eight tube chassis, two channels, reverb, tremolo, top mounted control panel, four inputs, seven knobs (v1, v2, tone 1, tone 2, s, i, r), two one-button footswitches, black ostrich grained leather covering, brown grille, 26 in. wide, 18 in. tall, 9.5 in. deep, mfg. 1965-66.

	N/A	$600 - 750	$400 - 500	

H440 – 70W, 2-12 in. Jensen special design speakers, guitar combo, 12 tube chassis, two channels, reverb, tremolo, top mounted control panel, four inputs, seven knobs (v1, v2, tone 1, tone 2, s, i, r), two one-button footswitches, black ostrich grained leather covering, brown grille, 32 in. wide, 24 in. tall, 9.5 in. deep, mfg. 1965-66.

	N/A	$650 - 800	$400 - 500	

This model featured two separate power amplifiers with one powering each speaker.

ELECTRIC SS AMPLIFIERS: H500 "RALLY STRIPE" SERIES

Like almost any other large amplifier company, the late 1960s marked their introduction into solid-state amplifiers. The H500 "Rally Stripe" Series are somewhat similar to Fender's solid-state amps from the late 1960s in they are much larger than they need to be and they feature a new contemporary look. Cabinets were covered in a black grained ostrich simulated leather, the grille cloth was a gray with three red (one wide, two narrow) rally stripes on the left side of the cabinet running vertically, and on larger models a chrome strip with the Harmony logo and model number ran horizontally.

There were two versions of the H500 Series. The first version complemented the H400 Series at the same time, so no new smaller combos were introduced at the same time. Models introduced were the H525, H535, H570, and H540 speaker cabinet. The H525 and H535 actually have hybrid chassis with tubes and silicon diodes. In 1969, the H400 Series was discontinued altogether, and H500 small combos appeared. Models introduced were the H510, H512, H515, H530, H545, and H550. The only model to survive the change was the H540 speaker cabinet. All of these models were entirely solid-state in design.

H500 – wattage unknown, 1-8 in. speaker, guitar combo, solid-state chassis, single channel, top chrome control panel, three inputs, two knobs (v, tone), black ostrich grained simulated leather covering, gray grille with red rally stripes, 15.75 in. wide, 15.75 in. tall, 7.75 in. deep, mfg. 1969-1971.

	N/A	$120 - 150	$75 - 95	

MSR/NOTES	100%	EXCELLENT	AVERAGE	LAST MSR

H510 – 5W, 1-10 in. Jensen speaker, guitar combo, solid-state chassis, single channel, tremolo, top chrome control panel, three inputs, four knobs (v, tone, s, i), one-button footswitch, black ostrich grained simulated leather covering, gray grille with red rally stripes, 18.75 in. wide, 15.75 in. tall, 7.75 in. deep, mfg. 1969-1971.

| | N/A | $135 - 175 | $85 - 110 | |

H512 – 5W, 1-10 in. Jensen speaker, guitar combo, solid-state chassis, single channel, reverb, tremolo, top chrome control panel, three inputs, five knobs (v, tone, s, i, r), two one-button footswitches, black ostrich grained simulated leather covering, gray grille with red rally stripes, 18.75 in. wide, 18 in. tall, 7.75 in. deep, mfg. 1969-1971.

| | N/A | $150 - 200 | $95 - 120 | |

H515 – 18W, 2-12 in. Jensen speakers, guitar combo, solid-state chassis, two channels, tremolo, top chrome control panel, four inputs, six knobs (v1, tone 1, v2, tone 2, s, i,), one-button footswitch, black ostrich grained simulated leather covering, gray grille with red rally stripes, 19.25 in. wide, 33.25 in. tall, 9.25 in. deep, mfg. 1969-1971.

| | N/A | $200 - 250 | $120 - 150 | |

H525 – 35W, 1-15 in. Jensen speaker, bass combo, hybrid chassis with four tubes and four silicon rectifiers, two channels, tremolo, front chrome control panel, three inputs, three knobs (v, t, b), black ostrich grained simulated leather covering, gray grille with red rally stripes, 19 in. wide, 27 in. tall, 9.25 in. deep, mfg. 1967-68.

| | N/A | $175 - 225 | $110 - 140 | |

H530 – 35W, 1-15 in. Jensen speaker, bass combo, solid-state chassis, two channels, tremolo, top chrome control panel, three inputs, three knobs (v, t, b), black ostrich grained simulated leather covering, gray grille with red rally stripes, 19.25 in. wide, 27 in. tall, 9.25 in. deep, mfg. 1969-1971.

| | N/A | $150 - 200 | $95 - 120 | |

H535 – 35W, 2-12 in. Jensen speakers, guitar piggyback unit, hybrid chassis with seven tubes and four silicon rectifiers, two channels, reverb, tremolo, front chrome control panel, four inputs, nine knobs (Ch.1: v, t, b, Ch.2: v, t, b, s, i, r), two one-button footswitches, black ostrich grained simulated leather covering, gray grille with red rally stripes, 20.625 in. wide, 45 in. tall, 11.5 in. deep, mfg. 1967-68.

| **Head & Cab** | N/A | $275 - 325 | $150 - 200 | |
| **Head Only** | N/A | $135 - 175 | $85 - 110 | |

H540 – speaker cabinet only with 4-10 in. Jensen speakers, matches as a secondary or remote speaker for the H515, H530, H545, and H550, black ostrich grained simulated leather, gray grille with red rally stripes, 16.625 in. wide, 48 in. tall, 11 in. deep, mfg. 1967-1971.

| | N/A | $150 - 200 | $95 - 120 | |

H545 – 25W, 2-12 in. Jensen speakers, guitar piggyback unit, solid-state chassis, two channels, reverb, tremolo, top chrome control panel, four inputs, nine knobs (Ch.1: v, t, b, Ch.2: v, t, b, s, i, r), two one-button footswitches, black ostrich grained simulated leather covering, gray grille with red rally stripes, 19.25 in. wide, 33.25 in. tall, 9.25 in. deep, mfg. 1969-1971.

| | N/A | $250 - 300 | $135 - 175 | |

H550 – 50W, 2-12 in. Jensen speakers, guitar piggyback unit, solid-state chassis, two channels, reverb, tremolo, front chrome control panel, four inputs, nine knobs (Ch.1: v, t, b, Ch.2: v, t, b, s, i, r), two one-button footswitches, black ostrich grained simulated leather covering, gray grille with red rally stripes, 20.5 in. wide, 45 in. tall, 11.5 in. deep, mfg. 1969-1971.

| **Head & Cab** | N/A | $275 - 325 | $150 - 200 | |
| **Head Only** | N/A | $135 - 175 | $85 - 110 | |

H570 – 70W, 2-12 in. Jensen speakers, guitar piggyback unit, solid-state chassis, two channels, reverb, tremolo, front chrome control panel, four inputs, nine knobs (Ch.1: v, t, b, Ch.2: v, t, b, s, i, r), two one-button footswitches, black ostrich grained simulated leather covering, gray grille with red rally stripes, 23 in. wide, 50 in. tall, 11.5 in. deep, mfg. 1967-68.

| **Head & Cab** | N/A | $300 - 350 | $175 - 225 | |
| **Head Only** | N/A | $150 - 200 | $95 - 120 | |

ELECTRIC SS AMPLIFIERS: 1970S MODELS

In 1972, Harmony discontinued production of all other amplifiers and introduced a new unnamed series that consisted of seven models. These amps were solid-state in design, covered in a deep blue vinyl covering with a transparent dark grille cloth, and cardboard was actually used in the cabinet. The **H1516** is a guitar combo, features 5.5W peak output power, 1-6 in. speaker, two inputs, and two knobs (v, tone). The **H1618** is a guitar combo, features 20W peak output power, 1-8 in. speaker, tremolo, three inputs, and four knobs (v, tone, s, depth). The **H1710** is a guitar combo, features 20W peak output power, 1-10 in. speaker, reverb, tremolo, three inputs, and five knobs (v, tone, s, depth, r). The **H1720** is a piggyback guitar unit, features 35W peak output power, 2-10 in. speakers, reverb, tremolo, three inputs, and five knobs (v, tone, s, depth, r). The **H1722** is a piggyback guitar unit, features 90W peak output power, 2-12 in. speakers, two channels, reverb, tremolo, four inputs, and nine knobs (Ch. 1: v, b, t, Ch. 2: v, b, t, s, i, r). The **H1812** is a piggyback bass unit, features 35W peak output power, 1-12 in. speaker, three inputs, and three knobs (v, b, t). The **H1815** is a piggyback bass unit, features 75W peak output power, 1-15 in. speaker, three inputs, and three knobs (v, b, t).

MSR/NOTES	100%	EXCELLENT	AVERAGE	LAST MSR

HARRY JOYCE

Amplifiers and speaker cabinets previously produced in England from 1993 to 2000.

Harry Joyce had been involved in electronics for most of his life. During WWII, a couple of Americans taught Joyce military-spec construction. This military-spec construction can be found in HIWATT amplifiers as Dan Reeves contracted Joyce to build HIWATT amps with this construction in the 1960s and 1970s. From then until 1993, Joyce worked for the British Ministry of Defense as an electrical contractor of sorts. In 1993, Joyce took his knowledge in military-spec construction and applied it to his own brand of amplifiers. These new amps were based on the old HIWATT design with significant improvements including an extra gain stage, redesigned transformers, and an effects loop. Joyce retired from the amp business in the fall of 2000, and died January 12, 2002.

In 2015, it was announced that a group led by President Kevin Wood, Head of Research & Development George Scholz, and consultant Charles Bertonazzi would launch Harry Joyce USA in Sarasota, FL. Both Scholz and Bertonazzi worked alongside Harry Joyce during his legendary career. The new company is dedicated to the legacy of Joyce and debuted with three amplifier models in its initial line, the HJ Custom 30, HJ Custom 50, and HJ Custom 100 head-units. HJ USA will soon be expanding their line to include combo amps, bass amps, and preamps. For more information visit the Harry Joyce USA website at http://harryjoyce.com

ELECTRIC TUBE AMPLIFIERS

Joyce produced three different variations of one model available as a head or combo unit. The H.J. Custom was available with 30W, 50W, or 100W output. Amps featured two channels and a tube chassis with preamp: 4 X ECC83/12AX7, power: 2 X EL34 (4 X EL34 for the 100W), and a silicon rectifier. The control panel featured four inputs, seven knobs (norm v, brill vol, b, t, m, p, MV) and an effects loop was on the rear control panel.

HARTKE

Amplifiers and speaker cabinets currently produced in Ashbury Park, NJ and overseas. Hartke amplifiers are distributed worldwide by Samson Technology Corp. in Hauppauge, NY. The Hartke trademark was established in 1984.

The Hartke Amplifier company was co-founded by Larry Hartke and Ron Lorman in 1984/85. In the late 1970s, Lorman was an engineer at the Bottom Line Club in New York City where he and Hartke began experimenting with aluminum cone drivers. Aluminum driver cone speakers gave bass a clearer sound with broader dynamics - something that bassists did not have access to previously. Bassist Jaco Pastorius heard a prototype, and suggested Hartke and Lorman build one for him. This first model was equipped with 8-10 in. aluminum cone driver speakers and a plate on it that states "THE FIRST HARTKE BASS CABINET, CUSTOM BUILT IN 1984 FOR JACO PASTORIUS." Shortly after this, many big name musicians were using more prototype cabinets that Hartke and Lorman were esentially giving away to get their name out. In 1985, the first Hartke production models were produced with the 410XL model (4-10 in. speakers). Since then, Hartke has expanded their line and they offer several models of bass amplifiers, bass cabinets, bass combo units, guitar amps, and acoustic amps. Hartke cabinets stand out because of their aluminum cones that can be seen from the front of the amp. They also have produced some solid-body bass guitars made of wood and aluminum. For more information, visit Hartke's website or contact them directly.

ACOUSTIC AMPLIFIERS

AC75
courtesy Hartke

AC150
courtesy Hartke

ACR5
courtesy Hartke

AC75 – 75W (50W for woofers, 25W for tweeter), 2-5 in. woofers and 1 2 X 4 in. ribbon tweeter, acoustic guitar combo, solid-state chassis, two channels (inst. and mic), 100 24-bit digital effects, front gold control panel, three inputs (two regular, one XLR), nine gold knobs (Ch. 1: g, b, t, Ch. 2: v, All: notch filter freq. and depth, digital effects select and level, MV), five-band EQ, RCA inputs, effects loop, direct out, phase switch, tilt-back cabinet design, brown covering, black metal grille, 40 lbs., mfg. summer 2006-disc.

$350	$225 - 275	$135 - 175	$450

MSR/NOTES	100%	EXCELLENT	AVERAGE	LAST MSR

AC150 – 150W (2 X 50W for woofers, 50W for tweeter), 4-5 in. woofers and 1 2 X 4 in. ribbon tweeter, acoustic guitar combo, solid-state chassis, two channels (inst. and mic), 100 24-bit digital effects, front gold control panel, three inputs (two regular, one XLR), nine gold knobs (Ch. 1: g, b, t, Ch. 2: v, All: notch filter freq. and depth, digital effects select and level, MV), five-band EQ, RCA inputs, effects loop, direct out, phase switch, tilt-back cabinet design, brown covering, black metal grille, 50 lbs., mfg. summer 2006-disc.

	$450	$275 - 325	$150 - 200	$590

The AC150 features three individual power amps with two powering two woofers each and the third powering the tweeter.

ACR5 – 50W, 1-6.5 in. woofer and 1 in. tweeter, acoustic guitar combo, solid-state chassis, two channels (inst. and mic), 24-bit digital effects, top black control panel, two inputs (one 1/4 in., one XLR), seven knobs, three-band EQ, aux. input, footswitch jack, top handle, brown covering, black mesh grille, 25 lbs., new 2016.

MSR $325	$250	$165 - 190	$80 - 100	

BASS AMPLIFIERS: HEAD UNITS

HA5500/HA5500C
courtesy Hartke

Kilo 1000
courtesy Hartke

TX600
courtesy Hartke

The HA3500 originally had a black control panel, and in the early 2000s, they changed to a silver control panel. In the late 2000s, Hartke went back to the classic black control panel on the HA3500 and HA5500 and changed the name of the model to the HA3500C and HA5500C, respectively.

HA1400 – 140W, head-unit only, solid-state combo, single channel, black front control panel, single input, five black knobs (v, l, l/m, l/h, h), contour switch, compression switch, effects loop, headphone jack, black metal covering, 13 lbs., disc. 2004.

	N/A	$150 - 200	$95 - 120	$300

HA2000 – 200W, head-unit only, solid-state and tube preamp (selectable), front black control panel, two inputs (passive/active), six black and silver knobs (pre-amp A & B, compression, contour low and high pass, MV) 10-band equalizer, black metal covering, 19.5 lbs., disc. 2005.

	N/A	$200 - 250	$120 - 150	$520

HA2500 – 250W at 4 ohms (180W at 8 ohms), head-unit only, solid-state and tube preamp (selectable), front black control panel, two inputs (passive/active), six black and silver knobs (pre-amp A & B, compression, contour low and high pass, MV) 10-band equalizer, black metal covering, 19.5 lbs., mfg. 2004-present.

MSR $325	$250	$140 - 180	$90 - 110	

HA3000 MILLENIUM SERIES – 300W, head-unit only, solid-state chassis, single channel, shape circuit, front black control panel, two inputs, seven black knobs (v, shape, i, l, m/l, m/h, h), direct XLR out, black covering with description on top of amp, 23 lbs., disc. 2005.

	N/A	$300 - 350	$175 - 225	$710

HA3500/HA3500C – 350W, head-unit configuration, solid-state and tube preamp (selectable), front black (1990s, late 2000s, HA3500C) or silver (early to mid-2000s, HA3500) control panel, two inputs (passive/active), six black and silver knobs, (pre-amp A & B, compression, contour low and high pass, MV), in/out switch, 10-band equalizer, black metal covering, 25 lbs., mfg. 1991-present.

MSR $520	$400	$260 - 300	$130 - 160	

HA4000 MILLENIUM SERIES – 400W, head-unit only, solid-state chassis, single channel, shape circuit, front black control panel, two inputs, 12 black knobs (v, shape, i, D-Bass, l, m/l, freq, bandwith, m/h, freq, bandwith, h), direct XLR out, black covering with description on top of amp, 26. 5 lbs., disc. 2005.

	N/A	$375 - 450	$225 - 275	$875

HA5000 (BI-AMP) – 500W (250W X 2), head-unit only, solid-state and tube preamp (selectable), front black control panel, two inputs (passive/active), eight black and silver knobs (pre-amp A & B, compression, contour low and high pass, MV, Crossover freq & balance) in/out switch, 10-band equalizer, black metal covering, 28.5 lbs., disc. 2005.

	N/A	$400 - 475	$275 - 325	$935

HA5500/HA5500C – 500W at 4 ohms (350W at 8 ohms), head-unit configuration, solid-state and tube preamp (selectable), front black (1990s, late 2000s, HA5500C) or silver (early to mid-2000s, HA5500) control panel, two inputs (passive/active), six black and silver knobs (pre-amp A & B, compression, contour low and high pass, MV), in/out switch, 10-band equalizer, black metal covering, 37 lbs., mfg. 2004-present.

MSR $650	$500	$325 - 375	$165 - 200	

HA7000 (BI-AMP) – 700W (350W X 2), head-unit only, solid-state and tube preamp (selectable), front black control panel, two inputs (passive/active), eight black and silver knobs (pre-amp A & B, compression, contour low and high pass, MV, Crossover freq & balance) in/out switch, 10-band equalizer, black metal covering, 29.5 lbs., disc. 2005.

	N/A	$550 - 625	$350 - 425	$1,250

HARTKE, cont. 391 **H**

MSR/NOTES	100%	EXCELLENT	AVERAGE	LAST MSR

KILO 1000 – 1000W bridged mono (2 X 500W stereo), three-space rack-mount bass head-unit, solid-state chassis, single channel, front dark gray control panel, single input, 11 black knobs (g, compressor, b, m, t, shape, OD, balance, v, select, direct out), 10-band graphic EQ with level control and on/off switch, tuner out jack, active/passive switch, mute switch, deep switch, brite switch, OD on/off switch, effects on/off switch, power switch, rear panel: four standard 1/4 in. speaker jacks (two per side), three Speakon jacks (two per side, one bridged), stereo preamp out, stereo power amp in, effects loop with stereo return, three footswitch jacks, XLR direct line out with ground/lift switch, tuner out jack, black casing, mfg. 2008-disc.

MSR $1,300	$1,000	$600 - 700	$375 - 450	

LH500 – 500W, two-space rack-mount bass head-unit, hybrid chassis with a single 12AX7 preamp tube, single channel, front dark gray control panel, two inputs (passive and active), four chrome knobs (v, b, m, t), brite switch, limiter switch, XLR balanced direct line out, power switch, rear panel: effects loop, four standard speaker jacks, dark gray casing, mfg. 2008-present.

MSR $455	$350	$225 - 275	$135 - 175	

LH1000 – 1000W bridged mono (2 X 500W stereo), two-space rack-mount bass head-unit, hybrid chassis with a single 12AX7 preamp tube, single channel, front dark gray control panel, two inputs (passive and active), five chrome knobs (v, b, m, t, power amp balance control), brite switch, limiter switch, XLR balanced direct line out, power switch, rear panel: effects loop, four standard speaker jacks and one Speakon jack, bridge switch, dark gray casing, mfg. 2008-present.

MSR $650	$500	$300 - 375	$175 - 225	

TX600 – 600W, lightweight bass head-unit, hybrid chassis with a single 12AX7 preamp tube, single channel, front black/orange control panel, two inputs (passive and active), seven black knobs (compressor, g, b, shape, freq., t, MV), mute switch, brite switch, aux. input, headphone jack, rear panel: preamp out, power amp in, XLR direct out with lift/ground switch, two external speaker jacks, cooling fan, power switch, side handle, black casing, 7 lbs., new 2016.

MSR $520	$400	$260 - 300	$130 - 160	

BASS AMPLIFIERS: KICKBACK COMBO SERIES

Kickback 12
courtesy Hartke

Kickback 15
courtesy Hartke

Kickback KB15
courtesy Hartke

KICKBACK 10 – 120W, 1-10 in. aluminum-cone driver, solid-state combo, single channel, shape control, front black control panel, single input, five black knobs (v, shape, l, m, h), direct XLR line out, headphone jack, stand up or "kickback" stance, black carpet covering, black metal grille, 30 lbs., disc. 2005.

	N/A	$200 - 250	$120 - 150	$570

KICKBACK 12 – 120W, 1-12 in. aluminum-cone driver, solid-state combo, single channel, shape control, front black control panel, single input, five black knobs (v, shape, l, m, h), direct XLR line out, headphone jack, stand up or "kickback" stance, black carpet covering, black metal grille, 42 lbs., disc.

	$350	$225 - 275	$135 - 175	$455

KICKBACK 15 – 120W, 1-15 in. aluminum-cone driver, solid-state combo, single channel, shape control, front black control panel, single input, five black knobs (v, shape, l, m, h), direct XLR line out, headphone jack, stand up or "kickback" stance, black carpet covering, black metal grille, 47 lbs., disc.

	$450	$275 - 325	$150 - 200	$585

KICKBACK KB12 – 500W, 1-12 in. aluminum-cone driver, Neodymium magnet, solid-state combo, single channel, shape control, front black control panel, single input, five black knobs (v, shape, b, m, t), direct XLR line out, headphone jack, stand up or "kickback" stance, black covering, black metal grille, 28.2 lbs., mfg. 2015-present.

MSR $550	$450	$295 - 325	$145 - 180	

KICKBACK KB15 – 500W, 1-15 in. aluminum-cone driver, Neodymium magnet, solid-state combo, single channel, shape control, front black control panel, single input, five black knobs (v, shape, b, m, t), direct XLR line out, headphone jack, stand up or "kickback" stance, black covering, black metal grille, 35.6 lbs., mfg. 2015-present.

MSR $670	$550	$350 - 400	$180 - 220	

MSR/NOTES	100%	EXCELLENT	AVERAGE	LAST MSR

BASS AMPLIFIERS: A COMBO SERIES

A-25
courtesy Hartke

A-35
courtesy Hartke

A-70
courtesy Hartke

A-25 – 25W, 1-8 in. aluminum cone speaker, solid-state chassis, front gray control panel, single input, six knobs (v, b, m, t, bright, limiter), RCA inputs, headphone jack, effects loop, black covering, black grille, mfg. 2003-present.

MSR $200	$140	$90 - 105	$45 - 55	

A-35 – 35W, 1-10 in. aluminum cone speaker, solid-state chassis, front gray control panel, single input, six knobs (v, b, m, t, bright, limiter), RCA inputs, headphone jack, effects loop, black covering, black grille, 37.4 lbs., mfg. 2003-present.

MSR $270	$200	$130 - 150	$65 - 80	

A-70 – 70W, 1-12 in. aluminum cone speaker, solid-state chassis, front gray control panel, two inputs, four knobs (v, b, t, limiter), seven-band EQ, RCA inputs, headphone jack, XLR line out, effects loop, tilt-back cabinet design, black covering, black grille, 44 lbs., mfg. 2003-present.

MSR $400	$280	$180 - 210	$90 - 110	

A-100 – 100W, 1-15 in. aluminum cone speaker, solid-state chassis, front gray control panel, two inputs, four knobs (v, b, t, limiter), seven-band EQ, RCA inputs, headphone jack, XLR line out, effects loop, tilt-back cabinet design, black covering, black grille, 50.7 lbs., mfg. 2003-present.

MSR $540	$380	$250 - 300	$150 - 200	

BASS AMPLIFIERS: B COMBO SERIES

The original B Combo series (Models B15, B20, B30, B60, B90, and B120) were replaced in 2004 with upgraded models (except the B120, which was disc. altogether) and a zero was added to each model number (B150, B200, B300, B600, and B900). Hartke also offered a **Bass-Gig Pack** that included a B-15 amp, a Hartke Bass Guitar (red or black finish), guitar strap, gig bag and an instrument cable that last retailed for $430.

B15 – 15W, 1-6.5 in. driver, solid-state combo, single channel, front light brown control panel, two inputs, four black knobs (v, b, m, h), effects loop, line out, headphone jack, black Tolex covering, black grille, mfg. 2002-03.

	N/A	$50 - 75	$35 - 45	$140

B20 – 20W, 1-8 in. driver, solid-state combo, single channel, front light brown control panel, two inputs, four black knobs (v, b, m, h), effects loop, line out, headphone jack, black Tolex covering, black grille, 23.2 lbs, disc. 2003.

	N/A	$70 - 90	$45 - 60	$170

B30 – 30W, 1-10 in. driver, solid-state combo, single channel, shape circuit, front light brown control panel, two inputs, five black knobs (v, shape, b, m, h), effects loop, line out, headphone jack, black Tolex covering, black grille, 32 lbs., disc. 2003.

	N/A	$95 - 120	$60 - 75	$220

B60 – 60W, 1-12 in. driver, solid-state combo, single channel, shape circuit, front light brown control panel, two inputs, five black knobs (v, shape, b, m, h), effects loop, line out, headphone jack, black Tolex covering, black grille, 47 lbs., disc. 2003.

	N/A	$150 - 200	$95 - 120	$370

B90 – 90W, 1-15 in. driver, solid-state combo, single channel, shape circuit, front light brown control panel, two inputs, five black knobs (v, shape, b, m, h), effects loop, line out, headphone jack, black Tolex covering, black grille, 62 lbs., disc. 2003.

	N/A	$225 - 275	$120 - 150	$500

B120 – 120W, 2-12 in. drivers, solid-state combo, single channel, shape circuit, front light brown control panel, two inputs, five black knobs (v, shape, b, m, h), effects loop, line out, headphone jack, casters, black Tolex covering, black grille, 74 lbs., disc. 2003.

	N/A	$275 - 325	$150 - 200	$620

B150 – 15W, 1-6.5 in. driver, solid-state combo, single channel, front black control panel, two inputs, four black knobs (v, b, m, h), effects loop, line out, headphone jack, black Tolex covering, black grille, 23 lb., mfg. 2004-disc.

	$100	$60 - 80	$40 - 50	$130

MSR/NOTES	100%	EXCELLENT	AVERAGE	LAST MSR

B150
courtesy Hartke

B300
courtesy Hartke

B600
courtesy John Beeson/The Music Shoppe

B200 – 20W, 1-8 in. driver, solid-state combo, single channel, front black control panel, two inputs, four black knobs (v, b, m, h), effects loop, line out, headphone jack, black Tolex covering, black grille, 25.5 lbs, mfg. 2004-disc.

	$130	$75 - 100	$50 - 65	$180

B300 – 30W, 1-10 in. driver, solid-state combo, single channel, shape circuit, front black control panel, two inputs, five black knobs (v, shape, b, m, h), effects loop, line out, headphone jack, black Tolex covering, black grille, 32 lbs., mfg. 2003-disc.

	$170	$100 - 125	$60 - 80	$235

B600 – 60W, 1-12 in. driver, solid-state combo, single channel, shape circuit, front black control panel, two inputs, five black knobs (v, shape, b, m, h), effects loop, line out, headphone jack, black Tolex covering, black grille, 39.5 lbs., mfg. 2004-disc.

	$230	$135 - 175	$85 - 110	$320

B900 – 90W, 1-15 in. driver, solid-state combo, single channel, shape circuit, front black control panel, two inputs, five black knobs (v, shape, b, m, h), effects loop, line out, headphone jack, black Tolex covering, black grille, 47.5 lbs., mfg. 2004-disc.

	$280	$150 - 200	$95 - 120	$390

BASS AMPLIFIERS: HYDRIVE COMBO SERIES

HyDrive 112C
courtesy Hartke

HyDrive 210C
courtesy Hartke

HyDrive 5410C
courtesy Hartke

HYDRIVE 112C – 250W, 1-12 in. HyDrive Neodymium hybrid cone driver with a 1 in. titanium compression driver, bass combo, solid-state chassis, single channel, front black/gray control panel, single input, eight knobs (level, compressor, shape freq., harmonics, brite, mix, b, t), seven-band graphic EQ, shape circuit on/off switch, bass attack overdrive circuit on/off switch, power switch, rear panel: standard speaker jack, footswitch jack, XLR direct line out with ground/lift and pre/post EQ switches, effects loop, RCA aux. inputs, kickback cabinet design, black covering, silver metal grille, mfg. 2008-disc.

	$550	$325 - 400	$175 - 225	$730

HYDRIVE 115C – 250W, 1-15 in. HyDrive Neodymium hybrid cone driver with a 1 in. titanium compression driver, bass combo, solid-state chassis, single channel, front black/gray control panel, single input, eight knobs (level, compressor, shape freq., harmonics, brite, mix, b, t), seven-band graphic EQ, shape circuit on/off switch, bass attack overdrive circuit on/off switch, power switch, rear panel: standard speaker jack, footswitch jack, XLR direct line out with ground/lift and pre/post EQ switches, effects loop, RCA aux. inputs, kickback cabinet design, black covering, silver metal grille, mfg. 2008-disc.

	$600	$375 - 450	$225 - 275	$800

HYDRIVE 210C – 250W, 2-10 in. HyDrive Neodymium hybrid cone drivers with a 1 in. titanium compression driver, bass combo, solid-state chassis, single channel, front black/gray control panel, single input, eight knobs (level, compressor, shape freq., harmonics, brite, mix, b, t), seven-band graphic EQ, shape circuit on/off switch, bass attack overdrive circuit on/off switch, power switch, rear panel: standard speaker jack, footswitch jack, XLR direct line out with ground/lift and pre/post EQ switches, effects loop, RCA aux. inputs, kickback cabinet design, black covering, silver metal grille, mfg. 2008-disc.

	$600	$375 - 450	$225 - 275	$800

MSR/NOTES	100%	EXCELLENT	AVERAGE	LAST MSR

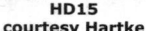

HD15
courtesy Hartke

HD25
courtesy Hartke

HD75
courtesy Hartke

HYDRIVE 5210C – 350W, 2-10 in. HyDrive Neodymium hybrid cone drivers with a 1 in. titanium high-freq. compression driver, hybrid chassis with a single 12AX7 preamp tube, single channel, front dark gray control panel, two inputs (passive and active), four chrome knobs (v, b, m, t), brite switch, limiter switch, XLR balanced direct line out, power switch, rear panel: effects loop, four standard speaker jacks, sealed enclosure, recessed metal handles, removable casters, black vinyl covering, perforated metal speaker grille, mfg. 2009-disc.

| MSR $910 | $650 | $425 - 500 | $250 - 300 | |

HYDRIVE 5410C – 500W, 4-10 in. HyDrive Neodymium hybrid cone drivers with a 1 in. titanium high-freq. compression driver, hybrid chassis with a single 12AX7 preamp tube, single channel, front dark gray control panel, two inputs (passive and active), four chrome knobs (v, b, m, t), brite switch, limiter switch, XLR balanced direct line out, power switch, rear panel: effects loop, four standard speaker jacks, sealed enclosure, recessed metal handles, removable casters, black vinyl covering, perforated metal speaker grille, mfg. 2009-disc.

| | $800 | $525 - 600 | $300 - 375 | $1,120 |

HD15 – 15W, 1-6.5 in. speaker, bass combo, solid-state chassis, single channel, top black control panel, single input, four knobs (v, b, m, t), three-band EQ, aux. input, headphone jack, power switch, top handle, black covering, black metal grille, 13.44 lbs., mfg. 2015-present.

| MSR $120 | $90 | $60 - 70 | $30 - 35 | |

HD25 – 25W, 1-8 in. speaker, bass combo, solid-state chassis, single channel, top black control panel, single input, four knobs (v, b, m, t), three-band EQ, aux. input, headphone jack, power switch, top handle, black covering, black metal grille, 28 lbs., mfg. 2014-present.

| MSR $165 | $130 | $85 - 100 | $40 - 50 | |

HD50 – 50W, 1-10 in. speaker, bass combo, solid-state chassis, single channel, top black control panel, single input, four knobs (v, b, m, t), three-band EQ, aux. input, headphone jack, power switch, top handle, black covering, black metal grille, 38 lbs., mfg. 2014-present.

| MSR $255 | $200 | $130 - 150 | $65 - 80 | |

HD75 – 75W, 1-12 in. speaker with 1 in. tweeter, bass combo, solid-state chassis, single channel, top black control panel, single input, four knobs (v, b, m, t), seven-band graphic EQ, aux. input, headphone jack, effects loop, power switch, top handle, black covering, black metal grille, 52 lbs., mfg. 2014-present.

| MSR $325 | $250 | $165 - 190 | $80 - 100 | |

HD150 – 150W, 1-15 in. speaker with 1 in. tweeter, bass combo, solid-state chassis, single channel, top black control panel, single input, four knobs (v, b, m, t), seven-band graphic EQ, aux. input, headphone jack, effects loop, XLR direct out jack, power switch, side handles, casters, black covering, black metal grille, 66 lbs., mfg. 2014-present.

| MSR $490 | $375 | $245 - 285 | $125 - 150 | |

BASS AMPLIFIERS: MISC. COMBO SERIES

HA1410 – 140W, 2-10 in. aluminum-cone drivers, solid-state chassis, single channel, front black control panel, single input, five black knobs (v, l, l/m, l/h, h), contour button, compression button, effects loop headphone jack, black carpet covering, black metal grille, 59 lbs., disc. 2002.

| | N/A | $325 - 400 | $200 - 250 | $700 |

HA1415 – 140W, 1-15 in. aluminum-cone driver, solid-state chassis, single channel, front black control panel, single input, five black knobs (v, l, l/m, l/h, h), contour button, compression button, effects loop headphone jack, black carpet covering, black metal grille, 59 lbs., disc. 2002.

| | N/A | $300 - 375 | $175 - 225 | $650 |

HA2115 – 200W, 1-15 in. aluminum-cone driver, solid-state and tube preamp (selectable), front black control panel, two inputs (passive/active), six black and silver knobs (pre-amp A & B, compression, contour low and high pass, MV) 10-band equalizer, black metal covering, 70 lbs., disc. 2002.

| | N/A | $425 - 500 | $275 - 325 | $950 |

MSR/NOTES	100%	EXCELLENT	AVERAGE	LAST MSR

VX3500
courtesy Hartke

AK410 Speaker Cabinet
courtesy Hartke

VX215
courtesy Hartke

HA2155 – 200W, 1-15 in. aluminum-cone driver & 1-5 in. high-frequency speaker, solid-state and tube preamp (selectable), front black control panel, two inputs (passive/active), six black and silver knobs (pre-amp A & B, compression, contour low and high pass, MV) 10-band equalizer, black metal covering, 76 lbs., disc. 2002.

	N/A	$550 - 650	$350 - 425	$1,250

VX2510 – 250W (HA2500 head), 2-10 in. paper cone drivers, high-frequency horn, solid-state and tube preamp (selectable), front black control panel, two inputs (passive/active), six black and silver knobs (pre-amp A & B, compression, contour low and high pass, MV) 10-band equalizer, black metal covering, 74.8 lbs., mfg. 2005-09.

	$600	$375 - 450	$225 - 275	$800

VX2515 – 250W (HA2500 head), 1-15 in. paper cone drivers, high-frequency horn, solid-state and tube preamp (selectable), front black control panel, two inputs (passive/active), six black and silver knobs (pre-amp A & B, compression, contour low and high pass, MV) 10-band equalizer, black metal covering, 76.6 lbs., mfg. 2005-09.

	$600	$375 - 450	$225 - 275	$800

VX3500 – 350W (HA3500 head), 4-10 in. aluminum-cone drivers, solid-state and tube preamp (selectable), front black control panel, two inputs (passive/active), six black and silver knobs (pre-amp A & B, compression, contour low and high pass, MV) 10-band equalizer, black metal covering, mfg. 2002-present.

MSR $1,000	$750	$475 - 550	$245 - 300	

BASS SPEAKER CABINETS: AK SERIES

AK115 SPEAKER CABINET – 300W, 1-15 in. paper cone driver with a 1 in. titanium compression driver, 8 ohm impedance, parallel Speakon and standard 1/4 in. speaker inputs, high-freq. attenuation switch, specially-tuned ported cabinet design, recessed side handles, black covering, black cloth grille with white piping, removable casters, 24 in. wide, 24 in. tall, 15 in. deep, mfg. 2009-present.

MSR $520	$400	$250 - 300	$135 - 175	

AK410 SPEAKER CABINET – 400W, 4-10 in. paper cone driver with a 1 in. titanium compression driver, 8 ohm impedance, parallel Speakon and standard 1/4 in. speaker inputs, high-freq. attenuation switch, dual-chambered sealed cabinet design, recessed side handles, black covering, black cloth grille with white piping, removable casters, 24 in. wide, 24 in. tall, 15 in. deep, mfg. 2009-present.

MSR $650	$500	$300 - 375	$175 - 225	

BASS SPEAKER CABINETS: VX SERIES

VX115 – 300W, 1-15 in. paper cone driver, high-freq. horn, 8 ohm impedance, 3/4 in. plywood construction, recessed handles, black carpet covering, black metal grille, 69 lbs., current mfg.

MSR $410	$300	$195 - 225	$100 - 120	

VX1508 – 350W, 1-15 in. and 2-8 in. paper cone drivers, high-freq. horn, 8 ohm impedance, 3/4 in. plywood construction, recessed handles, black carpet covering, black metal grille, 68 lbs., mfg. 2003-05.

	N/A	$250 - 300	$135 - 175	$585

VX210 – 200W, 2-10 in. paper cone drivers, high-freq. horn, 8 ohm impedance, 3/4 in. plywood construction, recessed handles, black carpet covering, black metal grille, 48 lbs., mfg. 2005-08.

	$200	$130 - 160	$75 - 100	$290

VX215 – 500W, 2-15 in. paper cone drivers, high-freq. horn, 4 ohm impedance, 3/4 in. plywood construction, recessed handles, black carpet covering, black metal grille, 83 lbs., mfg. 2003-08.

	$300	$180 - 230	$100 - 130	$420

MSR/NOTES	100%	EXCELLENT	AVERAGE	LAST MSR

410XL
courtesy Hartke

HyDrive 112
courtesy Hartke

HyDrive 210
courtesy Hartke

VX410/VX410A – 400W, 4-10 in. paper cone drivers, high-freq. horn, 8 ohm impedance, straight (VX410) or angled (VX410A, available 2002-05) cabinet, 3/4 in. plywood construction, recessed handles, black carpet covering, black metal grille, 70 lbs., mfg. 2002-08, reintroduced-present.

MSR $475	$350	$230 - 265	$115 - 140	

VX810 – 800W, 8-10 in. paper cone drivers, high-freq. horn, 4 ohm impedance, 3/4 in. plywood construction, recessed handles, rear-mounted casters, black carpet covering, black metal grille, 146 lbs., mfg. 2003-08.

	$500	$300 - 350	$175 - 225	$660

BASS SPEAKER CABINETS: XL SERIES

115XL – 200W, 1-15 in. aluminum cone driver, 8 ohm impedance, 3/4 in. plywood construction, recessed side handles, black carpet covering, black metal grille, 63 lbs., current mfg.

MSR $460	$350	$230 - 265	$115 - 140	

210XL – 200W, 2-10 in. aluminum cone driver, 8 ohm impedance, 3/4 in. plywood construction, recessed side handles, black carpet covering, black metal grille, 46 lbs., current mfg.

MSR $330	$250	$165 - 190	$80 - 100	

215XL – 400W, 2-15 in. aluminum cone driver, 4 ohm impedance, 3/4 in. plywood construction, recessed side handles, black carpet covering, black metal grille, 110 lbs., disc. 2008.

	$550	$350 - 425	$225 - 275	$740

410XL – 400W, 4-10 in. aluminum cone driver, 8 ohm impedance, 3/4 in. plywood construction, recessed side handles, black carpet covering, black metal grille, 88 lbs., current mfg.

MSR $525	$400	$260 - 300	$130 - 160	

810XL – 800W, 8-10 in. aluminum cone driver, 4 ohm impedance, 3/4 in. plywood construction, recessed side handles, rear-mounted casters, black carpet covering, black metal grille, 145 lbs., disc. 2009.

	$795	$500 - 600	$300 - 375	$1,040

2.5XL – 200W, 2-10 in. aluminum cone drivers and 1-5 in. high-freq. speaker, 8 ohm impedance, 3/4 in. plywood construction, recessed side handles, black carpet covering, black metal grille, 66 lbs., mfg. 1994-2008.

	$330	$200 - 250	$120 - 150	$440

4.5XL – 400W, 4-10 in. aluminum cone drivers and 1-5 in. high-freq. speaker, 8 ohm impedance, 3/4 in. plywood construction, recessed side handles, black carpet covering, black metal grille, 99 lbs., mfg. 1994-present.

MSR $700	$550	$350 - 400	$180 - 220	

BASS SPEAKER CABINETS: HYDRIVE SERIES (HX MODELS)

HYDRIVE 112 (HX112) – 300W, 1-12 in. HyDrive Neodymium hybrid cone driver with a 1 in. titanium compression driver, switchable 4 or 8 ohm impedance, parallel Speakon and standard 1/4 in. speaker inputs, high-freq. attenuation switch, specially-tuned ported cabinet design, black covering, silver metal grille, removable casters, 19 in. wide, 15 in. tall, 16 in. deep, 30.5 lbs., mfg. 2010-present.

MSR $510	$400	$260 - 300	$130 - 160	

HYDRIVE 115 (HX115) – 500W, 1-15 in. HyDrive Neodymium hybrid cone driver with a 1 in. titanium compression driver, 8 ohm impedance, parallel Speakon and standard 1/4 in. speaker inputs, high-freq. attenuation switch, specially-tuned ported cabinet design, black covering, silver metal grille, removable casters, 24 in. wide, 24 in. tall, 15 in. deep, 51 lbs., mfg. 2008-present.

MSR $780	$600	$400 - 450	$195 - 240	

MSR/NOTES	100%	EXCELLENT	AVERAGE	LAST MSR

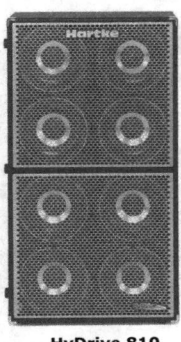

HyDrive 810
courtesy Hartke

Pro 2200
courtesy Hartke

210TP
courtesy Hartke

HYDRIVE 210 (HX210) – 500W, 2-10 in. HyDrive Neodymium hybrid cone driverS with a 1 in. titanium compression driver, 8 ohm impedance, parallel Speakon and standard 1/4 in. speaker inputs, dual-chamber sealed cabinet design, black covering, silver metal grille, removable casters, 49 lbs., mfg. 2015-present.

| MSR $650 | $500 | $325 - 375 | $165 - 200 | |

HYDRIVE 410 (HX410) – 1000W, 4-10 in. HyDrive Neodymium hybrid cone driver with a 1 in. titanium compression driver, 8 ohm impedance, parallel Speakon and standard 1/4 in. speaker inputs, high-freq. attenuation switch, dual-chamber sealed cabinet design, black covering, silver metal grille, removable casters, 24 in. wide, 24 in. tall, 15 in. deep, 68 lbs., mfg. 2008-present.

| MSR $950 | $700 | $450 - 525 | $230 - 280 | |

HYDRIVE 810 (HX810) – 2000W, 8-10 in. HyDrive Neodymium hybrid cone driver with a 1 in. titanium compression driver, 4 ohm impedance, parallel Speakon and standard 1/4 in. speaker inputs, high-freq. attenuation switch, quad-chamber sealed cabinet design, black covering, silver metal grille, large handle, steel casters, and kickplate for tilt-back transportation, 26 in. wide, 47.25 in. tall, 15.75 in. deep, 135 lbs., mfg. 2008-present.

| MSR $1,680 | $1,200 | $775 - 900 | $400 - 475 | |

BASS SPEAKER CABINETS: PROFESSIONAL SERIES

PRO 1800 – 600W, 1-18 in. paper cone driver, 4 ohm impedance, tuned four-port enclosure, 3/4 in. plywood construction, grab bar, casters, black carpet covering, black metal grille, 94 lbs., disc. 2008.

| | $440 | $290 - 340 | $175 - 225 | $600 |

PRO 2100 – 200W, 2-10 in. paper cone drivers, compression horn and driver, 4 ohm impedance, tuned dual-port enclosure, 3/4 in. plywood construction, recessed side handles, casters, angled cabinet, black carpet covering, black metal grille, 60.5 lbs., mfg. 2002-08.

| | $390 | $250 - 300 | $150 - 200 | $520 |

PRO 2200 – 300W, 2-12 in. paper cone drivers, compression horn and driver, 4 ohm impedance, tuned dual-port enclosure, 3/4 in. plywood construction, recessed side handles, casters, angled cabinet, black carpet covering, black metal grille, 74.3 lbs., mfg. 2002-08.

| | $440 | $275 - 325 | $175 - 225 | $590 |

PRO 4200 – 400W, 4-10 in. paper cone drivers, 1-2 in. titanium high-freq. driver, horn, 4 ohm impedance, tuned dual-port enclosure, 3/4 in. plywood construction, recessed side handles, black carpet covering, black metal grille, 117 lbs., disc. 2008.

| | $600 | $375 - 450 | $225 - 275 | $810 |

BASS SPEAKER CABINETS: TRANSPORTER SERIES

115TP – 150W, 1-15 in. aluminum cone driver, 8 ohm impedance, tuned dual-vent ported enclosure, 3/4 in. plywood construction, recessed side handles, black carpet covering, black metal grille, 51 lbs., disc. 2008.

| | $230 | $140 - 180 | $80 - 110 | $320 |

210TP – 150W, 2-10 in. aluminum cone drivers, 8 ohm impedance, tuned dual-vent ported enclosure, 3/4 in. plywood construction, recessed side handles, black carpet covering, black metal grille, 36 lbs., disc. 2008.

| | $150 | $85 - 110 | $50 - 70 | $200 |

410TP – 300W, 4-10 in. aluminum cone drivers, 8 ohm impedance, tuned dual-vent ported enclosure, 3/4 in. plywood construction, recessed side handles, black carpet covering, black metal grille, 65 lbs., disc. 2008.

| | $250 | $150 - 190 | $90 - 120 | $340 |

MSR/NOTES	100%	EXCELLENT	AVERAGE	LAST MSR

G15
courtesy Hartke

GT-100C Combo
courtesy Hartke

KM60
courtesy Hartke

ELECTRIC SS AMPLIFIERS: G SERIES

G10 – 10W, 6.5 in. speaker, guitar combo, solid-state chassis, single channel, front black control panel, single input, four knobs (crunch, v, b, t), headphone jack, black covering, gray grille, 9 lbs., mfg. 2006-disc.

	$60	$30 - 45	$15 - 25	$84

G15 – 15W, 1-8 in. speaker, guitar combo, solid-state chassis, two channels, front black control panel, single input, five knobs (v1, crunch, v2, b, t), CD input, headphone jack, optional footswitch, black covering, gray grille, 15 lbs., mfg. 2006-disc.

	$75	$40 - 60	$20 - 30	$125

* G15R – similar to the G15, except has a reverb circuit with reverb control for a total of six knobs, 17 lbs., mfg. summer 2006-disc.

	$90	$50 - 70	$30 - 40	$140

G30R – 30W, 1-12 in. speaker, guitar combo, solid-state chassis, two channels, reverb, front black control panel, single input, seven knobs (v1, crunch, v2, b, p, t, r), CD input, headphone jack, optional footswitch, black covering, gray grille, 26 lbs., mfg. summer 2006-disc.

	$150	$95 - 120	$60 - 75	$210

ELECTRIC SS AMPLIFIERS: GT SERIES

GT-60 – 60W, head-unit configuration, hybrid chassis, preamp: 12AX7, power: solid-state, two channels, reverb, front black control panel, single input, 10 knobs, effects loop, headphone jack, black covering, black grille, 24 lbs., mfg. 2006-08.

	$150	$95 - 120	$60 - 75	$210

* GT-60C Combo – similar to the GT-60 Head, except in combo configuration with 1-12 in. speaker, 39 lbs., mfg. 2004-08.

	$200	$130 - 160	$75 - 100	$280

* GT-60 Piggyback – piggyback unit consisting of the GT-60 Head and a mini 4-8 in. speaker cabinet, 67 lbs., mfg. 2004-08.

	$300	$175 - 225	$110 - 140	$420

GT-100 – 100W, head-unit only, hybrid chassis, preamp: 12AX7, power: solid-state, two channels, reverb, front black control panel, single input, 10 knobs, effects loop, headphone jack, black covering, black grille, 32 lbs., mfg. 2004-08.

	$200	$130 - 160	$75 - 100	$280

* GT-100C Combo – similar to the GT-100, except in combo form with 2-12 in. speakers, 59 lbs., mfg. 2004-08.

	$300	$175 - 225	$110 - 140	$420

GH410/GH410A SPEAKER CABINET – 120W mono (60W stereo), 4-10 in. speakers, straight (GH410) or angled (GH410A) cabinet, 3/4 in. plywood construction, recessed side handles, casters, black covering, gray grille, 46 lbs., mfg. 2003-05.

	N/A	$135 - 175	$85 - 110	$330

GH412/GH412A SPEAKER CABINET – 260W mono (130W stereo), 4-12 in. speakers, straight (GH412) or angled (GH412A) cabinet, 3/4 in. plywood construction, recessed side handles, casters, black covering, gray grille, 77 lbs., mfg. 2003-08.

	$250	$160 - 200	$100 - 130	$360

KEYBOARD AMPLIFIERS: KM SERIES

KM60 – 60W, 1-10 in. aluminum cone speaker, ceramic tweeter, keyboard combo, solid-state chassis, four channels, front gray control panel, six inputs (Ch. 1 mic on front only, four mono inputs and stereo aux. input on back), six knobs (Aux. in level, v1, v2, v3, v4, MV), seven-band graphic EQ, XLR balanced out, headphone jack, black covering, black metal grille, 43 lbs., mfg. 2006-disc.

	$300	$170 - 210	$110 - 140	$380

MSR/NOTES	100%	EXCELLENT	AVERAGE	LAST MSR

KM100 – 100W, 1-12 in. aluminum cone speaker, 1-1 in. titanium compression driver, keyboard combo, solid-state chassis, four channels, front gray control panel, six inputs (Ch. 1 mic on front only, four mono inputs and stereo aux. input on back), six knobs (Aux. in level, v1, v2, v3, v4, MV), seven-band graphic EQ, XLR balanced out, headphone jack, black covering, black metal grille, 59 lbs., mfg. 2006-disc.

$400	$225 - 275	$140 - 175		$500

KM200 – 200W, 1-15 in. aluminum cone speaker, 1-1 in. titanium compression driver, keyboard stereo combo, solid-state chassis, four channels, front/top gray control panel, nine inputs (two per channel, one mic input), nine knobs (v1, b1, t1, v2, v3, v4, headphone v, line out v, MV), seven-band graphic EQ, XLR balanced out, headphone jack, casters, tilt-back cabinet design, black covering, black metal grille, 75 lbs., mfg. 2004-disc.

$500	$300 - 350	$175 - 225		$640

HAYDEN

Amplifiers currently produced in Essex, England. Distributed in the U.S. by Musiquip, Inc. in Dorval, Quebec, Canada since mid-2011. Previously distributed by EMD Music in Lavergne, TN. Hayden is a division of Ashdown Design and Marketing Ltd.

The Hayden trademark was created by Ashdown engineering to offer a guitar-only amplifier line that compliments Ashdown's bass and acoustic amps. Ashdown used to offer the Peacemaker Series of guitar amplifiers, but these amplifiers are now built under the Hayden trademark. Hayden amps are all hand-built with high-quality components in England. For more information, visit Hayden's website.

CONTACT INFORMATION
HAYDEN
Ashdown Design & Marketing Ltd.
The Old Maltings, Hall Road, Heybridge
Maldon, Essex CM9 4NJ England
Phone No.: 01621 856010
www.haydenamps.com
info@haydenamps.com

U.S. Distributor: Musiquip Inc.
325 Bouchard Blvd.
Dorval, Quebec H9S 1A9 Canada
Phone No.: 615-218-0459
Phone No.: 866-832-8679
www.musiquip.com
info@musiquip.com

ELECTRIC TUBE AMPLIFIERS

Hayden's Peacemaker Series includes the **Peacemaker 40 Combo** (MSR $1,220), **Peacemaker 60 Head** (MSR $1,220), and the **Peacemaker 60 Combo** (MSR $1,350). The **Peacemaker 412A/412F** speaker cabinet (MSR $620) is available in an angled or flat front.

Hayden also produces a variety of hand-wired tube amplifiers. The **Petite Blonde/Petite 2** (MSR $1,180) features 2W, 1-10 in. Celestion speaker, and one 6V6 power tube. The **Essex Blonde 8** (disc.) has 8W, 1-12 in. speaker, and can be powered by a variety of power tubes. The **Petite Blonde/Petite 5** (MSR $2,050) has 5W power with 1-12 in. speaker, and can be switched from EL84 to 6V6 tubes. The **Essex Blonde 15** (disc.) has 15W, 1-12 in. speaker, and can be powered by a variety of power tubes. The Buxom Blonde (disc.) has 100W power and is powered by 4 X EL34 tubes. The **Cotton Club Blues** (disc.) features 30W, 1-12 in. speaker and can be powered by either 4 X 6L6 or 4 X 6V6 tubes. The **Cotton Club 7/15** (MSR $2,600) can be switched between 7W and 15W power and has 1-12 in. speaker and two channels. The **Cotton Club 15/30** (MSR $3,700) can be switched between 15W and 30W power and has 2-12 in. speakers and two channels. The **Speakeasy 8-28** (disc.) can be switched between 8W and 28W, has 2-12 in. speakers, and can be powered by a variety of power tubes. The **Speakeasy 50** is available as a head-unit (MSR $2,760) and a 1-12 in. combo (MSR $3,400) and features 50W power from 2 X EL34 tubes and two independent channels. The **Classic Lead 80** (MSR $3,100) is an 80W head driven by EL34 power tubes.

Speaker cabinets include the 2-12 cabinet (MSR $1,060) and the 4-12 cabinet (MSR $1,850).

HAYNES

Amplifiers previously built in Westbury, NY during the late 1950s and early 1960s.

Haynes amplifiers were built by the Amplifier Corporation of America (ACA) during the late 1950s and early 1960s. They produced one notable model - the **Jazz King 212 Combo**. This amp was solid-state in construction and featured reverb, phaser, tremolo, and two channels. In 1964, Unicord bought ACA and started building Univox-branded amplifiers. The Haynes trademark was discontinued at this same time. It's possible that Haynes and Univox may have some similarities in construction, but there is no evidence supporting that this ever happened. Any further information can be submitted directly to Blue Book Publications.

HEADSTRONG AMPLIFIERS

Amplifiers currently built in Asheville, NC since 2002. Distributed by Headstrong Amplifiers.

CONTACT INFORMATION
HEADSTRONG AMPLIFIERS
22 Herron Ave.
Asheville, NC 28806
Phone No.: 510-898-8123
www.headstrongamps.com
sales@headstrongamps.com

Wayne Jones and Jessica Winterbottom founded Headstrong Amplifiers in 2002. They produce tube head amps, combos, and speaker cabinets in a variety of configurations based on Fender blackface and brownface designs and cosmetics. Headstrong's first amps were based on Fender's tweed designs, and they produced these in 2002 and 2003. In 2004, they developed their first blackface replica amps with the Lil' King reverb which was the first replica based on a 1964 blackface Fender Princeton Reverb. Later in 2004, Headstrong introduced their second blackface design called the Royal Reverb based on the blackface Deluxe Reverb. The Prima Series was introduced. In mid-2006, Headstrong introduced their first original designs as part of the Prima Series, and the first model introduced was the Prima 30. In 2007, Headstrong introduced the first hand-wired replica of the 1963 brownface Fender Vibroverb. In 2008, Headstrong introduced the Lil King S and Wayne's brother Jesse took over cabinet production. All amps have hand-wired chassis and can be biased to use various power tubes. Their cabinets feature solid pine and finger joints and they have a unique look to them with diagonal slats for the grille openings. Amps start at $1,525. For more information, visit Headstrong's website or contact them directly.

HENRIKSEN AMPLIFIERS

Amplifiers currently produced in Arvada, CO. Previously produced in Golden, CO beginning in 2006.

Peter Henriksen started Henriksen Data Systems, Inc. in 1980 as a telecommunication and data processing equipment manufacturer, but in 2006, they began building guitar amplifiers full-time. Henriksen's **JazzAmp** is specifically voiced to be used with archtop jazz guitars, and are advertised as having pure and true reproduction of the guitar and guitarist's tone. The JazzAmp is available as a head-unit and several combos; prices start at $699 for the head and $899 for the combo. Henriksen also produces a **BluesAmp** that utilizes the same chassis as the JazzAmp but has a Ragin Cajun speaker with a tweeter suited for blues playing. Speaker cabinets are also available. For more information, visit their website or contact them directly.

CONTACT INFORMATION
HENRIKSEN AMPLIFIERS
6260 W. 52nd Ave.
Unit 109
Arvada, CO 80002
Phone No.: 303-674-0842
Fax No.: 303-674-0440
henriksenamplifiers.com
info@henriksenamplifiers.com

HERITAGE AMPLIFICATION

Amplifiers previously produced by the MacClane Corporation in Brentwood, TN between 2004 and 2008.

Heritage Amplifiers of Tennessee was formed by Malcolm MacDonald and Lane Zastrow in January, 2004. Lane Zastrow has experience from working with Mike Holland at Holland Amplifiers, and in January 2004, Zastrow leased the former Holland amplifier facility and turned it into a dedicated Heritage amplifier facility. Heritage actually used the same address and phone number as Holland Amplifiers.

Heritage Guitars and Heritage amplifiers are two different companies; however there is some affiliation between the two names. When Heritage was building amplifiers, they were linked to each others' websites, and they were marketed together at shows, etc. Heritage Amplifiers of Tennessee was completely owned by Maclane, which is different from Heritage Guitars.

All Heritage amplifiers are hand-wired, point-to-point, and they used custom-made transformers. Kenny Burrell has a signature amplifier as well. Heritage also had a Cabinet Works division that built boutique and reproduction cabinets for many popular manufacturers. Heritage stopped producing amplifiers in 2008.

ELECTRIC TUBE AMPLIFIERS

The **Kenny Burrell** model features 40W output and is available as a head-unit (disc. 2008, last MSR was $2,500), 1-12 in. speaker combo (MSR $2,600), 1-15 in. speaker combo (disc. 2008, last MSR was $2,800) or 2-10 in. (disc. 2005, last MSR was $2,495). This is the amp Kenny endorses and plays. The **Kenny Burrell Freedom** (previously the **KB30**) model is lightweight in design at 40 lbs., and comes in a head-unit (disc. 2008, last MSR was $2,250) and a 1-12 in. speaker combo (disc. 2008, last MSR was $2,400). The **Patriot 50** has 45W from either 2 X 6L6 or 2 X EL34 tubes and is available as a head-unit (disc. 2008, last MSR was $2,500), 1-12 in. speaker combo (disc. 2005, last MSR $2,195), or a 2-12 in. speaker combo (disc. 2008, last MSR was 2,750). The **Liberty** is Heritage's version of a classic American amp. It has 50W, reverb, and is available as a head-unit (disc. 2008, last MSR was $2,500), 1-15 in. speaker combo (disc. 2008, last MSR was $2,800), or a head and speaker cabinet half-stack (disc. 2008, last MSR was $3,220). The **Revolution 34** is based off of British amplifiers with EL34 power tubes. This model comes as a head (disc. 2005, last MSR was $2,195) or a head and 2-12 in. speaker cabinet (disc. 2005, last MSR was $2,595). The **Colonial** is based on a classic 50W design that can be used with 6L6 or EL34 tubes for either a tweed or plexi sound respectively. This amp is available as a head (disc. 2008, last MSR was $2,600) or a head and speaker cabinet piggyback (disc. 2008, last MSR was $3,460). The **Briton** is a 30W English-style amp with 4 X EL84 tubes and is available as a 1-12 in. speaker combo (disc. 2008, last MSR was $3,400). The **Briton II** is similar to the Briton but features a second channel and a master volume control instead of reverb. This model is available as a head (disc. 2008, last MSR was $2,600) or a head and speaker cabinet piggyback (disc. 2008, last MSR was $3,980). The **Victory** features 22W from 2 X 6V6 tubes and features two channels in the head version (disc. 2008, last MSR was $2,250) and one channel and a reverb circuit in the 1-12 in. speaker combo (disc. 2008, last MSR was $2,400). A head and speaker cabinet piggyback (disc. 2008, last MSR was $2,840) was also available.

HILGEN

Amplifiers previously produced in Hillside, NJ during the 1960s.

Hilgen amplifiers were built by Hilgen Manufacturing in Hillside, NJ. It is possible that these amps were built alongside or were similar to Ampeg and Sano amps of the same era. Hilgen produced mainly low to mid-wattage tube models with simple features. Models were numbered starting with the letter B for bass or T for guitar, the number 25, and followed in a type of numerical sequence. Known models include the **B2501**, **B2503**, **T2512**, and **T2513**. Any further information can be submitted directly to Blue Book Publications.

HIWATT

Amplifiers previously produced in England since 1964. The Bulldog series is produced in Asia. Distributed in the U.S. by Musical Distributors Group, LLC in Boonton, NJ. Previously distributed by Hiwatt Amplification in Chatsworth, CA and previously located in North Hollywood, CA.

The Hiwatt company was founded in 1964 by Dave Reeves in England. Harry Joyce was commissioned by Reeves to build military-spec chassis in Hiwatt amps. Hiwatt amps from the 1960s and 1970s are known for being very loud, but very well built. Pete Townshend was an early endorser (and early

CONTACT INFORMATION
HIWATT
HIWATT U.S. Office
21020 Superior St.
Chatsworth, CA 91311
Phone No.: 800-318-8599
Fax No.: 818-885-6797
www.hiwatt.com
info@hiwatt.com

U.S. Distributor: Musical Distributors Group
9 Mars Court, Suite C-3
Boonton, NJ 07005
Phone No.: 973-335-7888
Phone No.: 866-632-8346
Fax No.: 973-335-7779
www.musicaldistributors.com
sales@musicaldistributors.com

MSR/NOTES	100%	EXCELLENT	AVERAGE	LAST MSR

destroyer) of Hiwatt amps. 50W and 100W head models were first introduced with other wattages and combos to follow. Hiwatt didn't change much in their design or product line until Reeves died in 1981. Eric Dixon took over the company and started redesigning amps trying to save some costs along the way. One problem Hiwatt players encountered was the preamp and power tubes were mounted directly to the circuit board. The vibration and heat sometimes caused the circuit board to warp among other problems. The second generation of Hiwatt amps introduced in 1981 are noted for not being nearly as dependable as the earlier ones. Hiwatt discontinued their traditional line of amps by the late 1980s and replaced them with the new 2000 Series. These amps were produced through the early to mid-1990s with little fanfare. In the mid-1990s, Hiwatt was purchased by the Fernandes corporation of North Hollywood, CA (currently Chatsworth, CA). Starting in 1995, Hiwatt and Fernandes actually shared catalogs as well as booth space at shows. Fernandes decided to reissue models from Hiwatt's heyday in the 1960s and 1970s that were exact replications. Fernandes was also producing amps at this time, but by the end of the 1990s, Fernandes had halted all production on amplifiers and used Hiwatt for their amplifiers. In the 2000s, Hiwatt expanded their line to include everything from the entry level solid-state Bulldog Series to their hand-wired tube amps. By 2005, Hiwatt had a full line of reproduction amps based on 1970s models. For more information, visit Hiwatt's website or contact them directly. Early information courtesy: Aspen Pittman, *The Tube Amp Book*.

ELECTRIC TUBE AMPLIFIERS: EARLY HEAD UNITS

DR103 (CUSTOM HIWATT 100) – 100W, head-unit configuration, tube chassis, preamp: 3 X ECC83/12AX7, 1 X ECC81/12AT7, power: 4 X EL34/KT77, rectifier: 3 X BYX94, two channels, front black control panel, two or four inputs, seven black knobs (Norm v, Brilliant v, b, t, m, p, MV), black covering with white piping, mfg. mid-1960s-mid-1980s.

 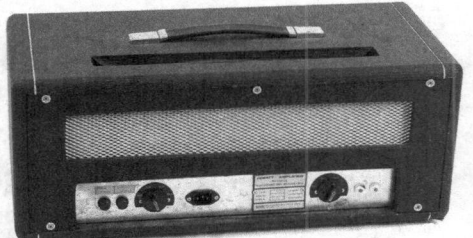

courtesy solidbodyguitar.com, Inc.　　　　courtesy solidbodyguitar.com, Inc.

1964-1969	N/A	$2,000 - 2,500	$1,100 - 1,400
1970-1981	N/A	$1,800 - 2,200	$1,000 - 1,250
1980S	N/A	$1,400 - 1,600	$850 - 1,000

DR504 (CUSTOM HIWATT 50) – 50W, head-unit only, all-tube chassis, preamp: 4 X ECC83/12AX7, power: 2 X EL34, rectifier: 3 X BYX94, two channels, front black control panel, two or four inputs (normal and bright), seven black knobs (norm v, brilliant v, b, t, m, p, MV), black covering with white piping, mfg. mid 1960s-mid 1980s.

courtesy solidbodyguitar.com, Inc.　　　　courtesy solidbodyguitar.com, Inc.

1964-1969	N/A	$2,000 - 2,500	$900 - 1,100
1970-1981	N/A	$1,400 - 1,700	$800 - 950
1980S	N/A	$1,200 - 1,450	$700 - 850

OL103 (HIWATT LEAD 100) – 100W, head-unit only, all-tube chassis, preamp: 4 X ECC83/12AX7, power: 4 X EL34/KT77, rectifier: 3 X BY127, two channels, front black control panel, two inputs (normal and bright), eight black knobs (OD, norm v, bright, b, m, t, p, MV), black covering with white piping, mfg. 1980s.

	N/A	$1,200 - 1,500	$700 - 850

OL504 (HIWATT LEAD 50) – 50W, head-unit only, all-tube chassis, preamp: 4 X ECC83/12AX7, power: 2 X EL34/KT77, rectifier: 3 X BY127, two channels, front black control panel, two inputs (normal and bright), eight black knobs (OD, norm v, bright, b, m, t, p, MV), black covering with white piping, mfg. 1980s.

	N/A	$1,000 - 1,200	$600 - 700

MSR/NOTES	100%	EXCELLENT	AVERAGE	LAST MSR

S100 MAXWATT – 100W, head-unit only, all-tube chassis, preamp: 5 X ECC83/12AX7, power: 4 X EL34/KT77, rectifier: 5 X BY127, two channels, front black control panel, four inputs (two normal and two bright), seven black knobs, black covering with white piping, mfg. 1980s.

	N/A	$1,200 - 1,500	$800 - 1,000	

DR201 (HIWATT 200) – 200W, head-unit configuration, tube chassis, preamp: 3 X ECC83/12AX7, 1 X ECC81/12AT7, power: 6 X EL34/KT77, solid-state rectifier, two channels, front black control panel, two inputs, seven black knobs (Norm v, Brilliant v, b, t, m, p, MV), black covering with white piping, mfg. late 1960s-mid-1980s.

1960S-1981	N/A	$2,000 - 2,500	$1,200 - 1,500	
1980S	N/A	$1,400 - 1,700	$850 - 1,000	

DR405 (HIWATT 400) – 400W, head-unit configuration, tube chassis, preamp: 4 X ECC83/12AX7, 1 X ECC81/12AT7, power: 8 X KT88, solid-state rectifier, two channels, front black control panel, two inputs, seven black knobs (Norm v, Brilliant v, b, t, m, p, MV), black covering with white piping, mfg. late 1960s-mid-1980s.

1960S-1981	N/A	$2,000 - 2,500	$1,200 - 1,500	
1980S	N/A	$1,750 - 2,250	$1,250 - 1,500	

ELECTRIC TUBE AMPLIFIERS: EARLY COMBO UNITS

LEAD HIWATT 30 – 30W, 1-12 in. speaker, guitar combo, all-tube chassis, preamp: 4 X 7025, power: 2 X EL84, single channel, front black control panel, single input, seven black knobs (MV, p, m, t, b, Brilliant v, Norm v), black covering, black grille, mfg. 1960s-mid-1970s.

Lead Hiwatt 30
courtesy Willie's American Guitars

	N/A	$1,500 - 2,000	$1,000 - 1,200	

SA112 (CUSTOM HIWATT 50) – 50W, 1-12 in. speaker, guitar combo, tube chassis, preamp: 4 X ECC83/12AX7, power: 2 X EL34/KT77, solid-state rectifier, two channels, front black control panel, two inputs, seven black knobs (MV, p, m, t, b, brilliant v, norm v), black covering, black speaker grille, mfg. mid-1970s-mid-1980s.

	N/A	$2,000 - 2,500	$1,200 - 1,500	

SA112FL (CUSTOM HIWATT 100) – 100W, 1-12 in. speaker, guitar combo, tube chassis, preamp: 4 X ECC83/12AX7, power: 4 X EL34/KT77, solid-state rectifier, two channels, front black control panel, two inputs, seven black knobs (MV, p, m, t, b, brilliant v, norm v), black covering, black speaker grille, mfg. mid-1970s-mid-1980s.

	N/A	$2,000 - 2,500	$1,200 - 1,500	

SA212 – 50W, 2-12 in. speakers, guitar combo, tube chassis, preamp: 4 X ECC83/12AX7, power: 2 X KT77, solid-state rectifier, two channels, front black control panel, two inputs, seven black knobs (MV, p, m, t, b, brilliant v, norm v), black covering, black speaker grille, mfg. 1980s.

	N/A	$2,500 - 3,000	$1,500 - 2,000	

SA212R – 100W, 2-12 in. speakers, guitar combo, tube chassis, preamp: 4 X ECC83/12AX7, power: 4 X KT77, solid-state rectifier, two channels, reverb, vibrato, front black control panel, four inputs, 10 black knobs (MV, vibrato depth, vibrato speed, r, p, m, t, b, brilliant v, norm v), black covering, black speaker grille, casters, mfg. 1980s.

	N/A	$2,750 - $3,250	$1,500 - 2,000	

ELECTRIC TUBE AMPLIFIERS: 2000 SERIES

The 2000 series amps were designed by Frank S. Levi, III and a design team at Hiwatt. These amps feature added controls and features such as reverb and vibrato, and single and dual-channel amps are available. The control panel features a 2000 logo with three wing-style graphics above it and the model name below.

D50L – 50W, head-unit configuration, tube chassis, preamp: 4 X ECC83/12AX7, power: 2 X EL34, solid-state rectifier, two channels, front black control panel, single input, 10 chickenhead knobs (Ch. 1: v, t, b, Ch. 2: OD, v, t, m, b, All: p, MV), effects loop, optional footswitch, black covering with white piping, mfg. late 1980s-early 1990s.

	N/A	$750 - 900	$525 - 625	

* D50LR Reverb – similar to the D50L, except has a reverb circuit with an additional tube and reverb control for a total of 11 knobs, mfg. late 1980s-early 1990s.

	N/A	$850 - 1,000	$575 - 675	

MSR/NOTES	100%	EXCELLENT	AVERAGE	LAST MSR

»**D50LCR Reverb Combo** – similar to the D50LR, except in combo configuration with 1-12 in. speaker and a black speaker grille, mfg. late 1980s-early 1990s.

N/A $1,000 - 1,200 $700 - 850

D100L – 100W, head-unit configuration, tube chassis, preamp: 4 X ECC83/12AX7, power: 4 X EL34, solid-state rectifier, two channels, front black control panel, single input, 10 chickenhead knobs (Ch. 1: v, t, b, Ch. 2: OD, v, t, m, b, All: p, MV), effects loop, optional footswitch, black covering with white piping, mfg. late 1980s-early 1990s.

N/A $850 - 1,000 $575 - 675

* **D100LR Reverb** – similar to the D100L, except has a reverb circuit with an additional tube and reverb control for a total of 11 knobs, mfg. late 1980s-early 1990s.

N/A $925 - 1,100 $625 - 725

S30LC COMBO – 30W, 1-12 in. Celestion speaker, guitar combo, tube chassis, preamp: 4 X ECC83/12AX7, power: 4 X EL84, solid-state rectifier, single channel, front black control panel, single input, five chickenhead knobs (Mv, b, m, t, g), black covering with white piping, mfg. early 1990s.

N/A $600 - 700 $375 - 450

S50L – 50W, head-unit configuration, tube chassis, preamp: 4 X ECC83/12AX7, power: 2 X EL34, solid-state rectifier, single channel, front black control panel, single input, six chickenhead knobs (g, t, m, b, p, MV), effects loop, black covering with white piping, mfg. late 1980s-early 1990s.

N/A $675 - 800 $450 - 525

* **S50LC Combo** – similar to the S50L, except in combo configuration with 1-12 in. speaker and a black speaker grille, mfg. early 1990s.

N/A $800 - 950 $550 - 650

S100L – 100W, head-unit configuration, tube chassis, preamp: 4 X ECC83/12AX7, power: 4 X EL34, solid-state rectifier, single channel, front black control panel, single input, six chickenhead knobs (g, t, m, b, p, MV), effects loop, black covering with white piping, mfg. late 1980s-early 1990s.

N/A $750 - 900 $525 - 625

PRE-1 PREAMP – preamp only, one-space rack-mount head configuration, tube chassis, preamp: 3 X ECC83/12AX7, two channels, front black control panel, single input, seven knobs (g1, g2, t, m, b, MV l, MV r), effects loop, optional footswitch, black casing, mfg. late 1980s-early 1990s.

N/A $425 - 500 $300 - 350

PW-50 POWER AMP – 100W (50W per side), power amp only, four-space rack-mount head configuration, tube chassis, power: 4 X EL34 (two per channel), two channels, four knobs (Ch. A: v, p, Ch. B: v, p), four inputs and four speaker outs (two per channel), black casing, mfg. late 1980s-early 1990s.

N/A $675 - 800 $450 - 525

ELECTRIC TUBE AMPLIFIERS: FIRST REISSUE SERIES

CUSTOM 20 – 20W, 1-10 in. Celestion speaker, tube chassis, single channel, front black control panel, single input, six black knobs (MV, p, m, t, b, v), effects loop, line out, black covering, black grille, mfg. 2002-04.

N/A $275 - 325 $150 - 200 $600

DC40 BULLDOG (CUSTOM HIWATT 50) – 40W (switchable to 12W), 1-12 in. Hiwatt speaker, tube chassis, preamp: 4 X 12AX7, 1 X 12AT7, power: 4 X EL84, two channels, front black control panel, single input, 12 black knobs (effects loop, p, Ch. 1: MV, t, m, b, g, Ch. 2: MV, t, m, b, g), line out, line level, black covering, gray grille, mfg. mid-1990s-2003.

N/A $600 - 700 $375 - 450 $1,299

DR103 (CUSTOM HIWATT 100) – 100W, head-unit configuration, tube chassis, preamp: 3 X 12AX7, 1 X 12AT7, power: 4 X EL34, two channels, front black control panel, four inputs, seven black chickenhead knobs (Norm v, Brilliant v, b, t, m, p, MV), black covering with white piping, mfg. mid 1990s-early 2000s.

N/A $1,100 - 1,300 $750 - 900

DR504 (CUSTOM HIWATT 50) – 50W, head-unit configuration, tube chassis, preamp: 3 X 12AX7, 1 X 12AT7, power: 2 X EL34, two channels, front black control panel, four inputs, seven black chickenhead knobs (Norm v, Brilliant v, b, t, m, p, MV), black covering with white piping, mfg. mid 1990s-early 2000s.

N/A $1,000 - 1,200 $700 - 850

SA112 BULLDOG CUSTOM – 50W, 1-12 in. Fane 75 speaker, tube chassis, preamp: 3 X 12AX7, 1 X 12AT7, power: 2 X EL34, single channel, front black control panel that reads, four inputs, seven black knobs (MV, p, m, t, b, brill. v, norm. v), black covering, gray grille, mfg. mid-1990s-early 2000s.

N/A $1,150 - 1,400 $800 - 950

MSR/NOTES	100%	EXCELLENT	AVERAGE	LAST MSR

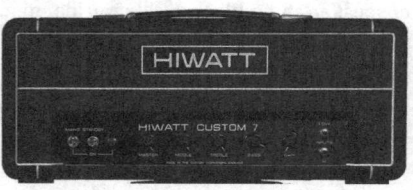

Custom 7 Head
courtesy Hiwatt

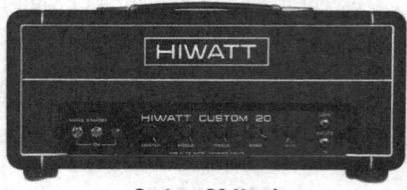

Custom 20 Head
courtesy Hiwatt

Custom 50 Head
courtesy Hiwatt

ELECTRIC TUBE AMPLIFIERS: CUSTOM HANDMADE SERIES

The Custom Handmade/Handwired Series was introduced in 2005, which represents Hiwatt's third reissue line. These amps are wired point-to-point with the specific military design that Dave Reeves used originally. Many of the popular amps produced many years ago are included in this series. In mid-2005, Hiwatt introduced Red and White coverings on all models in this series. A few models can be custom-ordered in Union Jack covering (red, white, and blue).

CUSTOM 7 HEAD – 7W, guitar head-unit, three-tube chassis, preamp: 2 X ECC83/12AX7, power: 1 X EL84, solid-state rectifier, single channel, front black control panel, two inputs, five black knobs (MV, m, t, b, h), power switch, standby switch, available in black covering with white piping, red covering with white piping, or white covering with black piping, mfg. 2007-disc.

	$1,750	$1,025 - 1,275	$650 - 775	$2,569

* Custom 7 1-10 Combo (SA-110) – similar to the Custom 7 Head, except in combo configuration with 1-10 in. speaker, mfg. 2007-disc.

	$1,970	$1,150 - 1,450	$725 - 875	$2,889

CUSTOM 20 HEAD (DR-20A) – 20W, head-unit configuration, tube chassis, preamp: 4 X ECC83/12AX7, power: 2 X EL84, solid-state rectifier, single channel, front black control panel, two inputs, five black knobs (g, b, t, m, MV), available in black covering with white piping, red covering with white piping, or white covering with black piping, mfg. 2005-present.

MSR $3,303	$2,400	$1,550 - 1,800	$775 - 950	

* Custom 20 2-10 Combo (SA-210) – similar to the Custom 20, except in combo configuration with 2-10 in. Fane speakers, mfg. 2005-present.

MSR $3,748	$2,700	$1,775 - 2,025	$875 - 1,075	

CUSTOM 50 HEAD (DR-504) – 50W, head-unit configuration, tube chassis, preamp: 4 X ECC83/12AX7, power: 2 X EL34, solid-state rectifier, single channel, front black control panel, four inputs, seven black knobs (Norm v, Bright v, b, t, m, p, MV), available in black covering with white piping, red covering with white piping, or white covering with black piping, mfg. 2005-present.

MSR $3,894	$2,800	$1,825 - 2,125	$925 - 1,125	

* Custom 50 1-12 Combo (SA-112) – similar to the Custom 50, except in combo configuration with 1-12 in. Fane speaker, mfg. 2005-present.

MSR $4,192	$3,050	$1,975 - 2,275	$975 - 1,225	

* Custom 50 2-12 Combo (SA-212) – similar to the Custom 50, except in combo configuration with 2-12 in. Fane speakers, mfg. 2005-present.

MSR $4,457	$3,250	$2,100 - 2,425	$1,050 - 1,300	

CUSTOM 100 (DR-103) – 100W, head-unit configuration, tube chassis, preamp: 4 X ECC83/12AX7, power: 4 X EL34, solid-state rectifier, single channel, front black control panel, four inputs, seven black knobs (Norm v, Bright v, b, t, m, p, MV), available in black covering with white piping, red covering with white piping, or white covering with black piping, mfg. 2005-present.

MSR $4,081	$2,950	$1,925 - 2,225	$950 - 1,175	

CUSTOM 200 HEAD (DR-201) – 200W, head-unit configuration, bass application, tube chassis, preamp: 3 X ECC83/12AX7, 1 X ECC81/12AT7, power: 4 X KT88, solid-state rectifier, single channel, front black control panel, four inputs, seven black knobs (Norm v, Bright v, b, t, m, p, MV), available in black covering with white piping, red covering with white piping, or white covering with black piping, mfg. 2005-present.

MSR $4,786	$3,450	$2,250 - 2,600	$1,125 - 1,375	

CUSTOM 400 HEAD (DR-405) – 400W, head-unit configuration, bass application, tube chassis, preamp: 4 X ECC83/12AX7, 1 X ECC81/12AT7, power: 6 X KT88, solid-state rectifier, single channel, front black control panel, four inputs, seven black knobs (Norm v, Bright v, b, t, m, p, MV), available in black covering with white piping, red covering with white piping, or white covering with black piping, mfg. 2005-present.

MSR $6,516	$4,700	$3,050 - 3,550	$1,525 - 1,900	

STUDIO STAGE HEAD (SSH) – 40W (switchable to 20W), head-unit configuration, tube chassis, preamp: 4 X ECC83/12AX7, power: 2 X EL34, solid-state rectifier, single channel, reverb, front black control panel, two inputs, six black knobs (MV, r, m, t, b, g), available in black covering with white piping, red covering with white piping, or white covering with black piping, mfg. 2006-present.

MSR $4,069	$2,950	$1,925 - 2,200	$950 - 1,175	

MSR/NOTES	100%	EXCELLENT	AVERAGE	LAST MSR

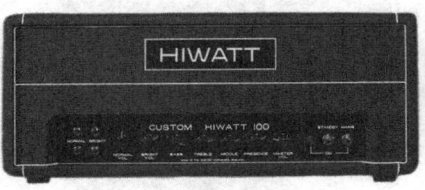
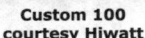

Custom 100
courtesy Hiwatt

Studio Stage Head
courtesy Hiwatt

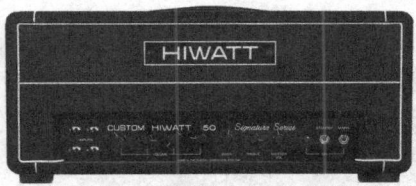

Pete Townshend Signature 50W Head
courtesy Hiwatt

* ***Studio Stage 2-12 Combo (SS-212)*** – similar to the Studio Stage, except in combo configuration with 2-12 in. Fane speakers, mfg. 2005-present.

| MSR $4,837 | $3,500 | $2,275 - 2,650 | $1,150 - 1,400 | |

DAVID GILMOUR SIGNATURE 50W HEAD (DG-504) – 50W, guitar head-unit, six-tube chassis, preamp: 4 X ECC83/12AX7, power: 2 X EL34, solid-state rectifier, single channel, front black control panel, four inputs, seven black knobs (Norm v, Bright v, b, t, m, p, MV), available in black covering with white piping, red covering with white piping, or white covering with black piping, mfg. 2007-disc.

| | $3,030 | $1,800 - 2,250 | $1,125 - 1,350 | $4,469 |

This model uses a specially linked input system where the gain of each channel can be altered to suit different styles.

DAVID GILMOUR SIGNATURE 100W HEAD (DG-103) – 100W, guitar head-unit, eight-tube chassis, preamp: 4 X ECC83/12AX7, power: 4 X EL34, solid-state rectifier, single channel, front black control panel, four inputs, seven black knobs (Norm v, Bright v, b, t, m, p, MV), available in black covering with white piping, red covering with white piping, or white covering with black piping, mfg. 2005-disc.

| | $3,250 | $1,900 - 2,400 | $1,200 - 1,450 | $4,779 |

This model uses a specially linked input system where the gain of each channel can be altered to suit different styles.

PETE TOWNSHEND SIGNATURE 50W HEAD (CP-504) – 50W, guitar head-unit, six-tube chassis, preamp: 4 X ECC83/12AX7, power: 2 X EL34, solid-state rectifier, four channels, front black control panel, four inputs, seven black knobs (v1, v2, v3, v4, t, b, MV), available in black covering with white piping, red covering with white piping, or white covering with black piping, mfg. 2007-disc.

| | $3,360 | $2,000 - 2,500 | $1,250 - 1,500 | $4,949 |

PETE TOWNSHEND SIGNATURE 100W HEAD (CP-103) – 100W, guitar head-unit, eight-tube chassis, preamp: 4 X ECC83/12AX7, power: 4 X EL34, solid-state rectifier, four channels, front black control panel, four inputs, seven black knobs (v1, v2, v3, v4, t, b, MV), available in black covering with white piping, red covering with white piping, or white covering with black piping, mfg. 2005-disc.

| | $3,360 | $2,000 - 2,500 | $1,250 - 1,500 | $4,949 |

ELECTRIC TUBE AMPLIFIERS: HI-GAIN SERIES

As of 2016, the Hi-Gain Series is no longer available in the USA but is still available for purchase in Europe.

HI-GAIN 50 HEAD – 50W, guitar head-unit, six-tube chassis, preamp: 4 X 12AX7, power: 2 X EL34, solid-state rectifier, two channels, front black control panel, single input, two white chickenhead knobs (Ch. 1 v with a push/pull bright switch, Ch. 2 v with a push/pull hi-gain switch) and six black chickenhead knobs (b, m, t, p, Ch. 2 level, MV), channel switch, power switch, standby switch, rear panel: four speaker jacks, footswitch jacks, black covering with white piping, mfg. 2007-present.

| MSR $2,789 | $1,900 | $1,125 - 1,400 | $700 - 825 | |

* ***Hi-Gain 50 2-12 Combo*** – similar to the Hi-Gain 50 Head, except in combo configuration with 2-12 in. speakers, black covering with white piping, gray grille cloth, mfg. 2007-present.

| MSR $3,379 | $2,300 | $1,350 - 1,700 | $850 - 1,000 | |

HI-GAIN 50 SER HEAD – 50W, guitar head-unit, six-tube chassis, preamp: 4 X 12AX7, power: 2 X EL34, solid-state rectifier, two channels, front black control panel, single input, two white chickenhead knobs (Ch. 1 v with a push/pull bright switch, Ch. 2 v with a push/pull hi-gain switch) and seven black chickenhead knobs (b, m, t, p, Ch. 2 level, r, MV), channel switch, power switch, standby switch, rear panel: four speaker jacks, two footswitch jacks, effects loop, black covering with white piping, mfg. 2007-present.

| MSR $2,939 | $2,000 | $1,175 - 1,475 | $725 - 875 | |

* ***Hi-Gain 50 SER 2-12 Combo*** – similar to the Hi-Gain 50 SER Head, except in combo configuration with 2-12 in. speakers, black covering with white piping, gray grille cloth, mfg. 2007-present.

| MSR $3,669 | $2,500 | $1,475 - 1,825 | $925 - 1,100 | |

HI-GAIN 100 HEAD – 100W, guitar head-unit, eight-tube chassis, preamp: 4 X 12AX7, power: 4 X EL34, solid-state rectifier, two channels, front black control panel, single input, two white chickenhead knobs (Ch. 1 v with a push/pull bright switch, Ch. 2 v with a push/pull hi-gain switch) and six black chickenhead knobs (b, m, t, p, Ch. 2 level, MV), channel switch, power switch, standby switch, rear panel: four speaker jacks, footswitch jacks, black covering with white piping, mfg. 2007-present.

| MSR $3,099 | $2,100 | $1,250 - 1,550 | $775 - 925 | |

MSR/NOTES	100%	EXCELLENT	AVERAGE	LAST MSR

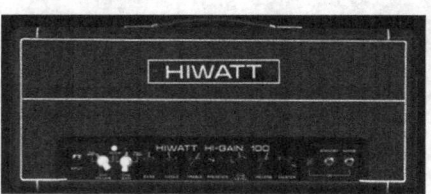

Hi-Gain 100 SER Head
courtesy Hiwatt

Bulldog 10
courtesy Hiwatt

Bulldog 20 Bass
courtesy Hiwatt

HI-GAIN 100 SER HEAD – 100W, guitar head-unit, eight-tube chassis, preamp: 4 X 12AX7, power: 4 X EL34, solid-state rectifier, two channels, front black control panel, single input, two white chickenhead knobs (Ch. 1 v with a push/pull bright switch, Ch. 2 v with a push/pull hi-gain switch) and seven black chickenhead knobs (b, m, t, p, Ch. 2 level, r, MV), channel switch, power switch, standby switch, rear panel: four speaker jacks, two footswitch jacks, effects loop, black covering with white piping, mfg. 2007-present.

| MSR $3,349 | $2,280 | $1,350 - 1,675 | $850 - 1,000 | |

HI-GAIN 4-12 SPEAKER CABINET – 300W, 4-12 in. speakers, designed for use with the Hi-Gain heads, black covering with white piping, gray grille cloth with HIWATT logo, mfg. 2007-present.

| MSR $1,279 | $870 | $525 - 625 | $325 - 400 | |

ELECTRIC SS AMPLIFIERS: BULLDOG SERIES

BULLDOG 10 (BD-10) – 10W, 1-6.25 in. speaker, solid-state chassis, front black control panel, single input, five black knobs (g, MV, t, m, b), headphone jack, black covering, gray grille, disc.

| | N/A | $40 - 50 | $20 - 30 | $100 |

BULLDOG 20 (BD-20) – 20W, 1-8 in. speaker, solid-state chassis, front black control panel, single input, six black knobs (g, MV, t, m, b, p), overdrive boost, headphone jack, black covering, gray grille, disc.

| | N/A | $50 - 60 | $25 - 35 | $120 |

BULLDOG 30 (BD-30R) – 30W, 1-10 in. speaker, solid-state chassis, two channels, front black control panel, two inputs, seven black knobs (g, MV, mic level, t, m, b, r), overdrive boost, headphone jack, CD in, black covering, gray grille, disc.

| | N/A | $70 - 90 | $45 - 60 | $160 |

BULLDOG 20 BASS (BD-20B) – 20W, 1-6 in. speaker, solid-state chassis, front black control panel, single input, five black knobs (v, t, m, b, MV), headphone jack, CD in, black covering, gray grille, disc.

| | N/A | $60 - 75 | $40 - 50 | $140 |

BULLDOG 30 BASS (BD-30B) – 30W, 1-10 in. speaker, solid-state chassis, front black control panel, single input, six black knobs (g, MV, t, m, b, c), headphone jack, external speaker out, black covering, gray grille, disc.

| | N/A | $80 - 95 | $50 - 65 | $180 |

ELECTRIC SS AMPLIFIERS: CUSTOM SERIES

CUSTOM 10 – 10W, 1-6 in. speaker, solid-state chassis, single channel, front black control panel, single input, three black knobs (g, fine, MV), distortion switch, headphone jack, black covering, gray grille, disc. 2004.

| | N/A | $40 - 50 | $20 - 30 | $100 |

CUSTOM 15B – 15W, 1-10 in. speaker, solid-state bass chassis, single channel, front black control panel, single input, five black knobs (MV, t, m, b, p), seven-band EQ, headphone jack, black covering, gray grille, disc. 2004.

| | N/A | $80 - 100 | $45 - 60 | $180 |

CUSTOM 20 – 20W, 1-8 in. speaker, solid-state chassis, single channel, front black control panel, single input, six black knobs (g, fine, t, m, b, MV), distortion switch, effects loop, headphone jack, black covering, gray grille, disc. 2004.

| | N/A | $65 - 80 | $40 - 50 | $150 |

CUSTOM 20 MINI-STACK – 20W, 2-10 in. speakers in separate cabinets (one per cabinet), solid-state chassis, single channel, front black control panel, single input, six black knobs (g, fine, t, m, b, MV), distortion switch, effects loop, headphone jack, black covering, gray grille, disc. 2004.

| | N/A | $175 - 225 | $95 - 125 | $400 |

MSR/NOTES	100%	EXCELLENT	AVERAGE	LAST MSR

SE4123
courtesy Savage Audio

Custom Handmade 2-12 Speaker Cabinet
courtesy Hiwatt

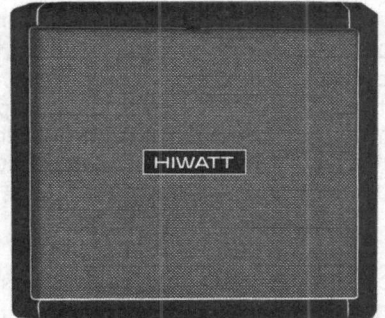

Custom Handmade 4-10 Bass Fane Speaker
Cabinet courtesy Hiwatt

SPEAKER CABINETS

In mid-2005, Hiwatt introduced optional Celestion speakers and Red and White coverings on all models in the Custom Hand-Made series. A few models can be custom-ordered in Union Jack covering (red, white, and blue).

SE4122 – 150W, 4-12 in. speakers, 16 or 4 ohm impedance, black covering, black grille covering, side recessed handles, mfg. 1970s-mid-1980s.

	N/A	$1,200 - 1,500	$850 - 1,000	

SE4123 – 100W, 4-12 in. speakers, 16 or 4 ohm impedance, black covering, gray (early models) or black grille covering, side recessed handles, mfg. mid-1960s-mid-1980s.

1964-1969	N/A	$1,400 - 1,750	$950 - 1,150	
1970-1981	N/A	$1,200 - 1,500	$850 - 1,000	
1980S	N/A	$800 - 1,000	$600 - 700	

CLASSIC 2-12 SPEAKER CABINET (SEC-2121) – 75W, 2-12 in. Celestion speakers, available in black covering with white piping, red covering with white piping, or white covering with black piping, mfg. 2005-present.

MSR $2,234	$1,625	$1,050 - 1,225	$525 - 650	

CLASSIC 4-12 SPEAKER CABINET (SEC-4123) – 150W, 4-12 in. Celestion speakers, available in black covering with white piping, red covering with white piping, or white covering with black piping, mfg. 2005-present.

MSR $1,489	$1,100	$700 - 825	$350 - 425	

CUSTOM HANDMADE 2-12 SPEAKER CABINET (SE-2121/SEF-2121) – 75W, 2-12 in. Fane speakers, available in black covering with white piping, red covering with white piping, or white covering with black piping, mfg. 2005-present.

MSR $2,459	$1,670	$975 - 1,225	$625 - 750	

CUSTOM HANDMADE 4-12 SPEAKER CABINET (SE-4123/SEF-4123) – 150W, 4-12 in. Fane speakers, available in black covering with white piping, red covering with white piping, or white covering with black piping, mfg. 2005-present.

MSR $2,949	$2,000	$1,175 - 1,475	$750 - 875	

CUSTOM HANDMADE 1-15 BASS SPEAKER CABINET (SE-115C) – 200W, 1-15 in. Celestion speaker, available in black covering with white piping, red covering with white piping, or white covering with black piping, mfg. 2005-06, reintroduced-present.

MSR $1,095	$800	$525 - 600	$260 - 325	

CUSTOM HANDMADE 4-10 BASS CELESTION SPEAKER CABINET (SE-410C) – 400W, 4-10 in. Celestion speakers, available in black covering with white piping, red covering with white piping, or white covering with black piping, mfg. 2005-present.

MSR $1,639	$1,200	$775 - 900	$375 - 475	

CUSTOM HANDMADE 4-10 BASS FANE SPEAKER CABINET (SE-410F) – 400W, 4-10 in. Fane speakers, available in black covering with white piping, red covering with white piping, or white covering with black piping, mfg. 2007-present.

MSR $3,899	$2,650	$1,550 - 1,950	$975 - 1,175	

CUSTOM HANDMADE 1-15/4-10 BASS CELESTION SPEAKER CABINET (SE-1510/SE-115410C) – 600W, 1-15 in. and 4-10 in. Celestion speakers, available in black covering with white piping, red covering with white piping, or white covering with black piping, mfg. 2005-present.

MSR $2,479	$1,800	$1,175 - 1,350	$575 - 725	

CUSTOM HANDMADE 1-15/4-10 BASS FANE SPEAKER CABINET (SE-1510/SE-115410F) – 600W, 1-15 in. and 4-10 in. Fane speakers, available in black covering with white piping, red covering with white piping, or white covering with black piping, mfg. 2007-present.

MSR $5,999	$4,070	$2,400 - 3,000	$1,500 - 1,800	

HOFFMAN AMPLIFIERS

Amplifiers previously produced in Sarasota, FL from 1993 to circa 2000. Hoffman currently runs an internet business selling tube amp parts in Pisgah Forest, NC since 2001.

CONTACT INFORMATION
HOFFMAN AMPLIFIERS
190 Lakeland Dr.
Pisgah Forest, NC 28768
www.hoffmanamps.com

Doug Hoffman currently runs an internet-only business selling tube amp parts and accessories, but he previously built amplifiers along with tube kits from 1993 to the early 2000s. Hoffman's amps consisted of 30W and 50W head units a 30W combo, and he also experimented with 50W and 100W heads. Dickie Betts was a customer of Hoffman's and had a 100W head built for him. Hoffman also runs a tube amp forum on his website along with a lot of tube amp information. For more information, visit Hoffman's website or contact him directly via mail.

HOHNER

Amplifiers previously produced overseas periodically from the 1970s through the 1990s. Previously distributed by Hohner/HSS.

The Hohner company was founded in 1857, and is currently the world's largest manufacturer and distributor of harmonicas. Hohner offers a wide range of solidly constructed musical instruments. The company has stayed contemporary with the current market by licensing designs and parts from Ned Steinberger, Claim Guitars (Germany), and Wilkinson hardware. Hohner started producing guitars in the 1970s, when they also started producing amplifiers. In 1986, HSS was established by Hohner to become a distributor to all of Hohner's products (guitars, drums, accessories, etc.). The last Hohner-branded amplifiers were produced in 1990s with the Panther series. Hohner introduced more brand names over the years, and amplifiers were moved to a different division to let Hohner concentrate on harmonicas and guitars. For more information on acoustic guitars, refer to the *Blue Book of Acoustic Guitars*. For more information on electric guitars refer to the *Blue Book of Electric Guitars*.

ELECTRIC SS AMPLIFIERS

Hohner produced several amplifiers during the 1970s, 1980s, and 1990s, but they never moved out of the entry-level to beginner category. Almost all amps have low wattages, small speakers, and relatively simple controls and features. The Sound Producer Series featured amps made in the 1980s. The Panther Series were also built in the 1980s, but some models lasted into the 1990s. Models in the Panther Series include the **P-12**, **P-20**, **P-25R**, and **P-200** with the last MSR on the Panther P-200 being $120. Most Hohner amplifiers are valued between $50 and $150 in the used market depending upon size and features.

HOLLAND

Amplifiers previously produced in Virginia Beach, VA from 1992 to 2000 and Brentwood, TN from 2000 to 2004. Previously distributed by L&M Amplifiers.

Holland Amplifiers was founded by Mike Holland on April 1, 1992 in Virginia Beach, VA while he was serving in the United States Navy. Mike worked on F14 fighter jets as a structural mechanic. On his kitchen table, using only all American components with specifications that were far above any other amp, Mike created the first Holland Tube Amplifier.

In 1998, Mike contacted Lane Zastrow, President of Lasar Music and former Vice President of Sales and Marketing for the Gibson Guitar Corporation, to handle sales and marketing for Holland Amplifiers. Lane and Mike then decided to become partners and formed L&M Amplifiers in July of 2000. In September of 2000, Holland moved its operations from Virginia Beach to Brentwood, Tennessee.

Holland Amplifiers were completely handmade with point-to-point wiring, whether it was a standard model or a custom amp. At their peak, Holland was producing over ten models and distributed them throughout the world, but in 2004, Holland stopped producing amplifiers with Mr. Zastrow, who converted the factory to a production facility for his Heritage Amplifier line. As Heritage, they produced a full line of amplifiers that featured some carryover from the Holland line including the Kenny Burrell model, and they even utilized the same address and phone number as Holland's. However, Heritage stopped producing amplifiers in 2008. In 2007, Holland founded Nashville Audio Research Laboratories International, LLC and renewed production of the Holland line.

ELECTRIC TUBE AMPLIFIERS

The Gibb was considered the flagship of the Holland line. This amp was created for East coast artist Gibb Droll. It features a 50W all tube chassis that was available in a head unit, or combo with 10 or 12 inch speakers. Holland described the amp as toned of blues sounds from the 1950s -1960s, and "reminiscent of ZZ Top." **The Jazz Amp** is another 50W with different power tubes, also available as a head-unit or combo. The Jazz is known for having lots of headroom and great clean power. The **Little Jimi** (last MSR $1,650) is a 35W or 50W amp with 2 X 5881 or 6L6 power tubes. This amp is more of a blues amp, which sounds like Hendrix, Clapton, and Stevie Ray Vaughn. The **Mini Jimi** (last MSR $1,365) is the same as the Little Jimi with more bite in a 1-12 in. speaker combo. The **Brentwood** (last MSR $2,400) and **Titan** (last MSR $2,300) amps are both 50W or 100W models in 2-12 in. speaker configurations. The **Kenny Burrell** is a 50W combo available in a 1-12 in. speaker combo (last MSR $2,400) and a 2-10 in. speaker combo (last MSR $2,300). Holland also produced the **Westside Andy Harmonica** amp, which is designed for harmonicas.

HOLMES

Amplifiers previously produced in Greensboro, NC and Greenville, MS from the late 1970s to the early 1990s.

Holmes built a variety of mainly solid-state amplifiers from the late 1970s through the late 1980s and possibly into the early 1990s. Harrison Holmes founded the company and they were reportedly first built in Greensboro, NC. In the 1980s, On-Site Music bought the company and changed the name to The Holmes Corporation. They also moved to Greensville, MS in the 1980s and went out of business in the late 1980s or early 1990s. Older models should have a logo with all capital letters, while newer models should have a logo with all lower-case letters and a large lower-case "h." James Lomenza of White Lion endorsed Holmes amps during the 1980s as well. Although Holmes put out several models, they seem to be best-known for their Tech Series line of amps. This series came in a variety of configurations and reviews seem to be favorable for a lower-priced amp. Any further information can be submitted directly to Blue Book Publications.

HONDO

Amplifiers previously produced in China, Korea, and/or Taiwan from the mid-1980s through the late 1990s or early 2000s. Acoustic and Electric guitars were produced in various Asian countries through 2005. Hondo is distributed by Musicorp International in Charleston, SC.

The Hondo guitar company was originally formed in 1969 when Jerry Freed and Tommy Moore of the International Music Corporation (IMC) of Fort Worth, TX, combined with the recently formed Samick company. IMC's intent was to introduce modern manufacturing techniques and American quality standards to the Korean guitar manufacturing industry.

The Hondo concept was to offer an organized product line and solid entry level market instruments at a fair market price. The original Korean products were classical and steel-string acoustic guitars, and in 1972, the first crudely-built Hondo electrics were introduced. However, two years later the product line took a big leap forward in quality under the new Hondo II logo. Hondo also began offering limited production guitars in Japan in 1974.

By 1975, Hondo had distributors in seventy countries worldwide, and they began producing other stringed instruments such as banjos and mandolins. In 1976, over 22,000 of the Bi-Centennial banjos were sold. The company also made improvements to the finish quality on their products, introduced scalloped bracing on acoustics, and began using a higher quality brand of tuning machines.

Hondo was one of the first overseas guitar builders to feature American-built DiMarzio pickups on the import instruments beginning in 1978. By this year, a number of Hondo II models featured designs based on classic American favorites. In 1979, over 790,000 Hondo instruments were sold worldwide. All guitar production returned to Korea in 1983, and at that point, the product line consisted of 485 different models!

In 1985, IMC acquired the major interest in the Charvel/Jackson company, and began dedicating more time and interest in the higher end guitar market. By 1987, Hondo had ceased operations and the trademark was put into hiatus. In 1989, Jerry Freed started the Jerry Freed International company, and acquired the rights to the Hondo trademark in 1991 (the "Est. 1969" tag line was added to the Hondo logo at this time). Freed began distribution of a new line of Hondo guitars. In 1993, the revamped company was relocated to Stuart, FL, and models were produced in China and Taiwan.

The Hondo Guitar Company was purchased by MBT International in 1995 and began offering Hondo guitars through their large Musicorp distribution catalog. MBT continued to offer a full line of entry-level acoustic guitars, electric guitars, and guitar amplifiers through the late 1990s and early 2000s. In 2005, MBT International/Musicorp was acquired by Kaman Music. The distribution side of the company is now solely referred to as Musicorp leaving the MBT trademark for their lighting and sound division. Shortly thereafter, Kaman/Musicorp phased out the Hondo brand in favor of their other trademarks including Arbor and J.B. Player. Currently, there are no Hondo-branded instruments available in the U.S. Sources: Tom Malm, MBT International, and Michael Wright, *Guitar Stories*, Volume One.

ELECTRIC SOLID-STATE AMPLIFIERS

Hondo also produced two mini-amps the **HA-97** and **HA-97S**, which are models that run on a nine-volt battery and turn your headphones into an amplifier. They have a 1/4 in. jack and three controls. Models listed here are split into two series. The first was produced circa late 1980s to the early 1990s and they can be distinguised by their black control panel with white trim and a logo mounted in the upper center of the grille. The second series was produced from circa the mid-1990s to the late 1990s and possibly into the 2000s. These amps have a black control panel with blue trim and a logo mounted in the upper left corner of the grille.

H10 – 8W, 1-4.75 in. speaker, guitar combo, solid-state chassis, single channel, front black control panel, single input, three knobs (v, b, t), headphone jack, black covering, black grille, mfg. mid-1990s-late 1990s.

	N/A	$30 - 40	$15 - 25	

H20 (FIRST VERSION) – 10W, 1-6.5 in. speaker, guitar combo, solid-state chassis, single channel, front black control panel, single input, three knobs (OD, v, tone), distortion switch, headphone jack, black covering, black grille, mfg. late 1980s-early 1990s.

	N/A	$35 - 50	$20 - 30	

H20 (SECOND VERSION) – 8W, 1-6.5 in. speaker, guitar combo, solid-state chassis, single channel, front black control panel, single input, two knobs (v, tone), distortion switch, headphone jack, black covering, black grille, mfg. mid-1990s-late 1990s.

	N/A	$35 - 50	$20 - 30	

H25B – 8W, 1-6.5 in. speaker, bass combo, solid-state chassis, single channel, front black control panel, one input, four knobs (v, t, m, b), headphone jack, black covering, black grille, mfg. mid-1990s-late 1990s.

	N/A	$35 - 50	$20 - 30	

MSR/NOTES	100%	EXCELLENT	AVERAGE	LAST MSR

H30 – 15W, 1-6.5 in. speaker, guitar combo, solid-state chassis, single channel, front black control panel, two inputs, five knobs (OD, v, l, m, h), distortion switch, headphone jack, black covering, black grille, mfg. late 1980s-early 1990s.

| | N/A | $40 - 60 | $25 - 35 | |

* **H30C Chorus** – similar to the H30, except has a chorus circuit with a dual purpose chorus control for a total of six knobs, mfg. late 1980s-early 1990s.

| | N/A | $50 - 75 | $30 - 40 | |

HB30 – 15W, 1-6.5 in. speaker, bass combo, solid-state chassis, single channel, front black control panel, two inputs, five knobs (v, l, m, h, p), headphone jack, line out, black covering, black grille, mfg. late 1980s-early 1990s.

| | N/A | $35 - 50 | $20 - 30 | |

HB35 – 20W, 1-8 in. speaker, bass combo, solid-state chassis, single channel, front black control panel, two inputs, five knobs (v, t, m, b, p), distortion switch, headphone jack, line out, black covering, black grille, mfg. mid-1990s-late 1990s.

| | N/A | $40 - 60 | $25 - 35 | |

H50 PRO – 25W, 1-8 in. speaker, guitar combo, solid-state chassis, two channels, front black control panel, two inputs, eight knobs (Ch. A: g, v, Ch. B: g, v, All: h, m, l, p), channel switch, effects loop, headphone jack, line out, line in, black covering, black grille, mfg. late 1980s-early 1990s.

| | N/A | $70 - 95 | $40 - 55 | |

HB70 – 35W, 1-8 in. speaker, bass/keyboard combo, solid-state chassis, single channel, front black control panel, two inputs, four knobs (v, l, m, h), headphone jack, line out, black covering, black grille, mfg. late 1980s-early 1990s.

| | N/A | $40 - 60 | $25 - 35 | |

H80 – 40W, 1-10 in. speaker, guitar combo, solid-state chassis, single channel, reverb, front black control panel, two inputs, eight knobs (OD, g, v, l, m, h, p, r), channel switch, headphone jack, line out, black covering, black metal grille, mfg. late 1980s-early 1990s.

| | N/A | $70 - 95 | $40 - 55 | |

H100SRC – 50W (stereo 25W X 2), 2-8 in. speaker, guitar combo, solid-state chassis, two channels, chorus, reverb, front black control panel, two inputs, 11 knobs (Ch. A: g, v, Ch. B: g, v, All: h, m, l, p, r, chorus depth, chorus rate), channel switch, chorus switch, headphone jack, line out, black covering, black grille, mfg. late 1980s-early 1990s.

| | N/A | $95 - 120 | $55 - 75 | |

HB100 – 50W, 1-10 in. speaker, bass/keyboard combo, solid-state chassis, single channel, front black control panel, two inputs, six knobs (v, l, m, h, p, MV), bright switch, effects loop, headphone jack, line out, black covering, black metal grille, mfg. late 1980s-early 1990s.

| | N/A | $70 - 95 | $40 - 55 | |

H160SRC – 80W (stereo 40W X 2), 2-10 in. speaker, guitar combo, solid-state chassis, two channels, chorus, reverb, front black control panel, two inputs, 11 knobs (Ch. A: g, v, Ch. B: g, v, All: h, m, l, p, r, chorus depth, chorus rate), channel switch, chorus switch, headphone jack, line out, black covering, black metal grille, mfg. late 1980s-early 1990s.

| | N/A | $120 - 150 | $70 - 95 | |

HOUND DOG

Amplifiers previously produced in Huntington Valley, PA from 1994 to 1998.

George Alessandro founded Hound Dog amps in 1994, but changed the name of his company to Alessandro in 1998. Alessandro only produced the Bloodhound and Redbone models with the brand Hound Dog between 1994 and 1998, and these models are currently available under the Alessandro brand. Please refer to Alessandro for more information on current models.

HUGHES & KETTNER

Amplifiers currently produced in St. Wendel, Germany. Hughes & Kettner is distributed in the U.S. by Yorkville Sound in Niagra Falls, NY. Previously distributed by Hughes & Kettner in Mt. Prospect, IL and the Pearl Corporation in Nashville, TN. The Hughes & Kettner trademark was established in 1985.

Hughes and Kettner was established in Germany in 1985. During the 1980s, a tube scare was looming around the corner where it was estimated that tubes would be no longer available and solid-state was going to be the only way to build amplifiers. However, Hughes & Kettner went to work designing a guitar amp that featured the three most important channels (clean, cruch, and overdrive), with effect devices as well. The first product was the **AS 64**, which was released in 1985 and is also considered one of the first modeling amps. The AS 64 could store 64 presets producing a number of different emulated amp sounds from one unit. Since then, they have expanded their line to include guitar and bass amplifiers in head and combo configurations. In 2006, the Pearl Drum Corporation became the exclusive U.S. distributor for Hughes & Kettner amplifiers, and in 2008, Yorkville Sound became the exclusive distributor. For more information, visit Hughes & Kettner's website or contact them or their distributor directly.

CONTACT INFORMATION
HUGHES & KETTNER
Factory
St. Wendel, Germany
www.hughes-and-kettner.com
info@hughes-and-kettner.com

U.S. Distributor: Yorkville Sound
4625 Witmer Industrial Estates
Niagra Falls, NY 14305
Phone No.: 716-297-2920
Fax No.: 716-297-3689
www.yorkville.com

MSR/NOTES	100%	EXCELLENT	AVERAGE	LAST MSR

ELECTRIC TUBE AMPLIFIERS: MISC. MODELS

Duotone Head
courtesy Hughes & Kettner

Duotone Combo
courtesy Hughes & Kettner

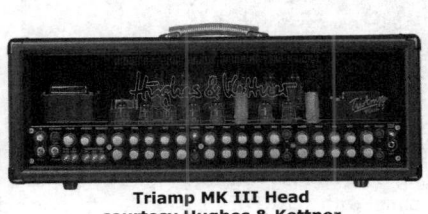

Triamp MK III Head
courtesy Hughes & Kettner

DUOTONE HEAD – 100W, head-unit only, all tube chassis, preamp: 5 X ECC83, power: 4 X EL34, dual channels, front silver control panel, single input, 13 silver knobs (Master: MV1, MV2, p, FX level, OD: b, m, t, MV, g, Clean: b, m, t, v) boost switch, effects loop, footswitch, black covering, clear front panel, disc.

	$2,760	$1,725 - 2,075	$1,200 - 1,450	$3,449

* *Duotone Combo* – similar to the Duotone Head except in combo form with 1-12 in. Celestion speaker, reverb, 50W output (2 X EL34), disc.

	$2,920	$1,850 - 2,200	$1,275 - 1,550	$3,649

* *Duotone Tommy Thayer Signature Head* – similar to the Duotone Head except has Dragon Skin covering, mfg. 2008-disc.

	$2,920	$1,850 - 2,200	$1,275 - 1,550	$3,649

EDITION TUBE 20 AC – 20W, 1-12 in. Eminence speaker combo, tube chassis, power: 2 X EL84, two channels, reverb, top black control panel, single input, seven white knobs (Clean: v, Lead: g, MV, All: b, m, t, r), effects loop, external speaker jack, black covering, brown grille, 35 lbs., mfg. 2004-07.

	$650	$350 - 425	$200 - 250	$759

EDITION TUBE 25TH ANNIVERSARY – 20W, 1-12 in. Celestion G12T-100 speaker, guitar combo, four-tube chassis, preamp: 2 X 12AX7, power: 2 X EL84, solid-state rectifier, two channels (clean and lead), reverb, top black control panel, single input, seven chrome knobs (r, t, m, b, lead Ch. MV, g, clean Ch. v), footswitch jack, rear panel: effects loop, extension speaker jack, black covering, black sparkle grille, mfg. 2010-disc.

	$700	$450 - 525	$275 - 325	$879

PURETONE – 25W, head-unit only, all tube Class A chassis, power: 2 X EL34, single channel, front silver control panel, single input, five silver knobs (growl, b, m, t, v), black covering, mfg. 2001-present.

MSR $2,750	$2,200	$1,425 - 1,700	$1,000 - 1,200	

* *Puretone Combo* – similar to the Puretone head except in combo form with 1-12 in. Celestion Vintage 30 speaker, mfg. 2001-disc.

	$2,760	$1,725 - 2,075	$1,200 - 1,450	$3,449

TRIAMP MK II HEAD – 100W, head-unit only, all tube chassis, power: 4 X EL34 or 4 X 6L6, three channels, front silver control panel, single input, 21 black knobs (t, b, m, MV, gA, gB, per channel, p, MV, FX mix), effects loop, possible reverb, black covering, clear front panel, disc.

	$3,470	$2,175 - 2,600	$1,525 - 1,850	$4,339

TRIAMP MK III HEAD – 150W, head-unit only, all tube chassis, power: 2 X EL34, 4 X 6L6, preamp: 1 X E83CC, 1 X 12AX7A-C, 7 X ECC83, six channels, front black control panel, single input, 33 chrome knobs (Each Channel: t, b, m, MV, g, All: v, presence, resonance), power switch, standby switch, six channel switches, MIDI learn switch, rear panel: effects loop with level control, MIDI in, MIDI out/thru, panel brightness control, preamp out, power amp in, noise gate level control, Red Box XLR DI out, four external speaker jacks, black covering, 48.5 lbs., mfg. 2015-present.

MSR $5,000	$4,000	$2,600 - 3,000	$1,300 - 1,600	

TRIAMP ALEX LIFESON SIGNATURE HEAD – 100W, head-unit only, all tube chassis, power: 4 X EL34 or 4 X 6L6, three channels, front black control panel with purple backlighting, single input, 21 black knobs (t, b, m, MV, gA, gB, per channel, p, MV, FX mix), effects loop, possible reverb, black covering, clear front panel, mfg. 2005-disc.

	$3,280	$2,050 - 2,450	$1,425 - 1,750	$4,099

TRILOGY HEAD – 100W, head-unit configuration, tube chassis, power: 4 X EL34, four channels (clean, crunch, lead, ultra lead), built-in MIDI features, front black control panel, single input, 18 knobs (All: MV, p, FX, Lead: t, m, b, MV ultra g, g, Crunch: t, m, b, MV, g, Clean: t, m, b, v), sparkle switch, boost switch, ultra lead switch, FX serial switch, MIDI learn switch, effects loop, includes four-button MIDI footswitch, black covering, clear front, 46 lbs., mfg. 2006-disc.

	$2,000	$1,250 - 1,500	$875 - 1,050	$2,499

MSR/NOTES	100%	EXCELLENT	AVERAGE	LAST MSR

Warp X Head
courtesy Hughes & Kettner

Zenamp Head
courtesy Hughes & Kettner

Zentera Head
courtesy Hughes & Kettner

WARP X HEAD – 120W, head-unit only, tube chassis, preamp: 4 X 12AX7/ECC83, power: 4 X 6L6, two channels, front control panel, single input, 13 knobs (Clean: p, t, m, b, v, Warp: MV, p, t, m, b, g, Master: v, FX level), effects loop, impedance selector, black covering, clear front panel with WARP logo, 45 lbs., mfg. 2004-disc.

| | **$2,000** | **$1,250 - 1,500** | **$875 - 1,050** | **$2,499** |

• Add $100 for Warp Factor pedal.

ZENAMP HEAD – 2 X 100W, head-unit only, 1 Sharc 32Bit Floating Point DSP, 16 Amp types, 30 presets, MIDI in/out/through, front blue control panel, single input, ten silver knobs (g, b, m, t, p, preset v, FX parameter, r, delay, MV) three black knobs for effects, black covering, 36 lbs., disc. 2005.

| | **N/A** | **$750 - 900** | **$500 - 600** | **$1,999** |

* Zenamp Combo – similar to the Zenamp head except in combo form with 2-12 in. Celestion speakers (1 Vintage 30 & 1 Rockdrive Junior), 2 X 60W output, 60 lbs., disc. 2005.

| | **N/A** | **$750 - 900** | **$500 - 600** | **$1,999** |

ZENTERA HEAD – 2 X 100W, head-unit only, 2 Sharc 32Bit Floating Point DSPs, 17 amp types, four effects groups, 128 presets, front silver control panel, single input, 15 silver knobs (g, amp type, b, m, t, p, v, preset, mod FX, delay, r, type, para1, para2, MV), digital control panel, black covering, 40 lbs., disc. 2007.

| | **$3,350** | **$2,150 - 2,550** | **$1,400 - 1,600** | **$3,899** |

* Zentera Combo – similar to the Zentura head except in combo form with 2-12 in. Celestion Vintage 30 speakers, and 2 X 120W output, 60 lbs., disc. 2007.

| | **$3,400** | **$2,200 - 2,600** | **$1,400 - 1,600** | **$3,999** |

ELECTRIC TUBE AMPLIFIERS: STATESMAN SERIES

STATESMAN DUAL 6L6 COMBO – 60W, 2-12 in. Eminence Rockdriver Cream speakers, guitar combo, four-tube chassis, preamp: 2 X 12AX7, power: 2 X 6L6, solid-state rectifier, two channels (clean and drive) with two modes (boost and twang), reverb, top black control panel, single input, 11 cream knobs (r, p, Drive Ch.: b, m, t, MV, g, Clean Ch.: b, m, t, v), boost switch, drive and clean channel select switches, twang switch, power switch, standby switch, rear panel: reverb balance, effects loop with -10dB and series/parallel switches, 2nd volume drive channel adjust, two footswitch jacks, four speaker jacks, two-button footswitch included, available in black or oxblood brown covering, brown grille, mfg. 2008-disc.

| | **$1,520** | **$950 - 1,150** | **$675 - 800** | **$1,899** |

STATESMAN DUAL EL34 HEAD – 50W, guitar head-unit, four-tube chassis, preamp: 2 X 12AX7, power: 2 X EL34, solid-state rectifier, two channels (clean and drive) with two modes (boost and twang), reverb, top black control panel, single input, 11 cream knobs (r, p, Drive Ch.: b, m, t, MV, g, Clean Ch.: b, m, t, v), boost switch, drive and clean channel select switches, twang switch, power switch, standby switch, rear panel: reverb balance, effects loop with -10dB and series/parallel switches, 2nd volume drive channel adjust, two footswitch jacks, four speaker jacks, two-button footswitch included, available in black or oxblood brown covering, brown grille, mfg. 2008-disc.

| | **$1,360** | **$850 - 1,025** | **$600 - 725** | **$1,699** |

STATESMAN DUAL EL84 COMBO – 20W, 1-12 in. Eminence Rockdriver Cream speaker, guitar combo, four-tube chassis, preamp: 2 X 12AX7, power: 2 X EL84, solid-state rectifier, two channels (clean and drive) with two modes (boost and twang), reverb, top black control panel, single input, seven cream knobs (r, b, m, t, Drive Ch. MV, g, Clean Ch. v), boost switch, drive and clean channel select switches, twang switch, power switch, rear panel: reverb balance, effects loop, two footswitch jacks, extension speaker jack, two-button footswitch included, available in black or oxblood brown covering, brown grille, mfg. 2008-disc.

| | **$1,090** | **$675 - 825** | **$475 - 575** | **$1,359** |

STATESMAN QUAD EL84 COMBO – 40W, 1-12 in. Eminence Rockdriver Cream speaker, guitar combo, six-tube chassis, preamp: 2 X 12AX7, power: 4 X EL84, solid-state rectifier, two channels (clean and drive) with two modes (boost and twang), reverb, top black control panel, single input, seven cream knobs (r, b, m, t, Drive Ch. MV, g, Clean Ch. v), boost switch, drive and clean channel select switches, twang switch, power switch, rear panel: reverb balance, effects loop, two footswitch jacks, extension speaker jack, two-button footswitch included, available in black or oxblood brown covering, brown grille, mfg. 2008-disc.

| | **$1,240** | **$775 - 925** | **$550 - 650** | **$1,549** |

STATESMAN 2-12 SPEAKER CABINET – 120W, 2-12 in. Eminence Rockdriver Cream speakers, 4/16 ohm impedance, two standard 1/4 in. jacks, available in black or oxblood brown covering, brown grille, mfg. 2008-disc.

| | **$650** | **$400 - 475** | **$275 - 325** | **$809** |

MSR/NOTES	100%	EXCELLENT	AVERAGE	LAST MSR

STATESMAN 4-12 SPEAKER CABINET – 240W, 4-12 in. Celestion Vintage 30 speakers, 4/16 ohm mono or 8 ohm stereo impedance, two standard 1/4 in. jacks, casters included, available in black or oxblood brown covering, brown grille, mfg. 2008-disc.

$1,030	$650 - 775	$450 - 550		$1,289

ELECTRIC TUBE AMPLIFIERS: SWITCHBLADE SERIES

The Switchblade Series of amplifiers features an all-tube chassis that features multi effects and a fully programmable preset section.

- **Add $200 for Tube Safety Control on all Switchblade models.**

**Switchblade Head
courtesy Hughes & Kettner**

**Switchblade Combo 50
courtesy Hughes & Kettner**

**Coreblade Head
courtesy Hughes & Kettner**

SWITCHBLADE HEAD – 100W, head-unit configuration, tube chassis, power: 4 X EL34, four switchable channels (clean, crunch, lead, ultra), reverb, digital effects, 128 presets, front black control panel, single input, 13 knobs (MV, r, FX v, FX feedback, FX time, FX select, MV, p, t, m, b, g, channel select), effects loop, MIDI footpedal included, black covering, black metal grille, 39 lbs., mfg. 2006-present.

MSR $1,400	$1,125	$725 - 850	$375 - 450	

SWITCHBLADE COMBO 50 – 50W, 1-12 in. Eminence speaker, guitar combo, tube chassis, power: 2 X EL34, four switchable channels (clean, crunch, lead, ultra), reverb, digital effects, 128 presets, front black control panel, single input, 13 knobs (MV, r, FX v, FX feedback, FX time, FX select, MV, p, t, m, b, g, channel select), effects loop, MIDI footpedal included, black covering, black grille with silver accents, 50 lbs., mfg. 2006-disc.

	$1,700	$1,050 - 1,275	$750 - 900	$2,119

SWITCHBLADE COMBO 100 – 100W, 2-12 in. Eminence speakers, guitar combo, tube chassis, power: 4 X EL34, four switchable channels (clean, crunch, lead, ultra), reverb, digital effects, 128 presets, front black control panel, single input, 13 knobs (MV, r, FX v, FX feedback, FX time, FX select, MV, p, t, m, b, g, channel select), effects loop, MIDI footpedal included, black covering, black grille with silver accents, 67 lbs., mfg. 2006-present.

MSR $2,500	$2,000	$1,200 - 1,450	$850 - 1,000	

COREBLADE HEAD – 100W, head-unit configuration, tube chassis, preamp: 3 X 12AX7, power: 4 X EL34, four switchable channels (clean, crunch, ultra 1, ultra 2), reverb, digital effects, 128 presets, front black control panel, single input, 14 knobs (MV, r, FX v, FX feedback, FX time, FX intensity, FX select, MV, p, resonance, t, m, b, g), channel selector switch, rear panel: effects loop, five external speaker jacks, MIDI in, MIDI thru, MIDI footpedal included, black covering, black metal grille, 40.25 lbs., mfg. 2009-present.

MSR $2,650	$2,125	$1,375 - 1,600	$700 - 850	

ELECTRIC TUBE AMPLIFIERS: TUBEMEISTER SERIES

**Tubemeister 18 Combo
courtesy Hughes & Kettner**

**Tubemeister 18-12 Combo
courtesy Hughes & Kettner**

**Tubemeister 36 Combo
courtesy Hughes & Kettner**

TUBEMEISTER 18 COMBO – 18W, 1-10 in. Celestion Custom speaker, guitar combo, four-tube chassis, preamp: 2 X 12AX7, power: 2 X EL84, two channels (clean and lead), top silver control panel, single input, seven chrome knobs (All: b, m, t, Lead Ch.: MV, g, Clean Ch.: g, MV), boost switch, channel select switch, power switch, standby switch, rear panel: reverb balance, effects loop, footswitch jack, one speaker jack with power soak control, black covering, black grille, mfg. 2011-present.

MSR $900	$700	$450 - 525	$230 - 280	

MSR/NOTES	100%	EXCELLENT	AVERAGE	LAST MSR

Tubemeister 36 Head
courtesy Hughes & Kettner

Tubemeister Deluxe 20 Head
courtesy Hughes & Kettner

Grandmeister 60 Head
courtesy Hughes & Kettner

TUBEMEISTER 18 HEAD – 18W, switchable to 5W/1W, guitar head unit, four-tube chassis, preamp: 2 X 12AX7, power: 2 X EL84, two channels (clean and lead), front silver control panel, single input, seven chrome knobs (All: b, m, t, Lead Ch.: MV, g, Clean Ch.: g, MV), boost switch, channel select switch, power switch, standby switch, rear panel: effects loop, footswitch jack, Red Box DI out, one speaker jack with power soak control, black covering, 11 lbs., mfg. 2011-present.

| MSR $750 | $500 | $325 - 375 | $165 - 200 | |

TUBEMEISTER 18-12 COMBO – 18W (switchable to 5W/1W), 1-12 in. Celestion Custom speaker, guitar combo, four-tube chassis, preamp: 2 X 12AX7, power: 2 X EL84, two channels (clean and lead), top silver control panel, single input, seven chrome knobs (All: b, m, t, Lead Ch.: MV, g, Clean Ch.: g, MV), boost switch, channel select switch, power switch, standby switch, rear panel: reverb balance, effects loop, footswitch jack, Red Box DI out, one speaker jack with power soak control, black covering, black grille, 34 lbs., mfg. 2014-present.

| MSR $1,000 | $800 | $525 - 600 | $260 - 325 | |

TUBEMEISTER 36 COMBO – 36W, switchable to 18W/5W/1W, 1-12 in. Celestion Vintage 30 speaker, guitar combo amp, seven-tube chassis, preamp: 3 X 12AX7, power: 4 X EL84, three channels (clean/crunch/lead), front silver control panel, single input, 12 chrome knobs (Lead Ch.: t, m, b, MV, g, Crunch Ch.: MV, g, Clean Ch.: t, m, b, g, MV), three channel select switches, power switch, standby switch, rear panel: effects loop, two footswitch jacks, Red Box DI out, reverb level control, one speaker jack with power soak control, MIDI in, black covering, black grille, 42.55 lbs., mfg. 2012-present.

| MSR $1,500 | $1,000 | $650 - 750 | $325 - 400 | |

TUBEMEISTER 36 HEAD – 36W, switchable to 18W/5W/1W, guitar head unit, seven-tube chassis, preamp: 3 X 12AX7, power: 4 X EL84, three channels (clean/crunch/lead), front silver control panel, single input, 12 chrome knobs (Lead Ch.: t, m, b, MV, g, Crunch Ch.: MV, g, Clean Ch.: t, m, b, g, MV), three channel select switches, power switch, standby switch, rear panel: effects loop, two footswitch jacks, Red Box DI out, reverb level control, one speaker jack with power soak control, MIDI in, black covering, 17 lbs., mfg. 2012-present.

| MSR $1,200 | $950 | $625 - 725 | $300 - 375 | |

TUBEMEISTER DELUXE 20 HEAD – 20W, switchable to 5W/1W, guitar head unit, four-tube chassis, preamp: 2 X 12AX7, power: 2 X EL84, two channels (clean and lead), 3-band EQ, cabinet emulation amp modeling, front black control panel, single input, seven chrome knobs (All: b, m, t, Lead Ch.: MV, g, Clean Ch.: g, MV), boost switch, channel select switch, power switch, standby switch, rear panel: effects loop, footswitch jack, Red Box DI out, one speaker jack with power soak control, black covering, 11 lbs., new 2016.

| MSR $880 | $700 | $450 - 525 | $230 - 280 | |

TUBEMEISTER DELUXE 40 HEAD – 40W, switchable to 18W/5W/1W, guitar head unit, seven-tube chassis, preamp: 3 X 12AX7, power: 4 X EL84, three channels (clean/crunch/lead), 3-band EQ, front black control panel, single input, 12 chrome knobs (Lead Ch.: t, m, b, MV, g, Crunch Ch.: MV, g, Clean Ch.: t, m, b, g, MV), three channel select switches, power switch, standby switch, rear panel: effects loop, two footswitch jacks, Red Box DI out, reverb level control, one speaker jack with power soak control, MIDI in, black covering, 17 lbs., new 2016.

| MSR $1,300 | $1,000 | $650 - 750 | $325 - 400 | |

GRANDMEISTER 36 HEAD – 36W, switchable to 18W/5W/1W, guitar head unit, seven-tube chassis, preamp: 3 X 12AX7, power: 4 X EL84, four channels (clean/crunch/lead/ultra), 3-band EQ, 128 user presets, front black control panel, single input, nine chrome knobs (MV, presence, resonance, r, t, m, b, v, g), channel selector switch, power switch, standby switch, noise gate switch, FX loop switch, store switch, FX access switch, boost switch, rear panel: effects loop, Red Box DI out, noise gate level control, one speaker jack with power soak control, MIDI in, MIDI out/thru, line out jack, black covering, 17 lbs., gig bag included, mfg. 2013-present.

| MSR $1,500 | $1,200 | $775 - 900 | $400 - 475 | |

TM 110 SPEAKER CABINET – 30W, 1-10 in. Celestion Ten 30 speaker, straight front, open back, top handle, designed for use with the Tubemeister Series heads, black covering, black grille, 14.55 lbs., mfg. 2013-present.

| MSR $250 | $200 | $130 - 150 | $65 - 80 | |

TM 112 SPEAKER CABINET – 60W, 1-12 in. Celestion Vintage 30 speaker, 16 ohms mono, straight front, closed back, top handle, designed for use with the Tubemeister Series heads, black covering, black grille, 29.8 lbs., mfg. 2011-present.

| MSR $380 | $300 | $195 - 225 | $100 - 120 | |

TM 212 SPEAKER CABINET – 120W, 2-12 in. Celestion Vintage 30 speakers, 16 ohms mono, straight front, closed back, top handle, designed for use with the Tubemeister Series heads, black covering, black grille, 43 lbs., mfg. 2013-present.

| MSR $750 | $600 | $400 - 450 | $195 - 240 | |

MSR/NOTES	100%	EXCELLENT	AVERAGE	LAST MSR

ELECTRIC SS AMPLIFIERS: ATTAX SERIES

The Attax series was produced from the mid-1990s to 2001. The **Tour Reverb** was available as either a combo or head unit. This model was good for 100W, reverb, and master volume. The **Club Reverb** was a simpler version of the Tour. This had 65W and not as many knobs. The **Metroverb** was a dual channel, 50W amp that could be used for many purposes. Again there were less controls on this model. All the combo units came equipped with Celestion 12 in. Rock Driver Junior speakers. Look for more information in upcoming editions.

ELECTRIC SS AMPLIFIERS: EDITION SERIES

Hughes & Kettner's DFX Edition Blue amps are still produced, but are not available in North America.

Edition Blue 15DFX
courtesy Hughes & Kettner

Edition Blue 30R
courtesy Hughes & Kettner

Edition Blue 60R
courtesy Hughes & Kettner

EDITION BLUE 15R – 15W, 1-8 in. Celestion speaker combo, solid-state chassis, two channels, top silver control panel with blue backlighting, single input, eight black knobs (Clean: v, Lead: g, MV, All: b, m, t, r, MV), CD in, headphone jack, black covering, black grille, mfg. 2003-07.

	$140	**$90 - 110**	**$60 - 75**	**$189**

* *Edition Blue 15DFX* – similar to the Edition Blue 15R, except has a digital effects section including chours, reverb, and two delays and 10 control knobs (Clean: v, Lead: g, MV, All: b, m, t, MV, FX select, FX level, reverb level), 18 lbs., mfg. 2006-present.

MSR N/A	**$190**	**$110 - 140**	**$70 - 90**	

EDITION BLUE 30R – 30W, 1-10 in. Jensen speaker combo, solid-state chassis, two channels, top silver control panel with blue backlighting, single input, eight black knobs (Clean: v, Lead: g, MV, All: b, m, t, r, MV), CD in, headphone jack, effects loop, black covering, black grille, mfg. 2003-05.

	N/A	**$135 - 175**	**$85 - 110**	**$299**

* *Edition Blue 30DFX* – similar to the Edition Blue 30R, except has a digital effects section including chours, reverb, and two delays and 10 control knobs (Clean: v, Lead: g, MV, All: b, m, t, MV, FX select, FX level, reverb level), 22 lbs., mfg. 2006-present.

MSR N/A	**$250**	**$150 - 200**	**$95 - 120**	

EDITION BLUE 60R – 60W, 1-12 in. Celestion speaker combo, solid-state chassis, two channels, top silver control panel with blue backlighting, single input, eight black knobs (Clean: v, Lead: g, MV, All: b, m, t, r, MV), CD in, headphone jack, effects loop, black covering, black grille, mfg. 2004-05.

	N/A	**$175 - 225**	**$100 - 135**	**$399**

* *Edition Blue 60DFX* – similar to the Edition Blue 60R, except has a digital effects section including chours, reverb, and two delays and 10 control knobs (Clean: v, Lead: g, MV, All: b, m, t, MV, FX select, FX level, reverb level), 32 lbs., mfg. 2006-present.

MSR N/A	**$350**	**$200 - 250**	**$120 - 150**	

EDITION SILVER 50 – 50W, 1-12 in. Celestion RockDriver Junior speaker combo, solid-state chassis, reverb, top silver control panel, eight knobs, CD in, effects loop, black covering, black grille, mfg. 2001-04.

	N/A	**$200 - 250**	**$120 - 150**	**$449**

ELECTRIC SS AMPLIFIERS: MISC. MODELS

MATRIX HALF-STACK – 100W, head and 4-12 in. Celestion RockDriver Ultra 65 speakers in a cabinet, solid-state chassis, Autostore digital FX Matrix, four channels, front black and chrome control panel, single input, 17 black knobs, channel selector switches, four-button footswitch, black covering, black grille, mfg. 2005-07.

	$1,025	**$575 - 675**	**$325 - 400**	**$1,199**

MATRIX 112 COMBO – 100W, 1-12 in. Celestion RockDriver Ultra 100 speaker combo, solid-state chassis, Autostore digital FX Matrix, four channels, front black and chrome control panel, single input, 17 black knobs, channel selector switches, four-button footswitch, black covering, black grille, mfg. 2005-07.

	$600	**$325 - 400**	**$200 - 250**	**$699**

MSR/NOTES	100%	EXCELLENT	AVERAGE	LAST MSR

Vortex Half Stack
courtesy Hughes & Kettner

Warp 7 Half Stack
courtesy Hughes & Kettner

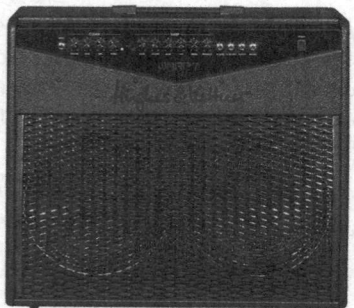

Warp 7 212 Combo
courtesy Hughes & Kettner

VORTEX HALF STACK – 80W, head-unit & speaker enclosure, solid-state chassis, dual channels, reverb, front silver V control panel, single input, nine black knobs (clean v, lead g, voicing, lead MV, b, m, t, r, MV), effects loop, speaker cabinet: 4-12 in. Celestion RockDriver Junior speakers, black covering, black grille, disc. 2004.

	N/A	$550 - 650	$325 - 400	$1,149

VORTEX 112 COMBO – 80W, 1-12 in. Celestion RockDriverJunior speaker combo, solid-state chassis, two channels, reverb, front silver V control panel, single input, nine black knobs (clean v, lead g, voicing, lead MV, b, m, t, r, MV), effects loop, black covering, black metal grille, mfg. 2004 only.

	N/A	$300 - 375	$175 - 225	$659

VORTEX 212 COMBO – 80W, 2-12 in. Celestion RockDriverJunior speaker combo, solid-state chassis, two channels, reverb, front silver V control panel, single input, nine black knobs (clean v, lead g, voicing, lead MV, b, m, t, r, MV), effects loop, black covering, black metal grille, mfg. 2004 only.

	N/A	$375 - 450	$200 - 250	$799

WARP 7 HALF STACK – 100W, head-unit only, solid-state chassis, dual channels, front black control panel, single input, ten black knobs (Clean: v, b, m, t, Warp: g, MV, b, m, t, p), effects loop, footswitch, black covering, mfg. 2002-05.

	N/A	$600 - 700	$375 - 450	$1,199

The price listed includes the speaker cabinet that comes with the head. The speaker cabinet is a 4-12 enclosure with 4-12 in. Celestion RockDriver Junior speakers.

WARP 7 112 COMBO – similar to the Warp 7 212 Combo except with 1-12 in. speaker, and 80W output, mfg. 2002-04.

	N/A	$300 - 375	$175 - 225	$649

WARP 7 212 COMBO – similar to the Warp 7 head unit except has 2-12 in. Celestion speakers, mfg. 2002-04.

	N/A	$375 - 450	$250 - 300	$849

BASS TUBE AMPLIFIERS: BASSBASE SERIES

Speaker cabinets designed specifically for use with the Bassbase series include the **BC118** (disc. 2007, last MSR was $1,169) handles 400W and has 1-18 in. speaker, the **BC215H** (disc. 2007, last MSR was $1,399) handles 600W and has 2-15 in. speakers with a horn, and the **BC410H** (disc. 2007, last MSR was $1,399) handles 600W and has 4-10 in. speakers with a horn.

BASSBASE 400 – 400W, rack-mount head-unit, tube preamp: 12AX7, solid-state power unit, Varimetric soundmodes, front silver control panel, single input, 11 black knobs, various lights and buttons, effects loop, disc. 2004.

	N/A	$675 - 800	$450 - 525	$1,499

BASSBASE 600 – 650W, rack-mount head-unit, 12AX7 preamp, solid-state power unit, varimetric soundmodes, front silver control panel, 15 black knobs, various lights and buttons, effects loop, dual fan cooling system, 41 lbs., disc. 2007.

Bassbase 600
courtesy Hughes & Kettner

$2,050	$1,150 - 1,400	$750 - 900	$2,429

BASS SS AMPLIFIERS: BASSFORCE SERIES

The Bassforce Series was produced from the mid-1990s to 2001. The **XXL Bassforce** was the top model with 300W in a combo or head unit version. It has 1-15 in. driver, and some cool controls including the EQ Matrix. The **XL Bassforce** has 200W, and most of the controls of the XXL. The **Bassforce L** has 100W output, and a basic control panel. All are of good quality and good for practice or performing. The Bassforce XXL is available as a head-unit and matching speaker cabinets are available. Earlier models feature a red covering and later models were switched to a black covering. Look for more information in upcoming editions.

MSR/NOTES	100%	EXCELLENT	AVERAGE	LAST MSR

BASS SS AMPLIFIERS: BASSKICK SERIES

BK100
courtesy Hughes & Kettner

BK200
courtesy Hughes & Kettner

BK300
courtesy Hughes & Kettner

BK100 – 100W, 1-15 in. Eminence speaker with HF horn, solid-state chassis, front blue control panel, single input, five black knobs (g, b, m, t, MV), effects loop, line out, headphone jack, black covering, dark gray metal grille, 55 lbs., mfg. 2006-07.

	$500	$300 - 350	$175 - 225	$669

BK200 – 200W, 1-15 in. Eminence speaker with switchable HF horn, solid-state chassis, single channel, compression, front blue control panel, two inputs, seven black knobs (g, compression, b, l/m, m/h, h, t, MV), effects loop, line out, headphone jack, black covering, dark gray metal grille, 70 lbs., mfg. 2006-07.

	$675	$425 - 500	$275 - 325	$899

BK300 – 300W, 1-15 in. Eminence speaker with switchable HF horn, solid-state chassis, single channel, compression, front blue control panel, two inputs, seven black knobs (g, compression, b, l/m, m/h, h, t, MV), effects loop, line out, headphone jack, black covering, dark gray metal grille, 79 lbs., mfg. 2006-07.

	$775	$475 - 550	$325 - 375	$1,049

BASS SS AMPLIFIERS: QUANTUM SERIES

• **Add $125 for Quantum Cordura Rolling Bag with wheels and grips on Quantum combo units.**

Quantum QC 310
courtesy Hughes & Kettner

Quantum QC 415
courtesy Hughes & Kettner

Quantum QC 421
courtesy Hughes & Kettner

QUANTUM QC 310 – 250W, 1-10 in. speaker, solid-state chassis, single channel, front blue/gray control panel, two inputs (active and passive), seven black knobs (g, b, l/m, h/m, t, tube growl, MV), headphone jack, tuner out, effects loop, line out, tilt-back cabinet, black covering, black metal grille, indented metal handles, 38.5 lbs., mfg. 2004-07.

	$999	$550 - 650	$325 - 400	$1,169

QUANTUM QC 412 – 400W, 1-12 in. speaker, solid-state chassis, single channel, front blue/gray control panel, two inputs (active and passive), seven black knobs (g, b, l/m, h/m, t, tube growl, MV), headphone jack, tuner out, effects loop, line out, tilt-back cabinet, black covering, black metal grille, indented metal handles, 43 lbs., mfg. 2004-07.

	$1,100	$600 - 725	$350 - 425	$1,299

QUANTUM QC 415 – 400W, 1-15 in. speaker, solid-state chassis, single channel, front blue/gray control panel, two inputs (active and passive), seven black knobs (g, b, l/m, h/m, t, tube growl, MV), headphone jack, tuner out, effects loop, line out, tilt-back cabinet, black covering, black metal grille, indented metal handles, 52 lbs., mfg. 2004-07.

	$1,200	$650 - 775	$400 - 475	$1,419

QUANTUM QC 421 – 400W, 2-10 in. speakers, solid-state chassis, single channel, front blue/gray control panel, two inputs (active and passive), seven black knobs (g, b, l/m, h/m, t, tube growl, MV), headphone jack, tuner out, effects loop, line out, tilt-back cabinet, black covering, black metal grille, indented metal handles, 63 lbs., mfg. 2004-07.

	$1,350	$750 - 900	$450 - 525	$1,599

MSR/NOTES	100%	EXCELLENT	AVERAGE	LAST MSR

Quantum QS 115 Pro Speaker Cabinet
courtesy Hughes & Kettner

Quantum QS 210 Pro Speaker Cabinet
courtesy Hughes & Kettner

Quantum QS 2115 Pro Speaker Cabinet
courtesy Hughes & Kettner

QUANTUM QT 600 HEAD – 600W, head-unit only, solid-state chassis, Dynavalve power amp, single channel, front black control panel, two inputs (active and passive), seven black knobs (g, b, l/m, h/m, t, tube growl, MV), headphone jack, tuner out, effects loop, line out, black covering, black front, 32 lbs., mfg. 2004-07.

	$1,475	$850 - 1,000	$500 - 600	$1,749

QUANTUM QS 115 PRO SPEAKER CABINET – 300W, 1-15 in. Dura Dome Neodynamium speaker, 8 ohm impedance, black covering, black metal grille, 51 lbs., mfg. 2004-07.

	$775	$425 - 500	$250 - 300	$919

QUANTUM QS 210 PRO SPEAKER CABINET – 450W, 2-10 in. Dura Cone Neodynamium speaker, 4 or 16 ohm impedance, black covering, black metal grille, 46 lbs., mfg. 2004-07.

	$775	$425 - 500	$250 - 300	$919

QUANTUM QS 410 PRO SPEAKER CABINET – 900W, 4-10 in. Dura Cone Neodynamium speaker, 8 ohm impedance, black covering, black metal grille, 70.5 lbs., mfg. 2004-07.

	$1,200	$700 - 800	$400 - 475	$1,419

QUANTUM QS 610 PRO SPEAKER CABINET – 1350W, 4-10 in. Dura Cone Neodynamium speaker, 5.3 ohm impedance, black covering, black metal grille, 101 lbs., mfg. 2004-07.

	$1,600	$900 - 1,050	$550 - 625	$1,899

QUANTUM QS 810 PRO SPEAKER CABINET – 1800W, 8-10 in. Dura Cone Neodynamium speaker, 4 ohm impedance, black covering, black metal grille, 137 lbs., mfg. 2004-07.

	$1,900	$1,100 - 1,350	$650 - 750	$2,249

QUANTUM QS 2115 PRO SPEAKER CABINET – 750W, 2-10 in. Dura Cone and 1-15 in. Dura Dome speaker Neodynamium, 2.8 ohm impedance, black covering, black metal grille, 75 lbs., mfg. 2004-07.

	$1,200	$650 - 775	$400 - 475	$1,419

SPEAKER CABINETS

CC 212 CAB
courtesy Hughes & Kettner

CC 412 CAB WA30
courtesy Hughes & Kettner

CC 412 CAB A25
courtesy Hughes & Kettner

CC 212 CAB – 100W, 2-12 in. Celestion speakers, 13-ply birch cabinet, Tolex covering, black with silver sparkle grille cloth, disc.

	$1,010	$625 - 750	$450 - 525	$1,259

CC 412 CAB A30/B30 – 240W, 4-12 in. Celestion Vintage 30 speakers, angled/straight design, 13-ply birch cabinet, Tolex covering, black with silver sparkle grille cloth, mfg. 2002-disc.

	$1,700	$1,050 - 1,275	$750 - 900	$2,119

These cabinets were also known as the CC 412 V30.

MSR/NOTES	100%	EXCELLENT	AVERAGE	LAST MSR

MC 412 CL CAB
courtesy Hughes & Kettner

MC 412 SE CAB
courtesy Hughes & Kettner

TC 412 A60 CAB
courtesy Hughes & Kettner

* *CC 412 CAB WA30* – similar to the CC 412 CAB, except has an oversized configuration which is taller and deeper for Nu-Metal, mfg. 2002-disc.

	$1,840	$1,150 - 1,375	$800 - 975	$2,299

CC 412 CAB A25/B25 – 100W, 4-12 in. Celestion Greenback speakers, stereo/mono output, angled/straight design, 13-ply birch cabinet, Tolex covering, black with silver sparkle grille cloth, disc.

	$1,700	$1,050 - 1,275	$750 - 900	$2,119

These cabinets were also known as the CC 412 A/B without the 25 suffix.

CC 412 ALEX LIFESON SIGNATURE – 100W, 4-12 in. Celestion Greenback speakers, meant for use with the Alex Lifeson Signature Head, Crocodile Tolex covering, black grille, mfg. 2005-disc.

	$1,700	$1,050 - 1,275	$750 - 900	$2,119

BC 215H CAB – 600W, 2-15 in. speakers, high frequency CD Horn, 8 Ohm bass cabinet, Tolex covering, black with silver sparkle grille cloth, disc. 2003.

	N/A	$500 - 600	$300 - 375	$1,099

BC 410H CAB – 600W, 4-10 in. speakers, high frequency CD Horn, 8 Ohm bass cabinet, Tolex covering, black with silver sparkle grille cloth, disc. 2003.

	N/A	$500 - 600	$300 - 375	$1,099

BC 118 CAB – 400W, 1-18 in. speaker, 8 Ohm bass cabinet, Tolex covering, black with silver sparkle grille cloth, disc. 2003.

	N/A	$375 - 450	$250 - 300	$849

VC 412 A25/B25 – 100W, 4-12 in. Celestion Greenback speakers, angled (VC 412 A25) or straight (VC 412 B25) design, plywood cabinet, Tolex covering, black with silver sparkle grille cloth, mfg. 2006-disc.

	$1,010	$625 - 750	$450 - 525	$1,259

VC 412 A30/B30 – 240W, 4-12 in. Celestion Vintage 30 speakers, angled (VC 412 A30) or straight (VC 412 B30) design, plywood cabinet, Tolex covering, black with silver sparkle grille cloth, mfg. 2006-disc.

	$1,010	$625 - 750	$450 - 525	$1,259

MC 412 CL CAB – 320W, 4-12 in. Celestion Classic Lead speakers, 8 ohms mono, angled design, removeable casters, black covering, black grille with silver Coreblade graphic, 114 lbs., current mfg.

MSR $1,500	$1,200	$775 - 900	$400 - 475	

MC 412 SE CAB – 320W, 4-12 in. Celestion Classic Lead speakers, 8 ohms mono, straight front, removeable casters, black covering, black metal grille with silver Coreblade graphic, 119 lbs., current mfg.

MSR $600	$400	$260 - 300	$130 - 160	

TC 412 A60 CAB – 240W, 4-12 in. Rockdriver Classic 60 speakers, 8 ohms mono, angled design, closed back, side handles, black covering, black grille, 91 lbs., current mfg.

MSR $1,400	$1,100	$725 - 825	$350 - 450	

HURRICANE TUBE AMPS

Amplifiers previously produced in Sarasota, FL beginning in 1998.

Gary Drouin and Rock Bottom founded the Hurricane Tube Amp company in 1998 to build custom tube guitar and harmonica amplifiers. Rock Bottom passed away in 2001, but Drouin still continued to produce amps. Any further information on Hurricane Tube Amps can be submitted directly to Blue Book Publications.

CONTACT INFORMATION
HURRICANE TUBE AMPS
1312 East Ave.
Sarasota, FL 34234
Phone No.: 941-906-1179

NOTES

I SECTION
IBANEZ

Amplifiers and speaker cabinets currently produced in Japan, China, and/or Korea. Distributed by Ibanez U.S.A. in Bensalem, PA.

The Ibanez trademark goes way back to 1932. They have been producing guitars for several years and they have been widely available in the U.S. since the 1960s. For more information on acoustic guitars, refer to the *Blue Book of Acoustic Guitars*. For more information on electric guitars, refer to the *Blue Book of Electric Guitars*.

Hoshino U.S.A. had tried amplifiers before they introduced the Ibanez line in the late 1990s. The first amps distributed by Hoshino were the IBZ brand that were made in Japan during the early 1980s. In the mid-1980s, Hoshino started distributing the Sundown brand, which were made in the U.S.A. In the mid-to late 1990s, Hoshino became the distributor of Laney amps that were primarily made in Britain. None of these brands ever took off with any success. Jon Romanowski decided to introduce a full line of Ibanez-branded amps that were to be built overseas. They started with small amps (Ibanez had been producing the IBZ amps in their JumpStart packages prior to 1998) and eventually moved up to larger models. In 2005, they introduced their first tube amplifier. For more information, visit Ibanez's website or contact them directly. Information courtesy, Paul Specth, Michael Wright, Jim Donahue, and Pat Lefferts of *Ibanez: The Untold Story*.

CONTACT INFORMATION
IBANEZ
Hoshino USA Inc.
1726 Winchester Road
Bensalem, PA 19020
Phone No.: 215-638-8670
Phone No.: 800-669-4226
Fax No.: 215-245-8583
www.ibanez.com

MSR/NOTES	100%	EXCELLENT	AVERAGE	LAST MSR

ELECTRIC GUITAR TUBE AMPLIFIERS: THERMION (TN) SERIES

TN120 THERMION HEAD – 120W, head-unit configuration, tube chassis, preamp: 5 X 12AX7, power: 4 X 6L6/6550, two channels, front black control panel, single input, 15 knobs (Vintage Ch.: g, three-way bright knob, b, m, t, p, MV, Hot Ch.: g, b, m, t, p, MV, effects loop bend and return), channel switch, hi/lo impedance switch, effects loop switch, dampening switch on hot channel, effects loop, three-button footswitchblack covering, black brushed black metal grille, 50 lbs., mfg. summer 2005-2009.

TN120 Thermion Head
courtesy Ibanez

TN412A Thermion Speaker Cabinet
courtesy Ibanez

TN412S Thermion Speaker Cabinet
courtesy Ibanez

$1,100	$625 - 775	$425 - 500	$1,467

TN412A/S THERMION SPEAKER CABINET – 280W, 4-12 in. Celestion Vintage 30 speakers, two inputs, stereo/mono switch, straight (TN412S) or angled (TN412A) design, 5/8 in. plywood construction, black covering, dark gray cane net grille, detachable casters, recessed handles, designed for use with the TN120 Thermion head, 105 lbs., mfg. summer 2005-2009.

$800	$475 - 550	$300 - 350	$1,067

ELECTRIC GUITAR TUBE AMPLIFIERS: TUBE SCREAMER (TSA) SERIES

TSA5TVR Tube Screamer Combo
courtesy Ibanez

TSA15H Tube Screamer Head
courtesy Ibanez

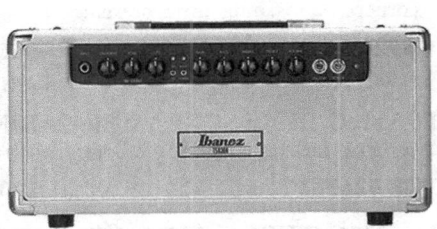

TSA30H Tube Screamer Head
courtesy Ibanez

MSR/NOTES	100%	EXCELLENT	AVERAGE	LAST MSR

TSA30 Tube Screamer Combo
courtesy Ibanez

TSA112C Tube Screamer Cabinet
courtesy Ibanez

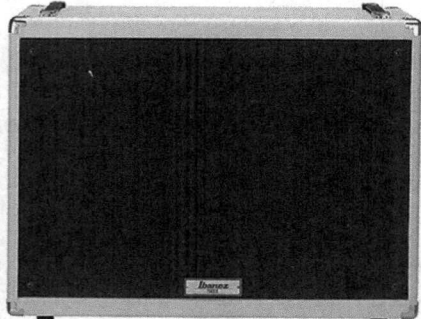

TSA212C Tube Screamer Cabinet
courtesy Ibanez

TSA5 TUBE SCREAMER COMBO – 5W, 1-10 in. Celestion speaker, guitar combo, two-tube chassis, preamp: 1 X 12AX7, power: 1 X 6V6, solid-state rectifier, single channel with genuine Tube Screamer built-in, top green control panel, single input, five black knobs (v, color, Tube Screamer: level, tone, OD), on/off Tube Screamer switch, rear panel: power switch, footswitch jack, external speaker jack, cream covering with chrome corners, black grille, mfg. 2012-2014.

	$250	$135 - 175	$80 - 105	$333

• Add $25 (MSR $33) for two-button footswitch (Model IFS1G).

TSA5TVR TUBE SCREAMER COMBO – 5W, 1-8 in. Jensen C8R speaker, guitar combo, two-tube chassis, preamp: 1 X 12AX7, power: 1 X 6V6GT, single channel with genuine Tube Screamer built-in, top white control panel, single input, seven black knobs (t, b, v, reverb, Tube Screamer: level, tone, OD), on/off Tube Screamer switch, power switch, footswitch, line out, headphone out, cream covering with turquoise edging, cream grille, 18 lbs., mfg. 2014-present.

MSR $533	$400	$260 - 300	$130 - 160

• Add $20 (MSR $27) for single-button footswitch (Model IFS1G).

TSA15H TUBE SCREAMER HEAD – 15W, guitar head-unit, four tube chassis, preamp: 2 X 12AX7, power: 2 X 6V6, solid-state rectifier, single channel with genuine Tube Screamer built-in, front black control panel, single input, six black knobs (Tube Screamer: OD, tone, level, Amp: b, t, v), standby switch, power switch, pentode (15W)/triode (5W) switch, footswitch jack, optional two-button Tube Screamer/6db boost footswitch, cream covering with chrome corners, mfg. 2010-present.

MSR $400	$300	$175 - 225	$100 - 130

• Add $30 (MSR $40) for two-button footswitch (Model IFS2G).

* TSA15 Tube Screamer Combo – similar to the TSA15H Tube Screamer Head, except in combo configuration with 1-12 in. Celestion Seventy/80 speaker, cream covering with chrome corners, and black grille, 33 lbs., mfg. 2012-present.

MSR $600	$450	$260 - 325	$160 - 200

• Add $30 (MSR $40) for two-button footswitch (Model IFS2G).

TSA30 TUBE SCREAMER COMBO – 30W, guitar combo, 1-12 in. Celestion speaker, five tube chassis, preamp: 3 X 12AX7, power: 2 X 6V6 or 2 X 6L6GC, solid-state rectifier, single channel with genuine Tube Screamer built-in, front black control panel, single input, eight black knobs (Tube Screamer: OD, tone, level, Amp: g, b, m, t, v), standby switch, power switch, pentode (15W)/triode (5W) switch, footswitch jack, optional two-button Tube Screamer/6db boost footswitch, cream covering with chrome corners, 39 lbs., mfg. 2010-present.

MSR $800	$600	$350 - 425	$200 - 250

• Add $30 (MSR $40) for two-button footswitch (Model IFS2G).

TSA30H TUBE SCREAMER HEAD – 30W, guitar head-unit, five tube chassis, preamp: 3 X 12AX7, power: 2 X 6L6GC, single channel with genuine Tube Screamer built-in, front green control panel, single input, eight black knobs (Tube Screamer: OD, tone, level, Amp: g, b, m, t, v), standby switch, power switch, footswitch jack, optional two-button Tube Screamer/6db boost footswitch, cream covering with chrome corners, 24 lbs., mfg. 2012-present.

MSR $600	$450	$260 - 300	$130 - 160

• Add $30 (MSR $40) for two-button footswitch (Model IFS2G).

TSA112C TUBE SCREAMER CABINET – 80W, 1-12 in. Celestion Seventy 80 speaker, 8 ohm impedance, cream covering with chrome corners, dark brown grille cloth, mfg. 2010-present.

MSR $267	$200	$110 - 140	$70 - 85

TSA212C TUBE SCREAMER CABINET – 160W, 2-12 in. Celestion Seventy 80 speaker, 16 ohm impedance, cream covering with chrome corners, dark brown grille cloth, 44 lbs., mfg. 2012-present

MSR $400	$300	$195 - 225	$100 - 120

| MSR/NOTES | 100% | EXCELLENT | AVERAGE | LAST MSR |

MIMX30 Amp Selection/Control Panel
courtesy Ibanez

MIMX65
courtesy Ibanez

MIMX150H
courtesy Ibanez

ELECTRIC GUITAR AMPLIFIERS: MIMX SERIES

MIMX30 – 30W, 1-10 in. speaker, guitar combo, solid-state chassis, fully digital programmable preamp with 11 amp models, 26 rhythm patterns and 18 digital effects, front angled silver control panel, single input, 11 chrome knobs (amp selection, g, b, m, t, FX 1 selector, FX mix, FX 2 selector, rhythm selector, rhythm level, MV), CD/MP3 input jack, headphone jack, footswitch jack, black covering, black grille, 19.4 lbs., mfg. summer 2008-2009.

| | $200 | $110 - 140 | $70 - 90 | $267 |

* **Add $30 (Last MSR was $40) for two button footswitch (Model IFS2M).**

MIMX65 – 65W, 1-12 in. speaker, guitar combo, solid-state chassis, fully digital programmable preamp with 11 amp models, 10 memory locations, 50 rhythm patterns and 13 digital effects, front angled silver control panel, single input, 11 chrome knobs, digital display, CD/MP3 input jack, headphone jack, footswitch jack, black covering, black grille, 37 lbs., mfg. 2007-2010.

| | $350 | $200 - 250 | $120 - 150 | $467 |

MIMX150H – 150W, guitar head-unit configuration, solid-state chassis, fully digital programmable preamp with 11 amp models, 10 memory locations, 50 rhythm patterns and 13 digital effects, front angled silver control panel, single input, 13 chrome knobs, digital display, footswitch jack, black covering, black grille, accessory compartment, 34 lbs., mfg. 2007-2010.

| | $400 | $225 - 275 | $130 - 170 | $533 |

IS412MCA/MCS MIMX SPEAKER CABINET – 320W, 4-12 in. speakers, 4 or 16 ohm impedance jacks, MDF baffle board, particle board back and sides, angled front (MCA) or straight front (MCS), side handles, black covering, black grille, 27.5 in. wide, 29.75 in. tall, 13.25 in. deep, 92 lbs., casters included, designed for use with the MIMX150H Head, mfg. 2007-2010.

| | $300 | $175 - 225 | $100 - 130 | $400 |

ELECTRIC GUITAR AMPLIFIERS: TONE BLASTER (TB) SERIES

TB stands for Tone Blaster, which was what the initial electric amplifiers were called by Ibanez. TB Series amplifiers produced between 1998 and 1999 feature a darker gray grille cloth and slightly different cosmetics.

TB15R
courtesy Ibanez

TB225C
courtesy Ibanez

TB100H
courtesy Ibanez

TB15R – 15W, 1-8 in. "Power Jam Jr." speaker combo, solid-state chassis, dual channels, front black control panel, single input, seven black knobs (v, g, v, b, m, t, level), headphone jack, CD input, black covering, gray grille cloth, mfg. 2000-06.

| | N/A | $50 - 70 | $30 - 40 | $130 |

* *TB15D* – similar to the TB15R, except has DSP, mfg. 2003-04.

| | N/A | $75 - 100 | $40 - 60 | $200 |

TB25 – 25W, 1-10 in. "Power Jam" speaker combo, solid-state chassis, single channel, switchable gain, front black control panel, single input, seven black knobs (g, v, v, b, m, t, level), headphone jack, footswitch, black covering, black grille cloth, mfg. 1998-99.

| | N/A | $60 - 80 | $35 - 50 | $170 |

MSR/NOTES	100%	EXCELLENT	AVERAGE	LAST MSR

TB25R – 25W, 1-10 in. "Power Jam" speaker combo, solid-state chassis, reverb, single channel, switchable gain, front black control panel, single input, seven black knobs (g, v, v, b, m, t, r), headphone jack, footswitch, black covering, gray grille cloth, mfg. 2000-06.

	N/A	$75 - 100	$40 - 60	$190

TB225C – 50W (2 X 25W stereo), 2-10 in. "Power Jam" speakers, dual channels, chorus, front black control panel, single input, 13 black knobs (Ch 1: b, m, t, v, Ch. 2: g, b, m, t, v, r, s, depth, MV), effects loop, footswitch, headphone jack, black covering, gray grille cloth, mfg. 2000-06.

	N/A	$175 - 225	$110 - 140	$400

TB50R – 50W, 1-12 in. "Power Jam" speaker, dual channels, front black control panel, single input, 11 black knobs (Ch. 1: g, b, m, t, v, Ch. 2: g, b, m, t, v, MV), effects loop, footswitch, headphone jack, black covering, gray grille cloth, mfg. 2001-06.

	N/A	$140 - 175	$85 - 110	$330

TB100H – 100W, head unit only, dual channels, reverb, front black control panel, single input, thirteen black knobs, effects loop, footswitch, headphone jack, black covering, gray grille cloth, mfg. 2003-06.

	N/A	$150 - 200	$95 - 120	$400

In summer 2005, a limited edition half-stack was introduced with dragon scale covering. This unit came with the TB100H head and a 4-12 in. speaker cabinet (last MSR $800).

* *TB100R* – similar to the TB100H, except in combo configuration with 2-12 in. speakers, mfg. 2003-05.

	N/A	$200 - 250	$120 - 150	$500

TB212 – 2-12 in. speaker cabinet, black covering, gray grille, mfg. 2003-05.

	N/A	$140 - 175	$85 - 110	$330

TB412A/S – 4-12 in.speaker cabinet, angled or straight (disc. 2006), black covering, gray grille, mfg. 2003-06.

	N/A	$175 - 225	$110 - 140	$400

ELECTRIC GUITAR AMPLIFIERS: TONE BLASTER EXTREME (TBX) SERIES

TBX15R
courtesy Ibanez

TBX65R
courtesy Ibanez

TBX150H
courtesy Ibanez

TBX15R – 15W, 8 in. speaker, guitar combo, solid-state chassis, two channels, reverb, front angled black control panel, single input, eight chrome knobs (Ch. 1: v, g, Ch. 2: v, g, All: l, m, h, r), CD/MP3 input jack, headphone jack, black covering, black grille, 20 lbs., mfg. 2007-2010.

	$100	$55 - 70	$35 - 45	$133

TBX30R – 30W, 1-10 in. speaker, guitar combo, solid-state chassis, two channels, reverb, front angled black control panel, single input, eight chrome knobs (Ch. 1: v, g, Ch. 2: v, g, All: l, m, h, r), CD/MP3 input jack, headphone jack, footswitch jack, black covering, black grille, 23 lbs., mfg. 2007-2011.

	$180	$100 - 125	$60 - 75	$240

TBX65R – 65W, 1-12 in. speaker, guitar combo, solid-state chassis, two channels, reverb, front angled black control panel, single input, 11 chrome knobs (Ch. 1: v, g, l, m, h, Ch. 2: v, g, l, m, h, All: r), CD/MP3 input jack, headphone jack, footswitch jack, black covering, black grille, 42 lbs., mfg. 2007-2011.

	$280	$160 - 200	$95 - 120	$373

TBX150H – 150W, guitar head unit, solid-state chassis, two channels, reverb, front angled black control panel, single input, 13 chrome knobs (Ch. 1: v, g, l, m, h, r, Ch. 2: v, g, l, m, h, r, All: hue), effects loop, CD/MP3 input jack, headphone jack, footswitch jack, black covering, 38 lbs., mfg. 2007-2012.

	$250	$135 - 175	$80 - 105	$333

• **Add $50 (MSR $67) for four-button footswitch (Model IFS4X).**

MSR/NOTES	100%	EXCELLENT	AVERAGE	LAST MSR

TBX150R – similar to the TBX150H, except in combo configuration with 2-12 in. speakers, black covering, black grille, 71 lbs., mfg. 2007-2012.

| | $380 | $225 - 275 | $120 - 150 | $507 |

• Add $50 (MSR $67) for four-button footswitch (Model IFS4X).

IS412CA/CS TBX SPEAKER CABINET – 320W, 4-12 in. speakers, 4 or 16 ohm impedance jacks, MDF baffle board, particle board back and sides, angled front (CA) or straight front (CS), side handles, black covering, black grille, 27.5 in. wide, 29.75 in. tall, 13.25 in. deep, 92 lbs., casters included, designed for use with the TBX150H, mfg. 2007-2012.

| | $250 | $135 - 175 | $80 - 105 | $333 |

ELECTRIC GUITAR AMPLIFIERS: MISC. MODELS

IBZ10/IBZ10G
courtesy Ibanez

IL15 Iron Label
courtesy Ibanez

GT10DX – 10W, 1-6 in. speaker combo, solid-state chassis, switchable gain, front black control panel, single input, six black konbs (level, v, clean: v, b, m, t), headphone jack, black covering, black grille, mfg. 1998-99.

| | N/A | $35 - 50 | $20 - 30 | $80 |

GT10DXR – similar to the GT10DX, except has reverb, mfg. 1998-99.

| | N/A | $45 - 60 | $30 - 40 | $110 |

IBZ10/IBZ10G – 10W, 1-6 in. speaker, solid-state chassis combo, single channel, front black control panel, single input, five black knobs (g, b, m, t, v), boost switch, power switch, headphone jack, CD input (later models), black covering, gray grille cloth, mfg. 2000-present.

| MSR $93 | $70 | $45 - 55 | $25 - 30 | |

This amp is part of the Jumpstart package, which comes with a guitar, amp, and distortion box all in one. The price reflects the amp only.

IBZ15GR – 15W, 1-6.5 in. speaker, solid-state chassis combo, single channel, reverb, front black control panel, single input, seven black knobs (normal Ch. v, Distortion Ch. g, Distortion Ch. v, b, m, t, r), channel switch, aux. in, headphone jack, power switch, black covering, black grille cloth, 10.9 in. wide, 12.5 in. tall, 7.5 in. deep, mfg. 2011-present.

| MSR $120 | $90 | $50 - 65 | $30 - 40 | |

IL15 IRON LABEL – 15W, guitar combo, 1-12 in. Celestion speaker, four tube chassis, preamp: 2 X 12AX7, power: 2 X EL84, two channels with independent 3-band EQ, front black control panel, single input, eleven black knobs (r, MV, clean/crunch: b, m, t, v, lead: gain, b, m, t, v), channel switch, fat switch, power switch, rear panel: effect loop, speaker out, external speaker out, footswitch jack, black covering, black grille, 37 lbs., mfg. 2014-present.

| MSR $667 | $500 | $325 - 375 | $165 - 200 | |

• Add $30 (MSR $40) for dual latching footswitch Model IFS2L.
• Add $20 (MSR $27) for single channel latching footswitch Model IFS1L.

WT80 WHOLETONE – 80W, 1-15 in. speaker, jazz combo amp, solid-state chassis, single channel, chorus, reverb, top chrome control panel, single input, eight black knobs (g, tone, t, m, b, chorus, r, MV), aux. input jack with volume control, power switch, headphone jack, black covering, black metal grille, mfg. 2011-2014.

| | $380 | $225 - 275 | $120 - 150 | $507 |

ACOUSTIC GUITAR AMPLIFIERS

TA stands for Troubadour, which was what the initial acoustic amplifiers were called by Ibanez.

GT10DXA – 10W, 1-6 in.speaker, solid-state chassis, single channel, chorus, brown control panel, single input, five black knobs (depth, b, m, t, v), headphone jack, brown covering, brown grille cloth, mfg. 1998-99.

| | N/A | $55 - 70 | $35 - 45 | $120 |

MSR/NOTES	100%	EXCELLENT	AVERAGE	LAST MSR

IBZ10A
courtesy Ibanez

T35 Troubadour
courtesy Ibanez

T35 Troubadour
courtesy Ibanez

IBZ10A – 10W, 1-6 in. speaker, solid-state chassis, single channel, chorus, brown control panel, single input, five black knobs (depth, b, m, t, v), headphone jack, brown covering, brown grille cloth, mfg. 2000-08.

	$90	$55 - 70	$35 - 45	$120

T10 TROUBADOUR – 10W, 1-6.5 in. speaker, acoustic guitar combo, solid-state chassis, single channel, chorus, top black control panel, single input, four knobs (middle shape, mix, v, chorus speed), chorus switch, RCA CD input, 1/4 in. line out, power switch, tilt bar, black covering, brown straw grille, 10.25 in. wide, 8.25 in. tall, 7.625 in. deep, 7.5 lbs., mfg. 2009-2012.

	$100	$60 - 75	$35 - 40	$133

T15 TROUBADOUR – 15W, 1-6.5 in. speaker, acoustic guitar combo, solid-state chassis, single channel, chorus, top black control panel, single input, three knobs (v, b, t), chorus switch, headphone out, power switch, tilt bar, black covering, brown straw grille, 6.4 lbs., mfg. 2013-present.

MSR $133	$100	$60 - 75	$35 - 40	

T20 TROUBADOUR – 20W, 1-8 in. speaker, acoustic guitar combo, solid-state chassis, two channels, chorus, reverb, internal limiter, top black control panel, two inputs (one 1/4 in. for guitar, one XLR for mic), 10 knobs (Mic Ch.: tone, v, Guitar Ch.: v, b, mid. freq., mid level, t, chorus speed, All: r, MV), natural/shaped guitar switch, chorus switch, RCA CD/Aux. input, power switch, tilt bar, black covering, brown straw grille, 12.375 in. wide, 10.5 in. tall, 9.5 in. deep, 14 lbs., mfg. 2009-2011.

	$200	$110 - 140	$70 - 85	$267

T30 TROUBADOUR – 30W, 1-8 in. speaker, acoustic guitar combo, solid-state chassis, two channels, chorus, reverb, top black control panel, black covering, brown straw grille, mfg. 2012-present.

MSR $267	$200	$110 - 140	$70 - 85	

T35 TROUBADOUR – 35W, 1-10 in. speaker, acoustic guitar combo, solid-state chassis, two channels, chorus, reverb, top black control panel, two inputs (one 1/4 in. for guitar, one XLR for mic), 11 knobs (Mic Ch.: tone, v, Guitar Ch.: v, b, mid. freq., mid level, t, chorus depth, chorus speed, All: r, MV), natural/shaped guitar switch, chorus switch, RCA CD/Aux. input, stereo balanced out, power switch, tilt bar, black covering, brown straw grille, 15 in. wide, 12.75 in. tall, 9.75 in. deep, 25 lbs., mfg. 2009-2011.

	$280	$160 - 200	$95 - 120	$373

T80 TROUBADOUR – 80W, 2-8 in. speakers, acoustic guitar combo, solid-state chassis, two channels, chorus, reverb, top black control panel, three inputs (two 1/4 in. for guitar, one XLR for mic), 14 knobs (Ch. 1: v, t, m, b, chorus, r, Ch. 2: v, t, m, b, chorus, r, All: notch filter, MV), power switch, line/mic level switch, phantom switch, phase switch, mute switch, headphone jack, aux. in jack, rear panel: stereo balanced out jack, tilt bar, black covering, brown straw grille, mfg. 2011 only.

	$380	$225 - 275	$120 - 150	$507

T80N TROUBADOUR – 80W, 1-10 in. speaker with a tweeter, acoustic guitar combo, solid-state chassis, two channels, chorus, reverb, top black control panel, four inputs (two 1/4 in. for guitar. two XLR for mics), 14 knobs (Ch. 1: v, t, m, b, chorus, r, Ch. 2: v, t, m, b, chorus, r, All: notch filter, MV), level switch and phantom switch for each channel, phase inverter, mute switch, headphone jack, aux. in jack with level control, rear panel: line out, footswitch jacks, black covering, brown straw grille, mfg. 2012-present.

MSR $400	$300	$175 - 225	$105 - 130	

T150S TROUBADOUR – 150W (75W per side stereo), 2-6.5 in. speakers, acoustic guitar combo, solid-state chassis, two channels, chorus, reverb, top black control panel, four inputs (two 1/4 in. for guitar. two XLR for mics), 14 knobs (Ch. 1: v, t, m, b, chorus, r, Ch. 2: v, t, m, b, chorus, r, All: notch filter, MV), level switch and phantom switch for each channel, phase inverter, mute switch, headphone jack, aux. in jack with level control, rear panel: line out, footswitch jacks, black covering, brown straw grille, mfg. 2012-present.

MSR $600	$450	$260 - 325	$160 - 200	

MSR/NOTES	100%	EXCELLENT	AVERAGE	LAST MSR

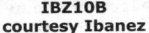

IBZ10B
courtesy Ibanez

P3110 Promethean Combo
courtesy Ibanez

P3115 Promethean Combo
courtesy Ibanez

TA20 TROUBADOUR – 20W, 1-8 in. speaker, solid-state chassis, single channel, reverb, chorus, front brown control panel, single input, eight brown knobs (v, b, m/h, m/l, t, d, s, r), line out, brown covering, brown grille, mfg. 2004-08.

	$170	$100 - 130	$70 - 85	$227

TA25(H) TROUBADOUR – 25W, 1-10 in. Ibanez speaker w/ tweeter, solid-state chassis, dual channels, front brown control panel, single input, eight white knobs (mic v, inst v, s, b, m/h, m/l, t, level), brown covering, brown cloth grille, mfg. 1999-2003.

	N/A	$135 - 175	$85 - 110	$300

TA35 TROUBADOUR – 35W, 1-10 in. speaker, solid-state chassis, two channels, reverb, chorus, front brown control panel, two inputs, 10 brown knobs (v, b, m/h, m/l, t, d, s, r, mic v, MV), line out, RCA inputs, tilt-back cabinet, brown covering, brown grille, mfg. 2004-08.

	$240	$140 - 170	$90 - 110	$320

TA225(C) TROUBADOUR – 50W (2 X 25 stereo), 2-10 in. "Power Jam" speakers, two tweeters, solid-state chassis, dual channels, chorus, reverb, front brown control panel, mic and instrument inputs, 13 white knobs (Mic: b, t, v, Instrument: b, two parametric, t, v, s, depth, level, MV), brown covering, brown cloth grille, mfg. 2000-08.

	$400	$240 - 290	$150 - 175	$533

BASS AMPLIFIERS: BT/IBZ SERIES

BT10 – 10W, 1-6.5 in. speaker, solid-state chassis combo, single channel, front black control panel, single input, five black knobs (v, b, m, t, p), headphone jack, black covering, black grille, mfg. 1998-99.

	N/A	$50 - 60	$30 - 40	$100

IBZ10B – 10W, 1-6 in. speaker, solid-state chassis combo, single channel, front black control panel, single input, five black knobs (v, b, m, t, p), headphone jack, CD input (later models), black covering, black grille, mfg. 2000-present.

MSR $93	$70	$45 - 55	$25 - 35	

BASS AMPLIFIERS: PROMETHEAN SERIES

P300H PROMETHEAN HEAD – 300W, ultralight bass head unit, solid-state chassis, single channel, front red control panel, single input, six red knobs (g, h, m, l, Phat, MV), limiter switch, aux. in jack, headphone jack, rear panel: XLR balanced line out, black casing, 11 in. wide, 10.4 in. deep, 2.2 in. tall, 6.4 lbs., mfg. 2012-present.

MSR $400	$300	$195 - 225	$100 - 120	

P500H PROMETHEAN HEAD – 250W @ 4 ohms (500W @ 8 ohms), ultralight bass head unit, solid-state chassis, single channel, peak limiting circuit, front red control panel, single input, five red knobs (g, l, h, vibe, MV), six-band graphic EQ, mute switch, vibe switch, headphone jack, aux. input, balanced XLR line out with ground lift switch, tuner out, footswitch jack, optional two-button mute and vibe control footswitch, black casing, 11 in. wide, 2.25 in. tall, 10.375 in. deep, 6.4 lbs., mfg. 2009-2011.

	$500	$300 - 375	$175 - 225	$667

* Add $25 (MSR $35) for gig bag (Model BGP500).
* Add $30 (MSR $40) for two-button footswitch (Model IFS2X).

P3110 PROMETHEAN COMBO – 300W, 1-10 in. speaker with tweeter, ultralight bass head unit, solid-state chassis, single channel, top red control panel, single input, six red knobs (g, h, m, l, Phat, MV), limiter switch, aux. in jack, headphone jack, rear panel: XLR balanced line out, external speaker out, tweeter on/off switch, 12.6 in. wide, 13.9 in. tall, 12 in. deep, 22 lbs., mfg. 2012-present.

MSR $467	$350	$230 - 265	$115 - 140	

P3115 PROMETHEAN COMBO – 300W, 1-15 in. speaker with a high-freq. dome tweeter and crossover, ultralight bass head unit, solid-state chassis, single channel, front red control panel, single input, six red knobs (g, h, m, l, Phat, MV), limiter switch, aux. in jack, headphone jack, rear panel: XLR balanced line out, tuner out, 17.7 in. wide, 14.4 in. tall, 21.7 in. deep, 37.4 lbs., mfg. 2012-present.

MSR $533	$400	$225 - 275	$130 - 170	

MSR/NOTES	100%	EXCELLENT	AVERAGE	LAST MSR

P5110 Promethean Combo
courtesy Ibanez

P110C Promethean Cabinet
courtesy Ibanez

P410C Promethean Cabinet
courtesy Ibanez

P5110 PROMETHEAN COMBO – 250W (500W with extension cab), 1-10 in. speaker with a tweeter, bass combo, solid-state chassis, single channel, peak limiting circuit, front red control panel, single input, five red knobs (g, l, h, vibe, MV), six-band graphic EQ, mute switch, vibe switch, headphone jack, aux. input, balanced XLR line out with ground lift switch, 0/-20 db level switch, pre/post EQ switch, tuner out, footswitch jack, optional two-button mute and vibe control footswitch, bottom ported cabinet, black covering, black metal grille, 12.75 in. wide, 12.75 in. tall, 18 in. deep, 26.8 lbs., mfg. 2009-2011.

	$700	$450 - 525	$250 - 300	$933

* Add $45 (MSR $60) for gig bag (Model BGP511).
* Add $30 (MSR $40) for two-button footswitch (Model IFS2X).

P5115K PROMETHEAN COMBO – 500W, 1-15 in. speaker with a tweeter, bass combo, solid-state chassis, single channel, peak limiting circuit, front red control panel, single input, five red knobs (g, l, h, vibe, MV), six-band graphic EQ, mute switch, vibe switch, headphone jack, aux. input, balanced XLR line out with ground lift switch, 0/-20 db level switch, pre/post EQ switch, tuner out, footswitch jack, optional two-button mute and vibe control footswitch, kick-back cabinet design, black covering, black metal grille, 13.1 in. wide, 30.3 in. tall, 14.8 in. deep, 26.8 lbs., mfg. 2011-2014.

	$900	$550 - 650	$325 - 375	$1,200

* Add $45 (MSR $60) for gig bag (Model BGP511).
* Add $30 (MSR $40) for two-button footswitch (Model IFS2X).

P5210 PROMETHEAN COMBO – 500W, 2-10 in. speakers with an HF dome tweeter, bass combo, solid-state chassis, single channel, peak limiting circuit, front red control panel, single input, five red knobs (g, l, h, vibe, MV), six-band graphic EQ, mute switch, vibe switch, headphone jack, aux. input, balanced XLR line out with ground lift switch, 0/-20 db level switch, pre/post EQ switch, tuner out, footswitch jack, optional two-button mute and vibe control footswitch, bottom ported cabinet, black covering, black metal grille, 13 in. wide, 30.25 in. tall, 14.75 in. deep, 54.6 lbs., mfg. summer 2009-2014.

	$900	$550 - 650	$325 - 375	$1,200

* Add $30 (MSR $40) for two-button footswitch (Model IFS2X).

P110C PROMETHEAN CABINET – 250W, 1-10 in. Neodymium speaker with a dome tweeter, bass cabinet, 8 ohm impedance, Speakon combo jack, bottom ported cabinet, black covering, black metal grille, 12.75 in. wide, 12.75 in. tall, 18 in. deep, 21 lbs., mfg. 2009-2010.

	$350	$200 - 250	$120 - 150	$467

P115C PROMETHEAN CABINET – 300W, 1-15 in. Neodymium speaker with a horn tweeter, bass cabinet, 8 ohm impedance, two Speakon combo jacks, bottom ported cabinet, recessed side handles, casters, black covering, black metal grille, 23.75 in. wide, 24.375 in. tall, 17.75 in. deep, 65 lbs., mfg. summer 2009-2010.

	$600	$350 - 425	$200 - 250	$800

P115CC PROMETHEAN CABINET – 250W, 1-15 in. Ceramic speaker with a horn tweeter, bass cabinet, 8 ohm impedance, recessed side handles, casters, black covering, black metal grille, 23.75 in. wide, 24.375 in. tall, 17.75 in. deep, mfg. 2011-present.

MSR $533	$400	$225 - 275	$130 - 170	

P210KC PROMETHEAN CABINET – 250W, 2-10 in. Ceramic speakers, bass cabinet, 8 ohm impedance, bottom ported kickback cabinet design, black covering, black metal grille, 23.75 in. wide, 24.375 in. tall, 17.75 in. deep, mfg. 2011-present.

MSR $467	$350	$200 - 250	$120 - 150	

P410C PROMETHEAN CABINET – 1000W, 4-10 in. Neodymium speaker with a horn tweeter, bass cabinet, 8 ohm impedance, two Speakon combo jacks, bottom ported cabinet, recessed side handles, casters, black covering, black metal grille, 23.75 in. wide, 24.375 in. tall, 17.75 in. deep, 82.5 lbs., mfg. summer 2009-2010.

	$900	$550 - 650	$325 - 375	$1,200

P410CC PROMETHEAN CABINET – 500W, 4-10 in. Ceramic speakers with a horn tweeter, bass cabinet, 8 ohm impedance, recessed side handles, casters, black covering, black metal grille, mfg. 2011-present.

MSR $667	$500	$300 - 375	$175 - 225	

MSR/NOTES	100%	EXCELLENT	AVERAGE	LAST MSR

BASS AMPLIFIERS: SOUNDWAVE (SW/SWX SERIES)

SW stands for Sound Wave, which was what the initial electric amplifiers were called by Ibanez. In summer, 2008 the new SBX Soundwave Series replaced the previous Soundwave Series.

SW20
courtesy Ibanez

SW100
courtesy Ibanez

SWX20
courtesy Ibanez

SW15 – 15W, 1-8 in. speaker, bass combo, solid-state chassis, single channel, front burgundy control panel, single input, four black knobs (v, t, m, b), aux. in, headphone jack, kickback cabinet design, black covering, black cloth grille, mfg. 2011-present.

MSR $133	**$100**	**$50 - 70**	**$30 - 40**	

SW20 – 20W, 1-8 in. speaker, solid-state chassis combo, single channel, front black control panel, five black knobs (v, b, m, t, p), headphone jack, CD inputs, black covering, black grille, mfg. summer 2001-mid-2008.

	$100	**$55 - 70**	**$35 - 45**	**$133**

SW25 – 25W, 1-10 in.speaker, solid state chassis combo, single channel, compression, front black control panel, six black knobs (v, threshold, b, l/m, m/h, t), headphone jack, line out, shelf port, black covering, black grille, mfg. 1998-99.

	N/A	**$75 - 100**	**$50 - 60**	**$180**

* ***SW25DX*** – similar to the SW25 except has a tuned front mounted port design, mfg. 2000-01.

	N/A	**$75 - 100**	**$50 - 60**	

SW35 (FIRST VERSION) – 35W, 1-10 in. speaker, solid-state chassis combo, limiter, front black control panel, single input, six black knobs (g, b, m, t, p, v), CD-input, headphone jack, line out, effects loop, tilt-back cabinet, black covering, black grille, mfg. summer 2001-mid-2008.

	$160	**$95 - 115**	**$65 - 80**	**$213**

SW35 (SECOND VERSION) – 35W, 1-10 in. speaker, bass combo, solid-state chassis, single channel, front burgundy control panel, single input, six black knobs (g, t, h/m, l/m, b, v), distortion switch, envelope switch, shape switch, mid level switch, line out jack, footswitch jack, aux. in with level control, headphone jack, kickback cabinet design, black covering, black metal grille, mfg. 2011-2014.

	$250	**$135 - 175**	**$80 - 105**	**$333**

SW65 – 65W, 1-12 in. speaker with piezo tweeter, solid-state chassis combo, limiter, black front control panel, single input, six black knobs (g, b, m, t, p, v), CD-inputs, headphone jack, line out, effects loop, black covering, black grille, mfg. summer 2001-mid-2008.

	$230	**$130 - 160**	**$75 - 100**	**$307**

SW80 – 80W, 1-15 in. speaker, bass combo, solid-state chassis, single channel, front burgundy control panel, single input, six black knobs (g, t, h/m, l/m, b, v), distortion switch, envelope switch, shape switch, mid level switch, line out jack, footswitch jack, aux. in with level control, headphone jack, kickback cabinet design, black covering, black metal grille, mfg. 2011-2014.

	$350	**$200 - 250**	**$120 - 150**	**$467**

SW100 – 100W, 1-15 in.speaker with piezo tweeter, solid-state chassis combo, limiter, black front control panel, single input, eight black knobs (g, b, m, select, t, p, FX mix, MV), RCA inputs, headphone jack, line out, effects loop, tilt-back cabinet, black covering, black grille, mfg. 2004-mid-2008.

	$350	**$200 - 250**	**$120 - 150**	**$467**

SWX20 – 20W, 1-8 in. speaker bass combo, solid-state chassis, single channel, auto compression circuit, front/top combination black control panel, single input, five white knobs (level, b, m, t, hue), bright switch, shape switch, CD/MP3 RCA inputs, headphone jack, black covering, black metal grille with Ibanez logo in upper left corner, 19 lbs., mfg. summer 2008-2010.

	$150	**$85 - 110**	**$50 - 65**	**$200**

SWX35 – 35W, 1-10 in. speaker bass combo, solid-state chassis, single channel, auto compression circuit, front/top combination black control panel, single input, six white knobs (level, b, m, t, hue, MV), bright switch, shape switch, CD/MP3 RCA inputs, headphone jack, line out, closed back cabinet with tilt-up system, black covering, black metal grille with Ibanez logo in upper left corner, 31.4 lbs., mfg. summer 2008-2010.

	$200	**$110 - 140**	**$65 - 85**	**$267**

MSR/NOTES	100%	EXCELLENT	AVERAGE	LAST MSR

SWX65
courtesy Ibanez

SWX100
courtesy Ibanez

SW115S Speaker Cabinet
courtesy Ibanez

SWX65 – 65W, 1-12 in. speaker bass combo with piezo horn tweeter, solid-state chassis, single channel, auto compression circuit, front/top combination black control panel, single input, six white knobs (level, b, m, t, hue, MV), bright switch, shape switch, tweeter on/off switch, effects loop, CD/MP3 RCA inputs, headphone jack, line out, closed back cabinet with tilt-up system, black covering, black metal grille with Ibanez logo in upper left corner, 44.5 lbs., mfg. summer 2008-2010.

$250	$140 - 175	$90 - 110		$333

SWX100 – 100W, 1-15 in. speaker bass combo with piezo horn tweeter, solid-state chassis, single channel, auto compression circuit, front/top combination black control panel, single input, six white knobs (level, b, m, t, hue, MV), bright switch, shape switch, tweeter on/off switch, effects loop, CD/MP3 RCA inputs, headphone jack, XLR direct line out with pre/post switch and ground lift switch, closed back bottom ported cabinet with casters, black covering, black metal grille with Ibanez logo in upper left corner, 53.4 lbs., mfg. summer 2008-2010.

$350	$200 - 250	$120 - 150		$467

SW115S SPEAKER CABINET – bass extension cabinet designed for use with the SW100, 1-15 in. speaker with piezo tweeter, closed back cabinet, casters, black covering, black grille, mfg. 2004-mid-2008.

$250	$150 - 190	$90 - 120		$333

IDOL

Amplifiers previously produced in Japan during the 1960s.

Idol produced amplifiers during the 1960s with their most notable models coming from the Hobby Series. Known models include the **Hobby 10**, **Hobby 20**, **Hobby 45**, and **Hobby 100** and prices on these amplifiers typically range between $100 and $200. Any further information on Idol amplifiers can be submitted directly to Blue Book Publications.

INDUSTRIAL AMPS

Amplifiers currently produced in York, PA since 2007.

Tony and JoAnn Niekrewicz build industrial-quality tube amplifiers in their York, PA shop. All amps are built one at a time with point-to-point construction using military spec and hospital grade components. Cabinets are constructed of 3/4 in. eleven-ply hardwood birch with 1/4 in. aluminum grilles, and the tubes are housed behind 1/4 in. glass. Needless to say, these amps are built very rugged for heavy use, but they also have a unique tone different than many other popular manufacturers. For more information, visit Industrial Amps' website or contact them directly.

CONTACT INFORMATION
INDUSTRIAL AMPS
472 Beck Rd.
York, PA 17403
Phone No.: 717-347-7419
Phone No.: 845-489-0688
www.industrialamps.com
tony@industrialamps.com

ELECTRIC TUBE AMPLIFIERS/SPEAKER CABINETS

All Industrial Amps' models come standard in white or black Tolex, but other colors are available upon request. The **Crunch 15** has 15W from 2 X 6V6 power tubes with a single channel and reverb. The Crunch 15 has a purple chassis and is available as a head unit (MSR $2,150) or a 1-12 in. combo (MSR $2,300). The **Overdrive 15** has 15W from 2 X 6V6 power tubes with a single overdrive channel. The Overdrive 15 has a yellow chassis and is available as a head unit (MSR $2,050) or a 1-12 in. combo (MSR $2,200). The **Blues 60** has 60W from either 2 X 6L6 or EL34 power tubes with two channels and reverb. The Blues 60 has a blue chassis and is available as a head unit (MSR $2,800) or a 2-12 in. combo (MSR $3,150). The **Rock 120** is Industrial Amps' flagship model and has 120W power from 4 X EL34 power tubes with two channels and reverb. The Rock 120 has a red chassis and is available as a head unit (MSR $2,900) or a 2-12 in. combo (MSR $3,250).

Speaker cabinets are available in 1-12 in. (MSR $700), 2-12 in. (MSR $900), 4-12 in. (MSR $1,450), or an extended 4-12 in. (MSR $1,650) configuration.

INTELLI ELECTRONICS INC.

Amplifiers currently produced in China. The Intelli headquarters is located in South Korea. Currently there is no U.S. Distributor.

Intelli Amplification is a Korean-based company that builds amplifiers and other products in China. Currently they have guitar and bass amplifiers in a number of different configurations. Most of the products are entry-level practice units, but there are some higher-end models. The amps are solid-state design, and have the basic controls that practice level amplifiers usually have. They also make rackmount power amplifiers.

ISP TECHNOLOGIES

Intelligent Signal Processing. Amplifiers currently produced in Waterford, MI since 2001. Distributed by ISP Technologies.

James Waller created Rocktron amplifiers in 1985. At Rocktron, he developed the HUSH Noise Reduction System, a line of DSP guitar rack products, and the Circle Surround stereo five-speaker matrix among other devices. In 2001, Waller sold Rocktron to GHS, but he took the engineering team with him and formed ISP (Intelligent Signal Processsing) Technologies in the same year. They produce a line of guitar amplifiers and speaker cabinets along with signal processors, PA speaker cabinets, subwoofers, and various other products. For more information, visit ISP's website or contact the company directly.

CONTACT INFORMATION
ISP TECHNOLOGIES
5479 Perry Drive, Suite B
Waterford, MI 48329
Phone No.: 248-673-7790
Fax No.: 248-673-7696
www.isptechnologies.com
sales@isptechnologies.com

ELECTRIC/BASS GUITAR AMPLIFIERS

For bass, ISP produces the **Beta Preamp** with two active EQs, compression, excitor, and the Decimator Noise Reduction. ISP also makes the Vector speaker cabinet series that are designed for use with the Theta guitar head and Beta bass preamp.

THETA HEAD – 300W, guitar head-unit, solid-state chassis, two channels (clean/distortion), Decimator Noise Reduction, digital reverb, front black control panel, single input, 29 black knobs, effects loop, black covering, black grille, 29 in. wide, 11.75 in. tall, 9 in. deep, 40 lbs., current mfg.

| MSR $2,100 | $1,750 | $1,000 - 1,250 | $675 - 800 |

THETA COMBO – 400W (100W/300W), 2-12 in. speakers (one Celestion speaker and one large excursion neo woofer), solid-state chassis, two channels (clean/distortion), Decimator Noise Reduction, digital reverb, front black control panel, single input, 29 black knobs, effects loop, black covering, black grille, 30 in. wide, 20 in. tall, 14 in. deep, 70 lbs., current mfg.

| MSR $2,479 | $2,100 | $1,200 - 1,450 | $750 - 900 |

NOTES

J SECTION

JACKSON

Amplifiers previously produced in Fort Worth, TX during the late 1980s and early 1990s.

The Charvel/Jackson Guitar company was founded in 1978 after Grover Jackson bought out Wayne Charvel's Guitar Repair shop in Azusa, California. As the bolt-neck custom-built Charvel guitars gained popularity with the up-and-coming West Coast rock musicians, it became a necessity that standardized models were established. By 1983, neck-through designs were introduced with the Jackson logo on the headstock. Jackson/Charvel was first licensed (in 1985) and later acquired (in 1986) by the International Music Company (IMC) of Fort Worth, Texas. It was around this time that Jackson introduced their first amplifiers. 1980s models include the Apogee 50 Combo and the JG tube head models. In 1994, they introduced the Reference series and listed the Apogee 50 Combo as well. There is speculation that early models were designed by Lee Jackson, Laney of England built them, and Jackson marketed them under their name. However, the newer Reference Series were advertised as being all made in the U.S. and designed by Steve Mauriello. In 1995, a Charvel/Jackson brochure advertised that they were going to introduce a Reference 30 model as well, but it is unlikely it ever went into production. By the mid-1990s, Jackson discontinued all production of amplifiers and hasn't produced any since. In 2002, FMIC (Fender) bought Jackson and currently produces and distributes Jackson guitars. Please refer to the *Blue Book of Electric Guitars* for more information on Jackson guitars.

MSR/NOTES	100%	EXCELLENT	AVERAGE	LAST MSR

ELECTRIC TUBE AMPLIFIERS

In 1995, Jackson advertised a new **Reference 30** amp in their "What's New For 1995" flyer, but there was no picture of the amp and it is unlikely it ever went into production.

APOGEE COMBO – 50W, 2-12 in. Celestion Vintage 30 speakers, guitar combo, tube chassis, preamp: 4 X 12AX7, power: 2 X 5881, front chrome control panel, single input, nine knobs (Ch. 1: v, l, m, h, Ch. 2: v, g, l, m, h), A/B voicing switch, effects loop, black Tolex covering, black speaker grille, 33 in. wide, 23 in. tall, 15 in. deep, 82 lbs., mfg. mid-1990s.

	N/A	$850 - 1,000	$600 - 700	$2,295

REFERENCE 50 – 50W, head-unit configuration, tube chassis, preamp: 4 X 12AX7, power: 2 X EL34, front black control panel, single input, nine knobs (Ch. 1: v, l, m, h, Ch. 2: v, g, l, m, h), effects loop, optional footswitch, black carpet covering, 23.5 in. wide, 12 in. tall, 14.5 in. deep, 39 lbs., mfg. mid-1990s.

	N/A	$425 - 500	$275 - 325	$1,295

* *Reference 50 Ltd.* – similar to the Reference 50, except has a triple plated chrome control panel and black Tolex covering with white piping, mfg. mid-1990s.

	N/A	$450 - 525	$300 - 350	$1,395

REFERENCE 100 – 100W, head-unit configuration, tube chassis, preamp: 4 X 12AX7, power: 4 X 5881, front black control panel, single input, nine knobs (Ch. 1: v, l, m, h, Ch. 2: v, g, l, m, h), A/B voicing switch, effects loop, optional footswitch, black carpet covering, 23.5 in. wide, 12 in. tall, 14.5 in. deep, 43 lbs., mfg. mid-1990s.

	N/A	$475 - 550	$300 - 350	$1,375

* *Reference 100 Ltd.* – similar to the Reference 100, except has a triple plated chrome control panel and black Tolex covering with white piping, mfg. mid-1990s.

	N/A	$500 - 600	$325 - 375	$1,475

SPEAKER CABINETS

T-1 – 280W, 4-12 in. Celestion G12-70 speakers, black Tolex covering with white piping, black grille, 31.5 in. wide, 32 in. tall, 17.5 in. deep, 99 lbs., mfg. mid-1990s.

	N/A	$300 - 350	$175 - 225	$750

This model matches the Reference Series Ltd. heads.

* *T-1V* – similar to the T-1, except has 120W and 4-12 in. Celestion Vintage 30 speakers, mfg. mid-1990s.

	N/A	$325 - 375	$200 - 250	$850

T-2 – 280W, 4-12 in. Celestion G12-70 speakers, black carpet covering with white piping, black metal grille, 31.5 in. wide, 32 in. tall, 17.5 in. deep, 99 lbs., mfg. mid-1990s.

	N/A	$250 - 300	$125 - 175	$650

This model matches the regular Reference Series heads.

* *T-2V* – similar to the T-2, except has 120W and 4-12 in. Celestion Vintage 30 speakers, mfg. mid-1990s.

	N/A	$275 - 325	$150 - 200	$750

MSR/NOTES	100%	EXCELLENT	AVERAGE	LAST MSR

JACKSON-GULDAN

Amplifiers previously produced in Columbus, OH between the 1940s and 1960s.

Jackson-Guldan was a violin company based in Columbus, OH between the 1920s and the 1960s. When lap steel and Hawaiian guitars became popular in the late 1930s and early 1940s, Jackson-Guldan introduced their own lap steels with amplifiers. Most models are small with low wattage and limited features. Examples seem to be similar to Oahu and early Gibson EH models. Any further information on Jackson-Guldan can be submitted directly to Blue Book Publications.

JAGUAR AMPLIFICATION

Amplifiers currently produced in Fallbrook, CA.

Jaguar builds handcrafted tube amps with the goal of combining great looks of an amplifier with a sound second to none. All amps are built in the U.S. with point-to-point wiring and the finest components available. Jaguar amplifiers are sold through a variety of select dealers. For more information, visit Jaguar's website or contact them directly.

CONTACT INFORMATION
JAGUAR AMPLIFICATION
PO Box 1479
Fallbrook, CA 92088
Phone No.: 760-518-4236
www.jaguaramplification.com
info@jaguaramplification.com

ELECTRIC TUBE AMPLIFIERS/SPEAKER CABINETS

The **Jaguar Twin** features the best of British and American sounds with 45W output from 2 X EL34 power tubes, a single channel, and a half-power switch. The Twin is available as a head-unit (MSR $2,399), 1-12 in. combo (MSR $2,899), or 2-12 in. combo (MSR $2,999). The **Jaguar Lead** is designed after the late 1970s master volume amps from Britain with 45W output from 2 X 6L6GC power tubes, a single channel, and a half-power switch. The Lead is available as a head-unit (MSR $2,399), 1-12 in. combo (MSR $2,899), or 2-12 in. combo (MSR $2,999). The **Jaguar Jr.** is a basic Class A all-tube amp with 17W output from 2 X EL84 power tubes and a single channel with volume, gain, and tone controls. The Jr. is available as a head-unit (MSR $2,199), 1-12 in. combo (MSR $2,499), or 2-12 in. combo (MSR $2,599). The **Jaguar 200** is an all-tube bass amp with 200W output from 4 X KT88 fan-cooled power tubes, a single channel, and a half-power switch. The 200 is only available as a head-unit (MSR $2,999) with a 4-10 in. speaker cabinet (MSR $1,399). The **Jaguar Retro** was introduced in 2009 and is based around the early 1960s "British Chime" sounds with 30W output from 4 X EL84 power tubes, a single channel, and a half-power switch. The Retro is available as a head-unit (MSR $2,299), 1-12 in. combo (MSR $2,699), or 2-12 in. combo (MSR $2,799). The **Jaguar 7** was introduced in 2010 and features 7W power, a single EL84 power tube, and only volume and tone controls. The Jaguar 7 is only available as a 1-10 in. combo (MSR $1,499).

Speaker cabinets are available in 1-12 in. (MSR $799), 2-10 in. (MSR $899), 2-12 in. (MSR $999), and 4-12 in. (MSR $1,499) configurations.

JAY TURSER

Amplifiers previously produced in Asia. Distributed by U.S. Music Corp. in Mundelein, IL. Previously distributed by American Music & Sound (AM&S) in Agoura Hills, CA.

The Jay Turser brand of guitars was created by Tommy Rizzi at Music Industries Corp. in the late 1990s. Initially, Jay Turser instruments consisted of student and entry-level guitars that were based on popular American designs. As the line expanded through the 2000s, mid-level guitars and original designs have been introduced and Jay Turser currently offers a wide variety of guitars and basses. Guitar amplifiers are no longer in production. For more information visit their website or contact them directly.

CONTACT INFORMATION
JAY TURSER
Distributed by U.S. Music Corp.
444 E. Courtland St.
Mundelein, IL 60060
Phone No.: 847-949-0444
Phone No.: 800-877-6863
Fax No.: 847-949-8444
www.jayturser.com
cservice@usmusiccorp.com

ELECTRIC SS AMPLIFIERS: EARLY MODELS

G-10 – 10W practice guitar amp, 1-6.5 in. speaker, five controls (g, MV, t, m, b), headphone jack, disc. 2003.

	N/A	$40 - 50	$25 - 35	$90

JG-10 – 20W lead guitar amp, 1-8 in. speaker, reverb, seven controls (g, MV, t, m, b, p, r), headphone jack, disc. 2003.

	N/A	$45 - 60	$30 - 40	$110

JG-30R – 30W lead guitar amp, 1-10 in. speaker, reverb, seven controls (g, MV, t, m, b, p, r), headphone jack, footswitch jack, disc. 2003.

	N/A	$95 - 120	$55 - 75	$210

JB-20 – 20W practice bass amp, 1-8 in. speaker, six controls (g, MV, t, m, b, c), headphone jack, disc. 2003.

	N/A	$50 - 65	$35 - 45	$120

JB-30 – 30W bass amp, 1-10 in. speaker, six controls (g, MV, t, m, b, c), headphone jack, ext. speaker jack, disc. 2003.

	N/A	$75 - 100	$45 - 60	$175

JZ-30X – 30W acoustic amp, 4-5 in. speakers, two channels, eleven controls, headphone jack, disc. 2003.

	N/A	$95 - 120	$55 - 75	$210

MSR/NOTES	100%	EXCELLENT	AVERAGE	LAST MSR

Classic-25RC
courtesy Jay Turser

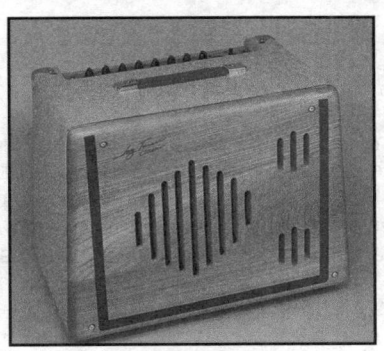
Classic-30RC
courtesy Jay Turser

GA-30B
courtesy Jay Turser

ELECTRIC SS AMPLIFIERS: CLASSIC SERIES

CLASSIC-10 – 10W practice guitar amp with rechargable battery, 1-6.5 in. speaker, solid-state chassis, top control panel, five controls (g, MV, t, m, b), headphone jack, inlaid wood front, tweed body, gold hardware, disc.

| MSR N/A | $80 | $50 - 60 | $30 - 40 | |

CLASSIC-25RC – 25W lead guitar amp, 1-10 in. Celestion speaker, solid-state chassis, reverb, tremolo, top control panel, nine controls (Overdrive: depth, master, MV, t, m, b, r, s, i), headphone jack, inlaid wood front, tweed body, gold hardware, disc.

| MSR N/A | $185 | $110 - 140 | $65 - 85 | |

CLASSIC-30B – 30W bass guitar amp, 1-10 in. Celestion speaker, solid-state chassis, top control panel, five controls (g, MV, t, m, b, c), headphone jack, inlaid wood front, tweed body, gold hardware, disc. 2006.

| | $175 | $110 - 130 | $65 - 80 | $240 |

CLASSIC-30RC – 30W acoustic guitar amp, 1-8 in. speaker with 2-3 in. tweeters, solid-state chassis, top control panel, eight controls (g, MV, t, m, b, r, s, i), headphone jack, inlaid wood front, tweed body, gold hardware, disc. 2005.

| | N/A | $120 - 150 | $75 - 95 | $250 |

ELECTRIC SS AMPLIFIERS: GA SERIES

GA-10TS – 10W, 1-6.5 in. speaker, solid-state chassis, single channel, built-in recording, front black and silver control panel, single input, five black knobs (g, l, MV, t, b), OD switch, recording circuit with knob and buttons, headphone jack, black covering, silver metal grille, mfg. 2006-disc.

| | $75 | $35 - 50 | $15 - 25 | |

GA-15DSPR – 15W, 1-8 in. speaker, solid-state chassis, single channel, built-in recording, front black and silver control panel, single input, five black knobs (g, MV, t, m, b), OD switch, recording circuit and DSP with one white knob and buttons, headphone jack, black covering, silver metal grille, mfg. 2006-disc.

| | $150 | $95 - 120 | $50 - 70 | |

GA-25DSPR – 25W, 1-10 in. speaker, solid-state chassis, single channel, built-in recording, front black and silver control panel, single input, six black knobs (g, level, MV, t, m, b), OD switch, recording circuit and DSP with one white knob and buttons, headphone jack, black covering, silver metal grille, mfg. 2006-disc.

| | $175 | $100 - 135 | $60 - 80 | |

GA-30B – 30W, 1-8 in. speaker, solid-state chassis, bass combo, single channel, front silver control panel, single input, six black knobs (g, MV, t, m, b, p), headphone jack, black covering, silver metal grille, mfg. 2006-disc.

| | $100 | $60 - 80 | $30 - 45 | |

JAZZKAT AMPLIFIERS

Amplifiers currently produced in New Jersey since the mid-2000s.

VMV (Vince, Marty, and Vic) Electric Instruments developed the JazzKat amplifier in the 2000s. These amps are designed especially for the Jazz musician. While there is only one basic design, they have made several variations out of it for use with guitars and basses. John Pizzarelli is their first major endorser. For more information, visit JazzKat's website or contact them directly.

CONTACT INFORMATION
JAZZKAT AMPLIFIERS
4057 Route 9 N., Suite 225
Howell, NJ 07731
Phone No.: 732-618-0825
www.jazzkatamps.com
vvg@jazzkatamps.com
ma@jazzkatamps.com

ELECTRIC JAZZ AMPLIFIERS

Models include the **GypsyKat** (disc.), **JazzKat**, **PhatKat** (MSR $1,099), **TomKat** (MSR $1,299), **TwinKat** (MSR $1,149), the **BluesKat** (MSR $999), **BassKat** (MSR $999), the **CoolKat**, and the **AcoustiKat**.

MSR/NOTES	100%	EXCELLENT	AVERAGE	LAST MSR

JBL

Speakers, speaker cabinets, and other pro-audio related equipment currently produced in Northridge, CA. The JBL trademark was established in 1946.

JBL was founded by James B. Lansing in 1946. Before JBL, speakers were produced under the name Lansing. In the amplifier industry, JBL is probably best known for their speakers, especially in Fender amps. Currently they produce a wide variety of speaker cabinets and other pro-audio products. They also offer components to replace many popular speaker sizes. For more information and a full history of Lansing/JBL, visit JBL's website or contact them directly.

JCA CIRCUITS

Amplifiers previously produced in Pottstown, PA.

Jason C. Arthur founded JCA Circuits in 1995, and he built his **GR 1.6** amplifier on a custom basis one at a time. The GR 1.6 has a completely original design that can produce many different tones, including many classic tones as well. The GR 1.6 is so versatile that Arthur states that his amp could replace a small fleet of medium powered combo amplifiers. All amps were built as they are ordered and were customized by the customer, but Arthur offered two "standard" models that have a combination of popular features. Prices started at $2,699 for the GR 1.6.

JET CITY AMPLIFICATION

Amplifiers currently produced in China since 2009. Distributed in the U.S. by Jet City Amplification in Woodinville, WA.

Amp designer Mike Soldano, Doug White, and Dan Gallagher formed Jet City Amplification to create a new line of affordable amplifiers based on Soldano's circuits. Jet City amps are designed by Soldano and the preamp is based on the Soldano SLO-100. For more information, visit Jet City's website or contact them directly.

ELECTRIC TUBE AMPLIFIERS

Jet City also advertises a 50W combo called the **JCA5212RC**, but it does not have a current MSR.

Jet City 20 Head
courtesy Jet City Amplification

Jet City 20 1-12 Combo
courtesy Jet City Amplification

Jet City 100 Head
courtesy Jet City Amplification

Jet City 50 Head
courtesy Jet City Amplification

Jet City THD Picovalve Head
courtesy Jet City Amplification

JET CITY 20 HEAD (JCA20H) – 20W, guitar head-unit, five-tube chassis, preamp: 3 X 12AX7, power: 2 X EL84, solid-state rectifier, single channel, front black control panel, single input, six knobs (preamp g, v, m, t, MV, p), power switch, standby switch, rear panel: three speaker jacks, black covering with a blue front panel, 19.5 in. wide, 9 in. tall, 9 in. deep, 21.3 lbs., mfg. 2009-present.

MSR $430	$335	$200 - 250	$120 - 150

JET CITY 20 1-12 COMBO (JCA2112RC) – 20W, 1-12 in. Jet City Custom Eminence speaker, seven-tube chassis, preamp: 5 X 12AX7, power: 2 X EL84, solid-state rectifier, single channel, reverb, top black control panel, single input, seven knobs (preamp g, r, v, m, t, MV, p), power switch, standby switch, rear panel: three speaker jacks, black covering with a black speaker grille and top blue front panel, 21 in. wide, 20 in. tall, 11 in. deep, 38.7 lbs., mfg. 2009-present.

MSR $500	$400	$250 - 300	$150 - 200

JET CITY 50 HEAD (JCA50H) – 50W, guitar head-unit, seven-tube chassis, preamp: 5 X 12AX7, power: 2 X 6L6, solid-state rectifier, two channels (normal and overdrive), front black control panel, single input, eight knobs (normal Ch. preamp g, overdrive Ch. preamp g, v, m, t, normal Ch. MV, overdrive Ch. MV, p), power switch, standby switch, rear panel: five speaker jacks, footswitch jack, effects loop, black covering with a blue front panel, single button footswitch included, 25 in. wide, 9.5 in. tall, 9.5 in. deep, 40 lbs., new 2010.

MSR $800	$600	$375 - 450	$225 - 275

MSR/NOTES	100%	EXCELLENT	AVERAGE	LAST MSR

JET CITY 100 HEAD (JCA100H) – 100W, guitar head-unit, nine-tube chassis, preamp: 5 X 12AX7, power: 4 X 6L6, solid-state rectifier, two channels (normal and overdrive), front black control panel, single input, eight knobs (normal Ch. preamp g, overdrive Ch. preamp g, v, m, t, normal Ch. MV, overdrive Ch. MV, p), power switch, standby switch, rear panel: five speaker jacks, footswitch jack, effects loop, black covering with a blue front panel, single button footswitch included, 25 in. wide, 9.5 in. tall, 9.5 in. deep, 40 lbs., mfg. 2009-present.

MSR $1,000 $800 $500 - 600 $300 - 350

JET CITY THD PICOVALVE HEAD – 5W (switchable to 2.5W), mini guitar head-unit, three-tube chassis, preamp: 2 X 12AX7, power: 1 X 6L6, solid-state rectifier, single channel, front black control panel, single input, five knobs (preamp g, t, m, b, MV), bright switch, 5W/2.5W switch, standby switch power switch, rear panel: three speaker jacks, black cage casing, 12.5 in. wide, 6.5 in. tall, 7 in. deep, 21 lbs., mfg. 2010-present.

MSR $355 $250 $160 - 200 $95 - 120

The PicoValve Head was designed by Andy Marshall of THD Electronics and is licensed by them.

SPEAKER CABINETS

2-12 Speaker Cabinet
courtesy Jet City Amplification

4-12 Speaker Cabinet
courtesy Jet City Amplification

1-12 Jetstream Isolation Cabinet
courtesy Jet City Amplification

1-12 SPEAKER CABINET (JCA12S) – 100W, 1-12 in. Jet City Custom Eminence speaker, 16 ohm impedance, single input, multi-ply hardwood construction, black covering with a black speaker grille and top front blue panel, 21 in. wide, 20 in. tall, 11 in. deep, 26.6 lbs., mfg. 2009-present.

MSR $249 $200 $120 - 150 $75 - 95

2-12 SPEAKER CABINET (JCA24S) – 200W mono (100W per side stereo), 2-12 in. Jet City Custom Eminence speaker, 8 ohm mono or 2 X 16 ohm stereo impedance, two inputs with mono/stereo switch, multi-ply hardwood construction, black covering with a black speaker grille and top front blue panel, 28 in. wide, 20 in. tall, 12 in. deep, 40.2 lbs., mfg. 2009-present.

MSR $400 $300 $175 - 225 $110 - 140

4-12 SPEAKER CABINET (JCA48S) – 400W mono (200W per side stereo), 4-12 in. Jet City Custom Eminence speaker, 8 ohm mono or 2 X 16 ohm stereo impedance, two inputs with mono/stereo switch, multi-ply hardwood construction, angled front, black covering with a black speaker grille, 28 in. wide, 28 in. tall, 14 in. deep, 69.5 lbs., mfg. 2009-present.

MSR $650 $500 $300 - 375 $175 - 225

1-12 JETSTREAM ISOLATION CABINET (ISO12) – 100W, 1-12 in. Jet City Custom Eminence speaker house in an isolation cabinet, 16 ohm impedance, single input, XLR and USB outputs, multi-ply hardwood construction, two-tone black and blue covering, new summer 2010.

MSR $500 $400 $250 - 300 $150 - 200

The isolation cabinet is designed to produce full volume guitar amp tones that can be controlled for home or studio recording and stage applications. By positioning a mic inside the cabinet with it closed, it sends out a full volume signal that can be controlled by the player.

JMI AMPLIFIERS

Jennings Musical Instruments. Amplifiers currently produced in Great Britain since 2004.

JMI (Jennings Musical Instruments) was created to revive the amplifiers based on Tom Jennings popular Vox designs of the early 1960s. Tom Jennings built the original AC Vox amps in the late 1950s and early 1960s, and JMI amplifiers are built to the original specifications of the early Vox designs. JMI amps also feature Vox-style black or fawn brown covering with the only cosmetic difference being the logo which reads "JMI" in the same "VOX" lettering. JMI recently began recreating various effects pedals that they produce in limited quantities, including the famous Rangemaster Treble Booster. For more information, visit JMI's website or contact them directly.

CONTACT INFORMATION
JMI AMPLIFIERS
Unit 1, Holmeroyd Road, Bentley Moor Lane, Adwick-Le-Street
Doncaster, South Yorkshire DN6 7BH
United Kingdom
Phone No.: +44 (0)1302 330429
Fax No.: +44 (0)1302 330437
www.jmiamplification.com
sales@jmiamplification.com

MSR/NOTES	100%	EXCELLENT	AVERAGE	LAST MSR

JOHNSON

Amplifiers currently produced in Asia since the mid-1990s. Distributed by the Music Link in Hayward, CA.

Johnson is a trademark used by the Music Link in the U.S. Johnson amplifiers (as well as guitars and other related accessories) are produced overseas and imported into the U.S. and other countries. Early efforts were aimed at the student or entry-level guitarists, but they have expanded recently with tube amplifiers and a half-stack unit. For more information, visit Johnson's website or contact them directly.

CONTACT INFORMATION
JOHNSON
Distributed by The Music Link
31067 San Clemente Street
Hayward, CA 94544
Phone No.: 415-570-0970
Fax No.: 415-570-0651
www.johnsongtr.com
info@johnsongtr.com

AMPLIFIERS

The earliest series of Johnson amplifiers was the JA Series. This series included guitar and bass amps with features running from a basic 10W amp to a 30W amp with delay. Models include the **JA-010**, **JA-025D**, **JA-025R**, **JA-050D**, **JA-050R**, **JA-050A** Acoustic, **JA-025B** Bass, and **JA-050B** Bass. Last MSR prices on these amps ran from $90 to $249.

Currently, Johnson has a full line of guitar, bass, acoustic, and keyboard amplifiers available. The **Loredo T25R** (MSR $400) is Johnson's first all-tube amplifier with 25W power, 2 X 12AX7 preamp tubes, and 2 X EL84 power tubes. The **Hybrid T15R** (MSR $240) features 15W output power, 1 X 12AX7, and a solid-state power section. The **Blueline** Series are solid-state guitar amps that feature models ranging from 20W up to 100W including the **BlueLine 20R** (MSR $240), **BlueLine 30R** (MSR $260), **BlueLine 50R** (MSR $340), and the **BlueLine 100R** (MSR $460). Johnson also offers the **Power 10** (MSR $90), **RepTone 15** (MSR $110), **RepTone 30R** (MSR $150), and the **Barn Burner** (disc. last MSR was $100). For acoustic guitars, Johnson offers the **Standard 15** (MSR $140) and the **Stage 50** (MSR $230). For bass guitars, Johnson features the **RepTone JA-015B** (MSR $130), the **RepTone JA-030B** (MSR $150), the **RepTone JA-060-B** (MSR $300), the **Stage 100** (disc. 2006, last MSR was $248), and the **Ultimate Garage Band Amp** (MSR $280).

Standard 15 Acoustic
courtesy Johnson

Standard Loredo T25R
courtesy Johnson

Blue Line 50R
courtesy Johnson

JOHNSON AMPLIFICATION

Amplifiers and other products produced in Sandy, UT since 1997. The Johnson trademark stopped producing modeling guitar amplifiers in July 2002.

John Johnson founded Johnson Amplification in 1997, which is part of the Harmon Music Group. They are known for producing tube integrated amp modeling with real tubes in the amp's modeling. Johnson also studied the frequency responses, and the EQ curves of vintage amplifiers to store data in modes for instant recall. Johnson stopped producing their current line of modeling amplifiers in July of 2002, but they still offer customer support and warranty options. The J-Station is still available, which is a digital device similar to the Line 6 POD. This unit contains different amp models, speaker cabinets, and other effects all in a portable, small package. Visit Johnson's website or contact them directly for more information.

CONTACT INFORMATION
JOHNSON AMPLIFICATION
8760 S. Sandy Parkway
Sandy, UT 84070
Phone No.: 801-566-8800
Fax No.: 801-566-7005
www.johnson-amp.com

ELECTRIC HYBRID AMPLIFIERS

The Johnson line of amplifiers were available with footswitches. The **J3** footswitch has three buttons that can flip through the different programmed presets. The J3 comes standard with the JM150 and JM250. The **JT3** is similar to the J3 with three buttons but has three presets only. This comes standard with the JT50 Mirage. The **J8** is a more advanced footswitch with eight buttons and a pedal. This is an option for the Marquis and Millenium series. The **J-12** footswitch has even more features for maxium foot control. There are 12 buttons and 2 pedals on this footcontroller that is compatible with the Millenium series.

* Add $50 for J3 footswitch on JT50 Mirage, JM60 Marquis, and JM120 Marquis Stereo.
* Add $75 for J8 footswitch.
* Add $100 for J12 footswitch.

JT50 MIRAGE – 50W, 1-12 in. speaker, guitar combo, V-Tube technology preamp, 12 amp models, single channel, top silver control panel, single input, 14 black knobs (MV, g, t, m, b, level, amp type, mod speed, mod depth, mod select, delay time, delay feedback, reverb, bank select), 21 user presets, reverb, effects loop, headphone/line out, optional J3 or J8 footswitch, black covering, gray grille, mfg. 1999-2002.

	N/A	$250 - 300	$150 - 200	$849

MSR/NOTES	100%	EXCELLENT	AVERAGE	LAST MSR

JM60 MARQUIS – 60W, 1-12 in. Johnson speaker, hybrid chassis, preamp: 1 X 12AX7 and solid-state, power: solid-state, 18 amp models, 27 user/27 factory presets, front gold control panel, single input, 12 black knobs (MV, g, t, m, b, level, mod speed, mod depth, delay level, delay feedback, r, bank select), effects loop, headphone jack, speaker out jack, optional J3 or J8 footswitch, black covering, gray grille, mfg. 1997-2002.

	N/A	$300 - 350	$175 - 225	$1,100

JM120 MARQUIS STEREO – 120W (2 X 60W Stereo), 2-12 in. Johnson speakers, guitar combo, hybrid chassis, preamp: 1 X 12AX7 and solid-state, power: solid-state, 18 amp models, 27 user/27 factory presets, front gold control panel, single input, 14 black knobs (MV, g, t, m, b, p, level, mod speed, mod depth, mod level, delay level, delay feedback, r, bank select), effects loop, headphone jack, optional J3 or J8 footswitch, black covering, gray grille, mfg. 1997-2002.

courtesy Zachary R. Fjestad   courtesy Zachary R. Fjestad

	N/A	$375 - 450	$250 - 300	$1,299

JM150 MILLENIUM – 150W (2 X 75 Stereo), 2-12 in. Celestion Vintage 30 speakers, guitar combo, hybrid chassis, preamp: 2 X 12AX7 and solid-state, power: solid-state, 36 amp models, S-DISC II processing, MIDI capable, front gold control panel, two inputs, 13 knobs (input level, g, t, m, b, level, contour, MV, mix/page, speed, depth, delay, r), five tone knobs have digital readouts, six amp effects buttons, six function buttons, six effects buttons, one large preset/effect wheel, large custom digital display, chromatic tuner, standard J3 or optional J12 footswitch, black covering, gray grille, mfg. 1997-2002.

	N/A	$500 - 600	$300 - 375	$2,100

* **Subtract 10% for no footswitch.**

JM250 MILLENIUM – 250W (2 X 125 Stereo), head-unit configuration, hybrid chassis, preamp: 2 X 12AX7 and solid-state, power: solid-state, 36 amp models, S-DISC II processing, MIDI capable, front gold control panel, two inputs, 13 knobs (input level, g, t, m, b, level, contour, MV, mix/page, speed, depth, delay, r), five tone knobs have digital readouts, six amp effects buttons, six function buttons, six effects buttons, one large preset/effect wheel, large custom digital display, chromatic tuner, standard J3 or optional J8 footswitch, black covering, gray grille, mfg. 1997-2002.

	N/A	$450 - 525	$275 - 325	$1,800

* **Subtract 10% for no footswitch.**

SPEAKER CABINETS

J112 SPEAKER CABINET – 30W, 1-12 in. Celestion Vintage 30 speaker, black covering, gray grille, mfg. 1997-2002.

	N/A	$100 - 150	$50 - 70	

J212 SPEAKER CABINET – 60W, 2-12 in. Celestion Vintage 30 speakers, designed for use with the JM150 or JM250, black covering, gray grille, mfg. 1997-2002.

	N/A	$200 - 250	$120 - 150	

J412 SPEAKER CABINET – 120W, 4-12 in. Celestion Vintage 30 speakers, straight or angled cabinet, designed for use with the JM250, black covering, gray grille, mfg. 1997-2002.

	N/A	$300 - 350	$150 - 200	

JOMAMA MUSIC, LLC

Amplifiers and speaker cabinets currently produced in New Mexico since 1994. Distributed by JoMama Music, LLC in Santa Fe, NM.

Joe Kelemen founded the Kelemen and JoMama brands in 1994, and they are both produced by JoMama Music, LLC. Earlier JoMama amps used thick linen grade phenolic turrent board construction, whereas all current amps use hand wired terminal strips and direct point to point construction. The current offereings include two high quality heads that weigh in at approximately 20 lbs. and can be set up using almost any 8-pin power tubes The **Road Runner** (MSR $1,970) is a single channel head built to deliver a wide variety of all tube clean & distorted tones. The Road Runner has a tight fixed biased power section featuring individual tube adjustments. The

CONTACT INFORMATION
JOMAMA MUSIC, LLC
3025 Cliff Palace
Santa Fe, NM 87507
Phone No.: 505-780-1173
kelemenamps.com
joe@kelemenamps.com

Raven (MSR $2,270) is a channel switching head with completely separate preamps designed to produce clean, compressed, and thick distortion through a cathode biased power tube section. Kelemen also has a 2-12 in. speaker cabinet (MSR $649) that features a semi-closed oval ported back and treble diffusers incorporated into the grille. For more information, visit Kelemen's website or contact them directly.

JUKE

Amplifiers currently produced in Troy, NH since 1989. Juke is distributed by Black Canyon Distributing at guitar shows. Juke is part of Warbler & Muse.

Gary R. Croteau founded Juke amplifiers in 1989. He builds all-tube guitar and harmonica amps that are based on the fundamentals of amplifiers built in the late 1950s and early 1960s. Croteau also used the Warbler brand on a series of amps in the 1990s. In 1997, Juke was introduced with Warbler on models, and by 2000, all models were strictly named Juke. Juke amplifiers feature top mounted chassis and a narrow-style cabinet with a trapezoid-shaped speaker grille opening. Models are available in a variety of configurations and options. In 2009, Croteau introduced four new models including the **Coda**, **Vamp**, **Rave**, and Juke-branded **Warbler**. Croteau works by himself and only produces about one amp a week. For more information, visit Juke's website or contact Croteau directly.

CONTACT INFORMATION

JUKE
Box 264
Troy, NH 03465
Phone No.: 603-242-6478
www.jukeamps.com
warbler@jukeamps.com

K SECTION
KALAMAZOO

Amplifiers previously produced in Kalamazoo, MI between 1965 and 1967. Kalamazoo was a house brand of Gibson.

Kalamazoo is a budget-brand (house-brand) name Gibson used between the 1930s and late 1960s. Gibson produced several budget-brands over the years, but Kalamazoo is considered one of the more collectible ones, because of the adjustable truss rods used in guitars after WWII.

When the economy was feeling the effects of the depression in the early 1930s, Guy Hart knew that lower priced instruments were going to sell better than the higher priced counterparts. Gibson started to introduce some budget lines that were Gibson-made guitars with a different label on the headstock. These guitars were nearly as good as authentic Gibsons except they didn't have the truss rod (or price tag). Like most Gibson guitars, Kalamazoo was not produced during WWII. In the late 1940s, Kalamazoo was introduced again and was reaffirmed as Gibson's in-house budget brand. The Kalamazoo name went away again in the 1950's as Gibson went through the roof in sales, and didn't need a budget line to get by. Kalamazoo was introduced again one more time in the mid-1960s with a line of electric guitars and amplifiers. By 1967, Kalamazoo amplifiers were phased out as all Gibson amplifier production moved out of house. It is possible some models were produced into the late 1960s at other factories as a 1968 catalog offers the entire line. However shipping totals only indicate amps shipped between 1965 and 1967. Kalamazoo was discontinued for good as Epiphone became the budget brand for Gibson in 1970. Sources: Walter Carter, *Gibson Guitars 100 Years of an American Icon*, George Gruhn and Walter Carter, *Gruhn's Guide to Vintage Guitars*, and *Gibson Shipment Totals*, and Wallace Marx Jr., *Gibson Amplifiers 1933-2008 - 75 Years of the Gold Tone*.

MSR/NOTES	100%	EXCELLENT	AVERAGE	LAST MSR

ELECTRIC TUBE AMPLIFIERS

The first Kalamazoo amps were released shortly after Gibson introduced the EH-100 in the late 1930s. The Kalamazoo **KEH** was very similar to the EH-100 and was initially housed in a Geib case with a dark olive covering. Later versions include a tan tweed covering with vertical silk-screened stripes and a circular speaker grille. By 1940, the KEH was nearly identical to the Gibson EH-100 with a bare wood cabinet. The KEH featured a single knob for volume and was powered by 42-type tubes with a 6V6 later on. The KEH was produced between circa 1938 and 1942. In 1947, the second Kalamazoo amp was introduced and was called the **KEA**. It featured a 10-inch speaker driven by 2 X 6V6 tubes and had a red leatherette covering with a white metal grille. The KEA was only produced for a short while. Kalamazoo was reintroduced in 1965 with the Model 1 and Model 2. Since Gibson amps were produced in the same factory at the same time, it is more than likely that Kalamazoo Models 1 and 2 are similar if not exactly the same in chassis as the Gibson Skylark GA-5 and GA-5T respectively.

Model 1
courtesy John Beeson/The Music Shoppe

Model 1
courtesy John Beeson/The Music Shoppe

Model 2
courtesy John Beeson/The Music Shoppe

BASS 30 – 30W, 2-10 in. speakers, bass combo, four tube chassis, preamp: unknown, power: 2 X 7591, solid-state rectifier, single channel, flip-out gray control panel, two inputs, three knobs (v, t, b), black covering, gray grille, 25.5 in. wide, 20 in. tall, mfg. 1965-67.

	N/A	$250 - 300	$120 - 150	

BASS 50 – 50W, 2-10 in. speakers, bass combo, tube chassis, tubes unknown, solid-state rectifier, single channel, flip-out gray control panel, two inputs, three knobs (v, t, b), black covering, gray grille, 25.5 in. wide, 20 in. tall, mfg. 1965-67.

	N/A	$275 - 325	$150 - 200	

MODEL 1 – ~5W, 1-10 in. speaker, guitar combo, three tube chassis, preamp: 12AX7, power: 6BQ5/EL84, rectifier: 6X4, single channel, front gray control panel, two inputs, two knobs (v, tone), gray covering, gray grille cloth, 21,387 shipped, 14 in. wide, 15.875 in. tall, mfg. 1965-67.

	N/A	$150 - 200	$95 - 120	

MODEL 2 – ~5W, 1-10 in. speaker, guitar combo, four tube chassis, preamp: 2 X 12AX7, power: 1 X 6BQ5/EL84, rectifier: 6X4, single channel, tremolo, front gray control panel, two inputs, three knobs (v, i, tone), gray covering, gray grille cloth, 32,285 shipped, 14 in. wide, 15.875 in. tall, mfg. 1965-67.

	N/A	$200 - 250	$120 - 150	

MSR/NOTES	100%	EXCELLENT	AVERAGE	LAST MSR

REVERB 12 – 12W, 1-10 in. speaker, guitar combo, five-tube chassis, preamp: 3 X 12AX7, power: 2 X EL84, solid-state rectifier, single channel, reverb, tremolo, front black control panel, two inputs, six black with silver face control knobs (loudness, t, b, f, d, r), RCA input on back panel, footswitch, black Tolex covering, white/black grille cloth, mfg. 1965-67.

courtesy David Chandler/R&R Guitars   courtesy David Chandler/R&R Guitars

N/A	$325 - 400	$175 - 225

ELECTRIC SS AMPLIFIERS

MODEL 3 – ~5W, 1-10 in. speaker, guitar combo, solid-state chassis, single channel, front silver control panel, two inputs, two knobs (v, tone), gray covering, gray grille cloth, 760 shipped, 13 in. wide, 16.125 in. tall, mfg. 1967 only.

N/A	$95 - 120	$50 - 70

MODEL 4 – ~5W, 1-10 in. speaker, guitar combo, solid-state chassis, single channel, tremolo, front silver control panel, two inputs, three knobs (v, i, tone), gray covering, gray grille cloth, 2,528 shipped, 13 in. wide, 16.125 in. tall, mfg. 1967 only.

N/A	$120 - 150	$70 - 95

KASHA AMPLIFIERS

Amplifiers and other guitar related products currently produced in California since 1988.

John Kasha started Kasha Amplifiers out of a store called ABK Rocks in 1987. In 1988, Kasha introduced the ROCKMOD to the public in Los Angeles, CA, which was one of the first all-tube guitar preamps in the industry. Kasha has established themselves as a producer of various guitar related products including guitar amplifiers, preamps, amplifier modifications, speaker cabinets, and guitar monitors. Currently, Kasha offers the ROCKMOD Series of guitar heads, the QUICKMOD that converts a single channel or dual channel guitar amplifier and adds a channel, and a variety of speaker cabinets/guitar monitors. For more information, visit Kasha's website.

CONTACT INFORMATION
KASHA AMPLIFIERS
Phone No.: 818-584-2299
www.kashaamplifiers.com
sales@kashaamplifiers.com

ROCKMOD Head
courtesy Kasha Amplifiers

ROCKMOD Robo Combo
courtesy Kasha Amplifiers

Brick
courtesy Kasha Amplifiers

KAY

Amplifiers currently produced in Asia. Distributed in the U.S. by the Kay Guitar Company in Newport Beach, CA. Amplifiers previously in Chicago, IL between the 1930s and the 1960s.

The Kay Musical Instrument Company roots go way back to 1890, when the Groeschel Company of Chicago started building bowl-back mandolins. In 1918, the Groeschel name was changed to the Stromberg-Voisenet Company, and incorporated in 1921. C.G. Stromberg was the vice-president, and the company started to produce guitars and banjos under the Mayflower trademark. Henry Kay Kuhrmeyer offered to use his middle name on the instruments, and Kay Kraft was born. Kuhrmeyer bought the company in 1928, and changed the name of the company to Kay Musical Instruments in 1931. At this time they started to mass-produce stringed instruments. At this point the company became a "house brand" company.

CONTACT INFORMATION
KAY
PO Box 8798
Newport Beach, CA 92658
www.kayguitar.com

| MSR/NOTES | 100% | EXCELLENT | AVERAGE | LAST MSR |

Early guitar amplification for the Stromberg company (before Kay) is thought to go way back to 1928. Electric amplification was just being explored and the quest for portable amplification was under development in the mid 1920s. The first Stromberg amplifier is thought to have a 12 in. Jensen speaker driven by old tubes (71A power tubes), and put out 3W. These amps were very basic and little is known about them.

When the economy rebounded in the mid-1930s, Kay (previously Stromberg), went back to developing a guitar amplifier. The depression had halted this research, but many advances had come to surface by 1939. When lap steels and electric guitars became popular and newer technology became available, Kay started to produce amplifiers again. In 1940, Sears, Roebuck, and Company placed its first order with Kay, signifying its entry into supplying large distributors. The first line of Kay amplifiers was introduced in 1952 and they produced tube amps consistently through 1962. In 1962, a new line of amps was introduced with transitorized chassis. The company was sold to Sydney Katz in 1955. By 1965, the guitar market was super-saturated and Kay was feeling the pinch of too much supply with not enough demand. Katz sold the company to Seeburg, a large jukebox manufacturer in Chicago. They owned the company for two years and sold to Valco guitars. Kay wanted to buy Valco but Bob Keyworth suggested the opposite; that they sell to Valco. Like many guitar manufacturers of this era, Kay fizzled towards the end of the 1960s, and Kay (and Valco) were out of business by 1970. However, the Kay name did not go away forever. The brand has been reintroduced several times since 1970 and all instruments and amplifiers are currently built in Asia. Kay produces one practice guitar the **GA20K** (MSR $80) and one practice bass amp **GB12K** (MSR $120). Kay history and model information courtesy: Michael Wright, *Guitar Stories: Volume 2*.

ELECTRIC TUBE AMPLIFIERS: EARLY MODELS

Before 1952 most amplifiers were not produced consistently and had odd or no model number designations. In 1952, the K prefix first appeared on amplifiers.

The first Kay amplifier, technically, can be dated back to 1928-29 as the Stromberg amp. As talked about in the heading, this amp was basic, used ancient tubes, and doesn't show up on the second-hand market too often. Kay didn't start putting their name on amplifiers until the late 1930s. In between this time there were some Ward, Oahu, and Gretsch amps made by Kay, which in turn were all made by Valco. In 1945, Kay debuted its first post-war amp. In 1947, the Model F475 High Fidelity Amp was released. In 1952, Kay's amplifier line expanded rapidly as they debuted the K series, which are listed here.

F475 HIGH FIDELITY AMP – wattage unknown, 1-12 in. speaker, guitar combo, five tube chassis, rear control panel, two inputs, two knobs (v, tone), mahogany cabinet with a curly maple front finished in sunburst, 14.5 in. wide, 18.5 in. tall, 8.25 in. deep, mfg. 1947-1951.

| | N/A | $400 - 500 | $250 - 300 | |

K300 – ~5W, 1-8 in. speaker, guitar combo, three tube chassis, single channel, rear control panel, two inputs, single volume knob, two-tone brown covering, light brown grille, mfg. 1952-56.

| | N/A | $200 - 250 | $100 - 150 | |

In 1955 or 56, the covering on this model changed to a solid green color and a refridgerator-style handle was added.

K600 – 16-20W, 1-12 in. Jensen speaker, guitar combo, seven tube chassis, two channels, rear control panel, three inputs, three knobs (inst. v, mic v, tone), brown covering, dark brown grille with rounded corners, 24 in. wide, 18 in. tall, 10 in. deep, mfg. 1952-56.

| | N/A | $300 - 375 | $200 - 250 | |

In 1955 or 56, the covering on this model changed to a two-tone light brown and green with a lighter grille and a refridgerator-style handle was added.

K615 – 16-20W, 1-15 in. Jensen speaker, guitar combo, seven tube chassis, two channels, rear control panel, three inputs, three knobs (inst. v, mic v, tone), brown covering, dark brown grille with rounded corners, 24 in. wide, 19 in. tall, 10 in. deep, mfg. 1952-56.

| | N/A | $350 - 425 | $200 - 275 | |

In 1955 or 56, the covering on this model changed to a two-tone light brown and green with a lighter grille and a refridgerator-style handle was added.

ELECTRIC TUBE AMPLIFIERS: K500 SERIES

The K500 Series feature all-tube chassis, a two-tone brown covered cabinet with the back and sides of the amp covered in dark brown and the front grille trim covered in light brown. A brown grille cloth with white swirls is used as well as a refridgerator-style handle. All chassis are mounted in the top and the control panel is in the back. These amps are considered the most desirable and collectible among Kay amplifiers.

K503 HOT-LINE SPECIAL – ~4W, 1-8 in. speaker, three-tube chassis, two channels, rear control panel, three inputs, two knobs (v, tone), two-tone brown covering, brown grille with swirls, refridgerator-style handle, 15.375 in. wide, 12.5 in. tall, mfg. 1957-1961.

| | N/A | $200 - 250 | $100 - 150 | |

K504 VIBRATO LEADER – ~5W, 1-8 in. speaker, four-tube chassis, two channels, vibrato, rear control panel, three inputs, four knobs (v, tone, s, i), footswitch jack, two-tone brown covering, brown grille with swirls, refridgerator-style handle, 17.25 in. wide, 14.75 in. tall, mfg. 1960-62.

| | N/A | $275 - 325 | $150 - 200 | |

MSR/NOTES	100%	EXCELLENT	AVERAGE	LAST MSR

K505 TWIN EIGHT HI-POWER – 12W, 2-8 in. speakers, guitar combo, five-tube chassis, preamp: 1 X 12AX7, 1 X 12AU7, power: 2 X 6V6, rectifier: 5Y3, two channels, rear control panel, four inputs, three knobs (v1, v2, tone), two-tone brown covering, brown grille with swirls, refridgerator-style handle, 16.5 in. wide, 20.5 in. tall, mfg. 1957-1961.

	N/A	$375 - 450	$200 - 250	

K506 VIBRATO 12 – 12W, 1-12 in. speaker, guitar combo, six-tube chassis, preamp: 2 X 12AX7, 1 X 12AU7, power: 2 X 6V6, rectifier: 5Y3, two channels, rear control panel, four inputs, five knobs (v1, v2, tone, s, i), two-tone brown covering, brown grille with swirls, refridgerator-style handle, 16.5 in. wide, 20.5 in. tall, mfg. 1960-62.

	N/A	$375 - 475	$200 - 250	

K507 TWIN TEN SPECIAL – 20W, 2-10 in. speakers, guitar combo, seven-tube chassis, two channels, rear control panel, four inputs, six knobs (Ch. 1: v, tone, Ch. 2: v, t, s, i), two-tone brown covering, brown grille with swirls, refridgerator-style handle, 24 in. wide, 20 in. tall, mfg. 1957-1961.

	N/A	$425 - 500	$300 - 350	

K515 HEAVY DUTY BASS AMP – 15W, 1-15 in. speaker, bass combo, seven-tube chassis, preamp: 4 X 12AX7, power: 2 X 6V6, rectifier: 5Y3, two channels, rear control panel, four inputs, six knobs (Ch. 1: v, tone, Ch. 2: v, t, s, i), two-tone brown covering, brown grille with swirls, refridgerator-style handle, 24 in. wide, 20 in. tall, mfg. 1957-1960.

	N/A	$350 - 425	$125 - 175	

K520 HEAVY DUTY BASS AMP – wattage unknown, 1-15 in. speaker, bass combo, five-tube chassis, preamp: 1 X 5879, 1 X 7199, power: 2 X 6L6, rectifier: 5U4, rear control panel, three inputs, two-tone brown covering, brown grille with swirls, refridgerator-style handle, 27 in. wide, 22 in. tall, 9.5 in. deep, mfg. 1961-62.

	N/A	$300 - 375	$200 - 250	

K550 – 12W, 2-8 in. speakers, guitar combo, five-tube chassis, preamp: 2 X 6EU7, power: 2 X 6V6, rectifier: 5Y3, two channels, reverb, rear control panel, four inputs, four knobs (v1, v2, tone, r), two-tone brown covering, brown grille with swirls, refridgerator-style handle, mfg. 1961-62.

	N/A	$300 - 375	$200 - 250	

ELECTRIC AMPLIFIERS: K700 SERIES

Generally speaking, all amps in the K700 series have solid-state chassis with the exception of the K703, which was the only model listed with a full-tube chassis. Some models may feature a hybrid chassis. A new two-tone covering was introduced with this series as well. A light brown is used on the sides with a dark brown strip in the middle. The chassis faces towards the top, the speaker grille is a dark brown that wraps around the top, and a new gold metal handle is introduced. Earlier models do not have a Kay logo in the lower right corner as newer models do. The K703 and K720 never adopted the new covering, but continued with the K500 series covering with a standard dark grille. These models are less desirable than the K500 series because they are solid-state in design.

K700 VANGUARD – wattage unknown, 1-8 in. speaker, solid-state chassis (four transistors, two diodes), single channel, top control panel, three inputs, two knobs (v, tone), two-tone brown/cream covering, brown grille, mfg. 1962-65.

	N/A	$120 - 150	$75 - 100	

K703 VALUE LEADER – 4W, 1-8 in. speaker, three tube chassis, preamp: 1 X 12AU6, power: 1 X 50L6, rectifier: 35Z5, single channel, rear control panel, three inputs, two knobs (v, tone), two-tone brown/cream covering, brown grille, gold metal handle, mfg. 1962-65.

courtesy Competition Music

courtesy Competition Music

	N/A	$200 - 250	$100 - 150	

| MSR/NOTES | 100% | EXCELLENT | AVERAGE | LAST MSR |

K704 VANGUARD – 5W, 1-8 in. speaker, solid-state chassis (7 transistors, 4 diodes), single channel, vibrato, top control panel, three inputs, four knobs (v, tone, s, i), two-tone brown/cream covering, brown grille, mfg. 1962-66.

courtesy John Beeson/The Music Shoppe

courtesy John Beeson/The Music Shoppe

N/A $120 - 150 $50 - 75

K705 VANGUARD – 10W, 1-10 in. speaker, solid-state chassis (7 transistors, 4 diodes), single channel, vibrato, top control panel, four inputs with three tone circuits, four knobs (v, tone, s, i), footswitch jack, two-tone brown/cream covering, brown grille, 20 in. wide, 17.125 in. tall, 9.5 in. deep, mfg. 1962-66.

N/A $125 - 175 $60 - 80

K706 VANGUARD – 15W, 1-15 in. speaker, solid-state chassis (8 transistors, 4 diodes), two channels, vibrato, top control panel, four inputs (two per channel), seven knobs (Ch. 1: v, tone, i, Ch. 2: v, tone, i, master vibrato speed control), two footswitch jacks (one footswitch included), two-tone brown/cream covering, brown grille, 20 in. wide, 17.125 in. tall, 9.5 in. deep, mfg. 1962-66.

N/A $150 - 180 $100 - 125

K707 GALAXIE I – 35W, 1-12 in. speaker, solid-state chassis (11 transistors, 8 diodes), two channels, vibrato, top control panel, six inputs (three per channel), seven knobs (Ch. 1: v, tone, i, Ch. 2: v, tone, i, master vibrato speed control), two footswitch jacks (one footswitch included), two-tone brown/cream covering, brown grille, 24 in. wide, 20.5 in. tall, 12 in. deep, mfg. 1962-66.

N/A $150 - 180 $100 - 125

K708 GALAXIE II – 35W, 1-12 in. speaker, removable chassis guitar piggyback configuration, solid-state chassis (11 transistors, 8 diodes), two channels, vibrato, top control panel, six inputs (three per channel), seven knobs (Ch. 1: v, tone, i, Ch. 2: v, tone, i, master vibrato speed control), two footswitch jacks (one footswitch included), cabinet with four removable legs that raises it 10.5 in., two-tone brown/cream covering, brown grille, 24 in. wide, 20 in. tall, 12 in. deep, mfg. 1962-66.

N/A $150 - 180 $100 - 125

K720 BASS AMPLIFIER – wattage unknown, 1-15 in. speaker, bass combo, solid-state chassis, single channel, rear control panel, three inputs, two knobs (v, tone), two-tone brown/cream covering, brown grille, 27 in. wide, 22 in. tall, 9.5 in. deep, mfg. 1962-66.

N/A $150 - 180 $100 - 125

ELECTRIC AMPLIFIERS: K750/K760 SERIES

Like the K700 Series, all amps in the K750/K760 series have solid-state chassis with the exception of the K754, which was the only model listed with a full-tube chassis. This series features black grain vinyl covering with gray grilles, front-facing angled silver (sometimes silver and black) control panels, a rubber handle, and true piggyback units were introduced. These are less desirable than the K700 series.

K750 BUDGET LEADER – ~5W, 1-8 in. speaker, guitar combo, solid-state chassis, single channel, front silver control panel, three inputs, two knobs (v, tone), black covering, gray grille, 16.25 in. wide, 16.375 in. tall, 6.5 in. deep, mfg. 1966-68.

N/A $60 - 80 $30 - 40

K752 VALUE LEADER – 5W, 1-8 in. speaker, guitar combo, solid-state chassis, single channel, front silver and black control panel, three inputs, two knobs (v, tone), black covering, gray grille, 17 in. wide, 14 in. tall, 7 in. deep, mfg. 1966-68.

N/A $60 - 80 $30 - 40

K754 TREMOLO – 5W, 1-8 in. speaker, guitar combo, hybrid chassis with three tubes and one transistor, single channel, front silver and black control panel, three inputs, three knobs (v, tone, s), black covering, gray grille, 18 in. wide, 16 in. tall, 8 in. deep, mfg. 1966-68.

N/A $100 - 125 $60 - 80

K755 TREMOLO – 10W, 1-8 in. speaker, guitar combo, solid-state chassis (9 transistors, 6 diodes), single channel, front silver and black control panel, three inputs, four knobs (v, tone, s, i), black covering, gray grille, 19 in. wide, 17 in. tall, 9.5 in. deep, mfg. 1966-68.

N/A $100 - 125 $60 - 80

MSR/NOTES	100%	EXCELLENT	AVERAGE	LAST MSR

K756 TREMOLO – 20W, 1-12 in. speaker, guitar combo, solid-state chassis (11 transistors, 6 diodes), two channels, tremolo, front silver control panel, four inputs, six knobs (Ch. 1: v, tone, s, i, Ch. 2: v, tone), black covering, gray grille, 21 in. wide, 18 in. tall, 9.5 in. deep, mfg. 1966-68.

	N/A	$100 - 125	$60 - 80	

K760 VALUE LEADER TREMOLO/REVERB – 20W, 1-12 in. speaker, guitar combo, solid-state chassis (13 transistors, 6 diodes), two channels, reverb, tremolo, front silver control panel, four inputs, seven knobs (Ch. 1: v, tone, s, i, r, Ch. 2: v, tone), black covering, gray grille, 21 in. wide, 18 in. tall, 9.5 in. deep, mfg. 1966-68.

	N/A	$150 - 180	$100 - 125	

K761 PROFESSIONAL REVERB/TREMOLO – 50W, 2-12 in. speakers, guitar combo, solid-state chassis (17 transistors, 6 diodes), two channels, reverb, tremolo, front silver control panel, four inputs, seven knobs (Ch. 1: v, t, b, s, i, r, Ch. 2: v, t, b), two footswitch jacks, black covering, gray grille, 25 in. wide, 21 in. tall, 9.5 in. deep, mfg. 1966-68.

	N/A	$175 - 225	$100 - 150	

Each component of the piggyback unit carried its own model number. The head-unit was K765, the regular speaker cabinet was K768, the tall remote speaker cabinet was K767, and the combination of the head and speaker cabinet was K765.

K765 PROFESSIONAL PIGGYBACK – 100W, 2-12 in. speakers, guitar piggyback configuration, solid-state chassis (17 transistors, 6 diodes), two channels, reverb, tremolo, front silver control panel, four inputs, seven knobs (Ch. 1: v, t, b, s, i, r, Ch. 2: v, t, b), two footswitch jacks, black covering, gray grille, 27 in. wide, 22 in. tall, 9.5 in. deep, mfg. 1966-68.

Head & Cab (K765)	N/A	$200 - 250	$120 - 150	
Head Only (K766)	N/A	$120 - 150	$70 - 95	
Remote Cab Only (K767)	N/A	$95 - 120	$50 - 75	
Cab Only (K768)	N/A	$70 - 95	$45 - 60	

Each component of the piggyback unit carried its own model number. The head-unit was K766, the regular speaker cabinet was K768, the tall remote speaker cabinet was K767, and the combination of the head and speaker cabinet was K765.

K770 DUAL PURPOSE GUITAR/BASS AMPLIFIER – 50W, 1-15 in. speaker, guitar and bass combo, solid-state chassis (12 transistors, 4 diodes), two channels (guitar and bass), front silver control panel, four inputs (two per channel), five knobs (Guitar: v, b, t, Bass: v, tone), black covering, gray grille, 22 in. wide, 27 in. tall, 9.5 in. deep, mfg. 1966-68.

	N/A	$175 - 225	$100 - 125	

K771 VALUE LEADER BASS AMPLIFIER – 20W, 1-12 in. speaker, bass combo, solid-state chassis (6 transistors, 4 diodes), single channel, front silver and black control panel, three inputs, two knobs (v, tone), black covering, gray grille, 25 in. wide, 21 in. tall, 9.5 in. deep, mfg. 1966-68.

	N/A	$125 - 175	$50 - 75	

KELEMEN

Amplifiers and speaker cabinets currently produced in New Mexico since 1994. Distributed by JoMama Music, LLC in Santa Fe, NM.

CONTACT INFORMATION
KELEMEN
3025 Cliff Palace
Santa Fe, NM 87507
Phone No.: 505-474-3616
www.kelemenamps.com
joe@kelemenamps.com

Joe Kelemen founded the Kelemen and JoMama brands in 1994, and they are both produced by JoMama Music, LLC. Earlier JoMama amps used thick linen grade phenolic turrent board construction, whereas all current amps use hand wired terminal strips and direct point to point construction. The current offerings include two high quality heads that weigh in at approximately 20 lbs. and can be set up using almost any 8-pin power tubes The **Road Runner** (MSR $1,970) is a single channel head built to deliver a wide variety of all tube clean and distorted tones. The Road Runner has a tight fixed biased power section featuring individual tube adjustments. The **Raven** (MSR $2,270) is a channel switching head with completely separate preamps designed to produce clean, compressed, and thick distortion through a cathode biased power tube section. Kelemen also has a 2-12 in. speaker cabinet (MSR $649) that features a semi-closed oval ported back and treble diffusers incorporated into the grille. For more information, visit Kelemen's website or contact them directly.

Raven Head
courtesy Joe Kelemen

Runner Head Rail
courtesy Joe Kelemen

MSR/NOTES	100%	EXCELLENT	AVERAGE	LAST MSR

KENDRICK AMPLIFIERS

Amplifiers currently produced in Kempner, Texas. Previously produced in Austin, TX.

CONTACT INFORMATION
KENDRICK AMPLIFIERS
531 County Road 3300
Kempner, TX 76539
Phone No.: 512-932-3130
Fax No.: 512-932-3135
www.kendrick-amplifiers.com
kendrick@kendrick-amplifiers.com

Gerald Weber started making Kendrick amps and has been making/building amplifiers since 1989. The company has expanded to producing guitars, as well as distributing several products, including Gerald's books and other items. Weber is also the author of *A Desktop Reference of Hip Vintage Guitar Amps*, *Tube Talk for the Guitarist and Tech*, *Tube Guitar Amplifier Essentials*, *All About Vacuum Tube Guitar Amplifiers*, and *Sound Advice from Gerald Weber*, all of which gather together numerous technical tips for tube amplifiers. Weber has also hosted and produced three Tube Amp Instructional DVDs - *Tube Guitar Amplifier Servicing and Overhaul*, *Understanding Vacuum Tube Guitar Amplifiers*, and *Tube Guitar Amplifier Forum* - each approximately 4 hours of material indexed with point and click navigation for easy review. Kendrick stopped taking orders on amplifiers between December 16, 2003 and 2005 as Gerald underwent surgery. Gerald also hosts his tube amp seminars, which have spread to many major cities. For more information, visit Kendrick's website or contact them directly.

ELECTRIC TUBE AMPLIFIERS: EARLY MODELS

Kendrick's original amplifier series, which never had an "official" name, was based on Fender narrow-panel tweeds from the late 1950s. Models are numbered after their chassis and speaker configuration. When these were produced in the early 1990s, they were considered some of the most exact replicas of Fender tweeds to date.

- **Add $250 for Kendrick-installed Reverb module.**

MODEL 118 – 5W, 1-8 in. Kendrick speaker, guitar combo, tube chassis, single channel, top control panel, two inputs, single volume knob, line level output, narrow panel-style tweed covering, brown grille, 13.5 in. wide, 12 in. tall, 7.5 in. deep, mfg. circa 1992-95, 2005-present.

MSR $895	$895	$600 - 700	$375 - 450	

This model is based on a 1959 Fender Champ.

MODEL 2000 – 40W, head-unit configuration, tube chassis, single channel, top control panel, narrow panel-style tweed covering, brown grille, 23.5 in. wide, 22.75 in. tall, 11 in. deep, mfg. circa 1989-1995.

	N/A	$1,200 - 1,500	$900 - 1,050	$1,395

* *Model 2210* – similar to the Model 2000, except in combo configuration with 2-10 in. speakers, 23.5 in. wide, 15 in. tall, 10 in. deep, mfg. circa 1992-95.

	N/A	$1,300 - 1,650	$850 - 1,000	$1,699

»*Model 2210B Bass* – similar to the Model 2210, except designed for bass use with 60W output, mfg. circa 1992-95.

	N/A	$1,300 - 1,650	$850 - 1,000	$1,799

* *Model 2212* – similar to the Model 2000, except in combo configuration with 2-12 in. speakers, 27 in. wide, 20 in. tall, 10 in. deep, mfg. circa 1992-95.

	N/A	$1,400 - 1,750	$950 - 1,100	$1,949

* *Model 2410* – similar to the Model 2000, except in combo configuration with 4-10 in. speakers, 23.5 in. wide, 22.75 in. tall, 11 in. deep, mfg. circa 1992-95.

	N/A	$1,400 - 1,750	$950 - 1,100	$1,899

MODEL 2112 – 25W, 1-12 in. Kendrick Blackframe speaker, guitar combo, tube chassis, power: 2 X 6V6, two channels, top control panel, four inputs, three knobs (v1, v2, tone), line level output, narrow panel-style tweed covering, brown grille, 20 in. wide, 15.75 in. tall, 9.5 in. deep, mfg. circa 1992-95.

	N/A	$1,000 - 1,250	$700 - 800	$1,199

This model is based on a 1958 Fender Deluxe.

* *Model 2112 Texas Crude* – similar to the Model 2112, except has 35W output and a slightly larger cabinet, 22 in. wide, 20 in. tall, 10.25 in. deep, mfg. circa 1992-95.

	N/A	$1,100 - 1,350	$750 - 850	$1,399

MODEL 4000 – 80W, head-unit configuration, tube chassis, power: 4 X 5881 (although amp can be biased for use with several other tubes) single channel, top control panel, six knobs, narrow panel-style tweed covering, brown grille, 23.5 in. wide, 22.75 in. tall, 11 in. deep, mfg. circa 1989-1995.

	N/A	$1,400 - 1,750	$900 - 1,050	$1,975

* *Model 4212* – similar to the Model 4000, except in combo configuration with 2-12 in. speakers, 27 in. wide, 20 in. tall, 10 in. deep, mfg. circa 1989-1995.

	N/A	$1,600 - 2,000	$1,000 - 1,200	$2,495

This model is based on the 1959 Fender Tweed amp Model 5F8A.

* *Model 4610* – similar to the Model 4000, except in combo configuration with 6-10 in. speakers, 23.5 in. wide, 35.75 in. tall, 11 in. deep, mfg. circa 1989-1995.

	N/A	$1,600 - 2,000	$1,000 - 1,200	$2,495

MSR/NOTES	100%	EXCELLENT	AVERAGE	LAST MSR

ELECTRIC TUBE AMPLIFIERS: TEXAS CRUDE SERIES

The Texas Crude series was introduced in 1994. This series featured more original designs rather than copies of Fender tweed models like previous amps. The styling on these amps feature a brown covering available in either the Austin (rectangular) or Beaumont (trapezoidal) cabinet. A copper/bronze medallion is located in the lower left of the grille.

GUSHER HEAD – 50W, head-unit configuration, tube chassis, two channels, top control panel, four inputs, six knobs (Norm v, bright v, t, m, b, p), effects loop, cathode/fixed bias switch, Austin or Beaumont cabinet style, brown covering, light brown grille, mfg. 1996-98, 2005-present.

MSR $2,295	$2,295	$1,400 - 1,750	$950 - 1,100	

* *Gusher 2-12 Combo* – similar to the Gusher Head, except in combo configuration with 2-12 in. speakers, mfg. 1996-98.

	N/A	$1,600 - 2,000	$1,000 - 1,200	$2,095

* *Gusher 4-10 Combo* – similar to the Gusher Head, except in combo configuration with 4-10 in. speakers, mfg. 1996-98.

	N/A	$1,600 - 2,000	$1,000 - 1,200	$2,095

LOW RIDER BASS AMP – 100W, 2-10 in. speakers, bass combo, tube chassis, single channel, top control panel, two inputs, effects loop, square cabinet with three slots above main speaker grille opening, brown covering, light brown grille, mfg. 1996-98.

	N/A	$1,200 - 1,500	$800 - 950	

PIPELINE REVERBERATION – reverb unit only, head-unit configuration, tube chassis, 1 X 12AX7, 1 X 12AT7, 1 X 6K6, single channel, top control panel, three knobs (dwell, tone, mix), footswitch, beaumont trapezoidal-shaped cabinet, tweed covering, light brown grille, mfg. 1994-2003, 2005-present.

MSR $895	$895	$600 - 700	$375 - 450	

This model is based on the Fender Reverb unit from the 1960s.

RIG HEAD – 35W, head-unit configuration, tube chassis, two channels, top control panel, four inputs, three knobs (Norm v, bright v, tone), line level out, Austin or Beaumont cabinet style, brown covering, light brown grille, mfg. 1994-98.

	N/A	$950 - 1,100	$700 - 800	$1,195

* *Rig 1-12 Combo* – similar to the Rig Head, except in combo configuration with 1-12 in. speaker, mfg. 1994-98.

	N/A	$1,100 - 1,300	$800 - 900	$1,595

* *Rig 2-10 Combo* – similar to the Rig Head, except in combo configuration with 2-10 in. speakers, mfg. 1994-98.

	N/A	$1,100 - 1,300	$800 - 900	$1,595

ROUGHNECK – 6W, 1-8 or 1-10 in. speaker, guitar combo, tube chassis, power: 1 X 6550 (although several other tubes can be used), single channel, top chrome control panel, two inputs, single volume knob, trapezoidal-shaped cabinet, tweed covering, light brown grille, mfg. 1994-2003, 2005-present.

MSR $995	$995	$600 - 725	$425 - 500	

SONNY BOY HARP AMP – 35W, 1-10 in. speaker, tube chassis, harmonica combo, preamp: 2 X 12AX7, power: 2 X 6L6, rectifier: GZ34, single channel, top control panel, four inputs, three knobs (grind v, extra grind v, tone), Beaumont trapezoidal-shaped cabinet, brown leatherette covering, light brown grille with five vertical slat openings, mfg. 1996-2003, 2005-present.

MSR $1,995	$1,995	$1,200 - 1,500	$800 - 950	

SPINDLETOP HEAD – 100W, head-unit configuration, tube chassis, two channels, top control panel, four inputs, six knobs (Norm v, bright v, t, m, b, p), effects loop, cathode/fixed bias switch, Austin or Beaumont cabinet style, brown covering, light brown grille, mfg. 1996-98, 2005-present.

MSR $2,695	$2,695	$1,600 - 1,950	$1,000 - 1,200	

This model is the same as the Gusher Head, except with 100W output.

* *Spindletop 2-12 Combo* – similar to the Spindletop Head, except in combo configuration with 2-12 in. speakers, mfg. 1996-98.

	N/A	$1,700 - 2,150	$1,100 - 1,350	$2,595

WILDCAT – 25W, head-unit configuration, tube chassis, two channels, top control panel, four inputs, three knobs (Norm v, bright v, tone), line level out, Austin or Beaumont cabinet style, brown covering, light brown grille, mfg. 1994-98.

	N/A	$850 - 1,000	$600 - 700	$995

* *Wildcat 1-12 Combo* – similar to the Wildcat Head, except in combo configuration with 1-12 in. speaker, mfg. 1994-98.

	N/A	$950 - 1,150	$700 - 800	$1,395

* *Wildcat 2-10 Combo* – similar to the Wildcat Head, except in combo configuration with 2-10 in. speakers, mfg. 1994-98.

	N/A	$950 - 1,150	$700 - 800	$1,395

MSR/NOTES	100%	EXCELLENT	AVERAGE	LAST MSR

ELECTRIC TUBE AMPLIFIERS: BLACK GOLD SERIES

The Black Gold series originally featured black covering and a gold plexi-style control panel, but several other covering colors are now available.

BLACK GOLD 5 – 5W, 1-10 in. speaker, guitar combo, tube chassis, power: 1 X 6L6, rectifier: GZ34, single channel, reverb, front gold control panel, single input, four knobs (v, t, b, r), various color coverings, dark brown grille, current mfg.

MSR $1,295	$1,295	$800 - 950	$600 - 700	

BLACK GOLD 15 – 15W, 2-10 in. speaker, guitar combo, tube chassis, two channels, reverb, front gold control panel, four input, six knobs (clean v, lead v, tone, three reverb knobs), various color coverings, dark brown grille, mfg. 1996-2003, 2005-present.

MSR $1,695	$1,695	$1,050 - 1,250	$750 - 900	

BLACK GOLD 35 1-12 COMBO – 35W, 1-12 in. speaker, guitar combo, tube chassis, two channels, reverb, front gold control panel, four input, six knobs (clean v, lead v, tone, three reverb knobs), various color coverings, dark brown grille, mfg. 1996-2003, 2005-present.

MSR $1,795	$1,795	$1,100 - 1,300	$775 - 925	

  * *Black Gold 35 2-10 Combo* – similar to the Black Gold 35 1-12 Combo, except has 2-10 in. speakers, mfg. 1996-2003, 2005-present.

MSR $1,795	$1,795	$1,100 - 1,300	$775 - 925	

  * *Black Gold 35 4-10 Combo* – similar to the Black Gold 35 1-12 Combo, except has 4-10 in. speakers, current mfg.

MSR $1,995	$1,995	$1,200 - 1,450	$850 - 1,000	

BLACK GOLD 50 2-12 COMBO – 50W, 2-12 in. speakers, guitar combo, tube chassis, two channels, reverb, front gold control panel, four input, six knobs (clean v, lead v, tone, three reverb knobs), various color coverings, dark brown grille, mfg. 1996-2003.

	N/A	$1,250 - 1,500	$850 - 1,000	

  * *Black Gold 50 4-10 Combo* – similar to the Black Gold 50 2-12 Combo, except has 4-10 in. speakers, mfg. 1996-2003.

	N/A	$1,250 - 1,500	$850 - 1,000	

ELECTRIC TUBE AMPLIFIERS: SPECIALTY/MISC. MODELS

Kendrick also produces specialty amps from time to time. Currently they offer the **Gerald Weber Signature** (see below), the **Specialty Blues Amp** (MSR $2,595), the **Specialty Canary Harp Amp** (MSR $2,095), and the **Specialty Jazz Amp** (MSR $3,295).

GERALD WEBER SIGNATURE – Gerald's signature amp, this model is completely designed by Gerald using his favorite (and best) components. A full description of this amp is available on Kendrick's website and it is well worth the read if you are interested in Kendrick Amplifiers. Current mfg.

MSR $7,995	$7,995	N/A	N/A	

K SPOT – 35W, 1-12 in. FANE Alnico Premium Speaker, six-tube chassis, preamp: 4 X 12AX7, power: 2 X 6L6, single channel, reverb, top control panel, 100 year old antique pine cabinet, lacquered tweed or Tolex covering, brown speaker grille with a large "K" across the entire front of the amp, mfg. 2007-present.

MSR $2,895	$2,895	$1,700 - 2,100	$1,100 - 1,300	

SPEAKER CABINETS

The "Model" series speaker cabinets are designed for use with the early model tube amps and they all have tweed covering. The Austin series speaker cabinets are designed for use with Austin-shaped (rectangular cabinets) head and combo units. The Beaumont series speaker cabinets are designed for use with Beaumont-shaped (trapezoidal-shaped) head and combo units.

MODEL 112 – 80W, 1-12 in. Kendrick speaker, 8 ohm impedance, tweed covering, brown grille, 20 in. wide, 15.75 in. tall, 9.5 in. deep, mfg. circa 1992-95.

	N/A	$375 - 450	$225 - 275	$529

This model is the same size as the 2112 combo.

MODEL 210 – 40W, 2-10 in. Kendrick speaker, 4 ohm impedance, tweed covering, brown grille, 23.5 in. wide, 15 in. tall, 10 in. deep, mfg. circa 1992-95.

	N/A	$425 - 500	$275 - 325	$555

This model is the same size as the 2210 combo.

MODEL 212 – 140W, 2-12 in. Kendrick speaker, 4 ohm impedance, tweed covering, brown grille, 27 in. wide, 20 in. tall, 10 in. deep, mfg. circa 1992-95.

	N/A	$500 - 600	$325 - 400	$699

This model is the same size as the 4212 combo.

MODEL 410 – 80W, 4-10 in. Kendrick speaker, 2 or 8 ohm impedance, tweed covering, brown grille, 23.5 in. wide, 22.75 in. tall, 11 in. deep, mfg. circa 1992-95.

	N/A	$550 - 650	$350 - 425	$749

MSR/NOTES	100%	EXCELLENT	AVERAGE	LAST MSR

MODEL 2410B POWERED SPEAKER CABINET – 40W, 4-10 in. Kendrick speaker, power amp only, tube chassis, tweed covering, brown grille, 23.5 in. wide, 22.75 in. tall, 12 in. deep, mfg. circa 1989-1995.

	N/A	$850 - 1,000	$600 - 700	$1,299

This model features a power tube section with no controls. It acts as a slave when plugged into the Model 2410 or Model 2210's preamp out jack.

AUSTIN 112 – wattage unknown, 1-12 in. speaker, brown covering, brown grille, mfg. circa 1996-98.

	N/A	$650 - 750	$475 - 550	$549

AUSTIN 212 – wattage unknown, 2-12 in. speakers, brown covering, brown grille, mfg. circa 1996-98.

	N/A	$850 - 1,000	$600 - 700	$749

AUSTIN 410 – wattage unknown, 4-10 in. speakers, brown covering, brown grille, mfg. circa 1996-98.

	N/A	$850 - 1,000	$600 - 700	$749

AUSTIN 412 – wattage unknown, 4-12 in. speakers, brown covering, brown grille, mfg. circa 1996-2003, 2005-present.

MSR $2,095	$2,095	$1,250 - 1,500	$900 - 1,050	

BEAUMONT 112 – wattage unknown, 1-12 in. speaker, brown covering, brown grille, mfg. circa 1996-98.

	N/A	$650 - 750	$475 - 550	$549

BEAUMONT 212 – wattage unknown, 2-12 in. speakers, brown covering, brown grille, mfg. circa 1996-2003, 2005-present.

MSR $1,395	$1,395	$850 - 1,000	$600 - 700	

KENT

Amplifiers previously produced in Korea and Japan between circa 1962 and 1968. Distributed in the U.S. by Buegeleisen & Jacobson of New York, NY, Maxwell Meyers in TX, Southland Musical Merchandise Corporation in NC, and Harris Fandel Corporation in Massachusetts.

The Kent trademark was used on a full line of acoustic guitars, solid body electric guitars, amplifiers, banjos, and mandolins imported into the U.S. market during the 1960s. Some of the earlier Kent guitars were built in Japan by either the Teisco company or Guyatone, but the quality level at this time is down at the entry or student level. The majority of the models were built in Korea and both tube and solid-state models were available. Source: Walter Murray, Frankenstein Fretworks; and Michael Wright, *Guitar Stories, Volume One*.

AMPLIFIERS

1475 – ~5W, 1-8 in. speaker, guitar combo, three tube chassis, single channel, front gold and black control panel, two inputs, single volume knob, slanted front cabinet, brown tweed Keratol covering, brown/silver grille, 12 in. wide, 15 in. tall, mfg. mid-1960s.

	N/A	$45 - 65	$30 - 40	

2198 – ~5W, 1-10 in. speaker, guitar combo, three tube chassis, single channel, front gold and black control panel, three inputs, two knobs (v, tone), slanted front cabinet, brown tweed Keratol covering, brown/silver grille, 14 in. wide, 17 in. tall, mfg. mid-1960s.

	N/A	$60 - 80	$40 - 50	

5999 – ~5W, 1-8 in. speaker, guitar combo, three tube chassis, single channel, tremolo, front gold and black control panel, three inputs, four knobs (v, tone, s, i), slanted front cabinet, brown tweed Keratol covering, brown/silver grille, 16 in. wide, 19.25 in. tall, mfg. mid-1960s.

	N/A	$70 - 95	$45 - 60	

6100/SL-11 AVANTI – 6W, 1-8 in. speaker, guitar combo, three tube chassis, two transistors, single channel, tremolo, front gold and black control panel, three inputs, four knobs (v, tone, s, i), slanted front cabinet, brown tweed Keratol covering, brown/silver grille, 19 in. wide, 19 in. tall, 9.5 in. deep, mfg. mid-1960s.

	N/A	$95 - 120	$50 - 75	

6101/SL-21 PROFESSIONAL – 12W, 1-12 in. speaker, guitar combo, four tube chassis, four transistors, two channels, tremolo, front gold and black control panel, four inputs, six knobs (Ch. 1: v, tone, Ch. 2: v, tone, s, i), slanted front cabinet, brown tweed Keratol covering, brown/silver grille, 23 in. wide, 19 in. tall, 9.5 in. deep, mfg. mid-1960s.

	N/A	$120 - 150	$70 - 95	

6102/SL-31 BASS – 40W, 2-12 in. speakers, guitar combo, five tube chassis, preamp: 2 X 12AX7, power: 2 X 7189, rectifier: 6CA4, single channel, top gold and black control panel, two inputs, two knobs (v, tone), brown tweed Keratol covering, brown/silver grille, 27 in. wide, 21.5 in. tall, 11 in. deep, mfg. mid-1960s.

	N/A	$150 - 200	$95 - 120	

KING AMPLIFICATION

Amplifiers previously produced in Los Gatos, CA and San Jose, CA.

Val King founded King Amplification in 2005, and he holds the principle that amplifiers with high-quality components and classic tone can still be built in the U.S. All amps feature tube chassis, are hand wired, and are so durable that King offers a three-year transferable warranty. In the late 2000s, King teamed up with Keith Holland Guitars and opened a store in Los Gatos, CA.

ELECTRIC TUBE AMPLIFIERS

The **Tigerhund 18** features 18W output power from 2 X 6V6 tubes, a single channel, effects loop, and is available as a head (MSR $1,750) or 1-12 in. or 2-10 in. speaker combo (MSR $1,950). The **Rocket 88** (MSR $2,650) is only available as a head and features 80W output from KT88 power tubes and has power scaling that allows the user to attenuate the output from 2W up to 80W. The **Uptown 33** features 33W output power from 2 X 6L6 tubes, two channels, reverb, and is available as a head (MSR $2,150) or a 1-12 in. or 2-10 in. speaker combo (MSR $2,450).

Tigerhund 18
courtesy King Amplification

Uptown 33
courtesy King Amplification

KINGSLEY AMPLIFIERS

Amplifiers currently produced in Maple Ridge, British Columbia, Canada since 1998.

CONTACT INFORMATION
KINGSLEY AMPLIFIERS
13051 248A Street
Maple Ridge, British Columbia V4R 2C7
Canada
Phone No.: 604 463-5201
www.kingsleyamplifiers.com
simon@kingsleyamplifiers.com

Simon Jarrett founded Kingsley Amplifiers in 1998. Jarrett is a professional guitarist that lives in Canada, but is originally from the UK. He graduated from the Guitar Institute in Los Angeles where he studied with several big names including Scott Henderson. Jarrett has repaired and modified tube amplifiers for many years as a side project, and he decided to start building his own amps to satisfy his needs/wants in a guitar amplifier. The Kingsley line uses tube chassis with Jarrett's own pre-amp design and other refinements. Jarrett focuses on the Deluxe Series and Overdrive Series. All models are available as a head-unit or combo, and speaker cabinets are also available. Prices start around $2,150 for head units, $2,300 for combos, and $575 for speaker cabinets. For more information, visit Kingsley's website or contact him directly.

KINGSTON

Amplifiers previously produced in Japan from 1958 to 1967. Distributed in the U.S. by Westheimer Importing Corporation in Chicago, IL.

The Kingston brand name was used by U.S. importer Westheimer Importing Corporation of Chicago, IL. Jack Westheimer, who was one of the original guitar importers and distributors, also served as president of Cort Musical Instruments in Northbrook, IL. The Kingston trademark was used on a product line of amplifiers, acoustic and solid body electric guitars, electric bass guitars, banjos, and mandolins imported into the U.S. market during the 1960s. It has been estimated that 150,000 guitars were sold in the U.S. during the 1960s. Some of the earlier Kingston guitars were built in Japan by either the Teisco company or Guyatone. Source: Michael Wright, *Guitar Stories, Volume One*.

AMPLIFIERS

Although thousands of amplifiers with the Kingston brand name were produced, the Cat, Cougar, and Lion series seem to be the most popular. The Cat Series were entry-level solid-state models with limited features. Used prices on these models fall between $40 and $60 typically. The Cougar Series were solid-state bass amps in a variety of configurations. Prices range between $50 and $150 for most models. The Lion Series were higher-end solid-state guitar models with various features and options. Prices on the Lion series typically range between $100 and $200.

KITCHEN-MARSHALL

Amplifiers previously produced in England by Marshall between circa 1965 and 1966.

Kitchen-Marshall is another trademark Marshall used for a private brand even though the amp is a Marshall in design. The Kitchen chain of music shops was located in North England in the mid- to late 1960s, and like CMI and Park, Kitchen Music came to Marshall to build amps for them. Marshall agreed, and built the amps under the name Kitchen-Marshall due to Marshall's exclusive distribution deal with Rose-Morris. Kitchen-Marshall-branded amps include guitar and P.A. amp heads along with 4-12 in. speaker cabinets. These amps look exactly like Marshalls, except they have a logo featuring "Kitchen" spelled before Marshall in the block logo. These amps are very rare today, and prices in the used marketplace have ranged between $5,000 and $7,500 for a JTM 45W head. Information courtesy: Michael Doyle, *The History of Marshall*.

KITTY HAWK

Amplifiers and speaker cabinets currently produced in Enschede, The Netherlands since the late 1980s. Previously produced in Germany during the late 1970s and 1980s.

CONTACT INFORMATION
KITTY HAWK
www.kittyhawkamps.com
mgfmusik@aol.com

In the late 1970s, two German brothers, Wolfram and Gundolf Roy, had a company called Applied Acoustics located in Bochum, West Germany. Applied Acoustics was the authorized importer/distributor for Mesa Boogie and Dumble amplifiers for the European market at the time.

In the early 1980s, the high U.S. Dollar rate and even higher shipping costs created very expensive prices for Mesa Boogie and Dumble amps to be distributed in Europe. Applied Acoustics made an agreement with Howard Dumble that he would ship amplifiers without a cabinet and speaker to save on shipping costs. Then, the combo-cabinets were handmade in Germany. At that time, a Mesa/Boogie Mark I was even more expensive than a Dumble Overdrive Special! Also, if customers wanted an added reverb or effects loop, Applied Acoustics was authorized by Dumble to make these adjustments. Therefore, a lot of technical details regarding Dumble amps were shared with Applied Acoustics.

Dumble hand-built each amp himself, and as Dumble amps gained popularity, worldwide lead-time for a completed amp increased dramatically. With a lead time of six to nine months, Applied Acoustics decided to build there own amp, the Kitty Hawk Amp. The first Kitty Hawk Amp is an exact copy of a silverface Dumble Overdrive Special, even using the same U.S.-made components.

When Dumble realized his amps were being copied, he immediately began to cover the preamp circuit with a thick layer of epoxy to protect his circuits so no one could see exactly what components he was using. He also halted distribution to Applied Acoustics, although the damage had already been done.

The Kitty Hawk Amp was the first direct copy of a Dumble Overdrive Special with a single master volume control and two pre-amp volume (or overdrive) controls. When Kitty Hawk decided to copy the blackface Overdrive Special with two master volumes, one for each channel, and two overdrive controls, they changed the name "Amp" to "Standard." The new Kitty Hawk was now called the Custom Series.

Kitty Hawks sold very well in Germany and the Netherlands, and they soon began copying the still expensive Mesa/Boogie Mark I, naming it the Kitty Hawk Junior. A successor, named the Kitty Hawk Model 4, was built sometime in 1984, and was based on a Mesa/Boogies Mark II.

The Kitty Hawk Amp, Standard, Custom Series, Junior and Model 4 all featured a Golden Eagle and handwritten fonts were used. High quality, mostly U.S-built, components were used in these amplifiers. The Amp, Standard and Custom had high quality hardwood cabinets and were available as combo or head-unit versions. A combo was also available equipped with an Electro Voice EVM-12L speaker. The junior was only available as a combo in hardwood or black Tolex, with an EVM-12L or Celestion speaker. Today, these amps continue to be very popular in Europe because of their distinguished sound and high quality.

In the mid-1980s the production quantities increased rapidly but the quality decreased. Some amps built in this period include the Junior Series 1, Supreme Series 1, Triumph Series 1, The Kid, M1, and M5.

In the late 1980s, the quality became so poor that several retailers refused to sell Kitty Hawk anymore, because of the high amount of problems. Poor quality as well as some legal problems forced Kitty Hawk to stop sales and production soon thereafter.

A Dutch Kitty Hawk dealer took over the production and brand name. These models do not have the Golden Eagle logo and are totally different amplifiers compared to the original ones.

Today, Kitty Hawk is still produced in small quantities in the Netherlands and is still sold in the Netherlands. In 1997,

Kitty Hawk Amp
courtesy Nick Meuwese

Kitty Hawk Model 4
courtesy Nick Meuwese

Kitty Hawk Supreme
courtesy Nick Meuwese

they featured the Apache guitar amps that were available in 50W, 100W, and 150W variations along with matching speaker cabinets. They have also produced preamps, power amps, and other accessories. These amplifiers, however, have nothing in common with the old Kitty Hawks. Many reviews indicate that Kitty Hawk did not produce any models during the late 1990s and early 2000s, but they are currently building again.

The author would like to thank Nick Meuwese for his contributions to the Kitty Hawk section.

ELECTRIC TUBE AMPS

Many Kitty Hawk Amps are bought, sold, and traded in Europe but there are some in the U.S. as well. The following values have been compiled from Euro prices and converted to U.S. dollars at the time of publication. The **Kitty Hawk Amp** is valued between $2,500 and $3,000, the **Kitty Hawk Standard Series** ranges between $1,750, and $2,300 depending on model (50/100 Watt, with or without reverb, with or without effects loop), the **Kitty Hawk Custom Series** ranges between $2,900 and $3,500 depending on model (50/100 Watt, with or without reverb, with or without effects loop), the **Kitty Hawk Junior** ranges between $1,450 and $1,850, the **Kitty Hawk Model 4** ranges between $1,450 and $1,850, and the **Kitty Hawk Supreme Series 1** ranges between $600 and $1,000.

KJL

Amplifiers and speaker cabinets currently produced in Gretna, LA. Previously produced in New Orleans, LA. Distributed by Acoustic Analysis Inc.

KJL was founded by Kenny Lannes in 1995. Lannes is an electric engineering professor at the University of New Orleans, and he decided to apply his knowledge to a line of amplifiers. All amps feature tube chassis, basic controls, and a large "KJL" logo on the front. The **Dirty 30** (MSR $999) is KJL's best-known model with 30W or 60W of power. A **15W Companion Head** (MSR $699) can utilize different tubes. The Clubowner Speaker Cabinet is also available (MSR $749). For more information, visit KJL's website or contact them directly.

CONTACT INFORMATION
KJL
Distributed by Acoustic Analysis, Inc.
1800 Franklin Ave.
Gretna, LA 70053
Phone No.: 228-326-3196
www.kjlamps.com
techsupport@kjlamps.com

Dirty 30 and Cabinet
courtesy KJL

Dirty 30
courtesy KJL

KMD

Amplifiers previously produced during the late 1980s. Distributed by Kaman Music in Bloomfield, CT.

KMD was distributed in the U.S. by Kaman Music and this name was used as their in-house amp company. KMD amplifiers can be identified by their round black metal grille covers with "kmd" in lower letters in the top center. Most amps appear to have been built in England, and a full range of amplifiers was available from a small solid-state combo model to large tube amps. Head units, combos, and speaker cabinets were all available. Endorsers included Al Di Meola and Ritchie Sambora.

KOCH

Amplifiers currently produced in Amersfoort, The Netherlands, since 1988. Koch amplifiers are distributed in the U.S. and Canada by StageTrix Products. Previously distributed by Audionova Inc. in Dorval, Québec, Canada and Eden Electronics in Montrose, MN.

Dolf Koch developed Koch amps in 1988. He runs an amplifier company that is dedicated to creating an amplifier that is perfectly tonally balanced. Amps are built with tube chassis. They also have a custom shop that can make modifications on a special request. Everything that goes into the amplifier is carefully constructed. For more information, visit Koch's website or contact the company directly.

CONTACT INFORMATION
KOCH
The Netherlands Factory
Distributed by Audionova, Inc.
Neonweg 27
Amersfoort, 3812 RG The Netherlands
Phone No.: 31-33-4634533
Fax No.: 31-33-465527
www.koch-amps.com
info@koch-amps.com

U.S. Distribution: Audionova, Inc.
2083 Chartier Ave.
Dorval, Québec H9P 1H3 Canada
Phone No.: 514-631-5787
Fax No.: 866-255-4010
www.audionova.ca
sales@audionova.ca

ELECTRIC TUBE AMPLIFIERS

Koch produces one preamp unit called the **Pedaltone** (MSR $1,145) that is equipped with 4 X 12AX7 tubes and has four channels. The **Load Box** (MSR $695) is a unit that reduces the sound output coming out of the amp (similar to the Marshall powerbreak). Since some amplifiers need to be run wide-open to get that sound, this will keep that sound but reduce the volume at different percentage levels. Between 2005 and 2006, Koch upgraded most of its models and labeled each one with a II on the end of the name. New features include a third channel, voicing switches, and an additional MV knob.

MSR/NOTES	100%	EXCELLENT	AVERAGE	LAST MSR

Load Box LB120
courtesy Koch

Pedaltone
courtesy Koch

Multitone 50 Head
courtesy Koch

Multitone 100 Combo
courtesy Koch

Powertone
courtesy Koch

CLASSICTONE 210 COMBO – 40W, 2-10 in. Koch VG10-25 speaker combo, six-tube chassis, preamp: 4 X 12AX7, power: 2 X EL34, two channels, vibrato, front black and chrome control panel, two inputs, 13 black knobs (Clean: v, b, m, t, OD: drive, v, b, m, t, All: d, s, p, r), effects loop, black covering, black and gray grille, disc. 2009.

	$2,850	$1,750 - 2,075	$1,225 - 1,475	$3,475

* *Classictone 410 Combo* – similar to the Classictone 210, except has 4-10 in. speakers, disc. 2009.

	$3,325	$2,025 - 2,425	$1,425 - 1,725	$4,050

MULTITONE 50 HEAD – 50W, head-unit only, all tube chassis, preamp: 1 X 12AX7WA, 2 X 12AX7, power: 1 X 12AX7, 2 X EL34 or 4 X 6V6, dual channels, front black and silver control panel, two inputs, 14 black knobs (Pre: b, m, t, v, drive, v, Post: g, v, p, b, m, t, Master: MV, r), effects loop, footswitch, black Tolex covering, gray grille cloth, disc. 2005.

	N/A	$1,200 - 1,500	$850 - 1,000	$2,295

* *Multitone 50 Combo* – similar to the Multitone 50 head except in combo form with 2-12 in. Koch/Jensen VG12-90 speakers, disc. 2005.

	N/A	$1,400 - 1,750	$950 - 1,150	$2,795

MULTITONE 50 II HEAD – 50W, head-unit only, six tube chassis, preamp: 4 X 12AX7, power: 2 X EL34, three channels, front black and silver control panel, two inputs, 15 black knobs (Pre: b, m, t, v, drive, v, Post: g, v, p, b, m, t, Master: rhythm MV, solo MV, r/FX mix), effects loop, recording out, footswitch, black Tolex covering, gray grille cloth, mfg. 2006-present.

MSR $3,025	$2,500	$1,500 - 1,800	$1,050 - 1,275	

* *Multitone 50 II Combo* – similar to the Multitone 50 II Head except in combo form with 2-12 in. Koch/Jensen VG12-90 speakers, mfg. 2006-present.

MSR $3,730	$3,075	$1,850 - 2,250	$1,300 - 1,575	

MULTITONE 100 HEAD – similar to the Multitone 50 except has 100W output from either 4 X EL34/6L6 or 2 X EL34 + 2 X 6L6, disc. 2005.

	N/A	$1,400 - 1,750	$950 - 1,150	$2,495

* *Multitone 100 Combo* – similar to the Multitone 100 head except in combo form with 2-12 in. Koch/Jensen VG12-90 speakers, disc. 2005.

	N/A	$1,600 - 2,000	$1,050 - 1,250	$2,995

MULTITONE 100 II HEAD – similar to the Multitone 50 II Head except has 100W output from 4 X EL34 tubes, mfg. 2006-present.

MSR $3,320	$2,750	$1,650 - 2,000	$1,150 - 1,400	

* *Multitone 100 II Combo* – similar to the Multitone 100 II Head except in combo form with 2-12 in. Koch/Jensen VG12-90 speakers, mfg. 2006-present.

MSR $4,035	$3,350	$2,000 - 2,00	$1,400 - 1,700	

POWERTONE – 120W, head-unit only, all tube chassis, preamp: 1 X 12AX7WA, 2 X 12AX7, power: 1 X 12AX7, 4 X EL34, dual channels, reverb, front black and silver control panel, two inputs, 14 black knobs (Clean: b, m, t, v, Gain: g, m, ultra g, v, p, b, m, t, Master: MV, r), effects loop, footswitch, black Tolex covering, silver metal grille, disc. 2004.

	N/A	$1,450 - 1,800	$1,000 - 1,200	$2,575

• **Add $150 for the 6550 tube option.**

This model is also available with 6550 power tubes (4).

MSR/NOTES	100%	EXCELLENT	AVERAGE	LAST MSR

POWERTONE II HEAD – 120W, head-unit only, eight tube chassis, preamp: 4 X 12AX7, power: 4 X EL34 or 4 X 6550, three channels, reverb, front black and silver control panel, two inputs, 15 black knobs (Clean: b, m, t, v, Gain: g, m, ultra g, v, p, b, m, t, Master: rhythm MV, solo MV, r), effects loop, recording out, footswitch, black Tolex covering, silver metal grille, mfg. 2005-present.

| MSR $3,395 | $2,800 | $1,700 - 2,050 | $1,200 - 1,450 | |

- Add 7.5% for 6550 power tubes (MSR $3,670).

* *Powertone II Combo* – similar to the Powertone II Head, except has 2-12 in. Koch VG12-90 speakers, 99 lbs., mfg. 2006-present.

| MSR $4,115 | $3,375 | $2,050 - 2,475 | $1,450 - 1,750 | |

- Add 5% for 6550 power tubes (MSR $4,435).

STUDIOTONE HEAD – 20W, guitar head-unit, Class A five-tube chassis, preamp: 3 X 12AX7, power: 2 X EL84, three channels, reverb, front black and chrome control panel, single input, seven black knobs (Clean: v, OD: v, drive, All: b, m, t, r), mid-shift and bright switches, power soak, speaker on/off switch, headphone jack, effects loop, black covering, gray grille, 22 lbs., mfg. 2006-present.

| MSR $1,760 | $1,450 | $875 - 1,050 | $625 - 750 | |

* *Studiotone 112 Combo* – similar to the Studiotone Head, except in combo configuration with 1-12 in. Koch VG12-60 speaker, 33 lbs., mfg. 2004-present.

| MSR $1,950 | $1,600 | $975 - 1,175 | $675 - 825 | |

STUDIOTONE XL HEAD – 40W (switchable to 20W), guitar head-unit, Class A seven-tube chassis, preamp: 3 X 12AX7, power: 4 X EL84, three channels, reverb, front black and chrome control panel, single input, eight black knobs (Clean: v, OD: g, v, OD+: v, All: b, m, t, r), three-position channel switch, three-way h/m/l OD+ switch, two-way mid-shift switch, three-way bright switch, rear panel: footswitch jack, effects loop, speaker simulated recording out with two voicing filters, two line out jacks, headphone jack, three speaker jacks, black covering, gray grille, two-button footswitch included, 12.75 in. wide, 7.125 in. tall, 7.125 in. deep, 26.4 lbs., mfg. 2009-present.

| MSR $2,195 | $1,825 | $1,100 - 1,325 | $775 - 925 | |

* *Studiotone XL 112 Combo* – similar to the Studiotone XL Head, except in combo configuration with 1-12 in. Koch VG12-60 speaker, 12.75 in. wide, 12 in. tall, 7.125 in. deep, 50.6 lbs., mfg. 2009-present.

| MSR $2,425 | $2,000 | $1,200 - 1,450 | $850 - 1,025 | |

SUPERNOVA HEAD – 120W (Model SN120) or 2 X 60W stereo (Model SN6060), guitar head unit, 12-tube chassis, preamp: 8 X 12AX7, power: 4 X EL34, solid-state rectifier, five channels (clean, crunch, gain, high gain, ultra gain), reverb, OTS, front gray control panel, two inputs (normal, bright/clean), 28 knobs (Ch. 1: v, b, m, t, Ch. 2: drive, v, b, m, t, Ch. 3: drive, v, p, b, m, t, Ch. 4: high g, v, Ch. 5: ultra g, v, Ch. 4/5: p, b, m, t, All: Master 1, Master 2, OTS drive, OTS v, r), four voicing switches (low, mid shift, bright, hi cut), channel switch, OTS switch, Master switch, reverb switch, four effects loop switches, speaker dampening switch, store switch, standby switch, rear panel: power switch, one regular footswitch jack, two MIDI footswitch jacks, tuner out jack, two serial effects loop, two parallel effects loops with level controls, multiple speaker jacks, black covering with a front black metal grille, optional two-button and six-button footswitches available, mfg. 2009-present.

| MSR $5,495 | $4,525 | $2,750 - 3,300 | $1,925 - 2,350 | |

- Add $135 (MSR $160) for a two-button footswitch (Model FS2).
- Add $400 (MSR $490) for a six-button footswitch (Model FS6).

TWINTONE – 50W, head-unit only, all tube chassis, preamp: 1 X 12AX7WA, 2 X 12AX7, power: 1 X 12AX7, 2 X EL34, dual channels, front black and silver control panel, dual inputs, ten black knobs (Clean: v, b, m, t, OD: g, v, p, b, m, t), footswitch, effects loop, headphone jack, black Tolex covering, gray grille, disc. 2005.

Twintone
courtesy Koch

Twintone Combo
courtesy Koch

| | N/A | $1,050 - 1,250 | $750 - 900 | $1,895 |

* *Twintone Combo* – similar to the Twintone Head, except in combo form with 1-12 in. Koch/Jensen VG12-90 speaker, disc. 2005.

| | N/A | $1,100 - 1,400 | $750 - 900 | $2,150 |

TWINTONE II HEAD – 50W, head-unit only, six tube chassis, preamp: 4 X 12AX7, power: 2 X EL34, three channels, front black and silver control panel, dual inputs, ten black knobs (Clean: v, b, m, t, OD: g, v, p, b, m, t), OD switch, recording out, solo/rhythm facility, footswitch, effects loop, headphone jack, black Tolex covering, gray grille, mfg. 2006-present.

| MSR $2,395 | $1,975 | $1,200 - 1,450 | $825 - 1,025 | |

* *Twintone II Combo* – similar to the Twintone II Head, except in combo form with 1-12 in. Koch/Jensen VG12-90 speaker, mfg. 2006-present.

| MSR $2,720 | $2,250 | $1,350 - 1,625 | $950 - 1,150 | |

MSR/NOTES	100%	EXCELLENT	AVERAGE	LAST MSR

SPEAKER CABINETS

TS 112 SPEAKER CABINET – 90W, 1-12 in. Koch/Jensen VG12-90 speaker, 8 ohm impedance, black covering, gray grille, 40 lbs., current mfg.

| MSR $965 | $790 | $475 - 575 | $325 - 400 | |

TS 212 SPEAKER CABINET – 180W, 2-12 in. Koch/Jensen VG12-90 speaker, closed back, 8 ohm impedance, vertical or horizontal arrangement, black covering, gray grille, 57 lbs., current mfg.

| MSR $1,225 | $1,000 | $625 - 725 | $425 - 500 | |

TS 412 SPEAKER CABINET – 360W, 4-12 in. Koch/Jensen VG12-90 speakers, closed back, 4 or 8 ohm impedance, straight or angled cabinet, black covering, gray grille, 99 lbs., current mfg.

| MSR $2,085 | $1,700 | $1,050 - 1,250 | $725 - 875 | |

This model is also available in a Deluxe version that is meant to be matched up with the Powertone Head.

KOMET AMPLIFICATION

Amplifiers currently produced in Baton Rouge, LA by Riverfront Music since 1998. Distributed by Ultra Sound Rehearsal Studio in New York, NY.

Holger Notzel and Michael Kennedy opened Riverfront Music in 1998 as an amp repair facility. Shortly thereafter, with Ken Fischer of Trainwreck notoriety, they founded Komet Amplification. Their first model, the Komet amp, is based on Trainwreck amps, but it is an entirely new chassis designed by Ken Fischer. Like Trainwreck, Komet amps are a simple design with a single channel, no reverb, no master volume, no effects loop, no footswitches, no transistors, and no chips. The chassis is built of solid aluminum, no printed circuits are used, and the cabinet is covered in a Tolex fabric. For more information, visit Komet's website or contact the company or distributor directly.

CONTACT INFORMATION
KOMET AMPLIFICATION
Riverfront Music, LLC
1865 Dallas Drive
Baton Rouge, LA 70806-1454
Phone No.: 225-926-1976
www.kometamps.com
kometamp@cox-internet.com

Distributor: Ultra Sound Rehearsal Studio
251 West 30th St. 6FE
New York, NY 10001-2810
Phone No.: 212-967-5626
www.ultrasoundrehearsal.com
ultrasound@ultrasoundrehearsal.com

ELECTRIC TUBE AMPS/SPEAKER CABINETS

The original **Komet Amplifier** (MSR $3,699) is based on Ken Fischer's Trainwreck design and puts out between 50W and 60W from 2 X EL34 power tubes, and has a six knob control panel layout with volume, treble, mid, bass, presence, and high cut. The **Komet 19** (MSR $2,295) is a 19W head powered by either 2 X EL84 or 2 X 6BQ5 power tubes and has a three knob control panel layout with a volume, saturation, and tone controls with a two-position bright switch. The Komet 19 is also available as a combo unit with 1-12 in. Celestion Heritage G12H-30 Greenback speaker. The **Concorde** (MSR $3,850) is a limited edition head enclosed in a baltic birch cabinet. The **Constellation 30** (MSR $3,499) is an original Komet design with two independent preamps. One preamp is based on a 6SN7 preamp tube and the other is based on a 12AX7 preamp tube. The channels can be blended by adjusting the individual volume controls for each preamp. Several speaker cabinets are also available with various speaker options.

KONA

Amplifiers currently produced in Asia since 2001. Distributed by M&M Merchandisers of Ft. Worth, TX.

Since 1976, M&M Merchandisers has been a national wholesaler of musical instruments and consumer electronics. Tiring of quality issues usually associated with the entry level guitars offered to them at the time, M&M decided to make a change to better serve their dealer base. In July of 2001, M&M introduced their Kona brand of import electric guitars, acoustic guitars, and guitar amplifiers (as well as Z.Z. Ryder and Trinity River acoustic guitars) to have better control over the quality and features offered. For more information contact M&M Merchandisers.

CONTACT INFORMATION
KONA
Distributed by M&M Merchandisers
1923 Bomar Ave.
Fort Worth, TX 76103
Phone No.: 800-299-9035
www.konaguitars.com
chuck@mmwholesale.com

ELECTRIC SOLID-STATE AMPLIFIERS

The **KA-10** (MSR $80) has 10W output with a five inch speaker. The **KA-15T** (MSR $100) has 10W output with a 5 inch speaker, two channels, and a built-in tuner. The **KA-20** (MSR $115) has 20W, 1-8 in. speaker and two channels. The **KA20REC** (MSR $265) is a 20W amp with an 8 inch speaker, and a digital recorder. The **KA-20TR** (MSR $180) has 20W, 1-8 in. speaker, reverb, and a built-in tuner. The **KA-35R** (MSR $225) has 35W output, 1-10 in. speaker, two channels, and reverb. The **KA35RM** (MSR $400) is a 35W amp with a 10 inch speaker, and has a built-in rhythm machine. The **KA-35DSP** (disc. last MSR was $300) has 35W, 1-8 in. speaker and digital signal processing. The **KA-4010RC** (MSR $490) has 40W, 2-10 in. speakers, chorus, and reverb. The **KAA-60** (MSR $466) is an acoustic amp with 60W, 1-10 in. speaker, two channels, reverb, and chorus. The **KCA15** (MSR $80) is a 10W amp with a 5 inch speaker, single channel, and is available in blue, red, or tweed covering. The **KCA25** (MSR $170) is a 20W amp with an 8 inch speaker, two channels, a built-in tuner, and is available in black, red, or tweed covering. The **KB-30** (MSR $200) is a bass amp with 30W and 1-10 in. speaker. The **KB-50** (MSR $260) is a larger bass amp with 50W of power, 1-12 in. speaker, and reverb. All amplifiers have the following features: volume, treble, and bass knobs, black Tolex covering, a black grille, silver control panel, top handle, and metal corners.

| MSR/NOTES | 100% | EXCELLENT | AVERAGE | LAST MSR |

KRANK

Amplifiers currently produced in Tempe, AZ, since 1996.

Tony Dow founded Krank Amps in 1996. They offer tube amplifier heads, combos and speaker cabinets. Their products are different than others because all products are entirely hand-built, the speaker cabinets are built out of solid wood, and they are loud! Krank has had several endorsers, but the most notable one was Dimebag Darrell. Dimebag Darrell endorsed the Revolution Head for a short while, until he was fatally shot onstage at a concert in December 2004. For more information, visit Krank's website or contact them directly.

CONTACT INFORMATION
KRANK
Chandler, AZ
Phone No.: 480-899-1264
Phone No.: 888-KRANK-IT
Fax No.: 480-968-6733
www.krankamps.com
tonykrank@krankamps.com

ELECTRIC TUBE AMPLIFIERS

CHADWICK SERIES II HEAD – 50W, guitar head-unit, six-tube chassis, preamp: 4 X 12AX7, power: 2 X 5881, two channels (Clean/Drive), front black control panel, single input, 11 knobs (Drive Ch.: g, envelope, v, t, m, b, Clean Ch.: g, v, t, m, b), push/pull series effects loop, line out, speaker impedance selector, voltage selector, available in Black, Blue, Red, or Silver Tolex covering, black Tolex or chrome metal grille, current mfg.

| MSR $2,199 | $1,500 | $950 - 1,150 | $600 - 700 |

- Add 7.5% for a chrome grille.
- Add 15% for Blue, Red, or Silver Tolex covering.

KRANKENSTEIN 100W HEAD – 100W, guitar head-unit, eight-tube chassis, preamp: 4 X 12AX7, power: 4 X 5881, two channels (Clean and Dime), front black control panel with green accents, single input, 13 knobs (MV, Master p, Dime Ch.: p, sweep, b, m, t, MV1, MV2, g, Clean Ch.: v, t, m, b), push/pull series effects loop with level control, line out, speaker impedance selector, voltage selector, available in Black Tolex covering, black grille, current mfg.

| MSR $2,599 | $1,700 | $1,150 - 1,400 | $750 - 900 |

This model was designed in conjunction with and voiced by the late Dimebag Darrell.

REVOLUTION 100W HEAD – 100W, guitar head-unit, eight-tube chassis, preamp: 4 X 12AX7, power: 4 X 5881, two channels (Kleen and Krank), front black control panel, single input, 12 knobs (Krank Ch.: p, sweep, b, m, t, MV1, MV2, g, Kleen Ch.: v, t, m, b), series effects loop, line out, speaker impedance selector, voltage selector, available in Black, Blue, Red, or Silver Tolex covering, black or chrome grille, current mfg.

| MSR $2,299 | $1,600 | $1,000 - 1,200 | $625 - 750 |

- Add 5% for a chrome grille.
- Add 10% for Blue, Red, or Silver Tolex covering.

* *Revolution 100W Combo* – similar to the Revolution 100W Head, except in combo configuration with 2-12 in. speakers, current mfg.

| MSR $2,499 | $1,900 | $1,100 - 1,350 | $700 - 850 |

- Add 5% for a chrome grille.
- Add 12.5% for Blue, Red, or Silver Tolex covering.

SPEAKER CABINETS

KRANKENSTEIN SPEAKER CABINET – unknown handling power, 4-12 in. Eminence Texas Heat speakers, solid wood construction, black Tolex covering, black metal grille, designed for use with the Krankenstein Head, current mfg.

| MSR $1,299 | $1,000 | $600 - 700 | $375 - 450 |

REVOLUTION SPEAKER CABINET – unknown handling power, 4-12 in. Eminence Legend V12 speakers, solid wood construction, available in Black, Blue, Red, or Silver Tolex covering, black or chrome metal grille, current mfg.

| MSR $1,299 | $1,000 | $600 - 700 | $375 - 450 |

- Add 15% for a chrome metal grille.
- Add 25% for Blue, Red, or Silver Tolex covering.

KUSTOM

Amplifiers previously produced in Chanute, KS from 1965 until circa mid-1980s. Kustom Amplifiers were reintroduced in 1994, and are currently produced today. Distributed by Hanser Music Group in Hebron, KY. Previously distributed by HHI located in Cincinnati, OH.

Bud Ross founded Kustom amps in 1965, but he used the famous Tuck-n-Roll covering as early as 1958. Kustom is most famous for their Tuck-n-Roll covering (although some musician's swear by the sound!) that is made of Naugahyde and feels like a squishy plastic. Amps came in seven sparkling finishes including black, Cascade (teal), dark blue, dark gray, red, and silver. By 1975, Ross had sold all of his stock in the company and Kustom stopped building Tuck-n-Roll models to focus on more tradtional designs. However, these amps were never well-received and after the company changed ownership a few times, Kustom was discontinued by the mid-1980s. Hanser Holdings Inc. (HHI, currently Hanser Music Group) bought Kustom out of bankruptcy in the late 1980s and they introduced new models in 1994. In 1999 and 2000, Kustom introduced their first Tuck-n-Roll models in almost 25 years.

CONTACT INFORMATION
KUSTOM
Distributed by Hanser Music Group
3015 Kustom Drive
Hebron, KY 41048
Phone No.: 859-817-7100
Fax No.: 859-817-7199
www.kustom.com
info@kustom.com

MSR/NOTES	100%	EXCELLENT	AVERAGE	LAST MSR

Currently Kustom offers a full line of guitar, acoustic, bass, keyboard, and PA amplifiers in a variety of configurations. A new toned-down Tuck-n-Roll series is also available with a tube chassis. For more information, visit Kustom's website or contact them directly.

KUSTOM IDENTIFICATION AND OVERVIEW

Correctly identifying a Kustom amp can be very difficult. They used several different numbering systems for the same amp. Chassis numbers, model numbers, and catalog numbers have all been used to identify Kustom amps. In the *Blue Book of Guitar Amplifiers*, we use the model number because it seems to be the most straight-forward, and most people seem to be familiar with this system. Often times, the chassis number will be used, but we do not use catalog numbers anywhere in this publication.

All models start with the letter K, which represents Kustom. The following two or three numbers indicate the power of the amp (i.e. 25, 50, 100, 150, 200, 250, 400, etc.). For models produced between 1966 and 1972, the number is approximately twice the amount of RMS power (and possibly numbered after peak power). For instance, the 100 has 50W RMS and 100W peak and the 200 has 100W RMS and 200W peak. Remember these are approximations and there may be some variations in the system. This number is followed by a dash and another number. This last number indicates the configuration of the amp. The following chart displays what each number represents.

1 - No effects (reverb, tremolo).	5 - PA application with reverb
2 - Reverb and tremolo.	6 - Combo with Selectone.
3 - Harmonic clip and boost.	7 - Combo with reverb, tremolo, and boost.
4 - Reverb, tremolo, harmonic clip, and boost.	8 - Combo with reverb, tremolo, and boost.

This model number system applies to head-units only. Speaker cabinets are named with chassis numbers. This system is based on the number and size of the speaker, the brand of the speaker, and the configuration in relation to the head-unit. The first three numbers are separated by a dash and indicate how many and what size speakers the cabinet consists of. Kustom used several different speakers in their cabinets including Altec Lansing, CTS, JBL, Jensen, and Kustom. These are all indicated by the first letter of the speaker name. The last number corresponds to head-unit the cabinet was sold with. This number will range from 1-4, but there is not any difference between speaker cabinets. For example, 1-15L-1 is a 1-15 in. JBL cabinet meant to be teamed up with a standard amp with no effects. A 3-15A-2 is a 3-15 in. Altec Lansing cabinet meant to be teamed up with an amp with reverb and tremolo.

Identifying series of Kustom amplifiers is a bit easier because they usually changed their entire lines all at once. Amplifiers can be grouped into general years if you don't know the exact specifications.

1966-1967: The Frankenstein Model. The early Kustom amps are easy to recognize because the heads have a large top covering in relation to the rest of the material. It makes the amp look like it has a forehead similar to Frankenstein. Models during this era do not have a number on the front. They simply read "Kustom" and the only model produced during this time was the K200.

1967-1971: This era of amplifiers are what most people are familiar with. They have a front face of equal size (no more forehead) and have the number of the amp underneath the Kustom logo. The 100 and 400 Series were introduced, and the 200 Series continued in production. These amps are generally the most desirable and collectible of Kustom amps.

1971-1974: The covering did not change, but the control panel did. It received a slanted design and the panel was divided up into different sections by white lines.The number followed the Kustom logo, instead of going under it. The models changed numbers as well. The 100, 200, and 400 were all discontinued and the 150, 250, 300, 500, and 600 were introduced. The speaker cabinets remained the same for the most part.

1974-late 1970s: The end of the Tuck-n-Roll models. After ownership changed in 1975, they dropped tuck and roll and opted for the more popular (and bland) black vinyl. The control panel was also changed to look more traditional. Models from this era are a bit similar to the Fender Silverface. All previous models were discontinued at this time and replaced by the Kustom I, II, III, and IV lead, and Bass I, II, III, and IV bass amps.

Late 1978-mid 1980s: The amp line completely changed again in the late 1970s and black Tolex was introduced - very similar to Fender. The logo was also changed to a large K. Kustom kept the same model nomenclature from the previous series, but they did change them a bit.

1994-present: New amps were introduced in 1994. In 1999, they tried a new line of Tuck-n-Roll amplifiers in a tube version, but they only lasted for a year. Currently, they have a entire line of amplifiers, including tube and solid-state models and another Tuck-n-Roll Series.

Naugahyde is the material used on Kustom's Tuck-n-Roll models from 1966 to 1975 and it came in many different colors. Black was the standard covering and brings the least in value. Black Tuck-n-Roll covering to Kustom amplifiers is like Sunburst finish is to Stratocasters. Optional coverings include Cascade (a blueish-green color), Silver, Gold, Red, Dark Blue, and Charcoal (a dark gray). Optional colors command a premium in the used market. Gold might be the rarest color seen.

ELECTRIC SS AMPLIFIERS: MISC. TUCK-N-ROLL MODELS

K-25-2 – 12W, 1-12 in. speaker combo, solid-state chassis, reverb, tremolo, front black control panel, two inputs, six black and silver knobs (v, b, t, r, s, i), tuck and roll covering (various colors), black grille, mfg. late 1960s-1972.

	100%	EXCELLENT	AVERAGE
Black	N/A	$250 - 300	$150 - 200
Color	N/A	$425 - 500	$275 - 325

MSR/NOTES	100%	EXCELLENT	AVERAGE	LAST MSR

K-50-2
courtesy Dave Rogers/Dave's Guitar Shop

2-150-1
courtesy Dave Rogers/Dave's Guitar Shop

K100-1 115 Piggyback
courtesy Dave Rogers/Dave's Guitar Shop

K-50-2 – 25W, 1-12 in. speaker combo, solid-state chassis, reverb, tremolo, front black control panel, two inputs, six black and silver knobs (v, b, t, r, s, i), tuck and roll covering (various colors), black grille, mfg. late 1960s-1972.

Black	N/A	$300 - 350	$175 - 225	
Color	N/A	$475 - 550	$300 - 350	

2-150-1 – 150W, head-unit only, solid-state chassis, front black control panel, dual channels, four inputs, eight black and silver knobs (Ch. 1: v, b, t, bright, Ch. 2: v, b, t, bright), tuck and roll covering (various colors), mfg. 1970s.

	N/A	$200 - 250	$125 - 175	

TRB-400 BASS AMP – 400W Bass amp, mfg. 1960s-1970s.

	N/A	$700 - 900	$500 - 600	

ELECTRIC SS AMPLIFIERS: K100 SERIES

K100-1 HEAD – 50W, head-unit only, solid-state Energizer chassis, two channels, front black control panel, two inputs, six knobs (Ch. 1: v, b, t, Ch. 2: v, b, t), tuck and roll covering, mfg. 1968-1972.

Black	N/A	$150 - 200	$95 - 125	
Color	N/A	$250 - 300	$100 - 150	

* **K100-1 115 Piggyback (Models 1-15A-1, 1-15J-1, 1-15L-1)** – similar to the K100-1 Head, except in head-unit configuration with 1-15 in. speaker cabinet (Altec Lansing, Jensen, or JBL speaker), tuck and roll covering, mfg. 1968-1972.

Black	N/A	$280 - 325	$140 - 175	
Color	N/A	$550 - 650	$325 - 400	

* **K100-1 212 Piggyback (Models 2-12A-1 and 2-12J-1)** – similar to the K100-1 Head, except in piggyback configuration with 2-12 in. Altec Lansing or Jensen speakers, tuck and roll covering, mfg. 1968-1972.

Black	N/A	$325 - 375	$160 - 195	
Color	N/A	$600 - 700	$350 - 450	

* **K100-1 115 Bass Piggyback (Model 1-15C)** – similar to the K100-1 Head, except in piggyback configuration with 1-15 in. CTS speaker, designed for bass application, tuck and roll covering, mfg. 1968-1972.

Black	N/A	$280 - 325	$140 - 175	
Color	N/A	$550 - 650	$325 - 400	

* **K100-1 115 Bass Piggyback (Model 1-D140F)** – similar to the K100-1 Head, except in piggyback configuration with 1-15 in. JBL speaker, designed for bass application, tuck and roll covering, mfg. 1968-1972.

Black	N/A	$280 - 325	$140 - 175	
Color	N/A	$600 - 700	$350 - 450	

* **K100-1 212 Bass Piggyback (Model 2-12C)** – similar to the K100-1 Head, except in piggyback configuration with 2-12 in. CTS speaker, designed for bass application, tuck and roll covering, mfg. 1968-1972.

Black	N/A	$325 - 400	$200 - 250	
Color	N/A	$600 - 700	$350 - 425	

K100-2 HEAD – 50W, head-unit only, solid-state Energizer chassis, single channel, reverb, tremolo, front black control panel, single input, six knobs (v, b, t, r, s, i), tuck and roll covering, mfg. 1968-1972.

Black	N/A	$200 - 250	$120 - 150	
Color	N/A	$325 - 400	$175 - 225	

MSR/NOTES	100%	EXCELLENT	AVERAGE	LAST MSR

K100-2 212 Piggyback
courtesy Dave Rogers/Dave's Guitar Shop

K100-C7 Combo
courtesy Dave Rogers/Dave's Guitar Shop

K100-C8 Combo
courtesy Dave Rogers/Dave's Guitar Shop

* ***K100-2 115 Piggyback (Models 1-15A-2, 1-15J-2, 1-15L-2)*** – similar to the K100-2 Head, except in head-unit configuration with 1-15 in. speaker cabinet (Altec Lansing, Jensen, or JBL speaker), tuck and roll covering, mfg. 1968-1972.

Black	N/A	$280 - 325	$140 - 175	
Color	N/A	$600 - 700	$350 - 425	

* ***K100-2 212 Piggyback (Models 2-12A-2 and 2-12J-2)*** – similar to the K100-2 Head, except in piggyback configuration with 2-12 in. Altec Lansing or Jensen speakers, tuck and roll covering, mfg. 1968-1972.

Black	N/A	$350 - 400	$170 - 210	
Color	N/A	$625 - 750	$425 - 500	

K100-5 HEAD – 50W, PA application, head-unit only, solid-state Energizer chassis, four channels, reverb, front black control panel, single input, 16 knobs (r, b, t, v per channel), tuck and roll covering, mfg. 1968-1972.

Black	N/A	$375 - 450	$190 - 235	
Color	N/A	$500 - 600	$255 - 325	

K100-C6 COMBO – 50W, 1-15 in. speaker combo, solid-state chassis, two channels, front black control panel, two inputs, six knobs, tuck and roll covering (various colors), black grille, mfg. 1968-1972.

Black	N/A	$275 - 325	$150 - 200	
Color	N/A	$500 - 600	$300 - 350	

K100-C7 COMBO – 100W, 2-12 in. speaker combo, solid-state chassis, two channels, reverb, tremolo, front black control panel, two inputs, 10 knobs, tuck and roll covering (various colors), black grille, casters, mfg. 1968-1972.

Black	N/A	$325 - 400	$200 - 250	
Color	N/A	$600 - 700	$375 - 450	

K100-C8 COMBO – 100W, 4-10 in. speaker combo, solid-state chassis, two channels, reverb, tremolo, front black control panel, two inputs, 10 black and silver knobs, tuck and roll covering (various colors), black grille, mfg. 1968-1972.

Black	N/A	$375 - 450	$250 - 300	
Color	N/A	$625 - 750	$425 - 500	

ELECTRIC SS AMPLIFIERS: K200 SERIES

K200-1 HEAD – 100W, head-unit only, solid-state chassis, two channels, front black control panel, four inputs, eight knobs, tuck and roll covering (various colors), mfg. 1966-1972.

Black	N/A	$240 - 280	$120 - 145	
Color	N/A	$350 - 400	$170 - 210	

* ***K200-1 215 Combo (Models 2-15A-1, 2-15J-1, 2-15L-1)*** – similar to the K200-1 Head, except in piggyback form with 2-15 in. Altec Lansing, Jensen, or JBL speakers, mfg. 1966-1972.

Black	N/A	$425 - 500	$215 - 265	
Color	N/A	$625 - 750	$325 - 400	

* ***K200-1 315 Combo (Models 3-15A-1, 3-15J-1, 3-15L-1)*** – similar to the K200-1 Head, except in piggyback form with 3-15 in. Altec Lansing, Jensen, or JBL speakers, mfg. 1966-1972.

Black	N/A	$500 - 600	$255 - 325	
Color	N/A	$675 - 800	$350 - 425	

MSR/NOTES	100%	EXCELLENT	AVERAGE	LAST MSR

K200-1 415 Combo (Models 4-15A-1, 4-15J-1, 4-15L-1) – similar to the K200-1 Head, except in piggyback form with 4-15 in. Altec Lansing, Jensen, or JBL speakers in two separate cabinets (2-15 in. speakers in each cabinet), mfg. 1966-1972.

Black	N/A	$550 - 650	$275 - 350	
Color	N/A	$725 - 850	$350 - 450	

K200-2 HEAD – 100W, head-unit only, solid-state chassis, two channels, reverb, front black control panel, four inputs, tuck and roll covering (various colors), mfg. 1966-1972.

Black	N/A	$225 - 275	$125 - 175	
Color	N/A	$300 - 375	$175 - 225	

K200-2 215 Combo (Models 2-15A-2, 2-15J-2, 2-15L-2) – similar to the K200-2 Head, except in piggyback form with 2-15 in. Altec Lansing, Jensen, or JBL speakers, mfg. 1966-1972.

Black	N/A	$425 - 500	$215 - 265	
Color	N/A	$550 - 650	$325 - 400	

K200-2 315 Combo (Models 3-15A-2, 3-15J-2, 3-15L-2) – similar to the K200-2 Head, except in piggyback form with 3-15 in. Altec Lansing, Jensen, or JBL speakers, mfg. 1966-1972.

Black	N/A	$475 - 550	$235 - 290	
Color	N/A	$600 - 700	$350 - 425	

K200-2 415 Combo (Models 4-15A-2, 4-15J-2, 4-15L-2) – similar to the K200-2 Head, except in piggyback form with 4-15 in. Altec Lansing, Jensen, or JBL speakers in two separate cabinets (2-15 in. speakers in each cabinet), mfg. 1966-1972.

Black	N/A	$500 - 575	$245 - 300	
Color	N/A	$625 - 750	$375 - 450	

K200-3 HEAD – 100W, head-unit only, solid-state chassis, two channels, harmonic clipper, boost, front black control panel, four inputs, ten knobs (Ch. 1: v, b, t, boost, Ch. 2: v, b, t, bright, boost v, selective boost), tuck and roll covering (various colors), mfg. 1966-1972.

Black	N/A	$300 - 350	$150 - 185	
Color	N/A	$425 - 500	$275 - 325	

K200-3 215 Combo (Models 2-15A-3, 2-15J-3, 2-15L-3) – similar to the K200-3 Head, except in piggyback form with 2-15 in. Altec Lansing, Jensen, or JBL speakers, mfg. 1966-1972.

Black	N/A	$425 - 500	$215 - 265	
Color	N/A	$500 - 600	$300 - 350	

K200-3 315 Combo (Models 3-15A-3, 3-15J-3, 3-15L-3) – similar to the K200-3 Head, except in piggyback form with 3-15 in. Altec Lansing, Jensen, or JBL speakers, mfg. 1966-1972.

Black	N/A	$500 - 600	$255 - 325	
Color	N/A	$600 - 700	$300 - 375	

K200-3 415 Combo (Models 4-15A-3, 4-15J-3, 4-15L-3) – similar to the K200-3 Head, except in piggyback form with 4-15 in. Altec Lansing, Jensen, or JBL speakers in two separate cabinets (2-15 in. speakers in each cabinet), mfg. 1966-1972.

Black	N/A	$550 - 650	$275 - 350	
Color	N/A	$700 - 825	$350 - 425	

K200-4 HEAD – 100W, head-unit only, solid-state chassis, two channels, reverb, tremolo, harmonic clipper, boost, front black control panel, four inputs, 16 knobs, tuck and roll covering (various colors), mfg. 1966-1972.

Black	N/A	$350 - 400	$170 - 210	
Color	N/A	$475 - 550	$300 - 350	

K200-4 215 Combo (Models 2-15A-4, 2-15J-4, 2-15L-4) – similar to the K200-4 Head, except in piggyback form with 2-15 in. Altec Lansing, Jensen, or JBL speakers, mfg. 1966-1972.

Black	N/A	$550 - 650	$275 - 350	
Color	N/A	$675 - 800	$425 - 500	

K200-4 315 Combo (Models 3-15A-4, 3-15J-4, 3-15L-4) – similar to the K200-4 Head, except in piggyback form with 3-15 in. Altec Lansing, Jensen, or JBL speakers, mfg. 1966-1972.

Black	N/A	$600 - 700	$300 - 375	
Color	N/A	$700 - 850	$475 - 550	

K200-4 415 Combo (Models 4-15A-4, 4-15J-4, 4-15L-4) – similar to the K200-4 Head, except in piggyback form with 4-15 in. Altec Lansing, Jensen, or JBL speakers in two separate cabinets (2-15 in. speakers in each cabinet), mfg. 1966-1972.

Black	N/A	$625 - 750	$325 - 400	
Color	N/A	$750 - 900	$500 - 575	

MSR/NOTES	100%	EXCELLENT	AVERAGE	LAST MSR

ELECTRIC SS AMPLIFIERS: K400 SERIES

K400-1 HEAD – 200W, head-unit only, solid-state chassis, two channels, front black control panel, four inputs, eight knobs, tuck and roll covering (various colors), mfg. 1968-1972.

Black	N/A	$250 - 300	$125 - 175	
Color	N/A	$325 - 400	$200 - 250	

* **K400-1 615 Combo (Models 6-15A-1, 6-15J-1, 6-15L-1)** – similar to the K400-1 Head, except in piggyback form with 6-15 in. Altec Lansing, JBL, or Jensen speakers, speakers are in two separate cabinets with 3-15 in. speakers in each one, head comes with a metal stand, mfg. 1968-1972.

Black	N/A	$475 - 550	$300 - 350	
Color	N/A	$600 - 700	$375 - 450	

* **K400-1 815 Combo (Models 8-15A-1, 8-15J-1, 8-15L-1)** – similar to the K400-1 Head, except in piggyback form with 8-15 in. Altec Lansing, JBL, or Jensen speakers, speakers are in two separate cabinets with 4-15 in. speakers in each one, head comes with a metal stand, mfg. 1968-1972.

Black	N/A	$500 - 600	$300 - 375	
Color	N/A	$625 - 750	$400 - 475	

K400-2 HEAD – 200W, head-unit only, solid-state chassis, two channels, reverb, tremolo, front black control panel, four inputs, tuck and roll covering (various colors), mfg. 1968-1972.

Black	N/A	$300 - 350	$150 - 200	
Color	N/A	$375 - 450	$200 - 250	

* **K400-2 615 Combo (Models 6-15A-2, 6-15J-2, 6-15-2)** – similar to the K400-2 Head, except in piggyback form with 6-15 in. Altec Lansing, JBL, or Jensen speakers, speakers are in two separate cabinets with 3-15 in. speakers in each one, head comes with a metal stand, mfg. 1968-1972.

Black	N/A	$500 - 600	$300 - 375	
Color	N/A	$625 - 750	$400 - 475	

* **K400-2 815 Combo (Models 8-15A-2, 8-15J-2, 8-15-2)** – similar to the K400-2 Head, except in piggyback form with 8-15 in. Altec Lansing, JBL, or Jensen speakers, speakers are in two separate cabinets with 4-15 in. speakers in each one, head comes with a metal stand, mfg. 1968-1972.

Black	N/A	$550 - 650	$325 - 400	
Color	N/A	$675 - 800	$425 - 500	

K400-3 HEAD – 200W, head-unit only, solid-state chassis, two channels, harmonic clipper, boost, front black control panel, four inputs, tuck and roll covering (various colors), mfg. 1968-1972.

Black	N/A	$300 - 350	$175 - 225	
Color	N/A	$375 - 450	$225 - 275	

* **K400-3 615 Combo (Models 6-15A-3, 6-15J-3, 6-15-3)** – similar to the K400-3 Head, except in piggyback form with 6-15 in. Altec Lansing, JBL, or Jensen speakers, speakers are in two separate cabinets with 3-15 in. speakers in each one, head comes with a metal stand, mfg. 1968-1972.

Black	N/A	$550 - 650	$325 - 400	
Color	N/A	$675 - 800	$425 - 500	

* **K400-3 815 Combo (Models 8-15A-3, 8-15J-3, 8-15-3)** – similar to the K400-3 Head, except in piggyback form with 8-15 in. Altec Lansing, JBL, or Jensen speakers, speakers are in two separate cabinets with 4-15 in. speakers in each one, head comes with a metal stand, mfg. 1968-1972.

Black	N/A	$600 - 700	$375 - 450	
Color	N/A	$725 - 850	$475 - 550	

K400-4 HEAD – 200W, head-unit only, solid-state chassis, two channels, reverb, tremolo, harmonic clipper, boost, front black control panel, four inputs, tuck and roll covering (various colors), mfg. 1968-1972.

Black	N/A	$350 - 425	$200 - 250	
Color	N/A	$450 - 525	$275 - 325	

* **K400-4 615 Combo (Models 6-15A-4, 6-15J-4, 6-15-4)** – similar to the K400-4 Head, except in piggyback form with 6-15 in. Altec Lansing, JBL, or Jensen speakers, speakers are in two separate cabinets with 3-15 in. speakers in each one, head comes with a metal stand, mfg. 1968-1972.

Black	N/A	$600 - 700	$375 - 450	
Color	N/A	$750 - 900	$475 - 550	

MSR/NOTES	100%	EXCELLENT	AVERAGE	LAST MSR

* **K400-4 815 Combo (Models 8-15A-4, 8-15J-4, 8-15-4)** – similar to the K400-4 Head, except in piggyback form with 8-15 in. Altec Lansing, JBL, or Jensen speakers, speakers are in two separate cabinets with 4-15 in. speakers in each one, head comes with a metal stand, mfg. 1968-1972.

Black	N/A	$650 - 750	$425 - 500	
Color	N/A	$800 - 950	$500 - 600	

ELECTRIC TUBE AMPLIFIERS: TUCK-N-ROLL/COUPE SERIES (RECENT MFG.)

The Tuck-n-Roll Series was reintroduced in 1999 with three new heads and four speaker cabinets. Unlike the Kustom amps of the late 1960s and early 1970s, these amps feature tube chassis and only red, blue, black, or charcoal coverings were available. Kustom offered four different speaker cabinet configurations to match the tuck and roll heads. All cabinets use Jensen speakers and can handle at least 100W. The cabinets are the TR212 (2-12 in.), TR215 (2-15 in.), TR410 (4-10 in.), and TR412 (4-12 in.). This series only lasted about a year. In 2005, Kustom introduced another Tuck-n-Roll line of amps, but this time only the area above the speaker featured this colorful covering. This series was designed by James Brown and features tube chassis.

* Add $20 (MSR $30) for a cover.

'36 Coupe 112
courtesy Kustom

'36 Coupe 210
courtesy Kustom

'72 Coupe Head
courtesy Kustom

TRT50H – 50W, head-unit only, all tube chassis, preamp: 4 X 12AX7, power: 2 X 6L6, dual channels, reverb, front black control panel, two inputs, 12 black and silver knobs (b, m, t, g, r, v, per channel), footswitch, tuck-n-roll covering (various colors), 38 lbs., mfg. circa 1999-2000.

N/A   N/A   N/A

TRT100H – 100W, head-unit only, all tube chassis, preamp: 4 X 12AX7, power: 4 X 6L6, dual channels, reverb, front black control panel, two inputs, 12 black and silver knobs (b, m, t, g, r, v, per channel), footswitch, tuck-n-roll covering (various colors), 42 lbs., mfg. circa 1999-2000.

N/A   N/A   N/A

TRB400H – 400W, bass head-unit only, tube/solid-state chassis, preamp: 1 X 12AX7, solid-state power supply, dual channels, chorous, compressor, front black control panel, two inputs, 16 black and silver knobs (voice, voice, ratio, depth, g, g, threshold, rate, 7-band equalizer, v), footswitch, tuck-n-roll covering (various colors), 42 lbs., mfg. circa 1999-2000.

N/A   N/A   N/A

'36 COUPE 112 – 36W, 1-12 in. KEI speaker, guitar combo, tube chassis, preamp: 4 X 12AX7, power: 2 X 6L6, two channels, reverb, top black control panel, nine black knobs, three-button footswitch, black covering with black, blue, charcoal, or red Tuck-n-Roll covering on front, mfg. 2005-disc.

$900 $525 - 600 $300 - 375 $1,150

* Add 10% for custom colors.

* **'36 Coupe 210** – similar to the '36 Coupe, except has 2-10 in. KEI Turbo speakers, mfg. 2007-disc.

$950 $525 - 625 $325 - 400 $1,200

* Add 10% for custom colors.

'72 COUPE HEAD – 72W, head-unit configuration, tube chassis, preamp: 4 X 12AX7, power: 4 X 6L6, two channels, reverb, top black control panel, 12 black knobs, three-button footswitch, black covering with black Tuck-n-Roll covering on front, mfg. 2006-disc.

$1,000 $550 - 650 $350 - 425 $1,250

* Add 10% for custom colors.

* **'72 Coupe Combo** – similar to the '72 Coupe Head, except in combo configuration with 2-12 in. KEI speakers, and black covering with black, blue, charcoal, or red Tuck-n-Roll covering on front, mfg. 2005-disc.

$1,100 $625 - 750 $375 - 450 $1,400

* Add 10% for custom colors.

SPORT COUPE – 18W, 1-10 in. KEI speaker, guitar combo, tube chassis, preamp: 12AX7s, power: 1 X 6L6, two channels, reverb, top black control panel, eight black knobs, three-button footswitch, black covering with blue Tuck-n-Roll covering on front, mfg. 2009-disc.

$800 $500 - 600 $300 - 375 $1,050

MSR/NOTES	100%	EXCELLENT	AVERAGE	LAST MSR

ELECTRIC TUBE AMPS: CONTENDER, DEFENDER, & DOUBLE CROSS SERIES

The Contender
courtesy Kustom

The Defender 112
courtesy Kustom

Double Cross Head
courtesy Kustom

THE CONTENDER – 18W, 1-8 in. Eminence speaker guitar combo, hybrid chassis with one 12AX7 preamp tube, single channel, front black control panel, single input, four chrome and black knobs (v, b, t, MV), bright switch, MV bypass switch, external speaker jack, black covering, black grille with white piping, deluxe leather handle, 13.25 in. wide, 13 in. tall, 7.5 in. deep, 12.25 lbs., mfg. 2008-disc.

	$170	$100 - 130	$60 - 80	$260

THE DEFENDER 5H – 5W, mini guitar head unit, two-tube chassis, preamp: 1 X 12AX7, power: 1 X EL84, solid-state rectifier, single channel, front black control panel, single input, single volume control, black casing, 12.375 in. wide, 5 in. tall, 7.25 in. deep, 7 lbs., mfg. 2010-present.

MSR $180	$110	$70 - 85	$35 - 45	

THE DEFENDER 112 – 50W, 1-12 in. KEI Epic speaker guitar combo, five-tube chassis, preamp: 3 X 12AX7, power: 2 X EL34 or 2 X 6L6GC, single channel, reverb, top black control panel, single input, eight black and chrome knobs (v, MV, b, m, t, r, p, boost), bright switch, MV bypass switch, external speaker jack, footswitch, black covering, black grille with white piping, deluxe leather handle, mfg. 2007-present.

MSR $850	$570	$325 - 400	$175 - 225	

THE DEFENDER V50 – 50W, 1-12 in. Celestion Vintage 30 speaker, guitar combo, six-tube chassis, preamp: 4 X 12AX7, power: 2 X EL34, solid-state rectifier, two channels, reverb, tremolo, vibrato, top control panel, XLR direct out with cabinet emulation, black covering, black/gray grille cloth, 22.75 in. wide, 20.5 in. tall, 10.75 in. deep, 48.5 lbs., mfg. 2010-disc.

	$800	$500 - 575	$300 - 350	$1,100

THE DEFENDER V100 – 100W, 2-12 in. Celestion Vintage 30 speakers, guitar combo, eight-tube chassis, preamp: 4 X 12AX7, power: 4 X EL34, solid-state rectifier, two channels, reverb, tremolo, vibrato, top control panel, XLR direct out with cabinet emulation, black covering, black/gray grille cloth, 27.25 in. wide, 21.25 in. tall, 10.75 in. deep, 68 lbs., mfg. 2010-disc.

	$1,000	$600 - 700	$375 - 450	$1,400

THE DEFENDER 1-12 SPEAKER CABINET – 30W, 1-12 in. speaker, 16 ohm impedance, plywood baffle board cabinet, designed for use with The Defender 5H head, black covering, gray/black "salt and pepper" grille cloth, 17.75 in. wide, 17 in. tall, 10 in. deep, 20.5 lbs., mfg. 2010-disc.

	$100	$50 - 75	$30 - 40	$145

DOUBLE CROSS HEAD – 100W, guitar head-unit configuration, 12 tube chassis, preamp: 5 X 12AX7, 1 X 12AT7, power: 6 X 6L6 or 6 X EL34, three channels (Rhythm, Lead I, Lead II), front dark gray control panel, two inputs (normal, tight), 21 chrome knobs (Rhythm Ch.: p, t, m, b, v, g, Lead I Ch.: p, t, m, b, v, g, Lead II Ch.: p, t, m, b, v, g, All: MV, boost, channel switch), drive and boost switches on the rhythm channel, effects loop, switchable tube bias, XLR direct out with slant/straight speaker cabinet emulation, five-button footswitch, black covering, silver grille with black metal inserts, 27 in. wide, 12 in. tall, 10.875 in. deep, 43 lbs., mfg. 2008-disc.

	$1,600	$900 - 1,050	$600 - 700	$2,100

ELECTRIC AMPS: MISC. MODELS

12 GAUGE – 10W, 1-12 in. speaker, guitar combo, solid-state chassis, single channel, top control panel, single input, seven knobs, RCA inputs, headphone jack, black covering, gray grille, mfg. 2006-disc.

	$130	$70 - 90	$45 - 60	$190

DOUBLE BARREL – 30W, 2-12 in. Kustom speakers guitar combo, solid-state chassis, two channels (Lead, Clean), delay, reverb, chorus, top black control panel, single input, seven chrome knobs (Lead Ch.: g, v, Clean Ch.: v, All: l, m, h, effect level), headphone jack, aux. in, line out jack, external speaker jack, black covering, black grille with white piping, deluxe leather handle, 26.25 in. wide, 17.25 in. tall, 10 in. deep, 35.25 lbs., mfg. 2008-disc.

	$220	$120 - 160	$75 - 95	$330

MSR/NOTES	100%	EXCELLENT	AVERAGE	LAST MSR

12 Gauge
courtesy Kustom

Double Barrel
courtesy Kustom

Tube 12
courtesy Kustom

TUBE 12 – 12W, 1-8 in. speaker, guitar combo, hybrid chassis, preamp: 1 X 12AX7 and solid-state, power: solid-state, single channel, top control panel, single input, four knobs (v, t, b, UK/USA tone switch), black covering, gray grille, disc.

$120	$60 - 80	$40 - 50		$170

ELECTRIC SS AMPLIFIERS: AURIS SERIES

In 2014, Kustom introduced the Auris Series. The Auris Series of Solid State Amplifiers includes the **5012FX** Combo, **60212FX** Combo, and the **60FXH** head unit.

ELECTRIC SS AMPLIFIERS: DUAL/QUAD SERIES

- Add $20 (MSR $30) for a cover.

Dual 30RC
courtesy Kustom

Quad 65 DFX 112 Combo
courtesy Kustom

Quad 100 DFX 212 Combo
courtesy Kustom

DUAL 30RC – 30W, 1-10 in. Celestion speaker, solid-state chassis, two channels, reverb, chorus, top control panel, eight black knobs, black covering, gray grille, mfg. 2004-disc.

$200	$110 - 140	$70 - 90		$300

DUAL 35FX – 30W, 1-10 in. Celestion speaker, solid-state chassis, two channels, eight 24-bit digital effects, top control panel, eight black knobs, black covering, gray grille, mfg. 2004-disc.

$250	$135 - 175	$85 - 105		$370

QUAD 65 DFX 112 COMBO – 65W, 1-12 in. speaker combo, solid-state chassis, two channels, eight 24-bit digital effects, top black control panel, single input, 11 knobs, black covering, gray grille, mfg. 2004-disc.

$300	$175 - 225	$110 - 140		$470

QUAD 100 HEAD – 100W, head-unit only, solid-state chassis, two channels, eight 24-bit digital effects, front black control panel, single input, 11 knobs, black covering, black front, mfg. 2004-disc.

$320	$175 - 225	$110 - 140		$480

* *Quad 100 DFX 212 Combo* – similar to the Quad 100 Head, except in combo form with 2-12 in. Celestion speakers, black covering, silver grille, mfg. 2004-disc.

$470	$275 - 325	$150 - 200		$700

QUAD 200 HEAD – 200W, head-unit only, solid-state chassis, two channels, eight 24-bit digital effects, front black control panel, single input, 11 knobs, black covering, black front, mfg. 2004-disc.

$420	$250 - 300	$135 - 175		$630

QUAD JR. HALF STACK – features the Quad100 Head with a special 4 ohm 4-12 in. speaker cabinet, mfg. 2006-disc.

$750	$425 - 500	$250 - 300		$1,100

MSR/NOTES	100%	EXCELLENT	AVERAGE	LAST MSR

ELECTRIC SS AMPLIFIERS: K/SOLO/DART/ARROW SERIES

Models produced before 2003 all have K model designations. In 2003, models that continued to the new series were changed to the Solo series. In 2005, the Solo Series changed to the Arrow Series. In 2006, the KGA10 became the Dart Series.

KGA10/Dart 10
courtesy John Beeson/The Music Shoppe

KGA16/Solo 16/Arrow 16
courtesy Kustom

KGA16R/Solo 16R/Arrow 16R
courtesy John Beeson/The Music Shoppe

KGA10/DART 10 – 10W, 1-6.5 in.speaker, solid-state chassis, voice control, single channel, top silver control panel, single input, three black and silver knobs (g, voice, v), headphone jack, overdrive switch, black covering, gray grille, disc.

	$70	$40 - 55	$20 - 30	$100

As part of Kustom's 40th Anniversary in 2006, the Dart was offered in a limited edition with tuck-n-roll covering in a variety of colors.

* KGA 10FX/DART 10FX – similar to the KGA10/Dart 10, except has digital effects, seven knobs, mfg. 2004-disc.

	$90	$50 - 70	$30 - 40	$135

KGA16/SOLO 16/ARROW 16 – 16W, 1-8in.Celestion speaker combo, solid-state chassis, single channel, top silver control panel, two inputs, six black and silver knobs (g, v, rhythm v, l, m, h), headphone jack, overdrive switch, black covering, gray grille, disc.

	$110	$60 - 85	$40 - 50	$165

* KGA16R/Solo 16R/Arrow 16R – similar to the KGA16/Solo 16/Arrow 16, except has reverb circuit with control for a total of seven knobs, disc.

	$140	$80 - 105	$50 - 65	$210

* Solo 16DFX/Arrow 16DFX – similar to the KGA16/Solo 16/Arrow 16, except has digital effects and eight knobs, mfg. 2004-disc.

	$170	$100 - 130	$60 - 80	$260

KGA30 – 30W, 1-10 in. Celestion speaker combo, solid-state chassis, reverb, chorus, single channel, top silver control panel, two inputs, eight black and silver knobs (g, v, rhythm v, l, m, h, r, chorus), headphone jack, overdrive switch, footswitch, black covering, gray grille, disc. 2004.

	N/A	$120 - 150	$75 - 95	$258

KGA65 – 65W, 1-12 in. Celestion speaker combo, solid-state chassis, digital effects, dual channels, top silver control panel, two inputs, 11 black and silver knobs (Lead: g, l, m, h, v, Rhythm b, m, t, v, digital effects level, program), eight preset effects, headphone jack, overdrive switch, footswitch, black covering, gray grille, footswitch, disc. 2004.

	N/A	$150 - 200	$95 - 120	$360

ELECTRIC SS AMPLIFIERS: KG SERIES

In 2010, Kustom introduced the KG Series of solid state amplifiers. In 2015, each of these amps were updated to a 2.0 version. This series of amps includes the **KG1**, **KG100FX112**, **KG100FX212**, **KG112FX**, **KG210FX**, **KG212FX**, and **KGBAT10** combo amps, as well as the **KG100HFX** head unit.

ELECTRIC SS AMPLIFIERS: PHASE (PH) SERIES

In 2014, Kustom introduced the Phase Series of Solid State amplifiers. This line of combo amps includes the **PH1012**, **PHTUBE12**, and the **PH2012R**.

ELECTRIC SS AMPLIFIERS: WAV SERIES

The WAV series are not described as modeling amps. They have a solid-state rhythm channel and four seperate, tube-driven lead channels.

WAV 1000 HEAD – 260W (2 X 130W Stereo), head-unit only, solid-state chassis, two channels, digital effects, front blue control panel, single input, eleven knobs, 45 tonal settings, digital display, footswitch, black covering, blue grille, mfg. 2004-05.

	N/A	$300 - 375	$175 - 225	$699

MSR/NOTES	100%	EXCELLENT	AVERAGE	LAST MSR

WAV 212 COMBO – 260W (2 X 130W Stereo), 2-12 in. Celestion speaker combo, solid-state chassis, two channels, digital effects, front blue control panel, single input, eleven knobs, 45 tonal settings, digital display, footswitch, black covering, blue grille, mfg. 2004-05.

	N/A	$400 - 475	$250 - 300	$899

WAV 412 SPEAKER CABINET – 4-12 in. Celestion speakers, black covering, blue grille, mfg. 2004-05.

	N/A	$300 - 375	$175 - 225	$699

ELECTRIC HYBRID AMPS: HV SERIES

- Add $23 (MSR $35) for a cover.
- Add $30 (MSR $45) for a one-button Tap/Tempo footswitch.
- Add $50 (MSR $75) for a three-button footswitch.

HV30
courtesy Kustom

HV100
courtesy Kustom

HV30T
courtesy Kustom

HV30 – 30W, 1-12 in. Celestion speaker guitar combo, hybrid chassis with one 12AX7 preamp tube, two channels (Rhythm, Lead), 16 programmable effects, top black control panel, single input, nine chrome knobs (Lead Ch.: g, v, Rhythm Ch.: g, v, All: b, m, t, effects level, effects select), effects loop, speaker emulated direct out, external speaker jack, aux. input, footswitch, black covering, black grille, 18.1 in. wide, 15.1 in. tall, 9.8 in. deep, 27 lbs., mfg. 2007-disc.

	$300	$175 - 225	$110 - 140	$460

HV65 – 65W, 1-12 in. Celestion speaker guitar combo, hybrid chassis with one 12AX7 preamp tube, two channels (Rhythm, Lead), 16 programmable effects, top black control panel, single input, 13 chrome knobs (Lead Ch.: g, v, b, m, t, Rhythm Ch.: g, v, b, m, t, All: boost v, effects level, effects select), effects loop, speaker emulated direct out, external speaker jack, aux. input, footswitch, black covering, black grille, 20.9 in. wide, 18.1 in. tall, 11.6 in. deep, 37 lbs., mfg. 2007-disc.

	$400	$225 - 275	$135 - 175	$600

HV100 – 100W, 2-12 in. Celestion speakers guitar combo, hybrid chassis with one 12AX7 preamp tube, two channels (Rhythm, Lead), 16 programmable effects, top black control panel, single input, 13 chrome knobs (Lead Ch.: g, v, b, m, t, Rhythm Ch.: g, v, b, m, t, All: boost v, effects level, effects select), effects loop, speaker emulated direct out, external speaker jack, aux. input, footswitch, black covering, black grille, 28 in. wide, 19 in. tall, 12.5 in. deep, 54 lbs., mfg. 2007-disc.

	$600	$350 - 425	$200 - 250	$850

HV20T – 20W, 1-10 in. Celestion speaker, guitar combo, hybrid chassis with a 12AX7 preamp tube, two channels, reverb, eight digital effects, top black control panel, single input, nine knobs (Lead Ch.: g, v, Rhythm Ch.: g, v, All: b, t, r, effects level, effects select), channel select switch, effects on/off switch, rear panel: effects loop, speaker emulated XLR direct line out, footswitch jack, headphone jack, aux. in jack, black covering with a black grille, two-button footswitch included, 17.25 in. wide, 14 in. tall, 8.25 in. deep, 21 lbs., mfg. 2009-disc.

	$300	$175 - 225	$110 - 140	$460

HV30T – 35W, 1-12 in. Celestion speaker, guitar combo, hybrid chassis with a 12AX7 preamp tube, two channels, 16 digital effects, top black control panel, single input, nine knobs (Lead Ch.: g, v, Rhythm Ch.: g, v, All: b, m, t, effects level, effects select), channel select switch, Lead Ch. gain boost switch, Rhythm Ch. bright switch, effects on/off switch, effects tap/tempo switch, rear panel: effects loop, speaker emulated XLR direct line out, footswitch jack, external speaker jack, headphone jack, aux. in jack, black covering with a black grille, two-button footswitch included, 19.75 in. wide, 17 in. tall, 9.5 in. deep, 27 lbs., mfg. 2009-disc.

	$400	$250 - 300	$135 - 175	$630

HV65T – 65W, 1-12 in. Celestion speaker, guitar combo, hybrid chassis with a 12AX7 preamp tube, two channels, 16 semi-programmable digital effects, top black control panel, single input, 13 knobs (Lead Ch.: g, v, b, m, t, Rhythm Ch.: g, v, b, m, t, All: boost v, effects level, effects select), channel select switch, Lead Ch. gain boost switch, Lead Ch. EQ mod switch, Rhythm Ch. bright switch, Rhythm overdrive switch, effects on/off switch, effects tap/tempo switch, rear panel: effects loop, speaker emulated XLR direct line out, two footswitch jacks, external speaker jack, headphone jack, aux. in jack, black covering with a black grille, 22.75 in. wide, 17.875 in. tall, 10.25 in. deep, 34.5 lbs., mfg. 2009-disc.

	$500	$300 - 375	$175 - 225	$750

MSR/NOTES	100%	EXCELLENT	AVERAGE	LAST MSR

HV100T HEAD – 100W, guitar head unit, hybrid chassis with a 12AX7 preamp tube, two channels, 16 semi-programmable digital effects, top black control panel, single input, 13 knobs (Lead Ch.: g, v, b, m, t, Rhythm Ch.: g, v, b, m, t, All: boost v, effects level, effects select), channel select switch, Lead Ch. gain boost switch, Lead Ch. EQ mod switch, Rhythm Ch. bright switch, Rhythm overdrive switch, effects on/off switch, effects tap/tempo switch, rear panel: effects loop, speaker emulated XLR direct line out, two footswitch jacks, external speaker jack, headphone jack, aux. in jack, black covering with a black grille, 27 in. wide, 11.5 in. tall, 10 in. deep, 30.5 lbs., mfg. 2009-disc.

	$480	$275 - 325	$150 - 200	$680

* HV100T Combo – similar to the HV100T Head, except in combo configuration with 2-12 in. Celestion speakers, 26 in. wide, 19 in. tall, 10.875 in. deep, 48.5 lbs., mfg. 2009-disc.

	$600	$375 - 450	$225 - 275	$900

ELECTRIC BASS AMPS: DEEP END SERIES

Deep End DE50 Combo
courtesy Kustom

Deep End DE100-210 Combo
courtesy Kustom

Deep End 115 Speaker Cabinet
courtesy Kustom

DEEP END 200HD HEAD – 200W, two-space rack-mount bass head unit, solid-state chassis, front silver control panel with black inserts, single input, nine chrome knobs (g, v, notch freq,. six-band EQ), XLR direct out, cd/tape input, effects loop, two speaker outputs, line out, black casing, mfg. 2007-08.

	N/A	$175 - 225	$110 - 140	$450

DEEP END 300HD HEAD – 300W, bass head-unit, hybrid chassis with a 12AX7 preamp tube and Organic Clipping power amp circuit, single channel, front black control panel, two inputs, five knobs (tube g, b, m, t, MV), two-band graphic EQ (low contour, high contour), tube display window, power switch, rear panel: effects loop, preamp out, power amp in, speaker-emulated XLR direct line out, black covering with a black grille, 23 in. wide, 11.5 in. tall, 10.5 in. deep, 36 lbs., mfg. 2009-disc.

	$380	$225 - 275	$135 - 175	$550

DEEP END DE50 COMBO – 50W, 1-10 in. Deep End speaker, bass combo, hybrid chassis with a 12AX7 preamp tube and Organic Clipping power amp circuit, single channel, front black control panel, two inputs, five knobs (tube g, b, m, t, MV), two-band graphic EQ (low contour, high contour), tube display window, power switch, rear panel: effects loop, preamp out, power amp in, speaker-emulated XLR direct line out, black covering with a black grille, 16.5 in. wide, 19 in. tall, 11.75 in. deep, 37.5 lbs., mfg. 2009-disc.

	$300	$185 - 235	$120 - 150	$500

DEEP END DE100-115 COMBO – 100W, 1-15 in. Deep End speaker with a piezo horn, bass combo, hybrid chassis with a 12AX7 preamp tube and Organic Clipping power amp circuit, single channel, front black control panel, two inputs, five knobs (tube g, b, m, t, MV), two-band graphic EQ (low contour, high contour), tube display window, power switch, rear panel: piezo horn on/off switch, effects loop, speaker-emulated XLR direct line out, tuner out jack, black covering with a black grille, 23 in. wide, 24.5 in. tall, 14 in. deep, 65.5 lbs., mfg. 2009-disc.

	$480	$300 - 350	$175 - 225	$740

DEEP END DE100-210 COMBO – 100W, 2-10 in. Deep End speakers with a piezo horn, bass combo, hybrid chassis with a 12AX7 preamp tube and Organic Clipping power amp circuit, single channel, front black control panel, two inputs, five knobs (tube g, b, m, t, MV), two-band graphic EQ (low contour, high contour), tube display window, power switch, rear panel: piezo horn on/off switch, effects loop, speaker-emulated XLR direct line out, tuner out jack, black covering with a black grille, 23 in. wide, 24.5 in. tall, 14 in. deep, 62 lbs., mfg. 2009-disc.

	$500	$300 - 375	$175 - 225	$800

DEEP END DE200-115 COMBO – 200W, 1-15 in. Eminence speaker with a compression horn, bass combo, hybrid chassis with a 12AX7 preamp tube and Organic Clipping power amp circuit, single channel, front black control panel, two inputs, five knobs (tube g, b, m, t, MV), two-band graphic EQ (low contour, high contour), tube display window, power switch, rear panel: compression horn on/off switch, effects loop, preamp out, power amp in, speaker-emulated XLR direct line out, tuner out jack, black covering with a black grille, 23 in. wide, 24.5 in. tall, 14 in. deep, 71 lbs., mfg. 2009-disc.

	$580	$350 - 425	$200 - 250	$850

MSR/NOTES	100%	EXCELLENT	AVERAGE	LAST MSR

DEEP END DE200-210 COMBO – 200W, 2-10 in. Eminence speakers with a compression horn, bass combo, hybrid chassis with a 12AX7 preamp tube and Organic Clipping power amp circuit, single channel, front black control panel, two inputs, five knobs (tube g, b, m, t, MV), two-band graphic EQ (low contour, high contour), tube display window, power switch, rear panel: compression horn on/off switch, effects loop, preamp out, power amp in, speaker-emulated XLR direct line out, tuner out jack, black covering with a black grille, 23 in. wide, 24.5 in. tall, 14 in. deep, 68 lbs., mfg. 2009-disc.

	$600	$375 - 450	$225 - 275	$900

DEEP END 115 SPEAKER CABINET – 250W, 1-15 in. Kustom speaker, 3 in. high freq. driver, 8 ohm impedance, side-mounted handles, black covering, black grille, 23.5 in. wide, 23.75 in. tall, 17.125 in. deep, 61.5 lbs., mfg. 2007-08.

	N/A	$120 - 150	$70 - 95	$300

DEEP END 115H SPEAKER CABINET – 250W, 1-15 in. Deep End speaker with a high freq. piezo horn, 8 ohm impedance, recessed side handles, removable casters, black covering, black grille, 23 in. wide, 23 in. tall, 17 in. deep, 55 lbs., mfg. 2009-disc.

	$260	$160 - 200	$100 - 130	$390

DEEP END 210H SPEAKER CABINET – 200W, 2-10 in. Deep End speakers with a high freq. piezo horn, 8 ohm impedance, recessed side handles, removable casters, black covering, black grille, 23 in. wide, 15.75 in. tall, 16.5 in. deep, 46.5 lbs., mfg. 2009-disc.

MSR $390	$260	$160 - 200	$100 - 130	

DEEP END 410 SPEAKER CABINET – 400W, 4-10 in. Kustom speakers, 3 in. high freq. driver, 8 ohm impedance, side-mounted handles, black covering, black grille, 23.5 in. wide, 23.75 in. tall, 17.125 in. deep, 59.4 lbs., mfg. 2007-08.

	N/A	$150 - 200	$95 - 120	$420

DEEP END 410H SPEAKER CABINET – 400W, 4-10 in. Deep End speakers with a high freq. piezo horn, 8 ohm impedance, recessed side handles, removable casters, black covering, black grille, 23 in. wide, 23 in. tall, 17 in. deep, 65 lbs., mfg. 2009-disc.

	$300	$175 - 225	$110 - 140	$500

DEEP END 810H SPEAKER CABINET – 800W, 8-10 in. Deep End speakers with a high freq. piezo horn, 4 ohm impedance, recessed side handles, built-in casters, tilt-bar and spring loaded bottom, black covering, black grille, 23 in. wide, 45.5 in. tall, 15.75 in. deep, 127 lbs., mfg. 2009-disc.

	$700	$400 - 475	$250 - 300	$1,000

ELECTRIC BASS AMPS: GROOVE SERIES

Groove 600H Head courtesy Kustom
Groove 1300H Head courtesy Kustom

Groove G-215H Speaker Cabinet courtesy Kustom

Groove G-810H John Moyer Speaker Cabinet courtesy Kustom

GROOVE 600H HEAD – 600W @ 2 ohms, two-space rack-mount bass head, solid-state chassis, front black control panel with silver borders, single input, five chrome knobs (g, b, m, h, MV), nine-band graphic EQ, mute switch, boost switch, tuner output, effects loop, Speakon outputs, two-button footswitch, black casing, 19 in. wide, 3.5 in. tall, 15.5 in. deep, 26 lbs., mfg. 2007-disc.

	$560	$325 - 400	$175 - 225	$830

* Add $80 (MSR $110) for headcase.

GROOVE 1200H HEAD – 1200W @ 2 ohms (750W @ 4 ohms, 450W @ 8 ohms), two-space rack-mount bass head, solid-state chassis, front silver control panel, single input, five chrome knobs (g, b, m, h, MV), nine-band graphic EQ, mute switch, boost switch, tuner output, effects loop, Speakon outputs, two-button footswitch, black casing, disc. 2007.

	N/A	$400 - 475	$250 - 300	$900

* Add $70 (Last MSR was $100) for headcase.

GROOVE 1300H HEAD – 1200W @ 2 ohms, two-space rack-mount bass head, solid-state chassis, front black control panel with silver borders, single input, five chrome knobs (g, b, m, h, MV), nine-band graphic EQ, mute switch, boost switch, tuner output, effects loop, Speakon outputs, two-button footswitch, black casing, 19 in. wide, 3.5 in. tall, 15.5 in. deep, 31 lbs., mfg. 2007-disc.

	N/A	$450 - 525	$275 - 325	$1,150

* Add $80 (MSR $110) for headcase.

MSR/NOTES	100%	EXCELLENT	AVERAGE	LAST MSR

GROOVE 115C COMBO – 600W, 1-15 in. Eminence speaker with a 1 in. compression horn, bass combo, solid-state chassis, front silver control panel, single input, five chrome knobs (g, b, m, h, MV), nine-band graphic EQ, mute switch, boost switch, tuner output, effects loop, Speakon outputs, two-button footswitch, removable casters, side-mounted handles, black covering, black metal grille, mfg. 2005-07.

	N/A	$550 - 625	$325 - 400	$1,199

GROOVE 210C COMBO – 600W, 2-10 in. Eminence speakers with a 1 in. compression horn, bass combo, solid-state chassis, front silver control panel, single input, five chrome knobs (g, b, m, h, MV), nine-band graphic EQ, mute switch, boost switch, tuner output, effects loop, Speakon outputs, two-button footswitch, removable casters, side-mounted handles, black covering, black metal grille, mfg. 2005-07.

	N/A	$550 - 625	$325 - 400	$1,199

GROOVE 310C COMBO – 1200W, 3-10 in. Eminence speakers with a 1 in. compression horn, bass combo, solid-state chassis, front silver control panel, single input, five chrome knobs (g, b, m, h, MV), nine-band graphic EQ, mute switch, boost switch, tuner output, effects loop, Speakon outputs, two-button footswitch, tilt back cabinet with wheels, side-mounted handles, black covering, black metal grille, mfg. 2005-07.

	N/A	$650 - 800	$425 - 500	$1,499

GROOVE G-115H SPEAKER CABINET – 450W, 1-15 in. Eminence speaker, 1 in. Eminence compression horn with level adjust, 8 ohm impedance, plywood construction, black covering, black grille, spring-loaded handles, removable casters, 24.25 in. wide, 24.625 in. tall, 20.125 in. deep, 70 lbs., mfg. 2009-disc.

	$600	$350 - 425	$200 - 250	$850

GROOVE G-215H SPEAKER CABINET – 700W, 2-15 in. Eminence speakers, horn with level adjust, 8 ohm impedance, plywood construction, black covering, black grille, spring-loaded handles, removable casters, 24.3 in. wide, 46.7 in. tall, 20 in. deep, 115 lbs., disc.

	$850	$500 - 600	$300 - 350	$1,230

GROOVE G-410H SPEAKER CABINET – 1000W, 4-10 in. Eminence speakers, horn with level adjust, 8 ohm impedance, plywood construction, black covering, black grille, spring-loaded handles, removable casters, 24.3 in. wide, 32.3 in. tall, 20.1 in. deep, 102 lbs., disc.

	$700	$400 - 475	$250 - 300	$1,000

GROOVE G-810H SPEAKER CABINET – 2000W, 8-10 in. Eminence speakers, horn with level adjust, 4 ohm impedance, plywood construction, black covering, black grille, spring-loaded handles, wheels and tilt-bar handle, 23.5 in. wide, 47 in. tall, 20 in. deep, 150 lbs., mfg. 2006-disc.

	$1,000	$625 - 750	$375 - 450	$1,550

GROOVE G-810H JOHN MOYER SPEAKER CABINET – 2000W, 8-10 in. Eminence speakers, horn with level adjust, 4 ohm impedance, plywood construction, black covering, black grille with custom silver skull and flame graphics, spring-loaded handles, wheels and tilt-bar handle, 23.5 in. wide, 47 in. tall, 20 in. deep, 150 lbs., mfg. 2008-disc.

	$1,200	$750 - 900	$450 - 525	$1,900

ELECTRIC BASS AMPS: KBA SERIES

KBA 16X
courtesy Kustom

KBA 30X
courtesy Kustom

KBA 200 115
courtesy Kustom

KBA 10X – 10W, 1-8 in. speaker bass combo, solid-state chassis, top silver control panel, single input, four chrome knobs (v, l, m, h), headphone jack, black covering, black metal grille, 13.2 in. wide, 11.3 in. tall, 8 in. deep, 15 lbs., disc.

	$80	$45 - 60	$25 - 35	$120

KBA 16X – 16W, 1-8 in. Celestion speaker bass combo, solid-state chassis, top silver control panel, single input, five chrome knobs (v, l/m, m/h, h), CD/Tape input jack, headphone jack, external speaker jack, black covering, black metal grille, 15.8 in. wide, 13 in. tall, 10 in. deep, 22 lbs., disc.

	$120	$70 - 95	$40 - 55	$180

* KBA 16X John Moyer Signature – similar to the KBA 16X, except has a custom John Moyer silver skull and flame graphic on the grille, mfg. 2008-disc.

	$140	$80 - 110	$50 - 65	$220

MSR/NOTES	100%	EXCELLENT	AVERAGE	LAST MSR

KBA 30X – 30W, 1-10 in. Celestion speaker bass combo, solid-state chassis, top silver control panel, single input, six chrome knobs (v, notch, l/m, m/h, h), CD/Tape input jack, headphone jack, external speaker jack, line out jack, black covering, black metal grille, 18.5 in. wide, 15.3 in. tall, 13 in. deep, 34 lbs., disc.

	$180	$110 - 140	$65 - 85	$270

KBA 35X DFX – 30W, 1-10 in. Celestion speaker bass combo, solid-state chassis, 8 24-bit digital effects, top silver control panel, single input, eight chrome knobs (v, notch, l/m, m/h, h, digital effects level, digital effects program), CD/Tape input jack, headphone jack, external speaker jack, line out jack, black covering, black metal grille, 18.5 in. wide, 15.3 in. tall, 13 in. deep, 34 lbs., disc.

	$260	$160 - 200	$100 - 130	$390

KBA 65X – 65W, 1-12 in. Celestion speaker bass combo, solid-state chassis, 8 24-bit digital effects, top silver control panel, single input, 11 chrome knobs (g, v, notch, six EQ knobs, digital effects level, digital effects program), CD/Tape input jack, XLR line out, headphone jack, external speaker jack, line out jack, black covering, black metal grille, 21 in. wide, 17.5 in. tall, 14.6 in. deep, 56 lbs., disc.

	$350	$220 - 270	$135 - 175	$530

KBA 100X – 100W, 1-15 in. Celestion speaker bass combo, solid-state chassis, 8 24-bit digital effects, top silver control panel, single input, 11 chrome knobs (g, v, notch, six EQ knobs, digital effects level, digital effects program), CD/Tape input jack, XLR line out, headphone jack, external speaker jack, line out jack, side-mounted handles, black covering, black metal grille, 24 in. wide, 17.5 in. tall, 14.6 in. deep, 68 lbs., disc.

	$440	$275 - 325	$150 - 200	$660

KBA 200 115 – 200W, 1-15 in. Eminence speaker bass combo, compression driver horn, solid-state chassis, top black control panel, single input, nine chrome knobs (g, v, notch, six EQ knobs), CD/Tape input jack, XLR line out, headphone jack, external speaker jack, line out jack, side-mounted handles, black covering, black metal grille, 20.75 in. wide, 28.25 in. tall, 24.25 in. deep, 63.6 lbs., mfg. 2007-disc.

	$450	$275 - 325	$150 - 200	$670

KBA 200 210 – 200W, 2-10 in. Eminence speakers bass combo, compression driver horn, solid-state chassis, top black control panel, single input, nine chrome knobs (g, v, notch, six EQ knobs), CD/Tape input jack, XLR line out, headphone jack, external speaker jack, line out jack, side-mounted handles, black covering, black metal grille, 20.75 in. wide, 28.25 in. tall, 24.25 in. deep, 73.1 lbs., mfg. 2007-disc.

	$500	$300 - 375	$175 - 225	$750

ELECTRIC BASS AMPS: KXB SERIES

In 2011, Kustom introduced the KXB Series of bass amplifiers. This line includes the **KXB1, KXB10, KXB100, KXB20,** and **KXB200** combo amps, as well as the **KXB500** and **KXB800** head units.

ACOUSTIC AMPLIFIERS

Models produced before 2003 feature black covering and a black grille. In 2003, brown covering and a brown grille was introduced, TH was added to the model names, and the KAA35THDFX model was added. In 2005, all models were changed to Sienna with their respective wattage. In 2014, the Sienna Pro Series of acoustic combos was added, including the **Sienna 16 Pro, Sienna 30 Pro, Sienna 35 Pro,** and **Sienna 65 Pro.**

KAA 16TH/Sienna 16
courtesy Kustom

KAA 30TH/Sienna 30
courtesy Kustom

KAA 65TH/Sienna 65
courtesy Kustom

KAA 16TH/SIENNA 16 – 16W, 1-8 in. Celestion speaker combo, solid-state chassis, reverb, chorus, top control panel, eight knobs (mic v, guitar v, l l/m, h/m, h, r), feedback filter, external speaker, headphone jack, black (early models) or brown covering, black (early models) or brown grille, disc. 2013.

	$130	$70 - 95	$45 - 60	$190

KAA 30TH/SIENNA 30 – 30W, 1-10 in. Celestion speaker combo, solid-state chassis, reverb, chorus, top control panel, eight knobs (mic v, guitar v, feedback freq., l, m, h, r, chorus), feedback filter, external speaker, headphone jack, black (early models) or brown covering, black (early models) or brown grille, disc. 2013.

	$160	$95 - 120	$60 - 80	$240

MSR/NOTES	100%	EXCELLENT	AVERAGE	LAST MSR

KAA 35TH DFX/SIENNA 35 – 30W, 1-10 in. Celestion speaker combo, solid-state chassis, eight 24-bit digital effects, top control panel, eight knobs, feedback filter, external speaker, headphone jack, brown covering, brown grille, mfg. 2003-2013.

	$220	$125 - 160	$80 - 100	$320

KAA 65TH/SIENNA 65 – 65W, 1-12 in. Celestion speaker combo, solid-state chassis, eight 24-bit digital effects, top control panel, eleven knobs (Mic: g, b, m, t, Inst: g, b, t, feedback, MV, FX level, FX program), feedback filter, external speaker, headphone jack, black (early models) or brown covering, black (early models) or brown grille, disc.

	$320	$175 - 225	$110 - 140	$470

SPEAKER CABINETS

Coupe 412A
courtesy Kustom

Pro 412A
courtesy Kustom

Quad ST 412A
courtesy Kustom

COUPE 112 – 75W, 1-12 in. KEI Turbo 12 speakers, 16 ohm impedance, Baltic birch construction, black covering, black grille, side-mounted handles, 26 in. wide, 22.5 in. tall, 14.5 in. deep, 37 lbs., mfg. 2008-disc.

	$450	$275 - 325	$150 - 200	$580

COUPE 212 – 75W, 1-12 in. KEI Turbo 12 speakers, 16 ohm impedance, Baltic birch construction, black covering, black grille, side-mounted handles, 26 in. wide, 22.5 in. tall, 14.5 in. deep, 37 lbs., mfg. 2008-disc.

	$580	$325 - 400	$200 - 250	$750

COUPE 412A/412B – 240W, 4-12 in. Celestion Vintage 30 speakers, 16 ohm impedance, Baltic birch construction, straight (412B) or angled (412A) cabinet, black covering, black grille, side-mounted handles, 30 in. wide, 30 in. tall, 14 in. deep, 96 lbs., disc.

	$1,100	$625 - 750	$375 - 450	$1,400

PRO 412A/412B – 260W, 4-12 in. Celestion G12P80 speakers, 8 ohm impedance, plywood construction angled (412A) or straight (412B) front, black covering, black grille with white piping, side-mounted handles, removable casters, 30 in. wide, 30 in. tall, 14 in. deep, 70.5 lbs., mfg. 2007-disc.

	$490	$300 - 350	$175 - 225	$730

QUAD ST 412A/412B – 260W, 4-12 in. Kustom speakers, 8 ohm impedance, plywood construction angled (412A) or straight (412B) front, black covering, brown grille with white piping, side-mounted handles, removable casters, 30 in. wide, 30 in. tall, 14 in. deep, 70.5 lbs., disc.

	$350	$200 - 250	$120 - 150	$530

* **Add $30 (MSR $43) for a cover.**

L SECTION
LAB SERIES

Amplifiers and speaker cabinets previously produced in Chicago, IL between 1977 and the early 1980s. Distributed by Gibson.

After Gibson discontinued production of all amplifiers in 1975, Norlin (Gibson's parent company at the time) looked for a new amp to complement their product lineup. They went to Moog, which was a division of Norlin to design a series of amps and in 1978 or 1979, the first Lab Series was born. These amps are all solid-state in design and had no reference to Gibson on them. The first series was met with lukewarm acceptance and the amps were discontinued by the end of 1979 to make way for the Lab Series 2. The second Lab Series was produced in the early 1980s and they feature a Gibson logo in the upper left corner of the grille. The Genesis Series was released at the same time as the Lab Series 2 and Genesis amps were meant to be the practice/entry-level models where the Lab Series were higher end. Information courtesy George Gruhn and Walter Carter, *Gruhn's Guide to Vintage Guitars*.

MSR/NOTES	100%	EXCELLENT	AVERAGE	LAST MSR

AMPLIFIERS: LAB SERIES

The L5, L7, and L9 all share the exact same chassis, and the L11 is very similar except it has 200W output instead of 100W.

L2 – 100W, 1-15 in. speaker cabinet, piggyback bass configuration, solid-state chassis, single channel, front black control panel, two inputs, seven knobs (v, b, freq., m, t, compressor, MV), deep switch, black covering, black grille, mfg. late 1970s.

Head & Cabinet	N/A	$300 - 350	$175 - 225	
Head Only	N/A	$175 - 225	$110 - 140	

L3 – 60W, 1-12 in. speaker, guitar combo configuration, solid-state chassis, single channel, front black control panel, two inputs, eight knobs (v, b, freq., m, t, r, compressor, MV), bright switch, black covering, black grille, mfg. late 1970s.

	N/A	$275 - 325	$150 - 200	

L4 – 200W, 2-15 in. speaker cabinet, piggyback bass configuration, solid-state chassis, two channels, front black control panel, two inputs, 11 knobs (Ch.1: v, b, m, t, Ch. 2: v, b, freq., m, t, compressor, MV), deep switch, black covering, black grille, mfg. late 1970s.

Head & Cabinet	N/A	$325 - 400	$200 - 250	
Head Only	N/A	$200 - 250	$120 - 150	

L5 – 100W, 2-12 in. speakers, guitar combo configuration, solid-state chassis, single channel, front black control panel, two inputs, 13 knobs (Ch. 1: v, b, m, t, Ch. 2: v, b, freq., m, t, multifilter, r, compressor, MV), bright switch, black covering, black grille, mfg. late 1970s.

	N/A	$350 - 425	$225 - 275	

L7 – 100W, 4-10 in. speakers, guitar combo configuration, solid-state chassis, single channel, front black control panel, two inputs, 13 knobs (Ch. 1: v, b, m, t, Ch. 2: v, b, freq., m, t, multifilter, r, compressor, MV), bright switch, black covering, black grille, mfg. late 1970s.

	N/A	$375 - 450	$250 - 300	

L9 – 100W, 1-15 in. speaker, guitar combo configuration, solid-state chassis, single channel, front black control panel, two inputs, 13 knobs (Ch. 1: v, b, m, t, Ch. 2: v, b, freq., m, t, multifilter, r, compressor, MV), bright switch, black covering, black grille, mfg. late 1970s.

	N/A	$325 - 400	$200 - 250	

L11 – 200W, 8-12 in. speakers, guitar piggyback configuration with 2 4-12 in. speaker cabinets, solid-state chassis, single channel, front black control panel, two inputs, 13 knobs (Ch. 1: v, b, m, t, Ch. 2: v, b, freq., m, t, multifilter, r, compressor, MV), bright switch, black covering, black grille, mfg. late 1970s.

Head & Two Cabs	N/A	$450 - 550	$300 - 350	
Head Only	N/A	$200 - 250	$120 - 150	

AMPLIFIERS: LAB SERIES 2

B79 – 70W, 1-15 in. speaker, bass combo configuration, solid-state chassis, mfg. early 1980s.

	N/A	$250 - 300	$150 - 200	

B120 – 120W, 1-15 in. speaker, bass combo or piggyback configuration, solid-state chassis, two channels, mfg. early 1980s.

	N/A	$300 - 350	$175 - 225	

GA60R-10 – 60W, 1-10 in. speaker, guitar combo configuration, solid-state chassis, mfg. early 1980s.

	N/A	$225 - 275	$140 - 175	

* ***GA60R Piggyback*** – similar to the GA60R-10, except in piggyback configuration with a 2-12 in. or 4-10 in. speaker cabinet, mfg. early 1980s.

	N/A	$300 - 350	$175 - 225	

* ***GA60R-12*** – similar to the GA60R-10, except has 1-12 in. speaker, mfg. early 1980s.

	N/A	$250 - 300	$150 - 200	

MSR/NOTES	100%	EXCELLENT	AVERAGE	LAST MSR

GA120R-10 – 120W, 4-10 in. speakers, guitar combo configuration, solid-state chassis, two channels, mfg. early 1980s.

	N/A	$325 - 400	$200 - 250	

* *GA120R-12* – similar to the GA120R-10, except has 2-12 in. speakers, mfg. early 1980s.

	N/A	$350 - 425	$225 - 275	

LACE MUSIC PRODUCTS

Amplifiers previously built overseas during the late 1990s. Previously distributed by AGI (Actodyne General Inc.) of Huntington Beach, CA. Lace still produces acoustic guitars, electric guitars, and pickups.

Lace Music Products was started in the family garage by Don Lace, Sr. in 1979. They first produced pickups and other electronics. In the mid-1990s, they introduced a line of amplifiers and in 1997, Lace ventured down the instrument building path with the ergonomically correct Lace Helix Twisted Neck. The Twisted Neck has a 20 degree twist that follows the natural twist of the player's hand as it travels up and down the fingerboard. Fender really put them on the map when many of their guitars featured Lace pickups. Currently, Lace focuses on acoustic guitars, electric guitars, and guitar picukps. For more information visit Lace's website, or contact the company directly.

CONTACT INFORMATION
LACE MUSIC PRODUCTS
5561 Engineer Drive
Huntington Beach, CA 92649
Phone No.: 714-898-2776
Fax No.: 714-893-1045
www.lacemusic.com
info@lacemusic.com

LAFAYETTE

Amplifiers previously produced in Japan during the 1960s and 1970s. Distributed by LaFayette Radio Electronics in Syosset, NY.

Lafayette amplifiers and guitars were imported to the U.S. and sold through LaFayette Radio Electronics catalogs. The LaFayette product line consisted of amplifiers, thinline acoustic/electric archtops, and solid body electric guitars and basses. Many models were built by Japan's Guyatone company, although some may also be Teisco models. Initially, only smaller practice/entry-level models were available, but by the late 1960s, a full line of small and large amps in a variety of configurations was available. Some models may look very similar to other Japanese brands (Kent for example) as they were built by the same company. Most amps are valued between $150 and $200. Source: Michael Wright, *Vintage Guitar Magazine*.

LANEY

Amplifiers currently produced in England since 1967. Lower end solid-state models may be produced in China. Laney's headquarters are currently located in Cradley Heath, West Midlands, England. Distributed in the U.S. by Musical Distributors Group, LLC in Boonton, NJ. Previously distributed by HSS (Hohner) in Glen Allen, VA and Chesbro Music.

Laney was founded in 1967 by amp enthusiast Lyndon Laney and salesman Bob Thomas in Birmingham, England. The first Laney amplifiers are modeled very close to the Marshall Plexi models of the late 1960s. Laney continued through the 1970s with their small lineup of amps, but they became very popular among heavy metal, especially with Tony Iommi of Black Sabbath. In the 1980s, Laney introduced the Advanced Overdrive Response (AOR) line of amps. In 1989, Laney bought the HH Amplification company to produce speakers and MOSFET power amps. In 1993, Laney teamed up with Ibanez to be the exclusive distributor in the U.S., and an entire new line of amps was introduced with the American in mind. Since then, Laney has produced the GH, VC, TT, and LC tube amplifiers along with a vast range of solid-state electric, acoustic, and bass amplifiers. Distribution in the U.S. has shifted hands several times with the Musical Distributors Group being the most recent. Prior to Musical Distributors Group, HSS and Chesbro Music were exclusive distributors. For more information, visit Laney's website or contact the distributor directly.

CONTACT INFORMATION
LANEY
Factory/Headquarters
Newlyn Road
Cradley Heath, West Midlands B64 6BE
England
www.laney.co.uk

U.S. Distributor: Musical Distributors Group
9 Mars Court, Suite C-3
Boonton, NJ 07005
Phone No.: 973-335-7888
Phone No.: 866-632-8346
Fax No.: 973-335-7779
www.musicaldistributors.com
sales@musicaldistributors.com

ELECTRIC TUBE AMPLIFIERS: EARLY MODELS

The early Plexi-style Laney amps typically have Supergroup on the control panel, but there is no reference to this in their catalogs. The LA model ID is typically not labeled on the amp. The wattage should be listed on the back and most amps came in 50W, 60W, 100W, or 200W configurations. In the 1980s, the Klipp and AOR amps were released. Look for more information in upcoming editions.

MODEL LA.60BL – 60W, head-unit lead/bass/organ configuration, tube chassis, preamp: 3 X ECC83, power: 2 X EL34, two channels, front control panel, four inputs, six knobs (p, b, m, t, g1, g2), black covering, 26.75 in. wide, 9.5 in. tall, 8.75 in. deep, mfg. circa 1967-1970s.

	N/A	$1,400 - 1,750	$900 - 1,100	

MSR/NOTES	100%	EXCELLENT	AVERAGE	LAST MSR

MODEL LA.100BL – 100W, head-unit lead/bass/organ configuration, tube chassis, preamp: 3 X ECC83, power: 4 X EL34, two channels, front control panel, four inputs, six knobs (p, b, m, t, g1, g2), black covering, 30 in. wide, 10 in. tall, 8.75 in. deep, mfg. circa 1967-1970s.

courtesy solidbodyguitar.com, Inc.   courtesy solidbodyguitar.com, Inc.

	100%	EXCELLENT	AVERAGE	
	N/A	$1,600 - 2,000	$1,100 - 1,350	

MODEL LA.200BL – 200W, head-unit lead/bass/organ configuration, tube chassis, preamp: 3 X ECC83, power: 4 X EL34, two channels, front control panel, four inputs, six knobs (p, b, m, t, g1, g2), black covering, 30 in. wide, 10.5 in. tall, 10 in. deep, mfg. circa 1967-1970s.

	N/A	$1,800 - 2,200	$1,200 - 1,500	

AOR100 SERIES II – 100W, head-unit only, all tube chassis, preamp: 4 X 12AX7, power: 4 X EL34, dual channels, front black control panel, two inputs, eight black knobs (p, b, m, t, v, clean channel preamp, OD v, OD channel preamp), effects loop, footswitch, black rough covering, mfg. 1980s.

	N/A	$600 - 700	$375 - 450	

ELECTRIC TUBE AMPLIFIERS: CURRENT PRODUCTION MODELS

CH100L
courtesy Laney

Cub 8
courtesy Laney

Cub 10
courtesy Laney

CH100TI Tony Iommi
courtesy Laney

CHROME-O-ZONE – 30W, 2-10 in. HH Special Edition, all tube chassis, 4 X EL84 outputs, dual channels, reverb, front chrome control panel, two inputs, 17 silver knobs, effects loop, footswitch, gray covering, black grille cloth, disc.

	N/A	N/A	N/A	

CUB 8 – 5W, 1-8 in. Celestion speaker, guitar combo, two-tube chassis, preamp: 1 X ECC83, power: 1 X 6V6GT, single channel, top brown control panel, two inputs (lo/hi), two cream chickenhead knobs (v, tone), power switch, black leatherette vinyl covering, brown/black woven grille cloth, mfg. 2010-disc.

	$220	$125 - 160	$75 - 100	$290

CUB 10 – 10W, 1-10 in. Celestion speaker, guitar combo, four-tube chassis, preamp: 2 X ECC83, power: 2 X 6V6GT, single channel, top brown control panel, two inputs (lo/hi), three cream chickenhead knobs (v, g, tone), power switch, black leatherette vinyl covering, brown/black woven grille cloth, mfg. 2010-present.

MSR $500	$250	$165 - 190	$80 - 100	

GH50L – 50W, head-unit only, all tube chassis, preamp: 12AX7s, power: 2 X 5881, dual channels, front silver control panel, two inputs, seven black chicken head knobs (p, b, m, t, MV, g, drive), various switches, effects loop, black covering, gray grille, mfg. mid-1990s-present.

MSR $1,700	$1,050	$625 - 775	$375 - 450	

GH100L – 100W, head-unit only, all tube chassis, preamp: 12AX7's, power: 4 X 5881, dual channels, front silver control panel, two inputs, seven black chicken head knobs (p, b, m, t, MV, g, drive), various switches, effects loop, black covering, gray grille, mfg. mid-1990s-present.

MSR $2,000	$1,200	$775 - 900	$400 - 475	

GH100TI TONY IOMMI – 100W, head-unit only, all tube chassis, 4 X EL34 output tubes, permanent gain channel, front silver control panel, two inputs, six black knobs (p, b, t, m, MV, g), effects loop, black covering, black metal grille, disc.

	$1,370	$825 - 975	$475 - 550	$1,850

This amp was designed specially for Tony Iommi and is in permanent gain. There are also special speaker cabinets for this that will be listed in the speaker cabinet section.

MSR/NOTES	100%	EXCELLENT	AVERAGE	LAST MSR

LC15
courtesy Laney

LC50-II Combo
courtesy Laney

TT100-212 Combo
courtesy Laney

LC15 – 15W, 1-10 in. HH Invader or Custom Celestion speaker, all tube chassis, preamp: 3 X ECC83, power: 2 X EL84, single channel, front silver control panel, two inputs, five black knobs (g, b, m, t, v), bright switch, black covering, gray grille, disc.

	$620	$375 - 450	$200 - 250	$830

* *LC15R Reverb* – similar to the LC15 except has reverb circuit, effects loop, and a footswitch, disc. 2007.

	N/A	$300 - 350	$175 - 225	$680

LC30-II – 30W, 1-12 in. HH Invader or Custom Celestion speaker, all tube Class AB chassis, preamp: 4 X ECC83, power: 4 X EL34, two channels, reverb, front silver control panel, two inputs, eleven black knobs (v, b, m, t, drive, MV, b, m, t, r, effects), bright switch, channel switch, effects loop, footswitch, black covering, gray grille, disc.

	$1,030	$625 - 725	$350 - 425	$1,400

LH50 – 50W, guitar head unit, six-tube Class AB chassis, preamp: 4 X ECC83, power: 2 X EL34, two channels, reverb, front silver control panel, two inputs, eleven black knobs (v, b, m, t, drive, MV, b, m, t, r, effects), bright switch, channel switch, effects loop, footswitch, black covering, gray grille, mfg. 2009-disc.

	$950	$625 - 725	$350 - 425	$1,400

* *LC50-II Combo* – similar to the LH50, except in combo configuration with 1-12 in. HH Invader or Custom Celestion speaker, disc.

	$1,180	$725 - 850	$400 - 475	$1,600

TT50H HEAD – 50W, head-unit only, tube chassis, preamp: ECC83s, power: 2 X EL34, three channels, reverb, front black control panel, single input, 22 knobs (Ch. 1: v, b, m, t, r, Ch. 2: v, drive, b, m, t, r, Ch. 3: v, drive, b, m, t, r, All: MV1, MV2, r, FX mix, p), various buttons, effects loop, line out, record out, speaker outs, black covering, mfg. 2002-disc.

	$1,480	$875 - 1,025	$500 - 575	$1,950

* *TT50-112 Combo* – similar to the TT50 Head, except in combo form with 1-12 in. Celestion speaker, mfg. 2002-disc.

	$1,750	$1,100 - 1,300	$625 - 725	$2,450

TT100H HEAD – 100W, head-unit only, tube chassis, preamp: ECC83s, power: 4 X EL34, three channels, reverb, front black control panel, single input, 22 knobs (Ch. 1: v, b, m, t, r, Ch. 2: v, drive, b, m, t, r, Ch. 3: v, drive, b, m, t, r, All: MV1, MV2, r, FX mix, p), various buttons, effects loop, line out, record out, speaker outs, black covering, mfg. 2002-disc.

	$1,680	$1,000 - 1,150	$550 - 650	$2,200

* *TT100-212 Combo* – similar to the TT100 Head, except in combo form with 2-12 in. Neodymium Vintage 30 speakers, mfg. 2002-disc.

	$2,050	$1,300 - 1,525	$725 - 875	$2,900

VC15-110 – 15W, 1-10 in. speaker, all tube Class AB chassis, preamp: 3 X ECC83, power: 2 X EL84, two channels, reverb, top silver control panel, two inputs, eight black knobs (clean v, drive, drive v, b, m, t, r, effects level), bright switch, channel switch, effects loop, footswitch, black covering, gray grille, mfg. 2006-disc.

	$680	$425 - 500	$225 - 275	$930

VC30-112 – 30W, 1-12 in. HH Invader or Celestion speaker, all tube Class A chassis, preamp: 3 X ECC83, power: 4 X EL84, two channels, reverb, top silver control panel, two inputs, eight black knobs (clean v, drive, drive v, b, m, t, r, effects level), bright switch, channel switch, effects loop, footswitch, black covering, gray grille, mfg. mid-1990s-disc.

	$970	$575 - 675	$325 - 400	$1,290

* *VC30-210* – similar to the VC30-12 except has 2-10 in. speakers, mfg. mid-1990s-disc.

	$1,100	$650 - 775	$350 - 425	$1,450

* *VC30-212* – similar to the VC30-12 except has 2-12 in. Custom Celestion speakers, mfg. mid-1990s-disc.

	$1,170	$700 - 825	$400 - 475	$1,550

MSR/NOTES	100%	EXCELLENT	AVERAGE	LAST MSR

VC50 – similar to the VC100 except has 50W output, mfg. mid-1990s-early 2000s.

	N/A	$600 - 700	$375 - 450	$1,400

VC100 – similar to the VH100R except is in combo form with 2-12 in. HH Premier Vintage 60W speakers, control panel reversed, disc.

	N/A	$725 - 850	$450 - 525	

VH100R – 100W, head-unit only, tube chassis, power: 4 X 5881, or EL34, dual channels, reverb, front silver control panel, two inputs, 17 black chicken head knobs, effects loop, footswitch, black covering, gray grille, mfg. mid-1990s-disc.

$1,680	$1,025 - 1,200	$575 - 675	$2,300

ELECTRIC TUBE AMPLIFIERS: IRONHEART SERIES

The Ironheart Series by Laney was launched in 2012. The Ironheart amps are extremely versatile and come in a variety of configurations for guitar players. The smallest amp is the 15W head and it climbs all the way up to a 120W head unit. Combo amps and speaker cabinets are also available in various sizes. USB connectivity is available on some models. For more information please visit Laney's website.

ELECTRIC TUBE AMPLIFIERS: LIONHEART SERIES

Lionheart L5T-112 Combo
courtesy Laney

Lionheart L20H Head
courtesy Laney

Lionheart L20T-410 Combo
courtesy Laney

LIONHEART L5 STUDIO HEAD – 5W, head unit only, four tube chassis, preamp: 3 X 12AX7, power: 1 X EL84, two channels (clean/drive), reverb, front chrome control panel, two inputs (lo/hi), eight white chickenhead knobs (clean v, drive, drive v, b, m, t, r, tone), bright switch, drive switch, standby switch, back panel: power switch, mains, three speaker outputs, effects loop, footswitch jack, USB connectivity, blue covering, light brown grille cloth, current mfg.

MSR $1,400	$700	$450 - 525	$230 - 280	

LIONHEART L5T-112 COMBO – 5W, 1-12 in. Celestion Heritage G12H speaker combo, four-tube chassis, preamp: 3 X 12AX7, power: 1 X EL84, two channels (clean/drive), reverb, top white control panel, two inputs (lo/hi), eight white chickenhead knobs (clean v, drive, drive v, b, m, t, r, tone), bright switch, drive switch, standby switch, back panel: power switch, mains, three speaker outputs, effects loop, footswitch jack, blue covering, light brown grille cloth, folding cabinet stand to tilt the cabinet back, mfg. 2007-present.

MSR $1,800	$950	$625 - 700	$300 - 375	

LIONHEART L20H HEAD – 20W, guitar head-unit, seven-tube chassis, preamp: 3 X 12AX7, power: 4 X EL84, two channels (clean/drive), reverb, top white control panel, two inputs (lo/hi), eight white chickenhead knobs (clean v, drive, drive v, b, m, t, r, tone), bright switch, drive switch, standby switch, back panel: power switch, mains, three speaker outputs, effects loop, footswitch jack, blue covering, light brown grille cloth, mfg. 2007-present.

MSR $1,700	$850	$550 - 650	$280 - 350	

* *Lionheart L20T-212 Combo* – similar to the Lionheart L20H Head, except in combo configuration with 2-12 in. Jensen P10-R speakers and a folding cabinet stand to tilt the cabinet back, current mfg.

MSR $2,000	$1,100	$725 - 825	$350 - 450	

Also available in 1-12 in. configuration (model L20T-112).

* *Lionheart L20T-410 Combo* – similar to the Lionheart L20H Head, except in combo configuration with 4-10 in. Jensen P10-R speakers and a folding cabinet stand to tilt the cabinet back, mfg. 2007-disc.

	$1,500	$900 - 1,050	$500 - 600	$2,000

LIONHEART L50H HEAD – 50W, guitar head-unit, eight-tube chassis, preamp: 3 X 12AX7, power: 5 X EL34, two channels (clean/drive), reverb, front chrome control panel, two inputs (lo/hi), nine white chickenhead knobs (clean v, drive, drive v, b, m, t, r, tone, dynamics), bright switch, drive switch, standby switch, back panel: power switch, mains, three speaker outputs, effects loop, footswitch jack, blue covering, light brown grille cloth, current mfg.

MSR $4,000	$1,800	$1,175 - 1,350	$575 - 725	

MSR/NOTES	100%	EXCELLENT	AVERAGE	LAST MSR

LIONHEART LT212 SPEAKER CABINET – 100W, 2-12 in. Celestion Heritage G12H speakers, closed back, two input jacks, marine-grade plywood construction, folding cabinet stand to tilt the cabinet back, blue covering, light brown grille cloth, mfg. 2007-present.

| MSR $1,600 | $800 | $525 - 600 | $260 - 325 | |

LIONHEART L412 SPEAKER CABINET – 120W, 4-12 in. Celestion Heritage G12H speakers, closed back, two input jacks, marine-grade plywood construction, blue covering, light brown grille cloth, current mfg.

| MSR $3,000 | $1,500 | $975 - 1,125 | $500 - 600 | |

ELECTRIC SS AMPLIFIERS: EXTREME (LX) SERIES

On amps with digital effects, the featured models include two reverbs, four delays, two chorus, flange, roatary speaker out, chorus/reverb, chorus/delay, flange/delay, and octave/delay.

LX35
courtesy Laney

LX65R Reverb
courtesy Laney

LX120 Twin Combo
courtesy Laney

LX12 – 12W, 1-6.5 in. speaker, guitar combo, solid-state chassis, single channel, front black control panel, single input, five knobs (g, b, m, t, v), CD input, headphone jack, black covering, black metal grille, mfg. 2006-disc.

| | $80 | $45 - 60 | $25 - 35 | $110 |

LX20 – 15W, 1-8 in. speaker, guitar combo, solid-state chassis, two channels, front black control panel, single input, six knobs (v, crunch, MV, b, m, t), channel switch, CD input, headphone jack, black covering, black metal grille, mfg. 2006-disc.

| | $110 | $60 - 80 | $35 - 50 | $150 |

* **LX20D** – similar to the LX20, except has digital effects processing with control for a total of seven knobs and RCA inputs, mfg. 2006-disc.

| | $170 | $95 - 120 | $55 - 75 | $230 |

* **LX20R Reverb** – similar to the LX20, except has a reverb circuit with control for a total of seven knobs, mfg. 2006-disc.

| | $140 | $75 - 95 | $45 - 60 | $180 |

LX35 – 30W, 1-10 in. speaker, guitar combo, solid-state chassis, two channels, front black control panel, single input, six knobs (v, crunch, MV, b, m, t), channel switch, XTS switch, RCA inputs, headphone jack, black covering, black metal grille, mfg. 2006-disc.

| | $170 | $95 - 120 | $55 - 75 | $230 |

* **LX35D** – similar to the LX35, except has digital effects processing with controls for a total of eight knobs, mfg. 2006-disc.

| | $250 | $140 - 175 | $80 - 110 | $330 |

* **LX35R Reverb** – similar to the LX35, except has a reverb circuit with control for a total of seven knobs, mfg. 2006-disc.

| | $210 | $115 - 145 | $65 - 85 | $280 |

LX65R REVERB – 65W, 1-12 in. Celestion speaker, guitar combo, solid-state chassis, two channels, reverb, front black control panel, single input, 10 knobs (Ch. 1: v, b, m, t, Ch. 2:crunch, MV, b, m, t, r), channel switch, XTS switch, RCA inputs, headphone jack, optional footswitch, black covering, black metal grille, mfg. 2006-disc.

| | $300 | $175 - 225 | $110 - 140 | $400 |

* **LX65D** – similar to the LX65R, except has digital effects processing with controls for a total of 11 knobs, mfg. 2006-disc.

| | $340 | $200 - 250 | $120 - 150 | $450 |

LX120 HEAD – 120W, head-unit configuration, solid-state chassis, two channels, reverb, front black control panel, single input, 11 knobs (Ch. 1: v, b, m, t, Ch. 2:crunch, MV, b, m, t, FX level, FX select), channel switch, XTS switch, RCA inputs, headphone jack, optional footswitch, black covering, black metal grille, mfg. 2006-disc.

| | $350 | $225 - 275 | $135 - 175 | $500 |

MSR/NOTES	100%	EXCELLENT	AVERAGE	LAST MSR

* *LX120 Twin Combo* – similar to the LX120 Head, except in combo configuration with 2-12 in. Celestion speakers, mfg. 2006-disc.

$500 $300 - 375 $175 - 225 $700

LX412A/LX412S SPEAKER CABINET – 200W, 4-12 in. Custom Rocket 50 speakers, 8 ohm impedance, straight (LX412S) or angled (LX412A) design, black covering, black metal grille, recessed handles, mfg. 2006-present.

MSR $655 $350 $225 - 275 $135 - 175

ELECTRIC SS AMPLIFIERS: HARD CORE SERIES

The Hard Core Series by Laney are the more affordable solid-state models for the more hard rock/heavy metal scene. These amps come in a variety of configurations for bass and guitar players. The small amp is the 30W with or without reverb and it climbs all the way up to a 120W head unit.

ELECTRIC SS AMPLIFIERS: LG SERIES

LG12
courtesy Laney

LG20R
courtesy Laney

LG35R
courtesy Laney

LG12 – 10W, 1-6.5 in. speaker, guitar combo, solid-state chassis, single channel, top black control panel, single input, five knobs (clean, crunch, b, m, t), headphone jack, CD input, black covering, dark gray grille, mfg. 2006-disc.

$80 $45 - 60 $25 - 35 $110

LG20R – 15W, 1-8 in. speaker, guitar combo, solid-state chassis, reverb, two channels, top black control panel, single input, seven knobs (clean, crunch, master, b, m, t, r), headphone jack, CD input, black covering, dark gray grille, mfg. 2006-disc.

$140 $75 - 95 $45 - 60 $180

LG35R – 30W, 1-10 in. speaker, guitar combo, solid-state chassis, reverb, two channels, top black control panel, single input, seven knobs (clean, crunch, master, b, m, t, r), scoop switch, headphone jack, RCA input, ext. speaker out, black covering, dark gray grille, mfg. 2006-disc.

$210 $115 - 145 $65 - 85 $270

ELECTRIC HYBRID AMPLIFIERS: LV SERIES

LV100
courtesy Laney

LV200
courtesy Laney

LV300 Twin Combo
courtesy Laney

LV100 – 65W, 1-12 in. Celestion Rocket 50 speaker, guitar combo, hybrid chassis with tube emulation circuitry, two channels, front black control panel, single input, 11 knobs (Clean: v, b, m, t, r, Drive: g, master, b, m, t r), VTS tone shaping, V scoop switch, bright switch, effects loop, ext. speaker out, headphone jack, two-button footswitch, black covering, dark gray grille, mfg. 2006-disc.

$350 $200 - 250 $120 - 150 $460

LV200 – 65W, 1-12 in. Celestion Super 65 speaker, guitar combo, hybrid chassis with 1 X ECC83 preamp tube, three channels, front black control panel, single input, 13 knobs (Clean: v, b, m, t, r, Drive 1: g, master, b, m, t r, Drive 2: g, master), VTS tone shaping, two V scoop switches, bright switch, effects loop, ext. speaker out, headphone jack, three-button footswitch, black covering, dark gray grille, mfg. 2006-disc.

$460 $275 - 325 $150 - 200 $620

MSR/NOTES	100%	EXCELLENT	AVERAGE	LAST MSR

LV300 HEAD – 120W, head-unit guitar configuration, hybrid chassis with 1 X ECC83 preamp tube, three channels, front black control panel, single input, 13 knobs (Clean: v, b, m, t, r, Drive 1: g, master, b, m, t r, Drive 2: g, master), VTS tone shaping, two V scoop switches, bright switch, effects loop, two speaker out, three-button footswitch, black covering, dark gray grille, mfg. 2006-disc.

	$400	$250 - 300	$135 - 175	$550

* *LV300 1-12 Combo* – similar to the LV300 Head, except in combo configuration with 1-12 in. Celestion Seventy 80 speaker, mfg. 2006-disc.

	$510	$300 - 375	$175 - 225	$680

* *LV300 Twin Combo* – similar to the LV300 Head, except in combo configuration with 2-12 in. Celestion Super 65 speakers, mfg. 2006-present.

MSR $1,200	$600	$400 - 450	$195 - 240	

LV412A/LV412S SPEAKER CABINET – 200W, 4-12 in. Celestion Rocket 50 speakers, 8 ohm impedance, angled (LV412A) or straight (LV412S) front design, black covering, dark gray grille, recessed handles, mfg. 2006-disc.

	$430	$275 - 325	$150 - 200	$580

ELECTRIC HYBRID AMPLIFIERS: TUBE FUSION (TF) SERIES

TF50 – 30W, 1-10 in. HH Vintage, dual channels, reverb, front slanted silver control panel, two inputs, seven silver knobs (v, drive, v, b, m, t, r), effects loop, footswitch, black covering, gray grille, disc.

	N/A	$135 - 175	$85 - 110	$330

TF100 – 50W, 1-10 in. HH Vintage, dual channels, reverb, front slanted silver control panel, single input, eleven silver knobs (v, b, m, t, drive, v, b, m, enhance, t, r), effects loop, footswitch, black covering, gray grille, disc.

	N/A	$200 - 250	$120 - 150	$480

TF200 – 65W, 1-12 in. HH Vintage, three channels, reverb, front slanted silver control panel, single input, fourteen silver knobs (v, b, m, t, drive, v, g, m, enhance, b, m, enhance, t, r), effects loop, footswitch, black covering, gray grille, disc.

	N/A	$275 - 325	$150 - 200	$630

TF300 – 120W, 1-12 in. HH Vintage, ECC83 preamp tube, three channels, reverb, front slanted silver control panel, single input, fifteen silver knobs (v, b, m, t, drive, v, enhance, g, m, enhance, b, m, enhance, t, r), effects loop, footswitch, black covering, gray grille, disc.

	N/A	$325 - 400	$200 - 250	$750

TF320 – 120W, 2-12 in. HH Vintage, ECC83 preamp tube, three channels, reverb, front slanted silver control panel, single input, fifteen silver knobs (v, b, m, t, drive, v, enhance, g, m, enhance, b, m, enhance, t, r), effects loop, footswitch, black covering, gray grille, disc.

	N/A	$375 - 450	$225 - 275	$840

TF400 – 120W, 2-12 in. HH Premier, ECC83 preamp tube, four channels, reverb, front slanted silver control panel, single input, 22 silver knobs, effects loop, footswitch, black covering, gray grille, disc.

	N/A	$400 - 475	$250 - 300	$860

TF500M – similar to the TF400 except has MIDI send and receive, disc.

	N/A	$425 - 500	$275 - 325	

TF700 – similar to the TF300 & TF320 except in head-unit only, disc.

	N/A	$250 - 300	$135 - 175	$550

TF800 – similar to the TF400 except in head-unit only, disc.

	N/A	$300 - 350	$175 - 225	

ELECTRIC HYBRID AMPLIFIERS: TUBE FUSION X (TFX) SERIES

TFX 1 – 50W, 1-10 in. Custom Celestion speaker, solid-state chassis, two channels, X-Factor DSP, front silver control panel, single input, 12 knobs, 16 DSP effects, black covering, black/gray grille, mfg. 2004-05.

	N/A	$225 - 275	$120 - 150	$500

TFX 2 – 65W, 1-12 in. Custom Celestion speaker, hybrid chassis, ECC83 preamp tube, three channels, X-Factor DSP, front silver control panel, single input, 15 knobs, 16 DSP effects, footswitch, black covering, black/gray grille, mfg. 2004-05.

	N/A	$300 - 375	$175 - 225	$700

TFX 3 – 120W, 1-12 in. Custom Celestion speaker, hybrid chassis, ECC83 preamp tube, three channels, X-Factor DSP, front silver control panel, single input, 17 knobs, 16 DSP effects, footswitch, black covering, black/gray grille, mfg. 2004-05.

	N/A	$350 - 425	$200 - 250	$800

* *TFX 3H* – similar to the TFX 3, except in head-unit only configuration, mfg. 2004-05.

	N/A	$300 - 350	$175 - 225	$650

* *TFX Twin* – similar to the TFX 3, except has 2-12 in. speakers, mfg. 2004-05.

	N/A	$400 - 475	$250 - 300	$900

MSR/NOTES	100%	EXCELLENT	AVERAGE	LAST MSR

TFX200 – 65W, 1-12 in. HH Vintage speaker combo, 1 X ECC83 preamp tube, three channels, digital processor, front silver control panel, single input, 15 silver knobs (v, b, m, t, effects, drive, drive v, g, master, enhance, b, m, t, effects, effects level), various buttons, black covering, gray grille, disc.

	N/A	$325 - 400	$200 - 250	$770

TFX300 – similar to the TFX200 except has 120 W output, disc.

	N/A	$375 - 450	$225 - 275	$880

TFX320 – similar to the TFX300 except has 2-12 in. speakers, disc.

	N/A	$425 - 500	$250 - 300	

TFX700 – similar to the TFX300 and TFX320 except in head unit version, disc.

	N/A	$300 - 375	$175 - 225	$700

TFX 412A/412S SPEAKER CABINET – 200W, 4-12 in. Custom Celestion speakers, straight or angled design, designed for use with the TFX3 Head, black covering, black/gray grille, mfg. 2004-05.

	N/A	$275 - 325	$150 - 200	$600

BASS AMPLIFIERS: NEXUS SERIES

Nexus-Tube Head
courtesy Laney

Nexus-FET Head
courtesy Laney

Nexus N115 Speaker Cabinet
courtesy Laney

Nexus NX410 Speaker Cabinet
courtesy Laney

NEXUS-TUBE HEAD – 400W, bass head unit, 12-tube chassis, preamp: 3 X ECC83, 1 X 12B7, power: 8 X KT88, solid-state rectifier, two channels (tube and FET), front black control panel, single input, 13 knobs (FET Ch. g, Tube Ch. g, level, All: b, t, lo/mid freq., lo/mid level, hi/mid freq., hi/mid level, compressor, p, deep, MV), six-band graphic EQ, input pad switch, FET power amp on/off switch, tube power amp on/off, graphic EQ on/off switch, compressor on/off switch, sub switch, standby switch, power switch, rear panel: fan on/off switch, three Neutrik combination Speakon/standard 1/4 in. speaker jacks, preamp out jack, power amp in jack, XLR direct out jack with ground/lift and pre/post EQ switches, effects loop, tuner out jack, footswitch jack, black covering, gray metal grille, five-button footswitch included, mfg. 2008-present.

MSR $3,500	$2,000	$1,300 - 1,500	$650 - 800	

NEXUS-FET HEAD – 650W, bass head unit, hybrid chassis with 2 X ECC83 preamp tubes and a MOS-FET power amp, two channels (tube and FET), front black control panel, single input, 13 knobs (FET Ch. g, Tube Ch. g, level, All: b, t, lo/mid freq., lo/mid level, hi/mid freq., hi/mid level, compressor, p, deep, MV), six-band graphic EQ, input pad switch, FET power amp on/off switch, tube power amp on/off, graphic EQ on/off switch, compressor on/off switch, sub switch, standby switch, power switch, rear panel: fan on/off switch, two Neutrik combination Speakon/standard 1/4 in. speaker jacks, preamp out jack, power amp in jack, XLR direct out jack with ground/lift and pre/post EQ switches, effects loop, tuner out jack, footswitch jack, black covering, gray metal grille, five-button footswitch included, mfg. 2008-present.

MSR $2,000	$1,300	$825 - 975	$475 - 550	

NEXUS NX115/NX210 SPEAKER CABINET – 800W, 1-15 or 2-10 in. Celestion Neodymium driver(s), 8 ohm impedance, two Neutrik combination speaker jacks, front ported cabinet, recessed side handles, black covering, black metal grille, mfg. 2008-present.

MSR $1,400	$600	$400 - 450	$195 - 240	

NEXUS NX410 SPEAKER CABINET – 800W, 4-10 in. Celestion Neodymium drivers, 8 ohm impedance, two Neutrik combination speaker jacks, front ported cabinet, recessed side handles, black covering, black metal grille, mfg. 2008-present.

MSR $1,900	$900	$575 - 675	$295 - 350	

NEXUS NX810 SPEAKER CABINET – 1600W, 8-10 in. Celestion Neodymium drivers, 4 or 8 ohm impedance, two Neutrik combination speaker jacks, front ported cabinet, recessed side handles, heavy duty road wheels, black covering, black metal grille, mfg. 2008-disc.

	$1,250	$775 - 925	$450 - 525	$1,750

BASS SS AMPLIFIERS: RICHTER SERIES

The Richter Bass series has changed series three times since its inception, but some models carry over with only cosmetic differences. The first Richter series was the RBW series and this lasted until about 2002. Between 2003 and 2004, the LR series of Richter basses was introduced. The RB Series was introduced in 2005 and is still in production today.

MSR/NOTES	100%	EXCELLENT	AVERAGE	LAST MSR

RB4
courtesy Laney

RB6
courtesy Laney

RB9
courtesy Laney

RB1 – 15W, 1-8 in. speaker, bass combo, solid-state chassis, front white control panel, single input, five knobs (g, b, m, t, v), compressor, limiter, CD input, headphone jack, black covering, black metal grille, mfg. 2005-present.

MSR $262	$200	$130 - 150	$65 - 80	

RB2 – 30W, 1-10 in. speaker, bass combo, solid-state chassis, front white control panel, two inputs, six knobs (g, b, freq., level, t, v), compressor, limiter, RCA input, headphone jack, ext. speaker jack, black covering, black metal grille, mfg. 2005-disc.

	$200	$110 - 140	$65 - 85	$260

RB3 – 65W, 1-12 in. Custom Celestion speaker, bass combo, solid-state chassis, front white control panel, two inputs, six knobs (g, b, freq., level, t, v), compressor, limiter, RCA input, headphone jack, ext. speaker jack, black covering, black metal grille, mfg. 2005-disc.

	$300	$160 - 210	$100 - 130	$390

RB4 – 160W, 1-15 in. Custom Celestion speaker, bass combo, solid-state chassis, front white control panel, two inputs, five knobs (g, enhance, b, t, v), seven-band graphic middle EQ, compressor, limiter, line out, XLR direct in, ext. speaker jack, black covering, black metal grille, mfg. 2005-present.

MSR $800	$470	$275 - 325	$150 - 200	

RBW200/LR2/RB5 – 120W, 1-12 in. Custom Celestion speaker with switchable horn, bass combo, solid-state chassis, front white control panel, two inputs, nine knobs (g, enhance, b, low para-mid with freq. and level, hi para-mid with freq. and level, t, v), compressor, limiter, line out, XLR direct in, ext. speaker jack, black covering, black metal grille, disc.

	$450	$250 - 300	$135 - 175	$600

RBW300/LR3/RB6 – 165W, 1-15 in. Custom Celestion speaker with switchable horn, bass combo, solid-state chassis, front white control panel, two inputs, nine knobs (g, enhance, b, low para-mid with freq. and level, hi para-mid with freq. and level, t, v), compressor, limiter, line out, XLR direct in, ext. speaker jack, tilt-back cabinet, black covering, black metal grille, current mfg.

MSR $900	$500	$300 - 350	$175 - 225	

LR5/RB7 – 300W, 2-10 in. Custom Celestion speaker with switchable horn, bass combo, solid-state chassis, front white control panel, two inputs, nine knobs (g, enhance, b, low para-mid with freq. and level, hi para-mid with freq. and level, t, v), compressor, limiter, line out, XLR direct in, ext. speaker jack, tilt-back cabinet, black covering, black metal grille, mfg. 2003-present.

MSR $1,000	$600	$350 - 425	$200 - 250	

LR4/RB8 – similar to the LR4H/RD9, except in combo configuration with 1-15 Celestion speaker with a switchable horn, mfg. 2003-present.

MSR $1,050	$620	$350 - 425	$200 - 250	

LR4H/RB9 – 300W, head-unit bass configuration, solid-state chassis, front white control panel, two inputs, five knobs (g, enhance, b, t, v), seven-band graphic middle EQ, compressor, limiter, line out, XLR direct in, ext. speaker jack, tilt-back cabinet, black covering, black metal grille, mfg. 2003-present.

MSR $700	$400	$225 - 275	$120 - 150	

RB115 SPEAKER CABINET – 250W, 1-15 in. Celestion custom driver, 8 ohm impedance, dual front ported, black covering, black metal grille, recessed side handles, mfg. 2005-present.

MSR $500	$320	$175 - 225	$110 - 140	

RB410 SPEAKER CABINET – 250W, 4-10 in. Celestion drivers plus a switchable high-frequency horn, 8 ohm impedance, black covering, black metal grille, recessed side handles, mfg. 2005-present.

MSR $800	$450	$250 - 300	$135 - 175	

MSR/NOTES	100%	EXCELLENT	AVERAGE	LAST MSR

ACOUSTIC AMPLIFIERS

LA30C
courtesy Laney

LA65C
courtesy Laney

LA65D
courtesy Laney

A1(PLUS) – 65W, 1-10 in. driver with a tweeter, acoustic combo, solid-state chassis, three channels, digital effects processing, front white control panel, three inputs, 16 knobs, headphone jack, tuned reflex dual ported tilt-back cabinet, black covering, black metal grille, mfg. 2005-present.

| MSR $900 | $450 | $275 - 325 | $150 - 200 | |

LA12C – 12W, 1-6.5 in. speaker with a coaxial tweeter, acoustic guitar combo, solid-state chassis, single channel, chorus, front brown control panel, single input, four black knobs (v, lo, mid, hi), chorus switch, aux. in. jack, headphone jack, power switch, brown covering, black metal grille, mfg. 2009-disc.

| | $100 | $50 - 75 | $30 - 40 | $140 |

LA20C – 20W, 1-8 in. speaker with a coaxial tweeter, acoustic guitar combo, solid-state chassis, single channel, chorus, reverb, anti-feedback circuitry, front brown control panel, single input, six black knobs (v, lo, mid freq., mid, hi, r), chorus switch, aux. in. jack, DI out jack, headphone jack, power switch, brown covering, black metal grille, mfg. 2009-present.

| MSR $350 | $170 | $95 - 120 | $55 - 75 | |

LA30C – 30W, 1-8 in. driver with a horn, acoustic combo, solid-state chassis, two channels, chorus, reverb, front brown control panel, three inputs (one mic, two inst.), seven knobs (Ch. 1: v, Ch. 2: v, b, freq., level, t, r), RCA inputs, insert socket, line out, brown leatherette covering, brown grille, disc. 2008.

| | N/A | $140 - 175 | $80 - 110 | $330 |

LA35C – 35W, 2-6.5 in. speakers with a coaxial tweeter, acoustic guitar combo, solid-state chassis, two channels, chorus, reverb, anti-feedback circuitry, front brown control panel, two inputs (combination XLR/standard 1/4 in. jacks), six black knobs (Ch. 1 v, Ch. 2 v, anti-feedback, chorus rate, chorus depth, r), four-band graphic EQ, Ch. 1 reverb switch, Ch. 2 input pad switch, Ch. 2 anti-feedback switch, Ch. 2 reverb switch, Ch. 2 chorus switch, aux. in. jack, DI out jack, headphone jack, rear panel: power switch, brown covering, black metal grille, mfg. 2009-present.

| MSR $500 | $250 | $150 - 190 | $95 - 120 | |

LA65C – 65W, 2-8 in. drivers with a horn, acoustic combo, solid-state chassis, two channels, chorus, reverb, front brown control panel, three inputs (one mic, two inst.), 12 knobs (Aux. Ch.: v, b, t, Inst. Ch.: g, b, t, All: anti-feedback freq., anti-feedback level, chorus rate, chorus depth, r, MV), RCA inputs, insert socket, line out, brown leatherette covering, brown grille, disc. 2008.

| | N/A | $175 - 225 | $110 - 140 | $430 |

LA65D – 65W, 2-8 in. speakers with a coaxial tweeter, acoustic guitar combo, solid-state chassis, two channels, digital chorus, digital reverb, anti-feedback circuitry, front brown control panel, two inputs (combination XLR/standard 1/4 in. jacks), 10 black knobs (Ch. 1 g, lo, hi, r, Ch. 2 g, anti-feedback, chorus rate, chorus depth, r, MV), four-band graphic EQ, Ch. 2 preshape switch, Ch. 2 input pad switch, Ch. 2 phase switch, Ch. 2 anti-feedback switch, Ch. 2 chorus shimmer switch, Ch. 2 chorus switch, aux. in. jack, rear panel: power switch, headphone jack, XLR DI out jack with ground/lift switch, effects loop with bypass switch, footswitch jack, brown covering, black metal grille, mfg. 2009-present.

| MSR $700 | $350 | $225 - 275 | $120 - 150 | |

SPEAKER CABINETS

GS112VE SPEAKER CABINET – 30W, 1-12 in. Celestion 70 Eighty, 8 ohm impedance, closed back, single jack input, black covering with white piping, dark gray grille, designed for use as an extension cabinet with the VC30-112 or VC30-210, current mfg.

| MSR $320 | $240 | $135 - 175 | $85 - 110 | |

GS210VE SPEAKER CABINET – 70W, 2-10 in. Jensen C10Q16 speakers, 8 ohm impedance, closed back, single jack input, black covering with white piping, dark gray grille, designed for use as an extension cabinet with the VC30-112 or VC30-210, current mfg.

| MSR $370 | $280 | $150 - 200 | $95 - 120 | |

MSR/NOTES	100%	EXCELLENT	AVERAGE	LAST MSR

GS412IA Speaker Cabinet
courtesy Laney

GS412LA Speaker Cabinet
courtesy Laney

TT412A Speaker Cabinet
courtesy Laney

GS212IE SPEAKER CABINET – 160W, 2-12 in. Celestion Seventy 80 speakers, 16 ohm mono or 8 ohm stereo impedance, closed back, two input jacks, black covering with white piping, dark gray grille, designed for use as an extension cabinet with the GH50L Head, mfg. 2008-present.

MSR $440	$330	$175 - 225	$110 - 140	

GS412 IA/IS SPEAKER CABINET – 320W, 4-12 in. Celestion 70 Eighty speakers, 16 ohm impedance, closed back, two input jacks, angled (IA) or straight (IS) front, black covering with white piping and chrome corners, dark gray grille, casters, recessed side handles, designed for use with the GH50L, GH100L, or the VH100R, current mfg.

MSR $750	$550	$300 - 375	$175 - 225	

GS412 LA/LS SPEAKER CABINET – 320W, 4-12 in. Celestion 70 Eighty speakers, 16 ohm impedance, closed back, two input jacks, angled (LA) or straight (LS) front, black covering with black chrome corners, black metal grille, casters, recessed side handles, designed for use with the GH100TI, current mfg.

MSR $750	$550	$300 - 375	$175 - 225	

TT412 A/S SPEAKER CABINET – 240W, 4-12 in. Celestion Vintage 30 speakers, 16 ohm impedance, closed back, two input jacks, angled (A) or straight (S) front, black covering with white piping and chrome corners, dark gray grille, casters, recessed side handles, designed for use with the TT50H and TT100H, current mfg.

MSR $1,100	$800	$500 - 575	$300 - 350	

LANYAO

Amplifiers and speaker cabinets currently produced in China. Currently, there is no U.S. Distributor.

Lanyao produces a full line of amplifiers including tube amps, solid-state amps, and speaker cabinets. A 100W tube head is available with 4-12 in. Celestion speaker cabinets. Many of the smaller solid-state amps have Killer on the grille, which indicates the series.

CONTACT INFORMATION
LANYAO
www.lanyao.com

LECTROLAB

Amplifiers previously produced during the 1960s, and reissued in the mid-2000s.

Lectrolab was originally a trademark/brand of amplifiers produced in the 1960s. While Lectrolab's origins are relatively unknown, it is speculated that they were their own company and not built by another amp manufacturer as some have suggested. Labels on the inside of various Lectrolab amps read: Lectrolab: Sound Projects, Chicago, Illinois, Venice, Florida" suggesting they were built in the U.S. These amps were available in 400, 600, 800, and 900 series with the higher number indicating higher wattage and features, and they were all offered with tube chassis. In the mid-2000s, the Lectrolab brand was revived as a reissue line built by Jim Benedict in Michigan. However, many customers reported quality issues with the new Lectrolab amps, and Benedict appears to not be building any more amps. Any further information about vintage or recent Lectrolab amplifiers can be submitted directly to Blue Book Publications.

LEE JACKSON

Amplifiers and other electronic products currently produced in Austin, TX since the 2000s. Amplifiers previously produced in Cape Girardeau, MO from 1993 to 1996 and Austin, TX during the late 1990s.

Lee Jackson has been involved in many different music companies over the years including B.C. Rich, Fender, Pignose, Metaltronix, Ampeg, and Harmony. Even though he has designed many amplifiers, he didn't produce his own until 1993. Harmony Music asked him to design some amplifiers and they would name the company around him. During his time with Harmony he produced XLS-1000 series first and the XLA-1000 followed shortly thereafter. The XLA-1000 amp was a direct copy of the amps that he had built for Zakk Wylde, Steve Vai, and George Lynch. Jackson made

CONTACT INFORMATION
LEE JACKSON
5701 West Slaughter Lane
A130
Austin, TX 78749
www.leejackson.com
info@leejackson.com

MSR/NOTES	100%	EXCELLENT	AVERAGE	LAST MSR

amplifiers up until 1996 when Horizon had some problems within the company, and they put the amp project on hold. As they tried to get Lee Jackson amplifiers going again in 2001, the stock market crashed and investors in the new amplifiers became very skeptical. This was bad news for Jackson as they were giving a presentation the day the market crashed. With the terrorist attacks on September 11, 2001, all the investors got really scared and pulled out all money and support. In 2002, Uponus Technologies developed a new computer chip to compress music files, which was very helpful with digital processing and recording. Later on in the 2000s, Jackson moved back to Austin and met some engineers from North Shore Circuit Designs. There, he has developed a new line of Lee Jackson amplifiers as well as guitar pedals. Current models include the **XLA-1000** 100W head, **XLS-1000** 50/100W head, and the **XLCS-1000** 50/100W combo. For more information, visit Lee Jackson's website or contact him directly.

LEGEND

Amplifiers previously produced in East Syracuse, NY between 1978 and 1985. Distributed by Legend Musical Instruments.

Legend Amplifiers were produced between 1978 and 1985 in Syracuse, NY. Legend has been considered one of the first boutique amplifier companies out there. They offered a wide variety of tube head-unit and combo amps and speaker cabinets. Some early models have the wicker-style front that early Mesa/Boogie amps feature. The G-50W and G-100W were probably their most popular series, and in 1984, the Model A Series III was introduced. By 1985 they had ceased production on all models and went out of business. Most head units are priced between $350 and $500 and combo units are between $400 and $600. Look for more information in further editions.

LEGION SOUND

Amplifiers and speaker cabinets previously produced in Asia. Distributed in the U.S. by Legion Sound/Madison in Loveland, CO.

Madison was founded by Andy Hitch in 2000, and is named after his daughter that was born the same year. They started out producing speakers and eventually moved on to building amplifiers as well. Legion Sound is the budget brand for Madison, and they produce a wide variety of solid-state guitar and bass amplifiers, speaker cabinets, and PA equipment. At the end of 2006, Madison announced that they would not be building anymore Legion combo guitar or bass amps, and are focusing on head units and speaker cabinets. In 2010, Madison closed their doors and halted production of all products, which included the Legion Sound brand as well.

LENAHAN ELECTRONICS

Amplifiers currently produced since the mid-2000s.

James Lenahan has been involved with electronics and the music industry for many years, and he built tube guitar amplifiers on the side as well. After spending many years in Los Angeles and working for Soldano and Ampeg, he moved back to Middle America in the mid-2000s and began building amplifeirs full-time under the Lenahan brand. Lenahan focuses on 50 watt amplifiers and his first two models include a regular 50 watt head and a master volume 50 watt head. Lenahan works by himself and everything is hand-built.

LESLIE

Amplifiers and speaker cabinets currently produced since the 1960s. Distributed by Hammond Suzuki USA, Inc. in Addison, IL.

CONTACT INFORMATION
LESLIE
Distributed by Hammond Suzuki USA, Inc.
743 Annoreno Drive
Addison, IL 60101 USA
Phone No.: 630-543-0277
Phone No.: 888-674-2623
Fax No.: 800-466-2286
www.hammondorganco.com
info@hammondorganco.com

Leslie is best-known for their rotating speaker cabinets that are mainly used with Hammond Organs. These rotating cabinets consist of two horns facing directly away from each other that are mounted on a motor that spins when turned on. The result is an echo/reverb/wah (think game show organ) sound that is almost impossible to reproduce with any current effect. Although Leslie is designed for use with organs, many guitar players have experimented with the unique sound. In 1991, the Suzuki Corporation in Japan bought Hammond and Leslie. Currently products are produced in both the Japan and U.S. factories and distributed in the U.S. by Hammond Suzuki USA, Inc. A full range of rotating speaker cabinets as well as a rotating speaker guitar amplifier and guitar speaker cabinet are currently available. For more information, visit Leslie's website or contact them directly.

ELECTRIC AMPLIFIERS/ROTATING SPEAKER CABINETS

Although Leslie produced several different models, they are all based on the rotating speaker design. Some popular models include the **Model 122A** (MSR $3,195), **Model 122XB**, **Model 147A**, **Model 525**, **Model 760** (disc.), **Model 820 Pro Line** (disc.), **Model 825** (disc.), **Model 971**, **Model 2101** (MSR $1,945), **Model 2121** (MSR $1,945), **Model 3300** (MSR $2,475), and **Model 3301** (MSR $1,295). Both tube and solid-state models were offered in a variety of wattages and speaker configurations. The current mfg. Leslies include models that can be used with new and old Hammond organs.

LESLIE 15 ROTATING SPEAKER CABINET — no power amp, 1-10 in. or 1-12 in. speaker, black Tolex covering, silver grille cloth, single input, mfg. 1960s-1970s.

N/A		$475 - 550	$300 - 350	

MSR/NOTES	100%	EXCELLENT	AVERAGE	LAST MSR

LESLIE 60 ROTATING SPEAKER CABINET – 45W, 2-10 in. speakers, black Tolex covering, silver grille cloth, mfg. 1960s-1970s.

Leslie 60 Rotating Speaker Cabinet
courtesy S.P. Fjestad

Leslie 60 Rotating Speaker Cabinet
courtesy S.P. Fjestad

	N/A	$550 - 650	$350 - 425	

G27 – 100W, 1-12 in. vintage V30 speaker, rotating speaker guitar cabinet with no pre- or power amplifier, rear black control panel, single input, two black knobs (slow rotor speed, fast rotor speed), power switch, two footswitch jacks (rotor on/off, rotor speed), black painted cabinet built with 3/4 in. MDF, protective corners, two folding handles, two-button FS-10TL footswitch included, 29.25 in. wide, 26.75 in. tall, 20.5 in. deep, 82 lbs., mfg. 2008-present.

MSR $1,575	$1,325	$950 - 1,100	$675 - 800	

G37 – 100W, 1-12 in. vintage V30 speaker, hybrid chassis with a tube preamp and solid-state power amp, rotating speaker guitar combo, two channels, rear black control panel, two inputs (high and low), nine black knobs (Clean Ch.: v, OD Ch.: g, v, contour, All: t, m, b, slow rotor speed, fast rotor speed), channel select switch, power switch, three footswitch jacks (channel select, rotor on/off, rotor speed), black painted cabinet built with 3/4 in. MDF, protective corners, two folding handles, two-button FS-10TL footswitch included, 29.25 in. wide, 26.75 in. tall, 20.5 in. deep, 85 lbs., mfg. 2008-present.

MSR $1,745	$1,500	$1,000 - 1,200	$725 - 850	

LINE 6

Amplifiers and other modeling devices currently produced in Agoura Hills, CA since 1996.

Michael Doidic and Marcus Ryle founded Line 6 in 1996 with the introduction of their first modeling guitar amplifier called the AxSys 212. Prior to creating Line 6, Doidic and Ryle both designed guitar effects and they wanted to create an amplifier that could produce a wide variety of amp sounds and effects. The AxSys 212 featured 28 amp models, 15 cabinet models, and a variety of rack- and stomp box-style effects all in one stand-alone amplifier! In 1998, Line 6 introduced the versatile POD, which was a kidney bean-shaped desktop modeling device that contained 32 amp models, 15 speaker cabinet models, 16 digital effects, and 36 user programmable channels and it could be used with headphones, an external amplifier, or for recording purposes. In 2000, they introduced the Bass POD, which was designed for bass guitars. In 2001, the Vetta Series was introduced, and in 2002 the Duoverb Series along with Line 6's first modeling guitar Variax were introduced. In 2003, the HD-147 Head, the Flextone III Series, and the Vetta II Series were introduced. In 2004, the Spider II Series replaced the Spider Series. In 2006, the Spider III Series replaced the Spider II Series with a few minor changes, and the LowDown Bass Series of bass amps was introduced. In 2008, the Spider Valve Series which was designed with Reinhold Bogner of Bogner Amplification introduced the first Line 6 tube modeling amplifiers. In 2009, the redesigned Spider IV Series was introduced along with an expanded LowDown Bass Series. For more information, visit Line 6's website or contact them directly.

CONTACT INFORMATION
LINE 6
26580 Agoura Road
Calabasas, CA 91302-1921
Phone No.: 818-575-3600
Fax No.: 818-575-3601
www.line6.com
Info@line6.com

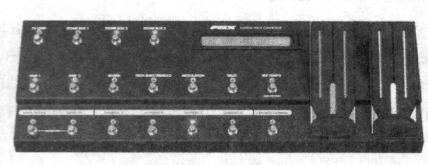

FBV Footcontroller
courtesy Line 6

FBV2 Footcontroller
courtesy Line 6

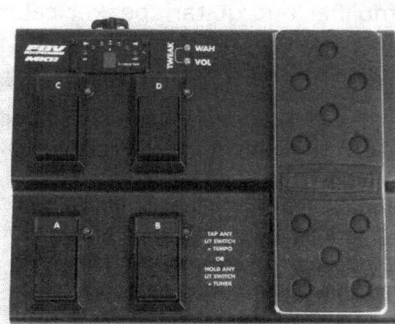

FBV Express MKII Footcontroller
courtesy Line 6

MSR/NOTES	100%	EXCELLENT	AVERAGE	LAST MSR

FOOTSWITCHES/FOOTPEDALS

FBV FOOTCONTROLLER – 18-button footswitch with two expression pedals and a backlit display, features dedicated channel switches, dedicated on/off effects switches, wah pedal, volume pedal, chromatic digital tuner, tap tempo, self powered through locking cable, compatible with the Spider II, Spider III, Vetta, Vetta II, HD-147, and LowDown Bass amplifiers, current mfg.

| MSR $600 | $400 | $250 - 300 | $135 - 175 | |

FBV2 FOOTCONTROLLER – two-button footswitch with buttons to scroll through the first bank of four presets, compatible with the Spider II, Spider III, Spider IV, Spider Valve, Vetta, Vetta II, Flextone III, HD-147, and LowDown Bass amplifiers, current mfg.

| MSR $49 | $35 | $20 - 25 | $10 - 15 | |

FBV EXPRESS MKII FOOTCONTROLLER – four-button footswitch with single pedal control, four channel switches, volume/wah pedal, chromatic tuner, FBV software for easy and unlimted mapping of FBV controls, self-powered by locking cable, USB jack, compatible with the Spider II, Spider III, Spider IV, Spider Valve, Vetta, Vetta II, Flextone III, HD-147, and LowDown Bass amplifiers, current mfg.

| MSR $140 | $100 | $50 - 75 | $30 - 40 | |

FBV SHORTBOARD MKII FOOTCONTROLLER – 13-button footswitch with one expression pedals and a backlit display, four channel switches, tap/tuner button, stomp, modulation, delay, and reverb effects buttons, fuction 1, function 2, and two directional buttons, wah/volume pedal, chromatic digital tuner, FBV software for easy and unlimted mapping of FBV controls, self-powered by locking cable, USB jack, compatible with the Spider II, Spider III, Spider IV, Spider Valve, Vetta, Vetta II, Flextone III, HD-147, and LowDown Bass amplifiers, current mfg.

| MSR $280 | $200 | $120 - 150 | $75 - 95 | |

ELECTRIC AMPLIFIERS: AMPLIFI SERIES

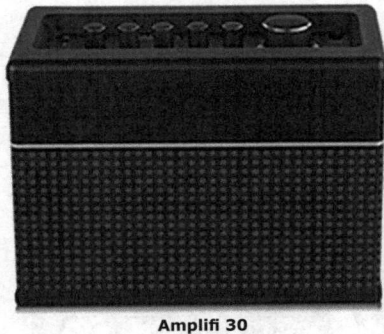

Amplifi 30
courtesy Line 6

Amplifi 75
courtesy Line 6

Amplifi 150
courtesy Line 6

AMPLIFI 30 – 30W, 4-2.5 in. speaker, stereo guitar combo, solid-state chassis, four onboard preset channels, 3-band EQ, 200 effects, top black control panel, single input, six black knobs (drive, b, m, t, r, v), tone switch, tap switch, Bluetooth switch, headphone jack, power switch, aux. in jack, USB connector, FBV pedal jack, compatible with Amplifi remote app, black covering, red grille, new 2016.

| MSR $430 | $300 | $195 - 225 | $100 - 120 | |

AMPLIFI 75 – 75W, 1-8 in. speaker, 2 drivers, 2 tweeters, stereo guitar combo, solid-state chassis, four user created preset channels, 3-band EQ, 100 effects, 70 guitar models, top black control panel, single input, seven black knobs (drive, b, m, t, FX, r, v), tone switch, tap switch, Bluetooth switch, headphone jack, power switch, aux. in jack, USB connector, FBV pedal jack, compatible with Amplifi remote app, black covering, red grille, 20.5 lbs., mfg. 2014-present.

| MSR $560 | $400 | $260 - 300 | $130 - 160 | |

AMPLIFI 150 – 150W, 1-12 in. speaker, 2 drivers, 2 tweeters, stereo guitar combo, solid-state chassis, four user created preset channels, 3-band EQ, 100 effects, 70 guitar models, top black control panel, single input, seven black knobs (drive, b, m, t, FX, r, v), tone switch, tap switch, Bluetooth switch, headphone jack, power switch, aux. in jack, USB connector, FBV pedal jack, compatible with Amplifi remote app, black covering, red grille, 35.6 lbs., mfg. 2014-present.

| MSR $700 | $500 | $325 - 375 | $165 - 200 | |

ELECTRIC AMPLIFIERS: AX2, DUOVERB, & HD SERIES

AX2 – 100W, 2-12 in. speakers, digital modeling guitar combo, solid-state chassis, single channel, 28 amp models, 15 cabinet models, rack-style and stomp box-style effects, front black control panel, guitar input, aux. input, nine black knobs (guitar v, aux. v, MV, drive, b, m, t, Ch. v, delay/reverb), digital display with 16 buttons for models, effects, and programming, MIDI in/out, stereo headphone/direct out jack, two internal speaker jacks, Cat5 footswitch jack, two 1/4 in. footswitch jacks (volume, wah), black Tolex covering, silver grille (early models) or black grille (later models), 28.5 in. wide, 21.25 in. tall, 11 in. deep, 63 lbs., mfg. 1996-2001.

| | N/A | $375 - 450 | $250 - 300 | |

MSR/NOTES	100%	EXCELLENT	AVERAGE	LAST MSR

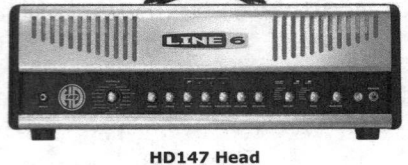

HD147 Head
courtesy Line 6

Duoverb Combo
courtesy Line 6

DUOVERB COMBO – 100W, 2-12 in. Custom Celestion speakers, modeling amp design, 16 amp models, dual amp capability, spring reverb, front black control panel, single input, seventeen white knobs, various switches, black covering, brown grille cloth, 63 lbs., mfg. fall 2002-04.

N/A	$425 - 500	$300 - 350	$1,800

DUOVERB HEAD – similar to the Duoverb combo except in head-unit version, 29 lbs., mfg. fall 2002-04.

N/A	$325 - 400	$200 - 250	

HD147 HEAD – 300W, head-unit configuration, solid-state chassis, four channels, 32 amp models, 12 programmable effects, 16 mix and match cabinet models, front black control panel, single input, eleven silver knobs (amp model select, drive, b, m, t, v, r, delay, mod select, MV), tap tempo select, gate and comp buttons, black side covering with chrome front/top/back, mfg. 2003-09.

$1,250	$850 - 950	$600 - 675	$1,750

ELECTRIC AMPLIFIERS: DT SERIES

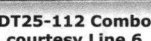

DT25 Head
courtesy Line 6

DT25-112 Combo
courtesy Line 6

DT25-112 Combo
courtesy Line 6

DT25-112 COMBO – 25W, 1-12 in. Celestion G12H90 speaker, modeling guitar combo, hybrid chassis, Preamp: 1 X 12AX7, Power 2 X EL84, two channels, four amp models (clean, crunch, chime, high-gain), top black control panel, single input, 15 black knobs (each channel: drive, b, m, t, presence, r, v, All: MV), channel switch, amp model selector, bias switch, standby switch, midi in/out, L6 link jacks, footswitch jack, power switch, effects loop, XLR direct out with ground/lift switch, five external speaker jacks, top handle, black covering, light brown grille, mfg. 2011-present.

MSR $1,400	$1,000	$650 - 750	$325 - 400

DT25 HEAD – 25W, modeling guitar head unit, hybrid chassis, Preamp: 1 X 12AX7, Power 2 X EL84, two channels, four amp models (clean, crunch, chime, high-gain), front black control panel, single input, 15 black knobs (each channel: drive, b, m, t, presence, r, v, All: MV), channel switch, amp model selector, bias switch, standby switch, midi in/out, L6 link jacks, footswitch jack, power switch, effects loop, XLR direct out with ground/lift switch, five external speaker jacks, top handle, black covering, mfg. 2011-present.

MSR $1,290	$900	$575 - 675	$295 - 350

DT25 SPEAKER CABINET – 90W, 8 ohm impedance, 1-12 in. Celestion G12H-90 speaker, straight front, designed for use with the DT25 Head, top handle, black covering, light brown grille, 25 in. wide, 21 in. tall, 15 in. tall., mfg. 2011-present.

MSR $420	$300	$195 - 225	$100 - 120

ELECTRIC AMPLIFIERS: FIREHAWK SERIES

FIREHAWK 1500 – 1500W, 2-5.5 in. drivers, 1-12 in. subwoofer, 1 in. high-freq. driver, modeling guitar combo, solid-state chassis, four preset channels, 3-band EQ, multi-effects, 200 amp/cab models, 128 built-in guitar models, top black control panel, single input, seven black knobs (drive, b, m, t, FX, r, v), model selector, tap switch, Bluetooth switch, two monitor in jacks with level control, effects loop, two XLR main out jack, MIDI in/out jacks, headphone jack, power switch, variax jack, USB connector, FBV pedal jack, top, black covering, silver grille, 63.1 lbs., new 2016.

MSR $1,400	$1,000	$650 - 750	$325 - 400

| MSR/NOTES | 100% | EXCELLENT | AVERAGE | LAST MSR |

Firehawk
courtesy Line 6

Flextone II
courtesy Line 6

Flextone III XL
courtesy Line 6

ELECTRIC AMPLIFIERS: FLEXTONE SERIES

FLEXTONE II – 60W, 1-12 in. speaker, digital modeling guitar combo, solid-state chassis, single channel, 32 amplifier models, 15 cabinet models, 16 digital effects, 4 user programmable channels (up to 36 presets with Floor Board), ToneTransfer compatible, top red control panel, single input, 10 black knobs (MV, amp model selector, drive, b, m, t, Ch. v, r, FX tweak, effects selector), manual button, four channel select buttons, save button, tap/tempo switch, rear panel: power switch, headphone jack, foot controller jack, effects loop, MIDI in/out, two 1/4 in. speaker jacks (internal/external), black covering with Line 6 logo, brown cloth grille, 23.5 in. wide, 18 in. tall, 10.5 in. deep, 47 lbs., disc. 2003.

N/A $175 - 225 $110 - 140

* **Flextone II Plus** – similar to the Flextone II, except has a dual power amp section that produces 100W when used with a 1-12 in. extension speaker cabinet, two XLR outputs with ground/lift and live/studio switches and two 1/4 in. speaker jacks (external, internal), 48 lbs., disc. 2003.

N/A $200 - 250 $120 - 150

* **Flextone II XL** – similar to the Flextone II, except has 100W output, 2-12 in. speakers, two XLR outputs with ground/lift and live/studio switches and two 1/4 in. speaker jacks (external, internal), 28.5 in. wide, 20.75 in. tall, 10.5 in. deep, 59 lbs., disc. 2003.

N/A $300 - 350 $175 - 225

FLEXTONE II HD HEAD – 200W, digital modeling guitar head, solid-state chassis, single channel, 32 amplifier models, 15 cabinet models, 16 digital effects, 4 user programmable channels (up to 36 presets with Floor Board), ToneTransfer compatible, front red control panel, single input, 10 black knobs (MV, amp model selector, drive, b, m, t, Ch. v, r, FX tweak, effects selector), manual button, four channel select buttons, save button, tap/tempo switch, power switch, rear panel: power switch, headphone jack, foot controller jack, effects loop, two XLR outputs (mono/stereo) with ground/lift and live/studio switches, MIDI in/out, two 1/4 in. speaker jacks (internal/external), black covering with Line 6 logo, 26 in. wide, 9.25 in. tall, 9 in. deep, 30 lbs., disc. 2003.

N/A $250 - 300 $135 - 175

FLEXTONE III – 75W, 1-12 in. speaker, guitar combo, solid-state chassis, four channels, 32 Vetta-based amp modules, 12 premium effects, 16 mix-n-match cab options, top black control panel, single input, 11 white knobs (amp model select, drive, b, m, t, p, v, r, delay, mod select, MV), tap tempo control, gate and comp buttons, black covering, brown grille, 47 lbs., mfg. 2003-06.

$500 $300 - 375 $200 - 250

* **Flextone III Plus** – similar to the Flextone III, except has 150W stereo output (75W mono) and stereo XLR speaker outs, 48 lbs., mfg. 2003-08.

$600 $350 - 425 $225 - 275 $840

* **Flextone III XL** – similar to the Flextone III, except has 150W stereo output (75W mono), 2-12 in. speakers, and stereo XLR speaker outs, 59 lbs., mfg. 2003-08.

$700 $425 - 500 $275 - 325 $980

FLEXTONE 112 SPEAKER CABINET – 60W, 1-12 in. speaker, 8 ohm impedance, designed for use with the Flextone II Plus, black covering, brown cloth grille, 23.5 in. wide, 18 in. tall, 11.25 in. deep, 34 lbs., disc. 2003.

N/A $120 - 150 $75 - 95

FLEXTONE 212S SPEAKER CABINET – 150W, 2-12 in. speakers, 4 or 8 ohm stereo/mono impedance, designed for use with the Flextone II HD, removable casters, black covering, brown cloth grille, 30.25 in. wide, 20 in. tall, 12 in. deep, 62 lbs., disc. 2003.

N/A $150 - 200 $95 - 120

FLEXTONE 412S/412SB SPEAKER CABINET – 300W, 4-12 in. speakers, switchable 2, 4, 8, or 16 ohm stereo/mono impedance, straight or angled front, designed for use with the Flextone II HD, metal handles, metal corners, removable casters, black covering, brown cloth grille, 29.75 in. wide, 29.25 in. tall, 14 in. deep, 78 lbs., disc. 2003.

N/A $200 - 250 $120 - 150

MSR/NOTES	100%	EXCELLENT	AVERAGE	LAST MSR

ELECTRIC AMPLIFIERS: SPIDER SERIES

SPIDER 112 – 50W, 1-12 in. speaker, digital modeling guitar combo, solid-state chassis, six Line 6 amp models (Clean, Blues, Recto, Twang, Crunch, Insane), seven digital effects (Delay, Ping-Pong, Tape Echo, Flanger, Chorus, Tremolo, Reverb), four user programmable channels, front red control panel, single input, 10 black knobs (amp model selector, drive, b, m, t, Ch. v, flange/chorus/tremolo effects, delay/ping-pong/tape echo effects, r, MV), four channel select buttons, tap button, Cat5 footswitch jack, headphone/direct out jack, power switch, black covering, black grille, 20.75 in. wide, 17.5 in. tall, 11 in. deep, 34 lbs., disc. 2003.

	N/A	$200 - 250	$120 - 150	$600

SPIDER 210 – 50W, (25W X 2 Stereo), 2-10 in. speakers, digital modeling guitar combo, solid-state chassis, six Line 6 amp models (Clean, Blues, Recto, Twang, Crunch, Insane), seven digital effects (Delay, Ping-Pong, Tape Echo, Flanger, Chorus, Tremolo, Reverb), four user programmable channels, front red control panel, single input, 10 black knobs (amp model selector, drive, b, m, t, Ch. v, flange/chorus/tremolo effects, delay/ping-pong/tape echo effects, r, MV), four channel select buttons, tap button, Cat5 footswitch jack, headphone/direct out jack, power switch, black covering, black grille, 23.5 in. wide, 17.5 in. tall, 11 in. deep, 38 lbs., disc. 2003.

	N/A	$275 - 325	$150 - 200	

SPIDER 212 – 100W, (50W X 2 Stereo), 2-12 in. speakers, digital modeling guitar combo, solid-state chassis, six Line 6 amp models (Clean, Blues, Recto, Twang, Crunch, Insane), seven digital effects (Delay, Ping-Pong, Tape Echo, Flanger, Chorus, Tremolo, Reverb), four user programmable channels, front red control panel, single input, 10 black knobs (amp model selector, drive, b, m, t, Ch. v, flange/chorus/tremolo effects, delay/ping-pong/tape echo effects, r, MV), four channel select buttons, tap button, Cat5 footswitch jack, headphone/direct out jack, power switch, black covering, black grille, 26.5 in. wide, 20.5 in. tall, 11 in. deep, 54 lbs., disc. 2003.

	N/A	$325 - 400	$175 - 225	$950

ELECTRIC AMPLIFIERS: SPIDER II/SPIDER III SERIES

In 2006, Line 6 introduced the updated Spider III series. These models are exactly the same as the Spider II Series except Line 6 had artists resound some of the amp mods and some slightly altered cosmetics were introduced. All amps follow the same pricing as the old models.

* **Add $250 for Floor Board controller.**

Spider II 15
courtesy Line 6

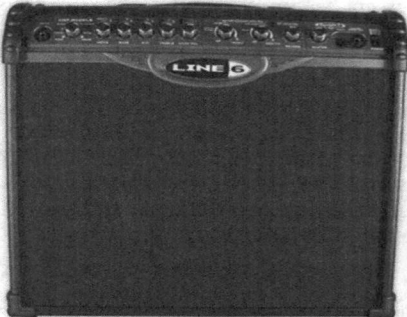

Spider II 75 112
courtesy Line 6

Spider II 150 212
courtesy Line 6

SPIDER II 15/SPIDER III 15 – 15W, 1-8 in. speaker combo, solid-state chassis, four channels, six digital effects, front black control panel, single input, eight knobs (drive, b, m, t, Channel v, two smart control FX buttons, MV), tap tempo select, black covering, black grille, mfg. 2004-08.

	$100	$50 - 75	$25 - 40	$200

SPIDER II 30/SPIDER III 30 – 30W, 1-12 in. speaker combo, solid-state chassis, four channels, six digital effects, front black control panel, single input, eight knobs (drive, b, m, t, Channel v, two smart control FX buttons, MV), tap tempo select, black covering, black grille, mfg. 2004-08.

	$200	$120 - 150	$70 - 95	$280

SPIDER II HD75/SPIDER III HD75 – 75W, head-unit guitar configuration, solid-state chassis, four channels, six digital effects, front black control panel, single input, eight knobs (drive, b, m, t, Channel v, two smart control FX buttons, MV), tap tempo select, black covering, black grille, mfg. 2005-08.

	$250	$150 - 190	$95 - 120	$350

SPIDER II 75 112/SPIDER III 75 112 – 75W, 1-12 in. speaker combo, solid-state chassis, four channels, 12 amp models, seven programmable effects, built-in tuner, front black control panel, single input, 10 knobs, (amp model select, drive, b, m, t, Channel v, two smart control FX buttons, r, MV), headphone/direct out jack, optional footswitch, black covering, black grille, mfg. 2004-08.

	$300	$175 - 225	$110 - 140	$420

SPIDER II 120 210/SPIDER III 120 210 – 120W, 2-10 in. speakers, guitar combo, solid-state chassis, four channels, 12 amp models, seven programmable effects, built-in tuner, front black control panel, single input, 10 knobs, (amp model select, drive, b, m, t, Channel v, two smart control FX buttons, r, MV), headphone/direct out jack, optional footswitch, black covering, black grille, mfg. 2004-08.

	$400	$250 - 300	$140 - 175	$600

MSR/NOTES	100%	EXCELLENT	AVERAGE	LAST MSR

SPIDER II 150 212/SPIDER III 150 212 – 150W, 2-12 in. speakers, guitar combo, solid-state chassis, four channels, 12 amp models, seven programmable effects, built-in tuner, front black control panel, single input, 10 knobs, (amp model select, drive, b, m, t, Channel v, two smart control FX buttons, r, MV), headphone/direct out jack, optional footswitch, black covering, black grille, mfg. 2004-08.

	$500	$300 - 375	$175 - 225	$700

SPIDER II HD 150/SPIDER III HD 150 – 150W, head-unit guitar configuration, solid-state chassis, four channels, 12 amp models, seven programmable effects, built-in tuner, front black control panel, single input, 10 knobs, (amp model select, drive, b, m, t, Channel v, two smart control FX buttons, r, MV), headphone/direct out jack, optional footswitch, black covering, black grille, mfg. 2004-08.

	$400	$250 - 300	$140 - 175	$560

ELECTRIC AMPLIFIERS: SPIDER IV SERIES

Spider IV 15
courtesy Line 6

Spider IV 30
courtesy Line 6

Spider IV 75
courtesy Line 6

SPIDER IV 15 – 15W, 1-8 in. speaker, modeling guitar combo, solid-state chassis, single channel, four amp models, six smart effects, four channels of user-created presets, built-in tuner, front black control panel, single input, eight chrome knobs (drive, b, m, t, v, flange/phaser/tremolo effects, sweep echo/tape echo/reverb effects, MV), four amp model buttons (clean, crunch, metal, insane), tuner/tap button, CD/MP3 input, headphone/recording out jack, FBV Cat5 footswitch jack, power switch, black covering, black cloth grille, 16 in. wide, 15 in. tall, 8.5 in. deep, 17 lbs., mfg. 2009-present.

MSR $200	$100	$50 - 80	$30 - 40	

SPIDER IV 30 – 30W, 1-12 in. Celestion speaker, modeling guitar combo, solid-state chassis, single channel, 12 amp models (clean, twang, blues, crunch, metal, insane), seven smart effects, four channels of user-created presets, built-in tuner, front black control panel, single input, 10 chrome knobs (amp model selector, drive, b, m, t, v, chorus flange/phaser/tremolo effects, delay/tape echo/sweep echo effects, r, MV), four user channel buttons, tuner/tap button, CD/MP3 input, headphone/recording out jack, FBV Cat5 footswitch jack, power switch, black covering, black cloth grille, 18.5 in. wide, 17.5 in. tall, 9.5 in. deep, 26 lbs., mfg. 2009-present.

MSR $330	$180	$115 - 135	$60 - 70	

SPIDER IV 75 – 75W, 1-12 in. Celestion speaker, modeling guitar combo, solid-state chassis, single channel, 16 amp models, 20 smart effects, over 300 presets selected by bands, nearly 200 song-based presets, four channels with 64 user-created presets, built-in tuner, front black control panel, single input, 11 chrome knobs (amp model selector, drive, b, m, t, Ch. v, gain/auto/pitch effects, chorus/phaser/tremolo effects, delay/tape echo/sweep echo effects, r, MV), manual button, four user channel buttons, tuner/tap button, quick loop button, digital display with selector control and directional selector, power switch, rear panel: CD/MP3 input, headphone/recording out jack, FBV Cat5 footswitch jack, black covering, black cloth grille, 20.75 in. wide, 19.25 in. tall, 11 in. deep, 36 lbs., mfg. 2009-present.

MSR $500	$270	$150 - 200	$95 - 120	

SPIDER IV 120 – 120W (60W X 2 stereo), 2-10 in. Celestion speakers, modeling guitar combo, solid-state chassis, single channel, 16 amp models, 20 smart effects, over 300 presets selected by bands, nearly 200 song-based presets, four channels with 64 user-created presets, built-in tuner, front black control panel, single input, 11 chrome knobs (amp model selector, drive, b, m, t, Ch. v, gain/auto/pitch effects, chorus/phaser/tremolo effects, delay/tape echo/sweep echo effects, r, MV), manual button, four user channel buttons, tuner/tap button, quick loop button, digital display with selector control and directional selector, power switch, rear panel: CD/MP3 input, headphone/recording out jack, FBV Cat5 footswitch jack, black covering, black cloth grille, 24 in. wide, 18.5 in. tall, 11 in. deep, 49 lbs., mfg. 2009-present.

MSR $670	$350	$225 - 275	$135 - 175	

SPIDER IV 150 – 150W (75W X 2 stereo), 2-12 in. Celestion speakers, modeling guitar combo, solid-state chassis, single channel, 16 amp models, 20 smart effects, over 300 presets selected by bands, nearly 200 song-based presets, four channels with 64 user-created presets, built-in tuner, front black control panel, single input, 11 chrome knobs (amp model selector, drive, b, m, t, Ch. v, gain/auto/pitch effects, chorus/phaser/tremolo effects, delay/tape echo/sweep echo effects, r, MV), manual button, four user channel buttons, tuner/tap button, quick loop button, digital display with selector control and directional selector, power switch, rear panel: CD/MP3 input, headphone/recording out jack, FBV Cat5 footswitch jack, black covering, black cloth grille, 27.5 in. wide, 21.5 in. tall, 11 in. deep, 54 lbs., mfg. 2009-present.

MSR $830	$450	$300 - 350	$175 - 225	

MSR/NOTES	100%	EXCELLENT	AVERAGE	LAST MSR

Spider IV 120
courtesy Line 6

Spider IV 150
courtesy Line 6

Spider Jam
courtesy Line 6

* *Spider IV 150 Head (HD 150)* – similar to the Spider IV 150, except in head-unit configuration, 27.5 in. wide, 10.75 in. tall, 11 in. deep, 30 lbs., mfg. 2009-present.

| MSR $670 | $350 | $225 - 275 | $135 - 175 | |

SPIDER 4-12 SPEAKER CABINET – 320W, 4-12 in. Celestion speakers, angled front, side-mounted recessed handles, designed for use with the Spider III 75 Head (HD 75), Spider III 150 Head (HD 150), and the Spider IV 150 Head (HD 150), black covering, black cloth grille, 27 in. wide, 28 in. tall, 11.5 in. deep, current mfg.

| MSR $420 | $300 | $150 - 200 | $95 - 120 | |

SPIDER JAM – 75W, 1-12 in. Celestion speaker, 1-2 in. tweeter, modeling guitar combo, solid-state chassis, single channel, 12 amp models, seven smart effects, over 200 artist-created presets, over 150 song-based presets, four channels with 36 user-created presets, built-in tuner, front gray control panel, single guitar input, CD/MP3 input, XLR input, 11 chrome knobs (input level, amp model selector, drive, b, m, t, Ch. v, chorus flange/phaser/tremolo effects, delay/tape echo/sweep echo effects, r, MV), headphone jack, FBV Cat5 footswitch jack, power switch, top gray control panel: record select button, drums button, inputs level button, settings tone button, digital display, record, play, and undo buttons, large selector knob, up/down/sideways selector, save button, rear panel: SD card input, POD quality direct/recording RCA jacks out, black covering, black cloth grille, mfg. 2008-present.

| MSR $830 | $375 | $240 - 280 | $120 - 150 | |

MICRO SPIDER – 6W, 1-6.5 in. speaker, modeling guitar combo, solid-state chassis, single channel, five amp models, six smart effects, five channels of user-created presets, built-in tuner, front gray control panel, single input, five chrome knobs (drive, b, m, t, Ch. v), four amp model buttons (clean, crunch, metal, insane), top/rear black control panelmic trim control, mic input, CD/MP3 input, headphone/recording out jack, chorus flange/phaser/tremolo effects control, sweep echo/tape echo/reverb effects knob, tuner/tap button, digital chromatic tuner, power switch, AC input, powered by six C batteries, black covering, black cloth grille, strap included, 9.5 in. wide, 10 in. tall, 7 in. deep, 7 lbs., mfg. 2009-present.

| MSR $250 | $135 | $75 - 100 | $45 - 60 | |

ELECTRIC AMPLIFIERS: SPIDER VALVE SERIES

The Spider Valve Series combines Line 6's modeling technology with a tube amplifier designed by Reinhold Bogner of Bogner Amplifiers.

SPIDER VALVE 112 MKII – 40W, 1-12 in. Celestion Vintage 30 speaker, tube modeling guitar combo, Class AB four-tube chassis, preamp: 2 X 12AX7, power: 2 X 6L6, single channel, 16 amp models, 20 smart effects, 128 user presets, quick loop, front black control panel, single input, 11 black knobs (amp model selector, drive, b, m, t, Ch. v, chorus flange/phaser/tremolo effects, delay/tape echo/sweep echo, r, MV, display knob), four channel select buttons, tap/tuner button, digital display with up/down/sideways selector, standby switch power switch, rear panel: MIDI in/out, FBV footswitch jack, XLR out, two 1/4 in. speaker out jacks, 1/4 in. preamp out, 1/4 in. power amp in, tuned three-quarter closed back cabinet, black covering, black cloth grille with "Line 6" and "Tube Amp Design By Bogner" logos, 22.5 in. wide, 22 in. tall, 11.25 in. deep, 45 lbs., mfg. 2009-disc.

| | $750 | $475 - 550 | $275 - 325 | $1,190 |

SPIDER VALVE 212 MKII – 40W, 2-12 in. Celestion Vintage 30 speakers, tube modeling guitar combo, Class AB four-tube chassis, preamp: 2 X 12AX7, power: 2 X 6L6, single channel, 16 amp models, 20 smart effects, 128 user presets, quick loop, front black control panel, single input, 11 black knobs (amp model selector, drive, b, m, t, Ch. v, chorus flange/phaser/tremolo effects, delay/tape echo/sweep echo, r, MV, display knob), four channel select buttons, tap/tuner button, digital display with up/down/sideways selector, standby switch power switch, rear panel: MIDI in/out, FBV footswitch jack, XLR out, two 1/4 in. speaker out jacks, 1/4 in. preamp out, 1/4 in. power amp in, tuned three-quarter closed back cabinet, black covering, black cloth grille with "Line 6" and "Tube Amp Design By Bogner" logos, 26.75 in. wide, 21.75 in. tall, 11.25 in. deep, 60 lbs., mfg. 2009-disc.

| | $900 | $550 - 650 | $325 - 400 | $1,400 |

SPIDER VALVE HEAD HD 100 MKII – 100W, tube modeling guitar head, Class AB six-tube chassis, preamp: 2 X 12AX7, power: 4 X 6L6, single channel, 16 amp models, 20 smart effects, 128 user presets, quick loop, front black control panel, single input, 11 black knobs (amp model selector, drive, b, m, t, Ch. v, chorus flange/phaser/tremolo effects, delay/tape echo/sweep echo, r, MV, display knob), four channel

MSR/NOTES	100%	EXCELLENT	AVERAGE	LAST MSR

Spider Valve 112 MKII
courtesy Line 6

Spider Valve 212 MKII
courtesy Line 6

Spider Valve Head HD 100 MKII
courtesy Line 6

select buttons, tap/tuner button, digital display with up/down/sideways selector, standby switch power switch, rear panel: MIDI in/out, FBV footswitch jack, XLR out, two 1/4 in. speaker out jacks, 1/4 in. preamp out, 1/4 in. power amp in, tuned three-quarter closed back cabinet, black covering, black cloth grille with "Line 6" and "Tube Amp Design By Bogner" logos, 25.75 in. wide, 10.75 in. tall, 9.5 in. deep, 35 lbs., mfg. 2009-disc.

	$900	$550 - 650	$325 - 400	$1,330

SPIDER VALVE 4-12 VS SPEAKER CABINET – 240W @ 16 or 4 ohms mono (120W @ 8 oms stereo), 4-12 in. Celestion Vintage 30 speakers, straight or slanted front, designed for use with the Spider Valve HD 100 Head, HD 147 Head, and the Vetta II Head, recessed side handles, black covering, black cloth grille with Line 6 logo, 29 in. wide, 30 in. tall, 15 in. tall, 83 lbs., current mfg.

MSR $970	$700	$425 - 500	$250 - 300	

ELECTRIC AMPLIFIERS: VETTA SERIES

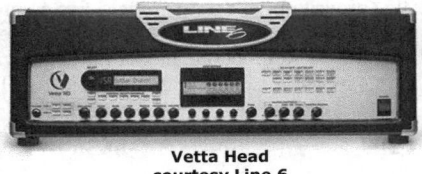

Vetta Head
courtesy Line 6

Vetta II Head
courtesy Line 6

Vetta II Combo
courtesy Line 6

VETTA HEAD – 200W, head-unit only, modeling amp, amp, effect, and cabinet models, front silver control panel, single input, 12 black knobs, various other buttons, black covering, 40 lbs., mfg. summer 2001-04.

	N/A	$850 - 1,000	$550 - 650	$2,400

VETTA COMBO – 100W, 2-12 in. Custom Celestion speakers, modeling amp, amp, effect, and cabinet models, front silver control panel, single input, 12 black knobs, various other buttons, brown/red, reddish grille cloth, covering, 65 lbs., mfg. summer 2001-04.

	N/A	$1,000 - 1,200	$675 - 800	$2,400

VETTA II HEAD – 300W, head-unit guitar configuration, 74 amp models, over 100 effects, 128 programmable channels, front black control panel, single input, 17 knobs, approx. 30 various buttons, two full digital screen readouts, black covering, 40 lbs., mfg. 2003-disc.

$1,700	$1,100 - 1,300	$950 - 1,050	$2,400

VETTA II COMBO – 300W, 2-12 in. speakers, 74 amp models, over 100 effects, 128 programmable channels, front black control panel, single input, 17 knobs, approx. 30 various buttons, two full digital screen readouts, black covering, 65 lbs., mfg. 2003-disc.

$1,700	$1,100 - 1,300	$950 - 1,050	$2,400

VETTA 212 SPEAKER CABINET – 150W, 2-12 in. Celestion speakers, 4 ohm mono or 8 ohm stereo impedance, designed for use with the Vetta Combo, black covering, black cloth grille, 29 in. wide, 20 in. tall, 10.125 in. deep, 50 lbs., disc. 2008.

$400	$250 - 300	$135 - 175	$600

BASS AMPLIFIERS: LOWDOWN SERIES

LOWDOWN HD400 HEAD – 400W, three-space rack-mount modeling bass head unit, solid-state chassis, single channel, five amp models (Clean, R&B, Rock, Brit, and Grind), five effects (Compressor, Envelope Filter, Octaver, Chorus, Synth, four programmable channels, front brushed chrome control panel with two chrome handles, two inputs (passive, active), 10 chrome knobs (amp model selector, drive, b, lo-mid, hi-mid, t, Ch. v, compressor, filter/octave/chorus effects, MV), deep switch, four channel memory buttons, tuner switch, rear panel: power switch, FBV Cat5 footswitch jack, headphone jack, XLR direct out, preamp out, two Speakon jacks, black casing, mfg. 2009-disc.

$400	$275 - 325	$150 - 200	$830

MSR/NOTES	100%	EXCELLENT	AVERAGE	LAST MSR

Lowdown HD400 Head
courtesy Line 6

Lowdown HD750 Head
courtesy Line 6

Lowdown LD150
courtesy Line 6

Lowdown LD400 Pro
courtesy Line 6

LOWDOWN HD750 HEAD – 750W @ 4 ohms (375W @ 8 ohms), three-space rack-mount modeling bass head unit, solid-state chassis, single channel, five amp models (Clean, R&B, Rock, Brit, and Grind), five effects (Compressor, Envelope Filter, Octaver, Chorus, Synth, four programmable channels, front brushed chrome control panel with two chrome handles, two inputs (passive, active), 10 chrome knobs (amp model selector, drive, b, lo-mid, hi-mid, t, Ch. v, compressor, filter/octave/chorus effects, MV), deep switch, four channel memory buttons, tuner switch, rear panel: power switch, FBV Cat5 footswitch jack, headphone jack, XLR direct out, preamp out, two Speakon jacks, black casing, mfg. 2009-disc.

$500	$300 - 375	$175 - 225	$1,200

LOWDOWN LD15 – 15W, 1-8 in. speaker, bass modeling combo, solid-state chassis, single channel, four amp models (Clean, R&B, Rock, Grind), four essential bass effects (Envelope Filter, Octaver, Chorus, Compressor), front black control panel, single input, eight chrome knobs (drive, b, l/m, h/m, t, opto compressor, Smart FX selector, MV), four amp model buttons, headphone jack, CD/MP3 input, black covering, black metal grille, 16 in. wide, 20 in. tall, 10 in. deep, mfg. 2009-disc.

$180	$100 - 130	$60 - 80	$252

LOWDOWN LD150 – 150W, 1-12 in. speaker bass combo, solid-state chassis, single channel, five programmable amp models, five essential bass effects, front black control panel, two inputs (passive/active), 10 chrome knobs (amp model selector, drive, b, l/m, h/m, t, v, opto compressor, Smart FX selector, MV), four channel memories, deep switch, headphone jack, preamp out, XLR direct out, aux. input, footswitch jack, chromatic tuner, bottom ported cabinet, tilt-back cabinet design, black covering, black grille, 17.5 in. wide, 21.5 in. tall, 16 in. deep, 48 lbs., mfg. 2006-disc.

$450	$275 - 325	$150 - 200	$630

LOWDOWN LD175 – 175W, 1-15 in. speaker bass combo, solid-state chassis, single channel, five programmable amp models, five essential bass effects, front black control panel, two inputs (passive/active), 10 chrome knobs (amp model selector, drive, b, l/m, h/m, t, v, opto compressor, Smart FX selector, MV), four channel memories, deep switch, headphone jack, preamp out, XLR direct out, aux. input, footswitch jack, chromatic tuner, bottom ported cabinet, side handles, black covering, black grille, 22 in. wide, 30 in. tall, 18 in. deep, 86 lbs., mfg. 2006-disc.

$500	$300 - 375	$175 - 225	$700

LOWDOWN LD300 PRO – 300W, 1-15 in. speaker bass combo with a horn, solid-state chassis, single channel, five programmable amp models, five essential bass effects, front black control panel, two inputs (passive/active), 10 chrome knobs (amp model selector, drive, b, l/m, h/m, t, v, opto compressor, Smart FX selector, MV), four channel memories, deep switch, headphone jack, preamp out, XLR direct out, aux. input, footswitch jack, chromatic tuner, bottom ported cabinet, side handles, black covering, black grille, 22 in. wide, 30 in. tall, 18 in. deep, 89 lbs., mfg. 2006-disc.

$500	$300 - 375	$175 - 225	$840

LOWDOWN LD400 PRO – 400W, 2-10 in. speakers, high-freq. compression driver, modeling bass combo, solid-state chassis, single channel, five amp models (Clean, R&B, Rock, Brit, and Grind), five essential bass effects (Compressor, Envelope Filter, Octaver, Chorus, Synth), four programmable user channels, front black control panel, two inputs (passive/active), 10 chrome knobs (amp model selector, drive, b, l/m, h/m, t, v, opto compressor, Smart FX selector, MV), four channel memories, deep switch, headphone jack, preamp out, XLR direct out, aux. input, footswitch jack, chromatic tuner, bottom ported cabinet, side handles, black covering, black grille, mfg. 2009-disc.

$600	$375 - 450	$225 - 275	$1,200

LOWDOWN STUDIO 110 – 75W, 1-10 in. speaker bass combo, solid-state chassis, single channel, top black control panel, seven chrome knobs, four programmable amp models, headphone jack, preamp out, XLR direct out, aux. input, black covering, black grille, 12 in. wide, 12 in. tall, 12 in. deep, 24 lbs., mfg. 2006-disc.

$300	$140 - 180	$80 - 110	$420

LOWDOWN 4-10 SPEAKER CABINET – 600W, 4-10 in. Eminence speakers, high-freq. compression driver horn, 8 ohm impedance, horn volume control, spring-loaded side handles, removable casters, black carpet covering, black metal grille, 29 in. wide, 28 in. tall, 19 in. deep, 68 lbs., mfg. 2009-disc.

$700	$425 - 500	$250 - 300	$980

LITTLE LANILEI 495 L

MSR/NOTES	100%	EXCELLENT	AVERAGE	LAST MSR

LITTLE LANILEI

Amplifiers currently produced in San Juan Capistrano, CA since 1997. Distributed by Mahaffay Amplifiers in San Juan Capistrano, CA.

Tris Mahaffay founded Songworks Systems and Products in 1990 as a home-based business to design and test amps and other electric products Mahaffay wanted to sell. In 1994, Tris and his friend Mike first walked the NAMM show to see what the market wanted and what they came up with was a small tube amp. In 1997, the first Little Lanilei amps (a Hawaiian name coined from Hawaiian shirts) debuted at the NAMM show. The grille is illustrated with a Hawaiian graphic design that really sticks out. The **Model 3350LT** (MSR $449) is the flagship of the company with 33W/50W output, 1-6.5 in. speaker, and a tube preamp all in a tiny combo. A clean version of the 3350LT is also offered called the **Super 50**. Lanilei also produces a 1/4 watt amp (MSR $369), reverb pedal, and rotating speaker cabinet called the **Rotary Wave** (MSR $399). In the late 2000s, Songworks Systems & Products became Mahaffay Amplifiers. For more information, visit Mahaffay Amplifiers' website or contact them directly.

CONTACT INFORMATION
LITTLE LANILEI
Mahaffay Amplifiers
26895 Aliso Creek Rd.
Suite 640
Aliso Viejo, CA 92656
Phone No.: 949-582-7720
Fax No.: 949-582-7720
www.mahaffayamps.com
info@mahaffayamps.com

LOCO

Amplifiers previously produced in Japan during the late 1970s and early 1980s.

Loco Amplifiers were produced in Japan and have appeared at least in a 1981 Loco catalog. These amps are budget/entry-level models known as the Micro Amp Series. Almost all models feature basic functions and come in a variety of configurations. Known examples include the **Model 4102**, **Model 2201**, **Model 4251**, **MX-60**, **MX-100**, **MX-100R**, **MXB-120** Bass, **Model 6000B** Bass, **Model 6162B** Bass, **Model 3301B** Bass, **Model 4381B** Bass, **Model 0251** speaker cabinet, and **Model 0381B** bass speaker cabinet. Used prices range between $25 and $150 depending upon configuration and condition. Very little other information is known. Any further information on Loco can be submitted directly to Blue Book Publications.

LONE WOLF AMPLIFICATION

Amplifiers previously produced starting in 2005.

Lone Wolf Amplification built their amplifiers to have killer tone regardless of the cost. All amplifiers were individually hand-built for the customer. They offered their Outlaw 18 amp was available as a head unit (MSR $2,195) or a combo (MSR $2,495). A 2-12 inch speaker cabinet was also available ($850).

LOUIS ELECTRIC AMPLIFIERS

Amplifiers currently produced in Bergenfield, NJ since 1993. Distributed by Louis Electric Amplifiers.

Louis Rosano started building Tweed Twin amps in 1992. Since then he has expanded to produce a full line of amplifiers based on classic designs by Fender and Marshall. Louis produces many of their own parts including hand-built speakers with a wood pulp fiber for the voice coil, hand-wound transformers, and pine cabinets. All-tube chassis are built and Louis features a variety of models with varying configurations. For more information, visit Louis' website or contact them directly.

CONTACT INFORMATION
LOUIS ELECTRIC AMPLIFIERS
260 Merritt Ave.
Bergenfield, NJ 07621
Phone No.: 908-276-1244
www.louiselectricamps.com
jim@louiselectricamps.com

L.R. BAGGS

Amplifiers currently produced in China since 2007. L.R. Baggs has been producing acoustic preamps, pickups, and other related accessories since 1975. Distributed by L.R. Baggs in Nipomo, CA.

Lloyd Baggs started out refinishing and refurbishing old Gibson and Washburn guitars in the early 1970s. In 1975, Baggs started the L.R. Baggs company to produce acoustic guitar pickups and electronics. The LB6 Series pickup was Baggs' first product that was also patented along with four other products. Today several large manufacturers including Gibson, Tacoma, Breedlove, and Larrivee use L.R. Baggs products in their instruments. In 2007, L.R. Baggs introduced their first stand alone guitar amplifier called the Core 1, which was later renamed the Acoustic Reference Amplifier. This amp was built after three years of research and has many unique features not found in any other product. For more information, visit L.R. Baggs' website or contact them directly.

CONTACT INFORMATION
L.R. BAGGS
483 N. Frontage Rd.
Nipomo, CA 93444
Phone No.: 805-929-3545
Fax No.: 805-929-2043
www.lrbaggs.com

ACOUSTIC AMPLIFIERS

ACOUSTIC REFERENCE AMPLIFIER – 200W, 1-8 in. custom honeycomb-diaphragm speaker that provides 140 degrees wide sound, solid-state chassis, two channels, reverb, top brown control panel, two inputs (one per channel with each one compatible with an XLR or regular 1/4 in. jack), 16 brown and white knobs (Ch. 1: g, notch, b, l/m, h/m, t, r, Ch. 2: g, notch, b, l/m, h/m, t, r, All: MV), two input voltage switches, two phase switches, two analog input meter gauges, mute switch with gain control, effects loop, unique curved cabinet design, two-tone wood (early models) or flamed maple (later models) panel sides, cream (early models) or bronze (later models) horizontal bar across the top, brown (early models) or black (later models) metal grille, 18 in. wide, 18 in. tall, 12 in. wide, 28 lbs., mfg. 2007-present.

MSR $1,599	$1,200	$700 - 850	$450 - 525

This model was initially called the Core 1.

NOTES

M SECTION
MACK AMPS

Amplifiers currently produced in Peachland, British Columbia, Canada. Previously produced in Toronto, Ontario, Canada.

Don Mackrill founded Mack Amps in 2005 because he wanted to offer a boutique amplifier to those who couldn't afford one. In 2005, Mackrill set out to design a simple, high-quality amp with boutique tone that could still be sold at a reasonable price. After a year of design work and prototyping, Mack Amps was incorporated in 2006 when they released their first amp called the Heatseeker HS-18. In 2007, Mack introduced the Heatseeker HS-36 and Skyraider, and in 2009, they introduced the Gem. Mackrill originally constructed every part of his amplifiers himself, but he now outsources the cabinets and chassis. However, Mackrill personally mounts every chassis into its cabinet and tests every amp before shipping it. Mack amps start at $449 for the GEM and $749 for the Heatseeker HS-18. Speaker cabinets are also available. For more information, visit Mack's website or contact Mackrill directly.

MADISON

Amplifiers and speaker cabinets previously produced in Loveland, CO between 2000 and 2010.

Madison was founded by Andy Hitch in 2000, and was named after his daughter that was born the same year. Madison started out producing speakers and eventually moved on to building amplifiers as well including guitar and bass amps, speaker cabinets, and raw speakers. Madison was built on the philosophy to build the best speakers and amps and are the best of everything. Madison also distributed the Legion Sound budget brand. In 2010, Madison closed its doors; however, Madison will continue to support their products and offer tech support.

ELECTRIC AMPLIFIERS/SPEAKER CABS

The **Divinity** (last MSR was $1,299) head amp features 100W, an all-tube chassis with 2 X 12AX7 and 2 X 12AT7 for preamp and 4 X EL34 for power, three independent channels, reverb, and an effects loop. Matching 412 straight and slant cabinets are also available (last MSR was $799-$1,149). The **Divinity 12 Combo** (disc. 2006, last MSR was $939) is the same as the Divinity head, except has 60W power from 2 X EL34 power tubes and is in combo configuration with 1-12 in. speaker. The **Omen** (disc., last MSR was $1,599) was introduced in 2007, and is an expansion of the Divinity with three channels and more controls. The **E-600** (disc. 2006, last MSR was $989) is a 600W hybrid bass amp with a 12AX7 preamp and solid-state power amp. The **Abraxas** (disc., last MSR was $1,799) bass head was introduced in 2007, and it is a hybrid bass amp with 1200W output! Several speaker cabinets are available for bass amps. Madison also offered PA speaker cabinets.

Divinity
courtesy Madison

Divinity 12 Combo
courtesy Madison

E600 Bass
courtesy Madison

MAD PROFESSOR AMPLIFICATION

Amplifiers currently produced in Tampere, Finland since 2002. Distributed in the U.S. by Musical Distribution Group in Riverdale, NJ. Previously distributed by MG Audio Sales.

Bjorn Juhl and Jukka Mönkkönen founded Mad Professor Amplification in 2002. They produce premium tube guitar amplifiers as well as a line of effects pedals. The **CS-40** was Mad Professor's first amplifier design and they have also introduced the **MP-101** and **MP-21 Old School** amps as well. All products are hand-built and constructed with only quality components. For more information, visit Mad Professor's website or contact them directly.

MAESTRO

Amplifiers previously produced in Kalamazoo, MI from 1955 to 1967. Distributed by Gibson.

Maestro was used by Gibson on their accordion amplifiers in the late 1950s and 1960s. Although they are listed as separate brands, there are many similarities between the two. They were listed in the same catalog, numbered the same as Gibson amps, and entered in the Gibson shipping ledger with all other Gibson amps. Gibson designated Maestro amps as accordion models, but most models had inputs for guitars anyway. When amp production moved out of Kalamazoo in 1967, Maestro production was discontinued. However, Maestro has appeared on other models in the 1970s. For information on Gibson amplifiers, see Gibson. Information courtsey George Gruhn and Walter Carter, *Gruhn's Guide to Vintage Guitars*.

ELECTRIC TUBE AMPLIFIERS

GA-1RT/GA-1RVT (MAESTRO) REVERB-ECHO – 8W, 1-8 in. speaker, three tube chassis, preamp: 1 X 12AX7, power: 1 X 6BM8, rectifier: 5Y3, single channel, tremolo, reverb, top mounted nickel control panel, two instrument inputs, two or three black chicken head knobs (v, s, r), tweed covering, brown grille, 2,183 shipped, mfg. 1961 only.

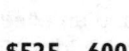
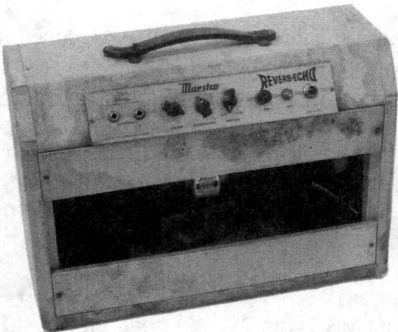

courtesy David Chandler/R&R Guitars   *courtesy David Chandler/R&R Guitars*

N/A	$525 - 600	$325 - 400

There were two variations of this amp as the GA-1RVT and the regular GA-1. Specs are unknown on these models, but the GA-1RVT has two knobs where the GA-1RT has three knobs. Both models were advertised with reverb, but the RVT is the only one that has a control for reverb.

GA-2RT (MAESTRO) DELUXE REVERB-ECHO – 16W, 1-12 in. Jensen speaker, eight tube chassis, preamp: 4 X 6EU7, 1 X 12AU7, power: 2 X 6V6, rectifier: 5Y3, two channels, top mounted nickel control panel, four inputs (two per channel), five black and silver knobs (v1, v2, tone, r, one dual purpose s, depth for tremolo), tweed covering, brown grille, 20 in. wide, 16 in. tall, 396 shipped, mfg. 1961 only.

N/A	$850 - 1,000	$600 - 700

GA-15RV (MAESTRO) – 14-16W output, 1-12 in. Jensen speaker, seven tube chassis, preamp: 3 X 6EU7, 1 X 12AU7, power: 2 X 6V6, rectifier: 5Y3, two channels, reverb, top chrome control panel, four inputs (two per channel), five black and silver knobs (v1, v2, t, b, r), dark covering, light grille, 135 shipped, mfg. 1961 only.

N/A	$725 - 850	$475 - 550

GA-16T VISCOUNT (MAESTRO) – 14W, 1-10 in. speaker, 5 tubes, preamp:2 X 12AX7, power: 2 X 6V6, 5Y3 rectifier, single channel, tremolo, top chrome control panel, three inputs, four black chicken head knobs (v, tone, depth, freq.), tweed covering, dark slanted grille cloth, mfg. 1959-1961.

N/A	$600 - 700	$375 - 450

GA-45T SATURN (MAESTRO STANDARD) – 14W, 4-8 in. Jensen speakers, designed for accordions, seven tube chassis: preamp: 2 X 5879, 1 X 6SQ7, 1 X 12AX7, power: 2 X 6V6, rectifier: 5Y3, two channels, tremolo, top control panel, four inputs (two per channel), six black knobs (v1, v2, b, t, trem depth, freq), two-tone gray covering, brown grille, 22 in. wide, 20 in. tall, 10.125 in. deep, 34 lbs., 2,161 shipped, mfg. 1955-1961.

courtesy Big Jim's Guitars   *courtesy Big Jim's Guitars*

N/A	$850 - 1,000	$600 - 700

In 1958, the output was increased to 16W, a new style was introduced with a two-tone deluxe ebony sharkskin/light patterned

MSR/NOTES	100%	EXCELLENT	AVERAGE	LAST MSR

tweed covering, and only "Maestro" logo above grille. In 1960, tweed covering was introduced with a dark brown grille with "Maestro" logo in upper right corner. This model is very similar to the GA-40, but it has separate treble and bass controls and a different speaker configuration.

* ***GA-45RV Saturn (Maestro)*** – similar to the GA-45T except has reverb instead of tremolo, 106 shipped, mfg. 1961 only.

| | N/A | $1,050 - 1,300 | $725 - 850 | |

GA-46 SUPER MAESTRO – 60W, 2-12 in. speakers, accordion combo, ten tube chassis, preamp: 3 X 7025, 2 X 5879, 1 X 6SN7, 1 X 6V6, power: 2 X 6550, rectifier: 5AR4, two channels, tremolo, top/rear control panel, four inputs (two per channel), eight black knobs (Ch. 1: v, b, t, s, depth, Ch. 2: v, b, t), chickenhead power knob, external speaker jack, included Gada-Kart four-wheel dolly, two tone dark gray/light tweed style, light brown grille with "Maestro Super" logo, metal handle with plastic middle, 20 in. wide, 20 in. tall, 10.5 in. deep, 62 lbs., 53 shipped, mfg. 1957-1961.

| | N/A | $1,600 - 2,000 | $1,050 - 1,300 | |

In 1960, a tweed covering was introduced, the Gada-Kart was no longer offered, and the handles were moved to the side.

GA-78 MAESTRO 30 – 30W (2 X 15W Stereo), 2-10 in. speakers, eight tube chassis, preamp: 4 X 6EU7, power: 4 X 6BQ5, two channels, top silver control panel, five inputs (four mono, one stereo), six black and silver knobs (Ch. 1: v, b, t, Ch. 2: v, b, t), stereo-mono switch, charcoal grey casing, brown grille, cabinet is set up so speakers face away from each other, 25.75 in. wide in back, 11 in. wide in front, 18.75 in. tall, 10.5 in. deep, 139 shipped, mfg. 1960-61.

| | N/A | $1,600 - 2,000 | $1,050 - 1,300 | |

* ***GA-78RV Maestro 30 Reverb*** – similar to the GA-78, except has a reverb circuit, nine-tube chassis, preamp: 3 X 6EU7, 1 X 7199, 1 X 12AU7, power: 4 X 6BQ5, reverb control for a total of seven knobs, 105 shipped, mfg. 1961 only.

| | N/A | $1,750 - 2,250 | $1,100 - 1,400 | |

* ***GA-78RVT Maestro 30 Reverb Tremolo*** – similar to the GA-78, except has a reverb and tremolo circuit, tube chassis unknown, 4 shipped, mfg. 1961 & 63 only.

| | N/A | $2,000 - 2,500 | $1,200 - 1,500 | |

GA-87 MAESTRO STEREO-ACCORDION – 35W, 2-12 in. speakers, eight tube chassis, preamp: 3 X 12AX7, power: 4 X 6BQ5, rectifier: GZ34, two channels, four inputs, seven knobs, tweed covering, brown grille with "Maestro Stereo" logo, metal handle with plastic middle, 22.75 in. wide, 22 in. tall, 13 in. deep, 13 shipped, mfg. 1960-61.

| | N/A | $1,750 - 2,250 | $1,100 - 1,400 | |

MAGNATONE

Amplifiers previously built in California between the 1940s and 1960s.

Magnatone was originally founded as the Dickerson Brothers in Los Angeles, California circa 1937. The company began building phonographs, lap steels, and amplifiers. In 1947, the company changed its name to Magna Electronics. They produced many amplifiers, but wanted a guitar to accompany it. In the early 1950s, they jumped on the bandwagon and began producing electric Spanish hollow-body guitars, which were designed by Paul Bigsby. In 1959, Magna merged forces with Estey Electronics. In 1966, Magnatone moved to Pennsylvania from Torrance. Magnatone continued to produce amplifiers in California during the 1950s and 1960s until Magnatone was bought out by a toy company in 1971.

ELECTRIC TUBE AMPLIFIERS

Magnatone produced many amplifiers during their existence. Information on every model is sketchy in parts. The model listings, typically, are three digit numbers. Amplifiers began being produced around 1937 when the Dickerson amplifiers were introduced with the **Student**, **Standard**, and **Semi De Luxe** models. These are probably the rarest of the Magnatone amplifiers and are hard to put a price on since there is little secondary market on them.

Models weren't typically numbered until circa 1951. Models up until this point were also named Oahu, Silver Grey, and the Gourley along with Magnatone. Around 1952, the models became all Magnatone brand with model numbers. It is estimated that Magnatone produced at least 35 different amplifiers during the 1950s, and probably more.

MODEL 280 (CUSTOM) – 50W, 2-12 in. speakers with 2-5 in. tweeters, tube chassis, preamp: 12AX7s, 6CG7s, 12HB7, power: 4 X 6973, two channels, stereo/vibrato, top black and white control panel, four inputs (two per channel), 11 knobs (Ch. 1: v, t, b, Ch. 2: v, t, b, remote, s, i, vibrato, speaker control), remote speaker jacks, bs, footswitch, brown covering, brown grille with two small "Vs" in lower right hand corner, mfg. 1957-early 1960s.

| | N/A | $1,000 - 1,250 | $675 - 800 | |

In the late 1950s, the Model 280 was replaced with the Model 280A, which introduced a mellow switch and an extra bright switch. The logo bar was also changed to be an overhang over the grille.

courtesy Willie's American Guitars

MSR/NOTES	100%	EXCELLENT	AVERAGE	LAST MSR

MODEL 111 STUDENT – 2.5W, 1-8 in. speaker, tube chassis, preamp: 12AX7, power: 50C5, single channel, rear brown control panel, two inputs, two white knobs (v, tone), brown covering, brown grille, mfg. 1955-59.

courtesy Barry Clark

courtesy Barry Clark

N/A $275 - 325 $150 - 200

MODEL M7 – 38W, 1-15 in. speaker & 3 in. midrange speaker, tube chassis, preamp: 7025, 12AU7, power: 2 X 7189A, single channel, top silver control panel, two inputs, three knobs (v, b, t), black covering, brown grille, mfg. 1964-66.

courtesy John Beeson/The Music Shoppe

courtesy John Beeson/The Music Shoppe

N/A $475 - 550 $275 - 325

MODEL M197-3-V VARSITY – 10W, 1-8 in. speaker, tube chassis, preamp: 6SJ7, power: 6V6, 5Y3 rectifier, single channel, rear control panel mounted on the bottom, two inputs, single volume control, brown or other covering, brown or other color grille with three separate panels, mfg. 1947-mid 1950s.

courtesy Shake Rag

courtesy Shake Rag

N/A $300 - 350 $175 - 225

• Add 25%-50% for custom coverings such as the "Mother of Toilet Seat."

This amp came in many variations with all of them having the same chassis. Some grilles were an ordinary square and some had two semi-circle bars splitting the grille into three pieces. Another variation is the Lelani model, which features a Hawaii style grille cloth and was teamed up with the Magnatone Lap Steel.

MODEL MP-1 – 27W, 1-12 in. speaker, tube chassis, preamp: 12AX7s, 12AU7s, power: 2 X 7189A, two channels, front silver control panel, four inputs, 11 knobs, black covering, light gray/tan grille, mfg. 1966-67.

N/A $425 - 500 $250 - 300

courtesy Shake Rag

MSR/NOTES	100%	EXCELLENT	AVERAGE	LAST MSR

MAKO

Amplifiers previously produced in Asia during the late 1980s. Distributed by Kaman Music in Bloomfield, CT.

Mako amps were imported and distributed by Kaman Music during the late 1980s. Mako amps are small, solid-state practice models with Fender Blackface cosmetic features. Known models include the **10 Piranha**, **15R**, **25**, **40**, and **50B** Bass. KMD and Mako were distributed about the same time by Kaman with Mako amps representing the lower-end models and KMD the mid- to higher end models. Used prices on these models are typically between $25 and $100.

MANN

Amplifiers previously produced in the early 1970s.

Mann amplifiers were produced in either the U.S. or Canada during the early 1970s and distributed by Great West Imports Ltd. in Canada. These amps feature tube chassis and are available in head and speaker cabinet configuration only. Amps came in a 35W lead (**BN001**), 50W lead (**BN002**), 50W bass (**BN003B**), and various other PA units. Any further information on MANN can be submitted directly to Blue Book Publications.

MARK BASS AMPLIFIERS

Amplifiers currently produced in San Giovanni Teatino, Italy since 2001.

Marco De Virgiliis founded Mark Bass Amplifiers in 2001. They build amplifiers with the concept of producing a high-quality bass amp that could meet the needs of professional bass players everywhere. Some features that make these amps stand out are they are lightweight, can handle low frequencies, and have a wide variety of speaker configurations. For more information visit Mark Bass' website or contact them directly.

CONTACT INFORMATION
MARK BASS AMPLIFIERS
Via Po, 52 San Giovanni
Teatino, 66020 Italy
Phone No.: 39 085-44-65-705
Fax No.: 39 085-44-07-399
www.markbass.it
info@markbass.it

BASS AMPLIFIERS

Mark Bass produces a wide variety of bass heads, combos, and speaker cabinets. The Combo series are numbered to their speaker configuration and feature the Little Mark amplifier. These combos come in 121 (1-12 in. speaker), 102 (2-10 in. speakers), 151 (1-15 in. speaker), the Traveler 102 (2-10 in. speakers vertically stacked), and the Mini Combo 121 (1-12 in. speaker in a small cabinet). Head units are available as the Little Mark (450W), Basic P501 (500W), Club S450 (500W), and the T-902 (1000W, 500W in stereo). Speaker cabinets are numbered like the combos and are available in the Traveler/Club or Standard Series.

MARLBORO SOUND WORKS/MARLBORO AMPLIFICATION

Amplifiers previously produced in Asia between the late 1970s and 1980s. Distributed by Musical Instrument Corporation in Syosset, NY.

Marlboro was imported and distributed by the Musical Instrument Corporation of America during the late 1970s and 1980s. The Marlboro line features a vast range of solid-state in various configurations for guitar and bass applications. By the early 1980s, the company was called strictly Marlboro Amplification and a new line of amps was introduced.

ELECTRIC SS AMPLIFIERS

Most Marlboro amplifiers can be found priced between $25 and $150 depending upon configuration and condition.

20A COMBO – 10W, 1-8 in. speaker, solid-state chassis, single channel, front control panel, two inputs, three knobs (v, b, t), black covering, dark grille, mfg. early 1980s.

	N/A	$20 - 30	$10 - 15	

30A COMBO – 10W, 1-8 in. speaker, solid-state chassis, single channel, reverb, front control panel, two inputs, four knobs (v, b, t, r), black covering, dark grille, mfg. early 1980s.

	N/A	$25 - 40	$10 - 20	

MARSHALL

Amplifiers currently produced in Milton Keynes, England, China, India, and Korea. Marshall is distributed in the U.S. by Marshall Amplification USA. The Marshall trademark was established circa 1962 in Hanwell, England.

CONTACT INFORMATION
MARSHALL
Marshall England
Denbigh Road Bletchley
Milton Keyes, MK1 1DQ England
www.marshallamps.com

Jim Marshall was born on July 29, 1923 in Kensington, England. Jim suffered tuberculosis of the bones, and spent most of his school years in a plaster cast up to his arms. He was only in school for three months and left at the age of 13 1/2. From here he started a variety of jobs, including working for his dad at a fish and chip shop, a scrap metal yard, a builder's merchant, a bakery, and was a salesman. Because of tuberculosis, he wasn't able to go into the forces for World War II. Instead he went to work at Cramic Engineering. He was able to explore his interest in engineering and electronics and used this engineering experience by working at Heston Aircraft in Middlesex as a tool maker in the late '40s.

Jim's interest in music started when he was 14, when he learned how to tap dance. Originally, Jim was a drummer and played in a band around 1942. In 1946, he started to take lessons to sharpen up his skills. By 1949, he felt he had learned enough and he started teaching drums to people including Mitch Mitchell of Jimi Hendrix fame. By 1960, Jim had made enough money to start his own business called Marshall's Music. Initially, Jim's shop was just for drums/drummers, but shortly thereafter Jim started to stock guitars and amps due to popularity in American instruments especially Fenders and Gibsons.

In 1960, Jim started to build bass and PA cabinets in his garage, because of the demand for a good bass amp. The first amps Jim built were 25W amps with either a 12 in., 15 in. or 18 in. speaker. Since Marshall's Music was buying other amplifiers and selling them, Ken Bran, the new service engineer, suggested that they start building their own amplifiers. Jim and Ken looked at Fenders since they were their favorites, and were going to try to make them better. The first Marshall amp was a 2-12 in. 50W lead. Speakers kept blowing on these first models, so they decided to add more speakers. This lead to the 4-12 in. cabinet, which became an industry standard.

Once these amps became available, orders began to pour in. By 1964 Marshall Amplifiers had expanded three times! The Marshall Amplifier factory in Hayes was 6,000 square feet with 16 people making 20 amplifiers a week. In order to distribute his amps beyond England, Jim signed an exclusive world-wide distribution agreement with Rose-Morris in 1965, which was to last for 15 years. Jim had been distributing to his friend Johnny Jones for some time, but this was lost after the exclusive contract with Rose-Morris. Jim then introduced Park, a new line of amplifiers, for Johnny to distribute. This led to a number of amps being built with different names (but the same Marshall chassis) during the late 1960s and early 1970s (see Park, Narb, Kitchen Marshall, CMI). In 1966, the factory was moved to Milton Keynes, England.

By the mid- to late 1960s, The British Invasion was in full swing, and bigger amps were becoming the hottest fad. Pete Townshend was an early customer for Marshall when he requested more power for a louder sound. Jim sent Ken to built a 100W amp and an 8-12 in. speaker cabinet. Jim built both of these but Townshend's roadies complained of achy backs (8 speaker cabinets are not light). Pete suggested cutting the 8-12 in. in half. Marshall took the 8-12 in. cabinet and split it into two 4-12 in. cabinets. The head-unit was then set on top to create the infamous Marshall stack, which is one of the most famous icons in rock amplification to date.

As Jimi Hendrix, The Who, Cream, Roy Orbison, and many others started to use Marshall Amplifiers, sales went through the roof. In just a few short years, Marshall had established themeselves as king of the rock guitar amplfier. By the 1970s, Marshall was experimenting with all kinds of products including bass amps, PA cabinets, and mixer designs. In 1981, Jim ended the 15 year deal with Rose-Morris and started to distribute on his own. The early 1980s presented a tough time for Marshall, as Britain was in a recession and they had been producing essentially the same model for over 15 years. In 1981, Marshall pulled around and released the JCM-800 series, which was an entirely new design but based on the original Marshall. In 1982, they released their 20th anniversary amplifiers. In 1984, Marshall was presented with the Queen's award for export, which meant they could use the Queen's Award logo on letterheads and any advertising. In 1985, Jim was invited to put his handprints in the sidewalk of Hollywood, along with him was Les Paul, Leo Fender, and Eddie Van Halen. In 1987, Marshall celebrated 25 years in amplification and 50 years in music by releasing the Silver Jubilee Series. In 1990, Marshall announced the long-awaited JCM-900 series. In 1992, Marshall celebrated 30 years of business with the 30th Anniversary Series.

HISTORY: 1993-PRESENT

In 1993, Marshall got the contract to build the reissue of the Vox AC-30, which Marshall was in direct competition with back in the '60s! In the early 1990s Marshall introduced Valvestate, which are hybrid amplifiers (tube preamp, solid-state power section) with the Marshall sound. In 1998, Marshall released the JCM-2000 Series that included two and three channel amplifiers. In 2006, they celebrated the 40th Anniversary of the JTM45/100 head with two limited edition stacks - the 40th Anniversary and the Jimi Hendrix Signature Stack. Marshall has also produced reissue and hand-wired models that are all based on original designs from the 1960s. Currently, Marshall offers a full range of tube, hybrid, and solid-state amplifiers including guitar amps, bass amps, and acoustic amps. Marshall also produces a line of effects pedals and their famous Powerbrake. Jim Marshall continues to regularly attend NAMM shows to sign posters, shirts, and calendars. In late 2010, Marshall announced that they were parting ways with longtime U.S. distributor Korg, and were going to distribute in the U.S. by themselves as Marshall USA. Jim Marshall passed away on April 5, 2012 at the age of 88 after a battle with cancer. For more information, visit Marshall's website or contact them directly. Source for Marshall History: Michael Doyle, *The History of Marshall: The Sound of Rock*.

DATING MARSHALL AMPLIFIERS

Dating Marshall amplifiers can be challenging, but most information is available to correctly identify the date. In 1969, Marshall started using both model codes and serial numbers, which are listed here. Marshall exclusively used Celestion speakers in their amps, and if the speaker is original, it can be dated with the Celestion speaker code (see section on Celestion speaker codes). Most amps underwent cosmetic changes during the same time, so most amps can be group in a certain period of manufacture by what they look like.

October 1962-December 1964 - No recorded serialization exists and the only known information is that numbers started at 1001 and ran numerically in sequence. At the beginning of 1964 they started with 2001. The serial numbers are stamped in the back panel of the chassis, with an occasional model number. Amps from this era are covered in black levant with a gray grille, feature an old block-style Marshall logo, and some chassis' are mounted offset.

January 1965-June 1969 - Serialization unknown from this period, but model codes are known. Plexiglass panels (hence the name Marshall Plexi) were used. Marshall started using their four-digit model system around this time and most models should have this on the chassis. Amps from this era are covered in black levant with a black front on heads or gray grille on combos, feature an old block-style Marshall logo, and all chassis' are mounted center.

Model Codes:	SP/ - Super PA
/A - 200W	ST/ - 100W Tremolo
SL/ - 100W Super Lead	S/ - 50W
SB/ - 100W Super Bass	T/ - 50W Tremolo

July 1969-September 1992 - The Marshall date coding system was introduced in 1969. The serial number is broken down into three different parts - the model code, serial number, and date code. The charts are listed for the model and date codes, and the serial number is simply the production ranking. These serial numbers are on the back of the chassis, except for the years 1979-1981 when they were on the front panel. The model code changed slightly from earlier models, and these codes were both used into the late 1970s. On date codes, they started at A in July 1969, which ran until December 1970. They then skipped the letter B and started with C in 1971. O, I, and Q weren't used since they looked too much like numbers. Up until 1983, the order is model code, serial number, then date code. In 1984, it changed to model code, date code, and serial number. Aluminum back panels were also introduced in 1969. Examples: SL/A G 10058 is a 100W Super Lead produced in 1975. RI 13590 Z is a reissue model produced in 1991 or 1992.

Model Codes:

A/ - 200W	SP/ - Super PA
RI - Reissue	ST/A - 100W Tremolo
SL/A - 100W Super Lead	S/A - 50W
SB/A - 100W Super Bass	T/A - 50W Tremolo

Date Codes:

A - 1969/1970	N - 1981
C - 1971	P - 1982
D - 1972	R - 1983
E - 1973	S - 1984
F - 1974	T - 1985
G - 1975	U - 1986
H - 1976	V - 1987
J - 1977	W - 1988
K - 1978	X - 1989
L - 1979	Y - 1990
M - 1980	Z - 1991/1992

October 1992-July 1997 - A new bar code was introduced along with the serial number applied by a sticker instead of being stamped on. This new system consists of nine numbers. The first two numbers indicate the last two numbers of year, the middle five are the five-digit serial number/production rank, and the last two indicate the week of the year (01-52). Example: 961018915 is amp number 10189 made in the 15th week of 1996. This is also the first time speaker cabinets were issued a serial number.

August 1997-Present - Marshall expanded on their previous idea with a bar code and added more information to the serial number. This new number contains two letters and 10 digits, wihch is applied to all amps and speaker cabinets. The first letter indicates the country of manufacture:

M - England	I - India
C - China	K - Korea

The next four digits indicate the complete four digit year of production (between 1997 and 1998, some models produced overseas may only have a two digit year). The next two digits indicate the week (01-52) of the respective year the amp was built. The last four digits indicate the serial number/production rank. The last digit indicates what voltage the amp is set for:

A - 230V (U.K.)	E - 220/60 (Europe)
B - 120/60 (U.S.)	F - 130/60 (Mexico)
C - 220/50 (Canada)	Z - used on models where there is no power such as speaker cabinets.
D - 105/50/60 (Japan)	

Examples: M-1999-34-1234-B indicates an amp built in the England production facility in the 34th week of 1999, is serial number 1234, and the voltage is set for U.S. use. C-2003-09-1560-E is an amp built in China in the ninth week of 2003 and the voltage is set for Europe use.

MARSHALL COVERING/GRILLE CLOTH/LOGOS

Mashall has used numerous vinyls and grille cloths over the years. For Marshall vinyl coverings, black has been the most popular. This has been offered on almost all the models since the beginning. There was a black on green that was used here and there in the late 1960s. In 1967 and 1968, orange, purple, red and blue Levant coverings were all offered in Marshall catalogs. A yellow and a silver were also available but are not known to exist. In 1975, the Levant coverings were changed to the new Elephant covering. Black was still standard on all models. Light brown, dark brown, red, and white Elephant coverings have been used on some models since then. Blue Levant covering was used on the 30th Anniversary Series, and Silver Levant was used on the Silver Jubilee Series. Black is now standard on all Marshall models. Marshall cloths have changed over the years as well. Marshall covering and grille cloth information courtesy Michael Doyle: *The History of Marshall.*

Coverings:

Black Levant: 1965-1974.

Black on Green: First appeared in 1966 and was occasionally used through the 1970s.

Black Elephant: 1975-Present.

Blue Levant: late 1960s, possibly early 1970s, and used on the 30th Anniversary Series in 1992.

Dark Brown Elephant: 1978-1982. Used on the Club & Country Series.

Light Brown Elephant: Used occasionally on amps since 1975.

Orange Levant: late 1960s-early 1970s.

Purple Levant: late 1960s-early 1970s.

Red Elephant: Used occasionally on amps since 1975.

Red Levant: late 1960s-early 1970s.

Silver: 1987, 2006. Used on Silver Jubilee amps in 1987 and on a limited DSL series in 2006. Possibly used on other models as well.

White Elephant: Used occasionally on amps since 1975.

Yellow Levant: offered in 1972 catalog, unknown if any exist.

Grille Cloth:

Black 1st Version: Light black, almost dark gray that faded very easily. Replaced the Chequerboard covering in 1976.

Black 2nd Version: Darker than the first version and doesn't fade as easily. Used since the late 1980s on almost all models.

Brown Basket Weave: Two-tone brown/dark brown weave. Primarily used on the Purple Levant cabinets between the late 1960s and early 1970s.

Brown Basket Weave Version 2: Two-tone light brown/dark brown weave used between 1968 and 1969.

Brown Bluesbreaker: Brown and white random pattern grille with horizontal brown lines, very rare, 1965-1968.

Chequerboard: Large black squares with smaller white squares crisscrossed used between 1972 and 1975, but examples were still used in the U.S. until 1981. Resembles a checkerboard.

Gray Basket Weave: Two-tone black and white weave used during the late 1960s and early 1970s. Also referred to as Salt & Pepper.

Gray Bluesbreaker: Black and white random pattern grille with horizontal black lines, 1965-1968.

Light Straw: Straw basketweave used on the Club & Country series between 1978 and 1982.

White with black accents: 1962-1965.

Logos:

1962-1964/65: Silver rectangle with maroon block letters in upper case.

1964/65: Gold rectangle with black block letters in upper case.

1965/66-Present: White script Marshall logo in lower case letters.

MARSHALL OVERVIEW: PLEASE READ!

Marshall amplifiers are some of the most desirable and collectible models on the market today. Early JTMs are bringing $15,000 and $20,000 is probably not far away. Early Bluesbreakers amps are also very collectible - watch for prices to keep climbing on these amps steadily. There are several factors that affect values on Marshalls. Unlike Fender, Ampeg, and Vox, Marshall heads and speaker cabinets were usually sold separately. Therefore, most pieces are listed and priced separately. However, matching or recommended heads and speaker cabinets from the same year in the same color are going to bring a premium over the two separate items listed individually. For instance, a Model 1959 Head and Model 1960 speaker cabinet listed separately are going to bring about $5,500 and $3,250 respectively. If they are both from 1967 and have matching colors, they could easily bring $15,000 -- about $5,000 more than when listed separately. Custom colors including blue, orange, purple, and red are also very desirable/collectible bringing 25-50% over the listed price. Keep in mind that each Marshall piece needs to be inspected individually and appraised accordingly if it is a matched set.

Most Marshall amps were voiced for a specific genre -- typically lead (guitar), bass, organ, and PA. Generally speaking the lead, bass, and organ amps had the same chassis and control panels and one could be used for another application. For example, many guitarists have used bass applications because of their lower sound (and cheaper price!). PA amps usually featured four volume knobs. Lead guitar applications are typically worth the most, followed by bass amps, organ amps, and PA amps.

Speaker cabinets that belong to no particular series are listed in the Speaker Cabinet section. All other cabinets that are part of an exclusive series will be listed within the amps.

ELECTRIC TUBE AMPLIFIERS: JTM 45 SERIES

This was Marshall's first line of amplifiers released in 1962. Since this was Marshall's first attempt at mass producing amplifiers, the cosmetics changed quite frequently. When parts would run out, they would just go out and buy whatever was handy. For a series of amps there are many different looking models that bear the same name. The electronics didn't change much except for small tweaks and occasional tube differences. JTM stands for Jim and Terry Marshall; Terry is Jim's son. The JTM-45 combo amps are known as the Bluesbreaker models and are listed under the Bluesbreaker Series.

MSR/NOTES	100%	EXCELLENT	AVERAGE	LAST MSR

JTM-45 (NO MODEL NUMBER) 45W LEAD – 45W, head unit only, lead guitar application, tube chassis, preamp: 3 X 7025, 2 X 6L6, GZ34 rectifier, two channels, front white control panel, 4 inputs, typically six knobs (p, b, m, t, high t (loudness 1), normal (loudness 2) black leather covering, brown grille, mfg. 1962-64.

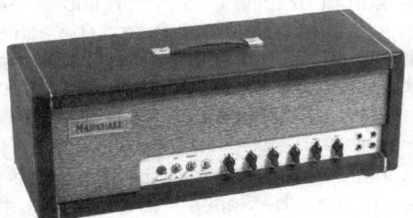

courtesy solidbodyguitar.com, Inc.   courtesy solidbodyguitar.com, Inc.   courtesy solidbodyguitar.com, Inc.

| | N/A | $10,000 - 12,000 | $7,000 - 8,500 | |

The first Marshall amplifier, very desirable and hard to find. The offset chassis is very rare.

JTM-45 (MODEL 1963) 50W PA – similar to the JTM-45 lead except Super PA version, 50W output, four channels, eight normal inputs, eight knobs (p, b, m, t, v1, v2, v3, v4), bears the name MK III on front panel, mfg. 1965-66.

| | N/A | $3,000 - 4,000 | $2,000 - 2,500 | |

JTM-45 (MODEL 1985) 45W PA – similar to the JTM-45 lead except PA version, 45W, output, bears the name MK II, mfg. 1965-66.

courtesy solidbodyguitar.com, Inc.   courtesy solidbodyguitar.com, Inc.

| | N/A | $4,000 - 5,000 | $2,500 - 3,000 | |

JTM-45 (MODEL 1986) 45W BASS – similar to the JTM MK II except in bass version, high treble and normal channels, mfg. 1965-66.

| | N/A | $5,000 - 6,000 | $3,000 - 4,000 | |

JTM-45 (MODEL 1987) 45W LEAD – similar to the JTM-45 MK II except in lead version, high treble and normal channels, mfg. 1965-66.

| | N/A | $6,250 - 7,500 | $4,000 - 5,000 | |

Also available with Tremolo as an option, model number T1987. This model replaced the original JTM-45 in 1965. The JTM-45 Model 1987 was replaced by the 50W Model 1987 in 1966.

JTM-45 (MODEL 1989) 45W ELECTRIC ORGAN – similar to the JTM MK II except designed for electric organs, mfg. 1965-66.

| | N/A | $5,000 - 6,000 | $3,000 - 4,000 | |

Also available with Tremolo as an option, model number T1989.

JTM-45 MODEL 1987 REISSUE (MODEL 2245) – 30W, head-unit only, tube chassis, preamp: 3 X ECC83, power: 2 X 5881, GZ34 rectifier, two channels, front gold control panel, four inputs, six knobs (p, b, m, t, v1, v2), black covering, 32 lbs., original reissue of the JTM-45 (Model 1987) re-released in 1989, mfg. 1989-present.

| 1989-1999 | N/A | $900 - 1,100 | $600 - 700 | |
| 2002-Present MSR $2,760 | $2,000 | $1,300 - 1,500 | $650 - 800 | |

JTM-45 LIMITED EDITION HALF STACK (MODEL 2255HS) – reissue of the original offset-chassis JTM-45 with matching 4-12 in. speaker cabinet, mfg. 2000-03.

| | N/A | $3,000 - 3,500 | $2,200 - 2,500 | $5,000 |

Back in 1962, three JTM-45 heads were built with an off-set chassis. Recently they went to work recreating this model piece by piece all hand-wired and made to look original. This model was a limited edition run of 300 half stacks that were numbered in sequence - 250 were sold in the U.S. with the remaining 50 sold in Japan.

ELECTRIC TUBE AMPLIFIERS: BLUESBREAKER SERIES

The Model 1961 and Model 1962 "Bluesbreakers" were the first combo amps produced by Marshall, and according to Jim Marshall were built as a request by Eric Clapton. Two models were designed, and designated the Model 1961 for the 4 X 10 in. and the Model 1962 for the 2 X 12 in. version. The Model 1961 was designed for guitar, to compete with the 4 X 10 in. Fender Bassman, and employed the Marshall Model 1987 lead chassis. The Model 1962 was designed for the bass and guitar and used the Marshall Model 1986 bass chassis. Eric Clapton is known for playing through a second series Model 1962 Bluesbreaker on John Mayall and the

MSR/NOTES	100%	EXCELLENT	AVERAGE	LAST MSR

Bluesbreakers album, which is where the nickname comes from. Both the Model 1961 and Model 1962 are comprised of two different versions, known as the Series I and Series II and the changes noted below between these two series are the same for both models.

The Series I was produced from late 1964-66 and features the nearly square proportioned and deeper cabinet designed by Jim Marshall. The Series I cabinet included the "White" (thin horizontal gray lines in a white background) grille cloth, changing in 1965 to the classic Gray Bluesbreaker or Pinstripe cloth that featured gray horizontal strips with a subtle snakeskin pattern. The earliest Bluesbreakers employed the gold block Marshall logo, changing around 1965 to the classic Marshall script logo. The Series I was essentially the JTM45 amplifier electronics, combined with multiple speakers in a single Baltic birch cabinet. Utilizing the Radiospares transformers, KT66 power tubes, and GZ34 tube rectification, the amp was rated at 30 to 35 watts. The 2 X 12 Model 1962 combo also included the early G12 Celestion Alnico speakers, which added a violin-like smoothness to the sound.

The Series II was introduced in mid-1965 while the Series I was still in production, and featured a revised cabinet designed by Marshall's chief engineer, Ken Bran. The overall appearance of the Series II cabinet is sleeker than the Series I, and it utilized the classic Marshall Bluesbreaker grille cloth and script logo. During the last six months of 1966, the amps were upgraded to a full 50 watts and were designated the JTM50 MKII (Model 1961) and the JTM50 MKIV (Model 1962). The electronics were revised and employed new EL34 power tubes, Drake transformers, and a solid-state rectifier. They were also equipped with Celestion Greenback Ceramic magnet speakers. During 1968, the physical appearance of the Bluesbreaker was revised with the new full-faced Basketweave grille cloth. Although these amps were still designated as Model 1961 (4 X 10), and Model 1962 (2 X 12), they are not considered the "classic" Bluesbreaker, nor a plexi unit.

Extension cabinets were also available of the Model 1962 (see the Speaker Cabinets section). For a complete history and technical overview of the Marshall Bluesbreaker, please refer to The Marshall Bluesbreaker - The Story of Marshall's First Combo by John R. Wiley. The author would like to thank John R. Wiley for the information in the Bluesbreaker section.

BLUESBREAKER MODEL 1961 – 30-35W (1964-mid-1966) or 50W (late 1966-1972), 4-10 in. Ceramic magnet speakers, guitar combo, seven-tube chassis (1964-mid-1966) including preamp: 4 X ECC83/12AX7, power: 2 X KT66, rectifier: GZ34 or six-tube chassis (late 1966-1972) including preamp: 4 X ECC83/12AX7, power: 2 X EL34, solid-state rectifier, two channels, tremolo, top gold control panel, four inputs (two per channel), eight knobs (p, b, m, t, v1, v2, s i), black covering, white or gray Bluesbreaker/Pinstripe (1964-early 1965), Marshall Bluesbreaker/Pinstripe (mid-1965-1968), or full-face Basketweave (1968-1972) grille cloth, mfg. late 1964-1972.

1964-1966 Series I	N/A	$7,500 - 9,000	$5,250 - 6,500
1966-1968 Series II	N/A	$7,000 - 8,500	$5,000 - 6,000
1969-1970	N/A	$6,000 - 7,500	$4,000 - 5,000
1971-1972	N/A	$4,000 - 5,000	$2,750 - 3,500

The Bluesbreaker was originally equipped with Radiospares transformers, and in circa 1965 Drake transformers began being phased in and the Marshall Bluesbreaker/Pinstripe grille cloth was used exclusively. During the second half of 1966 the upgraded JTM50 chassis was offered with a full 50 watt power rating, which utilized the EL34 power tubes, Drake transformers, and solid-state rectifier. In 1967, the JTM designation was changed to JMP for Jim Marshall Products. The control panel designations remained the same as above. By 1968, the Bluesbreaker was known as the JMP50, although it kept the same cabinet dimensions and control panel layout as the circa mid 1965/1966 Series II, but included the new Basketweave full-face grille cloth, introduced in 1968 and the revised electronics stated above.

BLUESBREAKER MODEL 1962 – 30-35W (1964-mid-1966) or 50W (late 1966-1972), 2-12 in. Alnico (1964-mid-1965) or Ceramic magnet (mid-1965-1972) speakers, guitar combo, seven-tube chassis (1964-mid-1966) including preamp: 4 X ECC83/12AX7, power: 2 X KT66, rectifier: GZ34 or six-tube chassis (late 1966-1972) including preamp: 4 X ECC83/12AX7, power: 2 X EL34, solid-state rectifier, two channels, tremolo, top gold control panel, four inputs (two per channel), eight knobs (p, b, m, t, v1, v2, s i), black covering, white or gray Bluesbreaker/Pinstripe (1964-early 1965), Marshall Bluesbreaker/Pinstripe (mid-1965-1968), or full-face Basketweave (1968-1972) grille cloth, mfg. late 1964-1972.

courtesy Savage Audio

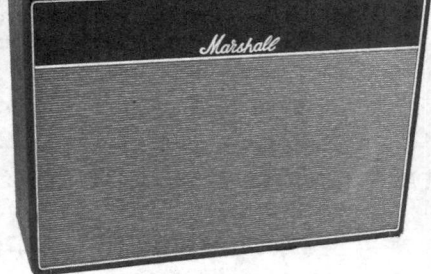
courtesy solidbodyguitar.com, Inc.

courtesy solidbodyguitar.com, Inc.

1964-1966 Series I	N/A	$9,500 - 11,000	$6,500 - 8,000
1966-1968 Series II	N/A	$8,500 - 10,500	$6,000 - 7,500
1969-1970	N/A	$6,750 - 8,500	$4,000 - 5,500
1971-1972	N/A	$5,500 - 7,000	$3,000 - 4,000

The Bluesbreaker was originally equipped with Radiospares transformers, and in circa 1965 Drake transformers began being phased in and the Marshall Bluesbreaker/Pinstripe grille cloth was used exclusively. During the second half of 1966 the upgraded JTM50 chassis was offered with a full 50 watt power rating, which utilized the EL34 power tubes, Drake transformers, and solid-state rectifier. In 1967, the JTM designation was changed to JMP for Jim Marshall Products. The control panel designations

MSR/NOTES	100%	EXCELLENT	AVERAGE	LAST MSR

remained the same as above. By 1968, the Bluesbreaker was known as the JMP50, although it kept the same cabinet dimensions and control panel layout as the circa mid 1965/1966 Series II, but included the new Basketweave full-face grille cloth, introduced in 1968 and the revised electronics stated above.

BLUESBREAKER MODEL 1962 REISSUE – 30W, 2-12 in. Celestion Greenback speakers, guitar combo, six-tube chassis, preamp:4 X ECC83 (one dedicated for Tremolo circuit), power: 2 X 5881, GZ34 rectifier, two channels, tremolo, top gold control panel, four inputs (two per channel), eight knobs (p, b, m, t, v1, v2, s, i), power switch, standby switch, two speaker jacks with impedance selector, mains voltage selector, black covering, reissue Bluesbreaker grille cloth, 67 lbs., a reissue of the late '60s Series II Model 1962 Bluesbreaker, mfg. 1989-1999, 2002-present.

1989-1999	N/A	$950 - 1,200	$700 - 800
2002-Present MSR $3,900	$2,700	$1,750 - 2,025	$875 - 1,100

ELECTRIC TUBE AMPLIFIERS: 18 & 20 WATT SERIES

This series of amps was debuted in the Summer of 1965, right around the same time as the 100 Watt heads. The 18 Watt amps were released first and then in 1967 were replaced by the 20 Watt amps. These two amps were identical as far as cosmetics, but the electronics inside were completely different. The 18 Watts are more desirable than the 20 Watts.

MODEL 1917 20W PA – 20W, 2-10 in. or 2-13 in. X 8 in. elliptical speakers, separate head and two cabinets, tube chassis, preamp: 2 X ECC83, power: 2 X EL84, solid-state rectifier, two channels, front gold control panel, four inputs, four knobs (Ch. 1: v, tone, Ch. 2: v, tone), black covering, brown grille, mfg. 1967-1973.

1968-1969	N/A	$3,500 - 4,500	$2,500 - 3,000
1970-1973	N/A	$3,000 - 3,750	$2,000 - 2,500

This model was sold as a set of one head and two cabinets. Price includes all parts.

MODEL 1958 18W LEAD COMBO – 18W, 2-10 in. speakers, lead application, tube chassis, preamp: 3 X ECC83, power: 2 X EL84, EZ81 rectifier, two channels, tremolo on first channel, top control panel, four inputs, six knobs (s,i, v1, tone1, v2, tone 2), black covering, gray and white striped cloth, mfg. 1965-68.

Non-Reverb	N/A	$5,000 - 6,500	$3,000 - 4,000
Reverb	N/A	$5,750 - 7,000	$4,500 - 5,250

Reverb was optional and included an ECC86 tube and knob.

MODEL 1958 20W LEAD COMBO – 20W, 2-10 in. speakers, lead application, tube chassis, preamp: 2 X ECC83, power: 2 X EL84, solid-state rectifier, two channels, tremolo on first channel, top control panel, four inputs, six knobs (s,i, v1, tone1, v2, tone 2), black covering, gray and white striped cloth, mfg. 1968-1973.

1968-1969	N/A	$4,500 - 5,750	$2,750 - 3,500
1970-1973	N/A	$3,500 - 4,500	$2,250 - 2,750

MODEL 1973 18W LEAD/BASS COMBO – 18W, 2-12 in. speakers, lead and bass application, tube chassis, preamp: 3 X ECC83, power: 2 X EL84, EZ81 rectifier, two channels, tremolo on first channel, top control panel, four inputs, six knobs (s,i, v1, tone1, v2, tone 2), black covering, gray and white striped cloth, mfg. 1966-68.

Model 1973 18W Lead/Bass Combo
courtesy solidbodyguitar.com, Inc.

Model 1973 18W Lead/Bass Combo
courtesy solidbodyguitar.com, Inc.

Model 1973 20W Lead/Bass Combo
courtesy Savage Audio

Non-Reverb	N/A	$6,750 - 8,000	$4,500 - 5,250
Reverb	N/A	$8,500 - 10,000	$5,500 - 7,000

Reverb was optional and included an ECC86 tube and knob.

MODEL 1973 20W LEAD/BASS COMBO – 20W, 2-12 in. speakers, lead and bass application, tube chassis, preamp: 2 X ECC83, power: 2 X EL84, solid-state rectifier, two channels, tremolo on first channel, top control panel, four inputs, six knobs (s,i, v1, tone1, v2, tone 2), black covering, gray and white striped cloth, mfg. 1968-1973.

1968-1969	N/A	$5,000 - 6,000	$3,000 - 3,750
1970-1973	N/A	$4,000 - 5,000	$2,500 - 3,250

MSR/NOTES	100%	EXCELLENT	AVERAGE	LAST MSR

* *Model 1973 20W Lead/Bass Head & Cab* – similar to the Model 1973 20W Lead/Bass, except is in separate head and cabinet with 1-12 in. speaker in a ported enclosure, mfg. 1973 only.

	N/A	$2,250 - 2,750	$1,400 - 1,750	

This model was never listed in the Marshall catalogs, and there is some confusion about what model number this really was. It has been seen as Model 2061, as well as the Model 1973.

MODEL 1974 18W LEAD/BASS COMBO – 18W, 1-12 in. speaker, lead and bass application, tube chassis, preamp: 3 X ECC83, power: 2 X EL84, EZ81 rectifier, two channels, tremolo on first channel, top control panel, four inputs, six knobs (s,i, v1, tone1, v2, tone 2), black covering, gray and white striped cloth, mfg. 1966-68.

Non-Reverb	N/A	$4,500 - 5,500	$3,000 - 3,750	
Reverb	N/A	$5,750 - 7,000	$3,750 - 4,500	

Reverb was optional and included an ECC86 tube and knob.

MODEL 1974 20W LEAD/BASS COMBO – 20W, 1-12 in. speaker, lead and bass application, tube chassis, preamp: 2 X ECC83, power: 2 X EL84, solid-state rectifier, two channels, tremolo on first channel, top control panel, four inputs, six knobs (s,i, v1, tone1, v2, tone 2), black covering, gray and white striped cloth, mfg. 1968-1973.

1968-1969	N/A	$4,000 - 5,000	$2,500 - 3,250	
1970-1973	N/A	$3,000 - 4,000	$2,000 - 2,500	

MODEL 2019 20W BASS HALF STACK – 20W, 4-10 in. speakers in a separate cabinet, bass application, tube chassis, preamp: 2 X ECC83, power: 2 X EL84, solid-state rectifier, two channels, top control panel, four inputs, four knobs (v1, tone1, v2, tone 2), black covering, gray and white striped cloth, mfg. 1968-1973.

1968-1969	N/A	$4,000 - 5,000	$2,500 - 3,250	
1969-1973	N/A	$3,000 - 4,000	$2,000 - 2,500	

MODEL 2022 20W LEAD HALF STACK – 20W, 4-10 in. speakers in a separate cabinet, lead application, tube chassis, preamp: 2 X ECC83, power: 2 X EL84, solid-state rectifier, two channels, top control panel, four inputs, four knobs (v1, tone1, v2, tone 2), black covering, gray and white striped cloth, mfg. 1968-1973.

1968-1969	N/A	$4,000 - 5,000	$2,500 - 3,250	
1969-1973	N/A	$3,000 - 4,000	$2,000 - 2,500	

Tremolo was an option on this model.

ELECTRIC TUBE AMPLIFIERS: 50W SERIES (1966-1981)

This series was introduced in 1966 and is an updated version of the JTM45. There were some tube changes amongst other electronics inside the amp, while the cosmetics on the outside changed as well. In 1967, the "JTM 50" and "MK II" labels had been replaced by JTM. In 1968, the steel chassis was introduced and the initials JMP (Jim Marshall Products) were added. In 1969, the Plexiglas panel were changed to gold aluminum. It should be noted that in the price lines, 1969 refers to models having Plexi panels and 1970 for the aluminum, even though an aluminum amp may have been produced in 1969. This series was discontinued in 1981, when the JCM-800 series was introduced.

* **Add 25-50% for covering colors other than black.**

MODEL 1963 50W PA – 50W, head unit only, PA application, tube chassis: preamp: 3 X 7025, power: 2 X 6550/EL34, solid-state rectifier, four channels, front control panel, eight inputs, eight knobs (p, b, m, t, v1, v2, v3, v4), black levant covering, brown or gray grille cloth, mfg. 1966-68.

	N/A	$3,000 - 4,000	$1,500 - 2,250	

MODEL 1964 50W LEAD/BASS – 50W, head unit only, lead and bass application, tube chassis: preamp: 3 X 7025, power: 2 X 6550/EL34, solid-state rectifier, two channels, front control panel, four inputs, six knobs (p, b, m, t, v1, v2), black levant covering, mfg. 1973-76.

	N/A	$900 - 1,100	$650 - 750	

This is the head-unit configuration of the Model 2100.

MODEL 1985 50W PA – 50W, head-unit only, PA application, tube chassis, preamp: 3 X 7025, power: 2 X 6550/EL34, two channels, front control panel, four inputs, six knobs (p, b, m, t, v1, v2), black Levant covering, mfg. 1966-68.

	N/A	$3,500 - 4,500	$2,000 - 2,500	

This is the PA version of the Model 1987 Lead.

MODEL 1986 50W BASS – 50W, head-unit only, bass application, tube chassis, preamp: 3 X 7025, power: 2 X 6550/EL34, two channels, front control panel, four inputs, six knobs (p, b, m, t, v1, v2), black Levant covering, mfg. 1966-1981.

1966-1969	N/A	$3,000 - 3,750	$2,000 - 2,500	
1969-1970	N/A	$2,000 - 2,500	$1,000 - 1,500	
1971-1972	N/A	$1,800 - 2,250	$1,200 - 1,500	
1971-1972	N/A	$1,800 - 2,250	$1,200 - 1,500	
1976-1981	N/A	$1,300 - 1,600	$700 - 800	

This is the Bass version of the Model 1987 Lead. Early models between 1966 and 1969 featured Plexi control panels.

MSR/NOTES	100%	EXCELLENT	AVERAGE	LAST MSR

MODEL 1987 50W LEAD – 50W, head-unit only, lead application, tube chassis, preamp: 3 X 7025, power: 2 X 6550/EL34, two channels, front control panel, four inputs, six knobs (p, b, m, t, v1, v2), black Levant covering, mfg. 1966-1981.

courtesy Savage Audio

courtesy Savage Audio

1966-1969	N/A	$3,000 - 3,500	$1,750 - 2,500
1969-1970	N/A	$2,000 - 2,500	$1,000 - 1,500
1971-1972	N/A	$1,750 - 2,250	$900 - 1,200
1971-1972	N/A	$1,750 - 2,250	$900 - 1,200
1976-1981	N/A	$1,200 - 1,500	$800 - 950

This model came from the original JTM 45 series. Tremolo was available as an option until 1975.

* *Model 1987S Reissue 50W Lead* – first reissue of the Model 1987 lead, mfg. 1988 only.

Head Only	N/A	$950 - 1,150	$675 - 800
Head & Cab	N/A	$1,100 - 1,400	$750 - 900

This reissue was available with a matching 4-12 in. cabinet with Celestion G12 75 speakers, and 70s Chequerboard cloth.

* *Model 1987X Reissue 50W Lead* – second Reissue of the Model 1987, with the Plexiglas panels, mfg. 1992-mid 1990s.

	N/A	$1,100 - 1,400	$675 - 800

* *Model 1987XL Reissue 50W Lead* – 50W, head-unit only, all-tube chassis, preamp: 3 X 12AX7/ECC83, power: 4 X EL34, GZ34 rectifier, two channels, front gold plexi control panel, four inputs, six knobs (p, b, m, t, v1, v2), true bypass Series FX effects loop, black Levant covering, third reissue of the 50W Lead Plexi produced between 1966 and 1969, 34 lbs., mfg. 2002-present.

MSR $3,000	$2,100	$1,375 - 1,575	$675 - 850

MODEL 1989 50W ORGAN – similar design to the Model 1987, except designed for organ applications, mfg. 1966-1975.

1966-1969	N/A	$3,750 - 4,500	$2,000 - 2,500
1969-1970	N/A	$2,750 - 3,500	$1,750 - 2,250
1971-1972	N/A	$1,800 - 2,250	$1,200 - 1,500
1973-1975	N/A	$1,400 - 1,750	$850 - 1,100

This model also came with tremolo as an option and sold as the Model T1989.

MODEL 2040 ARTIST 50W LEAD COMBO – 50W, 2-12 in. speakers, tube chassis, preamp: 3 X 7025, power: 2 X EL34/6550, lead application, two channels, reverb, four inputs, eight knobs (Ch. 1: r, v, b, t, Ch. 2: v, t, b, Both: p), black levant covering, Chequerboard cloth, mfg. 1971-78.

1971-1972	N/A	$1,750 - 2,250	$1,000 - 1,200
1973-1978	N/A	$1,500 - 2,000	$900 - 1,100

This model features a revised version of the 50W chassis with reverb.

MODEL 2041 ARTIST 50W LEAD HALF STACK – 50W, 2-12 in. speakers in a separate cabinet, tube chassis, preamp: 3 X 7025, power: 2 X EL34/6550, lead application, two channels, reverb, four inputs, eight knobs (Ch. 1: r, v, b, t, Ch. 2: v, t, b, Both: p), black levant covering, Chequerboard cloth, mfg. 1971-78.

1971-1972	N/A	$2,000 - 2,500	$1,400 - 1,750
1973-1978	N/A	$1,750 - 2,250	$1,100 - 1,400

MODEL 2048 ARTIST 50W LEAD – 50W, head-unit only, tube chassis, preamp: 3 X 7025, power: 2 X EL34/6550, lead application, two channels, reverb, four inputs, eight knobs (Ch. 1: r, v, b, t, Ch. 2: v, t, b, Both: p), black levant covering, Chequerboard cloth, mfg. 1971-78.

1971-1972	N/A	$1,300 - 1,700	$750 - 1,000
1973-1978	N/A	$1,000 - 1,200	$650 - 850

MODEL 2100 50W LEAD/BASS COMBO – 50W, 2-12 in. speakers, lead and bass application, tube chassis: preamp: 3 X 7025, power: 2 X 6550/EL34, solid-state rectifier, two channels, top control panel, four inputs, six knobs (p, b, m, t, v1, v2), black levant covering, black grille, mfg. 1973-76.

	N/A	$1,500 - 2,000	$1,000 - 1,200

This is the combo version of the Model 1964 head.

MSR/NOTES	100%	EXCELLENT	AVERAGE	LAST MSR

MODEL 2104 50W LEAD MV COMBO – 50W, 2-12 in. speakers, lead application, tube chassis, preamp: 3 X 7025, power: 2 X 6550/EL34, single channel, front control panel, four inputs, six knobs (p, b, m, t, v, MV), black Levant covering, black grille, mfg. 1975-1981.

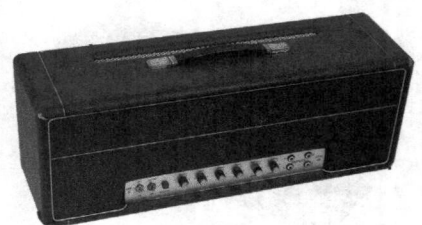

courtesy Savage Audio   *courtesy Savage Audio*

	N/A	$1,100 - 1,400	$700 - 850	

MODEL 2144 50W LEAD MV COMBO – similar to the Model 2104 except has reverb and boost, mfg. 1978 only.

	N/A	$1,400 - 1,700	$900 - 1,100	

MODEL 2187 50W ORGAN COMBO – similar to the model 1989 Organ except is the combo version with 2-12 in. speakers, mfg. 1974-1981.

1974-1978	N/A	$1,500 - 2,000	$950 - 1,200	
1979-1981	N/A	$1,200 - 1,500	$800 - 950	

MODEL 2204 50W LEAD MV – 50W, head-unit only, lead application, tube chassis, preamp: 3 X 7025, power: 2 X 6550/EL34, single channel, front control panel, four inputs, six knobs (p, b, m, t, v, MV), black Levant covering, mfg. 1975-1981.

	N/A	$1,200 - 1,500	$750 - 900	

ELECTRIC TUBE AMPLIFIERS: 100W SERIES (1966-1981)

The 100 Series project was launched in 1965. These amps had a lot more power than the 50W models and there was not anything out there at the time that could match it. The 100 Watt amplifiers were designed because of the demands for more power, but more importantly, Pete Townshend wanted them. These amps made their way onto the market in 1966 and were discontinued in 1981 with the introduction of the JCM-800 series. In 1969, the Plexiglas panel were changed to gold aluminum. It should be noted that in the price lines, 1969 refers to models having Plexi panels and 1970 for the aluminum, even though an aluminum amp may have been produced in 1969.

- **Add 25-50% for covering colors other than black.**

MODEL 1959 100W LEAD – 100W, head-unit only, lead application, tube chassis, preamp: 3 X 7025, power: 4 X 6550/EL34, two channels, front gold control panel, four inputs, six knobs (p, b, m, t, v1, v2), black Levant covering, mfg. 1966-1981.

1966-1969	N/A	$4,500 - 5,500	$3,000 - 3,750	
1969-1970	N/A	$2,750 - 3,500	$1,750 - 2,250	
1971-1972	N/A	$2,000 - 2,500	$1,000 - 1,500	
1973-1975	N/A	$1,750 - 2,250	$1,100 - 1,400	
1976-1981	N/A	$1,400 - 1,750	$850 - 1,050	

This model was known as the Super Lead. It was also available with tremolo in the model T1959. The tremolo option was discontinued in 1973.

* *Model 1959S Reissue 100W Lead* – first reissue of the 1970s Model 1959, mfg. 1988 only.

	N/A	$1,200 - 1,500	$725 - 850	

* *Model 1959X Reissue 100W Lead* – second reissue of the model 1959, based on the '60s Plexiglas models, mfg. 1991-93.

	N/A	$1,200 - 1,500	$725 - 850	

* *Model 1959SLP Reissue 100W Lead* – third reissue of the model 1959, mfg. 1993-1995

	N/A	$1,200 - 1,500	$725 - 850	

* *Model 1959SLPX Reissue 100W Lead* – 100W, head-unit only, all-tube chassis, preamp: 3 X 12AX7/ECC83, power: 4 X EL34, GZ34 rectifier, two channels, front gold plexi control panel, four inputs, six knobs (p, b, m, t, v1, v2), true bypass Series FX effects loop, black Levant covering, fourth reissue of the 100W "Super" Lead produced in the late 1960s/early 1970s, 45 lbs., mfg. 2002-present.

MSR $4,300	$3,000	$1,950 - 2,250	$975 - 1,200	

MODEL 1968 100W PA – 100W, head-unit only, PA application, tube chassis, preamp: 3 X 7025, power: 4 X 6550/EL34, four channels, front gold control panel, eight inputs, eight knobs (p, b, m, t, v1, v2, v3, v4), black Levant covering, mfg. 1966-1975.

1966-1969	N/A	$3,250 - 3,750	$1,750 - 2,250	
1969-1970	N/A	$2,500 - 3,000	$1,500 - 2,000	
1971-1972	N/A	$2,250 - 2,750	$1,200 - 1,500	
1971-1972	N/A	$2,250 - 2,750	$1,200 - 1,500	

Known as the "Super PA" amp.

MSR/NOTES	100%	EXCELLENT	AVERAGE	LAST MSR

MODEL 1992 100W BASS – 100W, head-unit only, bass application, tube chassis, preamp: 3 X 7025, power: 4 X 6550/EL34, two channels, front gold control panel, four inputs, six knobs (p, b, m, t, v1, v2), black Levant covering, mfg. 1966-1981.

1966-1969	N/A	$4,000 - 5,000	$2,500 - 3,250	
1969-1970	N/A	$2,750 - 3,250	$1,500 - 2,000	
1971-1972	N/A	$2,250 - 2,750	$1,400 - 1,750	
1973-1975	N/A	$1,500 - 2,000	$950 - 1,200	
1976-1981	N/A	$1,200 - 1,500	$750 - 950	

Known as the Super Bass amp. It was available with tremolo as the model T1992. This option was discontinued in 1972.

MODEL 2059 ARTIST 100W LEAD HALF STACK – 100W, 4-12 in. speakers in a separate cabinet, lead application, tube chassis, preamp: 3 X 7025, power:4 X EL34/6550, lead application, two channels, reverb, front control panel, four inputs, eight knobs (Ch. 1: r, v, b, t, Ch. 2: v, t, b, Both: p), black levant covering, mfg. 1971-78.

1971-1972	N/A	$2,250 - 2,750	$1,250 - 1,750	
1973-1978	N/A	$1,750 - 2,250	$1,000 - 1,250	

MODEL 2068 ARTIST 100W LEAD – 100W, head-unit only, lead application, tube chassis, preamp: 3 X 7025, power: 4 X EL34/6550, lead application, two channels, reverb, four inputs, eight knobs (Ch. 1: r, v, b, t, Ch. 2: v, t, b, Both: p), black levant covering, mfg. 1971-78.

1971-1972	N/A	$1,400 - 1,750	$850 - 1,100	
1973-1978	N/A	$1,100 - 1,400	$700 - 850	

MODEL 2103 100W LEAD MV COMBO – 100W, 2-12 in. speakers, lead application, tube chassis, preamp: 3 X 7025, power: 4 X 6550/EL34, single channel, top control panel, four inputs, six knobs (p, b, m, t, v, MV), black Levant covering, black grille, mfg. 1975-1981.

	N/A	$1,100 - 1,300	$700 - 900	

MODEL 2159 100W LEAD COMBO – 100W, 2-12 in. speakers, lead application, tube chassis, preamp: 3 X 7025, power: 4 X 6550/EL34, two channels, front gold control panel, four inputs, six knobs (p, b, m, t, v1, v2), black Levant covering, mfg. 1977-1981.

	N/A	$1,400 - 1,700	$1,000 - 1,200	

This model is the combo version of the Model 1959 Head.

MODEL 2203 100W LEAD MV – 100W, head-unit only, lead application, tube chassis, preamp: 3 X 7025, power:4 X 6550/EL34, single channel, front control panel, four inputs, six knobs (p, b, m, t, v, MV), black Levant covering, mfg. 1975-1981.

courtesy Savage Audio

courtesy Savage Audio

	N/A	$1,200 - 1,500	$850 - 1,000	

This was Marshall's first attempt at designing a master volume amp.

MODEL 2959 100W LEAD – 100W, Head unit only, tubes, reverb, boost, no master volume, foot switch for reverb, mfg. 1978-1980.

	N/A	$1,000 - 1,200	$700 - 850	

This model was the last introduced in the first 100 Watt series, and was discontinued shortly after its introduction. Only about 150 of these were made. This model was a combination of new features without master volume.

ELECTRIC TUBE AMPLIFIERS: 200W SERIES (1967-1974)

This series was introduced after the success of the 100 Watt heads and the increasing power race many amp companies were participating in. By the late 1960s and early 1970s, people were looking for more and more power and liked what many other companies were doing, so Marshall followed suit. These amps were first known as the Marshall 200, but in 1968 the name was changed to the Marshall Major. These models came in a lead, bass, and PA version. The series was discontinued in 1974.

• Add 25-50% for covering colors other than black.

MODEL 1966 200W PA – 200W, head unit only, PA application, tube chassis, preamp: 3 X ECC83/7025, power: 4 X KT88/6550, solid-state rectifier, four channels, small gold control panel, eight inputs, seven knobs (t, m, b, v1, v2, v3, v4), passive tone controls, black covering, mfg. 1968-1971.

1968-1969	N/A	$1,750 - 2,250	$1,200 - 1,500	
1969-1971	N/A	$1,250 - 1,750	$750 - 1,000	

MSR/NOTES	100%	EXCELLENT	AVERAGE	LAST MSR

MODEL 1967 200W LEAD – 200W, head unit only, lead application, tube chassis, preamp: 3 X ECC83/7025, power: 4 X KT88/6550, solid-state rectifier, one channel, small gold control panel, two inputs, three knobs (t, b, v), active tone controls, black covering, mfg. 1967-1974.

1967	N/A	$3,000 - 3,700	$2,000 - 2,500	
1968-1969	N/A	$2,750 - 3,500	$1,750 - 2,250	
1969-1970	N/A	$2,500 - 3,000	$1,500 - 2,000	
1971-1972	N/A	$2,000 - 2,500	$1,200 - 1,500	
1973-1974	N/A	$1,500 - 2,000	$950 - 1,200	

In 1968, the cosmetics were overhauled from the small chassis to the more conventional look, two channels were standard, four inputs, and passive tone controls were added.

MODEL 1978 200W BASS – similar to the Model 1967 Lead except was meant for Bass application, mfg. 1967-1974.

1967	N/A	$2,500 - 3,000	$1,500 - 2,000	
1968-1969	N/A	$2,500 - 3,000	$1,500 - 2,000	
1969-1970	N/A	$2,000 - 2,500	$1,200 - 1,500	
1971-1972	N/A	$1,500 - 2,000	$950 - 1,200	
1973-1974	N/A	$1,200 - 1,500	$750 - 950	

ELECTRIC TUBE AMPLIFIERS: 2000 SERIES (1981)

In April 1981, Marshall released new workhorse amps that had output of over 200W. At this time, these were the most powerful Marshalls built. Input for these amps came from many rock personalities, including AC/DC. These amps produced lots of power, and had features that many traditional Marshalls never fooled with. The 2000 series never caught on for a number of reasons, including their weight, cost, and technology that no one really knew how to use them. Only a few hundred are known to exist. These amps would evolve into the JCM-800 series to be released later in 1981.

2000 LEAD – 200W, head-unit only, lead application, tube chassis, preamp: 6 X ECC83/7025, power: 6 X 6550, two channels, two inputs, front control panel, eleven knobs (Ch. A: p, b, m, t, v, Ch. B: preamp g, t, m, m sweep, b, MV), effects loops on back that could be patched between channels, preamp jack for other systems, XLR jacks, standby and power were on the back, black covering, black grille, mfg. 1981 only.

	N/A	$1,100 - 1,400	$700 - 900	

2001 BASS – 300W, head-unit only, bass application, tube chassis, preamp: 3 X ECC83/7025, 3 X ECC81/12AT7, power: 8 X 6550, solid-state rectifier, two channels, front control panel, two inputs, eight knobs (Ch. A: gain, t, m, mid-frequecy select, b, Ch. B: gain, t, b), similar controls on the back to the 2000 Lead, footswitch, compression circuit, black covering, black grille, mfg. 1981 only.

	N/A	$1,100 - 1,400	$700 - 900	

ELECTRIC TUBE AMPLIFIERS: 9000 SERIES

These are Marshall "Rack amps." By the late '80s, a variety of people wanted a variety of products, even though the Marshall stack was still the standard. The Rack system was used by musicians that wanted to put all of their effects along with an amp into a rack box. This way there could be several effects within reach. There were some models that were strictly preamps, and there were models that were the power amps. The prototype was announced at the 1989 NAMM show, but the product was dramatically altered before it was released. All of the models were in black cases, 19 in. wide for rack-mounts, and labeled 9000. The first of this series ran through 1993 when a couple new models were released. The Models 9010 and 9030 were prototypes that were advertised, but never put into production.

ELECTRIC TUBE AMPLIFIERS: 30TH ANNIVERSARY SERIES

As Marshall had done with the 25/50 Anniversary (Silver Jubilee Series), they released a series of amps for the 30th Anniversary in 1992. This amp was the result of a triple-channel JCM-900 that wasn't ready for release when the Hi-Gain and Hi-Gain Dual Reverb were. They saved it for the 30 year anniversary, and released their most advanced amplifier to date. The first channel was for clean tone and by using a switch the sound could be switched from Marshall sound in the out to Fender sound pushed in. Channel 2 presented three different modes (A, B, & C), that could be used all together. The Lead/JTM 45, a 2203, and a JCM-900 could all be heard through this amp in channel 2. Channel 3 was a whole different animal with distortion like no other. All of these could be used through a footswitch. The power selection was also new. Not only was there a triode/peontode selection switch, but a new power selection switch was added. This allowed the selection between two or four tubes.

The series lasted for the better half of the 90s. For the year 1992, the amp was covered in Blue Levant vinyl, but after that it was changed to standard black like the JCM-900s. This series was discontinued in 1998, around the same time as the JCM-900 series. All of these models are meant for lead applications.

30TH ANNIVERSARY HEAD (MODEL 6100/6100B/6100LM) – 100W (switchable to 50W or 25W), head-unit only, 11 tube chassis, preamp: 7 X ECC83/12AX7, power: 4 X EL34, solid-state rectifier, three channels (clean, crunch, lead), MIDI, speaker emulator, front gold control panel, one input, 17 gold knobs, Ch. 1 controls: four knobs (b, m, t, v), mid-shift switch, bright switch, Ch. 2 controls: five knobs (b, m, t, v, g), Mode A/B/C selector switch, Ch. 3 controls: five knobs (b, m, t, v, g), contour switch, gain boost switch, Master controls: v, p, effects, effects loop, low volume switch, three MIDI channel switches with store button, low and high compensation input switches, rear panel: half power switch (100/50W), damping select switch, multiple outputs on back, effects loop with loop level switch, series/parallel switch, and FX

MSR/NOTES	100%	EXCELLENT	AVERAGE	LAST MSR

send trims, balanced XLR out with level control, footswitch jack, MIDI in, available in Blue Levant covering (1992 only) or black covering (1993-99), black cloth grille with white piping and a white script Marshall logo, mfg. 1992-99.

courtesy Ferris Wheel Music

courtesy Ferris Wheel Music

1992 Blue Covering	N/A	$950 - 1,200	$750 - 875	
1993-1999 Black Covering	N/A	$875 - 1,050	$700 - 850	$2,099

In 1994, Marshall modified the lead channel and changed the model name to the 6100LM.

* **30th Anniversary Head Limited Edition (Model 6100LE)** – similar to the 30th Anniversary Head (Model 6100) except has limited edition features, including brass plated chassis, valve caps, spring retainers, and transformer covers, and a signature plate mounted on the chassis with the serial number, available in Blue Levant covering only, limited edition run of 800 units, mfg. 1992 only.

	N/A	$1,200 - 1,500	$850 - 1,000	

* **30th Anniversary 1-12 Combo (Model 6101/6101B/6101LM)** – similar to the 30th Anniversary Head (Model 6100/6100B/6100LM), except in combo configuration with 1-12 in. Celestion G12 gold speaker or Electro-Voice EVM 12L (U.S. only) and a stacked control panel, available in Blue Levant covering (1992 only) or black covering (1993-97), black cloth grille with white piping and a white script Marshall logo, mfg. 1992-97.

1992 Blue Covering	N/A	$1,200 - 1,500	$850 - 1,000	
1993-1997 Black Covering	N/A	$950 - 1,200	$750 - 875	

In 1994, Marshall modified the lead channel and changed the model name to the 6101LM.

» **30th Anniversary 1-12 Combo Limited Edition (Model 6101LE)** – similar to the 30th Anniversary 1-12 Combo (Model 6101), except has limited edition features, including brass plated chassis, valve caps, spring retainers, and transformer covers, and a signature plate mounted on the chassis with the serial number, available in Blue Levant covering only, limited edition run of 500 units, mfg. 1992 only.

	N/A	$1,400 - 1,750	$900 - 1,100	

30TH ANNIVERSARY 1-12 SPEAKER CABINET (MODEL 6912/6912B) – 1-12 in. Celestion G12 gold speaker or Electro-Voice EVM 12L speaker (U.S. only), designed for use as an extension cabinet for the 30th Anniversary 1-12 Combo (Model 6101/6101B), available in blue covering (1992 only) or black covering (1992-97), black cloth grille with white piping and a white script Marshall logo, mfg. 1992-97.

1992 Blue Covering	N/A	$325 - 400	$200 - 250	
1993-1997 Black Covering	N/A	$300 - 350	$175 - 225	

* **30th Anniversary 1-12 Speaker Cabinet Limited Edition (Model 6912LE)** – similar to the 30th Annniversary 1-12 Speaker Cabinet (Model 6912), except has a brass-plated logo on the grille designed for use as an extension cabinet for the 30th Anniversary 1-12 Combo Limited Edition (Model 6101LE), available in blue covering only, mfg. 1992 only.

	N/A	$375 - 450	$225 - 275	

30TH ANNIVERSARY 4-12 SPEAKER CABINET (MODEL 6960A/6960B) – 4-12 in. Celestion G12 gold speakers or Electro-Voice EVM 12L speakers (U.S. only), angled (Model 6960A) or straight (Model 6960B) front, designed for use with the 30th Anniversary Head (Model 6100), blue covering, black grille with white piping and a white script Marshall logo, mfg. 1992-93.

	N/A	$625 - 750	$425 - 500	

* **30th Anniversary 4-12 Vintage Speaker Cabinet (Model 6960AV/6960BV)** – similar to the 30th Anniversary 4-12 Speaker Cabinet (Model 6960A/6960B), except has 4-12 in. Celestion Vintage 30 speakers, mfg. 1992-93.

	N/A	$625 - 750	$425 - 500	

* **30th Anniversary 4-12 Limited Edition Speaker Cabinet (Model 6960ALE/6960BLE)** – similar to the 30th Annniversary 4-12 Speaker Cabinet (Model 6960A/6960B), except has a brass-plated logo on the grille, designed for use with the 30th Anniversary Head Limited Edition (Model 6100LE), available in blue covering only, mfg. 1992 only.

	N/A	$675 - 800	$475 - 550	

ELECTRIC TUBE AMPLIFIERS: 35TH ANNIVERSARY SERIES

For their 35th Anniversary as a company, Marshall released the 35th Anniversary Series in 1997. The 35th Anniversary Series featured three models with a 50W head (Model 1987WSP), 100W head (Model 1959WSP, and a Bluesbreaker 2-12 Combo (Model 1962WSP). A 4-12 angled-front speaker cabinet (Model 1960AXWSP) with 4-12 in. 25W Celestion Greenback speakers and a "100" logo in the upper left-hand corner was also offered, but it was only sold with one of the two heads as a set. All models were produced with a white vinyl covering, gold piping, a gold script Marshall logo, and salt and pepper weave cloth grille. 250 of each model and 500 speaker cabinets were produced (250 speaker cabinets for each head). Unlike the 30th Anniversary Series, the 35th Anniversary amplifiers were only produced for one year in 1997.

35TH ANNIVERSARY 50W HALF-STACK (MODELS 1987WSP/1960AXWSP) – 50W, guitar head-unit (Model 1987WSP) with an angled front 4-12 in. speaker cabinet (Model 1960AXWSP), five-tube chassis, preamp: 3 X ECC83/12AX7, power: 2 X EL34, solid-state rectifier, two channels, front gold plexi control panel with "MK II" logo, four inputs (two per channel), six knobs (p, b, m, t, v1, v2), power switch, standby switch, rear gold plexi panel with "Super Lead 100W," two speaker jacks with impedance selector, mains voltage selector, white vinyl covering, salt and pepper weave cloth grille with gold piping and gold script Marshall logo, limited edition run of 250 sets, mfg. 1997 only.

| Half-Stack (Complete Set) | N/A | $1,800 - 2,200 | $1,150 - 1,400 | |
| Head Only | N/A | $1,050 - 1,200 | $775 - 900 | |

35TH ANNIVERSARY 100W HALF-STACK (MODELS 1959WSP/1960AXWSP) – 100W, guitar head-unit (Model 1959WSP) with an angled front 4-12 in. speaker cabinet (Model 1960AXWSP), seven-tube chassis, preamp: 3 X ECC83/12AX7, power: 4 X EL34, solid-state rectifier, two channels, front gold plexi control panel with "MK II" logo, four inputs (two per channel), six knobs (p, b, m, t, v1, v2), power switch, standby switch, rear gold plexi panel with "Super Lead 100W," two speaker jacks with impedance selector, mains voltage selector, white vinyl covering, salt and pepper weave cloth grille with gold piping and gold script Marshall logo, limited edition run of 250 sets, mfg. 1997 only.

| Half-Stack (Complete Set) | N/A | $2,250 - 2,750 | $1,400 - 1,700 | |
| Head Only | N/A | $1,200 - 1,450 | $850 - 1,000 | |

35TH ANNIVERSARY BLUESBREAKER (MODEL 1962WSP) – 30W, 2-12 in. Celestion Greenback speakers, seven-tube chassis, preamp: 4 X ECC83 (one dedicated for Tremolo circuit), power: 2 X 5881, GZ34 rectifier, two channels, tremolo, top gold control panel, four inputs (two per channel), eight knobs (p, b, m, t, v1, v2, s, i), power switch, standby switch, two speaker jacks with impedance selector, mains voltage selector, white vinyl covering, salt and pepper weave cloth grille with gold piping and gold script Marshall logo, commemorative grille cloth plaque, limited edition run of 250 units, mfg. 1997 only.

| | N/A | $1,600 - 1,900 | $1,050 - 1,300 | |

ELECTRIC TUBE AMPLIFIERS: ASTORIA SERIES

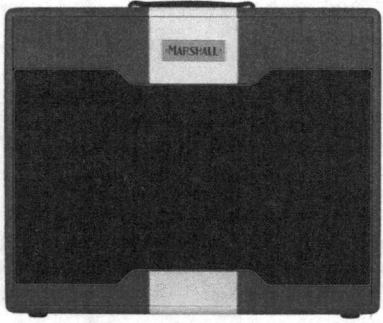

Astoria Classic Combo
courtesy Marshall

Astoria Custom Combo
courtesy Marshall

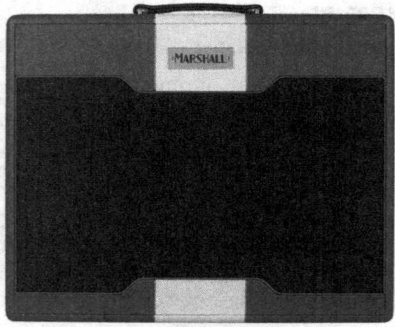

Astoria Dual Combo
courtesy Marshall

ASTORIA CLASSIC COMBO – 30W, 1-12 in. Celestion G12H-75 Creamback speaker combo, all-tube chassis, preamp: 3 X ECC83, power: 2 X KT66, rectifier: GZ34, single channel, 3-band EQ, top gray control panel, two inputs (high, low), six knobs (MV, senitivity, t, m, b, edge), standby switch, power switch, power reduction switch, five external speaker jacks, top handle, Green/White vinyl covering, black grille cloth, 21.25 in. tall, 23.62 in. wide, 10.23 in. deep, 60.62 lbs., mfg. 2015-present.

| MSR $4,400 | $3,000 | $1,950 - 2,250 | $975 - 1,200 | |

ASTORIA CLASSIC HEAD – 30W, guitar head unit, preamp: 3 X ECC83, power: 2 X KT66, rectifier: GZ34, single channel, 3-band EQ, front nickel control panel, two inputs (high, low), six knobs (MV, senitivity, t, m, b, edge), standby switch, power switch, power reduction switch, five external speaker jacks, top handle, Green/White vinyl covering, 11.41 in. tall, 23.62 in. wide, 9.05 in. deep, 36.37 lbs., mfg. 2015-present.

| MSR $3,800 | $2,700 | $1,750 - 2,025 | $875 - 1,075 | |

ASTORIA CLASSIC 112 SPEAKER CABINET – 75W, 1-12 in. Celestion Creamback G12H-75 speaker, 8 ohm, designed to accompany the Astoria series amp heads, Green/White vinyl covering, Black grille cloth, top handle, 20.89 in. tall, 23.62 in. wide, 10.23 in. deep, 37.47 lbs., mfg. 2015-present.

| MSR $1,150 | $850 | $550 - 625 | $275 - 350 | |

ASTORIA CUSTOM COMBO – 30W, 1-12 in. Celestion G12H-75 Creamback speaker combo, all-tube chassis, preamp: 4 X ECC83, power: 2 X KT66, rectifier: GZ34, single channel, 3-band EQ, top gray control panel, two inputs (high, low), six knobs (MV, gain, t, m, b, edge), standby switch, power switch, power reduction switch, effects loop with level control, loop switch, footswitch jack, five external speaker jacks, top handle, footswitch included, Red/White vinyl covering, black grille cloth, 21.25 in. tall, 23.62 in. wide, 10.23 in. deep, 60.62 lbs., mfg. 2015-present.

| MSR $4,600 | $3,200 | $2,075 - 2,400 | $1,050 - 1,275 | |

MSR/NOTES	100%	EXCELLENT	AVERAGE	LAST MSR

ASTORIA CUSTOM HEAD – 30W, guitar head unit, preamp: 4 X ECC83, power: 2 X KT66, rectifier: GZ34, single channel, 3-band EQ, front nickel control panel, two inputs (high, low), six knobs (MV, gain, t, m, b, edge), standby switch, power switch, power reduction switch, boost switch, effects loop with level control, footswitch jack, footswitch included, loop switch, five external speaker jacks, top handle, Red/White vinyl covering, 11.41 in. tall, 23.62 in. wide, 9.05 in. deep, 36.37 lbs., mfg. 2015-present.

MSR $4,000 $2,900 $1,875 - 2,175 $950 - 1,150

ASTORIA CUSTOM 112 SPEAKER CABINET – 75W, 1-12 in. Celestion Creamback G12H-75 speaker, 8 ohm, designed to accompany the Astoria series amp heads, Red/White vinyl covering, Black grille cloth, top handle, 20.89 in. tall, 23.62 in. wide, 10.23 in. deep, 37.47 lbs., mfg. 2015-present.

MSR $1,150 $850 $550 - 625 $275 - 350

ASTORIA DUAL COMBO – 30W, 1-12 in. Celestion G12H-75 Creamback speaker combo, all-tube chassis, preamp: 4 X ECC83, power: 2 X KT66, rectifier: GZ34, dual channel, 3-band EQ, top gray control panel, two inputs (high, low), eight knobs (MV, clean v, OD gain, OD v, t, m, b, edge), standby switch, power switch, power reduction switch, effects loop with level control, loop switch, footswitch jack, five external speaker jacks, top handle, footswitch included, Blue/White vinyl covering, black grille cloth, 21.25 in. tall, 23.62 in. wide, 10.23 in. deep, 60.62 lbs., mfg. 2015-present.

MSR $5,000 $3,400 $2,200 - 2,550 $1,100 - 1,350

ASTORIA DUAL HEAD – 30W, guitar head unit, preamp: 4 X ECC83, power: 2 X KT66, rectifier: GZ34, dual channel, 3-band EQ, front nickel control panel, two inputs (high, low), eight knobs (MV, clean v, OD v, OD gain, t, m, b, edge), standby switch, power switch, power reduction switch, effects loop with level control, footswitch jack, footswitch included, loop switch, five external speaker jacks, top handle, Blue/White vinyl covering, 11.41 in. tall, 23.62 in. wide, 9.05 in. deep, 36.37 lbs., mfg. 2015-present.

MSR $4,500 $3,100 $2,025 - 2,325 $1,000 - 1,250

ASTORIA DUAL 112 SPEAKER CABINET – 75W, 1-12 in. Celestion Creamback G12H-75 speaker, 8 ohm, designed to accompany the Astoria series amp heads, Blue/White vinyl covering, Black grille cloth, top handle, 20.89 in. tall, 23.62 in. wide, 10.23 in. deep, 37.47 lbs., mfg. 2015-present.

MSR $1,150 $850 $550 - 625 $275 - 350

ELECTRIC TUBE AMPLIFIERS: DSL SERIES

DSL15C Combo
courtesy Marshall

DSL15H Head
courtesy Marshall

DSL40C Combo
courtesy Marshall

DSL15C COMBO – 15W, 1-12 in. speaker, guitar combo, six-tube chassis, preamp: 4 X ECC83, power: 2 X 6V6, two channels, digital reverb, tone shift, front gold control panel, single input, nine gold knobs (Clean Ch.: g, v, OD Ch.: g, v, t All: t, m, b, presence, reverb), channel switch, power switch, rear panel: pentode/triode switch, speaker jacks, footswitch jack, footswitch included, black covering, black cloth grille with white piping and a white script Marshall logo, 18 in. wide, 19.5 in. tall, 9.75 in. deep, 37 lbs., mfg. 2012-present.

MSR $840 $600 $400 - 450 $195 - 240

DSL15H HEAD – 15W, guitar head unit, six-tube chassis, preamp: 4 X ECC83, power: 2 X 6V6, two channels, tone shift, front gold control panel, single input, eight gold knobs (Clean Ch.: g, v, OD Ch.: g, v, t All: t, m, b, presence), channel switch, power switch, rear panel: pentode/triode switch, speaker jacks, footswitch jack, footswitch included, black covering, black cloth grille with white piping and a white script Marshall logo, 19.7 in. wide, 9.5 in. tall, 9.2 in. deep, 22.5 lbs., mfg. 2012-present.

MSR $690 $500 $325 - 375 $165 - 200

DSL40C COMBO – 40W, 1-12 in. speaker, guitar combo, six-tube chassis, preamp: 4 X ECC83, power: 2 X 6V6, two channels, digital reverb, tone shift, front gold control panel, single input, eleven gold knobs (Clean Ch.: g, v, OD Ch.: g, v, All: t, m, b, presence, resonance, clean reverb, OD reverb), channel switch, clean/crunch switch, lead switch, standby switch, power switch, rear panel: pentode/triode switch, effects loop, speaker jacks, footswitch jack, footswitch included, black covering, black cloth grille with white piping and a white script Marshall logo, 24.45 in. wide, 19.29 in. tall, 9.92 in. deep, 50.48 lbs., mfg. 2012-present.

MSR $970 $700 $450 - 525 $230 - 280

MSR/NOTES	100%	EXCELLENT	AVERAGE	LAST MSR

DSL100H HEAD – 100W, guitar head unit, eight-tube chassis, preamp: 4 X ECC83, power: 4 X EL34, two channels, digital reverb, tone shift, front gold control panel, single input, eleven gold knobs (Clean Ch.: g, v, OD Ch.: g, v, All: t, m, b, presence, resonance, clean reverb, OD reverb), channel switch, clean/crunch switch, lead switch, standby switch, power switch, rear panel: pentode/triode switch, effects loop, speaker jacks, footswitch jack, footswitch included, black covering, black cloth grille with white piping and a white script Marshall logo, 29.2 in. wide, 10.8 in. tall, 9.5 in. deep, 53.4 lbs., mfg. 2012-present.

| MSR $1,250 | $900 | $575 - 675 | $295 - 350 | |

ELECTRIC TUBE AMPLIFIERS: HANDWIRED SERIES

The Marshall Handwired Series are reissues of the vintage-style Marshalls that were originally handwired.

Model 1958X Combo
courtesy Marshall

Model 1962HW Combo
courtesy Marshall

Model 2245THW Head
courtesy Marshall

MODEL 1958X COMBO – 18W, 2-10 in. Celestion G10-F15 Greenback speakers, guitar combo, five-tube chassis, preamp: 3 X ECC83, power: 2 X EL84, EZ81 rectifier, two channels, tremolo, top gold control panel, two inputs, six knobs (tone 1, tone 2, v1, v2, s, i), power switch, standby switch, black covering, black/gray grille cloth, 21.1 in. tall, 24.1 in. wide, 9.1 in. deep, 43 lbs., mfg. 2014-present.

| MSR $3,900 | $2,700 | $1,750 - 2,025 | $875 - 1,075 | |

MODEL 1959HW HEAD – 100W, head-unit guitar configuration, tube chassis, preamp: 3 X ECC83, power: 4 X EL34, solid-state rectifier, two channels, front gold control panel, four inputs, six knobs (p, b, m, t, v1, v2), black covering, black front with small gold stripes, white script Marshall logo, mfg. 2005-present.

| MSR $4,300 | $3,000 | $1,950 - 2,250 | $975 - 1,200 | |

MODEL 1960AHW/1960BHW HANDWIRED – 120W, 4-12 in. Celestion G12H-30 speakers, 16 ohm impedance, angled front (Model 1960AHW) or straight front (Model 1960AHW), black covering, gray grille with small gold Marshall script logo and "100" in upper left corner, mfg. 2005-present.

| MSR $2,300 | $1,500 | $975 - 1,125 | $500 - 600 | |

MODEL 1962HW COMBO – 30W, 2-12 in. Celestion G12-C Greenback speakers, guitar combo, six-tube chassis, preamp:4 X ECC83, power: 2 X KT66, GZ34 rectifier, two channels, tremolo, top gold control panel, four inputs (two per channel), eight knobs (p, b, m, t, v1, v2, s, i), power switch, standby switch, black covering, reissue Bluesbreaker grille cloth, 24.61 in. tall, 33 in. wide, 10.63 in. deep, 77 lbs., mfg. 2014-present.

| MSR $5,800 | $4,000 | $2,600 - 3,000 | $1,300 - 1,600 | |

MODEL 1973X COMBO – 18W, 2-12 in. Celestion G12-C Greenback speakers, guitar combo, five-tube chassis, preamp:3 X ECC83, power: 2 X EL84, EZ81 rectifier, two channels, tremolo, top gold control panel, two inputs, six knobs (tone 1, tone 2, v1, v2, s, i), power switch, standby switch, black covering, black/gray grille cloth, 23.39 in. tall, 27.96 in. wide, 9.3 in. deep, 50.7 lbs., mfg. 2014-present.

| MSR $4,200 | $2,800 | $1,825 - 2,100 | $900 - 1,125 | |

MODEL 1974X – 18W, 1-12 in. Celestion Greenback T1221 speaker combo, all-tube chassis, preamp: 3 X ECC83, power: 2 X EL84, rectifier: EZ81, two channels, tremolo, top gold control panel, four inputs, six knobs (s, i, Ch. 1: tone, v, Ch. 2: tone, v), Black Levant covering, Gray and White striped grille cloth, 42 lbs , mfg. summer 2004-present.

| MSR $3,900 | $2,700 | $1,750 - 2,025 | $875 - 1,075 | |

This model is based off of the 1966-68 Model 1974 1-12 in. combo.

MODEL 1974CX CABINET – 20W, 1-12 in. Celestion Greenback T1221 speaker, 16 ohm, hand-soldered, designed for the 1974X combo, Black Levant Covering, Black and White striped grille cloth, 31 lbs., mfg. summer 2004-present.

| MSR $1,280 | $900 | $575 - 675 | $295 - 350 | |

MODEL 2061X – 20W, head-unit only, tube chassis, preamp: 2 X ECC83, power: 2 X EL84, rectifier: solid-state, two channels, front gold control panel, four inputs, four knobs (Ch. 1: tone, v, Ch. 2: tone, v), Black Levant covering, 22 lbs., mfg. summer 2004-present.

| MSR $3,000 | $2,100 | $1,375 - 1,575 | $675 - 850 | |

This model is based off of the 1968-1973 Model 2061 Lead & Bass 20.

MODEL 2061CX CABINET – 60W, 1-12 in. Celestion G12H-30 speaker, 8 ohm, hand-soldered, designed for the 2061X head, Black Levant Covering, Black and White chequerboard grille cloth, 53 lbs., mfg. summer 2004-present.

| MSR $1,280 | $900 | $525 - 625 | $300 - 375 | |

MSR/NOTES	100%	EXCELLENT	AVERAGE	LAST MSR

MODEL 2245THW HEAD – 30W, head-unit guitar configuration, tube chassis, preamp: 4 X ECC83, power: 2 X KT66, solid-state rectifier, two channels, front gold control panel, four inputs, eight knobs (s, i, p, b, m, t, v1, v2), black covering, black front with small gold stripes, white script Marshall logo, 10.43 in. tall, 26.2 in. wide, 8.1 in. deep, 33.3 lbs., mfg. 2014-present.

| MSR $4,800 | $3,300 | $2,150 - 2,475 | $1,075 - 1,325 | |

ELECTRIC TUBE AMPLIFIERS: HAZE SERIES

HAZE MHZ 15 HEAD – 15W, guitar head-unit, five-tube chassis, preamp: 3 X ECC83, power: 2 X 6V6, solid-state rectifier, two channels, reverb, echo, vibe, chorus, front gold control panel, single input, nine knobs (effects adjust, effects depth, r, b, m, t, OD v, OD g, Clean v), power switch, effects switch, channel switch, bright switch, rear panel: emulated line out, two speaker jacks (16 ohm, 8 ohm), effects loop with on/off switch, footswitch jack, two-button footswitch included, black covering, gray grille with white piping and white script Marshall logo, 20.5 lbs., mfg. 2009-disc.

| | $600 | $350 - 425 | $200 - 250 | $840 |

HAZE MHZ 40C COMBO – 40W, 1-12 in. Celestion G12T-66 speaker, guitar combo, five-tube chassis, preamp: 3 X ECC83, power: 2 X EL34, solid-state rectifier, two channels, reverb, echo, vibe, chorus, front gold control panel, single input, 10 knobs (Normal Ch. v, OD Ch. v, OD Ch. g, t, m, b, p, r, effect depth, effects adjust), bright switch, boost switch (Normal Ch.), channel switch, boost switch (OD Ch.), effects switch, standby switch, power switch, rear panel: emulated line out, two speaker jacks (16 ohm, 8 ohm), effects loop with on/off switch, footswitch jack, two-button footswitch included, black covering, gray grille with white piping and white script Marshall logo, 44.7 lbs., mfg. 2009-disc.

| | $700 | $450 - 525 | $275 - 325 | $1,000 |

HAZE MHZ112 SPEAKER CABINET – 1-12 in. Celestion G12-66 Marquee speaker, closed back, straight or angled front, designed for use with the Haze MHZ 15 Head, black covering, dark gray grille cloth with white piping and white script Marshall logo, mfg. 2009-disc.

| | $250 | $135 - 175 | $80 - 105 | $350 |

ELECTRIC TUBE AMPLIFIERS: JCM600 SERIES

In 1997, the JCM600 Series was introduced to replace the short-lived JTM Series. Marshall decided against a 30W version for this series and they went back to Marshall basics with black covering, a black grille cloth, and white piping. The JCM600 was also a short-lived series as it was replaced by the JCM2000 Series of amps that featured the TSL60.

JCM600 HEAD (JCM600) – 60W, guitar head-unit, six-tube chassis, preamp: 4 X 12AX7, power: 2 X EL34, solid-state rectifier, two channels, reverb, front gold control panel, single input, 13 knobs (Clean Ch.: v, b, m, t, OD Ch.: g, v, b, m, t, All: effects mix, clean r, OD r, MV), channel switch, power switch, standby switch, two effects loop (series/parallel), two speaker outputs, master presence control, XLR line out with Marshall speaker emulation, black covering, black cloth grille with white script Marshall logo, mfg. 1997-99.

| | N/A | $400 - 500 | $300 - 350 | $1,049 |

* *JCM600 1-12 Combo (JCM601)* – similar to the JCM600 Head, except in combo configuration with 1-12 in. Marshall/Celestion Heritage speaker, mfg. 1997-99.

| | N/A | $400 - 500 | $300 - 375 | $1,149 |

* *JCM600 2-12 Combo (JCM602)* – similar to the JCM600 Head, except in combo configuration with 2-12 in. Marshall/Celestion Heritage speakers, mfg. 1997-99.

| | N/A | $500 - 600 | $325 - 400 | $1,249 |

JCM600 1-12 SPEAKER CABINET (JCMC12) – 70W, 1-12 in. Marshall/Celestion Heritage speaker, 16 ohm impedance, designed for use with the JCM600 Head or JCM600 1-12 Combo (JCM601), black covering, black cloth grille with a white script Marshall logo, mfg. 1997-99.

| | N/A | $175 - 225 | $110 - 140 | $349 |

JCM600 2-12 SPEAKER CABINET (JCMC212) – 140W, 2-12 in. Marshall/Celestion Heritage speakers, 16 ohm impedance, designed for use with the JCM600 2-12 Combo (JCM602), black covering, black cloth grille with a white script Marshall logo, mfg. 1997-99.

| | N/A | $225 - 275 | $135 - 175 | $549 |

JCM600 4-10 SPEAKER CABINET (JCMC410A/JCMC410B) – 120W, 4-10 in. Marshall/Celestion Heritage speakers, 16 ohm impedance, angled (JCMC410A) or straight (JCMC410B) front, recessed metal handles, designed for use with the JCM600 Head, black covering, black cloth grille with a white script Marshall logo, mfg. 1997-99.

| | N/A | $250 - 300 | $150 - 200 | $599 |

ELECTRIC TUBE AMPLIFIERS: JCM-800 SERIES (1981-1991)

This series was released in 1981 at the end of Rose-Morris' contract for distribution. The early '80s were tough times for the music industry, and Marshall felt the pinch that everyone else did. Ending the exclusive distribution deal with Rose Morris opened up some opportunities, but Marshall needed to spice up their line that had not changed since the late 1960s. Therefore, a new amp to bring them into the new decade was needed. The JCM-800 series which was named after Jim Marshall's license plate (JCM is James Charles Marshall) and was virtually identical to the Master Volumes and the Super Leads of the 1970s. The big change was the cosmetics of the amp. A new black cloth with white piping (spelling Marshall) and the control panel spanning the entire width of the amp. Jim's signature was also on the front with JCM 800 in bold, black letters. Basically, they took the old, familiar models and made them into the JCM-800 series. However, new combos were introduced with different designs and new models. In 1983 they brought on the first channel switching in their amps. The JCM-800 series lasted about 10 years and was replaced by the JCM-900 series. The good news around this time was no more Rose-Morris, which opened Marshall's opportunities up a lot.

MSR/NOTES	100%	EXCELLENT	AVERAGE	LAST MSR

Marshall produced the Limited Edition, Original Classic series of amps in 1986. This was supposed to be a line of reproduction amplifiers (like reissues) to the models they had produced in 1969. This was a great idea, however they didn't do enough research on what was original. First of all none of the original amps that were produced in 1969 (Model 1959 and Model 1987) were not offered in this new series. Instead, they produced the newer JCM-800 amps with reverb, channel-switching, and other non-original features. They covered these amps in an odd green vinyl that is nothing like that of 1969 and Checkerboard grille cloth that was unique to the early 1970s.

JCM-800 MODEL 1959 100W LEAD – 100W, head-unit only, lead application, tube chassis, preamp: 3 X ECC83/7025, power: 4 X EL34/6550 two channels, four inputs, six knobs (p, b, m, t, v1, v2), black covering, black cloth grille, mfg. 1981-1991.

| | N/A | $1,200 - 1,500 | $800 - 1,000 | |

This is the JCM-800 version of the Model 1959 Super Lead.

JCM-800 MODEL 1986 50W BASS – 50W, head-unit only, bass application, tube chassis, preamp: 3 X ECC83/7025, power: 2 X EL34/6550, front gold control panel, two inputs, six knobs (slope, b, m, mid-sweep, t, v), black covering, new black grille cloth, active tone circuit, mfg. 1981-87.

| | N/A | $1,200 - 1,500 | $800 - 1,000 | |

This is the JCM-800 version of the Model 1986 Bass.

JCM-800 MODEL 1987 50W LEAD – 50W, head-unit only, lead application, tube chassis, preamp: 3 X ECC83/7025, power: 2 X EL34/6550, solid-state rectifier, two channels, front gold control panel, four inputs, six knobs (p, b, m, t, v1, v2), black covering, black grille, mfg. 1981-1991.

| | N/A | $1,200 - 1,500 | $800 - 1,000 | |

This is the JCM-800 version of the Model 1987 lead.

JCM-800 MODEL 1992 100W BASS – 100W, head-unit only, bass application, tube chassis, 3 X ECC83/7025, power: 4 X EL34/6550, two channels, front gold control panel, four inputs, six knobs (slope, b, m, mid-sweep, t, v), active tone controls, black covering, black grille, mfg. 1981-86.

| | N/A | $1,200 - 1,500 | $800 - 1,000 | |

This is the JCM-800 version of the Model 1992.

JCM-800 MODEL 2203 100W LEAD MV – 100W, head-unit only, lead application, tube chassis, preamp: 3 X ECC83/7025, power: 4 X EL34/6550, solid-state rectifier, one channel, front gold control panel, two inputs (high and low), six knobs (presence, b, m, t, MV, preamp v), black covering, black grille, mfg. 1981-1990.

| | N/A | $1,300 - 1,600 | $775 - 900 | |

This is the JCM-800 version of the Model 2203.

JCM-800 MODEL 2203X REISSUE 100W LEAD – 100W, head-unit only, tube chassis, preamp: 3 X ECC83, power: 4 X EL34, solid-state rectifier, single channel, front gold control panel, two inputs, six knobs (p, b, m, t, MV, v), Series FX effects loop, black covering, black grille, reissue of the JCM-800 produced 1981-1990, 45 lbs., mfg. 2002-present.

| MSR $3,750 | $2,600 | $1,700 - 1,950 | $850 - 1,050 | |

JCM-800 MODEL 2204 50W LEAD MV – 50W, head-unit only, lead application, tube chassis, preamp: 3 X ECC83/7025, power: 2 X EL34/6550, solid-state rectifier, one channel, front gold control panel, two inputs (high and low), six knobs (p, b, m, t, MV, preamp v), black covering, black grille, mfg. 1981-1990.

| | N/A | $1,200 - 1,500 | $800 - 1,000 | |

This is the JCM-800 version of the Model 2204.

* *JCM-800 Model 2204S* – similar to the JCM-800 Model 2204, except is the mini-stack version with a 4-10 in. speaker cabinet, mfg. 1986-87.

| | N/A | $1,200 - 1,500 | $800 - 1,000 | |

JCM-800 MODEL 2205 50W LEAD – 50W, head-unit only, tube chassis, preamp: 5 X 7025, power: 2 X EL34/6550, solid-state chassis, two switchable channels, reverb, front gold control panel, one input, 11 knobs (p, v, r, Drive Ch.: b, m, t, v, g, Clean Ch.: b, t, v), effects loop, black covering, black grille, mfg. 1983-1990.

courtesy Ferris Wheel Music

courtesy Ferris Wheel Music

| | N/A | $1,200 - 1,500 | $800 - 1,000 | |

MSR/NOTES	100%	EXCELLENT	AVERAGE	LAST MSR

JCM-800 MODEL 2210 100W LEAD – 100W, head-unit only, tube chassis, preamp: 5 X 7025, power: 4 X EL34/6550, solid-state chassis, two switchable channels, reverb, front gold control panel, one input, 11 knobs (p, v, r, Drive Ch.: b, m, t, v, g, Clean Ch.: b, t, v), effects loop, black covering, black grille, mfg. 1983-1990.

N/A $1,200 - 1,500 $850 - 1,000

This was Marshall's first channel-switching amp and became very successful over the years.

JCM-800 MODEL 4010 50W LEAD MV 112 COMBO – 50W, 1-12 in. speaker, lead application combo, five-tube chassis, preamp: 3 X ECC83/7025, power: 2 X EL34/6550, solid-state rectifier, one channel, front gold control panel, two inputs (high and low), six knobs (p, b, m, t, MV, preamp v), black covering, black grille, mfg. 1981-1990.

courtesy Savage Audio   courtesy Savage Audio

N/A $1,300 - 1,500 $800 - 950

This is the 1-12 combo version of the JCM-800 Model 2204 Head.

JCM-800 MODEL 4103 100W LEAD MV 212 COMBO – 100W, 2-12 in. speakers, lead application, tube chassis, preamp: 3 X ECC83/7025, power: 4 X EL34/6550, solid-state rectifier, one channel, front gold control panel, two inputs (high and low), six knobs (p, b, m, t, MV, preamp v), black covering, black grille, mfg. 1981-1990.

N/A $1,350 - 1,600 $850 - 975

This is the 2-12 combo version of the JCM-800 Model 2203 Head.

JCM-800 MODEL 4104 50W LEAD MV 212 COMBO – 50W, 2-12 in. combo, lead application, tube chassis, preamp: 3 X ECC83/7025, power: 2 X EL34/6550, solid-state rectifier, one channel, front gold control panel, two inputs (high and low), six knobs (p, b, m, t, MV, preamp v), black covering, black grille, mfg. 1981-1990.

courtesy Savage Audio   courtesy Savage Audio

N/A $1,350 - 1,600 $850 - 975

This is the 2-12 combo version of the JCM-800 Model 2204 Head.

JCM-800 MODEL 4210 50W LEAD 112 COMBO – 50W, 1-12 in. speaker, tube chassis, preamp: 5 X 7025, power: 2 X EL34/6550, solid-state chassis, two switchable channels, reverb, front gold control panel, one input, 11 knobs (p, v, r, Drive Ch.: b, m, t, v, g, Clean Ch.: b, t, v), effects loop, black covering, black grille, mfg. 1982-1990.

N/A $1,100 - 1,400 $675 - 850

This is the 1-12 combo version of the JCM-800 Model 2205 Head.

JCM-800 MODEL 4211 100W LEAD 212 COMBO – 100W, 2-12 in. speakers, tube chassis, preamp: 5 X 7025, power: 4 X EL34/6550, solid-state chassis, two switchable channels, reverb, front gold control panel, one input, 11 knobs (p, v, r, Drive Ch.: b, m, t, v, g, Clean Ch.: b, t, v), effects loop, black covering, black grille, mfg. 1983-1990.

N/A $1,100 - 1,400 $675 - 850

This is the 2-12 combo version of the JCM-800 Model 2210 Head.

MSR/NOTES	100%	EXCELLENT	AVERAGE	LAST MSR

JCM-800 MODEL 4212 50W LEAD 212 COMBO – 50W, 2-12 in. speakers, tube chassis, preamp: 5 X 7025, power: 2 X EL34/6550, solid-state chassis, two switchable channels, reverb, front gold control panel, one input, 11 knobs (p, v, r, Drive Ch.: b, m, t, v, g, Clean Ch.: b, t, v), effects loop, black covering, black grille, mfg. 1983-1990.

	N/A	$1,100 - 1,400	$675 - 850	

This is the 2-12 combo version of the JCM-800 Model 2205 Head.

ELECTRIC TUBE AMPLIFIERS: JCM 900 SERIES (1990-1998)

JCM 900 100W Hi-Gain Master Volume Head
courtesy Dave Rogers/Dave's Guitar Shop

JCM 900 100W Hi-Gain Master Volume Head
courtesy Dave Rogers/Dave's Guitar Shop

The JCM-900 Series replaced the JCM-800 Series in 1990. This new series featured two basic models: the Hi-Gain Master Volume MK III and the Hi Gain Dual Reverb. The Hi-Gain Master Volume MKIII was the latest incarnation of the popular Models 2203 and 2004, while the Hi-Gain Dual Reverb was an updated version of the JCM 800 Models 2205 and 2210. Marshall responded to consumer demand at the time, and added more gain and distortion to this series as well as improved effects loops. The gain section featured two stages with two different knobs - the first one ranged from the standard 0 to 10, while the second knob added on to this by ranging from 10 to 20. Guitarist Nigel Tufnel of Spinal Tap is largely credited with coming up with the extra stage of gain. In the movie *This Is Spinal Tap*, Tufnel's Marshall has a gain knob that goes one beyond the normal highest point of ten to eleven. Marshall actually had Sir Christopher Guest (the actor who played Nigel Tufnel) at the Winter NAMM show in 1990 to introduce the new JCM 900 Series.

Other features of the JCM 900 Series include a series effects loop with adjustable levels, a high/low power switch that acts as a half-power switch by changing the tube's operation from pentode to triode, two line outputs including a direct out and a new recording compensated recording out, and new tube output protection fuses that would blow a fuse if a tube failed protecting the amp from damage.

Marshall also introduced a new numbering system for the JCM 900 Series that actually supplied information about the model's specifications instead of being a random number assignment. Like their previous numbering system, the new system featured four numbers, but that is where the similarities ended. The first number indicated which one of two chassis the amp featured with a 2 for the Hi-Gain Master Volume chassis and a 4 for the Hi-Gain Dual Reverb. The second and the third numbers indicated which one of two wattage outputs the amp had with 50 for 50 watts and 10 for 100 watts. The final number indicated the configuration of an amp: a 0 for a head-unit, a 1 for a 1-12 in. combo, or a 2 for a 2-12 in. combo.

The JCM 900 Series remained largely unchanged for their production run, aside from the two Hi-Gain Master Volume heads. In 1993, the Model 2100 and 2500 were updated by adding an extra preamp tube for more gain. These amps were called the SL-X, which stood for Super Lead Extended. These new SL-X amps were also referred to as MKIVs in Marshall's literature and price lists, but neither these nor the MKIII models (Models 2100 and 2500) had these markings anywhere on the amplifiers. The JCM 900 was discontinued after 1998 when it was replaced by the JCM 2000 Series that featured the new DSL (Dual Super Lead) and TSL (Triple Super Lead) heads.

JCM 900 50W HI-GAIN MASTER VOLUME HEAD (MODEL 2500, MKIII) – 50W (switchable to 25W), guitar head-unit, five-tube chassis, preamp: 3 X ECC83/12AX7, power: 2 X 5881, solid-state rectifier, pentode/triode output stage, two channels, front gold control panel, single input, eight knobs (p, b, m, t, Ch. B MV, Ch. A MV, gain sensitivity [10-20], preamp v [1-10]), footswitch jack, power switch, standby switch, rear panel: effects loop with loop level control, DI out, recording compensated DI out, two speaker jacks with impedance selector switch, high/low power mode switch, output valve protection fuse with LED, black vinyl covering, black cloth grille with white piping and a white script Marshall logo, mfg. 1990-92.

	N/A	$700 - 900	$500 - 575	

* **JCM 900 50W Hi-Gain Master Volume 1-12 Combo (Model 2501, MKIII)** – similar to the JCM 900 50W Head (Model 2500), except in combo configuration with 1-12 in. speaker, mfg. 1990-92.

	N/A	$850 - 1,050	$650 - 725	

* **JCM 900 50W Hi-Gain Master Volume 2-12 Combo (Model 2502, MKIII)** – similar to the JCM 900 50W Head (Model 2500), except in combo configuration with 2-12 in. speakers, mfg. 1990-92.

	N/A	$850 - 1,050	$650 - 725	

* **JCM 900 50W Hi-Gain Master Volume SL-X Head (Model 2500SL-X, MKIV)** – similar to the JCM 900 50W Head (Model 2500), except has an added ECC83/12AX7 preamp tube for added gain, mfg. 1993-98.

	N/A	$750 - 950	$525 - 600	$1,299

JCM 900 100W HI-GAIN MASTER VOLUME HEAD (MODEL 2100, MKIII) – 100W (switchable to 50W), guitar head-unit, seven-tube chassis, preamp: 3 X ECC83/12AX7, power: 4 X 5881, solid-state rectifier, pentode/triode output stage, two channels, front gold control panel, single input, eight knobs (p, b, m, t, Ch. B MV, Ch. A MV, gain sensitivity [10-20], preamp v [1-10]), footswitch jack, power switch, standby switch, rear panel: effects loop with loop level control, DI out, recording compensated DI out, two speaker jacks with impedance selector switch, high/low power mode switch, two output valve protection fuses with LEDs, black vinyl covering, black cloth grille with white piping and a white script Marshall logo, mfg. 1990-92.

N/A $750 - 900 $525 - 600

* **JCM 900 100W Hi-Gain Master Volume 1-12 Combo (Model 2101, MKIII)** – similar to the JCM 900 100W Head (Model 2100), except in combo configuration with 1-12 in. speaker, mfg. 1990-92.

N/A $800 - 950 $525 - 600

* **JCM 900 100W Hi-Gain Master Volume SL-X Head (Model 2100SL-X, MKIV)** – similar to the JCM 900 100W Head (Model 2100), except has an added ECC83/12AX7 preamp tube for added gain, mfg. 1993-98.

N/A $750 - 900 $525 - 600   **$1,299**

JCM 900 HI-GAIN DUAL REVERB 50W HEAD (MODEL 4500) – 50W (switchable to 25W), guitar head-unit, five-tube chassis, preamp: 3 X ECC83/12AX7, power: 2 X 5881/EL34, solid-state rectifier, pentode/triode output stage, two switchable channels, reverb, front gold control panel, single input, ten knobs (Master Ch B: v, r, Master Ch. A: v, r, All: p, b, m, t, Ch. B gain enhance/lead g, Ch. A g), footswitch jack, power switch, standby switch, rear panel: effects loop with loop level control, DI out, recording compensated DI out, two speaker jacks with impedance selector switch, high/low power mode switch, output valve protection fuse with LED, black vinyl covering, black cloth grille with white piping and a white script Marshall logo, mfg. 1990-98.

N/A $650 - 750 $475 - 550   **$1,249**

* **JCM-900 50W Hi-Gain Dual Reverb 1-12 Combo (Model 4501)** – similar to the JCM 900 50W Hi-Gain Dual Reverb Head (Model 4500), except in combo configuration with 1-12 in. speaker, mfg. 1990-98.

N/A $750 - 950 $500 - 575   **$1,349**

* **JCM-900 50W Hi-Gain Dual Reverb 2-12 Combo (Model 4502)** – similar to the JCM 900 50W Hi-Gain Dual Reverb Head (Model 4500), except in combo configuration with 2-12 in. speakers, mfg. 1990-98.

N/A $800 - 950 $625 - 700   **$1,499**

JCM 900 HI-GAIN DUAL REVERB 100W HEAD (MODEL 4100) – 100W (switchable to 50W), guitar head-unit, seven-tube chassis, preamp: 3 X ECC83/12AX7, power: 4 X 5881/EL34, solid-state rectifier, pentode/triode output stage, two switchable channels, reverb, front gold control panel, single input, ten knobs (Master Ch B: v, r, Master Ch. A: v, r, All: p, b, m, t, Ch. B gain enhance/lead g, Ch. A g), footswitch jack, power switch, standby switch, rear panel: effects loop with loop level control, DI out, recording compensated DI out, two speaker jacks with impedance selector switch, high/low power mode switch, two output valve protection fuses with LEDs, black vinyl covering, black cloth grille with white piping and a white script Marshall logo, mfg. 1990-98.

N/A $650 - 800 $450 - 550   **$1,399**

* **JCM-900 100W Hi-Gain Dual Reverb 1-12 Combo (Model 4101)** – similar to the JCM 900 100W Hi-Gain Dual Reverb Head (Model 4100), except in combo configuration with 1-12 in. speaker, mfg. 1990-98.

N/A $700 - 850 $500 - 600   **$1,499**

* **JCM-900 100W Hi-Gain Dual Reverb 2-12 Combo (Model 4102)** – similar to the JCM 900 100W Hi-Gain Dual Reverb Head (Model 4100), except in combo configuration with 2-12 in. speakers, mfg. 1990-98.

N/A $750 - 900 $525 - 650   **$1,599**

ELECTRIC TUBE AMPLIFIERS: JCM 2000 SERIES (1998-2008)

Marshall introduced the first JCM 2000 Series amps at the 1998 Winter NAMM Show. The Dual Super Lead (DSL) heads were based on the previous generation of the JCM 900 Hi Gain Dual Reverb models with more modern features including a deep button. Combo variations of the DSL followed in the summer of 1998, as well as the much anticipated Triple Super Lead (TSL) heads that featured three fully independent channels and a wide array of useful features. 60W variations of the TSL appeared in 1999. In 2006, Marshall introduced a Silver Limited Edition of the TSL100 Head and 1960A/B speaker cabinet that featured silver vinyl and a large check cloth grille with a black script Marshall logo. The JCM-2000 Series was produced for a majority of the 2000s when it was replaced by the JVM Series in 2008. Marshall stopped offering their JCM 2000 models in 2008, but the JCM 2000 Dual Super Lead 100W Head was still being sold by several retailers as either a half- or full-stack.

JCM 2000 DUAL SUPER LEAD 20W 1-12 COMBO (DSL201) – 20W, 1-12 in. speaker, guitar combo, eight-tube chassis, preamp: 4 X ECC83/12AX7, power: 2 X EL84, solid-state rectifier, three channels (Clean, Overdrive 1, Overdrive 2), reverb, front gold control panel, single input, 12 gold knobs (Clean Ch.: g, t, m, b, OD Ch.: g, v, t, m, b, All: FX mix, r, v), channel switch, standby switch, power switch, rear panel: parallel effects loop, speaker jacks, footswitch jack, footswitch included, black Levant covering, black cloth grille with white piping and a white script Marshall logo, 22.5 in. wide, 18 in. tall, 10.5 in. deep, 48.4 lbs., mfg. 1998-2001.

N/A $450 - 525 $300 - 350

MSR/NOTES	100%	EXCELLENT	AVERAGE	LAST MSR

JCM 2000 DUAL SUPER LEAD 40W 1-12 COMBO (DSL401) – 40W, 1-12 in. speaker, guitar combo, eight-tube chassis, preamp: 4 X ECC83/12AX7, power: 4 X EL84, solid-state rectifier, three channels (Clean, Overdrive 1, Overdrive 2), reverb, front gold control panel, single input, 12 gold knobs (Clean Ch.: g, t, m, b, OD Ch.: g, v, t, m, b, All: FX mix, r, v), channel switch, standby switch, power switch, rear panel: parallel effects loop, speaker jacks, footswitch jack, footswitch included, black Levant covering, black cloth grille with white piping and a white script Marshall logo, 22.5 in. wide, 18 in. tall, 10.5 in. deep, 44 lbs., mfg. 1998-2008.

	N/A	$700 - 800	$425 - 500	$1,580

JCM 2000 DUAL SUPER LEAD 50W HEAD (DSL50) – 50W, guitar head-unit, tube chassis, six-tube chassis, preamp: 4 X ECC83/12AX7, power: 2 X EL34, solid-state rectifier, two channels (Classic Gain, Ultra Gain), reverb, front gold control panel, single input, ten gold knobs (p, t, m, b, Ch. B r, Ch. A r, Ch. B v, Ch. B g, Ch. A v, Ch. A g), deep switch, tone switch, Ch. B Lead 1/Lead 2 switch, Ch. A clean/crunch switch, rear panel: series effects loop, speaker jacks, footswitch jack, footswitch included, black Levant covering, black cloth grille with white piping and a white script Marshall logo, 29.5 in. wide, 11.75 in. tall, 8.5 in. deep, 39.6 lbs., mfg. 1998-2008.

	N/A	$800 - 950	$500 - 600	$1,850

JCM 2000 DUAL SUPER LEAD 100W HEAD (DSL100) – 100W, guitar head-unit, tube chassis, eight-tube chassis, preamp: 4 X ECC83/12AX7, power: 4 X EL34, solid-state rectifier, two channels (Classic Gain, Ultra Gain), reverb, front gold control panel, single input, ten gold knobs (p, t, m, b, Ch. B r, Ch. A r, Ch. B v, Ch. B g, Ch. A v, Ch. A g), deep switch, tone switch, Ch. B Lead 1/Lead 2 switch, Ch. A clean/crunch switch, rear panel: series effects loop, speaker jacks, footswitch jack, footswitch included, black Levant covering, black cloth grille with white piping and a white script Marshall logo, 29.5 in. wide, 11.75 in. tall, 8.5 in. deep, 41.8 lbs., mfg. 1998-present.

MSR $2,000	$1,200	$850 - 1,000	$600 - 700	

* *JCM 2000 Dual Super Lead Silver Limited Edition 100W Head (DSL100SL)* – similar to the JCM 2000 Dual Super Lead 100W Head (DSL100), except has a silver control panel, silver vinyl covering, and a gray grille cloth with large black checkering, mfg. 2006 only.

	N/A	$1,000 - 1,200	$650 - 750	$2,310

This head has two matching speaker cabinets - the JCM1960ASL and BSL.

JCM 2000 TRIPLE SUPER LEAD 60W HEAD (TSL60) – 60W, guitar head-unit, tube chassis, six-tube chassis, preamp: 4 X ECC83/12AX7, power: 2 X EL34, solid-state rectifier, three channels (Clean, Crunch, Lead), reverb, front gold control panel, single input, 16 gold knobs (Clean Ch.: g, t, m, b, Crunch Ch.: g, v, Lead Ch.: g, v, t, m, b, Master: p, MV, FX mix, Clean Ch. r, OD r), two channel switches (Clean/OD, OD1/OD2) with LEDs, deep switch, shift switch, standby switch, power switch, rear panel: parallel effects loop, speaker jacks, footswitch jack, five-button footswitch with LEDs included, black Levant covering, black cloth grille with white piping and a white script Marshall logo, 29.5 in. wide, 11.75 in. tall, 8.625 in. deep, 48.4 lbs., mfg. 1999-2007.

	N/A	$900 - 1,050	$550 - 650	$2,000

* *JCM 2000 Triple Super Lead 60W 1-12 Combo (TSL601)* – similar to the JCM 2000 Triple Super Lead 60W Head (TSL60), except in combo configuration with 1-12 in. Celestion speaker, 22.5 in. wide, 18.875 in. tall, 10.5 in. deep, 65 lbs., mfg. 2000-07.

	N/A	$950 - 1,100	$600 - 700	$2,180

* *JCM 2000 Triple Super Lead 60W 2-12 Combo (TSL602)* – similar to the JCM 2000 Triple Super Lead 60W Head (TSL60), except in combo configuration with 2-12 in. Celestion speakers, 26.625 in. wide, 19.875 in. tall, 10.5 in. deep, 79.2 lbs., mfg. 2000-07.

	N/A	$1,000 - 1,200	$600 - 700	$2,280

JCM 2000 TRIPLE SUPER LEAD 100W HEAD (TSL100) – 100W, guitar head-unit, eight-tube chassis, preamp: 4 X ECC83/12AX7, power: 4 X EL34, solid-state rectifier, three channels (Clean, Crunch, Lead), reverb, front gold control panel, single input, 21 gold knobs (Clean Ch.: g, v, t, m, b, p, FX mix, r, Crunch Ch.: g, v, t, m, b, Lead Ch.: g, v, t, m, b, Crunch/Lead shared Ch.: p, FX mix, r), two channel switches (Clean/OD, OD1/OD2) with LEDs, mid boost switch, two deep switches, two tone switches, output mute switch, Virtual Power Reduction (VPR) switch, standby switch, power switch, rear panel: two effects loops with loop level switches, three speaker jacks with impedance selector, footswitch jack, XLR emulated line out, five-button footswitch with LEDs included, black Levant covering, black cloth grille with white piping and a white script Marshall logo, 29.5 in. wide, 11.75 in. tall, 8.5 in. deep, 49.5 lbs., mfg. 1998-2007.

	N/A	$1,000 - 1,200	$750 - 850	$2,300

* *JCM 2000 Triple Super Lead 100W 2-12 Combo (TSL122)* – similar to the JCM 2000 Triple Super Lead 100W Head (TSL100), except in combo configuration with 2-12 in. Celestion speakers, 26.625 in. wide, 19.875 in. tall, 10.5 in. deep, 67.1 lbs., mfg. 1998-2007.

	N/A	$1,350 - 1,550	$850 - 1,000	$3,000

JCM 2000 TRIPLE SUPER LEAD 2-12 SPEAKER CABINET (TSLC212) – 150W, 2-12 in. speakers (one Marshall/Celestion Vintage speaker and one Marshall/Celestion Heritage speaker), 16 ohm mono impedance, recessed side handles, black Levant covering, black cloth grille with white piping and a white script Marshall logo, mfg. 1998-2008.

	N/A	$400 - 475	$250 - 300	$940

JCM 2000 LIMITED EDITION SILVER SPEAKER CABINET (1960ASL/1960BSL) – 300W, 4-12 in. Celestion G12T75 speakers, silver vinyl covering, gray grille with large black checkered pattern, black script Marshall logo, designed for use with the JCM 2000 Dual Super Lead Silver Limited Edition 100W Head (DSL100SL), mfg. 2006 only.

	N/A	$575 - 650	$350 - 425	$1,265

MSR/NOTES	100%	EXCELLENT	AVERAGE	LAST MSR

ELECTRIC TUBE AMPLIFIERS: JTM SERIES

The JTM Series of the 1990s was designed as an affordable, portable, all-tube amplifier. Two chassis were offered in 30W and 60W power ratings and a variety of speaker configurations and cabinets were available. The JTM Series was relatively short-lived, which was attributed to many things including the odd combination of black covering and a gray grille and the fact that the 30W heads were not true modern two channel amplifiers.

JTM30 1-12 COMBO (JTM312) – 30W, 1-12 in. speaker, guitar combo, five-tube chassis, preamp: 3 X ECC83, power: 2 X 5881, solid-state rectifier, two channels, reverb, front gold control panel, single input, eight knobs (Ch. 1: v, Ch. 2: g, v, b, m, t, r, MV), channel switch, power switch, standby switch, emulated speaker output, effects loop, footswitch jack, black covering, gray cloth grille with a white script Marshall logo, mfg. 1995-98.

	N/A	$425 - 500	$275 - 325	$799

JTM30 2-10 COMBO (JTM310) – 30W, 2-10 in. speakers, guitar combo, five-tube chassis, preamp: 3 X ECC83, power: 2 X 5881, solid-state rectifier, two channels, reverb, front gold control panel, single input, eight knobs (Ch. 1: v, Ch. 2: g, v, All: b, m, t, r, MV), channel switch, power switch, standby switch, effects loop, footswitch jack, emulated speaker output, black covering, gray cloth grille with a white script Marshall logo, mfg. 1995-97.

	N/A	$475 - 550	$300 - 350	

JTM60 HEAD (JTM600) – 60W, guitar head-unit, six-tube chassis, preamp: 4 X ECC83, power: 2 X EL34, solid-state rectifier, two channels, reverb, front gold control panel, single input, 13 knobs (Ch. 1: v, b, m, t, Ch. 2: g, v, b, m, t, Master: effects, norm r, boost r, MV), channel switch, power switch, standby switch, footswitch jack, two effects loop (series and parallel), black covering, gray grille with a white script Marshall logo, mfg. 1996-97.

	N/A	$475 - 550	$300 - 350	

* *JTM60 1-12 Combo (JTM612)* – similar to the JTM60 Head (JTM600), except in combo configuration with 1-12 in. speaker, mfg. 1995-97.

	N/A	$500 - 600	$300 - 375	

* *JTM60 1-15 Combo (JTM615)* – similar to the JTM60 Head (JTM600), except in combo configuration with 1-15 in. speaker, mfg. 1995-97.

	N/A	$525 - 625	$300 - 375	

* *JTM60 2-12 Combo (JTM622)* – similar to the JTM60 Head (JTM600), except in combo configuration with 2-12 in. speakers, mfg. 1995-97.

	N/A	$550 - 650	$325 - 400	

* *JTM60 3-10 Combo (JTM610)* – similar to the JTM60 Head (JTM600), except in combo configuration with 3-10 in. speakers, mfg. 1995-97.

	N/A	$550 - 650	$325 - 400	

JTM 1-12 SPEAKER CABINET (JTMC12) – 70W, 1-12 in. speaker, designed for use with the JTM30 1-12 Combo (JTM312), JTM60 Head (JTM600), and JTM60 1-12 Combo (JTM612), black covering, gray grille cloth with a white script Marshall logo, mfg. 1995-97.

	N/A	$175 - 225	$110 - 140	

JTM 2-12 SPEAKER CABINET (JTMC212) – 140W, 2-12 in. speakers, designed for use with the JTM60 2-12 Combo (JTM622), black covering, gray grille cloth with a white script Marshall logo, mfg. 1995-97.

	N/A	$225 - 275	$135 - 175	

JTM 4-10 SPEAKER CABINET (JTMC410) – 120W, 4-10 in. speakers, designed for use with the JTM60 Head (JTM600), black covering, gray grille cloth with a white script Marshall logo, mfg. 1996-97.

	N/A	$250 - 300	$150 - 200	

ELECTRIC TUBE AMPLIFIERS: JVM SERIES

JVM205H HEAD – 50W, guitar head-unit, seven-tube chassis, preamp: 5 X ECC83, power: 2 X EL34, two independent channels (three modes per channel), reverb, front gold control panel, single input, 16 black and gold knobs (Clean/Crunch Ch.: v, b, m, t, g, r, OD Ch.: v, b, m, t, g, r, All: MV1, MV2, resonance, presence), clean/crunch switch, OD mode switch, reverb switch, MV switch, footswitch/MIDI program switch, effects loop switch, back panel: five speaker outputs (various ohm ratings), effects loop with level control, preamp out, power amp in, XLR line out, footswitch jack, MIDI in, MIDI thru, mains, programmable four-button footswitch, black covering, black grille with white piping, 19 in. wide, 7.875 in. tall, 5.5 in. deep, 38.5 lbs., mfg. 2008-present.

MSR $2,300	$1,600	$1,050 - 1,200	$525 - 650	

* *JVM205C Combo* – similar to the JVM205H Head, except in combo configuration with 2-12 in. Celestion speakers (one Celestion Vintage and one Celestion Heritage), 17.5 in. wide, 13 in. tall, 6.75 in. deep, 65 lbs., mfg. 2008-present.

MSR $2,850	$2,000	$1,200 - 1,450	$850 - 1,000	

* *JVM215C Combo* – similar to the JVM205H Head, except in combo configuration with 1-12 in. Celestion G12B speaker, 15.375 in. wide, 13 in. tall, 6.75 in. deep, 58.3 lbs., mfg. 2008-present.

MSR $2,698	$1,850	$1,200 - 1,400	$825 - 975	

MSR/NOTES	100%	EXCELLENT	AVERAGE	LAST MSR

JVM210H HEAD – 100W, guitar head-unit, nine-tube chassis, preamp: 5 X ECC83, power: 4 X EL34, two independent channels (three modes per channel), reverb, front gold control panel, single input, 16 black and gold knobs (Clean/Crunch Ch.: v, b, m, t, g, r, OD Ch.: v, b, m, t, g, r, All: MV1, MV2, resonance, presence), clean/crunch switch, OD mode switch, reverb switch, MV switch, footswitch/MIDI program switch, effects loop switch, back panel: five speaker outputs (various ohm ratings), effects loop with level control, preamp out, power amp in, XLR line out, footswitch jack, MIDI in, MIDI thru, mains, programmable four-button footswitch, black covering, black grille with white piping, 19 in. wide, 7.875 in. tall, 5.5 in. deep, 48.5 lbs., mfg. 2008-present.

| MSR $2,540 | $1,800 | $1,175 - 1,350 | $575 - 725 | |

* **JVM210C Combo** – similar to the JVM210H Head, except in combo configuration with 2-12 in. Celestion speakers (one Celestion Vintage and one Celestion Heritage), 17.5 in. wide, 13 in. tall, 6.75 in. deep, 76 lbs., mfg. 2008-present.

| MSR $3,150 | $2,200 | $1,425 - 1,650 | $725 - 875 | |

JVM410H HEAD – 100W, guitar head-unit, nine-tube chassis, preamp: 5 X ECC83, power: 4 X EL34, four independent channels (clean, crunch, OD1, OD2), reverb, front gold control panel, single input, 28 black and gold knobs (Clean Ch.: v, b, m, t, g, r, Crunch Ch.: v, b, m, t, g, r, OD1 Ch.: v, b, m, t, g, r, OD2 Ch.: v, b, m, t, g, r, All: MV1, MV2, resonance, presence), switch for each channel, reverb switch, MV switch, footswitch/MIDI program switch, effects loop switch, back panel: five speaker outputs (various ohm ratings), effects loop with level control, preamp out, power amp in, XLR line out, footswitch jack, MIDI in, MIDI thru, mains, programmable six-button footswitch, black covering, black grille with white piping, 19 in. wide, 7.875 in. tall, 5.5 in. deep, 48.5 lbs., mfg. 2007-present.

| MSR $3,550 | $2,500 | $1,625 - 1,875 | $825 - 1,000 | |

* **JVM410C Combo** – similar to the JVM410H Head, except in combo configuration with 2-12 in. Celestion speakers (one Celestion Vintage and one Celestion Heritage), 17.5 in. wide, 13 in. tall, 6.75 in. deep, 76 lbs., mfg. 2007-present.

| MSR $4,040 | $2,900 | $1,875 - 2,175 | $950 - 1,150 | |

JVMC212 SPEAKER CABINET – 140W, 2-12 in. Celestion Vintage 30 speakers, 16 ohm impedance, straight front, black covering, black grille, 26.77 in. wide, 19.69 in. tall, 10.63 in. deep, 46.3 lbs., mfg. 2010-present.

| MSR $1,170 | $850 | $550 - 625 | $275 - 350 | |

ELECTRIC TUBE AMPLIFIERS: LIMITED EDITION/SIGNATURE SERIES

For the JTM-45 series reissues, please refer to the JTM-45 series.

40TH ANNIVERSARY STACK/JTM 45/100 – 100W (2 X 50W), guitar piggyback configuration with two 4-12 in. speaker cabinets, tube chassis, preamp: 3 X ECC83, power: 4 X KT66, two channels, front gold control panel, four inputs (two normal and two high treble), six knobs (p, b, m, t, high treble v, normal v), power switch, standby switch, red pilot light, black levant covering with gold accents and an early Marshall-style logo, mfg. 2006 only.

| | $6,500 | N/A | N/A | $9,000 |

The JTM45/100 Stack was created to commemorate the 40th Anniversary of the 100W Marshall stack. The Chassis is based on the early Marshall models before the Model 1959 was introduced. This amp is sold as a full-stack only and includes the JTM45/100 head, one straight 4-12 speaker cabinet (Model 812B40), and one angled speaker cabinet (Model 812T40). Only 250 of these sets are slated for production and Jim Marshall has numbered each one individually.

DAVE MUSTAINE SPEAKER CABINET (MODEL 1960ADM/BDM) – 280W, 4-12 in. Celestion Vintage 30 speakers, 16/4 ohm mono or 8 ohm stereo impedance, recessed metal handles, black covering, black metal grille with white script Marshall logo and lower left-hand corner brushed aluminum plate signed by Dave Mustaine and Jim Marshall, mfg. 2009-disc.

| | $1,200 | $800 - 950 | $550 - 650 | $1,760 |

JCM SLASH SIGNATURE (MODEL 2555SL) – 100W (switchable to 50W), guitar head-unit, seven-tube chassis, preamp: 3 X 12AX7, power: 4 X EL34, solid-state rectifier, two channels, front gold control panel with Slash graphic, Jim Marshall signature, and Slash signature, single input, seven knobs (p, b, m, t, output master with push/pull channel switch, lead master, input gain with push/pull clip switch), power switch, standby switch, low output/high output switch, rear panel: footswitch jack, series effects loop, DI output jack, two speaker jacks with ohm selector, mains voltage selector, black snakeskin covering, black grille with white piping and a white script Marshall logo, limited edition run of 3,000 units, mfg. 1996-97.

| | N/A | $1,600 - 2,000 | $1,100 - 1,300 | |

This amp was designed around the Model 2555 Silver Jubilee produced in 1987 that Slash began using in earnst.

JCM SLASH SIGNATURE 4-12 SPEAKER CABINET (MODEL 1960ASL/BSL) – 280W, 4-12 in. 70W Celestion Vintage 30 speakers, mono/stereo operation, two input jacks, angled (1960ASL) or straight (1960BSL) front, black snakeskin covering, black grille cloth with white piping, a white script Marshall logo, and a gold Slash signature plate in the lower left-hand corner, mfg. 1996-97.

| | N/A | $425 - 500 | $250 - 300 | |

JOE SATRIANI JVM410HJS SIGNATURE HEAD – 100W, guitar head-unit, nine-tube chassis, preamp: 5 X ECC83, power: 4 X EL34, four independent channels (clean, crunch, OD1, OD2), noise gates, front gold control panel, single input, 28 black and gold knobs (Clean Ch.: v, b, m, t, g, gate threshold, Crunch Ch.: v, b, m, t, g, gate threshold, OD1 Ch.: v, b, m, t, g, gate threshold, OD2 Ch.: v, b, m, t, g, gate threhold, All: MV1, MV2, resonance, presence), switch for each channel, reverb switch, MV switch, footswitch/MIDI program switch, effects loop switch, back panel: five speaker outputs (various ohm ratings), effects loop with level control, preamp out, power amp in, XLR line out, footswitch jack, MIDI in, MIDI thru, mains, programmable six-button footswitch, black covering, black grille with white piping, 29.5 in. wide, 12.2 in. tall, 8.4 in. deep, 48.5 lbs., mfg. 2012-present.

| MSR $3,600 | $2,600 | $1,700 - 1,950 | $850 - 1,050 | |

MSR/NOTES	100%	EXCELLENT	AVERAGE	LAST MSR

KERRY KING JCM800 SIGNATURE HEAD (2203KK) – 100W, guitar head-unit, seven-tube chassis, preamp: 3 X ECC83, power: 4 X KT88, single channel, front gold control panel with Kerry King's and Jim Marshall's signatures, single input, eight black and gold knobs (p, b, m, t, MV, preamp v, gate/threshold, assault/intensity), "The Beast" switch (King's custom EQ curve and a variable gain boost), five speaker outputs, black covering, black grille with white piping and Slayer/Kerry King inspired graphics, 29.5 in. wide, 12.25 in. tall, 8.5 in. deep, 47.3 lbs., mfg. 2007-2012.

	$1,900	$1,200 - 1,400	$800 - 950	$2,700

LEMMY KILMISTER SUPERBASS SIGNATURE HEAD (MODEL 1992LEM) – 100W, bass application head-unit, seven-tube chassis, preamp: 3 X ECC83, power: 4 X EL34, solid-state rectifier, two channels, brushed gold aluminum control panel, four inputs (two per channel), six black knobs with gold inserts (p, b, m, t, v1, v2), power switch standby switch, rear panel: two speaker out jacks, output ohmselector, mains voltage selector, features Motorhead Ace Of Spades logo and Jim Marhsall's and Lemmy Kilmister signatures, black covering, black front with white piping, white script Marshall logo, and two gold-pained wooden crests with a five-point star inside them, red corner piece in lower right-hand corner, 34.5 lbs., mfg. 2008-2013.

	$3,000	$1,900 - 2,250	N/A	$4,200

MODEL 1959 LIMITED EDITION PURPLE PLEXI STACK – 100W, guitar head-unit (Model 1959LTD) with one angled front 4-12 in. speaker cabinet (Model 1982ALTD) and one straight front extra-tall 4-12 in. speaker cabinet (Model 1982BLTD), seven-tube chassis, preamp: 3 X ECC83/12AX7, power: 4 X EL34, solid-state rectifier, two channels, front gold plexi control panel with "MK II" logo, four inputs (two per channel), six knobs (p, b, m, t, v1, v2), power switch, standby switch, rear gold plexi panel with "Super Lead 100W" two speaker jacks with impedance selector, mains voltage selector, purple vinyl covering, light straw basket weave cloth grille with white piping and white script Marshall logo, limited edition run of 200 sets (100 for the U.S.), mfg. 1994 only.

Full Stack (Complete Set)	N/A	$3,000 - 3,500	$2,000 - 2,500	
Head Only	N/A	$1,600 - 2,000	$1,100 - 1,300	$4,000

The volume controls on the control panel were labeled "High Treble Loudness 1" and "Normal Loudness 2." This Marshall set has obtained a variety of nicknames including "Barney" because of the purple color and the "Hendrix Stack" because of the association with Jimi Hendrix and the extra tall base cabinet. This stack was only sold as a set.

RANDY RHOADS SIGNATURE HEAD (MODEL 1959RR) – 100W, lead application head-unit, seven-tube chassis, preamp: 3 X ECC83, power: 4 X EL34, solid-state rectifier, two channels, brushed gold aluminum control panel, four inputs (two per channel), six black knobs with gold inserts (p, b, m, t, v1, v2), power switch standby switch, rear panel: two speaker out jacks, output ohm selector, mains voltage selector, features image of Randy Rhoads and Jim Marhsall's and Randy Rhoads signatures, white covering, white front with white piping, black script Marshall logo, and black corners, 34.5 lbs., mfg. 2008-2013.

	$2,800	$1,800 - 2,100	$1,200 - 1,400	$4,000

SUPER 100JH JIMI HENDRIX SIGNATURE STACK – 100W (2 X 50W), guitar stack configuration with two pinstriped 4-12 in. Model 1982 speaker cabinets, tube chassis, preamp: 3 X ECC83, power: 4 X KT66, two channels, front gold control panel, four inputs (two normal and two high treble), six knobs (p, b, m, t, high treble v, normal v), power switch, standby switch, red pilot light, black levant covering with gold accents, mfg. 2006 only.

	N/A	$4,000 - 5,000	$3,000 - 3,500	$8,000

The Super 100JH Jimi Hendrix Signature Stack was created to commemorate the 40th Anniversary between Marshall and Jimi Hendrix. The Chassis is based on a circa 1966 model, just like what Jimi played in the late 1960s. This amp is sold as a full-stack only and includes the Super 100JH head and two Model 1982 speaker cabinets - one that is the extra-tall Model 1982B. Only 600 of these sets are slated for production.

ZAKK WYLDE SIGNATURE HEAD (2203ZW) – 100W, head-unit only, all tube chassis, 4 X 6550 power tubes, single channel, front custom control panel, two inputs, six gold knobs (presence, b, m, t, MV, v), black covering, TV fret cloth, mfg. 2002 only.

	N/A	$1,400 - 1,700	$1,200 - 1,350	$2,250

This amp is a reissue of the JCM-800 2203 made signature for Zakk. When shipped, it came equipped with Zakk Wylde guitar picks, a custom cover, and certificate of authenticity. There were only 600 made and they sold out within half a year. There are speaker cabinets to match up with this head that are listed in the Speaker Cabinet section.

ELECTRIC TUBE AMPLIFIERS: MA SERIES

MA50H HEAD – 50W, guitar head-unit, five-tube chassis, preamp: 3 X ECC83, power 2 X EL34, two channels, reverb, front gold brushed aluminum control panel, single input, 13 knobs (Clean Ch.: b, m, t, v, OD Ch.: crunch balance, g, b, m, t, v, All: r, resonance, p), channel switch, overdrive boost switch, power switch, standby switch, rear panel: three speaker jacks, footswitch jack, effects loop, black covering, black grille, 29.5 in. wide, 12.5 in. tall, 10 in. deep, 36 lbs., mfg. 2010-disc.

	$700	$425 - 500	$250 - 300	$950

* **MA50C Combo** – similar to the MA50H Head, except in combo configuration with 1-12 in. speaker, 25 in. wide, 20 in. tall, 10.625 in. deep, 50 lbs., mfg. 2010-disc.

	$750	$450 - 525	$275 - 325	$1,000

MA100H HEAD – 100W, guitar head-unit, seven-tube chassis, preamp: 3 X ECC83, power: 4 X EL34, two channels, reverb, front gold brushed aluminum control panel, single input, 13 knobs (Clean Ch.: b, m, t, v, OD Ch.: crunch balance, g, b, m, t, v, All: r, resonance, p), channel switch, overdrive boost switch, power switch, standby switch, rear panel: three speaker jacks, footswitch jack, effects loop, black covering, black grille, 29.5 in. wide, 12.5 in. tall, 10 in. deep, 40.5 lbs., mfg. 2010-disc.

	$800	$500 - 575	$300 - 350	$1,100

MSR/NOTES	100%	EXCELLENT	AVERAGE	LAST MSR

* **MA100C Combo** – similar to the MA100H Head, except in combo configuration with 2-12 in. speakers, 26.75 in. wide, 20 in. tall, 10.5 in. deep, 62.5 lbs., mfg. 2010-disc.

	$900	$550 - 650	$325 - 400	$1,250

M412A/M412B SPEAKER CABINET – 300W, 4-12 in. Eminence 12AX75 speakers, 16 ohm impedance, straight (M412B) or angled (M412A) front, black covering, black grille, 29.75 in. wide, 30 in. tall, 14.375 in. deep, 80 lbs., mfg. 2010-disc.

	$400	$250 - 300	$150 - 200	$550

ELECTRIC TUBE AMPLIFIERS: SILVER JUBILEE SERIES

The Silver Jubilee (25/50) series was introduced in 1987 to commemorate Jim Marshall's 25 years in amplification and 50 years in music. These amps were based on the 2203 and 2204 Master Volume models, but they did have other changes in the electronics as well. The wattage could be dropped (cut in half) by a switch when less sound was needed. There were three different gain modes as well. These amps were covered in silver vinyl (for the 25th Annniversary), and featured chrome-plated control panels. The Jubilee series was only produced for that year, 1987, and after that the name was changed to the Custom Series for the next year or so. These were discontinued in 1990, around the same time ast the JCM-800 series. The speaker cabinets are included here because they are exclusive to this series only. Essentially they were a 1960 cabinet in silver vinyl. These amps have recently become more collectible because of the added features they have over the JCM-800 series.

SILVER JUBILEE MODEL 2550 50W LEAD – 50W (switchable to 25W), head-unit only, lead application, tube chassis, preamp: 3 X ECC83/7025, power: 2 X EL34/6550, solid-state rectifier, pentode/triode output section, gain switching, front chrome control panel, one input, seven silver knobs, effects loop on back, silver covering, black grille, mfg. 1987-89.

	N/A	$1,950 - 2,400	$1,100 - 1,350	

In 1988, the silver covering, and chrome control panel was replaced with traditional black covering and gold control panel.

SILVER JUBILEE MODEL 2551A/B 412 SPEAKER CABINET – 4-12 in. Celestion G12 70 & 75 speakers, full size cabinet, silver covering, black grille, mfg. 1987-88.

	N/A	$700 - 900	$500 - 600	

SILVER JUBILEE MODEL 2551AV/BV 412 SPEAKER CABINET – 4-12 in. Celestion Vintage 30 speakers, full size cabinet, silver covering, black grille, mfg. 1987-88.

	N/A	$700 - 900	$500 - 600	

SILVER JUBILEE MODEL 2553 50W LEAD – 50W (switchable to 25W), head-unit only, lead application, tube chassis, preamp: 3 X ECC83/7025, power: 2 X EL34/6550, solid-state rectifier, pentode/triode output section, gain switching, front chrome control panel, one input, seven silver knobs, effects loop on back, silver covering, black grille, mfg. 1987 only.

	N/A	$1,900 - 2,300	$1,050 - 1,300	

This model is similar to the Model 2550, except is a smaller head-unit built for a mini-stack and was discontinued when the Custom Series was launched in 1988.

SILVER JUBILEE MODEL 2554 50W LEAD 112 COMBO – 50W (switchable to 25W), 1-12 in. speaker, lead application, tube chassis, preamp: 3 X ECC83/7025, power: 2 X EL34/6550, solid-state rectifier, pentode/triode output section, gain switching, front chrome control panel, one input, seven silver knobs, effects loop on back, silver covering, black grille, mfg. 1987-89.

	N/A	$2,000 - 2,400	$1,050 - 1,300	

In 1988, the silver covering, and chrome control panel was replaced with traditional black covering and gold control panel.

SILVER JUBILEE MODEL 2555 100W LEAD – 10W (switchable to 50W), head-unit only, lead application, tube chassis, preamp: 3 X ECC83/7025, power: 4 X EL34/6550, solid-state rectifier, pentode/triode output section, gain switching, front chrome control panel, one input, seven silver knobs, effects loop on back, silver covering, black grille, mfg. 1987-89.

	N/A	$2,000 - 2,500	$1,300 - 1,600	

In 1988, the silver covering, and chrome control panel was replaced with traditional black covering and gold control panel.

SILVER JUBILEE MODEL 2556A/B SPEAKER CABINET – 2-12 in. Celestion G12 70 & 75 speakers, small cabinet meant to match up to the 2553 Mini Head, silver covering, black grille, mfg. 1987-88.

	N/A	$550 - 700	$425 - 500	

SILVER JUBILEE MODEL 2556AV/BV SPEAKER CABINET – 2-12 in. Celestion Vintage 30 speakers, small cabinet meant to match up to the 2553 Mini Head, silver covering, black grille, mfg. 1987-88.

	N/A	$550 - 700	$425 - 500	

SILVER JUBILEE MODEL 2558 100W LEAD 212 COMBO – 50W (switchable to 25W), 1-12 in. speaker, lead application, tube chassis, preamp: 3 X ECC83/7025, power: 2 X EL34/6550, solid-state rectifier, pentode/triode output section, gain switching, front chrome control panel, one input, seven silver knobs, effects loop on back, silver covering, black grille, mfg. 1987-89.

	N/A	$1,900 - 2,400	$950 - 1,200	

In 1988, the silver covering, and chrome control panel was replaced with traditional black covering and gold control panel.

MSR/NOTES	100%	EXCELLENT	AVERAGE	LAST MSR

ELECTRIC TUBE AMPLIFIERS: VINTAGE MODERN SERIES

MODEL 2266 50W LEAD – 50W, guitar head-unit, eight-tube chassis, preamp: 4 X 12AX7, power: 2 X KT66, single channel, digital plate reverb, extra gain stage, front gold control panel, single input, eight gold and black knobs (r, MV, p, b, m, t, preamp detail, preamp body), mid-boost switch, dynamic range switch, back panel: footswitch jack, effects loop with two switches, two speaker outputs with an 8/16 ohm impedance selector switch, mains, footswitch, black covering, black grille with white piping, 29.5 in. wide, 12.25 in. tall, 9 in. deep, 39.6 lbs., mfg. 2007-2013.

	$1,500	$650 - 800	$425 - 550	$2,100

* *Model 2266 50W 212 Combo* – similar to the Model 2266 50W Lead Head, except in combo configuration with 2-12 in. G12C-25 Celestion Greenback speakers, 27.2 in. wide, 22.5 in. tall, 10.6 in. deep, 66 lbs., mfg. 2007-2013.

	$1,800	$750 - 900	$500 - 650	$2,500

MODEL 2466 100W LEAD – 100W, guitar head-unit, eight-tube chassis, preamp: 4 X 12AX7, power: 4 X KT66, single channel, digital plate reverb, extra gain stage, front gold control panel, single input, eight gold and black knobs (r, MV, p, b, m, t, preamp detail, preamp body), mid-boost switch, dynamic range switch, back panel: footswitch jack, effects loop with two switches, two speaker outputs with an 8/16 ohm impedance selector switch, mains, footswitch, black covering, black grille with white piping, 29.5 in. wide, 12.25 in. tall, 9 in. deep, 49.5 lbs., mfg. 2007-2013.

	$1,650	$700 - 850	$475 - 600	$2,350

MODEL 425A/425B SPEAKER CABINET – 100W, 4-12 in. G12C Celestion Greenback speakers, 16/4 ohm impedance mono (8 ohm impedance stereo), angled (425A) or straight (425B) front, black covering, black grille with white piping, 30.3 in. wide, 29.75 in. tall, 14.4 in. deep, 79 lbs. (425A) or 81.5 lbs. (425B), mfg. 2007-2013.

	$1,000	$525 - 650	$300 - 375	$1,455

ELECTRIC TUBE AMPLIFIERS: VINTAGE REISSUE SERIES

2555X Head Silver Jubilee Reissue
courtesy Marshall

JCM900 4100 Head Reissue
courtesy Marshall

Silver Jubilee 2551AV/2551BV 412
Reissue Speaker Cabinet courtesy Marshall

2555X HEAD SILVER JUBILEE REISSUE – 100W (switchable to 50W), head-unit only, tube chassis, preamp: 3 X ECC83, power: 4 X EL34, two channels, 3-band EQ, pentode/triode output section, gain switching, front chrome control panel, one input, seven silver knobs (presence, b, m, t, output MV, lead MV, input gain), five external speaker jacks, DI jack, footswitch jack, effects loop, silver covering, black grille, 9.05 in. tall, 29.53 in. wide, 12.2 in. deep, 48.72 lbs., mfg. 2015-present.

MSR $2,580	$1,900	$1,225 - 1,425	$625 - 750	

JCM900 4100 HEAD REISSUE – 100W, guitar head-unit, seven-tube chassis, preamp: 3 X ECC83/12AX7, power: 4 X 5881, pentode/triode output stage, two switchable channels, reverb, front gold control panel, single input, ten knobs (Master Ch B: v, r, Master Ch. A: v, r, All: p, b, m, t, Ch. B gain enhance/lead g, Ch. A g), single input, footswitch jack, power switch, standby switch, rear panel: effects loop with loop level control, DI out, recording compensated DI out, two speaker jacks with impedance selector switch, high/low power mode switch, two output valve protection fuses with LEDs, black vinyl covering, black cloth grille with white piping and a white script Marshall logo, 12.2 in. tall, 29.5 in. wide, 8.6, in. deep, 41.5 lbs., current mfg.

MSR $2,900	$2,100	$1,375 - 1,575	$675 - 850	

SILVER JUBILEE 2551AV/2551BV 412 REISSUE SPEAKER CABINET – 280W, 4-12 in. Celestion Vintage 30 speakers, 4/8/16 ohm impedance, angled (2551AV) or straight (2551BV) front, silver vinyl covering, black grille, 30.31 in. wide, 29.72 in. tall, 14.37 in. deep, 91.27 lbs., mfg. 2015-present.

MSR $1,800	$1,300	$850 - 975	$425 - 525	

ELECTRIC TUBE AMPLIFIERS: VALVE BASS SERIES (VBA)

VBA 400 HEAD – 400W, head-unit only, tube chassis, preamp: 3 X ECC83, 1 X ECC82, power: 8 X 6550, single channel, front black control panel, two inputs (passive, active), six knobs (MV, t, m, c, b, g), deep switch, bright switch, effects loop, fan cooled, Black covering, Black grille cloth, 79 lbs., disc.

	$2,700	$1,400 - 1,750	$950 - 1,100	$3,400

MSR/NOTES	100%	EXCELLENT	AVERAGE	LAST MSR

VBC 412 SPEAKER CABINET – 400W, 4-12 in. speakers, 4 ohm impedance, Black covering, Black grille cloth, 108 lbs., disc.

	$975	$600 - 700	$375 - 450	$1,380

VBC 810 SPEAKER CABINET – 640W, 8-10 in. speakers, 4 ohm impedance, Black covering, Black grille cloth, 158 lbs., disc.

	$1,900	$1,200 - 1,400	$800 - 950	$2,700

ELECTRIC TUBE AMPLIFIERS: MISC. MODELS

Model 2525C Mini Jubilee Combo
courtesy Marshall

Model 2525H Mini Jubilee Head
courtesy Marshall

Model 4001 Studio 15
courtesy Willie's American Guitars

85TH ANNIVERSARY HEAD (MODEL 1923) – 50W, guitar head-unit based on the DSL (Dual Super Lead) platform, six-tube chassis, preamp: 4 X ECC83, power: 2 X EL34, two channels, reverb, front gold control panel with faded British flag and Jim Marshall 85 logo, single input, 10 knobs (p, t, m, b, Ch. A r, Ch. B r, Ch. A v, Ch. A g, Ch. B v, Ch. B g), deep shift switch, tone shift switch, power switch, standby switch, rear panel: two footswitch jacks, effects loop, three speaker jacks, black covering, black speaker grille with white piping, white script Marshall logo, and Jim Marshall 85th Birthday gold plaque in upper left-hand corner, mfg. 2009-disc.

	$1,900	$1,200 - 1,450	$800 - 950	$2,700

* **85th Anniversary 2-12 Combo (Model 1923C)** – similar to the 85th Anniversary Head (Model 1923), except in combo configuration with 2-12 in. speakers (one Heritage, one Vintage), recessed metal handles, and Jim Marshall 85th Birthday gold plaque in lower left-hand corner, mfg. 2009-disc.

	$2,500	$1,400 - 1,750	$950 - 1,100	$3,350

CAPRI – 5W, 1-8 in. speaker combo, tube chassis, preamp: 1 X ECC83, power: 1 X EL84, front control panel, two inputs, volume and tone controls, red custom vinyl, white grille, mfg. 1966-67.

	N/A	$325 - 400	$200 - 250	

There were only around 100 of these made.

CLASS 5 – 5W, 1-10 in. Celestion G10F-15 speaker, guitar combo, three-tube chassis, preamp: 2 X ECC83, power: 1 X EL84, solid-state rectifier, single channel, top gold control panel, single input, four knobs (v, t, m, b), power switch, headphone jack, speaker/headphone switch, extension speaker jack, black covering, basketweave salt/pepper grille cloth with white script Marshall logo, 19.5 in. wide, 16.375 in. tall, 9 in. deep, 26.5 lbs., mfg. 2009-2014.

	$400	$250 - 300	$135 - 175	$560

MODEL 1930 POPULAR – 10W, 1-12 in. speaker combo, tube chassis, preamp: ECC83, power: 2 X ECL86, two channels, tremolo, four inputs (two per channel), six knobs (Ch. 1: v, t, Ch. 2: v, t, s, i), footswitch, mfg. 1972-73.

	N/A	$2,000 - 2,500	$1,400 - 1,700	

MODEL 2046 SPECIALIST – 25W, 1-15 in. speaker combo, tube chassis, preamp: ECL86, 2 X ECC83, power: 2 X EL34, single channel, reverb, tremolo, front control panel, two inputs, five knobs, black covering, chequerboard grille, mfg. 1971-73.

	N/A	$700 - 900	$500 - 600	

This model was the first Marshall amp to have a printed circuit board in the electronics. This was a model designed for a jazz application.

MODEL 2060 MERCURY – 5W, 1-12 in. speaker combo, hybrid design, preamp: solid-state, power: 1 X EL84, solid-state rectifier, one channel, two inputs, four knobs (s, i, tone, v), red or orange covering, chequerboard grille, Marshall logo on a piece of metal running across front of amp, mfg. 1972-73.

	N/A	$1,000 - 1,200	$700 - 850	

This model was available through mail order catalogs only.

MODEL 2150 – 100W, 1-12 in. speaker combo, tube chassis, preamp: unknown, power: 4 X EL34, dual channels, four inputs (two per channel), 7 knobs, Master volume, mfg. 1978-1980.

	N/A	$800 - 950	$575 - 700	

This model was the only Marshall amp to have four inputs with a Master Volume control. Rose-Morris called it the "Rock n' Roll Baby."

MSR/NOTES	100%	EXCELLENT	AVERAGE	LAST MSR

MODEL 2525C MINI JUBILEE COMBO – 20W (switchable to 5W), 1-12 in. Celestion G12M Greenback speaker, guitar combo amp, tube chassis, preamp: 3 X ECC83, power: 2 X EL34, pentode/triode output section, gain switching, front chrome control panel, one input, seven silver knobs (presence, b, m, t, output MV, lead MV, input g), five external speaker jacks, DI out jack, footswitch jack, effects loop, silver covering, black grille, 18.7 in. tall, 19.2 in. wide, 11 in. deep, 41.8 lbs., new 2016.

| MSR $2,050 | $1,500 | $975 - 1,125 | $500 - 600 | |

MODEL 2525H MINI JUBILEE HEAD – 20W (switchable to 5W), head-unit only, tube chassis, preamp: 3 X ECC83, power: 2 X EL34, pentode/triode output section, gain switching, front chrome control panel, one input, seven silver knobs (presence, b, m, t, output MV, lead MV, input g), five external speaker jacks, DI out jack, footswitch jack, effects loop, silver covering, black grille, 9.1 in. tall, 20 in. wide, 8.6 in. deep, 22 lbs., new 2016.

| MSR $1,800 | $1,300 | $850 - 975 | $425 - 525 | |

MODEL 3203 ARTIST – 30W, head-unit only, tube chassis, preamp: ECC83, power: 2 X EL34, solid-state tone network, front gold control panel, one input, nine knobs, black covering, black grille, mfg. 1986-1991.

| | N/A | $425 - 500 | $275 - 325 | |

This model is the same as the Model 4203 Combo except in a mini head-unit configuration, which is meant to be used in the mini-stack.

MODEL 3210 LEAD 100 MOSFET – 100W, head-unit only, dual channels, reverb, front gold control panel, nine knobs, black covering, mfg. 1984-1991.

| | N/A | $300 - 350 | $200 - 250 | |

This amp was the first in the mini-stack series, where 2 4-10 in. speaker cabinets could be teamed up with the head unit, but at an affordable price.

MODEL 4001 STUDIO 15 – 15W, 1-12 in. speaker combo, tube chassis, preamp: ECC83, power: 6V6, one channel, front gold control panel, one input, five gold knobs (gain, t, m, b, v), headphone jack, black covering, black grille, mfg. 1986-1992.

| | N/A | $675 - 875 | $475 - 550 | |

This Marshall amp was the first for the company in many ways. It was the first to have the 6V6 tubes, Clestion Vintage 30 speakers, and a headphone jack.

MODEL 4140 CLUB AND COUNTRY – 100W, 2-12 in. speakers, lead application, tube chassis, preamp: unknown, power: 4 X KT77, two channels, reverb, front gold control panel, four inputs, 10 knobs, brown oak (brown vinyl) covering, light brown (straw colored) grille, mfg. 1978-1982.

| | N/A | $850 - 1,000 | $600 - 700 | |

MODEL 4145 CLUB AND COUNTRY – 100W, 4-10 in. speakers, lead application, tube chassis, preamp: unknown, power: 4 X KT77, two channels, reverb, front gold control panel, four inputs, 10 knobs, brown oak (brown vinyl) covering, light brown (straw colored) grille, mfg. 1978-1982.

| | N/A | $850 - 1,000 | $600 - 700 | |

This amp was intended for the country musician.

MODEL 4150 CLUB AND COUNTRY BASS – 100W, 4-10 in. speakers, bass application, tube chassis, preamp: unknown, power: 4 X KT77, two channels, reverb, front gold control panel, four inputs, 9 knobs, brown oak (brown vinyl) covering, light brown (straw colored) grille, mfg. 1978-1982.

| | N/A | $750 - 900 | $525 - 600 | |

This amp was intended for the country musician.

MODEL 4203 ARTIST 112 COMBO – 30W, 1-12 in. speaker combo, tube chassis, preamp: ECC83, power: 2 X EL34, solid-state tone network, front gold control panel, one input, nine knobs, black covering, black grille, mfg. 1986-1991.

| | N/A | $525 - 650 | $300 - 350 | |

This model was designed around the model 3203 mini-stack.

ELECTRIC HYBRID AMPLIFIERS: JMD:1 SERIES

JMD50 HEAD – 50W, guitar head-unit, hybrid chassis with a digital preamp and 2 X EL34 power tubes, solid-state rectifier, four channels, 16 preamp digital selections, four digital delays, four digital mods, front gold brushed aluminum control panel, single input, 13 gold knobs (16-position pre-amp selector, g, b, m, t, v, mod adjust, mod depth, delay adjust, delay level, r, p, MV), footswitch/MIDI program switch, compare switch, Ext FX switch, delay/tap tempo switch, modulation switch, four channel switches, manual switch, power switch, standby switch, rear panel: effects loop, MIDI in and through, emulated line out jack, headphone jack, MP3/CD line in, black covering, black grille, footswitch included, 29.5 in. wide, 12.25 in. tall, 8.675 in. deep, 34 lbs., mfg. 2010-disc.

| | $1,000 | $600 - 725 | $325 - 400 | $1,350 |

MSR/NOTES	100%	EXCELLENT	AVERAGE	LAST MSR

* **JMD501 1-12 Combo** – similar to the JMD50 Head, except in combo configuration with 1-12 in. G12-70MD speaker, 25 in. wide, 20.675 in. tall, 10 in. deep, 49.5 lbs., mfg. 2010-disc.

	$1,150	$700 - 825	$400 - 475	$1,550

JMD100 HEAD – 100W, guitar head-unit, hybrid chassis with a digital preamp and 4 X EL34 power tubes, solid-state rectifier, four channels, 16 preamp digital selections, four digital delays, four digital mods, front gold brushed aluminum control panel, single input, 13 gold knobs (16-position pre-amp selector, g, b, m, t, v, mod adjust, mod depth, delay adjust, delay level, r, p, MV), footswitch/MIDI program switch, compare switch, Ext FX switch, delay/tap tempo switch, modulation switch, four channel switches, manual switch, power switch, standby switch, rear panel: effects loop, MIDI in and through, emulated line out jack, headphone jack, MP3/CD line in, black covering, black grille, footswitch included, 29.5 in. wide, 12.25 in. tall, 8.675 in. deep, 34 lbs., mfg. 2010-disc.

	$1,100	$650 - 775	$375 - 450	$1,500

* **JMD102 2-12 Combo** – similar to the JMD100 Head, except in combo configuration with 1-12 in. G12-70MD and 1-12 in. 12AX75 speakers, 27 in. wide, 20.875 in. tall, 10.25 in. deep, 66 lbs., mfg. 2010-disc.

	$1,200	$725 - 850	$425 - 500	$1,650

ELECTRIC HYBRID AMPLIFIERS: MODE FOUR SERIES

The Mode Four Series debuted at the Winter NAMM show in 2003. This amp was designed with the same intention that Jim Marshall used when the first JTM-45 was built. Jim listened to what players wanted and he delivered. 40 years later, the Mode Four Series is built on those same principles. This new amp has a massive 350W of power, more gain, more low-end, more head room, and the best cleans and crunches that Marshalls are known for. There are two separate amps in each unit with either clean or crunch selections for a total of four modes (hence the name).

MODE FOUR (MF 350) – 350W, head-unit only, hybrid chassis, single ECC83 tube in each amp, MF350 power section, reverb, front gold control panel, single input, 19 silver knobs (Ch. 1: g, v, r, FX, b, m, t, Ch. 2: g, v, r, FX, Tone Matrix, b, m, t, Both: resonance, p, solo level, MV), clean/crunch switches for each amp, tuner mute, effects loop, line out, six-button footswitch included, black covering, silver slanted stripe grille, 53 lbs., mfg. 2003-08.

courtesy Marshall   courtesy Marshall

	N/A	$900 - 1,050	$550 - 650	$2,000

MODE FOUR MF280 A/B SPEAKER CABINET – 280W, 4-12 in. speakers, 16 ohm impedance, designed for use with Mode Four head, angled front (MF280A) or straight front (MF280B), black covering, black grille with white script logo and Mode Four logo in lower left corner, mfg. 2003-08.

	N/A	$700 - 800	$425 - 500	$1,550

MODE FOUR MF400 A/B SPEAKER CABINET – 400W, 4-12 in. speakers, 16 ohm impedance, designed for use with Mode Four head, angled front (MF400A) or straight front (MF400B), black covering, black grille with white script logo and Mode Four logo in lower left corner, mfg. 2003-08.

	N/A	$700 - 800	$425 - 500	$1,550

VALVESTATE AMPLIFIERS (HYBRID): VALVESTATE SERIES I

Prior to 1991, Marshall never produced a "budget" amplifier line and Hybrid technology was also becoming popular among amplifier manufacturers. In 1991, Marshall introduced the Valvestate Series that featured a tube in the preamp section and a solid-state power amp. These amps were targeted for the musician that was on a budget, was entry-level, or didn't need the big power of their tube amps. The first Valvestate series came in four models with matching cabinets. In 1991, they introduced a 100W head with matching 4 X 12 cabinet, two power amps, and a mircro-stack. Models then followed in 1992 with the popular 8200 head-unit, and combo 8240. A new feature on this series, with the exception of the 10W model, was a contour knob. This knob worked with the mid-frequencies to go from metal to blues.

MODEL 8004 80W POWER AMP – 80W (40W X 2), power amp, rack mount, hybrid design, originally finished in black, but changed to gold in 1993, mfg. 1991-98.

	N/A	$100 - 150	$60 - 80	

MODEL 8008 160W POWER AMP – 160W (80W X 2), power amp, rack mount, hybrid design, dual volume controls, originally finished in black, but changed to gold in 1993, mfg. 1991-98.

	N/A	$150 - 200	$75 - 125	

MODEL 8010 10W 18 COMBO – 10W, 1-8 in. speaker combo, hybrid design with an ECC83 preamp tube, single channel, front gold control panel, one input, five gold knobs (g, MV, b, m, t) headphone jack, line output, black covering, black grille, mfg. 1991-98.

	N/A	$120 - 150	$75 - 95	

MSR/NOTES	100%	EXCELLENT	AVERAGE	LAST MSR

* **Model 8001 Micro Stack** – similar to the 8010, except in micro-stack version, mfg. 1991-98.

| | N/A | $275 - 325 | $150 - 200 | |

MODEL 8020 20W 110 COMBO – 20W, 1-10 in. speaker combo, hybrid design with an ECC83 preamp tube, dual channels, reverb, front gold control panel, one input, eight gold knobs (Norm: g, b, t, Boost: g, c, p, v, r), headphone jack line out, footswitch, black covering, black grille, mfg. 1991-98.

courtesy John Beeson/The Music Shoppe

courtesy John Beeson/The Music Shoppe

| | N/A | $100 - 125 | $60 - 80 | |

MODEL 8040 40W 112 COMBO – 40W, 1-12 in. speaker combo, hybrid design with an ECC83 preamp tube, dual channels, reverb, front gold control panel, one input, 10 gold knobs (Norm: g, b, m, t, Boost: g, c, b, t, v, r), preamp out, power amp in jacks, line out, footswitch, black covering, black grille, mfg. 1991-98.

| | N/A | $150 - 200 | $100 - 125 | |

MODEL 8080 100W 112 COMBO – 100W, 1-12 in. speaker, hybrid design with an ECC83 preamp tube, dual channels, reverb, two modes in each channel, front gold control panel, one input, 13 gold knobs (Norm: g, b, m, t, Boost: g, b, m, t, c, v, Master: effects, r, v) effects loop on front, footswitch, black covering, black grille, mfg. 1991-98.

| | N/A | $150 - 200 | $100 - 125 | |

MODEL 8100 100W HEAD – 100W, head-unit only, hybrid design with an ECC83 preamp tube, dual channels, reverb, two modes in each channel, front gold control panel, one input, 13 gold knobs (Norm: g, b, m, t, Boost: g, b, m, t, c, v, Master: effects, r, v) effects loop on front, footswitch, black covering, black grille, mfg. 1991-98.

| | N/A | $175 - 225 | $100 - 125 | |

The Model 8412 speaker cabinet (140W, 4-12 in. speakers) is made especially to fit the Model 8100 Head.

MODEL 8200 200W HEAD – 200W (100W X 2), head-unit only, hybrid design with an ECC83 preamp tube, dual channels, Overdrive 1/2 switch in boost, chorus, reverb, front gold control panel, one input, 17 gold knobs (Norm: g, b, m, t, Boost: gain, b, m, t, c, v, Master: effects, r, v, Chorus: rate and depth controls for Normal and Boost channels), various switches, effects loop, black covering, black grille, mfg. 1993-98.

| | N/A | $225 - 275 | $100 - 150 | |

There is a cabinet, Model 8222, to match the 8200 head listed in the cabinet section.

MODEL 8240 80W 212 COMBO – 80W (40W X 2), 2-12 in. speakers, hybrid design with an ECC83 preamp tube, dual channels, Overdrive 1/2 switch in boost, chorus, reverb, front gold control panel, one input, 17 gold knobs (Norm: g, b, m, t, Boost: gain, b, m, t, c, v, Master: effects, r, v, Chorus: rate and depth controls for Normal and Boost channels), various switches, effects loop, black covering, black grille, mfg. 1993-98.

| | N/A | $225 - 275 | $125 - 175 | |

MODEL 8280 160W 212 COMBO – 160W (80W X 2), 2-12 in. speakers, hybrid design with an ECC83 preamp tube, dual channels, Overdrive 1/2 switch in boost, chorus, reverb, front gold control panel, one input, 17 gold knobs (Norm: g, b, m, t, Boost: gain, b, m, t, c, v, Master: effects, r, v, Chorus: rate and depth controls for Normal and Boost channels), various switches, effects loop, black covering, black grille, mfg. 1993-98.

| | N/A | $250 - 300 | $150 - 200 | |

VALVESTATE AMPLIFIERS (HYBRID): VALVESTATE SERIES II

The first few models of the Valvestate second series was introduced in 1995 and the entire line was rolled out in 1996, replacing the original Valvestate Series. The second series was more user-friendly for guitarists and they were designed to sound even more like a tube amp. The Valvestate Series II was produced through 2000 when they were replaced by the AVT (Advanced Valvestate Technology) Series. Marshall also produced a two-space rack-mount Valvestate Power Amp called the **VS Pro 120/120**, but specifications and used values are unknown.

VS15 – 15W, 1-8 in. speaker, guitar combo, hybrid chassis with an ECC83 preamp and Valvestate power stage, single channel, front gold control panel, one input, six gold knobs (g1, g2, t, c, b, MV), headphone jack, line out jack, black covering, black grille cloth with white piping and white script Marshall logo, mfg. 1995-2000.

| | N/A | $95 - 120 | $50 - 75 | | $199 |

MSR/NOTES	100%	EXCELLENT	AVERAGE	LAST MSR

VS15R – similar to the VS 15, except has reverb and a reverb control for a total of seven knobs, mfg. 1995-2000.

| | N/A | $120 - 150 | $70 - 95 | $259 |

VS30R – 30W, 1-10 in. speaker, guitar combo, hybrid chassis with an ECC83 preamp tube and Valvestate power stage, two channels, reverb, front gold control panel, one input, nine gold knobs (Ch 1: v, b, t, Ch 2: g, b, c, t, v, r), channel switch, power switch, line out, headphone jack, footswitch jack, black covering, black grille cloth with white piping and white script Marshall logo, mfg. 1995-2000.

| | N/A | $150 - 200 | $95 - 125 | $399 |

VS65R – 65W, 1-12 in. speaker, guitar combo, hybrid chassis with an ECC83 preamp and Valvestate power stage, two channels, reverb, front gold control panel, single input, 11 gold knobs (Ch 1: v, b, m, t, Ch 2: g, b, c, t, v, FX mix, r), channel switch, effects loop, line out, headphone jack, footswitch, black covering, black grille cloth with white piping and white script Marshall logo, mfg. 1996-2000.

| | N/A | $250 - 300 | $125 - 175 | $599 |

VS100RH HEAD – 100W, guitar head-unit, hybrid chassis with an ECC83 preamp tube and Valvestate power stage, three channels, reverb, front gold control panel, single input, 15 gold knobs (Clean Ch.: v, b, m, t, OD 1 Ch.: g, v, OD2 Ch.: g, c, v, OD EQ: b, m,t, All: FX mix, clean r, OD r), Clean/OD channel switch, OD1/OD2 channel switch, tone shift switch, power dimension switch, FX loop level switch, effects loop, headphone jack, footswitch, black covering, black grille cloth with white piping and white script Marshall logo, mfg. 1996-2000.

| | N/A | $275 - 350 | $175 - 225 | $739 |

VS100R 1-12 Combo – similar to the VS100RH Head, except in combo configuration with 1-12 in. speaker, mfg. 1996-2000.

| | N/A | $300 - 375 | $175 - 225 | $789 |

VS102R 2-12 Combo – similar to the VS100RH Head, except in combo configuration with 2-12 in. speakers, mfg. 1998-2000.

| | N/A | $325 - 400 | $200 - 250 | |

VS230 – 60W (2 x 30W stereo), 2-10 in. speakers, guitar combo, hybrid chassis with an ECC83 preamp and Valvestate power stage, two channels, chorus, reverb, front gold control panel, one input, 11 gold knobs (Clean: v, b, t, OD: g, b, c, t, v, r, chorus s, chorus d), power switch, chorus switch, channel switch, headphone jack, stereo line out, black covering, black cloth grille with white piping and a white script Marshall logo, mfg. 1996-2000.

| | N/A | $200 - 250 | $120 - 150 | $749 |

VS232 – 60W (2 x 30W stereo), 2-12 in. speakers, guitar combo, hybrid chassis with an ECC83 preamp and Valvestate power stage, two channels, chorus, reverb, front gold control panel, one input, 11 gold knobs (Clean: v, b, t, OD: g, b, c, t, v, r, chorus s, chorus d), power switch, chorus switch, channel switch, headphone jack, stereo line out, black covering, black cloth grille with white piping and a white script Marshall logo, mfg. 1998-2000.

| | N/A | $225 - 275 | $130 - 160 | |

VS265 – 130W (2 x 65W stereo), 2-12 in. speakers, guitar combo, hybrid chassis with an ECC83 preamp tube and Valvestate power stage, three channels, chorus, reverb, front gold control panel, one input, 17 gold knobs (Clean Ch.: v, b, m, t, OD1 Ch.: g, v, OD2 Ch.: g, c, v, EQ: b, m, t, All: FX mix, clean r, overdrive r, s, d), Clean/OD channel switch, OD1/OD2 channel switch, tone shift switch, power dimension switch, power switch, rear panel: speaker jacks, emulated stereo line out, effects loop, headphone jack, black covering, black cloth grille with white piping and a white script Marshall logo, mfg. 1996-2000.

| | N/A | $375 - 450 | $250 - 300 | $1,049 |

VS112 SPEAKER CABINET – 80W, 1-12 in. speaker, 8 ohm mono impedance, designed for use with the VS100R 1-12 combo, black covering, black cloth grille with white piping and a white script Marshall logo, mfg. 1996-2000.

| | N/A | $150 - 200 | $95 - 120 | $369 |

VS212 SPEAKER CABINET – 160W, 2-12 in. speakers, mono/stereo impedance, designed for use with the VS265R 2-12 combo, black covering, black cloth grille with white piping and a white script Marshall logo, mfg. 1996-2000.

| | N/A | $200 - 250 | $120 - 150 | $499 |

VS412A/VS412B SPEAKER CABINET – 140W, 4-12 in. speakers, 8 ohm mono impedance, angled (VS412A) or straight (VS412B) front, designed for use with the VS100RH Head, black covering, black cloth grille with white piping and a white script Marshall logo, mfg. 1996-2000.

| | N/A | $300 - 350 | $175 - 225 | $679 |

VALVESTATE AMPLIFIERS (HYBRID): ADVANCED VALVESTATE TECH. (AVT) SERIES

The Advanced Valvestate Technology (AVT) series is built with the VS2000 series of chassis. These amps are even more advanced than the earlier Valvestates. The most noted addition is the digital effects touting. This lets the user use different digital effects in the amp. In 2006, Marshall introduced the AVTX Series. This series simply has updated cosmetics with the same chassis as the original AVT series. New style models will have an X on the end of the model name/number.

AVT 20(X) – 20W, 1-10 in. speaker, guitar combo, hybrid chassis with an ECC83 preamp and Valvestate power section, single channel, overdrive, reverb, front gold control panel, one input, six gold knobs (g, v, b, m, t, d), CD input, DI emulation input, headphone jack, external speaker jack, black covering, black grille, 31 lbs., mfg. 2000-07.

| | $325 | $200 - 250 | $120 - 150 | $449 |

This model was also available as a limited edition with white covering and checkered grille cloth.

MSR/NOTES	100%	EXCELLENT	AVERAGE	LAST MSR

AVT 50H(X)
courtesy Marshall

AVT150H(X)
courtesy Marshall

AVT 50(X) – 50W, 1-12 in. speaker, guitar combo, hybrid chassis with an ECC83 preamp and Valvestate power section, two channels, reverb, front gold control panel, one input, ten gold knobs (Clean: g, v, b, t, OD: g, v, b, m, t, r, d), CD and headphone jacks, effects loop, emulated DI output, footswitch, black covering, black grille, 42 lbs., mfg. 2000-07.

	N/A	$325 - 400	$200 - 250	$750

* **AVT 50H(X)** – similar to the AVT 50(X) except in head-unit configuration, 26 lbs., mfg. 2000-07.

	N/A	$300 - 350	$175 - 225	$650

AVT 100(X) – 100W, 1-12 in. speaker, guitar combo, hybrid chassis with an ECC83 preamp and Valvestate power section, three channels, reverb, 16 built in DFX (digital effects), front gold control panel, one input, 18 gold knobs (g and v for clean, OD1, and OD2 channels, b, m, t, for clean and overdrive, MV, p, mix, DFX mix, Adjust, and program selection knob), parallel effects loop, footswitch, black covering, black grille, 53 lbs., mfg. 2000-07.

	N/A	$300 - 375	$175 - 225	$950

AVT 150(X) – 150W, 1-12 in. speaker, guitar combo, hybrid chassis with an ECC83 preamp and Valvestate power section, four channels (Acoustic simulator, Clean, OD1, and OD2), reverb, front gold control panel, one input, 24 gold knobs (gain and voulme for Clean, OD1, and OD2, Ac. Sim and voulme for Acoustic, b, m, t, for clean and overdrive, master volume, presence, FX loop mix (2), DFX mix, adjust and program selection for clean and overdrive channels), effects loop, footswitch, black covering, black grille, 62 lbs., mfg. 2000-07.

	N/A	$300 - 375	$200 - 250	$1,050

* **AVT 150H(X)** – similar to the AVT 150(X) except in head-unit configuration, 35 lbs., mfg. 2000-07.

	N/A	$250 - 300	$150 - 200	$1,050

AVT 275(X) STEREO – 150W (2 X 75W Stereo), 2-12 in. speaker, guitar combo, hybrid chassis with an ECC83 preamp and Valvestate power section, four channels (Acoustic simulator, Clean, OD1, and OD2), The Clean and Overdrive channels are the same as the AVT 150, reverb, one input, 24 gold knobs (gain and volume for Clean, OD1, and OD2, Ac. Sim and volume for Acoustic, b, m, t, for clean and overdrive, master volume, presence, FX loop mix (2), DFX mix, adjust and program selection for clean and overdrive channels), effects loop, footswitch, black covering, gold control panel, black grille, 75 lbs., mfg. 2000-07.

	N/A	$375 - 475	$250 - 325	$1,300

AVT 112(X) SPEAKER CABINET – 100W, 1-12 in. speaker, 8 ohm, designed for use with the AVT 150, Black covering, Black grille cloth, mfg. 2000-07.

	N/A	$150 - 200	$95 - 120	$360

AVT 412 A/B(X) SPEAKER CABINET – 200W, 4-12 in. speakers, 8 ohm, straight or angled cabinet, designed for use with the AVT 50H(X) or AVT 150H(X), Black covering, Black grille cloth, mfg. 2000-07.

	N/A	$300 - 375	$175 - 225	$750

SOLID-STATE AMPLIFIERS: 5000 SERIES (EARLY MODELS)

MODEL 5002 "LEAD 20" – 20W, 1-10 in. speaker, guitar combo, solid-state chassis, single channel, front gold control panel, two inputs, five knobs (g, v, t, m, b), headphone jack, power switch, black covering, black grille, mfg. 1984-1991.

	N/A	$175 - 225	$85 - 105	

MODEL 5005 "LEAD 12" – 12W, 1-10 in. speaker, guitar combo, solid-state chassis, single channel, front gold control panel, two inputs, five knobs (g, v, t, m, b), headphone jack, power switch, black covering, black grille, mfg. 1984-1991.

	N/A	$150 - 200	$100 - 125	

SOLID-STATE AMPLIFIERS: CODE SERIES

CODE 25 COMBO – 25W, 1-10 in. speaker, digital guitar combo, solid-state chassis, single channel, reverb, 14 preamp models, four power amp models, eight speaker emulations, 24 digital effects, 3-band EQ, top gold control panel, single input, seven knobs (g, b, m, t, v, effects select, MV), tuner switch, Bluetooth switch, tap switch, store switch, power switch, MP3/line in, headphone jack, footswitch jack, digital tuner, USB connectivity, black covering, black grille with white script Marshall logo, 13.38 in. tall, 13.77 in. wide, 8.46 in. deep, 13.4 lbs., new 2016.

MSR $285	$200	$130 - 150	$65 - 80	

MSR/NOTES	100%	EXCELLENT	AVERAGE		LAST MSR

Code 50 Combo
courtesy Marshall

Code 100H Head
courtesy Marshall

Code 412 Speaker Cabinet
courtesy Marshall

CODE 50 COMBO – 50W, 1-12 in. speaker, digital guitar combo, solid-state chassis, single channel, reverb, 14 preamp models, four power amp models, eight speaker emulations, 24 digital effects, 3-band EQ, top gold control panel, single input, seven knobs (g, b, m, t, v, effects select, MV), tuner switch, Bluetooth switch, tap switch, store switch, power switch, MP3/line in, headphone jack, footswitch jack, digital tuner, USB connectivity, speaker emulation, LCD display, Bluetooth connectivity, black covering, black grille with white script Marshall logo, 17.3 in. tall, 20.8 in. wide, 11 in. deep, 28.6 lbs., new 2016.

MSR $375 $250 $165 - 190 $80 - 100

CODE 100 COMBO – 100W, 2-12 in. speakers, digital guitar combo, solid-state chassis, single channel, reverb, 14 preamp models, four power amp models, eight speaker emulations, 24 digital effects, 3-band EQ, top gold control panel, single input, eight knobs (g, b, m, t, v, MV, preset, edit), tuner switch, Bluetooth switch, tap switch, store switch, power switch, MP3/line in, headphone jack, footswitch jack, digital tuner, USB connectivity, speaker emulation, LCD display, Bluetooth connectivity, footswitch included, black covering, black grille with white script Marshall logo, 18.90 in. tall, 27.36 in. wide, 10.83 in. deep, 52.8 lbs., new 2016.

MSR $570 $400 $260 - 300 $130 - 160

CODE 100H HEAD – 100W, digital guitar head unit, solid-state chassis, single channel, reverb, 14 preamp models, four power amp models, eight speaker emulations, 24 digital effects, 3-band EQ, front gold control panel, single input, eight knobs (g, b, m, t, v, MV, preset, edit), tuner switch, Bluetooth switch, tap switch, store switch, power switch, MP3/line in, headphone jack, footswitch jack, digital tuner, USB connectivity, speaker emulation, LCD display, Bluetooth connectivity, footswitch included, black covering, black grille with white script Marshall logo, 8.5 in. tall, 23.22 in. wide, 11.81 in. deep, 24.25 lbs., new 2016.

MSR $500 $350 $230 - 265 $115 - 140

CODE 412 SPEAKER CABINET – 120W, 4-12 in. custom voiced speakers, 4 ohm mono impedance, angled front, black covering, black grille, 52.8 lbs., new 2016.

MSR $350 $250 $165 - 190 $80 - 100

SOLID-STATE AMPLIFIERS: G/MG SERIES

In summer 1998, Marshall discontinued their entry-level Park line of amps, and moved the models over to the Marshall line. Since these amps utilize solid-state electronics, Marshall was wary of putting his name on any solid-state product. After five years of the Park amps, Marshall decided that they had earned enough credentials and moved them into the Marshall line with the models **G10MKII**, **G15RCD**, **G30RCD**, and the **G215RCD**. In 1999, the **G50RCD**, **G80RCD**, **G100RCD**, and **MG412A** and **B** speaker cabinets were introduced along with a G15MS Micro Stack that featured a G15RCD in head configuration and two small speaker cabinets.

Marshall initially referred to these amplifiers as the Marshall Park Series. In 1999, they began calling them the MG Series, although they never had "MG" in the model name (aside from the speaker cabinets). The MG probably stands for the Marshall G Series, and this line of amps should be referred to as the MG II Series, since they were all replaced in 2002 with the MG III Series.

G10MKII – 10W, 1-6.5 in. speaker, guitar combo, solid-state chassis, single channels, front gold control panel, single input, three knobs (g, contour, v), boost switch, headphone jack, power switch, black covering, black grille cloth with white script Marshall logo, 11.4 in. wide, 11.4 in. tall, 6.7 in. deep, 9.9 lbs., mfg. summer 1998-2001.

     N/A $40 - 60 $20 - 30

G15RCD – 15W, 1-8 in. speaker, guitar combo, solid-state chassis, single channel (two gain stages), reverb, front gold control panel, single input, seven knobs (g1, g2, t, c, b, MV, r), headphone jack, line out, CD input, black covering, black grille cloth with white script Marshall logo, 14.8 in. wide, 14 in. tall, 7.9 in. deep, 14.3 lbs., mfg. summer 1998-2001.

     N/A $70 - 90 $40 - 55

* **G15MS Micro-Stack** – similar to the G15RCD except is in mini-stack configuration with a head and two 1-8 in. speaker cabinets (one angled, one straight), mfg. 1999-2001.

     N/A $200 - 250 $120 - 150

MSR/NOTES	100%	EXCELLENT	AVERAGE	LAST MSR

G30RCD – 30W, 1-10 in. speaker, guitar combo, solid-state chassis, two channels, reverb, front gold control panel, single input, nine knobs (Ch. 1: v, b, t, Ch. 2: g, b, c, t, v, r), channel switch, footswitch jack, line out, headphone jack, CD input, power switch, black covering, black grille cloth with white script Marshall logo, 18.7 in. wide, 15.6 in. tall, 8.7 in. deep, 25.3 lbs., mfg. summer 1998-2001.

| | N/A | $150 - 200 | $95 - 120 | |

G50RCD – 50W, 1-12 in. speaker, guitar combo, solid-state chassis, two channels, reverb, front gold control panel, single input, 10 knobs (Normal Ch.: g, b, m, t, Boost Ch.: g, c, b, t, v, r), boost switch, preamp out, power amp in, line out, footswitch jack, power switch, rear panel: effects loop, CD input, black covering, black grille cloth with white script Marshall logo, footswitch included, 20.9 in. wide, 18.1 in. tall, 10.6 in. deep, 44 lbs., mfg. 1999-2001.

| | N/A | $200 - 250 | $120 - 150 | |

G80RCD – 80W, 1-12 in. speaker, guitar combo, solid-state chassis, two channels, reverb, front gold control panel, single input, 13 knobs (Normal Ch.: g, b, m, t, Boost Ch.: g, b, m, t, c, v, All: effects level, r, MV), effects loop, channel switch, Normal Ch. clean/crunch switch, Boost Ch. OD1/OD2 switch, effects loop switch, line out, footswitch jack, power switch, rear panel: speaker out jacks, CD input, black covering, black grille cloth with white script Marshall logo, footswitch included, 22.4 in. wide, 18.1 in. tall, 10.6 in. deep, 55 lbs., mfg. 1999-2001.

| | N/A | $250 - 300 | $150 - 200 | |

G100RCD – 100W, guitar head unit, solid-state chassis, two channels, reverb, front gold control panel, single input, 13 knobs (Normal Ch.: g, b, m, t, Boost Ch.: g, b, m, t, c, v, All: effects level, r, MV), effects loop, channel switch, Normal Ch. clean/crunch switch, Boost Ch. OD1/OD2 switch, effects loop switch, line out, footswitch jack, power switch, rear panel: speaker out jacks, CD input, black covering, black grille cloth with white script Marshall logo, footswitch included, 22.4 in. wide, 9.1 in. tall, 10.6 in. deep, 39.6 lbs., mfg. 1999-2001.

| | N/A | $200 - 250 | $120 - 150 | |

G215RCD – 30W (2 X 15W stereo), 2-8 in. speakers, guitar combo, solid-state chassis, single channel (two gain stages), reverb, chorus, front gold control panel, single input, nine knobs (g1, g2, t, c, b, MV, r, chorus speed, chorus depth), chorus switch, line out, headphone jack, CD input, power switch, black covering, black grille cloth with white script Marshall logo, 19.3 in. wide, 14 in. tall, 9 in. deep, 22 lbs., mfg. summer 1998-2001.

| | N/A | $200 - 250 | $120 - 150 | |

MG412A/B SPEAKER CABINET – 120W, 4-12 in. speakers, 8 ohm impedance, angled (A) or straight (B) front, designed for use with the G and MG Series heads, available in black covering with a black grille and white script Marshall logo, cream covering with a basketweave grille and white script Marshall logo (recent models only), or red covering with a dark gray grille and white script Marshall logo (recent models only), mfg. 1999-present.

| MSR $450 | $260 | $175 - 225 | $110 - 140 | |

SOLID-STATE AMPLIFIERS: MGIII SERIES

In 2002, Marshall replaced the initial MG Series with the new MG Series that actually featured "MG" in the model name. Frequency Dependent Dampning (FDD) was introduced on all MG models and digital effects were introduced on a few. For the MG412A/B speaker cabinets, please refer to the G/MG Series.

MG10CD – 10W, 1-6.5 in. speaker, guitar combo, solid-state chassis, two channels, front gold control panel, single input, four knobs (Ch. 1: v, Ch. 2: g, v, contour), overdrive switch, CD input, headphone jack, power switch, black covering, black grille cloth with white script Marshall logo, 11.6 in. wide, 12.2 in. tall, 7.5 in. deep, 11 lbs., mfg. 2002-08.

| | N/A | $45 - 60 | $20 - 30 | $115 |

MG15CD – 15W, 1-8 in. speaker, guitar combo, solid-state chassis, two channels, front gold control panel, single input, six knobs (Clean Ch.: v, Od Ch.: g, v, All: b, c, t), overdrive switch, FDD switch, CD input/emulated line out, emulated headphone jack, power switch, black covering, black grille cloth with white script Marshall logo, 15 in. wide, 14.8 in. tall, 8.1 in. deep, 15.9 lbs., mfg. 2002-08.

| | N/A | $75 - 90 | $45 - 60 | $175 |

* **MG15CDR Reverb** – similar to the MG15CD, except has reverb with reverb control (total of seven knobs), mfg. 2002-08.

| | N/A | $85 - 110 | $55 - 65 | $199 |

»**MG15MSII Micro-Stack** – similar to the MG15CDR, except in mini-stack configuration with an MG15CDR head and two 1-10 in. speaker cabinets (one angled, one straight), mfg. 2006-08.

| | N/A | $180 - 230 | $110 - 140 | $430 |

MG15DFX – 15W, 1-8 in. speaker, guitar combo, solid-state chassis, two channels, digital effects (reverb, chorus, flange, delay), front gold control panel, single input, eight knobs (Clean Ch.: v, Od Ch.: g, v, All: b, c, t, effects preset/adjust, effects level), overdrive switch, FDD switch, CD input/emulated line out, emulated headphone jack, power switch, black covering, black grille cloth with white script Marshall logo, 15 in. wide, 14.8 in. tall, 8.1 in. deep, 15.9 lbs., mfg. 2002-08.

| | N/A | $100 - 130 | $60 - 80 | $249 |

The MG15DFX was also available as part of the RockBox (Last MSR was $280), which is an accessories package that comes with the amp. This package includes the MG15DFX, Marshall gig bag, instructional DVD, picks, strings, a string winder, and a tuner.

MSR/NOTES	100%	EXCELLENT	AVERAGE	LAST MSR

MG30DFX – 30W, 1-10 in. speaker, guitar combo, solid-state chassis, two channels, digital effects (reverb, chorus, flange, delay), front gold control panel, single input, 10 knobs (Clean Ch.: v, b, t, OD Ch.: g, b, c, t, v, All: effects preset/adjust, effects level), channel switch, FDD switch, footswitch jack, CD input, emulated line out/headphone jack, power switch, black covering, black grille cloth with white script Marshall logo, 18.75 in. wide, 16 in. tall, 9.5 in. deep, 21.1 lbs., mfg. 2002-08.

	N/A	$150 - 190	$90 - 110	$350

MG50DFX – 50W, 1-12 in. speaker, guitar combo, solid-state chassis, two channels, digital reverb, digital effects (chorus/delay, chorus, flange, delay), front gold control panel, single input, 13 knobs (Clean Ch.: g, b, m, t, OD Ch.: g, b, c, t, v, All: effects preset/adjust, effects level, r, MV), channel switch, FDD switch, emulated line out/headphone jack, power switch, rear panel: effects loop, CD input, footswitch jack, black covering, black grille cloth with white script Marshall logo, footswitch included, 20.375 in. wide, 19.625 in. tall, 10.75 in. deep, 35.2 lbs., mfg. 2002-08.

	N/A	$240 - 290	$125 - 165	$555

MG100HDFX HEAD – 100W, guitar head unit, solid-state chassis, two channels, digital reverb, digital effects (chorus/delay, chorus, flange, delay), front gold control panel, single input, 15 knobs (Clean Ch.: g, b, m, t, OD Ch.: g, b, m, t, c, v, All: effects preset/adjust, effects level, r, effects loop mix, MV), Clean Ch. clean/crunch switch, Clean Ch./OD Ch. switch, OD1/OD2 switch, FDD switch, CD input, emulated line out/headphone jack, power switch, rear panel: effects loop, footswitch jack, black covering, black grille cloth with white script Marshall logo, footswitch included, 23.5 in. wide, 10 in. tall, 10.625 in. deep, 28.2 lbs., mfg. 2002-08.

	N/A	$225 - 275	$135 - 175	$569

* **MG100DFX Combo** – similar to the MG100HDFX Head, except in combo configuration with 2-12 in. speakers, 23.25 in. wide, 21.875 in. tall, 10.75 in. deep, 49.3 lbs., mfg. 2002-08.

	N/A	$300 - 350	$175 - 225	$660

MG250DFX – 100W (50W x 2 stereo), 2-12 in. speakers, guitar combo, solid-state chassis, two channels, digital reverb, digital effects (chorus/delay, chorus, flange, delay), front gold control panel, single input, 13 knobs (Clean Ch.: g, b, m, t, OD Ch.: g, b, c, t, v, All: effects preset/adjust, effects level, r, MV), channel switch, FDD switch, emulated line out/headphone jack, power switch, rear panel: effects loop, CD input, footswitch jack, black covering, black grille cloth with white script Marshall logo, footswitch included, 26.375 in. wide, 19.625 in. tall, 10.75 in. deep, 48.4 lbs., mfg. 2002-08.

	N/A	$325 - 400	$200 - 250	$749

SOLID-STATE AMPLIFIERS: MG 4 SERIES

The MG 4 Series was introduced in 2009 with new features such as four digital effects and preset modes. The MG 4 Series can be distinguished by the large "MG" letters on the right-hand side of the control panel with an ink blot the features the model number. For the MG412 speaker cabinets, please refer to the G/MG Series category.

* Add $60 (MSR $80) for MG-4 four-button footswitch (compatible with models MG15FX, MG30FX, MG50FX, MG100FX, MG101FX, and MG102FX).

MG2FX – 2W, 1-6.5 in. speaker, guitar combo, solid-state chassis, single channel with ten voices, top gold control panel, single input, four dual purpose knobs (mode/bass, gain/treble, FX/reverb, volume/delay), tap/shift switch, MP3/line in, black covering, black grille with white script Marshall logo, mfg. 2010-present.

MSR $140	$100	$55 - 75	$30 - 40	

MG10 – 10W, 1-6.5 in. speaker, guitar combo, solid-state chassis, two channels (clean and overdrive), front gold control panel, single input, four knobs (clean v, g, OD v, contour), power switch, overdrive switch, MP3/line in, emulated headphone jack, black covering, black grille with white script Marshall logo, 10.6 lbs., mfg. 2009-present.

MSR $125	$70	$50 - 60	$30 - 40	

MG15 – 15W, 1-8 in. speaker, guitar combo, solid-state chassis, two channels (clean and overdrive), front gold control panel, single input, six knobs (clean v, g, OD v, b, m, t), overdrive switch, power switch, MP3/line in, emulated headphone jack, black covering, black grille with white script Marshall logo, 16.3 lbs., mfg. 2009-present.

MSR $150	$100	$60 - 80	$35 - 50	

MG15FX – 15W, 1-8 in. speaker, guitar combo, solid-state chassis, four channels, reverb, four digital effects (chorus, phaser, flanger, delay), front gold control panel, single input, eight knobs (g, OD b, m, t, r, v, effects select, MV), clean/crunch switch, overdrive switch, tap switch, store switch, power switch, MP3/line in, emulated headphone jack, tuner, footswitch jack, black covering, black grille with white script Marshall logo, 16.9 lbs., mfg. 2009-present.

MSR $250	$150	$95 - 120	$55 - 75	

* **MG15HFXMS Mini-Stack** – similar to the MG15FX, except in mini-stack configuration with a head unit and two speaker cabinets each containing 1-10 in. speaker, mfg. 2010-present.

MSR $510	$350	$200 - 250	$120 - 150	

MG30FX – 30W, 1-10 in. speaker, guitar combo, solid-state chassis, four channels, reverb, four digital effects (chorus, phaser, flanger, delay), front gold control panel, single input, eight knobs (g, OD b, m, t, r, v, effects select, MV), clean/crunch switch, overdrive switch, tap switch, store switch, power switch, MP3/line in, emulated headphone jack, footswitch jack, digital tuner, black covering, black grille with white script Marshall logo, 23.8 lbs., mfg. 2009-present.

MSR $350	$200	$120 - 150	$75 - 95	

MSR/NOTES	100%	EXCELLENT	AVERAGE	LAST MSR

MG50FX – 50W, 1-12 in. speaker, guitar combo, solid-state chassis, four channels, reverb, four digital effects (chorus, phaser, flanger, delay), front gold control panel, single input, nine knobs (g, OD b, m, t, r, v, effects select, delay, MV), clean/crunch switch, overdrive switch, reverb switch, FX switch, external effects loop switch, damping switch, store switch, power switch, emulated headphone/line out jack, digital tuner, footswitch jack, effects loop, black covering, black grille with white script Marshall logo, 36.5 lbs., mfg. 2009-present.

MSR $600	$380	$225 - 275	$120 - 150	

MG100HFX HEAD – 100W, guitar head unit, solid-state chassis, four channels, reverb, four digital effects (chorus, phaser, flanger, delay), front gold control panel, single input, nine knobs (g, OD b, m, t, r, v, effects select, delay, MV), clean/crunch switch, overdrive switch, reverb switch, FX switch, tap switch, external effects loop switch, damping switch, store switch, power switch, emulated headphone/line out jack, tuner, footswitch jack, effects loop, available in black covering with a black grille and white script Marshall logo, cream covering with a basketweave grille and white script Marshall logo, or red covering with a dark gray grille and white script Marshall logo, 25.1 lbs., mfg. 2009-present.

MSR $580	$360	$225 - 275	$120 - 150	

* **MG100FX 1-12 Combo (Model MG101FX)** – similar to the MG100FX Head, except in combo configuration with 1-12 in. speaker, 44 lbs., mfg. 2009-present.

MSR $700	$500	$300 - 375	$175 - 225	

* **MG100FX 2-12 Combo (Model MG102FX)** – similar to the MG100FX Head, except in combo configuration with 2-12 in. speakers, 49.3 lbs., mfg. 2009-present.

MSR $775	$550	$325 - 400	$200 - 250	

SOLID-STATE AMPLIFIERS: MG CARBON FIBRE SERIES

MG10CF
courtesy Marshall

MG15CFR
courtesy Marshall

MG30CFX
courtesy Marshall

MG10CF – 10W, 1-6.5 in. speaker, guitar combo, solid-state chassis, two channels (clean and overdrive), front chrome control panel, single input, four knobs (clean v, g, OD v, contour), power switch, overdrive switch, MP3/line in, emulated headphone jack, black carbon fibre covering, black grille with white script Marshall logo, 12.4 in. tall, 11.7 in. wide, 6.9 in. deep, 10.6 lbs., mfg. 2012-present.

MSR $104	$80	$50 - 60	$25 - 30	

MG15CF – 15W, 1-8 in. speaker, guitar combo, solid-state chassis, two channels (clean and overdrive), front chrome control panel, single input, six knobs (clean v, g, OD v, b, m, t), power switch, overdrive switch, MP3/line in, emulated headphone jack, black carbon fibre covering, black grille with white script Marshall logo, 15 in. tall, 14.9 in. wide, 8.1 in. deep, 16.3 lbs., mfg. 2012-present.

MSR $145	$100	$65 - 75	$35 - 40	

MG15CFR – 15W, 1-8 in. speaker, guitar combo, solid-state chassis, two channels (clean and overdrive), front chrome control panel, single input, seven knobs (clean v, g, OD v, b, m, t, r), power switch, overdrive switch, MP3/line in, emulated headphone jack, black carbon fibre covering, black grille with white script Marshall logo, 15 in. tall, 14.9 in. wide, 8.1 in. deep, 16.3 lbs., mfg. 2012-present.

MSR $170	$130	$85 - 100	$40 - 50	

MG15CFX – 15W, 1-8 in. speaker, guitar combo, solid-state chassis, four channels, front chrome control panel, single input, eight knobs (g, b, m, t, r, v, effect selector, MV), clean/crunch switch, OD1/OD2 switch, tap switch, store switch, footswitch jack, power switch, MP3/line in, emulated headphone jack, black carbon fibre covering, black grille with white script Marshall logo, 15 in. tall, 14.9 in. wide, 8.1 in. deep, 16.3 lbs., mfg. 2012-present.

MSR $210	$150	$100 - 115	$50 - 60	

MG15CFXMS – 15W, micro-stack configuration, guitar head-unit, 2 X 1-10 in. speaker cabinets, solid-state chassis, four channels, front chrome control panel, single input, eight knobs (g, b, m, t, r, v, effect selector, MV), clean/crunch switch, OD1/OD2 switch, tap switch, store switch, footswitch jack, power switch, MP3/line in, emulated headphone jack, black carbon fibre covering, black grille with white script Marshall logo, 37.8 in. tall, 15.1 in. wide, 9.44 in. deep, 41.22 lbs., mfg. 2012-present.

MSR $540	$400	$260 - 300	$130 - 160	

MG30CFX – 30W, 1-10 in. speaker, guitar combo, solid-state chassis, four channels, front chrome control panel, single input, eight knobs (g, b, m, t, r, v, effect selector, MV), clean/crunch switch, OD1/OD2 switch, tap switch, store switch, footswitch jack, power switch, MP3/line in, emulated headphone jack, black carbon fibre covering, black grille with white script Marshall logo, 16.5 in. tall, 18.9 in. wide, 8.9 in. deep, 23.8 lbs., mfg. 2012-present.

MSR $285	$200	$130 - 150	$65 - 80	

MSR/NOTES	100%	EXCELLENT	AVERAGE	LAST MSR

MG100HCFX
courtesy Marshall

MG101CFX
courtesy Marshall

MG102CFX
courtesy Marshall

MG50CFX – 50W, 1-12 in. speaker, guitar combo, solid-state chassis, four channels, front chrome control panel, single input, nine knobs (g, b, m, t, r, v, effect selector, delay MV), clean/crunch switch, OD1/OD2 switch, tap switch, external effects switch, damping switch, store switch, footswitch jack, power switch, MP3/line in, emulated headphone jack, external speaker jack, effects loop, black carbon fibre covering, black grille with white script Marshall logo, 16.5 in. tall, 18.9 in. wide, 8.1 in. deep, 23.8 lbs., mfg. 2012-present.

| | MSR $580 | $400 | $260 - 300 | $130 - 160 | |

MG100HCFX – 100W, guitar head-unit, solid-state chassis, four channels, front chrome control panel, single input, nine knobs (g, b, m, t, r, v, effect selector, delay MV), clean/crunch switch, OD1/OD2 switch, tap switch, external effects switch, damping switch, store switch, footswitch jack, power switch, MP3/line in, emulated headphone jack, external speaker jacks, effects loop, footswitch included, black carbon fibre covering, black grille with white script Marshall logo, 10 in. tall, 26.5 in. wide, 10.94 in. deep, 25.13 lbs., mfg. 2012-present.

| | MSR $520 | $350 | $235 - 270 | $115 - 145 | |

MG101CFX – 100W, 1-12 in. speaker, guitar combo, solid-state chassis, four channels, front chrome control panel, single input, nine knobs (g, b, m, t, r, v, effect selector, delay MV), clean/crunch switch, OD1/OD2 switch, tap switch, external effects switch, damping switch, store switch, footswitch jack, power switch, MP3/line in, emulated headphone jack, external speaker jack, effects loop, footswitch included, black carbon fibre covering, black grille with white script Marshall logo, 21.3 in. tall, 23.5 in. wide, 11.1 in. deep, 44.09 lbs., mfg. 2012-present.

| | MSR $720 | $500 | $325 - 375 | $165 - 200 | |

MG102CFX – 100W, 2-12 in. speakers, guitar combo, solid-state chassis, four channels, front chrome control panel, single input, nine knobs (g, b, m, t, r, v, effect selector, delay MV), clean/crunch switch, OD1/OD2 switch, tap switch, external effects switch, damping switch, store switch, footswitch jack, power switch, MP3/line in, emulated headphone jack, external speaker jack, effects loop, footswitch included, black carbon fibre covering, black grille with white script Marshall logo, 19.9 in. tall, 26.6 in. wide, 11.1 in. deep, 49.38 lbs., mfg. 2012-present.

| | MSR $790 | $600 | $400 - 450 | $195 - 240 | |

MG412ACF/MG412BCF SPEAKER CABINET – 120W, 4-12 in. Celestion speakers, 8 ohm impedance, angled (MG412ACF) or straight (MG412BCF) front, black carbon fibre covering, black grille, 26.5 in. wide, 26.25 in. tall, 14 in. deep, 63.93 lbs., mfg. 2012-present.

| | MSR $420 | $260 | $170 - 195 | $85 - 105 | |

SOLID-STATE AMPLIFIERS: ACOUSTIC SERIES

AS50D – 50W, 2-8 in. speakers with a tweeter, acoustic guitar combo, solid-state chassis, two channels, reverb, chorus, front cream control panel, three inputs, 12 knobs, Ch. 1 controls: 1/4 in. input, three knobs (v, b, t) Ch. 2 controls: 1/4 in. input, XLR input, link Channel switch, three knobs (v, b, t), All: Ch. 1/2 anti-feedback on/off button, six knobs (chorus speed, chorus depth, reverb/loop balance, reverb level, frequency, MV), power switch, rear panel: footswitch jack, stereo effects loop with level knob, stereo XLR DI out, stereo line out, Brown covering, Brown cloth grille with gold piping and white script Marshall logo, 21.36 in. wide, 16.37 in. tall, 10.27 in. deep, 35.27 lbs., mfg. 2012-present.

| | MSR $560 | $400 | $260 - 300 | $130 - 160 | |

AS50R – 50W, 2-8 in. speakers with a polymer dome tweeter, acoustic guitar combo, solid-state chassis, two channels (Acoustic, Microphone/Aux.), reverb, chorus, front cream control panel, three inputs, 12 knobs, Ch. 1 controls, 1/4 in. input, three knobs (v, b, t) Ch. 2 controls: RCA aux. inputs, XLR input, 1/4 in. input, three knobs (v, b, t), chorus on/off buttons for each channel, chorus speed, chorus depth, reverb/loop balance knob, reverb level, anti-feedback phase and notch buttons, anti-feedback freq. level, MV, power switch, rear panel: effects loop, DI out, line out, Brown covering, Brown cloth grille with gold piping and white script Marshall logo, 21.625 in. wide, 16.275 in. tall, 10 in. deep, 35.2 lbs., mfg. 1999-2006.

| | N/A | $250 - 300 | $125 - 175 | $550 |

AS80R – 80W (40W x 2 stereo), 2-10 in. speakers with a two polymer dome tweeters, acoustic guitar combo, solid-state chassis, three channels (Microphone, Magnetic/Aux., Transducer), reverb, chorus, front cream control panel, three inputs, 23 knobs, Ch. 1 controls: XLR input, phase switch, four knobs (v, l, m, h), Ch. 2 controls: 1/4 in. input, shift switch, four knobs (v, l, m, h), Ch. 3 controls: 1/4 in. input, input source switch, eight knobs (v, FBF1, FBF2, attack, l, m, freq., h), All: Ch. FX return, r, output volume, chorus resonance, chorus intensity, chorus rate, chorus modulation, chorus switch, power switch, rear panel: stereo line out, output phase switch, stereo effects loop, footswitch jack, Brown covering, Brown cloth grille with gold piping and white script Marshall logo, disc. 1999.

| | N/A | $275 - 325 | $150 - 200 | $1,199 |

MSR/NOTES	100%	EXCELLENT	AVERAGE	LAST MSR

AS100D – 100W (50W x 2 stereo), 2-8 in. speakers with a two polymer dome tweeters, acoustic guitar combo, solid-state chassis, four channels (Acoustic Ch. 1, Acoustic Ch. 2, Microphone, Aux.), reverb, chorus, front cream control panel, three inputs, 20 knobs, Ch. 1 controls: 1/4 in. input, phase switch, gain switch, five knobs (v, b, m, mid freq., t) Ch. 2 controls: 1/4 in. input, XLR input, link Channel 1 switch, contour switch, phase switch, phantom switch, three knobs (v, b, t), Ch. 3 controls: XLR input, phase switch phantom switch, five knobs (v, b, t, int. FX, ext. FX), Ch. 4 controls: RCA inputs, volume knob, All: Ch. 1/2 anti-feedback on/off button, anti-feedback depth switch, two anti-feedback knobs (Sweep 1, Sweep 2), Int. FX switch, Ext. FX switch, digital effects select knob, digital effects adjust, digital effects level, MV, power switch, rear panel: footswitch jack, stereo effects loop with level knob, stereo XLR DI out, stereo line out, Brown covering, Brown cloth grille with gold piping and white script Marshall logo, 23.75 in. wide, 20.875 in. tall, 10.625 in. deep, 46.2 lbs., mfg. 2004-present.

| MSR $1,000 | $700 | $450 - 525 | $250 - 300 | |

MISC. SS SIGNATURE MODELS

DAVE MUSTAINE MEGASTACK (MG15XFMSDM) – 15W, 2-10 in. speakers, mini-stack with a head unit and two speaker cabinets each containing 1-10 in. speaker, solid-state chassis, four channels, reverb, four digital effects (chorus, phaser, flanger, delay), front gold control panel, single input, eight knobs (distortion, l, m, h, r, v, effects select, MV), clean/crunch switch, overdrive switch, tap switch, store switch, power switch, MP3/line in, emulated headphone jack, tuner, footswitch jack, carbon fiber-style vinyl covering, black diamond stamped kick grilles with white script Marshall logo, mfg. 2010-disc.

| | $400 | $250 - 300 | $135 - 175 | $560 |

MG10 KERRY KING SIGNATURE (MG10KK) – 10W, 1-6.5 in. speaker combo, solid-state chassis, two channels, front red/black Kerry King control panel, single input, four knobs (Clean Ch.: v, OD Ch.: g, v, contour), CD input/emulated line out, headphone jack, Black covering, Black grille cloth, 11 lbs., mfg. 2008-09.

| | $100 | $55 - 75 | $30 - 40 | $140 |

ZAKK WYLDE LIMITED EDITION MICROSTACK (MG15MSZW) – 15W, guitar head-unit with two mini 1-10 in. speaker cabinets (one angled and one straight) creating a miniature full-stack, solid-state chassis, two channels, reverb, front gold control panel with custom Zakk Wylde bullseye graphics, single input, seven black and gold knobs (clean v, OD g, OD v, b, contour, t, r), channel switch, FDD switch, speaker emulated headphone jack, line out, CD input, black covering, dark gray grille cloth with white piping, mfg. 2007-09.

| | $350 | $225 - 275 | $135 - 175 | $499 |

BASS SS AMPLIFIERS: MB SERIES

MB15 COMBO – 15W, 1-8 in. speaker bass combo, solid-state chassis, two channels (modern/classic), front black control panel, single input, seven chrome knobs (Modern Ch.: v, compressor, Classic Ch.: g, v, All: b, voice, t), compression switch, CD input, line out jack, headphone jack, black covering, black metal grille, 15 in. wide, 14.5 in. tall, 9.5 in. deep, 26.5 lbs., mfg. 2007-2012.

| | $140 | $85 - 110 | $55 - 70 | $200 |

MB30 COMBO – 30W, 1-10 in. speaker bass combo, solid-state chassis, two channels (modern/classic), front black control panel, single input, eight chrome knobs (Modern Ch.: v, compressor, Classic Ch.: g, v, All: b, three-way voice shift, voice, t), compression switch, channel switch, CD input, headphone jack, series effects loop, emulated line out, limiter, optional footswitch, black covering, black metal grille, 17.25 in. wide, 15.75 in. tall, 10.25 in. deep, 32.5 lbs., mfg. 2007-2012.

| | $200 | $110 - 140 | $65 - 85 | $300 |

MB60 COMBO – 60W, 1-12 in. speaker bass combo, solid-state chassis, two channels (modern/classic), front black control panel, single input, 12 chrome knobs (Modern Ch.: v, b, mid-freq., m, t, compressor, Classic Ch.: g, v, b, three-way voice shift, voice, t), active/passive switch, compression switch, channel switch, boost switch, CD input, headphone jack, series effects loop, emulated line out, limiter, one-button footswitch included, black covering, black metal grille, 13.5 in. wide, 12.75 in. tall, 8.25 in. deep, 50.5 lbs., mfg. 2008-2012.

| | $450 | $300 - 350 | $175 - 225 | $700 |

MB150 COMBO – 150W, 1-15 in. speaker bass combo, solid-state chassis, two channels (modern/classic), front black control panel, single input, 12 chrome knobs (Modern Ch.: v, b, mid-freq., m, t, compressor, Classic Ch.: g, v, b, three-way voice shift, voice, t), active/passive switch, compression switch, channel switch, CD input, headphone jack, series effects loop, emulated line out, limiter, one-button footswitch included, black covering, black metal grille, 14.75 in. wide, 14.85 in. tall, 9 in. deep, 66 lbs., mfg. 2008-2012.

| | $600 | $375 - 450 | $225 - 275 | $850 |

MB450H HEAD – 300W @ 2 ohms (450W @ 4 ohms), bass head-unit configuration, solid-state chassis, two channels (modern/classic), front black control panel, single input, 15 chrome knobs (Modern Ch.: v, b, mid-freq., m, t, compressor, Classic Ch.: g, v, b, three-way voice shift, voice, t, All: blend, blend v, MV), active/passive switch, compression switch, channel switch, boost switch, blend switch, CD input, headphone jack, series effects loop, emulated line out, limiter, two-button footswitch included, black covering, black metal grille, 16 in. wide, 5.6 in. tall, 6 in. deep, 33 lbs., mfg. 2008-2012.

| | $500 | $300 - 375 | $175 - 225 | $700 |

* **MB4210 Combo** – similar to the MB450H, except in combo configuration with 2-10 in. speaker bass combo and a high freq. horn, 16 in. wide, 13.6 in. tall, 7.1 in. deep, 72.6 lbs., mfg. 2008-2012.

| | $700 | $425 - 500 | $275 - 325 | $1,000 |

* **MB4410 Combo** – similar to the MB450H, except in combo configuration with 4-10 in. speaker bass combo and a high freq. horn, 16 in. wide, 18.25 in. tall, 10.4 in. deep, 112.2 lbs., mfg. 2008-2012.

| | $850 | $525 - 600 | $300 - 375 | $1,200 |

MSR/NOTES	100%	EXCELLENT	AVERAGE	LAST MSR

MBC115 SPEAKER CABINET – 300W, 1-15 in. speaker with a high freq. horn and level adjust, 4 ohm impedance, one regular and one Speakon connectors, black covering, black metal grille, 16 in. wide, 16 in. tall, 10.4 in. deep, 70.4 lbs., mfg. 2008-2012.

	$400	$250 - 300	$135 - 175	$550

MBC410 SPEAKER CABINET – 600W, 4-10 in. speakers with a high freq. horn and level adjust, 4 ohm impedance, one regular and one Speakon connectors, black covering, black metal grille, 16 in. wide, 18.25 in. tall, 10.4 in. deep, 93.5 lbs., mfg. 2008-2012.

	$500	$300 - 350	$175 - 225	$700

MBC810 SPEAKER CABINET – 1200W, 8-10 in. speakers with a high freq. horn and level adjust, 4 ohm impedance, one regular and one Speakon connectors, black covering, black metal grille, 16 in. wide, 31.75 in. tall, 10.4 in. deep, 154 lbs., mfg. 2008-2012.

	$900	$550 - 650	$350 - 425	$1,250

PREAMPS/POWERAMPS

JMP-1 PREAMP – preamp only, one-space rack-mount guitar head-unit, two-tube chassis, preamp: 2 X ECC83, four channels (clean 1, clean 2, OD1, OD2), 100 programmable settings, front gold control panel, single input, output level knob, two two-digit digital displays, 16 buttons, data knob, headphone jack, parallel effects loop with a level switch, MIDI capabilities, optional footswitch, standard outputs, speaker emulated outputs, black casing, 10 lbs., disc. 2007.

	N/A	$875 - 1,025	$550 - 650	$1,980

* **Add $75 (MSR $175) for four-button MPM4E footswitch.**

EL34 100/100 POWERAMP – 200W (100W per side) power amp only, three-space rack-mount guitar head-unit, 12 tube chassis, predrives: 2 X ECC83, phase inverters: 2 X ECC81, power: 8 X EL34, two channels, front gold control panel with the controls mounted in the middle facing upwards, four knobs (Ch. A: v, p, Ch. B: v, p), two voicing switches (one per channel), optional footswitch, black casing, 45 lbs., disc.

	$1,900	$1,200 - 1,400	$800 - 950	$2,698

SPEAKER CABINETS

Marshall is given credit for developing the "stack," which is two speaker cabinets and a head-unit stacked on top of each other and the "half-stack" with one speaker cabinet with a head-unit amp on the top. Head-units and speaker cabinets were listed and sold separately - something that no other amp company had really done at this point. The user had several possibilities when it came to mixing and matching head-units with speaker cabinets.

As listed in the dating of Marshall Amplifiers earlier in the section, it can be done by the speakers if they are original. There are also cosmetic features that indicate the year as well. This will be helpful in idenitifying the year of the speaker cabinet.

1962-1966 - Marshall cabinets introduced and included a yellow material made of foam for an acoustic insulator.

1970-1971 - The black baffle board in the back was changed from plywood to chipboard. Chequerboard cloth replaced the basket-weave grille cloth.

1972-1973 - The metal grab handles on 4-12 in. models were changed to plastic ones.

1975 - Black grille cloth replace the Chequerboard cloth in the U.K. It changed over in the U.S.A. in 1981.

The speaker cabinets listed in this section are cabinets that were sold separately and not part of an exclusive series. For speaker cabinets that only apply to a certain series, refer to that series (i.e. AVT Series, Mode Four Series). Many speaker cabinets were available with a straight or angled front. When the same cabinet came in both versions, it is often noted by an A for angled and B for straight. Don't be confused with some models produced in the 1970s where the B suffix indicated caster cups. The Model 1960 is the most popular Marshall 4-12 in. speaker cabinet.

* **Add 25-50% for coverings in colors other than black.**

MODEL 1912 – 150W, 1-12 in. extension cab designed for use with the JCM900 1-12 in. combos, mfg. 1989-1998, 2013-present.

MSR $820	$600	$400 - 450	$195 - 240	

MODEL 1922 – 150W, 2-12 in. G12T75 speakers, extension cabinet designed for use with JCM900 2-12 in. combos, stereo/mono switching, similar to the model 1936, mfg. 1989-1998.

	N/A	$300 - 375	$150 - 200	

MODEL 1931A/1931B – 75W, 1-12 in. G12T75 speaker, angled cabinet, designed for use with the Model 3310, mfg. 1989-1991.

	N/A	$200 - 250	$120 - 150	

MODEL 1933 – 65W, 1-12 in.G12 65 speakers, extension cabinet designed for use with the JCM-800 Model 4010 and Model 4210 1-12 in. combos, mfg. 1984-89.

	N/A	$200 - 250	$120 - 150	

In 1986 the output was increased to 70W and the speakers were changed to G12M70s.

MODEL 1936 – 140W, 2-12 in., extension cabinets for full-sized heads, mfg. 1981-present.

MSR $1,090	$750	$475 - 550	$245 - 300	

* **Add $80 (MSR $1,170) for Celestion Vintage 30 speakers**

In 1986 the speakers were changed to G12T75s. Switches from 16 ohms Stereo to 8 ohms Mono.

MSR/NOTES	100%	EXCELLENT	AVERAGE	LAST MSR

Model 1960
courtesy solidbodyguitar.com, Inc.

Model 1960AC/1960BC
courtesy Marshall

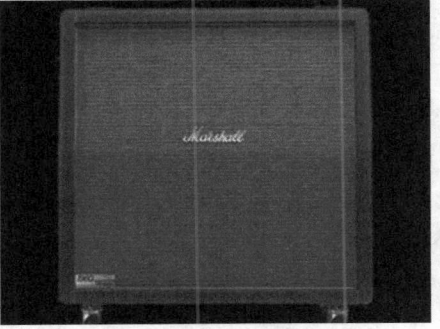

Model 1960AV/1960BV
courtesy Marshall

MODEL 1551 – 2-15 in. speakers, bass cabinet, mfg. date unknown.

	N/A	$325 - 400	$200 - 250	

MODEL 1960 – 60W, 4-12, lead/bass application, angled front cabinet for full-sized heads, mfg. 1964-1979.

	100%	EXCELLENT	AVERAGE
1964-1965	N/A	$2,750 - 3,500	$1,750 - 2,250
1966-1970	N/A	$2,500 - 3,000	$1,500 - 2,000
1971-1972	N/A	$1,750 - 2,250	$1,100 - 1,400
1973-1975	N/A	$1,200 - 1,500	$750 - 950
1976-1979	N/A	$950 - 1,200	$600 - 750

In 1965, the rated handling was increased to 75W. In 1970, the rated handling was increased to 100W and was changed to a lead-only application. The Model 1960 was the first production cabinet with 4-12 in. speakers and it only came as an angled front. In 1979, the Model 1960 came in two variations - the 1960A with an angled front and the new 1960B with a straight front (see Model 1960A/1960B).

MODEL 1960A/1960B – 260W, 4-12 in. G12 65 speakers, angled front (1960A) or straight front (1960B), designed for use with full-sized heads, mfg. 1979-present.

	100%	EXCELLENT	AVERAGE
1979-1982	N/A	$750 - 900	$500 - 600
1983-1985	N/A	$600 - 700	$425 - 500
1986-1989	N/A	$550 - 650	$375 - 450
1990-Present MSR $1,300	$950	$525 - 600	$325 - 400

In 1983, the output was raised to 280W and speakers were changed to G12M70s. In 1986, the output was raised to 300W and speakers were changed to G12T75s. In 1990 the cabinet was changed to mono/stereo switching speakers. The cabinets current impedance are 4/16 ohms for mono and 8 ohms for stereo.

* *Model 1960AC/1960BC* – similar to the 1960A/1960B except has 100W rated handling and 4-12 in. Classic 25 Greenback speakers, 16 ohms impedance, mfg. 1990-2008.

	N/A	$600 - 700	$350 - 425	$1,350

* *Model 1960AS/1960BS* – similar to the 1960A/1960B, except has 4-12 in. G12T75 speakers, designed for use with the reissue Model 1987S and Model 1959S heads, mfg. 1988 only.

	N/A	$600 - 750	$425 - 500	

* *Model 1960AV/1960BV* – similar to the Model 1960A/1960B except has 280W output, 4-12 in. Celestion Vintage 30 speakers, stereo/ mono switching, and 4/16 ohms mono/ 8 ohms stereo impedance, mfg. 1990-present.

MSR $1,750	$1,250	$800 - 925	$400 - 500

* *Model 1960AX/1960BX* – similar to the Model 1960A/1960B except has 100W rated handling, 4-12 in. mono Celestion Classic 25 speakers, reissue cabinet desiged for use with the 1987X and 1959X reissue heads, mfg. 1990-93, 2004-present.

	100%	EXCELLENT	AVERAGE
1990-1993	N/A	$600 - 750	$425 - 500
2004-Present MSR $1,800	$1,300	$675 - 800	$400 - 475

* *Model 1960ST* – similar to the 1960B except has 4-12 in. Celestion G12T75 speakers and features stereo/mono switching, mfg. 1989 only.

	N/A	$600 - 700	$425 - 500	

This cabinet was only available in straight front version (B). This was Marshall's first stab at a stereo 4-12 in. cabinet and was designed for use with the JCM-900 series.

MSR/NOTES	100%	EXCELLENT	AVERAGE	LAST MSR

* *Model 1960TV* – similar to the 1960B except has 100W output, 4-12 in. Celestion Classic 25 speakers, mono impedance, and an extra-tall cabinet design, 97 lbs., mfg. 1990-mid 1990s, 2004-present.

1990S	N/A	$600 - 750	$425 - 500	
MSR $1,800	$1,300	$675 - 800	$400 - 475	

MODEL 1961A/1961B – 150W, 2-12 in. Celestion G12T75 speakers, angled front (Model 1961A) or straight front (Model 1961B), extension cabinet designed for use with the Model 3315 head, mfg. 1988-1990.

	N/A	$300 - 350	$200 - 250	

MODEL 1965A/1965B – 140W, 4-10 in. speakers, angled front (Model 1965A) or straight front (Model 1965B), extension cabinet designed for use with the "mini-stack" Model 3210/3203 heads, mfg. 1984-1991.

	N/A	$375 - 450	$225 - 275	

MODEL 1966A/1966B – 150W, 2-12 in. Celestion G12 75 speakers, angled front (Model 1966A) or straight front (Model 1966B), extension cabinet designed for use with the "mini-stack" Model 3210/3203 heads, mfg. 1985-1991.

	N/A	$300 - 375	$175 - 225	

MODEL 1972 – 50W, 2-12 in. speakers, lead/bass/organ applications, extension cabinet designed for use with the Bluesbreaker Model 1962 combo, mfg. 1966-68.

1966	N/A	$2,000 - 2,500	$1,200 - 1,500	
1967-1968	N/A	$1,750 - 2,250	$1,100 - 1,400	

Initially in 1966, this cabinet was designed with two horizontal mounted speakers. In 1967, the speakers were changed to the more common vertical design. The horizontal cabinet is very rare.

MODEL 1982 – 100W, 4-12 in. speakers, lead/bass application, straight front, extension cabinet designed for use with full-sized heads, mfg. 1967-1980.

1967-1969	N/A	$2,000 - 2,500	$1,200 - 1,500	
1970-1972	N/A	$1,500 - 2,000	$950 - 1,200	
1973-1980	N/A	$1,200 - 1,500	$750 - 950	

This model is a high-powered version of the Model 1960. In 1970, the output was raised to 120W.

MODEL 1982A/1982B – 320W, 4-12 in. speakers, angled front (Model 1982A) or straight front (Model 1982B), high-powered extension cabinets designed for use with full-sized heads, mfg. 1981-1987.

	N/A	$600 - 750	$425 - 500	

In 1982, the output was raised to 400W.

MODEL 1990 – 80W, 8-10 in. speakers, extension cabinet designed for use with full-sized heads, mfg. 1967-1978.

1967-1969	N/A	$2,500 - 3,000	$1,500 - 2,000	
1970-1972	N/A	$2,000 - 2,500	$1,200 - 1,500	
1973-1978	N/A	$1,500 - 2,000	$950 - 1,200	

In 1973, the output was increased to 100W. This cabinet is a slightly smaller version of the 2034 speaker cabinet.

MODEL 2032 – 80W, 4-12 in. speakers, extension cabinet designed for use with full-sized heads, mfg. 1970-74.

	N/A	$950 - 1,200	$700 - 800	

In 1973, the output was increased to 100W. This cabinet is in similar size to the Model 2034 cabinet.

MODEL 2034 – 120W, 8-10 in. speakers, extension cabinet designed for use with full-sized heads, mfg. 1970-73.

	N/A	$2,250 - 2,750	$1,400 - 1,750	

This model along with the 1990 and 2032 are all in the same family. This model is a heavy-duty version of the Model 1990 and is slightly larger in size.

MODEL 2035B – 75W, 4-12 in. speakers and a horn, lead/organ application, mfg. 1970-74.

	N/A	$1,100 - 1,400	$750 - 900	

In 1973, the power was increased to 100W.

MODEL 2036B – 120W, 4-12 in. speakers and a horn, lead/organ application, mfg. 1970-74.

	N/A	$1,300 - 1,600	$850 - 1,100	

This model is the same as the Model 2035B with larger rated handling power.

MODEL 2038 – 60W, 4-10 in. speakers, extension cabinet for smaller amps, about the size of a 4-12 in. cabinet, mfg. 1972 only.

	N/A	$850 - 1,100	$550 - 700	

MODEL 2045 – 60W, 2-12 in. speakers, lead/bass/organ applications, extension cabinet designed for used with smaller amps, mfg. 1972-76.

	N/A	$750 - 950	$550 - 650	

MSR/NOTES	100%	EXCELLENT	AVERAGE	LAST MSR

MX112
courtesy Marshall

MX212
courtesy Marshall

MX412A/MX412B
courtesy Marshall

MODEL 2049 – 60W, 2-12 in. speakers, 4 foot tall extension cabinet designed for use with the 50W Artist series, mfg. 1973-77.

	N/A	$600 - 750	$425 - 500	

MODEL 2052 – 125W, 1-15 in. speaker, lead/organ application, horn loaded in rear with Powercel, extension cabinet designed for use with full-sized heads, mfg. 1973-79.

	N/A	$500 - 600	$325 - 400	

MODEL 2053/2053B – 100W, 1-12 in. speaker, lead/organ application, extension cabinet sized for a 4-12 in. with flared "picture frame" cosmetics, 2053B has caster cups, mfg. 1972-73.

	N/A	$550 - 650	$375 - 450	

MODEL 2054/2054B – 125W, 1-15 in. speaker, lead/organ application, extension cabinet with flared picture frame front, same size as a 4-12 in. cabinet, 2054B has caster cups, mfg. 1972-73.

	N/A	$475 - 550	$300 - 350	

MODEL 2064/2064B – 100W, 1-12 in. Powercel speaker, lead/organ application, straight front, extension cabinet designed for use with full-sized heads, 2064B has castor cups, mfg. 1973-75.

	N/A	$400 - 475	$275 - 325	

MODEL 2065/2065B – 125W, 1-15 in. Powercel speaker, lead/organ application, extension cabinet designed for use with full-sized heads, straight front, 2065B has caster cups, mfg. 1973-75.

	N/A	$425 - 500	$300 - 350	

MODEL 2069 – 120W, 4-12 in. speakers, tall extension cabinet designed for use with 100W Artist series, mfg. 1973-77.

	N/A	$800 - 1,000	$550 - 700	

MODEL 2196 – 100W, 2-12 in. 80W speakers, lead/bass application, 4 ohm impedance, extension cabinet designed for use with the Model 2195 head, mfg. 1976-1980.

	N/A	$475 - 550	$300 - 350	

MC212 – 130W, 2-12 in. Celestion Platform 65 speakers, 4 ohm mono impedance (8 ohm stereo impedance), black covering, black grille, 29.3 in. wide, 20.9 in. tall, 12.25 in. deep, 50.6 lbs., disc.

	$340	$180 - 230	$100 - 130	$450

MC412A/MC412B – 200W, 4-12 in. Celestion Platform 50 speakers, 16/4 ohm mono impedance (8 ohm stereo impedance), black covering, black grille, 30.25 in. wide, 29.75 in. tall, 14.4 in. deep, 75 lbs., disc.

	$600	$350 - 425	$175 - 225	$900

MX112 – 80W, 1-12 in. Celestion Seventy 80 speaker, 16 ohm impedance, straight front, black Tolex covering, black grille, 20.28 in. wide, 20.07 in. tall, 12.4 in. deep, 33 lbs., mfg. 2013-present.

MSR $330	$250	$165 - 190	$80 - 100	

MX212 – 160W, 2-12 in. Celestion Seventy 80 speakers, 8 ohm mono impedance, straight front, black Tolex covering, black grille, 29.53 in. wide, 21.46 in. tall, 12.40 in. deep, 50.7 lbs., mfg. 2013-present.

MSR $470	$350	$230 - 265	$115 - 140	

Also available in vertical configuration with angled front (Model MX212A).

MX412A/MX412B – 240W, 4-12 in. Celestion G12E-60 speakers, 16 ohm impedance, angled (MX412A) or straight (MX412B) front, black Tolex covering, black grille, 31.1 in. wide, 31.8 in. tall, 15.2 in. deep, 90.3 lbs., mfg. 2013-present.

MSR $650	$500	$325 - 375	$165 - 200	

MARTIN

Amplifiers previously built in Nazareth, PA in the early 1960s.

World renowned guitar company, Martin, tried their hand at building guitar amplifiers during the 1960s. Martin was founded in 1833 as an acoustic guitar company in New York. They moved to Nazareth, PA in 1939, where they have been ever since. Fast forward to the 1960s, when Martin began producing solid-body electric guitars and amplifiers. The amps lasted until the mid-1960s when the idea was retired due to lack of interest. However, Martin introduced amplifiers again under the Stinger brand in 1988 (see Stinger). For more information on acoustic guitars refer to the *Blue Book of Acoustic Guitars*. For more information on electric guitars, refer to the *Blue Book of Electric Guitars*.

ELECTRIC AMPLIFIERS

Models released in the 1960s include the 110T, 112T, SS140, and the portable #700. These amplifiers were introduced to be teamed up with the new Martin electric guitars at the time. Prices on early models are still relatively unknown.

MASCO

Amplifiers previously produced in Long Island, NY in the 1950s.

Masco made small amplifiers in the 1950s. The name MASCO stands for Mark Alan Sampson Company. They were generally small amps used for guitars, PAs, and even harps. Masco has been long out of business now, and little is known about the company and what they made. Any information on Masco or Masco amplifiers can be submitted directly to Blue Book Publications.

MATAMP

Amplifiers and speaker cabinets currently produced in Huddersfield, West Yorkshire, England. The Matamp trademark was established in the mid-1960s.

Mat Mathias moved to England from Germany during World War II and started working with electronics. Mathias started his own company and earned the nickname "The Radio Doctor" because he could fix just about anything to do with electronics. In 1958, he opened a recording studio when almost all musicians were using Vox amplifiers. Mathias began looking for an alternative sound and he began experimenting with his own circuits. The first Matamp Series 2000 was produced in 1963. In the late 1960s, Mathias partnered up with Clifford Cooper who owned the Orange Music Shop and they began to distribute Matamps in southern England. These amps were initially covered in black, but later models were covered in a bright orange vinyl. These were the first Orange amplifiers (see Orange). Peter Green of Fleetwood Mac was one of the first users of Matamps and Mathias toured with the band on their first U.S. tour. By 1973, the partnership between Mathias and Cooper dissolved and Mathias went back to building amps under the Matamp brand. He also built amps named after the color they were finished in including Red, Green, Blue, Black, and White. Mathias produced amplifiers through the 1970s and 1980s when he died in 1989. His sons inherited the company, but they soon sold it to Jeff Lewis, Mathias' long-time friend. Matamp still produces amps and speaker cabinets and many of the other brands that are named after colors are still produced. Much of their custom business is in the U.S. They currently offer a wide range of amplifiers and speaker cabinets. For more information, visit Matamp's website or contact them directly.

MATCHLESS

Amplifiers and speaker cabinets currently produced in Los Angeles, CA since 1999. Matchless amplifiers were previously produced in North Hollywood, CA from 1989 to 1994, Santa Fe Springs, CA from 1994 to 1997, and Pico Rivera, CA from 1997 to 1998.

The Matchless Amplifier Company was founded by Mark Sampson and Rick Perrotta in 1989. Mark was born and raised in Iowa where he built streetrods and racecars while playing in a band as a hobby. In the late 1980s, Mark and his family moved to the west coast. Mark then worked in various enterprises relating to music and instrument manufacture. Rick had an incredible collection of vintage radio and tube instruments. The two came together to form a partnership in 1989 to put together an amplifier. They spent two years forming the first prototype amplifier after extensive research and trial and error. Finally in 1991, they had an amp that wasn't too complicated to make or operate; therefore, creating a product that would be reliable, which became the 30W series. The first amp had features that the ones produced today still have, including: shock-mounted tubes, 1-watt resistors, and Teflon wiring. Mark stayed with the company until 1998, and Matchless went out of business in 1999. In 2000, Mark began doing freelance work and became involved with BadCat amplifiers. Late in 1999, Phil Jamison who had worked with Matchless prior, started producing Matchless amplifiers again under new ownership/managment. By 2000, new Matchless amplifiers started rolling off the line. All currently manufactured and most older models are made using point-to-point hand wiring, made in the U.S. Matchless uses this philosophy in their business: To build the best most versatile amplifier possible. For more information, visit Matchless' website or contact them directly.

ELECTRIC TUBE AMPLIFIERS: OVERVIEW

All Matchless amplifiers are available in custom colors at an additional charge. Colors include Crimson (red), Elk (tan), Green, White, Dark Burgundy, Grey, Sparkle White, Shower Curtain Black, and Shower Curtain Turquoise.

The first run of Marshall Amplifiers (1989-1998) by Mark Sampson generally are regarded as more collectible than recent amps.

MSR/NOTES	100%	EXCELLENT	AVERAGE	LAST MSR

Sampson has established himself as a premier amp builder in the 1990s and 2000s, and amps that he has built tend to bring a premium. Although several of the same models were produced in both eras, earlier models will bring more money than later models.

ELECTRIC TUBE AMPLIFIERS: 15W MODELS

All 15W amps made prior to January 1997 were in small cabinet size and had a full cloth grille front. In January, 1997, the cabinets were enlarged and started using the grille cloth they looked like the DC-30 amps. Head units first became available in 1997 and 2-12 in. combos were introduced in 1998.

HURRICANE HEAD (HR-HD) – 15W, head-unit only, all tube chassis, preamp: 2 X 12AX7, power: 2 X EL84, 5AR4 rectifier, single channel, tremolo, front black control panel, five control knobs (v, tone, s, depth, MV), various color covering, gray grille cloth, mfg. 1994-early 97.

| | N/A | $1,100 - 1,300 | $750 - 900 | $1,399 |

* *Hurricane 112 Combo (HR-112)* – similar to the Hurricane, except in combo form with 1-12 in. speaker, mfg. 1994-early 97.

| | N/A | $1,250 - 1,450 | $900 - 1,050 | $1,599 |

* *Hurricane 210 Combo (HR-210)* – similar to the Hurricane, except in combo form with 2-10 in. speakers, mfg. 1994-early 97.

| | N/A | $1,250 - 1,500 | $900 - 1,050 | $1,599 |

LIGHTNING HEAD (LG-HD) – 15W, head-unit guitar configuration, all tube chassis, preamp: 3 X 12AX7, power: 2 X EL84, 5AR4 rectifier, single channel, front black control panel, four control knobs (v, B, T, MV), various color covering, gray grille cloth, mfg. 1994-98, 2005-present.

| 1994-1997 | N/A | $1,100 - 1,300 | $750 - 900 | |
| 2005-Present MSR $2,113 | $1,700 | $1,100 - 1,275 | $550 - 675 | |

* *Lightning 112 (LG-112)* – similar to the Lightning 15 Head, except in combo configuration with 1-12 in. speaker, mfg. 1994-early 97, 2001-present.

Lightning 112
courtesy Willie's American Guitars

| 1994-1998 | N/A | $1,250 - 1,500 | $850 - 1,050 | |
| 2001-Present MSR $2,224 | $1,775 | $1,150 - 1,325 | $575 - 700 | |

* *Lightning 210 (LG-210)* – similar to the Lightning 112 except has 2-10 in. speakers, mfg. mid-1994-1998 and 2001-08.

| 1994-1998 | N/A | $1,300 - 1,600 | $900 - 1,100 | |
| 2001-2008 | $1,700 | $1,050 - 1,250 | $700 - 800 | $2,119 |

* *Lightning 212 (LG-212)* – similar to the Lightning 112 except has 2-12 in. speakers, mfg. 1998, 2001-present.

| 1998 | N/A | $1,500 - 1,800 | $1,050 - 1,200 | |
| 2001-Present MSR $2,447 | $1,950 | $1,275 - 1,475 | $625 - 775 | |

LIGHTNING REVERB HEAD (LG-15HDR) – 15W, head-unit guitar configuration, all tube chassis, preamp: 5 X 12AX7, power: 2 X EL84, 5AR4 rectifier, single channel, reverb, front black control panel, five control knobs (v, B, T, r, MV), various color covering, gray grille cloth, mfg. 1997-98, reintroduced 2006-08.

| 1997-1998 | N/A | $1,200 - 1,500 | $850 - 1,000 | |
| 2006-2008 | $1,900 | $1,100 - 1,300 | $750 - 850 | $2,389 |

* *Lightning Reverb 112 (LR-112/LG-112 Reverb)* – similar to the Lightning Reverb Head, except in combo configuration with 1-12 in. speaker, mfg. 1997-98, reintroduced 2003-present.

| 1997-1998 | N/A | $1,400 - 1,750 | $950 - 1,150 | |
| MSR $2,503 | $2,000 | $1,300 - 1,500 | $650 - 800 | |

* *Lightning Reverb 210 (LR-210/LG-210 REVERB)* – similar to the Lightning Reverb Head, except in combo configuration with 2-10 in. speakers, mfg. 1997-98, reintroduced 2003-08.

| 1997-1998 | N/A | $1,500 - 1,850 | $1,000 - 1,250 | |
| 2003-2008 | $1,900 | $1,100 - 1,300 | $750 - 850 | $2,369 |

MSR/NOTES	100%	EXCELLENT	AVERAGE	LAST MSR

* **Lightning Reverb 212 (LR-212/LG-212 REVERB)** – similar to the Lightning Reverb Head, except in combo configuration with 2-12 in. speakers, mfg. 1997-98, reintroduced 2003-present.

1997-1998	N/A	$1,600 - 2,000	$1,100 - 1,300	
MSR $2,726	$2,175	$1,425 - 1,625	$700 - 875	

NIGHTHAWK HEAD (NH-15) – 15W, head-unit configuration, all-tube chassis, preamp: 1 X 12AX7, power: 2 X EL84, single channel, front control panel, various color coverings, mfg. 2006-present.

MSR $2,113	$1,700	$1,100 - 1,275	$550 - 675	

* **Nighthawk 112 Combo (NH-112)** – similar to the Nighthawk Head, except in combo configuration with 1-12 in. speaker, mfg. 2003-present.

MSR $2,224	$1,775	$1,150 - 1,325	$575 - 700	

* **Nighthawk 210 Combo (NH-210)** – similar to the Nighthawk Head, except in combo configuration with 2-10 in. speakers, mfg. 2003-08.

MSR $2,119	$1,700	$1,050 - 1,250	$700 - 800	

* **Nighthawk 212 Combo (NH-212)** – similar to the Nighthawk Head, except in combo configuration with 2-12 in. speakers, mfg. 2003-present.

MSR $2,447	$1,950	$1,275 - 1,450	$625 - 775	

NIGHTHAWK 112 COMBO REVERB – 15W, 1-12 in. speaker combo, all-tube chassis, preamp: 2 X 12AX7, power: 2 X EL84, single channel, reverb, front control panel, various color coverings, mfg. 2003-05, 2009-present.

MSR $2,585	$2,075	$1,350 - 1,550	$675 - 825	

* **Nighthawk 210 Combo Reverb** – similar to the Nighthawk 112 Combo, except has 2-10 in. speakers, mfg. 2003-05.

	N/A	$1,150 - 1,350	$775 - 900	$2,549

* **Nighthawk 212 Combo Reverb** – similar to the Nighthawk 112 Combo, except has 2-12 in. speakers, mfg. 2003-05, 2009-present.

MSR $2,738	$2,200	$1,425 - 1,650	$700 - 875	

SPITFIRE HEAD (SP-HD) – 15W, head-unit only, all tube chassis, preamp: 2 X 12AX7, power: 2 X EL84, 5AR4 rectifier, single channel, front black control panel, three control knobs (v, tone, MV), various color covering, gray grille cloth, mfg. 1994-early 1997, 2009-present.

1994-1997	N/A	$1,000 - 1,200	$700 - 800	
2009-Present MSR $1,809	$1,450	$950 - 1,075	$475 - 575	

This amp was available as a head-unit for a short while in 1997. It was also available as a 2-10 in. combo for a while. The combos offer a slight premium over the head unit in value.

* **Spitfire 112 Combo (SP-112)** – similar to the Spitfire head, except with 1-12 in. speaker, mfg. 1994-early 97, 2003-present.

1994-1997	N/A	$1,200 - 1,400	$800 - 900	
MSR $1,909	$1,550	$850 - 1,000	$600 - 700	

» **Spitfire 112 Combo Reverb (SP-112R)** – similar to the Spitfire 112 Combo, except has reverb, mfg. 2005-present.

MSR $2,172	$1,725	$950 - 1,100	$650 - 750	

* **Spitfire 210 Combo (SP-210)** – similar to the Spitfire head, except with 2-10 in. speakers, mfg. 1994-early 97.

	N/A	$1,300 - 1,550	$950 - 1,100	$1,499

* **Spitfire 212 Combo (SP-212)** – similar to the Spitfire head, except with 2-12 in. speakers, mfg. 2005-present.

MSR $2,119	$1,700	$1,050 - 1,250	$700 - 800	

» **Spitfire 212 Combo Reverb (SP-212R)** – similar to the Spitfire 212 Combo, except has reverb, mfg. 2005-present.

MSR $2,384	$1,900	$1,100 - 1,300	$750 - 850	

THE BABY HEAD – 6W, guitar head unit, three-tube chassis, preamp: 1 X 12AX7, power: 1 X EL84, rectifier: 1 X 5AR4, single channel, top black control panel, single input, three cream chickenhead knobs (v, tone, MV), power switch, speaker out, available in various color coverings, mfg. 2009-present.

MSR $1,699	$1,375	$850 - 1,025	$600 - 700	

* **The Baby 112 Combo** – similar to The Baby Head, except in combo configuration with 1-12 in. speaker, mfg. 2009-present.

MSR $1,799	$1,450	$900 - 1,100	$625 - 750	

* **The Baby 2X8 Combo** – similar to The Baby Head, except in combo configuration with 2-8 in. speakers, mfg. 2009-present.

MSR $1,999	$1,600	$1,000 - 1,250	$675 - 825	

TORONADO – 15W, 1-12 in. speaker combo, all tube chassis, preamp: 2 X 12AX7, power: 2 X EL84, 5AR4 rectifier, single channel, tremolo, front black control panel, four control knobs (v, tone, s, depth), various color covering, gray grille cloth, mfg. 1994 only.

	N/A	$1,250 - 1,450	$900 - 1,000	$1,290

This amp was available identical to the Spitfire except with tremolo. This model was replaced by the Hurricane.

MSR/NOTES	100%	EXCELLENT	AVERAGE	LAST MSR

ELECTRIC TUBE AMPLIFIERS: 30W MODELS

SC-30 112 Combo
courtesy Dave Rogers/Dave's Guitar Shop

DC-30 212 Combo
courtesy Dave Rogers/Dave's Guitar Shop

30/15 HEAD – 30W, guitar head unit, seven-tube chassis, preamp: 2 X 12AX7, power: 4 X EL84, rectifier: 5AR4, single channel, optional reverb and tremolo, front black control panel, single input, three cream chickenhead knobs (v, tone, MV), power switch, standby switch, rear panel: 30/15W power switch, speaker jacks, optional effects loop, available in various color coverings, mfg. 2009-present.

MSR $2,098	$1,675	$1,100 - 1,250	$550 - 675	

- Add $50 for an effects loop.
- Add $250 for reverb.
- Add $250 for tremolo.

* 30/15 112 Combo – similar to the 30/15 Head, except in combo configuration with 1-12 in. speaker, mfg. 2009-present.

MSR $2,413	$1,925	$1,250 - 1,450	$625 - 775	

- Add $50 for an effects loop.
- Add $250 for reverb.
- Add $250 for tremolo.

* 30/15 212 Combo – similar to the 30/15 Head, except in combo configuration with 2-12 in. speakers, mfg. 2009-present.

MSR $2,549	$2,050	$1,275 - 1,525	$900 - 1,050	

- Add $50 for an effects loop.
- Add $250 for reverb.
- Add $250 for tremolo.

HC-30 HEAD – similar to the SC-30 in head-unit only, 50 lbs., mfg. 1991-98, 2000-present.

1991-1998	N/A	$1,750 - 2,250	$1,100 - 1,400	
2000-Present MSR $3,004	$2,400	$1,550 - 1,800	$775 - 950	

- Add $315 for reverb on currently produced models.

Current production models use only 2 X 12AX7 preamp tubes.

SC-30 112 COMBO – 30W, 1-12 in. speaker combo, all-tube chassis, preamp: 3 X 12AX7, EF86, power: 4 X EL84, 5AR4 or 2 X 5V4 rectifiers, two channels, front black control panel, four inputs, seven black knobs (Ch. 1: v, b, t, Ch. 2: v, tone, Both: Cut, MV), hi/lo power switch, impedance selector switch, various color coverings, gray grille cloth, 70 lbs., mfg. 1990-98, 2000-present.

1990-1998	N/A	$2,250 - 2,750	$1,500 - 1,800	
2000-Present MSR $3,468	$2,800	$1,800 - 2,075	$900 - 1,100	

- Add $315 for reverb on currently produced models.

This was the first production Matchless amp introduced in mid-1990. Early models used the 5AR4 rectifier. In 1992, burgundy became a color option and in 1993, a multitude of colors were available. Before 1993 effects loop was optional however few were produced with them. Current production models use only 2 X 12AX7 preamp tubes.

DC-30 212 COMBO – similar to the SC-30 except has 2-12 in. dissimilar speakers, 83 lbs., mfg. 1991-98, 2000-present.

1991-1998	N/A	$2,500 - 3,000	$1,600 - 2,000	
2000-Present MSR $3,778	$3,000	$1,975 - 2,275	$975 - 1,200	

- Add $315 for reverb on currently produced models.

This was the second production Matchless model. Current production models use only 2 X 12AX7 preamp tubes.

TC-30 210 COMBO – similar to the SC-30 except has 2-10 in. speakers, mfg. 1998 only.

	N/A	$2,350 - 2,850	$1,550 - 1,900	$3,449

410-C30 – similar to the SC-30 except has 4-10 in. speakers, mfg. 1991-93.

	N/A	$2,750 - 3,250	$1,800 - 2,200	$2,450

This amp was available on special order after 1993. It was replaced by a head unit with a 4-10 in. speaker cabinet.

MSR/NOTES	100%	EXCELLENT	AVERAGE	LAST MSR

RMC-30 – 30W, rack-mount head, all-tube chassis, preamp: 3 X 12AX7, 1 X EF86, power: 4 X EL84, 5AR4 or 2 X 5V4 rectifiers, two channels, front black control panel, four inputs, seven black knobs (Ch. 1: v, b, t, Ch. 2: v, tone, Both: Cut, MV), hi/lo power switch, impedance selector switch, light gray casing with black lettering, mfg. 1991-94.

	N/A	$1,500 - 1,750	$1,000 - 1,200	$1,890

RA-30 – 30W, power amp only, rack mount head, all-tube chassis, power: 4 X EL84, front chrome control panel, three ivory chicken head knobs (input level, brilliance, MV), mfg. 1998 only.

	N/A	$1,200 - 1,400	$950 - 1,100	

JOHN JORGENSEN SIGNATURE – 30W, 1-12 in. speaker combo, all tube Class A chassis, preamp: 1 X EF86, 4 X 12AX7, power: 4 X EL84, rectifier: 5AR4 or 2 X 5V4, single channel, front control panel, two inputs, seven white knobs (v, master tone, s, depth, r, cut, MV), hi/lo power switch, speaker phase switch, sparkle red, white, blue or silver covering, black grille cloth, mfg. 1997-98.

	N/A	$3,750 - 4,500	$2,500 - 3,000	

This amp was designed with John Jorgensen who was playing with Elton John at the time. It is the only Matchless amp to be made in the 30W configuration with reverb.

AVALON 30 – 30W (switchable to 15W), guitar head-unit, eight (non-reverb) or ten-tube (reverb) chassis, preamp: 3 X 12AX7 (non-reverb) or 5 X 12AX7 (reverb), power: 4 X EL84, rectifier: 1 X 5AR4, single channel, optional reverb, front black control panel, two inputs (hi/low), six black chickenhead knobs (v, b, t, cut, MV with push/pull, r), standby switch, power switch, rear panel: two speaker jacks, impedance selector, effects loop, available in various coverings, current mfg.

MSR $2,118	$1,700	$1,100 - 1,275	$550 - 675	

- Add $265 for reverb.
- Add $180 for plexiglass front panel.

* *Avalon 30 Combo* – similar to the Avalon 30, except in combo configuration with 1-12 in. Celestion G12H30 speaker, current mfg.

MSR $2,436	$1,950	$1,275 - 1,450	$625 - 775	

- Add $330 for reverb.

AVENGER 30 – 30W, head-unit only, all-tube chassis, preamp: 2 X 12AX7/ECC83, power: 4 X EL84/6BQ5, rectifier: 5AR4, single channel, front control panel, single input, six white chickenhead knobs (v, b, m, t, post, MV), hi/lo power switch, impedance switch, various color coverings, mfg. 2005-present.

MSR $2,967	$2,350	$1,350 - 1,650	$1,000 - 1,150	

* *Avenger 30 112 Combo* – similar to the Avenger 30, except in combo form with 1-12 in. speaker, mfg. 2005-present.

MSR $3,391	$2,700	$1,700 - 2,050	$1,100 - 1,300	

* *Avenger 30 212 Combo* – similar to the Avenger 30, except in combo form with 2-12 in. speakers, mfg. 2005-present.

MSR $3,705	$3,000	$1,850 - 2,225	$1,150 - 1,400	

* *Avenger 30 210/112 Combo* – similar to the Avenger 30, except in combo form with 2-10 in. and 1-12 in. speakers, mfg. 2005-08.

	$3,000	$1,800 - 2,100	$1,200 - 1,400	$3,729

AVENGER 30 REVERB – 30W, head-unit only, all-tube chassis, preamp: 4 X 12AX7/ECC83, power: 4 X EL84/6BQ5, rectifier: 5AR4, single channel, reverb, front control panel, single input, seven white chickenhead knobs (v, b, m, t, post, MV, r), hi/lo power switch, impedance switch, various color coverings, mfg. 2005-08.

	$2,350	$1,350 - 1,650	$1,000 - 1,150	$2,946

* *Avenger 30 112 Combo Reverb* – similar to the Avenger 30 Reverb, except in combo form with 1-12 in. speaker, mfg. 2005-08.

	$2,600	$1,600 - 1,900	$1,050 - 1,250	$3,264

* *Avenger 30 212 Combo Reverb* – similar to the Avenger 30 Reverb, except in combo form with 2-12 in. speakers, mfg. 2005-08.

	$2,900	$1,750 - 2,100	$1,100 - 1,300	$3,635

* *Avenger 30 210/112 Combo Reverb* – similar to the Avenger 30 Reverb, except in combo form with 2-10 in. and 1-12 in. speakers, mfg. 2005-08.

	$3,200	$1,950 - 2,300	$1,300 - 1,500	$3,979

ELECTRIC TUBE AMPLIFIERS: 35W MODELS

CLUBMAN 35 HEAD – 35W, head-unit only, all tube Class A chassis, three variations, current (3rd variation; see below for others) preamp: 2 X 12AX7, 1 X EF86, power: 2 X EL34, 5AR4 rectifier, single channel, front black control panel, two inputs, five white knobs (v, b, t, brilliance, MV), effects loop, various color covering, gray cloth grille, mfg. 1993-98, 2001-present.

1993-1998	N/A	$1,400 - 1,700	$950 - 1,150	
MSR $2,113	$1,700	$1,100 - 1,275	$550 - 675	

There were three variations of this amp produced (as far as electronics). The first variation had a tube chassis of 1 X 6AT6, 1 X 6SH7, 1 X 12AX7, 2 X EL34, and 1 X 5AR4 rectifier. The second variation featured 2 X 12AX7, 1 X 6SH7, 2 X EL34, and 1 X 5AR4 rectifier. The third variation is listed in the model description. By mid-1994, the Clubman 35 was using the third variation.

MSR/NOTES	100%	EXCELLENT	AVERAGE	LAST MSR

* *Clubman 35 Reverb Head* – similar to the Clubman 35, except has reverb circuit and knob, mfg. 2003-present.

| MSR $2,391 | $1,900 | $1,250 - 1,425 | $625 - 775 | |

COBRA HEAD – 35W, guitar head unit, 10-tube chassis, preamp: 4 X 12AX7, 1 X EF86, power: 4 X EL84, rectifier: 5AR4, single channel, reverb, tremolo, front black control panel, two inputs, seven cream chickenhead knobs (v, tone, tremolo speed, tremolo depth, cut MV), power switch, standby switch, rear panel: reverse speaker phase switch, hi/lo power switch, three-position rotary impedance selector, six-position rotary tone selector, available in various color coverings, mfg. 2009-present.

| MSR $3,323 | $2,650 | $1,600 - 2,000 | $1,050 - 1,300 | |

* *Cobra 112 Combo* – similar to the Cobra Head, except in combo configuration with 1-12 in. speaker, mfg. 2009-present.

| MSR $3,641 | $2,900 | $1,800 - 2,150 | $1,200 - 1,500 | |

* *Cobra 212 Combo* – similar to the Cobra Head, except in combo configuration with 2-12 in. speakers, mfg. 2009-present.

| MSR $3,995 | $3,200 | $2,000 - 2,400 | $1,300 - 1,650 | |

INDEPENDENCE – 35W, head-unit only, all-tube chassis, preamp: 2 X 12AX7, power: 2 X EL 34, rectifier: 5AR4, three switchable channels, front control panel, nine white chickenhead knobs (v1, tone, v2, v3, g, b, t, cut, MV), impedance selector, various color coverings, mfg. 2005-present.

| MSR $3,195 | $2,550 | $1,650 - 1,925 | $825 - 1,025 | |

- Add 7.5% for reverb (MSR $3,445).

* *Independence 112 Combo* – similar to the Independence Head, except in combo form with 1-12 in. speaker, mfg. 2005-present.

| MSR $3,526 | $2,825 | $1,750 - 2,125 | $1,150 - 1,400 | |

- Add 7.5% for reverb (MSR $3,776).

* *Independence 212 Combo* – similar to the Independence Head, except in combo form with 2-12 in. speakers, mfg. 2005-present.

| MSR $3,816 | $3,050 | $1,925 - 2,300 | $1,200 - 1,450 | |

- Add 7.5% for reverb (MSR $4,076).

KING COBRA HEAD – 35W, guitar head unit, eight-tube chassis, preamp: 4 X 12AX7, 1 X EF86, power: 2 X EL34, rectifier: 5AR4, single channel, reverb, tremolo, front black control panel, two inputs, seven cream chickenhead knobs (v, tone, tremolo speed, tremolo depth, cut MV), power switch, standby switch, rear panel: reverse speaker phase switch, hi/lo power switch, three-position rotary impedance selector, six-position rotary tone selector, available in various color coverings, mfg. 2009-present.

| MSR $3,323 | $2,650 | $1,600 - 2,000 | $1,050 - 1,300 | |

* *King Cobra 112 Combo* – similar to the King Cobra Head, except in combo configuration with 1-12 in. speaker, mfg. 2009-present.

| MSR $3,641 | $2,900 | $1,800 - 2,150 | $1,200 - 1,500 | |

* *King Cobra 212 Combo* – similar to the King Cobra Head, except in combo configuration with 2-12 in. speakers, mfg. 2009-present.

| MSR $3,955 | $3,200 | $2,000 - 2,400 | $1,300 - 1,650 | |

PHOENIX – 35W, head-unit only, all-tube chassis, preamp: 2 X 12AX7, 1 X EF86, power: 2 X EL84, 5AR4 rectifier, two channels, front black control panel, four inputs, seven black chickenhead knobs (Ch. 1: v, b, t, Ch. 2: v, tone, cut, MV), effects loop, various color coverings, mfg. 2003-present.

| MSR $2,967 | $2,350 | $1,400 - 1,700 | $900 - 1,100 | |

* *Phoenix 112 Combo* – similar to the Phoenix Head, except is in combo form with 1-12 in. speaker, mfg. 2003-present.

| MSR $3,391 | $2,700 | $1,600 - 1,950 | $1,050 - 1,300 | |

* *Phoenix 212 Combo* – similar to the Phoenix Head, except is in combo form with 2-12 in. speakers, mfg. 2003-present.

| MSR $3,705 | $2,950 | $1,800 - 2,150 | $1,150 - 1,400 | |

ELECTRIC TUBE AMPLIFIERS: 40W MODELS

BRAVE 112 – 40W, 1-12 in. speaker combo, all tube Class A chassis, preamp: 2 X 12AX7, power: 2 X EL34, 5AR4 rectifier, single channel, front black control panel, two inputs (high/lo), four knobs (v, b, t, MV), various color covering, gray cloth grille, mfg. 1997-98.

| | N/A | $1,200 - 1,500 | $850 - 1,000 | $2,249 |

This amp was a stripped down version of the Chieftain.

* *Brave 212* – similar to the Brave 112 except has 2-12 in. speakers, mfg. 1997-98.

| | N/A | $1,300 - 1,650 | $950 - 1,150 | $2,499 |

CHIEFTAIN CH-40 HEAD – 40W, head-unit only, all tube Class A chassis, preamp: 5 X 12AX7, power: 2 X EL34, 5AR4 rectifier, single channel, reverb, front black control panel, single input, seven white knobs (v, b, m, t, brilliance, MV, r), effects loop, switchable output impedance, various color covering, gray cloth grille, 50 lbs., mfg. 1994-98, 2001-present.

| 1994-1998 | N/A | $1,600 - 2,000 | $1,100 - 1,300 | |
| 2001-Present MSR $2,725 | $2,175 | $1,425 - 1,625 | $700 - 875 | |

MSR/NOTES	100%	EXCELLENT	AVERAGE	LAST MSR

* *Chieftan CH-112 Combo* – similar to the Chieftain CH-40 except in combo configuration with 1-12 in. speaker, 71 lbs., mfg. 1994-98, 2001-present.

1994-1998	N/A	$1,750 - 2,250	$1,150 - 1,400	
2001-Present MSR $3,059	$2,450	$1,600 - 1,825	$800 - 975	

* *Chieftan CH-210 Combo* – similar to the Chieftain CH-40 except in combo form with 2-10 in. speakers, 74 lbs., mfg. 1994-98, 2003-08.

1994-1998	N/A	$1,850 - 2,350	$1,200 - 1,500	
2003-2008	$2,350	$1,450 - 1,750	$900 - 1,100	$2,914

* *Chieftan CH-212 Combo* – similar to the Chieftain CH-40 except in combo form with 2-12 in. speakers, 85 lbs., mfg. 1994-98, 2001-present.

1994-1998	N/A	$2,000 - 2,500	$1,200 - 1,500	
2001-Present MSR $3,449	$2,750	$1,800 - 2,075	$900 - 1,100	

* *Chieftan CH-410 Combo* – similar to the Chieftain CH-40 except in combo form with 4-10 in. speakers, 92 lbs., mfg. 1994-98.

	N/A	$2,250 - 2,750	$1,400 - 1,750	$3,099

ELECTRIC TUBE AMPLIFIERS: 45W MODELS

BOLT 45 112 – 45W, 1-12 in. speaker combo with flip-top head design, all tube chassis with solid-state rectifier, preamp: 2 X 12AX7, power: 2 X EL34, 5U4 rectifier, single channel, front black control panel, five knobs (v, b, t, brilliance, MV), tube/s.s. rectifier switch, various color covering, gray cloth grille, mfg. 1997-98.

	N/A	$1,400 - 1,750	$950 - 1,150	$2,799

This amp was the guitar version of the Thunderman bass amp (see Bass amp section)

* *Bolt 45 115* – similar to the Bolt 45 112 except has 1-15 in. speaker, mfg. 1997-98.

	N/A	$1,400 - 1,750	$950 - 1,150	$2,799

ELECTRIC TUBE AMPLIFIERS: 85W AND HIGHER MODELS

CHIEF 100 – 100W, head-unit only, all tube chassis, preamp: 5 X 12AX7, power: 4 X EL34, single channel, reverb, front black control panel, single input, seven white knobs (v, b, m, t, brilliance, MV r), various color covering, brown grille (combo only), mfg. 1997-98.

	N/A	$1,750 - 2,250	$1,150 - 1,400	$2,799

This amp is a high-wattage version of the Chieftan.

* *Chief 100 212 Combo* – similar to the Chief 100 except in combo form with 2-12 in. speakers, mfg. 1997-98.

	N/A	$2,000 - 2,500	$1,300 - 1,600	$3,349

* *Chief 100 410 Combo* – similar to the Chief 100 except in combo form with 4-10 in. speakers, mfg. 1997-98.

	N/A	$2,250 - 2,750	$1,400 - 1,750	$3,349

HC-85 – 85W, head-unit only, all tube chassis, preamp: 3 X 12AX7, 1 X EF86, power: 4 X EL34, rectifier: 2 X 5R4, or 2 X 5U4, two channels, front black control panel, four inputs, seven black knobs (Ch. 1: v, b, t, Ch. 2: v, tone, Both: Cut, MV), hi/lo power switch, impedance selector switch, light gray vinyl covering (later other colors), gray grille cloth, mfg. 1991-93.

	N/A	$2,000 - 2,500	$1,300 - 1,600	$2,355

All of these models had a fan installed. In 1992 burgundy became a color option and in 1993, a multitude of colors were available. Before 1993 effects loop was optional. However, few were produced with them. This amp used the same cabinet as the HC-30.

HC-90 – similar to the HC-85 except has 90W output, mfg. 1993 only.

	N/A	$2,250 - 2,750	$1,400 - 1,750	

This model replaced the HC-85 before the Superchief 120 replaced this model. Only a handful of the HC-90s were built.

SUPERCHIEF 120 – 120W, head-unit only, all tube chassis, preamp: 3 X 12AX7, power: 4 X EL34, rectifier: 2 X 5U4, single channel, front black control panel, single input, six black knobs (v, b, m, t, brilliance, MV), hi/lo power switch, impedance selector switch, various color covering, gray grille cloth, mfg. 1994-98, 2005-08.

1994-1998	N/A	$1,400 - 1,850	$1,000 - 1,200	
2005-2008	$2,400	$1,300 - 1,650	$900 - 1,100	

ELECTRIC TUBE AMPLIFIERS: BASS AMPS "THUNDER AMPS"

THUNDERCHIEF – 200W, head-unit only, all-tube chassis, preamp: 2 X 12AX7, 1 X 12AU7, 1 X 12BH7, power: 4 X KT88, rectifier: 2 X 5U4, single channel, front black control panel, single input, six white knobs (input level, v, b, m, t, MV), deep switch, hi/lo switch, various color covering, gray grille cloth, mfg. 1994-98.

	N/A	$1,200 - 1,500	$850 - 1,000	

This amp was meant to be mated with 1-15 in. ported cab or a 4-10 in. closed back cabinet.

MSR/NOTES	100%	EXCELLENT	AVERAGE	LAST MSR

THUNDERMAN 45 – 45W, 1-15 in. or 2-10 in. speaker combo in a flip-top design, all tube chassis, preamp: 2 X 12AX7, power: 2 X 6L6, 5U4 rectifier, single channel, front black control panel, four knobs (v, b, t, sensitivity), compression switch, chrome cage over chassis, various color covering, black grille cloth, mfg. 1997-98.

	N/A	$1,400 - 1,750	$1,000 - 1,200	$2,349

This is a recording bass amp.

THUNDERMAN 100 – 100W, 1-15 in. or 2-10 in. speaker combo in a flip-top design, all tube chassis, preamp: 2 X 12AX7, power: 4 X 6L6, 5U4 rectifier, single channel, front black control panel, five knobs (v, b, t, sensitivity, definition), chrome cage over chassis, various color covering, black grille cloth, mfg. 1998 only.

	N/A	$1,600 - 2,000	$1,100 - 1,300	$3,249

This is the big brother of the Thunderman 45.

THUNDERMAN HEAD – 45W, bass head unit, all tube chassis, preamp: 2 X 12AX7, power: 2 X EL34, 5U4G rectifier, single channel, front black control panel, five knobs (response, v, b, t, brilliance), standbyswitch, power switch, top handle, metal corners, various color covering, cream grille cloth, 55 lbs., current mfg.

MSR $2,200	$1,750	$1,125 - 1,300	$575 - 700	

ELECTRIC TUBE AMPLIFIERS: SUPERLINER SERIES

The Superliner series are different than all other Matchless amps. All models in this series are made on a circuit board and not point-to-point wired. In addition, there are no internal lights or lights behind the logo like there are on other Matchless amps. The only covering available for this series was black.

CLIPPER – 15W, 1-12 in. or 2-10 in. speakers, Class A tube chassis, preamp: 12AX7, power: 2 X EL84, single channel, front black control panel, single input, five white chickenhead knobs (g, b, m, t, MV), black covering, gray grille, mfg. 1998 only.

	N/A	$850 - 1,000	$600 - 725	

SKYLINER – 15W, 1-12 in. or 2-10 in. speakers, Class A tube chassis, preamp: 5 X 12AX7, power: 2 X EL84, 5AR4 rectifier, two channels, front black control panel, single input, nine white chickenhead knobs (Ch. 1: g, b, m, t, MV, Ch. 2: g, b, t, MV), effects loop, black covering, gray grille, mfg. 1998 only.

	N/A	$1,000 - 1,200	$675 - 850	

* *Skyliner Reverb* – similar to the Skyliner 15, except for the addition of reverb (extra preamp tube and 10 controls), mfg. 1998 only.

	N/A	$1,150 - 1,400	$850 - 1,000	

SLIPSTREAM REVERB – 40W, 1-12 in. speaker, tube chassis, preamp: 6 X 12AX7, power: 2 X EL34, 5AR4 rectifier, single channel, front black control panel, single input, six white chickenhead knobs (g, b, m, t, MV, r), effects loop, black covering, gray grille, mfg. 1998 only.

	N/A	$1,200 - 1,500	$850 - 1,000	

STARLINER 40 – 40W, 2-12 in. speakers, tube chassis, preamp: 5 X 12AX7, power: 2 X EL34, 5AR4 rectifier, two channels, front black control panel, single input, nine white chickenhead knobs (Ch. 1: g, b, m, t, MV, Ch. 2: g, b, t, MV), effects loop, black covering, gray grille, mfg. 1998 only.

	N/A	$1,400 - 1,750	$950 - 1,150	

* *Starliner 40 Reverb* – similar to the Starliner 40, except for the addition of reverb (extra preamp tube and 10 controls), mfg. 1998 only.

	N/A	$1,550 - 1,900	$1,100 - 1,250	

EXTENSION SPEAKER CABINETS

AVALON 212 SPEAKER CABINET – 35W, 2-12 in. Celestion G12H30 speakers, 4 ohm impedance, open back design, various color covering, gray grille, 35 lbs., mfg. 2009-present.

MSR $799	$650	$425 - 500	$275 - 325	

EB-115 – 200W, 1-15 in. Celestion speaker, bass cabinet, 8 Ohm impedance, closed back, ported design, various color covering, gray grille, mfg. 1997-98.

	N/A	$425 - 500	$275 - 325	$799

Very few of these models were produced.

EB-410 – 300W capability, 4-10 in. Celestion speakers, 8 Ohm impedance, closed back, ported design, various color covering, gray grille, mfg. 1996-98.

	N/A	$500 - 600	$300 - 375	$999

Very few of these models were produced.

ES-210 – 70W, 2-10 in. Celestion speakers, 8 Ohm impedance, open back design, various color covering, gray grille, 43 lbs., mfg. 1993-98.

	N/A	$475 - 550	$300 - 350	$799

ES-410 – 140W, 4-10 in. Celestion speakers, 8 Ohm impedance, open back design, various color covering, gray grille, 55 lbs., mfg. 1993-98, 2003-present.

MSR $1,058	$850	$525 - 600	$325 - 400	

MSR/NOTES	100%	EXCELLENT	AVERAGE	LAST MSR

ES-412 – 120W, 4-12 in. Celestion speakers, 8 Ohm impedance, open back design, various color covering, gray grille, mfg. 1993-98, 2003-present.

| MSR $1,207 | $975 | $600 - 700 | $375 - 450 | |

* **ES-412D** – similar to the ES-412 except has a closed back, 99 lbs., mfg. 1993-98.

| | N/A | $600 - 700 | $375 - 450 | $1,249 |

ES-1012 – 120W, 2-12 in., & 2-10 in. Celestion speakers, 8 Ohm impedance, open back design, various color covering, gray grille, 89 lbs., mfg. 1993-98.

| | N/A | $625 - 750 | $425 - 500 | $1,139 |

ESD/ES-212 – 40W or 60W, 2-12 in. Celestion speakers, 4 Ohm impedance, open back design, various color covering, gray grille, 45 lbs., mfg. 1991-present.

| MSR $1,058 | $850 | $550 - 625 | $275 - 350 | |

ESS/ES-112 – 30W, 1-12 in. Celestion speaker, 8 Ohm impedance, open back design, various color covering, gray grille, 35 lbs., mfg. 1991-present.

| MSR $719 | $575 | $375 - 450 | $225 - 275 | |

* **ES-112 Mini** – similar to the ESS/ES-112, except in a mini cabinet configuration, various color covering, gray grille, 30 lbs., mfg. 2009-present.

| MSR $560 | $450 | $275 - 325 | $150 - 200 | |

MAVEN PEAL

Amplifiers and pedals built by Maven Peal Instruments, Inc. in Vermont since 1999.

Dave Zimmerman began building amps after he listened to Neil Young play the Fender Deluxe that had been modified. Dave noticed how the power supply was not producing enough power to drive the power tubes. He then developed and patented the Sag Circuit that allows players to adjust the amount of voltage the amp gets from the power supply, as well as the number of watts the amp is actually producing. This allows the amp to produce the distorted sound many players crave when an amp is run wide open at any volume. The Sag Control featured on all Maven Peal amps also includes a built-in power conditioner and line regulator. For more information visit Maven Peal's website or contact them directly. Information courtesy *The ToneQuest Report*.

CONTACT INFORMATION
MAVEN PEAL
PO Box 71
Strafford, VT 05072
Phone No.: 802-793-4847
www.mavenpeal.com
info@mavenpeal.com

ELECTRIC TUBE AMPLIFIERS

Maven Peal produces tube amplifiers and high end speaker enclosures. The **Zeeta** 0.5->20W (several variations, starts at $2,600) was Maven Peal's first amplifier, followed by the **Ganesha** 1->100W (starts at $3,250), the **Tuskadaro** 1->50W (starts at $2,950), and the **RG-88** 0.5->88W (starts at $3,500). Maven Peal also offered the highest quality naked clear pine 1-12 in., 2-12 in., and 4-12 in. speaker enclosures featuring Maven Peal's proprietary removable back design, giving players two enclosures in one box. The company has recently offered a new line of Impact Pedals, the first being the Howler ($219 retail) followed by the Microdot series ($199 and $189 retail).

MCINTOSH

Amplifiers previously produced in Binghamton, NY during the late 1940s and 1950s.

McIntosh amplifiers are very popular among hi-fi enthusiasts and in the recording studio. McIntosh amps featured unique transformers that they labeled Unity Coupled, which gave the amps high accuracy and durability. McIntosh amps typically came in head-unit configurations. Mono amps were available in from 30W to 75W and stereo amps were available from 30W per side to 75W per side. Any further information on McIntosh amplifiers can be submitted directly to Blue Book Publications. Initial information courtesy, Aspen Pittman, *The Tube Amp Book*.

MEGA AMPLIFIERS

Amplifiers currently produced in South Korea. Distributed in the U.S. by Guitar Jones, Inc. in Ponoma, CA. Mega is part of WooSung Chorus Industries.

Mega amplifiers are produced in Korea, and have just recently become available in the U.S. through Guitar Jones, Inc. in Ponoma, CA. Mega produces a wide variety of mainly budget/entry-level amplifiers, but they also produce a full tube series. Most retail prices range between $50 and $250. For more information visit Mega's website or contact Guitar Jones, Inc. directly.

CONTACT INFORMATION
MEGA AMPLIFIERS
www.megaamps.com

U.S. Distributor: Guitar Jones, Inc.
2300 S. Reservoir St., Suite 208
Pomona, CA 91766
Phone No.: 909-548-6855
Fax No.: 909-548-6856
www.wscmusic.com
info@guitarjonesusa.com

ELECTRIC AMPLIFIERS

Mega produces quite a few series including the DL, SL, ML, WL, SL, PL, GL, AL, and VL series. Within each of these series are about four amps that are for guitar and sometimes bass. They also have a line of acoustic amplifiers, the AC series, a line of tube amplifiers, the T series, and the mini-series. They also offer footswitches and effects for their products.

MESA/BOOGIE

Also Mesa Engineering. Amplifiers, speaker cabinets, and other electronic products currently produced in Petaluma, CA, since early 1969.

CONTACT INFORMATION
MESA/BOOGIE
1317 Ross Street
Petaluma, CA 94954 USA
Phone No.: 707-778-6565
Fax No.: 707-765-1503
www.mesaboogie.com
info@mesaboogie.com

Mesa Boogie was started by Randall Smith in the early 1970s. Randall had a life-altering experience as a young boy. He was working on a Boy Scout project and for a merit badge he had to go to his scout leader with some wood carvings. The leader took him into this shop, an electronics lab, cut up his wood carvings in a band saw, and told him "this is what I think of your projects and you!" The leader explained to Smith that he wouldn't want that showing up one day when he was making decent stuff and would ask himself, embarrassingly, "I did that?" Randall took an instant liking to the electronics lab, and began learning from his odd friend. He also took a liking to cars (Mercedes in particular). He would repair cars for friends.

In 1966, the hippie movement came through San Francisco, and music was the thing. Smith got a drumset to get into the scene and joined a band. One day an amp blew in the band and shortage of funds made fixing it at a shop not feasible. So Randall took a look at it and ended up fixing it in fifteen minutes. The band instantly thought they should open up a shop and Prune Music was then set up in N. Berkeley, California. Randall fixed amps in the back of the store and a lot of great artists would come in including the Grateful Dead, Jefferson Airplane, Big Brother, Quicksilver, and Santana. Randall also would modify amps for people, and as Smith states, "What started out as a joke became the foundation of the company." Barry Melton's roadies came in and wanted something to be done to make his Princeton amp "melt." Randall stripped the chassis, put a chassis from a 4-10 in. Fender Bassman, and carefully installed a 12 in. JBL D-120 speaker while at the same time the amp still looked stock. He got some regular customer to plug into it and was blown away by the new 60W Bassman/Princeton. Things really changed when Carlos Santana came in and played the concoction. Carlos is quoted as saying, "This little amp really boogies," which, ended up becoming the name of the company. It is estimated that 200 of these Princetons were converted before Fender stopped supplying Randall with transformers.

By 1970, Randall had left Prune Music, thinking that Prune would buy him out. He actually got zero money out of the deal and was out of a job, so he started fixing cars to get cash and would build amps at night. At this point he formed MESA Engineering as a company that suppliers would take seriously. He built amps for a while until Lee Michaels, an "equipment junkie," got his hands on these new Crown DC300 solid-state power amplifiers. Many companies had tried to make a preamp for this but they all had no tone. Randall was summoned where he worked his magic in the circuitry and came up with the winning combination. Randall had found something and thought it was for Carlos Santana himself. Carlos got an amp and people were coming after Randall wondering if the guy making amps in the shack was for real. The idea behind this amp was a cascading preamp, which is having the preamp stages lined up into each other that would produce enhanced distortion and gain.

The first amp Smith built from scratch was a snakeskin covered Boogie 130 Lead Head for English rocker Dave Mason of Winterland. Smith then began to develop a pre-amp design for Lee Michaels' new Crown DC 300 power amps. He ended up adding three variable gain controls at critical points within the circuit. Once Smith and Michaels tried the amp, they were blown away and Smith knew he was onto something. Smith, his wife, and a few friends began building the first Boogies by hand in his house during the early 1970s. These first amps were referred to as the Mark I but they didn't get labled until the second series (MKII) was released in the late 1970s. Smith estimates that 3,000 of these Mark I Boogies were built at his house.

In 1980, Smith moved to their current location in Petaluma, California. In 1980, they also introduced the Mark II-A, which was the first modern channel switching with separate rhythm and high-gain lead modes. Mesa and Smith continued to experiment and expand with the D-180 Rack-mount bass amp and the Mark II-B with an improved lead overdrive circuit and the first-ever effects loop in 1982. The revised Mark II-C+ was introduced in 1983 with the dual cascading lead stage. In circa 1985, the new Mark III Series was introduced with three independent channels. In 1986, they introduced the Quad and Studio preamps for rack systems that featured the first tuned recording outputs. In 1989, the Mark IV Series was introduced and became one of Mesa's most popular models until it was discontinued in 2008.

HISTORY 1990-PRESENT

In 1990, Mesa introduced the Dual Caliber Series, which started with the Studio .22 and ultimately evolved into the F-Series. In 1991, they introduced the Dual and Triple Rectifier Series, which featured multiple tube rectifiers. In 1994, they introduced Maverick and Blue Angel Series, which offered simpler features and more vintage sounds. In 1998, the Nomad Series was introduced with three independent channels.

In 2000, the Road King was introduced with four complete three-mode channels. In 2004, the Lone Star, Lone Star Special, and Stiletto Series were introduced. The Lone Star Series of amps were designed for blues players while the Stiletto Series were designed with the British EL34 sound in mind. In 2006, the Roadster, Stiletto Ace, and Titan V-12 bass amps were introduced. The Roadster features four channels with 12 modes! In 2007, the Express Series were introduced that featured lower wattages and simpler features with two channels and four modes. In 2008, they introduced the Fathom 600 (later changed to M6 Carbine) bass amplifier. In 2009, Mesa celebrated their 40th Anniversary with the introduction of the Mark V that incorporates elements of the legendary Mark I, Mark IIC+, and Mark IV amps all in one. They also introduced the Electra Dyne Series of amps that feature SimulClass 90W/45W power switching.

Mesa continues to innovate the guitar amplifier world. All of their products are built in the USA at their California workshop. For more information, visit Mesa's website or contact them directly. Early history courtesy Ritchie Flieger, *Amps!*

MSR/NOTES	100%	EXCELLENT	AVERAGE	LAST MSR

CUSTOM COLORS/OPTIONS

All amps and cabinets that come standard with vinyl are open for the above options. Most of these are custom ordered.

Mesa Boogie is responsible for some fine tube amplifiers in combos, heads, preamps, and power amps. The MK series is listed with the models from MK I up until MK IV. All the current amp combos and heads are listed. There are other preamps and power amps that Mesa builds that aren't listed yet. Look for more information on this and other discontinued models in upcoming editions of the *Blue Book of Guitar Amplifiers*.

- Add $109 for a Custom jute grille (Tan or Gold).
- Add $159 for a wicker grille.
- Add $179 for Custom vinyl covering (Gray, Wine, Vanilla, Blue, Cream, Cocoa, Emerald, Red, Purple, Silver, Zinc, Hot White, Orange, or Garnet).
- Add $349 for whole hide or Suede leather covering (heads, combos, and cabinets up to a 2-12 horizontal guitar and 1-15 bass).
- Add $449 for embossed custom leather covering (heads, combos, and cabinets up to a 2-12 horizontal guitar and 1-15 bass).
- Add $549 for premier exotic hardwood cabinet.
- Add $649 for premier exotic hardwood cabinet (Roadster, Lone Star, Ace, and Electra Dyne models).
- Add $699 for whole hide or Suede leather covering (cabinets including 2-12 vertical guitar, 4-10 guitar and all larger cabinets).
- Add $739 for premier maple hardwood cabinet.
- Add $839 for premier maple hardwood cabinet (Roadster, Lone Star, Ace, and Electra Dyne models).
- Add $899 for embossed custom leather covering (cabinets including 2-12 vertical guitar, 4-10 guitar and all larger cabinets).
- Add $1,069 (minimum) for private reserve hardwood cabinet.
- Add $1,169 (minimum) for private reserve hardwood cabinet (Roadster, Lone Star, Ace, and Electra Dyne models).

ELECTRIC TUBE AMPLIFIERS: BLUE ANGEL SERIES

BLUE ANGEL – 38W (switchable to 33W & 15W), head-unit only, all tube Class A chassis, preamp: 5 X 12AX7, power: 2 X 6V6, 4 X EL84, 5AR4 rectifier, single channel, reverb, front blue control panel, two inputs, six black knobs (v, t, m, b, r, progressive linkage), effects loop, fan cooled, black covering, black grille cloth, mfg. 1994-2003.

	N/A	$775 - 900	$375 - 475	$999

This model has a tube switching feature where either 6V6 or EL84 tubes can be used or they can be combined. A 2X10 Combo has been offered as well in the catalog but doesn't appear in any price lists.

* ***Blue Angel 1-12 Combo*** – similar to the Blue Angel head unit, except in combo configuration with 1-12 in. Celestion Custom 90 speaker, mfg. 1994-2003.

	N/A	$850 - 1,000	$425 - 525	$1,099

* ***Blue Angel 2-10 Combo*** – similar to the Blue Angel head unit, except in combo configuration with 2-10 in.speakers, mfg. mid-1990s.

	N/A	$925 - 1,100	$475 - 575	$999

* ***Blue Angel 4-10 Combo*** – similar to the Blue Angel head unit, except in combo configuration with 4-10 in. Jensen Vintage Alnico speakers, mfg. 1994-2003.

	N/A	$975 - 1,150	$500 - 600	$1,249

ELECTRIC TUBE AMPLIFIERS: DUAL CALIBER SERIES

DC-2 STUDIO CALIBER – 25W, guitar head-unit, eight-tube chassis, preamp: 6 X 12AX7, power: 2 X EL84, solid-state rectifier, two channels, three footswitch sounds, reverb, front black control panel, single input, 15 black numbered knobs (Ch. 1: g, t, m, b, p, r, MV, Ch. 2: g, t, m, b, p, r, MV, All: output level), footswitch jack, channel switch (rhythm/lead), standby switch, power switch, rear panel: ground switch, recording out jack, footswitch (reverb), effects loop send and return with FX mix knob, speaker mute switch, slave out jack with level, three speaker jacks (two 4 ohm, one 8 ohm), black covering, black grille cloth, short head width (18.625 in.), mfg. 1994-98.

	N/A	$550 - 650	$275 - 350	$599

* ***DC-2 Studio Caliber 1-12 Combo*** – similar to the DC-2 Studio Caliber, except in combo configuration with 1-12 in. Vintage Black Shadow Speaker, mfg. 1994-98.

	N/A	$600 - 700	$300 - 375	$649

DC-3 DUAL CALIBER – 35W, guitar head-unit, ten-tube chassis, preamp: 6 X 12AX7, power: 4 X EL84, solid-state rectifier, two channels, four switchable sounds, reverb, front black control panel, single input, 15 black numbered knobs (Ch. 1: g, t, m, b, p, r, MV, Ch. 2: g, t, m, b, p, r, MV, All: output level), five-band graphic EQ, footswitch jack, channel switch (rhythm/lead), standby switch, power switch, rear panel: five-way rotary EQ knob, footswitch (reverb/EQ), effects loop send and return with FX mix knob, select recording out jack, speaker mute switch, slave out jack with level, three speaker jacks (two 4 ohm, one 8 ohm), black covering, black grille cloth, short head width (18.625 in.), mfg. 1994-98.

	N/A	$600 - 700	$300 - 375	$699

* ***DC-3 Dual Caliber 1-12 Combo*** – similar to the DC-3 Dual Caliber, except in combo configuration with 1-12 in. Celestion Vintage 30 Speaker, mfg. 1994-98.

	N/A	$625 - 750	$325 - 400	$799

MSR/NOTES	100%	EXCELLENT	AVERAGE	LAST MSR

DC-5 DUAL CALIBER – 50W, guitar head-unit, eight-tube chassis, preamp: 6 X 12AX7, power: 2 X 6L6, solid-state rectifier, two channels, four switchable sounds, reverb, front black control panel, single input, 15 black numbered knobs (Ch. 1: g, t, m, b, p, r, MV, Ch. 2: g, t, m, b, p, r, MV, All: output level), five-band graphic EQ, footswitch jack, channel switch (rhythm/lead), standby switch, power switch, rear panel: five-way rotary EQ knob, footswitch (reverb/EQ), effects loop send and return with FX mix knob, select recording out jack, speaker mute switch, slave out jack with level, three speaker jacks (two 4 ohm, one 8 ohm), black covering, black grille cloth, medium head width (22.75 in.), slip cover included, mfg. 1993-98.

	N/A	$725 - 850	$350 - 450	$999

* ***DC-5 Dual Caliber 1-12 Combo*** – similar to the DC-5 Dual Caliber, except in combo configuration with 1-12 in. Celestion 90 Speaker, mfg. 1994-98.

	N/A	$775 - 900	$375 - 475	$1,099

DC-10 DUAL CALIBER – 100W (switchable to 60W), guitar head-unit, ten-tube chassis, preamp: 6 X 12AX7, power: 4 X 6L6, solid-state rectifier, two channels, four switchable sounds, reverb, front black control panel, single input, 15 black numbered knobs (Ch. 1: g, t, m, b, p, r, MV, Ch. 2: g, t, m, b, p, r, MV, All: output level), five-band graphic EQ, footswitch jack, channel switch (rhythm/lead), 100W/60W power switch, standby switch, power switch, rear panel: headphone jack, EQ assignment switch, recording out jack, footswitch (reverb), effects loop send and return with FX mix knob, speaker mute switch, slave out jack with level, five speaker jacks (two 4 ohm, two 8 ohm, and one 16 ohm), black covering, black grille cloth, long head width (27.375 in.), slip cover included, mfg. 1996-98.

	N/A	$775 - 900	$375 - 475	$1,149

* ***DC-10 Dual Caliber 2-12 Combo*** – similar to the DC-10 Dual Caliber, except in combo configuration with 2-12 in. Celestion 90 Speakers and casters, mfg. 1996-98.

	N/A	$850 - 1,000	$425 - 525	$1,399

CALIBER 1-12 WIDEBODY SPEAKER CABINET – matching speaker cabinet designed for use with the Dual Caliber series heads/cabinets with 1-12 in. Celestion 90 speaker, mfg. 1993-98.

	N/A	$215 - 250	$105 - 130	$249

CALIBER 2-12 VERTICAL SPEAKER CABINET – matching speaker cabinet designed for use with the DC-10 Dual Caliber with 2-12 in. Celestion 90 speakers and a 3/4 closed back, mfg. 1996-98.

	N/A	$300 - 350	$150 - 185	$499

ELECTRIC TUBE AMPLIFIERS: ELECTRA DYNE SERIES

**Electra Dyne Head
courtesy Mesa/Boogie**

**Electra Dyne 2-12 Combo
courtesy Mesa/Boogie**

ELECTRA DYNE HEAD – 90W (switchable to 45W), guitar head unit, eleven tube chassis, preamp: 7 X 12AX7, power: 4 X 6L6 or EL34, solid-state rectifier, single channel, three modes (clean, vintage lo, vintage hi), reverb, front black control panel, single input, six black knobs (MV, p, b, m, t, v), power switch, standby switch, three-way mode switch, footswitch jack, rear control panel: power select switch (90 or 45W), footswitch jack, reverb control knob with bypass and hi/low defeat switch, effects loop, slave out with level control, Bias switch (EL34/6L6), speaker out jacks with ohm switch, two-button footswitch, 17 in. aluminum chassis, available in 22.75 in. or 26.75 in. widths, black Taurus covering, black oval grille cloth, slip cover included, mfg. 2009-2013.

	$1,699	$1,025 - 1,225	$725 - 850	$1,699

* ***Electra Dyne Rackmount Head*** – similar to the Electra Dyne Head, except in rackmount head configuration, mfg. 2009-2013.

	$1,699	$1,025 - 1,225	$725 - 850	$1,699

* ***Electra Dyne 1-12 Combo*** – similar to the Electra Dyne Head, except in combo configuration with 1-12 in. speaker and casters, available in 22.75 in. or 26.75 in. (2009-2010) widths, mfg. 2009-2013.

	$1,849	$1,100 - 1,350	$775 - 925	$1,849

* ***Electra Dyne 2-12 Combo*** – similar to the Electra Dyne Head, except in combo configuration with 2-12 in. speakers and casters, mfg. 2009-2013.

	$1,949	$1,125 - 1,400	$800 - 950	$1,949

MSR/NOTES	100%	EXCELLENT	AVERAGE	LAST MSR

ELECTRA DYNE 1-12 23 SPEAKER CABINET – 90W, 1-12 in. Celestion 90 speaker, 8 ohm impedance, designed for use with the Electra Dyne heads and combos, available in Black Taurus covering with a black grille and silver piping, 23 in. wide, 18 in. tall, 11.75 in. deep, mfg. mid-2009-2013.

	$419	$250 - 300	$175 - 210	$419

ELECTRA DYNE 1-12 27 SPEAKER CABINET – 90W, 1-12 in. Celestion 90 speaker, 8 ohm impedance, designed for use with the Electra Dyne heads and combos, available in Black Taurus covering with a black grille and silver piping, 26.75 in. wide, 18 in. tall, 11.75 in. deep, mfg. mid-2009-2013.

	$439	$265 - 320	$185 - 220	$439

ELECTRA DYNE 2-12 SPEAKER CABINET – 120W, 2-12 in. Celestion V30 speakers, 8 ohm impedance, designed for use with the Electra Dyne heads and combos, available in Black Taurus covering with a black grille and silver piping, 26.75 in. wide, 18 in. tall, 11.75 in. deep, mfg. mid-2009-2013.

	$619	$375 - 450	$265 - 310	$619

ELECTRIC TUBE AMPLIFIERS: EXPRESS SERIES

Express 5:25 Plus Head
courtesy Mesa/Boogie

Express 5:25 Plus Rackmount Head
courtesy Mesa/Boogie

Express 5:25 Plus 1-12 Combo
courtesy Mesa/Boogie

EXPRESS 5:25 HEAD – 25W (Duo-Class power amp switchable to 5W), guitar head-unit, seven-tube chassis, preamp: 5 X 12AX7, power: 2 X EL84, two fully independent channels, reverb, front black control panel, single input, 14 black knobs (two of each knob per channel: g, t, m, b, r, MV, contour), channel switch, clean/crunch switch (Ch. 1), blues/burn switch (Ch. 2), two contour switches (one per channel), effects loop, four external switch jacks, 25W/5W switch, three-button footswitch, black covering, black grille, slip cover included, 19 in. wide, mfg. 2007-2012.

	$1,149	$675 - 825	$475 - 550	$1,149

* *Express 5:25 Rackmount Head* – similar to the Express 5:25 Head, except in rackmount head configuration, mfg. 2009-2012.

	$1,149	$675 - 825	$475 - 550	$1,149

* *Express 5:25 1-10 Combo* – similar to the Express 5:25 Head, except in combo configuration with 1-10 in. E50 speaker, mfg. 2007-2012.

	$1,249	$750 - 900	$525 - 600	$1,249

* *Express 5:25 1-12 Combo* – similar to the Express 5:25 Head, except in combo configuration with 1-12 in. speaker, mfg. 2008-2012.

	$1,299	$775 - 950	$550 - 650	$1,299

EXPRESS 5:25 PLUS HEAD – 25W (Duo-Class power amp switchable to 15W/5W), guitar head-unit, seven-tube chassis, preamp: 5 X 12AX7, power: 2 X EL84, two fully independent channels, 5-band EQ, reverb, front black control panel, single input, 15 black knobs (two of each knob per channel: g, t, m, b, r, MV, all: preset, depth, solo), channel switch, clean/crunch switch (Ch. 1), blues/burn switch (Ch. 2), two contour switches (one per channel), four EQ switches, effects loop, three external speaker jacks, two 25W/15W/5W switches, four-button footswitch, black covering, black grille, slip cover included, 19 in. wide, 9.25 in. tall, 11.25 in. deep, 27 lbs., mfg. 2012-present.

MSR N/A	$1,200	$775 - 900	$400 - 475	

* *Express 5:25 Plus Rackmount Head* – 25W (Duo-Class power amp switchable to 15W/5W), guitar head-unit, rackmount configuration, seven-tube chassis, preamp: 5 X 12AX7, power: 2 X EL84, two fully independent channels, 5-band EQ, reverb, front black control panel, single input, 15 black knobs (two of each knob per channel: g, t, m, b, r, MV, all: preset, depth, solo), channel switch, clean/crunch switch (Ch. 1), blues/burn switch (Ch. 2), two contour switches (one per channel), four EQ switches, effects loop, four external speaker jacks, two 25W/15W/5W switches, four-button footswitch, black covering, black grille, slip cover included, 19.13 in. wide, 7 in. tall, 9.5 in. deep, 16 lbs., mfg. 2012-present.

MSR N/A	$1,200	$775 - 900	$400 - 475	

* *Express 5:25 Plus 1-12 Combo* – 25W (Duo-Class power amp switchable to 15W/5W), guitar combo amp, 1-12 in. speaker, seven-tube chassis, preamp: 5 X 12AX7, power: 2 X EL84, two fully independent channels, 5-band EQ, reverb, front black control panel, single input, 15 black knobs (two of each knob per channel: g, t, m, b, r, MV, all: preset, depth, solo), channel switch, clean/crunch switch (Ch. 1), blues/burn switch (Ch. 2), two contour switches (one per channel), four EQ switches, effects loop, four external speaker jacks, two 25W/15W/5W switches, four-button footswitch, black covering, black grille, slip cover included, 19 in. wide, 17.75 in. tall, 11.25 in. deep, 45 lbs., mfg. 2012-present.

MSR N/A	$1,350	$875 - 1,000	$450 - 550	

Express 5:50 Plus Head
courtesy Mesa/Boogie

Express 5:50 Plus 1-12 Combo
courtesy Mesa/Boogie

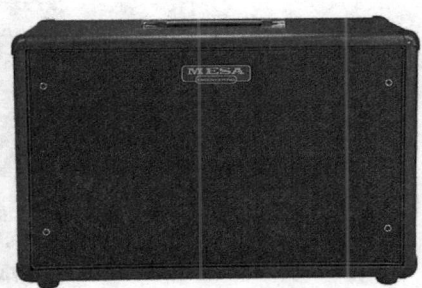

Express 2-12 Speaker Cabinet
courtesy Mesa/Boogie

EXPRESS 5:50 HEAD – 50W (Duo-Class power amp switchable to 5W), guitar head-unit, seven-tube chassis, preamp: 5 X 12AX7, power: 2 X 6L6, two fully independent channels, reverb, front black control panel, single input, 14 black knobs (two of each knob per channel: g, t, m, b, r, MV, contour), channel switch, clean/crunch switch (Ch. 1), blues/burn switch (Ch. 2), two contour switches (one per channel), effects loop, four external switch jacks, 50W/5W switch, three-button footswitch, black covering, black grille, slip cover included, available in medium head width (22.875 in.) or long head width (26.75 in.), mfg. 2007-2012.

$1,249 $750 - 900 $525 - 600 $1,249

* *Express 5:50 1-12 Combo* – similar to the Express 5:50 Head, except in combo configuration with 1-12 in. C90 speaker, mfg. 2007-2012.

$1,399 $850 - 1,025 $600 - 700 $1,399

* *Express 5:50 2-12 Combo* – similar to the Express 5:50 Head, except in combo configuration with 2-12 in. C90 speakers and casters, mfg. 2007-present.

MSR $1,499 $1,499 $900 - 1,075 $625 - 750

EXPRESS 5:50 PLUS HEAD – 50W (Duo-Class power amp switchable to 25W/5W), guitar head-unit, seven-tube chassis, preamp: 5 X 12AX7, power: 2 X 6L6, two fully independent channels, 5-band graphic EQ, reverb, front black control panel, single input, 15 black knobs (two of each knob per channel: g, t, m, b, r, MV, all: preset, depth, solo), channel switch, clean/crunch switch (Ch. 1), blues/burn switch (Ch. 2), two contour switches (one per channel), four EQ switches, effects loop, three external speaker jacks, two 50W/25W/5W switches, four-button footswitch, black covering, black grille, slip cover included, 22.88 in. wide, 9.88 in. tall, 11.75 in. deep, 38 lbs., mfg. 2012-present.

MSR N/A $1,300 $850 - 975 $425 - 525

* *Express 5:50 Plus 1-12 Combo* – 50W (Duo-Class power amp switchable to 25W/5W), guitar combo amp, 1-12 in. speaker, seven-tube chassis, preamp: 5 X 12AX7, power: 2 X 6L6, two fully independent channels, 5-band graphic EQ, reverb, front black control panel, single input, 15 black knobs (two of each knob per channel: g, t, m, b, r, MV, all: preset, depth, solo), channel switch, clean/crunch switch (Ch. 1), blues/burn switch (Ch. 2), two contour switches (one per channel), four EQ switches, effects loop, three external speaker jacks, two 50W/25W/5W switches, four-button footswitch, black covering, black grille, slip cover included, 22.8 in. wide, 19.5 in. tall, 11.75 in. deep, 54 lbs., mfg. 2012-present.

MSR N/A $1,450 $950 - 1,075 $475 - 575

EXPRESS 1-10 SPEAKER CABINET – 50W, 1-10 in. E50 speaker, 8 ohm impedance, designed for use with the Express heads and combos, black covering, black grille, mfg. 2007-2012.

$319 $190 - 230 $135 - 160 $319

EXPRESS 1-12 19 SPEAKER CABINET – 60W, 1-12 in. V30 speaker, 8 ohm impedance, designed for use with the Express heads and combos, black covering, black grille, 19 in. wide, mfg. 2008-2012.

$359 $215 - 260 $150 - 180 $359

EXPRESS 1-12 23 SPEAKER CABINET – 90W, 1-12 in. Celestion 90 speaker, 8 ohm impedance, designed for use with the Express heads and combos, black covering, black grille, 23 in. wide, mfg. 2007-2012.

$389 $235 - 285 $165 - 195 $389

EXPRESS 2-12 SPEAKER CABINET – 180W, 2-12 in. Celestion 90 speakers, 8 ohm impedance, designed for use with the Express heads and combos, black covering, black grille, mfg. 2007-2012.

$589 $350 - 425 $250 - 300 $589

ELECTRIC TUBE AMPLIFIERS: F-SERIES

F-30 – 30W, 1-12 in. Celestion Vintage 30 speaker combo, all tube Dyna-Watt chassis, preamp: 4 X 12AX7, power: 2 X EL84, two channels, reverb, front black control panel, single input, fourteen black knobs (g, b, m, t, r, MV per channel, pull bright, contour switch), effects loop headphone output, three button footswitch, black covering, black grille cloth, mfg. 2002-06.

N/A $575 - 675 $325 - 400 $949

MSR/NOTES	100%	EXCELLENT	AVERAGE	LAST MSR

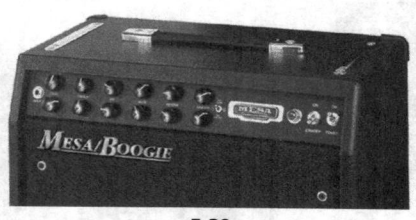

F-30
courtesy Mesa/Boogie

F-50
courtesy Mesa/Boogie

* F-30 Head – similar to the F-30 Combo, except in head-unit configuration, mfg. 2002-06.

	N/A	$500 - 600	$300 - 350	$899

F-50 – 50W, 1-12 in. Celestion Vintage 30 speaker combo, all tube Class A/B chassis, preamp: 4 X 12AX7, power: 2 X 6L6, two channels, reverb, front black control panel, single input, fourteen black knobs (g, b, m, t, r, MV per channel, pull bright, contour switch), effects loop headphone output, three button footswitch, black covering, black grille cloth, mfg. 2002-06.

	N/A	$650 - 800	$425 - 500	$1,099

* F-50 Head – similar to the F-50 Combo, except in head-unit configuration, mfg. 2002-06.

	N/A	$575 - 700	$350 - 425	$1,049

F-100 – 100W, 2-12 in. Celestion Vintage 30 speakers combo, all tube Class A/B chassis, preamp: 4 X 12AX7, power: 4 X 6L6, two channels, reverb, front black control panel, single input, fourteen black knobs (g, b, m, t, r, MV per channel, pull bright, contour switch), effects loop headphone output, three button footswitch, black covering, black grille cloth, casters, mfg. 2002-06.

	N/A	$800 - 950	$500 - 600	$1,399

* F-100 Head – similar to the F-100 Combo, except in head-unit configuration, mfg. 2002-06.

	N/A	$700 - 850	$450 - 525	$1,199

ELECTRIC TUBE AMPLIFIERS: HEARTBREAKER SERIES

HEARTBREAKER – 100W, head-unit only, all tube Class A/B chassis, preamp: 7 X 12AX7, power: 4 X 6L6, 5AR4 rectifier, two channels, black front control panel, two inputs, eleven black knobs (v, t, m, b, r per channel, overall level), half-power switch, various other switches and buttons, one button footswitch, crocodile skin covering, brown cloth grille, mfg. 1996-2002.

	N/A	$850 - 1,000	$550 - 650	$1,499

* Hearbreaker 2-12 Combo – similar to the Heartbreaker, except in combo form with 2-12 in. speakers, mfg. 1996-2002.

	N/A	$950 - 1,100	$600 - 700	$1,699

ELECTRIC TUBE AMPLIFIERS: LONE STAR SERIES

Lone Star 112 Combo
courtesy Mesa/Boogie

Lone Star Special 112 Combo
courtesy Mesa/Boogie

Lone Star (Classic) 4-10 Speaker Cabinet
courtesy Mesa/Boogie

In 2006, the Classic Series of speaker cabinets was changed to the Lone Star Series.

LONE STAR HEAD – 100W (switchable to 50W), head-unit, all tube Class A/B chassis, preamp: 5 X 12AX7, power: 4 X 6L6, rectifier: 1 X 5U4, two independent channels, front control panel, 14 knobs (g, t, m , b, p, r, MV for each channel), effects loop, two button footswitch included, available in Blue Bronco covering with a pewter grille (2003-06) or Black Taurus covering with a black grille and silver piping (2006-present), mfg. 2003-present.

MSR N/A	$1,799	$1,075 - 1,300	$775 - 900	

This model is available in either a long or medium scale. In 2007, this model was upgraded with the new Duo-Class power amp that allows power output in three settings (10W, 50W, and 100W).

* Lone Star Rackmount Head – similar to the Lone Star Head, except in rackmount configuration, mfg. 2009-present.

MSR N/A	$1,799	$1,075 - 1,300	$775 - 900	

MSR/NOTES	100%	EXCELLENT	AVERAGE	LAST MSR

* *Lone Star 112 Combo* – similar to the Lone Star Head, except has 1-12 in. Fillmore C90 speaker and casters, mfg. 2003-present.

| MSR N/A | $1,949 | $1,125 - 1,400 | $800 - 950 | |

* *Lone Star 212 Combo* – similar to the Lone Star Head, except has 2-12 in. Fillmore C90 speakers and casters, mfg. 2003-present.

| MSR N/A | $2,099 | $1,225 - 1,475 | $875 - 1,025 | |

* *Lone Star 410 Combo* – similar to the Lone Star Head, except has 4-10 in. Jensen Vintage Alnico speakers and casters, mfg. 2005-disc.

| | $2,099 | $1,275 - 1,525 | $900 - 1,050 | $2,099 |

LONE STAR SPECIAL HEAD – 30W (switchable to 15 or 5W), head-unit, all tube Class A chassis, preamp: 5 X 12AX7, power: 4 X EL84, 5Y3 rectifier, two independent channels, front control panel, 14 knobs (g, t, m , b, p, r, MV for each channel), effects loop, two-button footswitch included, available in black tarus covering with a black grille or Cocoa Bronco (brown) covering with a tan grille and cream Bronco control panel, mfg. 2004-present.

| MSR N/A | $1,699 | $1,025 - 1,225 | $725 - 850 | |

This model is available in either a long or medium scale.

* *Lone Star Special Rackmount Head* – similar to the Lone Star Special, except in rackmount configuration, mfg. 2009-present.

| MSR N/A | $1,699 | $1,025 - 1,225 | $725 - 850 | |

This model is available in either a long or medium scale.

* *Lone Star Special 112 Combo* – similar to the Lone Star Special Head, except has 1-12 in. Fillmore C90 speaker and casters, mfg. 2004-present.

| MSR N/A | $1,849 | $1,100 - 1,350 | $775 - 925 | |

• **Add $887 ($2,736) for Tan Western covering with Wicker grille.**

* *Lone Star Special 212 Combo* – similar to the Lone Star Special Head, except has 2-12 in. Fillmore C90 speakers and casters, mfg. 2004-present.

| MSR N/A | $1,999 | $1,125 - 1,400 | $800 - 950 | |

* *Lone Star Special 410 Combo* – similar to the Lone Star Special Head, except has 4-10 in. Jensen Vintage Alnico speakers and casters, mfg. 2005-disc.

| | $1,999 | $1,200 - 1,450 | $850 - 1,000 | $1,899 |

LONE STAR (CLASSIC) 1-10 SPEAKER CABINET – 50W, 1-10 in. Eminence 50 speaker, 8 ohm impedance, designed for use with the Lone Star heads and combos, available in Black Taurus covering with a black Twisted jute grille, slip cover included, 13.12 in. tall, 19.25 in. wide, 11.25 in. deep, 22 lbs., current mfg.

| MSR N/A | $350 | $225 - 260 | $115 - 140 | |

LONE STAR (CLASSIC) 1-12 19 SPEAKER CABINET – 90W, 1-12 in. Celestion 90 speaker, 8 ohm impedance, designed for use with the Lone Star heads and combos, available in Black Taurus covering with a black grille with silver piping, or LoneStar Special Cocoa/Cream with a tan jute grille, 19 in. wide, mfg. 2011-present.

| MSR N/A | $389 | $225 - 275 | $150 - 185 | |

LONE STAR (CLASSIC) 1-12 23 SPEAKER CABINET – 90W, 1-12 in. Celestion 90 speaker, 8 ohm impedance, designed for use with the Lone Star heads and combos, available in Black Taurus covering with a black grille with silver piping, LoneStar Blue with a pewter grille (disc. 2006), or LoneStar Special Cocoa/Cream with a tan jute grille, 23 in. wide, current mfg.

| MSR N/A | $419 | $250 - 300 | $175 - 210 | |

• **Add $179 ($598) for Teal covering with Cream grille.**

LONE STAR (CLASSIC) 1-12 27 SPEAKER CABINET – 90W, 1-12 in. Celestion 90 speaker, 8 ohm impedance, designed for use with the Lone Star heads and combos, available in Black Taurus covering with a black grille with silver piping, LoneStar Blue with a pewter grille (2005-06), or LoneStar Special Cocoa/Cream with a tan jute grille, 27 in. wide, mfg. 2005-disc.

| | $439 | $265 - 320 | $185 - 220 | $439 |

LONE STAR (CLASSIC) 2-12 SPEAKER CABINET – 180W, 2-12 in. Celestion 90 speakers, 8 ohm impedance, designed for use with the Lone Star heads and combos, available in Black Taurus covering with a black grille with silver piping, LoneStar Blue with a pewter grille (disc. 2006), or LoneStar Special Cocoa/Cream with a tan jute grille, mfg. 2003-present.

| MSR N/A | $619 | $375 - 450 | $265 - 310 | |

LONE STAR (CLASSIC) 4-10 SPEAKER CABINET – 100W, 4-10 in. Jensen Alnico speakers, 8 ohm impedance, designed for use with the Lone Star heads, available in Black Taurus covering with a black grille with silver piping, LoneStar Blue with a pewter grille (disc. 2006), or LoneStar Special Cocoa/Cream with a tan jute grille, mfg. 2003-present.

| MSR N/A | $800 | $525 - 600 | $260 - 325 | |

MSR/NOTES	100%	EXCELLENT	AVERAGE	LAST MSR

LONE STAR (CLASSIC) 4-12 SPEAKER CABINET – 360W, 4-12 in. Celestion 90 speakers, 8 ohm impedance, designed for use with the Lone Star heads, available in Black Taurus covering with a black grille with silver piping, LoneStar Blue with a pewter grille (2004-06), or LoneStar Special Cocoa/Cream with a tan jute grille, mfg. 2004-disc.

$979	$600 - 700	$425 - 500	$979

ELECTRIC TUBE AMPLIFIERS: MARK (MK) SERIES

JP-2C John Petrucci Head
courtesy Mesa/Boogie

JP-2C John Petrucci Rackmount Head
courtesy Mesa/Boogie

MK-1
courtesy Dave Rogers/Dave's Guitar Shop

The Mark (MK) Series are the first amplifiers produced by MESA. These were made famous by Carlos Santana after Randall Smith altered a Fender Princeton and Santana played it. These amps represent the company's early efforts and because of that, there are several variations of these models. Some amps may have the 5-band EQ, some may not. Some may have reverb, and others may not. Some models may only be 60W. Cabinets were covered in all different types of woods including maple and koa, and other coverings were available as well. Note that just because our description may not list a feature does not mean something is wrong with the nomenclature to the actual amp. The descriptions we list are the most common "standard" models that were produced.

The reverb, presence, and effects loop controls were mounted on the back of the chassis. Since reverb was optional on almost all models, the reverb control could be added with altering the front of the amp. There were speaker cabinets available to match up with the Mark Series. These were available as a 1-12 in. or 4-12 in. configuration.

JP-2C JOHN PETRUCCI HEAD – 60W/100W, guitar head unit, nine-tube chassis, preamp: 5 X 12AX7, power: 4 X 6L6, three switchable channels, 15 modes, spring reverb, front black control panel, single input, 18 black knobs (each channel: g, MV, p, t, m, b), EQ switch for each channel, dual five-band graphic EQ, standby switch, power switch, rear panel: reverb level knob for each channel, headphone jack, slave jack, four speaker jacks, effects loop, CabClone XLR DI jack, speaker on/off switch, closed back/open back/vintage switch, lift/ground switch, dB switch, footswitch jack, MIDI thru/out jack, MIDI in jack, store switch, 60W/100W switch, available in black covering with a black cloth grille, 9.25 in. tall, 18.75 in. wide, 10.87 in. deep, 40 lbs., new 2016.

MSR N/A	$2,500	$1,625 - 1,875	$825 - 1,000

• Add $1,000 for Limited Edition Autographed model featuring flame maple front panel and MOP Mesa logo.

* *JP-2C John Petrucci Rackmount Head* – 60W/100W, guitar head unit, rackmount configuration, nine-tube chassis, preamp: 5 X 12AX7, power: 4 X 6L6, three switchable channels, 15 modes, spring reverb, front black control panel, single input, 18 black knobs (each channel: g, MV, p, t, m, b), EQ switch for each channel, dual five-band graphic EQ, standby switch, power switch, rear panel: reverb level knob for each channel, headphone jack, slave jack, four speaker jacks, effects loop, CabClone XLR DI jack, speaker on/off switch, closed back/open back/vintage switch, lift/ground switch, dB switch, footswitch jack, MIDI thru/out jack, MIDI in jack, store switch, 60W/100W switch, available in black covering with a black cloth grille, 7 in. tall, 19.12 in. wide, 9.5 in. deep, 35 lbs., new 2016.

MSR N/A	$2,500	$1,625 - 1,875	$825 - 1,000

MK-1 – 60 or 100W, 1-12 in. speaker, guitar combo, eight-tube chassis, preamp: 4 X 12AX7, power: 4 X 6L6GC, two channels, optional reverb, front black control panel, two inputs, six black knobs (v1, v2, MV, t, b, m), optional five-band graphic EQ (later models), standy switch, power switch, rear panel: ground switch, slave out jack with level control, optional presence control, optional reverb control, speaker jacks, available in a wood cabinet with a wicker cane grille or white Tolex with a brown grille, includes serial numbers 1-2999, mfg. 1971-78.

1971-1974	N/A	$1,200 - 1,500	$750 - 900
1975-1978	N/A	$1,000 - 1,200	$675 - 800

• Add 50% for wood cabinet with a wicker cane grille.

These early Boogies are referred to as "Mark I" but this nomenculture isn't stamped anywhere on the amp and it wasn't called this until the Mark II was introduced in 1978. The Mark I has two channels, but they are not switchable - the cable must be plugged into one or the other inputs. Later models have a push/pull bright switch on the 1st volume knob and a push/pull boost switch on the 2nd volume knob. Reverb was optional and this did not become very common until later on. The five-band graphic EQ was introduced as an option later on as well. The rear control panel is very primitive with Dymo stick labeling the various controls and jacks.

MK-II(A)
courtesy Don's Music

MK-IIB
courtesy Savage Audio

MK-1 REISSUE – 100W, 1-12 in. Celestion Custom 90 speaker, guitar combo, nine-tube Class A/B chassis, 4 X 12AX7, 1 X 12AT7, power: 4 X 6L6, two modes, reverb, front black control panel, two inputs, six black knobs (v1, v2, MV, t, b, m), half power switch, effects loop, Imbuya hardwood or cream vinyl coverings wicker cane or brown cloth grille, mfg. 1989-2007.

| | N/A | $1,025 - 1,200 | $500 - 625 | $1,419 |

• Add 50% for wood cabinet with a wicker cane grille.

* *MK-1 Reissue Head* – similar to the MK-1 Reissue except in head-unit configuration, mfg. 1989-2007.

| | N/A | $850 - 1,000 | $425 - 525 | $1,319 |

• Add 50% for wood cabinet with a wicker cane grille.

MK-II(A) – 60 or 100W, 1-12 in. or optional 1-15 in. speaker, guitar combo, eight-tube chassis, preamp: 4 X 12AX7, power: 4 X 6L6GC, two switchable channels, optional reverb, front black control panel, single input, footswitch jack, seven black knobs (volume 1 with a push/pull bright switch, t with a push/pull shift switch, b, m, Master 1 with a push/pull gain boost switch, Lead Drive with a push/pull Lead switch, Lead Master with a push/pull bright switch), optional five-band graphic EQ with EQ in/out switch, standby switch, power switch, rear panel: mains selector, ground switch, slave out jack with level control, preamp out/power amp in jack, presence control, optional reverb control, speaker jacks, 60W/100W power switch, available in standard black Tolex covering with a black grille or custom hardwood cabinet with wicker grille, serial numbers 3000-5574, mfg. 1978-1980.

| 1-12 In. | N/A | $850 - 1,000 | $600 - 700 | |
| 1-15 In. | N/A | $750 - 900 | $500 - 600 | |

• Add 50% for wood cabinet with a wicker cane grille.

This amp is often referred to as the MK-IIA although that was never mentioned in Mesa's product information or on the amp itself. The Mark II along with a few late-model Mark I amps featured a silicon component called a Fetron that was used in place of one of the 12AX7 tubes. When a Fetron was installed, the amp also had a switch that allowed the user to configure the amp for use with either a Fetron or a regular tube. The Fetron was not very popular and was discontinued in the early 1980s.

* *MK-II(A) Head* – similar to the MK-II(A), except in head-unit configuration, mfg. 1978-1980.

| | N/A | $725 - 850 | $500 - 575 | |

* *MK-IIB* – similar to the MK-II(A), except has an effects loop and Mesa/Boogie's patented optional Simul-Class system, serial numbers 5,575-11,000, mfg. 1980-83.

| 1-12 In. | N/A | $900 - 1,050 | $625 - 725 | |
| 1-15 In. | N/A | $800 - 950 | $525 - 625 | |

• Add 50% for wood cabinet with a wicker cane grille.

Mesa/Boogie's patetened Simul-Class power tube system utilized two separate sets of power amp tubes instead of running all four the same way. In Simul-Class Two 6L6 tubes operate in Class AB pentode and two other 6L6 or EL34 power tubes operate in Class A triode. Simul-Class was optional on the Mark IIB, and models without it will have the standard 60W/100W power switch.

»*MK-IIB Head* – similar to the MK-IIB, except in head-unit configuration, mfg. 1983-1985.

| | N/A | $725 - 850 | $500 - 575 | |

* *MK-IIC/MK-IIC+* – similar to the MK-IIA and MK-IIB, except has quieter channel switching and a quieter reverb circuit (MK-IIC) and a more sensitive lead channel and improved effects loop (MK-IIC+), serial numbers 11,001-14,999, mfg. 1983-85.

MK-IIC 1-12 In.	N/A	$2,000 - 2,500	$1,400 - 1,600	
MK-IIC 1-15 In.	N/A	$2,200 - 2,800	$1,700 - 1,850	
MK-IIC+ 1-12 In.	N/A	$1,800 - 2,200	$1,000 - 1,200	
MK-IIC+ 1-15 In.	N/A	$2,100 - 2,400	$1,450 - 1,700	

• Add 50% for wood cabinet with a wicker cane grille.

The Mark IIC+ is widely considered to be Mesa's best sounding Mark amp and is the most collectible. While the MK-IIC and MK-IIC+ look identical on the outside, the difference between the two can be determined by a "+" hand-written in black above the power cord input on the rear panel for the MK-IIC+. Since this is such an easy forgery by someone simply putting this "+" on their MK-IIC themselves, we recommend contacting Mesa/Boogie directly to confirm the exact model of your amp. Mesa built about 1,400 MK-IIC amps before switching to the MK-IIC+, meaning serial numbers over approximately 12,401 are the MK-IIC+ models.

MSR/NOTES	100%	EXCELLENT	AVERAGE	LAST MSR

Mark IV 1-12 Combo
courtesy Mesa/Boogie

Mark V Head (40th Anniversary)
courtesy Mesa/Boogie

Mark V 1-12 Combo (40th Anniversary)
courtesy Mesa/Boogie

»MK-IIC/MK-IIC+ Head – similar to the MK-IIC/MK-IIC+, except in head-unit configuration, mfg. 1983-85.

MK-IIC	N/A	$1,050 - 1,200	$600 - 700	
MK-IIC+	N/A	$1,200 - 1,400	$700 - 850	

MK-III HEAD – 100W (switchable to 60W), guitar head-unit, nine-tube chassis, preamp: 5 X 12AX7, power: 4 X 6L6GC or 2 X 6L6GC and 2 X EL34, three switchable channels (Clean Rhythm, Crunch Rhythm, Lead), reverb, front black control panel, single input, seven black numbered knobs (v with pull bright for Rhythm channels, t with pull gain for Lead channel, b with pull low-end breath in Rhythm channels, m with pull channel switch to Crunch Rhythm channel, MV with pull deep switch, Lead Drive with pull channel switch to Lead channel, Lead Master with pull bright switch in Lead channel), five-band graphic EQ, footswitch jack, EQ auto/EQ in switch, standby switch, power switch, rear panel: ground switch, direct out, effects loop, presence control reverb control, three speaker jacks (two 4 ohm and one 8 ohm), tube switch, black covering, black grille, mfg. 1985-1999.

1985-1990	N/A	$900 - 1,100	$500 - 650	
1991-1999	N/A	$950 - $1,150	$550 - 700	

* MK-III 1-12 Combo – similar to the MK-III Head, except in combo configuration with 1-12 in. speaker, mfg. 1985-1999.

1985-1990	N/A	$1,000 - 1,200	$550 - 650	
1991-1999	N/A	$1,050 - $1,300	$600 - 700	

MARK IV (MK IV) HEAD – 85W, guitar head-unit, nin-tube chassis, preamp: 5 X 12AX7, power: 4 X 6L6, solid-state rectifier, Simul-Class power section, three channels (rhythm 1, rhyhtm 2, lead), reverb, front black control panel, single input, eighteen black knobs (Rhythm 1 g with pull bright switch, Rhythm 2 g with pull fat switch, Lead g with pull fat switch, Rhythm 1 t, Lead 2 t, Rhythm 1 and 2 b, Lead b, Rhythm 1 and 2 m, Lead m, Rhythm 2 t, Lead drive with pull bright switch, Rhythm 1 p, Rhythm 1 MV, Rhythm 2 p with push/pull, Rhythm 2 MV, Lead p with push/pull, Lead MV, output level with pull silent recording), five band graphic equalizer, graphic EQ switch, lead voicing switch, power switch, full power/tweed power switch, rear panel: reverb knob, reverb footswitch jack, Satellite send and EQ, effects loop with stereo return, effects loop switch, two auto assign switches, recording out jack with level control, slave out jack with level control, triode/pentode switch, Simul Class/Class A switch, Harmonics/mid-gain switch, three speaker out jacks (two 4 ohm, one 8 ohm), five-way rotary mode select switch, six external switching jacks, black vinyl covering, black grille, slip cover, available in short head width (18.625 in.), medium head width (22.5 in.), or rackmount configuration, mfg. 1990-2008.

	N/A	$1,225 - 1,450	$625 - 750	$1,899

The Mark IV is also available in a wood cabinet with a wicker grille. In 1994, this amp was redesigned and labeled the Mark IVB, which is what the version described here is.

* Mark IV 1-12 Combo – similar to the Mark IV Head, except in combo configuration with 1-12 in. Original EVM 12L speaker, mfg. 1990-2008.

	N/A	$1,350 - 1,600	$675 - 850	$1,999

* Mark IV 1-12 Widebody Combo – similar to the Mark IV Head, except in combo configuration with 1-12 in. Celestion Custom 90 speaker, mfg. 1990-2008.

	N/A	$1,350 - 1,600	$675 - 850	$1,999

MARK V HEAD (40TH ANNIVERSARY) – 90W (switchable to 45W or 10W), medium width guitar head unit, 12 tube chassis, preamp: 7 X 12AX7, power: 4 X 6L6, switchable 5U4/solid-state rectifier, three channels, three modes, reverb, front black control panel, single input, 23 black knobs, Channel 1 controls: g, MV, p, t, m, b, clean/fat/tweed mode switch, EQ on/footswitch switch, 90/45/10W switch, normal/bright switch, Channel 2 controls: g, MV, p, t, m, b, edge/crunch/Mark 1 mode switch, EQ on/footswitch switch, 90/45/10W switch, normal/bright switch, Channel 3 controls: g, MV, p, t, m, b, MK II C+/MK IV/Extreme mode switch, EQ on/footswitch switch, 90/45/10W switch, normal/bright switch, five-band slider EQ with three preset switches and three preset depth knobs, independent reverb knobs for each channel, tube/solid-state rectifier switches for Channels 1 and 2, pentode/triode rectifier switch for Channel 3, effects loop, eight-button footswitch, black Taurus covering, black grille cloth, 22.875 in. wide, mfg. 2009-present.

MSR N/A	$2,349	$1,275 - 1,600	$900 - 1,050	

• Also available with Cream/Black face plate ($2,428), Blue Bronco covering with Tan grille ($2,528), or Cream covering with Cream face plate ($2,528).

* Mark V 1-12 Combo (40th Anniversary) – similar to the Mark V Head (40th Anniversary), except in combo configuration with 1-12 in. C90 speaker, mfg. 2009-present.

MSR N/A	$2,499	$1,350 - 1,700	$950 - 1,125	

MARK V 25 HEAD – 25W (switchable to 10W), small width guitar head unit, eight-tube chassis, preamp: 6 X 12AX7, power: 2 X EL84, two channels, six modes, reverb, front black control panel, single input, 12 black knobs, Channel 1 controls: g, t, m, b, p, MV, clean/fat/crunch mode switch, EQ on/footswitch switch, 25/10W switch, Channel 2 controls: g, t, m, b, p, MV, Mark IIC/Mark IV/XTreme mode switch, EQ on/footswitch switch, 25/10W switch, five-band slider EQ, rear panel: effects loop, headphone jack, independent reverb knobs for each channel, footswitch, black Taurus covering, black grille cloth, 14 inches wide, mfg. 2014-present.

MSR N/A	$1,399	$775 - 925	$550 - 650	

- Also available with Black/Cream face ($1,478), Baby Blue with Cream grille ($1,578), Fawn with Gold grille ($1,578), Gold with Gold grille ($1,578), Teal with Cream grille ($1,578), Emerald with Wicker grille ($1,628), Black Floral with White grille ($1,898), Private Reserve Claro Flamed Walnut ($3,537), and Walnut with matching cabinet ($5,885).

MARK V 35 HEAD – 35W (switchable to 25W/10W), guitar head unit, ten-tube chassis, preamp: 6 X 12AX7, power: 4 X EL84, two channels, six modes, reverb, front black control panel, single input, 14 black knobs, Channel 1 controls: g, t, m, b, p, MV, solo, clean/fat/crunch mode switch, EQ on/footswitch switch, 35/25/10W switch, Channel 2 controls: g, t, m, b, p, MV, solo, Mark IIC/Mark IV/XTreme mode switch, EQ on/footswitch switch, 35/25/10W switch, five-band slider EQ, power switch, standby switch, rear panel: footswitch jack, effects loop, headphone jack, independent reverb knobs for each channel, three speaker jacks, DI jack, speaker power switch, closed back/open back/vintage switch, lift/ground switch, footswitch, black Taurus covering, black grille cloth, 9.12 in. tall, 18.87 inches wide, 10.87 in. deep, 27 lbs., mfg. 2015-present.

MSR N/A	$1,600	$1,050 - 1,200	$525 - 650	

* *Mark V 35 1-12 Combo* – 35W (switchable to 25W/10W), guitar combo amp, ten-tube chassis, preamp: 6 X 12AX7, power: 4 X EL84, two channels, six modes, reverb, front black control panel, single input, 14 black knobs, Channel 1 controls: g, t, m, b, p, MV, solo, clean/fat/crunch mode switch, EQ on/footswitch switch, 35/25/10W switch, Channel 2 controls: g, t, m, b, p, MV, solo, Mark IIC/Mark IV/XTreme mode switch, EQ on/footswitch switch, 35/25/10W switch, five-band slider EQ, power switch, standby switch, rear panel: footswitch jack, effects loop, headphone jack, independent reverb knobs for each channel, three speaker jacks, DI jack, speaker power switch, closed back/open back/vintage switch, lift/ground switch, footswitch, black Taurus covering, black grille cloth, 18.12 in. tall, 18.75 inches wide, 11.5 in. deep, 44 lbs., mfg. 2015-present.

MSR N/A	$1,800	$1,175 - 1,350	$575 - 725	

ELECTRIC TUBE AMPLIFIERS: MAVERICK SERIES

MAVERICK – 35W, head-unit only, all tube Class A chassis, preamp: 6 X 12AX7, power: 4 X EL84, 5AR4 rectifier, two channels, reverb, front black control panel, single input, 13 black knobs (v, t, m, b, r, MV per channel, output level), bright/fat switch, effects loop, fan cooled, one button footswitch, vanilla vinyl covering, tan grille cloth, mfg. 1994-2004.

	N/A	$700 - 850	$450 - 525	$1,149

* *Maverick 2-12 Combo* – similar to the Maverick Head, except in combo configuration with 2-12 in. Celestion Vintage 30 speakers, mfg. 1994-2004.

	N/A	$925 - 1,100	$475 - 575	$1,349

* *Maverick 4-10 Combo* – similar to the Maverick Head, except in combo configuration with 4-10 in. Jensen Vintage Alnico speakers, mfg. 1994-2004.

	N/A	$1,025 - 1,200	$500 - 625	$1,399

ELECTRIC TUBE AMPLIFIERS: NOMAD SERIES

NOMAD 45 – 45W, head-unit only, Dyna-Watt power, all tube chassis, preamp: 5 X 12AX7, power: 4 X EL84, three channels, six modes, reverb, front black control panel, single input, eighteen black knobs (g, master, p, t, m, b per channel, output, solo), effects loop, five button footswitch, black covering, black grille, short (18.625 in. width) or long (26.25 in. width) cabinet, mfg. 1998-2004.

	N/A	$525 - 625	$265 - 325	$1,149

* *Nomad 45 1-12 Combo* – similar to the Nomad 45, except in combo form with 1-12 in. Celestion Custom 90 speaker, mfg. 1998-2001.

	N/A	$550 - 650	$275 - 350	$999

* *Nomad 45 2-12 Combo* – similar to the Nomad 45, except in combo form with 2-12 in. Celestion Vintage 30 speakers, mfg. 1998-2004.

	N/A	$625 - 750	$325 - 400	$1,349

* *Nomad 45 4-10 Combo* – similar to the Nomad 45, except in combo configuration with 4-10 in. speakers, disc.

	N/A	$675 - 800	$350 - 425	

NOMAD 55 – 55W, head-unit only, all tube Class A/B chassis, preamp: 5 X 12AX7, power: 2 X 6L6, three channels, six modes, reverb, front black control panel, single input, eighteen black knobs (g, master, p, t, m, b per channel, output, solo), effects loop, five button footswitch, black covering, black grille, short (22.5 in. width) or long (26.25 in. width) cabinet, mfg. 1998-2003.

	N/A	$575 - 675	$285 - 350	$1,199

* *Nomad 55 1-12 Combo* – similar to the Nomad 55, except in combo form with 1-12 in. Celestion Custom 90 speaker, mfg. 1998-2003.

	N/A	$625 - 725	$300 - 375	$1,299

MSR/NOTES	100%	EXCELLENT	AVERAGE	LAST MSR

* *Nomad 55 2-12 Combo* – similar to the Nomad 55, except in combo form with 2-12 in. Celestion Custom 90 speakers, mfg. 1998-2003.

	N/A	$725 - 850	$350 - 450	$1,399

* *Nomad 55 4-10 Combo* – similar to the Nomad 55, except in combo form with 4-10 in. Jensen Vintage Alnico speakers, mfg. 1998-2003.

	N/A	$775 - 900	$375 - 475	$1,449

NOMAD 100 – 100W, head-unit only, all tube Class A/B chassis, preamp: 5 X 12AX7, power: 4 X 6L6, three channels, six modes, reverb, front black control panel, single input, eighteen black knobs (g, master, p, t, m, b per channel, output, solo), half power switch, effects loop, six button footswitch, black covering, black grille, medium (22.5 in. width) or long (26.25 in. width) cabinet, mfg. 1998-2004.

	N/A	$675 - 800	$350 - 425	$1,549

* *Nomad 100 1-12 Combo* – similar to the Nomad 100, except in combo form with 1-12 in. Celestion Custom 90 speaker, mfg. 1998-2001.

	N/A	$775 - 900	$375 - 475	$1,499

* *Nomad 100 2-12 Combo* – similar to the Nomad 55, except in combo form with 2-12 in. Celestion Custom 90 speakers, mfg. 1998-2004.

	N/A	$825 - 975	$425 - 500	$1,749

ELECTRIC TUBE AMPLIFIERS: RECTIFIER SERIES

Dual Rectifier Solo Head
courtesy Mesa/Boogie

Triple Rectifier Solo Head
courtesy Mesa/Boogie

Recto-Verb 25 Head
courtesy Mesa/Boogie

MINI RECTIFIER 25 HEAD – 25W (switchable to 10W), head-unit only, seven-tube Class A/B chassis, preamp: 5 X 12AX7, power: 2 X EL84, two channels, four modes, front black control panel, two inputs, 12 chrome knobs (Ch. 1: g, t, m, b, p, MV, Ch. 2: g, t, m, b, p, MV), footswitch jack, Ch. 1 clean/pushed mode switch, Ch. 2 vintage/modern mode switch, 25W/10W power switch for each channel, channel switch, power switch, standby switch, rear panel: effects loop with hard bypass switch, two speaker jacks, one button footswitch, black metal casing with a polished Silver diamond front, padded gig bag and strap included, 12.625 in. wide, 6.75 in. tall, 5.875 in. deep, 12 lbs., mfg. 2011-present.

MSR N/A	$999	$600 - 725	$425 - 500	

• **Add $49 ($1,048) for Blue or Red diamond plate models.**

SINGLE RECTIFIER SOLO 50 HEAD – 50W, head-unit only, all tube Class A/B chassis, preamp: 5 X 12AX7, power: 2 X 6L6, rectifier: 5U4, two channels, five modes, front black control panel, two inputs, 14 chrome knobs (Ch. 1: g, b, m, t, p, MV, Ch. 2: g, b, m, t, p, MV, output level, solo level), effects loop, two button footswitch, Black Taurus covering, black chassis, polished diamond front, mfg. 1998-disc.

1998-2001 Series I	N/A	$750 - 900	$525 - 600	
2001-Disc. Series II MSR $1,469	$1,469	$875 - 1,050	$600 - 700	$1,469

In 2000, this model was upgraded to Series II specifications.

DUAL RECTIFIER SOLO HEAD – 100W, head-unit only, all tube Class A/B chassis, preamp: 5 X 12AX7, power: 4 X 6L6, rectifiers: 2 X 5U4, three channels, eight modes, front black control panel, single input, 20 chrome knobs (Ch. 1: g, b, m, t, p, MV, Ch. 2: g, b, m, t, p, MV, Ch. 3: g, b, m, t, p, MV, output level, solo), Ch. 1 clean/pushed mode switch, Ch. 1 50W/100W power switch (2010-present), Ch. 2 Vintage/Raw/Modern mode switch, Ch. 2 50W/100W power switch (2010-present), Ch. 3 Vintage/Raw/Modern mode switch, Ch. 3 50W/100W power switch (2010-present), power switch, standby switch, rear panel: five speaker jacks, rectifier selector, bias switch, effects loop, five footswitchable jacks, tuner out jack (2010-present), Black Taurus covering, black chassis, black Taurus or polished diamond front, five button footswitch included, mfg. 1996-present.

1996-2000 Series I	N/A	$1,000 - 1,150	$675 - 800	
2000-Present Series II MSR N/A	$1,949	$1,150 - 1,375	$800 - 950	

• **Add $148 ($2,097) for a Special Edition "Blacked Out" face plate model.**

In 2000, this model was upgraded to Series II specifications, and in 2010 it was upgraded with Mesa Boogie's Multi-Watt channel assignable power amp, an improved effects loop, more channel assignable rectifier choices with Rectifier Tracking, a tuner out jack with Silent Tune, and a new footswitch.

TRIPLE RECTIFIER SOLO HEAD – 150W, head-unit only, all tube Class A/B chassis, preamp: 5 X 12AX7, power: 6 X 6L6, rectifiers: 3 X 5U4, three channels, eight modes, front black control panel, two inputs, 20 chrome knobs (Ch. 1: g, b, m, t, p, MV, Ch. 2: g, b, m, t, p, MV, Ch. 3: g, b, m, t, p, MV, output level, solo), Ch. 1 clean/pushed mode switch, Ch. 1 50W/150W power switch (2010-present), Ch. 2 Vintage/Raw/Modern mode switch, Ch. 2 50W/150W power switch (2010-present), Ch. 3 Vintage/Raw/Modern mode switch, Ch. 3 50W/150W power switch (2010-present), power switch, standby switch, rear panel: five speaker jacks, rectifier selector, bias switch, effects loop, five footswitchable jacks, tuner out jack (2010-present), Black Taurus covering, black chassis, black Taurus or polished diamond front, five button footswitch included, mfg. 1996-present.

1996-2000 Series I	N/A	$1,050 - 1,250	$725 - 850	
2000-Present Series II MSR N/A	$2,099	$1,200 - 1,475	$850 - 1,000	

MSR/NOTES	100%	EXCELLENT	AVERAGE	LAST MSR

**Recto-Verb 25 Rackmount Head
courtesy Mesa/Boogie**

**Recto-Verb 25 1-12 Combo
courtesy Mesa/Boogie**

**Mini Rectifier 1-12 Speaker Cabinet
courtesy Mesa/Boogie**

In 2000, this model was upgraded to Series II specifications, and in 2010 it was upgraded with Mesa Boogie's Multi-Watt channel assignable power amp, an improved effects loop, more channel assignable rectifier choices with Rectifier Tracking, a tuner out jack with Silent Tune, and a new footswitch.

RECT-O-VERB – 50W, head-unit only, all tube Class A/B chassis, preamp: 5 X 12AX7, power: 2 X 6L6, two channels, five modes, front black control panel, two inputs, 14 knobs (12 chrome, 2 black, Ch. 1: g, b, m, t, p, MV, Ch. 2: g, b, m, t, p, MV), two black knobs (output level, solo level), effects loop, bias select switch, two button footswitch, black covering, polished diamond front, mfg. 1998-2010.

1998-2001 Series I	N/A	$750 - 900	$525 - 600	
2001-Present Series II	N/A	$900 - 1,075	$625 - 750	$1,499

In 2001, this model was upgraded to Series II specifications.

* *Rect-O-Verb Combo* – similar to the Rect-O-Verb, except in combo configuration with 1-12 in. Celestion 90 speaker, mfg. 1998-2010.

1998-2001 Series I	N/A	$850 - 1,000	$600 - 700	
2001-Present Series II	N/A	$950 - 1,150	$675 - 800	$1,599

In 2001, this model was upgraded to Series II specifications.

RECTO-VERB 25 HEAD – 25W (switchable to 10W), head-unit only, eight-tube chassis, preamp: 6 X 12AX7, power: 2 X EL84, two channels, spring reverb, front black control panel, single input, 14 chrome knobs (Ch. 1: g, b, m, t, p, MV, Ch. 2: g, b, m, t, p, MV, rear: Ch. 1 reverb, Ch. 2 reverb), channel switch, power switch, standby switch, 25W/10W switch for each channel, clean/pushed switch, vintage/modern switch, footswitch jack, effects loop, external reverb jack, three external speaker jacks, one-button footswitch, black covering, cream/black grille, top handle, 7.5 in. tall, 17.5 in. wide, 9 in. deep, 19 lbs., mfg. 2014-present.

MSR N/A	$1,100	$725 - 825	$350 - 450

* *Recto-Verb 25 Rackmount Head* – 25W (switchable to 10W), head-unit only, rackmount configuration, eight-tube chassis, preamp: 6 X 12AX7, power: 2 X EL84, two channels, spring reverb, front black control panel, single input, 14 chrome knobs (Ch. 1: g, b, m, t, p, MV, Ch. 2: g, b, m, t, p, MV, rear: Ch. 1 reverb, Ch. 2 reverb), channel switch, power switch, standby switch, 25W/10W switch for each channel, clean/pushed switch, vintage/modern switch, footswitch jack, effects loop, external reverb jack, three external speaker jacks, one-button footswitch, black covering, cream/black grille, top handle, 6.88 in. tall, 19 in. wide, 9.5 in. deep, 17 lbs., mfg. 2014-present.

MSR N/A	$1,550	$1,000 - 1,150	$500 - 625

* *Recto-Verb 25 1-12 Combo* – 25W (switchable to 10W), guitar combo amp, 1-12 in. Fillmore 75 speaker, eight-tube chassis, preamp: 6 X 12AX7, power: 2 X EL84, two channels, spring reverb, front black control panel, single input, 14 chrome knobs (Ch. 1: g, b, m, t, p, MV, Ch. 2: g, b, m, t, p, MV, rear: Ch. 1 reverb, Ch. 2 reverb), channel switch, power switch, standby switch, 25W/10W switch for each channel, clean/pushed switch, vintage/modern switch, footswitch jack, effects loop, external reverb jack, three speaker jacks, one-button footswitch, black covering, cream/black grille, top handle, 17 in. tall, 19 in. wide, 11 in. deep, 41 lbs., mfg. 2014-present.

MSR N/A	$1,250	$800 - 925	$400 - 500

TREM-O-VERB HEAD – 100W, head-unit guitar configuration, 12 tube chassis, preamp: 6 X 12AX7, power: 4 X 6L6, rectifier: 2 X 5U4, two channels, reverb, tremolo, four modes, front black control panel, single input, 16 chrome knobs (master, r, p, b, m, t, g per channel, tremolo speed, tremolo depth), one black loop knob, two mode switches (one per channel), rear control panel: effects loop with send and mix levels, loop select, slave out with level control, external switching jacks, bold/spongy switch, black covering, black grille, mfg. 1993-2000.

	N/A	$1,000 - 1,200	$650 - 800

* *Trem-O-Verb Combo* – similar to the Trem-O-Verb Head, except in combo configuration with 2-12 in. speakers, mfg. 1993-2000.

	N/A	$1,100 - 1,350	$750 - 900

MINI RECTIFIER 1-12 SPEAKER CABINET – 60W, 1-12 in. Celestion Vintage 30 speaker, 8 ohm mono impedance, closed back, slant or straight front, designed for use with the Rectifier Series heads, black Tolex covering, black grille, slipcover included, recessed side handles, 19 in. tall, 18 in. wide, 11 in. deep, 32 lbs., mfg. 2012-present.

MSR N/A	$450	$295 - 325	$145 - 180

MSR/NOTES	100%	EXCELLENT	AVERAGE	LAST MSR

Rectifier 1-12 Speaker Cabinet
courtesy Mesa/Boogie

Rectifier 2-12 Horizontal Speaker Cabinet
courtesy Mesa/Boogie

Rectifier 4-12 Standards Speaker Cabinet
courtesy Mesa/Boogie

RECTIFIER 1-12 SPEAKER CABINET – 60W, 1-12 in. Celestion Vintage 30 speaker, 8 ohm impedance, closed back, designed for use with the Rectifier Series heads, black covering, black grille, current mfg.

| MSR N/A | $439 | $265 - 320 | $185 - 220 | |

RECTIFIER 2-12 COMPACT SPEAKER CABINET – 120W, 2-12 in. Celestion Vintage 30 speakers, 8 ohm impedance, closed back, designed for use with the Rectifier Series heads, black covering, black grille, slip cover included, 15.25 in. tall, 26.75 in. wide, 12.75 in. deep, 50 lbs., current mfg.

| MSR N/A | $600 | $400 - 450 | $195 - 240 | |

RECTIFIER 2-12 HORIZONTAL SPEAKER CABINET – 120W, 2-12 in. Celestion Vintage 30 speakers, 8 ohm impedance, closed back, designed for use with the Rectifier Series heads, black covering, black grille, 61 lbs., current mfg.

| MSR N/A | $649 | $375 - 450 | $265 - 310 | |

* Add $549 ($1,198) for Snake Skin covering with Vintage grille.

RECTIFIER 2-12 VERTICAL SPEAKER CABINET – 120W, 2-12 in. Celestion Vintage 30 speakers, 8 ohm impedance, closed back, vertical cabinet design with casters, designed for use with the Rectifier Series heads, black covering, black grille, 75 lbs., current mfg.

| MSR N/A | $699 | $400 - 475 | $275 - 325 | |

* Add $130 ($829) for Emerald Green with Wicker grille.
* Add $179 ($878) Blue Bronco with Tan grille or Cream with Cream grille.

RECTIFIER 4-10 SPEAKER CABINET – 100W, 4-10 in. Jensen Alnico speakers, 8 ohm impedance, tuned semi-open back, straight front, casters, designed for use with the Rectifier Series heads, black covering, black grille, 47 lbs., disc. 2003.

| | N/A | $475 - 550 | $325 - 400 | $499 |

RECTIFIER 4-12 STANDARD SPEAKER CABINET – 240W, 4-12 in. Celestion Vintage 30 speakers, 8 ohm mono/4 ohm stereo impedance, closed back, straight or slanted front, casters, designed for use with the Rectifier Series heads, black covering, black grille, 32.875 in. wide, 30.125 in. tall, 14.25 in. deep, 104 lbs. (slanted front) or 106 lbs. (straight front), current mfg.

| MSR N/A | $999 | $575 - 675 | $400 - 475 | |

* Add $79 ($1,078) for Grey/Black grille.

RECTO 4-12 TRADITIONAL SPEAKER CABINET – 240W, 4-12 in. Celestion Vintage 30 speakers, 8 ohm mono/4 ohm stereo impedance, closed back, straight or slanted front, casters, designed for use with the Rectifier Series heads, black covering, black grille, 29.875 in. wide, 30.25 in. tall, 14.25 in. deep, 99 lbs. (slanted front) or 101 lbs. (straight front), current mfg.

| MSR N/A | $1,000 | $575 - 675 | $400 - 475 | |

ELECTRIC TUBE AMPLIFIERS: ROAD KING SERIES

ROAD KING (II) – 120W (switchable to 100 or 50W), head-unit only, all tube chassis, preamp: 5 X 12AX7, power: 4 X 6L6 & 2 X EL34, rectifiers: 2 X 5U4, four independent channels, reverb, front black control panel, two inputs, 24 chrome knobs (Master, p, b, m, t, gper channel), reverb control for each channel on back, five position tube selector per channel, output and solo level controls, effects loop with mix and send levels, nine-button footswitch, black covering, black grille, mfg. 2001-present.

| MSR N/A | $2,749 | $1,650 - 2,000 | $1,175 - 1,375 | |

* Add $150 for the diamond plate front panel.

In 2006, this model was upgraded to Series II specifications with an improved channel selection and tube reverb that are from the Lonestar design. The front panel is the same, but the rear panel was redesigned with the four reverb knobs moved to each channel selection and the Loop 2 Mix buttons were eliminated. Series II models also do not have a footswitch mix knob.

* *Road King Combo (II)* – similar to the Road King head except has 2-12 in.Celestion Custom 90 speakers, mfg. 2001-present.

| MSR N/A | $3,049 | $1,800 - 2,150 | $1,250 - 1,475 | |

MSR/NOTES	100%	EXCELLENT	AVERAGE	LAST MSR

ROAD KING 2-12 SPEAKER CABINET – 150W (90W/60W per side), 1-12 in. Celestion 90 speaker (right side) and 1-12 in. Celestion Vintage 30 speaker (left side), 4 ohm mono or 8 ohm stereo impedance, dual cabinet design (left open back, right closed back), designed for use with the Road King Series combos, black covering, black grille, 30.125 in. wide, 17.5 in. tall, 14.25 in. deep, 63 lbs., mfg. 2003-present.

| MSR N/A | $699 | $425 - 500 | $300 - 350 | |

ROAD KING 4-12 SPEAKER CABINET – 300W (180W/120W per side), 2-12 in. Celestion 90 speakers (right side) and 2-12 in. Celestion Vintage 30 speakers (left side), 4 ohm mono or 8 ohm stereo impedance, dual cabinet design (left open back, right closed back), slanted or straight front, casters, designed for use with the Road King Series heads, black covering, black grille, 30.125 in. wide, 32.875 in. tall, 14.25 in. deep, 109 lbs. (slanted front) or 111 lbs. (straight front), mfg. 2003-present.

| MSR N/A | $1,049 | $600 - 725 | $425 - 500 | |

ELECTRIC TUBE AMPLIFIERS: ROADSTER SERIES

Roadster Head
courtesy Mesa/Boogie

Roadster 1-12 Speaker Cabinet
courtesy Mesa/Boogie

Roadster 2-12 Speaker Cabinet
courtesy Mesa/Boogie

ROADSTER HEAD – 100W (switchable to 50W), head-unit guitar configuration, 12 tube chassis, preamp: 6 X 12AX7, power: 4 X 6L6, rectifier: 2 X 5U4, four channels, 12 modes, reverb, front black control panel, single input, 26 chrome knobs (Master, p, b, m, t, g per channel, solo, output), three-way mode switch for each channel, back control panel: footswitch input with channel selector, speaker jacks, effects loop with level, four reverb knobs (one for each channel), three switches for each channel, direct out jack with level, black covering, mfg. 2006-present.

| MSR N/A | $2,249 | $1,250 - 1,575 | $750 - 950 | |

This model is a stripped-down version of the Road King with one effects loop instead of two, one set of speaker jacks instead of two, and only power switching between 6L6 tubes (no EL34s).

* *Roadster 1-12 Combo* – similar to the Roadster Head, except in combo configuration with 1-12 in. speaker, mfg. 2006-disc.

| | $2,099 | $1,500 - 1,800 | $800 - 1,000 | $2,099 |

* *Roadster 2-12 Combo* – similar to the Roadster Head, except in combo configuration with 2-12 in. speakers, mfg. 2006-present.

| MSR N/A | $2,549 | $1,450 - 1,800 | $875 - 1,100 | |

ROADSTER 1-12 SPEAKER CABINET – 60W, 1-12 in. Celestion Vintage 30 speaker, 8 ohm impedance, ported back, designed for use with the Roadster Series head and combos, black Taurus covering, black grille, 26.75 in. wide, 15.25 in. tall, 12.75 in. deep, 39 lbs., mfg. 2006-disc.

| | $439 | $265 - 320 | $185 - 220 | $439 |

ROADSTER 2-12 SPEAKER CABINET – 120W, 2-12 in. Celestion Vintage 30 speakers, 8 ohm impedance, closed back, designed for use with the Roadster Series head and combos, black Taurus covering, black grille, 26.75 in. wide, 15.25 in. tall, 12.75 in. deep, 50 lbs., mfg. 2006-disc.

| | $589 | $350 - 425 | $250 - 300 | $589 |

ELECTRIC TUBE AMPLIFIERS: ROCKET SERIES

ROCKET 44 – 44W, 1-12 in. speaker, guitar combo, eight tube chassis, preamp: 4 X 12AX7, power: 4 X EL84, solid-state rectifier, two channels, front black control panel, single input, eight black numbered knobs (Rhyhtm Ch.: g, MV, Lead Ch." g, MV, All: t, m, b, r), channel switch (lead/rhythm/contour), standby switch, power switch, rear panel: footswitch jack, recording out/headphone jack, effects loop with mix knob, speaker mute switch, three speaker jacks (two 4 ohm, one 8 ohm), black covering, black grille, mfg. 1999-2000.

| | N/A | $425 - 500 | $250 - 300 | |

ROCKET 440 – 44W, 4-10 in. speakers, guitar combo, eight tube chassis, preamp: 4 X 12AX7, power: 4 X EL84, solid-state rectifier, two channels, reverb, tremolo, front black control panel, single input, 11 black numbered knobs (Rhyhtm Ch.: g, MV, Lead Ch." g, MV, All: t, m, b, p, r, tremolo speed, tremolo depth), channel switch (lead/rhythm/contour), standby switch, power switch, rear panel: footswitch jack, recording out/headphone jack, effects loop with mix knob, speaker mute switch, three speaker jacks (two 4 ohm, one 8 ohm), black covering, black grille, mfg. 1999-2000.

| | N/A | $500 - 600 | $300 - 350 | |

ELECTRIC TUBE AMPLIFIERS: STILETTO SERIES

STILETTO ACE – 50W, all tube class A/B chassis, preamp: 5 X 12AX7, power: 2 X EL34, rectifier: 1 X 5U4, two channels, six modes, front chrome or copper control panel, single input, 14 black knobs (Master, p, b, m, t, g per channel, solo, output), tube rectifier tracking, available in black Tolex covering with black grille or Green Bronco covering with a tan grille, mfg. 2006-2012.

| | $1,679 | $800 - 1,000 | $500 - 650 | $1,679 |

MSR/NOTES	100%	EXCELLENT	AVERAGE	LAST MSR

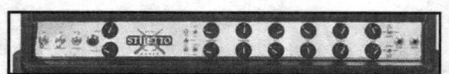

Stiletto Deuce (II) Panel
courtesy Mesa/Boogie

Stiletto 1-12 Speaker Cabinet
courtesy Mesa/Boogie

Stiletto 4-12 Speaker Cabinet
courtesy Mesa/Boogie

* ***Stilletto Ace 1-12 Combo*** – similar to the Stiletto Ace Head, except in combo configuration with 1-12 in. speaker, mfg. 2006-2012.

| | $1,829 | $875 - 1,100 | $600 - 750 | $1,829 |

* ***Stilletto Ace 2-12 Combo*** – similar to the Stiletto Ace Head, except in combo configuration with 2-12 in. speakers, mfg. 2006-2012.

| | $1,929 | $1,000 - 1,200 | $600 - 800 | $1,929 |

STILETTO DEUCE (II) – 100W (switchable to 50W), all tube class A/B chassis, preamp: 5 X 12AX7, power: 4 X EL34, rectifier: 2 X 5U4, two channels, three modes, front chrome control panel, single input, 14 black knobs (Master, p, b, m, t, g per channel, solo, output), tube rectifier tracking, black Tolex covering with front alligator skin covering, mfg. 2004-2012.

| | $1,889 | $1,100 - 1,350 | $775 - 925 | $1,889 |

In 2006, this model was upgraded to Series II specficiations.

STILETTO TRIDENT (II) – 150W (switchable to 50W), all tube class A/B chassis, preamp: 5 X 12AX7, power:6 X EL34, rectifier:3 X 5U4, two channels, six modes, front chrome control panel, single input, 14 black knobs (Master, p, b, m, t, g per channel, solo, output), tube rectifier tracking, various switches, black Tolex covering with front alligator skin covering, mfg. 2004-09.

| | N/A | $1,150 - 1,375 | $800 - 950 | $1,899 |

In 2006, this model was upgraded to Series II specficiations.

STILETTO 1-12 SPEAKER CABINET – 60W, 1-12 in. Celestion Vintage 30 speaker, 8 ohm impedance, closed back, designed for use with the Stiletto heads and cabinets, black Taurus covering, black grille with silver piping, mfg. 2006-2012.

| | $439 | $265 - 320 | $185 - 220 | $439 |

STILETTO 2-12 SPEAKER CABINET – 120W, 2-12 in. Celestion Vintage 30 speakers, 8 ohm impedance, closed back, horizontal configuration, designed for use with the Stiletto heads and cabinets, black Taurus covering, black grille with silver piping, mfg. 2006-2012.

| | $589 | $350 - 425 | $250 - 300 | $589 |

STILETTO 4-12 SPEAKER CABINET – 240W, 4-12 in. Celestion Vintage 30 speakers, 8 ohm mono/4 ohm stereo impedance, straight or slanted front, closed back, casters, designed for use with the Stiletto heads, black Taurus covering, black grille with silver piping, mfg. 2006-2012.

| | $949 | $575 - 675 | $400 - 475 | $949 |

ELECTRIC TUBE AMPLIFIERS: SUBWAY SERIES

SUBWAY BLUES – 20W, 1-10 in. speaker, guitar combo, six tube chassis, preamp: 4 X 12AX7, power: 2 X EL84, single channel, reverb, front black control panel, single input, five knobs (v, b, m, t, r), half power jack, fat/bright switch, effects loop, record out with mute switch, black covering, black grille, mfg. 1994-2000.

| | N/A | $500 - 600 | $255 - 325 | |

SUBWAY ROCKET – 20W, 1-10 in. speaker, guitar combo, six tube chassis, preamp: 4 X 12AX7, power: 2 X EL84, two channels, front black control panel, single input, eight knobs (Ch. 1: v, g, Ch. 2: v, g, t, m, b, c), effects loop, headphone jack, record out with mute switch, two-button footswitch, black covering, black grille, mfg. 1996-98.

| | N/A | $600 - 700 | $300 - 375 | |

* ***Subway Rocket Reverb*** – similar to the Subway Rocket, except has a reverb circuit with control, mfg. 1998-2000.

| | N/A | $600 - 700 | $300 - 375 | |

ELECTRIC TUBE AMPLIFIERS: TRANSATLANTIC/ROYAL ATLANTIC SERIES

TRANSATLANTIC TA-15 HEAD – 25W (switchable to 15W and 5W), guitar head unit, six-tube chassis, preamp: 4 X 12AX7, power: 2 X EL84, solid-state rectifier, two channels, front chrome control panel, single input, eight knobs (Ch. 1: v, t, b, cut/MV, Ch. 2: g, t, b, MV), Ch. 1 normal/top boost mode switch, Ch. 2 tweed/Hi 1/Hi 2 mode switch, channel switch, 5W/15W/25W power switch for each channel, power switch, standby switch, footswitch jack, black crinkle and platinum pearl powder casing, one-button footswitch included and gigbag with strap included, 12.375 in. wide, 5.875 in. tall, 6.75 in. deep, mfg. 2010-2015.

| | $899 | $550 - 650 | $375 - 450 | $899 |

MSR/NOTES	100%	EXCELLENT	AVERAGE	LAST MSR

TRANSATLANTIC TA-30 HEAD – 40W (switchable to 30W and 15W), guitar head unit, ten-tube chassis, preamp: 6 X 12AX7, power: 4 X EL84, solid-state rectifier, two channels, reverb, front chrome control panel, two inputs, ten knobs (Ch. 1: v, t, b, r, cut/MV, Ch. 2: g, t, b, r, MV), Ch. 1 normal/top boost mode switch, Ch. 2 tweed/Hi 1/Hi 2 mode switch, channel switch, 15W/30W/40W power switch for each channel, FX and reverb assignment switch for each channel, power switch, standby switch, footswitch jack, black crinkle and platinum pearl powder casing, two-button footswitch included and gigbag with strap included, 17.25 in. wide, mfg. 2011-2015.

	$1,499	$900 - 1,100	$625 - 750	$1,499

* *Transatlantic TA-30 Rackmount Head* – similar to the Transatlantic TA-30 Head, except in rackmount configuration, mfg. 2011-2015.

	$1,499	$900 - 1,100	$625 - 750	$1,499

* *Transatlantic TA-30 1-12 Combo* – similar to the Transatlantic TA-30 Head, except in combo configuration with 1-12 in. speaker, casters and slip cover included, black Taurus covering and choice of gray and black weave or black grille cloth, 22.875 in. width, mfg. 2011-2015.

	$1,649	$1,000 - 1,200	$700 - 825	$1,649

* *Transatlantic TA-30 2-12 Combo* – similar to the Transatlantic TA-30 Head, except in combo configuration with 2-12 in. speakers, casters and slip cover included, black Taurus covering and choice of gray and black weave or black grille cloth, 26.75 in. width, mfg. 2011-2015.

	$1,749	$1,050 - 1,275	$750 - 875	$1,749

ROYAL ATLANTIC RA-100 HEAD – 100W (power attenuator "multi soak" allows wattage ranging from 3W to 100W), guitar head unit, 11-tube chassis, preamp: 7 X 12AX7, power: 4 X EL84 or 6L6, solid-state rectifier, two channels/three modes, reverb, front chrome control panel, single input, 11 knobs (Ch. 1 "Clean": MV, b, m, t, g, Ch. 2 "Hi/Lo": MV hi, MV lo, b, m, t, g), power/half-power switch, standby switch, multi-soak switch, three-way channel/mode switch, footswitch jack, rear panel: slave out with level control, two speaker jacks with 4/8 ohm impedance selector, EL34/6L6 bias selector, reverb with level control, on/bypass switch, and mode switch, effects loop, fan speed switch, three channel assignable multi soak power attenuator controls, black Taurus covering with choice of gray and black weave or black grille cloth, two-button footswitch and slip cover included, 26.75 in. wide, mfg. 2011-2015.

	$1,899	$1,150 - 1,375	$800 - 950	$1,899

* *Royal Atlantic RA-100 2-12 Combo* – similar to the Royal Atlantic RA-100 Head, except in combo configuration with 2-12 in. speakers, casters and slip cover included, 26.75 in. width, mfg. 2011-2015.

	$2,149	$1,300 - 1,550	$925 - 1,075	$2,149

TRANSATLANTIC 1-10 SPEAKER CABINET – 50W, 1-10 in. E50 speaker, 8 ohm impedance, designed for use with the Transatlantic heads and combos, black Taurus covering, choice of gray and black weave or black grille cloth, 19 in. wide, 13 in. tall, 11 in. deep, 27 lbs., mfg. 2011-2015.

	$349	$210 - 250	$150 - 175	$349

TRANSATLANTIC 1-12 19 SPEAKER CABINET – 90W, 1-12 in. Celestion speaker, 8 ohm impedance, designed for use with the Transatlantic heads and combos, black Taurus covering, choice of gray and black weave or black grille cloth, 19 in. wide, 15 in. tall, 11 in. deep, 27 lbs., mfg. 2011-2015.

	$389	$235 - 285	$165 - 195	$389

TRANSATLANTIC 1-12 23 SPEAKER CABINET – 60W, 1-12 in. V30 speaker, 8 ohm impedance, designed for use with the Transatlantic heads and combos, black Taurus covering, choice of gray and black weave or black grille cloth, 23 in. wide, 18 in. tall, 11.75 in. deep, 36 lbs., mfg. 2011-2015.

	$419	$250 - 300	$175 - 210	$419

TRANSATLANTIC 2-12 SPEAKER CABINET – 180W, 2-12 in. Celestion 90 speakers, 8 ohm impedance, designed for use with the Transatlantic heads and combos, black Taurus covering, choice of gray and black weave or black grille cloth, 27 in. wide, 18 in. tall, 11.75 in. deep, 49 lbs., mfg. 2011-2015.

	$619	$375 - 450	$265 - 310	$619

PRE-AMP/POWER AMP MODELS

FORMULA PRE-AMP – pre-amp only, one-space rack mount head, five tube chassis: 5 X 12AX7, three channels, four modes (rhythm, boost, lead I, lead II), front black control panel, single input, 13 black knobs (Ch. 1: g with push/pull boost, t, m, b, MV, Ch. 2: g, t, m, b, p, MV, All: g, MV, output), five-band graphic EQ, footswitch jack, lo gain/high gain switch, EQ in/EQ Lead II/footswitch switch, mode switch, power switch, four-button footswitch included, black casing, mfg. 1998-2001.

	N/A	$425 - 500	$250 - 300	$799

RECTIFIER RECORDING PRE-AMP – pre-amp only, two-space rack mount head, six tube chassis: 6 X 12AX7, two channels, six modes (clean, fat, bright, raw, vintage, modern), front black control panel, single input, 15 chrome knobs (Ch. 1: g, t, m, b, p, MV, Ch. 2: g, t, m, b, p, MV, All: record output level, live output level, solo output level, clean/fat/bright mode switch, raw/vintage/modern mode switch, bright switch, pad switch, preamp voicing switch, channel switch, standby switch, power switch, rear panel: lift/ground switch, parallel effects loop with FX mix knob, stereo recording outputs, stereo live outputs, three external switch ports (modern, Ch. 1/Ch. 2, and Solo), additional input jack, two-button footswitch, black casing, mfg. 2002-present.

MSR N/A	$1,449	$850 - 1,025	$600 - 700	

MSR/NOTES	100%	EXCELLENT	AVERAGE	LAST MSR

Rectifier Recording Pre-Amp
courtesy Mesa/Boogie

Triaxis Programmable Pre-Amp
courtesy Mesa/Boogie

20/20 Dyna-watt Power Amp
courtesy Mesa/Boogie

TRIAXIS PROGRAMMABLE PRE-AMP – pre-amp only, one-space rackmount guitar head unit, five-tube chassis: 5 X 12AX7, single channel, eight modes (Vintage Fat Rhythm, Modern hyper-clean Rhythm, Vintage Mark I lead, Modified Higher Gain Mark I, British Lead, Mark IV Pentode Lead, Modified Mark IV Searing Lead), front black control panel, single stacked black knob (A/B output), 90 user presets, 128 MIDI program locations, complete digital display with push button controls, rear panel: full MIDI in, MIDI through, MIDI out, four footswitch jacks, stereo main and recording outputs, programmable effects loop with stereo returns, single input, black casing, mfg. 1991-present.

| MSR N/A | $1,999 | $1,200 - 1,450 | $850 - 1,000 | |

20/20 DYNA-WATT POWER AMP – 40W (20W per channel), one-space rackmount power amp guitar head, seven-tube chassis, preamp: 3 X 12AX7, power 4 X EL84, two channels (stereo output), front chrome (early models) or black (later models) control panel, four chrome (very early and later models) or black chrome (earlier models) knobs (Ch. 1: p, v, Ch. 2: v, p), power switch, standby switch, rear panel: two inputs (one for each channel), six speaker outputs (three for each channel, one 8 ohm, two 4 ohm), two slave outputs (one per channel), black casing, mfg. 1995-2010.

| | N/A | $600 - 725 | $425 - 500 | $999 |

50/50 STEREO POWER AMP – 100W (50W per channel), two-space rackmount power amp guitar head, seven-tube chassis, preamp: 3 X 12AX7, power 4 X 6L6, two channels (stereo output), front black control panel, four black numbered knobs (Ch. A: v, p, Ch. B: v, p), power switch, standby switch, hi/lo power switch, black casing, mfg. 1989-2001.

| | N/A | $550 - 650 | $375 - 450 | $699 |

RECTO 2: ONE HUNDRED POWER AMP – 200W (100W per channel), two-space rackmount power amp guitar head, eleven-tube chassis, preamp: 3 X 12AX7, power 8 X EL34/6L6, two channels (stereo output), two modes (Normal, Recto Preamp), Smart Power modern jack, front black control panel with silver insert, four chrome knobs (Ch. A: v, p, Ch. B: v, p), power switch standby switch, rear panel: four inputs (two per channel, one of each mode), EL34/6L6 bias switch, ground switch, Smart Power modern switch jack, six speaker outputs (three for each channel, one 8 ohm, two 4 ohm), black casing, mfg. 2002-disc.

| | $1,579 | $925 - 1,125 | $625 - 775 | $1,579 |

STEREO 2: FIFTY POWER AMP – 100W (50W per channel), two-space rackmount power amp guitar head, seven-tube chassis, preamp: 3 X 12AX7, power 4 X 6L6/EL34, two channels (stereo output), front black control panel, four chrome knobs (Ch. A: v, p, Ch. B: v, p), power switch standby switch, rear panel: two inputs (one per channel), 6L6/EL34 bias switch, ground switch, six speaker outputs (three for each channel, one 8 ohm, two 4 ohm), black casing, mfg. 2002-present.

| MSR N/A | $1,199 | $675 - 825 | $475 - 550 | |

STEREO SIMUL-CLASS 2: NINETY POWER AMP – 180W (90W per channel), two-space rackmount power amp guitar head, eleven-tube chassis, preamp: 3 X 12AX7, power 8 X 6L6, two channels (stereo output), Smart Power (Deep, Half Drive, Modern) line/instrument input select, front black control panel, four chrome (later models) or black chrome (earlier models) knobs (Ch. A: v, p, Ch. B: v, p), power switch standby switch, rear panel: two inputs (one per channel), line/instrument switch, ground switch, three external switch jacks (deep, modern, half drive), six speaker outputs (three for each channel, one 8 ohm, two 4 ohm), black casing, mfg. 1992-present.

| MSR N/A | $1,599 | $925 - 1,125 | $625 - 775 | |

ELECTRIC BASS AMPLIFIERS

BASIS M-2000 – 600W, bass two-space rack-mount head-unit, hybrid three-tube chassis, preamp: 3 X 12AX7, 12 tube-driven power Mos-Fets, two independent blendable channels, front black control panel, two inputs (active/passive), Vaccum Tube Channel controls: seven black knobs (g, t, m, b, MV, compression threshold, compression freq.), nine-band graphic EQ, EQ switch, bright/normal switch, hi gain/normal mix switch, compression ratio switch, Field Effect Channel controls: seven black knobs (MV, t, m, b, bass freq., compression threshold, compression freq.), nine-band graphic EQ, EQ switch, bright/normal switch, hi/lo bass shift switch, compression ratio switch, All: Channel mix knob, output level knob, power switch, rear panel: six external select EQ jacks, two XLR speaker outs, two 1/4 in. speaker outs, effects loop with mix knob, crossover level, and five-way rotary FX loop auto knob, XLR balance line out with level control and post/pre switch, tuner out, six-way rotary channel select switch, mute switch, footswitch jack, black casing, six-button footswitch included, mfg. 1995-2002.

| | N/A | $750 - 900 | $500 - 600 | $1,699 |

BASS 400+ – 500W, four space rack-mount head-unit only, all-tube chassis, preamp: 4 X 12AX7, power: 12 X 6L6, two channels, front black control panel, two inputs, six black knobs (m, b, t, MV, v1, v2), seven band EQ, effects loop with level control, fan cooled, black casing, mfg. 1988-2007.

| | N/A | $1,100 - 1,300 | $550 - 675 | $1,699 |

Bass Prodigy Four:88 Head
courtesy Mesa/Boogie

Bass Strategy Eight:88 Head
courtesy Mesa/Boogie

Bass Strategy Eight:88 Rackmount Head
courtesy Mesa/Boogie

BASS PRODIGY FOUR:88 HEAD – 250W/125W, head-unit only, all-tube chassis, preamp: 3 X 12AX7, power: 4 X KT88, single channel, front black control panel, one input, eight black knobs (g, b, m, t, voice, MV, DI level, solo), three-band EQ, active/bright switch, mute switch, 250W/125W switch, DI switch, lift/ground switch, power switch, standby switch, rear panel: mute jack, voice jack, solo jack, effects loop, tuner jack, slave jack, three speaker jacks, footswitch jack, DI XLR out jack, optional four-button footswitch, slipcover included, 7.5 in. tall, 16.25 in. wide, 9.5 in. deep, 29 lbs., top handle, black casing, mfg. 2013-present.

| MSR N/A | $1,800 | $1,175 - 1,350 | $575 - 725 | |

BASS STRATEGY EIGHT:88 HEAD – 465W/250W/125W, head-unit only, all-tube chassis, preamp: 3 X 12AX7, power: 8 X KT88, single channel, front black control panel, one input, eight black knobs (g, b, m, t, voice, MV, DI level, solo), three-band active/passive EQ, nine-band graphic EQ, active/bright switch, mute switch, 465W/250W/125W switch, EQ switch, DI switch, power switch, standby switch, rear panel: mute jack, voice jack, solo jack, EQ jack, effects loop, tuner jack, slave jack, five speaker jacks, footswitch jack, DI XLR out jack, DI lift/ground switch, loop ext. switch, optional five-button footswitch, slipcover included, 7.44 in. tall, 18.87 in. wide, 13.19 in. deep, 49 lbs., black casing, mfg. 2013-present.

| MSR N/A | $2,400 | $1,550 - 1,800 | $775 - 950 | |

* ***Bass Strategy Eight:88 Rackmount Head*** – 465W/250W/125W, head-unit only, rackmount configuration, all-tube chassis, preamp: 3 X 12AX7, power: 8 X KT88, single channel, front black control panel, one input, eight black knobs (g, b, m, t, voice, MV, DI level, solo), three-band active/passive EQ, nine-band graphic EQ, active/bright switch, mute switch, 465W/250W/125W switch, EQ switch, DI switch, power switch, standby switch, rear panel: mute jack, voice jack, solo jack, EQ jack, effects loop, tuner jack, slave jack, five speaker jacks, footswitch jack, DI XLR out jack, DI lift/ground switch, loop ext. switch, optional five-button footswitch, slipcover included, black casing, mfg. 2013-present.

| MSR N/A | $2,400 | $1,550 - 1,800 | $775 - 950 | |

BIG BLOCK 750 – 750W (@ 2Ohm), two-space rack-mount head unit, hybrid Simul-State chassis, preamp: 4 X 12AX7, 8 stage vacuum tube preamp, power: 20 tube driven MOSFETs, single channel, front black control panel, single input, nine knobs (OD, g, b, passive m, active m, freq., t, MV, OD Master), tuner output, two fan cooling system, black casing, disc.

| | $1,599 | $950 - 1,150 | $675 - 800 | $1,599 |

* ***Big Block 750 Head*** – similar to the Big Block 750, except in classic head configuration, black covering, mfg. 2005-disc.

| | $1,799 | $1,075 - 1,300 | $775 - 900 | $1,799 |

BIG BLOCK TITAN V12 – 1400W @ 2 ohms (1200W @ 4 ohms, 700W @ 8 ohms), three-space rack-mount head unit, hybrid Simul-State chassis, preamp: 4 X 12AX7, 8 stage vacuum tube preamp, power: 22 tube driven MOSFETs, two channels, front brushed aluminum control panel, two inputs, 20 knobs (OD, OD level, g, b, passive m, active m, freq., t, MV per channel, solo, output), tuner output, two fan cooling system, five-button footswitch, black casing, mfg. 2006-2010.

| | N/A | $1,025 - 1,225 | $725 - 850 | $1,699 |

* ***Big Block Titan V12 Head*** – similar to the Big Block Titan V12, except is mounted in a traditional cabinet, black covering, mfg. 2006-2010.

| | N/A | $1,100 - 1,350 | $775 - 925 | $1,849 |

BUSTER! BASS 200 HEAD – 200W, bass head-unit, nine-tube chassis, preamp: 3 X 12AX7, power: 6 X 6L6, solid-state rectifier, single channel, front black control panel, single input, five black knobs (v, t, m, b, MV), seven-band graphic EQ, EQ footswitch jack, EQ switch (on/off/footswitch), standby switch, power switch, rear panel: effects loop with blend knob, speaker mute switch, ground lift switch, XLR direct out, four speaker jacks (two 4 ohm, two 8 ohm), black covering, black grille, mfg. 1997-2001.

| | N/A | $500 - 600 | $300 - 350 | $999 |

* ***Buster! Bass 1-15 Combo*** – similar to the Buster! Bass 200 Head, except in combo configuration with 1-15 in. original EVM 15L speaker and an HF driver, recessed metal handles, and Tone Luggage Transport System, mfg. 1999-2001.

| | N/A | $600 - 750 | $350 - 425 | $1,299 |

* ***Buster! Bass 2-10 Combo*** – similar to the Buster! Bass 200 Head, except in combo configuration with 2-10 in. PAS speakers and an HF driver, recessed metal handles, and Tone Luggage Transport System, mfg. 1999-2001.

| | N/A | $600 - 750 | $350 - 425 | $1,299 |

M3 CARBINE – 300W @ 4 ohms (165W @ 8 ohms), bass two-space rackmount head, hybrid chassis with 1 X 12AX7 preamp tube and eight power MOSFETs, single channel, front black control panel, single input, six black knobs (g, b with push/pull deep switch, m, t, di level with a push/pull pre switch, MV with a push/pull mute switch), power switch, rear panel: two 1/4 in. speaker jacks, mute switch jack, tuner out jack, effects loop with bypass switch, XLR out with ground/lift switch, black casing, mfg. 2010-disc.

| | $899 | $575 - 675 | $375 - 450 | $899 |

MSR/NOTES	100%	EXCELLENT	AVERAGE	LAST MSR

* **M3 Carbine Head** – similar to the M3 Carbine, except in standard head configuration with black Bronco vinyl covering, available in regular and short widths, slip cover included, mfg. 2010-disc.

	$1,099	$650 - 800	$450 - 525	$1,099

* **M3 Carbine 1-12 Combo** – similar to the M3 Carbine, except in combo configuration with 1-12 in. PH Neo 300 speaker, tri port, player control, tilt and roll designed cabinet, black Bronco vinyl covering and black jute grille, slip cover included, mfg. 2010-disc.

	$1,249	$750 - 900	$525 - 600	$1,249

M6 CARBINE (FATHOM 600) – 600W @ 4 or 2 ohms (320W @ 8 ohms), bass two-space rackmount head, hybrid chassis with 1 X 12AX7 preamp tube and eight power MOSFETs, single channel, front black control panel, single input, seven black knobs (g, b with push/pull deep switch, m, five-way voice switch, t, di level with a push/pull pre switch, MV with a push/pull mute switch), active/passive input switch, power switch, rear panel: four voice function switch jacks, mute switch jack, two Speakon outs with ohm switch, tuner out jack, effects loop with bypass switch, XLR out with ground/lift switch, black casing, mfg. 2008-present.

MSR N/A	$1,300	$850 - 975	$425 - 525	

Mesa initially called this amp the Fathom 600, but another company outside the music industry was already using it for another product, so they decided to call it the M6 Carbine.

* **M6 Carbine Head (Fathom 600 Head)** – similar to the M6 Carbine (Fathom 600), except in standard head configuration with black Bronco vinyl covering, slip cover included, mfg. 2008-present.

MSR N/A	$1,500	$975 - 1,125	$475 - 600	

* **M6 Carbine 2-12 Combo (Fathom 600 2-12 Combo)** – similar to the M6 Carbine (Fathom 600), except in combo configuration with 2-12 in. PH Neo 300 speakers, tri port, player control, tilt and roll designed cabinet, black Bronco vinyl covering and black jute grille, slip cover included, mfg. 2008-2010.

	N/A	$850 - 1,025	$600 - 700	$1,399

M9 CARBINE – 900W @ 4 or 2 ohms (450W @ 8 ohms), bass two-space rackmount head, hybrid chassis with 1 X 12AX7 preamp tube and ten power MOSFETs, single channel, front black control panel, single input, eight black knobs (g, b with push/pull deep switch, m, t, threshold, ratio, five-way voice switch, MV with a push/pull mute switch), nine-band graphic EQ, active/passive input switch, graphic EQ on/off switch, comp on/off switch, power switch, rear panel: two Speakon outputs with impedance switch, footswitch jack, voice active/defeat switch, tuners out, effects loop, XLR direct out with pre/post and lift/ground switch, black casing, mfg. 2009-present.

MSR N/A	$1,550	$1,000 - 1,150	$500 - 625	

* **M9 Carbine Head** – similar to the M9 Carbine, except in standard head configuration with black Bronco vinyl covering, slip cover included, mfg. 2009-present.

MSR N/A	$1,750	$1,125 - 1,300	$575 - 700	

M-PULSE 360 – 360W, two-space rack-mount head unit, hybrid Simul-State chassis, preamp: 2 X 12AX7, 4 stage vacuum tube preamp, power: 12 tube driven power MOSFETs, single channel, compression, front brushed chrome control panel, two inputs, 18 chrome knobs (g, b, m, t, compression threshold, compression ratio, MV, Master solo, 10-band EQ), effects loop, four-button footswitch, black casing, mfg. 2000-04.

	N/A	$650 - 750	$425 - 500	$1,199

M-PULSE 600 – 600W, two-space rack-mount head unit, hybrid Simul-State chassis, preamp: 2 X 12AX7, 4 stage vacuum tube preamp, power: 12 tube driven power MOSFETs, single channel, compression, front brushed chrome control panel, two inputs, 18 chrome knobs (g, b, m, t, compression threshold, compression ratio, MV, Master solo, 10-band EQ), effects loop, four-button footswitch, black casing, mfg. 2000-disc.

	$1,599	$950 - 1,150	$675 - 800	$1,599

This model was improved in 2005.

* **M-Pulse 600 Head** – similar to the M-Pulse 600, except in classic head configuration, black covering, mfg. 2005-disc.

	$1,799	$1,075 - 1,300	$775 - 900	$1,799

SUBWAY D-800 HEAD – 800W (@ 4 ohms), lightweight bass head unit, solid-state chassis, single channel, front black control panel, single input, seven black knobs (input, voicing, bass, low mid, high mid, treble, MV), mute switch, active/passive switch, on/deep switch, rear panel: power switch, two speaker output jacks, impedance switch, headphone jack, aux input jack, XLR jack, EQ switch, Line/Mic switch, Lift/Ground switch, black casing, 3 in. tall, 10.6 in. wide, 11.12 in. deep, 5.5 lbs., mfg. 2015-present.

MSR N/A	$700	$450 - 525	$230 - 280	

VENTURE 600 – 600W, head unit only, hybrid Simul-State chassis, preamp: 2 X 12AX7, 4 stage vacuum tube preamp, power: 12 tube driven power MOSFETs, single channel, compression, front brushed chrome control panel, two inputs, 18 chrome knobs (g, b, m, t, compression threshold, compression ratio, MV, Master solo, 10-band EQ), effects loop, four-button footswitch, black covering, black grille, disc. 2005.

	N/A	$950 - 1,100	$625 - 725	$1,579

The head-unit has a removable grille that has two rack-spaces available for use. This model was improved in 2005.

* **Venture 600 115 Combo** – similar to the Venture 600, except in combo configuration with 1-15 in. speaker, tilt-back design, and casters, disc. 2005.

	N/A	$975 - 1,175	$625 - 725	$1,649

MSR/NOTES	100%	EXCELLENT	AVERAGE	LAST MSR

Subway D-800 Head
courtesy Mesa/Boogie

Venture 600
courtesy Mesa/Boogie

Venture 600 212 Combo
courtesy Mesa/Boogie

Walkabout
courtesy Mesa/Boogie

* *Venture 600 210 Combo* – similar to the Venture 600, except in combo configuration with 2-10 in. speakers, tilt-back design, and casters, disc. 2005.

| | N/A | $1,000 - 1,200 | $625 - 725 | $1,699 |

* *Venture 600 212 Combo* – similar to the Venture 600, except in combo configuration with 2-12 in. speakers, tilt-back design, and casters, mfg. 2005-09.

| | $1,699 | $1,025 - 1,225 | $725 - 850 | $1,699 |

WALKABOUT – 300W, two-space rack-mount head unit, hybrid Simul-State chassis, preamp: 2 X 12AX7, 4 stage vacuum tube preamp, power: eight tube driven power MOSFETs, single channel, front brushed chrome control panel, two inputs, 12 chrome knobs (g, b, m, t, DI level, MV, 6-band EQ), effects loop, black casing, 13 lbs., mfg. 2001-present.

| MSR N/A | $1,149 | $650 - 800 | $450 - 525 | |

In 2007, this model was upgraded.

* *Walkabout Head* – similar to the Walkabout, except in classic head configuration, black covering, mfg. 2005-present.

| MSR N/A | $1,349 | $775 - 925 | $550 - 650 | |

* *Walkabout Scout 112 Combo* – similar to the Walkabout Head, except in combo configuration with 1-12 in. Neodym speaker and driver, black vinyl covering, black grille, current mfg.

| MSR N/A | $1,600 | $1,050 - 1,200 | $525 - 650 | |

* *Walkabout Scout 115 Combo* – similar to the Walkabout Head, except in combo configuration with 1-15 in. Neodym speaker and driver, black vinyl covering, black grille, disc.

| | $1,549 | $900 - 1,100 | $600 - 700 | $1,549 |

GUITAR SPEAKER CABINETS

1-12 Three-Quarter Back Speaker Cabinet
courtesy Mesa/Boogie

1-12 Compact Thiele Speaker Cabinet
courtesy Mesa/Boogie

1-12 Compact Widebody Speaker Cabinet
Closed Back courtesy Mesa/Boogie

Currently, Mesa/Boogie offers many specific speaker cabinets to their respective series. However, they have and still produce a variety of speaker cabinets that can be used for a variety of applications. The Classic line of speaker cabinets was not initially designed for use specifically with the Lone Star Series, but when Mesa changed their covering on the Lone Star Series to black, they renamed the Classic speaker cabinets the Lone Star cabinets. Please refer to the Lone Star Series for information on the Classic line of speaker cabinets.

1-12 SPEAKER CABINET – 200W, 1-12 in. EVM 12L speaker, 8 ohm impedance, open back, black covering, black grille, disc. 2003.

| | N/A | $250 - 300 | $135 - 175 | $399 |

1-12 WIDEBODY SPEAKER CABINET – 200W, 1-12 in. EVM 12L speaker, 8 ohm impedance, extended width, open back, black covering, black grille, disc. 2003.

| | N/A | $250 - 300 | $135 - 175 | $419 |

1-12 THIELE SPEAKER CABINET – 200W, 1-12 in. EVM 12L speaker, 8 ohm impedance, extended width, closed back, ported front, black covering, black grille, disc. 2003.

| | N/A | $250 - 300 | $135 - 175 | $419 |

MSR/NOTES	100%	EXCELLENT	AVERAGE	LAST MSR

1-12 THREE-QUARTER BACK SPEAKER CABINET – 90W, 1-12 in. Celestion 90 speaker, 8 ohm impedance, tuned 3/4 closed back, black covering, black grille, 26.875 in. wide, 20.25 in. tall, 11.5 in. deep, 47 lbs., disc.

	$409	$250 - 300	$175 - 205	$409

2-12 THREE-QUARTER BACK SPEAKER CABINET – 180W, 2-12 in. Celestion 90 speakers, 8 ohm impedance, tuned 3/4 closed back, black covering, black grille, 26.625 in. wide, 17.125 in. tall, 12 in. deep, 48 lbs., disc.

	$589	$350 - 425	$250 - 300	$589

4-12 THREE-QUARTER BACK SPEAKER CABINET – 360W, 4-12 in. Celestion 90 speakers, 8 ohm impedance, tuned 3/4 closed back, black covering, black grille, disc. 2004.

	N/A	$475 - 550	$300 - 375	$849

1-12 COMPACT SPEAKER CABINET – 90W, 1-12 in. Celestion 90 speaker, 8 ohm impedance, opened back, black covering, black grille, 18.75 in. wide, 15.75 in. tall, 11 in. deep, 31 lbs., disc.

	$359	$215 - 260	$150 - 180	$359

1-12 COMPACT THIELE SPEAKER CABINET – 90W, 1-12 in. Celestion 90 speaker, 8 ohm impedance, closed back, ported front, black covering, black grille, 18.875 in. wide, 15.75 in. tall, 12.75 in. deep, 36 lbs., current mfg.

MSR N/A	$439	$265 - 320	$185 - 220	

• Also available in Black Floral with White grille ($888).

In late 2007, a WideBody version of the front-ported Thiele 1-12 Compact Speaker Cabinet was announced at a price of $469, but it is unknown how many, if any, were produced.

1-12 COMPACT WIDEBODY SPEAKER CABINET – 90W, 1-12 in. Celestion 90 speaker, 8 ohm impedance, opened back, black covering, black grille, 22.5 in. wide, 16.5 in. tall, 11.25 in. deep, 33 lbs., current mfg.

MSR N/A	$389	$235 - 285	$165 - 195	

* *1-12 Compact Widebody Speaker Cabinet Closed Back* – similar to the 1-12 Compact Widebody Speaker Cabinet, except has a closed back, mfg. 2009-present.

MSR N/A	$469	$300 - 350	$175 - 225	

• Add $179 ($648) for Cream Bronco covering with Tan grille, Gold Covering with Gold grille, or Wine Taurus with Tan grille.

BASS SPEAKER CABINETS

Powerhouse 1-15 Speaker Cabinet
courtesy Mesa/Boogie

Traditional Powerhouse 1-15 Speaker
Cabinet courtesy Mesa/Boogie

Traditional Powerhouse 2-10 Speaker
Cabinet courtesy Mesa/Boogie

POWERHOUSE 1-12 SPEAKER CABINET – 300W, 1-12 in. PH Neo speaker, tuned front ported, adj. HF driver, 8 ohm (optional 4 ohm) impedance, Player Control network featuring a three-point crossover, premium horn attenuator, instant reset horn protection and Speakon and 1/4 in. input and output jacks, AA Marine Grade baltic birch construction, recessed metal handles, Lexan corners, available in Black Bronco, Black Rhino, or Zinc Bronco vinyl covering, black or silver metal grille, 19.375 in. wide, 15.25 in. tall, 18.375 in. deep, 48 lbs., slip cover included, mfg. 2005-disc.

	$549	$325 - 400	$200 - 250	$549

* *RoadReady 1-12 Speaker Cabinet* – similar to the Powerhouse 1-12 Speaker Cabinet, except is enclosed in a roadcase cabinet, steel corners, aluminum edges, a removable front cover, recessed metal handles, and a black or silver metal grille, mfg. 2005-08.

	N/A	$500 - 625	$350 - 425	$849

POWERHOUSE 1-15 SPEAKER CABINET – 400W (disc. 2005) 600W (2006-present), 1-15 in. PH Neo speaker, tuned front ported (2004-present), adj. HF driver, 8 ohm (optional 4 ohm) impedance, Player Control network (2004-present) featuring a three-point crossover, premium horn attenuator, instant reset horn protection and Speakon and 1/4 in. input and output jacks, AA Marine Grade baltic birch construction, recessed metal handles, Lexan corners, removable Trak-Loc casters, available in Black Bronco, Black Rhino, or Zinc Bronco vinyl covering, black or silver metal grille, 19.375 in. wide, 19.375 in. tall, 19.75 in. deep, 72 lbs., slip cover included, mfg. 2000-present.

MSR N/A	$799	$475 - 575	$325 - 400	

MSR/NOTES	100%	EXCELLENT	AVERAGE	LAST MSR

Vintage Powerhouse 2-10 Speaker Cabinet
courtesy Mesa/Boogie

Powerhouse 2-12 Speaker Cabinet
courtesy Mesa/Boogie

Vintage Powerhouse 2-12 Speaker
Cabinet courtesy Mesa/Boogie

* **RoadReady 1-15 Speaker Cabinet** – similar to the Powerhouse 1-15 Speaker Cabinet, except is enclosed in a roadcase cabinet, steel corners, aluminum edges, a removable front cover, recessed metal handles, and a black or silver metal grille, disc. 2008.

	N/A	$650 - 775	$450 - 525	$1,069

* **Traditional Powerhouse 1-15 Speaker Cabinet** – 400W, 1-15 in. PH speaker, 8 ohm impedance, Speakon and 1/4 in. input and output jacks, AA Marine Grade baltic birch construction, recessed metal handles, removable casters, available in Black Rhino covering, black twisted jute grille with Silver piping, slip cover included, 24.25 in. wide, 19.37 in. tall, 19.75 in. deep, 68 lbs., mfg. 2012-present.

MSR N/A	$600	$400 - 450	$195 - 240	

* **Vintage Powerhouse 1-15 Speaker Cabinet** – similar to the Powerhouse 1-15 Speaker Cabinet, except has a black twisted jute cloth grille, mfg. 2007-disc.

	$799	$475 - 575	$325 - 400	$799

POWERHOUSE 2-10 SPEAKER CABINET – 600W, 1-12 in. PH speakers, tuned front ported (2004-present), adj. HF driver, 8 ohm (optional 4 ohm) impedance, Player Control network (2004-present) featuring a three-point crossover, premium horn attenuator, instant reset horn protection and Speakon and 1/4 in. input and output jacks, AA Marine Grade baltic birch construction, recessed metal handles, Lexan corners, available in Black Bronco, Black Rhino, or Zinc Bronco vinyl covering, black or silver metal grille, 24.5 in. wide, 16.5 in. tall, 19.75 in. deep, 69 lbs., slip cover included, mfg. 2000-present.

MSR N/A	$729	$450 - 525	$300 - 350	

* **RoadReady 2-10 Speaker Cabinet** – similar to the Powerhouse 2-10 Speaker Cabinet, except is enclosed in a roadcase cabinet, steel corners, aluminum edges, a removable front cover, recessed metal handles, and a black or silver metal grille, disc. 2008.

	N/A	$600 - 725	$425 - 500	$999

* **Traditional Powerhouse 2-10 Speaker Cabinet** – 400W, 2-10 in. PH speakers, adj. HF driver, 8 ohm impedance, switchable crossover, premium horn attenuator, Speakon and 1/4 in. input and output jacks, AA Marine Grade baltic birch construction, recessed metal handles, optional casters, available in Black Rhino covering, black twisted jute grille with Silver piping, slip cover included, 24.62 in. wide, 16.87 in. tall, 19.37 in. deep, 65 lbs., mfg. 2012-present.

MSR N/A	$600	$400 - 450	$195 - 240	

* **Vintage Powerhouse 2-10 Speaker Cabinet** – similar to the Powerhouse 2-10 Speaker Cabinet, except has a black twisted jute cloth grille, mfg. 2007-disc.

	$729	$450 - 525	$300 - 350	$729

POWERHOUSE 2-12 SPEAKER CABINET – 600W, 2-12 in. PH speakers, tuned front ported, adj. HF driver, 8 ohm (optional 4 ohm) impedance, Player Control network featuring a three-point crossover, premium horn attenuator, instant reset horn protection and Speakon and 1/4 in. input and output jacks, AA Marine Grade baltic birch construction, recessed metal handles, Lexan corners, removable Trak-Loc casters, available in Black Bronco, Black Rhino, or Zinc Bronco vinyl covering, black or silver metal grille, 24.5 in. wide, 25.125 in. tall, 19.75 in. deep, 78 lbs., slip cover included, mfg. 2004-present.

MSR N/A	$899	$525 - 650	$375 - 450	

* **RoadReady 2-12 Speaker Cabinet** – similar to the Powerhouse 2-12 Speaker Cabinet, except is enclosed in a roadcase cabinet, steel corners, aluminum edges, a removable front cover, recessed metal handles, and a black or silver metal grille, mfg. 2005-08.

	N/A	$675 - 825	$500 - 575	$1,139

* **Vintage Powerhouse 2-12 Speaker Cabinet** – similar to the Powerhouse 2-12 Speaker Cabinet, except has a black twisted jute cloth grille, mfg. 2007-disc.

	N/A	$525 - 650	$375 - 450	$879

MSR/NOTES	100%	EXCELLENT	AVERAGE	LAST MSR

**Powerhouse 2-15 Speaker Cabinet
courtesy Mesa/Boogie**

**Powerhouse 4-10 Speaker Cabinet
courtesy Mesa/Boogie**

**Traditional Powerhouse 4-10 Speaker
Cabinet courtesy Mesa/Boogie**

POWERHOUSE 2-15 SPEAKER CABINET – 600W (disc. 2005) or 1200W (2006-present), 1-15 in. PH Neo speakers, tuned front ported (2004-present), adj. HF driver, 8 ohm (optional 4 ohm) impedance, Player Control network (2004-present) featuring a three-point crossover, premium horn attenuator, instant reset horn protection and Speakon and 1/4 in. input and output jacks, AA Marine Grade baltic birch construction, tilt & roll transport system with rear glide rails, recessed metal handles, Lexan corners, casters, available in Black Bronco, Black Rhino, or Zinc Bronco vinyl covering, black or silver metal grille, 24.5 in. wide, 36.75 in. tall, 19.75 in. deep, 123 lbs., slip cover included, mfg. 2000-present.

MSR N/A	$1,199	$725 - 875	$500 - 600	

* **RoadReady 2-15 Speaker Cabinet** – similar to the Powerhouse 2-15 Speaker Cabinet, except is enclosed in a roadcase cabinet, steel corners, aluminum edges, a removable front cover, recessed metal handles, and a black or silver metal grille, disc. 2008.

	N/A	$850 - 1,025	$600 - 700	$1,409

* **Vintage Powerhouse 2-15 Speaker Cabinet** – similar to the Powerhouse 2-15 Speaker Cabinet, except has a black twisted jute cloth grille, mfg. 2007-disc.

	N/A	$725 - 875	$500 - 600	$1,199

POWERHOUSE 4-10 SPEAKER CABINET – 600W, 4-10 in. PH speakers, tuned front ported (2004-present), adj. HF driver, 8 ohm (optional 4 ohm) impedance, Player Control network (2004-present) featuring a three-point crossover, premium horn attenuator, instant reset horn protection and Speakon and 1/4 in. input and output jacks, AA Marine Grade baltic birch construction, recessed metal handles, Lexan corners, removable Trak-Loc casters, available in Black Bronco, Black Rhino, or Zinc Bronco vinyl covering, black or silver metal grille, 24.5 in. wide, 25.125 in. tall, 19.75 in. deep, 96 lbs., slip cover included, mfg. 2000-present.

MSR N/A	$1,099	$650 - 800	$475 - 550	

* **RoadReady 4-10 Speaker Cabinet** – similar to the Powerhouse 4-10 Speaker Cabinet, except is enclosed in a roadcase cabinet, steel corners, aluminum edges, a removable front cover, recessed metal handles, and a black or silver metal grille, disc. 2008.

	N/A	$825 - 1,000	$575 - 675	$1,359

* **Traditional Powerhouse 4-10 Speaker Cabinet** – 600W, 4-10 in. PH speakers, adj. HF driver, 8 ohm impedance, switchable crossover, premium horn attenuator, Speakon and 1/4 in. input and output jacks, AA Marine Grade baltic birch construction, recessed metal handles, removable casters, available in Black Rhino covering, black twisted jute grille with Silver piping, slip cover included, 24.62 in. wide, 25.37 in. tall, 19.37 in. deep, 85 lbs., mfg. 2012-present.

MSR N/A	$900	$575 - 675	$295 - 350	

* **Vintage Powerhouse 4-10 Speaker Cabinet** – similar to the Powerhouse 4-10 Speaker Cabinet, except has a black twisted jute cloth grille, mfg. 2007-2012.

	$1,099	$650 - 800	$475 - 550	$1,099

POWERHOUSE 4-12 SPEAKER CABINET – 1200W, 4-12 in. PH speakers, tuned front ported, adj. HF driver, 4 ohm (optional 8 ohm) impedance, Player Control network featuring a three-point crossover, premium horn attenuator, instant reset horn protection and Speakon and 1/4 in. input and output jacks, AA Marine Grade baltic birch construction, tilt & roll transport system with rear glide rails, recessed metal handles, Lexan corners, casters, available in Black Bronco, Black Rhino, or Zinc Bronco vinyl covering, black or silver metal grille, 24.5 in. wide, 45.25 in. tall, 19.75 in. deep, 136 lbs., slip cover included, mfg. 2004-present.

MSR N/A	$1,299	$775 - 950	$550 - 650	

* **RoadReady 4-12 Speaker Cabinet** – similar to the Powerhouse 4-12 Speaker Cabinet, except is enclosed in a roadcase cabinet, steel corners, aluminum edges, a removable front cover, recessed metal handles, and a black or silver metal grille, mfg. 2005-08.

	N/A	$900 - 1,100	$650 - 750	$1,519

* **Vintage Powerhouse 4-12 Speaker Cabinet** – similar to the Powerhouse 4-12 Speaker Cabinet, except has a black twisted jute cloth grille, mfg. 2007-disc.

	$1,299	$775 - 950	$550 - 650	$1,299

MSR/NOTES	100%	EXCELLENT	AVERAGE	LAST MSR

Powerhouse 6-10 Speaker Cabinet
courtesy Mesa/Boogie

Traditional Powerhouse 6-10 Speaker Cabinet
courtesy Mesa/Boogie

Powerhouse 8-10 Speaker Cabinet
courtesy Mesa/Boogie

POWERHOUSE 6-10 SPEAKER CABINET – 900W, 6-10 in. PH speakers, tuned front ported (2004-present), adj. HF driver, 4 ohm impedance, Player Control network (2004-present) featuring a three-point crossover, premium horn attenuator, instant reset horn protection and Speakon and 1/4 in. input and output jacks, AA Marine Grade baltic birch construction, tilt & roll transport system with rear glide rails, recessed metal handles, Lexan corners, casters, available in Black Bronco, Black Rhino, or Zinc Bronco vinyl covering, black or silver metal grille, 24.5 in. wide, 36.75 in. tall, 19.75 in. deep, 134 lbs., slip cover included, mfg. 2000-present.

| MSR N/A | $1,349 | $800 - 975 | $575 - 675 | |

* **RoadReady 6-10 Speaker Cabinet** – similar to the Powerhouse 6-10 Speaker Cabinet, except is enclosed in a roadcase cabinet, steel corners, aluminum edges, a removable front cover, recessed metal handles, and a black or silver metal grille, disc. 2008.

| | N/A | $950 - 1,150 | $675 - 800 | $1,579 |

* **Traditional Powerhouse 6-10 Speaker Cabinet** – 900W, 6-10 in. PH speakers, 4 ohm impedance, Speakon and 1/4 in. input and output jacks, AA Marine Grade baltic birch construction, recessed metal handles, tilt and roll transport system, available in Black Rhino covering, gray/black twisted jute grille with Silver piping, slip cover included, 26.25 in. wide, 35.25 in. tall, 16.25 in. deep, 117 lbs., mfg. 2012-present.

| MSR N/A | $1,100 | $725 - 825 | $350 - 450 | |

* **Vintage Powerhouse 6-10 Speaker Cabinet** – similar to the Powerhouse 6-10 Speaker Cabinet, except has a black twisted jute cloth grille, mfg. 2007-disc.

| | $1,349 | $800 - 975 | $575 - 675 | $1,349 |

POWERHOUSE 8-10 SPEAKER CABINET – 1200W, 8-10 in. PH speakers, tuned front ported (2004-present), adj. HF driver, 4 ohm (optional 8 ohm) impedance, Player Control network (2004-present) featuring a three-point crossover, premium horn attenuator, instant reset horn protection and Speakon and 1/4 in. input and output jacks, AA Marine Grade baltic birch construction, tilt & roll transport system with rear glide rails, recessed metal handles, Lexan corners, casters, available in Black Bronco, Black Rhino, or Zinc Bronco vinyl covering, black or silver metal grille, 24.5 in. wide, 45.25 in. tall, 19.75 in. deep, 173 lbs., slip cover included, mfg. 2000-present.

| MSR N/A | $1,699 | $1,025 - 1,225 | $725 - 850 | |

* **RoadReady 8-10 Speaker Cabinet** – similar to the Powerhouse 8-10 Speaker Cabinet, except is enclosed in a roadcase cabinet, steel corners, aluminum edges, a removable front cover, recessed metal handles, and a black or silver metal grille, disc. 2008.

| | N/A | $1,200 - 1,450 | $850 - 1,000 | $1,989 |

* **Traditional Powerhouse 8-10 Speaker Cabinet** – 1200W, 8-10 in. PH speakers, 4 ohm impedance, Speakon and 1/4 in. input and output jacks, AA Marine Grade baltic birch construction, recessed metal handles, tilt and roll transport system, available in Black Rhino covering, black twisted jute grille with Silver piping, slip cover included, 26.25 in. wide, 46 in. tall, 16.25 in. deep, 146 lbs., mfg. 2012-present.

| MSR N/A | $1,400 | $900 - 1,050 | $450 - 550 | |

* **Vintage Powerhouse 8-10 Speaker Cabinet** – similar to the Powerhouse 8-10 Speaker Cabinet, except has a black twisted jute cloth grille, mfg. 2007-disc.

| | $1,699 | $1,025 - 1,225 | $725 - 850 | $1,699 |

POWERHOUSE 1000/1200 SPEAKER CABINET – 1000W (disc. 2007) or 1200W (2008-present), 1-15 in. and 4-10 in. PH speakers, tuned front ported (2004-present), adj. HF driver, 4 ohm (optional 8 ohm) impedance, Player Control network (2004-present) featuring a three-point crossover, premium horn attenuator, instant reset horn protection and Speakon and 1/4 in. input and output jacks, AA Marine Grade baltic birch construction, tilt & roll transport system with rear glide rails, recessed metal handles, Lexan corners, casters, available in Black Bronco, Black Rhino, or Zinc Bronco vinyl covering, black or silver metal grille, 24.5 in. wide, 36.75 in. tall, 19.75 in. deep, 137 lbs., slip cover included, mfg. 2000-present.

| MSR N/A | $1,599 | $950 - 1,150 | $675 - 800 | |

* **RoadReady 1000/1200 Speaker Cabinet** – similar to the Powerhouse 1200 Speaker Cabinet, except is enclosed in a roadcase cabinet, steel corners, aluminum edges, a removable front cover, recessed metal handles, and a black or silver metal grille, disc. 2008.

| | N/A | $1,075 - 1,300 | $775 - 900 | $1,799 |

MSR/NOTES	100%	EXCELLENT	AVERAGE	LAST MSR

Scout Bass Radiator 1-12 Speaker Cabinet
courtesy Mesa/Boogie

Subway Ultra-Lite 1-12 Speaker Cabinet
courtesy Mesa/Boogie

Subway Ultra-Lite 1-15 Speaker Cabinet
Cabinet courtesy Mesa/Boogie

🎸 * *Vintage Powerhouse 1000/1200 Speaker Cabinet* – similar to the Powerhouse 1200 Speaker Cabinet, except has a black twisted jute cloth grille, mfg. 2007-disc.

	$1,599	$950 - 1,150	$675 - 800	$1,599

🎸 **SCOUT BASS RADIATOR 1-12 SPEAKER CABINET** – 300W, 1-12 in. Neodym speaker, 10 in. passive radiator, 4 ohm (or specially ordered 8 ohm) impedance, adj. HF driver, Player Control Network (2005-disc.) with selectable three-point crossover, premium horn attenuator, instant reset horn protection, Speakon and 1/4 in. inputs and outputs, AA Marine Grade baltic birch cabinet, black Bronco vinyl covering, leather corners, black twisted jute speaker grille, 16.5 in. wide, 20.25 in. tall, 15 in. deep, 37 lbs., mfg. summer 2003-disc.

	$649	$400 - 475	$275 - 325	$649

🎸 **SCOUT BASS RADIATOR 1-15 SPEAKER CABINET** – 300W, 1-15 in. Neodym speaker, 12 in. passive radiator, 4 ohm (or specially ordered 8 ohm) impedance, adj. HF driver, Player Control Network (2005-disc.) with selectable three-point crossover, premium horn attenuator, instant reset horn protection, Speakon and 1/4 in. inputs and outputs, AA Marine Grade baltic birch cabinet, black Bronco vinyl covering, leather corners, black twisted jute speaker grille, 17.25 in. wide, 23.25 in. tall, 19.75 in. deep, 43 lbs., mfg. summer 2003-disc.

	$799	$475 - 575	$325 - 400	$799

🎸 **SUBWAY ULTRA-LITE 1-12 SPEAKER CABINET** – 400W, 1-12 in. Neodymium speaker, 8 ohm pedance, designed for use with the Subway D-800 bass head, variable horn frequency, 1/4 in./Speakon combo inputs and outputs, Italian poplar construction, black Bronco vinyl covering, black grille, 19.25 in. wide, 15.25 in. tall, 18.25 in. deep, 33 lbs., mfg. 2015-present.

MSR N/A	$650	$425 - 475	$210 - 260	

🎸 **SUBWAY ULTRA-LITE 1-15 SPEAKER CABINET** – 400W, 1-15 in. Neodymium speaker, 8 ohm impedance, designed for use with the Subway D-800 bass head, variable horn frequency, 1/4 in./Speakon combo inputs and outputs, Italian poplar construction, black Bronco vinyl covering, black grille, 19.25 in. wide, 19.37 in. tall, 18.25 in. deep, 38 lbs., mfg. 2015-present.

MSR N/A	$750	$475 - 550	$245 - 300	

METALTRONIX

Amplifiers previously produced in Reseda, CA and Northridge, CA between 1983 and 1990.

Lee Jackson started Metaltronix amplifiers in 1983 out of the Harmony Music store in Reseda, CA. Jackson had worked at Fender prior to starting Metaltronix, and decided to start his own company in an effort to keep up with market trends faster then Fender could. He set up in a small area of the Harmony Music Store in Reseda, CA and started to produce custom hand-built tube amplifiers (very heavy metal). After Jackson ran an ad in *Guitar Player* magazine, orders came in through the roof and he had established himself as a tube amp manufacturer. Jackson soon took over the entire Harmony Music store and later moved to a new factory in Northridge, CA. In 1985, Jackson teamed up with a group of investors to form the Perfect Connection Corporation. During this time, he produced the widely successful SP-1000 (100W per side all-tube one rack space poweramp), and an all tube one-space rack unit preamp for guitars and basses. Metaltronix also produced the Blues '59 tube guitar amp at the request of Billy Gibbons (ZZ Top). In 1990, the investors Jackson had turned to in 1985 for support tried to buy the company out, but as things did not get straightened out in court, Metaltronix ceased production for good in 1990. Jackson then went to Ampeg and designed the VL Series of amps. Currently, Jackson produces amplifiers under the name Lee Jackson (see Lee Jackson).

METEORO

Amplifiers, speaker cabinets, and effects currently produced in Brazil since 1986. Distributed in the U.S. by Meteoro Amplifiers.

Meteoro has been producing guitar amplifiers since the mid-1990s in Brazil. They offer a full range of amplifiers including solid-state and tube designs available in guitar, bass, and acoustic configurations. Andreas Kisser, Derrik Green, and Paulo Xisto of Sepultura recently became endorsers of Meteoro amplifiers. For more information, visit Meteoro's website or contact them directly.

CONTACT INFORMATION
METEORO
Brazil
www.meteoroamplifiers.com

METROPOULOS AMPLIFICATION

Amplifiers currently produced in Burton, MI since 2004.

George Metropoulos founded Metropoulos in 2004 and he builds replica amplifers of 1960s Marshall Plexi heads and Bluesbreaker combos. All amps feature point-to-point wiring on circuit boards. For more information, visit Metropoulos' website or contact him directly.

CONTACT INFORMATION
METROPOULOS AMPLIFICATION
1045 Adamas Road
Burton, MI 48509
Phone No.: 810-614-3905
www.metropoulos.net
metroamp@gmail.com

MIGHTY MOE

Amplifiers previously produced in China. Distributed by Mighty Moe in San Rafael, CA.

Inventor/CEO Peter Bellak became tired of lugging around inadequate mini guitar amplifiers for his local group so he invented an amplifier that mounts on a guitar strap. The Mighty Moe is a 1W amplifier that is hard-wired to a boot leather strap that has a clean and overdrive channels. The guitar strap can be muted by plugging in headphones, it runs on a 9V battery, and the entire apparatus fits inside of a guitar case. Bellak was granted a U.S. patent for his design in 2005 and the Mighty Moe was introduced in summer, 2007. The Mighty Moe retails for $69.95. For more information, visit Mighty Moe's website or contact them directly.

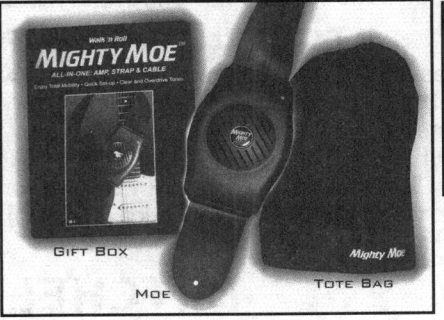

courtesy Mighty Moe

CONTACT INFORMATION
MIGHTY MOE
747 B Street, #2
San Rafael, CA 94901
Phone No.: 415-455-9268
Fax No.: 415-454-3743
www.mightymoe.com
peter@intimedesign.net

MILL HILL

Amplifiers and other audio equipment previously produced in Camarillo, CA during the late 1990s and early 2000s.

Mill Hill creations was founded by Johnathon E. Glynn in California. They produced four different models including the **Juma**, **Love**, **Summer**, and **Phoenix Rising**. These are all tube amplifiers that are small in size and are designed for small room performances and the like. Glynn also do restorations and modifications to other amplifiers and was known to do some hot-rodding. It is unknown if Glynn is still involved in amplifiers.

MILLS ACOUSTICS

Speaker cabinets previously produced in Mobile, AL.

Dave Mills and his small staff built high-quality guitar and bass speaker cabinets. Mills featured the Afterburner Series of speaker cabinets that were built with many unique qualities that separate them from other cabinets. Features included Celestion Vintage 30 and EV EVM-12L Black Label speakers, 13-ply baltic birch construction, slightly oversized dimensions, an internal "Afterburner" ported baffle, and a limited lifetime warranty. Guitar cabinets were available in 2-12 in. (Mach 212B, Last MSR $898) and a 4-12 in. (Afterburner 412A/412B, Last MSR $1,298) configurations. Bass cabinets were also available with the Afterburner 410B (Last MSR $1,198) and Afterburner 610B (Last MSR $1,398) with a choice of Eminence or Celestion bass drivers.

Speaker Cabinet 2-12
courtesy Mills Acoustic

Speaker Cabinet 4-12
courtesy Mills Acoustic

Speaker Cabinet 4-12
courtesy Mills Acoustic

MINDECH

Amplifiers currently produced in Korea and China. Currently there is no U.S. Distributor.

Mindech produces a wide range of mainly budget/entry-level solid-state amps, but they also make a tube line. The name Mindech comes from combining mind and echo. Currently there is no U.S. Distributor. They also make guitar/bass tuners. For more information, visit Mindech's website.

CONTACT INFORMATION
MINDECH
www.mindech.com
mindech@daum.net

MISSION AMPS

Amplifiers currently produced in Commerce City, CO since 1996.

CONTACT INFORMATION
MISSION AMPS
10671 Racine St.
Commerce City, CO 80022
Phone No.: 303-955-2412
www.missionamps.com
sales@missionamps.com

Bruce Collins founded Mission Amps in 1996. Not only do they produce their line of Aurora amps, but they are a repair shop with a full repair department, and they stock a wide variety of parts for tube amplifiers. They also produce tweed amp kits that the user puts together. The Aurora line of amps has a reminiscent look of mid-1950s Gibson GA-style amps but don't be fooled by that. They are tweaked like a high gain, vintage AC50 combined with a tweed Bassman and a little Plexi thrown in on top of that. All chassis come with a non-gain, signal-boosting foot switch and are available in reverb or non-reverb versions with or without an extra gain stage. For more information, visit Mission Amps' website or contact them directly.

ELECTRIC TUBE AMPLIFIERS

The Aurora model is available as the **MA-10 CB** (direct price is $999) with 8-10W output, 1-12 in. Jensen speaker, 6K6 power tubes, and a 5Y3 rectifier, the **MA-18 FB** (direct price is $1,049) with 16-18W output, 1-12 in. speaker, 6V6 power tubes, and a GZ34 rectifier, and the **MA-28 CB/FB** (direct price is $1,155) with 24-28W output, 1-12 in. Jensen or Mojo speaker, 6L6 power tubes, and a GZ34 rectifier. The Aurora Reverb models are available as the **MA-22R FB** (direct price is $1,549) with 18-22W, 1-12 in. Mojo speaker, 6V6 power tubes, and a GZ30 rectifier, the **MA-35R FB** (direct price is $1,645) with 32-36W, 1-12 in. Mojo speaker, 6L6 power tubes, and a GZ34 rectifier, the **MA-50R FB** (direct price is $1,730) with 42-50W, 1-12 in. Mojo speaker, 6L6 power tubes, and a GZ34 rectifier.

MITCHELL

Amplifiers previously produced in the U.S. during the late 1970s and early 1980s.

Mitchell amps are very similar to Mesa/Boogie amps of the same era (late 1970s and early 1980s) with their wicker style grille and other cosmetics. The most popular model appears to be the Pro-100 available in a head-unit and 1-12 in. speaker combo. This amp features a tube chassis and other standard features. Many reviews indicate that these amps are well-built and were known as poor man's Mesa/Boogies at the time. Any further information on Mitchell can be submitted directly to Blue Book Publications.

MOJAVE AMP WORKS

Amplifiers currently produced in Apple Valley, CA since 2002.

CONTACT INFORMATION
MOJAVE AMP WORKS
PO Box 1089
Apple Valley, CA 92307
Phone No.: 760-515-2578
www.mojaveampworks.com
info@mojaveampworks.com

Victor Mason founded Mojave Amp Works in 2002. Mojave produces quality tube amplifiers based mainly on popular British designs as well as speaker cabinets. Peter Frampton endorses the Mojave Coyote. For more information visit Mojave's website or contact them directly.

ELECTRIC TUBE AMPLIFIERS

The **Coyote** features 12W output power, 2 X EL84 power tubes, and a power dampening switch. It is available as a head-unit (MSR $2,100), 1-12 in. speaker combo (MSR $2,250 with a 30W Ceramic speaker, MSR $2,515 with a 15W Blue AlNiCo speaker), or 2-12 in. speaker combo (MSR $2,570 with 30W Ceramic speakers, MSR $2,995 with 15W Blue AlNiCo speakers, and $2,789 for one of each speaker). The **Sidewinder** features 30W output power, 4 X EL84 power tubes, and is basically a larger version of the Coyote. It is available as a head-unit (MSR $2,400), 1-12 in. speaker combo (MSR $2,510 with a 30W Ceramic speaker), or 2-12 in. speaker combo (MSR $2,730 with 30W Ceramic speakers, MSR $3,214 with 15W Blue AlNiCo speakers, and $2,995 for one of each speaker). The **Plexi 45** is based on the original Marshall JTM-45 chassis with Mojave's own modifications including either 6L6 or EL34 power tubes, a power dampening control, and line out with level. It is available as a head-unit (MSR $2,795), or 2-12 in. speaker combo (disc., last MSR was $3,125 with 30W Ceramic speakers, disc., last MSR was $3,285 with one 15W Blue AlNiCo and one 30W Ceramic speaker. The **Scorpion** features 50W output with 2 X EL34 power tubes, and a unique set of tone controls. It is available as a head-unit only (MSR $2,750). The **Peacemaker** features 100W output with 4 X EL34 power tubes, and is a larger version of the Scorpion. It is available as a head-unit only (MSR $3,125). 2-12 in. and 4-12 in. speaker cabinets are also available.

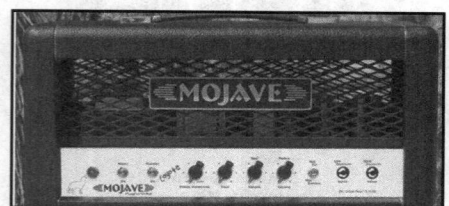

Coyote Head
courtesy Mojave Amp Works

Peacemaker Head
courtesy Mojave Amp Works

Plexi 45 Head
courtesy Mojave Amp Works

MONTGOMERY WARD

See Airline.

MOONEYES

Amplifiers previously produced overseas during the early 2000s. Distributed by Lace Music Products of Huntington Beach, CA.

Mooneyes amplifiers were developed after Dean Moon and his hot-rod automotive industry collaborated with Lace Music Products. Dean started a small speed shop in Santa Fe Springs, CA, and his logo is featured on several products around the world. Lace produced a Mooneyes small guitar amplifier in the early 2000s that was covered in yellow vinyl. Currently, the only product offered by Mooneyes/Lace is a yellow Mooneyes guitar cable. Lace has also produced amps under the names Lace and Rat Fink. For more information on Mooneyes, visit Lace's website or contact them directly.

CONTACT INFORMATION
MOONEYES
Distributed by Lace Music Products
5561 Engineer Drive
Huntington Beach, CA 92649
Phone No.: 714-898-2776
Fax No.: 714-893-1045
www.lacemusic.com
info@lacemusic.com

MOSRITE

Amplifiers previously produced in the mid- to late 1960s. Distributed by Mosrite in Bakersfield, CA.

After the success of Mosrite guitars during the 1960s, Mosrite Electronics introduced a line of solid-state amplifiers to complement the guitars. These amps featured a full solid-state chassis with transistors, reverb, tremolo, Mosrite's Fuzzrite, 15 in. Jensen or Altec Lansing speakers, and were covered in scuff-resistant black Tolex. Like all solid-state amps of this era, they are taller in design than they are wider. There were three models available with each having the same chassis/controls but different wattages and speaker configurations. Very few of these were probably produced, and they don't show up in the used marketplace very often.

MOTION SOUND

Amplifiers currently produced in Salt Lake City, UT, since 1994.

Motion Sound was established in 1994 by three people, one an electronics engineer and musician, one a mechanical engineer and the other a financial guy. John H. Fischer is the current president. At the 1995 NAMM show, they introduced the Pro-3 a rotating hybrid amplifier. This unit could produce the large sound of big rotating systems (such as a Leslie) in a much smaller model. Later on they started making products for guitars. In 2001, John Johnson joined the team to help market. Currently Motion Sound has these rotating horn units for all types of applications. For more information, visit Motion Sound's website or contact them directly.

CONTACT INFORMATION
MOTION SOUND
PO Box 25111
Salt Lake City, UT 84125
www.msamps.com
support@msamps.com

HYBRID AMPLIFIERS

Motion Sound built their foundation on rotating horn cabinets, built mainly as speaker cabinets. Later on they started building Keyboard amplifiers, and now they have entered the acoustic and electric guitar market. The Pro-3, which was their first amp, is still offered but as the **Pro-3T** model. Motion Sound compares it to the Leslie 147. All amps have a 12AX7 tube in the preamp circuit with a solid-state power amp. In 2006, the **Pro-3X** was introduced, which is a portable rotary horn amp designed for organ use.

The guitar amps offered by Motion Sound are the **AR-112**, which is a 100W electric rotary guitar amp with a 12 in. speaker and has reverb. The **SR-112** is a speaker cabinet that can be hooked up to the AR-112 or can be powered by any other amplifier as well. It features a 12 in. speaker that can handle 150W, and full rotary speed control of the unit. The **AG-110H** is an electric acoustic amplifier with a unique rotary speaker that can produce sound in several directions. The **SRV-212** is a speaker cabinet only with 2-12 in. Eminence speakers that provides 360 degrees of sound.

MOUNTAIN

Amplifiers previously produced in Vancouver, British Columbia, Canada, Antioch, CA, and Nevada between the 1990s and 2000s.

Mountain produced a line of portable 9V battery AC/DC operated amplifiers. These were small combo models with a single volume control, 6.5 in. speaker, and dimensions of 8.5 in. wide, 9.25 in. tall, and 5 in. deep. The cabinets were available in various color coverings including Ferrari Red, Creme, Lake Placid Blue, Desert Zolotone, and hand-crafted wood cabinets in Ribbon Mahogany, Pine, solid Bolivian Rosewood, Figured Walnut, Green Flame maple, Red Trans, Flame maple, and Bolivian rosewood with a maple front. The grille covering features a large MTN metal logo spanning the circle opening. These amps were designed for electric guitar use, but they also become increasingly popular for acoustic guitarists and harmonicas. Mountain's last model, a figured maple cabinet amp was last offered for $199.

courtesy S.P. Fjestad

MULTIVOX

Amplifiers previously produced in New York City, NY and Hauppauge, NY, between the late 1940s and 1984.

The Multivox company was started in the late 1940s by Peter Sorkin Music to manufacture amplifiers as a subsidiary to the company. The company produced amplifiers for many years until around 1984. They also produced some guitars and other products under the same name. A lot of products were produced in the same factory Multivox was in, just under different names, specifically Strad-O-Lin and Premier. The Multivox company produced many patents

MSR/NOTES	100%	EXCELLENT	AVERAGE	LAST MSR

as far as amplifiers, which included the "Organ-Tone Tremolo" circuit. In the 1960s Multivox broke away from the Sorkin company and in 1970 when Sorkin closed down, Multivox kept going. They produced amplifiers throughout the 1970s and stopped producing products in 1984. Further information on Multivox amplifiers can be submitted directly to Blue Book Publications.

AMPLIFIERS

Multivox started producing tube amplifiers in the late 1940s and by the time the company closed its doors in 1984, they were producing mostly solid-state amplifiers. Needless to say there are a lot of models and information between those 35 years. Most of the models that show up on today's market are the models that were built in the 1970s and 1980s. These amps can usually be landed in the range of $50 to $150 in excellent shape. These amps will typically show up in pawn shops and such for dirt cheap prices.

Early models include the Model 50 and Model 110. These two amps were introduced around 1948 and had an 8 in. and 10 in. speaker respectively. The Premier series was first introduced in the late 1940s with the models Premier 66 (17W, 1-12 in. speaker, tremolo), Premier 88, and the Premier 120 (20W, 1-12 in. speaker). From then on pretty much all Multivox amps were of the Premier series. More elaborate models that include higher-wattages, dual speakers, tremolo, etc, will add a premium over more basic models.

MUSICLORD

Amplifiers and speaker cabinets currently produced in the Pacific Northwest since 1984.

MusicLord was started in 1984 by Glen Huttenlocker and he is still president today. They produce amplifiers and speaker cabinets in a variety of colored coverings. MusicLord has expanded steadily since their birth in 1984 and their products are now distributed across the world. Alice in Chains, Queensryche, Tim Bachman, Randy Hansen, and Howard Leese of Paul Rodgers Band are just a few of the artists that use/have used MusicLord products. For more information visit MusicLord's website or contact them directly.

CONTACT INFORMATION
MUSICLORD
www.musiclord.com
glen@musiclord.com

MUSIC MAN

Amplifiers previously produced in Fullerton, CA, between 1972 and 1984.

The Music Man company was formed in March of 1972 by two ex-Fender executives, Tom Walker and Forrest White. They first started to produce amplifiers keeping Fender ideas in mind. Music Man produced some of the first hybrid amplifiers, but they are backwards to most modern design. Walker and White built their amplifiers with a solid-state preamp section (sometimes a single tube was used) and the power section was composed of tubes. The amps were very successful early and they decided to produce guitars as well. In 1976, they released their first guitar, designed and built by Leo Fender. After abiding by a ten year "no compete" clause in the sale of Fender in 1965, Music Man produced guitars up until 1979. Music Man made amplifiers throughout the 1970s and kept producing up until circa 1984. Ernie Ball bought out Music Man in 1984 and they stopped producing amplifiers around this time, but continued on with guitar production. For more information on Music Man guitars and Ernie Ball/Music Man guitars refer to the *Blue Book of Electric Guitars*.

OVERVIEW AND MODEL NOMENCLATURE

Identifying Music Man amplifiers is relatively easy because of their easy naming/numbering system and the model name/number was on the lower right corner of the speaker grille. Music Man also produced few designs in many configurations and models are pretty consistent over their 13 year history. All amps in this section were researched through old catalogs from 1975, 1980, 1982, and 1984, and the breakdown between model years is strictly based on assumption. From our research we found that the Sixty Five and One Thirty Series were produced circa 1972 through 1978, the Seventy Five, One Hundred, and One Fifty were produced 1978 through 1984, and the Fifty Series was produced between 1981 and 1984. Any further information on model year availability can be submitted directly to Blue Book Publications. Music Man amps are also becoming increasingly popular because of their unique hybrid design and the fact they were designed by all ex-Fender employees.

Music Man Numbering/Naming System:

All Music Man amps are named after their respective configuration. There are six general series that amps fall into and these are all named after the wattage: Fifty, Sixty Five, Seventy Five, One Hunderd, One Thirty, and One Fifty. A series of bass amps was also produced with a B suffix. Combo units were then numbered with their speaker configuration (112, 210, 212, 410, etc.). Head units had only the wattage listed. In the late 1970s, Music Man introduced their distortion and phasor amps. These were designated with an RD for reverb and distortion or an RP for reverb and phasor. Examples: 210 Seventy Five is a 75W combo amp with 2-10 in. speakers, the 410 HD One Thirty is a 130W amp with 4-10 in. speakers, the 115RP One Hundred is a 100W amp with 1-15 in. speaker and reverb and phasor effects.

ELECTRIC AMPLIFIERS: FIFTY SERIES

RD FIFTY HEAD – 50W, head-unit guitar configuration, tube chassis, preamp: 1 X 7025, power: 2 X 6L6, two channels, reverb, front black control panel, single input, eight knobs (Ch. 1: v, t, b, Ch. 2: v, t, b, g, r), bright/normal switch, channel switch, black covering, silver grille, mfg. circa 1981-83.

| N/A | $500 - 600 | $300 - 400 | |

MSR/NOTES	100%	EXCELLENT	AVERAGE	LAST MSR

* **RD 110 Fifty** – similar to the RD Fifty Head, except in combo configuration with 1-10 in. speaker, mfg. circa 1981-83.

N/A $600 - 750 $400 - 450

* **RD 112 Fifty** – similar to the RD Fifty Head, except in combo configuration with 1-12 in. speaker, mfg. circa 1981-83.

courtesy John Beeson/The Music Shoppe

courtesy John Beeson/The Music Shoppe

N/A $700 - 850 $450 - 550

ELECTRIC AMPLIFIERS: SIXTY FIVE SERIES

SIXTY FIVE HEAD – 65W, head-unit bass, organ, or piano configuration, hybrid chassis, preamp: 1 X 7025 and solid-state, power: 2 X 6L6 or 2 X 6CA7, two channels, front black control panel, four inputs, nine knobs (Ch. 1: v, t, m, b, Ch. 2: v, t, m, b, g), two bright switches, low freq. turnover switch, black covering, silver grille, 34 lbs., mfg. circa 1972-78.

N/A $450 - 550 $250 - 300

SIXTY FIVE HEAD REVERB – 65W, head-unit guitar configuration, hybrid chassis, preamp: 1 X 7025 and solid-state, power: 2 X 6L6 or 2 X 6CA7, two channels, reverb, tremolo, front black control panel, four inputs, 11 knobs (Ch. 1: v, t, b, Ch. 2: v, t, m, b, r, i, s, MV), bright switch, deep switch, black covering, silver grille, 40 lbs., mfg. circa 1972-78.

N/A $500 - 650 $300 - 400

* **112 Sixty Five** – similar to the Sixty Five Head Reverb, except in combo configuration with 1-12 in. speaker, 24.5 in. wide, 17 in. tall, 10.5 in. deep, 50 lbs., mfg. circa 1972-78.

N/A $600 - 750 $325 - 400

* **115 Sixty Five** – similar to the Sixty Five Head Reverb, except in combo configuration with 1-15 in. speaker, 24.5 in. side, 20.5 in. tall, 11 in. deep, 59 lbs., mfg. circa 1972-78.

N/A $600 - 750 $325 - 400

* **210 Sixty Five** – similar to the Sixty Five Head Reverb, except in combo configuration with 2-10 in. speakers, 24.5 in. wide, 15 in. tall, 10.5 in. deep, 53 lbs., mfg. circa 1972-78.

N/A $650 - 800 $350 - 425

* **212 Sixty Five** – similar to the Sixty Five Head Reverb, except in combo configuration with 2-12 in. speakers, two bright switches, and an additional mid-control in Ch. 1 for a total of 12 knobs, 26.5 in. wide, 19.5 in. tall, 11 in. deep, 60 lbs., mfg. circa 1972-78.

N/A $650 - 800 $350 - 425

* **410 Sixty Five** – similar to the Sixty Five Head Reverb, except in combo configuration with 4-10 in. speakers, 24.5 in. wide, 25.5 in. tall, 11 in. deep, 72 lbs., mfg. circa 1972-78.

N/A $650 - 800 $350 - 425

112 RD SIXTY FIVE – 65W, 1-12 in. speaker, guitar combo, hybrid chassis, preamp: solid-state, power: 2 X 6L6 or 2 X 6CA7, two channels, distortion, reverb, front black control panel, four inputs, eight knobs (g, MV, footswitch g, footswitch v, t, m, b, r), bright switch, deep switch, black covering, silver grille, 22.625 in. wide, 17 in. tall, 10.5 in. deep, 47 lbs., mfg. circa 1978-1984.

N/A $650 - 800 $350 - 425

112 RP SIXTY FIVE – 65W, 1-12 in. speaker, guitar combo, hybrid chassis, preamp: solid-state, power: 2 X 6L6 or 2 X 6CA7, single channel, phasor, reverb, front black control panel, two inputs, eight knobs (g, t, m, b, r, phasor i, phasor s, MV), bright switch, deep switch, black covering, silver grille, 22.625 in. wide, 17 in. tall, 10.5 in. deep, 47 lbs., mfg. circa 1978-1984.

N/A $650 - 800 $350 - 425

ELECTRIC AMPLIFIERS: SEVENTY FIVE SERIES

75 (SEVENTY FIVE HEAD) – 75W, head-unit bass, organ, or piano configuration, hybrid chassis, preamp: solid-state, power: 2 X 6L6, two channels, front black control panel, four inputs, nine knobs (Ch. 1: v, t, m, b, Ch. 2: v, t, m, b, g), two bright switches, low freq. turnover switch, black covering, silver grille, 22.7 in. wide, 8.5 in. tall, 10 in. deep, 34 lbs., mfg. circa 1978-1983.

N/A $400 - 500 $200 - 250

MSR/NOTES	100%	EXCELLENT	AVERAGE	LAST MSR

75R (SEVENTY FIVE HEAD REVERB) – 75W, head-unit guitar configuration, hybrid chassis, preamp: solid-state, power: 2 X 6L6, two channels, reverb, tremolo, front black control panel, four inputs, 11 knobs (Ch. 1: v, t, b, Ch. 2: v, t, m, b, r, i, s, MV), bright switch, deep switch, black covering, silver grille, 24.5 in. wide, 11 in. tall, 10 in. deep, 40 lbs., mfg. circa 1973-1981.

| | N/A | $450 - 575 | $225 - 275 | |

* **112 Seventy Five** – similar to the 75R (Seventy Five Head Reverb), except in combo configuration with 1-12 in. speaker, 24.5 in. wide, 17 in. tall, 10.5 in. deep, 50 lbs., mfg. circa 1978-1983.

| | N/A | $650 - 800 | $325 - 400 | |

* **210 Seventy Five** – similar to the 75R (Seventy Five Head Reverb), except in combo configuration with 2-10 in. speakers, 24.5 in. wide, 15 in. tall, 10.5 in. deep, 53 lbs., mfg. circa 1978-1983.

| | N/A | $650 - 800 | $325 - 400 | |

* **212 Seventy Five** – similar to the 75R (Seventy Five Head Reverb), except in combo configuration with 2-12 in. speakers, two bright switches, and an additional mid-control in Ch. 1 for a total of 12 knobs, 26.5 in. wide, 19.5 in. tall, 11 in. deep, 60 lbs., mfg. circa 1978-1983.

| | N/A | $700 - 850 | $475 - 575 | |

* **410 Seventy Five** – similar to the 75R (Seventy Five Head Reverb), except in combo configuration with 4-10 in. speakers, 24.5 in. wide, 25.5 in. tall, 11 in. deep, 72 lbs., mfg. circa 1978-1983.

| | N/A | $800 - 950 | $500 - 600 | |

ELECTRIC AMPLIFIERS: ONE HUNDRED SERIES

100 RD ONE HUNDRED HEAD – 100W, head unit guitar configuration, hybrid chassis, preamp: solid-state, power: 2 X 6L6 or 2 X 6CA7, two channels, distortion, reverb, front black control panel, four inputs, eight knobs (g, MV, footswitch g, footswitch v, t, m, b, r), bright switch, deep switch, black covering, silver grille, 22.625 in. wide, 8.5 in. tall, 8.5 in. deep, 38 lbs., mfg. circa 1978-1983.

| | N/A | $500 - 600 | $275 - 325 | |

* **112 RD One Hundred (EVM)** – similar to the RD 100 Head, except in combo configuration with 1-12 in. regular or Electro-Voice EVM speaker, 22.625 in. wide, 17 in. tall, 10.5 in. deep, 57 lbs., mfg. circa 1978-1984.

| | N/A | $650 - 800 | $350 - 425 | |

* **115 RD One Hundred (EVM)** – similar to the RD 100 One Hundred Head, except in combo configuration with 1-15 in. regular or Electro-Voice EVM speaker, 22.625 in. wide, 19.75 in. tall, 10.5 in. deep, 72 lbs., mfg. circa 1978-1983.

| | N/A | $700 - 900 | $450 - 550 | |

* **210 RD One Hundred** – similar to the RD 100 One Hundred Head, except in combo configuration with 2-10 in. speakers, 22.625 in. wide, 15.125 in. tall, 10.5 in. deep, 55 lbs., mfg. circa 1978-1983.

| | N/A | $700 - 900 | $450 - 550 | |

100 RP ONE HUNDRED HEAD – 100W, head unit guitar configuration, hybrid chassis, preamp: solid-state, power: 2 X 6L6 or 2 X 6CA7, single channel, phasor, reverb, front black control panel, two inputs, eight knobs (g, t, m, b, r, phasor i, phasor s, MV), bright switch, deep switch, black covering, silver grille, 22.625 in. wide, 8.5 in. tall, 8.5 in. deep, 37 lbs., mfg. circa 1978-1983.

| | N/A | $450 - 550 | $275 - 325 | |

* **112 RP One Hundred (EVM)** – similar to the RP 100 Head, except in combo configuration with 1-12 in. regular or Electro-Voice EVM speaker, 22.625 in. wide, 17 in. tall, 10.5 in. deep, 57 lbs., mfg. circa 1978-1984.

| | N/A | $600 - 750 | $350 - 425 | |

* **115 RP One Hundred (EVM)** – similar to the RP 100 One Hundred Head, except in combo configuration with 1-15 in. regular or Electro-Voice EVM speaker, 22.625 in. wide, 19.75 in. tall, 10.5 in. deep, 67 lbs., mfg. circa 1978-1984.

| | N/A | $650 - 800 | $350 - 425 | |

* **210 RP One Hundred** – similar to the RP 100 One Hundred Head, except in combo configuration with 2-10 in. speakers, 22.625 in. wide, 15.125 in. tall, 10.5 in. deep, 55 lbs., mfg. circa 1978-1983.

| | N/A | $650 - 800 | $350 - 425 | |

ELECTRIC AMPLIFIERS: ONE THIRTY SERIES

HD-130 (ONE THIRTY HEAD) – 130W, head-unit bass, organ, or piano configuration, hybrid chassis, preamp: 1 X 7025 and solid-state, power: 4 X 6CA7, two channels, front black control panel, four inputs, nine knobs (Ch. 1: v, t, m, b, Ch. 2: v, t, m, b, g), two bright switches, low freq. turnover switch, black covering, silver grille, 22.75 in. wide, 8.5 in. tall, 10 in. deep, 38 lbs., mfg. circa 1972-78.

| | N/A | $500 - 600 | $300 - 400 | |

HD-130R (ONE THIRTY HEAD REVERB) – 130W, head-unit guitar configuration, hybrid chassis, preamp: 1 X 7025 and solid-state, power: 4 X 6CA7, two channels, reverb, tremolo, front black control panel, four inputs, 11 knobs (Ch. 1: v, t, b, Ch. 2: v, t, m, b, r, i, s, MV), bright switch, deep switch, power switch, rear panel: ground switch, standby switch, two footswitch jacks (reverb, tremolo), two speaker jacks, black covering, silver grille, 24.5 in. wide, 11 in. tall, 10 in. deep, 45 lbs., mfg. circa 1972-78.

| | N/A | $550 - 700 | $275 - 325 | |

MSR/NOTES	100%	EXCELLENT	AVERAGE	LAST MSR

* **210 HD One Thirty** – similar to the HD-130R One Thirty Head Reverb, except in combo configuration with 2-10 in. speakers, 24.5 in. wide, 15 in. tall, 10.5 in. deep, 57 lbs., mfg. circa 1972-78.

	N/A	$650 - 800	$400 - 475	

* **212 HD One Thirty** – similar to the HD-130R One Thirty Head Reverb, except in combo configuration with 2-12 in. speakers, two bright switches, and an additional mid-control in Ch. 1 for a total of 12 knobs, 26.5 in. wide, 19.5 in. tall, 11 in. deep, 72 lbs., mfg. circa 1972-78.

	N/A	$700 - 900	$425 - 500	

* **410 HD One Thirty** – similar to the HD-130R One Thirty Head Reverb, except in combo configuration with 4-10 in. speakers, 24.5 in. wide, 25.5 in. tall, 11 in. deep, 75 lbs., mfg. circa 1972-78.

	N/A	$800 - 1,000	$550 - 650	

ELECTRIC AMPLIFIERS: ONE FIFTY SERIES

HD 150 (ONE FIFTY HEAD) – 150W, head-unit bass, organ, or piano configuration, hybrid chassis, preamp: solid-state, power: 4 X 6L6, two channels, front black control panel, four inputs, nine knobs (Ch. 1: v, t, m, b, Ch. 2: v, t, m, b, g), two bright switches, low freq. turnover switch, black covering, silver grille, 22.75 in. wide, 8.5 in. tall, 10 in. deep, 40 lbs., mfg. circa 1978-1983.

	N/A	$500 - 650	$250 - 300	

HD 150R (ONE FIFTY HEAD REVERB) – 150W, head-unit guitar configuration, hybrid chassis, preamp: solid-state, power: 4 X 6L6, two channels, reverb, tremolo, front black control panel, four inputs, 11 knobs (Ch. 1: v, t, b, Ch. 2: v, t, m, b, r, i, s, MV), bright switch, deep switch, black covering, silver grille, 24.5 in. wide, 11 in. tall, 10 in. deep, 40 lbs., mfg. circa 1978-1983.

	N/A	$550 - 700	$275 - 325	

* **115 HD One Fifty (EVM)** – similar to the HD 150R (One Fifty Head Reverb), except in combo configuration with 1-15 in. Electro-Voice EVM speaker, 24.5 in. wide, 20.5 in. tall, 11 in. deep, 76 lbs., mfg. circa 1978-1983.

	N/A	$650 - 775	$350 - 425	

* **210 HD One Fifty** – similar to the HD 150R (One Fifty Head Reverb), except in combo configuration with 2-10 in. speakers, 24.5 in. wide, 15 in. tall, 10.5 in. deep, 57 lbs., mfg. circa 1978-1983.

	N/A	$650 - 775	$350 - 425	

* **212 HD One Fifty (EVM)** – similar to the HD 150R (One Fifty Head Reverb), except in combo configuration with 2-12 in. regular or Electro-Voice EVM speakers, two bright switches, and an additional mid-control in Ch. 1 for a total of 12 knobs, 26.5 in. wide, 19.5 in. tall, 11 in. deep, 72 lbs. (92 lbs. with EVM speakers), mfg. circa 1978-1983.

	N/A	$700 - 850	$500 - 575	

* **410 HD One Fifty** – similar to the HD 150R (One Fifty Head Reverb), except in combo configuration with 4-10 in. speakers, 24.5 in. wide, 25.5 in. tall, 11 in. deep, 75 lbs., mfg. circa 1978-1983.

	N/A	$850 - 1,000	$600 - 700	

BASS AMPLIFIERS: BASS B SERIES

Even though Music Man produced heads that were designed for bass, organ, and piano use (75, HD-130, HD-150, RD100, etc.), they produced a line of amps in the early 1980s that were specifically designed for bass guitars called the B Series.

100 B HEAD – 100W, head-unit bass configuration, hybrid chassis, preamp: solid-state, power: 4 X 6L6, single channel, front black control panel, two inputs, 11 knobs, black covering, silver grille, mfg. circa 1981-83.

	N/A	$500 - 600	$275 - 325	

120 B HEAD – 80W, head-unit bass configuration, solid-state chassis, single channel, front black control panel, single inputs, eight knobs, black covering, silver grille, mfg. circa 1981-83.

	N/A	$450 - 550	$225 - 275	

* **112 B Combo** – similar to the 120 B Head, except in combo configuration with 1-12 in. speaker and a slanted front cabinet, mfg. circa 1981-83.

	N/A	$600 - 750	$400 - 500	

* **115 B Combo** – similar to the 120 B Head, except in combo configuration with 1-15 in. speaker and a slanted front cabinet, mfg. circa 1981-83.

	N/A	$700 - 850	$400 - 500	

SPEAKER CABINETS

Speaker cabinets were designed for use with specific models, but some cabinets can be used with other heads. For cabinets with the bottom-ported opening, the cabinet can be turned upside down and the grille switched to make it a top-ported cabinet. This was often used when two of the same cabinets were used together with one bottom-ported and top-ported.

115 RH SIXTY FIVE – 65W, 1-15 in. speaker, 8 ohm impedance, bottom ported cabinet (large opening below speaker grille for sound to escape), black covering, silver grille, 27.5 in. wide, 27.5 in. tall, 13.25 in. deep, 58 lbs., mfg. circa 1972-78.

	N/A	$200 - 250	$120 - 150	

This model was designed for use with Sixty Five Series models.

MSR/NOTES	100%	EXCELLENT	AVERAGE	LAST MSR

115 RH SEVENTY FIVE – 75W, 1-15 in. speaker, 8 ohm impedance, bottom ported cabinet (large opening below speaker grille for sound to escape), black covering, silver grille, 27.375 in. wide, 27.625 in. tall, 13 in. deep, 60 lbs., mfg. circa 1978-1981.

	N/A	$200 - 250	$120 - 150	

This model was designed for use with Seventy Five Series models.

115 RH ONE FIFTY EVM – 150W, 1-15 in. Electro-Voice speaker, 8 ohm impedance, bottom ported cabinet (large opening below speaker grille for sound to escape), black covering, silver grille, 27.375 in. wide, 27.625 in. tall, 13 in. deep, 70 lbs., mfg. circa 1978-1983.

	N/A	$250 - 300	$150 - 200	

This model was designed for use with One Fifty Series models.

118 RH ONE FIFTY EVM – 150W, 1-18 in. Electro-Voice speaker, 8 ohm impedance, bottom ported cabinet (large opening below speaker grille for sound to escape), black covering, silver grille, 27.375 in. wide, 31.875 in. tall, 16.5 in. deep, 94 lbs., mfg. circa 1978-1983.

	N/A	$300 - 350	$175 - 225	

This model was designed for use with One Fifty Series models.

210 RH ONE FIFTY (EVM) – 150W, 2-10 in. regular or Electro-Voice speakers, 4 ohm impedance, bottom ported cabinet (large opening below speaker grille for sound to escape), black covering, silver grille, 26.375 in. wide, 22.375 in. tall, 13 in. deep, 52 lbs., mfg. circa 1978-1983.

	N/A	$250 - 300	$150 - 200	

This model was designed for use with One Fifty Series models.

212 RH ONE THIRTY – 130W, 2-12 in. speakers, 4 ohm impedance, bottom ported cabinet (large opening below speaker grille for sound to escape), black covering, silver grille, 27.5 in. wide, 27.5 in. tall, 13.25 in. deep, 68 lbs., mfg. circa 1972-78.

	N/A	$275 - 325	$165 - 215	

This model was designed for use with One Thirty Series models.

212 RH ONE FIFTY (EVM) – 150W, 2-12 in. regular or Electro-Voice speakers, 4 ohm impedance, bottom ported cabinet (large opening below speaker grille for sound to escape), black covering, silver grille, 27.375 in. wide, 27.375 in. tall, 13 in. deep, 69 lbs. (89 lbs. with Electro-Voice speakers), mfg. circa 1978-1983.

	N/A	$300 - 350	$175 - 225	

This model was designed for use with One Fifty Series models.

412 B – 130W, 4-12 in. speakers, 8 ohm impedance, sealed cabinetblack covering, silver grille, 27.5 in. wide, 27.5 in. tall, 16.5 in. deep, 82 lbs., mfg. circa 1978-1983.

	N/A	$325 - 450	$250 - 300	

This model was designed for use with bass, organ, and piano application heads.

412 GS – 130W, 4-12 in. speakers, 8 ohm impedance, sealed cabinetblack covering, silver grille, 27.5 in. wide, 27.5 in. tall, 13.25 in. deep, 78 lbs., mfg. circa 1972-1983.

	N/A	$425 - 500	$275 - 325	

This model was designed for use with guitar application heads.

N SECTION
NADY

Amplifiers, speaker cabinets, and other audio products currently produced since 1976.

John Nady founded Nady Systems in 1996 as a wireless microphone manufacturer and designer. As one of the first wireless microphone producers in the market, Nady gained much notoriety in the music and pro audio industry during the late 1970s and 1980s, and by 1987, they had introduced the 101/201 Series that was available to the general public. In 1999, Nady introduced a full professional audio line including guitar amplifiers and speaker cabinets. Nady's guitar amp products include the **GTH-100** tube head with the **GAC-412** speaker cabinet, the **GTA-1260** combo tube amp, and the **WGA-15** wireless guitar amp. For more information, visit Nady's website or contact them directly.

CONTACT INFORMATION
NADY
870 Harbour Way South
Richmond, CA 94804
Phone No.: 510-652-2411
Fax No.: 510-652-5075
www.nady.com
support@nady.com

NARB

Amplifiers previously produced in England by Marshall during the mid-1970s. Distributed and sold through Sound City in London, England.

Narb was a trademark used on a line of amplifiers that Marshall produced for Sound City in Charing Cross Road, London. Sound City wanted to sell Marshall amps in the 1970s, but due to Marshall's exclusive distribution contract with Rose-Morris, they had to call the amps something other than Marshall. Narb, along with CMI, Park, and Kitchen Marshall were all brands Marshall produced for other dealers/distributors to not violate their Rose-Morris contract. The Narb name is derived from Ken Bran who was Jim Marshall's close associate for many years. First, they decided to use Bran, but they did not want to be confused with a breakfast cereal. Eventually they ended up spelling Ken's last name backwards and came up with Narb. Another theory that exists for Marshall introducing Narb amplifiers was to use up some old components around. However, there were less than fifty of these amps produced and they are extremely rare. History courtesy Michael Doyle, *The History of Marshall*.

MSR/NOTES	100%	EXCELLENT	AVERAGE	LAST MSR

ELECTRIC TUBE AMPLIFIERS

Since Narb amps were simply Marshalls with different logos, they are usually exact clones of a Marshall amp. They made a handful of amp heads, and a speaker cabinet with 4-12 in. speakers. Two examples had serial numbers of 0008 and 0011. Both of these models are 100W heads with tremolo, which is probably the same as the Model 1959T Marshall. Needless to say, pricing in the vintage market is very hard to determine because of rarity. The *Blue Book of Guitar Amplifiers* strongly suggests getting multiple opinions when either selling or buying a Narb.

100W TREMOLO – 100W, guitar head unit, eight-tube chassis, preamp: 4 X ECC83, power: 4 X EL34, solid-state rectifier, two channels, tremolo, front silver control panel, four inputs, eight black knobs (p, b, m, t, v1, v2, s, i), black covering, white piping, mfg. mid-1970s.

courtesy solidbodyguitar.com, Inc.   courtesy solidbodyguitar.com, Inc.

N/A   N/A   N/A

NATIONAL

Amplifiers previously produced in Chicago, IL under the company Valco between the late 1940s and early 1970s.

The National name goes way back to the early 1920s, when John and Rudy Dopyera started producing banjos in Southern California. Guitarist George Beauchamp approached the company with an idea on how to solve the lack of volume in the instruments of the Vaudevill Orchestra. His idea was to place an aluminum resonator in a guitar body to amplify the sound. With this idea, John Dopyera and four brothers formed National in 1925. This was the birth of possibly the greatest resonator guitar company.

National ran into financial hardship because of the Depression in the early 1930s. Louis Dopyera owned more than 50% of Dobro and bought out National in the early 1930s. He merged the two companies together and called it National-Dobro. In 1936, the company moved to Chicago, IL, where many companies were mass producing instruments (Kay, Harmony, etc.). Victor Smith, Al Frost, and Louis came together in 1943 to change the name of the company to VALCO (The initials of their three first names). Valco worked on war materials during WWII, and returned to start producing instruments afterwards.

Amplifiers first appeared in the 1930s and had a strikingly similar appearance to the acousic resonator instruments

MSR/NOTES	100%	EXCELLENT	AVERAGE	LAST MSR

that they also produced. Some of these amps are known as "chicken feet." In the early 1940s, National began to produce amps with their National badge as the front grille. They also had some models with elaborate designs on the grille, such as the moon and stars.

After the war, Valco began producing amplifiers under the name National. Valco also produced amplifiers for other companies including Super, Oahu, Gretsch and Airline. Most of these amps were built between the late 1940s and the 1960s, and there is plenty of crossover in designs between all the brands.

In 1969 or 1970, Valco went bankrupt and the assests were auctioned off. The rights to the National trademark were bought by Strum & Drum in Chicago, IL. However, Strum & Drum didn't have a factory to produce National instruments, so they took the Norma brand guitars and amplifiers and applied the National logo to some of them. Naturally, this did not last long and all National-branded amplifiers were gone by the early 1970s. In 1988, Don Young and McGregor Gaines revived the National trademark under National Reso-Phonic Guitars but they focus strictly on resonator guitars. Early company history courtesy Bob Brozeman, *The History And Artistry Of National Resonator Instruments*.

ELECTRIC TUBE AMPLIFIERS: 1940S/1950S MODELS

National never really had a designated series of amplifiers, so these amps are broken into their respective eras. Early models featured TV-style tweed coverings and rear or side-mounted control panels.

NATIONAL DOBRO 100 – 40W, 1-12 in. speaker, all tube chassis, single channel, three inputs, three knobs, brown wood covering, National badge style grille, mfg. 1940s.

  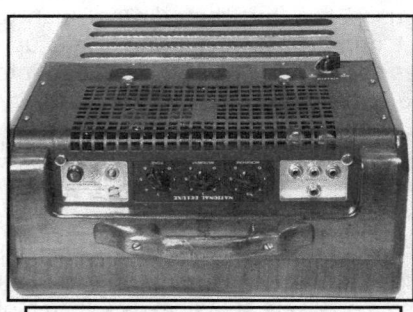

courtesy Blue Book Archives   courtesy Blue Book Archives   courtesy Blue Book Archives

N/A	$500 - 650	$250 - 300

The amp picture isn't stock from factory. The vibrato shown on the back panel was added sometime in the 1950s.

1202 – 18W, 2-8 in. speakers, five tube chassis, two channels, top chrome control panel, four inputs (three inst., one mic), four knobs (inst. v, mic v, t, b), tweed covering, brown suede rectangular grille with bird/National graphic, 18.75 in. wide, 15 in. tall, 10.5 in. deep, 23 lbs., mfg. circa 1950-mid-1950s.

N/A	$700 - 900	$400 - 500

1210 – 20-25W, 1-15 in. speaker, eight tube chassis, two channels, right side chrome control panel, four inputs (three inst., one mic), four knobs (inst. v, mic v, t, b), tweed covering, offset brown suede rectangular grille with zebra graphic, 24 in. wide, 20 in. tall, 10 in. deep, 36 lbs., mfg. circa 1950-mid-1950s.

N/A	$650 - 800	$400 - 500

1212 – 12W, 1-12 in. speaker, five tube chassis, single channel, rear chrome control panel, three inputs, unknown controls, tweed covering, brown suede grille with bird graphic, 15 in. wide, 18 in. tall, 8 in. deep, 20 lbs., mfg. circa 1950-mid-1950s.

N/A	$650 - 800	$400 - 500

1215 – 20-25W, 1-12 in. Jensen speaker, eight tube chassis, two channels, rear chrome control panel, four inputs (three inst., one mic), four knobs (inst. v, mic v, t, b), tweed covering, offset brown suede rectangular grille with zebra graphic, 17.625 in. wide, 20.5 in. tall, 8.75 in. deep, 31 lbs., mfg. circa 1950-mid-1950s.

N/A	$450 - 550	$200 - 250

1220 – 8W, 1-10 in. speaker, five tube chassis, single channel, rear chrome control panel, three inputs, two knobs (v, tone), tweed covering, brown suede grille, 15 in. wide, 14 in. tall, 7.5 in. deep, 18 lbs., mfg. circa 1950-mid-1950s.

N/A	$250 - 300	$125 - 175

1260 DELUXE – 20-24W, 1-12 in. speaker, eight tube chassis, single channel, rear chrome control panel, three inputs, controls unknown, tweed covering, brown grille with 50s style graphics, 20 lbs., mfg. circa 1952-mid-1950s.

N/A	$450 - 550	$175 - 225

* *1260T Deluxe Tremolo* – similar to the 1260 Deluxe, except has a tremolo circuit with a separate control panel that has speed and intensity controls, footswitch included, mfg. circa 1952-mid-1950s.

N/A	$500 - 600	$300 - 400

MSR/NOTES	100%	EXCELLENT	AVERAGE	LAST MSR

1275 – 12W, 1-10 in. speaker, five tube chassis, single channel, rear chrome control panel, three inputs, two knobs (v, tone), tweed covering, brown suede grille, 15 in. wide, 14.75 in. tall, 7.5 in. deep, 18 lbs., mfg. circa 1950-mid-1950s.

	N/A	$550 - 700	$300 - 400	

ELECTRIC TUBE AMPLIFIERS: LATE 1950S MODELS

In the mid- to late 1950s, National introduced an entire new line of amps that except for the 1201 and 1220 models, featured new two and three rectangle speaker baffle openings.

1201 WESTWOOD – 5W, 1-8 in. speaker, three tube chassis, single channel, top chrome control panel, two inputs, single volume control, tweed covering with a black center stripe around the cabinet, rectangular brown grille, 15.5 in. wide, 11.75 in. tall, 7.5 in. deep, 13 lbs., mfg. late 1950s.

	N/A	$400 - 500	$275 - 325	

1210 TWIN-TONE – 5W, 2-11 X 6 in. elliptical speakers, three tube chassis, single channel, top chrome control panel, three inputs, two knobs (v, tone), tweed covering with a black center stripe around the cabinet, three rectangle grille openings with the center a dark brown and larger and the two outer rectangles a light brown and smaller, 15.75 in. wide, 13 in. tall, 8.5 in. deep, 17 lbs., mfg. late 1950s.

	N/A	$525 - 650	$350 - 425	

1220 CHICAGOAN – 17W, 1-10 in. speaker, five tube chassis, single channel, top chrome control panel, three inputs, two knobs (v, tone), tweed covering with a black center stripe around the cabinet, rectangular brown grille, 15.75 in. wide, 15 in. tall, 8 in. deep, 19 lbs., mfg. late 1950s.

	N/A	$600 - 750	$400 - 500	

1224T TREMO-TONE – 17W, 2-11 X 6 in. speakers, six tube chassis, single channel, tremolo, top chrome control panel, three inputs, four knobs (v, tone, s, i), tweed covering with a black center stripe around the cabinet, two horizontal rectangular speaker grilles, bottom rectangle is larger and has a dark brown cloth with a bird graphic and the top rectangle is smaller and has a gold cloth, 15.5 in. wide, 17.5 in. tall, 8 in. deep, 23 lbs., mfg. late 1950s.

	N/A	$750 - 900	$525 - 600	

1230T SPORTSMAN – 35W, 2-10 in. speakers, seven tube chassis, two channels, tremolo, top chrome control panel, three inputs, four knobs (v1, v2, tone, s), optional footswitch, tweed covering with a black center stripe around the cabinet, two vertical rectangular speaker grilles, right rectangle is larger and has a dark brown cloth and the left rectangle is smaller and has a gold cloth, 20.75 in. wide, 18.5 in. tall, 8.5 in. deep, 32 lbs., mfg. late 1950s.

	N/A	$850 - 1,000	$600 - 700	

1240T AZTEC – 38W, 1-15 in. speaker, seven tube chassis, single channel, tremolo, top chrome control panel, four inputs, three knobs (v1, tone, s), optional footswitch, tweed covering with a black center stripe around the cabinet, two vertical rectangular speaker grilles, right rectangle is larger and has a dark brown cloth with a bird graphic and the left rectangle is smaller and has a gold cloth, 20.5 in. wide, 18.5 in. tall, 8.75 in. deep, 35 lbs., mfg. late 1950s.

	N/A	$800 - 1,000	$500 - 650	

1280T STAGE STAR – 40W, 4-11 X 6 in. speakers, seven tube chassis, two channels, tremolo, top chrome control panel, four inputs, five knobs (v1, v2, tone, s, i), optional footswitch, tweed covering with a black center stripe around the cabinet, two horizontal rectangular speaker grilles, bottom rectangle is larger and has a dark brown cloth and the top rectangle is smaller and has a gold cloth, 26 in. wide, 18.5 in. tall, 9.5 in. deep, 37 lbs., mfg. late 1950s.

	N/A	$1,100 - 1,400	$800 - 950	

ELECTRIC TUBE AMPLIFIERS: 1960S MODELS

In 1960 or 1961, National introduced a new line of amps that have become the most recognizable and popular. These amps followed suit with the style of the early 1960s by moving the control panel to the front of the amp. They were also named in conjuction with National's electric guitars at the time, including Glenwood, Newport, and Westwood.

BASS AMP 70/75 (N6475B) – 35W, 2-12 in. Jensen speakers, five tube chassis, single channel, front chrome control panel, two inputs, three knobs (v, tone, three-way range selector), black with random colored stitching covering, Saran light brown/gray grille, 27.625 in. wide, 18.75 in. tall, 9.5 in. deep, 55 lbs., mfg. circa 1960-67.

	N/A	$700 - 850	$450 - 550	

DYNAMIC 20 – 20W, 2-8 in. Jensen speakers, five tube chassis, preamp: 2 X 6EU7, power: 2 X 6973, rectifier: 5Y3GT, single channel, front chrome control panel, three inputs (one treble, two regular), two knobs (v, tone), black with random colored stitching covering, Saran light brown/gray grille, 20.375 in. wide, 13.5 in. tall, 8.5 in. deep, mfg. circa 1960-63.

	N/A	$650 - 800	$400 - 500	

Dynamis 20
courtesy George McGuire

MSR/NOTES	100%	EXCELLENT	AVERAGE	LAST MSR

GLENWOOD 90 (N6490TR) – 35W, 2-12 in. Jensen speakers, nine tube chassis, preamp: 3 X 6EU7, 2 X 12AX7, 1 X 6973 power: 2 X 6L6, rectifier: 5U4, two channels, reverb, tremolo, front chrome control panel, four inputs (on rear control panel, two per channel), eight knobs (Ch. 1: v, t, b, Ch. 2: r, i, v, b, t), chrome rear control panel with tremolo speed, tone switches, two one-button footswitches, black with random colored stitching covering, Saran light brown/gray grille, 27.375 in. wide, 18.75 in. tall, 9.5 in. deep, 47 lbs., mfg. circa 1960-67.

courtesy George McGuire

courtesy George McGuire

N/A	$1,000 - 1,200	$700 - 850		

GLENWOOD VIBRATO (N6499VR) – 70W, 2-12 in. Jensen speakers, 14 tube chassis, two channels, reverb, vibrato, front chrome control panel, four inputs (on rear control panel, two per channel), eight knobs (Ch. 1: v, t, b, Ch. 2: r, i, v, b, t), chrome rear control panel with vibrato speed, tone switches, two one-button footswitches, black with random colored stitching covering, Saran light brown/gray grille, 27.375 in. wide, 18.75 in. tall, 9.5 in. deep, 56 lbs., mfg. circa 1963-67.

N/A	$1,100 - 1,400	$700 - 900		

NEWPORT 40 (N6440T) – 17W, 2-10 in. Jensen speakers, six tube chassis, two channels, tremolo, front chrome control panel, four inputs (on rear control panel, two per channel), six knobs (Ch. 1: v, tone, Ch. 2: s, i, v, tone), chrome rear control panel with tone switches, one-button footswitch, black with random colored stitching covering, Saran light brown/gray grille, 23.625 in. wide, 16 in. tall, 8.5 in. deep, 26 lbs., mfg. circa 1963-67.

N/A	$650 - 800	$375 - 450		

NEWPORT 50 (N6450TR) – 17W, 2-10 in. Jensen speakers, all tube chassis, preamp: 4 X 12AX7, 1 X 6973, power: 2 X 6973, rectifier: 5Y3GT rectifier, two channels, reverb, tremolo, front chrome control panel, four inputs (on rear control panel, two per channel), six knobs (Ch. 1: v, tone, Ch. 2: r, i, v, tone), chrome rear control panel with tremolo speed, tone switches, two one-button footswitches, black with random colored stitching covering, Saran light brown/gray grille, 23.75 in. wide, 16 in. tall, 8.5 in. deep, 28 lbs., mfg. circa 1963-67.

courtesy George McGuire

courtesy George McGuire

N/A	$650 - 800	$375 - 450		

NEWPORT 97 (N6497T) – 35W, 1-15 in. Jensen speaker, six tube chassis, two channels, tremolo, rear chrome control panel, four inputs (on rear control panel, two per channel), six knobs (Ch. 1: v, tone, Ch. 2: s, i, v, tone), one-button footswitch, black with random colored stitching covering, Saran light brown/gray grille, 23.75 in. wide, 19 in. tall, 11.25 in. deep, 36 lbs., mfg. circa 1963-67.

N/A	$700 - 850	$475 - 575		

STUDIO 10 (N6410) – 5W, 1-8 in. Jensen speaker, three tube chassis, preamp: 12AX7, power: 6V6GT, rectifier: 5Y3GT, single channel, front chrome control panel, three inputs, one volume knob, black with random colored stitching covering, Saran light brown/gray grille, 15.625 in. wide, 11.625 in. tall, 7.5 in. deep, mfg. circa 1960-67.

Studio 10
courtesy George McGuire

N/A	$450 - 600	$200 - 250		

MSR/NOTES	100%	EXCELLENT	AVERAGE	LAST MSR

VAL-PRO 80 – 35W, 2-12 in. Jensen speakers, eight tube chassis, two channels, tremolo, front chrome control panel, four inputs (two per channel), eight knobs (Ch. 1: v, b, t, Ch. 2: v, b, t, s, i), black with random colored stitching covering, Saran light brown/gray grille, 27.75 in. wide, 18.75 in. tall, 9.5 in. deep, mfg. circa 1960-63.

	N/A	$1,000-1,250	$700 - 850	

VAL-TREM 40 – 17W, 2-10 in. Jensen speakers, six tube chassis, two channels, tremolo, front chrome control panel, four inputs (two per channel), six knobs (Ch. 1: v, tone, Ch. 2: v, tone, s, i), black with random colored stitching covering, Saran light brown/gray grille, 23.75 in. wide, 16 in. tall, 8.5 in. deep, mfg. circa 1960-63.

	N/A	$850 - 1,000	$500 - 600	

VAL-VERB 60 – 17W, 2-10 in. Jensen speakers, seven tube chassis, two channels, reverb, front chrome control panel, four inputs (on rear panel, two per channel), five knobs (Ch. 1: v, tone, Ch. 2: v, tone, r), black with random colored stitching covering, Saran light brown/gray grille, 23.75 in. wide, 16 in. tall, 8.5 in. deep, mfg. circa 1960-63.

	N/A	$1,000-1,250	$650 - 800	

WESTWOOD 16 (N6416T) – 5W, 2-8 in. Jensen speakers, four tube chassis, single channel, tremolo, front chrome control panel, two inputs, three knobs (v, s, i), optional footswitch, black with random colored stitching covering, Saran light brown/gray grille with National logo in lower right corner, 19.75 in. wide, 14 in. tall, 8.5 in. deep, 15 lbs., mfg. circa 1963-67.

	N/A	$700 - 850	$450 - 550	

WESTWOOD 22 (N6422TR) – 5W, 2-8 in. Jensen speakers, five tube chassis, single channel, reverb, tremolo, front chrome control panel, two inputs, four knobs (v, tone, s, r), optional footswitch, black with random colored stitching covering, Saran light brown/gray grille with National logo in lower right corner, 19.75 in. wide, 14 in. tall, 8.5 in. deep, 20 lbs., mfg. circa 1963-67.

	N/A	$750 - 900	$450 - 550	

ELECTRIC AMPLIFIERS: LATE 1960S AND 1970S MODELS

In circa 1968, National introduced an entirely new line of amps, and for the first time, they included piggyback models. The chassis were mainly tube, but some of the larger models used solid-state rectifiers. This series lasted through 1969 or 1970 when Valco went out of business. Models from this era include the **N6800**, **N6810**, **N6816**, **N6820**, **N6822**, **N6850**, **N6875**, **N6878**, **N6895**, **N6898**, and **N6899**. After Strum & Drum bought National out of bankruptcy in either 1969 or 1970, they introduced an enirely new line of amplifiers that were solid-state in design. These amps lasted through the early 1970s and were the last amps to feature National on them. Models include the **GA 920P**, **GA 927PB**, **GAX 945**, **GA 950P**, and **GA 960P**.

NAYLOR ENGINEERING

Amplifiers previously produced in Detroit, MI from 1994-1997. Currently produced in Dallas, TX since 2002.

CONTACT INFORMATION
NAYLOR ENGINEERING
PO Box 222058
Dallas, TX 75222-2058
Phone No.: 214-628-4710
www.naylorengineering.com
info@naylorengineering.com

Joe Naylor and Kyle Kurtz co-founded Naylor Engineering in the early 1990s. The company first produced J.F. Naylor speakers and in 1994 they started to produce amplifiers. Joe left the company to start Reverend Guitars in 1997 and left Kurtz with the share of the company. In 1999, David King purchased Naylor Engineering and moved the operation to Dallas, TX. From 1999 to 2002, King set up new manufacturing facilities and worked on producing the amplifiers to the original Naylor specifications. The first new Naylor amp was built in July, 2002 and Joe Naylor played it at the 2002 Arlington Guitar Show. The New Naylor amps are built the same way as they were originally because King received all the original engineering specifications, working models, component layout boards, assembly jigs, full line of cabinets, lots of component inventory, and other information. For more information visit Naylor's website or contact them directly.

COLOR OPTIONS

Naylor offers several different color options on their amplifiers and cabinets. The basic colors include: Black, Palomino Brown, and Aged Blonde. Custom colors are available at an additional charge. Contact Naylor for pricing information. These colors include: Blue Sparkle, Burgundy Sparkle, Cascade Sparkle, Charcoal Sparkle, Gold Sparkle, Green Sparkle, Hot Pink Sparkle, Silver Sparkle, Zodiac Sparkle, Black Chap (Real Leather), Brown Oily (Real Leather), Tweed, Red Tolex, Python (snake skin style), Grey Taurus, Tooled Leather, Purple levant (Marshall style), British Emerald, and Hot White.

- Add 10%-25% for custom color depending on the option.
- Add $80-90 (MSR $109-126) for cover.
- Add $75 (MSR $99) for a Special Design 1040 10 in. speaker.
- Add $90 (MSR $119) for a Special Design 50 12 in. speaker.

ELECTRIC TUBE AMPLIFIERS: DUEL SERIES

The Duel Series represents Naylor's two channel amps.

DUEL 38 HEAD – 38W, head-unit only, all tube chassis, preamp: 12AX7WBs, power: 5881s, two channels, front control panel, two inputs, six knobs (g, bite, b, m, t, p), effects loop, footswitch, various color coverings, 24.25 in. wide, 8.875 in. tall, 9.25 in. deep, 33 lbs., mfg. 1994-97, 2002-present.

MSR $2,149	$1,625	$950 - 1,150	$625 - 725	

Duel 60 Head
courtesy Naylor Engineering

Electra-verb 60 Head
courtesy Naylor Engineering

DUEL 38 1-12 COMBO – 38W, 1-12 in. speaker, all tube chassis, preamp: 12AX7WBs, power: 5881s, two channels, front control panel, two inputs, six knobs (g, bite, b, m, t, p), effects loop, footswitch, various color coverings, 24.25 in. wide, 17.625 in. tall, 10 in. deep, 48 lbs., mfg. 1994-97, 2002-present.

| MSR $2,349 | $1,775 | $1,050 - 1,250 | $650 - 775 | |

DUEL 38 2-10 COMBO – 38W, 2-10 in. speaker, all tube chassis, preamp: 12AX7WBs, power: 5881s, two channels, front control panel, two inputs, six knobs (g, bite, b, m, t, p), effects loop, footswitch, various color coverings, 24.25 in. wide, 17.625 in. tall, 10 in. deep, 55 lbs., 2002-present.

| MSR $2,399 | $1,800 | $1,075 - 1,275 | $675 - 800 | |

DUEL 38 2-12 COMBO – 38W, 2-12 in. speaker, all tube chassis, preamp: 12AX7WBs, power: 5881s, two channels, front control panel, two inputs, six knobs (g, bite, b, m, t, p), effects loop, footswitch, various color coverings, 26.5 in. wide, 20 in. tall, 10 in. deep, 56 lbs., mfg. 1994-97, 2002-present.

| MSR $2,549 | $1,925 | $1,150 - 1,400 | $750 - 875 | |

DUEL 60 HEAD – 60W, head-unit only, all tube chassis, preamp: 12AX7WBs, power: 5881s, two channels, front control panel, two inputs, six knobs (g, bite, b, m, t, p), effects loop, footswitch, various color coverings, 24.25 in. wide, 8.875 in. tall, 9.25 in. deep, 34 lbs., mfg. 1994-97, 2002-present.

| MSR $2,349 | $1,775 | $1,050 - 1,250 | $650 - 775 | |

DUEL 60 2-12 COMBO – 60W, 2-12 in. speaker, all tube chassis, preamp: 12AX7WBs, power: 5881s, two channels, front control panel, two inputs, six knobs (g, bite, b, m, t, p), effects loop, footswitch, various color coverings, 26.5 in. wide, 20 in. tall, 10 in. deep, 56 lbs., mfg. 1994-97, 2002-present.

| MSR $2,749 | $2,075 | $1,250 - 1,550 | $825 - 975 | |

ELECTRIC TUBE AMPLIFIERS: ELECTRA-VERB SERIES

The Electra-Verb series are Naylor's amps with reverb.

ELECTRA-VERB 38 HEAD – 38W, head-unit only, all tube chassis, preamp: 12AX7WBs, power: 5881s, one channel, reverb, front control panel, two inputs, six knobs (g, bite, b, m, t, r), effects loop, various color coverings, 24.25 in. wide, 8.875 in. tall, 9.25 in. deep, 36 lbs., mfg. 1994-97, 2002-present.

| MSR $2,149 | $1,625 | $950 - 1,150 | $625 - 725 | |

ELECTRA-VERB 38 1-12 COMBO – 38W, 1-12 in. speaker, all tube chassis, preamp: 12AX7WBs, power: 5881s, one channel, reverb, front control panel, two inputs, six knobs (g, bite, b, m, t, r), effects loop, various color coverings, brown or gray grille, 24.25 in. wide, 17.625 in. tall, 10 in. deep, 49 lbs., mfg. 1994-97, 2002-present.

| MSR $2,349 | $1,775 | $1,050 - 1,250 | $650 - 775 | |

ELECTRA-VERB 38 2-10 COMBO – 38W, 2-10 in. speaker, all tube chassis, preamp: 12AX7WBs, power: 5881s, one channel, reverb, front control panel, two inputs, six knobs (g, bite, b, m, t, r), effects loop, various color coverings, brown or gray grille, 24.25 in. wide, 17.625 in. tall, 10 in. deep, 55 lbs., mfg. 1994-97, 2002-present.

| MSR $2,399 | $1,800 | $1,075 - 1,275 | $675 - 800 | |

ELECTRA-VERB 38 2-12 COMBO – 38W, 2-12 in. speaker, all tube chassis, preamp: 12AX7WBs, power: 5881s, one channel, reverb, front control panel, two inputs, six knobs (g, bite, b, m, t, r), effects loop, various color coverings, brown or gray grille, 26.5 in. wide, 20 in. tall, 10 in. deep, 56 lbs., 55 lbs., mfg. 1994-97, 2002-present.

| MSR $2,549 | $1,925 | $1,150 - 1,400 | $750 - 875 | |

ELECTRA-VERB 60 HEAD – 60W, head-unit only, all tube chassis, preamp: 12AX7WBs, power: 5881s, one channel, reverb, front control panel, two inputs, six knobs (g, bite, b, m, t, r), effects loop, various color coverings, 24.25 in. wide, 8.875 in. tall, 9.25 in. deep, 38 lbs., mfg. 1994-97, 2002-present.

| MSR $2,349 | $1,775 | $1,050 - 1,250 | $650 - 775 | |

ELECTRA-VERB 60 2-12 COMBO – 60W, 2-12 in. speakers, all tube chassis, preamp: 12AX7WBs, power: 5881s, one channel, reverb, front control panel, two inputs, six knobs (g, bite, b, m, t, r), effects loop, various color coverings, brown or gray grille, 26.5 in. wide, 20 in. tall, 10 in. deep, 57 lbs., mfg. 1994-97, 2002-present.

| MSR $2,749 | $2,075 | $1,250 - 1,550 | $825 - 975 | |

MSR/NOTES	100%	EXCELLENT	AVERAGE	LAST MSR

Super Club 38 1-12 Combo
courtesy S.P. Fjestad

Super Club 38 1-12 Combo
courtesy S.P. Fjestad

412 Speaker Cabinet
courtesy Naylor Engineering

ELECTRIC TUBE AMPLIFIERS: SUPER SERIES

SUPER CLUB 38 HEAD – 38W, head-unit only, all tube chassis, preamp: 12AX7WBs, power: 5881s, single channel, front control panel, two inputs, six knobs (g, bite, b, m, t, p), effects loop, various color coverings, 24.25 in. wide, 8.875 in. tall, 9.25 in. deep, 33 lbs., mfg. 1994-97, 2002-present.

MSR $1,949	$1,475	$900 - 1,050	$575 - 675

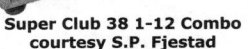

SUPER CLUB 38 1-12 COMBO – 38W, 1-12 in. speaker, all tube chassis, preamp: 12AX7WBs, power: 5881s, single channel, front control panel, two inputs, six knobs (g, bite, b, m, t, p), effects loop, various color coverings, brown grille, 24.25 in. wide, 17.625 in. tall, 10 in. deep, 47 lbs., mfg. 1994-97, 2002-present.

MSR $2,149	$1,625	$950 - 1,150	$625 - 725

SUPER CLUB 38 2-10 COMBO – 38W, 2-10 in. speakers, all tube chassis, preamp: 12AX7WBs, power: 5881s, single channel, front control panel, two inputs, six knobs (g, bite, b, m, t, p), effects loop, various color coverings, brown or gray grille, 24.25 in. wide, 17.625 in. tall, 10 in. deep, 55 lbs., mfg. 2002-present.

MSR $2,199	$1,650	$975 - 1,175	$650 - 750

SUPER CLUB 38 2-12 COMBO – 38W, 2-12 in. speakers, all tube chassis, preamp: 12AX7WBs, power: 5881s, single channel, front control panel, two inputs, six knobs (g, bite, b, m, t, p), effects loop, various color coverings, brown or gray grille, 26.5 in. wide, 20 in. tall, 10 in. deep, 56 lbs., mfg. 1994-97, 2002-present.

MSR $2,349	$1,775	$1,050 - 1,250	$650 - 775

SUPER DRIVE 60 HEAD – 60W, head-unit only, all tube chassis, preamp: 12AX7WBs, power: 5881s, single channel, front control panel, two inputs, six knobs (g, bite, b, m, t, p), effects loop, various color coverings, 24.25 in. wide, 8.875 in. tall, 9.25 in. deep, 35 lbs., mfg. 1994-97, 2002-present.

MSR $2,149	$1,625	$950 - 1,150	$625 - 725

SUPER DRIVE 60 2-12 COMBO – 60W, 2-12 in. speakers, all tube chassis, preamp: 12AX7WBs, power: 5881s, single channel, front control panel, two inputs, six knobs (g, bite, b, m, t, p), effects loop, various color coverings, brown or gray grille, 26.5 in. wide, 20 in. tall, 10 in. deep, 56 lbs., 56 lbs., mfg. 1994-97, 2002-present.

MSR $2,549	$1,925	$1,150 - 1,400	$750 - 875

SPEAKER CABINETS

112 SPEAKER CABINET – 1-12 in. Naylor Special Design 50 speaker, 16 Ohm impedance, birch plywood construction, various color coverings, brown or gray grille, 29 lbs., current mfg.

MSR $549	$425	$250 - 300	$150 - 200

210 SPEAKER CABINET – 2-10 in. Naylor Special Design 1040 speakers, 16 Ohm impedance, birch plywood construction, various color coverings, brown or gray grille, 36 lbs., current mfg.

MSR $599	$450	$275 - 325	$175 - 225

212 SPEAKER CABINET – 2-12 in. Naylor Special Design 50 speakers, 16 Ohm impedance, birch plywood construction, various color coverings, brown or gray grille, 56 lbs., current mfg.

MSR $799	$600	$375 - 450	$225 - 275

410 SPEAKER CABINET – 4-10 in. Naylor Special Design 1040 speakers, 8 Ohm impedance, birch plywood construction, various color coverings, brown or gray grille, 46 lbs., current mfg.

MSR $899	$675	$425 - 500	$250 - 300

412 SPEAKER CABINET – 4-12 in. Naylor Special Design 50 speakers, 16 Ohm impedance, birch plywood construction, various color coverings, brown or gray grille, 63 lbs., current mfg.

MSR $1,129	$850	$525 - 625	$300 - 375

MSR/NOTES	100%	EXCELLENT	AVERAGE	LAST MSR

NEMESIS

Amplifiers and speaker cabinets previously produced in China until 2009, and in Montrose, MN until the early 2000s. Nemesis was a division and distributed by U.S. Music Corporation in Mundelein, IL.

The Nemesis brand was Eden Electronics' budget line, and they offered a full line of bass amp heads, combos, and speaker enclosures that are designed in the U.S. but manufactured in China. Early Nemesis models were produced in the U.S., but all production eventually moved overseas. The first Nemesis amps featured a different style than their Eden counterparts while older models feature a large Nemesis logo. In 2005, the NC series was introduced, and the amps began to look more similar to other Eden amps. The new logo was very similar to the Eden logo with "David" replaced with "Nemesis." In 2008, much of the Nemesis line was overhauled with the RS Series, and in 2009, they changed the prefix of all Nemesis amps to "EN." In 2010, U.S. Music discontinued all Nemesis-branded amps and have introduced budget-line models within the Eden trademark.

HEAD UNITS

In 2009, Eden changed all the designations of their RS Heads from an RS prefix to an EN prefix, Eden also made some minor cosmetic changes to these amps, but electronically, they remained generally the same.

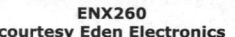

ENX260
courtesy Eden Electronics

NA650
courtesy Eden Electronics

RS400/EN400
courtesy Eden Electronics

ENX260 – 260/300W @ 4 ohms, compact head-unit bass configuration, solid-state chassis, single channel, front black control panel, single input, six knobs (g, enhance, b, m, h, MV), effects loop, stereo aux. inputs, tuner out, mute switch, XLR direct in with level control, headphone jack, optional footswitch, black casing, 8 in. wide, 2.5 in. tall, 9 in. deep, 3.8 lbs., mfg. 2009 only.

	$400	$275 - 325	$150 - 200	$600

NA320 – 320W at 4 ohms, head-unit only, FET solid-state chassis, single channel, front blue control panel, single input, eight knobs (g, enhance, level, freq., b, m, t, MV), compressor, effects loop, headphone jack, black casing, 15 lbs., mfg. 2005-08.

	$500	$275 - 325	$150 - 200	$620

NA600 – 630W at 2 ohms (440W at 4 ohms, 270W at 8 ohms), head-unit only, FET solid-state chassis, single channel, front blue control panel, single input, 10 knobs (g, edge, enhance, level, freq., b, m, t, DI level, MV), compressor, effects loop, headphone jack, black cabinet with vents, mfg. 1990s-2000s.

	N/A	$375 - 450	$200 - 250	

NA650 – 650W at 2 ohms, head-unit only, FET solid-state chassis, single channel, front blue control panel, single input, 10 knobs (g, edge, enhance, level, freq., b, m, t, DI level, MV), compressor, effects loop, headphone jack, black casing, 18 lbs., mfg. 2005-08.

	$700	$400 - 475	$225 - 275	$870

RS400/EN400 – 400W @ 4 ohms (800W peak), bass application, two-space head-unit, FET solid-state chassis, single channel, front black control panel, single input, nine knobs (g, distortion, enhance, semi parametric EQ: level and freq., b, m, t, MV), semi parametric EQ on/off switch, pre/post EQ switch, headphone jack, effects loop, direct in and level control, tuner out, recording out, ext. speaker out with on/off switch, optional footswitch, black casing, 15 lbs., mfg. 2008-09.

	$450	$300 - 350	$175 - 225	$700

RS700/EN700 – 700W @ 2 ohms (1400W peak), bass application, two-space head-unit, FET solid-state chassis, single channel, front black control panel, single input, 10 knobs (g, distortion, enhance, semi parametric EQ: level and freq., b, m, t, D.I. level, MV), gain boost switch, compressor bypass switch, mute switch, semi parametric EQ on/off switch, pre/post EQ switch, headphone jack, effects loop, direct in and level control, tuner out, recording out, ext. speaker out with on/off switch, optional footswitch, black casing, 17 in. wide, 11 in. deep, 25 lbs., mfg. 2008-09.

	$700	$450 - 525	$275 - 325	$1,000

COMBO UNITS

Early Nemesis combo units all featured the NA200 head unit with 225W power at 4 ohms. When the new NC series was introduced in 2005, the amps were outfitted with cosmetic changes and different amp sizes for the corresponding speaker configuration. In 2009, Eden changed all the designations of the small combos from an N prefix to an EN prefix, and on the large combos from an RS prefix to an EN prefix. Eden also made some minor cosmetic changes to these amps, but electronically, they remained generally the same.

EN8 MICRO – 15W, 1-8 in. speaker combo, bass application, solid-state chassis, single channel, front black control panel, single input, two black knobs (v, tone), headphone jack, power switch, black covering, black metal grille, mfg. 2008-09.

	$100	$55 - 75	$30 - 45	$150

MSR/NOTES	100%	EXCELLENT	AVERAGE	LAST MSR

N10/EN10
courtesy Eden Electronics

N28
courtesy Eden Electronics

NC410
courtesy Eden Electronics

N8JR/EN8JR – 25W, 1-8 in. speaker combo, bass application, solid-state chassis, single channel, front black control panel, single input, two black knobs (v, tone), headphone jack, tilt-back cabinet design, black covering, black metal grille, 14.5 in. wide, 16.5 in. tall, 11.5 in. deep, 19 lbs., mfg. 2008-09.

	$130	$75 - 100	$45 - 60	$190

N10/EN10 – 40W, 1-10 in. speaker combo, bass application, solid-state chassis, single channel, front black control panel, single input, five black knobs (g, b, m, t, MV), headphone jack, tilt-back cabinet design, black covering, black metal grille, 14.5 in. wide, 17.5 in. tall, 13 in. deep, 27 lbs., mfg. 2008-09.

	$200	$120 - 150	$70 - 95	$300

N12/EN12 – 150W, 1-12 in. speaker combo with a tweeter, bass application, solid-state chassis, single channel, front black control panel, single input, six black knobs (g, enhance, b, m, t, MV), headphone jack, tilt-back cabinet design, black covering, black metal grille, 18.5 in. wide, 20.5 in. tall, 13 in. deep, 43 lbs., mfg. 2008-09.

	$380	$225 - 275	$135 - 175	$570

N15/EN15 – 200W, 1-15 in. speaker combo with a tweeter, bass application, solid-state chassis, single channel, front black control panel, single input, six black knobs (g, enhance, b, m, t, MV), headphone jack, XLR line out jack, aux. in jack, tilt-back cabinet design, black covering, black metal grille, 18.5 in. wide, 25 in. tall, 17.25 in. deep, 45 lbs., mfg. 2008-09.

	$400	$250 - 300	$150 - 200	$600

N28 – 200W, 2-8 in. speaker combo with a tweeter, bass application, solid-state chassis, single channel, front black control panel, single input, six black knobs (g, enhance, b, m, t, MV), headphone jack, XLR line out jack, aux. in jack, tilt-back cabinet design, black covering, black metal grille, 18.5 in. wide, 20.5 in. tall, 15.5 in. deep, 41 lbs., mfg. 2008 only.

	$380	$240 - 290	$140 - 190	$550

NC115 – 250W at 4 ohms, 1-15 in. speaker combo, FET solid-state chassis, single channel, top blue control panel, single input, eight knobs (g, enhance, level, freq., b, m, t, MV), compressor, effects loop, headphone jack, black covering, black grille, 42 lbs., disc. 2006.

	$700	$425 - 500	$250 - 300	$930

NC210 – 250W at 4 ohms, 2-10 in. speaker combo with a tweeter, FET solid-state chassis, single channel, top blue control panel, single input, eight knobs (g, enhance, level, freq., b, m, t, MV), compressor, effects loop, headphone jack, black covering, black grille, 47 lbs., disc. 2006.

	$740	$450 - 525	$275 - 325	$980

NC212 – 320W at 4 ohms, 2-12 in. speaker combo with a tweeter, FET solid-state chassis, single channel, top blue control panel, single input, eight knobs (g, enhance, level, freq., b, m, t, MV), compressor, effects loop, headphone jack, black covering, black grille, 58 lbs., disc. 2007.

	$775	$475 - 550	$275 - 325	$1,030

NC410 – 320W at 4 ohms, 4-10 in. speaker combo with a tweeter, FET solid-state chassis, single channel, top blue control panel, single input, eight knobs (g, enhance, level, freq., b, m, t, MV), compressor, effects loop, headphone jack, black covering, black grille, 62 lbs., disc. 2007.

	$900	$525 - 625	$300 - 350	$1,190

NC810 – 400W at 4 ohms, 8-10 in. speaker combo with a tweeter, FET solid-state chassis, single channel, top blue control panel, single input, eight knobs (g, enhance, level, freq., b, m, t, MV), compressor, effects loop, headphone jack, black covering, black grille, 120 lbs., mfg. 2005-07.

	$1,300	$800 - 950	$500 - 600	$1,750

N8 – 40W @ 4 ohms, 1-18 in. speaker, bass combo, FET solid-state chassis, single channel, front silver control panel, two inputs, five knobs (g, b, m, t, MV), built-in compression, effects loop, headphone jack, black covering, black metal grille, 14.375 in. wide, 19.25 in. tall, 8.25 in. deep, 20 lbs., mfg. 2006-08.

	$130	$75 - 100	$45 - 65	$180

MSR/NOTES	100%	EXCELLENT	AVERAGE	LAST MSR

N12S Silver Series
courtesy Eden Electronics

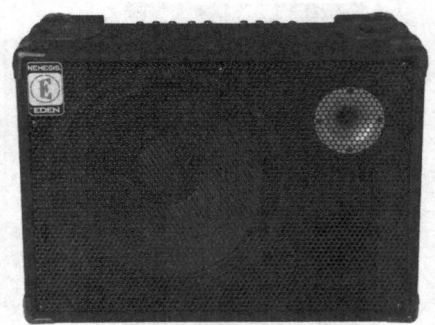

RS115/EN115
courtesy Eden Electronics

RS410/EN410
courtesy Eden Electronics

N10S SILVER SERIES – 80W at 8 ohms, 1-10 in. speaker combo with a tweeter, FET solid-state chassis, single channel, front silver control panel, single input, eight knobs (g, low balance, g, enhance, b, m, t, MV), compression, RCA inputs, headphone jack, black covering, black metal grille, 45 lbs., mfg. 2005-07.

	$380	$200 - 250	$120 - 150	$500

N12S SILVER SERIES – 175W at 8 ohms, 1-12 in. speaker combo with a tweeter, FET solid-state chassis, single channel, front silver control panel, single input, eight knobs (g, low balance, g, enhance, b, m, t, MV), compression, RCA inputs, headphone jack, black covering, black metal grille, 47 lbs., mfg. 2005-07.

	$400	$225 - 275	$130 - 170	$520

N15S SILVER SERIES – 175W at 8 ohms, 1-15 in. speaker combo with a tweeter, FET solid-state chassis, single channel, front silver control panel, single input, eight knobs (g, low balance, g, enhance, b, m, t, MV), compression, RCA inputs, headphone jack, black covering, black metal grille, 50 lbs., mfg. 2005-07.

	$475	$275 - 325	$150 - 200	$620

N28S SILVER SERIES – 175W at 8 ohms, 2-8 in. speaker combo with a tweeter, FET solid-state chassis, single channel, front silver control panel, single input, eight knobs (g, low balance, g, enhance, b, m, t, MV), compression, RCA inputs, headphone jack, black covering, black metal grille, 47 lbs., mfg. 2005-07.

	$440	$260 - 310	$140 - 190	$570

RS115/EN115 – 320W, 1-15 in. speaker and a T2004 tweeter, bass combo, FET solid-state chassis, single channel, top black control panel, single input, nine knobs (g, edge, enhance, semi parametric EQ: level and freq., b, m, t, MV), headphone jack, effects loop, direct in and level control, tuner out, recording out, ext. speaker out with on/off switch, optional footswitch, black covering, black metal grille, 24.75 in. wide, 17.25 in. tall, 16.25 in. deep, 44 lbs., mfg. 2006-09.

	$800	$500 - 600	$300 - 375	$1,150

RS210/EN210 – 320W, 2-10 in. speakers and a T2004 tweeter, bass combo, FET solid-state chassis, single channel, top black control panel, single input, nine knobs (g, edge, enhance, semi parametric EQ: level and freq., b, m, t, MV), headphone jack, effects loop, direct in and level control, tuner out, recording out, ext. speaker out with on/off switch, optional footswitch, black covering, black metal grille, 24.75 in. wide, 16.25 in. tall, 16.25 in. deep, 50 lbs., mfg. 2006-09.

	$840	$525 - 625	$325 - 400	$1,200

RS212/ES212 – 320W, 2-12 in. speakers and a T2004 tweeter, bass combo, FET solid-state chassis, single channel, top black control panel, single input, nine knobs (g, edge, enhance, semi parametric EQ: level and freq., b, m, t, MV), headphone jack, effects loop, direct in and level control, tuner out, recording out, ext. speaker out with on/off switch, optional footswitch, black covering, black metal grille, 24.75 in. wide, 24.75 in. tall, 16.25 in. deep, 58 lbs., mfg. 2006-09.

	$870	$550 - 650	$325 - 400	$1,250

RS410/EN410 – 320W, 4-10 in. speakers and a T2004 tweeter, bass combo, FET solid-state chassis, single channel, top black control panel, single input, nine knobs (g, edge, enhance, semi parametric EQ: level and freq., b, m, t, MV), headphone jack, effects loop, direct in and level control, tuner out, recording out, ext. speaker out with on/off switch, optional footswitch, black covering, black metal grille, 24.75 in. wide, 24.75 in. tall, 16.25 in. deep, 62 lbs., mfg. 2006-09.

	$910	$575 - 675	$350 - 425	$1,300

SPEAKER CABINETS

N115RS – 250W, 1-15 in. ES1560-8 speaker, T2004 tweeter, 8 ohm impedance, black covering, black metal grille, 24.75 in. wide, 17.25 in. tall, 16.25 in. deep, 42 lbs., mfg. 2008-09.

	$340	$200 - 250	$120 - 150	$500

MSR/NOTES	100%	EXCELLENT	AVERAGE	LAST MSR

NSP115
courtesy Eden Electronics

NSP212
courtesy Eden Electronics

EN410XST
courtesy Eden Electronics

N210RS – 300W, 2-10 in. ES1040XL16 speakers, T2004 tweeter, 8 ohm impedance, black covering, black metal grille, 24.75 in. wide, 16.25 in. tall, 16.25 in. deep, 47 lbs., mfg. 2008-09.

| | $400 | $225 - 275 | $135 - 175 | $550 |

N212RS – 400W, 2-10 in. ES1260-F8 speakers, T2004 tweeter, 4 ohm impedance, black covering, black metal grille, 24.75 in. wide, 24.75 in. tall, 16.25 in. deep, mfg. 2008-09.

| | $450 | $250 - 300 | $150 - 200 | $640 |

N410RS – 600W, 2-10 in. ES1040XL16 speakers, T2004 tweeter, 4 or 8 ohm impedance, black covering, black metal grille, 24.75 in. wide, 24.75 in. tall, 16.25 in. deep, 52 lbs., mfg. 2008-09.

| | $480 | $300 - 350 | $175 - 225 | $700 |

NSP115 – 250W, 1-15 in. speaker, 8 ohm impedance, black covering, black metal grille, side handles, 24.75 in. wide, 17.25 in. tall, 16.25 in. deep, 32 lbs., disc. 2007.

| | $420 | $225 - 275 | $135 - 175 | $520 |

NSP210 – 300W, 2-10 in. speakers, 4 or 8 ohm impedance, black covering, black metal grille, side handles, 24.75 in. wide, 16.25 in. tall, 16.25 in. deep, 35 lbs., disc. 2007.

| | $480 | $250 - 300 | $150 - 200 | $600 |

NSP212 – 350W, 2-12 in. speakers, 4 ohm impedance, black covering, black metal grille, side handles, 24.75 in. wide, 24.75 in. tall, 16.25 in. deep, 48 lbs., disc. 2007.

| | $500 | $275 - 325 | $175 - 225 | $620 |

NSP410 – 500W, 4-10 in. speakers, 4 or 8 ohm impedance, black covering, black metal grille, side handles, 24.75 in. wide, 24.75 in. tall, 16.25 in. deep, 61 lbs., disc. 2007.

| | $660 | $350 - 425 | $200 - 250 | $830 |

NSP810 – 800W, 8-10 in. speakers, 4 ohm impedance, black covering, black metal grille, side handles, 24.75 in. wide, 48.75 in. tall, 16.25 in. deep, 105 lbs., disc. 2007.

| | $995 | $550 - 650 | $325 - 400 | $1,240 |

EN115XST – 250W, 1-15 in. ES1560-8 speaker, T2004 tweeter, 8 ohm impedance, black covering, black metal grille, mfg. 2009 only.

| | $375 | $225 - 275 | $135 - 175 | $530 |

EN210XST – 200W, 2-10 in. ES1040XL16 speakers, T2004 tweeter, 8 ohm impedance, black covering, black metal grille, mfg. 2009 only.

| | $475 | $300 - 350 | $175 - 225 | $680 |

EN410XST – 400W, 4-10 in. ES1040XL16 speakers, T2004 tweeter, 4 or 8 ohm impedance, black covering, black metal grille, mfg. 2009 only.

| | $625 | $375 - 450 | $225 - 275 | $880 |

NOBLE

Amplifiers previously produced in Chicago, IL during the 1950s and 1960s. Distributed in the 1950s and early 1960s by Noble Accordions and in the mid- to late 1960s by Strum & Drum.

Don Noble of Noble Accordions produced a line of small to mid-sized tube amplifiers in the 1950s and 1960s. The earliest designs appear to be very close to mid-1950s Danelectro designs. It is possible that all Noble amps were built by Danelectro, but Valco and Supro may have also supplied amps. In the mid-1960s, Strum & Drum bought Noble and distributed their amplifiers through the rest of the 1960s. Any further information on Noble amplifiers can be submitted directly to Blue Book Publications.

MSR/NOTES	100%	EXCELLENT	AVERAGE	LAST MSR

NOLATONE AMPWORKS

Amplifiers currently produced in Cumming, GA.

CONTACT INFORMATION
NOLATONE AMPWORKS
4145 Hedgemoore Court
Cumming, GA 30041
Phone No.: 919-533-9151
www.nolatone.com
info@nolatone.com

Paul Sanders builds premium guitar tube amplifiers in his Cumming, GA shop. All Nolatone amplifiers are hand-built one-at-a-time using the highest quality components available, and Sanders pays special attention to soldering. Sanders was trained to solder at the US Navy Aviation community, and stresses how important it is to use the right amount when connecting components. Nolatone offers the CL "Chimey Limey," Junebug, Superbug, Rotten Johnny, and 22 Tango amps. Speaker cabinets are also available. For more information, visit Nolatone's website or contact Sanders directly.

NORMA

Amplifiers previously produced overseas between the late 1960s and the early 1970s. Distributed by Strum & Drum in Wheeling (Chicago), IL.

Norma was a brand used on imported amplifiers by Strum & Drum during the late 1960s and early 1970s. Strum & Drum bought National in 1970 and used both the names National and Norma on amplifiers, with Norma on smaller models and National on larger, more elaborate models. It is possible that there is some crossover between these two brands. Norma was phased out in the early 1970s, along with National amps. Norma models were built very cheaply and feature solid-state chassis with various features.

ELECTRIC SS AMPLIFIERS

GAP-2 STUDENT – 3W, 1-4 in. speaker, guitar combo, solid-state chassis, single channel, front control panel, one input, one volume knob, brown covering, light brown grille, mfg. late 1960s-early 1970s.

	N/A	$40 - 55	$25 - 35	

GA 93 MIGHTY MITE – 7.5W, 1-6 in. speaker, guitar combo, solid-state chassis, single channel, front control panel, two inputs, two knobs (v, tone), brown covering, dark brown grille, mfg. late 1960s-early 1970s.

	N/A	$55 - 75	$30 - 45	

GA 97T TREMOLO DELUXE – 15W, 1-8 in. speaker, guitar combo, solid-state chassis, single channel, tremolo, front control panel, three inputs, four knobs (v, tone, s, i), optional footswitch, brown covering, dark brown grille, mfg. late 1960s-early 1970s.

	N/A	$75 - 95	$45 - 60	

O SECTION
OAHU

Amplifiers previously produced by various manufacturers between the 1930 and the 1960s. Distributed by the Oahu Publishing Company of Cleveland, OH.

The Oahu Publishing Company started offering Hawaiian and Spanish style guitars, lap steels, sheet music, and other accessories in the 1930s. As their Hawiian electric guitars became popular in the late 1930s, Oahu began to distribute amplifiers as well. Note that Oahu never produced their own products - they were a house brand of sorts. Most amps were produced by Supro and other suppliers and branded with the Oahu name (similar to what Sears had Harmony and Kay do with their products). Although Oahu amps were designed and sold as Hawiian electric amps, the chassis were often the same of other Supro amps that were for use with regular guitars. Oahu has been reissued by other companies in recent years including Jester and Valco. Any information on Oahu amplifiers can be submitted directly to Blue Book Publications.

MSR/NOTES	100%	EXCELLENT	AVERAGE	LAST MSR

ELECTRIC TUBE AMPLIFIERS

OAHU HAWAIIAN EARLY MODELS – various configurations usually in small wattages and speaker combos, tube chassis, mfg. circa 1930s-1940s.

courtesy Harry Browning   courtesy Harry Browning

Low End Models	N/A	$175 - 225	$110 - 140	
High End Models	N/A	$250 - 300	$135 - 175	

MODEL 260K – 4.5W, 1-8 in. speaker, three tube chassis, single channel, top gold control panel, three inputs, two knobs (v, tone), yellow leatherette covering, black grille with Oahu graphic, 14.5 in. wide, 15.5 in. tall, 7.5 in. deep, 13.75 lbs., mfg. late 1950s-early 1960s.

	N/A	$200 - 250	$120 - 150	

MODEL 280K – 4.5W, 1-11 X 6 in. speaker, three tube chassis, single channel, top gold control panel, two inputs, one volume knob, white leatherette covering, black grille with Oahu graphic, 15.75 in. wide, 11.25 in. tall, 7.5 in. deep, 13 lbs., mfg. late 1950s-early 1960s.

	N/A	$150 - 200	$95 - 120	

This model was sold as a package with the Model 280K Electric Hawaiian guitar.

MODEL 413K – 14W, 1-10 in. speaker, five tube chassis, two channels, rear gold control panel, four inputs, three knobs (v1, v2, tone), white leatherette covering, black grille with Oahu graphic, 17.5 in. wide, 15 in. tall, 8 in. deep, 20 lbs., mfg. late 1950s-early 1960s.

	N/A	$250 - 300	$135 - 175	

MODEL 415K – 15W, 2-11 X 6 in. speakers, six tube chassis, two channels, tremolo, rear gold control panel, four inputs, five knobs (v1, v2, tone, s, i), optional footswitch, white leatherette covering, white and black or white gold grille, 20.5 in. wide, 19 in. tall, 8.5 in. deep, 29 lbs., mfg. late 1950s-early 1960s.

	N/A	$325 - 400	$175 - 225	

TONEMASTER 112 – 20W, 1-12 in. Rola speaker, all tube chassis: preamp: 1 X 6SL7, 1 X 1273, power: 2 X 6V6, 5Y3 rectifier, single channel, three input jacks, one volume and tone knob, light-bulb for a Oahu sign on amp, covering unknown, mfg. late 1940s-1950s.

	N/A	$300 - 350	$175 - 225	

TONEMASTER 230K – approx 10W, 1-8 in. speaker guitar combo, five tube chassis, preamp: 1 X 6SN7GT, 1 X 6SL7GT, power: 2 X 6V6GT, rectifier: 5Y3, two channels, rear bottom-mounted chassis/control panel, three inputs (two inst., one mic), three knobs (inst. v, mic. v, tone with on/off switch), available in two-tone brown/tan or two-tone black/white with blue/white grille covering, mfg. late 1940s-early 1960s.

	N/A	$300 - 350	$175 - 225	

MSR/NOTES	100%	EXCELLENT	AVERAGE	LAST MSR

JESTER REISSUE MODEL – a Jester reissue of a late 1950s or early 1960s Oahu model, other information and specs unknown.

courtesy Blue Book Archive

courtesy Blue Book Archive

courtesy Blue Book Archive

| | N/A | N/A | N/A | |

OBRIEN AMPLIFICATION

Amplifiers previously produced in Minneapolis (Columbia Heights), MN, during the 2000s.

Tim O'Brien became tired with channel switching amps where you either have A or B and nothing in between. He sat down and designed the first Obrien amp which used the patented Obrien Variable Gain. So instead of flipping a switch between two channels, an Obrien amp gives you everything in between. Obrien produced head units, combo units, and speaker cabinets. It appears that O'Brien is not producing amps anymore.

ELECTRIC TUBE AMPLIFIERS/SPEAKER CABINETS

The **Obrien Variable Gain** amplifier came in two version: 50W and 100W. The 50W has an eight tube chassis, preamp: 4 X 12AX7, 1 X 12AT7, power: 2 X 6L6, rectifier: 1 X 5AR4U, and the 100W has a nine-tube chassis, preamp: preamp: 4 X 12AX7, 1 X 12AT7, power: 4 X 6L6, and a solid-state rectifier. O'Brien amps were available as a 50W head (last MSR was $3,995), 100W head (last MSR was $4,395), 50W 2-12 in. speaker combo (last MSR was $4,995), 100W 2-12 in. speaker combo (last MSR was $5,295), and a 50W 4-10 in. speaker combo (last MSR was $5,395). Speaker cabinets were available in several configurations including 1-12 in. speaker (last MSR was $1,595), 2-12 in. speakers (last MSR was $1,995), and 4-12 in. speakers in a straight or slanted front (last MSR was $2,995). All amps and cabinets were covered in hand-stiched top grain black leather upholstery, and custom coverings were available.

OLIVER

Amplifiers previously produced in Westbury, NY from the late 1960s until the 1970s.

The Oliver Sound Company was started by Jess Oliver after he left Ampeg in 1966. Oliver started the company with Gene Andre who was a technician from Ampeg. Most Oliver amps were based off of Ampeg's designs, including an extension on the Portaflex. The Oliver Powerflex was probably their most popular design where an electric motor would elevate the head out of the speaker cabinet on a platform. Oliver also produced combo amps with a rotating speaker cabinet. Oliver received patents on the Powerflex, Orbital Power Projector, and the Electro-Vibe Pick-Up. Jess Oliver passed away on June 30, 2011. History courtesy: Gregg Hopkins & Bill Moore, *Ampeg: The Story Behind the Sound*.

ELECTRIC AMPLIFIERS

POWERFLEX (P-500) – ~60W, 1-15 in. or 2-15 in. speakers in a separate cabinet, all-tube chassis, preamp: 6EU7s, two channels, tremolo, reverb, head raised out of cabinet like Ampeg Portaflex, but raised by a motor, front brown control panel, nine knobs, black grille, silver grille, mfg. late 1960s-1970s.

W/Working Motor	N/A	$650 - 800	$350 - 450	
W/O Working Motor	N/A	$400 - 550	$200 - 300	

• Add $150 for 2-15 in. speaker cabinet.

OMEGA

Amplifiers previously produced in Japan during the 1960s.

Omega were Japanese-built amplifiers that were modeled very closely to Ampeg models. One example is an Omega model that is almost identical to the Ampeg R-12, with the only difference being that Japanese components were used to build it. These amps were covered in very cheap papery silver-gray material, and very inferior to real Ampeg models. There are other Omega models out there other than this R-12 copy, and if anybody has any information they can submit it directly to Blue Book Publications. Information courtesy Gregg Hopkins & Bill Moore, *Ampeg: The Story Behind the Sound*.

| MSR/NOTES | 100% | EXCELLENT | AVERAGE | LAST MSR |

ORANGE

Amplifiers currently produced in London, England, the U.S., Korea, and China since the mid-1990s. Orange amplfiers were previously produced from circa 1968 to 1981. Distributed in the U.S. by the Orange Musical Electronic Company Limited in Atlanta, GA.

The Orange amplifier trademark was established by Clifford Cooper in September of 1968. Cooper started a shop in London, England selling musical instruments, but being a young man and not widely known, he was unable to develop many dealerships within his shop. Cooper decided to build amplifiers himself if he couldn't establish any dealerships with manufacturers. Cooper hired some of the best engineers in the area to build amplifiers, including Mat Mathias, and he acquired some vinyl in the color orange that they started covering the amps in. Instead of naming the company Cooper, he named it after the color the amps sported, and Orange amplifiers was born. Mathias left Orange in 1973 and went on to produce amps under the Matamp, Green, Red, Blue, and White labels (see Matamp).

The success of these amplifiers was partly to do with the oddly colored vinyl, but they were also solid, well-built, good sounding amps. It really didn't take long for Orange amps to take off in the 1970s when solid-state products were being introduced. Solid-state was innovative and new at the time, but users still craved the tube sound and power that tube amps could produce. So, Orange began making PA units that were full of power, along with bass combos, large guitar amps, mixing boards, disco units, & other products. Orange had a full line of products throughout the 1970s.

The dawn of the 1980s signified Orange's demise. Solid-state amps were becoming a useful option and synthesizers became the new fad. Suddenly, Orange didn't have the following they once had and they stopped producing amps circa 1981. There is speculation that amps were produced sporadically during the 1980s, but most people consider 1981 to be the last year of Orange. In 1993, Orange was revived by the original founder, Clifford Cooper. The first amps appeared in 1994 and were reissues of the popular OR80 and OR120 models from the 1970s. In 1995, they released the V12 Combo and Hustler Combo. In 1997, Orange introduced the Oscillatory Transition Return (OTR) model, which was a completely new innovation for Orange. In 2000, Orange introduced a line of solid-state practice amps that are produced in Korea. Orange continues to produce a full line of guitar and bass amps that are produced in England, the U.S., and Korea. For more information, visit Orange's website or contact them directly. Source for Orange history: www.orange-amps.com by Mo Morgan the Media Manager at Orange in 2002.

CONTACT INFORMATION
ORANGE
World Headquarters
108 Ripon Way
Borehamwood, Hertfordshire WD6 2JA
England
Phone No.: +44 20 8905 2828
Fax No.: +44 20 8905 2868
www.orangeamps.com
info@omec.com

USA Distribution
2065 Peachtree Industrial Ct, Suite 208
Atlanta, GA 30341
Phone No.: 404-303-8196
Fax No.: 404-303-7176
www.orangeamps.com
info@orangeusa.com

ELECTRIC TUBE AMPLIFIERS: EARLY ORANGE MODELS

These are the original Orange models produced between circa 1968 and 1981. Extremely clean examples are very collectible and they bring a premium.

OR80 – 80W, head-unit only, all tube chassis, preamp: 3 X ECC83/7025, power: 2 X EL34, front silver control panel, two inputs (hi and lo), five black knobs (F.A.C., b, t, H.F. Drive, g), echo return and send jacks, orange vinyl covering, brown grille, mfg. 1968-1981.

Head Only	N/A	$1,200 - 1,500	$750 - 900
Head & One Cabinet	N/A	$2,250 - 2,750	$1,300 - 1,650

* *OR80 Combo* – similar to the OR80 Head, except in combo configuration with 2-12 in. speakers, mfg. 1968-1981.

	N/A	$1,750 - 2,150	$1,100 - 1,400

OR120 – 120W, head-unit only, all tube chassis, preamp: 3 X ECC83/7025, power: 4 X EL34, front white control panel, two inputs (hi and lo), five black knobs (F.A.C., b, t, H.F. Drive, g), echo return and send jacks, orange vinyl covering, mfg. 1968-1981.

courtesy Willie's American Guitars

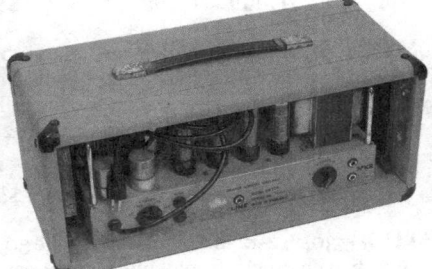
courtesy Willie's American Guitars

courtesy Willie's American Guitars

Head Only	N/A	$1,500 - 2,000	$950 - 1,200
Head & One Cabinet	N/A	$2,500 - 3,000	$1,500 - 2,000
Head & Two Cabinets	N/A	$3,250 - 4,000	$2,000 - 2,500

MSR/NOTES	100%	EXCELLENT	AVERAGE	LAST MSR

* **OR120 Combo** – similar to the OR120 Head, except in combo configuration with 2-12 in. speakers, mfg. 1968-1981.

	N/A	$2,000 - 2,500	$1,200 - 1,500	

* **OR120 Overdrive** – similar to the OR120 Head, except has an additional presence knob for a total of six knobs, mfg. 1970s.

	100%	EXCELLENT	AVERAGE	
Head Only	N/A	$1,500 - 2,000	$950 - 1,200	
Head & One Cabinet	N/A	$2,500 - 3,000	$1,500 - 2,000	
Head & Two Cabinets	N/A	$3,250 - 4,000	$2,000 - 2,500	

ELECTRIC TUBE AMPLIFIERS: AD SERIES

All AD Series amplifiers are designed in England and produced in the England and the U.S. with the exception of the AD5 that is built in China. Custom Shop amps are entirely hand-built to order in England, and air freighted to the USA.

AD5
courtesy Orange

AD30 Twin Channel Head
courtesy Orange

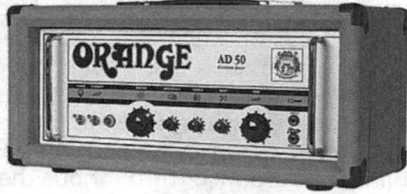

AD50 Custom Head
courtesy Orange

AD5 – 5W, 1-10 in. Celestion G10N-40 speaker, guitar combo, two-tube chassis, preamp: 1 X ECC83/12AX7, power: 1 X EL84, single channel, top white control panel, single input, two black knobs (v, tone), power switch, plywood cabinet, orange covering, brown cloth grille with Orange logo, made in China, mfg. early 2000s, reintroduced 2009-disc.

	$520	$300 - 350	$175 - 225	$649

AD15-10 – 15W, 1-10 in. Jensen Alnico speaker, guitar combo, five-tube Class A chassis, preamp: 2 X ECC83, power: 2 X EL84, GZ34 rectifier, single channel, top white control panel, single input, five black knobs (g, b, m, t, MV), standby, 8 and 16 Ohm external speaker jacks, orange vinyl covering, light brown grille, mfg. 2000-02.

	N/A	$500 - 600	$250 - 350	$1,059

AD15-12 – 15W, 1-12 in. Celestion Vintage 30 speaker, guitar combo, five-tube Class A chassis, preamp: 2 X ECC83, power: 2 X EL84, GZ34 rectifier, single channel, top white control panel, single input, five black knobs (g, b, m, t, MV), standby, 8 and 16 Ohm external speaker jacks, orange vinyl covering, light brown grille, 35 lbs., mfg. 2000-04.

	N/A	$550 - 650	$300 - 375	$1,199

AD30H HEAD – 30W, all tube chassis Class A head-unit, preamp: 2 X ECC83, power: 4 X EL84, GZ34 rectifier, single channel, front white control panel, two inputs, five black knobs (MV, t, m, b, g), standby, orange vinyl covering, 37 lbs., mfg. 2000-04.

	N/A	$550 - 650	$300 - 400	$1,199

AD30R COMBO – 30W, 2-12 in. Celestion Vintage 30 speakers, all tube Class A chassis, preamp: 2 X ECC83, power: 4 X EL84, GZ34 rectifier, single channel, reverb, front white control panel, two inputs, six black knobs (MV, r, t, m, b, g), standby, orange vinyl covering, brown grille, 81 lbs., mfg. 2000-05.

	N/A	$1,000 - 1,200	$550 - 650	

AD30 TWIN CHANNEL HEAD (AD30HTC) – 30W, guitar head-unit, nine-tube chassis, preamp: 4 X ECC83/12AX7, power: 4 X EL84, GZ34 rectifier, two channels, front white control panel with two chrome handles, single input, ten black knobs (Ch.1: MV, t, m, b, g, Ch.2: MV, t, m, b, g), power switch, standby switch, channel switch, rear panel: three speaker out jacks (one 16 ohm and two 8 ohm), channel footswitch jack, two HT fuses, orange covering with a black handle and black corners, 21.625 in. wide, 10 in. tall, 9.5 in. deep, 39.6 lbs., made in England and the USA, mfg. 2001-present.

MSR $2,300	$1,650	$1,075 - 1,250	$550 - 675	

AD30 TWIN CHANNEL COMBO (AD30TC) – 30W, 2-12 in. Celestion Vintage 30 speakers, guitar combo, nine-tube chassis, preamp: 4 X ECC83/12AX7, power: 4 X EL84, GZ34 rectifier, two channels, front white control panel with two chrome handles, single input, ten black knobs (Ch.1: g, b, m, t, MV, Ch.2: g, b, m, t, MV), power switch, standby switch, channel switch, rear panel: three speaker out jacks (one 16 ohm and two 8 ohm), channel footswitch jack, two HT fuses, orange covering with a black handle and black corners, brown cloth grille with Orange logo and symbol, 26 in. wide, 21.25 in. tall, 11.75 in. deep, 83.8 lbs., made in England and the USA, mfg. 2001-present.

MSR $3,180	$2,300	$1,300 - 1,550	$700 - 850	

MSR/NOTES	100%	EXCELLENT	AVERAGE		LAST MSR

AD50 CUSTOM HEAD (CUSTOM SHOP) – 50W (Class AB, switchable to 30W in Class A), guitar head-unit only, four-tube hand wired point-to-point chassis, preamp 2 X 12AX7/ECC83, power: 2 X EL34/6CA7, solid-state rectifier, single channel, front white control panel with two chrome handles, two inputs (high and low), five black knobs (MV, t, m, b, g), power switch, standby switch, footswitch EQ bypass, 8 & 16 Ohm speaker outputs, orange covering with a black handle and black corners, 21.625 in. wide, 10 in. tall, 9.5 in. deep, 46.2 lbs., made in England, mfg. 2002-disc.

	$2,840	$1,650 - 2,000	$850 - 1,050	

* **AD50 Custom Combo (AD50C, Custom Shop)** – similar to the AD50 Custom Head, except in combo configuration with 2-12 in. Celestion Heritage speakers, made in England, mfg. 2008-09.

	$4,099	$1,950 - 2,350	N/A	$4,099

AD140TC TWIN CHANNEL HEAD – 140W, head-unit only, all tube Class AB chassis, preamp: 4 X ECC83, power: 4 X EL34, dual channels, front white control panel, single input, ten black knobs (Ch. 1: MV, t, m, b, g, Ch. 2: MV, t, m, b, g), channel switch, orange vinyl covering, 55 lbs., mfg. 2001-06.

	$1,850	$1,100 - 1,300	$600 - 700	

AD200 BASS (AD200B, CUSTOM SHOP) – 200W, bass head-unit, six-tube hand wired point-to-point chassis, preamp: 1 X ECC81, 1 X ECC83, power: 4 X 6550, solid-state rectifier, single channel, front white control panel with two chrome handles, two inputs (high and low), five black knobs (MV, t, m, b, g), power switch, standby switch, orange covering with a black handle and black corners, 53 lbs., mfg. 2000-06.

	$2,279	$1,075 - 1,300	$625 - 750	

AD200 BASS MK3 (AD200B) – 200W, bass head-unit, seven-tube hand wired point-to-point chassis, preamp: 2 X ECC83, 1 X ECC81/12AT7, power: 4 X 6550/KT88, solid-state rectifier, single channel, front white control panel with two chrome handles, two inputs (passive/active), five black knobs (MV, t, m, b, g), power switch, standby switch, rear panel: slave out, three speaker jacks (two 4 ohm, one 8 ohm), two power tube failure fuses, orange covering with a black handle and black corners, 21.625 in. wide, 9.5 in. tall, 11 in. deep, 55 lbs., made in England and the USA, mfg. 2008-present.

MSR $3,300	$2,400	$1,350 - 1,650	$725 - 875	

ELECTRIC TUBE AMPLIFIERS: ROCKER/ROCKERVERB SERIES

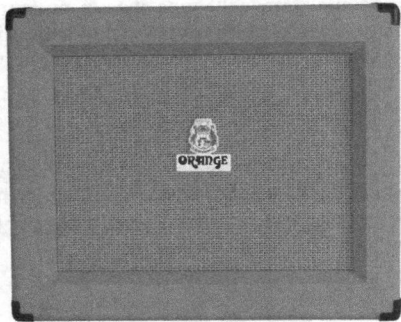

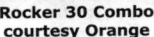

Rocker 30 Combo
courtesy Orange

Rockerverb 50 MK II Head
courtesy Orange

Rockerverb 50 Combo
courtesy Orange

ROCKER 30 HEAD (RK30HTC) – 30W, guitar head-unit, five-tube chassis, preamp: 3 X 12AX7/ECC83, power: 2 X EL34, solid-state rectifier, two channels (Natural, Dirty), front white control panel with two chrome handles, single input, six black knobs (Dirty v, h, m, l, Dirty g, Natural v), power switch, channel switch, rear panel: channel footswitch jack, three speaker outputs (two 8 ohm and one 16 ohm), orange covering with a black handle and black corners, 21.625 in. wide, 10 in. tall, 11 in. deep, 33 lbs., mfg. 2006-disc.

	$1,470	$800 - 1,000	$475 - 550	

ROCKER 30 COMBO (RK30TC) – 30W, 1-12 in. Celestion Vintage 30 speaker, guitar combo, five-tube chassis, preamp: 3 X 12AX7/ECC83, power: 2 X EL34, solid-state rectifier, two channels (Natural, Dirty), front white control panel with two chrome handles, single input, six black knobs (Natural v, Dirty g, l, m, h, Dirty v), power switch, channel switch, rear panel: channel footswitch jack, three speaker outputs (two 8 ohm and one 16 ohm), orange covering with a black handle and black corners, brown cloth grille with Orange logo, 20.5 in. wide, 17.75 in. tall, 11.75 in. deep, 52.8 lbs., mfg. 2004-disc.

	$1,570	$900 - 1,100	$500 - 600	

ROCKERVERB 50 HEAD (RK50HTC) – 50W, guitar head-unit only, ten-tube chassis, preamp: 4 X 12AX7/ECC83, 2 X 12AT7/ECC81, power: 4 X 6V6, solid-state rectifier, two channels, reverb, front white control panel with two chrome handles, single input, nine black knobs (Both: r, Dirty Ch.: v, t, m, b, g, Clean Ch.: t, b, v), power switch, channel switch, rear panel: tube-driven effects loop, footswitch jacks for channel and reverb, three speaker outputs (two 8 ohm and one 16 ohm), hi/low output damping switch, two output valve failure fuses, orange covering, 21.625 in. wide, 10 in. tall, 11 in. deep, 52.8 lbs., mfg. 2004-2010.

	$2,100	$1,200 - 1,450	$650 - 750	

MSR/NOTES	100%	EXCELLENT	AVERAGE	LAST MSR

Rockverb 50 MKIII 1-12 Combo
courtesy Orange

Rockerverb 50 MK III Combo
courtesy Orange

Rockerverb 50 MK III Head
courtesy Orange

ROCKERVERB 50 MK II HEAD (RK100HTC) – 50W, guitar head unit, nine-tube chassis, preamp: 4 X 12AX7/ECC83, 3 X 12AT7/ECC81, power: 2 X EL34 (6L6, KT88, or 6550 tubes may also be used), two channels (clean/dirty), reverb, front white control panel with original Orange hieroglyphic symbols, single input, 10 black knobs (Both: r, Dirty Ch.: v, t, m, b, g, Clean Ch.: t, m, b, v), channel switch, power/standby switch, rear panel: three speaker jacks, footswitch jack, effects loop, orange covering, 21.625 in. wide, 9.5 in. tall, 11 in. deep, 44 lbs., mfg. 2010-2015.

| | $2,100 | $1,200 - 1,450 | $650 - 750 | |

* *Rockerverb 50 MKII 1-12 Combo (RK50C112)* – similar to the Rockerverb 50 MK II Head, except in combo configuration with 1-12 in. speaker, orange covering, brown grille cloth with an orange logo and symbol, 21.625 in. wide, 20.5 in. tall, 11 in. deep, 66 lbs., mfg. 2010-disc.

| | $2,300 | $1,300 - 1,600 | $700 - 825 | |

* *Rockerverb 50 MKII 2-12 Combo (RK50C212)* – similar to the Rockerverb 50 MK II Head, except in combo configuration with 2-12 in. speakers, orange covering, brown grille cloth with an orange logo and symbol, 26 in. wide, 20.5 in. tall, 11 in. deep, 81.5 lbs., mfg. 2010-disc.

| | $2,550 | $1,450 - 1,800 | $800 - 950 | |

ROCKERVERB 50 MK III COMBO – 50W, 2-12 in. Celestion Vintage 30 speakers, guitar combo amp, eight-tube chassis, preamp: 4 X 12AX7/ECC83, 2 X 12AT7/ECC81, power: 2 X EL34, two channels (clean/dirty), reverb, top orange/black/white control panel with original Orange hieroglyphic symbols, single input, 10 black knobs, channel switch, power switch, standby switch, orange or black covering, light brown grille, side handles, 25.98 in. wide, 21.26 in. tall, 11 in. deep, 82.89 lbs., mfg. 2015-present.

| MSR $3,199 | $2,350 | $1,525 - 1,750 | $775 - 950 | |

ROCKERVERB 50 MK III HEAD – 50W, guitar head unit, eight-tube chassis, preamp: 4 X 12AX7/ECC83, 2 X 12AT7/ECC81, power: 2 X EL34, two channels (clean/dirty), reverb, front orange/black/white control panel with original Orange hieroglyphic symbols, single input, 10 black knobs, channel switch, power switch, standby switch, three external speaker jacks, three footswitch jacks, effects loop, orange or black covering, two front chrome handles, top black handle, 21.65 in. wide, 10.63 in. tall, 11 in. deep, 45.75 lbs., mfg. 2015-present.

| MSR $2,799 | $2,000 | $1,300 - 1,500 | $650 - 800 | |

ROCKERVERB 50 COMBO (RK50TC) – 50W, 2-12 in. Celestion Vintage 30 speakers, ten-tube chassis, preamp: 4 X 12AX7/ECC83, 2 X 12AT7/ECC81, power: 4 X 6V6, solid-state rectifier, two channels, reverb, front white control panel with two chrome handles, single input, nine black knobs (Both: r, Dirty Ch.: v, t, m, b, g, Clean Ch.: t, b, v), power switch, channel switch, rear panel: tube-driven effects loop, footswitch jacks for channel and reverb, three speaker outputs (two 8 ohm and one 16 ohm), hi/low output damping switch, two output valve failure fuses, side-mounted recessed handles, orange covering, brown speaker grille with Orange logo and symbol, 26 in. wide, 21.25 in. tall, 11.75 in. deep, 81.4 lbs., mfg. 2004-disc.

| MSR N/A | $2,520 | $1,400 - 1,750 | $750 - 900 | |

ROCKERVERB 100 HEAD (RK100HTC) – 100W, head-unit only, all-tube chassis, preamp: 4 X 12AX7/ECC83, 2 X 12AT7/ECC81, power: 4 X EL34/6CA7/6L6GC/KT88, 6550, two channels, reverb, front white control panel, single input, nine black knobs (Both: r, Dirty Ch.: v, t, m, b, g, Clean Ch.: t, b, v), channel switch, tube-driven effects loop, footswitch, orange covering, mfg. 2004-2010.

| | $2,300 | $1,300 - 1,600 | $700 - 825 | |

ROCKERVERB 100 MK II HEAD (RK100HTC) – 100W, guitar head unit, 11-tube chassis, preamp: 4 X 12AX7/ECC83, 3 X 12AT7/ECC81, power: 4 X EL34 (6L6, KT88, or 6550 tubes may also be used), two channels (clean/dirty), reverb, front white control panel with original Orange hieroglyphic symbols, single input, 10 black knobs (Both: r, Dirty Ch.: v, t, m, b, g, Clean Ch.: t, m, b, v), channel switch, power/standby switch, rear panel: three speaker jacks, footswitch jack, effects loop, orange covering, 21.625 in. wide, 9.5 in. tall, 11 in. deep, 50.5 lbs., mfg. 2010-present.

| MSR $3,200 | $2,350 | $1,525 - 1,750 | $775 - 950 | |

* Add $249 (MSR $3,449) for model with DIVO embedded mfg. 2012-present

MSR/NOTES	100%	EXCELLENT	AVERAGE	LAST MSR

ELECTRIC TUBE AMPLIFIERS: TINY TERROR SERIES

Dark Terror Head
courtesy Orange

Dual Dark 50 Head
courtesy Orange

Dual Dark 100 Head
courtesy Orange

DARK TERROR HEAD – 15W, portable guitar head-unit, five-tube chassis, preamp: 3 X 12AX7, power: 2 X EL84, solid-state rectifier, one channel, front black control panel, single input, three knobs v, shape, g), power switch, 15W/7W/standby switch, three speaker jacks (one 16 ohm and two 8 ohm), effects loop, black all-metal portable cabinet with top carrying handle, padded gig bag included, 15 lbs., mfg. 2011-present.

| MSR $829 | $650 | $425 - 475 | $210 - 260 | |

DUAL DARK 50 HEAD – 50W, portable guitar head-unit, ten-tube chassis, preamp: 5 X 12AX7, 1 X 12AT7, power: 4 X EL34, solid-state rectifier, two channels, front black control panel, single input, nine knobs, power switch, 50W/25W/standby switch, channel switch, three speaker jacks (one 16 ohm and two 8 ohm), effects loop, two footswitch jacks, black all-metal portable cabinet with top carrying handle, 46.3 lbs., mfg. 2014-present.

| MSR $3,199 | $2,300 | $1,500 - 1,725 | $750 - 925 | |

DUAL DARK 100 HEAD – 100W, guitar head-unit, ten-tube chassis, preamp: 5 X 12AX7, 1 X 12AT7, power: 4 X EL34, solid-state rectifier, two channels, front black control panel, single input, nine knobs, power switch, power-mode/standby switch, channel switch, output switch, three speaker jacks (one 16 ohm and two 8 ohm), effects loop, two footswitch jacks, black all-metal portable cabinet with top carrying handle, 52 lbs., mfg. 2014-present.

| MSR $3,399 | $2,500 | $1,625 - 1,875 | $825 - 1,000 | |

DUAL TERROR HEAD (DT30H) – 30W, portable guitar head-unit, eight-tube chassis, preamp: 4 X ECC83, power: 4 X EL84, solid-state rectifier, two channels, front white control panel, single input, six knobs (Ch. 1: v, tone, g, Ch. 2: v, tone, g), power switch, 30W/15W/7W switch, three speaker jacks (one 16 ohm and two 8 ohm), white all-metal portable cabinet with top carrying handle, padded gig bag included, made in China, mfg. 2009-present.

| MSR $1,139 | $900 | $575 - 675 | $295 - 350 | |

MICRO DARK HEAD – 20W, guitar head-unit, hybrid chassis, preamp: 1 X 12AX7, solid-state power, single channel, front black control panel, single input, three knobs (v, shape, g), power switch, headphone jack, one speaker jack, effects loop, black all-metal portable cabinet with top carrying handle, 1.72 lbs., mfg. 2015-present.

| MSR $249 | $190 | $125 - 140 | $60 - 75 | |

MICRO TERROR HEAD – 20W, guitar head-unit, hybrid chassis, preamp: 1 X 12AX7, solid-state power, single channel, front white control panel, single input, three knobs (v, tone, g), power switch, headphone jack, aux. in jack, one speaker jack, white all-metal portable cabinet with top carrying handle, 1.87 lbs., mfg. 2012-present.

| MSR $199 | $150 | $100 - 115 | $50 - 60 | |

TINY TERROR HEAD (TT15) – 15W, guitar head-unit, four-tube chassis, preamp: 2 X ECC83, power: 2 X EL84, solid-state rectifier, single channel, front white control panel, single input, three knobs (v, tone, g), power switch, 15W/7W/standby switch, three speaker jacks (one 16 ohm and two 8 ohm), white all-metal portable cabinet with top carrying handle, padded gig bag included, 12 in. wide, 6 in. tall, 5.25 in. deep, 13.25 lbs., made in China, mfg. 2007-present.

| MSR $769 | $600 | $400 - 450 | $195 - 240 | |

* Tiny Terror Hand Wired Edition Head (TTHW15H) – similar to the Tiny Terror Head, except is point-to-point handwired and includes a leather padded gig bag, made in England and the USA, mfg. 2009-disc.

| | $1,150 | $650 - 800 | $325 - 400 | |

* Tiny Terror Jim Root 4 Signature Head (TT15JR) – 15W, guitar head-unit, five-tube chassis, preamp: 3 X 12AX7, power: 2 X EL84, solid-state rectifier, single channel, front black control panel with orange logo/emblem and Jim Root signature, single input, five knobs (v, b, m, t, g), power switch, 15W/7W/standby switch, three speaker jacks (one 16 ohm and two 8 ohm), effects loop, black all-metal portable cabinet with top carrying handle, padded gig bag included, 12 in. wide, 7.48 in. tall, 6.1 in. deep, 12.45 lbs., mfg. 2012-present.

| MSR $899 | $700 | $450 - 525 | $230 - 280 | |

TINY TERROR 1-10 COMBO (TT15-10) – 15W, 1-10 in. Celestion G10N-40 speaker, guitar combo, four-tube chassis, preamp: 2 X ECC83, power: 2 X EL84, solid-state rectifier, single channel, top white control panel, single input, three knobs (v, tone, g), power switch, 15W/7W/standby switch, three speaker jacks (one 16 ohm and two 8 ohm), orange covering with a black handle and black corners, brown cloth grille with Orange logo, 37.4 lbs., made in China, mfg. 2010-disc.

| | $660 | $375 - 450 | $225 - 275 | $819 |

MSR/NOTES	100%	EXCELLENT	AVERAGE	LAST MSR

Tiny Terror Head
courtesy Orange

Tiny Terror 1-12 Combo
courtesy Orange

Terror Bass 500
courtesy Orange

TINY TERROR 1-12 COMBO (TT15C) – 15W, 1-12 in. Celestion G12H-30 speaker, guitar combo, four-tube chassis, preamp: 2 X ECC83, power: 2 X EL84, solid-state rectifier, single channel, top white control panel, single input, three knobs (v, tone, g), power switch, 15W/7W/standby switch, three speaker jacks (one 16 ohm and two 8 ohm), orange covering with a black handle and black corners, brown cloth grille with Orange logo, 37.4 lbs., made in China, mfg. 2009-disc.

	$860	$500 - 600	$300 - 350	$1,089

TERROR BASS 500 (BT500H) – 500W, portable guitar head-unit, two-tube hybrid chassis, preamp: 2 X 12AX7, Class D solid-state power section, solid-state rectifier, single channel, front white control panel, single input with active/passive switch, five knobs (v, t, m, b, g), power/standby switch, side panel: effects loop, XLR line out, rear panel: selectable 4 or 8 ohm impedance speaker outs, white all-metal portable cabinet with top carrying handle, padded gig bag included, made in China, mfg. 2009-disc.

	$860	$500 - 600	$300 - 350	$1,089

* *Terror Bass 1000 (BT1000H)* – similar to the Terror Bass 500, except has 1000W output, mfg. 2010-disc.

	$1,000	$600 - 700	$325 - 400	$1,275

ELECTRIC TUBE AMPLIFIERS: MISC. MODELS

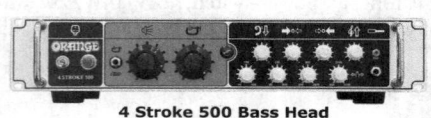

4 Stroke 500 Bass Head
courtesy Orange

Custom Shop 50 Head (CS50)
courtesy Orange

OR 15 Head (OR15H)
courtesy Orange

4 STROKE 300 BASS HEAD – 300W, bass head-unit, solid-state chassis, single channel, front white/black/orange control panel, single input, two black knobs, eight white knobs, pad switch, power switch, footswitch jack, XLR out, line out, cooling fan, two speaker out jacks, two front chrome handles, white covering, 20.83 lbs., new 2016.

MSR $1,279	$950	$625 - 725	$300 - 375	

4 STROKE 500 BASS HEAD – 500W, bass head-unit, solid-state chassis, single channel, front white/black/orange control panel, single input, two black knobs, eight white knobs, pad switch, power switch, footswitch jack, XLR out, line out, cooling fan, two speaker out jacks, two front chrome handles, white covering, 20.83 lbs., new 2016.

MSR $1,449	$1,100	$725 - 825	$350 - 450	

40th ANNIVERSARY OR50 HEAD – 50W, guitar head-unit, five-tube chassis, preamp: 3 X ECC83/12AX7, power: 2 X EL34, solid-state rectifier, single channel, pics only Plexiglass front panel with two chrome handles, single input, six black knobs (MV, high-freq. drive, t, m, b, g), power switch, standby switch, footswitch jack, rear panel: three speaker jacks (one 16 ohm, two 8 ohm), orange covering with a black handle and black corners, 21.625 in. wide, 10 in. tall, 9.5 in. deep, 46.2 lbs., made in England and the USA, mfg. 2009 only.

	$1,959	$1,000 - 1,250	N/A	$1,959

Orange also produced a 40th Anniversary Custom Shop Model OR50 that was limited to 40 units worldwide.

CUSTOM SHOP 50 HEAD (CS50) – 50W (Class AB, switchable to 30W in Class A), guitar head-unit only, four-tube chassis, preamp 2 X 12AX7/ECC83, power: 2 X EL34/6CA7, solid-state rectifier, single channel, front white control panel with two chrome handles, single input, six black knobs (MV, drive, t, m, b, g), power switch, standby switch, footswitch jack, rear panel: Class AB 50W/Class A 30W power switch, three speaker jacks (two 8 ohm and one 16 ohm), orange covering with a black handle and black corners, 21.625 in. wide, 10.63 in. tall, 9.5 in. deep, 40.9 lbs., made in England, mfg. 2013-present.

MSR $3,899	$2,800	$1,825 - 2,100	$900 - 1,125	

OR 15 HEAD (OR15H) – 15W (switchable to 7W), guitar head-unit, six-tube chassis, preamp: 3 X ECC83/12AX7, 1 X 12AT7, power: 2 X EL84, solid-state rectifier, single channel, pics only Plexiglass front panel with two chrome handles, single input, five black knobs (MV, t, m, b, g), power switch, standby switch, rear panel: three speaker jacks (one 16 ohm, two 8 ohm), effects loop, orange covering with a black handle and black corners, 15.75 in. wide, 8.27 in. tall, 7.09 in. deep, 17.77 lbs., made in England and the USA, mfg. 2012-present.

MSR $999	$700	$450 - 525	$230 - 280	

MSR/NOTES	100%	EXCELLENT	AVERAGE	LAST MSR

OR 50 Head (OR50H)
courtesy Orange

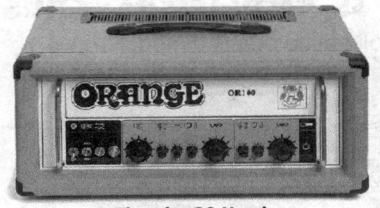

Thunder 30 Head
courtesy Orange

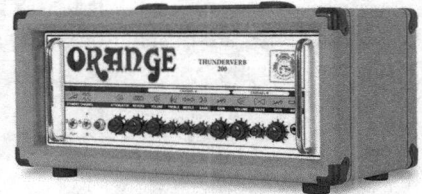

Thunderverb 200 Head
courtesy Orange

OR 50 HEAD (OR50H) – 50W, guitar head-unit, five-tube chassis, preamp: 3 X ECC83/12AX7, power: 2 X EL34, solid-state rectifier, single channel, pics only Plexiglass front panel with two chrome handles, single input, six black knobs (MV, high-freq. drive, t, m, b, g), power switch, standby switch, footswitch jack, rear panel: three speaker jacks (one 16 ohm, two 8 ohm), orange covering with a black handle and black corners, 21.625 in. wide, 10.63 in. tall, 9.5 in. deep, 40.9 lbs., made in England and the USA, mfg. 2012-present.

MSR $2,369 $1,700 $1,100 - 1,275 $550 - 675

OR 100 HEAD (OR100H) – 100W, guitar head-unit, nine-tube chassis, preamp: 4 X ECC83/12AX7, 1 X 12AT7, power: 4 X EL34, solid-state rectifier, two channels, pics only Plexiglass front panel with two chrome handles, single input, eight black knobs, power switch, standby switch, channel switch, footswitch jack, rear panel: three speaker jacks (one 16 ohm, two 8 ohm), orange covering with a black handle and black corners, 21.625 in. wide, 10.63 in. tall, 11.02 in. deep, 52.14 lbs., made in England and the USA, mfg. 2013-present.

MSR $2,999 $2,000 $1,300 - 1,500 $650 - 800

RETRO 50 HEAD (CUSTOM SHOP) – 50W (Class AB, switchable to 30W in Class A), guitar head-unit only, four-tube hand wired point-to-point chassis, preamp 2 X 12AX7/ECC83, power: 2 X EL34/6CA7, solid-state rectifier, single channel, front white control panel with two chrome handles, single input, five black knobs (MV, t, m, b, g), power switch, standby switch, footswitch gain switch, rear panel: Class AB 50W/Class A 30W power switch, three speaker jacks (two 8 ohm and one 16 ohm), orange covering with a black handle and black corners, 21.625 in. wide, 10 in. tall, 9.5 in. deep, 46.2 lbs., made in England, mfg. 2000-disc.

$2,400 $1,350 - 1,650 $725 - 875

* *Retro Combo (Retro 50C, Custom Shop)* – similar to the AD50 Custom Head, except in combo configuration with 2-12 in. Celestion Heritage speakers, made in England, mfg. 2008-09.

$4,099 $1,950 - 2,350   N/A $4,099

THUNDER 30 HEAD (TH30) – 30W, guitar head unit, eight-tube chassis, preamp: 2 X ECC83, 2 X ECC81, power: 4 X EL84, solid-state rectifier, two channels (clean/dirty), top white control panel with original Orange hieroglyphic symbols, single input, six black knobs (Clean Ch.: v, b, t, Dirty Ch.: g, shape, v), channel switch, full power/half power/standby switch, power switch, rear panel: three speaker jacks, footswitch jack, effects loop, orange vinyl covering, 21.625 in. wide, 9.5 in. tall, 9.5 in. deep, 33 lbs., mfg. 2010-present.

MSR $1,649 $1,200 $750 - 900 $500 - 600

* *Thunder 30 Combo (TH30)* – similar to the TH30 Head, except in combo configuration with 1-12 in. Celestion Vintage 30 speaker, orange vinyl covering, brown grille with orange logo and symbol, 21.625 in. wide, 20.5 in. tall, 11 in. deep, 53 lbs., mfg. 2010-present.

MSR $1,879 $1,375 $900 - 1,025 $450 - 550

THUNDER 100 HEAD (TH100) – 100W, switchable to 70/50/35W, guitar head unit, eight-tube chassis, preamp: 4 X ECC83, power: 4 X EL84, solid-state rectifier, two channels (clean/dirty), front white control panel with original Orange hieroglyphic symbols, single input, six black knobs (Clean Ch.: v, b, t, Dirty Ch.: g, shape, v), channel switch, full power/half power/standby switch, power switch, rear panel: three speaker jacks, footswitch jack, effects loop, orange vinyl covering, 33 lbs., mfg. 2011-present.

MSR $2,079 $1,500 $975 - 1,125 $500 - 600

THUNDERVERB 50 HEAD (MODEL TH50HTC) – 50W, guitar/bass head-unit, eight-tube chassis, preamp: 4 X ECC83/12AX7, 2 X ECC81/12AT7, power: 2 X 6550/KT88, two channels (A/B), reverb, front white control panel with two chrome handles, single input, 10 black knobs of various sizes (attenuator, r, Ch. A: v, t, m, b, g, Ch. B: v, shape, g), standby switch, channel switch, rear panel: effects loop, three footswitch jacks (channel, reverb, attenuator), three speaker jacks (two 8 ohm and one 16 ohm), power switch, orange covering with a black handle and black corners, 21.625 in. wide, 10 in. tall, 11 in. deep, 55 lbs., made in England and the USA, mfg. 2007-present.

MSR $3,210 $2,350 $1,525 - 1,750 $775 - 950

THUNDERVERB 200 HEAD (MODEL TH200HTC) – 200W, guitar/bass head-unit, 10-tube chassis, preamp: 4 X ECC83, 2 X ECC81, power: 4 X 6550/KT88, two channels (A/B), reverb, front white control panel with two chrome handles, single input, 10 black knobs of various sizes (attenuator, r, Ch. A: v, t, m, b, g, Ch. B: v, shape, g), standby switch, channel switch, rear panel: effects loop, three footswitch jacks (channel, reverb, attenuator), four speaker jacks, output power jack (100W/200W), mains, orange covering with a black handle and black corners, 21.75 in. wide, 10.25 in. tall, 11 in. deep, 66 lbs., made in England and the USA, mfg. 2007-present.

MSR $4,090 $2,940 $1,700 - 2,050 $900 - 1,100

MSR/NOTES	100%	EXCELLENT	AVERAGE	LAST MSR

ELECTRIC SS AMPLIFIERS: CRUSH SERIES

The Crush series are built in Korea and are solid-state practice models.

Crush 12
courtesy Orange

Crush 30R
courtesy Orange

Crush 35B Bass
courtesy Orange

CRUSH 10 (CR10) – 10W, 1-6 in. heavy-duty speaker, guitar combo, solid-state chassis, single channel, top white control panel, single input, six black knobs (l, m, h, MV, g2, g1), headphone jack, orange vinyl covering with black handle and black corners, light brown grille with Orange logo/emblem, 9 lbs., mfg. 2000-09.

	$75	$40 - 50	$25 - 35	$89

CRUSH 12 (CR12) – 12W, 1-6 in. heavy-duty speaker, guitar combo, solid-state chassis, single channel, top white control panel, single input, six black knobs (t, m, b, V, g, OD), headphone jack, power switch, orange or black vinyl covering with black handle and black corners, light brown grille with Orange logo/emblem, 10.4 lbs., mfg. 2014-present.

MSR $119	$100	$65 - 75	$35 - 40	

CRUSH 15 (CR15) – 15W, 1-8 in. heavy-duty speaker, guitar combo, solid-state chassis, single channel, top white control panel, single input, six black knobs (l, m, h, MV, g2, g1), gain switch, headphone jack, orange vinyl covering with black handle and black corners, light brown grille with Orange logo/emblem, 18 lbs., mfg. 2000-09.

	$100	$50 - 70	$35 - 45	$119

* **Crush 15 Reverb (CR15R)** – similar to the Crush 15 except has a reverb circuit and extra knob for reverb, mfg. 2000-09.

	$120	$60 - 85	$40 - 50	$149

CRUSH 30R (CR30R) – 30W, 1-10 in. heavy-duty speaker, guitar combo, solid-state chassis, single channel, top white control panel, two inputs (high/low), seven black knobs (r, l, m, h, v, level, g), gain switch, headphone jack, footswitch jack, orange vinyl covering with black handle and black corners, light brown grille with Orange logo/emblem, 20 lbs., mfg. 2003-09.

	$200	$110 - 135	$70 - 90	$249

CRUSH 20B BASS (CR20B) – 20W, 1-10 in. heavy-duty speaker, bass combo, solid-state chassis, single channel, top white control panel, single input, five black knobs (g, v, l, m, h), headphone jack, orange vinyl covering with a black handle and black corners, dark brown grille with Orange logo/emblem, 15 lbs., mfg. 2003-09.

	$140	$65 - 90	$45 - 55	$159

CRUSH 35B BASS (CR35B) – 35W, 1-12 in. heavy-duty speaker, bass combo, solid-state chassis, single channel, reverb, top white control panel, two inputs (high/low), five black knobs (g, v, l, m, h), headphone jack, line out jack, speaker out jack, orange vinyl covering with a black handle and black corners, dark brown grille with an Orange logo/emblem, 29 lbs., mfg. 2003-09.

	$200	$110 - 135	$70 - 90	$249

CRUSH PIX 12L (CR12L) – 12W, 1-6 in. heavy-duty speaker, guitar combo, solid-state chassis, single channel, top white control panel with original Orange hieroglyphic symbols, single input, six black knobs (l, m, h, MV, OD, g), aux. in/MP3 jack, headphone jack, available in orange or black vinyl covering with black handle and black corners, light brown grille with Orange logo/emblem, mfg. 2010-disc.

	$90	$50 - 60	$30 - 40	$109

CRUSH PIX 20L (CR20L) – 20W, 1-8 in. heavy-duty speaker, guitar combo, solid-state chassis, two channels (Clean, Dirty), top white control panel with original Orange hieroglyphic symbols, single input, six black knobs (l, m, h, Clean Ch. v, OD, Dirty Ch. g), aux. in/MP3 jack, headphone jack, available in orange or black vinyl covering with black handle and black corners, light brown grille with Orange logo/emblem, mfg. 2010-disc.

	$115	$60 - 80	$35 - 50	$139

* **Crush PiX 20LDX (CR20LDX)** – similar to the Crush PiX 20L, except has digital effects including reverb, delay, chorus, and tremolo, and a built-in tuner, mfg. 2010-disc.

	$160	$95 - 120	$55 - 75	$199

MSR/NOTES	100%	EXCELLENT	AVERAGE	LAST MSR

Crush Pro 60 (CR60C)
courtesy Orange

Crush Pro 120 Combo (CR120C)
courtesy Orange

Crush Pro 120 Head (CR120H)
courtesy Orange

CRUSH PIX 25BX (CR25BX) – 25W, 1-8 in. heavy-duty speaker, bass combo, solid-state chassis, single channel, top white control panel with original Orange hieroglyphic symbols, single input, five black knobs (v, h, m, l, g), headphone jack, line out, aux./MP3 in, available in orange or black vinyl covering with a black handle and black corners, black grille with Orange logo/emblem, mfg. 2010-present.

| MSR $210 | $180 | $95 - 120 | $55 - 75 | |

CRUSH PIX 35LDX (CR35LDX) – 35W, 1-10 in. heavy-duty speaker, guitar combo, solid-state chassis, two channels (Clean, Dirty), 16 digital effects, top white control panel with original Orange hieroglyphic symbols, two inputs, seven black knobs (l, m, h, Clean Ch. v, OD, Dirty Ch. g, digital effects), aux. in/MP3 jack, headphone jack, line out, built-in tuner, available in orange or black vinyl covering with black handle and black corners, light brown grille with Orange logo/emblem, mfg. 2010-disc.

| | $240 | $135 - 175 | $85 - 110 | $299 |

CRUSH PIX 50BX (CR50BXT) – 50W, 1-12 in. heavy-duty speaker, bass combo, solid-state chassis, single channel, top white control panel with original Orange hieroglyphic symbols, single input, five black knobs (v, h, m, l, g), headphone jack, speaker out, line out, CD RCA inputs, built-in tuner, available in orange or black vinyl covering with a black handle and black corners, black grille with Orange logo/emblem, mfg. 2010-present.

| MSR $330 | $270 | $175 - 205 | $90 - 110 | |

CRUSH PIX 100BX (CR100BXT) – 100W, 1-15 in. heavy-duty speaker, bass combo, solid-state chassis, single channel, top white control panel with original Orange hieroglyphic symbols, single input, eight black knobs (g, contour, p, t, h/m, l/m, b, v), peaker out, line out, aux. input, effects loop, XLR direct line out with ground/lift and pre/post EQ switches, built-in tuner, available in orange or black vinyl covering with a black handle and black corners, black grille with Orange logo/emblem, mfg. 2010-present.

| MSR $749 | $525 | $350 - 400 | $170 - 210 | |

CRUSH PRO 60 (CR60C) – 60W, 1-12 in. speaker, guitar combo, solid-state chassis, two channels, top white control panel, one input, ten black knobs, channel switch, power switch, orange vinyl covering with black handle and black corners, light brown grille with Orange logo/emblem, 44.64 lbs., mfg. 2013-present.

| MSR $699 | $500 | $325 - 375 | $165 - 200 | |

CRUSH PRO 120 COMBO (CR120C) – 120W, 2-12 in. speakers, guitar combo, solid-state chassis, two channels, top white control panel, one input, ten black knobs, channel switch, power switch, orange vinyl covering with black handle and black corners, light brown grille with Orange logo/emblem, 63.93 lbs., mfg. 2013-present.

| MSR $949 | $700 | $450 - 525 | $230 - 280 | |

CRUSH PRO 120 HEAD (CR120H) – 120W, guitar head unit, solid-state chassis, two channels, front white control panel, one input, ten black knobs, channel switch, power switch, effects loop, two footswitch jacks, two external speaker jacks, two front chrome handles, orange vinyl covering with black handle and black corners, 31.75 lbs., mfg. 2013-present.

| MSR $599 | $450 | $295 - 325 | $145 - 180 | |

MICRO CRUSH (CR3) – 1W, 1-4 in. speaker, miniature guitar combo, solid-state chassis, top white control panel, single input, two knobs (tone, v), overdrive button, built-in tuner, headphone jack, powered by 9V battery or power supply unit, orange covering, brown grille with Orange logo/emblem, mfg. 2007-present.

| MSR $89 | $69 | $30 - 40 | $15 - 25 | |

* Add $10 (MSR $15) for power supply unit.

MICRO CRUSH (CR6S) – 6W (2 X 3W stereo), 2-4 in. speakers, miniature stereo guitar combo, solid-state chassis, top white control panel, single input, four knobs (g, tone, v, aux. in level), overdrive button, aux. in jack, built-in tuner, headphone jack, powered by 9V battery or power supply unit, orange covering, brown grille with Orange logo/emblem, mfg. 2010-disc.

| | $90 | $50 - 65 | $30 - 40 | $110 |

* Add $10 (MSR $15) for power supply unit.

MSR/NOTES	100%	EXCELLENT	AVERAGE	LAST MSR

ELECTRIC SS BASS AMPLIFIERS: OB1 SERIES

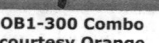

OB1-300 Combo
courtesy Orange

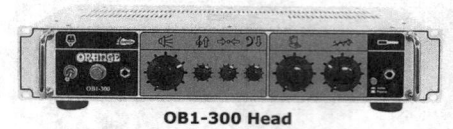

OB1-300 Head
courtesy Orange

OB1-500 Head
courtesy Orange

OB1-300 COMBO – 300W, 1-15 in. Eminence Neodymium speaker, 8 ohms, bass combo, solid-state chassis, single channel, front white/black/orange control panel, single input, six black knobs, active/passive switch, power switch, footswitch jack, XLR out, line out, cooling fan, two speaker out jacks, recessed side handles, orange or black vinyl covering with black corners, black grille with Orange logo/emblem, 65.37 lbs., new 2016.

MSR $1,839 $1,350 $875 - 1,000 $450 - 550

OB1-300 HEAD – 300W, bass head-unit, solid-state chassis, single channel, front white/black/orange control panel, single input, six black knobs, active/passive switch, power switch, footswitch jack, XLR out, line out, cooling fan, two speaker out jacks, two front chrome handles, white covering, 21 lbs., mfg. 2015-present.

MSR $999 $800 $525 - 600 $260 - 325

OB1-500 HEAD – 500W, bass head-unit, solid-state chassis, single channel, front white/black/orange control panel, single input, six black knobs, active/passive switch, power switch, footswitch jack, XLR out, line out, cooling fan, two speaker out jacks, two front chrome handles, white covering, 22.26 lbs., mfg. 2015-present.

MSR $1,099 $900 $575 - 675 $295 - 350

SPEAKER CABINETS

Orange also made other cabinets between 1967 and 1981.

49th Aniversary 4-12 Speaker Cabinet
courtesy Orange

1-8 Speaker Cabinet
courtesy Orange

1-15 Bass Speaker Cabinet
courtesy Orange

40th ANNIVERSARY 4-12 SPEAKER CABINET (PPC412-LTD) – 240W, 4-12 in. Celestion Vintage 30 70th Anniversary speakers, 16 ohm impedance, 18-ply birch faced marine plywood construction, side-mounted recessed handles, orange covering with black corners, brown cloth grille with Orange logo, emblem, and 40th Anniversary badge in lower right-hand corner, 30.75 in. wide, 29.125 in. tall, 15 in. deep, 110 lbs., made in USA, mfg. 2008 only.

                        $1,099 $525 - 625 $300 - 375 $1,099

1-8 SPEAKER CABINET (PPC108) – 20W, 1-8 in. speaker, 8 ohm impedance, orange covering, brown cloth grille with Orange logo, made in China, 7.7 lbs., mfg. 2012-present.

MSR $139 $100 $65 - 75 $35 - 40

1-12 SPEAKER CABINET (PPC112) – 60W, 1-12 in. Celestion Vintage 30 speaker, 16 ohm impedance, 18 ply birch faced marine plywood construction, orange covering, brown cloth grille with Orange logo, made in China, mfg. 2007-present.

MSR $469 $379 $210 - 250 $120 - 145

1-15 BASS SPEAKER CABINET (OBC115) – 400W, 1-15 in. Eminence speaker, 8 ohm impedance, side ported, heavy duty plywood cabinet, side-mounted recessed black handles, orange covering with black corners, dark brown covering with orange logo and emblem, 24.375 in. wide, 20 in. tall, 18.125 in. deep, 66 lbs., current mfg.

MSR $910 $660 $400 - 475 $200 - 250

MSR/NOTES	100%	EXCELLENT	AVERAGE	LAST MSR

**2-10 Bass Speaker Cabinet
courtesy Orange**

**2-12 Bass Speaker Cabinet
courtesy Orange**

**4-10 Speaker Cabinet
courtesy Orange**

2-10 BASS SPEAKER CABINET (OBC210) – 400W, 2-10 in. Eminence Legend speakers, 8 ohm impedance, heavy duty plywood cabinet, top handle, orange or black covering with black corners, black grille with orange logo and emblem, 24.375 in. wide, 13.8 in. tall, 13.4 in. deep, 42.43 lbs., mfg. 2015-present.

| MSR $1,099 | $800 | $525 - 600 | $260 - 325 | |

2-12 SPEAKER CABINET (PPC212) – 120W, 2-12 in. Eminence Custom (disc.) or Celestion Vintage 30 speakers, 16 ohm impedance, 18-ply birch faced marine plywood construction, side-mounted recessed handles, orange covering with black corners, brown cloth grille with Orange logo and emblem, 30.75 in. wide, 20.875 in. tall, 15 in. deep, 61.6 lbs., made in USA, current mfg.

| MSR $1,029 | $750 | $475 - 550 | $245 - 300 | |

* Subtract 10% for Eminence speakers.

2-12 Open Back Speaker Cabinet (PPC212OB) – similar to the 2-12 Speaker Cabinet (PPC212), except has an open back, designed for use/sized the same as the Rockerverb 50 Combo and the AD30 Twin Channel combo, 26 in. wide, 21.25 in. tall, 11.75 in. deep, 44 lbs., mfg. 2008-present.

| MSR $829 | $600 | $400 - 450 | $195 - 240 | |

2-12 Jim Root 4 Signature Speaker Cabinet (PPC212JR) – 120W, 2-12 in. Special Design Orange speakers, 16 ohm impedance, straight front, closed back, birch construction, side-mounted recessed handles, black covering with black corners, black grille with Jim Root Signature and Orange logo/emblem, 30.1 in. wide, 17.5 in. tall, 14.25 in. deep, 61 lbs., mfg. 2012-present.

| MSR $829 | $600 | $400 - 450 | $195 - 240 | |

2-12 BASS SPEAKER CABINET (OBC212) – 600W, 2-12 in. Eminence Neodymium speakers located one behind the other, 8 ohm impedance, heavy duty plywood cabinet, top handle, orange or black covering with black corners, black grille with orange logo and emblem, 21 in. wide, 19 in. tall, 15.1 in. deep, 55 lbs., mfg. 2015-present.

| MSR $949 | $750 | $475 - 550 | $245 - 300 | |

4-10 SPEAKER CABINET (PPC410) – 120W, 4-10 in. Celestion speakers, 16 ohm impedance, 13-ply birch faced marine plywood construction, side-mounted recessed handles, orange covering with black corners, brown cloth grille with Orange logo and emblem, 26 in. wide, 27.5 in. tall, 11.75 in. deep, 88 lbs., made in USA, mfg. 2010-disc.

| MSR N/A | $700 | $400 - 475 | $250 - 300 | |

4-10 BASS SPEAKER CABINET (OBC410) – 600W, 4-10 in. Eminence speakers, high-powered horn, 8 Ohm impedance, Speakon and 1/4 in. jacks, side ported, heavy duty plywood cabinet, side-mounted recessed black handles, orange covering with black corners, dark brown grille with Orange logo and emblem, 24.375 in. wide, 25.25 in. tall, 18.125 in. deep, 94.6 lbs., current mfg.

| MSR $1,379 | $1,000 | $600 - 700 | $300 - 375 | |

4-12 CRUSH PRO SPEAKER CABINET (CRPRO412) – 240W, 4-12 in. Voice Of The World speakers, 16 ohm impedance, 13-ply birch plywood construction, closed back, straight front, side-mounted recessed handles, orange covering with black corners, brown cloth grille with Orange logo and emblem, mfg. 2014-present.

| MSR $848 | $600 | $400 - 450 | $195 - 240 | |

4-12 SPEAKER CABINET (VINTAGE) – 4-12 in. speakers, straight front only, orange covering, brown grille, mfg. 1968-1981.

| | N/A | $750 - 1,000 | $500 - 650 | |

4-12 SPEAKER CABINET (PPC412) – 240W, 4-12 in. Eminence Custom (disc.) or Celestion Vintage 30 speakers, 16 ohm impedance, 18-ply birch faced marine plywood construction, side-mounted recessed handles, orange covering with black corners, brown cloth grille with Orange logo and emblem, 30.75 in. wide, 29.125 in. tall, 15 in. deep, 110 lbs., made in USA, current mfg.

| MSR $1,499 | $1,100 | $625 - 750 | $325 - 400 | |

* Subtract 10% for Eminence speakers.

MSR/NOTES	100%	EXCELLENT	AVERAGE	LAST MSR

4-12 Crush Pro Speaker Cabinet
courtesy Orange

8-10 Speaker Cabinet
courtesy Orange

Smart Power 410 Bass Cabinet
courtesy Orange

* **4-12 Slanted Speaker Cabinet (PPC412-A)** – similar to the 4-12 Speaker Cabinet (PPC412), except has an angled front, made in USA, mfg. 2008-present.

MSR $1,529	$1,100	$650 - 775	$350 - 425

* **4-12 Speaker Cabinet (PPC4X12HP)** – similar to the 4-12 Speaker Cabinet (PPC412), except has 400W, 4-12 in. Celestion G12K-100 speakers, and 8 ohm impedance, 122 lbs., made in USA, mfg. 2007-present.

MSR $1,529	$1,100	$650 - 775	$350 - 425

8-10 BASS SPEAKER CABINET (OBC810) – 1200W, 8-10 in. Eminence speakers, 4 ohm impedance, Speakon and 1/4 in. jacks, rear ported, heavy duty plywood cabinet, side-mounted recessed black handles, two heavy duty casters, orange covering with black corners, dark brown grille with Orange logo and emblem, mfg. 2010-present.

MSR $2,900	$2,100	$1,200 - 1,500	$625 - 750

SMART POWER 210 BASS CABINET (SP210) – 600W, 2-10 in. Neodymium speakers, 8 ohm impedance, two separated speaker compartments, bottom ported, orange covering with black corners, black grille with Orange logo, mfg. 2010-disc.

	$780	$475 - 550	$250 - 300

SMART POWER 212 BASS CABINET (SP212) – 600W, 2-12 in. Neodymium speakers, 8 ohm impedance, two separated speaker compartments, bottom ported, orange covering with black corners, black grille with Orange logo, mfg. 2010-disc.

MSR N/A	$870	$525 - 625	$275 - 325

SMART POWER 410 BASS CABINET (SP410) – 1200W, 4-10 in. Neodymium speakers, 8 ohm impedance, four separated speaker compartments, bottom ported, orange covering with black corners, black grille with Orange logo, mfg. 2010-disc.

	$1,250	$750 - 900	$375 - 450

ORPHEUM

Amplifiers previously produced in Japan during the 1950s and 1960s. Distributed by Maurice Lipsky Music in New York, NY.

Orpheum was a line of guitars and amps imported and distributed by the Maurice Lipsky Music Company in New York City, NY. These amps were produced in Japan during the late 1950s and early 1960s. Information on specific models is unknown at this point. There is also speculation that some early models were produced in the U.S. Any further information on Orpheum amps can be submitted directly to Blue Book Publications.

OVATION

Amplifiers previously produced in New Hartford, CT between the late 1960s and the early 1970s. Distributed by Kaman Music. The Ovation trademark was established in 1967.

Ovation are probably best known for their acoustic guitars with bowl backs and unique soundholes. Shortly after the company was incorporated, they tried their luck with guitar amplifiers to little avail. In 1972, they introduced solid-body electric guitars. These amplifiers were produced circa 1969-1971, and they produced guitar amps, bass amps, PA systems, and a wide variety of speaker cabinets. However, Ovation's amplifiers were similar in design to Acoustic as the speaker cabinet contained the power amp, and the preamp that acted as the head was separate. Oddly enough, amps were introduced before Ovation electric guitars appeared, but they were discontinued at almost the same time the electric guitars were introduced. For more information on Ovation electric guitars, refer to the *Blue Book of Electric Guitars*. For more information on Ovation acoustic guitars, refer to the *Blue Book of Acoustic Guitars*.

ELECTRIC AMPLIFIERS

LITTLE DUDE (K-6323-1) – 100W, 1-15 in. Ovation Standard speaker, solid-state chassis, 1 mid-range horn, reverb, bass and treble controls, mfg. circa 1969-1971.

	N/A	$200 - 250	$120 - 150

MSR/NOTES	100%	EXCELLENT	AVERAGE	LAST MSR

BIG DUDE (K-63XX-1) – 100W, 2-12 in. Ovation Standard speakers, solid-state chassis, 1 mid-range horn, reverb, bass and treble controls, mfg. circa 1969-1971.

	N/A	$250 - 300	$135 - 175	

OVERBUILT AMPLIFIERS

Amplifiers previously produced in West Hills, CA between 1999 and 2006.

Richard Seccombe founded Overbuilt Amplifiers in 1999 and is known to manufacture some of the world's finest and most musical guitar amplifiers. This is backed up by a lifetime transferable warranty. By end of 2006 Seccombe had produced 56 amplifiers spread out over four continents, with more than several players owning two or more.

Rick has designed, built, tested, repaired, and/or modified over 5,500 amplifiers, guitars and basses that have been in the hands and ears of artists and producers including, Rich Costey, John Scofield, Rick Holmstrom, Jimmie Vaughn, Scott McGill, Greg Martin, Joe Baressi, Dave Navarro, The Edge, Bob Rock, Peter Buck, Coco Montoya, Josh Abraham, Lemmy Kilmiester, Muse, Roger McGuinn, Scott Henderson, David Kahne, and thousands of others. He is also one of the very top technicians specializing in Matchless amplifiers and Rickenbacker guitars.

In the spring of 2006, Richard was hired by Dan Smith at Fender Musical Instruments as Guitar R&D Design Engineer. This position required that he stop taking orders for Overbuilt Amplifiers, but he still fully warrants his amplifiers to any owner and maintains service, repair, and modifications for all other brands of guitars and amplifiers.

ELECTRIC GUITAR AMPLIFIERS: HEADS & COMBO UNITS

Variations exist of most models produced because of custom orders and design refinements throughout the years, complete design specs exist for each variation. All amplifiers were available in either head or a wide variety of combo cabinet styles. Tolexed combo cabinets were available in 1-12 in. speaker, 1-10 & 1-12 in. speakers, 2-12 in. speakers, switchable 2-10 & 2-12 in. speakers, 4-12 in. speakers, 1-15 in. speakers, and 1-15 & 2-10 in. speakers. The Super Deluxe Bad Boy was the hardwood cabinet option which included combo's and heads. Most common cabs are Tolexed heads, the 2-12 in. speaker combo, and the 2-10 in. speaker combo. Cow brown is a factory favorite but all color options were available.

NOTES

_____

_____

_____

_____

_____

_____

_____

_____

_____

_____

_____

_____

_____

_____

_____

_____

_____

_____

_____

_____

_____

_____

P SECTION
PAC-AMP

Amplifiers previously produced by Magnatone from the late 1950s to the early 1960s.

Pac-Amp was a brand Magnatone used on a line of accordion amplifiers during the late 1950s and the early 1960s. Magnatone (Estey) built these amps, which were almost all clones of Magnatones, and put a Pac-Amp logo on the front. Essentially all Pac-Amp models should have a corresponding model with Magnatone. Exact models are unknown, but they did produce a copy of the popular Magnatone Model 280-A called the **Custom Model 382**. Any further information on Pac-Amp amps can be submitted directly to Blue Book Publications.

PALETTE AMPS

Amplifiers previously produced in Stillwater, OK.

Palette amps produced high-end tube amplifiers and hand-crafted wood cabinets. They had an in-house cabinet builder who hand picked all hard woods used in their cabinets. Aluminum chassis, grilles, nameplates, and hardware all accent the wood cabinets. In 2001, they made a dedicated Palette studio to test and develop their equipment. Head units, combo units, and speaker cabinets were all available.

AMPLIFIERS & SPEAKER CABINETS

Palette produced the **W1** tube amplifier that featured 30W output, an all-tube chassis, and only two controls (colour and intensity). The W1 was available as a head-unit (Last MSR $3,424), 1-15 in. ceramic Jensen speaker combo (Last MSR $4,593), or 2-10 in. speaker combo (Last MSR $4,593). Palette introduced the **Minuette**, which is a small combo unit with 1-10 in. speaker (Last MSR $2,783). Speaker cabinets were available with 1-15 in. ceramic Jensen speaker (Last MSR $1,961) or 2-10 in. speakers (Last MSR $1,961).

PANARAMIC

Amplifiers previously produced by Magnatone in the early 1960s and by Audio Guild in the late 1960s. Distributed by Ernest Deffner Musical Merchandise in New York, NY in the early 1960s.

Panaramic was a brand Magnatone used on a line of accordion amplifiers during the early 1960s. Magnatone (Estey) built these amps, which were almost all clones of Magnatones, and put a PANaramic logo on the front instead of Magnatone. Essentially all Panaramic models should have a corresponding model with Magnatone. Although Panaramic amps were specifically produced for Panaramic Accordions, the amps could also be used for guitars. In the late 1960s, the Panaramic brand was reintroduced on a line of amps produced by Audio Guild in Van Nuys, CA. Any further information on Panaramic amps can be submitted directly to Blue Book Publications.

ELECTRIC TUBE AMPLIFIERS

Panaramic amps are mostly based on the Magnatone Series that was produced between circa 1960 and 1963. These Magnatone amps feature brown coverings, light brown grilles, mainly rear-mounted control panels, and a speaker grille that slants upward but the cabinet is completely vertical (see Model 280 and Model 111 Student in the Magnatone section for this era's style). Panaramic amps were very similar in style, but they usually had a black or dark gray covering with a light gray grille. Known models include the **Model 1208**, **Model 1210**, **Model 1240**, and **Model 1262**. A reverb/echo unit called the Canyon was also available. Not much information is known about late 1960s models. Look for more information in further editions.

PARIS

Amplifiers previously produced in the 1960s. Distributed by the L.W. Hagelin Company in Minneapolis, MN.

Paris was a brand used by the L.W. Hagelin Company on a line of amps in the 1960s. L.W. Hagelin was a large wholesaler of musical instruments and they distributed acoustic guitars, electric guitars, mandolins, ukuleles, harmonicas, accordions, and other accessories. Little is known about who made Paris amps, but they were all solid-state in design. They produced a full range of models from student models to professional amps. Any further information on Paris amps can be submitted directly to Blue Book Publications.

ELECTRIC SS AMPLIFIERS

Paris produced the **PC-I Superior Student Amp**, **PC-II Power Tremolo Amp**, **PC-III Battery Powered Amp**, **PC-IV AC/DC Amp**, the **Mater II Professional Peformance Amp**, the **Professional Bass Amp**, the **Big Daddy Advanced Response Professional Amplifier**, the **President Dual-Feature Professional Amp**, and the **Magnificent 600** piggyback unit. Amps were covered in a black vinyl and had a silver grille that was very similar to the Fender Blackface design. Used prices on these amps range anywhere from $50 for the student amps to $100-$150 for the mid-range models, and $200-$250 for the top-end models.

PARK

Amplifiers previously produced by Marshall in England between circa 1965 and 1982, and in Asia from 1992 until 2000 in Asia. Distributed by Marshall.

Park amps were initially produced between 1965 and 1982. Marshall used the Park name for another line of amps outside the Rose-Morris distribution deal. Jonny Jones was the man to sell most of the early Marshall amps through his shop, Jones and Crossland. He became the top distributor in North England, and Jim appreciated everything he

MSR/NOTES	100%	EXCELLENT	AVERAGE	LAST MSR

had done. As Marshall began to expand business in 1964, Jim began looking for a big-time distributor, and in early 1965, Rose-Morris became the exclusive distributor of Marshall. Since no one else in England could distribute Marshall amps as of 1965, it left many large distributors out in the cold, including Johnny. As part of the new deal with Rose-Morris, Jim was allowed to build amps under different names for other distribution outlets. Originally, this new line of amps was going to be called Jones Amplifiers, but Jim didn't like the average Joe sound of the name. After having supper with Jones and his wife one night, Jim asked his wife what her maiden name was. She responded with Park and the name of the new line of amps was born. However, after a few months into the new Rose-Morris contract, Jim realized this deal with Jones wasn't as great as he had first thought. Jones sold these amps at wholesale and they were distributed by Cleartone Musical Instruments (CMI). Marshall grew in popularity throughout the 1960s, but people didn't associate the connection between Park and Marshall. Value in a brand name became very important as Marshall found out. Jones stopped wholesaling these amps in 1971, but Marshall continued to produce them as a brand for distributors outside of Rose-Morris. The Marshall/Rose-Morris exclusive distribution contract expired in 1981, and Jim took on distribution himself. Since there was no need for private branded amps anymore, Marshall discontinued producing Park models by 1982. The Park trademark was revived in 1992 on a line of solid-state budget amps built overseas for Marshall. Once again, Marshall noticed the importance in a brand name, and they introduced their own solid-state budget line in 2000 with the MG Series.

Park amplifiers were simply Marshall amps with different cosmetic features and a different logo on the front. The first Park amps were JTM 45s, and when Marshall started producing 50W and 100W models, Park followed suit. However, Marshall used Park to experiment with new designs throughout the 1970s, including some of the first solid-state models. Sources for Park History, Michael Doyle, *The History of Marshall*, and Rich Maloof, *Jim Marshall: The Father of Loud.*

MODEL IDENTIFICATION/OVERVIEW

Serial numbers on Park amplifiers aren't documented like they are on Marshall amps, so it is difficult to date by serial number. Cosmetic features are the best identifying feature as far as Park goes. The earliest Park amps have a top mounted control panel and a black and white grille. By 1967, the control panel was moved to the front, and the front was made of black vinyl. The Park logo is also a useful way in dating Park amplifiers. Early on the "P" in Park was separate and above the "ark," and there was no line connecting all the letters along the bottom. In the early seventies the enlongated "P" was connected with the rest of the letters along the top, and all letters were connected at the bottom with a line. The logo was also raised later on.

As far as the construction of Park amps, they are generally very similar if not identical to Marshall amps of the same model. Therefore, they usually sound and play the same as Marshall. However, they are not nearly as collectible as respective Marshall models because of the value in the Marshall brand and Park amps were generally sold at a lower price compared to Marshalls. We list as many models as we have found information on in this section, but there are additional models out there. As a general guide, Park amps are valued about 50-75% in proportion to Marshall. For example, a Marshall amp that is worth $2,500 may be worth between $1,500 and $2,000 as a Park amp with the same chassis. Keep in mind this is only a general guide!

ELECTRIC TUBE AMPLIFIERS: EARLY MODELS

* Add 25-50% for custom colors.

JTM45 (PARK) – 45W, head-unit only, all tube chassis, preamp: 12AX7, power: 2 X 5881, GZ34 rectifier, lead guitar application, dual channels, front or top black plexi control panel, four inputs, typically six knobs (p, b, m, t, high t, v), black covering, mfg. 1965-66.

courtesy solidbodyguitar.com, Inc.

courtesy solidbodyguitar.com, Inc.

	N/A	$4,750 - 6,000	$2,750 - 3,500	

This amp is essentially a Marshall JTM45 with a Park nametag. This amp was available as a top mount control panel or a front mount. The top-mount is rarer.

100W P.A. AMPLIFIER – 100W, head-unit only, all tube chassis, four channels, front black control panel, eight inputs (high and low for each channel), eight white knobs (v1, v2, v3, v4, b, m, t, brightness), 8 & 16 Ohm speaker output, black covering, mfg. 1966-1972.

	N/A	$2,750 - 3,500	$1,750 - 2,250	

* **50W P.A. Amplifier** – Similar to the 100W version except has 50W output and two less channels, mfg. 1966-1972.

	N/A	$2,500 - 3,000	$1,600 - 2,000	

100W BASS/LEAD/ORGAN – 100W, head-unit only, all tube chassis, two channels, front black control panel, four inputs (high and low for each channel, six white knobs (v1, v2, b, m, t, brightness), black covering, mfg. 1966-1972.

N/A $3,250 - 4,000 $2,000 - 2,500

* *50W Bass/Lead/Organ* – Similar to the 100W version except has 50W output, mfg. 1966-1972.

N/A $2,750 - 3,500 $1,750 - 2,250

ELECTRIC TUBE AMPLIFIERS: MODELS WITH NUMBER DESIGNATIONS

• Add 25-50% for custom colors.

MODEL 1001B 75W BASS – 75W, head-unit only, bass application, all tube chassis, two channels with first channel bass boosted, front silver control panel, four inputs (two per channel), 6 silver knobs (v1, v2, b, m, t, brightness), 4, 8, & 16 Ohm Speaker output, black covering, mfg. 1972-75.

N/A $1,600 - 2,000 $1,050 - 1,300

MODEL 1001L 75W LEAD – 75W, head-unit only, lead-application, all tube chassis, front silver control panel, four inputs (two per channel), 6 silver knobs (v1, v2, b, m, t, brightness), 4, 8, & 16 Ohm Speaker output, black covering, mfg. 1972-75.

courtesy solidbodyguitar.com, Inc.

courtesy solidbodyguitar.com, Inc.

N/A $2,000 - 2,500 $1,300 - 1,600

MODEL 1002B 150W BASS – 150W, head-unit only, bass application with first channel bass boosted, all tube chassis, front silver control panel (slightly offset), four inputs (two per channel), six silver knobs (v1, v2, b, m, t, brightness), 4, 8, & 16 Ohm speaker output, black covering, mfg. 1972-75.

N/A $1,750 - 2,250 $1,100 - 1,400

MODEL 1002L 150W LEAD – 150W, head-unit only, lead application with first channel treble boosted, all tube chassis, front silver control panel (slightly offset), four inputs (two per channel), six silver knobs (v1, v2, b, m, t, brightness), 4, 8, & 16 ohm speaker output, black covering, mfg. 1972-75.

N/A $2,000 - 2,500 $1,300 - 1,600

MODEL 1005B 100W BASS – 100W, head-unit only, bass application with first channel bass boosted, all tube chassis, front silver control panel, four inputs (two per channel), six silver knobs (v1, v2, b, m, t, brightness), 4, 8, & 16 ohm speaker output, black covering, mfg. 1972-75.

N/A $1,400 - 1,750 $950 - 1,150

MODEL 1005L 100W LEAD – 100W, head-unit only, lead application with first channel treble boosted, all tube chassis, front silver control panel, four inputs (two per channel), six silver knobs (v1, v2, b, m, t, brightness), 4, 8, & 16 ohm speaker output, black covering, mfg. 1972-75.

N/A $1,750 - 2,250 $1,100 - 1,400

MODEL 1206 50W LEAD – 50W, head-unit only, lead-application, all tube chassis, high-input gain, single channel, master volume, front silver control panel, two inputs, six silver knobs (v, MV, b, m, t, brightness), black covering, mfg. 1976-1982.

N/A $1,050 - 1,300 $750 - 900

MODEL 1207 100W LEAD – 100W, head-unit only, lead-application, all tube chassis, high-input gain, single channel, master volume, front silver control panel, two inputs, six silver knobs (v, MV, b, m, t, brightness), black covering, mfg. 1976-1982.

N/A $1,200 - 1,500 $850 - 1,000

MODEL 1210 100W LEAD (ROCK HEAD) – 100W, head-unit only, lead-application, all tube chassis, dual channels, front silver control panel, four inputs (two per channel), 7 knobs (g1, g2, t, m, b, brightness, MV), black covering, mfg. mid 1970s-early 1980s.

N/A $1,400 - 1,750 $950 - 1,150

This amp was derived from the Marshall 2159 100W combo. Supposedly, this was the "non-watered down" version of the 2159.

MODEL 1212 50 WATT LEAD COMBO – 50W, 2-12 in. speakers, all tube chassis combo, lead application, dual channels, reverb, top black control panel, two inputs, seven black and silver knobs (v1, v2, r, b, m, t, brightness), black covering, black and white grille cloth, mfg. 1975-78.

N/A $1,600 - 2,000 $1,050 - 1,300

MSR/NOTES	100%	EXCELLENT	AVERAGE	LAST MSR

MODEL 1213 100W LEAD COMBO – 100W, 2-12 in. speakers, all tube chassis combo, lead application, dual channels, reverb, top black control panel, two inputs, seven black and silver knobs (v1, v2, r, b, m, t, brightness), black covering, black and white grille cloth, mfg. 1975-78.

| | N/A | $1,750 - 2,250 | $1,100 - 1,400 | |

MODEL 1214 50W LEAD COMBO – 50W, 2-12 in. speakers, all tube chassis combo, lead application, single channel, master volume, top black control panel, two inputs, six black and silver knobs (v1, MV, b, m, t, brightness), black covering, black and white grille cloth, mfg. 1975-78.

| | N/A | $1,600 - 2,000 | $1,050 - 1,300 | |

MODEL 1215 100W LEAD COMBO – 100W, 2-12 in. speakers, all tube chassis combo, lead application, single channel, master volume, top black control panel, two inputs, six black and silver knobs (v1, MV, b, m, t, brightness), black covering, black and white grille cloth, mfg. 1975-78.

| | N/A | $1,750 - 2,250 | $1,100 - 1,400 | |

MODEL 1216 50W BASS – 50W, head-unit only, bass application, all tube chassis, dual channels, front silver control panel, four inputs, six silver knobs (v1, v2, b, m, t, brightness), black covering, mfg. 1975-1982.

| | N/A | $1,050 - 1,300 | $750 - 900 | |

MODEL 1217 100W BASS – 100W, head-unit only, bass application, all tube chassis, dual channels, front silver control panel, four inputs, six silver knobs (v1, v2, b, m, t, brightness), black covering, mfg. 1975-1982.

| | N/A | $1,200 - 1,500 | $850 - 1,000 | |

MODEL 1228 50W LEAD – 50W, head-unit only, lead application, all-tube chassis, dual channels, front silver control panel, four inputs (two per channel), six silver knobs (brightness, b, m, t, v1, v2), black covering, mfg. 1975-76.

| | N/A | $1,600 - 2,000 | $1,050 - 1,300 | |

MODEL 1229 100W LEAD – 100W, head-unit only, lead application, all-tube chassis, dual channels, front silver control panel, four inputs (two per channel), six silver knobs (brightness, b, m, t, v1, v2), black covering, mfg. 1975-76.

| | N/A | $1,750 - 2,250 | $1,100 - 1,400 | |

MODEL 1231 20W LEAD COMBO (VINTAGE 20LE) – 20W, 1-12 in. Celestion speaker, all tube chassis, preamp: 2 X ECC83, power: 2 X EL84, various knobs, brown vinyl covering, black and white grille cloth, mfg. mid 1970s.

| | N/A | $1,050 - 1,300 | $750 - 900 | |

MODEL 1238 50W BASS COMBO – 50W, 1-12 in. speaker, all-tube chassis, bass application, single channel, front silver control panel, two inputs, seven black and silver knobs (v, b, t, m1, m2, m3, e), black covering, black and white grille cloth, mfg. 1976-1982.

| | N/A | $1,200 - 1,500 | $850 - 1,000 | |

MODEL 1239 50W LEAD COMBO – 50W, 1-12 in. speaker, all-tube chassis, lead application, single channel, reverb, master volume, front silver control panel, two inputs, seven black and silver knobs (g, MV, t, m, b, brightness, r), black covering, black and white grille cloth, mfg. 1976-1982.

| | N/A | $1,050 - 1,300 | $750 - 900 | |

MODEL 1240 100W LEAD COMBO (ROCK COMBO) – 100W, 1-12 in. speaker, lead-application, all tube chassis, dual channels, front silver control panel, four inputs (two per channel), 7 knobs (g1, g2, t, m, b, brightness, MV), black covering, checkerboard grille, casters, mfg. mid 1970s-early 1980s.

| | N/A | $1,750 - 2,250 | $1,100 - 1,400 | |

MODEL 1273 20W LEAD COMBO REISSUE – reissue of the Vintage 20, mfg. 1980-82.

| | N/A | $950 - 1,200 | $650 - 800 | |

ELECTRIC SS AMPLIFIERS: (1965-1982)

In the mid-1970s, Marshall began to experiment with solid-state amplifiers, but affixed the Park logo to the first models. These solid-state Park amplifiers are mildly collectible because of their rarity.

1211 50 WATT LEAD COMBO – 50W, 2-12 in. speakers, solid-state combo, single channel, tremolo, front black control panel, two inputs (normal and bright), eight black and silver knobs (g1, g2, b, m, t, d, f, MV), black covering, black and white grille, mfg. mid-1970s.

| | N/A | $850 - 1,000 | $600 - 700 | |

1218 100 WATT LEAD – 100W, narrow head unit-only, solid-state chassis, single channel, front black control panel, two inputs, six black and silver knobs (g, t, m, b, brightness, MV), black covering, mfg. 1976-1982.

| | N/A | $600 - 750 | $375 - 450 | |

1230 8 WATT COMBO – 8W, 1-8 in. speaker, practice solid-state combo, single channel, various controls, mfg. 1977-1982.

| | N/A | $175 - 225 | $110 - 140 | |

MSR/NOTES	100%	EXCELLENT	AVERAGE	LAST MSR

ELECTRIC SS AMPLIFIERS: RECENT MFG. (1993-1998)

In the early 1990s, Marshall wasn't ready to introduce a line of Marshall-branded solid-state amps, but they knew to stay competitive, they needed to expand their offerings to a wider audience. In 1993, Marshall introduced a line of Korean-built solid-state budget amplifiers, but they labeled them with their old Park trademark for these new models. Models G10, G10R, and G25R were produced until 1996 when an updated line was introduced that featured a new "Park by Marshall" logo. These amps were produced through 1998 when Marshall decided that a budget solid-state line could survive under their own trademark. In summer 1998, all models moved to the Marshall line, but they remained the same electronically and cosmetically other than no Park markings. Please refer to the Marshall G/MG Series for additional models.

G10 – 10W, 1-8 in. speaker, guitar combo, solid-state chassis, single channel, front gold control panel, single input, six black knobs (g1, g2, t, m, b, r, MV), headphone jack, black covering, black grille with white script Park logo, mfg. 1993-96.

| | N/A | $50 - 75 | $30 - 40 | |

G10MKII (PG10MKII) – 10W, 1-6.5 in. speaker, guitar combo, solid-state chassis, single channels, front gold control panel, single input, three knobs (g, contour, v), boost switch, headphone jack, power switch, black covering, black cloth grille with white script Park by Marshall logo, 11.4 in. wide, 11.4 in. tall, 6.7 in. deep, 9.9 lbs., mfg. 1997-98.

| | N/A | $40 - 60 | $20 - 30 | $100 |

G10R – 10W, 1-8 in. speaker, guitar combo, solid-state chassis, reverb, single channel, front gold control panel, single input, seven black knobs (g1, g2, t, m, b, r, MV), headphone jack, black covering, black grille with white script Marshall logo, mfg. 1993-96.

| | N/A | $55 - 85 | $30 - 45 | |

G15RCD (PG15RCD) – 15W, 1-8 in. speaker, guitar combo, solid-state chassis, single channel (two gain stages), reverb, front gold control panel, single input, seven knobs (g1, g2, t, c, b, MV, r), headphone jack, line out, CD input, black covering, black cloth grille with white script Park by Marshall logo, 14.8 in. wide, 14 in. tall, 7.9 in. deep, 14.3 lbs., mfg. 1997-98.

| | N/A | $70 - 90 | $40 - 55 | $180 |

G25R – 25W, 1-10 in. speaker, guitar combo, solid-state chassis, reverb, two channels, front gold control panel, single input, seven black knobs (g1, v1, v2, t, m, b, r), channel switch, footswitch jack, headphone jack, black covering, black cloth grille with a white script Park logo, mfg. 1993-96.

| | N/A | $75 - 110 | $35 - 50 | |

G30RCD (PG30RCD) – 30W, 1-10 in. speaker, guitar combo, solid-state chassis, two channels, reverb, front gold control panel, single input, nine knobs (Ch. 1: v, b, t, Ch. 2: g, b, c, t, v, r), channel switch, footswitch jack, line out, headphone jack, CD input, power switch, black covering, black cloth grille with white script Park by Marshall logo, 18.7 in. wide, 15.6 in. tall, 8.7 in. deep, 25.3 lbs., mfg. 1997-98.

| | N/A | $150 - 200 | $95 - 120 | $260 |

G215RCD (PG215RCD) – 30W (2 X 15W stereo), 2-8 in. speakers, guitar combo, solid-state chassis, single channel (two gain stages), reverb, chorus, front gold control panel, single input, nine knobs (g1, g2, t, c, b, MV, r, chorus speed, chorus depth), chorus switch, line out, headphone jack, CD input, power switch, black covering, black cloth grille with white script Park by Marshall logo, 19.3 in. wide, 14 in. tall, 9 in. deep, 22 lbs., mfg. 1997-98.

| | N/A | $200 - 250 | $120 - 150 | $330 |

B25MKII (PB25MKII) – 25W, 1-10 in. speaker, bass combo, solid-state chassis, single channel, front black control panel, single input, five knobs (v, b, m, t, MV), headphone jack, black covering, black cloth grille with white script Park by Marshall logo, mfg. 1997-98.

| | N/A | $100 - 125 | $65 - 80 | $250 |

SPEAKER CABINETS

Like Marshall, Park offered speaker cabinets for use with their heads or combo units when applicable. Park speaker cabinets were also often sold as individual units - not as a head/cabinet package (although some distributors would sell their own half-stack and full-stack packages). Several Park speaker cabinets exist and most fall into a configuration of 1-18 in. speaker, 2-12 in. speakers, or 4-12 in. speakers. Usually the 4-12 in. cabinets have an A suffix to indicate an angled front or a B suffix for a straight front. Early Park speaker cabinets may feature a full-front angled cabinet, whereas later models from circa 1975-1982 feature a half-angled front cabinet (like all Marshall cabinets). Early models don't carry a model number on the speaker cabinet. There are other models intended for P.A. application (i.e. Model 1014, and Model 1015) but specs and pricing is unknown on these.

* **Add 25-50% for custom colors.**

MODEL 1008 4-12 LEAD – 100W, 4-12 in. Celestion 25W speakers, black or various color coverings, mfg. 1970s.

| | N/A | $1,600 - 2,000 | $1,050 - 1,300 | |

MODEL 1009 4-12 BASS – 100W, 4-12 in. Celestion 25W speakers, bass application, black or various color coverings, mfg. 1970s.

| | N/A | $1,400 - 1,750 | $950 - 1,150 | |

MODEL 1010 2-15 BASS/LEAD – 100W, 2-15 in. Celestion speakers, bass or lead application, straight front only, black or various color coverings, mfg. 1970s.

| | N/A | $1,200 - 1,500 | $850 - 1,000 | |

MODEL 1011 1-18 BASS – 100W, 1-18 in. 100W Celestion speaker, bass application, straight front only, black or various color coverings, mfg. 1970s.

| | N/A | $1,200 - 1,500 | $850 - 1,000 | |

MSR/NOTES	100%	EXCELLENT	AVERAGE	LAST MSR

MODEL 1209 2-12 BASS/LEAD – 100W, 2-12 in. 50W speakers, bass/lead application, mfg. 1976-1982.

	N/A	$1,050 - 1,300	$750 - 900	

MODEL 1222 4-12 LEAD – 100W, 4-12 in. speakers, lead application, available in black or various color coverings, mfg. 1976-1982.

	N/A	$1,200 - 1,500	$850 - 1,000	

MODEL 1223 4-12 LEAD – 120W, 4-12 in. heavy-duty speakers, lead application, available in black or various color coverings, mfg. 1976-1982.

	N/A	$1,200 - 1,500	$850 - 1,000	

PARKSONS

Amplifiers currently produced in Korea. Distributed by Paxphil in Korea.

Parksons produces a line of guitar amplifiers as well as acoustic guitars, electric guitars, basses, banjos, mandolins, and resonators. These amplifiers are mainly entry level instruments that retail for under $200. For more information, visit Parkson's website or contact them directly.

CONTACT INFORMATION
PARKSONS
Distributed by Paxphil
#207 Hyundai Bldg. 982-4
Yangcheon-Ku
Seoul, Shinwol-Dong Korea
Phone No.: 82-2-2607-8283/4
Fax No.: 82-2-2607-8285
www.paxphil.co.kr
ham@paxphil.co.kr

PAUL REED SMITH (PRS)

Amplifiers currently produced in Stevensville, MD since 2009 and in Korea since 2011. Previously produced in Annapolis, MD between circa 1989 and 1990. The PRS trademark was established in 1985.

CONTACT INFORMATION
PAUL REED SMITH (PRS)
380 Log Canoe Circle
Stevensville, MD 21666
Phone No.: 410-643-9970
www.prsguitars.com

Luthier Paul Reed Smith devised an electric guitar that became very influential in the 1980s. With the success of the electric guitars, Smith decided to move into other markets, including the amplifier business. Because of the tube scare during the late 1980s, Smith thought amps with solid-state chassis was the way to go. Eric Pritchard developed these amps with the Harmonic Generator circuit, which is where the amps got their name "HG." The HG Series of amps were first released in 1989, but despite initial good reviews, high prices and lack of interest in solid-state models, the project lasted less than a year. Only 350 units were shipped and they were discontinued in 1990.

As boutique tube amplifiers became popular in the late 1990s and early 2000s, Smith decided he wanted to offer a guitar amplifier again with a tube chassis. In 2006, Smith met amp designer/builder Doug Sewell at the Dallas Guitar Show and after getting to know each other, Smith asked Sewell to design a line of guitar amps for Paul Reed Smith. Sewell declined at first, but later on accepted the offer and began working for Smith full time in June 2008. At the 2009 NAMM Show, PRS introduced three new guitar amplifiers called the Original Sewell, Dallas, and Blue Sierra that were all covered in a gold/black paisley fabric covering. In mid-2009, PRS introduced two smaller amplifiers with a more traditional white covering called the 30 and the Sweet 16. In late 2011, PRS introduced the SE line of amps that are built in Korea. Source for early PRS amplifier history, Dave Burrluck, The *Paul Reed Smith Book*.

ELECTRIC SS AMPLIFIERS/SPEAKER CABINETS

The "Harmonic Generator" featured in all PRS amps added harmonics to the tone.

HG-70 – 70W, head-unit guitar configuration, solid-state chassis, two separate preamps to create a "Vintage American" and a "Vintage English" sound, two channels, reverb, front black control panel, single input, 14 black knobs (Rhythm Ch.: r, MV, bright, b, m, t, g, Solo Ch.: MV, p, b, m, t, gate, g), effects loop, speaker switching (16, 8, & 4 Ohm), XLR out, luminescent rear panel, black covering, black/green grille, mfg. 1989-1990.

	N/A	$500 - 600	$325 - 400	

HG-212 – 70W, 2-12 in. speakers, guitar combo, solid-state chassis, two separate preamps to create a "Vintage American" and a "Vintage English" sound, two channels, reverb, front black control panel, single input, 14 black knobs (Rhythm Ch.: r, MV, bright, b, m, t, g, Solo Ch.: MV, p, b, m, t, gate, g), effects loop, speaker switching (16, 8, & 4 Ohm), XLR out, luminescent rear panel, black covering, black/green grille, mfg. 1989-1990.

	N/A	$600 - 700	$425 - 500	

412 SPEAKER CABINET – 4-12 in. speakers, designed for use with the HG-70 head-unit or the HG-212 combo, mfg. 1989-1990.

	N/A	$450 - 525	$300 - 350	

ELECTRIC TUBE AMPLIFIERS: ARCHON SERIES

ARCHON 25 COMBO – 25W (switchable to 13W), 1-12 in. Celestion G12-75T speaker, guitar combo, eight-tube chassis, preamp: 6 X 12AX7, power: 2 x 5881, two channels, front black control panel, single input, 12 black knobs (Lead Ch.: v, t, m, b, Clean Ch.: v, t, m, b, All: p, d, Lead Ch. MV, Clean Ch. MV), channel switch, power switch, rear panel: effects loop, half-power switch, speaker jacks, footswitch jack, available in black Tolex covering with black grille cloth, black Tolex covering with wheat grille cloth, or gray tweed covering with brown grille cloth, mfg. 2015-present.

MSR N/A	$1,350	$800 - 1,000	$475 - 600	

MSR/NOTES	100%	EXCELLENT	AVERAGE	LAST MSR

ARCHON 50 HEAD – 50W (switchable to 25W), guitar head unit, eight-tube chassis, preamp: 6 X 12AX7, power: 2 x 6L6GC or EL34, two channels, front black control panel, single input, 12 black knobs (Lead Ch.: v, t, m, b, Clean Ch.: v, t, m, b, All: p, d, Lead Ch. MV, Clean Ch. MV), bright switches for each channel, channel switch, power switch, rear panel: effects loop, half-power switch, speaker jacks, footswitch jack, available in black Tolex covering with black grille cloth, black Tolex covering with wheat grille cloth, or gray tweed covering with brown grille cloth, 21.5 in. wide, 10.5 in tall, 10 in. deep, 33.5 lbs., mfg. 2014-present.

| MSR N/A | $1,600 | $1,000 - 1,250 | $600 - 750 | |

* *Archon 50 Combo* – similar to the Archon 50 Head, except in combo configuration with 1-12 in. Celestion G12-75T speaker, available in black Tolex covering with black grille cloth, black Tolex covering with wheat grille cloth, or gray tweed covering with brown grille cloth, 21.5 in. wide, 17 in tall, 10.5 in. deep, 47 lbs., mfg. 2014-present.

| MSR N/A | $1,650 | $1,025 - 1,300 | $625 - 775 | |

ARCHON 100 HEAD – 100W (switchable to 50W), guitar head unit, eight-tube chassis, preamp: 6 X 12AX7, power: 4 x 6L6GC or EL34, two channels, front black control panel, single input, 12 black knobs (Lead Ch.: v, t, m, b, Clean Ch.: v, t, m, b, All: p, d, Lead Ch. MV, Clean Ch. MV), bright switches for each channel, channel switch, power switch, rear panel: effects loop, half-power switch, speaker jacks, footswitch jack, available in black (stealth) covering with charcoal grille cloth, 21.5 in. wide, 10.5 in tall, 10 in. deep, 43 lbs., mfg. 2014-present.

| MSR N/A | $1,950 | $1,150 - 1,450 | $700 - 875 | |

ELECTRIC TUBE AMPLIFIERS: BLUE SIERRA, DALLAS, & ORIGINAL SEWELL SERIES

PRS offers numerous cosmetic options on their amps including custom covering and wood faceplate options. All of these options are price on request through PRS.

25th ANNIVERSARY HEAD – 50W, guitar head-unit, hand-wired to military spec, tube chassis, power: 2 X EL34, two channels (Treble/Bass), top black control panel, single input, seven black knobs (Treble Ch. g, Bass Ch. g, t, m, b, p, wattage attenuator), rear panel: power switch, standby switch, bias adjust, five speaker jacks, available in vintage green or paisley fabric covering, split front grille with PRS eagle logo, limited edition run of 100 amplifiers each one signed and numbered, mfg. 2010-disc.

| | $2,650 | N/A | N/A | $2,949 |

BLUE SIERRA HEAD – 50W or 100W, 2 (50W) or 4 (100W) X EL34 or 6L6 power tubes, single channel, optional reverb, top black control panel, single input, five black knobs (v, b, m, t, MV) or six black knobs (v, r, b, m, t, MV), bright switch, rear panel: power switch, standby switch, bias adjustments, five speaker jacks (two 4 ohm, two 8 ohm, one 16 ohm), black and gold paisley fabric covering, split black leather/brown cloth front grille, mfg. 2009 only.

| | $2,800 | $2,000 - 2,400 | N/A | $3,500 |

* **Add 10% (Last MSR was $3,835) for reverb.**
* **Add 10% (Last MSR was $3,875) for 100W output.**

The Blue Sierra has a gainy Texas sound that is voiced from a mix of English and American tone and clean to medium gain with big bass and sweet highs.

* *Blue Sierra 1-12 Combo* – similar to the Blue Sierra Head, except in combo configuration with 1-12 in. speaker, black and gold paisley fabric covering, split black leather/brown cloth front grille, mfg. 2009 only.

| | $3,150 | $2,150 - 2,600 | N/A | $3,920 |

* **Add 7.5% (Last MSR was $4,255) for reverb.**
* **Add 10% (Last MSR was $4,295) for 100W output.**

* *Blue Sierra 2-12 Combo* – similar to the Blue Sierra Head, except in combo configuration with 2-12 in. speakers, black and gold paisley fabric covering, split black leather/brown cloth front grille, mfg. 2009 only.

| | $3,275 | $2,250 - 2,750 | N/A | $4,085 |

* **Add 7.5% (Last MSR was $4,420) for reverb.**
* **Add 10% (Last MSR was $4,460) for 100W output.**

DALLAS HEAD – 50W or 100W, 2 (50W) or 4 (100W) X 6L6 power tubes, single channel. reverb, top black control panel, single input, six black knobs (v, r, b, m, t, MV), bright switch, rear panel: power switch, standby switch, bias adjustments, five speaker jacks (two 4 ohm, two 8 ohm, one 16 ohm), black and gold paisley fabric covering, split black leather/brown cloth front grille, mfg. 2009 only.

| | $3,000 | $2,100 - 2,500 | N/A | $3,675 |

* **Add 10% (Last MSR was $4,050) for 100W output.**

The Dallas features a clean '60s-style Texas sound with standard reverb and clean to medium/low gain.

* *Dallas 1-12 Combo* – similar to the Dallas Head, except in combo configuration with 1-12 in. speaker, black and gold paisley fabric covering, split black leather/brown cloth front grille, mfg. 2009 only.

| | $3,325 | $2,250 - 2,700 | N/A | $4,095 |

* **Add 10% (Last MSR was $4,470) for 100W output.**

* *Dallas 2-12 Combo* – similar to the Dallas Head, except in combo configuration with 2-12 in. speakers, black and gold paisley fabric covering, split black leather/brown cloth front grille, mfg. 2009 only.

| | $3,450 | $2,350 - 2,850 | N/A | $4,260 |

* **Add 10% (Last MSR was $4,845) for 100W output.**

MSR/NOTES	100%	EXCELLENT	AVERAGE	LAST MSR

ORIGINAL SEWELL HEAD – 50W or 100W, 2 (50W) or 4 (100W) X EL34 or 6L6 power tubes, single channel, optional reverb, top black control panel, single input, four black knobs (v, t, bass/boost, MV) or five black knobs (v, r, t, bass/boost, MV), bright switch, rear panel: power switch, standby switch, bias adjustments, five speaker jacks (two 4 ohm, two 8 ohm, one 16 ohm), black and gold paisley fabric covering, split black leather/brown cloth front grille, mfg. 2009 only.

	$2,800	$2,000 - 2,400	N/A	$3,500

- Add 10% (Last MSR was $3,835) for reverb.
- Add 10% (Last MSR was $3,875) for 100W output.

The Original Sewell has clean to medium/high gain with singing vocal tones, sweet midranges, a tighter bottom end, a musically sweet top, and is harmonically rich.

* **Original Sewell 1-12 Combo** – similar to the Original Sewell Head, except in combo configuration with 1-12 in. speaker, black and gold paisley fabric covering, split black leather/brown cloth front grille, mfg. 2009 only.

	$3,150	$2,150 - 2,600	N/A	$3,920

- Add 7.5% (Last MSR was $4,255) for reverb.
- Add 10% (Last MSR was $4,295) for 100W output.

* **Original Sewell 2-12 Combo** – similar to the Original Sewell Head, except in combo configuration with 2-12 in. speakers, black and gold paisley fabric covering, split black leather/brown cloth front grille, mfg. 2009 only.

	$3,275	$2,250 - 2,750	N/A	$4,085

- Add 7.5% (Last MSR was $4,420) for reverb.
- Add 10% (Last MSR was $4,460) for 100W output.

PRS RECORDING AMP HEAD – 50W, guitar head-unit, hand-wired to military spec, tube chassis, power: 2 X EL34, Cinemag output transformer, two channels (Treble/Bass), reverb, top black control panel, single input, seven cream knobs (Treble Ch. g, Bass Ch. g, t, m, b, MV, r), treble channel gain switch, bass channel gain switch, treble channel bright switch, overall gain switch, high cut switch, power amp extra gain switch, rear panel: power switch, standby switch, bias adjust, five speaker jacks, available in PRS Stealth covering with a faded charcoal maple face plate or paisley covering with a black gold figured maple face plate, limited edition run of 25 amplifiers each one signed and numbered, mfg. 2010-2011.

MSR $3,120	$2,850	N/A	N/A	

SUPER DALLAS – 50W, guitar head-unit, hand-wired to military spec, four-tube chassis, preamp: 2 X 12AX7, power: 2 X EL34, Cinemag output transformer, single channel, reverb, top black control panel, single input, six black knobs (v, t, m, b, r, MV), rear panel: power switch, standby switch, bias adjust, five speaker jacks, heavy duty Stealth black Tolex covering, split front grille, mfg. 2010-disc.

	$2,650	$1,525 - 1,900	$925 - 1,150	$2,949

ELECTRIC TUBE AMPLIFIERS: DAVID GRISSOM SERIES

DG Cutsom 30 Head
courtesy Paul Reed Smith

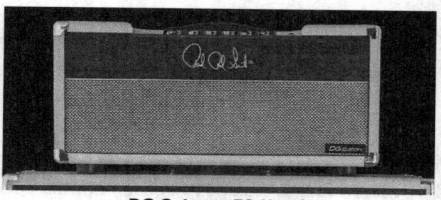

DG Cutsom 50 Head
courtesy Paul Reed Smith

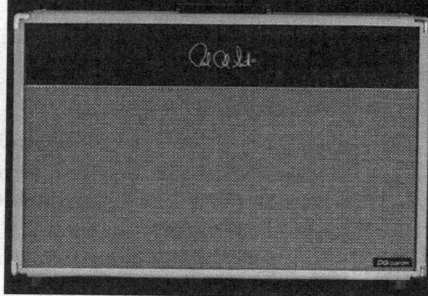

DG Cutsom 212 Speaker Cabinet
courtesy Paul Reed Smith

DG CUSTOM 30 HEAD – 30W, guitar head-unit, tube chassis, preamp: 3 X 12AX7, 1 X 12AT7, power: EL84 tubes, one channel, top black control panel, single input, six black knobs (v, reverb, t, m, b, MV), bright switch, rear panel: power switch, standby switch, five speaker jacks, available in blonde vinyl covering, split front with cherry mahogany fascia and blonde grille with DG Custom logo, mfg. 2013-present.

MSR N/A	$3,300	$2,150 - 2,475	$1,075 - 1,325	

DG CUSTOM 50 HEAD – 50W, guitar head-unit, tube chassis, preamp: 3 X 12AX7, 1 X 12AT7, power: EL34 tubes, one channel, top black control panel, single input, six black knobs (v, reverb, t, m, b, MV), bright switch, rear panel: power switch, standby switch, five speaker jacks, available in blonde vinyl covering, split front with cherry mahogany fascia and blonde grille with DG Custom logo, mfg. 2013-present.

MSR N/A	$3,400	$2,200 - 2,550	$1,100 - 1,350	

DG CUSTOM 212 SPEAKER CABINET – 120W, 2-12 in. Celestion Vintage 30 speakers, 8 ohm impedance, open back, solid pine construction, designed for use with the DG Custom amps, blonde vinyl covering, split front with cherry mahogany fascia and blonde grille, mfg. 2013-present.

MSR N/A	$700	$425 - 475	$210 - 260	

MSR/NOTES	100%	EXCELLENT	AVERAGE	LAST MSR

ELECTRIC TUBE AMPLIFIERS: HXDA SERIES

HXDA 30 Head
courtesy Paul Reed Smith

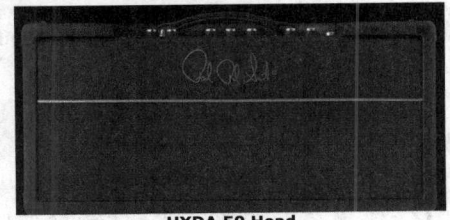

HXDA 50 Head
courtesy Paul Reed Smith

HXDA 30 COMBO – 30W, 1-12 in. speaker, guitar combo amp, tube chassis, preamp: 3 X 12AX7, power: 2 X 6L6, one channel, top black control panel, single input, seven black knobs (HXDA g, Bass g, t, m, b, p, MV), three HX/DA switches, rear panel: power switch, standby switch, bias adjust, five speaker jacks, available in black covering, black grille with PRS eagle logo, mfg. 2012-present.

| MSR N/A | $3,200 | $2,075 - 2,400 | $1,050 - 1,275 | |

HXDA 30 HEAD – 30W, guitar head-unit, tube chassis, preamp: 3 X 12AX7, power: 2 X 6L6, one channel, top black control panel, single input, seven black knobs (HXDA g, Bass g, t, m, b, p, MV), three HX/DA switches, rear panel: power switch, standby switch, bias adjust, five speaker jacks, available in black covering, split front grille with PRS eagle logo, mfg. 2012-present.

| MSR N/A | $3,000 | $1,950 - 2,250 | $975 - 1,200 | |

HXDA 50 HEAD – 50W, guitar head-unit, tube chassis, preamp: 3 X 12AX7, power: 2 X el34, one channel, top black control panel, single input, 3-band EQ, seven black knobs (HXDA g, Bass g, t, m, b, p, MV), three HX/DA switches, rear panel: power switch, standby switch, bias adjust, five speaker jacks, available in black covering, split front grille with PRS eagle logo, mfg. 2012-present.

| MSR N/A | $3,200 | $2,075 - 2,400 | $1,050 - 1,275 | |

ELECTRIC TUBE AMPLIFIERS: SE SERIES

SE 20 HEAD – 20W, guitar head-unit, six-tube chassis, preamp: 2 X 12AX7, 2 X 12AT7, power: 2 X "JJ" 6V6, solid-state rectifier, two channels (clean/lead), reverb, front white control panel, single input, 11 black knobs (Lead Ch.: v, t, m, b, Clean Ch.: v, t, m, b, All: r, Lead MV, Clean MV), channel switch, bright switch for each channel, power/standby switch, rear panel: effects loop, two speaker jacks, impedance selector, heavy duty Stealth black vinyl, black metall grille, mfg. 2012-disc.

| | $900 | $525 - 650 | $325 - 400 | $985 |

* SE 20 Combo – similar to the SE 20 Head, except in combo configuration with 1-12 in. PRS/Eminence speaker, heavy duty Stealth black vinyl, black cloth grille, mfg. 2012-disc.

| | $975 | $550 - 700 | $350 - 425 | $1,075 |

SE 30 HEAD – 30W, guitar head-unit, six-tube chassis, preamp: 2 X 12AX7, 2 X 12AT7, power: 2 X "Tungsol" 5881, solid-state rectifier, two channels (clean/lead), reverb, front gray control panel, single input, 11 black knobs (Lead Ch.: v, t, m, b, Clean Ch.: v, t, m, b, All: r, Lead MV, Clean MV), channel switch, bright switch for each channel, power/standby switch, rear panel: effects loop with level control, bias adjust, two speaker jacks, impedance selector, heavy duty Stealth black vinyl, black metal grille, mfg. 2012-disc.

| | $925 | $550 - 675 | $350 - 425 | $1,020 |

* SE 30 Combo – similar to the SE 30 Head, except in combo configuration with 1-12 in. PRS/Eminence speaker, heavy duty Stealth black vinyl, black cloth grille, mfg. 2012-disc.

| | $1,000 | $550 - 700 | $350 - 425 | $1,099 |

SE 50 HEAD – 50W, guitar head-unit, six-tube chassis, preamp: 2 X 12AX7, 2 X 12AT7, power: 2 X "JJ" EL34, solid-state rectifier, two channels (clean/lead), reverb, front purple control panel, single input, 11 black knobs (Lead Ch.: v, t, m, b, Clean Ch.: v, t, m, b, All: r, Lead MV, Clean MV), channel switch, bright switch for each channel, power/standby switch, rear panel: effects loop with level control, bias adjust, two speaker jacks, impedance selector, heavy duty Stealth black vinyl, black metal grille, mfg. 2012-disc.

| | $1,000 | $550 - 700 | $350 - 425 | $1,099 |

* SE 50 Combo – similar to the SE 50 Head, except in combo configuration with 1-12 in. PRS/Eminence speaker, heavy duty Stealth black vinyl, black cloth grille, mfg. 2012-disc.

| | $1,150 | $650 - 825 | $400 - 500 | $1,255 |

SE 2X12 SPEAKER CABINET – 2-12 in. PRS/Eminence speakers, 8 ohm impedance, closed back, 5/8 inch plywood construction, black vinyl covering, black cloth grille, mfg. 2012-disc.

| | $380 | $225 - 275 | $135 - 170 | $419 |

ELECTRIC TUBE AMPLIFIERS: TUXEDO SERIES

PRS offers numerous cosmetic options on their amps including custom covering and wood faceplate options. All of these options are price on request through PRS.

MSR/NOTES	100%	EXCELLENT	AVERAGE	LAST MSR

DALLAS II HEAD – 50W, guitar head unit, six-tube chassis, preamp: 2 X 12AX7, 2 X 12AT7, power: 2 X 6L6, solid-state rectifier, single channel, reverb, front black control panel, single input, six black knobs (v, r, t, m, b, MV), power/standby switch, black and white leather "tuxedo" covering with a partial metal grille, mfg. 2010 only.

	$1,950	$1,050 - 1,300	$700 - 825	$2,145

* *Dallas II 1-12 Combo* – similar to the Dallas II Head, except in combo configuration with 1-12 in. speaker, black and white leather "tuxedo" covering with a black grille, mfg. 2010 only.

	$2,120	$1,150 - 1,450	$775 - 925	$2,330

PRS 30 HEAD – 30W, guitar head unit, eight-tube chassis, preamp: 2 X 12AX7, 2 X 12AT7, power: 4 X EL84, solid-state rectifier, single channel, reverb, front black control panel, single input, six black knobs (v, r, t, m, b, MV), power/standby switch, black and white leather "tuxedo" covering with a partial metal grille, mfg. mid-2009-disc.

	$1,600	$950 - 1,200	$575 - 725	$1,759

* *PRS 30 1-12 Combo* – similar to the PRS 30 Head, except in combo configuration with 1-12 in. speaker, black and white leather "tuxedo" covering with a black grille, mfg. 2010-disc.

	$1,860	$1,125 - 1,400	$675 - 850	$2,040

SWEET 16 HEAD – 16W, guitar head unit, six-tube chassis, preamp: 2 X 12AX7, 2 X 12AT7, power: 2 X 6V6, solid-state rectifier, single channel, reverb, front black control panel, single input, six black knobs (v, r, t, m, b, MV), power/standby switch, black and white leather "tuxedo" covering with a partial metal grille, mfg. mid-2009-disc.

	$1,350	$800 - 1,000	$475 - 600	$1,479

* *Sweet 16 1-12 Combo* – similar to the Sweet 16 Head, except in combo configuration with 1-12 in. speaker, black and white leather "tuxedo" covering with a black grille, mfg. 2010-disc.

	$1,530	$925 - 1,150	$550 - 700	$1,685

TWO CHANNEL "C" HEAD – 50W, guitar head unit, power: 2 X EL34, solid-state rectifier, two channels (clean/lead), reverb, front black control panel, single input, 11 black knobs (Lead Ch.: v, t, m, b, Clean Ch.: v, t, m, b, All: r, Lead MV, Clean MV), channel switch, bright switch for each channel, power/standby switch, rear panel: effects loop with send and return levels, bias jacks, two speaker jacks, impedance selector, footswitch jack, heavy duty Stealth black covering with a partial black metal grille, mfg. 2011-disc.

	$1,800	$1,050 - 1,300	$650 - 800	$1,999

TWO CHANNEL "H" HEAD – 50W, guitar head unit, power: 2 X 6L6, solid-state rectifier, Heyboer transformer, two channels (clean/lead), reverb, front black control panel, single input, 11 black knobs (Lead Ch.: v, t, m, b, Clean Ch.: v, t, m, b, All: r, Lead MV, Clean MV), channel switch, bright switch for each channel, power/standby switch, rear panel: effects loop with send and return levels, bias jacks, two speaker jacks, impedance selector, footswitch jack, heavy duty Stealth black covering with a partial black metal grille, mfg. 2011-disc.

	$1,500	$875 - 1,100	$525 - 650	$1,649

* *Two Channel "H" Combo* – similar to the Two Channel "H" Head, except in combo configuration with 1-12 in. Celestion Vintage 30 speaker, black covering, black cloth grille, mfg. 2011-disc.

	$1,650	$950 - 1,200	$575 - 725	$1,819

ELECTRIC TUBE AMPLIFIERS: TWO-CHANNEL CUSTOM SERIES

2 Channel Custom 20 Head
courtesy Paul Reed Smith

2 Channel Custom 50 Head
courtesy Paul Reed Smith

2 Channel Custom 20 Combo
courtesy Paul Reed Smith

2 Channel Custom 50 Combo
courtesy Paul Reed Smith

2 CHANNEL CUSTOM 20 COMBO – 20W, guitar combo amp, 1-12 in. speaker, power: 3 X 12AX7, 2 X 12AT7, 1 X 12DW7, power: 5881 tubes, two channels (clean/lead), reverb, front black control panel, single input, 12 black knobs (Lead Ch.: v, t, m, b, MV, Clean Ch.: v, t, m, b, MV, All: r, presence), channel switch, bright switch for each channel, power/standby switch, rear panel: effects loop with send and return levels, bias jacks, lead jack, clean jack, two speaker jacks, impedance selector, footswitch jack, heavy duty Stealth black covering with a black grille, mfg. 2013-present.

MSR N/A	$1,600	$1,050 - 1,200	$525 - 650	

* Add $149 (MAP $1,749) for Charcoal Maple option

MSR/NOTES	100%	EXCELLENT	AVERAGE	LAST MSR

2 CHANNEL CUSTOM 20 HEAD – 20W, guitar head unit, power: 3 X 12AX7, 2 X 12AT7, 1 X 12DW7, power: 5881 tubes, two channels (clean/lead), reverb, front black control panel, single input, 12 black knobs (Lead Ch.: v, t, m, b, MV, Clean Ch.: v, t, m, b, MV, All: r, presence), channel switch, bright switch for each channel, power/standby switch, rear panel: effects loop with send and return levels, bias jacks, lead jack, clean jack, two speaker jacks, impedance selector, footswitch jack, heavy duty Stealth black covering with a partial black grille, mfg. 2013-present.

| MSR N/A | $1,450 | $950 - 1,075 | $475 - 575 | |

2 CHANNEL CUSTOM 50 COMBO – 50W, guitar combo amp, 1-12 in. speaker, power: 3 X 12AX7, 2 X 12AT7, 1 X 12DW7, power: 6L6 tubes, two channels (clean/lead), reverb, front black control panel, single input, 12 black knobs (Lead Ch.: v, t, m, b, MV, Clean Ch.: v, t, m, b, MV, All: r, presence), channel switch, bright switch for each channel, power/standby switch, rear panel: effects loop with send and return levels, bias jacks, lead jack, clean jack, two speaker jacks, impedance selector, footswitch jack, heavy duty Stealth black covering with a black grille, mfg. 2013-present.

| MSR N/A | $1,900 | $1,225 - 1,425 | $625 - 750 | |

• Add $299 (MAP $2,199) for Paisley covering with Maple front.

2 CHANNEL CUSTOM 50 HEAD – 50W, guitar head unit, power: 3 X 12AX7, 2 X 12AT7, 1 X 12DW7, power: 6L6 tubes, two channels (clean/lead), reverb, front black control panel, single input, 12 black knobs (Lead Ch.: v, t, m, b, MV, Clean Ch.: v, t, m, b, MV, All: r, presence), channel switch, bright switch for each channel, power/standby switch, rear panel: effects loop with send and return levels, bias jacks, lead jack, clean jack, two speaker jacks, impedance selector, footswitch jack, heavy duty Stealth black covering with a partial black grille, mfg. 2013-present.

| MSR N/A | $1,750 | $1,125 - 1,300 | $575 - 700 | |

• Add $149 (MAP $1,899) for Charcoal Maple grille. Add $299 (MAP $2,049) for Paisley covering with Maple grille.

SPEAKER CABINETS

1-12 TUXEDO SPEAKER CABINET – 1-12 in. Celestion Vintage 30 speaker, designed for use with the 30 and Sweet 16 amps, black and white leather "tuxedo" covering with a black cloth grille, mfg. mid-2009-disc.

| | $500 | $325 - 400 | $200 - 250 | $549 |

2-12 TUXEDO SPEAKER CABINET – 2-12 in. Celestion Vintage 30 speakers, 8 ohm impedance, designed for use with the Dallas II amp heads, black and white leather "tuxedo" covering with a black cloth grille, mfg. 2010-disc.

| | $700 | $425 - 500 | $275 - 325 | $769 |

2-12 RECORDING AMP SPEAKER CABINET – 120W, 2-12 in. Celestion Vintage 30 speakers, 8 ohm impedance, closed back, solid pine construction, designed for use with the PRS Recording Amp Head, available in PRS Stealth covering with a faded charcoal maple face plate or paisley covering with a black gold figured maple face plate, mfg. 2010-2011.

| MSR $855 | $770 | $450 - 550 | $275 - 350 | |

2-12 STEALTH SPEAKER CABINET – 120W, 2-12 in. Celestion Vintage 30 speakers, 8 ohm impedance, closed or open back, solid pine construction, designed for use with the Blue Sierra, Dallas, and Original Sewell amps, black and gold paisley fabric covering, split black leather/brown cloth front grille, mfg. 2009-present.

| MSR N/A | $975 | $625 - 725 | $325 - 400 | |

4-10 STEALTH SPEAKER CABINET – 120W, 4-10 in. Celestion G10 speakers, 8 ohm impedance, open back, solid pine construction, designed for use with the Blue Sierra, Dallas, and Original Sewell heads, black and gold paisley fabric covering, split black leather/brown cloth front grille, mfg. 2009-present.

| MSR N/A | $1,175 | $750 - 875 | $375 - 475 | |

4-12 STEALTH SPEAKER CABINET – 4-12 in. Celestion Vintage 30 speakers, 16 ohm impedance, open back, solid pine construction, designed for use with the Blue Sierra, Dallas, and Original Sewell heads, black and gold paisley fabric covering, split black leather/brown cloth front grille, mfg. 2010-present.

| MSR N/A | $1,175 | $750 - 875 | $375 - 475 | |

PEARCE

Amplifiers previously produced between the 1980s and early 1990s.

Dan Pearce produced a variety of rack mounted pre-amps, power amps, guitar amps, bass amps, and speaker cabinets from the 1980s through the early 1990s. Such notables as Billy Sheehan, Ronnie Montrose, and Allan Holdsworth used these amplifiers. These units were very well built but were very expensive and didn't sell very well. It is rumored that some Pearce extension speaker cabinets featured Eden speakers. Any further information on Pearce amps can be submitted directly to Blue Book Publications.

PEAVEY

Amplifiers, speaker cabinets, and other electronics currently produced in Meridian and Leaksville, MS, and overseas. Peavey Electronics are distributed by the Peavey Electronics Corporation of Meridian, MS. The Peavey trademark was established in 1965.

Hartley Peavy grew up in Meridian, MS and spent time working in his father's music store repairing record players. While he was in high school, he gained recognition, locally, for guitar amplifiers he built by hand. Before college graduation, he decided to go into business for himself and Peavey Electronics was established in 1965 out

CONTACT INFORMATION
PEAVEY
5022 Hartley Peavey Drive
Meridian, MS 39305
Phone No.: 601-483-5365
Fax No.: 601-486-1278
www.peavey.com
humanresources@peavey.com

MSR/NOTES	100%	EXCELLENT	AVERAGE	LAST MSR

of the basement of his parents' house. The first amps Hartley began producing were P.A. system amps and cabinets. The young Peavey's company took off in a hurry and the first shop was built in 1968 along with hiring another staff member. By 1970, there were 150 people working for Peavey! At this time they were still making P.A. amps primarily, but guitar and bass amps were becoming popular as well.

After a decade of making amplifiers, Peavey emerged as a guitar builder as well. Throughout the 1980s and 1990s, Peavey nailed the market at the perfect time. The tube scare of the 1980s couldn't have come at a better time as they were producing all solid-state amps. In the 1990s, Peavey released the EVH5150, which was an amplifier developed in conjunction with Edward Van Halen. This amp has been one of Peavey's most successful amplifiers and later on they released a series of guitars with Van Halen. In the mid-2000s, Peavey introduced their Custom Shop, which allowed customers to personally customize guitars and amplifiers.

Hartley is still president of Peavey Electronics and they are still based in Meridian, MS. They offer a full line of electric guitar, bass guitar, acoustic guitar, and keyboard amplifiers as well as PA systems, power amps, preamps, mics, and a variety of other electronics. For more information on Peavey electric guitars, refer to the *Blue Book of Electric Guitars*. For more information on Peavey acoustic guitars, refer to the *Blue Book of Acoustic Guitars*. For more general information, visit Peavey's website or contact them directly.

ELECTRIC TUBE AMPLIFIERS: 5150 SERIES

The 5150 series was developed with Eddie Van Halen. All 5150 products have Eddie's signature on them, and were built to his specifications.

(EVH) 5150 HEAD – 120W (16, 8, or 4 Ohms), head-unit only, all tube chassis, preamp: 5 X 12AX7, power: 4 X 6L6GC, dual channels, front silver control panel, two inputs, nine black knobs (rhythm pre g, lead g, l, m, h, rhythm post g, lead post g, resonance, p), bright and crunch switches, effects loop, preamp out, footswitch, black covering, black metal grille, 48 lbs., mfg. 1995-2004.

 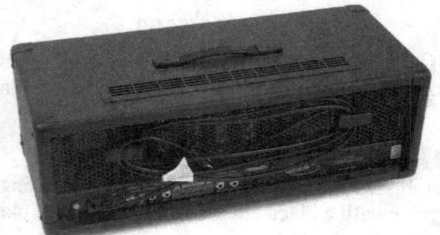

courtesy Dave Rogers/Dave's Guitar Shop   courtesy Dave Rogers/Dave's Guitar Shop

	N/A	$750 - 900	$500 - 600	$1,300

This model was originally called the EVH 5150, but the EVH was dropped from the model designation in 1994.

5150 II HEAD – 120W (16, 8, or 4 Ohms), head-unit only, all tube chassis, preamp: 6 X 12AX7, power: 4 X 6L6GC, dual channels, front silver control panel, two inputs, 14 black knobs (Rhythm: pre, l, m, h, post, Lead: pre, l, m, h, post, resonance & p per channel), bright and crunch switches, effects loop, preamp out, black covering, footswitch, black metal grille, 48.3 lbs., mfg. 2000-04.

	N/A	$700 - 850	$475 - 550	$1,350

5150 212 COMBO – - 60W, 2-12 in. Sheffield 1200 speakers, all tube chassis combo, preamp: 5 X 12AX7, power: 4 X 6L6GC, dual channels, top silver control panel, two inputs, nine black knobs (rhythm pre g, lead g, l, m, h, rhythm post g, lead post g, resonance, p), bright and crunch switches, effects loop, preamp out, footswitch, black covering, black metal grille, 84.5 lbs., mfg. 1995-2004.

	N/A	$475 - 550	$235 - 290	$1,300

5150 412 SPEAKER CABINET – 300W, 4-12 in. Sheffield 1200 speakers, 16 Ohm impedance, straight or slanted front, stackable configuration, black covering, black grille, 90 lbs., mfg. 1992-2004.

	N/A	$325 - 400	$200 - 250	$850

This model is also available in a slanted version as the model 412ES.

ELECTRIC TUBE AMPLIFIERS: 6505 SERIES

The 6505 was renamed from the 5150. Peavey renamed the amp in honor of their 40th Anniversary from 1965 to 2005.

6505 HEAD – 120W, head-unit only, tube chassis, preamp: 5 X 12AX7, power: 4 X 6L6GC, two channels, front silver control panel, two inputs, nine black chickenhead knobs (Ch. 1: pre g, post g, Ch. 2: pre g, post g, All: l, m, h, resonance, p), effects loop, preamp out, footswitch, black covering, black metal grille, 48 lbs., mfg. 2005-present.

MSR $1,350	$900	$575 - 675	$295 - 350	

6505+ Head – similar to the 6505 Head, except has an individual EQ for each channel, 14 black chickenhead knobs (Rhythm: pre g, l, m, h, post g, resonance, presence, Lead: pre g, l, m, h, post g, resonance, presence), 48.3 lbs., mfg. 2005-present.

MSR $1,700	$1,000	$650 - 750	$325 - 400	

MSR/NOTES	100%	EXCELLENT	AVERAGE	LAST MSR

6505 Head
courtesy Peavey

6505+ Head
courtesy Peavey

6505 212 Combo
courtesy Peavey

6505+ 212 Combo
courtesy Peavey

* 6505 MH – similar to the 6505 head, except in a smaller, more portable package, - 20W, head-unit only, tube chassis, preamp: 3 X 12AX7, power: 2 X EL84, two channels, front silver control panel, one input, ten black chickenhead knobs, effects loop, preamp out, footswitch, black covering, black metal grille, 17 lbs., mfg. 2015-present.

| MSR $600 | $500 | $325 - 375 | $165 - 200 | |

6505 212 COMBO – 60W, 2-12 in. Sheffield 1200 speaker combo, tube chassis, preamp: 5 X 12AX7, power: 2 X 6L6, two channels, reverb, front silver control panel, two inputs, 10 black chickenhead knobs (Rhythm: pre g, post g, Lead: pre g, post g, All: l, m, h, resonance, p, r), effects loop, preamp out, footswitch, black covering, black metal grille, 84.5 lbs., mfg. 2005-disc.

| | $1,200 | $725 - 850 | $400 - 475 | $1,600 |

6505+ 112 COMBO – 60W, 1-12 in. Sheffield speaker, guitar combo, seven-tube chassis, preamp: 5 X 12AX7, power: 2 X 6L6GC, solid-state rectifier, two channels (rhythm, lead), reverb, front silver control panel, single input, fifteen black knobs (Rhythm Ch.: pre g, l, m, h, post g, resonance, p, Lead Ch.: pre g, l, m, h, post g, resonance, p, master r), channel switch, rhythm channel crunch switch, rear panel: effects loop, speaker outs, XLR DI out, sealed back cabinet, black covering, black grille with lighted Peavey logo, 25.5 in. wide, 23.3 in. tall, 11.2 in. deep, 64.2 lbs., mfg. 2009-present.

| MSR $800 | $650 | $350 - 425 | $200 - 250 | |

6505 412 SPEAKER CABINET – 300W, 4-12 in. Sheffield 1200 speakers, 16 ohm impedance, locking XLR or 1/4 in. inputs, straight or angled front, plywood construction, recessed handles, casters, black covering, black grille with 6505 logo, straight: 96 lbs., angled: 90 lbs., mfg. 2005-present.

| MSR $1,200 | $800 | $525 - 600 | $260 - 325 | |

6534+ HEAD – 120W, head-unit only, 10-tube chassis, preamp: 6 X 12AX7, power: 4 X EL34, solid-state rectifier, two channels (rhythm/lead), front silver control panel, two inputs, 14 black chickenhead knobs (Rhythm Ch.: pre g, l, m, h, post g, resonance, p, Lead Ch.: pre g, l, m, h, post g, resonance, p), channel switch, Clean Ch. bright switch, Clean Ch. crunch switch, rear panel: effects loop, preamp out, footswitch jack, black covering, black metal grille, 28.75 in. wide, 14 in. tall, 13.25 in. deep, 48.3 lbs., mfg. 2009-present.

| MSR $1,700 | $1,300 | $850 - 975 | $425 - 525 | |

ELECTRIC TUBE AMPLIFIERS: CLASSIC SERIES

The entire Classic Series is available as a special order with Classic Tweed or custom coverings.

Blues Classic
courtesy S.P. Fjestad

Classic 20 MH (Minihead)
courtesy Peavey

Classic 30
courtesy Peavy

BLUES CLASSIC – 50W, 1-15 in. speaker combo, tube chassis, preamp: 3 X 12AX7, power: 4 X EL84, two channels, reverb, top chrome control panel, two inputs, nine black knobs (p, v, t, m, b, r, post g, pre g, MV), effects loop, tweed covering, brown grille cloth, mfg. 1994-95.

| | N/A | $325 - 400 | $200 - 250 | $800 |

MSR/NOTES	100%	EXCELLENT	AVERAGE	LAST MSR

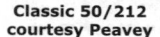

Classic 50/212
courtesy Peavey

Classic 50/410
courtesy Peavey

Classic 212 Speaker Cabinet
courtesy Peavey

CLASSIC 20 – 15W, 1-10 in. speaker, tube chassis, preamp: 2 X 12AX7, power: 2 X EL84, single channel, top chrome control panel, single input, five black knobs (v, MV, b, m, t), headphone jack, tweed covering, brown grille, mfg. 1994-97.

	N/A	$200 - 250	$120 - 150	$330

CLASSIC 20 MH (MINIHEAD) – 20W, minihead-unit only, all tube chassis, preamp: 3 X 12AX7/ECC83, power: 2 X EL84, dual channels, front chrome control panel, single input, seven black knobs (v, pre g, post g, b, m, t, r), footswitch, xlr out, usb out, brown tweed covering, 16.75 lbs., mfg. 2015-present.

MSR $600	$500	$325 - 375	$165 - 200	

CLASSIC 30 – 30W, 1-12 in. Blue Marvel speaker, all tube chassis, preamp: 3 X 12AX7, power: 4 X EL84, two channels, reverb, top chrome control panel, single input, seven black knobs (normal v, pre gain, post gain, r, b, m, t), effects loop, optional footswitch, brown or black tweed covering, brown or black grille, mfg. 1994-present.

MSR $1,000	$700	$450 - 525	$230 - 280	

This model in black vinyl covering and a black grille is known as the Classic 30 BT.

* *Classic 30 Head* – similar to the Classic 30, except in head-unit configuration, available in Black or Tweed covering, mfg. summer 2005-09.

	N/A	$300 - 350	$175 - 225	$650

* *Classic 30 Limited Edition Signature Series* – similar to the Classic 30 except has quilted maple cabinet, with a hand-painted, hand-sanded finish, 36.4 lbs., mfg. 2002-05.

	N/A	$625 - 750	$350 - 425	$1,400

CLASSIC 50 HEAD – 50W, head-unit only, all tube chassis, preamp: 3 X 12AX7, power: 4 X EL84, dual channels, reverb, front chrome contol panel, two inputs (normal and bright), nine black knobs (p, v, t, m, b, r, post g, pre g, MV), effects loop, footswitch, brown or black tweed covering, 43 lbs., mfg. 1992-2004.

	N/A	$325 - 400	$200 - 250	$750

Black vinyl covering was introduced in the 2000s.

* *Classic 50/212* – similar to the Classic 50 head except in combo form with 2-12 in. Blue Marvel speakers, brown or black tweed covering, brown or black grille, 59.6 lbs., mfg. 1990-present.

MSR $1,150	$900	$525 - 600	$300 - 375	

Black covering was introduced in the 2000s (known as the Classic 50/212 BT).

* *Classic 50/410* – similar to the Classic 50 head except in combo form with 4-10 in. Blue Marvel speakers, tweed covering with brown cloth grille or black vinyl covering with black grille (2006-present), 62.8 lbs., mfg. 1990-present.

MSR $1,250	$1,000	$550 - 650	$325 - 400	

CLASSIC 100 HEAD – 100W, head-unit only, all tube chassis, preamp: 3 X 12AX7, power: 8 X EL84, dual channels, reverb, front chrome control panel, two inputs (normal and bright), nine black knobs (p, v, t, m, b, r, post g, pre g, MV), effects loop, footswitch, brown tweed covering, brown grille, mfg. 1994-2000.

	N/A	$325 - 400	$200 - 250	$750

CLASSIC 400 HEAD – 400W, head-unit only, all tube chassis, preamp: 5 X 12AX7, 12AT7, power: 8 X 6550, dual channels, front chrome contol panel, single input, 12 black knobs, compression, effects loop, footswitch, brown tweed covering, brown grille, mfg. 1996-97.

	N/A	$700 - 800	$300 - 400	$1,600

DELTA BLUES 115 – 30W, 1-15 in. Blue Marvel speaker, all tube chassis, preamp: 3 X 12AX7, power: 4 X EL84, reverb, tremolo, two channels, top chrome control panel, single input, nine black knobs (normal v, pre gain, post gain, r, b, m, t, i, s), effects loop, optional footswitch, tweed covering, brown grille, 46.3 lbs., mfg. 1994-present.

MSR $1,050	$850	$550 - 625	$275 - 350	

MSR/NOTES	100%	EXCELLENT	AVERAGE	LAST MSR

🎸 *** Delta Blues 210 BT/TWEED** – similar to the Delta Blues in circuitry, except has 2-10 in. Blue Marvel speakers, black or brown tweed covering, black or brown grille covering, 52 lbs., mfg. 1999-present.

MSR $1,050	$850	$550 - 625	$275 - 350	

CLASSIC 112E SPEAKER CABINET – 75W, 1-15 in. Sheffield 1230 speaker, 16 Ohm impedance, tweed covering, brown grille, mfg. 1994-2000.

	N/A	$120 - 150	$70 - 95	$260

This cabinet is designed for use with the Classic 30 Combo.

CLASSIC 115E SPEAKER CABINET – 75W, 1-15 in. speaker, 16 Ohm impedance, tweed covering, brown grille, mfg. 1992-97.

	N/A	$120 - 150	$70 - 95	$270

🎸 **CLASSIC 212 SPEAKER CABINET** – 150W, 2-12 in. Blue Marvel speakers, 16 ohm impedance, mono only, closed removable back, single input jack, side handles, available in tweed covering with a brown grille or black Tolex covering with a silver grille, mfg. summer 2005-09.

	N/A	$250 - 300	$125 - 175	$600

CLASSIC 410E SPEAKER CABINET – 200W (100W per side in stereo), 4-10 in. speakers, 16 Ohm impedance mono 8 Ohm stereo, tweed covering, brown grille, mfg. 1992-97.

	N/A	$150 - 200	$95 - 125	$360

CLASSIC 410TX SPEAKER CABINET – 700W, bass application, 4-10 in. Kelvar speakers, horn-loaded tweeter with level control, 8 Ohm impedance, crossover, chrome plated hardware, tweed covering, brown grille, mfg. 1996-97.

	N/A	$225 - 275	$100 - 150	$550

CLASSIC 412E/412ES SPEAKER CABINET – 300W (150 per side in stereo), 4-12 in. Sheffield 1230 speakers, stereo or mono operation, stackable configuration, straight or angled front, brown or black tweed covering, black or brown grille, 89.4 lbs., mfg. 1996-2003.

	N/A	$325 - 375	$175 - 225	$680

CLASSIC 810TX SPEAKER CABINET – 800W, bass application, 8-10 in. Kelvar speakers, horn-loaded tweeter with level control, 4 Ohm impedance, crossover, chrome plated hardware, tweed covering, brown grille, casters, mfg. 1996-97.

	N/A	$375 - 450	$200 - 250	$850

ELECTRIC TUBE AMPLIFIERS: CUSTOM SHOP MODELS

Peavey currently offers three models through their Custom Shop. The **Studio Special** is a 1.5W tube amp head. The **Sensation 20**, has 20W, a single channel, and is available as a head-unit, 1-12 in. combo, or 2-12 in. combo. The **Masterpiece 50** has 50W, two channels, and is available as a head-unit, 1-12 in. combo, or 2-12 in. combo.

ELECTRIC TUBE AMPLIFIERS: JOE SATRIANI (JSX) SERIES

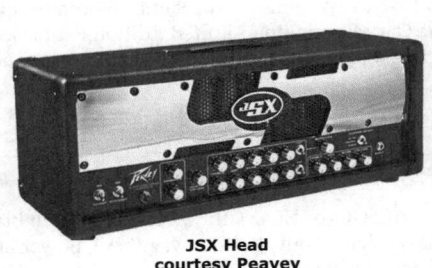

JSX Head
courtesy Peavey

JSX 212 Combo
courtesy Peavey

JSX Mini Colossal
courtesy Peavey

🎸 **JSX HEAD** – 120W, head-unit only, tube chassis, preamp: 4 X 12AX7, power: 4 X EL34 or 4 X 6L6GS, three switchable channels, front black control panel, single input, 18 knobs (Clean: t, m, b, v, Crunch: t, m, b, v, g, Ultra: t, m, b, v, g, All: resonance, presence, MV), effects loop with levels, line out with level control, footswitch, black covering, black grille with brushed chrome design, 54.3 lbs., mfg. 2005-2010.

	N/A	$750 - 850	$475 - 550	$1,680

🎸 **JSX 212 COMBO** – 120W, 2-12 in. JSX speakers, tube chassis, preamp: 4 X 12AX7, power: 4 X EL34 or 4 X 6L6GS, three switchable channels, front black control panel, two inputs, 19 knobs (Clean: t, m, b, v, Crunch: t, m, b, v, g, Ultra: t, m, b, v, g, All: resonance, presence, MV, r, noise gate), effects loop with levels, line out with level control, footswitch, black covering, black grille, mfg. 2005-2010.

	N/A	$850 - 1,000	$550 - 650	$1,940

🎸 **JSX MINI COLOSSAL** – 5W, 1-8 in. C8R-type speaker, guitar combo, tube chassis, preamp: 1 X 12AX7, power: 1 X EL34, single channel, tremolo, front black control panel, single input, four knobs (v, tone, s, d), effects loop, Power Sponge control (0-5W), mic-simulated XLR direct out with ground lift, black covering, black grille, mfg. 2007-09.

	N/A	$275 - 325	$150 - 200	$600

MSR/NOTES	100%	EXCELLENT	AVERAGE	LAST MSR

JSX 412 SPEAKER CABINET – 400W, 4-12 in. Custom JSX speakers, 16 ohm impedance mono (8 ohm stereo), voiced direct-out crossover, straight or slanted configuration, side handles, black covering, black grille, mfg. summer 2005-2010.

	$750	$425 - 500	$275 - 325	$980

ELECTRIC TUBE AMPLIFIERS: PENTA SERIES

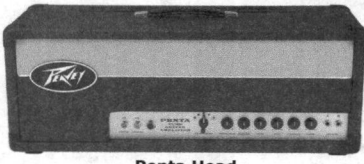

Penta Head
courtesy Peavey

Gary Rossington Limited Edition Penta
courtesy Peavey

Penta 412 Speaker Cabinet
courtesy Peavey

Gary Rossington Limited Edition Penta
412 Speaker Cabinet courtesy Peavey

PENTA HEAD – 140W, head-unit only, tube chassis, preamp: 4 X 12AX7, power: 4 X EL34, single channel, offset front gold control panel, two inputs, six black knobs (p, MV, b, m, t, g), five-way EQ/gain switch, green covering, brown grille and black covering, mfg. 2005-09.

	N/A	$375 - 450	$190 - 235	$1,600

PENTA 212 COMBO – 70W, 2-12 in. speakers, guitar combo, tube chassis, preamp: 4 X 12AX7, power: 2 X EL34, single channel, reverb, offset front gold control panel, two inputs, six black knobs (p, MV, b, m, t, g), five-way EQ/gainswitch, effects loop, green covering, brown grille, mfg. 2006-07.

	N/A	$550 - 650	$275 - 350	$1,800

PENTA 412 SPEAKER CABINET – 4-12 in. speakers, 1/2 in. poplar sides, 11-ply birch baffle, casters, designed to be used with the Penta head, green covering, brown weave grille cloth, mfg. 2005-09.

	N/A	$325 - 375	$160 - 195	$950

GARY ROSSINGTON LIMITED EDITION PENTA HEAD – 140W, guitar head-unit, eight-tube chassis, preamp: 4 X 12AX7, power: 4 X EL34, solid-state rectifier, single channel, offset front gold control panel, two inputs, six black knobs (p, MV, b, m, t, g), five-way EQ/gain chickenhead knob, maroon covering, maroon and black front panel with a white trim line and Peavey logo, 57.4 lbs., mfg. 2009-disc.

	N/A	$750 - 900	$450 - 525	$1,700

The Gary Rossington Limited Edition Penta Head features custom USA transformers and ceramic tube sockets.

GARY ROSSINGTON LIMITED EDITION PENTA 412 SPEAKER CABINET – 300W, 4-12 in. speakers, 16 ohm mono/8 ohm stereo impedance, 1/2 in. poplar sides, 11-ply birch baffle, casters, designed for use with the Gary Rossington Limited Edition Penta Gead, maroon covering, black cloth grille with white piping, centered Peavey logo, and Gary Rossington signature badge in lower right corner, 90.5 lbs., mfg. 2009-disc.

	N/A	$450 - 525	$275 - 325	$1,000

ELECTRIC TUBE AMPLIFIERS: TRIPLE XXX SERIES

TRIPLE XXX HEAD – 120W, head-unit only, all tube chassis, preamp: 4 X 12AX7, power: 4 X 6L6GC (or EL34), three channels, front black control panel, single input, 15 silver knobs (Clean: v, b, m, t, Crunch: hair, body, bottom, v, g, Ultra: hair, body, bottom, v, g, MV), power amp switch, effects loop, line out, 16, 8, or 4 Ohms speaker outputs, footswitch, black covering, brushed aluminum face with lady graphics, 50.7 lbs., mfg. 2001-09.

	N/A	$500 - 600	$255 - 325	$1,540

TRIPLE XXX II HEAD – 120W, head-unit only, all tube chassis, preamp: 4 X 12AX7, power: 4 X 6L6GC (or EL34), three channels, front black control panel, two inputs, 14 knobs (Clean: v, b, m, t, Rhythm: g, v, b, m, t, Lead: g, v, b, m, t), FAT switch and adjustable noise gate control on Rhythm and Lead channels, resonance and presence control, power amp switch, effects loop, line out, 16, 8, or 4 Ohms speaker outputs, footswitch, black covering, brushed aluminum face, 55.9 lbs., mfg. 2011-present.

MSR $1,500	$1,200	$775 - 900	$400 - 475	

TRIPLE XXX 112 COMBO – 60W, 1-12 in. Triple XXX 30 speaker, all tube chassis, preamp: 4 X 12AX7, power: 2 X 6L6GC (or EL34), three channels, reverb, front black control panel, single input, 16 silver knobs (Clean: v, b, m, t, Crunch: g, v, bottom, body, hair, Ultra: g, v, bottom, body, hair, MV, r), power amp switch, effects loop, line out, footswitch, 16, 8, or 4 Ohms speaker outputs, black covering, black and silver grille, brushed aluminum face, 60 lbs., mfg. 2003-05.

	N/A	$575 - 675	$350 - 425	$1,300

MSR/NOTES	100%	EXCELLENT	AVERAGE	LAST MSR

Triple XXX Super 40
courtesy Peavey

Triple XXX Super 40 EFX
courtesy Peavey

Triple XXX 412 Speaker Cabinet
courtesy Peavey

TRIPLE XXX 212 COMBO – 120W (16, 8, or 4 ohms), 2-12 in. Triple XXX chrome-plated speakers, all tube chassis, preamp: 4 X 12AX7, power: 4 X 6L6GC (or EL34), three channels, reverb, front black control panel, single input, 16 silver knobs (Clean: v, b, m, t, Crunch: g, v, bottom, body, hair, Ultra: g, v, bottom, body, hair, MV, r), power amp switch, effects loop, line out, footswitch, 16, 8, or 4 ohms speaker outputs, black covering, black and silver grille, brushed aluminum face, 85.3 lbs., mfg. 2002-05.

	N/A	$675 - 800	$450 - 500	$1,500

TRIPLE XXX SUPER 40 – 40W, 1-12 in. Triple XXX 30 speaker, all tube chassis, preamp: 4 X 12AX7, power: 2 X 6L6GC (or EL34), two channels with boost, front black control panel, single input, 13 silver knobs (Clean: g, v, b, m, t, r, Crunch & Lead:g, v, bottom, body, body, e, r, Both: v boost), effects loop, line out, footswitch, 16, 8, or 4 Ohms speaker outputs, black covering, black and silver grille, brushed aluminum face, 52.6 lbs., mfg. 2003-05.

	N/A	$500 - 575	$300 - 350	$1,100

* *Triple XXX Super 40 EFX* – similar to the Triple XXX Super 40, except has nine programmable digital effects, 53.7 lbs., mfg. 2003-05.

	N/A	$525 - 625	$300 - 375	$1,200

TRIPLE XXX 212 SPEAKER CABINET – 2-12 in. Triple XXX speakers, 16 Ohm impedance mono, 8 Ohm stereo, stackable configuration, straight front, black covering, black and silver grille, 55.4 lbs., mfg. 2003-05.

	N/A	$250 - 300	$125 - 175	$550

TRIPLE XXX 412 SPEAKER CABINET – 4-12 in. Triple XXX speakers, stackable configuration, straight or angled front, black covering, black and silver grille, 96/95 lbs., mfg. 2001-09.

	N/A	$375 - 450	$200 - 250	$880

ELECTRIC TUBE AMPLIFIERS: ULTRA SERIES

ULTRA 60 HEAD – 60W, head-unit only, tube chassis, preamp: 4 X 12AX7, power: 2 X 6L6GC, reverb, three channels, front silver control panel, two inputs, 13 black knobs (MV, r, Lead/Cruch Ch.: egde, body, bottom, v1, g1, v2, g2, Clean: h, m, l, v), bs, gs, effects loop, 4, 8, or 16 Ohm speaker output, footswitch, black covering, black metal grille, mfg. 1991-94.

	N/A	$235 - 275	$115 - 145	$700

ULTRA PLUS (ULTRA 120) – 120W, head-unit only, tube chassis, preamp: 4 X 12AX7, power: 4 X 6L6GC, reverb, three channels, front silver control panel, two inputs, 13 black knobs (MV, r, Lead/Cruch Ch.: egde, body, bottom, v1, g1, v2, g2, Clean: h, m, l, v), bs, gs, effects loop, logo changes color for different channels, 4, 8, or 16 Ohm speaker output, footswitch, black covering, black metal grille, mfg. 1991-2001.

	N/A	$350 - 400	$170 - 210	$1,000

From 1991-94, this model was known as the Ultra 120.

ULTRA 112 – 60W, 1-12 in. Sheffield 1230 speaker, tube chassis, preamp: 4 X 12AX7, power: 2 X 6L6GC, reverb, three channels, front silver control panel, two inputs, 13 black knobs (MV, r, Lead/Cruch Ch.: egde, body, bottom, v1, g1, v2, g2, Clean: h, m, l, v), bs, gs, effects loop, logo changes color for different channels, 4, 8, or 16 Ohm speaker output, footswitch, black covering, black metal grille, mfg. 1998-2001.

	N/A	$235 - 275	$115 - 145	$900

ULTRA 212 – 60W, 2-12 in. Sheffield 1230 speakers, tube chassis, preamp: 4 X 12AX7, power: 2 X 6L6GC, reverb, three channels, front silver control panel, two inputs, 13 black knobs (MV, r, Lead/Cruch Ch.: egde, body, bottom, v1, g1, v2, g2, Clean: h, m, l, v), bs, gs, effects loop, logo changes color for different channels, footswitch, black covering, black metal grille, mfg. 1998-2001.

	N/A	$300 - 350	$150 - 185	$960

ULTRA 410 – 60W, 4-10 in. Blue Marvel speakers, tube chassis, preamp: 4 X 12AX7, power: 2 X 6L6GC, reverb, three channels, front silver control panel, two inputs, 13 black knobs (MV, r, Lead/Cruch Ch.: egde, body, bottom, v1, g1, v2, g2, Clean: h, m, l, v), bs, gs, effects loop, logo changes color for different channels, footswitch, black covering, black metal grille, mfg. 1998-2001.

	N/A	$300 - 350	$150 - 185	$1,000

MSR/NOTES	100%	EXCELLENT	AVERAGE	LAST MSR

ELECTRIC TUBE AMPLIFIERS: VALVEKING SERIES

**Valveking 100 Head
courtesy Peavey**

**Valveking 112 Combo (20 Watt)
courtesy Peavey**

**Valveking 212 Combo
courtesy Peavey**

VALVEKING MICROHEAD – 20W, head-unit only, tube chassis, preamp: 3 X 12AX7, power: 2 X EL84, one channels, reverb, front black control panel, one inputs, 8 white knobs, effects loop, black covering, black metal grille, 14.6 lbs., mfg. 2014-present.

| MSR $550 | $425 | $280 - 325 | $140 - 170 | |

VALVEKING ROYAL 8 – 5W, 1-8 in. speaker, two tube Class A chassis, preamp: 1 X 12AX7/ECC83, power: 1 X 6BQ5/EL84, single channel, front black control panel, two inputs, three knobs (g, tone, MV), headphone jack, black covering, black/gray grille, mfg. 2006-09.

| | N/A | $110 - 140 | $60 - 85 | $250 |

VALVEKING 100 HEAD – 100W, head-unit only, tube chassis, preamp: 3 X 12AX7, power: 4 X 6L6, two channels, reverb, front black control panel, two inputs, 12 black knobs, effects loop, paralleled speaker jacks, black covering, black metal grille, mfg. 2005-present.

| MSR $900 | $600 | $400 - 450 | $195 - 240 | |

VALVEKING 112 COMBO (50 WATT) – 50W, 1-12 in. ValveKing speaker, tube chassis, preamp: 3 X 12AX7, power:2 X 6L6, two channels, reverb, front black control panel, two inputs, 10 black knobs, effects loop, black covering, gray cloth grille, mfg. 2005-present.

| MSR $900 | $600 | $400 - 450 | $195 - 240 | |

* ***ValveKing 112 Combo (20 Watt)*** – similar to the ValveKing 112 Combo (50 Watt), except features 20 Watt, power: 2 x EL84, and is 37.6 lbs., mfg. 2014-present.

| MSR $750 | $550 | $375 - 425 | $180 - 225 | |

VALVEKING 212 COMBO – 100W, 2-12 in. ValveKing speakers, tube chassis, preamp: 3 X 12AX7, power:4 X 6L6, two channels, reverb, front black control panel, two inputs, 12 black knobs, effects loop, black covering, gray cloth grille, mfg. 2005-present.

| MSR $880 | $650 | $375 - 450 | $225 - 275 | |

VALVEKING 412 SPEAKER CABINET – 400W, 4-12 in. ValveKing speakers, 16 ohm mono impedance (8 ohm stereo), stereo/mono switch, side handles, slant or straight configuration, black covering, gray cloth grille, mfg. 2005-present.

| MSR $580 | $450 | $275 - 325 | $150 - 200 | |

112 EXTENSION CABINET – 40W, 1-12 in. Blue Marvel speaker, closed back, black covering, black grille, 27.8 lbs., current mfg.

| MSR $200 | $130 | $85 - 100 | $40 - 50 | |

ELECTRIC TUBE AMPLIFIERS: WINDSOR SERIES

WINDSOR HEAD – 100W, head-unit guitar configuration, seven tube chassis, preamp: 3 X 12AX7, power: 4 X EL34, solid-state rectifier, single channel, front gold control panel, two inputs, eight knobs (preamp v, b, m, t, MV, resonance, p, Class A-A/B texture), effects loop, two button footswitch, black covering, brown grille, mfg. 2006-disc.

| | $400 | $250 - 300 | $135 - 175 | $530 |

WINDSOR STUDIO – 15W, 1-12 in. Blue Marvel speaker, guitar combo, three tube chassis, preamp: 2 X 12AX7/ECC83, power: 2 X EL34 (6L6GC, 6550, 6CA7, KT88, and KT66 tubes can also be used without rebiasing), solid-state rectifier, single channel, reverb, front gold control panel, two inputs, six knobs (preamp v, b, m, t, MV, r, MV), effects loop, Power Sponge power attenuator, two button footswitch, black covering, brown grille, mfg. 2007-disc.

| | $400 | $250 - 300 | $135 - 175 | $600 |

WINDSOR 412 SPEAKER CABINET – 300W, 4-12 in. UK speakers, 16 ohm impedance, straight or slanted front, black covering, black grille, 92 lbs., mfg. 2006-disc.

| | $280 | $175 - 225 | $110 - 140 | $450 |

MSR/NOTES	100%	EXCELLENT	AVERAGE	LAST MSR

ELECTRIC TUBE AMPLIFIERS: MISC. MODELS

3120 Head
courtesy Peavey

Butcher Head
courtesy Peavey

Jack Daniel's JD30T Combo
courtesy Peavey

3120 HEAD – 120W, guitar head unit, eight-tube chassis, preamp: 4 X 12AX7, power: 4 X EL34, solid-state rectifier, three channels (clean, rhythm, lead), front black control panel, single input, 15 black knobs (Clean Ch.: t, m, b, v, Rhythm Ch.: t, m, b, v, g, Lead Ch.: t, m, b, v, g, MV), three-way channel switch, power switch, standby switch, rear panel: effects loop with send level and return level, remote switch jack, bias adjustments, three-way damping switch (tight, mid, loose), two speaker jacks with three-way impedance switch (16, 8, 4 ohm), line out with level control, polarity switch, footswitch included, black covering, black metal grille, mfg. 2009-present.

MSR $1,330	$1,000	$600 - 700	$350 - 425	

BRAVO 112 – 25W, 1-12 in. speaker, tube chassis, preamp: 3 X 12AX7, power: 2 X 6BQ5/EL84, two channels, reverb, front black control panel, two inputs, 10 knobs (Ch. 1: level, l, m, h, Ch. 2: pre g, post g, bottom, body, edge, r), effects loop, speaker jacks, footswitch, black covering, black grille, mfg. 1991-94.

	N/A	$250 - 300	$135 - 175	$400

BUTCHER HEAD – 100W, guitar head unit, nine-tube chassis, preamp: 5 X 12AX7, power: 4 X EL34, solid-state rectifier, two channels, front black control panel, single input, 14 white chickenhead knobs (All: p, MV2, MV1, Clean Ch.: v, b, m, t, g, Crunch Ch.: v, b, m, t, g, punch), MV1/MV2 master volume switch, two boost switches (one per channel), channel switch, power switch standby switch, rear panel: effects loop with send and return level controls, MIDI Footswitch in jack, XLR Microphone Simulated Direct Interface (MSDI) jack with ground/lift switch, level control, and three-position bright/normal/dark tone switch, two speaker jacks with impedance selector switch, 100W/50W half-power switch, black covering, footswitch included, 54.25 lbs., mfg. 2010-present.

MSR $1,500	$1,200	$675 - 800	$400 - 475	

DEUCE – 120W, 2-12 in. speakers, hybrid chassis, preamp: solid-state, power: 4 X 6L6, solid-state rectifier, two channels, front black control panel, four inputs (effects, parallel, series, normal), 11 black knobs (Effects Ch.: g, t, m, b, d, rate, Norm Ch.: g, t, b, Both: r, MV), speaker outs, mfg. early 1970s.

	N/A	$215 - 250	$105 - 130	

DEUCE II – 120W, 2-12 in. speakers, hybrid chassis, preamp: solid-state, power: 4 X 6L6, solid-state rectifier, two channels, front black control panel, four inputs (two bright, two normal), nine black knobs (g1, g2, b, m, t, r, d, rate, MV), speaker outs, optional footswitch, mfg. mid-1970s-early 1980s.

	N/A	$275 - 325	$150 - 200	

DEUCE VT SERIES – 120W, 2-12 in. speakers, hybrid chassis, preamp: solid-state, power: 4 X 6L6, solid-state rectifier, two channels, front control panel, four inputs, 12 knobs (Ch. 1: pre g, t, b, post g, Ch. 2: pre g, b, m, t, post g, color, rate, r), speaker outputs, preamp in/out, black covering, black grille, mfg. 1980s.

	N/A	$275 - 325	$150 - 200	

DUEL 212 – 120W, 2-12 in. speakers, tube chassis, two channels, reverb, front silver control panel, two inputs, 15 knobs (Ch. 1: g, l, m, h, Ch. 2: pre g, post g, l, m, h, r, s, i, resonance, p, MV), effects loop, speaker jacks, preamp out, black covering, black metal grille, 80 lbs., mfg. 1994-98.

	N/A	$350 - 425	$225 - 275	$1,000

ENCORE 65 – 65W, 1-12 in. speaker, tube chassis, preamp: 3 X 12AX7, 12AT7, power: 2 X 6L6GC, solid-state rectifier, reverb, front black control panel, two inputs, eight knobs (pre g, pump, post g, l, m, h, r, p), speaker jacks, power amp in, preamp out, optional footswitch, black covering, black grille, mfg. 1980s.

	N/A	$250 - 300	$135 - 175	

FESTIVAL – similar to the Deuce II, except in head-unit configuration, mfg. mid-1970s-early 1980s.

	N/A	$150 - 200	$95 - 120	

HERITAGE – 130W, 2-12 in. speakers, hybrid chassis, preamp: solid-state, power: 4 X 6L6, phaser, reverb, two channels, front black control panel, two inputs, 15 black knobs (Ch. 1: pre g, saturation, post g, l, m, h, p, Ch. 2: pre g, post g, l, paramid/shift, h, phase d, phase range), effects loop, optional footswitch, black covering, black grille, mfg. 1980s.

	N/A	$170 - 200	$85 - 105	

JACK DANIEL'S JD30T COMBO – 30W, 1-12 in. Jack Daniel's speaker, chrome-plated tube chassis, preamp: 3 X 12AX7, power: 4 X EL84, two channels, reverb, top control panel, single input, seven knobs (pre g, post g, l, m, h, r), effects loop, black covering, black grille, 39 lbs., mfg. 2005-present.

MSR $900	$700	$400 - 475	$250 - 300	

MSR/NOTES	100%	EXCELLENT	AVERAGE	LAST MSR

MACE VT SERIES – similar to the Duece VT, except has 160W output, 6 X 6L6 power tubes, mfg. 1980s.

	N/A	$255 - 300	$130 - 160	

PROWLER – 45W, 1-12 in. speaker, tube chassis, preamp: 3 X 12AX7, power: 2 X 6L6, two channels, reverb, front control panel, two inputs, 10 knobs (Ch. 1: v, l, m, h, Ch. 2: g, v, bottom, body, edge, r), external speaker jack, footswitch, black covering, black grille, mfg. 1999-2001.

	N/A	$250 - 300	$135 - 175	$600

RANGER 212 – 120W, 2-12 in. Blue Marvel speakers, tube chassis, preamp: 4 X 12AX7, power: 4 X 6L6, two channels, reverb, front black control panel, two inputs, 15 knobs (Ch. 1: g, l, m, h, Ch. 2: pre g, post g, l, m, h, r, s, i, resonance, p, MV), effects loop, speaker jacks, preamp out, footswitch, black covering, black grille, mfg. 1999-2000.

	N/A	$375 - 450	$250 - 300	$1,000

This is basically the Duel 212 with a new name and cosmetic change.

ROAD MASTER (VINTAGE TUBE SERIES) – 160W, guitar head-unit, 12-tube chassis, preamp: 4 X 12AX7, 2 X 12AT7, power: 6 X 6L6GC, two channels (normal/lead), front black control panel, two inputs (high gain, low gain), 13 knobs (Lead Ch.: pre g with pull boost, pump, post g with pull smooth, l, m, h with pull thick, r, Normal Ch.: pre g with pull bright, post g with push/pull channel switch, l, m, h with pull thick, p), power switch standby switch, rear panel: ground lift switch, two speaker jacks, power amp in, pre-amp out, footswitch jack, hum balance adjust, black covering, black grille with silver sides and Peavey logo, mfg. 1980s.

	N/A	$375 - 450	$225 - 275	

TRIUMPH 60 – 60W, 1-12 in. speaker, tube chassis, preamp: 4 X 12AX7, 12AT7, power: 2 X 6L6GC, solid-state rectifier, reverb, three channels, front control panel, two inputs, 10 knobs (Ultra: pre g, post g, Crunch: pre g, post g, Clean: g, All: l, m, h, p, r), effects loop, 4 and 8 Ohm speaker outputs, black covering, mfg. 1988-1991.

	N/A	$250 - 300	$135 - 175	

* ***Triumph 60 Head*** – similar to the Triumph 60, except in head-unit configuration, mfg. 1987-1991.

	N/A	$175 - 225	$110 - 140	

TRIUMPH 120 – 120W, 1-12 in. speaker, tube chassis, preamp: 4 X 12AX7, 12AT7, power: 4 X 6L6GC, solid-state rectifier, reverb, three channels, front control panel, two inputs, 10 knobs (Ultra: pre g, post g, Crunch: pre g, post g, Clean: g, All: l, m, h, p, r), effects loop, 4 and 8 Ohm speaker outputs, black covering, mfg. 1988-1991.

	N/A	$300 - 350	$175 - 225	

* ***Triumph 120 Head*** – similar to the Triumph 120, except in head-unit configuration, mfg. 1987-1991.

	N/A	$200 - 250	$120 - 150	

TRIUMPH PAG 60 – 60W, 1-12 in. speaker, tube chassis, preamp: 4 X 12AX7, power: 2 X 6L6GC, solid-state rectifier, reverb, three channels, front control panel, two inputs, 13 knobs (Clean: g, l, m, h, Crunch: pre g, post g, Ultra: pre g, post g, bottom, body, e, r, MV), effects loop, 4 and 8 Ohm speaker outputs, black covering, mfg. 1991-93.

	N/A	$275 - 325	$150 - 200	$700

TRIUMPH PAG 120 – 120W, 1-12 in. speaker, tube chassis, preamp: 4 X 12AX7, power: 4 X 6L6GC, solid-state rectifier, reverb, three channels, front control panel, two inputs, 13 knobs (Clean: g, l, m, h, Crunch: pre g, post g, Ultra: pre g, post g, bottom, body, e, r, MV), effects loop, 4 and 8 Ohm speaker outputs, black covering, mfg. 1991-93.

	N/A	$300 - 375	$175 - 225	$800

VTM 60 – 60W, head-unit only, tube chassis, preamp: 4 X 12AX7, power: 2 X 6L6GC, single channel, front black control panel, two inputs, six knobs (pre g, post g, l, m, h, p) eight individual response modifications, effects loop, 4, 8, or 16 Ohm speaker outputs, black covering, black grille, mfg. 1987-1993.

	N/A	$250 - 300	$135 - 175	$600

VTM 120 – 120W, head-unit only, tube chassis, preamp: 4 X 12AX7, power: 4 X 6L6GC, single channel, front black control panel, two inputs, six knobs (pre g, post g, l, m, h, p) eight individual response modifications, effects loop, 4, 8, or 16 Ohm speaker outputs, black covering, black grille, mfg. 1987-1993.

	N/A	$300 - 350	$175 - 225	$700

ELECTRIC SS AMPLIFIERS: EARLY MODELS

BANDIT – 50W, 1-12 in. speaker, solid-state chassis, two channels, reverb, front black control panel, two inputs, nine knobs (Ch. 1: pre g, sat., post g, Ch. 2: g, l, m, h, p, r), preamp out, power amp in, optional footswitch, black covering, black grille, mfg. 1975-1980s.

	N/A	$170 - 200	$85 - 105	

RENOWN – 160W, 2-12 in. speakers, solid-state chassis, two channels, reverb, front black control panel, two inputs, 14 knobs (Ch. 1: pre g, sat., post g, l, m, h, p, Ch. 2: pre g, post g, l, paramid, shift, h, r), speaker jacks, power amp in, preamp out, footswitch, mfg. late 1970s-1980s.

	N/A	$255 - 300	$130 - 160	

SPECIAL – 120W, 1-12 in. speaker, solid-state chassis, two channels, reverb, front black control panel, two inputs, nine knobs (Ch.1: pre g, sat., post g, Ch. 2: pre g, l, m, h, p, r), speaker outputs, power amp in, preamp out, optional footswitch, black covering, black grille, mfg. late 1970s-1980s.

	N/A	$215 - 250	$105 - 130	

MSR/NOTES	100%	EXCELLENT	AVERAGE	LAST MSR

ELECTRIC SS AMPLIFIERS: 1980S MFG.

AUDITION 20 – 12W, 1-8 in. speaker, solid-state chassis, single channel, front black control panel, single input, five knobs (pre g, post g, l, m, h), headphone jack, preamp out, black covering, black grille, mfg. 1980s.

	N/A	$45 - 50	$20 - 25	

AUDITION 30 – 30W, 1-12 in. speaker, solid-state chassis, front black control panel, two inputs, five knobs (pre g, post g, l, m, h), saturation button, thick button, preamp out, headphone jack, black covering, black grille, mfg. 1980s.

	N/A	$45 - 55	$25 - 30	

AUDITION PLUS – 20W, 1-8 in. speaker, solid-state chassis, single channel, front black control panel, two inputs, six knobs (pre g, supersat, post g, l, m, h), preamp out, headphone jack, black covering, black grille, mfg. 1980s.

	N/A	$55 - 65	$30 - 35	

BACKSTAGE – 20W, 1-10 in. speaker, solid-state chassis, two channels, reverb, front black control panel, two inputs, seven knobs (pre g, sat., post g, l, m, h, r), black covering, black grille, 23 lbs., mfg. 1980s.

	N/A	$50 - 60	$25 - 30	

BACKSTAGE PLUS – 35W, 1-10 in. speaker, solid-state chassis, two channels, reverb, front black control panel, two inputs, seven knobs (pre g, sat., post g, l, m, h, r), headphone jack, preamp out/power amp in, optional footswitch, black covering, black grille, mfg. 1980s.

	N/A	$55 - 65	$30 - 35	

BACKSTAGE 30 – 18W, 1-10 in. speaker, solid-state chassis, two channels, front black control panel, two inputs, five knobs (pre g, l, m, h, post g), black covering, black grille, mfg. 1980s.

	N/A	$45 - 50	$20 - 25	

BACKSTAGE 50 – 50W, 1-10 in. speaker, solid-state chassis, two channels, reverb, front black control panel, two inputs, seven knobs (normal g, sat., post g, l, m, h, r), effects loop, optional footswitch, black covering, black grille, mfg. 1980s.

	N/A	$85 - 100	$45 - 55	

BANDIT 65 – 65W, 1-12 in. speaker, solid-state chassis, two channels, reverb, front black control panel, two inputs, nine knobs (Ch. 1: pre g, sat., post g, Ch. 2: g, l, m, h, p, r), power amp in, preamp out, optional footswitch, black covering, black grille, mfg. 1980s.

	N/A	$100 - 120	$50 - 65	

BANDIT 75 – 75W, 1-12 in. speaker, solid-state chassis, two channels, reverb, front black control panel, two inputs, nine knobs (Ch. 1: level, Ch. 2: supersat, post g, l, m, h, p, r), effects loop, power amp in, preamp out, optional footswitch, black covering, black grille, mfg. 1980s.

	N/A	$130 - 150	$65 - 80	

JAZZ CLASSIC – 210W, 1-15 in. speaker, solid-state chassis, DDT compression, front black control panel, two inputs, nine knobs (Ch. 1: pre g, sat., post g, Ch. 2: g, l, m/shift, h, p, r), power amp out, preamp in, line out, footswitch, black covering, black grille, mfg. 1980s.

	N/A	$175 - 225	$110 - 140	

RAGE – 12W, 1-8 in. speaker, solid-state chassis, two channels, front black control panel, single input, six black knobs (v, pre g, post g, l, m, h), headphone jack, preamp out, black covering, black grille, mfg. 1980s.

	N/A	$40 - 45	$20 - 25	

SPECIAL 130 – 130W, 1-12 in. speaker, solid-state chassis, two channels, reverb, front black control panel, two inputs, nine knobs (Ch.1: pre g, sat., post g, Ch. 2: pre g, l, m, h, p, r), speaker outputs, power amp in, preamp out, optional footswitch, black covering, black grille, mfg. 1980s.

	N/A	$170 - 200	$85 - 105	

SPECIAL 150 – 150W, 1-12 in. speaker, solid-state chassis, two channels, reverb, front black control panel, two inputs, eight knobs (Ch.1: pre g, Ch. 2: sat., post g, l, m, h, p, r), effects loop, speaker outputs, power amp in, preamp out, optional footswitch, black covering, black grille, mfg. 1980s.

	N/A	$215 - 250	$105 - 130	

STUDIO PRO – 20W, 1-12 in. speaker, solid-state chassis, reverb, front black control panel, two inputs, seven knobs (pre g, sat., post g, l, m, h, r), power amp in, preamp out, line out, optional footswitch, black covering, black grille, mfg. 1980s.

	N/A	$170 - 200	$85 - 105	

STUDIO PRO 40 – 40W, 1-10 or 1-12 in. speaker, solid-state chassis, reverb, front black control panel, two inputs, seven knobs (pre g, sat., post g, l, m, h, r), power amp in, preamp out, line out, optional footswitch, black covering, black grille, mfg. 1980s.

	N/A	$170 - 200	$85 - 105	

STUDIO PRO 50 – 50W, 1-10 or 1-12 in. speaker, solid-state chassis, reverb, front black control panel, two inputs, seven knobs (pre g, sat., post g, l, m, h, r), power amp in, preamp out, line out, optional footswitch, black covering, black grille, mfg. 1980s.

	N/A	$170 - 200	$85 - 105	

STUDIO PRO 60 – 50W, 1-12 in. speaker, solid-state chassis, reverb, front black control panel, two inputs, seven knobs (pre g, supersat, post g, l, m, h, r), effects loop, headphone jack, optional footswitch, black covering, black grille, mfg. 1980s.

	N/A	$170 - 200	$85 - 105	

MSR/NOTES	100%	EXCELLENT	AVERAGE	LAST MSR

ELECTRIC SS AMPLIFIERS: CHORUS MODELS

AUDITION CHORUS – 20W (2 X 10W per channel), 2-6 in. speakers, solid-state chassis, two channels, chorus, front black control panel, two inputs, seven knobs (pre g, supersat, post g, l, m, h, chorus rate/depth), chorus and channel select, headphone jack, black covering, black grille, mfg. 1980s-1990.

	N/A	$85 - 100	$45 - 55	

BACKSTAGE CHORUS 208 – 50W (2 X 25W per channel), 2-8 in. speakers, solid-state chassis, two channels, chorus, front black control panel, two inputs, 12 knobs (Ch. 1: pre g, l, m, h, Ch. 2: supersat, post g, bottom, body, edge, r chorus rate, chorus d), chorus and channel select, headphone jack, black covering, black grille, mfg. 1991-97.

	N/A	$120 - 150	$75 - 95	$360

CLASSIC CHORUS 130 – 130W (2 X 65W per channel), 2-12 in. speakers, solid-state chassis, two channels, chorus, vibrato, front black control panel, two inputs, 13 knobs (Ch. 1: pre g, sat., post g, Ch. 2: pre g, l, m, h, r chorus rate, chorus d, vib d, vib rate), channel select, bs, preamp in/out, black covering, black grille, mfg. 1980s.

	N/A	$200 - 250	$120 - 150	

CLASSIC CHORUS 212 – 150W (2 X 75W per channel), 2-12 in. Scorpion speakers, solid-state chassis, two channels, chorus, front black control panel, two inputs, 13 knobs (Ch. 1: pre g, l, m, h, p, Ch. 2: supersat, post g, bottom, body, edge, r chorus rate, chorus d), channel select, bs, shift switch, gain switch, preamp in/out, black covering, black grille, mfg. 1980s-1997.

	N/A	$250 - 300	$135 - 175	$670

STEREO CHORUS 212 – 130W (2 X 65W per channel), 2-12 in. Scorpion speakers, solid-state chassis, three channels, chorus, front black control panel, two inputs, 17 knobs (Ch. 1: pre g, l, m, h, p, Ch. 2: supersat, post g, Ch. 3: supersat, post g, bottom, body, edge, r select, r level, chorus rate, chorus d, MV), preamp in/out, four-button footswitch, black covering, black grille, mfg. 1980s-1997.

	N/A	$275 - 325	$140 - 170	$900

Earlier models may only have 15 knobs with the body and MV knobs missing.

STEREO CHORUS 400 – 200W (2 X 100W per channel), 2-12 in. speakers, solid-state chassis, two channels, chorus, front black control panel, three inputs, 14 knobs (Ch. 1: pre g, sat., post g, h/l, m/shift, p, Ch. 2: pre g, post g, h/l, m/shift, p, chorus, vibrato, r), many knobs are dual purpose, preamp in/out, black covering, black grille, mfg. 1980s.

	N/A	$235 - 275	$115 - 145	

STUDIO PRO 70 – 70W (2 X 35W), 1-12 in. speaker, solid-state chassis, two channels, reverb, front black control panel, two inputs, eight knobs (Ch. 1: pre g, sat., post, g, Ch. 2: g, l/m, h/p, chorus, r), some knobs are dual purpose, channel select, bs, thick switch, line outs, optional footswitch, black covering, black grille, mfg. 1980s.

	N/A	$135 - 175	$85 - 110	

STUDIO CHORUS 210 – 70W (2 X 35W), 2-10 in. speaker, solid-state chassis, two channels, reverb, front black control panel, two inputs, 13 knobs (Ch. 1: pre g, l, m, h, p, Ch. 2: supersat, post g, bottom, body, edge, r, chorus rate, chorus depth), channel select, gs, line outs, three-button footswitch, black covering, black grille, mfg. 1980s-1997.

	N/A	$175 - 225	$110 - 140	$500

Early models may not have the body control in the EQ.

ELECTRIC SS AMPLIFIERS: TRANSFORMER SERIES

TRANSFORMER 112 – 50W, 1-12 in. Blue Marvel speaker, solid-state chassis, TransTube preamp & power amp, 24-bit processing, 12 amp models, 32 presets, front blue control panel, two inputs, 14 black knobs (preset selector, amp mod, pre g, l, m, h, post g, r, rate, depth, feedback, level), built in tuner, effects loop, headphone jack, footswitch, black covering, black grille, mfg. 2001-05.

	N/A	$350 - 425	$200 - 250	$800

TRANSFORMER 212 – 100W (50W per side stereo), 2-12 in. Blue Marvel speakers, solid-state chassis, TransTube preamp & power amp, 24-bit processing, 12 amp models, 32 presets, front blue control panel, two inputs, 14 black knobs (preset selector, amp mod, pre g, l, m, h, post g, r, rate, depth, feedback, level), built in tuner, effects loop, headphone jack, footswitch, black covering, black grille, 54 lbs., mfg. 2001-05.

	N/A	$475 - 550	$250 - 325	$1,050

ELECTRIC SS AMPLIFIERS: TRANSTUBE SERIES

In late 1994, Peavey introduced their new Transtube series. These amps are meant to sound like a tube amp using solid-state technology. These amps are not more models that claim they really capture the tube sound. Peavey has had several years in research and they feel that they have "bridged the gap" between tube and transistor (solid-state) amplifiers, hence the name. This technology was applied to all of their solid-state amplifiers that were produced before to create an entirely new series.

In 2001, Peavey revamped the cosmetics on the Transtube series and called all amps the Transtube II. The electronics are still the same but the trim on the bottom was changed from silver to red, the grille was changed to a lighter black, and the control panel was gray with a black background.

MSR/NOTES	100%	EXCELLENT	AVERAGE	LAST MSR

Audition
courtesy Peavey

Backstage II
courtesy Peavey

Bandit 112
courtesy Peavey

AUDITION – 7W, 1-4 in. speaker, guitar combo, solid-state chassis with TransTube technology, two channels, front black control panel, single input, three black knobs (v, h, l), channel switch, headphone jack, power switch, black covering, black grille, 6.5 lbs., current mfg.

MSR $65	$50	$35 - 40	$15 - 20	

AUDITION 110 – 25W, 1-10 in. Blue Marvel speaker, solid-state Transtube design, two channels, reverb, front black control panel, single input, 7 black knobs (Clean: v, Lead: pre g, post g, Both: l, m, h, r), CD/tape input, headphone jack, external speaker jack, footswitch, black covering, black grille, mfg. 1995-2000.

	N/A	$70 - 80	$35 - 40	$200

BACKSTAGE II – 10W, 1-6 in. speaker, guitar combo, solid-state chassis with TransTube technology, two channels, front black control panel, single input, four black knobs (Overdrive, v, h, l), channel switch, tape/CD input, headphone jack, power switch, black covering, black grille, current mfg.

MSR $85	$65	$40 - 50	$20 - 25	

BANDIT 112 – 100/80W, 1-12 in. Sheffield 1230 speaker, solid-state Transtube design, two channels, reverb, front blue control panel, two inputs, 12 black knobs (Clean: v, l, m, h, Lead: pre g, l, m, h, post g, r, p, MV), T-Dynamics control, effects loop, footswitch, black covering, black grille, 45 lbs., mfg. 1995-present.

MSR $500	$400	$260 - 300	$130 - 160	

BLAZER 158 – 15W, 1-8 in. Blue Marvel speaker, solid-state Transtube design, reverb, two channels, front black control panel, single input, seven black knobs (v, pre g, post g, l, m, h, r), headphone jack, CD/tape input, black covering, black grille, 15 lbs., mfg. 1995-2005.

	N/A	$60 - 80	$35 - 50	$160

ENVOY 110 – 40W, 1-10 in. Blue Marvel speaker, solid-state Transtube design, two channels, reverb, front black control panel, two inputs, 10 black knobs (Clean: v, l, m, h, Lead: pre g, l, m, h, post g, r), preset T-Dynamics, headphone jack, external speaker jack, footswitch, black covering, black grille, 22 lbs., mfg. 1995-present.

MSR $329	$300	$195 - 225	$100 - 120	

EXPRESS 112 – 65W, 1-12 in. Sheffield speaker, solid-state Transtube design, two channels, reverb, front black control panel, two inputs, 11 black knobs (Clean: v, l, m, h, Lead: pre g, l, m, h, post g, r, T-Dynamics control), effects loop, footswitch, black covering, black grille, 33 lbs., mfg. 1995-2000.

	N/A	$150 - 200	$95 - 120	$400

RAGE 158 – 15W, 1-8 in. Blue Marvel speaker, solid-state Transtube design, two channels, front black control panel, single input, six black knobs (v, pre g, post g, l, m, h), headphone jack, CD/tape input, black covering, black grille, 14 lbs., mfg. 1995-2006.

	N/A	$50 - 60	$25 - 30	$150

RAGE 258 – 25W, 1-8 in. Blue Marvel speaker, solid-state Transtube design, two channels, front black control panel, single input, six black knobs (v, pre g, post g, l, m, h), headphone jack, CD/tape input, black covering, dark gray grille, 14 lbs., mfg. 2007-present.

MSR $160	$130	$85 - 100	$40 - 50	

REVOLUTION 112 – 100W, 1-12 in. Sheffield speaker, solid-state Transtube design, three channels, reverb, front black control panel, two inputs, 14 black knobs (Clean: v, l, m, h, Lead/Ultra: pre g1, post g1, pre g2, post g2, bottom, body e, r, p, T-Dynamics control), effects loop, footswitch, black covering, black grille, 46 lbs., mfg. 2001-02.

	N/A	$190 - 225	$95 - 120	$600

SOLO – 25W, 1-8 in. Blue Marvel speaker, solid-state Transtube design, two channels (mic and inst.), front black control panel, two standard inputs and one mic input, four black knobs (mic. v, inst. v, l, h), tape output, AC/DC operation, black covering, black grille with horizontal silver bars, 13 lbs., mfg. 2005-present.

MSR $200	$140	$90 - 110	$50 - 60	

MSR/NOTES	100%	EXCELLENT	AVERAGE	LAST MSR

Special 212
courtesy Dave Rogers/Dave's Guitar Shop

Special 212
courtesy Dave Rogers/Dave's Guitar Shop

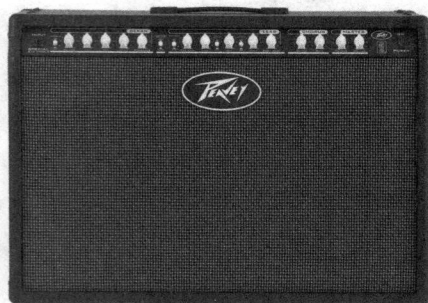

Special Chorus 212
courtesy Peavey

SPECIAL 212 – 200W, 2-12 in. Sheffield speakers, solid-state Transtube design, three channels, reverb, front black control panel, two inputs, 18 black knobs (Clean: v, l, m, h, Crunch: pre g, l, m, h, post g, Lead: pre g, l, m, h, post g, r, resonance, p, T-Dynamics control), effects loop, footswitch, black covering, black grille, 65 lbs., mfg. 1995-2005.

	N/A	$215 - 250	$105 - 130	$740

Circa 2000, the control panel was altered where the EQ was combined on the Crunch and Lead channels and the knob count was reduced to 16.

SPECIAL CHORUS 212 – 100W, 2-12 in. Peavey Blue Marvel speakers, solid-state Transtube design, two channels (clean and lead), reverb, front black control panel, one input, 14 white knobs (Clean: v, l, m, h, presence, Lead: pre g, l, m, h, post g, Chorus: depth, rate) Master Reverb, Master Volume, effects loop, footswitch, black covering, black grille, 38.58 lbs., mfg. 2011-present.

MSR $500	$350	$230 - 265	$115 - 140	

STUDIO PRO 112 – 65W, 1-12 in. Blue Marvel speaker, solid-state Transtube design, two channels, reverb, front black control panel, two inputs, 11 black knobs (Clean: v, l, m, h, Lead: pre g, l, m, h, post g, r, T-Dynamics control), effects loop, footswitch, black covering, black grille, 33 lbs., mfg. 1995-2005.

	N/A	$130 - 150	$65 - 80	$380

TRANSCHORUS 210 – 100W (2 X 50W), 2-10 in. Blue Marvel speakers, solid-state Transtube chassis, three channels, reverb, front black control panel, two inputs, 15 black knobs (Clean: v, l, m, h, Crunch: pre g, post g, Lead: pre g, post g, l, m, h, r, chorus rate, chorus d, T-Dynamics), power amp input, preamp out, headphone jack, footswitch, black covering, black grille, mfg. 1999-2000.

	N/A	$235 - 275	$115 - 145	$600

ELECTRIC SS AMPLIFIERS: TRANSTUBE EFX SERIES

Transtube 110 EFX
courtesy Peavey

Transtube 112 EFX
courtesy Peavey

Transtube 212 EFX
courtesy Peavey

TRANSTUBE 100 HEAD EFX – 100W, head-unit only, solid-state chassis with digital processing, front black and red control panel, two inputs, 15 knobs (Ch. 1: v, l, m, h, Ch. 2: pre g, l, m, h, post g, EFX, r, delay, p, resonance, T. Dynamics), nine digital effects, black covering, 40.4 lbs., mfg. 2003-04.

	N/A	$300 - 350	$175 - 225	$700

TRANSTUBE 110 EFX – 40W, 1-10 in. Blue Marvel speaker, solid-state chassis with digital processing, front black and red control panel, single input, nine knobs (v, pre g, post g, l, m, h, EFX, r, delay), nine digital effects, black covering, black grille, 23 lbs., mfg. 2003-07.

	N/A	$180 - 230	$110 - 140	$400

TRANSTUBE 112 EFX – 65W, 1-12 in. Blue Marvel speaker, solid-state chassis with digital processing, front black and red control panel, single input, 13 knobs (Ch. 1: v, l, m, h, Ch. 2: pre g, l, m, h, post g, EFX, r, delay, T. Dynamics), nine digital effects, black covering, black grille, 33.4 lbs., mfg. 2002-07.

	N/A	$250 - 300	$125 - 175	$550

MSR/NOTES	100%	EXCELLENT	AVERAGE	LAST MSR

TRANSTUBE 212 EFX – 100W, 2-12 in. Blue Marvel speakers, solid-state chassis with digital processing, front black and red control panel, single input, 15 knobs (Ch. 1: v, l, m, h, Ch. 2: pre g, l, m, h, post g, EFX, r, delay, p, resonance, T. Dynamics), nine digital effects, black covering, black grille, 53 lbs., mfg. 2002-07.

	N/A	$300 - 375	$175 - 225	$700

TRANSTUBE 258 EFX – 25W, 1-8 in. Blue Marvel speaker, solid-state chassis with digital processing, two channels, front black and red control panel, single input, nine knobs (v, pre g, post g, l, m, h, EFX, r, delay), nine digital effects, black covering, black grille, 16 lbs., mfg. 2002-07.

	N/A	$110 - 140	$60 - 80	$240

This model used to be the Transtube 208 with 20W of power.

ELECTRIC SS AMPLIFIERS: VYPYR SERIES

The Vypyr Series is a line of digital modeling amps that are available in two distinct configurations: solid-state chassis and hybrid chassis. The Vypyr 15, Vypyr 30, Vypyr 75, and Vypyr 100 all utilize a solid-state chassis while the Vypyr 60, Vypyr 120 Head, and Vypyr 120 Combo have a hybrid chassis with one preamp tube and a tube power section. All amps feature 24 amp models and 11 rack effects. All models besides the Vypyr 15 also have 11 stompbox effects. All effects can be edited and presets can be stored - 12 with the amp and up to 400 with the optional Sanpera footswitch.

- Add $120 (MSR $146) for Sanpera I footswitch.
- Add $230 (MSR $288) for Sanpera II footswitch.

Vypyr 60
courtesy Peavey

Vypyr 100
courtesy Peavey

Vypyr 120 Combo
courtesy Peavey

VYPYR 15 – 15W, 1-8 in. speaker, digital modeling guitar combo amp, solid-state chassis with TransTube technology, single channel, 24 amp channel models, 11 rack effects, 12 programmable presets, front blue and dark gray control panel, single input, eight chrome knobs (amp model selector, effects selector, pre gain/effects parameter 1, low/effects parameter 2, mid/delay feedback, high/delay level, post gain/reverb, MV), seven buttons for presets, aux. input, headphone/recording out jack, power switch, black covering, dark gray grille cloth, mfg. 2008-2014.

	$100	$60 - 80	$40 - 50	$170

VYPYR 30 – 30W, 1-12 in. speaker, digital modeling guitar combo amp, solid-state chassis with TransTube technology, single channel, 24 amp channel models, 11 stompbox effects, 11 rack effects, 12 programmable presets, front blue and dark gray control panel, single input, nine chrome knobs (stompbox selector, amp model selector, effects selector, pre gain/effects & stompbox parameter 1, low/effects & stompbox parameter 2, mid/delay feedback, high/delay level, post gain/reverb, MV), seven buttons for presets, aux. input, headphone/recording out jack, power switch, MIDI in/out, chromatic tuner, optional Sanpera footswitch, black covering, dark gray grille cloth, mfg. 2008-2014.

	$200	$120 - 150	$75 - 95	$280

* *Vypyr 30 Head* – similar to the Vypyr 30 Combo, except in head-unit configuration, mfg. 2010-2014.

	$180	$100 - 135	$60 - 80	$250

VYPYR 60 – 60W, 1-12 in. speaker, digital modeling guitar combo amp, hybrid chassis with three tubes, preamp: 1 X 12AX7, power: 2 X 6L6GC, single channel, 24 amp channel models, 11 stompbox effects, 11 rack effects, 12 programmable presets, front cream and dark gray control panel, single input, nine chrome knobs (stompbox selector, amp model selector, effects selector, pre gain/effects & stompbox parameter 1, low/effects & stompbox parameter 2, mid/delay feedback, high/delay level, post gain/reverb, MV), seven buttons for presets, aux. input, USB recording out, headphone/recording out jack, power switch, MIDI in/out, chromatic tuner, optional Sanpera footswitch, black covering, dark gray grille cloth, mfg. 2008-2014.

	$450	$275 - 325	$150 - 200	$600

VYPYR 75 – 75W, 1-12 in. speaker, digital modeling guitar combo amp, solid-state chassis with TransTube technology, single channel, 24 amp channel models, 11 stompbox effects, 11 rack effects, 12 programmable presets, front blue and dark gray control panel, single input, ten chrome knobs (stompbox selector, amp model selector, effects selector, pre gain/effects & stompbox parameter 1, low/effects & stompbox parameter 2, mid/delay feedback, high/delay level, post gain/reverb, MV, power sponge attentuator), seven buttons for presets, aux. input, USB recording out, headphone/recording out jack, power switch, MIDI in/out, chromatic tuner, optional Sanpera footswitch, black covering, dark gray grille cloth, mfg. 2008-2014.

	$300	$175 - 225	$110 - 140	$400

MSR/NOTES	100%	EXCELLENT	AVERAGE	LAST MSR

VYPYR PRO 100
courtesy Peavey

VYPYR VIP 1
courtesy Peavey

VYPYR VIP 3
courtesy Peavey

VYPYR 100 – 100W, 2-12 in. speakers, digital modeling guitar combo amp, solid-state chassis with TransTube technology, single channel, 24 amp channel models, 11 stompbox effects, 11 rack effects, 12 programmable presets, front blue and dark gray control panel, single input, ten chrome knobs (stompbox selector, amp model selector, effects selector, pre gain/effects & stompbox parameter 1, low/effects & stompbox parameter 2, mid/delay feedback, high/delay level, post gain/reverb, MV, power sponge attentuator), seven buttons for presets, aux. input, USB recording out, headphone/recording out jack, power switch, MIDI in/out, chromatic tuner, optional Sanpera footswitch, black covering, dark gray grille cloth, mfg. 2008-2014.

	$400	$275 - 325	$150 - 200	$600

VYPYR 120 HEAD – 120W, digital modeling guitar head unit, hybrid chassis with five tubes, preamp: 1 X 12AX7, power: 4 X 6L6GC, single channel, 24 amp channel models, 11 stompbox effects, 11 rack effects, 12 programmable presets, front cream and dark gray control panel, single input, nine chrome knobs (stompbox selector, amp model selector, effects selector, pre gain/effects & stompbox parameter 1, low/effects & stompbox parameter 2, mid/delay feedback, high/delay level, post gain/reverb, MV), seven buttons for presets, aux. input, USB recording out, headphone/recording out jack, power switch, MIDI in/out, chromatic tuner, optional Sanpera footswitch, black covering, dark gray grille cloth, mfg. 2008-2014.

	$550	$300 - 375	$175 - 225	$700

* *Vypyr 120 Combo* – similar to the Vypyr 120 Head, except in combo configuration with 2-12 in. speakers, mfg. 2008-2014.

	$650	$350 - 425	$225 - 275	$800

VYPYR 30 112 SPEAKER CABINET – 40W, 1-12 in. speaker, 16 ohm impedance, designed for use with the Vypyr 30 Head, black covering, black grille, 56.5 lbs., mfg. 2010-2014.

	$130	$75 - 100	$45 - 60	$200

VYPYR PRO 100 – 100W, 1-12 in. speaker, digital modeling guitar combo amp, solid-state chassis with TransTube technology using four stages of analog gain, single channel, over 100 different amp, effect, stompbox, and instrument models, silver control panel, single input, ten black knobs (model 1, model 2, model 3, model 4, pre gain, low, medium, high, post gain, MV), MP3/CD/aux. input, bi-directional USB connector, headphone/recording out jack, power switch, MIDI in/out, effects loop, optional Sanpera footswitch, black covering, black grille cloth, 37.92 lbs., mfg. 2014-present.

MSR $800	$600	$400 - 450	$195 - 240	

VYPYR VIP 1 – 20W, 1-8" in. speaker, digital modeling guitar combo amp with variable instrument capabilities, solid-state chassis with TransTube technology, Acoustic/Bass Guitar simulation, single channel, 16 presets, 25 amp accessible effects, 36 on board amp models, 6 bass amp models, 6 acoustic amp models, on board looper, tap tempo, silver control panel, single input, eight black knobs (pre gain, low, medium, high, post gain, MV, instrument/stomp selector, amplifier selector), MP3/CD/aux. input, bi-directional USB connector, headphone out jack, MIDI in/out, chromatic tuner, optional Sanpera footswitch, black covering, black grille cloth, 20 lbs., mfg. 2013-present.

MSR $200	$130	$85 - 100	$40 - 50	

VYPYR VIP 2 – 40W, 1-12" in. speaker, digital modeling guitar combo amp with variable instrument capabilities, solid-state chassis with TransTube technology, 10 instrument models, Acoustic/Bass Guitar simulation, single channel, 16 presets, 26 amp accessible effects, 36 on board amp models, 6 bass amp models, 6 acoustic amp models, on board looper, tap tempo, silver control panel, single input, eight black knobs (pre gain, low, medium, high, post gain, MV, instrument/stomp selector, amplifier selector), MP3/CD/aux. input, bi-directional USB connector, headphone out jack, MIDI in/out, chromatic tuner, optional Sanpera footswitch, black covering, black grille cloth, 29 lbs., mfg. 2013-present.

MSR $300	$200	$130 - 150	$65 - 80	

VYPYR VIP 3 – 100W, 1-12" in. speaker, digital modeling guitar combo amp with variable instrument capabilities, solid-state chassis with TransTube technology, 10 instrument models, Acoustic/Bass Guitar simulation, single channel, 16 presets, 26 amp accessible effects, 36 on board amp models, 6 bass amp models, 6 acoustic amp models, over 400 amp accessible presets, on board looper, tap tempo, silver control panel, single input, eight black knobs (pre gain, low, medium, high, post gain, MV, instrument/stomp selector, amplifier selector), MP3/CD/aux. input, bi-directional USB connector, headphone out jack, MIDI in/out, chromatic tuner, optional Sanpera footswitch, black covering, black grille cloth, 29.39 lbs., mfg. 2013-present.

MSR $400	$300	$195 - 225	$100 - 120	

MSR/NOTES	100%	EXCELLENT	AVERAGE	LAST MSR

ELECTRIC SS AMPLIFIERS: WIGGY SERIES

WIGGY – 100W (16, 8, or 4 Ohm), semi-circle shaped head-unit only, solid-state Transtube design, two channels, reverb, front silver control panel meant to emulate a car dashboard, two inputs, controls are gain (RPM), master volume (MPH), Batt, oil, and temp for 3-band equalizer, presence and T-Dynamics control, various lights and knobs, effects loop, footswitch, lighted control panel, purple covering, 31 lbs., mfg. 2001-04.

	N/A	$425 - 500	$215 - 265	$1,100

WIGGY 212 ENCLOSURE – 150W (75W per side stereo), 2-12 in. Sheffield 1230 speakers, 16 ohm impedance stereo, 8 ohm mono, straight front, purple covering, silver trapezoidal grille, 59 lbs., mfg. 2001-04.

	N/A	$225 - 275	$135 - 175	$550

ELECTRIC SS AMPLIFIERS: XXL/SUPREME SERIES

XXL
courtesy Peavey

XXL 212 Combo
courtesy Peavey

Supreme XL Head
courtesy Peavey

XXL – 100W (switchable to 50 or 25W), head-unit only, solid-state Transtube design, three channels, reverb, front black control panel, single input, 16 silver knobs (Clean: v, h, m, l, Crunch: edge, body, bottom, v, g, Ultra: h, m, l, v, g, MV, r), effects loop, footswitch, black covering, silver striped grille, 40 lbs., mfg. 2002-07.

	N/A	$375 - 450	$200 - 250	$820

XXL 212 COMBO – 100W (switchable to 50 or 25W), 2-12 in. Blue Marvel speakers, solid-state Transtube design, three channels, reverb, front black control panel, single input, 16 silver knobs (Clean: v, h, m, l, Crunch: edge, body, bottom, v, g, Ultra: h, m, l, v, g, MV, r), effects loop, footswitch, black covering, silver striped bar and black cloth grille, 59 lbs., mfg. 2003-05.

	N/A	$375 - 450	$250 - 300	$870

XXL 212 SPEAKER CABINET – 150W, 2-12 in. Blue Marvel speakers, closed back, stereo or mono operation, casters, straight front, black covering, black grille, 47 lbs., mfg. 2003-05.

	N/A	$135 - 175	$85 - 110	$320

XXL 412 SPEAKER CABINET – 300W, 4-12 in. Blue Marvel speakers, closed back, stereo or mono operation, casters, straight or angled front, black covering, black grille, 98/97 lbs., disc. 2005.

	N/A	$225 - 275	$135 - 175	$540

SUPREME – 100W (16, 8, or 4 Ohm), head-unit only, solid-state Transtube design, two channels, reverb, front black control panel, two inputs, 12 black knobs (Clean: v, l, m, h, Lead: pre g, l, m, h, post g, r, p, T-Dynamics control), effects loop, footswitch, black covering, black grille, mfg. 1999-2002.

	N/A	$225 - 275	$120 - 150	$570

SUPREME XL HEAD – 100W (switchable to 50 or 25W), head-unit only, solid-state Transtube design, two channels, reverb, front black control panel, two inputs, 12 silver knobs (Clean: v, l, m, h, Lead: pre g, l, m, h, post g, r, p, T-Dynamics control), effects loop, two-button footswitch, black covering, reversible chrome faceplate, 38 lbs., mfg. 2003-06.

	N/A	$250 - 300	$125 - 175	$550

SUPREME XL 412 SPEAKER CABINET – 300W, 4-12 in. Blue Marvel speakers, closed back, stereo or mono operation, casters, straight or angled front, black covering, black grille, 98/97 lbs., mfg. 2006-disc.

$350	$200 - 250	$120 - 150	$480

ELECTRIC HYBRID AMPLIFIERS

ARTIST/ARTIST 240 – 120W, 1-12 in. speaker, guitar combo, hybrid chassis with a solid-state preamp and 4 X 6L6GC power tubes, two channels, front black control panel, four inputs (bright, series, parallel, normal), seven knobs (v1, v2, b, m, t, r, MV), power switch, line power switch, main speaker output jack, external speaker jack, Din jack for optional Automix footswitch, black covering, black grille, mfg. 1975-1980s.

	N/A	$250 - 300	$135 - 175	

MSR/NOTES	100%	EXCELLENT	AVERAGE	LAST MSR

CLASSIC VTX – 65W, 2-12 in. Scorpion speakers, guitar combo, hybrid chassis, preamp: solid-state, power: 2 X 6L6, two channels (normal, lead), phase, reverb, front black control panel, two inputs (high gain, low gain), 11 knobs (Lead Gain: pre with pull bright, saturation, post, Norm gain: pre with pull bright, All: l, m, h with pull thick, p, phase depth, phase range with pull set, r), rear panel: ground switch, main speaker jack, aux. jack, DIN Automix footswitch jack, power amp in , pre-amp out, black covering, black metal grille, 26.25 in. wide, 20 in. tall, 11 in. deep, 64 lbs., mfg. 1980s.

	N/A	$200 - 250	$120 - 150	

STEEL AMPLIFIERS/SPEAKER CABINETS

NASHVILLE 112 – 80W, 1-12 in. Blue Marvel speaker, digital power amp, front black control panel, eight black knobs (pre g, l, m, shift, h, p, r, master g), pre-EQ patch loop send and return, footswitch, black covering, black grille, 43 lbs., mfg. 2003-present.

MSR $900	$700	$450 - 525	$230 - 280	

For the Matching speaker cabinet refer to the Speaker Cabinet section.

NASHVILLE 400 – 210W, 1-15 in. Black Widow speaker, solid-state chassis, single channel, DDT compression, front black control panel, two inputs, eight knobs (pre g, post g, l, m, shift, h, p, r), effects loop, power amp in. preamp out, mfg. 1980s-2000.

	N/A	$375 - 450	$190 - 235	$630

NASHVILLE 1000 – 300W, 1-15 in. Black Widow 1501-4SB speaker, digtial power amp, front black control panel, eight black knobs (pre g, l, m, shift, h, p, r, master g), pre-EQ patch loop send and return, footswitch, black covering, black grille, 57 lbs., mfg. 1999-2009.

	N/A	$375 - 450	$190 - 235	$1,200

NASHVILLE 112E SPEAKER CABINET – 350W, 1-12 in. Black Widow 1203-4 speaker, two input jacks, open-back, black covering, black grille, mfg. 1994-98.

	N/A	$120 - 150	$75 - 95	$260

NASHVILLE 115E SPEAKER CABINET – 250W, 1-15 in. Black Widow 1501-4 speaker, two input jacks, open-back, black covering, black grille, mfg. 1996-98.

	N/A	$135 - 175	$85 - 110	$300

SESSION 400/LTD – 200W, 1-15 in. JBL speaker, solid-state chassis, single channel, tremolo, front black control panel, two inputs, 10 knobs (v, p, t, m, m shift, b, r, depth, rate, MV), booster jack, optional footswitch, black covering, black grille, mfg. late 1970s-1980s.

	N/A	$375 - 450	$250 - 300	

Peavey also made an LTD amp, which is identical to the Session 400, except it has a smaller cabinet.

SESSION 400 LIMITED – 200W, 1-15 in. Black Widow speaker, solid-state chassis, single channel, tremolo, front black control panel, two inputs, eight knobs (pre g, l, m, m shift, h, p, p/sensitivity, r), 3 effects loops, optional footswitch, black covering, black grille, mfg. late 1980s-1998.

	N/A	$350 - 425	$225 - 275	$690

* *Session 400 Limited Wedge* – similar to the Session 400 Limited, except is in a slant wedge cabinet at 30 degrees and has a protective metal grille, mfg. 1980s-1993.

	N/A	$350 - 425	$225 - 275	$700

SESSION 500 – 250W, 1-15 in. speaker, solid-state chassis, single channel, front black control panel, two inputs, 13 knobs (pre g, level, edge, l, paramid, m shift, h, p, post g, r, phase color, phase rate, r, crossover), power amp in, preamp outs, optional footswitch, black covering, black grille, mfg. 1980-late 1980s.

	N/A	$375 - 450	$250 - 300	

ACOUSTIC AMPLIFIERS

ECOUSTIC 110 EFX – Biamped (30W to lows/mids, 10W to highs), 1-10 in. Blue Marvel coax speaker, solid state chassis, two channels, reverb, front brown control panel, instrument input, and mic input, five brown knobs (level 1, level 2, 2 inst. FX, mic FX), 2 four-band equalizers, various buttons, brown covering, brown grille cloth, 39 lbs., mfg. 2003-disc.

	N/A	$275 - 325	$150 - 200	$600

ECOUSTIC 112 – 100W, 1-12 in. Blue Marvel co-axial speaker, solid state chassis, two channels, reverb, front brown control panel, instrument input, and mic input, seven brown knobs (inst. level, nostch, r, mic. level, r, r, p), 2 five-band equalizers, various buttons, brown covering, brown grille cloth, mfg. 1996-2002.

	N/A	$250 - 300	$135 - 175	$650

ECOUSTIC 112 EFX – Biamped (100W to lows/mids, 25W to highs), 1-12 in. Blue Marvel co-axial speaker, solid state chassis, three channels, reverb, front brown control panel, instrument input, and mic input, ten brown knobs (level 1, level 2, 2 inst. FX, mic FX, Aux. Ch.: level, h, l, MV, r), 2 five-band equalizers, various buttons, brown covering, brown grille cloth, 62 lbs., mfg. 2003-disc.

	N/A	$400 - 475	$225 - 275	$900

MSR/NOTES	100%	EXCELLENT	AVERAGE	LAST MSR

Ecoustic 110 EFX
courtesy Peavey

Ecoustic E20
courtesy Peavey

Ecoustic E110
courtesy Peavey

RENO 400 – 210W, 1-15 in. Scorpion speaker, solid-state chassis, front black control panel, two inputs, eight knobs (pre g, post g, l, m, shift, h, p, r), effects loop, power amp in, preamp out, optional footswitch, black covering, black grille, mfg. 1980s-1992.

	N/A	$150 - 175	$75 - 90	$600

ECOUSTIC E20 – 20W, 1-8 in. speaker, acoustic guitar combo, solid state chassis, two channels, top black and gold control panel, two inputs (one per channel), six black knobs (Ch. 1: level, l, h, Ch. 2: level, l, h), headphone jack, black covering, black metal grille with gold accents, 16.25 lbs., mfg. 2010-present.

MSR $180	$140	$90 - 105	$45 - 55	

ECOUSTIC E208 – 20W, 2-8 in. speakers, acoustic guitar combo, solid state chassis, two channels, chorus, reverb, top black and gold control panel, two inputs (one 1/4 in. for Ch. 1, one combination XLR/standard 1/4 in. for Ch. 2), 10 black knobs (Ch. 1: level, l, h, chorus, Ch. 2: level, l, m, h, r, MV), chorus on/off switch, headphone jack, black covering, black metal grille with gold accents, 24.25 lbs., mfg. 2010-present.

MSR $250	$200	$95 - 120	$50 - 70	

ECOUSTIC E110 – 100W, 1-10 in. speaker with 1-3 in. high-freq. horn, acoustic guitar combo, solid state chassis, two channels, chorus, delay, reverb, front black and gold control panel, two combination 1/4 in./XLR inputs (one per channel), six black chickenhead knobs (Ch. 1: g, notch filter, Ch. 2: g, l, h, MV), three regular digital effects knobs (chorus, delay, reverb), Ch. 1 nine-band graphic EQ, mute switch, phase reverse switch, four digital effects switches: channel switch, parameter switch, tuner out jack, rear panel: power switch, footswitch jack, XLR line out with ground/lift switch, black covering, black metal grille with gold accents, mfg. 2010-present.

MSR $600	$500	$325 - 375	$165 - 200	

BASS AMPLIFIERS: BAM SERIES

BAM 210 – 500W, 2-10 in. cast frame woofers, horn-loaded tweeter, solid-state modeling amp, effects, front black control panel, single input, 14 black knobs (input trim, input preset, compressor squeeze, level, model selector, pre g, l, m, shift, h, post g, effects adj, depth, MV), various buttons and switches, on two wheel casters with dolly handle (adjustable like a suitcase), 97 lbs., mfg. 2001-04.

	N/A	$425 - 500	$250 - 300	$1,600

BAM HEAD – 500W, head-unit only, solid-state modeling amp, effects, front black control panel, single input, 14 black knobs (input trim, input preset, compressor squeeze, level, model selector, pre g, l, m, shift, h, post g, effects adj, depth, MV), various buttons and switches, mounted in its own rack enclosure, mfg. 2001-04.

	N/A	$325 - 400	$200 - 250	$1,170

BASS AMPLIFIERS: HEADLINER SERIES

Headliner 115 Speaker Cabinet
courtesy Peavey

Headliner 210 Speaker Cabinet
courtesy Peavey

Headliner 410 Speaker Cabinet
courtesy Peavey

HEADLINER 115 SPEAKER CABINET – 500W, 1-15 in. Sheffield driver, 8 ohm impedance, two 1/4 in. and one NL4 four-pin inputs, recessed side handles, black carpet covering, black metal grille, 63 lbs., mfg. 2010-present.

MSR $370	$250	$150 - 200	$95 - 120	

MSR/NOTES	100%	EXCELLENT	AVERAGE	LAST MSR

HEADLINER 210 SPEAKER CABINET – 400W, 2-10 in. drivers, 8 ohm impedance, two 1/4 in. and one NL4 four-pin inputs, recessed side handles, black carpet covering, black metal grille, 52 lbs., mfg. 2010-present.

MSR $380	$200	$120 - 150	$75 - 95	

HEADLINER 410 SPEAKER CABINET – 800W, 4-10 in. drivers, 8 ohm impedance, two 1/4 in. and one NL4 four-pin inputs, recessed side handles, black carpet covering, black metal grille, 72 lbs., mfg. 2010-present.

MSR $500	$300	$175 - 225	$110 - 140	

HEADLINER 1000 BASS HEAD – 1000W RMS (1500W peak), rack-mount head-unit bass configuration, solid-state chassis, front brushed aluminum/black control panel, one input, five knobs (pre gain, l, h, compressor, v), seven-band graphic EQ with bypass, mute switch, bright switch, contour switch, crunch switch, active/passive switch, power switch, headphone jack, parallel external speaker jacks, effect loop, remote switch jack, XLR DI out jack with ground/lift switch and post/pre switch, black casing, 2.8 in. tall, 17.38 in. wide, 12.5 in. deep, 10 lbs., mfg. 2015-present.

MSR $580	$450	$295 - 325	$145 - 180	

BASS AMPLIFIERS: MAX SERIES

Max 160 Head
courtesy Peavey

Max 450 Head
courtesy Peavey

Max 700 Head
courtesy Peavey

MAX 160 HEAD – 160W @ 4 ohms (100W @ 8 ohms), head-unit only, solid-state chassis, front black control panel, single passive/active input, seven black knobs (pre g, c, l, m, m shift, h, MV), post EQ effects loop, black Tolex covering, 24 lbs., mfg. 2003-07.

	N/A	$190 - 240	$120 - 150	$400

MAX 450 HEAD – 450W @ 2 ohms (300W @ 4 ohms, 170Wat 8 ohms), head-unit only, solid-state chassis, front black control panel, single passive/active input, seven black knobs (pre g, c, l, m, m shift, h, MV), post EQ effects loop, line out, black Tolex covering, 41 lbs., mfg. 2003-06.

	N/A	$275 - 325	$150 - 200	$600

MAX 700 HEAD – 700W @ 2 ohms (475W @ 4 ohms, 275W @ 8 ohms), head-unit only, solid-state chassis, front black control panel, single passive/active input, nine black knobs (pre g, c, l, m, m shift, h, 2 crossover knobs, MV), post EQ effects loop, line outblack Tolex covering, 52.5 lbs., mfg. 2003-06.

	N/A	$350 - 425	$200 - 250	$800

MAX 110 COMBO – 20W, 1-10 in. speaker, solid-state chassis, DDT speaker protection, front black control panel, single input, four knobs (g, h, m, l), tape/CD input, headphone jack, black covering, black grille, mfg. 2004-present.

MSR $300	$250	$165 - 190	$80 - 100	

MAX 112 COMBO – 35W, 1-12 in. speaker, solid-state chassis, DDT speaker protection, Hypervent ported enclosure technology, front black control panel, single input, four knobs (g, h, m, l), tape/CD input, headphone jack, black covering, black grille, mfg. 2004-present.

MSR $350	$300	$195 - 225	$100 - 120	

MAX 115 COMBO – 50W, 1-15 in. speaker, solid-state chassis, DDT speaker protection, Hypervent ported enclosure technology, front black control panel, single input, four knobs (g, h, m, l), tape/CD input, headphone jack, black covering, black grille, mfg. 2004-present.

MSR $400	$350	$230 - 265	$115 - 140	

MAX 126 COMBO – 10W, 1-6.5 in. speaker, solid-state chassis, front black control panel, single input, four knobs (g, v, h, l), tape/CD input, headphone jack, black covering, black grille, mfg. 2004-present.

MSR $150	$80	$40 - 60	$20 - 30	

MAX 158 COMBO – 15W, 1-8 in. speaker, solid-state chassis, front black control panel, single input, four knobs (v, h, m, l), tape/CD input, headphone jack, black covering, black grille, mfg. 2004-present.

MSR $170	$140	$90 - 105	$45 - 55	

BASS AMPLIFIERS: MICHAEL ANTHONY SERIES

MA-118 CABINET – 1600W, 1-18 in. Low Rider bass woofer, 8 ohm impedance, two 1/4 in. and one 4 four-pin connector, recessed side handles, black covering, black metal grille, 81.35 lbs., mfg. 2013-present.

MSR $1,000	$800	$525 - 600	$260 - 325	

MSR/NOTES	100%	EXCELLENT	AVERAGE	LAST MSR

MA-410 Cabinet
courtesy Peavey

MA-810 Cabinet
courtesy Peavey

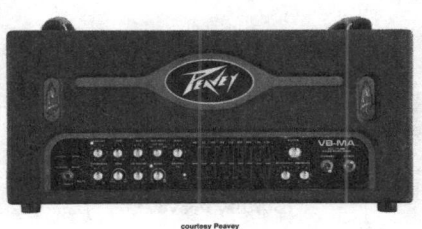

courtesy Peavey

VA-MA Head
courtesy Peavey

MA-410 CABINET – 800W, 4-10 in. ceramic magnet woofer, single 1 in. horn tweeter, 8 ohm impedance, two 1/4 in. and one 4 four-pin connector, recessed side handles, black covering, black metal grille, 81 lbs., mfg. 2013-present.

| MSR $1,000 | N/A | $675 - 800 | $350 - 425 | |

MA-810 CABINET – 800W, 8-10 in. ceramic magnet speakers, 8 ohm impedance, 4 2x10 chambers, switchless stereo or mono operation, recessed side handles, black covering, black metal grille, 144 lbs., mfg. 2013-present.

| MSR $1,200 | $1,000 | $650 - 750 | $325 - 400 | |

VB-MA HEAD – 300W, bass head-unit, 14 tube chassis, preamp: 2 X 12AT7, 4 X 12AX7, power: 8 X EL34, two channels, front red and black control panel, single input, eleven knobs (v, OD, l, t, m, OD volume, mid shift, blend, h, MV, r, p), nine-band graphic EQ, 15 dB pad switch, bright switch, mute switch, compression control, low cut switch, graphic EQ switch, standby switch, power switch, buffered tuner send, master effects loop, two top-mounted handles, black covering, mfg. 2013-present.

| MSR $3,000 | $2,000 | $1,300 - 1,500 | $650 - 800 | |

BASS AMPLIFIERS: MISC. HEAD UNITS

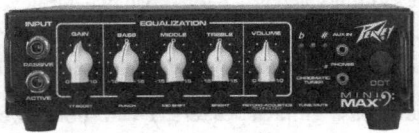

Minimax
courtesy Peavey

Minimega
courtesy Peavey

DELTABASS – 160W, head-unit only, solid-state chassis, DDT speaker protection with switch, single channel, front black and red control panel, seven black knobs (pre-g, c, l, m, m-shift, h, v), tuner output, XLR output, effects loop, disc. 2002.

| | N/A | $175 - 225 | $110 - 140 | $400 |

FIREBASS 700 – 700W, head-unit only, solid-state chassis, DDT speaker protection with switch, single channel, front black and red control panel, ten black knobs (pre-g, c, l, m, m-shift, h, v, line out level, freq, balance), tuner output XLR output, X over outs, effects loop, disc. 2002.

| | N/A | $325 - 400 | $200 - 250 | $760 |

NITROBASS – 450W, head-unit only, solid-state chassis, DDT speaker protection with switch, single channel, front black and red control panel, eight black knobs (pre-g, c, l, m, m-shift, h, v, line out level), tuner output XLR output, effects loop, disc. 2002.

| | N/A | $250 - 300 | $150 - 200 | $590 |

MINIMAX – 500W, head-unit only, solid-state chassis, DDT speaker protection pre-gain control with TransTube gain boost, active and passive inputs, front black control panel, five white knobs (g, b, m, t, v,), chromatic tuner, two .25 in. outputs, effects loop, mfg. 2014-present.

| MSR $550 | $350 | $230 - 265 | $115 - 140 | |

MINIMEGA – 1000W, head-unit only, solid-state chassis, gain control with punch button, single input, 4-band EQ, front black control panel, eight black knobs (g, comp, l, low mid, high mid, h, kosmos, v), tuner output, two .25 in. outputs, headphone jack, DI output, MIDI footswitch input, effects loop, mfg. 2014-present.

| MSR $800 | $600 | $400 - 450 | $195 - 240 | |

BASS AMPLIFIERS: PRO SERIES

In 2004, Blue Marvel speakers were officially introduced in the speaker cabinets. Before they were just listed as a high-performance cast frame speaker. In 2007, a new series of Pro amps was introduced and all the speaker cabinets were redesigned with a black metal grille and slightly different cosmetics.

PRO 500 HEAD – 500W @ 2 ohms (350W @ 4 ohms), rackmount head unit, tube preamp, solid-state power amp, DDT compression, black control panel, single input, 14 knobs (pre g, post g, l, h, contour, three low knobs, three mid knobs, three high mid knobs, MV), tuner send, effects loop, footswitch, 26 lbs., mfg. 2002-06.

| | N/A | $500 - 600 | $350 - 425 | $1,050 |

MSR/NOTES	100%	EXCELLENT	AVERAGE	LAST MSR

Pro 500 Head
courtesy Peavey

Pro 115 Speaker Cabinet
courtesy Peavey

Pro 410 Speaker Cabinet
courtesy Peavey

PRO 1600 HEAD – 1600W mono operation (800W per side stereo) Bi-Amp, rackmount head unit, tube preamp, solid-state power amp, DDT compression, black control panel, single input, 16 knobs (pre g, post g, l, contour, 2 low knobs, 2 mid knobs, 2 high mid knobs, h, boost, MV, crossover mode, crossover freq., crossover balance), tuner send, effects loop, footswitch, mfg. 2004 only.

| N/A | $900 - 1,050 | $600 - 700 | $2,000 |

PRO 2000 HEAD – 2000W @ 4 ohms mono (1500W @ 8 ohms mono, 1000W per channel stereo @ 2 ohms, 750W per channel stereo @ 4 ohms), rackmount head bass configuration, hybrid chassis with tube and solid-state components, front brushed aluminum/black control panel, single input, 12 knobs (pre-amp blend, solid-state pre gain, tube pre gain, l, m, h, mid-freq., Q, Freq., mode, balance, MV), XLR direct in, black casing, 25 lbs., mfg. 2006-09.

| N/A | $850 - 1,000 | $575 - 700 | $1,800 |

PRO 115 SPEAKER CABINET – 700W, 1-15 in. high performance cast frame bass guitar speakers, 1-1 in.horn tweeter, level and overload, protection, black carpet covering, silver metal grille, casters, 69 lbs., mfg. 2002-07.

| N/A | $350 - 425 | $200 - 250 | $800 |

PRO 210 SPEAKER CABINET – 700W, 2-10 in. high performance cast frame bass guitar speakers, 1-1 in. horn tweeter, level and overload, protection, black carpet covering, silver metal grille, casters, 58 lbs., mfg. 2002-06.

| N/A | $350 - 425 | $200 - 250 | $800 |

PRO 410 SPEAKER CABINET – 1400W, 4-10 in. high performance cast frame bass guitar speakers, 1-1 in. horn tweeter, level and overload protection, black carpet covering, silver metal grille, casters, 96 lbs., mfg. 2002-07.

| N/A | $450 - 525 | $300 - 350 | $1,000 |

PRO 810 SPEAKER CABINET – 2800W, 8-10 in. high performance cast frame bass guitar speakers, 1-1 in. horn tweeter, level and overload protection, black carpet covering, silver metal grille, tilt-back wheels, 160 lbs., mfg. 2003-07.

| N/A | $850 - 950 | $550 - 650 | $1,850 |

BASS AMPLIFIERS: TOUR COMBO SERIES

The Peavey series of bass combos has been produced for several years. For the most part, the chassis have remained the same. The cosmetics and the speakers have changed over the years. Here is a chart that may help you identify what year your amplifier may be.

1980s-early 1990s: Models have silver strips running vertically on the grille Upper End models have Black Widow or Scorpion speakers.

1990s-1999: TKO and TNT have new style black covering, black grille with old logo, and model name listed at bottom of grille on silver strip.

1990s-1996: Minx 100, Basic 60/112, and Microbass have 1980s style black covering, silver bars running vertically on each side of grille, and blue line on the bottom of the control panel. In 1996, all models would be updated to look like the TKO and TNT models. Some later models in the 1990s may have Sheffield speakers.

2000-2002: Blue Marvel speakers introduced, cosmetics were changed to a black control panel with red outlines, new style Peavey logo and triangle logo at bottom.

2003-2008: Cosmetics slightly changed with the old Peavey logo and the triangle removed from the bottom.

2009-Present: An entirely new cabinet and cosmetics were introduced. The control panel was moved to the top, while a new kick-back cabinet design and an all black metal grille with a lighted Peavey logo were introduced.

BASIC 60/112 – 75W, 1-12 in. speaker, solid-state chassis, DDT speaker protection, single channel, front black control panel, single input, six black knobs (pre-g, l, l/m, m/h, h, v), bright/normal switch, active/passive switch, headphone jack, external speaker jack, effects loop, black covering, black metal grille, 45 lbs., mfg. 1980s-2005.

| N/A | $150 - 200 | $95 - 120 | $380 |

In 1996, Peavey changed the model name from the Basic 60 to the Basic 112. Earlier models have 50W output power.

MSR/NOTES	100%	EXCELLENT	AVERAGE	LAST MSR

**Microbass
courtesy Peavey**

**Tour TKO 115 (Second Version)
courtesy Peavey**

**Tour TNT 115 (Second Version)
courtesy Peavey**

COMBO 115 – 300W, 1-15 in. speaker, solid-state chassis, DDT speaker protection, ported enclosure, active crossover, single channel, chorus, front black control panel, two inputs, five black knobs (v, l, h, crossover frequency, v), seven-band equalizer, bright/normal switch, normal/contour switch, active/passive switch, headphone jack, external speaker jack, effects loop, black covering, black metal grille, 100 lbs., mfg. 1980s-2008.

	N/A	$350 - 425	$175 - 225	$800

Older models have 210W output power.

MICROBASS – 20W, 1-8 in. speaker, solid-state chassis, DDT compression, single channel, front black control panel, single input, four black knobs (g, l, m, h), headphone jack, external speaker jack, black covering, black metal grille, 20 lbs., mfg. 1980s-2005.

	N/A	$50 - 75	$30 - 40	$180

MINX 110 – 35W, 1-10 in. speaker, solid-state chassis, DDT speaker protection, single channel, front black control panel, single input, four black knobs (g, l, m, h), headphone jack, external speaker jack, effects loop, black covering, black metal grille, 33 lbs., mfg. 1980s-2005.

	N/A	$120 - 150	$75 - 95	$300

TKO 115 (FIRST VERSION) – 100W, 1-15 in. speaker, solid-state chassis, DDT speaker protection, ported enclosure, single channel, front black control panel, single input, four black knobs (pre-g, l, h, v), seven-band equalizer, bright/normal switch, normal/contour switch, active/passive switch, headphone jack, external speaker jack, effects loop, black covering, black metal grille, 72 lbs., mfg. 1980s-2008.

courtesy Ryan Muetzel

courtesy Ryan Muetzel

	N/A	$250 - 300	$125 - 175	$550

Earlier models have 75W output power.

TOUR TKO 115 (SECOND VERSION) – 400W, 1-15 in. speaker with a high-freq. tweeter, solid-state chassis, top gray and black control panel, single input, active/passive pickup type switch, pre-gain knob, bright switch, contour switch, low EQ knob, graphic EQ switch, seven-band graphic EQ, high EQ knob, MV, DDT speaker protection switch, headphone jack, rear panel: XLR DI out, powered speaker out, effects loop, kick-back cabinet design, side-mounted recessed metal handles, black metal grille with lighted Peavey logo, mfg. 2009-present.

MSR $650	$475	$300 - 350	$155 - 190	

TNT 115 (FIRST VERSION) – 200W, 1-15 in. speaker, solid-state chassis, DDT speaker protection, ported enclosure, single channel, chorus, front black control panel, single input, four black knobs (pre-g, l, h, v), seven-band equalizer, bright/normal switch, normal/contour switch, active/passive switch, headphone jack, external speaker jack, effects loop, black covering, black metal grille, 85 lbs., mfg. 1980s-2009.

	N/A	$325 - 375	$175 - 225	$660

Earlier models have 150W output power.

MSR/NOTES	100%	EXCELLENT	AVERAGE	LAST MSR

TOUR TNT 115 (SECOND VERSION) – 600W, 1-15 in. speaker with a high-freq. tweeter, solid-state chassis, single channel, compressor, top gray and black control panel, single input, active/passive pickup type switch, pre-gain knob, bright switch, contour switch, crunch switch, low EQ knob, graphic EQ switch, seven-band graphic EQ, high EQ knob, compression knob, compression switch, MV, DDT speaker protection switch, headphone jack, rear panel: XLR DI out, powered speaker Speakon jack, effects loop, tweeter on/off switch, kick-back cabinet design, side-mounted recessed metal handles, footswitch included, black covering, black metal grille with lighted Peavey logo, mfg. 2009-present.

MSR $780 $600 $400 - 450 $195 - 240

BASS AMPLIFIERS: TOUR HEAD/SPEAKER CABINET SERIES

Tour VB-2
courtesy Peavey

Tour 210 Speaker Cabinet
courtesy Peavey

Tour 410 Speaker Cabinet
courtesy Peavey

Tour 700 Head
courtesy Peavey

TOUR VB-2 – 225W, head-unit configuration, nine tube chassis, preamp: 2 X 12AX7, 1 X 12AT7, power: 6 X EL34, solid-state rectifier, two switchable channels, resonance, front brushed aluminum control panel, two inputs, eight black knobs (clean g, OD v, l, m, h, MV, r, p), channel select, mid-shift switch, effects loop, tuner send jack, mute switch, footswitch, black covering, black metal grille, handles on top, mfg. 2007-disc.

N/A $500 - 575 $325 - 375 $1,100

TOUR 450 HEAD – 450W @ 4 ohms (300W @ 8 ohms), rack-mount head-unit bass configuration, solid-state chassis, front brushed aluminum/black control panel, two inputs, six knobs (pre gain, contour, l, h, post gain, octaver), nine-band graphic EQ with bypass, mute switch, bright switch, DDT compression with switch, black casing, mfg. 2006-disc.

$420 $250 - 300 $150 - 200 $580

TOUR 700 HEAD – 700W @ 4 ohms (500W @ 8 ohms), rack-mount head-unit bass configuration, solid-state chassis, front brushed aluminum/black control panel, two inputs, six knobs (pre gain, contour, l, h, post gain, octaver), nine-band graphic EQ with bypass, mute switch, bright switch, DDT compression with switch, black casing, mfg. 2006-disc.

$500 $300 - 350 $175 - 225 $650

TOUR 115 SPEAKER CABINET – 400W, 1-15 in. driver with 1-1 in. tweeter, 8 ohm impedance, parallel Neutrik and 1/4 in. input jacks, plywood construction, bottom ported cabinet that angles out in the middle, black Tolex covering with metal corners, black speaker grille with silver vertical strips on edge, 56 lbs., mfg. 2006-09.

N/A $275 - 325 $150 - 200 $600

TOUR 210 SPEAKER CABINET – 400W, 2-10 in. drivers with 1-1 in. tweeter, 8 ohm impedance, parallel Neutrik and 1/4 in. input jacks, plywood construction, bottom ported cabinet that angles out in the middle, black Tolex covering with metal corners, black speaker grille with silver vertical strips on edge, 46 lbs., mfg. 2006-disc.

$450 $275 - 325 $150 - 200 $600

TOUR 215 SPEAKER CABINET – 800W, 2-15 in. drivers with 1-1 in. tweeter, 4 ohm impedance, parallel Neutrik and 1/4 in. input jacks, plywood construction, bottom ported cabinet that angles out in the middle, black Tolex covering with metal corners, black speaker grille with silver vertical strips on edge, mfg. 2006-09.

N/A $400 - 475 $250 - 300 $900

TOUR 410 SPEAKER CABINET – 1600W, 4-10 in. drivers with 1-1 in. tweeter, 8 ohm impedance, parallel Neutrik and 1/4 in. input jacks, plywood construction, bottom ported cabinet that angles out in the middle, black Tolex covering with metal corners, black speaker grille with silver vertical strips on edge, 67 lbs., mfg. 2006-09.

N/A $350 - 425 $225 - 275 $800

TOUR 810 SPEAKER CABINET – 3200W, 8-10 in. drivers with 1-1 in. tweeter, 8 ohm impedance, parallel Neutrik and 1/4 in. input jacks, plywood construction, bottom ported cabinet that angles out in the middle, black Tolex covering with metal corners, black speaker grille with silver vertical strips on edge, 95 lbs., mfg. 2007-09.

N/A $450 - 525 $275 - 325 $1,000

BASS AMPLIFIERS: VB SERIES

The VB Series was announced in 2007, but was not actually listed in the price list until 2009.

MSR/NOTES	100%	EXCELLENT	AVERAGE	LAST MSR

VB-810 Speaker Cabinet courtesy Peavey

412EX Speaker Cabinet courtesy Peavey

115BX/BVX BW/TVX 115 EX Bass Speaker Cabinet courtesy Peavey

VB-3 BASS HEAD – 300W, bass head-unit, 13 tube chassis, preamp: 2 X 12AT7, 3 X 12AX7, power: 8 X EL34, two channels, front black control panel, single input, ten knobs (v, OD, l, m, h, compression, mid-shift, MV, r, p), nine-band graphic EQ, channel switch, 15 dB pad switch, bright switch, mute switch, compression switch, low cut switch, graphic EQ switch, standby switch, power switch, rear panel: tuner out jack, XLR line out with level control, EQ pre/post switch, and ground/lift switch, light dimming control, remote switch jack, effects loop, power amp in, pre-amp out, two Speakon jacks with three-way impedance selector (8, 4, or 2 ohm), two top-mounted handles, black covering, black front with lighted blue accent trim, mfg. 2009-disc.

	$1,800	$1,150 - 1,350	$650 - 800	$2,500

VB-810 SPEAKER CABINET – 800W, 8-10 in. custom designed ceramic magnet speakers divided into four individual 2-10 in. chambers, switchless stereo or mono operation, side mounted recessed metal handles, black bedliner covering, black cloth grille, 134.5 lbs., mfg. 2009-disc.

	$800	$475 - 550	$250 - 300	$1,050

GUITAR SPEAKER CABINETS: MISC. SERIES

112SX GUITAR – 75W, 1-12 in. Sheffield speaker, closed back, black covering, black grille, 36.4 lbs., disc. 2005.

	N/A	$135 - 175	$85 - 110	$300

412EX SPEAKER CABINET – 300W, 4-12 in. speakers, 16 ohm impedance, slanted front, recessed side handles, casters, designed for use with the 3120 Head, black covering, black grille cloth, 29.75 in. wide, 32 in. tall, 14.125 in. deep, 91.5 lbs., mfg. 2009-disc.

	$350	$225 - 275	$125 - 150	$500

430A/430B SPEAKER CABINET – 120W, 4-12 in. Stephens Tru-Sonic V30 speakers, 16 ohm impedance, 1/4 in. inputs with stereo/mono selection switch, straight (430B) or angled (430A) front, 18-ply baltic birch construction, heavy-duty casters, black covering, black grille with Stephens logo, straight: 98.7 lbs., angled: 96.2 lbs., mfg. 2010-present.

MSR $1,300	$800	$525 - 600	$260 - 325	

PX300 – 300W digital powered amplifier, 1-15 in. 1501-4 Black Widow speaker, can be used to add stereo capability to amps or as an extension speaker, disc. 2003.

	N/A	$375 - 450	$250 - 300	$850

112-6 SPEAKER CABINET – 25W, 1-12 in. Celestion Greenback 25 speaker, convertible back, straight front, 8/16 ohms mono, one 1/4 in. input, metal corners, top handle, black Tolex covering, black grille with white piping, 33 lbs., current mfg.

MSR $400	$300	$195 - 225	$100 - 120	

212-6 SPEAKER CABINET – 120W, 2-12 in. Celestion Greenback 25 speakers, convertible back, straight front, 8/16 ohms, two 1/4 in. inputs, metal corners, top handle, black Tolex covering, black grille with white piping, 43.6 lbs., current mfg.

MSR $500	$400	$260 - 300	$130 - 160	

BASS SPEAKER CABINETS: TX/TXF/TVX SERIES

The TVX Series has been around for several years and for the most part, the chassis haven't changed. The only thing that has really changed are the cosmetics and model designations. This chart should help you date or identify your speaker cabs.

1980s-1991: Known as simply the Bass Enclosure Series. Models are listed as the 115, 210, etc.

1992-1998: Models are changed to TX Series.

1999-2001: Model designation is changed to the TXF series for only certain models including the 210 TXF, 410TXF, and 412TXF. Cosmetics on these models have the new style Peavey logo and triangle logo at bottom of the grille.

2001-02: All models receive the TVX designation. Cosmetics are the same as the TXF with the new Peavey logo and triangle at bottom of the grille.

2003-06: Models receive a cosmetic makeover with the old Peavey logo and removal of the triangle of the bottom of the grille.

2006-Present: Models are renamed the TVX-EX series with minimal changes. The TVX-810 is disc.

MSR/NOTES	100%	EXCELLENT	AVERAGE	LAST MSR

115BX SPEAKER CABINET – 400W, 1-15 in. Scorpion, ported enclosure, 4 Ohm impedance, closed back cabinet, black covering, black grille, mfg. 1980s-2001.

	N/A	$120 - 150	$70 - 95	$300

• **Add $40 for Model 115TXR, which has a two-space rack spot above the speaker cab.**

This model was disc. in 2001 when the 115BVX was only offered with the Black Widow speaker.

115BX/BVX BW/TVX 115 EX BASS SPEAKER CABINET – 400W, 1-15 in. Black Widow, ported enclosure, 4 or 8 ohm impedance, closed back cabinet, black covering, black grille, 86 lbs., current mfg.

MSR $430	$330	$175 - 225	$125 - 150	

In 2000, this model was changed to the 115BVX BW, and the grille had the triangle logo placed at the bottom. By 2002/03, the triangle was removed and the old Peavey logo was introduced. In 2006, this model was renamed the TVX 115 EX.

210TVX/TVX 210 EX BASS SPEAKER CABINET – 175W, 2-10 in. Sheffield speakers, 1 dome tweeter, ported enclosure, 4 Ohm impedance, closed back cabinet, black covering, black grille, 62 lbs., mfg. 1980s-present.

MSR $370	$270	$150 - 200	$95 - 120	

• **Add $40 for Model 210TXR, which has a two-space rack spot above the speaker cab.**

410TVX/TVX 410 EX BASS SPEAKER CABINET – 350W, 4-10 in. Sheffield speakers, one-horn loaded tweeter, 4 or 8 Ohm impedance, closed back cabinet, black covering, black grille, 98 lbs., mfg. 1980s-present.

MSR $540	$400	$225 - 275	$120 - 150	

412TVX BASS SPEAKER CABINET – 350W, 4-12 in. Sheffield speakers, one-horn loaded tweeter, 4 Ohm impedance, closed back cabinet, black covering, black grille, 129.1 lbs., mfg. 1999-2004.

	N/A	$350 - 425	$200 - 250	$840

810TVX BASS SPEAKER CABINET – 400W, 8-10 in. Sheffield speakers, one-horn loaded tweeter, 4 ohm impedance, closed back cabinet, black covering, black grille, 161.7 lbs., mfg. 1980s-2006.

	N/A	$475 - 550	$325 - 375	$1,000

1516 SPEAKER CABINET – 400W, 1-15 in. Black Widow speaker, 2-8 in. special design speakers, black covering, black metal grille, mfg. 1980s-1997.

	N/A	$200 - 250	$100 - 150	$500

1820 SPEAKER CABINET – 700W, 1-15 in. Black Widow speaker, 2-10 in. Scorpion speakers, black covering, black metal grille, mfg. 1980s-1997.

	N/A	$250 - 300	$125 - 175	$620

PENN

Amplifiers currently produced in New Jersey since 1994.

Billy Penn is the owner and founder of the Penn Instrument Company. Penn is a boutique amplifier company that produces fine tube amplifiers that can be finished in fine wood cabinets. All amplifiers are built in the USA, and they are inspected and signed by Billy Penn, himself. For more information visit Penn's website or contact them directly.

CONTACT INFORMATION
PENN
1 Executive Dr.
Unit 1L
Toms River, NJ 08755
Phone No.: 848-218-0362
www.pennalizer.com
pennalizer@gmail.com

AMPLIFIERS

Penn offers two different options for their amplifiers. The Standard Series feature Penn's standard production models. This is a combo amp with 1-12 in. speaker and 40W output that retails for $2,400. The Custom Series allows the customer to start from a platform and build the amp from there. Basic platforms include a 5W amp with 1-8 in. speaker (MSR $799), a 15-20W amp with 1-12 in. speaker (MSR $1,899), a 30-50W amp with 1-12 in. speaker (MSR $2,099), and a 100W amp with 2-12 in. speakers (MSR $2,399).

**Signature Series 1-12
courtesy Penn**

**Custom Series 2X10B
courtesy Penn**

**Custom Series CS30
courtesy Penn**

MSR/NOTES	100%	EXCELLENT	AVERAGE	LAST MSR

PHIL JONES BASS

Amplifiers and other audio products currently produced in St. Louis, MO since 2003. Phil Jones Bass is a division of American Acoustic Development (AAD).

Phil Jones Bass represents some of the finest sound in bass amplification. Phil Jones fell in love with the bass guitar at the early age of 13. Ever since then, he has been involved in playing bass guitar and building his own equipment. In 1990, he moved from England to the U.S., and worked for Boston Acoustics for a short while. In 1994, he developed Platinum Audio, which specialized in building hi-fi home speakers and studio monitors. In 1998, he founded American Acoustic Development, which also specializes in hi-fi speakers and other products. Circa 2003, Phil took what had worked so well for professional audio and presented it to the bass guitar player. Phil Jones now produces bass amplifiers that are of the upmost quality. Some of the features that are unique to Phil Jones are their 5 in. driver speakers (some cabinets have 24 of them!) and the versatility in their sounding (equilization, etc.). For more information please refer to their website.

CONTACT INFORMATION
PHIL JONES BASS
A division of American Acoustic Development
8509 Mid County Industrial Dr.
St. Louis, MO 63114
Phone No.: 314-814-3383
Fax No.: 636-536-1338
www.pjbworld.com
info@philjonespuresound.com

AMPLIFIERS/SPEAKER CABINETS

Phil Jones produces both tube and solid-state amplifiers. The solid-state combo amps include the **Briefcase** and the **Six-Pak**. The Briefcase has 110W output through 2-5 in. drivers. The Six-Pak features the M-500 power uni (720W) through 6-5 in. drivers. The **M-500** has 720W output and a variety of features. The **M-1000** has 1400W output using MOSFET power. The M-1000 is also available as a slave unit.

The most impressive unit that Phil Jones produces may be the **T-500**. This amp pushes 650W of power from tubes! These tubes are not the ordinary ones you can find regularly on the street. These are Svetlana 813 "beam power transmitter tetrodes." They claim to put out as much power as 12 X 6550 conventional tubes.

Phil Jones also makes speaker cabinets in a variety of sizes. All their cabinets feature their 5 in. Piranha drivers. These come in 6, 8, 9, 16, and 24 speaker configurations.

PIGNOSE

Amplifiers currently produced in Las Vegas, NV since 1972. Distributed by Pignose Amplifiers.

Pignose amplifiers have been around since 1972. A kid went to a distributor in Oakland with this prototype amp that was built in a wooden box. The idea of a portable, battery operated amp wasn't taken by storm from the distributor in Oakland. He later gave a prototype to Terry Kath of Chicago who took interest in the idea. The volume knob kept coming loose and he brought it to his tech. The rubber knob was melted and when it was fixed, Terry said that it looked like a pig's nose. Some of the first models were produced with these "pignose" knobs, and there only two of them known in existence. The Pignose amp was one of the first on the market that was completely portable. Now Pignose offers amps that are run strictly on DC battery power along with a rechargeable model. Not only are these amps novel ideas, they are also fairly cheap. They also offer a wide range of products, including tube models. For further information, visit Pignose's website or contact them directly.

CONTACT INFORMATION
PIGNOSE
570 W. Cheyenne Ave
Suite 80
North Las Vegas, NV 89030
Phone No.: 702-648-2444
Phone No.: 1-888-369-0824
Fax No.: 702-648-2440
www.pignoseamps.com
hchatt@aol.com

ELECTRIC AMPLIFIERS

Pignose also produces the **PG-10** practice guitar amp (MSR $80), **PG-20** practice guitar amp (MSR $110), and **PB-30** practice bass amp (MSR $160).

7-100
courtesy Pignose

7-200 Hog 20
courtesy Pignose

7-300 Hog 30
courtesy Pignose

7-100 – original Pignose amplifier, brown covering, black round speaker with logo across it, single "pignose" knob, silver accents with latch, mfg. 1972-present.

	100%	EXCELLENT	AVERAGE
1972-1995	N/A	$50 - 75	$30 - 40
1996-Present MSR $120	$80	$40 - 60	$20 - 30

MSR/NOTES	100%	EXCELLENT	AVERAGE	LAST MSR

* *7-100 Special Edition* – similar to the 7-100, except in limited edition configuration with tweed covering, current mfg.

MSR $138	$90	$50 - 70	$25 - 35	

7-200 HOG 20 – 20W, 1-6.5 in. speaker, solid-state chassis, front black control panel, two inputs (one in front, one in back), three knobs (v, tone, sqeal), "pignose" knob, headphone jack, rechargable battery, brown leatherette covering, black grille, 15 lbs., current mfg.

MSR $190	$150	$85 - 110	$50 - 70	

7-300 HOG 30 – 30W, bass, acoustic, or keyboard application, 1-8 in. speaker, solid-state chassis, front black control panel, two inputs (one in front, one in back), five knobs (v, MV, t, m, b), "pignose" knob, headphone jack, line out, rechargable battery, brown Pignose Tolex covering, black metal grille, 28 lbs., current mfg.

MSR $260	$180	$100 - 135	$60 - 80	

30/60 – 30W, 1-12 in. speaker, solid-state chassis, single channel, front black control panel, two inputs, five knobs (v, MV, t, m, b), effects loop, brown Pignose covering, black grille, mfg. late 1970s-1980s.

	N/A	$120 - 150	$75 - 95	

B-100V – 100W, bass amplifier, 1-15 in. speaker, tube chassis, preamp: 2 X 12AX7, power: 4 X 6L6GC, single channel, front black control panel, single input, five black knobs (v, p, t, m, b), effects loop, speaker outputs, black Tolex covering, black grille, 66 lbs., disc. 2005.

	N/A	$375 - 450	$225 - 275	$899

* *B-100VH Head* – similar to the B100V, except in head-unit configuration, 31 lbs., disc. 2005.

	N/A	$300 - 350	$175 - 225	$699

G-40V – 40W, 1-10 in. speaker, tube chassis, preamp: 3 X 12AX7, power: 2 X 6L6, single channel, front black control panel, single input, six black knobs (v, MV, p, t, m, b), speaker outputs, brown Pignose Tolex covering, black grille, 24 lbs., mfg. 2002-09.

	$320	$175 - 225	$120 - 150	$550

G-60VR – 60W, 1-12 in. speaker, tube chassis, preamp: 4 X 12AX7, power: 2 X 6L6, single channel, reverb, front black control panel, single input, seven black knobs (v, MV, p, t, m, b, r), effects loop, speaker outputs, black Tolex covering, black grille, 44 lbs., disc. 2009.

	$530	$325 - 400	$200 - 250	$850

* *G-60VRH Head* – similar to the G-60VR, except in head-unit configuration, 34 lbs., disc. 2009.

	$470	$290 - 340	$175 - 225	$750

PIONEER

Amplifiers previously produced by Danelectro in the 1950s.

Pioneer amplifiers were produced by Danelectro and distributed by Continental Music. Very little is known about Pioneer, but they produced almost exact clones of Danelectro amplifiers from the 1950s. A 1956 Pioneer catalog actually has Danelectro in plain sight on some pictures. Any further information on Pioneer amps can be submitted directly to Blue Book Publications.

ELECTRIC TUBE AMPLIFIERS

Pioneer produced at least two different series of amplifiers. The first series featured four models with a two-tone covering that is unique. The speaker grilles are round or oval in style and the covering is split around the grille - the left side and bottom of the cabinet is covered in a dark covering and the right and top side is covered in a light covering. Models from this era include the **Model 15**, **Model 25**, **Model 30**, and **Model 50**. In the mid-1950s, Pioneer amps with more traditional stylings were introduced. This series included all models from the previous series with minor changes. Four other models were advertised, but they all feature Danelectro model names and it is unknown if any models under the Pioneer exist. These models include **The Commando**, **The Master-Slave** system, **The Cadet**, and **The Corporal**.

PLEXI

See Cornell.

PLUSH

Amplifiers and speaker cabinets previously produced in the late 1960s and early 1970s.

Plush was founded circa 1968 in New York City, and they built mainly tube amps that were covered in a variation of the Tuck N' Roll covering Kustom was famous for using. This covering has been found in several variations, but the most common appears to be a criss-cross pattern with buttons in the junctions, similar to the pattern found in older couches, loveseats, chairs, etc. In 1971, they opened a new factory in California and by 1974, they filed Chapter 11 bankruptcy. There is also a lot of speculation that Plush Amplifiers and Earth Sound Research (ESR) are one in the same company. The theory is Plush started out building amplifiers in New York, they built a second factory on the West Coast in Los Angeles, and as the East Coast factory went under, the amps in the West Coast were renamed Earth Sound Research. Currently, there is no proof that Plush and ESR were the same company, built the same amps,

MSR/NOTES	100%	EXCELLENT	AVERAGE	LAST MSR

or operated in the same building. There seems to be a lot of crossover between these two names, and any additional information can be submitted directly to Blue Book Publications.

AMPLIFIERS

Plush produced the Vagrant series of guitar and bass amplifiers early on. It appears that Plush used the same head unit with several different speaker cabinet combinations for a number of variations. Guitar models were noted by an EV prefix and bass models were noted by a VB prefix. 15 in. Jensen and Electro-Voice speakers were used most often. Plush also offered the Bruiser, which was a large unit designed for PA applications. By 1970, Plush was producing the 1000 and 1060 series of guitar and bass amplifiers. Values on the 1000 and 1060 series of amplifiers range between $300 and $450 in excellent condition.

POLYTONE

Amplifiers previously produced in North Hollywood, CA.

The Polytone company was started in 1968 by Tommy Gumina. The motto for Polytone was "Made by Musicians for Musicians." Tommy started to build small, portable amps with the "Polytone" sound. The Mini-Brute line of amps debuted in 1976. Since then they worked with musicians to build products to the highest industry standards. The Mini-Brute series was still the most popular to the company and have produced many different versions of the amp.

Baby-Brute
courtesy S.P. Fjestad

Baby-Brute
courtesy S.P. Fjestad

ELECTRIC AMPLIFIERS

MEGA-BRUTE – 100W, 1-8 in. speaker, solid-state chassis, two channels, Sonic Circuit, reverb, top control panel, single input, nine knobs, effects loop, headphone jack, external speaker jack, black covering, black steel grille, 22 lbs., current mfg.

courtesy Dave Rogers/Dave's Guitar Shop

courtesy Dave Rogers/Dave's Guitar Shop

MSR $995	$995	$500 - 600	$300 - 350	

The Mega-Brute is also available in bass configuration (MSR $950).

* *Mega Brain/Mini Brain* – similar to the Mega Brute, except in head-unit configuration, 8 lbs., current mfg.

MSR $995	$995	$500 - 600	$300 - 350	

MIGHTY-BRUTE – 100W, 2-4 in. speakers, solid-state chassis, two channels, Sonic Circuit, reverb, top control panel, single input, headphone jack, external speaker jack, black covering, black steel grille, 12 in. wide, 8 in. tall, 8.5 in. deep, 12 lbs., new 2010.

MSR $795	$795	$425 - 500	$250 - 300	

MINI-BRUTE II – 110W, 1-12 in. speaker, solid-state chassis, two channels, reverb, top control panel, effects loop, headphone jack, external speaker jack, black covering, black steel grille, 30 lbs., current mfg.

MSR $1,045	$1,045	$550 - 650	$300 - 375	

MSR/NOTES	100%	EXCELLENT	AVERAGE	LAST MSR

MINI-BRUTE III – wattage unknown, 1-15 in. speaker, solid-state chassis, single channel, top silver control panel, two inputs, three knobs (v, b, t), black covering, black steel grille, mfg. 1990s.

	N/A	$425 - 500	$250 - 300	

MINI-BRUTE IV – 110W, 1-15 in. speaker, solid-state chassis, two channels, reverb, top control panel, effects loop, headphone jack, external speaker jack, black covering, black steel grille, 36 lbs., current mfg.

MSR $1,050	$1,050	$550 - 650	$300 - 375	

MINI-BRUTE V – 140W, 1-12 in. or 1-15 in. speaker and horn, solid-state chassis, two channels, reverb, top control panel, four inputs, effects loop, headphone jack, external speaker jack, black covering, black steel grille, 36 lbs., current mfg.

MSR $1,150	$1,150	$600 - 700	$325 - 400	

MINI +2 – 140W, 1-12 in. speaker, solid-state chassis, two channels, reverb, top control panel, single input, headphone jack, external speaker jack, black covering, black steel grille, new 2010.

MSR $1,175	$1,175	$625 - 750	$350 - 425	

The Mini +2 is also available in bass configuration (MSR $1,125).

SONIC BASS I – 140W, 1-15 in. speaker with horn, solid-state chassis, two channels, Sonic Circuit, top control panel, preamp out, headphone jack, external speaker jack, black covering, black steel grille, 36 lbs., current mfg.

MSR $995	$995	$500 - 600	$300 - 350	

This model replaced the Mini-Brute III.

SONIC BASS II – 140W, 1-15 in. speaker with two horns, solid-state chassis, two independent channels, Sonic Circuit, top control panel, preamp out, headphone jack, external speaker jack, black covering, black steel grille, new 2010.

MSR $1,095	$1,095	$575 - 675	$325 - 400	

TAURUS ELITE – keyboard amplifier, 1-15 in. speaker, solid-state chassis, 3 channels, reverb, chorus, top control panel, 6 inputs, effects loop, preamp out, black covering, black steel grille, wheels, 38 lbs., current mfg.

MSR $1,195	$1,195	$625 - 750	$350 - 425	

TAURUS STEREO BASS – 280W (140W per side stereo), 1-15 in. and 2-8 in. speakers and 2 horns, solid-state chassis, preamp 1 drives the 15 in. and preamp 2 drives the 2-8 in. and 2 horns, two channels, four inputs, effects loop, available in light gray or black carpeting, black steel grille, current mfg.

MSR $1,650	$1,650	$800 - 1,000	$500 - 600	

PORT CITY AMPLIFICATION

Amplifiers and speaker cabinets currently produced in Swannanoa, NC. Previously produced in Rocky Point, NC.

CONTACT INFORMATION
PORT CITY AMPLIFICATION
Swannanoa, NC 28778
Phone No.: 336-577-1810
www.portcityamps.com

Port City Amplification produces a full line of speaker cabinets called the Wave Series, a line of amplifiers, and tube kits. The Wave Series of speaker cabinets are available in 1-12 in., 2-12 in., and 4-12 in. speaker configurations and are unique in design. There is a sound reflector plate inside the cabinet that allows the sound to project not only from the speaker, but from other places inside the cabinet that are otherwise lost. The outside of the cabinets also have a unique design and are available in various colors. Port City also offers a series of amps based on the Blackface Fender Bassman. This amp is available as a head-unit with speaker cabinet or a 2-12 in. speaker combo. For more information, visit Port City Amplification's website or contact them directly.

PREMIER

Amplifiers previously produced in New York City, NY, from the late 1930s-1973/74.

Premier was the brand name of the Louis Sorkin Music Company. They started producing amplifiers in the late 1930s, World War II halted production of any products, and they came with vigor to the 1947 NAMM show. They advertised the new "Premier Multivox Amplifier with Push-Button tuning." These new amplifiers were manufactured by Multivox with the Premier name on them. It's obvious to tell that these two companies as later Multivox models are exact copies, even the model name to Premier's models. Premier focused more on the guitars that they built during their existence.

They made amplifiers with random designs and applications. Such early models were the 76, 88, and the 120, which would become Multivox later. Premier manufactured amplifiers until the late 1960s. Premier officially stopped guitar production in 1973-74. No more amplifiers were made after this time.

ELECTRIC TUBE AMPLIFIERS

Multivox conveniently numbered most of their amplifiers, which makes them easier to identify. Amplifier production began around 1946 (not counting pre-war) and models at this time had lyre grilles. In the early 1960s a dark brown/light brown two-tone covering was introduced (similar to Gibson amps of the same era). In the late 1960s the amps were covered in a dark woodgrain. The 1940 and 1950 model Premiers that are not listed are quite more desirable than the 1960 models.

MSR/NOTES	100%	EXCELLENT	AVERAGE	LAST MSR

PREMIER 50 – ~5-8W, 1-8 in. speaker, guitar combo, three or four tube chassis, top control panel, three inputs, two knobs (v, tone), various coverings and grilles, mfg. circa 1947-1965.

| | N/A | $325 - 400 | $200 - 250 | |

There are at least seven variations of the Premier 50. The first model featured all brown covering, an upside down trapezoid-shaped grille with no logo, a rear-mounted control panel and only one volume knob. In late 1940s or early 1950s, a two-tone brown cabinet with a trapezoid-shaped grille, a "Premier" logo above the grille, and two knobs (v, tone) were introduced. Another variation in the 1950s includes a square cabinet with a lighter two-tone brown covering and larger trapezoid-shaped grille with a white Premier graphic. The late 1950s dawned another version of the 50 with a tall cabinet finished in a dark/light two-tone brown with a small upside down trapezoid-shaped grille with the "Premier" logo under it. By the early 1960s, a new two-tone brown covering was introduced with a slightly larger light trapezoid-shaped grille with the "Premier" logo and two large circle graphics. The sixth variation brought the introduction of a square speaker grille and a new two-tone brown/woodgrain cabinet. The last known version was covered in a woodgrain vinyl and narrow edge front with "Premier" in the upper left corner.

PREMIER 71 – ~20W, 1-12 in. Jensen speaker and two tweeters, eight tube chassis, two channels, tremolo, top control panel, four inputs, six knobs (Ch. 1: v, tone, Ch. 2: v, b, t, trem speed), available in various coverings, mfg. late 1950s-mid-1960s.

| | N/A | $800 - 1,000 | $500 - 600 | |

There are at least three variations of the Premier 71.

PREMIER 75 – 75W, piggy-back unit with speaker cabinet with 1-8 in. and 1-15 in. speakers, two channels, front control panel, four inputs, nine knobs (independent brightness, v, b, t controls, dual controlled tremolo), wood-grain vinyl covering, 28 lbs. (head), 53 lbs. (speaker cabinet), mfg. mid-1960s.

| | N/A | $575 - 700 | $325 - 400 | |

Price includes both the head and speaker cabinet. There were extension speaker cabinets available that can add $150-$200 to the price.

PREMIER 76 – 17W, 1-12 in. Jensen speaker, eight tube chassis, two channels, tremolo, top control panel, four inputs, six knobs (Ch. 1: v, tone, Ch. 2: v, b, t, trem speed), designed in a two-part case that when not in use it would snap together and when in use it would sit apart as two wedges, two-tone woodgrain/tweed covering, music-style grille graphic, mfg. late 1950s-mid-1960s.

| | N/A | $650 - 800 | $425 - 500 | |

PREMIER 88 – 45W, 1-15 in. speaker and two tweeters, ten-tube chassis, two channels, tremolo, top control panel, six inputs, four knobs (v1, v2, s, i), eight push-button tone system with off switch, designed in a two-part case that when not in use it would snap together and when in use it would sit apart as two tall boxes, two-tone woodgrain/tweed covering, fan guard metal grille, mfg. late 1950s-mid-1960s.

| | N/A | $750 - 900 | $500 - 600 | |

PREMIER 110 – 10W, 1-10 in. speaker, five tube chassis, two channels, top control panel, three inputs, three knobs (v1, v2, tone), available in various coverings and grilles, mfg. circa early 1950s-mid-1960s.

courtesy Shaped Music

courtesy Shaped Music

| | N/A | $475 - 550 | $300 - 350 | |

The earliest 110 models have a finished wood cabinet with a bottom-mounted chassis. The most common and possibly the only other variation is known as the "overbite." This model features two-tone woodgrain/tweed with the top part of the amp extending over the speaker creating an overhang. The grille is trapezoid-shaped with a music-style graphic on the front.

PREMIER 120 – ~12-25W, 1-12 in. Jensen speaker, tube chassis, two channels, tremolo, top control panel, four inputs (v1, v2, tone, trem. speed), wood-grain vinyl covering, mfg. late 1950s-mid-1960s.

| | N/A | $500 - 600 | $350 - 425 | |

There are at least five variations of the Premier 120. The first version appears to be the same as the Premier 110 with the overhang above the front grille. By 1960, a new round speaker grille was introduced with a "fan guard" protector over the speaker. Another version features a trapezoid grille with the "Premier" logo with two large circle graphics. In the early to mid-1960s, six knobs were introduced with separate volume and tone controls along with speed and intensity controls for the tremolo. Later variations include a two-tone woodgrain/tweed combo with a trapezoid grille and an all woodgrain model with a large square speaker grille.

MSR/NOTES	100%	EXCELLENT	AVERAGE	LAST MSR

PREMIER TWIN 8 – 8-10W, 2-8 in. speakers, guitar combo, three tube chassis, power: 7591, top control panel, three inputs, three knobs (v, tone, trem. speed), two-tone wood-grain vinyl/tweed (earlier models) or wood-grain (later models) covering, mfg. late 1950s-mid-1960s.

courtesy Shaped Music

courtesy Shaped Music

	N/A	$650 - 800	$425 - 500	

There are two main variations of this amp. The first has a two-tone brown cabinet with an odd-shaped grille that looks like a widow's peak and the "Premier" logo in the center of the top peak. The second version features two-tone woodgrain/tweed with a square grille.

PREMIER TWIN 12-R – 22W, 2-12 in. Jensen speakers, seven tube chassis, two channels, reverb, top control panel, four inputs, six knobs, wood-grain vinyl covering, mfg. 1960s.

	N/A	$700 - 850	$475 - 550	

There are two main variations of this amp. The first has a two-tone brown cabinet with an odd-shaped grille that looks like a widow's peak and the "Premier" logo in the center of the top peak. The second version features two-tone woodgrain/tweed with a square grille.

PREMIER COMBO TWIN 12 – 100W, 2-12 in. speakers, two channels, tremolo, top control panel, six controls, wood-grain vinyl covering, mfg. 1960s.

	N/A	$625 - 750	$425 - 500	

PREMIER 100R-C – 25W, 1-12 in. Jensen speaker, two channels, reverb, tremolo, top control panel, three inputs, volume, tone, reverb, and tremolo controls, wood-grain vinyl covering, 37 lbs., mfg. 1960s.

	N/A	$550 - 650	$325 - 400	

PREMIER G2R – 10W, 1-12 in. speaker, two channels, tremolo, reverb, top control panel, four inputs, volume, tone, and tremolo controls, wood-grain vinyl covering, 23 lbs., mfg. 1960s.

	N/A	$300 - 350	$175 - 225	

B-160 – 25W Bass amp, 1-12 in. Jensen speaker, top control panel, two inputs, three knobs (v, b, t), wood-grain vinyl covering, 28 lbs., mfg. 1960s.

	N/A	$425 - 500	$250 - 300	

B-220 – 35W Bass amp, 1-15 in. Jensen speaker, 2 X 7591 power tubes, top control panel, two inputs, three knobs (v, b, t), wood-grain vinyl covering, 36 lbs., mfg. 1960s.

	N/A	$475 - 550	$275 - 325	

PRIME

Amplifiers previously produced in Korea and China between the early 1990s and the mid-2000s.

Prime amplifiers was a trademark of guitar amplifiers originally imported and distributed by Music Industries in Floral Park, NY. Prime amps are primarily budget/entry-level models that are available in acoustic, electric, and bass configurations. Jay Turser eventually overtook the Prime brand, and Jay Turser is currently controlled by U.S. Music Corp.

ELECTRIC GUITAR AMPLIFIERS

Prime also makes keyboard and professional audio amplifiers.

CA-30RC – 30W, acoustic amplifier, 1-8 in. speaker, 2-3 in. tweeters, solid state chassis acoustic combo, reverb, chorus, single channel, front black control panel, single input, eight black and yellow knobs, mic input, oak cabinet, black grille, disc.

$150	$80 - 110	$40 - 60		$220

The CAT-30 is similar to the CA-30RC, except has a tweed covering and retailed for $200.

CA-60RC – 60W, acoustic amplifier, 2-6.5 in. speakers, 2-3 in. tweeters, solid state chassis acoustic combo, reverb, chorus, single channel, front black control panel, single input, eight black and yellow knobs, five-band equalizer, mic input, oak cabinet, black grille, disc.

$285	$200 - 250	$150 - 175		$400

MSR/NOTES	100%	EXCELLENT	AVERAGE	LAST MSR

CB-50 – 50W, bass amplifier, 1-6 in. speaker, solid-state chassis, single channel, front control panel, four-band EQ, black covering, black grille, disc.

	$210	$120 - 150	$60 - 80	$300

CG-25RC – 25W, 1-8 in. speaker guitar combo, solid-state chassis, single channel, reverb, chorus, front silver control panel, two inputs, nine black knobs, three band equalizer, separate mic volume, black covering, black grille, disc.

	$150	$80 - 105	$40 - 60	$210

CG-40RC – 40W, 1-12" speaker guitar combo, solid-state chassis, single channel, reverb, chorus, front silver control panel, two inputs, nine black knobs, three band equalizer, separate mic volume, black covering, black grille, disc.

	$210	$120 - 150	$70 - 90	$300

PGA-10 – 10W, practice amplifier, 1-6.5 in. speaker, solid-state chassis, single channel, front black control panel, single input, five knobs (g, MV, t, m, b), headphone jack, black covering, black grille, disc.

	$65	$35 - 45	$15 - 25	$90

PBA-20 – 20W, bass practice amplifier, 1-8 in. speaker, solid-state chassis, single channel, front control panel, four-band EQ, black covering, black grille, disc.

	$95	$50 - 65	$30 - 40	$130

PRITCHARD AMPS

Amplifiers currently produced in Berkely Springs, WV since 2004.

Pritchard Amps has a histroy tracing back to Paul Reed Smith when PRS produced amplifiers for a short while in the late 1980s and early 1990s. Pritchard was involved in this and after the PRS amps were discontinued he was convinced that he could create that great tube sound with solid-state components (a feat every amp manufacturer has tried at some point). Deja Vu Audio was born and they started developing this idea. Later on the company changed the name to Pritchard to what it is today.

CONTACT INFORMATION
PRITCHARD AMPS
340 Pritchard Lane
Berkeley Springs, WV 25411
Phone No.: 304-258-9113
Phone No.: 877-762-6665
Fax No.: 304-258-4673
www.pritchardamps.com
eric@pritchardamps.com

Pritchard Amps is not like any other amplifier company. Pritchard is based on years and years of research about the problem and answer of the philosophical dichotomy between engineers and musicians. Pritchard's patented XGPA technology is lyrical, warm, fat, full-bodied, resilient, responsive, and quite alive. Their products are also unique because they singularly combine versatility with great tone and keep that great tone at low levels. They have a big sound and get it from a small, light package. Pritchard has more patents, which is a measure of uniqueness, in this niche than anyone in the world. For more information refer to their website or contact them directly.

ELECTRIC AMPLIFIERS

All Pritchard amplifiers are available in the same speaker cabinets. This means that every speaker cabinet can be used with every amp. The **Dagger Series** comes in three different versions. The Black Dagger, the Blood Dagger, and the Jade Dagger are all priced the same and the difference between the three has mainly to do with the voicing options. The Dagger series is priced like this: 1-12 TB $2,000, 1-12 CB $2,100, 1-12/2-5 $2,225, 1-15 TB $2,100, 2-8/1-5 TB $2,150, 4-10 TB $2,400, 4-12 TB $2,550, and the head-unit is $1,775. The **Sword of Satori** series has two channels and is priced like this: 1-12 TB $2,225, 1-12 CB $2,325, 1-12/2-5 $2,425, 1-15 TB $2,325, 2-8/1-5 TB $2,350, 4-10 TB $2,625, 4-12 TB $2,750, and the head-unit is $2,000. The **Sultry Margaux** series has two mixing channels and is priced like this: 1-12 TB $2,225, 1-12 CB $2,325, 1-12/2-5 $2,425, 1-15 TB $2,325, 2-8/1-5 TB $2,350, 4-10 TB $2,625, 4-12 TB $2,750, and the head-unit is $2,000. The **Gold Estoc** series is the top of the line and has two channels and is priced like this: 1-12 TB $2,350, 1-12 CB $2,475, 1-12/2-5 $2,575, 1-15 TB $2,475, 2-8/1-5 TB $2,500, 4-10 TB $2,750, 4-12 TB $2,900, and the head-unit is $2,150.

Extension cabinets are available with a 1-12 in. speaker for $525 and 1-15 in. speaker for $850.

Sword of Satori 1-12/2-5 TB
courtesy Pritchard Amps

Sword of Satori 1-12
courtesy Pritchard Amps

Sword of Satori 4-10
courtesy Pritchard Amps

Q SECTION
QSC AUDIO PRODUCTS

Amplifiers and other products currently produced in Costa Mesa, CA since 1968.

QSC was developed in 1968 from two people running into each other and becoming friends. Barry Andrews broke down on his motorcycle in California and while waiting for it to get fixed, he struck up a conversation with Pat Quilter working in a garage. Barry was a cabinet maker while Pat was designing and building amplifiers. Shortly thereafter Pat needed help with his business and he called Barry. This was the roots for the small company that was named Quilter's Sound Company. Later it would be renamed QSC Audio Products, Inc.

The early years of QSC were that of a small company building guitar amplifiers and other items of the same caliber. In the late 1970s, they took a look at the market and decided to focus on building power amplifiers. This is when the business really took off. In 1978, Pat developed the AC Coupled Amplifier Circuit. In 1982, the Series three and Series One models were released. A lot of their units could be used for guitars, but they were starting to branch out to pro audio, such as theaters.

Currently they offer several amplifiers in high wattages, and in several different industries. Visit the QSC website and see what the new 81,000 square foot facility is producing today. For a full company history or more information, visit QSC's website.

CONTACT INFORMATION
QSC AUDIO PRODUCTS
1675 MacArthur Blvd.
Costa Mesa, CA 92626
Phone No.: 714-754-6161
Phone No.: 800-854-4079
Fax No.: 714-754-6173
www.qsc.com
info@qsc.com

AMPLIFIERS

QSC produces amplifiers for a variety of configurations. Although QSC power amps are designed for cinema, installation, and live sound reinforcement, many guitarists and bassists use them because they are lightweight and the have a lot of power for their small size. The PLX, RMX, and MX (disc.) Series are most appropriate for guitar and bass applications. QSC also manufactures the HPR Series that is a range of powered sound reinforcement speakers for entertainers.

QUANTUM

Amplifiers previously built overseas during the 1980s. Distributed by DME of Indianapolis, IN.

Quantum was a brand used on a line of amplifiers during the 1980s that was imported and distributed by DDE. They produced a variety of budget/economy amps with generally low wattages and small speaker configurations. Chorus and reverb effects were options on some models. The most popular appears to be the Terminator models. Used prices on these amplifiers are generally between $50-$100 in excellent condition. Any further information on Quantum amps can be submitted directly to Blue Book Publications.

QUIDLEY GUITAR AMPLIFIERS

Amplifiers previously produced in Wilmington, NC.

Ed Quidley built electric guitar tube amplifiers in his Wilmington, NC shop. For more information, visit his website or contact him directly.

CONTACT INFORMATION
QUIDLEY GUITAR AMPLIFIERS
110 Trail in the Pines
Wilmington, NC 28409
Phone No.: 910-350-0155
www.quidleyamps.com

QUILTER

Amplifiers currently produced in the U.S. since the 2010s. Previously produced between the late 1960s and early 1970s in Costa Mesa, CA. Distributed by the Quilter Sound Company.

Pat Quilter began building amplifiers in 1967 as the Quilter Sound Company (QSC). Along with Barry Andrews and later John Andrews, Quilter produced a line of solid-state amplifiers and speaker cabinets that were similar to the large applications that were popular during this era (i.e. Kustom, Earth Sound Research, EBS, etc.). After building guitar amplifiers proved to be unsuccessful in the 1970s, they began focusing on power amps and speaker cabinets (QSC). In the 2010s, Pat Quilter began building Quilter Sound amps again near the QSC factory.

ELECTRIC *SS* AMPLIFIERS

Quilter produced the **255** and **455** units with the 655 as an option. The 255 featured 75W output and is designed for guitar and bass use. The 455 featured 150W output and is also designed for guitar or bass use. The **655** option added 50% more power to the RMS rating. The **PA 1000** head featured 150W and eight channels for PA use. Speaker cabinets were available in 12 in. and 15 in. configurations with Eminence or Altec speakers.

R SECTION
RAEZER'S EDGE

Speaker cabinets currently built in Pewaukee, WI. Previously produced in Hartland, WI and Swarthmore, PA.

Rich Raezer builds quality speaker cabinets for bass and guitar applications. He started buliding these cabinets, because there were very few small speaker cabinets that would produce big sounds in the industry. Performers were getting sick of carrying around heavy speaker cabinets, and there was a demand for a lightweight design. After a lot of research and development, Rich found the perfect ratio, between the cabinet being small enough without sacrificing the sound. Raezer's Edge has also teamed up with Acoustic Image to provide amplifiers with their cabinets. This new series of cabinets features a spot that can hold the Acoustic Image Clarus amp. Most cabinets are covered in black with a brown strip at the bottom that has two sound port holes. Prices on cabinets start around $625. For more information visit Raezer's Edge's website or contact them directly.

CONTACT INFORMATION
RAEZER'S EDGE
W290 N3808 Fox Field Ct.
Pewaukee, WI 53072
Phone No.: 262-563-3343
www.raezers-edge.com
sales@raezers-edge.com

RANDALL

Amplifiers currently produced in the U.S. and overseas since the late 1960s. Previously produced in California and other locations. Distributed by U.S. Music Corp. in Buffalo Grove, IL.

Don Randall worked with Leo Fender in the 1940s when Fender was a new company. Don was responsible for designing many amps for Fender. Eventually, Don broke away and started his own company. He wanted to design and experiment with some more radical designs that Fender never allowed. Don started Randall amplifiers in the late 1960s. Since then they have produced a full line of guitar amps, bass amps, speaker cabinets, and other accessories. Randall uses a lot of hybrid chassis with tube and solid-state components. They also have produced the very successful MTS module system where programmed modules are interchangeable. Doug Reynolds is the current director of Randall, and they are distributed by U.S. Music Corp, which also represents Washburn, Parker, and Eden. For more information, visit Randall's website or contact them directly.

CONTACT INFORMATION
RANDALL
A division of U.S. Music Corp.
1000 Corporate Grove Drive
Buffalo Grove, IL 60089
Phone No.: 847-949-0444
Phone No.: 800-877-6863
Fax No.: 847-949-8444
www.randallamplifiers.com
guitar.support@usmusiccorp.com

ELECTRIC TUBE AMPLIFIERS

Randall has been producing amplifiers since the 1970s. They have produced several models over the years, but there is very little information about them. Look for more models in further editions of the *Blue Book of Guitar Amplifiers*.

RG50TC (First Version) courtesy Randall

RG50TC (Second Version) courtesy Randall

RH50T Head courtesy Randall

EOD88 Element of Doom Head courtesy Randall

RT30 – 35W, 2-12 in. speakers Celestion Vintage 30, Class A tube chassis, power: 4 X EL84, two channels, front black control panel, 10 white chicken head knobs (Ch. 1: v, b, m, t, Ch. 2: g, MV, b, m, t, p), black covering, black cloth grille, mfg. mid-1990s.

N/A	$300 - 400	$150 - 225	

RG50TC – 50W, 1-12 in. Celestion Seventy 80 speaker combo, tube chassis, preamp: 4 X 12AX7, power: 2 X EL34, two channels, front silver control panel, two inputs, 12 knobs (Ch. 1: g1, g2, b, m, t, level, Ch. 2: level, b, m, t, All: r, MV), effects loop, line out, footswitch, black covering, black grille, mfg. 2005-09.

$630	$375 - 450	$200 - 250	$900

* RH50T Head – similar to the RG50TC, except in head-unit configuration, mfg. summer 2005-09.

$580	$325 - 400	$175 - 225	$800

RGT-100(ES) HEAD – 100W, head-unit only, all-tube chassis, preamp: 4 X 12AX7, 12AT7, power: 4 X 6L6, reverb, two channels, front control panel, two inputs, nine knobs, black covering, black grille, mfg. late 1980s-early 1990s.

N/A	$200 - 275	$100 - 150	

* RGT-100HT Head – similar to the RG-100 Head, except in rack-mount configuration, blue control panel, mfg. 1980s-early 1990s.

N/A	$175 - 200	$75 - 125	

MSR/NOTES	100%	EXCELLENT	AVERAGE	LAST MSR

* **RGT-100 112 Combo** – similar to the RGT-100 Head, except in combo configuration with 1-12 in. Celestion speaker, mfg. 1980s-early 1990s.

	N/A	$225 - 300	$125 - 175	

EOD88 ELEMENT OF DOOM HEAD – 88W, head-unit only, all-tube chassis, preamp: 12AX7 tubes, power: KT88 tubes, three gain modes, front black control panel, single input, eight knobs (fuzz, g, b, m, t, depth, presence, MV), standby switch, power switch, effect loop, external speaker out, top handle, limited edition red covering, 34.6 lbs., mfg. 2015-present.

MSR $1,500	$1,000	$650 - 750	$325 - 400	

ELECTRIC AMPLIFIERS: MTS SERIES

The MTS series is Randall's way of modeling an amp. Instead of having all the different amp types in a digital computer inside the amplifier, Randall has introduced modules that plug into the amp chassis. Each chassis has 2 X 12AX7 preamp tubes along with 5 controls (g, b, m, t, MV). This way each "modeled" sound has its own chassis and the settings will never change like you do on a normal modeling amp. Each module can be quickly removed by two screws and pulled out through the front of the amp. The module acts as the control panel for the amplifier.

All amplifiers are listed and sold without any modules included. Each standard module retails for $250. The different types are as following: Tweed, Blackface, DLX, SL+, Plexi, JTM, Recto (disc. 2006), Ultra, Modern (disc. 2005), Clean, Brown, Top Boost, XTC, Ultra Lead (2006-present), Ultra XL (2006-present), and Treadplate (2006-present). In summer 2005, signature modules were introduced. The George Lynch Signature series includes the Super V, Brahma, Mr. Scary, and the Grail. The Dan Donegan (Disturbed) Signature series includes the 1086. The Kirk Hammett (Metallica) Signature Series was introduced in 2008 and includes the KH1, KH2, and KH3 (the RM100KH come pre-loaded with all three modules). Each signature module retails for $300.

RM4 Preamp
courtesy Randall

RM20B Combo
courtesy Randall

RM50(B) Combo
courtesy Randall

RM4 PREAMP – preamp only, two-space rack-mount head, four modules, tube chassis, preamp: 3 X 12AX7, four independent channels, front black control panel, two knobs (effects, MV), effects loop, four-button MIDI footswitch, black casing, disc..

	$630	$325 - 400	$175 - 225	$750

RM20HB HEAD – 18W, head-unit, guitar configuration, tube chassis, power: 2 X EL84, single channel, one module spot, front control panel, single input, nine knobs (boost g, boost level, p, density, five module knobs), effects loop, footswitch, available in black covering with a black grille, Palomino (brown covering with a brown grille, RM20HP/RM20HCRP, available 2007-2011), or black covering with a Palomino grille (RM20HBP, 2008-2011), mfg. 2006-2011.

	$700	$375 - 450	$225 - 275	$800

• **Add $175 - 200 for each module; price listed does not include modules.**

RM20B COMBO – 18W, 1-12 in. Celestion Greenback speaker, guitar combo, tube chassis, power: 2 X EL84, single channel, one module spot, front control panel, single input, nine knobs (boost g, boost level, p, density, five module knobs), effects loop, footswitch, available in black covering with a black grille, Palomino (brown covering with a brown grille, RM20P/RM20CRP, 2007-2011), or black covering with a Palomino grille (RM20BP, 2008-2011), mtg. 2005-2011.

	$770	$425 - 500	$250 - 300	$900

• **Add $175 - 200 for each module; price listed does not include modules.**

RM50HB HEAD – 50W, head-unit only, 2 module hybrid chassis, power tubes: 2 X 6L6, reverb, front black control panel, 14 knobs (MV, effects, density, presence, 10 module knobs), effects loop, footswitch, available in black covering with a black (RM50HB) or silver (RM50HS) grille, Palomino (brown covering with a brown grille, RM50HP/RM50HCRP, 2007-2011), or black covering with a Palomino grille (RM50HBP, 2008-2011), mfg. 2004-2011.

	$1,030	$550 - 650	$325 - 400	$1,200

• **Add $175 - 200 for each module; price listed does not include modules.**

This model is also availble with pre-loaded modules.

MSR/NOTES	100%	EXCELLENT	AVERAGE	LAST MSR

RM50(B) COMBO – 50W, 1-12 in. Celestion G12T-75 speaker, two module hybrid chassis, power tubes: 2 X 6L6, reverb, front black control panel, 14 knobs (MV, effects, density, presence, 10 module knobs), effects loop, footswitch, available in black covering with a black (RM50B) or silver (RM50S) grille, Palomino (brown covering with a brown grille, RM50P/RM50CRP, 2007-2011), or black covering with a Palomino grille (RM50BP, 2008-2011), 62 lbs., mfg. 2002-2011.

	$1,070	$600 - 700	$375 - 450	$1,250

* Add $175 - 200 for each module; price listed does not include modules.

This model is also availble with pre-loaded modules.

RM80(B) COMBO – 80W, 2-12 in. Celestion G12T-75 speaker, 2 module hybrid chassis, power tubes: 2 X 6550, reverb, front black control panel, 14 knobs (MV, effects, density, presence, 10 module knobs), effects loop, footswitch, black covering, silver or black (RM80B) cloth grille, 73 lbs., mfg. 2003-04.

	N/A	$625 - 750	$400 - 475	$1,200

* Add $175 - 200 for each module; price listed does not include modules.

RM100(B)/RM100S HEAD – 100W, head-unit only, 3 module hybrid chassis, power tubes:4 X EL34 or 4 X 6L6, front black control panel, 19 knobs (MV, effects, density, presence, 15 module knobs), effects loop, footswitch, available in black covering with a black (RM100BR) or silver (RM100S) grille, Palomino (brown covering with a brown grille, RM100P/RM100CRP, 2007-2011), or black covering with a Palomino grille (RM100BP, 2008-2011), cloth grille, mfg. 2003-2011.

	$1,280	$725 - 850	$475 - 550	$1,500

* Add $175 - 200 for each module; price listed does not include modules.

In 2005, the RM100B was changed to the RM100S and MTS models became available pre-loaded with certain modules. There is no discount for a pre-loaded cabinet. This model is also available with a metal grille front (Model RM100M). In 2006, the RM100BR was introduced with black retro cosmetics.

RM100C COMBO – 100W, 2-12 in. Celestion G12T-75 speakers, two module hybrid chassis, power tubes: 4 X EL34, three channels, reverb, front black control panel, 14 knobs (MV, effects, density, presence, 10 module knobs), effects loop, footswitch, available in black covering with a black grille (RM100C), Palomino (brown covering with a brown grille, RM100CP/RM100CCRP, 2007-2011), or black covering with a Palomino grille (RM100CBP, 2008-2011), mfg. 2005-2011.

	$1,530	$850 - 1,000	$550 - 650	$1,800

* Add $175 - 200 for each module; price listed does not include modules.

This model is also availble with pre-loaded modules.

RM100LB LYNCH BOX – 100W, head-unit only, three module hybrid chassis, power tubes: 4 X EL34 front black control panel, 19 knobs (MV, effects, density, presence, 15 module knobs), effects loop, footswitch, available in Dark Forest Alligator vinyl covering with an alligator front and gold Lynch box logo or a black vinyl front with a silver Lynch box logo (2008-09), mfg. 2006-2011.

	$1,360	$750 - 900	$500 - 575	$1,600

* Add $225 - 250 for each George Lynch signature module; price listed does not include modules.

RM100KH KIRK HAMMETT – 100W, head-unit only, three module hybrid chassis, power tubes: 4 X JJ6L6GC, includes three Hammett modules (KH1 Clean, KH2 Rhythm, KH3 Hi-Gain) front black control panel, 19 knobs (MV, effects, density, presence, 15 module knobs), effects loop, footswitch, all solid maple construction with a AAAA flame maple top finished in Trans. Black finish, mfg. 2008-2011.

	$2,050	$1,100 - 1,350	$650 - 800	$2,400

* Add $225 - 250 for each Kirk Hammett signature module; price listed does not include modules.

ELECTRIC AMPLIFIERS: RD/DIAVLO SERIES

RD1C Combo
courtesy Randall

RD1H Head
courtesy Randall

RD5C Combo
courtesy Randall

RD1C COMBO – 1W, 4 ohms, combo amp, 1-8 in. RS8-35-8 speaker, all-tube chassis, preamp: 12AX7, power 12AU7, single channel, top rear control panel, single input, three black knobs (g, v, t), power switch, effect loop, XLR out, speaker out, top handle, black covering, black metal grille, 24.25 lbs., mfg. 2013-present.

MSR $450	$300	$195 - 225	$100 - 120	

MSR/NOTES	100%	EXCELLENT	AVERAGE	LAST MSR

RD20C Combo
courtesy Randall

RD40C Combo
courtesy Randall

RD45H Head
courtesy Randall

RD1H HEAD – 1W, head-unit only, all-tube chassis, preamp: 2 X 12AX7, power: 1 X 12AU7, single channel, front black control panel, single input, three black knobs (g, t, v), power switch, effect loop, XLR out jack, speaker out jack, black covering, top handle, black metal grille, 12.1 lbs., mfg. 2013-present.

| MSR $375 | $250 | $165 - 190 | $80 - 100 | |

RD5C COMBO – 5W, 4 ohms, combo amp, 1-10 in. RS10-30-8 speaker, all-tube chassis, preamp: 12AX7, power 6V6, single channel, top rear control panel, single input, three black knobs (g, v, t), power switch, effect loop, XLR out, speaker out, top handle, black covering, black metal grille, 28.66 lbs., mfg. 2013-present.

| MSR $525 | $300 | $195 - 225 | $100 - 120 | |

RD5H HEAD – 5W, head-unit only, all-tube chassis, preamp: 2 X 12AX7, power: 1 X 6V6, single channel, front black control panel, single input, three black knobs (g, t, v), power switch, effect loop, XLR out jack, speaker out jack, black covering, top handle, black metal grille, 14.33 lbs., mfg. 2013-present.

| MSR $450 | $300 | $195 - 225 | $100 - 120 | |

RD20C COMBO – 20W, 4/8/16 ohms, combo amp, 1-12 in. RD12-50-8 speaker, all-tube chassis, preamp: 12AX7, power: 6V6, dual channel, top black control panel, single input, eight black knobs (OD g, OD v, Clean g, b, m, t, presence, MV), power switch, standby switch, effect loop, XLR out, speaker out, top handle, black covering, black metal grille, mfg. 2015-present.

| MSR $900 | $600 | $400 - 450 | $195 - 240 | |

RD20H HEAD – 20W, head-unit only, all-tube chassis, preamp: 4 X 12AX7, power: 2 X 6L6, dual channels, front black control panel, single input, eight black knobs (clean g, OD g, OD v, b, m, t, presence, MV), standby switch, power switch, effect loop, XLR out jack, speaker out jacks, footswitch included, black covering, top handle, black metal grille, metal corners, 26.46 lbs., mfg. 2013-present.

| MSR $750 | $475 | $300 - 350 | $155 - 190 | |

RD40C COMBO – 40W, 4/8/16 ohms, combo amp, 1-12 in. RD12-50-8 speaker, all-tube chassis, preamp: 12AX7, power: 6V6, dual channel, front black control panel, single input, eight black knobs (OD g, OD v, Clean g, b, m, t, presence, MV), power switch, standby switch, effect loop, XLR out, speaker out, top handle, footswitch included, black covering, black metal grille, 50 lbs., mfg. 2013-present.

| MSR $1,050 | $650 | $425 - 475 | $210 - 260 | |

RD45H HEAD – 45W, head-unit only, all-tube chassis, preamp: 4 X 12AX7, power: 2 X 6L6, two channels, front black control panel, single input, eight black knobs (clean g, OD gaon, OD v, b, m, t, presence, MV), standby switch, power switch, effect loop, XLR out jack, speaker out jacks, footswitch included, black covering, top handle, black metal grille, metal corners, 30.8 lbs., mfg. 2013-present.

| MSR $900 | $600 | $400 - 450 | $195 - 240 | |

RD100H HEAD – 100W, head-unit only, all-tube chassis, preamp: 12AX7 tubes, power: 6L6 tubes, three channels, front black control panel, single input, eleven black knobs, standby switch, power switch, effect loop, XLR out jack, speaker out jacks, footswitch included, black covering, top handle, black metal grille, metal corners, 44.1 lbs., mfg. 2013-present.

| MSR $1,350 | $900 | $575 - 675 | $295 - 350 | |

RD110-D SPEAKER CABINET – 30W, 1-10 in. RS10-30-8 speaker, 8 ohms, straight front, angled baffle, metal corners, black covering, black steel grille, 22 lbs., mfg. 2013-present.

| MSR $225 | $150 | $100 - 115 | $50 - 60 | |

RD112-V30 SPEAKER CABINET – 65W, 1-12 in. Celestion Vintage 30 speaker, 8 ohms, straight front, angled baffle, metal corners, black covering, black steel grille, 39.7 lbs., mfg. 2013-present.

| MSR $450 | $280 | $180 - 210 | $90 - 110 | |

MSR/NOTES	100%	EXCELLENT	AVERAGE	LAST MSR

**RD212 Speaker Cabinet
courtesy Randall**

**RD212-UV Speaker Cabinet
courtesy Randall**

**RD412D Speaker Cabinet
courtesy Randall**

RD212 SPEAKER CABINET – 130W or 160W, 2-12 in. Celestion Vintage 30 or RS12-80-16 speakers, 8 ohms mono, 16 ohms stereo, straight front, angled baffle, metal corners, casters included, black covering, black steel grille, 63.5 lbs., mfg. 2013-present.

MSR $825 $550 $350 - 400 $180 - 220

RD212-UV SPEAKER CABINET – 140W, upright configuration, 2-12 in. Celestion V-type 70watt speakers, 8 ohms mono, slanted front, metal corners, casters included, recessed side handles, black covering, black metal grille, mfg. 2013-present.

MSR $900 $600 $400 - 450 $195 - 240

* *RD212-UV-RED Speaker Cabinet* – 140W, upright configuration, 2-12 in. Celestion V-type 70watt speakers, 8 ohms mono, slanted front, metal corners, casters included, recessed side handles, red covering, black metal grille, designed to pair with the EOD88 head unit, mfg. 2015-present.

MSR $900 $600 $400 - 450 $195 - 240

RD212-V30 SPEAKER CABINET – 120W, 2-12 in. Celestion V30 speakers, 8 or 16 ohms, straight front, metal corners, casters included, recessed side handles, black covering, black metal grille, 63.5 lbs., mfg. 2013-present.

MSR $825 $500 $325 - 375 $160 - 200

RD412A SPEAKER CABINET – 260W or 320W, 4-12 in. Celestion Vintage 30 or RS12-80-16 speakers, 8 ohms mono, 16 ohms stereo, angled front, metal corners, casters included, black covering, black steel grille, 94.8 lbs., mfg. 2013-present.

MSR $900 $600 $400 - 450 $195 - 240

RD412D SPEAKER CABINET – 260W or 320W, 4-12 in. Celestion Vintage 30 or RS12-80-16 speakers, 8 ohms mono, 16 ohms stereo, straight front, angled baffle, metal corners, casters included, black covering, black steel grille, 94.8 lbs., mfg. 2013-present.

MSR $900 $600 $400 - 450 $195 - 240

RD412-V SPEAKER CABINET – 280W, 4-12 in. Celestion V-Type 70watt speakers, 16 ohms mono, straight front, angled baffle, metal corners, casters included, black covering, black steel grille, 94.8 lbs., mfg. 2013-present.

MSR $1,200 $800 $525 - 600 $260 - 325

* *RD412-V-RED Speaker Cabinet* – 280W, 4-12 in. Celestion V-Type 70watt speakers, 16 ohms mono, straight front, angled baffle, metal corners, casters included, red covering covering, black steel grille, designed to be paired with the EOD88 head unit, mfg. 2015-present.

MSR $1,200 $800 $525 - 600 $260 - 325

RD412-V30 SPEAKER CABINET – 240W, 4-12 in. Celestion V30 speakers, 8 or 16 ohms, straight front, angled baffle, metal corners, casters included, black covering, black steel grille, 94.8 lbs., mfg. 2013-present.

MSR $1,275 $850 $550 - 625 $275 - 350

ELECTRIC AMPLIFIERS: RG/RH/G2/G3 SERIES

In 2006, a new Valve-Dynamic power circuit with a 12AT7 tube-driven MOSFET circuit was introduced on all models, and they all received the new G3 model designation. In 2008, the preamp circuit was completely redesigned utilizing the tone circuits of the Randall T2 and V2 amps, the Overdrive controls were slightly changed (level, r, t, sweep, m, b, G2, G1), and they all received the new G3 Plus designation.

The RG series was discontinued in 2009 and reintroduced in 2013.

RG8 SPEAKER CABINET (MINI-CAB) – 35W, 1-8 in. RS8-35-8 speaker, 8 ohms mono, straight front, black covering, black steel grille, steel corners, metal logo, 14.3 lbs., mfg. 2013-present.

MSR $105 $70 $45 - 55 $25 - 30

MSR/NOTES	100%	EXCELLENT	AVERAGE	LAST MSR

RG8 Speaker Cabinet (Mine-Cab)
courtesy Randall

RG30 Combo
courtesy John Beeson/The Music Shoppe

RG80 Combo
courtesy Randall

RG30 COMBO – 30W, 1-10 or 1-12 in. speaker, solid-state chassis, reverb, single channel, front black control panel, two inputs, five black knobs (v, r, t, b, MV), black covering, black cloth grille with orange stripe under control panel, mfg. late 1980s-early 1990s.

	N/A	$150 - 225	$75 - 125	

RG75 COMBO – 75W, 1-12 in. Custom 80W Celestion speaker, solid-state chassis, two channels, reverb, front black control panel, single input, 13 black knobs, line out, headphone jack, two-button footswitch, black covering, black grille, disc. 2003.

	N/A	$250 - 300	$175 - 205	$450

RG75G2/G3/G3 PLUS COMBO – 75W, 1-12 in. Celestion Seventy 80 speaker, solid-state chassis, two channels, three modes, contour, reverb, front black control panel, single input, 14 black knobs, line out, headphone jack, four-button footswitch, black covering, black grille, 51 lbs., mfg. 2004-09.

$350	$250 - 300	$135 - 175	$730

In 2006, this model was upgraded to the G3 with a new Valve-Dynamic power circuit with a 12AT7 tube-driven MOSFET circuit. In 2008, this model was upgraded to the G3 Plus with a new preamp circuit and revised control panel.

* RG75DG2/G3/G3 Plus Combo – similar to the RG75G2, except has 16 digital effects, 15 black knobs, and a slightly revised control panel, 54 lbs., mfg. 2004-09.

$375	$275 - 325	$150 - 200	$750

In 2006, this model was upgraded to the G3 with a new Valve-Dynamic power circuit with a 12AT7 tube-driven MOSFET circuit. In 2008, this model was upgraded to the G3 Plus with a new preamp circuit and revised control panel.

RG80 COMBO – 80W, 1-12 in. RS12-80-8 speaker, solid-state chassis, two channels, reverb, front black control panel, single input, nine black knobs, line out, headphone jack, effects loop, two-button footswitch, top handle, black covering, black metal grille, 40.1 lbs., mfg. 2013-present.

MSR $406	$250	$165 - 190	$80 - 100	

RG100SC COMBO – 100W, 2-12 in. Custom 80W Celestion speakers, solid-state chassis, two channels, stereo chorus, reverb, front black control panel, single input, 15 black knobs, line out, headphone jack, two-button footswitch, black covering, black grille, disc. 2003.

	N/A	$300 - 350	$175 - 225	$580

RG100SCG2/G3/G3 PLUS COMBO – 75W, 1-12 in. Celestion Seventy 80 speaker, solid-state chassis, two channels, three modes, contour, reverb, front black control panel, single input, 14 black knobs, line out, headphone jack, four-button footswitch, black covering, black grille, 51 lbs., mfg. 2004-09.

$400	$325 - 375	$200 - 250	$930

In 2006, this model was upgraded to the G3 with a new Valve-Dynamic power circuit with a 12AT7 tube-driven MOSFET circuit. In 2008, this model was upgraded to the G3 Plus with a new preamp circuit and revised control panel.

RG200G3/G3 PLUS COMBO – 200W, 2-12 in. Celestion G12T-100 speakers, hybrid chassis with Valve Dynamic power and a 12AT7 tube-driven power circuit, two channels, three modes, reverb, front black control panel, single input, 14 black knobs (Clean Ch.: b, m, t, r, level, OD Ch.: level, r, contour, b, m, t, g2, g1, MV), effects loop with level, line out, four-button footswitch, black covering, black grille, mfg. 2006-09.

$550	$375 - 450	$225 - 275	$1,050

In 2008, this model was upgraded to the G3 Plus with a new preamp circuit and revised control panel.

* RG200DG3/DG3 Plus Combo – similar to the RG200G3 Combo, except has digital effects, and effects knobs instead of reverb and an additional effects select knob for a total of 15 knobs, mfg. 2006-09.

$575	$400 - 475	$250 - 300	$1,100

In 2008, this model was upgraded to the G3 Plus with a new preamp circuit and revised control panel.

| MSR/NOTES | 100% | EXCELLENT | AVERAGE | LAST MSR |

RG212 Speaker Cabinet
courtesy Randall

RG1003H Head
courtesy Randall

RG1503-212 Combo
courtesy Randall

RG212 SPEAKER CABINET – 100W, 2-12 in. RS12-50-16 speakers, 8 ohms mono, straight front, black covering, black steel grille, steel corners, metal logo, casters included, 51.8 lbs., mfg. 2013-present.

| MSR $420 | $280 | $180 - 210 | $90 - 110 | |

RG230SC COMBO – 40W (2 X 20W stereo), 2-10 in. Randall Jaguar speakers, solid-state chassis, two channels, chorus, reverb, front black control panel, single input, eleven black knobs, line out, headphone jack, black covering, black grille, disc. 2003.

| | N/A | $175 - 225 | $110 - 140 | $380 |

RG412 SPEAKER CABINET – 200W, 4-12 in. RS12-50-8 speakers, 8 ohms mono, straight front, black covering, black steel grille, steel corners, metal logo, casters included, 81.57 lbs., mfg. 2013-present.

| MSR $569 | $350 | $230 - 265 | $115 - 140 | |

RG1003H HEAD – 100W, head-unit only, solid-state chassis, three channels, spring reverb, front black control panel, single input, twelve black knobs, headphone jack, auxillary input, speaker outputs, effects loop, XLR line out, footswitch included, black covering, 32 lbs., mfg. 2013-present.

| MSR $450 | $300 | $195 - 225 | $100 - 120 | |

RG1503H HEAD – 150W, head-unit only, solid-state chassis, three channels, spring reverb, front black control panel, single input, twelve black knobs, headphone jack, auxillary input, speaker outputs, effects loop, XLR line out, footswitch included, black covering, 33 lbs., mfg. 2013-present.

| MSR $600 | $400 | $260 - 300 | $130 - 160 | |

RG1503-212 COMBO – 150W, 2-12 in. RS12-80-8 speakers, solid-state chassis, three channels, front black control panel, single input, 14 black knobs (Gain, Volume for each channel, b, m, t, presence, reverb, MV), power switch, effects loop, line out, speaker out, four-button footswitch, top handle, caster included, black covering, black metal grille, 72.75 lbs., mfg. 2013-present.

| MSR $812 | $500 | $325 - 375 | $165 - 200 | |

RG3003H HEAD – 300W, head-unit only, solid-state chassis, three channels, front black control panel, single input, twelve black knobs, headphone jack, auxillary input, speaker outputs, effects loop, XLR line out, footswitch included, black covering, 34.2 lbs., mfg. 2013-present.

| MSR $750 | $500 | $325 - 375 | $165 - 200 | |

RH100 HEAD – 100W, head-unit only, solid-state chassis, two channels, reverb, front black control panel, single input, 13 black knobs, headphone jack, two-button footswitch, black covering, black grille, 45 lbs., disc. 2003.

| | N/A | $250 - 300 | $135 - 175 | $450 |

RH100G2 HEAD – 100W, head-unit only, solid-state chassis, two channels, three modes, reverb, front black control panel, single input, 14 black knobs, headphone jack, four-button footswitch, black covering, black metal grille, 31 lbs., mfg. 2004-05.

| | N/A | $225 - 275 | $120 - 150 | $530 |

RH150G3/G3 PLUS HEAD – 150W, head-unit, guitar configuration, hybrid chassis with Valve-Dynamic power and a 12AT7 tube-driven power circuit, two channels, three modes, reverb, front black control panel, single input, 14 black knobs (Clean Ch.: b, m, t, r, level, OD Ch.: level, r, contour, b, m, t, g2, g1, MV), effects loop with level, line out, four-button footswitch, black covering, black metal grille, mfg. 2006-09.

| | $450 | $275 - 325 | $150 - 200 | $750 |

In 2008, this model was upgraded to the G3 Plus with a new preamp circuit and revised control panel.

* **RH150DG3/G3 Plus Head** – similar to the RG150G3 Head, except has digital effects, and effects knobs instead of reverb and an additional effects select knob for a total of 15 knobs, mfg. 2007-09.

| | $500 | $300 - 350 | $175 - 225 | $830 |

In 2008, this model was upgraded to the G3 Plus with a new preamp circuit and revised control panel.

MSR/NOTES	100%	EXCELLENT	AVERAGE	LAST MSR

RH150G3 Head
courtesy Randall

RH200SC Head
courtesy Randall

RH300G3 Head
courtesy Randall

RH200SC HEAD – 200W, head-unit only, solid-state chassis, two channels, reverb, front silver control panel, single input, 13 black knobs, headphone jack, two-button footswitch, black covering, black grille, 44 lbs., mfg. 2003 only.

	N/A	$275 - 325	$200 - 250	$600

RH200SCG2 HEAD – 200W, head-unit only, solid-state chassis, two channels, three modes, reverb, contour, front black control panel, single input, 16 black knobs, voicing switch, five-button footswitch, black covering, black grille, 35 lbs., mfg. 2004-05.

	N/A	$300 - 350	$175 - 225	$650

RH300G3/G3 PLUS HEAD – 300W, head-unit, guitar configuration, hybrid chassis with Valve-Dynamic power and a 12AT7 tube-driven power circuit, two channels, three modes, reverb, front black control panel, single input, 14 black knobs (Clean Ch.: b, m, t, r, level, OD Ch.: level, r, contour, b, m, t, g2, g1, MV), effects loop with level, line out, four-button footswitch, black covering, black metal grille, mfg. 2006-09.

$600	$350 - 425	$200 - 250	$930

ELECTRIC AMPLIFIERS: SIGNATURE SERIES

The Colossus Series was designed with Paul Stanley of Kiss. The Warhead Series was designed with Dimebag Darrell of Pantera and was his signature series.

George Lynch LB-15 Combo
courtesy Randall

KH15 Kirk Hammett
courtesy Randall

KH75 Kirk Hammett
courtesy Randall

COLOSSUS HEAD – 300W, head-unit only, solid-state chassis, two channels, front black control panel, single input, eight black and silver knobs (v, b, m, t per channel), effects loop, footswitch, black covering with white piping, disc. 2002.

	N/A	$500 - 600	$300 - 375	

GEORGE LYNCH HEADHUNTER LIMITED EDITION HEAD – 50W, head-unit only, all-tube chassis, preamp: Tung Sol 12AX7 tubes, power: Electro Harmonix 6CA7 tubes, single channels, front black control panel, single input, six aluminum knobs (g, b, m, t, presence, wattage), standby switch, power switch, rear panel: line out with level control, five speaker out jacks, MOR boost pedal included, top handle, faux snake skin covering, metal corners, limited to 45 hand signed/numbered units, mfg. 2015-present.

MSR $5,000	$2,500	$1,625 - 1,875	$825 - 1,000	

GEORGE LYNCH LB-15 COMBO – 15W, 8 ohms, combo amp, SP8 speaker, solid state chassis, dual channels, front silver control panel, single input, seven black knobs (clean level, OD gain, OD level, b, m, t, MV), headphone jack, power switch, CD/tape input, black covering, metal corners, top handle, gray/black mesh grille, 14.3 lbs., mfg. 2015-present.

MSR $195	$120	$80 - 90	$40 - 50	

KH15 KIRK HAMMETT – 15W, 1-6.5 in. Randall Jaguar speaker combo, solid-state chassis, two channels, front black control panel, single input, seven black knobs (Clean v, OD g, OD v, b, m, t, MV), headphone jack, tape/CD input, black leatherette covering, black cloth grille with large Kirk Hammett signature emblem in lower right corner, mfg. 2008-present.

MSR $178	$100	$65 - 75	$35 - 40	

KH75 KIRK HAMMETT – 75W, 1-12 in. Celestion Seventy 80 speaker, combo amp, solid-state chassis, two channels, front black control panel, single input, thirteen black knobs (Overdrive: gain 1, gain 2, b, m, contour, t, v, Lead: b, m, t, v, Master: v, reverb), headphone jack, power switch, gain switch, channel switch, ground lift, two external speaker jacks, spring reverb, footswitch, effects loop, CD input, black leatherette covering, black cloth grille with large Kirk Hammett signature emblem in lower left corner, 55 lbs., mfg. 2009-present.

MSR $712	$450	$295 - 325	$145 - 180	

MSR/NOTES	100%	EXCELLENT	AVERAGE	LAST MSR

**KH103 Kirk Hammett Head
courtesy Randall**

**KH412-V30 Kirk Hammett Speaker
Cabinet courtesy Randall**

**Nuno Bettencourt NB 412 Speaker
Cabinet courtesy Randall**

KH103 KIRK HAMMETT HEAD – 120W, head-unit only, all-tube chassis, preamp: 9 X 12AX7, power: 4 X 6L6, three channels, front black control panel, single input, twenty-three knobs (MV1, MV 2, each channel: g, v, b, m, t, depth, presence), seven MIDI functions per channel, standby switch, power switch, rear panel: midi in jack, midi thru jack, two effect loops, output jack with volume control, five external speaker out jacks, RF3 footswitch included, dual side handles, black covering, silver grille, mfg. 2015-present.

MSR $3,500	$2,000	$1,300 - 1,500	$650 - 800	

KH120RHS KIRK HAMMETT HALF-STACK – 120W, head-unit with a 200W 4-12 in. Celestion Rocket speaker cabinet, solid-state chassis, two channels, reverb, front black control panel, single input, 13 black knobs (OD Ch.: G1, G2, b, m, c, t, v, Clean Ch.: b, m, t, v, All: MV, r), headphone jack, Series EFX loop, tape/CD input, footswitch included, black leatherette covering, black grille cloth, speaker cabinet has a large Kirk Hammett signature emblem in the lower right corner, mfg. 2008-present.

MSR $1,300	$850	$500 - 600	$300 - 350	

KH412-V30 KIRK HAMMETT SPEAKER CABINET – 240W, 4-12 in. Celestion V30 speakers, parallel mono inputs 16 ohms, straight front, black covering, black grille, 122 lbs., new 2016.

MSR $1,750	$1,000	$650 - 750	$325 - 400	

NUNO BETTENCOURT NB-15 COMBO – 15W, 8 ohms, combo amp, SP8 speaker, solid state chassis, dual channels, front gold control panel, single input, seven black knobs (clean v, OD drive, OD volume, b, m, t, MV), headphone jack, power switch, CD/tape input, black covering, metal corners, top handle, gold/black mesh grille, 14.3 lbs., mfg. 2010-present.

MSR $178	$120	$80 - 90	$40 - 50	

NUNO BETTENCOURT NB 412 SPEAKER CABINET – 100W, 4-12 in. Celestion Greenback speakers, 8 ohms, straight front, black covering, black/gold mesh grille, 90.4 lbs., mfg. 2009-2015.

	$1,000	$650 - 750	$325 - 400	$1,625

NUNO BETTENCOURT NB KING-100 HEAD – 100W, head-unit only, all-tube chassis, power: 4 X E34L, dual channels, front gold control panel, single input, thirteen knobs (MV, OD: b, m, t, level, drive, solo: level, drive, clean: b, m, t, level, drive), standby switch, power switch, VU meter, rear panel: MIDI in/through, power tube bias section, effect loop, black covering, top handle, black mesh grille, metal corners, 50 lbs., mfg. 2009-2015.

	$1,500	$975 - 1,125	$500 - 600	$3,000

NUNO BETTENCOURT NB KING-112 COMBO – 30W, 8 ohms, combo amp, 1-12 in. Celestion Greenback speaker, all-tube chassis, power: 4 X EL84, three channels, top gold control panel, single input, thirteen black knobs (MV, clean: drive, v, t, m, b, OD: drive, v, t, m, b, solo: drive, v), standby switch, power switch, VU meter, rear panel: footswitch/MIDI in/thru jacks, external speaker out, effects loop, black covering, metal corners, top handles, gold/black mesh grille, 74.3 lbs., mfg. 2009-present.

MSR $2,000	$1,250	$825 - 950	$400 - 500	

OLA ENGLUND SATAN HEAD – 120W, head-unit only, all-tube chassis, preamp: 6 X 12AX7, power: 2 X 6L6, 2 X KT88, two channels, front black control panel, dual inputs, sixteen knobs (depth, presence, MV, channel 1: girth, grind, gain, sweep, v, b, m, t, channel 2: gain, v, b, m, t), standby switch, power switch, kill switch, bright switch, shift switch, rear panel: footswitch jacks, effect loop, XLR output jack, 1/4 in. out jack, five external speaker out jacks, RF2 footswitch included, top handle, black covering, black metal grille, metal corners, mfg. 2014-present.

MSR $2,995	$1,625	$1,050 - 1,225	$525 - 650	

OLA ENGLUND SATAN 412 SPEAKER CABINET – 270W, 4-12 in. X-pattern Celestion V30 speakers, 4/16 ohms mono, 8 ohms stereo, straight front, black covering, black grille, 63.5 lbs., mfg. 2015-present.

MSR $1,600	$900	$575 - 675	$295 - 350	

RS215W SPEAKER CABINET – 400W, 2-15 in. Jaguar speakers, 8 Ohm mono impedance, straight front, black covering, stainless steel and metal grille cosmetics, disc. 2004.

	N/A	$300 - 375	$175 - 225	$1,000

MSR/NOTES	100%	EXCELLENT	AVERAGE	LAST MSR

Scott Ian Nullifer EN120 Head
courtesy Randall

Scott Ian Nullifer Speaker Cabinet
courtesy Randall

V2N Michael Amott Ninja
courtesy Randall

RS412W SPEAKER CABINET – 280W, 4-12 in. Celestion V30 speakers, 4 stereo/8 mono, straight front, black covering, stainless steel and metal grille cosmetics, disc. 2004.

	N/A	$325 - 400	$200 - 250	$1,100

SCOTT IAN NULLIFER EN120 HEAD – 120W, head-unit only, all-tube chassis, preamp: 6 X 12AX7, power: 4 X 6L6, two channels, front black control panel, dual input, sixteen knobs (depth, presence, MV, channel 1: lo gain, high gain, gain, boost, v, b, m, t, channel 2: gain, v, b, m, t), standby switch, power switch, effect loop, footswitch included, dual side handles, black covering, metal front/rear grilles, mfg. 2014-present.

MSR $2,700	$1,800	$1,175 - 1,350	$575 - 725	

SCOTT IAN NULLIFER SPEAKER CABINET – 100W, 4-12 in. Celestion Greenback speakers, 8 ohms, straight front, black covering, steel grille with star logo, casters included., mfg. 2014-present.

MSR $1,787	$1,100	$725 - 825	$350 - 450	

V2BC CHRISTIAN OLDE WOLBERS ARCHETYPE – 480W @ 2 ohms (400W @ 4 ohms, 280W @ 8 ohms), head-unit, guitar configuration, hybrid Valve Dynamic chassis, preamp: 3 X 12AX7, power: 12AT7 tube-driven MOSFET, three channels, front black control panel, single input, 16 black knobs (Ch. 1: g, level, Ch. 2: g, l, b, m, t, p, Ch. 3: g, b, m, t, level, All: MV, density, p), six-band graphic EQ, MIDI assignable series of parallel effects loop, slave out with level control, direct out, footswitch, silver leatherette covering, black grille with red accents, mfg. 2006-2010.

	$1,250	$700 - 850	$425 - 500	$1,800

V2N MICHAEL AMOTT NINJA – 480W @ 2 ohms (400W @ 4 ohms, 280W @ 8 ohms), head-unit, guitar configuration, hybrid Valve Dynamic chassis, preamp: 3 X 12AX7, power: 12AT7 tube-driven MOSFET, three channels, front chrome control panel, single input, 16 black knobs (Ch. 1: g, level, Ch. 2: g, l, b, m, t, p, Ch. 3: g, b, m, t, level, All: MV, density, p), six-band graphic EQ, MIDI assignable series of parallel effects loop, slave out with level control, direct out, footswitch, silver leatherette covering, silver grille, mfg. 2008-2010.

	$1,250	$700 - 850	$425 - 500	$1,800

WARHEAD COMBO – 150W, 2-12 in. Celestion Vintage 30 speakers, same chassis as the head, black covering, side handles, black metal grille, disc. 2004.

	N/A	$550 - 650	$325 - 400	$1,400

WARHEAD HEAD – 300W, head-unit only, solid-state chassis, two channels, front black control panel, single input, 14 black and silver knobs, 9-band equalizer, 16 D.D. EFX, 6 equalizer knobs, independent gain and master, effects loop, footswitch, black covering, black metal grille, disc. 2004.

	N/A	$475 - 550	$300 - 350	$1,300

WARHEAD X2 – 300W, head-unit only, solid-state chassis, two channels, front black control panel, single input, 10 black knobs, active density and presence controls, effects loop, footswitch, black covering, brushed chrome front panel, mfg. 2004 only.

	N/A	$475 - 550	$300 - 350	$1,300

ELECTRIC AMPLIFIERS: THRASHER/667 SERIES

667 HEAD – 120W, head-unit only, all-tube chassis, preamp: 9 X 12AX7, power: 4 X 6L6, six channels (three sets of two channels), front black control panel, single input, twenty-nine knobs (MV1, MV 2, each set of channels: g1, v1, g2, v2, b, m, t, depth, presence), six channel switches, six bright switches, three TSS switches, seven MIDI functions per channel, standby switch, power switch, rear panel: midi in jack, midi thru jack, two effect loops with level controls, output jack with volume control, five external speaker out jacks, dual top handles, black covering, black/silver grille, mfg. 2014-present.

MSR $3,745	$2,500	$1,625 - 1,875	$825 - 1,000	

THRASHER 50 HEAD – 50W, head-unit only, all-tube chassis, preamp: 4 X 12AX7, power: 2 X 6L6, dual channels, front black control panel, single input, twelve knobs (channel 1: low g, high g, g, b, m, t, channel 2: g, v, tone, power: depth, presence, MV), standby switch, power switch, boost switch, channel switch, effect loop, black covering, top handle, black/silver metal grille, metal corners, 59.5 lbs., mfg. 2015-present.

MSR $1,500	$1,000	$650 - 750	$325 - 400	

MSR/NOTES	100%	EXCELLENT	AVERAGE	LAST MSR

667 Head
courtesy Randall

Thrasher 50 Head
courtesy Randall

Thrasher 120 Head
courtesy Randall

THRASHER 120 HEAD – 120W, head-unit only, all-tube chassis, four mode, dual channels, front black control panel, dual inputs, sixteen knobs (channel 1: low g, high g, g, boost, v, b, m, t, channel 2: g, v, b, m, t, power: depth, presence, MV), standby switch, power switch, boost switch, bright switch, channel switch, effect loop, black covering, two top handles, black/silver metal grille, metal corners, 59.5 lbs., mfg. 2013-present.

| MSR $2,700 | $1,500 | $975 - 1,125 | $500 - 600 | |

THRASHER 212 SPEAKER CABINET – 200W, 2-12 in. Celestion G12H-100 speakers, 8 ohms mono, 16 ohms stereo, angled front, black covering, black steel grille, steel corners, metal logo, recessed side handles, casters included, 63.5 lbs., mfg. 2013-present.

| MSR $900 | $600 | $400 - 450 | $195 - 240 | |

THRASHER 412A SPEAKER CABINET – 400W, 4-12 in. Celestion G12H-100 speakers, 16 or 4 ohms mono, 16 ohms stereo, angled front, black covering, black steel grille, steel corners, metal logo, recessed side handles, casters included, 110.2 lbs., mfg. 2013-present.

| MSR $1,462 | $900 | $575 - 675 | $295 - 350 | |

THRASHER 412S SPEAKER CABINET – 400W, 4-12 in. Celestion G12H-100 speakers, 16 or 4 ohms mono, 16 ohms stereo, straight front, black covering, black steel grille, steel corners, metal logo, recessed side handles, casters included, 110.2 lbs., mfg. 2013-present.

| MSR $1,462 | $900 | $575 - 675 | $295 - 350 | |

ELECTRIC AMPLIFIERS: X/RX SERIES

The X Series was replaced by the RX series in summer, 2004.

RX15
courtesy Randall

RX15M
courtesy Randall

RG15XM – 15W, 1-6.5 in. speaker, solid-state chassis, two channels, front black control panel, single input, five black knobs (g, v, t, m, b), line out jack, headphone jack, black covering, black metal grille, disc. 2003.

| | N/A | $40 - 50 | $20 - 30 | $100 |

* *RG15RXM* – similar to the RG15XM, except has reverb, disc. 2003.

| | N/A | $55 - 70 | $30 - 40 | $140 |

RG25RXM – 25W, 1-8 in. speaker, solid-state chassis, reverb, two channels, front black control panel, single input, seven black knobs (v, g, t, m, b, MV, r) effects loop, line out jack, headphone jack, black covering, black metal grille, disc. 2003.

| | N/A | $70 - 90 | $40 - 55 | $180 |

RX15 – 12W, 1-6.5 in. speaker combo, solid-state chassis, two channels, front black control panel, single input, (clean level, OD g, OD level, b, m, t, MV), headphone jack, black covering, black grille, mfg. 2004-07.

| | $75 | $40 - 55 | $25 - 35 | $100 |

* *RX15M* – similar to the RX15, except has 15W output and a black metal grille, mfg. 2008-2011.

| | $100 | $55 - 75 | $30 - 45 | $140 |

RX20R – 20W, 1-10 in. Celestion speaker combo, solid-state chassis, two channels, reverb, front silver control panel, black covering, black grille, mfg. 2004-07.

| | $135 | $70 - 95 | $45 - 60 | $180 |

MSR/NOTES	100%	EXCELLENT	AVERAGE	LAST MSR

RX25RM
courtesy Randall

RX50D
courtesy Randall

RX120RH Head
courtesy Randall

RX20D – 20W, 1-10 in. Celestion speaker combo, solid-state chassis, two channels, 16 DFX, front silver control panel, black covering, black grille, mfg. 2004-07.

	$190	$110 - 140	$70 - 90	$250

RX25RM – 25W, 1-10 in. Randall Jaguar speaker combo, solid-state chassis, reverb, front black control panel, single input, eight black knobs (clean level, OD g, OD level, b, m, t, MV, r), headphone jack, Series EFX loop, tape/CD input, footswitch included, black leatherette covering, black metal grille, mfg. 2008-2011.

	$170	$95 - 120	$50 - 70	$220

RX30D – 30W, 1-12 in. Celestion speaker combo, solid-state chassis, two channels, 16 DFX, front silver control panel, black covering, black grille, mfg. 2004-07.

	$250	$145 - 175	$95 - 125	$330

RX35DM – 35W, 1-12 in. Randall Jaguar speaker combo, solid-state chassis, 15 digital effects, front black control panel, single input, nine black knobs (clean level, OD g, OD level, b, m, t, MV, EFX level, EFX select), headphone jack, Series EFX loop, tape/CD input, footswitch included, black leatherette covering, black metal grille, mfg. 2008-2011.

	$250	$140 - 180	$85 - 110	$350

RX50D – 50W, 1-12 in. Jaguar speaker, guitar combo, solid-state chassis, two channels, 16 digital effects, front black control panel, single input, 13 knobs (Clean Ch.: level, t, m, b, OD Ch.: g, t, m, b, contour, level, All: MV, effects select, effects level), headphone jack, two-button footswitch, black covering, black grille, mfg. 2006-07.

	$360	$200 - 250	$120 - 150	$480

RX75R – 75W, 1-12 in. Jaguar speaker, guitar combo, solid-state chassis, two channels, reverb, front black control panel, single input, 12 knobs (Clean Ch.: level, t, m, b, OD Ch.: g, t, m, b, contour, level, All: MV, r), headphone jack, two-button footswitch, black covering, black grille, mfg. 2006-07.

	$340	$190 - 240	$110 - 140	$450

RX75RG2 – 75W, 1-12 in. Randall Jaguar speaker combo, solid-state chassis, two channels (three modes), reverb, front black control panel, single input, fourteen black knobs (OD Ch.: g1, g2, t, m, b, c, r, level, Clean Ch.: level, r, t, m, b, All: MV), headphone jack, Series EFX loop, slave output with level, footswitch included, black leatherette covering, black cloth grille, mfg. 2008-2011.

	$400	$250 - 300	$150 - 200	$550

RX120DHS HALF-STACK – 120W, head-unit with speaker cabinet, 4-12 in. Jaguar speakers, solid-state chassis, two channels, 16 digital effects, front black control panel, single input, 13 knobs (Clean Ch.: level, t, m, b, OD Ch.: g, t, m, b, contour, level, All: MV, effects select, effects level), headphone jack, two-button footswitch, black covering, black grille, mfg. 2006-2011.

	$630	$375 - 450	$225 - 275	$950

RX120RH HEAD – 120W, guitar head-unit, solid-state chassis, two channels, reverb, front black control panel, single input, 12 knobs (Clean Ch.: level, t, m, b, OD Ch.: g, t, m, b, contour, level, All: MV, r), headphone jack, two-button footswitch, black covering, black grille, mfg. 2006-present.

MSR $487	$300	$200 - 250	$120 - 150	

* **RX120R Combo** – similar to the RX120RH, except in combo configuration with 2-12 in. Jaguar speakers, mfg. 2006-07.

	$430	$250 - 300	$150 - 190	$580

* **RX120RHS Half-Stack** – similar to the RX120RH, except in half-stack configuration with a speaker cabinet loaded with 4-12 in. Jaguar speakers, mfg. 2006-2011.

	$500	$300 - 375	$175 - 225	$850

V2XM – 35W, 1-12 in. Randall Jaguar speaker combo, solid-state chassis, reverb, front black control panel, single input, seven black knobs (clean level, OD g, OD level, b, m, t, MV), three-band graphic EQ, headphone jack, Series EFX loop, tape/CD input, footswitch included, black leatherette covering, black metal grille, mfg. 2008-2011.

	$250	$135 - 175	$85 - 110	$300

MSR/NOTES	100%	EXCELLENT	AVERAGE	LAST MSR

VMX30 – 30W, 1-12 in. Randall Jaguar speaker combo, solid-state chassis, two channels, front silver control panel, single input, seven black knobs (Clean level, OD g, OD level, b, m, t, MV), three-band graphic EQ, effects loop, headphone jack, RCA inputs, black covering, black grille, mfg. 2005-07.

	$165	$95 - 120	$55 - 75	$220

ELECTRIC AMPLIFIERS: XL SERIES

T2 Head
courtesy Randall

V2 Head
courtesy Randall

CYCLONE – 300W, head-unit only, solid-state chassis, two channels, reverb, front black control panel, single input, 13 black knobs, nine-band graphic equalizer, effects loop, black covering, black grille, two-button footswitch, disc. 2004.

	N/A	$475 - 550	$275 - 325	$1,200

T2 HEAD – 500W @ 2 ohms (400W @ 4 ohms, 280W @ 8 ohms), head-unit, guitar configuration, hybrid Valve Dynamic chassis, preamp: 3 X 12AX7, power: 12AT7 tube-driven MOSFET, two channels, front black control panel, single input, 10 black knobs (Ch. 1: g, level, Ch. 2: g, l, All: b, mid range, mid sweep, t, density, p), MIDI assignable series of parallel effects loop, slave out with level control, direct out, footswitch, available in black or silver (2008-2011) covering, black grille, mfg. 2006-2011.

	$1,000	$600 - 700	$350 - 425	$1,500

TITAN – 300W, head-unit, solid-state chassis, two channels, reverb, front black control panel, single input, nine black knobs, effects loop, two-button footswitch, black covering, black grille, disc. 2005.

	N/A	$425 - 500	$250 - 300	$950

V2 HEAD – 480W @ 2 ohms (400W @ 4 ohms, 280W @ 8 ohms), head-unit, guitar configuration, hybrid Valve Dynamic chassis, preamp: 3 X 12AX7, power: 12AT7 tube-driven MOSFET, three channels, front black control panel, single input, 16 black knobs (Ch. 1: g, level, Ch. 2: g, l, b, m, t, p, Ch. 3: g, b, m, t, level, All: MV, density, p), six-band graphic EQ, MIDI assignable series of parallel effects loop, slave out with level control, direct out, footswitch, available in black or silver (2008-2011) leatherette covering, black grille, mfg. 2006-2011.

	$1,100	$650 - 800	$400 - 475	$1,700

VMAX – 300W, head-unit only, hybrid design, dual preamps (one solid-state, one tube), solid-state power amp, front silver control panel, single input, 17 black knobs, six-band graphic equalizer, effects loop, five-button footswitch, black covering, black grille, disc. 2005.

	N/A	$600 - 700	$375 - 450	$1,400

BASS AMPLIFIERS

All the current bass amps produced are listed along with a brief description of the older RB series. Randall's earlier bass amps typically carried the RB model prefix. These amps were found in combo units as well as heads. Such examples of models are the RB-60, RB-35, and RBA-500ES head unit. These units can be usually found in the price range of $100-300.

RB30XM – 30W, 1-10 in. speaker, solid-state combo, front black control panel, two inputs (active/passive), five black knobs, effects loop, headphone jack, black covering, black metal grille, disc. 2003.

	N/A	$80 - 100	$60 - 70	$160

RB100 – 100W, 1-15 in. Eminence Legend speaker, solid-state combo, single channel, front silver control panel, single input, eight black knobs, nine-band graphic equalizer, effects loop, balanced XLR out, headphones, black carpet covering, black metal grille, disc. 2003.

	N/A	$450 - 525	$350 - 400	$850

RB200/115 – 200W, 1-15 in. Eminence Legend speaker, solid-state combo, single channel, front silver control panel, single input, eight black knobs, nine-band graphic equalizer, effects loop, balanced XLR out, headphones, black carpet covering, black metal grille, disc. 2003.

	N/A	$500 - 600	$375 - 450	$1,000

RB200/410 – same as the RB200/15 in circuitry has 4-10 in. Eminence Coaxial speakers, disc. 2003.

	N/A	$575 - 675	$475 - 525	$1,100

RB300 – 300W, two-space rack-mount bass head-unit, solid-state chassis with Valve-Dynamic power, single channel, front black control panel, single input, 11 black knobs (OD, OD level, comp. pre g, b, m, contour, t, MV, Valve-Dynamic bottom, Valve-Dynamic definition, OD switch, lo cut switch, mute switch, comp. switch, headphone jack, back panel: four speaker outputs (two 1/4 in. and two Speakon), footswitch jack, XLR direct out with level control, effects loop, tuner output, black casing, mfg. 2007-2010.

	$700	$425 - 500	$250 - 300	$950

RB500 – similar to the RB300, except has 500W output, mfg. 2007-2010.

	$950	$550 - 625	$325 - 400	$1,250

MSR/NOTES	100%	EXCELLENT	AVERAGE	LAST MSR

RB750 – similar to the RB300, except has 750W output, mfg. 2007-2010.

	100%	EXCELLENT	AVERAGE	LAST MSR
	$1,250	$700 - 850	$450 - 525	$1,700

RX35BM – 35W, 1-12 in. Randall Jaguar speaker bass combo, solid-state chassis, single channel, front black channel panel, two inputs (high/low), four knobs (v, b, m, t), RCA inputs, headphone jack, Series EFX loop, black leatherette covering, black metal grille, mfg. 2008-2011.

	100%	EXCELLENT	AVERAGE	LAST MSR
	$200	$120 - 150	$75 - 95	$280

SPEAKER CABINETS

These speaker cabinets are universal for many of the Randall heads. If the speaker cabinet series is specific to another series, such as the Warhead, then they would be listed in the Warhead series. Along with the speaker cabinets listed here, there are two isolation cabinets available. These are speaker cabinets that are meant for live recording with a microphone, essentially a recording studio in a box. This cabinet blocks out outside sounds to make recording possible. They are available for guitar for $500 and for bass for $500.

R112CBG
courtesy Randall

R212CB
courtesy Randall

R412CB
courtesy Randall

R112CS/R112CB/R112CP – 60W, 1-12 in. Celestion V30 speakers, 8 Ohm mono, angled front, available in black covering with a Vintage Silver grille (R112CS, disc.), black (R112CB), or Palomino (R112CP/R112CBP, 2008-2011) grille cloth, mfg. 2003-2011.

	100%	EXCELLENT	AVERAGE	LAST MSR
	$360	$200 - 250	$100 - 150	$480

R112CBG/R112CPG/R112CBPG – 25W, 1-12 in. Celestion Greenback speaker, 8 ohm impedance, 3/4 in. birch plywood construction, deep cabinet design for low end response, available in black covering with black (R112CBG) or Palomino (R112CBPG, 2008-2011) cloth grille, or Palomino (brown covering with brown cloth grille, R112CPG/R112CRPG, 2007-2011), mfg. 2006-2011.

	100%	EXCELLENT	AVERAGE	LAST MSR
	$360	$190 - 240	$120 - 150	$480

R(S)125CX – 260W, 2-12 in. Custom 80W Celestion and 1-15 in. Eminence woofer speakers, 4 Ohm impedance, straight front, black covering, metal grille, 85 lbs., mfg. 2004-09.

	100%	EXCELLENT	AVERAGE	LAST MSR
	$450	$250 - 300	$150 - 200	$750

RS125XL SPEAKER CABINET – 220W, 2-12 in. Celestion V30 and 1-15 in. Eminence Legend speakers, 8 Ohm mono impedance, straight front, angled baffle, black covering, black cloth grille, 90 lbs., mfg. 2004-2011.

	100%	EXCELLENT	AVERAGE	LAST MSR
	$700	$425 - 500	$250 - 300	$1,000

R212CS/R212CB/R212CP – 120W, 2-12 in. Celestion V30 speakers, 8 ohm mono impedance, straight front, available in black covering with a silver (disc., R212CS), black (R212CB), or brown (R212CBP) grille cloth or Palomino (RG212CRP, brown covering with a brown grille cloth, 2007-2011), 47 lbs., disc.

	100%	EXCELLENT	AVERAGE	LAST MSR
	$580	$325 - 400	$175 - 225	$800

R212CX – 160W, 2-12 in. Custom 80W Celestion speakers, 4/16 mono/8 stereo, straight front, black covering, metal grille, 47 lbs., disc. 2009.

	100%	EXCELLENT	AVERAGE	LAST MSR
	$300	$175 - 225	$110 - 140	$450

R212NXT – 160W, 2-12 in. Celestion Neodymium speakers, 4/16 mono/8 stereo, angled or straight front, black covering, black grille cloth, 35 lbs., mfg. 2004-2011.

	100%	EXCELLENT	AVERAGE	LAST MSR
	$600	$325 - 400	$175 - 225	$850

The black grille was introduced in 2004.

R412CBR – 200W, 4-12 in. Celestion Greenback speakers, 8 ohm mono impedance, single input jack, straight front, angled baffle, black covering with silver pin-striping and black retro cosmetics, mfg. 2006-07.

	100%	EXCELLENT	AVERAGE	LAST MSR
	$880	$500 - 575	$300 - 350	$1,100

MSR/NOTES	100%	EXCELLENT	AVERAGE	LAST MSR

R412CXM
courtesy Randall

R412NXT
courtesy Randall

RA412XL
courtesy Randall

R412CS/R412CB/RA412CS/R412CP/R412CBP – 280W, 4-12 in. Celestion V30 speakers, 4/16 ohm impedance mono (8 ohm impedance stereo), angled or straight front, available in black covering with a silver (R412CS/RA412CS), black (R412CB, 2004-08), or Palomino (R412CBP, 2008-disc.) grille cloth, Palomino (brown covering with brown grille cloth, R412CP/R412CRP, 2007-disc), 96 lbs., disc.

	$850	$500 - 575	$300 - 350	$1,250

R412CXM – 320W, 4-12 in. Custom 80W Celestion speakers, 4 ohm stereo/8 ohm mono impedance, straight front, angled baffle, black covering, metal grille, 96 lbs., disc. 2006.

	$575	$325 - 400	$225 - 275	$750

R412CXP – 320W, 4-12 in. Celestion Seventy 80 speakers, 8 ohm mono impedance (4 ohm stereo impedance), birch construction, straight front, angled baffle, black covering, black grille cloth, designed for use with the RH300G3 head, Made in U.S.A., mfg. 2007 only.

	$600	$325 - 400	$225 - 275	$750

R412JX – 300W, 4-12 in. Eminence Jaguar 75W speakers, 8 ohm impedance, straight front, angled baffle, black covering, metal grille, mfg. 2005-06.

	$490	$300 - 350	$175 - 225	$650

R412NXT – 320W, 4-12 in. Celestion Neodymium speakers, 4/16 mono/8 stereo, angled or straight front, black covering, black grille cloth, 68 lbs., mfg. 2004-2011.

	$900	$525 - 675	$325 - 400	$1,300

The black grille was introduced in 2004.

R412XLTX/RS412XLTX/RS412XLX – 280W, 2-12 in. Celestion Vintage 30 speakers and 2-12 in. Celestion G12T-75 speakers, 4/16 ohm mono impedance (8 ohm stereo impedance), straight front, angled front (RS412XLTX only), Mic Eliminator XLR outputs, black covering, black cloth (RS412XLR) or black metal (R412XLTX/RS412XLTX) grille, mfg. 2006-2011.

	$880	$525 - 600	$325 - 375	$1,300

• **Subtract 5% for black cloth grille (Models RS412XLR).**

R412XLT SPEAKER CABINET – 280W, 4-12 in. Celestion V30 speakers, 4/16 mono/8 stereo, straight front, angled baffle, black covering, black metal grille, 98 lbs., disc.

	$920	$525 - 600	$325 - 375	$1,150

RA412XL100/RS412XL100/R412XLT100/RS412XLT100 – 400W, 4-12 in. 4-12 in. Celestion G12H-100 speakers, 4/16 ohm mono impedance (8 ohm stereo impedance), straight front, angled front (RS412XLT100 only), Mic Eliminator XLR outputs, black covering, black cloth (RA412XL100/RA412XL100) or black metal (RA412XLT100/RS412XLT100) grille, mfg. 2007-disc.

	$920	$525 - 600	$325 - 375	$1,150

RA412XL/RS412XL SPEAKER CABINET – 280W, 4-12 in. Celestion V30 or G12T-75 speakers, 4/16 mono/8 stereo, angled or straight front, black covering, black grille cloth, 96/98 lbs., disc.

	$880	$500 - 575	$300 - 350	$1,250

• **Add 5% (MSR $1,100) for oversized cabinet (Model RS412XXL).**

RA412XLT/RS412XLT SPEAKER CABINET – 280W, 4-12 in. Celestion V30 or G12T-75 speakers, 4/16 mono/8 stereo, angled or straight front, black covering, black metal grille, 98/100 lbs., disc.

	$880	$500 - 575	$325 - 375	$1,300

• **Add 5% (MSR $1,350) for oversized cabinet (Model RS412XXLT).**

RC212-V30 SPEAKER CABINET – 130W, 2-12 in. Celestion Vintage 30's speakers, 8 ohms, straight front, black covering, black cloth grille, casters included, USA made, baltic birch construction, 77.5 lbs., mfg. 2013-present.

MSR $1,219	$750	$475 - 550	$245 - 300	

MSR/NOTES	100%	EXCELLENT	AVERAGE	LAST MSR

RC412-V30 Speaker Cabinet
courtesy Randall

USM-RV412A Angled Speaker Cabinet
courtesy Randall

USM-RV412S Straight Speaker Cabinet
courtesy Randall

RC412-V30 SPEAKER CABINET – 260W, 4-12 in. Celestion Vintage 30's speakers, 8 or 16 ohms, straight front, black covering, black cloth grille, casters included, USA made, baltic birch construction, 96 lbs., mfg. 2013-present.

| MSR $1,625 | $1,000 | $650 - 750 | $325 - 400 | |

RS412KHX/100 KIRK HAMMETT CABINET – 270W/400W, either 4-12 in. Celestion G12H-100 speakers or 2-12 in. Celestion Vintage 30 and 2-12 in. Celestion G12T-75 speakers, 4/16 ohm impedance mono 8 ohm impedance stereo, straight front, AAAA flame maple veneer finished in Trans. Black, black grille cloth with a large Kirk Hammett signature emblem in lower right corner, mfg. 2008-2012.

| | $1,100 | $625 - 725 | $375 - 450 | $1,400 |

RS412LB GEORGE LYNCH CABINET – 240W, 4-12 in. Lynch Signature Super V speakers, 8 ohm impedance, straight front, Forest Green Alligator vinyl covering with gold accents, brown grille, mfg. 2006-2012.

| | $1,050 | $600 - 700 | $375 - 450 | $1,300 |

RS412XC – 320W, 4-12 in. Celestion 80W speakers, 8 ohm mono impedance (4 ohm stereo impedance), birch construction, straight front, black covering, black grille cloth, designed for use with the RH150G3 heads, mfg. 2007-09.

| | $450 | $250 - 300 | $150 - 200 | $800 |

RX412 – 200W, 4-12 in. Randall 50W Jaguar speakers, 8 ohm impedance, straight front, black covering, black grille cloth, designed for use with the RX120 heads, mfg. 2007-present.

| MSR $568 | $350 | $200 - 250 | $120 - 150 | |

USM-RV112GB SPEAKER CABINET – 25W, 1-12 in. Celestion G12M-25 Greenback speaker, 8 ohms, straight front, top handle, black covering, black cloth grille, 37 lbs., mfg. 2010-present.

| MSR $487 | $300 | $195 - 225 | $100 - 120 | |

USM-RV212 SPEAKER CABINET – 120W, 2-12 in. Celestion Vintage 30 speakers, 4/16 ohms mono, 8 ohms stereo, straight front, recessed side handles, black covering, black cloth grille, 68.78 lbs., mfg. 2010-present.

| MSR $812 | $550 | $350 - 400 | $180 - 220 | |

USM-RV412 SPEAKER CABINET – 240W, 4-12 in. speakers in an X-pattern, 2 Celestion Vintage 30 speakers, 2 Celestion G12T-75 speakers, 4/16 ohms mono, 8 ohms stereo, straight front, recessed side handles, black covering, black cloth grille, 97 lbs., mfg. 2013-present.

| MSR $1,381 | $850 | $550 - 625 | $275 - 350 | |

USM-RV412A ANGLED SPEAKER CABINET – 240W, 4-12 in. Celestion Vintage 30 speakers, 4/16 ohms mono, 8 ohms stereo, angled front, removable casters, black covering, black cloth grille, 100.31 lbs., mfg. 2013-present.

| MSR $1,381 | $850 | $550 - 625 | $275 - 350 | |

USM-RV412S STRAIGHT SPEAKER CABINET – 240W, 4-12 in. Celestion Vintage 30 speakers, 4/16 ohms mono, 8 ohms stereo, straight front, removable casters, black covering, black cloth grille, 100.31 lbs., mfg. 2013-present.

| MSR $1,381 | $850 | $550 - 625 | $275 - 350 | |

BASS SPEAKER CABINETS

RB115XL/RB115XLT SPEAKER CABINET – 300W, 1-15 in. Basslite Neodynium speaker, 8 ohm impedance, single 1/4 in. input, 11-ply void free birch construction, black covering, black cloth (RB115XL) or black metal (RB115XLT) grille, mfg. 2007-disc.

| | $520 | $300 - 350 | $175 - 225 | $800 |

RB410XL/RB410XLT SPEAKER CABINET – 800W, 4-10 in. Custom Eminence speakers and a tweeter with a level control, 8 ohm impedance, single 1/4 in. and two Speakon inputs, 11-ply void free birch construction, black covering, black cloth (RB410XL) or black metal (RB410XLT) grille, mfg. 2007-disc.

| | $730 | $425 - 500 | $275 - 325 | $1,200 |

MSR/NOTES	100%	EXCELLENT	AVERAGE	LAST MSR

RB412XL/RB412XLT SPEAKER CABINET – 600W, 4-12 in. Basslite Neodynium speakers and a tweeter with a level control, 8 ohm impedance, single 1/4 in. and two Speakon inputs, 11-ply void free birch construction, black covering, black cloth (RB412XL) or black metal (RB412XLT) grille, mfg. 2007-2011.

	100%	EXCELLENT	AVERAGE	LAST MSR
	$830	$500 - 575	$325 - 375	$1,300

RB810XL/RB810XLT SPEAKER CABINET – 1600W, 8-10 in. Custom Eminence speakers and a tweeter with a level control, 4 ohm impedance, single 1/4 in. and two Speakon inputs, 11-ply void free birch construction, black covering, black cloth (RB810XL) or black metal (RB810XLT) grille, mfg. 2007-2011.

	100%	EXCELLENT	AVERAGE	LAST MSR
	$1,030	$600 - 700	$350 - 425	$1,600

RAT FINK

RF-40
courtesy Rat Fink

Amplifiers previously produced between 2002 and 2005. Distributed by Lace Music Products in Huntington Beach, CA.

Rat Fink is a series of amplifiers and guitars that are based on characters that were created by "Big Daddy" Ed Roth. These products were released at the Winter NAMM show in 2002 with an animated video of these characters playing in the Lace booth featuring the new amps and guitars. Rat Fink has appeared more on show cars and other related memorabilia. Ken Mitchroney has painted designs on Rat Fink guitars as well.

ELECTRIC AMPLIFIERS

RF-15 – 15W, 1-6 in. speaker, solid-state chassis, front silver control panel, single input, 6 black knobs (g, MV, t, m, b, r), headphone jack, red vinyl covering, gray grille with Rat Fink graphics, mfg. 2002-05.

	100%	EXCELLENT	AVERAGE	LAST MSR
	N/A	$70 - 95	$35 - 50	$169

RF-40 – 40W, 1-12 in. speaker, solid-state chassis, chorus, reverb, tremolo, two channels, front silver control panel, two inputs, 10 black knobs, mic input send and return, headphone jack, footswitch, red vinyl covering, gray grille with Rat Fink graphics, mfg. 2002-05.

	100%	EXCELLENT	AVERAGE	LAST MSR
	N/A	$175 - 225	$110 - 140	$399

RED

See MatAmp.

RED BEAR

Amplifiers previously produced in St. Petersburg, Russia during the mid-1990s. Distributed by Gibson and Novik LTD.

Red Bear amplifiers were designed by Sergei Novikov, who was one of the best tube amp experts in Russia at the time. These amps were mainly produced in Russia, but an ad indicates that speaker cabinets were built in the U.S., and it is unknown if they were produced in the U.S. or not. They were distributed in the U.S. by Gibson during the mid-1990s, but the distribution deal was disc. in 1997 or 1998. Red Bear amps were all-tube amps available in head-units, combos, and speaker cabinets. They came primarily in 60W and 120W versions. A red "Red Bear" logo with the r from Bear reversed and a star between the Red and Bear was placed center on the amp. Any further information can be submitted directly to Blue Book Publications.

REEVES AMPLIFICATION

Amplifiers currently produced in Cincinnati, OH since 2002.

Bill Jansen founded Reeves amplifiers in 2002, and they are based on the military-spec Hiwatt amps of the 1960s and 1970s. Dave Reeves founded Hiwatt back in the 1960s and Jansen named his company after him. Besides the Reeves logo and other slight modifications, Reeves 100 and 200 series amps are identical to Hiwatt amps. Reeves has also released more amps that vary from the original Hiwatt design, but they are still built with the same high quality. For more information, visit Reeve's website or contact them directly.

CONTACT INFORMATION
REEVES AMPLIFICATION
11122 Luschek Drive
Cincinnati, OH 45241
Phone No.: 513-451-1071
www.reevesamps.com
reevesamps@fuse.net

ELECTRIC TUBE AMPLIFIERS

CUSTOM 6 HEAD – 6W, head-unit, guitar configuration, two-tube chassis, preamp: 12AX7, power: EL34, single channel, top black control panel, two inputs, four chickenhead knobs (v, t, m, b), headphone jack, multiple speaker jacks, line out jack, black, red, or cream Tolex coverings, 20 in. wide, 8 in. tall, 8 in. deep, mfg. 2005-present.

MSR/NOTES	100%	EXCELLENT	AVERAGE	
MSR $659	$659	$450 - 525	$300 - 350	

Custom 6 Combo – similar to the Custom 6 Head, except in combo configuration with 1-12 in. speaker, silver grille, 20 in. wide, 17 in. tall, 9.9375 in. deep, mfg. 2004-present.

MSR/NOTES	100%	EXCELLENT	AVERAGE	
MSR $799	$799	$525 - 625	$350 - 425	

MSR/NOTES	100%	EXCELLENT	AVERAGE	LAST MSR

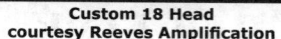

Custom 18 Head
courtesy Reeves Amplification

Custom 30 Head
courtesy Reeves Amplification

Custom 6 Combo
courtesy Reeves Amplification

CUSTOM 10 HG HEAD – 10W, guitar head unit, three tube chassis, preamp: 2 X 12AX7, power: 1 X EL34, single channel, front control panel, single input, five knobs (MV, b, m, t, g), various speaker out jacks, available in Black, Orange, or White finish, 20 in. wide, 8.625 in. tall, 8 5/16 in. deep, mfg. 2008-present.

| MSR $999 | $999 | $650 - 775 | $450 - 525 | |

* *Custom 10 HG Combo* – similar to the Custom 10 HG, except in combo configuration with 1-12 in. speaker, 22 in. wide, 19 in. tall, 10.5 in. deep, mfg. 2008-present.

| MSR $1,149 | $1,149 | $775 - 925 | $525 - 600 | |

CUSTOM 12 HEAD – 12W, head-unit, guitar configuration, three tube chassis, preamp: 12AX7, power: 2 X EL34, single channel, top black control panel, two inputs, four chickenhead knobs (v, t, m, b), headphone jack, multiple speaker jacks, line out jack, black, red, or cream Tolex coverings, 20 in. wide, 8 in. tall, 8 in. deep, mfg. 2005-present.

| MSR $779 | $779 | $525 - 625 | $325 - 400 | |

* *Custom 12 Combo* – similar to the Custom 12 Head, except in combo configuration with 1-12 in. speaker, silver grille, 20 in. wide, 17 in. tall, 9.9375 in. deep, mfg. 2005-present.

| MSR $899 | $899 | $600 - 725 | $425 - 500 | |

CUSTOM 18 HEAD – 20W, head-unit, guitar configuration, five tube chassis, preamp: 3 X 12AX7, power: 2 X EL84, solid-state rectifier, single channel, front black control panel, two inputs, seven chickenhead knobs (power scale, cut, drive, t, m, b, g), gain switch, bright/mid switch, speaker outs, black, red, or cream Tolex coverings, 26 in. wide, 9 in. tall, 8.25 in. deep, mfg. 2005-present.

| MSR $1,599 | $1,599 | $1,000 - 1,250 | $750 - 850 | |

* *Custom 18 1-12 Combo* – similar to the Custom 18 Head, except in combo configuration with 1-12 in. speaker, 21.625 in. wide, 21 in. tall, 11.75 in. deep, mfg. 2005-present.

| MSR $1,799 | $1,799 | $1,150 - 1,400 | $775 - 900 | |

* *Custom 18 2-12 Combo* – similar to the Custom 18 Head, except in combo form with 2-12 in. speakers, 27 in. wide, 20.5 in. tall, 11.375 in. deep, mfg. 2005-09.

| | $1,939 | $1,250 - 1,500 | $850 - 1,000 | $1,939 |

CUSTOM 30 HEAD (MKII) – 30W, head-unit, guitar configuration, seven-tube chassis, preamp: 4 X 12AX7, 1 X 12AT7, power: 2 X EL84/KT66, solid-state rectifier, single channel, reverb, front black control panel, two inputs, eight chickenhead knobs (g, v, b, m, t, r, cut, power scale), footswitch, black, red, or cream Tolex coverings, 25.1875 in. wide, 10.875 in. tall, 11.25 in. deep, mfg. 2005-present.

| MSR $1,999 | $1,999 | $1,350 - 1,600 | $900 - 1,050 | |

In 2009, Reeves updated the Custom 30 to MKII specifications with a lead boost variable control on the back panel, a boost switch mounted on the back panel, and a fixed bias power tube section.

* *Custom 30 1-12 Combo (MKII)* – similar to the Custom 30 Head, except in combo configuration with 1-12 in. speaker, 21.75 in. wide, 22 in. tall, 11.875 in. deep, mfg. 2005-present.

| MSR $2,299 | $2,299 | $1,400 - 1,750 | $950 - 1,100 | |

* *Custom 30 2-12 Combo* – similar to the Custom 30 Head, except in combo configuration with 2-12 in. speakers, 27 in. wide, 20.5 in. tall, 11.375 in. deep, mfg. 2005-09.

| | $2,349 | $1,450 - 1,800 | $975 - 1,125 | $2,349 |

CUSTOM 50 HEAD – 50W, head-unit only, tube chassis, preamp: 4 X 12AX7, power: 2 X EL34, two channels, front black control panel, four inputs, seven black chickenhead knobs (v1, v2, b, t, m, p, MV), black covering (custom colors optional), 25.1875 in. wide, 10.875 in. tall, 11.25 in. deep, mfg. 2002-present.

| MSR $1,799 | $1,799 | $1,150 - 1,400 | $775 - 900 | |

MSR/NOTES	100%	EXCELLENT	AVERAGE	LAST MSR

* *Custom 50 1-12 Combo* – similar to the Custom 50 Head, except in combo configuration with 1-12 in. speakers, 21.75 in. wide, 22 in. tall, 11.875 in. deep, mfg. 2005-present.

| MSR $2,029 | $2,029 | $1,400 - 1,750 | $950 - 1,100 | |

* *Custom 50 2-12 Combo* – similar to the Custom 50 Head, except in combo configuration with 2-12 in. Fane speakers, mfg. 2004-05.

| | N/A | $1,600 - 1,900 | $1,000 - 1,300 | $2,459 |

* *Custom 50 PS Head* – similar to the Custom 50 Head, except has Reeves' Power Scaling circuit with an additional Power Scaling knob on the front, mfg. 2008-present.

| MSR $2,099 | $2,149 | $1,350 - 1,650 | $900 - 1,050 | |

» *Custom 50PS 1-12 Combo* – similar to the Custom 50PS Head, except in combo configuration with 1-12 in. speaker, 21.75 in. wide, 22 in. tall, 11 in. deep, mfg. 2009-present.

| MSR $2,329 | $2,329 | $1,450 - 1,800 | $975 - 1,125 | |

CUSTOM 50 'JIMMY' – 50W, guitar head-unit, six-tube chassis, preamp: 3 X 12AX7, 1 X 12AT7, power: 2 X EL34, solid-state rectifier, single channel, front black control panel, two inputs, seven black chickenhead knobs (input v, balance, b, m, t, p, MV), power switch, standby switch, rear panel: footswitch jack for volume cut switch, two speaker jacks with impedance selector, resonance level control, black covering (custom colors optional), 25.1875 in. wide, 10.875 in. tall, 11.25 in. deep, footswitch included, mfg. 2009-present.

| MSR $1,999 | $1,999 | $1,350 - 1,600 | $900 - 1,050 | |

The Custom 50 'Jimmy' is a faithful recreation of Jimmy Page's Hiwatt that used between circa 1969 and 1971.

CUSTOM 100 'JIMMY' – 100W, guitar head-unit, eight-tube chassis, preamp: 3 X 12AX7, 1 X 12AT7, power: 4 X EL34, solid-state rectifier, single channel, front black control panel, two inputs, seven black chickenhead knobs (input v, balance, b, m, t, p, MV), power switch, standby switch, rear panel: footswitch jack for volume cut switch, two speaker jacks with impedance selector, resonance level control, black covering (custom colors optional), 25.1875 in. wide, 10.875 in. tall, 11.25 in. deep, footswitch included, mfg. 2009-present.

| MSR $2,199 | $2,199 | $1,400 - 1,700 | $950 - 1,100 | |

The Custom 50 'Jimmy' is a faithful recreation of Jimmy Page's Hiwatt that he used between circa 1969 and 1971.

CUSTOM 100 HEAD – 100W, head-unit only, tube chassis, preamp: 4 X 12AX7, power: 4 X EL34, two channels, front black control panel, four inputs, seven black chickenhead knobs (v1, v2, b, t, m, p, MV), black covering (custom colors optional), 25.1875 in. wide, 10.875 in. tall, 11.25 in. deep, mfg. 2002-present.

| MSR $2,099 | $2,099 | $1,350 - 1,650 | $900 - 1,050 | |

CUSTOM 200 HEAD – 200W, head-unit only, tube chassis, preamp: 4 X 12AX7, 12AT7, power: 4 X KT88, two channels, front black control panel, four inputs, seven black chickenhead knobs (v1, v2, b, t, m, p, MV), black covering (custom colors optional), mfg. 2002-05.

| | N/A | $1,600 - 1,900 | $900 - 1,100 | $2,459 |

CUSTOM 225 BASS HEAD – 225W, bass head-unit, eight-tube chassis, preamp: 3 X 12AX7, 1 X 12AT7, power: 4 X KT88, solid-state rectifier, two channels, front black control panel, two inputs, seven black chickenhead knobs (normal v, bright v, b, m, t, p, MV), passive/active switch, speaker impedance switch, balanced XLR line out, black covering with white piping, 24 in. wide, 11.8125 in. tall, 11.625 in. deep, mfg. fall 2007-present.

| MSR $2,499 | $2,299 | $1,500 - 1,850 | $1,000 - 1,200 | |

CUSTOM LEAD HEAD – 60W, guitar head-unit, five-tube chasis, preamp: 3 X 12AX7, power: 2 X EL34, single channel, front control panel, single input, eight knobs (Norm v, Bright v, t, m, b, p, d, power scale), three-way voice switch (stock, round, shimmer), speaker outs, available in Black, Orange, or White covering, 25 in. wide, 10.25 in. tall, 11.125 in. deep, mfg. 2008-09.

| | $1,949 | $1,250 - 1,500 | $850 - 1,000 | $1,949 |

* *Custom Lead High Gain Head* – similar to the Custom Lead Head, except has an extra 12AX7 tube in the preamp stage and a gain knob on the back of the amp, gain stage is switched in/out by a switch on the back of the amp or by footswitch, mfg. 2008-09.

| | $2,199 | $1,400 - 1,700 | $950 - 1,100 | $2,199 |

SIGNATURE CP504 50W – 50W, head-unit only, tube chassis, preamp: 5 X 12AX7, power: 2 X EL34, single channel, front black control panel, four inputs, seven black chickenhead knobs (v1, v2, v3, v4, b, t, MV), black covering (custom colors optional), 25.1875 in. wide, 10.875 in. tall, 11.25 in. deep, mfg. 2005-present.

| MSR $1,899 | $1,899 | $1,200 - 1,450 | $825 - 975 | |

This model is based on the Custom 100 Head, which was made famous by the group, The Who. There are four separate inputs rated at normal sensitivity with 4 separate volume controls.

SIGNATURE CP103 100W – similar to the Signature CP103 50W, except has 100W output with 4 X EL34 tubes, mfg. 2002-present.

| MSR $1,999 | $1,999 | $1,350 - 1,600 | $850 - 1,000 | |

This model is based on the Custom 100 Head, which was made famous by the group, The Who. There are four separate inputs rated at normal sensitivity with 4 separate volume controls.

MSR/NOTES	100%	EXCELLENT	AVERAGE	LAST MSR

STUDIO/STAGE MKII HEAD – 40W (switchable to 20W in Studio mode), head-unit only, Class A tube chassis, preamp: 3 X 12AX7, 12AT7, power: 4 X EL84, solid-state rectifier, reverb, single channel with boost, front black control panel, two inputs, six black chickenhead knobs (g, b, t, m, r, MV), black covering, mfg. 2002-05.

	N/A	$1,300 - 1,500	$650 - 850	$1,999

* *Studio/Stage MKII Combo* – similar to the Reeves Studio/Stage Head, except in combo configuration with 2-12 in. Fane speakers, mfg. 2002-05.

	N/A	$1,600 - 1,900	$900 - 1,100	$2,459

SUPER '78 50W HEAD – 50W, guitar head-unit, six-tube chassis, preamp: 4 X 12AX7, power: 2 X EL34, solid-state rectifier, two channels, front black control panel, single input, seven black chickenhead knobs (g, drive, b, m, t, cut, MV), rear panel: two speaker jacks with impedance selector, resonance level control, black covering (custom colors optional), 25.1875 in. wide, 10.875 in. tall, 11.25 in. deep, 47 lbs., mfg. 2009-present.

MSR $1,799	$1,799	$1,150 - 1,400	$775 - 900	

The Super '78 is designed to sound like Eddie Van Halen's tone from the late 1970s.

SUPER '78 100W HEAD – 100W, guitar head-unit, eight-tube chassis, preamp: 4 X 12AX7, power: 4 X EL34, solid-state rectifier, two channels, front black control panel, single input, seven black chickenhead knobs (g, drive, b, m, t, cut, MV), rear panel: two speaker jacks with impedance selector, resonance level control, black covering (custom colors optional), 25.1875 in. wide, 10.875 in. tall, 11.25 in. deep, 49 lbs., mfg. 2009-present.

MSR $1,999	$1,999	$1,350 - 1,600	$900 - 1,050	

The Super '78 is designed to sound like Eddie Van Halen's tone from the late 1970s.

SPEAKER CABINETS

In 2004, Vintage Purple speakers were introduced as an option for speaker cabinets. These retail for less than the Fane speakers. Cabinets are also available without speakers.

2-12 SPEAKER CABINET – 150W, 2-12 in. Fane speakers, 8 Ohm impedance, 3/4 in. marine birch plywood, available in black or custom colors, gray grille, mfg. 2002-06.

	$895	$550 - 650	$325 - 400	$895

* *2-12 Speaker Cabinet Vintage Purple* – similar to the 2-12 Speaker Cabinet, except has Vintage Purple speakers, mfg. 2004-present.

MSR $799	$799	$500 - 575	$300 - 375	

4-12 SPEAKER CABINET – 150W, 4-12 in. Fane speakers, 16 Ohm impedance, 3/4 in. marine birch plywood, available in black or custom colors, gray grille, mfg. 2002-06.

	$1,165	$675 - 800	$425 - 500	$1,165

* *4-12 Speaker Cabinet Vintage Purple* – similar to the 4-12 Speaker Cabinet, except has Vintage Purple speakers, mfg. 2004-present.

MSR $999	$999	$625 - 725	$400 - 475	

REINHARDT AMPLIFICATION

Amplifiers previously produced in Evington, VA.

Reinhardt Amplification was created after the founder wanted to create the tone he heard in his head. He built a few amps for himself and followed that with models for a few friends. When he made the first commercial sale, he went into business exclusively building amps. Reinhardt amps were mainly based on English designs with EL34 and EL84 power tubes. The cabinets all featured a unique style with different striping and two-tone coverings. Reinhardt also produced amps for each individual person, which means all models were custom built.

ELECTRIC TUBE AMPLIFIERS

Reinhardt's original and most popular amp is the **18** (Head Unit: last MSR $1,695, 1-12 Combo: last MSR $1,875). The **Titan** (Head Unit: last MSR $1,850, 1-12 Combo: last MSR $2,025) is the bigger brother of the 18 and features 36W of power from 4 X EL84 power tubes. The **Sentinel** (Head Unit: last MSR $1,950, Combo: last MSR $2,125) is based on Marshall's popular Bluesbreaker model of the late 1960s with KT66 power tubes. The **MI-6** (Head Unit: last MSR $1,695, 1-12 Combo: 1,875) is based on the chassis of the 18, except it uses 6V6 power tubes., The **Jester** (disc., last price for a Head Unit: last MSR $1,875) puts out about 40W from 4 X EL84 power tubes. The **Vintage 50** (Head Unit: last MSR $1,875, 1-12 Combo: last MSR $2,050) is based on Marshall's 50W models from the late 1960s and early 1970s. The **Vintage 100** (Head Unit: last MSR $2,295) features twice the power of the Vintage 100 and is based on Marshall's 100W heads. The **JKC 33** (Head Unit: last MSR $1,875, 1-12 Combo: last MSR $2,050) is based on the Vintage 50 chassis, but only puts out 33W that is designed for club use. The **Ampzilla** is Reinhardt's newest model (Head Unit: last MSR $1,875, 1-12 Combo: last MSR $2,050) is a high-gain amp. The **Storm** (Head Unit: last MSR $1,875, 1-12 Combo: last MSR $2,050) is based on Marshall's late 1970s and 1980s JCM-style amps. The **SHG** (Head Unit: last MSR $1,995, 1-12 Combo: last MSR $2,170) stands for Serious High Gain amp and it has two more gain stages than the Storm. The **Sonoma** (Head Unit: last MSR $2,795) is based on the Bluesmaster and Overdive amps built by Howard Dumble. The **Sultan** (Head Unit: last MSR $1,995, 1-12 Combo: last MSR $2,170) is based on a Trainwreck Liverpool model and was inspired by Mark Knopfler. The **Talyn** (Head Unit: last MSR $2,100) is another Knopfler-inspired amp based on the Trainwreck Rocket. The Mr. Clean is based on a Fender blackface Super and is available in 20W (Head Unit: last MSR $1,895), 40W (Head Unit: last MSR $1,995),

MSR/NOTES	100%	EXCELLENT	AVERAGE	LAST MSR

and 80W (Head Unit: last MSR $2,095) configurations. The Fat Albert was created to try and capture the sound from Jimmy Page playing at the Royal Albert Hall in 1970. It is available in 50W (Head Unit: last MSR $2,095) and 100W (Head Unit: last MSR $2,295) configurations. A **Bass amp** (Head Unit: last MSR $2,650) is also available.

Reinhardt offers a variety of speaker cabinet configurations with prices starting at $495 for 1-12 in. speaker, $695 for 2-12 in. speakers, and $995 for 4-12 in. speakers.

REVEREND

Amplifiers previously produced in Warren, MI between 1997 and 2005. Distributed by Reverend.

Joe Naylor and Dennis Kager left Naylor Engineering to start Reverend in 1997. Joe Naylor founded Naylor Engineering in the early 1990s, and produced several tube amplifiers. Dennis Kager had roots with Ampeg and worked with Joe at Naylor. Together they produced a tube amplifier at a workingman's price. In 2005, Reverend stopped producing amplifiers to focus on their guitar line. Originally, Naylor was a factory direct order company, which eliminated dealers, distributors, and other middle men. For more information on Reverend electric guitars, refer to the *Blue Book of Electric Guitars*.

ELECTRIC TUBE AMPLIFIERS

Goblin 5/15
courtesy Reverend

Hellhound 40/60 Combo
courtesy Reverend

Kingsnake 20/60 Combo
courtesy Reverend

GOBLIN 5/15 – 15W (switchable to 5W), 1-10 in. All-Tone 1025 speaker, tube chassis, preamp: 4 X 12AX7, power: 2 X 6V6, front black control panel, single input, seven black knobs (g, v, t, m, b, r, p), 3-position schizo switch, black vinyl covering, brown checkerboard grille cloth, 22 lbs., mfg. 2002-05.

	N/A	$325 - 400	$200 - 250	$749

• Add $45 for cover.

HELLHOUND 40/60 HEAD – 60W (switchable to 40W), head-unit only, all-tube chassis, preamp: 4 X 12AX7, power: 2 X 6L6, single channel, front black control panel, single input, schizo switch (US to UK), seven black knobs (g, v, t, m, b, p, r), effects loop, black custom tooled vinyl, gray/white peppered grille cloth, 24.5 lbs., mfg. 1997-2003.

	N/A	$375 - 450	$225 - 275	$849

HELLHOUND 40/60 COMBO – similar to the Hellhound in circuitry, has 1-12 in. Alltone 1250 speaker, 36 lbs., mfg. 1997-2003.

	N/A	$425 - 525	$250 - 325	$949

• Add $25 for cover.

KINGSNAKE 20/60 COMBO – 60W (switchable to 20W), 1-12 in. Jensen Neo 100 speaker, tube chassis, preamp: 4 X 12AX7, power: 2 X 6L6GC, front black control panel, single input, seven black knobs (g, v, t, m, b, r, p), 3-position schizo switch, black vinyl covering, brown checkerboard grille cloth, 32 lbs., mfg. 2004-05.

	N/A	$425 - 525	$250 - 325	$999

• Add $50 for cover.

SPEAKER CABINETS

112 GUITAR CABINET – 1-12 in. Alltone 1250 speaker, 8 Ohm, compact open back, black custom tooled vinyl, gray/white peppered grille, 24 lbs., mfg. 1997-2003.

	N/A	$175 - 225	$100 - 150	$399

• Add $20 for Blonde covering.

This cabinet matches up with the Hellhound 1-12 in. combo or head.

410 GUITAR CABINET – 4-10 in. Alltone 1030 speakers, 8 Ohm, compact open back, black custom tooled vinyl, gray/white peppered grille, 45 lbs., mfg. 1997-2002.

	N/A	$200 - 250	$150 - 175	$399

This cabinet matches the Hellhound head.

MSR/NOTES	100%	EXCELLENT	AVERAGE	LAST MSR

REX

Amplifiers previously produced circa 1930s-1960s. Distributed by Gretsch.

The Rex brand name has appeared on several amplifiers as well as electric guitars (Rex seems to be a very popular name for Japanese companies). The most notable Rex amps were budget brands that were probably built by some of the large amp suppliers including Harmony, Kay, and Valco. In the 1950s, Gretsch used Rex as their student/value model brand. Any further information on Rex amps can be submitted directly to Blue Book Publications.

RHINO

Amplifiers previously produced in El Paso, Texas, between 2000 and circa 2005.

Robert Turner founded Rhino in 2000 and was the president of the company. In 2002, Michael Spitzer started working with Rhino Amps as a technical advisor. A long time friend of Yngwie's and "gearhead guru" for his fanclub, Spitzer was also Yngwie Malmsteen's manager from 2000-02. It was during this time that plans were discussed to design a signature model amplifier based on Yngwie's specifications, which resulted in the Black Star YJM-50. Rhino produced high-wattage high-gain amplifiers that were available in either head or combo configurations. Unfortunately, broken promises and unreliable customer service ultimately led to Rhino's demise. There is no evidence that Rhino is still producing amplifiers currently, but there is no contact information. Reviews on Rhino amps detail the horror stories many users have experienced with customer service and wait times on amps. Unfortunately, no other information is available and any further info on Rhino can be submitted directly to Blue Book Publications.

ELECTRIC TUBE AMPLIFIERS

THE BABY RHINO – 100W (switchable to 50W), head-unit only, all tube chassis, preamp: 4 X 12AX7, power: 4 X 6V6, two channels, reverb, definition, front black control panel, single input, eight black knobs, effects loop, line out, speaker impedance control, black covering, black metal grille, mfg. circa 2000-05.

	N/A	$300 - 350	$150 - 200	$672

THE BAD BOY – 100W (switchable to 50W), head-unit only, all tube chassis, preamp: 5 X 12AX7, 1 X 12AT7, power: 4 X 6L6/EL34, two channels, reverb, definition, front black control panel, single input, nine black knobs, effects loop, line out, speaker impedance control, black covering, silver metal grille, mfg. circa 2000-05.

	N/A	$425 - 500	$250 - 300	$995

The Bad Boy had its own speaker cabinets available in 2-12 in. speakers (Last MSR $468) or 4-12 in. speaker (Last MSR $722) configurations.

* ***The Bad Boy Combo*** – similar to the Bad Boy Head, except in combo configuration with 2-12 in. speakers, mfg. circa 2000-05.

	N/A	$475 - 550	$275 - 325	$1,270

THE BEAST – 100W (switchable to 50W), head-unit only, all tube chassis, preamp: 5 X 12AX7, 1 X 12AT7, power: 4 X 6L6/EL34, two channels, reverb, front black control panel, single input, 13 black knobs, effects loop, line out, speaker impedance control, black covering, black metal grille, mfg. circa 2000-05.

	N/A	$425 - 500	$250 - 300	$1,060

The Beast had its own speaker cabinets available in 2-12 in. speaker (Last MSR $468) or 4-12 in. speaker (Last MSR $722) configurations.

* ***The Beast Combo*** – similar to the Beast Head, except in combo configuration with 2-12 in. speakers, mfg. circa 2000-05.

	N/A	$475 - 550	$275 - 325	$1,343

BLACK STAR YJM-50 – 50W, head-unit only, preamp: 4 X 12AX7, power: 2 X EL34, overdrive, noise reduction, and Powerator circuits, front silver control panel, single input, nine black knobs, black covering and black grille, mfg. 2002-05.

	N/A	$500 - 600	$300 - 350	$1,249

This model was available with 4-12 in. speaker cabinets.

* ***Black Star YJM-50 Combo*** – similar to the Black Star YJM-50 Head, except in combo configuration with 2-12 in. speakers, mfg. circa 2002-05.

	N/A	$550 - 650	$325 - 400	$1,343

THE TEXAS TONE RANGER – 100W (switchable to 50W), 2-12 in. speakers, guitar combo, all tube chassis, preamp: 5 X 12AX7, 1 X 12AT7, power: 4 X 6L6/EL34, two channels, reverb, definition, front black control panel, single input, 12 black knobs, effects loop, line out, speaker impedance control, brown covering, black metal grille, mfg. circa 2000-05.

	N/A	$550 - 650	$325 - 400	$1,421

The Texas Tone Ranger could use a 2-12 in. extension speaker cabinet (Last MSR $468).

| MSR/NOTES | 100% | EXCELLENT | AVERAGE | LAST MSR |

RICKENBACKER

Amplifiers previously produced in Santa Ana, CA between the 1930s and the late 1980s.

CONTACT INFORMATION
RICKENBACKER
3895 South Main Street
Santa Ana, CA 92707
Phone No.: 714-545-5574
Fax No.: 714-754-0135
www.rickenbacker.com
info@rickenbacker.com

The Rickenbacker company has been producing instruments that date back to 1931. In 1925, John Dopyera (and brothers) joined up with George Beauchamp and Adolph Rickenbacker. They formed National and started to build resonator guitars. Dopyera left the company and Rickenbacker, Beauchamp, and Dopyera's nephew, Paul Barth, started to build electric lap steel guitars. Beauchamp left in the late 1920s and the company was in the hands of Rickenbacker and Barth. In 1931, they started building aluminum versions of the electric Frying Pan prototype. Rickenbacker was added to the headstock around 1933, and the company was born. Shortly thereafter in the 1930s, amplifiers were introduced as companions to their new electric Hawaiian lap steel guitars. Rickenbacker produced various models in the 1930s and 1940s, but didn't introduce a formal amplifier line until circa 1953 with the M Series. This was the same time that F.C. Hall bought Rickenbacker. The M Series were widely popular and produced into the early to mid-1960s when they were replaced by the B Series. In the late 1960s, they introduced the odd Transonic series, which featured solid-state chassis. Various tube and solid-state models were produced in the 1970s and the TR Series appeared in the late 1970s. In the mid-1980s, Rickebacker bought the Road trademark (Bob Ross of Kustom fame) and produced amplifiers under Rickenbacker/Road. In the late 1980s, they produced the RG series of solid-state amps, which represented the last amplifiers by Rickenbacker. They currently focus on acoustic and electric models. For more information on acoustic guitars, refer to the *Blue Book of Acoustic Guitars*. For more information on electric guitars, refer to the *Blue Book of Electric Guitars*.

GENERAL INFORMATION/MISC. MODELS

Before Rickenbacker released the official M Series, they produced various amps in the 1930s and 1940s. These models include the M-10, M-11, and M-12 that all predated the first M series and feature wood cabinets, the Model 59, which was sold with the Model 59 Hawaiian steel, the 200A Rhythm amp, and a 1948 model that was sold with another Hawaiian model. After the TR series, the R Road series models were introduced in the mid-1980s. These amps are slightly based on the previous TR Series, but they feature the "Road" trademark that was owned by Bob Ross of Kustom fame. Rickenbacker produced their last line of amps in the late 1980s with the RG Series that were once again based on the previous TR and R model designs.

On early models, the number has nothing to do with the wattage of the amp. An "A" suffix usually indicates tremolo. A "D" suffix usually indicates a piggyback unit.

ELECTRIC TUBE AMPLIFIERS: B SERIES

Most of the models in the B Series were either carry overs or modified versions of the M Series, which can be seen by their similar model numbers. For example the M14A became the B-14A, the M-15 became the B-15, etc. The B-16 Supersonic is probably the most popular model because of its similarities to the Fender Bassman. In the 1970s, Rickenbacker introduced three new tube amplifiers: the B-115, B-212, and B-410. These had little to do with the 1960s models but were labeled part of the B Series anyway.

B-9 – ~5W, 1-10 in. Jensen speaker, three tube chassis, preamp: 1 X 7025, power: 1 X 6V6, rectifier: 5Y3, single channel, front control panel, four inputs, two gray knobs (v, tone), silver covering, silver grille cloth, mfg. mid-1960s.

| N/A | $400 - 500 | $275 - 325 |

* **B-9A** – similar to the B-9, except has a 12 in. Jensen speaker, tremolo circuit, four tube chassis (2 X 7025 preamp), and a tremolo speed control for a total of three knobs, mfg. mid-1960s.

| N/A | $400 - 500 | $250 - 300 |

B-14A – wattage unknown, 1-12 in. Jensen speaker, all-tube chassis, preamp: 3 X 12AX7, power: 2 X 6V6, rectifier: 5Y3, two channels, tremolo, front control panel, four inputs, five gray knobs (tone, s, d, v2, v1), silver covering, silver grille cloth, mfg. mid-1960s.

courtesy Savage Audio

courtesy Savage Audio

| N/A | $600 - 750 | $400 - 500 |

MSR/NOTES	100%	EXCELLENT	AVERAGE	LAST MSR

B-15 – wattage unknown, 1-15 in. Jensen speaker plus a tweeter, tube chassis, two channels, front control panel, four inputs, four gray knobs (v1, v2, b, t), silver covering, silver grille cloth, mfg. mid-1960s.

	N/A	$600 - 750	$400 - 500	

* **B-15A** – similar to the B-15, except has tremolo with speed and depth controls, mfg. mid-1960s.

	N/A	$675 - 775	$450 - 550	

»**B-15AD** – similar to the B-15A, except in piggyback configuration, mfg. mid-1960s.

	N/A	$700 - 850	$500 - 575	

* **B-15AE** – similar to the B-15, except has tremolo with speed and depth controls, and Ek-O-Tone with controls, mfg. mid-1960s.

	N/A	$600 - 750	$400 - 500	

* **B-15D** – similar to the B-15, except in piggyback configuration, mfg. mid-1960s.

	N/A	$650 - 775	$400 - 500	

B-16 SUPERSONIC – wattage unknown, 4-10 in. Jensen speakers, seven tube chassis, preamp: 3 X 12AX7, 1 X 12AU7, power: 2 X 6L6, rectifier: 5AR4, two channels, front control panel, four inputs, five gray knobs (v1, v2, b, t, Brillante), silver covering, silver grille cloth, mfg. mid-1960s.

	N/A	$750 - 900	$500 - 600	

* **B-16A Supersonic** – similar to the B-16 Supersonic, except has tremolo with speed and depth controls, and an eight tube chassis (4 X 12AX7), mfg. mid-1960s.

	N/A	$800 - 1,000	$550 - 650	

»**B-16AD Supersonic** – similar to the B-16A Supersonic, except in piggyback configuration, mfg. mid-1960s.

	N/A	$800 - 1,000	$550 - 650	

* **B-16AE Supersonic** – similar to the B-16 Supersonic, except has tremolo with speed and depth controls, and Ek-O-Tone with controls, mfg. mid-1960s.

	N/A	$850 - 1,050	$600 - 700	

* **B-16D Supersonic** – similar to the B-16 Supersonic, except in piggyback configuration, mfg. mid-1960s.

	N/A	$850 - 1,050	$600 - 700	

B-22D – wattage unknown, 2-15 in. speakers plus two tweeters, tube chassis, two channels, front control panel, inputs and controls unknown, silver covering, silver grille cloth, mfg. mid-1960s.

	N/A	$750 - 900	$500 - 600	

B-115 – wattage unknown, 1-15 in. speaker, bass combo, tube chassis, seven tube chassis, preamp: 2 X 7025, 1 X 12AT7, power: 4 X 6L6, solid-state rectifier, two channels, front silver control panel, four inputs, various knobs, black covering, black grille, mfg. 1970s.

	N/A	$500 - 600	$300 - 375	

B-212 – wattage unknown, 2-12 in. speaker, guitar combo, tube chassis, nine tube chassis, preamp: 3 X 7025, 1 X 12AT7, 1 X 12AU7, power: 4 X 6L6, solid-state rectifier, two channels, front silver control panel, four inputs, 12 knobs (Ch. 1: v, t, m, b, Ch. 2: v, t, m, b, r, s, i, MV), bright switches, black covering, black grille, mfg. 1970s.

	N/A	$500 - 600	$300 - 400	

B-410 – wattage unknown, 4-10 in. speakers, guitar combo, tube chassis, nine tube chassis, preamp: 3 X 7025, 1 X 12AT7, 1 X 12AU7, power: 4 X 6L6, solid-state rectifier, two channels, front silver control panel, four inputs, 12 knobs (Ch. 1: v, t, m, b, Ch. 2: v, t, m, b, r, s, i, MV), bright switches, black covering, black grille, mfg. 1970s.

	N/A	$600 - 750	$350 - 450	

ELECTRIC TUBE AMPLIFIERS: M SERIES

The M Series was produced between circa 1953 and the early 1960s (exact dates unknown).

M-8
courtesy John Beeson/The Music Shoppe

M-11
courtesy Working Man's Music

MSR/NOTES	100%	EXCELLENT	AVERAGE	LAST MSR

M-8 – ~5W, 1-8 in. speaker, all-tube chassis, preamp: 6AV6 (12AX7 or 12AU7 may have been used as well), power: 6V6, rectifier: 5Y3, single channel, back control panel, two inputs, single volume knob with on/off switch, gray covering, brown grille, 13.5 in. wide, 12.25 in. tall, 6.25 in. deep, mfg. circa 1957-early 1960s.

| | N/A | $425 - 500 | $300 - 350 | |

Some models may be covered in a cream Tolex with a brown handle.

M-11 – ~10W, 1-12 in. speaker, five tube chassis, preamp: 2 X 6SC7, power: 2 X 6V6, rectifier: 5Y3, two channels, top control panel, three inputs (mic, two inst.), three knobs (v1, v2, tone), gray covering, brown grille, mfg. early 1950s-early 1960s.

| | N/A | $600 - 750 | $400 - 450 | |

Early models have a square cabinet with rounded corners (18.5 in. wide, 16 in. tall, 9 in. deep), and later models have a wider, rectangular cabinet with sharp corners (22 in. wide, 16 in. tall, 9 in. deep).

* ***M-11A*** – similar to the M-11, except has a tremolo circuit, six tube chassis, tremolo speed control for a total of four knobs, and a one-button footswitch, mfg. circa 1956-late 1950s.

| | N/A | $650 - 800 | $450 - 550 | |

M-12 – ~10W, 2-12 in. speakers, five tube chassis, preamp: 2 X 6SC7, power: 2 X 6V6, rectifier: 5Y3, two channels, top control panel, three inputs (early models) or four inputs (later models), three knobs (v1, v2, tone), gray covering, brown grille, 26.5 in. wide, 18.5 in. tall, 9.75 in. deep, mfg. circa 1957-early 1960s.

| | N/A | $650 - 800 | $450 - 550 | |

M-14A – ~10W, 1-12 in. speaker, six tube chassis, preamp: 3 X 6SC7, power: 2 X 6V6, rectifier: 5Y3, two channels, tremolo, top control panel, four inputs, four knobs (v1, v2, tone, tremolo speed), gray covering, brown grille, 22 in. wide, 16 in. tall, 9 in. deep, mfg. circa late 1950s-early 1960s.

| | N/A | $650 - 800 | $450 - 550 | |

This model replaced the M-11A and in most respects it is exactly the same as the M-11A except has four inputs and a wider cabinet with square corners.

M-15 – wattage unknown, 1-15 in. Jensen speaker, seven tube chassis, preamp: 4 X 6SC7, power: 2 X 6L6, rectifier: 5AR4, two channels, top control panel, four inputs, four knobs (v1, v2, t, b), gray covering, brown grille, mfg. circa 1953-early 1960s.

| | N/A | $700 - 850 | $500 - 575 | |

Early models have a square cabinet with rounded corners (22.25 in. wide, 19.5 in. tall, 11.5 in. deep), and later models have a wider, rectangular cabinet with sharp corners (26.5 in. wide, 19.5 in. tall, 9.5 in. deep).

* ***M-15A*** – similar to the M-15, except has a tremolo circuit, eight tube chassis, tremolo speed and intensity controls for a total of six knobs, and a one-button footswitch, mfg. circa 1956-late 1950s.

| | N/A | $800 - 950 | $600 - 700 | |

M-16 BASS – ~50W, 4-10 in. Jensen speaker, seven tube chassis, two channels, top control panel, four inputs, four knobs (v1, v2, t, b), gray covering, brown grille, 26.5 in. wide, 21.5 in. tall, 8.5 in. deep, mfg. late 1950s-early 1960s.

| | N/A | $800 - 950 | $550 - 650 | |

M-22 – wattage unknown, 2-15 in. speakers, eight tube chassis, three channels, top control panel, six inputs (two normal, two bass, one Variable Reluctance High Fidelity Phono, one for high fidelity FM tuner or Crystal pickup), six knobs (v1, v2, v3, t, b, Brillante), gray covering, brown grille, optional leg extensions, 32.25 in. wide, 24 in. tall, 11.75 in. deep, mfg. late 1950s-early 1960s.

| | N/A | $700 - 850 | $450 - 550 | |

M-23 – wattage unknown, 3-12 in. speakers, eight tube chassis, three channels, top control panel, six inputs (two normal, two bass, one Variable Reluctance High Fidelity Phono, one for high fidelity FM tuner or Crystal pickup), six knobs (v1, v2, v3, t, b, Brillante), gray covering, brown grille, optional leg extensions, 32.25 in. wide, 24 in. tall, 11.75 in. deep, mfg. late 1950s-early 1960s.

| | N/A | $700 - 850 | $500 - 600 | |

M-30 EK-O-SOUND – wattage unknown, 1-12 in. Jensen speaker, 11 tube chassis, two channels, echo effect, top control panel, two inputs, six knobs (inst. Ch. v, echo Ch. v, echo input, secondary echo level, echo decay, tone), slanted rear cabinet, gray covering, brown grille, 22 in. wide, 21 in. tall, 10.5 in. deep, mfg. late 1950s-mid-1960s.

| | N/A | $3,000 - 3,750 | $2,000 - 2,500 | |

M-88 – ~5W, 1-8 in. speaker, three tube chassis, preamp: 6AV6 (12AX7 or 12AU7 may have been used as well), power: 6V6, rectifier: 5Y3, single channel, back control panel, two inputs, two knobs (v, tone), gray covering, brown grille, 18 in. wide, 15 in. tall, 8.25 in. deep, mfg. circa 1953-early 1960s.

| | N/A | $400 - 500 | $250 - 300 | |

MODEL 98 – wattage unknown, 3-8 in. Jensen speakers, five tube chassis, one top control panel with three knobs (v1, v2, tone), and pilot lights, one rear control panel with four inputs, accessory 110V outlet, input jack switch, gray covering, brown grille, 25 in. wide, 13.5 in. tall, 9 in. deep, mfg. circa 1955-early 1960s.

| | N/A | $650 - 775 | $400 - 500 | |

MSR/NOTES	100%	EXCELLENT	AVERAGE	LAST MSR

ELECTRIC SS AMPLIFIERS: TRANSONIC SERIES

Bob Rissi, who worked for Fender and designed their first solid-state amps, designed the Transonic Series for Rickenbacker in the mid- to late 1960s. These were not very popular at the time because of their complexity, price, and the fact that they were solid-state. Today, they are very collectible, and bring the most money of any Rickenbacker amps - tube or solid-state. A Transonic 70 without fuzz and basic controls and only 2-12 in. speakers was also available.

TRANSONIC 100 – 200W peak power, 1-15 in. or 2-12 in. speakers, guitar combo, solid-state chassis, two channels, fuzz, reverb, tremolo, top/rear wood grain control panel, top control panel features nine knobs (Ch. 1: v, t, b, trem. speed, trem. depth, r, Ch. 2: v, t, b), six Rick-O-Select tone selector switches (pierce, hollow, and mellow for each channel), fuzz on/off switch, UV meter, and eight lights for various functions, rear control panel features four inputs (two standard, two custom with brilliant switch), volume pedal jack, fuzz control, fuzz pedal footswitch input, Rick-O-Gain output, various power switches, black covering, multi-colored brown and green crisscross weave grille with Rickenbacker and Transonic logos, mfg. late 1960s.

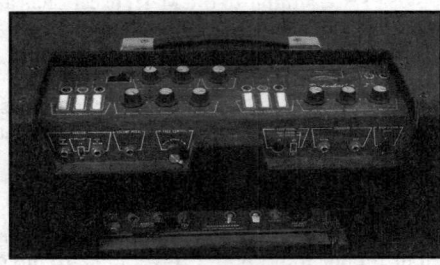

courtesy Dave Rogers/Dave's Guitar Shop

courtesy Dave Rogers/Dave's Guitar Shop

courtesy Dave Rogers/Dave's Guitar Shop

	N/A	$1,100 - 1,400	$750 - 900	

TRANSONIC 200 – 350W peak power, 2-15 in., 4-12 in., or 2-12 in. and 1-15 in. speakers, guitar piggyback configuration, solid-state chassis, two channels, fuzz, reverb, tremolo, top/rear wood grain control panel, top control panel features nine knobs (Ch. 1: v, t, b, trem. speed, trem. depth, r, Ch. 2: v, t, b), six Rick-O-Select tone selector switches (pierce, hollow, and mellow for each channel), fuzz on/off switch, UV meter, and eight lights for various functions, rear control panel features four inputs (two standard, two custom with brilliant switch), volume pedal jack, fuzz control, fuzz pedal footswitch input, Rick-O-Gain output, various power switches, includes metal cart/stand with wheels and allows the cabinet to tilt in various directions, black covering, multi-colored brown and green crisscross weave grille with Rickenbacker and Transonic logos, mfg. late 1960s.

	N/A	$1,400 - 1,700	$900 - 1,100	

ELECTRIC SS AMPLIFIERS: TR SERIES

The TR Series was produced between circa 1977 and 1984. They are all solid-state amps available in various configurations from 7W to 100W. The TR7 is a very popular practice/student amp in the used market.

TR7 – 7W, 1-10 in. speaker, guitar combo, solid-state chassis, tremolo, front black and silver control panel, two inputs, six knobs (v1, v2, t, b, s, i), black grained vinyl covering, black grille, mfg. circa 1977-1984.

	N/A	$125 - 175	$75 - 95	

TR14 – 14W, 1-10 in. speaker, guitar combo, solid-state chassis, reverb, front black and silver control panel, two inputs, six knobs (v, b, m, t, r, distortion), black grained vinyl covering, black grille, mfg. circa 1983-84.

	N/A	$150 - 200	$95 - 120	

TR25 – 25W, 1-12 in. speaker, guitar combo, solid-state chassis, reverb, tremolo, front black and silver control panel, two inputs, eight knobs (v, b, m, t, r, s, i, distortion), black grained vinyl covering, black or silver grille, mfg. circa 1979-1984.

	N/A	$300 - 375	$200 - 250	

TR35B BASS – 35W, 1-15 in. speaker, bass combo, solid-state chassis, front black and silver control panel, two inputs, four knobs (v, b, m, t), preamp in/out, black grained vinyl covering, black or silver grille, mfg. circa 1980-84.

	N/A	$300 - 375	$200 - 250	

TR50BH HEAD – 50W, head unit, bass configuration, solid-state chassis, two channels, front black and silver control panel, five inputs (one stereo), eight knobs (Ch. 1: v, b, t, Ch. 2: distort, b, m, t, v), black grained vinyl covering, black or silver grille, mfg. circa 1980-84.

	N/A	$200 - 250	$95 - 120	

* **TR50B Combo** – similar to the TR50BH Head, except in combo configuration with 1-15 in. speaker, mfg. circa 1980-84.

	N/A	$250 - 300	$120 - 150	

TR50GH HEAD – 50W, head unit, guitar configuration, solid-state chassis, two channels, front black and silver control panel, five inputs (one stereo), eight knobs (Ch. 1: v, b, t, Ch. 2: distort, b, m, t, v), black grained vinyl covering, black or silver grille, mfg. circa 1980-84.

	N/A	$200 - 250	$95 - 120	

MSR/NOTES	100%	EXCELLENT	AVERAGE	LAST MSR

* *TR50G Combo* – similar to the TR50GH Head, except in combo configuration with 4-10 in. speakers, mfg. circa 1980-84.

| | N/A | $250 - 300 | $135 - 175 | |

TR75GT – 75W, 2-12 in. speakers, guitar combo, solid-state chassis, two channels, front black and silver control panel, four inputs, 10 knobs (Ch. 1: v, b, m, t, Ch. 2: v, b, t, p, r, distortion), black grained vinyl covering, black or silver grille, mfg. circa 1977-1984.

| | N/A | $300 - 375 | $200 - 250 | |

TR100BH HEAD – 100W, head unit, bass configuration, solid-state chassis, two channels, front black and silver control panel, five inputs (one stereo), eight knobs (Ch. 1: v, b, m, t, Ch. 2: distort, b, m, t, p, v), black grained vinyl covering, black or silver grille, mfg. circa 1977-1984.

| | N/A | $225 - 275 | $110 - 140 | |

TR100GH HEAD – 100W, head unit, guitar configuration, solid-state chassis, two channels, front black and silver control panel, five inputs (one stereo), 10 knobs (Ch. 1: v, b, m, t, Ch. 2: distort, b, m, t, p, v), black grained vinyl covering, black or silver grille, mfg. circa 1977-1984.

| | N/A | $225 - 275 | $110 - 140 | |

* *TR100G Combo* – similar to the TR100GH Head, except in combo configuration with 4-10 in. speakers, mfg. circa 1977-1984.

| | N/A | $350 - 425 | $150 - 200 | |

* *TR100GT Combo* – similar to the TR100GH Head, except in combo configuration with 2-12 in. speakers, mfg. circa 1977-1984.

| | N/A | $350 - 425 | $200 - 250 | |

RISSON AMPLIFIERS

Amplifiers currently produced since the late 1990s or early 2000s in California. Previously produced in Orange County, CA between 1972 and the mid-1980s.

CONTACT INFORMATION
RISSON AMPLIFIERS
Phone No.: 714-743-9111
www.rissonamplifiers.com
rissonamplifiers@earthlink.net

Bob Rissi originally produced Risson amplifiers between the 1970s and 1980s in California. Rissi gained notoriety when he worked at Fender between 1961 and 1967 and designed their first solid-state amps. He also worked at Rickenbacker between 1967 and the late 1970s, and he designed the Transonic solid-state series. Even though these were not successful lines, they were way ahead of their time and it showed what Rissi could do. He produced both tube and solid-state models in a variety of configurations. The most popular Risson amp appears to be the LTA 120 head that was tube powered. Risson also produced solid-state amps that sounded very good - unlike many solid-state amps of that era. Notable players that currently use or have used Risson Amplifiers include Slash, Joe Walsh, Glen Campbell, Roger McGuinn, Rick Nelson, Al Perkins, Nikki Sixx, Rick Vito, Love Song, The Way, Parable, and Walter Egan. Rissi left the amp industry to pursue a career in computers in the mid-1980s. When Rissi stopped building, he had a supply of parts on hand that he put in storage. Recently, he decided to build a limited quantity of Risson amps with these old parts that are called the Marvell Series. For more information, visit Risson's website or contact him directly.

ELECTRIC TUBE AMPLIFIERS: MARVELL SERIES

Bob Rissi is currently building the Marvell Series of amps that are built out of parts he has had in storage for several years. There are two basic models offered in a half-stack configuration with a head and 1-12 in. speaker cabinet and a self-contained combo unit with a 1-12 in. speaker. Both models are available in two versions. The first version is entirely point-to-point wired and the second features a circuit board for the tone circuit but is otherwise entirely wired point-to-point. Features include 6W or 12W output, an all tube chassis (preamp: 2 X 7025, power: 2 X 6AQ5), single channel, two inputs, and six knobs (v, MV, t, m, b, p). The sound of the amp features a 1960 full-bodied tone with smooth overtones, a clean 1950s Tweed sound, and when pushed with Master Volume it sounds like a late 1960s/early 1970s British overdrive. The Marvell is available in the following configurations: Marvell Head point-to-point wired ($2,000), Marvell Head tone circuit board ($1,600), Marvell 1-12 in. Celestion speaker combo point-to-point ($2,800), and Marvell 1-12 in. Celestion speaker combo tone circuit board ($2,400).

* **Add $500 for 12W power amp.**
* **Add $550 for 4-8 in. speaker cabinet.**
* **Add $200 for JBL speakers (each).**

Marvell Combo
courtesy Risson Amplifiers

Marvell Combo
courtesy Risson Amplifiers

Marvell Head 48 with Cabinet
courtesy Risson Amplifiers

MSR/NOTES	100%	EXCELLENT	AVERAGE	LAST MSR

RIVERA

Amplifiers currently produced in Burbank, CA. Previously produced in Sun Valley, CA, Arleta, CA and Slymar, CA. The Rivera R&D trademark was established in 1976.

CONTACT INFORMATION
RIVERA
508 South Varney
Burbank, CA 91502
Phone No.: 818-767-4600
Fax No.: 818-394-2097
www.rivera.com
sales@rivera.com

Rivera R&D was founded by Paul Rivera in 1976. Paul started in a repair shop in New York City repairing amplifiers, and he also modified amplifiers for many famous musicians. In 1972, he moved to California where he continued to modify and started to help design new amplifiers. In 1976, Rivera Research Development & Co. was formed, and the first client of the company was Yamaha. Paul then worked with Fender in the early 1980s, trying to turn their amplifier division around. He designed the Super Champ, Concert, and Twin Reverb II for Fender.

In 1985, Paul began producing his own amplifiers, and the first design was the rack-mount TBR-1. Ever since then, amplifier production has expanded rapidly. They offer many products now, including combo amps, amp heads, and speaker cabinets. Not only does Rivera build quality components but they are built to withstand road wear. Paul's son, Paul Rivera Jr. works at Rivera now, and many members of their staff have worked there for many years. For more information, visit Rivera's website or contact them directly.

ELECTRIC TUBE AMPLIFIERS: GENERAL INFORMATION & TUBE RACK SERIES

Rivera has produced quite a few models over the years. Some of the models that have been recently discontinued include the Bonehead Series. This was a 100W head that was aimed to be built for a half or a full-stack. The Jake and Rake amps were also recently discontinued. Look for more information on these models and pricing in upcoming editions of the *Blue Book of Guitar Amplifiers*.

Rivera used to make a Tube Rack series that was known as the TBR series. TBR-1M, TBR-2SL, and the TBR-3 were some of the models that used to be available. The TBR-3 and TBR-5 were strictly power amps. There is more information on these out of production amps on the Rivera website.

Fandango 55W 212 Combo
courtesy Rivera

Knucklehead Reverb 55 Top
courtesy Rivera

Knucklehead Reverb 100
courtesy Rick Wilkiewicz

ELECTRIC TUBE AMPLIFIERS: FANDANGO SERIES

• Add $299 for balanced input for Taylor T5 guitar.

FANDANGO 55W TOP – 55W, guitar head-unit, seven-tube chassis, preamp: 5 X 12AX7, power: 2 X EL34, two channels, reverb, front black control panel, two inputs, 13 black knobs (v, b, m, t, MV per channel, r, p, focus), effects loop with level controls, three-button footswitch, available in Black, Blonde, British Vintage Green, Cobalt Blue, Ruby, or Two-Tone Palomino (brown/light brown) coverings, various grille cloth colors, current mfg.

MSR N/A	$2,099	$1,200 - 1,450	$800 - 950

* *Fandango 55W 112 Combo* – similar to the Fandango Top, except in combo configuration with 1-12 in. G12T-75 speaker, 65 lbs., current mfg.

MSR N/A	$2,299	$1,300 - 1,600	$900 - 1,050

* *Fandango 55W 212 Combo* – similar to the Fandango Top, except in combo configuration with 2-12 in. G12T-75 speakers, 73 lbs., current mfg.

MSR N/A	$2,499	$1,350 - 1,675	$950 - 1,100

* *Fandango 100W Top* – similar to the Fandango 55W Top, except has 100W output with 4 X EL34 power tubes, current mfg.

MSR N/A	$2,299	$1,300 - 1,600	$900 - 1,050

* *Fandango 100W 212 Combo* – similar to the Fandango 100W Top, except in combo configuration with 2-12 in. Celestion G12T-75 speakers, 80 lbs., current mfg.

MSR N/A	$2,699	$1,550 - 1,900	$1,050 - 1,250

FANDANGO 212 SPEAKER CABINET – unknown wattage, 2-12 in. Celestion G12T-75 speakers, closed back, available in Black, Blonde, British Vintage Green, Cobalt Blue, Ruby, or Two-Tone Palomino (brown/light brown) coverings, various grille cloth colors, disc. 2008.

	$799	$500 - 575	$325 - 400

MSR/NOTES	100%	EXCELLENT	AVERAGE	LAST MSR

FANDANGO 412 SPEAKER CABINET – unknown wattage, 4-12 in. Celestion G12T-75 speakers, closed back, available in Black, Blonde, British Vintage Green, Cobalt Blue, Ruby, or Two-Tone Palomino (brown/light brown) coverings, various grille cloth colors, disc. 2008.

	$999	$650 - 725	$400 - 475	

ELECTRIC TUBE AMPLIFIERS: KNUCKLEHEAD SERIES

- Add $250 for balanced input for Taylor T5 guitar.

KNUCKLEHEAD REVERB 55 TOP – 55W, head-unit only, all tube chassis, preamp: 5 X 12AX7, power: 2 X 6L6GC or EL34, three channels, reverb, front black control panel, single input, 17 black knobs (Ch. 1: g, t, m, b, MV, Ch. 2/3: Ch. 2 g, Ch. 3 g, b, m, t, Ch. 2 MV, Ch. 3 MV, All: Ch. 1 r, Ch. 2/3 r, sub level, focus, p), push/pull channel switches in the gain knobs, various other push/pull functions in knobs, back panel: effects loop with send level, return level, and loop blend, sub out, recording out, impedance selector switch, two speaker jacks, vintage/modern power class switch, output power switch, black covering, black metal grille, 36 lbs., disc. 2001.

	N/A	$1,200 - 1,500	$850 - 1,000	$1,495

* *Knucklehead Reverb 55 Top W/ MIDI* – similar to the Knucklehead Reverb 55, except has MIDI capabilities, mfg. 2003-present.

MSR N/A	$2,399	$1,400 - 1,750	$1,000 - 1,150	

* *Knucklehead Reverb 55 112 Combo* – similar to the Knucklehead Reverb 55 Top, except in combo configuration with 1-12 in. Celestion V-30 or G12T-75 speaker, current mfg.

MSR N/A	$2,899	$1,650 - 2,000	$1,150 - 1,350	

* *Knucklehead Reverb 55 212 Combo* – similar to the Knucklehead Reverb 55 Top, except in combo configuration with 2-12 in. Celestion V-30 or G12T-75 speakers, mfg. 2005-present.

MSR N/A	$3,099	$1,800 - 2,150	$1,200 - 1,400	

* *Knucklehead Reverb 100 Top* – similar to the Knucklehead Reverb 55 except has 100W output with 4 power tubes, disc. 2002.

	N/A	$1,300 - 1,600	$900 - 1,050	$1,795

» *Knucklehead Reverb 100 Top W/ MIDI* – similar to the Knucklehead Reverb 100, except has MIDI capabilities, mfg. 2003-present.

MSR N/A	$2,699	$1,550 - 1,900	$1,050 - 1,250	

» *Knucklehead Reverb 100 212 Combo* – similar to the Knucklehead Reverb 100 Top, except in combo configuration with 2-12 in. Celestion V-30 or G12T-75 speakers, current mfg.

MSR N/A	$3,099	$1,750 - 2,100	$1,250 - 1,450	

KNUCKLEHEAD REVERB II 100 TOP – 100W, head-unit only, all tube chassis, preamp: 5 X 12AX7, power: 4 X 6L6GC or EL34, three channels, reverb, front black control panel, single input, 12 black knobs, various boosts and knobs, black covering, black metal grille, mfg. 2002-05.

	N/A	$1,150 - 1,400	$750 - 900	

KNUCKLEHEAD K-TRÉ 55 REVERB 112 COMBO – 55W, 1-12 in. Celestion speaker guitar combo, seven-tube chassis, preamp: 5 X 12AX7, power: 2 X EL34, two channels, reverb, front black control panel, single input, 11 black knobs, various boosts and knobs, assignable effects loop, black covering, black metal grille, mfg. 2007-present.

MSR N/A	$2,399	$1,350 - 1,650	$950 - 1,100	

* *Knucklehead K-TRÉ 55 Reverb 212 Combo* – similar to the Knucklehead K-TRÉ 55 112 Combo, except has 2-12 in. Celestion speakers, mfg. 2007-present.

MSR N/A	$2,599	$1,450 - 1,800	$1,000 - 1,200	

KNUCKLEHEAD K-TRÉ 120 TOP – 120W, head-unit, guitar configuration, all tube chassis, preamp: 5 X 12AX7, power: 4 X EL34, two channels, reverb, front black control panel, single input, 11 black knobs, various boosts and knobs, assignable effects loop, black covering, black metal grille, mfg. 2006-present.

MSR N/A	$2,199	$1,250 - 1,500	$850 - 1,000	

* *Knucklehead K-TRÉ Reverb 120 Top* – similar to the Knucklehead K-TRÉ 120 Top, except has a reverb circuit, mfg. 2007-present.

MSR N/A	$2,399	$1,350 - 1,650	$950 - 1,100	

» *Knucklehead K-TRÉ Reverb 120 212 Combo* – similar to the Knucklehead K-TRÉ 120 Reverb Top, except is in combo configuration with 2-12 in. Celestion speakers, mfg. 2007-present.

MSR N/A	$2,699	$1,600 - 1,950	$1,100 - 1,300	

KNUCKLEHEAD K212 SPEAKER CABINET – unknown wattage, 2-12 in. Celestion Vintage 30 speakers, stackable enclosure, designed for use with Knucklehead head units and combos, black covering, gray grille, current mfg.

MSR N/A	$899	$525 - 600	$325 - 400	

KNUCKLEHEAD K412B/K412T SPEAKER CABINET – unknown wattage, 4-12 in. Celestion Vintage 30 speakers, straight front (K412B) or angled front (K412T), designed for use with the Knucklehead head-units, black covering, gray grille, current mfg.

MSR N/A	$1,099	$650 - 750	$400 - 475	

MSR/NOTES	100%	EXCELLENT	AVERAGE	LAST MSR

MICK THOMPSON SIGNATURE 100W KNUCKLEHEAD REVERB TOP (KR-7) – 100W, guitar head-unit, nine-tube chassis, preamp: 5 X 12AX7, power: 4 X EL34, three channels, reverb, front black control panel, single input, 17 black knobs, various boosts and knobs, voiced in conjunction with Paul Rivera by Mick Thompson of Slipknot, gray covering, black metal grille with "seven" logo in upper right corner, mfg. 2007-present.

| MSR N/A | $2,999 | $1,700 - 2,050 | $1,200 - 1,400 | |

MICK THOMPSON SIGNATURE KNUCKLEHEAD K412B-MT/K412T-MT SPEAKER CABINET – unknown wattage, 4-12 in. Celestion G12K100 speakers, straight front (K412B-MT) or angled front (K412T-Mt), designed for use with the Mick Thompson Signature Knucklehead head-units, gray covering, black cloth grille with a "seven" logo in the upper right corner, mfg. 2006-present.

| MSR N/A | $1,199 | $750 - 875 | $500 - 575 | |

ELECTRIC TUBE AMPLIFIERS: M/S PRO SERIES

All amps listed in this section are usually available on a custom built to order basis. Therefore, expect some variations in the following listings due to custom orders/modifications. The S120 amp is the only all-tube stereo amp available.

BM100-115DE M100 DUANE EDDY SIGNATURE COMBO – 100W, 1-15 in. JBL speaker combo, nine-tube chassis, preamp: 5 X 12AX7, power: 4 X EL34, two channels, slavemaster, reverb, front black control panel, two inputs, 15 black knobs (Ch. 1: v, b, m, t, MV, Ch. 2: v, t, m, b, MV, All: r, SM g, SM level, focus, p), effects loop with levels, slavemaster, disc. 2008.

| | $2,299 | $1,350 - 1,650 | $950 - 1,100 | |

M-60 TOP – 60W, guitar head-unit, seven-tube chassis, preamp: 5 X 12AX7, power: 2 X EL34, two channels, slavemaster, reverb, front black control panel, two inputs, 15 black knobs (Ch. 1: v, b, m, t, MV, Ch. 2: v, t, m, b, MV, All: r, SM g, SM level, focus, p), effects loop with levels, slavemaster, black Tolex covering with a gray grille or black carpet covering with a black metal grille, mfg. 1990-2008.

| | $1,699 | $1,050 - 1,250 | $675 - 800 | |

* **M-60 112 Combo** – similar to the M-60 Top, except in combo configuration with 1-12 in. Celestion G12T-75 speaker, mfg. 1990-2008.

| | $1,899 | $1,150 - 1,375 | $750 - 900 | |

* **M-60 410 Combo** – similar to the M-60 Top, except in combo configuration with 4-10 in. Eminence speakers, disc. 2008.

| | $2,099 | $1,250 - 1,500 | $850 - 1,000 | |

* **M-100 Top** – similar to the M-60 Top, except has 100W output and 4 X EL34 power tubes, mfg. 1990-2008.

| | $1,899 | $1,150 - 1,375 | $750 - 900 | |

»**M-100 112 Combo** – similar to the M-100 Top, except in combo configuration with 1-12 in. EV speaker, mfg. 1990-2008.

courtesy Rick Wilkiewicz

courtesy Rick Wilkiewicz

| | $2,199 | $1,300 - 1,600 | $900 - 1,050 | |

»**M-100 212 Combo** – similar to the M-100 Top, except in combo configuration with 2-12 in. Celestion G12T-75 speakers, disc. 2008

| | $2,299 | $1,350 - 1,650 | $950 - 1,100 | |

»**M-100 410 Combo** – similar to the M-100 Top, except in combo configuration with 4-10 in. Eminence speakers, disc. 2008.

| | $2,299 | $1,350 - 1,650 | $950 - 1,100 | |

S-120 TOP – 120W (2 X 60W stereo), guitar head-unit, ten-tube chassis, preamp: 6 X 12AX7, power: 4 X EL34, two channels, slavemaster, reverb, chorus, front black control panel, two inputs, 15 black knobs (Ch. 1: v, b, m, t, MV, Ch. 2: v, t, m, b, MV, r, SM g, SM level, chorus speed, chorus depth), several push/pull functions on various knobs, back panel: (one set of the following controls for each channel [power class switch, two speaker outputs, speaker impedance selector, line out switch], hum adjust, two footswitch jacks, effects loop two sends (regular, slavemaster) and three returns (slavemaster, A, B), black covering, gray grille, mfg. 1990-disc.

| | $2,099 | $1,250 - 1,500 | $850 - 1,000 | |

The S-120 Top was still produced by Rivera as of 2010, but was offered as a Reissue Limited Edition with a MAP/Street price of $2,999.

MSR/NOTES	100%	EXCELLENT	AVERAGE	LAST MSR

* **S-120 210 Combo** – similar to the S-120 Top, except in combo configuration with 2-10 in. Eminence speakers, disc. 2008.

| | $2,299 | $1,350 - 1,650 | $950 - 1,100 | |

* **S-120 212 Combo** – similar to the S-120 Top, except in combo configuration with 2-12 in. Celestion G12T-75 speakers, disc. 2008.

| | $2,399 | $1,400 - 1,750 | $1,000 - 1,150 | |

C112 SPEAKER CABINET – 80W, 1-12 in. Celestion G12T-75 speaker, 8 ohm mono impedance, open back cabinet, black covering, gray grille, disc.

| | $499 | $300 - 350 | $175 - 225 | |

C210 SPEAKER CABINET – 140W, 2-10 in. Eminence speakers, 4 ohm mono/8 ohm stereo impedance, open back cabinet, black covering, gray grille, disc.

| | $549 | $325 - 400 | $200 - 250 | |

C212 SPEAKER CABINET – 160W, 2-12 in. Celestion G12T-75 speakers, 4 ohm mono/8 ohm stereo impedance, open back cabinet, black covering, gray grille, disc.

| | $799 | $475 - 575 | $250 - 300 | |

C410 SPEAKER CABINET – 280W, 4-10 in. Eminence speakers, 8 ohm mono/16 ohm stereo impedance, open back cabinet, black covering, gray grille, disc. 2008.

| | $599 | $350 - 425 | $250 - 300 | |

ELECTRIC TUBE AMPLIFIERS: QUIANA SERIES

• **Add $299 for balanced input for Taylor T5 guitar.**

QUIANA 50W TOP – 50W, guitar head-unit, all tube chassis, preamp: 5 X 12AX7, power: 2 X 6L6, two channels, reverb, top black control panel, two inputs, 13 black knobs (Ch. 1: v, b, m, t, MV, Ch. 2: v, t, m, b, MV, All: r, p, focus), various push/pull controls on knobs, back panel: vintage/modern switch, two speaker jacks, line out jack, impedance selector switch, FS-7 footswitch jack, effects loop with send level and return level, available in standard Ruby covering or optional custom colors and standard Vintage blonde grille cloth or optional custom colors, current mfg.

| MSR N/A | $2,199 | $1,300 - 1,550 | $800 - 950 | |

* **Quiana 50W 112 Combo** – similar to the Quiana 55W Top, except in combo configuration with 1-12 in. Celestion Vintage 30 speaker, 65 lbs., current mfg.

| MSR N/A | $2,299 | $1,300 - 1,600 | $900 - 1,050 | |

* **Quiana 50W 212 Combo** – similar to the Quiana 55W Top, except in combo configuration with 2-12 in. Celestion Vintage 30 speakers, current mfg.

| MSR N/A | $2,499 | $1,400 - 1,750 | $1,000 - 1,150 | |

* **Quiana 50W 410 Combo** – similar to the Quiana 55W Top, except in combo configuration with 4-10 in. Eminence speakers, disc. 2008.

| | $2,299 | $1,350 - 1,650 | $950 - 1,100 | |

* **Quiana 100W Top** – similar to the Quiana 50W Top, except has 100W output with 4 X 6L6 tubes, current mfg.

| MSR N/A | $2,399 | $1,400 - 1,700 | $900 - 1,050 | |

» **Quiana 100W 212 Combo** – similar to the Quiana 100W Top, except in combo configuration with 2-12 in. Celestion Vintage 30 speakers, current mfg.

| MSR N/A | $2,699 | $1,550 - 1,900 | $1,050 - 1,250 | |

QUIANA 212 SPEAKER CABINET – unknown wattage, 2-12 in. Celestion Vintage 30 speakers, closed back, designed for use with the Quiana head unit and combos, disc. 2008.

| | $799 | $500 - 575 | $325 - 400 | |

QUIANA 412 SPEAKER CABINET – unknown wattage, 2-12 in. Celestion Vintage 30 speakers, closed back, designed for use with the Quiana head unit and combos, disc. 2008.

| | $999 | $650 - 725 | $400 - 475 | |

ELECTRIC TUBE AMPLIFIERS: R SERIES

THIRTY TWELVE (R30-112 COMBO) – 30W, 1-12 in. Celestion G12L-55 speaker guitar combo, seven-tube chassis, preamp: 5 X 12AX7, power: 2 X EL34, two channels, reverb, front black control panel, two inputs, 11 black knobs (Ch. 1: v, b, m, t, MV, Ch. 2: v, t, m, b, MV, All: r), various push/pull controls on knobs, back panel: two speaker jacks, line out jack, FS-7 footswitch jack, effects loop with send and return level controls, black covering, black grille cloth, mfg. 1993-2006.

| | $1,299 | $775 - 875 | $550 - 625 | |

FIFTY FIVE TWELVE (R55-112 COMBO) – 55W, 1-12 in. Celestion G12L-85 speaker guitar combo, seven-tube chassis, preamp: 5 X 12AX7, power: 2 X EL34, two channels, reverb, front black control panel, two inputs, 12 black knobs (Ch. 1: v, b, m, t, MV, Ch. 2: v, t, m, b, MV, All: r, p), various push/pull controls on knobs, back panel: two speaker jacks, line out jack, FS-7 footswitch jack, effects loop with send and return level controls, black covering, black grille cloth, mfg. 1993-2006.

| | $1,499 | $900 - 1,050 | $650 - 750 | |

MSR/NOTES	100%	EXCELLENT	AVERAGE	LAST MSR

HUNDRED DUO TWELVE (R100-212A COMBO) – 100W, 2-12 in. Celestion G12L-85 speakers, guitar combo, nine-tube chassis, preamp: 5 X 12AX7, power: 4 X EL34, two channels, reverb, front black control panel, two inputs, 12 black knobs (Ch. 1: v, b, m, t, MV, Ch. 2: v, t, m, b, MV, All: r, p), various push/pull controls on knobs, back panel: two speaker jacks, line out jack, FS-7 footswitch jack, effects loop with send and return level controls, black covering, black grille cloth, mfg. 1993-2006.

	$2,099	$1,350 - 1,550	$875 - 975	

ELECTRIC TUBE AMPLIFIERS: CLUBSTER/PUBSTER SERIES

CLUBSTER 25 110 COMBO – 25W, 1-10 in. Rivera Vintage Gold speaker guitar combo, four-tube chassis, preamp: 2 X 12AX7, power: 2 X 6V6GT, two channels, reverb, front black control panel, single input, 10 black knobs (Ch. 1: v, b, m, t, MV, Ch. 2: MV2, v, t, b, All: r, p), push/pull gain switch on Ch. 1 bass knob, push/pull channel switch on Ch. 2 v knob, push/pull bright switch on Ch. 2 treble knob, back panel: two speaker out jacks, line out jack, power amp in, preamp out, black covering, gray grille, mfg. 2005-present.

MSR N/A	$1,049	$625 - 725	$400 - 475	

* **Clubster 25 112 Combo** – similar to the Clubster 25 110 Combo, except has 1-12 in. Rivera Vintage Gold speaker, mfg. 2007-disc.

	$1,099	$675 - 800	$425 - 500	

* **Clubster 25 Doce 112 Combo** – 25W, 1-12 in. Celestion 70/80 speaker guitar combo, four-tube chassis, preamp: 2 X 12AX7, power: 2 X 6V6, two channels, reverb, front black control panel, two inputs, 10 black knobs, footswitch jack, top handle, metal corners, black covering, gray grille, current mfg.

MSR N/A	$1,100	$725 - 825	$350 - 450	

* **Clubster 45 112 Combo** – similar to the Clubster 25 110 Combo, except has 45W output, 1-12 in. Rivera Vintage Gold speaker combo, and 2 X EL34 power tubes, mfg. 2005-present.

MSR N/A	$1,249	$725 - 850	$475 - 550	

CLUBSTER ROYALE TOP – 50W, guitar head-unit, five-tube chassis, preamp: 3 X 12AX7, power: 2 X EL34, solid-state rectifier, two channels, reverb, front black control panel, two inputs, 10 black knobs (Ch. 1: v, b, m, t, MV, Ch. 2: v, t, b, All: r, p), various push/pull functions in the knobs, footswitch jack, power switch standby switch, rear panel: effects loop with return level, line out jack, external speaker jack, available in standard pearl white or black covering with a vintage gold grille or optional custom color coverings and grilles, mfg. 2009-disc.

	$1,299	$775 - 925	$500 - 575	

* **Clubster Royale 112 Combo** – similar to the Clubster Royale Top, except in combo configuration with 1-12 in. speaker, current mfg.

MSR N/A	$1,599	$1,050 - 1,200	$525 - 650	

PUBSTER 25 110 COMBO – 25W, 1-10 in. Rivera Vintage Gold speaker guitar combo, four-tube chassis, preamp: 2 X 12AX7, power: 2 X 6V6GT, two channels, reverb, front black control panel, single input, nine black knobs (v, g, b, m, t, MV1, MV2, r, p), push/pull boost switch on gain knob, back panel: two speaker out jacks, line out jack, power amp in, preamp out, black covering, gray grille, mfg. 2005-disc.

	$949	$550 - 650	$350 - 425	

* **Pubster 45 112 Combo** – similar to the Pubster 25 110 Combo, except has 45W output, 1-12 in. Rivera Vintage Gold speaker combo, and 2 X EL34 power tubes, mfg. 2005-present.

MSR N/A	$1,099	$675 - 800	$425 - 500	

ELECTRIC TUBE AMPLIFIERS: VENUS SERIES

The Venus 6 Series marks Rivera's first amplifier with Class A circuitry.

VENUS 3 15W TOP – 15W, guitar head-unit, class A four-tube chassis, preamp: 2 X 12AX7, power: 2 X 6V6GT, solid-state rectifier, single channel, reverb, front black control panel, single input, seven black knobs (Ch. 1: v, b, m, t, MV, r, p), various push/pull controls on knobs, back panel: vintage/modern switch, two speaker jacks, line out jack, impedance selector switch, assignable effects loop with send level and return level, available in standard pearl white or black covering with a vintage gold grille or optional custom color coverings and grilles, mfg. 2009-present.

MSR N/A	$1,500	$975 - 1,125	$500 - 600	

* **Venus 3 15W 110 Combo** – similar to the Venus 3 15W Top, except in combo configuration with 1-10 in. Celestion Vintage Gold speaker, mfg. 2009-present.

MSR N/A	$1,600	$1,050 - 1,200	$525 - 650	

* **Venus 3 15W 112 Combo** – similar to the Venus 3 15W Top, except in combo configuration with 1-12 in. Celestion G12H speaker, mfg. 2009-present.

MSR N/A	$1,800	$1,175 - 1,350	$575 - 725	

VENUS 5 30W TOP – 30W, guitar head-unit, class A seven-tube chassis, preamp: 5 X 12AX7, power: 2 X 6L6, solid-state rectifier, two channels, reverb, front black control panel, two inputs, 12 black knobs (Ch. 1: g, b, m, t, MV, Ch. 2: g, t, m, b, All: r, p), various push/pull controls on knobs, back panel: vintage/modern switch, two speaker jacks, line out jack, impedance selector switch, footswitch jack, assignable effects loop with send level and return level, available in standard pearl white or black covering with a vintage gold grille or optional custom color coverings and grilles, FS-7R footswitch included, mfg. 2009-present.

MSR N/A	$2,200	$1,425 - 1,650	$725 - 875	

MSR/NOTES	100%	EXCELLENT	AVERAGE	LAST MSR

* *Venus 5 30W 112 Combo* – similar to the Venus 5 30W Top, except in combo configuration with 1-12 in. Celestion G12H speaker, mfg. 2009-present.

| | $2,400 | $1,550 - 1,800 | $775 - 950 | |

* *Venus 5 30W 212 Combo* – similar to the Venus 5 30W Top, except in combo configuration with 2-12 in. Celestion G12H speakers, mfg. 2009-present.

| MSR N/A | $2,600 | $1,700 - 1,950 | $850 - 1,050 | |

VENUS 6 35W TOP – 35W, guitar head-unit, class A nine-tube chassis, preamp: 5 X 12AX7, power: 4 X 6V6GT, solid-state rectifier, two channels, reverb, front black control panel, two inputs, 13 black knobs (Ch. 1: v, b, m, t, MV, Ch. 2: v, t, m, b, MV, All: r, p, focus), various push/pull controls on knobs, back panel: vintage/modern switch, two speaker jacks, line out jack, impedance selector switch, FS-4 footswitch jack, assignable effects loop with send level and return level, available in standard pearl white or black covering with a vintage gold grille or optional custom color coverings and grilles, mfg. 2007-present.

| MSR N/A | $2,500 | $1,625 - 1,875 | $825 - 1,000 | |

* *Venus 6 35W 112 Combo* – similar to the Venus 6 35W Top, except in combo configuration with 1-12 in. Celestion G12H speaker, mfg. 2007-present.

| MSR N/A | $2,700 | $1,750 - 2,025 | $875 - 1,075 | |

* *Venus 6 35W 212 Combo* – similar to the Venus 6 35W Top, except in combo configuration with 2-12 in. Celestion G12H speakers, mfg. 2007-present.

| MSR N/A | $2,900 | $1,875 - 2,175 | $950 - 1,150 | |

VENUS DEUX 25W TOP – 25W, guitar head-unit, five-tube chassis, preamp: 3 X 12AX7, power: 2 X 6V6, one channel, reverb, front black control panel, one input, seven black knobs (v, t, m, b, reverb, focus, presence), various push/pull controls on knobs, back panel: two speaker jacks, line out jack, footswitch jack, power amp in, preamp in, black covering, top handle, metal corners, footswitch included, current mfg.

| MSR N/A | $1,300 | $850 - 975 | $425 - 525 | |

* *Venus Deux 25W 112 Combo* – 25W, 1-12 in. Eminence speaker guitar combo, five-tube chassis, preamp: 3 X 12AX7, power: 2 X 6V6, one channel, reverb, front black control panel, one input, seven black knobs (v, t, m, b, reverb, focus, presence), various push/pull controls on knobs, back panel: two speaker jacks, line out jack, footswitch jack, power amp in, preamp in, black covering, top handle, metal corners, footswitch included, current mfg.

| MSR N/A | $1,500 | $975 - 1,125 | $500 - 600 | |

VENUS 112 SPEAKER CABINET – 80W, 1-12 in. Celestion G12H, Vintage 30, or G12T-75 speaker, 8 ohm impedance, open back construction, available in standard pearl white or black covering with a vintage gold grille or optional custom color coverings and grilles, mfg. 2009-disc.

| | $599 | $350 - 425 | $200 - 250 | |

VENUS 212 SPEAKER CABINET – 160W, 2-12 in. Celestion G12H, Vintage 30, or G12T-75 speakers, 4 ohm mono or 8 ohm stereo impedance, open back construction, available in standard pearl white or black covering with a vintage gold grille or optional custom color coverings and grilles, mfg. 2009-disc.

| | $799 | $475 - 575 | $250 - 300 | |

ELECTRIC TUBE AMPLIFIERS: MISC. MODELS

CHUBSTER 40W – 40W, 1-12 in. Celestion G12L-55 speaker guitar combo, seven-tube chassis, preamp: 5 X 12AX7, power: 2 X EL34, two channels, reverb, front black control panel, two inputs, 12 black knobs (Ch. 1: v, b, m, t, MV, Ch. 2: Ch. 1: v, b, m, t, MV All: r, p), various push/pull controls on knobs, back panel: two speaker jacks, line out jack, FS-7 footswitch jack, effects loop with send and return level controls, available in standard Ruby covering or optional custom colors and standard Vintage blonde grille cloth or optional custom colors, 45 lbs., mfg. 2000-present.

| MSR N/A | $1,800 | $1,175 - 1,350 | $575 - 725 | |

* *Chubster 55W* – similar to the Chubster 40W, except has 55W output, 56 lbs., mfg. 2000-present.

| MSR N/A | $1,899 | $1,100 - 1,300 | $725 - 850 | |

SUPREMA 55W 112 COMBO – 55W, 1-12 in. Celestion Vintage 30 speaker guitar combo, seven-tube chassis, preamp: 5 X 12AX7, power: 2 X EL34, two channels, reverb, front black control panel, two inputs, 12 black knobs (Ch. 1: v, b, m, t, MV, Ch. 2: Ch. 1: v, b, m, t, MV All: r, p), various push/pull controls on knobs, back panel: two speaker jacks, line out jack, FS-7 footswitch jack, effects loop with send and return level controls, available in standard Black covering or optional custom colors and standard Tri-Tone Silver/Black grille cloth or optional custom colors, 70 lbs., mfg. 2000-disc.

| MSR N/A | $2,099 | $1,250 - 1,500 | $850 - 1,000 | |

* *Suprema 55W 115 Combo* – similar to the Suprema 55W 112 Combo, except has 1-15 in. speaker, mfg. 2000-01.

| | N/A | $1,250 - 1,500 | $850 - 1,000 | |

MSR/NOTES	100%	EXCELLENT	AVERAGE	LAST MSR

"JAZZ" SUPREMA 55 112 COMBO – 55W, 1-12 in. Celestion G12-80 speaker, jazz guitar combo, tube chassis, preamp: 12AX7s, power: 2 X EL34, solid-state rectifier, two channels, reverb, front black control panel, two inputs, 12 knobs (Ch. 1: v, b, m, t, MV, Ch. 2: v, t, m, b, MV, All: r, p), various push/pull knob functions, power switch, standby switch, rear panel: two speaker jacks, line out jack, footswitch jack, effects loop with send and return levels, brown leatherette covering, brown grille cloth, mfg. 2007-present.

| MSR N/A | $1,699 | $1,050 - 1,250 | $675 - 800 | |

"JAZZ" SUPREMA 55 115 COMBO – 55W, 1-15 in. Jensen Alnico speaker, jazz guitar combo, tube chassis, preamp: 12AX7s, power: 2 X EL34, solid-state rectifier, two channels, reverb, front black control panel, two inputs, 12 knobs (Ch. 1: v, b, m, t, MV, Ch. 2: v, t, m, b, MV, All: r, p), various push/pull knob functions, power switch, standby switch, rear panel: two speaker jacks, line out jack, footswitch jack, effects loop with send and return levels, brown leatherette covering, brown grille cloth, mfg. 2007-present.

| MSR N/A | $1,899 | $1,150 - 1,350 | $750 - 900 | |

ACOUSTIC/ELECTRIC TUBE AMPLIFIERS: SEDONA SERIES

- Add $299 for balanced input for Taylor T5 guitar.

SEDONA 55W TOP – 55W, guitar head-unit, seven-tube chassis, preamp: 5 X 12AX7, power: 2 X EL34, two channels, reverb, front brown control panel, two inputs (high gain/low gain), 14 black knobs (Ch. 1: v, b, m, t, MV, Ch. 2: v, b, m, t, MV, All: r, p, anti-feedback level, anti-feedback freq.), back panel: two speaker jacks, two tweeter jacks, impedance selector switch, FS-7 footswitch jack, effects loop with send and return level knobs, XLR direct line out with level control, Brown Tolex covering, Di-Tone Brown/Cream grille cloth, current mfg.

| MSR N/A | $2,200 | $1,425 - 1,650 | $725 - 875 | |

* *Sedona 55W 112 Combo* – similar to the Sedona 55 Top, except in combo configuration with 1-12 in. JBL speaker and a high-power dome tweeter, current mfg.

| MSR N/A | $2,599 | $1,550 - 1,900 | $1,050 - 1,250 | |

»*Sedona 55W C 112 Combo* – similar to the Sedona 55 112 Combo, except has 1-12 in. Celestion G12T75 speaker and a high-power dome tweeter, current mfg.

| MSR N/A | $2,599 | $1,450 - 1,800 | $1,000 - 1,200 | |

* *Sedona 100W Top* – similar to the Sedona 55W Top, except has 100W output and 4 X EL34 power tubes, current mfg.

| MSR N/A | $2,399 | $1,350 - 1,650 | $950 - 1,100 | |

»*Sedona 100W 115 Combo* – similar to the Sedona 100W Top, except in combo configuration with 1-15 in. JBL speaker and a high-power dome tweeter, disc.

| | $2,899 | $1,700 - 2,050 | $1,200 - 1,400 | |

SEDONA LITE – 55W, 1-12 in. Neodymium driver with a liquid-cooled dome tweeter, guitar combo, four-tube chassis, preamp:2 X 12AX7, power: 2 X EL34, two channels, reverb, front brown control panel, two inputs, 12 brown knobs (Ch. 1: v, t, m, b, Ch. 2: v, t, m, b, All: r, p, 2 anti-feedback level, anti-feedback freq.), back panel: two speaker jacks, effects loop with send and return level knobs, direct line out with level control, Brown Tolex covering, Di-Tone Brown/Cream grille cloth, mfg. 2005-present.

| MSR N/A | $1,900 | $1,225 - 1,425 | $625 - 750 | |

* *Sedona Lite 25W 110 Combo* – 25W, 1-10 in. Custom Rivera speaker with a liquid-cooled dome tweeter, guitar combo, four-tube chassis, preamp: 2 X 12AX7, power: 2 X 6V6, two channels, reverb, front brown control panel, two inputs, 12 brown knobs (Ch. 1: v, t, m, b, Ch. 2: v, t, m, b, All: r, p, anti-feedback level, anti-feedback freq.), back panel: two speaker jacks, effects loop with send and return level knobs, direct line out with level control, Brown Tolex covering, Di-Tone Brown/Cream grille cloth, current mfg.

| MSR N/A | $1,800 | $1,175 - 1,350 | $575 - 725 | |

SEDONA 112 SPEAKER CABINET – unknown wattage, 1-12 in. JBL speaker and a high-power dome tweeter, designed for use with the Sedona head unit and combos, brown covering, brown grille cloth, disc.

| MSR N/A | $949 | $575 - 675 | $375 - 450 | |

SEDONA 115 SPEAKER CABINET – unknown wattage, 1-15 in. JBL speaker and a high-power dome tweeter, designed for use with the Sedona head unit and combos, brown covering, brown grille cloth, disc.

| MSR N/A | $1,249 | $750 - 875 | $475 - 550 | |

POWERED SUBWOOFERS

LOS LOBOTTOM SUB 1 – 300W, 1-12 in. JBL powered subwoofer, black or blonde Tolex covering, silver/black or blonde grille cloth, disc. 2006.

| | $999 | $650 - 750 | $450 - 525 | |

LOS LOBOTTOM SUB 2 – 500W, 1-12 in. JBL powered subwoofer, black or blonde Tolex covering, silver/black or blonde grille cloth, disc. 2005.

| | N/A | $850 - 1,000 | $600 - 700 | |

K312 SUB 1 – 300W (Sub 1), 1-12 in. JBL powered subwoofer, 2-12 in. Vintage Celestion 30 Speakers, black or blonde Tolex covering, silver/black or blonde grille cloth, disc. 2005.

| | N/A | $850 - 1,000 | $600 - 700 | |

RMS AUDIO

Amplifiers previously produced overseas. Distributed in the U.S. by Musicorp in North Charleston, SC.

Revolutionary Media Systems (RMS) was a brand used by Musicorp (previously MBT International) that made a handful of guitar and bass amplifiers along with various other electronics. Originally, they built their speaker cabinets in the U.S.A, but other products are built overseas. Among their other products were P.A. mixers, microphones, and audio snakes. For guitar and bass amplifiers, they offered the Standard and Pro Drive Series. The Standard series were smaller wattage amps that were used more for the beginner and practice. The Pro-Drive series were sounded more for the performing musician. These amps were available in wattages up to 100 and chorus amps were available. Bass amps were also available in both series, and all products were priced competitively.

ROAD

Amplifiers previously produced in Fort Scott, KS during the mid-1970s.

Road amps was founded by Bob Ross of Kustom after he sold the company. Road Electronics, Inc. was located in Fort Scott, KS and they produced a variety of high-end solid-state amps. Rickenbacker bought Road in the early 1980s, and used their products/designs/jigs to produce Rickenbacker amps. Some amps feature both Road and Rickenbacker logos on the amp. Any further information on Road amps can be submitted directly to Blue Book Publications.

AMPLIFIERS

The Model 440-218 Bass that advertised "for the first time, solid-state design that provides true tube sound with transistor reliablity." The amp listed at $1,195, and features a separate head unit and speaker cabinet with 250W output.

ROCCAFORTE

Amplifiers currently produced in Brea, CA since 1993.

Doug Roccaforte was never satisified with the sound of most amps, and he started modifying them in order to make them sound better. His first attempts were usually Fenders that he would soup up into a Marshall chassis. The first amp was a 1978 or 1979 Marshall 50W Master Lead that he rebuilt with a completely different circuit. A friend named Mark Dickerson really liked the tone of the modified amp and told Doug that he thought he should be able to sell them. He started by building mainly custom orders, before Roccaforte really got going in the 1990s. Roccaforte currently has a full line of standard production amps. Endorsers include Cesar Rosas, Marc Ford, Steve Stevens, Ben Harper, and Billy Morrison. Doug is also a tube amp repairman. For more information, visit Roccaforte's website or contact him directly. Initial information courtesy of *Tonequest Magazine*, August, 2002.

CONTACT INFORMATION
ROCCAFORTE
678 Oleander
Brea, CA 92821
Phone No.: 949-981-6095
www.roccaforteamps.com
roccaforteamps@aol.com

ELECTRIC TUBE AMPLIFIERS

Roccaforte models include the **Custom 18**, **Custom 30**, **Custom 40**, **Custom 80**, **Denelle 45R**, **Hi-Gain 30**, **Hi-Gain 100**, **Jenelle 80/100**, and **Rockie 30** Head. Two speaker cabinets are also offered with 2-12 in. speakers and 4-12 in. speakers. Roccaforte also offered the Flame Series that are wood cabinets in an attractive solid flame maple wood, and custom inlay. In 2006, Roccaforte introduced the DRRS Head, which is available by custom order only.

ROCKTRON

Amplifiers currently produced in Battle Creek, MI since 1985. Rocktron is a division of the GHS corporation.

James Waller created Rocktron in 1985. Notable products include the HUSH Noise Reduction System, a line of DSP guitar rack products, and the Circle Surround stereo five-speaker matrix among other devices. In 2001, Waller sold Rocktron to GHS, and they currently produced a full line of tube, solid-state, and hybrid amplifiers. Effects pedals, preamps, and other devices are also available. For more information, visit Rocktron's website or contact them directly.

CONTACT INFORMATION
ROCKTRON
A division of GHS Corporation
2813 Wilber Ave.
Battle Creek, MI 49015
Phone No.: 800-388-4447
Fax No.: 800-860-6913
www.rocktron.com
info@rocktron.com

ELECTRIC TUBE AMPLIFIERS: VENDETTA SERIES

The Vendetta is the current tube series offered by Rocktron. This amp was designed by Bruce Egnator. It features a 100W output and EL34 output tubes. There are numerous controls on the amp, as it has four channels. It is available as a combo unit or a head unit that can be played through the matching 4-12 in. speaker cabinet (Vintage Celestion 30 speakers).

VENDETTA 100W HEAD – 100W, head-unit only, tube chassis, power: 4 X EL34, four channels, front chrome control panel, single input, 20 black knobs (Ch. 1&2: g1, g2, b, m, t, p, MV1, MV2, Ch. 3&4: g3, g4, b, m, t, p, MV3, MV4, All: MV, p, effects, density), MIDI footswitch, effects loop, black covering, metal grille, current mfg.

MSR $1,899 $1,580 $1,000 - 1,200 $675 - 800

MSR/NOTES	100%	EXCELLENT	AVERAGE	LAST MSR

VENDETTA 100W COMBO – 100W, 2-12 in. Vintage Celestion 30 speaker combo, tube chassis, power: 4 X EL34, four channels, front chrome control panel, single input, 20 black knobs (Ch. 1&2: g1, g2, b, m, t, p, MV1, MV2, Ch. 3&4: g3, g4, b, m, t, p, MV3, MV4, All: MV, p, effects, density), MIDI footswitch, effects loop, black covering, metal grille, disc. 2007.

	N/A	$1,100 - 1,350	$725 - 850	$1,999

VENDETTA 412 SPEAKER CABINET – 4-12 in. Vintage Celestion 30 speakers, straight or angled cabinet design, black covering, black cloth grille, current mfg.

MSR $799	$600	$375 - 450	$250 - 300	

ELECTRIC SS AMPLIFIERS: RAMPAGE SERIES

RAMPAGE R-10 – 10W, 1-6 in. Velocity speaker, solid-state chassis, front black control panel, single input, four black knobs (g, level, t, b), overdrive switch, headphone jack, black covering, silver grille, disc. 2006.

	$70	$40 - 50	$20 - 30	$99

RAMPAGE R-20 – 20W, 1-8 in. Velocity speaker, solid-state chassis, AGX technology, two channels, front black control panel, single input, seven black knobs (Ch. 1: g, level, Ch. 2: level, t, m, b, r), overdrive switch, headphone jack, black covering, silver grille, disc. 2006.

	$100	$60 - 80	$35 - 50	$159

RAMPAGE R-50C – 50W (2 X 25W stereo), 2-8 in. Velocity speakers, solid-state chassis, AGX technology, reverb, chorus, two channels, front black control panel, two inputs, 11 black knobs (Ch. 1: g, level, Ch. 2: g, level, t, m, b, p, r, chorus depth, chorus rate), headphone jack, footswitch, black covering, silver grille, disc. 2006.

	$200	$125 - 150	$70 - 90	$299

RAMPAGE R-50DSP – 50W, 2-8 in. Velocity speaker combo, solid-state chassis, DSP effects, two channels, front black control panel, two inputs, ten knobs (Ch. 1: g, level, Ch. 2: g, level, All: b, m, t, p, effects, speaker), CD input, black covering, 26 lbs., disc. 2005.

	N/A	$150 - 200	$95 - 120	$399

RAMPAGE R-80DSP – 80W, 1-12 in. Velocity speaker combo, solid-state chassis, DSP effects, two channels, front black control panel, two inputs, eight knobs (g, level, MV, b, m, t, effects mix, effects control), CD input, black covering, gray grille, 38 lbs., disc. 2005.

	N/A	$200 - 250	$120 - 150	$499

RAMPAGE R-120DSP – 120W, 2-10 in. Velocity speaker combo, solid-state chassis, DSP effects, two channels, front black control panel, two inputs, eight knobs (g, level, MV, b, m, t, effects mix, effects control), CD input, black covering, gray grille, 45 lbs., disc. 2005.

	N/A	$250 - 300	$135 - 175	$559

RAMPAGE RT-80 – 80W, 1-12 in. Velocity speaker combo, solid-state chassis, two channels, reverb, front black control panel, two inputs, seven knobs (Ch. 1 g, Ch. 2 g, MV, r, b, m, t), chromatic tuner, effects loop, headphone jack, black covering, gray grille, 38 lbs., disc. 2006.

	$280	$150 - 200	$95 - 125	$399

RAMPAGE RT-122C – 120W (60W per side stereo), 2-12 in. Velocity speaker combo, solid-state chassis, two channels, reverb, chorus, front black control panel, two inputs, nine knobs (Ch. 1 g, Ch. 2 g, MV, r, rate, depth, b, m, t), chromatic tuner, effects loop, headphone jack, black covering, gray grille, 55 lbs., disc. 2005.

	N/A	$275 - 325	$150 - 200	$579

ELECTRIC SS AMPLIFIERS: REPLITONE SERIES

The Replitone series are Rocktron's modeling amplifiers. They are strictly solid-state amps with no tube circuits, just digital technology.

REPLITONE 112 – 60W, 1-12 in. speaker, solid-state chassis with Digital Tube Replication (DTR) technology, front black control panel, single input, 12 black knobs (MV, preset, amp selector, g, l, b, m, t, r, delay, effect level, effect select, 30 programmable presets, MIDI interface, stereo 24-bit digital effects, 16 amplifier mods, black covering, silver grille, disc. 2007.

	$500	$350 - 425	$200 - 250	$799

REPLITONE 212 – 120W (2 x 60 stereo), 2-12 in. speakers, solid-state chassis with Digital Tube Replication (DTR) technology, front black control panel, single input, 12 black knobs (MV, preset, amp selector, g, l, b, m, t, r, delay, effect level, effect select, 30 programmable presets, MIDI interface, stereo 24-bit digital effects, 16 amplifier mods, black covering, silver grille, disc. 2007.

	$650	$450 - 525	$275 - 350	$999

ELECTRIC BASS SS AMPLIFIERS: RAMPAGE SERIES

RAMPAGE BASS 10 – 10W, 1-5.5 in. speaker, practice guitar combo, solid-state chassis, single channel, front black control panel, single input, three knobs (v, t, b), headphone jack, CD/MP3 aux. input jack, power switch, black covering, black grille, mfg. 2007-disc.

	$70	$40 - 55	$20 - 30	$109

RAMPAGE BASS 15 – 15W, 1-7 in. speaker, practice bass combo, solid-state chassis, single channel, front black control panel, single input, four knobs (v, b, m, t), headphone jack, CD/MP3 aux. input jack, power switch, black covering, black grille, mfg. 2007-disc.

	$90	$55 - 70	$30 - 40	$135

MSR/NOTES	100%	EXCELLENT	AVERAGE	LAST MSR

RAMPAGE BASS 20 (RB-20) – 20W, 1-8 in. speaker combo, solid-state chassis, single channel, front black control panel, single input, five knobs (MV, t, m, b, p), line out, headphone jack, black covering, gray grille (disc. 2005) or black grille (2006-disc.), disc.

	$130	$80 - 100	$50 - 65	$189

RAMPAGE BASS 30 (RB-30) – 30W, 1-10 in. speaker combo, solid-state chassis, single channel, front black control panel, single input, five knobs (MV, t, m, b, p), line out, headphone jack, black covering, gray grille (disc. 2005) or black grille (2006-disc.), disc.

	$160	$95 - 120	$60 - 75	$239

RAMPAGE BASS 60 (RB-60) – 60W, 1-12 in. speaker combo, solid-state chassis, single channel, front black control panel, two inputs, six knobs (g, t, m1, m2, b, MV), line out, headphone jack, black covering, gray grille (disc. 2005) or black grille (2006-disc.), disc.

	$230	$130 - 170	$80 - 105	$329

RAMPAGE BASS 100 (RB-100) – 100W, 1-15 in. speaker combo with a tweeter, solid-state chassis, single channel, front black control panel, two inputs, six knobs (g, t, m1, m2, b, MV), line out, headphone jack, black covering, gray grille (disc. 2005) or black grille (2006-present), current mfg.

MSR $618	$400	$270 - 300	$135 - 165	

BASS 200 – 200W, 1-15 in. speaker, bass combo, solid-state chassis, single channel, front silver control panel, two inputs, nine knobs (g, shape, b, m/l, m, m/h, h, compressor, MV), deep switch, bright switch, EQ bypass switch, compressor on/off switch, effects loop, line out jack, power switch, black covering, black grille, mfg. 2006-present.

MSR $830	$550	$350 - 425	$180 - 220	

RODGERS AMPLIFIERS

Amplifiers currently produced in Naples, FL since 1993.

Larry Rodgers founded Rodgers Amplifiers in 1993. He builds hand-made tube amps, constructs vintage cabinets, and restores vintage amps. He has a full supply of electronic parts, sound boards, coverings, and speakers in stock. For more information, contact Rodgers directly.

CONTACT INFORMATION
RODGERS AMPLIFIERS
3824 Exchange Ave.
Naples, FL 34104
Phone No.: 239-649-8799
www.rodgersamplifiers.com
ljrodgers@embarqmail.com

ROGUE

Instruments currently produced in China and/or Korea since the mid-1990s. Distributed by Musician's Friend in Medford, OR.

Musician's Friend distributes a full line of guitars, amplifiers, and other music related products through their mail order catalog. Musician's Friend introduced Rogue as their imported trademark on a line of guitars and amplifiers. For further information, visit Musician's Friend's website or contact them directly.

CONTACT INFORMATION
ROGUE
PO Box 4370
Medford, OR 97501
Phone No.: 800-391-8762
www.musiciansfriend.com

ELECTRIC GUITAR AMPLIFIERS

GS-50R – 50W, 1-12 in. speaker, solid-state chassis, reverb, two channels, front silver control panel, two inputs, nine black knobs (Ch. 1: g, v, Ch. 2: g, v, t, m, b, p, r), effects loop, headphone jack, black covering, black grille, 40 lbs., disc.

	$175	$100 - 130	$50 - 75	$380

GS-100R – 100W, 2-12 in. speaker, solid-state chassis, reverb, two channels, front silver control panel, two inputs, nine black knobs (Ch. 1: g, v, Ch. 2: g, v, t, m, b, p, r), effects loop, headphone jack, black covering, black grille, 65 lbs., disc.

	$225	$120 - 150	$70 - 90	$480

RG65R – 65W, 1-12 in. speaker, solid-state chassis, reverb, two channels, front black control panel, two inputs, eight black knobs (v1, g, v2, t, m, b, r, MV), bright switch, boost switch, effects loop, black covering, black grille, 43 lbs., disc.

	$200	$150 - 175	$80 - 110	$399

RG120R – 120W, 2-12 in. speaker, solid-state chassis, reverb, two channels, front black control panel, two inputs, eight black knobs (v1, g, v2, t, m, b, r, MV), bright switch, boost switch, effects loop, black covering, black grille, disc.

	$250	$150 - 190	$95 - 125	$499

ROLAND

Amplifiers and other audio equipment currently produced in Japan and China since 1974. Roland Amplifiers are distributed in the U.S. by Roland Corporation U.S. in Los Angeles, CA.

The Roland company was founded in Japan in 1974. They are known as one of the premier synthesizer builders in the world today. They started out with keyboards and other synthesizers and later moved on to building amplifiers and guitars. They have produced a number of amplifiers over the years in a different variety of applications. One of Roland's designs was to build a guitar with a synthesizer sort of built into it. This worked with a guitar with 10 buttons on it that plugged into a Roland unit where the sounds

CONTACT INFORMATION
ROLAND
5100 S. Eastern Ave.
Los Angeles, CA 90040-2938
Phone No.: 323-890-3700
Fax No.: 323-890-3701
www.rolandus.com

MSR/NOTES	100%	EXCELLENT	AVERAGE	LAST MSR

could be processed. The problem with this is that you would have to buy both the guitar and synthesizer together as a package for either one to work.

Today Roland produces several items in the music industry. They produce amplifiers, mixers, digital drum sets, effects, pedals, and other products. They have produced both tube and solid-state amps during the 1980s and 1990s. At the 2002 Summer NAMM show, Roland re-released their Cube 15 and their Cube 30, which are little solid-state guitar amps, but the effects on them are unbelievable. For more information, visit Roland's website or contact them directly.

ELECTRIC TUBE AMPLIFIERS: BOLT SERIES

BOLT-30 – 30W, 1-12 in. speaker, tube chassis, preamp: 12AT7, power: 2 X 7391, reverb, two channels, front black control panel, two inputs, eight black knobs (v1, v2, MV, v3, b, m, t, r), effects loop, black vinyl covering, brown grille, mfg. 1980s.

	N/A	$200 - 250	$120 - 150	

Part of the preamp stage is solid-state as well as the single 12AT7. The tube drives the reverb, while the rest is solid-state.

BOLT-60 – 60W, 1-12 in. speaker, tube chassis, preamp: 12AT7, power: 2 X 6L6, reverb, two channels, front black control panel, two inputs, eight black knobs (v1, v2, MV, v3, b, m, t, r), effects loop, black vinyl covering, brown grille, mfg. 1980s.

	N/A	$250 - 300	$150 - 200	

Part of the preamp stage is solid-state as well as the single 12AT7. The tube drives the reverb, while the rest is solid-state.

BOLT-100 – 100W (switchable to 60W), 1-12 in. speaker, tube chassis, preamp: 12AT7, power: 4 X 6L6, reverb, two channels, front black control panel, two inputs, nine black knobs (v1, v2, MV, v3, b, m, t, p, r), effects loop, black vinyl covering, brown grille, mfg. 1980s.

	N/A	$300 - 350	$175 - 225	

Part of the preamp stage is solid-state as well as the single 12AT7. The tube drives the reverb, while the rest is solid-state.

ELECTRIC SS AMPLIFIERS: CUBE SERIES

Roland has produced the Cube series in two different eras, but they are essentially the same amplifiers with the same purpose. The first series of the Cube was produced from the late 1970s until sometime in the 1980s and had a brown covering. At the Summer 2002 NAMM show, they reintroduced the Cube series with the Cube 30. In 2003 and 2004 they have expanded the series to several models and this time they have a black covering. In 2006, the Cube 15, Cube 20, and Cube 30 were all upgraded with the new power squeezer switch and received an X model suffix.

Cube-01
courtesy Roland

Cube 10GX
courtesy Roland

Cube 20XL Bass
courtesy Roland

CUBE-01 – 10W, 1-8 in. speaker, guitar combo, solid-state chassis, one channel, three COSM amp models, top control panel, single input, six knobs (g, v, b, m, t, r), power switch, rear panel: recording out/headphone jack, aux. in jack, top handle, black covering, silver metal grille, 10.375 lbs., mfg. 2015-present.

MSR $149	$120	$80 - 90	$40 - 50	

CUBE 10GX – 10W, 1-8 in. speaker, guitar combo, solid-state chassis, one channel, three COSM amp models, EFX section, top control panel, single input, six knobs (g, v, b, m, t, EFX selector, power switch, rear panel: recording out/headphone jack, aux. in jack, top handle, black covering, silver metal grille, 10.375 lbs., mfg. 2014-present.

MSR $169	$130	$85 - 100	$40 - 50	

CUBE 15(X) – 15W, 1-8 in. speaker, solid-state combo, two channels, overdrive, distortion, metal and metal stack sounds, 3-band equalizer, black covering, top control panel, black grille, mfg. 2002-disc.

	$99	$60 - 80	$40 - 50	$139

In 2006, a power squeeze switch was introduced (Model Cube 15X).

CUBE 20 – 20W, 1-8 in. speaker, solid-state chassis, reverb, two channels, top black control panel, two inputs, six black knobs (v, t, m, b, r, MV), brown covering, black grille, mfg. late 1970s-1980s.

	N/A	$135 - 175	$85 - 110	

MSR/NOTES	100%	EXCELLENT	AVERAGE	LAST MSR

Cube 30(X)
courtesy Dave Rogers/Dave's Guitar Shop

Cube 60 (Recent Mfg)
courtesy Roland

Cube 60XL Bass
courtesy Roland

CUBE 20X(GX) – 20W, 1-8 in. speaker, solid-state combo, two channels, DSP circuit, six COSM guitar amp models, EFX section, top control panel, single input, nine knobs (v, b, m, t, EFX select/level, delay/reverb, COSM select, g, v), Power Squeezer switch, optional footswitch, black covering, top control panel, silver metal grille, mfg. 2006-present.

| MSR $255 | $200 | $110 - 140 | $60 - 85 | |

In 2013, the Cube 20X was upgraded to the Cube 20GX with IOS connectivity via the i-CUBE LINK.

CUBE 20XL BASS – 20W, 1-8 in. speaker, solid-state bass combo, one channel, six COSM bass amp models, EFX section, top control panel, single input, nine knobs (comp/drive, b, m, t, EFX select/level, delay/reverb, COSM select, g, v), tuner switch, shape switch, Power Squeezer switch, recording out/phone jack, optional footswitch, top handle, black covering, top control panel, black metal grille, 20.72 lbs., mfg. 2011-present.

| MSR $265 | $220 | $145 - 165 | $70 - 90 | |

CUBE 30(X) – 30W, 1-10 in. speaker, solid-state combo, two channels, DSP circuit, 8 COSM guitar amp models, EFX section, top control panel, single input, nine knobs, black covering, top control panel, silver metal grille, mfg. 2002-disc.

| | $260 | $140 - 180 | $90 - 115 | $345 |

In 2006, a power squeeze switch was introduced (Model Cube 30X).

CUBE 30 BASS – 30W, 1-10 in. speaker, solid-state chassis, DSP circuit, 7 COSM bass amp models, top control panel, black covering, black metal grille, 20.5 lbs., mfg. 2003-disc.

| | $300 | $175 - 225 | $110 - 140 | $353 |

CUBE 40 – 40W, 1-10 in. speaker, solid-state combo, two channels, various knobs and buttons, effects loop, black covering, black grille, mfg. late 1970s-1980s.

| | N/A | $175 - 225 | $110 - 140 | |

CUBE 40GX – 40W, 1-10 in. speaker, guitar combo, solid-state chassis, three channels, 10 COSM amp models, EFX section, top control panel, single input, 11 knobs (Clean Ch. v, Lead Ch. g, v, All: b, m, t, EFX selector, delay/looper selector, r, amp selector, MV), clean switch, lead switch, solo switch, tuner mute switch, i-cube link input, rear panel: two footswitch jacks, recording out/headphone jack, top handle, black covering, silver metal grille, 20.75 lbs., mfg. 2013-present.

| MSR $323 | $250 | $165 - 190 | $80 - 100 | |

CUBE 60 – 60W, 1-12 in. speaker, solid-state combo, two channels, top control panel, two inputs, seven knobs (g1, g2, MV, b, m, t, r), effects loop, gray covering, black grille, mfg. late 1970s-1980s.

| | N/A | $225 - 275 | $120 - 150 | |

CUBE 60 (RECENT MFG) – 60W, 1-12 in. speaker, solid-state chassis, two channels, DSP circuit, 9 COSM amp models, EFX section, top control panel, 10 knobs, black covering, silver metal grille, 32 lbs., mfg. 2004-08.

| | $400 | $225 - 275 | $135 - 175 | $499 |

CUBE 60XL BASS – 60W, 1-10 in. speaker, solid-state bass combo, one channel, eight COSM bass amp models, EFX section, top control panel, single input, 11 knobs (comp/drive, b, m, t, EFX select/level, delay/looper, reverb, COSM select, g, v, solo v), tuner switch, shape switch, Power Squeezer switch, recording out/phone jack, three footswitch jacks, line out jack, DI XLR out, aux. in, top handle, black covering, top control panel, black metal grille, 35.71 lbs., mfg. 2011-present.

| MSR $533 | $400 | $260 - 300 | $130 - 160 | |

CUBE 80X(GX) – 80W, 1-12 in. speaker, guitar combo, solid-state chassis, two channels, DSP circuit, 10 COSM amp models, EFX section, top control panel, single input, 12 knobs (Clean Ch. v, Lead Ch. g, v, All: b, m, t, p, EFX selector, delay/looper selector, r, amp selector, MV), tap switch, clean ch. bright switch, tuner mute switch, channel switch, solo switch, rear panel: three footswitch jacks with selector switch, external speaker jack, recording out/headphone jack, line out jack, aux. in jack, black covering, silver metal grille, mfg. 2009-present.

| MSR $529 | $400 | $225 - 275 | $135 - 175 | |

In 2013, this model was upgraded to the GX version which includes i-CUBE LINK interface for IOS connectivity.

MSR/NOTES	100%	EXCELLENT	AVERAGE	LAST MSR

Cube 100 Bass
courtesy Roland

Cube 120XL Bass
courtesy Roland

Cube Street EX
courtesy Roland

CUBE 100 – 100W, 1-12 in. speaker, solid-state chassis, two channels, top-mounted control panel, various knobs, brown covering, black grille, mfg. late 1970s-1980s.

	N/A	$250 - 300	$150 - 200	

CUBE 100 BASS – 100W, 1-12 in. speaker, solid-state chassis, DSP circuit, 8 COSM bass amp models, top control panel, single input, ten knobs, black covering, black metal grille, 37.5 lbs., mfg. 2004-disc.

	$450	$275 - 325	$150 - 200	$603

CUBE 120XL BASS – 120W, 1-12 in. speaker, solid-state bass combo, one channel, eight COSM bass amp models, EFX section, top control panel, single input, 12 knobs (comp/drive, b, low-m, high-m, t, EFX select/level, delay/looper, reverb, COSM select, g, v, solo v), tuner switch, shape switch, recording out/phone jack, three footswitch jacks, ext. speaker jack, DI XLR out, aux. in, top handle, black covering, top control panel, black metal grille, 43.43 lbs., mfg. 2011-present.

MSR $792	$600	$400 - 450	$195 - 240	

CUBE LITE – 10W, 3-3 in. speaker, solid-state chassis, three COSM guitar amp models, top control panel, single input, five knobs, headphone jack, aux. in, i-Cube link, available in black with silver grille, 3.75 lbs., mfg. 2013-present.

MSR $221	$170	$110 - 130	$55 - 70	

CUBE STREET – 5W (2 X 2.5W stereo), 2-6.5 in. speakers, stereo practice guitar combo, solid-state chassis, two channels (mic/line and guitar/instrument), six digital effects, eight COSM guitar amp models, top control panel, two inputs (one per channel), 12 knobs (Ch. 1: v, b, t, delay/reverb, Ch. 2: amp selector, g, v, b, m, t, EFX selector, delay/reverb), mic/line input selector, onboard tuner/tuner mute switch, stereo aux. in jack, headphone jack, power switch, rear panel: two footswitch jacks, operates on both AC or battery power, available in black or red covering, silver metal grille, 11.5 lbs., mfg. 2009-present.

MSR $408	$300	$195 - 225	$100 - 120	

CUBE STREET EX – 50W, 2-8 in. speakers, battery powered guitar combo and PA, solid-state chassis, four channels, digital effects, five COSM guitar amp models, top control panel, two inputs, 14 knobs, stereo line in jacks, headphone jack, aux. in jack, stereo line out jacks, power switch, rear panel: two footswitch jacks, operates on both AC or battery power, available in black covering, silver metal grille, 16.4 lbs., mfg. 2014-present.

MSR $699	$500	$325 - 375	$165 - 200	

MICROCUBE(GX) – 2W, 1-5 in. speaker, solid-state chassis, DSP circuit, 7 COSM guitar amp models, top control panel, single input, six knobs, headphone jack, runs on both AC or battery power, available in black, red (2007-present), or white (2007-present) covering, silver metal grille, 7.5 lbs., mfg. 2004-present.

MSR $194	$150	$100 - 115	$50 - 60	

In 2013, this model was upgraded to the GX version with i-CUBE LINK IOS connectivity.

MICROCUBE RX – 5W (2 X 2.5W stereo), 4-4 in. speakers, stereo practice guitar combo, solid-state chassis, single channel, digital effects, rhythm guide, top control panel, single input, 10 knobs (amp selector, g, v, b, m, t, EFX selector, delay/reverb, rhythm guide selector, rhythm guide volume), input boost switch, tuner switch, rhythm guide start/stop, tap/temp, and variation switches, power switch, rear panel: footswitch jack, recording out/headphone jack, stereo and mono aux. in jacks, operates on both AC or battery power, available in black covering, silver metal grille, 14 lbs., mfg. 2008-disc.

	$250	$150 - 200	$95 - 120	$342

MICROCUBE BASS RX – 5W (2 X 2.5W stereo), 4-4 in. speakers, stereo practice bass combo, solid-state chassis, single channel, digital effects, rhythm guide, top control panel, single input, 10 knobs (amp selector, g, v, b, m, t, EFX selector, delay/reverb, rhythm guide selector, rhythm guide volume), input boost switch, tuner switch, rhythm guide start/stop, tap/temp, and variation switches, power switch, rear panel: footswitch jack, recording out/headphone jack, stereo and mono aux. in jacks, operates on both AC or battery power, available in black covering, silver metal grille, 15 lbs., mfg. 2008-present.

MSR $382	$280	$180 - 210	$90 - 110	

MSR/NOTES	100%	EXCELLENT	AVERAGE	LAST MSR

MOBILE CUBE – 5W (2 X 2.5W stereo), 2-4 in. speakers, stereo auxillary combo amp, solid-state chassis, two channels (mic and keyboard/instrument/guitar), chorus, delay, reverb, top control panel, five knobs (mic v, amp selector, instrument v, tone, delay/reverb), side panel: three inputs (mono mic, stereo keyboard/instrument), aux in and RCA inputs, operates on both AC or battery power, available in black covering, silver metal grille, 5.5 lbs., mfg. summer 2008-present.

MSR $246	$180	$115 - 135	$60 - 70	

ELECTRIC SS AMPLIFIERS: BLUES CUBE (BC) SERIES

Blues Cube Artist 112
courtesy Roland

Blues Cube Hot
courtesy Roland

Blues Cube Tour
courtesy Roland

BC-30 – 30W, 1-12 in. speaker, solid-state combo, two channels (normal/lead), top control panel, various knobs, cream covering, brown grille cloth, made in the U.S.A., mfg. 1995-2005.

	N/A	$150 - 200	$95 - 120	$379

* **BC-30/210** – similar to the BC-30, except has 2-10 in. speakers, mfg. 1995-2005.

	N/A	$175 - 225	$110 - 140	$479

BC-60 – 60W, 1-12 in. speaker, solid-state combo, two channels, reverb, top control panel, various knobs, cream covering, brown grille cloth, made in the U.S.A., mfg. 1995-2005.

	N/A	$200 - 250	$120 - 150	$599

* **BC-60/310** – similar to the BC-30, except has 3-10 in. speakers, mfg. 1995-2005.

	N/A	$250 - 300	$150 - 200	$779

BLUES CUBE ARTIST 112 – 80W, 1-12 in. speaker, solid-state combo, two channels, top black control panel, two inputs, 11 knobs (Clean: v, Crunch: g, v, All: b, m, t, tremolo, r, presence, MV, power control), power switch, channel switch, dual tone switch, boost switch per channel, tone switch per channel, tap switch, loop switch, USB output, three footswitch jacks, headphone jack, line out, effect loop, top handle, available in vintage blonde covering with dark gray grille cloth, 35.31 lbs., mfg. 2015-present.

MSR $1,169	$900	$575 - 675	$295 - 350	

BLUES CUBE ARTIST 212 – 85W, 2-12 in. speakers, solid-state combo, two channels, top black control panel, two inputs, 11 knobs (Clean: v, Crunch: g, v, All: b, m, t, tremolo, r, presence, MV, power control), power switch, channel switch, dual tone switch, boost switch per channel, tone switch per channel, tap switch, loop switch, USB output, three footswitch jacks, headphone jack, line out, effect loop, top handle, available in vintage blonde covering with dark gray grille cloth, 46.3 lbs., mfg. 2015-present.

MSR $1,689	$1,300	$850 - 975	$425 - 525	

BLUES CUBE HOT – 30W, 1-12 in. speaker, solid-state combo, one channel with boost, top black control panel, single input, seven knobs (v, b, m, t, r, MV, power control), power switch, boost switch, tone switch, USB output, footswitch jack, headphone jack, line out, top handle, available in black covering with silver grille cloth or vintage blonde covering with dark gray grille cloth, 27.8 lbs., new 2016.

MSR $699	$500	$325 - 375	$165 - 200	

BLUES CUBE STAGE – 60W, 1-12 in. speaker, solid-state combo, two channels, top black control panel, two inputs, nine knobs (Clean: v, Crunch: g, v, All: b, m, t, r, MV, power control), power switch, channel switch, dual tone switch, boost switch per channel, tone switch per channel, USB output, footswitch jack, headphone jack, line out, top handle, available in vintage blonde covering with dark gray grille cloth, 30.87 lbs., mfg. 2014-present.

MSR $899	$700	$450 - 525	$230 - 280	

BLUES CUBE TOUR – 100W, head unit, solid-state chassis, two channels, front black control panel, two inputs, thirteen knobs (Clean: v, b, m, t, Crunch: g, v, b, m, t, All: r, presence, MV, power control), power switch, boost switch, tone switch, channel switch, dual tone switch, USB output, footswitch jack, headphone jack, line out, external speaker jack, XLR line out, top handle, vintage blonde covering, 17.64 lbs., mfg. 2015-present.

MSR $1,949	$1,500	$975 - 1,125	$500 - 600	

MSR/NOTES	100%	EXCELLENT	AVERAGE	LAST MSR

Blues Cube 410 Speaker Cabinet
courtesy Roland

GA-112
courtesy Roland

GA-212
courtesy Roland

BLUES CUBE 410 SPEAKER CABINET – 100W, 4-10 in. speakers, guitar speaker cabinet, 4-ohms, open back, straight front, casters included, recessed side handles, vintage blonde covering, dark gray grille, 56.44 lbs., mfg. 2015-present.

MSR $1,819 $1,400 $900 - 1,050 $450 - 550

ELECTRIC SS AMPLIFIERS: GA SERIES

GA-112 – 100W, 1-12 in. speaker, guitar combo, solid-state chassis, four channels, COSM amp modeling, front control panel, two inputs, eight knobs, five channel switches, rear panel: two footswitch jacks, two effect loops, two main in jacks, line out jack, tuner out jack, top handle, black covering, silver metal grille, mfg. 2013-2015.

$1,000 $650 - 750 $325 - 400 $1,299

GA-212 – 200W, 2-12 in. speaker, guitar combo, solid-state chassis, four channels, COSM amp modeling, front control panel, two inputs, eight knobs, five channel switches, rear panel: two footswitch jacks, two effect loops, two main in jacks, line out jack, tuner out jack, top handle, casters, black covering, silver metal grille, mfg. 2013-2015.

$1,200 $775 - 900 $400 - 475 $1,549

ELECTRIC SS AMPLIFIERS: JAZZ-CHORUS (JC) SERIES

JC-40 Jazz Chorus
courtesy Roland

JC-90 Jazz Chorus
courtesy Roland

JC-120 Jazz Chorus
courtesy Savage Audio

JC-40 JAZZ CHORUS – 400W, 2-10 in. speakers, solid-state combo, distortion, reverb, chorus, vibrato, front black control panel, two inputs, nine black and silver knobs (v, t, m, b, distortion, r, depth,s, vib/chorus), rear panel: headphone jack, two line out jacks, effects loop, three footswitch jacks, black covering, black and silver grille, 34.83 lbs., mfg. 2015-present.

MSR $779 $600 $400 - 450 $195 - 240

JC-50 JAZZ CHORUS – 50W, 1-12 in. speaker, solid-state combo, single channel, distortion, reverb, chorus, vibrato, front black control panel, two inputs, seven black and silver knobs (v, t, b, distortion, r, s, d), black covering, black and silver grille, 40 lbs., mfg. 1980s-1990s.

N/A $300 - 350 $175 - 225

JC-55 JAZZ CHORUS – 50W (2 X 25W Stereo), 2-8 in. speakers, solid-state combo, distortion, reverb, chorus, front black control panel, two inputs, eight black and silver knobs (v, b, m, t, distortion, r, chorus rate, depth), black covering, black and silver grille, 25.5 lbs., mfg. 1980s-1990s.

N/A $325 - 375 $200 - 250

JC-60 JAZZ CHORUS – 60W, 1-12 in. speaker, solid-state combo, single channel, distortion, reverb, chorus, vibrato, front black control panel, two inputs, eight black and silver knobs (v, t, m, b, distortion, r, s, d), chorus/vibrato switch, line out jack, external speaker jack, black covering, black and silver grille, 44 lbs., mfg. 1980s-1990s.

N/A $325 - 400 $200 - 250

MSR/NOTES	100%	EXCELLENT	AVERAGE	LAST MSR

JC-77 JAZZ CHORUS – 70W (2 X 35W Stereo), 2-10 in. speakers, solid-state combo, distortion, reverb, chorus, front black control panel, two inputs, nine black and silver knobs (v, b, m, high t, t, distortion, r, chorus rate, depth), chorus switch, black covering, black and silver grille, 42 lbs., mfg. 1980s-1990s.

	N/A	$325 - 400	$200 - 250	

JC-90 JAZZ CHORUS – 80W (2 X 40W Stereo), 2-10 in. speakers, solid-state combo, distortion, reverb, chorus, front black control panel, two inputs, ten black and silver knobs (v, b, m, high t, t, distortion, r, chorus rate, depth), black covering, black and silver grille, disc. 2006.

	$560	$350 - 425	$200 - 250	$799

JC-120 JAZZ CHORUS – 120W (2 X 60W Stereo), 2-12 in. speakers, solid-state combo, distortion, reverb, chorus, vibrato, front black control panel, two inputs, 13 black and silver knobs (v, b, m, high t, t, distortion, r, chorus rate, depth, s, i), black covering, black and silver grille, mfg. 1975-present.

	100%	EXCELLENT	AVERAGE	
1975-1979	N/A	$600 - 750	$375 - 450	
1980-1999	N/A	$600 - 700	$350 - 425	
2000-Present MSR $1,599	$1,000	$550 - 650	$325 - 400	

* *JC-120H* – similar to the JC-120, except in head-unit configuration, 34 lbs., disc 1995.

	N/A	$425 - 500	$275 - 325	

JC-160 JAZZ CHORUS – 120W (2 X 60W Stereo), 4-10 in. speakers, solid-state combo, distortion, reverb, chorus, vibrato, front black control panel, two inputs, 12 black and silver knobs (2v, 2b, 2m, distortion, r, s, i), black covering, black and silver grille, 77 lbs., disc 1995/1996.

	N/A	$550 - 650	$325 - 400	

ELECTRIC SS AMPLIFIERS: SPIRIT SERIES

SPIRIT 10 – 10W, 1-10 in. speaker, solid-state chassis, two channels, front black control panel, two inputs, five knobs (v, MV, b, m, t), line out jack, headphone jack, black covering, black or gray grille, mfg. 1980s.

	N/A	$120 - 150	$70 - 95	

SPIRIT 25 – 25W, 1-12 in. speaker, solid-state chassis, reverb, two channels, front black control panel, two inputs, six knobs (v, MV, b, m, t, r), line out jack, headphone jack, black covering, black or gray grille, mfg. 1980s.

	N/A	$135 - 175	$85 - 110	

SPIRIT 50 – 50W, 1-12 in. speaker, solid-state chassis, reverb, two channels, front black control panel, two inputs, six knobs (v, MV, b, m, t, r), line out jack, headphone jack, preamp in/outs, power in/outs, black covering, black or gray grille, mfg. 1980s.

	N/A	$175 - 225	$110 - 140	

ELECTRIC SS AMPLIFIERS: V-GUITAR SERIES

VGA-3
courtesy Roland

VGA-7
courtesy Roland

VGA-3 – 50W, 1-12 in. speaker, digital solid-state chassis, 11 COSM digital amp models, 10 digital memories presets, front black control panel, single input, 11 black and silver knobs, various buttons and switches, black covering, black grille cloth, disc. 2005.

	N/A	$275 - 325	$150 - 200	$649

VGA-5 – 65W, 1-12 in. speaker, digital solid-state chassis, 11 COSM digital amp models, 10 digital memories presets, front silver control panel, two input, 16 black and silver knobs, various buttons and switches, effects-loop, casters, black covering, black grille cloth, disc. 2005.

	N/A	$325 - 400	$200 - 250	$999

VGA-7 – 130W (2 X 65 Stereo), 2-12 in. speaker, digital solid-state chassis, 20 COSM digital amp models, 26 guitar models, 80 digital memory presets, front silver control panel, two input, a whole bunch of black and silver knobs, various buttons and switches, effects-loop, casters, black covering, black grille cloth, disc. 2005.

	N/A	$500 - 600	$300 - 350	$1,699

MSR/NOTES	100%	EXCELLENT	AVERAGE	LAST MSR

ACOUSTIC SS AMPLIFIERS

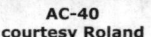

AC-40
courtesy Roland

AC-60
courtesy Roland

AC-100
courtesy Roland

AC-33 – 30W (15W per side stereo, 20W and 10W per side stereo in DC operation), 2-5 in. speakers, portable acoustic combo amplifier, solid-state chassis, two channels (guitar, mic/line), chrous, reverb, top black control panel, three inputs (Guitar Ch. 1: 1/4 in., Mic/Line Ch.: XLR and 1/4 in.), nine knobs (Guitar Ch.: v, b, m, t, Mic/Line Ch.: v, b, t, All: reverb/ambience, MV), three-way chorus switches for each channel, anti-feedback switch, Looper with two buttons and three LEDs, headphone jack, power switch, rear panel: DC input, looper footswitch jack, chorus/reverb footswitch jack, two line outs, RCA and 1/8 in. aux. in jacks with level control, black covering, black grille, bottom stand, runs on either AC or 8 AA battery DC power, mfg. 2010-present.

MSR $557	$400	$250 - 300	$135 - 175	

  • Add $27 (MSR $584) for Rosewood covering/grille.

AC-40 – 40W, 2-6.5 in. speakers, portable acoustic combo amplifier, solid-state chassis, two channels (guitar, mic/line), chrous, reverb, top black control panel, three inputs (Guitar Ch. 1: 1/4 in., Mic/Line Ch.: XLR and 1/4 in.), 11 knobs (Guitar Ch.: v, b, m, t, r Mic/Line Ch.: v, b, m, t, r, All: MV), three-way chorus switches for each channel, anti-feedback switch, power switch, rear panel: DC input, headphone jack, two line outs, 1/8 in. aux. in jacks with level control, footswitch jack, black covering, black grille, 11.68 lbs., mfg. 2013-present.

MSR $485	$375	$245 - 285	$125 - 150	

AC-60 – 60W (2 X 30W), 2-6.5 in. speakers, solid-state chassis, two channels, chorus, reverb, top black control panel, two inputs (one per channel), 12 black and silver knobs, anti-feedback system, black covering, black grille cloth, mfg. 2003-present.

MSR $667	$500	$275 - 325	$175 - 225	

AC-90 – 90W (45W X 2 stereo), 2-8 in. speakers and 2-3 X 2 in. tweeters, acoustic chorus guitar combo, solid-state chassis, two channels (guitar, mic/live), chorus, delay, reverb, top black control panel, two inputs (guitar, mic/live), 12 black and silver knobs (guitar Ch.: v, b, m, t, mic/live Ch.: v, b, m, t, chorus, reverb/delay, anti-feedback, MV), pickup switch (guitar Ch.), shape switch (guitar Ch.), two chorus switches (one per Ch.), phantom power switch (mic/live Ch.), select switch (mic/live Ch.), anti-feedback switch, mute switch, power switch, headphone jack, back panel: L/R XLR line outs, mono 1/4 in. line out, sub woofer out, RCA and two 1/4 in. aux. in jacks, DI out/tuner out, two footswitch jacks, black covering, black grille, 18.3125 in. wide, 12.875 in. tall, 12.9375 in. deep, 25.7 lbs., mfg. 2007-present.

MSR $937	$700	$425 - 500	$275 - 325	

AC-100 – 100W (50W, 2 X 25W), 1-12 in. plus 2-5 in. speakers, solid-state chassis, two channels, chorus, reverb, front gold control panel, four inputs (two per channel), 14 black and gold knobs, anti-feedback system, brown covering, brown grille cloth, mfg. 1995-2005.

	N/A	$500 - 600	$300 - 350	$1,195

MOBILE AC – 5W, 2-4 in. speakers, portable acoustic combo amplifier, solid-state chassis, one channel, top black control panel, three inputs (Guitar/Mic/Audio), five knobs (audio v, mic v, guitar v, tone, reverb), chorus switch, wide switch, power switch, headphone jack, RCA jacks, black covering, black grille, 5.56 lbs., mfg. 2012-present.

MSR $262	$130	$85 - 100	$40 - 50	

BASS SS AMPLIFIERS

DB-500 – 160W, 1-12 in. speaker + horn tweeter, solid-state chassis, digital COSM modeling, D-Chorus effect, shape controls, 2 programmable memories, top control panel, various knobs and buttons, black covering, gray grille, disc. 2005.

	N/A	$450 - 525	$275 - 325	$999

DB-700 – 250W, 1-15 in. speaker + horn tweeter, solid-state chassis, digital COSM modeling, D-Chorus effect, shape controls, 2 programmable memories, top control panel, various knobs and buttons, black covering, gray grille, disc. 2005.

	N/A	$550 - 650	$325 - 400	$1,299

DB-900 – 320W, 7-speaker cabinet including 4-10 in., 2-12 in. and a horn tweeter, solid-state chassis, digital COSM modeling, D-Chorus effect, shape controls, 2 programmable memories, front control panel, various knobs and buttons, black covering, gray grille, disc. 2005.

	N/A	$850 - 1,000	$600 - 700	$1,999

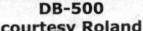

DB-500
courtesy Roland

DB-700
courtesy Roland

D-Bass 115
courtesy Roland

D-BASS 115 – 300W, 1-15 in. speaker plus a tweeter, Feed Forward Processing, Bi-Amp solid-state chassis, COSM preamp models, single channel, front silver control panel, two inputs (piezo and normal), 10 knobs (g, amp model type, compression, b, m, mid-freq., t, tweeter level, effect blend, v), mute switch, pickup switch, rear control panel: footswitch jack, sub out, line out, effects loop, tuner out, balanced XLR out, recessed handles, casters, black covering, black grille, 55 lbs., mfg. 2006-disc.

$1,300	$725 - 850	$425 - 500	$1,599

D-BASS 210 – 400W, 2-10 in. speakers plus a tweeter, Feed Forward Processing, Bi-Amp solid-state chassis, COSM preamp models, single channel, front silver control panel, two inputs (piezo and normal), 10 knobs (g, amp model type, compression, b, m, mid-freq., t, tweeter level, effect blend, v), mute switch, pickup switch, rear control panel: footswitch jack, sub out, line out, effects loop, tuner out, balanced XLR out, recessed handles, black covering, black grille, 51 lbs., mfg. 2006-disc.

$1,500	$850 - 1,000	$550 - 650	$1,899

D-BASS 115X POWERED SPEAKER CABINET – 300W, 1-15 in. speaker plus a tweeter, powered cabinet only - no preamp, Bi-Amp solid-state chassis, rear control panel, single input, three knobs (v, sub freq., tweeter level), sub/full range switch, sub out, recessed handles, casters, black covering, black grille, 55 lbs., mfg. 2006-disc.

$1,200	$675 - 800	$400 - 475	$1,499

NOTES

S SECTION
SADOWSKY AUDIO

Amplifiers previously produced in Holland, and speaker cabinets previously produced in Boston, MA between 2005 and 2007.

Roger Sadowsky, a noted East Coast repairman and luthier, has been providing quality customizing and repairs in his shop since 1979. Sadowsky currently produces archtop jazz electric guitars, solidbody electric guitars, and electric basses. For more information on electric guitars, refer to the *Blue Book of Electric Guitars*. In 2005, he introduced a line of bass amps to complement his electric bass line. Sadowsky came up with the idea and initial concept and brought them to noted amp manufacturers to design and build it. The **SA200** tube bass amp head was the first amp project, and it was designed and built by Dolf Koch of Koch Amplification in Holland. The speaker cabinets **SA210** and **SA410** designed for use with the SA200 are built by Jim Bergantino in Boston, MA. Sadowsky also had plans for a guitar amp line, but it appears that it never materialized.

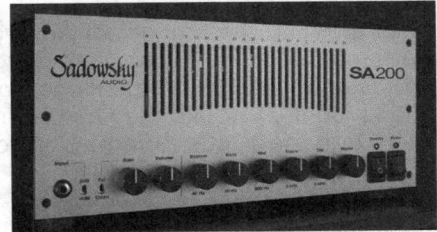

SA200
courtesy Sadowsky Audio

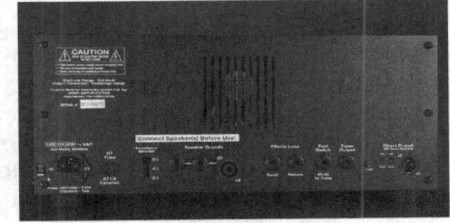

SA200
courtesy Sadowsky Audio

SAMAMP

Amplifiers currently produced in Vestavia Hills, AL since 2004.

Amp builder Sam Timberlake first started playing music when he was six years old, and while he was learning how to play guitar, he became interested in guitar tone. This led Timberlake to begin experimenting with tube amplifiers, vacuum tubes, reference guides, and schematics and he started to fix and modify old tube amplifiers. Timberlake attended Auburn University where he played in a band and worked as a guitar and amp tech for The Guitar Shoppe. After graduation, he moved to Birmingham, AL and began repairing guitar amplifiers for local guitar shops. Timberlake's reputation as an amp repairman grew and he soon earned the nickname of "Amp Sam." In October 2004, Timberlake developed the Variable Amplitude Clipping (V.A.C.) circuit and applied for a patent. This prototype became the first Samamp called the VAC 45. Several other models followed and Timberlake continues to develop and produce a variety of tube amplifiers. All amplifiers are hand wired point to point with Class A tube circuitry. For more information, visit his website or contact him directly.

ELECTRIC TUBE AMPLIFIERS

The **VAC 23** ($1,200) features 23W (switchable to 3, 5, 11, or 18W), 1-12 in. speaker, 6V6 power tubes, and a push/pull gain switch in the volume knob. The **VAC 25** ($1,400) has a British-style sound and features 25W (switchable to 3, 5, 11, or 18W), 1-12 in. speaker, 6V6 power tubes, and a variety of push/pull switches in the preamp. The **VAC 30R** ($1,200) is housed in a circular cabinet and features 30W (switchable to 3, 6, 12, or 20W), 1-12 in. speaker, 6V6GT power tubes, and five controls (g, MV, t, m, b). The **VAC 40 Head** ($1,500) has the same gain and volume preamps of the VAC 25 except with 40W output (switchable to 4, 9, 20, or 30W) and 6L6GC power tubes. The **VAC 45** ($1,800) has the same gain and volume preamps of the VAC 25 except with 45W output (switchable to 5, 15, or 30W) and 6L6GC power tubes.

SAM ASH

Amplifiers previously produced by Oliver Amplifiers in Brooklyn, NY, Linden, NJ, and/or Westbury Long Island, NY in the late 1960s and early 1970s.

Sam Ash opened the first Sam Ash store in 1924. Since then they have grown into several stores selling guitars, amplifiers, basses, and a variety of musical related products. By the mid-1960s, Ash decided to introduce their own line of amplifiers. Since they didn't have their own factory, they took the route that was very popular in the 1950s and 1960s, and had another company build amps with the Sam Ash name on the front. Oliver Amplifiers privately branded some of their popular models with Sam Ash. Jess Oliver, who started Oliver Amplifiers, worked several years during Ampeg's golden era from the mid-1950s through the mid-1960s. Sam Ash is currently run by his grandson, Richard Ash, and they have over forty-five Sam Ash music retail stores across the country. Currently, they do not produce or brand any Sam Ash amplifiers. Information courtesy, Gregg Hopkins and Bill Moore, Ampeg: *The Story Behind The Sound*.

SAMSON TECHNOLOGIES

Amplifiers, effects pedals, and other audio equipment currently distributed in Hauppauge, NY. Previously located in Syosset, NY. The Samson trademark was established in 1980.

Samson Technologies was founded in 1980, and they currently distribute Hartke, Zoom, Samson Audio, Samson Wireless, and Armoured Cable. Samson first started producing wireless microphones and instrument systems. Their wireless mics were very affordable and extremely successful early on leading to Samson's rapid expansion in audio electronics. In the mid-1980s, they became a distributor of Hartke bass amplifiers (see Hartke). In 1993, they became a distributor of Zoom amplifiers and effects pedals. They currently have a full line of audio products available. For more information, visit their website.

CONTACT INFORMATION
SAMSON TECHNOLOGIES
45 Gilpin Avenue
Hauppauge, NY 11788
Phone No.: 631-784-2200
Fax No.: 631-784-2201
www.samsontech.com
info@samsontech.com

SANO

Amplifiers previously produced in New Jersey in the 1960s.

Sano was founded by ex-Ampeg amp builder, Stanley Michael. Everett Hull, the founder of Ampeg, and Stanley went different ways in 1948. In 1952, Stanley helped develop the Sano Accordion Pickup and Matched Amplifier, which was distributed by the Major Music Company in Irvington, NJ. Stanley took his experience from Ampeg and applied it to his new company. The first amps released were accordion models, just like they had been at Ampeg. In the late 1950s, Sano introduced several amplifiers and produced them into the 1960s. Information courtesy: Gregg Hopkins and Bill Moore, *Ampeg: The Story Behind the Sound*.

ELECTRIC AMPLIFIERS

Sano is known for their Ampeg-style amplifiers that are not high-gain, meaning they were really designed for accordion use and not for guitars - a practice Ampeg was famous for. Amps that were produced in the 1950s and early 1960s were all tube based, but Sano released at least one solid-state model in the late 1960s. Sano amps are built with quality parts and generally sound good, just like Ampeg, but they do not command the premium that Ampegs do. Most tube models can be found between $200 and $400 depending upon configuration/condition.

SAVAGE AUDIO

Amplifiers currently produced in Savage, MN (a suburb of Minneapolis) since 1994.

Savage Audio was started by Jeff Krumm in his basement in 1991. Since then, the company has evolved into an amp fix-it shop where they specialize in tube amps but they also fix solid-state models as well. The repair shop at Savage Audio can do almost anything from repair, to rebuilding, to restoration. In 1994, Krumm started building Savage-branded tube amps, becoming an early player in the boutique niche. The Macht 6 is actually based on the original design of the DeArmond amplifier, and the Blitz 50 is designed after the Marshall Bluesbreaker. Notable artists include Beck, Doyle Bramhall, Peter Buck, Jeff Tweedy, and Adam Levy. For more information, visit Savage's website or contact them directly.

CONTACT INFORMATION
SAVAGE AUDIO
4813 West 124th St.
Savage, MN 55378
Phone No.: 952-894-1022
Fax No.: 952-894-1536
www.savageamps.com
info@savageaudio.com

ELECTRIC TUBE AMPLIFIERS

Savage offers a full range of amplifiers, available in multiple configurations. Aside from the Blitz 50, which utilizes Class A/B design, all Savage amplifiers boast Class A circuit design and highest-quality components to provide optimum performance. The **Macht 6** and **Macht 12x** were introduced in circa 2003 and feature 6 and 12 watts of single-ended power, respectively. The Macht 6 is available as a head-unit ($1,299) and a 1-12 in. combo ($1,399), as well as the Macht 12x: head unit ($1,499) and a 1-12 in. combo ($1,599). The **Rohr 15** was introduced in 1994, has 15W Class A output, two input channels (Bright and Normal), and 2 X EL84 power tubes. The Rohr 15 is available as a head-unit ($2,399), 1-12 in. combo ($2,599), 2-10 in. combo ($2,699), and 2-12 in. combo ($2,799). The **Gläs 30** was also introduced in 1994, has 30W Class A output, two input channels (Bright and Normal), uses 4 X EL84 power tubes. The Gläs 30 is available as a head-unit ($2,599), 1-12 in. combo ($2,799), 2-10 in. combo ($2,899), and 2-12 in. combo ($2,999). The **Blitz 50** was introduced in 1996, has 50W output, two input channels (Bright and Normal), uses 2 X EL34 power tubes, and is available as a head-unit ($2,799) or 2-12 in. combo ($2,999). The **Schatten 19** ($1,899) and **Schatten 38** ($2,299) are new amplifiers driven by EL84 power tubes and feature simple controls with a volume control, three-way tone selector, and variable tone-cut control. All amps and cabinets are available in a variety of colors and coverings. Contact Savage directly to discuss what is the right amp for the customer.

Blitz 50
courtesy Savage Audio

Gläs 30
courtesy Savage Audio

Rohr 15
courtesy Savage Audio

MSR/NOTES	100%	EXCELLENT	AVERAGE	LAST MSR

SCEPTRE

Amplifiers previously produced in Hamilton, Ontario, Canada during the 1960s and early 1970s.

Sceptre produced tube amplifiers in Hamilton, Ontario, which is a suburb of Toronto, Ontario in Canada. Most of their amps were based on popular American designs, especially on Fender Blackface and Silverface-era models. Known models include the **Challenger**, **Cougar**, **Custom Dart**, **Marauder Bass**, and **Signet**. Most Sceptre amplifiers are priced between $50 and $250 depending upon condition and configuration. Any further information on Sceptre amplifiers can be submitted directly to Blue Book Publications.

SCHECTER

Amplifiers, speaker cabinets, and other electronics currently produced in USA and China. Schecter electronics are distributed by Schecter Amplification of Sun Valley, CA.

Schecter is widely known for producing electric guitars but debuted an amplifier line in 2013.

CONTACT INFORMATION
SCHECTER
10953 Pendleton St.
Sun Valley, CA 91352
Phone No.: 800-660-6621
Fax No.: 818-846-2727
www.schecterguitars.com
info@schecterguitars.com

AMPLIFIERS

Hellraiser 100 Stage Head
courtesy Schecter

Hellraiser Depth Charge 4x12 Sub Cabinet
courtesy Schecter

Hellraiser USA 4x12 Speaker Cabinet
courtesy Schecter

HELLRAISER 100 STAGE HEAD – 100W, guitar head-unit, eight tube chassis, preamp: 4 X EI12AX7EH, power: 4 X EL34-B, two channels, front black control panel, two inputs, 15 chrome knobs (Master: volume, presence, boost, gate/noise reduction, focus, Lead: t, m, b, v, gain, Clean: t, m, b, v, gain,) standby switch, power switch, footswitch jack, direct out, metal corners, top handle, black covering, black grille, 43 lbs., mfg. 2013-present.

| MSR $1,599 | $775 | $500 - 575 | $250 - 300 | |

HELLRAISER 100 USA 2x12 COMBO AMP – 100W, guitar combo amp, baltic burch construction, 2-12 in. Celestion Vintage 30's speakers, eight tube chassis, preamp: 4 X EI12AX7EH, power: 4 X EL34-B, two channels, front black control panel, two inputs, 16 chrome knobs (Master: volume, presence, reverb, loop, gain/noise reduction, focus, Lead: t, m, b, v, gain, Clean: t, m, b, v, gain,) standby switch, power switch, footswitch jack, direct out, metal corners, top handle, black covering, black grille, 65 lbs., made in USA, mfg. 2013-present.

| MSR $2,399 | $1,200 | $775 - 900 | $375 - 475 | |

HELLRAISER DEPTH CHARGE 4X12 SUB CABINET – 240W, 3-12 in. Celestion Seventy 80 P1280 speakers, 1-12in. 200-watt sub powered by internal amp, 4 ohm 200-watt impedance, pocket handles, removeable casters, metal corners, slant or straight configuration, black covering, black grille, mfg. 2013-present.

| MSR $899 | $425 | $275 - 325 | $135 - 170 | |

HELLRAISER DLX 4x12 SPEAKER CABINET – 320W, 4-12 in. Celestion Seventy 80 P1280 speakers, 16 ohm impedance (8 ohm per side), pocket handles, removeable casters, metal corners, slant or straight configuration, black covering, black grille, 96 lbs., mfg. 2014-present.

| MSR $699 | $350 | $230 - 265 | $115 - 140 | |

HELLRAISER STAGE 4X12 SPEAKER CABINET – 240W, 4-12 in. Celestion Vintage 30's 16 ohm speakers, 16 ohm impedance (8 ohm per side), pocket handles, removeable casters, metal corners, slant or straight configuration, black covering, black grille, 96 lbs., mfg. 2013-present.

| MSR $1,149 | $550 | $375 - 425 | $180 - 225 | |

HELLRAISER USA 4x12 SPEAKER CABINET – 240W, baltic burch construction, 4-12 in. Celestion Vintage 30's 16 ohm speakers, 16 ohm impedance (8 ohm per side), mono or stereo operation, pocket handles, removeable casters, metal corners, slant or straight configuration, black covering, black grille, made in USA, 96 lbs., mfg. 2013-present.

| MSR $1,399 | $700 | $450 - 525 | $230 - 280 | |

MSR/NOTES	100%	EXCELLENT	AVERAGE	LAST MSR

SYNYSTER GATES HELLWIN STAGE 4X12 SPEAKER CABINET – 240W, 4-12 in. Celestion Vintage 30's 16 ohm speakers, 16 ohm impedance (8 ohm per side), pocket handles, removeable casters, metal corners, slant or straight configuration, black covering, black grille, 96 lbs., mfg. 2013-present.

MSR $1,199	$600	$400 - 450	$195 - 240	

SYNYSTER GATES HELLWIN USA 4x12 SPEAKER CABINET – 240W, baltic burch construction, 4-12 in. Celestion Vintage 30's 16 ohm speakers, 16 ohm impedance (8 ohm per side), wired for mono or stereo operation, pocket handles, removeable casters, metal corners, slant configuration, black covering, black grille, 96 lbs., made in USA, mfg. 2013-present.

MSR $1,499	$725	$475 - 550	$235 - 290	

SCHERTLER

Amplifiers and other electronics produced in Medrisio, Switzerland since the early 1980s. Distributed in the U.S. by Schertler USA Inc. in Kirkland, WA.

CONTACT INFORMATION
SCHERTLER
Factory/Headquarters — Via Beroldingen 18, Medrisio, CH-6850 Switzerland, Phone No.: +41 91 630 07 10, Fax No.: +41 91 630 07 11, www.schertler.com, info@schertlergroup.com
U.S. Distributor: Schertler USA Inc. — 218 Main Street, #110, Kirkland, WA 98033-6108, Phone No.: 425-822-0102, Fax No.: 425-822-0739, www.schertlerusa.com, info@schertlerusa.com

Schertler was founded in the early 1980s, and they started by producing acoustic transducers. Since then, they have expanded to offer pickups, preamps, amplifiers, speakers, and guitars. Their amplifiers are designed for acoustic guitars. Their amplifiers are built on biamplification technology, where two power amplifiers are used. Their two models include the **Unico** and the **David**. They also have loudspeakers and acoustic preamps available. For more information visit their website or contact them directly.

SCHREYER AUDIO

Amplifiers currently produced in Carlsbad, CA.

CONTACT INFORMATION
SCHREYER AUDIO
2720 Loker Ave. W., #S, Carlsbad, CA 92010, Phone No.: 760-213-8939, www.schreyeraudio.com, eschreyer@schreyeraudio.com

Earl Schreyer founded Schreyer Audio, and they produce a tube head-unit and combo amplifiers. All amps are point-to-point hand wired and are built to maintain the authenticity and quality of their predecessors. Amplifiers currently produced include the EDS-45 and the Sage 7 models. Discontinued models include the EOT-18, the Kraken, Moonlight Twin, Sage 14, Santa Cruz, and the Roadhouse. Amplifiers range between $1,100 and $2,158. Schreyer also builds stand alone reverb and tremolo units that start around $570. Speaker cabinets start at $858. For more information, visit Schreyer Audio's website or contact them directly.

SELMER

Amplifiers previously produced in London, England between the late 1940s and the mid-1980s.

Selmer dates back to before the Franco-Prussian war in the 1800s. Henry Selmer developed a clarinet that was much better than anything else that was out there at the time, which became the first Selmer instrument. Ben Davis formed the Selmer instrument company after meeting with Selmer in the early 1930s. By the time World War II came around, Selmer was the largest producer of instruments in the U.K. The company really took off in the 1950s and 1960s when amplifiers became widely available.

Selmer amps go back to when they took over a small company named RMS. They produced amps under this name for a while in the late 1940s and early 1950s. Selmer then began putting their own names on amps. The company went through some changes and by the 1970s things started to dissipate. By the mid-1970s, amp production had been discontinued all together. Selmer still produces musical instruments, but focuses more in the woodwind and brass industry. The author would like to thank Tim Fletcher and Steve Russell for contributing information to this section.

ELECTRIC TUBE AMPLIFIERS

CONSTELLATION TWENTY – 20W, 2-12 in. speakers, guitar combo, six tube chassis, preamp: 1 X ECC82, 2 X ECC83, power: 2 X EL34, rectifier: GZ34, two channels, tremolo, top gold control panel, four inputs, six knobs (v1, v2, b, t, trem. speed, trem. depth), one-button

courtesy solidbodyguitar.com, Inc.

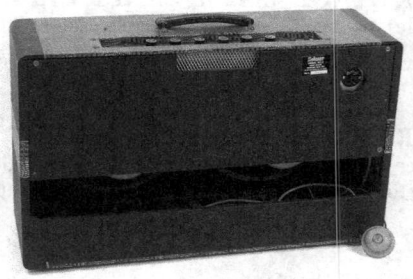

courtesy solidbodyguitar.com, Inc.

MSR/NOTES	100%	EXCELLENT	AVERAGE	LAST MSR

footswitch, two-tone croc-skin/black covering, brown grille with large Selmer logo in lower left corner, 28 in. wide, 17 in. tall, 9 in. deep, mfg. circa 1963-65.

| | N/A | $1,200 - 1,500 | $800 - 1,000 | |

SELECTORTONE AUTOMATIC – 25W, 1-15 in. speaker guitar combo, six-tube chassis, preamp: 1 X ECC83, 2 X EF86, power: 2 X EL34, rectifier: GZ34, two channels, tremolo, top gold control panel, four inputs (two per channel), six knobs (Ch. 1: v, tone, Ch. 2: v, tone, trem s, trem depth), six push button tone/effects controls, two-tone gray/blue cabinet, gray grille, "Selmer" script logo in center of grille (early models) or "Selmer" badge logo in upper right corner of grille (later models), mfg. 1961-63.

| | N/A | $750 - 900 | $475 - 550 | |

ZODIAC TWIN THIRTY – 30W, 2-12 in. speakers, guitar combo, eight tube chassis, preamp: 2 X EF86, 3 X ECC83, power: 2 X EL34, rectifier: GZ34, two channels, tremolo, top gold control panel, four inputs, six knobs (Ch. 1: v, tone, Ch. 2: v, tone, trem. speed, trem. depth), six push-button tone settings, "blinking-eye" tremolo light indicator, two-tone croc-skin/black covering, brown grille with large Selmer logo in lower left corner, mfg. circa 1963-65.

courtesy solidbodyguitar.com, Inc.

courtesy solidbodyguitar.com, Inc.

| | N/A | $2,000 - 2,500 | $1,200 - 1,500 | |

ZODIAC TWIN FIFTY – 50W, 2-12 in. speakers, guitar combo, eight tube chassis, preamp: 2 X EF86, 3 X ECC83, power: 2 X EL34, rectifier: GZ34, two channels, tremolo, top gold control panel, four inputs, six knobs (Ch. 1: v, tone, Ch. 2: v, tone, trem. speed, trem. depth), six push-button tone settings, "blinking-eye" tremolo light indicator, two-tone croc-skin/black covering, brown grille with large Selmer logo in lower left corner, mfg. circa 1963-65.

| | N/A | $2,000 - 2,500 | $1,200 - 1,500 | |

SEYMOUR DUNCAN

Amplifiers previously produced in Santa Barbara, CA between the mid-1980s and early 1990s. The Seymour Duncan trademark was established in 1978.

Seymour Duncan is both a guitar player and guitar repairman. He is probably most noted for the pickups he has made over the past two decades. Early in life he learned how to play guitar and became a noted musician. His first experience winding a pickup came when his Tele's lead pickup broke and he rewound it on a 33 1/3 RPM record player. He spent time with musicians including Les Paul and Roy Buchanan, and he realized it was his pickups that were keeping him from getting that tone. He moved to England as a suggestion by Les Paul and learned all about pickups. He fixed and rewound pickups for many notables including Jimmy Page and Pete Townshend, among others. Seymour moved back to the states in the mid-1970s, and along with more experience, started his own company. Seymour Duncan pickups was established in 1978 with Cathy Carter Duncan.

Shortly after they started producing pickups, they began producing amplifiers. Seymour Duncan produced both tube and solid-state designs. One of the innovations that they had at Seymour was the Convertible series, where the amps were capable of holding interchangeable modules, for all kinds of different amp sounds. For one reason or another, they only produced amplifiers for about a decade. By the early 1990s, amp production had been phased out and production was focused on pickups. Today Seymour Duncan has over 60 employees and produces some of the finest pickups out on the market.

ELECTRIC TUBE AMPLIFIERS

84-40 COMBO – 40W, 1-12 in. speaker, tube chassis, preamp: 1 X 12AX7, power: 4 X EL84, two channels, front black control panel, single input, eight black knobs, black covering, black grille, mfg. 1980s.

| | N/A | $300 - 350 | $175 - 225 | |

84-50 COMBO – 50W, 1-12 in. speaker, tube chassis, preamp: 1 X 12AX7, power: 4 X EL84, two channels, three boost stages, front black control panel, single input, eight black knobs, black covering, black grille, mfg. 1980s.

| | N/A | $325 - 400 | $200 - 250 | |

* **84-50 Head** – similar to the 84-50, except in head-unit only, mfg. 1980s.

| | N/A | $225 - 275 | $120 - 150 | |

MSR/NOTES	100%	EXCELLENT	AVERAGE	LAST MSR

CONVERTIBLE 60 – 60W, 1-12 in. Celestion speaker, tube chassis, preamp: 2 X 12AX7, power: 2 X EL34, two channels, reverb, space for two amp modules, front black control panel, two inputs, eight black knobs, black covering, black grille, mfg. 1980s.

	N/A	$325 - 375	$200 - 250	

* *Convertible 60 Head* – similar to the Convertible 60, except in head-only configuration, mfg. 1980s.

	N/A	$250 - 300	$100 - 150	

CONVERTIBLE 100 – 100W, 1-12 in. Celestion speaker, tube chassis, preamp: 3 X 12AX7, power: 4 X EL34, five amp module with preamp tube for each, two channels, reverb, front black control panel, two inputs, 13 black knobs (OD, MV, t, m, b, r per channel, wattage selector), black covering, black grille, mfg. 1980s.

	N/A	$425 - 500	$250 - 300	

* *Convertible 100 4-12 In. Speakers* – similar to the Convertible 100W, except has 4-12 in. speakers, mfg. 1980s.

	N/A	$500 - 600	$250 - 350	

* *Convertible 100 Head* – similar to the Convertible 100W, except in head-only configuration, mfg. 1980s.

	N/A	$350 - 425	$200 - 250	

CONVERTIBLE 2000 – 100W, 1-12 in. Celestion speaker, all-tube chassis with 5 interchangable preamp modules, power: 4 X EL34, front black control panel, 13 black knobs, black covering, black grille, mfg. 1980s.

	N/A	$600 - 800	$425 - 500	

* *Convertible 2000 Head* – similar to the Convertible 2000, except in head-only configuration, mfg. 1980s.

	N/A	$450 - 550	$275 - 325	

KTG-2100 – 100W, rack-mount head, all-tube chassis, preamp: 2 X 12AX7, 2 X 12AU7, power: 4 X KT88, two channels, front control panel, six knobs (v, p, dynamics for each channel), black casing, 30 lbs., mfg. 1980s.

	N/A	$425 - 500	$250 - 300	

SOLID-STATE AMPLIFIERS

BASS 400 – 400W, head-unit only, solid-state chassis, front control panel, single input, eight knobs (v, 7-band EQ), effects loop, black casing, mfg. 1980s.

	N/A	$250 - 300	$135 - 175	

BASS 400 X 2 – 600W bridge, 400W per channel in bi-amp mode, head-unit only, solid-state chassis, front control panel, single input, 11 knobs (v, 7-band EQ, crossover, MV, MV), effects loop, black casing, 36 lbs., mfg. 1980s.

	N/A	$325 - 400	$175 - 225	

SG SYSTEMS

Amplifiers previously produced in Lincolnwood, IL during the 1970s. Distributed by the Chicago Musical Instrument Co. (CMI).

SG Systems amplifiers was another division of Norlin-owned CMI. At the time, Norlin also owned Gibson and it is possible that these amps were either copies of Gibsons, Norlin used these as a separate line from Gibson, or they had nothing to do with each other. Regardless, they were built by CMI and they usually featured hybrid chassis, but it is possible some of them are entirely solid-state. The amps were covered in an odd "durable" metal casing that made the amps look like road cases. Almost all models were equipped with casters because they were so heavy. They also featured an "SG" logo in the lower right hand that actually looked more like an "SE." SG mainly produced guitar, bass, and PA systems with matching speaker cabinet. Any further information on SG Systems can be submitted directly to Blue Book Publications.

SHO-BUD

Amplifiers previously built in the U.S. during the early 1970s. Distributed through the Gretsch Guitar company catalog between 1972 and 1975; possibly as late as 1979.

While this company is best known for their pedal steel guitars, the company did produce a number of amplifiers. Sho-Bud amplifiers were produced in the Gretsch (Baldwin) factory in the early 1970s, and distributed through Grestch. Sho-Bud amps came in both tube and solid-state designs. Any further information on Sho-Bud can be submitted directly to Blue Book Publications.

SIEGMUND

Amplifiers currently produced in Tehachapi, CA, since 1993.

Luthier/amp builder Chris Siegmund produces amplifiers along with other custom guitars (acoustic, electric, and resophonic). The current line of amplifiers includes the Midnight Blues, Midnight Special, Diamond, and Muddy Buddy series. These are all tube amplifiers that are open for custom options as far as tone and other features. Visit Siegmund's website or contact them directly to get a list of options and features that they have to offer.

CONTACT INFORMATION
SIEGMUND
Tehachapi, CA
Phone No.: 661-823-4104
Fax No.: 661-823-4104
www.siegmundguitars.com
chris@siegmundguitars.com

MSR/NOTES	100%	EXCELLENT	AVERAGE	LAST MSR

SILVERTONE

Amplifiers previously produced in Korea in the 2000s. Amplifiers previously produced in the U.S. from the early 1940s through circa 1972. Distributed by the Samick Corporation in Gallatin, TN.

Silvertone is a company that never actually produced or had a factory to build amplifiers (or guitars). Amplifiers were made by the Danelectro company, which also produced solid body guitars for Silvertone. Silvertone was the brand name for Sears and Roebuck that was used between 1941 and 1970. The acoustic instruments and other guitars were usually made by Harmony, Valco, and Kay. Silvertone amps for the most part were made by Danelectro. Since Silvertone amps were typically sold out of the Sears and Roebuck mail order catalog, they were entry-level models. Silvertone guitars were known as house-brand instruments, and amplifiers can be thought of in the same way. Danelectro closed its doors around 1969, and naturally all amplifier production was finished. Silvertone was terminated after Sears and Roebuck stopped selling their instruments and amps in the catalog. In the early 2000s, Samick revived the Silvertone trademark with a new line of guitar amplifiers and guitars. For more information visit Silvertone's website or contact them directly.

CONTACT INFORMATION
SILVERTONE
Distributed by Samick Music Corporation
1329 Gateway Drive
Gallatin, TN 37066
Phone No.: 615-206-0077
www.silvertoneclassic.com
info@silvertoneguitar.com

GENERAL INFORMATION

Silvertone often added or changed models as a series. This guide should help date an amplifier and what features it may have.

1947: The first amp by Silvertone appears as the Model 1302. Little information is known about it except it has 3W, an 8 in. speaker, and two-tone brown covering.

1948-1953: Models include the 1339, 1340, 1342, 1344, and 1346. Each amp has its own unique color scheme.

1953-1957: Models include the 1330, 1331, 1333, 1334, 1335, and 1336. All amps are different than ther predecessors except the 1330 which is the same as the 1339. All amps have the tan covering with simulated alligator sides.

1956: The 1337 is introduced and has a simple brown color. This model is disc. in 1957.

1957-1959: Models include the 1390, 1391, 1392, 1394, and 1396. Amps once again have unique color combinations. The 1390 is the same as the 1330, but receives the name Meteor.

1959-1961: Models include the 1430, 1431, 1432, 1433, and 1434. The 1430 is the same as the 1390 once again. All the other amps have the same circuitry as the amps previously built. All amps except the 1430 feature the gray or black covering with the wrap around light grille.

1961-1964: Models include the 1430, 1471, 1472, 1473 and 1474. The chassis are carried over once again and the 1430 finally retains the same number. These amps feature the "TV" style with the controls on the 1472 and 1473 mounted vertically on the right side of the amp.

1964-1966: Models include the 1430, 1481, 1482, 1483, 1484, and new 1485. Chassis are different than the previous series and the larger amps come in piggyback configuration. They still have the "TV" style look to them, without the chassis.

1966-1972: The 1481 and 1482 survive until the late 1960s. The 1430 is replaced by the 1459. Solid-state amps make their appearance around this time.

Model 4707 Organ
courtesy Austin Thomerson

Model 4707 Organ
courtesy Austin Thomerson

ELECTRIC TUBE AMPLIFIERS

Silvertone amplifiers were budget, entry level, practice instruments when they were first produced, and they still are today. Silvertone amps are basically Danelectro amplifiers with a different name on them. This means that Danelectro descriptions will match most Silvertone descriptions (funny how that works). In some ways you can cross reference Danelectro with Silvertone (just a helpful hint). Silvertone amplifiers were typically numbered with a four-digit identification.

MODEL 1304 – approx. 18W, 1-12 in. Jensen speaker, guitar combo, five-tube chassis, preamp: 1 X 12SJ7, 1 X 12SN7GT, power: 2 X 6L6G, rectifier: 5U4, single channel, tremolo, rear top maroon control panel, three inputs, four knobs (v, t, b, tremolo), two-tone oxblood red/gray fabric covering, round speaker cutout with a silver fabric grille, leather handle, mfg. late 1940s.

N/A	$450 - 550	$300 - 350

The Model 1304 was the precursor and evolved into the Model 1344 in 1950.

MODEL 1330 – 3W, 1-6 in. speaker, 3 tubes, single input, single volume control, tan leatherette covering, 9 lbs., mfg. 1953-57.

N/A	$175 - 225	$110 - 140

This model is the same as the Model 1339 with cosmetic changes.

MSR/NOTES	100%	EXCELLENT	AVERAGE	LAST MSR

MODEL 1331 – 8W, 1-8 in. speaker, single channel, two inputs, two knobs (v, tone), tan simulated leather covering with brown alligator trim, 16 lbs., mfg. 1953-57.

| | N/A | $200 - 250 | $120 - 150 | |

MODEL 1333 – 12W, 1-12 in. speaker, six tube chassis, two channels, tremolo, three inputs, five knobs (v1, v2, tone, trem strength, speed), tan simulated leather covering with brown alligator trim, 20 lbs., mfg. 1953-57.

| | N/A | $450 - 600 | $275 - 350 | |

MODEL 1334 – 15W, 1-12 in. speaker, seven tube chassis, two channels, tremolo, four inputs, seven knobs (v1, v2, b, m, t, trem strength, speed), footswitch, tan simulated leather covering with brown alligator trim, 36 lbs., mfg. 1953-57.

| | N/A | $500 - 650 | $275 - 350 | |

MODEL 1335 – 25W, 1-15 in. speaker, seven tube chassis, two channels, tremolo, six inputs, eight knobs (v1, v2, b1, t1, b2, t2, trem strength, speed), footswitch, tan simulated leather covering with brown alligator trim, 39 lbs., mfg. 1953-57.

| | N/A | $525 - 650 | $300 - 400 | |

MODEL 1336 – 50W, 2-12 in. speakers, nine tube chassis, power: 4 X 6L6, two channels, tremolo, six inputs, eight knobs (v1, v2, b1, t1, b2, t2, trem strength, speed), footswitch, tan simulated leather covering with brown alligator trim, 45 lbs., mfg. 1953-57.

| | N/A | $600 - 700 | $375 - 450 | |

MODEL 1337 – 30W, 8-8 in. speakers, nine tube chassis, two channels, tremolo, six inputs, eight knobs (Ch. 1: v, b, t, Ch. 2.: v, b, t, trem speed, strength), footswitch, suitcase style amp where there are four speakers in each halve, the sides may be separated, mfg. 1956-57.

| | N/A | $500 - 600 | $300 - 375 | |

This model is similar to the Danelectro Commando.

MODEL 1339 – 3W, 1-6 in. speaker, 3 tube chassis, single channel, two inputs, one volume knob, maroon leatherette covering, 10 lbs., mfg. 1948-1953.

| | N/A | $175 - 225 | $110 - 140 | |

MODEL 1340 – 5W, 1-6 in. speaker, 3 tube chassis, single channel, two inputs, two knobs (v, tone), brown and white leatherette covering, 16 lbs., mfg. 1948-1953.

| | N/A | $200 - 250 | $120 - 150 | |

MODEL 1342 – 10W, 1-12 in. speaker, 5 tube chassis, two channels, three inputs, four knobs (v1, tone1, v2, tone2), green and beige leatherette covering, 26 lbs., mfg. 1948-1953.

| | N/A | $400 - 500 | $225 - 300 | |

MODEL 1344 – 15W, 1-12 in. speaker, seven-tube chassis, two channels, three inputs, six knobs (v1, t1, b1, v2, t2, b2), maroon leatherette covering, 29 lbs., mfg. 1948-1953.

| | N/A | $450 - 550 | $325 - 375 | |

MODEL 1346 – 30W, 2-12 in. speakers, eight tube chassis, power: 4 X 6L6, two channels, tremolo, four inputs, eight knobs (v1, t1, b1, v2, t2, b2, trem strength, speed), tan leatherette covering, speaker grille divided into two sections, 34 lbs., mfg. 1948-1953.

| | N/A | $600 - 700 | $375 - 450 | |

MODEL 1390 METEOR – 3W, 1-6 in. speaker, 3 tubes, single input, single volume control, tan leatherette covering, 9 lbs., mfg. 1957-59.

| | N/A | $200 - 250 | $110 - 140 | |

This model is the same as the Model 1330.

MODEL 1391 – 5W, 1-8 in. speaker, 3 tube chassis, single channel, two inputs, two knobs (v, tone), cream covering, dark grille, mfg. 1957-59.

| | N/A | $275 - 325 | $150 - 200 | |

MODEL 1392 – 10W, 1-12 in. speaker, six tube chassis, two channels, tremolo, top control panel, five knobs (v1, v2, tone, trem strength, speed), footswitch, brown covering, brown grille, mfg. 1957-59.

courtesy Blue Book Archive · courtesy Blue Book Archive

| | N/A | $400 - 500 | $250 - 300 | |

MSR/NOTES	100%	EXCELLENT	AVERAGE	LAST MSR

MODEL 1394 – 15W, 1-15 in. speaker, seven tube chassis, two channels, tremolo, top control panel, four inputs, seven knobs (v1, v2, t, m, b, trem strength, speed), footswitch, brown covering, brown grille, mfg. 1957-59.

	N/A	$400 - 475	$225 - 275	

MODEL 1396 – 50W, 2-12 in. speaker, nine tube chassis, 4 X 6L6 power, two channels, tremolo, top control panel, six inputs, eight knobs (v1, t1, b1, v2, t2, b2, trem strength, speed), footswitch, brown covering, brown grille, mfg. 1957-59.

	N/A	$600 - 700	$375 - 450	

MODEL 1430 METEOR – 3W, 1-6 in. speaker, 3 tubes, single input, single volume control, tan leatherette covering, 9 lbs., mfg. 1959-1966.

	N/A	$200 - 250	$110 - 140	

This model is the same as the Model 1390.

MODEL 1431 – 5W, 1-8 in. speaker, 3 tube chassis, single channel, two inputs, two knobs (v, tone), light gray covering, white grille that wraps around the front, mfg. 1959-1961.

	N/A	$200 - 250	$120 - 150	

MODEL 1432 – 10W, 1-12 in. speaker, six tube chassis, two channels, tremolo, top control panel, six knobs (mic. v, mic. tone, inst. v, inst. tone, tremolo strength, tremolo speed), footswitch, dark gray tweed effect covering, white grille that wraps around, 23 lbs., mfg. 1959-1961.

	N/A	$400 - 500	$275 - 325	

MODEL 1433 – 15W, 1-15 in. speaker combo, all tube chassis, preamp: 2 X 12AX7, 1 X 6AU6, 1 X 6CG7, power: 2 X 6L6, rectifier: 5Y3, tremolo, top control panel, four input jacks, seven knobs (v1, v2, 3 tone, s, i), gray covering, wheat grille that wraps around the front sides, 38 lbs., mfg. 1959-1961.

	N/A	$450 - 550	$250 - 300	

MODEL 1434 – 50W, 2-12 in. speaker, nine tube chassis, 4 X 6L6 power, two channels, tremolo, top control panel, six inputs, eight knobs (v1, t1, b1, v2, t2, b2, trem strength, speed), footswitch, brown covering, brown grille, 45 lbs., mfg. 1959-1961.

	N/A	$625 - 775	$375 - 450	

MODEL 1448 GUITAR & AMP – 3W, 1-6 in. speaker, three tube chassis, guitar case with built in amp, single channel, two knobs (v, tone), black case with gray grille, red lining inside, guitar included is a single pickup model, mfg. 1963-69.

Case Only	N/A	$150 - 200	$95 - 120	
Case & Guitar	N/A	$500 - 600	$300 - 375	

In 1967, the guitar was replaced with the Hornet body shape. The Guitar is a Model 1448 as well as the amplifier. For information on the guitar refer to the *Blue Book of Electric Guitars*.

MODEL 1457 GUITAR & AMP – 5W, 1-8 in. speaker, four tube chassis, guitar case with built in amp, single channel, tremolo, four knobs (v, tone, s, strength), footswitch, black case with gray grille, red lining inside, guitar included is a double pickup model, mfg. 1963-69.

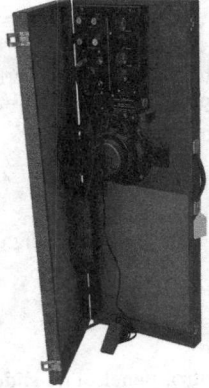

courtesy Savage Audio

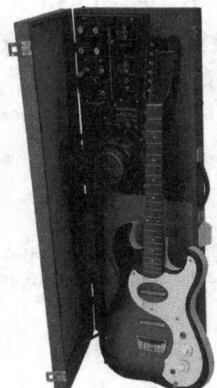

courtesy Savage Audio

courtesy Savage Audio

Case Only	N/A	$200 - 250	$120 - 150	
Case & Guitar	N/A	$650 - 800	$400 - 475	

In 1967, the guitar was replaced with the Hornet body shape. The Guitar is a Model 1457 as well as the amplifier. For information on the guitar refer to the *Blue Book of Electric Guitars*.

MODEL 1459 – 3W, 1-8 in. speaker, 3 tube chassis, single channel, front silver control panel, two inputs, two knobs (v, tone), black vinyl covering, gray grille, 12 lbs., mfg. late 1960s.

	N/A	$200 - 250	$110 - 140	

MODEL 1471 – 5W, 1-8 in. speaker, 3 tube chassis, single channel, two inputs, two knobs (v, tone), black leatherette covering, white grille, 15 lbs., mfg. 1961-63.

	N/A	$300 - 375	$150 - 200	

MSR/NOTES	100%	EXCELLENT	AVERAGE	LAST MSR

MODEL 1472 – 10W, 1-12 in. speaker combo, all tube chassis, preamp: 2 X 12AX7, 6AU6, power: 2 X 6L6, rectifier: 6X4, two channels, tremolo, vertical mounted chassis/control panel on right side of amp, three inputs on back of chassis, six knobs (Mic: v, tone, Inst.: v, tone, trem strength, speed), footswitch, black leatherette covering, white grille, 26 lbs., mfg. 1961-63.

	N/A	$450 - 575	$300 - 375	

MODEL 1473 BASS/ACCORDION – 25W, 6 tube chassis, two channels, vertically left-mounted chassis, four inputs, seven knobs, black leatherette covering, white grille, 40 lbs., mfg. 1961-63.

	N/A	$550 - 700	$350 - 425	

MODEL 1474 – 50W, 2-12 in. speaker, 10 tube chassis, 4 X 6L6GC power, two channels, tremolo, reverb, front control panel, four inputs, nine knobs (v1, t1, b1, v2, t2, b2, trem strength, speed, r), footswitch, black leatherette covering, white grille, 54 lbs., mfg. 1961-63.

	N/A	$750 - 950	$500 - 600	

MODEL 1481 – 5W, 1-8 in. speaker, 3 tube chassis, single channel, two inputs, two knobs (v, tone), gray leatherette covering, white grille, 13 lbs., mfg. 1964-68.

	N/A	$325 - 400	$200 - 250	

MODEL 1482 – 15W, 1-12 in. speaker, six tube chassis, two channels, tremolo, chassis mounted vertically on the right side of amp, three inputs, six knobs (v1, v2, tone1, tone2, speed, strength), gray leatherette covering, silver grille, 26 lbs., mfg. 1964-68.

	N/A	$500 - 600	$300 - 375	

MODEL 1483 PIGGYBACK – 23W, 1-15 in. speaker, head is separate but mounts in the back of cabinet, 6 tube chassis, two channels, front control panel, four inputs, six knobs (v1, b1, t1, v2, b2, t2), gray vinyl covering, white grille, mfg. 1964-66.

	100%	EXCELLENT	AVERAGE	
Head Only	N/A	$300 - 375	$200 - 250	
Head & Cab	N/A	$600 - 700	$425 - 500	

MODEL 1484 TWIN TWELVE PIGGYBACK – ~50W, 2-12 in. speakers, head is separate but mounts in the back of cabinet, 8 tube chassis, power: 4 X 6L6, 5 rectifiers, two channels, reverb, tremolo, front silver control panel, four inputs, nine knobs (Ch. 1: v, b, t, Ch. 2: v, b, t, r, trem strength, speed), gray vinyl covering, white grille, mfg. 1964-66.

Head Only	N/A	$375 - 475	$250 - 300	
Head & Cab	N/A	$800 - 1,000	$575 - 650	

MODEL 1485 PIGGYBACK – 120W (80 RMS), 6-10 in. speakers, head is separate but mounts in the back of cabinet, 10 tube chassis, power: 4 X 6L6, 5 rectifiers, two channels, reverb, tremolo, front silver control panel, four inputs, nine knobs (Ch. 1: v, b, t, Ch. 2: v, b, t, r, trem strength, speed), gray vinyl covering, white grille, mfg. 1964-66.

Head Only	N/A	$400 - 500	$275 - 325	
Head & Cab	N/A	$1,200 - 1,450	$775 - 900	

ELECTRIC SS AMPLIFIERS

MODEL 1463 – 100W, 2-12 in. speakers, head is separate but mounts in the back of cabinet, solid-state chassis, tremolo, reverb, two channels, front silver control panel, four inputs, ten knobs (Ch. 1: v, b, t, Ch. 2: v, b, t, speed, strength, r drive, r depth), black vinyl covering, gray grille, mfg. late 1960s.

Head Only	N/A	$120 - 150	$75 - 95	
Head & Cab	N/A	$300 - 400	$150 - 200	

MODEL 1464 BASS – 35W, 1-15 in. speaker, head is separate but mounts in the back of cabinet, solid-state chassis, single channel, front control panel, two inputs, three knobs (v, b, t), black vinyl covering, gray grille, mfg. late 1960s.

Head Only	N/A	$150 - 200	$100 - 125	
Head & Cab	N/A	$375 - 475	$225 - 275	

XL125 – 50W, 2-12 in. speakers, piggyback combo, solid-state chassis, reverb, tremolo, front white control panel, nine slider knobs, black covering, gray grille, mfg. late 1960s-early 1970s.

Head Only	N/A	$95 - 125	$50 - 75	
Head & Cab	N/A	$250 - 300	$135 - 175	

SIMMS-WATTS

Amplifiers previously produced in London, England between the late 1960s and mid-1970s.

Simms-Watts started producing amplifiers in the late 1960s that are very similar to Marshall and Hiwatt amps of that era. A large "simms-watts" logo in all lower case identifies these amps easily. They produced both guitar and PA head amplifiers with matching speaker cabinets. The 100W guitar head featured two channels, but had separate volume and tone controls for each channel. They went out of business circa 1976 and their amps are pretty rare today. Any further information can be submitted directly to Blue Book Publications.

SMF

Sonic Machine Factory. Amplifiers previously produced in Newport Beach, CA between circa 2002 and 2005.

SMF stands for Sonic Machine Factory, LLC, which was founded in 2002 by Rick Hamel. Rick was working in San Diego with his line of SIB effects pedals, and Mark Sampson of Matchless fame was consulted to engineer these amps. All amplifiers were hand-assembled in California. SMF stopped producing amps around 2005 after approximately 300 of them were produced. Mark Sampson moved on to build Star amplifiers and it is unknown what Rick Hamel is doing today.

ELECTRIC TUBE AMPLIFIERS

The **15 Watter** combo (last MSR $1,749) has 1-12 in. Celestion speaker, 2 X EL84 power output tubes, and a footswitch. The 15 is also available as a head-unit (last MSR $1,539) and a compact combo (last MSR $1,629). The **35 Watter** features 2 X EL34 tubes, reverb, and is available as a head-unit (last MSR $1,929), 1-12 in. Celestion speaker combo (last MSR $2,199), and a compact combo (last MSR $2,079). Both the 15 and the 35 have two channels (Clean and Hi-Gain), and a Sonic Hatch tunable cabinet. The front of these amps have their own look to them as well, with a sort of an off-set oval grille cloth.

A single channel model is available as the **Formean 12W** with 2X EL84 power tubes, digital echo, delay, and is available as a head-unit (last MSR $1,069), 1-12 in. speaker combo (last MSR $1,219), or a 1-12 in. speaker combo without echo and delay (last MSR $1,219).

There are also speaker cabinets available with a **1X12 SMF MOD** (last MSR $719) with 1-12 in. speaker that can handle 30W, and **2X12 SMF MOD** (last MSR $879) with 2-12 in. speakers that can handle 60W. Burgundy, Turquoise, Red, Green, or Gray color coverings were optional.

SMICZ AMPLIFICATION

Amplifiers, speaker cabinets, and other tube-amp related accessories produced in Bristol, CT.

Bob Smicz founded Smicz Amplification to produce both tube amps and the TAD tube adapter. The TAD tube adapter allows the player to use smaller tubes for low wattage applications. This adapter plugs into the power tube socket in an amp and the small tube plugs into the adapter. Smicz also produces the PORTABLuEs series of tube amps that operate on AC or DC power with an internal battery.

SMOKEY AMPLIFIERS

Amplifiers currently produced in Flagstaff, AZ since the mid-1990s.

Smokey Amplifiers are built by Bruce Zinky and Zinky Amplifiers. Smokey specializes in building mini-amps into old cigarette packs. They also offer a model in a translucent polycarbonate box and a custom artist series. Smokey has various used cigarette packs on hand, but to ensure the customer can get their brand, Smokey encourages them to send in their own pack. The polycarbonate amp retails for $32, the recycled cigarette pack amp for $34, and the custom artist series for $32. For more information, visit Smokey's website or contact them directly.

CONTACT INFORMATION
SMOKEY AMPLIFIERS
PO Box 3973
Flagstaff, AZ 86003
Phone No.: 928-225-0400
www.smokeyamps.com
info@zinky.com

SNIDER AMPLIFICATION

Amplifiers currently produced in San Diego, CA since 1999.

Jeff Snider runs an amp repair shop in San Diego and has been fixing and building his own tube amplifiers for several years. In the late 1990s, he started to produces amps with his own name on the logo. His amps are typically built in collaboration with other people, and named after states including California and New Jersey. For more information, refer to Snider's website.

CONTACT INFORMATION
SNIDER AMPLIFICATION
www.snideramps.com
snideramps@cox.net

SOLDANO

Amplifiers currently produced in Seattle, WA since 1987.

Soldano amplifiers have been in the works for more than two decades, but serious production didn't start until 1988. Michael Soldano has been working and building things from the ground up ever since he was a kid. At twenty-one he began playing guitar, and because of a shortage of cash while going to college, he built his own amplifier. His first amp was a Bassman copy that would pretty much blow up every night. He started fixing it and found that they were fun to actually work on. Mike's knowledge of amplifiers really took off when he picked up some tube books from the library where his mom worked. They were throwing them away as they thought tube technology was obsolete. Doug Roberts helped Mike build his first amp in 1980. The first amp wasn't much but it was a learning experience. He was building an amp on a chassis that he named Mr. Science. After he had saved enough money he bought a Mesa Boogie MK II. He decided that it needed some modifications and started a five year building process to make the "ultimate guitar amp." Mike moved to L.A. from Seattle and back with very little success. He had a couple SOL-100, which were the Super Overdrive Lead 100W amp, and had sold a few to friends and players. Tony Antidormi started working for Mike and tried to get the amp out on the music scene. Mike took a job as a roadie for a gig. When he got done with that gig, word had been spread like wildfire about the Soldano amp. The rest, like they say, is history. In 1987 and 1988 some big names bought Soldano amps, like Eric Clapton, and Mark Knopfler of Dire Straits. Later on came the Soldano/Caswell motorized preamp. Business has boomed ever since.

CONTACT INFORMATION
SOLDANO
4233 21st Avenue West
Seattle, WA 98199
Phone No.: 206-781-4636
Fax No.: 206-781-5173
www.soldano.com
info@soldano.com

MSR/NOTES	100%	EXCELLENT	AVERAGE	LAST MSR

Currently Soldano produces a full line of amplifiers that have proved to be some of the best amplifiers on the market. Solidbodyguitars.com is a dealer of Soldano and sell them only because they are "the best amps out there." They now make a full range of head-units, combo amps, and speaker cabinets. In 2009, Soldano and a few others introduced a new line of amplifiers under the Jet City Amplification trademark that are based on famous Soldano circuits but produced overseas. Soldano history courtesy of Ritchie Flieger, *Amps!*

ELECTRIC TUBE AMPLIFIERS

There are various series for all types of electric guitar amplification in the Soldano line. The color of an amp is also an option. They do come standard in black, red, snakeskin, and purple. For a fee custom colors can be used on both the head units and speaker cabinets.

- Add $100-150 for custom colors.

Astroverb Head
courtesy Soldano

Hot Rod 50 Head & 4-12 Speaker Cabinet
courtesy Soldano

Hot Rod 50+ Head & 4-12 Speaker Cabinet
courtesy Soldano

ASTROVERB HEAD – 20W, guitar head-unit, seven-tube chassis, preamp: 5 X 12AX7, power: 2 X EL84, solid-state rectifier, single channel, reverb, front silver control panel, single input, seven black knobs (preamp v, r, b, m, t, v, p), power switch, rear panel: two speaker jacks, available in standard black covering, optional color covering also available, black or silver grille cloth, 17.5 in. wide, 10 in. tall, 9 in. deep, 25 lbs., mfg. 1997-present.

| MSR $1,540 | $1,300 | $850 - 975 | $425 - 525 | |

* *Astroverb 16 112 Combo* – similar to the Astroverb Head, except in combo configuration with 1-12 in. speaker, 17.5 in. wide, 17.5 in. tall, 10 in. deep, 38 lbs., mfg. 1997-present.

| MSR $1,760 | $1,500 | $975 - 1,125 | $500 - 600 | |

* *Astroverb 16 212 Combo* – similar to the Astroverb Head, except in combo configuration with 2-12 in. speakers, 17.5 in. wide, 29 in. tall, 12 in. deep, 57 lbs., mfg. 1997-present.

| MSR $1,980 | $1,675 | $1,100 - 1,250 | $550 - 675 | |

AVENGER 50W HEAD – 50W, head-unit only, all-tube chassis, power: 2 X 5881/6L6, single channel (SLO Overdrive channel), front black control panel, two inputs, seven knobs (preamp g, b, m, t, MV, p, depth), power switch, standby switch, rear panel: two speaker jacks with three-way impedance selector, available in standard black covering or optional color coverings, black/silver metal grille, 25 in. wide, 9.5 in. tall, 9.5 in. deep, 40 lbs., mfg. 2008-present.

| MSR $2,270 | $1,925 | $1,250 - 1,450 | $625 - 775 | |

* *Hot Rod Avenger 50W Head* – similar to the Avenger 50W Head, except has an effects loop, mfg. 2008-present.

| MSR $2,450 | $2,075 | $1,350 - 1,550 | $675 - 825 | |

AVENGER 100W HEAD – 100W, head-unit only, all-tube chassis, power: 4 X 5881/6L6, single channel (SLO Overdrive channel), front black control panel, two inputs, seven knobs (preamp g, b, m, t, MV, p, depth), power switch, standby switch, rear panel: two speaker jacks with three-way impedance selector, available in standard black covering or optional color coverings, black/silver metal grille, 25 in. wide, 9.5 in. tall, 9.5 in. deep, 42 lbs., mfg. 2003-present.

| MSR $2,380 | $2,025 | $1,325 - 1,525 | $650 - 800 | |

* *Hot Rod Avenger 100W Head* – similar to the Avenger 100W Head, except has an effects loop, mfg. 2008-present.

| MSR $2,560 | $2,175 | $1,425 - 1,625 | $700 - 875 | |

DECATONE HEAD – 100W, guitar head-unit, all tube chassis, three channels (clean, crunch, overdrive), front black control panel, single input, 12 black knobs (Clean Ch. preamp, Crunch Ch. preamp, OD Ch. preamp, b, m, t, Clean Ch. v, Crunch Ch. v, OD Ch. v, p, depth, MV), three bright switches (one per channel), power switch, standby switch, rear panel: two speaker jacks with a three-way impedance selector, footswitch jack, effects loop with mix level, available in standard black covering, optional color coverings also available, black metal grille, 25 in. wide, 9.5 in. tall, 9.5 in. deep, 40 lbs., mfg. 1998-present.

| MSR $3,850 | $3,300 | $2,125 - 2,450 | $1,075 - 1,300 | |

* *Decatone 212 Combo* – similar to the Decatone, except in combo configuration with 2-12 in. speakers, disc. 2003.

| | N/A | $1,950 - 2,350 | $1,350 - 1,600 | $3,179 |

| MSR/NOTES | 100% | EXCELLENT | AVERAGE | LAST MSR |

Lucky 13 Head 100 & 4-12 Speaker Cabinet
courtesy Soldano

SLO 100 Head & 4-12 Speaker Cabinet
courtesy Soldano

HOT ROD 25TH ANNIVERSARY HEAD – 25W, guitar head-unit, all tube chassis, preamp: 5 x 12AX7, power: 2 X 6L6, two channels (normal, overdrive), front silver control panel, one input, eight black knobs (Normal Ch. preamp, OD Ch. preamp, b, m, t, Normal Ch. MV, OD Ch. MV, p,), power switch, standby switch, rear panel: two speaker jacks with three-way impedance selector, footswitch jack, effects loop, available in standard black covering or optional color covering, black metal grille, footswitch included, 17.5 in. wide, 8.5 in. tall, 9.5 in. deep, 29 lbs., mfg. 2012-present.

| MSR $2,800 | $2,375 | $1,550 - 1,775 | $775 - 950 | |

HOT ROD 50/HOT ROD 50XL HEAD – 50W, guitar head-unit, all tube chassis, two channels (normal, overdrive), front silver control panel, two inputs, six black knobs (preamp v, b, m, t, MV, p), power switch, standby switch, rear panel: two speaker jacks with three-way impedance selector, effects loop, available in standard black covering or optional color covering, black metal grille, 25 in. wide, 9.5 in. tall, 9.5 in. deep, disc. 2008.

| | $1,375 | $900 - 1,050 | $650 - 750 | $1,600 |

* *Hot Rod 50 212 Combo* – similar to the Hot Rod 50, except in combo configuration with 2-12 in. speakers, disc. 2003.

| | N/A | $1,000 - 1,200 | $700 - 800 | $1,739 |

HOT ROD 50+/HOT ROD 50+XL HEAD – 50W, guitar head-unit, all tube chassis, two channels (normal, overdrive), front silver control panel, two inputs, nine black knobs (Normal Ch. preamp, OD Ch. preamp, b, m, t, Normal Ch. MV, OD Ch. MV, p, depth), power switch, standby switch, rear panel: two speaker jacks with three-way impedance selector, footswitch jack, effects loop, available in standard black covering or optional color covering, black metal grille, 25 in. wide, 9.5 in. tall, 9.5 in. deep, 40 lbs., current mfg.

| MSR $3,080 | $2,600 | $1,700 - 1,975 | $850 - 1,050 | |

* *Hot Rod 50+ 212 Combo* – similar to the Hot Rod 50, except in combo configuration with 2-12 in. speakers, disc. 2003.

| | N/A | $1,450 - 1,750 | $1,000 - 1,150 | $2,459 |

HOT ROD 100+ HEAD – 100W, guitar head-unit, all tube chassis, two channels (normal, overdrive), front silver control panel, two inputs, nine black knobs (Normal Ch. preamp, OD Ch. preamp, b, m, t, Normal Ch. MV, OD Ch. MV, p, depth), power switch, standby switch, rear panel: two speaker jacks with three-way impedance selector, footswitch jack, effects loop, available in standard black covering or optional color covering, black metal grille, 25 in. wide, 9.5 in. tall, 9.5 in. deep, 42 lbs., current mfg.

| MSR $3,190 | $2,700 | $1,750 - 2,025 | $875 - 1,075 | |

LUCKY 13 HEAD 50 – 50W, guitar head-unit, all tube chassis, power: 2 X 5881, two channels (classic vintage, overdrive), reverb, front black control panel, single input, 12 black knobs (Clean Ch.: v, m, b, t, r, OD Ch.: g, b, m, t, r, v, All: p), Clean Ch. bright switch, power switch standby switch, rear panel: three speaker jacks, footswitch jack, available in standard black covering or optional color coverings, black grille cloth, 26 in. wide, 11 in. tall, 9.5 in. deep, 43 lbs., mfg. 2000-present.

| MSR $3,200 | $2,700 | $1,775 - 2,050 | $875 - 1,100 | |

* *Lucky 13 Combo 50* – similar to the Lucky 13 Head 50 except in combo configuration with 2-12 in. speakers, 26 in. wide, 23 in. tall, 10.5 in. deep, 75 lbs., mfg. 2000-present.

| MSR $3,400 | $2,900 | $1,875 - 2,175 | $950 - 1,150 | |

LUCKY 13 HEAD 100 – 100W, guitar head-unit, all tube chassis, power: 4 X 5881, two channels (classic vintage, overdrive), reverb, front black control panel, single input, 12 black knobs (Clean Ch.: v, m, b, t, r, OD Ch.: g, b, m, t, r, v, All: p), Clean Ch. bright switch, power switch standby switch, rear panel: three speaker jacks, footswitch jack, available in standard black covering or optional color coverings, black grille cloth, 26 in. wide, 11 in. tall, 9.5 in. deep, 50 lbs., mfg. 2000-present.

| MSR $3,300 | $2,800 | $1,825 - 2,100 | $900 - 1,125 | |

* *Lucky 13 Combo 100* – similar to the Lucky 13 Head 100, except in combo configuration with 2-12 in. speakers, 26 in. wide, 23 in. tall, 10.5 in. deep, 78 lbs., mfg. 2000-present.

| MSR $3,500 | $3,000 | $1,925 - 2,225 | $975 - 1,200 | |

REVERB-O-SONIC 212 COMBO – 50W, 2-12 in. speakers, guitar combo, all tube chassis, two channels (clean, crunch/blues), reverb, front silver control panel, single input, nine black knobs (Clean Ch. preamp, Crunch Ch. v, r, b, m, t, Clean Ch. MV, Crunch Ch. MV, p), power switch, standby switch, rear panel: speaker jacks, footswitch jack, effects loop, available in standard black covering or optional color coverings, black or silver cloth grille, 26 in. wide, 20 in. tall, 10.5 in. deep, current mfg.

| MSR $3,200 | $2,700 | $1,775 - 2,050 | $875 - 1,100 | |

MSR/NOTES	100%	EXCELLENT	AVERAGE	LAST MSR

SLO 100 HEAD – 100W, guitar head-unit, all tube chassis, two channels (normal, overdrive), front silver control panel, single input, eight knobs (Normal Ch. preamp, OD Ch. preamp, b, m, t, Normal Ch. MV, OD Ch. MV, p), bright switch, channel switch, power switch, standby switch, rear panel: two speaker jacks with three-way impedance selector, line out with level control, footswitch jack, effects loop, available in standard black covering or optional color coverings, black metal grille, 25 in. wide, 9.5 in. tall, 9.5 in. deep, 42 lbs., mfg. 1988-present.

| MSR $5,000 | $4,250 | $2,750 - 3,200 | $1,375 - 1,700 | |

* **SLO 100 212 Combo** – similar to the SLO 100, except in combo configuration with 2-12 in. speakers, disc.

| | N/A | $2,400 - 2,900 | $1,650 - 1,950 | |

SOLDANO 44 – 50W, 1-12 in. Eminence Legend speaker, seven-tube chassis, preamp: 5 X 12AX7, power: 2 X 5881, single channel (SLO crunch), reverb, front black control panel, single input, eight black knobs (preamp, r, b, m, t, Normal v, Lead v, p), power switch, standby switch, available in standard blue covering or optional color coverings, black grille, 17.5 in. wide, 17.5 in. tall, 10 in. deep, mfg. 2009-present.

| MSR $2,750 | $2,325 | $1,525 - 1,750 | $750 - 925 | |

SPEAKER CABINETS

Soldano features several speaker cabinet options to be teamed up with the head unit amplifiers. Cabinets can be bought empty or equipped with Soldano speakers. Earlier models feature Eminence Legend speakers. The configurations consist of 4-12 in. or 2-12 in. cabinets in either straight or angled fronts.

1-12 IN. CABINET – 2-12 in. speaker cabinet, various color coverings, black grille, current mfg.

| MSR $750 | $650 | $425 - 475 | $205 - 255 | |

2-12 IN. CABINET – 2-12 in. speaker cabinet, various color coverings, black grille, current mfg.

| MSR $1,045 | $900 | $575 - 675 | $290 - 350 | |

4-12 IN. CABINET – 4-12 in. speaker cabinet, available in slant or straight front, various color coverings, black grille, current mfg.

| MSR $1,600 | $1,350 | $875 - 1,025 | $450 - 550 | |

LUCKY 2-12 IN. CABINET – 2-12 in. speaker cabinet, designed for use with the Lucky Head, various color coverings, black grille, current mfg.

| MSR $1,100 | $925 | $600 - 700 | $300 - 375 | |

LUCKY 4-12 IN. CABINET – 4-12 in. speaker cabinet, designed for use with the Lucky Head, various color coverings, black grille, current mfg.

| MSR $1,700 | $1,450 | $950 - 1,075 | $475 - 575 | |

SONAX

Amplifiers previously produced in Canada circa 1972-73. Distributed by Gretsch.

After Gretsch amplifiers were discontinued in the late 1960s, Baldwin wanted to introduce a new line of models. They had Yorkville Sound of Traynor fame in Canada build a line of amps that were called Sonax. These amps were solid-state in design and available in bass or guitar configurations. The Sonax line lasted less than two years when Baldwin/Gretsch discontinued the line. For more information on Gretsch amplifiers see the Gretsch section.

ELECTRIC SS AMPLIFIERS

530B (MODEL 7814) – 20W, 1-12 in. speaker, bass combo, solid-state chassis, single channel, front black control panel, two inputs, three knobs (v, t, b), black covering, black grille, 20.875 in. wide, 24.625 in. tall, 11.875 in. deep, mfg. circa 1972-73.

| | N/A | $150 - 200 | $95 - 120 | |

550B (MODEL 7816) – 40W, 1-15 in. speaker, bass combo, solid-state chassis, single channel, front black control panel, two inputs, four knobs (v, t, m, b), bright switch, black covering, black grille, 20.875 in. wide, 29.625 in. tall, 12.25 in. deep, mfg. circa 1972-73.

| | N/A | $200 - 250 | $120 - 150 | |

720G (MODEL 7802) – 15W, 2-8 in. speakers, guitar combo, solid-state chassis, single channel, reverb, front black control panel, two inputs, four knobs (v, t, b, r), black covering, black grille, 25.125 in. wide, 17.75 in. tall, 10 in. deep, mfg. circa 1972-73.

| | N/A | $200 - 250 | $120 - 150 | |

730G (MODEL 7804) – 25W, 2-10 in. speakers, guitar combo, solid-state chassis, single channel, reverb, tremolo, front black control panel, two inputs, five knobs (v, t, b, r, trem. speed), tremolo on/off switch, black covering, black grille, 27 in. wide, 20.25 in. tall, 11.125 in. deep, mfg. circa 1972-73.

| | N/A | $275 - 325 | $150 - 200 | |

750G (MODEL 7806) – 40W, 2-12 in. speakers, guitar combo, solid-state chassis, two channels, reverb, tremolo, front black control panel, two inputs, 10 knobs (Ch. 1: v, t, b, Ch. 2: v, t, m, b, r, s, i), two treble boost switches, optional footswitch, black covering, black grille, 30.125 in. wide, 20.375 in. tall, 11.25 in. deep, mfg. circa 1972-73.

| | N/A | $325 - 400 | $200 - 250 | |

775G (MODEL 7808) – 53W, 4-10 in. speakers, guitar combo, solid-state chassis, two channels, reverb, tremolo, front black control panel, two inputs, 10 knobs (Ch. 1: v, t, b, Ch. 2: v, t, m, b, r, s, i), two treble boost switches, optional footswitch, black covering, black grille, 30.125 in. wide, 27 in. tall, 11.75 in. deep, mfg. circa 1972-73.

| | N/A | $325 - 400 | $200 - 250 | |

SONGWORKS SYSTEMS & PRODUCTS

See Little Lanilei.

SONIC CORD

Amplifiers previously produced in Pawtucket, RI between 1999 and the mid-2000s.

Sonic Cord produced their first amp, the **Bantam**, in 1998 that attracted several musicians in the Boston area and soon Sonic Cord was fixing up studios and the like with their products. In 2000, Sonic Cord helped put the stage together for the Museum of Fine Arts in a piece called "Dangerous Curves: Art of the Guitar." In 2002, they became public and started selling more models of amps, and they attended their first NAMM show in 2003. Sonic Cord stopped producing amplifiers in the mid-2000s.

ELECTRIC TUBE AMPLIFIERS

The **Toad** model was available in a 112 or 115 Combo (last price was $759), and a 112 Combo with a P12N (last price was $799). The **SWW** was disc. in 2003 and last retailed for $1,500. The **Bantam** was available as a head unit (last price was $699) 1-12 in. combo (last price was $789), or 1-15 in. combo ($1,800, disc. 2003). The **SWW/Bantam** 112 retailed last for $525 (disc. 2003). There was a bass amp **Classic** model available for $999.

SONNY JR.

Amplifiers currently produced in Tolland, CT since 1996.

Sonny Jr. has been playing harmonicas since 1974, and after thirty years of playing and studying tone, he decided to apply this knowledge to his own line of harmonica amplifiers. Sonny's amps resemble Fender's narrow panel tweed amps from the 1950s; however, the chassis and speaker configurations are all voiced for harmonica use. Amplifiers are typically in stock and they work hard to keep their lead time down to a week or two. For more information, visit Sonny Jr.'s website or contact him directly.

CONTACT INFORMATION
SONNY JR.
Phone No.: 203-230-8839
www.sonnyjr.com
sonnytone@aol.com

HARMONICA AMPLIFIERS

Sonny Jr. currently produces two models. The **Sonny Jr. 410** (MSR $1,795) is based on a '59 Bassman but features more superior parts, including paper-in-oil capacitors, custom built transformers, and an extra package of tubes and patch cable so the amp can be used in any room setting. The **Cruncher** (MSR $1,595) features 35W, 1-12 in. (Weber P12Q) and 2-8 in. speakers (P8Q and P8R). Gary Smith and Dave Barrett currently endorse this model.

Cruncher
courtesy Sonny Jr.

Cruncher
courtesy Sonny Jr.

SOUNDBOARD

Amplifiers previously produced in Kaukauna, WI.

Soundboards are acoustic amplifiers hand assembled by luthier Bruce Petros in Wisconsin. These amps are carefully built and tested to ensure great sound and reliability. Instead of having a standard grille cloth covering the speaker, these amps have a real spruce soundboard where the sound is aimed to. This replicates what a real acoustic guitar does instead of using the harsh overtones that a speaker produces. The soundboard actually has a soundhole that is about the size of one on a guitar. Essentially these amps replicate the sound of an acoustic guitar the most accurately with a wood soundboard.

ACOUSTIC AMPLIFIERS

The Acoustic Soundboard 2nd Generation amp Series 2 Model HC 125/M was the most recent amp on the market. This is an 85W amplifier with two channels, separate gain controls, a seven-band Timbre control equalizer, and effects loop. It is available in a brown vinyl covering, or in Dovetailed oak, and the controls and general color is brown . Speaker cabinets are also available to match up with the respective amp. The original Acoustic Soundboard amp was discontinued circa 2002. The combo amp in a wood cabinet (last MSR $2,650) and in vinyl for (last MSR $2,400). Currently Petros has discontinued their Soundboard amplifier line and is focused on producing their custom guitars.

SOUND CITY

Amplifiers previously produced in England from circa 1965 through the late 1970s.

The roots of Sound City date back to 1875. The parent company of Sound City was formed then as John E. Dallas and Sons, Ltd. (JED). JED grew in the musical instrument area, and circa early 1960s, they entered into consumer electronics. This division was called Dallas Musical Ltd. In 1965, Dallas bought Arbiter Electronics, and the new partnership was called Dallas Arbiter, Ltd. Arbiter owned three music shops before Dallas acquired them. They decided to start producing sound reinforcement equipment and it was first built in one of those three music shops that was named Sound City. This is how the amp acquired the name. All products produced by Arbiter featured the Sound City name or some close variation of it.

Sound City amps have a reputation of being HIWATT copies. There is some truth to this as it was reported that Sound City and HIWATT were produced in the same location for a short period. Dave Reeves actually designed some of Sound City's first amplifiers. Pete Townshend of The Who played through Sound City amplifiers as well. Information courtesy: Unofficial Sound City website.

ELECTRIC TUBE AMPLIFIERS

CONCORD COMBO – 35-40W, 2-12 in. speakers, guitar combo, seven-tube chassis, preamp: 3 X 12AX7, 2 X 12AT7, power: 2 X EL34, solid-state rectifier, two channels, reverb, front silver control panel, four inputs (two per channel, low gain/high gain), seven slider controls (Ch. 1: v, t, b, Ch. 2: v, t, b, All: r), two brilliant switches (one per channel), output level meter, power switch, standby switch, black vinyl covering, cream/oxblood basketweave grille cloth, mfg. early 1970s.

N/A	$800 - 1,000	$475 - 600

MODEL L50 (SOUND CITY 50 PLUS) – 50W, head-unit, guitar configuration, tube chassis, preamp: 3 X 7025, 1 X 12AT7, power: EL34, two channels, front silver control panel, four inputs, five multi-colored knobs (v1, v2, t, m, b), black covering, mfg. 1970-late 1970s.

N/A	$800 - 1,000	$550 - 700

Later models may not have colored knobs. The covering may also be a different color than black as tan and others were used.

MODEL L120 (SOUND CITY 120) – 120W, head-unit, guitar configuration, tube chassis, preamp: 3 X 7025, 1 X 12AT7, power: 4 X EL34, two channels, front silver control panel, six inputs, (two inputs per channel, two for slave inputs), six multi-colored knobs (v1, v2, t, m, b, p), black covering, mfg. 1970-late 1970s.

N/A	$950 - 1,200	$650 - 800

Later models may not have colored knobs. The covering may also be a different color than black as tan and others were used.

MODEL L-200 PLUS (SOUND CITY 200 PLUS) – 200W, head-unit, guitar configuration, all tube chassis, preamp: 4 X 7025, 1 X 12AT7, power: 4 X 6550, two channels, front chrome control panel, six inputs (two inputs per channel, two slave inputs), six knobs (v1, v2, t, m, b, p), black covering, mfg. 1970s.

courtesy John Beeson/The Music Shoppe

courtesy John Beeson/The Music Shoppe

N/A	$950 - 1,200	$650 - 800

SOUND ENHANCER

Amplifiers currently produced in California since 2006. Previously produced in Waxahachie, TX, between 2002 and 2005. Distributed by Sound Enhancer in The Woodlands, TX.

Harold N. Smith Jr. is the president of Sound Enhancer and the company is a family owned business. Sound Enhancer is possibly the only trademark in the book whose amplifier doesn't run on electricity. The Sound Enhancer is a hollow black box that acts as a stand for a guitar amplifier, and the Mainfold Horn Technology amplifies the amplifier that is sitting on the Sound Enhancer. The guitar amp is angled upward and sound resonates inside the box. The sound is then projected out of the opening in the front right underneath the amplifier. The Sound Enhancer is great for isolating the amps volume as it keeps volume levels under control by sending all sound waves forward. If the back of an amp is left open, the secondary sound wave causes phase cancellation, thus destroying tone. The Sound Enhancer solves this problem. For more information, visit Sound Enhancer's website or contact them directly.

AMPLIFIERS

Sound Enhancer offers their amplifiers in five different sizes, and each size allows a six inch variation in the size of the actual guitar amplifier. The **Mini** Model (MSR $159) is 17 in. wide and is designed for extra small amps such as the Fender Champ. The **E-SM** (MSR $219) is 22.5 in. wide and is designed for small amps such as the Fender Princeton. The **E-MD** (MSR $224) is 24.5 in. wide and is designed for mdeium-sized amps such as the Fender Deluxe or Deluxe Reverb. The **E-LG** (MSR $229) is 26.5 in. wide and is designed for large amps such as the Fender Twin or Twin Reverb. The **E-XL** (MSR $234) is 28.5 in. wide and is designed for extra large amps such as Marshall Blues Breakers, Vox AC-30s, and Roland JC-120s.

**Model E-SM
courtesy Sound Enhancer**

**Model E-SM
courtesy Sound Enhancer**

SOUNDKING

Amplifiers and other audio equipment currently produced in Ningbo, China. Currently, there is no U.S. Distributor.

SoundKing produces a full line of electronic equipment. They make power amps, preamps and guitar amplifier combos. Along with these guitar products they have mixers, speakers, speaker cabinets, stands, cables, and other accessories. Among their amplifiers are the Professional series. The power units are of different wattages and mostly rack-mounts. The guitar combos are small practice units along with some larger (50W) models. For more information, visit Soundking's website.

CONTACT INFORMATION
SOUNDKING
818# Chenxin Rd.
Yinzhou Investment Industry Park
Ningbo, 315105 China
Phone No.: 86-574-88235195
Fax No.: 86-574-88235763
www.soundking.com
sales@soundking.com

SOVTEK

Amplifiers previously produced in Russia between circa 1992 and 2000. Distributed by Electro-Harmonix.

Mike Matthews started the New Sensor Corporation in Russia in the late 1980s. The first brand of tubes he produced were under the Sovtek brand. In circa 1992, Sovtek released a line of tube guitar amplifiers that were produced through the late 1990s. Sovtek continues to produce tubes, but they do not produce any amplifiers. For more information on Mike Matthews and Electro-Harmonix, see the Electro-Harmonix section.

ELECTRIC TUBE AMPLIFIERS

Sovtek produced the Mig Series of tube amps during its existence. These amps were available as a 30W head, 50W head, 60W head, 100W head, 100W bass amp head, and a 50W Midget combo. Used prices on these amplifiers generally fall between $300 and $500 depending upon condition/configuration.

**Midget Combo
courtesy John Beeson/The Music Shoppe**

**Midget Combo
courtesy John Beeson/The Music Shoppe**

SPECIMEN PRODUCTS

Amplifiers currently produced in Chicago, IL since 1993.

Ian Schneller started using the Specimen Products name in 1981 on art pieces and sculptures. In 1984, he started to build custom guitars and basses, and in 1994, he introduced tube amplifiers. Schneller is best-known for his Horn Amp, which is reminiscent of early record players with the large horn-style speaker. He also builds a variation of this amp as a speaker only for instrument or hi-fi applications. Prices start at $5,000 for the Horn Amp and $2,300 for a single Horn Speaker. For more information, visit Specimen's website or contact him directly.

CONTACT INFORMATION
SPECIMEN PRODUCTS
1240 N. Homan Ave.
Chicago, IL 60651
Phone No.: 773-489-4830
www.specimenproducts.com
ian@specimenproducts.com

SPEEDSTER

Amplifiers previously produced in Gig Harbor, WA from 1995-2000 and 2003-early 2010s.

Speedster amps were built for a while in the late 1990s, and because of their popularity were reintroduced to the market in 2003. These amps feature some interesting designs. These amps look a little like an old radio from the 1930s or 1940s. They also have great circuitry with tubes and other effects. The cabinets were available in many different colors and wood grains. They made some anniversary models for such occasions as the 100th Anniversary of NAMM.

ELECTRIC TUBE AMPLIFIERS

Models include the **25W Deluxe** and the **Class A 40**. All models come with a head unit and a separate speaker cabinet. The 25W Deluxe features 2 X 6V6 power tubes, 1-12 in Eminence speaker, reverb, and an adjustable tube bias with an illuminated meter. The Class A 40 is a Class A-wired amp with EL84 power tubes, 2-12 in. Eminence speakers, and an engraved anodized faceplate.

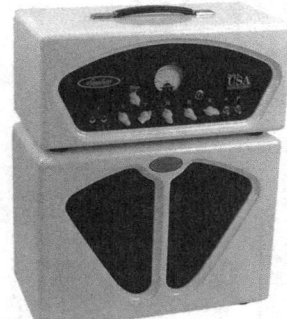

25W Deluxe
courtesy solidbodyguitar.com, Inc.

25W Deluxe
courtesy solidbodyguitar.com, Inc.

Class A 40
courtesy Speedster

SQUIER

Amplifiers previously produced in Mexico, Korea, and China. Distributed by the Fender Musical Instrument Company in Scottsdale, AZ.

Squier instruments began in 1983 in Matsumoto, Japan at the Fugi Fen Gakki. Fender had established Fender Japan in 1982 in conjunction with Kanda Shokai and Yamano music. This trademark came from the V.C. Squier company that produced strings in the 1950s. Fender later aquired the trademark in 1965 and it remained unused until 1982. The Squier name was originally going to be for the European market, but Fender quickly realized that they could use it in the U.S. for an entry level brand of instruments. They first started producing guitars that were all Fender designs, built overseas that could be sold cheaply. Shortly after this they started producing small solid-state amplifiers. Among the most popular Squier amps are the Champ series, based off the popular line by Fender. Squier amplifiers only appear now in the Strat-Pak and Bass-Pak. These are all-in-one packages where you get the guitar, amp, strings, cord, strap, picks, and a video. Currently these packages include Fender amps. For more information, visit Squier's website or contact them directly.

ELECTRIC SS AMPLIFIERS

Fender produced a line of amps in the late 1980s and early 1990s called the Squier series. This brings up the argument again if these are Fender amps with a Squier logo on them, or are they Squier amps produced by Fender? More research is underway and look for further information in upcoming editions. The Strat-Pak and Bass-Pak are currently including Fender amps. As of now Fender is no longer producing any amps with a Squier logo.

BP-15 (NO. 023-5000-000) – 15W, bass amplifiers, 1-8 in. speaker, solid-state chassis, front black control panel, single input, four black knobs (v, l, m, h), headphone jack, speaker-out, black vinyl covering, silver grille, mfg. 2000-02.

	100%	EXCELLENT	AVERAGE	LAST MSR
	N/A	$55 - 70	$30 - 40	$140

CHAMP 15 – 15W, 1-8 in. speaker, solid-state chassis, front black control panel, two inputs, six black knobs (g, v, t, m, b, p), overdrive switch, effects loop, headphone jack, black Tolex covering, silver grille, mfg. 1990s.

	100%	EXCELLENT	AVERAGE	LAST MSR
	N/A	$40 - 60	$20 - 30	

* *Champ 15 GR* – similar to the Champ 15, except has reverb and reverb knob, mfg. 1990s.

	100%	EXCELLENT	AVERAGE	LAST MSR
	N/A	$45 - 65	$25 - 35	

SA-10 ACOUSTIC (NO. 238-9000) – 10W, 1-6 in. speaker, acoustic combo configuration, solid-state chassis, single channel, front black control panel, single input, three knobs (v, t, b), headphone jack, brown covering, wheat brown grille, mfg. 2006-disc.

	100%	EXCELLENT	AVERAGE	LAST MSR
	$80	$45 - 60	$20 - 30	$133

MSR/NOTES	100%	EXCELLENT	AVERAGE	LAST MSR

SIDEKICK SP-10 (NO. 023-1000-049) – 10W, 1-6 in. speaker, solid-state chassis, front black control panel, single input, three black knobs (v, t, b), overdrive switch, black Tolex covering, silver grille, disc.

Sidekick SP-10
courtesy John Beeson/The Music Shoppe

Sidekick SP-10
courtesy John Beeson/The Music Shoppe

	100%	EXCELLENT	AVERAGE	LAST MSR
	$50	$25 - 40	$10 - 15	$80

STAGE

Amplifiers previously produced in the U.S. during the mid-1970s. Distributed by Unicord, Inc. in Westbury, NY.

Stage amplifiers were owned by Unicord who was the same company that owned Univox. More than likely, Univox built these amplifiers and Unicord put a Stage logo on them. These amps were of solid-state design, and they came in a variety of configurations. Any further information on Stage amplifiers can be submitted directly to Blue Book Publications.

ELECTRIC SS AMPLIFIERS

There were quite a few models produced with the Stage name and they all featured black covering, black grilles, and red logos indicating the model number. For guitar, models include the Mirco Series, the **25**, the **65**, the **400/112**, the **400/210**, the **720/115**, the **720/212**, and the **720/410**. For bass guitars, models include the Micro Series, the **252**, the **450**, and the **750**. Keyboard and PA amplifiers were also available. Used prices on most models are between $100 and $300 depending upon condition/configuration.

STANDEL

Amplifiers originally produced in Temple City, CA from 1953 to 1967 and from 1968 to 1973 in El Monte, CA. Production resumed in 1997 in Glendale, CA by Requisite Audio Engineering from 1997 to 2007. Currently, Standel amplifiers are being handcrafted in Ventura, CA.

CONTACT INFORMATION
STANDEL
Phone No.: 818-437-0779
www.standelamps.com
danny@standelamps.com

The Standel company was founded by Bob Crooks, an electronics engineer, in 1953. Crooks learned electronics from correspondence courses and began working for Lockheed. After a while he was promoted to engineer in charge of their electronics to build amplifiers. Crooks had a radio repair business that was called Standard Electronics where they derived the name of the company from. Bob was approached by Paul Bigsby to design an amplifier for his pedal steel guitars. After many failed attempts the 25L15 was eventually perfected with the first one going to Speedy West. Within a few months, musicians Joe Maphis, Merle Travis, and Chet Atkins were all playing Standel amplifiers and continued to use them for their entire careers. The first brochure for Standel amplifiers was published in 1954.

Crooks began experimenting with semi-conductors in 1961 and within two years had developed a hybrid tube and solid-state amplifier. The company was successful in the 1960s as they beat Fender to the punch by releasing a solid-state amp by 1964. Solid-state Standels were played by Wes Montgomery, Pete Drake and Buddy Emmons. The 1970s proved to be very unlucky for Standel as they had parts and components that faulted often. This led to erosion of the Standel quality reputation. Crooks sold the company to Gibson Guitars distributor, Chicago Musical Instruments and worked for them for two years designing the SG Systems line of amplifiers. Later Crooks worked

Studio X
courtesy George McGuire

Studio X
courtesy George McGuire

at Barcus Berry where he designed the Sonic Maximizer, which was a unit that compensated for speaker errors by modifying the signal going into the amplifier. The product is still being produced by the BBE Sound Corporation in Long Beach, California. Bob Crooks passed away in 1999.

Standel amplifiers are back in business producing the amplifiers that made them famous in the first place. Danny "Sage" McKinney is now the current owner and president of the company and producing amplifiers after a 25 year absence from the music industry. For more information, visit Standel's website. Source: Willie Moseley, *Vintage Guitar Magazine*, Deke Dickerson, and Danny McKinney.

ELECTRIC TUBE AMPLIFIERS

Bob Crooks first started building amplifiers out of his garage in 1953. The first model (and most popular) was the **25L15**. These amplifiers were typically completely custom made from the speaker size to the color of covering. This is the model that Standel re-released when they came back in the late 1990s. The unique thing about Standel amplifiers is that they beat the big companies to the punch with several designs, including the piggyback and the front mounted control panel. Other models from this era include the **10L8** and **15L12**. Prices on these early amps need to be evaluated on a case by case basis as almost every one will be different than another. Used pricing has been seen from anywhere between $7,000 to $14,000.

ELECTRIC SS AMPLIFIERS

Standel started producing solid-state models in circa 1963/64, which was before Fender, Vox, and Ampeg flirted with solid-state designs. They produced amplifiers throughout the 1960s until faulty parts and the amps started failing. Models from this era include the Imperial Series, the Artist Series, the Custom Series, and the Studio Series. Around 1972, Standel sold the company and stopped producing amplifiers shortly thereafter. Standel remained out of production until the late 1990s, when they revived the name, just in time for the original founder, Bob Crooks to develop the 25L15 reissue prototype and see its re-release. Solid-state amps from the 1960s are typically priced between $400 and $600 depending upon condition/configuration.

STAR

Amplifiers previously produced in Los Angeles, CA from 2003-2016.

Star amplifiers were designed by Mark Sampson of Matchless and SMF notoriety. Sampson has been involved in guitar amplifiers since the early 1980s, and has been building amps since the late 1980s when he started Matchless. Star amps are built on all the knowledge Samson has learned over the years, and the result are some of the best Class A amps on the market. All Star amps have Class A tube chassis, Teflon coated point-to-point wired chassis (no circuit boards), tube rectifiers, and other quality building features. Star offered a wide range of amps with reverb and effects loop.

ELECTRIC TUBE AMPLIFIERS

The **Blues Star** amp comes in 15W or 30W variations, features a single channel, and is available as a head-unit or combo. The Blues Star 15W head retails for $3,029, the 15W 1-12 in. combo retails for $3,299, the 30W head retails for $3,449, and the 30W 1-12 in. combo retails for $3,749. The **Gain Star** amp comes in 15W or 30W variations, features two channels, has an effects loop, and is available as a head-unit or combo. The Gain Star 15W head retails for $3,029, the 15W 1-12 in. combo retails for $3,299, the 30W head retails for $3,449, and the 30W 1-12 in. combo retails for $3,749. The **Sirius Reverb** amp comes in 15W or 30W variations, features two channels, has reverb on channel one, an effects loop on channel two, and is available as a head-unit or combo. The Sirius Reverb 15W head retails for $3,449, the 15W 1-12 in. combo retails for $3,749, the 30W head retails for $3,859, and the 30W 1-12 in. combo retails for $4,159. The **Super Nova** (MSR $2,929) was introduced in 2006 and features a 15W chassis with reverb in a smaller, ligher cabinet with 1-12 in. speaker. Speaker cabinets are also available as the ST112 (MSR $829) with 1-12 in. speaker, and the ST212 (MSR $1,029) with 2-12 in. speakers.

STEPHENS AUDIO

Amplifiers previously produced in Taylorsville (Salt Lake City), UT. Distributed by Stephens Audio.

Stephens Audio produced tube amplifiers that were built with quality and will not break your wallet. They produce dthe Molasses model, which has 15 tubes in it! They also had speaker boxes, smaller tube amps, pocket sized amps, and their own switch cable.

ST. GEORGE

Amplifiers previously produced in Japan during the mid- to late 1960s.

The St. George trademark was a brand name used by U.S. importer Buegeleisen & Jacobson of New York, New York. It has also been reported that amplifiers bearing the St. George label were imported by the WMI Corporation of Los Angeles, CA. St. George produced tube amplifiers and it is possible that some solid-state models exist. Generally, they are of low to mid-quality and are priced between $200 and $400 depending upon condition/configuration (source: Michael Wright, *Guitar Stories, Volume One*).

STINGER

Amplifiers previously produced in Korea during the late 1980s. Distributed in the U.S. by Martin in Nazareth, PA.

After Martin stopped building solid body electric guitars in the U.S. in 1982, they decided to introduce a Korean line of electric instruments in 1985. These guitars were branded Stinger, and were set up and inspected at Martin's factory in Nazareth, PA. Designs were based on popular American models including Strats, Teles, and Fender basses. In 1988, they introduced a line of amplifiers called the FX Series, which featured about four models. Information courtesy *Michael Wright, Guitar Stories, Volume 2*.

ELECTRIC SS AMPLIFIERS

The Stinger FX series featured seven models. The **FX-1** and **FX-1R** featured 10W and reverb on the second model. The **FX-1R** was also available as a mini-stack. The **FX-3B** was a 15W bass amp. The **FX-3C** featured 30W, 1-12 in. speaker, and chorus. The **FX-30RC** featured 65W, 1-12 in. speaker, reverb, and chorus. The **FX-6B** was a 60W bass amp with 1-15 in. speaker. Used prices on these models are typically between $75 and $200 depending on condition/configuration.

SUNN

Amplifiers previously produced in Portland, Oregon and in Kentucky. Sunn is now owned by Fender Musical Instrument Corporation of Scottsdale, Arizona, but they currently do not produce any models under the name Sunn.

The Sunn Amplifier company was founded by Norm Sundholm and his brother Conrad. Norm played bass in the band the Kingsmen. He played through a Fender Bandmaster, but needed more power out of it. He changed speakers with improvement, but later changed the actual amp to a Hi-Fi amplifier, leaving only the cabinet the original part of the Bandmaster. So he figured he could build the box and get the components for much chepaer than what a Fender cost. Norm bought the parts to build the box and would buy the power amp from Dynakits. His first amplifiers were named BAMCO, which stood for Burke Aarons Music Company. Enter Norm's brother Conrad, who knew a little about woodworking. Conrad (Con for short) built some amps after school for Norm, as he was on the road with the Kingsmen. They started putting Sunn on the amplifiers for the first time and Sunn Musical Equipment Company was born. They chose Sunn rather than Sun because of Sun Tachometers in all the cars that could be a problem. This idea came from Barry Curtis.

In 1965, Con hired the first full time employee, and in late 1965 they decided they needed a factory to build amps. They moved to Tualtain, Oregon, which was right outside Portland. Their building was actually an old public swimming pool that had gone out of business. They filled in the hole with dirt, cemented it over and it became the factory. Employees included Jim Peterson and Gene Matheny, and later Bob Teneyck as an engineer.

In 1969, the brothers of the company began to disagree, and Con bought out Norm's part of the company. However, in three years Con sold Sunn to Hartzell. When Hartzell took over they moved the factory to Williamstown, Kentucky so they would be closer to Cinncinnati and the east coast. Amps were heavy and speaker cabinets were only coming from Kentucky (the amplifiers were still produced in Oregon). They ended up moving back to Oregon in the late 1970s where they manufactured amps until the company was sold to a rebuilding Fender organization in 1987. Fender took Sunn and put them in mothballs until Fender became reorganized in their own name. Either Fender took a long time to reorganize or they forgot about Sunn amps, never producing them until 1998. Sunn amplifiers were mainly for the bass players like they had been in the seventies. By 2002, the Sunn name did not appear on amplifiers as Fender put their own name on Sunn amps. Fender bass amps are now Sunn in disguise (courtesy Ritchie Fliegler: *Amps!*).

ELECTRIC TUBE AMPLIFIERS: VINTAGE AMPS (1965-1987)

The Sunn amplifiers are split up into two sections, vintage and non-vintage. No tube amplifiers were manufactured during the 1980s and early 1990s making a big gap between the series. This makes it easy to date them and tell the difference.

100S (FIRST VERSION) – 60W head-unit, came with speaker cabinet loaded with 1-15 in. JBL speaker and a high frequency horn, all-tube chassis, preamp:1 X 7025, 1 X 12AU7, 1 X 6AN8, power: 2 X 6550 (or KT-88, 6CA7), rectifier: GZ34, single channel, front silver control panel, two inputs (hi and lo), three black knobs (v, b, t), black covering, silver grille, 150 lbs., (amp and cabinet), mfg. late 1960s.

	100%	EXCELLENT	AVERAGE
Head & Cabinet	N/A	$800 - 1,000	$500 - 600
Head Only	N/A	$325 - 400	$200 - 250

100S (SECOND VERSION) – 60W, 1-15 in. JBL speaker with a high freq. horn, guitar piggyback configuration, all-tube chassis, preamp: 1 X 12AX7, 1 X 12AU7, 1 X 6AN8, power: 2 X 6550, rectifier: GZ34, single channel, reverb, tremolo, front silver control panel, four inputs (two bright, two normal), seven black knobs (v, t, b, contour, vibrato depth, vibrato rate, r), mid boost switch, standby switch, polarity switch, power switch, black covering, silver grille, head dimensions: 24 in. wide, 9.5 in. tall, 9.5 in. deep, cabinet dimensions: 24 in. wide, 42 in. tall, 15 in. deep, casters, 150 lbs., (amp and cabinet), mfg. late 1960s-mid 1970s.

	100%	EXCELLENT	AVERAGE
Head & Cabinet	N/A	$950 - 1,250	$600 - 750
Head Only	N/A	$425 - 500	$250 - 300

200S – 60W, 2-15 in. JBL speakers, bass piggyback configuration, all-tube chassis, preamp: 1 X 12AX7, 1 X 6AN8 (or 7199, 6CA7), power: 2 X 6550 (or KT-88), rectifier: GZ34, single channel, front silver control panel, two inputs (hi and lo), three black knobs (v, b, t), black covering, silver grille, head dimensions: 24 in. wide, 9.5 in. tall, 9.5 in. deep, cabinet dimensions: 24 in. wide, 42 in. tall, 15 in. deep, casters, 150 lbs., (amp and cabinet), mfg. late 1960s-mid 1970s.

	100%	EXCELLENT	AVERAGE
Head & Cabinet	N/A	$950 - 1,250	$600 - 750
Head Only	N/A	$425 - 500	$250 - 300

1000S – 120W, 2-15 in. JBL speakers and one JBL LE100S high-freq. driver and horn, guitar piggyback configuration, nine tube chassis, preamp: 1 X 7025, 1 X 12AU7, 1 X 6AN8, power: 4 X KT88/6550, rectifier: 2 X GZ34, single channel, reverb, vibrato, front silver control panel, two inputs (two bright, two normal), seven black knobs (v, b, t, contour, rate, depth, r), midboost switch, standby switch, polarity switch, power switch, black covering, silver grille, head dimensions: 30 in. wide, 10 in. tall, 9.5 in. deep, cabinet dimensions: 30 in. wide, 48 in. tall, 15 in. deep, casters, 200 lbs., (amp and cabinet), mfg. late 1960s-mid 1970s.

	100%	EXCELLENT	AVERAGE
Head & Cabinet	N/A	$1,100 - 1,400	$700 - 850
Head Only	N/A	$500 - 600	$300 - 375

MSR/NOTES	100%	EXCELLENT	AVERAGE	LAST MSR

1200S – 120W, 6-12 in. speakers, guitar piggyback configuration, eight tube chassis, preamp: 1 X 7025, 1 X 6AN8, power: 4 X KT88/6550, rectifier: 2 X GZ34, single channel, reverb, vibrato, front silver control panel, two inputs (two bright, two normal), seven black knobs (v, b, t, contour, rate, depth, r), midboost switch, standby switch, polarity switch, power switch, black covering, silver grille, head dimensions: 30 in. wide, 10 in. tall, 9.5 in. deep, cabinet dimensions: 30 in. wide, 48 in. tall, 15 in. deep, casters, 200 lbs. (amp and cabinet), mfg. late 1960s-mid 1970s.

Head & Cabinet	N/A	$1,200 - 1,500	$800 - 1,000	
Head Only	N/A	$500 - 600	$300 - 375	

2000S – 120W, 2-15 in. JBL speakers, bass piggyback configuration, all-tube chassis, preamp: 1 X 12AX7, 1 X 6AN8 (or 7199, 6CA7), power: 2 X 6550/KT-88, rectifier: 2 XGZ34, single channel, front silver control panel, four inputs (two bright, two normal), four black knobs (v, b, t, contour), black covering, silver grille, head dimensions: 30 in. wide, 10 in. tall, 9.5 in. deep, cabinet dimensions: 30 in. wide, 48 in. tall, 15 in. deep, casters, 200 lbs. (amp and cabinet), mfg. late 1960s-mid 1970s.

Head & Cabinet	N/A	$1,100 - 1,400	$700 - 850	
Head Only	N/A	$500 - 600	$300 - 375	

MODEL T – 100W head-unit only, all-tube chassis, preamp: 3 X 12AX7, power: 4 X 6550, dual channels (normal and bright), front silver control panel, five inputs (normal and bright), seven black knobs (norm v, bright v, b, m, t, p, MV), black covering, silver grille, mfg. late 1960s-mid 1970s.

	N/A	$1,200 - 1,500	$800 - 1,000	

SOLARUS – 40W, 2-12 in. speakers, guitar piggyback configuration, six tube chassis, preamp: 1 X 12AX7, 1 X 12AU7, 1 X 7199, power: 2 X EL34, rectifier: GZ34, single channel, reverb, vibrato, front silver control panel, four inputs (two normal, two bright), seven knobs (v, t, b, contour, vibrato depth, vibrato rate, r), midboost switch, standby switch, polarity switch, power switch, black covering, gray grille, head dimensions: 24 in. wide, 9.5 in. tall, 9.5 in. deep, cabinet dimensions: 24 in. wide, 29 in. tall, 11.5 in. deep, 75 lbs., mfg. late 1960s-1970s.

	N/A	$600 - 700	$375 - 450	

SONARO – 40W, 1-15 in. speaker, bass piggyback configuration, six tube chassis, preamp: 1 X 12AX7, 1 X 7199, power: 2 X EL34, rectifier: GZ34, single channel, front silver control panel, two inputs, three knobs (v, t, b), standby switch, polarity switch, power switch, black covering, gray grille, head dimensions: 24 in. wide, 9.5 in. tall, 9.5 in. deep, cabinet dimensions: 24 in. wide, 29 in. tall, 11.5 in. deep, 75 lbs., mfg. late 1960s-1970s.

	N/A	$475 - 550	$300 - 350	

SONIC I – 30W, 1-15 in. JBL D130F speaker, bass piggyback configuration, five tube chassis, preamp: 1 X 12AX7, 1 X 7199, power: 2 X EL34, rectifier: GZ34, single channel, front silver control panel, two inputs, three knobs (v, t, b), standby switch, polarity switch, power switch, black covering, gray grille, head dimensions: 24 in. wide, 9.5 in. tall, 9.5 in. deep, cabinet dimensions: 24 in. wide, 24 in. tall, 15 in. deep, 120 lbs., mfg. late 1960s.

	N/A	$625 - 750	$400 - 475	

* **SONIC I-40** – similar to the Sonic 1, except has a JBL D-140-F speaker, mfg. late 1960s.

	N/A	$650 - 800	$425 - 500	

SONIC II – 30W, 2-15 in. JBL D130F speakers, bass piggyback configuration, five tube chassis, preamp: 1 X 12AX7, 1 X 6AN8, power: 2 X KT88, rectifier: GZ34, single channel, front silver control panel, two inputs, three knobs (v, t, b), standby switch, polarity switch, power switch, black covering, gray grille, head dimensions: 24 in. wide, 9.5 in. tall, 9.5 in. deep, cabinet dimensions: 24 in. wide, 42 in. tall, 15 in. deep, mfg. late 1960s.

	N/A	$800 - 1,000	$500 - 600	

SPECTRUM I – 30W, 1-15 in. JBL D130F speaker, piggyback unit, all-tube chassis, preamp: 1 X 12AX7, 1 X 7199, power: 2 X EL34, rectifier: GZ34, single channel, front silver control panel, two inputs, four black knobs (v, t, b, c), standby switch, polarity switch, power switch, black covering, gray grille, head dimensions: 24 in. wide, 9.5 in. tall, 9.5 in. deep, cabinet dimensions: 24 in. wide, 38 in. tall, 11.5 in. deep, mfg. late 1960s.

	N/A	$625 - 750	$400 - 475	

SPECTRUM II – 60W, 2-15 in. JBL D130F speakers, piggyback unit, all-tube chassis, preamp: 1 X 12AX7, 1 X 6AN8, power: 2 X KT88, rectifier: GZ34, single channel, front silver control panel, two inputs, four black knobs (v, t, b, c), standby switch, polarity switch, power switch, black covering, gray grille, head dimensions: 24 in. wide, 9.5 in. tall, 9.5 in. deep, cabinet dimensions: 24 in. wide, 38 in. tall, 11.5 in. deep, mfg. late 1960s.

	N/A	$800 - 1,000	$500 - 600	

ELECTRIC/BASS AMPLIFIERS: RECENT MFG. (1998-2001)

300T (NO. 021-3302-000) – 300W, bass amplifier, head-unit only, tube chassis, preamp: 3 X 12AX7WA, 12AT7, power: 6 X 6550C, two channels, front black control panel, single input, 11 black knobs, 10-band graphic EQ, effects loop, compression, three-button footswitch, black Tolex covering, black metal grille, 75 lbs., mfg. 1998-2001.

	N/A	$650 - 800	$350 - 450	

MSR/NOTES	100%	EXCELLENT	AVERAGE	LAST MSR

1200S (NO. 021-3300-000) – 1200W, two-space rack-mount head, hybrid chassis (tube preamp, solid-state power), two channels, front black control panel, 11 black knobs, 10-band graphic EQ, several white buttons, effects loop, compression, three button footswitch, black metal casing, 32 lbs., mfg. 1998-2001.

	N/A	$550 - 650	$300 - 400	$1,300

215 BASS SPEAKER CABINET (NO. 021-1674-000) – 300W, 2-15 in. Eminence speakers, 8 Ohm impedance, black Tolex covering, black metal grille, casters, 87 lbs., mfg. 1998-2001.

	N/A	$225 - 300	$125 - 175	$600

410H BASS SPEAKER CABINET (NO. 021-1673-000) – 300W, 4-10 in. Eminence speakers, piezo high freq. horn and control, 8 Ohm impedance, black Tolex covering, black metal grille, casters, 97 lbs., mfg. 1998-2001.

	N/A	$250 - 325	$150 - 200	$630

MODEL T (NO. 021-3303-000) – 100W (switchable to 25W), head-unit only, tube chassis, two channels, front silver control panel, single input, 10 black knobs (Ch. 1: v, t, b, m, Ch. 2: g, t, b, m, v, p), effects loop, footswitch, black Tolex covering, black metal grille, 75 lbs., mfg. 1998-2001.

	N/A	$600 - 700	$375 - 450	$1,400

MODEL T 412 SPEAKER CABINET (NO. 021-1675-000) – 300W, 4-12 in. Celestion G12 T-75 speakers, black Tolex covering, silver grille, casters, 97 lbs., mfg. 1998-2001.

	N/A	$325 - 400	$200 - 250	$750

T50C (NO. 021-3304-000) – 50W (switchable to 12.5W), 1-12 in. Celestion G12T-75 speaker, tube chassis, preamp: 7 X 12AX7, 12AT7, power: 2 X 6L6GC, two channels, front silver control panel, single input, 11 black knobs (Ch. 1: v, t, b, m, Ch. 2: g, t, b, m, v, p, r), effects loop, three-button footswitch, black Tolex covering, black metal grille, 70 lbs., mfg. 1998-2001.

	N/A	$700 - 850	$400 - 550	$1,700

T50C 112 SPEAKER CABINET (NO. 021-1676-000) – 75W, 1-12 in. Celestion G12 T-75 speaker, 16 Ohm impedance, black Tolex covering, silver grille, casters, 42 lbs., mfg. 1998-2001.

	N/A	$125 - 175	$75 - 100	$350

ELECTRIC SS AMPLIFIERS

Sunn had pretty much gone completely solid-state by the mid-1970s. About the only amp that survived the transistor stage was the Model T. In the late 1970s, Sunn produced the Alpha and Beta series of amps in various configurations. In the 1980s, Sunn produced the SL series of guitar amps as well as various other guitar and bass models.

SL 160 – 60W, 1-12 in. speaker combo, solid-state chassis, two channels, reverb, front control panel, two inputs, nine black knobs (level A, drive, level B, b, m, m-freq, t, r, MV), power switch, extension speaker jack, headphone jack, effects loop, footswitch, black covering, black grille, mfg. mid 1980s.

	N/A	$275 - 325	$150 - 200	

SL 260 – 60W, 2-12 in. speaker combo, solid-state chassis, two channels, reverb, front control panel, two inputs, nine black knobs (level A, drive, level B, b, m, m-freq, t, r, MV), power switch, extension speaker jack, headphone jack, effects loop, footswitch, black covering, black grille, mfg. mid-1980s.

	N/A	$325 - 400	$175 - 225	

SOLOS II – 120W, 2-12 in. Sunn, 2-12 in. Vega, or 1-15 in. JBL speakers, guitar combo, solid-state chassis, two channels, reverb, vibrato, chrome control panel, four inputs (two per channel, one normal, one brite), 11 knobs (Ch. 1: v, t, m, b, Ch. 2: v, t, m, b, r, vibrato rate, vibrato depth), two treble boost switches (one per channel), X20 switch, power switch, polarity switch, rear panel, extension speaker jack, pre amp out jack, power amp in jack, two footswitch jacks, black covering, silver grille, mfg. early 1970s.

	N/A	$450 - 550	$275 - 350	

SUPERTONE

Amplifiers previously sold by Sears & Roebuck. Amplifiers were made by various companies.

Supertone is another brand name trademark that was used by Sears & Roebuck between 1914 and 1941. These amplifiers were manufactured by a number of different companies including Harmony, which was a subsidiary of Sears. Sears used the Supertone trademark on a full range of amplifiers, guitars, lap steels, banjos, mandolins and ukuleles. In 1940, Jay Krause, the president of the company at the time, bought Harmony from Sears by acquiring the controlling stock, and continued to expand the company's production. In 1941, Sears retired the Supertone name in favor of the Silvertone trademark, which was brand new. Harmony produced amps and guitars for Sears with other names. Supertone made a handful of amplifiers during the 1930s and 1940s.

| MSR/NOTES | 100% | EXCELLENT | AVERAGE | LAST MSR |

SUPRO

Amplifiers currently produced by Absara Audio LLC in Port Jefferson Station, NY. Previously produced by Zinky Amplifiers in Flagstaff, AZ. Distributed by KMC Music since mid-2015. Previously produced by the National Dobro company (Valco) between circa 1935 and 1969.

CONTACT INFORMATION
SUPRO
Absara Audio LLC
200 Wilson St.
Bldg F
Port Jefferson Station, NY 11776
Phone No.: 631-331-7447
www.suprousa.com

U.S. Distributor: KMC Music
310 Newberry Road
Bloomfield, CT 06002
Phone No.: 855-417-8677
www.kmcmusic.com
info@kamanmusic.com

The Supro trademark was the budget brand of the National Dobro company (See NATIONAL or VALCO), who also supplied Montgomery Wards with Supro models under the Airline trademark. National offered budget versions of their designs under the Supro brand name beginning in 1935.

When National moved to Chicago in 1936, the Supro name was used on wood-bodied lap steels, amplifiers, and electric Spanish arch top guitars. The first solid body Supro electrics were introduced in 1952, and the fiberglass models began in 1962.

In 1962, Valco Manufacturing Company name was changed to Valco Guitars, Inc. (the same year that fiberglass models debuted). Kay purchased Valco in 1967, so there are some Kay-built guitars under the Supro brand name. Kay went bankrupt in 1968, and both the Supro and National trademarks were acquired by Strum & Drum in Chicago, IL. The National name was used on a number of Japanese-built imports, but the Supro name was never reused until recently.

Archer's Music of Fresno, California bought the rights to the Supro name in the early 1980s. They marketed a number of Supro guitars constructed from new old stock (N.O.S.) parts for a limited period of time. In 2004, Bruce Zinky of Zinky started producing guitars and amps under the Supro name again. In 2014, Absara Audio LLC acquired the rights to the Supro brand from former Fender amp designer and longtime Pigtronix associate Bruce Zinky and they introduced a new line of vintage inspired Supro amplifiers. In mid-2015, KMC Music announced Absara Audio LLC as the exclusive distributor in the U.S. For more information, visit Supro's website or contact them directly. Source for early history: Michael Wright, *Vintage Guitar Magazine.*

OVERVIEW/GENERAL INFORMATION

There are over a hundred different models produced with the Supro name on them, and there are probably more that aren't documented. Since nobody has written a book strictly on Supro guitars/amplifiers, and they are a budget brand of National, not a lot of information exists on individual models. Almost all information has come from old catalogs, but there are significant gaps in between years, especially before 1957. Every attempt has been made to accurately describe/represent information from the following models. The good news about Supro amps, is that style changes usually only happened with cosmetics and the chassis were left unchanged. This means the same chassis could be used in over five amps - all with different styles. For example, the Model 1606 Super has at least five style changes in the 1950s and 1960s, but besides a speaker size change and a possible tube change, the chassis remained untouched.

Up to 1957: Individual year changes are unknown at this point. Supro generally used a black and white (salt & pepper) tweed style covering with various grille shapes and sizes. Supro also used plastic and leatherette coverings. Several variations could exist during these years.

1958-1959: Rhino Hide-style covering was introduced. This was a black and white mixture that looked gray when combined. Dark grilles with Supro logos in the lower right corner were standard. A white strip of covering ran around the middle of the amp (top, sides, bottom) to give a two-tone-style covering. Control panels were mounted on the top or rear. It is possible that this type of style was introduced before 1958, but we have no catalog to back this up.

1960-1961: The same type of Rhino Hide covering carried over from the 1950s, but the grille was changed to a light silver color, the "Supro" logo was mounted on the covering itself - not the grille, and most amps had a larger "forehead" section above the speaker to allow for logo placement. Most models carried over from before as well.

1961-1963: Rhino Hide covering still used, but advertised as Tolex - possibly more durable then earlier models. The front of the amp changed again with a narrow strip of uniform width along the entire front of the amp making the grille cloth span almost the entire front. "Supro" logo was mounted in upper left corner of grille. These were the last of the 1000 series amps.

1964-1969: Rhino Hide covering still used, but all renumbered models (6000 series) - some are carryovers, some are new names but old amps, and some are of entirely new design. In 1964, some amps came standard in red, blue, or white colored cabinets and these command a premium. In 1966, the first piggyback amps appear and some models feature the new front control panel that is turquoise and blue. Amps that feature the new control panel also have a black vinyl covering with a silver grille. Amps from the mid-1960s are generally referred to as the most collectible and desirable amps by Supro. Most of these are listed in the current edition.

ELECTRIC TUBE AMPLIFIERS: 1964 REISSUE SERIES

1622RT TREMO-VERB COMBO – 25W, combo amp, 1-10 in. Supro CR10 speaker, all-tube chassis, preamp: 4 X 12AX7, 1 X 12AT7, power: 2 X 6973, single channel, top silver control panel, single input, six knobs (v, t, b, reverb, speed, depth), standby switch, power switch, top handle, blue rhino Tolex covering, gray mesh grille, 30 lbs., mfg. 2015-present.

| MSR $1,750 | $1,300 | $850 - 975 | $425 - 525 |

MSR/NOTES	100%	EXCELLENT	AVERAGE	LAST MSR

**1624T Dual-Tone Combo
Supro**

**S6420 Thunderbolt Combo
Supro**

**1695T Black Magick Combo
Supro**

1624T DUAL-TONE COMBO – 24W, combo amp, 1-12 in. Supro DT12 speaker, all-tube chassis, preamp: 4 X 12AX7EH, power: 2 X 6973, dual channels, top silver control panel, dual input, six knobs (v1, t1, v2, t2,speed, depth), standby switch, power switch, top handle, blue rhino Tolex covering, gray mesh grille, 34 lbs., mfg. 2014-present.

MSR $1,595	$1,200	$775 - 900	$400 - 475

1690T CORONADO COMBO – 35W, combo amp, 2-10 in. Supro CR10 speakers, all-tube chassis, preamp: 4 X 12AX7, 1 X 12AT7, power: 2 X 6L6, 5U4 tube rectifier, dual channels, top silver control panel, two inputs, six knobs (v1, t1, v2, t2, speed, depth), standby switch, power switch, top handle, blue rhino Tolex covering, gray mesh grille, 45 lbs., mfg. 2015-present.

MSR $1,795	$1,350	$875 - 1,000	$450 - 550

S6420 THUNDERBOLT COMBO – 35W, combo amp, 1-15 in. Supro TB15 speaker, all-tube chassis, preamp: 2 X 12AX7, power: 2 X 6L6, 5U4GB tube rectifier, single channel, top silver control panel, dual input (hi, lo), two knobs (v, tone), standby switch, power switch, top handle, blue rhino Tolex covering, gray mesh grille, 45 lbs., mfg. 2014-present.

MSR $1,595	$1,200	$775 - 900	$400 - 475

ELECTRIC TUBE AMPLIFIERS: CLASSIC SERIES

1695T BLACK MAGICK COMBO – 25W, combo amp, 1-12 in. Supro BD12 speaker, all-tube chassis, preamp: 4 X 12AX7, power: 2 X 6973, dual channels, top gold control panel, two inputs, five knobs (v1, v2, tone, speed, depth), tremolo jack, standby switch, power switch, top handle, blue rhino Tolex covering, gray mesh grille, new 2016.

MSR $1,995	$1,500	$975 - 1,125	$500 - 600

ELECTRIC TUBE AMPLIFIERS: EARLY MODELS

BANTAM (S6511) – 4W, 1-8 in. Jensen speaker, two tube chassis, preamp: 1 X 12AX7, power: 1 X 50L6, solid-state rectifier (one diode), single channel, rear control panel, two inputs, single on/off volume knob, gray/black rhino-style covering, off-white grille with black stripes and "Supro" logo in upper left corner, 14.875 in. wide, 11 in. tall, 5.5 in. deep, 7.5 lbs., mfg. mid- to late 1960s.

	N/A	$325 - 400	$200 - 250

BIG STAR (S6651) – 35W, 2-12 in. Jensen speakers, guitar combo, seven tube chassis, preamp: 5 X 12AX7, power: 2 X 6L6, solid-state rectifier (four diodes), two channels, reverb, tremolo, front turquoise/chrome control panel with "Supro" logo, four inputs, seven knobs (Ch. 1: v, tone, Ch. 2: v, tone, r, i, s), power switch, standby switch, line reverse switch, two footswitch inputs, black covering, silver grille, 26.75 in. wide, 22.5 in. tall, 9.5 in. deep, 44 lbs., mfg. mid- to late 1960s.

	N/A	$900 - 1,100	$550 - 650

COMBO TREMOLO (S6497) – 35W, 1-15 in. Jensen speaker, six tube chassis, preamp: 3 X 12AX7, power: 2 X 6L6GC, rectifier: 5U4G, two channels, tremolo, rear or top control panel, four inputs, six knobs (Ch. 1: v, tone, Ch. 2: v, tone, i, s), gray rhino covering, off-white grille with black stripes with "Supro" logo in upper left corner, 23.625 in. wide, 19 in. tall, 11.25 in. deep, 38 lbs., mfg. 1964-68.

	N/A	$700 - 850	$475 - 600

CORSICA (S6622) – ~5W, 1-12 in. Jensen speaker, guitar combo, six tube chassis, preamp: 4 X 12AX7, power: 1 X 6V6, rectifier: 5Y3, two channels, reverb, tremolo, front turquoise/chrome control panel with "Supro" logo, three inputs, four knobs (v, tone, r, trem. speed), two footswitch inputs, black covering, silver grille, 17.75 in. wide, 23 in. tall, 8.5 in. deep, 27 lbs., mfg. mid- to late 1960s.

	N/A	$475 - 600	$275 - 350

DUAL-TONE TREMOLO (S6424/S6524) – 17W, 1-12 in. Jensen speaker, six tube chassis, preamp: 3 X 12AX7, power: 2 X 6973, rectifier: 5Y3, two channels, tremolo, four inputs, six knobs (Ch. 1: v, tone, Ch. 2: v, tone, i, s), gray rhino covering, off-white grille with black stripes and "Supro" logo in upper left corner, 23.625 in. wide, 16 in. tall, 8.5 in. deep, 26 lbs., mfg. 1964-68.

	N/A	$700 - 850	$500 - 600

MSR/NOTES	100%	EXCELLENT	AVERAGE	LAST MSR

GALAXY (S6688) – 35W, 2-12 in. Jensen speakers, guitar combo, six tube chassis, preamp: 4 X 12AX7, power: 2 X 6L6, solid-state rectifier (four diodes), two channels, tremolo, front turquoise/chrome control panel with "Supro" logo, four inputs, six knobs (Ch. 1: v, tone, Ch. 2: v, tone, i, s), power switch, standby switch, line reverse switch, one footswitch jack, black covering, silver grille, 26.75 in. wide, 22.5 in. tall, 9.5 in. deep, 40 lbs., mfg. mid- to late 1960s.

| | N/A | $600 - 750 | $375 - 450 | |

ROYAL REVERB (S6450) – 17W, 2-10 in. Jensen speakers, nine tube chassis, preamp: 5 X 12AX7, 1 X 6EU7, power: 2 X 6973, rectifier: 5U4, two channels, reverb, tremolo, top control panel, four inputs, seven knobs (Ch. 1: v, tone, Ch. 2: v, tone, r, i, s), gray rhino-style covering, off-white grille with black stripes and "Supro" logo in upper left corner, 23.625 in. wide, 16 in. tall, 8.5 in. deep, 38.5 lbs., mfg. 1964-66.

| | N/A | $850 - 1,000 | $550 - 650 | |

SPORTSMAN (S6698) – 35W, 2-12 in. Jensen speakers, guitar piggyback configuration, seven tube chassis, preamp: 5 X 12AX7, power: 2 X 6L6, solid-state rectifier (four diodes), two channels, reverb, tremolo, front turquoise/chrome control panel with "Supro" logo, four inputs, seven knobs (Ch. 1: v, tone, Ch. 2: v, tone, r, i, s), power switch, standby switch, line reverse switch, black covering, silver grille with "Supro" logo in upper left corner, head dimensions: 26.75 in. wide, 9.5 in. tall, 9.5 in. deep, cabinet dimensions: 32.125 in. wide, 20.5 in. tall, 11.5 in. deep, 65 lbs. overall weight, mfg. mid- to late 1960s.

| | N/A | $850 - 1,000 | $550 - 650 | |

SUPER SIX (S6606) – 4.5W, 1-8 in. Jensen speaker, guitar combo, three tube chassis, preamp: 1 X 12AX7, power: 1 X 6V6, rectifier: 5Y3, single channel, front chrome control panel with Supro logo in center, three inputs, two knobs (volume with on/off, tone), gray/black rhino-style covering, off-white grille with black stripes, 13.5 lbs., mfg. mid- to late 1960s.

courtesy John Beeson/The Music Shoppe   *courtesy John Beeson/The Music Shoppe*

| | N/A | $275 - 350 | $150 - 200 | |

SUPREME (S6400) – 17W, 1-10 in. Jensen speaker, five tube chassis, preamp: 2 X 12AX7, power: 2 X 6973, rectifier: 5Y3, single channel, top control panel, three inputs, two knobs (v with on/off power switch, tone), gray rhino-style covering, silver grille with "Supro" logo in upper left corner, 19.25 in. wide, 14 in. tall, 8.5 in. deep, 22.5 lbs., mfg. 1964-68.

| | N/A | $650 - 775 | $400 - 500 | |

STATESMAN (S6699) – 70W, 2-12 in. Jensen speakers, guitar piggyback configuration, 10 tube chassis, preamp: 6 X 12AX7, power: 4 X 6L6, solid-state rectifier (four diodes), two channels, reverb, tremolo, front turquoise/chrome control panel, four inputs, nine knobs (Ch. 1: v, t, b, Ch. 2: v, t, b, r, i, s), two high/low tone switches (one per channel), power switch, standby switch, line reverse switch, black covering, silver grille with Supro logo in upper left corner, head dimensions: 26.75 in. wide, 9.5 in. tall, 9.5 in. deep, cabinet dimensions: 32.125 in. wide, 20.5 in. tall, 11.5 in. deep, 70 lbs. overall weight, mfg. mid- to late 1960s.

| | N/A | $700 - 850 | $475 - 550 | |

TAURUS (S6625) – ~75W, 2-12 in. Jensen speakers, bass piggyback configuration, six tube chassis, preamp: 2 X 12AX7, power: 4 X 6L6, solid-state rectifier (four silicon diodes), single channel, front turquoise/chrome control panel, three inputs, three knobs (v, tone, three-way tone selector), power switch, standby switch, line reverse switch, dark gray covering, silver grille with Supro logo in upper left corner, head dimensions: 26.75 in. wide, 9.5 in. tall, 9.5 in. deep, cabinet dimensions: 32.125 in. wide, 23.5 in. tall, 11.5 in. deep, 65 lbs. overall weight, mfg. mid- to late 1960s.

| | N/A | $750 - 900 | $500 - 600 | |

THUNDERBOLT BASS (S6420) – 35W, 1-15 in. Jensen speaker, four tube chassis, preamp: 2 X 12AX7, power: 2 X 6L6GC, solid-state rectifier, single channel, two inputs, two knobs (v, tone), gray/black rhino-style covering, silver grille with Supro logo in upper right corner, 23.75 in. wide, 19 in. tall, 11.25 in. wide, 38 lbs., mfg. mid- to late 1960s.

| | N/A | $1,200 - 1,500 | $800 - 1,000 | |

Jimmy Page used this model early on in his career.

TREMO-VERB (S6422/S6522) – ~10W, 1-10 in. Jensen speaker, six tube chassis, preamp: 4 X 12AX7, power: 1 X 6U6, rectifier: 5Y3GT, single channel, reverb, tremolo, top control panel, three inputs, six knobs (v1, tone, v2, reverb i, s), gray rhino-style covering (Model S6522) or red vinyl covering (Model S6422), silver grille with "Supro" logo in upper left corner, 19.25 in. wide, 14 in. tall, 8.5 in. deep, 20 lbs, mfg. 1964-68.

| | N/A | $600 - 750 | $400 - 500 | |

• **Add 10-25% for red vinyl covering (Model S6422).**

MSR/NOTES	100%	EXCELLENT	AVERAGE	LAST MSR

TROJAN TREMOLO (S6616) – 5W, 1-10 in. Jensen speaker, four tube chassis, preamp: 2 X 12AX7, power: 1 X 6V6, rectifier: 5Y3, single channel, front turquoise/chrome control panel with "Supro" logo, two inputs, three knobs (v, tone, trem. speed), one footswitch jack, black covering, silver grille, 15.75 in. wide, 20 in. tall, 7.5 in. deep, 19 lbs., mfg. mid- to late 1960s.

N/A $400 - 500 $225 - 275

VIBRA-VERB (S6498/S6598) – 35W, 2-12 in. Jensen speakers, eight tube chassis, preamp: 4 X 12AX7, 1 X 6DR7, power: 2 X 6L6GC, rectifier: 5U4, two channels, reverb, vibrato, top control panel, four inputs, seven knobs (Ch. 1: v, tone, Ch. 2: v, tone, r, i, s), gray rhino-style covering, silver grille with "Supro" logo in upper left corner, 27.625 in. wide, 18.75 in. tall, 9.5 in. deep, 42 lbs, mfg. mid 1965-66.

N/A $1,200 - 1,500 $800 - 1,000

ELECTRIC TUBE AMPLIFIERS: RETRO SERIES

1642RT Titan Combo
courtesy Supro

1650RT Royal Reverb Combo
courtesy Supro

1675RT Rhythm Master Combo
courtesy Supro

1642RT TITAN COMBO – 50W, combo amp, 1-10 in. Supro HP10 speaker, all-tube chassis, preamp: 4 X 12AX7, 1 X 12AT7, power: 2 X 6L6, single channel, top silver control panel, single input, six knobs (v, t, b, reverb, speed, depth), standby switch, power switch, top handle, blue rhino Tolex covering, gray mesh grille, 53 lbs., new 2016.

MSR $1,995 $1,500 $975 - 1,125 $500 - 600

1648RT SATURN REVERB COMBO – 15W, combo amp, 1-12 in. Supro DT12 speaker, all-tube chassis, preamp: 4 X 12AX7, 1 X 12AT7, power: 2 X 6973, 5U4 rectifier, single channel, top silver control panel, single input, six knobs (v, t, b, reverb, speed, depth), standby switch, power switch, top handle, blue rhino Tolex covering, gray mesh grille, 40 lbs., mfg. 2015-present

MSR $1,890 $1,400 $900 - 1,050 $450 - 550

1650RT ROYAL REVERB COMBO – 35W/45W/60W, combo amp, 2-10 in. Supro CR10 speakers, all-tube chassis, preamp: 4 X 12AX7, 1 X 12AT7, power: 2 X 6L6, 5U4 tube rectifier, single channels, top silver control panel, single input, six knobs (v, t, b, reverb, speed, depth), 3-way rectifier switch, standby switch, power switch, top handle, blue rhino Tolex covering, gray mesh grille, 65 lbs., mfg. 2015-present.

MSR $1,995 $1,500 $975 - 1,125 $500 - 600

1668RT JUPITER COMBO – Switchable 30W or 45W/60W, combo amp, 1-12 in. Supro HP12 speaker, all-tube chassis, preamp: 4 X 12AX7, 1 X 12AT7, power: 2 X 6L6, 5U4 rectifier, single channel, three modes, top silver control panel, single input, six knobs (v, t, b, reverb, speed, depth), rectifier switch, standby switch, power switch, top handle, blue rhino Tolex covering, gray mesh grille, new 2016.

MSR $2,150 $1,600 $1,050 - 1,200 $525 - 650

1675RT RHYTHM MASTER COMBO – Switchable 30W or 45W/60W, combo amp, 1-15 in. Supro TB15 speaker, all-tube chassis, preamp: 4 X 12AX7, 1 X 12AT7, power: 2 X 6L6, 5U4 rectifier, single channel, three modes, top silver control panel, single input, six knobs (v, t, b, reverb, speed, depth), rectifier switch, standby switch, power switch, top handle, blue rhino Tolex covering, gray mesh grille, 60 lbs., new 2016.

MSR $2,150 $1,600 $1,050 - 1,200 $525 - 650

S6420+ THUNDERBOLT PLUS COMBO – 35W/45W/60W, combo amp, 1-15 in. Supro TB15 speaker, all-tube chassis, preamp: 2 X 12AX7, power: 2 X 6L6, 5U4GB tube rectifier, single channel, top silver control panel, dual input (hi, lo), two knobs (v, tone), 3-way rectifier switch, standby switch, power switch, top handle, blue rhino Tolex covering, gray mesh grille, 45 lbs., mfg. 2014-present.

MSR $1,735 $1,300 $850 - 975 $425 - 525

SUZUKI

Amplifiers previously produced overseas.

Suzuki makes all kinds of products, similar to the Yamaha corporation. During the 1990s and the 2000s, they sporadically produced a number of amplifiers from beginner models such as the SG-10 (10W, 1-6 in. speaker), all the way up to a 100W amp covered in tweed. Electric and acoustic guitars have also been available. They currently offer band instruments, pianos, and harmonicas.

MSR/NOTES		100%	EXCELLENT	AVERAGE		LAST MSR

SWANPRO

Amplifiers previously produced in Conifer, CO from 2004-2012.

Bob Swanson founded Swanpro amplifiers because he wanted to develop his own sound. He had grown up in the 1970s listening to rock n' roll and all the amplifiers that were associated with it. Rack units took over in the 1980s, but Bob was back to tube amps by the early 1990s; however, they didn't sound as good as he had remembered. He started to tinker with old amps and after hundreds of amps in experience, he started his own company in 2004. The Swanpro Recording Club Series were designed to be used in the recording studio with a mic in front of them. The RCS 20 and RCS40 were the last amps available on the market.

SWR

Amplifiers most recently produced in Corona, CA and Mexico from 2003-2013. Previously produced in Sun Valley, CA between 1984 and 2003. Previously distributed by Fender Musical Instruments Corporation in Scottsdale, AZ beginning in 2003. In 2013, (FMIC) discontinued production of all SWR products.

SWR was founded in 1984 by Steve W. Rabe (SWR are his initials). The company was formed with the idea that their products would serve the creative needs of musicians beyond their expectations. Daryl Jamison was the last president/CEO at the company. They have grown from a company that started with a power amp in 1984 to having a half-dozen lines of amps. They specialized in bass amplication and acoustic amps. In 2002, they won two awards from the MIPA (Musikmesse International Press Award) for making the best bass cabinets in the world and for the Mo' Bass soundstation. In 2003, Fender Musical Instrument Corporation (FMIC) took over as the owners for SWR. Like Gretsch, Guild, and Jackson, FMIC is now responsible for representing SWR.

DATING INFORMATION

We do not have serialization information at this point. However we do have some points in production that can help to date your amplifier. This is also a guide to show whether a certain model may have received upgrades or changes without noting in the model listings.

1984: The first model, the PB-200, as a rack-mount unit was released.

1985: The second model, the SM-400 was released.

1986: The third model, the SS-180 rack-mount unit was released.

1987: The PB-200 was upgraded and changed to the ST-220.

1996: The Pro Series speaker grilles were changed from triangular bronze to the black and silver square punch.

1999: The Pro Series front control panels were changed from black to chrome, and the speaker grille was changed from a powder coat to chrome.The Workingman's series grilles were changed from black and silver to red and navy blue.

2002: The Pro Series front control panels were changed from chrome to a brushed aluminum with the dome logo. The Workingman's series grilles were changed from red and navy blue to midnight blue with the dome logo.

Information courtesy SWR.

ACOUSTIC AMPLIFIERS

For the Blonde on Blonde model, refer to the speaker cabinet section in SWR.

**California Blonde II
courtesy SWR**

**Natural Blonde
courtesy SWR**

**Strawberry Blonde II
courtesy SWR**

CALIFORNIA BLONDE (NO. 446-0000-000) – 120W, 1-12 in. plus a tweeter acoustic combo, solid-state chassis, two channels, reverb, front brown control panel, instrument and mic input, 13 cream knobs, effects loop, headphone jack, XLR direct out, tuner out, cream covering, brown metal grille, mfg. 1996-2005.

	100%	EXCELLENT	AVERAGE	LAST MSR
	N/A	$500 - 600	$300 - 350	$1,143

CALIFORNIA BLONDE II (NO. 440-6000-010) – 160W, 1-12 in. Celestion speaker plus an Eminence tweeter, acoustic combo, solid-state chassis, two channels, reverb, front brown control panel, instrument and mic input, 13 cream knobs, effects loop, headphone jack, XLR direct out, tuner out, cream covering, brown metal grille, 51 lbs., mfg. 2006-disc.

100%	EXCELLENT	AVERAGE	LAST MSR
$800	$500 - 600	$300 - 375	$1,150

MSR/NOTES	100%	EXCELLENT	AVERAGE	LAST MSR

NATURAL BLONDE (NO. 446-0600-000) – 200W, 2-8 in. Celestion speakers, 1-5 in. Ultimate Sound speaker (rear-firing), and a Foster horn, designed for use as an acoustic bass amp, solid-state chassis with SWR preamp and Aural Enhancer, two channels, front black control panel, two inputs (one regular 1/4 in. and one combo 1/4 in./XLR), 16 black knobs (Ch. 1: g, Aural Enhancer, t, m, b, effects blend, Ch. 2: g, Aural Enhancer, t, m, b, effects blend, Bass Intensifier: freq., level, All: compression, MV), mute switches, input switches, phase reverse switches, back panel: effects loop and line outs (1/4 in. and XLR) for each channel, summed 1/4 in. and XLR line out, tuner out, XLR ground lift switch, built-in wheels and telescoping handle, Blonde textured vinyl covering, black steel grille with overall level and horn level controls, 15.5 in. wide, 25.75 in. tall, 15 in. deep, 53 lbs., mfg. summer 2007-disc.

$1,075	$650 - 800	$425 - 500		$1,550

STRAWBERRY BLONDE (NO. 446-0400-000) – 80W, 1-10 in. plus a tweeter acoustic combo, solid-state chassis, single channel, reverb, front strawberry-colored control panel, single input, eight cream knobs, effects loop, headphone jack, XLR direct out, cream covering, cream metal grille, mfg. 1996-2006.

N/A	$300 - 350	$175 - 225		$714

STRAWBERRY BLONDE II (MEX. MFG. NO. 446-0400-010) – 90W, 1-10 in.speaker plus a tweeter, acoustic combo, solid-state chassis, single channel, reverb, front strawberry-colored control panel, single input, eight cream knobs, effects loop, headphone jack, XLR direct out, cream covering, cream metal grille, 16 in. wide, 18.75 in. tall, 13.75 in. deep, 40 lbs., mfg. 2007-disc.

$650	$400 - 475	$250 - 300		$950

ELECTRIC BASS AMPS: PRO SERIES (HEAD UNITS)

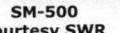

SM-500
courtesy SWR

SM-1500
courtesy SWR

Bass 550X
courtesy SWR

PB-200 – 200W, rack-mount head, solid-state chassis, front black control panel, eleven black knobs, 4-band EQ, black casing, mfg. 1984-87.

N/A	$500 - 600	$275 - 350		$799

SM-400 – 400W, rack-mount head, solid-state chassis, black control panel, 12 knobs, 4-band EQ, effects loop, limiter, electronic crossover, black casing, mfg. 1985-1993.

N/A	$650 - 800	$400 - 500		$1,299

* **SM-400S** – similar to the SM-400, except has 500W output, an internal cooling fan, and a transparency control, mfg. 1993-99.

N/A	$600 - 700	$325 - 400		$1,299

SM-500 (NO. 440-0300-000) – 500W (250W per side stereo), rack-mount head unit only, tube preamp, solid-state power amp, single channel, front black control panel, two inputs (passive and active), 11 black knobs, four-band equalizer, lots of speaker and line outs, black casing, 2-space rack mount, 20 lbs., disc. 2009.

$1,400	$850 - 1,000	$550 - 625		$1,950

SM-900 BLACK FACE PURPLE SCREEN – 800W mono, 350W per channel stereo, rack-mount head, solid-state chassis, purple control panel, 15 knobs, effects loop, limiter, electronic crossover, 24 lbs., mfg. 1991-99.

N/A	$850 - 1,050	$500 - 600		

SM-900 (NO. 440-0100-000) – 900W (400W per side stereo), rack-mount head unit only, tube preamp, solid-state power amp, single channel, limiter, crossover, front black control panel, two inputs (passive and active), 17 black knobs, switchable equalizers, lots of speaker and line outs, footswitch, black casing, 2-space rack mount, 26 lbs., disc.

$1,800	$1,075 - 1,300	$650 - 800		$2,500

SM-1500 (U.S. MFG. NO. 440-0140-000) – 1500W (750W per side stereo), three-space rack-mount head unit, tube preamp, solid-state power amp, single channel, limiter, crossover, front black control panel, two inputs (passive and active), 19 black knobs, switchable equalizers, lots of speaker and line outs, footswitch, black casing, 19 in. wide, 5.5 in. tall, 19.5 in. deep, 67 lbs., mfg. 2007-disc.

$2,250	$1,350 - 1,650	$875 - 1,050		$3,200

SS-180 – 180W (2 or 4 Ohm) or 120W (8 Ohm), rack-mount head, hybrid chassis, tube preamp, solid-state power amp, black control panel, ten black knobs, black casing, mfg. 1986 only.

N/A	$350 - 425	$200 - 250		$699

ST-220 – 220W, rack-mount head, solid-state chassis, black control panel, eleven knobs, 4-band EQ, adjustable crossover, limiter, black casing, 13.5 lbs., mfg. 1987-1998.

N/A	$375 - 450	$225 - 275		$999

MSR/NOTES	100%	EXCELLENT	AVERAGE	LAST MSR

Bass 350X
courtesy SWR

Bass 550X
courtesy SWR

Bass 750X
courtesy SWR

BASIC 350 – same as the Bass 350 except for chassis venting, mfg. 1993-94.

	N/A	$550 - 650	$400 - 450	$849

This was what the Bass 350 started out as. There was a copyright issue with another company with the same name so they changed the model nomenclature.

BASS 350 – 350W, rack-mount head unit only, tube preamp, solid-state power amp, single channel, limiter, front black and silver control panel, two inputs (passive and active), eight black knobs, lots of speaker and line outs, effects loop, black casing, 2-space rack mount, 16.5 lbs., mfg. 1994-2002.

	N/A	$500 - 600	$400 - 450	$999

From 1994 to 1999, the control panel was burgundy.

BASS 350X (NO. 440-0900-000) – similar to the Bass 350 except has SubWave circuitry and one more control knob, silver casing, mfg. 2002-09.

	$900	$525 - 625	$325 - 400	$1,200

BASS 550X (NO. 440-0700-000) – 550W, rack-mount head unit only, tube preamp, solid-state power amp, Sub Wave circuitry, single channel, limiter, front black and silver control panel, two inputs (passive and active), nine black knobs, lots of speaker and line outs, effects loop, black casing, two-space rack mount, mfg. 2003-09.

	$1,100	$650 - 775	$425 - 500	$1,500

BASS 750 – 750W, rack-mount head unit only, tube preamp, solid-state power amp, single channel, limiter, front black and silver control panel, two inputs (passive and active), nine black knobs, lots of speaker and line outs, effects loop, black casing, 2-space rack mount, 33 lbs., mfg. 1999-2002.

	N/A	$800 - 900	$700 - 750	$1,499

BASS 750X (NO. 440-0500-000) – similar to the Bass 750 except has SubWave circuitry (with overdrive), and one more control knob, silver casing, mfg. 2002-present.

MSR $1,900	$1,350	$800 - 975	$525 - 625	

ELECTRIC BLUE/BABY BLUE HEAD – 160W (120W @ 4 Ohms), head-unit only, tube preamp, solid-state power amp, single channel, front blue control panel, single input, seven black knobs, effects loop, headphone jack, tuner out, black carpet covering, 12 lbs., mfg. 1990-93, 1998-2002.

	N/A	$400 - 475	$275 - 325	$849

This model was originally named the Electric Blue as a head version of the Baby Blue. The head came with a mini road case. The amp was reintroduced in 1998 due to popular demand, but was named the Baby Blue Head.

HEADLITE (NO. 441-5000-000) – 400W, lightweight bass head-unit, hybrid chassis with a single 12AX7 preamp tube, single channel, front black control panel, single input, seven knobs (g, aural enhancer with push defeat switch, bass freq./level, mid freq./level, treble freq./level, effects blend/compressor level, MV), input pad switch, mute switch, shift switch, rear panel: power switch, Speakon speaker jack, preamp out jack, footswitch jack, XLR and 1/4 in. direct line out with level control and ground/lift and pre/post EQ switches, effects loop, black casing with chrome rails, optional two-button footswitch, 8.5 in. wide, 1.75 in. tall, 9.75 in. deep, 3.75 lbs., mfg. 2010-disc.

	$700	$450 - 525	$250 - 300	$1,000

MO' BASS – 900W (400W per side stereo), rack-mount head unit only, tube preamp, solid-state power amp, single channel, chorus, overdrive, front silver control panel, two inputs (passive and active), 23 silver knobs, headphone jack, lots of speaker and line outs, blue casing, 3-space rack mount, 29 lbs., mfg. 2000-03.

	N/A	$1,100 - 1,300	$950 - 1,000	$1,999

• Add $250 for master footswitch (Mo' Control).

ELECTRIC BASS AMPS: COMBO UNITS

BABY BABY BLUE (NO. 442-0500-000) – same chassis as the Baby Blue Head, in combo form with 1-10 in. speaker and a tweeter, silver metal grille, 39 lbs., disc. 2008.

	$950	$600 - 700	$350 - 425	$1,350

BABY BLUE – 120W, 2-8 in. speakers and 1-5 in. tweeter, solid-state chassis, front blue control panel, seven black knobs, black covering, black metal grille, 45 lbs., mfg. 1990-93.

	N/A	$650 - 800	$400 - 500	

| MSR/NOTES | 100% | EXCELLENT | AVERAGE | LAST MSR |

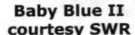

Baby Blue II
courtesy SWR

Black Beauty First Version
courtesy SWR

Black Beauty Second Version
courtesy SWR

BABY BLUE II – same chassis as the Baby Blue Head, in combo form with 2-8 in. speakers and a tweeter, silver metal grille, 45 lbs., mfg. 1993-2002.

| | N/A | $650 - 750 | $425 - 500 | $1,399 |

BASIC BLACK – 100W, 1-15 in. speaker, Le Son TLX-1 piezo tweeter, rear port, solid-state chassis, top control panel, seven knobs, black covering, black metal grille, 50 lbs., mfg. 1992-99.

| | N/A | $425 - 500 | $250 - 300 | $1,000 |

BLACK BEAUTY FIRST VERSION (NO. 442-0300-000) – 350W, 1-15 in. speaker + a tweeter, tube preamp, solid-state power amp, single channel, front black control panel, single input, nine black knobs, black vinyl covering, black metal grille, 95 lbs., mfg. 2002-mid-2009.

| | $1,150 | $750 - 900 | $475 - 575 | $1,650 |

* **Add $75 for chrome grille.**

BLACK BEAUTY SECOND VERSION (NO. 442-0300-000) – 400W @ 4 ohms (525W @ 2.67 ohms with an 8 ohm extension speaker or 650W @ 2 ohms with a 4 ohm extension speaker), 1-15 in. custom-designed SWR speaker, one Foster horn tweeter, hybrid chassis with 1 X 12AX7 preamp tube, solid-state power amp, single channel, built-in tuner, front black control panel: tuning mute, two inputs (1/4 in. passive and 1/4 in. active), gain control, preamp clip LED, Aural Enhancer control, Subwave on/off switch with LED, Subwave control, bass control, mid-range level control, mid-range freq. control, treble control, compressor control with LED, MV with power amp clip LED, DI Line/ Direct/Direct+Subwave sliding switch, DI Mute/Line sliding switch, DI Ground Lift sliding switch, DI Pad control, headphone jack, effects blend control, power switch with LED, rear panel: 1/4 in. internal speaker jack, Speakon and 1/4 in. external speaker jacks, 1/4 in. tuner out, 1/4 in. footswitch jack, effects loop, DI outputs, horn attenuator, front slot ported 5/8 in. seven-ply Meranti plywood cabinet, black carpeting covering with Stack Lock corners, chrome stamped steel grille, 22.5 in. wide, 26.5 in. tall, 18.5 in. deep, 105 lbs., two-button footswitch included, mfg. summer 2009-disc.

| | $1,200 | $750 - 925 | $475 - 575 | $2,150 |

REDHEAD – wattage unknown, 2-10 in. P.A.S. speakers with Foster horn, solid-state chassis, front red control panel, nine black knobs, various buttons and controls, black covering, black metal grille, mfg. 1988-1996.

| | N/A | $800 - 1,000 | $500 - 600 | $1,799 |

SILVERADO – 220W, 4-8 in. P.A.S. speakers with Piezo tweeter, solid-state chassis, front control panel, eight white knobs, effects loop, compressor, limiter, headphone jack, black covering, black metal grille, 70 lbs., mfg. 1994-97.

| | N/A | $600 - 750 | $350 - 450 | $1,299 |

SILVERADO II – 350W, 2-12 in. SWR speakers with Foster horn, solid-state chassis, otherwise similar to the Silverado, black covering, black metal grille, 90 lbs., mfg. 1997-98.

| | N/A | $550 - 700 | $350 - 450 | $1,299 |

SILVERADO SPECIAL – 350W, 2-12 in. SWR speakers with Foster horn, solid-state chassis, front chrome control panel, eight white knobs, effects loop, limiter, headphone jack, black carpet covering, gray metal grille, 93 lbs., mfg. 1998-2002.

| | N/A | $700 - 900 | $400 - 500 | $1,599 |

SPELLBINDER BLUE (NO. 442-0500-010) – 160W, 1-10 in. Eminence Neodymium speaker and one Custom Eminence Supertweeter, bass combo, hybrid chassis with one 12AX7 preamp tube, single channel, front blue control panel, single Neutrick (XLR or 1/4 in.) input jack, eight black knobs (g, aural enhancer, b, m, t, effects blend, compression, MV), phantom power switch, input pad switch, phase switch, EQ in/out switch, effects bypass switch, mute switch, rear panel: Speakon speaker jack, internal speaker on/off switch, effects loop, headphone jack, tuner out jack, balanced outs (XLR and 1/4 in.), line out pad, XLR ground lift switch, line/direct switch, horn level attenuator, black carpet covering with heavy duty corners, chrome stamped steel grille, 15.375 in. wide, 19.5 in. tall, 14.5 in. deep, 26.5 lbs., mfg. late 2008-disc.

| | $1,000 | $625 - 775 | $400 - 475 | $1,450 |

MSR/NOTES	100%	EXCELLENT	AVERAGE	LAST MSR

Spellbinder Blue
courtesy SWR

Redhead
courtesy SWR

SUPER REDHEAD/REDHEAD (NO. 442-0100-000) – 350W, 2-10 in. speaker plus a tweeter, tube preamp, solid-state power amp, single channel, front red control panel, single input, nine black knobs, black vinyl covering, black metal grille, front black cover also serves as a tilt-back floor stand, 80 lbs., mfg. 1988-disc.

	100%	EXCELLENT	AVERAGE	LAST MSR
	$1,650	$1,000 - 1,250	$650 - 775	$2,350

In 2008 for the 20th Anniversary of the Super Redhead, SWR updated and upgraded this model. Changes include a new control panel with ten knobs, 400W output, and the model was just called the Redhead.

ELECTRIC BASS AMPS: LA SERIES

LA 10
courtesy SWR

LA 12
courtesy SWR

LA 15
courtesy SWR

LA 8 – 30W, 1-8 in. speaker, solid-state chassis, top control panel, four knobs, side handles, black covering, black grille, 20 lbs., disc.

	100%	EXCELLENT	AVERAGE	LAST MSR
	N/A	$110 - 140	$70 - 90	$300

LA 10 (NO. 449-0300-000) – 35W, 1-10 in. speaker with tweeter, solid-state chassis, pre-set Aural Enhancer, top control panel, four knobs (v, l, m, h), headphone jack, CD input, edgemount handles, black covering, silver grid-style grille, 26 lbs., disc.

	100%	EXCELLENT	AVERAGE	LAST MSR
	$250	$150 - 190	$95 - 120	$380

LA 12 (NO. 449-0200-000) – 60W, 1-12 in. speaker with tweeter, solid-state chassis, pre-set Aural Enhancer, top control panel, four knobs (v, l, m, h), headphone jack, CD input, line out, edgemount handles, black covering, silver grid-style grille, 39 lbs., disc.

	100%	EXCELLENT	AVERAGE	LAST MSR
	$300	$175 - 225	$110 - 140	$500

LA 15 (NO. 449-0000-000) – 100W, 1-15 in. speaker with tweeter, solid-state chassis, pre-set Aural Enhancer, top control panel, four knobs (v, l, m, h), headphone jack, CD input, line out, edgemount handles, black covering, silver grid-style grille, 47 lbs., disc.

	100%	EXCELLENT	AVERAGE	LAST MSR
	$350	$200 - 250	$120 - 150	$575

ELECTRIC BASS AMPS: WORKINGMAN'S/WORKING PRO SERIES

WORKINGMAN'S 160 – 160W, rack-mount only, solid-state chassis, limiter, compressor, front control panel, two inputs, 10 black knobs, black covering, 14 lbs., mfg. 1994-99.

	100%	EXCELLENT	AVERAGE	LAST MSR
	N/A	$225 - 275	$125 - 175	$499

This model was upgraded and changed to the Workingman's 2004 in 1999.

WORKINGMAN'S 300 – 340W, rack-mount only, solid-state chassis, limiter, compressor, front control panel, two inputs, 5 black knobs, 5-band EQ, black covering, 18 lbs., mfg. 1994-99.

	100%	EXCELLENT	AVERAGE	LAST MSR
	N/A	$300 - 350	$150 - 200	$649

This model was upgraded and changed to the Workingman's 4004 in 1999.

MSR/NOTES	100%	EXCELLENT	AVERAGE	LAST MSR

Working Pro 10
courtesy SWR

Working Pro 12
courtesy SWR

Working Pro 2X10C
courtesy SWR

WORKINGMAN'S 2004 (NO. 44-50400-000) – 200W, head-unit only, solid-state chassis, single channel, limiter, compression, front black control panel, two inputs, nine silver knobs, headphone jack, tuner out jack, black rough covering, 27 lbs., mfg. 1999-2005.

	N/A	$275 - 325	$150 - 200	$643

From 1999-2002, the control panel was blue with a red logo.

WORKINGMAN'S 4004 (NO. 44-50200-000) – 400W, head-unit only, solid-state chassis, single channel, limiter, compression, front black control panel, two inputs, five silver knobs, five-band equalizer, headphone jack, tuner out jack, black rough covering, 33 lbs., mfg. 1999-2005.

	N/A	$375 - 450	$200 - 250	$857

From 1999-2002, the control panel was blue with a red logo.

WORKINGMAN'S 8004 T/O/P (NO. 44-50000-000) – 750W, head-unit only, solid-state chassis, single channel, limiter, compression, front black control panel, two inputs, nine silver knobs, headphone jack, tuner out jack, black rough covering, 49 lbs., mfg. 2002-04.

	N/A	$500 - 600	$300 - 350	$1,143

WORKINGMAN'S/WORKING PRO 10 (NO. 44-52400-000) – 80W, 1-10 in. plus a tweeter combo, solid-state chassis, single channel, limiter, compression, top black control panel, two inputs, six black knobs, headphone jack, tuner out jack, effects loop, black rough covering, black metal grille, 32 lbs., disc.

$450	$300 - 375	$175 - 225	$650

WORKINGMAN'S/WORKING PRO 12 (NO. 44-52200-000) – 100W, 1-12 in. and a tweeter combo, solid-state chassis, single channel, limiter, compression, top black control panel, two inputs, seven black knobs, headphone jack, tuner out jack, effects loop, black rough covering, black metal grille, 50 lbs., disc.

$550	$350 - 425	$225 - 275	$800

Models produced before 2002 had a different situated control panel as it was set back on top of the cabinet.

WORKINGMAN'S/WORKING PRO 15 (NO. 44-52000-000) – 160W, 1-15 in. and a tweeter combo, solid-state chassis, single channel, limiter, compression, top black control panel, two inputs, nine black knobs, headphone jack, tuner out jack, effects loop, black rough covering, black metal grille, 70 lbs., disc.

$700	$500 - 575	$300 - 350	$1,000

Models produced before 2002 had a different situated control panel as it was set back on top of the cabinets.

WORKINGMAN'S/WORKING PRO 2X10C (NO. 44-52600-000) – 260W, 2-10 in. and a tweeter combo, solid-state chassis, single channel, limiter, compression, top black control panel, two inputs, five silver knobs, five-band EQ, headphone jack, tuner out jack, effects loop, black rough covering, black metal grille, disc.

$900	$575 - 675	$350 - 425	$1,300

WORKING PRO 400 (NO. 44-50200-010) – 400W at 4 ohms (250W at 8 ohms), rack-mount head-unit only, solid-state chassis, front black control panel, single input, eleven black knobs, limiter, effects loop, black casing, two-button footswitch included, 25 lbs., mfg. 2005-disc.

$650	$425 - 500	$250 - 300	$950

WORKING PRO 700 (NO. 44-50000-010) – 700W at 4 ohms (450W at 8 ohms), rack-mount head-unit only, solid-state chassis, front black control panel, single input, eleven black knobs, limiter, effects loop, black casing, two-button footswitch included, 25 lbs., mfg. 2005-disc.

$800	$500 - 600	$300 - 350	$1,150

PREAMPS & POWER AMPS

SWR also produced the GT Preamp specially for Groove Tubes between 1984 and 1994. This amp is the preamp version of the Studio 220 and has GT on the front.

MSR/NOTES	100%	EXCELLENT	AVERAGE	LAST MSR

Working Pro 400
courtesy SWR

Working Pro 700
courtesy SWR

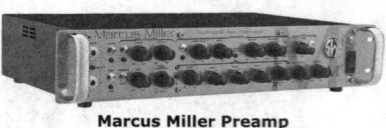

Marcus Miller Preamp
courtesy SWR

Power 750
courtesy SWR

Golight 1X15
courtesy SWR

GRAND PRIX – preamp only, rack-mount head, solid-state chassis, black control panel, nine knobs, black casing, 5.25 lbs., mfg. 1991-2001.

N/A	$350 - 450	$225 - 275	$799

AMPLITE POWER AMP (NO. 441-5050) – 400W, power amp only, single channel, front black control panel, single input, single volume knob, power amp meter, rear panel: power switch, two Speakon speaker jacks, pass-through jack, Neutrik combo input jack, black casing with chrome rails, 8.5 in. wide, 1.75 in. tall, 9.75 in. deep, 3 lbs., mfg. 2010-disc.

$550	$350 - 425	$200 - 250	$800

INTERSTELLAR OVERDRIVE PREAMP BLUE & CHROME FACE – preamp only, rack mount head-unit, blue or chrome control panel, two inputs, eight black knobs, four LED lights, single rack-mount space, 7 lbs., mfg. 1993-2002.

N/A	$375 - 475	$200 - 275	$849

The control panel was blue from 1993 to 1999 and chrome from June 1999, to May 2002.

INTERSTELLAR OVERDRIVE PREAMP (NO. 440-5100-000) – preamp only, rack mount head-unit, silver and black control panel, two inputs, eight black knobs, four LED lights, single rack-mount space, 10 lbs., mfg. 2002-06.

$700	$475 - 550	$325 - 400	$1,000

MARCUS MILLER PREAMP (NO. 440-5200-000) – preamp only, two-space rack-mount bass head, hybrid chassis with 2 X 12AX7 preamp tubes, single channel, front light blue anodized aluminum control panel with two chrome handles, 16 black knobs, front panel controls: two selectable inputs, mute switch, Bass Intensifier on/off switch, level knob, and cutoff knob, Compression on/off switch, threshold, ratio, comp position, attack, and release knobs, Boost on/off switch with level/comp blend knob, Pad on/off switch, gain knob, Aural Enhancer knob, five EQ knobs (b, semi-parametric EQ with l, m, h, and t), effects blend, MV, power switch, rear panel: XLR and 1/4 in. preamp out with ground lift switch, Tube DI with XLR and 1/4 in. out and ground lift switch, phase switch, and three-way direct compressor output switch, effects loop, footswitch jack, tuner out jack, aux. input jack, black casing, four-button footswitch (controls for Bass Intensifier, EQ Bypass, Effects Loop, and Boost) included, 19 in. wide, 3.5 in. tall, 11.125 in. deep, 13 lbs., mfg. summer 2008-disc.

$900	$550 - 675	$350 - 425	$1,300

POWER 750 (NO. 440-5500-000) – 750W power amp only, rack mount head-unit, silver and black control panel, single volume knob, four LED lights, silver casing, 32 lbs., disc.

$1,050	$650 - 800	$400 - 475	$1,500

This model received a facelift in 2002, older models are going to have polished look, the new one has ribs.

STEREO 800 – 800W mono, 350W per channel stereo, power amp only, rack-mount head, solid-state chassis, two channels, front black control panel, two volume controls, black casing, mfg. 1991-2001.

N/A	$575 - 675	$300 - 375	$1,249

SPEAKER CABINETS: GOLIGHT SERIES

GOLIGHT 1X15 (NO. 441-5900-000) – 350W, 1-15 in. custom SWR neodymium speaker, horn tweeter, 8 ohm impedance, input panel with tweeter attenuator, two 1/4 in. and two Speakon input/output jacks, specially-tuned bottom front slot port, spring-loaded rubber grip handles, gray Ozite carpeting with Stack Lock corners, black stamped steel grille, 23.25 in. wide, 20.25 in. tall, 18.5 in. deep, 45 lbs., mfg. 2009-disc.

$650	$425 - 500	$225 - 275	$900

GOLIGHT 2X10 (NO. 441-5700-800) – 400W, 2-10 in. custom SWR Eminence neodymium speakers, Foster horn tweeter, 8 ohm impedance, horn protection circuit, input panel with tweeter attenuator, two 1/4 in. and two Speakon input/output jacks, specially-tuned bottom front slot port, spring-loaded rubber grip handles, gray Ozite carpeting with Stack Lock corners, black stamped steel grille, 23 in. wide, 15.75 in. tall, 16.5 in. deep, 38 lbs., mfg. 2009-disc.

$650	$425 - 500	$225 - 275	$900

MSR/NOTES	100%	EXCELLENT	AVERAGE	LAST MSR

Golight 2X10
courtesy SWR

Golight 4X10
courtesy SWR

Marcus Miller Golight 4X10
courtesy SWR

GOLIGHT 4X10 (NO. 441-5500-400/800) – 800W, 4-10 in. custom SWR Eminence neodymium speakers, Foster horn tweeter, 4 ohm (No. 441-5500-400) or 8 ohm (No. 441-5500-800) impedance, horn protection circuit, input panel with tweeter attenuator, two 1/4 in. and two Speakon input/output jacks, specially-tuned bottom front slot port, spring-loaded rubber grip handles, removable casters, gray Ozite carpeting with Stack Lock corners, black stamped steel grille, 25.25 in. wide, 23 in. tall, 18.375 in. deep, 56 lbs., mfg. 2009-disc.

	$900	$575 - 675	$350 - 425	$1,300

MARCUS MILLER GOLIGHT 4X10 (NO. 441-5510-400) – 800W, 4-10 in. custom SWR Eminence neodymium speakers, Foster horn tweeter, 4 ohm impedance, horn protection circuit, input panel with tweeter attenuator, two 1/4 in. and two Speakon input/output jacks, sealed non-ported cabinet design, spring-loaded rubber grip handles, removable casters, gray Ozite carpeting with Stack Lock corners, black stamped steel grille, 23 in. wide, 23.5 in. tall, 18.375 in. deep, 55 lbs., mfg. 2009-disc.

	$900	$575 - 675	$350 - 425	$1,300

SPEAKER CABINETS: PRO & CUSTOM PRO SERIES

12-PACK ROCK BOX (NO. 447-1200-000) – 400W+, 2-12 in. drivers, ported cabinet, removable caster wheels, brown leatherish covering, black metal grille, 63 lbs., mfg. 2002-05.

	N/A	$350 - 425	$225 - 275	$714

12-STACK ROCK BOX (NO. 447-1000-000) – 800W+, 4-12 in. drivers, ported cabinet, removable caster wheels, brown leatherish covering, black metal grille, 107 lbs., mfg. 2002-05.

	N/A	$475 - 550	$325 - 375	$1,000

BABY BLUE MONITOR – 200W, 2-8 in. Bag End speakers, Bag End cone tweeter, 8 Ohm impedance, black covering, mfg. 1990-97.

	N/A	$250 - 300	$125 - 175	

In 1993, this model was upgraded to the Baby Blue Monitor II with changes including: 250W, 4 ohm impedance, and 2-8 in. Celestion speakers. The way to tell the difference between these two is to look at the speakers. If the surrounds are foam then it is the earlier version. If the surrounds have the accordion/bellow style then it is the newer model.

BASIC 2-WAY – 250W, 1-15 in. P.A.S. speaker with piezo tweeter, 8 Ohm impedance, black covering, black metal grille, 59 lbs., mfg. 1992-98.

	N/A	$275 - 325	$175 - 225	$599

BASS MONITOR 12 (NO. 447-0800-000) – 250W, 1-12 in. Bag End or Eminence speaker, LeSon Piezo tweeter, tilt-back cabinet design, black covering, black metal grille, 33 lbs., mfg. 1994-2003.

	N/A	$175 - 225	$100 - 150	$399

BIG BEN (NO. 447-1200-000/447-0600-000) – 400W, 1-18 in. subwoofer, 8 ohm, black covering, chrome metal grille, 73 lbs., disc.

	$675	$425 - 500	$250 - 300	$950

BIG BERTHA (NO. 447-0000-000) – 700W, 2-15 in. P.A.S. or Foster speakers, high-frequency tweeter, 4 Ohm impedance, caster wheels, black covering, chrome metal grille, 98 lbs., mfg. 1998-2003.

	N/A	$600 - 700	$475 - 525	$1,299

This model was featured in an advertisement for SWR with Derek Smalls from Spinal Tap.

BIGFOOT – 500W, 2-12 in. Bag End speakers, Le Son ferro-electric tweeter, 4 Ohm impedance, black covering, gray metal grille, mfg. 1994-97.

	N/A	$350 - 425	$225 - 275	$729

GOLIATH I – 400W, 4-10 in. speakers with high-end tweeter, 8 Ohm impedance, 3/4 in. 7 ply construction, black carpet covering, black metal grille, 90 lbs., mfg. 1987-1990.

	N/A	$650 - 800	$400 - 500	$999

MSR/NOTES	100%	EXCELLENT	AVERAGE	LAST MSR

Goliath III
courtesy SWR

Goliath Senior
courtesy SWR

Son of Bertha
courtesy SWR

GOLIATH II – 500W, 4-10 in. speakers with high-end tweeter, 8 Ohm impedance, redesigned crossover, black carpet covering, black metal grille, 90 lbs., mfg. 1990-1996.

| | N/A | $600 - 750 | $350 - 450 | $999 |

GOLIATH III (NO. 441-0500-400/800/410/810) – 700W, 4-10 in. speakers + a tweeter, 4 or 8 Ohm, black covering, chrome metal grille, 89 lbs., disc.

| | $900 | $575 - 675 | $350 - 425 | $1,300 |

GOLIATH JUNIOR I – 200W, 2-10 in. speakers with high-end tweeter, 4 Ohm impedance, black carpet covering, black grille, mfg. 1987-1990.

| | N/A | $400 - 500 | $175 - 250 | $649 |

GOLIATH JUNIOR II – 200W, 2-10 in. speakers with high-end tweeter, 4 Ohm impedance, redesigned crossover, input panel, black carpet covering, black grille, mfg. 1990-1996.

| | N/A | $350 - 450 | $150 - 200 | $649 |

GOLIATH JUNIOR III (NO. 441-0700-400/800/410/810) – 350W, 2-10 in. speaker plus a tweeter, 4 or 8 ohm, black covering, chrome metal grille, 55 lbs., disc.

| | $650 | $400 - 475 | $225 - 275 | $900 |

GOLIATH SENIOR (NO. 440-1300-000) – 1,000W, 6-10 in. speakers + a tweeter, 4 Ohm, black covering, chrome metal grille, 115 lbs., disc.

| | $1,200 | $750 - 900 | $425 - 500 | $1,700 |

HENRY JUNIOR 4X8 – 250W, 4-8 in. custom P.A.S. speakers with piezo tweeter, 8 Ohm impedance, black covering, black metal grille, 55 lbs., mfg. 1994-97.

| | N/A | $325 - 400 | $200 - 250 | $699 |

HENRY THE 8X8 (NO. 447-0200-000) – 480W, 8-8 in. drivers, high-frequency tweeter, 4 Ohm, black covering, chrome metal grille, 100 lbs., disc.

| | $1,000 | $625 - 725 | $375 - 450 | $1,400 |

MEGOLIATH (NO. 441-0100-000/010) – 1,200W, 8-10 in. speakers + a tweeter, 8 or 4 Ohm, black covering, chrome metal grille, 154 lbs., disc.

| | $1,500 | $950 - 1,150 | $600 - 700 | $2,150 |

A.K.A. "The Chiropractors special," luckily there are wheels and handles to move it along. The *Blue Book of Guitar Amplifiers* doesn't suggest carrying it up the stairs by yourself.

SON OF BERTHA (NO. 441-0900-000/010) – 350W, 1-15 in. speaker + a tweeter, black covering, chrome metal grille, 60 lbs., disc.

| | $650 | $400 - 475 | $225 - 275 | $900 |

TRIAD 1 (NO. 447-0400-000) – 400W, 1-15 in. driver, 1-10 in. driver, high-frequency tweeter, 4 ohm, black covering, chrome metal grille, 80 lbs., disc.

| | $800 | $500 - 600 | $300 - 350 | $1,150 |

SPEAKER CABINETS: WORKINGMAN'S/WORKING PRO SERIES

In 2005, the Workingman's speaker cabinets were revised a bit and renamed the Working Pro to match up with the new heads. Changes were mainly cosmetic including a chrome-powdercoat stamped-steel vibration free grille. Components were basically the same as the old models.

MSR/NOTES	100%	EXCELLENT	AVERAGE	LAST MSR

Working Pro 1X15T
courtesy SWR

Working Pro 2X10T
courtesy SWR

Baja Blonde
courtesy SWR

WORKINGMAN'S/WORKING PRO 1X10T (NO. 445-6800-000) – 100W, 1-10 in. driver, high-frequency tweeter, ported front slot, black covering, black metal grille, 26 lbs., disc. 2005.

| | N/A | $140 - 175 | $90 - 110 | $286 |

This cabinet matches perfectly up with the Workingman's/Working Pro 10 combo amp.

WORKINGMAN'S 1X12T – 200W, 1-12 in. Celestion speaker, Le-Son Piezo tweeter, 8 Ohm impedance, front slot port, black covering, black metal grille, 38 lbs., mfg. 1995-96.

| | N/A | $150 - 200 | $75 - 100 | $349 |

WORKINGMAN'S/WORKING PRO 1X15T (NO. 445-6600-000/010) – 200W, 1-15 in. driver, high-frequency tweeter, ported front slot, black covering, black metal grille, 45 lbs., disc.

| $400 | $275 - 325 | $150 - 200 | $575 |

WORKINGMAN'S/WORKING PRO 2X10T (NO. 445-6400-000/010) – 200W, 2-10 in. drivers, high-frequency tweeter, ported front slot, black covering, black metal grille, 60 lbs., disc.

| $400 | $275 - 325 | $150 - 200 | $575 |

WORKINGMAN'S 2X12T – 250W, 2-12 in. Celestion speakers, high-frequency tweeter, 8 Ohm impedance, 3-way switch for horn, black covering, gray "Texas Bar Proof" metal grille, 55 lbs., mfg. 1995-99.

| | N/A | $300 - 350 | $175 - 225 | $649 |

WORKINGMAN'S/WORKING PRO 4X10T (NO. 445-6200-000/010/410) – 400W, 4-10 in. drivers, high-frequency tweeter, 4 ohm (No. 445-6200-410) or 8 ohm (No. 445-6200-000/010) impedance, ported front slot, black covering, black metal grille, 97 lbs., disc.

| $550 | $350 - 425 | $225 - 275 | $800 |

WORKINGMAN'S/WORKING PRO TOWER (NO. 445-600-000) – 800W, 8-10 in. drivers, high-frequency tweeter, ported front slot, black covering, black metal grille, 110 lbs., mfg. 2002-04.

| | N/A | $500 - 600 | $300 - 350 | $1,214 |

SPEAKER CABINETS: ACOUSTIC SERIES

BAJA BLONDE (NO. 446-0300-000) – 80W output, 200W handling capacity, 1-12 in. Celestion speaker with a SWR tweeter, 8 ohm impedance, horn attenuator, inputs, blonde textured vinyl covering, brown metal grille, 35 lbs., mfg. 2006-09.

| $450 | $275 - 325 | $150 - 200 | $650 |

This model replaced the Blonde on Blonde and is designed to be used as an extension cabinet to the California Blonde II or a personal monitoring system.

BLONDE ON BLONDE (NO. 44-60200-000) – 80W, 1-12 in. speaker with a high-frequency tweeter, volume control, horn on/off switch, speaker jack, cream covering, brown metal grille, mfg. 1998-2005.

| | N/A | $300 - 375 | $175 - 225 | $714 |

This unit is capable of giving the acoustic series stereo output as well as a monitoring system.

NATURAL BLONDE – 200W, 1-12 in. Custom Celestion speaker with tweeter, 8 Ohm impedance, bottom slot port, blonde covering, brown metal grille, 37 lbs., mfg. 1997-98.

| | N/A | $300 - 375 | $175 - 225 | $449 |

NOTES

T SECTION
TAKT

Amplifiers previously produced in Japan during the 1960s.

Takt amplifiers were built in Japan (manufacturer unknown) and sold throughout various outlets in the U.S., possibly including Woolworth. All amps that appear in the used market are from the GA series that includes models GA-9, GA-10, GA-11, GA-12, GA-14, and GA-15. Most amps feature tube chassis, but solid-state models are reported to have existed. In the used market, these amps are generally priced between $50 and $100 depending on condition/configuration. Any further information on Takt amplifiers can be submitted directly to Blue Book Publications.

TALOS

Instruments previously produced in Springfield, VA.

Talos amps were built by Bill Thalmann and Doug Weisbrod in Virgina, and they first started experimenting with this design in the early 2000s. The Talos Basic Amp steers away from models that have numerous controls and switches to produce a versatile and complex sound from very simple controls. The Basic Amp has only two knobs and four switches, which leaves the guitar to shape more of the tone. Talos amps were hand-built one at a time, feature tube chassis, and were available in a head or a combo unit. The head starts at (Last MSR $2,400) and the combo at (Last MSR $3,000). Options were available such as custom wood cabinets and a tweeter. Speaker cabinets were also available.

The Basic
courtesy Talos

The Basic
courtesy Talos

The Basic Control Panel
courtesy Talos

TASCAM

Amplifiers currently produced in Japan since 2006. Distributed by Tascam in Montebello, CA.

Tascam has been producing audio electronic products since 1953, and they have been involved in pro-audio guitar gear since the 1970s. They are best-known for their computer recording, professional audio, DJ/producer equipment, and other audio electronics. In 2006, they applied some of their technology to a guitar amplifier, the **GA-100CD**. This amp features Tascam's Neo TubeT technology, which makes it sound like a tube amp, a 60W amp section, a 40W (20W X 2) CD playback amp section, 1-12 in. speaker for the amp, and 2-5 in. speakers for CD playback. The GA-100CD also features DSP effects, an effects loop, and a CD trainer section. The CD trainer allows the user to play along with a CD, speed up the tempo of the CD without changing pitch, and a guitar cancel. This is a perfect application for the CDs that many guitar magazines and books offer that only have the rhythm section. A small version called the GA-30CD was added in 2007. For more information, visit Tascam's website or contact them directly.

CONTACT INFORMATION
TASCAM
7733 Telegraph Rd.
Montebello, CA 90640
Phone No.: 323-727-7617
www.tascam.com

MSR/NOTES	100%	EXCELLENT	AVERAGE	LAST MSR

GUITAR AMPLIFIERS

GA-30CD – 30W (15W for amplifier, 15W [7.5W x 2 stereo] for CD player and built-in guitar effects), 1-6.5 in. speaker (amplifier) and 2-3 in. speakers (CD player and built-in guitar effects), solid-state chassis, two channels, built-in CD player, top/front black control panel, single input, 7 black knobs on front (g, b, m, t, r, center v, side v), three black effects knobs on top, 1/8 in. line in jack, headphone jack, digital displays with various buttons for CD playback and guitar effects, black covering, silver metal grille with blue baffle, 15 in. wide, 13.5 in. tall, 10 in. deep, 30.5 lbs., mfg. 2007-present.

MSR/NOTES	100%	EXCELLENT	AVERAGE
MSR $429	$250	$150 - 200	$95 - 120

courtesy Tascam

MSR/NOTES	100%	EXCELLENT	AVERAGE	LAST MSR

GA-100CD – 100W (60W for amplifier, 40W [20W x 2 stereo] for CD player and built-in guitar effects), 1-12 in. RockReady speaker (amplifier) and 2-5 in. full range speakers (CD player and built-in guitar effects), Neo Tube solid-state chassis, two channels, built-in CD player, top silver control panel, two inputs (high/low), 16 black knobs (Clean Ch.: g, v, b, m, t, OD Ch.: g, v, b, m, t, All: main MV, sub MV, three effects knobs, r), two digital displays with various buttons for CD playback and guitar effects, back panel: two footswitch jacks, effects loop, RCA line in, RCA line out, headphone jack, black covering, silver metal grille with blue baffle, 32.2 in. wide, 21.6 in. tall, 13.5 in. deep, 79.4 lbs., mfg. 2006-present.

courtesy Tascam

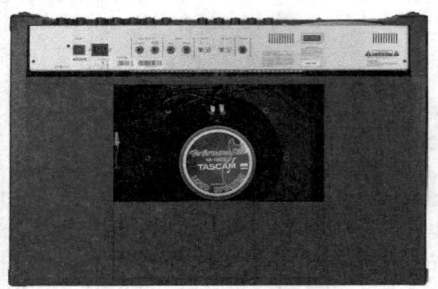

courtesy Tascam

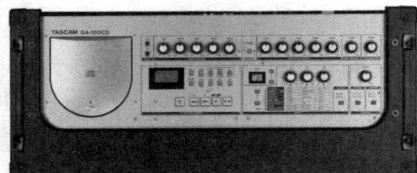

courtesy Tascam

MSR $875 $525 $375 - 450 $225 - 275

TC ELECTRONIC

Amplifiers and speaker cabinets currently produced since the mid-2000s. TC Electronics was founded in 1976 and is based in Risskov, Denmark.

Brothers Kim and John Rishøj founded TC Electronics in 1976 building mainly guitar effects pedals. Frustrated with the lack of quality in effects pedals during the 1970s the Rishøjs set out to make pedals better. They later expanded into rack-mounted equipment and became an industry leader in digital signal processing. In the 2000s, they introduced their first bass amplifiers. They currently offer bass amp heads, combos, and speaker cabinets and they continue to produce a variety of guitar effects and processors. For more information, visit TC Electronics website or contact them directly.

TECAMP (CHINA)

Amplifiers currently produced in China. Distributed in the U.S. by the Sino-Amp Company in Los Angles, CA.

Tecamp amplifiers are produced by the Sino-Amp Company, which are built in Tianjin, China. The amps are distributed in the U.S. by Sino-Amp that is located in Los Angeles. They produce a full line of guitar and bass amplifiers that are mainly budget/entry-level models. They also produce building mixers, speaker cabinets, and monitors. For more information visit Tecamp's website or contact them directly.

TECAMP (GERMANY)

Amplifiers currently produced in Germany and in Austin, TX.

TecAmp produces bass amps and cabinets in Germany. In 2014, TecAmp announced they would also begin building some of their models in Austin, TX. These amps are considered high-end products and come in a variety of configurations. Amps are available in MOSFET solid-state or tube configurations. For more information, visit TecAmp's website or contact them directly.

TECH 21

Amplifiers currently produced in New York City, NY since 1989. Distributed by Tech 21.

Tech 21 is a company that produces many different products, including guitar amplifiers. Their most popular line of amplifiers are probably the Trademark series. These are amps that come in a variety of configurations. They can produce many different wattages and have a great channel switching feature. They also offer the Bronzewood and Landmark series. Tech 21 has several different effects and pedals including a Randy Bachman signature overdrive called the American Woman. There are also several SansAmp units available. For more information, visit Tech 21's website or contact them directly.

MSR/NOTES	100%	EXCELLENT	AVERAGE	LAST MSR

GUITAR/BASS AMPLIFIERS

BASS POWER ENGINE 60 – 60W, powered bass cabinet, 1-12 in. custom speaker, analog chassis, front black control panel, single input, four black knobs (level, l, m, h), speaker out, XLR out, black scuff-proof finish, chrome plated steel grille, 35 lbs., disc. 2007.

	$370	$200 - 250	$120 - 150	$485

BRONZEWOOD 60 – 60W, acoustic amp, 1-12 in. Celestion speaker, HF horn, analog SansAmp chassis, two channels, top stainless steel control panel, guitar and mic inputs, 16 black knobs, effect loop, headphone out, XLR out, brown crocodile-embossed vinyl cabinet, black grille, 38 lbs., current mfg.

MSR $715	$540	$325 - 375	$200 - 250	

LANDMARK 60 – 60W, bass amp, 1-12 in. speaker, analog SansAmp chassis, front black control panel, single input, seven black knobs (drive, p, blend, b, m, t, level), headphone jack, effect loop, speaker out, XLR out, front-ported cabinet, black scuff-proof covering, chrome plated steel grille, 36 lbs., disc. 2008.

	$495	$275 - 325	$150 - 200	$655

LANDMARK 120 – 120W, bass amp, 1-15 in. custom Eminence Neodymium speaker, analog SansAmp chassis, front black control panel, single input, seven black knobs (drive, p, blend, b, m, t, level), headphone jack, effect loop, speaker out, XLR out, black scuff-proof covering, chrome plated steel grille, disc. 2008.

	$575	$325 - 400	$200 - 250	$765

LANDMARK 300 – 300W, bass amp, 2-space rack-mount head, analog SansAmp chassis, two channels, front gray control panel, single input, 12 black knobs (Ch.1: drive, b, p, blend, t, level, Ch.2: drive, b, m, mid-shift, t, level), XLR output, effects loop, tuner output, speaker out, black casing, 21 lbs., mfg. 2003-present.

MSR $1,035	$775	$450 - 525	$275 - 325	

LANDMARK 600 – 600W, bass amp, three-space rack-mount head, analog SansAmp chassis, two channels, front gray control panel, single input, 12 black knobs (Ch.1: drive, b, p, blend, t, level, Ch.2: drive, b, m, mid-shift, t, level), XLR output, effects loop, tuner output, speaker out, black casing, 40 lbs., disc. 2006.

	$1,200	$700 - 900	$450 - 550	$1,595

POWER ENGINE 60 112 – 60W, powered cabinet, 1-12 in. Celestion speaker, analog chassis, top stainless steel control panel, 1/4 in. and XLR input, four black knobs (level, l, m, h), speaker out, XLR out, black vinyl covering, wheat grille, 33 lbs., current mfg.

MSR $455	$340	$190 - 240	$100 - 140	

* *Power Engine 60 212* – similar to the Power Engine 60 112, except has 2-12 in. Celestion speakers, 39 lbs., mfg. 2007-09.

	$475	$275 - 325	$150 - 200	$605

* *Power Engine 60 410* – similar to the Power Engine 60 112, except has 4-10 in. custom Eminence speakers, 43 lbs., mfg. 2007-present.

MSR $805	$610	$325 - 400	$200 - 250	

TRADEMARK 10 – 10W, 1-8 in. speaker, analog SansAmp GT2 chassis, reverb, top stainless steel control panel, single input, six black knobs, effects loop, headphone jack, black covering, wheat grille, 12 lbs., disc. 2006.

	$300	$175 - 225	$100 - 140	$395

• Add $45 for optional gig bag.

TRADEMARK 30 – 30W, 1-10 in. speaker, analog SansAmp GT2 chassis, reverb, top stainless steel control panel, single input, six black knobs, effects loop, headphone jack, black vinyl covering, wheat grille, mfg. 2005-present.

MSR $520	$320	$225 - 275	$135 - 175	

• Add $45 for optional gig bag.

TRADEMARK 60 112 – 60W, 1-12 in. Celestion speaker, analog SansAmp chassis, two channels, reverb, top stainless steel control panel, single input, ten black knobs, effects loop, headphone jack, three button footswitch, black vinyl covering, wheat grille, 35 lbs., current mfg.

MSR $695	$610	$325 - 400	$200 - 250	

* *Trademark 60 212* – similar to the Trademark 60 112, except has 2-12 in. Celestion speakers, 47 lbs., mfg. 2006-09.

	$700	$425 - 500	$250 - 300	$935

» *Trademark 60 212C* – similar to the Trademark 60 212, except has 2-12 in. Celestion Neodymium speakers, 42 lbs., mfg. 2006 only.

	$825	$475 - 550	$300 - 350	$1,095

* *Trademark 60 410* – similar to the Trademark 60 112, except has 4-10 in. custom Eminence speakers, 46 lbs., mfg. 2006-present.

MSR $1,150	$870	$475 - 550	$300 - 350	

TRADEMARK 120 – 120W, 2-12 in. Celestion speakers, stereo, analog SansAmp chassis, three channels, reverb, top stainless steel control panel, single input, 18 black knobs, effects loop, headphone jack, six button footswitch, black vinyl covering, wheat grille, 50 lbs., disc. 2006.

	$750	$450 - 550	$275 - 325	$995

MSR/NOTES	100%	EXCELLENT	AVERAGE	LAST MSR

TRADEMARK 300 – 300W, two-space rack-mount head, stereo, analog SansAmp chassis, three channels, front stainless steel control panel, single input, 18 black knobs, effects loop, headphone jack, six button footswitch, black covering, stainless steel decorative panel on front, 37 lbs., mfg. 2003-06.

	$750	$450 - 550	$275 - 325	$995

A vintage-style version in all vinyl is also available at no additional charge.

SPEAKER CABINETS

2X12TM – 300W, 2-12 in. Eminence speakers, closed-back cabinet, black vinyl covering, black grille, disc. 2009.

	$420	$225 - 275	$135 - 175	$550

4X12TM – 320W, 4-12 in. Celestion speakers, closed-back straight or slanted cabinet, black vinyl covering, wheat grille, current mfg.

MSR $795	$600	$350 - 450	$200 - 250	

4X12TMS – 320W, 4-12 in. Celestion speakers, closed-back straight or slanted cabinet, black vinyl covering, black grille, current mfg.

MSR $795	$600	$350 - 450	$200 - 250	

B115 – 300W, 1-15 in. Eminence Neodymium speaker, rear vented cabinet, black scuff-proof covering, chrome plated steel grille, 48 lbs., current mfg.

MSR $765	$575	$325 - 400	$200 - 250	

B410 – 400W, 4-10 in. cast-frame custom speakers, rear vented cabinet, black scuff-proof covering, chrome plated steel grille, 70 lbs., current mfg.

MSR $765	$575	$325 - 400	$200 - 250	

TEISCO

Amplifiers previously produced in Japan between 1956 and 1973. Teisco amplifiers were distributed in the U.S. by Westheimer Musical Instruments of Evanston, Illinois.

In 1946, Mr. Atswo Kaneko and Mr. Doryu Matsuda founded the Aoi Onpa Kenkyujo company, makers of the guitars bearing the Teisco and other trademarks (the company name roughly translates to the **Hollyhock Soundwave or Electricity Laboratories**). The Teisco name was chosen by Mr. Kaneko, and was used primarily in domestic markets. Early models include lap steel and electric-Spanish guitars. By the 1950s, the company was producing slab-bodied designs with bolt-on necks along with guitar amplifiers. In 1956, the company name was changed to the Nippon Onpa Kogyo Co., Ltd. - but the guitars still stayed Teisco!

As the demand for guitars in the U.S. market began to expand, Mr. Jack Westheimer of WMI Corporation of Evanston, Illinois started to import Japanese guitars and amplifiers in the late 1950s, perhaps circa 1958. WMI began importing the Teisco-built Kingston guitars in 1961, and also used the Teisco Del Rey trademark extensively beginning in 1964. Other Teisco-built guitars had different trademarks (a rebranding technique), and the different brand names will generally indicate the U.S. importer/distributor. The Japanese company again changed names, this time to the Teisco Co. Ltd. The Teisco line included all manners of solid body and semi-hollowbody guitars, and their niche in the American guitar market (as entry level or beginner's guitars) assured steady sales.

In 1967, the Kawai Corporation purchased the Teisco company. Not one to ruin a good thing, Kawai continued exporting the Teisco line to the U.S. (although they did change some designs through the years) until 1973. Due to the recent popularity in the Teisco name, Kawai actually produced some limited edition Teisco Spectrum Five models lately in Japan, although they were not made available to the U.S. market (Source: Michael Wright, *Vintage Guitar Magazine*).

TUBE AMPLIFIERS

CHECKMATE 10 – 10W, 1-12 in. speaker, all-tube chassis, tremolo, reverb, mfg. 1960s.

	N/A	$200 - 250	$120 - 150	

CHECKMATE 17 – approx 15W, 1-10 in. speaker, all-tube chassis, preamp: 2 X 12AX7, power: EL84, rectifier: 6X4, tremolo, reverb, two inputs, four knobs (v, tone, tremolo, r), mfg. 1960s.

	N/A	$200 - 250	$120 - 150	

CHECKMATE 25 – approx 25W, 1-15 in. and 1-2 in. speaker, all-tube chassis, two channels, preamp: 3 X 12AX7, 12AU7, power: 2 X 7819, reverb, tremolo, three inputs, six knobs (v, t, b, d, s, r), mfg. 1960s.

	N/A	$225 - 275	$120 - 150	

SOLID-STATE AMPLIFIERS

CHECKMATE 10 – 5W, 1-6 in. speaker, solid-state chassis, top control panel, two inputs, two knobs (v, tone), black cabinet, black grille, mfg. late 1960s.

	N/A	$75 - 100	$45 - 60	

MSR/NOTES	100%	EXCELLENT	AVERAGE	LAST MSR

CHECKMATE 22 – approx 50W, head and cabinet unit, 2-10 in. speaker, solid-state chassis, tremolo, reverb, two inputs, four knobs (v, tone, tremolo, r), headphone jack, line out, mfg. 1960s.

	N/A	$120 - 150	$75 - 95	

CHECKMATE 30 – approx 8W, 1-6 in. speaker, solid-state chassis, tremolo, two inputs, four knobs (v, tone, s, i), footswitch, uniquely built amplifier in it sits on three legs and is circular, the amp is in the bottom section and the speaker faces upward, brown woodgrain finish with chrome trim, mfg. 1960s.

courtesy solidbodyguitar.com, Inc.

courtesy solidbodyguitar.com, Inc.

	N/A	$375 - 450	$225 - 275	

CHECKMATE 66 – approx 10W, 2-6 in. speakers, solid-state chassis, tremolo, reverb, two inputs, four knobs (v, tone, tremolo, r), headphone jack, line out, mfg. 1960s.

	N/A	$100 - 135	$60 - 80	

CHECKMATE 88 – approx 10W, 2-8 in. speakers, solid-state chassis, tremolo, reverb, two inputs, four knobs (v, tone, tremolo, r), headphone jack, line out, mfg. 1960s.

	N/A	$120 - 150	$75 - 95	

TELE-STAR

Amplifiers previously produced in Japan between the late 1960s and 1983.

The Tele-Star trademark was distributed in the U.S. by the Tele-Star Musical Instrument Corporation in New York, NY. Tele-Star offered a full range of acoustic, thinline acoustic/electric hollow body, and solid body electric guitars and basses. They also offered select guitar amplifiers. Many were built by Kawai of Japan. Source: Michael Wright, *Vintage Guitar Magazine*.

TENEYCK

Amplifiers previously produced in Ashbury Park, NJ during the late 1960s. Distributed by Mid-Eastern Industries, Inc. in Ashbuy Park, NJ.

Teneyck amplifiers were produced by Mid-Eastern Industries, Inc. in Ashbury, NJ. They feature all solid-state chassis, which were the technology of the future at the time. Teneyck produced the G series of amplifiers until 1966, and in 1967 introduced the T series of amplifiers, which were very similar to the G series. Models were available as guitar amps, bass amps, and satellite speaker cabinets. Known models includes the **G1000, G2000, G3000, B3000, GB4000, GB4000, S4000, GB5000, B5000, GB6000, T220, TT250, T290, T295, T330, T350, T440, T450, T510, T550,** and **T660**. Any further information on Teneyck amplifiers can be submitted directly to Blue Book Publications.

THD ELECTRONICS

Amplifiers currently produced in Seattle, WA since 1987.

Andy Marshall founded THD Electronics in 1987. THD specializes in tube amplification and other products that have to deal with tube amps including the Hot Plate, which is a power attenuator that allows the player to use full distortion at a reduced volume, and a Yellow Jacket converter, which is a class A tube adaptor. THD released the BiValve 30 at the 2002 Summer NAMM show. They also make other amps, speaker cabinets, and tube converters. For more information visit THD's website or contact them directly.

ELECTRIC TUBE AMPLIFIERS

• Add $175 for polished chrome cage.

MSR/NOTES	100%	EXCELLENT	AVERAGE	LAST MSR

UNIVALVE 15 HEAD (UNI15) – 15W, head-unit only, class A tube chassis, preamp: 2 X 12AX7 (or optional 12AT7, 12AU7, 12AY7, 12AZ7), power: 1 X 6L6 (or optional EL34, 6550, KT66, KT77, KT88, KT90), single channel, front chrome control panel, five knobs (v, t, b, attitude, hot plate attenuator), full power switch, high v/low v switch, standby switch, power switch, available in a black metal cage head unit, black or a colored (blue, gold, purple, or red) rack-mount unit, or a traditional head-unit in black, cream, or paisley covering (new 2010), current mfg.

MSR $1,195	$1,000	$675 - 800	$425 - 500	

- Add 5% (MSR $1,260) for black rackmount equipment.
- Add 10% (MSR $1,320) for colored (blue, gold, green, purple, or red) rackmount equipment.
- Add 30% for a standard head-unit in black covering.
- Add 32.5% for a standard head-unit in cream or paisley covering.

* *Univalve 15 Lefty* – similar to the Univalve 15 except in "lefty" configuration, only 100 made of limited edition run, disc. 2003.

	N/A	$750 - 900	$475 - 550	$1,045

* *Univalve 15 112 Combo (112U15C)* – similar to the Univalve 15 Head, except in combo configuration with 1-12 in. speaker, black covering, brown grille, current mfg.

MSR $1,895	$1,600	$1,050 - 1,250	$650 - 800	

* *Univalve 15 210 Combo (210U15C)* – similar to the Univalve 15 Head, except in combo configuration with 2-10 in. speakers, black covering, brown grille, mfg. 2002-disc.

	N/A	$1,100 - 1,300	$675 - 825	$1,774

* *Univalve 15 212 Combo (212U15C)* – similar to the Univalve 15 Head, except in combo configuration with 2-12 in. speakers, black covering, brown grille, disc.

	N/A	$1,150 - 1,350	$700 - 850	$1,794

BIVALVE 30 HEAD (BIV30) – 30W, head-unit only, class A four tube chassis, preamp: 2 X 12AX7 (or optional 12AT7, 12AU7, 12AY7, 12AZ7), power: 2 X 6L6 (or optional EL34, 6550, KT66, KT77, KT88, KT90), single channel, front chrome control panel, five knobs (v, t, b, attitude, hot plate attenuator), full power switch, high v/low v switch, standby switch, power switch, available in a black metal cage head unit, black or a colored (blue, gold, purple, or red) rack-mount unit, or traditional head-unit available in black, cream or paisley covering (new 2010), current mfg.

MSR $1,795	$1,525	$1,000 - 1,150	$650 - 750	

- Add 5% (MSR $1,860) for black rackmount equipment.
- Add 7.5% (MSR $1,920) for colored (blue, green, gold, purple, or red) rackmount equipment.
- Add 20% for a standard head-unit in black covering.
- Add 22.5% for a standard head-unit in cream or paisley covering.

* *Bivalve 30 112 Combo (112B30C)* – similar to the Bivalve 30 Head, except in combo configuration with 1-12 in. speaker, black covering, brown grille, current mfg.

MSR $2,495	$2,100	$1,350 - 1,600	$850 - 1,000	

* *Bivalve 30 210 Combo (210B30C)* – similar to the Bivalve 30 Head, except in combo configuration with 2-10 in. speakers, black covering, brown grille, mfg. 2002-disc.

	N/A	$1,400 - 1,650	$875 - 1,025	$2,274

* *Bivalve 30 212 Combo (212B30C)* – similar to the Bivalve 30 Head, except in combo configuration with 2-12 in. speakers, black covering, brown grille, disc.

	N/A	$1,450 - 1,700	$900 - 1,050	$2,294

FLEXI 50 – 50W, head-unit only, class A/B five tube chassis, preamp: 3 X 12AX7 (or optional 12AT7, 12AU7, 12AY7, 12AZ7, 12DW7, 12BH7, ECC81, ECC82, and ECC83), power: 2 X EL34 (or optional 6L6, 6V6, 6CA7, 6550, 8417, KT66, KT77, KT88, KT90, KT100, and EL84 with Yellow Jacket adapter), single channel, front gold control panel, single input, eight knobs (v, t, m, b, g, tone, MV, cut), high/low switch, bright switch, boost switch, MV on/off switch, 50W/20W switch, standby switch, power switch, available in a black metal cage head unit, black or a colored (blue, gold, purple, or red) rack-mount unit, or traditional head-unit available in black, cream, or paisley covering (new 2010), 45 lbs., mfg. 2004-present.

MSR $2,395	$2,000	$1,300 - 1,550	$800 - 950	

- Add 2.5% (MSR $2,460) for black rackmount equipment.
- Add 5% (MSR $2,520) for colored (blue, gold, green, purple, or red) rackmount equipment.
- Add 15% for a standard head-unit in black covering.
- Add 17.5% for a standard head-unit in cream or paisley covering.

* *Flexi 50 112 Combo* – similar to the Flexi 50 Head, except in combo configuration with 1-12 in. speaker, black covering, brown grille, current mfg.

MSR $3,095	$2,600	$1,750 - 2,000	$1,100 - 1,300	

SPEAKER CABINETS

212 SPEAKER CABINET – wattage unknown, 2-12 in. speakers, available in Black, Brown, Creme, or Paisley covering, brown grille, 26.5 in. wide, 18 in. tall, 11 in. deep, 45 lbs., current mfg.

MSR $799	$675	$450 - 525	$250 - 300	

- Add 7.5% (MSR $849) for Brown, Creme, or Paisley covering.

MSR/NOTES	100%	EXCELLENT	AVERAGE	LAST MSR

412 SPEAKER CABINET – wattage unknown, 4-12 in. speakers, slot-port in rear, black covering, brown grille, current mfg.

MSR $1,249 $1,000 $675 - 825 $425 - 500

THUNDERFUNK

Amplifiers previously produced in the 1990s.

Thunderfunk produced amplifiers in the early 1990s that were very large and heavy. Despite what the name suggests, these amplifiers were guitar amps rather than bass amps.

TITANO

Amplifiers previously produced by Magnatone during the early 1960s.

Titano was a brand Magnatone used on a line of accordion amplifiers during the early 1960s. Magnatone (Estey) built these amps, which were almost all clones of Magnatones, and put a Titano logo on the front. Essentially all Titano models should have a corresponding model with Magnatone. Although these amps were designed for accordions, guitars could be used as well. Known models include the **Custom 160R**, **Custom 262R**, **Model 383**, **Custom 415**, and **Custom 415R**. Any further information on Titano amps can be submitted directly to Blue Book Publications.

TOKAI

Amplifiers previously produced in Japan.

Tokai amplifiers are very good Fender and other popular American replicas produced during the 1950s and 1960s. These models are becoming increasingly collectible and are starting to bring some higher dollars. There are a few websites out there dedicated to Tokai instruments. Lawsuits have been filed against Tokai because of their strikingly close copies of popular instruments (note the similarity in the Tokai logo versus Fender). Tokai no longer produces amplifiers. They still build guitars, but they are original designs only.

TA-35
courtesy Rick Wilkiewicz

TA-35
courtesy Rick Wilkiewicz

TONE KING

Amplifiers currently designed in Baltimore, MD and produced in Rohnert Park, CA. Previously produced in Baltimore, MD and New York, NY.

Mark Bartel founded Tone King in 1993. They produced amps for a short while in New York, but moved to Baltimore, MD in 1994. Tone King amps are all designed by Bartel at his shop in Baltimore, MD and then hand built one at a time by the Tone King build team in California. For more information visit Tone King's website or contact them directly.

CONTACT INFORMATION
TONE KING
619 Martin Ave.
Suite 6
Rohnert Park, CA 94928
www.toneking.com
info@premierbuildersguild.com

ELECTRIC TUBE AMPLIFIERS

Previous models include the Meteor Series, Comet Series, Galaxy Series, Continental Series, and Imperial Series. These older amps have a vintage-style look to them. The Imperial, Continental, and Galaxy models were produced from 1993 to 1997. The **Imperial** featured 20W output, 1-12 in. speaker, reverb, and tremolo. The **Continental** was introduced in 1994 and featured 40W output (switchable to 20W), reverb, and tremolo and was available in a 1-12 in. combo or head unit with a 2-12 in speaker cabinet. The **Galaxy** was introduced in 1995 and featured 60W output (switchable to 30W), reverb, tremolo, and came in head-unit configuration with a 4-12 in. speaker cabinet.

In 1997, the **Comet Series** was introduced and all other models were discontinued. The Comet was available in a 20W (Comet 20A), or 40W (Comet 40A, 40B) version. The Comet 20A was a combo unit with 1-12 in. speaker. The Comet 40A featured a 1-12 in. combo and the 40B featured a 2-12 in. cabinet. These amps had a cosmetic change as well with the controls mounted on the top. They were also the first to feature an effects loop. This line was produced until 2003.

In 2003, The **Meteor Series** was introduced. Four configurations were available: Meteor 15A (15W), Meteor 20A (20W), Meteor 30A (30W), and the Meteor 40A (40W). All models came in combo form with 1-12 in. speaker, and featured tremolo, reverb, and two channels. This series was discontinued circa 2005 in favor of the Meteor Series II.

In 2005, the **Meteor Series II** was introduced. These amps are available in 15W, 20W, 30W, and 40W configurations. Head-units, 1-12 in. combos, and 2-12 in. combos are available in most configurations. Prices are between $2,150 and $2,450 for all models. Extension speaker cabinets are also available. Custom hemp-cone speakers are used in their products.

In 2010, the **Metropolitan** was introduced.

TONEMASTER

Amplifiers previously produced by Magnatone during the late 1950s and early 1960s.

Tonemaster was a brand Magnatone used on a line of accordion amplifiers during the late 1950s and the early 1960s for the Imperial Accordion Company in Chicago, IL. Magnatone (Estey) built these amps, which were almost all clones of Magnatones, and put a Tonemaster logo on the front instead of Magnatone. Essentially all Tonemaster models should have a corresponding model with Magnatone. Although Tonemaster amps were specifically produced for Imperial Accordions, the amps could also be used for guitars. Known models include the **Custom 62**, **Custom 261**, **Custom 381**, and **Model 214**. Any further information on Tonemaster amps can be submitted directly to Blue Book Publications.

TONE TUBBY

Speakers and speaker cabinets currently produced in San Francisco, CA. Previously produced in San Rafael, CA.

> **CONTACT INFORMATION**
> **TONE TUBBY**
> 554 Clayton St.
> #170285
> Haight Ashbury, CA 94117
> Phone No.: 415-479-8822
> www.tonetubby.com
> info@tonetubby.com

John Harrison is the man in charge at Tone Tubby. John has been reconing speakers since 1973. The Tone Tubby speaker came about when a customer brought in an old Vox Bulldog speaker to be reconed. John did his thing with it and the customer went nuts. The speaker caught on shortly thereafter. Tone Tubby has also revolutionized speakers by using hemp paper for the speaker cone. Hemp is a more durable material and does not rip as fast as paper does. Tone Tubby has also taken their speakers and fitted them into speaker cabinets. Customers no longer have to mess with reconing speakers in an old amp, or replacing old speakers. Tone Tubby has several other speakers available. For more information and availability, visit Tone Tubby's website or contact them directly.

SPEAKER CABINETS

Ceramic Tone Tubby speakers are available in a 1-12 in. cabinet (MSR $485), a 2-10 in. cabinet (MSR $595), a 2-12 in. cabinet (MSR $645), a 4-10 in. cabinet (MSR $945), and a 4-12 in. cabinet (MSR $1,095). Alnico Tone Tubby speakers are available in a 1-12 in. cabinet (MSR $575), a 2-10 in. cabinet (MSR $795), a 2-12 in. cabinet (MSR $850), a 4-10 in. cabinet (MSR $1,350), and a 4-12 in. cabinet (MSR $1,450). Combination Alnico/Ceramic speaker cabinets are available in 4-10 in. (MSR $1,175) and 4-12 in. (MSR $1,195) variations. Bass cabinets are also available as a 1-15 in. cab (MSR N/A), 2-10 in. cab (MSR $595), and a 4-10 in. cab (MSR $895).

TONY BRUNO CUSTOM AMPLIFIERS

Custom amplifiers currently produced in Woodside, NY.

> **CONTACT INFORMATION**
> **TONY BRUNO CUSTOM AMPLIFIERS**
> *Ultra Sound Music Inc.*
> 251 West 30th St., 6th Floor
> New York, NY 10001
> Phone No.: 212-967-5626
> Fax No.: 212-736-3287
> www.brunoamps.com
> ultrasound@ultrasoundrehearsal.com

Tony Bruno owns and produces Tony Bruno Custom Amplifiers. He builds amplifiers so that they sound absolutely perfect to him before they leave the factory. Each amplifier is tested by him with point-to-point wiring and components checked individually. He also takes each amp before it leaves and plays it in a band to make sure that it has the right tone. If an amp isn't cutting it, he takes it apart and makes adjustments to his liking. Each Bruno amp leaves the shop with that "Bruno tone." Tony has over one thousand designs to his name and has won awards for his amplifiers. Bruno offers "standard production" models, but almost every amp is specifically designed for the customer. For more information, visit Bruno's website or contact him directly.

TOP HAT

Amplifiers currently produced in North Carolina since 2010. Previously produced in Anaheim, CA between 1994 and 2004 and in Fuquay-Varina, NC between 2005 and 2009.

> **CONTACT INFORMATION**
> **TOP HAT**
> 252 Northlands Dr.
> Cary, NC 27519
> Phone No.: 919-817-5614
> www.tophatamps.com
> tophatamps@aol.com

Brian Gerhard founded Top Hat amplifiers in 1994. They produced all-tube, hand-built, point-to-point wired chassis guitar amps. Top Hat was located in Anaheim, CA from 1994 to 2004, and in 2005, they relocated to North Carolina. Most Top Hat amps are available in different color coverings and grille cloths. For more information, visit Top Hat's website or contact them directly.

ELECTRIC TUBE AMPLIFIERS: PORTLY CADET & PRINCE ROYALE SERIES

PORTLY CADET (MODEL TC-PC) – 5W, 1-8 in. speaker, guitar combo, three-tube chassis, preamp: 1 X 12AX7, power: 1 X 6V6, rectifier: 5Y3, single channel, top control panel, single volume knob, boost and bright switches, various color covering, gray or brown grille, 15 in. wide, 13 in. tall, 7.5 in. deep, 15 lbs., mfg. 1999-2004.

100%	EXCELLENT	AVERAGE	LAST MSR
N/A	$525 - 600	$325 - 400	$799

MSR/NOTES	100%	EXCELLENT	AVERAGE	LAST MSR

PRINCE ROYALE (MODEL TC-PR) – 5W, 1-8 in. speaker, guitar combo, three-tube chassis, preamp: 1 X EF86, power: 1 X EL84, rectifier: 5Y3, single channel, top control panel, single volume knob, boost and bright switches, various color covering, gray or brown grille, 15 in. wide, 13 in. tall, 7.5 in. deep, 15 lbs., mfg. 2000-02.

	N/A	$525 - 600	$325 - 400	$849

ELECTRIC TUBE AMPLIFIERS: FLAGSHIP SERIES

AMBASSADOR 35 HEAD (MODEL TH-A35) – 35W, head-unit, guitar configuration, all tube Class A chassis, power: 4 X 6V6, single channel, reverb, front black control panel, two inputs, eight white chicken head knobs, various color covering, disc.

	$2,200	$1,250 - 1,500	$850 - 1,000	$2,749

* *Ambassador 35 Combo (Model TC-A35)* – similar to the Ambassador 35 Head, except in combo configuration with 2-12 in. speakers, disc.

	$2,500	$1,350 - 1,650	$950 - 1,100	$3,129

AMBASSADOR 50 HEAD (MODEL TH-A50) – 50W, head-unit only, all tube Class AB chassis, power tubes: 2 X 6L6, one channel, reverb, front black control panel, two inputs, eight white chicken head knobs, various color covering, disc.

	$2,200	$1,250 - 1,500	$850 - 1,000	$2,749

* *Ambassador 50 Combo (Model TC-A50)* – similar to the Ambassador 50 Head, except in combo configuration with 2-12 in. speakers, disc.

	$2,500	$1,350 - 1,650	$950 - 1,100	$3,129

AMBASSADOR 100 HEAD (MODEL TH-A100) – 100W, head-unit only, all tube Class AB chassis, power: 4 X 6L6, single channel, reverb, front black control panel, two inputs, eight white chicken head knobs, various color coverings, disc.

MSR N/A	$2,300	$1,300 - 1,550	$875 - 1,025	

* *Ambassador 100 Combo (Model TC-A100)* – similar to the Ambassador 100 Head, except in combo configuration with 2-12 in. speakers, disc.

MSR N/A	$2,600	$1,400 - 1,750	$950 - 1,100	

EMPLEXADOR 50 HEAD (MODEL TH-E50) – 50W, head-unit only, all tube Class AB chassis, two channels, reverb, front black control panel, two inputs, eight white chicken head knobs, various color coverings, current mfg.

MSR $2,699	$2,175	$1,150 - 1,400	$750 - 900	

* *Emplexador 50 Combo (Model TC-E50)* – similar to the Emplexador 50 Head, except in combo configuration with 2-12 in. speakers, current mfg.

MSR $3,199	$2,550	$1,300 - 1,600	$925 - 1,075	

* *Emplexador 100 Head (Model TC-E100)* – similar to the Emplexador 50 TH-E50, except has 100W output, current mfg.

MSR $2,849	$2,275	$1,475 - 1,700	$750 - 900	

KING ROYALE HEAD (MODEL TH-K35) – 35W, head-unit only, all tube Class A chassis, power tubes: 4 X EL84, GZ34, 5AR4 rectifier, two channels, front black control panel, four inputs (two per channel), eight white chicken head knobs, various color covering, current mfg.

MSR $2,649	$2,125	$1,375 - 1,600	$700 - 850	

* *King Royale Combo (Model TC-K35)* – similar to the King Royale 35 Head, except in combo configuration with 2-12 in. speakers, current mfg.

MSR $3,049	$2,450	$1,600 - 1,825	$800 - 975	

ELECTRIC TUBE AMPLIFIERS: CLUB SERIES

CLUB BAJO 115 COMBO (MODEL TC-B115) – 40W, 1-15 in. speaker, bass combo, all tube Class A chassis, preamp: 1 X 12AY7, 1 X 12AX7, 1 X 12AU7, power: 2 X 6L6, one channel, top black control panel, two inputs, six white chicken head knobs, various color covering, disc. 2002.

	N/A	$850 - 1,000	$550 - 700	$1,649

* *Club Bajo 212 Combo (Model TC-B212)* – similar to the Club Bajo 115 Combo, except has 2-12 in. speakers, disc 2002.

	N/A	$900 - 1,050	$575 - 725	$1,899

The Club Bajo is also available as a custom order with 2-10 in. or 4-10 in. speakers.

CLUB DELUXE 112 COMBO (MODEL TC-D1) – 20W, 1-12 in. speaker, guitar combo, all tube Class A chassis, power: 2 X 6V6, one channel, top black control panel, two inputs, six white chicken head knobs, various color covering, disc. 2006.

	$1,325	$700 - 850	$475 - 550	$1,650

* *Club Deluxe 212 Combo (Model TC-D2)* – similar to the Club Deluxe 112 Combo, except has 2-12 in. speakers, disc. 2006.

	$1,550	$850 - 1,000	$600 - 700	$1,924

CLUB ROYALE 112 COMBO (MODEL TC-R1) – 20W, 1-12 in. speaker, guitar combo, all tube Class A chassis, power: 2 X EL34, one channel, top black control panel, two inputs, six white chicken head knobs, various color coverings, current mfg.

MSR $1,949	$1,550	$1,000 - 1,150	$500 - 625	

MSR/NOTES	100%	EXCELLENT	AVERAGE	LAST MSR

* *Club Royale 212 Combo (Model TC-R2)* – similar to the Club Royale 112 Combo except has 2-12 in. speakers, current mfg.

| MSR $2,149 | $1,725 | $1,125 - 1,300 | $550 - 700 | |

CLUB SUPER DELUXE 112 COMBO (MODEL TC-SD1) – 40W, 1-12 in. speaker, bass combo, all tube Class A chassis, preamp: 1 X 12AY7, 1 X 12AX7, 1 X 12AU7, power: 2 X 7591, one channel, top black control panel, two inputs, six white chicken head knobs, various color coverings, mfg. 2002-current.

| MSR $2,049 | $1,650 | $1,075 - 1,225 | $525 - 650 | |

* *Club Super Deluxe 212 Combo (Model TC-SD2)* – similar to the Club Super Deluxe 112 Combo, except has 2-12 in. speakers, mfg. 2002-present.

| MSR $2,249 | $1,800 | $1,175 - 1,350 | $575 - 725 | |

The Club Super Deluxe is available with 2-10 in. and 4-10 in. speaker configurations, which is a custom order. Essentially the Club Super Deluxe replaced the Club Bajo.

CLUB SUPER 33 112 COMBO – 33W, 1-12 in. Celestion Heritage G12H30 speaker, combo amp, all tube Class A chassis, preamp: 2 X 12AX7, 1 X EF86, power: 2 X EL34, one channel with boost, top control panel, six knobs, various color coverings, current mfg.

| MSR $2,149 | $1,725 | $1,125 - 1,300 | $550 - 700 | |

* *Club Super 33 212 Combo* – 33W, 2-12 in. Celestion Heritage G12H30 speaker, combo amp, all tube Class A chassis, preamp: 2 X 12AX7, 1 X EF86, power: 2 X EL34, one channel with boost, top control panel, six knobs, various color coverings, current mfg.

| MSR $2,349 | $1,875 | $1,225 - 1,400 | $600 - 750 | |

ELECTRIC TUBE AMPLIFIERS: CUSTOM SERIES

SUPREME 16 – 16W, head-unit only, all tube Class A aluminum chassis, two channels, front black control panel, four inputs, six cream knobs, bright/fat switch, power switch, standby switch, various color coverings, current mfg.

| MSR $1,999 | $1,600 | $1,050 - 1,200 | $525 - 650 | |

VANDERBILT 33 – 33W, head-unit only, all tube Class A aluminum chassis, two channels, front black control panel, four inputs, six cream knobs, bright/fat switch, power switch, standby switch, various color coverings, current mfg.

| MSR $2,349 | $1,875 | $1,225 - 1,400 | $600 - 750 | |

CUSTOM 112 SPEAKER CABINET – 1-12 in. Celestion Alnico Blue or Celestion Heritage G12H speaker cabinet, available in a variety of colors, current mfg.

| MSR $699 | $550 | $350 - 400 | $180 - 220 | |

CUSTOM 212 SPEAKER CABINET – 2-12 in. Celestion Alnico Blue or Celestion Heritage G12H speaker cabinet, available in a variety of colors, current mfg.

| MSR $1,099 | $875 | $575 - 650 | $285 - 350 | |

SPEAKER CABINETS

Standard speakers in these cabinets are Celestion G12H, but Celestion Greenback, Vintage 30 and Jensen C12N speakers are available as options. For more information on speaker choices contact Top Hat directly.

- **Add $20 for casters on cabinets.**

SC-112 – 1-12 in. speaker (Celestions are standard, others are optional), available in a variety of colors, current mfg.

| MSR $579 | $475 | $300 - 350 | $175 - 225 | |

SC-212 – 2-12 in. speakers (Celestions are standard, others are optional), closed or open back cabinet, available in a variety of colors, current mfg.

| MSR $849 | $675 | $400 - 475 | $250 - 300 | |

SC-410 – 4-10 in. Jensen P10R speakers, available in a variety of colors, disc.

| MSR N/A | $750 | $425 - 500 | $275 - 325 | |

SC-412 – 4-12 in. speakers, available in a variety of colors, current mfg.

| MSR $1,149 | $925 | $550 - 650 | $350 - 425 | |

TORRES ENGINEERING

Amplifiers currently produced in Grass Valley, CA. Previously produced in San Carlos, CA.

Dan Torres founded Torres Engineering as a tube amp company. Along with selling tubes, tube kits, and other tube related accessories, Dan has built some amps under his own name as well. Tube amp kits are available for the customer to build his or her own amp. Torres is also the author of *Inside Tube Amps: The Book on Tube Amps Technology*. For more information, visit Torre's website or contact him directly.

CONTACT INFORMATION
TORRES ENGINEERING
2036 Nevada City Hwy.
#317
Grass Valley, CA 95945
www.torresengineering.stores.yahoo.net
torresengineering@yandex.com

| MSR/NOTES | 100% | EXCELLENT | AVERAGE | LAST MSR |

TRACE ELLIOT

Amplifiers currently produced in Essex, England since the late 1970s. Distributed in the U.S. by Peavey in Meridian, MS since 2005. Previously distributed in the U.S. by Kaman Music in Bloomfield, CT between 1993 and 1997, and by Gibson in Nashville, TN between the late 1990s or early 2000s and 2004.

CONTACT INFORMATION
TRACE ELLIOT
U.S. Distributor: Peavey
5022 HWY 493 North
Meridian, MS 39305
Phone No.: 877-856-9243
Fax No.: 601-486-1278
www.traceelliot.com
customerservice@traceelliot.com

Factory/Headquarters
Great Folds Road, Oakley Hay
Corby, Northants NN18 9ET England
Phone No.: +44 0 1536-424740
Fax No.: +44 0 1536-747222

Trace Elliot is probably most noted for their bass amplifiers, and they advertise themselves as "The original bass amplification specialist." The company was formed in the late 1970s in a small music shop located in Essex, England. Trace Elliot noticed that bass players were looking for an amp that simply wasn't available at the time, so they set out to develop one. This new amp was one that had flexibility and power along with quality components that were reliable. Trace Elliot nailed the bass amp market, then looked to expand to other industries, including acoustic and electric guitar amplifiers. Trace Elliot has been produced consistently since the 1970s, but distribution in the U.S. is another story. Gibson became the distributor of Trace Elliot, in the 2000s, which lasted through 2004. By 2004, the only two products Gibson listed were two acoustic amplifiers. In 2005, Peavey took over North American distribution, and Trace introduced an entirely new line of amps that are based on the seven and twelve-band graphic equalizers they are famous for. For more information, visit Trace Elliot's website or contact them directly.

Tramp
courtesy John Beeson/The Music Shoppe

Tramp
courtesy John Beeson/The Music Shoppe

BASS AMPLIFIERS: 7-BAND SERIES

AH150-7 – 150W, head-unit only, solid-state chassis, single channel, front black control panel, two inputs (passive and active), three black knobs, seven-band equalizer, various buttons, compression, black covering, green accents, disc. 2003.

| | N/A | $325 - 400 | $200 - 250 | |

AH300-7 – 300W, head-unit only, solid-state chassis, single channel, front black control panel, two inputs (passive and active), three black knobs, seven-band equalizer, various buttons, compression, black covering, green accents, disc. 2003.

| | N/A | $425 - 500 | $275 - 325 | |

AH500-7 – 500W, head-unit, bass configuration, solid-state chassis, MOSFET power section, single channel, front black control panel, single input, three knobs (input gain, compressor level, output gain), seven-band graphic EQ, six buttons (hi/lo, pre shape, pre/post, graphic EQ on/off, compressor on/off, mute, effects loop, tuner out, XLR direct out, direct out, black covering, mfg. 2005-present.

| MSR $1,500 | $1,200 | $675 - 775 | $425 - 500 | |

712 – 300W, 1-15 in. speaker combo, solid-state chassis, single channel, front black control panel, two inputs (passive and active), three black knobs, seven-band equalizer, various buttons, compression, black covering, green accents, black metal grille, disc. 2003.

| | N/A | $500 - 600 | $300 - 350 | |

715 – 150W, 1-15 in. speaker combo, solid-state chassis, single channel, front black control panel, two inputs (passive and active), three black knobs, seven-band equalizer, various buttons, compression, black covering, green accents, black metal grille, disc. 2003.

| | N/A | $425 - 500 | $275 - 325 | |

715 (CURRENT MFG.) – 200W, 1-15 in. Celestion speaker, bass combo, solid-state chassis, MOSFET power section, single channel, front black control panel, single input, three knobs (input gain, compressor level, output gain), seven-band graphic EQ, six buttons (hi/lo, pre shape, pre/post, graphic EQ on/off, compressor on/off, mute, effects loop, tuner out, XLR direct out, direct out, black covering, black metal grille, mfg. 2005-present.

| MSR $1,350 | $950 | $600 - 700 | $375 - 450 | |

715X (CURRENT MFG.) – 500W, 1-15 in. Celestion speaker, bass combo, solid-state chassis, MOSFET power section, single channel, front black control panel with vents on either side, single input, three knobs (input gain, compressor level, output gain), seven-band graphic EQ, six buttons (hi/lo, pre shape, pre/post, graphic EQ on/off, compressor on/off, mute, effects loop, tuner out, XLR direct out, direct out, black covering, black metal grille, mfg. 2005-present.

| MSR $1,500 | $1,050 | $675 - 775 | $425 - 500 | |

MSR/NOTES	100%	EXCELLENT	AVERAGE	LAST MSR

7210H COMBO – 300W, 2-10 in. speaker combo, HF horn, solid-state chassis, single channel, front black control panel, two inputs (passive and active), three black knobs, seven-band equalizer, various buttons, compression, black covering, green accents, black metal grille, disc. 2003.

	N/A	$500 - 600	$300 - 350	

7215 COMBO – 300W, 1-15 in. speaker combo, solid-state chassis, single channel, front black control panel, two inputs (passive and active), three black knobs, seven-band equalizer, various buttons, compression, black covering, green accents, black metal grille, disc. 2003.

	N/A	$500 - 600	$300 - 350	

BASS AMPLIFIERS: 12-BAND SERIES

AH300-12 – 300W, head-unit only, solid-state chassis, single channel, front black control panel, two inputs (passive and active), seven black knobs, 12-band equalizer, various buttons, compression, black covering, green accents, disc. 2003.

	N/A	$475 - 550	$300 - 350	

AH500-12 – 500W, head-unit only, solid-state chassis, single channel, front black control panel, two inputs (passive and active), seven black knobs, 12-band equalizer, various buttons, compression, black covering, green accents, disc. 2003.

	N/A	$500 - 600	$300 - 375	

AH1000-12 – 1000W, head-unit only, solid-state chassis, single channel, front black control panel, two inputs (passive and active), seven black knobs, 12-band equalizer, various buttons, compression, black covering, green accents, disc. 2003.

	N/A	$550 - 650	$325 - 400	

AH1000-12 (CURRENT MFG.) – 1000W (500W X 2), head-unit, bass configuration, solid-state chassis, MOSFET power section, single channel, front black control panel, single input, six knobs (input gain, drive, blend, low band, high band, output gain), seven-band graphic EQ, six buttons (hi/lo, pre shape, pre/post, graphic EQ on/off, compressor on/off, effects loop on/off, mute), effects loop, tuner out, XLR direct out, direct out, black covering, mfg. 2005-present.

MSR $2,300	$1,600	$1,000 - 1,200	$650 - 800	

122H COMBO – 300W, 2-10 in. speaker combo, HF horn, solid-state chassis, single channel, front black control panel, two inputs (passive and active), seven black knobs, 12-band equalizer, various buttons, compression, black covering, green accents, black metal grille, disc. 2003.

	N/A	N/A	N/A	

1210H COMBO – 300W, 4-10 in. speaker combo, HF horn, solid-state chassis, single channel, front black control panel, two inputs (passive and active), seven black knobs, 12-band equalizer, various buttons, compression, black covering, green accents, black metal grille, disc. 2003.

	N/A	N/A	N/A	

1210 (CURRENT MFG.) – 500W, 2-10 in. speakers, bass combo, solid-state chassis, MOSFET power section, single channel, front black control panel with side vents, single input, six knobs (input gain, drive, blend, low band, high band, output gain), seven-band graphic EQ, six buttons (hi/lo, pre shape, pre/post, graphic EQ on/off, compressor on/off, effects loop on/off, mute), effects loop, tuner out, XLR direct out, direct out, black covering, black metal grille, mfg. 2005-present.

MSR $1,900	$1,350	$850 - 1,000	$550 - 650	

1215 COMBO – 300W, 1-15 in. speaker combo, solid-state chassis, single channel, front black control panel, two inputs (passive and active), seven black knobs, 12-band equalizer, various buttons, compression, black covering, green accents, black metal grille, disc. 2003.

	N/A	N/A	N/A	

1215 (CURRENT MFG.) – 500W, 1-15 in. speaker, bass combo, solid-state chassis, MOSFET power section, single channel, front black control panel with side vents, single input, six knobs (input gain, drive, blend, low band, high band, output gain), seven-band graphic EQ, six buttons (hi/lo, pre shape, pre/post, graphic EQ on/off, compressor on/off, effects loop on/off, mute), effects loop, tuner out, XLR direct out, direct out, black covering, black metal grille, mfg. 2005-present.

MSR $1,800	$1,275	$800 - 950	$525 - 625	

BASS AMPLIFIERS: V-TYPE SERIES

Trace Elliot makes tube powered bass amplifiers. These hogs put out 400W of power (The V-8 model) from eight, yes eight KT88 fan cooled power tubes, and have seven X ECC83 or 12AX7 preamp tubes with 1 X EM84 display tube. The controls are fairly basic with gain controls, a three knob EQ section, and compressor knobs. Along with this model there is a V-Type 300H, which is a hybrid model with a tube preamp section powered by MOSFET.

ACOUSTIC AMPLIFIERS

TA-50R – 50W, 2-5 in. speakers, acoustic combo, solid-state chassis, two channels, digital reverb, front black control panel, eight knobs, five-band graphic EQ, black covering, black metal grille, disc. 2004.

	N/A	$375 - 450	$225 - 275	$1,249

TA-100R – 100W, 4-5 in. speakers, acoustic combo, solid-state chassis, two channels, digital reverb, front black control panel, eight knobs, five-band graphic EQ, black covering, two black metal grilles with the control panel splitting them, disc. 2004.

	N/A	$500 - 600	$300 - 350	$1,799

MSR/NOTES	100%	EXCELLENT	AVERAGE	LAST MSR

SPEAKER CABINETS

1028H – 400W, 2-10 in. Celestion speakers with a high freq. horn, compact size, black covering, black metal grille, mfg. 2005-present.

| MSR $850 | $600 | $375 - 450 | $225 - 275 | |

1048H – 800W, 4-10 in. Celestion speakers with a high freq. horn, black covering, black metal grille, mfg. 2005-present.

| MSR $1,300 | $925 | $575 - 675 | $350 - 425 | |

1518 – 500W, 1-15 in. Celestion speaker with a high freq. horn, black covering, black metal grille, mfg. 2005-present.

| MSR $800 | $575 | $350 - 425 | $200 - 250 | |

1518C – 300W, 1-15 in. Celestion speaker with a high freq. horn, compact cabinet, black covering, black metal grille, mfg. 2005-present.

| MSR $700 | $495 | $300 - 375 | $175 - 225 | |

TRAINWRECK

Amplifiers previously produced in Colonia, NJ between the early 1980s and 2006.

Ken Fischer started Trainwreck Amplifiers in circa 1980. Fischer has a long history in the tube amp business, and he is considered to be one of the most knowledgeable persons in the industry. After working for the Navy in the technical service departments and Ampeg during their heyday, he opened an amp repair shop in New Jersey. Fischer has always been interested in Vox amplifiers, especially the famed AC-30. After building a reputation of repairing, modifying, and restoring amps, he was encouraged by many customers to start building his own models. The first amp he designed was the **Liverpool 30** - a variation built on the Vox AC-30 chassis with 4 X EL84 tubes. The two other models he produced are the **Rocket** (2 X EL84 power tubes) and the **Express** (2 X EL34 or 2 X 6V6 power tubes).

The Trainwreck name, according to Aspen Pittman, comes from his handle (nickname) in his motorcycle riding group as he drove like a "Trainwreck." All amps come as head units finished in hardwood cabinets. Fischer does not build combos because he prefers keeping the electronics and speakers separate to reduce interference. The hardwood cabinets are unique in themselves, as they are entirely hand-built and they feature engravings on the control panel. The controls typically include five knobs (v, t, m, b, p) and a bright switch. Fischer designs are very simple with few controls, as complexity often distorts the original tone. Trainwreck amps are also "serial-numbered" with a woman's name instead of a number. Each amp has a different name, and at one point, Fischer could remember every one he had built.

Fischer estimated that he built four or five amps a year, and very few have been produced in the past. Because of the amount of time invested in each amp and the overall quality in Trainwreck amps, they are very expensive. Used models have sold for between $20,000 and $30,000! Many collectors and players consider this to be the Holy Grail of guitar amplifiers. Each model should be evaluated individually, and currently there is no set pricing for individual models. Fischer passed away on December 23, 2006 after a long battle with a chronic illness that left him very frail. He produced less and less in later years and built amps specifically for close friends. Before he passed away, Fischer estimates that there are about one hundred true Trainwreck amplifiers out there.

In the late 1990s, Fischer was approached by Holger Notzel and Michael Kennedy from Riverfront Music in Baton Rouge, LA. They wanted to build a Trainwreck-style amp themselves, and they asked Fischer if they could do it. Fischer agreed and supplied them with a design of Trainwreck. Notzel and Kennedy produced a prototype that was well-received as a Trainwreck-sounding amp. Fischer allowed the boys from Louisiana to produce amps commercially, and they named the new company Komet Amplification. Currently, there is a licensing agreement between Trainwreck and Komet to produce Trainwreck-style amps in different cabinets (see Komet Amplification). Information courtesy Aspen Pittman, *The Tube Amp Book: Deluxe Revised Edition*.

Express
courtesy solidbodyguitar.com, Inc.

Express
courtesy solidbodyguitar.com, Inc.

MSR/NOTES	100%	EXCELLENT	AVERAGE	LAST MSR

TRAVELER GUITAR

Amplifiers previously produced in Redlands, CA. Instruments produced since 1992.

Designer J. Corey Oliver offers a full scale travel-style guitar that is only 28 in. overall length (full size 24.75 in. fret board), and 2 in. thick. In 2005, Traveler developed an amplifier with the same idea of their traveler guitar. The amplifier is small and light, but it also sounds and plays great. It features a 4-hour-life rechargable battery, a flip up thin speaker with 360 degree sound dispersion, and eight built-in effects. Traveler has discontinued their amplifier line. For more information, visit Traveler Guitar's website or contact them directly.

CONTACT INFORMATION
TRAVELER GUITAR
325 Alabama St., #8
Redlands, CA 92373
Phone No.: 909-307-2626
Phone No.: 800-476-1591
Fax No.: 909-307-2628
www.travelerguitar.com
travel@travelerguitar.com

AMPLIFIERS

The FlipTone V.25 is a portable amplifier with many features. It has NXT flat panel speakers by Fane Acoustics, 25 power output, three-band EQ, eight built-in effects, RCA inputs, and 360 degree sound dispersion. This amp was released in July, 2005 and retails for $699 with a MAP/Street price of $500.

TRAYNOR

Amplifiers currently produced in Canada and in China since the early 1960s. Distributed by the Yorkville Group in Niagra Falls, NY.

Pete Traynor has been making amplifiers since 1963. He had been a musician for many years and had fixed his own amplifier during his stint. He started off in Toronto, Canada making amplifiers until he moved to Nova Scotia in the late 1970s. Many different bands have played through Traynor amplifiers. Today Traynor amps are still built by Yorkville Sound. All old Traynor amps are tube designed with various features and functions. Traynor amps have a wide variety of solid state and tube amps. For more information, visit Traynor's website or contact them directly.

CONTACT INFORMATION
TRAYNOR
A division of Yorkville Sound
4625 Witmer Industrial Estate
Niagra Falls, NY 14305
Phone No.: 716-297-2920
Fax No.: 716-297-3689
www.traynoramps.com
sales@yorkville.com
550 Granite Court
Pickering, Ontario L1W 3Y8 Canada
Phone No.: 905-837-8481
Fax No.: 905-839-5776
www.traynoramps.com
canada@yorkville.com

ELECTRIC TUBE AMPLIFIERS: 1960S-1970S MFG.

MARK II BASS MASTER HEAD – 60W, head-unit only, all-tube chassis, power: 2 X EL34, two channels, front black control panel, four inputs (two per channel), six knobs (v1, v2, t, b, resonance, presence), black covering, gray grille, mfg. 1970s.

	N/A	$500 - 600	$300 - 375	

MARK III HEAD – 100W, head-unit only, all-tube chassis, preamp: 5 X 12AX7, power: 4 X EL84, two channels, reverb, tremolo, front black control panel, four inputs (two per channel), 12 knobs (Ch.1: v, t, m, b, Ch. 2: v, t, m, b, r, s, i, MV), black covering, gray grille, mfg. 1970s.

	N/A	$625 - 750	$400 - 475	

MARK III COMBO – 100W, 2-12 in. speakers, all-tube chassis, preamp: 5 X 12AX7, power: 4 X EL84, two channels, reverb, tremolo, front black control panel, four inputs (two per channel), 12 knobs (Ch.1: v, t, m, b, Ch. 2: v, t, m, b, r, s, i, MV), black covering, gray grille, mfg. 1970s.

	N/A	$750 - 900	$500 - 600	

YBA-1 BASS MASTER – 50W, head-unit designed for bass use, five-tube chassis, preamp: 3 X 12AX7, power: 2 X EL34, solid-state rectifier, two channels, front black control panel, four inputs (two per channel), six black and silver knobs (v1, v2, t, b, range expander l, range expander h), operate/standby switch, black covering, gray grille, mfg. late 1960s-1970s.

	N/A	$475 - 550	$300 - 350	

YBA-2 BASS MATE – 15W, 1-15 in. speaker, all-tube chassis, preamp: 12AX7s, power: 2 X 6V6, top control panel, two inputs, two knobs (v, tone), black covering, gray grille, mfg. late 1960s-1970s.

	N/A	$500 - 600	$300 - 375	

ELECTRIC TUBE AMPLIFIERS: CUSTOM SPECIAL SERIES

CUSTOM SPECIAL 50 HEAD (YCS50H) – 50W (switchable to 15W), head-unit, guitar configuration, six-tube chassis, preamp: 3 X 12AX7, 1 X 12AT7, power: 2 X EL34, two channels, reverb, front chrome control panel, single input, 18 knobs (Ch. 1: g, boost level, v, t, m, b, effects, r, Ch. 2: g, v, t, m, b, effects, r, All: p, resonance, MV), USA/Britain switch, channel select switch, modern switch, scoop switch, parallel and in-line effects loop, direct out and headphone jack with level, tuner out, power amp in, preamp out, 50/15W power switch, black covering, chrome grille, mfg. 2007-present.

MSR $1,150	$800	$500 - 575	$300 - 350	

* ***Custom Special 50 Combo (YCS50)*** – similar to the Custom Special 50 Head, except in combo configuration with 1-12 in. Celestion Vintage 30 speaker, a bronze control panel, Nubtex black leatherette covering, and an oatmeal brown grille, mfg. 2007-disc.

	$920	$525 - 600	$325 - 400	$1,149

MSR/NOTES	100%	EXCELLENT	AVERAGE	LAST MSR

Custom Special 50 Combo
courtesy Traynor

Custom Special 90 Combo
courtesy Traynor

YCS412AV2 Speaker Cabinet
courtesy Traynor

»*Custom Special 90 Combo (YCS90)* – similar to the Custom Special 50 Combo, except has 90W output, 2-12 in. Celestion G12 Century Neodymium speakers, and a 90W/25W power switch, mfg. 2007-disc.

	$1,080	$600 - 700	$375 - 450	$1,349

CUSTOM SPECIAL 100 HEAD (YCS100/YCS100H2) – 100W, head-unit, guitar configuration, eight tube chassis, preamp: 3 X 12AX7, 1 X 12AT7, power: 4 X EL34, three channels, reverb, front chrome control panel, single input, 25 knobs (g, v, t, m, b, r, effects per channel, All: p, resonance, solo level, MV), effects loop with level control, direct out and headphone jack with level, tuner out, power amp in, preamp out, 100/30W power switch, black covering, chrome grille, mfg. 2006-present.

MSR $1,450	$1,050	$675 - 775	$350 - 425	

YCS412 SPEAKER CABINET – 240W, 4-12 in. Celestion Vintage 30 speakers, 4/16 ohm stereo impedance, 2/8 ohm mono impedance, black covering, black grille, removable casters, designed for use with the Custom Special 50 Head and Custom Special 100 Head, mfg. 2006-present.

MSR $1,000	$725	$475 - 550	$235 - 290	

YCS412AV2 SPEAKER CABINET – 300W, 4-12 in. Celestion G12-T75 speakers, 4/16 ohm mono impedance, 2/8 ohm stereo impedance, angled front, black covering, tan grille, removable casters, 101.5 lbs., mfg. 2012-present.

MSR $1,000	$750	$475 - 550	$245 - 300	

ELECTRIC TUBE AMPLIFIERS: CUSTOM VALVE SERIES

Custom Valve 20
courtesy Traynor

Custom Valve 40
courtesy Traynor

Custom Valve 80
courtesy Traynor

CUSTOM VALVE 20 (YCV20) – 15W, 1-12 in. Celestion speaker, all tube class A chassis: 3 X 12AX7, 2 X EL84, two channels, separate controls for each channel, eleven black chickenhead knobs, reverb, various switches and inputs, black Tolex covering, silver grille, 35 lbs., disc. 2007.

MSR $699	$560	$325 - 375	$200 - 250	

• Wine Red covering model (YCV20WR) is still available (MSR $990).

CUSTOM VALVE 40 (YCV40) – 40W, 1-12 in. Celestion speaker, two channels, all tube chassis: 3 X 12AX7WA, 2 X 5881 WXT, separate controls for each channel, eleven black chickenhead knobs, reverb, various switches and inputs, black Tolex covering, silver grille, 46 lbs., current mfg.

MSR $1,020	$750	$500 - 575	$245 - 300	

• Add $30 for Wine Red covering (YCV40WR, MSR $1,050).

* *Custom Valve 40T (YCV40T)* – similar to the Custom Valve 40, except has 2-10 in. Celestion speakers, disc. 2009.

	$750	$425 - 500	$275 - 325	$929

CUSTOM VALVE 50 BLUE/BLACK (YCV50BLUE/YCV50B) – 50W, 1-12 in. Celestion Vintage 30 speaker, all tube chassis: 3 X 12AX7WA, 2 X EL34, two channels, separate controls for each channel, eleven black chickenhead knobs, reverb, various switches and inputs, blue or black Tolex covering, black grille, 50 lbs., mfg. 2005-present.

MSR $1,080	$800	$525 - 600	$260 - 325	

MSR/NOTES	100%	EXCELLENT	AVERAGE	LAST MSR

CUSTOM VALVE 80 (YCV80) – 80W, 2-12 in. Celestion speakers, two channels, seven tube chassis, preamp: 3 X 12AX7, power: 4 X 5881, separate controls for each channel, eleven black chickenhead knobs, reverb, various switches and inputs, black Tolex covering, silver grille, 65 lbs., current mfg.

| MSR $1,400 | $1,000 | $650 - 750 | $325 - 400 | |

* Custom Valve 80Q (YCV80Q) – similar to the Custom Valve 80, except has 4-10 in. Celestion Tube 10 speakers, disc.

| | $1,000 | $550 - 650 | $350 - 425 | $1,249 |

YCX12 SPEAKER CABINET – 1-12 in. Celestion 70/80 speaker, 8 Ohm impedance, 7-ply .75 in. plywood construction, 2 .25 in. inputs, black covering, silver grille, 30 lbs., current mfg.

| MSR $400 | $300 | $195 - 225 | $100 - 120 | |

YCX12WR/YCX12B/YCX12 BLUE SPEAKER CABINET – 1-12 in. Celestion Vintage 30 speaker, 8 ohm impedance, seven-ply 3/4 in. plywood construction, two 1/4 in. inputs, available in Black or Blue covering with a black grille or Wine Red covering with an oatmeal brown grille, 34.5 lbs., current mfg.

| MSR $450 | $350 | $220 - 255 | $110 - 135 | |

YCX212 SPEAKER CABINET – 2-12 in. Celestion 70/80 speakers, 4 Ohm impedance, 7-ply 3/4 in. plywood construction, 2 1/4 in. inputs, black covering, silver grille, 39.7 lbs., disc.

| | $345 | $200 - 250 | $150 - 150 | $429 |

ELECTRIC TUBE AMPLIFIERS: HORSES SERIES

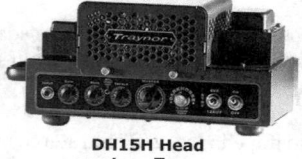

DH15H Head
courtesy Traynor

DH40H Head
courtesy Traynor

DHX12 Speaker Cabinet
courtesy Traynor

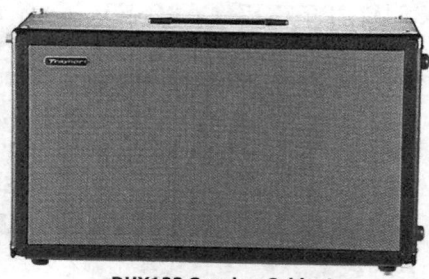

DHX122 Speaker Cabinet
courtesy Traynor

DH15H HEAD – 15W, head-unit, guitar configuration, five-tube chassis, preamp: 2 X 12AX7, power: 2 X 6V6, 1 X 12AU7, one channels, front black control panel, single input, four knobs (g, b, t, MV), UK/USA switch, power tube selector switch, power switch, three external speaker jacks, black covering, black grille, 11 lbs., mfg. 2011-present.

| MSR $650 | $500 | $325 - 375 | $165 - 200 | |

DH40H HEAD – 40W, head-unit, guitar configuration, five-tube chassis, preamp: 2 X 12AX7, power: 2 X EL84, 1 X 12AU7, one channel, front black control panel, two input, four knobs (g, b, t, MV), UK/USA switch, bias/standby switch, power switch, two external speaker jacks, impedance switch, power amp in, preamp out, footswitch jack, black covering, black grille, 15.9 lbs., mfg. 2011-present.

| MSR $700 | $550 | $350 - 400 | $180 - 220 | |

DHX12 SPEAKER CABINET – 25W, 1-12 in. Celestion Greenback G12M speaker, 16 ohm impedance, black covering, silver grille, top handle, metal corners, designed for use with the DH15H Head, mfg. 2011-present.

| MSR $440 | $325 | $215 - 250 | $105 - 130 | |

DHX212 SPEAKER CABINET – 50W, 2-12 in. Celestion Greenback G12M speakers, 8 ohm impedance, black covering, silver grille, top handle, metal corners, designed for use with the DH40H Head, mfg. 2011-present.

| MSR $670 | $500 | $325 - 375 | $165 - 200 | |

INTERNATIONAL SERIES

The Traynor International Series are amplifiers that are manufactured in Korea under Yorkville's design. These amps are smaller, made with the beginner in mind.

BASS MATE 10 (TBM 10) – 10W, 1-8 in. speaker, solid-state chassis, front black control panel, two inputs, five knobs (v, h, m, l, p), black or cream covering, silver or black grille, 18 lbs., disc.

| | $105 | $50 - 70 | $30 - 40 | $129 |

MSR/NOTES	100%	EXCELLENT	AVERAGE	LAST MSR

Bass Mate 25
courtesy Traynor

Guitar Mate 20
courtesy Traynor

Reverb Mate 40
courtesy Traynor

BASS MATE 25 (TBM 25) – 25W, 1-10 in. speaker, solid-state chassis, front black control panel, two inputs, six knobs (v, h, h/m, l/m, l, p), black or cream covering, silver or black grille, 24 lbs., disc.

	$135	$70 - 95	$35 - 50	$169

GUITAR MATE 15 (TGM15) – 15W, 1-8 in. speaker, solid-state chassis, front black control panel, single input, four knobs (v, b, m, t), overdrive switch, black or cream covering, silver or black grille, 13 lbs., disc. 2007.

	$75	$40 - 55	$20 - 30	$89

GUITAR MATE 20 (TGM20) – 20W, 1-8 in. speaker, solid-state chassis, two channels, chorus, front black control panel, single input, eight knobs (Ch.1: v, g, Ch. 2: v, g, b, m, t, chorus), footswitch, black or cream covering, silver or black grille, 18 lbs., disc. 2007.

	$110	$50 - 75	$30 - 40	$139

REVERB MATE 30 (TRM30) – 30W, 1-10 in. speaker, solid-state chassis, two channels, reverb, front black control panel, single input, nine knobs (Ch.1: v, g, Ch. 2: v, g, h, m, l, p, r), footswitch, black or cream covering, silver or black grille, 21 lbs., disc. 2007.

	$125	$60 - 85	$35 - 50	$155

REVERB MATE 40 (TRM40) – 40W, 2-8 in. speakers, solid-state chassis, two channels, reverb, chorus, front black control panel, two input, 11 knobs (Ch.1: v, g, Ch. 2: v, g, h, m, l, p, r, 2 chorus), footswitch, black or cream covering, silver or black grille, 34 lbs., disc.

	$240	$125 - 160	$75 - 100	$299

STUDIO MATE 10 (TSM10) – 10W, 1-6 in. speaker, solid-state chassis, front black control panel, single input, three knobs (v, b, t), overdrive switch, black covering, silver grille, disc.

	$80	$40 - 55	$25 - 35	$99

TRAVEL MATE 10 (TVM10) – 15W, 1-6.5 in. speaker and a tweeter, rechargable battery powered and designed for use as a guitar amp, PA system, or CD/MP3 use, solid-state chassis, two channels, rear/top black control panel, two inputs (Ch. 1: Speakon, Ch. 2: regular 1/4 in.), six black knobs (Ch. 1 v, Ch. 2 v, All: b, l/m, h/m, t), aux. RCA inputs, headphone jack, AC charger included, wedge cabinet design, black covering, black metal grille, 13.75 in. wide, 11.75 in. tall, 10.25 in. deep, mfg. 2007-present.

MSR $250	$190	$125 - 145	$60 - 75	

TRAVEL MATE 50 (TVM50) – 50W, 1-10 in. speaker and a 2 in. tweeter, rechargable battery powered and designed for use as a guitar amp, PA system, or CD/MP3 use, solid-state chassis, two channels, rear/top black control panel, two inputs (Ch. 1: Speakon, Ch. 2: regular 1/4 in.), seven black knobs (Ch. 1 v, Ch. 1 tone, Ch. 2 g, v, b, m, t), aux. RCA inputs, headphone jack, AC charger included, wedge cabinet design, black covering, black metal grille, 19.6 in. wide, 13.5 in. tall, 13 in. deep, 31 lbs., mfg. 2010-present.

MSR $380	$280	$180 - 210	$90 - 110	

TUBE MATE 30 (TTM) – 30W, 1-10 in. speaker, hybrid chassis (tube pre-amp), reverb, front black control panel, two inputs, seven knobs (v, g, h, m, l, p, r), footswitch, black covering, silver grille, 26 lbs., disc. 2006.

	$225	$120 - 150	$65 - 85	$279

ELECTRIC SS AMPLIFIERS: DYNAGAIN SERIES

DYNAGAIN 10 (DG10) – 10W, 1-8 in. Celestion speaker, guitar combo, solid-state chassis, single channel, top black control panel, single input, four knobs (v, b, m, t), OD switch, RCA inputs, headphone jack, black covering, black grille, mfg. 2006-disc.

	$95	$50 - 65	$30 - 40	$119

DYNAGAIN 15 (DG15) – 15W, 1-10 in. Celestion speaker, guitar combo, solid-state chassis, two channels, top black control panel, two inputs, seven knobs (Ch. 1: v, g, Ch. 2: v, b, m, t, MV), channel switch, RCA inputs, headphone jack, black covering, black grille, mfg. 2006-disc.

	$145	$75 - 100	$45 - 60	$179

MSR/NOTES	100%	EXCELLENT	AVERAGE	LAST MSR

Dynagain 30 D
courtesy Traynor

Dynagain 65
courtesy Traynor

Dynabass 200 115 Combo
courtesy Traynor

* ***Dynagain 15 Reverb (DG15R)*** – similar to the Dynagain 15, except has a reverb circuit with a reverb control for a total of seven knobs, mfg. 2006-disc.

	$170	$95 - 120	$50 - 70	$209

DYNAGAIN 30 D (DG30D) – 30W, 1-12 in. Celestion speaker, guitar combo, solid-state chassis, two channels, digital reverb, digital effects, top black control panel, two inputs, 10 knobs (Ch. 1: v, g, Ch. 2: v, b, m, t, All: MV, r, effects select, effects level), channel switch, RCA inputs, headphone jack, black covering, black grille, mfg. 2006-disc.

	$255	$135 - 175	$75 - 100	$319

DYNAGAIN 60R (DG60R) – 60W, 1-12 in. Celestion speaker guitar combo, solid-state chassis, two channels, reverb, top control panel, two inputs (high/lo), 13 black knobs (Ch. 1: g, v, t, m, b, Ch. 2: g, v, t, m, b, All: c, MV, r), Ch. 1 boost switch, Ch. 2 bright switch, channel switch, headphone jack, external speaker jack with internal speaker defeat switch, power amp in, preamp out, two footswitch jacks (Channel select/boost and reverb), black covering, silver grille, mfg. 2007-disc.

	$385	$200 - 250	$120 - 150	$479

DYNAGAIN 65 (DG65R) – 65W, 1-12 in. Eminence speaker combo, solid-state chassis, two channels, spring reverb or digital effects with digital spring reverb, top control panel, two inputs (high/lo), 13 black knobs (Ch. 1: g, v, t, m, b, Ch. 2: g, v, t, m, b, All: c, MV, r), Ch. 1 boost switch, Ch. 2 bright switch, channel switch, headphone jacks, effects loop, external speaker jack, black covering, black grille, mfg. 2005-06.

	$560	$300 - 375	$175 - 225	$699

BASS AMPLIFIERS: DYNABASS SERIES

Tube Bass 200 Head (YBA200)
courtesy Traynor

Tube Bass 300 Head (YBA300)
courtesy Traynor

TUBE BASS 200 HEAD (YBA200) – 200W, head-unit only, all-tube chassis, preamp: 2 X 12AX7, 12AU7, power: 4 X 6550, front black control panel, two inputs, eight knobs (g, t, m, range, b, scoop, resonance, MV), black covering, black grille, 41 lbs., mfg. 2004-present.

MSR $1,300	$950	$625 - 700	$300 - 375	

In 2007, the YBA200 was upgraded to Series II with DynaBass cosmetics.

TUBE BASS 300 HEAD (YBA300) – 300W, head-unit only, all-tube chassis, preamp: 3 X 12AX7, 12AU7, power: 12 X 6L6, front black control panel, two inputs, six knobs (g, t, m, freq., b, MV), deep switch, bright switch, resonance switch, standby switch, power switch, effect loop, XLR DI line out, tuner jack, 3 external speaker jacks, black covering, black grille, 51 lbs., mfg. 2011-present.

MSR $1,800	$1,350	$875 - 1,000	$450 - 550	

YBX1510 SPEAKER CABINET – 400W, 1-15 in., 2-10 in., and a 1 in. driver speakers, 4 Ohm impedance, black covering, black grille, 78 lbs., mfg. 2004-06.

	$480	$275 - 325	$150 - 200	$599

DYNABASS 50 COMBO (DB50) – 50W, 1-10 in. speaker bass combo, solid-state chassis, single channel, front black control panel, single input, four chrome knobs (v, b, m, t), aux. RCA inputs, XLR line out, Nubtex black leatherette covering, black metal grille, side tiltback cabinet design, 16 in. tall, 13 in. wide, 11 in. deep, 18 lbs., mfg. 2007-disc.

	$280	$150 - 200	$95 - 120	$349

MSR/NOTES	100%	EXCELLENT	AVERAGE	LAST MSR

Dynabass 400 Head
courtesy Traynor

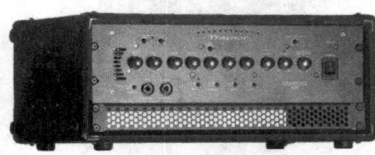

Dynabass 800 Head
courtesy Traynor

Dynabass TC115 Speaker Cabinet
courtesy Traynor

Dynabass TC115 Neo Speaker Cabinet
courtesy Traynor

DYNABASS 100 COMBO (DB100) – 100W, 1-15 in. speaker bass combo, solid-state chassis, single channel, front black control panel, two inputs, five chrome knobs (v, b, m, t, scoop), aux. RCA inputs, XLR line out, Nubtex black leatherette covering, black metal grille, side tiltback cabinet design, 21 in. tall, 17 in. wide, 13 in. deep, 30 lbs., mfg. 2007-disc.

	$375	$200 - 250	$120 - 150	$469

DYNABASS 200 115 COMBO (DB200) – 200W, 1-15 in. speaker and piezo tweeter bass combo, solid-state chassis, single channel, front black control panel, two inputs, six chrome knobs (v, b, l/m, m/h, t, scoop), limiter switch, direct line out pre/post switch, effects loop, XLR line out, external speaker jack, headphone jack, Nubtex black leatherette covering, black metal grille, built-in side metal handles, removable casters, mfg. 2007-disc.

	$600	$325 - 400	$200 - 250	$749

* *DynaBass 200 210 Combo (DB200T)* – similar to the DynaBass 200 115 Combo, except has 2-10 in. speakers, mfg. 2007-disc.

	$630	$350 - 425	$225 - 275	$789

DYNABASS 400 HEAD (DB400H) – 400W, bass head-unit, hybrid chassis with switchable tube/solid-state preamp, single channel, front black control panel, two inputs (passive/active), 10 chrome knobs (tube g, tube drive, b, l/m, parametric mid, m/h, t, scoop, effects level, MV), three small black knobs (compression, effects blend, parametric mid freq.), tube/solid-state preamp switch, mute switch, limiter switch, direct line out pre/post switch, effects loop, XLR line out, external speaker jack, headphone jack, Nubtex black leatherette covering, black metal grille, built-in side metal handles, mfg. 2007-disc.

	$760	$425 - 500	$250 - 300	$949

* *DynaBass 400 115 Combo (DB400)* – similar to the DynaBass 400 Head, except is in combo configuration with 1-15 in. speaker and a tweeter, mfg. 2007-disc.

	$960	$550 - 625	$325 - 400	$1,199

* *DynaBass 400 210 Combo (DB400T)* – similar to the DynaBass 400 Head, except is in combo configuration with 2-10 in. speakers and a tweeter, mfg. 2007-disc.

	$1,000	$550 - 650	$350 - 425	$1,249

DYNABASS 800 HEAD (DB800H) – 800W, bass head-unit, hybrid chassis with switchable tube/solid-state preamp, single channel, front black control panel, two inputs (passive/active), 10 chrome knobs (tube g, tube drive, b, l/m, parametric mid, m/h, t, scoop, effects level, MV), four small black knobs (compression, effects blend, parametric mid freq., bass resonance), tube/solid-state preamp switch, mute switch, limiter switch, direct line out pre/post switch, effects loop, XLR line out, external speaker jack, headphone jack, Nubtex black leatherette covering, black metal grille, built-in side metal handles, mfg. 2007-present.

MSR $1,130	$800	$525 - 600	$260 - 325	

DYNABASS TC115 SPEAKER CABINET – 400W, 1-15 in. speaker, 8 ohm impedance, four inputs (two 1/4 in. and two Speakon), solid plywood construction, built-in side handles, removable casters, Nubtex Black leatherette covering, black metal grille, 24 in. wide, 18.25 in. tall, 18.5 in. deep, 60 lbs., mfg. 2007-present.

MSR $579	$425	$280 - 325	$140 - 170	

* *Dynabass TC115 Neo Speaker Cabinet* – 400W, 1-15 in. Eminence Neodymium speaker, 8 ohm impedance, four inputs (two 1/4 in. and two Speakon), solid plywood construction, built-in side handles, removable casters, Black covering, black metal grille, 24.5 in. wide, 18.25 in. tall, 18.5 in. deep, 39.2 lbs., mfg. 2013-present.

MSR $650	$475	$300 - 350	$155 - 190	

DYNABASS TC210 SPEAKER CABINET – 400W, 2-10 in. speakers and 1-1 in. tweeter with L-Pad, 8 ohm impedance, four inputs (two 1/4 in. and two Speakon), solid plywood construction, built-in side handles, Nubtex Black leatherette covering, black metal grille, 24 in. wide, 16 in. tall, 18.5 in. deep, 55.5 lbs., mfg. 2007-present.

MSR $640	$475	$300 - 350	$155 - 190	

MSR/NOTES	100%	EXCELLENT	AVERAGE	LAST MSR

Dynabass TC410 Speaker Cabinet
courtesy Traynor

Dynabass TC410 Neo Speaker Cabinet
courtesy Traynor

Dynabass TC1510 Speaker Cabinet
courtesy Traynor

DYNABASS TC410 SPEAKER CABINET – 800W, 4-10 in. speakers and 1-1 in. tweeter with L-Pad, 8 ohm impedance, four inputs (two 1/4 in. and two Speakon), solid plywood construction, built-in side handles, removable casters, Nubtex Black leatherette covering, black metal grille, 24 in. wide, 28 in. tall, 18.5 in. deep, 90.4 lbs., mfg. 2007-present.

MSR $1,000	$725	$475 - 550	$235 - 290	

* ***Dynabass 410 Neo Speaker Cabinet*** – 800W, 4-10 in. Eminence Neodymium speakers, 40W 1in. tweeter, 8 ohm impedance, four inputs (two 1/4 in. and two Speakon), solid plywood construction, built-in side handles, removable casters, Black covering, black metal grille, 24.5 in. wide, 28 in. tall, 18.5 in. deep, 59.1 lbs., mfg. 2013-present.

MSR $1,100	$800	$525 - 600	$260 - 325	

DYNABASS TC808 SPEAKER CABINET – 800W, 8-8 in. speakers and 1-1 in. tweeter with L-Pad, 4 ohm impedance, four inputs (two 1/4 in. and two Speakon), solid plywood construction, built-in side handles, two fixed casters for tilt-back transportation, metal top, side, and bottom handles, Nubtex Black leatherette covering, black metal grille, 23 in. wide, 36 in. tall, 17 in. deep, mfg. 2007-disc.

	$760	$425 - 500	$275 - 325	$949

DYNABASS TC810 SPEAKER CABINET – 1600W mono (800W stereo), 8-10 in. speakers, 4 ohm (mono) or 8 ohm (stereo) impedance, four inputs (two 1/4 in. and two Speakon), solid plywood construction, built-in side handles, two fixed casters for tilt-back transportation, metal top, side, and bottom handles, Nubtex Black leatherette covering, black metal grille, 26.25 in. wide, 49 in. tall, 16 in. deep, 156.5 lbs., mfg. 2007-present.

MSR $1,450	$1,050	$700 - 800	$350 - 425	

DYNABASS TC1510 SPEAKER CABINET – 600W, 1-15 in. and 2-10 in. speakers, 1-1 in. tweeter with L-Pad, 4 ohm impedance, four inputs (two 1/4 in. and two Speakon), solid plywood construction, built-in side handles, removable casters, Nubtex Black leatherette covering, black metal grille, mfg. 2007-present.

MSR $900	$650	$425 - 500	$215 - 265	

DNBH DYNABLOCK HEAD – 400W, bass head-unit, solid-state chassis, single channel, front black control panel, two inputs (passive/active), seven black knobs (g, b, l/mid, h/mid, t, low expander, MV), tuner jack, mute switch, power switch, XLR line out pre/post switch and ground switch, effects loop, two external speaker jacks, headphone jack, black covering, built-in side metal handles, mfg. 2012-present.

MSR $800	$600	$400 - 450	$195 - 240	

BASS AMPLIFIERS: SMALL BLOCK SERIES

SB110 Combo
courtesy Traynor

SB112 Combo
courtesy Traynor

SB115
courtesy Traynor

SB110 COMBO – 120W, 1-10 in. speaker and tweeter bass combo, solid-state chassis, two channel, top black control panel, two inputs, six knobs (g, b, l/m, h/m, t, low expander), XLR line out, tweeter switch, headphone jack, black covering, black metal grille, top handle, 21 lbs., mfg. 2013-present.

MSR $570	$400	$260 - 300	$130 - 160	

MSR/NOTES	100%	EXCELLENT	AVERAGE	LAST MSR

SB112 COMBO – 200W, 1-12 in. speaker and tweeter bass combo, solid-state chassis, two channel, top black control panel, two inputs, six knobs (g, b, l/m, h/m, t, low expander), XLR line out, tweeter switch, headphone jack, black covering, black metal grille, top handle, 25 lbs., mfg. 2013-present.

| MSR $630 | $450 | $295 - 325 | $145 - 180 | |

SB115 COMBO – 200W, 1-15 in. speaker and tweeter bass combo, solid-state chassis, two channel, top black control panel, two inputs, six knobs (g, b, l/m, h/m, t, low expander), XLR line out, tweeter switch, headphone jack, black covering, black metal grille, top handle, 31 lbs., mfg. 2013-present.

| MSR $700 | $500 | $325 - 375 | $165 - 200 | |

SB200H HEAD – 200W, bass head-unit, solid-state chassis, single channel, front black control panel, two inputs (passive/active), six black knobs (g, b, l/mid, h/mid, t, low expander), mute switch, power switch, XLR line out with pre/post switch and ground/lift switch, external speaker jack, headphone jack, aux. in jack, headphone jack, black covering, 1.5 lbs., mfg. 2014-present.

| MSR $400 | $300 | $195 - 225 | $100 - 120 | |

SB500H HEAD – 500W, bass head-unit, solid-state chassis, single channel, front black control panel, two inputs (passive/active), seven knobs (g, b, l/mid, h/mid, t, low expander, MV), mute switch, tuner jack, headphone jack, power switch, XLR line out with pre/post switch and ground/lift switch, two external speaker jacks, effects loop, black covering, 4 lbs., mfg. 2014-present.

| MSR $600 | $450 | $300 - 350 | $150 - 185 | |

ACOUSTIC AMPLIFIERS: AM SERIES

These amps are the same as the AM models under Yorkville, they just have different cosmetics and a Traynor logo on the front.

AM50T
courtesy Traynor

AM100T
courtesy Traynor

AM150T
courtesy Traynor

AM50T – 50W, 1-8 in.woofer, tweeter, solid-state chassis, two channels, reverb, front black control panel, three inputs (Ch. 1: 1/4 in., Ch. 2: XLR and 1/4 in.), six knobs (Ch. 1: g, l, h, freq., Ch. 2: g, All: r), Ch. 1 notch filter, line out jack, wedge design, brown leatherette covering, light brown grille, 23 lbs., mfg. 2006-09.

| | $480 | $250 - 300 | $150 - 200 | $599 |

AM100T – 100W, 2-6.5 in. speakers, 1-3.75 in. tweeter, two channels with separate gain controls, 32 preset ART digital effects processor, front black control panel, three inputs (Ch. 1: 1/4 in., Ch. 2: XLR and 1/4 in.), nine knobs (Ch. 1: g, l, m, h, freq., Ch. 2: g, All: MV, effects select, effects v), Ch. 1 notch filter switch, Ch. 2 effects defeat switch, line out jack, effects loop, wedge or upright design, brown leatherette covering, light brown grille, 25 lbs., mfg. 2006-09.

| | $590 | $325 - 400 | $200 - 250 | $729 |

AM150T – 150W stereo, 2-8 in. speakers, horn, tweeter, two channels with separate gain controls, 32 preset ART digital effects processor, front black control panel, three inputs (Ch. 1: 1/4 in., Ch. 2: XLR and 1/4 in.), nine knobs (Ch. 1: g, l, m, h, freq., Ch. 2: g, All: MV, effects select, effects v), Ch. 1 notch filter switch, Ch. 2 effects defeat switch, two 1/4 in. and one XLR line out jacks, effects loop, wedge or upright design, brown leatherette covering, light brown grille, 36 lbs., mfg. 2006-disc.

| | $700 | $375 - 450 | $225 - 275 | $869 |

AM CUSTOM – 225W stereo, 1-8 in. speaker, 2-2 in. tweeters, three channels with separate gain controls, 24-bit digital effects processor, top brown control panel, three inputs (Ch. 1: 1/4 in., Ch. 2: SpeakOn, Channel 3: mic,) Aux. input, RCA inputs, twenty knobs (All Channels: g, b, l/m, h/m, t, feedback notch, AUX: gain, All: MV), Channel 1/2 effects select and effects mix switches, Channel 3 effects select and effects mix switches, one 1/4 in. and one XLR line out jacks, footswitch jack, brown leatherette covering, light brown grille, 35 lbs., mfg. 2010-present.

| MSR $1,400 | $1,000 | $650 - 750 | $325 - 400 | |

AM STANDARD – 150W stereo, 2-6.5 in. speakers, 2-1 in. tweeters, two channels, 24-bit digital effects processor, front brown control panel, two inputs, 16 knobs (Ch. 1: g, b, l/m, h/m, t, notch, fx select, fx modify, fx mix, Ch. 2: g, b, t, fx select, fx modify, fx mix, ALL: MV), two 1/4 in. and one XLR line out jacks, footswitch jack, RCA jacks, effects loop, brown leatherette covering, light brown grille, 27.5 lbs., mfg. 2013-present.

| MSR $1,000 | $725 | $475 - 550 | $235 - 290 | |

AM STUDIO – 65W stereo, 1-8 in. speaker, 1 in. tweeter, two channels, 24-bit digital effects processor, front brown control panel, two inputs, 10 knobs (Ch. 1: g, b, t, notch, Ch. 2: g, tone, fx select, fx modify, fx mix, ALL: MV), 1/4 in. line out jack, footswitch jack, RCA jacks, brown leatherette covering, light brown grille, 23.5 lbs., mfg. 2012-present.

| MSR $800 | $600 | $400 - 450 | $195 - 240 | |

MSR/NOTES	100%	EXCELLENT	AVERAGE	LAST MSR

MISC. MODELS

YBX212 SPEAKER CABINET – 150W, 2-12 in. Celestion Vintage 30 speakers, vertical configuration, 8 ohm impedance, angled front, black covering, silver grille, recessed side handles, mfg. 2013-present.

MSR $650	$500	$325 - 375	$165 - 200	

YGL 1 COMBO – 15W, 1-12 in. Celestion Greenback speaker, all tube chassis, Preamp: 2 X 12AX7, Power: 2 X EL84, one channel, single input, six black knobs (g, b, m, t, v, reverb), power switch, amp in jack, amp out jack, footswitch jack, two speaker jacks, top handle, black covering, silver grille, 35 lbs., mfg. 2011-present.

MSR $880	$625	$400 - 475	$205 - 250	

YGL 2 COMBO – 30W, 1-12 in. Celestion Vintage 30 speaker, all tube chassis, Preamp: 3 X 12AX7, Power: 4 X EL84, two channels, single input, eight black knobs (Clean V, OD g, OD v, b, m, t, MV, reverb), power switch, amp in jack, amp out jack, footswitch jack, two speaker jacks, top handle, black covering, silver grille, 45 lbs., mfg. 2011-present.

MSR $1,200	$850	$550 - 625	$275 - 350	

TRUE TONE

Amplifiers previously produced in Chicago, IL during the 1960s. Distributed by Western Auto.

True Tone amplifiers were built by some of the large guitar/amp manufacturers in the Chicago area including Kay and Harmony. These amps were branded True Tone and sold by the Western Auto company. They also produced guitars. Any further information on True Tone can be submitted directly to Blue Book Publications.

TUBE WORKS

Amplifiers previously produced in Scottsdale, AZ and Denver, CO between circa 1991 and 2004. Distributed by Genz Benz.

Tube Works is a company out of Arizona that produces amplifers and the famous Tube Works "Tube Driver" guitar pedal. Tube Works was founded in the late 1970s with the Tube Works guitar pedal designed to give the warm feeling of a tube amplifier run through a footswitch. In circa 1991, they introduced their first guitar amplifiers that included both tube and solid-state designs. In 1997, Tube Works was acquired by Genz Benz of Scottsdale, AZ. Genz Benz was acquired by Kaman Music in late 2003, and they phased out the Tube Works brand in 2004.

TUSC

Amplifiers previously produced in Central Islip, NY during the late 1970s and early 1980s.

Tusc produced the Prestige Series that were programmable tube amplifiers. These amps feature analog circuits that store featured distortion, EQ, and other effects settings. There is no digital readout on these amps, and everything is controlled by a series of switches, knobs, and other controls. Amps were available as head units, combos, and speaker cabinets. They were covered in black and had a black grille with a large "TUSC" logo in the lower left corner. Any further information on Tusc amplifiers can be submitted directly to Blue Book Publications.

TWILIGHTER

Amplifiers previously produced by Magnatone during the late 1950s and early 1960s.

Twilighter was a brand Magnatone used on a line of amplifiers during the late 1950s and the early 1960s for LoDuca Brothers in Milwaukee, WI. The LoDuca Brothers were a major distribution company in the 1960s. Magnatone (Estey) built these amps, which were almost all clones of Magnatones, and put a Twilighter logo on the front instead of Magnatone. Essentially all Twilighter models should have a corresponding model with Magnatone. Known models include the **Model 213R**, **Troubadour Model 213**, and **Custom 260**. Any further information on Twilighter amps can be submitted directly to Blue Book Publications.

TWO-ROCK AMPLIFIERS

Amplifiers currently produced in Rohnert Park, CA. Previously produced in Cotati, CA. Designed and produced by K&M Analog Designs. The K&M Analog Designs trademark was established in 1999.

CONTACT INFORMATION
TWO-ROCK AMPLIFIERS
A Division of K&M Analong Designs
619 Martin Avenue, Suite 6
Rohnert Park, CA 94928
Phone No.: 707-584-8663
www.two-rock.com
joe@two-rock.com

K & M Analog Designs, LLC was founded in 1999 by Bill Krinard and Joe Mloganoski. Both have long histories in music, sound, and electronic design. Their collaboration is driven by their desire to produce the best sounding guitar amplifiers available, and began with listening to, playing, and tweaking many of the fine production tube amplifiers of the last sixty years.

The Two-Rock current product line includes the **Custom Reverb Signature**, **Overdrive Signature**, **Classic Reverb**, **Custom Clean**, **Jet**, and **Jet Signature**, **Classic Series** 1, 2, and 3, and two buffered effects loop interface units. Today, there are dealers and distributors across the United States (including Hawaii), in Canada, Asia, Europe, and South America. For more information visit Two-Rock's website or contact them directly.

U SECTION
UGLY AMPS

Amplifiers currently produced in Los Angeles, CA since 2003.

Steve O'Boyle builds custom guitar amps and cabinets designed for the working musician. All amps are hand-built in the U.S. yet remain affordable by sticking to strong simple circuits instead of complex designs. Ugly's first two amps were the **Ugly 18** that is an 18-watt amp loosely based on the Marshall 18 watt design, and the **Whirley** that is an original design. O'Boyle has also introduced the **Ugly 33** that is a big brother of the Ugly 18. For more information including pricing, visit Ugly's website or contact O'Boyle directly.

CONTACT INFORMATION
UGLY AMPS
Phone No.: 717-744-8459
Phone No.: 877-522-2102
www.uglyamps.com
steve@uglyamps.com

ULTRASOUND

Amplifiers currently produced in Des Moines, IA and overseas.

UJC Electronics, the former parent company of Ultrasound, was founded in 1985. They produce a vast range of products including smoke detectors, pest control devices, digital recording devices, and LED lighting systems. In 1991, Greg Farres came to work for UJC and his expertise in guitar amplifier circuitry inspired the first Ultrasound AG-50 amp. UJC and Farres saw a need for an acoustic amplifier that would replicate the exact tone of the guitar. Ultrasound now has a full line of acoustic guitar amplifiers and accessories. In late 2007, Dean Markley bought Ultrasound, and they are now a wholly-owned subsidiary of Dean Markley. All amps are designed and set up in their Des Moines factory, and a select few are entirely produced in the U.S. For more information, visit Ultrasound's website or contact them directly.

CONTACT INFORMATION
ULTRASOUND
2150 Delavan Dr., Suite 11
West Des Moines, IA 50265
Phone No.: 888-993-5091
Fax No.: 888-993-4550
www.ultrasoundamps.com
info@ultrasoundamps.com
17505 N. 79th Ave.
Suite 307
Glendale, AZ 85308

MSR/NOTES	100%	EXCELLENT	AVERAGE	LAST MSR

ACOUSTIC AMPLIFIERS

AG-30
courtesy Ultrasound

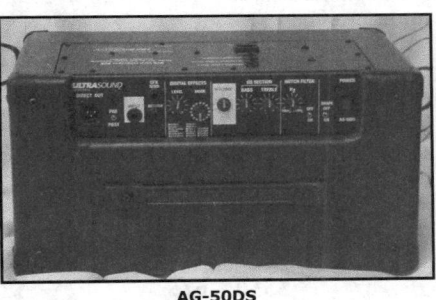
AG-50DS
courtesy Jason Scheuner

AG-50DS2
courtesy S.P. Fjestad

AG-30 – 30W, 1-8 in. speaker plus a 2 in. tweeter, solid-state chassis, sweepable notch filter, top black control panel, single input, four black knobs (v, b, t, notch), effects loop, line out, direct out, headphone jack, brown leatherette covering, black or brown grille, 20 lbs., current mfg.

MSR $276	$200	$120 - 150	$75 - 95	

AG-50 – 50W, 2-8 in. speakers plus a 2 in. tweeter, solid-state chassis, sweepable notch filter, top black control panel, single input, four black knobs (v, b, t, notch), effects loop, line out, brown leatherette covering, black grille, disc. 2001.

	N/A	$225 - 275	$175 - 200	

* *AG-50R* – similar to the AG-50, except has reverb circuit with knob, disc. 2001.

	N/A	$275 - 325	$200 - 225	

AG-50DS – 50W, 2-8 in. speakers plus a 2 in. tweeter, solid-state chassis, single channel, sweepable notch filter, digital effects, top black control panel, two inputs (mic & instrument), six black knobs (digital effect level & mode, level, b, t, notch), effects loop, line out, brown leatherette covering, black grille, disc. 2001.

	N/A	$400 - 450	$300 - 350	

AG-50DS2 – 50W, 2-8 in. speakers plus a 2 in. tweeter, solid-state chassis, dual channels, sweepable notch filter, digital effects, top black control panel, two inputs (mic & instrument), ten black knobs (Mic: b, t, level, Inst: digital effect level & mode, level, b, t, notch, MV), effects loop, line out, direct out, headphone jack, brown leatherette covering, black or brown grille, 24 lbs., disc. 2004.

	N/A	$350 - 400	$350 - 300	$696

AG-50DS3 – 50W, 2-8 in. speakers, solid-state chassis, two channels, sweepable notch filter, digital effects, top black control panel, two inputs, ten black knobs (Ch. 1: b, t, v, Inst: FX level, FX mode, v, b, t, notch, MV), effects loop, line out, direct out, headphone jack, light brown leatherette covering, brown grille, 18 in. wide, 13 in. tall, 11 in. deep, 24 lbs., mfg. 2004-06.

$550	$325 - 400	$200 - 250		$768

MSR/NOTES	100%	EXCELLENT	AVERAGE	LAST MSR

AG-50DS4 – 50W, 2-8 in. speakers, solid-state chassis, two channels, sweepable notch filter, 16 digital effects, top black control panel, two inputs, ten black knobs (Ch. 1: b, t, v, Inst: v, b, t, notch, All: FX level, FX mode, MV), notch switch, shape switch, FX channel switch, effects loop, line out, direct out, headphone jack, RCA inputs with level control, light brown leatherette covering, brown grille, 18 in. wide, 13 in. tall, 11 in. deep, 24 lbs., mfg. 2006-present.

| MSR $499 | $450 | $275 - 325 | $150 - 200 | |

AG-100 – 100W, 4-8 in. speakers plus a 2 in. tweeter, solid-state chassis, sweepable notch filter, top black control panel, single input, four black knobs (v, b, t, notch), effects loop, line out, brown leatherette covering, black grille, disc. 2001.

| | N/A | $300 - 350 | $175 - 200 | |

* *AG-100R* – similar to the AG-100, except has reverb circuit with knob, disc. 2001.

| | N/A | $375 - 425 | $250 - 300 | |

AG-100B – 100W, bass amp, 4-6 in. speakers, tweeters, solid-state chassis, top control panel, five knobs (r, b, t, notch filter, v), direct out, brown leatherette covering, black grille, disc.

| | N/A | $325 - 400 | $175 - 250 | |

AG-100DS – 100W, 4-8 in. speakers plus a 2 in. tweeter, solid-state chassis, single channel, sweepable notch filter, digital effects, top black control panel, two inputs (mic & instrument), six black knobs (digital effect level & mode, level, b, t, notch), effects loop, line out, brown leatherette covering, black grille, disc. 2001.

| | N/A | $500 - 550 | $400 - 450 | |

AG-100DS2 – 100W, 4-8 in. speakers plus a 2 in. tweeter, solid-state chassis, dual channels, sweepable notch filter, digital effects, top black control panel, two inputs (mic & instrument), ten black knobs (Mic: b, t, level, Inst: digital effect level & mode, level, b, t, notch, MV), effects loop, line out, direct out, headphone jack, brown leatherette covering, black or brown grille, disc. 2004.

| | N/A | $450 - 500 | $300 - 350 | $872 |

CP-100 – 100W, 1-8 in. speaker plus a high-freq. super tweeter, solid-state chassis, two channels, sweepable notch filter, 16 digital effects, top black control panel, two inputs, ten black knobs (Ch. 1: b, t, v, Inst: v, b, t, notch, All: FX level, FX mode, MV), notch switch, shape switch, FX channel switch, effects loop, line out, direct out, headphone jack, RCA inputs with level control, light brown leatherette covering, brown grille, 16 in. wide, 12 in. tall, 11 in. deep, 30 lbs., mfg. 2006-present.

| MSR $799 | $600 | $375 - 450 | $250 - 300 | |

PAMM (PREAMP MINI MIXER) – Preamp only, solid-state chassis, four inputs, 13 black knobs, tape/cd in, main out, cased in a black box, disc. 2003.

| | N/A | $75 - 100 | $45 - 60 | $230 |

PRO 100 – 100W, 1-10 in. speaker and 1 HF tweeter, solid-state chassis, two channels, feedback control, top control panel, two instrument inputs and one mic, 16 digital effects, effects loop, three direct outs, three line outs, ground lift, tilt-back legs, brown leatherette covering, black grille, 50 lbs., disc. 2008.

| | $850 | $550 - 625 | $325 - 400 | $1,178 |

PRO 200 – 200W, 2-8 in. speakers and 2 HF tweeters, solid-state chassis, two channels, feedback control, top control panel, two instrument inputs and one mic, 16 digital effects, effects loop, three direct outs, three line outs, ground lift, tilt-back legs, brown leatherette covering, black grille, 55 lbs., disc. 2008.

| | $1,175 | $725 - 850 | $450 - 525 | $1,618 |

EXTENSION SPEAKER CABINETS

AG-50E – 50W powered extension speaker cabinet, 2-8 in. speakers, top control panel, single volume control, brown leatherette covering, black grille, disc.

| | $340 | $200 - 250 | $120 - 150 | $478 |

AG-100E – 100W powered extension speaker cabinet, 2-8 in. speakers, top control panel, single volume control, brown leatherette covering, black grille, disc. 2005.

| | N/A | $300 - 350 | $225 - 250 | $557 |

This model is also available as the model G-100-UL/EQ, which features a six band graphic equalizer.

UNIQUE

Amplifiers previously produced by Laub Manufacturing in Mequon, WI during the early 1960s. Distributed by Magnatone.

Unique was a brand Magnatone used on a line of amplifiers during the late 1950s and the early 1960s that were built by Laub Manufacturing in Mequon, WI. Apparently, Magnatone only supplied the design/chassis on Unique amps and Laub built them as a private brand. Unique amps are all Magnatones in design, but they have slightly different cosmetics than other private branded Magnatones. Known models include the **Model 260** and **Model 460**. Any further information on Unique amps can be submitted directly to Blue Book Publications.

UNIVOX

Amplifiers previously produced in the United States and Japan between founded circa 1964 and the late 1970s. Distributed by the Merson Musical Supply Company of Westbury, NY.

Univox amplifiers were in circa 1964, and early models were completely made in the U.S. as tube amplifiers with Jensen speakers. By late 1968, Univox started using Japanese parts to assemble their amplifiers in American made cabinets. By 1971, Univox was offering several different designs and solid-state models were introduced as part of the regular line. Univox produced amplifiers under the Univox name until the late 1970s. By 1980, all amplifiers were produced by Westbury, the company that had supplied the cabinets for Univox. Westbury amps were made up until 1982. Univox was purchased by Korg in 1985. Univox amplifiers were introduced as budget/entry-level solid-state models in the 1990s as well. Early history courtesy: Michael Wright, *Guitar Stories* Volume One.

U3R Pro erb Delay Bos
courtesy John Beeson/The Music Shoppe

U3R Pro erb Delay Bos
courtesy John Beeson/The Music Shoppe

ELECTRIC TUBE AMPLIFIERS

U45 – 10W, 1-12 in. Jensen speaker, guitar combo, four tube chassis, preamp: 1 X 12AX7, 1 X 6BM8, power: 1 X 6BM8, rectifier: 6X4, single channel, tremolo, top control panel, three inputs, three knobs (v, tone, trem. speed), footswitch jack, dark covering, light grille, 16.5 in. wide, 15.25 in. tall, 18 lbs., mfg. mid-1960s.

	N/A	$150 - 200	$95 - 120

U75 – 12W, 2-10 in. Jensen speakers, guitar combo, five tube chassis, single channel, tremolo, top control panel, three inputs, three knobs (v, tone, trem. speed), one-button footswitch, dark covering, dark grille, 23.5 in. wide, 15.25 in. tall, 25 lbs., mfg. mid-1960s.

	N/A	$175 - 225	$110 - 140

U155-R – 18W, 1-12 in. Jensen speaker, guitar combo, eight tube chassis, single channel, reverb, tremolo, top control panel, three inputs, five knobs (v, tone, s, i, r), two-button footswitch, dark covering, light grille, 19 in. wide, 19.5 in. tall, 35 lbs., mfg. mid-1960s.

	N/A	$250 - 300	$135 - 175

U-255R – 40W, 2-12 in. Jensen speakers, guitar combo, five tube chassis, preamp: 2 X 12AX7, 1 X 12AT7, power: 2 X 6973, solid-state rectifier, single channel, reverb, tremolo, front chrome control panel, three inputs, five knobs (v, tone, r, s, i), black covering, black grille, mfg. late 1960s-early 1970s.

	N/A	$325 - 400	$200 - 250

U305-R – 30W, 1-15 in. Jensen speaker, guitar combo, eight tube chassis, two channels, reverb, tremolo, top control panel, four inputs, seven knobs (Ch. 1: v, tone, Ch. 2: v, tone, s, i, r), ext. speaker jack, two-button footswitch, dark covering, light grille, 23 in. wide, 23 in. tall, 42 lbs., mfg. mid-1960s.

	N/A	$325 - 400	$200 - 250

U1226 LEAD – 60W, head-unit, eight-tube chassis, preamp: 3 X 12AX7, 2 X 12AU7, 1 X 6AN8, power: 2 X 6L6GC, solid-state rectifier, two channels, reverb, tremolo, front blue control panel, four inputs (two per channel), nine knobs (v1, v2, b, m, t, p, r, s, i), power switch, rear panel: two speaker jacks, speaker impedance, switch, reverb adjust, reverb footswitch jack, tremolo footswitch jack, dark blue vinyl side covering and light blue front vinyl covering, red/blue grille cloth, mfg. 1969-1971.

	N/A	$325 - 400	$200 - 250

ELECTRIC SS AMPLIFIERS

BT505 BASS – 50W, 1-15 in. speaker, bass combo, solid-state chassis, single channel, front chrome control panel, three inputs, four knobs (v, t, b, balance), closed back, dark covering, light grille, 21.75 in. wide, 23.75 in. tall, 14.5 in. deep, 45 lbs., mfg. mid-1960s.

	N/A	$275 - 325	$150 - 200

U-65R – 20W, 1-12 in. speaker, guitar combo, solid-state chassis, single channel, reverb, tremolo, front black control panel, three inputs, four knobs (v, tone, r, trem. speed), footswitch jack, black covering, black grille, mfg. late 1960s-early 1970s.

	N/A	$150 - 200	$95 - 120

UB-250 – 50W, 1-15 in. Eminence speaker, bass piggyback configuration, solid-state chassis, single channel, front black control panel, two inputs, two knobs (v, tone), black covering, black grille, mfg. late 1960s-early 1970s.

	N/A	$150 - 200	$95 - 120

U.S. MUSIC CORP.

Distributor/parent company of a variety of brands located in Buffalo Grove, IL.

U.S. Music Corp. is the distributor and parent company of a variety of trademarks including Marshall, Washburn, Parker, Oscar Schmidt, Hagstrom, Jay Turser, Eden Electronics, Randall Amplification, Soundtech, Vinci, and GWL. In August 2009, JAM Industries of Canada acquired U.S. Music Corp.

CONTACT INFORMATION
U.S. MUSIC CORP.
1000 Corporate Grove Dr.
Buffalo Grove, IL 60089
Phone No.: 847-949-0444
Phone No.: 800-877-6863
Fax No.: 847-949-8444
www.usmusiccorp.com
guitar.support@usmusiccorp.com

NOTES

V SECTION
VALCO

Amplifiers previously produced between the early 1940s and late 1960s in Chicago, IL. A majority of Valco's business was supplying amps to other companies including National, Supro, Gretsch, Airline, and Oahu.

Louis Dopyera bought out the National company, and as he owned more than 50% of the stock in Dobro, Dopyera merged the two companies back together (as National Dobro). In 1936, Dopyera moved the company to Chicago, IL. Chicago was home to many of the mass production instrument companies such as Harmony, Kay, Washburn and Regal. Major wholesalers and retailers like the Tonk Bros., Lyon & Healy, and Sears & Roebuck were also based there. In 1943, Victor Smith, Al Frost, and Louis Dopyera (the three owners of Dobro-National), changed the name of the company to VALCO (the initials of their three first names: V-A-L company). Valco produced war materials during World War II, and returned to instrument/amplifier production in the mid-1940s.

Although Valco produced thousands of amplifiers, very few appear with a Valco name on them. Valco produced most of their amplifiers for sale under another name. Amps were built for National (their flagship line), Supro (a budget brand of National), and other manufacturers including Airline, Gretsch, and Oahu. Valco probably produced more Supro amps than any other single brand. In the late 1960s, Kay bought Valco and continued for a short while as Kay/Valco Guitars, Inc. when they went out of business in 1969 or 1970. The Strum & Drum Music Company of Chicago, IL bought the Kay and National trademarks, but Valco was never used again. A few amplifiers appeared with National on them, but they were completely gone by the early 1970s. Information courtesy: Aspen Pittman, *The Tube Amp Book*, Deluxe Revised Edition.

Since Valco produced for so many companies and mass production was very cost-effective, the same amp can appear in five different brands. The only differences include the brand's unique cosmetics and logo. For example, a Supro, National, and Gretsch all look very different from the outside, but it is possible that the chassis are identical. This is helpful when it comes to identifying and evaluating amps that are not individually listed. If an Airline amp isn't listed, the Supro version can serve as a general guide to its features and approximate value. This may take quite a bit of research since there doesn't seem to be any pattern to the numbering/naming system. Currently, there is no cross reference between brands, but look for more information in upcoming editions. Refer to the Supro, National, Gretsch, Airline, and Oahu sections for more individual model listings.

VALVETRAIN AMPLIFICATION

Amplifiers currently produced in Altamonte Springs (Orlando), FL. Previously produced in Sorrento, FL.

Valvetrain Amplifiers was founded by Rick Gessner in Orlando, FL. They build all-tube guitar amps that are mainly based on the narrow-panel Fender tweed style from the mid- to late 1950s. Several models are copies of the popular Fender models with slight modifications (the Classic Series), but Valvetrain also offers their own series of models (Valvetrain Series). Custom shop amps and signature series models are also available. Valvetrain offers a service called Tortured Tweed, where they age the tweed covering on an amp sort of like the Relic series from Fender. For more information, visit Valvetrain's website or contact them directly.

Classic 205
courtesy Valvetrain Amplification

Classic 338
courtesy Valvetrain Amplification

Valvetone 1530
courtesy Valvetrain Amplification

ELECTRIC TUBE AMPLIFIERS

Valvetrain offers the most Classic Series models. The **Classic 105 Po' Boy** (MSR $499) is based on the Fender Champ. The **Classic 205** is based on the mid-1950s Fender Princeton and is available as a head-unit (MSR $649), or 1-8 in. speaker combo (MSR $699). The **Classic 205 Tall Boy** is based on the Classic 205 chassis with a tall cabinet and is available as a 1-10 in. speaker combo (MSR $749) or 1-12 in. speaker combo (MSR $799). The **Classic 315** is based on the late-1950s Deluxe and is available as a head-unit (MSR $1,299), 1-12 in. combo (MSR $1,499), or a Big-Box combo with various speaker sizes (MSR starting at $1,649). A Classic 315 Harp amp (MSR $1,499) is also available that is specifically designed for harps. The Classic 535 is based on the late 1950s Fender Super and starts at $1,699).

The Valvetrain Valvetone Series are Fender narrow-panel tweed-inspired models that Valvetrain has designed for what they want in an amp. The **Valvetone 414** is a mix of the Vox AC30, Matchless Spitfire, and Fender Deluxe from the late 1950s, with 14W, 2 X

6V6 power tubes, and is available as a head (MSR $1,399), 1-12 in. speaker combo (MSR $1,599), or Big Box combo with various speaker sizes (MSR starting at $1,749). The **Valvetone 1530** is loosely based on the late 1950s Fender Deluxe with a master volume control and uses either 6V6 or 6L6 tubes for different power ratings. This model is available as a head (MSR $1,399), 1-12 in. speaker combo (MSR $1,599), or Big Box combo with various speaker sizes (MSR starting at $1,749). The **SpringThing** (MSR $749) is a reverb unit, similar to Fender's reverb unit from the 1960s.

Valvetrain has also produced signature models including the **Golden Eagle 315** for Joe Walsh and the **PowerTrain 338** for Pat Travers. Speaker cabinets are available in a variety of speaker configurations and they start at $549.

VEGA

Banjos currently built by the Deering Banjo Company. Originally, Vega guitars and amps were produced in Boston, MA and instruments were later produced in Korea.

The predecessor company to Vega was founded in 1881 by Swedish immigrant Julius Nelson, C. F. Sunderberg, Mr. Swenson, and several other men. Nelson was the foreman of a 20-odd man workforce (which later rose to 130 employees during the 1920s banjo boom). Nelson, and his brother Carl, gradually bought out the other partners, and incorporated in 1903 as Vega (which means star). In 1904, Vega acquired banjo maker A.C. Fairbanks & Company after Fairbanks suffered a fire, and Fairbank's David L. Day became Vega's general manager.

Vega built banjos under the Bacon trademark, named after popular banjo artist Frederick J. Bacon. Bacon set up his own production facility in Connecticut in 1921, and a year later wooed Day away from Vega to become the vice president in the newly reformed Bacon & Day Company. While this company marketed several models of guitars, they had no facility for building them. It is speculated that the Bacon & Day guitars were built by the Regal company of Chicago, IL.

In the mid-1920s, Vega began marketing a guitar called the Vegaphone. By the early 1930s, Vega started concentrating more on guitar production, and less on banjo making. Vega debuted its Electrovox electric guitar and amplifier in 1936, and an electric volume control foot pedal in 1937. Vega is reported to have built over 40,000 guitars during the 1930s.

In the 1940s, Vega continued to introduce models such as the Duo-Tron and the Supertron; and by 1949 had become both a guitar producer and a guitar wholesaler as it bought bodies built by Harmony. Vega also produced various amplifiers during the 1950s and 1960s, many of which featured tube chassis. The A series of amps produced in the late 1950s and early 1960s appear to be the most popular. In 1970, Vega was acquired by the C.F. Martin Company for its banjo operations. Martin soon folded Vega's guitar production, and applied the trademark to a line of imported guitars. Ten years later, Martin sold the Vega trademark rights to a Korean guitar production company (source: Tom Wheeler, *American Guitars*).

VERO AMPS

Amplifiers currently produced in Joliet, IL since 1998.

The Vero Amplifier company was formed in 1997 in Joliet, IL. The company has taken guitar amps and brought them to an artistic level. Their amps typically feature an elaborate wooden cabinet with old-school tube technology chassis. Vero also lets the customer design the amp to his or her specs, therefore making each amplifier entirely custom. Vero now has standard production models, but they still follow the custom feel that the older amps had. For more information, visit Vero Amp's website or contact them directly.

CONTACT INFORMATION
VERO AMPS
22436 S. River Road
Joliet, IL 60431 USA
Phone No.: 815-467-7093
www.veroamps.com
info@veroamps.com

GUITAR AMPLIFIERS

The Paramount and Paramount Club models are special order only. They feature bird's-eye maple and mahogany woods and have the traditional tube electronics inside. The Paramount lists at $8,000. The Paramount Club has a trans. finish, a gold bezel on the front, and lists for $7,800. Add $1,000 for a hand engraved top.

20TH CENTURY LIMITED – 25W, 1-12 in. or 1-15 in. speaker, tube chassis, 7591 power tubes only, top control panel, five knobs, line out, rounded front top cabinet, round speaker grille with stylized V, 42 lbs., current mfg.

MSR $1,940	$1,940	$1,100 - 1,300	$750 - 900

- **Add $100 for 1-15 in. speaker.**

CHICAGO ZEPHYR – 45W, 1-15 in., 2-10 in., 2-12 in. or 4-10 in. speakers, all tube chassis: 12AX7 preamp, 6L6GC power tubes, GZ34 rectifier, reverb, top control panel, six knobs, rounded front top cabinet, unique grille shape with Vero logo in the middle, current mfg.

MSR $2,350	$2,350	$1,400 - 1,700	$900 - 1,100

- **Add $25 for 1-15 in. speaker.**
- **Add $200 for 2-12 in. speakers.**
- **Add $250 for 4-10 in. speakers.**

VESTA FIRE

Amplifiers previously produced in Japan during the 1980s. Distributed by Shiino Musical Instruments and Midco International.

Vesta Fire mainly produced preamps, power amps, and effects pedals in Japan. They were first distributed by Shiino Musical Instruments and Midco International distributed them later. Any further information on Vesta Fire can be submitted directly to Blue Book Publications.

MSR/NOTES	100%	EXCELLENT	AVERAGE	LAST MSR

VHT AMPLIFICATION

Amplifiers currently produced in Burbank, CA since 2003. Previously produced in Sun Valley, CA. Distributed in the U.S. by The Music Link and internationally by AXL in Hayward, CA. The VHT trademark was established in 1989.

CONTACT INFORMATION
VHT AMPLIFICATION
31067 San Clemente Street
Hayward, CA 94544
Phone No.: 415-570-0970
Fax No.: 415-570-0651
www.vhtamp.com
info@vhtamp.com

Steven Fryette founded VHT amplifiers in 1989, and they are hand built in California by Fryette and his crew. Steven feels that a guitarist is born with their own tone and it takes a certain product, such as the amplifier, to develop the sound so the world can hear. This is what VHT amplifiers were created to do. VHT are all-tube amplifiers that come in head and combo units. Not only are these units hand checked before they leave the factory, but they are checked by the president himself! VHT relocated to Burbank, California in 2003. In 2009, Fryette sold the VHT brand to The Music Link, but he continues to build the same models under the Fryette brand, while The Music Link has introduced new VHT-branded models. For more information visit VHT's website or contact them directly.

ELECTRIC TUBE AMPLIFIERS: DELIVERANCE SERIES

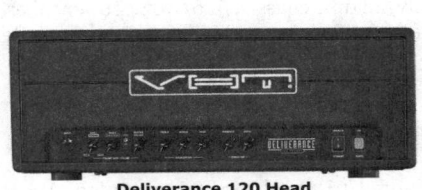

**Deliverance 120 Head
courtesy VHT Amplification**

**Deliverance 412 Speaker Cabinet
courtesy VHT Amplification**

DELIVERANCE 60 HEAD (KT60H/D60H) – 60W, head-unit only, tube chassis, preamp: 4 X 12AX7, power: 2 X KT88, single channel, front black control panel, single input, eight black knobs (g1, g2, MV, t, m, b, p, d), gain switch, impedance selector switch, black covering, mfg. 2005-present.

MSR $1,895	$1,525	$850 - 1,000	$550 - 650

* *Deliverance 60 Combo (Model KT60C/D60C)* – similar to the Deliverance 60, except in combo configuration with 2-12 in. VHT designed P50E speakers, mfg. 2005-present.

MSR $2,895	$2,325	$1,250 - 1,500	$850 - 1,000

DELIVERANCE 120 HEAD (KT120H/D120H) – 120W, head-unit only, tube chassis, preamp: 4 X 12AX7, power: 4 X KT88, single channel, front black control panel, single input, eight black knobs (g1, g2, MV, t, m, b, p, d), gain switch, impedance selector switch, black covering, mfg. 2005-present.

MSR $2,395	$1,925	$1,100 - 1,300	$675 - 800

DELIVERANCE 212 SPEAKER CABINET (K212-P50E/D212-P50E) – 100W, 2-12 in. VHT designed P50E speakers, straight front, charcoal black vinyl, black grille, mfg. 2005-present.

MSR $995	$800	$450 - 525	$275 - 325

DELIVERANCE 412 SPEAKER CABINET (K412-P50E/D412-P50E) – 200W, 4-12 in. VHT designed P50E speakers, 16 ohm mono or 8 ohm stereo impedance, straight front, charcoal black vinyl, black grille, mfg. 2005-present.

MSR $1,295	$1,050	$600 - 700	$350 - 425

ELECTRIC TUBE AMPLIFIERS: PITTBULL SERIES

PITTBULL FIFTY/CL HEAD (G-50-CL) – 50W, head-unit only, all tube chassis, 6L6/EL34 power tubes, 5U4 tube rectifiers, two channels, front black control panel, two inputs, 13 black knobs, various buttons, half power mode, variable line out, effects loop, footswitch, cover, black or spruce vinyl covering, black grille, current mfg.

MSR $2,495	$2,000	$1,150 - 1,350	$700 - 850

• Add 9% for optional EQ. Add 13% for reverb.

PITTBULL FIFTY/ST HEAD (G-5034-L) – 50W, head-unit only, all tube chassis, EL34 power tubes, two channels, reverb, front black control panel, two inputs, 11 black knobs, effects loop, variable line out, class A switch, footswitch, black or spruce vinyl, black grille with white piping, disc. 2005.

	N/A	$1,050 - 1,250	$650 - 750	$2,095

• Add 10% for optional EQ.

MSR/NOTES	100%	EXCELLENT	AVERAGE	LAST MSR
* *Pittbull Fifty/Twelve 2-12 Combo (C-5034-L)* – similar to the Pittbull Fifty/ST Head, except has 2-12 in. speakers, disc. 2005.				
	N/A	$1,150 - 1,350	$750 - 850	$2,395
• Add 8% for optional EQ.				

PITTBULL FORTY-FIVE HEAD (G-5084-T) – 45W, head-unit only, all-tube chassis, EL84 power tubes, two channels, reverb, front ivory control panel, two inputs, 11 black chicken-head knobs, effects loop, line out, footswitch, black, spruce, or ivory vinyl covering, black grille, disc. 2005.

	N/A	$900 - 1,050	$550 - 650	$1,895

* *Forty-Five 1-12 in. Combo (C-5084-T)* – similar to the Forty Five head in chassis, has 1-12 in. speaker, and no master controls, disc. 2005.

	N/A	$1,000 - 1,200	$650 - 750	

* *Forty-Five 2-10 in. Combo (C-5084-TW10)* – similar to the Forty Five head in chassis, has 2-10 in. Jensen speakers, disc. 2005.

	N/A	$1,100 - 1,300	$700 - 800	$2,295

* *Forty-Five 2-12 in. Combo (C-5084-TW12)* – similar to the Forty Five head in chassis, has 2-12 in. speakers, disc. 2005.

	N/A	$1,100 - 1,300	$700 - 800	$2,295

PITTBULL HUNDRED/CL HEAD (G-100-CL) – 100W, head-unit only, all tube chassis, 6L6/EL34 power tubes, 5U4 tube rectifiers, two channels, front black control panel, two inputs, 13 black knobs, various buttons, half power mode, variable line out, effects loop, footswitch, cover, black or spruce vinyl covering, black grille, current mfg.

MSR $2,995	$2,400	$1,300 - 1,600	$850 - 1,000	
• Add 7% for optional EQ.				
• Add 10% for reverb.				

* *Pittbull Hundred/CLX Head (G-100-CLX)* – similar to the Pittbull Hundred/CL Head, except is part of the Master Built series that is fully tested and signed by Steven Fryette, mfg. 2006-present.

MSR $4,295	$3,450	$2,000 - 2,500	N/A	

PITTBULL SUPER THIRTY (C-3084-S) – 30W, 1-12 in. speaker combo, all tube Class A chassis, EL84 power tubes, two channels, front black control panel, nine black chicken head knobs, various buttons, effects loop, line out, footswitch, black covering, black grille with white piping, disc. 2005.

	N/A	$675 - 800	$425 - 500	$1,449

PITTBULL ULTRA-LEAD HEAD (G-100-UL) – 120W, head-unit only, all tube chassis, KT-88 power tubes, three channels, front black control panel, two inputs, 14 black knobs, various buttons, half power mode, variable line out, effects loop, footswitch, cover, black or spruce vinyl covering, black grille, current mfg.

MSR $3,995	$3,200	$1,800 - 2,200	$1,150 - 1,400	
• Add 5% for optional EQ.				

This model is also available with an optional 6-band graphic equalizer and 3-spring Accutronics reverb.

PREAMPS/POWER AMPS

TWO/FIFTY/TWO POWER AMPLIFIER (G-2502-S) – 100W (50W per channel stereo), power amp only, two-space rack-mount head-unit, four-tube chassis: 4 X EL34, front anodized aluminum control panel, six black knobs (Ch. A: v, p, depth, Ch. B: v, p, depth), switchable voicing, fan speed switch, lower-power mode, black casing, current mfg.

MSR $1,295	$1,050	$575 - 675	$350 - 425	

TWO/NINETY/TWO POWER AMPLIFIER (G-2902-S) – 190W (95W per channel stereo, switchable to 60W per channel), power amp only, two-space rack-mount head-unit, four-tube chassis: 4 X KT88, front anodized aluminum control panel, six black knobs (Ch. A: v, p, depth, Ch. B: v, p, depth), switchable voicing, fan speed switch, lower-power mode, black casing, 13 in. deep, 35 lbs., current mfg.

MSR $1,595	$1,275	$700 - 850	$450 - 525	

SPEAKER CABINETS: FAT BOTTOM SERIES

FAT BOTTOM 212 SPEAKER CABINET (MODEL 212FB-P50E) – 100W, 2-12 in. VHT designed P50E speakers, straight front, available in black or spruce vinyl covering, black grille, current mfg.

MSR $995	$800	$450 - 525	$275 - 325	

FAT BOTTOM 412 SPEAKER CABINET (MODEL 412/412S-P50E) – 200W, 4-12 in. VHT designed P50E speakers, 16 ohm mono or 8 ohm stereo impedance, straight (412-P50E) or angled (412S-P50E) front, available in black or spruce vinyl covering, black grille, current mfg.

MSR $1,295	$1,050	$600 - 700	$350 - 425	

MSR/NOTES	100%	EXCELLENT	AVERAGE	LAST MSR

VICTORIA

Amplifiers currently produced in Naperville, IL, since 1993.

Mark Baier is the president and founder of Victoria amplifiers. Mark set out in 1993, to recreate the 1950s Fender amps. Victoria have made tweed amplifiers that are close to the original Fender tweeds. They are not Fenders inside out, and they have had several modern updates to make them some of the finest amps out there. The Victoriette and Victorilux were released in 2001 when Mark gave in to the request/demand for amps with tremolo and reverb. A few new amps that stray a bit from the original Fenders debuted between 2003 and 2004. Victoria also builds amplifiers that are built to order and more speaker options are available. For more information contact Victoria directly.

CONTACT INFORMATION
VICTORIA
Business Office
1504 Newman Court
Naperville, IL 60560
Phone No.: 630-369-3527
Fax No.: 630-527-2221
www.victoriaamp.com
sambisbee@spcglobal.net

Shop Address
10 S. 059 Schoger Rd, Suite 30 & 32
Naperville, IL 60564
Phone No.: 630-820-6400

ELECTRIC TUBE AMPLIFIERS

Victoria offers a full range of the Fender-era tweed amps. Victoria amps are very easy to figure out what you have under the hood by the model name and vice versa (If you know what is under the hood, you know what model it is!). The model number is made up of the wattage, the number of speakers, the size of the speakers, and if there is tremolo.

59 TREMOLUX STYLE – 18W, 1-12 in. Jensen P12Q speakers, all-tube chassis, 2 X 6L6 power tubes, top control panel, tweed covering, brown grille, mfg. 2004-05.

	N/A	$1,200 - 1,400	$700 - 850	$2,395

518 – 5W, 1-8 in. Jensen P8R or C8R speaker, all-tube chassis, top control panel, tweed covering, brown grille, modeled after the 5F1 Champ, mfg. 1993-present.

MSR $1,149	$925	$575 - 675	$375 - 450	

5112 – 5W, 1-12 in. Jensen P12R speaker, all-tube chassis, top control panel, tweed covering, brown grille, mfg. 2004-present.

MSR $1,249	$1,000	$650 - 750	$425 - 500	

20112 – 20W, 1-12 in. Jensen P12R speaker, all-tube chassis, top control panel, tweed covering, brown grille, modeled after the Narrow Panel Deluxe, mfg. 1993-present.

MSR $2,095	$1,675	$1,050 - 1,250	$700 - 825	

35115 – 35W, 1-15 in. Eminence speaker, all-tube chassis, top control panel, tweed covering, brown grille, modeled after the Narrow Panel Pro, mfg. 1993-present.

MSR $2,729	$2,175	$1,375 - 1,650	$900 - 1,075	

35210 – 35W, 2-10 in. Jensen P10R speakers, all-tube chassis, top control panel, tweed covering, brown grille, modeled after the Narrow Panel Super, mfg. 1993-present.

MSR $2,729	$2,175	$1,375 - 1,650	$900 - 1,075	

35310 – 35W, 3-10 in. Jensen P10R speakers, all-tube chassis, top control panel, tweed covering, brown grille, modeled after the Narrow Panel Bandmaster, mfg. 1993-present.

MSR $2,829	$2,275	$1,425 - 1,700	$950 - 1,125	

45410 – 45W, 4-10 in. Jensen P10R speakers, all-tube chassis, top control panel, tweed covering, brown grille, modeled after the Narrow Panel Bassman, mfg. 1993-present.

courtesy Dave Rogers/Dave's Guitar Shop

courtesy Dave Rogers/Dave's Guitar Shop

MSR $2,950	$2,375	$1,475 - 1,775	$975 - 1,175	

50212 – 50W, 2-12 in. Jensen P12Q speakers, all-tube chassis, top control panel, tweed covering, brown grille, modeled after the Narrow Panel Twin, mfg. 1993-present.

MSR $2,950	$2,375	$1,475 - 1,775	$975 - 1,175	

MSR/NOTES	100%	EXCELLENT	AVERAGE	LAST MSR

80212 – 80W, 2-12 in. Jensen P12N speakers, all-tube chassis, top control panel, tweed covering, brown grille, modeled after the late '50s Narrow Panel Twin, mfg. 1993-present.

MSR $3,495	$2,800	$1,750 - 2,100	$1,150 - 1,400	

DOUBLE DELUXE – 30/40W, 2-12 in. Jensen P12Q speakers, all-tube chassis, 4 X 6V6GT power tubes, 5Y3 or 5AR4 rectifier, top control panel, tweed covering, brown grille, modeled after two Deluxes in one cabinet, mfg. 1993-present.

MSR $2,829	$2,275	$1,425 - 1,700	$950 - 1,125	

REGAL – 12W, 1-10 in. Jensen P10Q or1-12 in. Eminence Legend speakers, all-tube chassis,Class A design, 6L6 power tube, reverb, tremolo, top control panel, tweed covering, brown grille, mfg. 2004-06.

	$1,925	$1,200 - 1,400	$700 - 850	$2,395

REGAL II – 35W, 1-15 in. Weber Custom Alnico speaker guitar combo, seven-tube chassis, preamp: 3 X 12AX7, 1 X 12AT7, power: 2 X 5881 (many other power tubes work as well), rectifier: 1 X 5U4GB, single channel, reverb, tremolo, top brown control panel, two inputs, six white chickenhead knobs (v, t, b, r, s, i), power and standby switches, available in laquered tweed or vanilla white Tolex covering, brown grille, 22.5 in. wide, 20.5 in. tall, 10.5 in. deep, mfg. 2007-present.

MSR $2,995	$2,400	$1,500 - 1,800	$1,000 - 1,200	

The Regal II features the new "Adaptive Transformer Technology" where several tube configurations can be used and the output of the amp can range from 5W to 35W. Other optional speakers are available as well.

TREM D'LA TREM – 14W, 1-15 in. Eminence Legend speaker guitar combo, six-tube chassis, preamp: 2 X 12AX7, 1 X 12AY7, power: 2 X 6V6GT, rectifier: 1 X 5U4GB, two channels (normal/bright), top chrome control panel, four inputs (two per channel), five black knobs (Normal Ch. v, Bright Ch. v, tone, trem. speed, trem. depth), power and standby switches, single button footswitch, tweed covering, narrow panel era brown grille, modeled after the mid-1950s Model 5E9-A Tremolux, 23 in. wide, 21.5 in. tall, 10.5 in. deep, mfg. 2005-present.

MSR $2,695	$2,150	$1,350 - 1,625	$875 - 1,075	

VICTORIETTE – 20W, 1-12 in. Jensen P12Q, 1-12 in. Eminence Legend, or 2-10 in. Jensen P10R speakers, all-tube chassis, reverb, tremolo, top control panel, brown Tolex covering, brown grille, modeled after a cross between a Blackface Deluxe and a Class A British amp, mfg. 2001-present.

MSR $2,749	$2,200	$1,400 - 1,675	$925 - 1,100	

VICTORILUX – 35W, 2-12 in. Jensen P12Q, 2-12 in. Eminence Legend, 3-10 in. Jensen P10R, or 1-15 in. Eminence speakers, all-tube chassis, 2 X 6L6 or 4 X EL84 power tubes, reverb, tremolo, top control panel, brown Tolex covering, brown grille, modeled after the Deluxe Reverb and Super Reverb, mfg. 2001-present.

MSR $2,949	$2,375	$1,475 - 1,775	$975 - 1,175	

The 6L6 power tubes are only available with a 3-10 in. speaker cabinet.

VIVI-TONE

Instruments previously built in Kalamazoo, MI during the 1930s.

After pioneering such high quality instruments for Gibson in the 1920s (such as the F-5 Mandolin), designer/ engineer/builder Lloyd Loar founded the Vivi-Tone company to continue exploring designs too radical for Gibson. It is rumored that Loar designed a form of stand-up bass that was amplified while at Gibson, but this prototype was never developed into a production model.

Loar, along with partners Lewis A. Williams and Walter Moon started Vivi-Tone in 1933. Loar continued building his pioneering designs, such as an acoustic guitar with sound holes in the rear, but failed to find commercial success. However, it is because of his early successes at Gibson that researchers approach the Vivi-tone designs with some wonderment instead of discounting the radical ideas altogether. Vivi-Tone produced some small amplifiers for use with their electric designs. Source: Tom Wheeler, *American Guitars*.

VOLTMASTER

Amplifiers previously produced in Plano, TX during the late 1990s and early 2000s.

Matt Iddings produced Voltmaster amplifiers during the late 1990s in Plano, TX. Most of his amps were custom amps built at the request of customers. Amps featured all-tube chassis and various other controls. The cabinets are trapezoid-shaped, which Matt called "Deco-Trapezoid." Any further information on Voltmaster amps can be submitted directly to Blue Book Publications.

VOODOO

Amplifiers currently produced in Horseheads, NY. Previously produced in Ithaca, NY.

Voodoo amps was created in 1998, by Trace Allen Davis. He started building amplifiers, like so many other musicians do, searching for the perfect tone. Voodoo's single goal is to "craft more flexible and reliable ways to achieve great tone and vintage tones as well as high gain while always maintaining articulation and definition at all times." Voodoo has amps based on all different types of other models such as the Marshall Plexi 50 and 100W heads. For more information contact Voodoo directly.

CONTACT INFORMATION
VOODOO
315 Daniel Zenker Dr.
IST Center BLDG 202
Horseheads, NY 14845
Phone No.: 607-256-0465
Fax No.: 607-330-0272
www.voodooamps.com
info@voodooamps.com

MSR/NOTES	100%	EXCELLENT	AVERAGE	LAST MSR

**V-Plex 50 Watt
courtesy Voodoo**

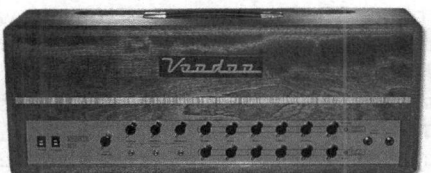

**WD Witchdoctor 100 Watt
courtesy Voodoo**

ELECTRIC TUBE AMPLIFIERS

HEX-50 – 50W, head-unit only, all-tube chassis, 6 X 12AX7 preamp, 2 X EL34 power, two channels, front control panel, one input, 16 knobs, effects loop, speaker impedance selector on back, footswitch, Tolex or wood covering, current mfg.

MSR $2,195	$1,800	$1,100 - 1,300	$650 - 850

HEX-100 – 100W, head-unit only, all-tube chassis, 6 X 12AX7 preamp, 4 X EL34 power, two channels, front control panel, one input, 16 knobs, effects loop, speaker impedance selector on back, footswitch, Tolex or wood covering, current mfg.

MSR $2,395	$2,000	$1,200 - 1,400	$700 - 900

V-PLEX 25 WATT HEAD – 25W, head-unit only, all-tube chassis, 3 X 12AX7 preamp, 2 X EL34 power, two channels, front Plexi control panel, four inputs, six knobs (p, t, m, b, Ch. 1 v, Ch. 2 v), speaker impedance selector on back, Tolex or wood covering, current mfg.

MSR $1,999	$1,500	$950 - 1,150	$550 - 750

- Add 5% (MSR $2,099) for Master Volume.

* V-Plex 25Watt Combo – similar to the V-Plex 25 Watt Head, except in combo configuration with 1-12 in. Celestion Vintage 30 speaker, current mfg.

MSR $2,499	$1,900	$1,150 - 1,350	$675 - 875

- Add 5% (MSR $2,599) for Master Volume.

V-PLEX 50 WATT – 50W, head-unit only, all-tube chassis, 3 X 12AX7 preamp, 2 X EL34 power, two channels, front Plexi control panel, four inputs, six knobs (p, t, m, b, Ch. 1 v, Ch. 2 v), speaker impedance selector on back, Tolex or wood covering, current mfg.

MSR $2,099	$1,600	$1,000 - 1,200	$600 - 800

- Add 5% (MSR $2,199) for Master Volume.

V-PLEX 100 WATT – 100W, head-unit only, all-tube chassis, 3 X 12AX7 preamp, 4 X EL34 power, two channels, front Plexi control panel, four inputs, six knobs (p, t, m, b, Ch. 1 v, Ch. 2 v), speaker impedance selector on back, Tolex or wood covering, current mfg.

MSR $2,399	$1,800	$1,100 - 1,300	$650 - 850

- Add 5% (MSR $2,499) for Master Volume.

WD WITCHDOCTOR 50 WATT – 50W, head-unit only, all-tube chassis, 6 X 12AX7 preamp, 2 X EL34 power, two channels, front control panel, one input, 16 knobs, effects loop, speaker impedance selector on back, footswitch, Tolex or wood covering, current mfg.

MSR $2,195	$1,800	$1,100 - 1,300	$650 - 850

WD WITCHDOCTOR 100 WATT – 100W, head-unit only, all-tube chassis, 6 X 12AX7 preamp, 4 X EL34 power, two channels, front control panel, one input, 16 knobs, effects loop, speaker impedance selector on back, footswitch, Tolex or wood covering, current mfg.

MSR $2,395	$2,000	$1,200 - 1,400	$700 - 900

SPEAKER CABINETS

2-12 IN. CABINET – 50W (2-12 in. Celestion Greenbacks), 120W (2-12 in. Celestion Vintage 30s), or 150W (2-12 in. Celestion GT75s), birch plywood construction, current mfg.

MSR $689	$540	$325 - 400	$200 - 250

- Add $35 for Celestion Vintage 30s or Greenback speakers.

4-12 IN. CABINET – 100W (4-12 in. Celestion Greenbacks), 240W (4-12 in. Celestion Vintage 30s), or 300W (4-12 in. Celestion GT75s), birch plywood construction, current mfg.

MSR $899	$725	$400 - 500	$225 - 275

- Add $80 for Celestion Vintage 30s or Greenback speakers.

VOX

Amplifiers currently produced in China, Vietnam, and Indonesia. Previously produced in Erith, Kent, England. Vox Amplification is distributed in England and through the U.S.A. in Melville, NY by Vox Amplification (Korg). The Vox trademark was established circa 1957 in Dartford, Kent.

The Vox Amplifier company was started by Tom Jennings and Dick Denney. Tom Jennings was born on February 28, 1917 in Hackney England. After school he began playing the piano and accordion. As World War II raged on, he was called up to duty in 1940, but discharged

CONTACT INFORMATION
VOX
U.S. Distributor: Korg USA
316 S. Service Road
Melville, NY 11747
Phone No.: 631-390-6500
www.voxamps.co.uk

medically in 1941. He then went to work in a munitions plant where he and fellow colleagues learned to entertain themselves musically. This is where he was inspired to go into music and did so after the war was over. In 1944, he formed his own business trading accordians and other musical instruments. In 1946, his co-worker back at the ammunition plant, Dick Denney, came to work with Jennings. Denney was into amplifying instruments and set out to make an amplifier for a Hawaiian guitar. Denney and Jennings went their different ways as the war ended and many war-industry workers were laid-off.

Tom kept on with the small business and hired a new electric technician. Shortly thereafter the Univox, a portable piano/accordion, was released. With the slow growing of the Univox and Jennings being a successful business man, the Jennings Organ Company was started in 1951. Jennings made organs and the Univox throughout the 1950s when he decided that a new line of products was necessary. Dick Denney had employed himself in radio and electronics as a repairer and an engineer. He also developed an amplifier during his sickness, which restricted him from working on a normal basis. One of Denney's buddies took this new 15W amp down to Jennings shop and Tom was very interested. Jennings ended up hiring Denney as the chief design engineer for Jenning's new company to be called Vox. After ten years of hardly talking to each other, Tom and Dick were now in the process of releasing the first Vox amplifier. Denney's 15W amp would become the Vox AC15.

As Rock & Roll exploded into Britain in 1958, Vox picked up a couple of endorsers like Cliff Richard and The Shadows. Later in 1958, Vox released two new amps without the vibrato that the AC-15 had. In late 1959, Vox released the infamous AC-30 that was designed to compete directly with the popular American Fender Twin. The AC-30 became an unqualified success until the Beatles began using it. The Beatles had been using Vox amps since their inception, and one day Brian Epstein traded in their AC-15s for the bigger AC-30s. Vox enjoyed much success with The Beatles as endorsers and sales roared through the early 1960s. Amps were produced and sold solely in England through the early 1960s as well. Due to financial difficulties in the mid-1960s, Jennings sold Vox to the Royston Group in 1964.

Under new ownership, Vox appeared to be destined for success, especially with the guitar boom of the 1960s and The Beatles as endorsers. The Thomas Organ Company arranged a deal to produce Vox tube amps in the United States at their factory between 1964 and 1965 so importing them wouldn't be an issue. They also introduced solid-state amps in 1966, which were also produced in the U.S. for a short time. However, Vox was unable to remain competitive with other amplifier companies such as Marshall as guitar players were requesting more power. After a fire in 1966 at the factory, and declining numbers, Tom Jennings resigned from Vox in 1967. Shortly thereafter Royston was liquidated and Corinthian Securities took over. This proved to be a bad ownership, as Corinthian had no connection with the previous staff and they discontinued almost all of the amplifiers in the catalog, and the few that remained were manufactured in Japan. This ownership didn't last long and Stolec bought them out in 1970. CBS-Arbiter bought out Vox again in 1972 for the third change of ownership in as many years.

When CBS-Arbiter took over it looked like things may change around for Vox. The return of the Vox organs came along with many new amplifiers and effects. But the 1970s had its toll on Vox, as it did with other manufacturers as well. CBS took a loss during the 1970s and were forced to sell again, this time to the long-time distributor of Marshall, Rose-Morris. RM had just lost the rights of Marshall and were looking for something to get them back with amplifiers. The company name was now called Vox Ltd. Rose Morris released quite a bit of new products including the Venue Series and the Q Series, and in a sense kept Vox going through the tough 1980s. Dick Denney endorsed the new AC-30 Limited Edition Reissue that was released in 1990. In 1992, Rose-Morris sold the company to Korg, who also distributes Marshall in the U.S. In 1993, Vox introduced an accurate reissue of the original AC30. Tube amps from most of the 1990s were built by Marshall, but all production has shifted to China. Vox continues to produce a wide variety of amplifiers including tube reissues, solid-state practice amps, and digital modeling amps. For more information, visit Vox's website or contact them directly. Source: David Petersen & Dick Denney, Vox: The Vox Story.

DATING VOX AMPLIFIERS

The only way to date Vox amplifiers is to know when and what models were made during certain times. Since ownership has changed so many times over this manufacturer's lifespan, the serialization records haven't survived through today. Cosmetics and a niche for looking at Vox amps is the best way to date amps so far. It should be noted that Vox has made U.S. and British amps. Some were special only to the U.S. or Britain and others were equivalents of each other. Make sure to take note as not to mix things up.

Here is a list of changes that happened during the years as far as cosmetics, and other features that can be detected by looking at it.

COVERING - Vox started making amps with Blonde covering in 1958. Some of the early coverings were a two-tone gray/cream. Blond covering was used until around 1962 when dark covering was introduced. There have been some models found in 1961 and 1962 that had black, red or blue samples. Cabinets remained covered in dark covering up until current.

GRILLES - In 1958 the original grille cloth was brown latticed however a plain cloth is known to exist. The brown latticed covering was in use until 1964 when it was changed to black latticed. The black grille covering is in use today.

CONTROL PANELS - The original Vox control panel was black with gold legend. This was used for two years between 1958 and 1959. In 1960, the panel was changed to a copper and this lasted until 1964. In 1965, a dark gray panel was introduced with a metallic legend. In 1978, the control panel was changed to a spray paint/screen print legend with the same color.

FEATURES ON THE AMP - There are other certain features on the amp that were changed throughout the years that help identify the approximate year.

1958 - At the beginning of 1958, amps had small letters for the Vox emblem, a small Jennings embossing on the frame, round control knobs, a small 10 or 15 badge on the lower left, Audiom speakers, brass ventilators, and a handle.

1959 - Knobs were now pointer (chicken head knobs), all models have 4 inputs, an "A J.M.I. Product" legend appears between the input jacks, otherwise same as 1958.

MSR/NOTES	100%	EXCELLENT	AVERAGE	LAST MSR

1960 - 6-input models with three channels, otherwise same as 1958.

1961 - Blue "Vox" speakers in amplifiers, a J.M.I Product logo on lower right part of control panel.

1962 - Top Boost models made their first appearance. These models would have treble and bass controls on the back.

1963 - Injection-molded vents introduced, dark covering varies in texture from smooth to rough, quite random.

1964 - Top Boost controls now part of the control panel, corner protectors added to cabinet, and hardware injection molding.

1965 - Black speaker cloth introduced, speakers in lead models are changed to a silver color, and the mains switch is changed to a 5-way rotary.

1966 - Black ventilators introduced.

1967 - Solid-state amplifiers begin to take off.

1968 - "A Vox Product" logo introduced on control panel, the GZ34 rectifier is replaced with a solid-state system.

1969-1991 - Information is tough to come by with all of the changes in ownership over the years. Research still underway.

ELECTRIC TUBE AMPLIFIERS: AC SERIES, EARLY MODELS (1950S-1970S)

The AC-30 model was originally known as the AC-30/4, which meant it only had four input jacks. It was changed in 1960 to the AC-30/6 with six jacks. Early models of the AC-30 have Audiom 60 speakers. Later models have Celestion Model G12 speakers made especially for Vox. This model was also available later with 2-15" Vox Celestion speakers. In 1963, dark covering was introduced. The Original Top-Boost AC-30 came from a separate bass and treble control mounted on the back of the amp separately from the control panel.

AC-2/AC-4 – 3.5W, 1-8 in. Elac speaker, tubes: preamp: 1 X 7025, 1 X 6267, power: 1 X EL84, rectifier: 6V4, single channel, tremolo, top control panel, two inputs, three black pointer knobs (v, tone, s), blond or brown covering, brown grille, mfg. 1960-1965.

courtesy John Beeson/The Music Shoppe   courtesy John Beeson/The Music Shoppe

	N/A	$1,200 - 1,500	$725 - 900	

This model was originally called the AC-2 until late 1961 when it was changed to the AC-4.

AC-10 – 12W, 1-10 in. Vox speaker, tube chassis: preamp: 1 X EF86, 1 X ECF82, 1 X ECC83/12AX7, power: 2 X EL84, rectifier: EZ81, two channels, tremolo, top control panel, four input jacks, five knobs (vol, tone, s, depth), blond or brown covering, brown grille, mfg. 1958-1965.

	N/A	$2,200 - 2,750	$1,325 - 1,650	

* AC-10 Twin – similar to the AC-10 except has 2-10 in. speakers, mfg. 1962-65.

courtesy solidbodyguitar.com, Inc.   courtesy solidbodyguitar.com, Inc.

	N/A	$2,600 - 3,250	$1,575 - 1,950	

»AC-10 Reverb Twin – similar to the AC-10 Twin, except in piggyback configuration with a separate head and 2-10 in. speaker cabinet, a seven-tube chassis, preamp: 1 X 12AX7/ECC83, 3 X 12AU7/ECC82, power: 2 X EL84, rectifier: EZ31, and reverb with a reverb control, mfg. 1963-65.

	N/A	$2,800 - 3,500	$1,675 - 2,100	

MSR/NOTES	100%	EXCELLENT	AVERAGE	LAST MSR

AC-15 – 15W, 1-12 in. Vox Celestion speaker, guitar combo, eight-tube chassis, preamp: 1 X EF86, 3 X 12AX7/ECC83, 1 X 12AU7/ECC82, power: 2 X EL84, rectifier: EZ81, two channels, vibrato, top control panel, four inputs, six knobs (vibrato speed, vib/trem, Ch. 1 v, Ch. 2 v, brilliance, top cut), blond covering, brown grille, mfg. 1958-1965.

| | N/A | $3,550 - 4,200 | $1,775 - 2,200 | |

* **AC-15 Twin** – similar to the AC-15, except has 2-12 in. speakers, mfg. 1961-65.

| | N/A | $4,100 - 4,800 | $2,050 - 2,500 | |

AC-30/4 TWIN – 30W, 2-12 in. Vox Celestion Alnico speakers, guitar combo, 10-tube chassis: preamp: 1 X EF86, 3 X 12AX7 (ECC83), 1 X 12AU7 (ECC82), power: 4 X EL84, rectifier: GZ34 (5AR4), two channels, vibrato/tremolo, top control panel, four inputs (two per channel), six black pointer knobs (vib/trem speed, vib/trem depth, Ch. 1 v, Ch. 2 v, Ch. 1 brilliance, Ch. 2 top cut), blond covering, brown grille, mfg. 1960-61.

| | N/A | $6,000 - 7,500 | $3,600 - 4,500 | |

AC-30/6 TWIN – 30W, 2-12 in. Vox Celestion Alnico speakers, guitar combo, 10-tube chassis: preamp: 4 X 12AX7 (ECC83), 1 X 12AU7 (ECC82), power: 4 X EL84, rectifier: GZ34 (5AR4), three channels, vibrato/tremolo, top control panel, six inputs (two per channel, vib/trem, normal, brilliant), six black pointer knobs (vib/trem speed, vib/trem depth, three volumes, one per channel, tone), blond covering, brown grille, mfg. 1961-1972.

 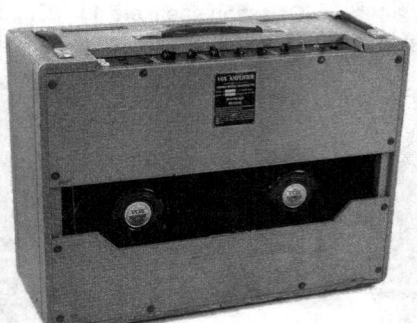 

courtesy solidbodyguitar.com, Inc.　　courtesy solidbodyguitar.com, Inc.　　courtesy Savage Audio

	100%	EXCELLENT	AVERAGE	
1960-1963	N/A	$4,300 - 5,000	$2,400 - 2,700	
1964-1966	N/A	$3,500 - 4,000	$1,800 - 2,250	
1967-1969	N/A	$3,000 - 3,500	$1,650 - 2,000	
1970s	N/A	$2,500 - 3,000	$1,300 - 1,650	

The AC-30/4 and AC-30/6 were produced concurrently in 1961, but the AC-30/4 was quickly discontinued in favor of the AC-30/6. Several variations of the AC-30/6 were produced including bass, normal, and treble models that were all voiced differently for their application.

* **AC-30/6 Super Twin** – similar to the AC-30/6 except in a piggyback version with a separate head and 2-12 in. Vox Clesetion speaker cabinet, mfg. 1962-67.

| 1962-1963 | N/A | $3,200 - 4,000 | $1,925 - 2,400 | |
| 1964-1967 | N/A | $2,600 - 3,250 | $1,550 - 1,950 | |

»**AC-30/6 Super Twin Reverb I** – similar to the AC-30/6 Super Twin except has reverb with an additional 2 X 12AX7 (7025) preamp tubes for a total of 6 X 12AX7 (7025), mfg. mid-1960s.

| | N/A | $3,500 - 4,250 | $2,200 - 2,750 | |

»**AC-30/6 Super Twin Reverb II** – similar to the AC-30/6 Super Twin except has two separate speaker cabinets and reverb with an additional 2 X 12AX7 (7025) preamp tubes for a total of 6 X 12AX7 (7025), mfg. mid-1960s.

| | N/A | $3,500 - 4,250 | $2,200 - 2,750 | |

* **AC-30/6 Twin Top Boost** – - similar to the AC-30/6 Twin, except has an additional treble and volume controls driven by an additional 12AX7 preamp tube, mfg. 1961-1972.

1961-1963	N/A	$4,000 - 5,000	$2,500 - 3,300	
1964-1966	N/A	$3,250 - 4,000	$2,100 - 2,650	
1967-1969	N/A	$2,700 - 3,250	$1,750 - 2,200	
1970s	N/A	$2,250 - 2,750	$1,400 - 1,750	

The Top Boost unit was initially an aftermarket add-on offered by Vox and the bass and treble controls were mounted on a small vertical white control panel on the back of the amplifier. Starting in 1963, the Top Boost unit became available as part of the actual control panel.

»**AC-30/6 Super Twin Top Boost** – similar to the AC-30/6 Twin Top Boost except in piggyback configuration with a separate head and speaker cabinet, mfg. 1961-mid 1960s.

| | N/A | $4,000 - 5,000 | $2,500 - 3,300 | |

MSR/NOTES	100%	EXCELLENT	AVERAGE	LAST MSR

»*AC-30/6 Super Twin Top Boost Reverb* – similar to the AC-30/6 Super Twin Top Boost except has reverb, mfg. 1961-mid 1960s.

| | N/A | $4,250 - 5,250 | $2,650 - 3,350 | |

AC-50 SUPER TWIN – 50W, Piggyback with a 2-12 in. cabinet with a mid-range horn, tubes: preamp: 3 X 7025, 12AU7, power: 2 X EL34, 5AR4 rectifier, dual channels, top control panel, four input jacks, six black knobs (2v, 2b, 2t one for each channel), black covering, dark grille, mfg. 1964-1973.

courtesy solidbodyguitar.com, Inc.   courtesy solidbodyguitar.com, Inc.

| | N/A | $1,700 - 2,000 | $850 - 1,050 | |

This model was originally aimed for the bassist.

AC-100 SUPER DELUXE – 100W, Piggyback, cabinet contains 4-12 in. Vox Celestion Alnico speakers and 2 midrange horns, tubes: preamp: 7025, 2 X 12AU7, power: 4 X EL34, one channel, top control panel, two inputs, three black knobs (v, b, t), black covering, dark grille, mfg. 1964-late 1960s.

| | N/A | $2,125 - 2,500 | $1,075 - 1,325 | |

This model was meant to be used with the new Beatle speaker cabinet.

AC-120 – 120W, 2-12 in. heavy-duty speakers, tube combo with 4 X EL34 power tubes, dual channels, reverb, distortion, top control panel, four inputs (two normal, two bright), 14 black knobs (v1, v2, b, m, t, presence, five band harmonic balance knobs, distortion, r, MV), brown covering, brown diagonal grille, mfg. 1975-late 1970s.

| | N/A | $1,000 - 1,300 | $750 - 900 | |

ELECTRIC TUBE AMPLIFIERS: AC SERIES, RECENT MODELS (1990S-2000S)

AC-15 TOP BOOST (1990S PRODUCTION) – 15W, 1-12 in. Bulldog speaker, tube combo, preamp: 5 X ECC83, ECC82, power: 2 X EL84, 5Y3 rectifier, single channel, top control panel, two inputs, seven black pointer knobs (v, t, b, reverb, s, depth, MV), black covering, diagonal brown grille, mfg. 1996-2002.

| | N/A | $750 - 900 | $600 - 700 | $1,375 |

* Add $150 for chrome stand.
* Add $35 for cover.

* *AC-15TBX* – similar to the AC-15 Top Boost, except has 1-12 in. Celestion G12 Alnico Vox "blue" speaker, mfg. 1996-2002.

| | N/A | $800 - 950 | $625 - 725 | $1,675 |

* Add $150 for chrome stand. Add $35 for cover.

AC-30 LIMITED EDITION – 36W combo, 2-12 in. Vox Celestion Alnico speakers, tubes: preamp: 7 X 7025, 12AU7 power: 4 X EL84, three channels, vibrato/tremolo, top control panel, six inputs (two per channel, vib/trem, normal, brilliant), eight black pointer knobs (vib/trem speed, vib/trem depth, three volumes, one per channel, b, t, cut), blond or brown covering, brown grille, mfg. 1990-91.

| | N/A | $1,875 - 2,200 | $925 - 1,150 | |

These models were available in a blonde or dark finish covering. There is a label inside indicating the 30th anniversary of the AC-30 inside. These amplifiers were built to commemorate the original AC-30 of the early 1960s.

* *AC-30 TB Collector* – similar to the AC-30 Limited Edition, except finished in a mahogany cabinet, mfg. 1990-91.

| | N/A | $1,875 - 2,200 | $925 - 1,150 | |

* *AC-30TBR (Reverb)* – similar to the AC-30, except has reverb with reverb controls, mfg. 1990-91.

| | N/A | $2,200 - 2,500 | $1,200 - 1,500 | |

* *AC-30 Top Boost Vintage Head and Speaker Cabinet* – similar in chassis to the AC-30 Limited Edition, is a head-unit that sits atop a 4-12 in. speaker cabinet, available in blonde or black covering, mfg. 1990-91.

| | N/A | $2,200 - 2,500 | $1,250 - 1,500 | |

AC-30/6 TOP BOOST (1993-2004 MFG.) – 33W, 2-12 in.G12M-25W "Greenback" speakers, tube combo, preamp: 5 X ECC83, ECC82, power, 4 X EL84 (class A), GZ34 rectifier, three channels, vibrato/tremolo, top control panel, six inputs (three per channel), eight black pointer knobs (v for each channel, vib/trem speed, vib/trem, b, t, cut), black covering, diagonal brown grille, three handles, mfg. 1993-2004.

| | N/A | $1,200 - 1,400 | $850 - 975 | $2,600 |

MSR/NOTES	100%	EXCELLENT	AVERAGE	LAST MSR

* *AC-30/6 TBX* – similar to the AC-30/6 Top Boost except has 2-12 in. Celestion G12 "blue" speakers, mfg. 1993-2004.

	N/A	$1,500 - 1,700	$1,000 - 1,150	$3,200

- Add $200 for the Chrome stand.
- Add $45 for cover.

ELECTRIC TUBE AMPLIFIERS: AC4 SERIES (RECENT MFG.)

AC-4 Combo (AC4TV)
courtesy Vox

AC-4 Head (AC4TVH)
courtesy Vox

AC-4 Mini Combo (AC4TVMINI)
courtesy Vox

AC-4 COMBO (AC4TV) – 4W, 1-10 in. Celestion VX10 speaker, guitar combo, two-tube chassis, preamp: 1 X 12AX7, power: 1 X EL84, solid-state rectifier, single channel, top black control panel, single input, three white chickenhead knobs (v, tone, three-way output power knob [4W, 1W, or 1/4W]), power switch, external speaker jack, white covering, brown diagonal Vox grille cloth with Vox logo in upper right hand corner, 13.75 in. wide, 14.75 in. tall, 8.5 in. deep, 19.8 lbs., mfg. summer 2009-present.

MSR $350	$325	$210 - 240	$105 - 130	

AC-4 HEAD (AC4TVH) – 4W, guitar head-unit, two-tube chassis, preamp: 1 X 12AX7, power: 1 X EL84, solid-state rectifier, single channel, top black control panel, single input, three white chickenhead knobs (v, tone, three-way output power knob [4W, 1W, or 1/4W]), power switch, external speaker jack, white covering, brown diagonal Vox grille cloth with Vox logo in upper right hand corner, mfg. summer 2009-disc.

	$200	$130 - 160	$85 - 110	$300

AC-4 MINI COMBO (AC4TVMINI) – 4W (switchable to 1W or 1/10W), 1-6.5 in. Vox Original speaker, guitar combo, two-tube chassis, preamp: 1 X 12AX7, power: 1 X EL84, solid-state rectifier, single channel, top black control panel, single input, three white chickenhead knobs (v, tone, three-way output power knob [4W, 1W, or 1/10W]), power switch, external speaker jack, white covering, brown diagonal Vox grille cloth with Vox logo in upper right hand corner, 10.25 in. wide, 11 in. tall, 6.75 in. deep, 13.5 lbs., mfg. 2011-disc.

	$200	$120 - 150	$75 - 95	$300

V112TV SPEAKER CABINET – 1-12 in. Celestion VX12 speaker, 16 ohm impedance, designed for use with the AC4 Head (AC4TVH), white covering, brown diagonal grille cloth with Vox logo in upper right-hand corner, mfg. summer 2009-disc.

MSR $250	$170	$95 - 120	$65 - 75	

ELECTRIC TUBE AMPLIFIERS: AC CLASSIC PLUS SERIES

AC50 Classic Plus Combo (AC50CP2)
courtesy Vox

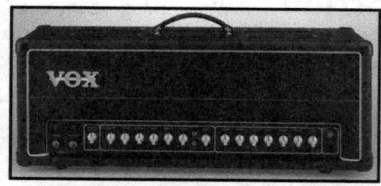
AC100 Classic Plus Combo (AC100CPH)
courtesy Vox

AC50 CLASSIC PLUS HEAD (AC50CPH) – 50W, guitar head-unit, six-tube chassis, preamp: 4 X 12AX7/ECC83, power: 2 X EL34B, two channels, reverb, front black control panel, single input, 15 white chickenhead knobs (Ch. 1: g, t, m, b, tone cut, r, v, Ch. 2: g, t, m, b, p, r, v, All: MV), channel switch, bright switch, fat switch, power and standby switches, effects loop with selectable level control and bypass switching, balanced XLR line out, unbalanced 1/4 in. line out, two-button footswitch, black covering with white piping, 27.6 in. wide, 10.4 in. tall, 11.2 in. deep, 48.5 lbs., mfg. 2007-08.

	N/A	$650 - 775	$425 - 500	$1,450

MSR/NOTES	100%	EXCELLENT	AVERAGE	LAST MSR

* **AC50 Classic Plus Combo (AC50CP2)** – similar to the AC50 Classic Plus Head (AC50CPH), except in combo configuration with 2-12 in. Vox original design speakers and a brown diamond grille, 27.6 in. wide, 21.3 in. tall, 10.4 in. deep, 77.2 lbs., mfg. 2007-08.

	N/A	$750 - 900	$500 - 575	$1,750

AC100 CLASSIC PLUS HEAD (AC100CPH) – 100W, guitar head-unit, eight-tube chassis, preamp: 4 X 12AX7/ECC83, power: 4 X EL34B, two channels, reverb, front black control panel, single input, 15 white chickenhead knobs (Ch. 1: g, t, m, b, tone cut, r, v, Ch. 2: g, t, m, b, p, r, v, All: MV), channel switch, bright switch, fat switch, power and standby switches, effects loop with selectable level control and bypass switching, balanced XLR line out, unbalanced 1/4 in. line out, two-button footswitch, black covering with white piping, 27.6 in. wide, 10.4 in. tall, 11.2 in. deep, 55.1 lbs., mfg. 2007-09.

	N/A	$700 - 850	$500 - 550	$1,650

ELECTRIC TUBE AMPLIFIERS: AC CUSTOM CLASSIC/CUSTOM SERIES

AC10 Custom Combo (Model AC10C1)
courtesy Vox

AC15 Custom Classic (Model CC1)
courtesy Vox

AC-15 Custom Twin (AC15C2)
courtesy Vox

AC4 CUSTOM COMBO (MODEL AC4C1) – 4W, 1-12 in. Celestion VX12 speaker, guitar combo, three-tube chassis, preamp: 2 X 12AX7, power: 1 X EL84, single channel, top black control panel with tan accents, single input, four knobs (g, b, t, v), power switch, black covering, brown diamond grille cloth, 15.98 in. wide, 17.76 in. tall, 8.31 in. deep, 23.37 lbs., mfg. 2012-present.

MSR $500	$350	$230 - 265	$115 - 140	

Also available in Limited Edition models featuring red, blue, or tan covering.

AC10 CUSTOM COMBO (MODEL AC10C1) – 10W, 1-10 in. Celestion VX10 speaker, guitar combo, four-tube chassis, preamp: 2 X 12AX7, power: 2 X EL84, single channel, reverb, 2-band EQ, top black control panel with tan accents, single input, five knobs (g, b, t, reverb, v), power switch, black covering, brown diamond grille cloth, 20.47 in. wide, 16.14 in. tall, 8.27 in. deep, 27.1 lbs., mfg. 2015-present.

MSR $650	$450	$295 - 325	$145 - 180	

• Also available in Limited Edition Tan covering.

AC15 CUSTOM CLASSIC (MODEL CC1) – 15W, 1-12 in. Wharfedale GSH12-30 speaker, guitar combo, tube chassis, preamp: 2 X 12AX7/ECC83, power: 2 X 6BQ5/EL84, solid-state rectifier, single channel, reverb, tremolo, top black control panel, single input, seven black chickenhead knobs (MV, trem depth, trem speed, r, b, t, v), footswitch, impedance selector, effects loop, Black covering, Brown Diamond grille, 48 lbs., mfg. 2006-09.

	N/A	$400 - 475	$250 - 300	$899

* **AC-15 Custom Classic (Model CC1X)** – similar to the AC-15 Custom Classic (Model CC1), except has a Celestion Blue 15W AlNiCo speaker, mfg. 2006-09.

	N/A	$600 - 700	$350 - 425	$1,300

AC-15 CUSTOM (AC15C1) – 15W, 1-12 in. Celestion G12M Greenback speaker, guitar combo, five-tube chassis, preamp: 3 X 12AX7, power: 2 X EL84, two channels, reverb, tremolo, top dark gray control panel with tan accents, two inputs (normal, top boost), nine black knobs (Normal Ch.: v, Top Boost Ch.: v, t, b, All: r, trem speed, trem depth, Master tone cut, MV), power switch, standby switch, rear panel: external speaker jack, extension speaker jack, footswitch jack, black covering, brown diamond grille cloth, 23.75 in. wide, 18 in. tall, 10.5 in. deep, 48.5 lbs., optional two-button footswitch, mfg. 2010-present.

MSR $882	$625	$400 - 475	$205 - 250	

• Add $40 (MSR $50) for two-button footswitch (Model VFS2A).

Also available in Limited Edition models featuring Tan, Red, or Blue covering.

* **AC-15 Custom Twin (AC15C2)** – similar to the AC-15 Custom (AC15C1), except has 2-12 in. Celestion G12M Greenback speakers, 27.65 in. wide, 22 in. tall, 10.5 in. deep, 66.5 lbs., optional two-button footswitch, mfg. 2011-present.

MSR $1,120	$800	$475 - 575	$275 - 350	

• Add $40 (MSR $50) for two-button footswitch (Model VFS2A).

MSR/NOTES	100%	EXCELLENT	AVERAGE	LAST MSR

AC15 Custom Head (Model AC15CH)
courtesy Vox

AC30 Custom Classic (Model CC2X)
courtesy Vox

AC30 Custom Head (Model AC30CH)
courtesy Vox

AC15 CUSTOM HEAD (MODEL AC15CH) – 15W, guitar head unit, five-tube chassis, preamp: 3 X 12AX7, power: 2 X EL84, two channels, reverb, tremolo, top dark gray control panel with tan accents, two inputs (normal, top boost), nine black knobs (Normal Ch.: v, Top Boost Ch.: v, t, b, All: r, trem speed, trem depth, Master tone cut, MV), power switch, standby switch, rear panel: external speaker jack, extension speaker jack, footswitch jack, black covering, brown diamond grille cloth, 24.02 in. wide, 11.18 in. tall, 10.5 in. deep, 33.73 lbs., optional two-button footswitch, new 2016.

MSR $800	$600	$400 - 450	$195 - 240	

AC30 CUSTOM CLASSIC (MODEL CC1) – 30W, 1-12 in. NeoDog speaker combo, tube chassis, preamp: 3 X 12AX7/ECC83, power: 4 X 6BQ5/EL34, rectifier: GZ34, two channels, tremolo, reverb, top red control panel, two inputs, ten black chickenhead knobs (Normal: v, Top Boost: v, t, b, All: r tone, r mix, s, d, tone cut, MV), footswitch, impedance selector, effects loop, Black covering, Brown Diamond grille, mfg. summer 2004-06.

	N/A	$625 - 725	$375 - 450	$1,400

* *AC30 Custom Classic (Model CC2)* – similar to the AC30 CC1, except has 2-12 in. Celestion GSH12-30 speakers, 70.5 lbs., mfg. 2004-09.

	N/A	$725 - 850	$450 - 525	$1,650

* *AC30 Custom Classic (Model CC2X)* – similar to the AC30 CC1, except has 2-12 in. Celestion Blue 15W Alnico speakers, 70.5 lbs., mfg. 2004-09.

	N/A	$1,000 - 1,300	$750 - 900	$2,500

* *AC30 Custom Classic Head (Model CCH)* – similar to the AC30 CC1, except in head-unit configuration, 41.9 lbs., mfg. 2004-09.

	N/A	$575 - 675	$325 - 400	$1,250

AC-30 CUSTOM (AC30C2) – 30W, 2-12 in. Celestion G12M Greenback speakers, guitar combo, seven-tube chassis, preamp: 3 X 12AX7, power: 4 X EL84, two channels, reverb, tremolo, top pink control panel with white accents, four inputs (two normal, two top boost), ten black knobs (Normal Ch.: v, Top Boost Ch.: v, t, b, All: r tone, r level, trem speed, trem depth, Master tone cut, MV), power switch, standby switch, rear panel: effects loop, external speaker jack, extension speaker jack, footswitch jack, black covering, brown diamond grille cloth, 27.65 in. wide, 21.9 in. tall, 10.5 in. deep, 71 lbs., optional two-button footswitch, mfg. 2010-present.

MSR $1,540	$1,100	$725 - 825	$350 - 450	

• Add $40 (MSR $50) for two-button footswitch (Model VFS2A).

* *AC-30 Custom Twin (AC30C2X)* – similar to the AC-30 Custom (AC30C2), except has 2-12 in. Celestion Blue Alnico speakers, 73.6 lbs., optional two-button footswitch, mfg. 2010-disc.

	$1,500	$850 - 1,050	$525 - 625	$2,000

• Add $40 (MSR $50) for two-button footswitch (Model VFS2A).

AC30 CUSTOM HEAD (MODEL AC30CH) – 30W, guitar head unit, five-tube chassis, preamp: 3 X 12AX7, power: 2 X EL84, two channels, reverb, tremolo, top red control panel, four inputs (normal high, normal low, top boost high, top boost low), ten black knobs (Normal Ch.: v, Top Boost Ch.: v, t, b, All: r tone, r level, trem speed, trem depth, Master tone cut, MV), power switch, standby switch, rear panel: external speaker jack, extension speaker jack, footswitch jack, black covering, brown diamond grille cloth, 27.76 in. wide, 11.18 in. tall, 10.5 in. deep, 41.48 lbs., optional two-button footswitch, new 2016.

MSR $1,200	$900	$575 - 675	$295 - 350	

• Also available in Limited Edition model with Blue covering.

AC30BM BRIAN MAY LIMITED EDITION – 30W, 2-12 in. Celestion Blue 15W AlNiCo speakers, tube chassis, preamp: 2 X 12AX7/ECC83, power: 4 X 6BQ5/EL34, rectifier: GZ34, single channel, top red control panel with Brian May's signature, single input, single volume knob, half-power switch, footswitch for boost switch, Black covering, Brown Diamond grille, 70.5 lbs., mfg. 2006-08.

	N/A	$1,400 - 1,700	$900 - 1,100	$3,000

Only 500 of these amps were scheduled to be produced.

MSR/NOTES	100%	EXCELLENT	AVERAGE	LAST MSR

**AC-4 Hand Wired Combo (AC4HW1)
courtesy Vox**

**AC15 Heritage Handwired Combo
(AC15H1TV) courtesy Vox**

**AC30 Heritage Handwired Combo (AC30H2)
courtesy Vox**

ELECTRIC TUBE AMPLIFIERS: AC HAND-WIRED SERIES

AC-4 HAND WIRED COMBO (AC4HW1) – 4W, 1-12 in. Celestion G12M Greenback speaker, guitar combo, three-tube chassis, preamp: 2 X 12AX7, power: 1 X EL84, single channel, top black control panel, two inputs (high/low), four cream knobs (v, t, b, MV), Top Boost hot/cool switch, power switch, rear panel: external speaker jack, footswitch jack, fawn vinyl covering, brown diamond grille cloth, 15.94 in. wide, 17.72 in. tall, 10.25 in. deep, 29.74 lbs., single-button VFS1 footswitch and dust cover included, mfg. 2012-present.

| MSR $1,100 | $800 | $525 - 600 | $260 - 325 | |

AC15 HERITAGE HANDWIRED HEAD (AC15HTVH) – 15W, guitar head-unit, seven-tube chassis, preamp: 1 X EF86, 3 X 12AX7/ECC83, power: 2 X EL84, rectifier: 1 X EZ81, two channels (EF86/Top Boost), top black control panel, two inputs, six white chickenhead knobs (Ch. 1: v, three-way brilliance, Ch. 2: v, t, b, All: top cut), bass shift switch, pentode/triode EF86 mode switch, O/P pentode/triode (15W/7.5W) switch, power switch, speaker impedance selector switch, vintage "TV-style" cabinet, cream vinyl covering, brown diamond grille with pre-1960 Vox logo, 31.5 lbs., mfg. 2007-2010.

| | N/A | $600 - 700 | $350 - 425 | $1,300 |

This amp combines several tones from the amps of the early 1960s Vox era.

* *AC15 Heritage Handwired Combo (AC15H1TV)* – similar to the AC15H1TV Head, except in combo configuration with 1-12 in. Celestion Alnico Blue speaker, 20.75 in. wide, 20.75 in. tall, 10.375 in. deep, 49.6 lbs., mfg. 2007-2010.

| | N/A | $850 - 1,000 | $575 - 650 | $1,900 |

»*AC15 Heritage Handwired Combo Limited Edition (AC15H1TVL)* – similar to the AC15H1TV Heritage Combo, except features an oiled cabinet, 54 lbs., mfg. 2007-08.

| | N/A | $1,150 - 1,400 | $725 - 850 | $2,700 |

Only 200 of these amplifiers are scheduled for production. It also comes with a copy of the book *Vox: The JMI Years* by Jim Elyea.

AC-15 HANDWIRED COMBO (AC15HW1) – 15W, 1-12 in. Celestion G12M Greenback speaker, guitar combo, six-tube chassis, preamp: 3 X ECC83/12AX7, power: 2 X EL84, rectifier: EZ81, two channels (normal and top boost), top brown control panel, four inputs (two per channel, high/low), six cream knobs (Normal Ch.: v, Top Boost Ch.: v, t, b, All: tone cut, MV), Normal Ch. bright switch, Top Boost hot/cool switch, MV bypass switch, power switch, standby switch, rear panel: external speaker jack, extension speaker jack, footswitch jack, fawn vinyl covering, brown diamond grille cloth, 24 in. wide, 21.65 in. tall, 10.25 in. deep, 49 lbs., single-button VFS1 footswitch and dust cover included, mfg. 2011-present.

| MSR $1,820 | $1,300 | $850 - 975 | $425 - 525 | |

* *AC-15 Handwired Combo (AC15HW1X)* – similar to the AC-15 Handwired Combo (AC15HW1), except has 1-12 in. Celestion Alnico Blue speaker, 50.25 lbs., single-button VFS1 footswitch and dust cover included, mfg. 2011-disc.

| $1,450 | $850 - 1,050 | $500 - 625 | $2,000 |

AC-30 HAND-WIRED HEAD – 30W, head-unit only, all hand-wired tube chassis, preamp: 5 X ECC83, power: 4 X EL84, rectifier: GZ34, reverb, tremolo, top maroon control panel, two inputs, nine knobs (v, t, m, tone cut, s, d, r, tone, MV), black covered cabinet, brown VOX style grille, mfg. 2003-04.

| | N/A | $1,500 - 1,800 | N/A | $3,250 |

* *AC-30 Hand-Wired Combo* – similar to the AC-30 Head, except in combo version with 2-12 in. speakers, mfg. 2003-04.

| | N/A | $1,900 - 2,300 | N/A | $4,000 |

• Add $150 for chrome stand.
• Add $35 for cover.

AC30 HERITAGE HANDWIRED HEAD (AC30HH) – 30W, guitar head-unit, nine-tube chassis, preamp: 1 X EF86, 3 X 12AX7/ECC83, power: 4 X EL84, rectifier: 1 X GZ34, two channels (EF86/Top Boost), top black control panel, two inputs, six white chickenhead knobs (Ch. 1: v, three-way brilliance, Ch. 2: v, t, b, All: top cut), bass shift switch, pentode/triode EF86 mode switch, O/P pentode/triode (30W/15W) switch, power switch, speaker impedance selector switch, vintage "TV-style" cabinet, cream vinyl covering, brown diamond grille with pre-1960 Vox logo, 23.9 in. wide, 11.7 in. tall, 10.2 in. deep, 44.1 lbs., mfg. 2008-2010.

| | N/A | $700 - 850 | $425 - 500 | $1,599 |

This amp combines several tones from the amps of the early 1960s Vox era.

MSR/NOTES	100%	EXCELLENT	AVERAGE	LAST MSR

* **AC30 Heritage Handwired Combo (AC30H2)** – similar to the AC30HH Head, except in combo configuration with 1-12 in. Celestion Alnico Blue speaker, 27.4 in. wide, 22.2 in. tall, 10.2 in. deep, 75.2 lbs., mfg. 2008-2010.

	N/A	$1,150 - 1,400	$800 - 950	$2,599

»**AC30 Heritage Handwired Combo Limited Edition (AC30H2)** – similar to the AC30H2 Heritage Combo, except features an oiled cabinet, 76.1 lbs., mfg. 2008-2010.

	N/A	$1,600 - 1,950	$1,000 - 1,200	$3,599

Only 200 of these amplifiers were scheduled for production. It also came with a copy of the book *Vox: The JMI Years* by Jim Elyea.

AC-30 HANDWIRED HEAD (AC30HWHD) – 30W, guitar head-unit, eight-tube chassis, preamp: 3 X ECC83/12AX7, power: 4 X EL84, rectifier: GZ34, two channels (normal and top boost), top brown control panel, four inputs (two per channel, high/low), six cream knobs (Normal Ch.: v, Top Boost Ch.: v, t, b, All: tone cut, MV), Normal Ch. bright switch, Top Boost hot/cool switch, MV bypass switch, power switch, standby switch, rear panel: external speaker jack, extension speaker jack, footswitch jack, fawn vinyl covering, brown diamond grille cloth, 27.75 in. wide, 9.85 in. tall, 10.25 in. deep, 41.5 lbs., single-button VFS1 footswitch, dust cover, and speaker cable included, mfg. 2011-present.

MSR $1,750	$1,300	$750 - 925	$450 - 550	

* **AC-30 Handwired Combo (AC30HW2)** – similar to the AC-30 Handwired Head (AC30HWHD), except in combo configuration with 2-12 in. Celestion G12M Greenback speakers, 27.75 in. wide, 21.65 in. tall, 10.25 in. deep, 68 lbs., single-button VFS1 footswitch and dust cover included, mfg. 2011-present.

MSR $2,380	$1,700	$1,100 - 1,275	$550 - 675	

»**AC-30 Handwired Combo (AC30HW2X)** – similar to the AC-30 Handwired Combo (AC30HW2), except has 2-12 in. Celestion Blue Alnico speakers, 70.5 lbs., single-button VFS1 footswitch and dust cover included, mfg. 2011-disc.

	$2,000	$1,125 - 1,400	$675 - 850	$2,600

ELECTRIC TUBE AMPLIFIERS: AV SERIES

AV15 Combo
courtesy Vox

AV30 Combo
(AC15H1TV) courtesy Vox

AV60 Combo
courtesy Vox

AV15 COMBO – 15W, 1-8 in. Vox original speaker, guitar combo, one-tube chassis, 1 X 12AX7 in both preamp and power stages, single channel, eight preamp circuits, reverb, top black control panel with tan accents, single input, eight black knobs (preamp circuit selector, g, t, m, b, v, power level, effect selector), bright switch, fat switch, bias switch, reactor switch, power switch, enclosed back, black covering, gray grille cloth, 17.72 in. wide, 14.84 in. tall, 9.21 in. deep, 16.9 lbs., new 2016.

MSR $310	$230	$150 - 175	$75 - 90	

AV30 COMBO – 30W, 1-10 in. Vox original speaker, guitar combo, two-tube chassis, preamp: 1 X 12AX7, power: 1 X 12AX7, dual channel, eight preamp circuits, reverb, top black control panel with tan accents, single input, fourteen black knobs (each channel: preamp circuit selector, g, t, m, b, v, all: power level, effect selector), bright switch, fat switch, bias switch, reactor switch, power switch, channel switch, footswitch jack, aux in, headphone in, enclosed back, black covering, gray grille cloth, 20.2 in. wide, 18.66 in. tall, 9.71 in. deep, 26.46 lbs., new 2016.

MSR $440	$325	$215 - 250	$105 - 130	

AV60 COMBO – 60W, 1-12 in. Vox original speaker, guitar combo, two-tube chassis, preamp: 1 X 12AX7, power: 1 X 12AX7, dual channel, eight preamp circuits, reverb, top black control panel with tan accents, single input, fourteen black knobs (each channel: preamp circuit selector, g, t, m, b, v, all: power level, effect selector), bright switch, fat switch, bias switch, reactor switch, power switch, channel switch, footswitch jack, aux in, headphone in, enclosed back, black covering, gray grille cloth, 23.23 in. wide, 19.33 in. tall, 10.71 in. deep, 36.6 lbs., new 2016.

MSR $570	$425	$280 - 325	$140 - 170	

ELECTRIC TUBE AMPLIFIERS: U.S. MODELS PRODUCED 1965-1966

The following models are tube amps produced by the Thomas Organ Company in California beginning in 1965 and lasting through 1966 when all models were converted to solid-state chassis.

MSR/NOTES	100%	EXCELLENT	AVERAGE	LAST MSR

BERKELEY SUPER REVERB (V-8) – ~17W, 2-10 in. Celestion (early models) or Vox Gold Bulldog speakers, guitar piggyback unit, seven-tube chassis: preamp: 3 X 12AX7 (ECC83), 1 X 12AU7 (ECC82), power: 2 X EL84, rectifier: EZ81, single channel, reverb, tremolo, top mounted control panel, two input jacks, six black knobs (v, t, b, r, trem s, trem depth), power switch, rear panel: 3rd input jack, footswitch jack, external speaker jack, aux. outlet, line reverse, black covering, brown diagonal grille, mfg. 1965-66.

	N/A	$1,000 - 1,250	$600 - 750	

The circuitry of the Berkeley Super Reverb V-8 was based on the Vox AC-15 circuitry with reverb. The Berkeley Super Reverb and Cambridge Reverb are very similar to each other, except the Berkeley Super Reverb is a piggyback unit and the Cambridge Reverb is a combo.

CAMBRIDGE REVERB (V-3/V103) – ~17W, 1-10 in. Celestion (early models) or Vox Gold Bulldog speaker, guitar combo, seven-tube chassis: preamp: 3 X ECC83, 1 X ECC82, power: 2 X EL84, rectifier: EZ81, single channel, reverb, tremolo, top mounted control panel, two input jacks, six black knobs (v, t, b, r, trem s, trem depth), power switch, rear panel: 3rd input jack, footswitch jack, external speaker jack, aux. outlet, line reverse, black covering, brown diagonal grille, mfg. 1965-66.

	N/A	$875 - 1,100	$525 - 650	

The circuitry of the Cambridge Reverb V-3/V103 was based on the Vox AC-15 circuitry with reverb. The Cambridge Reverb and Pacemaker are very similar to each other, except the Cambridge Reverb has reverb and the Pacemaker does not.

PACEMAKER (V-2/V102) – ~17W, 1-10 in. Celestion (early models) or Vox Gold Bulldog speaker, guitar combo, five-tube chassis: preamp: 2 X ECC83, power: 2 X EL84, rectifier: EZ81, single channel, tremolo, top mounted control panel, three input jacks, five black knobs (v, t, b, trem s, trem depth), power switch, rear panel: footswitch jack, external speaker jack, aux. outlet, black covering, brown diagonal grille, mfg. 1965-66.

	N/A	$800 - 1,000	$475 - 600	

The circuitry of the Pacemaker V-2 was based on the Vox AC-15 circuitry.

PATHFINDER (V-1/V101) – ~6W, 1-8 in. Vox Gold Bulldog speaker, guitar combo, four-tube chassis, preamp: ECC83, power: 1 X EL84, rectifier: EZ80, single channel, tremolo, top mounted control panel, two input jacks, five knobs (v, t, b, trem s, trem depth), power switch, rear panel: footswitch jack, line reverse switch, black covering, brown diagonal grille, mfg. 1965-66.

courtesy Savage Audio   *courtesy Savage Audio*

	N/A	$900 - 1,050	$450 - 550	

The circuitry of the Pathfinder V-1/V101 was based on the Vox AC-4 circuitry.

STUDENT – ~2W, 1-7 in. Vox speaker, guitar combo, three-tube chassis, preamp: 35W4, power: 1 X 12AU6, rectifier: 50C5, single channel, front mounted control panel, two input jacks, single volume knob with on/off switch, black covering, black diagonal grille, mfg. 1965-66.

	N/A	$250 - 300	$150 - 190	

ELECTRIC TUBE AMPLIFIERS: V (V-15 & V-125) SERIES

These amplifiers were the first efforts of Rose-Morris. The Escort Series (solid-state) debuted at the same time. Since these models were released in England and didn't get over to the U.S. much, very little are showing up in the American market.

V-15 – 15W, 2-10 in. speakers, guitar combo, five-tube chassis, preamp: 2 X ECC83, 1 X ECC81, power: 2 X EL84, single channel, top mounted control panel, two input jacks, five black knobs (v, t, m, b, MV), black covering, brown diagonal grille, mfg. 1980-mid-1980s.

	N/A	$425 - 500	$250 - 300	

V-125 LEAD – 125W, guitar head-unit, eight-tube chassis, preamp: 2 X ECC83, 1 X ECC82, 1 X ECC81, power: 4 X EL34, single channel, top mounted control panel, two input jacks (one normal, one brilliant), six control knobs (v, sensitivity, three equalizer knobs, MV), black covering, brown diagonal grille, mfg. 1980-mid 1980s.

	N/A	$425 - 500	$250 - 300	

* **VR212 Speaker Cabinet** – 2-12 in. speakers, designed for use with the V-125 Lead head-unit, mfg. 1980-mid 1980s.

	N/A	$250 - 300	$150 - 200	

* **V-125 Climax** – similar to the V-125 except in combo configuration with 2-12 in. speakers and has a distortion circuit with a distortion knob in place of sensitivity, mfg. 1979-mid 1980s.

	N/A	$500 - 600	$300 - 375	

MSR/NOTES	100%	EXCELLENT	AVERAGE	LAST MSR

* ***V-125 Bass*** – similar to the V-125 except has cabinets with 1-15 in. speakers, and the equalizer consists of the frequencies of 50, 100, 250, 500, and 1500 Hz, mfg. 1980-mid 1980s.

N/A	$600 - 750	$425 - 500	

ELECTRIC TUBE AMPLIFIERS: BRUNO SERIES

The Bruno Series was designed in conjunction with Tony Bruno of Tony Bruno Custom Amplifiers. Unique features of the Bruno Series include a quartet of 6V6 power tubes for an American sound and an Accutronics reverb unit driven by one 12AX7 and one 12AT7 tubes.

**Bruno (TB35C1)
courtesy Vox**

**Bruno (TB35C2)
courtesy Vox**

BRUNO (TB35C1) – 35W, 1-12 in. Celestion G12-65 speaker, guitar combo, nine-tube chassis, preamp: 3 X ECC83/12AX7, 1 X 12AX7, 1 X 12AT7, power: 4 X 6V6, solid-state rectifier, single channel, reverb, top black control panel, two inputs (high/low), six white knobs (v, t, m, b, r, MV), macho switch, tight bass boost switch, MV bypass switch, power switch, standby switch, rear panel: external speaker jack, extension speaker jack, footswitch jack, black covering, black diamond grille, 23.625 in. wide, 22.25 in. tall, 10.25 in. deep, 63.5 lbs., single-button VFS-1 footswitch and dust cover included, mfg. 2011-disc.

$1,200	$675 - 850	$400 - 500	$1,600

* ***Bruno (TB35C2)*** – similar to the Bruno (TB35C1), except has 2-12 in. Celestion G12-65 speakers, 27.375 in. wide, 22.25 in. tall, 10.25 in. deep, 73.8 lbs., single-button VFS-1 footswitch and dust cover included, mfg. 2011-disc.

$1,400	$800 - 1,000	$475 - 600	$1,900

ELECTRIC TUBE AMPLIFIERS: CONCERT SERIES

This series was introduced after the Venue series. The first model in the Concert series, The Concert 501, was basically a 50W version of the Dual 100 in the Venue series.

CONCERT 501 – 50W, 1-12 in. speaker, guitar combo, nine tube chassis, preamp: 5 X 7025, power: 4 X EL84, two channels, reverb, gain, front black control panel, two inputs (hi and lo), eleven black and white control knobs (Ch. 1: v, b, m, t, Ch. 2: gain, b, m, t, v, Both: r, MV), effects loop, extension speaker jack, headphone jack, black covering, black grille, mfg. 1984-87.

N/A	$475 - 550	$300 - 350	

* ***Concert 501/2*** – similar to the Concert 501, except has 2-10 in. speakers, mfg. 1984-87.

N/A	$475 - 550	$300 - 350	

CONCERT 100 – 100W, head-unit with two cabinets consisting of 4-12 in. speakers in each, eight tube chassis, preamp: 4 X 7025, power: 4 X EL34, single channel, front black control panel, two input jacks, six control knobs (gain, t, m, b, MV, presence), output jacks for speakers, black covering, diagonal black grille cloth, mfg. 1986-87.

Head Only	N/A	$300 - 350	$175 - 225
Speaker Cab	N/A	$200 - 250	$120 - 150
Head & Two Cabinet	N/A	$800 - 1,000	$550 - 650

This model was also available for a short time with blond covering in 1964.

ELECTRIC TUBE AMPLIFIERS: NIGHT TRAIN SERIES

LIL' NIGHT TRAIN (NT2H) – 2W, guitar head-unit, three-tube chassis, preamp: 2 X 12AX7, power: 1 X 12AU7, solid-state rectifier, single channel, front black control panel, single input, four white chickenhead knobs (g, t, b, v), bright/thick preamp switch, power switch, rear panel: one speaker jack, headphone jack, "armored lunchbox" chrome mirror metal casing with Vox logo and carrying handle, 8.75 in. wide, 4.625 in. tall, 4.625 in. deep, 11.6 lbs., speaker cable included, mfg. 2011-disc.

$250	$150 - 200	$95 - 120	$400

The Chassis of the Night Train NT15H is based on Vox's AC15.

MSR/NOTES	100%	EXCELLENT	AVERAGE	LAST MSR

Lil' Night Train (NT2H)
courtesy Vox

Night Train 15 Combo (NT15C1)
courtesy Vox

Night Train 15 Head Second Version
(NT15H-G2) courtesy Vox

NIGHT TRAIN 15 COMBO (NT15C1) – 15W, guitar combo amp, 1-12 in. speaker, five-tube chassis, preamp: 3 X 12AX7, power: 2 X EL84, solid-state rectifier, dual channel, top black control panel, single input, eight cream chickenhead knobs (bright g, girth g, girth v, t, m, b, master reverb, master volume), thick switch, bright/girth switch, dark switch, standby switch, power switch, top handle, black covering, black grille, 19.49 in. wide, 16.14 in. tall, 10.24 in. deep, 38.58 lbs., mfg. 2014-present.

MSR $720	$500	$325 - 375	$175 - 210	

Also available in Limited Edition version with Vox Classic covering (Model NT15C1-CL).

NIGHT TRAIN 15 HEAD FIRST VERSION (NT15H) – 15W, guitar head-unit, four-tube chassis, preamp: 2 X 12AX7/ECC83, power: 2 X EL84/6BQ5, solid-state rectifier, single channel, front black control panel, single input, five white chickenhead knobs (g, t, m, b, v), bright/thick preamp switch, pentode (15W)/standby/triode (7.5W) operating switch, power switch, two speaker jacks, "armored lunchbox" chrome mirror metal casing with Vox logo and carrying handle, 12.125 in. wide, 7 in. tall, 6.25 in. deep, 17 lbs., padded carrying case included, mfg. 2009-2013.

	$500	$325 - 375	$175 - 210	$700

The Chassis of the Night Train NT15H is based on Vox's AC15.

NIGHT TRAIN 15 HEAD SECOND VERSION (NT15H-G2) – 15W, guitar head-unit, five-tube chassis, preamp: 3 X 12AX7, power: 2 X EL84, solid-state rectifier, dual channel, front black control panel, single input, eight cream chickenhead knobs (bright g, girth g, girth v, t, m, b, master reverb, master volume), thick switch, bright/girth switch, dark switch, standby switch, power switch, three speaker jacks, footswitch jack, effect loop, top handle, black covering, black metal grille, 14.57 in. wide, 7.1 in. tall, 6.10 in. deep, 16 lbs., padded carrying case included, mfg. 2014-present.

MSR $699	$500	$325 - 375	$175 - 210	

NIGHT TRAIN 50 HEAD FIRST VERSION (NT50H) – 50W, guitar head-unit. six-tube chassis, preamp: 4 X 12AX7, power: 2 X EL34, solid-state rectifier, two channels (Bright/Girth), front black control panel, single input, 11 white chickenhead knobs (Bright Ch.: g, t, m, b, Girth Ch.: g, t, m, b, v, Master: tone cut, MV), channel switch, Bright Ch. thick switch, master tight switch, standby switch, power switch, rear panel: three speaker jacks, effects loop, footswitch jack, "armored lunchbox" chrome mirror metal casing with Vox logo and carrying handle, 18 in. wide, 9.25 in. tall, 6.875 in. deep, 26.8 lbs., speaker cable included, mfg. 2011-2013.

	$700	$425 - 525	$250 - 325	$1,000

NIGHT TRAIN 50 HEAD SECOND VERSION (NT50H-G2) – 50W, guitar head-unit. five-tube chassis, preamp: 3 X 12AX7, power: 2 X EL34, solid-state rectifier, two channels (Bright/Girth), front black control panel, single input, 12 cream chickenhead knobs (Bright Ch.: g, t, m, b, Girth Ch.: g, t, m, b, v, Master: reverb, tone cut, MV), channel switch, thick switch, standby switch, power switch, rear panel: three speaker jacks, effects loop, footswitch jack, speaker emulated D.I. jack, top handle, black covering, black metal grille, 17.72 in. wide, 8.46 in. tall, 6.5 in. deep, 26.9 lbs., speaker cable included, mfg. 2014-present.

MSR $979	$700	$450 - 525	$230 - 280	

ELECTRIC SS AMPLIFIERS: AC SERIES

Vox tried its first transistor amp with the T-60, which was a bass amp. They took the AC-30 and made it a solid-state, and issued a couple new AC amps that were solid-state as well.

AC-30 SOLID-STATE – 40W, 2-12 in. speakers, guitar combo, solid-state chassis, tremolo, top control panel, six inputs (three per channel), seven black control knobs (v1, v2, v3, t, b, tone, s), tremolo on/off, footswitch for tremolo, black covering, diagonal brown grille, mfg. 1975-1980s.

	N/A	$1,650 - 2,000	$1,100 - 1,350	

T-60 BASS – 60W, Piggyback, cabinet with 1-15 in. Vox Celestion Alnico HD and 1-12 in. Vox Celestion Alnico, solid-state, single channel, rear control panel, four input jacks, three knobs (v, t, b), black covering, black diagonal grille, mfg 1964-67.

	N/A	N/A	N/A	

MSR/NOTES	100%	EXCELLENT	AVERAGE	LAST MSR

ELECTRIC SS AMPLIFIERS: U.S. MODELS PRODUCED 1965-1970

When the Thomas Organ Company began producing Vox amplifiers in the U.S., most of their first models were tube amps including the Pathfinder (V-1), Pacemaker (V-2), Cambridge Reverb (V-3), and Berkeley Super Reverb (V-8). They also introduced a few solid-state Vox amplifiers including the Essex Bass (V-4), and the U.S. line would shortly evolve into an entirely solid-state offering. All U.S.-built tube models (except the Student model) feature a solid-state version that are in most cases quite similar to each other.

Kensington Bass (V1043)
courtesy John Beeson/The Music Shoppe

Pacemaker
courtesy S.P. Fjestad

Pathfinder
courtesy John Beeson/The Music Shoppe

BEATLE POWER STAK (V1262) – 120W, 8-12 in. speakers, guitar piggyback unit with two 4-12 in. speaker cabinets, three channels, reverb, tremolo, nine top control panel knobs (Normal Ch.: v, b, t, Brilliant Ch.: v, b, t, Bass Ch.: v, Tone X, power switch), Normal Ch. top boost switch, Brilliant Ch. mid boost switch, rear panel: six knobs (trem speed, trem depth, repeat percussion, three-way MRB effects switch, three-way reverb channel select, reverb level), footswitch jack, line reverse switch, aux. outlet, E tuner, black covering, brown diagonal grille, five-button footswitch included, black vinyl covering, Vox diamond grille cloth, mfg. 1969-1970.

	N/A	N/A	N/A	

Rarity precludes accurate pricing on this model. The Beatle Power Stak is known for being a very unstable amp structurally, and is prone to collapsing upon itself because the speaker cabinets were so shallow.

BERKELEY II (V1081) – ~17W, 2-10 in. Vox Gold Bulldog speakers, guitar piggyback unit, solid-state chassis, single channel, reverb, tremolo, top mounted control panel, two input jacks, six black knobs (v, t, b, r, trem s, trem depth), power switch, rear panel: 3rd input jack, footswitch jack, external speaker jack, aux. outlet, line reverse, black covering, brown diagonal grille, mfg. 1966-67.

	N/A	$725 - 850	$350 - 450	

BERKELEY III (V1081) – ~17W, 2-10 in. Vox Gold Bulldog speakers, guitar piggyback unit, solid-state chassis, two channels, reverb, tremolo, top/rear mounted control panel, four input jacks (two per channel), six top panel black knobs (Ch. 1: v, t, b, Ch. 2: v, t, b), power switch, rear panel: three knobs (r, trem s, trem depth), footswitch jack, aux. outlet, line reverse, E tuner, black covering, brown diagonal grille, mfg. 1968-69.

	N/A	$900 - 1,050	$450 - 550	

BUCKINGHAM (V12/V112/V1121/V1122/V1123) – 35W, 2-12 in. Vox Bulldog speakers, guitar piggyback, solid-state chassis, three channels (normal, brilliant, bass), reverb, tremolo, top/rear control panel, six inputs (two per channel), nine top control panel knobs (Normal Ch.: v, b, t, Brilliant Ch.: v, b, t, Bass Ch.: v, Tone X, power switch), Normal Ch. top boost switch, Brilliant Ch. mid boost switch, rear panel: five knobs (trem speed, trem depth, three-way MRB effects switch, three-way reverb channel select, reverb level), footswitch jack, E tuner switch (Model V1123 only), line reverse switch, aux. outlet, black covering, brown grille, chrome roller stand and footswitch included, mfg. 1965-69.

	N/A	$850 - 1,000	$425 - 525	$695 for V1122 and

$725 for the V1121

The Buckingham Models V12 and V112 had two separate footswitches and footswitch jacks. When the V1122 was introduced in 1966, it featured a new three-button footswitch that consolidated the previous two. The V1121 featured a distortion booster that could only be controlled by footswitch and this amp came equipped with a four-button footswitch. The V1123 was introduced in 1967 and featured an E tuner. The Buckingham is the same as the Viscount in piggyback configuration.

CAMBRIDGE REVERB (V1031/V1032) – ~17W, 1-10 in. Vox Gold Bulldog speaker, guitar combo, solid-state chassis, single channel, reverb, tremolo, top mounted control panel, two input jacks, six black knobs (v, t, b, r, trem s, trem depth), power switch, rear panel: 3rd input jack, footswitch jack, external speaker jack, aux. outlet, line reverse, E tuner switch (Model V1032 only, 1967-69), black covering, brown diagonal grille, mfg. 1966-69.

	N/A	$575 - 700	$275 - 350	$229

In 1967, an E tuner was added to the Cambridge Reverb and the model number was switched from V1031 to V1032. The Cambridge Reverb and Pacemaker are very similar to each other, except the Cambridge Reverb has reverb and the Pacemaker does not.

ESSEX BASS (V-4/V1041/V1042/V1043) – 35W (V-4/V-1041/V-1042) or 50W (V-1043), 2-12 in. Vox Bulldog bass speakers, bass combo, solid-state chassis, single channel, top mounted control panel, two input jacks, two controls (v, Tone-X), power switch, line reverse switch, black covering, brown diagonal grille, chrome roller stand and single-button footswitch for Tone-X control (V-1042/V-1043 only) included, mfg. 1965-68.

	N/A	$550 - 650	$275 - 350	

Models V-4 and V-1041 are identical electronically. The Model V-1042 featured a single-button footswitch to activiate the Tone-X control, and the Model V-1043 boosted the output to 50W.

MSR/NOTES	100%	EXCELLENT	AVERAGE	LAST MSR

KENSINGTON BASS (V124/V1241) – 22W, 1-15 in. Oxford/Vox speaker, bass combo, solid-state chassis, top mounted control panel, single channel, two input jacks, two controls (v, Tone-X), power switch, line reverse switch, G-tuner (Model V1241 only), chrome roller stand and single-button footswitch included, black covering, brown diagonal grille, mfg. 1967-69.

| | N/A | $625 - 750 | $325 - 400 | |

PACEMAKER (V1021/V1022) – 17W, 1-10 in. speaker, guitar combo, solid-state chassis, single channel, tremolo, top mounted control panel, three input jacks, six control knobs (v, b, t, m, s, depth tremolo), pedal jack, aux. speaker jack, line reverse switch, built in E-tuner (Model V1022, 1967-69), black covering, brown diagonal grille, mfg. 1966-69.

| | N/A | $375 - 450 | $225 - 275 | $150 |

In 1967, an E tuner was added to the Pacemaker and the model number was switched from V1021 to V1022.

PATHFINDER (V1011) – ~10W, 1-8 in. Vox Gold Bulldog speaker, guitar combo, solid-state chassis, single channel, tremolo, top mounted control panel, two input jacks, five knobs (v, t, b, trem s, trem depth), power switch, rear panel: footswitch jack, line reverse switch, black covering, brown diagonal grille, mfg. 1966-69.

| | N/A | $400 - 500 | $200 - 250 | $110 |

ROYAL GUARDSMAN (V13/V113/V1131/V1132/V1133) – 60W, 2-12 in. Vox Celestion speakers and a high-freq. horn, guitar piggyback, solid-state chassis, three channels (normal, brilliant, bass), reverb, tremolo, top/rear control panel, six inputs (two per channel), nine top control panel knobs (Normal Ch.: v, b, t, Brilliant Ch.: v, b, t, Bass Ch.: v, Tone X, power switch), Normal Ch. top boost switch, Brilliant Ch. mid boost switch, rear panel: five knobs (trem speed, trem depth, three-way MRB effects switch, three-way reverb channel select, reverb level), footswitch jack, E tuner switch (Model V1133 only), line reverse switch, aux. outlet, black covering, brown grille, chrome roller stand and footswitch included, mfg. 1965-68.

| | N/A | $1,300 - 1,600 | $750 - 950 | |

Last MSR was $895 for the V1132 and $925 for the V1131.

The Royal Guardsman Models V13 and V113 had two separate footswitches and footswitch jacks. When the V1132 was introduced in 1966, it featured a new three-button footswitch that consolidated the previous two. The V1131 featured a distortion booster that could only be controlled by footswitch and this amp came equipped with a four-button footswitch. The V1133 was introduced in 1967 and featured an E tuner.

SCORPION (V116) – 60W, 4-10 in. Vox Gold Bulldog speakers, guitar combo, solid-state chassis, two channels, reverb, tremolo, top/rear mounted control panel, four input jacks (two per channel), six top panel black knobs (Ch. 1: v, t, b, Ch. 2: v, t, b), power switch, rear panel: three knobs (r, trem s, trem depth), footswitch jack, aux. outlet, line reverse, E tuner, black covering, brown diagonal grille, removable casters, mfg. 1968-69.

| | N/A | $550 - 700 | $350 - 425 | |

The Scorpion appears that it was built out of parts from already existing Vox amplifiers. The cabinet is the same as the Royal Guardsman and the chassis is the same as the Berkeley III.

SOVEREIGN (V117) – 60W, 4-12 in. Vox Bulldog speakers, bass piggyback unit, solid-state chassis, two channels (Normal/Bass), top mounted control panel, four inputs (two per channel), six knobs (Normal Ch.: v, b, t, Bass Ch.: v, Tone-X, power switch), Normal Ch. top boost switch, rear panel: footswitch jack, line reverse switch, aux. outlet, black covering, brown diagonal grille, chrome roller stand and single-button footswitch included, mfg. 1967-69.

| | N/A | $525 - 650 | $325 - 400 | $669 |

When the Westminster (V1181) was updated to 120W and a built-in G tuner (V1182), the original Westminster chassis became the Sovereign. In 1968, the Sovereign was renamed the Westminster Power Stak and was sold in pairs of speaker cabinets along with the Beatle (V1143) head.

SUPER BEATLE (V14/V114/V1141) – 120W, piggyback, 4-12 in. Vox Bulldog speakers and two high-freq. horn, guitar piggyback, solid-state chassis, three channels, tremolo, reverb, top/rear control panel, six inputs (two per channel), nine top control panel knobs (Normal Ch.: v, b, t, Brilliant Ch.: v, b, t, Bass Ch.: v, Tone X, power switch), Normal Ch. top boost switch, Brilliant Ch. mid boost switch, rear panel: five knobs (trem speed, trem depth, three-way MRB effects switch, three-way reverb channel select, reverb level), two footswitch jacks (V14/V114) or one footswitch jack (V1141), line reverse switch, aux. outlet, black covering, brown diagonal grille, two footswitches (V14/V114) or one four button footswitch (V1141) and chrome stand included, mfg. 1966-67.

| | N/A | $3,400 - 4,000 | $1,700 - 2,100 | $1,225 |

The V1141 featured a distortion booster that could only be controlled by footswitch and this amp came equipped with a four-button footswitch.

* ***Super Beatle (V1142)*** – similar to the Super Beatle (V14/V114/V1141), except the separate footswitches are consolidated into one three-button footswitch, mfg. 1966-67.

| | N/A | $3,400 - 4,000 | $1,700 - 2,100 | $1,195 |

* ***Beatle (V1143)*** – similar to the Super Beatle model (V14/V114/V1141), except has a Repeat Percussion tremolo effect with an additional knob on the back panel and an E tuner, five-button footswitch included, mfg. 1967-1970.

| | N/A | $2,400 - 3,000 | $1,450 - 1,800 | |

This model was designated the V1143J or the V1143A. Each designated what speakers the amp contained. The J indicated JBL and the A stood for Altec Lansing speakers.

MSR/NOTES	100%	EXCELLENT	AVERAGE	LAST MSR

VISCOUNT (V1151/V1152/V1153/V1154) – 35W, 2-12 in. Vox Bulldog speakers, guitar combo, solid-state chassis, three channels (normal, brilliant, bass), reverb, tremolo, top/rear control panel, six inputs (two per channel), nine top control panel knobs (Normal Ch.: v, b, t, Brilliant Ch.: v, b, t, Bass Ch.: v, Tone X, power switch), Normal Ch. top boost switch, Brilliant Ch. mid boost switch, rear panel: five knobs (trem speed, trem depth, three-way MRB effects switch, three-way reverb channel select, reverb level), footswitch jack, E tuner switch (Model V1154 only), line reverse switch, aux. outlet, black covering, brown grille, chrome roller stand and footswitch included, mfg. 1966-69.

	N/A	$725 - 850	$350 - 450	

WESTMINSTER (V118/V1181) – 60W, 1-18 in. Vox Bulldog speaker, bass piggyback unit, solid-state chassis, two channels (Normal/Bass), top mounted control panel, four inputs (two per channel), six knobs (Normal Ch.: v, b, t, Bass Ch.: v, Tone-X, power switch), Normal Ch. top boost switch, rear panel: footswitch jack, line reverse switch, aux. outlet, black covering, brown diagonal grille, chrome roller stand and single-button footswitch included, mfg. 1965-67.

	N/A	$600 - 700	$300 - 375	$850

When the Westminster (V1181) was updated to 120W and a built-in G tuner (V1182), the original Westminster chassis became the Sovereign.

* *Westminster (V1182)* – similar to the Westminster (V1181), except has 120W output and a G tuner, mfg. 1968-69.

	N/A	$600 - 700	$350 - 425	

» *Westminster Power Stak (V1261)* – similar to the Westminster (V1182), except has two 4-12 in. speaker cabinets mfg. 1969-1970.

	N/A	N/A	N/A	

Rarity on this model precludes accurate pricing.

ELECTRIC SS AMPLIFIERS: 4 & 7 SERIES

This was the first dedicated series developed for solid-state. This happened when Jennings sold Vox to Royston and they were looking to get into the solid-state market. The 7 series were designed for guitar amps and the 4 series were for bass amps. These amps were used by a few endorsers, but the overall market rejected them and were discontinued shortly thereafter. The circuitry between the 4 and 7 Series are very similar, and there are four variations for each line. Many of these amplifiers were sold and distributed in England and never made it over to North America.

4120 – 120W, Piggyback, 2 cabinets with 4-12 in. G12H25 W speakers and 2-10 in. Celestion speakers, solid-state, dual channels, bottom front control panel, two inputs, eight knobs (v, b, t, m, v, b, t, m), bright switch, boost switch, black covering, diagonal black covering, mfg. 1966-mid 1970s.

	N/A	$475 - 550	$300 - 350	

* *460* – similar to the 4120 except has 60W output, and a speaker configuration of 4-12 in., 2-12 in. or 2-10 in. speakers, mfg. 1966-mid 1970s.

	N/A	$375 - 450	$200 - 250	

* *430* – similar to the 460 except has 30W output, mfg. 1966-mid 1970s.

	N/A	$300 - 350	$175 - 225	

* *415* – similar to the 460 except has 15W output, mfg. 1966-mid 1970s.

	N/A	$250 - 300	$140 - 175	

7120 – 120W, Piggyback, 4-12 in. Vox Celestion Aninco speakers and two Midax HF horns in a cabinet, solid-state, dual channels, front control panel, four input jacks, eight knobs (Ch.1: v, t, m, b Ch. 2: v, t, m, b), black covering, diagonal black covering, mfg. 1966-mid 1970s.

	N/A	$500 - 600	$300 - 375	

This model was also available in a 2-cabinet system.

* *760* – similar to the 7120 except has 60W output, cabinet with 2-12 in. Celestion G12H 25W speakers and 2-10 in. Celestion 10W speakers, mfg. 1966-68.

	N/A	$425 - 500	$250 - 300	

730 – 30W, 2-12 in. or 2-10 in. speakers, Piggyback, solid-state, dual channels, front control panel, four input jacks, six knobs (Ch. 1: v, t, b, Ch. 2: v, t, b), bright and boost switches, black covering, diagnoal black grille, mfg. 1966-68

	N/A	$325 - 400	$175 - 225	

* *715* – similar to the 730 except with 15W output, mfg. 1966-68.

	N/A	$300 - 350	$175 - 225	

ELECTRIC SS AMPLIFIERS: BRITISH VIRTUOSO & DYNAMIC MODELS

VIRTUOSO – 30W, 2-10 in. speakers, solid-state combo, dual channels, tremolo, reverb, distortion, top control panel, four input jacks, 14 control knobs (Ch. 1: v, b, t, Ch. 2: v, b, t, bright switch, mid-range (MRB) switch, mid-range select, s, trem depth, reverb switch, reverb depth, distortion knob), three button footswitch, black covering, brown diagonal grille, mfg. 1966-1970s.

	N/A	$925 - 1,100	$475 - 575	

MSR/NOTES	100%	EXCELLENT	AVERAGE	LAST MSR

* *Conqueror* – similar to the Virtuoso, except is in piggyback form, with a 2-12 in. speaker cabinet, mfg. 1966-1970s.

| | N/A | $1,100 - 1,300 | $550 - 675 | |

* *Defiant* – similar to the Conqueror, except has 50W output and the cabinet contains a Midax with the speakers, mfg. 1966-1970s.

| | N/A | $1,625 - 1,900 | $800 - 1,000 | |

* *Supreme* – similar to the Defiant, except has 100W, a cabinet with 4-12" speakers and 2 Midax, and has a Watchdog limiter, mfg. 1966-1970s.

| | N/A | $1,775 - 2,100 | $900 - 1,100 | |

DYNAMIC BASS – 30W, piggyback, cabinet with 1-15 in. speaker, solid-state, dual channels, distortion switch, top control panel, four input jacks, eight control knobs (v1, v2, t, b, Tone-X, distortion, mid-range switch, mid-range select), black covering, brown diagonal grille, mfg. 1966-1970s.

| | N/A | $600 - 700 | $300 - 375 | |

* *Foundation Bass* – similar to the Dynamic Bass, except has 50W output and a cabinet with 1-18" speaker, mfg. 1966-1970s.

| | N/A | $725 - 850 | $350 - 450 | |

* *Super Foundation Bass* – similar to the Foundation Bass, except has 100W output, mfg. 1966-1970s.

| | N/A | $800 - 950 | $400 - 500 | |

ELECTRIC SS AMPLIFIERS: DA (DIGITAL AMPLIFIER) SERIES

DA5
courtesy Vox

DA10
courtesy Vox

DA15
courtesy Vox

DA5 – 5W, 1-6.5 in. speaker, guitar combo, solid-state chassis, digital effects, top black control panel, single input, six knobs (style select, g, tone, MV, edit knob, effects select), tap switch, bypass switch, aux. input, mic. input, headphone jack, line out, available in Black with a silver grille (2006-07), Black with a black grille (2008-present), Green with a black grille (2006-07), Pink with a silver grille (2006-07), Red with a silver or black grille (2006-07), White with a black grille, or Classic black covering with a brown diamond grille, runs on AC/DC power or 6 C Cell batteries, 8 lbs., 10.5 in. wide, 10.5 in. tall, 7 in. deep, 7.75 lbs., mfg. 2006-disc.

| | $140 | $80 - 100 | $50 - 65 | $190 |

DA10 – 10W, 2-6.5 in. speaker guitar combo, solid-state chassis, digital effects, top black control panel, single input, six knobs (style select, g, tone, MV, edit knob, effects select), tap switch, bypass switch, aux. input, mic. input, headphone jack, line out, available with black covering and a metal diamond grille or Classic black vinyl covering with brown diamond covering grille, runs on AC/DC power or 6 C Cell batteries, 15.25 in. wide, 12.375 in. tall, 7.25 in. deep, 16.5 lbs., mfg. 2008-disc.

| | $200 | $110 - 140 | $70 - 90 | $270 |

DA15 – 15W, 1-8 in. speaker, guitar combo, solid-state chassis, digital effects, top black control panel, single input, nine knobs (style select, g, v, t, m, b, MV, edit knob, effects select), programmable channel section, tap switch, bypass switch, headphone jack, line out, available in Black finish, silver grille, 22 lbs., mfg. 2006-08.

| | N/A | $95 - 120 | $60 - 75 | $230 |

DA20 – 20W, 2-8 in. speaker guitar combo, solid-state chassis, digital effects, top black control panel, single input, six knobs (style select, g, tone, MV, edit knob, effects select), tap switch, bypass switch, aux. input, mic. input, headphone jack, line out, available with black covering and a metal diamond grille or Classic black vinyl covering with brown diamond covering grille, runs on AC/DC power or 6 C Cell batteries, 18.25 in. wide, 14.875 in. tall, 9 in. deep, 22.5 lbs., mfg. 2008-disc.

| | $250 | $135 - 175 | $90 - 115 | $330 |

ELECTRIC SS AMPLIFIERS: ESCORT SERIES

ESCORT 30 – 30W, 1-12 in. speaker, solid-state combo, three channels, distortion, top-mounted control panel, three input jacks, seven black chicken head knobs (v1, v2, v3, fuzz intensity, t, m, b) footswitch for fuzz (distortion), brown covering, brown diagonal grille, mfg. 1970s.

| | N/A | $300 - 350 | $135 - 175 | |

* *Escort Super Twin 30* – similar to the Escort 30, except has 2-5 in. speakers, mfg. 1970s.

| | N/A | $550 - 650 | $325 - 400 | |

MSR/NOTES	100%	EXCELLENT	AVERAGE	LAST MSR

ESCORT BATTERY – 3W, 1-5.5 in. speaker, solid-state combo, single channel, top control panel, two input jacks (one normal, one brilliant), two control knobs (v, tone), black covering, brown diagonal grille, mfg. 1970s.

	N/A	$350 - 400	$175 - 225	

This amp was modeled after the ever so popular AC-30 but in mini-form.

* *Escort Battery/Mains* – similar to the Escort Battery, except has an output socket that feeds a signal into the main amplifier (i.e. AC-30), has third control knobs which is a supply selector, mfg. 1970-mid 70s.

courtesy Dave Rogers/Dave's Guitar Shop   courtesy Dave Rogers/Dave's Guitar Shop

	N/A	$200 - 250	$75 - 100	

ESCORT 50 – 50W, 1-12 in. speaker, solid-state combo, single channel, top control panel, two input jacks, five control knobs (v, t, m, b, harmonics), black covering, brown diagonal grille, mfg. 1970-mid 70s.

	N/A	$350 - 400	$175 - 225	

ELECTRIC SS AMPLIFIERS: VENUE SERIES

BASS 100 – 100W, 1-15 in. speaker, solid-state combo, single channel, front black control panel, two input jacks, four black and white knobs (v, t, m, b), effects loop, extension speaker jack, headphone jack, black covering, black grille, mfg. mid 1980s.

	N/A	$275 - 325	$150 - 200	

* *Bass 50* – similar to the Bass 100, except has 50W output and 1-12 in. speaker, no extension speaker jack, mfg. mid-1980s.

	N/A	$225 - 275	$135 - 175	

BUSKER – 4W, 1-8 in. speaker, solid-state combo, single channel, front black control panel, two input jacks, four black knobs (v, m, t, MV), headphone jack, operable on AC or DC, black covering, black grille, mfg. mid 1980s.

	N/A	$150 - 200	$95 - 120	

This model is essentially the Escort now in the Venue series.

DUAL 100 – 100W, 1-12 in. speaker, solid-state combo, dual switchable channels, reverb, gain, front black control panel, two inputs (hi and lo), eleven black and white control knobs (Ch. 1: v, b, m, t, Ch. 2: gain, b, m, t, v, Both: r, MV), extension speaker jack, headphone jack, black covering, black grille, mfg. mid-1980s.

	N/A	$325 - 400	$200 - 250	

GT-100 – 100W, 1-12 in. and H.F. horn, solid-state combo, dual channels, reverb, front control panel, three input jacks (two for Ch. 2), 12 control knobs (Ch. 1: v, mid sweep, m, t, b, Ch. 2: v, mid sweep, m, t, b, r, MV), footswitch for lots of controls, extension speaker jack, headphone jack, black covering, black grille, mfg. mid 1980s.

	N/A	$325 - 400	$200 - 250	

KEYBOARD 100 – 100W, 1-15 in. speaker and a H.F. horn, solid-state combo, three channels, reverb, six input jacks (three per channel), 12 black and white knobs (v, b, & t for each channel, presence, r, MV), effects loop, footswitch, extension speaker jack, headphone jack, black covering, black grille, mfg. mid-1980s.

	N/A	$275 - 325	$150 - 200	

LEAD 30 – 30W, 1-10 in. speaker, solid-state combo, single channel, reverb, front mounted control panel, two input jacks, six black control knobs (v, t, m, b, r, MV), slave jack, headphone jack, black covering, black grille, mfg. mid-1980s.

	N/A	$200 - 250	$120 - 150	

LEAD 100 – 100W, 1-12 in. speaker, solid-state combo, single channel, reverb, overdrive, front black control panel, two input jacks, seven black and white knobs (v, t, m, b, r, overdrive, MV), footswitch for overdrive and reverb, black covering, black grille, mfg. mid-1980s.

	N/A	$300 - 350	$175 - 225	

* *Lead 50* – similar to the Lead 100, except has 50W output and no overdrive circuit, mfg. mid-1980s.

	N/A	$250 - 300	$150 - 200	

MSR/NOTES	100%	EXCELLENT	AVERAGE	LAST MSR

PA-120 – 120W, piggyback unit, two cabinets with 1-12 in. speaker and a H.F. horn in each, solid-state, four channels, reverb, front control panel, eight input jacks (two per channel), 15 control knobs (v, t, & b for each channel, presence, r, MV), effects loop, footswitch, headphone jack, black covering, black grille, mfg. mid-1980s.

	N/A	$325 - 400	$200 - 250	

ELECTRIC SS AMPLIFIERS: Q SERIES

BASS 100 MOSFET – 100W, 1-15 in. speaker, solid-state combo, single channel, front black control panel, two inputs, eight black knobs (three compressors, b, mid-freq, mid, t, MV), five-band equalizer, effects loop, extension speaker jack, headphone jack, black covering, black grille, mfg. 1988-1990.

	N/A	$250 - 300	$135 - 175	

GT 100 MOSFET – 100W, 1-12 in. and H.F. horn, solid-state combo, dual channels, reverb, front control panel, three input jacks (two for Ch. 2), 12 control knobs (Ch. 1: v, mid sweep, m, t, b, Ch. 2: v, mid sweep, m, t, b, r, MV), footswitch for lots of controls, extension speaker jack, headphone jack, black covering, black grille, mfg. 1988-1990.

	N/A	$300 - 350	$175 - 225	

KB 50 MOSFET – 50W, 1-12 in. speaker, solid-state combo, reverb, three channels, front black control panel, six input jacks (two per channel), 14 black knobs (v, mid-freq, mid & b for each channel, r, MV), effects loop, extension speaker jack, headphone jack, black covering, black grille, mfg. 1988-1990.

	N/A	$250 - 300	$135 - 175	

LEAD 100 MOSFET – 100W, 1-12 in. speaker, solid-state combo, dual channels, reverb, front black control panel, three input jacks, eight black knobs (v1, v2, t, mid-freq, mid, b, MV, r), five-band equalizer, effects loop, extension speaker jack, headphone jack, black covering, black grille, mfg. 1988-1990.

	N/A	$275 - 325	$150 - 200	

ELECTRIC SS AMPLIFIERS: PATHFINDER SERIES (CURRENT MFG.)

These are small practice amplifiers that were introduced in 1999. These are solid-state amps that are affordable to have in your bedroom to practice with. The Pathfinders have all of the features that the larger amps have but in a smaller package.

Pathfinder 10
courtesy Vox

Pathfinder 15R
courtesy Vox

PATHFINDER 10 (V9106) – 10W, 6.5 in. speaker, guitar combo, solid-state, clean/overdrive switch, top control panel, one input, four black pointer knobs (gain, v, b, t), headphone jack, black covering, brown diagonal grille, mfg. 2001-03, reintroduced 2008-present.

MSR $112	$80	$50 - 60	$25 - 30	

Also available in Limited Editon models with Union Jack or Classic Red coverings.

PATHFINDER 15 (V9168) – 15W, 1-8 in. speaker, guitar combo, solid-state, clean/overdrive switch, tremolo, top control panel, one input, six black pointer knobs (gain, v, b, t, s, d), headphone jack, footswitch, black covering, brown diagonal grille, mfg. 1999-2003.

	N/A	$70 - 80	$45 - 55	$150

* Add $25 for cover.

* *Pathfinder 15R (V9168R)* – similar to the Pathfinder 15, except has reverb and an extra control on panel for reverb, mfg. 1999-disc.

	$120	$75 - 95	$50 - 60	$175

* Add $25 for cover.
* Add $30 for footswitch.

* *Pathfinder 15SMR* – similar to the Pathfinder 15R, except is a mini-stack, tremolo, and has 2-10 in. speakers, mfg. 2003 only.

	N/A	$175 - 225	$100 - 125	$399

* Add $35 for footswitch.

PATHFINDER BASS (PB10) – 10W, 2-5 in. speakers, bass combo, solid-state chassis, single channel, top red control panel, single input, four black pointer knobs (drive, t, b, v), bright switch, headphone jack, power switch, black covering, black diagonal grille, 15 in. wide, 11 in. tall, 6.75 in. deep, 12.3 lbs., mfg. 2011-present.

MSR $120	$100	$55 - 75	$35 - 45	

MSR/NOTES	100%	EXCELLENT	AVERAGE	LAST MSR

VX I Combo
courtesy Vox

VX II Combo
courtesy Vox

Mini 3 Combo
courtesy Vox

ELECTRIC SS AMPLIFIERS: VX SERIES

VX I COMBO – 15W, 6.5 in. speaker, guitar combo, solid-state, top control panel, one input, 11 models, eight effects, eight black knobs (amp selector, gain, v, b, t, power level, modulation selector, delay/reverb selector), program button, tap button, power button, aux in jack, headphone jack, black covering, black diagonal grille, 13.94 in. wide, 12.32 in. tall, 7.56 in. deep, 8.38 lbs., mfg. 2015-present.

MSR $140	$100	$65 - 75	$35 - 40	

VX II COMBO – 30W, 8 in. speaker, guitar combo, solid-state, top control panel, one input, 11 models, eight effects, eight black knobs (amp selector, gain, v, b, t, power level, modulation selector, delay/reverb selector), program button, tap button, power button, aux in jack, headphone jack, USB port, black covering, black diagonal grille, 13.94 in. wide, 12.32 in. tall, 7.56 in. deep, 8.38 lbs., mfg. 2015-present.

MSR $210	$150	$100 - 115	$50 - 60	

ELECTRIC SS AMPLIFIERS: MISC. MODELS

MINI 3 COMBO – 3W, 1-5 in. speaker, AC/DC powered, solid-state chassis, 11 amps, 8 effects (4 effects, 4 delay/reverb), top black control panel, single input, mic input, eight black knobs (amp model selector, g, tone, MV, effects trim, delay/reverb send, effects selector, delay/reverb selector), tap/tuner switch, power switch, aux. in jack, headphone jacks, available in traditional Vox black covering with a brown grille (MINI3CL), Black covering with a black grille (MINI3), Ivory covering with a black grille (MINI3IV), or Racing Green covering with a black grille (MINI3RG), 10.5 in. wide, 10.5 in. tall, 7 in. deep, 7.75 lbs., AC adaptor and strap included, mfg. 2011-present.

MSR $156	$120	$80 - 90	$40 - 50	

MINI 5 RHYTHM COMBO – 5W, 1-6.5 in. speaker, AC or battery powered, solid-state chassis, 11 amps, 8 effects, top black control panel, single input, mic input, eleven knobs (amp model selector, g, tone, MV, effects trim, effect send, effect selector 1, effect selector 2, rhythm selector, rhythm tempo, rhythm level), power switch, aux. in jack, headphone jack, black covering, silver metal grille, 10.59 in. wide, 10.51 in. tall, 7 in. deep, 7.72 lbs., AC adaptor and strap included, mfg. 2014-present.

MSR $200	$160	$105 - 120	$50 - 65	

VALVEREACTOR VR15 – 15W, 1-8 in. speaker, Hybrid design, 1 X ECC83 (12AX7) tube, two channels, front black control panel, single input, five black chickenhead knobs (Normal: v, OD: g, v, b, t), Black covering, Brown Diamond grille, 18 lbs., mfg. summer 2004-05.

	N/A	$110 - 140	$65 - 80	$260

VALVEREACTOR VR30R – 30W, 1-10 in. speaker, hybrid design, 1 X ECC83 (12AX7) tube, two channels, reverb, front black control panel, single input, five black chickenhead knobs (Normal: v, b, t, OD: g, v, b, t, MV, r), Black covering, Brown Diamond grille, 29 lbs., mfg. summer 2004-05.

	N/A	$150 - 200	$95 - 120	$400

VBM1 BRIAN MAY SIGNATURE – 10W, 1-6.5 in. Custom voiced full range speaker, top black control panel, three knobs (g, tone, v), single input, booster output, external speaker and headphone jacks, white covering, brown Vox grille, 12 lbs., mfg. 2003-05.

	N/A	$95 - 115	$65 - 75	$200

This amp has a built in booster pedal that can reproduce Brian May's sound.

ELECTRIC HYBRID AMPLIFIERS: CAMBRIDGE SERIES

The Cambridge Series featured hybrid chassis with a single preamp tube in the preamp stage and a solid-state power section.

CAMBRIDGE 15 (9310) – 15W, 1-8 in. Vox/Celestion Bulldog speaker, hybrid design, 1 X 12AX7 preamp, solid-state power section, single channel, tremolo, top control panel, one input, six black pointer knobs (gain, v, t, b, s, d), footswitch, headphone jack, black covering, black diagonal grille, mfg. 1999-2000.

	N/A	$150 - 175	$100 - 125	

MSR/NOTES	100%	EXCELLENT	AVERAGE	LAST MSR

CAMBRIDGE 30 REVERB (9310) – 30W, 1-10 in. Vox/Celestion Bulldog speaker, hybrid design, 1 X 12AX7 preamp, solid-state power section, dual channels, gain, tremolo, reverb, top control panel, one input, 10 black pointer knobs (Ch 1: v, t, b, Ch 2: gain, t, b, v, Both: s, d, reverb), footswitch, headphone jack, line output, extra speaker jack, black covering, black diagonal grille cloth, mfg. 1999-2002.

	N/A	$200 - 250	$150 - 175	$399

* *Cambridge 30 Reverb Twin (9320)* – similar to the Cambridge 30 Reverb, except has 2-12 in. speakers, mfg. 1999-2000.

	N/A	$225 - 275	$150 - 200	

ELECTRIC HYBRID AMPLIFIERS: VALVE REACTOR SERIES

VALVE REACTOR AC15VR – 15W, 1-12 in. Celestion VX12 speaker, guitar combo, hybrid chassis with a single 12AX7 tube that operates in both pre- and power amp stages, Valve Reactor circuitry, two channels (Normal, Overdrive), reverb, top blue control panel, single input, seven black knobs (Normal Ch.: v, OD Ch.: g, v, All: b, t, r, MV), channel switch, OD1/OD2 style switch, power switch, rear panel: external speaker jack, footswitch jack, black covering, brown diamond grille cloth, 23.75 in. wide, 18 in. tall, 10.5 in. deep, optional two-button VFS2 footswitch, mfg. 2010-present.

MSR $500	$380	$200 - 250	$120 - 150	

• Add $40 (MSR $50) for two-button footswitch (Model VFS2).

VALVE REACTOR AC30VR – 30W, 2-12 in. Celestion VX12 speaker, guitar combo, hybrid chassis with a single 12AX7 tube that operates in both pre- and power amp stages, Valve Reactor circuitry, two channels (Normal, Overdrive), reverb, top blue control panel, single input, 11 black knobs (Normal Ch.: v, b, t, OD Ch.: g, v, b, m, t, All: tone cut, r, MV), channel switch, OD1/OD2 style switch, power switch, rear panel: external speaker jack, footswitch jack, black covering, brown diamond grille cloth, 27.625 in. wide, 21.875 in. tall, 10.5 in. deep, optional two-button VFS2 footswitch, mfg. 2010-present.

MSR $800	$550	$325 - 400	$200 - 250	

• Add $40 (MSR $50) for two-button footswitch (Model VFS2).

ELECTRIC HYBRID AMPLIFIERS: VALVETRONIX SERIES

The Valvetronix series was debuted at the Winter NAMM 2002, as a digital modeling amp. With the digital features and the power of Vox amps a person is able to create an unlimited number of possibilities in sound. Smaller models were introduced in 2004, with the AD15VT, AD30VT, and at the Summer NAMM 2004 show, the AD50VT. In 2008, Vox introduced a variation of each Valvetronix amp that featured 11 heavier new amp models. These amps were labeled as the XL Series that stood for Extreme Lead. In 2009, Vox discontinued all their current models and replaced them with similar new models that incorporated 22 amp models, eliminating the need for two separate amps with 11 models each. These models were simply called "VT" models. In 2011, Vox introduced their next series of Valvetronix amps with the VT Plus Series. These amps feature 33 amp models along with 99 user presets.

AD15VT – 15W, 1-8 in. speaker combo, digital preamp with 1 X 12AX7 tube, 11 amp models, 11 effects, two channels, eight black chicken head knobs, various buttons, top mount control panel, black covering, brushed chrome grille, 22 lbs., mfg. 2004-08.

	N/A	$120 - 150	$70 - 90	$279

* *AD15VT-XL* – similar to the AD15VT, except has 11 different amp models voiced after distorted/high-gain amps, and has a dark gray covering with a black metal grille, mfg. 2008 only.

	N/A	$135 - 175	$90 - 115	$330

AD30VT – 30W, 1-10 in. speaker, stereo guitar combo, digital preamp with 1 X 12AX7 tube, 11 amp models, 11 effects, two channels, eight black chicken head knobs, various buttons, top mount control panel, black covering, brushed chrome grille, 26 lbs., mfg. 2004-08.

	N/A	$140 - 190	$85 - 115	$350

* *AD30VT-XL* – similar to the AD30VT, except has 11 different amp models voiced after distorted/high-gain amps, and has a dark gray covering with a black metal grille, mfg. 2008 only.

	N/A	$175 - 225	$110 - 140	$430

AD50VT – 50W, 1-12 in. Celestion speaker, guitar combo, digital preamp with 1 X 12AX7 tube, 11 amp models, 11 effects, two channels, eight black chicken head knobs, various buttons, top mount control panel, black covering, brushed chrome grille, 44 lbs., mfg. 2004-08.

	N/A	$225 - 275	$120 - 170	$540

* *AD50VT-212* – similar to the AD50VT, except in combo configuration with 2-12 in. Celestion speakers, 51 lbs., mfg. 2007-08.

	N/A	$250 - 325	$130 - 180	$650

»*AD50VT2-XL* – similar to the AD50VT212, except has 11 different amp models voiced after distorted/high-gain amps, and has a dark gray covering with a black metal grille, mfg. 2008 only.

	N/A	$300 - 350	$175 - 225	$670

AD60VTX – 60W, 1-12 in. Custom voiced Celestion combo, digital preamp, 12AX7 power section, 16 amp models, 21 effects, top blue control panel, two inputs (high and low), nine black pointer knobs (pedal, amp type, gain, v, t, m, b, presence, master), modulation, delay and reverb effects, programming, black covering, diagonal black grille cloth, 43 lbs., mfg. 2001-06.

	N/A	$475 - 575	$300 - 375	$1,049

• Add $35 for cover.
• Subtract $125 for Celestion speaker (Model AD60VT).

In 2003, Celestion speakers were disc. making only Neodog speakers available.

MSR/NOTES	100%	EXCELLENT	AVERAGE	LAST MSR

AD100VTH
courtesy Vox

VT30
courtesy Vox

* ***AD60VTH*** – similar to the AD60VT, except in head-unit configuration, 35 lbs., mfg. 2002-05.

	N/A	$350 - 450	$200 - 250	$799

• **Add $15 for cover.**

AD100VT – 100W, 2-12 in. Vox speakers, guitar combo, digital preamp with 1 X 12AX7 tube, 11 amp models, 11 effects, two channels, eight black chicken head knobs, various buttons, top mount control panel, black covering, brushed chrome grille, 64 lbs., mfg. 2006-08.

	N/A	$350 - 425	$200 - 250	$830

* ***AD100VTH*** – similar to the AD100VT, except in head-unit configuration, mfg. 2006-08.

	N/A	$240 - 290	$135 - 175	$549

* ***AD100VT-XL*** – similar to the AD100VT, except has 11 different amp models voiced after distorted/high-gain amps, and has a dark gray covering with a black metal grille, mfg. 2008 only.

	N/A	$325 - 400	$200 - 250	$840

AD120VTX – similar to the AD60VT, except has 120W output, and 2-12 in. Custom voiced Celestion speakers, 58 lbs., mfg. 2001-06.

	N/A	$600 - 750	$400 - 500	$1,499

• **Add $40 for cover.**
• **Add $160 for footswitch controller (VC-4).**
• **Add $70 for Passive Volume Pedal footswitch controller.**
• **Add $325 for dual footswitch controller (VC-12).**
• **Add $150 for chrome stand.**
• **Subtract $125 for Celestion speakers (Model AD120VT).**

In 2003, Celestion speakers were disc. making only Neodog speakers available.

* ***AD120VTH*** – similar to the AD120VTX, except in head-unit configuration, 40 lbs., mfg. 2002-06.

	N/A	$525 - 575	$300 - 350	$1,099

• **Add $15 for cover.**

VT15 – 15W, 1-8 in. speaker, guitar combo, hybrid chassis with Vox Valve Reactor circuit including 1 X 12AX7 tube, single channel, 22 amp models, 11 effects, 66 presets and eight user program presets, top black control panel, single input, eight white chickenhead knobs (amp model select, g, v, t, m, b, r, MV), amp select switch, preset mode button, manual mode button, five user program buttons (bank and one for each of the four channels), black effects knob selector, effects button, effects level, effects bypass, power switch, black covering, split front with black covering on the top third and a silver Vox logo and a silver metal grille on the bottom two-thirds with Valvetronix logo, 16.875 in. wide, 15.5 in. tall, 8.875 in. deep, 22 lbs., mfg. 2009-2010.

	N/A	$120 - 150	$75 - 95	$280

VT20+ (VT20PLUS) – 30W, 1-8 in. speaker, guitar combo, hybrid chassis with Vox Valve Reactor circuit including 1 X 12AX7 tube, single channel, 33 amp models, 25 effects (11 pedal effects, 11 mod/delay effects, 3 reverb types), 99 presets and eight user program presets, top black control panel, single input, eight white chickenhead knobs (amp model select, g, v, t, m, b, MV, power level), preset mode button, amp select switch, five user program buttons (bank and one for each of the four channels), pedal effects knob selector, pedal knob, mod/delay effect knob, mod/delay depth knob, tap switch, reverb knob, aux. in jack, headphone jack, rear panel: power switch, footswitch jack, black covering, split front with black covering on the top third and a silver Vox logo and a black cloth grille on the bottom two-thirds with Valvetronix logo, 16.875 in. wide, 14.75 in. tall, 8.75 in. deep, 19.5 lbs., mfg. 2011-present.

MSR $246	$180	$115 - 135	$60 - 70	

Also available in Limited Edition Classic VOX color scheme.

VT30 – 30W, 1-10 in. speaker, guitar combo, hybrid chassis with Vox Valve Reactor circuit including 1 X 12AX7 tube, single channel, 22 amp models, 11 effects, 66 presets and eight user program presets, top black control panel, single input, eight white chickenhead knobs (amp model select, g, v, t, m, b, r, MV), amp select switch, preset mode button, manual mode button, five user program buttons (bank and one for each of the four channels), black effects knob selector, effects button, effects level, effects bypass, power switch, black covering, split front with black covering on the top third and a silver Vox logo and a silver metal grille on the bottom two-thirds with Valvetronix logo, 18 in. wide, 17 in. tall, 8.875 in. deep, 26.5 lbs., mfg. 2009-2010.

	N/A	$170 - 205	$95 - 110	$375

MSR/NOTES	100%	EXCELLENT	AVERAGE	LAST MSR

VT40+ (VT40PLUS) – 60W, 1-10 in. speaker, guitar combo, hybrid chassis with Vox Valve Reactor circuit including 1 X 12AX7 tube, single channel, 33 amp models, 25 effects (11 pedal effects, 11 mod/delay effects, 3 reverb types), 99 presets and eight user program presets, top black control panel, single input, eight white chickenhead knobs (amp model select, g, v, t, m, b, MV, power level), preset mode button, amp select switch, five user program buttons (bank and one for each of the four channels), pedal effects knob selector, pedal knob, mod/delay effect knob, mod/delay depth knob, tap switch, reverb knob, aux. in jack, headphone jack, rear panel: power switch, footswitch jack, black covering, split front with black covering on the top third and a silver Vox logo and a black cloth grille on the bottom two-thirds with Valvetronix logo, 16.875 in. wide, 16 in. tall, 8.75 in. deep, 24 lbs., mfg. 2011-2015.

	$250	$150 - 200	$95 - 120	$400

VT50 – 50W, 1-12 in. speaker, guitar combo, hybrid chassis with Vox Valve Reactor circuit including 1 X 12AX7 tube, single channel, 22 amp models, 11 effects, 66 presets and eight user program presets, top black control panel, single input, eight white chickenhead knobs (amp model select, g, v, t, m, b, r, MV), amp select switch, preset mode button, manual mode button, five user program buttons (bank and one for each of the four channels), black effects knob selector, effects button, effects level, effects bypass, power switch, external speaker jack, black covering, split front with black covering on the top third and a silver Vox logo and a silver metal grille on the bottom two-thirds with Valvetronix logo, mfg. 2009-2010.

	N/A	$250 - 300	$135 - 160	$540

VT80+ (VT80PLUS) – 120W, 1-12 in. speaker, guitar combo, hybrid chassis with Vox Valve Reactor circuit including 1 X 12AX7 tube, single channel, 33 amp models, 25 effects (11 pedal effects, 11 mod/delay effects, 3 reverb types), 99 presets and eight user program presets, top black control panel, single input, eight white chickenhead knobs (amp model select, g, v, t, m, b, MV, power level), preset mode button, amp select switch, five user program buttons (bank and one for each of the four channels), pedal effects knob selector, pedal knob, mod/delay effect knob, mod/delay depth knob, tap switch, reverb knob, aux. in jack, headphone jack, rear panel: power switch, footswitch jack, black covering, split front with black covering on the top third and a silver Vox logo and a black cloth grille on the bottom two-thirds with Valvetronix logo, 17.75 in. wide, 17.25 in. tall, 10.25 in. deep, 31 lbs., mfg. 2011-2015.

	$350	$230 - 265	$115 - 140	$475

VT100 – 100W, 2-12 in. speakers, guitar combo, hybrid chassis with Vox Valve Reactor circuit including 1 X 12AX7 tube, single channel, 22 amp models, 11 effects, 66 presets and eight user program presets, top black control panel, single input, eight white chickenhead knobs (amp model select, g, v, t, m, b, r, MV), amp select switch, preset mode button, manual mode button, five user program buttons (bank and one for each of the four channels), black effects knob selector, effects button, effects level, effects bypass, power switch, effects loop, external speaker jack, black covering, split front with black covering on the top third and a silver Vox logo and a silver metal grille on the bottom two-thirds with Valvetronix logo, mfg. 2009-2010.

	N/A	$400 - 475	$225 - 275	$900

VT120+ (VT120PLUS) – 150W, 2-12 in. speakers, guitar combo, hybrid chassis with Vox Valve Reactor circuit including 1 X 12AX7 tube, single channel, 33 amp models, 25 effects (11 pedal effects, 11 mod/delay effects, 3 reverb types), 99 presets and eight user program presets, top black control panel, single input, eight white chickenhead knobs (amp model select, g, v, t, m, b, MV, power level), preset mode button, amp select switch, five user program buttons (bank and one for each of the four channels), pedal effects knob selector, pedal knob, mod/delay effect knob, mod/delay depth knob, tap switch, reverb knob, aux. in jack, headphone jack, rear panel: power switch, footswitch jack, black covering, split front with black covering on the top third and a silver Vox logo and a black cloth grille on the bottom two-thirds with Valvetronix logo, 26.75 in. wide, 20.125 in. tall, 10.25 in. deep, 47.5 lbs., mfg. 2011-present.

MSR $900	$550	$350 - 425	$200 - 250	

VTX150 NEODYMIUM – 150W, 1-12 in. Celestion Vox NeoDog Neodymium speaker, guitar combo, hybrid chassis with Vox Valve Reactor circuit including 1 X EL84 tube, single channel, 44 amp models, 25 effects (11 pedal effects, 11 mod/delay effects, 3 reverb types), 132 presets and eight user program presets, top cream control panel, single input, eight white chickenhead knobs (amp model select, g, v, t, m, b, MV, power level), preset mode button, amp select switch, five user program buttons (bank and one for each of the four channels), pedal effects knob selector, pedal knob, mod/delay effect knob, mod/delay depth knob, tap switch, reverb knob, aux. in jack, headphone jack, rear panel: power switch, effects loop, footswitch jack, extension speaker jack, Vox Bus jack, footswitch jack, black covering, split front with black covering on the top third and a silver Vox logo and a black cloth grille on the bottom two-thirds with "Valvetronix Pro" logo, 17.75 in. wide, 17.25 in. tall, 10.25 in. deep, 26.7 lbs., mfg. 2011-disc.

	$800	$475 - 575	$275 - 350	$1,099

* Add $60 (MSR $84) for five-button footswitch (Model VFS5).

ELECTRIC HYBRID AMPLIFIERS: VTX SERIES

VT20X COMBO – 20W, 1-8 in. speaker, guitar combo, hybrid chassis with Vox multi-stage circuit including 1 X 12AX7 tube, single channel, 11 amp models, 13 onboard effects, 33 presets, top black control panel, single input, nine knobs (amp model select, g, t, m, b, v, power level, effect value 1, effect value 2), preset mode button, five user program buttons (bank and one for each of the four channels), pedal one button, pedal two button, reverb button, amp select button, bias shift button, tap switch, aux. in jack, headphone jack, USB jack, power switch, footswitch jack, black covering, black cloth grille, 16.14 in. wide, 13.66 in. tall, 8.86 in. deep, 16.09 lbs., new 2016.

MSR $245	$180	$115 - 135	$60 - 70	

MSR/NOTES	100%	EXCELLENT	AVERAGE	LAST MSR

VT20X Combo
courtesy Vox

VT40X Combo
courtesy Vox

VT100X Combo
courtesy Vox

VT40X COMBO – 40W, 1-10 in. speaker, guitar combo, hybrid chassis with Vox multi-stage circuit including 1 X 12AX7 tube, single channel, 11 amp models, 13 onboard effects, 33 presets, top black control panel, single input, nine knobs (amp model select, g, t, m, b, v, power level, effect value 1, effect value 2), preset mode button, five user program buttons (bank and one for each of the four channels), pedal one button, pedal two button, reverb button, amp select button, bias shift button, tap switch, aux. in jack, headphone jack, USB jack, footswitch jack, power switch, black covering, black cloth grille, 18.19 in. wide, 13.66 in. tall, 15.91 in. deep, 20.94 lbs., new 2016.

| MSR $340 | $250 | $165 - 190 | $80 - 100 | |

VT100X COMBO – 100W, 1-12 in. speaker, guitar combo, hybrid chassis with Vox multi-stage circuit including 1 X 12AX7 tube, single channel, 11 amp models, 13 onboard effects, 33 presets, top black control panel, single input, nine knobs (amp model select, g, t, m, b, v, power level, effect value 1, effect value 2), preset mode button, five user program buttons (bank and one for each of the four channels), pedal one button, pedal two button, reverb button, amp select button, bias shift button, tap switch, aux. in jack, headphone jack, USB jack, footswitch jack, power switch, black covering, black cloth grille, 23.62 in. wide, 19.25 in. tall, 10.52 in. deep, 41.67 lbs., new 2016.

| MSR $490 | $350 | $230 - 265 | $115 - 140 | |

ACOUSTIC SS AMPLIFIERS: AGA SERIES

AGA70 – 70W, 1-6.5 in. speaker, acoustic guitar combo, hybrid chassis with a 12AU7 preamp tube, two channels (normal/tube pre), chorus, reverb, top black control panel, two 1/4 in. inputs (one per channel), and two XLR mic inputs (one per channel), 14 cream knobs (Normal Ch.: v, b, m, t, color, r, Pre Tube Ch.: v, b, m, t, color, r, All: anti feedback, MV), two gain (low/high) switches (one per channel), two phantom switches (one per channel), two chorus switches (one per channel), mute switch, rear panel: power switch, footswitch jack, XLR direct out, tuner out jack, stereo line in jacks, aux. in jack, black covering, black grille cloth, 12.75 in. wide, 13 in. tall, 10.25 in. deep, 22.3 lbs., optional two-button footswitch, mfg. 2011-disc.

| | $400 | $250 - 300 | $150 - 190 | $550 |

AGA150 – 150W, 1-6.5 in. speaker, 1 in. dome type tweeter, acoustic guitar combo, hybrid chassis with a 12AU7 preamp tube, two channels (normal/tube pre), chorus, reverb, top black control panel, two 1/4 in. inputs (one per channel), and two XLR mic inputs (one per channel), 14 cream knobs (Normal Ch.: v, b, m, t, color, r, Pre Tube Ch.: v, b, m, t, color, r, All: anti feedback, MV), two gain (low/high) switches (one per channel), two phantom switches (one per channel), two chorus switches (one per channel), mute switch, rear panel: power switch, footswitch jack, XLR direct out, tuner out jack, stereo line in jacks, aux. in jack, black covering, black grille cloth, 14.75 in. wide, 13 in. tall, 10.25 in. deep, 26.9 lbs., optional two-button footswitch, mfg. 2011-disc.

| | $600 | $350 - 425 | $200 - 250 | $750 |

BASS SS AMPLIFIERS: T SERIES

From 2000 to 2006, Vox had a series of amps specifically made for bass guitars. The T-60 is derived from the amp back in the 1960s.

T-15 – 15W, 1-8 in. Vox speaker combo, solid-state, single channel, top control panel, one instrument input, tape/CD input, four black pointer knobs (v, t, m, b), headphone jack, black covering, diagonal brown grille, mfg. 2002-03.

| | N/A | $85 - 105 | $60 - 70 | $175 |

T-25 – 25W, 1-10 in. Vox speaker and horn combo, solid-state, single channel, top control panel, two inputs (high and low), five black knobs (v, t, high-mid, mid-low, b), "bassilator switch," black covering, diagonal brown grille, mfg. 2000-03.

| | N/A | $125 - 145 | $85 - 95 | $270 |

* **Add $35 for cover.**

T-60 – 60W, 1-12 in. with horn combo, solid-state, single channel, top control panel, two inputs (active and passive), five black knobs (v, t, high-mid, low-mid, b) "bassilator switch," headphone jack, FX loop, external speaker jack, black covering, brown diagonal grille, mfg. 2001-05.

| | N/A | $210 - 240 | $130 - 155 | $450 |

* **Add $40 for cover.**

MSR/NOTES	100%	EXCELLENT	AVERAGE	LAST MSR

V212BN
courtesy Vox

V212C Speaker Cabinet
courtesy Vox

V412BN
courtesy Vox

SPEAKER CABINETS

AD212 – 160W mono, 80W stereo max inputs, 2-12 in. Neodog speakers by Celestion, matches up with the Valvetronix series, 43 lbs., mfg. 2002-07.

	N/A	$300 - 350	$150 - 200	$650

• Add $30 for cover.

AD412 – 320W mono, 160W stereo max inputs, 4-12 in. Neodog speakers by Celestion, matches up with the Valvetronix series, 84 lbs., mfg. 2002-05.

	N/A	$600 - 700	$350 - 425	$1,299

• Add $50 for cover.

CV212LTD – 2-12 in. speaker cabinet to match up with the Hand-Wired AC-30 head, mfg. 2003-04.

	N/A	$600 - 750	$375 - 450	$1,350

V110NT – 30W, 1-10 in. Celestion VX10 speaker, designed for use with the Lil' Night Train Head (NT2H), rounded corners, black covering, black grille cloth with white piping and Vox logo in upper center, 16.5 in. wide, 11.75 in. tall, 6.25 in. deep, 11.6 lbs., mfg. 2011-disc.

$130	$75 - 100	$45 - 60	$250

V112HTV HERITAGE SPEAKER CABINET – 1-12 in. Celestion Alnico Blue speaker, cream vinyl covering, brown diamond grille with pre-1960s logo, 32 lbs., mfg. 2007-2010.

	N/A	$400 - 475	$250 - 300	$900

V112NT – 1-12 in. Celestion Greenback speaker, designed for use with the Night Train Head (NT15H), rounded corners, black covering, black grille cloth with white piping and Vox logo in upper center, mfg. 2009-present.

MSR $350	$250	$140 - 175	$90 - 110

V212BN – 2-12 in. GSH12-30 speakers, Black covering, Brown Diamond Grille, designed for use with the AC30 Custom Classic, 44 lbs., mfg. 2004-09.

	N/A	$200 - 250	$120 - 150	$450

V212BNX – 2-12 in. Celestion Blue Alnico speakers, Black covering, Brown Diamond Grille, designed for use with the AC30 Custom Classic, 44 lbs., mfg. 2004-09.

	N/A	$600 - 700	$375 - 450	$1,300

V212C SPEAKER CABINET – 2-12 in. Celestion G12M Greenback speakers, 16 ohms, Black covering, Brown Diamond Grille, designed for use with the AC15CH and AC30CH Custom Heads, 49.61 lbs., new 2016.

MSR $620	$450	$295 - 325	$145 - 180

V212H HERITAGE SPEAKER CABINET – 2-12 in. Celestion Alnico Blue speakers, cream vinyl covering, brown diamond grille with pre-1960s logo, 27.4 in. wide, 22.2 in. tall, 10.2 in. deep, 44.1 lbs., mfg. 2008-2010.

	N/A	$675 - 800	$425 - 500	$1,499

V212HWX HANDWIRED SPEAKER CABINET – 30W, 2-12 in. Celestion Alnico Blue speakers, cream vinyl covering, brown diamond grille, 27.75 in. wide, 21.65 in. tall, 10.25 in. deep, 44.8 lbs., dust cover included, mfg. 2011-present.

MSR $1,500	$1,100	$650 - 800	$400 - 500

V212NT – 60W, 2-12 in. Celestion G12H Anniversary model speakers, designed for use with the Night Train 50 (NT50H), rounded corners, black covering, black grille cloth with white piping and Vox logo in upper center, 27.5 in. wide, 20 in. tall, 10 in. deep, 43 lbs., mfg. 2011-present.

MSR $700	$500	$300 - 375	$175 - 225

MSR/NOTES	100%	EXCELLENT	AVERAGE	LAST MSR
V412BK – 4-12 in. Vox speakers, black grille, mfg. 2006-08.				
	N/A	$225 - 275	$135 - 175	$499
V412BL – 320W mono (160W stereo), 4-12 in. GSH12-30 Celestion speakers, designed for use with the Valvetronix Head, blue grille, 83 lbs., mfg. 2005-2010.				
	N/A	$325 - 400	$190 - 225	$750
V412BN – 4-12 in. GSH12-30 speakers, Black covering, Brown Diamond Grille, designed for use with the AC30 Custom Classic, 97 lbs., mfg. 2004-09.				
	N/A	$325 - 400	$200 - 250	$750

VVT AMPS

Vintage Vacuum Tubes. Amplifiers currently produced in Waldorf, MD.

Tony Albany and the guys at VVT Amps produce a wide range of tube amplifiers. They specialize in the Earthquake and Raptor models. They have produced a Lindy Fralin signature model and they are currently working on a Rick Derringer signature. They also make tweed amps that can be professionally aged by them (like a Fender Relic). Most amps and cabinets are available in tweed or custom hardwood cabinets. For more information, visit VVT's website or contact them directly.

CONTACT INFORMATION
VVT AMPS
520 University Drive
Waldorf, MD 20602
Phone No.: 240-222-3830
www.vvtamps.com
vvtamps@vvtamps.com

W SECTION
WALLER AMPLIFICATION

Amplifiers previously produced in Clarkston, MI during the early 2000s. Distributed by ISP Technologies.

James Waller created Rocktron amplifiers in 1985. At Rocktron, he developed the HUSH Noise Reduction System, a line of DSP guitar rack products, and the Circle Surround stereo five-speaker matrix among other devices. In 2001, Waller sold Rocktron to GHS, but he took the engineering team with him and formed ISP (Intelligent Signal Processsing) Technologies in the same year. At first, they used the Waller name on their guitar amplifiers and guitar related speaker cabinets. By 2004, they were only using ISP Technologies as a brand name on their products. The Theta is the only model to be produced with both a Waller and ISP brand name on it. For more information on current ISP products see ISP Technologies.

WARBLER

Amplifiers previously produced in Troy, NH during the 1990s.

Gary R. Croteau founded Juke amplifiers in 1989. He builds all-tube guitar and harmonica amps that are based on the fundamentals of amplifiers built in the late 1950s and early 1960s. Croteau also used the Warbler brand on a series of amps in the 1990s. In 1997, Juke was introduced with Warbler on models, and by 2000, all models were strictly named Juke. See Juke for more information.

WARWICK

Amplifiers currently produced in Markneukirchen, Germany by Warwick GmbH & Co., Musicequipment KG since 1982 and China since the 2000s. Distributed exclusively in the U.S. by U.S. Music Corp. in Buffalo Grove, IL. Previously distributed by Dana B. Goods in Ventura, CA and Hanser Music Group in Hebron, KY.

Hans Peter Wilfer, son of Framus' Frederick Wilfer, established the Warwick trademark in 1982 in Erlangen (Bavaria). Wilfer literally grew up in the Framus factories of his father, and learned all aspects of construction and production 'right at the source.' The high quality of Warwick basses quickly gained notice with bass players worldwide.

In 1995, Warwick moved to Markneukirchen (in the Saxon Vogtland) to take advantage of the centuries of instrument-making traditions. Construction of the new plant provided the opportunity to install new state-of-the-art machinery to go with the skilled craftsmen. The Warwick company continues to focus on producing high quality bass guitars.

Recently Warwick established an amplifier line to team up with their basses. They have taken tube and solid-state technology and combined them to create the best sound that they could. Like they have from the beginning, Warwick works with musicians to develop the best amplifiers they can. Warwick focused on keeping the controls simple, which can be seen on the control panel. They now have a full line of bass amps that are available in head units, combos, and speaker enclosures are available. For more information, visit Warwick's website or contact them directly.

MSR/NOTES	100%	EXCELLENT	AVERAGE	LAST MSR

ELECTRIC BASS AMPLIFIERS: HEAD UNITS

Warwick also produces the Pro Tube IX but it is not available in the U.S. The W that appears on the grille of most Warwick amplifiers may not be on earlier models. Keep in mind that Warwick has kept certain models only for distribution outside of the U.S., but later introduced them. We indicate that the year produced is actually the year it has been available in the U.S.

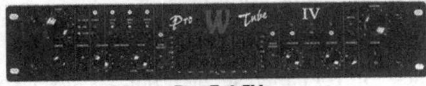
Pro Fet IV
courtesy Warwick

Quad IV
courtesy Warwick

Quad VI
courtesy Warwick

PRO FET II – 250W, two-space rack-mount head-unit only, MOSFET solid-state chassis, single channel, front black control panel, single input, eight silver knobs, various buttons, effects loop, black casing, mfg. 1997-2002.

N/A	$300 - 375	$200 - 250		$599

PRO FET 3.2 (III) – 300W, two-space rack-mount head-unit, bass configuration, MOSFET solid-state chassis, single channel, front black control panel, single input, eight silver knobs (g, comp. rate, cont. grade, b, l/m, m/h, t, MV), various buttons, effects loop, black casing, mfg. 2003-present.

MSR $549	$440	$250 - 300	$135 - 175	

PRO FET IV – 400W, two-space rack-mount head-unit only, MOSFET solid-state chassis, single channel, front black control panel, single input, three silver knobs, eight-band equalizer, various buttons, effects loop, black casing, mfg. 1997-2007.

	$400	$225 - 275	$120 - 150	$499

MSR/NOTES	100%	EXCELLENT	AVERAGE	LAST MSR

PRO FET 5.1 – 500W, two-space rack-mount head-unit, bass configuration, MOSFET solid-state chassis, single channel, front black control panel, single input, eight silver knobs (g, comp. rate, cont. grade, b, l/m, m/h, t, MV), various buttons, effects loop, black casing, mfg. 2005-present.

MSR $649	$525	$300 - 325	$175 - 225	

QUAD IV – 400W, two-space rack-mount head-unit only, all-tube preamp, MOSFET solid-state power amp, single channel, front black control panel with silver grilles, single input, seven silver knobs, various buttons, effects loop, black casing, silver handles, mfg. 2003-06.

	$725	$400 - 475	$250 - 300	$899

QUAD VI – 600W, two-space rack-mount head-unit only, all-tube preamp, MOSFET solid-state power amp, single channel, front black control panel with silver grilles, single input, seven silver knobs, various buttons, effects loop, black casing, silver handles, mfg. 2000-04.

	N/A	$900 - 1,100	$650 - 750	$1,999

QUADRUPLET – preamp only, one space rack-mount head, tube preamp circuit, single channel, front black control panel, single input, seven silver knobs, effects loop, headphone jack, various buttons, black casing, mfg. 1998-2003.

	N/A	$450 - 550	$300 - 350	$999

TUBEPATH 5.1 – 500W, two space rack-mount head-unit, bass configuration, hybrid chassis with an all-tube preamp, MOSFET power amp, single channel, front black control panel, single input, seven chrome knobs (g, contour, b, mid 1, mid2, t, MV), various switches, black casing, mfg. 2005-present.

MSR $2,399	$1,925	$1,100 - 1,300	$675 - 800	

TUBEPATH 10.1 – 1000W, two space rack-mount head-unit, bass configuration, hybrid chassis with an all-tube preamp, MOSFET power amp, single channel, front black control panel, single input, seven chrome knobs (g, contour, b, mid 1, mid2, t, MV), various switches, black casing, mfg. 2005-present.

MSR $2,699	$2,175	$1,200 - 1,450	$725 - 875	

X-TREME 5.1 – 500W, rack-mount unit (2 space), MOSFET power, compressor, 12 knobs, five switches, single input, footswitch control, black metal front with handles, mfg. 2005-present.

MSR $1,799	$1,450	$800 - 950	$525 - 600	

X-TREME 10.1 – 1000W, rack-mount unit (2 space), MOSFET power, compressor, 12 knobs, five switches, single input, footswitch control, black metal front with handles, mfg. 2004-present.

MSR $2,199	$1,775	$1,000 - 1,150	$650 - 750	

ELECTRIC BASS AMPLIFIERS: COMBO UNITS

BLUE CAB 15 – 15W, 1-8 in. speaker, bass combo, solid-state chassis, front control panel, single input, four knobs (v, b, m, t), headphone jack, tilt-back legs, black covering, black grille with "W" logo, mfg. 2006-present.

MSR $189	$150	$80 - 100	$50 - 70	

BLUE CAB 20 – 20W, 1-10 in. speaker, solid-state chassis, front control panel, two inputs, four knobs (v, b, m, t), headphone jack, effects loop, tilt-back legs, black covering, black grille with W on it, mfg. 2004-06.

	$200	$120 - 150	$75 - 100	$279

BLUE CAB 30 – 30W, 1-12 in. speaker, solid-state chassis, front control panel, two inputs, five knobs (v, b, m, t, aux. v), auxillary input, headphone jack, effects loop, tilt-back legs, black covering, black grille with W on it, 46 lbs., mfg. 2004-present.

MSR $239	$190	$100 - 130	$60 - 80	

BLUE CAB 60 – 60W, 1-12 in. speaker, bass combo, solid-state chassis, front control panel, two inputs, five knobs (v, b, m, t, aux. v), RCA inputs, effects loop, headphone jack, tilt-back legs, fan cooled, black covering, black grille with "W" logo, mfg. 2006-present.

MSR $299	$240	$130 - 170	$80 - 105	

CL COMBO – 150W, 1-12 in. speaker with horn, solid-state chassis, single channel, front black control panel, single input, six silver knobs, various buttons, effects loop, black covering, black or gray metal grille with large "W," wheels with retractable luggage handle, mfg. 1997-present.

MSR $899	$725	$400 - 475	$250 - 300	

In 2005, Neodymium speakers and a gray metal grille with a black "W" were introduced.

CCL COMBO – 250W, 1-15 in. speaker with horn, solid-state chassis, single channel, front black control panel, single input, eight silver knobs, various buttons, effects loop, black covering, black or gray metal grille with large "W," wheels with retractable luggage handle, mfg. 1997-present.

MSR $1,099	$895	$500 - 575	$300 - 375	

In 2005, Neodymium speakers and a gray metal grille with a black "W" were introduced.

* *CCL210 Combo* – similar to the CCL Combo, except has 2-10 in. speakers, mfg. 2003-present.

MSR $1,199	$975	$525 - 625	$325 - 400	

In 2005, Neodymium speakers and a gray metal grille with a black "W" were introduced.

MSR/NOTES	100%	EXCELLENT	AVERAGE	LAST MSR

SWEET 15 – 150W, 1-15 in. speaker, solid-state chassis, single channel, front black control panel, single input, six silver knobs (b, ml, mh, t, v, MV), effects loop, low and high boost switches, black covering, black metal grille with W on it, mfg. 2003-06.

	$375	$200 - 250	$120 - 150	$449

SWEET 15.2 – 150W, 1-15 in. speaker with high-freq. switchable horn, solid-state chassis, single channel, front black control panel, single input, two silver knobs (g, MV), eight-band graphic EQ, low and high boost switches, mute switch, effects loop, line out, headphone jack, black covering, black metal grille with W on it, mfg. 2006-present.

MSR $629	$500	$300 - 350	$175 - 225	

SWEET 25.1 – 250W, 1-15 in. and 1-8 in. speakers with high-freq. switchable horn, solid-state chassis, single channel, front black control panel, single input, eight silver knobs (g, comp. adj., cont. adj, b, l/m, m/h, t, MV), deep and bright switches, effects loop, line out, tuner out, black covering, black metal grille with W on it, mfg. 2006-present.

MSR $899	$725	$400 - 475	$250 - 300	

TAKE 12 – 80W, 1-12 in. speaker, solid-state chassis, single channel, front black control panel, single input, six silver knobs (b, ml, mh, t, v, MV), effects loop, black covering, black metal grille with W on it, mfg. 2003-present.

MSR $429	$340	$175 - 225	$110 - 140	

SPEAKER CABINETS

115 PRO – 400W handling, ported cabinet, 1-15 in. speaker, black covering, black metal grille with large "W" logo, mfg. 1997-present.

MSR $529	$425	$225 - 275	$120 - 150	

211 PRO – 400W handling, ported cabinet, 2-10 in. speakers, black covering, black metal grille with large "W" logo, current mfg.

MSR $539	$425	$225 - 275	$120 - 150	

410 PRO – 300W handling, ported cabinet, 4-10 in. speakers, black covering, black metal grille with large "W" logo, mfg. 1997-2005.

	N/A	$240 - 290	$130 - 160	$549

411 PRO – 600W handling, ported cabinet, 4-10 in. speakers with horn, black covering, black metal grille with large "W" logo, mfg. 1997-present.

MSR $789	$640	$350 - 425	$175 - 225	

611 PRO – 900W handling, ported cabinet, 6-10 in. speakers with horn, black covering, black metal grille with large "W" logo, mfg. 2005-present.

MSR $999	$800	$450 - 525	$275 - 325	

TERMINATOR – 450W handling, ported cabinet, 2-15 in., 2-10 in. speakers and a horn, bandpass design, black covering, black metal grille with large "W" logo, mfg. 1997-2002.

	N/A	$700 - 850	$450 - 550	$1,499

WA XV (SUB III) – 300W slave cabinet for cabinets, 1-15 in. speaker, black covering, black metal grille with large "W" logo, disc. 2005.

	N/A	$575 - 675	$350 - 425	$1,299

When this was reintroduced in 2004, it was renamed the Sub III.

WASHBURN

Amplifiers currently produced in China, Korea, and/or Japan. Washburn is a division of and distributed by U.S. Music Corp in Buffalo Grove, IL.

CONTACT INFORMATION
WASHBURN
1000 Corporate Grove Dr.
Buffalo Grove, IL 60089
Phone No.: 847-949-0444
Phone No.: 800-877-6863
Fax No.: 847-949-8444
www.washburn.com
guitar.support@usmusiccorp.com

The Washburn trademark was originated by the Lyon & Healy company of Chicago, Illinois. George Washburn Lyon and Patrick Joseph Healy were chosen by Oliver Ditson, who had formed the Oliver Ditson Company, Inc. in 1835 as a musical publisher. Ditson was a primary force in music merchandising, distribution, and retail sales on the East Coast. In 1864 the Lyon & Healy music store opened for business. The late 1800s found the company ever expanding from retail, to producer, and finally distributor. The Washburn trademark was formally filed for in 1887, and the name applied to quality stringed instruments produced by a manufacturing department of Lyon & Healy.

Lyon & Healy were part of the Chicago musical instrument production conglomerate that produced musical instruments throughout the early and mid-1900s. As in business, if there is demand, a successful business will supply. Due to their early pioneering of mass production, the Washburn facility averaged up to one hundred instruments a day! Lyon & Healy/Washburn were eventually overtaken by the Tonk Bros. company, and the Washburn trademark was eventually discarded.

When the trademark was revived in 1964, the initial production of acoustic guitars came from Japan. Washburn electric guitars were re-introduced to the American market in 1979, and featured U.S. designs on Japanese-built instruments. Production of the entry level models was switched to Korea during the mid to late 1980s. As the company gained a larger foothold in the guitar market, American production was reintroduced in the late 1980s as well. Grover Jackson (ex-Jackson/Charvel) was instrumental in introducing new designs for Washburn for the Chicago series in 1993.

MSR/NOTES	100%	EXCELLENT	AVERAGE	LAST MSR

Washburn introduced amplifiers sometime in the 1980s. The exact release date wasn't available to us, but in literature the PG series was available until 1991. Washburn then discontinued all amplifiers until 1995 when the Vintage Guitar series was released along with a single acoustic amp. These models lasted a single year. Washburn then reorganized and came out with the BD (Bad Dog) series in 2000. The WA line of acoustic amplifiers were released in 2001, and more BD amps debuted in 2002. For more information, visit Washburn's website or contact them directly. Information courtesy: John Teagle, Washburn: *Over One Hundred Years of Fine Stringed Instruments.*

ACOUSTIC AMPLIFIERS

WA20
courtesy Washburn

WA30
courtesy Washburn

AG80 FESTIVAL – 80W, acoustic amp, 1-12 in. and 1-5 in. speakers, piezo tweeter, solid-state chassis, two channels, reverb, front gold control panel, two inputs, 24 black chickenhead knobs, tape input, contour, notch filter, XLR inputs, brown covering, brown grille, mfg. 1995 only.

	N/A	$350 - 425	$200 - 250	$750

WA20 – 12W 1-6.5 in. speaker, acoustic combo, solid state chassis, front control panel, single input, five knobs (v, b, m, t, c) headphone jack, brown covering, wedge-shaped cabinet, brown metal grille, mfg. 2001-present.

MSR $213	$120	$75 - 95	$40 - 55	

WA30 – 30W, 1-6.5 in. speaker, acoustic combo, solid state chassis, reverb, chorus, front control panel, single input, nine knobs, XLR output, headphone jack, effects loop, brown covering, wedge-shaped cabinet, brown metal grille, mfg. 2001-present.

MSR $534	$300	$175 - 225	$105 - 130	

GUITAR AMPLIFIERS: BD SERIES

The BD Series stands for the Bad Dog series.

BD12
courtesy Washburn

BD25R
courtesy Washburn

BD30B
courtesy Washburn

BD12 – 12W, electric amplifier, 1-6.5 in. speaker, solid-state chassis, front silver control panel, single input, five knobs (g, v, t, m, b), headphone jack, black cabinet, silver metal grille, mfg. 2000-05.

	N/A	$35 - 55	$15 - 25	$100

* **Add $25 for reverb (Model BD12R, extra reverb knob).**

BD25R – 25W, electric amplifier, 1-8 in. speaker, solid-state chassis, two channels, reverb, front silver control panel, single input, seven knobs (Ch. 1 v, Ch. 2 v, t, m, b, MV, r), headphone jack, effects loop, black cabinet, silver metal grille, mfg. 2000-05.

	N/A	$75 - 100	$40 - 55	$180

* *BD25FX* – similar to the BD25R, except has a digital effect section with an EFX-SEL knob, mfg. 2002-03.

	N/A	$105 - 135	$60 - 80	$250

BD30B – 30W, bass amplifier, 1-10 in. speaker, solid-state chassis, single channel, front silver chrome control panel, two inputs, five knobs (v, b, m, t), effects loop, headphone jack, black covering, silver metal grille, mfg. 2000-05.

	N/A	$70 - 90	$35 - 50	$160

MSR/NOTES	100%	EXCELLENT	AVERAGE	LAST MSR

BD40R – 40W, electric amplifier, 1-12 in. speaker, solid-state chassis, two channels, reverb, front silver control panel, single input, nine knobs, single switch, headphone jack, effects loop, speaker outs, black cabinet, silver metal grille, mfg. 2002-04.

	N/A	$105 - 135	$60 - 80	$250

BD75B – 75W, bass amplifier, 1-15 in. speaker with a piezo tweeter, solid-state chassis, compression, single channel, front silver chrome control panel, two inputs, four knobs and 7-band EQ, effects loop, headphone jack, black covering, silver metal grille, mfg. 2002-04.

	N/A	$150 - 200	$85 - 110	$370

BD75R – 75W, electric amplifier, 1-12 in. speaker, solid-state chassis, two channels, reverb, front silver control panel, single input, 13 knobs, two switches, headphone jack, effects loop, speaker outs, black cabinet, silver metal grille, mfg. 2002-04.

	N/A	$145 - 195	$80 - 110	$350

GUITAR AMPLIFIERS: PG SERIES

Washburn also made a PG50H and PG100H, which were both head units and featured 50 and 100 watts, respectively. They retailed last for $350 and $450, but little is known about them. 4-12 in. speaker cabinets were also available at a last retail of $450.

PG12 – 12W, 1-8 in. speaker, basic features, headphone jack, black covering, black grille, mfg. late 1980s-1992.

	N/A	$40 - 60	$15 - 25	$120

PG15 – 15W, 1-8 in. speaker, solid-state chassis, reverb, front black control panel, single input, six knobs (v, OD, MV, t, m, b), headphone jack, black covering, black grille, mfg. late 1980s-1992.

	N/A	$50 - 75	$25 - 35	$150

* **Add $20 for reverb.**

PG30B – 30W, bass amp, 1-12 in. speaker, solid-state chassis, front black control panel, two inputs, five knobs (v, MV, t, m, b), headphone jack, line out, black covering, black grille, mfg. late 1980s-1991.

	N/A	$120 - 150	$70 - 90	$300

PG35R – 35W, 1-10 in. speaker, solid-state chassis, reverb, front black control panel, single input, seven knobs (v, OD, MV, t, m, b, r), headphone jack, line out, black covering, black grille, mfg. late 1980s-1992.

	N/A	$100 - 140	$50 - 70	$270

PG55R – 55W, 1-12 in. speaker, solid-state chassis, reverb, front black control panel, single input, seven knobs (v, OD, MV, t, m, b, r), headphone jack, line out, black covering, black grille, mfg. late 1980s-1992.

	N/A	$150 - 200	$95 - 120	$360

PG65B – 65W, bass amp, 1-15 in. speaker, solid-state chassis, front black control panel, two inputs, five knobs (v, MV, t, m, b), headphone jack, line out, extra speaker jack, black covering, black grille, mfg. late 1980s-1991.

	N/A	$170 - 220	$95 - 120	$430

PG65C – 65W, 2-10 in. speakers, solid-state chassis, chorus, reverb, front black control panel, headphone jack, line out, footswitch, black covering, black grille, mfg. late 1980s-1991.

	N/A	$175 - 225	$110 - 140	$480

GUITAR AMPLIFIERS: VINTAGE GUITAR SERIES

VGA15 THE SOUTH SIDE JR. – 15W, guitar amp, 1-8 in. speaker, solid-state chassis, top chrome control panel, five knobs, tweed covering, brown grille, mfg. 1995 only.

	N/A	$80 - 110	$40 - 60	$180

VGA30 THE SOUTH SIDE – 30W, guitar amp, 1-10 in. speaker, solid-state chassis, top chrome control panel, five knobs, tweed covering, brown grille, mfg. 1995 only.

	N/A	$100 - 150	$50 - 70	$270

VBA15 THE BASS KING JR. – 15W, bass amp, 1-10 in. speaker, solid-state chassis, top chrome control panel, five knobs, tweed covering, brown grille, mfg. 1995 only.

	N/A	$90 - 120	$45 - 65	$220

VBA30 THE BASS KING – 30W, bass amp, 1-12 in. speaker, solid-state chassis, top chrome control panel, five knobs, tweed covering, brown grille, mfg. 1995 only.

	N/A	$125 - 175	$70 - 95	$300

WATKINS

Amplifiers currently produced in England.

Watkins Electric Music (WEM) was established by Charlie Watkins in the 1950s. He and his brother opened a record shop in London with his brother in 1949. In 1951, they moved across town and started to sell guitars and accordions. Charlie's

CONTACT INFORMATION
WATKINS
wemwatkins.co.uk
watkins@wemwatkins.co.uk

brother opened up his own shop in 1957 to build and design an electric guitar. In the late 1950s, the first amplifiers, the Westminster and Dominator, were built. In 1958 the Watkins Copicat Echo was developed. They produced thousands of these units and many of them are still in use today. In the 1960s, Watkins continued to produce the Copicat as well as their line of amplifiers. In 1966, the Slave P.A. system was introduced. By the late 1960s and early 1970s, WEM started to appear on the products instead of Watkins. There were a wide variety of WEM amplifiers produced in the 1970s that were offered at an affordable price.

The Watkins Dominator amp and Copicat Echo unit are now being reproduced. There are no current U.S. prices on them, just British pounds. Visit www.wemwatkins.co.uk for more information on Watkins, WEM, and new models. Information courtesy of Charlie Watkins.

ELECTRIC AMPLIFIERS

DOMINATOR – 17W, 2-10 in. speakers that face away from each other, tube chassis including 2 X EL84 power tubes, top control panel that wraps around back, four inputs, six knobs, beige and green cabinet, two beige color grilles-one for each speaker, mfg. late 1950s-1960s.

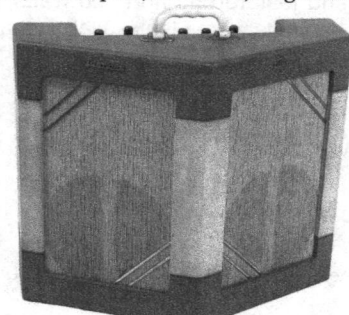

courtesy solidbodyguitar.com, Inc.   courtesy solidbodyguitar.com, Inc.

N/A	$1,500 - 2,000	$950 - 1,200

JOKER – 30W, 1-12 in. Hi-Fi speaker and a Hi-Fi horn, tube chassis with 4 X EL84 power tubes, built in Copicat, two-tone cabinet, rectangular grille, mfg. 1960s.

N/A	$700 - 900	$400 - 500

WESTMINSTER – smaller amplifier estimated 5-10W, 1-8 in. or 1-10 in. speaker, top control panel, two inputs, five knobs, 2-color cabinet, square grille, mfg. 1960s.

N/A	$500 - 650	$300 - 400

WEM

See WATKINS

WEM stands for Watkins Electric Music. W.E.M. had a number of amplifiers and speaker equipment produced during the mid 1970s. The company has remained the same under Charlie Watkins, but in the late 1960s and early 1970s the amplifiers and P.A. equipment started to appear with WEM on the label. These amps were produced and England and many of them have stayed over there. A few may appear in the U.S., but until more have been circulated it is difficult to price these amps accurately. Some of the more popular models were the Dominator and the Westminster (mainly because of their popularity in the 1960s. Look for more information or updates in further editions of the *Blue Book of Guitar Amplifiers.*

WESTBURY

Amplifiers previously produced overseas.

Westbury is a company that produced both guitars and amplifiers in the early 1980s. They were part of Korg (Marshall, and ex-Parker), and produced overseas. Korg owns (owned) the trademark but hasn't produced any models in quite some time. Back in the 1980s the company was apparently called Unicord and they produced the Westbury amp.

ELECTRIC AMPLIFIERS

Some examples of Westbury amplifiers include the DG1000 with either 2-10 in. or 2-12 in. speakers. These amps were solid-state and had general features of amps. They are typically found used in excellent condition from $200 - 350 and in average condition $100 - 200.

WEST LABORATORIES

Amplifiers previoulsy produced in Okemos, MI, Flint, MI and Lansing, MI between 1965 and 2015.

Dave West started producing West amplifiers in 1965. He operated a small Hi-Fi shop in Flint, MI that sold McIntosh, Dynaco, Acoustic Research, and Klipsch brands. Dick Wagner of the Bossmen came in and wanted to get JBL speakers. West arranged a meeting with the JBL rep and ordered a large amount of JBL speakers, which was a huge financial risk at the time. One day, a Sunn amp was shipped to his shop and he took the amp apart to inspect it. He realized he had all the components inside the amp, so why not try to produce them under his own name and make some money. West Laboratories moved to Lansing, MI in the late 1960s, and continued to produce amplifiers until 1972. In 2005, West started West Laboratories again featuring different amps then he produced in the 1960s and early 1970s. Most amps are custom orders.

WHITE (FENDER)

Amplifiers previously produced by Fender in the late 1950s. Distributed by Fender.

White is one of the first and only private-branded names by Fender. The White name was used on a line of a steel guitars with matching amps (these were sold together as a set, much like many steel guitars and amps at the time). The White amp is almost identical in design to the Fender Princeton narrow panel tweed model, but they were covered in a gray vinyl with a dark grille and a small White logo in the upper left corner. Fender named these guitars and amps White in appreciation of Forrest White, who was the plant manager at the time. They were probably sold to non-Fender dealers, so they could sell a Fender product without violating Fender authorized dealer's territory. Information courtesy John Teagle and John Sprun, *Fender Amps: The First Fifty Years*.

WHITE (MATAMP)

See MatAmp.

WILDER

Amplifiers previously produced in Chicago, IL during the late 1960s and early 1970s.

Wilder amplifiers were produced by Wilder Engineering Products in Chicago, IL from about 1965 to 1971. They produced a wide range of solid-state guitar, bass, and PA application amps. Since these amps were built and distributed in Chicago, they were very popular in the midwest. Models include the **Model 120-A**, **Model 120-RB**, **Model 150 RV**, **Model 150 RV Super Classic**, **The Wild One 210 RVPA**, and various speaker cabinets. Any further information on Wilder amps can be submitted directly to Blue Book Publications.

WIZARD AMPLIFICATION, INC.

Amplifiers and speaker cabinets currently produced in Cornwall, Ontario and White Rock, British Columbia, Canada.

CONTACT INFORMATION
WIZARD AMPLIFICATION, INC.
www.wizardamplification.com
admin@wizardamplification.com

Wizard Amplification Inc. is a Canadian company dedicated to the design and manufacturing of high-end tube amplifiers and speaker cabinets. Construction consists of military type turrent boards, true point to point soldering, premium capacitors and metal film resistors for stability and tolerance. Fully welded and polished 14 gauge nickel and brass plated steel chassis support high quality built transformers. Lexan control panels dress these amplifiers and high grade potentiometers control them. Heavy duty sockets are fitted with matched sets of high grade tubes. Hand wired to military specifications and zero compromise in construction assures ultimate reliability in the studio and on the road. All speaker cabinets are made of 100% Baltic birch. Recessed steel handles, high quality speaker mounting hardware, aluminum jack plates with Switchcraft jacks, and high grade Tolex covering add to the ruggedness that make all Wizard speaker durable. For more information, visit their website.

GUITAR AMPLIFIERS & SPEAKER CABINETS

The Wizard **Vintage Classic** is a high-end alternative to the mid-sixties Marshall Plexi. The Wizard **Modern Classic** is a Hi-Gain foot-switching version of the Vintage Classic. Wizard offers 2-12 speaker combo versions of both the Vintage Classic and the Modern Classic. The Wizard **Classic Bass Amplifier** is available in 50 - 100 - 300 watt models. Wizard Amplification produces a

Vintage Classic
courtesy Wizard Amplification, Inc.

2-12 Combo
courtesy Wizard Amplification, Inc.

Modern Classic
courtesy Wizard Amplification, Inc.

full line of speaker cabinets for Guitar applications loaded with "Wizard Rock 20" guitar speakers, "Wizard Alnico Black" guitar speakers, Celestion Greenback speakers, and Celestion Alnico Gold speakers. Loaded in Wizard Bass are cabinets are the historic Wizard Bass 8032 10 in. bass speaker, and Wizard custom designed 12 in. and 15 in. bass speakers.

WOODSON

Amplifiers previously produced in Bartlesville, OK and Bolivar, MO during the 1970s.

Woodson produced various guitar, bass, and PA amps with solid-state chassis during the 1970s. Very little is known about the company and history, and further information on Woodson amplifiers can be submitted directly to Blue Book Publications.

WORKHORSE

Amplifiers previously produced by Visual Sound in Spring Hill, TN during the mid-2000s.

Bob Weil founded Visual Sound in 1994 with the Visual Volume pedal. It all started in 1988, when he bought a volume pedal that left much to desire. Since there wasn't a product on the market that Bob was looking for, he decided to learn how to build his own. The Visual Volume was his first pedal, but the Jeckyll & Hyde pedal really put Visual on the amp. In the early 2000s, Bob and chief engineer R.G. Keen designed a line of tube amplifiers called the Workhorse Series. Models include the **Pony 30W** with 1-12 in. speaker and the **Stallion 60W** with 2-12 in. speakers. Visual Sound does not produce guitar amplifiers anymore, but they do produced a full line of guitar effects pedals.

WORKING DOG

See Alessandro.

Y SECTION
YAMAHA

Amplifiers currently produced in U.S., Taiwan, and Indonesia. Distributed in the U.S. by the Yamaha Corporation of America, located in Buena Park, CA. Amplifiers previously produced in Japan. Yamaha company headquarters is located in Hamamatsu, Japan.

Yamaha has a tradition of building musical instruments for over 100 years. The first Yamaha solid body electric guitars were introduced to the American market in 1966. While the first series relied on designs based on classic American favorites, the second series developed more original designs. In the mid-1970s, Yamaha was recognized as the first Asian brand to emerge as a prominent force equal to the big-name US builders.

Production shifted to Taiwan in the early 1980s as Yamaha built its own facility to maintain quality. In 1990, the Yamaha Corporation of America (located in Buena Park, California) opened the Yamaha Guitar Development (YGD) center in North Hollywood, California. The Yamaha Guitar Development center focuses on design, prototyping, and customizing both current and new models. The YGD also custom builds and maintains many of the Yamaha artist's instruments. The center's address on Weddington Street probably was the namesake of the Weddington series instruments of the early 1990s. Recently Yamaha released the DG-1000 & DG100-212 digital guitar amplifiers. Currently, the only amplifier Yamaha produces is the GA-15 practice amp that is part of Yamaha's Gigmaker package. The Yamaha company is active in producing a full range of musical instruments, including band instruments, stringed instruments, bass amplifiers, and P.A. equipment. For more information, visit Yamaha's website or contact them directly.

CONTACT INFORMATION
YAMAHA
Yamaha Corporation of America
6600 Orangethorpe Ave.
Buena Park, CA 90620
Phone No.: 714-522-9011
Phone No.: 800-322-4322
Fax No.: 714-522-9587
www.usa.yamaha.com

MSR/NOTES	100%	EXCELLENT	AVERAGE	LAST MSR

ELECTRIC TUBE AMPLIFIERS

T50 HEAD – 50W, head unit only, rack mount, all tube chassis, designed by Soldano, mfg. early 1990s.

	N/A	$325 - 400	$200 - 250	$949

T50C COMBO – similar to the T-50, except is in combo form with 1-12 in. Celestion speaker, mfg. early 1990s.

	N/A	$425 - 500	$275 - 325	$1,049

T100 HEAD – 100W, head unit only, rack mount, all tube chassis, designed by Soldano, mfg. early 1990s.

	N/A	$375 - 450	$225 - 275	$1,099

T100C COMBO – similar to the T-100, except is in combo form with 1-12 in. Celestion speaker, mfg. early 1990s.

	N/A	$475 - 550	$300 - 375	$1,249

ELECTRIC GUITAR AMPLIFIERS

Yamaha has also produced a few speaker cabinets over the years. Keep in mind that several of these models may have different variations such as different knob configurations and the addition or subtraction of reverb or tremolo. Often times these factors do not affect the value. Yamaha also produced the GA-10 practice amp. New price on this models is typically around $25.

DG60-112 – 60W, 1-12 in. Eminence speaker, solid-state chassis, 2 channels, reverb, front red control panel, eighteen black knobs, two inputs, effects loop, line out, speaker mute, black covering, black grille, 40 lbs., mfg. 1999-2002.

	N/A	$300 - 350	$175 - 225	

* ***DG60FX-112*** – similar to the DG60-112, except has a DG-Stomp as its preamp section and has a footswitch to select separate patches and on-board effects, 37 lbs., mfg. 2000-02.

	N/A	$375 - 450	$250 - 300	

DG80-112 – 80W, 1-12 in. Celestion speaker, solid-state chassis, eight-amp types, 128 presets, three reverbs, front red control panel, ten motorized black knobs, two inputs, digital display with buttons, effects loop, line out, speaker simulator, black covering, brown grille, 55 lbs., mfg. 1998-2002.

	N/A	$475 - 550	$300 - 350	

DG80-210 – 80W, 2-10 in. Celestion V10-60 speakers, solid-state chassis, eight amp types, 128 presets, three reverbs, front red control panel, ten motorized black knobs, two inputs, digital display with buttons, effects loop, line out, speaker simulator, black covering, brown grille, 57 lbs., mfg. 2000-02.

	N/A	$475 - 550	$300 - 350	

DG100-212 – 100W, 2-12 in. Celestion Vintage 30 speakers, solid-state chassis, eight-amp types, 128 presets, three reverbs, front red control panel, ten motorized black knobs, two inputs, digital display with buttons, effects loop, line out, speaker simulator, removable caster wheels, black covering, brown grille, 73 lbs., mfg. 1998-2002.

	N/A	$625 - 750	$450 - 525	

DG130H – 130W, head-unit only, solid-state chassis, eight-amp types, 128 presets, three reverbs, front red control panel, ten motorized black knobs, two inputs, digital display with buttons, effects loop, XLR output, speaker simulator, black covering, black grille, 40 lbs., mfg. 1999-2002.

	N/A	$450 - 525	$275 - 325	

MSR/NOTES	100%	EXCELLENT	AVERAGE	LAST MSR

DG1000 – 100W, head-unit rack mount, solid-state chassis, eight amp types, 128 presets, three reverbs, front control panel, ten motorized black knobs, two inputs, digital display with buttons, effects loop, XLR output, speaker simulator, mfg. 1999-2001.

	N/A	$375 - 450	$250 - 300	

F-20 – 20W, 20cm speaker, solid-state chassis, two channels, front black control panel, six knobs, single input, black covering, black grille, disc. 2003.

	N/A	$60 - 80	$35 - 50	$150

F-20B – 20W bass amp, 25cm speaker, solid-state chassis, active/passive switching, front black control panel, five knobs, single input, black covering, black grille, disc. 2003.

	N/A	$75 - 100	$45 - 60	$170

G50-112 – 50W, 1-12 in. speakers, solid-state chassis, single channel, front black control panel, two inputs (high and low), seven black and silver knobs, black covering, black grille, mfg. 1983-1992.

courtesy S.P. Fjestad   courtesy S.P. Fjestad

	N/A	$225 - 275	$135 - 175	

G50-210 – 50W, 2-10 in. speakers, solid-state chassis, reverb, tremolo, front control panel, two inputs, ten knobs (v, b, m, t, b, dist., r, s, i, pre-set v), black covering, black grille, mfg. 1983-1992.

	N/A	$250 - 300	$150 - 200	

G100-112 – 100W, 1-12 in. speaker, solid-state chassis, tremolo, reverb, front control panel, two inputs, 10 knobs (v, b, m, t, b, dist., r, s, i, pre-set v), black covering, black grille, mfg. 1983-1992.

	N/A	$250 - 300	$150 - 200	

G100-210 – 100W, 2-10 in. speakers, solid-state chassis, tremolo, reverb, front control panel, two inputs, 10 knobs (v, b, m, t, b, dist., r, s, i, pre-set v), black covering, black grille, mfg. 1983-1992.

	N/A	$275 - 325	$175 - 225	

G100-212 – 100W, 2-12 in. speakers, solid-state chassis, tremolo, reverb, front control panel, two inputs, 10 knobs (v, b, m, t, b, dist., r, s, i, pre-set v), black covering, black grille, mfg. 1983-1992.

	N/A	$300 - 350	$200 - 250	

HY10GIII – 10W, 1-8 in. speaker, solid-state chassis, portable design, mfg. 1988-early 1990s.

	N/A	$75 - 100	$40 - 60	

JX-20 – 20W, 1-10 in. speaker, solid-state chassis, single channel, reverb, front brown control panel, two inputs (high and low), five knobs (v, MV, t, b, r), brown covering, brown grille, mfg. 1980s-1990s.

courtesy S.P. Fjestad   courtesy S.P. Fjestad

	N/A	$150 - 200	$95 - 120	

MSR/NOTES	100%	EXCELLENT	AVERAGE	LAST MSR

JX-30 – 30W, 1-10 in. speaker, solid-state chassis, reverb, distortion, front control panel, two inputs, six knobs, brown covering, brown grille, mfg. 1983-1992.

	N/A	$175 - 225	$110 - 140	

JX-30B – 30W, bass amp, mfg. 1980s-1990s.

	N/A	$175 - 225	$110 - 140	

JX-35 – 40W, 1-12 in. speaker, solid state chassis, reverb, pull-style gain, front control panel, two inputs, six knobs (v, MV, t, m, b, r), headphone jack, brown covering, brown grille, mfg. 1980s-1990s.

	N/A	$200 - 250	$120 - 150	

TA SERIES – series of guitar amps that were mainly wedge shaped. This series had a variety of models and configurations. These were some of the first amps produced by Yamaha starting in the late 1960s and lasted to the early 1970s.

	100%	EXCELLENT	AVERAGE	
Small Models	N/A	$100 - 200	$50 - 95	
Large Models	N/A	$200 - 300	$120 - 150	

THR5 – 10W (2 X 5W), 2-3.15 in. speakers, guitar modeling combo, solid-state chassis, five amp models (Modern, Brit Hi, Lead, Crunch, Clean), eight effects (chorus, flanger, phaser, tremolo, delay, delay/reverb, spring reverb, hall reverb), single channel, top control panel, single input, seven black knobs (amp model selector, g, MV, tone, effect selector/level, delay/reverb selector/level, v), power switch, tap/tuner button, headphone jack, aux. in jack, USB connection, cream metal casing, slotted speaker grille, AC/DC operation, 10.675 in. wide, 6.5 in. tall, 4.75 in. deep, AC adapter, USB cable, stereo mini cable, and DVD included, new 2012.

MSR $330	$200	$135 - 170	$80 - 100	

THR10 – 10W (2 X 5W), 2-3.15 in. speakers, guitar modeling combo, solid-state chassis, eight amp models (Modern, Brit Hi, Lead, Crunch, Clean, Bass, Acoustic, Flat), eight effects (chorus, flanger, phaser, tremolo, delay, delay/reverb, spring reverb, hall reverb), single channel, top control panel, single input, 10 black knobs (amp model selector, g, MV, b, m, t, effect selector/level, delay/reverb selector/level, guitar output, USB/Aux. output), five user memory buttons, power switch, tap/tuner button, headphone jack, aux. in jack, USB connection, cream metal casing, slotted speaker grille, AC/DC operation, 14.175 in. wide, 7.25 in. tall, 5.5 in. deep, 6.2 lbs., AC adapter, USB cable, stereo mini cable, and DVD included, new 2012.

MSR $460	$300	$180 - 225	$110 - 135	

VR4000 – 50W, 2-12 in. speakers, solid-state chassis, stereo, two channels, chorus, reverb, front black control panel, sixteen black knobs, two effects loop, black covering, black grille, footswitch available, mfg. 1988-1992.

	N/A	$300 - 350	$175 - 225	

VR6000 – 100W, 2-12 in. speakers, solid-state chassis, stereo, two channels, chorus, reverb, front black control panel, sixteen black knobs, two effects loop, black covering, black grille, footswitch available, mfg. 1988-1992.

	N/A	$325 - 400	$200 - 250	

YTA/YTB SERIES – series of guitar and bass amps produced in the mid 1970s that came in a variety of configurations. Pricing depends upon how much power and how big the speaker is.

	100%	EXCELLENT	AVERAGE	
Small Models	N/A	$150 - 250	$75 - 120	
Large Models	N/A	$250 - 450	$150 - 200	

ELECTRIC BASS AMPLIFIERS: BBT SERIES

BBT 500H BASS HEAD – 500W, head-unit, bass configuration, solid-state digital chassis, DSP, 11 amp models, front black and gray control panel, single input, 11 knobs (input level, sound type select, comp., g, MV, b, l/m, m, m/h, t, output), effects loop, line out with level, tuner out, headphone jack, MIDI in/out, fan cooled, black casing, 11 lbs., disc. 2006

	N/A	$350 - 425	$225 - 275	$950

* ***BBT 500-110 Combo*** – similar to the BBT 500H Bass Head, except in combo configuration with 1-10 in. speaker, disc. 2006.

	N/A	$600 - 700	$375 - 450	$1,400

* ***BBT 500-115 Combo*** – similar to the BBT 500H Bass Head, except in combo configuration with 1-15 in. speaker, disc. 2006.

	N/A	$700 - 800	$450 - 525	$1,600

BBT 110S SPEAKER CABINET – wattage unknown, 1-10 in. speaker, 4 ohm impedance, bottom ported, black covering, black metal grille, disc. 2006.

	N/A	$175 - 225	$110 - 140	$450

BBT 210S SPEAKER CABINET – wattage unknown, 2-10 in. speakers, 4 ohm impedance, bottom ported, black covering, black metal grille, disc. 2006.

	N/A	$250 - 300	$135 - 175	$600

BBT 410S SPEAKER CABINET – wattage unknown, 4-10 in. speakers, 4 ohm impedance, bottom ported, black covering, black metal grille, disc. 2006.

	N/A	$325 - 400	$200 - 250	$800

MSR/NOTES	100%	EXCELLENT	AVERAGE	LAST MSR

YORKVILLE

Amplifiers previously produced in Pickering, Ontario, Canada between the mid-1960s and 2007. Other audio equipment is currently produced. The Yorkville trademark was founded in 1963. Yorkville products are distributed in the U.S. by Yorkville Sound Inc. in Niagra Falls, NY.

CONTACT INFORMATION
YORKVILLE
4625 Witmer Industrial Estate
Niagra Falls, NY 14305
Phone No.: 716-297-2920
Fax No.: 716-297-3689
www.yorkville.com
info@yorkville.com

Pete Traynor built the first Traynor bass amplifier while he was a repairman in the back of the shop Long & McQuade in 1963. Soon after, Jack Long started the Yorkville Sound company and began selling Traynor's bass amplifier along with a few other products. The company expanded quickly and by 1963 Yorkville was building PA colums, and by 1965 they became incorporated as a company. In the mid-1960s, Yorkville products became available in the U.S., and by the early 1970s, they became available in Europe. Between the 1970s and the late 1990s, Yorkville mainly focused on pro audio and other related products, but they did also offer various guitar and bass amplifiers.

By 2007, the Yorkville Group had divided the Yorkville and Traynor brands so they each served just one industry. Currently, all guitar and instrument related amplifiers are branded Traynor, and all other pro audio, mixing equipment, and misc. speaker cabinets are branded Yorkville. Also, the acoustic line of amplifiers that Yorkville was producing under their own name were given new cosmetics and moved to the Traynor line. For more information, visit their website, or contact them directly.

AM50
courtesy Yorkville

AM100
courtesy Yorkville

AM150
courtesy Yorkville

ACOUSTIC GUITAR AMPLIFIERS

In 2006, Yorkville discontinued this series, but introduced the exact same models with different cosmetics under the Traynor Brand (see Traynor).

AM50 – 50W, 1-8 in. woofer, tweeter, two channels, reverb, front black control panel, six knobs, notch filter, wedge design, black carpet covering, black metal grille, 23 lbs., disc. 2005.

	N/A	$250 - 300	$150 - 200	$449

AM100 – 100W, 2-6.5 in. speakers, tweeter, two channels with separate gain controls, 32 preset ART digital effects processor, front black control panel, nine knobs, notch filter, wedge or upright design, black carpet covering, black metal grille, 25 lbs., disc. 2005.

	N/A	$325 - 400	$200 - 250	$589

AM150 – 150W stereo, 2-8 in. speakers, horn, tweeter, two channels with separate gain controls, 32 preset ART digital effects processor, front black control panel, nine knobs, notch filter, wedge or upright design, black carpet covering, black metal grille, 25 lbs., disc. 2005.

	N/A	$375 - 450	$225 - 275	$699

BASS GUITAR AMPLIFIERS

BM50 – 50W, 1-10 in. speaker combo, solid-state chassis, front silver control panel, four knobs, single input, line out, headphone jack, blue textured covering, metal grille covering, 26 lbs., disc. 2003.

	N/A	$135 - 175	$85 - 110	$309

BM100 – 100W, 1-15 in. speaker combo, solid-state chassis, front silver control panel, four knobs, single input, effects loop, line out, headphone jack, blue textured covering, metal grille covering, 45 lbs., disc. 2003.

	N/A	$175 - 225	$110 - 140	$399

BM200 – 200W, 1-15 in. speaker combo with a tweeter, solid-state chassis, front silver control panel, five knobs, single input, effects loop, line out, headphone jack, blue textured covering, metal grille covering, 57 lbs., disc. 2003.

	N/A	$225 - 275	$135 - 175	$499

* **BM200T** – similar to the BM200, except has 2-10 in. speakers with a tweeter, disc. 2003.

	N/A	$275 - 325	$150 - 200	$599

MSR/NOTES	100%	EXCELLENT	AVERAGE	LAST MSR

XM50(C)
courtesy Yorkville

XM200(C)
courtesy Yorkville

XS400(C)
courtesy Yorkville

BM400 – 400W, 1-15 in. speaker combo with a tweeter, solid-state chassis, front silver control panel, two knobs, 10-band graphic equalizer, two inputs, effects loop, line out, blue textured covering, metal grille covering, 80 lbs., disc. 2003.

	N/A	$425 - 500	$275 - 325	$959

* **BM400H** – similar to the BM400, except in head-unit rack-mount configuration, black casing, disc. 2003.

	N/A	$325 - 375	$200 - 250	$699

XM50(C) – 50W, 1-10 in. speaker, solid-state chassis, single channel, front control panel, four knobs (v, b, m, t), RCA inputs, headphone jack, black carpet covering, chrome grille, 30 lbs., mfg. 2003-07.

	$320	$175 - 225	$110 - 140	$399

• Add $25 for regular black covering (Model XM50, disc. 2004).

XM100(C) – 100W, 1-15 in. speaker, solid-state chassis, single channel, front control panel, two inputs, five knobs (v, b, m, t, scoop), RCA inputs, effects loop, XLR output, headphone jack, black carpet covering, chrome grille, 50.5 lbs., mfg. 2003-07.

	$400	$225 - 275	$135 - 175	$499

• Add $25 for regular black covering (Model XM100, disc. 2004).

XM200(C) – 200W, 1-15 in. speaker and tweeter, solid-state chassis, single channel, front control panel, two inputs, six knobs (v, b, lm, hm, t, scoop), limiter, RCA inputs, effects loop, XLR output, headphone jack, black carpet covering, chrome grille, 60.5 lbs., mfg. 2003-07.

	$480	$275 - 325	$150 - 200	$599

• Add 15% for regular black covering (Model XM200).

* **XM200T(C)** – similar to the XM200, except has 2-10 in. speakers with a tweeter, mfg. 2003-07.

	$575	$300 - 375	$175 - 225	$719

• Add 15% for regular black covering (Model XM200T).

XS400(C) – 400W, 1-15 in. speaker and piezo tweeter, hybrid chassis (12AX7 in preamp), single channel, front control panel, two inputs, ten silver knobs, compressor, effects loop, XLR output, black carpet covering, gray grille, 80 lbs., mfg. 2003-07.

	$850	$475 - 550	$275 - 325	$1,049

• Add 10% for regular black covering (Model XS400).

* **XS400T(C)** – similar to the XS400C, except has 2-10 in. speakers with a piezo tweeter, mfg. 2004-07.

	$895	$500 - 575	$300 - 350	$1,099

• Add 10% for regular black covering (Model XS400T).

* **XS400H** – similar to the XS400C, except in head-unit configuration (rack mount), mfg. 2003-07.

	$590	$300 - 375	$200 - 250	$729

XS800H – 800W, head-unit only, similar to the XS400 head-unit, mfg. 2004-07.

	$850	$475 - 550	$275 - 325	$1,049

SPEAKER CABINETS

XC115X(C) – 300W, 1-15 in. speaker, 8 ohm impedance, black carpet covering, gray grille, 52 lbs., mfg. 2003-07.

	$290	$150 - 200	$95 - 120	$359

• Add 20% for regular black covering (Model XC115X).

XC115 – 300W, 1-15 in. speaker and piezo tweeter, 8 ohm impedance, black covering, gray grille, 63 lbs., mfg. 2003-07.

	$360	$200 - 250	$120 - 150	$449

MSR/NOTES	100%	EXCELLENT	AVERAGE	LAST MSR

XC115
courtesy Yorkville

XC410
courtesy Yorkville

XC808
courtesy Yorkville

XC210 – 300W, 2-10 in. speakers and 1-1 in. horn, 8 ohm impedance, black covering, gray grille, 63 lbs., mfg. 2003-07.

	$400	$225 - 275	$135 - 175	$499

XC410 – 500W, 4-10 in. speakers and 1-1 in. horn, 8 ohm impedance, black covering, gray grille, 89 lbs., mfg. 2003-07.

	$560	$300 - 375	$175 - 225	$699

XC808 – 800W, 8-8 in. speakers and a Motorola tweeter, 4 ohm impedance, black covering, gray grille, 113 lbs., mfg. 2004-07.

	$720	$400 - 475	$250 - 300	$899

Z SECTION
ZAPP

Amplifiers previously produced in the 1970s.

Not much is known about Zapp, the amplifier company. They produced amplifiers during the 1970s, when small practice amplifiers were beginning to take off. A couple small solid-state models exist, but information is scarce on them. These amps had solid-state chassis and typically had 6 in. or 8 in. speakers. The cabinets were made out of particle board and the controls featured one tone and one volume knob. The best part of these amplifiers is that they were made in the U.S.A. They were developed by Bob Archigian and were available through Red Tree Music in Mamaranic, NY. There was a total of 250 produced. It is possible that some other variations may be out there, but for the most part all of these amps are the small practice type. However, there appears to be increasing interest in these amps. Further information on Zapp amplifiers can be submitted directly to Blue Book Publications.

ELECTRIC GUITAR AMPLIFIERS

SMALL PRACTICE AMP – 6 or 8 in. speaker, particle board cabinet, one volume and one tone knob, mfg. 1970s.

	N/A	$60 - 80	$30 - 50

- **Add $20 for 8 in. speaker.**

Z-50 – 10W, 1-8 in. speaker, solid state chassis, reverb, tremolo, front black control panel, two inputs, five knobs (v, tone, s, i, r), black covering, black grille, mfg. early 1980s.

	N/A	$75 - 100	$35 - 55

ZETA

Amplifiers previously built in Oakland, CA during the late 1980s and early 1990s. Distributed by Zeta Music Systems, Inc. of Oakland, CA. The Zeta trademark was established in 1982.

Zeta currently offers quality acoustic/electric violins, and a MIDI violin synthesizer in addition to the current Crossover models of electric bass. They also produced a line of solid-state amplifiers during the late 1980s and early 1990s. Not much information is known about these amplifiers and any further info can be submitted directly to Blue Book Publications. For electric Zeta guitars, refer to the *Blue Book of Electric Guitars*.

ZINKY

Amplifiers currently produced in Flagstaff, AZ since 1999. Distributed by Zinky Electronics.

Bruce Zinky founded Zinky Electronics in 1999. They build tube amps, speaker cabinets, and other electronic related products. Zinky also produces the Smokey guitar amp that is built into empty cigarette packs (see Smokey Amplifiers), and they have also revived the Supro name with a line of tube amps. Zinky currently offers the SuperFly and the Blue Velvet models. The Blue Velvet models are actually covered in a crushed blue velvet material. For more information, visit Zinky's website or contact them directly.

CONTACT INFORMATION
ZINKY
PO Box 3973
Flagstaff, AZ 86003
Phone No.: 928-225-0400
www.zinky.com
info@zinky.com

ZOOM

Amplifiers previously produced in Japan during the mid-2000s. Distributed in the USA by Samson Technologies of Syssonet, N.Y.

The roots of Zoom go back to 1983 when the company was named simply to stand out in the alphabet by starting with Z. The first seven years the company was in business, they helped other manufacturers developing electronic musical devices and MIDI applications. In 1990, Zoom released the 9002 Multi-Effect processor, which could be mounted on a guitar strap, when at the time the only processor was in a rack unit. This product broke into the public and Zoom hasn't looked back since. They have kept ahead of the times by releasing many products before any other company did. Zoom made products mainly for rack units and the like for many years. In 1994, they released a series of foot pedals that featured multi-effects, and in 1996 released the Zoom 505 pedals. After many years of success with effects, Zoom released the Zoom Fire Series of guitar amplifiers in 2003. Zoom produced amplifiers through the late 2000s, but they currently do not produce guitar amps, instead they are focusing on effects.

MSR/NOTES	100%	EXCELLENT	AVERAGE	LAST MSR

ELECTRIC GUITAR AMPLIFIERS

FIRE 15 – 15W, 1-8 in. speaker, guitar combo, solid state chassis, black and silver control panel, 11 modeling types, 17 effect programs, five effect modules, 20 user presets, seven knobs, several buttons, and a digital display, black Tolex, black screen, disc. 2003.

	N/A	$90 - 120	$40 - 60	

FIRE 18 – 18W, 1-8 in. speaker, guitar combo, solid-state chassis, black and silver control panel, 11 modeling types, 17 effect programs, five effect modules, 20 user presets, seven knobs, several buttons, and a digital display, black Tolex, black screen, mfg. 2004-08.

$140	$95 - 120	$50 - 75	$230

- **Add 20% for built in microphone (Model Fire 18M, Last MSR was $280).**

MSR/NOTES	100%	EXCELLENT	AVERAGE	LAST MSR

FIRE 30 – 36W, 1-10 in. speaker, guitar combo, solid-state chassis, black and silver control panel, 22 modeling types, 19 effect programs, seven effect modules, 30 user presets, 10 knobs, several buttons, digital display, black Tolex, black screen, disc. 2003.

	N/A	$130 - 160	$70 - 95	

FIRE 36 – 36W, 1-10 in. speaker, black and silver control panel, 22 modeling types, 19 effect programs, seven effect modules, 30 user presets, 10 knobs, several buttons, digital display, black Tolex, black screen, mfg. 2004-08.

	$210	$150 - 180	$80 - 110	$350

* Add 15% for built in microphone (Model Fire 36M, Last MSR was $400).

ZT AMPLIFIERS

Amplifiers currently produced in Berkeley, CA since 2008.

Ken Kantor founded ZT Amplifiers in 2008 and is the president. ZT builds amplifiers that are compact, innovative, and affordable - they are made by musicians for musicians. In 2009, they introduced their flagship amp called the **Lunchbox** (MSR $290) that is compact yet fully professional and has an output of 200W. ZT also offers an acoustic version of the Lunchbox called the **Lunchbox Acoustic** (MSR $549) and the **Club** (MSR $599) that shares the same circuit as the Lunchbox but has a 12 inch speaker. An extension speaker cabinet called the **Lunchbox Cab** (MSR $199) is also available. For more information, visit ZT Amplifiers' website or contact them directly.

CONTACT INFORMATION
ZT AMPLIFIERS
2329 4th Street
Berkeley, CA 94710
Phone No.: 510-704-1868
www.ztamplifiers.com
info@ztamplifiers.com

NOTES

GUITAR AMP REFERENCES/ RECOMMENDED READING

GENERAL GUITAR AMPLIFIER BOOKS

The Amp Book - A Guitarist's Introductory Guide to Tube Amplifiers, Brosnac, Donald, 64 pages, Westport, CT, The Bold Strummer, Ltd., 1987. This is a very early book about tubes, and as far as I can tell one of the first. The Amp Book contains sections about history, construction, speakers, how to use, and information about several amp manufacturers.

AMPS! The Other Half of Rock 'n' Roll, Fliegler, Ritchie, Milwaukee, WI, Hal Leonard Publishing Corporation, 1993. Fliegler writes one of the first books with both tube and solid-state designs. Several amp companies are identified including Fender, Vox, Ampeg, and Marshall as well as many manufacturers who hadn't had a lot of ink prior including Mesa/Boogie, HiWatt, Orange, Matchless, Soldano, Rivera, and Sunn. Ritchie also covers several transistor "dinosaurs" from the early days including Kustom, Acoustic, and the Rickenbacker Transonic.

The Art of the Amplifier, Doyle, Michael, 80 pages, Milwaukee, WI, Hal Leonard Publishing Corporation, 1996. More of a picture book than anything else, The Art of the Amplifier is printed entirely in color with little text. Doyle covers over 20 guitar amplifier manufacturers including Dumble, Conrad-Johnson, McIntosh, and Olympus III. This book pays tribute to amplifier pioneers and innovators.

Blue Book of Guitar Amplifiers, 5th edition, 840 pages, 2016, Minneapolis, MN, Blue Book Publications, Inc. What good is an old edition once a new one is released? As far as information, nothing. However, if you are interested in how values have changed (up or down) you can compare values between the current edition and older editions. Historic pricing can also be tracked through our online subscriptions back to 2005. Visit our website for more information.

The Bonehead's Guide To Amps (Guitar World Presents), Hilton, Dominic, 80 pages, Milwaukee, WI, Hal Leonard Publishing Corporation, 1999. Just like the "Idiot's Guide to (insert subject here)," the Bonehead's Guide To Amps can speak to all levels of people including novices and pros. Without too much technical jargon and unknown terms, the Bonehead's Guide is very easy to follow, especially for somebody who is just learning about guitar amplifiers.

The Complete Guide to Guitar and Amp Maintenance, A Practical Manual for Every Guitar Player, Fliegler, Richie, 80 pages, Milwaukee, WI, Hal Leonard Publishing Corporation, 1994. Fliegler, author of AMPS!, provides a complete illustrated manual for the guitar and guitar amplifier user. In the guitar amplifier section, Fliegler covers troubleshooting, capacitors, tube bias, wattage, fuses, solid-state amps (briefly), and speakers/ speaker cabinets. Unlike many tube amp books, this one contains several black and white images, which are very helpful for the do-it-yourselfer.

Dave Funk's Tube Amp Workbook, Complete Guide to Vintage Tube Amplifiers Volume 1 - Fender, Funk, Dave, 422 pages, Waukegan, IL Thunderfunk Labs, Inc. 1996. Fender junkies, this book is for you. Funk's workbook contains everything you need to know about tube amplifiers, especially about Fender. Over 250 schematics are included as well.

A Desktop Reference of Hip Vintage Guitar Amps, Weber, Gerald, 512 pages, Pflugerville, TX, Kendrick Books, 1994. This book is a compilation of all the articles Gerald Weber wrote for Vintage Guitar up to the time of publication in 1994. Anybody who has heard of Weber or Kendrick knows how much this guy is involved in amps. Topics include popular guitar amplifiers, mods for your amplifier, and tube schematics.

Inside Tube Amps, The Book on Tube Amps Technology, Torres, Dan, 310 pages, San Mateo, CA, Sparpco, Inc., 1995. Torres provides the reader with all the information about tube amplifiers you may ever need. The last part of his book gives a step-by-step process on how to build your own tube amp. Torres also writes with a sense of humor and on a level most people enjoy.

The Tube Amp Book, Deluxe Revised Edition, Pittman, Aspen, 188 pages plus a CD-ROM, San Francisco, CA, Backbeat Books, 2003. Aspen may be the best tube amp guy out there, and for those who disagree with me, think about the information he provides that many others don't take the time to do! Pittman founded GT Electronics, builds some of the only American-made tubes, and publishes a book on the side! The Deluxe Revised Edition of the Tube Amp Book is actually the sixth edition, but Pittman went above and beyond with this book. It contains history on over fifty tube amp manufacturers, amp mods, tube reference, and tube schematics. Since paper is expensive and publishing endless pages on schematics doesn't make much sense, Aspen provides hundreds of schematics in .pdf form on a CD-ROM!

INDIVIDUAL GUITAR AMPLIFIER MANUFACTURERS

Ampeg - The Story Behind the Sound, Hopkins, Gregg & Bill Moore, Milwaukee, WI, Hal Leonard Publishing Corporation, 1999. This is the first comprehensive book on Ampeg guitar amplifiers, as well as all related accessories and off- brands. Hopkins and Moore present the history of Ampeg from start to present, a complete listing of models with specs and tube listings, and several pictures including a color section. This book also includes information on the Oliver brand.

The Burns Book, Day, Paul, Westport, CT, The Bold Strummer, Ltd., 1990. Many Burns amplifiers never ended up in the U.S.A., but the few that have often bring confusion to the consumer as he or she does not know what it is. The Burns Book gives a complete history of Burns guitars as well as amplifiers.

Epiphone - The Complete History, Carter, Walter, Milwaukee, WI, Hal Leonard Publishing Corporation, 1995. Carter does a great job of outlining Epiphone with a complete history and several catalogs and price lists for model identification. Since the bulk of Epiphone amps are really Gibsons, very little information has been written. However, price lists in this book provide interesting information.

The Fender Amp Book, Morrish, John, 96 pages, San Francisco, CA, Miller Freeman Books, 1995. This book is similar in design to several of Tony Bacon and Paul Day's books on various guitars (see Gibson Les Paul, Rickenbacker, etc.). The first 2/3 of the book is an illustrated history of Fender amps in chronological order, and the last 1/3 is a complete reference section.

Fender Amps - The First Fifty Years, Teagle, John & John Sprung, 256 pages, Milwaukee, WI, Hal Leonard Publishing Corporation (in cooperation with Fender), 1995. Just as the title suggests, this book features the first fifty years of Fender guitar amplifiers. The authors include a history of Fender, dating information, and a color section helpful in identifying Fender amps. The amp section, which composes most of the book, is organized by model name in chronological order.

The Soul of Tone - Celebrating 60 Years of Fender Amps, Wheeler, Tom, 512 pages, Milwaukee, WI, Hal Leonard Publishing Corporation, 2007. This beautiful, full-color, hardcover book is the definitive history on Fender amplifiers from the beginning up through 2006. With a foreword by Keith Richards and several interviews, this book is a must-read for any Fender amp enthusiast. Wheeler focuses more on the history instead of technical reference information, and the pictures are outstanding.

Gibson Amplifiers 1933-2008 - 75 Years of the Gold Tone, Marx, Wallace Jr., Minneapolis, MN, Blue Book Publications, 2008. Blue Book Publications was thrilled to publish the first book solely on Gibson amplifiers. Author Marx chronicles the entire history of Gibson amps back when guitar amplification was in its infant stages during the late 1920s and early 1930s all the way to Gibson's current Gold Tone amps. A reference section includes detailed information on all Gibson, Lab Series, and SG Systems amps as well as a CD-ROM including Gibson's Amplifier Master Service Book in PDF format! A 16-page full color section completes the one and only book on Gibson amps.

Gibson Shipment Totals 1937-1979, 192 pages, Meiners, Larry, Chicago, IL, Flying Vintage Publications, 2001. Meiners' book on Shipment Totals contains shipping dates for all Gibson Amplifiers produced between 1937 and 1979. It also includes shipping totals for Gibson's other instruments including guitars, basses, mandolins, and banjos. Currently out of print.

Gruhn's Guide to Vintage Guitars - An Identification Guide for American Fretted Instruments, 3rd Edition, Gruhn, George & Walter Carter, San Francisco, CA, Backbeat Books, 2010. Most collectors, dealers, and guitar enthusiasts (including me) have a copy of this book on their desk. Gruhn's book is considered to be the gospel to many people when it comes to identifying American made guitars and amplifiers, and most of the time I agree. As far as amplifiers, Gruhn only covers Fender and Gibson, but his book is best used as a cross reference as descriptions aren't as detailed as some people would like. The new 3rd Edition is organized much better as well for easy reference.

Guitars from Neptune, (Danelectro), Bechtoldt, Paul & Doug Tulloch, Backporch Publications, 1995. All you old timers thought no one would ever care enough about Danelectro to write a book - well you were wrong! Danelectros are becoming extremely collectible and Silvertones are also on the rise. Tulloch gives a basic outline of Danelectro instruments and provides several catalogs and price lists.

Guitar Stories Volume One, Wright, Michael, 312 pages, Bismarck, ND, Vintage Guitar Inc., 1995 and Guitar Stories Volume Two, Wright, Michael, 262 pages, Bismarck, ND, Vintage Guitar Inc., 2000. Michael Wright has been writing for Vintage Guitar for several years now, and is one of the most accomplished writers I have ever read. I especially like these two books because they cover the oddball stuff. Let's face it, information about Fender, Marshall, Ampeg, and Vox amplifiers is not tough to come by. Kay, Alamo, Premier, and other brands of that caliber do not show up very readily, but these are all covered by Wright in his Guitar Stories. These books contain both histories and scanned catalogs that are helpful to identify amplifiers.

The High Performance Marshall Handbook, A Guide to Great Marshall Amplifier Sounds, Boehnlein, John "Dutch," 64 pages, Westport, CT, The Bold Strummer, Ltd., 1994. Just like cars, people enjoy modifying or "souping" their amplifier up to get more sound or gain out of it. This book describes and illustrates how to get the most sound out of your Marshall amplifier.

A History of Marshall Valve Guitar Amplifiers, The Sound of Rock, Doyle, Michael, 68 pages, Westport, CT, The Bold Strummer, Ltd., 1990. This is Doyle's first history of Marshall, which at the time was a very good book. There are several black and white photos and charts to help identify Marshall amps. However, the book he wrote three years later takes Marshall amplifiers to the next level.

The History of Marshall, The Illustrated Story of "The Sound of Rock," Doyle, Michael, 254 pages, Milwaukee, WI, Hal Leonard Publishing Corporation, 1993. The first complete history of Marshall is a good one. Doyle includes a complete history, a complete model listing, and two color sections. The first color section is extremely helpful in identifying Marshall variations, colors, and grille cloths, and the second color section is composed of old catalogs, which is very helpful in identifying vintage Marshalls. Most individual Marshall listings in the Blue Book of Guitar Amplifiers were composed from Doyle's book.

Jim Marshall, The Father of Loud, Maloof, Rich, 256 pages, San Francisco, CA, Backbeat Books, 2004. Although all books written about Marshall Amplifiers are ultimately about Jim Marshall, this book is specifically written about him. This recent book contains many new images and text written by a different author than previous Marshall books. Several extras are included in this book such as dating Marshall amps, Jim Marshall's Top 11 (not 10) amplifiers, and testimonies from several big personalities.

The Marshall Bluesbreaker - The Story of Marshall's First Combo, Wiley, John R., 144 pages, Minneapolis, MN, Blue Book Publications, 2010. Several books exist on Jim Marshall and his amplifiers, but this is the first book about the most famous and collectible combo amp - the Marshall Bluesbreaker. Author John Wiley chronicles the entire history of the development of Marshall's JTM45 chassis into a combo guitar unit all the way to the reissues produced today. A complete guide reference section, 16-page color section, and a chapter describing how to convert a standard Bluesbreaker reissue into a Clapton-spec Bluesbreaker are all included!

Music Man 1978-1982 (and then some)!! The Other Side of the Story, Green, Frank W/M, 112 pages, Anaheim, CA, Centerstream Publishing, LLC, 2007. Music Man was mainly a three-person team including Leo Fender, Forrest White, and Tom Walker. This book is dedicated to Tom Walker and mainly covers the years between 1978 and 1982, and also covers the transition of Music Man to Ernie Ball. This is the only book on Music Man amps and guitars!

The PRS Guitar Book - A Complete History of Paul Reed Smith Guitars, Burrluck, Dave, updated edition, San Francisco, CA, Backbeat Books, 2002. A few of you may have heard of PRS amps and an even fewer number of you may remember PRS amps from the late 1980s and 1990s, but are these transistor dinosaurs actually mentioned in the PRS book? Absolutely! Burrluck writes about two paragraphs on the PRS models (which is plenty!) and covers everything you would want to know. The rest of the PRS book is pretty informative too!

Vox Amplifiers - The JMI Years, Elyea, Jim, 682 pages. It took Elyea over five years, but he has assembled the ultimate history on Vox amps from the Jennings Musical Instruments era. This 10 inch by 12 inch full-color hardcover sells for $85, but for 682 pages of information and pictures, it seems well worth the price.

The Vox Story - A Complete History of the Legend, Petersen David & Dick Denney, 168 pages, Westport, CT, The Bold Strummer, Ltd., 1993. Without this book, many people would only know about the AC series by Vox and forget they produced hundreds of cool models during the 1960s and 1970s. The Vox Story provides a complete history of Vox, a complete listing of models, and history about Vox guitars. This is the one and only book for Vox guitar amplifiers.

PERIODICALS

For those of you who love guitars, amplifiers, and related gear, keep reading for good news! The following list of periodicals represents several extensions for guitar related information beyond the *Blue Book of Guitar Amplifiers*. Most magazines charge for an annual subscription, but many of their websites offer information for no charge or even a digital edition. Feel free to peruse any of the following magazines that pique your interest for further information. We've included a little information about each periodical and what makes it unique.

In addition to the regular publications put out by these publishers, many offer Special Edition (i.e., yearly buyers' guides, new product reviews, market overviews, etc.) magazines that are released annually, or bi-annually. We have included them whenever possible, but if you are curious about some other features, do not hesitate to contact the publisher directly.

ACOUSTIC GUITAR

Acoustic Guitar magazine is probably the best-known periodical dedicated entirely to acoustic guitars. Typical features include exclusive interviews, acoustic guitar and related accessories reviews, and tablature. Acoustic Guitar also has several unique exclusives that are worth checking out.

501 Canal Blvd., Suite J
Richmond, CA 94804-3505
Phone 510-215-0010
Fax 510-231-5824
Website: www.acousticguitar.com
Email: help@acousticguitarservice.com

AMERICAN LUTHERIE

American Lutherie is the quarterly journal of the Guild of American Lutherie (GAL). The GAL is a non-profit, tax exempt educational organization formed in 1972 designed to function as an information sharing system. This journal contains information about the GAL as well as feature articles from members of the GAL and other unique articles. In order to receive this magazine, you need to be a member of the GAL and it is published quarterly.

8222 South Park
Tacoma, WA 98408
Phone: 253-472-7853
Website: www.luth.org
Email: tim@luth.org

Published quarterly, must be a member of the GAL to receive. A yearly membership to the GAL is $51 in the USA.

BASS PLAYER

Bass Player is published by the same company that publishes Guitar Player, and their formats are very similar. Features include interviews with famous bassists, product reviews, lessons, and other exclusives.

NewBay Media LLC
1111 Bayhill Drive, Suite 125
San Bruno, CA 94066
Phone: 650-238-0260
Fax: 650-238-0261
Website: www.bassplayer.com
Email: bassplayer@pcspublink.com

Published monthly with an extra issue in December. A 12-month subscription is $18.99 and a 24-month subscription is $26.99 in the USA.

EQ

EQ magazine is the industry leader in all products related to recording studios, DJ products, and any other sound-related field. Features include interviews with industry professionals, record producers, and soundboard managers, product reviews, and lessons.

NewBay Media LLC
1111 Bayhill Drive, Suite 125
San Bruno, CA 94066
Phone: 650-238-0260
Fax: 650-238-0261
Email: eqmag@musicplayer.com

Published monthly. A 12-month subscription is $15, a 24-month subscription is $25, and a 36-month subscription is $35 in the USA.

THE FRETBOARD JOURNAL

The Fretboard Journal is one of the only scholarly-type journals available in the guitar industry. It features exclusive in-depth articles about players, builders, and other stories. The Fretboard Journal is published quarterly and was first published in 2005.

2221 NW 56th Street, Suite 101
Seattle, WA 98107
Phone: 206-706-3252
Fax: 650-238-0261
Website: www.fretboardjournal.com
Email: subscriptions@fretboardjournal.com

Published quarterly. A one-year subscription is $40 (4 issues), and a two-year subscription is $75 (8 issues).

GUITAR AFICIONADO

Guitar Aficionado was introduced in 2009 and is a guitar magazine heavily involved in cross marketing for the upper class. While most of the magazine is geared toward guitars, they also have features about cars, watches, and liquor to name a few. Guitar Aficionado is published quarterly by the staff of Guitar World.

149 5th Ave., 9th Floor
New York, NY 10010
Phone: 800-456-6441
Website: www.guitaraficionado.com

Published quarterly. A one-year (4 issues) subscription is $24.95 in the USA.

GUITAR DIGEST

Guitar Digest is a newspaper format magazine that is based in the Ohio region. Although this magazine may seem like the "poor man's option," GD offers exclusive interviews, product reviews, classifieds, and other features you can't find anywhere else such as the *EncycloMedia Man* by Mike Overly.

PO Box 66
The Plains, OH 45780
Phone: 740-797-3351 or 740-592-4614
Website: www.guitardigest.com

Published quarterly. A six-issue (one-and-a-half year) subscription is $10 in the USA.

GUITAR PLAYER

Guitar Player is one of the most coveted guitar magazines on the market, and they have one of the largest circulations of any guitar magazine. Features include exclusive interviews, lessons, product reviews, and a large selection of ads with new gear. Although Guitar Player does not have a tablature section, there are plenty of riffs and licks you can learn.

NewBay Media LLC
28 East 28th Street, 12th floor
New York, NY 10016
Phone: (212) 378-0400
Fax: (212) 378-0470
Website: www.guitarplayer.com
Email: guitarplayer@sfsdayton.com

Published monthly. A 12-month subscription is $14.99 and a 24-month subscription is $22.99 in the USA.

GUITAR WORLD

Guitar World established themselves with their tablature listings. At first three entire songs were tabbed out, and now they offer five full tabbed songs in each issue. Guitar World has also become an industry leader with many big-name interviews and product reviews. Guitar World publishes the Buyers Guide twice a year as well as Guitar World Legends periodically that are usually tributes to individual bands or genres.

28 East 28th Street, 12th floor
New York, NY 10016
Phone: (212) 378-0400
Fax: (212) 378-0470
Website: www.guitarworld.com

Published monthly with a magazine and an optional CD. A 12-month subscription is $12 and with a CD is $24.95 in the USA

JAZZTIMES

A magazine published almost monthly that is dedicated to jazz music as well as jazz guitars.

Madavor Media
25 Braintree Hill Office Park, Suite 404
Braintree, MA 02184
Phone: 877-252-8139
Website: www.jazztimes.com
Email: CustomerService@JazzTimes.us

Published ten times a year plus the Annual Jazz Education Guide. A one year subscription is $28 in the USA.

JUST JAZZ GUITAR

Just Jazz Guitar is a magazine published quarterly that is dedicated to jazz music and jazz players. Features include arrangements, lessons, interviews, and other exclusives.

560 Bridgewater Drive
Atlanta, GA 30328
Phone: 404-250-9298
Fax: 404-250-9951
Website: www.justjazzguitar.com
Email: justjazzguitar@mindspring.com

Published four times a year. A four-issue (one year) subscription is $44 in the USA.

MMR (MUSICAL MERCHANDISE REVIEW)

MMR is a trade magazine for the musical industry. They report industry happenings, sales figures, and reports of NAMM, the musical industry trade show. MMR is heavily involved with musical dealers.

Timeless Communications, Corp.
6000 S. Eastern Ave. Suite J-14
Las Vegas, NV 89119
Phone: 702-479-1879
Fax: 702-554-5340
Website: www.mmrmagazine.com

Published monthly. A 12-month subscription is $32 and a 24-issue (two year) subscription is $40 in the USA.

THE MUSIC AND SOUND RETAILER

The Music and Sound Retailer is a news magazine designed for musical instrument and sound product merchandisers. In a sense, it is another trade magazine that features industry news, new products, and editorial reviews and advice from their staff reviews.

Testa Communications
25 Willowdale Ave.
Port Washington, NY 11050-3779
Phone: 516-767-2500
Fax: 516-767-9335
Website: www.msretailer.com

Published Monthly. A 12-issue (one year) subscription is $18 in the USA. Subscriptions are free to music retailers.

MUSIC INC.

Music Inc. is a trade magazine targeted towards music retailers. Any music retailer with proper credentials can receive the magazine for free and any other person interested can subscribe for a fee. Music Inc. focuses on growth and success in the music retail industry with interviews, product reviews, and popular market trends.

102 N. Haven
Elmhurst, IL 60126-2932
Toll Free: 800-554-7470
Phone: 630-941-2030
Fax: 630-941-3210
Website: www.musicincmag.com
Email: subscriptions@musicincmag.com

Published Monthly except for April. An 11-issue (one year) subscription is $50 and a 22 issue (two year) subscription is $90 in the USA. Subscriptions are free to music retailers.

THE MUSIC TRADES

The Music Trades is one of the oldest magazines published in the music industry, and they cater specifically to the music trade. Music Trades publishes a lot of industry sales data and analysis, along with many "top 10" style lists for manufacturers. They also heavily cover the NAMM industry trade shows. The Purchaser's Guide supplements the November issue each year with hundreds of products available.

80 West Street
Englewood, NJ 07631
Toll-Free: 800-423-6530
Phone: 201-871-1965
Fax: 201-871-0455
Website: www.musictrades.com
Email: music@musictrades.com

Published monthly. A 12-month subscription is $23 and a 24-month subscription is $38 in the USA.

PREMIER GUITAR

Premier Guitar has established itself as one of the largest guitar magazines currently available. Content in each issue includes several product reviews specifically aimed toward the higher-end market, exclusive interviews, and monthly editorial columns by several leading figures in the music industry. PG also publishes a digital edition of their print magazine that has set the industry standard for digital guitar magazines.

Gearhead Communications, LLC
Three Research Center
Marion, IA 52302
Toll free: 877-704-4327
Phone: 319-447-5550
Fax: 319-447-5599
Email: info@premierguitar.com
Website: www.premierguitar.com

Published monthly. A 12-month subscription is $24.95 and a 24-issue (two year) subscription is $39.95 in the USA.

THE TONEQUEST REPORT

As the name Tonequest suggests, they are "The Player's Guide to Ultimate Tone," which pretty much sums it up. Although the subscription price may seem somewhat steep, you will not get a lot of this information or interviews from any other source. Tonequest is very serious when it comes to tone and they only highlight the high-end guitar, amp, and effect pedal builders that are really making a difference. The *Blue Book of Guitar Amplifiers* references Tonequest mainly because of their extensive interviews with some of the best builders in the country.

Mountainview Publishing LLC
PO Box 717
Decatur, GA 30031-0717
Phone: 877-629-8663
Fax: 404-377-0604
Website: www.tonequest.com
Email: tonequest1@aol.com

Published monthly. A 12-month subscription is $89 in the USA.

VINTAGE GUITAR MAGAZINE

Vintage Guitar may publish the most popular magazine on vintage guitars, amplifiers, and related accessories. Features of this magazine include vintage product reviews/research, exclusive interviews, guitar collections, want ads, and updates in vintage guitar pricing. Vintage Guitar also publishes the *Vintage Guitar Price Guide* every fall.

PO Box 7301
Bismarck, ND 58507
Toll-Free: 800-844-1197
Phone: 701-255-1197
Fax: 701-255-0250
Website: www.vintageguitar.com
Email: subscribe@vintageguitar.com

Published monthly. A 12-month subscription is $24.95, and a 24-month subscription is $46.95 in the USA.

ENTHUSIASTS WEBSITES

In today's era of the Internet and websites, there is an abundance of information available. The problem with the Internet is you can get published with very little credentials (as opposed to getting a book printed). However, the Internet does provide places for people to submit information, discuss guitar amplifier-related topics, and shop for guitar amps whenever they want. The *Blue Book of Guitar Amplifiers* encounters and references several of these websites on a regular basis. Once again, take all information with a grain of salt - just because somebody has it posted online does not mean it is factual!

WWW.HARMONYCENTRAL.COM

Harmony Central is the largest music-based review site. Anybody can submit a review on a guitar, bass, amp, or any other music-related item. The only problem on this website (besides spelling) is that there a lot of errors from people selling gear they either don't have, can't see, or can't properly describe. If you have something you are trying to find information on, this is a good place to start, but make sure you read all listings.

WWW.VINTAXE.COM

This website has a lot of features with vintage guitars, but my favorite aspects are the catalog listings. For $50 a year, you can view any of the catalogs vintaxe has scanned in (there are thousands of pages). Anyone who is interested in vintage guitar and amp catalogs should visit this site.

WWW.SCHEMATICHEAVEN.NET

Schematics are posted all over the Internet, but I have found that this website has a good selection in many areas. Several Fender, Marshall, and Ampeg schematics are available, but they also include many "bargain bin" amplifier schematics such as Harmony, Kay, Supro, etc. All files are in Adobe Acrobat format.

WWW.REVERB.COM

Reverb is the largest online musical instrument buying and selling site out there. Many dealers, as well as individual sellers, post their gear on this site as it offers a user-friendly interface and receives a lot of web traffic.

WWW.GBASE.COM

Gbase is very similar to Reverb. Although many sellers list their gear on both sites, it's always best to search each individual site to make sure you aren't missing out on a great deal.

WWW.EBAY.COM

What isn't on eBay these days? Collectors have found eBay a great place to snatch up deals, but the site is also useful to search for oddities that people have for sale. There is a lot of bad information on eBay, so beware as to what you read. Remember that pictures are worth a thousand words.

WWW.MYGEAR.COM

Many guitarists and players have become frustrated with eBay and other monopolistic online marketplace policies, so myGear.com was founded as an instrument-only eBay-style site. The best part of the site is that it is free!

WWW.MUSICIANSFRIEND.COM

The Blue Book of Guitar Amplifiers always supports your local guitar and guitar amplifier dealer, but Musician's Friend has the largest database of new/used guitars and amplifiers on the Internet. Usually, Musician's Friend posts the MSR and the selling price, which is right at or around MAP (Minimum Advertised Price). An image usually accompanies model listings, making this a great site to research new and used gear from your home.

WWW.DUCKSDELUXE.COM

This website has been around for many years and contains a lot of guitar-related information. Some highlights include a thoroughly updated guitar show database, serialization charts, and other helpful identification features.

Several other manufacturer-specific websites exist as well. Instead of listing all of them here (as they do come and go), we suggest using an Internet search engine to try to find the brand you are interested in. Some known sites and suggested searches include:

Fender	**Marshall**	**Sound City**
Gibson	**Rickenbacker**	**Sunn**
Magnatone	**Selmer**	**Traynor**

Suggested Search Engines:

Google	**Yahoo**	**Bing**	**Ask**

INDEX

# #

A

INDEX

INDEX

INDEX

INDEX

INDEX

INDEX

INDEX

INDEX

INDEX

INDEX

INDEX

INDEX

INDEX